THE BANTAM NEW COLLEGE
SPANISH & ENGLISH DICTIONARY

COMPREHENSIVE: More than 70,000 words and phrases in education, business, travel, science, history, literature, art and music, social sciences, law, medicine, diplomacy, international affairs, matters of everyday life . . . American and British usage. Hundreds of neologisms.

AUTHORITATIVE: Based on reliable spoken and written sources and organized to achieve the utmost clarity, precision, and convenience.

EASY TO USE: All words are found in one single alphabet for each language, including proper names and abbreviations.

A NEW LANDMARK
IN SPANISH-ENGLISH DICTIONARIES
FOR THE MODERN USER OF WORDS!

THE BANTAM NEW
COLLEGE DICTIONARY SERIES

Edwin B. Williams, General Editor

Edwin B. Williams, A.B., A.M., Ph.D., Doct. d'Univ., LL.D, L.H.D. was chairman of the Department of Romance Languages, dean of the Graduate School, and provost of the University of Pennsylvania. He was a member of the American Philosophical Society and the Hispanic Society of America and the author of *The Bantam New College Spanish & English Dictionary* and the Scribner's (formerly the Holt) *Spanish and English Dictionary* and many other works on the Spanish, Portuguese and French languages.

THE BANTAM NEW COLLEGE
SPANISH & ENGLISH
DICTIONARY

DICCIONARIO
INGLÉS y ESPAÑOL

BY EDWIN B. WILLIAMS
Professor of Romance Languages
University of Pennsylvania

BANTAM BOOKS
TORONTO • NEW YORK • LONDON • SYDNEY • AUCKLAND

THE BANTAM NEW COLLEGE
SPANISH & ENGLISH DICTIONARY
A Bantam Book / November 1968
39 printings through April 1986

Library of Congress Catalog Card Number: 68-29099

ISBN 0-553-26088-X

Published simultaneously in the United States and Canada

---

*Bantam Books are published by Bantam Books, Inc. Its trade-
mark, consisting of the words "Bantam Books" and the portrayal of a rooster, is Registered in U.S. Patent and Trademark
Office and in other countries. Marca Registrada. Bantam
Books, Inc., 666 Fifth Avenue, New York, New York 10103.*

PRINTED IN THE UNITED STATES OF AMERICA

KR   48 47 46 45 44 43 42 41 40 39

CONTENTS

PREFACE

This book is based on primary spoken and written sources. It is designed for speakers of either language who wish to find words or the meanings of words in the foreign language. Its purpose is, therefore, fourfold. It gives to the English-speaking user (1) the Spanish words he needs to express his thoughts in Spanish and (2) the English meanings of Spanish words he needs to understand Spanish, and to the Spanish-speaking user (3) the English words he needs to express his thoughts in English and (4) the Spanish meanings of English words he needs to understand English.

In order to accomplish the purpose of (1) and (3), discriminations are provided in the source language except that, because of the special facility with which the subject of the verb can be shown in Spanish and because of the convenience of showing the object with personal a, discriminations in the form of subject and/or object are given in Spanish on the English-Spanish side as well as on the Spanish-English side. For the purpose of (2) and (4) discriminations are not needed and are not given because the user will always have the context of what he hears or reads to guide him. However, some glosses whose purpose is not to show discrimination but rather to elaborate on the meaning of what may be judged to be an unfamiliar or obscure word or expression in the user's native language are provided in that language.

All words are treated in a fixed order according to the parts of speech and the functions of verbs; and meanings with subject, usage, and regional labels come after more general meanings.

In order to facilitate the finding of the meaning and use sought for, changes within a vocabulary entry in part of speech and function of verb, in irregular inflection, in the gender of Spanish nouns, and in the pronunciation of English words are marked with parallels instead of the usual semicolons.

Periods are omitted after labels and grammatical abbreviations and at the end of vocabulary entries.

The feminine form of a Spanish adjective used as a noun (or a Spanish feminine noun having identical spelling with the feminine form of an adjective) which falls alphabetically in a separate position from the adjective is treated in that position and is listed again as a cross reference under the adjective.

PRÓLOGO

Hemos basado este libro en fuentes originales del lenguaje hablado y escrito. Está destinado a los hablantes de uno u otro idioma que buscan palabras o significados de palabras en el idioma extranjero. Tiene, por lo tanto, los cuatro siguientes propósitos: al usuario de habla inglesa le suministra (1) las palabras españolas que necesita para expresar su pensamiento en español y (2) los significados ingleses de las palabras españolas que necesita para comprender el español; y al usuario de habla española le suministra (3) las palabras inglesas que necesita para expresar su pensamiento en inglés y (4) los significados españoles de las palabras inglesas que necesita para comprender el inglés.

Para lograr los propósitos indicados bajo los números (1) y (3), se suministran diferenciaciones (es decir, distinciones entre dos o más significados de una palabra) en la lengua-fuente; pero, dada la facilidad con que el sujeto del verbo puede indicarse en español y dada la conveniencia de destacar el objeto del verbo con la preposición a, las diferenciaciones consistentes en el sujeto o el objeto, o ambos, se dan en español tanto en la parte de inglés-español como en la parte de español-inglés. Para los propósitos indicados bajo los números (2) y (4) no se necesitan diferenciaciones y no se dan, porque el usuario siempre tendrá como guía el contexto de lo que oye o lee. Con todo, algunas glosas que no tienen por objeto indicar diferenciaciones sino más bien dilucidar el sentido de lo que parece ser una palabra o expresión raras u obscuras en la lengua nativa del usuario, se indican en esta lengua.

Los vocablos se tratan consecutivamente de acuerdo con las partes de la oración y las funciones verbales; y los significados marcados con calificativos de tema, uso y país van después de los significados más generales.

Para facilitar la búsqueda del significado y el uso deseados, los cambios en la parte de la oración y función verbal, en la flexión, en el género de los nombres españoles y en la pronunciación de las palabras inglesas van señalados con doble raya vertical, en vez del punto y coma de costumbre.

Se han omitido los puntos después de los calificativos y abreviaturas gramaticales y al fin de los artículos.

La forma femenina de un adjetivo español usado como sustan-

The gender of Spanish nouns is shown on both sides of the Dictionary except that the gender of masculine nouns ending in -o, feminine nouns ending in -a, -dad, -tad, -tud, -ión, and -umbre, masculine nouns modified by an adjective ending in -o, and feminine nouns modified by an adjective ending in -a is not shown on the English-Spanish side.

Numbers referring to the model conjugations of Spanish verbs are placed before the abbreviations indicating the part of speech. The complete list of model verbs includes models of all verbs that show a combination of two types of irregularity, e.g., esforzar, seguir, teñir.

Proper nouns and abbreviations are listed in their alphabetical position in the main body of the Dictionary. Thus España and español do not have to be looked up in two different parts of the book. And all subentries are listed in strictly alphabetical order.

The centered period is used in vocabulary entries of irregularly inflected words to mark off the final syllable that has to be detached before the syllable showing the inflection is added, e.g., lá·piz m (pl -pices) and falsi·fy ['fɔlsɪ ˌfaɪ] v (pret & pp -fied).

There are three kinds of compound words in English: (1) solid, e.g., steamboat, (2) hyphenated, e.g., long-range, and (3) spaced, e.g., high school. In this Dictionary the pronunciation of all English simple words is shown in a new adaptation of the symbols of the International Phonetic Alphabet and in brackets. The pronunciation of English compound words is not shown provided the pronunciation of the components is shown where they appear as independent vocabulary entries, except that the accentuation of solid and hyphenated compounds is indicated in the vocabulary entry itself, e.g., fall'out', the IPA pronunciation of fall and out being shown where these words appear as independent vocabulary entries.

Since vocabulary entries are not determined on the basis of etymology, homographs are included in a single entry. When the pronunciation of an English homograph changes, this is shown in the proper place after parallels.

E.B.W.

The author wishes to express his gratitude to many persons who have worked with him in lexicographical research and development and who helped him directly in the compilation of this book and particularly to the following: Paul Aguilar, William Beigel, Henry H. Carter, Eugenio Chang-Rodríguez, R. Thomas Douglass, David Louis Gold, Allison Gronberg, James E. Iannucci, Christopher Stavrou, Roger J. Steiner, John C. Traupman, and José Vidal.

tivo (o de un sustantivo femenino que se escribe lo mismo que la forma femenina de un adjetivo), que cae alfabéticamente en lugar apartado del adjetivo, se trata en este lugar y se consigna otra vez bajo el adjetivo con una referencia a la palabra traducida anteriormente.

El género de los nombres españoles aparece en ambas partes del Diccionario; pero no aparece en la parte de inglés-español el género de los nombres masculinos que terminan en -o, los nombres femeninos que terminan en -a, -dad, -tad, -tud, -ión y -umbre, los nombres masculinos modificados por un adjetivo que termina en -o ni los nombres femeninos modificados por un adjetivo que termina en -a.

Los números que se refieren a los modelos de conjugación de los verbos españoles van antes de las abreviaturas que indican la parte de la oración. La lista completa de los modelos de conjugación incluye muchos que muestran una combinación de dos irregularidades, p.ej., **esforzar, seguir, teñir.**

Los nombres propios y las abreviaturas se consignan en su propio lugar alfabético en el texto del Diccionario. No hay, pues, que buscar **España** y **español** en dos partes distintas del libro. Y todos los artículos secundarios van colocados en riguroso orden alfabético.

Se usa el punto divisorio en los artículos de palabras de flexión irregular para señalar la sílaba final que debe separarse antes de agregar la sílaba que denota la flexión, p.ej., **lá·piz** (*pl* **-pices**) y **falsi·fy** [ˈfɔlsɪˌfaɪ] *v* (*pret & pp* **-fied**).

Hay tres clases de palabras compuestas en inglés: (1) las sólidas, p.ej., **steamboat,** (2) las escritas con guión, p.ej., **long-range** y (3) las separadas en dos o más elementos, p.ej., **high school.** En este Diccionario se muestra la pronunciación de todas las palabras inglesas simples por medio de una nueva adaptación de los símbolos del Alfabeto fonético internacional y entre corchetes. No se muestra la pronunciación de las palabras inglesas compuestas cuando la pronunciación de los componentes consta en los lugares donde aparecen como artículos independientes, si bien la acentuación de las palabras compuestas sólidas y las escritas con guión se indica en la voz alfabetizada misma, p.ej., **fall'out',** pues la pronunciación de **fall** y **out** va indicada según el Alfabeto fonético internacional en los lugares donde estas palabras aparecen como artículos independientes.

Como la constitución de los artículos no se ha determinado a base de su etimología, se incluyen bajo un mismo artículo todos los homógrafos de una palabra. Cuando varía la pronunciación de un homógrafo inglés, se indica en su propio lugar después de la doble raya vertical.

E.B.W.

Labels and Grammatical Abbreviations
Calificativos y abreviaturas gramaticales

abbr abbreviation—abreviatura

(acronym) acrónimo—a word formed from the initial letters or syllables of a series of words—palabra formada de las letras o sílabas iniciales de una serie de palabras

adj adjective—adjetivo

adv adverb—adverbio

(aer) aeronautics—aeronáutica

(agr) agriculture—agricultura

(alg) algebra—álgebra

(Am) Spanish American—hispano-americano

(anat) anatomy—anatomía

(archaic) arcaico

(archeol) archeology—arqueología

(archit) architecture—arquitectura

(Arg) Argentine—argentino

(arith) arithmetic—aritmética

art article—artículo

(arti) artillery—artillería

(astr) astronomy—astronomía

(aut) automobiles—automóviles

(bact) bacteriology—bacteriología

(bb) bookbinding—encuadernación

(Bib) Biblical—bíblico

(billiards) billar

(biochem) biochemistry—bioquímica

(biol) biology—biología

(Bol) Bolivian—boliviano

(bowling) bolos

(bot) botany—botánica

(box) boxing—boxeo

(Brit) British—británico

(CAm) Central American—centroamericano

(cards) naipes

(carp) carpentry—carpintería

(chem) chemistry—química

(chess) ajedrez

(Chile) Chilean—chileno

(Col) Colombian—colombiano

(coll) colloquial—familiar

(com) commercial—comercial

comp comparative—comparativo

cond conditional—condicional

conj conjunction—conjunción

(C-R) Costa Rican—costarriqueño

(Cuba) Cuban—cubano

(culin) cooking—cocina

def definite—definido

dem demonstrative—demostrativo

(dent) dentistry—odontología

(dial) dialectal—dialectal

(eccl) ecclesiastical—eclesiástico

(econ) economics—economía

(Ecuad) Ecuadorian—ecuatoriano

(educ) education—educación

(elec) electricity—electricidad

(electron) electronics—electrónica

(El Salv) El Salvador

(ent) entomology—entomología

f feminine noun—nombre femenino

(fa) fine arts—bellas artes

fem feminine—femenino

(fencing) esgrima

(feud) feudalism—feudalismo

(fig) figurative—figurado

fpl feminine noun plural—nombre femenino plural

fsg feminine noun singular—nombre femenino singular

fut future—futuro

(geog) geography—geografía

(geol) geology—geología

(geom) geometry—geometría

ger gerund—gerundio

(gram) grammar—gramática

(Guat) Guatemalan—guatemalteco

(heral) heraldry—heráldica

(hist) history—historia

(Hond) Honduran—hondureño

(hort) horticulture—horticultura

(hum) humorous—jocoso

(hunt) hunting—caza

(ichth) ichthyology—ictiología

imperf imperfect—imperfecto

impers impersonal—impersonal

impv imperative—imperativo

ind indicative—indicativo

indecl indeclinable—indeclinable

indef indefinite—indefinido

inf infinitive—infinitivo

(ins) insurance—seguros

interj interjection—interjección

interr interrogative—interrogativo

intr intransitive verb—verbo intransitivo

invar invariable—invariable

(iron) ironical—irónico

(Lat) Latin—latín

(law) derecho

(letterword) a word in the form of an abbreviation which is pronounced by sounding the names of its letters in succession and which functions as a part of speech—palabra en forma de abreviatura la cual se pronuncia haciendo sonar el nombre de cada letra consecutivamente y que funciona como parte del discurso

(log) logic—lógica

m masculine noun—nombre masculino

(mach) machinery—maquinaria

(mas) masonry—albañilería

masc masculine—masculino

(math) mathematics—matemática

(mech) mechanics—mecánica

(med) medicine—medicina

(metal) metallurgy—metalurgia

(meteor) meteorology—meteorología

(Mex) Mexican—mejicano

mf masculine or feminine noun according to sex—nombre masculino o nombre femenino según el sexo

(mil) military—militar

(min) mining—minería

(mineral) mineralogy—mineralogía

(mountaineering) alpinismo

(mov) moving pictures—cine

mpl masculine noun plural—nombre masculino plural

msg masculine noun singular—nombre masculino singular

(mus) music—música

(myth) mythology—mitología

m & f masculine and feminine noun without regard to sex—nombre masculino y femenino sin tener en cuenta el sexo
(naut) nautical—náutico
(nav) naval—naval militar
neut neuter—neutro
(obs) obsolete—desusado
(obstet) obstetrics—obstetricia
(opt) optics—óptica
(orn) ornithology—ornitología
(paint) painting—pintura
(Pan) Panamanian—panameño
(Para) Paraguayan—paraguayo
(pathol) pathology—patología
pers personal—personal
(Peru) Peruvian—peruano
(pharm) pharmacy—farmacia
(philol) philology—filología
(philos) philosophy—filosofía
(phonet) phonetics—fonética
(phot) photography—fotografía
(phys) physics—física
(physiol) physiology—fisiología
pl plural—plural
(poet) poetical—poético
(pol) politics—política
poss possessive—posesivo
pp past participle—participio pasado
(P-R) Puerto Rican—puertorriqueño
prep preposition—preposición
pres present—presente
pret preterit—pretérito
pron pronoun—pronombre
(psychol) psychology—sicología
(rad) radio—radio
ref reflexive verb—verbo reflexivo
reflex reflexive—reflexivo
rel relative—relativo

(rhet) rhetoric—retórica
(rr) railway—ferrocarril
s substantive—substantivo
(SAm) South American—sudamericano
(scornful) despreciativo
(sculp) sculpture—escultura
(S-D) Santo Domingo—República Dominicana
(sew) sewing—costura
sg singular—singular
(slang) jerga
spl substantive plural—substantivo plural
ssg substantive singular—substantivo singular
subj subjunctive—subjuntivo
super superlative—superlativo
(surg) surgery—cirugía
(surv) surveying—agrimensura
(taur) bullfighting—tauromaquia
(telg) telegraphy—telegrafía
(telp) telephony—telefonía
(telv) television—televisión
(tennis) tenis
(theat) theater—teatro
(theol) theology—teología
tr transitive verb—verbo transitivo
(typ) printing—imprenta
(Urug) Uruguayan—uruguayo
v verb—verbo
var variant—variante
v aux auxiliary verb—verbo auxiliar
(Ven) Venezuelan—venezolano
(vet) veterinary medicine—veterinaria
(vulg) vulgar—grosero
(W-I) West Indian—antillano
(zool) zoology—zoología

PART ONE

Spanish-English

Spanish Pronunciation

The Spanish alphabet has twenty-eight letters. Note that **ch, ll,** and **ñ** are considered to be separate single letters and are so treated in the alphabetization of Spanish words. While **rr** is considered to be a distinct sign for a particular sound, it is not included in the alphabet and, except in syllabification—notably for the division of words at the end of a line—, is not treated as a separate letter, perhaps because words never begin with it.

These twenty-eight letters plus the sign **rr** are listed below with their names and a description of their sounds.

LETTER	NAME	SOUND
a	a	Like **a** in English **father**, e.g., **casa, fácil.**
b	be	When initial or preceded by **m**, like **b** in English **book**, e.g., **boca, combate.** When standing between two vowels and when preceded by a vowel and followed by **l** or **r**, like **v** in English **voodoo** except that it is formed with both lips, e.g., **saber, hablar, sobre.** It is generally silent before **s** plus a consonant and often dropped in spelling, e.g., **oscuro** for **obscuro.**
c	ce	When followed by **e** or **i**, like **th** in English **think** in Castilian and like **c** in English **cent** in American Spanish, e.g., **acento, cinco.** When followed by **a, o, u,** or a consonant, like **c** in English **come**, e.g., **cantar, como, cubo, acto, creer.**
ch	che	Like **ch** in English **much**, e.g., **escuchar.**
d	de	Generally, like **d** in **dog**, e.g., **diente, rendir.** When standing between two vowels, when preceded by a vowel and followed by **r**, and when final, like **th** in English **this**, e.g., **miedo, piedra, libertad.**
e	e	At the end of a syllable, like **a** in English **fate**, but without the glide the English sound sometimes has, e.g., **beso, menos.** When followed by a consonant in the same syllable, like **e** in English **met**, e.g., **perla, selva.**
f	efe	Like **f** in English **five**, e.g., **flor, efecto.**
g	ge	When followed by **e** or **i**, like **h** in English **home**, e.g., **gente, giro.** When followed by **a, o, u,** or a consonant, like **g** in English **go**, e.g., **gato, gota, agudo, grande.**
h	hache	Always silent, e.g., **hombre, alcohol.**
i	i	Like **i** in English **machine**, e.g., **camino, ida.** When preceded or followed by another vowel, it has the sound of English **y**, e.g., **tierra, reina.**
j	jota	Like **h** in English **home**, e.g., **jardín, junto.**
k	ka	Like English **k**, e.g., **kilociclo.**
l	ele	Like **l** in English **laugh**, e.g., **lado, ala.**
ll	elle	Somewhat like **lli** in **William** in Castilian and like **y** in English **yes** in American Spanish, e.g., **silla, llamar.**
m	eme	Like **m** in English **man**, e.g., **mesa, amar.**
n	ene	Generally, like **n** in English **name**, e.g., **andar, nube.** Before **v**, like **m** in English **man**, e.g., **invierno, enviar.** Before **c** [k] and **g** [g], like **n** in English **drink**, e.g., **finca, manga.**

3

LETTER	NAME	SOUND
ñ	eñe	Somewhat like **ni** in English **onion**, e.g., **año, enseñar.**
o	o	At the end of a syllable, like **o** in English **note,** but without the glide the English sound sometimes has, e.g., **boca, como.** When followed by a consonant in the same syllable, like **o** in English **organ,** e.g., **poste, norte.**
p	pe	Like **p** in English **pen,** e.g., **poco, aplicar.** It is often silent in **septiembre** and **séptimo.**
q	cu	Like **c** in English **come.** It is always followed by **ue** or **ui,** in which the **u** is silent, e.g., **querer, quitar.** The sound of English **qu** is represented in Spanish by **cu,** e.g., **frecuente.**
r	ere	Strongly trilled, when initial and when preceded by **l, n,** or **s,** e.g., **rico, alrededor, honra, israelí.** Pronounced with a single tap of the tongue in all other positions, e.g., **caro, grande, amar.**
rr	erre	Strongly trilled, e.g., **carro, tierra.**
s	ese	Generally, like **s** in English **say,** e.g., **servir, casa, este.** Before a voiced consonant (**b, d, g [g], l, r, m, n**), like **z** in English **zero,** e.g., **esbelto, desde, rasgar, eslabón, mismo, asno.**
t	te	Like **t** in English **stamp,** e.g., **tiempo, matar.**
u	u	Like **u** in English **rude,** e.g., **mudo, puño.** It is silent in **gue, gui, que,** and **qui,** but not in **güe** and **güi,** e.g., **guerra, guisa, querer, quitar,** but **agüero, lingüístico.** When preceded or followed by another vowel, it has the sound of English **w,** e.g., **fuego, deuda.**
v	ve or uve	Like Spanish **b** in all positions, e.g., **vengo, invierno, uva, huevo.**
x	equis	When followed by a consonant, like **s** in English **say,** e.g., **expresar, sexto.** Between two vowels, like **gs,** e.g., **examen, existencia, exótico;** and in some words, like **s** in **say,** e.g., **auxilio, exacto.** In **México** (for **Méjico**), like Spanish **j.**
y	ye or i griega	In the conjunction **y,** like **i** in English **machine.** When standing next to a vowel or between two vowels, like **y** in English **yes,** e.g., **yo, hoy, vaya.**
z	zeda or zeta	Like **th** in English **think** in Castilian and like **c** in English **cent** in American Spanish, e.g., **zapato, zona.**

SPANISH—ENGLISH

A

A, a (a) *f* first letter of the Spanish alphabet

a *prep* at; for, to; on, upon; in, into; by; from; **a decir verdad** to tell the truth; **a la española** in the Spanish manner; **a lo que parece** as it seems; **a no ser por** if it weren't for; **a saberlo yo** if I had known it; **oler a** to smell of

abacería *f* grocery store

abace·ro -ra *mf* grocer

abad *m* abbot

abadejo *m* codfish; (orn) kinglet; (ent) Spanish fly

abadesa *f* abbess

abadía *f* abbacy; abbey

abaje·ño -ña *adj* (Mex) coastal, lowland || *mf* (Mex) lowlander

abaje·ro -ra *adj* (Arg) lower, under || *f* (Arg) bellyband, bellystrap; (Arg) saddlecloth

abaji·no -na *adj* (Col, Chile) northern || *mf* (Col, Chile) northerner

abajo *adv* down, underneath; downwards; downstairs; **abajo de** down; **más abajo** lower down; **río abajo** downstream || *interj* down with . . . !

abalanzar §60 *tr* to hurl || *ref* to rush; to venture; (*un caballo*) to rear

abalizar §60 *tr* to mark with buoys || *ref* (naut) to take bearings

abalorio *m* glass bead

abaluartar *tr* to bulwark

abanderado *m* colorbearer

abanderar *tr* (*un buque*) to register

abanderizar §60 *tr* to organize into bands || *ref* to band together; (Chile, Peru) to join up

abandonar *tr* to abandon, to forsake || *intr* to give up || *ref* to abandon oneself; to give up

abandonismo *m* defeatism

abandonista *adj* & *mf* defeatist

abandono *m* abandon, abandonment; neglect; forlornness; yielding, giving up

abanicar §73 *tr* to fan

abanico *m* fan; fanlight; (coll) sword; **abanico de chimenea** fire screen

abaniquear *tr* to fan

abaniqueo *m* fanning; gesticulations

abanto *adj* skittish (*bull*)

abaratar *tr* to cheapen; (*precios*) to lower || *intr* & *ref* to get cheap

abarca *f* sandal

abarcar §73 *tr* to embrace; to encompass; to surround; (Am) to corner, monopolize

abarloar *tr* (naut) to bring alongside || *ref* to snuggle up

abarquillar *tr* & *ref* to curl up

abarrotar *tr* to bar; to bind, to fasten; to jam, to pack, to stuff; to overstock || *ref* (Am) to become a glut on the market

abarrote *m* (naut) packing; **abarrotes** (Am) groceries; (Am) hardware

abarrotería *f* (Guat) grocery store; (CAm) hardware store

abarrote·ro -ra *mf* (Am) grocer

abastecer §22 *tr* to supply, to provide

abastecimiento *m* supplying; supplies, provisions

abasto *m* supply; abundance; **dar abasto** to be sufficient

abatanar *tr* to full

abatí *m* (Arg, Para) corn; (Arg, Para) corn whiskey

abati·do -da *adj* downcast; abject, contemptible || *f* abatis

abatir *tr* to lower; to knock down; to shoot down; to take apart; to humble; to discourage || *intr* (aer) to drift, (naut) to have leeway || *ref* to be discouraged; to be humbled; to drop, fall; to swoop down

abdicar §73 *tr* & *intr* to abdicate

abdomen *m* abdomen

abecé *m* A B C

abecedario *m* A B C's

abedul *m* birch

abeja *f* bee; **abeja maestra** or **abeja reina** queen bee

abejar *m* apiary, beehive

abejarrón *m* bumblebee

abeje·ro -ra *mf* beekeeper

abejorro *m* bumblebee

abertura *f* aperture; opening; crack, slit; cove; openness, frankness

abeto *m* fir tree; hemlock; **abeto del Norte**, **abeto falso** spruce tree

abier·to -ta *adj* open; frank

abigarra·do -da *adj* motley, variegated

abigeo *m* horse thief, cattle thief

abijar *tr* (Col) to sic

abiselar *tr* to bevel

abismar *tr* to cast down; to humble; to spoil, ruin || *ref* to sink; to cave in; to be humbled; to give in; to lose oneself; (Am) to be surprised

abismo *m* abyss, chasm

ablandabre·vas *m* (*pl* -vas) or **ablandahi·gos** *m* (*pl* -gos) good-for-nothing

ablandar *tr* to soften; to soften up; to soothe; to loosen || *intr* (*el tiempo*) to moderate || *ref* to soften; to relent; (*el tiempo*) to moderate

ablativo *m* ablative

aboba·do -da *adj* stupid, stupid-looking

abobar *tr* to make stupid || *ref* to grow stupid

aboca·do -da adj (vino) mild, smooth; vulnerable; **abocado a** verging on

abocar §73 tr to bite; to pour; to bring near ‖ intr to enter ‖ ref to approach; to have an interview

abocinar tr to give a flare to ‖ intr to fall on the face ‖ ref to flare

abochornar tr to overheat; to make blush ‖ ref to blush; to wilt

abofetear tr to slap in the face

abogacía f law, legal profession

abogaderas fpl (CAm) specious arguments

abogado m lawyer; **abogado de secano** quack lawyer; **abogado firmón** lawyer who will sign anything; **abogado trampista** shyster

abogar §44 intr to plead; **abogar por** to advocate, to back

abolengo m ancestry, descent; inheritance

abolir §1 tr to revoke, to repeal

abolladura f dent; bump, bruise; embossing

abollar tr to bump, to bruise; to dent; to stun; to emboss ‖ ref to get bumped, get bruised; to dent, be dented

abollonar tr to emboss

abombar tr to make convex; (coll) to stun, confound ‖ ref to rot, to decompose

abominación f abomination

abominar tr to detest, abominate ‖ intr — **abominar de** to abominate

abona·do -da adj trustworthy; apt, likely ‖ mf subscriber; (al gas, electricidad, etc.) consumer; (a una localidad en el teatro) season-ticket holder; (al ferrocarril) commuter

abonanzar §60 intr (el tiempo) to clear up; (el viento) to abate

abonar tr to vouch for; to certify; to improve; to fertilize; **abonar en cuenta a** to credit to the account of ‖ intr (el tiempo) to clear up ‖ ref to subscribe

abonaré m promissory note

abono m subscription; credit; installment; voucher; fertilizer, manure

abordar tr to approach; to accost; to undertake, to plan; (naut) to board; (naut) to run afoul of; (naut) to dock ‖ intr to run afoul; (naut) to put into port

aborígenes mpl aborigines

aborrascar §73 ref to get stormy

aborrecer §22 tr to abhor, detest, hate; to bore ‖ ref to get bored

aborrecible adj abhorrent, hateful

aborrega·do -da adj (nubes) fleecy; (cielo) mackerel

abortar tr & intr to abort

aborto m abortion

abotagar §44 ref to become bloated, to swell up

abotonador m buttonhook

abotonar tr to button ‖ intr to bud

abovedar tr to arch, to vault

abozalar tr to muzzle

abra f cove; vale; fissure; (Mex) clearing

abrasar tr to set fire to, to burn; to parch; to nip; to squander; to shame ‖ intr to burn ‖ ref to burn; to become parched; (fig) to be burning up

abrasi·vo -va adj & m abrasive

abrazadera f clasp, clip, clamp; (typ) bracket

abrazar §60 tr to embrace, to clasp; to include; to take in ‖ ref (dos personas) to embrace

abrazo m embrace, hug

abrebo·cas m (pl -cas) mouth prop, mouth gag

abrebote·llas m (pl -llas) bottle opener

abrecar·tas m (pl -tas) knife, letter opener

abreco·ches m (pl -ches) doorman

abrela·tas m (pl -tas) can opener

abreos·tras m (pl -tras) oyster knife

abrevadero m watering place, drinking trough

abrevar tr to water; to wet, soak; to irrigate; to size ‖ ref to drink

abreviación f abridgment, abbreviation, shortening; hastening

abreviar tr to abridge; to abbreviate; to shorten; to hasten ‖ intr to be quick; **abreviar con** to make short work of

abreviatura f abbreviation; **en abreviatura** (coll) in a hurry

abridor m opener; grafting knife; **abridor de guantes** glove stretcher

abrigadero m windbreak

abrigar §44 tr to shelter; to protect; (esperanzas, sospechas) to harbor ‖ ref to take shelter; to wrap oneself up

abrigo m shelter; aid, support; cover, wrap; overcoat; (naut) harbor; **abrigo antiaéreo** air-raid shelter; **abrigo de entretiempo** topcoat, spring-and-fall coat; **al abrigo de** sheltered from, protected from; sheltered by, protected by; (ropa) **de mucho abrigo** heavy

abril m April

abrir m opening; **en un abrir y cerrar de ojos** (coll) in the twinkling of an eye ‖ §83 tr to open; to unlock, unfasten; (el apetito) to whet; (el bosque) (Am) to clear ‖ intr to open ‖ ref to open; **abrirse a** or **con** to unbosom oneself to

abrochador m buttonhook

abrochar tr to button, to hook, to fasten

abrojo m thistle, thorn; **abrojos** reef, hidden rocks

abrótano m southernwood

abruma·dor -dora adj crushing, oppressing; overwhelming

abrumar tr to crush, oppress; to overwhelm; to annoy ‖ ref to become foggy

abrup·to -ta adj abrupt, steep; rough, rugged

absceso m abscess

absenta f absinth

ábsida f or **ábside** m apse

absoluta f dogmatic statement; (mil) discharge

absolutamente *adv* absolutely; (Am) by no means

absolu·to -ta *adj* absolute; (coll) arbitrary || *m* absolute; **en absoluto** absolutely not || *f* see **absoluta**

absolvederas *fpl* — **tener buenas absolvederas** (coll) to be an indulgent confessor

absolver §47 & §83 *tr* to absolve; to solve, to answer

absorbente *adj* absorbent; (*interesante*) absorbing

absorber *tr* to absorb; to use up; to attract

absor·to -ta *adj* absorbed; entranced

abste·mio -mia *adj* abstemious

abstener §71 *ref* to abstain

abstinente *adj* abstinent

abstracción *f* abstraction; absorption, deep thought; **hacer abstracción de** to leave out, to disregard

abstrac·to -ta *adj* abstract

abstraer §75 *tr* to abstract || *intr* — **abstraer de** to do without, leave aside || *ref* to be abstracted or absorbed; **abstraerse de** to do without, leave aside

abstraí·do -da *adj* absorbed in thought; withdrawn

abstru·so -sa *adj* abstruse

absurdidad *f* absurdity

absur·do -da *adj* absurd || *m* absurdity

abuchear *tr* & *intr* to boo, to hoot

abuela *f* grandmother; **cuénteselo a su abuela** (coll) tell that to the marines

abuelo *m* grandparent; grandfather; **abuelos** grandparents; ancestors

abulta·do -da *adj* bulky, massive

abultar *tr* to enlarge; to exaggerate || *intr* to be bulky

abundamiento *m* abundance; **a mayor abundamiento** with greater reason

abundante *adj* abundant

abundar *intr* to abound

abur *interj* (coll) good-bye!, so long!

aburri·do -da *adj* bored; tiresome

aburrir *tr* to bore, tire || *ref* to become bored

abusar *intr* to go too far; **abusar de** to abuse; to impose on; to overindulge in

abusión *f* superstition

abusi·vo -va *adj* abusive

abuso *m* abuse; imposition

abyec·to -ta *adj* abject

A.C. *abbr* **año de Cristo**

acá *adv* here, around here; **acá y allá** here and there; **de ayer acá** since yesterday; **¿de cuándo acá?** since when?; **desde entonces acá** since then; **más acá** here closer; **muy acá** right here

acaba·do -da *adj* complete, perfect; worn-out, exhausted || *m* finish

acabar *tr* to end, finish, complete || *intr* to end; to die; **acabar con** to put an end to; to end in; **acabar de** to finish; to have just, e.g., **acaba de salir** he has just left; **acababa de salir** he had just left; **acabar por** to end in; to end by; **no acabar de decidirse** to be unable to make up one's mind || *ref* to end; to be ex-

hausted; to be all over; to run out of, e.g., **se me acabó el café** I have run out of coffee

acabóse *m* (coll) limit, last straw

acacia *f* acacia; **acacia falsa** locust tree

academia *f* academy

académi·co -ca *adj* academic || *mf* academician

acaecer §22 *intr* to happen, to occur

acaecimiento *m* happening, occurrence

acalora·do -da *adj* heated; warm; fiery, excited

acalorar *tr* to heat, to warm; to incite, to encourage; to stir up || *ref* to become heated; to warm up

acallar *tr* to quiet, to silence; to pacify

acampada *f* camp

acampar *tr* (*las mieses la lluvia o el viento*) to beat down, to blow over

acampamento *m* camp, encampment

acampana·do -da *adj* bell-shaped

acampar *tr, intr* & *ref* to encamp

acanalar *tr* to groove; to flute; to channel; to corrugate

acantila·do -da *adj* rocky; steep, precipitous || *m* cliff, bluff

acantonamiento *m* cantonment

acantonar *tr* to canton, to quarter || *ref* to be quartered; **acantonarse en** to limit one's activities to

acaparar *tr* to corner; to monopolize; to hoard

acaramela·do -da *adj* candied; (coll) smooth, honey-tongued

acarar *tr* to bring face to face

acarear *tr* to bring face to face; to face, to brave

acariciar *tr* to caress; (*una ilusión*) to cherish

acarraladura *f* (Chile, Peru) run (*in stockings*)

acarreadi·zo -za *adj* transportable

acarrear *tr* to cart, transport, carry along; to cause, occasion || *ref* to incur, to bring upon oneself

acarreo *m* cartage, drayage; conveyance

acartonar *ref* (coll) to shrivel up, become wizened

acasera·do -da *adj* (Chile, Peru) home-loving; (*parroquiano*) (Chile, Peru) regular || *mf* (Chile, Peru) stay-at-home, homebody; (Chile, Peru) regular customer

acaso *m* chance, accident; **al acaso** at random || *adv* maybe, perhaps; **por si acaso** in case of need, just in case

acatar *tr* to respect, to hold in awe; to observe

acatarrar *tr* to chill, give a cold to; (Chile, Mex) to bother, annoy || *ref* to catch cold; (Am) to get tipsy

acaudala·do -da *adj* rich, well-to-do

acaudalar *tr* to acquire, to accumulate

acaudillar *tr* to lead, to command; to direct

acceder *intr* to accede; to agree

accesible *adj* accessible

accesión *f* accession; acquiescence; access, entry

accésit *m* second prize, honorable mention

acceso *m* access, approach; attack, fit, spell; **acceso prohibido** no admittance

acceso·rio -ria *adj* accessory ‖ *m* accessory, fixture, attachment; **accesorios** (theat) properties

accidenta·do -da *adj* agitated; restless; rough, uneven ‖ *mf* victim, casualty

accidental *adj* accidental; acting, pro-tempore, temporary

accidentar *tr* to injure, hurt ‖ *ref* to faint

accidente *m* accident; (*del terreno*) roughness, unevenness; fainting spell

acción *f* action; gesture; (*parte del capital de una sociedad*) share; stock certificate; **acción crecedera** growth stock; **acción de gracias** thanksgiving; **acción liberada** stock dividend

accionar *tr* to drive ‖ *intr* to gesticulate

accionista *mf* shareholder, stockholder

acebo *m* holly tree

acebuche *m* wild olive

acecinar *tr* to dry-cure, to dry-salt; (*el salmón o el arenque*) to kipper ‖ *intr* to shrivel up

acechar *tr* to watch, to spy on

acecho *m* watching, spying; **al acecho** or **en acecho** on the watch, spying

acedar *tr* to turn sour; to embitter ‖ *ref* to turn sour; to wither

acedía *f* sourness; crabbedness; heart-burn

ace·do -da *adj* sour, tart; crabbed

aceitar *tr* to oil; to grease

aceite *m* oil; olive oil; **aceite de hígado de bacalao** cod-liver oil; **aceite de linaza** linseed oil; **aceite de pie de buey** neat's-foot oil; **aceite de ricino** castor oil; **aceite mineral** coal oil

aceite·ro -ra *adj* oil ‖ *mf* oiler; oil dealer ‖ *f* oilcan; oil cup; **aceiteras** cruet stand

aceito·so -sa *adj* oily, greasy

aceituna *f* olive

aceituno *m* olive tree

acelerador *m* accelerator

acelerar *tr & ref* to accelerate; to hasten, hurry

acelga *f* Swiss chard

acémila *f* beast of burden, pack animal; (coll) dolt; (coll) drudge

acendra·do -da *adj* refined; stainless, spotless

acendrar *tr* to refine; to purify, make stainless

acento *m* accent; **acento de altura** pitch accent; **acento ortográfico** written accent, accent mark; **acento prosódico** stress accent, tonic accent

acentuar §21 *tr* to accent; to accentuate, emphasize

aceña *f* water-driven flour mill

acepción *f* meaning

acepillar *tr* to plane; to brush; to smooth

aceptable *adj* acceptable

aceptación *f* acceptance

aceptar *tr* to accept; to agree

acequia *f* irrigation ditch; (Bol, Col, Peru) stream, rivulet

acera *f* sidewalk

acera·do -da *adj* steel, steely; (fig) cutting, biting, sharp

acerar *tr* to steel, to harden; to line with a sidewalk ‖ *ref* to harden; to steel oneself

acer·bo -ba *adj* sour, bitter; harsh

acerca *adv* — **acerca de** about, with regard to

acercamiento *m* approach, rapprochement

acercar §73 *tr* to bring near or nearer ‖ *ref* to approach, to come near or nearer

acería *f* steel mill

acerico *m* small cushion; pincushion

acero *m* steel; sword; courage, spirit

acérri·mo -ma *adj* all-out; (*enemigo*) bitter

acerrojar *tr* to bolt

acerta·do -da *adj* fit, right; skillful, sure; well-aimed

acertante *mf* winner

acertar §2 *tr* to hit; to hit upon; to figure out correctly; to find; to do right ‖ *intr* to be right; to succeed; to guess right; **acertar a** to happen to; to succeed in; **acertar con** to come upon; to find

acertijo *m* conundrum, riddle

acervo *m* heap; assets, estate; shoal; store, fund, hoard

acetato *m* acetate

acéti·co -ca *adj* acetic

acetificar §73 *tr & ref* to acetify

acetileno *m* acetylene

acetona *f* acetone

acia·go -ga *adj* unlucky, ill-fated, evil

acíbar *m* aloes; bitterness, sorrow

acicalar *tr* to polish, to burnish; to dress, to dress up ‖ *ref* to get all dressed up

acicate *m* long-pointed spur; incentive, stimulus

acidez *f* acidity

acidificar §73 *tr & ref* to acidify

áci·do -da *adj* acid, tart, sour ‖ *m* acid

acierto *m* lucky hit, good shot; good guess; tact, prudence; ability, skill; accuracy; success

aci·mut *m* (*pl* -**muts**) azimut

aclamación *f* acclaim, applause

aclamar *tr & intr* to acclaim, to hail, to cheer

aclarar *tr* to brighten, to clear; to rinse; to explain ‖ *intr* to get bright; to clear up; to dawn

aclarato·rio -ria *adj* explanatory

aclimatar *tr & ref* to acclimate

acobardar *tr* to cow, intimidate ‖ *ref* to be frightened

acocear *tr* to kick; to trample upon, to ill-treat

acocil *m* Mexican crayfish; **estar como un acocil** (Mex) to blush, to be abashed

acoda·do -da *adj* elbow-shaped

acodar *tr* (*el brazo*) to lean; to prop; (hort) to layer ‖ *ref* to lean

acodillar *tr* to bend at an angle ‖ *ref* to double up; to bend, to crumple

acoger §17 *tr* to receive, to welcome;

to accept || *ref* to take refuge; to resort

acogida *f* reception, welcome; meeting place, confluence; refuge, shelter; **dar acogida a** (com) to honor

acolada *f* accolade

acolchar *tr* to quilt, to pad

acolchi *m* (Mex) red-winged blackbird

acólito *m* acolyte; altar boy

acollador *m* (naut) lanyard

acomedi·do -da *adj* (Am) obliging

acometer *tr* to attack; to undertake; (*el sueño, la enfermedad, el deseo a una persona*) to overcome

acometida *f* attack; (*p.ej., de una línea eléctrica*) house connection

acomodación *f* accommodation

acomodadi·zo -za *adj* accommodating, obliging

acomoda·do -da *adj* convenient, suitable; comfort-loving; well-to-do

acomoda·dor -dora *adj* accommodating, obliging || *mf* usher

acomodar *tr* to accommodate; to usher; to reconcile; to suit; to furnish, to supply || *intr* to be suitable, be convenient || *ref* to comply; to come to terms; to hire out; to make oneself comfortable

acomodo *m* arrangement, adjustment; lodgings; job, position; (Chile) neatness, tidiness

acompañamiento *m* accompaniment; escort, retinue; (theat) extras, supernumeraries

acompañanta *f* female companion or escort; accompanist

acompañante *m* companion; accompanist

acompañar *tr* to accompany; to escort; to enclose; to sympathize with

acompasa·do -da *adj* rhythmic; slow; easy-going; cautious

aconchar *tr* to push to safety; (naut) to beach, run aground || *ref* to take shelter; (naut) to run aground; (Chile) to form a deposit

acondiciona·do -da *adj* conditioned; **bien acondicionado** well-disposed; in good condition; **mal acondicionado** ill-disposed; in bad condition

acondicionador *m* conditioner; **acondicionador de aire** air conditioner

acondicionamiento *m* conditioning; **acondicionamiento del aire** air conditioning

acondicionar *tr* to condition; to put in condition; to repair; to season || *ref* to qualify; to find a job

acongojar *tr* to grieve, to afflict || *ref* to grieve

aconsejable *adj* advisable

aconsejar *tr* to advise, to counsel, to warn || *ref* to seek advice, to get advice

acontecer §22 *intr* to happen, to occur

acontecimiento *m* happening, event

acopiar *tr* to gather together

acopio *m* gathering; stock; abundance

acoplado *m* (Arg, Chile, Urug) trailer trolley car

acoplamiento *m* coupling; joint; connection

acoplar *tr* to couple; to join; to connect; to hitch; to reconcile || *ref* to be reconciled; to mate; to be intimate

acoquinar *tr* to intimidate

acoraza·do -da *adj* armored, armorplated; (coll) contrary || *m* battleship

acorazar §60 *tr* to armor-plate

acorchar *tr* to line with cork; to turn into cork || *ref* to get spongy; to wither, shrivel; to become corky or pithy; to get numb

acorchetar *tr* to bracket

acordar §61 *tr* to agree upon; to authorize; to reconcile; to make level or flush; to remind of; to tune || *intr* to agree; to blend || *ref* to be agreed, come to an agreement; to remember; **acordarse de** to remember

acorde *adj* agreed, in accord; in tune || *m* accord; (mus) chord

acordeón *m* accordion

acordonar *tr* to cord, to lace; (*monedas*) to knurl, to mill; to rope off

acornar §61 *tr* gore; to butt

acornear *tr* to gore; to butt

acorralar *tr* to corral, to corner; to intimidate

acortar *tr* to shorten; to reduce; to slow down; to check, to stop || *ref* to become shorter; to hold back; to be timid; to slow down; to shrink

acosar *tr* to harass; to pester

acostar §61 *tr* to lay down; to put to bed; (naut) to bring alongside || *ref* to lie down; to go to bed

acostumbra·do -da *adj* accustomed; customary, usual

acostumbrar *tr* to accustom || *intr* to be accustomed || *ref* to accustom oneself; to become accustomed

acotación *f* boundary mark; marginal note; elevation mark

acotamiento *m* boundary mark; marginal note; elevation mark; stage direction

acotar *tr* to mark off, to map; to annotate; to admit, to accept; to check; to vouch for; to select; to mark elevations on

acotillo *m* sledge hammer

acre *adj* acrid; austere; biting, mordant

acrecentamiento *m* increase, growth; promotion

acrecentar §2 *tr* to increase; to promote || *ref* to increase; to bud, to blossom

acreditar *tr* to accredit; to credit; to get a reputation for || *ref* to get a reputation, to prove oneself

acree·dor -dora *adj* accrediting; deserving || *mf* creditor; **acreedor hipotecario** mortgagee

acribar *tr* to sift; to riddle

acribillar *tr* to riddle; (coll) to harass, to plague, to pester

acriminar *tr* to incriminate; to exaggerate

acrimonio·so -sa *adj* acrid; acrimonious

acriollar *ref* (Am) to acquire Spanish American ways

acrisolar *tr* to purify, to refine; to reveal, to bring out

acrobacia *f* acrobatics

acróbata *mf* acrobat

acrobatismo *m* acrobatics

acrónimo *m* acronym

acrópo·lis *f* (*pl* **-lis**) acropolis

acróstico *m* acrostic

acta *f* minutes; certificate; **acta notarial** affidavit; **actas** proceedings, transactions; **levantar acta** to write up the minutes

actitud *f* attitude; **en actitud de** getting ready to

activar *tr* to activate; to hasten, to expedite

actividad *f* activity

acti·vo -va *adj* active ‖ *m* (com) assets; (com) credit side

acto *m* act; ceremony, function; commencement; thesis; **acto continuo** right afterward; **acto seguido** right afterward; **acto seguido de** right after; **hacer acto de presencia** to honor with one's presence

actor *m* actor; agent; **primer actor** leading man

ac·triz *f* (*pl* **-trices**) actress; **primera actriz** leading lady

actuación *f* acting, performance; action; operation; behavior

actual *adj* present, present-day; up-to-date ‖ *m* current month

actualidad *f* present time; timeliness; **actualidades** current events; newsreel; **actualidad escénica** theater news; **actualidad gráfica** news in pictures

actualizar §60 *tr* to bring up to date

actualmente *adv* at present, at the present time

actuante *mf* participant

actuar §21 *tr* to actuate ‖ *intr* to act; to perform

actua·rio -ria *mf* actuary

acuaplano *m* aquaplane

acuarela *f* water color

acuario *m* aquarium

acuartelar *tr* to billet, to quarter

acuáti·co -ca *adj* aquatic

acuatizaje *m* (aer) alighting on water; (*de nave espacial*) splashdown

acuatizar §60 *intr* (aer) to alight on water

acucia *f* zeal, diligence; yearning

acuciar *tr* to goad, to prod; to harass; to yearn for

acuclillar *ref* to squat, to crouch

acuchilla·do -da *adj* knife-shaped; schooled by experienced; (*vestido*) slashed

acuchillar *tr* to stab; to stab to death; to slash

acudir *intr* to come up, to respond; to apply; to hang around; to come to the rescue

acueducto *m* aqueduct

acuerdo *m* accord; agreement; memory; **de acuerdo con** in accord with; **de común acuerdo** with one accord; **estar en su acuerdo** to be in one's

right mind; **ponerse de acuerdo** to come to an agreement; **recobrar su acuerdo** to come to; **tomar un acuerdo** to make a decision; **volver en su acuerdo** to come to; to change one's mind

acuitar *tr* & *intr* to grieve

acullá *adv* yonder, over there

acumulador *m* storage battery

acumular *tr* to accumulate, to gather; to store up ‖ *intr* & *ref* to accumulate, to gather

acunar *tr* to rock; to cradle

acuñación *f* coining, minting; wedging

acuñar *tr* to coin, to mint; to wedge; to key, to lock; (typ) to quoin

acuo·so -sa *adj* watery; juicy

acurrucar §73 *ref* to squat, to crouch; to huddle

acusación *f* accusation

acusa·do -da marked ‖ *mf* accused

acusar *tr* to accuse; to show; (*recibo de una carta*) to acknowledge ‖ *ref* to confess

acusati·vo -va *adj* & *m* accusative

acuse *m* acknowledgment

acústi·co -ca *adj* acoustic ‖ *f* acoustics

achacar §73 *tr* to impute, to attribute

achaco·so -sa *adj* ailing, sickly

achaparra·do -da *adj* stocky; stubby; chubby

achaparrar *ref* to become stunted

achaque *m* sickliness, indisposition; excuse, pretext; matter, subject; weakness; (coll) monthlies

achatar *tr* to flatten

achica·do -da *adj* childish; abashed, disconcerted

achicador *m* scoop

achicar §73 *tr* to make smaller; to humble; to bail, to bail out

achicoria *f* chicory

achicharrar *tr* to scorch; to bedevil ‖ *ref* to get scorched

achispa·do -da *adj* tipsy

achispar *tr* to make tipsy ‖ *ref* to get tipsy

achuchar *tr* to incite; to crumple, crush; to jostle ‖ *ref* (Arg, Urug) to shiver, have a chill

adagio *m* adage

adalid *m* chief; guide, leader; champion

adama·do -da *adj* womanish; chic, stylish

adamar *ref* to become effeminate

adán *m* (coll) dirty, ragged fellow, lazy, careless fellow ‖ **Adán** *m* Adam

adaptación *f* adaptation

adaptar *tr* to adapt

adarga *f* oval or heart-shaped leather shield

adarvar *tr* to bewilder, to stun

A. de C. *abbr* año de Cristo

adecentar *tr* to clean up, to tidy up ‖ *ref* (coll) to put on a clean shirt, to dress up

adecua·do -da *adj* fitting, suitable

adecuar *tr* to fit, to adapt

adefesio *m* (coll) nonsense; (coll) outlandish outfit; (coll) queer-looking fellow

adehala *f* gratuity, extra

adehesar *tr* to convert into pasture

adelanta·do -da *adj* precocious; bold, forward; (*reloj*) fast; **por adelantado** in advance || *m* provincial governor

adelantamiento *m* anticipation; advancement, promotion, progress

adelantar *tr* to move forward; to outstrip, get ahead of; to advance; to promote; to improve || *intr* to advance; to improve; to be fast || *ref* to move forward; to gain, be fast

adelante *adv* ahead; forward; **más adelante** farther on; later || *interj* go ahead!; come in!

adelanto *m* advance, progress, improvement; advancement; payment in advance

adelfa *f* oleander

adelgazar §60 *tr* to make thin; to taper; to purify; to argue subtly about; to weaken, lessen || *intr & ref* to get thin; to taper

ademán *m* attitude; gesture; **ademanes** manners; **en ademán de** getting ready to; **hacer ademán de** to make a move to

además *adv* moreover, besides; **además de** in addition to, besides

adentellar *tr* to sink one's teeth into

adentrar *intr & ref* to go in; **adentrarse en el mar** to go farther out to sea

adentro *adv* inside; **mar adentro** out at sea; **ser muy de adentro** to be like a member of the family; **tierra adentro** inland || **adentros** *mpl* inmost being, inmost thoughts; **en** or **para sus adentros** to oneself, to himself, etc.

adep·to -ta *adj* initiated || *mf* follower

aderezar §60 *tr* to dress, adorn; to cook; (*una tela*) to starch; to season; to repair; to lead; (*bebidas*) to mix; (*vinos*) to blend || *ref* to dress, get ready

aderezo *m* dressing; seasoning, condiment; starch; finery; equipment; set of jewelry

adestrar §2 *tr & ref* var of **adiestrar**

adeuda·do -da *adj* indebted, in debt

adeudar *tr* to owe; to be liable for; to charge || *intr* to become related by marriage || *ref* to run into debt

adeudo *m* debt, indebtedness; customs duty; charge, debit

adherencia *f* adhesion; **tener adherencias** to have connections

adherente *adj* adherent || *m* adherent; **adherentes** accessories

adherir §68 *intr & ref* to adhere; to stick

adhesión *f* adherence, adhesion

adhesi·vo -va *adj* adhesive

adición *f* addition; (*en un café o restaurante*) check

adicionar *tr* to add; to add to

adic·to -ta *adj* devoted; supporting || *mf* supporter, follower

adiestrar *tr* to train; to teach; to lead, to guide || *ref* to train, to practice

adietar *tr* to put on a diet

adinera·do -da *adj* wealthy, well-to-do

adiós *m* adieu, good-bye || *interj* adieu!, good-bye!

aditamento *m* addition; accessory

aditi·vo -va *adj & m* additive

adivinación *f* prophecy; guessing, divination; **adivinación del pensamiento** mind reading

adivina·dor -dora *mf* guesser; good guesser; **adivinador del pensamiento** mind reader

adivinaja *f* (coll) riddle, puzzle

adivinanza *f* riddle; guess

adivinar *tr* to prophesy; to guess, to divine; (*un enigma*) to solve; (*el pensamiento ajeno*) to read

adivi·no -na *mf* fortuneteller; guesser

adjetivo *m* adjective

adjudicar §73 *tr* to adjudge, to award || *ref* to appropriate

adjuntar *tr* to join, connect; to add; to enclose

adjun·to -ta *adj* added, attached; enclosed || *mf* associate || *m* adjunct; adjective

adminículo *m* aid, auxiliary; gadget; meddler; **adminículos** emergency equipment

administración *f* administration, management; headquarters

administra·dor -dora *mf* administrator, manager; **administrador de correos** postmaster

administrar *tr* to administer, to manage

admiración *f* admiration; wonder; exclamation mark

admira·dor -dora *mf* admirer

admirar *tr* to admire; to surprise || *ref* to wonder; **admirarse de** to wonder at

admisible *adj* admissible

admisión *f* admission; (mach) intake

admitir *tr* to admit; to allow; to accept, recognize; to agree to

adobar *tr* to repair, restore; to dress, prepare; to cook, stew; (*carne, pescado*) to pickle; (*pieles*) to tan

adobe *m* adobe

adobo *m* repairing; dressing; cooking; pickling; tanning; pickled meat or fish

adocena·do -da common, ordinary

adoctrinar *tr* to indoctrinate, to teach, to instruct

adolecer §22 *intr* to fall sick; **adolecer de** to suffer from || *ref* — **adolecerse de** (archaic) to sympathize with, feel sorry for

adolescencia *f* adolescence

adolescente *adj & mf* adolescent

adonde *conj* where, whither

adónde *adv* where, whither

adopción *f* adoption

adoptar *tr* to adopt

adoquín *m* paving stone, paving block; (coll) blockhead

adoquina·do -da *adj* paved with cobblestones || *m* cobblestone paving

adorable *adj* adorable

adoración *f* adoration, worship; **Adoración de los Reyes** Epiphany

adora·dor -dora *mf* adorer, worshiper || *m* suitor

adorar *tr & intr* to adore, to worship

adormecer §22 *tr* to put to sleep || *ref* to go to sleep; to get sleepy

adormeci·do -da *adj* sleepy, drowsy; numb; calm

adormilar *ref* to doze, to drowse

adornar *tr* to adorn; (*un cuento*) to embroider

adornista *mf* decorator

adorno *m* adornment, decoration; **adorno de escaparate** window dressing

adosar *tr* to lean; to push close

adquirir §40 *tr* to acquire; **adquirir en propiedad** to buy, to purchase

adquisición *f* acquisition

adrede *adv* on purpose

Adriáti·co -ca *adj & m* Adriatic

adscribir §83 *tr* to attribute; to assign

adscripción *f* attribution; assignment

aduana *f* customhouse; **aduana seca** inland customhouse

aduane·ro -ra *adj* customhouse; customs || *m* customhouse officer, customs inspector

aduar *m* Arab settlement; gipsy camp; Indian ranch

adueñar *ref* to take possession

adujar *tr* (naut) to coil || *ref* (naut) to curl up

adular *tr* to flatter, to fawn on

adu·lón -lona *adj* (coll) fawning, groveling || *mf* (coll) fawner

adúltera *f* adulteress

adulterar *tr* to adulterate || *intr* to commit adultery || *ref* to become adulterated, to spoil

adulterio *m* adultery

adúlte·ro -ra *adj* adulterous || *m* adulterer || *f* see **adúltera**

adul·to -ta *adj* & *mf* adult

adulzar §60 *tr* to sweeten; (*metales*) to soften

adunar *tr* to join, bring together

adus·to -ta *adj* grim, stern, gloomy; scorching hot

advenedi·zo -za *adj* strange; foreign || *mf* stranger; foreigner; outsider; parvenu, upstart; nouveau riche

advenimiento *m* advent, coming; accession; **esperar el santo advenimiento** (coll) to wait in vain

advenir §79 *intr* to come, arrive; to happen

adverbio *m* adverb

adversa·rio -ria *mf* adversary

adversidad *f* adversity

advertencia *f* observation; notice, remark; warning; preface

adverti·do -da *adj* capable, clever, wide-awake

advertir §68 *tr* to notice, observe; to notify, warn; to point out || *ref* to become aware

Adviento *m* (eccl) Advent

adyacente *adj* adjacent

aeración *f* aeration; ventilation; air conditioning

aére·o -a *adj* air, aerial; overhead, elevated; airy, light, fanciful

aéroatómi·co -ca *adj* air-atomic

aerodinámi·co -ca *adj* aerodynamic || *f* aerodynamics

aeródromo *m* aerodrome, airdrome; **aeródromo de urgencia** emergency-landing field

aeroespacial *adj* aerospace

aerofumigación *f* crop dusting

aeromedicina *f* aviation medicine

aeromodelismo *m* model-airplane building

aeromodelista *mf* model-airplane builder

aeromodelo *m* model airplane

aeromotor *m* windmill; airplane motor

aeromoza *f* air hostess, stewardess

aeronauta *mf* aeronaut

aeronáuti·co -ca *adj* aeronautic || *f* aeronautics

aeronave *f* airship; **aeronave cohete** rocket ship

aeropista *f* landing strip

aeroplano *m* aeroplane

aeroposta *f* air mail

aeropostal *adj* air-mail

aeropropulsor *m* airplane engine; **aeropropulsor por reacción** jet engine

aeropuerto *m* airport

aeroscala *f* transit point

aerosol *m* aerosol

aeroste·ro -ra *adj* aviation || *m* flyer; airman

aeroterrestre *adj* air-ground

aerovía *f* airway

afable *adj* affable, friendly, agreeable

afama·do -da *adj* noted, famous

afamar *tr* to make famous || *ref* to become famous

afán *m* hard work; eagerness, zeal; task; worry

afanar *tr* to press, hurry || *intr* to strive, toil || *ref* to strive, toil; to busy oneself

afano·so -sa *adj* hard, laborious; hard-working

afarolar *ref* (Am) to make a fuss, to get excited

afear *tr* to deface, to disfigure; to blame

afeblecer §22 *intr* to grow feeble, to get thin

afección *f* affection, fondness; (med) affection

afectación *f* affectation

afecta·do -da *adj* affected; **estar afectado de** (*p.ej., los riñones*) to have (*e.g., kidney*) trouble

afectar *tr* to affect; (Am) to hurt, to injure || *ref* to be moved, be stirred

afecti·vo -va *adj* emotional

afec·to -ta *adj* fond; kind; affected; **afecto a** fond of; (*un empleo, un servicio, etc.*) attached to; **afecto de** suffering from || *m* affection, fondness; emotion

afectuo·so -sa *adj* affectionate; kind

afeitado *m* shave; **afeitado a ras** close shave

afeitar *tr* to shave; to adorn; (*la cara*) to paint || *ref* to shave; to paint

afeite *m* cosmetics, rouge, make-up

afeminación *f* effeminacy

afemina·do -da *adj* effeminate

afeminar *tr* to effeminate ‖ *ref* to become effeminate

aferra·do -da *adj* stubborn, obstinate

aferrar *tr* to seize; to catch; to hook; (naut) to moor; (naut) to furl ‖ *ref* to interlock, hook together; to cling; to insist

Afganistán, el Afghanistan

afga·no -na *adj* & *mf* Afghan

afianzar §60 *tr* to guarantee, vouch for; to bail; to fasten; to prop up; to grasp; to support ‖ *ref* to hold fast, to steady oneself

afición *f* fondness, liking, taste; ardor, zeal; fans, public

aficiona·do -da *adj* fond; amateur; aficionado a fond of ‖ *mf* amateur; fan, follower

aficionar *tr* to win, to win the attachment of ‖ *ref* — aficionarse a or de to become fond of; to become a follower of, become a fan of

afiebra·do -da *adj* feverish

afi·jo -ja *adj* affixed ‖ *m* affix

afila·do -da *adj* sharp; tapering; pointed; peaked

afilador *m* grinder, sharpener; razor strop

afilalápi·ces *m* (*pl* -ces) pencil sharpener

afilar *tr* to grind, to sharpen; (*una navaja de afeitar*) to strop; (Arg & Urug) to flirt with ‖ *ref* to sharpen, get sharp; to taper, get thin

afiliar §77 & regular *tr* to affiliate, take in ‖ *ref* — afiliarse a to join

afiligranar *tr* to filigree; to adorn, embellish

afilón *m* knife sharpener; razor strop

afín *adj* near, bordering; like, similar; related ‖ *mf* relative by marriage

afinador *m* tuner; tuning hammer, tuning key

afinar *tr* to purify, refine, perfect; to trim; to tune

afincar §73 *intr* & *ref* to buy up real estate

afinidad *f* affinity; por afinidad by marriage

afirmar *tr* to strengthen, secure, fasten; to assert ‖ *ref* to hold fast; to steady oneself

afirmati·vo -va *adj* & *f* affirmative

aflicción *f* affliction; sorrow, grief

afligir §27 *tr* to afflict, to grieve ‖ *ref* to grieve

aflojar *tr* to slacken, to let go; to loosen ‖ *intr* to slacken, to slow up; to abate, lessen ‖ *ref* to come loose; to slacken

aflora·do -da *adj* flour; fine, elegant

aflorar *tr* to sift ‖ *intr* to crop out

afluencia *f* flowing; affluence, abundance; crowd, jam, rush; fluency

afluente *adj* flowing; abundant; fluent ‖ *m* tributary

afluir §20 *intr* to flow; to pour, to flock

afmo. *abbr* afectísimo

afofar *tr* to make fluffy, make spongy

afonizar §60 *tr* & *ref* to unvoice

aforar *tr* to gauge, to measure; to appraise

aforismo *m* aphorism

afortuna·do -da *adj* fortunate; happy

afrancesa·do -da *adj* & *mf* Francophile

afrecho *m* bran

afrenta *f* affront

afrentar *tr* to affront ‖ *ref* to be ashamed

África *f* Africa

africa·no -na *adj* & *mf* African

afrodisía·co -ca *adj* & *m* aphrodisiac

afrontar *tr* to bring face to face; to defy ‖ *ref* — afrontarse con to confront, to meet face to face

afuera *adv* outside ‖ *interj* clear the way!, look out! ‖ afueras *fpl* outskirts, environs

agachadiza *f* snipe; hacer la agachadiza (coll) to duck

agachar *tr* to lower, bend down ‖ *ref* to crouch, to squat; to cower; (SAm) to give in, yield

agalla *f* gallnut; (*de pez*) gill; (*de ave*) ear lobe; agallas (coll) courage, guts

ágape *m* banquet, love feast

agarrada *f* (coll) brawl, fight, scrap

agarra·do -da *adj* (coll) stingy, tight ‖ *f* see agarrada

agarrar *tr* to grab, to grasp; to take hold of; (coll) to get, obtain ‖ *intr* to take hold; to take root; to stick ‖ *ref* to grapple; to have a good hold; to worry; agarrarse a to take hold of, to cling to

agarrochar *tr* to jab with a goad

agarrotar *tr* to garrote; to bind, to tie up ‖ *ref* to become numb

agasajar *tr* to regale, to lionize, to make a fuss over

agasajo *m* kindness, attention; lionization; favor, gift; treat; party

agavillar *tr* to bind or tie in sheaves ‖ *ref* to band together

agazapar *tr* (coll) to grab, to nab ‖ *ref* (coll) to crouch; (coll) to hide

agencia *f* agency; bureau; (Chile) pawn shop; agencia de noticias news agency

agenciar *tr* to manage to bring about; to promote ‖ *ref* to manage

agenda *f* notebook

agente *m* agent; policeman; agente de policía policeman; agente viajero traveling salesman, commercial traveler

agigantar *tr* to make huge ‖ *ref* to become huge

ágil *adj* agile; flexible, light

agilitar *tr* & *ref* to limber up

agita·do -da *adj* agitated, excited; (*mar*) rough; exalted

agitar *tr* to agitate; to shake; to wave; to stir ‖ *intr* to agitate ‖ *ref* to be agitated; to shake; to wave; to get excited; (*el mar*) to get rough

aglomeración *f* agglomeration; crowd; built-up area

aglomerado *m* briquet, coal briquet

aglutinar *tr* to stick together ‖ *ref* to cake

agnósti·co -ca *adj* & *mf* agnostic

agobiar *tr* to overburden; to exhaust, oppress

agolpar *ref* to flock, to throng

agonía *f* agony, throes of death; agony, anguish; yearning; craving

agonizar §60 *tr* (*al moribundo*) to assist, to attend; (coll) to harass || *intr* to be in the throes of death

agorar §3 *tr* to augur, foretell

agore•ro -ra *adj* fortunetelling; ill-omened; superstitious || *mf* fortuneteller

agostar *tr* to burn up, to parch || *ref* to dry up; (*la esperanza, la felicidad*) to fade away

agostero *m* harvest helper

agosto *m* August; harvest; harvest time; **hacer su agosto** to make hay while the sun shines

agota•do -da *adj* exhausted; sold out; out of print

agotar *tr* to exhaust, to wear out, to use up || *ref* to become exhausted, to be used up; to go out of print; to run out

agracia•do -da *adj* charming, graceful; nice, pretty || *mf* winner

agradable *adj* agreeable

agradar *tr* to please || *intr* to be pleasing || *ref* to be pleased

agradecer §22 *tr* to thank; **agradecerle a uno una cosa** to thank someone for something

agradeci•do -da *adj* thankful, grateful; rewarding

agradecimiento *m* thanks, gratitude

agrado *m* agreeableness, graciousness; pleasure, liking

agrandar *tr* to enlarge || *ref* to grow larger

agranelar *tr* (*cuero*) to grain, to pebble

agrapar *tr* to clamp

agrariense *adj & mf* agrarian

agra•rio -ria *adj* agrarian

agravar *tr* to weigh down; to aggravate; to exaggerate; to oppress || *ref* to get worse

agraviar *tr* to wrong, offend || *ref* to take offense

agravio *m* wrong, offense; **agravios de hecho** assault and battery

agravio•so -sa *adj* offensive, insulting

agraz *m* (*pl* **agraces**) sour grape; sourgrape juice; (coll) bitterness, displeasure; **en agraz** prematurely

agredir §1 *tr* to attack, assault

agregado *m* aggregate; concrete block; attaché; (Arg) tenant farmer

agregar §44 *tr* to add; to attach; to appoint || *ref* to join

agremiado *m* union member

agremiar *tr* to unionize

agresión *f* aggression

agresi•vo -va *adj* aggressive

agre•sor -sora *adj* aggressive || *mf* aggressor

agreste *adj* country, rustic; wild, rough; uncouth

agriar §77 & *regular tr* to make sour; to exasperate || *ref* to turn sour; to become exasperated

agrícola *adj* agricultural || *mf* farmer

agricultura *f* agriculture

agridulce *adj* bittersweet

agriera *f* (Chile) heartburn; **agrieras** (Col) cruet stand

agrietar *tr & ref* to crack

agrimensor *m* surveyor

agrimensura *f* surveying

agringar §44 *ref* (Am) to act like a gringo

a•grio -gria *adj* sour, acrid; uneven, rough; brittle || **agrios** *mpl* citrus fruit

agronomía *f* agronomy

agropecua•rio -ria *adj* land-and-cattle, farm

agrumar *tr & ref* to curd, to clot

agrupar *tr & ref* to group, to cluster

agrura *f* sourness; unpleasantness; **agruras** citrus fruit

agua *f* water; (*de un tejado*) slope; **agua abajo** downstream; **agua arriba** upstream; **agua bendita** holy water; **agua corriente** running water; **agua de Colonia** eau de Cologne; **agua de marea** tidewater; **agua gaseosa** carbonated water; **agua oxigenada** hydrogen peroxide; **aguas** mineral springs; (*de sedas; de piedras preciosas*) water, sparkle; **aguas mayores** equinoctial tide; feces; **aguas menores** ordinary tide; urination; **cubrir aguas** to have under roof; **entre dos aguas** under water, under the surface of the water; (coll) undecided

aguacate *m* avocado, alligator pear

aguacero *m* shower

aguada *f* source of water; water color; watering station

aguade•ro -ra *adj* water || *m* watering place

agua•do -da *adj* watery; thin, watered; (Am) weak, washed out, limp; (Am) dull, insipid || *f* see **aguada**

agua•dor -dora *mf* water carrier || *m* paddle, bucket

aguafies•tas *mf* (*pl* **-tas**) kill-joy, wet blanket, crapehanger

aguafortista *mf* etcher

aguafuerte *f* etching; **grabar al aguafuerte** to etch

aguaje *m* watering place; tidal wave; strong current; (*de buque*) wake

aguamala *f* jellyfish

aguamanil *m* ewer, wash pitcher; washstand

aguama•nos *m* (*pl* **-nos**) water for washing hands; washstand

aguamarina *f* aquamarine

aguanie•ves *f* (*pl* **-ves**) wagtail

aguano•so -sa *adj* watery, soaked

aguantar *tr* to hold up, sustain; to bear, endure, tolerate; to hold back, control || *intr* to last, to hold out || *ref* to restrain oneself; to keep quiet; **aguantarse las lágrimas** to swallow one's tears

aguante *m* patience; endurance; strength, vigor

aguar §10 *tr* to water; to spoil, to mar || *ref* to become watery; to fill up with water; to be spoiled

aguardar *tr* to await, to wait for; to grant time to || *intr* to wait; **aguardar a que** to wait until

aguardentera *f* liquor bottle, brandy flask

aguardentería *f* liquor store

aguardento·so -sa *adj* brandy; (*voz*) whiskey

aguardiente *m* brandy; spirituous liquor; **aguardiente de caña** rum; **aguardiente de manzana** applejack

aguardo *m* hunter's blind

aguasar *ref* (Arg & Chile) to become countrified

aguazal *m* swamp, pool

agudeza *f* acuteness, acuity; sharpness; witticism; **agudeza visual** visual acuity

agu·do -da *adj* acute; sharp; keen; witty

agüero *m* augury; omen; forecast

aguerri·do -da *adj* inured, hardened

aguijada *f* goad, spur; prod

aguijar *tr* to goad, spur, prod || *intr* to hurry along

aguijón *m* goad, spur; sting; thorn; stimulus; **dar coces contra el aguijón** to kick against the pricks

aguijonear *tr* to goad, incite; to sting

águila *f* eagle; **ser un águila** to be wide-awake, be a wizard

agule·ño -ña *adj* aquiline; sharp-featured

aguilón *m* (*de grúa*) boom, jib; (*del tejado*) gable

aguinaldo *m* Christmas gift, Epiphany gift; Christmas carol

aguja *f* needle; hatpin; steeple, spire; (*del reloj*) hand; **aguja de gancho** crochet needle; **aguja de hacer media** knitting needle; **aguja de zurcir** darning needle; **agujas** (rr) switch; **buscar una aguja en un pajar** to look for a needle in a haystack

agujerear *tr* to make a hole in, to pierce, to perforate

agujero *m* hole; pincushion

agujeta *f* (*de la jeringa*) needle; shoestring; **agujetas** stitches, twinges

agusanar *ref* to get wormy; to become worm-eaten

aguzanie·ves *f* (*pl* -ves) wagtail

aguzar §60 *tr* to sharpen; to incite, stir up; to stare at; (*las orejas*) to prick up

ah-chís *interj* kerchoo!

aherrojar *tr* to fetter, to shackle; to oppress

aherrumbrar *tr & ref* to rust

ahí *adv* there; **de ahí** hence; **por ahí que** hence; **por ahí** that way

ahija·do -da *mf* godchild; protégé || *m* godson || *f* goddaughter

ahilar *ref* to faint from hunger; to waste away; to grow poorly; to turn sour

ahincar §73 *tr* to urge, press; to importune || *ref* to hasten

ahínco *m* earnestness, zeal, eagerness

ahitar *tr* to cloy, to surfeit, to stuff

ahí·to -ta *adj* surfeited, stuffed; fed up, disgusted || *m* surfeit; indigestion

ahoga·do -da *adj* drowned; smothered; sunk; close, unventilated; **mate ahogado** stalemate; **perecer ahogado** to

drown; **verse ahogado** (coll) to be swamped

ahogar §44 *tr* to drown; to suffocate, smother; (*cal*) to slake; (*plantas*) to soak; to oppress; to extinguish; to stalemate || *ref* to drown; to suffocate; to drown oneself

ahogo *m* shortness of breath; great sorrow; stringency

ahondar *tr* to make deeper; to go deep into || *intr* to go deep, go deeper

ahora *adv* now; presently; **ahora bien** now then, so then; **ahora mismo** right now; **por ahora** for the present

ahorcajar *ref* to sit astride

ahorcar §73 *tr* to hang || *ref* to hang, be hanged; to hang oneself

ahorra·do -da *adj* saving, thrifty

ahorrar *tr* to save; to spare || *ref* to save or spare oneself

ahorrati·vo -va *adj* saving, thrifty; stingy || *f* economy

ahorro *m* economy; **ahorros** savings

ahuchar *tr* to hoard

ahuecar §73 *tr* to hollow, hollow out; to loosen, fluff up; **ahuecar la voz** to speak in deep and solemn tones || *ref* to be puffed up

ahumar *tr* to smoke || *intr* to be smoky || *ref* to get smoked up; to look or taste smoky; (coll) to get drunk

ahusar *tr & ref* to taper

ahuyentar *tr* to put to flight; to scare away || *ref* to flee, run away

aira·do -da *adj* angry; wild; depraved

airar §4 *tr* to anger || *ref* to get angry

aire *m* air; **al aire libre** in the open air; **darse aires** to put on airs

airear *tr* to air, aerate, ventilate || *ref* to get aired; to catch cold

airón *m* aigrette, panache; gray heron

airo·so -sa *adj* airy; drafty; graceful, light; resplendent; successful

aislación *f* insulation

aislacionista *adj & mf* isolationist

aislador *m* insulator

aislamiento *m* isolation; (elec) insulation

aislar §4 *tr* to isolate; to detach, separate; (elec) to insulate || *ref* to live in seclusion

ajar *m* garlic field || *tr* to crumple, to muss; (*marchitar*) to wither; to tamper with; to abuse, ill-treat || *ref* to get mussed; to wither

ajedrea *f* (bot) savory

ajedrecista *mf* chess player

ajedrez *m* chess; chess set

ajenjo *m* (*Artemisia*) wormwood; (*licor*) absinthe; (*sinsabores y penas*) (fig) wormwood, bitterness; **ajenjo del campo** or **ajenjo mayor** (*Artemisia absinthium*) wormwood

aje·no -na *adj* another's; extraneous, foreign; different; contrary; free; insane; uninformed; **lo ajeno** what belongs to someone else

ajetrear *tr* to drive, harass || *ref* to bustle about; to fidget

ajetreo *m* bustle, fuss

ají *m* (*pl* ajíes) chili; chili sauce; po-

nerse como un ají (Chile) to turn red as a tomato

ají·mez *m* (*pl* **-meces**) mullioned window

ajo *m* garlic; garlic clove; garlic sauce

ajorca *f* bracelet, anklet

ajornalar *tr* to hire by the day ‖ *ref* to hire out by the day

ajuar *m* housefurnishings; trousseau

ajuiciar *tr* to bring to one's senses ‖ *ref* to come to one's senses

ajusta·do -da *adj* just, right; tight, close-fitting

ajustar *tr* to adapt, to fit, to adjust; to hire; to arrange; to reconcile; to fasten; to settle ‖ *intr* to fit ‖ *ref* to fit; to hire out; to be hired; to come to an agreement

ajuste *m* fit; fitting, adjustment; hiring; arrangement; reconciliation; settlement; agreement

ajusticiar *tr* to execute, to put to death

ala *f* wing; (*del sombrero*) brim; (*de puerta, mesa, etc.*) leaf; (*de pez*) fin; (*de hélice*) blade; (football) end; **ahuecar el ala** (coll) to beat it; **ala en flecha** (aer) sweptback wing; **alas** boldness, courage; **volar con sus propias alas** to stand on one's own feet

Alá *m* Allah

alabanza *f* praise

alabar *tr* to praise ‖ *ref* to boast

alabarda *f* halberd

alabardero *m* halberdier; hired applauder, claqueur

alabastro *m* alabaster

álabe *m* drooping branch; bucket, paddle; cog

alabear *tr & ref* to warp

alacena *f* cupboard, wall closet; (naut) locker; (Mex) booth, stall

alacrán *m* scorpion

ala·do -da *adj* winged

alamar *m* frog (*button and loop on a garment*)

alambica·do -da *adj* precious, oversubtle, fine-spun; begrudged

alambicar §73 *tr* to distill; to refine to excess

alambique *m* still, alembic; (*de laboratorio*) retort; **por alambique** sparingly

alambrada *f* chicken wire; wire mesh; (mil) barbed wire; (elec) wiring

alambrado *m* chicken wire; wire mesh; wire fence; (elec) wiring; (mil) wire entanglement

alambraje *m* (elec) wiring

alambrar *tr* to fence with wire; to string with wire; to wire

alambre *m* wire; **alambre cargado** live wire; **alambre de púas** barbed wire; **alambre sin aislar** bare wire

alambrera *f* wire screen; wire cover

alameda *f* poplar grove; mall, shaded walk

álamo *m* poplar; **álamo de Italia** Lombardy poplar; **álamo negro** black poplar; **álamo temblón** aspen

alampar *ref* to have a craving

alancear *tr* to lance, to spear

alano *m* mastiff, great Dane

alarde *m* display, ostentation; (mil) review; **hacer alarde de** to make a show of; to boast of

alardear *intr* to boast, brag, show off

alardo·so -sa *adj* showy, ostentatious

alargar §44 *tr* to extend, lengthen, stretch; to hand; to increase; to let out ‖ *ref* to go away, withdraw; to grow longer; to be long-winded

alarido *m* howl, shout, yell, whoop

alarma *f* alarm; (aer) alert; **alarma aérea** air-raid warning; **alarma de incendios** fire alarm; **alarma de ladrones** burglar alarm

alarmar *tr* to alarm; to alert ‖ *ref* to become alarmed

alarmista *mf* alarmist

alastrar *tr* (*las orejas*) to throw back; (naut) to ballast ‖ *ref* to lie flat, to cower

ala·zán -zana *adj* sorrel, reddish-brown ‖ *m* sorrel horse

alba *f* dawn, daybreak

albacea *m* executor ‖ *f* executrix

albahaguero *m* flowerpot

alba·nés -nesa *adj & mf* Albanian

albañal *m* sewer, drain

albañil *m* mason, bricklayer

albañilería *f* masonry

albarán *m* rent sign; bulletin; (com) check list

albarca *f* sandal

albarda *f* packsaddle

albardilla *f* (*tejadillo sobre los muros*) coping; shoulder pad

albaricoque *m* apricot

albaricoquero *m* apricot tree

alba·tros *m* (*pl* **-tros**) albatross

albayalde *m* white lead

albear *intr* to turn white; (Arg) to get up at dawn

albedrío *m* free will; fancy, caprice, pleasure; **libre albedrío** free will

albéitar *m* veterinarian

alberca *f* pond, pool; tank, reservoir; **en alberca** roofless

albérchigo *m* clingstone peach

albergar §44 *tr* to shelter, to harbor; to house ‖ *intr & ref* to take shelter; to take lodgings

albergue *m* shelter, refuge; lodging; den, lair

albero *m* dishcloth, dishrag; white earth

al·bo -ba *adj* (poet) white ‖ *f* see **alba**

albóndiga *f* meat ball, fish ball

albor *m* whiteness; dawn

alborada *f* dawn; morning serenade; reveille

alborear *intr* to dawn

albor·noz *m* (*pl* **-noces**) terry cloth; burnoose; cardigan; beach robe

alborota·do -da *adj* hasty, rash; noisy; rough

alborota·dor -dora *mf* agitator, rioter

alborotapue·blos *m* (*pl* **-blos**) (coll) rabble rouser; (coll) gay noisy person

alborotar *tr* to agitate, arouse, stir up ‖ *intr* to make a racket ‖ *ref* to get excited; to riot; (*la mar*) to get rough

alboroto *m* agitation, disturbance;

noise, riot; **alborotos (CAm)** candied popcorn; **armar un alboroto** to raise a racket

alborozar §60 *tr* to gladden, to cheer, to overjoy, to elate

alborozo *m* joy, merriment, elation

albricias *fpl* reward for good news; reward given on the occasion of some happy event; **en albricias de** as a token of || *interj* good news!, congratulations!

albufera *f* saltwater lagoon

ál•bum *m* (*pl* **-bumes**) album; **álbum de recortes** scrapbook

albumen *m* albumen

albúmina *f* albumin

albuminar *tr* (phot) to emulsify

albur *m* risk, chance

alcachofa *f* artichoke

alcahue•te -ta *mf* bawd, procurer, go-between; screen, fence; (coll) schemer; (coll) gossip

alcahuetear *tr* to procure; to harbor || *intr* to pander

alcaide *m* governor, warden, jailer

alcalde *m* mayor, chief burgess; **alcalde de monterilla** small-town mayor; **tener el padre alcalde** to have a friend at court

alcaldesa *f* mayoress

álcali *m* alkali

alcali•no -na *adj* alkaline

alcallería *f* pottery

alcana *f* henna

alcance *m* reach, scope, extent; range; pursuit; capacity; late news; import; coverage; brains, intelligence; **al alcance de** within reach of, within range of; **alcance de la vista** eyesight, eyeshot; **alcance del oído** earshot; **dar alcance a** to catch up with

alcancía *f* child's bank; bin, hopper

alcanfor *m* camphor

alcantarilla *f* sewer; culvert

alcantarillar *tr* to sewer

alcanza•do -da *adj* needy, hard up

alcanzar §60 *tr* to reach; to overtake, catch up to; to grasp; to obtain; to understand; to live through || *intr* to succeed; (*un arma de fuego*) to carry; to manage; to suffice

alcaravea *f* caraway

alcázar *m* fortress; castle, royal palace; quarterdeck

alce *m* elk, moose

alcista *adj* bullish || *mf* (fig) bull

alcoba *f* bedroom; **alcoba de respeto** master bedroom

alcohol *m* alcohol

alcohóli•co -ca *adj* & *mf* alcoholic

alcor *m* hill, elevation, eminence

alcornoque *m* cork oak; (coll) blockhead

alcorque *m* cork-soled shoe; trench for water around a tree

alcorza *f* sugar paste, sugar icing; **ser una alcorza (Arg)** to be highly emotional

alcurnia *f* ancestry, lineage

alcuza *f* olive-oil can

aldaba *f* knocker, door knocker; bolt, crossbar; latch; hitching ring; **aldaba**

dormida deadlatch; **tener buenas aldabas** to have pull

aldabonazo *m* knock on the door

aldea *f* village, hamlet

aldea•no -na *adj* village; rustic || *mf* villager

aleación *f* alloy

alear *tr* to alloy || *intr* to flap the wings; to flap one's arms; to convalesce

aleccionar *tr* to teach, instruct; to train, to coach

aleda•ño -ña *adj* bordering || *m* border, boundary

alegar §44 *tr* to allege; to declare, assert || *intr* (Col, Hond) to quarrel

alegoría *f* allegory

alegóri•co -ca *adj* allegoric(al)

alegrar *tr* to cheer, gladden; (*un fuego*) to stir || *ref* to be glad, to rejoice; (coll) to get tipsy

alegre *adj* glad; bright, gay; cheerful, light-hearted; careless; fast, spicy; **alegre de cascos** scatterbrained

alegría *f* cheer, joy, gladness; brightness, gaiety

aleja•do -da *adj* distant, remote

alejandri•no -na *adj* & *mf* Alexandrine

alejar *tr* & *ref* to move aside, to move away

alelar *tr* to make stupid || *ref* to grow stupid

aleluya *m* & *f* hallelujah || *m* Easter time || *f* doggerel; daub; **aleluya navideña** Christmas card || *interj* hallelujah!

ale•mán -mana *adj* & *mf* German

Alemania *f* Germany

alenta•do -da *adj* brave, spirited; proud, haughty; (Am) well, healthy || *f* deep breath

alentar §2 *tr* to encourage, to cheer up || *intr* to breathe || *ref* to take heart; to get well, to recover

alerce *m* larch

alergia *f* allergy

alero *m* eaves

alerón *m* aileron

alerta *adv* on the alert || *interj* watch out!, look out! || *m* (mil) alert; (mil) watchword

alertar *tr* to alert

aler•to -ta *adj* alert, watchful, vigilant

alesaje *m* bore

alesna *f* awl

aleta *f* small wing; (*de pez*) fin; (*de hélice*) blade

aletargar §44 *tr* to benumb; to put to sleep || *ref* to get drowsy, fall asleep

aletear *intr* to flap the wings; to flap, flip, flutter

aleve *adj* treacherous, perfidious

alevosía *f* treachery, perfidy

alevo•so -sa *adj* treacherous, perfidious

alfabetizar §60 *tr* to alphabetize; to teach reading and writing to

alfabeto *m* alphabet

alfaneque *m* buzzard

alfanje *m* cutlass

alfarería *f* pottery

alfarero *m* potter

alféizar m splay; embrasure

alfeñicar §73 tr to candy, to ice || ref (coll) to grow thin; (coll) to be affected, to be finical

alfeñique m almond-flavored sugar paste; (coll) affectation, prudery; (coll) thin, delicate person, weakling

alfé·rez m (pl -reces) (mil) second lieutenant; (mil) subaltern (Brit); **alférez de fragata** (nav) ensign; **alférez de navío** (nav) lieutenant (j.g.)

alfil m bishop

alfiler m pin; **alfiler de corbata** stickpin, scarfpin; **alfiler de madera** clothespin; **alfiler de seguridad** safety pin; **alfileres** pin money

alfilerar tr to pin, to pin up

alfiletero m pincase, needlecase

alfombra f carpet; rug

alfombrar tr to carpet

alforfón m buckwheat

alforja f shoulder bag; traveling supplies; **pasarse a la otra alforja** (coll) to go too far, take too much liberty

alforza f pleat, tuck

al·foz m (pl -foces) outskirts; dependence; mountain pass

alga f alga; **alga marina** seaweed; **algas** algae

algaida f brush, thicket; sandbank

algalia f civet; catheter

algarabía f Arabic; (coll) gibberish, jabber; (coll) hubbub, uproar

algarada f outcry; uproar

algarroba f carob bean

algarrobo m carob

algazara f Moorish battle cry; din, uproar

álgebra f algebra

algebrai·co -ca adj algebraic

álgi·do -da adj cold, icy, frigid

algo pron indef something; anything; **algo por el estilo** something of the sort || adv somewhat, a little, rather

algodón m cotton; **algodón pólvora** guncotton; **estar criado entre algodones** to be brought up in comfort

algodoncillo m milkweed

algodono·so -sa adj cottony

alguacil m bailiff; mounted police officer at the head of the processional entrance of the bullfighters

alguien pron indef somebody, someone

algún adj indef apocopated form of **alguno**, used only before masculine singular nouns and adjectives

algu·no -na adj indef some, any; not any; **alguna vez** sometimes; ever || pron indef someone; **algunos** some

alhaja f jewel, gem; **buena alhaja** a bad egg, a sly fellow

alharaca f fuss, ado, ballyhoo; **hacer alharacas** to make a fuss

alharaquien·to -ta adj fussy, noisy

alhe·lí m (pl -líes) gillyflower (Matthiola incana); wallflower (Cheiranthus)

alheña f henna; blight, mildew

alheñar tr to henna; to blight, mildew || ref (el pelo) to henna

alhucema f lavender

alhumajo m pine needles

alia·do -da adj allied || mf ally

aliaga f furze, gorse

alianza f alliance; wedding ring; (Bib) covenant

aliar §77 tr to ally || ref to ally, become allied; to form an alliance

alias adv & m alias

alicaí·do -da adj failing, weak; (coll) crestfallen, discouraged

alicates mpl pliers

aliciente m inducement, incentive

alienar tr to alienate; to enrapture

aliento m breath, breathing; courage, spirit; **dar aliento a** to encourage; **de mucho aliento** arduous, difficult, endless; **nuevo aliento** second wind; **sin aliento** out of breath

alifafe m (coll) complaint, indisposition

aligerar tr to lighten; to alleviate, to ease; to hasten; to shorten

aligustre m privet

alijador m lighter; lighterman; sander

alijar tr to unload, to lighten; to sandpaper

alimaña f varmint, small predacious animal

alimentar tr to feed, nourish; (p.ej., esperanzas) to cherish, foster || ref to feed, to nourish oneself

alimenti·cio -cia adj alimentary, nourishing

alimento m food, nourishment; encouragement; **alimentos** foodstuffs; allowance; alimony

alindar tr to mark off; to embellish, to prettify || intr to border, be contiguous

alinear tr & ref to align, to line up

aliñar tr to dress, to season

aliño m dressing, seasoning

aliquebra·do -da adj (coll) crestfallen

alisar tr to smooth; to polish, to sleek; to iron lightly

aliso m alder tree

alistar tr to list; to enlist, to enroll; to stripe || ref to enlist, to enroll; to get ready

aliteración f alliteration

aliviar tr to alleviate, to relieve, to soothe; to remedy; to lighten; to hasten || ref to get better, to recover

alivio m alleviation, relief; remedy

aljaba f quiver

aljama f mosque; synagogue; Moorish quarter; ghetto

aljamía f Spanish of Moors and Jews; Spanish written in Arabic characters

aljez m gypsum

aljibe m water tender, tank barge; oil tanker; cistern

aljófar m imperfect pearl; (fig) dewdrops

aljofifa f floor mop

aljofifar tr to mop

alma f soul, heart, spirit; (persona) living soul; crux, heart; sweetheart; (de carril) web; (de cañón) bore; (de escalera) newel; **dar el alma,**

entregar el alma, rendir el alma to give up the ghost

almacén *m* warehouse; store, department store; storehouse; (phot) magazine

almacenaje *m* storage

almacenar *tr* to store; to store up, to hoard

almacenista *mf* storekeeper || *m* warehouseman

almáciga *f* seedbed, tree nursery

almádana *f* spalling hammer

almagre *m* red ocher

almajara *f* (hort) hotbed

almanaque *m* almanac; calendar

almeja *f* clam

almena *f* merlon

almenaje *m* battlement

almendra *f* almond; (*de cualquier fruto drupáceo*) kernel; **almendra amarga** bitter almond; **almendra de Málaga** Jordan almond; **almendra tostada** burnt almond

almendrado *m* macaroon

almendro *m* almond tree

almiar *m* haystack, hayrick

almíbar *m* simple syrup; fruit juice; **estar hecho un almíbar** (coll) to be as sweet as pie

almibarar *tr* to preserve in syrup; (*sus palabras*) to honey || *intr* to candy

almidón *m* starch; (Am) paste; **almidón de maíz** cornstarch

almidona·do -da *adj* starched; (coll) spruce, dapper; (coll) stiff, prim

almidonar *tr* to starch

alminar *m* minaret

almiranta *f* admiral's wife; flagship

almirante *m* admiral

almi·rez *m* (*pl* **-reces**) brass mortar

almizcle *m* musk

almizclera *f* muskrat

almizclero *m* musk deer

almohada *f* pillow; **consultar con la almohada** to sleep it over

almohadilla *f* cushion; pad; (Chile) pincushion

almohaza *f* currycomb

almohazar §60 *tr* to currycomb

almoneda *f* auction; clearance sale

almonedar *tr* to auction

almorranas *fpl* piles, hemorrhoids

almorta *f* grass pea

almorzar §35 *tr* to lunch on || *intr* to lunch, have lunch

almuecín *m* or **almuédano** *m* muezzin

almuerzo *m* lunch

alna·do -da *mf* stepchild

aloca·do -da *adj* mad, wild, reckless || *mf* madcap

alocar §73 *tr* to drive crazy

alocución *f* address, speech

áloe *m* or **aloe** *m* aloe; aloes

alojar *tr* to lodge; to quarter, billet || *intr* & *ref* to lodge; to be quartered or billeted

alondra *f* lark

aloquecer §22 *ref* to go crazy, to lose one's mind

alosa *f* shad

alpargata *f* hemp sandal, espadrille

alpende *m* tool shed; lean-to, penthouse

Alpes *mpl* Alps

alpestre *adj* alpine

alpinismo *m* mountain climbing

alpi·no -na *adj* alpine

alpiste *m* canary seed, birdseed; **quedarse alpiste** (coll) to be disappointed

alquería *f* farmhouse

alquibla *f* kiblah

alquiladi·zo -za *adj* & *mf* hireling

alquilar *tr* to rent, to let, to hire || *ref* to hire out; to be for rent

alquiler *m* rent, rental, hire; **alquiler de coches** car-rental service; **alquiler sin chófer** drive-yourself service; **de alquiler** for rent, for hire

alquilona *f* cleaning woman, charwoman

alquimia *f* alchemy

alquitarar *tr* to distill

alquitrán *m* tar; **alquitrán de hulla** coal tar

alquitranado *m* tarpaulin

alquitranar *tr* to tar

alrededor *adv* around; **alrededor de** around; about, approximately || **alrededores** *mpl* environs, surroundings, outskirts

Alsacia *f* Alsace

alsacia·no -na *adj* & *mf* Alsatian

alta *f* discharge from hospital; (mil) certificate of induction into active service; **dar de alta** to discharge from the hospital; **darse de alta** to join, be admitted; (mil) to report for duty

altane·ro -ra *adj* towering; arrogant, haughty

altar *m* altar; **altar mayor** high altar; **conducir al altar** to lead to the altar

alta·voz *m* (*pl* **-voces**) loudspeaker

altea *f* (bot) marsh mallow

alteración *f* alteration; disturbance; uneven pulse; altercation, quarrel

alterar *tr* to alter; to disturb; to agitate, upset; to falsify; to lessen || *ref* to alter; to be disturbed; to be agitated; to lessen; (*el pulso*) to flutter

altercación *f* or **altercado** *m* argument, wrangle, bickering

altercar §73 *intr* to argue, bicker, wrangle

alternar *tr* & *intr* to alternate; **alternar con** to go around with

alternativa *f* choice, option; admission as a matador; **no tener alternativa** to have no choice

alter·no -na *adj* alternate

alteza *f* sublimity || **Alteza** *f* (*tratamiento*) Highness

altibajo *m* downward thrust; **altibajos** uneven ground; ups and downs

altillo *m* hillock; (*oficina en una tienda o taller*) balcony; (Arg, Ecuad) attic, garret

altimetría *f* altimetry

altiplanicie *f* tableland

altitud *f* altitude; height

altivez *f* or **altiveza** *f* arrogance, haughtiness, pride

alti·vo -va *adj* haughty, proud; high, lofty

al·to -ta *adj* high; upper; top; loud;

(horas) late; **ponerse tan alto** to take offense, to be hoity-toity ‖ *m* height, altitude; story, floor; stop, halt; **de alto a bajo** from top to bottom; **hacer alto** to stop; **pasar por alto** to overlook, disregard ‖ *f see* **alta** ‖ **alto** *adv* high up; loud; aloud ‖ **alto** *interj* halt!

altoparlante *m* loudspeaker

altozanero *m* (Col) public errand boy

altozano *m* hill, knoll; upper part of town; (CAm, Col, Ven) parvis

altruísta *adj* altruistic ‖ *mf* altruist

altura *f* height, altitude; high seas; juncture, point, stage; (mus) pitch; (naut) latitude; **a estas alturas** at this juncture; **a la altura de** (naut) off; **estar a la altura de** to be up to, to be equal to; to be abreast of; **por estas alturas** (coll) around here

alucinación *f* hallucination

alud *m* avalanche

aludi·do -da *adj* above-mentioned

aludir *intr* to allude

alumbra·do -da *adj* lighted; enlightened; (coll) tipsy ‖ *m* lighting; lighting system

alumbramiento *m* lighting; childbirth, accouchement

alumbrar *tr* to light, illuminate; (*a los ciegos*) to give sight to; to enlighten; (*aguas subterráneas*) to discover and bring to the surface ‖ *intr* to have a child ‖ *ref* (coll) to get tipsy

alumbre *m* alum

aluminio *m* aluminum

alumnado *m* student body

alum·no -na *mf* (*niño criado como si fuera hijo*) foster child; (*discípulo*) pupil, student; **alumno mimado** teacher's pet

alunizaje *m* lunar landing

alunizar §60 *intr* to land on the moon

alusión *f* allusion

álveo *m* bed of a stream, river bed

alvéolo *m* alveolus; (*de diente*) socket; (*de rueda de agua*) bucket

alza *f* rise, advance, increase; **jugar al alza** to bull the market

alzada *f* height (*e.g., of a horse*)

alzado *m* lump sum, cash settlement; front elevation; (bb) quire, gathering

alzapaño *m* curtain holder; tieback

alzaplé *m* snare, trap

alzaprima *f* crowbar, lever; (*de instrumento de arco*) (mus) bridge

alzaprimar *tr* to pry, pry up; to arouse, stir up

alzapuer·tas *m* (*pl* -tas) (archaic) dumb player, supernumerary

alzar §60 *tr* to raise, lift, hoist; to pick up; (*la hostia*) to elevate; to hide, lock up; (*naipes*) to cut; (bb) to gather ‖ *ref* to rise, to get up; to revolt; **alzarse con** to abscond with

alzaválvu·las *m* (*pl* -las) tappet

allá *adv* there, over there; back there; **allá** en over in; back in; **el más allá** the beyond; **más allá** farther on, farther away; **más allá de** beyond; **por allá** thereabouts; that way

allanar *tr* to level, smooth, flatten;

(*una dificultad*) to iron out, to overcome, to get around; (*una casa*) to break into; the subdue ‖ *intr* to level off ‖ *ref* to tumble down; to yield, to submit; to humble oneself

allega·do -da *adj* near, close; related; partisan ‖ *mf* relative; partisan

allegar §44 *tr* to collect, gather; to reap ‖ *intr* to approach ‖ *ref* to approach; to be attached, be a follower, agree

allende *adv* beyond; **allende de** besides, in addition to ‖ *prep* beyond

allí *adv* there; **allí dentro** in there; **por allí** that way; around there

ama *f* housekeeper; housewife, lady of the house; landlady, proprietress; **ama de casa** housewife; **ama de cría** or **de leche** wet nurse; **ama de llaves** housekeeper; **ama seca** dry nurse

amable *adj* amiable, kind, obliging; (*digno de ser amado*) lovable

ama·do -da *adj* & *mf* beloved

ama·dor -dora *adj* fond, loving ‖ *mf* lover

amadrigar §44 *tr* to welcome, receive with open arms ‖ *ref* to burrow; to go into seclusion

amaestrar *tr* to teach, to coach; (*a los animales*) to train

amagar §44 *tr* to show signs of, to threaten; to feint ‖ *intr* to look threatening

amago *m* threat, menace; sign, indication; feint

amainar *tr* to lessen; (naut) to lower, shorten ‖ *intr* to subside, die down; to lessen; to yield ‖ *ref* to lessen; to yield

amalgama *f* amalgam

amalgamar *tr* & *ref* to amalgamate

amamantar *tr* to nurse, to suckle

amancebamiento *m* cohabitation, concubinage, liaison

amancebar *ref* to cohabit, to live in concubinage

amancillar *tr* to stain, spot; to sully, to tarnish

amanecer *m* dawn, daybreak ‖ *v* §22 *intr* to dawn, to begin to get light; to begin to appear; to get awake, to start the day

amanecida *f* dawn, daybreak

amanera·do -da *adj* mannered, affected

amansar *tr* (*a un animal*) to tame; (*a un caballo*) to break; to soothe, to appease

amante *adj* fond, loving ‖ *mf* lover

amaño *m* skill, cleverness, dexterity; trick; **amaños** tools, implements

amapola *f* poppy

amar *tr* to love

amaraje *m* alighting on water

amarar *intr* to alight on water

amargar §44 *tr* to make bitter; to embitter; (*una tertulia, una velada*) to spoil ‖ *intr* & *ref* to become bitter; to become embittered

amar·go -ga *adj* bitter; sour; distressing ‖ **amargos** *mpl* bitters

amargura *f* bitterness; sorrow, grief

amarillear *intr* to turn yellow, to show yellow

amarillecer §22 *intr* to become yellow

amarillen·to -ta *adj* yellowish

amariliez *f* yellowness

amari·llo -lla *adj* & *m* yellow

amarra *f* mooring cable; **amarras** support, protection; **soltar las amarras** (naut) to cast off

amarrar *tr* to moor; to lash, to tie up; (*las cartas*) to stack

amartelar *tr* to make love to; to make jealous || *ref* to fall in love; to become jealous

amartillar *tr* to hammer; (*un arma de fuego*) to cock

amasar *tr* to knead; to mix; to massage; (*dinero*) to amass; to concoct

amatista *f* amethyst

Amazonas *m* Amazon

ambages *mpl* ambiguity, quibbling; **sin ambages** straight to the point

ámbar *m* amber

Amberes *f* Antwerp

ambición *f* ambition

ambicionar *tr* to strive for, to be eager for

ambicio·so -sa *adj* ambitious; eager; **ambicioso de figurar** social climber

ambiente *m* atmosphere

ambi·gú *m* (*pl* -gúes) buffet supper; bar, refreshment bar

ambigüedad *f* ambiguity

ambi·guo -gua *adj* ambiguous; (*género*) (gram) common

ámbito *m* boundary, limit; compass, scope

ambladura *f* amble

amblar *intr* to amble

am·bos -bas *adj* & *pron indef* both; **ambos a dos** both, both together

ambrosía *f* ragweed

ambulancia *f* ambulance; **ambulancia de correos** mail car, railway post office

ambulante *adj* itinerant, traveling || *m* railway mail clerk

amedrentar *tr* to frighten, to scare

amelona·do -da *adj* melon-shaped; (coll) mentally retarded; (coll) lovesick

amén *interj* amen! || *m* amen || *adv* — **amén de** (coll) aside from; (coll) in addition to

amenaza *f* threat, menace

amenazar §60 *tr* to threaten, menace

amenguar §10 *tr* to lessen, to diminish; to belittle; to dishonor

amenidad *f* amenity

amenizar §60 *tr* to make pleasant, to brighten, to cheer

ame·no -na *adj* agreeable, pleasant

amento *m* catkin

América *f* America; **la América Central** Central America; **la América del Norte** North America; **la América del Sur** South America; **la América Latina** Latin America

americana *f* sack coat, jacket

americanizar §60 *tr* to Americanize

america·no -na *adj* & *mf* American; Spanish American || *f* see **americana**

amerizar §60 *intr* to alight on water

ametralladora *f* machine gun

ametrallar *tr* to machine-gun

amiba *f* amoeba

amiga *f* friend; mistress; schoolmistress; girls' school

amigable *adj* amicable, friendly

amigacho *m* (coll) chum, crony, pal

amígdala *f* tonsil

amigdalitis *f* tonsillitis

ami·go -ga *adj* friendly; fond || *mf* friend; sweetheart; **amigo del alma** bosom friend || *f* see **amiga**

amigote *m* (coll) chum, crony, pal

amilanar *tr* to terrify, intimidate

aminorar *tr* to lessen, to diminish

amistad *f* friendship; liaison; **hacer las amistades** (coll) to make up; **romper las amistades** (coll) to fall out, become enemies

amistar *tr* to bring together || *ref* to become friends

amisto·so -sa *adj* friendly

amnistía *f* amnesty

amnistiar §77 *tr* to amnesty, to grant amnesty to

amo *m* head of family; landlord, proprietor; boss; **ser el amo del cotarro** (coll) to rule the roost

amoblar §61 *tr* to furnish

amodorrar *ref* to get drowsy; to fall asleep; to grow numb

amohinar *tr* to annoy, irritate, vex

amojonar *tr* to mark off with landmarks

amoladera *f* grindstone, whetstone

amolar §61 *tr* to grind, sharpen; (coll) to bore, to annoy

amoldar *tr* to mold; to model, to pattern, to fashion; to adjust, adapt

amonestación *f* admonition; marriage banns

amonestar *tr* to admonish, to warn; to publish the banns of

amoníaco *m* ammonia

amontonar *tr* to heap, pile; to accumulate; to hoard || *ref* to collect, to gather; to crowd; (coll) to get angry; (Mex) to gang up

amor *m* love; **al amor del agua** with the current; obligingly; **al amor de la lumbre** by the fire, in the warmth of the fire; **amores** love affair; **amor propio** amour-propre; conceit; **por amor de** for the sake of

amorata·do -da *adj* livid, black-and-blue

amordazar §60 *tr* to muzzle; to gag

amorío *m* (coll) love-making; (coll) love affair

amoro·so -sa *adj* loving, affectionate, amorous

amortajar *tr* to shroud; (carp) to mortise

amortecer §22 *tr* to deaden, to muffle || *ref* to die away, become faint

amortiguador *m* shock absorber; door check; (*de automóvil*) bumper; **amortiguador de luz** dimmer; **amortiguador de ruido** muffler

amortiguar §10 *tr* to deaden, to muffle; to soften, tone down; to dim; to damp; (*un golpe*) to cushion; (*ondas electromagnéticas*) to damp

amortizar §60 *tr* to amortize; (*una deuda*) to pay off

amoscar §73 *ref* (coll) to get peeved; (Mex) to blush, be embarrassed

amotina·do -da *adj* mutinous, rebellious || *mf* mutineer, rebel, rioter

amotinar *tr* to stir up; to incite to mutiny || *ref* to rise up, mutiny, rebel

amover §47 *tr* to discharge, dismiss

amovible *adj* removable, detachable

amparar *tr* to shelter, protect || *ref* to seek shelter; to protect oneself

amparo *m* shelter, protection, refuge; stall; aid, favor

amperio *m* ampere

amperio-hora *m* (*pl* **amperios-hora**) ampere-hour

ampliación *f* amplification; (phot) enlargement

ampliar §77 *tr* to amplify, enlarge; to widen; (phot) to enlarge

amplificador *m* amplifier

amplificar §73 *tr* to amplify; to expand, enlarge; to magnify

am·plio -plia *adj* ample; spacious, roomy

amplitud *f* amplitude; roominess

ampo *m* dazzling white; snowflake

ampolla *f* blister; bubble; cruet; bulb, light bulb

ampollar *tr* & *ref* to blister

ampolleta *f* vial; sandglass, hourglass; bulb, light bulb; cruet

ampulosidad *f* bombast, pomposity

ampulo·so -sa *adj* bombastic, pompous

amputar *tr* to amputate

amueblar *tr* to furnish

amujera·do -da *adj* effeminate

amuleto *m* amulet, charm

amurallar *tr* to wall, to wall in

amurcar §73 *tr* to gore

amusgar §44 *tr* (*las orejas el toro, el caballo*) to throw back

anacardo *m* cashew; cashew nut

anacronismo *m* anachronism

ánade *mf* duck

anadear *intr* to waddle

anadeo *m* waddle, waddling

anales *mpl* annals

analfabetismo *m* illiteracy

analfabe·to -ta *adj* & *mf* illiterate

análi·sis *m* & *f* (*pl* -sis) analysis; **análisis gramatical** parsing; **análisis ocupacional** job analysis

analista *mf* analyst; annalist

analíti·co -ca *adj* analytic(al)

analizar §60 *tr* to analyze; **analizar gramaticalmente** to parse

analogía *f* analogy; similarity

análo·go -ga *adj* analogous; similar

ana·ná *m* (*pl* -naes) pineapple

ananás *m* pineapple

anaquel *m* shelf

anaranja·do -da *adj* & *m* (*color*) orange

anarquía *f* anarchy

anárqui·co -ca *adj* anarchic(al)

anarquista *mf* anarch, anarchist

anatema *m* & *f* anathema; curse

anatomía *f* anatomy

anatómi·co -ca *adj* anatomic(al) || *mf* anatomist

anatomista *mf* anatomist

anca *f* croup, haunch; buttock, rump; **a ancas** or **a las ancas** mounted behind another person

ancianidad *f* old age

ancia·no -na *adj* old, aged || *m* old man; (eccl) elder || *f* old woman

ancla *f* anchor; **echar anclas** to cast anchor; **levar anclas** to weigh anchor

anclar *intr* to anchor

anclote *m* kedge, kedge anchor

ancón *m* bay, cove

áncora *f* anchor

ancorar *intr* to anchor

an·cho -cha *adj* wide, broad; full, ample; loose, loose-fitting || *m* width, breadth

anchoa *f* anchovy

anchura *f* width, breadth; fullness, ampleness; looseness; comfort, ease

anchuro·so -sa *adj* wide, broad; spacious, roomy

andada *f* thin, hard-baked cracker; **andadas** (*de conejos y otros animales*) tracks; **volver a los andadas** to revert to one's old tricks

andaderas *fpl* gocart, walker

anda·do -da *adj* gone by, elapsed; frequented, trodden; worn, used; ordinary || *m* (Am) gait || *f* see **andada**

andadores *mpl* leading strings

andadura *f* pace, gait; amble; (Mex) mount

Andalucía *f* Andalusia

anda·luz -luza *adj* & *mf* Andalusian

andaluzada *f* (coll) tall story, exaggeration, fish story

andamiaje *m* scaffolding

andamio *m* scaffold; platform

andanada *f* (naut) broadside; (taur) covered upper section; (coll) scolding; (fig) fusillade

andante *adj* walking; errant, wandering

andanza *f* wandering, rambling; fate, fortune

andar *m* gait, pace, walk || §5 *tr* (*p.ej., dos millas*) to go; (*un camino*) to go down or up || *intr* to go, to walk; to run; to travel; to act, to behave; (*p.ej., un reloj*) to go, to run, to work; to be, to feel; to go by, to pass, to elapse; to go (*to bear up, to last*), e.g., **anduve diez horas sin comer** I went ten hours without eating || *ref* to go by, to pass, to elapse; to go away; **andarse sin** to go without

andarie·go -ga *adj* wandering, roving; swift, fleet

andas *fpl* litter; stretcher; bier

andén *m* railway platform; quay; footpath

Andes *mpl* Andes

andi·no -na *adj* Andean

andraje·ro -ra *mf* ragpicker

andrajo *m* rag, tatter; ragamuffin, scalawag

andrajo·so -sa *adj* ragged, raggedy, in tatters

andurriales *mpl* byways, out-of-the-way place

anea *f* cattail, bulrush

aneblar §2 *tr* to cloud; to becloud || *ref* to become clouded; to get dark

anécdota *f* anecdote

anegar §44 *tr* to flood; to drown || *ref* to become flooded; to drown

ane·jo -**ja** *adj* annexed; accessory || *m* annex; dependency; supplement

anemia *f* anaemia

anémi·co -**ca** *adj* anaemic

anestesia *f* anaesthesia

anestesiar *tr* anaesthetize

anestési·co -**ca** *adj & m* anaesthetic

aneurisma *m & f* aneurysm

anexar *tr* to annex

ane·xo -**xa** *adj* annexed; accessory || *m* annex; dependency

anfi·bio -**bia** *adj* amphibious

anfiteatro *m* amphitheater

anfitrión *m* (coll) host

anfitriona *f* (coll) hostess

ánfora *f* (Am) voting urn, ballot box

anfractuo·so -**sa** *adj* winding, tortuous

angarillas *fpl* handbarrow; panniers; cruet stand

ángel *m* angel; **ángel custodio** or **de la guarda** guardian angel; **ángel patudo** (coll) wolf in sheep's clothing; **tener ángel** to have great charm

angelical or **angéli·co** -**ca** *adj* angelic(al)

angina *f* angina; **angina de pecho** angina pectoris

angloparlante *adj* English-speaking || *mf* speaker of English

anglosa·jón -**jona** *adj & mf* Anglo-Saxon

angos·to -**ta** *adj* narrow

anguila *f* eel; **angullas** (*para botar un barco al agua*) ways; **escurrirse como una anguila** to be as slippery as an eel

angular *adj* angular

ángulo *m* angle; corner

angulo·so -**sa** *adj* (*facciones*) angular

angustia *f* anguish, distress, grief

angustia·do -**da** *adj* distressed, grieved

angustiar *tr* to distress, afflict, grieve

angustio·so -**sa** *adj* distressed, grieved; worrisome

anhelar *tr* to crave, to want badly || *intr* to pant; to yearn; **anhelar por** to long for

anhélito *m* hard breathing

anhelo *m* craving; yearning, longing

anhelo·so -**sa** *adj* eager, yearning; breathless, panting

anhi·dro -**dra** *adj* anhydrous

Aníbal *m* Hannibal

anidar *tr* to harbor, to shelter || *intr & ref* to nestle, make a nest; to live

anilina *f* aniline

anilla *f* curtain ring; (*en la gimnasia*) ring; hoop

anillo *m* ring; cigar band; **anillo de compromiso** or **de pedida** engagement ring; **anillo sigilar** signet ring

ánima *f* soul; (*de arma de fuego*) bore

animación *f* animation; liveliness; bustle, movement

anima·do -**da** *adj* animated, lively

animador *m* (*de un café-cantante*) master of ceremonies

animal *adj & m* animal

animar *tr* to enliven; to encourage; to strengthen; to drive || *ref* to take heart, feel encouraged

ánimo *m* mind, spirit; courage, valor, energy; attention, thought

animosidad *f* animosity, ill will

animo·so -**sa** *adj* brave, courageous; spirited; ready, disposed

aniña·do -**da** *adj* babyish, childish

anión *m* anion

aniquilar *tr* to annihilate, destroy || *ref* to be annihilated; to decline, waste away; to be humbled

anís *m* anise; anise-flavored brandy

aniversa·rio -**ria** *adj & m* anniversary

anoche *adv* last night

anochecer *m* nightfall, dusk || *v* §22 *intr* to grow dark; to arrive or happen at nightfall; to end the day; to go to sleep || *ref* to get dark; to get cloudy; (coll) to slip away

anochecida *f* nightfall, dusk

anodi·no -**na** *adj* innocuous, ineffective, harmless

ánodo *m* anode

anomalía *f* anomaly

anóma·lo -**la** *adj* anomalous

anonadar *tr* to annihilate, destroy; to overwhelm; to humble

anóni·mo -**ma** *adj* anonymous || *m* anonymity; **guardar** or **conservar el anónimo** to preserve one's anonymity

anormal *adj* abnormal

anotar *tr* to annotate; to note, jot down; to point out

anquilosa·do -**da** *adj* stiff-jointed; old-fashioned

ánsar *m* goose; wild goose

ansia *f* anxiety, anguish; eagerness; **ansias** (Ven) nausea

ansiar §77 & *regular tr* to long for, yearn for || *intr* to be madly in love

ansiedad *f* anxiety, worry; pain

ansio·so -**sa** *adj* anxious; anguished; longing; covetous

ant. *abbr* **anticuado**

anta *f* elk

antagonismo *m* antagonism

antaño *adv* last year; of yore, long ago

antárti·co -**ca** *adj* antarctic

ante *prep* before, in the presence of; in front of; at, with || *m* elk; buff

antea·do -**da** *adj* buff; (Mex) damaged, shopworn

anteanoche *adv* the night before last

anteayer *adv* the day before yesterday

antebrazo *m* forearm

antecámara *f* antechamber, anteroom

antecedente *adj* antecedent || *m* antecedent; **antecedentes** antecedents

anteceder *tr* to precede, to go before

antece·sor -**sora** *mf* predecessor; ancestor

antedatar *tr* to antedate

antedi·cho -**cha** *adj* aforesaid, above-mentioned

antelación *f* previousness, anticipation

antemano — **de antemano** in advance, beforehand

antena *f* (ent) antenna; (rad) antenna, aerial; **en antena** on the air; **llevar a las antenas** to put on the air

antenombre *m* title, honorific

anteojera *f* spectacle case; blinker, blinder

anteojo *m* eyeglass; spyglass; **anteojos** eyeglasses, spectacles; binoculars; blinkers

antepasa·do -da *adj* before last || **antepasados** *mpl* ancestors

antepecho *m* railing, guardrail; parapet; window sill

antepenúltima *f* antepenult

anteponer §54 *tr* to place in front; to prefer

anteportada *f* half title, bastard title

anteportal *m* porch, vestibule

antepuerta *f* portière

antepuerto *m* entrance to a mountain pass; (naut) outer harbor

anterior *adj* front; previous; earlier

antes *adv* before; sooner, soonest; rather; previously; **antes bien** rather; on the contrary; **antes de** before; **antes (de) que** before; **cuanto antes** as soon as possible

antesala *f* antechamber; (*p.ej., de médico*) waiting room; **hacer antesala** to dance attendance

antiaére·o -a *adj* anti-aircraft

antiartísti·co -ca *adj* inartistic

antibéli·co -ca *adj* antiwar

anticartel *adj* antitrust

anticientífi·co -ca *adj* unscientific

anticipación *f* preparation, anticipation; **con anticipación** in advance

anticipa·do -da *adj* future; advance; **por anticipado** in advance

anticipar *tr* to anticipate, hasten; to move ahead || *ref* to happen early; **anticiparse a** to anticipate, to get ahead of

anticipo *m* anticipation; advance payment, down payment; retaining fee

anticoncepti·vo -va *adj* & *m* contraceptive

anticongelante *m* antifreeze

anticonstitucional *adj* unconstitutional

anticua·do -da *adj* antiquated; old-fashioned; obsolete

anticua·rio -ria *adj* antiquarian || *mf* antiquarian, antiquary; antique dealer

anticuerpo *m* antibody

antideporti·vo -va *adj* unsportsmanlike

antiderrapante *adj* nonskid

antideslizante *adj* nonskid

antideslumbrante *adj* antiglare

antidetonante *adj* & *m* antiknock

antídoto *m* antidote

antieconómi·co -ca *adj* uneconomic(al)

antier *adv* (coll) the day before yesterday

antiesclavista *adj* antislavery || *mf* abolitionist

anti-faz *m* (*pl* **-faces**) veil, mask

antífona *f* anthem

antigás *adj invar* gas (*e.g., mask, shelter*)

antigramatical *adj* ungrammatical

antigualla *f* antique; (coll) relic, antique; (coll) has-been

antiguar §10 *intr* & *ref* to attain seniority

antigüedad *f* antiquity; seniority; (*mueble u otro objeto de arte antiguos*) antique; **antigüedades** antiquities; antiques

anti·guo -gua *adj* old; ancient; antique; former || *mf* veteran; senior

antihigiéni·co -ca *adj* unsanitary

antílope *m* antelope

antilla·no -na *adj* & *mf* West Indian **Antillas** *fpl* Antilles

antimonio *m* antimony

antiobre·ro -ra *adj* antilabor

antiparras *spl* (coll) spectacles

antipatía *f* dislike, antipathy

antipáti·co -ca *adj* disagreeable, uncongenial

antipatrióti·co -ca *adj* unpatriotic

antiproyectil *adj* antimissile

antirresbaladi·zo -za *adj* nonskid

antisemíti·co -ca *adj* anti-Semitic

antisépti·co -ca *adj* & *m* antiseptic

antisono·ro -ra *adj* soundproof

antisoviéti·co -ca *adj* anti-Soviet

antitanque *adj* antitank

antíte·sis *f* (*pl* **-sis**) antithesis

antitoxina *f* antitoxin

antojadi·zo -za *adj* capricious, whimsical

antojar *ref* to seem; to fancy; to seem likely; to have a notion to + *inf*; to take a fancy to + *inf*

antojo *m* caprice, fancy, whim; snap judgment; birthmark; **antojos** moles, warts; **a su antojo** as one pleases

antología *f* anthology

antónimo *m* antonym

antorcha *f* torch; **antorcha a soplete** blowtorch

antracita *f* anthracite

ántrax *m* anthrax

antro *m* cave, cavern; (fig) den

antropología *f* anthropology

antruejo *m* carnival

anual *adj* annual

anualidad *f* annuity; year's pay; annual occurrence

anuario *m* yearbook; directory; bulletin, catalogue; **anuario telefónico** telephone directory

anublar *tr* to cloud; to dim, darken; to blight, to wither || *ref* to become cloudy; to be withered; (*las esperanzas de uno*) to fade away

anudar *tr* to tie, fasten, knot; to unite; to resume || *ref* to get knotted; to be united; to fade away, to wilt, to fail

anuente *adj* consenting

anular *tr* to annul; to nullify; to remove, to discharge || *ref* to be passed over

anunciar *tr* to announce; to advertise || *intr* to advertise

anunciante *mf* advertiser

anuncio *m* announcement; advertisement

anverso *m* obverse

anzuelo *m* fishhook; **picar en el anzuelo** or **tragar el anzuelo** to swallow the bait, swallow the hook

añadi·do -da adj additional ‖ m false hair, switch

añadidura f addition; extra weight, extra measure; **de añadidura** extra, in the bargain; **por añadidura** besides

añadir tr to add; to increase

añafil m straight Moorish trumpet

añagaza f bird call; decoy, lure; trap, trick

añe·jo -ja adj aged; stale; musty, rancid

añicos mpl bits, pieces; **hacer añicos** to tear to pieces, to break to pieces; **hacerse añicos** (coll) to wear oneself out

añil m indigo; bluing

añilar tr to dye with indigo; (la ropa blanca) to blue

año m year; **año bisiesto** leap year; **año económico** fiscal year; **año lectivo** school year; **año luz** (pl **años luz**) light-year; **años** birthday; **cumplir . . . años** to be . . . years old

añoranza f longing, sorrow

añorar tr to long for, to sorrow for; to grieve over ‖ intr to yearn; to sorrow, to grieve

año·so -sa adj aged, old

aojada f (Col) skylight; (Col) transom

aojar tr to cast the evil eye on, to jinx

aojo m evil eye, jinx

aovar intr to lay eggs

ap. abbr **aparte, apóstol**

apabilar tr to trim

apabullar tr (coll) to mash, crush; (coll) to squelch

apacentar §2 tr & ref to pasture, to graze; to feed

apacible adj gentle, mild; calm

apaciguamiento m pacification, appeasement

apaciguar §10 tr to pacify, to appease ‖ ref to calm down

apachurrar tr to crush, squash, mash

apadrinar tr to sponsor; to act as godfather for; to back, support; to second

apagabron·cas m (pl **-cas**) bouncer

apagador m extinguisher; (de piano) damper

apagaincen·dios m (pl **-dios**) fire extinguisher

apagar §44 tr to extinguish, to put out; (la luz, la radio) to turn off; (la cal) to slake; (el sonido) to damp, to muffle; (el fuego del enemigo) to silence; (la sed) to quench; (el dolor) to deaden ‖ ref to go out; to subside, calm down, fade away

apagón m blackout

apalabrar tr to bespeak; to consider ‖ ref to agree

apalancar §73 tr to raise with a lever or crowbar

apalear tr to shovel; to beat; to pile up

apandar tr (coll) to steal

apantallar tr (elec) to shield, to screen; (Am) to dazzle, amaze

apañar tr to grasp; to pick up; to steal; to repair, to mend; (coll) to wrap up ‖ ref (coll) to be handy

apañuscar §73 tr (coll) to crumple, to

rumple; (coll) to steal; (CAm, Col, Ven) to jam, to crowd

aparador m sideboard, buffet; showcase; workshop

aparar tr to prepare; to adorn; to block; (las manos, la falda, el pañuelo, la capa) to hold out

aparato m apparatus; ostentation, show; exaggeration; radio set; television set; telephone; airplane; camera; bandage, application; (theat) scenery, properties; **aparato auditivo** hearing aid; **aparato de relojería** clockwork; **aparatos sanitarios** bathroom fixtures; **ponerse al aparato** to go or to come to the phone

aparato·so -sa adj showy, pompous, ostentatious

aparcamiento m parking; parking space

aparcar §44 tr & intr to park

aparcería f partnership, sharecropping

aparce·ro -ra mf partner, sharecropper; (Arg) customer

aparear tr to pair, to match; to mate ‖ ref to pair; to mate

aparecer §22 intr & ref to appear; to show up

aparecido m ghost, specter

aparejador m builder

aparejar tr to prepare; to prime, to size; to harness

aparejo m preparation; harness, set, kit; priming, sizing; (mas) bond; **aparejos** tools, implements, equipment

aparentar tr to feign, pretend; to look, to look to be

aparente adj apparent, seeming; evident; right, proper

aparición f apparition

apariencia f appearance, aspect; sign, indication; **salvar las apariencias** to save face

aparqueamiento m parking

aparquear tr & intr to park

aparqueo m parking

aparragar §44 ref (Am) to crouch, to squat; (CAm) to loll, to sprawl

apartadero m siding, side track; turnout

aparta·do -da adj distant, remote; aloof; (camino) side, back; different ‖ m side room; post-office box; vocabulary entry; section

apartamento m apartment, apartment house

apartar tr to take aside; to separate; to push away; to shunt; (el ganado) to sort ‖ ref to separate; to move away, keep away, stand aside; to withdraw; to get divorced; to give up

aparte adv apart, aside; **aparte de** apart from ‖ prep apart from ‖ m (theat) aside

apasiona·do -da adj passionate; devoted, tender, loving; sore

apasionar tr to impassion, appeal deeply to; to afflict ‖ ref to become impassioned; to be stirred up; to fall madly in love

apatía f apathy

apáti·co -ca *adj* apathetic

apatusco *m* (coll) ornament, finery

apdo. *abbr* **apartado**

apeadero *m* horse block; flag stop, wayside station; platform; temporary quarters

apear *tr* to help dismount, to help down; to bring down; to remove; to overcome; to prop up ‖ *ref* to dismount, get off; to back down; to stop, to put up

apechugar §44 *intr* to push with the chest; **apechugar con** (coll) to make the best of

apedazar §60 *tr* to mend, to patch; to cut or tear to pieces

apedrear *tr* to stone; to stone to death; to pit; to speckle ‖ *intr* to hail ‖ *ref* to be damaged by hail; to be pitted

apegar §44 *ref* to become attached, grow fond

apego *m* attachment, fondness

apelación *f* (coll) medical consultation; (coll) remedy, help; (law) appeal

apelar *intr* to appeal, make an appeal; to have recourse; to refer

apeldar *tr* — **apeldarlas** (coll) to flee, run away

apelmazar §60 *tr* to squeeze, compress ‖ *ref* to cake

apelotonar *tr* to form into a ball ‖ *ref* to form a ball; to curl up

apellidar *tr* to call, to name; to proclaim

apellido *m* name; surname, last name, family name; **apellido de soltera** maiden name

apenar *tr* & *ref* to grieve

apenas *adv* hardly, scarcely; **apenas si** hardly, scarcely ‖ *conj* no sooner, as soon as

apéndice *m* appendage; (anat) appendix

apendicitis *f* appendicitis

apercancar §73 *ref* (Chile) to get moldy, to mildew

apercibir *tr* to prepare; to provide; to warn; to perceive; (coll) to collect ‖ *ref* to get ready; to be provided; **apercibirse de** to notice

apergaminar *ref* (coll) to dry up, to become yellow and wrinkled

aperitivo *m* appetizer

aperla·do -da *adj* pearly

apero *m* tools, equipment, outfit; (Am) riding gear

aperrear *tr* to set the dogs on; to harass, plague, pester

apersogar §44 *tr* to tether

apersona·do -da *adj* — **bien apersonado** presentable; **mal apersonado** unpresentable

apersonar *ref* to appear in person; to have an interview

apertura *f* opening

apesadumbrar or **apesarar** *tr* & *ref* to grieve

apestar *tr* to infect with the plague; to corrupt; (coll) to sicken, to nauseate; to infest ‖ *intr* to stink ‖ *ref* to be infected with the plague

apesto·so -sa *adj* stinking, foul-smelling; pestilent; sickening

apetecer §22 *tr* to hunger for, to thirst for, to crave

apetecible *adj* desirable, tempting

apetencia *f* hunger, appetite, craving

apetito *m* appetite

apetito·so -sa *adj* tasty; tempting; gourmand

ápex *m* apex

apiadar *tr* to move to pity; to take pity on ‖ *ref* to have pity

ápice *m* apex; bit, whit; crux; **estar en los ápices de** (coll) to be up in

apilar *tr* & *ref* to pile, to pile up

apimpollar *ref* to sprout, to put forth shoots

apiñar *tr* & *ref* to crowd, to jam

apio *m* celery

apisonadora *f* road roller

apisonar *tr* to tamp; to roll

aplacar §73 *tr* to placate, appease, pacify; (*la sed*) to quench

aplanar *tr* to smooth, make even; (coll) to astonish ‖ *ref* to collapse; to become discouraged

aplanchar *tr* to iron

aplanetizar §60 *intr* to land on another planet

aplastar *tr* to flatten, crush, smash; (coll) to dumbfound

aplaudir *tr* & *intr* to applaud

aplauso *m* applause; **aplausos** applause

aplazar §60 *tr* to postpone; to convene; to summon

aplicación *f* appliance, application; diligence

aplica·do -da *adj* industrious, studious; applied

aplicar §73 *tr* to apply; to attribute ‖ *ref* to apply; to apply oneself

aplomar *tr* to plumb; to make straight or vertical ‖ *intr* to be vertical ‖ *ref* to collapse; (Chile) to be embarrassed; (Mex) to be slow, be backward

aplomo *m* aplomb, poise, self-possession; gravity

apoca·do -da *adj* diffident, timid, irresolute; humble, lowly

apocar §73 *tr* to cramp, contract; to narrow; to humble, belittle

apodar *tr* to nickname; to make fun of

apodera·do -da *adj* empowered, authorized ‖ *m* proxy; attorney

apoderar *tr* to empower, to authorize ‖ *ref* — **apoderarse de** to seize, grasp; to take possession of

apodo *m* nickname

apofoní· *f* ablaut

apogeo *m* apogee; (fig) height, apogee

apolilla·do -da *adj* moth-eaten, mothy

apolilladura *f* moth hole

apolillar *tr* (*la polilla, p.ej., las ropas*) to eat ‖ *ref* to become moth-eaten

apología *f* eulogy

apoltronar *ref* to loaf around; to loll, to sprawl

apontizaje *m* deck-landing

apontizar §60 *intr* to deck-land

apoplejía *f* apoplexy

apopléti·co -ca *adj* & *mf* apoplectic

aporcar §73 *tr* (*las hortalizas*) to hill

aporrear tr to beat, to club, to cudgel; to annoy ‖ ref to drudge, to slave

aportación f contribution; dowry

aportar tr to contribute; to bring; to lead; (como dote) to bring ‖ intr to show up; to reach port

aporte m contribution

aposentar tr to put up, to lodge ‖ ref to take lodging

aposento m lodging; room; inn

apostadero m stand, post; naval station

apostar tr to post, to station ‖ §61 tr to bet, to wager ‖ intr to bet; to compete

apostilla f note, comment

apóstol m apostle

apóstrofe m & f apostrophe (words addressed to absent person)

apóstrofo m apostrophe (written sign)

apostura f neatness, spruceness; bearing, carriage

apoyabra·zos m (pl -zos) armrest

apoyali·bros m (pl -bros) book end

apoyar tr to support, hold up; to lean, rest; to abet, back ‖ intr & ref to lean, rest, be supported

apoyatura f (mus) grace note

apoyo m support, prop; backing, approval

apreciable adj appreciable; estimable

apreciación f appraisal

apreciar tr to appreciate; to appraise; to esteem

aprecio m appreciation, esteem

aprehender tr to apprehend, catch; to think, conceive

aprehensión f apprehension

aprehensi·vo -va adj apprehensive

aprehensor m captor

apremiar tr to press, urge; to compel, force; to hurry; to harass; (a un deudor) to dun ‖ intr to be urgent

apremio m pressure; urgency; compulsion; oppression; surtax for late payment. (demanda de pago) dun

aprender tr & intr to learn

apren·diz diza mf apprentice; **aprendiz de imprenta** printer's devil

aprendizaje m apprenticeship; **pagar el aprendizaje** (coll) to pay for one's inexperience

aprensar tr to press; to oppress

aprensión f apprehension; misgiving, prejudice

aprensi·vo -va adj apprehensive

apresar tr to grasp, to seize; to capture

aprestador m primer

aprestar tr to prepare; (tejidos) to process; to prime; to size ‖ ref to get ready

apresto m preparation; equipment; priming; sizing

apresurar tr & ref to hurry, to hasten

apretadera f strap, rope; **apretaderas** (coll) pressure

apreta·do -da adj compact, tight; close, intimate; dense, thick; difficult, dangerous; (coll) mean, stingy; **estar muy apretado** (coll) to be in a bad way

apretar §2 tr to tighten; to squeeze; to

pinch; to hug; to harass, to importune; to afflict, to beset; (un botón) to press; (los puños) to clench; (los dientes) to grit; (la mano) to shake ‖ intr to pinch; to insist; to get worse; to push hard, press forward; **apretar a correr** to start running; **apretar con** (coll) to close in on ‖ ref to grieve, be distressed; to crowd

apretón m pressure, squeeze; struggle; dash, run; **apretón de manos** handshake

apretura f crush, jam; tightness; fix, trouble; need, want

aprietarropa m clothespin

aprieto m crush, jam; fix

aprisa adv fast, quickly

aprisco m sheepfold

aprisionar tr to imprison; to bind, tie; to shackle

aprobación f approbation, approval; pass, passing grade

aproba·do -da adj excellent ‖ m pass

aprobar §61 tr & intr to approve; to pass

aprontar tr to hand over without delay; to expedite

apropia·do -da adj appropriate, fitting, proper

apropiar tr to hand over; to fit, adapt ‖ ref to appropriate; to preëmpt

aprovechable adj available, usable

aprovecha·do -da adj thrifty; stingy; diligent; well-spent ‖ mf opportunist

aprovechar tr to make good use of, take advantage of; (una caída de agua) to harness ‖ intr to be useful; to progress, improve ‖ ref — **aprovecharse de** to avail oneself of, to take advantage of

aprovisionar tr to provision, supply, furnish

aproxima·do -da adj approximate, rough

aproximar tr to bring near; to approximate ‖ ref to come near; to approximate

aptitud f aptitude; suitability

ap·to -ta adj apt; suitable

apuesta f bet, wager

apues·to -ta adj neat, spruce, elegant ‖ f see **apuesta**

apulgarar ref to become mildewed

apuntador m (theat) prompter

apuntalar tr to prop up, underpin

apuntar tr to point; to point at; to aim; to aim at; to take note of; to sharpen; to stitch, to darn, to patch; to correct; to prompt; to stake, to put up; (theat) to prompt ‖ intr to begin to appear; to dawn ‖ ref (el vino) to begin to turn sour; to register; (coll) to get tipsy

apunte m note; rough sketch; stake; (coll) rogue, rascal; (theat) cue

apuñalar tr & intr to stab

apuñear tr to punch

apura·do -da adj needy, hard up; difficult, dangerous; (coll) hurried, rushed

apurar tr to purify, refine; to clear up, verify; to finish; to drain, use up, exhaust; to hurry, press; to annoy ‖ *ref* to worry, grieve; to exert oneself, to strive

apuro *m* need, want; grief, sorrow; (Am) haste, urgency; **apuros** financial embarrassment

aquejar *tr* to grieve, afflict

aquel, aquella *adj dem* (*pl* **aquellos, aquellas**) that, that . . . yonder

aquél, aquélla *pron dem* (*pl* **aquéllos, aquéllas**) that; that one, that one yonder; the one; the former ‖ *m* (coll) charm, appeal

aquelarre *m* witches' Sabbath

aquello *pron dem* that; that thing, that matter

aquende *adv* on this side ‖ *prep* on this side of

aquerenciar *ref* to become fond or attached

aquí *adv* here; **aquí dentro** in here; **de aquí en adelante** from now on; **por aquí** this way

aquiescencia *f* acquiescence

aquietar *tr* to quiet, to calm

aquilatar *tr* to assay; to check; to refine

Aquiles *m* Achilles

aquilón *m* north wind

ara *f* altar; altar slab; **en aras de** for the sake of

árabe *adj* Arab, Arabian; (archit) Moresque ‖ *mf* Arab, Arabian ‖ *m* (idioma) Arabic

Arabia, la Arabia

arábi·go -ga *adj* Arabian, Arabic ‖ *m* (idioma) Arabic; **estar en arábigo** (coll) to be Greek

aracanga *f* macaw

arado *m* plow

Aragón *m* Aragon

arago·nés -nesa *adj & mf* Aragonese

arancel *m* tariff

arancela·rio -ria *adj* tariff, customs

arándano *m* whortleberry; **arándano agrio** cranberry

arandela *f* bobèche; (mach) washer

araña *f* spider; chandelier

arañar *tr* to scratch; to scrape; (coll) to scrape together

arañazo *m* scratch

araño *m* scratching

aráquida *f* peanut

arar *tr* to plow

arbitraje *m* arbitration

arbitrar *tr & intr* to arbitrate; to referee; to umpire

arbitra·rio -ria *adj* arbitrary

arbitrio *m* free will; means, ways; **arbitrios** excise taxes

arbitrista *mf* wild eyed dreamer

árbi·tro -tra *mf* arbiter; referee ‖ *m* umpire

árbol *m* tree; axle, shaft; **árbol del caucho** rubber plant; **árbol de levas** camshaft; **árbol de mando** drive shaft; **árbol de Navidad** Christmas tree; **árbol motor** drive shaft

arbola·do -da *adj* wooded; (mar) high ‖ *m* woodland

arboleda *f* grove

arbollón *m* sewer, drain

arbotante *m* flying buttress

arbusto *m* shrub

arca *f* chest, coffer; tank; ark; **arca de agua** water tower; **arca de la alianza** ark of the covenant; **arca de Noé** ark, Noah's ark

arcada *f* arcade; archway; stroke of bow; **arcadas** retching

arcai·co -ca *adj* archaic

arcaísmo *m* archaism

arcaizante *adj* obsolescent

arcángel *m* archangel

arca·no -na *adj & m* secret

arcar §73 *tr* to arch

arce *m* maple tree

arcilla *f* clay; **arcilla figulina** potter's clay

arco *m* arch; (de cuna o mecedor) rocker; (elec, geom) arc; (mus) bow; **arco iris** rainbow; **arco triunfal** triumphal arch; memorial arch

arcón *m* large chest; bin, bunker

archiduque *m* archduke

archienemigo *m* archenemy

archipiélago *m* archipelago; (coll) mass, entanglement ‖ **Archipiélago** *m* Aegean Sea

archiva·dor -dora *mf* file clerk ‖ *m* filing cabinet; letter file

archivar *tr* to file; to file away; (coll) to hide away

archivero *m* city clerk

archivo *m* archives; files; filing; (Col) office

ardentía *f* heartburn; (en las olas de la mar) phosphorescence

arder *tr* to burn ‖ *intr* to burn; to blaze; **estar que arde** to be coming to a head ‖ *ref* to burn up

ardid *m* artifice, trick, wile

ardi·do -da *adj* burnt-up; bold, intrepid; (Am) angry

ardiendo *adj invar* burning

ardiente *adj* ardent; fiery, passionate; burning, hot

ardilla *f* squirrel; **ardilla de tierra** gopher; **ardilla ladradora** prairie dog; **ardilla listada** chipmunk

ardillón *m* gopher

ardite *m* old Spanish coin of little value; **no me importa un ardite** I don't care a hang; **no valer un ardite** (coll) to be not worth a straw

ardor *m* ardor; eagerness, fervor, zeal; vehemence; courage, dash

ardoro·so -sa *adj* fiery, enthusiastic; balky, restive

ar·duo -dua *adj* arduous, difficult

área *f* area; small plot

arena *f* sand; grit; arena; **arena movediza** quicksand; **arenas** arena; (pathol) stones

arenal *m* sandy place; quicksand

arenga *f* harangue

arengar *tr & intr* to harangue

arenis·co -ca *adj* sandy, gritty; sand ‖ *f* sandstone

areno·so -sa *adj* sandy

arenque *m* herring

areómetro *m* hydrometer

arepa *f* (Am) corn griddle cake

arete *m* eardrop, earring

arfada *f* (naut) pitching

arfar *intr* (naut) to pitch

argadijo or **argadillo** *m* bobbin, reel; (coll) restless fellow

argado *m* prank, trick, artifice

argamasa *f* mortar

argamasar *tr* to mortar, to plaster; (*los materiales de construcción*) to mix

árgana *f* (mach) crane; **árganas** panniers

Argel *f* Algiers

Argelia *f* Algeria

argeli·no -na *adj & mf* Algerian

argentar *tr* to silver

argenti·no -na *adj & mf* Argentine, Argentinean || **la Argentina** Argentina, the Argentine

argolla *f* large iron ring; (*que se pone en la nariz a un animal*) ring; (Am) engagement ring

argonauta *m* Argonaut

argucia *f* subtlety; trick

argüir §6 *tr* to argue, argue for; to prove; to accuse || *ref* to argue, to dispute

argumenta·dor -dora *adj* argumentative || *mf* arguer

argumentar *tr* to argue for; to prove || *intr & ref* to argue, dispute

argumento *m* argument

aria *f* (mus) aria

aridez *f* aridity, dryness

ári·do -da *adj* arid; (*aburrido, falto de interés*) dry

ariete *m* battering ram; **ariete hidráulico** hydraulic ram

arimez *m* projection

a·rio -ria *adj & mf* Aryan || *f* see **aria**

aris·co -ca *adj* churlish, surly, evasive; (*caballo*) vicious

arista *f* edge; (*intersección de dos planos*) ridge; (*del grano de trigo*) beard; **arista de encuentro** (archit) groin

aristocracia *f* aristocracy

aristócrata *mf* aristocrat

aristocráti·co -ca *adj* aristocratic

Aristóteles *m* Aristotle

aristotéli·co -ca *adj & mf* Aristotelian

aritméti·co -ca *adj* arithmetical || *mf* arithmetician || *f* arithmetic

arlequín *m* harlequin

arma *f* arm, weapon; **alzarse en armas** to rise up, rebel; **arma blanca** steel blade; **arma corta** pistol; **arma de fuego** firearm; **jugar a las armas** to fence; **sobre las armas** under arms

armada *f* fleet, armada; navy

armadía *f* raft, float

armadijo *m* trap, snare

arma·do -da *adj* armed; (*hormigón*) reinforced || *f* see **armada**

arma·dor -dora *mf* assembler || *m* recruiter of fishermen and whalers

armadura *f* armor; framework; skeleton; (elec) armature; (*de imán*) keeper

armamento *m* armament

armar *tr* to arm; (*un arma*) to load; (*una bayoneta*) to fix; to mount, assemble; to build; to equip; (*el hormigón*) to reinforce; (*una nave*) to fit out; (*caballero*) to dub; (coll) to start, stir up; **armarla** (coll) to start

a row || *ref* to arm oneself; to get ready; (Am) to balk

armario *m* closet, wardrobe; **armario botiquín** medicine cabinet; **armario de luna** wardrobe with mirror; **armario frigorífico** refrigerator

armatoste *m* hulk

armazón *f* frame; assemblage; skeleton

armella *f* screw eye, eyebolt

arme·nio -nia *adj & mf* Armenian || **Armenia** *f* Armenia

armería *f* arms shop; arms museum; arms

armero *m* gunsmith; (*para las armas*) rack

armiño *m* ermine

armisticio *m* armistice

armonía *f* harmony

armóni·co -ca *adj & m* harmonic || *f* harmonica; **armónica de boca** mouth organ

armonio·so -sa *adj* harmonious

armonizar §60 *tr & intr* to harmonize

arnés *m* armor, coat of mail; harness; **arneses** harness, trappings; outfit, equipment; accessories

aro *m* hoop; rim; **aro de émbolo** piston ring

aroma *m* aroma, fragrance

aromáti·co -ca *adj* aromatic

arpa *f* harp

arpar *tr* to claw, scratch; to tear, rend

arpegio *m* arpeggio

arpeo *m* grappling iron

arpía *f* harpy; (coll) shrew, jade

arpillera *f* burlap, sackcloth

arpista *mf* harpist

arpón *m* harpoon

arponear *tr & intr* to harpoon

arqueada *f* (mus) bow

arquear *tr* to arch; (*la lana*) to beat; (*una nave*) to gauge; to audit || *intr* to retch || *ref* to bow

arqueología *f* archeology

arquería *f* arcade

arquero *m* archer, bowman

arquitecto *m* architect

arquitectóni·co -ca *adj* architectural

arquitectura *f* architecture

arrabal *m* suburb; **arrabales** outskirts

arracada *f* earring with pendant

arracimar *ref* to cluster, to bunch

arraiga·do -da *adj* deep-rooted; property-owning, landed

arraigar §44 *tr* to establish, to strengthen || *intr* to take root || *ref* to take root; to become settled

arraigo *m* taking root; stability; property, real estate

arramblar *tr* to cover with sand or gravel; to sweep away

arrancadero *m* starting point

arrancar §73 *tr* to root up, pull out, pull up; to snatch, to wrest; (*lágrimas*) to draw forth || *intr* to start; to set sail; (coll) to leave; to originate

arranque *m* pull; fit, impulse; jerk; sudden start; sally, outburst; (aut) start, starter; **arranque a mano** (aut) hand cranking; **arranque automático** (aut) self-starter

arrapiezo *m* rag, tatter; (coll) whippersnapper

arras *fpl* earnest money, pledge; dowry

arrasar *tr* to level; to wreck, to demolish; to fill to the brim || *intr* to clear up || *ref* to clear up; to fill up

arrastra-do -da *adj* (coll) mean, crooked || *mf* (coll) wretch, crook

arrastrar *tr* to drag, drag along; to drag down; to impel || *intr* to drag, to trail; to crawl, creep || *ref* to drag, to trail; to crawl, creep; to drag on; to cringe

arrastre *m* drag; crawl; washout; influence; haulage; (*influencia política y social*) (Cuba, Mex) drag

arrayán *m* myrtle

arre *interj* gee!, get up!

arreador *m* muleteer; (SAm) whip

arrear *tr* to drive || *intr* (coll) to hurry || *ref* to lose all one's money

arrebata-do -da *adj* rash, reckless; (*color del rostro*) flushed, ruddy

arrebatar *tr* to snatch; to carry away; to attract; to move, to stir || *ref* to be carried away, to be overcome

arrebatiña *f* scuffle, scramble; andar a la arrebatiña (coll) to scramble

arrebato *m* rage, fury; ecstasy, rapture

arrebol *m* (*de las nubes*) red; (*de las mejillas*) rosiness; (*afeite*) rouge; arreboles red clouds

arrebozar $60 *tr* to muffle || *ref* to muffle one's face

arrebujar *tr* to jumble together; to wrap || *ref* to wrap oneself up

arreciar *intr & ref* to grow worse; to become more violent; to grow stronger

arrecife *m* stone-paved road; dike; reef; arrecife de coral coral reef

arredrar *tr* to drive back; to frighten || *ref* to draw back; to shrink; to be frightened

arregazar $60 *tr* to tuck up

arreglar *tr* to adjust, regulate, settle; to arange; to fix, repair || *ref* to adjust, settle; to arrange; to conform; arreglárselas (coll) to manage, to make out

arreglo *m* adjustment, regulation; settlement; arrangement; order, rule; agreement; con arreglo a in accordance with

arregostar *ref* (coll) to take a liking

arregosto *m* (coll) liking, taste

arrellanar *ref* to loll, to sprawl; to like one's work

arremangar *tr* (*las mangas*) to turn up; (*la ropa*) to tuck up || *ref* to turn up one's sleeves; to tuck up one's dress; (coll) to take a firm stand

arremeter *tr* to attack, assail; (*un caballo*) to spur || *intr* to attack; to be offensive to look at; arremeter contra to light into, sail into

arremetida *f* attack; (*de un caballo*) sudden start; push; short, wild run

arremolinar *ref* to crowd, mill around; to whirl

arrendajo *m* (orn) jay; (coll) mimic

arrendar §2 *tr* to rent; (*una caballería*) to tie || *ref* to rent, be rented

arreo *m* adornment; (SAm) drove; arreos harness, trappings

arrepenti-do -da *adj* repentant || *mf* penitent

arrepentimiento *m* repentance

arrepentir §68 *ref* to repent, be repentant; arrepentirse de (*p.ej., un pecado*) to repent

arrequives *mpl* finery; (coll) attendant circumstances

arresta-do -da *adj* bold, daring

arrestar *tr* to arrest || *ref* to rush boldly

arresto *m* arrest; boldness, daring; bajo arresto under arrest

arrezagar $44 *tr* to tuck up

arriada *f* flood

arriar §77 *tr* to flood; (naut) to lower, to strike; (naut) to slacken || *ref* to be flooded

arriba *adv* up, upward; above; upstairs; uptown; on top; arriba de up; de arriba abajo from top to bottom; com beginning to end; superciliously; más arriba farther up; río arriba upstream || *interj* up with . . . !

arribada *f* arrival (by sea); de arribada (naut) emergency

arribar *intr* to put into port; to arrive; (naut) to fall off to leeward; to recover, make a comeback

arribista *adj & mf* parvenu, upstart

arribo *m* arrival

arricete *m* shoal, bar

arriendo *m* rent, rental; lease

arriero *m* muleteer

arriesga-do -da *adj* dangerous, risky; bold, daring

arriesgar $44 *tr* to risk, jeopardize || *ref* to take a risk

arrimadillo *m* wainscot

arrimar *tr* to bring close, move up; (*un golpe*) to give; to abandon, neglect; to give up; to get rid of || *ref* to come close, move up; to snuggle up; to lean; to depend

arrinconar *tr* to corner; to put aside; to abandon, neglect; to get rid of || *ref* to live in seclusion

arrisca-do -da *adj* enterprising; brisk, spirited; craggy

arriscar §73 *tr* to risk || *ref* to take a risk; (*las reses*) to plunge over a cliff

arrisco *m* risk

arrivista *adj & mf* parvenu, upstart

arrizar §60 *tr* to reef

arroba *f* Spanish weight of about 25 pounds

arrobar *tr* to entrance, to enrapture || *ref* to be enraptured

arrobo *m* ecstasy, rapture

arroce-ro -ra *adj* rice || *mf* rice grower; rice merchant

arrocinar *tr* to bestialize || *ref* to become bestialized; to fall madly in love

arrodajar *ref* (CAm) to squat down with one's legs crossed

arrodillar *ref* to kneel, to kneel down

arrogancia *f* arrogance

arrogante *adj* arrogant
arrogar §44 *tr* to adopt ‖ *ref* to arrogate to oneself
arrojadi·zo -za *adj* for throwing, projectile
arroja·do -da *adj* bold, fearless, rash
arrojalla·mas *m* (*pl* -mas) flame thrower
arrojar *tr* to throw, to hurl; to emit; to bring forth; to yield ‖ *ref* to rush, rush forward
arrojo *m* boldness, fearlessness, rashness
arrollado *m* (elec) coil
arrolla·dor -dora *adj* sweeping, devastating
arrollamiento *m* winding
arrollar *tr* to roll; to roll up; to wind, to coil, (*al enemigo*) to rout; to dumbfound; (coll) to knock down, to run over
arropar *tr* to wrap, to wrap up ‖ *ref* to bundle up
arrope *m* grape syrup; honey syrup
arropía *f* taffy
arrostrar *tr* to face; to like ‖ *intr* — **arrostrar con** or **por** to face, to resist ‖ *ref* to rush into the fight
arroyada *f* gully; flood, freshet
arroyo *m* stream, brook; gutter; street; (*de lágrimas, sangre, etc.*) stream
arroz *m* rice
arrufar *tr* to sic, to incite
arruga *f* wrinkle; crease, rumple
arrugar §44 *tr* to wrinkle; to crease, rumple, (*la frente*) to knit ‖ *ref* to wrinkle; to crease, rumple; to shrink, shrivel
arruinar *tr* to ruin ‖ *ref* to go to ruin
arrullar *tr* to sing to sleep, to lull to sleep; (coll) to court, to woo ‖ *intr* to coo ‖ *ref* to coo; (*las palomas*) to bill
arrullo *m* billing and cooing; lullaby
arrumaje *m* stowage; ballast
arrumar *tr* to stow ‖ *ref* to become overcast
arrumbar *tr* to cast aside, to neglect; to silence; (*una costa*) to determine the lay of ‖ *intr* (naut) to take bearings ‖ *ref* to get seasick; (naut) to take bearings
arsenal *m* arsenal, armory; dockyard, shipyard
arsénico *m* arsenic
art. *abbr* **artículo**
arte *m & f* art; trick; knack; fishing gear; **artes y oficios** arts and crafts; **bellas artes** fine arts; **no tener arte ni parte en** to have nothing to do with
artefacto *m* artifact; appliance, device, contrivance; **artefactos de alumbrado** lighting fixtures; **artefactos sanitarios** bathroom fixtures
artemisa *f* sagebrush
arteria *f* artery
artería *f* craftiness, cunning
arte·ro -ra *adj* crafty, cunning, sly
artesa *f* trough; Indian canoe
artesanía *f* craftsmanship
artesa·no -na *mf* artisan, craftsman ‖ *f* craftswoman

artesón *m* kitchen tub; coffer, caisson (in ceiling)
árti·co -ca *adj* arctic
articulación *f* articulation; (*de huesos*) joint; **articulación universal** universal joint
articular *tr* to articulate
articulista *mf* feature writer
artículo *m* article; item; joint; (*en un diccionario*) entry; **artículo de fondo** leader, editorial; **artículos de consumo** consumers' goods; **artículos de deporte** sporting goods; **artículos de primera necesidad** basic commodities; **artículos para caballeros** men's furnishings
artífice *mf* artificer; craftsman
artificial *adj* artificial
artificio *m* artifice; workmanship; appliance, device; cunning; trick, ruse
artificio·so -sa *adj* ingenious, skillful; cunning; scheming, deceptive
artilugio *m* (coll) contraption, jigger
artillería *f* artillery
artillero *m* artilleryman, gunner
artimaña *f* trap; (coll) trick, cunning
artista *mf* artist
artísti·co -ca *adj* artistic
artolas *fpl* mule chair, cacolet
artríti·co -ca *adj & mf* arthritic
artritis *f* arthritis
arúspice *m* diviner, soothsayer
arveja *f* vetch, tare; (Chile) pea
arzobispo *m* archbishop
arzón *m* saddletree; **arzón delantero** saddlebow; **arzón trasero** cantle
as *m* ace; **as de fútbol** football star; **as de la pantalla** movie star; **as del volante** speed king
asa *f* handle; juice; **en asas** with arms akimbo
asa·do -da *adj* roasted; **bien asado** well done, **poco asado** rare ‖ *m* roast
asador *m* spit
asadura *f* entrails
asalaria·do *mf* wage earner
asaltar *tr* to assail, to assault, to storm; to overtake, overcome
asalto *m* assault, attack; (box) round; (mil) storm; **tomar por asalto** to take by storm
asamblea *f* assembly
asar *tr* to roast ‖ *ref* to be burning up
asbesto *m* asbestos
ascendencia *f* ancestry
ascendente *adj* ascending; up
ascender §51 *tr* to promote ‖ *intr* to ascend, go up; to be promoted; **ascender a** to amount to
ascendiente *adj* ascending; up ‖ *mf* ancestor ‖ *m* ascendancy, upper hand
ascensión *f* ascension, ascent
ascenso *m* ascent; promotion
ascensor *m* elevator; freight elevator
ascensorista *mf* elevator operator
aseta *f* ascetic
ascéti·co -ca *adj* ascetic
asco *m* disgust, nausea, loathing; **dar asco** (coll) to turn the stomach; **estar hecho un asco** (coll) to be filthy; **hacer ascos de** (coll) to turn one's nose

up at; **ser un asco** (coll) to be contemptible; (coll) to be worthless

ascua f ember, live coal; **estar sobre ascuas** (coll) to be on needles and pins || **ascuas** interj (coll) ouch!

asea·do -da adj clean, neat, tidy

asear tr & ref to clean up, tidy up

asechamiento m or **asechanza** f snare, trap

asechar tr to set a trap for

asediar tr to besiege; to harass

asedio m siege

asegundar tr to repeat right away

aseguración f insurance policy

asegura·dor -dora mf insurer, underwriter

asegurar tr to fasten, secure; to assure; to assert; to seize; to imprison; (garantizar por un precio contra determinado accidente o pérdida) to insure || ref to make sure; to take out insurance

asemejar tr to make like; to compare; to resemble || ref to be similar

asenso m assent; **dar asenso a** to believe

asentada f sitting; **de una asentada** at one sitting

asentaderas fpl (coll) buttocks

asentadillas — a asentadillas sidesaddle

asenta·do -da adj sedate; stable || f see asentada

asentador m strap, razor strap

asentar §2 tr to seat; to place; to establish; to tamp down, to level; to hone, sharpen; to note down; (un golpe) to impart; (en la mente de uno) to impress; to affirm; to suppose || intr to be becoming || ref to sit down; to be established, to establish oneself; to settle

asentimiento m assent

asentir §68 intr to assent

aseo m cleanliness, neatness, tidiness; care; toilet

asépti·co -ca adj aseptic

aseptizar §60 tr to purify, make aseptic

asequible adj accessible, obtainable

aserción f assertion

aserradero m sawmill

aserra·dor -dora mf sawyer; (coll) fiddler || f power saw

aserraduras fpl sawdust

aserrar §2 tr to saw

aserrín m sawdust

aserto m assertion

asesinar tr to assassinate, to murder

asesinato m assassination, murder

asesi·no -na adj murderous || mf assassin, murderer

asesorar tr to advise || ref to seek advice; to get advice

asestar tr to aim; to shoot; (un golpe) to deal

aseveración f assertion, declaration

aseverar tr to assert, to declare

asfaltar tr to asphalt

asfalto m asphalt

asfixia f asphyxiation

asfixiar tr to asphyxiate

así adv so, thus; **así . . . como** both . . . and; **así como** as soon as; as well as;

así que as soon as; with the result that; **así y todo** even so, anyhow; **por decirlo así** so to speak; **y así sucesivamente** and so on

Asia f Asia; **el Asia Menor** Asia Minor

asiáti·co -ca adj & mf Asian, Asiatic

asidero m handle; occasion, pretext

asi·duo -dua adj assiduous; frequent, persistent

asiento m seat; site; (de un edificio) settling; (de una botella, una silla, etc.) bottom; sediment; list, roll; wisdom, maturity; **asiento de rejilla** cane seat; **asiento lanzable** (aer) ejection seat; **asientos** buttocks; **planchar el asiento** (Am) to be a wallflower; **tome Vd. asiento** have a seat

asignación f assignment; salary; allowance

asignar tr to assign

asignatura f course, subject

asila·do -da mf inmate

asilar tr to shelter; to place in an asylum; to silo || ref to take refuge; to be placed in an asylum

asilo m asylum; shelter, refuge; (para menesterosos) home; **asilo de huérfanos** orphan asylum; **asilo de locos** insane asylum; **asilo de pobres** poorhouse

asilla f fastener; collarbone; **asillas** shoulder pole

asimetría f asymmetry

asimilar tr to compare; to take in || intr to be alike || ref to assimilate; asimilarse a to resemble

asimismo adv also, likewise

asir §7 tr to grasp, seize || intr to take root || ref to take hold; to fight, to grapple. **asirse a** or **de** to cling to

Asiria f Assyria

asi·rio -ria adj & mf Assyrian

asistencia f attendance; assistence; reward; audience, persons present; welfare, social work; (Mex) sitting room, parlor; **asistencias** allowance, support

asistenta f charwoman, cleaning woman

asistente adj attendant; present || m assistant, helper; bystander, spectator, person present; (mil) orderly

asistir tr to assist, help; to attend; to serve, wait on || intr to be present; **asistir a** to be present at, to attend

asma f asthma

asna f she-ass, jenny ass; **asnas** rafters

asnal adj donkey; (coll) brutish

asno m ass, donkey, jackass

asociación f association

asocia·do -da adj associated; associate || mf associate, partner

asociar tr to associate; to take as partner || ref to become associated; to become a partner; to become partners

asolamiento m razing, destruction

asolar tr to parch, burn || ref to become parched || §61 tr to raze, destroy

asolear tr to sun || ref to bask; to get sunburned

asomar *tr* (*p.ej., la cabeza*) to show, to stick out ‖ *intr* to begin to show or appear; to show ‖ *ref* to show, to appear; to stick out; to get tipsy

asombradi·zo -za *adj* timid, shy

asombrar *tr* to shade; (*un color*) to darken; to frighten; to astonish, amaze ‖ *ref* to be frightened; to be astonished, be amazed

asombro *m* fright; astonishment

asombro·so -sa *adj* astonishing, amazing

asomo *m* mark, token, sign; appearance; **ni por asomo** nothing of the kind, not by a long shot

asordar *tr* to deafen

aspa *f* X-shaped figure; reel; (*de molino de viento*) wheel, vane; propeller blade

aspar *tr* to reel; to crucify; to annoy, harass ‖ *ref* to writhe; to take great pains

aspaviento *m* fuss, excitement

aspecto *m* aspect

aspereza *f* harshness; roughness; bitterness, sourness; gruffness

asperjar *tr* to sprinkle; to sprinkle with holy water

áspe·ro -ra *adj* harsh; rough; bitter; gruff

áspid *m* asp

aspirador *m* vacuum cleaner; **aspirador de gasolina** (aut) vacuum tank

aspirante *m* applicant, candidate; **aspirante a cabo** private first class; **aspirante de marina** midshipman

aspirar *tr* to suck in, draw in; to inhale ‖ *intr* to aspire; to inhale, to breathe in

aspirina *f* aspirin

asquear *tr* to loathe ‖ *ref* to be nauseated

asquero·so -sa *adj* disgusting, loathsome; nauseating; squeamish

asta *f* spear; shaft; flagpole, staff, mast; antler; (*de toro*) horn; **a media asta** at half-mast; **dejar en las astas del toro** (coll) to leave high and dry

asta·do -da *adj* horned ‖ *m* bull

ástato *m* astatine

aster *m* aster

asterisco *m* asterisk

astil *m* handle; shaft

astilla *f* chip, splinter

astillar *tr* & *ref* to chip, splinter

Astillejos *mpl* (astr) Castor and Pollux

astillero *m* dockyard, shipyard

astro *m* star, heavenly body; (fig) star, leading light

astrología *f* astrology

astronauta *m* astronaut

astronáuti·co -ca *adj* astronautic ‖ *f* astronautics

astronave *f* spaceship; **astronave tripulada** manned spaceship

astronomía *f* astronomy

astronómi·co -ca *adj* astronomic(al)

astróno·mo -ma *mf* astronomer

astro·so -sa *adj* ill-fated; vile, contemptible; (coll) ragged, shabby

astucia *f* cunning, craftiness; trick

asturia·no -na *adj* & *mf* Asturian

astu·to -ta *adj* astute, cunning; tricky

asueto *m* day off; (coll) leisure

asumir *tr* to assume, take on

asunción *f* assumption

asunto *m* subject, matter; affair, business; theme; **asuntos internacionales** world affairs

asurar *tr* to burn; to parch; to harass, worry

asurcar §73 *tr* to furrow, to plow

asustadi·zo -za *adj* scary, skittish

asustar *tr* to scare, frighten

atabal *m* kettledrum; timbrel

ataca·do -da *adj* irresolute, undecided; mean, stingy

atacar §73 *tr* to attack; to attach, fasten; to pack, jam; (*un barreno*) to tamp; to corner, to contradict ‖ *intr* to attack

ata·do -da *adj* timid, shy; weak, irresolute; insignificant; cramped ‖ *m* pack, bundle, roll

ataguía *f* cofferdam

atajar *tr* to stop, intercept, interrupt; to partition off ‖ *intr* to take a short cut ‖ *ref* to be abashed

atajo *m* short cut; (*en un escrito*) cut

atalaya *m* guard, lookout ‖ *f* watchtower; elevation

atalayar *tr* to watch from a watchtower; to spy on

atanquía *f* depilatory ointment

atañer §70 *tr* to concern

ataque *m* attack

atar *tr* to tie, fasten

ataracea *f* marquetry, inlaid work

atarantar *tr* to stun, daze

atardecer *m* late afternoon ‖ *v* §22 *intr* to draw toward evening; to happen in the late afternoon

atarea·do -da *adj* busy

atarear *tr* to give an assignment to; to overload with work ‖ *ref* to toil, to work hard, to keep busy

atarjea *f* sewer

atarugar §44 *tr* to peg, to wedge; to plug; to stuff, to fill; (coll) to silence, shut up ‖ *ref* (coll) to become confused

atasajar *tr* to slash, hack; (*carne*) to jerk

atascadero *m* mudhole; (fig) pitfall

atascar §73 *tr* to stop, to stop up, clog, obstruct ‖ *ref* to get stuck; to stuff oneself; to clog, get clogged

atasco *m* sticking, clogging; obstruction

ataúd *m* casket, coffin

ataujía *f* damascene work

ataujiar §77 *tr* to damascene

ataviar §77 *tr* to dress, adorn, deck out

atavío *m* dress, adornment; **atavíos** finery, frippery, chiffons

atediar *tr* to tire, bore

ateísmo *m* atheism

ateísta *mf* atheist

atelaje *m* harness

atemorizar §60 *tr* to frighten

atemperar *tr* to soften, moderate, temper; to adjust, adapt

Atenas *f* Athens

atención *f* attention; **en atención a** in view of

atender §51 *tr* to attend to; to heed, pay attention to; to take care of; (*a los parroquianos*) to wait on

atener §71 *ref* — **atenerse a** to abide by, to rely on

ateniense *adj* & *mf* Athenian

atenta·do -da *adj* moderate, prudent; cautious || *m* attempt, assault

atentar *tr* to attempt, to try to commit || *intr* — **atentar a** or **contra** (*p.ej., la vida de una persona*) to attempt || §2 *ref* to grope

aten·to -ta *adj* attentive; courteous, polite || *f* favor (*letter*)

atenuar §21 *tr* to extenuate

ate·o -a *adj* & *mf* atheist

aterciopela·do -da *adj* velvety

ateri·do -da *adj* stiff, numb with cold

aterrada *f* landfall

aterrajar *tr* to thread, to tap

aterraje *m* landing

aterrar *tr* to terrify || §2 *tr* to destroy, demolish; to cover with earth || *intr* to land || *ref* to stand inshore

aterrizaje *m* landing; **aterrizaje a ciegas** blind landing; **aterrizaje aplastado** or **en desplome** pancake landing; **aterrizaje forzoso** emergency landing

aterrizar §60 *intr* to land

aterronar *tr* to make lumpy || *ref* to cake, to lump

aterrorizar §60 *tr* to terrify

atesorar *tr* to treasure; to hoard; (*virtudes, perfecciones*) to possess

atesta·do -da *adj* stuffed, jammed; obstinate, stubborn || *m* certificate

atestar *tr* (law) to attest || §2 & *regular tr* to jam, pack, stuff, cram; (coll) to stuff

atestiguar §10 *tr* to attest, testify, depose

atezar §60 *tr* to tan; to blacken || *ref* to become tanned, become sunburned

atiborrar *tr* to stuff || *ref* (coll) to stuff, stuff oneself

atiesar *tr* to stiffen; to tighten || *ref* to become stiff; to become tight

atildar *tr* to mark with a tilde, dash, or accent mark; to point out; to find fault with; to tidy up, to trim, to adorn

atina·do -da *adj* careful, keen, wise

atinar *tr* to find, come upon || *intr* to guess, guess right; to be right; to manage

atisbadero *m* peephole

atisbar *tr* to watch, spy on

atisbo *m* glimpse, look, peek

atizar §60 *tr* to stir, to poke; to snuff; to rouse; (*p.ej., un puntapié*) to let go

Atlánti·co -ca *adj* & *m* Atlantic

at·las *m* (*pl* **-las**) atlas

atleta *mf* athlete

atleticismo *m* athletics

atléti·co -ca *adj* athletic || *f* athletics

atmósfera *f* atmosphere

atmosféri·co -ca *adj* atmospheric

atoar *tr* (naut) to tow

atocinar *tr* (*un cerdo*) to cut up; to make into bacon; (coll) to murder ||

ref to get angry; to fall madly in love

atocha *f* esparto

atolondra·do -da *adj* confused; scatterbrained

atolondrar *tr* to confuse, bewilder

atolladero *m* mudhole; obstacle, difficulty

atollar *intr* & *ref* to get stuck, to get stuck in the mud

atómi·co -ca *adj* atomic

átomo *m* atom

atóni·to -ta *adj* astounded, aghast

atontar *tr* to stun; to confuse, bewilder

atorar *tr* to clog, obstruct || *intr* & *ref* to stick, get stuck; to choke

atormentar *tr* to torment; to torture

atornillar *tr* to screw, screw on

atortolar *tr* to rattle, scare, intimidate

atosigar §44 *tr* to poison; to harass || *ref* to be in a hurry

atrabanca·do -da *adj* overworked; (Mex) hasty, rash; (Ven) deep in debt

atrabancar §73 *tr* & *intr* to rush through

atrabilia·rio -ria *adj* irascible, grouchy

atracador *m* hold-up man

atracar §73 *tr* to hold up; to bring up; (naut) to bring alongside, to dock; (coll) to stuff || *intr* (naut) to come alongside, to dock || *ref* (coll) to stuff; (Am) to quarrel

atracción *f* attraction; amusement

atraco *m* holdup

atracón *m* (coll) stuffing, gluttony; (Am) fight; (Am) push, shove

atracti·vo -ca *adj* attractive || *m* attraction; attractiveness

atraer §75 *tr* to attract

atragantar *tr* to choke down || *ref* to choke; atragantarse con to choke on

atraillar §4 *tr* to leash; to master, subdue

atrampar *ref* to fall into a trap; to be stopped up; to stick; to get stuck

atrancar §73 *tr* to bar; to obstruct || *intr* (coll) to stride; (coll) to read falteringly || *ref* to get stuck; (*una ventana*) to stick; (Mex) to stick to one's opinion

atrapamos·cas *m* (*pl* **-cas**) flytrap; (bot) Venus'-flytrap

atrapar *tr* (coll) to trap, to catch; to get, to land, to net

atrás *adv* back, backward; behind; before; previously; **atrás de** back of, behind; **hacerse atrás** to back up, move back; **hacia atrás** backwards; the other way

atrasa·do -da *adj* late; (*reloj*) slow; needy; back; retarded; in arrears; **atrasado de medios** short of funds; **atrasado de noticias** behind the times

atrasar *tr* to slow down; to retard; to set back, to turn back; to delay; to leave behind; to postdate || *intr* to be slow || *ref* to be slow; to lose time; to lag, to stay behind; to be late; to be in debt

atraso *m* delay, slowness; backwardness; lag; **atrasos** arrears, delinquency

atravesar §2 *tr* to cross, to go across; to pierce; to pass through, go through; to put crosswise; to stake, wager ‖ *ref* to butt in; to fight, wrangle; to get stuck

atrayente *adj* attractive

atreguar §10 *tr* to give a truce to; to grant an extension to ‖ *ref* to agree to a truce

atrever *ref* to dare; **atreverse con** or **contra** to be impudent toward

atrevi-do -da *adj* bold, daring; impudent

atrevimiento *m* boldness, daring; impudence

atribuir §20 *tr* to attribute, ascribe ‖ *ref* to assume

atribular *tr* & *ref* to grieve

atributo *m* attribute

atril *m* lectern; music stand

atrincherar *tr* to entrench ‖ *ref* to dig in

atrio *m* hall, vestibule; court, courtyard; parvis

atri-to -ta *adj* contrite

atrocidad *f* atrocity; (coll) enormity

atrofia *f* atrophy

atrofiar *tr* & *ref* to atrophy

atrojar *tr* (*granos*) to garner; (Mex) to befuddle

atrona-do -da *adj* reckless, thoughtless

atronar §61 *tr* to deafen; to stun ‖ *intr* to thunder

atropella-do -da *adj* brusk, violent; hasty; tumultuous

atropellar *tr* to trample; to knock down; to run over; to disregard; to do hurriedly ‖ *intr* & *ref* to act hastily or recklessly

atropello *m* trampling; knocking down; running over; abuse, insult; outrage

a-troz *adj* (*pl* -**troces**) atrocious; (coll) huge, enormous

atto. *abbr* atento

atufar *tr* to anger, irritate ‖ *ref* to get angry; (*el vino*) to turn sour

atún *m* tuna

aturdi-do -da *adj* reckless, harebrained

aturdir *tr* to stun; to perplex, bewilder

atusar *tr* to trim; to smooth ‖ *ref* to dress fancily; (*el bigote*) to twist

audacia *f* audacity

au-daz *adj* (*pl* -**daces**) audacious

audición *f* audition; hearing; concert; listening

audiencia *f* audience, hearing; audience chamber; royal tribunal; provincial high court

audífono *m* hearing aid; earphone

audiofrecuencia *f* audio frequency

audiómetro *m* audiometer

auditor *m* judge advocate; **auditor de guerra** judge advocate (*in army*); **auditor de marina** judge advocate (*in navy*)

auditorio *m* (*concurso de oyentes*) audience; (*local*) auditorium

auge *m* height, acme; boom; vogue; **estar en auge** to be booming

augur *m* augur

augurar *tr* to augur; (Am) to wish ‖ *intr* to augur

augurio *m* augury; (Am) wish

augus-to -ta *adj* august

aula *f* classroom, lecture room; **aula magna** assembly hall

aulaga *f* gorse, furze

aullar §8 *intr* to howl

aullido *m* howl, howling

aúllo *m* howl

aumentar *tr* to augment, increase, enlarge; to promote; (coll) to exaggerate ‖ *intr* & *ref* to augment, increase

aumento *m* augmentation, increase, enlargement; promotion; **ir en aumento** to be on the increase

aun *adv* even; **aun cuando** although

aún *adv* still, yet

aunar §8 *tr* & *ref* to join, unite; to combine, mix

aunque *conj* although, though

aúpa *interj* up!; **de aúpa** (coll) swanky; **los de aúpa** (taur) the picadors

aupar §8 *tr* (coll) to help up; (coll) to extol

aura *f* gentle breeze; breath; popularity; turkey vulture

áure-o -a *adj* gold, golden

aureola *f* halo, aureole

auricular *m* earpiece, receiver; **auricular de casco** headpiece

auriga *m* (poet) coachman, charioteer

aurora *f* aurora, dawn; roseate hue

ausencia *f* absence

ausentar *tr* to send away ‖ *ref* to absent oneself

ausente *adj* absent; absent-minded ‖ *mf* absentee

auspiciar *tr* (Am) to sponsor, foster, back

auspicio *m* auspice; **bajo los auspicios de** under the auspices of

auste-ro -ra *adj* austere; harsh; honest; penitent

Australia *f* Australia

australia-no -na *adj* & *mf* Australian

Austria *f* Austria

austria-co -ca *adj* & *mf* Austrian

austro *m* south wind

auténtica *f* certificate; certification

autenticar §73 *tr* to authenticate

auténti-co -ca *adj* authentic; real ‖ *f* see **auténtica**

autillo *m* tawny owl

auto *m* edict; short Biblical play; miracle play; auto; **auto de prisión** commitment, warrant for arrest; **auto sacramental** play in honor of the Sacrament

autoamortizable *adj* self-liquidating

autobanco *m* drive-in bank

autobiografía *f* autobiography

autobombo *m* self-glorification

autobús *m* autobus, bus

autocamión *m* motor truck

autocráti-co -ca *adj* autocratic(al)

autócto-no -na *adj* native, indigenous

autodefensa *f* self-defense

autodeterminación *f* self-determination

autodidac-to -ta *adj* self-taught

autodisciplina *f* self-discipline

autódromo *m* automobile race track

auto-escuela *f* driving school

autógena *f* welding

autogobierno *m* self-government

autografiar §77 *tr* to autograph
autógra·fo -fa *adj* & *m* autograph
autoguia·do -da *adj* self-guided, homing
automación *f* automation
autómata *m* automaton
automáti·co -ca *adj* automatic
automatización *f* automation
automóvil *m* automobile
automovilista *mf* motorist
autonomía *f* autonomy; cruising radius
autóno·mo -ma *adj* autonomous, independent
autopiano *m* player piano
autopista *f* turnpike, automobile road
autopsia *f* autopsy
au·tor -tora *mf* author; (*de un crimen*) perpetrator || *f* authoress
autoridad *f* authority; pomp, display
autorita·rio -ria *adj* & *mf* authoritarian
autoriza·do -da *adj* authoritative
autorizar §60 *tr* to authorize; to legalize; to exalt
autorretrato *m* self-portrait
autoservicio *m* self-service
autostop *m* hitchhiking; **viajar en autostop** to hitchhike
autostopista *mf* hitchhiker
auto-teatro *m* drive-in movie theater
autovía *m* railway motor coach || *f* turnpike, automobile road
auxiliar *adj* auxiliary || *mf* auxiliary; aid, helper; substitute teacher || *v* §77 & *regular* *tr* to aid, help, assist; (*a un moribundo*) to attend
auxilio *m* aid, help, assistance; **acudir en auxilio a** or **de** to come to the aid of; **auxilio en carretera** road service; **primeros auxilios** first aid
avahar *tr* to steam; to breathe warmth on || *intr* to steam, give off vapor || *ref* to steam, give off vapor; to warm one's hands with one's breath
aval *m* endorsement; countersignature
avalancha *f* avalanche
avalorar *tr* to estimate; to encourage
avaluación *f* appraisal, valuation
avaluar §21 *tr* to appraise, to estimate
avalúo *m* appraisal, valuation
avance *m* advance; advance payment; (com) balance; (com) estimate; (mov) preview
avante *adv* (naut) fore
avanza·do -da *adj* advanced; **avanzado de edad** advanced in years || *f* outpost, advance guard
avanzar §60 *tr* to advance, extend; to propose || *intr* & *ref* to advance; to approach
avanzo *m* balance sheet; estimate
avaricia *f* avarice
avaricio·so -sa *adj* avaricious
avarien·to -ta *adj* avaricious || *mf* miser
ava·ro -ra *adj* miserly || *mf* miser
avasallar *tr* to subject, subjugate, enslave || *ref* to submit
ave *f* bird; fowl; **ave canora** songbird; **ave de corral** barnyard fowl; **ave de mal agüero** Jonah, jinx; **ave de paso** bird of passage; **ave de rapiña** bird of prey; **ave fría** lapwing; **ave zancuda** wading bird

avecinar *tr* to bring near || *ref* to approach; to take up residence
avecindar *tr* to domicile || *ref* to become a resident
avejentar *tr* & *ref* to age prematurely
avejigar §44 *tr*, *intr* & *ref* to blister
avellana *f* hazelnut
avellanar *tr* to countersink || *ref* to shrivel, shrivel up
avellano *m* hazel, hazel tree
avemaría *f* Hail Mary, Ave Maria; **al avemaría** at sunset; **en un avemaría** (coll) in a jiffy; **saber como el avemaría** (coll) to have a thorough knowledge of
avena *f* oats
avenar *tr* to drain
avenate *m* gruel, oatmeal gruel
avenencia *f* agreement; deal, bargain
avenida *f* avenue; allée; flood, freshet; gathering, assemblage
aveni·do -da *adj* — **bien avenido** in agreement; **mal avenido** in disagreement || *f* see **avenida**
avenimiento *m* agreement; reconciliation
avenir §79 *tr* to reconcile, bring together || *ref* to be reconciled, to agree; to compromise; to correspond
aventa·dor -dora *mf* winnower || *m* fan
aventaja·do -da *adj* excellent, outstanding; advantageous
aventajar *tr* to advance; to put ahead; to excel || *ref* to advance, win an advantage; to excel
aventar §2 *tr* to fan; to winnow; to scatter to the winds; to blow; (coll) to drive away || *ref* to swell up; (coll) to flee, run away
aventón *m* (Guat, Mex, Peru) push, shove; (*llevada gratuita*) (Mex) free ride; **pedir aventón** (Mex) to hitchhike
aventura *f* adventure; danger, risk
aventura·do -da *adj* hazardous, venturesome
aventurar *tr* to adventure, to venture, to hazard || *ref* to adventure, to take a risk; to venture, to risk
aventure·ro -ra *adj* adventuresome, adventurous || *m* adventurer, soldier of fortune || *f* adventuress
avergonzar §9 *tr* to shame; to embarrass || *ref* to be ashamed; to be embarrassed
avería *f* aviary; breakdown, failure; (com) damage; (naut) average
averiar §77 *tr* to damage || *ref* to suffer damage; to break down
averiguable *adj* ascertainable
averiguar §10 *tr* to ascertain, to find out
aversión *f* aversion, dislike; **cobrar aversión a** to take a dislike for
aves·truz *m* (*pl* -truces) ostrich
avezar §60 *tr* to accustom || *ref* to become accustomed
aviación *f* aviation
avia·dor -dora *mf* aviator, flyer || *m* aviator, airman; (mil) airman; **aviador postal** air-mail pilot || *f* aviatrix, airwoman
aviar §77 *tr* to make ready, prepare;

(coll) to equip, provide; **estar, encontrarse** or **quedar aviado** (coll) to be in a mess, be in a jam || *ref* to hurry; (aer) to take off

avia·triz f (pl **-trices**) aviatrix

avidez f avidity, greediness

ávi·do -da adj avid, greedy, eager

aviejar tr & ref to age prematurely

aviento m winnowing fork, pitchfork

avie·so -sa adj crooked, distorted; evil-minded, perverse

avilantar ref to be insolent

avilantez f insolence; meanness

avillana·do -da adj rustic, boorish

avillanar tr to debase, make boorish || *ref* to become boorish

avinagra·do -da adj (coll) vinegarish, sour, crabbed

avinagrar tr to sour || *ref* to become sour; to turn into vinegar

avío m provision; arrangement; (Am) load; **¡al avío!** let's go!; avíos equipment, tools, outfit; **avíos de pescar** fishing tackle

avión m airplane; (orn) martin; **avión birreactor** twin-jet plane; **avión de caza** pursuit plane; **avión a chorro, avión de propulsión a chorro** or **a reacción** jet plane

avión-correo m mailplane

avioneta f small plane; **avioneta de alquiler** taxiplane

avisaco·ches m (pl **-ches**) car caller

avisa·do -da adj prudent, wise; **mal avisado** rash, thoughtless

avisa·dor -dora adj warning || mf informer; adviser || m electric bell; **avisador de incendio** fire alarm

avisar tr to advise, inform; to warn; to report on

aviso m advice, information; warning; care, prudence; dispatch boat; (Am) advertisement; **sobre aviso** on the lookout

avispa f wasp

avispa·do -da adj (coll) brisk, wide-awake

avispar tr to spur; (coll) to stir up || *ref* to fret, worry

avispón m hornet

avistar tr to descry || *ref* to meet, have an interview

avituallar tr to supply, provision || *ref* to take in supplies

avivar tr to brighten, enlive, revive || *intr* & *ref* to brighten, revive

avizor adj watchful, alert || m watcher; **avizores** (slang) eyes

avizorar tr to watch, spy on || *ref* to hide and watch, to spy

ax interj ouch!, ow!

axioma m axiom

axiomáti·co -ca adj axiomatic

ay interj ay!, alas! **¡ay de mí!** woe is me! || m sigh

aya f nurse, governess

ayer adj & m yesterday

ayo m tutor

ayuda m valet; **ayuda de cámara** valet de chambre || f help, aid; enema

ayudanta f assistant; **ayudanta de cocina** kitchenmaid

ayudante m aid, assistant; adjutant; **ayudante de campo** aide-de-camp

ayudar tr to aid, help, assist

ayunar intr to fast

ayu·no -na adj fasting; uninformed; **en ayunas** or **en ayuno** fasting; before breakfast; uninformed; missing the point || m fast, fasting

ayuntamiento m town or city council; town or city hall; sexual intercourse

azabacha·do -da adj jet, jet-black

azabache m jet; **azabaches** jet trinkets

aza·cán -cana adj menial || mf drudge || m water carrier

azada f hoe

azadón m hoe; grub hoe; **azadón de peto** or **de pico** mattock

azadonar tr to hoe

azafata f air hostess, stewardess; lady of the queen's wardrobe

azafate m wicker tray

azafrán m saffron

azafrana·do -da adj saffron

azafranar tr to saffron

azahar m orange or lemon blossom

azar m chance, hazard; accident, misfortune; fate, destiny; losing card; losing throw: **(persona o cosa que traen mala suerte)** Jonah

azarar ref to go awry; to get rattled

azaro·so -sa adj hazardous, risky; unlucky

ázi·mo -ma adj unleavened

azófar m brass

azoga·do -da adj fidgety, restless || m quicksilver foil; **temblar como un azogado** (coll) to shake like a leaf

azogar §44 tr (un espejo) to silver || *ref* to have mercury poisoning; (coll) to shake, become agitated

azogue m quicksilver; market place; (coll) mirror

azor m goshawk

azorar tr to abash; to excite, stir up

Azores fpl Azores

azotar tr to whip, to scourge; to beat; to flail; to beat down upon

azote m whip; lash; (fig) scourge; **azotes y galeras** (coll) tiresome fare

azotea f flat roof, roof terrace

azteca adj & mf Aztec

azúcar m sugar; **azúcar de caña** cane sugar; **azúcar de remolacha** beet sugar

azucarar tr to sugar, to sugarcoat; (coll) to sugar over

azucare·ro -ra adj sugar || m sugar bowl

azucena f Madonna lily, white lily

azufrar tr to sulphur

azufre m sulfur; brimstone

azul adj & m blue; **azul marino** navy blue

azular tr to color blue, to dye blue

azulear intr to turn blue

azulejar tr to tile, to cover with tiles

azulejo m glazed colored tile; (orn) roller; (orn) indigo bunting; (orn) bee eater

azuzar §60 tr to sic; (coll) to tease, incite

B, b (be) *f* second letter of the Spanish alphabet

B. *abbr* Beato, Bueno

baba *f* drivel, spittle, slobber; (*de culebras, peces, etc.*) slime

babear *intr* to slobber, to drivel; to froth, foam

babel *m & f* (coll) bedlam, confusion; **estar en babel** (coll) to be daydreaming

babero *m* bib

Babia *f* — **estar en Babia** (coll) to be daydreaming

babieca *adj* (coll) silly, simple ‖ *mf* (coll) simpleton

Babilonia *f* (*imperio*) Babylonia; (*ciudad*) Babylon

babilóni·co -ca *adj* Babylonian

babilo·nio -nia *adj & mf* Babylonian ‖ *f* see **Babilonia**

bable *m* Asturian dialect; patois

babor *m* (naut) port

babosa *f* slug

babosear *tr* to slobber over ‖ *intr* to slobber

babo·so -sa *adj* slobbery; (*con las damas*) (coll) mushy ‖ *m* (CAm) scoundrel ‖ *f* see **babosa**

babucha *f* slipper, mule

babuino *m* baboon

bacalao or **bacallao** *m* codfish

baceta *f* (cards) widow

bacía *f* basin, vessel; shaving dish

bacilo *m* bacillus

bacín *m* chamber pot

Baco *m* Bacchus

bacteria *f* bacterium

bacteria·no -na *adj* bacterial

bacteriología *f* bacteriology

bacteriólo·go -ga *mf* bacteriologist

báculo *m* staff; crook; (fig) staff, comfort; **báculo pastoral** crozier

bache *m* hole, rut; blip; **bache aéreo** air pocket

bachi·ller -llera *adj* garrulous ‖ *mf* garrulous person ‖ **bachiller** *mf* bachelor

bachillerar *tr* to confer the bachelor's degree on ‖ *ref* to receive the bachelor's degree

bachillerato *m* baccalaureate, bachelor's degree

bachillerear *intr* (coll) to babble, prattle

bachillería *f* (coll) babble, prattle; (coll) gossip

badajo *m* clapper

badana *f* (dressed) sheepskin; **zurrarle a uno la badana** (coll) to tan someone's hide

badén *m* gully, gutter

badil *m* fire shovel

badulaque *m* (coll) nincompoop

bagaje *m* beast of burden; (mil) baggage

bagatela *f* trinket; triviality; (Chile, Peru) pinball

bagazo *m* waste pulp, bagasse

bagre *adj* (Bol, Col) showy, gaudy; (CAm) sly, slick; (SAm) coarse, ill-bred; (Mex) stupid ‖ *m* catfish

bahía *f* bay

bahorrina *f* (coll) slop; (coll) riffraff

bailable *adj* for dancing ‖ *m* ballet

bailadero *m* dance floor, dance hall

baila·dor -dora *mf* dancer

bailar *tr* (*p.ej.*, *un vals*) to dance; (*un trompo*) to spin ‖ *intr* to dance; to spin; to wobble

baila·rín -rina *mf* dancer ‖ *f* ballerina; **bailarina ombliguista** (coll) belly dancer

baile *m* dance; ball; ballet; **baile de etiqueta** dress ball, formal dance; **baile de los globos** bubble dance; **baile de máscaras** masked ball, masquerade ball; **baile de San Vito** (pathol) Saint Vitus's dance; **baile de trajes** costume ball, fancy-dress ball

baja *f* (*de los precios*) fall, drop; (*en la guerra*) casualty; **dar baja** to go down, decline; **dar de baja** to drop; (mil) to mark absent; **darse de baja** to drop out; **jugar a la baja** to bear the market

bajaca *f* (Ecuad) hair ribbon

bajada *f* descent; slope; downspout; (rad) lead-in wire

bajagua *f* (Mex) cheap tobacco

bajamar *f* low tide

bajar *tr* to lower, take down; to bring down; (*la escalera*) to go down, descend; **to humble** ‖ *intr* to come down, to go down; to get off ‖ *ref* to bend down; to get off; to humble oneself

bajel *m* ship, vessel

bajeza *f* humbleness, lowliness; meanness, baseness

bajío *m* shoal, sandbank; pitfall; (Am) lowland

bajista *adj* bearish ‖ *mf* (fig) bear

ba·jo -ja *adj* low, under, lower; short; mean, base; lowly, humble; (mus) bass ‖ *m* shoal, sandbank; (mus) bass ‖ *f* see **baja** ‖ **bajo** *adv* down; low, in a low voice ‖ **bajo** *prep* under

bajón *m* bassoon; (*en el caudal, la salud, etc.*) (coll) decline, loss

bajonista *mf* bassoon player

bajorrelieve *m* bas-relief

bala *f* bullet; bale; **bala fría** spent bullet; **bala perdida** stray bullet

balaca *f* (Am) boasting, show

balada *f* ballad; (mus) ballade

bala·dí *adj* (*pl* -díes) trivial, paltry

baladro *m* scream, shout, outcry

baladronada *f* boast, boasting

baladronear *intr* to boast, to brag

bálago *m* chaff

balance *m* balance, balance sheet; rocking, swinging; hesitation, doubt; (*de una nave*) rolling

balancear *tr* to balance ‖ *intr & ref* to rock, to swing; to hesitate, to waver; (*la nave*) to roll

balancín *m* balance beam; singletree; rocker arm; seesaw

balandra f sloop
balandrán m cassock
balanza f scales, balance; comparison, judgment; **balanza de pagos** balance of payments
balar intr to bleat; (coll) to pine
balastar tr to ballast
balasto m ballast
balaustre m baluster, banister
balay m (Am) wicker basket
balazo m shot; bullet wound
balbucear tr to stammer ‖ intr to stammer, stutter; to babble, to prattle
balbucir §1 tr & intr var of **balbucear**
Balcanes, los the Balkans
balcarrotas fpl (SAm) sideburns; (Mex) locks falling over sides of face
balcón m balcony
baldar tr to cripple; to incapacitate; to inconvenience; to trump
balde m bucket, pail; **de balde** free, gratis; over, in excess; **en balde** in vain
baldear tr to wash with pails of water; (una excavación) to bail out
baldí·o -a adj uncultivated; idle, lazy; careless; useless, vain; unfounded ‖ m untilled land
baldón m insult; blot, disgrace
baldonar tr to insult; to stain, disgrace
baldosa f floor tile, paving tile; flagstone
baldra·gas m (pl **-gas**) (coll) jellyfish
balduque s red tape, wrapping tape
balear adj Balearic ‖ tr to shoot at, to shoot, to shoot to death
balido m bleat, bleating
balísti·co -ca adj ballistic
baliza f buoy, beacon; danger signal
balizaje m (aer) airway lighting; (naut) buoys
balizar §60 tr to mark with buoys; to mark off
balnea·rio -ria adj bathing ‖ m watering place, spa
balompié m football, soccer
balón m football; bale; balloon
baloncesto m basketball
balota f ballot
balotar intr to ballot
balsa f pool, puddle; raft; float; corkwood; **balsa salvavidas** life float
bálsamo m balsam, balm
balsear tr to cross by raft; to ferry across
balsero m ferryman
bálti·co -ca adj Baltic
baluarte m bulwark
ballena f whale; whalebone; (de corsé) stay
ballesta f crossbow; spring, auto spring
ba·llet m (pl **-llets**) ballet
bambalinas fpl (theat) flies, borders
bambolear intr to sway, reel, wobble
bambolla f (coll) hulk; (coll) show, sham; (coll) show-off
bam·bú m (pl **-búes**) bamboo
banana f banana; (rad) plug
banane·ro -ra adj banana ‖ m banana tree
banano m banana tree
banas fpl (Mex) banns
banasta f hamper, large basket

banca f bench; banking; stand, fruit stand; (en el juego) bank; **banca de hielo** iceberg; **hacer saltar la banca** to break the bank
banca·rio -ria adj banking, bank
bancarrota f bankruptcy; **hacer bancarrota** to go bankrupt
bancarrote·ro -ra adj & mf bankrupt
banco m bench; bank; (de peces) school; **banco de ahorros** savings bank; **banco de hielo** iceberg; **banco de liquidación** clearing house
banda f band; ribbon; faction, party; flock; border, edge; bank, shore; (de la mesa de billar) cushion; **banda de rodamiento** (aut) tread; **banda de tambores** drum corps; **irse a la banda** (naut) to list
bandada f flock, covey; (de gente) (coll) flock
bandaje m tire
bandazo m swerving; (naut) lurch
bandear tr (Am) to go through, to pierce; (Am) to pursue; (Am) to make love to ‖ ref to manage
bandeja f tray; (Am) dish, platter
bandera f flag, banner; **con banderas desplegadas** with flying colors
banderilla f (taur) banderilla; **poner una banderilla a** (coll) to taunt; (coll) to hit for a loan
banderín m (mil) color corporal; recruiting post
banderola f streamer, pennant; (Am) transom
bandido m bandit
bando m proclamation; faction, side
bandolera f bandoleer; female bandit; **en bandolera** across the shoulders
bandolero m highwayman, brigand
bandurria f Spanish lute
banquero m banker
banqueta f stool, footstool; (Guat, Mex) sidewalk
banquete m banquet
banquetear tr, intr & ref to banquet
banquisa f floe, iceberg
bañadera f (Am) bathtub
bañado m chamber pot; (Am) marshland
baña·dor -dora adj bathing ‖ mf bather ‖ m bathing suit
bañar tr to bathe; to dip; to coat by dipping ‖ ref to bathe
bañera f bathtub
bañista mf bather; frequenter of a spa or seaside resort
baño m bath; bathing; bathroom; bathtub; **baño de asiento** sitz bath; **baño de ducha** shower bath; **baños** bathing place; spa
bao m (naut) beam
baptista adj & mf Baptist
baptisterio m baptistery
baque m thud, thump; bump, bruise
baquelita f bakelite
ba·quet m (pl **-quets**) bucket seat
baqueta f ramrod; drumstick; **correr baquetas** or **pasar por baquetas** to run the gauntlet
baquía f (Am) knowledge of the road, paths, rivers, etc. of a region; (Am) manual skill

baquia·no -na *adj* (Am) skillful, expert ‖ *mf* (Am) scout, pathfinder, guide

báqui·co -ca *adj* Bacchic

bar *m* bar; cocktail bar

barahunda *f* uproar, tumult

baraja *f* (*de naipes*) deck, pack; gang, mob; confusion, mix-up

barajadura *f* shuffling; dispute, quarrel

barajar *tr* (*naipes*) to shuffle; to jumble, to mix ‖ *intr* to shuffle; to fight, quarrel ‖ *ref* to get jumbled or mixed

baranda *f* railing; (*de la mesa de billar*) cushion

barandilla *f* balustrade, railing

barata *f* cheapness; barter; (Mex) bargain sale; (Chile, Peru) cockroach

baratija *f* trinket

baratillo *m* second-hand goods; second-hand shop; bargain counter

bara·to -ta *adj* cheap ‖ *m* bargain sale; **dar de barato** (coll) to admit for the sake of argument; **de barato** gratis, free ‖ *f* see **barata** ‖ **barato** *adv* cheap

báratro *m* (poet) hell

baratura *f* cheapness

baraúnda *f* uproar, tumult

barba *f* (*parte de la cara*) chin; (*pelo en ella*) beard; (*del papel*) deckle edge; (*de ave*) gill, wattle; **barba española** Spanish moss; **barbas** whiskers; **hacer la barba a** to shave; to bore, annoy; (Mex) to fawn on; **llevar por la barba** to lead by the nose; **mentir por la barba** (coll) to tell fish stories ‖ *m* (theat) old man

barbacoa *f* barbecue; (Col) kitchen cupboard; (Peru) attic

barbada *f* lower jaw of horse; bridle curb ‖ **la Barbada** Barbados

barbar *intr* to grow a beard; to strike root

barbaridad *f* barbarism; outrage; piece of folly; (coll) large amount; **¡qué barbaridad!** how awful!, what nonsense!

barbarie *f* barbarity, barbarism

barbarismo *m* illiteracy; outrage; (gram) barbarism

bárba·ro -ra *adj* barbaric; barbarous ‖ *mf* barbarian

barbear *tr* to reach with the chin; to be as high as ‖ *intr* to reach the same height; **barbear con** to be as high as

barbechar *tr* to plow for seeding; to fallow

barbecho *m* fallow; **firmar como en un barbecho** (coll) to sign with one's eyes closed

barbería *f* barber shop

barberil *adj* barber

barbe·ro -ra *mf* barber; (Mex) flatterer

barbilampi·ño -ña *adj* smooth-faced, beardless; beginning, green

barbilla *f* tip of chin; (*de pluma*) barb; (*de pez*) wattle

bar·bón -bona *adj* bearded ‖ *m* greybeard; solemn old fellow; billy goat

barboquejo *m* chin strap

barbotar *tr* & *intr* to mutter, to mumble

barbu·do -da *adj* bearded, long-bearded, heavy-bearded ‖ *m* shoot, sucker

barbullar *tr* & *intr* to blabber

barca *f* small boat; bark

barcia *f* chaff

barco *m* boat, ship; **barco de carga** cargo boat; **barco náufrago** shipwreck

barchi·lón -lona *mf* (Ecuad, Peru) nurse, orderly; (Arg, Bol, Peru) quack

barda *f* thatch; bard, horse armor

bardana *f* burdock

bardar *tr* to thatch; (*un caballo*) to bard

bardo *m* bard

bargueño *m* carved inlaid secretary

bario *m* barium

barjuleta *f* haversack

barloventear *intr* to wander around; to turn to windward

barlovento *m* windward

bar·niz *m* (*pl -nices*) varnish; (*de la loza, la porcelana, etc.*) glaze; gloss, polish; (*conocimientos superficiales*) smattering; (aer) dope

barnizar §60 *tr* to varnish

barómetro *m* barometer; **barómetro aneroide** aneroid barometer

barón *m* baron

baronesa *f* baroness

barquero *m* boatman

barquilla *f* (naut) log; (naut) log chip; (aer) nacelle

barquillero *m* waffle iron; harbor boatman

barquillo *m* cone; waffle

barquín *m* bellows

barra *f* bar; (*de dinamita*) stick; (*en el tribunal*) barr... , railing; **barra colectora** (elec) bus bar; **barra de labios** or **para los labios** lipstick; **barra imantada** bar magnet; **barras paralelas** (sport) parallel bars

barrabasada *f* (coll) fiendish prank, mean trick

barraca *f* cabin, hut; cottage; (Am) storage shed

barracón *m* barracks; fair booth

barragana *f* concubine

barranca *f* gorge, ravine, gully

barranco *m* gorge, ravine, gully; difficulty, obstruction; (Am) cliff, precipice

barrar *tr* to daub, to smear

barrear *tr* to barricade; to bar shut

barredera *f* street sweeper

barre·dor -dora *mf* sweeper; **barredora de alfombras** carpet sweeper; **barredora de nieve** snowplow

barredura *f* sweeping; **barreduras** sweepings

barremi·nas *m* (*pl -nas*) mine sweeper

barrena *f* auger, drill, gimlet; (*espiga para taladrar*) bit; (aer) spin; **barrena picada** (aer) tail spin; **entrar en barrena** (aer) to go into a spin

barrenar *tr* to drill; (*un buque*) to scuttle; to blast; to upset, to frustrate; to violate

barrende·ro -ra *mf* sweeper

barreno *m* large drill; drill hole; blast

hole; pride, vanity; (Chile) mania, pet idea; **dar barreno a** (*un buque*) to scuttle

barreño *m* earthen dishpan

barrer *tr* to sweep, to sweep away; to graze || *intr* to sweep; **barrer hacia dentro** to look out for oneself

barrera *f* barrier; barricade; (mil) barrage; crockery cupboard; tollgate; (rr) crossing gate; (taur) fence around inside of ring; (taur) first row of seats; **barrera de arrecifes** barrier reef; **barrera de paso a nivel** (rr) crossing gate

barriada *f* district, quarter

barrica *f* cask, barrel

barriga *f* belly; (*de una vasija, una pared, etc.*) bulge

barri·gón -gona or **barrigu·do -da** *adj* big-bellied

barril *m* barrel

barrilero *m* cooper, barrel maker

barrio *m* ward, quarter; suburb; **barrio bajo** slums; **barrio comercial** shopping district, business district; **el otro barrio** the other world; **estar vestido de barrio** (coll) to be dressed in house clothes

barro *m* mud; clay; earthenware; pimple; (coll) money; (Arg, Urug) blunder

barro·co -ca *adj & m* baroque

barro·so -sa *adj* muddy; pimply

barrote *m* heavy bar; bolt; cross brace

barruntar *tr* to guess; to sense

barrunto *m* guess, conjecture; sign, token, foreboding

bartola *f* (coll) belly; **a la bartola** (coll) lazily

bartolina *f* (CAm, W-I) jail, dungeon

bártulos *mpl* household tools; **liar los bártulos** (coll) to pack up one's belongings

barullo *m* confusion, tumult

basar *tr* to base; to build || *ref* **basarse en** to base one's judgment on, to rely on

basca *f* nausea, squeamishness; (coll) fit of temper, tantrum

basco·so -sa *adj* nauseated, squeamish

báscula *f* scales; platform scale

base *f* base; basis; **a base de** on the basis of

bási·co -ca *adj* basic

Basilea *f* Basle, Basel

basílica *f* basilica

basilisco *m* basilisk; **estar hecho un basilisco** (coll) to be in a rage

basquear *intr* to be nauseated

bastante *adj* enough || *adv* enough; fairly, rather || *m* enough

bastar *intr* to be enough, to suffice; to abound, be more than enough || *ref* to be self-sufficient

bastardilla *f* italics

bastar·do -da *adj & mf* bastard

bastidor *m* frame; stretcher; (theat) wing; **entre bastidores** behind the scenes

bastilla *f* hem

bastillar *tr* to hem

bas·to -ta *adj* coarse, rough; uncouth

|| *m* packsaddle; (*naipe*) club; **el basto** the ace of clubs

bastón *m* stick, staff; cane, walking stick; baton; **bastón de esquiar** ski pole or stick

bastoncillo *m* small stick; (*de la retina*) rod

bastonear *tr* to cane, to beat

basura *f* sweepings; rubbish, litter, refuse; horse manure

basurero *m* trash can; rubbish dump; rubbish collector

bata *f* smock; dressing gown, wrapper; **bata de baño** bathrobe

batacazo *m* thud, bump

bataclán *m* (Cuba) burlesque show

bataclana *f* (Cuba) showgirl, stripteaser

batahola *f* (coll) racket, hubbub

batalla *f* battle; (*de un vehículo*) wheel base; (*de la silla de montar*) seat; (paint) battle piece; **batalla campal** pitched battle; **librar batalla** to do battle

batallar *intr* to battle, to fight; to hesitate, to waver

bata·llón -llona *adj* (*cuestión*) controversial, moot || *m* battalion

batata *f* sweet potato; (Arg) timidity

bate *m* baseball bat

batea *f* tray; flat-bottomed boat; (rr) flatcar

bateador *m* batter

batear *tr & intr* to bat

batel *m* small boat

batelero *m* boatman

batería *f* battery; footlights; **batería de cocina** kitchen utensils

bati·do -da *adj* (*camino*) beaten; (*tejido*) moiré || *m* batter; milk shake; (rad) beat || *f* battue; combing, search

batidor *m* beater; scout, ranger; **batidor de huevos** egg beater; **batidor de oro** goldbeater

batidora *f* beater, mixer

batiente *m* jamb; (*hoja de puerta*) leaf, door; (*de piano*) damper; wash, place where surf breaks

batihoja *m* goldbeater; sheet-metal worker

batimiento *m* beating; (phys) beat

batín *m* smoking jacket

batintín *m* Chinese gong

batir *tr* to beat; to batter, beat down; (*las alas*) to flap; (*manos*) to clap; (*las olas*) to ply; **batir tiendas** (mil) to strike camp

bato *m* simpleton, rustic

batuque *m* (Arg) uproar, rumpus, jamboree; **armar un batuque** (Arg) to raise a rumpus

baturrillo *m* hodgepodge

batuta *f* (mus) baton; **llevar la batuta** (coll) to boss the show

baúl *m* trunk; **baúl mundo** large trunk; **baúl ropero** wardrobe trunk

bauprés *m* bowsprit

bautismo *m* baptism; **bautismo de aire** first flight

bautista *adj* Baptist || *mf* Baptist; baptizer; **el Bautista** John the Baptist

bautisterio *m* baptistery

bautizar §60 *tr* to baptize; (*el vino*) (coll) to water

bautizo *m* baptism; christening party

báva·ro -ra *adj* & *mf* Bavarian

Baviera *f* Bavaria

baya *f* berry

bayeta *f* baize

ba·yo -ya *adj* bay ‖ *m* bay horse ‖ *f* see **baya**

bayoneta *f* bayonet

bayonetear *tr* (Am) to bayonet

baza *f* trick; **meter baza en** (coll) to butt into

bazar *m* bazaar

ba·zo -za *adj* yellowish-brown ‖ *m* yellowish brown; spleen ‖ *f* see **baza**

bazofia *f* refuse, offal, garbage

bazuca *f* bazooka

bazucar §73 *tr* to stir, to shake; to tamper with

be *m* baa

beata *f* lay sister

beatería *f* cant, hypocrisy

beatificar §73 *tr* to beatify

beatísi·mo -ma *adj* most holy

bea·to -ta *adj* blessed; pious, devout; bigoted, prudish ‖ *mf* beatified person; devout person; bigot; (coll) churchgoer ‖ *f* see **beata**

bebé *m* baby; doll

bebede·ro -ra *adj* (archaic) drinkable ‖ *m* watering place; (Col, Ecuad, Mex) watering trough

bebedi·zo -za *adj* drinkable ‖ *m* potion, philter

bebe·dor -dora *adj* drinking ‖ *mf* drinker; hard drinker

beber *m* drink, drinking ‖ *tr* & *intr* to drink; **beber de** or **en** to drink out of ‖ *ref* to drink, drink up; (*p.ej., un libro*) to drink in

bebestible *adj* drinkable ‖ *m* drink

bebezón *f* (Col) drunk, spree

bebible *adj* drinkable

bebi·do -da *adj* tipsy, unsteady ‖ *f* drink

bebistrajo *m* (coll) dose, mixture

beborrotear *intr* (coll) to tipple

beca *f* scholarship, fellowship; (*de los colegiales*) sash

becacina *m* snipe, whole snipe

becacina *f* snipe, great snipe

becada *f* woodcock

beca·rio -ria *mf* scholar, fellow

becerra *f* snapdragon

becerrillo *m* calfskin

bece·rro -rra *mf* yearling calf ‖ *m* calfskin ‖ *f* see **becerra**

becuadro *m* (mus) natural sign

bedel *m* beadle

befa *f* jeer, flout, scoff

befar *tr* to jeer at, to scoff at ‖ *intr* (*un caballo*) to move the lips

be·fo -fa *adj* blobber-lipped; knock-kneed ‖ *m* (*de animal*) lip ‖ *f* see **befa**

béisbol *m* baseball

bejuco *m* cane, liana

beldad *f* beauty

beldar §2 *tr* to winnow

belén *m* crèche; (coll) bedlam, confusion; (coll) madhouse; (coll) gossip ‖ **Belén** Bethlehem

bel·fo -fa *adj* (*labio*) blobber; blobber-lipped ‖ *m* (*de animal*) lip; blobber lip

belga *adj* & *mf* Belgian

Bélgica *f* Belgium

bélgi·co -ca *adj* Belgian ‖ *f* see **Bélgica**

belicista *mf* warmonger

béli·co -ca *adj* warlike

belico·so -sa *adj* bellicose

beligerante *adj* & *mf* belligerent

belitre *adj* low, mean ‖ *m* scoundrel

bella·co -ca *adj* cunning, sly; wicked ‖ *mf* scoundrel

bellaquear *intr* to cheat, be crooked; (SAm) to be stubborn; (SAm) to rear

bellaquería *f* cunning, slyness; wickedness

belleza *f* beauty; **belleza exótica** glamour girl

be·llo -lla *adj* beautiful, fair

bellota *f* acorn; carnation bud

bem·bo -ba *adj* (Am) thick-lipped; (Mex) simple, silly ‖ *mf* (*persona*) (Am) thicklips

bemol *adj* & *m* (mus) flat; **tener bemoles** (coll) to be a tough job

bencina *f* benzine

bendecir §11 *tr* to bless; to consecrate; **bendecir la mesa** to say grace

bendición *f* benediction, blessing; godsend, (*en la mesa*) grace; **bendiciones** wedding ceremony; **echar la bendición a** (coll) to have nothing more to do with

bendi·to -ta *adj* blessed, saintly; simple, silly; happy; (*agua*) holy; **como el pan bendito** (coll) as easy as pie ‖ *m* simple-minded soul

benedicite *m* grace; **rezar el benedícite** to say grace

benedicti·no -na *adj* & *mf* Benedictine ‖ *m* benedictine

beneficencia *f* beneficence; charity, welfare; social service

beneficia·do -da *mf* person or charity receiving the proceeds of a benefit performance

beneficiar *tr* to benefit; (*la tierra*) to cultivate; (*una mina*) to work, to exploit; (*minerales*) to process, to reduce; (*una región del país*) to serve; to season; (Am) to slaughter ‖ *ref* — **beneficiarse de** to take advantage of

beneficia·rio -ria *mf* beneficiary

beneficio *m* benefit; profit, gain, yield; (*de una mina*) exploitation; smelting, ore reduction; benefit performance; **a beneficio de** for the benefit of; on the strength of

beneficio·so -sa *adj* beneficial, profitable

benéfi·co -ca *adj* charitable, benevolent

benemé·ri·to -ta *adj* & *mf* worthy; **benemérito de la patria** national hero

beneplácito *m* approval, consent

benevolencia *f* benevolence

benévo·lo -la *adj* benevolent, kindhearted

bengala *f* Bengal light; (aer) flare

benignidad f benignity, mildness, kindness; (del tiempo) mildness

benig·no -na adj benign, mild, kind; (tiempo) clement, mild

benjamín m baby (the youngest child)

beodez f drunkenness

beo·do -da adj & mf drunk

berbi·quí m (pl -quíes) brace; **berbiquí y barrena** brace and bit

berenjena f eggplant

berenjenal m eggplant patch; (coll) predicament, jam, fix

bergante m scoundrel, rascal

bergantín m (naut) brig; **bergantín goleta** (naut) brigantine

berilio m beryllium

berkelio m berkelium

berli·nés -nesa adj Berlin || mf Berliner

bermejear intr to turn bright red; to look bright red

berme·jo -ja adj vermilion, bright-red

berme·jón -jona adj red, reddish

bermellón m vermilion

berrear intr to bellow, to low; to bawl, yowl

berrenchín m (coll) rage, tantrum

berrido m bellow; scream, yowl

berrín m (coll) touchy person, cross child

berrinche m (coll) tantrum, conniption

berro m water cress

berza f cabbage

berzal m cabbage patch

besalamano m announcement, written in the third person and marked B.L.M. (kisses your hand)

besamanos m levee, reception at court; throwing kisses

besar tr to kiss; (coll) to graze || ref (coll) to bump heads together

beso m kiss; **beso sonado** buss

bestia adj stupid || mf dunce || f beast; **bestia de carga** beast of burden

bestial adj beastly; (coll) terrific

besucar §73 tr & intr (coll) to keep on kissing

besu·cón -cona adj (coll) kissing || mf (coll) kisser

besuquear tr & intr (coll) to keep on kissing

betabel m (Mex) beet

betún m bitumen, pitch; shoe polish

bezo m blubber lip; proud flesh

bezu·do -da adj thick-lipped

biberón m nursing bottle

Biblia f Bible

bíbli·co -ca adj Biblical

bibliófi·lo -la mf bibliophile

bibliografía f bibliography

bibliógra·fo -fa mf bibliographer

biblioteca f library; **biblioteca de consulta** reference library; **biblioteca de préstamo** lending library

biblioteca·rio -ria mf librarian

bibliotecnia f bookmaking

bicameral adj bicameral

bicarbonato m bicarbonate

bicicleta f bicycle

bichero m boat hook

bicho m bug, insect; vermin; animal;

fighting bull; simpleton; brat; **bicho viviente** (coll) living soul; **mal bicho** scoundrel; ferocious bull

bidón m (bote, lata) can; (tonel de metal) drum

biela f connecting rod

bielda f winnowing rack; winnowing

bieldar tr to winnow

bieldo m winnowing pitch rake

bien adv well; readily; very; indeed; **ahora bien** now then; **bien como** just as; **bien que** although; **más bien** rather; somewhat; **no bien** as soon as; scarcely || s welfare; property; darling; **bienes** wealth, riches, possessions; **bienes de fortuna** worldly possessions; **bienes dotales** dower; **bienes inmuebles** real estate; **bienes muebles** personal property; **bienes raíces** real estate; **bienes relictos** estate; **bienes semovientes** livestock; **bien público** commonweal; **en bien de** for the sake of

bienal adj biennial

bienama·do -da adj dearly beloved

bienandanza f happiness, prosperity

bienaventura·do -da adj happy, blissful; blessed; simple

bienaventuranza f happiness, bliss; blessedness

bienestar m well-being, welfare

bienhabla·do -da adj well-spoken

bienhada·do -da adj fortunate, lucky

bienhe·chor -chora adj beneficent || m benefactor || f benefactress

bienintenciona·do -da adj well-meaning

bienio m biennium

bienquerencia f affection, fondness

bienquistar tr to bring together, reconcile

bienvenida f safe arrival; welcome; **dar la bienvenida a** to welcome

bienveni·do -da adj welcome || f see bienvenida

bienvivir intr to live in comfort; to live decently, properly

bif·tec m (pl -tecs) beefsteak

bifurcar §73 tr to branch, to fork

bigamia f bigamy

bíga·mo -ma adj bigamous || mf bigamist

bigornia f two-horn anvil

bigote m mustache; **bigotes** (del gato) whiskers; **tener bigotes** (coll) to have a mind of one's own

bilingüe adj bilingual

bilis f bile; **descargar la bilis** to vent one's spleen

billar m billiards; billiard table; billiard room; **billar romano** pinball

billete m ticket; note, bill; **billete de abono** season ticket; commutation ticket; **billete de banco** bank note; **billete de ida y vuelta** round-trip ticket; **billete kilométrico** mileage ticket; **medio billete** half fare

billetero m billfold; ticket agent

billón m (U.S.A.) trillion; (Brit) billion

bimotor adj twin-motor || m twin-motor plane

biofísi·co -ca adj biophysical || f biophysics

biografía f biography
biógra·fo -**fa** mf biographer
biología f biology
biólo·go -**ga** mf biologist
biombo m folding screen
bióxido m dioxide
bioquími·co -**ca** adj biochemical || mf biochemist || f biochemistry
bipartición f fission, splitting
biplano m biplane
biplaza m (aer) two-seater
birimbao m jews'-harp
birlar tr to knock down, to shoot down; (coll) to outwit; **birlar algo a alguien** (coll) to snitch something from someone
birlocha f kite
Birmania f Burma
birma·no -**na** adj & mf Burmese
birreta f biretta, red biretta
birrete m mortarboard, academic cap
bis interj encore! || m encore
bisabue·lo -**la** mf great-grandparent || m great-grandfather || f great-grandmother
bisagra f hinge
bisar tr to repeat
bisbisar tr (coll) to mutter, mumble
bisecar §73 tr to bisect
bisel m bevel edge
biselar tr to bevel
bisies·to -**ta** adj leap
bismuto m bismuth
bisnie·to -**ta** mf great-grandchild || m great-grandson || f great-granddaughter
biso·jo -**ja** adj squint-eyed, cross-eyed
bisonte m bison; buffalo
biso·ño -**ña** adj green, inexperienced || mf greenhorn, rookie
bisté m or **bistec** m beefsteak
bisun·to -**ta** adj dirty, greasy
bisutería f costume jewelry
bitácora f binnacle
bitoque m bung; (CAm) sewer; (Mex) spigot
Bizancio Byzantium
bizanti·no -**na** adj & mf Byzantine
bizarría f gallantry, bravery; magnanimity
biza·rro -**rra** adj gallant, brave; magnanimous
bizcar §73 tr to wink || intr to squint
biz·co -**ca** adj squint-eyed, cross-eyed
bizcocho m biscuit; cake, sponge cake; hardtack; bisque
bizma f poultice
bizmar tr to poultice
biznie·to -**ta** mf var of **bisnieto**
bizquear intr to squint
bizquera f squint
blanca f steel blade; **sin blanca** (coll) penniless
blanca·zo -**za** adj (coll) whitish
blan·co -**ca** adj white; (tez) fair; (fuerza) water; (arma) steel; (cobarde) (coll) yellow; blank || m (persona) white; (coll) coward || m (color) white; blank; target; aim, object; interval; white heat; blank form; **dar en el blanco** to hit the mark; **en blanco** (hoja) blank; **hacer blanco** to hit the mark; **quedarse en**

blanco to not get the point; to be disappointed || f see **blanca**
blancor m whiteness
blancura f whiteness; purity
blancuz·co -**ca** adj whitish; dirty-white
blandear tr to persuade; to brandish || intr & ref to yield, give in
blandengue adj (coll) soft, colorless
blandir §1 tr, intr & ref to brandish
blan·do -**da** adj bland, soft; indulgent; flabby; sensual; (coll) cowardly; (ojos) (coll) tender
blandón m wax candle; candlestick
blandura f blandness, softness; tolerance; flabbiness; sensuality; flattery; mild weather; (coll) cowardice
blanquear tr to whiten, bleach; to blanch; to whitewash; to tin || intr to turn white
blanqueci·no -**na** adj whitish
blanqui·llo -**lla** adj white, whitish || m (Guat, Mex) egg; (Chile, Peru) white peach
blanqueci·no -**na** adj whitish
blasfemar intr to blaspheme, to curse
blasfemia f blasphemy
blasfe·mo -**ma** adj blasphemous || mf blasphemer
blasón m (ciencia de los escudos de armas; escudo de armas) heraldry; (heral) charge; (fig) glory, honor
blasonar tr to emblazon; (fig) to emblazon, to extol || intr to boast; **blasonar de** to boast of being
bledo m straw; **no me importa un bledo** or **no se me da un bledo de ello** that doesn't matter a rap to me
blindaje m armor; (elec) shield
blindar tr to armor, armor-plate; (elec) to shield
b.l.m. abbr besa la mano
bloc m (pl bloques) pad
blon·do -**da** adj blond, fair, flaxen, light; (Arg) curly || f blond lace
bloque m block; (de papel) pad; **bloque de hormigón** concrete block
bloquear tr to blockade; (un coche, un tren) to brake; (créditos) to freeze
bloqueo m blockade; (de crédito) freezing; **bloqueo vertical** (telv) vertical hold
b.l.p. abbr besa los pies
blusa f blouse, smock; (de mujer) shirtwaist; (Col) jacket
boardilla f dormer window; garret
boato m show, pomp
bobada f folly, piece of folly
bobali·cón -**cona** adj simple, silly || mf simpleton, nitwit
bobear intr to talk nonsense; to dawdle, loiter around
bobería f folly, nonsense
bóbilis: de bóbilis (coll) free, for nothing; (coll) without effort
bobina f bobbin; (elec) coil; **bobina de chispas** spark coil; **bobina de encendido** ignition coil, spark coil; **bobina de sintonía** tuning coil
bobinar tr to wind
bo·bo -**ba** adj simple, foolish, stupid || mf simpleton, fool || m (archaic) clown, jester

boca *f* mouth; speech; taste, flavor; (*del estómago*) pit; **a boca de jarro** immoderately; at close range; **boca de agua** hydrant; **boca de dragón** (bot) snapdragon; **boca de riego** hydrant; **buscarle a uno la boca** to draw someone out; **decir con la boca chica** (coll) to offer as a mere formality; **no decir esta boca es mía** (coll) to not say a word

bocacalle *f* street entrance

boca-caz *m* (*pl* **-caces**) spillway

bocadillo *m* tape, ribbon; snack, bite; farmer's snack in the field; sandwich

bocadito *m* little bit; (Cuba) cigarillo (*cigaret wrapped in tobacco*)

bocado *m* bite, morsel; bit; **bocado de Adán** Adam's apple; **no tener para un bocado** (coll) to not have a cent

bocal *m* narrow-mouthed pitcher; (*de un puerto*) narrows

bocallave *f* keyhole

bocamanga *f* cuff, wristband

bocanada *f* (*de líquido*) swallow; (*de humo*) puff; (*de viento*) gust; boasting

bocartear *tr* to crush, to stamp

bocera *f* smear on lips

boceto *m* sketch, outline; wax model, clay model

bocina *f* horn, trumpet; auto horn; phonograph horn; (Am) ear trumpet

bocio *m* goiter

bocoy *m* large barrel

bocha *f* bowling ball

boche *m* small hole in ground for boys' game; (Ven) slight, snub

bochinche *m* uproar, tumult, row

bochorno *m* sultry weather; blush, embarrassment, shame

bochorno-so -sa *adj* sultry, stuffy; embarrassing, shameful

boda *f* marriage, wedding; **bodas de Camacho** banquet, lavish feast

bodega *f* wine cellar; dock warehouse; granary; (*de nave*) hold; (coll) cellar; (*hombre que bebe mucho*) (coll) tank; (Am) grocery store

bodegón *m* hash house, beanery; saloon; still life

bodegue-ro -ra *mf* cellarer; (Am) grocer

bodijo *m* (coll) unequal match; (coll) simple wedding

bodoque *m* lump; (coll) dunce, dolt; (Mex) bump, lump

bodoquera *f* peashooter

bóer *mf* Boer

bofe *m* (coll) lung; (P-R) cinch, snap; **echar el bofe** or **los bofes** (coll) to drudge, to grind; **bofes** lights (*of sheep, etc.*)

bofetada *f* slap in the face

boga *mf* rower ‖ *f* vogue, fashion; rowing

bogar §44 *intr* to row

bogavante *m* lobster

bohardilla *f* dormer window; garret

bohe-mio -mia *adj* & *mf* Bohemian

bohío *m* (Am) hut, shack

boicotear *tr* to boycott

boicoteo *m* boycott, boycotting

boina *f* beret

boj *m* boxwood

boja *f* southernwood

bojar *tr* to measure the perimeter of; (*el cuero*) to scrape clean ‖ *intr* to measure

bola *f* ball; marble; bowling; shoe polish; shoeshine; (cards) slam; lie, deceit; (Mex) brawl, riot; **bola de alcanfor** moth ball; **bola de cristal** crystal ball; **bola de nieve** snowball; **bola rompedora** wrecking ball; **bolas** Gaucho lasso tipped with balls; **dejar que ruede la bola** to let things take their course; **raspar la bola** (Chile) to clear out, beat it

bolada *f* (*de una bola*) throw; (Am) luck, opportunity; (Arg) billiard stroke; (Chile) dainty, tidbit; (Guat, Mex) lie, fib

bolazo *m* hit with a ball; **de bolazo** (coll) hurriedly, right away; (Mex) at random

bolchevique *adj* & *mf* Bolshevik

bolchevismo *m* Bolshevism

boleada *f* (Arg) hunting with bolas; (Mex) shoeshine; (Peru) flunking

bolear *tr* (coll) to throw; (Arg) to catch with bolas; (*zapatos*) (Mex) to shine; (SAm) to kick out, to flunk ‖ *intr* to play for fun; to lie; to boast ‖ *ref* (Arg, Urug) to rear and fall backwards; (Arg, Urug) to upset; (Arg, Urug) to blush

bole·ro -ra *mf* bolero dancer ‖ *m* bolero (*dance; music; jacket*); (Mex) bootblack ‖ *f* bowling alley; **bolera encespada** bowling green

boleta *f* pass, permit, admission ticket; (mil) billet; (Am) ballot

boletería *f* (Am) ticket office

boletín *m* bulletin; ticket; form; press release

boleto *m* (Am) ticket

boliche *m* bowling; bowling alley; (SAm) hash house

bólido *m* fireball, bolide

bolígrafo *m* ball-point pen

bolillo *m* bobbin for making lace; frame for stiffening lace cuffs

Bolivia *f* Bolivia

bolivia-no -na *adj* & *mf* Bolivian

bolo *m* ninepin, tenpin; dunce, blockhead; (*de escalera*) newel; (cards) slam; **bolos** bowling, ninepins, tenpins; **jugar a los bolos** to bowl

Bolonia *f* Bologna

bolsa *f* purse, pocketbook; pouch; stock exchange, stock market; (*en el vestido*) bag, pucker; grant, award; **bolsa de agua caliente** hot-water bottle; **bolsa de hielo** ice bag; **bolsa de trabajo** employment bureau; **hacer bolsa** (*un vestido*) to bag; **jugar a la bolsa** to play the market

bolsear *tr* (Arg, Bol, Urug) to jilt; (Am) to pick the pocket of; (Chile) to sponge on

bolsillo *m* pocket; purse, pocketbook

bolsista *m* broker, stockbroker; (CAm, Mex) pickpocket

bolso *m* purse, pocketbook; **bolso de mano** handbag

bollo *m* bun, roll; bump, lump; dent; (*en un vestido*) puff; (*en adorno de tapicería*) tuft; **bollo de crema** cream puff

bomba *f* pump; bomb; fire engine; lamp globe; high hat; firecracker; soap bubble; bombshell; **a prueba de bombas** bombproof; **bomba atómica** atomic bomb; **bomba cohete** rocket bomb; **bomba de hidrógeno** hydrogen bomb; **bomba de incendios** fire engine; **bomba de profundidad** depth bomb; **bomba de sentina** bilge pump; **bomba rompedora** blockbuster; **bomba volante** buzz bomb; **caer como una bomba** (coll) to fall like a bombshell; (coll) to burst in unexpectedly

bombachas *fpl* loose-fitting baggy trousers

bombardear *tr* & *intr* to bomb; to bombard; **bombardear en picado** to dive-bomb

bombardeo *m* bombing; bombarding; **bombardeo en picado** dive bombing

bombardero *m* bomber; bombardier

bomba-reloj *f* time bomb

bombazo *m* bomb explosion; bomb hit; bomb damage

bombear *tr* to bomb; to ballyhoo, to puff up; (Am) to pump; (SAm) to reconnoiter; (Col) to fire, dismiss || *ref* to camber, bulge

bombero *m* fireman; pumpman

bombilla *f* bulb, light bulb; lamp chimney; (Am) tube for sucking up maté; **bombilla de destello** flash bulb

bombillo *m* trap, stench trap; (naut) pump

bombista *m* lamp maker; (*el que da bombos*) (coll) booster

bom·bo -ba *adj* (coll) astounded, stunned; (W-I) lukewarm || *m* bass drum; ballyhoo; (naut) barge, lighter; **dar bombo a** (coll) to ballyhoo, puff up; **irse al bombo** (Arg) to fail || *f* see **bomba**

bombón *m* bonbon, candy

bombona *f* carboy

bombonera *f* candy box

bona·chón -chona *adj* (coll) good-natured, kind, simple

bonancible *adj* (*tiempo*) fair; (*mar*) calm; (*viento*) moderate

bonanza *f* fair weather, calm seas; prosperity, boom; rich ore pocket

bona·zo za *adj* (coll) kind-hearted

bondad *f* kindness; favor; **tener la bondad de** to have the kindness to

bondado·so -sa *adj* kind, generous

bonete *m* cap, hat; candy bowl

boniato *m* sweet potato

bonificar §73 *tr* to improve; to give a discount on

boni·to -ta *adj* pretty, nice; pretty good

bono *m* bond; food voucher

boñiga *f* manure, cow dung

boqueada *f* gasp of death

boquear *tr* to pronounce, utter || *intr* to gasp

---

boquerel *m* nozzle

boquete *m* gap, breach, opening

boquiabier·to -ta *adj* open-mouthed

boquian·cho -cha *adj* wide-mouthed

boquiangos·to -ta *adj* narrow-mouthed

boquihun·di·do -da *adj* hollow-mouthed

boquilla *f* (*de instrumento de viento*) mouthpiece; (*de pipa*) stem; (*de cigarro*) tip; (*de aparato de alumbrado*) burner; cigar holder, cigarette holder; (*de manguera*) nozzle; opening in irrigation canal; opening at bottom of trouser leg

boquirro·to -ta *adj* (coll) garrulous

boquiverde *adj* (coll) obscene, smutty

bórax *m* borax

borbollar or **borbollear** *intr* to bubble up

borbollón *m* bubbling; **a borbollones** impetuously

borborigmos *mpl* rumbling of the bowels

borbotar *intr* to bubble up, bubble over

borce·guí *m* (*pl* **-guíes**) high shoe

borda *f* hut; (naut) gunwale; **arrojar, echar** or **tirar por la borda** to throw overboard

bordada *f* (naut) tack; **dar bordadas** (naut) to tack; to pace to and fro

bordado *m* embroidery

bordadura *f* embroidery

bordar *tr* to embroider

borde *m* border, edge; fringe; rim; **borde de la acera** curb; **borde del mar** seaside

bordear *tr* to border || *intr* to go on the edge; (naut) to tack

bordo *m* (naut) board; (naut) side; (naut) tack; (Guat, Mex) dam, dike; **a bordo** (naut) on board; **al bordo** (naut) alongside; **de alto bordo** seagoing; distinguished, important

bordón *m* (*de tambor*) snare; pilgrim's staff; pet word; burden, refrain

bordonear *intr* to grope along with a stick; to go around begging

borgoña *m* Burgundy (*wine*) || **la Borgoña** Burgundy

borgo·ñón -ñona *adj* & *mf* Burgundian

boricua or **borinque·ño -ña** *adj* & *mf* Puerto Rican

borla *f* tassel; powder puff; **tomar la borla** to take a higher degree, to take the doctor's degree

borne *m* binding post; (*de la lanza*) tip

bornear *tr* to bend, to twist; (*sillares pesados*) to set in place || *intr* to swing at anchor || *ref* to warp

borra *f* fuzz, nap, lint

borrachera *f* drunkenness; spree, binge; great exaltation; (coll) piece of folly; **pegarse una borrachera** to go on a binge

borrachín *m* drunkard

borra·cho -cha *adj* drunk; (*habitualmente*) drinking || *mf* drunkard

borrador *m* blotter, day book; rough draft; (Am) eraser

borradura *f* striking out, scratching out

borraj *m* borax

borrajear *tr & intr* to scribble; to doodle

borrar *tr* to scratch out, cross out; to erase, rub out; to darken, obscure; to blot, to smear

borrasca *f* storm, tempest; upset, setback

borrasco·so -sa *adj* stormy

borregos *mpl* (coll) fleecy clouds

borrica *f* she-ass; (coll) stupid woman

borrico *m* ass, donkey; sawhorse; (coll) stupid fellow, ass

borricón *m* or **borricote** *m* (coll) drudge

borrón *m* blot; rough draft; blemish; (fig) blot, stain

borronear *tr* to scribble

borro·so -sa *adj* blurred, smudgy, fuzzy; muddy, thick

boruca *f* noise, clamor, uproar

borujo *m* lump, clump

boscaje *m* woodland; (paint) woodland scene

bosque *m* forest, woodland; **bosque maderable** timberland

bosquejar *tr* to sketch, to outline; to make a rough model of

bosquejo *m* sketch, outline; rough model

bostezar §60 *intr* to yawn, gape

bostezo *m* yawn, yawning

bota *f* shoe, boot; leather wine bag; liquid measure (*125 gallons or 516 liters*); **bota de agua** gum boot; **bota de montar** riding boot; **ponerse las botas** (coll) to hit the jack pot, come out on top

botador *m* boat pole; punch, nailset

botadura *f* launching

botafuego *m* (coll) hothead, firebrand

botalón *m* (naut) boom; **botalón de foque** (naut) jib boom

botáni·co -ca *adj* botanical || *mf* botanist || *f* botany

botanista *mf* botanist

botar *tr* to throw, hurl; to throw away, throw out; (*un buque*) to launch; (*el timón*) to shift; (Am) to fire, dismiss; (Am) to squander || *intr* to jump; to bounce || *ref* (*un caballo*) to buck

botarate *m* madcap, wild man; (Am) spendthrift

bote *m* boat, small boat; can, jar, pot; bounce; blow, thrust; (Mex) jug, jail; **bote de paso** ferryboat; **bote de porcelana** apothecary's jar; **bote de remos** rowboat; **bote de salvamento** or **bote salvavidas** lifeboat; **de bote en bote** (coll) crowded, jammed; **de bote y voleo** (coll) thoughtlessly

botella *f* bottle

botica *f* drug store; medicine

botica·rio -ria *mf* druggist, apothecary

botija *f* earthenware jug with short narrow neck; (CAm, Ven) hidden treasure; **decirle a uno botija verde** (Cuba) to let someone have it, to tell someone off; **estar hecho una botija** (*un niño*) (coll) to be cross and scream; (*una persona*) (coll) to be fat, be pudgy

botijo *m* earthenware jar with spout and handle

botín *m* booty, plunder, spoils; spat, legging; (Chile) sock

botina *f* shoe, high shoe

botiquín *m* medicine kit, first-aid kit; medicine chest; first-aid station; (Ven) saloon

bo·to -ta *adj* (*sin filo o punta*) blunt, dull; (fig) dull, slow || *m* leather bag || *f* see bota

botón *m* button; (*de mueble o puerta*) knob; (*de reloj de bolsillo*) stem; (bot) bud; (elec) push button; **botón de oro** buttercup; **botón de puerta** doorknob; **botones** *msg* bellboy, bellhop

bou *m* fishing with a dragnet between two boats

bóveda *f* dome, vault; crypt; (aut) cowl; **bóveda celeste** canopy of heaven

boxeador *m* boxer; (Mex) brass knuckles

boxear *intr* to box

boxeo *m* boxing

bóxer *m* brass knuckles

boxibalón *m* punching bag

boya *f* buoy; **boya salvavidas** life buoy

boyante *adj* buoyant; lucky, successful; (*que no cala lo que debe calar*) (naut) light

boyera or **boyeriza** *f* ox stable

boyerizo or **boyero** *m* ox driver

bozal *adj* simple, stupid; (*negro*) just brought in || *m* muzzle; head-harness bells; (Am) headstall

bozo *m* down on upper lip; lips, mouth; headstall

B.p. *abbr* Bendición papal

Br. *abbr* bachiller

bracear *intr* to swing the arms; to swim with overhead strokes; to struggle

brace·ro -ra *adj* arm, hand; thrown with the hand || *m* man who offers his arm to a lady; day laborer; **de bracero** arm in arm

bra·co -ca *adj* pug-nosed

braga *f* diaper, clout; hoisting rope; **bragas** panties, step-ins; breeches; **calzarse las bragas** (coll) to wear the pants

bragadura *f* crotch

braga·zas *m* (*pl* -zas) (coll) easy mark, henpecked fellow

braguero *m* (*para hernias*) truss; (*entrepiernas*) crotch

bragueta *f* fly

bragui·llas *m* (*pl* -llas) (coll) brat

brama *f* rut, mating, mating time

bramante *adj* bellowing, roaring || *m* packthread, twine

bramar *intr* to bellow, roar; (*el viento*) to howl; to rage, storm

bramido *m* bellow, roar; howling; raging

brasa *f* live coal, red-hot coal

brasero *m* brazier; (Col) bonfire; (Mex) hearth, fireplace

Brasil, el Brazil

brasile·ño -ña *adj & mf* Brazilian

bravata *f* bravado, bragging; **echar bravatas** to talk big

bravear *intr* to talk big, to four-flush
braveza *f* bravery; ferocity; *(de los elementos)* fury, violence
bravi·o -a *adj* ferocious; wild, untamed, uncultivated; crude, unpolished; *(mar)* rough, wild; *(terreno)* rough, rugged
bra·vo -va *adj (valiente)* brave; fine, excellent; fierce, savage, wild; *(mar)* rough; magnificent; angry, mad; *(perro)* vicious; *(toro)* game; (coll) boasting; *(chili)* (coll) strong || *interj* bravo!
bravu·cón -cona *adj* (coll) four-flushing || *mf* (coll) fourflusher
bravura *f* bravery; fierceness; gameness; bravado, boasting
braza *f* fathom
brazada *f* stroke, pull *(with the arm)*; **brazada de pecho** breast stroke
brazado *m* armful, armload
brazal *m* arm band; **brazal de luto** mourning band
brazalete *m* bracelet
brazo *m* arm; *(de animal)* foreleg; **a brazo partido** hand to hand *(i.e., without weapons)*; **asidos del brazo** arm in arm; **brazo derecho** right-hand man; **brazos** hands, workmen; backers; **hecho un brazo de mar** dressed to kill
brea *f* tar, wood tar; calking substance; packing canvas; **brea seca** rosin
brear *tr* to annoy, mistreat, beat; to tar
brebaje *m* beverage, drink
brécol *m* or **brécoles** *mpl* broccoli
brecha *f* opening; *(en un muro)* breach; breakthrough
brega *f* fight, struggle, quarrel; trickery; drudgery
bregar §44 *intr* to strive, struggle, toil
breña *f*, **breñal** *m* or **breñar** *m* rocky thicket
bresca *f* honeycomb
Bretaña *f* Brittany; **la Gran Bretaña** Great Britain
brete *m* fetters, shackles; tight squeeze, fix
bretones *mpl* Brussels sprouts
breva *f* early fig; cinch, snap
breval *m* early-fig tree
breve *adj* brief, short; **en breve** shortly, soon
brevedad *f* brevity, shortness; **a la mayor brevedad** as soon as possible
brevete *m* note, mark
brezal *m* heath, moor
brezo *m* heath, heather
briba *f* loafing; **andar a la briba** to loaf around
bri·bón -bona *adj* loafing, crooked || *mf* loafer, crook
bribonada *f* loafing, crookedness
bribonear *intr* to loaf around, to be crooked
brida *f* bridle
brigada *f* brigade; gang, squad; warrant officer
brillante *adj* bright, brilliant, shining || *m* diamond, gem
brillantez *f* brilliance
brillar *intr* to shine; to sparkle

brillazón *f* (Arg, Bol, Urug) pampa mirage
brillo *m* brightness, brilliance; sparkle; **sacar brillo a** to shine
brillo·so -sa *adj (que brilla por el mucho uso)* shiny; (Am) shining, brilliant
brin *m* canvas
brincar §73 *tr* to bounce up and down; to skip, skip over || *intr* to jump, to leap; (coll) to be touchy, get angry easily
brinco *m* bounce; jump, leap; **en dos brincos** or **en un brinco** in an instant
brindador *m* toaster
brindar *tr* to invite; to offer; **brindar a uno con una cosa** to offer someone something || *intr* — **brindar a** or **por** to drink to, to toast || *ref* — **brindarse a** to offer to
brin·dis *m (pl* -dis) invitation, treat; toast
brío *m* spirit, enterprise; elegance; **cortar los bríos a** to cut the wings of
brio·so -sa *adj* spirited, lively, enterprising; elegant
brisa *f* breeze; residue of pressed grapes
brisera *f* or **brisero** *m* (Am) glass lamp shade *(for candles)*
británi·co -ca *adj* British, Britannic
brita·no -na *adj* British || *mf* Briton, Britisher
brizna *f* chip, particle; (Ven) drizzle
brl. *abbr* **barril**
broca *f* reel, spindle; drill, bit
brocado *m* brocade
brocal *m (de pozo)* curbstone; *(de bota)* mouthpiece; *(de banqueta)* (Mex) curb
brocamantón *m* diamond brooch
bróculi *m* broccoli
brocha *f* brush; loaded dice; **de brocha gorda** house *(painter)*; (coll) crude, heavy-handed
brochada *f* stroke with a brush; rough sketch
brochazo *m* stroke with a brush
broche *m* clasp, clip, fastener; *(conjunto de dos piezas)* hook and eye; (Chile) paper clip; **broche de oro** punch line; **broche de presión** snap, catch; **broches** (Ecuad) cuff buttons
brocheta *f* skewer
broma *f* joke, jest; fun; shipworm; **bromas aparte** joking aside; **en broma** in fun, jokingly; **gastar una broma a** to play a joke on
bromear *intr* & *ref* to joke, jest; to have a good time
bromhídri·co -ca *adj* hydrobromic
bromista *adj* joking || *mf* joker
bromo *m* bromine
bromuro *m* bromide
bronca *f* (coll) row, quarrel; (coll) rough joke, poor joke; **armar una bronca** (coll) to start a row
bronce *m* bronze; **bronce de cañón** gun metal
broncea·do -da *adj* bronze; tanned, sunburned || *m* bronzing; bronze finish; tan, sunburn

broncear *tr, intr & ref* to bronze; to tan, sunburn

bron·co -ca *adj* coarse, rough; gruff, crude; (*voz*) harsh, hoarse || *f* see **bronca**

bronquitis *f* bronchitis

broquel *m* buckler, shield; (fig) shield

broqueta *f* skewer

brota *f* bud, shoot

brotadura *f* budding, sprouting; gushing; (*de la piel*) eruption, rash

brotar *tr* to bring forth, to produce || *intr* to bud, sprout; to gush; (*la piel*) to break out

brote *m* bud, shoot; outbreak; (*de petróleo*) gush, spurt

broza *f* (*maleza*) underbrush; (*hojas, ramas, cortezas*) brushwood; (*desperdicio*) trash, rubbish; printer's brush

bruces — dar or caer de bruces to fall on one's face

bruja *f* witch, sorceress; barn owl; (*mujer fea*) hag; (*mujer de mala vida*) prostitute; (W-I) spook

brujear *tr* (*bestias salvajes*) (Ven) to hunt || *intr* to practice witchcraft

brujería *f* witchcraft, sorcery, magic

brujo *m* sorcerer, wizard

brújula *f* (*flechilla*) magnetic needle; (*instrumento*) compass; (*agujero para la puntería*) sight; **perder la brújula** to lose one's touch

brujulear *tr* (*las cartas*) to uncover gradually; (coll) to suspect

brulote *m* fire ship; (Arg, Chile, Bol) vulgarity, insult

bruma *f* fog, mist

brumo·so -sa *adj* foggy, misty

bruñido *m* burnish, polish; burnishing

bruñir §12 *tr* to burnish, to polish; to put rouge on; (CAm) to annoy

brus·co -ca *adj* brusque, gruff; sudden; (*curva*) sharp

bruselas *fpl* tweezers || **Bruselas** Brussels

brusquedad *f* brusqueness, gruffness; suddenness; (*de una curva*) sharpness

brutal *adj* brutal; sudden; (coll) huge, terrific; (coll) stunning

brutalidad *f* brutality; stupidity; (coll) tremendous amount

bruteza *f* brutality; (archaic) roughness

bru·to -ta *adj* brute; rough, coarse; stupid; gross || *mf* (*persona*) brute; blockhead || *m* (*animal*) brute

bu *m* (*pl* búes) (coll) bugaboo; **hacer el bu a** (*coll*) to scare, frighten

bucear *intr* to dive, be a diver; to delve, search

buceo *m* diving

bucle *m* curl, lock

buche *m* (*de ave*) craw, crop, maw; (*de líquido*) mouthful; (*del vestido*) bag, pucker; (*para secretos*) bosom; (coll) belly; (Ecuad) high hat; (Guat, Mex) goiter; **sacar el buche a** (coll) to make (*someone*) open up

budín *m* pudding

buen *adj* var of **bueno**, used before masculine singular nouns

buenamente *adv* with ease; gladly, willingly; conveniently

buenaventura *f* fortune, good luck; (*adivinación*) fortune; **decirle a uno la buenaventura** to tell someone his fortune

bue·no -na *adj* good; kind; (*sano*) well; (*tiempo*) good, fine; **a buenas** willingly; **¡buena es ésa** (or **ésta**)! (coll) that's a good one; **de buenas a primeras** all of a sudden; from the start; **¿de dónde bueno?** (coll) where have you been?, what's new?

buey *m* ox, bullock, steer

búfa·lo -la *mf* buffalo

bufanda *f* muffler, scarf

bufar *intr* to snort

bufete *m* writing desk; law office; (*de un abogado*) clients; law practice; (Am) refreshment; (Col) bedpan; **abrir bufete** to open a law office

bufido *m* snort

bu·fo -fa *adj* comic; (Ven) spongy || *mf* buffoon

bu·fón -fona *adj* clownish || *m* clown, buffoon; jester; peddler

bufonada *f* buffoonery; sarcasm

bufonería *f* buffoonery; peddling

bufones·co -ca *adj* clownish; coarse, crude

bugui-bugul *m* boogie-woogie

buharda *f* dormer; dormer window; garret

buhardilla *f* dormer window; garret

buho *m* eagle owl; (coll) shy fellow

buhonería *f* peddler's kit; peddler's wares

buhonero *m* peddler, hawker

buitre *m* vulture

buje *m* axle box, bushing

bujería *f* gewgaw, trinket

bujía *f* candle; candlestick; candle power; (*de motor de explosión*) spark plug

bulbo *m* bulb

bulevar *m* boulevard

bulevardero *m* boulevardier, man about town

Bulgaria *f* Bulgaria

búlga·ro -ra *adj & mf* Bulgarian

bulto *m* bulk, volume; bust, statue; parcel, piece of baggage; bump, swelling; pillowcase; form, mass; **a bulto** broadly, by guess; **buscar el bulto a** (coll) to keep after; **de bulto** evident; **escurrir** or **huir el bulto** (coll) to duck

bulla *f* noise; crowd; loud argument

bullaje *m* crush, mob (*of people*)

bullanga *f* racket, disturbance

bullebulle *mf* (coll) busybody, bustler

bullicio *m* brawl, riot, uprising; (*rumor que hace mucha gente*) rumble

bullicio·so -sa *adj* brawling, riotous; rumbling || *mf* rioter

bullir §13 *tr* to move || *intr* to boil; to abound; to bustle, to hustle; to swarm; to move, to stir; (coll) to be restless || *ref* to move, to stir

buniato *m* sweet potato

buñuelo *m* cruller, fritter, bun; (coll) botch, bungle

buque *m* ship, vessel; (*de una nave*)

hull; (de cualquier cosa) capacity; (C-R) doorframe; **buque almirante** admiral; **buque cisterna** tanker; **buque de guerra** warship; **buque de vapor** steamer, steamship; **buque de vela** sailboat; **buque escucha** vedette; **buque escucha** training ship; **buque fanal** or **buque faro** lightship; **buque mercante** merchantman, merchant vessel; **buque portaminas** mine layer; **buque tanque** tanker; **buque velero** sailing vessel

burbuja f bubble

burbujear intr to bubble

burdégano m hinny

burdel m brothel, disorderly house

Burdeos Bordeaux

bur·do -da adj coarse, rough

burear tr (Col) to fool || intr to have fun

burga f hot springs

bur·gués -guesa adj middle-class, bourgeois; (antiartístico) bourgeois || m middle-class man || f middle-class woman

burguesía f middle class, bourgeoisie; **alta burguesía** upper middle class; **pequeña burguesía** lower middle class

burla f hoax, trick; joke; ridicule; **burlas aparte** joking aside; **de burlas** in fun, for fun

burladero m safety island, safety zone; (en las plazas de toros) covert; (en los túneles) safety niche; hiding place

burla·dor -dora adj joking; deceptive || mf wag, prankster, practical joker || m seducer, libertine

burlar tr to make fun of; to deceive; to disappoint; to outwit, frustrate; (a una mujer) to seduce || intr to scoff || ref to joke; **burlarse de** to make fun of

burlería f derision, mockery; deception, trick; scorn, derision; fish story

burles·co -ca adj (coll) funny, comic, burlesque

burlete m weather stripping

bur·lón -lona adj joking || mf joker || m mockingbird

bu·ró m (pl -rós) writing desk; (Mex) night table

burócrata mf jobholder, bureaucrat

burra f she-ass; stupid woman; drudge (woman)

burrajear tr & intr to scribble; to doodle

burra·jo -ja adj (Mex) coarse, stupid || m dung (used as fuel)

bu·rro -rra adj (coll) stupid, asinine || m donkey, jackass; sawbuck, sawhorse; (Mex) stepladder; **burro cargado de letras** (coll) learned jackass; **burro de carga** (coll) drudge || f see **burra**

bursátil adj stock-market

busca f search; **en busca de** in search of

buscani·guas m (pl -guas) (Col) snake

buscapié m (para dar a entender algo) hint; (para averiguar algo) feeler || **busca·piés** m (pl -piés) snake

buscaplei·tos m (pl -tos) (Am) troublemaker

buscar §73 tr to seek, to hunt, to look for; (Mex) to provoke; **buscar tres pies al gato** to be looking for trouble || ref to take care of oneself; **buscársela** (coll) to manage to get along; (coll) to ask for it

buscareta f wren

buscarrui·dos mf (pl -dos) (coll) troublemaker

buscavi·das mf (pl -das) (coll) snoop, busybody; (coll) go-getter

bus·cón -cona adj searching; cheating || mf seeker; thief, cheat; (min) prospector || f loose woman

busi·lis m (pl -lis) (coll) trouble; **ahí está el busilis** (coll) that's the trouble; **dar en el busilis** (coll) to hit the nail on the head

búsqueda f search, hunt

busto m bust

butaca f armchair, easy chair; orchestra seat

butifarra f Catalonian sausage; (coll) loose sock, loose stocking; (Peru) ham and salad sandwich

bution·do -da adj lewd, lustful

buz m (pl buces) kiss of gratitude and reverence; lip; **hacer el buz** (archaic) to bow and scrape

buzo m diver

buzón m plug, stopper; mailbox, letter box; (agujero para echar las cartas) slot, letter drop; **buzón de alcance** special-delivery box; late-collection slot

C

C, c (ce) f third letter of the Spanish alphabet

c. abbr **capítulo, compañía, corriente, cuenta**

c abbr **caja, cargo, contra, corriente**

cabal adj exact; full, complete, perfect; **no estar en sus cabales** to be not in one's right mind || adv exactly; completely || interj right!

cábala f intrigue; divination

cabalgada f raid on horseback; gathering of riders

cabalgador m rider, horseman

cabalgadura f mount, horse; beast of burden

cabalgar §44 intr to go horseback riding

cabalgata f cavalcade

caballa *f* mackerel

caballada *f* drove of horses; (Am) nonsense, stupidity

caballaje *m* stud service

caballazo *m* (Am) collision of two horses, trampling by a horse; (Chile, Peru) bitter attack

caballerango *m* (Mex) stableman

caballeresco -ca *adj* chivalric, knightly; gentlemanly

caballerete *m* (coll) dude

caballería *f* mount, horse, mule; cavalry; chivalry, knighthood; **andarse en caballerías** (coll) to fall all over oneself in compliments; **caballería andante** knight-errantry; **caballería mayor** horse, mule; **caballería menor** ass, donkey

caballeriza *f* stable; stable hands

caballerizo *m* groom, stableman

caballe-ro -ra *adj* riding, mounted; stubborn ‖ *m* knight, nobleman; gentleman; mister; horseman, cavalier, rider; **armar caballero** to knight; **caballero andante** knight errant; **caballero de industria** crook, adventurer, sharper; **Caballero de la triste figura** Knight of the Rueful Countenance (*Don Quijote*); **ir caballero en** to ride

caballerosidad *f* chivalry, gentlemanliness

caballerote *m* boorish fellow, cad

caballete *m* (*bastidor para sostener un cuadro o pizarra*) easel; (*de tejado*) ridge, hip; (*lomo de tierra*) ridge; (*artificio usado como soporte*) trestle, sawbuck, horse; (*de la nariz*) bridge; chimney cap; (*del ave*) breastbone; little horse

caballista *m* horseman; mounted smuggler ‖ *f* horsewoman

caballito *m* little horse; merry-go-round; **caballito del diablo** dragonfly

caballo *m* horse; (*en ajedrez*) knight; playing card (*figure on horseback equivalent to queen*); **a caballo** on horseback; **a caballo de** astride; **a caballo regalado no se le mira el diente** never look a gift horse in the mouth; **caballo blanco** (*persona que da dinero para una empresa dudosa*) angel; **caballo de batalla** battle horse; (*de una controversia*) gist, main point; (*aquello en que uno sobresale*) forte, strong point; **caballo de carreras** race horse; **caballo de fuerza** French horsepower, metric horsepower; **caballo de tiro** draft horse; **caballo de Troya** Trojan horse; **caballo de vapor** French horsepower, metric horsepower; **caballo de vapor inglés** horsepower; **caballo mecedor** rocking horse, hobbyhorse; **caballo padre** stallion; **caballo semental** stallion

caballu-no -na *adj* horse, horselike

cabaña *f* cabin, hut; drove, flock; livestock; pastoral scene; (Arg) cattle-breeding ranch

cabañuelas *fpl* (Arg, Bol) first summer rains; (Mex) winter rains

caba-ret *m* (*pl* -rets) cabaret

cabecear *tr* (*un libro*) to put a headband on; (*el vino*) to put a new foot on ‖ *intr* to nod; to bob the head; (*en señal de negación*) to shake the head; (*los caballos*) to toss the head; (*la caja de un carruaje*) to lurch; (*un buque*) to pitch

cabeceo *m* (*de la cabeza*) nod, bob, shake; (*de la caja del carruaje*) lurching; (*del buque*) pitch, pitching

cabecera *f* (*de cama, mesa, etc.*) head; bedside; headboard; headwaters; (*de una casa, un campo*) end; (*del capítulo de un libro*) heading; (*de periódico*) headline; capital, county seat; bolster, pillow; (typ) headpiece, vignette; **cabecera de cartel** top billing; **cabecera de puente** (mil) bridgehead

cabecilla *mf* (coll) scalawag ‖ *m* ringleader ‖ *f* **cabecilla de alfiler** pinhead

cabellar *intr* to grow hair; to put on false hair ‖ *ref* to put on false hair

cabellera *f* head of hair; foliage; (*del cometa*) coma; (bot) mistletoe

cabello *m* hair; **cabello de Venus** maidenhair; **cabellos de ángel** cotton candy; **en cabello** with the hair down; **en cabellos** bareheaded; **traído por los cabellos** far-fetched

cabellu-do -da *adj* hairy

caber §14 *intr* to fit, to go; to have enough room; to be possible; to happen, to befall; **no cabe duda** there is no doubt; **no cabe más** that's the limit; **no caber de** to be bursting with; **no caber en sí** to be beside oneself, to be puffed up with pride; **todo cabe** anything can be expected of

cabestrar *tr* to put a halter on

cabestrillo *m* sling

cabestro *m* halter; **llevar** or **traer del cabestro** (coll) to lead by the halter; (fig) to lead by the nose

cabeza *f* head; chief city, capital; **cabeza de chorlito** (coll) scatterbrains; (Arg) forgetful person; **cabeza de motín** ringleader; **cabeza de playa** beachhead; **cabeza de puente** bridgehead; **cabeza de turco** butt, scapegoat; **cabeza mayor** head of cattle; **cabeza menor** head of sheep, goats, etc.; **de cabeza** headfirst; on end; on one's own; by heart; **ir cabeza abajo** (coll) to go downhill; **irse de la cabeza** to go out of one's mind; **mala cabeza** headstrong person; **por su cabeza** on one's own; **romperse la cabeza** (coll) to rack one's brains

cabezada *f* butt with the head; blow on the head; (*de buque*) pitch, pitching; (*de bota*) instep; (*de libro*) headband; **dar cabezadas** to nod; (*un buque*) to pitch

cabezal *m* pillow, cushion; bolster

cabezo *m* hillock; summit, peak; reef

cabe-zón -zona *adj* big-headed; stubborn; (*licor*) (Chile) strong ‖ *m* (*en la ropa*) hole for the head; tax register

cabezonada *f* (coll) stubbornness

cabezu·do -da *adj* big-headed; (coll) headstrong; (*vino*) heady

cabezuela *f* little head; (*harina gruesa del trigo*) middling; cornflower

cabida *f* room, space, capacity; influence, pull; **tener cabida en** to be included in

cabildear *intr* to lobby

cabildeo *m* lobbying

cabildero *m* lobbyist

cabildo *m* chapter (*of a cathedral*); chapter meeting; town hall

cabina *f* cabin; (*locutorio del teléfono*) booth; bathhouse, dressing room

cabio *m* rafter; joist

cabizba·jo -ja *adj* crestfallen, downcast

cable *m* cable; rope, hawser; **cable de remolque** towline; **cable de retén** guy wire

cablegrafiar §77 *tr & intr* to cable

cablegráfi·co -ca *adj* cable

cablegrama *m* cablegram

cabo *m* end, tip; (*punta de tierra que penetra en el mar*) cape; (*mango*) handle; small bundle; small piece; boss, foreman, cord, rope, cable; (mil) corporal; **al cabo** finally, at last; **al cabo de** at the end of; **atar cabos** (coll) to put two and two together; **Cabo de Buena Esperanza** Cape of Good Hope; **Cabo de Hornos** Cape Horn; **cabos** (*de caballo*) paws, nose, and mane; eyes, eyebrows, and hair; clothing; **cabo suelto** (coll) loose end; **estar al cabo de** (coll) to be well informed about; **llevar a cabo** to carry out, to accomplish

cabotaje *m* coasting trade

cabra *f* goat; nanny goat; (Chile) light two-wheel carriage; (Chile) sawbuck; (Col, Cuba, Ven) trick, gyp, loaded dice; **cabras** light clouds

cabrahigo wild fig

cabrería *f* goat stable; goat-milk dairy

cabre·ro -ra *mf* goatherd

cabrestante *m* capstan

cabrilla *f* sawbuck, sawhorse; (ichth) grouper; **cabrillas** skipping stones; (*olas blancas en el mar*) whitecaps

cabrillear *intr* (*el mar*) to be covered with whitecaps; to shimmer

cabrio *m* rafter; joist

cabri·o -a *adj* goat; goatish ‖ *m* herd of goats

cabriola *f* caper; somersault; **dar cabriolas** to cut capers

cabriolear *intr* to caper, frisk, prance

cabritilla *f* kid, kidskin

cabrito *m* kid; **cabritos** (Chile) popcorn

cabrón *m* buck, billy goat; (coll) complaisant cuckold; (Chile) pimp

cabronada *f* (coll) shamelessness; (coll) shameless forbearance

cabru·no -na *adj* goat

cacahuate *adj* (Mex) pocked ‖ *m* peanut

cacahuete *m* peanut

cacahuete·ro -ra *mf* peanut vendor

cacalote *m* (Mex) raven; (CAm, Mex) candied popcorn; (Cuba) break, blunder

cacao *m* chocolate tree; cocoa, chocolate; **pedir cacao** (Am) to call quits; **tener mucho cacao** (Guat) to have a lot of pep

cacaraña *f* pit, pock

cacarear *tr* (coll) to crow over, boast of ‖ *intr* (*la gallina*) to cackle; (*el gallo*) to crow

cacareo *m* (*de la gallina*) cackling; (*del gallo*) crowing; (*de una persona*) (coll) crowing, boasting

cacatúa *f* cockatoo

cacea *f* trolling; **pescar a la cacea** to troll

cacear *tr* to stir with a dipper or ladle ‖ *intr* to troll

cacería *f* hunting; hunting party; (*animales cobrados en la caza*) bag; hunting scene

cacerola *f* casserole, saucepan

cacique *m* Indian chief; bossy fellow; (*en asuntos políticos*) (coll) boss; (Chile) lazy lummox; **cacique veranero** Baltimore oriole, hangbird

caciquismo *m* bossism

caco *m* thief, pickpocket; (coll) coward

cacto *m* cactus

cacumen *m* summit; acumen, keen insight

cacha·co -ca *adj* (SAm) sporty ‖ *m* (SAm) sport, dude

cachada *f* (Am) thrust or wound made with the horns

cachalote *m* sperm whale

cachar *tr* to break to pieces; (*la madera*) to slit, split; (Arg, Ecuad, Urug) to make fun of; (Am) to butt with the horns; (Chile) to grasp, understand

cacharpari *m* (Arg, Bol, Peru) send-off party

cacharro *m* crock, earthen pot; piece of crockery; piece of junk; (CAm, W-I) jail; (Col) trinket

cachaza *f* (coll) sloth, phlegm; rum; (Am) first froth on cane juice when boiled

cachazu·do -da *adj* (coll) slothful, phlegmatic ‖ *mf* (coll) sluggard

cachear *tr* to frisk

cacheo *m* frisking

cachete *m* slap in the face; cheek; swollen cheek; dagger

cachetero *m* dagger; dagger man

cacheti·na *f* (coll) brawl, fistfight

cachicuer·no -na *adj* horn-handled

cachillada *f* brood, litter

cachimba *f* (*para fumar*) (Am) pipe; (Arg, Urug) well, spring; (Chile) revolver

cachimbo *m* (*para fumar*) (Am) pipe; (Cuba) sugar mill; **chupar cachimbo** (Ven) to smoke a pipe; (*un niño*) (Ven) to suck its finger

cachiporra *f* billy, bludgeon

cachivache *m* good-for-nothing; **cachivaches** broken pottery; pots and pans; junk, trash

cacho *m* slice, piece; (*mercadería que no se vende*) (Chile) drug on the market

cachón m (*ola de agua*) breaker; splash of water; **cachones** surf

cachon·do -da adj (*perra*) in rut; sexy

cacho·rro -rra mf cub, whelp, pup ‖ m little pistol

cachucha f rowboat; cap; Andalusian dance

cachuela f gizzard; fricassee of pork

cachu·pín -pína mf (CAm, Mex) Spanish settler in Latin America

cada adj each; every; **cada vez más** more and more; **cada vez que** whenever

cadalso m stand, platform; (*para la ejecución de un reo*) scaffold

cadarzo m floss, floss silk

cadáver m corpse, cadaver

cadavéri·co -ca adj cadaverous

cadena f chain; **cadena de presidiarios** chain gang; **cadena perpetua** life imprisonment

cadencia f cadence, rhythm

cadencio·co -sa adj rhythmical

cadenero m (surv) lineman

cadera f hip

cadete m (mil) cadet; (Arg, Bol) apprentice (*without pay*), errand boy

cadillo m burdock

cadmio m cadmium

caducar §73 intr to be in one's dotage; to be worn out; to lapse, expire

caedi·zo -za adj tottery, ready to fall over ‖ m (Am) lean-to

caer §15 intr to fall; to droop; to fall due; to be, be found; to fade; (*el sol, el día, el viento*) to decline; to happen; **caer a** to face, overlook; **caer bien** to fit; to be becoming; (coll) to make a hit; **caer de plano** to fall flat; **caer en** (*cierto día*) to come on, fall on, happen on; (*cierta página*) to be found on; **caer en cama** to fall ill; **caer en favor** to be in favor; **caer en la cuenta** to catch on, get the point; **caer en que** to realize that; **caer mal** to fit badly; to be unbecoming; (coll) to fall flat; **no caigo** (coll) I don't get it ‖ ref to fall, fall down; to be, be found; **caerse de su peso**, **caerse de suyo** to be self-evident; **caerse muerto de** (*p.ej., alegría, miedo, risa*) to be overcome with

café adj (Am) tan ‖ m coffee; coffee tree; coffee house; café; (Arg) reprimand; (Mex) tantrum; **café cantante** night club; **café de maquinilla** drip coffee; **café solo** black coffee

cafetal m coffee plantation

cafetera f coffee pot; (Arg) jalopy; **cafetera eléctrica** electric percolator

cafetería f cafeteria

cafete·ro -ra adj coffee ‖ mf coffee dealer; coffee-bean picker ‖ f see cafetera

cafeto m coffee tree

cagar §44 tr (coll) to spot, stain, spoil ‖ intr to defecate; ‖ ref to defecate; to be scared

cagatin·ta m or **cagatin·tas** m (pl -tas) office drudge, penpusher

ca·gón -gona adj (coll) cowardly ‖ mf (coll) coward

caída f fall; spill, tumble; drop; failure; blunder, slip; (*de una cortina*) hang; **a la caída de la noche** at nightfall; **a la caída del sol** at sunset; **caída de agua** waterfall; **caída radiactiva** fallout; **caídas** coarse wool; (coll) witticisms

caí·do -da adj fallen; (*cuello*) turndown; (*párpado, hombro*) drooping; dejected, crestfallen; **caído en desuso** obsolete ‖ **caídos** mpl interest due; **los caídos** (*en la guerra*) the fallen ‖ f see caída

caimán m alligator; (coll) schemer

Caín m Cain; **pasar las de Caín** (coll) to have a frightful time

Cairo, El Cairo

caja f box; case, chest, coffer; (*de caudales*) safe, strongbox; (*para dinero contante*) cashbox; (*dinero contante*) cash; (*ataúd*) casket, coffin; (*de reloj de bolsillo*) case; (*donde se pagan las cuentas en los hoteles*) desk; cashier's desk; (*del aparato de radio o televisión*) cabinet; (*de coche*) body; (*tambor*) drum; (*de fusil*) stock; (*de ascensor, de escalera*) shaft, well; (mach) housing; (typ) case; **caja alta** upper case; **caja baja** lower case; **caja clara** snare drum; **caja de ahorros** savings bank; **caja de cambio de marchas** transmission-gear box; **caja de caudales** safe; **caja de cigüeñal** crankcase; **caja de colores** paintbox; **caja de embalaje** packing box or case; **caja de enchufe** (elec) outlet; **caja de engranajes** gear case; **caja de fuego** firebox; **caja de fusibles** fuse box; **caja de ingletes** miter box; **caja de menores** petty cash; **caja de registro** manhole; **caja de reloj** watchcase; **caja de seguridad** safe; safe-deposit box; **caja de sorpresa** jack-in-the-box; **caja de velocidades** transmission-gear box; **caja fuerte** safe, bank vault; **caja postal de ahorros** postal savings bank; **caja registradora** cash register; **despedir** or **echar con cajas destempladas** (coll) to send packing, to give the gate

caje·ro -ra mf boxmaker; (*en un banco*) cashier, teller; (*en un hotel*) desk clerk

cajeta f little box; tobacco box; **de cajeta** (CAm, Mex) fine

cajetilla f pack (*of cigarettes*)

cajetín m rubber stamp; (typ) box

cajista mf compositor

cajón m large box, bin; (*caja movible de un mueble*) drawer; (*que se cierra con llave*) locker; (*que sirve de tienda*) booth, stall; (Chile) booth, gully; (Mex) dry-goods store; (SAm) coffin; **cajón de aire comprimido** caisson; **cajón de sastre** (coll) odds and ends; (coll) muddlehead; **ser de cajón** (coll) to be in vogue, be the thing

cal f lime; **cal apagada** slaked lime; **cal viva** quicklime; **de cal y canto** (coll) strong, tough

cala f calla lily; cove, inlet; (*de fruta*)

sample slice; *(de buque)* hold; suppository

calabacear *tr (a un alumno)* (coll) to flunk; *(una mujer a un pretendiente)* (coll) to jilt

calabacera *f* calabash, pumpkin, squash

calabaza *f* calabash, gourd, pumpkin, squash; (coll) dolt; **dar calabaza a** *(un alumno)* (coll) to flunk; *(un pretendiente)* (coll) to jilt

calabo·bos *m (pl* -**bos**) (coll) steady drizzle

calabocero *m* jailer, warden

calabozo *m* dungeon; cell, prison cell

calada *f* soaking; *(del ave de rapiña)* swoop; (coll) scolding

calado *m* openwork, drawn work; fretwork; *(del agua)* depth; (naut) draught

calafatear *tr* to calk

calafateo *m* calking

calamar *m* squid

calambre *m* cramp

calamidad *f* calamity

calamita *f* magnetic needle

calamito·so -**sa** *adj* calamitous

cálamo *m* reed, stalk; (poet) pen; (poet) flute, reed

calamoca·no -**na** *adj (algo embriagado)* (coll) tipsy; *(chocho)* (coll) doddering

calaña *f* nature, kind; pattern; fan

calar *tr* to pierce; to soak; to wedge; to cut open work in; *(un melón)* to cut a plug in; *(la bayoneta)* to fix; *(un puente levadizo)* to lower; *(las redes de pesca)* to lower in the water; *(un buque cierta profundidad)* to draw; *(a una persona o las intenciones de una persona)* to size up, to see through; (Arg) to stare at ‖ *ref* to get soaked, get drenched; *(introducirse)* to slip in; *(el ave de rapiña)* to swoop down; to miss fire; *(el sombrero)* to pull down tight; *(las gafas)* to stick on; **calarse hasta los huesos** to get soaked to the skin

cala·to -**ta** *adj* (Peru) naked; (Peru) penniless

calavera *m* daredevil; libertine ‖ *f* skull; *(imitación de la calavera)* death's-head; (Mex) tail light

calaverada *f* recklessness, daredeviltry; (Am) escapade

calaverear *tr* to spoil, make ugly ‖ *intr* (coll) to act recklessly; (Am) to go on a spree

calcado *m* tracing

calcañal *m* or **calcañar** *m* heel

calcar §73 *tr* to trace; to copy, imitate; to tread on

calce *m* wedge; iron tire; iron tip; *(de un documento)* (CAm, Mex, P-R) bottom, foot

calceta *f* stocking; fetter, shackle; **hacer calceta** to knit

calcetería *f* hosiery; hosiery shop

calcete·ro -**ra** *mf* hosier; stocking mender

calcetín *m* sock

calcificar §73 *tr & ref* to calcify

calcio *m* calcium

calco *m* tracing; copy, imitation

calcula·dor -**dora** *adj* calculating; *(egoísta, interesado)* (fig) calculating ‖ *mf* calculator ‖ *f* calculating machine

calcular *tr & intr* to calculate; *(suponer)* (fig) to calculate

cálculo *m* calculation; (math, pathol) calculus; **cálculo biliar** gallstone; **cálculo renal** kidney stone

calchona *f* (Chile) goblin, bogey; (Chile) witch, old hag

calda *f* heating, warming; **caldas** hot springs

caldeamiento *m* heating

caldear *tr* to heat; to weld ‖ *ref* to get hot; to get overheated

caldeo *m* heating; welding

caldera *f* boiler; pot, kettle; (Arg) coffee pot, teapot

calderero *m* boilermaker

calderilla *f* holy-water vessel; copper coin; small change; mountain currant

caldero *m* kettle, pot; *(reloj de bolsillo)* (Arg) turnip

calderón *m* caldron; *(signo)* (mus) pause, hold

caldo *m* broth; sauce, gravy, dressing; salad dressing; (Mex) syrup; (Mex) sugar-cane juice; **caldo de la reina** eggnog; **caldos** wet goods

calefacción *f* heating; **calefacción por agua caliente** hot-water heat; **calefacción por aire caliente** hot-air heat

calefactor *m* heater man; (electron) heater, heater element

calefón *m* (Arg) hot-water heater

calendar *tr* to date

calendario *m* calendar; **hacer calendarios** (coll) to meditate; (coll) to make wild predictions

calenta·dor -**dora** *adj* heating ‖ *m* heater; warming pan; *(reloj de bolsillo)* (coll) turnip; **calentador a gas** gas heater; **calentador de agua** water heater

calentamiento *m* heating

calentar §2 *tr* to heat; to warm; to beat; (Chile) to bore, annoy; **calentar la silla** *(detenerse demasiado)* to warm a chair ‖ *ref* to heat up, run hot; to warm oneself; to warm up; *(estar en celo las bestias)* to be in heat; (Chile, Ven) to become annoyed, get angry

calentón *m* (coll) warm-up; **darse un calentón** (coll) to stop and warm up

calentura *f* fever, temperature

calenturien·to -**ta** *adj* feverish; exalted; (Chile) consumptive

calenturón *m* high fever

calenturo·co -**sa** *adj* feverish

calera *f* limekiln; limestone quarry

calesa *f* chaise

caleta *f* cove, inlet

caletre *m* (coll) judgment, acumen

calibrador *m* calipers; **calibrador de alambre** wire gauge

calibrar *tr* to calibrate; to gauge

calibre *m* caliber; gauge; bore, diameter

calicanto *m* rubble masonry

cali·có *m* (*pl* **-cós**) calico

calidad *f* quality; condition, term; rank, nobility; importance; **a calidad de que** provided that; **en calidad de** in the capacity of

cáli·do -da *adj* warm, hot

calidoscopio *m* kaleidoscope

calientaca·mas *m* (*pl* **-mas**) bed warmer

calienta·piés *m* (*pl* **-piés**) foot warmer

caliente *adj* hot; fiery, vehement; (*en celo*) hot; **caliente de cascos** hotheaded; **en caliente** while hot; at once

califa *m* caliph

califato *m* caliphate

calificación *f* qualification; (*nota en un examen*) grade, mark; rating, standing

calificar §73 *tr* to qualify; to certify; to ennoble; (*un examen*) to mark; (*en los registros electorales*) (Chile) to register ‖ *ref* (archaic) to prove one's noble birth; (*en los registros electorales*) (Chile) to register

calificati·vo -va *adj* qualifying ‖ *m* (*nota en la escuela*) grade, mark; (*en un diccionario*) usage label

California *f* California; **la Baja California** Lower California

caligrafía *f* penmanship

calina *f* haze

calino·so -sa *adj* hazy

Calíope *f* Calliope

calipso *m* calypso ‖ **Calipso** *f* Calypso

calistenia *f* calisthenics

calisténi·co -ca *adj* calisthenic

cá·liz *m* (*pl* **-lices**) chalice; **cáliz de dolor** cup of sorrow

cali·zo -za *adj* lime, limestone ‖ *f* limestone

calma *f* calm; calm weather; quiet, tranquillity; slowness; (*cesación*) letup, suspension; **calma chicha** dead calm; **calmas ecuatoriales** doldrums; **en calma** in suspension; (*mercado*) steady; (*mar*) calm, smooth

calmante *adj* soothing; pain-relieving ‖ *m* sedative

calmar *tr* to calm, sooth ‖ *intr* to grow calm; to abate ‖ *ref* to calm down

calmazo *m* dead calm

cal·mo -ma *adj* barren, treeless; fallow, uncultivated ‖ *f* see **calma**

calmo·so -sa *adj* calm; (coll) slow, lazy

calmu·do -da *adj* calm; (*viento*) (naut) light; (*tiempo*) (naut) mild

caló *m* gypsy slang, underworld slang

calofriar §77 *ref* to become chilled

calofrío *m* chill

calor *m* heat; warmth; (fig) warmth, enthusiasm; **hace calor** it is hot, it is warm; **tener calor** (*una persona*) to be hot, be warm

calorífe·ro -ra *adj* heat ‖ *m* heater, furnace; heating system; foot warmer

calorífu·go -ga *adj* heatproof; fireproof

caloro·so -sa *adj* warm, hot; (fig) warm, enthusiastic, hearty

calotear *tr* (Arg) to gyp, cheat

calpul *m* (Guat) gathering, meeting; (Hond) Indian mound

caluma *f* (Peru) gorge in the Andes; (Peru) Indian hamlet

calumnia *f* calumny, slander

calumniar *tr* to slander

calumnio·so -sa *adj* slanderous

caluro·so -sa *adj* warm, hot; (fig) warm, enthusiastic, hearty

calva *f* bald spot; bare spot, clearing; (*en un tejido*) worn spot

calvario *m* (*sufrimiento moral*) cross; (coll) series of misfortures; (coll) string of debts ‖ **Calvario** *m* Calvary; Stations of the Cross

calvero *m* clearing; clay pit

calvez *f* or **calvicie** *f* baldness

cal·vo -va *adj* bald; barren, bare ‖ *f* see **calva**

calza *f* wedge; (coll) stocking; **calzas** hose, breeches, tights; **en calzas prietas** (coll) in a tight fix

calzada *f* highway, causeway; (S-D) sidewalk

calzado *m* footwear, shoes

calzador *m* shoehorn

calzar §60 *tr* to shoe, put shoes on; to provide with shoes; (*cierto tamaño de zapatos, guantes, etc.*) to wear, to take; (*un zapato a una persona*) to fit; to wedge; (*una rueda*) to block, scotch; (*la pata de una mesa*) to block up; to tip or trim with iron; (*plantas*) (hort) to hill ‖ *intr* (Arg) to get the place sought; **calzar bien** to wear good footwear; **calzar mal** to wear poor footwear ‖ *ref* to get; (*zapatos, guantes*) to put on, to wear; to put one's shoes on; (*a una persona*) (coll) to dominate, to manage

calzo *m* wedge; chock, skid

calzón *m* trousers, pants; **calzones** trousers, breeches; **calzarse los calzones** to wear the pants

calzonarias *fpl* (Col) suspenders

calzona·zos *m* (*pl* **-zos**) (coll) jellyfish; (coll) henpecked husband

calzoncillos *mpl* underdrawers

callada *f* (naut) abatement, lull; **a las calladas** or **de callada** (coll) on the quiet; **dar la callada por respuesta** to give no answer

calla·do -da *adj* silent; mysterious, secret ‖ *f* see **callada**

callampa *f* (Chile) felt hat; (Chile) large ear; (Chile) mushroom

callana *f* (SAm) Indian baking bowl; (*reloj de bolsillo*) (Chile) turnip; (Chile) behind; (Chile, Peru) flowerpot

callao *m* pebble

callar *tr* to silence; to not mention; (*un secreto*) to keep; to calm, quiet ‖ *intr* & *ref* to become silent, keep silent; to keep quiet, keep still; **callarse la boca** (coll) to shut up, to clam up

calle *f* street; **calle de travesía** cross street; **calle mayor** main street; **dejar en la calle** (coll) to deprive of one's livelihood

calleja *f* side street, alley; (coll) subterfuge, pretext

callejear *intr* to walk around the streets, to ramble around

calleje·ro -ra *adj* street; gadabout ‖ *m*

street guide; list of addresses of newspaper subscribers

callejón m alley, lane; **callejón sin salida** blind alley

callejuela f side street, alley; (coll) subterfuge, pretext

callicida m corn cure

callo m callus; (*en el pie*) corn; **callos** tripe

callo·so -sa adj callous

cama f bed; (*para las bestias*) bedding, litter; **cama imperial** four-poster; **cama turca** day bed; **guardar cama** to be sick in bed

camachuelo m (orn) bullfinch

camada f brood, litter; layer, stratum; (*de ladrones*) den

camafeo m cameo

camaleón m chameleon

cámara f chamber; hall; (*cuerpo legislador*) house, chamber; (*aparato fotográfico*) camera; (*tubo de goma del neumático*) inner tube; (*del arma de fuego*) chamber, breech; (*para cartuchos*) magazine; board, council; (*mueble donde se conservan los alimentos*) icebox; (*evacuación*) bowels; (aer) cockpit; **cámara agrícola** grange; **cámara ardiente** funeral chamber; **cámara de compensación** clearing house; **cámara de fuelle** folding camera; **cámara de las máquinas** (naut) engine room; **Cámara de los Comunes** House of Commons; **Cámara de los Lores** House of Lords; **cámara de oxígeno** oxygen tent; **Cámara de Representantes** House of Representatives; **cámara frigorífica** cold-storage room; **cámara indiscreta** candid camera; **cámaras** loose bowels

camarada m comrade

camarera f waitress; chambermaid; maid; (*en los barcos*) stewardess; (*que sirve a una reina o princesa*) lady in waiting

camarero m waiter; valet; (*en un barco o avión*) steward

camarilla f clique, coterie, cabal; palace coterie

camarín m boudoir; (theat) dressing room

cámaro m var of **camarón**

camarógrafo m cameraman

camarón m shrimp, prawn; (CAm, Col) tip, gratuity; (Ven) nap; **ponerse como un camarón** (Am) to blush

camarote m stateroom, cabin

camasquin·ce mf (pl -ces) (coll) meddlesome person, kibitzer

cambalachar tr & intr var of **cambalachear**

cambalache m exchange, swap; (Arg) second-hand shop

cambalachear tr to swap, exchange, trade off || intr to swap, exchange

cambiadis·cos m (pl -cos) record changer

cambiante adj changing; fickle; iridescent || **cambiantes** mpl iridescence

cambiar tr to change; to exchange || intr to change; **cambiar de** (*p.ej.,*

sombreros, ropa, trenes) to change; **cambiar de marcha** to shift gears || ref to change

cambiavía m (Am) switch; (Am) switchman

cambio m change; exchange; rate of exchange; (aut) shift; (rr) switch; **cambio de marchas, cambio de velocidades** gearshift; **en cambio** on the other hand

cambista mf moneychanger; banker || m (Arg) switchman

cambullón m (Mex, Col, Ven) barter, exchange; (Chile) subversion; (Peru) scheming, trickery

camelar tr (coll) to flirt with; (coll) to cajole, to tease

camelo m (coll) flirtation; (coll) joke; (coll) false rumor

camellero m camel driver

camello m camel

camellón m drinking trough; flower bed

came·ro -ra adj bed || mf maker of bedding || m (Col) highway

camilla f stretcher; couch; round table with heater underneath; (Mex) clothing store

camillero m stretcher-bearer

caminante mf walker; traveler on foot || m groom attending his master's horse

caminar tr (*cierta distancia*) to walk || intr to walk; to go; to travel, to journey; to behave

caminata f (coll) long walk, hike; (coll) outing, jaunt

camine·ro -ra adj road, highway

camino m road, way; (*viaje*) journey; (*tira larga que se pone en mesas o pisos*) (SAm) runner; **a medio camino** (entre) halfway (between); **camino de** on the way to; **camino de herradura** bridle path; **camino de hierro** railway; **camino de ruedas** wagon road; **Camino de Santiago** Way of St. James (*Milky Way*); **camino de sirga** towpath; **camino de tierra** dirt road; **camino real** highroad; **camino trillado** beaten path; **echar camino adelante** to strike out

camión m truck, motor truck; (Mex) bus; **camión volquete** dump truck

camionaje m trucking

camione·ro -ra adj truck || m trucker, teamster

camioneta f light truck

camión-grúa m tow truck

camionista m trucker, teamster

camisa f (*de hombre*) shirt; (*de mujer*) chemise; (*de la culebra*) slough; (*de un libro*) jacket; (*para papeles*) folder; (*de una pieza mecánica*) jacket, casing; (*de un horno de fundición*) lining; **camisa de agua** water jacket; **camisa de dormir** nightshirt; **camisa de fuerza** strait jacket; **cambiarse la camisa** to become a turncoat

camisería f haberdashery; shirt factory

camise·ro -ra mf haberdasher; shirt maker

camiseta f undershirt; (de traje de baño) top
camisola f stiff shirt
camisolín m dickey, shirt front
camón m bay window; **camón de vidrios** glass partition
camorra f (coll) quarrel, row; **armar camorra** (coll) to raise Cain, to raise a row; **buscar camorra** (coll) to be looking for trouble
camorrista adj (coll) quarrelsome || mf (coll) quarrelsome person
camote m (Mex) sweet potato; (Am) onion; (Chile) lie, fib; (Chile, Peru) sweetheart; (Arg, Ecuad) blockhead; (Mex) churl; (El Salv) black-and-blue mark; **tomar un camote** (Am) to become infatuated
camotear tr (Arg) to filch, to snitch; (Guat) to bother || intr (Mex) to wander around aimlessly
campal adj pitched (battle)
campamento m camp; encampment
campana f bell; (para la protección de plantas) bell glass, bell jar; (de las guarniciones de alumbrado eléctrico) canopy; **campana de buzo** diving bell; **por campana de vacante** (Mex) rarely, seldom
campanada f stroke of a bell, ring of a bell; scandal
campanario m belfry, steeple
campanear tr (las campanas) to ring || intr to ring the bells || ref (coll) to strut
campanero m bell ringer; bell founder
campanil adj bell || m belfry, bell tower
campanilla f hand bell; door bell; bubble; (anat) uvula; **de (muchas) campanillas** (coll) of great importance
campano m cowbell
campante adj (coll) proud, satisfied; (coll) outstanding
campanu·do -da adj bell-shaped; pompous, high-sounding
campaña f campaign; cruise; countryside
campar intr to camp; to excel, stand out
campear intr to go to pasture; (las sementeras) to turn green; to stand out, excel; to reconnoiter; (Am) to ride through the fields to check the cattle
campecha·no -na adj (coll) frank, good-natured, cheerful || f (Mex) mixed drink; (Ven) hammock
campeche m logwood
campeón m champion; **campeón de venta** best seller
campeona f championess
campeonato m championship
campe·ro -ra adj unsheltered, in the open
campesi·no -na adj country, rural, peasant || mf peasant, farmer || m countryman || f countrywoman
campestre adj country, rural
campiña f countryside, open country
campo m (terreno sembradío; sitio o foco de varias actividades) field; (en oposición a la ciudad) country; ground, background; (campamento)

(mil) camp; **a campo travlesa** across country; **campo de batalla** battle-field; **campo de juego** playground; **campo de tiro** range, shooting range; **campo santo** cemetery; **levantar el campo** (mil) to break camp; **quedar en el campo** to fall in battle
camposanto m cemetery
camuesa f pippin (apple)
camueso m pippin (tree)
camuflaje m camouflage
camuflar tr to camouflage
can m dog; (de arma de fuego) trigger
cana f grey hair; **echar una cana al aire** (coll) to cut loose, to step out; **peinar canas** (coll) to be getting old
Canadá, el Canada
canadiense adj & mf Canadian
canal m (cauce artificial) canal; (estrecho en el mar) channel; (anat) duct, canal; (telv) channel; **Canal de la Mancha** English Channel; **Canal de Panamá** Panama Canal; **Canal de Suez** Suez Canal; **canal alimenticio** alimentary canal || f channel; (conducto del tejado) gutter; (estría) flute, groove; pipe; (de un libro) fore edge
canalización f (de agua o gas) mains, pipes; ductwork; (elec) wiring; **canalización de consumo** (elec) house current
canalizar §60 to channel; to pipe; (elec) to wire
canalizo m (naut) waterway, fairway
canalón m rain-water spout; shovel hat; **canalones** ravioli
canalla m (coll) churl, scoundrel || f (coll) riffraff, canaille
canallada f (coll) dirty trick, meanness
canana f cartridge belt
canapé m sofa, couch
Canarias fpl Canaries
cana·rio -ria adj & mf Canarian || m canary, canary bird || fpl see **Canarias**
canasta f basket, hamper
canastilla f basket; (ropa para el niño que ha de nacer) layette; (equipo de novia) (dial) trousseau
canastillo m basket-weave tray
canasto m hamper || **canastos** interj confound it!
cáncamo m eyebolt; **cáncamo de argolla** ringbolt
cancanear intr (coll) to loaf around; (Am) to stammer
cancel m storm door; (Am) folding screen
cancela f door of ironwork
cancelar tr to cancel; (una deuda) to pay off
cáncer m cancer
cancero·so -sa adj cancerous
cancilla f lattice gate
canciller m chancellor
cancillería f chancellery
canción f song; poem, lyric poem; **canción de amor** love song; **canción de cuna** cradlesong, lullaby; **canción típica** folk song; **volver a la misma canción** to sing the same old song
cancionero m songbook; anthology

cancionista *mf* popular singer

canco *m* (Chile) flowerpot; (Chile) earthen jug; (Chile) chamber pot; (Bol) buttock; **cancos** (Chile) woman's broad hips

cancón *m* (coll) bugaboo; **hacer un cancón a** (Mex) to try to bluff

cancha *f* field, ground; race track; golf links; tennis court; cockpit; (Urug) path, way; **estar en su cancha** (Arg, Chile, Urug) to be in one's element; **tener cancha** (Arg) to have pull || *interj* gangway!

canche *adj* (Col) tasteless, poorly seasoned; (CAm) blond

candado *m* padlock

candar *tr* to lock, to padlock

candela *f* candle; candlestick; fire, light; **con la candela en la mano** at death's door

candelabro *m* candelabrum

candelecho *m* elevated hut for watching the vineyard

candelero *m* candlestick; brass olive-oil lamp; fishing torch

candelilla *f* catkin; (Arg, Chile) will-o'-the-wisp; (Am) glowworm

candida·to -ta *mf* candidate

candidatura *f* candidacy; list of candidates; voting paper

candidez *f* whiteness; innocence

cándi·do -da white; simple, innocent

candil *m* open olive-oil lamp

candilejas *fpl* footlights

candon·go -ga *adj* fawning, slick; loafing, shirking || *mf* fawner, flatterer; loafer, shirker || *f* fawning; teasing

candonguear *tr* (coll) to kid, tease || *intr* (coll) to scheme to get out of work

candor *m* innocence, ingenuousness

caneca *f* glazed earthen bottle

cane·co -ca *adj* (Arg, Bol) tipsy || *f* see **caneca**

canela *f* cinnamon; (*cosa fina*) (coll) peach

canela·do -da *adj* cinnamon-colored

cane·lo -la *adj* cinnamon || *m* (*árbol*) cinnamon || *f* see **canela**

canelón *m* rain-water spout; large icicle; cinnamon candy

cane·sú *m* (*pl* -**súes**) (*prenda*) guimpe; (*pieza de una prenda*) yoke

cangilón *m* jug, jar, bucket; (*de draga*) bucket, scoop; (Am) rut, track

cangrejo *m* crab

cangrena *f* gangrene

cangrenar *ref* to have gangrene

canguro *m* kangaroo

caníbal *adj* & *mf* cannibal

canica *f* (*bolita*) marble; (*juego*) marbles

canicle *f* whiteness (*of hair*)

canícula *f* dog days || **Canícula** *f* Dog Star

caniculares *mpl* dog days

cani·jo -ja *adj* (coll) weak, sickly || *mf* (coll) weakling

canilla *f* shank (*of leg*); (*espita, grifo*) tap; bobbin, spool; (Mex) strength

cani·no -na *adj* canine || *m* canine, canine tooth || *f* excrement of dogs

canje *m* exchange

canjear *tr* to exchange

ca·no -na *adj* gray; gray-haired; hoary, old || *f* see **cana**

canoa *f* canoe; launch

canoe·ro -ra *mf* canoeist

canon *m* canon

canóni·co -ca *adj* canonical || *f* rules of canonical life

canóniga *f* (coll) nap before eating; (coll) drunk

canónigo *m* canon

canonizar §60 *tr* to canonize; to approve

canonjía *f* (coll) sinecure

cano·ro -ra *adj* (*voz*) melodious; (*ave*) song, sweet-singing

cano·so -sa *adj* gray-haired

canotié *m* straw hat, skimmer

cansa·do -da *adj* tired, weary; exhausted, worn-out; tiresome

cansancio *m* tiredness, fatigue

cansar *tr* to tire, weary; to bore || *intr* be tiresome || *ref* to tire, get tired

cantable *adj* tuneful, singable || *m* (*del libreto de una zarzuela*) lyric; (*de una zarzuela*) musical passage

canta·dor -dora *mf* singer of popular songs

cantaletear *tr* (Am) to say over and over again; (Am) to make fun of

cantalupo *m* cantaloupe

cantante *adj* singing || *mf* singer

cantar *m* song, singing; chant; **Cantar de los Cantares** Song of Songs || *tr* to sing; to chant; to sing of; **cantarlas claras** (coll) to speak out || *intr* to sing; to chant; (coll) to creak, squeak; (coll) to squeal, to peach; **cantar de plano** (coll) to make a full confession

cántara *f* jug, pitcher

cantárida *f* Spanish fly

canta·rín -rina *adj* (*voz*) melodious; (coll) fond of singing || *mf* singer || *m* professional singer

cántaro *m* jug, pitcher; jugful; ballot box; **llover a cántaros** to rain pitchforks

canta·triz *f* (*pl* -**trices**) singer

cantera *f* quarry; talent, genius

cántico *m* canticle

cantidad *f* quantity; amount; sum; **cantidad de movimiento** (mech) momentum

cantiga *f* poem of the troubadours

cantilena *f* ballad, song; **salir con la misma cantilena** (coll) to sing the same old song

cantimplora *f* siphon; carafe, decanter; (*frasco para llevar bebida*) canteen; (Col) powder flask; (Guat) mumps

cantina *f* cantine; lunchroom, station restaurant; (Am) barroom

cantinera *f* camp follower

cantinero *m* bartender

canto *m* song; singing; (*división del poema épico*) canto; (*de notas iguales y uniformes*) chant; (*extremidad*) edge; (*esquina*) corner; (*de cuchillo*) back; (*de pan*) crust; stone, pebble; **canto de corte** cutting edge; **canto del cisne** swan song

cantonera *f* corner reinforcement; corner table, corner shelf; streetwalker

cantonero *m* corner loafer

can·tor -tora *adj* singing; (*pájaro*) song || *mf* singer || *m* chanter; minstrel; poet, bard

canto·so -sa *adj* rocky, stony

canturrear *tr & intr* to hum

canturreo *m* hum, humming

canzonetista *mf* popular singer

caña *f* cane; reed; stalk, stem; (*del brazo o la pierna*) long bone; (*de bota o media*) leg; wineglass; **caña de azúcar** sugar cane; **caña de pescar** fishing rod

cañada *f* glen, ravine, gully; cattle path; (*Am*) brook

cañamazo *m* canvas, burlap; embroidered canvas

cañamiel *f* sugar cane

cáñamo *m* hemp

cañamones *mpl* birdseed

cañaveral *m* canebrake; sugar-cane plantation

cañería *f* pipe; pipe line; piping; **cañería maestra** gas main, water main

cañero *m* pipe fitter, plumber; (*Am*) sugar-cane dealer; (*SAm*) cheat; (*SAm*) bluffer

cañista *m* pipe fitter, plumber

caño *m* pipe, tube; gutter, sewer; ditch; (*chorro*) spurt, jet; (*canal angosto*) channel; organ pipe; (*río pequeño*) (Col) stream

cañón *m* (*pieza de artillería*) cannon; (*valle estrecho*) canyon; (*de arma de fuego; de pluma*) barrel; (*pluma de ave*) quill; (*de escalera*) well; (*de columna; de ascensor*) shaft; organ pipe; (Col) trunk of tree; **cañón de campaña** fieldpiece; **cañón de chimenea** flue, chimney flue; **cañón obús** howitzer

cañonear *tr* to cannonade, to shell

cañutazo *m* (coll) gossip

caoba *f* mahogany

caos *m* chaos

caóti·co -ca *adj* chaotic

cap. *abbr* **capitán, capítulo**

capa *f* cloak, cape, mantle; (*de pintura*) coat; (*lo que cubre*) bed, layer; (*apariencia, pretexto*) (fig) cloak, mask; **capa del cielo** canopy of heaven; **andar de capa caída** to be on the decline, to be in a bad way; (*comedia*) **de capa y espada** cloak-and-sword; (*intriga, espionaje*) **de capa y espada** cloak-and-dagger; **so capa de** under the guise of

capacidad *f* capacity

capacitar *tr* to enable, qualify; to empower || *ref* to become qualified

capacha *f* fruit basket; (SAm) jail

capacho *m* fruit basket; hamper; (*de albañil*) hod

capar *tr* to geld, castrate; to curtail

caparazón *m* caparison; horse blanket; nose bag; (*de crustáceo*) shell

caparrosa *f* vitriol

capa·taz *m* (*pl* -**taces**) overseer, foreman, boss

ca·paz *adj* (*pl* -**paces**) (*grande*) capacious, spacious; (*que tiene cierta aptitud; diestro, instruido*) capable; **capaz de** capable of; with a capacity

of; **capaz para** competent in; qualified for; with room for

capcio·so -sa *adj* crafty, deceptive

capea *f* amateur free-for-all bullfight

capear *tr* (*al toro*) to challenge; (*el mal tiempo*) to weather; (coll) to deceive, take in || *intr* (naut) to lay to; (Guat) to play hooky

capellán *m* chaplain

capeo *m* capework (*of bullfighter*)

caperucita *f* little pointed hood; **Caperucita Roja** Little Red Ridinghood

caperuza *f* pointed hood; chimney cap

capilla *f* (*parte de una iglesia con altar*) chapel; (*de los reos de muerte*) death house; (*pliego suelto*) proof sheet; cowl, hood, cape; **estar en capilla** to be in the death house; (coll) to be on pins and needles; **estar expuesto en capilla ardiente** to be on view, to lie in state

capiller *m* churchwarden, sexton

capillo *m* baby cap; baptismal cap; hood; cocoon; (*del cigarro*) filler

capirotazo *m* fillip

capirote *m* hood; doctor's cap and hood; cardboard or paper cone (*worn on head*); fillip

capitación *f* poll tax

capital *adj* capital; main, principal; paramount; (*enemigo*) mortal || *m* (*dinero que produce renta*) capital; (*dinero que se presta para producir renta*) principal || *f* capital

capitalismo *m* capitalism

capitalista *adj* capitalistic || *mf* capitalist; shareholder, investor

capitalizar §60 *tr* to capitalize; (*los intereses devengados*) to compound

capitán *m* captain; leader; **capitán de bandera** flag captain; **capitán de corbeta** (nav) lieutenant commander; **capitán del puerto** harbor master

capitana *f* flagship

capitanear *tr* to captain; to lead, to command

capitanía *f* captaincy; (mil) company

capitel *m* (*de una iglesia*) spire; (*de una columna*) capital

capitolio *m* capitol

capítula *f* chapter (*of Scriptures*)

capitular *tr* to accuse; to agree on || *intr* to capitulate

capitulear *intr* (Arg, Chile, Peru) to lobby

capituleo *m* (Arg, Chile, Peru) lobbying

capitulero *m* (Arg, Chile, Peru) political henchman, lobbyist

capítulo *m* chapter; chapter house; subject, matter; errand; main point; **ganar capítulo** (coll) to win one's point; **llamar a capítulo** to take to task, call to account; **perder capítulo** (coll) to lose one's point

ca·pó *m* (*pl* -**pós**) hood (*of auto*)

capolar *tr* to cut to pieces, chop up

ca·pón -pona *adj* castrated || *m* eunuch; (*pollo*) capon; bundle of firewood; (*golpe*) (coll) fillip || *f* shoulder strap

caponera *f* coop for fattening capons; place of welcome; (*cárcel*) (coll) coop, jail

caporal *m* chief, leader; (Am) foreman (*on cattle ranch*)

capota *f* bonnet; (aer) cowling; (aut) top

capotaje *m* (aer) nosing over

capotar *intr* to upset; (aer) to nose over

capote *m* cape, cloak; (coll) frown, scowl; (Chile, Mex) beating; **capote de monte** poncho; **de capote** (Mex) on the sly; **dar capote a** (coll) to flabbergast; (*un rezagado*) (coll) to leave hungry; **decir para su capote** to say to oneself; **echar un capote** (coll) to turn the conversation

capotear *tr* (*al toro*) to challenge; (*dificultades*) to evade, duck; (coll) to beguile, take in; (*una obra teatral*) to cut, make cuts in

Capricornio *m* Capricorn

capricho *m* caprice, whim, fancy

capricho‧so -sa *adj* capricious, whimsical; willful

caprichu‧do -da *adj* (coll) capricious, whimsical

cápsula *f* capsule; (*de botella*) cap

capsular *tr* to cap

captación *f* capture; (*de las aguas de un río*) harnessing; (rad) tuning in, picking up

captar *tr* to catch; (*la confianza de una persona*) to win; (*las aguas de un río*) to harness; (*las ondas radiofónicas*) to tune in, to pick up; (*lo que uno dice*) to get, grasp ‖ *ref* to attract, win

captura *f* capture, catch

capturar *tr* to capture, catch

capucha *f* cowl, hood; circumflex accent

capuchina *f* garden nasturtium, Indian cress; Capuchin nun; confection of egg yolks

capucho *m* cowl, hood

capuchón *m* lady's cloak and hood; (*de una plumafuente*) cap; (aut) valve cap

capullo *m* cocoon; coarse spun silk; bud; **capullo de rosa** rosebud

capuzar §60 *tr* to throw in headfirst; (*un buque*) to overload at the bow

caqui *adj* khaki ‖ *m* khaki; Japanese persimmon

caquinos *mpl* (Mex) guffaw, outburst of laughter

cara *f* face; look, countenance; façade, front; (*de disco de fonógrafo*) side; **a cara descubierta** openly; **a cara o cruz** heads or tails; **cara a** facing; **cara al público** with an audience; **cara de acelga** (coll) sallow face; **cara de ajo** (coll) vinegar face; **cara de hereje** (*persona de feo aspecto*) (coll) fright, baboon; **cara de vinagre** (coll) vinegar face; **dar la cara** to take the consequences; **de cara** in the face; facing; **echar a cara o cruz** to flip a coin; **hacer cara a** to stand up to; **tener buena cara** to look well, to look good; **tener mala cara** to look ill, to look bad

cárabe *m* amber

carabina *f* carbine; (coll) chaperon

caracol *m* snail; snail shell; (*de pelo*) curl; (*trazado en espiral*) spiral; (*del oído*) cochlea

carácter *m* (*pl* **caracteres**) character; (*marca que se pone a las reses*) brand

característi‧co -ca *adj* characteristic ‖ *m* (theat) old man ‖ *f* characteristic; (theat) old woman

caracteriza‧do -da *adj* distinguished

caracterizar §60 *tr* to characterize; to confer a distinction on; (*un personaje en la escena*) to interpret ‖ *ref* to dress and make up for a role

caramba *interj* confound it!; upon my word!

carámbano *m* icicle

carambola *f* carom; (coll) double shot; (coll) trick, cheating

carambolear *intr* to carom ‖ *ref* (coll) to get tipsy

caramelo *m* caramel; drop, lozenge

carantamaula *f* (coll) ugly false face; (*persona*) (coll) ugly mug

carantoña *f* (coll) ugly false face; **carantoñas** (coll) adulation, fawning

carátula *f* mask; (*profesión de actor*) stage, theater; (Am) title page; (*de reloj*) (Mex, Guat) face

caravana *f* caravan; (*casa rodante*) trailer

caravanera *f* caravansary

caray *m* var of carey

carbohielo *m* dry ice

carbóli‧co -ca *adj* carbolic

carbón *m* (*de leña*) charcoal; (*de piedra*) coal; (*electrodo de carbono de la lámpara de arco o la pila*) carbon; black crayon; (*honguillo parásito*) smut; **carbón de buja** cannel coal, jet coal; **carbón tal como sale** run-of-mine coal

carboncillo *m* charcoal, charcoal pencil

carbonera *f* bunker, coal bunker; coalbin; (Col) coal mine

carbonería *f* coalyard

carbone‧ro -ra *adj* coal, charcoal; coaling ‖ *mf* coaldealer; charcoal burner ‖ *f* see **carbonera**

carbonilla *f* fine coal; (*en los cilindros*) carbon

carbonizar §60 *tr* to char

carbono *m* carbon

carbunclo *m* (*piedra*) carbuncle; (pathol) carbuncle

carbunco *m* (pathol) carbuncle

carbúnculo *m* (*piedra*) carbuncle

carburador *m* carburetor

carburo *m* carbide

carcacha *f* (Mex) jalopy

carcaj *m* quiver

carcajada *f* outburst of laughter

cárcel *f* jail, prison; (*para oprimir dos piezas de madera encoladas*) clamp

carcele‧ro -ra *adj* jail ‖ *m* jailer, warden

carcoma *f* woodworm, borer; anxiety, worry; spendthrift

carcomer *tr* to bore, gnaw away at; to undermine, to harass ‖ *ref* to become worm-eaten

cardán *m* universal joint

cardenal *m* cardinal; cardinal bird; black-and-blue mark

cardenillo 61 carnal

cardenillo *m* verdigris
cárde·no -na *adj* purple; dapple-gray; *(agua)* opaline
cardia·co -ca *adj* cardiac ‖ *mf (persona que padece del corazón)* cardiac ‖ *m (remedio)* cardiac
cardinal *adj* cardinal
cardo *m* thistle
cardume *m* school *(of fish)*
carear *tr* to bring face to face; to compare ‖ *intr* — **carear a** to overlook ‖ *ref* to meet face to face
carecer §22 *intr* — **carecer de** to lack, need, be in want of
carecimiento *m* lack, need, want
carencia *f* lack, need, want
carente *adj* — **carente de** lacking
careo *m* meeting; confrontation
care·ro -ra *adj* (coll) dear, expensive
carestía *f* scarcity, want, dearth; high prices; **carestía de la vida** high cost of living
careta *f* mask; **careta antigás** gas mask
carey *m* hawksbill turtle; tortoise shell
carga *f* load, loading; *(mercancías que se transportan)* freight, cargo; *(peso u obligación que pesan sobre una persona)* burden; *(de substancia explosiva, de electricidad, de soldados contra el enemigo)* charge; charge, responsibility, obligation; **carga de familia** dependent; **carga de punta** (elec) peak load; **carga útil** pay load; **echar la carga a** to put the blame on; **volver a la carga** to keep at it
cargaderas *fpl* (Col) suspenders
cargadero *m* loading platform; freight station
carga·do -da *adj* loaded; *(cielo)* overcast, cloudy; *(atmósfera, tiempo)* close, sultry; *(alambre eléctrico)* hot, charged; *(café, té)* strong; *(rato, hora)* busy; **cargado de años** along in years; **cargado de espaldas** round-shouldered, stoop-shouldered
cargador *m* loader, stevedore; carrier, porter; *(de acumulador)* charger
cargamento *m* load; (naut) loading; (naut) cargo, shipment
cargante *adj* (coll) boring, annoying, tiresome
cargar §44 *tr (un peso, mercancías; un carro, un mulo, un barco; un horno; un arma de fuego; a una persona)* to load; *(a una persona con un peso u obligación)* to burden; *(un acumulador; al enemigo)* to charge; *(a una persona)* to charge with; to entrust with; (coll) to annoy, bore, weary; **cargar en cuenta a** *(una persona)* to charge to the account of; **cargar** *(a una persona)* **de** to charge with; to burden with ‖ *intr* to load; *(el viento)* to turn; to crowd; to incline, tip; *(el acento)* to fall; (coll) to eat too much, drink too much; **cargar con** to pick up; to walk away with; *(un fusil)* to shoulder; to take on; **cargar sobre** to rest on; to bother, pester; to devolve on ‖ *ref (el cielo)* to become overcast; *(el viento)* to turn; (coll) to become an-

noyed, be bored; **cargarse de** to have a lot of; *(lágrimas)* to be bathed in
cargáréme *m* receipt, voucher
cargazón *f* loading; *(en el estómago, la cabeza, etc.)* heaviness; mass of heavy clouds; (Arg) clumsy job; (Chile) good crop
cargo *m* job, position; duty, responsibility; burden, weight; management; *(falta que se atribuye a uno; cantidad que uno debe y la acción de anotarla)* charge; **a cargo de** in charge of; **cargo de conciencia** sense of guilt; **girar a cargo de** to draw on; **hacerse cargo de** to take charge of; to realize, become aware of; to look into; **librar a cargo de** to draw on; **vestir el cargo** to look the part
cargosear *tr* (Arg, Chile) to pester
cargo·so -sa *adj* annoying, bothersome; onerous, costly
carguero *m* (naut) freighter; (Arg, Urug) beast of burden
cariaconteci·do -da *adj* (coll) downcast, woebegone
cariar §77 *tr & intr* to decay
cariátide *f* caryatid
Caribdis *f* Charybdis
caribe *adj* Caribbean ‖ *m* savage, brute
caricatura *f (descripción o figura grotescas; retrato festivo)* caricature; *(retrato festivo)* cartoon
caricaturista *mf* caricaturist; cartoonist
caricaturizar §60 *tr* to caricature; to cartoon
caricia *f* caress; endearment
caridad *f* charity; **la caridad bien ordenada empieza por uno mismo** charity begins at home
caries *f* decay, tooth decay; caries
carilla *f (de colmenero)* mask; *(de libro)* page
carille·no -na *adj* full-faced
carillón *m* carillon
carine·gro -gra *adj* swarthy
cariño *m* love, affection; loved one; (Chile) gift, present; **cariños** caresses, endearments; (Arg) greetings
cariño·so -sa *adj* loving, affectionate
caripare·jo -ja *adj* (coll) stone-faced, impassive
carirraí·do -da *adj* brazen-faced, shameless
carita *f* little face; **dar** or **hacer carita** *(una mujer coqueta)* (Mex) to smile back
caritati·vo -va *adj* charitable
cariz *m (de la atmósfera, el tiempo)* appearance, look; *(de un asunto)* (coll) look, outlook; *(de la cara de uno)* (coll) look; **mal cariz** black look, scowl
carlinga *f* (aer) cockpit
Carlomagno *m* Charlemagne
Carlos *m* Charles
carlota *f* pudding; **carlota rusa** charlotte russe ‖ **Carlota** *f* Charlotte
carmen *m* song, poem; house and garden *(in Granada)*
carmesí *(pl -síes) adj & m* crimson
carnada *f* bait; (coll) bait, trap
carnal *adj* carnal; *(hermano)* full; *(primo)* first

carne *f* (*parte blanda del cuerpo humano y del animal*) flesh; (*la comestible del animal*) meat; **carne de cañón** cannon fodder; **carne de cerdo asada** roast pork; **carne de cordero** lamb; **carne de gallina** goose flesh; **carne de horca** gallows bird; **carne de res** beef; **carne de ternera** veal; **carne de vaca asada** roast of beef; **carne de venado** venison; **carne fiambre** cold meat; **carne sin hueso** (coll) cinch, snap; **carne y sangre** flesh and blood; **cobrar carnes** (coll) to put on flesh; **en carnes** naked; **en vivas carnes** stark-naked

carnear *tr* (Arg, Chile, Urug) to butcher, slaughter; (Arg, Urug) to stab; (Chile) to take in, swindle

carnero *m* sheep; (*carne de este animal*) mutton; (*osario*) charnel house; family vault; (*persona que no tiene voluntad propia*) (Arg, Chile) sheep; **cantar para el carnero** (Arg, Bol, Urug) to die; **no hay tales carneros** there's no truth to it

car·net *m* (*pl* **-nets**) notebook; membership card; (Arg) dance card; **carnet de chófer** driver's license; **carnet de identidad** identification card

carnicería *f* butcher shop, meat market; (fig) carnage, massacre

carnice·ro -ra *adj* carnivorous; bloodthirsty ‖ *mf* butcher

carnosidad *f* fleshiness, corpulence; (*excrecencia carnosa anormal*) proud flesh

carno·so -sa *adj* fleshy; meaty, fat

ca·ro -ra *adj* (*de subido precio; amado, querido*) dear ‖ *f* see **cara** ‖ **caro** *adv* dear

carpa *f* carp; (Am) awning, tent; (Am) stand at a fair; **carpa dorada** goldfish

carpanta *f* (coll) raging hunger

carpeta *f* (*cubierta para mesas*) table cover; (*par de cubiertas para documentos*) letter file, portfolio; (*factura*) invoice; (Col) accounting department; (Peru) writing desk

carpintería *f* carpentry; carpenter shop; **carpintería de taller** millwork

carpintero *m* carpenter; woodpecker; **carpintero de carreta** wheelwright

carra·co -ca *adj* (coll) old, decrepit ‖ *f* (*barco viejo*) tub, hulk; (*instrumento de madera para producir un ruido desagradable*) rattle; (*berbiquí*) ratchet drill ‖ **la Carraca** Cádiz navy yard

carraspear *intr* to be hoarse

carraspera *f* hoarseness

carrera *f* (*paso del que corre*) run; (*lucha de velocidad*) race; (*sitio para correr*) race track; (*espacio recorrido corriendo*) course, stretch; (*curso de la vida, profesión*) career; (*calle*) avenue, boulevard; (*raya, crencha*) part (in hair); (*en las medias*) run; (*hilera*) row, line; (*viga*) rafter, girder; (*movimiento del émbolo del motor*) stroke; **a carrera abierta** at full speed; **carrera a pie** foot race; **carrera ascendente** upstroke; **carrera de baquetas** gantlet; **carrera de caballos** horse race; **carrera de campanario** steeplechase; **carrera de obstáculos** obstacle race; steeplechase; **carrera de relevos** relay race; **carrera descendente** downstroke; **carrera de vallas** hurdle race; **carreras** horse racing, turf

carrerista *adj* horsy ‖ *mf* racegoer; auto racer; bicycle racer ‖ *m* outrider ‖ *f* (slang) streetwalker

carreta *f* cart; **carreta de bueyes** oxcart

carrete *m* reel, spool; fishing reel; (elec) coil

carretear *tr* to cart, haul; (*un carro, una carreta*) to drive; (aer) to taxi ‖ *intr* (aer) to taxi

carretera *f* highway, road; **carretera de peaje** turnpike; **carretera de vía libre** expressway, limited-access highway

carretería *f* carts; wagon work; carting business; wagon shop

carrete·ro -ra *adj* wagon, carriage ‖ *m* wheelwright; teamster; charioteer; **jurar como un carretero** (coll) to swear like a trooper ‖ *f* see **carretera**

carretilla *f* wheelbarrow; baggage truck; (*para enseñar a los niños a andar*) gocart; (*buscapiés*) snake, serpent; (Arg, Chile, Urug) jaw; **carretilla de mano** handcart; **carretilla elevadora** lift truck; **de carretilla** (coll) offhand

carretón *m* cart, wagon, dray; gocart; (rr) truck; (Am) covered wagon

carricoche *m* covered wagon

carricuba *f* street sprinkler

carril *m* (*barra de acero en el ferrocarril*) rail, track; (*huella*) track, rut; (*hecho por el arado*) furrow; lane, path; (Chile) train; (Chile, P-R) railroad; **carril de toma** third rail

carrilera *f* track, rut

carrilero *m* (Peru) railroader

carrillera *f* jaw; chin strap

carrillo *m* cheek, jowl; pulley; **comer a dos carrillos** (coll) to eat like a glutton; (coll) to have two sources of income; (coll) to play both sides

carrizo *m* ditch reed

carro *m* cart, wagon; (mach) carriage; (Am) car, auto; **carro alegórico** float; **carro blindado** armored car; **carro correo** mail car; **carro de asalto** tank; **carro de combate** combat car, tank; **carro de equipajes** baggage car; **carro de mudanza** moving van; **carro de riego** street sprinkler; **carro frigorífico** refrigerator car; **carro fúnebre** hearse; **Carro mayor** Big Dipper; **Carro menor** Little Dipper; **carro romano** chariot; **pare Vd. el carro** hold your horses

ca·rró *m* (*pl* **-rrós**) diamond

carrocería *f* (*de automóvil*) body

carrocha *f* eggs (*of insect*)

carromato *m* covered wagon

carro·ño -ña *adj* & *f* carrion

carroza *f* coach, carriage; **carroza alegórica** float; **carroza fúnebre** hearse

carruaje *m* carriage

carta f (*comunicación escrita*) letter; (*constitución escrita de un país*) charter; (*naipe*) card, playing card; map; **carta aérea** air-mail letter; **carta blanca** carte blanche; **carta certificada** registered letter; **carta de marear** (naut) chart; **carta de naturaleza** naturalization papers; **carta general** form letter; **carta por avión** air-mail letter; **poner las cartas boca arriba** to put one's cards on the table

cartabón m carpenter's square

cartagi-nés -nesa adj & mf Carthaginian

Cartago f Carthage

cartapacio m notebook; schoolboy's satchel; writing book; (*papeles contenidos en una carpeta*) file, dossier

cartear intr to play low cards (*in order to see how the game stands*) || ref to write to each other

cartel m show bill, poster, placard; cartel, trust; (*pasquín*) lampoon; (*de toreros*) bill, line-up; (*del torero*) fame, reputation; **cartel de teatro** bill, show bill; **dar cartel a** (coll) to headline; **se prohibe fijar carteles** post no bills; **tener cartel** (coll) to be the rage

cartela f card; bracket

cartelera f billboard; (*en los periódicos*) amusement page, theater section

cartelero m billposter

cartelón m show bill

carteo m finessing; exchange of letters

cárter m (mach) housing; **cárter de engranajes** gearcase; **cárter del cigüeñal** crankcase

cartera f portfolio; pocket flap; **cartera de bolsillo** billfold, wallet

cartería f sorting room

carterista m pickpocket, purse snatcher

cartero m letter carrier, postman

cartilagino-so -sa adj gristly

cartílago m gristle

cartilla f primer, speller, reader; notebook; (*de la caja de ahorros*) deposit book; **cartilla de racionamiento** ration book

cartivana f (bb) hinge, joint

cartón m cardboard, pasteboard; cardboard box; **cartón de yeso y fieltro** plasterboard; **cartón picado** stencil; **cartón tabla** wallboard

cartoné — en cartoné (bb) in boards, bound in boards

cartucho m cartridge

cartulina f fine cardboard

casa f (*edificio para habitar*) house; (*hogar, domicilio*) home; (*establecimiento comercial o industrial*) firm, concern; (*familia*) household; (*escaque*) square; **a casa** home, homeward; **casa consistorial** town hall, city hall; **casa de azotea** penthouse; **casa de campo** country house; **casa de caridad** poorhouse; **casa de citas** house of assignation; **casa de correos** post office; **casa de empeños** pawnshop; **casa de expósitos** foundling home; **casa de fieras** menagerie; **casa**

de **huéspedes** boarding house; **casa de juego** gambling house; **casa de locos** madhouse; **casa de modas** dress shop; **casa de moneda** mint; **casa de préstamos** pawnshop; **casa de salud** private hospital; **casa de socorro** first-aid station; **casa de vecindad** or **de vecinos** apartment house, tenement house; **casa editorial** publishing house; **casa matriz** main office; **casa pública** brothel; **casa real** royal palace; royal family; **casas baratas** low-cost housing; **casa solar** or **solariega** ancestral mansion, manor house; **casa y comida** board and lodging; **¡convida la casa!** the drinks are on the house!; **en casa** home, at home; **ir a buscar casa** to go house hunting; **poner casa** to set up housekeeping

casaca f dress coat; (coll) marriage contract; (Guat, Hond) lively whispered conversation; **volver la casaca** (coll) to become a turncoat

casade·ro -ra adj marriageable

casa·do -da adj married || mf married person

casal m country place; (Arg) pair, couple

casamente·ro -ra adj matchmaking || mf matchmaker

casamiento m marriage; wedding

casapuerta f entrance hall, vestibule

casaquilla f jacket

casar tr to marry; to marry off; to match; to harmonize; (law) to annul, repeal || intr to marry, get married || ref to marry, get married; **no casarse con nadie** (coll) to get tied up with nobody

casatienda f store and home combined

cascabel m sleigh bell, jingle bell; rattlesnake; **ponerle cascabel al gato** (coll) to bell the cat

cascabelear intr to jingle; (coll) to act tactlessly

cascabeleo m jingle

cascabele·ro -ra adj (coll) tactless, thoughtless || mf (coll) featherbrain || m baby's rattle

cascabillo m jingle bell; chaff, husk; cup of acorn

cascada f cascade, waterfall

cascajo m pebble; gravel, rubble; (coll) broken jar; (coll) piece of junk; **estar hecho un cascajo** (coll) to be old and worn-out, to be a wreck

cascanue·ces m (pl **-ces**) nutcracker

cascar §73 tr to crack, break, split; (coll) to beat, strike, hit || ref to crack, break, split

cáscara f hull, peel, rind, shell; bark, crust; **cáscara rueda** (Arg) ring-around-a-rosy; **ser de la cáscara amarga** (coll) to be wild and flighty; (coll) to hold advanced views; (Mex) to be determined

cascarón m eggshell

cascarra·bias mf (pl **-bias**) (coll) crab, grouch

casco m (*pieza que sirve para proteger la cabeza del soldado, el bombero, etc.*) helmet; (*uña de las caba-*

llerías) hoof; (*pedazo de vasija rota*) potsherd; (*capa de la cebolla*) coat, shell; (*del sombrero*) crown; (*cuerpo de la nave*) hull; (*de un barco inservible*) hulk; (*barril, pipa*) barrel, tank, cask, vat; (*pieza del teléfono*) headset, headpiece; bottle; (*mach*) shell, casing; (*gajo de la naranja*) (Arg, Col, Chile) slice; (*Peru*) chest, breast; **casco de población** or **casco urbano** city limits; **romperse los cascos** (coll) to rack one's brain

casera *f* landlady; housekeeper

casería *f* country place; (Am) customers

caserío *m* country house; small settlement, hamlet

case•ro -ra *adj* homemade; homeloving; (*remedio*) household; house, home; (*sencillo*) homely || *mf* owner, proprietor; renter; caretaker; janitor; (Am) huckster; (Am) vendor || *m* landlord || *f* see **casera**

caseta *f* (*casa sin piso alto*) cottage; (*de una feria*) stall, booth; bathhouse

casi *adv* almost, nearly; **casi nada** next to nothing; **casi nunca** hardly ever

casilla *f* hut, shack, shed; cabin, lodge; stall, booth; (*escaque*) square; (*compartimiento en un mueble*) pigeonhole; (*división del papel rayado*) column, square; (*taquilla*) ticket office; (*de locomotora o camión*) cab; (Bol, Chile, Peru, Urug) post-office box; (Ecuad) water closet; (Cuba) bird trap; **sacarle a uno de sus casillas** (coll) to jolt someone out of his old habits; (coll) to drive someone crazy

casille•ro -ra *mf* (rr) crossing guard || *m* filing cabinet, set of pigeonholes

casino *m* casino; club; clubhouse

caso *m* case; chance; event; **caso de conformidad** in case you agree; **caso que** in case; **de caso pensado** deliberately, on purpose; **en todo caso** at all events; **hacer al caso** (coll) to be to the purpose; **hacer caso de** (coll) to take into account, pay attention to; **hacer caso omiso de** to pass over in silence, not mention; **no venir al caso** to be beside the point; **poner por caso** to take as an example; **venir al caso** to be just the thing

casorio *m* (coll) hasty marriage, unwise marriage

caspa *f* dandruff, scurf

cáspita *interj* well, well!, upon my word!

caspo•so -sa *adj* full of dandruff

casquete *m* (*cubierta que se ajusta al casco de la cabeza*) skullcap; skull, cranium; (*pieza de la armadura que cubre el casco de la cabeza*) helmet; (*pieza del teléfono*) headset

casquillo *m* butt, cap, tip; bushing, sleeve; ferrule; (Am) horseshoe

casquiva•no -na *adj* (coll) scatterbrained

casta *f* caste; kind, quality; breed, race

castaña *f* chestnut; (*moño*) knot, chi-

gnon; demijohn; **castaña de Indias** horse chestnut; **castaña de Pará** Brazil nut

castañeta *f* castanet; snapping of the fingers

castañetear *tr* (*los dedos*) to snap, to click; (*p.ej., una seguidilla*) to click off with the castanets || *intr* to click; (*los dientes*) to chatter

casta•ño -ña *adj* chestnut, chestnutcolored; (*p.ej., pelo*) brown; (*p.ej., ojos*) hazel || *m* chestnut tree; **castaño de Indias** horse chestnut || *f* see **castaña**

castañuela *f* castanet; **estar como unas castañuelas** (coll) to be bubbling over with joy

castella•no -na *adj & mf* Castilian || *m* Castilian, Spanish (*language*) || *f* chatelaine

casticidad *f* purity, correctness (*in language*)

casticismo *m* purism

castidad *f* chastity

castiga•dor -dora *mf* punisher || *m* (coll) seducer, Don Juan

castigar §44 *tr* to punish, chastise; (*la carne*) to mortify; (*los gastos*) to cut down, curtail; (*obras, escritos*) to correct, emend; (*un tornillo*) (Mex) to tighten

castigo *m* punishment, chastisement

Castilla *f* Castile; **Castilla la Nueva** New Castile; **Castilla la Vieja** Old Castile

castillo *m* castle; (*montura sobre un elefante*) howdah; **castillo en el aire** castle in Spain, castle in the air; **castillo de naipes** house of cards; **castillo de proa** forecastle

casti•zo -za *adj* chaste, pure, correct; pure-blooded; real, regular

cas•to -ta *adj* chaste, pure || *f* see **casta**

castor *m* beaver

castrar *tr* to castrate; (*una planta*) to prune, cut back; to weaken

casual *adj* casual, accidental, chance

casualidad *f* accident, chance; chance event; **por casualidad** by chance

casuca or **casucha** *f* shack, shanty

casulla *f* chasuble

cata *f* tasting; taste, sample

catacal•dos *mf* (*pl* -dos) (coll) rolling stone; (coll) busybody

catacumba *f* catacomb

cata•lán -lana *adj & mf* Catalan, Catalonian

catalejo *m* spyglass

catalogar §44 *tr* to catalogue

catálogo *m* catalogue

Cataluña *f* Catalonia

cataplasma *f* poultice; **cataplasma de mostaza** mustard plaster

catapulta *f* catapult

catapultar *tr* to catapult

catar *tr* to taste, sample; to check, examine; to be on the look out for

catarata *f* cataract, waterfall; (pathol) cataract

catarro *m* (*inflamación de las membranas mucosas*) catarrh; (*resfriado*) head cold

catástrofe *f* catastrophe

catavino *m* cup for tasting wine

catavi·nos *m* (*pl* -nos) winetaster; (*borracho*) (coll) rounder

catear *tr* to hunt, look for; (*a un alumno*) to flunk; (Am) to explore; (*una casa*) (Am) to search

catecismo *m* catechism

cátedra *f* chair, professorship; academic subject; teacher's desk; classroom; **poner cátedra** to hold forth

catedral *f* cathedral

catedrático *m* university professor

categoría *f* category; status, standing; class, kind; condition, quality; **de categoría** prominent

caterva *f* throng, crowd

catéter *m* catheter

cateterizar §60 *tr* to catheterize

cátodo *m* cathode

católi·co -ca *adj* catholic; Catholic; **no estar muy católico** (coll) to be under the weather || *mf* Catholic; **católico romano** Roman Catholic

catorce *adj & pron* fourteen || *m* fourteen; (*en las fechas*) fourteenth

catorcea·vo -va *adj & m* fourteenth

catorza·vo -va *adj & m* fourteenth

catre *m* cot; **catre de tijera** folding cot

catrecillo *m* campstool, folding canvas chair

ca·trín -trina *adj* (CAm, Mex) sporty, swell || *mf* (CAm, Mex) sport, dude

caucasia·no -na *or* **caucási·co -ca** *adj & mf* Caucasian

Cáucaso *m* Caucasus

cauce *m* river bed; channel, ditch, trench

caución *f* precaution; (law) bail, security

caucionar *tr* to guard against; (law) to give bail for

cauchal *m* rubber plantation

caucho *m* rubber; rubber plant; (Col) rubber raincoat; **caucho esponjoso** foam rubber; **cauchos** (*chanclos*) (Am) rubbers

caudal *adj* of great volume || *m* (*de agua*) volume; abundance; wealth

caudalo·so -sa *adj* of great volume; abundant; rich, wealthy

caudillo *m* chief, leader; military leader; caudillo, head of state

causa *f* cause; (law) suit, trial; (Chile) bite, snack; (Peru) potato salad; **a** or **por causa de** on account of, because of

causa·dor -dora *adj* causing || *mf* (*persona*) cause

causante *mf* (*persona*) cause; (law) principal, constituent; (Mex) taxpayer

causar *tr* to cause

causear *tr* (Chile) to get the best of || *intr* (Chile) to have a bite

causeo *m* (Chile) bite, snack

cáusti·co -ca *adj* caustic

cautela *f* caution

cautelo·so -sa *adj* cautious, guarded

cauterizar §60 *tr* to cauterize

cautín *m* soldering iron

cautivar *tr* to take prisoner; to attract, win over; (*encantar*) to captivate

cautiverio *m* or **cautividad** *f* captivity

cauti·vo -va *adj & mf* captive

cau·to -ta *adj* cautious

cavar *tr* to dig, dig up || *intr* (*una herida*) to go deep; (*el caballo*) to paw; **cavar en** to study thoroughly, to delve into

caverna *f* cavern, cave

cavidad *f* cavity

cavilar *tr* to brood over || *intr* to worry, fret

cavilo·so -sa *adj* suspicious, mistrustful; (CAm) gossipy; (Col) touchy

cayado *m* (*de pastor*) crook; (*de obispo*) crozier

cayo *m* key, reef; **Cayo Hueso** Key West; **Cayos de la Florida** Florida Keys

caz *m* (*pl* caces) flume, millrace

caza *m* pursuit plane, fighter; **caza de reacción** jet fighter || *f* chase, hunt; hunting; (*animales que se cazan*) game; **a caza de** on the hunt for; **caza al hombre** man hunt; **caza de grillos** fool's errand, wild-goose chase; **ir de caza** to go hunting

cazaautógra·fos *mf* (*pl* -fos) autograph seeker

caza·dor -dora *adj* hunting || *m* hunter; huntsman; **cazador de alforja** trapper; **cazador de cabezas** head-hunter; **cazador de dotes** fortune hunter; **cazador furtivo** poacher || *f* huntress; hunting jacket; jacket

cazanoti·cias (*pl* -cias) *m* newshawk || *f* newshen

cazar §60 *tr* to chase; to hunt; to catch; (*en un descuido o error*) (coll) to catch up; (*un descuido o error*) (coll) to catch; (*adquirir con maña*) (coll) to wangle; (*con halagos o engaños*) to take in || *intr* to hunt

cazarreactor *m* jet fighter

cazcalear *intr* (coll) to buzz around

cazo *m* dipper, ladle; glue pot; (*de cuchillo*) back

cazuela *f* earthen casserole; stew; (archaic) gallery for women; (SAm) chicken stew

cazu·rro -rra *adj* (coll) sullen, surly

cazuz *m* ivy

C. de J. *abbr* **Compañía de Jesús**

cebada *f* barley

cebadera *f* nose bag

cebador *m* (mach) primer

cebar *tr* (*a un animal*) to fatten; (*un horno*) to feed; (*un arma de fuego, una bomba, un carburador*) to prime; (*una pasión, la esperanza*) to nourish; (*atraer*) to lure; (*un clavo, un tornillo*) to make catch, make take hold; (*un anzuelo*) to bait || *intr* (*un clavo, un tornillo*) to catch, take hold || *ref* (*una enfermedad, una epidemia*) to rage; **cebarse en** to be absorbed in; to vent one's fury on

cebo *m* fattening; feed; bait; lure; (*carga de un arma de fuego*) primer; priming

cebolla *f* onion; bulb; (*del velón*) oil receptacle

cebra *f* zebra

ce·bú *m* (*pl* -búes) zebu

ceca *f* mint; **de Ceca en Meca** or **de la Ceca a la Meca** hither and thither, from pillar to post

cecear *intr* to lisp

ceceo *m* lisp, lisping

cecina *f* dried beef

cedazo *m* sieve

ceder *tr* to yield, cede, give up ‖ *intr* to yield, give way, give in; to slacken, relax; to go down, decline

cedro *m* cedar; **cedro de Virginia** juniper, red cedar

cédula *f* (*de papel*) slip; form, blank; rent sign; certificate, document; **cédula de vecindad** or **cédula personal** identification papers

cedulón *m* proclamation, public notice; (*pasquín*) lampoon

céfiro *m* zephyr

cegar §66 *tr* to blind; (*un agujero*) to plug, stop up; (*una puerta, una ventana*) to wall up ‖ *intr* to go blind; to be blinded ‖ *ref* to be blinded

cegato -ta *adj* (coll) dim-sighted, weak-eyed

ceguedad *f* blindness

ceguera *f* blindness

Ceilán Ceylon

cella-nés -nesa *adj* & *mf* Ceylonese

ceja *f* (*pelo sobre la cuenca del ojo*) eyebrow; edge, rim; cloud cap; (Am) clearing for a road; **arquear las cejas** to raise one's eyebrows; **fruncir las cejas** to knit one's brow; **quemarse las cejas** to burn the midnight oil

cejar *intr* to back up; to turn back; to slacken

cejijun-to -ta or ceju-do -da *adj* beetle-browed; (coll) scowling

celada *f* ambush; trap, trick

celador *m* guard (*e.g., in a museum*); (elec) lineman; (Urug) policeman

celaje *m* cloud effect; skylight, transom; (Am) ghost

celar *tr* to see to; to watch over, to keep an eye on; to hide; to carve

celda *f* cell; **celda de castigo** solitary confinement

celdilla *f* cell; niche

celebración *f* celebration; applause; (*de una reunión*) holding

celebrante *m* (*sacerdote*) celebrant

celebrar *tr* to celebrate; (*una reunión*) to hold; (*aprobar*) to welcome; (*un matrimonio*) to perform; (*misa*) to say ‖ *intr* (*decir misa*) to celebrate; to be glad ‖ *ref* to take place, be held; to be celebrated

célebre *adj* celebrated, famous; (coll) funny, witty; (Am) pretty

celebridad *f* (*fama; persona*) celebrity

celeridad *f* speed, swiftness

celeste *adj* celestial; sky-blue

celestial *adj* celestial, heavenly; (coll) stupid, silly

celestina *f* procuress, bawd

celestinaje *m* procuring, pandering

celibato *m* celibacy; (coll) bachelor

célibe *adj* celibate, single, unmarried ‖ *mf* celibate, single person ‖ *m* bachelor ‖ *f* spinster

celinda *f* mock orange

celo *m* zeal; envy; (*impulso reproductivo en las bestias*) heat, rut; **celos** jealousy

celofán *m* or **celofana** *f* cellophane

celosía *f* (*celotipia*) jealousy; (*enrejado de listoncillos*) lattice window, jalousie

celo-so -sa *adj* (*que tiene celo*) zealous; (*que tiene celos*) jealous; fearful, distrustful; (naut) unsteady

celotipia *f* jealousy

celta *adj* Celtic ‖ *mf* Celt ‖ *m* (*idioma*) Celtic

célti-co -ca *adj* Celtic

célula *f* cell

celuloide *m* celluloid; **llevar al celuloide** to put on the screen

cellisca *f* sleet, sleet storm

cellisquear *intr* to sleet

cementerio *m* cemetery

cemento *m* cement; concrete; **cemento armado** reinforced concrete

cena *f* supper; dinner ‖ **la Cena** the Last Supper

cena-dor -dora *mf* diner-out ‖ *m* arbor, bower, summerhouse

cenaduría *f* (Mex) supper club

cenagal *m* quagmire

cenago-so -sa *adj* muddy, miry

cenaoscu-ras *mf* (*pl* -ras) (coll) recluse; (coll) skinflint

cenar *tr* to have for supper, have for dinner ‖ *intr* to have supper, have dinner

cencerrada *f* tin-pan serenade

cencerrear *intr* to keep jingling; to rattle, jangle; (coll) to play out of tune

cencerro *m* cowbell; **a cencerros tapados** (coll) cautiously

cendal *m* gauze, sendal

cenefa *f* edging, trimming, border

cenicero *m* ash tray

ceni-cien-to -ta *adj* ashen, ash-gray ‖ **la Cenicienta** Cinderella

cenit *m* zenith

ceniza *f* ash; ashes; **cenizas** ashes; **huir de las cenizas y caer en las brasas** to jump from the frying pan into the fire

ceni-zo -za *adj* ashen, ash-gray ‖ *f* see ceniza

cenojil *m* garter

cenote *m* (Mex) deep underground water reservoir

censo *m* census; **levantar el censo** to take the census

censor *m* censor; **censor jurado de cuentas** certified public accountant

censura *f* censure; censoring; gossip; **censura de cuentas** auditing

censurar *tr* (*criticar, reprobar*) to censure; (*formar juicio de*) to censor

centauro *m* centaur

centa-vo -va *adj* hundredth ‖ *m* hundredth; cent

centella *f* flash of lightning; flash of light; spark; (*de ingenio, de ira*) (fig) spark, flash

centellar or centellear *intr* to flash, to spark; to glimmer, gleam, twinkle

centenar *m* hundred; **a centenares** by the hundreds

centena·rio -ria *adj* centennial ‖ *mf* centenarian ‖ *m* centennial
cente·no -na *adj* hundredth ‖ *m* rye
centési·mo -ma *adj & m* hundredth
centígra·do -da *adj* centigrade
centímetro *m* centimeter
cénti·mo -ma *adj* hundredth ‖ *m* hundredth; centime
centinela *mf (persona)* watch, guard ‖ *m & f (soldado)* sentinel, sentry; **hacer de centinela** to stand sentinel
centípedo *m* centipede
central *adj* central ‖ *m* sugar mill, sugar refinery ‖ *f* headquarters, main office; powerhouse; (telp) exchange, central; **central de correos** main post office; **central de teléfonos** telephone exchange
centralizar §60 *tr & ref* to centralize
centrar *tr* to center
céntri·co -ca *adj* center, central; *(próximo al centro de la ciudad)* downtown
centro *m* center; middle; business district, downtown; club; object, goal, purpose; **centro de mesa** centerpiece; **centro docente** educational institution; **pegar centro** (CAm) to hit the bull's-eye
Centro América *f* Central America
centroamerica·no -na *adj & mf* Central American
cénts. *abbr* céntimos
ceñi·do -da *adj* tight, tight-fitting; lithe, svelte; thrifty
ceñidor *m* belt, girdle, sash
ceñir §72 *tr* to gird; to girdle; to fasten around the waist; to fasten, to tie; to abridge, shorten; to surround; *(la espada)* to gird on; (mil) to besiege ‖ *ref (reducirse en los gastos)* to tighten one's belt; *(a pocas palabras)* to restrict oneself; to adapt oneself; **ceñirse a** *(p.ej., un muro)* to hug, keep close to
ceño *m* frown; *(del cielo, las nubes, el mar)* threatening look; *(cerco, aro)* hoop, ring, band; **arrugar el ceño** to knit one's brow; **mirar con ceño** to frown at
ceño·so -sa or **ceñu·do -da** *adj* beetle-browed; frowning, grim, gruff
cepa *f (de árbol)* stump; *(de la cola del animal)* stub; *(de la vid)* vine-stalk; *(de una familia o linaje)* strain; **de buena cepa** of well-known quality
cepillar *tr* to plane; to brush; to smooth
cepillo *m (instrumento para alisar la madera)* plane; *(utensilio para limpieza)* brush; *(cepo para limosnas)* charity box, poor box; (CAm, Mex) flatterer; **cepillo de cabeza** hairbrush; **cepillo de dientes** toothbrush; **cepillo de ropa** clothesbrush; **cepillo de uñas** nail brush
cepo *m (de limosnas)* poor box; *(rama de árbol)* bough, branch; *(trampa)* snare, trap; *(del yunque)* stock; *(para devanar la seda)* reel; clamp, vise; *(para asegurar a un reo)* stocks, pillory; **¡cepos quedos!** (coll) quiet!, stop it!
cera *f* wax; **cera de abejas** beeswax;

cera de los oídos earwax; **cera de lustrar** polishing wax; **cera de pisos** floor wax; **ceras** honeycomb; **ser como una cera** to be wax in one's hands
cerámi·co -ca *adj* ceramic
cerbatana *f* peashooter; ear trumpet; (coll) spokesman, go-between
cerca *m* (coll) close-up; **tener buen cerca** (coll) to look good at close quarters ‖ *f* fence, wall; **cerca viva** hedge ‖ *adv* near; **cerca de** near, close to; about; to, at the court of; **de cerca** closely; at close range
cercado *m* fence, wall; walled-in garden or field
cercanía *f* nearness, proximity; **cercanías** neighborhood, vicinity
cerca·no -na *adj* close, near; adjoining, neighboring; *(que debe acontecer en breve)* early
cercar §73 *tr* to fence in, wall in; to encircle, surround; to crowd around; (mil) to besiege
cercenar *tr* to clip, trim; to curtail; to cut out
cerciorar *tr* to inform, assure ‖ *ref* to find out; **cerciorarse de** to ascertain, find out about
cerco *m (aro, anillo)* hoop, ring; *(marco de puerta o ventana)* casing, frame; *(círculo que aparece alrededor del sol o la luna)* halo; *(reunión de personas)* circle, group; fence, wall; (mil) siege; **poner cerco a** (mil) to lay siege to
cerda *f* bristle, horsehair; *(hembra del cerdo)* sow
cerdear *intr* to be weak in the forelegs; *(las cuerdas de un instrumento)* to rasp, to grate; (coll) to hold back, look for excuses
Cerdeña *f* Sardinia
cerdo *m* hog; *(persona sucia)* (coll) pig, swine; *(hombre sin cortesía)* (coll) cad, ill-bred fellow; **cerdo de muerte** pig to be slaughtered; **cerdo de vida** pig not old enough to be slaughtered; **cerdo marino** porpoise
cerdo·so -sa *adj* bristly
cereal *adj & m* cereal
cerebro *m* brain; *(seso, inteligencia)* brain, brains
ceremonia *f* ceremony; formality; **de ceremonia** formal; **hacer ceremonias** to stand on ceremony; **por ceremonia** as a matter of form
ceremonio·so -sa *adj* ceremonious, punctilious; *(que gusta de ceremonias)* formal
cereza *f* cherry
cerezo *m* cherry tree
cerilla *f* wax taper; wax match
cerillera *f* or **cerillero** *m* match box
cerneja *f* fetlock
cerner §51 *tr* to sift; *(el horizonte)* to scan ‖ *intr* to bud, blossom; to drizzle ‖ *ref* to waddle; *(el ave)* to soar, to hover; *(un mal)* to threaten; **cernerse sobre** *(amenazar)* to hang over
cernícalo *m* (orn) sparrow hawk; (coll) ignoramus, (coll) jag, drunk

cernir §28 *tr* to sift

cero *m* zero; **ser un cero a la izquierda** (coll) to not count, to be a nobody

cerote *m* shoemaker's wax; (coll) fear

cerotear *tr* (*el hilo*) to wax ‖ *intr* (Chile) to drip

cerra·do -da *adj* closed; close; incomprehensible; (*cielo*) cloudy, overcast; (*barba*) thick; (*curva*) sharp; (coll) quiet, reserved, secretive; (coll) dense, stupid

cerradura *f* lock; closing, locking; **cerradura embutida** mortise lock

cerrajería *f* locksmith business; hardware; hardware store

cerrajero *m* locksmith; hardware dealer; (*el que trabaja el hierro frío*) ironworker

cerrar §2 *tr* to close, shut; to lock; to bolt; (*el puño*) to clench; to enclose; (*la radio*) to turn off; **cerrar con llave** to lock ‖ *intr* to close, to shut; (*la noche*) to fall; **cerrar con** (*el enemigo*) to close in on; **cerrar en falso** (*una puerta, cerradura, etc.*) to not catch ‖ *ref* to close, to shut; to lock; **cerrarse en falso** to not heal right

cerrazón *f* gathering storm clouds; (Arg) heavy fog

cerre·ro -ra *adj* free, loose; untamed; haughty; (Mex) rough, unpolished; (*café*) (Ven) bitter

cerril *adj* rough, uneven; wild, untamed; (coll) boorish, rough

cerrillar *tr* to knurl, to mill

cerro *m* hill, hillock; (*entre dos surcos*) ridge; (*espinazo*) backbone; (*del animal*) neck; **en cerro** bareback; **echar por los cerros de Úbeda** (coll) to talk nonsense; **por los cerros de Úbeda** (coll) off the beaten path

cerrojo *m* bolt; **cerrojo dormido** dead bolt

certamen *m* literary competition; contest, match

certe·ro -ra *adj* certain, sure, accurate; well-informed; (*tiro*) well-aimed; (*tirador*) good, crack

certeza *f* certainty

certidumbre *f* certainty; sureness

certificación *f* certification; certificate

certifica·do -da *adj* registered ‖ *m* registered letter, registered package; certificate; **certificado de estudios** transcript

certificar §73 *tr* to certify; (*una carta*) to register

certitud *f* certainty

cerval *adj* deer; (*miedo*) intense

cervato *m* fawn

cervecería *f* brewery; beer saloon

cervece·ro -ra *adj* beer ‖ *mf* brewer

cerveza *f* beer; **cerveza a presión** draught beer; **cerveza de marzo** bock beer

cer·viz *f* (*pl* -**vices**) cervix; nape of the neck; **bajar** or **doblar la cerviz** to humble oneself; **levantar la cerviz** to raise one's head, become proud; **ser de dura cerviz** to be ungovernable

cesación *f* cessation, suspension

cesante *adj* retired, out of office ‖ *mf* pensioner

cesantía *f* retirement; dismissal (*of a public official*)

cesar *intr* to stop, cease

César *m* Caesar

cese *m* ceasing; notice of retirement; **cese de alarma** all-clear; **cese de fuego** ceasefire

césped *m* lawn, sward; sod, turf

cesta *f* basket; (*para jugar a la pelota*) wicker scoop; **cesta de costura** sewing basket; **cesta para compras** market basket

cesto *m* basket; washbasket; **cesto de la colada** clothesbasket, washbasket; **estar hecho un cesto** (coll) to be overcome with sleep; **ser un cesto** (coll) to be crude and ignorant

cetrería *f* falconry

cetrero *m* falconer

cetri·no -na *adj* (*tez*) sallow; jaundiced, melancholy

cetro *m* scepter; (*para aves*) perch, roost; (eccl) verge; **cetro de bufón** bauble; **cetro de locura** fool's scepter; **empuñar el cetro** to ascend the throne

cf. *abbr* **confesor**

cg. *abbr* **centigramo**

C.I. *abbr* **cociente intelectual**

cía. *abbr* **compañía**

cía *f* hipbone

cianamida *f* cyanamide

cianuro *m* cyanide

ciar §77 *intr* to back up; to back water; to ease up

ciborio *m* ciborium

cicatear *intr* (coll) to be stingy

cicate·ro -ra *adj* (coll) stingy ‖ *mf* (coll) miser, niggard

cica·triz *f* (*pl* -**trices**) scar

cicatrizar §60 *tr* to heal; (*una impresión dolorosa*) (Arg) to heal ‖ *ref* to heal; to scar

Cicerón *m* Cicero

ciclamor *m* Judas tree; **ciclamor del Canadá** redbud

cicli·co -ca *adj* cyclic(al)

ciclismo *m* bicycle racing

ciclista *mf* bicyclist; bicycle racer

ciclo *m* cycle; series (of lectures); (*en las escuelas*) (Arg, Urug) term

ciclón *m* cyclone

cicuta *f* hemlock

cidra *f* citron (*fruit*)

cidrada *f* citron (*candied rind*)

cidro *m* citron (*tree or shrub*)

cie·go -ga *adj* blind; blocked, stopped up; **más ciego que un topo** blind as a bat ‖ *mf* blind person ‖ *m* blind man ‖ *f* blind woman; **a ciegas** blindly; thoughtlessly; without looking

cielo *m* sky, heavens; (*clima, tiempo*) skies, climate, weather; (*de una cama*) canopy; (*mansión de los bienaventurados*) Heaven; **a cielo abierto** in the open air, outdoors; **a cielo descubierto** openly; **a cielo raso** in the open air, outdoors; in the country; **cielo de la boca** roof of the mouth; **cielo máximo** (aer) ceiling;

cielo raso ceiling; **llovido del cielo** heaven-sent, manna from heaven

cielorraso *m* ceiling

ciem·piés *m* (*pl* **-piés**) centipede

cien *adj* hundred, a hundred, one hundred

ciénaga *f* swamp, marsh, mudhole

ciencia *f* science; knowledge; learning; **a ciencia cierta** with certainty

cieno *m* mud, mire, silt

cieno·so -sa *adj* muddy, miry, silty

ciento *adj* & *m* hundred, a hundred, one hundred; **por ciento** per cent

cierne *m* budding, blossoming; **en cierne** in blossom; only beginning

cierrarrenglón *m* marginal stop

cierre *m* closing; shutting; snap, clasp, fastener; latch, lock; (*de una tienda, de la Bolsa*) close; (*paro de trabajo*) shutdown; **cierre cremallera** zipper; **cierre de portada** metal shutter (*of store front*); **cierre de puerta** door check; **cierre hermético** weather stripping; **cierre relámpago** zipper

cierro *m* closing; shutting; (Chile) fence, wall; (Chile) envelope

cier·to -ta *adj* certain; a certain; (*acertado, verdadero*) true; (*seguro*) sure; **por cierto** for sure || **cierto** *adv* surely, certainly

cierva *f* hind

ciervo *m* deer, stag, hart

cierzo *m* cold north wind

cifra *f* (*número*) cipher; (*escritura secreta*) code; (*enlace de dos o más letras empleado en sellos*) device, monogram, emblem; abbreviation; amount, sum; **en cifra** in code; in brief; mysteriously

cifrar *tr* to cipher, to code; to abridge; to calculate; **cifrar la dicha en** to base one's happiness in; **cifrar la esperanza en** to place one's hope in || *ref* to be abridged; **cifrarse en** to be based on

cifrario *m* (com) code

cigarra *f* harvest fly, locust

cigarrera *f* cigar case; cigar girl

cigarrería *f* cigar store, tobacco store

cigarre·ro -ra *mf* cigar maker; cigar dealer || *f* see **cigarrera**

cigarrillo *m* cigarette; **cigarrillo con filtro** filter cigarette

cigarro *m* cigar; **cigarro de papel** cigarette; **cigarro puro** cigar

cigoñal *m* well sweep; (*del motor de explosión*) crankshaft

cigüeña *f* stork; crank, winch

cigüeñal *m* var of **cigoñal**

cilicio *m* haircloth, hair shirt

cilindrada *f* piston displacement

cilindrar *tr* to roll

cilíndri·co -ca *adj* cylindrical

cilindro *m* cylinder; roll, roller; (Mex) barrel organ, hand organ

cima *f* (*de árbol*) top; (*de montaña*) top, summit; **dar cima a** to complete, to carry out; **por cima** (coll) at the very top

cimarra *f* — **hacer cimarra** (Arg, Chile) to play hooky

cima·rrón -rrona *adj* (*animal*) (Am) wild, untamed; (*planta*) (Am) wild;

(*esclavo*) (Am) fugitive; (*marinero*) (Am) lazy; (*mate*) (Arg, Urug) black, bitter

cimarro·near *intr* (Arg, Urug) to drink black maté || *ref* (*el esclavo*) (Am) to flee, run away

címbalo *m* cymbal

cimbel *m* decoy pigeon, stool pigeon

cimborio or **cimborrio** *m* dome

cimbrar or **cimbrear** *tr* to brandish; to swing, sway; to bend; (coll) to thrash, beat || *ref* to swing, sway; to shake

cimbre·ño -ña *adj* flexible, pliant; lithe, willowy

cimentar §2 *tr* to found, establish; to lay the foundations of

cime·ro -ra *adj* top, uppermost

cimiento *m* foundation, groundwork; basis, source

cimitarra *f* scimitar

cinabrio *m* cinnabar

cinanquia *f* quinsy

cinc *m* (*pl* **cinces**) zinc

cincel *m* chisel, graver

cincelar *tr* to chisel, engrave

cinco *adj* & *pron* five; **las cinco** five o'clock || *m* five; (*en las fechas*) fifth; **¡choque Vd. esos cinco!** or **¡vengan esos cinco!** put it here!, shake!; **decirle a uno cuántas son cinco** (coll) to tell someone what's what

cincograbado *m* zinc etching

cincuenta *adj*, *pron* & *m* fifty

cincuenta·vo -va *adj* & *m* fiftieth

cincha *f* cinch; **a revienta cinchas** at breakneck speed; (Am) reluctantly

cinchar *tr* to cinch; to band, to hoop

cincho *m* girdle, sash; iron hoop; iron tire

cine *m* movie; **cine en colores** color movies; **cine hablado** talkie; **cine mudo** silent movie; **cine parlante** talkie; **cine sonoro** sound movie

cineasta *mf* motion-picture producer; movie fan || *m* movie actor || *f* movie actress

cinedrama *m* screenplay

cinelandia *f* (coll) movieland

cinema *m* var of **cine**

cinematografiar §77 *tr* & *intr* to cinematograph, to film

cinematógrafo *m* cinematograph; motion picture; motion-picture projector; motion-picture theater

cinematurgo *m* scriptwriter

cinescopio (telv) *m* kinescope

cineteatro *m* movie house

cinéti·co -ca *adj* kinetic || *f* kinetics

cínga·ro -ra *adj* & *mf* gypsy

cíni·co -ca *adj* cynical; impudent; slovenly, untidy || *mf* cynic || *m* Cynic

cinismo *m* cynicism; impudence

cinta *f* ribbon; (*tira de papel, celuloide, etc.*) tape; film; measuring tape; (*borde de la acera*) curb; fillet, scroll; **cinta aislante** electric tape, friction tape; **cinta de medir** tape measure; **cinta de teleimpresor** ticker tape; **cinta grabada de televisión** video tape; **cinta perforada** punched tape

cintillo *m* hatband; fancy hat cord; ring set with a gem; (*borde de la acera*) (P-R) curb; (Am) hair ribbon

cinto *m* belt, girdle; waist

cintura *f* (*parte estrecha del cuerpo humano sobre las caderas*) waist; waistline; (*de una chimenea*) throat; **meter en cintura** (coll) to bring to reason

cinturón *m* belt, sash; sword belt; **cinturón de asiento** seat belt; **cinturón salvavidas** (naut) safety belt

cipo *m* milestone; signpost; memorial pillar

cipote *adj* (Col, Ven) stupid; (Guat) chubby ‖ *mf* (Hond, El Salv, Ven) brat

ciprés *m* cypress

circo *m* circus

circón *m* zircon

circonio *m* zirconium

circuito *m* circuit; (*de carreteras, ferrocarriles, etc.*) network; race track; **corto circuito** (elec) short circuit

circulación *f* circulation; traffic; **circulación rodada** vehicular traffic

circular *adj* circular ‖ *f* circular, circular letter ‖ *tr & intr* to circulate

círculo *m* circle; club; clubhouse

circuncidar *tr* to circumcise; to clip, curtail

circundante *adj* surrounding

circundar *tr* to surround, go around

circunferencia *f* circumference

circunflejo -ja *adj* circumflex

circunlocución *f* or **circunloquio** *m* circumlocution

circunnavegación *f* circumnavigation

circunnavegar §44 *tr* to circumnavigate

circunscribir §83 *tr* to circumscribe ‖ *ref* to hold oneself down; to be held down

circunscripción *f* circumscription; district, subdivision

circunspec-to -ta *adj* circumspect

circunstancia *f* circumstance

circunstancia-do -da *adj* circumstantial, detailed

circunstancial *adj* circumstantial

circunstanciar *tr* to circumstantiate, to describe in detail

circunstante *adj* surrounding; present ‖ *mf* bystander, onlooker

circunveci-no -na *adj* neighboring

circunvolar §61 *tr* to fly around

cirial *m* (eccl) processional candlestick

ciriga-llo -lla *mf* gadabout

ciríli-co -ca *adj* Cyrillic

cirio *m* wax candle

Ciro *m* Cyrus

ciruela *f* plum; **ciruela claudia** greengage; **ciruela pasa** prune

ciruelo *m* plum, plum tree; (coll) stupid fellow

cirugía *f* surgery; **cirugía cosmética, decorativa** or **estética** face lifting

ciruja-no -na *mf* surgeon

ciscar §73 *tr* to soil, dirty ‖ *ref* (coll) to soil one's clothes, to have an accident

cisco *m* culm; (coll) row, disturbance

cisma *m* schism; discord, disagree-

ment; (Arg) worry, concern; (Col) gossip; (Col) fastidiousness

cismáti-co -ca *adj* schismatic; dissident; (Col) gossipy; (Col) fastidious ‖ *mf* schismatic; dissident

cisne *m* swan; (Arg) powder puff

cisterna *f* cistern; reservoir

cita *f* date, appointment, engagement; (*mención, pasaje textual*) citation, quotation; **cita a ciegas** blind date; **cita previa** by appointment; **darse cita** to make a date

citación *f* citation, quotation; (*ante un juez*) citation, summons

citar *tr* to make a date with, have an appointment with; to cite, to quote; (*ante un juez*) to cite, to summon; (*al toro*) to incite, provoke ‖ *ref* to make a date, have an appointment

cítara *f* (mus) zither

ciudad *f* city; city council; **la ciudad Condal** Barcelona; **la ciudad del Apóstol** Santiago de Compostela; **la ciudad del Betis** Seville; **la ciudad del Cabo** Capetown or Cape Town; **la ciudad de los Califas** Cordova; **la ciudad de los Reyes** Lima, Peru; **la ciudad de María Santísima** Seville; **la ciudad Imperial** or **Imperial ciudad** Toledo

ciudadanía *f* citizenship

ciudada-no -na *adj* city; citizen; civic ‖ *mf* citizen; urbanite

ciudadela *f* citadel; (Cuba) tenement house

cívi-co -ca *adj* civic; city; domestic; public-spirited

civil *adj* civil; civilian ‖ *mf* civilian ‖ *m* guard, policeman

civilidad *f* civility

civilista *adj* civil-law ‖ *mf* authority on civil law; (Chile) antimilitarist

civilización *f* civilization

civilizar §60 *tr* to civilize

civismo *m* good citizenship

cizalla *f* shears; metal shaving, metal clipping; **cizalla de guillotina** gate shears, guillotine shears; **cizallas** shears

cizallar *tr* to shear

cizaña *f* darnel; contamination, corruption; discord; **sembrar cizaña** to sow discord

clac *m* (*pl* **claques**) opera hat, claque, crush hat; (*sombrero de tres picos*) cocked hat

clamar *tr* to cry out for ‖ *intr* to cry out; **clamar contra** to cry out against; **clamar por** to cry out for

clamor *m* clamor, outcry; (*toque de difuntos*) knell, toll; fame

clamorear *tr* to clamor for ‖ *intr* to clamor; (*tocar a muerto*) to toll

clamoreo *m* clamoring; tolling

clamoro-so -sa *adj* clamorous; loud, noisy

clan *m* clan

clandestinista *mf* (Guat) bootlegger

clandesti-no -na *adj* clandestine

claque *f* claque, hired clappers

clara *f* white of egg; bald spot; (*de un trozo de tela*) thin spot; (*en el tiempo lluvioso*) break, let-up

claraboya f (*ventana en el techo*) skylight; (*en la parte alta de la pared*) transom; (*esp. en las iglesias la parte superior de la nave que tiene una serie de ventanas*) clerestory

clarear tr to brighten, light up || intr (*empezar a amanecer*) to get light, to dawn; (*el mal tiempo*) to clear up || ref (*una tela*) to show through; (coll) to show one's hand

clarecer §22 ref to dawn

clarete m claret

claridad f clarity; clearness; brightness; fame, glory; blunt remark; **claridades** plain language

clarido·so -sa adj (CAm, Mex) blunt, rude, plain-spoken

clarificar §73 tr to clarify; to brighten, light up; (*lo que estaba turbio*) to clear

clarín m clarion; fine cambric; (Chile) sweet pea

clarinada f clarion call; (coll) uncalled-for remark

clarinete m clarinet

clarión m chalk

clarividencia f clairvoyance; clear-sightedness

clarividente adj clairvoyant; clear-sighted || mf clairvoyant

cla·ro -ra adj clear; (*de color*) light; (*pelo*) thin, sparse; (*té*) weak; famous, illustrious; (*cerveza*) light; a las claras publicly, openly, frankly || m gap; (*en el bosque*) glade, clearing; space, interval; (*ventana u otra abertura*) light; (*claraboya*) skylight; (*en las nubes*) break; **claro de luna** brief moonlight; **de claro en claro** evidently; from one end to the other; **pasar la noche de claro en claro** to not sleep all night; **poner o sacar en claro** to explain, clear up; (*un borrador*) to copy || f see **clara** || **claro** adv clearly || **claro** interj sure!, of course!; ¡claro está!, ¡claro que sí! sure!, of course!

claror m brightness; **claror de luna** moonlight, moonglow

claru·cho -cha adj (coll) watery, thin

clase f class; classroom; **clase alta** upper class; **clase baja** lower class; **clase media** middle class; **clase obrera** working class; **clases non-commissioned** officers, warrant officers; **clases pasivas** pensioners

clasicista mf classicist

clási·co -ca adj classical || mf classicist || m classic

clasificador m filing cabinet

clasificar §73 tr to classify; to class; to sort; to file || ref to class

clasismo m segregation

clasista mf segregationist

claudicar §73 intr (*cojear*) to limp; (*obrar defectuosamente*) to bungle; (coll) to back down

claustral adj cloistral

claustro m cloister; (*junta de la universidad*) faculty

cláusula f (*de un contrato u otro documento*) clause; (gram) sentence

clausula·do -da adj (*estilo*) choppy || m series of clauses

clausular tr to close, finish, conclude

clausura f confinement; seclusion; enclosure; adjournment

clausurar tr (*una asamblea, un tribunal, etc.*) to close, to adjourn; (*un comercio por orden gubernativa*) to suspend, to close up

clava f club

clavadista mf (Mex) diver

clava·do -da adj studded with nails; exact, precise; (*reloj*) stopped; sharp, e.g., a las siete **clavadas** at seven o'clock sharp || m (Mex) dive

clavar tr to nail; (*un clavo*) to drive; (*una daga, un punzón*) to stick; (*una piedra preciosa*) to set; (*los ojos, la atención*) to fix; (*a un caballo al herrarlo*) to prick; (coll) to cheat || ref to prick oneself; (coll) to get cheated; (Mex) to dive; **clavárselas** (CAm) to get drunk

clave m harpsichord || f (*de un enigma, código, etc.*) key; (*piedra con que se cierra el arco*) (archit) keystone; (mus) clef

clavel m carnation, pink; **clavel de ramillete** sweet william; **clavel reventón** double-flowered carnation

clavelón m marigold

clavellina f carnation, pink

clave·ro -ra mf keeper of the keys || m clove tree || f nail hole

claveta f peg, wooden peg

clavetear tr to stud; to tip, put a tip on; to wind up, settle

clavicordio m clavichord

clavícula f clavicle, collarbone

clavija f pin, peg, dowel; (elec) plug; (mus) peg; **apretarle a uno las clavijas** (coll) to put the screws on someone

clavillo or **clavito** m brad, tack; (*que sujeta las hojas de unas tijeras*) pin, rivet; clove

clavo m nail; (*capullo seco de la flor del clavero*) clove; migraine; keen sorrow; (*artículo que no se vende*) (Arg, Bol, Chile) drug on the market; (Col) bad deal; (Hond, Mex) rich vein of ore; (Ven) heartburn; **clavo de alambre** wire nail; **clavo de especia** (*flor*) clove; **clavo de herrar** horseshoe nail; **dar en el clavo** (coll) to hit the nail on the head

clemátide f clematis

clemencia f clemency

clemente adj clement, merciful

cleptóma·no -na mf kleptomaniac

clerecía f clergy

clerical adj & m clerical

clericato m or **clericatura** f priesthood

clerigalla f (*contemptuous*) priests

clérigo m cleric, priest; **clérigo de misa y olla** (coll) priestlet

clerizonte m shabby-looking priest; fake priest

clero m clergy

cleró·fobo -ba adj priest-hating || mf priest hater

cliché m (*lugar común*) cliché

cliente mf (*parroquiano de una tienda*)

customer; (de un abogado) client; (de un médico) patient; (de un hotel) guest
clientela f customers; clientele; patronage, protection; practice
clima m climate; country, region; clima artificial air conditioning
climatizar §60 tr to air-condition
clíni·co -ca adj clinical || mf clinician || f clinic; private hospital; clínica de reposo nursing home, convalescent home
cliqueteo m clicking
clisar tr (typ) to plate
clisé m (plancha clisada) cliché, plate; (phot) plate; (lugar común) cliché
clo m cluck; decir clo (Chile) to kick the bucket; hacer clo clo (la gallina clueca) to cluck
cloaca f sewer
clocar §81 intr to cluck
cloquear intr to cluck
cloqueo m cluck, clucking
clorhídri·co -ca adj hydrochloric
cloro m chlorine
clorofila f chlorophyll
cloroformizar §60 tr to chloroform
cloroformo m chloroform
cloruro m chloride
club m (pl clubs) club; club náutico yacht club
clubista mf club member
clue·co -ca adj broody; (coll) decrepit
c.m.b., C.M.B. abbr cuyas manos beso
coa f (Mex) hoe; (Chile) thieves' jargon
coacción f coercion, compulsion
coaccionar tr to coerce, compel
coacervar tr to pile up
coactar tr to coerce, compel
coadunar tr & ref to mix together
coadyuvar tr & intr to help, aid, assist
coagular tr & ref (la sangre) to coagulate; (la leche) to curdle
coágulo m clot
coalición f coalition
coalla f woodcock
coartada f alibi
coartar tr to limit, restrict
coba f (coll) hoax; (coll) flattery
cobalto m cobalt
cobarde adj cowardly; timid; (vista) dim, weak || mf coward
cobardear intr to act cowardly; to be timid
cobardía f cowardice; timidity
cobayo m guinea pig
cobertera f lid; bawd, procuress
cobertizo m shed; (tejado saledizo) covered balcony, penthouse
cobertor m bedcover, bedspread; lid
cobertura f cover; covering; (garantía metálica) coverage
cobija f curved tile; top, lid; short mantilla; (W-I) guano roof; cobijas (Am) bedclothes
cobijar tr to cover; to shelter, protect
cobijo m covering; shelter, protection; (hospedaje sin manutención) lodging
cobra f team of mares used in threshing; (hunt) retrieval
cobra·dor -dora adj (perro) retrieving || mf collector; trolley conductor

cobranza f collecting; (hunt) retrieval
cobrar tr (lo perdido) to recover; (lo que otro le debe) to collect; (un cheque) to cash; (cierto precio) to charge; to acquire, get; (una cuerda) to pull in; (hunt) to retrieve; (pedir, reclamar) (Am) to dun; cobrar afición a to take a liking for; cobrar al número llamado (telp) to reverse the charges; cobrar ánimo to take courage; cobrar carnes to put on flesh; cobrar fuerzas to gain strength || intr to get hit || ref to recover, to come to
cobre m copper; copper or brass kitchen utensils; batir el cobre (coll) to hustle, to work with a will; cobres (mus) brasses
cobre·ño -ña adj copper
cobrero m coppersmith
cobri·zo -za adj coppery
cobro m collection; recovery; cobro contra entrega collect on delivery; en cobro in a safe place
coca f (en una cuerda) kink; (coll) head; de coca (Mex) free; (Mex) in vain
cocaína f cocaine
cocción f cooking, baking; (de objetos cerámicos) baking, burning
cocear intr to kick; (resistir) (coll) to balk, rebel
cocer §16 tr to cook; to boil; (pan; ladrillos) to bake; to digest || intr to cook; to boil; to ferment || ref to suffer a long time
coci·do -da adj cooked || m Spanish stew
cociente m quotient; cociente intelectual intelligence quotient
cocina f (pieza) kitchen; (arte) cooking, cuisine; (aparato) stove; cocina de presión pressure cooker; cocina económica kitchen range
cocinar tr to cook || intr to meddle
cocine·ro -ra mf cook
cocinilla m (coll) meddler || f kitchenette; chafing dish; cocinilla sin fuego fireless cooker
coco m cocoanut; (moño) topknot, chignon; (duende) (coll) bogeyman; (gesto, mueca) (coll) face, grimace; (sombrero hongo) (Col, Ecuad) derby hat; hacer cocos (coll) to make a face; (los enamorados) (coll) to make eyes
cocodrilo m crocodile
cócora adj (coll) boring, tiresome || mf (coll) bore, pest
coco·so -sa adj worm-eaten
cocotero m cocoanut palm or tree
coctel m or cóctel m cocktail; cocktail party
coctelera f cocktail shaker
cocuma f (Peru) roast corn on the cob
cochambre m (coll) dirty, stinking thing, pigsty
cochambro·so -sa adj (coll) dirty, stinking
coche m carriage; coach; car; taxi; (puerco) hog; caminar en el coche de San Francisco to go or to ride on shank's mare; coche bar (rr) club

car; **coche bomba** fire engine; **coche celular** Black Maria, prison van; **coche de alquiler** cab, hack; **coche de carreras** racing car; **coche de correos** mail car; **coche de plaza** or **de punto** cab, hack; **coche de serie** (aut) stock car; **coche fúnebre** hearse
coche-cama m (pl **coches-camas**) sleeping car
cochecillo m baby carriage; **cochecillo para inválidos** wheelchair; **cochecillo para niños** baby carriage
coche-comedor m (pl **coches-comedores**) (rr) diner, dining car
coche-correo m (pl **coches-correo**) (rr) mail car
coche-fumador m (pl **coches-fumadores**) (rr) smoker, smoking car
coche-habitación m (pl **coches-habitación**) trailer
cochera f coach house; livery stable; carbarn; garage
cochería f (Arg, Chile) livery stable
coche·ro -ra adj easy to cook ‖ m coachman, driver; **cochero de punto** cabby, hackman ‖ f see **cochera**
cocherón m coach house; (depósito de locomotoras) roundhouse
coche-salón m (pl **coches-salón**) (rr) parlor car
cochevira f lard
cochina f sow; (mujer sucia y desaliñada) trollop
cochinada f (coll) piggishness, filthiness; (coll) dirty trick
cochinillo m sucking pig
cochi·no -na adj (coll) piggish, filthy; (tacaño) (coll) stingy; (Ven) cowardly ‖ m hog; (persona muy sucia) (coll) pig, dirty person ‖ f see **cochina**
cochite hervite adj, adv & m (coll) helter-skelter
cochitril m pigsty; (coll) den, hovel
cochura f batch of dough
codadura f (hort) layer
codal adj elbow ‖ m prop, shoring
codazo m poke, nudge; **dar codazo a** (Mex) to tip off
codear tr (SAm) to sponge on ‖ intr to elbow, elbow one's way ‖ ref to hobnob, to rub elbows
codelincuencia f complicity
codelincuente mf accomplice
codera f elbow patch; elbow itch
códice m codex
codicia f covetousness, greed, cupidity
codiciar tr to covet
codicilo m codicil
codicio·so -sa adj covetous, greedy; (laborioso) hard-working
codificar §73 tr to codify
código m code; **código penal** criminal code
codillo m (de animal) knee; (estribo) stirrup; (de un tubo) elbow; (de la rama cortada) stump
codo m elbow; **dar de codo a** to nudge; (coll) to spurn; **empinar el codo** (coll) to crook the elbow; **hablar por los codos** (coll) to talk too much
codor·niz f (pl **-nices**) quail
coeducación f coeducation

coeficiente adj & m coefficient
coetáne·o -a adj & mf contemporary
coexistencia f coexistence
coexistir intr to coexist
cofa f (naut) top; **cofa de vigía** (naut) crow's-nest
cofrade mf member, fellow member ‖ m brother ‖ f sister
cofradía f brotherhood, sisterhood; association, fraternity
cofre m coffer, chest, trunk
cogedor m dustpan; coal shovel, ash shovel
coger §17 tr to catch, seize, take hold of: to collect, gather, pick; to overtake; to surprise; to hold ‖ intr to be, to be located; to fit ‖ ref to get caught; to cling; to get involved
cogida f (coll) collecting, gathering, picking; (taur) hook
cogollo m (de la lechuga) heart; (de la berza) head; (de una planta) shoot; (del árbol) top; (lo mejor) cream, pick
cogote m back of the neck
cogotera f havelock
cogotu·do -da adj thick-necked; (coll) proud, stiff-necked; (SAm) moneyed
cogulla f cowl, frock; **cogulla de fraile** (bot) monkshood
cohabitar intr to live together; (el hombre y la mujer) to cohabit
cohechar tr to bribe; to plow just before sowing ‖ intr to take a bribe
cohecho m bribe
coherede·ro -ra mf coheir ‖ f coheiress
coherente adj coherent
cohesión f cohesion
cohete m (fuego artificial) rocket, skyrocket; (motor a reacción) rocket; (coll) fidgety person; **cohete de señales** (aer) flare; **cohete lanzador** booster rocket
cohibente adj (elec) nonconducting
cohibi·do -da adj timid, self-conscious
cohibir tr to check, restrain, inhibit; (Mex) to oblige
cohombro m cucumber
cohonestar tr to gloss over, to rationalize
coima f rake-off paid to operator of a gambling table; concubine; (SAm) bribe
coincidencia f coincidence
coincidir intr to coincide; to happen at the same time; to be at the same time (at a given place); to agree
coito m coition, coitus
coja f lame woman; (coll) lewd woman
cojear intr to limp; (una mesa, una silla) to wobble; (adolecer de algún vicio) to slip, lapse, have a weakness
cojera f (anormalidad del que cojea) lameness; (movimiento del que cojea) limp
cojijo m bug, insect; (coll) peeve
cojijo·so -sa adj peevish
cojín m cushion
cojincillo m pad
cojinete m cushion; sewing cushion; (mach) bearing; **cojinete de bolas** ball bearing; **cojinete de rodillos** roller bearing

co·jo **-ja** *adj* lame, crippled; (*mesa, silla*) wobbly; (*pierna*) game || *mf* lame person, cripple || *f* see **coja**

cojón *m* testicle

cok *m* var of **coque**

col. *abbr* **colonia, columna**

col *f* cabbage; **col de Bruselas** Brussels sprouts

cola *f* (*de animal, de ave, de cometa*) tail; (*de un vestido*) train, trail; (*de personas que esperan turno*) queue; (*extremidad posterior*) tail end, rear end; (*de una clase de alumnos*) bottom; (*pasta fuerte*) glue; **cola del pan** bread line; **cola de milano** or **de pato** dovetail; **cola de pescado** isinglass; **cola de retazo** size, sizing; **hacer cola** to queue, to stand in line

colaboración *f* collaboration; (*en un periódico, coloquio, etc.*) contribution

colaboracionista *mf* collaborationist

colabora·dor **-dora** *adj* collaborating || *mf* collaborator; contributor

colaborar *intr* to collaborate; (*en un periódico, coloquio, etc.*) to contribute

colación *f* (*cotejo; refacción ligera*) collation; (*de un grado de universidad*) conferring; parish land; **sacar a colación** to mention, to bring up; **traer a colación** to bring up; to adduce as proof; to bring up irrelevantly

colacionar *tr* to collate; to compare; (*un beneficio*) to confer

colactánea *f* foster sister

colactáneo *m* foster brother

colada *f* washing powder; wash; (*garganta entre montañas*) gulch; cattle run; **todo saldrá en la colada** (coll) it will all come out in the wash; (coll) the day of reckoning will come

coladera *f* strainer; (Mex) sewer

coladero *m* strainer; cattle run; narrow pass

colador *m* strainer, colander

colapez *f* or **colapiscis** *f* isinglass

colapso *m* breakdown, collapse; **colapso nervioso** nervous breakdown

colar *tr* (*un grado universitario*) to confer || §61 *tr* (*un líquido*) to strain; to bleach in hot lye, to buck; (*metales*) to cast; (*una moneda falsa*) (coll) to pass off; **colar el hueso por** (coll) to squeeze through || *intr* to run, to ooze; to squeeze through; to come in, slip in; (coll) to drink wine; **colar a fondo** to sink; **no colar** (*una cosa*) (coll) to not be believed || *ref* to seep, seep through; to slip in, slip through; to make a slip; to lie; **colarse de gorra** (coll) to crash the gate

colateral *adj* collateral || *mf* (*pariente*) collateral || *m* (com) collateral

colcrén *m* cold cream

colcha *f* quilt, counterpane, bedspread

colchón *m* mattress; **colchón de aire** air mattress; **colchón de muelles** bedspring, spring mattress; **colchón de plumas** feather bed

coleada *f* wag (*of the tail*); (Mex, Ven) throwing the bull by twisting its tail

colear *tr* (taur) to grab by the tail; (*la res*) (Mex, Ven) to throw by twisting the tail; (Col, Ven) to nag, harass; (Guat) to trail after; (*reprobar en un examen*) (Chile) to flunk || *intr* to wag the tail; (aer) to fishtail; (coll) to stay alive, to keep going; (*los últimos vagones de un tren*) (Am) to sway; **colear en** (*cierta edad*) (CAm, W-I) to border on, be close to; **todavía colea** (coll) it's not over yet

colección *f* collection

coleccionar *tr* to collect

coleccionista *mf* collector

colecta *f* collection for charity; (eccl) collect

colectar *tr* to collect; (*obras antes sueltas*) to collect in one volume

colecti·cio **-cia** *adj* new, untrained, green; (*tomo*) omnibus

colecti·vo **-va** *adj* collective

colector *m* collector; catch basin; (elec) commutator; (aut) manifold

colega *mf* colleague || *m* confrere

colegial *m* schoolboy

colegiala *f* schoolgirl

colegiatura *f* scholarship; (Mex) tuition

colegio *m* school, academy; (*sociedad de hombres de una misma profesión*) college (*e.g., of cardinals, electors*)

colegir §57 *tr* to gather, collect; to conclude, infer

cólera *m* cholera || *f* anger, wrath; (*bilis*) bile; **montar en cólera** to fly into a rage

coléri·co **-ca** *adj* choleric, irascible

colesterol *m* cholesterol

coleta *f* pigtail; (*del torero*) cue, queue; (coll) postscript; **cortarse la coleta** to quit the bull ring; to quit, retire; **tener** or **traer coleta** to have serious consequences

coletero *m* wren

coleto *m* buff jacket; (coll) body, one's body, oneself; **decir para su coleto** (coll) to say to oneself; **echarse al coleto** (coll) to eat up, drink up; (coll) to read from cover to cover

colgadero *m* hanger, hook; clothes rack

colgadizo *m* lean-to, penthouse; projection over a door, canopy

colga·do **-da** *adj* pending, unsettled; **dejar colgado** (coll) to disappoint, frustrate; **quedarse colgado** (coll) to be disappointed, frustrated

colgador *m* clothes hanger, coat hanger

colgajo *m* rag, tatter

colgante *adj* hanging, dangling; (*puente*) suspension || *m* drop, pendant; (archit) festoon; (P-R) watch fob

colgar §63 *tr* to hang; to impute, attribute; (*a un alumno*) to flunk; (*a un reo*) (coll) to hang || *intr* to hang, hang down, dangle; to droop; (telp) to hang up; **colgar de** to hang from, hang on; to depend on

colí·bri *m* (*pl* **-bríes**) humming bird

cóli·co **-ca** *adj* & *m* colic || *f* upset stomach

coliche *m* (coll) at-home, open house

coliflor *f* cauliflower

coligar §44 *ref* to join forces, make common cause

colilla *f* butt, stump, stub

co·lín -lina *adj* (*caballo o yegua*) bobtailed || *m* bobwhite; **colín de Virginia** bobwhite || *f* see **colina**

colina *f* hill, knoll

colindante *adj* adjacent, contiguous

colindar *intr* to be adjacent

colino·so -sa *adj* hilly

colirio *m* eyewash

coliseo *m* coliseum

colisión *f* collision; bruise, bump

colista *mf* (coll) person standing in line

colma·do -da *adj* abundant, plentiful || *m* food store, grocery store; seafood restaurant

colmar *tr* to fill up; (*las esperanzas de uno*) to fulfill; to overwhelm; **colmar de** to shower with, overwhelm with

colmena *f* beehive

colmenar *m* apiary

colmene·ro -ra *mf* beekeeper

colmillo *m* eyetooth, canine tooth; (*del elefante*) tusk; **tener el colmillo retorcido** (coll) to cut one's eyeteeth

col·mo -ma *adj* brimful, overflowing || *m* overflow; thatch, thatch roof; (*de un sorbete*) topping; **eso es el colmo** (coll) that's the limit; **para colmo de** to top off

colocación *f* (*acción de poner una persona o cosa en un lugar*) location; (*disposición de una cosa respecto del lugar que ocupa*) placement; (*inversión de dinero*) investment; (*empleo*) position, employment, job

colocar §73 *tr* to place, put; (*una trampa*) to set || *ref* to get placed, find a job; (*venderse*) to sell

colodra *f* milk bucket; drinking horn; (*bebedor de vino*) (coll) toper

colofón *m* colophon

colofonia *f* rosin

coloide *adj & m* colloid

colon *m* colon; (gram) main clause

Colón *m* Columbus

colonia *f* colony; cologne; silk ribbon; housing development; (W-I) sugar plantation || **Colonia** *f* Cologne; **la Colonia del Cabo** Cape Colony

colonial *adj* colonial; overseas || **coloniales** *mpl* imported foods

colonizar §60 *tr & intr* to colonize

colono *m* colonist, settler; tenant farmer; (W-I) owner of sugar plantation

coloquial *adj* colloquial

coloquialismo *m* colloquialism

coloquio *m* colloquy, talk, conference

color *m* color; (*substancia para pintar*) paint; (*para pintarse el rostro*) rouge; **colores** (*bandera*) colors; (*persona*) **de color** colored; (*zapatos*) tan; **sacar los colores a** to make blush; **so color de** under color of, under pretext of; **verlo todo de color de rosa** to see everything through rose-colored glasses

colora·do -da *adj* red, reddish; (*libre, obsceno*) off-color; (*aparentemente justo y razonable*) specious; **ponerse colorado** to blush

colorado·te -ta *adj* (coll) ruddy, sanguine

colorante *adj & m* coloring

colorar *tr* to color; to dye; to stain

colorear *tr* to color; (fig) to color, excuse, palliate || *ref* (*la cereza, el tomate, etc.*) to redden, turn red

colorete *m* rouge; **ponerse colorete** to put on rouge

colorir §1 *tr* to color; (fig) to color, to palliate || *intr* to take on color

colosal *adj* colossal

coloso *m* colossus

columbrar *tr* to discern, descry, glimpse; to guess

columna *f* column; **quinta columna** fifth column

columnata *f* colonnade

columnista *mf* columnist

columpiar *tr* to swing || *ref* to swing; to seesaw; (coll) to swing, swagger

columpio *m* swing; **columpio de tabla** seesaw

colusión *f* collusion

collada *f* mountain pass; (naut) steady blow

collado *m* hill, height

collar *m* necklace; dog collar, horse collar; (*aro de hierro asegurado al cuello del malhechor*) collar, band; (*plumas del cuello de ciertas aves*) frill, ring; (*cadena que rodea el cuello como insignia*) cord, chain; (mach) collar

collera *f* horse collar; chain gang; **colleras** (Arg, Chile) cuff links

co·llón -llona *adj* (coll) cowardly || *mf* (coll) coward

coma *m* (pathol) coma || *f* comma; (*en inglés se emplea el punto en aritmética para separar los enteros de las fracciones decimales*) decimal point

comadre *f* mother or godmother (*with respect to each other*); gossip (*woman*); friend, neighbor (*woman*)

comadrear *intr* (coll) to gossip, go around gossiping

comadreja *f* weasel

comadrería *f* (coll) gossip, idle gossip

comadre·ro -ra *adj* (coll) gossipy || *mf* (coll) gossip

comadrón *m* accoucheur

comadrona *f* midwife

comandancia *f* command; commander's headquarters; (mil) majority

comandante *m* commander, commandant; (mil) major

comandar *tr* (mil, nav) to command

comando *m* (mil) command; **comando a distancia** remote control

comarca *f* district, region, country

comarcar §73 *tr* to plant in a line at regular intervals || *intr* to border, be contiguous

comato·so -sa *adj* comatose

comba *f* bend, curve; warp, bulge; skipping rope; **saltar a la comba** to jump rope, to skip rope

combar *tr* to bend, curve || *ref* to bend, curve; to warp, bulge; to sag

combate *m* combat, fight; **combate revancha** (box) return bout; **fuera de**

combate hors de combat; (box) knockout

combatiente *adj & m* combatant

combatir *tr* to combat, fight; to beat, beat upon ‖ *intr & ref* to combat, fight, struggle

combinación *f* combination; (*de trenes*) connection

combinar *tr & ref* to combine

com·bo -ba *adj* bent, curved, crooked; warped ‖ *m* trunk or rock to stand wine casks on ‖ *f see* **comba**

combustible *adj* combustible ‖ *m* (*substancia que arde con facilidad*) combustible; (*substancia que sirve para calentar, cocinar, etc.*) fuel

combustión *f* combustion

comede·ro -ra *adj* eatable ‖ *m* manger, feed trough; (Mex) haunt, hangout; **limpiarle a uno el comedero** (coll) to deprive someone of his bread and butter

comedia *f* drama, play; theater; comedy; (fig) farce; **comedia cómica** (*drama de desenlace festivo*) comedy; **hacer la comedia** (coll) to pretend, make believe

comedian·te -ta *mf* (coll) hypocrite ‖ *m* actor, comedian ‖ *f* actress, comedienne

comedi·do -da *adj* courteous, polite; moderate; (Am) obliging, accommodating

comedimiento *m* courtesy, politeness; moderation

comediógra·fo -fa *mf* playwright

comedir §50 *ref* to be courteous; to restrain oneself, be moderate; (Am) to be obliging; **comedirse a** (Am) to offer to, to volunteer to

comedón *m* blackhead

come·dor -dora *adj* heavy-eating ‖ *m* dining room; restaurant, eating place; dining-room suite; **comedor de beneficencia** soup kitchen

comején *m* termite

comendador *m* prelate, prior; knight commander; (*de una orden militar*) commander

comensal *mf* dependent, servant; table companion

comentar *tr* to comment on ‖ *intr* to comment; (coll) to gossip

comentario *m* comment, commentary; **comentarios** (coll) talk, gossip

comentarista *mf* commentator

comento *m* comment, commentary; deceit, falsehood

comenzar §18 *tr & intr* to commence, begin, start

comer *m* eating, food ‖ *tr* to eat; to feed on; to gnaw away; to consume; (*alguna renta*) to enjoy; to itch; (*una pieza en el juego de damas*) to take; **comer vivo** (coll) to have it in for; **sin comerlo ni beberlo** (coll) without having anything to do with it; **tener qué comer** (coll) to have enough to live on ‖ *intr* to eat; to dine, to have dinner; to itch ‖ *ref* to eat up; (*las uñas*) to bite; (*el dinero*) (coll) to consume, eat up; (*omitir*) to skip,

skip over; **comerse unos a otros** (coll) to be at loggerheads

comerciable *adj* marketable; sociable

comercial *adj* commercial, business

comerciante *mf* merchant, trader, dealer; **comerciante al por mayor** wholesaler; **comerciante al por menor** retailer

comerciar *intr* to trade, to deal

comercio *m* commerce, trade, business; store, shop; business center; commerce, intercourse; **comercio de artículos de regalo** gift shop; **comercio exterior** foreign trade

comestible *adj* eatable ‖ *m* food, foodstuff

cometa *m* comet ‖ *f* kite

cometer *tr* (*un crimen, una falta*) to commit; (*un negocio a una persona*) to commit, to entrust; (*figuras retóricas*) to employ

cometido *m* assignment, duty; commitment

comezón *f* itch

comicastro *m* ham, ham actor

comicios *mpl* polls; **acudir a los comicios** to go to the polls

cómi·co -ca *adj* comic, comical; dramatic ‖ *mf* actor; comedian; **cómico de la legua** strolling player, barnstormer ‖ *f* actress; comedienne

comida *f* (*alimento*) food; (*el que se toma a horas señaladas*) meal; (*el principal de cada día*) dinner; **comida corrida** (Mex) table d'hôte

comidilla *f* (coll) hobby; **la comidilla del pueblo** (coll) the talk of the town

comienzo *m* beginning, start; **a comienzos de** around the beginning of

comilitona *f* (coll) spread, feast

comi·lón -lona *adj* (coll) heavy-eating ‖ *mf* (coll) hearty eater ‖ *f* (coll) hearty meal, spread

comillas *fpl* quotation marks

cominear *intr* (*el hombre*) (coll) to fuss around like a woman

comiquear *intr* to put on amateur plays

comiquillo *m* ham, ham actor

comisar *tr* to seize, confiscate

comisario *m* commissary; commissioner; **comisario de a bordo** purser

comisión *f* commission; committee; (*recado*) errand

comisiona·do -da *mf* commissioner ‖ *m* committeeman

comisionar *tr* to commission

comiso *m* seizure, confiscation; confiscated goods

comisura *f* corner (*e.g., of lips*)

comité *m* committee

comitente *mf* constituent

comitiva *f* retinue, suite; procession

como *adv* as, like; so to speak, as it were ‖ *conj* as; when; if; so that; as soon as; as long as; inasmuch as; **así como** as soon as; **como no** unless; **como que** because, inasmuch as; **como quien dice** so to speak; **tan luego como** as soon as

cómo *adv* how; why; what; **¿a cómo es . . .?** how much is . . .?; **¿cómo no?** why not?

cómoda *f* bureau, commode, chest

comodidad _f_ comfort; convenience; advantage, interest

comodín _m_ joker, wild card; gadget, jigger; excuse, alibi

cómo•do -da _adj_ handy, convenient; comfortable ‖ _f_ see **cómoda**

como•dón -dona _adj_ (coll) comfort-loving, self-indulgent, easy-going

compac•to -ta _adj_ compact

compadecer §22 _tr_ to pity, feel sorry for ‖ _ref_ to harmonize; **compadecerse con** to harmonize with; **compadecerse de** to pity, feel sorry for

compadraje _m_ clique, cabal

compadrar _intr_ to become a godfather; to become friends

compadre _m_ father or godfather (_with respect to each other_); friend, companion

compadrear _intr_ (coll) to be close friends; (Arg, Urug) to brag, show off

compadrería _f_ close companionship

compadrito _m_ (Arg) bully

compaginar _tr_ to arrange, put in order ‖ _ref_ to fit, agree; to blend

companage _m_ snacks, cold cuts

compañerismo _m_ companionship

compañe•ro -ra _mf_ companion; partner; mate; **compañero de cama** bedfellow; **compañero de cuarto** roommate; **compañero de juego** playmate; **compañero de viaje** fellow traveler ‖ _f_ (_esposa_) helpmeet

compañía _f_ company; society; **compañía de desembarco** (nav) landing force; **hacerle compañía a una persona** to keep someone company

compañón _m_ testicle; **compañón de perro** orchid

comparación _f_ comparison

comparar _tr_ to compare

comparati•vo -va _adj_ comparative

comparecencia _f_ (law) appearance

comparecer §22 _intr_ (law) to appear

compareado _m_ (law) summons

comparsa _mf_ (theat) supernummerary, extra ‖ _f_ supernummeraries, extras

compartimiento _m_ distribution, division; compartment

compartir _tr_ to distribute, divide; to share

compás _m_ (_brújula_) compass; (_instrumento para trazar curvas_) compass or compasses; rule, measure; (mus) time, measure; (mus) bar, measure; (mus) beat; **a compás** (mus) in time; **compás de calibres** calipers; **compás de división** dividers; **llevar el compás** (mus) to keep time

compasible _adj_ compassionate; pitiful

compasión _f_ compassion; **¡por compasión!** for pity's sake!

compasi•vo -va _adj_ compassionate

compatri•cio -cia or **compatriota** _mf_ fellow countryman, compatriot

compeler _tr_ to compel

compendiar _tr_ to condense, to summarize

compendio _m_ compendium; **en compendio** in a word

compendio•so -sa _adj_ compendious

compensación _f_ compensation; (com) clearing, clearance

compensar _tr_ to compensate; to compensate for ‖ _intr_ to compensate ‖ _ref_ to be compensated for

competencia _f_ (_aptitud_) competence; (_rivalidad_) competition; dispute; area, field; **de la competencia de** in the domain of; **sin competencia** unmatched (_prices_)

competente _adj_ competent; reliable

competer _intr_ to be incumbent

competición _f_ competition

competi•dor -dora _adj_ competing ‖ _mf_ competitor

competir §50 _intr_ to compete

compilación _f_ compilation

compilar _tr_ to compile

compinche _mf_ (coll) chum, crony, pal

complacencia _f_ complacency

complacer §22 _tr_ to please, to humor ‖ _ref_ to be pleased, take pleasure

complaciente _adj_ obliging; indulgent

comple•jo -ja _adj_ & _m_ complex; **complejo de inferioridad** inferiority complex

complementar _tr_ to complement

complemento _m_ complement; completion; perfection; accessory; **complemento directo** (gram) direct object

completar _tr_ to complete; to perfect

comple•to -ta _adj_ complete; (_autobús, tranvía_) full

complexión _f_ constitution

complexiona•do -da _adj_ — **bien complexionado** strong, robust; **mal complexionado** weak, frail

comple•xo -xa _adj_ complex

complica•do -da _adj_ complicated, complex

complicar §73 _tr_ to complicate; to involve ‖ _ref_ to become complicated; to become involved

cómplice _mf_ accomplice, accessory

complicidad _f_ complicity

com•plot _m_ (_pl_ **-plots**) plot, intrigue

compone•dor -dora _mf_ composer, compositor; typesetter; arbitrator; repairer ‖ _m_ stick, composing stick; **amigable componedor** mediator, umpire

componenda _f_ compromise, settlement, reconciliation

componente _adj_ component, constituent ‖ _m_ component, constituent; member ‖ _f_ (mech) component

componer §54 _tr_ to compose; to compound; to mend, repair; to pacify, reconcile; to arrange, put in order; (coll) to restore, strengthen; (_huesos dislocados_) (Am) to set; (Col) to bewitch ‖ _ref_ to compose oneself; to get dressed; to make up, become friends again; (_pintarse el rostro_) to make up; **componérselas** (coll) to make out, to manage

comportable _adj_ bearable, tolerable

comportamiento _m_ behavior, conduct

comportar _tr_ to support; (Am) to bring about, entail ‖ _ref_ to act, behave

comporte _m_ behavior; carriage, bearing

composición _f_ composition; agreement; (_circunspección_) composure, restraint; **hacer una composición de lugar** to carefully lay one's plans

compositi·vo -va *adj* (gram) combining

composi·tor -tora *mf* composer ‖ *m* (Arg, Urug) horse trainer, trainer of fighting cocks

compostura *f* composition; agreement; (*circunspección*) composure, restraint; repair, repairing, mending; (*aseo*) neatness; adulteration; (Arg, Urug) training

compota *f* compote, preserves; **compota de frutas** stewed fruit; **compota de manzanas** applesauce

compotera *f* (*vasija*) compote

compra *f* purchase, buy; shopping; **compra al contado** cash purchase; **compra a plazos** installment buying; **hacer compras, ir de compras** to go shopping

compra·dor -dora *mf* purchaser, buyer; shopper

comprar *tr* to purchase, to buy; (*sobornar*) to buy off ‖ *intr* to shop

compraventa *f* dealing, business, bargain, trading; resale

comprender *tr* (*entender*) to understand; (*entender; abrazar*) to comprehend; (*contener, incluir*) to comprise

comprensible *adj* comprehensible, understandable

comprensión *f* understanding, comprehension; inclusion

comprensi·vo -va *adj* understanding; comprehensive; **comprensivo de** inclusive of

compresa *f* (med) compress; **compresa higiénica** sanitary napkin

compresión *f* compression

comprimido *m* tablet

comprimir *tr* to compress; to restrain, repress; to flatten

comprobación *f* checking, verification; proof

comprobante *adj* proving ‖ *m* certificate, voucher, warrant; proof; claim check

comprobar §61 *tr* to check, verify; to prove

comprometer *tr* to compromise, endanger, jeopardize; to force, to oblige; (*un negocio a un tercero*) to entrust ‖ *ref* to promise; to commit oneself; to become engaged

comprometi·do -da *adj* awkward, embarrassing; engaged to be married

comprometimiento *m* commitment, promise; predicament, awkward situation; compromise

compromiso *m* commitment, promise; appointment, engagement; predicament, awkward situation; betrothal

compuerta *f* hatch, half door; floodgate, sluice

compues·to -ta *adj* & *m* composite, compound

compulsar *tr* to collate; to make an authentic copy of

compungi·do -da *adj* remorseful

compungir §27 *tr* to make remorseful ‖ *ref* to feel remorse

compurgar §44 *tr* (*el reo la pena*) (Mex) to finish serving

computador *m* computer

computar *tr* & *intr* to compute

cómputo *m* computation, calculation

comulgante *mf* (eccl) communicant

comulgar §44 *tr* to administer communion to ‖ *intr* to take communion

comulgatorio *m* communion rail, altar rail

común *adj* common ‖ *m* community; water closet; toilet; **el común de las gentes** the general run of people; **por lo común** commonly

comunal *adj* common; community ‖ *m* community

comune·ro -ra *adj* popular ‖ *m* shareholder

comunicación *f* communication; connection

comunicado *m* communiqué; letter to the editor; official announcement

comunica·dor -dora *adj* communicating

comunicante *mf* communicant, informant

comunicar §73 *tr* to communicate; to notify, inform; to connect, put into communication ‖ *intr* to communicate ‖ *ref* to communicate; to communicate with each other

comunicati·vo -va *adj* communicative

comunidad *f* community

comunión *f* communion; political party; sect

comunismo *m* communism

comunista *mf* communist

comunistizar §60 *tr* to convert to communism ‖ *ref* to become communistic

comunizar §60 *tr* to communize

con *prep* with; to, towards; in spite of; **con que** and so; whereupon; **con tal (de) que** provided that; **con todo** however, nevertheless

conato *m* effort, endeavor; (*delito que no llegó a consumarse*) attempt

cónca·vo -va *adj* concave

concebible *adj* conceivable

concebir §50 *tr* & *intr* to conceive

conceder *tr* to concede, admit; to grant

concejal *m* alderman, councilman; **concejales** city fathers

concejo *m* town council; town hall; council meeting; (*expósito*) foundling

concentrar *tr* & *ref* to concentrate

concéntri·co -ca *adj* concentric

concepción *f* conception

concepto *m* concept; opinion, judgment; (*dicho ingenioso*) conceit, witticism; point of view; **en concepto de** under the head of; **tener buen concepto de** or **tener en buen concepto** to have a high opinion of, to hold in high esteem

conceptuar §21 *tr* to deem, to judge, to regard

conceptuo·so -sa *adj* witty, epigrammatic

concerniente *adj* relative

concernir §28 *tr* to concern

concertar §2 *tr* to concert; to mend, repair; (*un casamiento; la paz*) to arrange; (*huesos dislocados*) to set; (*poner de acuerdo*) to reconcile; (*un pacto*) to conclude; to harmonize ‖ *intr* to concert; to agree ‖ *ref* to come to terms, become reconciled; to agree

concertino *m* concertmaster

concertista *mf* (mus) manager; (mus) performer, soloist

concesión *f* concession, admission; grant

concesionario *m* licensee; (*comerciante*) dealer

concesi•vo -va *adj* concessive

conciencia *f* (*conocimiento que uno tiene de su propia existencia*) consciousness; (*sentimiento del bien y del mal*) conscience; (*conocimiento*) awareness; **cobrar conciencia de** to become aware of; **en conciencia** in all conscience

concienzu•do -da *adj* conscientious; thorough

concierto *m* concert, harmony; (*función de música*) concert; (*composición de música*) concerto

concilia•dor -dora *adj* conciliatory

conciliar *tr* to conciliate, to reconcile || *ref* (*el respeto, la estima, etc.*) to conciliate, to win

concilio *m* (eccl) council

conci•so -sa *adj* concise

concitar *tr* to stir up, incite, agitate

conciudada•no -na *mf* fellow citizen

concluir §20 *tr* to conclude; to convince || *intr & ref* to conclude, to end

conclusión *f* conclusion

concluyente *adj* conclusive, convincing

concomitar *tr* to accompany, go with

concordancia *f* concordance; (gram, mus) concord

concordar §61 *tr* to harmonize; to reconcile; to make agree || *intr* to agree

concordia *f* concord; **de concordia** by common consent

concre•to -ta *adj* concrete

concubina *f* concubine

concubio *m* (archaic) bedtime

concuñada *f* sister-in-law

concuñado *m* brother-in-law

concurrencia *f* (*acaecimiento de varios sucesos en un mismo tiempo*) concurrence; (*competencia comercial*) competition; (*ayuda*) assistance; crowd, gathering, attendance

concurrente *adj* concurrent; competing || *mf* competitor, contender, entrant

concurri•do -da *adj* crowded, full of people; well-attended

concurrir *intr* to concur; to gather, meet, come together; to compete, contend; to coincide; **concurrir con** (*p.ej., dinero*) to contribute

concursante *mf* contender

concursar *tr* to declare insolvent || *intr* to contend, to compete

concurso *m* contest, competition; (*de gente*) concourse, crowd, throng; backing, coöperation; show, exhibition; **concurso de acreedores** meeting of creditors; **concurso de belleza** beauty contest; **concurso hípico** horse show

concusión *f* concussion; extortion, shakedown

concha *f* (*de molusco o crustáceo*) shell; (*cada una de las dos partes del caparazón de los moluscos bivalvos*) half shell; (*en que se sirve el pescado*) scallop; (*carey*) tortoise shell; oyster; shellfish; horseshoe bay; (theat) prompter's box; **concha de peregrino** scallop shell; (zool) scallop; (*ostras*) **en su concha** on the half shell; **tener muchas conchas** (coll) to be sly, cunning

conchabanza *f* comfort; (coll) collusion, cabal

conchabar *tr* to join, unite; (Am) to hire || *ref* (coll) to gang up; (Am) to hire out

conchabero *m* (Col) pieceworker

condado *m* county; earldom

conde *m* count, earl; gypsy chief

condecoración *f* decoration

condecorar *tr* to decorate

condena *f* sentence; penalty, jail term; **condena judicial** conviction

condenación *f* condemnation; (*la eterna*) damnation

condena•do -da *adj* condemned; damned; (Chile) shrewd, clever || *mf* sentenced person; **los condenados** the damned

condenar *tr* to condemn; to convict; (*a la pena eterna*) to damn; (*p.ej., una ventana*) to shut off, to block up; (*una habitación*) to padlock || *ref* to condemn oneself, confess one's guilt; (*a la pena eterna*) to be damned

condensar *tr* to condense || *ref* to condense, be condensed

condesa *f* countess

condescendencia *f* acquiescence, compliance

condescender §51 *intr* to acquiesce, comply; **condescender a** to accede to

condescendiente *adj* acquiescent, obliging

condición *f* condition, state; position, situation; standing; nature, character, temperament; **a condición (de) que** on condition that; **en buenas condiciones** in good condition, in good shape; **tener condición** to have a bad temper

condicional *adj* conditional

condimentar *tr* to season

condimento *m* condiment, seasoning

condiscípulo *m* fellow student

condolencia *f* condolence

condoler §47 *ref* to condole; **condolerse de** to sympathize with, feel sorry for, commiserate with

condonar *tr* to condone, overlook

conducción *f* conveyance, transportation; guiding, leading; (aut) drive, driving; **conducción a la derecha** right-hand drive; **conducción a la izquierda** left-hand drive; **conducción interior** closed car

conducente *adj* conducive

conducir §19 *tr* to conduct; to manage, direct; to guide, lead; to convey, transport; to drive; to employ, hire || *intr* to lead; to conduce || *ref* to conduct oneself, behave

conducta *f* conduct; management, direction; guidance; conveyance; conduct, behavior

conducto *m* pipe; conduit; (anat) duct, canal; agency, intermediary, channel; **por conducto de** through

conduc•tor -tora *adj* conducting || *mf* driver, motorist; (*cobrador en un vehículo público*) (Am) conductor || *m & f* (elec & phys) conductor; **buen conductor, buena conductora** good conductor; **mal conductor, mala conductora** bad or poor conductor || *m* (rr) engineman, engine driver

conectar *tr* to connect

conejera *f* burrow, warren; (coll) joint, dive

conejillo *m* young rabbit; **conejillo de Indias** guinea pig

conejo *m* rabbit

conexión *f* connection

conexionar *tr* to connect; to put in touch || *ref* to connect; to make contacts

confabulación *f* collusion, connivance

confabular *ref* to connive, scheme, plot

confección *f* making, preparation, confection; tailoring; ready-made suit; **confección a medida** suit made to order; **de confección** ready-made

confeccionar *tr* (*ropa*) to make; (*una receta*) to make up, concoct

confeccionista *mf* ready-made clothier

confederación *f* confederacy; alliance

confedera•do -da *adj & mf* confederate

confederar *tr & ref* to confederate

conferencia *f* (*reunión para tratar asuntos internacionales, etc.*) conference; (*plática para tratar de algún negocio*) interview; (*disertación en público o en la universidad*) lecture; **conferencia telefónica** (telp) long-distance call

conferenciante *mf* conferee; lecturer

conferenciar *intr* to confer, hold an interview

conferencista *mf* (Arg) lecturer

conferir §68 *tr* to confer, award, bestow; to discuss; to compare || *intr* to confer

confesante *mf* confessor

confesar §2 *tr*, *intr & ref* to confess

confesión *f* confession; denomination, faith, religion

confe•so -sa *adj* confessed; (*judío*) converted || *mf* converted Jew || *m* lay brother

confesonario *m* confessional

confesor *m* confessor

confiable *adj* reliable, dependable

confia•do -da *adj* unsuspecting; haughty, self-confident

confianza *f* confidence; self-confidence, self-assurance; familiarity; secret deal; **de confianza** reliable

confianzu•do -da *adj* (coll) overconfident; (Am) overfamiliar

confiar §77 *tr* to confide, entrust; to strengthen the confidence of || *intr & ref* to confide, trust; **confiar or confiarse de** or **en** to confide in, trust in; to rely on

confidencia *f* confidence; secret

confidencial *adj* confidential

confiden•te -ta *adj* trustworthy, faith-

ful || *mf* confident || *m* spy; informer; secret agent; love seat

configurar *tr* to shape, form

confín *m* confine, border, boundary; **los confines** the confines

confina•do -da *adj* exiled || *m* prisoner

confinamiento *m* confinement; abutment

confinar *tr* to exile; to confine || *intr* to border

confirmar *tr* to confirm

confiscar §73 *tr* to confiscate

confita•do -da *adj* hopeful, confident; (*bañado de azúcar*) candied

confitar *tr* (*frutas*) to candy; (*en almíbar*) to preserve; (*endulzar*) to sweeten

confite *m* candy, bonbon, confection; **confites** confectionery

confitera *f* candy box; candy jar

confitería *f* confectionery; confectionery store

confite•ro -ra *mf* confectioner || *f* see **confitera**

confitura *f* preserves, confiture; **confituras** confectionery

conflagración *f* conflagration

conflagrar *tr* to set fire to

conflicto *m* conflict; (*apuro*) fix, jam

confluencia *f* confluence

confluir §20 *intr* to flow together; to crowd, gather

conformador *m* hat block

conformar *tr* to shape; (*un sombrero*) to block || *intr & ref* to conform, to comply, to yield, to agree

conforme *adj* in agreement || *adv* depending on circumstances; fine, O.K.; **conforme a** according to || *conj* as, in proportion as; as soon as || *m* approval

conformidad *f* conformance, conformity; resignation

confort *m* comfort

confortable *adj* comfortable; comforting

confortante *adj* comforting; tonic || *mf* comforter || *m* tonic

confr. *abbr* **confesor**

confricar *tr* to rub

confrontar *tr* (*poner en presencia; cotejar*) to confront || *intr* to border; to agree || *ref* to get along, to agree; **confrontarse con** (*hacer frente a*) to confront

confundir *tr* to confuse; (*turbar, dejar desarmado*) to confound || *ref* to become confused; (*en la muchedumbre*) to get lost

confusión *f* confusion

confutar *tr* to confute

congelador *m* freezer

congelar *tr* to congeal, freeze; (*créditos*) (fig) to freeze || *ref* to congeal, freeze

congenial *adj* congenial (*having the same nature*)

congeniar *intr* to be congenial, to get along well

congéni•to -ta *adj* congenital

congestión *f* congestion

congestionar *tr* to congest || *ref* to congest, become congested

conglobar tr to lump together

congoja f anguish, grief

congojo·so -sa adj distressing; distressed

congosto m narrow mountain pass

congraciar tr to win over || ref to ingratiate oneself; **congraciarse con** to get into the good graces of

congratulación f congratulation

congratular tr to congratulate || ref to congratulate oneself, to rejoice

congregación f congregation; **la Congregación de los fieles** the Roman Catholic Church

congregar §44 tr to bring together || ref to congregate, to come together

congresal m (Arg, Chile) congressman

congresista mf delegate; member of congress || m congressman

congreso m (asamblea legislativa) congress; (reunión para deliberar sobre intereses comunes) meeting, convention

congrio m conger eel

cóni·co -ca adj conical

conjetura f conjecture, guess

conjeturar tr & intr to conjecture, guess

conjugación f conjugation

conjugar §44 tr to conjugate; to combine

conjunción f conjunction; combination

conjuntamente adv together

conjuntista m chorus man || f chorus girl

conjunti·vo -va adj conjunctive; subjunctive

conjun·to -ta adj joined, combined, united || m whole, entirety, ensemble; unit; group; (theat) chorus; **de conjunto** general; **en conjunto** as a whole; **en su conjunto** in its entirety

conjura or **conjuración** f conspiracy, plot

conjuramentar tr to swear in || ref to take an oath

conjurar tr to swear in; to conjure, entreat; to conjure away, to exorcise || intr to conspire, plot || ref to conspire, join in a conspiracy

conjuro m (invocación supersticiosa) conjuration; adjuration; entreaty

conllevar tr (los trabajos) to share in bearing; (a una persona) to tolerate, stand for; (las adversidades) to suffer

conmemorar tr to commemorate, memorialize

conmigo pron with me, with myself

conmilitón m fellow soldier

conminar tr to threaten

conmoción f commotion; concussion; shock

conmove·dor -dora adj touching, moving, stirring

conmover §47 tr to touch, move, affect; to stir, stir up; to shake, upset || ref to be touched, be moved

conmutación f commutation

conmutador m (elec) change-over switch

conmutar tr to commute

connivencia f connivance; **estar en connivencia** to connive

cono m cone; **cono de proa** nose cone; **cono de viento** (aer) wind cone, wind sock

conoce·dor -dora adj knowledgeable || mf expert, connoisseur

conocer §22 tr to know; to meet, get to know; to tell, to distinguish; (law) to try || intr to know; **conocer de** or **en** to know, have knowledge of || ref to know oneself; to know each other; to meet, meet each other

conoci·do -da adj known, well-known, familiar; distinguished, prominent || mf acquaintance

conocimiento m knowledge; understanding; acquaintance; consciousness; (com) bill of lading; **con conocimiento de causa** knowingly, with full knowledge; **conocimiento de embarque** (com) bill of lading; **conocimientos** knowledge; **hablar con pleno conocimiento de causa** to know what one is talking about; **perder el conocimiento** to lose consciousness; **por su real conocimiento** (Arg) for real money; **recobrar el conocimiento** to regain consciousness; **venir en conocimiento de** to come to know

conque adv and so || m (coll) condition, terms

conquista f conquest

conquista·dor -dora adj conquering || m conqueror; (ladrón de corazones) lady-killer

conquistar tr to conquer; (ganar la voluntad de) to win over

consabi·do -da adj well-known; above-mentioned

consagrar tr to consecrate; to devote; to dedicate; (una nueva palabra) to authorize || ref to devote oneself; to make a name for oneself

consciente adj conscious

conscripción f conscription

conscripto m conscript, draftee

consecución f obtaining, getting

consecuencia f (correspondencia lógica entre sus elementos) consistency; (acontecimiento que resulta necesariamente de otro) consequence; **en consecuencia** accordingly; **guardar consecuencia** to remain consistent; **traer a consecuencia** to bring in

consecuente adj (que tiene proporción consigo mismo) consistent; (que sigue en orden a otra cosa) consecutive

consecuti·vo -va adj consecutive

conseguir §67 tr to get, obtain; **conseguir + inf** to succeed in + ger

conseja f story, fairy tale; cabal

conseje·ro -ra adj advisory || mf advisor, counselor; councilor

consejo m advice, counsel; board; council; **consejos** advice; **un consejo** a piece of advice

consenso m consensus

consenti·do -da adj spoiled, pampered; (marido) indulgent

consenti·dor -dora adj acquiescent; pampering || mf acquiescent person; (de niños) pamperer || m cuckold

consentimiento *m* consent

consentir §68 *tr* to allow; to admit; to pamper, to spoil ‖ *intr* to consent; to come loose; **consentir** + *inf* to think that + *ind*; **consentir con** to be indulgent toward; **consentir en** to consent to ‖ *ref* to begin to crack up; (Arg) to be proud

conserje *m* janitor, concierge

conserva *f* preserves; preserved food; pickles; (naut) convoy; **conservas alimenticias** canned goods; **llevar en su conserva** (naut) to convoy; **navegar en (la) conserva** (naut) to sail in a convoy

conservación *f* conservation; preservation; self-preservation; maintenance, upkeep

conserva·dor -dora *adj* preservative; (pol) conservative ‖ *mf* conservative ‖ *m* curator

conservar *tr* to conserve, keep, maintain; to preserve ‖ *ref* to take good care of oneself; to keep

conservati·vo -va *adj* conservative, preservative

conservatorio *m* (*p.ej., de música*) conservatory; (Arg) private school; (Chile) hothouse, greenhouse

conservera *f* cannery; (Mex) preserve dish

conservería *f* canning

conserve·ro -ra *adj* canning ‖ *mf* canner ‖ *f* see **conservera**

considerable *adj* considerable; large, great, important

consideración *f* consideration; **ser de consideración** to be of importance, be of concern; **someter a consideración** to take under advisement

considera·do -da *adj* (*que guarda consideración a los demás*) considerate; (*digno de respeto*) respected, esteemed; (*que obra con reflexión*) cautious, prudent

considerando *conj* & *m* whereas

considerar *tr* to consider; to treat with consideration

consigna *f* slogan; watchword; (mil) orders; (rr) checkroom

consignación *f* consignment

consignar *tr* to consign; to assign; to state in writing, to set forth

consignatario *m* consignee

consigo *pron* with him, with her, with them, with you; with himself, with herself, with themselves, with yourself or yourselves

consiguiente *adj* consequential; **ir or proceder consiguiente** to act consistently ‖ *m* consequence; **por consiguiente** consequently, therefore

consilia·ro -ria *mf* advisor, counselor

consistencia *f* consistence, consistency

consistente *adj* consistent

consistir *intr* to consist; **consistir en** (*estar compuesto de*) to consist of; (*residir en*) to consist in

consistorio *m* consistory; town council; town hall

conso·cio -cia *mf* copartner; companion, fellow member

consola *f* console, console table; bracket

consolación *f* consolation

consolar §61 *tr* to console

consolidar *tr* to fund, refund; to strengthen; to repair

consommé *m* consommé

consonancia *f* consonance; rhyme

consonante *adj* consonantal; rhyming ‖ *m* rhyme ‖ *f* consonant

consonar §61 *intr* to be in harmony; to rhyme

cónsone *adj* harmonious ‖ *m* (mus) chord

consorcio *m* consortium; partnership; fellowship

consorte *mf* consort, mate, spouse; partner, companion; **consortes** (law) colitigants; (law) accomplices

conspi·cuo -cua *adj* outstanding, prominent

conspiración *f* conspiracy

conspirar *intr* to conspire

constancia *f* constancy; certainty, proof

constante *adj* constant; steady, regular; sure, certain ‖ *f* constant

constar *intr* to be clear, be certain; to be on record; to have the right rhythm; **constar de** to consist of; **hacer constar** to state, make known; **y para que conste** in witness whereof

constatación *f* proof

constatar *tr* to prove, establish, show

constelación *f* constellation; climate, weather; epidemic

consternar *tr* to depress, dismay

constipación *f* or **constipado** *m* cold, cold in the head

constipar *tr* (*los poros*) to stop up ‖ *ref* to catch cold

constitución *f* constitution

constituir §20 *tr* to constitute; to establish, found; **constituir en** to force into ‖ *ref* — **constituirse en** to set oneself up as

constituti·vo -va *adj* & *m* constituent

constituyente *adj* (*para dictar o reformar la constitución*) constituent

constreñir §72 *tr* to constrain, force, compel; to constrict, compress

construcción *f* construction; building, structure; **construcción de buques** shipbuilding

construc·tor -tora *adj* construction ‖ *mf* builder, constructor; **constructor de buques** shipbuilder

construir §20 *tr* to build, to construct

consuegro *m* fellow father-in-law (*with respect to the father of one's son-in-law or daughter-in-law*), father-in-law of one's child

consuelda *f* comfrey; **consuelda real** field larkspur; **consuelda sarracena** goldenrod

consuelo *m* consolation; joy, delight; **sin consuelo** inconsolably; (coll) to excess

consueta *m* (theat) prompter

consuetudina·rio -ria *adj* customary, usual

cónsul *m* consul

consulado *m* consulate; consulship; (*casa u oficina*) consulate

consular *adj* consular
consulta *f* consultation; opinion; reference
consultación *f* consultation
consultar *tr* to consult; to take up, discuss; to advise || *intr* to consult, confer
consulti·vo -va *adj* advisory
consul·tor -tora *mf* consultant
consultorio *m* doctor's office
consuma·do -da *adj* consummate || *m* consommé
consumar *tr* to consummate; to fulfill, carry out
consumición *f* consumption; drink (*in bar or restaurant*)
consumi·do -da *adj* (coll) thin, weak, emaciated; (coll) fretful
consumi·dor -dora *mf* consumer; customer (*in bar or restaurant*)
consumir *tr* to consume; to exhaust; (coll) to harass, wear down || *ref* to consume, waste away; to long, yearn
consumo *m* consumption; drink (*in bar or restaurant*); customers; **consumos** octroi
consunción *f* consumption; (pathol) consumption
consuno *adv* — **de consuno** together, in accord
consunti·vo -va *adj* consumptive; (*crédito*) consumer
contabilidad *f* accounting, bookkeeping
contabilista *mf* accountant, bookkeeper
contabilizadora *f* computer
contabilizar §60 *tr* to enter in the ledger
contable *adj* countable || *mf* accountant, bookkeeper
contactar *intr* to contact, be in contact
contacto *m* contact; **ponerse en contacto con** to get in touch with
conta·do -da *adj* scarce, rare; **al contado** cash, for cash; **contados** a few; **de contado** right away; **por de contado** of course
contador *m* counter; accountant; (*que mide el agua, gas, electricidad*) meter; (law) receiver; **contador de abonado** house meter; **contador kilométrico** speedometer; **contador público titulado** certified public accountant
contaduría *f* accountancy; accountant's office; box office for advanced sales
contagiar *tr* to infect; to corrupt
contagio *m* contagion
contagio·so -sa *adj* contagious
contaminación *f* contamination
contaminar *tr* to contaminate; (*un texto*) to corrupt; (*la ley de Dios*) to break
contante *adj* (*dinero*) ready
contar §61 *tr* to count; to regard, consider; to tell, relate; **contar . . . años to be . . . years old; dejarse contar diez** (box) to take the count; **tiene sus horas contadas** his days are numbered || *intr* to count; **a contar desde** beginning with; **contar con** to count on, rely on; to reckon with; to expect to
contemplación *f* contemplation; leniency, condescension

contemplar *tr* to contemplate; to be lenient to || *intr* to contemplate
contemporáne·o -a *adj* contemporaneous, contemporary || *mf* contemporary
contemporizar §60 *intr* to temporize
contención *f* containment; contention, strife; (law) suit, litigation
contencio·so -sa *adj* contentious
contender §51 *intr* to contend
contendiente *mf* contender, contestant
contener §71 *tr* to contain || *ref* to contain oneself
conteni·do -da *adj* moderate, restrained || *m* content, contents
contenta *f* gift or treat; indorsement; (mil) certificate of good conduct; (law) release
contentadi·zo -za *adj* easy to please
contentamiento *m* contentment
contentar *tr* to content; (com) to indorse; (Am) to reconcile
conten·to -ta *adj* content, contented, glad || *m* content, contentment; **a contento** to one's satisfaction; **no caber de contento** (coll) to be beside oneself with joy || *f* see **contenta**
contera *f* tip, metal tip
contesta *f* (Am) answer; (Mex) chat
contestación *f* answer; argument, debate; **mala contestación** (coll) back talk
contestar *tr* to answer || *intr* to answer; to agree
contexto *m* interweaving; context
conticinio *m* dead of night
contienda *f* contest, dispute, fight
contigo *pron* with thee, with you
conti·guo -gua *adj* contiguous, adjoining
continencia *f* continence
continental *adj* continental
continente *adj* continent || *m* (*cosa que contiene en sí a otra*) container; (*aire del semblante, compostura del cuerpo*) mien, bearing; (*gran extensión de tierra rodeada por los océanos*) continent
contingencia *f* contingency
contingente *adj* contingent || *m* contingent; share, quota
continuar §21 *tr* & *intr* to continue; **continuará** to be continued
continuidad *f* continuity
conti·nuo -nua *adj* continuous, continual; (mach) endless || **continuo** *adv* continuously
contonear *ref* to strut, swagger
contoneo *m* strut, swagger
contorcer §74 *ref* to writhe
contorno *m* contour, outline; **contornos** environs, neighborhood
contorsión *f* contorsion
contra *prep* against; toward, facing || *m* (*concepto opuesto*) con || *f* trouble, inconvenience; (*al comprador*) (Cuba) gift, extra; (Chile) antidote; **llevar la contra a** (coll) to disagree with
contraalmirante *m* rear admiral
contraatacar §73 *tr* & *intr* to counterattack
contraataque *m* counterattack

contrabajo m contrabass, double bass
contrabajón m double bassoon
contrabalancear tr to counterbalance
contrabalanza f counterbalance
contrabandear intr to smuggle
contrabandista adj smuggling; contraband || mf smuggler, contrabandist
contrabando m smuggling, contraband; **meter de contrabando** to smuggle, smuggle in
contrabarrera f second row of seats (in bull ring)
contracalle f parallel side street
contracarril m (rr) guardrail
contracción f contraction; (reducción del ritmo normal de los negocios) recession; (al estudio) (Chile, Peru) concentration
contracepti·vo -va adj & m contraceptive
contracorriente f countercurrent, cross-current; (entre aguas) undertow
contrachapado m plywood
contradecir §24 tr to contradict
contradicción f contradiction
contradic·tor -tora adj contradictory || mf contradicter
contradic·rio -ria adj contradictory
contraer §75 tr to contract; (deudas) to incur; (el discurso o idea) to condense || ref to contract; to shrink; (Chile, Peru) to concentrate, apply oneself
contraescalón m riser (of stairway)
contraespía mf counterspy
contraespionaje m counterespionage
contrafallar tr & intr to overtrump
contrafallo m overtrump
contrafigura f counterpart
contrafuero m infringement, violation
contrafuerte m abutment, buttress
contragolpe m counterstroke; kickback; (box) counter
contrahace·dor -dora adj counterfeiting; fake || mf counterfeiter; fake; impersonator
contrahacer §39 tr to counterfeit, copy, imitate; to fake; to impersonate; (un libro) to pirate || ref to pretend to be
contra·haz f (pl -haces) wrong side
contrahe·cho -cha adj counterfeit, fake; deformed
contrahechura f counterfeit, fake
contrahuella f riser (of stairway)
contralor m comptroller
contralto mf contralto (person) || m contralto (voice)
contraluz f view against the light; **a contraluz** against the light
contramaestre m foreman; (naut) boatswain; **segundo contramaestre** boatswain's mate
contramandar tr to countermand
contramandato m countermand
contramano adv — **a contramano** in the wrong direction, the wrong way
contramarcha f countermarch; reverse
contramarchar intr to countermarch; to go in reverse
contraofensiva f counteroffensive
contraorden f cancellation
contraparte f counterpart

contrapasar intr to go over to the other side
contrapelo adv — **a contrapelo** against the hair, against the grain; the wrong way; **a contrapelo de** against, counter to
contrapesar tr to offset, counterbalance
contrapeso m counterweight; counterbalance; (para completar el peso de carne, etc.) makeweight
contraponer §54 tr to set opposite; to oppose; to compare
contraproducente adj self-defeating, unproductive
contraprueba f second proof
contrapuerta f storm door; vestibule door
contrapuntear tr to sing in counterpoint; to taunt, be sarcastic to || ref to taunt each other
contrapunto m counterpoint
contrapunzón m nailset, punch
contrariar §77 tr to counteract, to oppose; to annoy, provoke
contrariedad f opposition; interference; annoyance, bother
contra·rio -ria adj opposite, contrary; harmful || mf enemy, opponent, rival || m opposite, contrary; **al contrario** on the contrary; **de lo contrario** otherwise
contrarreferencia f cross reference
Contrarreforma f Counter Reformation
contrarregistro m (para comprobar si algún género ha pasado por la frontera) double check; (de una experiencia científica) control
contrarréplica f (law) rejoinder
contrarrestar tr to resist, counteract; (la pelota) to return
contrarrevolución f counterrevolution
contrasentido m misinterpretation; mistranslation; nonsense
contraseña f countersign; baggage check; **contraseña de salida** (mov, theat) check
contrastar tr to resist; (las pesas y medidas) to check || intr to resist; to contrast
contraste m resistance; contrast; assayer; assayer's office; (naut) sudden shift in the wind
contratar tr to contract for; to hire, engage
contratiempo m misfortune, disappointment, setback
contratista mf contractor
contrato m contract
contratreta f counterplot
contratuerca f lock nut, jam nut
contraveneno m counterpoison, antidote
contravenir §79 intr to act contrary; **contravenir a** to contravene, act counter to
contraventana f window shutter
contravidriera f storm sash
contrayente mf contracting party (to a marriage)
contribución f contribution; tax; **contribución de sangre** military service;

contribución industrial excise tax; **contribución territorial** land tax
contribui·dor -dora *mf* contributor; taxpayer
contribuir §20 *tr & intr* to contribute
contribuyente *mf* contributor; taxpayer
contrición *f* contrition
contrincante *m* competitor, rival; fellow candidate
contristar *tr* to sadden
contri·to -ta *adj* contrite
control *m* control, check
controlar *tr* to control, check
controversia *f* controversy
controvertible *adj* controversial, controvertible
controvertir §68 *tr* to controvert
contubernio *m* cohabitation; evil alliance
contumacia *f* contumacy; (law) contempt
contu·maz *adj* (*pl* **-maces**) contumacious; germ-bearing; (law) guilty of contempt of court
contumelia *f* contumely
contundente *adj* bruising; impressive, convincing
contundir *tr* to bruise
conturbar *tr* to trouble, worry, upset
contusión *f* contusion
contusionar *tr* (Chile) to bruise
convalecencia *f* convalescence
convalecer §22 *intr* to convalesce, recover
convaleciente *adj & mf* convalescent
convalidar *tr* to confirm
conveci·no -na *adj* neighboring || *mf* neighbor
convencer §78 *tr* to convince
convencimiento *m* conviction
convención *f* (*acuerdo; conformidad; asamblea*) convention; (Am) political convention
convencional *adj* conventional
convenible *adj* docile, compliant; (*precio*) fair, reasonable
conveniencia *f* (*comodidad*) convenience; (*acuerdo, convenio*) agreement; fitness, suitability; (*formas sociales*) propriety; domestic employment; **conveniencias** income, property
conveniencie·ro -ra *adj* (coll) comfort-loving
conveniente *adj* (*cómodo*) convenient; fit, suitable; advantageous; proper
convenio *m* pact, covenant, treaty
convenir §79 *intr* to agree; (*concurrir, juntarse*) to convene; to be suitable, be becoming; to be important, to be necessary; **conviene a saber** to wit, namely || *ref* to agree, come to an agreement
conventillo *m* (SAm) tenement house
convento *m* convent, monastery; **convento de religiosas** convent
converger §17 or **convergir** §27 *intr* to converge; to concur
conversa *f* (coll) chat, conversation
conversación *f* conversation
conversacional *adj* conversational

conversar *intr* to converse; to live, dwell
conversión *f* conversion
conver·so -sa *adj* converted || *mf* convert || *m* lay brother || *f* see **conversa**
convertible *adj* convertible || *m* (aut) convertible
convertir §68 *tr* to convert; to turn || *ref* to convert; to be converted; **convertirse en** to turn into, become
conve·xo -xa *adj* convex
convic·to -ta *adj* convicted, found guilty
convidado -da *mf* guest || *f* (coll) treat
convidar *tr* to invite; to treat; to move, incite; **convidarle a uno con alguna cosa** to treat someone to something || *ref* to offer one's services
convincente *adj* convincing
convite *m* invitation; treat, banquet, party; **convite a escote** Dutch treat
convivir *intr* to live together
convocar §73 *tr* to convoke, call together; (*p.ej., una huelga*) to call; to acclaim
convoy *m* convoy; escort; cruet stand; (rr) train
convoyar *tr* to convoy
convulsionar *tr* to convulse
conyugal *adj* conjugal
cónyuge *mf* spouse, consort || **cónyuges** *mpl* couple, husband and wife
co·ñac *m* (*pl* **-ñacs** or **-ñaques**) cognac
cooperación *f* coöperation
cooperar *intr* to coöperate
cooperati·vo -va *adj* coöperative
coordena·do -da *adj* coördinate || *f* (math) coördinate
coordinante *adj* (gram) coördinating
coordinar *tr & intr* to coördinate
copa *f* (*acuerdo; conformidad*) goblet, wineglass; (*del sombrero*) crown; brazier; vase; drink; sundae; playing card, representing a bowl, equivalent to heart; (*del dolor*) (fig) cup; (sport) cup
copar *tr* (*la puesta equivalente a todo el dinero de la banca*) to cover; (*todos los puestos en una elección*) to sweep; (mil) to cut off and capture
copartícipe *mf* copartner, joint partner
copear *intr* to sell wine or liquor by the glass; (coll) to tipple
copero *m* cabinet for wineglasses
copete *m* (*cabello levantado sobre la frente*) pompadour; (*de plumas; de una montaña*) crest; (*de un caballo*) forelock; (*de lana, cabello, plumas, etc.*) tuft; (*de un mueble*) top, finial; (*de un sorbete*) topping; **de alto copete** aristocratic, important; **tener mucho copete** to be high-hat
copetu·do -da *adj* tufted; high, lofty; (coll) high-hat
copia *f* plenty, abundance; copy; **copia al carbón** carbon copy; **copia fiel** true copy
copiador *m* copier, copying machine
copiante *mf* copier, copyist
copiar *tr* to copy, copy down
copiloto *m* copilot
copio·so -sa *adj* copious, abundant

copista *mf* copier, copyist

copla *f* couplet; ballad, popular song; **coplas** (coll) verse, poetry; **coplas de ciego** (coll) doggerel

cople·ro **-ra** *mf* vendor of ballads; poetaster

coplista *mf* poetaster

copo *m* bundle of cotton, flax, hemp, etc. to be spun; **copo de nieve** snowflake; **copos de jabón** soap flakes

copón *m* ciborium, pyx

copo·so **-sa** *adj* bushy, flaky, woolly

copu·do **-da** *adj* bushy, thick

copular *ref* to copulate

coque *m* coke

coqueluche *f* whooping cough

coqueta *adj* coquettish ‖ *f* coquette, flirt; (W-I) dressing table

coquetear *intr* to coquette, to flirt; to try to please everybody

coquetería *f* coquetry, flirting; affectation

coque·tón **-tona** *adj* (coll) coquettish, kittenish ‖ *m* (coll) flirt, lady-killer

coracha *f* leather bag

coraje *m* anger; mettle, spirit

coraju·do **-da** *adj* (coll) ill-tempered; (Arg) brave, courageous

coral *adj* (mus) choral ‖ *m* (mus) chorale; (*zoófito; esqueleto calizo del zoófito; color*) coral; **corales** coral beads

corambre *f* hides, skins

Corán *m* Koran

coranvo·bis *m* (*pl* **-bis**) (coll) fat solemn look

coraza *f* armor; cuirass; (sport) guard

corazón *m* heart; (*centro de una cosa*) core; **de corazón** heartily; **hacer de tripas corazón** to pluck up courage

corazonada *f* impulsiveness; hunch, presentiment; (coll) entrails

corbata *f* necktie, cravat; scarf; **corbata de mariposa, corbata de lazo** bow tie; **corbata de nudo corredizo** four-in-hand tie

corbatín *m* bow tie

corbeta *f* corvette

Córcega *f* Corsica

corcel *m* steed, charger

corcova *f* hump, hunch

corcova·do **-da** *adj* humpbacked, hunchbacked ‖ *mf* humpback, hunchback

corcovar *tr* to bend

corcovear *intr* to buck; (Am) to grumble; (Mex) to be afraid

corcha *f* cork bark; cork bucket (*for cooling wine*)

corchea *f* (mus) quaver, eighth note

corche·ro **-ra** *adj* cork ‖ *f* cork bucket (*for cooling wine*)

corcheta *f* eye (*of hook and eye*)

corchete *m* snap; hook and eye; hook (*of hook and eye*); (*signo*) bracket; **corchete de presión** snap fastener

corcho *m* cork; cork, cork stopper; cork wine cooler; cork box; cork mat; **corcho bornizo, corcho virgen** virgin cork

cordada *f* (mountaineering) party of two or three men roped together

cordaje *m* cordage; (naut) rigging

cordal *adj* wisdom (*tooth*) ‖ *m* (mus) tailpiece

cordel *m* cord, string; (distance of) five steps; cattle run; **a cordel** in a straight line

cordelejo *m* string; **dar cordelejo a** to make fun of; (Mex) to keep putting off

cordera *f* ewe lamb; (*mujer dócil y humilde*) (fig) lamb

cordería *f* cordage

corderillo *m* lambskin

corderi·no **-na** *adj* lamb ‖ *f* lambskin

cordero *m* lamb; lambskin; (*hombre dócil y humilde*) (fig) lamb

corderuna *f* lambskin

cordial *adj* cordial; (*dedo*) middle ‖ *m* cordial

cordialidad *f* cordiality

cordillera *f* chain of mountains

cordobana *f* — **andar a la cordobana** (coll) to go naked

cordón *m* lace; (*de cuerda o alambre*) strand; cordon; milled edge of coin; (*de monje*) rope belt; **cordón umbilical** umbilical cord

cordoncillo *m* rib, ridge; braid; (*de monedas*) milling

cordura *f* prudence, wisdom

Corea *f* Korea; **la Corea del Norte** North Korea; **la Corea del Sur** South Korea

corea·no **-na** *adj & mf* Korean

corear *tr* to compose for a chorus; to accompany with a chorus; to join in singing; to agree obsequiously with

coreografía *f* choreography

coriáce·o **-a** *adj* leathery

Corinto *f* Corinth

corista *m* choir priest; (theat) chorus man ‖ *f* chorus girl, chorine

cori·to **-ta** *adj* naked; bashful, timid

cormorán *m* cormorant

cor·nac *m* (*pl* **-nacs**) or **cornaca** *m* mahout

cornada *f* hook with horns; goring; (*en la esgrima*) upward thrust

cornadura or **cornamenta** *f* (*del toro, la vaca, etc.*) horns; (*del ciervo*) antlers

cornamusa *f* bagpipe

córnea *f* cornea

cornear *tr* to butt; to gore

corneja *f* daw, crow

cornejo *m* dogwood

córne·o **-a** *adj* horn, horny ‖ *f* see **córnea**

corneta *f* bugle; swineherd's horn; **corneta acústica** ear trumpet; **corneta de llaves** cornet, cornet-à-pistons; **corneta de monte** huntinghorn

cornisa *f* cornice

cornisamento *m* (archit) entablature

corno *m* horn; dogwood; **corno inglés** (mus) English horn

Cornualles Cornwall

cornucopia *f* cornucopia; sconce with mirror

cornu·do **-da** *adj* horned, antlered; cuckold ‖ *m* cuckold

coro *m* chorus; choir; choir loft; **a**

coros alternately; **de coro** by heart; **hacer coro a** to echo

corolario *m* corollary

corona *f* (*cerco de metal; moneda; dignidad real; parte visible de una muela*) crown; (*cerco de flores*) garland, wreath; (*aureola*) halo; (*de eclesiástico*) tonsure; (*la que corresponde a un título nobiliario*) coronet; **corona nupcial** bridal wreath

coronación *f* coronation

coronamento or **coronamiento** *m* coronation; completion, termination; (archit) coping; (naut) taffrail

coronar *tr* to crown; to complete, finish; to top, surmount; (checkers) to crown

coronel *m* colonel

coronelía *f* colonelcy

coronilla *f* (*de la cabeza*) crown; **andar** or **bailar de coronilla** (coll) to be hard at it; **estar hasta la coronilla** (coll) to be fed up

corpiño *m* bodice, waist; (Arg) brassière

corporación *f* corporation

corporal *adj* corporal, bodily

corpu·do -da *adj* corpulent

corpulen·to -ta *adj* corpulent

corpúsculo *m* corpuscle; particle

corral *m* corral, stockyard; barnyard; fishpound; theater; **corral de madera** lumberyard; **corral de vacas** (coll) pigpen; **hacer corrales** (coll) to play hooky

correa *f* strap, thong; (aer, mach) belt; **besar la correa** (coll) to eat humble pie; **correa de seguridad** (aer, aut) safety belt

corrección *f* (*acción de corregir; reprensión*) correction; (*calidad de correcto*) correctness

correcti·vo -va *adj* & *m* corrective

correc·to -ta *adj* correct

correc·tor -tora *mf* corrector; **corrector de pruebas** proofreader

corredera *f* track, slide; slide valve; (*del trombón*) slide; (naut) log; (naut) log line; (*puerta*) de corredera sliding

corredi·zo -za *adj* slide; sliding; (*nudo*) slip

corre·dor -dora *adj* running || *mf* runner || *m* corridor; porch, gallery; (*el que interviene en compras y ventas de efectos comerciales, etc.*) broker; (mil) scout; **corredor de apuestas** bookmaker

corregidor *m* Spanish magistrate; chief magistrate of Spanish town

corregir §57 *tr* to correct; to temper, moderate || *intr* (W-I) to have a bowel movement || *ref* to mend one's ways

correlación *f* correlation

correlacionar *tr* & *intr* to correlate

correlati·vo -va *adj* & *m* correlative

correncia *f* bashfulness; (coll) looseness of the bowels

corrienti·o -a *adj* running; (coll) free, easy || *f* (coll) looseness of the bowels

corren·tón -tona *adj* jolly, full of fun

corrento·so -sa *adj* (Am) swift, rapid

correo *m* mail; post office; mail train; postman; courier; **correo aéreo** air mail; **correo urgente** special delivery; **echar al correo** to mail, to post

correo·so -sa *adj* leathery, tough

correr *tr* (*un caballo*) to run, to race; (*un riesgo*) to run; to travel over; to overrun; (*una cortina*) to draw; (*un toro*) to fight; to chase, pursue; to auction; to confuse; (Am) to throw out; **correrla** (coll) to run around all night || *intr* to run; to race; to pass, elapse; to circulate, be common talk; to be current; **a todo correr** at full speed; **correr a** to sell for; **correr a cargo de** or **por cuenta de** to be the business of; **correr con** to be on good terms with; to be in charge of; (*mes*) **que corre** current || *ref* (*a derecha o a izquierda*) to turn; to be confused; to be embarrassed, be ashamed; to slide, glide; (*una bujía, un color*) to run; to go too far

correría *f* short trip, excursion; foray, raid

correspondencia *f* correspondence; contact, communication; agreement, harmony; (*en el metro*) connection; (*en una carretera*) interchange

corresponder *intr* to correspond; (*dos habitaciones*) to communicate; **corresponder a** (*un beneficio, el afecto de una persona*) to return, reciprocate; to concern; to be up to || *ref* (*comunicarse por escrito*) to correspond; (*dos cosas*) to correspond with each other; to be in agreement; to be attached to each other

correspondiente *adj* corresponding; correspondent; respective || *mf* correspondent

corresponsal *mf* correspondent

corretaje *m* brokerage

corretear *tr* (Am) to harass, pursue; (CAm) to drive away; (Chile) to speed up || *intr* (coll) to race around

correveidi·le *mf* (*pl* -le) (coll) gossip; (coll) go-between

corrida *f* run; bullfight; (*carrera de entrenamiento de un caballo*) (Am) trial run; **corrida de banco** (Am) run on the bank; **corrida de toros** bullfight

corri·do -da *adj* (*peso, medida*) in excess; (*letra*) cursive; continued, unbroken; abashed, ashamed; (coll) worldly-wise, sophisticated || *m* overhang; (Am) street ballad || *f* see **corrida**

corriente *adj* (*agua*) running; (*actual*) current; common, ordinary; regular; well-known; fluent || *adv* all right, O.K. || *m* current month; **al corriente** on time; informed, aware, posted || *f* current, stream; (elec) current; **corriente de aire** draft; **Corriente del Golfo** Gulf Stream; **ir contra la corriente** to go against the tide

corrillo *m* circle, clique

corrimiento *m* running; sliding; watery

discharge; embarrassment, shyness; landslide; (Am) rheumatism

corro m (cerco de gente; espacio circular) ring; (juego de niñas) ring-around-a-rosy; **corro de brujas** fairy ring; **hacer corro** to make room

corroborar tr to corroborate; to strengthen

corroer §62 tr & ref to corrode

corromper tr to corrupt; to spoil; to rot; to seduce; to bribe; (coll) to annoy || intr to smell bad || ref to become corrupted; to spoil; to rot

corrosión f corrosion

corrosi·vo -va adj & m corrosive

corrugar §44 tr to shrink; to wrinkle

corrupción f corruption; seduction; bribery; stench

corruptela f corruption

corruptible adj corruptible; (p.ej., frutas) perishable

corrusco m (coll) crust of bread

corsa f (naut) day's run

corsario m corsair

corsé m corset

cor·so -sa adj & mf Corsican || m (naut) privateering; (SAm) drive, promenade || f see **corsa**

corta f clearing, cutting, felling

cortaalam·bres m (pl -bres) wire cutter

cortabol·sas m (pl -sas) (coll) pickpocket

cortacésped m lawn mower

cortaciga·rros m (pl -rros) cigar cutter

cortacircui·tos m (pl -tos) (elec) fuse

cortacorriente m (elec) change-over switch

cortada f (Am) cut, cutting

cortadillo m drinking cup

corta·do -da adj (estilo) choppy; (SAm) hard up || f see **cortada**

corta·dor -dora adj cutting || mf cutter || m butcher || f cutting machine

cortafrío m cold chisel

cortafuego s fire wall

cortahie·los m (pl -los) icebreaker

cortalápi·ces m (pl -ces) pencil sharpener

cortante adj cutting, sharp || m butcher; butcher knife

cortapape·les m (pl -les) paper cutter

cortapi·cos m (pl -cos) (ent) earwig; **cortapicos y callares** (coll) little children should be seen and not heard

cortaplu·mas m (pl -mas) penknife

cortapu·ros m (pl -ros) cigar cutter

cortar tr to cut; to trim; to chop; to cut off; to cut out, omit; to cut short; to cut up; to carve; (la corriente; la ignición) to cut off || intr to cut; (el viento, el frío) to be cutting; **cortar de vestir** to cut cloth; (coll) to gossip || ref to become speechless; (la leche) to curdle, turn sour; (la piel) to chap, to crack

cortarregión m marginal stop

cortaú·ñas m (pl -ñas) nail clipper

cortavi·drios m (pl -drios) glass cutter

cortaviento m windshield

corte m cut; cutting; (filo de un arma, cuchillo, etc.; borde de un libro)

edge; cross section; (de un vestido) cut, fit; piece of material; **corte de pelo** haircut; **corte de pelo a cepillo** crew cut; **corte de traje** suiting || f (de un rey) court; (corral) yard; stable, fold; (tribunal de justicia) (Am) court; **Cortes** Parliament; **darse cortes** (SAm) to put on airs; **hacer la corte a** to pay court to; **la Corte** the Capital (Madrid)

cortedad f shortness; smallness; lack; bashfulness

cortejar tr to escort, attend, court; to court, to woo

cortejo m courting; courtship; (séquito) cortege; gift, treat; (coll) beau

cortera f (Chile) streetwalker

cortero m (Chile) day laborer

cortés adj courteous, polite, courtly

cortesana f courtesan

cortesa·no -na adj courtly, courteous || m courtier || f see **cortesana**

cortesía f courtesy, politeness, courtliness; gift, favor; (inclinación de la cabeza o el cuerpo en señal de respeto) curtsy; (de una carta) conclusion; **hacer una cortesía** to make a bow; to curtsy

corteza f bark; peel, rind, skin; (de pan) crust; coarseness; (envoltura exterior de un órgano) cortex; **corteza cerebral** cortex

cortijo m farm, farmhouse

cortil m barnyard

cortina f curtain; **correr la cortina** to pull the curtain aside; **cortina de hierro** iron curtain; **cortina de humo** smoke screen

cortinal m fenced-in field

cortinilla f shade, window shade

cortisona f cortisone

cor·to -ta adj short; dull; bashful, shy; speechless; **a la corta o a la larga** sooner or later; **desde muy corta edad** from earliest childhood || f see **corta**

cortocircuitar tr & ref (elec) to short-circuit

cortocircuito m (elec) short circuit

cortometraje m (mov) short

corva f ham, back of knee; (vet) curb

corvejón m gambrel, hock; (orn) cormorant

cor·vo -va adj arched, bent, curved || m hook || f see **corva**

cor·zo -za mf roe deer

cosa f thing; **cosa de** a matter of; **cosa de cajón** a matter of course; **cosa de mieles** (coll) something fine; **cosa de nunca acabar** endless bore; **cosa de oír** something worth hearing; **cosa de risa** something to laugh at; **cosa de ver** something worth seeing; **cosa nunca vista** (coll) something unheard-of; **cosa que** (Am coll) so that; **cosa rara** strange to say; **como si tal cosa** (coll) as if nothing had happened; **en cosa de** in a matter of; **no . . . gran cosa** not much; **no haber**

tal cosa to be not so; **otra cosa** something else; **¿qué cosa?** what's new?

cosa•co -ca *adj & mf* Cossack ‖ *m* Cossack (*horseman*)

coscolina *f* (Mex) loose woman

cos•cón -cona *adj* sly, crafty

cosecha *f* crop, harvest; harvest time; **cosecha de vino** vintage; **de su cosecha** (coll) out of one's own head

cosechar *tr* to harvest, reap ‖ *intr* to harvest

coseche•ro -ra *mf* harvester, reaper; vintner

cose-pape•les *m* (*pl* -les) stapler

coser *tr* to sew; to join, unite closely; **coser a preguntas** to riddle with questions; **coser a puñaladas** to cut to pieces ‖ *intr* to sew; **ser coser y cantar** (coll) to be a cinch ‖ *ref* — **coserse con** or **contra** to be closely attached to

cosméti•co -ca *adj & m* cosmetic

cósmi•co -ca *adj* cosmic

cosmonauta *mf* cosmonaut

cosmopolita *adj & mf* cosmopolitan

cosmos *m* cosmos; (bot) cosmos

coso *m* enclosure for bullfighting

cosquillas *fpl* tickling, ticklishness; **buscarle a uno las cosquillas** (coll) to try to irritate a person; **no sufrir cosquillas** or **tener malas cosquillas** (coll) to be touchy

cosquillear *tr* to tickle; to tease, taunt; to stir up the curiosity of; to scare ‖ *intr* to tickle ‖ *ref* to be curious; to enjoy oneself

cosquilleo *m* tickling, tickling sensation

cosquillo•so -sa *adj* ticklish; (*que se ofende fácilmente*) touchy

costa *f* coast, shore; cost, price; **a toda costa** at all costs; **Costa Brava** Mediterranean coast in province of Gerona, Spain; **Costa Firme** Spanish Main; **costa marítima** seacoast; **costas** (law) costs

costado *m* side; (*del ejército*) flank; (Mex) station platform; **costados** ancestors, stock

costal *m* bag, sack; **costal de los pecados** human body (*full of sin*); **estar hecho un costal de huesos** (coll) to be nothing but skin and bones

costanera *f* slope; **costaneras** rafters

costane•ro -ra *adj* sloping; coastal ‖ *f* see **costanera**

costanilla *f* short steep street

costar §61 *intr* to cost; **cueste lo que cueste** cost what it may

costarricense or **costarrique•ño -ña** *adj & mf* Costa Rican

coste *m* cost; **a coste y costas** at cost

costear *tr* to pay for, to defray the cost of; to sail along the coast of ‖ *intr* to sail along the coast ‖ *ref* to pay; to pay one's way

coste•ño -ña *adj* sloping; coastal

coste•ro -ra *adj* coastal

costilla *f* rib; (coll) wealth; **costillas** back, shoulders

costillu•do -da *adj* heavy-set, broad-shouldered

costo *m* cost; **costo de la vida** cost of living; **costo, seguro y flete** cost, insurance, and freight

costo•so -sa *adj* costly, expensive; grievous

costra *f* scab, scale; (*moco de una vela*) snuff

costro•so -sa *adj* scabby, scaly

costumbre *f* custom, habit; **de costumbre** usual; usually; **tener por costumbre** to be in the habit of

costumbrista *mf* critic of manners and customs

costura *f* sewing, needlework; dressmaking; (*unión de dos piezas cosidas*) seam; **alta costura** fashion designing, haute couture

costurera *f* seamstress, dressmaker

costurero *m* sewing table

cota *f* coat of arms; coat of mail

cotarrera *f* (coll) gossipy woman

cotarro *m* night shelter (*for beggars and tramps*); **alborotar el cotarro** (coll) to raise a row

cotejar *tr* to compare, collate

cotejo *m* comparison, collation

cotidia•no -na *adj* daily, everyday

cotilla *f* (coll) gossip, tattletale

cotín *m* (sport) backstroke

cotización *f* quotation; dues

cotizante *adj* dues-paying

cotizar §60 *tr* to quote; to prorate ‖ *intr* to collect dues; to pay dues

coto *m* price; fixed price; term, limit

cotón *m* printed cotton

cotona *f* (Am) work shirt

cotonía *f* dimity

cotorra *f* parrot; parakeet; magpie; (coll) chatterbox; (Mex) night shelter

cotorrear *intr* (coll) to gossip, gabble

cotufa *f* Jerusalem artichoke; delicacy, tidbit; **hacer cotufas** (Bol) to be fastidious; **pedir cotufas en el golfo** (coll) to ask for the moon

coturno *m* buskin

covacha *f* cave; (Am) cubbyhole; (Am) shanty; (Am) doghouse

covachuelista *m* (coll) clerk, government clerk

coxcojita *f* hopscotch; **a coxcojita** hippety-hop

coy *m* (naut) hammock

coyunda *f* strap for yoking oxen; sandal string; marriage; tyranny

coyuntura *f* joint, articulation; (*sazón, oportunidad*) juncture

coz *f* (*pl* **coces**) kick; big end; ebb; (coll) insult; **dar coces contra el aguijón** to kick against the pricks

c.p.b., **C.P.B.** *abbr* cuyos pies beso

cps. *abbr* compañeros

crabrón *m* hornet

crac *m* (*ruido seco*) crack; crash; **hacer crac** to crash, to fail

cráneo *m* cranium, skull

crápula *f* drunkenness, debauchery; riffraff

crapulo•so -sa *adj* drunken; vicious, evil

crascitar *intr* to crow, croak

cra·so -sa *adj* fat, greasy, thick; *(ignorancia)* crass, gross

cráter *m* crater

creación *f* creation

crea·dor -dora *adj* creative || *mf* creator

crear *tr* to create; to appoint; to found || *ref* to make for oneself, to build up; to trump up

creati·vo -va *adj* creative

crecede·ro -ra *adj* growth; large enough to allow for growth

crecepelo *m* hair restorer

crecer §22 *intr* to grow; to increase; *(el río)* to rise, swell; *(la luna)* to wax || *ref* to grow; to take on more authority; to get bolder

creces *fpl* growth, increase; excess, extra; **con creces** amply, in abundance

crecida *f* freshet, flood

creciente *adj* growing, increasing || *f* — **creciente de la luna** waxing of the moon, crescent; **creciente del mar** high tide, flood tide

crecimiento *m* growth, increase

credenciales *fpl* credentials

crédito *m* credit

credo *m* creed; credo; **con el credo en la boca** (coll) with one's heart in one's mouth; **en un credo** (coll) in a trice

crédu·lo -la *adj* credulous

creederas *fpl* — **tener buenas creederas** (coll) to be gullible

creencia *f* belief; *(crédito que se presta a un hecho)* credence; *(secta)* creed

creer §43 *tr & intr* to believe; **¡ya lo creo!** (coll) I should say so! || *ref* to believe; to believe oneself to be

creíble *adj* believable, credible

crema *f* cream; cold cream; shoe polish; (gram) diaeresis; **crema de menta** crème de menthe; **crema desvanecedora** vanishing cream

cremación *f* cremation

cremallera *f* rack; zipper

cremato·rio -ria *adj & m* crematory

crémor *m* cream of tartar

cremo·so -sa *adj* creamy

crencha *f* part *(in hair)*; hair on each side of part

crepitar *intr* to crackle

crepuscular *adj* twilight

crepúsculo *m* twilight

cresa *f* maggot

crespar *tr & ref* to curl

cres·po -pa *adj* curly; curled; angry, irritated; stylish, conceited; *(estilo)* turgid || *m* (Am) curl

crespón *m* crape; **crespón fúnebre** crape; mourning band

cresta *f* crest; **cresta de gallo** cockscomb; (bot) cockscomb

creta *f* chalk || **Creta** *f* Crete

cretense *adj & mf* Cretan

cretona *f* cretonne

creyente *adj* believing || *mf* believer

creyón *m* crayon

cría *f* brood, litter; breeding; raising, rearing; nursing

criada *f* female servant, maid; **criada de casa, criada de servir** housemaid

criadero *m* nursery, tree nursery; fish hatchery; oyster bed

criadilla *f* testicle; potato

cria·do -da *adj* — **bien criado** well-bred; **mal criado** ill-bred || *mf* servant || *f* see **criada**

cria·dor -dora *mf* breeder || *f* wet nurse

criamiento *m* care, upkeep

crianza *f* raising, rearing; nursing; *(urbanidad)* breeding, manners; **buena crianza** good breeding; **mala crianza** bad breeding

criar §77 *tr* to raise, rear, bring up; to breed; to grow; to nurse, nourish; to fatten; to create; to foster

criatura *f* *(toda cosa creada; persona que debe su cargo o situación a otra)* creature; little child, little creature

criba *f* screen, sieve

cribar *tr* to screen, sieve

cribo *m* screen, sieve

cric *m* (pl **crics**) jack

crimen *m* crime; **crimen de lesa majestad** lese majesty

criminal *adj & mf* criminal

criminar *tr* to accuse, incriminate

crimino·so -sa *adj & mf* criminal

crines *fpl* mane

crío *m* (coll) baby, infant

crio·llo -lla *adj & mf* Creole

cripta *f* crypt

crisálida *f* chrysalis

crisantemo *m* chrysanthemum

cri·sis *f* (pl **-sis**) crisis; *(pánico económico)* depression, slump; mature judgment; **crisis del servicio doméstico** servant problem; **crisis de llanto** crying fit; **crisis de vivienda** housing shortage; **crisis ministerial** cabinet crisis; **crisis nerviosa** fit of nerves

crisma *f* (coll) head, bean

crisol *m* crucible

crispar *tr* to cause to twitch || *ref* to twitch

crispatura *f* twitch, twitching

crispir *tr* to grain, to marble

cristal *m* crystal; glass; pane of glass; mirror, looking glass; **cristal cilindrado** plate glass; **cristal de reloj** watch crystal; **cristal de roca** rock crystal; **cristal hilado** glass wool, spun glass; **cristal tallado** cut glass

cristalera *f* China closet; sideboard; glass door

cristalería *f* glassworks, glass store; glassware; glass cabinet

cristali·no -na *adj* crystalline || *m* lens, crystalline lens

cristalizar §60 *tr & ref* to crystallize

cristianar *tr* (coll) to baptize, christen

cristiandad *f* Christendom

cristianismo *m* Christianity

cristianizar §60 *tr* to Christianize

cristia·no -na *adj & mf* Christian || *m* soul, person; Spanish; (coll) watered wine

Cristo *m* Christ; crucifix; **donde Cristo dió las tres voces** (coll) in the middle of nowhere

Cristóbal *m* Christopher

criterio *m* criterion

crítica *f* *(juicio sobre una obra literaria, etc.; censura de la conducta de al-*

guno) criticism; (*arte de juzgar una obra literaria, etc.*) critique; gossip

criticar §73 *tr* & *intr* to criticize

crí•ti•co -ca *adj* critical; (*criticón*) (Am) critical (*faultfinding*) || *mf* critic || *f* see **crítica**

criti•cón -cona *adj* (coll) critical, faultfinding || *mf* (coll) critic, faultfinder

critiquizar §60 *tr* to overcriticize

crizneja *f* braid of hair

croar *intr* to croak

croata *adj* & *mf* Croatian

crocante *m* almond brittle, peanut brittle

crocitar *intr* to crow, croak

croco *m* crocus

croché *m* crochet

crochet *m* (box) hook

croma•do -da *adj* chrome || *m* chromium plating

cromar *tr* to chrome

cromo *m* chromium

cromosoma *m* chromosome

crónica *f* chronicle; news chronicle, feature story

cróni•co -ca *adj* chronic; longstanding; (*vicio*) inveterate || *f* see **crónica**

cronista *mf* chronicler; reporter, feature writer; **cronista de radio** newscaster

cronología *f* chronology

cronometra•dor -dora *mf* (sport) timekeeper

cronometraje *m* (sport) clocking, timing

cronómetro *m* chronometer; stop watch

croqueta *f* croquette

cro•quis *m* (*pl* -quis) sketch

croscitar *intr* to crow, croak

crótalo *m* rattlesnake; castanet

cruce *m* crossing; crossroads, intersection; exchange (*e.g., of letters*); (*avería*) crossed wires, short circuit; **cruce a nivel** grade crossing; **cruce en trébol** cloverleaf intersection

crucero *m* crossroads; railroad crossing; (*archit*) transept; (*aer, naut*) cruise, cruising; (*nav*) cruiser; **crucero a nivel** grade crossing

crucial *adj* crucial

crucificar §73 *tr* to crucify

crucifijo *m* crucifix

crucifixión *f* crucifixion

crucigrama *m* crossword puzzle

cruda *f* (Mex) hangover

crudeza *f* crudeness, rawness; (*del agua*) hardness; harshness, roughness; (coll) blustering; **crudezas** undigested food

cru•do -da *adj* crude, raw; (*agua*) hard; harsh, rough; (*tiempo*) raw; (*lienzo*) unbleached; **estar crudo** (P-R) to be rusty; (Mex) to have a hangover || *f* see **cruda**

cruel *adj* cruel

crueldad *f* cruelty

cruen•to -ta *adj* bloody

crujía *f* corridor, hall; hospital ward; block of houses; (naut) midship gangway; **crujía de piezas** suite of

rooms; **sufrir una crujía** (coll) to have a hard time of it

crujido *m* creak; crackle; clatter; chatter; rustle

crujir *intr* to creak; to crackle; to clatter; to chatter; to rustle; to crunch

crup *m* croup

crustáce•o -a *adj* crustaceous || *m* crustacean

cruz *f* (*pl* **cruces**) cross; (*de una moneda*) tails; (typ) dagger; **Cruz del Sur** Southern Cross; **¡cruz y raya!** (coll) that's enough!; **de la cruz a la fecha** from beginning to end

cruzada *f* (*expedición contra los infieles; propaganda contra un vicio*) crusade; crossroads, intersection

cruza•do -da *adj* crossed; (*de raza mixta*) cross; double-breasted || *m* (*el que toma parte en una cruzada*) crusader; (*caballero de una orden militar*) knight; twill || *f* see **cruzada**

cruzar §60 *tr* to cross; (*la tela*) to twill; (*cartas*) to exchange; to crossbreed; (naut) to cruise, cruise over || *intr* to cross; to cruise || *ref* to cross each other, to cross one's another's path; (*alistarse para una cruzada*) to take the cross; **cruzarse con** (*otro automóvil*) to pass; **cruzarse de brazos** (*estar ocioso*) to cross one's arms

cs. *abbr* **céntimos, cuartos**

cte. *abbr* **corriente**

c/u *abbr* **cada uno**

cuad. *abbr* **cuadrado**

cuaderna *f* (naut) frame

cuaderno *m* notebook; folder; **cuaderno de bitácora** (naut) logbook; **cuaderno de hojas cambiables or sueltas** loose-leaf notebook

cuadra *f* hall, large room; stable; dormitory, ward; croup, rump; (Am) block

cuadra•do -da *adj* square; square-shouldered; perfect || *m* square; (*regla*) rule, (*en las medias*) clock; **de cuadrado** perfectly; (*que se mira frente a frente*) full-faced

cuadragési•mo -ma *adj* & *m* fortieth

cuadrangular *adj* quadrangular || *m* home run

cuadrángu•lo -la *adj* quadrangular || *m* quadrangle

cuadrante *m* quadrant; (*de reloj*) face, dial; **cuadrante solar** sundial

cuadrar *tr* to square; to please; (*al toro*) (taur) to square off, to line up || *ref* to square; to stand at attention; (coll) to take on a serious air

cuadrilla *f* group, party; crew, gang

cuadrillazo *m* (SAm) surprise attack

cuadrillo *m* (*saeta*) bolt (*arrow*)

cuadrimotor *m* four-motor plane

cua•dro -dra *adj* square || *m* square; (*lienzo, pintura*) painting, picture; (*marco de pintura, ventana, etc.*) frame; (*de jardín*) patch, flower bed; staff, personnel; (mil) cadre; (sport) team; (theat) scene; (coll) sight, mess; **a cuadros** checked; **cuadro de costumbres** sketch of manners and customs; **cuadro de distribución** switchboard; **cuadro indicador** score board; **cuadro vivo** tableau; **en cuadro** square, e.g., **ocho pulgadas en cuadro** eight inches square; (coll) topsy-turvy; **quedarse en cuadro** to be all alone in the world; (mil) to be skeletonized ‖ *f* see **cuadra**

cuadrúpe·do -da *adj & m* quadruped

cuádruple *adj & m* quadruple

cuadruplicar §73 *tr & ref* to quadruple

cuajada *f* curd

cuajado *m* mincemeat

cuajar *tr* to curd, curdle, thicken, jelly; (coll) to please, to suit ‖ *intr* (coll) to take hold, catch on, jell, take shape; (Mex) to chatter, prattle ‖ *ref* to curd, curdle, thicken, jelly; to sleep sound; (coll) to become crowded

cuajo *m* curd; (Mex) chatter, prattle; (en la escuela) (Mex) recess

cual *adj rel & pron rel* such as; **el cual** which; who; **lo cual** which; **por lo cual** for which reason ‖ *adv* as ‖ *prep* like

cuál *adj interr & pron interr* which, what; which one

cualidad *f* quality, characteristic, trait

cualquier *adj indef* (*pl* **cualesquier**) apocopated form of **cualquiera**, used only before masculine nouns and adjectives

cualquiera (*pl* **cualesquiera**) *pron indef* anyone; **cualquiera que** whichever; whoever ‖ *adj indef* any ‖ *adj rel* whichever ‖ *m* (persona poco importante) nobody

cuan *adv* as

cuán *adv* how, how much

cuando *conj* when; although; in case; since; **aun cuando** even if, even though; **cuando más** at most; **cuando menos** at least; **cuando mucho** at most; **cuando quiera** whenever; **de cuando en cuando** from time to time ‖ *prep* (coll) at the time of

cuándo *adv* when; **cuándo . . . cuándo** sometimes . . . sometimes; **¿de cuándo acá?** since when?; how come?

cuantía *f* quantity; importance; **delito de mayor cuantía** felony; **delito de menor cuantía** misdemeanor; **de mayor cuantía** first-rate; **de menor cuantía** second-rate, of little importance

cuantiar §77 *tr* to estimate, appraise

cuánti·co -ca *adj* quantum

cuantio·so -sa *adj* large, substantial

cuan·to -ta *adj rel & pron rel* as much as, whatever, all that which; **cuantos** as many as, all those who, everybody who; **unos cuantos** some few ‖ *cuanto adv* as soon as; as long as; **cuanto antes** as soon as possible; **cuanto más . . . tanto más** the more . . . the more; **cuanto más que** all the more because; **en cuanto** as soon as; while; insofar as; **en cuanto a** as to, as for; **por cuanto** inasmuch as; **por cuanto . . . por tanto** inasmuch as . . . therefore ‖ **cuan·to** *m* (*pl* **-ta**) quantum

cuán·to -ta *adj interr & pron interr* how much; **cuántos** how many ‖

cuánto *adv* how, how much; how long; how long ago; **cada cuánto** how often

cuáque·ro -ra *adj & mf* Quaker

cuarenta *adj, pron & m* forty

cuarenta·vo -va *adj & m* fortieth

cuarentena *f* forty; quarantine; forty days, forty months, forty years; **poner en cuarentena** to quarantine; to withhold one's credence in

cuaresma *f* Lent

cuaresmal *adj* Lenten

cuarta *f* fourth, fourth part; (de la mano) span; (CAm, W-I) horse whip

cuartago *m* nag, pony

cuartear *tr* to divide in four parts; to divide; (la aguja) (naut) to box; (CAm, W-I) to whip ‖ *ref* to crack, split; (taur) to step aside, dodge

cuartel *m* quarter; (de una ciudad) section, ward; (terreno) lot; flower bed; (mil) barracks; (buen trato) (mil) quarter; (armazón de tablas para cerrar la escotilla) (naut) hatch; (coll) house, home; **cuartel de bomberos** engine house, firehouse; **cuarteles** (mil) quarters; **cuartel general** (mil) headquarters

cuartelada *f* mutiny, military uprising

cuarte·rón -rona *mf* quadroon ‖ *m* quarter; (de puerta) panel; (de ventana) shutter

cuarteto *m* quartet

cuartilla *f* sheet of paper

cuar·to -ta *adj* fourth; quarter ‖ *m* fourth; quarter; room, bedroom; quarter-hour; **cuarto creciente** (de la luna) first quarter; **cuarto de aseo** lavatory; **cuarto de baño** bathroom; **cuarto de dormir** bedroom; **cuarto de estar** living room; **cuarto delantero** (de la res) forequarter; **cuarto de los niños** nursery; **cuarto de luna** quarter; **cuarto menguante** (de la luna) last quarter; **cuarto obscuro** (phot) darkroom; **cuartos** (coll) money, cash; **cuarto trasero** (p.ej., de vaca) rump ‖ *f* see **cuarta**

cuarzo *m* quartz

cuate -ta *adj* (Mex) twin; (Mex) like ‖ *mf* (Mex) twin; (Mex) pal

cuatrilli·zo -za *mf* quadruplet

cuatrinca *f* foursome

cuatro *adj & pron* four; **las cuatro** four o'clock ‖ *m* four; (en las fechas) fourth; (de voces) quartet; **más de cuatro** (coll) quite a number

cuatrocien·tos -tas *adj & pron* four hundred ‖ **cuatrocientos** *m* four hundred

cuba *f* cask, barrel; tub, vat; (persona de mucho vientre) (coll) tub; (persona que bebe mucho) (coll) toper; **cuba de riego** street sprinkler

cuba·no -na *adj & mf* Cuban

cubeta *f* keg, cask; pail; bowl, toilet bowl; (del termómetro) cup; (chem, phot) tray; (Mex) high hat

cubicaje *m* piston displacement, cylinder capacity

cubicar *tr* (elevar al cubo) to cube; to measure the volume of; to have a piston displacement of

cúbico 93 cuenta

cúbi·co -ca *adj* cubic; (*raíz*) cube
cubierta *f* cover; envelope; roof; (*de un libro*) paper cover; (*de un neumático*) casing, shoe; (*del motor de un coche*) hood; (naut) deck; **bajo cubierta separada** under separate cover; **cubierta de aterrizaje** (nav) flight deck; **cubierta de cama** bedcover; **cubierta de mesa** table cover; **cubierta de paseo** (naut) promenade deck; **cubierta de vuelo** (nav) flight deck; **cubierta principal** (naut) main deck; **entre cubiertas** (naut) between decks
cubiertamente *adv* secretly
cubier·to -ta *adj* covered; (*cielo*) overcast ‖ *m* cover, roof, shelter; (*servicio de mesa para una persona*) cover; knife, fork, and spoon; table d'hôte, prix fixe; **a cubierto de** under cover of; protected from; **bajo cubierto** under cover, indoors ‖ *f* see **cubierta**
cubil *m* (*de fieras*) lair, den; (*de arroyo*) bed
cubilete *m* (*de cocinero*) copper mold; dicebox; mince pie; (Am) high hat; (SAm) scheming, wirepulling
cubo *m* bucket; (*de rueda*) hub; (*de un candelero; de una llave de caja*) socket; cube; (mach) barrel, drum; (math) cube; (Arg) finger bowl
cubreasiento *m* seat cover
cubrecama *f* counterpane, bedcover
cubrecorsé *m* corset cover
cubrefuego *m* curfew
cubrelibro *m* jacket
cubrenuca *f* havelock
cubrerrueda *f* mudguard
cubresexo *m* G-string
cubretablero *m* (aut) cowl
cubretetera *f* cozy, tea cozy
cubrir §83 *tr* to cover, cover over, cover up ‖ *ref* to cover oneself; to be covered; to put one's hat on; (*el cielo*) to become overcast; (*satisfacer una deuda*) to cover
eucaña *f* greased pole to be climbed in a game; (coll) cinch
cucañe·ro -ra *mf* (coll) loafer, parasite
cucar §73 *tr* to wink; to make fun of; (*la caza*) to sight; (Am) to incite, stir up ‖ *intr* (*el ganado*) to go off on a run (*when bitten by flies*)
cucaracha *f* roach, cockroach
cucarache·ro -ra *adj* (W-I) sly, tricky; (W-I) amorous, lecherous
cucarda *f* cockade
cuclillas — en cuclillas squatting, crouching
cuclillo *m* cuckoo; (coll) cuckold
cu·co -ca *adj* sly, tricky; (coll) cute ‖ *mf* (coll) sly person ‖ *m* bogeyman; cuckoo
cu·cú *m* (*pl* -cúes) cuckoo (*call*)
cuculla *f* cowl, hood
cucurucho *m* paper cone, ice-cream cone; **hacer cucurucho a** (Chile) to deceive, take in
cuchara *f* spoon; (*cazo*) dipper, ladle; (*para áridos; para achicar el agua en los botes*) scoop; (*de albañil*) trowel; (Mex) pickpocket; **cuchara de sopa** tablespoon; **media cuchara**

(coll) ordinary fellow; (Am) fellow with heavy accent; (Mex) mason's helper; **meter su cuchara** to butt in
cucharada *f* spoonful; ladleful; scoop
cucharear *tr* to spoon, ladle out
cucharetear *intr* (coll) to stir the pot, stir with a spoon; (coll) to meddle
cucharilla *f* teaspoon; (*de soldador*) ladle
cucharón *m* large spoon; soup ladle, dipper; scoop; **despacharse con el cucharón** (coll) to look out for number one
cuchichear *intr* to whisper
cuchilla *f* knife; (*hoja de arma blanca de corte*) blade; (*de patín de hielo*) runner; (*cerro escarpado*) hogback; (*de interruptor*) (elec) blade; (poet) sword; **cuchilla de carnicero** butcher knife, cleaver
cuchillada *f* slash, gash, hack; **cuchilladas** fight, quarrel; **dar cuchillada** (*un actor o un teatro*) (coll) to be the hit of the town
cuchillería *f* cutlery; cutler's shop
cuchillero *m* cutler
cuchillo *m* knife; (*en un vestido*) gore; (naut) triangular sail; **cuchillo de trinchar** carving knife; **cuchillo de vidriero** putty knife; **pasar a cuchillo** to put to the sword
cuchitril *m* hovel, den
cuchufieta *f* (coll) joke, fun, wisecrack
cuchufietear *intr* (coll) to joke, make fun, wisecrack
cuelga *f* fruit hung up for keeping; (coll) birthday present
cuelgaca·pas *m* (*pl* -pas) cloak hanger
cuello *m* (*del cuerpo*) neck; (*de una prenda*) collar; shirt collar; **cuello almidonado** stiff collar; **cuello de camisa** shirtband; **cuello de cisne** gooseneck; **cuello de pajarita** or **doblado** wing collar; **levantar el cuello** (coll) to get back on one's feet again
cuenca *f* wooden bowl; (*del ojo*) socket; basin, river basin; **cuenca de polvo** dust bowl
cuenco *m* earthen bowl; hollow
cuenta *f* count, calculation; account; (*factura*) bill; (*en un restaurante*) check; (*del rosario*) bead; **abonar en cuenta a** to credit to the account of; **a cuenta** or **a buena cuenta** on account; **adeudar en cuenta a** to charge to the account of; **a fin de cuentas** after all; **caer en la cuenta** (coll) to get the point; **cargar en cuenta a** to charge to the account of; **correr por cuenta de** to be the responsibility of, to be under the administration of; **cuenta corriente** current account; **cuenta de gastos** expense account; **cuenta de la vieja** (coll) counting on one's fingers; **cuentas del gran capitán** overdrawn account; **cuentas galanas** (coll) illusions; **darse cuenta de** to realize, become aware of; **de cuenta** of importance; **más de la cuenta** too long; too much; **pedir cuentas a** to bring to account; **por la cuenta** apparently;

por mi cuenta to my way of thinking; **tomar por su cuenta** to take upon oneself; **vamos a cuentas** (coll) let's settle this

cuentacorrentista *mf* depositor

cuentago·tas *m* (*pl* -tas) dropper, medicine dropper

cuentakilóme·tros *m* (*pl* -tros) odometer

cuente·ro -ra *adj* (coll) gossipy || *mf* (coll) gossip

cuentista *adj* (coll) gossipy || *mf* story teller; short-story writer; (coll) gossip

cuento *m* story, tale; short story; prop, support; tip, point; (*cómputo*) count; (coll) gossip, evil talk; (coll) disagreement; **cuento de hadas** fairy tale; **cuento del tío** (SAm) gyp, swindle; **cuento de nunca acabar** (coll) endless affair; **cuento de penas** (coll) hard-luck story; **cuento de viejas** old wives' tale; **Cuentos de Calleja** collection of nursery stories; **dejarse de cuentos** (coll) to come to the point; **estar en el cuento** to be well-informed; **¡puro cuento!** pure fiction!; **sin cuento** countless; **traer a cuento** to bring up; **venir a cuento** (coll) to be opportune; **vivir del cuento** to live by one's wits

cuerda *f* cord, rope; watch spring; winding a watch or clock; (*acción de ahorcar*) hanging; fishing line; (aer, anat, geom) chord; (mus) string; **acabarse la cuerda** to run down, e.g., **se acabó la cuerda** the watch ran down; **bajo cuerda** secretly, underhandedly; **cuerda de presos** chain gang; **cuerda de remolcar** tow rope; **cuerda de tripa** (mus) catgut; **cuerda tirante** tight rope; **dar cuerda a** to give free rein to; (*un reloj*) to wind; **sin cuerda** unwound, run-down

cuer·do -da *adj* wise, prudent; sane || *f* see **cuerda**

cuerna *f* antler; horns

cuerno *m* horn; (mus) horn; **cuerno de caza** huntinghorn; **cuerno inglés** (mus) English horn

cuero *m* (*pellejo de buey*) hide; (*después de curtido*) leather; wineskin; **cuero cabelludo** scalp; **cuero en verde** rawhide; **en cueros** stark-naked

cuerpear *intr* (Arg) to duck, dodge

cuerpo *m* body; (*parte del vestido hasta la cintura*) waist; (*talle, aspecto*) build; (*de escritos, leyes, etc.*) corpus; corps, staff; (mil) corps; **cuerpo a cuerpo** hand to hand; **cuerpo celeste** heavenly body; **cuerpo compuesto** (chem) compound; **cuerpo de aviación** air corps; **cuerpo de baile** corps of ballet; **cuerpo de bomberos** fire brigade, fire company; **cuerpo de ejército** army corps; **cuerpo de redacción** editorial staff; **cuerpo simple** (chem) simple substance; **dar con el cuerpo en tierra** (coll) to fall flat on the ground; **de cuerpo entero** full-length; **de medio**

cuerpo half-length; **descubrir el cuerpo** to drop one's guard; **en cuerpo** or **en cuerpo de camisa** in shirt sleeves; **estar de cuerpo presente** to be on view, to lie in state; **hacer del cuerpo** (coll) to have a movement of the bowels

cueru·do -da *adj* (Am) thick-skinned; (Am) annoying, boring; (Am) bold, shameless

cuervo *m* raven; **cuervo marino** cormorant; **cuervo merendero** rook

cuesco *m* (*de la fruta*) stone; (*del molino de aceite*) millstone; (coll) windiness

cuesta *f* hill, slope, grade; charity drive; **cuesta abajo** downhill; **cuesta arriba** uphill; **llevar a cuestas** (coll) to be burdened with

cuestión *f* question; dispute, quarrel; matter; **cuestión batallona** much-debated question; **cuestión palpitante** burning question; **en cuestión de** in a matter of

cuestionable *adj* questionable

cuestionar *tr* to question || *intr* (Arg) to argue

cuestionario *m* questionnaire

cuestua·rio -ria or **cuestuo·so -sa** *adj* profitable, lucrative

cuetear *ref* (Col) to blow up, explode; (Col) to die, kick the bucket; (Mex) to get drunk

cueva *f* cave; cellar; (*de ladrones, fieras, etc.*) den

cufi·fo -fa *adj* (Chile) tipsy

cugulla *f* cowl

cui·co -ca *adj* (Am) foreign, outside || *m* (Mex) cop, policeman

cuidado *m* care, concern, worry; **¡cuidado con . . .!** beware of . . .!, look out for!; **de cuidado** dangerously; **estar de cuidado** (coll) to be dangerously ill; **pierda Vd. cuidado** don't worry; **salir de su cuidado** (*una mujer*) to be delivered; **tener cuidado** to beware, be careful

cuidadora *f* (Mex) governess, chaperon

cuidado·so -sa *adj* careful, concerned, worried; watchful

cuidar *tr* to take care of, to watch over || *intr* — **cuidar de** to take care of, to care for; to care to || *ref* to take care of oneself; **cuidarse de** to care about; to be careful to

cuita *f* trouble, worry; longing, yearning

cuja *f* bedstead

culata *f* buttock, haunch; (*de la escopeta*) butt; (*de imán*) keeper, yoke; **culata de cilindro** cylinder head

culatazo *m* kick, recoil

culebra *f* snake; (*del alambique*) coil; **culebra de anteojos** cobra; **culebra de cascabel** rattlesnake; **saber más que las culebras** (coll) to be foxy

culebrear *intr* to wriggle; to wind, meander; to zigzag

culebrón *m* (coll) foxy fellow; (Mex) poor farce

cule·co -ca *adj* (Am) self-satisfied; (Am) madly in love

cu·lí *m* (*pl* -líes) coolie

culina·rio -ria *adj* culinary
culipandear *intr* & *ref* (CAm, W-I) to welsh, be evasive
culminar *intr* to culminate
culo *m* seat, behind, backside; (*de animal*) buttocks; (*de un vaso*) bottom; **culo de mal asiento** (coll) fidgety person; **volver el culo** (coll) to run away
culote *m* base
culpa *f* blame, guilt, fault; **echar la culpa a** to put the blame on; **tener la culpa** to be wrong, to be to blame
culpable *adj* blamable, guilty, culpable
culpa·do -da *adj* guilty ‖ *mf* culprit
culpar *tr* to blame, censure, accuse ‖ *ref* to take the blame
cultedad *f* fustian, affectation
culteranismo *m* euphuism, Gongorism
cultiparlar *intr* to speak in a euphuistic manner
cultismo *m* learned word; cultism, Gongorism
cultivar *tr* to cultivate; to till
cultivo *m* cultivation; **cultivo de secano** dry farming
cul·to -ta *adj* cultivated, cultured; (*vocablo*) learned ‖ *m* worship; cult; **culto a la personalidad** personality cult
cultura *f* culture, cultivation
culturar *tr* to cultivate, to till
cumbre *adj* top, greatest ‖ *f* summit; acme, pinnacle
cúmel *m* kümmel
cumiche *m* (CAm) baby (*youngest member of family*)
cúmplase *m* approval, O.K.
cumplea·ños *m* (*pl* **-ños**) birthday
cumpli·do -da *adj* full; perfect; (*en muestras de urbanidad*) correct ‖ *m* correctness; courtesy; present
cumplimentar *tr* to compliment; to pay a complimentary visit to; to carry out, execute; (*un cuestionario*) to fill out
cumplimente·ro -ra *adj* (coll) effusive, obsequious
cumplimiento *m* (*muestra de urbanidad*) compliment; (*conducta decorosa*) correctness; fulfillment; perfection; **por cumplimiento** as a matter of pure formality
cumplir *tr* to fulfill, perform, execute; **cumplir años** to have a birthday; **cumplir . . . años** to be . . . years old ‖ *intr* to fall due; to expire; to keep one's promise; to finish one's service in the army; **cumplir con** to fulfill; to fulfill one's obligation to; **cumplir por** to act on behalf of; to pay the respects of ‖ *ref* to be fulfilled, to come true; to fall due; **cúmplase** approved
cumquibus *m* (coll) wherewithal
cúmulo *m* heap, pile, lot
cuna *f* cradle
cundido *m* olive, vinegar, and salt for shepherds; olive oil, cheese, and honey to make children eat
cundir *intr* to spread; to swell, puff up; to increase

cunear *tr* to cradle, rock in a cradle ‖ *intr* (coll) to rock, swing, sway
cune·co -ca *mf* (Ven) baby (*youngest member of family*)
cuneta *f* gutter, ditch
cuña *f* wedge; (typ) quoin; **ser buena cuña** (coll) to take up a lot of room
cuñada *f* sister-in-law
cuñado *m* brother-in-law
cuñete *m* keg
cuño *m* die; stamp; mark
cuota *f* quota, share; fee, dues; tuition fee
cupé *m* coupé
cupo *m* quota, share; (Mex) capacity
cupón *m* coupon
cúpula *f* cupola; dome
cuquillo *m* cuckoo
cura *m* curate; (coll) priest; **este cura** (*yo*) (coll) yours truly (*I*) ‖ *f* cure; care, treatment; **cura de aguas** water cure; **cura de almas** care of souls; **cura de hambre** starvation diet; **cura de reposo** rest cure; **cura de urgencia** first aid; **no tener cura** (coll) to be hopeless, be incorrigible
curaca *m* (SAm) boss, chief ‖ *f* (Bol, Peru) priest's housekeeper
curación *f* cure, treatment
curade·ro -ra *mf* caretaker ‖ *m* (law) guardian
curande·ro -ra *mf* quack, healer
curar *tr* (*a un enfermo*) to treat; (*sanar*) to cure, to heal; (*curtir*) to cure; (*la madera*) to season; (*una herida*) to dress ‖ *intr* to cure; to recover; **curar de** to take care of; to recover from; to mind, pay attention to ‖ *ref* to cure; to cure oneself; to get well, to recover; (Am) to get drunk; **curarse de** to recover from, get over; **curarse en salud** to be forewarned
curati·vo -va *adj* & *f* curative
curda *f* (coll) jag, drunk
cureña *f* gun carriage
curia *f* (hist) curia; (*de rey*) court; (*conjunto de abogados*) bar
curiales·co -ca *adj* hairsplitting, legalistic
curiosear *tr* (coll) to pry into ‖ *intr* (coll) to snoop; (coll) to browse around
curiosidad *f* curiosity; (*objeto de arte raro y curioso*) curio; neatness, tidiness; care, carefulness
curio·so -sa *adj* curious; neat, tidy; careful ‖ *mf* busybody ‖ *m* (Ven) healer, medical man
currinche *m* (coll) cub reporter; (coll) hit playwright
cu·rro -rra *adj* (coll) flashy, sporty ‖ *m* (coll) sport, dandy
curruca *f* (orn) whitethroat; **curruca de cabeza negra** blackcap, warbler
curruta·co -ca *adj* (coll) dudish, sporty; (Am) chubby ‖ *m* (coll) dude, sport ‖ *f* (coll) chic dame
cursa·do -da *adj* skilled, experienced; (*asignatura*) taken
cursante *mf* student
cursar *tr* (*una materia, estudios*) to take, to study; (*conferencias*) to attend; (*una carta*) to forward; (*un*

paraje) to frequent, to haunt ‖ *intr* to study; to be current

curseria *f* cheapness, flashiness, vulgarity; flashy lot of people

cursi *adj* cheap, flashy, vulgar, loud ‖ *m* sporty guy ‖ *f* flashy dame

cursien·to -ta *adj* (Am) diarrheic

cursilería *f* cheapness, flashiness, vulgarity; flashy lot of people

cursillo *m* refresher course; short course of lectures

cursi·vo -va *adj* cursive; italic ‖ *f* cursive; italics

curso *m* course; academic year, school year; price, quotation, current rate; **curso académico** academic year; **curso legal** legal tender; **cursos** loose bowels; **dar curso a** to give way to; to forward

cursor *m* slide; sliding contact; **cursor de procesiones** marshal

curtiduría *f* tannery

curtiembre *f* (Am) tannery

curtir *tr* (*las pieles*) to tan; (*el cutis de una persona*) to tan, sunburn; to

harden, to inure; **estar curtido en** to be skilled in, be expert in ‖ *ref* to become tanned, sunburned; to become hardened; to be weather-beaten

curva *f* curve; bend

curvadura *f* painful exhaustion

cur·vo -va *adj* curved, bent ‖ *f* see **curva**

cusca *f* (Col) jag, drunk; (Mex) prostitute, slut

cúspide *f* (*de montaña*) peak; (*de diente*) cusp; apex, tip, top

custodia *f* custody, care; (*de un preso*) guard; (eccl) monstrance

custodiar *tr* to guard, watch over

custodio *m* custodian; guard

cususa *f* (CAm) rum

cu·tí *m* (*pl* **-tíes**) bedtick, ticking

cutícula *f* cuticle

cutio *m* work, labor

cu·tis *m* (& *f*) (*pl* **-tis**) skin, complexion; **cutis anserina** goose flesh

cu·yo -ya *adj rel* whose

c/v *abbr* **cuenta de venta**

Ch

Ch, ch (che) *f* fourth letter of the Spanish alphabet

chabacanada or **chabacanería** *f* crudeness, coarseness, vulgarity

chabaca·no -na *adj* crude, coarse, vulgar ‖ *m* (Mex) apricot tree

chabola *f* shack, shanty; (mil) foxhole

chacal *m* jackal

chacanear *tr* (Chile) to spur, goad on; (Chile) to annoy, bother

chacare·ro -ra *mf* (SAm) farm laborer, field worker; (Col) quack doctor; (Urug) gossip

chacarrachaca *f* (coll) row, racket

chacolotear *intr* to clatter

chacota *f* laughter, racket; **hacer chacota de** (coll) to make fun of

chacotear *intr* to laugh and make a racket

chacra *f* (Am) farm house; (Am) small farm; (Am) sown field

chacua·co -ca *adj* (Am) ugly, crude, boorish ‖ *m* (CAm) cigar butt; (CAm) cheap cigar

cháchara *f* (coll) chatter, idle talk; **chácharas** (coll) trinkets, junk

chacharear *intr* (coll) to chatter

chafallar *tr* (coll) to botch

chafandín *m* conceited ass

chafar *tr* to rumple, muss; to flatten; (coll) to cut short; (Chile) to dismiss, send off

chafarrinar *tr* to blot, stain

chafarrinón *m* blot, stain; **echar un chafarrinón a** (coll) to insult, throw mud at

chafián *m* chamfer

chaflanar *tr* to chamfer

chal *m* shawl

cha·lán -lana *adj* horse-dealing ‖ *mf*

horse dealer; horse trader ‖ *m* (Am) broncobuster, horsebreaker ‖ *f* scow, flatboat

chalanear *tr* (*un negocio*) to pull off shrewdly; (*un caballo*) (Am) to break; (Arg) to take advantage of ‖ *intr* to horse-trade

chalanería *f* horse trading

chalanes·co -ca *adj* horse-trading

chaleco *m* vest, waistcoat

chalupa *f* small two-master; launch, lifeboat; (Mex) corncake

chama·co -ca *mf* (Mex) youngster, urchin

chamago·so -sa *adj* (Mex) dirty, filthy; (Mex) botched

chamarasca *f* brushwood; brush fire

chamarille·ro -ra *mf* junk dealer, second-hand dealer ‖ *m* gambler

chamari·llón -llona *mf* poor card player

chamarra *f* sheepskin jacket

chamarreta *f* loose jacket; (Am) square poncho

chamba *f* fluke, scratch

chambelán *m* chamberlain; (Mex) atomizer, spray

chambergo *m* (orn) bobolink; (Arg) soft hat

chambe·rí *adj* (*pl* **-ríes**) (Peru) showy, flashy

cham·bón -bona *adj* (coll) awkward, clumsy; (coll) lucky

chambonada *f* (coll) awkwardness, clumsiness; (coll) stroke of luck

chambonear *intr* to foozle

chambra *f* blouse; (Ven) din, uproar

chambrana *f* trim (*around a door*)

chamburgo *m* (Col) stagnant water, puddle

chamico *m* jimson weed; **dar chamico a** (SAm) to bewitch

chamorrar *tr* (coll) to shear

champán *m* sampan; (coll) champagne

champaña *m* champagne

cham·pú *m* (*pl* -púes) shampoo

chamuscar §73 *tr* to singe, scorch; (Mex) to undersell

chamusco *m* singe, scorch

chamusquina *f* singeing; (coll) fight, row, quarrel; **oler a chamusquina** (coll) to look like a fight; (coll) to smack of heresy

chancar §73 *tr* (Am) to crush; (Am) to beat, beat up; (Am) to botch

chancear *intr & ref* to joke, jest

chance·ro -ra *adj* joking, jesting

chanciller *m* chancellor

chancla *f* old shoe; house slipper

chancleta *mf* (coll) good-for-nothing ‖ *f* slipper; (Ven) accelerator

chanclo *m* overshoe, rubber

chancha *f* cheat, lie; (Chile) slut; **hacer la chancha** (Bol, Col, Chile) to play hooky

chanche·ro -ra *mf* (Arg, Chile) pork butcher

chan·cho -cha *adj* (Am) dirty, filthy ‖ *m* (Am) pig ‖ *f* see **chancha**

chanchulle·ro -ra *mf* (coll) crook

changador *m* (SAm) errand boy

changarro *m* (Mex) small shop

chan·go -ga *adj* (Chile) dull, stupid; (Mex) sly, crafty ‖ *mf* (Mex) monkey ‖ *m* (Arg) house boy

chan·guí *m* (*pl* -guíes) (coll) trick, deception

chantaje *m* blackmail

chantajista *mf* blackmailer

chantar *tr* to put on; (SAm) to throw hard; (Urug) to keep waiting ‖ *ref* (*p.ej.*, *el sombrero*) to clap on

chantre *m* cantor, precentor

chanza *f* joke, jest

chapa *f* sheet, plate; (*hoja fina de madera*) veneer; (*en las mejillas*) flush; (coll) good sense, judgment; (Chile) lock, bolt; **chapa de circulación** (aut) license plate; **chapas** flipping coins

chapa·do -da *adj* plated; veneered; **chapado a la antigua** old-fashioned

chapalear *intr* (*el agua; las manos y los pies en el agua*) to splash; (*la herradura floja*) to clatter

chapar *tr* to cover or line with sheets of metal; to veneer

chaparrear *intr* to pour

chapa·rro -rra *mf* (Mex) child, little one; (Mex) runt ‖ *m* scrub oak

chaparrón *m* downpour

chapea·do -da *adj* lined with sheets of metal; veneered ‖ *m* plywood; veneer

chapear *tr* to cover or line with sheets of metal; to veneer

chapista *m* tinsmith, tinman

chapitel *m* (*remate de torre*) spire; (*capitel de columna*) capital

chapodar *tr* to trim, clear of branches; to curtail

chapotear *tr* to sponge, moisten ‖ *intr* to splash

chapucear *tr & intr* to botch, bungle

chapuce·ro -ra *adj* crude, rough;

clumsy, bungling ‖ *mf* bungler; amateur ‖ *m* blacksmith; junk dealer

chapurrar *tr & intr* to jabber

chapurreo *m* jabber

cha·puz *m* (*pl* -puces) duck, ducking

chapuzar §60 *tr, intr & ref* to duck

chaqué *m* cutaway coat, morning coat

chaqueta *f* jacket

chaquetilla *f* short jacket; (Ecuad) lady's vest

chaquetón *m* reefer, pea jacket

charamusca *f* (Am) brushwood, firewood; (Mex) candy twist

charanga *f* (mil) brass band

charangue·ro -ra *adj* crude, rough; bungling, clumsy ‖ *mf* bungler

charca *f* pool

charco *m* puddle

charla *f* (coll) talk, chat; (coll) talk, lecture; (coll) chatter, prattle

charla·dor -dora *adj* (coll) garrulous; (coll) gossipy ‖ *mf* (coll) chatterbox; (coll) gossip

charlar *intr* (coll) to talk, chat; (coll) to chatter, prattle

charla·tán -tana *adj* garrulous; gossipy ‖ *mf* chatterbox; gossip; charlatan

charlatanería *f* garrulity, loquacity

charlatanismo *m* charlatanism; garrulity, loquacity

charnela *f* (*de puerta; de molusco*) hinge; (mach) knuckle

charol *m* varnish; patent leather; (Am) lacquered tray; **calzarse las de charol** (Arg, Urug) to hit the jackpot; **darse charol** (coll) to blow one's own horn

charola·do -da *adj* shiny

charolar *tr* to varnish, to lacquer

charpa *f* pistol belt; (*cabestrillo*) sling

charquear *tr* (*carne de vaca*) (Am) to jerk; (Am) to slash, cut to pieces

charqui *m* (Am) jerked beef

charrada *f* country dance; boorishness; (coll) tawdry ornamentation

charretera *f* epaulet; garter, (*del aguador*) (coll) shoulder pad

charriada *f* (Mex) rodeo

cha·rro -rra *adj* coarse, ill-bred; flashy, loud, showy; Salamanca ‖ *mf* peasant; Salamanca peasant ‖ *m* broad-brimmed hat; Mexican cowboy

chasca *f* brushwood

chascar §73 *tr* (*la lengua*) to click; (*algún manjar*) to crunch; (*engullir*) to swallow ‖ *intr* to crack, crackle

chascarrillo *m* (coll) funny story

chas·co -ca *adj* (Arg, Bol) crinkly, crinkly-haired ‖ *m* joke, trick; disappointment; **dar un chasco a** to play a trick on; **llevar or llevarse (un) chasco** to be disappointed

chas·cón -cona *adj* (Bol, Chile) disheveled; (Bol, Chile) bushy-haired; (Bol, Chile) clumsy, unskilled

cha·sis *m* (*pl* -sis) chassis

chasquear *tr* (*un látigo*) to crack; to play a trick on; to disappoint ‖ *intr* to crack ‖ *ref* to be disappointed

chasqui *m* (SAm) messenger, courier

chasquido *m* crack; crackle

chata *f* barge, scow; flatcar; bedpan

chatarra *f* iron slag; junk, scrap iron

chatarrería f junk yard

chatarre-ro -ra mf junk dealer, scrap-iron dealer

cha-to -ta adj flat; flat-nosed; blunt; (Am) commonplace; (Am) disappointed || m (coll) wineglass || f see **chata**

chatre adj (Chile, Ecuad) all dressed up

cha-val -vala adj (coll) young || m (coll) lad || f (coll) lass

chaveta f cotter pin; **perder la chaveta** (coll) to go out of one's head

chayote m (Am) chayote, vegetable pear; (Am) dunce, fool

chazar §60 tr (la pelota) to stop; (el sitio donde paró la pelota) to mark

che interj (SAm) say!, hey!

che-co -ca adj & mf Czech

checoeslova-co -ca adj & mf Czecho-Slovak

Checoeslovaquia f Czecho-Slovakia

checoslova-co -ca adj & mf Czecho-Slovak

Checoslovaquia f Czecho-Slovakia

chechén m (Mex) poison ivy

chécheres mpl (Am) trinkets, junk

chelín m shilling

cheque m check; **cheque de viajeros** traveler's check

chica f lass, little girl; girl; (coll) my dear; **chica de cita** call girl; **chica de la vida alegre** party girl

chicalote m Mexican poppy

chicle m (Am) chewing gum

chiclear intr (Mex) to chew gum

chi-co -ca adj small, little; young || mf child, youngster || m lad, little boy; (coll) young fellow; (coll) old man; (Am) hand, turn || f see **chica**

chicolear intr to pay compliments, to flirt || ref (Arg, Peru) to enjoy oneself

chico-te -ta mf husky youngster || m (coll) cigar; (Am) cigar stub; (Am) whip

chicue-lo -la adj small, little || m little boy || f little girl

chicha f corn liquor; **no ser ni chicha ni limonada** (coll) to be good for nothing

chícharo m (Am) pea; (Col) poor cigar; (Mex) apprentice

chicharra f harvest fly; (coll) chatterbox; **cantar la chicharra** (coll) to be hot and sultry

chicharrón m residue of hog's fat; burnt meat; (coll) sunburned person; (Am) wrinkled person

chichear tr & intr to hiss

chi-chón -chona adj (CAm) easy; (SAm) joking; (Guat) large-breasted || m lump, bump on the head

chifla f hissing, whistling; paring knife; **estar de chifla** (Mex) to be in a bad humor

chifla-do -da adj (coll) daffy, nutty || mf (coll) crackbrain, nut

chifladura f (coll) daffiness, nuttiness; (coll) whim, wild idea

chiflar tr (a un actor) to hiss; (vino o licor) to gulp down; (el cuero) to pare || intr to whistle; (las aves) (Guat, Mex) to sing || ref to go crazy

chifle m whistle; (para cazar aves) bird call; powder flask

chiflido m whistle, hiss

chifión m (SAm) cold blast of air; (Am) rapids; (Am) slide of loose stone

chilaba f jelab, jellaba

Chile m Chile

chile-no -na adj & mf Chilean

chilla f fox call, hare call; clapboard; (Chile) small fox; (Mex) top gallery

chillar intr to shriek; to squeak; to hiss, sizzle; (los colores) to scream || ref (Am) to take offense

chillido m shriek, scream

chi-llón -llona adj shrill, high-pitched; (coll) screaming; (color) loud

chimenea f chimney, smokestack; fireplace, hearth; stovepipe hat; (naut) funnel

chimpancé m chimpanzee

china f Chinese woman; china, porcelain; pebble; (Am) nursemaid; (Col) spinning top || **China** f China

chinche mf (coll) bore, tiresome person || m (clavito de cabeza chata) thumbtack || f (insecto) bedbug; **caer** or **morir como chinches** to die like flies

chinchorre-ro -ra adj (coll) gossipy, mischievous

chincho-so -sa adj (coll) boring, tiresome

chinero m china closet

chines-co -ca adj Chinese || **chinescos** mpl (mus) bell tree

chingar §44 tr (coll) to tipple; (CAm) to bob, dock; (CAm, Mex) to bother, annoy || ref (coll) to tipple; (Am) to fail

chin-go -ga adj (CAm) short; (CAm) dull, blunt; (CAm) naked

chinguirito m (Am) cheap rum; (Am) swig of liquor

chi-no -na adj & mf Chinese || m (idioma) Chinese; (Col) boy, newsboy; (Mex) curl || f see **china**

chipichipi m (Am) drizzle, mist

Chipre f Cyprus

chiquero m pigsty; bull pen

chiquillada f childish prank

chiqui-to -ta adj small, little || mf little one || m (de vino) snifter; (Arg) moment, instant || f five cents; **no andarse con** or **en chiquitas** (coll) to talk right off the shoulder

chiribita f spark; daisy; **chiribitas** (coll) spots before the eyes

chiribitil m garret; cubbyhole

chirimbolos mpl (coll) utensils, vessels

chirimía f hornpipe

chiripa f (billiards) fluke, scratch; (coll) stroke of luck

chirivía f parsnip

chirle adj (coll) insipid, tasteless

chirlo m slash or scar on the face

chirlota f (Mex) meadow lark

chirona f (coll) jail, jug

chirriar §77 intr to creak, squeak; to shriek; to hiss, sizzle; to sing or play out of tune || ref (Col) to go on a spree; (Col) to shiver

chirrido m creak, squeak; shriek; hiss, sizzle

chis interj sh-sh!; ¡chis, chis! pst!

chischás m clash of swords

chisguete m (coll) swig of wine; (coll) squirt

chisme m piece of gossip; (coll) trinket; **chisme de vecindad** (coll) idle talker; **chismes** gossip; articles; **chismes de aseo** toilet articles

chismear intr to gossip

chismo·so -sa adj gossipy, catty || mf gossip

chispa f spark; (pequeña cantidad) drop; lightning; (fig) sparkle, wit; (coll) drunk, spree; (Col) rumor; **coger una chispa** (coll) to go on a drunk; **chispa de entrehierro** (elec) jump spark; **chispas** sprinkle (of rain); **dar chispa** (Guat, Mex) to work, to click; **echar chispas** (coll) to blow up, hit the ceiling

chispeante adj sparkling

chispear intr to spark; to sparkle; to drizzle, to sprinkle

chis·po -pa adj (coll) tipsy || m (coll) swallow, drink || f see **chispa**

chisporrotear intr to spark, to sputter

chispo·so -sa adj sputtering, sparking

chisquero m pocket lighter

chistar intr to speak, say something; **no chistar** to not say a word

chiste m joke; witticism; **caer en el chiste** (coll) to get the point; **dar en el chiste** (coll) to hit the nail on the head

chistera f fish basket; (coll) top hat

chisto·so -sa adj funny; witty || mf funny person; wit

chita f anklebone; quoits; **a la chita callando** (coll) quietly, secretly; **dar en la chita** (coll) to hit the nail on the head

chiticalla mf (persona que no revela lo que sabe) (coll) clam || f (coll) secret

chito interj hush!, sh-sh!

chivato m kid, young goat; (soplón) (coll) squealer; (Bol) apprentice, helper; (Chile) cheap rum

chi·vo -va mf kid || m billy goat || f nanny goat

chocante adj shocking; coarse, crude; (Col) annoying; (Mex) disagreeable

chocar §73 tr to shock, annoy, irritate; to surprise; (vasos) to clink; (coll) to please; ¡**choque Vd. esos cinco!** (coll) shake! || intr to shock; to collide; to clash, fight

chocarre·ro -ra adj coarse, crude || mf crude joker

choclo m wooden overshoe; (Mex) low shoe; (SAm) tender ear of corn

chocolate m chocolate

chocha f woodcock

chochear intr to be in one's dotage; (coll) to dote, be infatuated

chochera f dotage; (Arg, Peru) favorite

cho·chez f (pl -checes) dotage; doting act or remark

cho·cho -cha adj doting; doddering || m stick of cinnamon candy; **chochos** candy to quiet a child || f see **chocha**

chófer m chauffeur

chofeta f fire pan (for lighting cigars)

cho·lo -la adj (Am) half-breed (Indian and white); (Am) half-civilized (Indian) || mf (Am) Indian; (Am) half-breed; (Am) half-civilized Indian; (Chile) coward; (SAm) darling

cholla f (coll) noodle, head; (coll) ability, brains

chomite m (Mex) coarse wool; (Mex) woolen skirt

chopo m black poplar; (coll) gun, rifle; **chopo de Italia** Lombardy poplar; **chopo del Canadá** or **de Virginia** cottonwood; **chopo lombardo** Lombardy poplar

choque m shock; collision, impact; clash, conflict, skirmish; (elec) choke, choke coil

choricería f sausage shop

chorizo m smoked pork sausage

chorlito m plover, golden plover; (coll) scatterbrains

chorrear intr to gush, spurt, spout; to drip; to trickle

chorrera f spout, channel; cut, gulley; rapids; lace front, jabot; (Arg) string, stream

chorrillo m constant stream; **irse por el chorrillo** (coll) to follow the current; **tomar el chorrillo de** (coll) to get the habit of

chorro m jet, spurt; stream, flow; **a chorros** in abundance; **chorro de arena** sandblast

chotaca·bras m (pl -bras) goatsucker

chotear tr (Am) to make fun of; (Guat) to keep an eye on

choteo m (Am) jeering, mocking

choza f hut, cabin, lodge

chubasco m squall, shower; (fig) temporary setback; **chubasco de agua** rainstorm; **chubasco de nieve** blizzard

chubasco·so -sa adj stormy, threatening

chucruta f sauerkraut

chucha f (coll) female dog, bitch; (coll) drunk, jag; (Col) opossum; (Col) body odor

chuchaque m (Ecuad) hangover

chuchear tr (caza menor) to trap || intr to whisper

chuchería f knickknack, trinket; delicacy, tidbit

chu·cho -cha adj (CAm) mean, stingy; (fruto) (Col) watery; (Col) wrinkled || m (coll) dog || f see **chucha**

chue·co -ca adj (Mex) twisted, bent; (SAm) bow-legged; (Mex) crippled || m (Mex) dealing in stolen goods || f stump; hockey; hockey ball

chufa f groundnut

chufletear intr (coll) to joke, jest

chula f flashy dame (in lower classes of Madrid)

chulada f light-hearted remark; vulgarity

chul·co -ca mf (Bol) baby (youngest child)

chulear tr to tease; (Mex) to flirt with

chuleta f chop, cutlet; (coll) slap, smack; (de los estudiantes) (coll) crib, pony; **chuleta de cerdo** pork chop; **chuleta de ternera** veal chop; **chuletas** sideburns, side whiskers

chu·lo -la *adj* flashy, sporty; foxy, slick; (Guat, Mex) pretty, cute ‖ *m* sporty fellow (*in lower classes of Madrid*); pimp, procurer; gigolo; butcher's helper; (taur) attendant on foot ‖ *f* see **chula**

chumbera *f* prickly pear

chunga *f* (coll) jest, fun

chunguear *ref* (coll) to jest, joke

chupa *f* frock, coat; (Arg) drunk, jag; (Arg) tobacco pouch

chupa·do -da *adj* (coll) thin, skinny; (Am) drunk; (*falda*) (Am) tight ‖ *f* suck; pull (*on a cigar*)

chupador *m* teething ring, pacifier

chupaflor *m* (Mex, Ven) hummingbird

chupamirto *m* (Mex) hummingbird

chupar *tr* to suck; (*la hacienda ajena*) to milk, sap; (coll) to absorb ‖ *intr* to suck ‖ *ref* to get thin, lose strength; (*los labios*) to smack

chupatin·tas *mf* (*pl* -tas) (coll) office drudge

chupete *m* (*para un niño*) pacifier; (Am) lollipop; **de chupete** (coll) fine, splendid

chu·pón -pona *mf* (coll) swindler ‖ *m* (bot) sucker, shoot; (mach) plunger

chupópte·ro -ra *mf* (coll) sponger

chuquisa *f* (Chile, Peru) prostitute

churrasco *m* (Am) barbecue

churrasquear *tr* (Am) to barbecue

churre *m* (coll) filth, dirt, grease

churrete *m* dirty spot (*on hands or face*)

churrigueres·co -ca *adj* churrigueresque; loud, flashy, tawdry

chu·rro -rra *adj* (*lana*) coarse; (*carnero*) coarse-wooled ‖ *m* coarse-wooled sheep; fritter; (coll) botch

churrulle·ro -ra *adj* gossipy, loquacious ‖ *mf* gossip, chatterbox

churrusco *m* burnt piece of bread

churumbela *f* hornpipe, flageolet; (Am) maté cup; (Col) worry, anxiety; (Col, Ecuad) pipe

churumo *m* (coll) substance (*money, brains, etc.*)

chus *interj* here! (*to call a dog*); **no decir chus ni mus** (coll) to not say boo

chus·co -ca *adj* droll, funny; (Peru) ill-mannered; (*perro*) (Peru) mongrel

chusma *f* galley slaves; mob, rabble

chuza *f* (Mex) strike (*in bowling*)

D

D, d (de) *f* fifth letter of the Spanish alphabet

D. *abbr* don

D.ª *abbr* doña

daca give me, hand over; **andar al daca y toma** (coll) to be at cross purposes

dactilógra·fo -fa *mf* typist, typewriter ‖ *m* typewriter

dactilograma *m* fingerprint

dádiva *f* gift, present

dadivo·so -sa *adj* liberal, generous

da·do -da *adj* given; **dado que** provided, as long as ‖ *m* die; **cargar los dados** to load the dice; **dados dice**; **el dado está tirado** the die is cast

daga *f* dagger

dalia *f* dahlia

dama *f* lady, dame; maid-in-waiting; (*en el juego de damas*) king; (*en el ajedrez y los naipes*) queen; (theat) leading lady; concubine, mistress; **dama joven** (theat) young lead; **damas** checkers; **señalar dama** (*en el juego de damas*) to crown a man

damajuana *f* demijohn

damasquina·do -da *adj & m* damascene

damasquinar *tr* to damascene

damasqui·no -na *adj* damascene

damero *m* checkerboard

damisela *f* young lady; courtesan

damnación *f* damnation

damnificar §73 *tr* to damage, hurt

da·nés -nesa *adj* Danish ‖ *mf* Dane ‖ *m* (*idioma*) Danish

dáni·co -ca *adj* Danish

Danubio *m* Danube

danza *f* dance; dancing; dance team; **danza de cintas** Maypole dance; **danza de figuras** square dance; **meter en la danza** (coll) to drag in, involve

danza·dor -dora *mf* dancer

danzar §60 *tr* to dance ‖ *intr* to dance; (coll) to butt in

danza·rín -rina *mf* dancer; (coll) meddler, scatterbrain

dañable *adj* harmful; reprehensible

daña·do -da *adj* bad, wicked; spoiled

dañar *tr* to hurt, damage, injure; to spoil ‖ *ref* to be damaged; to spoil

dañi·no -na *adj* harmful, destructive, noxious; wicked

daño *m* damage, harm; (Arg) witchcraft; **a daño de** on the responsibility of; **daños y perjuicios** (law) damages; **en daño de** to the detriment of; **hacer daño** to be harmful; **hacer daño a** to hurt; **hacerse daño** to hurt oneself; to get hurt

daño·so -sa *adj* harmful, injurious

dar §23 *tr* to give; to cause; to hit, strike; (*el reloj la hora*) to strike; (*cartas*) to deal; (*un paseo*) to take; (*los buenos días*) to wish; (*un film*) to show; (*una capa de pintura*) to put on, apply; **dar a conocer** to make known; **dar a luz** to bring out, publish; **dar cuerda a** (*un reloj*) to wind; **dar curso a** to circulate; **dar de beber a** to give something to drink to; **dar de comer a** to give something to eat to; **dar la razón a** to admit that (someone) is right; **dar prestado** to lend; **dar palmadas** to clap the hands; **dar por** to consider as; **dar que hablar** to cause talk; to stir up criticism; **dar que hacer** to cause annoyance or trouble; **dar que pensar** to give food for thought; to give rise to suspicion ‖ *intr* to take place; to hit, strike; (*el reloj; dos, tres, etc. horas*) to strike; to tell, intimate; **dar a** to overlook; **dar con** to run into; **dar contra** to run against, strike against; **dar de sí** to stretch, to give; **dar en** to overlook; to hit; to run into; to fall into; to be bent on; (*un chiste*) to catch on to; **dar sobre** to overlook; **dar tras** to pursue hotly ‖ *ref* to give oneself up; to give in, yield; to occur, be found; **darse a** to devote oneself to; **darse a conocer** to make a name for oneself, make oneself known; to get to know each other; **darse cuenta de** to realize, become aware of; **darse la mano** to shake hands; **dárselas de** to pose as; **darse por aludido** to take the hint; **darse por entendido** to show an understanding; to show appreciation; **darse por ofendido** to take offense; **darse por vencido** to give up, to acknowledge defeat

dardo *m* dart; cutting remark

dares y tomares *mpl* (coll) quarrels, disputes

dársena *f* basin, dock, inner harbor

data *f* date; (*en una cuenta*) item; **de larga data** of long standing; **estar de mala data** (coll) to be in a bad humor

datar *tr & intr* to date; **datar de** to date from

dátil *m* date

datilera *f* date, date palm

dati•vo -va *adj & m* dative

dato *m* datum; basis, foundation

de *prep* of; from; about; **acompañado de** accompanied by; **cubierto de** covered with; **de noche** in the nighttime; **de no llegar nosotros a la hora** if we do not arrive on time; **más de** more than; **tratar de** to try to

deán *m* (eccl) dean

debajo *adv* below, underneath; **debajo de** below, under

debate *m* debate; altercation, argument

debatir *tr & intr* to debate; to fight, argue ‖ *ref* to struggle

debe *m* debit

debelar *tr* to conquer, vanquish

deber *m* duty; (*deuda*) debt; homework, school work; **últimos deberes** last rites ‖ *tr* to owe ‖ *v aux* to have to, ought to, must, should; **deber de** must, most likely ‖ *ref* to be committed; **deberse a** to be due to

debidamente *adv* duly

debi•do -da *adj* due, owed; proper, right; **debido a** due to

débil *adj* weak

debilidad *f* weakness, debility

debilitar *tr & ref* to weaken

débito *m* debt; debit; responsibility

debutar *intr* to make one's start, appear for the first time

decadencia *f* decadence

decadente *adj & mf* decadent

decaer §15 *intr* to decay, decline, fail, weaken; (naut) to drift from the course

decampar *intr* (mil) to decamp

decanato *m* deanship

decano *m* dean

decanta•do -da *adj* puffed-up, overrated

decapitar *tr* to decapitate

decelerar *tr, intr, & ref* to decelerate

decencia *f* decency

decenio *m* decade

dece•no -na *adj & m* tenth

decentar §2 *tr* to cut the first slice of; to begin to damage ‖ *ref* to get bedsores

decente *adj* decent, proper; decentlooking

decepción *f* disappointment

decepcionar *tr* to disappoint

decidi•do -da *adj* decided, determined

decidir *tr* to decide; to persuade ‖ *intr & ref* to decide

deci•dor -dora *adj* facile, fluent, witty

decimal *adj & m* decimal

déci•mo -ma *adj & m* tenth

decimocta•vo -va *adj* eighteenth

decimocuar•to -ta *adj* fourteenth

decimono•no -na *adj* nineteenth

decimonove•no -na *adj* nineteenth

decimoquin•to -ta *adj* fifteenth

decimosépti•mo -ma *adj* seventeenth

decimosex•to -ta *adj* sixteenth

decimoterce•ro -ra *adj* thirteenth

decimoter•cio -cia *adj* thirteenth

decir *m* say-so; **al decir de** according to ‖ §24 *tr* to say; to tell; (*disparates*) to talk; **como si dijéramos** so to speak, in a manner of speaking; **decir entre sí** to say to oneself; **decirle a uno cuántas son cinco** (coll) to tell a person what's what; **decir para sí** to say to oneself; **decir por decir** to talk for talk's sake; **decir que no** to say no; **decir que sí** to say yes; **decírselo a una persona deletreado** (coll) to spell it out to a person; **es decir** that is to say; **mejor dicho** rather; **¡por algo se lo dije!** I told you so!; **por decirlo así** so to speak ‖ *intr* to suit, fit; **¡diga!** (*al contestar el teléfono*) hello! ‖ *ref* to be said; to be called; **se dice** it is said, they say

decisión *f* decision

decisi•vo -va *adj* decisive

declamar *tr & intr* to declaim

declaración *f* declaration; (*en bridge*) bid

declarante *mf* declarant, deponent; (*en el juego de bridge*) bidder

declarar *tr* to declare; (*en bridge*) to bid; (law) to depose ‖ *ref* to declare oneself; to break out, take place

declarati•vo -va *adj* declarative

declinación *f* declination; fall, drop; decline; (gram) declension

declinar *tr & intr* to decline

declive *m* descent, declivity, slope

declividad *f* declivity
decollaje *m* (aer) take-off
decollar *intr* (aer) to take off
decomisar *tr* to seize, confiscate
decomiso *m* seizure, confiscation
decoración *f* decoration; memorizing; (theat) set, scenery; **decoraciones** (theat) scenery; **decoración interior** interior decoration
decorado *m* decoration; (theat) décor, scenery; memorizing
decora·dor -dora *mf* decorator
decorar *tr* to decorate; to memorize
decoro *m* decorum; honor, respect; decency, propriety
decoro·so -sa *adj* decorous; respectful; decent
decrecer §22 *intr* to decrease, grow smaller, grow shorter
decrepitar *intr* to crackle
decrépi·to -ta *adj* decrepit
decretar *tr* to decree
decreto *m* decree
decurso *m* course; **en el decurso de** in the course of
dechado *m* sample, model, example; (*labor de las niñas*) sampler
dedada *f* touch, spot; **dar una dedada de miel a** (coll) to feed the hopes of
dedal *m* thimble
dedalera *f* foxglove
dedeo *m* (mus) finger dexterity
dedicación *f* dedication
dedicar §73 *tr* to dedicate; to devote; to autograph ‖ *ref* to devote oneself
dedicatoria *f* dedication
dedil *m* fingerstall
dedillo *m* little finger; **saber** or **tener al dedillo** (coll) to have at one's finger tips, to have a thorough knowledge of
dedo *m* finger; toe; (coll) bit; **alzar el dedo** (*en señal de dar palabra*) (coll) to raise one's hand; **coger se los dedos** (coll) to burn one's fingers; **dedo auricular** little finger; **dedo cordial, de en medio,** or **del corazón** middle finger; **dedo gordo** thumb; big toe; **dedo índice** index finger, forefinger; **dedo meñique** little finger; **dedo mostrador** forefinger; **dedo pulgar** thumb; big toe; **estar a dos dedos de** (coll) to be within an ace of; **irse de entre los dedos** (coll) to slip between the fingers; **tener en la punta de los dedos** (coll) to have at one's finger tips
deducción *f* deduction; drawing off
deducir §19 *tr* (*concluir*) to deduce; (*rebajar*) to deduct; (law) to allege
defecar §73 *intr* to defecate
defección *f* defection
defeccionar *intr* & *ref* (Chile) to defect
defecti·vo -va *adj* defective
defecto *m* defect; shortage, lack; **en defecto de** for lack of
defectuo·so -sa *adj* defective; lacking
defender §51 *tr* to defend; to protect; to delay, interfere with
defensa *f* defense; fender, guard; (*del toro*) horn; (*del elefante*) tusk; (*del automóvil*) (Am) bumper; **defensa marítima** (Arg) sea wall; **defensa propia** self-defense

defensi·vo -va *adj* & *f* defensive
defen·sor -sora *adj* defending ‖ *mf* defender; (law) counsel for the defense
deferencia *f* deference
deferente *adj* deferential
deferir §68 *tr to* delegate ‖ *intr* to defer
deficiencia *f* deficiency
deficiente *adj* deficient
défi·cit *m* (*pl* -cits) deficit
deficita·rio -ria *adj* deficit
definición *f* definition; decision, verdict
defini·do -da *adj* definite; sharp, defined
definir *tr* to define; to settle, determine
definiti·vo -va *adj* definitive; **en definitiva** after all, in short
deflación *f* deflation
deflector *m* baffle
deformación *f* deformation; (rad) distortion
deformar *tr* to deform; to disfigure; to distort
deforme *adj* deformed
deformidad *f* deformity; gross error
defraudar *tr* to defraud, to cheat; (*las esperanzas de una persona*) to defeat; (*la claridad del día*) to cut off
defuera *adv* outside; **por defuera** on the outside
defunción *f* decease, demise
degeneración *f* (*acción y efecto de degenerar*) degeneration; (*estado de degenerado; depravación*) degeneracy
degenera·do -da *adj* & *mf* degenerate
degenerar *intr* to degenerate
deglutir *tr* & *intr* to swallow
degollar §3 *tr* to cut the throat of; to kill, massacre; (*un vestido*) to cut low in the neck; (*el actor una obra dramática*) to butcher, to murder; (coll) to become obnoxious to
degradante *adj* degrading
degradar *tr* to degrade; (mil) to break
degüello *m* throat-cutting; massacre; (*de un arma*) neck; **tirar a degüello** (coll) to try to harm
degustar *tr* (*probar*) to taste; (*percibir con deleite el sabor de*) to savor
dehesa *f* pasture land, meadow; (taur) range
deidad *f* deity
deificar §73 *tr* to deify
dejación *f* abandonment; (CAm, Chile, Col) negligence
dejadez *f* laziness; negligence; slovenliness; low spirits
deja·do -da *adj* lazy; negligent; slovenly; dejected
dejamiento *m* laziness; negligence; indolence, languor, indifference
dejar *tr* to leave; to abandon; to let, allow, permit; **dejar caer** to drop, let fall; **dejar feo** (coll) to slight; **dejar fresco** (coll) to leave in the lurch; **dejar por** + *inf* or **que** + *inf* to leave (*something*) to be + *pp*, e.g., **hemos dejado dos manuscritos por corregir** or **que corregir** we left two manuscripts to be corrected ‖ *intr* to stop; **dejar de** to stop, to cease; to fail to ‖ *ref* to be slovenly, to neglect oneself; (*una barba*) to grow; **dejarse de**

(disparates) to cut out; *(preguntas)* to stop asking; *(dudas)* to put aside; **dejarse ver** to show up; to be evident

dejillo m *(gusto que deja alguna comida)* aftertaste; *(acento regional)* local accent

dejo m *(gusto que deja alguna comida)* aftertaste; abandonment; slovenliness, neglect; local accent; *(placer o disgusto que queda después de hecha una cosa)* (fig) aftertaste

delación f accusation, denunciation

delantal m apron

delante adv before, ahead, in front; **delante de** before, ahead of, in front of

delantera f front; front row; advantage, lead; cowcatcher; **coger** or **tomar la delantera a** to get ahead of; to get a start on; **delanteras** overalls

delante·ro -ra adj front, foremost, first || f see **delantera**

delatar tr to accuse, denounce

delega·do -da mf delegate

delegar §44 tr to delegate

deleitable adj delectable, enjoyable

deleitar tr & ref to delight

deleite m delight

deleito·so -sa adj delightful

deletrear tr & intr to spell; to decipher

deletreo m spelling

deleznable adj *(poco durable)* perishable; *(que se rompe fácilmente)* crumbly, fragile; *(que se desliza con facilidad)* slippery

delfín m *(primogénito del rey de Francia)* dauphin; *(mamífero cetáceo)* dolphin

delgadez f thinness, leanness; delicateness, lightness; perspicacity

delga·do -da adj thin, lean; delicate, light; sharp, perspicacious; *(terreno)* poor, exhausted || adv — **hilar delgado** (coll) to hew close to the line; (coll) to split hairs

deliberar tr & intr to deliberate

delicadeza f delicacy, delicateness; scrupulousness

delica·do -da adj delicate; scrupulous

delicia f delight

delicio·so -sa adj delicious, delightful

delincuencia f guilt, criminality

delincuente adj guilty, criminal || mf criminal

delineante mf designer || m draughtsman

delinquir §25 intr to transgress, be guilty

deliquio m faint, swoon; weakening

delirante adj delirious

delirar intr to be delirious, rant, rave; to talk nonsense

delirio m delirium; nonsense

delito m crime; **delito de incendio** arson; **delito de lesa majestad** lese majesty; **delito de mayor cuantía** (law) felony; **delito de menor cuantía** (law) misdemeanor

deludir tr to delude

demacra·do -da adj emaciated, wasted, thin

demago·go -ga mf demagogue

demanda f demand, petition; charity box; lawsuit; undertaking; *(del Santo Grial)* quest; **en demanda de** in search of; **tener demanda** to be in demand

demanda·do -da mf (law) defendant

demandante mf (law) complainant, plaintiff

demandar tr to ask for, request; (law) to sue || intr (law) to sue, bring suit

demarcar §73 tr to demarcate

demás adj — **el demás** ... the other ..., the rest of the ...; **estar demás** to be useless, to be in the way; **lo demás** the rest; **por lo demás** furthermore, besides || pron others; **los demás** the others, the rest || adv besides; **por demás** in vain; too, too much

demasía f excess, surplus; daring, boldness; evil, guilt, wrong; insolence; **en demasía** excessively, too much

demasia·do -da adj & pron too much; **demasia·dos -das** too many || **demasiado** adv too, too much, too hard

demasiar §77 intr (coll) to go too far

demediar §1 tr to divide in half; to use up half of; to reach the middle of || intr to be divided in half

demente adj insane || mf lunatic

democracia f democracy

demócrata mf democrat

democráti·co -ca adj democratic

demoler §47 tr to demolish

demolición f demolition

demonía·co -ca adj demoniacal

demonio m demon, devil; **estudiar con el demonio** (coll) to be full of devilishness

demora f delay

demorar tr & ref to delay

demostración f demonstration

demostra·dor -dora mf demonstrator || m hand *(of clock)*

demostrar §61 tr to demonstrate

demostrati·vo -va adj demonstrative

demudar tr to change, alter; to disguise, cloak || ref to change countenance, to color

denegación f denial, refusal

denegar §66 tr to deny, to refuse

denegrecer §22 tr to blacken || ref to turn black

dengo·so -sa adj affected, finicky, overnice; (Col) strutting

dengue m affectation, finickiness, overniceness; (Col) strut, swagger

denguear ref (Col) to strut, swagger

denigrar tr to defame, revile; to insult

denominación f denomination

denoda·do -da adj bold, daring

denostar §61 tr to abuse, insult, mistreat

denotar tr to denote

densidad f density; darkness, confusion

den·so -sa adj dense; dark, confused; crowded, thick, close

denta·do -da adj toothed; *(sello de correo)* perforated || m gear; teeth

dentadura f set of teeth; **dentadura artificial** or **postiza** denture

dental adj & f dental

dentellada f bite; tooth mark

dentellar intr *(los dientes)* to chatter

dentellear tr to nibble, nibble at

dentera f (coll) envy; (coll) eagerness;

dentera to set the teeth on edge; to make the mouth water

dentición f teething

dentífri·co -ca adj (pasta, polvos) tooth || m dentifrice

dentista mf dentist

dentistería f dentistry

dentística f (Chile) dentistry

dentro adv inside, within; **dentro de** inside, within; **dentro de poco** shortly; **por dentro** on the inside

denuedo m bravery, courage, daring

denuesto m abuse, insult, mistreatment

denuncia f denunciation; report; proclamation

denunciar tr to denounce; to report; (la guerra) to proclaim

deparar tr to furnish, provide; to offer, present

departamento m department; (rr) compartment; (piso) (Am) apartment; naval district (in Spain)

departir intr to chat, converse

depauperación f impoverishment; exhaustion, weakening

depauperar tr to impoverish; to exhaust, weaken

dependencia f dependence, dependency; branch, branch office; relationship, friendship; accessory; personnel

depender intr to depend; **depender de** to depend on; to be attached to, to belong to

dependienta f female employee, clerk

dependiente adj dependent; branch || mf employee, clerk

deplorable adj deplorable

deplorar tr to deplore

deponer §54 tr to depose; to set aside, remove; (las armas) to lay down || intr to depose; (evacuar el vientre) to have a movement; (CAm, Mex) to vomit

deportación f deportation

deporta·do -da mf deportee

deportar tr to deport

deporte m sport; outdoor recreation

deportista mf sport fan || m sportsman || f sportswoman

deporti·vo -va adj sport, sports

depositante mf depositor

depositar tr to deposit; (la esperanza, la confianza) to put, place; (el equipaje) to check; (a una persona en seguro) to commit; to store || ref to deposit, settle

deposita·rio -ria mf trustee; (de un secreto) repository || m public treasurer

depósito m deposit; depot, warehouse; tank, reservoir; (de libros en una biblioteca) stack; (mil) depot; **depósito comercial** bonded warehouse; **depósito de agua** reservoir; **depósito de cadáveres** morgue; **depósito de cereales** grain elevator; **depósito de equipajes** (rr) checkroom; **depósito de gasolina** (aut) gas tank; **depósito de locomotoras** roundhouse; **depósito de municiones** munition dump

depravación f depravity, depravation

deprava·do -da adj depraved

depravar tr to deprave || ref to become depraved

deprecar §73 tr to entreat, implore

depreciación f depreciation

depreciar tr & ref to depreciate

depresión f depression; drop, dip; (en un muro) recess

deprimir tr to depress; to press down; to push in; to belittle; to humiliate || ref to be depressed; (la frente de una persona) to recede

depurar tr to purify, cleanse; to purge

derecha f right hand; right-hand side; (pol) right; **a la derecha** on the right, to the right

derechamente adv rightly; straight, direct; properly; wisely

derechazo m blow with the right; (box) right

dereche·ro -ra adj right, just

derechista adj rightist || mf rightist, right-winger

dere·cho -cha adj right; right-hand; right-handed; straight; upright, standing || m right; law; exemption, privilege; road, path; (de tela, papel, tabla) right side; **derecho consuetudinario** common law; **derecho de gentes** law of nations, international law; **derecho de subscripción** (a una nueva emisión de acciones) (com) right; **derecho de tránsito** or **paso** right of way; **derecho internacional** international law; **derecho penal** criminal law; **derechos** dues, fees, taxes; (de aduana) duties; **derechos de almacenaje** storage, cost of storage; **derechos de autor** royalty; **derechos del hombre** rights of man; **derechos de propiedad literaria** or **derechos reservados** copyright; **según derecho** by right, by rights || f see **derecha** || **derecho** adv straight, direct; rightly

deriva (aer, naut) drift; **ir a la deriva** (naut) to drift, to be adrift

derivado m by-product

derivar tr to derive || intr & ref to derive, be derived; (aer, naut) to drift

derogar §44 tr to abolish, destroy, repeal

derrabar tr to dock, cut off the tail of

derrama·do -da adj extravagant, lavish

derramamiento m pouring, spilling; shedding; spreading; lavishing, wasting

derramar tr to pour, to spill; (sangre) to shed; to spread, publish abroad; (dinero) to lavish, waste || ref to run over, overflow; to spread, scatter; (una corriente, un río) to open, empty; (la plumafuente) to leak

derrame m pouring, spilling; (de sangre) shed, shedding; spread, scattering; lavishing, wasting; overflow; leakage; slope; chamfering; (pathol) discharge; effusion

derredor m circumference; **al** or **en derredor** around, round about

derrelicto m (naut) derelict

derrelinquir §25 tr to abandon, forsake

derrenga·do -da adj crooked, out of shape; crippled, lame

derrengar §44 or §66 tr to bend, make crooked; to cripple

derreniego *m* (coll) curse

derreti·do **-da** *adj* madly in love; *(mantequilla)* drawn || *m* concrete

derretimiento *m* thawing, melting; intense love, passion

derretir §50 *tr* to thaw, melt; *(la mantequilla)* to draw; *(la hacienda)* to squander || *ref* to thaw, melt; to fall madly in love; to be quite susceptible; (coll) to be worried, be impatient

derribar *tr* to destroy, tear down, knock down; to wreck; *(un árbol)* to fell; to bring down, shoot down; to overthrow; to humiliate || *ref* to fall down, tumble down; to throw oneself on the ground

derribo *m* demolition, wrecking; *(de un árbol)* felling; overthrow; *(de un avión enemigo)* bringing down; **derribos** debris, rubble

derrocadero *m* rocky precipice

derrocar §73 or §81 *tr* to throw or hurl from a height; to ruin, wreck, tear down; to bring down, humble, overthrow

derrocha·dor **-dora** *mf* wastrel, squanderer

derrochar *tr* to waste, squander

derroche *m* wasting, squandering, extravagance

derrota *f* defeat, rout; road, route, way; *(de embarcación)* course

derrotadamente *adv* shabbily, poorly

derrotar *tr* to rout, put to flight; to wear out; to ruin || *ref* (naut) to drift from the course

derrotero *m* course, route; ship's course

derrotismo *m* defeatism

derrotista *adj* & *mf* defeatist

derrubiar *tr* & *ref* to wash away, wear away

derrubio *m* washout

derruir §20 *tr* to tear down, demolish

derrumbadero *m* crag, precipice; hazard, risky business

derrumbamiento *m* headlong plunge; cave-in, collapse; **derrumbamiento de tierra** landslide

derrumbar *tr* to throw headlong || *ref* to plunge headlong; to collapse, cave in, crumble

derrumbe *m* precipice; landslide; cave-in

derviche *m* dervish

desabonar *ref* to drop one's subscription

desabono *m* cancellation of subscription; discredit, disparagement

desabor *m* insipidity, tastelessness

desabotonar *tr* to unbutton || *intr* to blossom, bloom

desabri·do **-da** *adj* insipid, tasteless; gruff, surly; *(tiempo)* unsettled

desabrigar §44 *tr* to uncover, bare || *ref* to bare oneself; to undress

desabrir *tr* to give a bad taste to; to displease, to embitter

desabrochar *tr* to unclasp, unbutton, unfasten || *ref* (coll) to unbosom oneself

desacalorar *ref* to cool off

desacatamiento *m* incivility, disrespect

desacatar *tr* to treat disrespectfully

desacato *m* incivility, disrespect, contempt; *(para con las cosas sagradas)* profanation

desacelerar *tr* & *ref* to decelerate

desacerta·do **-da** *adj* mistaken, wrong

desacertar §2 *intr* to be mistaken, be wrong

desacierto *m* error, mistake, blunder

desacomoda·do **-da** *adj* inconvenient; out of work; in straightened circumstances

desacomodar *tr* to inconvenience; to discharge, dismiss

desacomodo *m* discharge, dismissal

desaconseja·do **-da** *adj* ill-advised

desaconsejar *tr* to dissuade

desacordar §61 *tr* to put out of tune || *ref* to get out of tune; to become forgetful

desacorde *adj* out of tune; incongruous

desacostumbra·do **-da** *adj* unusual

desacostumbrar *tr* to break of a habit

desacreditar *tr* to discredit; to disparage

desacuerdo *m* discord, disagreement; error, mistake; unconsciousness; forgetfulness

desadaptación *f* maladjustment

desadeudar *tr* to free of debt || *ref* to get out of debt

desadormecer §22 *tr* to awaken; to free of numbness || *ref* to get awake; to shake off the numbness

desadorna·do **-da** *adj* unadorned, plain; bare, uncovered

desadverti·do **-da** *adj* unnoticed; inattentive

desadvertimiento *m* inadvertence

desafección *f* dislike

desafec·to **-ta** *adj* adverse, hostile; opposed || *m* dislike

desaferrar *tr* to unfasten, loosen; to make *(a person)* change his mind; *(las áncoras)* to weigh

desafiar §77 *tr* to challenge, defy, dare; to rival, compete with

desafición *f* dislike

desaficionar *tr* to cause to dislike

desafilar *tr* to make dull || *ref* to become dull

desafina·do **-da** *adj* flat, out of tune

desafío *m* challenge, dare; rivalry, competition

desafora·do **-da** *adj* colossal, huge; disorderly, outrageous

desafortuna·do **-da** *adj* unfortunate

desafuero *m* excess, outrage

desagracia·do **-da** *adj* ungraceful, graceless

desagradable *adj* disagreeable

desagradar *tr* & *intr* to displease || *ref* to be displeased

desagradeci·do **-da** *adj* ungrateful

desagradecimiento *m* ungratefulness

desagrado *m* displeasure

desagraviar *tr* to make amends to, to indemnify

desagravio *m* amends, indemnification

desagregación *f* disintegration

desagregar §44 *ref* to disintegrate

desaguadero *m* drain, outlet; *(ocasión de continuo gasto)* (fig) drain

desaguar §10 *tr* to drain, empty; to

squander, waste || *intr* to flow, empty || *ref* to drain, be drained

desagüe *m* drainage, sewerage; drain, outlet

desaguisa·do -da *adj* illegal || *m* offense, outrage, wrong

desahijar *tr* (*las crías del ganado*) to wean || *ref* (*las abejas*) to swarm

desahogadamente *adv* freely; comfortably, easily; impudently

desahoga·do -da *adj* brazen, forward; roomy; in comfortable circumstances

desahogar §44 *tr* to relieve, comfort; (*deseos, pasiones*) to give free rein to || *ref* to take it easy, get comfortable; to unbosom oneself, open up one's heart; to get out of debt; **desahogarse en** (*denuestos*) to burst forth in

desahogo *m* brazenness; ample room; comfort; outlet, relief; comfortable circumstances

desahuciar *tr* to deprive of hope; to evict, oust, dispossess || *ref* to lose all hope

desahucio *m* eviction, ousting, dispossession

desaira·do -da *adj* unattractive, unprepossessing; unsuccessful

desairar *tr* to slight, snub, disregard

desaire *m* slight, snub, disregard; unattractiveness, lack of charm

desajustar *tr* to put out of order || *ref* to get out of order; to disagree

desalabanza *f* belittling, disparagement

desalabar *tr* to belittle, disparage

desala·do -da *adj* eager, in a hurry

desalar *tr* to desalt; to clip the wings of || *ref* to hasten, rush; **desalarse por** to be eager to

desalentar §2 *tr* to put out of breath; to discourage || *ref* to become discouraged

desalforjar *ref* to loosen one's clothing

desaliento *m* discouragement

desalinización *f* desalinization

desaliña·do -da *adj* slovenly, untidy; careless, slipshod

desaliño *m* slovenliness, untidiness; carelessness, neglect

desalma·do -da *adj* cruel, inhuman

desalojar *tr* to oust, evict; (*al enemigo*) to dislodge; (*el camino*) to clear || *intr* to leave, move away, move out

desalquila·do -da *adj* vacant, unrented

desalterar *tr* to calm, quiet

desalumbra·do -da *adj* dazzled, blinded; confused, unsure of oneself

desamable *adj* unlikeable, unlovable

desamar *tr* to dislike, hate, detest

desamarrar *tr* to untie, unfasten; (naut) to unmoor

desamistar *ref* to fall out, become estranged

desamor *m* dislike, coldness; hatred

desamorrar *tr* to make (*a person*) talk

desamparar *tr* to abandon, forsake; to give up

desamparo *m* abandonment, desertion; helplessness

desamueblado·do -da *adj* unfurnished

desandar §5 *tr* to retrace, go back over

desandraja·do -da *adj* ragged, in tatters

desangrar *tr* to bleed; to drain; (fig) to

bleed, impoverish || *ref* to lose a lot of blood

desanimación *f* discouragement, downheartedness

desanima·do -da *adj* discouraged, downhearted; (*reunión*) lifeless, dull

desanimar *tr* to discourage, dishearten || *ref* to become discouraged

desánimo *m* discouragement

desanublar *tr & ref* to clear up, brighten up

desanudar *tr* to untie; to disentangle

desapacible *adj* unpleasant, disagreeable

desapadrinar *tr* to disavow; to disapprove

desaparecer §22 *intr & ref* to disappear

desapareci·do -da *adj* missing; extinct || **desaparecidos** *mpl* missing persons

desaparecimiento *m* disappearance

desaparejar *tr* to unharness, unhitch; (naut) to unrig

desaparición *f* disappearance; (Ven) death

desapasiona·do -da *adj* dispassionate, impartial

desapego *m* dislike, coolness, indifference

desapercibi·do -da *adj* unprepared; wanting; unnoticed

desapiada·do -da *adj* merciless, pitiless

desaplica·do -da *adj* idle, lazy

desapodera·do -da *adj* headlong, impetuous; violent, wild; excessive

desapoderar *tr* to dispossess; to deprive of power || *ref* — **desapoderarse de** to lose possession of, give up possession of

desapolillar *tr* to free of moths || *ref* (coll) to expose oneself to the weather

desapreciar *tr* to depreciate

desaprecio *m* depreciation

desaprender *tr* to unlearn

desaprensión *f* composure, nonchalance

desapretar §2 *tr* to slacken, loosen; (typ) to unlock

desaprobación *f* disapproval

desaprobar §61 *tr & intr* to disapprove

desapropiar *tr* to divest || *ref* — **desapropiarse de** to divest oneself of

desaprovecha·do -da *adj* unproductive; indifferent, lackadaisical

desaprovechar *tr* to not take advantage of || *intr* to slip back

desarmable *adj* dismountable

desarmador *m* hammer (*of gun*); (Mex) screwdriver

desarmar *tr* to disarm; to dismount, dismantle, take apart; (*la cólera*) to temper, calm || *intr & ref* to disarm

desarme *m* disarmament; dismantling, dismounting

desarraigar §44 *tr* to uproot, dig up; to expel, drive out

desarregla·do -da *adj* out of order; slovenly, disorderly; intemperate

desarrollar *tr & intr* to develop; to unroll, unfold || *ref* to develop; to unroll, unfold; to take place

desarrollo *m* development; unrolling, unfolding

desarropar *tr & ref* to undress

desarrugar §44 *tr & ref* to unwrinkle

desarzonar *tr* to unsaddle, unhorse

desasea·do -da *adj* dirty, unclean, slovenly

desasentar §2 *tr* to remove; to displease || *ref* to stand up

desaseo *m* dirtiness, uncleanliness, slovenliness

desasir §7 *tr* to let go, let go of || *ref* to come loose; to let go; **desasirse de** to let go of; to give up, get free of

desasosegar §66 *tr* to disquiet, worry, disturb

desasosiego *m* disquiet, worry

desastra·do -da *adj* disastrous; unfortunate, wretched; ragged, shabby

desastre *m* disaster; **ir al desastre** to go to rack and ruin

desastro·so -sa *adj* disastrous

desatacar §73 *tr* to unbuckle, untie

desatar *tr* to untie, undo, unfasten; to solve, unravel || *ref* to come loose; to free oneself; (*la tempestad*) to break loose; to forget oneself, go too far; **desatarse en** (*denuestos*) to burst forth in

desatascar §73 *tr* to pull out of the mud; (*un conducto obstruído*) to unclog; (*a una persona de un apuro*) to extricate

desataviar §77 *tr* to disarray, undress

desatavío *m* disarray, undress, slovenliness

desate *m* (*de palabras*) flood; **desate del vientre** loose bowels

desatención *f* inattention; discourtesy, disrespect

desatender §51 *tr* to slight, disregard, pay no attention to

desatenta·do -da *adj* wild, disorderly, extreme

desaten·to -ta *adj* inattentive; discourteous, disrespectful

desatina·do -da *adj* wild, disorderly; foolish, nonsensical || *mf* fool

desatinar *tr* to bewilder, confuse || *intr* to talk nonsense, to act foolishly; to lose one's bearings

desatino *m* folly, nonsense; awkwardness, loss of touch

desatolondrar *tr* to bring to || *ref* to come to one's senses

desatollar *tr* to pull out of the mud

desatornillar *tr* to unscrew

desatraillar §4 *tr* to unleash

desatrampar *tr* to unclog

desatrancar §73 *tr* to unbar, unbolt; to unclog

desatufar *ref* to get out of the close air; to cool off, quiet down

desautoriza·do -da *adj* unauthorized

desavenencia *f* disagreement, discord

desavenir §79 *tr* to cause disagreement among || *ref* to disagree; **desavenirse con** to differ with, disagree with

desaventura *f* misfortune

desaviar §77 *tr* to mislead, lead astray

desayuna·do -da *adj* — **estar desayunado** to have had breakfast

desayunar *intr* to breakfast || *ref* to breakfast; **desayunarse con** to have breakfast on; **desayunarse de** to get the first news of

desayuno *m* breakfast

desazón *f* insipidity, tastelessness; annoyance, displeasure; discomfort

desazonar *tr* to make tasteless; to annoy, displease || *ref* to feel ill

desbancar §73 *tr* to win the bank from; to cut out, to supplant

desbandada *f* — **a la desbandada** helterskelter, in confusion

desbandar *ref* to run away; to disband; to desert

desbarajustar *tr* to put out of order || *ref* to get out of order, break down

desbarata·do -da *adj* (coll) debauched, corrupt || *mf* (coll) libertine

desbaratar *tr* to destroy, spoil, ruin; to squander, waste; (mil) to rout, throw into confusion || *intr* to talk nonsense || *ref* to be unbalanced

desbarrancadero *m* (Am) precipice

desbastar *tr* to smooth off; to waste, weaken; (*a una persona inculta*) to polish || *ref* to become polished

desbautizar §60 *ref* (coll) to lose one's temper

desbeber *intr* (coll) to urinate

desbloquear *tr* to relieve the blockade of; (*crédito*) to unfreeze

desboca·do -da *adj* (*pieza de artillería*) wide mouthed; (*herramienta*) nicked; (*caballo*) runaway; (*persona*) (coll) foul-mouthed

desbocar §73 *tr* to break the mouth of, break the spout of || *intr* (*un río*) to empty; (*una calle*) to run, open, end || *ref* (*un caballo*) to run away, to break loose; to curse, swear

desbordamiento *m* overflow

desbordar *tr* to overwhelm || *intr* & *ref* to overflow

desbozalar *tr* to unmuzzle

desbravar *tr* to tame, break in || *intr* & *ref* to abate, moderate; to cool off, calm down

desbrozar §60 *tr* to clear of underbrush, to clear of rubbish

desbulla *f* oyster shell

desbulla·dor -dora *mf* oyster opener || *m* oyster fork

desbullar *tr* (*la ostra*) to open

descabal *adj* incomplete, imperfect

descabalgar §44 *intr* to dismount, alight from a horse

descabella·do -da *adj* disheveled; rash, wild

descabellar *tr* to muss, dishevel

descabeza·do -da *adj* crazy, rash, wild

descabezar §60 *tr* to behead; (*un árbol*) to top; (*una dificultad*) (coll) to get the best off; **descabezar el sueño** to doze, snooze || *intr* to border || *ref* to rack one's brains

descabullir §13 *ref* to sneak out, slip away; to refuse to face the facts

descacharra·do -da *adj* (CAm) dirty, slovenly, ragged

descaecer §22 *intr* to decline, lose ground

descaecimiento *m* weakness; depression, despondency

descalabazar §60 *ref* (coll) to rack one's brain

descalabra·do -da *adj* banged on the

head; **salir descalabrado** to come out the loser, to be worsted

descalabrar *tr* to bang on the head; to knock down || *ref* to bang one's head

descalabro *m* misfortune, setback, loss

descalificar §73 *tr* to disqualify

descalzar §60 *tr* (*las botas, los guantes*) to take off; (*a una persona*) to take the shoes or stockings off; to undermine || *ref* to take one's shoes or stockings off; to take one's gloves off; (*las botas, los guantes*) to take off; (*el caballo*) to lose a shoe

descal·zo -za *adj* barefooted; seedy, down at the heel

descamar *ref* to scale, scale off

descaminadamente *adv* off the road, on the wrong track

descaminar *tr* to mislead, lead astray || *ref* to get lost; to run off the road

descamino *m* going astray; leading astray; nonsense; contraband, smuggled goods

descamisa·do -da *adj* shirtless, ragged || *m* wretch, ragamuffin

descampa·do -da *adj* free, open || *m* open country

descansadero *m* resting place, stopping place

descansa·do -da *adj* rested, refreshed; calm, restful

descansar *tr* to rest, relieve; (*la cabeza, el brazo*) to rest, lean || *intr* to rest; to lean; to not worry; (*yacer en el sepulcro*) to rest; **descansar en** to trust in

descanso *m* rest; peace, quiet; (*de la escalera*) landing; (theat) intermission; (Chile) toilet

descantillar *tr* to chip off; to deduct

descañonar *tr* to pluck; to shave against the grain; (coll) to gyp

descapiruzar §60 *tr* (Col) to muss, rumple, crumple

descapotable *adj* & *m* (aut) convertible

descara·do -da *adj* barefaced, brazen, saucy

descarar *ref* to be impudent; **descararse a** to have the nerve to

descarga *f* unloading; (*de un arma de fuego*) discharge; (com) discount; (elec) discharge; **descarga de aduana** customhouse clearance

descargar §44 *tr* to unload; (*de una deuda u obligación*) to free; (*un arma de fuego*) to discharge; (*un golpe*) to strike, to deal; (elec) to discharge || *intr* to unload; (*un río*) to empty; (*una calle, paseo*) to open; (*una nube en lluvia*) to burst || *ref* to unburden oneself; to resign; **descargarse con or en uno de algo** to unload something on someone; **descargarse de** to get rid of; to resign from; (*una imputación, un cargo*) to clear oneself of

descargo *m* unloading; (*de una obligación*) discharge; (*del cargo que se hace a uno*) release, acquittal; receipt

descargue *m* unloading

descariño *m* coolness, indifference

descarnadamente *adv* right off the shoulder, bluntly

descarnar *tr* to remove the flesh from; to chip; to wear away; to detach from earthly matters || *ref* to lose flesh

descaro *m* brazenness, effrontery

descarriar §77 *tr* to mislead, to lead astray || *ref* to go wrong, to go astray

descarrilamiento *m* derailment

descarrilar *intr* to jump the track; (coll) to wander from the point || *ref* to jump the track

descartable *adj* disposable

descartar *tr* to cast aside, reject; to discard || *ref* to shirk, evade; **descartarse de** (*un compromiso*) to shirk, evade

descarte *m* casting aside, rejection; discarding; (*cartas desechadas*) discard; shirking, evasion

descasar *tr* to divorce; to disturb, disarrange

descascar §73 *tr* to husk, shell, peel || *ref* to break to pieces; to jabber, talk too much

descascarar *tr* to shell, peel || *ref* to shell off, peel off

descascarillar *tr* & *ref* to shell, peel

descasta·do -da *adj* ungrateful, ungrateful to one's family

descaudala·do -da *adj* ruined, penniless

descendencia *f* descent

descendente *adj* descendent, descending; (tren) down

descender §51 *tr* to bring down, lower; (*la escalera*) to descend, to go down || *intr* to descend, go down; to flow, run; to decline

descendiente *mf* descendant

descenso *m* descent; (*de temperatura*) drop; decline

descentralizar §60 *tr* to decentralize

desceñi·do -da *adj* loose-fitting, loose

descepar *tr* to pull up by the roots; to extirpate, exterminate

descerebrar *tr* to brain

descerraja·do -da *adj* (coll) corrupt, evil, wicked

descifrar *tr* to decipher, to decode, to figure out

desclasificar §73 *tr* to disqualify

descocer §16 *tr* to digest

descoco *m* (coll) impudence, insolence

descocholla·do -da *adj* (Chile) ragged

descolar *tr* to dock, crop; (*a un empleado*) (CAm) to discharge, fire; (Mex) to slight, snub

descolgar §63 *tr* to unhook; to take down, lower; (*el auricular*) to pick up || *ref* to come down, come off; to show up suddenly; **descolgarse con** (coll) to blurt out

descolón *m* (Mex) slight, snub

descolorar *tr* & *ref* to discolor, to fade

descolori·do -da *adj* faded, off color

descollante *adj* prominent, outstanding; chief, main

descollar §61 *intr* to tower, stand out; (fig) to excel, stand out

descomedi·do -da *adj* immoderate, excessive; rude, discourteous

descomedir §50 *ref* to be rude, be discourteous

descomer *intr* to have a bowel movement

descómo·do -da *adj* inconvenient

descompasa·do -da *adj* extreme, excessive

descompletar *tr* to break (*a set or series*)

descomponer §54 *tr* to decompose; to disturb, disorganize; to put out of order; to set at odds ‖ *ref* to decompose; (*una persona, la salud de una persona*) to fall to pieces; (*el tiempo*) to change for the worse; (*el rostro*) to become distorted; (*un aparato*) to get out of order; to lose one's temper; **descomponerse con** to get angry with

descomposición *f* decomposition; disorder, disorganization; discord

descompostura *f* decomposition; disorder, untidiness; brazenness

descompresión *f* decompression

descompues·to -ta *adj* out of order; brazen, discourteous; irritated; (Am) drunk

descomulgar §44 *tr* to excommunicate

descomunal *adj* huge, colossal, enormous, extraordinary

desconcerta·do -da *adj* out of order; disconcerted, baffled, bewildered; slovenly; unbridled

desconcertar §2 *tr* to put out of order; to disturb, upset; (*un hueso*) to dislocate; to disconcert, bewilder

desconcierto *m* disrepair; disorder; mismanagement; confusion; discomfiture; disagreement; lack of restraint; loose bowels

desconchabar *tr* (Am) to dislocate ‖ *ref* (Am) to become dislocated; (Am) to disagree, fall out

desconchado *m* scaly part of wall; (*en la porcelana*) chip

desconchar *tr* & *ref* to chip, chip off; to scale off

desconectar *tr* to detach; to disconnect

desconfia·do -da *adj* distrustful, suspicious

desconfianza *f* distrust

desconfiar §77 *intr* to lose confidence; **desconfiar de** to lose confidence in, to distrust

desconformar *intr* to dissent, disagree ‖ *ref* to not go well together

descongelar *tr* to melt; to defrost; (com) to unfreeze

desconocer §22 *tr* to not know; to disavow, disown; to not recognize; to slight, ignore; to not see ‖ *ref* to be unknown; to be quite changed, be unrecognizable

desconocidamente *adv* unknowingly

desconoci·do -da *adj* unknown; strange, unfamiliar; ungrateful ‖ *mf* unknown, unknown person

desconsentir §68 *tr* to not consent to

desconsidera·do -da *adj* ill-considered; inconsiderate

desconsola·do -da *adj* disconsolate, downhearted; (*estómago*) weak

desconsuelo *m* disconsolateness, grief; upset stomach

descontaminación *f* decontamination

descontar §61 *tr* to discount; to deduct;

to take for granted; **dar por descontado que** to take for granted that

descontentadi·zo -za *adj* hard to please

desconten·to -ta *adj* & *m* discontent

descontinuar §21 *tr* to discontinue

desconvenir §79 *intr* to disagree; to not go together, to not match; to not be suitable ‖ *ref* to disagree

desconvidar *tr* to cancel an invitation to; (*lo prometido*) to take back

descopar *tr* to top (*a tree*)

descorazonar *tr* to discourage

descorchar *tr* to remove the bark from; (*una botella*) to uncork; to break into

descornar §61 *tr* to dehorn ‖ *ref* (coll) to rack one's brains

descorrer *tr* to run back over; (*una cortina, un cerrojo*) to draw ‖ *intr* & *ref* to flow, run off

descortés *adj* discourteous, impolite

descortesía *f* discourtesy, impoliteness

descortezar §60 *tr* to strip the bark from; to take the crust off; (coll) to polish ‖ *ref* (coll) to become polished

descoser *tr* to unstitch, to rip ‖ *ref* to loose one's tongue; (coll) to break wind

descosi·do -da *adj* disorderly, wild; indiscreet; desultory ‖ *m* wild man; rip, open seam

descote *m* low neck

descoyuntar *tr* to dislocate; to bore, annoy ‖ *ref* (*p.ej., el brazo*) to throw out of joint

descrédito *m* discredit

descreer §43 *tr* to disbelieve; to discredit ‖ *intr* to disbelieve

descreí·do -da *adj* disbelieving, unbelieving ‖ *mf* disbeliever, unbeliever

descriar §77 *ref* to spoil; to waste away

describir §83 *tr* to describe

descripción *f* description

descripti·vo -va *adj* descriptive

descto. *abbr* descuento

descuadrar *intr* to disagree; **descuadrar con** (Mex) to displease

descuajar *tr* to liquefy, dissolve; to uproot; to discourage ‖ *ref* to liquefy; to drudge

descuartizar §60 *tr* to tear to pieces; to quarter

descubierta *f* open pie; inspection; reconnoitering; (naut) scanning the horizon; **a la descubierta** openly; in the open; reconnoitering

descubiertamente *adv* clearly, openly

descubier·to -ta *adj* bareheaded; (*campo*) bare, barren; (*expuesto a reconvenciones*) under fire ‖ *m* deficiency, shortage; exposition of the Holy Sacrament; **al descubierto** in the open; unprotected; (*sin tener disponibles las acciones que se venden*) short, e.g., **vender al descubierto** to sell short ‖ *f* see **descubierta**

descubri·dor -dora *mf* discoverer ‖ *m* (mil) scout

descubrimiento *m* discovery

descubrir §83 *tr* to discover; to uncover, lay open, reveal; to invent; (*p.ej., una estatua*) to unveil ‖ *ref* to take off one's hat, uncover; to be discovered; to open one's heart

descuello *m* excellence, superiority; great height; haughtiness

descuento *m* discount; deduction, rebate

descuerar *tr* (Chile) to skin, flay; (Chile) to discredit, flay

descuerno *m* (coll) slight, snub

descuida·do -da *adj* careless, negligent; slovenly, dirty; off guard

descuidar *tr* to overlook, neglect; to divert, distract, relieve ‖ *ref* to be careless, not bother; to be diverted

descuide·ro -ra *mf* sneak thief

desculdo *m* carelessness, negligence, neglect; slip, mistake, blunder; oversight; **al descuido** with studied carelessness; **en un descuido** (Am) when least expected

desculta·do -da *adj* carefree

desde *prep* since, from; after; **desde ahora** from now on; **desde entonces** since then, ever since; **desde hace** for, e.g., **estoy aquí desde hace cinco días** I've been here for five days; **desde luego** at once; of course; **desde que** since

desdecir §24 *intr* to slip back; to be out of harmony ‖ *ref* — **desdecirse de** to take back, retract

desdén *m* scorn, disdain; **al desdén** with studied neglect

desdenta·do -da *adj* toothless

desdeñar *tr* to scorn, disdain ‖ *ref* to be disdainful; **desdeñarse de** to loathe, despise; to not deign to

desdeño·so -sa *adj* scornful, disdainful

desdicha *f* misfortune; indigence

desdicha·do -da *adj* unfortunate, unlucky; poor, wretched; (coll) backward, timid

desdinerar *tr* to impoverish

desdoblar *tr & intr* to unfold, spread open; to split, divide

desdorar *tr* to remove the gold or gilt from; to tarnish, sully; to disparage

desdoro *m* tarnish, blemish, blot; disparagement

deseable *adj* desirable

desear *tr* to desire, wish

desecar §73 *tr & ref* to dry; to drain

desechable *adj* disposable

desechar *tr* to discard, to throw out, to cast aside; to underrate; to blame, censure; (*la llave de una puerta*) to turn

desecho *m* remainder; offal, rubbish; castoff; scorn, contempt; (Am) short cut; **desecho de hierro** scrap iron

desegregación *f* desegregation

desollar *tr* to unseal

desembalaje *m* unpacking

desembalar *tr* to unpack

desembarazar §60 *tr* to free, clear, empty, open ‖ *ref* to free oneself; to be cleared, be emptied; **desembarazarse de** to get rid of

desembarazo *m* naturalness, lack of restraint; (Am) delivery, childbirth; **con desembarazo** naturally, readily

desembarcadero *m* wharf, pier, landing

desembarcar §73 *tr* to unload, debark, disembark ‖ *intr* to land, debark, disembark; (*de un carruaje*) to get out,

alight; (*la escalera al plano bajo*) to end ‖ *ref* to land, debark, disembark

desembarco *m* landing, debarkation, disembarkation; (*de la escalera*) landing

desembarque *m* unloading, debarkation, disembarkation

desembocadura *f* (*de una calle*) opening, outlet; (*de un río*) mouth

desembocar §73 *intr* (*una calle*) open, to end; (*un río*) to flow, empty

desembolsar *tr* to disburse, pay out

desembolso *m* disbursement, payment

desembragar §44 *tr* (*el motor*) to disengage ‖ *intr* to throw the clutch out

desembrague *m* disengagement, clutch release

desembravecer §22 *tr* to tame; to calm, quiet, pacify

desembriagar §44 *tr & ref* to sober up

desembrollar *tr* to untangle, unravel

desemejante *adj* — **desemejante de** dissimilar from or to, unlike; **desemejantes** dissimilar, unlike

desemejar *tr* to change, disfigure ‖ *intr* to be different, not look alike

desempacar §73 *tr* to unpack, unwrap ‖ *ref* to cool off, calm down

desempalagar §44 *tr* to rid of nausea ‖ *ref* to get rid of nausea

desempañar *tr* (*el vidrio*) to wipe the steam or smear from; to take the diaper off

desempapelar *tr* to unwrap; (*una pared, una habitación*) to scrape the wallpaper from

desempaquetar *tr* to unpack; to unwrap

desempatar *tr* to break the tie between; (*los votos*) to break the tie in

desempate *m* breaking a tie

desempedrar §2 *tr* to remove the paving stones from; (*un sitio empedrado*) (coll) to pound; **ir desempedrando la calle** (coll) to dash down the street

desempeñar *tr* (*un papel*) to play a rôle; (*un cargo*) to fill, perform; (*a uno de un empeño*) to disengage; (*un deber*) to discharge; to free of debt; to take out of hock ‖ *ref* to get out of a jam; to get out of debt

desempeño *m* acting, performance; disengagement; (*de un deber*) discharge; payment of a debt; taking out of hock

desempernar *tr* to unbolt

desemplea·do -da *adj & mf* unemployed

desempleo *m* unemployment

desempolvorar *tr* to dust; to renew, take up again ‖ *ref* to brush up

desempolvorar *tr* to dust, dust off

desencadenar *tr* to unchain, unleash ‖ *ref* to break loose

desencajar *tr* to dislocate; to disconnect ‖ *ref* to get out of joint; (*el rostro*) to be contorted

desencaminar *tr* to lead astray, mislead

desencantamiento *m* disenchantment, disillusion

desencantar *tr* to disenchant, disillusion

desencantarar *tr* (*nombres o números*) to draw; (*un nombre o nombres*) to exclude from balloting

desencanto *m* disenchantment, disillusion

desencarecer §22 *tr* to lower the price of ‖ *intr* & *ref* to come down in price

desencerrar §2 *tr* to release, set free; to disclose, reveal

desencoger §17 *tr* to unfold, spread out ‖ *ref* to relax, shake off one's timidity

desencolar *tr* to unglue ‖ *ref* to become unglued

desenconar *tr* to take the soreness out of; to calm down

desenchufar *tr* to unplug, to disconnect

desendiosar *tr* to bring down a peg

desenfadaderas *fpl* — **tener buenas desenfadaderas** (coll) to be resourceful

desenfada·do -da *adj* free, easy, unconstrained

desenfado *m* ease, naturalness; relaxation, calmness

desenfoca·do -da *adj* out of focus

desenfrena·do -da *adj* unbridled, wanton, licentious

desenfrenar *tr* to unbridle ‖ *ref* to yield to temptation; to fly into a passion; (*la tempestad, el viento*) to break loose

desenfreno *m* unruliness, wantonness, licentiousness

desenfundar *tr* to take out of its sheath, bag, pillowcase, etc.

desenganchar *tr* to unhook, uncouple, unfasten, disengage; to unhitch

desenganche *m* unhooking, disengaging; unhitching

desengañar *tr* to disabuse, undeceive; to disillusion; to disappoint

desengaño *m* disabusing; disillusionment; disappointment; plain fact, plain truth

desengrana·do -da *adj* out of gear

desengranar *tr* to unmesh; to disengage, throw out of gear

desengraso *m* (Chile) dessert

desenlace *m* outcome, result; (*de un drama, novela, etc.*) dénouement

desenlazar §60 *tr* to untie; to solve; (*el nudo de un drama*) to unravel

desenmarañar *tr* to disentangle; (*una cosa obscura*) to unravel

desenmascarar *tr* to unmask ‖ *ref* to take one's mask off

desenojar *tr* to appease, to free of anger ‖ *ref* to calm down; to be amused

desenredar *tr* to disentangle; to clear up ‖ *ref* to extricate oneself

desenredo *m* disentanglement; (*de un drama, novela, etc.*) dénouement

desenrollar *tr* to unroll, unwind, unreel

desensartar *tr* to unstring, unthread

desensillar *tr* to unsaddle (*a horse*)

desentablar *tr* to disrupt; to break off (*a bargain, friendship, etc.*)

desentender §51 *ref* — **desentenderse de** to take no part in, to not participate in; to affect ignorance of, pretend to be unaware of

desenterrar §2 *tr* to dig up; to disinter; (fig) to unearth, dig up; (fig) to recall to mind

desentona·do -da *adj* out of tune, flat

desentonar *tr* to humble, bring down a peg ‖ *intr* to be out of tune; to be out of harmony ‖ *ref* to talk loud and disrespectfully

desentono *m* dissonance, false note; loud tone of voice

desentornillar *tr* to unscrew

desentrampar *ref* (coll) to get out of debt

desentrañar *tr* to disembowel; to figure out, unravel ‖ *ref* to give away all that one has

desentrena·do -da *adj* out of training

desentronizar §60 *tr* to dethrone; to strip of influence

desentumecer §22 *tr* to relieve of numbness ‖ *ref* to be relieved of numbness

desenvainar *tr* to unsheathe; (*las uñas el animal*) to show, stretch out; (coll) to bare, uncover, show

desenvoltura *f* naturalness, ease of manner, offhandedness; fluency; lewdness, boldness (*chiefly in women*)

desenvolver §47 & §83 *tr* to unfold, unroll, unwrap; to unwind; to unravel, clear up; to develop ‖ *ref* to unroll; to unwind; to develop, evolve; to extricate oneself; to be forward

desenvuel·to -ta *adj* free and easy, offhand; fluent; brazen, bold, lewd

deseo *m* desire, wish

deseo·so -sa *adj* desirous, anxious

desequilibra·do -da *adj* unbalanced

desequilibrar *tr* to unbalance ‖ *ref* to become unbalanced

desequilibrio *m* disequilibrium, imbalance; derangement, mental instability

deserción *f* desertion

desertar *tr* & *intr* to desert

desertor *m* deserter

deservicio *m* disservice

desesperación *f* despair; **ser una desesperación** to be unbearable

desespera·do -da *adj* despairing, desperate ‖ *mf* desperate person

desesperanza *f* hopelessness

desesperanza·do -da *adj* hopeless

desesperanzar §60 *tr* to discourage ‖ *ref* to lose hope

desesperar *tr* to drive to despair; (coll) to exasperate ‖ *intr* to lose hope; (coll) to be exasperated ‖ *ref* to be desperate, lose all hope

desestancar §73 *tr* to open up, to unclog; to make free of duty; to open the market to

desestimar *tr* to hold in low regard; to refuse, reject

deséxito *m* failure

desfachata·do -da *adj* (coll) brazen, impudent

desfachatez *f* (coll) brazenness, impudence

desfalcar §73 *tr* & *intr* to embezzle

desfalco *m* embezzlement

desfallecer §22 *tr* to weaken ‖ *intr* to grow weak; to faint, faint away; to lose courage

desfalleci·do -da *adj* weak; faint

desfallecimiento *m* weakness; fainting; discouragement

desfavorable *adj* unfavorable

desfigurar *tr* to disfigure; to distort,

misrepresent; to disguise; to change, alter || *ref* to look different

desfiladero *m* defile, pass

desfilar *intr* to defile, parade, file by

desfile *m* review, parade

desflorar *tr* to deflower; to mention in passing

desfogar §44 *tr* (*un horno*) to vent; (*la cal*) to slake; (*una pasión*) to give free rein to || *intr* (*una tempestad*) to break into rain and wind || *ref* to give vent to one's anger

desfondar *tr* to stave in; (*una nave*) to bilge; (*agr*) to trench-plow

desforestar *tr* to deforest

desgaire *m* slovenliness; disdain, scorn; **al desgaire** scornfully; carelessly, with affected carelessness

desgajar *tr* to tear off; to split off || *ref* to come off, to come loose; to arise, originate; to separate, break away

desgana *f* lack of appetite; indifference; boredom; **a desgana** unwillingly, reluctantly

desgarba·do -da *adj* ungainly, uncouth

desgarrar *tr* to tear, rend; (*la flema*) to cough up || *ref* to tear oneself away

desgarro *m* tear, rent; brazenness, effrontery; boasting, bragging; (Chile, Col) phlegm, mucus

desgastar *tr* to wear away, wear down; to weaken, spoil || *ref* to wear away; to grow weak, decline

desgaste *m* wear, wearing away

desgoberna·do -da *adj* ungovernable, uncontrollable

desgobernar §2 *tr* to misgovern; (*un hueso*) to dislocate || *intr* (naut) to steer poorly || *ref* to twist and turn in dancing

desgobierno *m* misgovernment; dislocation

desgonzar §60 *tr* to unhinge; to disconnect

desgracia *f* misfortune; (*acontecimiento adverso*) mishap; (*pérdida de favor*) disfavor, disgrace; (*aspereza en el trato*) gruffness; (*falta de gracia*) lack of charm; **correr con desgracia** to have no luck; **por desgracia** unfortunately

desgracia·do -da *adj* unfortunate; unattractive, unpleasant; disagreeable || *mf* wretch, unfortunate

desgraciar *tr* to displease; to spoil || *ref* to spoil; to fail; to fall out, to disagree

desgranar *tr* (*el maíz*) to shell; (*un racimo*) to pick the grapes from || *ref* (*piezas ensartadas*) to come loose

desgreñar *tr* to dishevel || *ref* to get disheveled; to pull each other's hair

deshabita·do -da *adj* unoccupied

deshabituar §21 *tr* to break of a habit

deshacer §39 *tr* to undo; to untie; to take apart; to wear away, consume, destroy; to melt; to put to flight, to rout; (*un tratado o negocio*) to violate || *ref* to get out of order; to vanish, disappear; **deshacerse de** to get rid of; **deshacerse en** (*cumplidos*) to lavish; (*lágrimas*) to burst into; **deshacerse por** to strive hard to

desharrapa·do -da *adj* ragged, in rags

deshebillar *tr* to unbuckle

deshebrar *tr* to unravel, unthread

deshecha *f* sham, pretense; dismissal; **hacer la deshecha** to feign, pretend; (Mex) to pretend lack of interest

deshelar §2 *tr* to thaw, melt; to defrost; (aer) to deice || *intr* to thaw, melt

desthereda·do -da *adj* disinherited; underprivileged

desheredar *tr* to disinherit || *ref* to be a disgrace to one's family

desherrar §2 *tr* to unchain, unshackle; (*a una caballería*) to unshoe

desherrumbrar *tr* to remove the rust from

deshidratar *tr* to dehydrate

deshielo *m* thaw, melting; defrosting

deshilachar *ref* to fray

deshila·do -da *adj* in a file; **a la deshilada** in single file; secretly || *m* openwork, drawn work

deshilar *tr* to unweave; (*reducir a hilos*) to shred || *ref* to fray; to get thin

deshilvana·do -da *adj* disconnected, desultory

deshincar §73 *tr* to pull up, to pull out

deshinchar *tr* to deflate; (*la cólera*) to give vent to || *ref* (*un tumor*) to go down; (*una persona orgullosa*) (coll) to become deflated

deshojar *tr* to strip of leaves; to tear the pages out of || *ref* to lose the leaves

deshollejar *tr* (*la uva*) to peel, skin; (*las habichuelas*) to shell

deshollina·dor -dora *mf* chimney sweep; (coll) curious observer || *m* long-handled brush or broom

deshones·to -ta *adj* immodest, indecent; improper

deshonor *m* dishonor; disgrace

deshonorar *tr* to dishonor; to degrade; to disfigure

deshonra *f* dishonor; disrespect; **tener a deshonra** to consider improper

deshonrabue·nos *mf* (*pl* -nos) (coll) slanderer; (coll) black sheep

deshonrar *tr* to disgrace; (*a una mujer*) to seduce; to insult

deshonro·so -sa *adj* disgraceful, improper, discreditable

deshora *f* wrong time; **a deshora** at the wrong time, inopportunely; suddenly, unexpectedly

deshuesar *tr* (*la carne de un animal*) to bone; (*la fruta*) to stone, to take the pits out of

deshumedecer §22 *tr* to dehumidify

desidia *f* laziness, indolence

desidio·so -sa *adj* lazy, indolent || *mf* lazy person

desier·to -ta *adj* desert; deserted || *m* desert; wilderness

designar *tr* to designate; (*un trabajo*) to plan

designio *m* design, plan, scheme

desigual *adj* unequal; unlike; rough, uneven; difficult; inconstant

desigualar *tr* to make unequal || *ref* to become unequal; (*aventajarse*) to get ahead

desigualdad f inequality; roughness, unevenness

desilusión f disillusionment; disappointment

desilusionar tr to disillusion; to disappoint || ref to become disillusioned; to be disappointed

desimanar or **desimantar** tr to demagnetize

desimpresionar tr to undeceive

desinclina·do -da adj disinclined

desinencia f (gram) termination, ending

desinfectante adj & m disinfectant

desinfectar or **desinficionar** tr to disinfect

desinflación f deflation

desinflamar tr to take the soreness out of

desinflar tr to deflate; to let the air out of; (a una persona) (coll) to deflate

desintegración f disintegration

desintegrar tr & ref to disintegrate

desinterés m disinterestedness

desinteresa·do -da adj (imparcial) disinterested; (poco interesado) uninterested

desinteresar ref to lose interest

desintonizar §60 tr (rad) to tune out; (rad) to put out of tune

desistir intr to desist

desjarretar tr to hamstring; (coll) to bleed to excess

desjuicia·do -da adj lacking judgment, senseless

desjuntar tr to disjoin, separate

deslabonar tr to unlink; to disconnect || ref to come loose; to withdraw

deslastrar tr to unballast

deslava·do -da adj faded, colorless; barefaced || mf barefaced person

deslavar tr to wash superficially; to fade, to take the life out of

desleal adj disloyal; unfair

deslealtad f disloyalty

deslechar tr (Col) to milk

desleír §58 tr to dissolve; to dilute; (los colores, la pintura) to thin; (sus pensamientos) to express too diffusely || ref to dissolve; to become diluted

deslengua·do -da adj foul-mouthed, shameless

desliar §77 tr to untie, undo; to unravel || ref to come untied

desligar §44 tr to untie, unbind; to disentangle; to excuse || ref to come untied, come loose

deslindar tr to mark the boundaries of; to distinguish; to define, explain

des·liz m (pl -lices) sliding; (superficie lisa) slide; slip, blunder; peccadillo, indiscretion

deslizade·ro -ra adj slippery || m slippery place; launching way

deslizadi·zo -za adj slippery

deslizador m (aer) glider

deslizar §60 tr to slide; (decir por descuido) to let slip || intr to slide; to slip; to glide || ref to slide; to slip; to glide; to slip away, sneak away; (un reparo) to slip out; (caer en una flaqueza) to slide back, to backslide

deslomar tr to break or strain the back of || ref to break or strain one's back;

no deslomarse (coll) to not strain oneself

desluci·do -da adj quiet, lackluster; dull, undistinguished

deslucir §45 tr to tarnish; to deprive of charm, deprive of distinction; to discredit

deslumbramiento m dazzle, glare; bewilderment, confusion

deslumbrante adj dazzling; bewildering, confusing

deslumbrar tr to dazzle; to bewilder, confuse

deslustra·do -da adj dull, flat, dingy; (vidrio) ground, frosted

deslustrar tr to tarnish; to dull, dim; (el vidrio) to frost; to discredit || ref to tarnish

deslustre m tarnishing; dulling, dimming; discredit; (del vidrio) frosting

deslustro·so -sa adj ugly, unbecoming

desmadejar tr to enervate, weaken

desmagnetizar §60 tr to demagnetize

desmán m excess, misconduct; misfortune, mishap

desmanchar tr (Chile) to clean of spots

desmanda·do -da adj disobedient, unruly

desmandar tr to cancel, countermand || ref to misbehave; to go away, keep apart; to get out of control

desmanear tr to unfetter, unshackle

desmantela·do -da adj dilapidated

desmantelar tr to dismantle; (naut) to unmast; (naut) to unrig

desmaña f awkwardness, clumsiness

desmaña·do -da adj awkward, clumsy

desmaya·do -da adj faint, languid, weak; unconscious; (color) dull

desmayar tr to depress, discourage || intr to lose heart, be discouraged; to falter || ref to faint

desmayo m depression, discouragement; faint, fainting fit; weeping willow

desmedi·do -da adj excessive; boundless, limitless

desmedir §50 ref to go too far, be impudent

desmedra·do -da adj weak, run-down

desmedrar tr to impair || intr & ref to decline, deteriorate

desmejorar tr to impair, spoil || intr & ref to decline, go into a decline

desmelenar tr to muss, dishevel, rumple

desmembrar §2 tr to dismember

desmemoria f forgetfulness

desmemoria·do -da adj forgetful

desmemoriar ref to become forgetful

desmentida f contradiction; **dar una desmentida a** to give the lie to

desmentir §68 tr to belie, give the lie to; to conceal || intr to be out of line || ref to contradict oneself

desmenudear tr & intr (Col) to sell at retail

desmenuzar §60 tr to crumble; to chop up; to examine in detail; to criticize harshly || ref to crumb, crumble

desmerece·dor -dora adj unworthy

desmerecer §22 tr to be unworthy of || intr to decline in value; **desmerecer de** to compare unfavorably with

desmesura f excess, lack of restraint

desmesura·do -da *adj* excessive, disproportionate; insolent || *mf* insolent person

desmigajar *tr* & *ref* to crumble, break up

desmigar §44 *tr* & *ref* to crumble, crumb

desmilitarizar §60 *tr* to demilitarize

desmirria·do -da *adj* (coll) exhausted, emaciated, run-down

desmochar *tr* (*un árbol*) to top; (*al toro*) to dehorn; (*una obra artística*) to cut

desmodular *tr* to demodulate

desmola·do -da *adj* toothless

desmontable *adj* demountable

desmontar *tr* (*un terreno*) to level; (*un bosque*) to clear; to dismantle, dismount, take apart, knock down; (*las piezas de artillería del enemigo*) to knock out; (*al jinete del caballo*) to unhorse, to throw; (*un arma de fuego*) to uncock || *ref* to dismount, alight

desmoralizar §60 *tr* to demoralize

desmoronadi·zo -za *adj* crumbly

desmoronar *tr* to wear away || *ref* to wear away; to crumble, decline

desmotadera *f* burler; **desmotadera de algodón** cotton gin

desmotar *tr* (*la lana*) to burl; (*el algodón*) to gin

desmovilizar §60 *tr* to demobilize

desmurador *m* mouser

desnatadora *f* cream separator

desnatar *tr* to skim; to remove the slag from; to take the choicest part of

desnaturalizar §60 *tr* to denaturalize; (*el alcohol*) to denature; to alter, pervert

desnivel *m* unevenness; difference of level

desnivelar *tr* to make uneven || *ref* to become uneven

desnudar *tr* to undress; to strip, lay bare; (*la espada*) to draw || *ref* to undress, get undressed; to become evident; **desnudarse de** to get rid of

desnudez *f* nakedness; bareness

desnu·do -da *adj* naked, nude; bare; destitute, penniless || **el desnudo** the nude

desnutrición *f* undernourishment, malnutrition

desnutri·do -da *adj* undernourished

desobedecer *tr* & *intr* to disobey

desobediencia *f* disobedience

desobediente *adj* disobedient

desocupación *f* unemployment; idleness, leisure

desocupa·do -da *adj* unemployed; idle; free, unoccupied, vacant, empty || *mf* unemployed person

desocupar *tr* to empty, vacate || *intr* (*una mujer*) (coll) to be delivered || *ref* to become empty, vacated; to become unemployed, become idle

desodorante *adj* & *m* deodorant

desodorizar §60 *tr* to deodorize

desoír §48 *tr* to not hear, to pretend not to hear

desolación *f* desolation

desola·do -da *adj* desolate, disconsolate

desolar §61 *tr* to desolate, lay waste || *ref* to be desolate, be disconsolate

desoldar §61 *tr* to unsolder || *ref* to come unsoldered

desolla·do -da *adj* (coll) brazen, impudent

desollar §61 *tr* to skin, flay; to harm, hurt; **desollar vivo** (*hacer pagar mucho más de lo justo*) (coll) to fleece, to skin alive; (*murmurar acerbamente de*) (coll) to flay

desopilar *ref* to roar with laughter

desopinar *tr* to defame, discredit

desorbita·do -da *adj* (Am) popeyed; (Am) crazy

desorbitar *ref* to pop wide-open

desorden *m* disorder

desordena·do -da *adj* disorderly, unruly

desordenar *tr* to put out of order || *ref* to get out of order; to be unruly; to go too far

desoreja·do -da *adj* (coll) infamous, degraded; (*que canta mal*) (Peru) off tune; (Cuba) shameless; (Cuba) spendthrift, prodigal; (Guat) stupid; (Chile) without handles

desorganizar §60 *tr* to disorganize

desorientar *tr* to lead astray; to confuse

desovar *intr* to spawn

desove *m* spawning; spawning season

desovillar *tr* to unravel, disentangle; to encourage

desoxidar *tr* to deoxidize; to clean of rust

despabiladeras *fpl* snuffers

despabila·do -da *adj* wide-awake

despabilar *tr* (*una candela*) to snuff, to trim; (*la hacienda*) to dissipate; (*una comida*) to dispatch; (*robar*) to snitch; (*matar*) to dispatch || *ref* to brighten up; to wake up; (Am) to leave, disappear

despacio *adv* slow, slowly; at leisure; (Arg, Chile) in a low voice

despacio·so -sa *adj* slow, easy-going

despachaderas *fpl* (coll) surly reply; (coll) resourcefulness

despacha·do -da *adj* (coll) brazen, impudent; (coll) quick, resourceful

despachante *m* (Arg) clerk; **despachante de aduana** (Arg) customhouse broker

despachar *tr* to send, to ship; to dispatch, expedite; to discharge, dismiss; to decide, settle; to sell; (*a los parroquianos*) to wait on; (*la correspondencia*) to attend to; to hurry; (*matar*) (coll) to dispatch, to kill || *intr* to hurry; to make up one's mind; to work, be employed || *ref* to hurry; (*una mujer*) to be delivered; to speak out

despacho *m* shipping; dispatch, expedition; discharge, dismissal; (*tienda*) store, shop; (*aposento para el estudio*) study; (*aposento para los negocios*) office; (*comunicación por telégrafo o teléfono*) dispatch; (Chile) attic; **despacho de billetes** ticket office; **despacho de localidades** box office; **estar al despacho** to be pending; **tener buen despacho** to be expeditious

despachurrar *tr* to crush, smash, squash; *(dejar sin tener que replicar)* (coll) to squelch; *(lo que uno trata de decir)* (coll) to butcher, murder

despampanante *adj* (coll) stunning, terrific

despampanar *tr (las vides)* to prune, to trim; (coll) to astound || *intr* (coll) to give vent to one's feelings || *ref* to fall and hurt oneself

despancar §73 *tr* to husk *(corn)*

desparejar *tr (dos cosas que forman pareja)* to break, separate *(a pair)*

desparpajar *tr* to tear apart || *intr* (coll) to rant, rave || *ref* (coll) to rant, rave; (CAm, Mex, W-I) to wake up

desparramar *tr* to scatter, spread; *(el agua)* to spill; *(la hacienda)* to squander || *ref* to scatter, spread; to make merry

despartir *tr* to divide, part, separate; to reconcile

despatarrada *f* (coll) split *(in dancing)*; **hacer la despatarrada** (coll) to stretch out on the floor pretending to be ill or injured

despatarrar *tr* to dumbfound || *ref* (coll) to open one's legs wide, to fall down with legs outspread; (coll) to lie motionless; to be dumbfounded

despavorido -da *adj* terrified

despea·do -da *adj* footsore

despear *ref* to get sore feet

despecti·vo -va *adj* contemptuous; (gram) pejorative

despecha·do -da *adj* spiteful, enraged

despechar *tr* to spite, enrage; *(destetar)* (coll) to wean || *ref* to be enraged; to despair, lose hope

despecho *m* spite; despair; (Am) weaning; **a despecho de** despite, in spite of; **por despecho** out of spite

despechugar §44 *tr* to carve the breast of || *ref* (coll) to go with bare breast, to bare one's breast

despedazar §60 *tr* to break to pieces; *(la honra de uno)* to ruin; *(el alma de una persona)* to break || *ref* to break to pieces; **despedazarse de risa** (coll) to split one's sides laughing

despedida *f* farewell, leave-taking; *(de una carta)* close, conclusion; *(copla final)* envoi

despedir §50 *tr* to throw; to emit, send forth; to discharge, dismiss; *(al que sale de la casa)* to see off; *(un mal pensamiento)* to banish; **despedir en la puerta** to see to the door || *ref* to take leave, say good-by; to give up one's job; **despedirse a la francesa** to take French leave; **despedirse de** to take leave of, say good-by to

despega·do -da *adj* (coll) gruff, surly

despegar §44 *tr* to loosen, unglue, unseal; to open; to separate, detach || *intr* (aer) to take off || *ref* to come off; **despegarse con** to be unbecoming to

despego *m* dislike, indifference

despegue *m* (aer) take-off

despeina·do -da *adj* unkempt

despeja·do -da *adj (frente)* wide; *(día,* **cielo)** clear, cloudless; bright, sprightly; *(en el trato)* unconstrained

despejar *tr* to clarify, explain; to free; *(una incógnita)* (math) to find || *ref* to brighten up, cheer up; *(el cielo, el tiempo; una situación difícultosa)* to clear up; *(un borracho)* to sober up

despejo *m* ease, naturalness; talent, intelligence, understanding

despeluzar §60 *tr* to muss the hair of; to make the hair of *(a person)* stand on end || *ref (el pelo)* to stand on end

despeluznante *adj* hair-raising, horrifying

despellejar *tr* to skin, flay; (coll) to slander, malign

despenar *tr* to console; (coll) to kill; (Chile) to deprive of hope

despender *tr* to spend, squander; *(el tiempo)* to waste

despensa *f* pantry; food supplies; day's marketing; stewardship; (naut) storeroom

despensero *m* butler, steward; (naut) storekeeper

despeñade·ro -ra *adj* precipitous || *m* precipice; danger, risk

despeñadi·zo -za *adj* precipitous

despeñar *tr* to hurl, throw, push || *ref* to hurl oneself, jump; to fall headlong; *(en vicios, pecados, pasiones)* to plunge downward

despeño *m* plunge; headlong fall; ruin, failure, collapse; (coll) loose bowels

despepitar *tr* to seed, remove the seeds from || *ref* to rush around madly, to go around screaming; **despepitarse por** (coll) to be mad about

desperdicia·do -da *adj* wasteful, prodigal || *mf* spendthrift, prodigal

desperdiciar *tr* to waste, squander; *(la ocasión de aprovechar una cosa)* to miss, to lose

desperdicio *m* waste, squandering; **desperdicios** waste; waste products; by-products; rubbish; **no tener desperdicio** (coll) to be excellent, to be useful

desperdigar §44 *tr* to separate, scatter

desperecer §22 *ref* to long eagerly

desperezar §60 *ref* to stretch, to stretch one's arms and legs

desperfecto *m* blemish, flaw, imperfection

desperna·do -da *adj* footsore, weary

desperta·dor -dora *mf* awakener || *m* alarm clock; warning

despertar §2 *tr* to awaken; to arouse, stir || *intr & ref* to awaken, wake up

despestañar *tr* to pluck the eyelashes of || *ref* to look hard, strain one's eyes

despiada·do -da *adj* cruel, pitiless

despichar *tr* to squeeze dry; (Col, Chile) to crush, flatten || *intr* (coll) to croak, die

despidiente *m* stick placed between a hanging scaffold and wall; **despidiente de agua** flashing

despido *m* layoff, discharge

despier·to -ta *adj* wide-awake, alert; **soñar despierto** to daydream

despilfarra·do -da *adj* wasteful; ragged || *mf* prodigal; raggedy person

despilfarrar *tr* to squander, waste ‖ *ref* (coll) to spend recklessly

despilfarro *m* squandering, waste, extravagance; slovenliness

despintar *tr* to remove the paint from; to disfigure, distort, spoil; **no despintarle a uno los ojos** to not take one's eyes from a person ‖ *intr* to decline, slip back; **despintar de** to be unworthy of ‖ *ref* to fade, wash off; **no despintársele a uno** (coll) to not fade from one's memory

despiojar *tr* to delouse; (coll) to free from poverty

despique *m* revenge

despistar *tr* to outwit, to throw off the track ‖ *ref* to run off the track, run off the road

desplacer *m* displeasure ‖ §22 *tr* to displease

desplantar *tr* to uproot; to throw out of plumb ‖ *ref* to get out of plumb; to lose one's upright posture

desplaya-do -da *adj* broad, open, wide ‖ *m* (Arg) wide sandy beach

desplayar *tr* to widen, spread out ‖ *ref* (*el mar*) to recede from the beach

desplaza-do -da *adj* displaced ‖ *mf* displaced person

desplazar §60 *tr* (*cierto peso de agua*) to displace; to move, to transport ‖ *ref* to move

desplegar §66 *tr* to unfold, spread; to display; to explain; (mil) to deploy ‖ *ref* to unfold, spread out; (mil) to deploy

despliegue *m* unfolding, spreading out; display; (mil) deployment

desplomar *tr* to throw out of plumb ‖ *ref* to get out of plumb; to collapse, tumble; to fall down in a faint; (*un trono*) to crumble; (aer) to pancake

desplome *m* leaning; collapse, tumbling; falling in a faint; downfall; (aer) pancaking

desplumar *tr* to pluck; (*dejar sin dinero*) (coll) to fleece ‖ *ref* to molt

despoblado *m* wilderness, deserted spot

despoblar §61 *tr* to depopulate; to lay waste; to clear, lay bare

despojar *tr* to strip, despoil, divest; to dispossess ‖ *ref* to undress; **despojarse de** to divest oneself of; (*ropa*) to take off

despojo *m* dispoilment; dispossession; booty, plunder, spoils; prey, victim; **despojos** scraps, leavings; mortal remains; second-hand building materials

despolarizar §60 *tr* to depolarize

despolvar *tr* to dust

despolvorear *tr* to dust, dust off; to scatter

desportillar *tr* to chip, nick ‖ *ref* to chip, chip off

desposa-do -da *adj* handcuffed; newly married ‖ *mf* newlywed

desposar *tr* to marry ‖ *ref* to be betrothed, get engaged; to get married

desposeer §43 *tr* to dispossess ‖ *ref* — **desposeerse de** to divest oneself of

desposorios *mpl* betrothal, engagement; marriage, nuptials

déspota *m* despot

despóti-co -ca *adj* despotic

despotismo *m* despotism

despotricar §73 *intr* & *ref* to rave, rant

despreciable *adj* contemptible, despicable

despreciar *tr* to scorn, despise; to slight, snub; to overlook, forgive; to reject ‖ *ref* — **despreciarse de** to not deign to

despreciati-vo -va *adj* contemptuous, scornful

desprecio *m* scorn, contempt; slight, snub

desprender *tr* to loosen, unfasten, detach; to emit, give off; (chem) to liberate ‖ *ref* to come loose, to come off; to issue, come forth; **desprenderse de** to give up, part with; to be deduced from

desprendi-do -da *adj* generous, disinterested

desprendimiento *m* loosening, detachment; emission, liberation; generosity, disinterestedness; landslide; (chem) liberation

despreocupación *f* relaxation; impartiality

despreocupa-do -da *adj* relaxed, unconcerned; impartial; indifferent

despreocupante *adj* relaxing

despreocupar *ref* to relax; **despreocuparse de** to forget about, be unconcerned about

desprestigiar *tr* to disparage, run down ‖ *ref* to lose caste, lose one's standing, to lose face

desprestigio *m* disparagement; loss of standing, discredit

despreveni-do -da *adj* off one's guard; **coger a uno desprevenido** to catch someone unawares

desproporciona-do -da *adj* disproportionate

despropósito *m* absurdity, nonsense

desproveer §43 & §83 *tr* to deprive

desprovis-to -ta *adj* destitute; **desprovisto de** lacking, devoid of

después *adv* after, afterwards; **después de** after; **después (de) que** after

despulli-do -da *adj* ground (*glass*)

despumar *tr* to skim

despuntar *tr* to dull, blunt; (*un cabo o punta*) (naut) to double, round ‖ *intr* to begin to sprout; (*empezar a amanecer*) to dawn; to stand out ‖ *ref* to get dull

desquiciar *tr* to unhinge; to shake loose, upset; to unsettle, perturb; to overthrow, undermine

desquitar *tr* to recover, retrieve; to compensate ‖ *ref* to retrieve a loss; to get revenge, get even

desquite *m* recovery, retrieval; retaliation, revenge; (sport) return match

desrazonable *adj* unreasonable

desrielar *intr* (Am) to jump the track

destaca-do -da *adj* outstanding, distinguished

destacamiento *m* (mil) detachment; (mil) detail

destacar §73 *tr* to highlight, point up; to emphasize; to make stand out;

(mil) to detach; (mil) to detail ‖ *intr* to stand out, be conspicuous ‖ *ref* to stand out, to project; (fig) to stand out

destajar *tr* to arrange for, establish the terms for; (*la baraja*) to cut; (Am) to carve up

destaje·ro -ra or **destajista** *mf* piece-worker, jobber; free lance

destajo *m* piecework; job, contract; **a destajo** by the piece, by the job; free-lancing; **hablar a destajo** (coll) to talk too much

destapar *tr* to open, uncover, take the lid off; to uncork, unplug; to reveal ‖ *ref* to get uncovered; to throw off the covers; to unbosom oneself

destaponar *tr* to uncork, unplug; (*una botella; las fosas nasales*) to unstop

destartala·do -da *adj* tumble-down, ramshackle

destazar §60 *tr* to carve up

destechar *tr* to unroof

destejar *tr* to remove the tiles from; to leave unprotected

destejer *tr* to unbraid, unknit, unweave; to upset, disturb

destellar *tr* & *intr* to flash

destello *m* flash, beam, sparkle

destempla·do -da *adj* disagreeable, unpleasant; inharmonious, out of tune; indisposed; (*clima; pulso*) irregular

destemplanza *f* unpleasantness; discord; indisposition; (*del pulso*) irregularity; (*del tiempo*) inclemency; excess

destemple *m* dissonance; indisposition; disorder, disturbance

desteñir §72 *tr* to discolor ‖ *intr* & *ref* to fade

desternillante *adj* sidesplitting

desternillar *ref* — **desternillarse de risa** to split one's sides with laughter

desterra·do -da *adj* exiled ‖ *mf* exile

desterrar §2 *tr* to exile, to banish; (fig) to banish

destetar *tr* to wean ‖ *ref* — **destetarse con** to have known since childhood

destete *m* weaning

destiempo *m* — **a destiempo** untimely

destiento *m* surprise, shock

destierro *m* exile; backwoods

destilación *f* distillation

destiladera *f* still; scheme, stratagem

destilar *tr* to distill; to filter; to exude ‖ *intr* to drip

destilatorio *m* distillery; (*alambique*) still

destilería *f* distillery

destinación *f* destination

destinar *tr* to destine; to assign, designate

destinata·rio -ria *mf* addressee; consignee; (*de homenaje, aplausos*) recipient

destino *m* (*lugar a donde va una persona o una remesa*) destination; (*suerte, encadenamiento fatal de los sucesos*) fate, destiny; employment; place of employment; **con destino a** bound for

destituir §20 *tr* to deprive; to dismiss, discharge

destorcer §74 *tr* to untwist, straighten ‖

ref to become untwisted; (naut) to drift

destornilla·do -da *adj* rash, reckless, out of one's head

destornillador *m* screwdriver

destornillar *tr* to unscrew ‖ *ref* to lose one's head, go berserk

destoser *ref* to cough (*artificially, to attract attention*)

destrabar *tr* to loosen, untie, detach

destraillar §4 *tr* to unleash

destral *m* hatchet

destreza *f* skill, dexterity

destripacuen·tos *m* (*pl* **-tos**) (coll) butter-in

destripar *tr* to disembowel, to gut; to crush, mangle; (coll) to spoil (*a story by telling its outcome*)

destripaterro·nes *m* (*pl* **-nes**) (coll) clod-hopper

destriunfar *tr* to force to play trump

destrocar §81 *tr* to swap back again

destronar *tr* to dethrone; to overthrow

destroncar §73 *tr* to chop down; to chop off; to ruin; to exhaust, wear out

destrozar §60 *tr* to shatter, break to pieces; to destroy; to squander; (*al ejército enemigo*) to wipe out

destrozo *m* havoc, destruction; rout, annihilation, defeat

destrucción *f* destruction

destructi·vo -va *adj* destructive

destructor *m* (nav) destroyer

destruir §20 *tr* to destroy ‖ *ref* (alg) to cancel each other

desuellaca·ras *m* (*pl* **-ras**) (coll) sloppy barber; (coll) scoundrel

desuello *m* skinning, flaying; shamelessness; (*precio excesivo*) (coll) highway robbery

desuncir §36 *tr* to unyoke

desunir *tr* to disunite; to take apart ‖ *ref* to disunite; to come apart

desusa·do -da *adj* obsolete, out of use; uncommon, unusual; **estar desusado** (*perder la práctica*) to be rusty

desuso *m* disuse; **caído en desuso** obsolete

desvaí·do -da *adj* lank, ungainly; (*color*) dull

desvainar *tr* to shell

desvali·do -da *adj* helpless, destitute

desvalijar *tr* (*una valija, baúl, etc.*) to rifle; to rob, wipe out

desvalorar *tr* to devalue

desvalorizar §60 *tr* to devalue

desván *m* garret, loft

desvanecedor *m* (phot) mask

desvanecer §22 *tr* to dispel, dissipate; (*una conspiración*) to break up; (*la sospecha*) to banish; (phot) to mask ‖ *ref* to disappear, vanish, evanesce; to evaporate; to faint, faint away, swoon; (rad) to fade

desvanecimiento *m* disappearance, evanescence; dissipation; pride, vanity; faintness, fainting spell; (phot) masking; (rad) fading, fadeout

desvaria·do -da *adj* delirious, raving

desvariar §77 *intr* to be delirious, to rave, to rant

desvarío *m* delirium, raving; absurdity,

nonsense, extravagance; whim, caprice; inconstancy

desvela•do -da *adj* wakeful, sleepless; watchful, vigilant; anxious, worried

desvelar *tr* to keep awake, not let sleep || *ref* to keep awake, go without sleep; to be watchful, be vigilant; **desvelarse por** to be anxious about, be worried about

desvelo *m* wakefulness, sleeplessness; watchfulness, vigilance; anxiety, worry, concern

desvenar *tr* to strip (*tobacco*)

desvencija•do -da *adj* rickety, ramshackle

desvencijar *tr* to break, tear apart || *ref* to go to rack and ruin

desvendar *tr* to unbandage, to undress

desventaja *f* disadvantage

desventajo•so -sa *adj* disadvantageous

desventura *f* misfortune

desventura•do -da *adj* unfortunate; faint-hearted; stingy

desvergonza•do -da *adj* shameless, impudent

desvergüenza *f* shamelessness, impudence

desvestir §50 *tr* & *ref* to undress

desviación *f* deviation, deflection; detour; (rad, telv) drift

desviacionismo *m* deviationism

desviacionista *mf* deviationist

desviadero *m* (rr) siding, turnout

desvia•do -da *adj* devious

desviar §77 *tr* to deviate, deflect; to turn aside; to dissuade; to parry, ward off; (rr) to switch || *ref* to deviate, deflect; to turn aside; to branch off; to be dissuaded

desvío *m* deviation, deflection; coldness, indifference; detour; (rr) siding, sidetrack

desvirgar §44 *tr* to deflower, ravish

desvirtuar §21 *tr* to weaken, spoil, impair

desvivir *ref* — **desvivirse por** to be crazy about; **desvivirse por** + *inf* to be eager to + *inf*, to do one's best to + *inf*

desvolvedor *m* wrench

desvolver §47 & **§83** *tr* to alter, change; (*la tierra*) to turn up; (*una tuerca o tornillo*) to loosen, unscrew

detall *m* — **al detall** at retail

detalladamente *adv* in detail

detallar *tr* to detail, tell in detail; to retail, sell at retail

detalle *m* detail; (Am) retail; **ahí está el detalle** that's the point

detallista *mf* retailer; person fond of details

detección *f* detection

detectar *tr* to detect

detective *m* detective

detector *m* detector; **detector de mentiras** lie detector

detención *f* detention, detainment; delay; care, thoroughness

detener §71 *tr* to detain; to stop; to arrest; to keep, retain; (*el aliento*) to hold || *ref* to stop; to linger, tarry

detenidamente *adv* carefully, thoroughly

deteni•do -da *adj* careful, thorough;

hesitant, timid; stingy, mean || *mf* person held in custody

detenimiento *m* var of **detención**

detergente *adj* & *m* detergent

deteriorar *tr* & *ref* to deteriorate

deterioro *m* deterioration

determinación *f* determination; decision

determina•do -da *adj* determined, resolute; (*artículo*) (gram) definite

determinar *tr* to determine; to cause, to bring about || *ref* to decide

detestar *tr* to detest; to curse; **detestar** + *inf* to hate to + *inf*

detonar *intr* to detonate

detraer §75 *tr* to withdraw, take away, detract; to defame, vilify

detrás *adv* behind; **detrás de** behind, back of; **por detrás** behind; behind one's back; **por detrás de** behind the back of

detrimento *m* harm, detriment

deuda *f* debt; indebtedness

deu•do -da *mf* relative || *m* kinship || *f* see **deuda**

deu•dor -dora *adj* indebted || *mf* debtor; **deudor hipotecario** mortgagor; **deudor moroso** delinquent (*in payment*)

devalar *intr* (naut) to drift from the course

devaluación *f* devaluation

devanar *tr* to wind, to roll; (*un cuento*) to unfold || *ref* (CAm, Mex, W-I) to roll with laughter; (CAm, Mex, W-I) to writhe in pain

devanear *intr* to talk nonsense; to loaf around

devaneo *m* nonsense; loafing; flirtation

devastación *f* devastation

devastar *tr* to devastate

develar *tr* to reveal; (*p.ej., una estatua*) to unveil

devengar §44 *tr* (*salarios*) to earn; (*intereses*) to draw, to earn

devoción *f* devotion

devolución *f* return, restitution

devolver §47 & **§83** *tr* to return, give back, send back; to pay back; (coll) to vomit || *ref* (Am) to return, come back

devorar *tr* to devour

devo•to -ta *adj* devout; devoted; devotional || *mf* devotee; devout person || *m* object of worship

D.F. *abbr* **Distrito Federal**

d/f *abbr* **días fecha**

dho. *abbr* **dicho**

día *m* day; daytime; daylight; **al día** per day; up to date; **al otro día** on the following day; **buenos días** good morning; **dar los días a** to wish (*someone*) many happy returns of the day; **de día** in the daytime, in the daylight; **día de años** birthday; **día de ayuno** fast day; **día de carne** meat day; **día de engañabobos** December 28th, day when practical jokes are played on unsuspecting people; **día de inauguración** (fa) private view; **día de la raza** Columbus Day; **día del juicio** judgment day; **día de los caídos** Memorial Day; **día de los difuntos**

All Souls' Day; **día de ramos** Palm Sunday; **día de Reyes** Epiphany; **día de todos los santos** All Saints' Day; **día de trabajo** workday; weekday; **día de vigilia** fast day; **día festivo** holiday; **día laborable** workday, weekday; **día lectivo** school day; **día puente** day off between two holidays; **el día de Año Nuevo** New Year's Day; **el día menos pensado** (coll) when least expected; **el mejor día** some fine day; **en cuatro días** in a few days; **en pleno día** in broad daylight; **en su día** in due time; **ocho días** a week; **poner al día** to bring up to date; **quince días** two weeks, a fortnight; **tener sus días** to be up in years; **un día sí y otro no** every other day; **vivir al día** to live from hand to mouth

diabetes f diabetes
diabéti·co -ca adj & mf diabetic
diablillo m imp
diablo m devil; (Chile) ox-drawn log drag; **ahí será el diablo** (coll) there will be the devil to pay; **diablo cojuelo** tricky devil; **diablos azules** (Am) delirium tremens
diablura f devilment, deviltry, mischief
diabóli·co -ca adj devilish, diabolical
diaconisa f deaconess
diácono m deacon
diacríti·co -ca adj diacritical
diadema f diadem; (adorno femenino) tiara
diáfa·no -na adj diaphanous
diafragma m diaphragm
diagno·sis f (pl -sis) diagnosis
diagnosticar §73 tr to diagnose
diagonal adj diagonal || f diagonal, bias
diagrama m diagram
dialecto m dialect
diálogo m dialogue
diamante m diamond
diametral or **diamétri·co -ca** adj diametrical
diámetro m diameter
diana f bull's-eye; (mil) reveille; **hacer diana** to hit the bull's-eye
diantre m (coll) devil || interj (coll) the devil!, the deuce!
diapasón m tuning fork; pitch pipe; (p.ej., del violín) finger board; **bajar el diapasón** (coll) to lower one's voice, to change one's tune
diapositiva f slide, lantern slide
dia·rio -ria adj daily || m diary; daily, daily paper; **diario hablado** newscast
diarismo m (Am) journalism
diarrea f diarrhea
diástole f diastole
diatermia f diathermy
dibujante mf sketcher, illustrator || m draftsman
dibujar tr to draw, sketch, design; to outline || ref to be outlined; to appear, show
dibujo m drawing, sketch, design; outline; **dibujo al carbón** charcoal drawing; **dibujo animado** animated cartoon; **no meterse en dibujos** (coll) to attend to one's business
di·caz adj (pl -caces) sarcastic, witty

dicción f diction; word
diccionario m dictionary
diciembre m December
dicloruro m dichloride
dicotomía f dichotomy; (entre médicos) split fee
dictado m dictation; **escribir al dictado** to take dictation; (lo que otro dicta) to take down
dictador m dictator
dictadura f dictatorship
dictáfono m dictaphone
dictamen m dictum, judgment, opinion
dictar tr to dictate; (una ley) to promulgate; to inspire, suggest; (una conferencia) (Am) to give, deliver (a lecture)
dicterio m taunt, insult
dicha f happiness; luck; **por dicha** by chance
dicharache·ro -ra adj (coll) obscene, vulgar
dicharacho m (coll) obscenity, vulgarity; (coll) wisecrack
di·cho -cha adj said; **dicho y hecho** no sooner said than done; **mejor dicho** rather; **tener por dicho** to consider settled || m saying; promise of marriage, one's word; witticism; (coll) insult; **dicho de las gentes** (coll) talk, hearsay, gossip || f see **dicha**
dicho·so -sa adj happy; lucky, fortunate; annoying, tiresome
didácti·co -ca adj didactic
diecinueve adj & pron nineteen || m nineteen; (en las fechas) nineteenth
diecinueveavo -va adj & m nineteenth
dieciocha·vo -va adj & m eighteenth
dieciocho adj & pron eighteen || m eighteen; (en las fechas) eighteenth
dieciséis adj & pron sixteen || m sixteen; (en las fechas) sixteenth
dieciseisa·vo -va adj & m sixteenth
diecisiete adj & pron seventeen || m seventeen; (en las fechas) seventeenth
diecisietea·vo -va adj & m seventeenth
diente m tooth; (de elefante y otros animales) tusk, fang; (de peine, sierra, rastrillo) tooth; (de rueda dentada) cog; **dar diente con diente** (coll) to shake all over; **decir entre dientes** (coll) to mutter, to mumble; **diente canino** eyetooth, canine tooth; **diente de león** dandelion; **estar a diente** (coll) to be famished; **tener buen diente** (coll) to be a hearty eater; **traer entre dientes** (coll) to have a grudge against; (coll) to talk about
diére·sis f (pl -sis) diaeresis; (señal que indica la metafonía) umlaut
dies·tro -tra adj right; handy, skillful; shrewd, sly; favorable; **a diestro y siniestro** wildly, right and left || m expert fencer; bullfighter on foot; matador; halter, bridle || f right hand; **juntar diestra con diestra** to join forces
dieta f diet; **dietas** per diem; **estar a dieta** to diet, be on a diet
dietario m family budget
dietista mf dietitian

diez *adj & pron* ten; **las diez** ten o'clock || *m* ten; (*en las fechas*) tenth
diezmar *tr* (*causar gran mortandad en*) to decimate; (*pagar el diezmo de*) to tithe
diezmo *m* tithe
difamación *f* defamation, vilification
difamar *tr* to defame, to vilify
diferencia *f* difference; **a diferencia de** unlike; **partir la diferencia** to split the difference
diferenciar *tr* to differentiate || *intr* (*discordar*) to differ, dissent || *ref* (*distinguirse una cosa de otra*) to differ, be different
diferente *adj* different
diferir §68 *tr* to defer, postpone, put off || *intr* to differ, be different
difícil *adj* difficult; hard; hard to please
difícilmente *adv* with difficulty
dificultad *f* difficulty; (*reparo que se opone a una opinión*) objection
dificultar *tr* to make difficult; to consider difficult || *intr* to raise objections || *ref* to become difficult
dificultoso -**sa** *adj* difficult, troublesome; objecting; (coll) ugly, homely
difidencia *f* distrust
difidente *adj* distrustful
difteria *f* diphtheria
difundir *tr* to diffuse; to spread, disseminate; to divulge, publish; to broadcast || *ref* to diffuse; to spread
difunto -**ta** *adj & mf* deceased; **difunto de taberna** dead-drunk || *m* corpse
difuso -**sa** *adj* diffuse; extended; wordy
digerible *adj* digestible
digerir §68 *tr* to digest; **no digerir** to not bear, to not stand || *intr* to digest
digestible *adj* digestible
digestión *f* digestion
digestivo -**va** *adj & m* digestive
digesto *m* (law) digest
dígito *m* digit
dignación *f* condescension
dignar *ref* to deign, to condescend
dignatario *m* dignitary, official
dignidad *f* dignity; bishop, archbishop
dignificar §73 *tr* to dignify
digno -**na** *adj* worthy; fitting, suitable; (*grave, decoroso*) dignified
digresión *f* digression
dije *m* amulet, charm, trinket; (*persona de excelentes cualidades*) (coll) jewel; (coll) person all dressed-up; (coll) handy person
dilacerar *tr* to tear to pieces; (*la honra, el orgullo*) to damage
dilación *f* delay
dilapidar *tr* to squander
dilatación *f* expansion; serenity
dilatar *tr* to dilate, expand; to defer, postpone; (*p.ej., la fama*) to spread || *ref* to dilate, expand; to spread; to be wordy; (Am) to delay
dilección *f* true love
dilecto -**ta** *adj* dearly beloved
dilema *m* dilemma
diletante *adj & mf* dilettante
diligencia *f* diligence; step, démarche; errand; dispatch, speed; stagecoach; **hacer una diligencia** to do an errand; (coll) to have a bowel movement

diligente *adj* diligent; quick, ready
dilucidar *tr* to elucidate, explain
dilución *f* dilution
diluido -**da** *adj* dilute
diluir §20 *tr* to dilute; to thin || *ref* to dilute; to melt; to dissolve
diluviar *intr* to rain hard, to pour
diluvio *m* deluge
dimanar *intr* to spring up; **dimanar de** to spring from, originate in
dimensión *f* dimension
dimes *mpl* — **andar en dimes y diretes con** (coll) to bicker with
diminutivo -**va** *adj & m* (gram) diminutive
diminuto -**ta** *adj* tiny, diminutive; defective
dimisión *f* resignation
dimisorias *fpl* — **dar dimisorias a** (coll) to discharge, to fire
dimitir *tr* to resign, resign from || *intr* to resign
din *m* (coll) dough, money
Dinamarca *f* Denmark
dinamarqués -**quesa** *adj* Danish || *mf* Dane || *m* Danish (*language*)
dinámico -**ca** *adj* dynamic
dinamita *f* dynamite
dinamitar *tr* to dynamite
dínamo *f* dynamo
dinasta *m* dynast
dinastía *f* dynasty
dindán *m* ding-dong
dinerada *f* or **dineral** *m* large sum of money
dinero *m* money; currency; wealth; **dinero contante** cash; **dinero contante y sonante** ready cash, spot cash; **dinero de bolsillo** pocket money
dineroso -**sa** *adj* moneyed, wealthy
dintel *m* lintel, doorhead
diócesi *f* or **diócesis** *f* (*pl* -**sis**) diocese
diodo *m* diode
dios *m* god; **Dios mediante** God willing; **¡por Dios!** goodness!, for heaven's sake; **¡válgame Dios!** bless me!; **¡vaya con Dios!** off with you!
diosa *f* goddess
diploma *m* diploma
diplomacia *f* diplomacy
diplomado -**da** *adj & mf* graduate
diplomar *tr & ref* (Am) to graduate
diplomático -**ca** *adj* diplomatic || *mf* diplomat
diptongar §44 *tr & ref* to diphthongize
diptongo *m* diphthong
diputación *f* congress; commission
diputado -**da** *mf* deputy, representative
diputar *tr* to commission, delegate; to designate
dique *m* dike, jetty; dry dock; check, stop; **dique seco** dry dock
dirección *f* direction; (*señas en una carta*) address; administration, management; directorship; (aut) steering; **de dirección única** one-way; **dirección a la derecha** right-hand drive; **dirección a la izquierda** left-hand drive; **perder la dirección** to lose control of the car
directivo -**va** *adj* managing || *mf* director, manager || *f* management
directo -**ta** *adj* direct; straight

direc·tor -tora *adj* directing, guiding; managing, governing || *mf* director, manager; (*de un periódico*) editor; (*de una escuela*) principal; (*de una orquesta*) conductor; **director de escena** stage manager; **director de funeraria** funeral director; **director gerente** managing director

directorio *m* directorship; directory

dirigente *mf* leader, head, executive

dirigible *adj & m* dirigible

dirigir §27 *tr* to direct; to manage; (*un automóvil*) to steer; (*una carta; la palabra*) to address; (*una obra*) to dedicate || *ref* to go, to betake oneself; to turn; **dirigirse a** to address; to apply to

dirimir *tr* to dissolve, annul; (*una dificultad*) to solve; (*una controversia*) to settle, mediate

discar §73 *tr & intr* to dial

disceptar *intr* to discuss, debate

discerniente *adj* discerning

discernir §28 *tr* to discern; to distinguish

disciplina *f* discipline; **disciplinas** scourge, whip

disciplina·do -da *adj* disciplined; (*flores*) many-colored

disciplinar *tr* to discipline; to teach; to scourge, whip

disciplinazo *m* lash

discípu·lo -la *mf* disciple; pupil

disco *m* disk; (*del gramófono*) record, disk; (sport) discus; **disco de cola** (rr) taillight; **disco de goma** (*para un grifo*) washer (*for a spigot*); **disco de identificación** identification tag; **disco de larga duración** long-playing record; **disco de señales** (rr) semaphore; **disco selector** (telp) dial; **siempre el mismo disco** (coll) the same old song

discóbolo *m* discus thrower

discófi·lo -la *mf* record lover, discophile

disco·lo -la *adj* ungovernable, wayward

disconforme *adj* disagreeing

discontinuar §21 *tr* to discontinue

discordancia *f* discordance

discordar §61 *intr* to be out of tune; to disagree

discorde *adj* discordant, disagreeing; (mus) discordant, out of tune

discordia *f* discord

discoteca *f* record cabinet; record library

discreción *f* discretion; wit; witticism; **a discreción** at discretion; (mil) unconditionally

discrepancia *f* discrepancy; dissent

discrepar *intr* to differ, to disagree

discretear *intr* to try to be clever, to try to sparkle

discre·to -ta *adj* (*juicioso*) discreet; (*discontinuo*) discrete; witty

discrimen *m* risk, hazard; difference

discriminación *f* discrimination

discriminar *tr* to discriminate against || *intr* to discriminate

discriminato·rio -ria *adj* discriminatory

disculpa *f* excuse, apology

disculpar *tr* to excuse; (coll) to pardon, overlook || *ref* to apologize; **disculparse con** to apologize to; **disculparse de** to apologize for

discurrir *tr* to contrive, invent; to guess, conjecture || *intr* to ramble, roam; to occur, take place; to discourse; to reason; to pass, elapse

discursi·vo -va *adj* meditative

discurso *m* discourse, speech; (*paso del tiempo*) course; **discurso de sobremesa** after-dinner speech

discusión *f* discussion

discutible *adj* debatable

discutir *tr* to discuss || *intr* to discuss; to argue

disecar §73 *tr* to dissect; (*un animal muerto*) to stuff; (*una planta*) to mount

diseminar *tr* to disseminate; to scatter || *ref* to scatter

disensión *f* (*oposición*) dissent; (*contienda*) dissension

disentería *f* dysentery

disentir §68 *intr* to dissent

diseñar *tr* to draw, sketch; to design, outline

diseño *m* drawing, sketch; design, outline

disertar *intr* to discourse, discuss

diser·to -ta *adj* fluent, eloquent

disfavor *m* disfavor

disforme *adj* formless; monstrous, ugly

disforzar §35 *ref* (Peru) to be prudish, be finical

dis·fraz *m* (*pl* -**fraces**) disguise; (*traje de máscara*) costume, fancy dress

disfrazar §60 *tr* to disguise || *ref* to disguise oneself; to wear fancy dress, to masquerade, to dress in costume

disfrutar *tr* to enjoy, to use || *intr* — **disfrutar de** to enjoy, to use; **disfrutar con** to enjoy, take enjoyment in

disfrute *m* enjoyment, use

disgregar §44 *tr & intr* to disintegrate, break up

disgusta·do -da *adj* tasteless, insipid; sad, sorrowful; disagreeable; (Mex) hard to please

disgustar *tr* to displease || *ref* to be displeased; to fall out, become estranged

disgusto *m* displeasure; annoyance, unpleasantness; grief, sorrow; difference, quarrel; **a disgusto** against one's will

disidencia *f* dissidence; (*de una doctrina*) dissent

disidente *adj* dissident || *mf* dissident, dissenter

disidir *intr* to dissent

disíla·bo -ba *adj* dissyllabic || *m* dissyllable

disímil *adj* dissimilar

disimilar *tr & ref* to dissimilate

disimula·do -da *adj* sly, underhanded; **a lo disimulado** or **a la disimulada** underhandedly; **hacer la disimulada** (coll) to feign ignorance

disimular *tr* to dissemble, dissimulate, hide, conceal; to overlook, pardon || *intr* to dissemble, dissimulate

disimulo *m* dissembling, dissimulation; indulgence

disipación *f* dissipation

disipa·do -da *adj* dissipated; spendthrift || *mf* debauchee; spendthrift

disipar *tr* to dissipate || *ref* to be dissipated; to disappear, evanesce

dislate *m* nonsense

dislocar §73 *tr* to dislocate || *ref* to dislocate; to be dislocated

disloque *m* (coll) tops, top notch

disminuir §20 *tr, intr & ref* to diminish

disociar *tr* to dissociate

disolución *f* dissolution; disbandment; (*relajación de costumbres*) dissoluteness, dissipation

disolu·to -ta *adj* dissolute || *mf* debauchee

disolver §47 & §83 *tr* to dissolve; to disband; to destroy, ruin || *intr & ref* to dissolve

disonancia *f* dissonance

disonar §61 *intr* to be dissonant, lack harmony, disagree; to cause surprise; to sound bad

dispar *adj* unlike, different; (*que no hace juego*) odd

disparada *f* (Am) sudden flight; **a la disparada** (Am) like a shot, in mad haste; **de una disparada** (Arg) right away; **tomar la disparada** (Arg) to take to one's heels

disparadero *m* trigger

disparador *m* trigger; (*de reloj*) escapement; **poner en el disparador** (coll) to drive mad

disparar *tr* to throw, hurl; to shoot, to fire || *intr* to rant, talk nonsense || *ref* to dash away, rush away; (*un caballo*) to run away; (*una escopeta*) to go off; to be beside oneself

disparata·do -da *adj* absurd, nonsensical; frightful

disparatar *intr* to talk nonsense; to act foolishly

disparate *m* folly, nonsense; blunder, mistake; (coll) outrage

dispare·jo -ja *adj* unequal, different, uneven, disparate; rough, broken

disparidad *f* disparity

disparo *m* shot, discharge; nonsense; (mach) release, trip; **cambiar disparos** to exchange shots

dispendio *m* waste, extravagance

dispendio·so -sa *adj* expensive

dispensar *tr* to excuse, to pardon; to exempt; to dispense; to dispense with

dispensario *m* dispensary; **dispensario de alimentos** soup kitchen

dispepsia *f* dyspepsia

dispersar *tr & ref* to disperse

displicente *adj* disagreeable; cross, fretful, peevish

disponer §54 *tr* to dispose, arrange; to direct, order || *intr* to dispose; **disponer de** to dispose of, have at one's disposal || *ref* to prepare, get ready; to get ready to die, make one's will

disponible *adj* available, disposable

disposición *f* disposition, arrangement, layout; inclination; preparation; disposal; predisposition; state of health; elegance; **estar a la disposición de** to be at the disposal of, be at the service

of; **última disposición** last will and testament

dispositivo *m* appliance, device

dispues·to -ta *adj* ready, prepared; comely, graceful; clever, skillful; **bien dispuesto** well-disposed; well, in good health; **mal dispuesto** ill-disposed, unfavorable; ill, indisposed

disputa *f* dispute; fight, struggle; **sin disputa** beyond dispute

disputar *tr* to dispute, to question; to argue over; to fight for || *intr* to dispute; to debate, to argue; to fight

disquero -ra *mf* record dealer

distancia *f* distance; **a distancia** at a distance; **a larga distancia** long-distance; **tomar distancia** to stand aside, to stand off

distante *adj* distant

distar *intr* to be distant, be far; to be different

distender §51 *tr* to distend; (*p.ej., las piernas*) to stretch || *ref* to distend; to relax; (*un reloj*) to run down

distensión *f* distension; relaxation of tension

distinción *f* (*honor, prerrogativa*) distinction; (*diferencia*) distinctness; **a distinción de** unlike

distingui·do -da *adj* distinguished; refined, urbane, smooth

distinguir §29 *tr* to distinguish; to give distinction to; to make out

distinti·vo -va *adj* distinctive || *m* badge, insignia; distinction; distinctive mark

distin·to -ta *adj* distinct; different; **distintos** various, several

distorsión *f* distortion

distracción *f* distraction; (*licencia en las costumbres*) dissipation; (*substracción de fondos*) embezzlement

distraer §73 *tr* to distract; to amuse, divert, entertain; to seduce; to embezzle

distraí·do -da *adj* absent-minded, distracted; licentious, dissolute; (Chile, Mex) untidy, careless

distribución *f* distribution; electric supply system; timing gears, valve gears

distribui·dor -dora *adj* distributing || *mf* distributor || *m* (aut) distributor; slide valve; **distribuidor automático** vending machine

distribuir §20 *tr* to distribute

distrito *m* district; (rr) section; **distrito electoral** precinct; **distrito postal** zone, postal zone

disturbar *tr* to disturb

disturbio *m* disturbance

disuadir *tr* to dissuade

disyunti·vo -va *adj* disjunctive || *f* dilemma

disyuntor *m* circuit breaker

dita *f* bond, surety

diuca *m* (Arg, Chile) teacher's pet || *f* (Arg, Chile) finch (*Fringilla diuca*)

diur·no -na *adj* day, daytime

diva *f* goddess; (mus) diva

divagación *f* digression; wandering

divagar §44 *intr* to digress; to ramble, wander

diván *m* divan

divergir §27 *intr* to diverge
diversidad *f* diversity; abundance
diversificación *f* diversification
diversificar §73 *tr & ref* to diversify
diversión *f* diversion
diver·so -sa *adj* diverse, different; diversos several, various, divers
diverti·do -da *adj* amusing, funny; (Am) tipsy
divertimiento *m* diversion, amusement
divertir §68 *tr* to divert; to amuse ‖ *ref* to enjoy oneself, have a good time
dividendo *m* dividend
dividir *tr* to divide ‖ *ref* to divide, be divided; to separate
divieso *m* boil
divinidad *f* divinity; (*persona dotada de gran belleza*) beauty
divinizar §60 *tr* to deify; to exalt, extol
divi·no -na *adj* divine
divisa *f* badge; emblem; motto; goal, ideal; currency, foreign exchange
divisar *tr* to descry, espy
división *f* division
divisor *m* (math) divisor; **máximo común divisor** greatest common divisor; **divisor de voltaje** (rad) voltage divider
divisoria *f* dividing line; (geog) divide
di·vo -va *adj* godlike, divine ‖ *m* god; (mus) opera star ‖ *f* see **diva**
divorciar *tr* to divorce ‖ *ref* to divorce, get divorced
divorcio *m* divorce; divergency (*in opinion*); (Col) jail for women
divulgación *f* divulging, disclosure; popularization
divulgar §44 *tr* to divulge, disclose; to popularize
D.ⁿ *abbr* **don**
dobladillar *tr* to hem
dobladillo *m* hem
dobla·do -da *adj* rough, uneven; stocky, thickset; double-dealing ‖ *m* (mov) dubbing
doblaje *m* (mov) dubbing
doblar *tr* to double; to fold, to crease; to bend; (*una esquina*) to turn, to round; (*un promontorio*) to double; (*una película, generalmente en otro idioma*) to dub; (bridge) to double; (Mex) to shoot down ‖ *intr* to turn; (*tocar a muerto*) to toll; (mov, theat) to double, stand in; (bridge) to double ‖ *ref* to double; to fold, to crease; to bend; to bow, to stoop; to give in, yield
doble *adj* double; heavy, thick; stocky, thickset; deceitful, two-faced ‖ *adv* double, doubly ‖ *mf* (mov, theat) double, stand-in ‖ *m* double; fold, crease; (*toque de difuntos*) toll, knell; (*suma que se paga por la prórroga de una operación a plazos en la bolsa*) margin; **al doble** doubly
doblegar §44 *tr* to fold; to bend; (*una espada*) to brandish, flourish; to sway, dominate ‖ *ref* to fold; to bend; to give in, to yield
doblete *adj* medium ‖ *m* (*piedra falsa; cada una de dos palabras que poseen un mismo origen*) doublet; (bridge) doubleton

do·blez *m* (*pl* **-bleces**) fold, crease; (*del pantalón*) cuff; duplicity, double-dealing
doce *adj & pron* twelve; **las doce** twelve o'clock ‖ *m* twelve; (*en las fechas*) twelfth
doce·vo -va *adj & m* twelfth
docena *f* dozen; **docena del fraile** baker's dozen
docencia *f* (Arg) teaching; (Arg) teaching staff
docente *adj* educational, teaching
dócil *adj* docile; soft, ductile
doc·to -ta *adj* learned ‖ *mf* scholar
doc·tor -tora *mf* doctor ‖ *f* (coll) bluestocking
doctorado *m* doctorate
doctoran·do -da *mf* candidate for the doctor's degree
doctorar *tr* to grant the doctor's degree to ‖ *ref* to get the doctor's degree
doctrina *f* doctrine; teaching, instruction; learning; catechism; preaching the Gospel
doctrinar *tr* to teach, instruct
doctrino *m* orphan (*in orphanage*); **parecer un doctrino** (coll) to look scared
documentación *f* documentation; **documentación del buque** ship's papers
documental *adj* documentary ‖ *m* (mov) documentary
documentar *tr* to document
documento *m* document; **documento de prueba** (law) document
dogal *m* (*para atar las caballerías*) halter; (*para ahorcar a un reo*) noose, halter, hangman's rope; **estar con el dogal a la garganta** or **al cuello** (coll) to be in a tight spot
dogmáti·co -ca *adj* dogmatic
do·go -ga *mf* bulldog
dolamas *fpl* or **dolames** *mpl* hidden defects of a horse; (Am) complaints, aches and pains
dolar §61 *tr* to hew
dólar *m* dollar
dolencia *f* ailment, complaint
doler §47 *tr* to ache, to pain; to grieve, distress; **dolerle a uno el dinero** (coll) to hate to spend money ‖ *intr* to ache, to hurt, to pain ‖ *ref* to complain; to feel sorry; to repent
doliente *adj* sick, ill; aching, suffering; sad, sorrowful ‖ *mf* sufferer, patient ‖ *m* mourner
dolo *m* deceit, fraud, guile
dolor *m* ache, pain; grief, sorrow; regret, repentance; **dolor de cabeza** headache; **dolor de muelas** toothache; **dolor de oído** earache; **dolor de yegua** (CAm) lumbago; **estar con dolores** to be in labor
dolori·do -da *adj* sore, painful; grieving, disconsolate
doloro·so -sa *adj* painful; sorrowful, sad
dolo·so -sa *adj* deceitful, guileful
domador *m* horsebreaker; animal tamer
domar *tr* to tame, to break; to master
domeñar *tr* to master, subdue
domesticar §73 *tr* to domesticate; to tame

domésti·co -ca *adj* domestic, household || *mf* domestic, servant

domiciliar *tr* to domicile, settle; (*una carta*) (Mex) to address || *ref* to be domiciled, to take up one's residence

domicilio *m* domicile, home; dwelling, house; **domicilio social** home office, company office

dominación *f* domination; (mil) eminence, high ground

dominante *adj* dominant; (*mandón*) domineering || *f* (mus) dominant

dominar *tr* to dominate; to check, restrain, subdue; (*una ciencia, un idioma*) to master || *intr* to dominate; (*mandar imperiosamente*) to domineer || *ref* to restrain oneself

dómine *m* (coll) schoolmaster, Latin teacher; (coll) pedant

domingo *m* Sunday; **domingo de ramos** Palm Sunday; **domingo de resurrección** Easter Sunday; **guardar el domingo** to keep the Sabbath

dominguillo *m* tumbler

dominica·no -na *adj* & *mf* Dominican

dominio *m* dominion; domain; (*de una ciencia, de un idioma*) mastery; (*del aire*) supremacy

domi·nó *m* (*pl* -nós) (*traje*) domino; (*juego*) dominoes; (*fichas*) set of dominoes

dom.º *abbr* **domingo**

domo *m* dome

dompedro *m* four-o'clock

don *m* gift, present; talent, natural gift; Don (*Spanish title used before masculine Christian names*); **don de acierto** knack for doing the right thing; **don de errar** knack for doing the wrong thing; **don de gentes** charm, social grace; **don de lenguas** linguistic facility; **don de mando** ability to lead, generalship

dona *f* gift, present; **donas** wedding presents from the bridegroom to the bride

donación *f* gift, bequest; endowment

donada *f* lay sister

donado *m* lay brother

dona·dor -dora *mf* donor

donaire *m* charm, grace; witticism; cleverness

donairo·so -sa *adj* charming, graceful; witty; clever

donar *tr* to donate, to give

doncel *adj* mild, mellow || *m* (*joven noble aun no armado caballero*) bachelor; (*hombre virgen*) virgin

doncella *f* maiden, virgin; housemaid; lady's maid; maid of honor; (Col, Ven) felon, whitlow

doncellez *f* maidenhood, virginity

doncellona or **doncellueca** *f* spinster, maiden lady

donde *conj* where; wherever; in which; **donde no** otherwise; **por donde quiera** anywhere, everywhere || *prep* (Am) at or to the house, office, or store of

dónde *adv* where; **a dónde** where, whither; **de dónde** from where, whence; **por dónde** which way; for what cause, for what reason

dondequiera *adv* anywhere; **dondequiera que** wherever

dondiego *m* four-o'clock; **dondiego de día** morning-glory; **dondiego de noche** four-o'clock

donillero *m* sharper, smoothy

donjuán *m* four-o'clock

donosidad *f* charm, grace, wit

dono·so -sa *adj* charming, graceful, witty

donostiarra *adj* San Sebastian || *mf* native or inhabitant of San Sebastian

donosura *f* charm, grace, wit

doña *f* Doña (*Spanish title used before feminine Christian names*)

doñear *intr* (coll) to hang around women

doquier or **doquiera** *conj* wherever; **por doquier** everywhere

dorada *f* (ichth) gilthead

doradillo *m* fine brass wire

dora·do -da *adj* golden; gilt || *m* gilt, gilding; **dorados** bronze trimmings (*on furniture*) || *f* see **dorada**

dorar *tr* to gold-plate; to gild; (*tostar ligeramente*) to brown; (*paliar*) to sugar-coat || *ref* to turn golden; to turn brown

dormi·lón -lona *adj* (coll) sleepy || *mf* (coll) sleepyhead || *f* reclining armchair; (Mex) headrest; (Ven) sleeping gown; (Am) mimosa; **dormilonas** pearl earrings

dormir §30 *tr* to put to sleep; (*p.ej., una borrachera*) to sleep off || *intr* to sleep; to spend the night || *ref* to sleep; to fall asleep; (*entorpecerse, p.ej., el pie*) to go to sleep

dormirlas *m* hide-and-seek

dormitar *intr* to doze, nap

dormitorio *m* bedroom; (*muebles propios de esta habitación*) bedroom suit

dorsal *m* (sport) number (*worn on shirt*)

dorso *m* back

dos *adj* & *pron* two; **las dos** two o'clock || *m* two; (*en las fechas*) second

dosal·bo -ba *adj* (*horse*) with two white feet

doscien·tos -tas *adj* & *pron* two hundred || **doscientos** *m* two hundred

dosel *m* canopy, dais

doselera *f* valance, drapery

dosificación *f* dosage

dosificar §73 *tr* (*un medicamento*) to dose, to give in doses

do·sis *f* (*pl* -sis) dose

dos-pie·zas *m* (*pl* -zas) two-piece bathing suit

dotación *f* (*de una mujer; de una fundación*) endowment; (nav) complement; (aer) crew; (*de remeros*) (sport) crew; staff, personnel

dotar *tr* to give a dowry to; to endow; (*un buque*) to man; (*una oficina*) to staff; to equip; to fix the wages for

dote *m* & *f* dowry, marriage portion || *m* (*en el juego de naipes*) stack of chips || *f* endowment, talent, gift; **dotes de mando** leadership

dovela *f* voussoir

doza·vo -va *adj* & *m* twelfth

d/p *abbr* **días plazo**

dracma *f* (*moneda griega*) drachma; (*peso farmacéutico*) dram

draga *f* dredge; (*barco*) dredger

dragado *m* dredging

dragami·nas *m* (*pl* **-nas**) mine sweeper

dragar §44 *tr* to dredge

dragón *m* dragon; (*planta*) snapdragon; (*soldado*) dragoon

dragonear *intr* (Am) to flirt; (Am) to boast; **dragonear de** (Am) to boast of being; (Am) to pretend to be, to pass oneself off as

drama *m* drama

dramáti·co -ca *adj* dramatic || *mf* (*autor*) dramatist; actor || *f* (*arte y género*) drama

dramatizar §60 *tr* to dramatize

dramaturgo *m* dramatist

drásti·co -ca *adj* drastic

dren *m* drain

drenaje *m* drainage

drenar *tr* to drain

driblar *tr & intr* to dribble

dril *m* drill; duck; **dril de algodón** denim

driza *f* (naut) halyard

dro. *abbr* **derecho**

droga *f* drug; annoyance, bother; deceit, trick; (Chile, Mex, Peru) bad debt; (Cuba) drug on the market; **drogas milagrosas** wonder drugs

drogado *m* doping

drogar §44 *tr* to dope

droguería *f* drug store; drug business; (*comercio de substancias usadas en química, industria, medicina, bellas artes*) drysaltery (Brit)

drogue·ro -ra *mf* druggist; drysalter (Brit)

droguista *mf* druggist; (coll) crook, cheat; (Arg) toper, drunk

droláti·co -ca *adj* droll, snappy

dromedario *m* dromedary; big heavy animal; (coll) brute (*person*)

druida *m* druid

dúa *f* (min) gang of workmen

dual *adj & m* dual

dualidad *f* duality; (Chile) tie vote

ducado *m* duchy, dukedom; (*moneda antigua*) ducat; **gran ducado** grand duchy

dúctil *adj* ductile; easy to handle

ducha *f* (*chorro de agua en una cavidad del cuerpo*) douche; (*chorro de agua sobre el cuerpo entero*) shower bath; (*lista en los tejidos*) stripe; **ducha en alfileres** needle bath

duchar *tr* to douche; to give a shower bath to || *ref* to douche; to take a shower bath

du·cho -cha *adj* experienced, expert, skillful || *f* see **ducha**

duda *f* doubt; **sin duda** doubtless, no doubt, without doubt

dudable *adj* doubtful

dudar *tr* to doubt; to question || *intr* to hesitate; **dudar de** to doubt

dudo·so -sa *adj* doubtful; dubious

duela *f* stave (*of barrel*)

duelista *m* duelist

duelo *m* (*combate entre dos*) duel; grief, sorrow; bereavement, mourning; (*los que asisten a los funerales*) mourners; **batirse en duelo** to duel, to fight a duel; **duelos** hardships; **sin duelo** in abundance

duende *m* elf, goblin; gold cloth, silver cloth; (coll) restless daemon; **tener duende** (coll) to be burning within

due·ño -ña *mf* owner, proprietor; **dueño de sí mismo** one's own master; **ser dueño de** to be master of; to be at liberty to, be free to || *m* master, landlord || *f* mistress, landlady, housekeeper; duenna; matron; **dueña de casa** housewife

duermevela *f* (coll) doze, light sleep; (*sueño fatigoso e interrumpido*) fitful sleep

dula *f* common pasture land; land irrigated from common ditch

dulce *adj* sweet; (*agua*) fresh; (*metal*) soft, ductile; gentle, mild, pleasant; (*manjar*) tasteless, insipid || *m* candy; piece of candy; preserves; **dulce de almíbar** preserved fruit; **dulces** candy

dulcera *f* candy dish, preserve dish

dulcería *f* candy store, confectionery store

dulce·ro -ra *adj* (coll) sweet-toothed || *mf* confectioner || *f* see **dulcera**

dulcificar §73 *tr* to sweeten; to appease, mollify || *ref* to sweeten, turn sweet

dulcinea *f* (coll) sweetheart; (coll) ideal

dulzaina *f* flageolet

dulza·rrón -rrona *adj* (coll) cloying, sickening

dulzura *f* sweetness; pleasantness, kindliness; (*del clima*) mildness; endearment, sweet word

duna *f* dune

dun·do -da *adj* (CAm, Col) simple, stupid || *mf* (CAm, Col) simpleton

dúo *m* duet, duo

duodéci·mo -ma *adj & m* twelfth

duodeno *m* duodenum

duplica·do -da *adj & m* duplicate; **por duplicado** in duplicate

duplicar §73 *tr* to duplicate; to double; to repeat

duplicata *f* duplicate

duplicidad *f* (*falsedad*) duplicity; (*calidad de doble*) doubleness

du·plo -pla *adj & m* double

duque *m* duke; **gran duque** grand duke

duquesa *f* duchess; **gran duquesa** grand duchess

dura *f* (coll) durability; **de dura** or **de mucha dura** (coll) strong, durable

durable *adj* durable, lasting

duración *f* duration, endurance; (*espacio de tiempo del uso de una cosa*) life

durade·ro -ra *adj* durable, lasting

durante *prep* during, for

durar *intr* to last; to remain; (*la ropa*) to last, to wear, to wear well

durazno *m* peach; peach tree

dureza *f* hardness; harshness, roughness; **dureza de corazón** hardheartedness; **dureza de oído** hardness of hearing; **dureza de vientre** constipation

durmiente *adj* sleeping || *mf* sleeper || *m* girder, sleeper, stringer; (Am) tie, railroad tie; (Ven) steel bar

du•ro -ra *adj* hard; (*huevo*) hard-boiled; harsh, rough; cruel; stubborn, obstinate; unbearable; strong, tough; stingy; (*tiempo*) stormy; **duro de corazón** hard-hearted; **duro de oído** hard of hearing; **estar muy duro con** to be hard on; **ser duro de pelar** (coll) to be hard to put across; (coll) to be hard to deal with || *m* dollar (*Spanish coin worth five pesetas*) || *f* see **dura** || **duro** *adv* hard

dux *m* (*pl* **dux**) doge

d/v *abbr* **días vista**

E

E, e (e) *f* sixth letter of the Spanish alphabet

e *conj* (used before words beginning with *i* or *hi* not followed by a vowel) and

ea *interj* hey!

ebanista *m* cabinetmaker, woodworker

ebanistería *f* cabinetmaking, woodwork; cabinetmaker's shop

ébano *m* ebony

ebriedad *f* drunkenness

e•brio -bria *adj* drunk; (*p.ej., de ira*) blind || *mf* drunk

ebrio•so -sa *adj* drinking || *mf* drinker

ebullición *f* boiling

eccema *m* & *f* eczema

ecléc•ti•co -ca *adj* & *mf* eclectic

eclesiásti•co -ca *adj* & *m* ecclesiastic

eclipsar *tr* to eclipse; (fig) to outshine || *ref* to be in eclipse; (fig) to disappear

eclipse *m* eclipse

eclip•sis *f* (*pl* **-sis**) var of **elipsis**

eclisa *f* (rr) fishplate

eco *m* echo; (*del tambor*) rumbling; **hacer eco** to echo; to attract attention; **tener eco** to be well received, to catch on

economato *m* stewardship; commissary, company store, coöperative store

economía *f* economy; want, poverty; **economía política** economics; **economías** savings

económi•co -ca *adj* economic; (*que gasta poco; poco costoso*) economical; cheap; miserly, niggardly

economista *mf* economist

economizar §60 *tr* to economize, to save; to avoid || *intr* to economize, save; to skimp

ecónomo *m* steward, trustee; supply priest

ecuación *f* equation

ecuador *m* equator || **el Ecuador** Ecuador

ecuánime *adj* calm, composed; impartial

ecuanimidad *f* equanimity; impartiality

ecuatoria•no -na *adj* & *mf* Ecuadoran, Ecuadorian

ecuestre *adj* equestrian

ecuméni•co -ca *adj* ecumenic(al)

eczema *m* & *f* eczema

echacan•tos *m* (*pl* **-tos**) (coll) good-for-nothing

echacuer•vos *m* (*pl* **-vos**) (coll) pimp, procurer; (coll) cheat

echada *f* cast, throw; man's length; (Arg, Mex) boast, hoax

echadero *m* place to stretch out

echadi•zo -za *adj* discarded, waste; spying || *mf* foundling || *m* spy

echa•do -da *adj* stretched out; (C-R) lazy, indolent || *f* see **echada**

echar *tr* to throw, throw away, throw out; to issue, emit; to publish; to discharge, dismiss; to swallow; (*p.ej., agua*) to pour; (*p.ej., un cigarrillo*) to smoke; (*la baraja*) to deal; (*una partida de cartas*) to play; (*una llave*) to turn; (*un discurso*) to deliver; (*un drama*) to put on; (*maldiciones*) to utter; (*pelo, dientes, nuevos*) to grow, put forth; (*impuestos*) to impose, to levy; (*la buenaventura*) to tell; (*precio, distancia, edad, etc.*) to ascribe, attribute; (*una mirada*) to cast; (*sangre*) to shed; (*la culpa*) to lay; (*una mano*) to lend; **echar abajo** to demolish, destroy; to overthrow; **echar a pasear** (coll) to dismiss unceremoniously; **echar a perder** to spoil, to ruin; **echar a pique** to sink; **echar de menos** to miss; **echarla de** (coll) to claim to be, boast of being; **echarlo todo a rodar** (coll) to upset everything; (coll) to hit the ceiling || *intr* — **echar a** to begin to; to burst out (*e.g., crying*); **echar a perder** to spoil, to ruin; **echar de ver** to notice, to happen to see; **echar por** (*un empleo, un oficio*) to go into, take up; (*la derecha, la izquierda*) to turn toward; (*un camino*) to go down || *ref* to throw oneself; to lie down, stretch out; (*el viento*) to fall; (*un abrigo*) to throw on; (*una gallina*) to set; **echarse a** to begin to; **echarse a morir** (coll) to give up in despair; **echarse a perder** to spoil, to be ruined; **echarse atrás** to back out; **echarse de ver** to be easy to see; **echárselas de** to claim to be, to boast of being; **echarse sobre** to rush at, fall upon

echazón *f* jettison, jetsam

echiquier *m* Exchequer

edad *f* age; **edad crítica** change of life; **edad de quintas** draft age; **edad escolar** school age; **Edad Media** Middle Ages; **edad viril** prime of life; **mayor edad** majority; **menor edad** minority

edecán *m* aide-de-camp

edición *f* edition; publication; **la segun-**

da edición de (coll) the spit and image of

edicto m edict

edificación f construction, building; buildings; (*inspiración con el buen ejemplo*) edification, uplift

edificante adj edifying

edificar §73 tr to construct, build; (*dar buen ejemplo a*) to edify, to uplift

edificio m edifice, building

editar tr to publish

edi·tor -tora adj publishing || mf publisher

editorial adj publishing; editorial || m editorial || f publishing house

editorialista mf (Am) editorial writer

editorializar §60 intr (Urug) to editorialize

edredón m eider down

educación f education

educacional adj educational

educa·dor -dora mf educator

educan·do -da mf pupil, student

educar §73 tr to educate; (*los sentidos*) to train; (*al niño o el adolescente*) to rear, to bring up

educati·vo -va adj educational

EE.UU. abbr **Estados Unidos**

efectismo m sensationalism

efectista adj sensational, theatrical || mf sensationalist

efectivamente adv actually, really; as a matter of fact

efecti·vo -va adj actual, real; (*empleo, cargo*) regular, permanent; (*vigente*) effective; **hacer efectivo** to carry out; (*un cheque*) to cash; **hacerse efectivo** to become effective || m cash; **efectivo en caja** cash on hand

efecto m effect; end, purpose; article; (*en el juego de billar*) English; **a ese efecto** for that purpose; **al efecto** for the purpose; **con efecto** or **en efecto** indeed, as a matter of fact; **efecto útil** efficiency, output; **llevar a efecto** or **poner en efecto** to put into effect, to carry out; **surtir efecto** to work, to have the desired effect

efectuar §21 tr to carry out, to effect, to effectuate || ref to take place

efervescencia f effervescence

efervescente adj effervescent

eficacia f efficacy

efi·caz adj (pl -caces) efficacious, effectual; efficient

eficiencia f efficiency

eficiente adj efficient

efigie f effigy

efíme·ro -ra adj ephemeral

efugio m evasion, subterfuge

efusión f effusion; (*manifestación de afectos muy viva*) warmth, effusiveness; **efusión de sangre** bloodshed

efusi·vo -va adj effusive

égida f aegis

egip·cio -cia adj & mf Egyptian

Egipto m Egypt

eglantina f sweetbriar

eglefino m haddock

égloga f eclogue

egoísmo m egoism

egoísta adj egoistic || mf egoist

egotismo m egotism

egotista adj egotistic(al) || mf egotist

egre·gio -gia adj distinguished, eminent

egresar intr (Am) to graduate

egreso m departure; (Am) graduation

eje m (*pieza alrededor de la cual gira un cuerpo*) axle, shaft; (*línea que divide en dos mitades; línea recta alrededor de la cual se supone que gira un cuerpo*) axis; (fig) core, crux; **eje de balancín** rocker, rockershaft; **eje de carretón** axletree; **eje motor** drive shaft

ejecución f execution

ejecutante mf performer

ejecutar tr to execute; to perform

ejecutivamente adv expeditiously

ejecuti·vo -va adj urgent, pressing; insistent; executive || m (Am) executive

ejecu·tor -tora adj executive || mf executor; **ejecutor de la justicia** executioner; **ejecutor testamentario** executor (*of a will*) || f — **ejecutora testamentaria** executrix

ejemplar adj exemplary || m pattern, model; (*de una obra impresa*) copy; precedent; (*caso que sirve de escarmiento*) example; **ejemplar de cortesía** complimentary copy; **ejemplar muestra** sample copy; **sin ejemplar** unprecedented; as a special case

ejemplarizar §60 tr (Am) to set an example to; (Am) to exemplify

ejemplificar §73 tr to exemplify

ejemplo m example, instance; **por ejemplo** for example, for instance; **sin ejemplo** unexampled

ejercer §78 tr (*la medicina*) to practice; (*la caridad*) to show, exercise; (*una fuerza*) to exert || intr to practice; **ejercer de** to practice as, to work as

ejercicio m exercise; drill, practice; (*de un cargo u oficio*) tenure; (*uso constante*) exertion; (*año económico*) fiscal year; **hacer ejercicio** to take exercise; (mil) to drill

ejercitar tr to exercise; to practice; to drill, to train || ref to exercise; to practice

ejército m army; **ejército permanente** standing army; **los tres ejércitos** the three arms of the service

ejido m commons

ejote m (CAm, Mex) string bean

el, la (pl **los, las**) art def the || pron dem that, the one; **el que** who, which, that; he who, the one that

él pron pers masc he, it; him, it

elabora·do -da adj elaborate; finished

elaborar tr to elaborate; (*una teoría*) to work out; (*el metal, la madera*) to fashion, to work

elación f magnanimity, nobility; (*de estilo y lenguaje*) pomposity

elástica f knit undershirt; **elásticas** (Ven) suspenders

elasticidad f elasticity

elásti·co -ca adj elastic || m elastic; (Am) bedspring || f see **elástica**

eléboro m hellebore

elección f election; choice

electi·vo -va adj elective

elec·to -ta adj elect

electorado m electorate

electorero _m_ henchman, heeler
electricidad _f_ electricity
electricista _mf_ electrician
eléctrico -ca _adj_ electric(al)
electrificar §73 _tr_ to electrify
electrizar §60 _tr_ to electrify
electro _m_ electromagnet
electroafeitadora _f_ electric shaver
electrocutar _tr_ to electrocute
electrodo _m_ electrode
electrodomésti·co -ca _adj_ electric-household
electróge·no -na _adj_ generating electricity ‖ _m_ electric generator
electroimán _m_ electromagnet
electrólisis _f_ electrolysis
electrólito _m_ electrolyte
electromagnéti·co -ca _adj_ electromagnetic
electromo·tor -tora or **-triz** _adj_ (_pl_ **-tores -toras -trices**) electromotive
electrón _m_ electron
electróni·co -ca _adj_ electronic ‖ _f_ electronics
electrostáti·co -ca _adj_ electrostatic
electrotecnia _f_ electrical engineering
electrotipar _tr_ to electrotype
electrotipo _m_ electrotype
elefante _m_ elephant; **elefante blanco** (fig) (SAm) white elephant
elegancia _f_ elegance; style, stylishness
elegante _adj_ elegant; stylish ‖ _mf_ fashion plate
elegía _f_ elegy
elegía·co -ca _adj_ elegiac
elegible _adj_ eligible
elegir §57 _tr_ to elect; to choose, select
elemental _adj_ (_primordial; simple, no compuesto_) elemental; (_que se refiere a los principios de una ciencia o arte; de fácil comprensión_) elementary
elemento _m_ element; (_de una pila o batería_) cell; **elemento de compuestos** (gram) combining form; **estar en su elemento** to be in one's element
elenco _m_ catalogue, list, table; (theat) (Am) cast
elevación _f_ elevation; **elevación a potencias** (math) involution
eleva·do -da _adj_ elevated, high; lofty, sublime
elevador _m_ (Am) elevator; **elevador de granos** (Am) grain elevator
elevar _tr_ to elevate, to lift; (math) to raise ‖ _ref_ to ascend, rise; to be exalted; to become conceited
elfo _m_ elf
elidir _tr_ to eliminate; (_una vocal_) to elide
eliminar _tr_ to eliminate; to strike out
elipse _f_ (geom) ellipse
elip·sis _f_ (_pl_ **-sis**) (gram) ellipsis
elípti·co -ca _adj_ (geom & gram) elliptic(al)
elisión _f_ elision
elocución _f_ public speaking, elocution
elocuencia _f_ eloquence
elocuente _adj_ eloquent
elogiable _adj_ praiseworthy
elogiar _tr_ to praise, eulogize
elogio _m_ praise, eulogy

elogio·so -sa _adj_ (Am) laudatory, glowing
elote _m_ (Mex, Guat) ear of corn; **coger asando elotes** (CAm) to catch in the act; **pagar los elotes** (CAm) to be the goat
elucidar _tr_ to elucidate
eludir _tr_ to elude, evade, avoid
ella _pron pers fem_ she, it; her, it; (coll) the trouble
ello _pron pers neut_ it; (coll) the trouble; **ello es que** the fact is that ‖ _m_ (psychoanalysis) id
E.M. _abbr_ **Estado Mayor**
emancipar _tr_ to emancipate
embadurnamiento _m_ daub, daubing
embadurnar _tr_ to daub
embaír §1 _tr_ to deceive, take in, hoax
embajada _f_ embassy; ambassadorship; (iron) fine proposition
embajador _m_ ambassador; **embajadores** ambassador and wife
embajadora _f_ ambassadress
embalaje _m_ packing; package; (sport) sprint
embalar _tr_ to pack ‖ _intr_ (sport) to sprint ‖ _ref_ (_el motor_) to race; (sport) to sprint
embaldosado _m_ tile paving
embaldosar _tr_ to pave with tile
embalsamar _tr_ to embalm; to perfume
embalsar _tr_ to dam, to dam up
embalse _m_ dam; damming; backwater
embanastar _tr_ to put in a basket; to pack, jam, overcrowd
embanquetar _tr_ (Mex) to line with sidewalks
embarazada _adj fem_ pregnant ‖ _f_ pregnant woman
embarazar §60 _tr_ (_estorbar_) to embarrass; to obstruct; to make pregnant ‖ _ref_ to be embarrassed, be encumbered; to become pregnant
embarazo _m_ embarrassment; obstruction; awkwardness; pregnancy
embarazo·so -sa _adj_ embarrassing, troublesome
embarbillar _tr_ to rabbet
embarcación _f_ boat, ship; embarkation (_of passengers_)
embarcadero _m_ pier, wharf; (rr) (Am) platform; **embarcadero de ganado** (Arg) loading chute; **embarcadero flotante** landing stage
embarcador _m_ shipper
embarcar §73 _tr_ to ship ‖ _intr_ to entrain ‖ _ref_ to embark, to ship; to get involved
embarco _m_ embarkation (_of passengers_)
embargar §44 _tr_ to embargo; to paralyze; (law) to seize, attach
embargo _m_ embargo; indigestion; (law) seizure, attachment; **sin embargo** however, nevertheless
embarnizar §60 _tr_ to varnish
embarque _m_ shipment, embarkation (_of freight_)
embarrada _f_ (Am) blunder
embarrancar §73 _tr, intr & ref_ to run into a ditch; (_una nave_) to run aground
embarrar _tr_ to splash with mud; to

smear, stain; (CAm, Mex) to involve in a shady deal; **embarrarla** (Arg) to spoil the whole thing

embarrilar tr to barrel, put in barrels

embarullar tr (coll) to muddle, make a mess of; (coll) to bungle, botch

embastar tr to baste, to stitch

embate m blow, attack; (del mar) beating, dashing; (de viento) gust; **embates de la fortuna** hard knocks

embaucar §73 tr to trick, bamboozle, swindle

embaula·do -da adj crowded, packed, jammed

embaular §8 tr to put in a trunk; (coll) to jam, pack in

embayar ref (Ecuad) to fly into a rage

embazar §60 tr to dye brown; to hinder, obstruct; to astound, dumbfound || ref to get bored; to be upset, get sick at the stomach

embebecer §22 tr to entertain, amuse, fascinate, enchant

embeber tr to absorb, soak up; to soak; to contain, include; to embed; to contract, shrink || intr to contract, shrink || ref to be enchanted, be enraptured; to become absorbed or immersed; to become well versed

embebi·do -da adj (vocal) elided; (columna) engaged

embelecar §73 tr to cheat, dupe, bamboozle

embeleco m cheating, fraud; (coll) bore; **embelecos** cuteness

embeleñar tr to dope, stupefy; to enchant, bewitch

embelesar tr to charm, enrapture, fascinate

embeleso m charm, fascination, delight

embellece·dor -dora adj embellishing, beautifying || m (aut) hubcap || f beautician

embellecer §22 tr to embellish, beautify

embellecimiento m embellishment, beautification

embermejecer §22 tr to dye red; to make blush || ref to blush

emberrinchar ref (coll) to fly into a rage

embestida f attack, assault; (detención intempestiva) (coll) buttonholing

embesti·dor -dora mf (coll) beat, sponger

embestir §50 tr to attack, assail; to strike; (coll) to buttonhole, waylay || intr to attack, to charge, to rush

embetunar tr to blacken; to cover with tar

embicar §73 tr (Mex) to turn upside down, to tilt || intr (Arg, Chile) to run aground

emblandecer §22 tr to soften; to placate, mollify || ref to soften, to yield

emblanquecer §22 tr to whiten; to bleach || ref to turn white

emblema m emblem

emblemáti·co -ca adj emblematic(al)

embobar tr to amaze, fascinate || ref to stand gaping

embocadero m mouth, outlet

embocadura f nozzle; (de río) mouth; (del freno; de instrumento de viento)

mouthpiece; (de cigarrillo) tip; (del vino) taste; stage entrance

embocar §73 tr to catch in the mouth; to put in the mouth; to take on, undertake; (coll) to gulp down; (coll) to try to put over || intr & ref to enter, pass

embolada f stroke

embolado m bull with wooden balls on horns; (theat) minor role; (coll) trick, hoax

embolar tr (los cuernos del toro) to put wooden balls on; (el calzado) to shine

embolia f embolism

émbolo m (mach) piston; **émbolo buzo** (mach) plunger

embolsar tr to pocket, take in

embonar tr (Am) to fertilize; (Am) to suit, be becoming to

emboquillar tr (los cigarrillos) to put tips on; (una galería o túnel) to cut an entrance in; (las junturas entre los ladrillos) (Chile) to point, to chink

emborrachar tr to intoxicate || ref to get drunk; (los colores de una tela) to run

emborrar tr to stuff, pad, wad; (coll) to gulp down

emborrascar §73 tr to stir up, irritate || ref to get stormy; (un negocio) to fail; (la veta de una mina) (Arg, CAm, Mex) to peter out

emborronar tr to blot; to scribble

emboscada f ambush, ambuscade

emboscado m draft dodger

emboscar §73 tr (tropas para sorprender al enemigo) to ambush || ref to ambush, lie in ambush; to shirk, take an easy way out

embota·do -da adj blunt, dull; (Chile) black-pawed

embotadura f bluntness, dullness

embotar tr to blunt, to dull; to dull, weaken; (el tabaco) to put in a jar

embotella·do -da adj (discurso) prepared || m bottling; (del tráfico) bottleneck

embotellamiento m bottling; traffic jam

embotellar tr to bottle; (un negocio) to tie up; (nav) to bottle up

embotijar tr (un suelo) to underlay with jugs || ref (coll) to swell up with anger

embovedar tr to vault, vault over; to put in a vault

emboza·do -da adj muffled up || mf person muffled up to eyes

embozar §60 tr to muffle up to the eyes; (p.ej., a un perro) to muzzle; to disguise || ref to muffle oneself up to the eyes

embozo m muffler, cloak held over the face; fold back (of bed sheet); cunning, dissimulation; **quitarse el embozo** (coll) to drop one's mask

embragar §44 tr (el motor) to engage || intr to throw the clutch in

embrague m clutch; engagement

embravecer §22 tr to enrage, make angry || ref to get angry; (el mar) to get rough

embraveci·do -da *adj* angry; rough, wild

embrear *tr* to tar, cover with tar; to calk with tar

embregar §44 *ref* to wrangle

embriagar §44 *tr* to intoxicate, make drunk; to enrapture || *ref* to get drunk

embriaguez *f* drunkenness; rapture

embridar *tr* to bridle; to check, restrain

embriología *f* embriology

embrión *m* embryo

embroca *f* poultice

embrocar §73 *tr* to empty; (*el toro al torero*) to catch between the horns || *ref* (C-R) to fall on one's face; (Mex) to put on over the head

embrollar *tr* to tangle, muddle, embroil

embrollo *m* entanglement, muddle, embroilment; deception, trick

embromar *tr* to joke with, play jokes on; (Am) to bore, annoy || *ref* (Am) to be bored, be annoyed

embrujar *tr* to bewitch

embrutecer §22 *tr* to brutify, stupefy

embuchado *m* pork sausage; subterfuge; (*de la urna electoral*) stuffing (of ballot box)

embudar *tr* to put a funnel in; to trick, trap

embudista *adj* tricky, scheming || *mf* schemer

embudo *m* funnel; trick; (mil) shell hole; **embudo de bomba** (mil) bomb crater

embullar *tr* to stir up, excite, key up || *ref* to become excited, keyed up

emburujar *tr* to jumble, pile up || *ref* (Am) to wrap oneself up

embuste *m* lie, falsehood, trick; **embustes** baubles, trinkets; (*del niño*) cuteness

embuste·ro -ra *adj* lying, false, tricky || *mf* liar, cheat

embuti·do -da *adj* inlaid, flush || *m* inlay, marquetry; pork sausage; (Am) lace insertion

embutir *tr* to stuff, pack tight; to insert; to inlay; to set flush; (*una hoja de metal*) to fashion, to hammer into shape || *ref* to squeeze in; (coll) to stuff oneself

emergencia *f* emergence; incident

emerger §17 *intr* to emerge; (*un submarino*) to surface

emersión *f* emersion; (*de un submarino*) surfacing

eméti·co -ca *adj* & *m* emetic

emigración *f* emigration; migration

emigra·do -da *mf* émigré

emigrante *adj* & *mf* emigrant

emigrar *intr* to emigrate; to migrate

eminencia *f* eminence

eminente *adj* eminent

emisa·rio -ria *mf* emissary || *m* outlet

emisión *f* (acción de exhalar; acción de lanzar ondas luminosas, etc.) emission; (*títulos creados de una vez*) (com) issue; (*acción de emitir títulos nuevos*) (com) issuance; (rad) broadcast; **emisión seriada** (rad) serial

emi·sor -sora *adj* emitting; broadcasting || *m* (rad) transmitter || *f* broadcasting station

emitir *tr* to emit, send forth; to issue, give out; (*p.ej., opiniones*) to utter, express; (com) to issue; (rad) to broadcast

emoción *f* emotion

emocional *adj* emotional

emocionante *adj* moving, touching; thrilling, exciting

emocionar *tr* to move, stir; to thrill

emoti·vo -va *adj* emotional

empacadi·zo -za *adj* (Arg) touchy

empaca·do -da *adj* (Arg) gruff, grim

empacar §73 *tr* to pack, to crate || *ref* to be stubborn; (*un animal*) (Am) to balk, get balky

empa·cón -cona *adj* (Am) stubborn; (Am) balky

empacha·do -da *adj* backward, fumbling

empachar *tr* to hinder, embarrass; to disguise; to surfeit, upset the stomach of || *ref* to blush, be embarrassed; to be upset, have indigestion

empacho *m* hindrance; embarrassment, bashfulness; indigestion

empacho·so -sa *adj* sickening; shameful

empadronar *tr* to register, to take the census of || *ref* to register, be registered in the census

empalagar §44 *tr* to cloy, pall, surfeit; to bore, to weary

empalago·so -sa *adj* cloying, sickening, mawkish; boring, annoying; fawning

empalar *tr* impale

empalizada *f* palisade, stockade, fence

empalizar §60 *tr* to fence in

empalmar *tr* to splice, connect, join, couple; to combine || *intr* to connect, make connections; **empalmar con** to connect with; to follow, succeed

empalme *m* splice, connection, joint, coupling; combination; (elec) joint; (rr) connection, junction

empanada *f* pie; fraud

empanadilla *f* pie

empana·do -da *adj* unlighted, unventilated || *f* see **empanada**

empanar *tr* to crumb, to bread; (*las tierras*) to sow with wheat

empantanar *tr* to flood; to obstruct

empaña·do -da *adj* dim, misty; blurred, fogged; (*voz*) flat

empañar *tr* (*a las criaturas*) to swaddle; to blur, fog, dim, dull; to tarnish, sully || *ref* to blur, fog, dim, dull

empañetar *tr* (Am) to plaster

empapar *tr* to soak; to soak up, absorb; to drench || *ref* to soak; to be soaked; to become imbued; (coll) to be surfeited

empapelado *m* papering, paper hanging; wallpaper; paper lining

empapela·dor -dora *mf* paper hanger

empapelar *tr* to wrap in paper; to paper, line with paper; to wallpaper; (coll) to bring a criminal charge against

empaque *m* packing; (coll) look, appearance, mien; stiffness, stuffiness; (Am) brazenness

empaquetadura *f* gasket

empaquetar *tr* to pack; to jam, stuff ‖ *ref* to pack; to pack in; (coll) to dress up

empareda·do -da *mf* recluse ‖ *m* sandwich

emparedar *tr* to wall in, to confine

emparejar *tr* to pair, to match; to smooth, make level; to even, make even; (*una puerta*) to close flush ‖ *intr* to come up, come abreast; **emparejar con** to catch up with ‖ *ref* to pair, to match

emparentar §2 *intr* to become related by marriage; **emparentar con** (*buena gente*) to marry into the family of; (*una familia rica*) to marry into

emparrado *m* arbor, bower

emparrillar *tr* to grill

empasta·dor -dora *mf* (Am) bookbinder

empastadura *f* (Am) binding

empastar *tr* (*un diente*) to fill; (*un libro*) to bind with stiff covers; (Am) to convert into pasture land ‖ *ref* (Chile) to be overgrown with weeds

empaste *m* (*de diente*) filling; stiff binding

empastelar *tr* (typ) to pie

empatar *tr* (*en la votación y los juegos*) to tie; (Am) to join, connect; (Am) to tie, fasten ‖ *intr* to tie ‖ *ref* to tie; **empatársela a una persona** to be a match for someone; **empatárselo a una persona** (Guat, Hond) to put it over on someone

empate *m* tie, draw; (Col) penholder; (Ven) waste of time

empavar *tr* (Ecuad) to annoy; (Peru) to kid, to razz

empavesado *m* (naut) dressing, bunting

empavesar *tr* to bedeck with flags and bunting; (*un buque*) to dress; (*un monumento*) to veil ‖ *ref* to become overcast

empavonar *tr* to blue; (Am) to grease, spread grease over ‖ *ref* (CAm) to dress up

empecina·do -da *adj* (Am) stubborn

empederni·do -da *adj* hardened, inveterate; hard-hearted

empedra·do -da *adj* cloud-flecked; pock-marked; (*caballo*) dark-spotted ‖ *m* stone paving

empedrar §2 *tr* to pave with stones; to bespatter

empegado *m* tarpaulin

empegar §44 *tr* to coat with pitch, to dip in pitch; (*el ganado lanar*) to mark with pitch

empeine *m* instep; (*de la bota*) vamp; (*enfermedad cutánea*) tetter; (*región central del hipogastrio*) pubes

empelotar *ref* (coll) to get all tangled up; (coll) to get into a row; (Am) to take all one's clothes off; (Mex, W-I) to fall madly in love

empella *f* vamp

empellar *tr* to push, shove

empeller §31 *tr* to push, shove

empellón *m* push, shove; **a empellones** pushing, roughly

empenachar *tr* to adorn with plumes

empeña·do -da *adj* (*disputa*) bitter, heated; **no empeñado** noncommitted

empeñar *tr* (*dar en prenda*) to pawn; (*una lucha*) to launch, begin; (*prendar, hipotecar*) to pledge; (*la palabra*) to pledge; to force, compel ‖ *ref* to commit oneself, bind oneself; to go into debt; (*una lucha, una disputa*) to begin, to start; **empeñarse en** to engage in; to persist in, insist on

empeñe·ro -ra *mf* (Mex) pawnbroker

empeño *m* pledge, engagement, commitment; (*prenda*) pawn; pawnshop; persistence, insistence; eagerness, perseverance; effort, endeavor; pledge, backer, patron; favor, protection; **con empeño** eagerly

empeño·so -sa *adj* (Am) eager, persistent

empeorar *tr* to impair, make worse ‖ *intr & ref* to get worse, deteriorate

empequeñecer §22 *tr* (*hacer más pequeño*) to make smaller, to dwarf; (*amenguar la importancia de*) to belittle ‖ *ref* to get smaller, to dwarf

emperador *m* emperor; **los emperadores** the emperor and empress

empera·triz *f* (*pl* -trices) empress

emperchar *tr* to hang on a clothes rack

emperejilar *tr & ref* (coll) to dress up, to spruce up

emperezar §60 *tr* to delay, put off ‖ *intr & ref* to get lazy

empericar §73 *ref* (Col, Ecuad) to get drunk; (Mex) to blush

emperifollar *tr & ref* to dress up gaudily

empernar *tr* to bolt

empero *conj* but, however, yet

emperrar *ref* (coll) to get stubborn

empezar §18 *tr & intr* to begin

empicar §73 *ref* to become infatuated

empicotar *tr* to pillory

empiema *m* empyema

empina·do -da *adj* high, lofty; steep; stiff, stuck-up ‖ *f* (aer) zoom, zooming; **irse a la empinada** (*un caballo*) to rear

empinar *tr* to raise, lift; to tip over; (aer) to zoom; (*el codo*) (coll) to crook ‖ *intr* to be a toper ‖ *ref* to stand on tiptoe; (*un caballo*) to rear; to tower, rise high; (aer) to zoom

empingorota·do -da *adj* influential; (coll) proud, haughty

empingorotar *tr* (coll) to put on top ‖ *ref* (coll) to climb up, get up; (coll) to be stuck-up

empíre·o -a *adj & m* empyrean

empíri·co -ca *adj* empiric(al) ‖ *mf* empiricist

empizarrado *m* slate roof

empizarrar *tr* to roof with slate

emplastar *tr* to put a plaster on; to put make-up on; (*un negocio*) to tie up, obstruct ‖ *ref* to put make-up on; to smear oneself up

emplásti·co -ca *adj* sticky

emplasto *m* plaster, poultice

emplazamiento *m* emplacement, location; (law) summons

emplazar §60 *tr* to place, locate; to summon, to summons

emplea·do -da *mf* employee; (*de ofi-*

cina, de tienda) clerk; **empleado pú-blico** civil servant

emplear *tr* to employ; to use; (*el dinero*) to invest; **estarle a uno bien empleado** (coll) to serve someone right || *ref* to be employed; to busy oneself; **empleárselo mal** (coll) to act up, to misbehave

empleo *m* employ, employment; use; job, position, occupation

empleomania *f* (coll) eagerness to hold public office

empléoma·no -na *mf* (Am) public officeholder, bureaucrat

emplomar *tr* to lead; to line with lead; (*un techo*) to cover with lead; to put a lead seal on; (*un diente*) (Arg) to fill

emplumar *tr* to put a feather on; to adorn with feathers; to tar and feather; (Hond) to thrash; **emplumarlas** (Col) to beat it || *intr* to fledge, grow feathers

emplumecer §22 *intr* to fledge, grow feathers

empobrecer §22 *tr* to impoverish || *intr & ref* to become poor

empodrecer §22 *intr & ref* to rot

empolva·do -da *adj* (Mex) rusty

empolvar *tr* to cover with dust; (*el rostro*) to powder || *ref* to get dusty; (*el rostro*) to powder; (Mex) to get rusty

empolla·do -da *adj* primed for an examination

empollar *tr* (*huevos*) to brood, hatch; (*estudiar con mucha detención*) (coll) to bone up on || *intr* (coll) to grind, be a grind; **empollar sobre** (coll) to bone up on || *ref* to hatch; to bone up on

empo·llón -llona *mf* (coll) grind

emponcha·do -da *adj* (SAm) poncho-wearing; (SAm) crafty, hypocritical; (SAm) suspicious-looking

emponzoñar *tr* to poison; to corrupt

emporcar §81 *tr* to soil, to dirty

empotra·do -da *adj* built-in; recessed

empotrar *tr* to embed, recess, fasten in a wall || *intr & ref* to fit, interlock

emprende·dor -dora *adj* enterprising

emprender *tr* to undertake; **emprenderla con** (coll) to squabble with, have it out with; **emprenderla para** (coll) to set out for

empreñar *tr* to make pregnant || *ref* to become pregnant

empresa *f* enterprise, undertaking; company, concern, firm; device, motto; (*la parte patronal*) management; **empresa anunciadora** advertising agency; **empresa de tranvías** traction company; **pequeña empresa** small business

empresarial *adj* managerial

empresa·rio -ria *mf* contractor; business leader, industrialist; manager; promoter; theatrical manager; **empresario de circo** showman; **empresario de pompas fúnebres** undertaker; **empresario de publicidad** advertising man; **empresario de teatro** impresario, theater manager

emprestar *tr* to borrow

empréstito *m* loan, government loan

empujar *tr* to push, to shove; to replace || *intr* to push, to shove

empujatierra *f* bulldozer

empuje *m* push; (*fuerza o presión ejercidas por una cosa sobre otra*) thrust; (*espíritu emprendedor*) enterprise, push

empujón *m* hard push, shove; **tratar a empujones** (coll) to push around

empuñadura *f* (*de la espada*) hilt; (coll) first words of a story; (*de bastón o paraguas*) (Am) handle

empuñar *tr* to seize, grasp, clutch; (*un empleo o puesto*) to obtain; (*la mano*) (Chile) to clench; (Bol) to punch; **empuñar el bastón** (fig) to seize the reins

emular *tr & intr* to emulate; **emular con** to emulate, vie with

ému·lo -la *adj* emulous || *mf* rival

emulsión *f* emulsion

emulsionar *tr* to emulsify

en *prep* at; in; into; by; on; of, e.g., **pensar en** to think of

enaceitar *tr* to oil || *ref* to get oily, get rancid

enagua *f* petticoat; (Am) skirt; **enaguas** petticoat

enagüillas *fpl* kilt, short skirt

enajenación *f* alienation; estrangement; rapture; (*distracción*) absent-mindedness; **enajenación mental** mental derangement

enajenar *tr* (*la propiedad, el dominio; a un amigo*) to alienate, estrange; to enrapture, to transport || *ref* to be enraptured, to be transported; **enajenarse de** to dispossess oneself of; (*un amigo*) to become alienated from

enaltecer §22 *tr* to exalt, extol

enamoradi·zo -za *adj* susceptible

enamora·do -da *adj* lovesick; (*propenso a enamorarse*) susceptible || *mf* sweetheart || *m* lover

enamorar *tr* to make love to; to enamor, captivate || *ref* to fall in love

enamoricar §73 *ref* (coll) to trifle in love

enangostar *tr & ref* to narrow

ena·no -na *adj* dwarfish || *mf* dwarf

enarbolar *tr* to hoist, hang out; (*una espada*) to brandish || *ref* to get angry; (*el caballo*) to rear

enarcar §73 *tr* to arch; (*los toneles*) to hoop || *ref* to become confused, be bashful; (*el caballo*) (Mex) to rear

enardecer §22 *tr* to inflame, excite || *ref* to get excited; (*una parte del cuerpo*) to become inflamed, get sore

enarenar *tr* to throw sand on || *ref* (naut) to run aground

enastar *tr* (*una herramienta*) to put a handle on; (*una bandera*) to put a shaft on

encabalgamiento *m* gun carriage; trestlework; (*en el verso*) enjambment

encabalgar §44 *tr* to provide with horses || *intr* to lean, to rest

encaballar *tr* to overlap; (typ) to pie

encabezamiento *m* heading; (*fórmula con que comienza un documento*) opening words; tax list; tax rate; **encabezamiento de factura** billhead

encabezar §60 *tr* (*un escrito*) to put a heading or title on; to head; to register; (*vinos*) to fortify

encabritar *ref* (*un caballo*) to rear; (*un buque*) to shoot up, pitch up; (*un avión*) to nose up

encadenar *tr* to chain, put in chains; to brace, buttress; to bind, tie together; to tie down

encajar *tr* to fit, fit in, make fit; to insert, put in; (*un golpe*) to give, let go; (*dinero*) to put away; (*un chiste*) to tell at the wrong time; to palm off; to throw, hurl; **encajar una cosa a uno** to foist something on someone, to palm something off on someone || *intr* to fit; (*una puerta*) to close right || *ref* to squeeze one's way; (*una prenda de vestir*) to put on; (coll) to butt in, to intrude

encaje *m* (*tejido de mallas*) lace; (*labor de taracea*) inlay, mosaic; recess, groove; fitting, matching; insertion; appearance, look

encaje·ro -ra *mf* lacemaker; lace dealer

encajonado *m* cofferdam

encajonar *tr* to box, crate, case; to squeeze in || *ref* (*un río*) to narrow, narrow down; to squeeze in, squeeze through

encalambrar *ref* (Am) to get cramps

encalar *tr* (*espolvorear con cal*) to lime, sprinkle with lime; (*blanquear con cal*) to whitewash

encalma·do -da *adj* (*mercado de valores*) dull, quiet; (*mar, viento*) becalmed

encalvecer §22 *intr* to get bald

encalladero *m* sand bank, shoal

encallar *intr* to run aground; to fail, get stuck

encallecer §22 *intr* (*la piel*) to become callous || *ref* to become callous; (fig) to become callous, become hardened

encamar *tr* to spread out on the ground || *ref* (coll) to take to bed; (*el grano*) to droop, bend over

encaminar *tr* to direct, show the way to; (*sus esfuerzos, su atención*) to direct || *ref* to set out

encanalar *tr* to channel, to pipe

encandecer §22 *tr* to make white-hot

encandila·do -da *adj* (*sombrero*) cocked; (coll) stiff, erect

encandilar *tr* to daze, befuddle; (*un fuego*) to stir || *ref* (*los ojos*) to flash

encanecer §22 *intr & ref* to turn gray; to get old; to become moldy

encanta·do -da *adj* (coll) absent-minded, distracted; (*casa*) (coll) rambling

encanta·dor -dora *adj* charming, enchanting || *mf* charmer || *f* enchantress

encantamiento *m* charm, enchantment

encantar *tr* to charm, enchant, bewitch

encante *m* auction sale; auction house

encanto *m* charm, enchantment, spell

encantusar *tr* (coll) to coax, wheedle

encañada *f* gorge, ravine

encañar *tr* (*el agua*) to pipe; (*las tie-*

rras) to drain; (*las plantas*) to prop up; to wind on a spool

encañizada *f* reed fence; weir

encañonar *tr* to pipe; to wind on a spool; (*un pliego*) (typ) to tip in

encaperuzar §60 *tr* to put a hood on || *ref* to put on one's hood

encapotar *tr* to cloak || *ref* to frown; to cloud over, become overcast

encaprichar *ref* to insist on getting one's way; to become infatuated

encaracolado *m* spiral ornament, spiral work

encara·do -da *adj* — **bien encarado** well-featured; **mal encarado** ill-featured

encaramar *tr* to raise up, lift up; to praise, extol; (coll) to elevate, exalt || *ref* to climb, get on top; to rise, to tower; (Am) to blush

encarar *tr* to aim, point; (*una dificultad*) to face || *intr & ref* to come face to face

encarcelar *tr* to incarcerate, imprison, jail; (*piezas de madera recién encoladas*) to clamp; to plaster in || *ref* to stay indoors

encarecer §22 *tr* (*el precio*) to raise; to raise the price of; to extol; to urge; to overrate || *intr & ref* to rise, to rise in price

encarecidamente *adv* earnestly, insistently, eagerly

encarga·do -da *mf* agent, representative; **encargado de negocios** chargé d'affaires

encargar §44 *tr* (*mercancías*) to order; (*confiar*) to entrust; to urge, to warn || *ref* to take charge, be in charge

encargo *m* assignment, job, charge; (*pedido*) order; warning; **como de encargo** or **ni de encargo** (coll) just the thing, as if made to order

encariñar *tr* to awaken love in || *ref* — **encariñarse con** to become fond of, become attached to

encarnación *f* incarnation, embodiment

encarna·do -da *adj* red; flesh-colored; (*de forma humana*) incarnate

encarnar *tr* to incarnate, to embody; (*el anzuelo*) to bait || *intr* to become incarnate; (*una herida*) to heal over

encarnecer §22 *intr* to put on flesh

encarniza·do -da *adj* bloodshot; bloody, fierce, bitter, hard-fought

encarnizar §60 *tr* to anger, provoke || *ref* to get angry; to become fierce; **encarnizarse con** or **en** to be merciless to

encaro *m* aim; stare; blunderbuss

encarrilar *tr* to put back on the rails; to set right, to put on the right track; to guide, direct

encarruja·do -da *adj* wrinkled; (*pelo*) kinky; (*terreno*) (Mex) rough

encartar *tr* to enroll, register; to outlaw; (*un naipe*) to slip in || *ref* to be unable to discard

encartonar *tr* to cover with cardboard; (*libros*) to bind in boards

encasar *tr* (*un hueso dislocado*) to set (*a broken bone*)

encasillado *m* set of pigeonholes; (*lista*

de candidatos apoyados por el gobierno) government slate; (SAm) checkerwork

encasillar *tr* to pigeonhole; to sort out, classify; (*el gobierno a un candidato*) to slate

encasquetar *tr* (*un sombrero*) to stick on the head; (*una idea*) to drive in; to force on

encasquillar *tr* to put a tip on; (*un caballo*) (Am) to shoe ‖ *ref* to stick, get stuck

encastilla·do -da *adj* haughty, proud

encastillar *tr* to fortify with castles; to pile up ‖ *ref* to stick, get stuck; to take to the hills; to stick to one's opinion

encastrar *tr* to engage, to mesh

encastre *m* engaging, meshing; groove, socket; insert

encauchar *tr* to cover with rubber, line with rubber

encausar *tr* to prosecute, to sue, to bring to trial

encáusticar §73 *tr* to wax

encáustico *m* floor wax, furniture polish

encauzar §60 *tr* (*una corriente*) to channel; to guide, direct

encavar *ref* to hide, burrow

encebollado *m* beef stew with onions

encelar *tr* to make jealous ‖ *ref* to get jealous; to be in rut

encella *f* cheese mold

encenagar §44 *ref* to get covered with mud; to wallow in vice

encencerrar *tr* (*al ganado*) to put a bell on

encendajas *fpl* kindling, brush

encendedor *m* lighter; **encendedor de bolsillo** pocket lighter

encender §51 *tr* to light, kindle; to ignite, set fire to; (*la luz, la radio*) to turn on; (*la lengua*) to burn; to stir up, excite ‖ *ref* to catch fire, to ignite; to become excited; to blush

encendi·do -da *adj* bright, high-colored; red, flushed; keen, enthusiastic ‖ *m* ignition

encenizar §60 *tr* to cover with ashes ‖ *ref* to get covered with ashes

encepar *tr* to put in the stocks ‖ *intr* & *ref* to take deep root

encera·do -da *adj* wax, wax-colored; (*huevo*) boiled ‖ *m* oilcloth; tarpaulin; (*pizarra*) blackboard

encerar *tr* to wax ‖ *intr* & *ref* (*el grano*) to ripen, turn yellow

encerotar *tr* (*el hilo*) to wax

encerradero *m* sheepfold; (taur) bull pen

encerrar §2 *tr* to shut in; to lock in, lock up; to contain, include; to encircle; to imply ‖ *ref* to lock oneself in; to go into seclusion; **encerrarse con** to be closeted with

encespedar *tr* to sod

encía *f* gum

encíclica *f* encyclical

enciclopedia *f* encyclopedia

enciclopédi·co -ca *adj* encyclopedic

encierro *m* locking up, confinement; inclusion; encirclement; lockup, prison;

solitary confinement; retirement, retreat; (taur) bull pen

encima *adv* above, overhead, on top; at hand, here now; besides, in addition; **de encima** (Chile) in the bargain; **echarse encima** to take upon oneself; **encima de** on, upon; above, over; **por encima** hastily, superficially; **por encima de** above, over; in spite of; **quitarse de encima** to get rid of, to shake off

encina *f* holm oak, evergreen oak

encinta *adj* pregnant

encintado *m* curb

encintar *tr* to trim with ribbons; to provide with curbs

enclaustrar *tr* to cloister; to hide away

enclavar *tr* to nail; to pierce, transfix; (*el pie del caballo*) to prick; (coll) to cheat

enclave *m* enclave

enclavijar *tr* to dowel; (*un instrumento*) to peg

enclenque *adj* sickly, feeble

enclíti·co -ca *adj* & *m* enclitic

enclocar §81 *intr* & *ref* to brood

encofrado *m* planking, timbering; (*para el hormigón*) form

encoger §17 *tr* to shrink, shrivel; to discourage; to draw in ‖ *intr* to shrink, shrivel ‖ *ref* to shrink, shrivel; to be discouraged; to be bashful; (*humillarse*) to cringe; (*en la cama*) to curl up; **encogerse de hombros** to shrug one's shoulders

encogi·do -da *adj* bashful, timid

encogimiento *m* shrinkage; crouch; bashfulness, timidity; **encogimiento de hombros** shrug

encojar *tr* to cripple, to lame ‖ *ref* to become lame; (coll) to feign illness

encolar *tr* to glue; (*la superficie que ha de pintarse*) to size; (*el vino*) to clarify; (*p.ej., una pelota*) to throw out of reach

encolerizar §60 *tr* to anger ‖ *ref* to get angry

encomendar §2 *tr* to commend, entrust, commit; to knight ‖ *ref* to commend oneself; to send regards

encomiar *tr* to praise, extol

encomienda *f* charge, commission; commendation, praise; favor, protection; knight's cross; royal land grant (*with Indian inhabitants*); (Am) parcel post; (Mex) fruit stand

encomio *m* encomium

enconamiento *m* soreness; rancor, ill will

enconar *tr* to make sore, inflame; to aggravate, irritate ‖ *ref* to get sore, become inflamed; (*una herida; el ánimo de uno*) to rankle, to fester

enconchar *ref* (Am) to draw back into one's shell, keep aloof

encono *m* rancor, ill will; (Col, Chile, Mex, W-I) soreness

encono·so -sa *adj* sore, sensitive; harmful; rancorous

encontra·do -da *adj* opposite, facing; contrary; hostile; **estar encontrados** to be at odds

encontrar *tr* to encounter, to meet; (*ha-*

llar) to find ‖ *intr* to meet; to collide ‖ *ref* to meet, meet each other; to be, be situated; to find oneself; **encontrarse con** to meet, run into

encontrón *m* bump, jolt, collision

encopeta‧do -da *adj* aristocratic, of noble descent; conceited, boastful

encorajar *tr* to encourage ‖ *ref* to fly into a rage

encorajinar *ref* (coll) to fly into a rage; (Chile) to break up, go to ruin

encorchar *tr* (*botellas*) to cork; (*abejas*) to hive

encordar §61 *tr* (*un violín, una raqueta*) to string; to wrap, wind up with rope

encordelar *tr* to string; to tie with strings

encornudar *tr* to cuckold, make a cuckold of ‖ *intr* to grow horns

encorralar *tr* to corral

encortinar *tr* to curtain

encorvada *f* stoop, bending over; **hacer la encorvada** (coll) to malinger

encorvar *tr* to bend over ‖ *ref* to stoop, bend over; to be partial, be biased

encovar §61 *tr & ref* to hide away

encrespar *tr* to curl; (*el pelo*) to make stand on end; (*plumas*) to ruffle; (*las olas*) to stir up; to irritate, anger ‖ *ref* to curl; to bristle, stand on end; (*el mar, las olas*) to get rough; to get involved; to bristle, get angry

encresta‧do -da *adj* proud, haughty

encrucijada *f* crossroads, street intersection; ambush, snare, trap

encrudecer §22 *tr* to make raw; to aggravate

encuadernación *f* bookbinding; (*taller*) bindery; **encuadernación a la holandesa** half binding

encuaderna‧dor -dora *mf* bookbinder

encuadernar *tr* to bind; **sin encuadernar** unbound

encuadrar *tr* (*encerrar en un marco o cuadro*) to frame; (*incluir dentro de sí*) to encompass; (*encajar*) to insert, fit in; (Arg) to summarize

encuadre *m* film adaptation; (mov & telv) frame

encubar *tr* to put in a cask or vat; (min) to shore up

encubierta *f* fraud, deception

encubrimiento *m* concealment; (law) complicity

encubrir §83 *tr* to hide, conceal ‖ *ref* to hide; to disguise oneself

encuentro *m* encounter, meeting; clash, collision; (*hallazgo*) find; **encuentro fronterizo** border clash; **llevarse de encuentro** (CAm, Mex, W-I) to knock down, run over; (CAm, Mex, W-I) to drag down to ruin; **mal encuentro** foul play; **salir al encuentro a** to go to meet; to get ahead of; to take a stand against

encuerar *tr* (Am) to strip of clothes; (Am) to fleece ‖ *ref* (Am) to strip, get undressed

encuesta *f* inquiry; (*cuestionario para conocer la opinión pública*) poll, survey

encuitar *ref* to grieve

encumbra‧do -da *adj* high, lofty; sublime; influential

encumbramiento *m* height, elevation; exaltation

encumbrar *tr* to raise, elevate; to exalt ‖ *ref* to rise; to be exalted; to be proud; to be flowery, use flowery speech; (*subir una cosa a mucha altura*) to tower

encunar *tr* to cradle; to catch between the horns

encurtido *m* pickle

encurtir *tr* to pickle

enchapado *m* veneer

enchapar *tr* to veneer

encharcar §73 *tr* to make a puddle of; (*el estómago*) to upset ‖ *ref* to turn into a puddle; to wallow in vice

enchavetar *tr* to key

enchilada *f* (Guat, Mex) corn cake with tomato sauce seasoned with chili

enchilado *m* (Cuba, Mex) shellfish stew with chili sauce

enchinar *tr* to pave with pebbles; (Mex) to curl ‖ *ref* (Mex) to get goose flesh

enchispar *tr* (Am) to make drunk ‖ *ref* (Am) to get drunk

enchivar *ref* (Col, Ecuad, CAm) to fly into a rage

enchufar *tr* (*un tubo o caño*) to fit; (*dos tubos o caños*) to connect, connect together; (*dos negocios*) to merge; (elec) to connect, plug in ‖ *intr* to fit ‖ *ref* to merge

enchufe *m* fitting; (*de tubo o caño*) male end; (*de dos tubos*) joint; (elec) connector; (elec) plug; (elec) receptacle; (coll) sinecure, easy job; **tener enchufe** (coll) to have pull, to have a drag

enchufismo *m* (coll) spoils system

enchufista *m* (coll) spoilsman

ende *adv* — **por ende** therefore

endeble *adj* feeble, weak; worthless

endecha *f* dirge

endechadera *f* hired mourner

endemia *f* endemic

endémi‧co -ca *adj* endemic

endemonia‧do -da *adj* possessed of the devil; furious, wild; (coll) devilish

endentar §2 *tr & intr* to mesh

endentecer §22 *intr* to teethe

enderezar §60 *tr* to stand up; to straighten; to direct; to put in order; to regulate ‖ *intr* to go straight ‖ *ref* to stand up, straighten up; to head, make one's way; to go straight; (aer) to flatten out, to level off

endeuda‧do -da *adj* indebted

endeudar *ref* to run into debt; to acknowledge one's indebtedness

endevota‧do -da *adj* pious, devout; fond, devoted

endiabla‧do -da *adj* devilish; deformed, ugly; mean, wicked; (Arg) difficult, complicated

endilgar §44 *tr* (coll) to send, direct; (coll) to spring, unload

endiosar *tr* to deify ‖ *ref* to get stuck-up; to get absorbed

endominga‧do -da *adj* Sunday; all dressed up

endomingar §44 *ref* to get dressed in one's Sunday best

endosante *mf* endorser

endosar *tr* (*un documento de crédito*) to endorse; (*una cosa poco grata*) to unload

endosata·rio -ria *mf* endorsee

endoso *m* endorsement

endriago *m* fabulous monster

endri·no -na *adj* sloe-colored ‖ *m* (*arbusto*) sloe, blackthorn ‖ *f* (*fruto*) sloe

endrogar §44 *ref* (Am) to run into debt

endulzar §60 *tr* to sweeten; to make bearable

endura·dor -dora *adj* saving, stingy

endurar *tr* to harden; to delay, put off; (*tolerar*) to endure; to save, spare ‖ *ref* to get hard

endurecer §22 *tr* to harden; (*robustecer, acostumbrar*) to inure

endureci·do -da *adj* hard, strong; inured; hard-hearted; tenacious, obstinate

enebrina *f* juniper berry

enebro *m* juniper

enecha·do -da *adj & mf* foundling

eneldo *m* dill

enema *f* enema

enemiga *f* enmity, hatred

enemi·go -ga *adj* enemy; hostile ‖ *mf* enemy, foe; **el enemigo malo** the Evil One ‖ *f* see **enemiga**

enemistad *f* enmity

enemistar *tr* to make an enemy of; to make enemies of ‖ *ref* to become enemies

energía *f* energy; power

enérgi·co -ca *adj* energetic

energúme·no -na *adj* fiendish ‖ *mf* crazy person, wild person

enero *m* January

enervar *tr* to enervate; to weaken

enési·mo -ma *adj* nth

enfadadi·zo -za *adj* peevish, irritable

enfadar *tr* to annoy, bother; to anger

enfado *m* annoyance, bother; anger

enfado·so -sa *adj* annoying, disagreeable

enfaldar *ref* to tuck up one's skirt

enfardar *tr* to bale, to pack

énfa·sis *m* (*pl* -sis) emphasis; bombast, affected speech

enfasizar §60 *tr* to emphasize

enfáti·co -ca *adj* emphatic; affected

enfermar *tr* to make sick ‖ *intr* to get sick

enfermedad *f* sickness, illness, disease

enfermera *f* nurse; **enfermera ambulante** visiting nurse

enfermería *f* infirmary

enfermero *m* male nurse

enfermi·zo -za *adj* sickly; (*clima*) unhealthy

enfer·mo -ma *adj* sick, ill; (*enfermizo*) sickly; **enfermo de amor** lovesick ‖ *mf* patient

enfermo·so -sa *adj* (Am) sickly

enfiestar *ref* (Am) to have a good time

enfilar *tr* to line up; (*p.ej., perlas*) to string; to aim; to go down, to go up; (mil) to enfilade ‖ *intr* to bear

enfisema *m* emphysema

enflaquecer §22 *tr* to make thin; to weaken ‖ *intr* to get thin; to flag, slacken ‖ *ref* to get thin, lose weight

enflauta·do -da *adj* (coll) pompous, inflated

enflautar *tr* to blow up, inflate; (coll) to cheat

enfocar §73 *tr* to focus; (fig) to size up

enfoque *m* focus, focusing; (fig) approach (*to a problem*)

enfoscar §73 *tr* to trim with mortar; to patch with mortar; to darken, make dark ‖ *ref* to become sullen, become grouchy; to become absorbed in business; to become overcast

enfrailar *tr* to make a friar or monk of ‖ *ref* to become a friar or monk

enfranque *m* shank

enfrascar §73 *tr* to bottle ‖ *ref* to become involved, intangled; to be sunk in work; to have a good time

enfrenar *tr* (*un caballo*) to bridle; (*un tren*) to brake; to check

enfrentar *tr* to put face to face; (*p.ej., al enemigo*) to face ‖ *intr* to be facing ‖ *ref* to meet face to face; **enfrentarse con** to stand up to; to cope with

enfrente *adv* opposite, in front; **enfrente de** opposite, in front of; opposed to

enfriadera *f* bottle cooler, ice pail

enfriar §77 *tr* to cool, to chill; (Am) to kill ‖ *intr & ref* to cool off

enfundar *tr* to sheathe, to put in a case; to stuff; (*un tambor*) to muffle

enfurecer §22 *tr* to infuriate, anger ‖ *ref* to rage

enfurruñar *ref* (coll) to sulk

engalanar *tr* to adorn, deck out, dress

engalla·do -da *adj* straight, erect; haughty

enganchar *tr* to hook; (*un caballo*) to hitch; (*un coche de ferrocarril*) to couple; to recruit; to inveigle ‖ *intr* to get caught ‖ *ref* to get caught; (mil) to enlist

enganche *m* hook; hooking; hitching; coupling; inveigling; recruiting; enlisting; (rr) coupler

engañabo·bos *mf* (*pl* -bos) (coll) bamboozler

engaña·dor -dora *adj* deceptive; (*simpático*) winsome

engañar *tr* to deceive, cheat, fool; (*el tiempo*) to while away; (*el sueño, el hambre*) to ward off; to wheedle ‖ *ref* to be mistaken

engañifa *f* (coll) deception, trick

engaño *m* deception, deceit, fraud; mistake; falsehood; **llamarse a engaño** to back out because of fraud

engaño·so -sa *adj* deceptive

engargantar *tr* (*un ave*) to stuff the throat of ‖ *intr & ref* to mesh, to engage

engarzar §60 *tr* to link, string, wire; to curl; to enchase; (Col) to hook

engastar *tr* to enchase, mount, set

engaste *m* enchasing, mounting, setting

engatusar *tr* (coll) to coax, wheedle; to inveigle

engendrar tr to beget, engender; (geom) to generate

engendro m foetus; botch, bungle; (criatura informe) runt, stunt; **mal engendro** (coll) young tough

engolfar intr to go far out in the ocean ‖ ref to go far out in the ocean; to become deeply involved; to be lost in thought

engoma·do -da adj (Chile) all dressed up ‖ m (CAm) hangover

engomar tr to gum ‖ ref (Am) to have a hangover

engorda f (Am) fattening; (Am) animals being fattened

engordar tr to fatten ‖ intr to get fat; (coll) to get fat, get rich

engorro m bother, nuisance, obstacle

engorro·so -sa adj annoying

engoznar tr to hinge, to hang on a hinge

engranaje m gear, gears, teeth; (fig) link, connection; **engranaje de distribución** (aut) timing gears; **engranaje de tornillo sin fin** worm gear

engranar tr to gear, to mesh; to throw into gear ‖ intr to gear, to mesh

engrandecer §22 tr to amplify, enlarge, magnify; to exalt, extol; to enhance

engrane m gear; mesh

engranerar tr (el grano) to store

engrapar tr to clamp, to cramp

engrasador m grease cup; **engrasador de pistón** grease gun

engrasar tr to grease; to smear with grease

engrase m greasing; grease

engravar tr to spread gravel over

engredar tr to chalk, to clay

engreí·do -da adj conceited, vain

engreimiento m conceit, vanity

engreír §58 tr to make conceited; (Am) to spoil, pamper ‖ ref to become conceited

engreña·do -da adj disheveled

engrescar §73 tr to incite to fight; to incite to merriment ‖ ref to pick a fight; to join in the fun

engrifar tr to curl, to crisp ‖ ref to curl up; to stand on end; (un caballo) to rear

engrillar tr to shackle, fetter ‖ ref (las patatas) to sprout

engringar §44 ref to act like a foreigner

engrosar §61 tr to broaden; to enlarge ‖ intr to get fat ‖ ref to broaden; to swell, get bigger

engrudar tr to paste

engrudo m paste

engualdrapar tr to caparison

enguapear ref (Mex) to get drunk

enguirnaldar tr to garland, to wreathe; to trim, bedeck

engullir §13 tr to gulp down

engurrio m sadness, melancholy

enhebrar tr (una aguja) to thread; (perlas) to string; (mentiras) (coll) to rattle off

enhestar §2 tr to stand upright, to erect; to hoist, lift up

enhies·to -ta adj upright, straight, erect

enhilar tr to thread; to direct; to line up; (ideas) to marshal ‖ intr to set out

enhorabuena adv safely, luckily; **enhorabuena que** thank heavens that ‖ f congratulations; **dar la enhorabuena a** to congratulate

enhoramala adv unluckily, under an unlucky star; **nacer enhoramala** to be born under an unlucky star; **vete enhoramala** go to the devil

enhornar tr to put into the oven

enigma m enigma, riddle, puzzle

enigmáti·co -ca adj enigmatic(al)

enjabonar tr to soap, to lather; (adular) (coll) to soft-soap; (reprender) (coll) to upbraid

enjaezar §60 tr to harness, put trappings on

enjalbegado m whitewashing

enjalbegar §44 tr to whitewash; (el rostro) to paint ‖ ref to paint the face

enjambrar intr (las abejas) to swarm; to multiply in great numbers

enjambre m swarm

enjaretado m grating, lattice work

enjarrar ref (C-R, Mex) to stand with arms akimbo

enjaular tr to cage; (coll) to jail, lock up

enjergar §44 tr (coll) to launch, get started, to start on a shoestring

enjoyar tr to adorn with jewels; to set with precious stones; to adorn

enjuagadien·tes m (pl -tes) mouthwash

enjuagar §44 tr to rinse, rinse out

enjuague m rinse; rinsing water; mouthwash; rinsing cup; (coll) plot

enjugador m drier; clotheshorse

enjugama·nos m (pl -nos) towel, hand towel

enjugaparabri·sas m (pl -sas) windshield wiper

enjugar §44 tr (secar) to dry; (el sudor) to wipe, wipe off; (lágrimas) to wipe away; (deudas, un déficit) to wipe out ‖ ref to lose weight

enjuiciamiento m procedure; prosecution, suit; trial; judgment, sentence

enjuiciar tr to prosecute, to sue; to try; to judge

enjundio·so -sa adj fatty, greasy; solid, substantial

enju·to -ta adj (tiempo, clima; ojos) dry; lean, skinny; quiet, stolid ‖ **enjutos** mpl brushwood; (para excitar la gana de beber) tidbits

enlabiar tr to entice, take in; to press one's lips against

enlace m connection, linking; relationship; betrothal, engagement; marriage; (mil, phonet) liaison; (rr) connection, junction

enlaciar tr, intr & ref to wither, wilt, shrivel; to rumple

enladrillado m brickwork; bricklaying; brick paving

enladrillar tr to pave with bricks

enlajado m (Ven) flagstone

enlajar tr (Ven) to pave with flagstones

enlardar tr to baste

enlatado m canning

enlatar tr to can; (Am) to roof with tin, to line with tin

enlazar §60 tr to connect, to link; to lace; (un animal con el lazo) to lasso

|| *intr* (*p.ej., dos trenes*) to connect || *ref* to be connected, to be linked; to connect; to get married; to become related by marriage

enlechar *tr* to grout

enlistonado *m* lathing, lath

enlistonar *tr* to lath

enlodar *tr* to muddy, smear with mud; to plaster with mud; to seal with mud; (fig) to sling mud at

enloquecer §22 *tr* to drive crazy || *intr* to go crazy

enloquecimiento *m* insanity, madness

enlosado *m* flagstone paving

enlosar *tr* to pave with flagstone

enlozar §60 *tr* (Am) to enamel

enlozado *m* (Am) enamelware

enlucido *m* plaster, coat (*of plaster*)

enlucir §45 *tr* (*una pared*) to plaster; (*la plata*) to polish

enlutar *tr* to put in mourning, to hang with crape; to darken, sadden || *ref* to dress in mourning

enmaderar *tr* to cover with boards; to build the framework for

enmagrecer §22 *tr* to make thin || *intr & ref* to get thin

enmalecer §22 *tr* to spoil || *ref* to get full of weeds, to be overgrown with weeds

enmarañar *tr* to entangle; to confuse || *ref* to become entangled; to become overcast, get cloudy

enmarcar §73 *tr* to frame

enmarchitar *tr & ref* to wither

enmaridar *intr & ref* to take a husband

enmarillecer §22 *ref* to turn yellow, to turn pale

enmasar *tr* (*tropas*) to mass

enmascarar *tr* to mask; to camouflage || *ref* to put on a mask; to masquerade

enmasillar *tr* to putty

enmendación *f* emendation

enmendar §2 *tr* (*corregir*) to emend; (*reformar*) to amend; (*resarcir*) to make amends for || *ref* to amend, to mend one's ways, to go straight

enmienda *f* (*corrección*) emendation; (*propuesta de variante*) amendment; (*satisfacción del daño hecho*) amends

enmohecer §22 *tr* to make moldy; to rust; to neglect || *ref* to get moldy; to rust; (*la memoria*) to get rusty; to fade away

enmontar *ref* (CAm, Mex, Col, Ven) to become overgrown with brush

enmudecer §22 *tr* to hush, to silence || *intr* to hush up, keep quiet; to become dumb, lose one's voice

enmuescar §73 *tr* to notch; (carp) to mortise

ennegrecer §22 *tr* to blacken, dye black || *ref* to turn black; (*el porvenir*) to be black

ennoblecer §22 *tr* to ennoble; to glorify, enhance

ennoblecimiento *m* ennoblement; glory, splendor; (*grandeza de alma*) nobility

enodio *m* fawn, young deer

enojada *f* (Mex) fit of anger

enojadi·zo -za *adj* irritable, ill-tempered

enojar *tr* to anger; to annoy, vex || *ref* to get angry; **enojarse con** or **contra** to get angry with (*a person*); **enojarse de** to get angry at (*a thing*)

enojo *m* anger; annoyance, bother

eno·jón -jona *adj* (Chile, Ecuad, Mex) irritable, ill-tempered

enojo·so -sa *adj* annoying, bothersome

enorgullecer §22 *tr* to fill with pride, make proud || *ref* to be proud; **enorgullecerse de** to pride oneself on

enorme *adj* enormous, huge

enquiciar *tr* (*una puerta, una ventana*) to hang; to fasten, make firm

enrabiar *tr* to enrage || *intr* to have rabies || *ref* to become enraged

enramar *tr* (*ramos*) to intertwine; to adorn with branches || *intr* to sprout branches || *ref* to hide in the branches

enranciar *tr* to make rancid || *ref* to get rancid

enrarecer §22 *tr* to rarefy; to make scarce || *intr* to become scarce || *ref* to rarefy; to become scarce

enrarecimiento *m* (*p.ej., del aire*) thinness; scarceness, scarcity

enrasar *tr* to make flush; to grade, to level || *intr* to be flush

enratonar *ref* (coll) to get sick from eating mice; (Ven) to have a hangover

enredadera *adj* (*planta*) climbing || *f* climbing plant, vine

enreda·dor -dora *mf* (coll) gossip, busybody

enredar *tr* to catch in a net; (*redes, una trampa*) to set; to tangle up; to involve, to entangle; (*una pelea*) to start; to intertwine, interweave; to endanger, compromise || *intr* to romp around, to be frisky || *ref* to get tangled up; to get involved, become entangled; (coll) to have an affair

enredijo *m* entanglement

enredo *m* tangle; involvement, entanglement, complication; restlessness, friskiness; mischievous lie; (*de una novela, un drama*) plot; (*trato ilícito de hombre y mujer*) liaison

enre·dón -dona *adj* scheming || *mf* schemer

enredo·so -sa *adj* entangled, complicated; difficult

enrejado *m* grating, trellis, latticework; iron railing; grill; openwork embroidery

enrejar *tr* to grate, lattice; (*una ventana*) to put a grate on; to fence with an iron grating; (*ladrillos, tablas*) to pile alternately crosswise; (Mex) to darn

enrielar *tr* to make into ingots; (Am) to lay rails on; (Am) to put on the tracks; (Am) to put on the right track

enriquecer §22 *tr* to enrich || *intr & ref* to get rich

enrisca·do -da *adj* craggy, full of cliffs

enrizar §60 *tr & ref* to curl

enrocar §73 *tr & intr* (chess) to castle

enrodrigar §44 *tr* to prop, prop up

enrojar *tr* to redden, make red; (*el*

horno) to heat up ‖ *ref* to redden, turn red

enrojecer §22 *tr* to make red; to make red-hot; to make blush ‖ *intr* to blush ‖ *ref* to turn red; to get red-hot; to flush; to get sore, get inflamed

enromar *tr* to make dull, make blunt

enronquecer §22 *tr* to make hoarse ‖ *intr* & *ref* to get hoarse

enronquecimiento *m* hoarseness

enroque *m* (chess) castling

enroscar §73 *tr* to coil, twist; to screw in ‖ *ref* to coil, twist

enrubiar *tr* to bleach, make blond ‖ *ref* to turn blond

enrubio *m* bleaching; bleaching lotion

enrular *tr* & *ref* (Arg) to curl

ensacar §73 *tr* to bag, put in a bag

ensaimada *f* twisted coffee cake

ensalada *f* salad; hodgepodge; fiasco, flop

ensaladera *f* salad bowl

ensalmar *tr* (*un hueso*) to set; to treat or heal by incantation

ensalmo *m* incantation, spell; **como por ensalmo** as if by magic

ensalzar §60 *tr* to exalt, elevate, extol

ensamblar *tr* to assemble, join, fit together; **ensamblar a cola de milano** or **a cola de pato** to dovetail

ensanchador *m* glove stretcher

ensanchar *tr* to widen, to enlarge; (*una prenda ajustada*) to ease, let out; (*el corazón*) to unburden ‖ *intr* & *ref* to be proud and haughty

ensanche *m* widening, extension; (*de una calle*) extension; suburban development; allowance (*for enlargement of garment*)

ensandecer §22 *intr* to go crazy

ensangrenta·do -da *adj* bloody, gory

ensangrentar §2 *tr* to bathe in blood; to stain with blood ‖ *ref* to rage, to go wild; (*p.ej., las manos*) to bloody, make bloody

ensañar *tr* to anger, enrage ‖ *ref* to be cruel, be merciless; (*una enfermedad*) to rage

ensartar *tr* (*una aguja*) to thread; (*cuentas*) to string; to stick; (coll) to rattle off ‖ *ref* to squeeze in

ensayar *tr* to try, try on, try out; (*un espectáculo*) to rehearse; (*minerales*) to assay; to teach, train; to test ‖ *ref* to practice

ensaye *m* assay

ensayista *mf* essayist; (Chile) assayer

ensayo *m* trying, trial; testing, test; (*género literario*) essay; (*de minerales*) assay; exercise, practice; (theat) rehearsal; **ensayo general** dress rehearsal

ensenada *f* inlet, cove

enseña *f* standard, ensign

enseña·do -da *adj* trained, informed; (*perro de caza*) trained

enseñanza *f* teaching; education, instruction; (*ejemplo que sirve de experiencia*) lesson; **enseñanza superior** higher education

enseñar *tr* to teach; to train; to show, point out ‖ *intr* to teach

enseñorear *ref* to control oneself; **enseñorearse de** to take possession of

enseres *mpl* utensils, equipment, household goods

enseriar *ref* (Am) to become serious

ensillar *tr* to saddle

ensimismamiento *m* absorption in thought, deep thought

ensimismar *ref* to become absorbed in thought; (Chile, Ecuad, Peru) to be proud, be boastful

ensoberbecer §22 *tr* to make proud ‖ *ref* to become proud; (*el mar, las olas*) to swell, get rough

ensoberbecimiento *m* haughtiness

ensombrecer §22 *tr* to darken ‖ *ref* to get dark; to become sad and gloomy

ensoña·dor -dora *adj* dreamy ‖ *mf* dreamer

ensopar *tr* to dip, to dunk; (Am) to soak, to drench

ensordece·dor -dora *adj* deafening

ensordecer §22 *tr* to deafen; (*una consonante sonora*) to unvoice ‖ *intr* to become deaf; to play deaf, to not answer ‖ *ref* to unvoice

ensortijar *tr* to curl, make curly; (*la nariz de un animal*) to ring, put a ring in ‖ *ref* to curl

ensuciar *tr* to dirty, soil; to stain, smear; to defile, sully ‖ *ref* to soil oneself; to take bribes

ensueño *m* dream; daydream

entablado *m* flooring; wooden framework

entablar *tr* to board, board up; (*un hueso roto*) to splint; (*una conversación*) to start; (*p.ej., una batalla*) to launch; (*un pleito*) to bring; (*las piezas del ajedrez y de las damas*) to set up ‖ *ref* (*el viento*) to settle

entable *m* boarding; (*en los juegos de ajedrez y damas*) position of men; (Col) business, undertaking

entablillar *tr* (*un hueso roto*) to splint

enta·blón -blona *adj* (Peru) blustering, bragging ‖ *mf* (Peru) bully

entalegar §44 *tr* to bag, put in a bag; (*dinero*) to hoard

entalladura *f* carving, sculpture; engraving; slot, groove, mortise; cut, incision (*in a tree*)

entallar *tr* to carve, to sculpture; to engrave; to notch; to groove, mortise; (*un traje*) to fit, to tailor ‖ *intr* to take shape; (*el vestido*) to fit; (coll) to go well, be fitting

entallecer §22 *intr* & *ref* to shoot, to sprout

entapizar §60 *tr* to tapestry, to hang with tapestry; to cover with a fabric; to overgrow, to spread over

entarimado *m* parquet, inlaid floor, hardwood floor

entarimar *tr* to parquet, to put an inlaid floor on ‖ *ref* (coll) to put on airs

entarugar §44 *tr* to pave with wooden blocks ‖ *ref* (*el sombrero*) (Ven) to stick on

ente *m* being; (coll) guy, queer duck

enteca·do -da or **ente·co -ca** *adj* sickly, frail

enteleri·do -da *adj* shaking with cold, shaking with fright; (Am) sickly, frail

entena *f* lateen yard

entenado -da *mf* stepchild || *m* stepson || *f* stepdaughter

entendederas *fpl* (coll) brains; **tener malas entendederas** (coll) to have no brains

entende·dor -dora *adj* understanding, intelligent || *mf* understanding person; **al buen entendedor, pocas palabras** a word to the wise is enough

entender *m* understanding, opinion || §51 *tr* to understand; to intend, mean || *intr* — **entender de** to be a judge of; to be experienced as; **entender de razón** to listen to reason; **entender en** to be familiar with, to deal with || *ref* to be understood; to be meant; to have a secret understanding; **entenderse con** to get along with; to concern; (*una mujer*) to have an affair with

entendi·do -da *adj* expert, skilled; informed; **no darse por entendido** to take no notice, to pretend not to understand; **los entendidos** informed sources; **un entendido en** a well-informed person in

entendimiento *m* understanding

entenebrecer §22 *tr* to darken; to confuse || *ref* to get dark; to become confused

entera·do -da *adj* informed, posted; (Chile) conceited; (Chile) intrusive, meddlesome || *mf* insider

enterar *tr* to inform, acquaint; (Am) to pay; (Arg, Chile) to complete || *intr* (Chile) to get better; (Chile) to drift along || *ref* to find out; (Am) to recover; **enterarse de** to find out about, to become aware of

entereza *f* entirety, completeness; wholeness; perfection; fairness; constancy, fortitude; strictness

enteri·zo -za *adj* in one piece

enternece·dor -dora *adj* moving, touching

enternecer §22 *tr* to move, to touch || *ref* to be moved to pity

enternecimiento *m* pity, compassion

ente·ro -ra *adj* entire, whole, complete; honest, upright; firm, energetic; sound, vigorous; (*tela*) strong, heavy || *m* (arith) integer; (Am) payment; (Chile) balance; **por entero** entirely, wholly, completely

enterrador *m* gravedigger

enterramiento *m* burial, interment; (*hoyo*) grave; (*monumento*) tomb

enterrar §2 *tr* to bury, inter; to outlive, survive || *ref* to hide away

entesar §2 *tr* to stretch, make taut

entibar *tr* to prop up, shore up || *intr* to rest, lean

entibiar *tr* to cool off; to temper, moderate || *ref* to cool off, cool down

entidad *f* entity; importance, consequence, moment; body, organization

entierro *m* burial, interment; (*hoyo*) grave; (*monumento*) tomb; funeral; funeral cortege; buried treasure

entintar *tr* to ink; to ink in; to stain with ink; to dye

entoldar *tr* to cover with awnings; to adorn with hangings || *ref* to get cloudy, become overcast; to swell with pride

entomología *f* entomology

entonación *f* intonation; blowing of bellows

entona·do -da *adj* arrogant; haughty; harmonious, in tune

entonar *tr* to intone; to sing in tune; (*el órgano*) to blow; (*colores*) to harmonize; to tone, tone up; (*alabanzas*) to sound || *intr* to sing in tune || *ref* to be puffed up with pride

entonces *adv* then || *m* — **por aquel entonces** at that time

entonelar *tr* to put in barrels, put in casks

entongar §44 *tr* (Mex, W-I) to pile up, pile in rows; (Col) to drive crazy

entono *m* intoning; arrogance, haughtiness

entontecer §22 *tr* to make foolish, make stupid || *intr* & *ref* to become foolish, become stupid

entorchado *m* bullion; **ganar los entorchados** to win one's stripes

entorna·do -da *adj* ajar, half-closed

entornar *tr* to half-close; (*los ojos*) to squint; (*una puerta*) to leave ajar; (*volcar*) to upset || *ref* to upset

entornillar *tr* to twist, to screw up

entorpecer §22 *tr* to stupefy; to obstruct, delay; to benumb; (*una cerradura, una ventana*) to make stick || *ref* to stick, get stuck

entortar §61 *tr* to bend, make crooked; to knock out the eye of || *ref* to bend, get crooked

entrada *f* entrance, entry; admission; arrival; income, receipts; admission ticket; entrance hall; (*número de personas que asisten a un espectáculo*) house; (*producto de cada función*) gate; (*amistad en alguna casa*) entree; (*naipes que guarda un jugador*) hand; (*de una comida*) entree; (*visita breve*) (coll) short call; (Col) down payment; (Mex) attack, onslaught; (elec) input; **dar entrada a** to admit; to give an opening to; (*un buque*) to give the right of entry to; **entrada de taquilla** gate; **entrada general** top gallery; **entrada llena** full house; **mucha entrada** good house, good turnout; **se prohibe la entrada** no admittance

entra·do -da *adj* (Chile) officious, self-assertive; **entrado en años** advanced in years || *f* see **entrada**

entra·dor -dora *adj* (Mex) lively, energetic; (*enamoradizo*) (Am) susceptible; (Chile) officious, self-assertive

entrama·do -da *adj* half-timbered || *m* timber framework

entram·bos -bas *adj* & *pron indef* both; **entrambos a dos** both

entrampar *tr* to ensnare, trap; to trick, deceive; (coll) to overload with debt || *ref* to get trapped; to be tricked; (coll) to run into debt

entrante *adj* entering; (*p.ej., tren*) inbound, incoming; (*próximo, que viene*) next || *mf* entrant; **entrantes y salientes** (coll) hangers-on

entraña *f* internal organ; (fig) heart, center; **entrañas** entrails; (fig) heart, feeling; (fig) disposition, temper

entrañable *adj* close, intimate

entrañar *tr* to put away deep, bury deep; to involve; (*malos pensamientos*) to harbor || *ref* to go deep into; to be buried deep; to be close, be intimate

entrapajar *tr* to wrap up, to bandage

entrar *tr* to bring in; to overrun, invade; to influence || *intr* to enter, go in, come in; (*un río*) to empty; (*el viento, la marea*) to rise; to attack; to begin; **entrar a matar** (taur) to go in for the kill; **entrar en** to enter, enter into, go into; to fit into; to adopt, take up; **que entra** next

entre *prep* (*en medio de*) between; (*en el número de*) among; (*en el intervalo de*) in the course of; **entre manos** at hand; **entre mí** to myself; **entre que** while; **entre tanto** meanwhile; **entre Vd. y yo** between you and me

entreabier-to -ta *adj* half-open; (*puerta*) ajar

entreabrir §83 *tr* to half-open; to leave ajar

entreacto *m* entr'acte

entreca-no -na *adj* graying, grayish

entrecarril *m* (Ven) gauge

entrecejo *m* space between the eyebrows; frown; **fruncir el entrecejo** to frown; **mirar con entrecejo** to frown at

entrecoger §17 *tr* to catch, seize; to press hard, to hold down

entrecoro *m* chancel

entrecorta-do -da *adj* broken, intermittent

entrecortar *tr* to break in on, keep interrupting

entre·cruz *m* (*pl* **-cruces**) interweaving

entrecruzar §60 *tr* & *ref* to intercross; to interweave, interlace; to interbreed

entrecubiertas *fpl* between-decks

entrechocar §73 *ref* to collide, to clash

entredicho *m* interdiction, prohibition; (law) injunction; (Bol) alarm bell; **poner en entredicho** to cast doubt upon

entredós *m* (*tira de encaje*) insertion; (typ) long primer

entrefilete *m* short feature, special item

entrefi·no -na *adj* medium

entrega *f* delivery; (*p.ej., de una plaza fuerte*) surrender; (*cuaderno de un libro que se vende suelto*) fascicle; (*de una revista*) issue, number; **por entregas** in instalments

entregar §44 *tr* to deliver; to hand over, surrender; to fit in, insert; **entregarla** (coll) to die || *ref* to give in, surrender; to abandon oneself; to devote oneself; **entregarse de** to take possession of, take charge of

entrehierro *m* (elec) spark gap; (phys) air gap

entrelazar §60 *tr* to interlace, interweave

entremediar *tr* to put between

entremedias *adv* in between; in the meantime; **entremedias de** between; among

entremés *m* hors d'œuvre, side dish; short farce (*inserted in an auto or performed between two acts of a comedia*)

entremesear *tr* (*una conversación*) to enliven

entremeter *tr* to put in, to insert || *ref* to meddle, intrude, butt in

entremeti-do -da *adj* meddling, meddlesome || *mf* meddler, intruder, busybody

entremezclar *tr* & *ref* to intermingle, intermix

entremorir §30 & §83 *intr* to flicker, die out

entrenador *m* (sport) coach, trainer, handler

entrenamiento *m* (sport) coaching, training

entrenar *tr* & *ref* (sport) to coach, to train

entrepaño *m* (*de una puerta*) panel; (*espacio entre dos columnas, etc.*) pier; shelf

entreparecer §60 *ref* to show through

entrepiernas *fpl* crotch; patches in the crotch of trousers; (Chile) bathing trunks

entrepuentes *mpl* between-decks; (naut) steerage

entrerrenglonar *tr* to write between the lines

entrerriel *m* gauge

entrerrisa *f* giggle

entrerrosca *f* (mach) nipple

entresacar §73 *tr* to pick, pick out, select; to cull, sift; (*árboles; el pelo*) to thin out

entresijo *m* secret; mystery; **tener muchos entresijos** to be mysterious, to be hard to figure out

entresuelo *m* mezzanine, entresol

entretallar *tr* to carve, to engrave; to carve in bas-relief; to do openwork in; to intercept

entretanto *adv* meantime, meanwhile || *m* meanwhile; **en el entretanto** in the meantime

entretecho *m* (Arg, Chile, Urug) attic, garret

entretejer *tr* to interweave

entretela *f* interlining

entretelar *tr* to interline

entretención *f* (Am) amusement, entertainment

entretener §71 *tr* to amuse, entertain; (*el tiempo*) to while away; to maintain, keep up; to put off, delay; (*el dolor*) to allay; (*el hambre*) to stave off (*by taking a bite before mealtime*); to try to get one's mind off || *ref* to amuse oneself, to be amused

entreteni-do -da *adj* amusing, entertaining; (rad) continuous, undamped || *f* kept woman; **dar la entretenida a** or **dar con la entretenida a** to stall off by constant talk

entretenimiento *m* amusement, entertainment; upkeep, maintenance

entretiempo *m* in-between season; **de entretiempo** spring-and-fall (*coat*)

entreventana *f* pier

entrever §80 *tr* to glimpse, descry, catch a glimpse of; to guess, suspect

entreverar *tr* to mix || *ref* (Arg) to get all mixed together; (*dos grupos de caballería*) (Arg) to clash in hand-to-hand combat

entrevía *f* gauge

entrevista *f* interview

entrevistar *ref* to have an interview

entristecer §22 *tr* to sadden, make sad || *ref* to sadden, become sad

entrojar *tr* to store in a granary

entrometer *tr* & *ref* var of **entremeter**

entrometi-do -da *adj* & *mf* var of **entremetido**

entronar *tr* to enthrone

entroncamiento *m* connection, relationship; (*de caminos, ferrocarriles*) (Am) junction

entroncar §73 *tr* to prove relationship between || *intr* to be related; (*dos caminos, ferrocarriles, etc.*) (Am) to connect

entronerar *tr* (*una bola de billar*) to pocket

entronizar §60 *tr* to enthrone; to exalt; to popularize || *ref* to be puffed up with pride

entronque *m* connection, relationship; (*de caminos, ferrocarriles*) (Am) junction

entruchar *tr* (coll) to decoy, to trick

entru·chón -chona *adj* (coll) tricky || *mf* (coll) trickster

entuerto *m* wrong, harm, injustice

entumecer §22 *tr* to make numb || *ref* (*un miembro*) to get numb, to go to sleep; (*el mar*) to swell, get rough

entupir *tr* to stop up, clog; to pack tight || *ref* to get stopped up, get clogged

enturbiar *tr* to stir up, make muddy; to confuse, upset

entusiasmar *tr* to enthuse, make enthusiastic || *ref* to enthuse, become enthusiastic

entusiasmo *m* enthusiasm; inspiration

entusiasta *adj* enthusiastic || *mf* enthusiast

entusiásti·co -ca *adj* enthusiastic

enumerar *tr* to enumerate

enunciar *tr* to enunciate, to enounce

enunciati·vo -va *adj* (gram) declarative

envainar *tr* to sheathe

envalentonar *tr* to embolden, make bold || *ref* to pluck up, take courage

envanecer §22 *tr* to make vain || *ref* to become vain, get conceited

envanecimiento *m* vanity, conceit

envarar *tr* to make numb, to stiffen

envasar *tr* (*p.ej., trigo*) to pack, to sack; (*p.ej., vino*) to bottle; (*p.ej., pescado*) to can; (*una espada*) to thrust, poke; (*mucho vino*) to put away || *intr* to tipple

envase *m* container; bottle, jar; can; packing; bottling; canning; **envase de hojalata** tin can

envedijar *ref* to get tangled; (coll) to come to blows

envejecer §22 *tr* to age, make old || *intr* & *ref* to age, grow old; to get out of date

envejeci·do -da *adj* old, aged; experienced, tried

envenenar *tr* to poison; (*llenar de amargura*) to envenom, embitter; (*las palabras o conducta de una persona*) to put an evil interpretation on || *ref* to take poison

enverdecer §22 *intr* to turn green

envergadura *f* (*de las alas abiertas del ave*) spread; (*ancho de una vela*) breadth; (aer) span, wingspread; (fig) compass, spread, reach

envés *m* wrong side; (*del cuerpo humano*) back

enviado *m* envoy

enviar §77 *tr* to send; (*mercancías*) to ship; **enviar a buscar** to send for; **enviar a paseo** (coll) to send on his way, to dismiss without ceremony; **enviar por** to send for

enviciar *tr* to corrupt, vitiate; (*mimar*) to spoil || *intr* to have many leaves and little fruit || *ref* to become addicted; **enviciarse con** *o* **en** to addict oneself to, become addicted to

envidar *tr* to bid against, to bet against || *intr* to bid, to bet

envidia *f* envy; desire

envidiable *adj* enviable

envidiar *tr* to envy, to begrudge; to desire, want

envidio·so -sa *adj* envious; greedy, covetous || *mf* envious person

envilecer §22 *tr* to debase, vilify, revile || *ref* to degrade oneself

envío *m* sending; (*de mercancías*) shipment; (*de dinero*) remittance; (*en una obra*) autograph, inscription

envirota·do -da *adj* stiff, stuck-up

envite *m* bet; bid, offer, invitation; push, shove; (*apuesta adicional a un lance o suerte*) side bet; **al primer envite** right off, at the start

enviudar *intr* (*una mujer*) to become a widow; (*un hombre*) to become a widower

envoltorio *m* bundle; (*defecto en el paño*) knot

envoltura *f* cover, wrapper, envelope; swaddling clothes

envolver §47 & §83 *tr* to wrap, wrap up; (*hilo, cinta*) to wind, roll up; (*al niño*) to swaddle; to imply, mean; to involve; to envelop; (*dejar cortado y sin salida en la disputa*) to floor; (mil) to encircle || *ref* to become involved; to have an affair

enyerbar *tr* (Col, Chile, Mex) to bewitch || *ref* (Am) to be covered with grass; (Mex) to fall madly in love; (Mex) to take poison

enyesar *tr* to plaster; to put in a plaster cast; (*la tierra, el vino*) to gypsum

enyugar §44 *tr* to yoke

enzima *f* enzyme

enzolvar *tr* (Mex) to clog, stop up

epazote *m* (CAm, Mex) Mexican tea

E.P.D. *abbr* en paz descanse

epénte·sis *f* (*pl* -sis) epenthesis

eperlano *m* smelt

épica *f* epic poetry

epice·no **-na** *adj* (gram) epicene, common

épi·co **-ca** *adj* epic ‖ *m* epic poet ‖ *f* see épica

epicúre·o **-a** *adj* epicurean ‖ *mf* epicurean, epicure

epidemia *f* epidemic

epidémi·co **-ca** *adj* epidemic

epidemiología *f* epidemiology

epidermis *f* epidermis; **tener la epidermis fina** or **sensible** (coll) to be touchy

Epifanía *f* Epiphany, Twelfth-day

epígrafe *m* epigraph; inscription; head-line, title; device, motto

epilepsia *f* epilepsy

epilépti·co **-ca** *adj* & *mf* epileptic

epilogar §44 *tr* to sum up, summarize

episcopalista *adj* & *mf* Episcopalian

episodio *m* episode

epistemología *f* epistemology

epístola *f* epistle

epitafio *m* epitaph

epíteto *m* epithet

epitomar *tr* to epitomize

epítome *m* epitome

E.P.M. *abbr* **en propia mano**

época *f* epoch; **hacer época** to be epoch-making

epopeya *f* epic, epic poem

equidad *f* equity; (*templanza habitual*) equableness; (*moderación en el precio*) reasonableness

equiláte·ro **-ra** *adj* equilateral

equilibrar *tr* to balance, equilibrate; (*el presupuesto*) to balance ‖ *ref* to balance, equilibrate

equilibrio *m* equilibrium, balance, equipoise; (*del presupuesto*) balancing; **equilibrio político** balance of power

equilibrista *mf* balancer, ropedancer

equinoccial *adj* equinoctial

equinoccio *m* equinox

equipaje *m* baggage; piece of baggage; equipment; (naut) crew; **equipaje de mano** hand baggage

equipar *tr* to equip

equiparar *tr* to compare

equi·pier *m* (*pl* -piers) teammate

equipo *m* equipment, outfit; crew, gang; (sport) team; **equipo de novia** trousseau; **equipo de urgencia** first-aid kit

equitación *f* horsemanship, riding

equitati·vo **-va** *adj* fair, equitable; (*tranquilo*) equable

equivalente *adj* & *m* equivalent

equivaler §76 *intr* to be equal, be equivalent

equivocación *f* mistake; mistakenness

equivoca·do **-da** *adj* mistaken, wrong

equivocar §73 *tr* (*una cosa por otra*) to mistake, to mix ‖ *ref* to be mistaken, to make a mistake; to be wrong; **equivocarse con** to be mistaken for; **equivocarse de** to be wrong in, take the wrong . . .

equívo·co **-ca** *adj* equivocal, ambiguous ‖ *m* equivocation, ambiguity; pun

equivoquista *mf* equivocator; punster

era *f* era, age; threshing floor; vegetable patch, garden bed

eral *m* two-year-old bull

erario *m* state treasury

erección *f* erection; foundation, establishment

eremita *m* hermit

ergástulo *m* dungeon, slave prison

ergio *m* erg

erguir §33 *tr* to raise; to straighten up ‖ *ref* to straighten up; to swell with pride

erial *adj* unplowed, uncultivated ‖ *m* unplowed land, uncultivated land

erigir §27 *tr* to erect, build; to found, establish; (*a nueva condición*) to elevate ‖ *ref* — **erigirse en** to be elevated to; to set oneself up as

eriza·do **-da** *adj* bristling, bristly, spiny

erizar §60 *tr* to make stand on end, cause to bristle ‖ *ref* to stand on end, to bristle

erizo *m* (*mamífero*) hedgehog; (*zurrón espinoso de la castaña*) bur, thistle; (*púas de hierro que coronan lo alto de una muralla*) cheval-de-frise; (*persona de carácter áspero*) (coll) curmudgeon; **erizo de mar** (zool) sea urchin

ermita *f* hermitage

ermita·ño **-ña** *mf* hermit

erogación *f* (*de bienes o caudales*) distribution; (Am) expenditure; (Peru, Ven) gift, charity; (Mex) outlay

erogar §44 *tr* to distribute; (Ecuad) to contribute; (Mex) to cause

erosión *f* erosion

erosionar *tr* & *ref* to erode

erradicar §73 *tr* to eradicate

erra·do **-da** *adj* mistaken, wrong

errar §34 *tr* to miss ‖ *intr* to err, to be mistaken, to be wrong; to wander ‖ *ref* to be mistaken, to be wrong

errata *f* erratum; printer's error

erróne·o **-a** *adj* erroneous

error *m* error, mistake; **error de pluma** clerical error; **salvo error u omisión** barring error or omission

eructar *intr* to belch; (coll) to brag

eructo *m* belch, belching

erudición *f* erudition, learning

erudi·to **-ta** *adj* erudite, learned ‖ *mf* scholar, savant; **erudito a la violeta** egghead, highbrow

erugino·so **-sa** *adj* rusty

erumpir *intr* (*un volcán*) to erupt

erupción *f* eruption

esbel·to **-ta** *adj* slender, lithe, willowy

esbirro *m* bailiff, constable; (*el que ejecuta órdenes injustas*) myrmidon, henchman

esbozar §60 *tr* to sketch, outline

esbozo *m* sketch, outline

escabechar *tr* to pickle; (*el pelo, la barba*) to dye; (*reprobar en un examen*) (coll) to flunk; (coll) to stab to death ‖ *ref* to dye one's hair; (*el pelo, la barba*) to dye

escabeche *m* pickle; pickled fish; hair dye

escabel *m* stool; footstool; (*para medrar*) stepping stone
escabio·so **-sa** *adj* mangy
escabro·so **-sa** *adj* scabrous, risqué; scabrous, uneven, rough, harsh
escabuche *m* weeding hoe
escabullir §13 *ref* to slip away, sneak away; to slip out, wiggle out
escafandra *f* diving suit; **escafandra espacial** space suit
escafandrista *mf* diver
escala *f* (*escalera de mano*) ladder, stepladder; (*línea graduada de instrumento*) scale; (*de buque*) call; (*de avión*) stop; (*puerto donde toca una embarcación*) port of call; (*serie de las notas musicales*) scale; **en escala de uno a** on a scale of; **en grande escala** on a large scale; **escala móvil** (*de salarios*) sliding scale; **hacer escala** (naut) to call
escalada *f* scaling, climbing; breaking in; escalation
escalador *m* climber; (*ladrón*) burglar, housebreaker
escalación *f* escalation
escalafón *m* roster, roll, register
escalar *tr* (*subir, trepar*) to scale; to break in, to burglarize; (*la compuerta de la acequia*) to open || *intr* to climb; (naut) to call || *ref* to escalate
escalato·rres *m* (*pl* **-rres**) steeplejack, human fly
escalda·do **-da** *adj* (coll) cautious, scared, wary; (*mujer*) (coll) lewd, loose
escaldar *tr* to scald; to make red hot || *ref* to get scalded; to chafe
escalera *f* stairs, stairway; (*la portátil*) ladder; (*de naipes*) sequence; (*en el póker*) straight; **de escalera abajo** from below stairs, from the servants'; **escalera de caracol** winding stairway; **escalera de escape** fire escape; **escalera de husillo** winding stairway; **escalera de incendios** fire escape; **escalera de mano** ladder; **escalera de salvamento** fire escape; **escalera de tijera** or **escalera doble** ladder; **escalera excusada** or **falsa** private stairs; **escalera extensible** extension ladder; **escalera hurtada** secret stairway; **escalera mecánica**, **móvil** or **rodante** escalator, moving stairway
escalerilla *f* low step; car step; (*en las medias*) runner; (*de naipes*) sequence; thumb index
escalfar *tr* (*huevos*) to poach; (*el pan*) to bake brown
escalinata *f* stone steps, front steps
escalo *m* burglary, breaking in
escalofría·do **-da** *adj* chilly
escalofrío *m* chill
escalón *m* step, rung; (*grada de la escalera*) tread; (fig) step, echelon, grade; (*paso con que uno adelanta sus pretensiones*) (fig) stepping stone; (mil) echelon; (rad) stage
escalonar *tr* to space out, spread out; (*las horas de trabajo*) to stagger; (mil) to echelon
escalope *m* (*loncha delgada de carne*) scallop (*thin slice of meat*)

escalpar *tr* to scalp
escalpelo *m* scalpel
escama *f* scale; fear, suspicion
escamar *tr* (*los peces*) to scale; (coll) to frighten || *ref* to be frightened
escamondar *tr* to trim, to prune
escamo·so **-sa** *adj* scaly
escamotea·dor **-dora** *mf* prestidigitator; swindler
escamotear *tr* to whisk out of sight, cause to vanish; (*una carta*) to palm; to swipe, to snitch
escampada *f* (coll) clear spell, break in rain
escampar *tr* to clear out || *intr* to stop raining; to ease up; **¡ya escampa!** (coll) there you go again! || *ref* — **escamparse del agua** (Am) to get in out of the rain
escampavía *f* (naut) cutter, revenue cutter
escamujar *tr* (*un árbol, esp. un olivo*) to prune; (*ramas*) to clear out
escanciar *tr* (*vino*) to pour, to serve, to drink || *intr* to drink wine
escandalizar §60 *tr* to scandalize || *ref* to be scandalized; to be outraged, be exasperated
escándalo *m* scandal; **causar escándalo** to make a scene
escandalo·so **-sa** *adj* scandalous; noisy, riotous; (Am) loud, flashy
escandallo *m* (naut) sounding lead; (*del contenido de varios envases*) testing, sampling; cost accounting
escandina·vo **-va** *adj* & *mf* Scandinavian
escandir *tr* (*versos*) to scan
escansión *f* scansion; (telv) scanning
escaño *m* settle, bench with a back; (*en las Cortes*) seat; (Am) park bench; (Guat) nag
escañuelo *m* footstool
escapada *f* escape, flight; short trip, quick trip
escapar *tr* to free, to save; (*un caballo*) to drive hard || *intr* to escape; to flee, run away; **escapar en una tabla** to have a narrow escape || *ref* to escape; to flee, run away; (*el gas, el agua*) to leak; **escapársele a uno** to let slip; to not notice
escaparate *m* show window; (*armario con cristales*) cabinet; (Am) wardrobe, clothes closet
escaparatista *mf* window dresser
escapatoria *f* escape, getaway; (*de atenciones, deberes, etc.*) (fig) escape; (*efugio, pretexto*) (coll) evasion, subterfuge
escape *m* escape; flight; (*de gas, agua*) leak; (*de reloj*) escapement; (aut) exhaust valve; (aut) exhaust, exhaust pipe; **a escape** at full speed, on the run; **escape de rejilla** (rad) grid leak; **escape libre** (aut) cutout
escápula *f* shoulder blade, scapula
escaque *m* square; **escaques** chess
escarabajear *tr* (coll) to bother, worry, harass || *intr* to swarm, crawl; to scrawl, scribble
escarabajo *m* black beetle; (*imperfec-*

ción en los tejidos) flaw; *(persona pequeña)* (coll) runt

escaramuza *f* skirmish

escaramuzar §60 *intr* to skirmish

escarapela *f (divisa en forma de lazo)* cockade; dispute ending in hair pulling

escarapelar *intr* & *ref* to quarrel, to wrangle

escarbadien-tes *m (pl -tes)* toothpick

escarbar *tr (el suelo)* to scratch, scratch up; *(la lumbre)* to poke; *(los dientes, los oídos)* to pick; to pry into

escarcha *f* frost, hoarfrost

escarchar *tr (confituras)* to frost, put frosting on; *(la tierra del alfarero)* to dilute with water; to spangle ‖ *intr —* escarcha there is frost

escardar or **escardillar** *tr* to weed, weed out

escardillo *m* weeding hoe

escariar *tr* to ream

escarlata *adj* scarlet ‖ *f* scarlet fever

escarlatina *f* scarlet fever

escarmentar §2 *tr* to make an example of ‖ *intr* to learn one's lesson

escarmiento *m* example, lesson, warning; caution, wisdom; punishment

escarnecer §22 *tr* to scoff at, make fun of

escarnio *m* scoff, scoffing

escarola *f* endive

escarpa *f* scarp, escarpment; (Mex) sidewalk

escarpa-do -da *adj* steep; abrupt, craggy

escarpia *f* hooked spike

escarpín *m* pump

escasear *tr* to give sparingly; to cut down on, to avoid; to bevel ‖ *intr* to be scarce

escase-ro -ra *adj* sparing; saving, frugal; stingy ‖ *mf* skinflint

escasez *f (falta de una cosa)* scarcity; *(pobreza)* need, want; *(mezquindad)* stinginess

esca-so -sa *adj (poco abundante)* scarce; *(no cabal)* scant; *(muy económico)* parsimonious, frugal; *(tacaño)* stingy; *(oportunidad)* dim, slim, slight; estar escaso de to be short of

escatimar *tr* & *intr* to scrimp

escena *f (parte del teatro donde se representan las obras)* stage; *(subdivisión de un acto)* scene; incident, episode; **poner en escena** to stage

escenario *m* stage; *(disposición de la representación)* setting; *(guión de un cine)* scenario; *(antecedentes de una persona o cosa)* background

escenarista *mf* scenarist

escéni-co -ca *adj* scenic

escenificar §73 *tr* to adapt for the stage

escépti-co -ca *adj* sceptic(al) ‖ *mf* sceptic

Escila *f* Scylla; **entre Escila y Caribdis** between Scylla and Charybdis

Escipión *m* Scipio

escisión *f* (biol) fission; (surg) excision

esclarecer §22 *tr* to light up, brighten; to explain, elucidate; to ennoble ‖ *intr* to dawn

esclareci-do -da *adj* noble, illustrious

esclavitud *f* slavery

esclavización *f* enslavement

esclavizar §60 *tr* to enslave

escla-vo -va *adj* & *mf* slave

escla-vón -vona *adj* & *mf* Slav

esclusa *f* lock; floodgate; **esclusa de aire** caisson

esclusero *m* lock tender

escoba *f* broom

escobada *f* sweep; sweeping

escobar *tr* to sweep with a broom

escobazar §60 *tr* to sprinkle with a wet broom

escobén *m* (naut) hawse

escobilla *f* brush, whisk; gold and silver sweepings; (elec) brush

escocer §16 *intr* to smart, sting ‖ *ref* to hurt; to chafe, become chafed

esco-cés -cesa *adj* Scotch, Scottish ‖ *mf* Scot ‖ *m* Scotchman; *(whisky; dialecto)* Scotch; **los escoceces** the Scotch, the Scottish

Escocia *f* Scotland; **la Nueva Escocia** Nova Scotia

escofina *f* rasp

escofinar *tr* to rasp

escoger §17 *tr* to choose, pick out

escogi-do -da *adj* choice, select

escolar *adj* school ‖ *m* pupil

escolaridad *f* schooling, school attendance; curriculum

escolimo-so -sa *adj* (coll) impatient, gruff, restless

escolta *f* escort

escoltar *tr* to escort

escollar *intr* (Arg) to run aground on a reef; (Arg, Chile) to fail

escollera *f* jetty, breakwater

escollo *m (peñasco a flor de agua)* reef, rock; *(peligro)* pitfall; *(obstáculo)* stumbling block

escombrar *tr* to clear out

escombro *m (pez)* mackerel; **escombros** debris, rubble, rubbish

esconder *tr* to hide, conceal; to harbor, contain ‖ *ref* to hide; to lurk

escondi-do -da *adj* hidden; **a escondidas** secretly; **a escondidas de** without the knowledge of

escondite *m* hiding place; *(juego de muchachos)* hide-and-seek; **jugar al escondite** to play hide-and-seek

escondrijo *m* hiding place

escopeta *f* shotgun; **escopeta blanca** gentleman hunter; **escopeta de caza** fowling piece; **escopeta de viento** air rifle; **escopeta negra** professional hunter

escopetazo *m* gunshot; gunshot wound; bad news, blow

escoplear *tr* to chisel

escoplo *m* chisel

escorbuto *m* scurvy

escoria *f* dross, scoria, slag; (fig) dross, dregs

escorial *m* cinder bank, slag dump

escorpión *m* scorpion

escorzar §60 *tr* to foreshorten

escorzo *m* foreshortening

escota *f* (naut) sheet

escota-do -da *adj* low-neck ‖ *m* low neck

escotadura *f* low neck, low cut in neck

escotar *tr* to cut to fit; to draw water

from, to drain; to cut low in the neck || *intr* to go Dutch

escote *m* low neck; (*encajes en el cuello de una vestidura*) tucker; **ir a escote** or **pagar a escote** to go Dutch

escotilla *f* (naut) hatchway, scuttle

escotillón *m* hatch, trap door, scuttle; (theat) trap door

escozor *m* burning, smarting, stinging; grief, sorrow

escriba *m* scribe

escribanía *f* court clerkship; desk; writing materials

escribano *m* court clerk; lawyer's clerk

escribiente *mf* clerk, office clerk; **escribiente a máquina** typist

escribir §83 *tr & intr* to write || *ref* to enroll, enlist; to write to each other; **no escribirse** to be impossible to describe

escriño *m* casket, jewel case; straw basket

escri·to -ta *adj* streaked || *m* writing; (law) brief, writ; **poner por escrito** to write down, put in writing

escri·tor -tora *mf* writer

escritorio *m* writing desk; office; **escritorio ministro** kneehole desk, office desk; **escritorio norteamericano** rolltop desk

escritura *f* writing; script, handwriting, longhand; (law) deed, indenture; (law) sworn statement; **escritura al tacto** touch typewriting || **Escritura** *f* Scripture; **Sagrada Escritura** Holy Scripture, Holy Writ

escriturar *tr* to notarize; (*p.ej., a un actor*) to book || *ref* (taur) to sign up for a fight

escrnía. *abbr* **escribanía**

escrno. *abbr* **escribano**

escrófula *f* scrofula

escrúpulo *m* scruple

escrupulo·so -sa *adj* scrupulous; exact

escrutar *tr* to scrutinize; (*los votos*) to count

escrutinio *m* scrutiny; counting of votes

escuadra *f* (*pequeño número de personas o de soldados*) squad; (*pieza de metal para asegurar las ensambladuras*) angle iron; (*de carpintero*) square; (*de dibujante*) triangle; (nav) squadron

escuadrar *tr* (carp) to square

escuadrilla *f* (aer) squadron

escuadrón *m* (mil) squadron

escualidez *f* squalor

escuáli·do -da *adj* squalid

escualor *m* squalor

escucha *mf* listener || *m* (mil) scout, vedette || *f* listening; (*en un convento*) chaperon; **estar de escucha** (coll) to eavesdrop

escuchar *tr* to listen to; (*atender a*) to heed; (*radiotransmisiones*) to monitor || *intr* to listen || *ref* to like the sound of one's own voice

escudar *tr* to shield

escudero *m* esquire; nobleman; lady's page

escudete *m* escutcheon; (*refuerzo en la ropa*) gusset; (*planchuela delante de la cerradura*) escutcheon, escutcheon plate

escudilla *f* bowl

escudo *m* shield; buckler; (*delante de la cerradura*) escutcheon plate; **escudo de armas** coat of arms; **escudo térmico** (*de una cápsula espacial*) heat shield

escudriñar *tr* to scrutinize

escuela *f* school; **escuela de artes y oficios** trade school; **escuela de párvulos** kindergarten; **escuela de verano** summer school; **escuela dominical** Sunday school; **Escuela Naval Militar** Naval Academy; **hacer escuela** to be the leader of a school (*of thought*)

escuelante *mf* (Mex) schoolteacher || *m* (Mex) schoolboy || *f* (Mex) schoolgirl

escuerzo *m* toad

escue·to -ta *adj* free, unencumbered; bare, unadorned

escuintle *adj* (Mex) sickly || *m* (*perro*) (Mex) mutt; (Mex) brat

esculcar §73 *tr* (dial & Am) to frisk

esculpir *tr & intr* to sculpture, to carve; to engrave

escultismo *m* outdoor activities

escultista *m* outdoorsman

escultor *m* sculptor

escultora *f* sculptress

escultura *f* sculpture

escultural *adj* sculptural; statuesque

escupidera *f* cuspidor; (Am) chamber pot

escupidura *f* spit; fever blister

escupir *tr & intr* to spit

escurrepla·tos *m* (pl -tos) dish rack

escurridero *m* drainpipe; drainboard; slippery spot

escurridi·zo -za *adj* slippery

escurri·do -da *adj* narrow-hipped; (Am) abashed, confused

escurridor *m* colander

escurriduras *fpl* dregs, lees

escurrir *tr* (*una vasija; un líquido; la vajilla*) to drain; to wring, wring out; **escurrir el bulto** (coll) to duck || *intr* to drip, ooze, trickle; to slide, to slip || *ref* to drip, ooze, trickle; to slide, to slip; to slip away; (*un reparo*) to slip out

esdrúju·lo -la *adj* accented on the antepenult || *m* word or verse accented on the antepenult

ese, esa *adj dem* (pl **esos, esas**) that (*near you*) || **ese** *f* sound hole (*of violin*); **hacer eses** to reel, stagger

ése, ésa *pron dem* (pl **ésos, ésas**) that (*near you*); **ésa** your city

esencia *f* essence; **esencia de pera** banana oil; **quinta esencia** quintessence

esencial *adj & m* essential

esfera *f* sphere; (*del reloj*) dial

esféri·co -ca *adj* spherical || *m* football

esfinge *f* sphinx; spiteful woman

esforza·do -da *adj* brave, vigorous, enterprising

esforzar §35 *tr* to strengthen, to invigorate; to encourage || *ref* to exert oneself; to strive

esfuerzo *m* effort, exertion, endeavor; courage, vigor, spirit

esfumar *tr* to stump ‖ *ref* to disappear, fade away

esgarrar *tr* (*la flema*) to try to cough up ‖ *intr* to clear the throat

esgrima *f* fencing

esgrimidura *f* fencing

esgrimir *tr* to wield, to brandish; (*un argumento*) to swing ‖ *intr* to fence

esgrimista *mf* (Arg, Chile, Peru) fencer; (Chile) swindler, panhandler

esguazar §60 *tr* to ford

esguazo *m* fording; ford

esguince *m* dodge, duck; (*gesto de disgusto*) frown; twist, sprain, wrench

eslabón *m* (*de cadena*) link; (*hierro acerado para sacar fuego de un pedernal*; *cilindro de acero para afilar cuchillos*) steel

eslabonar *tr* to link; to link together, to string together ‖ *intr* to link

eslálom *m* slalom

esla·vo -va *adj* Slav, Slavic ‖ *mf* Slav ‖ *m* (*idioma*) Slavic

esla·vón -vona *adj* & *mf* Slav

eslogan *m* (*consigna usada en fórmulas publicitarias*) slogan

eslora *f* (naut) length

eslova·co -ca *adj* & *mf* Slovak

esmaltar *tr* to enamel; to embellish

esmalte *m* enamel; **esmalte para las uñas** nail polish

esmera·do -da *adj* careful, painstaking

esmeralda *f* emerald

esmerar *tr* to polish, to shine; to examine, to check ‖ *ref* to take pains, to do one's best

esmeril *s* emery

esmeriladora *f* emery wheel

esmerilar *tr* to grind or polish with emery

esmero *m* care, neatness

esmoladera *f* grindstone

esmoquin *m* tuxedo, dinner coat

esnob *adj* snobbish ‖ *mf* (*pl* **esnobs**) snob

esnobismo *m* snobbery, snobbishness

esnobista *adj* snobbish

eso *pron dem* that; **a eso de** about; **eso es** that's it; that is; **por eso** for that reason; therefore

esófago *m* esophagus

espaciador *m* space bar

espacial *adj* space, spatial

espaciar §77 (Arg, Chile) & *regular tr* to space; to spread, scatter ‖ *ref* to expatiate; to amuse oneself, to relax

espacio *m* space; **espacio de chispa** spark gap; **espacio exterior** outer space; **espacio libre** (*entre dos cosas*) clearance; **espacio muerto** (*en el cilindro de un motor*) clearance; **por espacio de** in the space of

espacio·so -sa *adj* spacious, roomy; slow, deliberate

espada *m* swordsman; (taur) matador ‖ *f* sword; playing card (*representing a sword*) equivalent to spade; **entre la espada y la pared** between the devil and the deep blue sea

espadachín *m* swordsman; (*amigo de pendencias*) bully

espadaña *f* cattail, bulrush, reed mace; (*campanario*) bell gable

espadilla *f* (*remo que se usa como timón*) scull; (*aguja para sujetar el pelo*) bodkin; red insignia of Order of Santiago

espadín *m* rapier

espadón *m* (coll) brass hat

espalar *tr* to shovel

espalda *f* back; **a espaldas de uno** behind one's back; **de espaldas a** with one's back to; **tener buenas espaldas** to have broad shoulders; **volver las espaldas a** to turn a cold shoulder to

espaldar *m* (*de silla*) back; (*enrejado para plantas*) trellis, espalier

espaldarazo *m* slap on the back; (*ceremonia para armar caballero*) accolade; **dar el espaldarazo a** to accept, approve

espalera *f* trellis, espalier

espantada *f* (*de un animal*) sudden flight; (*desistimiento ocasionado por el miedo*) cold feet

espantadi·zo -za *adj* shy, skittish, scary

espantajo *m* scarecrow; (*persona fea*) fright

espantamos·cas *m* (*pl* **-cas**) (*para poner a los caballos*) fly net; (*aparato para asustar a las moscas*) fly chaser

espantapája·ros *m* (*pl* **-ros**) scarecrow

espantar *tr* to scare, frighten; to scare away ‖ *ref* to get scared; to be surprised, to marvel

espanto *m* fright, terror; (*amenaza*) threat; (Am) ghost

espanto·so -sa *adj* frightening, terrifying

España *f* Spain; **la Nueva España** New Spain (*Mexico in the early days*)

espa·ñol -ñola *adj* Spanish; **a la española** in the Spanish manner ‖ *mf* Spaniard ‖ *m* (*idioma*) Spanish; **los españoles** the Spanish ‖ *f* Spanish woman

españolizar §60 *tr* to make Spanish, to Hispanicize; to translate into Spanish ‖ *ref* to become Spanish

esparadrapo *m* sticking plaster

esparaván *m* spavin

esparavel *m* mortarboard

esparcimiento *m* spreading, scattering, dissemination; diversion, relaxation; frankness, openness

esparcir §36 *tr* to spread, scatter; to divert, relax ‖ *ref* to spread, scatter; to disperse; to take it easy, to relax

espárrago *m* asparagus; (*perno*) stud bolt; awning pole

esparrancar §73 *ref* to spread one's legs wide apart

esparta·no -na *adj* & *mf* Spartan

esparto *m* esparto grass

espasmo *m* spasm

espasmódi·co -ca *adj* spasmodic

espásti·co -ca *adj* spastic

espato *m* spar; **espato flúor** fluor spar

espátula *f* spatula; putty knife

especia *f* spice

especia·do -da *adj* spicy

especial *adj* especial, special

especialidad *f* speciality; (*ramo a que se consagra una persona o negocio*) specialty

especialista *mf* specialist

especializar §60 *tr, intr & ref* to specialize

especiar *tr* to spice

especie *f (categoría de la clasificación biológica)* species; *(clase, género)* sort, kind; *(caso, asunto)* matter; *(chisme, cuento)* news, rumor; appearance, pretext, show; remark; **en especie** in kind; **soltar una especie** to try to draw someone out

especie·ro -ra *mf* spice dealer ǁ *m* spice box

especificar §73 *tr* to specify; to itemize

especifi·co -ca *adj* specific ǁ *m* specific; patent medicine

espécimen *m (pl* **especímenes)** specimen

especio·so -sa *adj (engañoso)* specious, nice, neat, perfect

especiota *f* (coll) hoax, wild idea

espectáculo *m* spectacle; **dar un espectáculo** to make a scene; **espectáculo de atracciones** side show

especta·dor -dora *mf* witness; spectator

espectral *adj* ghostly

espectro *m* specter, phantom, ghost; (phys) spectrum

especular *tr* to check, examine; to contemplate ǁ *intr* to speculate

espejear *intr* to sparkle

espejismo *m* mirage

espejo *m* mirror, looking glass; model; **espejo de cuerpo entero** full-length mirror, pier glass; **espejo de retrovisión** rear-view mirror; **espejo de vestir** full-length mirror, pier glass; **espejo retrovisor** rear-view mirror

espelunca *f* cave, cavern

espeluznante *adj* hair-raising

espera *f* wait, waiting; *(puesto para cazar)* blind, hunter's blind; composure, patience, respite; delay; (law) stay; **no tener espera** to be of the greatest urgency

esperanza *f* hope; **tener puesta su esperanza en** to pin one's faith on

esperanza·do -da *adj* hopeful *(having hope)*

esperanza·dor -dora hopeful *(giving hope)*

esperanzar §60 *tr* to give hope to

esperanzo·so -sa *adj* hopeful, full of hope

esperar *tr (aguardar)* to wait for, to await; *(tener esperanza de conseguir)* to expect, to hope for; **ir a esperar** to go to meet ǁ *intr* to wait; to hope; **esperar + inf** to hope to + *inf*; **esperar a que** to wait until; **esperar desesperando** to hope against hope; **esperar en** to put one's hope in; **esperar que** to hope that; **esperar sentado** to have a good wait

esperinque *m* smelt

esperma *f* sperm

espesar *m* depth, thickness *(of woods)* ǁ *tr* to thicken; *(un tejido)* to weave tighter ǁ *ref* to thicken, to get thick or thicker

espe·so -sa *adj* thick; dirty, greasy

espesor *m* thickness; *(de un fluido, gas, masa)* density

espesura *f* thickness; *(matorral)* thicket;

(cabellera muy espesa) shock of hair; dirtiness, greasiness

espetar *tr* to skewer; to pierce, pierce through; **espetar algo a** to spring something on ǁ *ref* to be solemn, be pompous; (coll) to settle down

espetón *m (hurgón)* poker; *(asador)* skewer, spit; jab, poke

espía *mf* spy; (coll) squealer ǁ *f* (naut) warping; *(cuerda)* (naut) warp

espiar §77 *tr* to spy on ǁ *intr* to spy; (naut) to warp

espichar *tr* to prick; *(dinero)* (Chile) to cough up; (Chile, Peru) to tap ǁ *intr* (coll) to die ǁ *ref* (Mex, W-I) to get thin

espiche *m (arma o instrumento puntiagudo)* prick; (naut) peg, bung

espichón *m* stab, prick

espiga *f* (bot) ear, spike; peg, pin, tenon; *(clavo sin cabeza)* brad; *(badajo)* clapper; *(de una llave)* stem

espigar §44 *tr* to glean; to tenon, to dowel ǁ *intr (los cereales)* to form ears ǁ *ref* to grow tall, to shoot up

espigón *m* sharp point, spur; *(mazorca)* ear of corn; *(cerro puntiagudo)* peak; breakwater

espina *f* thorn, spine; *(de los peces)* fishbone; doubt, uncertainty; sorrow; (anat) spine; **dar mala espina a** (coll) to worry; **espina de pescado** herringbone; **espina de pez** fishbone; **espina dorsal** spinal column; **estar en espinas** (coll) to be on pins and needles

espinaca *f* spinach; **espinacas** spinach

espinal *adj* spinal

espinapez *m* herringbone; thorny matter, difficulty

espinar *m* thorny spot; (fig) thorny matter ǁ *tr* to prick; *(árboles)* to protect with thornbushes; to hurt, offend

espinazo *m* backbone; *(de un arco)* keystone

espinel *m* trawl, trawl line

espineta *f* spinet

espinilla *f (de la pierna)* shin, shinbone; *(granillo en la piel)* blackhead

espino *m* hawthorn; **espino artificial** barbed wire; **espino negro** blackthorn

espinochar *tr (el maíz)* to husk

espino·so -sa *adj* thorny; *(pez)* bony; *(difícil)* (fig) thorny, knotty

espiocha *f* pickaxe

espión *m* spy

espionaje *m* spying, espionage

espira *f* turn

espiración *f* breathing; exhalation

espiral *adj* spiral ǁ *f (línea curva que da vueltas alrededor de un punto)* spiral; *(del reloj)* hairspring; *(de humo)* curl, wreath

espirar *tr* to breath; to encourage ǁ *intr* to breathe; to exhale, expire; *(el viento)* (poet) to blow gently

espiritismo *m* espiritualism

espiritu·so -sa *adj* spirited, lively; *(licor)* spirituous

espíritu *m* spirit; *(mente)* mind; *(aparecido, fantasma)* ghost, spirit; **espíritu de equipo** teamwork; **Espíritu Santo** Holy Ghost, Holy Spirit; **dar, despe-**

dir, **exhalar** or **rendir el espíritu** to give up the ghost

espiritual *adj* spiritual; sharp, witty

espiritualismo *m* spiritualism

espita *f* tap, cock; (coll) tippler

espitar *tr* to tap

esplendidez *f* splendor, magnificence

espléndi·do -da *adj* splendid, magnificent; generous, open-handed; (poet) brilliant, radiant

esplendor *m* splendor

esplendoro·so -sa *adj* resplendent

espliego *m* lavender

esplín *m* melancholy

espolada *f* prick with spur; **espolada de vino** (coll) shot of wine

espolear *tr* to spur, to spur on

espoleta *f* fuse; (*hueso*) wishbone

espolón *m* (*del gallo, una montaña, un buque de guerra*) spur; dike, jetty, mole, cutwater; (*prominencia córnea de las caballerías*) fetlock; (*sabañón*) chilblain

espolvorear *tr* (*quitar el polvo de; esparcir el polvo sobre*) to dust; (*el azúcar*) to sprinkle

esponja *f* sponge; (*sablista*) (coll) sponge, sponger; **beber como una esponja** (coll) to drink like a fish; **tirar la esponja** (coll) to throw in (or up) the sponge

esponja·do -da *adj* proud, puffed-up; (coll) fresh, healthy

esponjar *tr* to puff up, make fluffy ‖ *ref* to puff up, become fluffy; (coll) to be puffed up, be conceited; (coll) to look fresh and healthy

esponjo·so -sa *adj* spongy

esponsales *mpl* betrothal, engagement

espontanear *ref* to make a clean breast of it; to open one's heart

espontáne·o -a *adj* spontaneous ‖ *m* (taur) spectator who jumps into the ring to take on the bull

espora *f* spore

esporádi·co -ca *adj* sporadic

esposa *f* wife; **esposas** handcuffs, manacles

esposar *tr* to handcuff, to manacle

espo·so -sa *mf* spouse ‖ *m* husband ‖ *f* see **esposa**

espuela *f* spur; **echar la espuela** (coll) to take a nightcap; **espuela de caballero** delphinium, rocket larkspur; **espuela de galán** nasturtium

espuerta *f* two-handled esparto basket

espulgar §44 *tr* to delouse; to scrutinize

espuma *f* foam; (*en un vaso de cerveza; saliva parecida a la espuma*) froth; (*película de impurezas en la superficie de un líquido*) scum; **crecer como espuma** (coll) to grow like weeds; (coll) to have a meteoric rise; **espuma de caucho** foam rubber; **espuma de jabón** lather; **espuma de mar** meerschaum.

espumadera *f* skimmer

espumajear *intr* to froth at the mouth

espumajo·so -sa *adj* foamy, frothy

espumante *adj* foaming; (*vino*) sparkling

espumar *tr* to skim ‖ *intr* to foam, to froth; (*el jabón*) to lather; (*el vino*) to sparkle; to increase rapidly

espumarajo *m* froth, frothing at the mouth

espumilla *f* voile; (CAm, Ecuad) meringue

espumo·so -sa *adj* foamy, frothy; (*cubierto de una película*) scummy; (*jabonoso*) lathery; (*vino*) sparkling

espu·rio -ria *adj* spurious

espurrear or **espurriar** *tr* to squirt with water from the mouth

esputar *tr* & *intr* to spit

esputo *m* spit, saliva

esq. *abbr* **esquina**

esqueje *m* cutting, slip

esquela *f* note; announcement; death notice; **esquela amorosa** billet-doux

esquelétí·co -ca *adj* skeleton; skeletal, thin, wasted

esqueleto *m* skeleton; (CAm, Mex) blank form; (Chile) sketch, outline

esquema *m* scheme, diagram

es·quí *m* (*pl* -**quís**) ski; skiing; **esquí acuático** water ski; water skiing; **esquí remolcado** skijoring

esquia·dor -dora *adj* ski ‖ *mf* skier

esquiar §77 *intr* to ski

esquiciar *tr* to sketch

esquicio *m* sketch

esquifar *tr* (naut) to fit out, to man

esquife *m* skiff

esquismo *m* skiing

esquila *f* sheepshearing; hand bell

esquilar *tr* to shear, to fleece

esquilimo·so -sa *adj* (coll) fastidious, squeamish

esquilmar *tr* to harvest; (*las plantas el jugo de la tierra*) to drain, exhaust; (*una fuente de riqueza*) to drain, squander, use up; to carry away, steal

esquilmo *m* harvest, farm produce; (Mex) farm scrapings

esquilmo·so -sa *adj* (coll) fastidious

esquimal *adj* & *mf* Eskimo

esquina *f* corner; (SAm) corner store; **a la vuelta de la esquina** around the corner; **doblar la esquina** to turn the corner; **hacer esquina** (*un edificio*) to be on the corner; **las cuatro esquinas** puss in the corner

esquina·do -da *adj* sharp-cornered; difficult, unsociable

esquinar *tr* to be on the corner of; to put in the corner; to alienate ‖ *intr* — **esquinar con** to be on the corner of ‖ *ref* — **esquinarse con** to fall out with

esquinazo *m* (coll) corner; (Arg, Chile) serenade; **dar esquinazo a** (coll) to give the slip to, to shake off

esquinencia *f* quinsy

esquinera *f* (Am) corner piece (*of furniture*)

esquirla *f* splinter

esquirol *m* scab, strikebreaker

esquisto *m* schist

esquite *m* (CAm, Mex) popcorn

esquivar *tr* to avoid, evade, shun; to dodge ‖ *ref* to withdraw; to dodge

esquivez *f* aloofness, gruffness

esqui·vo -va *adj* aloof, gruff

estable *adj* stable, permanent; full-time ‖ *mf* regular guest, permanent guest

establecer §22 *tr* to establish, to institute ‖ *ref* to settle, take up residence; to start a business, to open an office

establecimiento *m* establishment; place of business; decree, ordinance, statute

establo *m* stable

estaca *f* stake, picket, pale; cudgel, club; (*clavo largo*) spike; (hort) cutting

estacada *f* stockade, palisade; dueling ground; **dejar en la estacada** to leave in the lurch; **quedarse en la estacada** to succumb on the field of battle, to fall in a duel; to fail; to lose out

estacar §73 *tr* to stake, to stake off; to tie to a stake ‖ *ref* to stand stiff

estación *f* (*cada una de las cuatro divisiones del año*) season; (*sitio en que paran los trenes; radioemisora*) station; (*lugar en que se hace alto en un paseo, etc.*) stop; **estación balnearia** bathing resort; **estación de cabeza** (rr) terminal; **estación de carga** freight station; **estación de empalme** junction; **estación de gasolina** gas station, filling station; **estación de la seca** dry season; **estación de paso** (rr) way station; **estación de radiodifusión** broadcasting station; **estación de seguimiento** tracking station; **estación de servicio** service station; **estación difusora** or **emisora** broadcasting station; **estación gasolinera** gas station, filling station; **estación telefónica** telephone exchange

estacional *adj* seasonal

estacionamiento *m* stationing; parking; parking lot

estacionar *tr* to station; to stand, to park ‖ *intr* to stand, to park ‖ *ref* to station oneself; to be stationary; to stand, to park; **se prohíbe estacionarse** no standing, no parking

estaciona·rio -ria *adj* stationary

estada *f* stay, stop

estadía *f* (*ante un pintor*) sitting; (com) demurrage; (Am) stop, stay

estadio *m* stadium; phase, stage; (*longitud*) furlong

estadista *mf* (*perito en estadística*) statistician ‖ *m* statesman

estadística *f* statistics

estadísti·co -ca *adj* statistical ‖ *m* (Am) statistician ‖ *f* see **estadística**

estadiunense *adj* American, United States ‖ *mf* American

estadi·zo -za *adj* (*aire*) heavy, stifling; (*agua*) stagnant

estado *m* state; state, condition, status; statement, report; **en estado de buena esperanza** or **en estado interesante** in the family way; **estado civil** marital status; **estado de ánimo** state of mind; **estado de cuentas** (com) statement; **estado libre asociado** commonwealth; **estado llano** commons, common people; **estado mayor** (mil) staff; **estado mayor conjunto** joint chiefs of staff; **estado mayor general** general staff; **Estados Unidos** *msg* the United States; **estado tapón** buffer state; **es-**

tar en estado de guerra to be under martial law; **los Estados Unidos** *mpl* the United States; **tomar estado** to take a wife; to go into the church

estado-policía *m* (*pl* **estados-policías**) police state

estadounidense or **estadunidense** *adj* American, United States ‖ *mf* American

estafa *f* swindle, trick; (*estribo*) stirrup

estafar *tr* to swindle, trick; to overcharge

estafeta *f* post, courier; post office; diplomatic mail

estallar *intr* to burst; to explode; (*un incendio, una revolución; la guerra*) to break out; (*la ira*) to break forth

estallido *m* report, crash, explosion; crack; (*p.ej., de la guerra*) outbreak; **dar un estallido** to crash, explode

estambre *m* (*hebras de lana e hilo formado de ellas*) worsted; (bot) stamen; **estambre de la vida** course or thread of life

estampa *f* stamp, print, engraving; press, printing; footstep, track; aspect, appearance; **dar a la estampa** to publish, bring out; **parecer la estampa de la herejía** (coll) to be a sight, be a mess; **la propia estampa de** the very image of

estampado *m* printing, stamping; printed fabric, cotton print

estampar *tr* to stamp, to print, to engrave; (*en el ánimo*) to fix, engrave; (*p.ej., el pie*) to leave a mark of; (bb) to tool; (*arrojar con fuerza*) (coll) to dash, to slam

estampida *f* report, crash, explosion; (Am) stampede

estampido *m* report, crash, explosion; **estampido sónico** (aer) sonic boom

estampilla *f* (*sello con letrero para estampar*) stamp; (*sello con una firma en facsímile*) rubber stamp; (*sello de correos o fiscal*) (Am) stamp

estampillar *tr* to stamp; to rubber-stamp

estanca·do -da *adj* stagnant; (fig) stagnant, dead

estancar §73 *tr* to stanch; to stem, check; (*un negocio*) to suspend, hold up; to corner; to monopolize ‖ *ref* to become stagnant, to become choked up

estancia *f* stay, sojourn; (*aposento*) living room; day in hospital; cost of day in hospital; (*mil*) bivouac; (Arg, Urug, Chile) cattle ranch; (Col) small country place; (Ven) truck farm

estanciero *m* (Am) rancher, cattle raiser

estan·co -ca *adj* stanch, watertight ‖ *m* government monopoly; cigar store, government store (*for sale of tobacco, matches, postage stamps, etc.*); archives; (Ecuad) liquor store

estándar *m* standard

estandardizar §60 or **estandarizar** §60 *tr* to standardize

estandarte *m* banner, standard

estandartizar §60 *tr* to standardize

estanque *m* basin, reservoir; pond, pool

estanque·ro -ra *mf* storekeeper, tobacconist; (Ecuad) saloonkeeper ‖ *m* reservoir tender

estanquillo *m* cigar store, government store (*for sale of tobacco, matches, postage stamps, etc.*); (Col, Ecuad) bar, saloon; (Mex) booth, stand

estante *adj* located, being; settled, permanent ‖ *m* shelf; shelving; bookcase, open bookcase

estantería *f* shelves, shelving; book stack

estañar *tr* to tin; to tin-plate; to solder; (Ven) to hurt, injure; (Ven) to fire

estaño *m* tin

estaquilla *f* peg, dowel, pin; (*clavo pequeño sin cabeza*) brad; (*clavo largo*) spike

estaquillar *tr* to peg, dowel; to nail

estar §37 *v aux* (*to form progressive form*) to be, e.g., **están aprendiendo el español** they are learning Spanish ‖ *intr* to be; to be in, be home; to be ready; **¿a cuántos estamos?** what day of the month is it?; **¡está bien!** O.K.!, all right!; **estar a** to cost, sell at; **estar bien** to be well; **estar bien con** to be on good terms with; **estar de** to be (*on a temporary basis*); **estar de más** (coll) to be in the way; (coll) to be unnecessary; (coll) to be idle; **estar de viaje** to be on a trip; **estar mal** to be sick, be ill; **estar mal con** to be on bad terms with; **estar para** to be about to; **estar por** to be for, be in favor of; to be about to; to have a mind to; to remain to be + *pp*; **estar sobre sí** to be wary, be on one's guard ‖ *ref* (*p.ej., en casa*) to stay; (*p.ej., quieto*) to keep

estarcido *m* stencil

estarcir §36 *tr* to stencil

estatal *adj* state

estáti·co -ca *adj* static; dumbfounded, speechless

estatificar §73 *tr* to nationalize

estatizar §60 *tr* (Am) to nationalize

estatua *f* statue; **quedarse hecho una estatua** (coll) to stand aghast

estatuir §20 *tr* to order, decree; to establish, prove

estatura *f* stature

estatuta·rio -ria *adj* statutory

estatuto *m* statute

estay *m* (naut) stay; **estay mayor** (naut) mainstay

este, esta *adj dem* (*pl* **estos, estas**) this ‖ *m* east; east wind

éste, ésta *pron dem* (*pl* **éstos, éstas**) this one, this one here; the latter; **ésta** this city

estela *f* (*de un buque*) wake; (*de cohete, humo, cuerpo celeste, etc.*) trail

estepa *f* steppe

estera *f* mat; matting; **cargado de esteras** (coll) out of patience

esterar *tr* to cover with matting ‖ *intr* (coll) to bundle up for the cold

estercolar *m* dunghill ‖ §61 *tr* to dung, to manure

estercolero *m* manure pile, dunghill; manure collector

estereofóni·co -ca *adj* stereophonic, stereo

estereoscópi·co -ca *adj* stereoscopic, stereo

estereotipa·do -da *adj* stereotyped

estéril *adj* (*que no produce nada*) sterile; (*inútil, vano*) futile

esterilizar §60 *tr* to sterilize ‖ *ref* to become sterile

esterlina *adj fem* (*libra*) sterling (*pound*)

esternón *m* breastbone

estero *m* tideland; estuary; (Arg) swamp, marsh; (Chile) stream; (Col, Ven) pool, puddle

estertor *m* death rattle; (*ruido en ciertas enfermedades, perceptible por la auscultación*) stertor, râle; **estertor agónico** death rattle

esteta *mf* aesthete ‖ *f* beautician

estéti·co -ca *adj* aesthetic ‖ *f* aesthetics

estetoscopio *m* stethoscope

estiaje *m* low water

estiba *f* (naut) stowage

estibador *m* stevedore, longshoreman

estibar *tr* to pack, to stuff; (naut) to stow

estiércol *m* dung, manure

esti·gio -gia *adj* Stygian ‖ **Estigia** *f* Styx

estigma *m* stigma

estigmatizar §60 *tr* to stigmatize

estilar *tr* (*una escritura*) to draw up in proper form; to be given to ‖ *intr* & *ref* to be in fashion

estilete *m* (*puñal*) stiletto

estilo *m* style; **por el estilo like** that, of the kind; **por el estilo de** like; **estilo directo** (gram) direct discourse; **estilo indirecto** (gram) indirect discourse

estilográfica *f* fountain pen

estima *f* esteem; (naut) dead reckoning

estimable *adj* estimable; considerable; appreciable, computable; esteemed

estimación *f* esteem, estimation; estimate, evaluation

estimar *tr* (*tener en buen concepto*) to esteem; (*apreciar, valuar*) to estimate; to think, believe; to appreciate, thank; to be fond of, to like; **estimar en poco** to hold in low esteem

estimativa *f* judgment; instinct

estimulante *adj* & *m* stimulant

estimular *tr* to stimulate

estímulo *m* stimulus

estío *m* summer

estipendio *m* stipend; wages

estípti·co -ca *adj* styptic; constipated; mean, stingy

estipular *tr* to stipulate

estiradamente *adv* scarcely, hardly; violently

estira·do -da *adj* conceited, stuck-up; prim, neat; tight, closefisted

estirar *tr* (*alambre, metal*) to draw; (*planchar ligeramente*) to iron lightly; (*un escrito, discurso, cargo, etc.*) (fig) to stretch out; (*el dinero*) (fig) to stretch ‖ *ref* to stretch; to put on airs

estirón *m* jerk, tug; **dar un estirón** (coll) to grow up in no time

estirpe *f* race, stock, lineage; *(linaje)* strain, pedigree

estival *adj* summer

esto *pron dem* that; **en esto** at this point; **por esto** for this reason

estocada *f* thrust, stab, lunge; *(herida)* stab, stab wound; *(cosa que ocasiona dolor)* blow

Estocolmo *f* Stockholm

estofa *f* brocade; quality, kind

estofado *m* stew

estoi·co -ca *adj* & *mf* stoic

estóli·do -da *adj* stupid, imbecile

estómago *m* stomach; **estómago de avestruz** iron digestion; **tener buen estómago** or **mucho estómago** (coll) to be thick-skinned; (coll) to have an easy conscience

estopa *f* *(de lino o cáñamo)* tow; *(de calafatear)* (naut) oakum; **estopa de acero** steel wool; **estopa de algodón** cotton waste

estopilla *f* *(tela muy sutil)* lawn; *(tela ordinaria de algodón)* cheesecloth

estoque *m* rapier; sword lily, gladiola

estoquear *tr* to stab with a rapier

estor *m* blind, shade, window shade

estorbar *tr* to hinder, obstruct; to inconvenience, bother, annoy ‖ *intr* (coll) to be in the way

estorbo *m* hindrance, obstruction; inconvenience, bother, annoyance

estorbo·so -sa *adj* hindering; bothersome, annoying

estornino *m* starling; **estornino de los pastores** grackle, myna

estornudar *intr* to sneeze

estornudo *m* sneeze, sneezing

estrado *m* *(tarima del trono)* dais; lecture platform; (archaic) lady's drawing room; **estrados** courtrooms, law courts; **citar para estrados** to subpoena

estrafala·rio -ria *adj* (coll) queer, eccentric, odd; (coll) sloppy, sloppily dressed ‖ *mf* (coll) screwball

estragar §44 *tr* to spoil, damage, vitiate

estrago *m* damage, ruin, havoc

estrambote *m* tail *(of sonnet)*

estrambóti·co -ca *adj* (coll) odd, queer

estrangul *m* (mus) reed, mouthpiece

estrangular *tr* & *ref* to strangle, to choke

estraperlear *intr* to deal in the black market

estraperlista *adj* black-market ‖ *mf* black-market dealer

estraperlo *m* black market

estrapontín *m* folding seat, jump seat

estratagema *f* stratagem; craftiness

estratega *m* strategist

estrategia *f* strategy; **alta estrategia** grand strategy

estratégi·co -ca *adj* strategic(al) ‖ *m* strategist

estratificar §73 *tr* & *ref* to stratify

estrato *m* stratum, layer

estratosfera *f* stratosphere

estraza *f* rag; brown paper

estrechar *tr* *(reducir a menor ancho)* to narrow; *(apretar)* to tighten; to press,

pursue; to force, compel; to hug, embrace; to squeeze; **estrechar la mano a** to shake hands with ‖ *ref* to narrow down; to contract; to hug, embrace; *(reducir los gastos)* to retrench; **estrecharse en** to squeeze in; **estrecharse la mano** *(dos personas)* to shake hands

estrechez *f* narrowness; rightness; *(amistad íntima)* closeness, intimacy; austerity, strictness; poverty, want, need; trouble, jam; **estrechez de miras** narrow outlook, narrow-mindedness; **hallarse en gran estrechez** to be in dire straits

estre·cho -cha *adj* narrow; tight; close, intimate; austere, strict; stingy, tight; poor, needy; mean ‖ *m* *(paso angosto en el mar)* strait; fix, predicament

estrechura *f* narrowness; tightness; closeness, intimacy; austerity, strictness; trouble, predicament

estregar §66 *tr* to rub hard; to scour

estregón *m* hard rub

estrella *f* star; (typ) asterisk, star; (mov & theat) star; *(hado, destino)* (fig) star; **estrella de los Alpes** edelweiss; **estrella de mar** starfish; **estrella de rabo** comet; **estrella filante** or **fugaz** shooting star; **estrella fulgurante** (astr) flare star; **estrella polar** polestar; **estrella vespertina** evening star; **ver las estrellas** (coll) to see stars

estrella·do -da *adj* *(cielo)* starry; starspangled; star-shaped; *(huevos)* fried

estrellamar *m* starfish

estrellar *adj* star ‖ *tr* to star, to spangle with stars; *(huevos)* to fry; to shatter, dash to pieces ‖ *ref* to be spangled with stars; to crash; **estrellarse con** to clash with

estrellón *m* large star; *(fuego artificial)* star; (Am) smash-up

estremecer §22 *tr* to shake; *(el aire)* to rend; (fig) to shake, upset ‖ *ref* to shake, tremble, shiver, shudder

estrena *f* *(regalo que se da en señal de agradecimiento)* handsel; first use

estrenar *tr* to use for the first time, to wear for the first time; *(un drama)* to perform for the first time; *(un cine)* to show for the first time; to try out for the first time ‖ *ref* to make the day's first transaction; to appear for the first time; *(un drama, un cine)* to open

estrenista *mf* first-nighter

estreno *m* beginning, debut; première, first performance; first use

estre·nuo -nua *adj* strenuous, vigorous, enterprising

estreñimiento *m* constipation

estreñir §72 *tr* to constipate

estrépito *m* racket, crash; fuss, show

estrepito·so -sa *adj* loud, noisy, boisterous; notorious; shocking

estría *f* flute, groove

estriar §77 *tr* to flute, groove

estribar *intr* to lean, rest; to be based, to depend

estriberón *m* stepping stone

estribillo *m* *(de un poema)* burden, refrain; pet word, pet phrase

estribo *m* (*de coche*) step; (*de automóvil*) running board; (*apoyo para el pie*) footboard; (*para el pie del jinete*) stirrup; abutment, buttress; (fig) foundation, support; **perder los estribos** to fly off the handle, to lose one's head

estribor *m* starboard

estricnina *f* strychnine

estricote *m* (Ven) riotous living; **al estricote** hither and thither

estric·to -ta *adj* strict, severe, rigorous; proper, punctual; (*sentido de una palabra*) narrow

estrictura *f* (pathol) stricture

estrige *f* barn owl; (*Athene noctua*) little owl

estro *m* poetic inspiration; (*de animal*) rut, heat

estrofa *f* strophe

estroncio *m* strontium

estropajo *m* mop; dishcloth; **servir de estropajo** (coll) to be forced to do the dirty work; (coll) to be treated with indifference

estropajo·so -sa *adj* (coll) raggedy, slovenly; (*carne*) (coll) tough, leathery; (coll) spluttering

estropear *tr* to spoil, ruin, damage; to abuse, mistreat; to cripple, maim || *ref* to spoil, go to ruin; to fail

estropicio *m* (coll) breakage; (coll) havoc, ruin; (coll) fracas, rumpus

estructura *f* structure

estruendo *m* noise, crash, boom; confusion, uproar; pomp, show; fame

estruendo·so -sa *adj* noisy, booming

estrujar *tr* to squeeze; to press, crush, mash; to bruise; to rumple; (coll) to drain, exhaust

estuante *adj* hot, burning

estuario *m* estuary; tideland

estucar §73 *tr* to stucco

estuco *m* stucco; **estuco de París** plaster of Paris

estuche *m* case, box; (*caja y utensilios que se guardan en ella*) kit; casket, jewel case; (*para tijeras*) sheath, **estuche de afeites** compact, vanity case; **ser un estuche** (coll) to be a handy fellow

estudia·do -da *adj* affected, studied

estudiantado *m* student body

estudiante *mf* student

estudiantil *adj* student

estudiar *tr* to study; (*la lección a una persona*) to hear (*someone's lesson*) || *intr* to study; **estudiar para . . .** to study to become . . .

estudio *m* study; (*aposento*) studio; (mus) étude; **altos estudios** advanced studies

estudio·so -sa *adj* studious || *m* student, scholar

estufa *f* stove; steam cabinet, steam room; foot stove; (*invernáculo*) hothouse

estul·to -ta *adj* stupid, silly, foolish

estupefac·to -ta *adj* stupefied, dumbfounded

estupen·do -da *adj* stupendous; (coll) famous, distinguished

estúpi·do -da *adj* stupid || *mf* dolt

estupor *m* stupor; surprise, amazement

estuprar *tr* to rape, violate

estupro *m* rape, violation

estuque *m* stucco

esturión *m* sturgeon

etapa *f* stage; **a etapas pequeñas by easy stages**

éter *m* ether

etére·o -a *adj* ethereal

eternidad *f* eternity

eternizar §60 *tr* to prolong endlessly || *ref* to be endless, be interminable

eter·no -na *adj* eternal

éti·co -ca *adj* ethical || *f* ethics

etileno *m* ethylene

etilo *m* ethyl

étimo *m* etymon

etimología *f* etymology

etíope *adj* & *mf* Ethiopian

etiópi·co -ca *adj* & *m* Ethiopic

etiqueta *f* (*marbete*) tag, label; (*ceremonial que se debe observar*) etiquette; (*ceremonia en la manera de tratarse*) formality; **de etiqueta** formal, full-dress; **de etiqueta menor** semiformal; **estar de etiqueta** to have become cool toward each other

etiquetar *tr* to tag, to label

etiquete·ro -ra *adj* formal, ceremonious; full of compliments

etiquez *f* (pathol) consumption

étni·co -ca *adj* ethnic(al); (gram) gentilic

etnografía *f* ethnography

etnología *f* ethnology

E.U.A *abbr* **Estados Unidos de América**

eucalipto *m* eucalyptus

Eucaristía *f* Eucharist

eufemismo *m* euphemism

eufemísti·co -ca *adj* euphemistic

eufonía *f* euphony

eufóni·co -ca *adj* euphonic, euphonious

euforia *f* euphoria; endurance, fortitude

eufuísmo *m* euphuism

eufuísti·co -ca *adj* euphuistic

eugenesia *f* eugenics

eunuco *m* eunuch

euritmia *f* regular pulse

euro *m* east wind

Europa *f* Europe

europe·o -a *adj* & *mf* European

eutanasia *f* euthanasia

eutrapelia *f* moderation; lightheartedness; simple pastime

evacuación *f* evacuation; **evacuación de basuras** garbage disposal

evacuar §21 & *regular tr* to evacuate; (*un trámite*) to transact; (*una visita*) to pay; (*un encargo, un asunto*) to do, carry out; **evacuar el vientre** to have a movement of the bowels || *intr* to evacuate; to have a movement of the bowels

evadi·do -da *adj* escaped || *mf* escapee

evadir *tr* to avoid, evade, elude || *ref* to evade; to escape, to flee

evaluar §21 *tr* to evaluate; to value

evangéli·co -ca *adj* evangelic(al)

evangelio *m* (coll) gospel, gospel truth || **Evangelio** *m* Gospel, Evangel

evangelista *m* Gospel singer or chanter;

(Mex) public writer, penman ‖ **Evangelista** *m* Evangelist

evaporar *tr* & *ref* to evaporate

evaporizar §60 *tr, intr* & *ref* to vaporize

evasión *f* (*efugio, evasiva*) evasion; (*fuga*) escape

evasi·vo -va *adj* evasive ‖ *f* loophole, pretext, excuse

evento *m* chance, happening, contingency; (Col) sports event; **a todo evento** in any event

eventual *adj* contingent; (*emolumentos; gastos*) incidental

eventualidad *f* eventuality, contingency; uncertainty

evidencia *f* evidence, obviousness; (*prueba judicial*) (Am) evidence; **evidencia moral** moral certainty

evidenciar *tr* to show, make evident

evidente *adj* evident, obvious

evitable *adj* avoidable

evitación *f* avoidance; prevention

evitar *tr* to avoid, shun; (*p.ej., el polvo*) to keep off; to prevent; **evitar** + *inf* to avoid + *ger*; to save from + *ger*, e.g., **la luz de la luna nos evitó tener que encender los faroles** the light of the moon saved us from having to light the lights

evo *m* (poet) age, aeon; (theol) eternity

evocar §73 *tr* to evoke; (*p.ej., los demonios*) to invoke

evolución *f* evolution; change, development (*of one's point of view, plans, conduct, etc.*)

evolucionar *intr* to evolve; to change, develop; (mil & nav) to maneuver

ex *adj* ex- (*former*), e.g., **el ex presidente** the ex-president

ex abrupto *adv* brashly ‖ *m* brash remark

exacción *f* (*de impuestos, deudas, multas, etc.*) exaction, levy; (*cobro injusto*) extortion

exacerbar *tr* to exacerbate, aggravate

exactitud *f* exactness; punctuality

exac·to -ta *adj* exact; punctual, faithful ‖ **exacto** *interj* right!

exactor *m* tax collector

exagerar *tr* to exaggerate

exalta·do -da *adj* exalted; extreme, hotheaded; wrought-up; radical

exaltar *tr* to exalt; to extol ‖ *ref* to be wrought-up, get excited

examen *m* examination; **examen de ingreso** entrance examination; **sufrir un examen** to take an examination

examinar *tr* to examine; to inspect ‖ *ref* to take an examination; **examinarse de ingreso** to take entrance examinations

exangüe *adj* bloodless; (coll) weak, exhausted; (coll) dead

exánime *adj* (*sin vida*) lifeless; (*desmayado*) faint, in a faint, lifeless

exasperar *tr* to exasperate

Exc.ª *abbr* Excelencia

excandecer §22 *tr* to incense, enrage

excarcelación *f* release

excarcelar *tr* (*a un preso*) to release

excavadora *f* power shovel

excavar *tr* to excavate; to loosen soil around

excedente *adj* excess; excessive; on leave ‖ *m* excess, surplus

exceder *tr* (*ser mayor que*) to exceed; (*aventajar*) to excel ‖ *ref* to go too far, go to extremes; **excederse a sí mismo** to outdo oneself

excelencia *f* excellence, excellency; **por excelencia** par excellence; **Su Excelencia** Your Excellency

excelente *adj* excellent

excel·so -sa *adj* lofty, sublime ‖ **el Excelso** the Most High

excéntrica *f* eccentric

excentricidad *f* eccentricity

excéntri·co -ca *adj* eccentric; (*barrio*) outlying ‖ *mf* eccentric ‖ *f* see **excéntrica**

excepción *f* exception; **a excepción de** with the exception of

excepcional *adj* exceptional

excepto *prep* except

exceptuar §21 *tr* to except; (*eximir*) to exempt

excerpta or **excerta** *f* excerpt

excesi·vo -va *adj* excessive; excess

exceso *m* excess; **exceso de equipaje** excess baggage; **exceso de peso** excess weight; **exceso de velocidad** speeding

excitable *adj* excitable

excitación *f* excitement; excitation

excitante *adj* & *m* stimulant

excitar *tr* to excite, stir up, stimulate ‖ *ref* to become excited

exclamación *f* exclamation

exclamar *tr* & *intr* to exclaim

exclaustrar *tr* (*a un religioso*) to secularize

excluir §20 *tr* to exclude

exclusión *f* exclusion; **con exclusión de** to the exclusion of

exclusiva *f* rejection, turndown; sole right, monopoly; (*anticipación de una noticia por un periódico*) news beat

exclusive *adv* exclusively ‖ *prep* exclusive of, not counting

exclusivista *adj* exclusive, clannish ‖ *mf* snob

exclusi·vo -va *adj* exclusive ‖ *f* see **exclusiva**

Exc.mo *abbr* Excelentísimo

ex combatiente *m* ex-serviceman

excomulgar §44 *tr* to excommunicate; (coll) to ostracize, banish

excomunión *f* excommunication

excoriar *tr* to skin ‖ *ref* to skin oneself; (*p.ej., el codo*) to skin

excrementar *intr* to have a bowel movement

excremento *m* excrement

exculpar *tr* to exculpate, exonerate

excursión *f* excursion, outing

excursionista *mf* excursionist, tourist

excusa *f* excuse; **a excusa** secretly; **excusa es decir** it is unnecessary to say

excusabaraja *f* basket with lid

excusable *adj* excusable; avoidable

excusadamente *adv* unnecessarily

excusa·do -da *adj* exempt; unnecessary; private, set apart; (*puerta*) side ‖ *m* toilet

excusa·lí *m* (*pl* -**líes**) small apron

excusar *tr* to excuse; to exempt; to avoid; to prevent; to make unnecessary; **excusar** + *inf* to not have to + *inf* ‖ *ref* to excuse oneself; to apologize; **excusarse de** + *inf* to decline to + *inf*

exención *f* exemption

exencionar *tr* to exempt

exentamente *adv* freely; frankly, simply

exentar *tr* to exempt

exen·to -ta *adj* exempt; open, unobstructed; free, disengaged

exequias *fpl* obsequies

exfolia·dor -dora *adj* (Am) tear-off

exhalación *f* exhalation; flash of lightning; shooting star; fume, vapor; **como una exhalación** (coll) like a flash of lightning

exhalar *tr* to exhale, emit; (*suspiros, quejas*) to breathe forth; **exhalar el último suspiro** to breathe one's last ‖ *ref* to exhale; (*con el ejercicio violento del cuerpo*) to breathe hard; to hurry; to crave

exhausti·vo -va *adj* exhaustive

exhaus·to -ta *adj* exhausted; (coll) wasted away

exheredar *tr* to disinherit

exhibición *f* exhibition; exhibit

exhibir *tr* to exhibit; (Mex) to pay ‖ *ref* (coll) to make oneself evident

exhilarante *adj* exhilarating; (*gas*) laughing

exhortar *tr* to exhort

exhumar *tr* to exhume

exigencia *f* exigency, requirement

exigente *adj* exigent, demanding

exigir §27 *tr* to exact, require, demand

exi·guo -gua *adj* meager, scanty

exila·do -da *adj & mf* (Am) exile

exi·mio -mia *adj* choice, select, superior; distinguished

eximir *tr* to exempt

existencia *f* existence; **en existencia** in stock; **existencias** (com) stock

existente *adj* existing, extant; in stock

existir *intr* to exist

exitazo *m* smash hit

exitista *adj* (Arg) me-too ‖ *mf* (Arg) me-tooer

éxito *m* (*resultado feliz*) success; (*canción, cine, etc. que ha tenido mucho éxito*) hit; (*resultado de un negocio*) outcome, result; **éxito de librería** best seller; **éxito de taquilla** box-office hit, good box office; **éxito de venta** best seller; **éxito rotundo** smash hit

exito·so -sa *adj* (Arg) successful

ex li·bris *m* (*pl* **-bris**) bookplate

éxodo *m* exodus; **éxodo de técnicos** brain drain

exonerar *tr* to exonerate, to relieve; to discharge, dismiss; **exonerar el vientre** to have a movement of the bowels

exorar *tr* to beg, entreat

exorbitante *adj* exorbitant

exorcizar §60 *tr* to exorcise

exornar *tr* to adorn, embellish

exóti·co -ca *adj* exotic; striking, stunning, glamorous

expandir *tr & ref* (Arg, Chile) to expand, extend, spread

expansión *f* expansion; (*manifestación efusiva*) expansiveness; (*difusión de una opinión*) spread; rest, recreation

expansionar *ref* to expand; to open one's heart; to relax, take it easy

expansi·vo -va *adj* expansive

expatria·do -da *adj & mf* expatriate

expectación *f* expectancy

expectativa *f* expectation; **estar en la expectativa de** to be expecting, to be on the lookout for

expectorar *tr & intr* to expectorate

expedición *f* (*excursión para realizar una empresa*) expedition; (*remesa*) shipment; (*de un certificado, títulos, etc.*) issuance; (*agilidad, facilidad*) expedition

expedi·dor -dora *mf* sender, shipper

expediente *m* expedient; makeshift, apology; (*agilidad, facilidad*) expedition; (*todos los papeles correspondientes a un asunto*) dossier; (law) action, proceedings; **expediente académico** (educ) record

expedienteo *m* red tape

expedir §50 *tr* to send, ship, remit; (*títulos*) to issue; (*despachar, cursar*) to expedite

expeditar *tr* (Am) to expedite

expediti·vo -va *adj* expeditious

expedi·to -ta *adj* ready; clear, open, unencumbered

expeler *tr* to expel, eject

expende·dor -dora *mf* dealer, retailer; ticket agent; **expendedor de moneda falsa** distributor of counterfeit money

expendeduría *f* cigar store (*for sale of state-monopolized articles*)

expender *tr* to spend; to dispense; to sell at retail; (*moneda falsa*) to circulate

expendio *m* (Am) shop, store; (Am) retail; (Mex) cigar store

expensar *tr* (Chile, Guat, Mex) to pay the cost of

expensas *fpl* expenses

experiencia *f* (*enseñanza que se adquiere con la práctica o con el vivir; suceso en que uno ha participado, cosa que uno ha experimentado*) experience; (*ensayo, experimento*) experiment

experimenta·do -da *adj* experienced

experimentar *tr* to experience, undergo, feel; to test, try, try out ‖ *intr* to experiment

experimento *m* experiment

exper·to -ta *adj & m* expert

expiación *f* expiation, atonement; purification

expiar §77 *tr* to expiate, atone for; to purify

expirar *intr* to expire

explanación *f* grading, leveling; explanation

explanada *f* esplanade

explanar *tr* to grade, to level; to explain

explayar *tr* to enlarge, extend ‖ *ref* to spread out, extend; to go for an outing; to expatiate, talk at length; **explayarse con** to unbosom oneself to

explicación *f* explanation

explicar §73 *tr* to explain; (*exponer*) to expound; (*exculpar*) to explain away; (*una clase*) to teach || *intr* to explain || *ref* to explain oneself; to understand, make out

explicati·vo -va *adj* explanatory

explíci·to -ta *adj* explicit

exploración *f* exploration; (mil) scouting; (telv) scanning

explora·dor -dora *mf* explorer || *m* boy scout; (mil) scout

explorar *tr* to explore; (mil) to scout; (telv) to scan

explosión *f* explosion; (*de gases en un motor*) combustion

explosi·vo -va *adj & m* explosive || *f* (phonet) explosive

explotación *f* operation, running; exploitation

explotar *tr* to operate, to run; (*una mina*) to work; to exploit || *intr* to explode

exponente *m* exponent

exponer §54 *tr* to expose; (*explicar*) to expound; (*a un niño recién nacido*) to abandon || *intr* to display, show, exhibit; (eccl) to expose the Host || *ref* to expose oneself; to be on view

exportación *f* exportation, export; (*mercaderías que se exportan*) exports

exporta·dor -dora *mf* exporter

exportar *tr & intr* to export

exposición *f* exposition; (*a un peligro; con relación a los puntos cardinales*) exposure; (phot) exposure; (rhet) exposition; **exposición universal** world's fair

exposímetro *m* light meter

expósi·to -ta *mf* foundling

exposi·tor -tora *mf* exhibitor

exprés *m* express train; (Mex) express company

expresa·do -da *adj* above-mentioned

expresamente *adv* express, expressly

expresar *tr* to express || *ref* to express oneself

expresión *f* expression; (*acción de exprimir*) squeezing; (*zumo exprimido*) juice; **expresiones** regards

expresi·vo -va *adj* expressive; kind, affectionate

expre·so -sa *adj* express || *m* (*tren muy rápido; correo extraordinario*) express; (Am) express company

exprimidera *f* squeezer; **exprimidera de naranjas** orange squeezer

exprimi·do -da *adj* lean, skinny; stiff, stuck-up; affected, prim, prudish

exprimidor *m* wringer; squeezer; **exprimidor de ropa** clothes wringer

exprimir *tr* to squeeze, press; (*p.ej., la ropa blanca*) to wring, wring out; (*extraer apretando*) to express

ex profeso *adv* on purpose

expropiar *tr* to expropriate

expues·to -ta *adj* dangerous, hazardous

expugnar *tr* to take by storm

expulsanie·ves *m* (*pl* -ves) snowplow

expulsar *tr* to expel

expulsión *f* expulsion

expurgar §44 *tr* to expurgate

exquisi·to -ta *adj* exquisite

extasiar §77 **& regular** *ref* to go into ecstasy

éxta·sis *m* (*pl* -sis) ecstasy

extáti·co -ca *adj* ecstatic

extemporal *adj* unseasonable

extemporáne·o -a *adj* unseasonable; untimely, inopportune

extender §51 *tr* to extend, to stretch out, to spread out; to spread; (*un documento*) to draw up || *ref* to extend, to stretch out; to spread; **extenderse a** or **hasta** to amount to

extendidamente *adv* at length, in detail

extensión *f* extension; (*vasta superficie, p.ej., del océano*) expanse; (*alcance, importancia*) extent; extending

extensi·vo -va *adj* extensive; **hacer extensivos a** to extend (*e.g., good wishes*) to

exten·so -sa *adj* extensive, extended, vast; **por extenso** at length, in detail

extenuar §21 *tr* to weaken, emaciate

exterior *adj* exterior, outer, outside; foreign || *m* exterior, outside; appearance, bearing; **al exterior** or **a lo exterior** on the outside; outwardly; **del exterior** from abroad; **en el exterior** on the outside; abroad; **en exteriores** (mov) on location

exterioridad *f* externals, outward appearance; **exterioridades** pomp, show

exteriorista *adj* outgoing, outgiving || *mf* extrovert

exteriorizar §60 *tr* to reveal || *ref* to unbosom one's heart

exterminar *tr* to exterminate

exterminio *m* extermination

exter·no -na *adj* external || *mf* day pupil

extinción *f* extinction; cancellation, elimination

extinguir §29 *tr* to extinguish, put out; to wipe out, put an end to; to fulfil, carry out; (*un plazo, un tiempo*) to spend, to serve || *ref* to be extinguished, go out; to come to an end

extin·to -ta *adj* (*volcán*) extinct; (Am) deceased || *mf* (Am) deceased

extintor *m* fire extinguisher; **extintor de espuma** foam extinguisher; **extintor de granada** fire grenade

extirpar *tr* to extirpate, to eradicate

extorno *m* premium adjustment (*based on change in policy*)

extorsión *f* extortion; harm, damage

extorsionar *tr* to harm, damage; (Am) to extort

extra *adj* extra; **extra de** (coll) in addition to, besides || *mf* (theat) extra || *m* (*de un periódico*) extra; (coll) extra, bonus

extracción *f* extraction; (*en la lotería*) drawing numbers; **extracción de raíces** (math) evolution

extractar *tr* (*un escrito*) to abstract

extracto *m* (*de un escrito*) abstract; (pharm) extract

extracurricular *adj* extracurricular

extradición *f* extradition

extraer §75 *tr* to extract; to pull; (*la raíz*) (math) to extract

extrafuerte *adj* heavy-duty

extralimitar *ref* to go too far

extramural *adj* extramural

extranjerismo *m* borrowing

extranje·ro -ra *adj* foreign, alien ‖ *mf* foreigner, alien; **extranjero enemigo** enemy alien ‖ *m* foreign country; **al extranjero** abroad; **del extranjero** from abroad; **en el extranjero** abroad

extrañar *tr* to banish, expatriate; to surprise; to find strange; (Am) to miss ‖ *ref* to be surprised; to refuse

extrañeza *f* strangeness, peculiarity; *(desavenencia)* estrangement; wonder, surprise

extra·ño -ña *adj* foreign; *(raro, singular)* strange; extraneous; **extraño a** unconnected with ‖ *mf* foreigner

extraoficial *adj* unofficial

extraordina·rio -ria *adj* extraordinary; extra, special ‖ *m* extra dish; special mail; *(de un periódico)* extra

extrapla·no -na *adj* extra-flat

extrapolar *tr & intr* to extrapolate

extrarradio *m* outer edge of town

extrasensorial *adj* extrasensory

extravagancia *f (singularidad, ridiculez)* extravagance, wildness, folly

extravagante *adj (singular, ridículo)* extravagant, wild, foolish; *(correspondencia en la casa de correos)* in transit

extravia·do -da *adj* lost, misplaced; astray, gone astray; *(lugar)* out-of-the-way

extraviar §77 *tr* to lead astray, mislead; to mislay, misplace ‖ *ref* to get lost, go astray; to go wrong; to get out of line

extravío *m* going astray; loss; misleading; misconduct; misplacement

extrema *f (escasez grande)* (coll) extremity; *(de la vida)* (coll) end, last moment

extremar *tr* to carry far, carry to the limit ‖ *ref* to strive hard

extremaunción *f* extreme unction

extreme·ño -ña *adj* frontier

extremidad *f* extremity; end, tip; **extremidades** *(pies y manos)* extremities; **la última extremidad** one's last moment

extremista *mf* extremist

extre·mo -ma *adj* extreme; utmost; critical, desperate ‖ *m* extremity; *(de la calle)* end; *(del dedo)* tip; *(punto último)* extreme; great care; *(de una conversación, una carta)* point; winter pasture; **al extremo de** to the point of; **de extremo a extremo** from one end to the other; **hacer extremos** to be demonstrative, to gush ‖ *f* see **extrema**

extremo·so -sa *adj* extreme, forthright; effusive, gushy, demonstrative

extrínse·co -ca *adj* extrinsic

extroverti·do -da *mf* extrovert

exuberante *adj* exuberant; luxuriant

exudar *tr & intr* to exude

exultante *adj* exultant

exultar *intr* to exult

exvoto *m* votive offering

eyacular *tr & intr* to ejaculate

F

F, f (efe) *f* seventh letter of the Spanish alphabet

f.a.b. *abbr* franco a bordo

fabada *f* pork-and-bean stew *(in Asturias)*

fábrica *f* factory, plant; building, masonry; (eccl) vestry

fabricación *f* manufacture; **fabricación en serie** mass production

fabricante *mf* manufacturer

fabricar §73 *tr* to manufacture; to devise, invent; to fabricate

fabril *adj* factory

fabriquero *m* manufacturer; charcoal burner; churchwarden

fábula *f* fable; *(p.ej., de un drama)* plot, story; rumor, gossip; *(mentira)* story, lie; *(objeto de murmuración)* talk of the town

fabulario *m* book of fables

fabulo·so -sa *adj* fabulous

facción *f* faction; feature; battle; **estar de facción** (mil) to be on duty; **facciones** features

facciona·rio -ria *adj* factional

faceta *f* facet

facetada *f* (Mex) flat joke

face·to -ta *adj* (Mex) affected; (Mex) finicky ‖ *f* see **faceta**

facial *adj* facial

fácil *adj* easy; pliant, yielding; likely; loose, wanton

facilidad *f* facility, ease, easiness; **facilidades de pago** easy payments

facilitar *tr* to facilitate, to expedite; to furnish, supply

facili·tón -tona *adj* (coll) bumbling, brash ‖ *mf* (coll) bumbler

facinero·so -sa *adj* wicked ‖ *mf* villain

facistol *m* choir desk

facón *m* (Arg, Urug) gaucho knife

facsímile *m* facsimile

factible *adj* feasible

factor *m* factor; commission merchant; baggageman; freight agent

factoría *f* trading post; (Ecuad, Peru) foundry; (Mex) factory

factura *f* invoice, bill; workmanship; **factura simulada** pro forma invoice; **según factura** as per invoice

facturación *f* invoicing, billing; *(del equipaje)* checking

facturar *tr* to invoice, to bill; *(el equipaje)* to check

facultad *f* faculty; *(de la universidad)* school; knowledge, skill; power; **facultad de altos estudios** graduate school

facultar *tr* to empower, to authorize
facultati·vo -va *adj* faculty; optional ‖ *m* doctor, physician
facundia *f* eloquence, fluency
facun·do -da *adj* eloquent, fluent
facha *mf* (*adefesio*) (coll) sight ‖ *f* look, appearance; **facha a facha** face to face
fachada *f* façade; (*de un libro*) title page; (coll) look, build, bearing; **hacer fachada con** to overlook, to look out on
facha·do -da *adj* — **bien fachado** good-looking ‖ *f* see **fachada**
fachenda *m* (coll) boaster, show-off ‖ *f* (coll) boasting
fachendear *intr* (coll) to boast, to show off
fachendista, fachen·dón -dona, fachen-do·so -sa *adj* (coll) boastful ‖ *mf* (coll) boaster, show-off
fachinal *m* (Arg) marshland
fada *f* fairy, witch
faena *f* work; toil; chore, task, job; (taur) windup; (taur) stunt, trick; (mil) fatigue, fatigue duty; (Guat, Mex, W-I) extra work, overtime; (Ecuad) morning work in the field; (Chile) gang of farm hands
faenero *m* (Chile) farm hand
Faetón *m* Phaëthon
fagot *m* bassoon
faisán *m* pheasant
faja *f* sash, girdle; bandage; band, strip; newspaper wrapper; (*de carretera*) lane; (*de tierra*) strip; **faja central or divisoria** median strip; **faja medical** supporter
fajar *tr* to wrap; to bandage; to swaddle; (*un periódico o revista*) to put a wrapper on; (Am) to beat, thrash; (Am) to attack ‖ *ref* to put on a sash
fajardo *m* meat pie
fajín *m* sash
fajina *f* fagot; fire wood; (mil) call to quarters
fajo *m* bundle; (*de papel moneda*) roll; (Am) swig; (Mex) blow; (Mex) leather belt; **fajos swaddling clothes**
falacia *f* deception; deceitfulness
falange *f* phalanx
falangia *f* daddy-longlegs
fa·laz *adj* (*pl* **-laces**) deceitful; deceptive
falba·lá *m* (*pl* **-laes**) gore; flounce, ruffle
falce *m* sickle; falchion
falda *f* skirt, dress; (*regazo*) lap; flap, fold; (*del sombrero*) brim; foothill; (*mujer*) (coll) skirt; **cosido a las faldas de** tied to the apron strings of
falde·ro -ra *adj* skirt; (*perro*) lap; lady-loving ‖ *m* lap dog
faldillas *fpl* skirts, coattails
faldón *m* coattail; shirttail; saddle flap
falible *adj* fallible
falsada *f* swoop (*of bird of prey*)
falsa·rio -ria *adj* lying ‖ *mf* falsifier, crook; liar
falsear *tr* to falsify; to counterfeit; to forge; (*la verdad*) to distort; (*una cerradura*) to pick; to bevel ‖ *intr* to sag, to buckle; to give, give way
falsedad *f* falsity; (*mentira*) falsehood

falsete *m* falsetto; plug, tap; door (*between rooms*)
falsetista *f* falsetto
falsía *f* falsity, treachery; unsteadiness
falsificación *f* falsification; fake; counterfeit; forgery
falsificar §73 *tr* to falsify; to fake; to counterfeit; to forge
falsilla *f* guide lines
fal·so -sa *adj* false; counterfeit; (*caballo*) vicious ‖ *m* patch; **coger en falso** (Mex) to catch in a lie; **envidar en falso** to bluff
falta *f* fault; lack, want; misdeed; absence; (*ausencia de la clase*) cut; (sport) fault; **a falta de** for want of; **echar en falta** to miss; **falta de ortografía** misspelling; **hacer falta** to be needed; to be lacking; **hacerle falta a uno** to need, e.g., **le hacen falta a Juan estos libros** John needs these books; to miss, e.g., **Vd. me hace mucha falta** I miss you very much; **sin falta** without fail
faltar *intr* to be missing, be lacking, be wanting; to fall short; to run out; to be absent; to fail; to die; to lack; to need, e.g., **me falta dinero** I lack money, I need money; **faltar a la clase** to cut class; **faltar a la verdad** to fail to tell the truth; **faltar a una cita** to fail to keep an appointment; **faltar . . . para** to be . . . to, e.g., **faltan cinco minutos para las dos** it is five minutes to two; **faltar poco para** to come near; **faltar por** to remain to be, e.g., **faltan por escribir dos cartas** two letters remain to be written
fal·to -ta *adj* short, lacking; (*peso o medida*) short; (Arg) dull, stupid; (Col) proud, vain; **falto de** short of ‖ *f* see **falta**
fal·tón -tona *adj* (coll) dilatory, remiss; (Arg) simple-minded
falto·so -sa *adj* (coll) addlebrained; (Col) quarrelsome; (CAm, Mex) disrespectful
faltriquera *f* pocket; handbag; **faltriquera de reloj** watch fob; **rascarse la faltriquera** (coll) to cough up
falúa *f* barge, tender
falucho *m* felucca
falla *f* failure, breakdown; defect; (geol) fault; (Mex) baby's bonnet
fallar *tr* to trump; to judge, pass judgment on ‖ *intr* to fail, to miss; to misfire; to sag, weaken; to break down; to judge, pass judgment
falleba *f* espagnolette
fallecer §22 *intr* to die; to fail, expire
falleci·do -da *adj* deceased, late
falli·do -da *adj* unsuccessful; bankrupt; (*deuda*) uncollectible
fallir §13 *intr* to fail; (Ven) to go bankrupt
fa·llo -lla *adj* (Chile) silly, simple; **estar fallo a** to be out of (*cards of a suit*) ‖ *m* short suit; decision; judgment, verdict; **tener fallo a or de** to be out of ‖ *f* see **falla**
fama *f* fame; reputation; rumor; (Chile) bull's-eye; **correr fama** to be ru-

mored; **es fama** it is said, it is rumored

faméli·co -ca *adj* famished, starving

familia *f* family

familiar *adj* familiar; family; (*sin ceremonia*) informal; (*lenguaje, estilo*) colloquial || *m* member of the family; member of the household; acquaintance; **familiar dependiente** dependent

familiaridad *f* familiarity

familiarizar §60 *tr* to familiarize || *ref* to become familiar; to become too familiar; to familiarize oneself

famo·so -sa *adj* famous; (*excelente*) (coll) famous; (*formidable*) (coll) some, e.g., **famoso sujeto** some guy

fámu·lo -la *mf* (coll) servant

fanal *m* beacon, lighthouse; lantern; bell glass, bell jar; lamp shade

fanáti·co -ca *adj* fanatic(al) || *mf* fanatic; (sport) fan

fanatismo *m* fanaticism

fanega *f* 1.58 bu.; **fanega de tierra** 1.59 acres

fanfarria *f* fanfare; (coll) blustering

fanfa·rrón -rrona *adj* (coll) blustering, bragging; (coll) flashy || *mf* (coll) blusterer, braggart

fanfarronada *f* (coll) bluster, bravado

fanfarronear *intr* (coll) to bluster, to brag

fanfarronería *f* (coll) blustering, bragging, sword rattling

fanfurriña *f* (coll) pet, peeve

fango *m* mud, mire; **llenar de fango** (fig) to sling mud at

fango·so -sa *adj* muddy; sticky, gooey

fantasear *tr* to dream of || *intr* to fancy, to daydream; **fantasear de** to boast of being

fantasía *f* fantasy; fancy; conceit, vanity; imagery; **con fantasía** (Arg) hard; **de fantasía** fancy, imitation; **tocar por fantasía** (Ven) to play by ear

fantasio·so -sa *adj* (coll) vain, conceited

fantasma *m* phantom, ghost; stuffed shirt; (telv) ghost; **fantasma magnético** magnetic curves || *f* scarecrow, hobgoblin

fantas·món -mona *adj* (coll) conceited || *mf* (coll) conceited person || *m* (coll) stuffed shirt; (coll) scarecrow

fantásti·co -ca *adj* fantastic; fancy; conceited

fantoche *m* puppet, marionette; (coll) nincompoop, whippersnapper

faquín *m* street porter, errand boy

fara·lá *m* (*pl* **-laes**) ruffle, flounce; (coll) frill

faramalla *mf* (coll) cheat, swindler || *f* (coll) jabber, claptrap; (coll) bluff, fake; (Chile) bragging

faramalle·ro -ra or **farama·llón -llona** *adj* (coll) scheming, swindling || *mf* (coll) schemer, swindler

farándula *f* (*baile*) farandole; (coll) gossip, scheming; (coll) theater people; (*de gente*) (Arg) crush, milling

farandulear *intr* (coll) to boast, to show off

Faraón *m* Pharaoh

faraute *m* herald, messenger; interpreter; (*actor*) prologue; (coll) busybody

fardel *m* bag, bundle; (coll) sloppy person

fardo *m* bundle, package

farfa·lá *m* (*pl* **-laes**) ruffle, flounce

farfullar *tr* (*p.ej., una lección*) (coll) to sputter through; (*p.ej., una tarea*) (coll) to stumble through || *intr* (coll) to sputter

faringe *f* pharynx

fariseo *m* pharisee; Pharisee; (coll) lanky good-for-nothing

farmacéuti·co -ca *adj* pharmaceutical || *mf* pharmacist

farmacia *f* pharmacy, drug store; **farmacia de guardia** drug store open all night

fármaco *m* drug, medicine

faro *m* lighthouse, beacon; floodlight; (aut) headlight; (fig) beacon; **faro piloto** (aut) spotlight; **faros de carretera** (aut) bright lights; **faros de cruce** (aut) dimmers; **faros de población** or **de situación** (aut) parking lights

farol *m* lamp, light; lantern; street light; (rr) headlight; (coll) conceited fellow; (Bol) bay window; **farol de tope** (naut) headlight

farola *f* lighthouse; street lamp, lamp-post

farolear *intr* (coll) to boast, brag

farole·ro -ra *adj* (coll) boasting || *mf* (coll) boaster || *m* lamplighter

farolillo *m* heartseed; Canterbury bell; **farolillo veneciano** Chinese lantern, Japanese lantern

farota *f* (coll) minx, vixen

farotear *intr* (Col) to romp around, make a racket

faro·tón -tona *adj* (coll) brazen, cheeky || *mf* (coll) cheeky person

farra *f* salmon trout; (SAm) revelry

fárrago *m* hodgepodge

farro *m* grits

farru·co -ca *adj* (coll) bold, fearless; (coll) ill-humored || *mf* (coll) Galician abroad, Asturian abroad

farru·to -ta *adj* (Arg, Bol, Chile) sickly

farsa *f* farce; humbug

farsante *adj* & *mf* (coll) fake, fraud, humbug

fas — por fas o por nefas rightly or wrongly, in any event

fascinante *adj* fascinating

fascinar *tr* to fascinate, to bewitch; to cast a spell on, cast the evil eye on

fascismo *m* fascism

fascista *adj* & *mf* fascist

fase *f* phase

fastidiar *tr* to bore, annoy; to cloy, sicken; to disappoint || *ref* to get bored; to suffer, be a victim

fastidio *m* boredom, annoyance; distaste, nausea

fastidio·so -sa *adj* boring, annoying; cloying, sickening; annoyed, displeased

fas·to -ta *adj* happy, blessed || *m* pomp, show

fastuo·so -sa *adj* vain, pompous; magnificent

fatal *adj* fatal; bad, evil; (law) unextendible

fatalidad *f* fatality; misfortune

fatalismo *m* fatalism

fatalista *mf* fatalist

fatalmente *adv* fatally; inevitably; unfortunately; badly, poorly

fatídi·co -ca *adj* ominous, fateful

fatiga *f* fatigue; hard breathing; **fatigas** hardship

fatigar §44 *tr* to fatigue, tire, weary; to annoy, bother || *ref* to get tired

fatigo·so -sa *adj* fatiguing, tiring; (coll) trying, tedious

fa·tuo -tua *adj* fatuous; conceited || *mf* simpleton

fauces *fpl* (anat) fauces; (fig) jaws, mouth

fauna *f* fauna

fauno *m* faun

faus·to -ta *adj* happy, fortunate || *m* pomp, magnificence

fausto·so -sa *adj* magnificent

fau·tor -tora *mf* abettor; accomplice

favor *m* favor; **a favor de** under cover of; by means of; in favor of; **hágame Vd. el favor de** do me the favor to; **por favor** please; **vender favores** to peddle influence

favorable *adj* favorable

favorecer §22 *tr* to favor; to flatter

favoritismo *m* favoritism

favori·to -ta *adj* & *mf* favorite

fayanca *f* unstable posture

faz *f* (*pl* **faces**) face; aspect, look; (*de monedas o medallas*) obverse; **faces** cheeks; **faz a faz** face to face

F.C. *abbr* **ferrocarril**

fe *f* faith; testimony, witness; certificate; **¡a fe mía!** upon my faith!; **dar fe de** to certify; **en fe de lo cual** in witness whereof; **fe de erratas** list of errata; **hacer fe** to be valid; **la fe del carbonero** simple faith

fealdad *f* ugliness

Febe *f* Phoebe

feble *adj* weak, sickly; (*moneda, aleación*) lacking in weight or fineness

Febo *m* Phoebus

febrero *m* February

febril *adj* feverish

fécula *f* starch

feculen·to -ta *adj* starchy; fecal

fecundar *tr* to fecundate, to fertilize

fecun·do -da *adj* fecund, fertile

fecha *f* date; **con fecha de** under date of; **de larga fecha** of long standing; **hasta la fecha** to date

fechador *m* (Chile, Mex) canceler, postmark

fechar *tr* to date

fechoría *f* misdeed, villainy

federación *f* federation

federal *adj* & *mf* federal

federar *tr* & *ref* to federate

Federico *m* Frederick

feéri·co -ca *adj* fairy

fehaciente *adj* authentic

feldespato *m* feldspar

felicidad *f* felicity, happiness; luck

felicitar *tr* to felicitate, congratulate, wish happiness to

feli·grés -gresa *mf* parishioner, church member

feligresía *f* parish; congregation

Felipe *m* Philip

fe·liz *adj* (*pl* **-lices**) happy; lucky; (*oportuno*) felicitous

fe·lón -lona *adj* perfidious, treacherous || *mf* wicked person

felonía *f* perfidy, treachery

felpa *f* plush; (coll) drubbing; (coll) severe reprimand

felpu·do -da *adj* plushy, downy || *m* mat, door mat

femenil *adj* feminine, womanly

femeni·no -na *adj* feminine; (*sexo*) female || *m* feminine

fementi·do -da *adj* false, treacherous

feminismo *m* feminism

fenecer §22 *tr* to finish, to close || *intr* to come to an end; to die

Fenicia *f* Phoenicia

feni·cio -cia *adj* & *mf* Phoenician || *f* see **Fenicia**

fé·nix *m* (*pl* **-nix** or **-nices**) phoenix

fenobarbital *m* phenobarbital

fenomenal *adj* phenomenal

fenómeno *m* phenomenon; (coll) monster, freak

fe·o -a *adj* ugly || *m* (coll) slight; **hacer un feo a** (coll) to slight || **feo** *adv* (Arg, Col, Mex) bad, e.g., **oler feo** to smell bad

feo·te -ta *adj* ugly, hideous

feral *adj* cruel, bloody

fe·raz *adj* (*pl* **-races**) fertile

féretro *m* bier

feria *f* weekday; market; fair; day off; (Mex) change; (CAm) extra; **revolver la feria** (coll) to upset the applecart

ferial *adj* week (*day*); market (*day*) || *m* market; fair

feriante *adj* fair-going || *mf* fairgoer

feriar *tr* to buy, to sell; to give, present; (Mex) to give change for

feri·no -na *adj* wild, savage; (*tos*) whooping (*cough*)

fermentación *f* ferment; fermentation

fermentar *tr* & *intr* to ferment

fermento *m* ferment

ferocidad *f* ferocity, fierceness

ferósti·co -ca *adj* (coll) irritable; (coll) hideous

fe·roz *adj* (*pl* **-roces**) ferocious, fierce

férre·o -a *adj* iron

ferrería *f* ironworks, foundry

ferretear *tr* to trim with iron; to work in iron

ferretería *f* ironworks; hardware; hardware store

ferrete·ro -ra *mf* hardware dealer

ferrocarril *m* railroad, railway; **ferrocarril de cremallera** rack railway, mountain railroad

ferrocarrile·ro -ra *adj* (Am) railroad, rail || *m* (Am) railroader

ferrotipo *m* tintype

ferrovia·rio -ria *adj* railroad, rail || *m* railroader

fértil *adj* fertile

fertilizar §60 *tr* to fertilize

férula *f* flexible splint; ferule; **estar bajo la férula de** to be under the thumb of

férvi·do -da *adj* fervid; *(fiebre; sed)* burning

ferviente *adj* fervent

fervor *m* fervor, zeal

fervoro·so -sa *adj* ardent, zealous

festejar *tr* to fete, honor, entertain; to celebrate; to court, to woo; (Mex) to beat, thrash

festejo *m* feast, entertainment; celebration; courting, wooing; (Peru) revelry; **festejos** public festivities

festín *m* feast, banquet

festinar *tr* (Am) to hurry through; (CAm) to entertain

festival *m* festival, music festival

festividad *f* festivity; feast day; witticism

festi·vo -va *adj* festive, gay; witty; *(digno de celebrarse)* solemn

festón *m* festoon

festonear *tr* to festoon

fetiche *m* fetish

féti·do -da *adj* fetid, foul

feto *m* fetus

feú·co -ca or **feú·cho -cha** *adj* hideous, repulsive

feudal *adj* feudal

feudalismo *m* feudalism

feudo *m* fief; **feudo franco** freehold

fiable *adj* trustworthy

fiado *m* — **al fiado** on credit; **en fiado** on bail

fia·dor -dora *mf* bail; **salir fiador por** to go bail for ‖ *m* fastener; catch, pawl; (Chile, Ecuad) chin strap

fiambre *adj* cold, cold-served; *(noticias)* old, stale ‖ *m* cold lunch, cold food; stale news; (Arg) dull party; **fiambres** cold cuts

fiambrera *f* dinner pail, lunch basket

fiambrería *f* (Arg) delicatessen store

fianza *f* guarantee, surety; bond; bail; **fianza carcelera** bail

fiar §77 *tr* to entrust, confide; to guarantee; to give credit to; to sell on credit ‖ *intr* & *ref* to trust

fiasco *m* fiasco

fibra *f* fiber; (fig) fiber, strength, vigor; **fibras del corazón** heartstrings

fibro·so -sa *adj* fibrous

ficción *f* fiction

ficciona·rio -ria *adj* fictional

fice *m* (ichth) hake

ficti·cio -cia *adj* fictitious

ficha *f* chip; counter; domino; filing card; police record; (elec) plug; **ficha catalográfica** index card; **llevar ficha** to have a police record; **ser una buena ficha** (Am) to be a sly fox

ficha·dor -dora *mf* file clerk

fichar *tr* to file; to play, to move; (coll) to black-list; (Cuba) to cheat ‖ *intr* (Col) to die

fichero *m* card index, filing cabinet

fidedig·no -na *adj* reliable, trustworthy

fideicomisa·rio -ria *mf* trustee

fideicomiso *m* trusteeship

fidelería *f* (Arg, Ecuad, Peru) vermicelli factory, noodle factory

fidelidad *f* fidelity; punctiliousness; **alta fidelidad** (rad) high fidelity

fideo *m* (coll) skinny person; (Arg) joke; (Arg) confusion, disorder; **fideos** vermicelli

Fidias *m* Phidias

fiducia·rio -ria *adj* & *mf* fiduciary

fiebre *f* fever; **fiebre del heno** hay fever; **fibre tifoidea** typhoid fever

fiel *adj* faithful; exact; punctilious; honest, trustworthy ‖ *m* inspector of weights and measures; *(en las balanzas)* pointer; *(de las tijeras)* pin; **fiel de romana** inspector of weights in a slaughterhouse; **los fieles** the faithful

fielato *m* inspector's office; octroi

fieltro *m* felt; felt hat; felt rug

fiera *f* wild animal; *(persona)* fiend; (taur) bull; **ser una fiera para** (coll) to be a fiend for

fierabrás *m* (coll) spitfire, little terror

fierecilla *f* shrew

fiereza *f* fierceness; cruelty; deformity

fie·ro -ra *adj* fierce, wild; cruel; deformed, ugly; huge, tremendous; **echar** or **hacer fieros** to bluster ‖ *f* see **fiera**

fiesta *f* feast, holy day; holiday; celebration, festivity; **estar de fiesta** (coll) to be in a holiday mood; **fiesta de la hispanidad** or **fiesta de la raza** Columbus Day; **fiesta de todos los santos** All Saints' Day; **fiesta onomástica** saint's day, birthday; **fiestas** holiday, vacation; **hacer fiesta** to take off *(from work)*; **hacer fiestas a** to act up to, to fawn on; **la fiesta brava** bullfighting; **no estar para fiestas** (coll) to be in no mood for joking; **por fin de fiestas** to top it off; **se acabó la fiesta** (coll) let's drop it

fieste·ro -ra *adj* merry, gay ‖ *mf* merrymaker, party-goer

figón *m* cheap restaurant

figura *f* figure; face, countenance; *(naipe)* face card; (mus) note; (theat) character; **figura retórica** figure of speech; **hacer figura** to cut a figure

figuración *f* representation; (Arg) status, social standing

figura·do -da *adj* figurative

figurar *tr* to depict, trace, represent; to feign ‖ *intr* to figure, to be in the limelight ‖ *ref* to figure, to imagine

figurati·vo -va *adj* figurative, representative

figurería *f* face, grimace

figurilla *mf* (coll) silly little runt ‖ *f* figurine

figurín *m* dummy, model; fashion plate

figurina *f* figurine

figurita *mf* (coll) silly little runt

figurón *m* (coll) stuffed shirt; **figurón de proa** (naut) figurehead

fija *f* hinge; trowel; *(caballo)* (Peru) sure bet; **la fija** (coll) sure thing

fijacarte·les *m* (*pl* **-les**) billposter

fijación *f* fixing, fastening; posting; **fijación de precios** price fixing

fijado *m* (phot) fixing

fija·dor -dora *adj* fixing ‖ *m* carpenter who installs doors and windows; fixing bath; sprayer; (mas) pointer; hair set, hair spray

fijamárge·nes *m* (*pl* **-nes**) margin stop

fijapeina·dos m (pl -**dos**) hair set, hair spray

fijar tr to fix; to fasten; (*carteles*) to post; (*una fecha; los cabellos; una imagen fotográfica; los precios; la atención; una hora, una cita*) to fix; (*residencia*) to establish; to paste, glue || ref to settle; to notice; **fijarse en** to notice; to pay attention to; to be intent on

fijeza f firmness, stability; steadfastness; **mirar con fijeza** to stare at

fi·jo -ja adj fixed; firm, solid, secure, fast; sure, determined; **de fijo** surely || f see **fija**

fil m — **estar en fil** or **en un fil** to be alike; **fil derecho** leapfrog

fila f row, line; file; (*línea que los soldados forman de frente*) rank; (coll) dislike, hatred; **cerrar las filas** (mil) to close ranks; **en fila** in single file; **en filas** (mil) in active service; **fila india** single file, Indian file; **llamar a filas** (mil) to call to the colors; **pasarse a las filas de** to go over to; **romper filas** (mil) to break ranks

filamento m filament

filantropía f philanthropy

filántro·po -pa mf philanthropist

filar tr (naut) to pay out slowly

filarmóni·co -ca adj philharmonic

filatelia f philately

filatelista mf philatelist

filatería f fast talking; wordiness

filate·ro -ra adj fast-talking; wordy || mf fast talker; great talker

file·no -na adj (coll) cute, tiny

filete m (*de carne o pescado*) filet or fillet; (*asador*) spit; edge, rim; narrow hem; (*de tornillo*) thread; snaffle bit; (archit, bb) fillet; (typ) rule, fancy rule

filetear tr to fillet; (*un tornillo*) to thread; (bb) to tool

filiación f filiation; description, characteristics; (mil) regimental register

filial adj filial || f affiliate, branch

filiar §77 tr to register || ref to enroll

filibustero m filibuster, buccaneer

filigrana f filigree; (*en el papel*) watermark

filipi·no -na adj Filipine, Filipino || mf Filipino || **Filipinas** fpl Philippines

Filipo m Philip (*of Macedonia*)

Filis f Phyllis

filiste·o -a adj & mf Philistine || m tall, fat fellow

film m (pl **films** or **filmes**) film

filmar tr to film

filo m edge; ridge; dividing line; (CAm, Mex) hunger; **al filo de** at, at about; **dar filo a** to sharpen; **filo del viento** direction of the wind; **pasar al filo de la espada** to put to the sword; **por filo** exactly

filobús m trolley bus, trackless trolley

filocomunista adj & mf procommunist

filología f philology

filólo·go -ga mf philologist

filón m seam, vein; (fig) gold mine

filo·so -sa adj (Am) sharp

filosofía f philosophy

filosófi·co -ca adj philosophic(al)

filóso·fo -fa mf philosopher

filote m (Col) corn silk; (Col) ear of green corn

filtración f filtering; leak; (fig) leak, loss

filtrado m filtrate

filtrar tr to filter || intr to leak; to ooze || ref to filter; (*el dinero*) to leak away, to disappear

filtro m filter; (*brebaje para conciliar el amor*) philter, love potion

filu·do -da adj (SAm) sharp-edged

filván m featheredge

fimo m dung, manure

fin m end; aim, purpose, end; **a fin de** to, in order to; **a fin de que** in order that, so that; **a fines de** toward the end of, late in; **al fin** finally; **al fin del mundo** far, far away; **al fin y a la postre** or **al fin y al cabo** after all, in the end; **dar fin a** to put an end to; **fin de semana** weekend; **por fin** finally, in short; **sin fin** endless; endlessly; **un sin fin de** no end of

fina·do -da adj deceased, late || mf deceased

final adj final || m end; (mus) finale; **por final** finally || f (sport) finals; **final de partido** windup

finalidad f end, purpose

finalista mf finalist

finalizar §60 tr to end, terminate; (*una escritura*) (law) to execute || intr to end, terminate

financiación f financing

financiar tr to finance

financie·ro -ra adj financial || mf financier

finanzas fpl finances

finar intr to die || ref to yearn

finca f property, piece of real estate; farm, ranch; **buena finca** (coll) sly fellow

fincar §73 tr (P-R) to cultivate, to farm || intr to buy up real estate; (Col) to reside, rest, be based || ref to buy up real estate

fincha·do -da adj (coll) vain, conceited

fi·nés -nesa adj Finnic; Finnish || mf Finn || m (*idioma uraliano*) Finnic; (*idioma de Finlandia*) Finnish

fineza f fineness; kindness, courtesy; token of affection, favor

fingi·do -da adj fake, sham; false, deceitful

fingir §27 tr & intr to feign, pretend, fake || ref to pretend to be

finiquitar tr (*una cuenta*) to settle, to close; (coll) to finish, wind up

finiquito m settlement, closing; **dar finiquito a** to settle, close; (coll) to finish, wind up

finíti·mo -ma adj bordering, neighboring

fini·to -ta adj finite

finlan·dés -desa adj Finnish || mf Finn, Finlander || m Finnish

Finlandia f Finland

fi·no -na adj fine; (*ligero, casi transparente*) sheer; (*esbelto*) thin, slender; (*paño, papel, etc.*) thin; (*agua*) pure; polite, courteous; shrewd, cunning

finta f feint

finura f fineness, excellence; politeness, courtesy

finústi·co -ca adj (coll) overobsequious

firma f signature; signing; firm; firm name; mail to be signed; **con mi firma** under my hand; **firma en blanco** blank check

firmamento m firmament

firmante adj signatory ‖ mf signer, signatory

firmar tr & intr to sign

firme adj firm, steady; solid, hard; staunch, unswerving ‖ adv firmly, steadily ‖ m roadbed; **de firme** hard, e.g., **llover de firme** to rain hard

firmeza f firmness; constancy, fortitude

firmón m shyster who signs anything

fiscal adj fiscal, treasury ‖ m treasurer; district attorney; busybody

fiscalizar §60 tr to control, inspect; to prosecute; to pry into

fisco m state treasury, exchequer

fisga f fish spear; prying, snooping; banter, raillery

fisgar §44 tr to harpoon, fish with a spear; to pry into ‖ intr to pry, to snoop; to mock, to jeer ‖ ref to mock, to jeer

fis·gón -gona mf (coll) mocker, jester; (coll) snooper, busybody

físi·co -ca adj physical; (Mex, W-I) finicky, prudish ‖ mf physicist ‖ m physique ‖ f physics

fisiología f physiology

fisiológi·co -ca adj physiological

fisión f fission

fisionable adj fissionable

fisonomía f physiognomy

fistol m sly fellow; (Mex) necktie pin

fisura f (anat, min) fissure; **fisura del paladar** cleft palate

fla·co -ca adj thin, skinny; feeble, weak, frail; insecure, unstable ‖ m weak spot

flacu·cho -cha adj (coll) skinny

flagrante adj occurring, actual; **en flagrante** in the act

flamante adj bright, flaming; brand-new, spick-and-span

flameante adj flamboyant

flamear intr to flame; to flare up (with anger); to flutter, to wave

flamen·co -ca adj Flemish; buxom; Andalusian gypsy; (coll) flashy, snappy, gypsyish ‖ mf Fleming ‖ m (idioma) Flemish; Andalusian gypsy dance, song, or music; (orn) flamingo

fláme·o -a adj flamelike

flamíge·ro -ra adj (poet) flaming; (archit) flamboyant

flan m custard

flanco m side, flank; **coger por el flanco** to catch off guard

Flandes f Flanders

flanquear tr to flank

flaquear intr to weaken, flag; to become faint; to become discouraged

flaqueza f thinness, skinniness; weakness; instability

flato m gas; (Am) gloominess, melancholy

flato·so -sa adj flatulent, windy; (Am) gloomy, melancholy

flauta f flute

flautín m piccolo

flautista mf flautist, flutist

flebitis f phlebitis

fleco m fringe; ragged edge; **flecos** bangs

flecha f arrow; (aer) sweepback

flechar tr (el arco) to draw; (a una persona) to wound with an arrow, to kill with an arrow; (coll) to infatuate

flechero m archer, bowman

fleje m iron strap, iron hoop

flema f phlegm

flemáti·co -ca adj phlegmatic(al)

flemón m gumboil

flequillo m bangs

Flesinga f Flushing

fletante m shipowner; (Arg, Chile, Ecuad) conveyancer

fletar tr (una nave) to charter; (ganado) to load; (bestias de carga, carros, etc.) (Arg, Chile, Ecuad, Mex) to hire ‖ ref (Arg) to sneak in, slip in; (Cuba, Mex) to beat it, clear out

flete m (naut) freight, cargo; (Arg, Bol, Col, Urug) race horse; **salir sin flete** (Col, Ven) to beat it

flexible adj flexible; (sombrero) soft ‖ m soft hat; (elec) flexible cord

flexo m gooseneck lamp

flinflanear intr to tinkle

flirt m flirting

flirtear intr to flirt

flojear intr to ease up, to idle; to flag, weaken

flojedad f slackness, looseness; limpness; laziness; weakness

flojel m fluff, nap; down, soft feathers

flo·jo -ja adj slack, loose; limp; languid, lazy; weak; (precios) sagging; (viento) light; lax, careless

flor f flower; (de árbol frutal) blossom; (del cuero) grain; (fig) compliment, bouquet; **a flor de** even with, flush with; **a flor de agua** at water level; **decir flores a** to flatter; to flirt with; **flor de la edad** bloom of youth; **flor de la vida** prime of life; **flor del campo** wild flower; **flor de lis** (escudo de armas de Francia) lily, fleur-de-lis; **flor de mano** paper flower, artificial flower; **la flor de la canela** the tops; **la flor y nata de** the cream of

flora f flora

floral adj floral

florcita f (Am) little flower; **andar de florcita** (Arg, Bol, Chile, Urug) to stroll around with a flower in one's buttonhole, to take it easy

florear tr to flower, decorate with flowers; (los naipes) to stack; (harina) to bolt ‖ intr (la punta de la espada) to quiver; to twang away on a guitar; (coll) to throw bouquets

florecer §22 intr to flower, to blossom, to bloom; (prosperar) to flourish ‖ ref to become moldy

floreciente adj flowering, florescent; flourishing

florenti·no -na *adj & mf* Florentine
floreo *m* idle talk; bright remark; *(de la punta de la espada)* quivering; *(de la guitarra)* twanging; *(mus)* flourish; **andarse con floreos** (coll) to beat about the bush
florera *f* flower girl
florería *f* (Am) flower shop
flore·ro -ra *adj* flattering, jesting ‖ *mf* flatterer, jester; florist ‖ *m (vaso para flores)* vase; *(maceta con flores)* flowerpot; flower stand, jardiniere; *(cuadro, pintura)* flower piece ‖ *f* see **florera**
florescencia *f* florescence
floresta *f* woods, woodland; grove; rural setting; anthology
florete *m (esgrima)* fencing; *(espadín)* foil
floretear *tr* to decorate with flowers ‖ *intr* to fence
flori·do -da *adj* flowery, full of flowers; choice, select
florilegio *m* anthology
floripondio *m* (SAm) angel's-trumpet
florista *mf* florist
floristería *f* flower shop
florón *m* large flower; finial; rosette; (typ) tailpiece, vignette
flota *f* fleet
flotación *f* buoyancy
flotador *m* float
flotaje *m* log driving
flotante *adj* floating; *(barba)* flowing ‖ *m* (Col) braggart
flotar *intr* to float; *(una bandera)* to wave
flote *m* floating; **a flote** afloat
fluctuar §21 *intr* to fluctuate; to bob up and down; to wave; to waver; to be in danger
fluente *adj* fluent, flowing; *(hemorroides)* bleeding
fluidez *f* fluidity
flúi·do -da *adj* fluid; *(estilo, lenguaje)* fluent ‖ *m* fluid
fluir §20 *intr* to flow
flujo *m* flow, flux; *(acceso de la marea)* floodtide; **flujo de risa** fit of noisy laughter; **flujo de vientre** loose bowels; **flujo y reflujo** ebb and flow
fluor *m* fluorine
fluorescencia *f* fluorescence
fluorescente *adj* fluorescent
fluorhídri·co -ca *adj* hydrofluoric
fluorización *f* fluoridation
fluorizar §60 *tr* to fluoridate
fluoroscopio *m* fluoroscope
fluoruro *m* fluoride
flux *m (en el póker)* flush; (Am) suit of clothes; **estar en flux** (Am) to be penniless; **hacer flux** (coll) to blow in everything without settling accounts; **tener flux** (Am) to be lucky
fluxión *f (acumulación morbosa de humores)* congestion; *(enrojecimiento de la cara y el cuello)* flush; *(constipado de narices)* cold in the head; **fluxión de muelas** swollen cheek; **fluxión de pecho** pneumonia
foca *f* seal
focal *adj* focal

foco *m* focus; *(de vicios)* center; *(de un absceso)* core; electric light
fodo·lí *adj (pl* **-líes)** meddlesome
fodon·go -ga *adj* (Mex) dirty, slovenly
fe·fo -fa *adj* soft, fluffy, spongy
fogaje *m (contribución)* hearth money; (Arg) fire, blaze; (Arg, Mex) rash, eruption; (Am) blush, flush
fogata *f* blaze, bonfire
fogón *m* cooking stove; *(de máquina de vapor)* firebox
fogonazo *m* powder flash
fogonero *m* fireman, stoker
fogosidad *f* fire, spirit, dash
fogo·so -sa *adj* fiery, spirited
fol. *abbr* folio
folgo *m* foot muff
foliar *tr* to folio
folio *m* folio; **al primer folio** right off; **de a folio** (coll) enormous; **en folio** folio
folklore *m* folklore
follaje *m* foliage; gaudy ornament; *(palabrería)* fustian
follar *tr* to shape like a leaf ‖ §61 *tr* to blow with bellows
folletín *m* newspaper serial *(printed at bottom of page)*; pamphlet
folleto *m* brochure, pamphlet, tract
fo·llón -llona *adj* careless, indolent, lazy; arrogant, cowardly ‖ *mf* lazy loafer, knave ‖ *m* noiseless rocket
fomentar *tr* to foment; to foster, encourage, promote; to warm
fonda *f* inn, restaurant; (Chile) refreshment stand
fondeadero *m* anchorage
fondea·do -da *adj* (Am) well-heeled
fondear *tr (un buque)* to search; to scrutinize, examine closely ‖ *intr* to cast anchor ‖ *ref* (Am) to save up for a rainy day
fondillos *mpl* seat *(of trousers)*
fondista *mf* innkeeper
fondo *m* bottom; *(de un cuarto, una tienda)* back, rear; *(del mar, de una piscina, etc.)* floor; *(de un cilindro, barril, etc.)* head; background; *(de una casa)* depth; *(de un paño)* ground; *(caudal)* fund; *(lo esencial)* bottom; **a fondo** thoroughly; **bajos fondos sociales** underworld, scum of the earth; **colar a fondo** to sink; **dar fondo** to cast anchor; **echar a fondo** to sink; **en el fondo** at bottom; **estar en fondos** to have funds available; **fondo de amortización** sinking fund; **fondos** *(caudales, dinero)* funds; **irse a fondo** to go to the bottom; *(un negocio)* to fail; **tener buen fondo** to be good-natured
fonducho *m* cheap eating house
fonéti·co -ca *adj* phonetic
fono *m* (Chile) earphone
fonocaptor *s* pickup
fonógrafo *m* phonograph
fonología *f* phonology
fontanería *f* plumbing; water-supply system
fontane·ro -ra *adj* fountain ‖ *m* plumber, tinsmith
foque *m* (naut) jib; (coll) piccadilly collar

foraji·do -da *adj* fugitive || *mf* fugitive, outlaw, bandit

foráne·o -a *adj* foreign, strange; offshore

foraste·ro -ra *adj* outside, strange; foreign || *mf* outsider, stranger

forbante *m* freebooter

forcejar or **forcejear** *intr* to struggle, resist, contend

forceju·do -da *adj* strong, husky, robust

fór·ceps *m* (*pl* **-ceps**) forceps

forestal *adj* forest

forja *f* forge; forging; silversmith's forge; foundry, ironworks; mortar

forjar *tr* to forge; to build with stone and mortar; to roughcast; (*mentiras*) to forge || *ref* to forge; to hatch, think up

forma *f* form, shape; way; (*de un libro*) format; **de forma que** so that, with the result that; **tener buenas formas** to have a good figure

formación *f* formation; **formación de palabras** word formation

formal *adj* formal, ceremonious; express, definite; reliable; sedate; serious

formalidad *f* formality; reliability; seriousness

formar *tr* to form; to shape, to fashion; to train, educate || *intr* to form; to form a line, to stand in line || *ref* to form; to form a line, to stand in line; to take form, to grow, to develop

formato *m* format

formidable *adj* formidable

formidolo·so -sa *adj* scared, frightened; frightful, horrible

fórmula *f* formula; prescription; **por fórmula** as a matter of form

formular *tr* to formulate

formulario *m* form, blank; **formulario de pedido** order blank

forni·do -da *adj* husky, sturdy, robust

foro *m* forum; (*abogacía*) bar; (*del escenario*) back, rear

forraje *m* forage, fodder

forrajear *tr & intr* to forage

forrar *tr* to line; (*un vestido*) to face; (*un libro, un paraguas*) to cover; (*un lienzo*) to stretch || *ref* (Guat, Mex) to stuff oneself

forro *m* lining; cover, covering; (naut) sheathing, planking; **forro de freno** brake lining; **ni por el forro** (coll) not by a long shot

fortalecer §22 *tr* to fortify, strengthen

fortaleza *f* fortitude; strength, vigor; fortress, stronghold

fortificación *f* fortification

fortificante *m* tonic

fortificar §73 *tr* to fortify

fortín *m* small fort; bunker

fortui·to -ta *adj* fortuitous

fortuna *f* fortune; **correr fortuna** (naut) to ride the storm; **de fortuna** makeshift; **por fortuna** fortunately; **probar fortuna** to try one's luck

fortunón *m* (coll) windfall

forza·do -da *adj* forced; (*p.ej., entrada*) forcible; (*sonrisa*) (fig) forced; (*trabajos*) hard || *m* galley slave

forzar §35 *tr* to force

forzo·so -sa *adj* unavoidable; strong, husky; (*trabajos*) hard; (*aterrizaje; marcha*) forced || *f* — **hacer la forzosa a** (coll) to put the squeeze on

forzu·do -da *adj* strong, husky, robust

fosa *f* grave; (aut) pit; **fosa de los leones** (Bib) lions' den

fosar *tr* to dig a ditch around

fos·co -ca *adj* dark; cross, sullen; (*tiempo*) threatening

fosfato *m* phosphate

fosforera *f* matchbox

fosforescente *adj* phosphorescent

fósforo *m* (*cuerpo simple*) phosphorus; match; **fósforo de seguridad** safety match

fósil *adj & m* fossil

foso *m* hole, pit; (*que rodea un castillo o fortaleza*) moat; (theat & aut) pit

fotingo *m* (Am) jalopy, jitney

foto *f* (coll) photo; **foto fija** (phot) still

fotodrama *m* photoplay

fotofija *m* photo-finish camera

fotogéni·co -ca *adj* photogenic

fotograbado *m* photoengraving

fotografía *f* (*arte*) photography; (*imagen, retrato*) photograph; photograph gallery

fotografiar §77 *tr & intr* to photograph

fotógra·fo -fa *mf* photographer

fotómetro *m* light meter

fotoperiodismo *m* photojournalism

fotopila *f* solar battery

fotostatar *tr & intr* to photostat

fotóstato *m* photostat

fototubo *m* phototube

fra. *abbr* **factura**

frac *m* (*pl* **fraques**) full-dress coat, tails, swallow-tailed coat

fracasar *intr* to fail; to break to pieces

fracaso *m* failure; breakdown, crash

fracción *f* fraction

fraccionar *tr* to divide up; to break up

fracciona·rio -ria *adj* fractional

fractura *f* fracture; breaking open, breaking in

fracturar *tr* to fracture; to break open, break in || *ref* (*p.ej., un brazo*) to fracture

fragancia *f* fragrance; good reputation

fragante *adj* fragrant; **en fragante** (archaic) in the act

fragata *f* frigate; **fragata ligera** corvette

frágil *adj* fragile; (*quebradizo; que cae fácilmente en el pecado*) frail; (Mex) poor, needy

fragmento *m* fragment

fragor *m* crash, roar, thunder

fragoro·so -sa *adj* noisy, thundering

fragosidad *f* roughness, unevenness; (*de un bosque*) thickness, denseness; rough road

frago·so -sa *adj* rough, uneven; thick, dense; noisy, thundering

fragua *f* forge

fraguar §10 *tr* to forge; to hatch, scheme; (*mentiras*) to forge || *intr* to forge; (*la cal, el cemento*) to set

fraile *m* friar, monk; **fraile de misa y olla** (coll) friarling; **fraile rezador** praying mantis

frambesia *f* (pathol) yaws

frambuesa *f* raspberry

frambueso *m* raspberry bush

francachela *f* (coll) feast, spread; (coll) carousal, high time; (Arg) excessive familiarity

francalete *m* strap with buckle

fran·cés -cesa *adj* French; **despedirse a la francesa** (coll) to take French leave ‖ *m* Frenchman; (*idioma*) French ‖ *f* Frenchwoman

francesada *f* French remark; French invasion of Spain in 1808

francesilla *f* French roll; (bot) turban buttercup

Francia *f* France

Francisca *f* Frances

francisca·no -na *adj* & *mf* Franciscan

Francisco *m* Francis

francmasón *m* Freemason

francmasonería *f* Freemasonry

fran·co -ca *adj* generous, liberal; outspoken, candid, frank; (*camino*) free, open; (*suelo*) loamy; free, gratis; Frankish; **franco a bordo** free on board; **franco de porte** postpaid ‖ *mf* Frank ‖ *m* franc; (*idioma*) Frankish

francolín *m* black partridge

franco·te -ta *adj* (coll) frank, wholehearted

francotirador *m* sniper

franela *f* flannel

frangente *m* accident, mishap

frangir §27 *tr* to break up, break to pieces

frangollar *tr* (coll) to bungle, to botch

frangollo *m* porridge; mash for cattle; (coll) bungle, botch

franja *f* fringe; strip, band; (opt) fringe

franjar *tr* to fringe

franquear *tr* to exempt; to cross, go over; to grant; to free, enfranchise; (*un camino*) to open, to clear; (*una carta*) to frank, pay the postage for; **a franquear en destino** postage will be paid by addressee ‖ *ref* to yield; **franquearse con** to open one's heart to

franqueo *m* freeing, liberation; postage; **franqueo concertado** postage permit

franqueza *f* generosity; candidness, frankness; freedom

franquía *f* (naut) sea room; **en franquía** (naut & fig) in the open

franquicia *f* franchise; exemption, tax exemption; **franquicia postal** franking privilege

franquista *mf* Francoist

frasca *f* leaves, twigs, brush; (Guat, Mex) high jinks

frasco *m* flask; (*p.ej., de aceitunas*) jar

frase *f* phrase; (*oración cabal*) sentence; idiom; **frase hecha** saying, proverb; cliché; **gastar frases** (coll) to talk all around the subject

frasear *tr* to phrase ‖ *intr* (coll) to talk all around the subject

frasquera *f* bottle frame, liquor case

fratás *m* plastering trowel

fraternal *adj* brotherly, fraternal

fraternidad *f* fraternity, brotherhood

fraternizar §60 *intr* to fraternize

frater·no -na *adj* brotherly, fraternal

fraude *m* fraud

fraudulen·to -ta *adj* fraudulent

fray *m* Fra

frecuencia *f* frequency; **alta frecuencia** high frequency; **baja frecuencia** low frequency; **con frecuencia** frequently

frecuentar *tr* (*ir con frecuencia a*) to frequent; to keep up, repeat

frecuente *adj* frequent; (*usual*) common

fregadero *m* sink, kitchen sink

frega·do -da *adj* (Am) annoying, bothersome; (SAm) stubborn; (Am) cunning; (P-R) brazen ‖ *m* scrubbing; mopping; (coll) mess

frega·dor -dora *mf* dishwasher

fregar §66 *tr* (*restregar*) to rub; (*restregar para limpiar*) to scrub, to scour; (*el pavimento*) to mop; (*los platos*) to wash; (Am) to annoy, bother

fregasue·los *m* (*pl* -los) mop, floor mop

fre·griz *f* (*pl* -trices) var of fregona

fre·gón -gona *adj* (Am) annoying, bothersome; (Am) brazen ‖ *f* (*criada que friega el pavimento*) scrub woman; (*criada que lava la vajilla*) dishwasher, scullery maid

freiduría *f* fried-fish shop

freír §58 & §83 *tr* to fry; (coll) to bore to death ‖ *intr* to fry; **dejarle a uno freír en su aceite** (coll) to let someone stew in his own juice ‖ *ref* to fry; (coll) to be bored to death; **freírsele a** a to try to fool, to scheme to deceive

fréjol *m* kidney bean

frenar *tr* to bridle, to check, hold back; (*un automóvil, tren*) to brake

frene·sí *m* (*pl* -síes) frenzy

frenéti·co -ca *adj* frantic; mad, furious; wild

frenillo *m* muzzle; **no tener frenillo en la lengua** (coll) to not mince one's words

freno *m* (*parte de la brida*) bit; (*aparato para parar el movimiento de los vehículos*) brake; (fig) brake, check, curb; **freno de contrapedal** coaster brake; **morder el freno** to champ the bit

frenología *f* phrenology

frentazo *m* (Mex) rebuff

frente *m* & *f* (*de un edificio*) front ‖ *m* (mil) front, front line; **al frente de** at the head of, in charge of ‖ *f* brow, forehead; face, front; head; **a frente** straight ahead; **arrugar la frente** to knit the brow; **de frente** straight ahead; abreast; **en frente de** in front of; against, opposed to; **frente a** in front of; compared with

freo *m* channel, strait

fresa *f* strawberry; (*de fresadora*) cutter

fresado *m* milling, millwork

fresadora *f* milling machine

fresal *m* strawberry patch

fresar *tr* to mill

fresca *f* fresh air; cool part of the day; (coll) blunt remark, piece of one's mind

fresca·chón -chona *adj* bouncing, buxom; (*viento*) brisk

fresca·les *mf* (*pl* -les) (coll) forward sort of person

frescamente adv recently; cheekily, brazenly

fres·co -ca adj (acabado de hacer o suceder) fresh; (moderadamente frío) cool; (pintura) fresh, wet; (tela, vestido) light; calm, unruffled; buxom, ruddy; (coll) cheeky, fresh; **estar fresco** (coll) to be in a fine pinch; **quedarse tan fresco** (coll) to show no offense, to be indifferent or unconcerned || m coolness; fresh air; fresh bacon; (fa) fresco; (Am) cool drink; **al fresco** in the open air; in the night air; **hace fresco** it is cool; **tomar el fresco** to go out for some fresh air || f see **fresca**

frescor m freshness; cool, coolness

fresco·te -ta adj (coll) plump and rosy

frescura f freshness; cool, coolness; unconcern, offhand manner; sharp reply; (coll) cheek, impudence

fresno m ash tree; (madera) ash

fresquera f meat closet, food cabinet, icebox

fresquería f (Am) ice-cream parlor, soft-drink store

fresque·ro -ra mf fish dealer; (Peru) soft-drink vendor || f see **fresquera**

freudismo m Freudianism

freza f dung; spawning; hole made by game

frialdad f coldness; carelessness, laxity; stupidity; (pathol) frigidity; (pathol) impotence; (fig) coolness, coldness

friáti·co -ca adj chilly; awkward, stupid; (ropa) cold

fricar §73 tr to rub

fricasé m fricassee

fricción f rubbing; massage; (pharm) rubbing liniment; (phys) friction

friccionar tr to rub; to massage

friega f rubbing, massage; (Am) annoyance, bother; (Am) flogging, whipping

frigidez f frigidity; coldness

frigi·do -da adj frigid; cold

frigorífero m freezing chamber

frigorífi·co -ca adj refrigerating; cold-storage || m refrigerator; (Arg, Urug) packing house, cold-storage plant

frijol m bean, kidney bean; **frijol de media luna** Lima bean; **¡frijoles!** (W-I) absolutely no!

frijolear tr (Guat) to annoy, molest

frijolizar §60 tr (Peru) to bewitch

frí·o -a adj cold; dull, weak, colorless; (fig) cold, cool || m cold; **fríos** (Am) chills and fever; **coger frío** to catch cold; **hace frío** it is cold; **tener frío** (una persona) to be cold; **tomar frío** to catch cold

friole·ro -ra adj chilly || f trifle, trinket; snack, bite

frisar tr to rub; to fit, fasten; (naut) to calk || intr to agree, get along; **frisar con** or **en** to border on

friso m dado, wainscot; (archit) frieze

fri·són -sona adj & mf Frisian

fritada f fry

fri·to -ta adj fried; (coll) bored to death || m fry; (Ven) daily bread

fritura f fry

frívo·lo -la adj frivolous; trifling

fronda f leaf; (del helecho) frond; sling-shaped bandage; **frondas** frondage, foliage

frondo·so -sa adj leafy; woodsy

frontalera f yoke pad

frontera f frontier, border; front, façade

fronteri·zo -za adj frontier, border; facing, opposite

fronte·ro -ra adj frontier, border; facing, opposite; front || f see **frontera**

frontín m (Mex) flip, fillip

fron·tis m (pl -tis) front, façade

frontispicio m frontispiece; (coll) face

frontón m (encima de puertas o ventanas) gable, pediment; pelota court; pelota wall; handball court

frotamiento m rubbing; (phys) friction

frotar tr to rub; to chafe || ref to rub

fro·tis m (pl -tis) (bact) smear

fructuo·so -sa adj fruitful

frugal adj (en comer y beber) temperate; (no muy abundante) frugal

fruición f enjoyment, satisfaction; (del mal ajeno) evil satisfaction

fruiti·vo -va adj enjoyable

frunce m shirr, shirring, gathering

frunci·do -da adj grim, gruff, stern; (Chile) temperate; (Chile) sad, gloomy || m shirr, shirring, gathering

fruncir §36 tr to wrinkle, pucker, pleat; (la frente) to knit; (los labios) to curl, to purse; (la verdad) to twist, disguise; to shirr, to gather || ref to affect modesty, to be shocked

fruslería f trifle, trinket; (coll) futility, triviality

frusle·ro -ra adj futile, trivial, trifling || m rolling pin

frustrar tr to frustrate, to thwart

fruta f fruit; **fruta del tiempo** fruit in season; **fruta de sartén** fritter, pancake; **frutas** fruit; **frutas agrias** citrus fruit

frutal adj fruit || m fruit tree

frutería f fruit store

frute·ro -ra adj fruit || mf fruit dealer || m fruit dish; tray of imitation fruit

frutilla f (del rosario) bead; Chilean strawberry; gumdrop

fruto m (bot & fig) fruit; **fruto de bendición** legitimate offspring; **frutos** produce; **sacar fruto de** to derive benefit from

fu interj faugh!, fie!; (del gato) spit!; **ni fu ni fa** (coll) neither this nor that

fucilazo m heat lightning, sheet lightning

fuego m fire; (para encender un cigarrillo) light; (de arma de fuego) firing; lighthouse, beacon; hearth, home; rash, eruption; sore, fever blister; **abrir fuego** to open fire; **echar fuego** (coll) to blow up, hit the ceiling; **¡fuego!** fire!; **fuego fatuo** will-o'-the-wisp; **fuego graneado** or **nutrido** drumfire; **fuegos artificiales** fireworks; **hacer fuego** to fire, to shoot; **marcar a fuego** to brand; **pegar fuego a** to set fire to, to set on fire; **poner a fuego y sangre** to lay waste; **prenderse fuego** to catch on fire; **romper fuego** to open fire; to stir up a row; **tocar a fuego** to sóund the fire alarm

fuelle *m* fold, pucker, wrinkle; (*instrumento para soplar*) bellows; (*cubierta de coche*) folding carriage top; wind clouds; (*persona soplona*) (coll) gossip, talebearer

fuente *f* fountain, spring; public hydrant; font, baptismal font; platter, tray; (fig) source; **beber en buenas fuentes** (coll) to have good sources of information; **fuente de gasolina** gasoline pump; **fuente de sodas** soda fountain; **fuente para beber** drinking fountain; **fuentes termales** hot springs

fuer *m* — **a fuer de** as a, by way of

fuera *adv* out, outside; away, out of town; **desde fuera** from the outside; **fuera de** outside of; away from; out of; aside from; in addition to; **fuera de que** aside from the fact that; **fuera de sí** beside oneself; **por fuera** on the outside

fuere·ño -ña *mf* (Mex) hick, stranger

fuero *m* law, statute; code of laws; jurisdiction; exemption, privilege; **fuero interior** conscience, inmost heart; **fueros** (coll) pride, arrogance

fuerte *adj* strong; hard; loud; heavy; **hacerse fuerte** to stick to one's guns; (mil) to hole up, to dig in ‖ *adv* hard; loud ‖ *m* fort, fortress; forte, strong point

fuerza *f* force, strength, power; (*de un ejército*) main body; literal meaning; (phys) force; **a fuerza de** by dint of, by force of; **a la fuerza** forcibly, by force; **a viva fuerza** by main strength; **fuerza aérea** air force; **fuerza de agua** water power; **fuerza de sangre** animal power; **fuerza mayor** (law) force majeure, act of God; **fuerza motriz** motive power; **fuerza pública** police; **fuerza viva** kinetic energy; **hacer fuerza** to strain, struggle; to carry weight; **por fuerza** perforce, necessarily; **ser fuerza** + *inf* to be necessary to + *inf*

fuete *m* (Am) whip

fufar *intr* (el gato) to spit

fuga *f* flight; (*salida de un gas o líquido*) leak; ardor, vigor; (mus) fugue; **darse a la fuga** to take flight, to run away; **poner en fuga** to put to flight

fugar §44 *ref* to flee, escape, run away

fu·gaz *adj* (*pl* -**gaces**) fleeting, passing; (*estrella*) shooting

fugiti·vo -va *adj & mf* fugitive

fugui·llas *m* (*pl* -**llas**) (coll) hustler

fula·no -na *mf* so-and-so

fulcro *m* fulcrum

fulgor *m* brilliance, radiance

fulgurar *intr* to flash

fulmicotón *m* guncotton

fulminar *tr* to strike with lightning; to strike dead; (*censuras, amenazas, etc.*) to thunder; (*balas o bombas*) to hurl

fullería *f* trickery, cheating

fulle·ro -ra *adj* crooked, cheating ‖ *mf* crook, cheat; **fullero de naipes** cardsharp

fumada *f* puff, whiff

fumadero *m* smoking room; **fumadero de opio** opium den

fuma·dor -dora *adj* smoking ‖ *mf* smoker

fumar *tr* to smoke ‖ *intr* to smoke; **fumar en pipa** to smoke a pipe; **se prohibe fumar** no smoking ‖ *ref* (coll) to squander; (coll) to stay away from; (*la clase*) (coll) to cut

fumarada *f* (*de humo*) puff; (*de tabaco*) pipeful

fumigación *f* fumigation; **fumigación aérea** crop dusting

fumigar §44 *tr* to fumigate

fumista *m* stove or heater repairman; stove or heater dealer

fumistería *f* stove or heater shop

fumo·so -sa *adj* smoky

funámbu·lo -la *mf* ropewalker

función *f* function; duty, office, function; (*espectáculo teatral*) show, performance; **entrar en funciones** to take office, take up one's duties; **función benéfica** charitable performance; **función de aficionados** amateur performance; **función de títeres** puppet show; **función secundaria** side show

funcional *adj* functional

funcionario *m* functionary, public official, civil servant

funcione·ro -ra *adj* (coll) officious, fussy

fund. *abbr* **fundador**

funda *f* case, sheath, envelope, slip; (*para una espada*) scabbard; (*para proteger los muebles*) slip cover; **funda de almohada** pillowcase; **funda de asientos** seat cover; **funda de gafas** spectacle case

fundación *f* foundation

fundadamente *adv* with good reason; on good authority

funda·dor -dora *adj* founding ‖ *mf* founder

fundamental *adj* fundamental

fundamentar *tr* to lay the foundations of

fundamento *m* foundation; (*razón, motivo*) grounds, reason; basis; reliability, sense; (Col) skirt

fundar *tr* to found, to base ‖ *ref* — **fundarse en** to be based on; to base one's opinion on

fundente *adj* molten ‖ *m* flux

fundería *f* foundry

fundible *adj* fusible

fundición *f* (*acción de fundir*) founding; (*fábrica*) foundry; (*herrería*) forge; (*hierro colado*) cast iron; (typ) font

fundidor *m* founder, foundryman

fundir *tr* (*p.ej., metales*) to found; (*campanas, estatuas*) to cast; (*derretir para purificar*) to smelt; (*colores*) to mix; (*un filamento eléctrico*) to burn out ‖ *intr* to smelt ‖ *ref* to melt; to fuse; (*un filamento eléctrico*) to burn out; (fig) to fuse, merge; (Am) to fail, founder

fúnebre *adj* (*marcha, procesión*) funeral; (*triste*) funereal

funeral *adj* funeral; (*triste, lúgubre*)

funereal ‖ *m* funeral; **funerales** funeral

funerala — **a la funerala** (mil) with arms inverted (*as a token of mourning*)

funera·rio -ria *adj* funeral ‖ *m* mortician, funeral director ‖ *f* (*empresa*) undertaking establishment; (*local*) funeral home, funeral parlor

funes·to -ta *adj* ill-fated; sad, sorrowful; (*p.ej., influencia*) baneful

fungir §27 *intr* (CAm, Mex) to act, function

fungo *m* (pathol) fungus

fungo·so -sa *adj* fungous

funicular *adj* & *m* funicular

fuñique *adj* awkward; dull, tiresome

furgón *m* wagon, truck; (rr) freight car, boxcar; (rr) caboose

furgoneta *f* light truck, delivery truck

furia *f* fury

furibun·do -da *adj* furious, frenzied

furio·so -sa *adj* furious; (*muy grande*) terrific, tremendous

furor *m* rage, furor; **hacer furor** to be all the rage

furti·vo -va *adj* furtive; sneaky; poaching

furúnculo *m* boil

fusa *f* (mus) demisemiquaver

fus·co -ca *adj* dark

fusela·do -da *adj* streamlined

fuselaje *m* fuselage

fusible *adj* fusible ‖ *m* (elec) fuse

fusil *m* gun, rifle

fusilar *tr* to shoot, execute; (coll) to plagiarize

fusilazo *m* (*tiro de fusil*) gunshot, rifle shot; (*relámpago sin ruido*) heat lightning, sheet lightning

fusilería *f* rifle corps; rifles, guns; (*descarga*) fusillade

fusión *f* fusion; melting; **fusión de empresas** (com) merger

fusionar *tr* & *ref* to fuse, to merge

fusta *f* brushwood, twigs; teamster's whip

fustán *m* fustian; (Am) cotton petticoat; (Ven) skirt

fuste *m* wood, timber; shaft, stem; (fig) importance, substance

fustigar §44 *tr* to whip, lash; to rebuke harshly

fútbol *m* football; soccer; **fútbol asociación** soccer

fútil *adj* futile, trifling, inconsequential

futilidad *f* futility

futre *m* (SAm) dandy, dude

futu·ro -ra *adj* future ‖ *m* future; (gram) future; (coll) fiancé; **futuros** (com) futures ‖ *f* fiancée

G

G, g (ge) *f* eighth letter of the Spanish alphabet

G. *abbr* **gracia**

gaba·cho -cha *adj* & *mf* Pyrenean; (coll) Frenchy ‖ *m* (coll) Frenchified Spanish (*language*)

gabán *m* overcoat

gabardina *f* gabardine; raincoat with belt

gabarra *f* barge, lighter

gabarro *m* (*en una piedra*) nodule; (*en un tejido*) flaw, defect; mistake

gabinete *m* cabinet; (*de médico, abogado, etc.*) office; studio, study; laboratory; (Col) glassed-in balcony; **de gabinete** armchair, theoretical; **gabinete de aseo** washroom; **gabinete de lectura** reading room

gablete *m* gable

gacela *f* gazelle

gaceta *f* government journal; (Am) newspaper; **mentir más que la gaceta** to lie like a trooper

gacetilla *f* town talk, gossip column; short item

gacetillero *m* gossip columnist

gacetista *mf* newspaper reader; newsmonger

gacha *f* watery mass; (Col, Ven) earthenware bowl; **gachas** mush, pap; porridge; (coll) mud; **gachas de avena** oatmeal; **hacerse unas gachas** to be mushy

ga·cho -cha *adj* turned down; flopping;

(*sombrero*) slouch; **a gachas** on all fours ‖ *f* see **gacha**

gachumbo *m* (SAm) hard fruit shell

gachu·pín -pina *mf* (CAm, Mex) Spanish settler in Latin America

gaéli·co -ca *adj* Gaelic ‖ *mf* Gael ‖ *m* Gaelic (*language*)

gafa *f* clamp; (*enganche de los anteojos*) temple; **gafas** glasses; **gafas de sol** or **gafas para sol** sunglasses

gafe *m* (coll) jinx, hoodoo

ga·fo -fa *adj* claw-handed; (Am) footsore ‖ *f* see **gafa**

gaguear *intr* (Am) to stutter

gaita *f* hornpipe; hurdy-gurdy; (coll) chore, hard task; (coll) neck; **gaita gallega** bagpipe

gaite·ro -ra *adj* (coll) flashy, gaudy ‖ *m* piper, bagpipe player

gajes *mpl* wages, salary; **gajes del oficio** cares of office, occupational annoyances

gajo *m* broken branch; (*de un racimo de uvas*) small stem; (*división interior de ciertas frutas*) slice; (*de horca*) tine, prong; (*ramal de montes*) spur; (Am) curl

gala *f* fine clothes; (*lo más selecto*) choice, cream; (Am) tip, fee; **de gala** full-dress; **hacer gala de** to glory in; **llevarse la gala** to win approval

galafate *m* slick thief

galai·co -ca *adj* Galician

galán *m* good-looking fellow; lover,

gallant, ladies' man; (*el que sirve de escolta a una dama*) escort, cavalier; (theat) leading man; **galán joven** (theat) juvenile; **primer galán** (theat) leading man

galancete *m* (theat) juvenile

gala·no -na *adj* elegant, graceful; spruce, smartly dressed; rich, tasteful

galante *adj* (*con las damas*) gallant; (*con los caballeros*) flirtatious; (*mujer*) wanton, loose

galantear *tr* to court, woo, make love to; to sue, entreat

galantería *f* gallantry; charm, elegance; generosity

galanura *f* charm, elegance

galápago *m* pond tortoise; (*del arado*) moldboard; light saddle; ingot

galardón *m* reward, recompense

galardonar *tr* to reward, recompense

galaxia *f* galaxy

galeón *m* (naut) galleon

galeote *m* galley slave

galera *f* covered wagon; women's jail; (*de hospital*) ward; (naut & typ) galley

galerada *f* wagonload; (typ) galley; (typ) galley proof

galería *f* gallery; **galería de tiro** shooting gallery; **galerías** department store; **hablar para la galería** (coll) to play to the gallery

galerna *f* stormy wind from the northwest (*on the northern coast of Spain*)

Gales *f* Wales; **el país de Gales** Wales; **la Nueva Gales del Sur** New South Wales

ga·lés -lesa *adj* Welsh || *m* Welshman; Welsh (*language*) || *f* Welsh woman

gal·go -ga *adj* (Col) sweet-toothed || *m* greyhound || *f* greyhound bitch; rolling stone; mange, rash

Galia, **la** Gaul

gálibo *m* template, pattern; (rr) gabarit

galicismo *m* Gallicism

gáli·co -ca *adj* Gallic || *m* syphilis; syphilitic

galillo *m* uvula; (coll) gullet

galimatí·as *m* (*pl* -as) (coll) gibberish, nonsense; (coll) confusion

galiparla *f* Frenchified Spanish

ga·lo -la *adj* Gaulish || *mf* Gaul || *m* Gaulish (*language*)

galocha *f* clog, wooden shoe

galón *m* braid, galloon; (*medida para líquidos*) gallon; (mil) chevron, stripe

galopar *intr* to gallop

galope *m* gallop; **a galope** at a gallop; in great haste; **a galope tendido** on the run

galopea·do -da *adj* (coll) hasty, sketchy || *m* (coll) beating, punching

galopear *intr* to gallop

galopillo *m* scullion, kitchen boy

galopín *m* ragamuffin; (*hombre taimado*) wise guy; (naut) cabin boy

galpón *m* (SAm) iron shed; (Col) tile works

galvanizar §60 *tr* to electroplate; to galvanize

galvanoplastia *f* electroplating

galladura *f* tread (*of egg*)

gallardete *m* streamer, pennant

gallardía *f* gallantry; elegance; nobility; generosity

gallar·do -da *adj* gallant; elegant; noble; generous; (*temporal*) fierce

gallear *intr* to stand out, excel; (coll) to shout, yell, threaten

galle·go -ga *adj* & *mf* Galician

gallera *f* cockpit

galleta *f* hardtack, ship biscuit; cracker; little pitcher; (coll) slap

gallina *adj* chicken-hearted || *mf* chicken-hearted person || *f* hen; **estar como gallina en corral ajeno** (coll) to be like a fish out of water; **gallina ciega** blindman's buff; **gallina de Guinea** guinea fowl

gallinería *f* poultry shop; cowardice

galline·ro -ra *mf* poultry dealer || *m* hencoop, henhouse; poultry basket; top gallery; babel, madhouse

gallipavo *m* turkey; (coll) sour note

gallito *m* (*el que figura sobre los demás*) somebody; **gallito del lugar** cock of the walk

gallo *m* cock, rooster; (coll) false note, sour note; (coll) boss; frog in the throat; **gallo de bosque** wood grouse; **gallo de pelea** gamecock; **tener mucho gallo** (coll) to be cocky

gallofa *f* vegetables; French roll; talk, gossip

gallofear *intr* to beg, bum, loaf around

gallofe·ro -ra *adj* begging, loafing || *mf* beggar, loafer

gama *f* doe, female fallow deer; (mus & fig) gamut

gamberrismo *m* gangsterism, rowdyism

gambe·rro -rra *adj* & *mf* libertine || *m* hoodlum, tough, rowdy

gambeta *f* crosscaper; caper, prance

gambito *m* gambit

gamo *m* buck, male fallow deer

gamón *m* asphodel

gamonal *m* field of asphodel; (Am) boss

gamuza *f* chamois

gana *f* desire; will; **darle a uno la gana de** to feel like, e.g., le da la gana de trabajar he feels like working; **de buena gana** willingly; **de gana** in earnest; willingly; **de mala gana** unwillingly; **tener ganas de** to feel like, to have a mind to

ganadería *f* cattle, livestock; brand, stock; cattle raising; cattle ranch

ganade·ro -ra *adj* cattle, livestock || *mf* cattle breeder; cattle dealer || *m* cattleman

ganado *m* cattle, livestock; **ganado caballar** horses; **ganado cabrío** goats; **ganado lanar** sheep; **ganado mayor** large farm animals (*cows, bulls, horses, and mules*); **ganado menor** small farm animals (*sheep, goats, pigs*); **ganado menudo** young cattle; **ganado moreno** swine; **ganado ovejuno** sheep; **ganado porcino** swine; **ganado vacuno** cattle

gana·dor -dora *adj* winning; earning; (coll) hard-working || *mf* winner; earner

ganancia *f* gain, profit; (Guat, Mex)

extra, bonus; **ganancias y pérdidas** profit and loss

ganancial *adj* profit

ganancio•so -sa *adj* gainful, profitable; earning || *mf* earner

ganapán *m* errand boy; (coll) boor

ganapierde *m & f* giveaway

ganar *tr* (*dinero trabajando*) to earn; (*la victoria luchando*) to win; (*beneficios en los negocios*) to gain; (*a una persona en una contienda*) to beat, defeat; (*aventajar*) to excel; (*la voluntad de una persona*) to win over; (*alcanzar*) to reach; **ganar algo a alguien** to win something from someone; **ganar de comer** to earn a living || *intr* to earn; (*mejorar*) to improve || *ref* to win over; **ganarse la vida** to earn a livelihood

ganchero *m* log driver; (Chile) odd-jobber; (Ecuad) gentle mount

ganchillo *m* crochet needle; crochet, crochet work; **hacer ganchillo** to crochet

gancho *m* hook; shepherd's crook; coaxer; procurer, pimp; (Am) hairpin; (Col, Ecuad) lady's saddle; **gancho de botalones** (naut) gooseneck; **echar el gancho a** (coll) to hook in, to land; **tener gancho** (*una mujer*) (coll) to have a way with the men

gandaya *f* (coll) bumming, loafing

gandujar *tr* to pleat, shirr

gan•dul -dula *adj* (coll) loafing, idling || *mf* (coll) loafer, idler

gandulear *intr* (coll) to loaf, idle

ganforro -rra *mf* (coll) scoundrel

ganga *f* bargain

ganglio *m* ganglion

gangocho *m* (Am) burlap

gango•so -sa *adj* snuffling, nasal

gangrena *f* gangrene

gangrenar *tr & ref* to gangrene

ganguear *intr* to snuffle, talk through the nose

gangue•ro -ra *adj* (coll) bargain-hunting; (coll) self-seeking || *mf* (coll) bargain hunter

gano•so -sa *adj* desirous; (*caballo*) (Chile) spirited, fiery

gan•so -sa *mf* (coll) dope, dullard || *m* goose; gander; **ganso bravo** wild goose || *f* female goose

Gante Ghent

ganzúa *f* (*garfio*) picklock, lock pick; (*persona*) picklock; (coll) pumper (*of secrets*)

gañán *m* farm hand; rough, husky fellow

gañido *m* yelp; croak

gañir §12 *intr* (*el perro*) to yelp; (*p.ej., el cuervo*) to croak

garabatear *tr* to scribble || *intr* to hook; to beat about the bush; to scribble

garabato *m* hook; pothook; scribbling; weeding hoe; (*bozal*) muzzle; (*de una mujer*) (coll) winsomeness; **garabato de carnicero** meathook; **garabatos** wiggling of hands and fingers

garabato•so -sa *adj* full of scrawls; (coll) winsome

garage *m* or **garaje** *m* garage

garagista *m* garage man

garambaina *f* gaudy trimming; **garambainas** simpering, smirking; (coll) scribble

garante *adj* responsible || *mf* guarantor, voucher

garantía *f* guarantee, guaranty

garantir §1 *tr* to guarantee

garantizar §60 *tr* to guarantee

garañón *m* stud jackass; stud camel; (Am) stallion

garapiña *f* icing, sugar-coating; (Am) iced pineapple drink

garapiñar *tr* to ice, to sugar-coat; to candy

garapiñera *f* ice-cream freezer

garbanzo *m* chickpea; **garbanzo negro** (fig) black sheep

garbillar *tr* to sieve, screen, riddle

garbillo *s* sieve, screen; riddled ore

garbo *m* jauntiness, grace, fine bearing; generosity

garbo•so -sa *adj* jaunty, graceful, spruce, sprightly; generous

gardu•ño -ña *mf* (archaic) sneak thief || *f* stone marten, beech marten

garete *m* — **al garete** (naut) adrift

garfa *f* claw

garfio *m* hook, gaff

gargajear *intr* to cough up phlegm, to hawk

gargajo *m* phlegm

garganta *f* throat; (*de un río, una vasija, etc.*) neck, throat; (*del pie*) instep; (*entre montañas*) ravine, gorge; (*del arado*) sheath; (*de una polea*) groove; (archit) shaft; **tener buena garganta** to have a good voice

gargantear *intr* to warble

gargantilla *f* necklace

gárgara *f* gargling; **gárgaras** (*líquido*) (Am) gargle; **hacer gárgaras** to gargle

gargarear *intr* (Am) to gargle

gargarismo *m* gargling; (*líquido*) gargle

gargarizar §60 *intr* to gargle

gárgola *f* gargoyle

garguero *m* gullet; (*caña del pulmón*) windpipe

garita *f* sentry box; porter's lodge; (*de una fortificación*) watchtower; railroad-crossing box; privy (*with one seat*); **garita de centinela** sentry box; **garita de señales** (rr) signal tower

garito *m* gambling den

garlito *m* fish trap; (coll) trap, snare

garlopa *f* jack plane, trying plane

garra *f* claw, talon; catch, hook; **caer en las garras de** (coll) to fall into the clutches of

garrafa *f* carafe, decanter; **garrafa corchera** demijohn

garrafal *adj* awful, terrible

garrafiñar *tr* (coll) to snatch

garrafón *m* carboy, demijohn

garramar *tr* (coll) to snitch

garranchuelo *m* crab grass

garrapata *f* cattle tick, sheep tick; (mil) disabled horse; (Chile) little runt; (Mex) slut

garrapatear *intr* to scrawl, scribble

garrapato *m* pothook, scrawl; **garrapatos** scrawl

garri•do -da *adj* handsome, elegant

garroba *f* carob bean

garrocha f goad; (sport) pole

garrotazo m blow with a club

garrote m club, cudgel; garrote (*method of execution; iron collar used for such execution*); (Mex) brake; **dar garrote a** to garrote

garrote·ro -ra adj (Chile) stingy ‖ m (Mex) brakeman

garrotillo m croup

garrucha f pulley, sheave

gárru·lo -la adj chirping; (*hablador*) garrulous; (*arroyo*) babbling; (*viento*) rustling

garúa f (Am) drizzle

garuar §21 intr (Am) to drizzle

garulla f (coll) mob, rabble

garza f heron; **garza real** gray heron

gar·zo -za adj blue ‖ f see garza

garzón m boy, youth; suitor; woman chaser

gas m gas; **gas de alumbrado** illuminating gas; **gas exhilarante** or **hilarante** laughing gas; **gas lacrimógeno** tear gas

gasa f gauze, chiffon; (*tira de gasa negra con que se rodea el sombrero en señal de luto*) hatband

Gascuña f Gascony

gasear tr to gas

gaseo·so -sa adj gaseous ‖ f soda water, carbonated water

gasificar §73 tr to gasify; to exalt, elate ‖ ref to gasify

gasista m gas fitter; (Chile) gasworker

gasoducto m gas pipe line

gasógeno m gas generator, gas producer; mixture of benzine and alcohol used for lighting and cleaning

gas-oil m diesel oil

gasolina f gasoline

gasolinera f motor boat; gas station, filling station

gasómetro m gasholder, gas tank

gastadero m waste

gasta·do -da adj worn-out; used up; spent; (*chiste*) (coll) crummy, corny

gasta·dor -dora adj & mf spendthrift ‖ m convict; (mil) sapper, pioneer

gastadura f worn spot

gastar tr (*dinero, tiempo*) to spend; (*en cosas inútiles*) to waste; (*echar a perder con el uso*) to wear out; (*consumir*) to use up; (*p.ej., una barba*) to wear; (*un coche*) to keep; **gastarlas** (coll) to act, behave ‖ intr to spend ‖ ref to wear; to wear out; to become used up; to waste away

gasto m cost, expense; wear; **gastos de conservación** or **de entretenimiento** upkeep; **gastos de explotación** operating expenses; **gastos menudos** petty expenses; **hacer el gasto** (coll) to do most of the talking; (coll) to be the subject of conversation; **hacer frente a los gastos** to meet expenses; **meterse en gastos con** to go to the expense of

gasto·so -sa adj wasteful, extravagant

gástri·co -ca adj gastric

gastronomía f gastronomy

gastróno·mo -ma mf gourmet

gata f she-cat; low-hanging cloud; (coll) Madrid woman; (Mex) maid, servant girl; **a gatas** on all fours, on hands and knees

gatada f catty act

gatatumba f (coll) faked attention, fake emotion, faked pain

gatazo m (coll) gyp

gatea·do -da adj catlike; grained, striped ‖ m crawling, climbing; (coll) scratching, clawing

gatear tr (coll) to scratch, claw; (coll) to snitch ‖ intr to crawl, to climb

gatera f cathole; (naut) hawsehole

gatería f (coll) cats; (coll) gang of toughs; (coll) fake humility

gate·ro -ra adj full of cats ‖ mf cat lover ‖ f see gatera

gates·co -ca adj (coll) catlike, feline

gatillo m (*de arma de fuego*) trigger; (coll) little pickpocket

gato m cat; tomcat; (*instrumento para levantar pesos*) jack, lifting jack; (coll) sly fellow; (coll) sneak thief; (coll) native of Madrid; **gato montés** wildcat; **gato rodante** dolly; **vender gato por liebre** (coll) to gyp, cheat

gauchada f (SAm) sly trick; (SAm) good turn

gauchaje m (SAm) gathering of Gauchos

gauches·co -ca adj Gaucho

gau·cho -cha adj (SAm) Gaucho; (Arg, Chile) sly, crafty ‖ m (SAm) Gaucho; (SAm) good horseman ‖ f (Arg) mannish woman; (Arg) loose woman

gaultería f wintergreen

gaveta f drawer, till

gavia f ditch, drain; (*ave*) gull; (min) gang of basket passers; (naut) topsail

gavilán m sparrow hawk; (*de la pluma*) nib; (*en la escritura*) hair stroke; (Am) ingrowing nail

gavilla f sheaf, bundle; gang

gaviota f sea gull

gavota f gavotte

gaya f colored stripe; (*ave*) magpie

gayar tr to trim with colored stripes

ga·yo -ya adj gay, bright, showy ‖ m (orn) jay ‖ f see gaya

gayola f cage; (coll) jail

gayomba f Spanish broom

gazapa f (coll) lie

gazapatón m (coll) blunder, slip

gazapera f rabbit warren; (coll) gang, gang of thugs; (coll) brawl, row

gazapo m young rabbit; sly fellow; slip, boner, blunder; (*de actor*) fluff

gazmiar tr (*oliendo*) to sniff; (*comiendo*) to nibble ‖ ref (coll) to complain

gazmoñada or **gazmoñería** f prudishness, priggishness

gazmoñe·ro -ra or **gazmo·ño -ña** adj prudish, priggish, strait-laced, demure ‖ mf prude, prig

gaznápiro m gawk, boob, bumpkin

gaznate m gullet; (Mex) fritter

gazpacho m cold vegetable soup; (Hond) leftovers

gazuza f (coll) hunger

Gedeón m Gideon

gehena m Gehenna

géiser m geyser

gel m gel

gelatina *f* gelatine
gema *f* gem; (bot) bud
geme·lo -la *adj & mf* twin; **gemelos** twins; binoculars; cuff links; **gemelos de campo** field glasses; **gemelos de teatro** opera glasses ‖ **Gemelos** *mpl* (astr) Gemini
gemido *m* moan, groan; wail, whine; howl, roar
Géminis *m* (astr) Gemini
gemiquear *intr* (Chile) to whine
gemir §50 *intr* to moan, groan; to wail, whine; to howl, roar
gen *m* gene
genciana *f* gentian
gendarme *m* (Am) policeman
genealogía *f* genealogy
generación *f* generation
genera·dor -dora *adj* generating ‖ *m* generator
general *adj* general; common, usual; **en general** or **por lo general** in general ‖ *m* general; **general de brigada** brigadier, brigadier general; **generales de división** major general ‖ **generales** *fpl* general information, personal data
generala *f* general's wife; call to arms
generalato *m* generalship
generalidad *f* generality; majority; **la generalidad de** the general run of
generalísimo *m* generalissimo
generalizar §60 *tr & intr* to generalize ‖ *ref* to become generalized
generar *tr* to generate
genéri·co -ca *adj* generic; (*artículo*) definite; (*nombre*) common; showing gender
género *m* kind, sort; way, manner; cloth, material; (biol, log) genus; (gram) gender; **de género** genre; **género chico** one-act play, one-act operetta; **género de punto** knit goods, knitwear; **género humano** humankind; **género ínfimo** light vaudeville; **género novelístico** fiction; **género picaresco** burlesque; **géneros** goods, merchandise, material; **géneros de pieza** yard goods; **géneros para vestidos** dress goods
genero·so -sa *adj* generous; highborn; noble, magnanimous; (*vino*) rich, full
géne·sis *f* (*pl* -sis) genesis ‖ **el Génesis** (Bib) Genesis
genéti·co -ca *adj* genetic ‖ *f* genetics
genial *adj* inspired, genius-like; pleasant, agreeable; temperamental
geniazo *m* (coll) fiery temper
genio *m* (*índole, carácter*) temperament, disposition; (*don altísimo de invención; persona que lo posee; espíritu tutelar, deidad pagana*) genius; fire, spirit
genital *adj* genital ‖ **genitales** *mpl* genitals
geniti·vo -va *adj & m* genitive
genocida *adj* genocidal ‖ *mf* genocide
genocidio *m* genocide
Génova *f* Genoa
geno·vés -vesa *adj & mf* Genoese
gente *f* people; (*parentela, familia*) folks; race, nation; troops; **gente baja** lower classes, rabble; **gente bien**

nice people; **gente de bien** decent people; **gente de capa parda** country people; **gente de coleta** (coll) bullfighters; **gente de color** colored people; **gente de la cuchilla** (coll) butchers; **gente de la vida airada** bullies; underworld; **gente del bronce** bright, lively people; **gente del rey** convicts; **gente de mal vivir** toughs, underworld; **gente de mar** seafaring people; **gente de paz** (*palabras con las cuales se contesta al que pregunta ¿quién?*) friend; **gente de pluma** (coll) clerks; **gente de su majestad** convicts; **gente de trato** tradespeople; **gente forzada** convicts; **gente menuda** (coll) small fry; (coll) common people
gentecilla *f* (coll) mob, rabble
gentil *adj* heathen, gentile; elegant, genteel; noble ‖ *mf* heathen, pagan
gentileza *f* elegance, gentility, courtesy; gallantry; show, splendor; (*hidalguía*) nobility
gentilhombre *m* (*pl* **gentileshombres**) gentleman; messenger to the king; my good man; **gentilhombre de cámara** gentleman in waiting
gentili·cio -cia *adj* national; family; (gram) gentile
gentilidad *f* heathendom
gentío *m* crowd, mob
gentualla or **gentuza** *f* (coll) rabble, riffraff
genui·no -na *adj* genuine
geofísi·co -ca *adj* geophysical ‖ *mf* geophysicist ‖ *f* geophysics
geografía *f* geography
geográfi·co -ca *adj* geographic(al)
geógra·fo -fa *mf* geographer
geología *f* geology
geológi·co -ca *adj* geologic(al)
geólo·go -ga *mf* geologist
geómetra *mf* geometrician
geometría *f* geometry; **geometría del espacio** solid geometry
geométri·co -ca *adj* geometric(al)
geopolíti·co -ca *adj* geopolitical ‖ *f* geopolitics
geranio *m* geranium
gerencia *f* management; manager's office
gerente *m* manager, director; **gerente de publicidad** advertising manager; **gerente de ventas** sales manager
geriatría *f* geriatry
geriatra *adj* geriatrical ‖ *mf* geriatrician
geriátri·co -ca *adj* geriatrical
germanía *f* gypsy slang, cant of thieves
germanizar §60 *tr* to Germanize
germen *m* germ; **germen plasma** germ plasm
germicida *adj* germicidal ‖ *m* germicide
germinal *adj* germ; germinal
germinar *intr* to germinate
gerontología *f* gerontology
gerundio *m* gerund; present participle; bombastic writer or speaker
gestación *f* gestation
gestear *intr* to make faces
gesticular *intr* to make a face, to make faces; (*hacer ademanes*) to gesticulate

gestión f step, measure; management; action, proceeding, negotiation

gestionar tr to promote, pursue; to manage; to negotiate

gesto m face; wry face, grimace; look, appearance; (movimiento, ademán) gesture

ges·tor -tora adj managing ‖ m manager

gestu·do -da adj (coll) cross-looking

ghetto m ghetto

giba f hump; (coll) annoyance

giga f jig

giganta f giantess

gigante adj giant ‖ m giant; (en las procesiones) giant figure

gigantes·co -ca adj gigantic

gigantez f giant size

gigantilla f large-headed masked figure; little fat woman

gigan·tón -tona mf huge giant ‖ m giant figure

gigote m chopped-meat stew; **hacer gigote** (coll) to chop up

gimnasia f gymnastics; **gimnasia sueca** Swedish movements, setting-up exercises

gimnasio m gymnasium; secondary school, academy

gim·vsta mf gymnast

gim·ásti·co -ca adj gymnastic ‖ f gymnastics

gimotear intr (coll) to whine

gimoteo m (coll) whining

ginebra f gin; (de voces) buzz, din; confusion, disorder ‖ **Ginebra** f Geneva

ginebri·no -na adj & mf Genevan

ginecología f gynecology

ginecólo·go -ga mf gynecologist

ginesta f Spanish broom

gira f var of jira

gira·do -da mf drawee

gira·dor -dora mf drawer

giralda f weathercock (in the form of person or animal)

girándula f girandole

girar tr (una visita) to pay; (com) to draw ‖ intr to turn; to rotate, gyrate; to trade; (com) to draw

girasol m sunflower; sycophant

girato·rio -ria adj revolving ‖ f revolving bookcase

gi·ro -ra adj (Guat) drunk; (Mex) cocky ‖ m turn; rotation; revolution; course, trend, turn; turn of phrase; boast, threat; gash, slash; line of business; trade; (com) draft; **giro a la vista** sight draft; **giro postal** money order ‖ f see gira

girofié m clove

giroscopio m gyroscope

gis m (Col) slate pencil

gitana f gypsy woman, gypsy girl

gitanada f gypsy trick; fawning, flattery

gitanería f band of gypsies; gypsy life; fawning, flattery

gitanes·co -ca adj gypsyish

gita·no -na adj gypsy; flattering; sly, tricky ‖ mf gypsy ‖ m Gypsy (language) ‖ f see gitana

glacial adj glacial; (zona) frigid; (fig) cold, indifferent

glaciar m glacier

glándula f gland; **glándula cerrada** ductless gland

glasé m glacé silk

glasea·do -da adj glossy, shiny

glicerina f glycerin

global adj total; global, world-wide

globo m globe; (aparato que, lleno de un gas, se eleva en el aire) balloon; (bomba de lámpara) globe, lamp shade; **globo del ojo** eyeball; **globo sonda** trial balloon; **lanzar un globo sonda** (fig) to send up a trial balloon

glóbulo m globule; (physiol) corpuscle; **glóbulo rojo** red cell

gloria f glory; **ganar la gloria** to go to glory; **oler a gloria** (coll) to smell heavenly; **saber a gloria** (coll) to taste heavenly

gloriar §77 tr to glorify ‖ intr to recite the rosary ‖ ref to glory

glorieta f arbor, bower, summerhouse; public square; traffic circle

glorificar §73 tr to glorify ‖ ref to glory

glorio·so -sa adj glorious; boastful

glosa f gloss

glosa·dor -dora adj commenting ‖ mf commentator

glosar tr to gloss; to audit; (Col) to scold ‖ intr to find fault

glosario m glossary

glóti·co -ca adj glottal

glo·tón -tona adj gluttonous ‖ mf glutton

glotonería f gluttony

glucosa f glucose

gluglú m (del agua) gurgle, glug; (del pavo) gobble; **hacer gluglú** to gurgle, to glug

gluglutear intr to gobble

gnomo m gnome

gob. abbr gobierno

gobernación f governing; government; department of the interior; (Arg) territory

goberna·dor -dora adj governing ‖ m governor

gobernalle m rudder, helm

gobernante adj governing ‖ mf ruler ‖ m (coll) self-appointed head

gobernar §2 tr to govern; to guide, direct; to control, rule; (un buque) to steer ‖ intr to govern; to steer

goberno·so -sa adj (coll) orderly

gobierno m government; governor's office, governorship; management; control, rule; guidance; (de un buque) navigability; **de buen gobierno** (buque) navigable; **gobierno de monigotes** puppet government; **gobierno doméstico** housekeeping; **gobierno exilado** government in exile; **para su gobierno** for your guidance; **servir de gobierno** (coll) to serve as a guide

goce m enjoyment

go·do -da adj Gothic ‖ mf Goth; Spanish noble; (Arg, Chile) Spaniard

gofio m (Am) roasted corn meal

gol m goal

gola f gullet

goldre m quiver

goleta f schooner

golf m golf

golfán *m* white water lily

golfista *mf* golfer

gol·fo -fa *mf* ragamuffin ‖ *m* gulf; open sea; **golfo de Méjico** Gulf of Mexico; **golfo de Vizcaya** Bay of Biscay

Gólgota, el (Bib) Golgotha

golilla *f* gorget, ruff; magistrate's collar; pipe flange; *(de los caños de barro)* collar, sleeve; *(del gallo)* (Am) erectile bristles

golondrina *f* swallow

golosina *f* delicacy, tidbit; eagerness, appetite; trifle

golosinear *intr* to go around eating candy

golo·so -sa *adj* sweet-toothed; *(glotón)* gluttonous; *(apetitoso)* tasty

golpe *m* blow, stroke, hit; bump, bruise; heartbeat; crowd, throng, flock; *(del bolsillo)* flap; *(pestillo)* bolt, latch; *(de licor)* shot; surprise, wonder; *(infortunio)* blow; witticism; **dar golpe** to make a hit; **de golpe** all at once, suddenly; **de golpe y porrazo** slambang; **de un golpe** at one stroke; **golpe de ariete** water hammer; **golpe de estado** coup d'état; **golpe de fortuna** stroke of fortune; **golpe de gracia** coup de grâce; **golpe de mano** surprise attack; **golpe de mar** surge; **golpe de ojo** glance; **golpe de teatro** dramatic turn of events; **golpe de tos** fit of coughing; **golpe de vista**, glance, look; view; **golpe en vago** miss, flop; **golpe mortal** deathblow; **no dar golpe** to not raise a hand, not do a stroke of work

golpear *tr* to strike, hit, beat; to bump, bruise ‖ *intr* to beat, strike; *(el reloj)* to tick; *(el motor de combustión interna)* to knock

golpete *m* door catch, window catch

golpetear *tr & intr* to beat; to rattle

golpismo *m* government by coup d'état

gollería *f* delicacy, dainty; **pedir gollerías** (coll) to ask for too much

gollete *m* throat, neck; *(de botella)* neck

goma *f* gum, rubber; *(tira de goma elástica)* rubber band; *(neumático)* tire; **goma arábiga** gum arabic; **goma de borrar** eraser, rubber; **goma de mascar** chewing gum; **goma espumosa** foam rubber; **goma laca** shellac

gomecillo *m* (coll) blind man's guide

gomia *f* bugaboo; (coll) waster; (coll) glutton

gomo·so -sa *adj* gum; gummy ‖ *m* dude, dandy

góndola *f* gondola

gondolero *m* gondolier

gongo *m* gong

gonorrea *f* gonorrhea

gordal *adj* large-size

gordia·no -na *adj* Gordian

gordi·flón -flona or **gordin·flón -flona** *adj* (coll) chubby, pudgy, fatty ‖ *mf* (coll) fatty

gor·do -da *adj* fat, plump; fatty, greasy; coarse; big, large; whopping big; *(agua)* hard ‖ *m* fat, suet; (coll) first prize *(in lottery)* ‖ **gordo** *adv* — **hablar gordo** (coll) to talk big

gordura *f* fatness, plumpness, stoutness, corpulence; fat, grease

gorgojo *m* grub, weevil; (coll) dwarf, runt; **gorgojo del algodón** boll weevil

gorgojo·so -sa *adj* grubby

gorgón *m* (Col) concrete

gorgonear *intr (el pavo)* to gobble

gorgoritear *intr* (coll) to trill

gorgorito *m* (coll) trill

gorgotear *intr* to burble, gurgle

gorgotero *m* peddler, hawker

gorigori *m* (coll) lugubrious funeral chant

gorila *f* gorilla

gorjear *intr* to warble, trill ‖ *ref (el niño)* to gurgle

gorra *f* cap; bumming, sponging; **andar de gorra** to sponge; **colarse de gorra** (coll) to crash the gate; **gorra de visera** cap; **vivir de gorra** to live on other people

gorrada *f* tipping the hat

gorrear *intr* (Ecuad) to sponge

gorretada *f* tipping the hat

gorrión *m* sparrow; **gorrión triguero** bunting

gorrista *adj* sponging ‖ *mf* sponger

gorro *m* cap, bonnet; baby's bonnet; **gorro de dormir** nightcap

go·rrón -rrona *adj* sponging ‖ *mf* sponger ‖ *m* pivot; journal, gudgeon

gota *f* drop; (pathol) gout; **gotas** touch of rum or brandy in coffee; **sudar la gota gorda** (coll) to work one's head off

gotear *intr* to drip, dribble; *(llover a gotas espaciadas)* to sprinkle

gotera *f* drip, dripping; mark left by dripping; *(en el techo)* leak; *(adorno de una cama)* valance; **estar lleno de goteras** (coll) to be full of aches and pains; **es una gotera** (coll) it's a constant drain; **goteras** (coll) aches, pains; (Col) environs, outskirts

góti·co -ca *adj* Gothic; noble, illustrious ‖ *m* Gothic

goto·so -sa *adj* gouty ‖ *mf* gout sufferer

gozar §60 *tr (poseer)* to enjoy ‖ *intr* to enjoy oneself; **gozar de** *(poseer)* to enjoy ‖ *ref* to enjoy oneself; to rejoice

gozne *m* hinge

gozo *m* joy, enjoyment; **no caber en sí de gozo** (coll) to be beside oneself with joy; **saltar de gozo** to leap with joy

gozo·so -sa *adj* joyful; **gozoso con** or **de** joyful over

gozque *m* or **gozquejo** *m* little yapping dog

grabación *f (de disco)* recording; **grabación sobre cinta** tape recording

grabado *m* engraving; print, cut, picture; *(de disco)* recording; **grabado en madera** wood engraving, woodcut; **grabado fuera de texto** inset, insert

graba·dor -dora *adj* recording ‖ *mf* engraver ‖ *f* recorder; **grabadora de cinta** tape recorder

grabadura *f* engraving

grabar *tr* to engrave; *(un sonido, una canción, un disco, etc.)* to record;

grabar en or **sobre cinta** to tape-record || *ref* to become engraved

gracejada *f* (CAm, Mex) cheap comedy, clownishness

gracejar *intr* to be engaging, be witty; to joke

gracejo *m* lightness, winsome manner, charm; (CAm, Mex) clown

gracia *f* witticism, witty remark, joke; grace; gracefulness; favor; pardon; (*de un chiste*) point; (coll) name; **caer en gracia a** to be pleasing to; **de gracia** gratis; **decir dos gracias a** (coll) to tell someone a thing or two; **en gracia a** because of; **gracia de Dios** daily bread; air and sunshine; **gracias** thanks; **¡gracias!** thanks!; **gracias a** thanks to; **¡gracias a Dios!** thank heavens!; **hacer gracia** to be pleasing; **hacer gracia de algo a uno** to exempt or free someone from something; **hacerle a uno gracia** to strike someone as funny; **¡linda gracia!** nonsense!; **tener gracia** to be funny, be surprising

graciable *adj* kind, gracious; easy to grant

grácil *adj* thin, small, slender

gracio·so -sa *adj* (*que tiene donaire, gracia*) graceful; (*afable, fino*) gracious; (*agudo, chistoso*) funny, witty; (*que se da de balde*) free, gratis || *mf* comic || *m* gracioso (*gay, comic character in Spanish comedy*)

grada *f* step, stair; row of seats; grandstand; altar step; (agr) harrow; (*plano inclinado sobre el cual se construyen los barcos*) slip; **gradas** stone steps; (Chile, Peru) atrium; **gradas al aire libre** bleachers

gradar *tr* (agr) to harrow

gradería *f* stone steps; row of seats; bleachers; **gradería cubierta** grandstand

gradiente *m* (phys) gradient || *f* (Am) slope, gradient

grado *m* step; grade; degree; (*título que se da en las universidades*) degree; (*sección en las escuelas*) grade, form, class; (mil) rank; **de buen grado** willingly; **de grado en grado** by degrees; **de grado o por fuerza** willy-nilly; **en sumo grado** to a great extent; **mal de mi grado** unwillingly, against my wishes

graduación *f* graduation; (*de las bebidas espirituosas*) strength; (mil) rank

gradual *adj* gradual

graduan·do -da *mf* (*persona próxima a graduarse en la universidad*) graduate (*candidate for a degree*)

graduar §21 *tr* to graduate, to grade; (*un grifo, una válvula, etc.*) to regulate; to appraise, estimate || *ref* to graduate

grafía *f* graph

gráfi·co -ca *adj* graphic(al); printing; illustrated; picture, camera || *m* diagram || *f* graph

grafito *m* graphite

grafospasmo *m* writer's cramp

gragea *f* colored candy; sugar-coated pill

grajear *intr* (*los cuervos*) to caw; (*los niños*) to gurgle

grajien·to -ta *adj* (Am) foul-smelling

gra·jo -ja *mf* rook, crow; (coll) chatter-box || *m* (Am) body odor

gral. *abbr* **general**

gramática *f* grammar; **gramática parda** (coll) shrewdness, mother wit

gramatical *adj* grammatical

gramáti·co -ca *adj* grammatical || *mf* grammarian || *f* see **gramática**

gramil *m* marking gauge, gauge

gramo *m* gram

gramófono *m* gramophone

gramola *f* console phonograph; portable phonograph

gran *adj* apocopated form of **grande**, used only before nouns of both genders in the singular

grana *f* seed; seeding; seeding time; red; **dar en grana** to go to seed

granada *f* pomegranate; (*proyectil explosivo*) grenade; **granada de mano** hand grenade; **granada de metralla** shrapnel; **granada extintora** fire extinguisher, fire grenade

granadero *m* grenadier

granadilla *f* passionflower

granadina *f* grenadine

grana·do -da *adj* choice, select; mature, expert || *m* pomegranate; **granado blanco** rose of Sharon || *f* see **granada**

granalla *f* filings

granangular *adj* wide-angle

granate *m* *adj invar* & *m* garnet

Gran Bretaña, la Great Britain

grande *adj* big, large; great || *m* grandee

grandeza *f* bigness, largeness; greatness; (*tamaño*) size; (*magnificencia*) grandeur; grandees; grandeeship

grandi·llón -llona *adj* (coll) oversize, overgrown

grandio·so -sa *adj* grandiose, grand

grandor *m* size

granea·do -da *adj* spattered; (*fuego*) heavy and continuous

granear *tr* to sow; (*la pólvora; una piedra litográfica*) to grain; to stipple

granel — a granel in bulk, loose; at random; lavishly

granelar *tr* (*el cuero*) to grain

granero *m* granary

granete *m* center punch

granífu·go -ga *adj* hail-dispersing

granito *m* granite

granizada *f* hailstorm; (Arg, Chile) iced drink

granizar §60 *tr* (*p.ej., golpes*) to hail; to sprinkle || *intr* to hail

granizo *m* hail

granja *f* farm, grange; dairy; country place

granjear *tr* to earn, gain; to win, win over || *ref* to win, win over

granjería *f* husbandry; gain, profit

granje·ro -ra *mf* farmer; merchant, trader

grano *m* grain; (*baya*) berry; (*baya de la uva*) grape; (*tumorcillo en la piel*) pimple; (*peso*) grain; **grano de belleza** beauty spot; **grano de café** coffee bean; **granos** (*fruto de los cereales*) grain; **ir al grano** (coll) to come to the point

granuja *m* scoundrel; (*muchacho vagabundo*) (coll) waif || *f* loose grape; grapeseed

granujo *m* (coll) pimple

granular *adj* granular; pimply || *tr & ref* to granulate

gránulo *m* granule

grapa *f* clamp, clip, staple

grasa *f* fat, grease; (*polvo*) pounce; (Mex) shoe polish; **grasa de ballena** blubber; **grasas** slag

grasien·to -ta *adj* greasy

grasilla *f* pounce

gra·so -sa *adj* fatty, greasy || *m* fattiness, greasiness || *f* see **grasa**

grasones *mpl* wheat porridge

graso·so -sa *adj* greasy; (pathol) fatty

grata *f* wire brush; (*carta*) favor

gratificar §73 *tr* to gratify; to reward, recompense; to tip, to fee

gratín *m* — **al gratín** au gratin

gratis *adv* gratis

gratisda·to -ta *adj* free, gratis

gratitud *f* gratitude

gra·to -ta *adj* pleasing, free; (Bol, Chile) grateful || *f* see **grata**

gratui·to -ta *adj* gratuitous; free, gratis

grava *f* gravel; crushed stone

gravamen *m* burden, obligation; encumbrance, lien; assessment

gravar *tr* to burden, encumber; to assess

grave *adj* grave, serious, solemn; hard, difficult; (*que pesa*) heavy; (*sonido*) grave, deep, low; (*música*) majestic, noble; (*negocio*) important; (*enfermedad*) serious; (*acento*) grave; paroxytone

gravedad *f* gravity; seriousness; **de gravedad** seriously; gravely; **gravedad nula** weightlessness, zero gravity

gravedo·so -sa *adj* heavy, pompous

gravidez *f* pregnancy

grávi·do -da *adj* pregnant

gravitación *f* gravitation

gravitar *intr* to gravitate; **gravitar sobre** to weigh down on

gravo·so -sa *adj* burdensome, onerous, costly; boring, tiresome

graznar *intr* to caw, to croak; to cackle; (*al cantar*) to cackle

graznido *m* caw, croak; cackle; (*canto que disuena mucho*) (fig) cackle

Grecia *f* Greece

grecia·no -na *adj* Grecian

gre·co -ca *adj & mf* Greek

greda *f* clay, fuller's earth

grega·rio -ria *adj* (*que vive confundido con otros*) gregarious; slavish, servile

gregoria·no -na *adj* Gregorian

gremial *adj* guild; trade-union, union || *m* guildsman; union member

gremio *m* guild, corporation; trade union, union; association, society

greña *f* confusion, entanglement; (*de cabello*) shock, tangled mop; **andar a la greña** (coll) to get into a hot argu-

ment; (*dos mujeres*) (coll) to pull each other's hair

greñu·do -da *adj* bushy-headed, shock-headed

gres *m* sandstone; stoneware

gresca *f* tumult, uproar; row, quarrel

grey *f* (*de ganado menor*) flock; group, party; nation, people; (*de fieles*) flock, congregation

grie·go -ga *adj* Greek || *mf* Greek || *m* (*idioma*) Greek; **hablar en griego** (coll) to not make sense

grieta *f* crack, crevice, chink; (*en la piel*) chap

grieta·do -da *adj* crackled || *m* crackleware

grietar *ref* to crack, split; (*la piel*) to become chapped

gri·fo -fa *adj* (*pelo*) kinky, tangled; (*letra*) script; (W-I) colored; (Mex) drunk; (Col) conceited || *mf* (W-I) colored person; (Mex) drunk || *m* faucet, spigot, tap, cock; (myth) griffin; (Peru) gas station

grilla *f* female cricket; (rad) grid; (Col) fight, quarrel; (SAm) annoyance, bother; **¡ésa es grilla!** (coll) you expect me to believe that!

grillar *intr* (*el grillo*) to chirp || *ref* (*las semillas, bulbos, etc.*) to sprout

grillete *m* fetter, shackle

grillo *m* (*insecto*) cricket; (*brote tierno*) sprout, shoot; **grillos** fetters, shackles

grima *f* fright, horror; **dar grima** to grate on the nerves

grin·go -ga *mf* (disparaging) foreigner; (*anglosajón*) (Am) gringo || *m* (coll) gibberish

griñón *m* (*toca de monja*) wimple; (*melocotón*) nectarine

gripe *f* grippe

gris *adj* gray; dull, gloomy || *m* gray; **hacer gris** (*el tiempo*) (coll) to be sharp, be brisk

grisáce·o -a *adj* grayish

gri·sú *m* (*pl* -**súes**) firedamp

grita *f* shouting; hubbub, uproar; **dar grita a** (coll) to hoot at

gritar *intr* to shout, cry out

gritería *f* shouting, outcry, uproar

grito *m* cry, shout; scream, shriek; **el último grito** (coll) the latest thing, all the rage; **poner el grito en el cielo** (coll) to raise the roof, to scream wildly

gro. *abbr* **género**

Groenlandia *f* Greenland

grosella *f* currant; **grosella silvestre** gooseberry

grosellero *m* currant bush; **grosellero silvestre** gooseberry bush

grosería *f* grossness, coarseness; churlishness, rudeness; stupidity; vulgarity

grose·ro -ra *adj* gross, coarse; churlish, rude; stupid; vulgar || *mf* churl, boor

grosor *m* thickness, bulk

grosura *f* fat, suet, tallow; meat diet; coarseness, vulgarity

grotes·co -ca *adj* grotesque

grúa *f* crane, derrick; **grúa de bote** (naut) davit; **grúa de auxilio** wrecking crane; **grúa de caballete** gantry crane

grúa-remolque *m* tow truck
grue·so -sa *adj* big, thick, bulky, heavy; coarse, ordinary; stout, fat; (*mar*) rough, heavy; **en grueso** in gross, in bulk || *f* (*doce docenas*) gross
grulla *f* (orn) crane
grumete *m* ship's boy, cabin boy
grumo *m* clot, curd; bunch, cluster
grumo·so -sa *adj* clotty, curdly
gruñido *m* (*de cerdo*) grunt; (*de perro cuando amenaza*) growl; (*de persona*) grumble; (*de puerta*) creak; (coll) grumble, scolding
gruñir §12 *intr* (*el cerdo*) to grunt; (*el perro*) to growl; (*una persona*) to grumble; (*una puerta*) to creak
gru·ñón -ñona *adj* (coll) grumpy, grumbly || *mf* (coll) crosspatch
grupa *f* croup, rump
grupada *f* squall
grupal *adj* group
grupo *m* group; (mach & elec) unit
gruta *f* grotto
grutes·co -ca *adj* & *m* (fa) grotesque
Gruyère *m* Swiss cheese
gte. *abbr* gerente
guaca *f* (Bol, Peru) Indian tomb; (Am) hidden treasure
guacal *m* (Am) crate
guacama·yo -ya *adj* (P-R) flashy, sporty || *m* (Am) macaw
guachapear *tr* to splash with the feet; to bungle, botch || *intr* to clank, clatter
guachinan·go -ga *adj* (Am) flattering, sly || *mf* (disparaging term used by Cubans) Mexican
gua·cho -cha *adj* (SAm) homeless, orphan; (SAm) odd, unmatched
guadal *m* (Am) bog, swamp; (Am) sand hill, dune
Guadalupe *m* Guadeloupe
guadama·cí *m* (*pl* -cíes) embossed leather
guadaña *f* scythe
guadañadora *f* mowing machine
guadañar *tr* to cut with a scythe
guadarnés *m* harness room; harness man
guagua *f* trifle; (SAm) baby; (W-I) bus; (Col) paca
guajada *f* (Mex) nonsense, folly
guaje *adj* (Hond, Mex) foolish, stupid || *m* (Hond, Mex) calabash, gourd; (CAm) piece of junk
guají·ro -ra *mf* (W-I) peasant, yokel
guajolote *m* (Am) turkey; (Mex) simpleton
gualda *f* (bot) weld, dyer's rocket
gual·do -da *adj* yellow || *f* see gualda
gualdrapa *f* housing, trappings; (coll) dirty rag hanging from clothes
gualdrapear *tr* to line up head to tail || *intr* (*las velas*) to flap
Gualterio *m* Walter
guanaco *m* (SAm) dope, simpleton; (SAm) tall lanky fellow; (zool) guanaco
guanajo *m* (W-I) boob, dunce; (Am) turkey
guano *m* (Am) palm tree; (Am) bird manure
guante *m* glove; **arrojar el guante** to throw down the gauntlet; **echar un**

guante to pass the hat; **guantes** tip, fee; **recoger el guante** to take up the gauntlet; **salvo el guante** (coll) excuse my glove
guantelete *m* gauntlet
guantería *f* glove shop
guapear *intr* (coll) to bluster, to swagger; (coll) to dress to kill
guape·tón -tona *adj* (coll) handsome; (coll) flashy, sporty; (coll) bold, fearless || *m* (coll) bully, tough
guapeza *f* (coll) good looks; (coll) flashiness, sportiness; (coll) boldness, daring; (coll) bravado
gua·po -pa *adj* (coll) handsome, good-looking; (coll) flashy, sporty; (coll) bold, daring || *m* (*hombre pendenciero*) bully; gallant, lady's man
guapura *f* (coll) good looks
guarache *m* (Mex) leather sandal; (Mex) tire patch
guarapo *m* sugar-cane juice; (Am) fermented juice of sugar cane
guarda *mf* guard, custodian || *m* (Arg) trolley-car conductor; **guarda de la aduana** customhouse officer; **guarda forestal** forest ranger || *f* guard, custody; (*de la ley*) observance; (*de la espada*) guard; (*de la cerradura*) ward; (bb) flyleaf
guardabarrera *mf* (rr) gatekeeper
guardaba·rros *m* (*pl* -rros) fender, mudguard, dashboard
guardabosque *m* gamekeeper; forest ranger; (Am) shortstop
guardabrisa *m* windshield; (naut) glass candle shade
guardacantón *m* spur stone
guardacarril *m* (rr) railguard
guardacar·tas *m* (*pl* -tas) letter file
guardaco·ches *m* (*pl* -ches) car watcher
guardacos·tas *m* (*pl* -tas) revenue cutter, coast guard cutter; **guardacostas** *mpl* (*servicio*) coast guard
guarda·dor -dora *adj* guarding, protecting; mindful, observant; stingy || *m* guardian, keeper; observer
guardaespal·das *m* (*pl* -das) bodyguard
guardafango *m* fender, mudguard
guardafre·nos *m* (*pl* -nos) (rr) brakeman, flagman
guardafuego *m* fender, fireguard
guardagu·jas *m* (*pl* -jas) (rr) switchman
guardajo·yas *m* (*pl* -yas) jewel case
guardalado *m* railing, parapet
guardalmacén *m* warehouseman; (Cuba) country station master
guardamalleta *f* valance
guardameta *m* goalkeeper
guardamue·bles *m* (*pl* -bles) warehouse, furniture warehouse
guardanieve *m* snowshed
guardapelo *m* locket
guardapolvo *m* (*sobretodo ligero*) duster; (*resguardo para preservar del polvo*) cover, cloth; (*del reloj*) inner lid; (*sobre una puerta o ventana*) hood
guardapuerta *f* storm door
guardar *tr* to guard; to watch over; to protect; to put away; to show, observe; to save, e.g., **¡Dios guarde a**

la Reina God save the Queen ‖ *intr* to keep, to save; **¡guarda!** look out!, watch out! ‖ *ref* to be on one's guard; **guardarse de** to look out for, watch out for, guard against

guardarraya *f* (C Am, W-I) boundary line, property line

guardarropa *mf* keeper of the wardrobe ‖ *m* (*armario donde se guarda la ropa*) wardrobe; (*local destinado a la custodia de ropa en establecimientos públicos*) checkroom, cloakroom; check boy ‖ *f* check girl, hat girl

guardarropía *f* (theat) wardrobe

guardasilla *f* chair rail

guardaventana *f* storm window

guardavía *m* (rr) trackwalker, lineman

guardavida *m* lifeguard

guardavientos *m* (*pl* -tos) (*abrigo contra los vientos*) windbreak; (*mitra de chimenea*) chimney pot

guardavivo *m* bead, corner bead

guardería *f* guard, guardship; **guardería infantil** day nursery

guardesa *f* woman guard

guardia *m* guard, guardsman; **guardia civil** rural policeman; **guardia marina** midshipman, middy; **guardia urbano** policeman ‖ *f* (*cuerpo de hombres armados; manera de defenderse en la esgrima*) guard; (naut) watch; **de guardia** on duty; on guard; **guardia civil** rural police; **guardia de asalto** shock troops; **guardia de corps** (mil) bodyguard; **guardia de cuartillo** (naut) dogwatch; **guardia suiza** Swiss Guards

guardián **-diana** *mf* guardian ‖ *m* watchman

guardilla *f* attic; attic room

guardoso **-sa** *adj* careful, neat, tidy; (*que ahorra mucho*) thrifty; (*mezquino*) stingy

guarecer §22 *tr* to take in, give shelter to; to keep, preserve; (*a un enfermo*) to treat ‖ *ref* to take refuge, take shelter

guarida *f* den, lair; shelter; haunt, hangout, hide-out

guarismo *m* cipher, figure

guarnecer §22 *tr* to trim, adorn; to equip, provide; to bind, to edge; (*joyas*) to set; to stucco, to plaster; (*frenos*) to line; (*un cojinete*) to bush; (*una plaza fuerte*) to man, garrison; (culin) to garnish

guarnición *f* trimming; equipping; binding, edging; (*de joyas*) setting; stuccoing, plastering; (*de la espada*) guard; (*de frenos*) lining; (*del émbolo*) packing; (*tropa que guarnece un lugar*) garrison; (culin) garnish; **guarniciones** fixtures, fittings; (*de la caballería*) harness

guarnicionar *tr* to garrison

guarnicionero *m* harness maker

guarro **-rra** *mf* hog

guasa *f* (coll) heaviness, churlishness; (coll) joking, kidding

guasca *f* (Am) rawhide; (Am) whip; **dar guasca a** (Am) to whip, thrash

guasería *f* (SAm) coarseness, crudity; (Chile) timidity

guaso **-sa** *adj* (SAm) coarse, crude, uncouth ‖ *mf* (Chile) peasant ‖ *f* see **guasa**

guasón **-sona** *adj* (coll) heavy, churlish; (coll) funny, comical ‖ *mf* (coll) dullard, churl; (coll) joker, kidder

guata *f* wadding, padding; (Arg, Chile, Peru) belly, paunch; (*de una pared*) (Chile) bulging, warping; (Ecuad) boon companion; **echar guata** (Chile) to prosper

guatemalteco **-ca** *adj & mf* Guatemalan

guáter *m* (coll) toilet, water closet

guau *m* (*ladrido del perro*) bowwow; (bot) woodbine, Virginia creeper; **guau guau** (*perro*) bowwow ‖ *interj* bowwow!

guay *interj* — **¡guay de mí!** (poet) woe is me!

guayaba *f* guava, guava apple

guayabo *m* guava tree; (Am) lie, trick

guayaco *m* lignum vitae

Guayana *f* Guiana

gubernamental *adj* governmental; (*defensor*) strong-government

gubernativo **-va** *adj* governmental

gubia *f* gouge

guedeja *f* shock of hair; lion's mane

guerra *f* war, warfare; billiards; **Gran guerra** Great War; **guerra a muerte** war to the death; **guerra bacteriana** germ warfare; **guerra de guerrillas** guerrilla warfare; **guerra de las dos Rosas** War of the Roses; **guerra de los Cien Años** Hundred Years' War; **guerra del Transvaal** Boer War; **guerra de ondas** radio jamming; **guerra de Troya** Trojan War; **guerra fría** cold war; **Guerra Mundial** World War; **guerra relámpago** blitzkrieg; **hacer la guerra** to wage war

guerreador **-dora** *adj* warring ‖ *mf* warrior

guerrear *intr* to war, wage war, fight; to struggle, resist

guerrero **-ra** *adj* war, warlike; warring; (coll) mischievous ‖ *m* fighter ‖ *m* warrior, soldier, fighting man ‖ *f* tight-fitting military jacket

guerrilla *f* band of skirmishers; guerrilla band; guerrilla warfare

guerrillear *intr* to skirmish; to wage guerrilla warfare

guerrillero *m* guerrilla

guía *mf* guide, leader; adviser ‖ *m* (mil) guide ‖ *f* guide; guidance; directory; (*del viajero*) guidebook; (*caballo*) leader; (*de la bicicleta*) handle bar; (*del bigote*) turned-up end; (*de la sierra*) fence; marker; shoot, sprout; (mach) guide; (rr) timetable; **guías** reins; **guía sonora** sound track; **guía telefónica** telephone directory

guiadera *f* (mach) guide

guiar §77 *tr* to guide, to lead; (*un automóvil*) to steer, to drive; to pilot; (*una planta, una vid*) to train ‖ *intr* to shoot, to sprout ‖ *ref* — **guiarse por** to be guided by, to go by

guija *f* pebble; grass pea

guijarro *m* cobble, cobblestone

guijeño **-ña** *adj* pebbly; hard-hearted

guijo *m* gravel
guijo•so -sa *adj* gravelly; pebbly
guillame *m* rabbet plane
Guillermo *m* William
guillotina *f* guillotine; paper cutter
guillotinar *tr* to guillotine
guimbalete *m* pump handle
guinda *f* sour cherry
guindal *m* sour cherry tree
guindaleza *f* (naut) hawser
guindar *tr* to hoist, raise; (coll) to win; (*ahorcar*) (coll) to hang, to string up
guindilla *m* (coll) policeman, cop; Guinea pepper
guindo *m* sour cherry tree
guindola *f* (naut) boatswain's chair; (naut) life buoy
guinea *f* (*moneda*) guinea
guineo *m* small banana
guinga *f* gingham
guiña *f* (Col, Ven) bad luck
guiñada *f* wink; (naut) yaw
guiñapo *m* rag, tatter; ragamuffin
guiñar *tr* (*el ojo*) to wink ‖ *intr* to wink; (naut) to yaw ‖ *ref* to wink at each other
guiño *m* wink; hacer guiños a to make eyes at; hacerse guiños to make faces at each other
guión *m* banner, standard; cross (*carried before prelate in procession*); (*signo ortográfico*) hyphen; (*signo ortográfico largo*) dash; (mil) guidon; (mov & theat) scenario; (rad & telv) script; (mus) repeat sign; guión de montaje (mov) cutter's script; guión de rodaje (mov) shooting script
guionista *mf* (mov) scenarist; (mov) scriptwriter; (mov) subtitle writer
guirigay *m* (coll) gibberish; (coll) confusion, hubbub
guirindola *f* frill, jabot
guirlache *m* almond brittle, peanut brittle
guirnalda *f* garland, wreath
guisa *f* way, manner, wise; a guisa de in the manner of, like
guisado *m* stew, meat stew

guisante *m* pea; guisante de olor sweet pea
guisar *tr* to cook; to stew; to arrange, prepare ‖ *intr* to cook
guiso *m* dish
guisote *m* hash
guita *f* twine; (coll) dough, money
guitarra *f* guitar
guitarrista *mf* guitarist
gui•tón -tona *mf* tramp, bum
gula *f* gluttony; gorging, guzzling
gulo•so -sa *adj* gluttonous; guzzling
gumía *f* Moorish poniard
gurrumi•no -na *adj* weak, puny ‖ *m* henpecked husband ‖ *f* uxoriousness
gusanear *intr* to swarm
gusanera *f* nest of worms; (coll) ruling passion
gusanien•to -ta *adj* wormy, grubby
gusanillo *m* small worm; twist stitch; (*de la barrena*) spur; matar el gusanillo (coll) to take a shot of liquor before breakfast
gusano *m* worm; gusano de luz glowworm; gusano de seda silk worm; gusano de tierra earthworm
gusano•so -sa *adj* wormy, grubby
gusarapo *m* waterworm, vinegar worm
gustación *f* tasting; taste
gustar *tr* to taste; to try, sample; to please, be pleasing to; to like, e.g., me gustan estas peras I like these pears ‖ *intr* to like, e.g., como Vd. guste as you like; gustar de to like; to like to
gustillo *m* slight taste, touch
gusto *m* taste; flavor; liking; caprice, whim; pleasure; a gusto as you like it; con mucho gusto with pleasure, gladly; encontrarse a gusto or estar a gusto to like it (*e.g., in the country*); tanto gusto so glad to meet you
gusto•so -sa *adj* tasty; agreeable, pleasant; ready, willing, glad
gutapercha *f* gutta-percha
gutural *adj* guttural

H

H, h (hache) *f* ninth letter of the Spanish alphabet
haba *f* bean, broad bean; (*simiente del café y el cacao*) bean; ser habas contadas (coll) to be a sure thing
Habana, La Havana
haber *m* salary, wages; credit, credit side; haberes property, wealth ‖ *v* §38 *tr* to have; to get, get hold of ‖ *v aux* to have, e.g., lo he visto a menudo I have seen it often; haber de + *inf* to be to + *inf*, e.g., ha de llegar a mediodía he is to arrive at noon ‖ *v impers* there to be, e.g., ha habido tres personas allí there were three people there; haber que + *inf* to be necessary to + *inf*; no hay de qué

you're welcome, don't mention it ‖ *ref* to behave oneself; habérselas con to deal with; to have it out with
habichuela *f* kidney bean; habichuela verde string bean
hábil *adj* skillful, capable; (*día*) work
habilidad *f* skill, ability, capability; (*lo que se ejecuta con gracia*) feat; (*enredo, embuste*) scheme, trick
habilido•so -sa *adj* skillful
habilitación *f* qualification; backing, financing; equipping, outfitting; habilitaciones fixtures
habilitar *tr* to qualify; to back, finance; to equip, fit out; (*en un examen*) to pass
habitable *adj* inhabitable

habitación f habitation; (edificio donde se habita) house, home, dwelling; (aposento de la casa o el hotel) room; (donde vive una especie vegetal o animal) habitat

habitante mf (de una casa) dweller, occupant; (de una población) inhabitant

habitar tr to inhabit, live in; (una casa, un piso) to occupy || intr to live

hábito m garment, dress; habit, custom; **ahorcar los hábitos** (coll) to doff the cassock, to leave the priesthood; (coll) to change jobs; **el hábito no hace al monje** clothes don't make the man

habitua·do -da mf habitué

habitual adj habitual; regular, usual

habituar §21 tr to accustom || ref to become accustomed

habitud f relationship, connection; custom, habit

habla f speech; **al habla** speaking

habla·dor -dora adj talkative; gossipy || mf talker, chatterbox; gossip

habladuría f cut, sarcasm; **andar con habladurías** to go around gossiping

hablante adj speaking || mf speaker

hablar tr (una lengua) to speak, to talk; (disparates) to talk || intr to speak, to talk; **es hablar por demás** it's wasted talk; **estar hablando** (una pintura, una estatua) to be almost alive; **hablar claro** to talk straight from the shoulder

hablilla f story, piece of gossip

hablista mf speaker, good speaker

hacede·ro -ra adj feasible, practicable

hacenda·do -da adj landed, property-owning || mf landholder, property owner; (Am) cattle rancher; (Am) plantation owner

hacendar §2 tr (el dominio de bienes raíces) to pass on || ref to buy property in order to settle down

hacende·ro -ra adj thrifty

hacendista m economist, fiscal expert; man of independent means

hacendo·so -sa adj hard-working, thrifty

hacer §39 tr (crear, producir, formar) to make; (ejecutar, llevar a cabo) to do; (un baúl) to pack; (un papel) to play; (un mandato) to give; (un drama) to act, perform; to pretend to be; (una pregunta) to ask; **hace ago**, e.g., **hace un mes** a month ago; **hacer + inf** to have + inf, e.g., **le hice tomar un libro en la biblioteca** I had him get a book at the library; to make + inf, e.g., **el médico me hizo guardar cama** the doctor made me stay in bed; to have + pp, e.g., **hará construir una casa** he will have a house built; **hacer . . . que** to be . . . since, e.g., **hace un año que yo estuve aquí** it is a year since I was here; to be for . . ., e.g., **hace un año que estoy aquí** I have been here for a year; for expressions like **hacer frío** to be cold, see the noun || intr to act; **hacer a** to fit; **hacer al caso** (coll) to be to the purpose; **hacer como que + ind** to pretend to + inf; **hacer de to** act as, to work as; **hacer por** to try to || ref to become, get to be, grow; **hacerse a** to become accustomed to; **hacerse a un lado** to step aside; **hacerse con** to make off with; **hacerse chiquito** (coll) to sing small; **hacérsele a uno difícil** to strike one as difficult; **hacerse viejo** to grow old; (coll) to kill time

hacia prep toward; (cierta hora o época) about, near; **hacia abajo** downward; **hacia adelante** forward; **hacia arriba** upward; **hacia atrás** backward; (coll) the wrong way; **hacia dentro** inward; **hacia fuera** outward

hacienda f farmstead, landed estate, country property; property, possessions; (Arg) cattle, livestock; (Am) ranch; **hacienda pública** public finance, federal income; **haciendas** household chores

hacina f pile, heap; shock, stack

hacinar tr to pile, heap, stack

hacha f axe; (hacha pequeña) hatchet; torch, firebrand; four-wick wax candle; **hacha de armas** battleaxe

hachazo m blow with an axe

hachear tr & intr to hew, hack, or chop with an axe

hachero m torchbearer; (candelero) torch stand; (leñador) woodcutter

hachich m or **hachís** m hashish

hacho m torch; (sitio elevado cerca de la costa) beacon, beacon hill

hada f fairy; (mujer que encanta por su belleza, gracia, etc.) charmer; **hada madrina** fairy godmother

hadar tr (determinar el hado) to predestine, foreordain; (pronosticar) to foretell; (encantar) to charm, cast a spell on

hado m fate, destiny

haiga m (slang) flashy auto; (slang) sport

halagar §44 tr (lisonjear) to flatter; (demostrar cariño a) to cajole, fawn on; (agradar) to gratify, please

halago m flattery; cajolery; gratification; **halagos** flattery, blandishments

halagüe·ño -ña adj flattering; fawning; gratifying, pleasing; bright, rosy, promising

halar tr (naut) to haul, to pull

halcón m falcon

halconear intr (la mujer) to chase after men

halconería f falconry

halconero m falconer

halda f skirt; **poner haldas en cinta** (coll) to pull up one's skirts to run; (coll) to roll up one's sleeves

halieto m fish hawk, osprey

hálito m breath; vapor; (poet) gentle breeze

halitosis f halitosis

halo m halo

halógeno m halogen

halterio m dumbbell

haluro m halide

hallar tr to find; (averiguar) to find out, discover || ref to find oneself; to be; **hallarse bien con** to be satisfied with; **hallárselo todo hecho** to never have to turn a hand; **no hallarse** to feel uncomfortable, to not like it

hallazgo *m* (*cosa hallada*) find; (*acción de hallar*) finding, discovery; (*premio al que ha hallado una cosa perdida*) reward, finder's reward, e.g., **diez dólares de hallazgo** ten dollars reward

hallulla *f* bread baked on embers or hot stones; (Chile) fine bread

hamaca *f* hammock

hamamelina *f* witch hazel

hambre *f* hunger; (*escasez general de comestibles*) famine; **matar de hambre** to starve to death; **morir de hambre** to starve to death, die of starvation; **pasar hambre** to go hungry; **tener hambre** to be hungry

hambrear *tr & intr* to starve, to famish

hambrien·to -ta *adj* hungry, starving

hambruna *f* (SAm) mad hunger; (Ecuad) starvation

hamburguesa *f* hamburger sandwich

hamo *m* fishhook

hampa *f* underworld life; denizens of the underworld

hampes·co -ca *adj* underworld

hampón *m* bully, tough

hangar *m* (aer) hangar

hara·gán -gana *adj* idling, loafing, lazy || *mf* idler, loafer

haraganear *intr* to idle, to loaf, to hang around

harapien·to -ta *adj* ragged, tattered

harapo *m* rag, tatter; **andar** or **estar hecho un harapo** (coll) to go around in rags

harapo·so -sa *adj* ragged, tattered

harén *m* harem

harina *f* (*especialmente del trigo*) flour; (*de cualquier grano*) meal; **estar metido en harina** (coll) to be deeply absorbed; (coll) to be fat and heavy; **harina de avena** oatmeal; **harina de maíz** corn meal; **ser harina de otro costal** (coll) to be a horse of another color

harine·ro -ra *adj* flour || *m* flour dealer; flour bin

harino·so -sa *adj* floury, mealy

harnear *tr* (Col, Chile) to sift

harnero *m* sieve

ha·rón -rona *adj* lazy || *mf* lazy loafer

harpillera *f* burlap, sackcloth

hartar *tr* to stuff, to cram; to satisfy, to satiate; to tire, to bore; to overwhelm, deluge || *intr* to have one's fill || *ref* to stuff; to be satiated; to tire, be bored

hartazgo or **hartazón** *m* fill, bellyful; **darse un hartazgo** (coll) to eat one's fill; **darse un hartazgo de** (coll) to have or to get one's fill of

har·to -ta *adj* full, fed up; very much; **harto de** full of, fed up with, sick of || *harto adv* enough; very, quite

hartura *f* fill, satiety; full satisfaction; abundance

hasta *adv* even || *prep* until, till; to, as far as; down to, up to; as much as; **hasta ahora** up till now; **hasta aquí** so far; **hasta después** (coll) so long, good-by; **hasta la vista** or **hasta luego**

so long, good-by; **hasta mañana** see you tomorrow; **hasta más no poder** to the utmost; **hasta no más** to the utmost; **hasta que** until, till

hastial *m* gable end; (*hombrón rústico*) bumpkin

hastiar §77 *tr* to surfeit, sicken, cloy; (*fastidiar*) to bother, annoy, bore

hastío *m* surfeit, loathing, disgust; bother, annoyance, boredom

hataca *f* large wooden ladle; (*cilindro para extender la masa*) rolling pin

hatajo *m* small herd, small flock; (*p.ej., de disparates*) (coll) lot, flock

hato *m* (*de ganado vacuno*) herd; (*de ovejas*) flock; (*de ropa*) pack, bundle; (*de gente*) clique, ring; (*de gente malvada*) gang; everyday outfit; (*de disparates*) flock, lot; (Am) cattle ranch; **liar el hato** (coll) to pack up, pack one's baggage; **revolver el hato** (coll) to stir up trouble

haya *f* beech tree; (*madera*) beech || **La Haya** The Hague

hayaca *f* (Ven) mince pie

hayo *m* (Col) coca; (Col) coca leaves (*mixed for chewing*)

hayuco *m* beechnut, mast

haz *m* (*pl* **haces**) bunch, bundle; (*de leña*) fagot; (*de mieses*) sheaf; (*de rayos*) beam, pencil; (*de soldados*) file || *f* (*pl* **haces**) face; (*de la tierra*) surface; (*de paño o tela*) right side; (*de un edificio*) façade, front; **a sobre haz** on the surface; **ser de dos haces** to be two-faced

hazaña *f* feat, exploit, deed

hazañería *f* fuss

hazañe·ro -ra *adj* fussy

hazaño·so -sa *adj* gallant, courageous

hazmerreír *m* (coll) laughingstock, butt

he *adv* behold, lo and behold; **he aquí** here is, here are; **he allí** there is, there are

hebilla *f* buckle

hebra *f* thread; fiber; (*en la madera*) grain; (*del discurso*) (fig) thread; **de una hebra** (Chile) all at once; **pegar la hebra** (coll) to strike up a conversation; (coll) to keep on talking

hebre·o -a *adj & mf* Hebrew || *m* (*idioma*) Hebrew; (coll) usurer

hebro·so -sa *adj* fibrous, stringy

hecatombe *f* hecatomb

hechicera *f* witch, sorceress; (*mujer que por su belleza cautiva*) enchantress

hechicería *f* witchcraft, sorcery, wizardry; (fig) fascination, charm

hechice·ro -ra *adj* bewitching, charming, enchanting; magic || *mf* sorcerer, magician; charmer, enchanter || *m* wizard, sorcerer || *f see* **hechicera**

hechizar §60 *tr* to bewitch, cast a spell on; (fig) to bewitch, charm, enchant || *intr* to practice sorcery; (fig) to be charming, to enchant

hechi·zo -za *adj* fake, artificial; (*de quita y pon*) detachable; made, manufactured; (*producto*) (Am) local, home || *m* spell, charm; magic, sorcery; (fig) magic, sorcery, glamour; (fig) charmer; **hechizos** (*de una mujer*) charms

he·cho -cha *adj* accustomed; finished; turned into; (*traje*) ready-made; (*llegado a la edad adulta*) full-grown || *m* act, deed; fact; event; (*hazaña*) feat; **de hecho** in fact; **en hecho de verdad** as a matter of fact; **estar en el hecho de** to catch on to; **hecho consumado** fait accompli || **hecho** *interj* all right!, OK!

hechura *f* form, shape, cut, build; creation, creature; workmanship; (Chile) drink, treat; **hechuras** cost of making; **no tener hechura** to be impracticable

heder §51 *tr* to bore, annoy, tire || *intr* to stink, to reek

hediondez *f* stench, stink

hedion·do -da *adj* stinking, smelly; annoying, boring; obscene, filthy, dirty || *m* bean trefoil; skunk

hedor *m* stench, stink

helada *f* freezing; (*escarcha*) frost; **helada blanca** hoarfrost

heladera *f* refrigerator; (Chile) ice-cream tray

heladería *f* (Am) ice-cream parlor

hela·do -da *adj* cold, icy; (*pasmado por el miedo, la sorpresa, etc.*) frozen; (*esquivo, indiferente*) cold, chilly; (*cubierto de azúcar*) (Ven) iced || *m* cold drink; (*manjar*) water ice; (*sorbete*) ice cream; **helado al corte** brick ice cream || *f* see **helada**

hela·dor -dora *adj* freezing || *f* ice-cream freezer

helar §2 *tr* to freeze; to harden, congeal; to dumbfound; to discourage || *intr* to freeze || *ref* to freeze; to harden, congeal, set; (*cubrirse de hielo*) to ice

helecho *m* fern

heléni·co -ca *adj* Hellenic

hele·no -na *adj* Hellenic || *mf* Hellene

helero *m* glacier

hélice *f* helix; (*de un buque*) screw, propeller; (*de un avión*) propeller

helicóptero *m* helicopter

helio *m* helium

heliotropo *m* heliotrope

helipuerto *m* heliport

hematíe *m* red cell

hembra *adj invar* (*animal, planta, herramienta*) female; weak, thin, delicate || *f* female; (*del corchete*) eye; (*tuerca*) nut; **hembra de terraja** (mach) die

hembraje *m* (SAm) females of a flock or herd

hembrilla *f* (mach) female part or piece; (*armella*) eyebolt

hemeroteca *f* periodical library

hemiciclo *m* (*semicírculo*) hemicycle; (*gradería semicircular*) amphitheater; (*espacio central del salón de sesiones de las Cortes*) floor

hemisferio *m* hemisphere

hemistiquio *m* hemistich

hemofilia *f* hemophilia

hemoglobina *f* hemoglobin

hemorragia *f* hemorrhage

hemorroides *fpl* hemorrhoids

hemóstato *m* hemostat

henal *m* hayloft

henar *m* hayfield

henchir §50 *tr* to fill; (*un colchón*) to stuff; (*a una persona, p.ej., de favores*) to heap, to shower || *ref* to be filled; to stuff, to stuff oneself

hendedura *f* crack, split, cleft

hender §51 *tr* to crack, split, cleave; (*el aire, las ondas*) to cleave; to make one's way through || *ref* to crack, to split

hendidura *f* crack, split, cleft

henil *m* hayloft, haymow

henna *f* henna

heno *m* hay

heñir §72 *tr* to knead; **hay mucho que heñir** (coll) there's still a lot of work to do

heraldía *f* heraldry

heráldi·co -ca *adj* heraldic || *f* heraldry

heraldo *m* herald

herbáce·o -a *adj* herbaceous

herbajar *tr* & *intr* to graze

herbaje *m* herbage

herba·rio -ria *adj* herbal || *m* (*libro*) herbal; (*colección*) herbarium

herbicida *m* weed killer

herbo·so -sa *adj* grassy

hercúle·o -a *adj* herculean

heredad *f* country estate

heredar *tr* & *intr* to inherit; **heredar a** to inherit from

herede·ro -ra *mf* heir, inheritor; owner of an estate; **heredero forzoso** heir apparent || *m* heir || *f* heiress

heredita·rio -ria *adj* hereditary

hereje *mf* heretic

herejía *f* heresy; insult, outrage; (coll) outrageous price

herencia *f* heritage, inheritance; (*transmisión de caracteres biológicos*) heredity; (*patrimonio de un difunto*) estate

heréti·co -ca *adj* heretic(a')

herida *f* injury, wound; insult, outrage; **renovar la herida** to open an old sore; **tocar en la herida** to sting to the quick

heri·do -da *adj* hurt, wounded; (*ofendido*) hurt || *mf* injured person, wounded person; **los heridos** the injured, the wounded || *f* see **herida**

herir §68 *tr* to injure, hurt, wound; (*ofender*) (fig) to hurt; (*golpear*) to strike; (*el sol sobre*) to beat down upon; (*un instrumento de cuerda*) to play; (*la cuerda de un instrumento*) to pluck; to touch, to move

hermana *f* sister; **hermana de leche** foster sister; **hermana política** sister-in-law; **media hermana** half sister

hermanar *tr* to match, to mate; to combine, join; to harmonize || *ref* to match; to become attached as brothers or sisters or brother and sister

hermanastra *f* stepsister

hermanastro *m* stepbrother

hermandad *f* brotherhood; sisterhood; close friendship; close relationship

herma·no -na *adj* (*p.ej.,* *idioma*) sister || *mf* companion, mate || *m* brother; **hermano de leche** foster brother; **hermano político** brother-in-law; **hermanos** brother and sister; brothers and sisters; **hermanos siameses** Siamese twins; **medio hermano** half brother; **primo hermano** first cousin || *f* see **hermana**

hermétl·co -ca *adj* hermetic(al); airtight; impenetrable; tight-lipped

hermosear *tr* to beautify, to embellish

hermo·so -sa *adj* beautiful; (*caballero*) handsome

hermosura *f* beauty; (*mujer hermosa*) belle, beauty

hernia *f* hernia

héroe *m* hero

herol·co -ca *adj* heroic; (*remedio*) desperate

heroína *f* heroine; (pharm) heroin

heroísmo *m* heroism

herrada *f* wooden bucket

herrador *m* horseshoer

herradura *f* horseshoe; **mostrar las herraduras** (*un caballo*) to kick, be vicious; (coll) to show one's heels

herraje *m* hardware, ironwork

herramental *adj* tool || *m* toolbox, tool bag

herramienta *f* tool; set of tools; (coll) teeth; (coll) horns

herrar §2 *tr* (*guarnecer con hierro*) to fit with hardware; (*un caballo*) to shoe; (*marcar con hierro candente*) to brand; (*un barril*) to hoop

herrería *f* forge, blacksmith shop; blacksmithing; ironworks; rumpus

herrero *m* blacksmith; **herrero de grueso** ironworker; **herrero de obra** steelworker

herrete *m* tip, metal tip

herretear *tr* to tip, put a metal tip on

herrín *m* rust

herrón *m* (*tejo de hierro horadado*) quoit; (*arandela*) washer

herrumbre *f* rust; (*honguillo parásito*) rust, plant rot

herrumbro·so -sa *adj* rusty

herventar §2 *tr* to boil

hervidero *m* boiling; bubbling spring; (*en el pecho*) rattle; (*de gente*) swarm

hervidor *m* boiler, cooker

hervir §68 *intr* to boil; (*el mar; una persona encolerizada*) to boil, to seethe; to swarm, to teem

hervor *m* boil, boiling; (*de la juventud*) fire, restlessness; **alzar el hervor** to begin to boil

hervoro·so -sa *adj* ardent, fiery, impetuous

heteróclí·to -ta *adj* irregular; unconventional

heterodinar *tr* to heterodyne

heterodí·no -na *adj* heterodyne

heterodo·xo -xa *adj* heterodox

heterogeneidad *f* heterogeneity

heterogéne·o -a *adj* heterogeneous

hexámetro *m* hexameter

hez *f* (*pl* **heces**) (fig) scum, dregs; **heces** lees, dregs; feces, excrement

hiato *m* hiatus

hibisco *n* hibiscus

hibridación *f* hybridization

hibridar *tr & intr* to hybridize

híbri·do -da *adj & m* hybrid

hidal·go -ga *adj* noble, illustrious || *m* nobleman || *f* noblewoman

hidalguez *f* or **hidalguía** *f* nobility

hidra *f* hydra

hidratar *tr & ref* to hydrate

hidrato *m* hydrate

hidráuli·co -ca *adj* hydraulic || *f* hydraulics

hidroala *m* (*vehículo mixto de buque y avión*) hydrofoil

hidroaleta *f* (*miembro alar del hidroala*) hydrofoil

hidroavión *m* hydroplane

hidrocarburo *m* hydrocarbon

hidroeléctri·co -ca *adj* hydroelectric

hidrófí·lo -la *adj* (*algodón*) absorbent (*cotton*)

hidrofobia *f* hydrophobia

hidrófu·go -ga *adj* waterproof

hidrógeno *m* hydrogen

hidropesía *f* dropsy

hidróxido *m* hydroxide

hiedra *f* ivy

hiel *f* bile, gall; (fig) gall, bitterness, sorrow; **echar la hiel** (coll) to strain, to overwork

hielo *m* ice; (fig) coldness, coolness; **hielo flotante** drift ice, ice pack; **hielo seco** dry ice; **romper el hielo** (*quebrantar la reserva*) to break the ice

hiena *f* hyena

hienda *f* dung

hierba *f* grass; (*especialmente la que tiene propiedades medicinales*) herb; **hierba de la plata** honesty; **hierba del asno** evening primrose; **hierba de París** truelove; **hierba gatera** catnip; **hierba pastel** woad; **hierbas** grass, pasture; herb poison; (coll) years of age (*said of animals*); **mala hierba** weed; (coll) wayward young fellow

hierbabuena *f* mint

hierro *m* iron; (*marca candente que se pone a los ganados*) brand; **hierro colado** cast iron; **hierro colado en barras** pig iron; **hierro de desecho** scrap iron; **hierro de marcar** branding iron; **hierro dulce** wrought iron; **hierro fundido** cast iron; **hierro galvanizado** galvanized iron; **hierro ondulado** corrugated iron; **hierros** irons, fetters; **llevar hierro a Vizcaya** to carry coals to Newcastle

higa *f* baby's fist-shaped amulet; (coll) scorn, contempt; **dar higa** to miss fire; **no dar dos higas por** (coll) to not give a rap for

hígado *m* liver; **echar los hígados** (coll) to strain, to overwork; **hígados** guts, courage; **malos hígados** (coll) hatred, grudge

higiene *f* hygiene

higiéni·co -ca *adj* hygienic

higo *m* fig; **higo chumbo** prickly pear; **higo paso** dried fig; **no valer un higo** (coll) to be not worth a continental

higuera *f* fig tree; **higuera chumba** prickly pear

hija *f* daughter; **hija política** daughter-in-law

hijas·tro -tra *mf* stepchild || *m* stepson || *f* stepdaughter

hi·jo -ja *mf* child; (*de un animal*) young; **hijo de bendición** legitimate child; good child; **hijo de la cuna**

foundling; **hijo del amor** love child; **hijo de leche** foster child ‖ *m* son; **cada hijo de vecino** (coll) every man Jack, every mother's son; **hijo del agua** good sailor; good swimmer; **hijo de su padre** (coll) chip off the old block; **hijo de sus propias obras** self-made man; **hijo político** son-in-law; **hijos** children; descendants ‖ *f* see **hija**

hijodalgo *m* (pl **hijosdalgo**) nobleman

hijuela *f* little girl, little daughter; *(tira de tela)* gore; branch drain; side path

hijuelero *m* rural postman

hijuelo *m* shoot, sucker

hila *f* row, line; *(acción de hilar)* spinning; **a la hila** in single file; **hilas** *(hebras para curar heridas)* lint

hilacha *f* shred, fraying; **hilacha de acero** steel wool; **hilacha de algodón** cotton waste; **hilacha de vidrio** spun glass; **hilachas** lint; **mostrar la hilacha** (Arg) to show one's worst side

hilachos *mpl* (Mex) rags, tatters

hilacho·so -sa *adj* frayed, raggedy

hilada *f* row, line; (mas) course

hilado *m* spinning; *(hilo)* yarn, thread

hila·dor -dora *adj* spinning ‖ *mf* spinner ‖ *f* spinning machine

hilandería *f* spinning; spinning mill

hilande·ro -ra *adj* spinning ‖ *m* spinning mill

hilar *tr & intr* to spin; **hilar delgado** to hew close to the line; **hilar largo** to drag on

hilarante *adj* laughable; *(gas)* laughing

hilaza *f* yarn, thread; lint; **descubrir la hilaza** (coll) to show one's true nature

hilera *f* row, line; fine thread, fine yarn; *(parhilera)* ridgepole; (mil) file

hilo *m* thread; *(hebras retorcidas)* yarn; *(alambre)* wire; *(de perlas)* string; *(de agua)* thin stream; *(de luz)* beam; linen, linen fabric; *(de un discurso, de la vida)* (fig) thread; **hilo bramante** twine; **hilo de la muerte** end of life; **hilo de masa** (aut) ground wire; **hilo de medianoche** midnight sharp; **hilo dental** dental floss; **hilo de tierra** (elec) ground wire; **irse al hilo** or **tras el hilo de la gente** to follow the crowd; **manejar los hilos** to pull strings; **perder el hilo de** to lose the thread of

hilván *m* basting, tacking; basting stitch; (Chile) basting thread; (Ven) hem; **hablar de hilván** (coll) to jabber along

hilvanar *tr* to baste, to tack; to sketch, outline; *(hacer con precipitación)* (coll) to hurry; (Ven) to hem ‖ *intr* to baste, to tack

himnario *m* hymnal, hymn book

himno *m* hymn; **himno nacional** national anthem

hin *m* neigh, whinny

hincadura *f* driving, thrusting, sticking

hincapié *m* stamping the foot; **hacer hincapié en** (coll) to lay great stress on, to emphasize

hincar §73 *tr* to drive, thrust, stick, sink; *(la rodilla)* to go down on, to

fall on ‖ *ref* to kneel, kneel down; **hincarse de rodillas** to go down on one's knees

hincha *mf* (sport) fan, rooter ‖ *f* (coll) grudge, ill will

hinchable *adj* inflatable; *(goma de mascar)* bubble

hincha·do -da *adj* swollen; swollen with pride; *(estilo, lenguaje)* pompous, high-flown ‖ *m* *(de un neumático)* inflation ‖ *f* (sport) fans, rooters

hinchar *tr* to swell; to inflate; *(un neumático)* to pump up; to exaggerate, embroider ‖ *ref* to swell; to swell up, become puffed up *(with pride)*

hinchazón *f* swelling; vanity, conceit; *(del estilo, lenguaje)* bombast

hinchismo *m* (sport) fans, rooters

hin·dú -dúa (pl **-dúes -dúas**) *adj & mf* Hindoo, Hindu

hiniesta *f* Spanish broom

hinojo *m* fennel; **de hinojos** on one's knees

hipar *intr* to hiccup; *(los perros cuando siguen la caza)* to pant, to snuffle; *(gimotear)* to wimper; to be worn out; **hipar por** to long for; to long to

hiperacidez *f* hyperacidity

hipérbola *f* (geom) hyperbola

hipérbole *f* (rhet) hyperbole

hiperbóli·co -ca *adj* (geom & rhet) hyperbolic

hipersensible *adj* *(alérgico)* hypersensitive

hipertensión *f* hypertension, high blood pressure

hípi·co -ca *adj* horse, equine

hipnosis *f* hypnosis

hipnóti·co -ca *adj* hypnotic ‖ *mf* hypnotic ‖ *m* *(medicamento que provoca el sueño)* hypnotic

hipnotismo *m* hypnotism

hipnotista *mf* hypnotist

hipnotizar §60 *tr* to hypnotize

hipo *m* hiccup; longing, desire; **tener hipo contra** to have a grudge against; **tener hipo por** to desire eagerly

hipocondría·co -ca *adj & mf* hypochondriac

hipocresía *f* hypocrisy

hipócrita *adj* hypocritical ‖ *mf* hypocrite

hipodérmi·co -ca *adj* hypodermic

hipódromo *m* hippodrome, race track

hipopótamo *m* hippopotamus

hiposulfito *m* hyposulfite

hipoteca *f* mortgage; **¡buena hipoteca!** (coll) you may believe it, if you want to!

hipotecar §73 *tr* to mortgage

hipoteca·rio -ria *adj* mortgage

hipotenusa *f* hypotenuse

hipóte·sis *f* (pl **-sis**) hypothesis

hipotéti·co -ca *adj* hypothetic(al)

hiriente *adj* cutting, stinging

hirsu·to -ta *adj* hairy, bristly; (fig) brusque, gruff

hirviente *adj* boiling

hisopear *tr* to sprinkle with holy water

hisopo *m* (bot) hyssop; aspergillum, sprinkler of holy water; (Am) paint brush, shaving brush

hispalense *adj & mf* Sevillian

hispáni·co -ca *adj* Hispanic
hispanista *mf* Hispanist
hispa·no -na *adj* Spanish; Spanish American ‖ *mf* Spaniard; Spanish American
hispanohablante *adj* Spanish-speaking ‖ *mf* speaker of Spanish
híspi·do -da *adj* bristly, spiny
histéri·co -ca *adj* hysteric(al)
histerismo *m* hysteria
histología *f* histology
historia *f* history; story, tale; **de historia** (coll) notorious, infamous; **dejarse de historias** (coll) to come to the point; **historia de lagrimitas** (coll) sob story; **historias** (coll) gossip, meddling; **pasar a la historia** to become a thing of the past; **picar en historia** to turn out to be serious
historia·do -da *adj* richly adorned; overadorned; *(cuadro, dibujo)* storied
historial *adj* historical ‖ *m* record, dossier
historiar §77 & *regular tr* to tell the history of; to tell the story of; *(un suceso histórico)* (fa) to depict
históri·co -ca *adj* historic(al)
historieta *f* anecdote, brief story; **historieta gráfica** comic strip
histrión *m* actor; juggler, buffoon
histrióni·co -ca *adj* histrionic
hita *f* brad; landmark, milestone
Hno. *abbr* Hermano
hoba·chón -chona *adj* (coll) lumpish
hocicar §73 *tr* to nuzzle, to root; (coll) to keep on kissing ‖ *intr* to nuzzle, to root; to run into a snag; *(la proa)* (naut) to dip
hocico *m* snout; *(de una persona)* (coll) snout; sour face; **caer de hocicos** (coll) to fall on one's face; **meter el hocico en todo** (coll) to poke one's nose into everything; **poner hocico** (coll) to make a face
hogaño *adv* (coll) this year; (coll) at the present time
hogar *m* fireplace, hearth; furnace; home; family life; *(hoguera)* bonfire
hogare·ño -ña *adj* home-loving ‖ *mf* homebody, stay-at-home
hogaza *f* large loaf of bread
hoguera *f* bonfire
hoja *f* *(de planta, libro, mesa, muelle, puerta plegadiza, etc.; pétalo de flor)* leaf; *(de planta acuática)* pad; *(de papel)* sheet; blank sheet; *(de cuchillo, sierra, espada, etc.)* blade; *(hojuela de metal)* foil; *(de persiana)* slat; *(del patín)* runner; **doblar la hoja** (coll) to change the subject; **hoja clínica** clinical chart; **hoja de afeitar** razor blade; **hoja de embalaje** packing slip; **hoja de encuadernador** (bb) end paper; **hoja de estaño** tin foil; **hoja de estudios** tran-

script; **hoja de guarda** (bb) flyleaf; **hoja del anunciante** tear sheet; **hoja de lata** tin, tin plate; **hoja de nenúfar** lily pad; **hoja de paga** pay roll; **hoja de parra** fig leaf; **hoja de pedidos** order blank; **hoja de rodaje** (mov) shooting record; **hoja de ruta** waybill; **hoja de servicios** service record; **hoja de trébol** cloverleaf *(intersection)*; **hoja maestra** master blade *(of spring)*; **hojas del autor** (typ) advance sheets; **hoja suelta** leaflet, handbill; (bb) flyleaf; **hoja volante** leaflet, handbill
hojalata *f* tin, tin plate
hojalatería *f* tinsmith's shop; tinwork
hojalatero *m* tinsmith, tinner
hojaldre *m* & *f* puff paste
hojarasca *f* dead leaves; trash, rubbish; bluff, vain show
hojear *tr* to leaf through ‖ *intr* to scale off; *(las hojas de los árboles)* to flutter
hojita *f* leaflet; **hojita de afeitar** razor blade
hojo·so -sa *adj* leafy
hojuela *f* *(hoja de otra compuesta)* leaflet; *(fruta de sartén)* pancake; *(hoja muy delgada de metal)* foil; **hojuela de estaño** tin foil
hola *interj* hey!, hello!
Holanda *f* Holland
holan·dés -desa *adj* Dutch; **a la holandesa** (bb) half-bound ‖ *mf* Hollander ‖ *m* Dutchman; *(idioma)* Dutch ‖ *f* Dutch woman
holga·chón -chona *adj* (coll) lazy, idle ‖ *mf* (coll) loafer, idler
holgadero *m* hangout
holga·do -da *adj* idle, unoccupied; *(vestido)* loose, full, roomy; *(que vive con bienestar)* fairly well-off
holganza *f* idleness, leisure; pleasure, enjoyment
holgar §63 *intr* to idle, be idle; to take it easy, to rest up; to not fit, be too loose; to be unnecessary, be of no use; to be glad ‖ *ref* to be glad; to be amused
holga·zán -zana *adj* idle, lazy ‖ *mf* idler, loafer
holgazanear *intr* to idle, loaf, bum around
hol·gón -gona *adj* pleasure-loving ‖ *mf* loafer, lizard
holgorio *m* (coll) fun, merriment
holgura *f* looseness, fulness; enjoyment, merriment; comfort, easy circumstances; (mach) play
holocausto *m* holocaust
hollar §61 *tr* to tread on, to trample on
hollejo *m* hull, peel, skin
hollín *m* soot
hollinar *tr* (Chile) to cover with soot
hollinien·to -ta *adj* sooty
hombracho *m* big husky fellow
hombrada *f* manly act
hombradía *f* manliness, courage
hombre *m* man; (coll) husband, man; (coll) my boy, old chap; **buen hombre** good-natured fellow; **¡hombre al agua!** or **¡hombre a la mar!** man overboard!; **hombre bueno** arbiter,

referee; **hombre de bien** honorable
man; **hombre de buenas prendas** man
of parts; **hombre de dinero** man of
means; **hombre de estado** statesman;
hombre de letras man of letters;
hombre de mundo man of the world;
hombre de suposición man of straw;
hombre hecho grown man || *interj*
man alive!, upon my word!
hombre-anuncio *m* sandwich man
bombrear *tr* (Arg) to carry on the
shoulders; (Mex) to aid, back || *intr*
to try to be somebody; (*una mujer*)
to be mannish; **hombrear con** to try
to equal
hombrecillo *m* little man; (*lúpulo*) hop
hombrera *f* (*del vestido*) shoulder;
shoulder pad; epaulet
hombre-rana *m* (*pl* **hombres-ranas**)
frogman
hombría *f* manliness; **hombría de bien**
honor, probity
hombrillo *m* (*de la camisa*) yoke;
shoulder piece
hombro *m* shoulder; **arrimar el hombro**
to lend a hand, put one's shoulder to
the wheel; **encoger los hombros** to let
one's shoulders droop; **encogerse de
hombros** to shrug one's shoulders; to
crouch, to shrink with fear; to not
answer; **mirar por encima del hombro** to look down upon; **salir en hombros** to be carried off on the shoulders of the crowd
hombru-no -na *adj* (coll) mannish
homenaje *m* homage; (feud) homage;
(Chile) gift, favor; **homenaje de boca**
lip service; **rendir homenaje a** to
swear allegiance to
homeópata *mf* homeopath
homeopatía *f* homeopathy
homicida *adj* homicidal || *mf* homicide
homicidio *m* homicide
homilía *f* homily
homogeneidad *f* homogeniety
homogeneizar §60 *tr* to homogenize
homogéne-o -a *adj* homogeneous
homologación *f* confirmation, ratifica-
tion; (sport) validation
homologar §44 *tr* to confirm, ratify; (*un
récord*) (sport) to validate
homóni-mo -ma *adj* homonymous; of
the same name || *mf* namesake || *m*
homonym
homosexual *adj & mf* homosexual
homúnculo *m* (coll) guy, little runt
honda *f* sling
hondazo *m* blow with a sling
hondear *tr* (naut) to sound
hondillos *mpl* patches in the crotch of
pants
hon-do -da *adj* deep; (*terreno*) low || *m*
bottom || *f* see **honda** || **hondo** *adv*
deep
hondón *m* (*de la aguja*) eye; (*de un
vaso*) bottom; lowland
hondonada *f* lowland, ravine
hondura *f* depth, profundity; **meterse
en honduras** (coll) to go beyond
one's depth
hondure-ño -ña *adj & mf* Honduran
honestidad *f* decency; chastity; mod-

esty; honesty, probity; fairness, reasonableness
hones-to -ta *adj* decent; chaste, pure;
modest; honest, upright; (*precio*)
fair, reasonable
hongo *m* fungus, mushroom; (*sombrero*) bowler, derby
honor *m* honor; **en honor a la verdad**
as a matter of fact, to tell the truth;
hacer honor a to do honor to; (*la
firma*) to honor
honorable *adj* honorable
honora-rio -ria *adj* honorary || *s* fee,
honorarium
honorífi-co -ca *adj* honorific
honra *f* honor; **tener a mucha honra**
to be proud of
honradez *f* honesty, integrity
honra-do -da *adj* honorable
honrar *tr* to honor || *ref* to feel hon-
ored
honrilla *f* — **por la negra honrilla** out
of concern for what people will say
honro-so -sa *adj* honorable
hopo *m* tuft, shock (*of hair*); bushy
tail; **seguir el hopo a** (coll) to keep
right after
hora *f* hour; (*momento determinado
para algo*) time; **a la hora** on time; **a
la hora de ahora** right now; **a la hora
en punto** on the hour; **a las pocas
horas** within a few hours; **dar hora**
to fix a time; **dar la hora** (*el reloj*)
to strike; **de última hora** up-to-date;
most up-to-date; (*noticias*) late; **en
buen hora** or **en hora buena** safely,
luckily; all right; **en mal hora** or **en
hora mala** unluckily, in an evil hour;
fuera de horas after hours; **hasta
altas horas** until late into the night;
hora de acostarse bedtime; **hora de
aglomeración** rush hour; **hora de
comer** mealtime; **hora deshorada**
fatal hour; **hora de verano** daylight-
saving time; **hora de verdad** (taur)
kill; **hora legal** or **oficial** standard
time; **hora punta** peak hour; rush
hour; **horas de consulta** office hours
(*of a doctor*); **horas de ocio** leisure
hours; **horas de punta** rush hour; **horas extraordinarias de trabajo** overtime
horadar *tr* to drill, bore, pierce
hora-rio -ria *adj* hour || *m* hour hand;
clock; (*de ferrocarriles*) timetable;
horario escolar roster
horca *f* (*para levantar la paja*) pitchfork; (*para ahorcar a un condenado*)
gallows, gibbet; (*de ajos, cebollas,
etc.*) string
horcajadas — **a horcajadas** astride,
astraddle
horcajadillas — **a horcajadillas** astride,
astraddle
horcajadura *f* crotch
horcajo *m* (*confluencia de dos ríos*)
fork; (*para mulas*) yoke
horcón *m* pitchfork; forked prop (*for
fruit trees*); (Am) upright, prop
horchata *f* orgeat
horda *f* horde
horizontal *adj & f* horizontal
horizonte *m* horizon

horma f form, mold; shoe tree; hat block; **hallar la horma de su zapato** (coll) to meet one's match

hormiga f ant; (*enfermedad que causa comezón*) itch

hormigón m concrete; **hormigón armado** reinforced concrete

hormigonera f concrete mixer

hormigo·so -sa adj ant; full of ants; ant-eaten; (*picante*) itchy

hormiguear intr (*ponerse en movimiento gente o animales*) to swarm; (*experimentar una sensación de hormigas corriendo por el cuerpo*) to crawl, to creep; to abound, to teem

hormiguero m anthill; (*de gente*) swarm, mob

hormillón m hat block

hormón m or **hormona** f hormone

hornacina f niche

hornada f (*cantidad que se cuece de una vez en un horno*) batch, bake; (*conjunto de individuos de una misma promoción*) crop

hornazo m Easter cake filled with hard-boiled eggs; Easter gift to Lenten preacher

horne·ro -ra mf baker

hornilla f kitchen grate; pigeonhole

hornillo m kitchen stove; hot plate; (*de la pipa de fumar*) bowl

horno m oven, furnace; (*para cocer ladrillos*) kiln; **alto horno** blast furnace; **horno de cal** limekiln; **horno de fundición** smelting furnace; **horno de ladrillero** brickkiln

horóscopo m horoscope; **sacar un horóscopo** to cast a horoscope

horqueta f pitchfork; fork, prop; (*ángulo agudo en un río*) (Arg) bend

horquilla f pitchfork; (*de bicicleta*) fork; (*de microteléfono*) cradle; (*alfiler para sujetar el pelo*) hairpin

hórreo m granary; (in Asturias and Galicia) crib or granary raised on pillars (*to protect grain from mice and dampness*)

horrible adj horrible

horripilante adj hair-raising, blood-curdling

horror m horror; **tener horror a** to have a horror of

horrorizar §60 tr to horrify

horroro·so -sa adj horrid; (coll) hideous, ugly

hortaliza f vegetable

hortela·no -na adj garden || mf gardener

hortera m (coll) clerk, helper || f wooden bowl

hortícola adj horticultural

horticul·tor -tora mf horticulturist

horticultura f horticulture

hos·co -ca adj dark, dark-skinned; sullen, grim, gloomy

hospedaje m lodging

hospedar tr to lodge || ref to lodge, stop, put up

hospedería f hospice; inn, hostelry

hospede·ro -ra mf innkeeper

hospicio m hospice; poorhouse; orphan asylum

hospital m hospital; **estar hecho un hos-**

pital (*una persona*) (coll) to be full of aches and pains; (*una casa*) (coll) to be turned into a hospital; **hospital de la sangre** poor relations; **hospital de primera sangre** (mil) field hospital; **hospital robado** (coll) bare house

hospitala·rio -ria adj hospitable

hospitalidad f hospitality; (*estancia del enfermo en el hospital*) hospitalization

hospitalizar §60 tr to hospitalize

hosquedad f darkness; sullenness, grimness, gloominess

hostería f inn, hostelry

hostia f sacrificial victim; wafer; (eccl) wafer, Host

hostigar §44 tr to scourge; to harass; to pester; (Am) to cloy, surfeit

hostigo·so -sa adj (Am) cloying, sickening

hostil adj hostile

hostilidad f hostility

hostilizar §60 tr to antagonize; (*al enemigo*) to harry, harass

hotel m (*establecimiento donde se da comida y alojamiento por dinero*) hotel; (*casa particular lujosa*) mansion

hotele·ro -ra adj hotel || mf hotelkeeper

hoy adv & s today; de hoy a mañana any time now; **de hoy en adelante** from now on; **hoy día** nowadays

hoya f hole, pit, ditch; (*sepultura*) grave; valley; (*almáciga*) seedbed; (Am) river basin

hoyanca f potter's field

hoyo m hole; grave; pockmark

hoyo·so -sa adj full of holes

hoyuelo m dimple; (*juego de muchachos*) pitching pennies

hoz f (pl **hoces**) sickle; narrow pass, defile; **de hoz y de coz** (coll) headlong, recklessly

hozar §60 tr & intr to nuzzle, to root

hta. abbr **hasta**

huacal m var of **guacal**

huachinango m (Mex) red snapper

hucha f workingman's chest; (*alcancía*) toy bank; (*dinero ahorrado*) savings, nest egg

huchear intr to cry, shout

hue·co -ca adj hollow; (*mullido*) soft, fluffy, spongy; (*voz*) deep, resounding; vain, conceited; (*estilo, lenguaje*) affected, pompous || m hollow; interval; (*en un muro, una hilera de coches, etc.*) opening; (*empleo sin proveer*) (coll) opening; **hueco de la axila** armpit; **hueco de escalera** stair well

huélfago m (vet) heaves

huelga f (*ocio*) rest, leisure, idleness; recreation; pleasant spot; (*cesación del trabajo en señal de protesta*) strike; (mach) play; **huelga de brazos caídos** sit-down strike; **huelga de hambre** hunger strike; **huelga patronal** lockout; **huelga sentada** sit-down strike; **ir a la huelga** or **ponerse en huelga** to go on strike

huelguista mf striker

huella f track, footprint; trace, mark; rut; (*acción de hollar*) tread, tread-

ing; (*peldaño en que se asienta el pie*)
tread; **huella dactilar** or **digital**
fingerprint; **huella de sonido** sound
track; **seguir las huellas de** to follow
in the footsteps of

huérfa·no -na *adj* orphan; orphaned;
alone, deserted ‖ *mf* orphan; (Chile,
Peru) foundling

hue·ro -ra *adj* rotten; (fig) empty, hollow; (Guat, Mex) blond; **salir huero**
(coll) to flop, to turn out bad ‖ *mf*
(Guat, Mex) blond

huerta *f* vegetable garden; fruit garden;
irrigated region

huerte·ro -ra *mf* (Arg, Peru) gardener

huerto *m* (*de árboles frutales*) orchard;
(*de verduras*) kitchen garden

huesa *f* grave

huesillo *m* (Chile, Peru) sun-dried
peach

hueso *m* bone; (*de ciertas frutas*)
stone, pit; drudgery; **a otro perro
con ese hueso** (coll) tell that to the
marines; **calarse hasta los huesos** to
get soaked to the skin; **hueso de la
alegría** crazy bone, funny bone;
hueso de la suerte wishbone; **hueso
duro de roer** (coll) a hard nut to
crack; **la sin hueso** (coll) the tongue;
no dejarle a uno un hueso sano (coll)
to beat someone up; (coll) to pick
someone to pieces; **no poder con sus
huesos** (coll) to be all in; **soltar la
sin hueso** (coll) to talk too much;
(coll) to pour forth insults; **tener los
huesos molidos** (coll) to be all fagged
out

hueso·so -sa *adj* bony

hués·ped -peda *mf* (*persona alojada en
casa ajena*) guest; (*persona que hos-
peda a otra en su casa*) host; (*mesonero*) innkeeper, host

hueste *f* followers; (*ejército*) army, host

huesu·do -da *adj* bony, big-boned

hueva *f* roe, fish roe

hueve·ro -ra *mf* egg dealer ‖ *f* eggcup;
oviduct

huevo *m* egg; **huevo a la plancha** fried
egg; **huevo al plato** shirred egg;
huevo del té tea ball; **huevo de zurcir**
darning egg or gourd; **huevo duro**
hard-boiled egg; **huevo escalfado**
poached egg; **huevo estrellado** or
frito fried egg; **huevo pasado por
agua** soft-boiled egg; **huevos revueltos** scrambled eggs

huída *f* flight; (*de un líquido*) leak;
(*ensanche en un agujero*) flare, splay;
(*de caballo*) shying

huidi·zo -za *adj* fugitive; evasive

huincha *f* (SAm) tape; (SAm) tape
measure

huipil *m* (Mex) colorful poncho worn
by Indian women

huir §20 *tr* to flee, avoid, shun; (*el
cuerpo*) to duck ‖ *intr* to flee; (*el
tiempo*) to fly; (*de la memoria*) to
slip ‖ *ref* to flee

hule *m* (*tela impermeable*) oilcloth;
rubber; (taur) blood, goring

hulear *intr* (CAm) to gather rubber

hulla *f* coal; **hulla azul** tide power; wind

power; **hulla blanca** white power,
water power

hullera *f* colliery, coal mine

humanidad *f* humanity; (coll) fatness

humanista *adj* & *mf* humanist

humanita·rio -ria *adj* & *mf* humanitarian

huma·no -na *adj* (*perteneciente al hombre*) human; (*compasivo, misericordioso; civilizador*) humane

humareda *f* cloud of smoke

humeante *adj* smoking, smoky; steamy;
reeking

humear *tr* (SAm) to fumigate ‖ *intr* to
smoke; to steam, to reek; to put on
airs; (*reliquias de un alboroto,
enemistad, etc.*) to last, persist

humectador *m* humidifier

humedad *f* humidity, dampness, moisture

humedecer §22 *tr* to humidify, dampen,
moisten, wet

húme·do -da *adj* humid, damp, moist

humero *m* smokestack, chimney

húmero *m* humerus

humildad *f* humility

humilde *adj* humble

humilladero *m* calvary, road shrine;
prie-dieu

humillante *adj* humiliating

humillar *tr* (*abatir el orgullo de*) to
humble; (*avergonzar*) to humiliate;
(*la cabeza*) to bow; (*el cuerpo, las
rodillas*) to bend ‖ *ref* to humble
oneself; to cringe, grovel

humo *m* smoke; steam, fume; **a humo
de pajas** (coll) lightly, thoughtlessly;
bajar los humos a (coll) to humble,
take down a peg; **echar más humo
que una chimenea** to smoke like a
chimney; **humos** airs, conceit;
hearths, homes; **irse todo en humo** to
go up in smoke; **tragar el humo** to
inhale; **vender humos** to peddle
influence

humor *m* humor; **de mal humor** out of
humor; **estar de humor para** to be
in the humor for; **seguir el humor a**
to humor

humorismo *m* humor, humorousness

humorista *mf* humorist

humorísti·co -ca *adj* humorous

humo·so -sa *adj* smoky

hundible *adj* sinkable

hundir *tr* to sink; to plunge; (*abrumar*)
to overwhelm; to confound, confute;
to destroy, ruin ‖ *ref* to sink; to collapse; to settle, cave in; to come to
ruin; (coll) to disappear, vanish

húnga·ro -ra *adj* & *mf* Hungarian ‖ *m*
(*idioma*) Hungarian

Hungría *f* Hungary

hupe *m* punk

huracán *m* hurricane

huraña *f* shyness, unsociability

hura·ño -ña *adj* shy, unsociable

hurgar §44 *tr* to poke; (fig) to stir up,
incite; **peor es hurgallo** (i.e., **hur-
garlo**) better keep hands off ‖ *intr* to
poke ‖ *ref* (*la nariz*) to pick

hurgón *m* poker; (coll) thrust, stab

hurgonazo *m* (*con hurgón*) poke; (coll)
jab, stab, thrust

hurgonear *tr* to poke; (coll) to jab, to stab at

hurgonero *m* poker

hu·rón -rona *adj* (coll) shy, diffident || *mf* (coll) prier, snooper; (coll) shy person, diffident person || *m* ferret

huronear *tr* to ferret, hunt with a ferret; (coll) to ferret out

huronera *f* ferret hole; (coll) lair, hiding place

hurtadillas — a hurtadillas by stealth, on the sly; **a hurtadillas de** unbeknown to

hurtar *tr* to steal; (*en pesos y medidas*) to cheat; (*el suelo*) to wear away; to plagiarize; **hurtar el cuerpo** to dodge, to duck || *ref* to withdraw, to hide

hurto *m* thieving; theft; **a hurto** stealthily, on the sly; **coger con el hurto en las manos** to catch with the goods

husma *f* snooping; **andar a la husma** to go around snooping

husmear *tr* to scent, to smell out; (coll) to pry into || *intr* (*la carne*) to smell bad, to become gamy

husmo *m* gaminess, high odor; **estar al husmo** (coll) to wait for a chance

huso *m* (*para hilar*) spindle; (*para devanar*) bobbin; (*cilindro del torno*) drum; **huso horario** time zone; **ser más derecho que un huso** (coll) to be as straight as a ramrod

huta *f* hunter's blind

huy *interj* ouch!

huyente *adj* (*frente*) receding; (*ojeada*) shifty

I

I, i (i) *f* tenth letter of the Spanish alphabet

ib. *abbr* **ibídem**

ibéri·co -ca *adj* Iberian

ibe·ro -ra *adj & mf* Iberian

íbice *m* ibex

ice·berg *m* (*pl* -bergs) iceberg

iconoclasia *f* or **iconoclasmo** *m* iconoclasm

iconoclasta *mf* iconoclast

iconoscopio *m* (telv) iconoscope

ictericia *f* jaundice

icterici·do -da *adj* jaundiced

ictiología *f* ichthyology

ida *f* going; departure; rashness; sally; trail; **de ida y vuelta** round-trip; **idas y venidas** comings and goings

idea *f* idea; **mudar de idea** to change one's mind

ideal *adj & m* ideal

idealista *adj & mf* idealist

idealizar $60 *tr* to idealize

idear *tr* to think up, to devise

idemista *adj* yes-saying || *mf* yes sayer

idénti·co -ca *adj* identic(al); (*muy parecido*) very similar

identidad *f* identity, sameness

identificación *f* identification

identificar $73 *tr* to identify

ideología *f* ideology

idíli·co -ca *adj* idyllic

idilio *m* idyll

idioma *m* language; (*modo particular de hablar*) idiom, speech

idiomáti·co -ca *adj* idiomatic; language, linguistic

idiosincrasia *f* idiosyncrasy

idiota *adj* idiotic || *mf* idiot

idiotez *f* idiocy

idiotismo *m* ignorance; (*idiotez*) idiocy; (gram) idiom

í·do -da *adj* wild, scatterbrained; (Am) drunk || **los idos** the dead || *f see* **ida**

idolatrar *tr* to idolize

idolatría *f* idolatry; (*amor excesivo a una persona*) idolization

ídolo *m* idol

idoneidad *f* fitness, suitability

idóne·o -a *adj* fit, suitable

idus *mpl* ides

iglesia *f* church; **entrar en la iglesia** to go into the church; **llevar a la iglesia** to lead to the altar

iglesie·ro -ra *adj* (Arg) church-going || *mf* (Arg) church goer

igna·ro -ra *adj* ignorant

ignominio·so -sa *adj* ignominious

ignorancia *f* ignorance

ignorante *adj* ignorant || *mf* ignoramus

ignorar *tr* to not know, be ignorant of

igno·to -ta *adj* unknown

igual *adj* equal; (*liso, llano*) smooth, even, level; (*no variable*) firm, constant, equable; indifferent; **me es igual** it makes no difference to me || *m* equal; equal sign; **al igual de** like, after the fashion of; **al igual que** as; while, whereas; **en igual de** instead of

iguala *f* equalization; agreement

igualación *f* equalization; agreement

igualar *tr* to equal; (*alisar, allanar*) to smooth, to even, to level; to make equal, to match; to deem equal || *intr & ref* to be equal

igualdad *f* equality; smoothness, evenness; **igualdad de ánimo** equanimity

igualmente *adv* likewise; **igualmente que** the same as

ijada *f* (*de animal*) flank; (*del cuerpo humano*) loin; (*dolor en estas partes*) stitch; **tener su ijada** to have its weak side or point

ijadear *intr* to pant

ijar *m* flank; loin

ilegal *adj* illegal

ilegible *adj* illegible

ilegíti·mo -ma *adj* illegitimate

ile·so -sa *adj* unscathed, unharmed

iletra·do -da *adj* unlettered, uncultured

ilíci·to -ta *adj* illicit, unlawful

ilimita·do -da *adj* limitless

ilitera·to -ta *adj* illiterate

ilógi·co -ca *adj* illogical

iludir *tr* to elude, evade

iluminación *f* illumination
iluminar *tr* to illuminate, light, light up || *ref* to light up, brighten
ilusión *f* illusion; (*esperanza infundada*) delusion; enthusiasm, zeal; dream; **forjarse** or **hacerse ilusiones** to kid oneself, to indulge in wishful thinking
ilusionar *tr* to delude || *ref* to have illusions, to indulge in wishful thinking; to be enraptured, be beguiled
ilusionista *mf* prestidigitator, magician
ilusi·vo -va *adj* illusive
ilu·so -sa *adj* deluded, misguided; (*propenso a ilusionarse*) visionary
iluso·rio -ria *adj* illusory
ilustración *f* illustration; enlightenment; illustrated magazine
ilustra·do -da *adj* illustrated; learned, informed; enlightened
ilustrar *tr* (*adornar con grabados alusivos al texto*) to illustrate; to make illustrious, make famous; to explain, elucidate; to enlighten || *ref* to become famous; to be enlightened
ilustre *adj* illustrious
imagen *f* image; picture
imaginación *f* imagination
imaginar *tr*, *intr* & *ref* to imagine
imagina·rio -ria *adj* imaginary
imaginati·vo -va *adj* imaginative || *f* imagination; understanding
imaginería *f* fancy colored embroidery; carving or painting of religious images
imán *m* magnet; (fig) loadstone; **imán de herradura** horseshoe magnet; **imán inductor** (elec) field magnet
imanar or **imantar** *tr* to magnetize
imbatible *adj* unbeatable
imbécil *adj* & *mf* imbecile
imbecilidad *f* imbecility
imberbe *adj* beardless
imbornal *m* drain hole
imborrable *adj* indelible; ineffaceable; unforgettable
imbuir §20 *tr* to imbue
imitación *adj* and *invar* imitation || *f* imitation; **a imitación de** in imitation of; **de imitación** imitation, fake
imita·do -da *adj* imitated; mock, sham; imitation
imitar *tr* to imitate
impaciencia *f* impatience
impacientar *tr* to make impatient || *ref* to get impatient
impaciente *adj* impatient
impacto *m* impact, hit; (*señal que deja el proyectil*) mark; **impacto directo** direct hit
impar *adj* odd, uneven; (*que no tiene igual*) unmatched || *m* odd number
imparcial *adj* impartial; (*que no entra en ningún partido*) nonpartisan
impartir *tr* to distribute, impart
impás *m* finesse
impasible *adj* impassible, impassive
impávi·do -da *adj* dauntless, fearless, intrepid
impecable *adj* impeccable
impedancia *f* impedance
impedi·do -da *adj* disabled, crippled, paralytic

impedimento *m* impediment, obstacle, hindrance
impedir §50 *tr* to hinder, prevent
impeler *tr* to impel; to spur, incite
impenetrable *adj* impenetrable
impenitente *adj* & *mf* impenitent
impensable *adj* unthinkable
impensa·do -da *adj* unexpected
imperar *intr* to rule, reign, command
imperati·vo -va *adj* & *m* imperative
imperceptible *adj* imperceptible
imperdible *m* safety pin
imperdonable *adj* unpardonable, unforgivable
imperecede·ro -ra *adj* imperishable, undying
imperfección *f* imperfection
imperfec·to -ta *adj* & *m* imperfect
imperial *adj* imperial || *f* imperial, roof (*of a coach or bus*)
imperialista *adj* & *mf* imperialist
impericia *f* unskillfulness, inexpertness
imperio *m* empire; dominion, sway
imperio·so -sa *adj* (*que manda con imperio*) imperious; (*indispensable*) imperative
imperi·to -ta *adj* unskilled, inexpert
impermeable *adj* impermeable; waterproof || *m* raincoat
impersonal *adj* impersonal
impertérri·to -ta *adj* dauntless, intrepid
impertinencia *f* impertinence; irrelevance; fussiness
impert·nente *adj* impertinent; (*que no viene al caso*) irrelevant; (*nimiamente susceptible*) fussy || **impertinentes** *mpl* lorgnette
impetrar *tr* to beg, beg for; to obtain by entreaty
ímpetu *m* impetus; force; haste
impetuo·so -sa *adj* impetuous
impiedad *f* (*falta de religión*) impiety; (*falta de compasión*) pitilessness
impí·o -a *adj* (*irreligioso*) impious; (*falto de compasión*) pitiless
impla *f* wimple
implacable *adj* relentless
implantar *tr* to implant; to introduce
implicar §73 *tr* (*envolver*) to implicate; (*incluir en esencia*) to imply || *intr* to stand in the way
implíci·to -ta *adj* implicit, implied
implorar *tr* to implore
implume *adj* featherless
imponente *adj* imposing || *mf* depositor, investor
imponer §54 *tr* (*la voluntad de uno, silencio, tributos*) to impose; (*dinero a rédito*) to invest; (*dinero en depósito*) to deposit; to instruct; to impute falsely || *intr* to dominate, command respect || *ref* (*responsabilidades*) to assume; to command attention, command respect; **imponerse a** to dominate, command the respect of; **imponerse de** to learn, to find out
imponible *adj* taxable
impopular *adj* unpopular
impopularidad *f* unpopularity
importación *f* importation; import; imports
importa·dor -dora *mf* importer
importancia *f* importance; (*extensión,*

tamaño) size; **ser de la importancia de** to be the concern of
importante *adj* important; large
importar *tr* (*introducir en un país*) to import; to amount to; to involve, imply; to concern ‖ *intr* to import; to be important; to matter
importe *m* amount
importunar *tr* to importune
importu·no **-na** *adj* (*molesto*) importunate; (*fuera de sazón*) inopportune
imposibilita·do **-da** *adj* paralyzed, disabled
imposibilitar *tr* to make impossible ‖ *ref* to become paralyzed, become disabled
imposible *adj* impossible
imposición *f* (*de la voluntad de uno*) imposition; burden; imposture; (*de dinero*) deposit; (*typ*) make-up
impos·tor **-tora** *mf* impostor; slanderer
impostura *f* imposture
impotable *adj* undrinkable
impotencia *f* impotence
impotente *adj* impotent
impracticable *adj* impracticable, impassable; impractical
impregnar *tr* to impregnate, to saturate
impremedita·do **-da** *adj* unpremeditated
imprenta *f* printing; printing shop; (*lo que se publica impreso*) printed matter; (*máquina para imprimir o prensar; conjunto de periódicos o periodistas*) press
imprentar *tr* (*la ropa*) (Chile) to press, to iron; (Ecuad) to mark
imprescindible *adj* indispensable, essential
impresentable *adj* unpresentable
impresión *f* (*efecto producido en el ánimo; señal que una cosa deja en otra por presión*) impression; (*acción de imprimir*) printing; (*los ejemplares de una edición*) edition, issue; (phot) print; **impresión dactilar** or **digital** fingerprint
impresionable *adj* impressionable
impresionante *adj* impressive
impresionar *tr* to impress; (*un disco fonográfico*) to record; (phot) to expose ‖ *intr* to make an impression ‖ *ref* to be impressed
impreso *m* printed paper or book; **impresos** printed matter
impre·sor **-sora** *mf* printer
imprevisible *adj* unforeseeable
imprevisión *f* improvidence, lack of foresight
imprevi·sor **-sora** *adj* improvident
imprevis·to **-ta** *adj* unforeseen, unexpected ‖ **imprevistos** *mpl* emergencies, unforeseen expenses
imprimar *tr* to prime
imprimir *tr* (*respeto, miedo; movimiento*) to impart ‖ §83 *tr* to stamp, imprint, impress; (*un disco fonográfico*) to press; (typ) to print
improbable *adj* improbable
improbar §61 *tr* to disapprove
improbidad *f* dishonesty; hardness, arduousness
impro·bo **-ba** *adj* dishonest; (*trabajo*) arduous

improcedente *adj* wrong; unfit, untimely
improducti·vo **-va** *adj* unproductive; unemployed
impronunciable *adj* unpronounceable
improperar *tr* to insult, revile
improperio *m* insult, affront
impropi·cio **-cia** *adj* unpropitious
impro·pio **-pia** *adj* improper; (*ajeno*) foreign
impróspe·ro **-ra** *adj* unsuccessful
impróvi·do **-da** *adj* unprepared
improvisación *f* improvisation; meteoric rise; (mus) impromptu
improvisadamente *adv* suddenly, unexpectedly; extempore
improvisar *tr* & *intr* to improvise
improvi·so **-sa** *adj* unforeseen, unexpected
imprudencia *f* imprudence; **imprudencia temeraria** criminal negligence
imprudente *adj* imprudent
impudicia *f* immodesty
impúdi·co **-ca** *adj* immodest
impues·to **-ta** *adj* informed ‖ *m* tax; **impuesto sobre la renta** income tax
impugnar *tr* to impugn, to contest
impulsar *tr* to impel; to drive
impulsión *f* impulse, drive
impulsi·vo **-va** *adj* impulsive
impulso *m* impulse
impune *adj* unpunished
impunidad *f* impunity
impureza *f* impurity
impu·ro **-ra** *adj* impure
imputar *tr* to impute; to credit on account
inabordable *adj* unapproachable
inacabable *adj* endless, interminable
inaccesible *adj* inaccessible
inacción *f* inaction
inacentua·do **-da** *adj* unaccented
inactividad *f* inactivity
inacti·vo **-va** *adj* inactive
inadecua·do **-da** *adj* inadequate; unsuited
inadvertencia *f* inadvertence, oversight
inadverti·do **-da** *adj* inadvertent, unwitting; careless, thoughtless; unseen, unnoticed
inagotable *adj* inexhaustible
inaguantable *adj* unbearable
inalámbri·co **-ca** *adj* wireless
inalcanzable *adj* unattainable
inamisto·so **-sa** *adj* unfriendly
inamovible *adj* irremovable; undetachable; (*incorporado*) built-in
inamovilidad *f* irremovability; tenure, permanent tenure
inane *adj* inane
inanición *f* starvation
inanima·do **-da** *adj* inanimate, lifeless
inapelable *adj* unappealable; unavoidable
inapetencia *f* loss of appetite
inapreciable *adj* inappreciable; imperceptible
inarmóni·co **-ca** *adj* unharmonious
inarrugable *adj* wrinkle-free
inarticula·do **-da** *adj* inarticulate
inartísti·co **-ca** *adj* inartistic
inasequible *adj* unattainable; unobtainable

inastillable *adj* nonshatterable, shatter-proof

inatacable *adj* unattackable; **inatacable por** resistant to

inaudi·to -ta *adj* unheard-of; outrageous

inauguración *f* inauguration; (*de una estatua*) unveiling

inaugural *adj* inaugural

inaugurar *tr* to inaugurate; (*p.ej., una estatua*) to unveil

inaveriguable *adj* unascertainable

inca *mf* Inca

incai·co -ca *adj* Inca, Incan

incalificable *adj* unqualifiable; (*infame, atroz*) unspeakable

incambiable *adj* unchangeable

incandescente *adj* incandescent

incansable *adj* untiring, indefatigable

incapacitar *tr* to incapacitate; (*law*) to declare incompetent

inca·paz *adj* (*pl* **-paces**) incapable, unable; not large enough; stupid; (*law*) incompetent; (*coll*) frightful, unbearable

incasable *adj* unmarriageable; opposed to marriage; (*por su fealdad*) unable to find a husband

incautar *ref* — **incautarse de** to hold until claimed; (*law*) to seize, to attach

incau·to -ta *adj* unwary, heedless

incendajas *fpl* kindling

incendiar *tr* to set on fire ‖ *ref* to catch fire

incendia·rio -ria *adj* incendiary ‖ *mf* incendiary, firebug

incendio *m* fire; (fig) fire, passion

incensar §2 *tr* to incense, to burn incense before; (fig) to flatter

incensario *m* censer, incense burner

incenti·vo -va *adj & m* incentive

inceremonio·so -sa *adj* unceremonious

incertidumbre *f* uncertainty, incertitude

incesante *adj* unceasing

incesto *m* incest

incestuo·so -sa *adj* incestuous

incidencia *f* incidence; **por incidencia** by chance

incidente *adj* incident; incidental ‖ *m* incident

incidir *tr* to make an incision in ‖ *intr* — **incidir en culpa** to fall into guilt; **incidir en** or **sobre** to strike, to impinge on

incienso *m* incense; (*olíbano*) frankincense

incier·to -ta *adj* uncertain

incineración *f* incineration; (*de cadáveres*) cremation

incinerar *tr* to incinerate; (*cadáveres*) to cremate

incipiente *adj* incipient

incisión *f* incision; (*mordacidad en el lenguaje*) incisiveness, sarcasm

incisi·vo -va *adj* incisive; biting, sarcastic

inci·so -sa *adj* (*estilo del escritor*) choppy ‖ *m* comma; clause; sentence

incitar *tr* to incite

incivil *adj* rude, impolite

incivilizu·do -da *adj* uncivilized

inclemencia *f* inclemency; **a la inclemencia** in the open, without shelter

inclemente *adj* inclement

inclinación *f* inclination; bent, leaning, propensity; nod, bow

inclinar *tr, intr & ref* to incline; to bend, to bow

incli·to -ta *adj* illustrious, renowned

incluir §20 *tr* to include; (*en una carta*) to inclose

inclusa *f* foundling home

incluse·ro -ra *mf* (coll) foundling

inclusión *f* inclusion; friendship

inclusive *adv* inclusive, inclusively ‖ *prep* including

inclusi·vo -va *adj* inclusive

inclu·so -sa *adj* inclosed ‖ *f* see **inclusa** ‖ **incluso** *adv* inclusively; (*hasta, aun*) even ‖ **incluso** *prep* including

incobrable *adj* uncollectible; irrecoverable

incógni·to -ta *adj* (*no conocido*) unknown; (*que no se da a conocer*) incognito ‖ *mf* (*persona*) incognito ‖ *m* (*condición de no ser conocido*) incognito; **de incógnito** (*sin ser conocido*) incognito ‖ *f* (math & fig) unknown quantity

incoherente *adj* incoherent

íncola *m* inhabitant

incolo·ro -ra *adj* colorless

incólume *adj* unharmed, safe

incombustible *adj* incombustible, fireproof; cold, indifferent

incomerciable *adj* unmarketable

incomible *adj* uneatable, inedible

incomodar *tr* to inconvenience, to disturb

incomodidad *f* inconvenience; annoyance, discomfort

incómo·do -da *adj* inconvenient; annoying, uncomfortable ‖ *m* inconvenience; discomfort

incomparable *adj* incomparable

incompartible *adj* unsharable

incompasi·vo -va *adj* pitiless, unsympathetic

incompatible *adj* incompatible; (*acontecimientos, citas, horas de clase, etc.*) conflicting

incompetente *adj* incompetent

incompetible *adj* unmatchable

incomple·to -ta *adj* incomplete

incomponible *adj* unmendable, beyond repair

incomprable *adj* unpurchasable

incomprensible *adj* incomprehensible

incomunicación *f* isolation, solitary confinement

inconcebible *adj* inconceivable

inconclu·so -sa *adj* unfinished

inconcluyente *adj* inconclusive

inconcu·so -sa *adj* undeniable

incondicional *adj* unconditional

incone·xo -xa *adj* unconnected; (*inaplicable*) irrelevant

inconfidente *adj* distrustful

inconfundible *adj* unmistakable

incon·gruo -grua *adj* incongruous

inconocible *adj* unknowable

inconquistable *adj* unconquerable; (*que no se deja vencer con ruegos y dádivas*) unbending, unyielding

inconsciencia *f* unconsciousness; unawareness

inconsciente adj unconscious; unaware; **lo inconsciente** the unconscious

inconsecuencia f (falta de consecuencia o correspondencia en dichos y hechos) inconsistency

inconsecuente adj inconsistent; (que no se deduce de otra cosa) inconsequential

inconsidera·do -da adj inconsiderate

inconsiguiente adj inconsequential, illogical

inconsistencia f (falta de cohesión) inconsistency

inconsistente adj inconsistent

inconsolable adj inconsolable

inconstante adj inconstant

inconstitucional adj unconstitutional

inconsútil adj seamless

incontable adj countless, innumerable

incontenible adj irrepressible

incontestable adj incontestable

incontinente adj incontinent ‖ adv at once, instantly

incontrastable adj invincible; inconvincible; (argumento) unanswerable

incontrovertible adj incontrovertible

inconveniencia f inconvenience; unsuitability; impoliteness; impropriety

inconveniente adj inconvenient; unsuitable; impolite; improper ‖ m drawback, disadvantage; objection

incordio m (coll) bore, nuisance

incorporación f incorporation, embodiment

incorpora·do -da adj (el que estaba echado) sitting up; (montado en la construcción) built-in

incorporar tr to incorporate, embody ‖ ref to incorporate; (el que estaba echado) to sit up; **incorporarse a** to join

incorrec·to -ta adj incorrect

incrédu·lo -la adj incredulous ‖ mf disbeliever, doubter

increíble adj incredible

incremento m increment, increase

increpar tr to chide, to rebuke

incriminar tr to incriminate; (un delito, falta, defecto) to exaggerate the gravity of

incruen·to -ta adj bloodless

incrustar tr to incrust; (embutir por adorno) to inlay

incubadora f incubator

incubar tr & intr to incubate ‖ ref (fig) to be brewing

incuestionable adj unquestionable

inculcar §73 tr to inculcate ‖ ref to become obstinate

inculpable adj blameless, guiltless

inculpar tr to accuse, to blame

incultivable adj untillable

incul·to -ta adj uncultivated, untilled; uncultured; (estilo) coarse, sloppy

incumbencia f incumbency, duty, obligation, province

incumbir intr — **incumbir a** to be incumbent on

incumplimiento m nonfulfillment

incunable m incunabulum

incurable adj & mf incurable

incuria f carelessness, negligence

incurio·so -sa adj careless, negligent

incurrir intr — **incurrir en** to incur

incursión f incursion, inroad, raid

indagación f investigation, research

indagar §44 tr to investigate

indebidamente adv unduly

indebi·do -da adj undue; wrong

indecencia f indecency

indecente adj indecent

indecible adj unspeakable, unutterable

indeci·so -sa adj undecided, indecisive; (contorno, forma) vague, obscure

indeclinable adj unavoidable; (gram) indeclinable

indecoro·so -sa adj improper

indefectible adj unfailing

indefendible adj indefensible

indefen·so -sa adj defenceless, undefended

indefinible adj indefinable

indefini·do -da adj indefinite; limitless; vague

indeleble adj indelible

indelibera·do -da adj unpremeditated

indelica·do -da adj indelicate

indemne adj unharmed, undamaged

indemnidad f (seguridad contra un daño) indemnity

indemnización f (compensación) indemnity, indemnification; **indemnización por despido** severance pay

indemnizar §60 tr to indemnify

independencia f independence

independiente adj & mf independent

independizar §60 tr to free, to emancipate ‖ ref to become independent

indescriptible adj indescribable

indeseable adj & mf undesirable

indesea·do -da adj unwanted

indesmallable adj runproof

indestructible adj indestructible

indetermina·do -da adj indeterminate; (gram) indefinite

indevo·to -ta adj impious; not fond, not devoted

India f wealth, riches; **Indias Occidentales** West Indies; **la India** India

indiana f printed calico

india·no -na adj & mf Spanish American; East Indian; West Indian ‖ m man back from America with great wealth; **indiano de hilo negro** (coll) skinflint ‖ f see **indiana**

indicación f indication; **por indicación de** at the direction of

indica·do -da adj appropriate, advisable; **muy indicado** just the thing, just the person

indica·dor -dora adj indicating, pointing ‖ m indicator; gauge; (de tránsito) traffic signal

indicar §73 tr to indicate

indicati·vo -va adj & m indicative

índice m index; **índice de libros prohibidos** (eccl) Index; **índice de materias** table of contents; **índice en el corte** thumb index

indiciar tr to betoken, indicate; to surmise, suspect

indicio m sign, token, indication; **indicios vehementes** circumstantial evidence

indiferente adj indifferent; (que no importa) immaterial

indígena *adj* indigenous || *mf* native
indigente *adj* indigent
indigestar *ref* to be indigestible; (coll) to be disliked, to be unbearable
indigestible *adj* indigestible
indigestión *f* indigestion
indignación *f* indignation
indigna·do -da *adj* indignant
indignar *tr* to anger, to provoke || *ref* to become indignant
indignidad *f* (*falta de mérito*) unworthiness; (*acción reprobable*) indignity
indig·no -na *adj* unworthy
índigo *m* indigo
in·dio -dia *adj* & *mf* Indian || *f* see **india**
indirec·to -ta *adj* indirect || *f* hint, innuendo; **indirecta del padre Cobos** broad hint
indiscernible *adj* indiscernible
indiscre·to -ta *adj* indiscreet
indisculpable *adj* inexcusable
indiscutible *adj* undeniable
indisoluble *adj* indissoluble
indispensable *adj* unpardonable; indispensable
indisponer §54 *tr* (*alterar la salud de*) to indispose, upset; to disturb, to upset; **indisponer a uno con** to set someone against, to prejudice someone against || *ref* to become indisposed; **indisponerse con** to fall out with
indisponible *adj* unavailable
indispues·to -ta *adj* indisposed
indistintamente *adv* indistinctly; indiscriminately, without distinction
indistin·to -ta *adj* indistinct
individual *adj* individual; (*habitación en un hotel; partido de tenis*) single
individualidad *f* individuality
indivi·duo -dua *adj* individual; indivisible || *mf* (*persona indeterminada*) (coll) individual || *m* (*cada persona*) individual; (*miembro de una corporación*) member, fellow
indócil *adj* unteachable; headstrong, unruly
indocumenta·do -da *adj* unidentified; unqualified || *mf* nobody (*person of no account*)
indochi·no -na *adj* & *mf* Indo-Chinese || **la Indochina** Indochina
indoeurope·o -a *adj* & *m* Indo-European
índole *f* kind, class; nature, disposition, temper
indolente *adj* stolid, impassive; (*perezoso*) indolent
indolo·ro -ra *adj* painless
indoma·do -da *adj* untamed
indone·sio -sia *adj* & *mf* Indonesian || **la Indonesia** Indonesia
inducción *f* induction
inducido *m* (*de dínamo o motor*) (elec) armature
inducir §19 *tr* to induce
inductor *m* (*de dínamo o motor*) (elec) field
indudable *adj* doubtless
indulgente *adj* indulgent
indultar *tr* to pardon; to free, exempt
indulto *m* pardon; exemption

indumentaria *f* clothing, dress; historical study of clothing
indumento *m* clothing, dress
industria *f* industry; **de industria** on purpose
industrial *adj* industrial || *m* industrialist
industrializar §60 *tr* to industrialize
industriar *tr* to teach, instruct, train || *ref* to get along, to manage
industrio·so -sa *adj* industrious
inédi·to -ta *adj* unpublished; new, novel, unknown
inefable *adj* ineffable
ineficacia *f* inefficacy
inefi·caz *adj* (*pl* -caces) inefficacious, ineffectual
inelegible *adj* ineligible
ineludible *adj* inescapable
inen·rr..ble *adj* indescribable
inencogible *adj* unshrinkable
inencontr..ble *adj* unobtainable
inequidad *f* inequity
inequívo·co -ca *adj* unmistakable
inerci.. *f* inertia
inerme *adj* unarmed
inerte *adj* inert; slow, sluggish
inescrupulo·so -sa *adj* unscrupulous
inescrutable or **inescudriñable** *adj* inscrutable
inespera·do -da *adj* unexpected, unforeseen; unhoped-for
inestable *adj* unstable
inevitable *adj* unavoidable, inevitable
inexactitud *f* inaccuracy, inexactness
inexac·to -ta *adj* inaccurate, inexact
inexcusable *adj* inexcusable, unpardonable; unavoidable; indispensable
inexorable *adj* inexorable
inexperiencia *f* inexperience
inexplicable *adj* inexplicable, unexplainable
inexplica·do -da *adj* unexplained, unaccounted-for
inexplora·do -da *adj* unexplored; (mar) uncharted
inexpresable *adj* inexpressible
inexpues·to -ta *adj* (phot) unexposed
inexpugnable *adj* impregnable; firm, unshakable
inextinguible *adj* unextinguishable; perpetual, lasting; (sed) unquenchable; (risa) uncontrollable
inextirpable *adj* ineradicable
infalible *adj* infallible
infamación *f* defamation
infamar *tr* to defame, discredit
infame *adj* infamous; (coll) vile, frightful || *mf* scoundrel
infamia *f* infamy
infancia *f* infancy
infan·do -da *adj* odious, unmentionable
infanta *f* female child; infanta (*any daughter of a king of Spain; wife of an infante*)
infante *m* male child; infante (*any son of a king of Spain who is not heir to the throne*); (mil) infantryman; **infante de coro** choirboy
infantería *f* infantry; **infantería de marina** m rines, marine corps
infantil *adj* infant, infantile, childlike; innocent

infatigable *adj* indefatigable
infatuar §21 *tr* to make vain ‖ *ref* to become vain
infaus·to -ta *adj* fatal, unlucky
infección *f* infection
infeccionar *tr* to infect
infeccio·so -sa *adj* infectious
infectar *tr* to infect
infec·to -ta *adj* foul, corrupt; infected; fetid
infecun·do -da *adj* sterile, barren
infe·liz (*pl* **-lices**) *adj* unhappy; (coll) simple, good-hearted ‖ *m* wretch, poor soul
inferior *adj* inferior; lower; **inferior a** inferior to; lower than; less than; smaller than ‖ *m* inferior
inferioridad *f* inferiority
inferir §68 *tr* to infer; to lead to, to entail; (*una herida*) to inflict; (*una ofensa*) to cause, offer
infernáculo *tr* hopscotch
infernal *adj* infernal
infernar §2 *tr* to damn; to irritate, annoy
infernillo *m* chafing dish
infestar *tr* infest ‖ *ref* to become infested
inficionar *tr* to infect ‖ *ref* to become infected
infidelidad *f* infidelity; (*conjunto de infieles*) unbelievers
infidente *adj* faithless, disloyal
infiel (*falto de fidelidad*) unfaithful; (*no exacto*) inaccurate, inexact; (*no cristiano*) infidel ‖ *mf* infidel
infierno *m* hell; **en el quinto infierno** or **en los quintos infiernos** (coll) far, far away
infijo *m* (gram) infix
infiltrar *tr & ref* to infiltrate
infi·mo -ma *adj* lowest; humblest, most abject; meanest, vilest
infinidad *f* infinity
infiniti·vo -va *adj & m* infinitive
infini·to -ta *adj* infinite ‖ *m* infinite; (math) infinity ‖ **infinito** *adv* greatly, very much
infirme *adj* infirm
inflación *f* inflation; (*vanidad*) conceit
inflado *m* inflation (*of a tire*)
inflamable *adj* inflammable, flammable
inflamación *f* ignition, inflammation; ardor, enthusiasm; (pathol) inflammation
inflamar *tr* to set on fire; to inflame ‖ *ref* to catch fire; to become inflamed
inflar *tr* to inflate; to exaggerate; to puff up with pride ‖ *ref* to inflate; to be puffed up with pride
inflexible *adj* inflexible; unyielding, unbending
inflexión *f* inflection; **inflexión vocálica** (*metafonía*) umlaut
inflexionar *tr* to umlaut
infligir §27 *tr* to inflict
influencia *f* influence
influenciar *tr* to influence
influenza *f* influenza
influir §20 *intr* to have influence; to have great weight; **influir en** or **sobre** to influence
influjo *m* influence; rising tide

influyente *adj* influential
información *f* information; (law) judicial inquiry, investigation; **informaciones testimonial**
informal *adj* (*que no se ajusta a las reglas debidas*) informal; unreliable
informar *tr & intr* to inform ‖ *ref* to inquire, find out
informati·vo -va *adj* informational; (*sección de un periódico*) news
informe *adj* shapeless, formless; misshapen ‖ *m* piece of information; report; **informes** information; **informes confidenciales** inside information
infortuna·do -da *adj* unfortunate, unlucky
infortunio *m* misfortune; (*acaecimiento desgraciado*) mishap
infracción *f* infraction, infringement
infraconsumo *m* underconsumption
infrac·to -ta *adj* unperturbable
infraestructura *f* substructure; (rr) roadbed
inframundo *m* underworld
infrarro·jo -ja *adj & m* infrared
infrascri·to -ta *adj* undersigned; hereinafter mentioned
infrecuente *adj* infrequent
infringir §27 *tr* to infringe, to break, to violate
infructuo·so -sa *adj* fruitless, unfruitful
ínfulas *fpl* conceit, airs; **darse ínfulas** to put on airs
infunda·do -da *adj* unfounded, groundless, baseless
infundio *m* (coll) lie, fib
infundir *tr* to infuse, to instill
infusión *f* infusion; (*acción de echar agua sobre el que se bautiza*) sprinkling; **estar en infusión para** (coll) to be all set for
ingeniar *tr* to think up ‖ *ref* to manage; **ingeniarse a** or **para** to manage to; **ingeniarse para ir viviendo** to manage to get along
ingeniería *f* engineering
ingeniero *m* engineer; **ingeniero de caminos, canales y puertos** government civil engineer
ingenio *m* talent, creative faculty; talented person; cleverness, skill, wit; (*artificio mecánico*) apparatus, device; (*del encuadernador*) paper cutter; engine of war; **afilar** or **aguzar el ingenio** to sharpen one's wits; **ingenio de azúcar** sugar refinery
ingeniosidad *f* ingenuity; wittiness
ingenio·so -sa *adj* (*dotado de ingenio; hecho con ingenio*) ingenious; (*agudo, sutil*) witty
ingéni·to -ta *adj* innate, inborn
ingente *adj* huge, enormous
ingenuidad *f* ingenuousness
inge·nuo -nua *adj* ingenuous
ingerir §68 *tr & ref* var of **injerir**
Inglaterra *f* England; **la Nueva Inglaterra** New England
ingle *f* groin
in·glés -glesa *adj* English; **a la inglesa** in the English manner ‖ *m* Englishman; (*idioma*) English; **el inglés medio** Middle English; **los ingleses** the English ‖ *f* Englishwoman

ingramatical *adj* ungrammatical

ingratitud *f* ingratitude, ungratefulness

ingra·to -ta *adj* (*desagradecido*) ungrateful; (*desagradecido; desagradable, áspero; improductivo*) thankless ‖ *mf* ingrate

ingravidez *f* lightness, tenuousness; (*gravedad nula*) weightlessness

ingrávi·do -da *adj* light, tenuous; weightless

ingrediente *m* ingredient

ingresa·do -da *mf* new student

ingresar *tr* to deposit ‖ *intr* to enter, become a member; (*beneficios*) to come in ‖ *ref* (Mex) to enlist

ingreso *m* entrance; admission; **ingresos** income, revenue

ingri·mo -ma *adj* (Am) solitary, alone

inhábil *adj* unable; unskillful; unfit, unqualified

inhabilidad *f* inability; unskillfulness; unfitness

inhabilitar *tr* to disable, to disqualify, to incapacitate

inhabita·do -da *adj* uninhabited

inhabitua·do -da *adj* unaccustomed

inherente *adj* inherent

inhibir *tr* to inhibit

inhospitala·rio -ria *adj* inhospitable

inhóspi·to -ta *adj* inhospitable

inhumanidad *f* inhumanity

inhuma·no -na *adj* inhuman, inhumane; (Chile) filthy

iniciación *f* initiation

inicial *adj & f* initial

iniciar *tr* to initiate ‖ *ref* to be initiated

iniciativa *f* initiative

ini·cuo -cua *adj* wicked, iniquitous

iguala·do -da *adj* unequaled

ininteligente *adj* unintelligent

ininteligible *adj* unintelligible

ininterrumpi·do -da *adj* uninterrupted

iniquidad *f* iniquity

injerencia *f* interference, meddling

injerir §68 *tr* to insert, introduce; (hort) to graft; (*alimentos*) (Am) to take in ‖ *ref* to interfere, meddle, intrude

injertar *tr* (hort & surg) to graft

injerto *m* (hort & surg) graft

injuria *f* offense, insult; abuse, wrong; damage, harm

injuriar *tr* to offend, insult; to abuse, to wrong; to harm, damage

injurio·so -sa *adj* offensive, insulting; abusive; harmful; (*lenguaje*) profane

injusticia *f* injustice

injustifica·do -da *adj* unjustified

injus·to -ta *adj* unjust

inmacula·do -da *adj* immaculate

inmanejable *adj* unmanageable; unhandy

inmarcesible *adj* unfading

inmaterial *adj* immaterial

inmaturo -ra *adj* immature

inmediación *f* immediacy; proximity; nearness; **inmediaciones** neighborhood, outskirts

inmediatamente *adv* immediately; **inmediatamente que** as soon as

inmedia·to -ta *adj* immediate; close, adjoining, next; next above; next below; (*pago*) prompt; **venir a las in-**

mediatas (coll) to get into the thick of the fight

inmejorable *adj* superb, unsurpassable

inmemorial *adj* immemorial

inmen·so -sa *adj* immense

inmensurable *adj* immesurable

inmereci·do -da *adj* undeserved

inmergir §27 *tr* to immerse

inmersión *f* immersion

inmigración *f* immigration

inmigrante *mf* immigrant

inmigrar *intr* to immigrate

inminente *adj* imminent

inmiscuir §20 & regular *tr* to mix ‖ *ref* to meddle, to interfere

inmobilia·rio -ria *adj* real-estate

inmoble *adj* motionless; firm, constant

inmodera·do -da *adj* immoderate

inmodes·to -ta *adj* immodest

inmódi·co -ca *adj* excessive

inmoral *adj* immoral

inmortal *adj* immortal, deathless ‖ *mf* immortal

inmortalizar §60 *tr* to immortalize

inmovilizar §60 *tr* to immobilize; (*un caudal*) to tie up

inmueble *m* property, piece of real estate; **inmuebles** real estate

inmun·do -da *adj* dirty, filthy

inmune *adj* immune

inmunizar §60 *tr* to immunize

inmutar *tr* to change, alter; to disturb, upset ‖ *ref* to change, alter; to change countenance; **sin inmutarse** without batting an eye

inna·to -ta *adj* innate, inborn; natural

innatural *adj* unnatural

innavegable *adj* (*río*) unnavigable; (*embarcación*) unseaworthy

innecesa·rio -ria *adj* unnecessary

innegable *adj* undeniable

innoble *adj* ignoble

inno·cuo -cua *adj* harmless

innovación *f* innovation

innovar *tr* to innovate

innumerable *adj* innumerable

inocencia *f* innocence

inocentada *f* (coll) simpleness; (coll) blunder; (Ecuad) April Fools' joke

inocente *adj & mf* innocent; **coger por inocente** to make an April fool of

inocen·tón -tona *adj* (coll) simple, gullible ‖ *mf* (coll) gull, dupe

inoculación *f* inoculation

inocular *tr* to inoculate; to contaminate, to pervert

inodo·ro -ra *adj* odorless ‖ *m* deodorizer; (*excusado que funciona con agua corriente*) toilet

inofensi·vo -va *adj* inoffensive

inolvidable *adj* unforgettable

inope *adj* impecunious

inopia *f* indigence

inoportu·no -na *adj* inopportune, untimely

inorgáni·co -ca *adj* inorganic

inortodo·xo -xa *adj* unorthodox

inoxidable *adj* (*acero*) stainless; inoxidizable

inquietante *adj* disquieting, upsetting

inquietar *tr* to disquiet, to worry; to stir up, excite

inquie·to -ta *adj* anxious, worried

inquietud *f* disquiet, worry, concern
inquili·no -na *mf* tenant, renter
inquina *f* aversion, dislike, ill will
inquirir §40 *tr* to inquire, inquire into
inquisición *f* inquiry; inquisition
insabible *adj* unknowable
insaciable *adj* insatiable
insania *f* insanity
insa·no -na *adj* insane; imprudent
insatisfe·cho -cha *adj* unsatisfied
inscribir §83 *tr* to inscribe; (law) to record ‖ *ref* to enroll, register
inscripción *f* inscription; enrollment, registration
insecticida *adj* & *m* insecticide
insecto *m* insect
insegu·ro -ra *adj* insecure, unsafe; uncertain
insensa·to -ta *adj* foolish, stupid
insensible *adj* callous, hard-hearted, unfeeling; imperceptible
inseparable *adj* inseparable; undetachable ‖ *mf* inseparable ‖ *m* lovebird
insepul·to -ta *adj* unburied
inserción *f* insertion
inserir §68 *tr* to insert; (*injertar*) to graft, engraft
insertar *tr* to insert
inservible *adj* useless
insidia *f* snare, ambush; plotting
insidiar *tr* to ambush, to waylay; to trap, to trick
insidio·so -sa *adj* insidious
insigne *adj* noted, famous, renowned
insignia *f* badge, decoration, insignia; banner, standard
insignificante *adj* insignificant
insince·ro -ra *adj* insincere
insinuación *f* insinuation, hint
insinuante *adj* engaging, slick, crafty
insinuar §21 *tr* to insinuate; to suggest, to hint at ‖ *ref* to creep in, to slip in; to ingratiate oneself; to flow, to run; **insinuarse en** to work one's way in
insípi·do -da *adj* insipid, vapid
insistir *intr* to insist
insi·to -ta *adj* inbred, innate
insociable *adj* unsociable
insolencia *f* insolence
insolentar *tr* to make insolent ‖ *ref* to become insolent
insolente *adj* insolent
insóli·to -ta *adj* unusual
insoluble *adj* insoluble
insolvencia *f* insolvency
insomne *adj* sleepless
insomnio *m* insomnia
insondable *adj* fathomless; inscrutable
insonorizar §60 *tr* to soundproof
insono·ro -ra *adj* soundproof
insospecha·do -da *adj* unsuspected
insostenible *adj* untenable
inspección *f* inspection; inspectorship
inspeccionar *tr* to inspect
inspiración *f* inspiration; inhalation
inspirante *adj* inspiring
inspirar *tr* & *intr* to inspire; (*atraer a los pulmones*) to inhale, to breathe in ‖ *ref* to be inspired
instalación *f* plant, factory; outfit, equipment; arrangements, fittings; installment; **instalación sanitaria** plumbing

instalar *tr* to install ‖ *ref* to settle
instantáne·o -a *adj* instantaneous ‖ *f* snapshot
instante *m* instant, moment; **al instante** right away, immediately; **por instantes** uninterruptedly; any time
instantemente *adv* insistently, urgently
instar *tr* to press, to urge ‖ *intr* to be pressing, to be urgent
instaurar *tr* to restore; to reëstablish
instigar §44 *tr* to instigate
instilar *tr* to instill
instinti·vo -va *adj* instinctive
instinto *m* instinct
institución *f* institution; **instituciones** (*de un Estado*) constitution; (*de una ciencia, arte, etc.*) principles
instituir §20 *tr* to institute, found
instituto *m* institute; (*de una orden religiosa*) rule, constitution; **instituto de segunda enseñanza** or **de enseñanza media** high school
institu·triz *f* (*pl* -**trices**) governess
instrucción *f* instruction; education
instructi·vo -va *adj* instructive
instruc·tor -tora *mf* teacher, instructor ‖ *m* (mil) drillmaster ‖ *f* instructress
instruí·do -da *adj* well-educated; well-posted
instruir §20 *tr* to instruct; (*un proceso o expediente*) to draw up
instrumentar *tr* to instrument
instrumentista *mf* instrumentalist
instrumento *m* instrument; (*persona que se emplea para alcanzar un resultado*) tool; **instrumento de cuerda** (mus) stringed instrument; **instrumento de viento** (mus) wind instrument
insubordina·do -da *adj* insubordinate
insubstituíble *adj* irreplaceable
insudar *intr* to drudge
insuficiente *adj* insufficient
insufrible *adj* insufferable
insula *f* island; one-horse town
insular *adj* insular ‖ *mf* islander
insulina *f* insulin
insulsez *f* tastelessness; dullness, heaviness
insul·so -sa *adj* tasteless; dull, heavy
insultar *tr* to insult ‖ *ref* to faint, swoon
insulto *m* insult; fainting spell
insume *adj* expensive
insumergible *adj* unsinkable
insuperable *adj* insurmountable
insurgente *adj* & *mf* insurgent
insurrección *f* insurrection
intac·to -ta *adj* intact, untouched
intachable *adj* blameless, irreproachable
integración *f* integration
integridad *f* integrity; virginity
ínte·gro -gra *adj* integral, whole; honest
intelecto *m* intellect
intelectual *adj* & *mf* intellectual
intelectualidad *f* intellectuality; (*conjunto de los intelectuales de un país o región*) intelligentsia
inteligencia *f* intelligence; **estar en inteligencia con** to be in collusion with
inteligente *adj* intelligent; trained, skilled
inteligible *adj* intelligible

intemperancia *f* intemperance
intemperante *adj* intemperate
intemperie *m* inclement weather; **a la intemperie** in the open, unsheltered
intempestivo -va *adj* unseasonable, inopportune, untimely
intención *f* intention; (*cautelosa advertencia*) caution; (*instinto dañino de un animal*) viciousness; **con intención** deliberately, knowingly; **de intención** on purpose
intendencia *f* intendance; (SAm) mayoralty
intendente *m* intendant; quartermaster general; (SAm) mayor
intensar *tr & ref* to intensify
intensidad *f* intensity
intensificar §73 *tr & ref* to intensify
intensión *f* intensity
intensivo -va *adj* intensive
intenso -sa *adj* intense
intentar *tr* to try, to attempt; to intend; to try out
intento *m* intent, purpose; **de intento** on purpose
intentona *f* (coll) rash attempt (*e.g., to rob, escape, etc.*)
interacción *f* interaction
interamericano -na *adj* inter-American
intercalar *tr* to intercalate, to insert
intercambiar *tr & ref* to interchange
intercambio *m* interchange, exchange
interceder *intr* to intercede
interceptar *tr* to intercept
interceptor -tora *mf* interceptor || *m* trap; separator; (aer) interceptor
interdecir §24 *tr* to interdict, forbid
interés *m* interest; **intereses creados** vested interests; **poner a interés** to put out at interest
interesado -da *adj* interested || *mf* interested party
interesante *adj* interesting
interesar *tr* to interest; to involve || *intr* to be interesting || *ref* — **interesarse en** or **por** to be interested in, take an interest in
interescolar *adj* interscholastic, intercollegiate
interfecto -ta *adj* murdered || *mf* victim of murder
interferencia *f* interference
interferir §68 *tr* to interfere with || *intr* to interfere
interfono *m* intercom
interín *adv* meanwhile || *conj* (coll) while, as long as || *s* (*pl* **interines**) temporary incumbency
interinar *tr* to fill temporarily, to fill in an acting capacity
interino -na *adj* temporary, acting, interim
interior *adj* interior, inner, inside; home, domestic || *m* interior, inside; mind, soul; **interiores** entrails, insides
interioridad *f* inside; **interioridades** inside story, private matters
interjección *f* interjection
interlinear *tr* to interline; (typ) to space, to lead
interlocutor -tora *mf* speaker, party; interviewer

intermediario -ria *adj & mf* intermediary || *m* (com) middleman
intermedio -dia *adj* intermediate || *m* interval, interim; (mus) intermezzo; (theat) intermission, entr'acte
intermitente *adj* intermittent
internacional *adj* international
internacionalizar §60 *tr* to internationalize
internado -da *mf* (mil) internee || *m* boarding school
internamiento *m* internment
internar *tr* to send inland; to intern || *intr* to move inland || *ref* to move inland; to take refuge, to hide; to insinuate oneself; **internarse en** to go deeply into
internista *mf* internist
interno -na *adj* internal; inside || *mf* boarding-school student; **interno de hospital** intern
interpelar *tr* to seek the protection or aid of; to interrogate; to interpellate
interpolar *tr* to interpolate; to interpose; to interrupt briefly
interponer §54 *tr* to interpose; to appoint as mediator || *ref* to intervene, intercede
interprender *tr* to take by surprise
interpresa *f* surprise action; surprise seizure
interpretar *tr* to interpret
intérprete *mf* interpreter
interrogación *f* interrogation; question mark
interrogar §44 *tr & intr* to question, interrogate
interrumpir *tr* to interrupt
interruptor *m* (elec) switch; **interruptor automático** (elec) circuit breaker; **interruptor del encendido** (aut) ignition switch; **interruptor de resorte** (elec) snap switch
intersección *f* (geom) intersection
intersticio *m* interstice; interval
intervalo *m* interval
intervención *f* intervention; inspection; (*de cuentas*) audit, auditing; (surg) operation; **intervención de los precios** price control; **no intervención** nonintervention
intervenir §79 *tr* to take up, work on; to inspect, supervise; (*cuentas*) to audit; (*un teléfono*) to tap; (surg) to operate on || *intr* to mediate, intervene, intercede; to participate; to happen
interventor *m* election supervisor; (com) auditor
interviú *m* (*pl* **-viús**) interview
interviewar *tr* to interview
intestado -da *adj & mf* intestate
intestino -na *adj* internal; domestic || *m* intestine; **intestino delgado** small intestine; **intestino grueso** large intestine
intimación *f* announcement, notification
intimar *tr* to announce || *intr & ref* to become well-acquainted, to become intimate
intimidad *f* intimacy; (*parte íntima o personal*) privacy
intimidar *tr* intimidate

ínti·mo -ma *adj* intimate; (*más interno*) innermost
intitular *tr* to entitle ‖ *ref* to use a title; to be called
intocable *mf* untouchable
intolerante *adj & mf* intolerant
inton·so -sa *adj* unshorn; ignorant; (*libro o revista*) uncut ‖ *mf* ignoramus
intoxicar §73 *tr* to poison, intoxicate
intracruzamiento *m* inbreeding
intranquilidad *f* uneasiness, worry
intranquilizar §60 *tr* to make uneasy, worry
intranquil·lo -la *adj* uneasy, worried
intransigente *adj & mf* intransigent, diehard
intransiti·vo -va *adj* intransitive
intratable *adj* unmanageable; impassable; unsociable
intrepidez *f* intrepidity
intrépi·do -da *adj* intrepid
intriga *f* intrigue
intrigar §44 *tr* (*excitar la curiosidad de*) to intrigue ‖ *intr* to intrigue ‖ *ref* to be intrigued
intrinca·do -da *adj* intricate
intrincar §73 *tr* to complicate; to confuse, bewilder
intríngu·lis *m* (*pl* **-lis**) (coll) hidden motive, mystery
intrínse·co -ca *adj* intrinsic(al)
introducción *f* introduction
introducir §19 *tr* to introduce; to insert, put in ‖ *ref* to gain access; to meddle, interfere, intrude
introito *m* (*de un escrito o una oración*) introduction; (*de un poema dramático*) prologue; (eccl) introit
introspecti·vo -va *adj* introspective
introverti·do -da *mf* introvert
intruso -sa *adj* intrusive ‖ *mf* intruder, interloper
intuición *f* intuition
intuir §20 *tr* to guess, to sense
intuito *m* view, glance, look; **por intuito de** in view of
inundación *f* flood, inundation
inundar *tr* to flood, to inundate
inurba·no -na *adj* discourteous, unmannerly
inusita·do -da *adj* (*no ordinario*) unusual; obsolete, out of use
inusual *adj* unusual
inútil *adj* useless
invadir *tr* to invade
invalidar *tr* to invalidate
invalidez *f* invalidity
inváli·do -da *adj & mf* invalid
invariable *adj* invariable
invasión *f* invasion
inva·sor -sora *mf* invader
invectiva *f* invective
invectivar *tr* to inveigh against
invencible *adj* invincible
invención *f* invention; finding, discovery; deception
invendible *adj* unsalable
inventar *tr* to invent
inventariar §77 **& regular** *tr* to inventory
inventario *m* inventory

inventi·vo -va *adj* inventive ‖ *f* inventiveness
invento *m* invention
inven·tor -tora *adj* inventive ‖ *mf* inventor
inverecun·do -da *adj* shameless, brazen
inverisímil *adj* improbable, unlikely
invernáculo *m* greenhouse, hothouse, conservatory
invernada *f* wintertime; (SAm) pasture land; (Ven) torrential rain
invernadero *m* greenhouse, hothouse; winter resort; winter pasture
invernal *adj* winter ‖ *m* cattle shed (*in winter-pasture land*)
invernar §2 *intr* to winter; to be winter
inverni·zo -za *adj* winter; wintery
inverosímil *adj* improbable, unlikely
inversión *f* inversion; (*de dinero*) investment; (gram) inverted order
inversionista *adj* investment ‖ *mf* investor
inver·so -sa *adj* inverse, opposite; **a or por la inversa** on the contrary
invertebra·do -da *adj & m* invertebrate
inverti·do -da *adj* inverted ‖ *mf* invert
invertir §68 *tr* to invert; (*dinero*) to invest; (*tiempo*) to spend; to reverse
investidura *f* investment, investiture; station, standing
investigación *f* investigation, research
investigar §44 *tr* to investigate ‖ *intr* to research
investir §50 *tr* — **investir con** or **de** (*poner en posesión de*) to invest with
invetera·do -da *adj* inveterate, confirmed
invic·to -ta *adj* unconquered
invidencia *f* blindness
invidente *adj* blind ‖ *mf* blind person
invierno *m* winter; (Am) rainy season
invisible *adj* invisible ‖ *m* (Mex) hair net; **en un invisible** in an instant
invitación *f* invitation
invita·do -da *mf* guest
invitar *tr* to invite
invocar §73 *tr* to invoke
involunta·rio -ra *adj* involuntary
invulnerable *adj* invulnerable
inyección *f* injection
inyecta·do -da *adj* bloodshot, inflamed
inyectar *tr* to inject ‖ *ref* to become congested; to become inflamed
ionizar §60 *tr* to ionize ‖ *ref* to be ionized
ir §41 *intr* to go; to be becoming, to fit, to suit; to be at stake; **ir a + inf** to be going to + *inf* (*to express futurity*); **ir a buscar** to go get, to go for; **ir a parar en** to end up in; **ir con cuidado** to be careful; **ir con miedo** to be afraid; **ir con tiento** to watch one's step; **ir de caza** to go hunting; **ir de pesca** to go fishing; **lo que va de** so far (as); **¡qué va!** of course not!; **¡vaya!** the deuce!; **what a . . .!** ‖ *ref* to go away; to leak; to wear away; to get old; to break to pieces
ira *f* anger, wrath, ire
iracun·do -da *adj* angry, wrathful, irate
Irak, el Irak or Iraq
Irán, el Iran

ira·nés -nesa or ira·nio -nia *adj & mf* Iranian

ira·qués -quesa or iraquiano -na *adj & mf* Iraqui

iris *m* (*pl* iris) (*del ojo*) iris; rainbow

Irlanda *f* Ireland

irlan·dés -desa *adj* Irish ‖ *m* Irishman; (*idioma*) Irish; los irlandeses the Irish ‖ *f* Irishwoman

ironía *f* irony

iróni·co -ca *adj* ironic(al)

ironizar §60 *tr* to ridicule

irracional *adj* irrational

irradiar *tr* to radiate, to irradiate; (*difundir*) to broadcast ‖ *intr* to radiate

irrazonable *adj* unreasonable

irreal *adj* unreal

irrealidad *f* unreality

irrebatible *adj* irrefutable

irreconocible *adj* unrecognizable

irrecuperable *adj* irretrievable

irrecusable *adj* unimpeachable

irredimible *adj* irredeemable

irreemplazable *adj* irreplaceable

irreflexión *f* rashness, thoughtlessness

irreflexi·vo -va *adj* rash, thoughtless

irregular *adj* irregular ‖ *m* (mil) irregular

irregularidad *f* irregularity; embezzlement

irreligio·so -sa *adj* irreligious

irrellenable *adj* nonrefillable

irremediable *adj* irremediable

irremisible *adj* unpardonable

irreparable *adj* irreparable

irreprimible *adj* irrepressible

irreprochable *adj* irreproachable

irresistible *adj* irresistible

irresoluble *adj* unworkable, unsolvable

irrespetuo·so -sa *adj* disrespectful

irresponsable *adj* irresponsible

irresuel·to -ta *adj* hesitant, wavering

irreverente *adj* irreverent

irrigación *f* irrigation

irrigar §44 *tr* to irrigate

irrisible *adj* laughable, absurd

irrisión *f* derision, ridicule; (coll) laughingstock

irritante *adj & m* irritant

irritar *tr* to irritate ‖ *ref* to become exasperated

irrompible *adj* unbreakable

irrumpir *intr* to burst in; irrumpir en to burst into

irrupción *f* sudden attack; invasion

isi·dro -dra *mf* (coll) hick, jake, yokel

isla *f* island; (*manzana de casas*) block; isla de seguridad safety island, safety zone; islas Baleares Balearic Islands; islas Canarias Canary Islands; islas de Barlovento Windward Islands; islas de Sotavento Leeward Islands; Islas Filipinas Philippine Islands

Islam, el Islam

islan·dés -desa *adj* Icelandic ‖ *mf* Icelander ‖ *m* (*idioma*) Icelandic

Islandia *f* Iceland

isle·ño -ña *adj* island ‖ *mf* islander; (Cuba) Canarian

isleta *f* isle

isósce·les *adj* (*pl* -les) isosceles

isótopo *m* isotope

israe·lí (*pl* -líes) *adj & mf* Israeli

israelita *adj & mf* Israelite

istmo *m* isthmus

Italia *f* Italy

italia·no -na *adj & mf* Italian

itáli·co -ca *adj* Italic; (typ) italic ‖ *f* (typ) italics

itinera·rio -ria *adj & m* itinerary

izar §60 *tr* (naut) to hoist, to haul up

izquierda *f* left hand; left-hand side; (pol) left; a la izquierda left, on the left, to the left

izquierdear *intr* to go wild, to go astray, to go awry

izquierdista *adj* leftist ‖ *mf* leftist, left-winger

izquierdizante *adj* leftish

izquier·do -da *adj* left; left-hand; left-handed; crooked; levantarse del izquierdo to get out of bed on the wrong side ‖ *f* see izquierda

J

J, j (jota) *f* eleventh letter of the Spanish alphabet

jabalcón *m* strut, brace

jaba·lí *m* (*pl* -líes) wild boar

jabalina *f* javelin; wild sow

jabardillo *m* (*de insectos*) noisy swarm; (coll) noisy throng

jabeque *m* (naut) xebec; (coll) gash in the face

jabón *m* soap; cake of soap; dar jabón a (coll) to softsoap; dar un jabón a (coll) to upbraid, to reprimand; jabón de afeitar shaving soap; jabón de Castilla Castile soap; jabón de tocador or de olor toilet soap; jabón de sastre soapstone, French chalk; jabón en polvo soap powder

jabonado *m* soaping; (*ropa lavada o por lavar*) wash

jabonadura *f* soaping; dar una jabonadura a (coll) to lambaste, to upbraid; jabonaduras soapy water; soapsuds

jabonar *tr* to soap; (coll) to reprimand

jaboncillo *m* cake of toilet soap; jaboncillo de sastre soapstone, French chalk

jabone·ro -ra *adj* soap; (*toro*) yellowish, dirty-white ‖ *mf* soapmaker; soap dealer ‖ *f* soap dish

jabonete *m* cake of toilet soap

jabono·so -sa *adj* soapy, lathery

jaca *f* pony, jennet

jacal *m* (Guat, Mex, Ven) hut, shack

jácara *f* merry ballad; gay song and

dance; night revelers; (coll) story, argument; (coll) fake, hoax, lie; (coll) annoyance, bother

jacarear *intr* (coll) to go serenading, to go singing in the street; (coll) to be disagreeable

jáca·ro -ra *adj & m* braggart ‖ *f* see jácara

jacinto *m* hyacinth

jaco *m* nag, jade; gray parrot

jactancia *f* boasting, bragging

jactancio·so -sa *adj* boastful, bragging

jactar *ref* to boast, to brag; **jactarse de** to boast of

jade *m* jade

jadeante *adj* panting

jadear *intr* to pant

jadeo *m* panting

ja·ez *m* (*pl* **-eces**) harness, piece of harness; ilk, stripe, kind; **jaeces** trappings

jaguar *m* jaguar

jagüel *m* (Arg) reservoir

jaharrar *tr* to plaster

jalar *tr* (coll) to pull; (Am) to flirt with ‖ *intr* (Am) to get out, to beat it ‖ *ref* (Am) to get drunk

jalbegar §44 *tr* to whitewash; (*el rostro*) to paint ‖ *ref* to paint the face

jalbegue *m* whitewash; whitewashing, paint, make-up

jalda·do -da *adj* bright-yellow

jalea *f* jelly; **hacerse una jalea** (coll) to be madly in love

jalear *tr* (*a los que bailan y cantan*) to animate with clapping and shouting; (*a los perros*) to incite, urge on; (Chile) to tease, pester ‖ *intr* to dance the jaleo ‖ *ref* to have a noisy time; to swing and sway

jaleo *m* cheering, shouting; jamboree; jaleo (*vivacious Spanish solo dance*)

jalis·co -ca *adj* (Guat, Mex) drunk ‖ *m* (Mex) straw hat

jalma *f* small packsaddle

jalón *m* surveying rod, range pole; (Guat, Mex) swig of liquor; (CAm) beau; **jalón de mira** leveling rod

jalonar *tr* to stake out, mark out

jalonear *tr* (Mex) to pull, to jerk

jalonero *m* (surv) rodman

jamaica *m* Jamaica rum ‖ *f* (Mex) charity fair

jamaica·no -na *adj & mf* Jamaican

jamaiqui·no -na *adj & mf* (Am) Jamaican

jamar *tr* (coll) to eat

jamás *adv* never; ever

jamba *f* jamb

jambaje *m* doorframe, window frame

jamelgo *m* (coll) jade, nag

jamete *m* samite

jamón *m* ham

jamona *f* (coll) fat middle-aged woman

jamugas *fpl* mule chair

ánda·lo -la *adj & mf* Andalusian

Jantipa or **Jantipe** *f* Xanthippe

Japón, el Japan

japo·nés -nesa *adj & mf* Japanese ‖ *m* (*idioma*) Japanese

jaque *m* (*lance del ajedrez*) check; (coll) bully; **dar jaque a** to check; **dar jaque mate a** to checkmate; **en**

jaque in check; **estar muy jaque** (coll) to be full of pep; **jaque mate** checkmate; **tener en jaque** to hold a threat over the head of ‖ *interj* check!

jaquear *tr* to check; (*al enemigo*) to harass

jaqueca *f* sick headache; **dar una jaqueca a** (coll) to bore to death

jaqueco·so -sa *adj* boring, tiresome

jaquemar *m* jack (*figure which strikes a clock bell*)

jarabe *m* syrup; sweet drink; **jarabe de pico** (coll) lip service, idle promise

jarana *f* (coll) merrymaking; (coll) rumpus; (coll) carousal, spree; (coll) trick, deceit; (Am) jest, joke; (Am) small guitar; **ir de jarana** (coll) to go on a spree

jaranear *tr* (CAm, Col) to swindle, cheat ‖ *intr* (coll) to go on a spree; (coll) to raise a rumpus; (Am) to joke

jarane·ro -ra *adj* merrymaking; gay, merry ‖ *mf* merrymaker, reveler

jarano *m* sombrero

jarcia *f* fishing tackle; (coll) jumble, mess; **jarcias** tackle, rigging; **jarcia trozada** junk (*old cable*)

jardín *m* garden, flower garden; (baseball) field, outfield; (naut) privy, latrine; **jardín central** (baseball) center field; **jardín de la infancia** kindergarten; **jardín derecho** (baseball) right field; **jardín izquierdo** (baseball) left field

jardinera *f* jardiniere, flower stand; basket carriage; summer trolley car, open trolley car

jardinería *f* gardening

jardine·ro -ra *mf* gardener; **jardinero adornista** landscape gardener ‖ *m* (baseball) fielder, outfielder ‖ *f* see jardinera

jardinista *mf* landscape gardener

jarea *f* (Mex) hunger

jarear *intr* (Bol) to stop for a rest ‖ *ref* (Mex) to flee, run away; (Mex) to swing, to sway; (Mex) to die of starvation

jareta *f* (sew) casing

jari·fo -fa *adj* showy, spruce, natty

jaro·cho -cha *adj* brusk, bluff ‖ *m* insulting fellow; Veracruz peasant

jarope *m* syrup; (coll) nasty potion

jarra *f* jug, jar, water pitcher; **de jarras** or **en jarras** with arms akimbo

jarrete *m* hock, gambrel

jarretera *f* garter

jarro *m* pitcher; **echar un jarro de agua (fría) a** to pour cold water on

jarrón *m* (*vaso para adornar chimeneas, consolas, etc.*) vase; (*sobre un pedestal*) urn

jaspe *m* jasper

jaspea·do -da *adj* marbled, speckled ‖ *m* marbling, speckling

jaspear *tr* to marble, speckle

jateo *m* foxhound

ja·to -ta *mf* calf

Jauja *f* Cockaigne; **¿estamos aquí o en Jauja?** (coll) where do you think you are?; **vivir en Jauja** (coll) to live in the lap of luxury

jaula *f* cage; (*embalaje de listones de madera*) crate; (Mex) open freight car; (Cuba, P-R) police wagon; **jaula de locos** insane asylum, madhouse

jauría *f* pack (*of hounds*)

java·nés -nesa *adj & mf* Javanese ‖ *m* (*idioma*) Javanese

Javier *m* Xavier

jazmín *m* jasmine; **jazmín de la India** gardenia

jazz *m* jazz

J.C. *abbr* Jesucristo

jebe *m* alum; (SAm) rubber

jedive *m* khedive

jefa *f* female head or leader; **jefa de ruta** hostess (*on a bus*)

jefatura *f* headship, leadership; (*de policía*) headquarters

jefe *m* chief, head, leader; (*de una tribu*) chieftain; **jefe de cocina** chef; **jefe de coro** choirmaster; **jefe de equipajes** (rr) baggage master; **jefe de estación** stationmaster; **jefe del estado** chief of state; **jefe del gobierno** chief executive; **jefe de redacción** editor in chief; **jefe de ruta** guide; **jefe de tren** (rr) conductor; **quedar jefe** (Chile) to gamble away everything

jején *m* gnat, sandfly

jenabe *m* or **jenable** *m* mustard

jengibre *m* ginger

Jenofonte *m* Xenophon

jeque *m* sheik

jerarca *m* hierarch, head

jerarquía *f* hierarchy; **de jerarquía** important

jeremiada *f* jeremiad

jerez *m* sherry

jerga *f* coarse cloth; straw mattress; (*lenguaje especial de ciertos oficios; lenguaje difícil de entender*) jargon

jergón *m* straw mattress; (coll) ill-fitting clothes; (*persona torpe y estúpida*) (coll) lummox

Jericó Jericho

jerife *m* shereef

jerigonza *f* (*lenguaje especial de ciertos oficios; lenguaje difícil de entender*) jargon; (*lenguaje vulgar, caló*) slang; (coll) piece of folly

jeringa *f* syringe; (*para inyectar materias blandas en una máquina*) gun; (coll) annoyance, plague; **jeringa de engrase** or **grasa** grease gun

jeringar §44 *tr* to syringe; to inject; to give an enema to; (coll) to plague

jeringazo *m* injection, shot; squirt

jeringuilla *f* (*jeringa pequeña*) syringe; (bot) mock orange

Jerjes *m* Xerxes

jeroglífi·co -ca *adj & m* hieroglyphic

Jerónimo *m* Jerome

jer·sey *m* (*pl* **-seis**) jersey, sweater

Jerusalén Jerusalem

Jesucristo *m* Jesus Christ

jesuíta *adj & m* Jesuit

jesuíti·co -ca *adj* Jesuitic(al)

Jesús *m* Jesus; (*imagen del niño Jesús*) bambino; **en un decir Jesús** in an instant; **¡Jesús, María y José!** my gracious!

jeta *f* hog's snout, pig face; (*rostro de una persona*) (coll) phiz, mug; **estar con tanta jeta** (coll) to make a long face; **poner jeta** (coll) to pucker one's lips

jetu·do -da *adj* thick-lipped; (coll) grim, gruff

Jhs. *abbr* Jesús

jíba·ro -ra *mf* (W-I) white peasant

jibia *f* cuttlefish

jícara *f* chocolate cup; (CAm, Mex, W-I) calabash cup

jifia *f* swordfish

jilguero *m* linnet, goldfinch

jineta *f* (zool) genet

jinete *m* rider, horseman

jinetear *tr* (*caballos cerriles*) (Am) to break in ‖ *intr* to show off one's horsemanship

jinglar *intr* to swing, to rock

jingoísmo *m* jingoism

jingoísta *adj & mf* jingo

jipa·to -ta *adj* (Am) pale, wan; (Am) insipid, tasteless; (Guat) drunk

jipijapa *m* Panama hat ‖ *f* jipijapa; strip of jipijapa straw

jira *f* strip of cloth; outing, picnic; trip, tour; swing, political trip

jirón *m* rag, tatter, shred; (*de una falda*) facing; pennant; bit, drop, shred; **hacer jirones** to tear to shreds

jitomate *m* (Mex) tomato

joco·so -sa *adj* jocose, jocular

jocotal *m* (CAm, Mex) Spanish plum (*tree*)

jocote *m* (CAm, Mex) Spanish plum (*fruit*)

jocoyote *m* (Mex) baby (*youngest child*)

jofaina *f* washbowl, basin

jolgorio *m* (coll) fun, merriment

jonrón *m* (baseball) home run

Jordán *m* Jordan (*river*); **ir al Jordán** (coll) to be born again

Jordania *f* Jordan (*country*)

jorda·no -na *adj & mf* Jordanian

jorguín *m* sorcerer, wizard

jorguina *f* sorceress, witch

jorguinería *f* sorcery, witchcraft

jornada *f* journey, trip, stage; day's journey; (*horas del trabajo diario del obrero*) workday; (*tiempo que dura la vida de un hombre*) lifetime; battle; (*muerte*) passing; summer residence of diplomat or diplomatic corps; event, occasion; undertaking; (mil) expedition; (*de un drama*) (archaic) act; **a grandes** or **largas jornadas** by forced marches; **al fin de la jornada** in the end; **caminar por sus jornadas** to proceed with circumspection; **hacer mala jornada** to get nowhere; **jornada ordinaria** full time

jornal *m* day's work; day's pay; **a jornal** by the day; **jornal mínimo** minimum wage

jornalero *m* day laborer

joroba *f* hump; (coll) annoyance, bother

joroba·do -da *adj* humpbacked, hunchbacked; (coll) annoyed, bothered ‖ *mf* humpback, hunchback

jorobar *tr* (coll) to annoy, pester

jorongo *m* (Mex) poncho; (Mex) woolen blanket

jota *f* (*letra del alfabeto*) J; **jota** (*Spanish folk dance and music*); jot, iota, tittle; vegetable soup; **sin faltar una jota** (coll) with not a whit left out

joven *adj* young; **ser joven de esperanzas** (coll) to have a bright future ‖ *mf* youth, young person; **de joven** as a youth, as a young man, as a young woman

jovial *adj* jovial

joya *f* jewel; (*brocamantón*) diamond brooch; (*agasajo*) gift, present; (*persona o cosa de mucha valía*) (fig) jewel, gem; **joya de familia** heirloom; **joyas** jewelry; trousseau; **joyas de fantasía** costume jewelry

joyante *adj* glossy

joyelero *m* jewel case, casket

joyería *f* (*conjunto de joyas*) jewelry; jewelry shop; jewelry trade

joye·ro -ra *mf* jeweler ‖ *m* jewel case, casket

Juan *m* John; **Buen Juan** (coll) sap, easy mark; **Juan Español** the Spanish people, the typical Spaniard; **San Juan Bautista** John the Baptist

Juana *f* Jane, Jean, Joan; **Juana de Arco** Joan of Arc, Jeanne d'Arc; **juanas** glove stretcher

juanete *m* bunion; high cheekbone

jubilación *f* retirement; (*renta de la persona jubilada*) pension, retirement annuity

jubila·do -da *adj* retired ‖ *mf* retired person, pensioner

jubilar *tr* to retire, to pension; (coll) to throw out ‖ *intr* to rejoice; to retire, be pensioned ‖ *ref* to rejoice; to retire, be pensioned; (Col) to decline, go to pieces; (CAm, Ven) to play hooky; (Cuba, Mex) to become a past master

jubileo *m* (coll) much coming and going, great doings; (eccl) jubilee; **por jubileo** (coll) once in a long time

júbilo *m* jubilation

jubilo·so -sa *adj* jubilant, joyful

jubón *m* jerkin

judaísmo *m* Judaism

judería *f* (*raza judaica*) Jewry; (*barrio de los judíos*) ghetto

judía *f* Jewess; kidney bean, string bean; **judía de careta** black-eyed bean; **judía de la peladilla** Lima bean

judicatura *f* judicature; (*cargo de juez*) judgeship

judicial *adj* judicial, judiciary

judí·o -a *adj* Jewish ‖ *mf* Jew ‖ *f see* **judía**

juego *m* (*acción de jugar*) play, playing; (*ejercicio recreativo en el cual se gana o se pierde*) game; (*vicio de jugar*) gambling; (*lugar donde se ejecutan ciertos juegos*): (bowling) alley; (tennis) court; (baseball) field; (*tantos necesarios para ganar la partida*) game; (*de muebles*) suit, suite; (*de café*) service; (*de vajilla*) set; (*de luces, colores, aguas*) play; (mach) play; (*p.ej., de diplomacia*) (fig) game; **a juego** to match, e.g., **una silla a juego** a chair to match; **conocer el**

juego de to see through, to have the number of; **en juego** at hand; **hacer juego** to match; **hacer juego con** to match, to go with; **juego de alcoba** bedroom suit; **juego de azar** game of chance; **juego de bolas** (mach) ball bearing; **juego de campanas** chimes; **juego de comedor** dining-room suit; **juego de envite** gambling game, game played for money; **juego de escritorio** desk set; **juego de la cuna** cat's cradle; **juego de la pulga** tiddlywinks; **juego del corro** ring-around-a-rosy; **juego del salto** leapfrog; **juego del tres en raya** tick-tack-toe played with movable counters or pebbles; **juego de manos** legerdemain, sleight of hand; (coll) roughhousing; **juego de niños** (*cosa muy fácil*) child's play; **juego de palabras** play on words, pun; **juego de pelota** ball game; **pelota**; **juego de piernas** footwork; **juego de por ver** (Chile) game played for fun; **juego de prendas** game of forfeits, forfeits; **juego de suerte** game of chance; **juego de tejo** shuffleboard; **juego de timbres** glockenspiel; **juego de vocablos** or **voces** play on words, pun; **juego limpio** fair play; **juego público** gambling house; **juegos de sociedad** parlor games; **juegos malabares** juggling; flimflam; **juego sucio** foul play; **no ser cosa de juego** to be no laughing matter; **por juego** in fun, for fun; **verle a uno el juego** to be on to someone

juerga *f* (coll) carousal, spree; **juerga de borrachera** (coll) drinking bout, binge; **ir de juerga** (coll) to go on a spree

juerguista *mf* (coll) carouser, reveler

jue·ves *m* (*pl* -ves) Thursday; **Jueves Santo** Maundy Thursday

juez *m* (*pl* jueces) judge; **juez de guardia** coroner; **juez de instrucción** examining magistrate; **juez de paz** justice of the peace; **juez de salida** (sport) starter; **juez de tiempo** (sport) timekeeper

jugada *f* (*lance*) play, throw, stroke, move; **mala jugada** dirty trick

juga·dor -dora *mf* player; gambler; **jugador de manos** prestidigitator; **jugador de ventaja** sharper

jugar §42 *tr* (*p.ej., un naipe, una partida de juego*) to play; (*una espada*) to wield; (*arriesgar*) to stake, to risk; (*las manos, los dedos*) to move; **jugarle a uno las bebidas** to match someone for the drinks ‖ *intr* to play; to gamble; (*hacer juego dos cosas*) to match; (*intervenir*) to figure, participate; **jugar a** (*p.ej., los naipes, el tenis*) to play; **jugar con** (*un contrario*) to play; (*una persona; los sentimientos de una persona*) to toy with; to match; **jugar en** to have a hand in ‖ *ref* (*p.ej., la vida*) to risk; to be at stake; **jugarse el todo por el todo** to stake all, to shoot the works

jugarreta *f* (coll) bad play, poor play; (coll) mean trick, dirty trick

juglar *m* minstrel, jongleur; (*bufón*) (archaic) juggler

juglaría *f* minstrelsy

jugo *m* (*p.ej., de la naranja*) juice; (*de la carne*) gravy; (*líquido orgánico*) juice; (fig) gist, essence, substance; **en su jugo** (culin) au jus; **jugo de muñeca** (coll) elbow grease

jugo·so -sa *adj* juicy; substantial, important

juguete *m* toy, plaything; (*burla*) joke, jest; (theat) skit; **de juguete** toy, e.g., **soldado de juguete** toy soldier; **juguete de movimiento** mechanical toy; **por juguete** for fun, in fun

juguetear *intr* to frolic, romp, sport

juguete·ro -ra *adj* toy ‖ *mf* toy dealer ‖ *m* whatnot, étagère

juguete-sorpresa *m* (*pl* **juguetes-sorpresa**) jack-in-the-box

jugue·tón -tona *adj* playful, frolicsome, frisky

juicio *m* judgment; (law) trial; **estar en su cabal juicio** to be in one's right mind; **estar fuera de juicio** to be out of one's mind; **juicio de Dios** (hist) ordeal; **pedir en juicio** (law) to sue

juicio·so -sa *adj* judicious, wise

julepe *m* julep; (coll) scolding; (Am) scare, fright

julepear *tr* (coll) to scold; (coll) to whip; (SAm) to scare, frighten; (Mex) to weary, tire out

julio *m* July

julo *m* lead cow, lead mule

jumen·to -ta *mf* ass, donkey

juncal *adj* willowy, rushy; (fig) willowy, lissome

juncia *f* sedge; **vender juncia** (coll) to boast, brag

junco *m* (*embarcación china*) junk; (bot) rush, bulrush; **junco de Indias** (bot) rattan; **junco de laguna** (bot) rush, bulrush

junco·so -sa *adj* rushy, full of rushes

jungla *f* jungle

junio *m* June

junípero *m* juniper

junquera *f* rush, bulrush

junquillo *m* jonquil

junta *f* meeting, conference; board, council; junction, union; joint, seam; (*empaquetadura*) gasket; (*arandela*) washer; **junta de comercio** board of trade; **junta de charnela** (mach) knuckle; **junta de sanidad** board of health; **junta universal** (mach) universal joint

juntamente *adv* together; at the same time

juntar *tr* to join, unite; to gather, gather together; (*una puerta*) to half-close ‖ *ref* to gather together; to go along; to copulate

jun·to -ta *adj* joined, united; **jun·tos -tas** together ‖ *f* see **junta** ‖ **junto** *adv* together; at the same time; **junto a** near, close to; **junto con** along with, together with; **todo junto** at the same time, all at once

juntura *f* junction; (*p.ej., de una cañería; de un hueso*) joint; connection, coupling

jura *f* oath

jura·do -da *adj* (*enemigo*) sworn ‖ *m* (*conjunto de ciudadanos encargados de determinar la culpabilidad del acusado; conjunto de examinadores de un certamen*) jury; (*cada uno de los expresados individuos*) juror, juryman

juramentar *tr* to swear in ‖ *ref* to take an oath, to be sworn in

juramento *m* oath; (*voto, reniego*) curse, swearword; **prestar juramento a** to swear to; **tomar juramento a** to swear in

jurar *tr* to swear; (*la verdad de una cosa*) to swear to; to swear allegiance to ‖ *intr* (*pronunciar un juramento*) to swear, take an oath; (*echar votos o reniegos*) to swear, to curse; **jurar + inf** to swear to + *inf* ‖ *ref* to swear; **jurársela** or **jurárselas a uno** (coll) to have it in for someone, to swear to get even with someone

jure·ro -ra *mf* (SAm) false witness

jurídi·co -ca *adj* juridical

jurisconsulto *m* (*el que escribe sobre el derecho*) jurist; (*jurisperito*) legal expert

jurisdicción *f* jurisdiction

jurisperito *m* jurist, legal expert

jurisprudencia *f* jurisprudence

jurista *mf* jurist

juro *m* right of perpetual ownership; **de juro** inevitably, for sure

justa *f* joust, tournament

justamente *adv* just, just at that time; justly; (*ajustadamente*) tightly

justar *intr* to joust, to tilt

justicia *f* justice; (*castigo de muerte*) execution; **de justicia** justly, deservedly; **hacer justicia a** to do justice to; **ir por justicia** to go to court, to bring suit

justicie·ro -ra *adj* just, fair; stern, righteous

justificable *adj* justifiable

justifica·do -da *adj* (*hecho*) just, right; (*persona*) just, upright

justificante *m* voucher, proof

justificar §73 *tr* to justify; (typ) to justify

justillo *m* jerkin, waist

justipreciar *tr* to estimate, appraise

jus·to -ta *adj* just; right, exact; (*apretado*) tight ‖ *mf* just person ‖ *f* see **justa** ‖ **justo** *adv* just; right, in tune; tight; (*con estrechez*) in straitened circumstances

Jutlandia *f* Jutland

ju·to -ta *mf* Jute

juvenil *adj* juvenile, youthful

juventud *f* youth; young people

juzgado *m* court of law; courtroom; court of one judge

juzgar §44 *tr & intr* to judge; **a juzgar por** judging by; **juzgar de** to judge, pass judgment on

K

K, k (ka) *f* twelfth letter of the Spanish alphabet
kermesse *f* var of **quermés**
keroseno *m* kerosene, coal oil
kg. *abbr* **kilogramo**
kilate *m* var of **quilate**
kilo *m* kilo, kilogram
kilociclo *m* kilocycle
kilogramo *m* kilogram
kilometraje *m* kilometrage, distance in kilometers
kilométri·co -ca *adj* kilometric; (coll) interminable, long-drawn-out

kilómetro *m* kilometer
kilovatio *m* kilowatt
kilovatio-hora *m* (*pl* **kilovatios-hora**) kilowatt-hour
kimono *m* var of **quimono**
kinescopio *m* (telv) kinescope
kiosco *m* var of **quiosco**
kirieleisón *m* (coll) dirge; **cantar el kirieleisón** (coll) to beg mercy
km. *abbr* **kilómetro**
kph. *abbr* **kilómetros por hora**
kv. *abbr* **kilovatio**
kv-h *abbr* **kilovatio-hora**

L

L, l (ele) *f* thirteenth letter of the Spanish alphabet
la *art def fem* of **el** || *pron pers fem* her, it; you || *pron dem* that, the one; **la que** who, which, that; she who, the one that
laberinto *m* labyrinth, maze
labia *f* (coll) fluency, smoothness
labial *adj* & *f* labial
labio *m* lip; (fig) edge, lip; **chuparse los labios** to smack one's lips; **labio leporino** harelip; **leer en los labios** to lip-read
labiolectura *f* lip reading
labio·so -sa *adj* (Am) fluent, smooth
labor *f* labor, work; (*cultivo de los campos*) farming, tilling; (*obra de coser, bordar, etc.*) needlework, fancywork, embroidery; **hacer labor** to match; **labor blanca** linen work, linen embroidery; **labor de ganchillo** crocheting
laborable *adj* workable; arable, tillable; (*día*) work
laborante *m* journeyman; political henchman
laborar *tr* to work || *intr* to scheme
laboratorio *m* laboratory
laborio·so -sa *adj* (*trabajador*) laborious, industrious; (*trabajoso*) laborious, arduous
laborismo *m* British Labour Party
laborista *adj* Labour || *mf* Labourite
labra *f* carving
labrada *f* fallow ground (*to be sown the following year*)
labrade·ro -ra *adj* arable, tillable
labra·do -da *adj* wrought, fashioned; carved; figured, embroidered || *m* carving; **labrado de madera** wood carving || *f* see **labrada**
labra·dor -dora *adj* work; farm || *mf* farmer; (*campesino*) peasant || *m* plowman; **el Labrador** Labrador
labrantí·o -a *adj* farm || *m* farmland
labranza *f* farming; farm, farmland
labrar *tr* to work, to fashion; (*la piedra, la madera*) to carve; (*arar*) to

plow; (*construir o mandar construir*) to build; to till, to cultivate; to cause, bring about || *intr* to make a lasting impression
labrie·go -ga *mf* peasant
laca *f* lacquer; shellac; **laca de uñas** nail polish; **lacas** lacquer ware
lacayo *m* lackey, footman
lacear *tr* to tie with a bow; to adorn with bows; (*la caza*) to drive within shot; (*la caza menor*) to trap, to snare
lacería *f* poverty, want; trouble, bother; leprosy
lacerio·so -sa *adj* poor, needy
lacero *m* lassoer; poacher; dogcatcher
la·cio -cia *adj* faded, withered; languid; (*cabello*) lank, straight
lacóni·co -ca *adj* laconic
lacra *f* fault, defect; (*señal dejada por una enfermedad*) mark, remains; (Am) sore; (Am) scab
lacrimóge·no -na *adj* tear, tear-producing
lacrimo·so -sa *adj* lachrymose, tearful
lactar *tr* to suckle
lácte·o -a *adj* milky
lacustre *adj* lake
ladear *tr* to tip, to tilt; to bend, to lean; (*un avión*) to bank || *intr* to tip, to tilt; to bend, to lean; to turn away, turn off; (*la aguja de brújula*) to deviate || *ref* to tip, to tilt; to bend, to lean; to be equal, be even; (Chile) to fall in love; **ladearse a** (*un dictamen, un partido*) to lean to or toward
ladeo *m* tipping, tilting; bending, leaning; inclination, bent
lade·ro -ra *adj* side, lateral || *f* hillside
ladilla *f* crab louse; **pegarse como ladilla** (coll) to stick like a leech
ladi·no -na *adj* crafty, sly, cunning; polyglot
lado *m* side; direction; (*del hilo telefónico*) end; **al lado** nearby; **dejar a un lado** to leave aside; **de lado** square, e.g., **diez centímetros de lado** ten centimeters square; **de otro lado**

on the other hand; **de un lado** on the one hand; **echar a un lado** to cast aside; to finish up; **hacer lado** to make room; **hacerse a un lado** to step aside; **lados** backers, advisers; **mirar de lado** or **de medio lado** to look askance at; to sneak a look at; **ponerse al lado de** to take sides with; **por el lado de** in the direction of; **tirar por su lado** to pull for oneself

ladrar tr (p.ej., injurias) to bark ‖ intr to bark

ladrido m bark, barking; (coll) slander, blame

ladrillador m bricklayer

ladrillal m brickyard

ladrillo m brick; (azulejo) tile; (p.ej., de chocolate) cake; **ladrillo de fuego** or **ladrillo refractario** firebrick

la·drón -drona adj thievish, thieving ‖ mf thief ‖ m sluice gate; **ladrón de corazones** heartbreaker, lady-killer

ladronera f den of thieves; thievery; (alcancía) child's bank

ladronerío m (Arg) gang of thieves; (Arg) wave of thieving

ladronzue·lo -la mf petty thief

lagaña f var of legaña

lagar m wino press; olive press; (establecimiento) winery

lagarta f female lizard; (ent) gypsy moth; (coll) sly woman

lagartija f green lizard; wall lizard

lagarto m lizard; (coll) sly fellow; **lagarto de Indias** alligator

lago m lake

lagotear tr & intr to flatter, to wheedle

lágrima f tear; (de cualquier licor) drop; **beberse las lágrimas** (coll) to hold back one's tears; **deshacerse en lágrimas** to weep one's eyes out; **lágrimas de cocodrilo** crocodile tears; **llorar a lágrima viva** to shed bitter tears

lagrimear intr to weep easily, to be tearful; (los ojos) to fill

lagrimo·so -sa adj tearful; (ojos) watery

laguna f (lago pequeño) lagoon; (hueco, omisión) lacuna, gap

laical adj lay

laicismo m secularism

laja f slab, flagstone

lama f mud, ooze, slime; pond scum

lambrija f earthworm; (coll) skinny person

lamedero m salt lick

lame·dor -dora adj licking ‖ mf licker ‖ m syrup; **dar lamedor** (coll) to lose at first in order to take in one's opponent

lamedura f lick, licking

lamentable adj lamentable

lamentación f lamentation

lamentar tr, intr & ref to lament, to mourn

lamento m lament

lamento·so -sa adj lamentable; plaintive

lamer tr to lick; to lap, lap against; (las llamas un tejado) to lick ‖ ref (p.ej., los dedos) to lick

lame·rón -rona adj (coll) sweet-toothed

lametada f lap, lick

lámina f sheet, plate, strip; (plancha grabada) engraving; (pintura en cobre) copper plate; (figura estampada) cut, picture, illustration

laminador m rolling mill

laminar tr to laminate; (el hierro, el acero) to roll

lampadario m floor lamp

lámpara f lamp, light; (mancha en la ropa) grease spot, oil spot; (rad) vacuum tube; **atizar la lámpara** (coll) to fill up the glasses again; **lámpara de alcohol** spirit lamp; **lámpara de arco** arc lamp, arc light; **lámpara de bolsillo** flashlight; **lámpara de carretera** (aut) bright light; **lámpara de cruce** (aut) dimmer; **lámpara de pie** floor lamp; **lámpara de sobremesa** table lamp; **lámpara de socorro** trouble light; **lámpara de soldar** blowtorch; **lámpara de techo** ceiling light; (aut) dome light; **lámpara inundante** floodlight; **lámpara testigo** pilot light

lamparilla f rushlight; aspen

lampi·ño -ña adj beardless; hairless

lampista mf lamplighter ‖ m tinsmith, plumber, glazier, electrician

lana f wool; **lana de acero** steel wool; **lana de ceiba** kapok; **lana de escorias** mineral wool, rock wool; **lana de vidrio** glass wool

lance m cast, throw; (en la red) catch, haul; (accidente en el juego) play, move, stroke; (ocasión crítica) chance, pass, juncture; incident, event; (riña) row, quarrel; (taur) capework; **de lance** cheap; secondhand; **echar buen lance** (coll) to have a break; **lance de honor** affair of honor, duel; **tener pocos lances** (coll) to be dull and uninteresting

lancero m lancer, spearman, pikeman

lanceta f (surg) lancet

lancinante adj piercing

lancha f barge, lighter; flagstone, slab; (naut) longboat; (nav) launch; (Ecuad) mist, fog; (Ecuad) frost; **lancha automóvil** launch, motor launch; **lancha de auxilio** lifeboat (stationed on shore); **lancha de carreras** speedboat; **lancha de desembarco** (nav) landing craft; **lancha salvavidas** lifeboat (on shipboard)

lanchar intr (Ecuad) to get foggy; (Ecuad) to freeze

lan·dó m (pl -dós) landau

landre f swollen gland; hidden pocket

lanería f wool shop; **lanerías** woolens, woolen goods

langosta f (insecto) locust; (crustáceo) lobster, spiny lobster

langostera f lobster pot

langostín m or **langostino** m prawn (Peneus)

langostón m green grasshopper

languidecer §22 intr to languish

languidez f languor

lángui·do -da adj languid, languorous

lano·so -sa adj woolly

lanu·do -da adj woolly; (Ecuad, Ven) coarse, ill-bred

lanza f lance, pike; (de la manguera) nozzle; (palo de coche) wagon pole

lanzabom·bas m (pl **-bas**) (aer) bomb release; (mil) trench mortar

lanzacohe·tes m (pl **-tes**) rocket launcher

lanzadera f shuttle; **parecer una lanzadera** (coll) to buzz around

lanza·do -da adj sloping; (salida de una carrera) (sport) running (start)

lanza·dor -dora mf thrower; **lanzador de lodo** (fig) mudslinger || m launcher; (aer) jettison gear; (baseball) pitcher

lanzaespu·mas m (pl **-mas**) foam extinguisher

lanzalla·mas m (pl **-mas**) flame thrower

lanzamiento m throw, hurl, fling, launch; (de un buque) launching; (de un cohete) shot, launch; (p.ej., de víveres) (aer) airdrop; (de bombas) (aer) release; (de paracaidistas) (aer) jump; (law) dispossession; (naut) steeve

lanzami·nas m (pl **-nas**) (nav) mine layer

lanzapla·tos m (pl **-tos**) trap

lanzar §60 tr to throw, hurl, fling; (un proyecto, un cohete, maldiciones, una ofensiva, un producto nuevo, un buque) to launch; (una mirada) to cast; to vomit, to throw up; (flores, hojas una planta) to put forth; (una advertencia) to toss, toss out; (aer) to airdrop; (bombas) (aer) to release; (law) to dispossess || ref to launch, launch forth; to throw oneself; to dash, to rush; (aer) to jump; (sport) to sprint

lanzatorpe·dos m (pl **-dos**) (nav) torpedo tube

laña f clamp; rivet

lañar tr to clamp; (objetos de porcelana) to rivet

lapicero m pencil holder; mechanical pencil

lápida f tablet, stone; **lápida sepulcral** gravestone

lapidar tr to stone to death

lá·piz m (pl **-pices**) (grafito) black lead; (barrita que sirve para escribir) pencil, lead pencil; **lápiz de labios** lipstick; **lápiz de pizarra** slate pencil; **lápiz de plomo** graphite; **lápiz estíptico** styptic pencil; **lápiz labial** lipstick

lapizar §60 tr to mark or line with a pencil

la·pón -pona adj Lapp || mf Lapp, Laplander || m (idioma) Lapp

Laponia f Lapland

lapso m lapse

laquear tr to lacquer

lardo·so -sa adj greasy, fatty

larga f long billiard cue; **dar largas a** to postpone, to put off

largamente adv at length, extensively; in comfort; generously; long, for a long time

largar §44 tr to get go, release; to ease, slack; (naut) to unfurl; (coll) to utter; (un golpe) (coll) to deal, strike, give; (Col) to give || ref to move away; to get away, sneak away, beat it; to take to sea; (el ancla) to come loose

lar·go -ga adj long; abundant; liberal, generous; quick, ready; (coll) shrewd, cunning; (naut) loose, slack; **a la larga** in the long run, in the end; **a lo largo** lengthwise; at great length; far away; **a lo largo de** along; along with; throughout; in the course of; (el mar) far out in; **a lo más largo** at most; **hacerse a lo largo** to get out in the open sea; **largo de lengua** loose-tongued; **largo de uñas** light-fingered; **pasar de largo** to pass without stopping; to take a quick look; to miss; **ponerse de largo** to come out, make one's debut; **vestir de largo** to wear long clothes || m length || f see **larga** || **largo** adv at length, at great length; abundantly || **largo** interj get out of here!

largometraje m full-featured film, full-length movie

largor m length

larguero m (palo, madero) stringer; (almohada larga) bolster; (aer) longeron

largueza f length; liberality, generosity

larguiru·cho -cha adj (coll) gangling, lanky

largura f length

lárice m larch tree

laringe f larynx

larínge·o -a adj laryngeal

laringitis f laryngitis

laringoscopio m laryngoscope

larva f larva; mask; (duende) hobgoblin

lascar §73 tr (naut) to pay out, to slacken; (Mex) to scratch, to bruise; (un objeto de porcelana) (Mex) to chip

lascivia f lasciviousness

lasci·vo -va adj lascivious; playful

la·so -sa adj tired, exhausted; weak, wan

lástima f pity; (quejido) complaint; **contar lástimas** to tell a hard-luck story; **dar lástima** to be pitiful; **es lástima (que)** it is a pity (that); **estar hecho una lástima** to be a sorry sight; **hacer lástima** to be pitiful; **llorar lástimas** (coll) to put on a show of tears; **poner lástima** to be pitiful; **¡qué lástima!** what a pity!, what a shame!; **¡qué lástima de saliva!** (coll) what a waste of breath!

lastimar tr to hurt, injure; to hurt, offend; to bruise || ref to hurt oneself; to bruise oneself; to complain

lastime·ro -ra adj hurtful, injurious; pitiful, sad, doleful

lastimo·so -sa adj pitiful

lastra f slab, flagstone

lastrar tr (aer & naut) to ballast

lastre m (aer & naut) ballast; (fig) wisdom, maturity; (coll) food; (rr) (Chile) ballast

lat. abbr **latín, latitud**

lata f (hojalata) tin, tin plate; (envase) tin, tin can; (madero sin pulir) log; (tabla delgada) lath; (coll) annoyance, bore; **dar la lata a** (coll) to pester; **estar en la lata** (Col) to be penniless

latebra f hiding place

latebro·so -sa *adj* furtive, secretive

latente *adj* latent

lateral *adj* lateral

latido *m* (*del perro*) yelp; (*del corazón*) beat, throb; (*dolor*) pang, twinge

latifundio *m* large neglected landed estate

latigazo *m* lash; crack of whip; (*reprensión áspera*) lashing

látigo *m* whip, horsewhip; cinch strap

latiguear *tr* (Am) to lash, to whip || *intr* to crack a whip

latiguillo *m* small whip; (*del actor u orador*) claptrap

latín *m* Latin; **latín de cocina** dog Latin, hog Latin; **latín rústico** or **vulgar** Vulgar Latin; **saber latín** or **mucho latín** (coll) to be very shrewd

latinajo *m* (coll) dog Latin, hog Latin; (coll) Latin word or phrase (*slipped into the vernacular*)

latinar or **latinear** *intr* to use Latin

lati·no -na *adj* Latin; (naut) lateen || *mf* Latin

Latinoamérica *f* Latin America

latinoamerica·no -na *adj* Latin-American || *mf* Latin American

latir *tr* (Ven) to annoy, bore, molest || *intr* (*el perro*) to bark, yelp; (*el corazón*) to beat, throb; **me late que** (Mex) I have a hunch that

latitud *f* latitude

la·to -ta *adj* broad || *f* see **lata**

latón *m* brass; (Cuba) garbage pail

lato·so -sa *adj* annoying, boring || *mf* bore

latrocinio *m* thievery; thievishness

laucha *f* (Arg, Chile) mouse

laúd *m* (mus) lute; (zool) leatherback turtle

laudable *adj* laudable

láudano *m* laudanum

laudato·rio -ria *adj* laudatory

laudo *m* (law) finding, decision

láurea *f* laurel wreath

laurea·do -da *adj* & *mf* laureate

laurean·do -da *mf* graduate, candidate for a degree

laurear *tr* to trim or adorn with laurel; to crown with laurel; to decorate, honor, reward

laurel *m* laurel; (*de la victoria*) laurels; **dormirse sobre sus laureles** to rest or sleep on one's laurels

láure·o -a *adj* laurel || *f* see **láurea**

lauréola *f* crown of laurel, laurel wreath; (*aureola*) halo

lava *f* lava; (min) washing

lavable *adj* washable

lavabo *m* washstand; washroom, lavatory

lavaca·ras *mf* (*pl* **-ras**) (coll) fawner, flatterer, bootlicker

lavaco·ches *m* (*pl* **-ches**) car washer

lavade·dos *m* (*pl* **-dos**) finger bowl

lavadero *m* laundry; (*tabla de lavar*) washboard; (*a orillas de un río*) washing place; (Guat, Mex, SAm) placer

lava·do -da *adj* (coll) brazen, fresh, impudent || *m* wash, washing; **lavado a seco** dry cleaning; **lavado cerebral** or **de cerebro** brain-washing; **lavado químico** dry cleaning

lava·dor -dora *mf* washer || *m* (phot) washer || *f* washing machine; **lavadora de platos** or **de vajilla** dishwasher

lavadura *f* washing; (*agua sucia; rozadura de una cuerda*) washings

lavafru·tas *m* (*pl* **-tas**) fruit bowl, finger bowl

lavama·nos *m* (*pl* **-nos**) (*pila con caño y llave*) washstand; (*jofaina*) washbowl

lavanda *f* lavender

lavandera *f* laundress, laundrywoman, washerwoman; (orn) sandpiper

lavandero *m* launderer, laundryman

lavándula *f* lavender

lavao·jos *m* (*pl* **-jos**) eyecup

lavaparabri·sas *m* (*pl* **-sas**) windshield washer

lavapla·tos (*pl* **-tos**) *mf* (*persona*) dishwasher || *m* (*aparato*) dishwasher; (Chile) kitchen sink

lavar *tr* & *ref* to wash

lavativa *f* enema; (coll) annoyance, bore

lavatorio *m* washing; washstand; toilet; (*ceremonia de lavar los pies*) maundy; (med) wash, lotion; (Am) washroom

lavazas *fpl* dirty water, wash water

laxante *adj* & *m* laxative

laxar *tr* to ease, to slack; (*el vientre*) to loosen

la·xo -xa *adj* lax, slack; (fig) lax, loose

laya *f* spade; kind, quality

layar *tr* to spade, dig with a spade

lazada *f* bowknot

lazar §60 *tr* to lasso

lazarillo *m* blind man's guide

lazari·no -na *adj* leprous || *mf* leper

lázaro *m* raggedy beggar; **estar hecho un lázaro** to be full of sores

lazo *m* bow, knot, tie; lasso, lariat; snare, trap; bond, tie; **armar lazo a** (coll) to set a trap for; **caer en el lazo** (coll) to fall into the trap; **lazo de amor** truelove knot; **lazo de unión** (fig) tie, bond

Ldo. *abbr* **Licenciado**

le *pron pers* to him, to her, to it; to you; him; you

leal *adj* loyal, faithful; reliable, trustworthy || *m* loyalist

lealtad *f* loyalty; reliability, trustworthiness

le·brel -brela *mf* whippet, small greyhound

lebrillo *m* earthen washtub

lebrón *m* large hare; (coll) coward; (Mex) slicker

lección *f* lesson; (*interpretación de un pasaje*) reading; **dar la lección** to recite one's lesson; **echar** or **señalar lección** to assign the lesson; **tomar una lección a** to hear the lesson of

leccionista *mf* private tutor

lecti·vo -va *adj* school (*e.g., day*)

lec·tor -tora *adj* reading || *mf* reader || *m* foreign-language teacher; (*empleado que anota el consumo registrado por el contador de agua, gas o* *electricidad*) meter reader; **lector mental** mind reader

lectura *f* reading; broad culture; public lecture; college subject; (*interpretación de un pasaje*) reading; (elec) playback; (typ) pica; **lectura de la mente** mind reading

lechada *f* grout; whitewash; (*para hacer papel*) pulp; (CAm, Mex, W-I) whitewash

lechar *tr* (Am) to milk; (CAm, Mex, W-I) to whitewash

leche *f* milk; **estar con la leche en los labios** to lack experience, to be young and inexperienced; **leche de manteca** buttermilk; **leche desnatada** skim milk; **leche en polvo** milk powder

lechecillas *fpl* sweetbread

lechera *f* milkmaid, dairymaid; (*vasija para guardar la leche*) milk can; (*vasija para servir la leche*) milk pitcher

lechería *f* dairy, creamery

leche·ro -ra *adj* (*que da leche*) milch; (*perteneciente a la leche*) milk; (*cicatero*) (coll) stingy || *m* milkman, dairyman || *f* see **lechera**

lecho *m* bed; (*especie de sofá*) couch; (*cauce de río*) bed; layer, stratum; **abandonar el lecho** to get up (*from illness*); **lecho de plumas** (fig) feather bed

le·chón -chona *adj* (coll) filthy, sloppy || *mf* suckling pig; (*persona sucia, desaseada*) (coll) pig || *m* pig || *f* sow

lecho·so -sa *adj* milky || *m* papaya (*tree*) || *f* papaya (*fruit*)

lechuga *f* lettuce; head of lettuce; (*fuelle formado en la tela*) frill; **lechuga romana** romaine lettuce

lechugui·no -na *adj* stylish, sporty || *m* dandy || *f* stylish young lady

lechuza *f* barn owl, screech owl; (coll) owllike woman

lechu·zo -za *adj* owlish; (*muleto*) yearling || *m* bill collector; summons server; (coll) owllike fellow || *f* see **lechuza**

leer §43 *tr* to read || *intr* to read; to lecture; **leer en to read** (*someone's thoughts*) || *ref* to read, e.g., **este libro se lee con facilidad** this book reads easily

leg. *abbr* **legal, legislatura**

lega *f* lay sister

legación *f* legation

legado *m* (*don que se hace por testamento*) legacy; (*enviado diplomático*) legate

legajo *m* file, docket, dossier

legal *adj* legal; faithful, prompt, right

legalidad *f* legality; faithfulness, promptness

legalizar §60 *tr* to legalize; to authenticate

légamo *m* slime, ooze

legamo·so -sa *adj* slimy, oozy

legaña *f* rheum (*on edge of eyelids*)

legaño·so -sa *adj* gummy

legar §44 *tr* to bequeath, to will

legata·rio -ria *mf* legatee

legenda·rio -ria *adj* legendary

legible *adj* legible

legión *f* legion

legislación *f* legislation

legisla·dor -dora *adj* legislating || *mf* legislator

legislar *intr* to legislate

legislati·vo -va *adj* legislative

legislatura *f* session of a legislature; (Am) legislature

legista *m* law professor; law student

legitimar *tr* to legitimate; to legitimize

legitimidad *f* legitimacy

legíti·mo -ma *adj* legitimate

le·go -ga *adj* lay; uninformed || *m* layman; lay brother || *f* see **lega**

legua *f* league; **a leguas** far, far away

leguleyo *m* pettifogger

legumbre *f* (*hortaliza*) vegetable; (bot) legume; (Chile) vegetable stew

leíble *adj* legible, readable

leída *f* reading

leí·do -da *adj* well-read; **leído y escribido** (coll) posing as learned || *f* see **leída**

lejanía *f* distance, remoteness

leja·no -na *adj* distant, remote; (*pariente*) distant

lejía *f* lye; wash water; (coll) severe rebuke

lejiadora *f* washing machine

lejos *adv* far; **a lo lejos** in the distance; **de lejos** or **desde lejos** from a distance || *m* glimpse; look from afar; **tener buen lejos** to look good at a distance

le·lo -la *adj* stupid, inane

lema *m* motto, slogan; theme

len *adj* soft, flossy

lena *f* spirit, vigor; breathing

lencería *f* linen goods, dry goods; linen closet; dry-goods store

lence·ro -ra *mf* linen dealer, dry-goods dealer

lendrera *f* fine-toothed comb

lendro·so -sa *adj* nitty, lousy

lene *adj* (*suave al tacto*) soft; (*ligero*) light; kind, agreeable

lengua *f* (anat) tongue; (*idioma*) language, tongue; (*de tierra, de fuego, de zapato; badajo de campana; lengua de un animal usada como alimento*) tongue; **buscar la lengua a** (coll) to pick a fight with; **dar la lengua** (coll) to chew the rag; **hacerse lenguas de** (coll) to rave about; **írsele a** (*uno*) **la lengua** (coll) to blab; **lengua madre** or **matriz** mother tongue (*language from which another is derived*); **lengua materna** mother tongue (*language acquired by reason of nationality*); **morderse la lengua** to hold one's tongue; **tener en la lengua** (coll) to have on the tip of one's tongue; **tener la lengua gorda** (coll) to talk thick; (coll) to be drunk; **tener mala lengua** (coll) to be blasphemous; (coll) to have an evil tongue; **tener mucha lengua** (coll) to be a great talker; **tirar de la lengua a** (coll) to draw out; **tomar en lenguas** (coll) to gossip about; **tomar lengua** or **lenguas** to pick up news

lenguado *m* sole

lenguaje *m* language

lengua·raz (*pl* **-races**) *adj* foul-mouthed, scurrilous; polyglot ‖ *mf* linguist
len·guaz *adj* (*pl* **-guaces**) garrulous
lengüeta *f* (*de la balanza*) pointer, needle; (*del zapato*) tongue; (anat) epiglottis; (carp) tongue; (*de un instrumento de viento*) (mus) reed; (Chile) paper cutter; (Mex) petticoat fringe; (SAm) chatterbox
lengüetada *f* licking, lapping
lengüetear *intr* to stick the tongue out; to flicker, to flutter; (Am) to jabber, to rant
lengüilar·go -ga *adj* (coll) foul-mouthed, scurrilous
lengüisu·cio -cia *adj* (Mex, P-R) foul-mouthed, scurrilous
lenidad *f* lenience
lenocinio *m* pandering, procuring
lente *m* & *f* lens; **lente de aumento** magnifying glass; **lente de contacto** or **lente invisible** contact lens; **lentes** *mpl* nose glasses; **lentes de nariz** or **de pinzas** pince-nez
lenteja *f* lentil; (*del reloj*) bob, pendulum bob
lentejuela *f* sequin, spangle
lentitud *f* slowness
len·to -ta *adj* slow; sticky; (*fuego*) low
leña *f* firewood, kindling wood; **cargar de leña** (coll) to give a drubbing to; **llevar leña al monte** to carry coals to Newcastle
leña·dor -dora *mf* woodcutter ‖ *m* woodsman
leñame *m* lumber, timber; stock of firewood
leñero *m* wood merchant; wood purchaser; (*sitio donde se guarda la leña*) woodshed
leño *m* (*madera*) wood; (*tronco de árbol, limpio de ramas*) log; (coll) sap, blockhead; (poet) ship, vessel; **dormir como un leño** to sleep like a log
leño·so -sa *adj* woody
león *m* lion
leona *f* lioness
leona·do -da *adj* tawny, fulvous
leonera *f* lion cage, den of lions; (coll) dive, gambling joint; (coll) junk room, lumber room
leonero *m* lion keeper; (coll) keeper of a gambling joint
leontina *f* watch chain
leopardo *m* leopard
leopoldina *f* watch fob; (mil) Spanish shako
leotardo *m* leotard
lepe *m* (Ven) flip in the ear; **saber más que Lepe** to be wide-awake
leperada *f* (CAm, Mex) coarseness, vulgarity
lepisma *f* (ent) silver fish, fish moth
lepori·no -na *adj* hare, harelike
lepra *f* leprosy
leprosería *f* leper house
lepro·so -sa *adj* leprous ‖ *mf* leper
ler·do -da *adj* slow, dull; coarse, crude
lesbianismo *m* lesbianism
les·bio -bia *adj* & *mf* Lesbian ‖ *f* (*mujer homosexual*) Lesbian, lesbian
lesión *f* harm, hurt; (pathol) lesion

lesionar *tr* to harm, hurt, injure
lesi·vo -va *adj* harmful, injurious
lesna *f* awl
le·so -sa *adj* hurt, harmed, injured; wounded; offended; perverted; (SAm) simple, foolish
leste *m* (naut) east
letal *adj* lethal, deadly
letame *m* manure
letanía *f* litany; (*enumeración seguida*) (coll) litany
letárgi·co -ca *adj* lethargic
letargo *m* lethargy
letargo·so -sa *adj* lethargic
le·tón -tona *adj* Lettish ‖ *mf* Lett ‖ *m* (*idioma*) Lettish, Lett
Letonia *f* Latvia
letra *f* (*del alfabeto*) letter; (*modo de escribir propio de una persona*) hand, handwriting; (*de una canción*) words, lyric; (com) draft; (typ) type; (*sentido material*) (fig) letter; **a la letra** (*al pie de la letra*) to the letter; **a letra vista** (com) at sight; **bellas letras** belles lettres; **cuatro letras** or **dos letras** (*esquela, cartita*) a line; **en letras de molde** in print; **escribir en letra de molde** to print; **las letras y las armas** the pen and the sword; **letra a la vista** (com) sight draft; **letra de cambio** (com) bill of exchange; **letra de imprenta** (typ) type; **letra de mano** handwriting; **letra de molde** printed letter; **letra menuda** fine print; (fig) cunning; **letra muerta** dead letter; **letra negrilla** (typ) boldface; **letra redonda** or **redondilla** (typ) roman; **letras** (*literatura*) letters; (coll) a few words, a line; **primeras letras** elementary education, three R's
letra·do -da *adj* learned, lettered; (coll) pedantic ‖ *m* lawyer
letrero *m* sign, notice; (*p.ej., en una botella*) label
letrina *f* privy, latrine; (*cloaca*) sewer; (*cosa sucia*) (fig) cesspool
letrista *mf* lyricist, writer of lyrics (*for songs*); calligrapher, engrosser
leucemia *f* leukemia
leucorrea *f* leucorrhea
leudar *tr* to leaven, to ferment with yeast ‖ *ref* (*la masa con la levadura*) to rise
leu·do -da *adj* leavened, fermented
leva *f* weighing anchor; (mach) cam; (mil) levy
levada *f* (*de la espada, el florete, etc.*) flourish; (*de los astros*) rise; (*del émbolo*) stroke
levadi·zo -za *adj* (*puente*) lift
levadura *f* leaven; leavening; yeast; (*tabla*) board; **levadura comprimida** yeast cake; **levadura de cerveza** brewer's yeast; **levadura en polvo** baking powder
levantaco·ches *m* (*pl* **-ches**) auto jack
levantada *f* rising, getting up (*from bed or from sickbed*)
levantamiento *m* rise, elevation; insurrection, revolt, uprising; **levantamiento del cadáver** inquest; **levantamiento del censo** census taking; **le-**

vantamiento de planos surveying

levantar *tr* to raise, to lift, to elevate; to agitate, rouse, stir up; (*una sesión*) to adjourn; (*la mesa*) to clear; (*la voz*) to raise; (*el campo*) to break; (*gente para el ejército; un sitio; fondos*) to raise; (*el ancla*) to weigh; to straighten up; to build, construct, erect; to establish, found; **levantar casa** to break up housekeeping; **levantar planos** to make a survey || *ref* to rise; (*de la cama*) to get up; (*de una silla*) to stand up; to straighten up; (*sublevarse*) to rise up, rebel

levantaválvu·las *m* (*pl* -las) valve lifter

levantaventana *m* sash lift

levante *m* east; (*viento*) levanter || **Levante** *m* (*países de la parte oriental del Mediterráneo*) Levant; northeastern Mediterranean shores of Spain, especially around Valencia, Alicante, and Murcia

levantí·no -na *adj* Levantine; of the northeastern Mediterranean shores of Spain || *mf* Levantine; native or inhabitant of the northeastern Mediterranean shores of Spain

levar *tr* (*el ancla*) to weigh || *ref* to set sail

leve *adj* (*de poco peso*) light; slight, trivial, trifling

levedad *f* lightness; trivialness

leviatán *m* (Bib & fig) leviathan

levita *m* deacon || *f* coat, frock coat

levitón *m* heavy frock coat

léxi·co -ca *adj* lexical || *m* lexicon; (*caudal de voces de un autor*) vocabulary; (*conjunto de vocablos de una lengua o dialecto*) wordstock

lexicografía *f* lexicography

lexicográfi·co -ca *adj* lexicographic(al)

lexicógra·fo -fa *mf* lexicographer

lexicología *f* lexicology

lexicón *m* lexicon

ley *f* law; loyalty, devotion; norm, standard; (*de un metal*) fineness; **a ley de caballero** on the word of a gentleman; **de buena ley** sterling, genuine; **ley de la selva** law of the jungle; **ley del menor esfuerzo** line of least resistance; **ley marcial** martial law; **ley seca** dry law; **tener o tomar ley a** to become devoted to; **venir contra una ley** to break a law

leyenda *f* legend

leyente *adj* reading || *mf* reader

lezna *f* awl

lía *f* plaited esparto rope; **lías** lees, dregs

llanza *f* (Chile) account, credit (*in a store*)

liar §77 *tr* to tie, bind; to tie up, wrap up; (*un cigarrillo*) to roll; (coll) to embroil, to involve; **liarlas** (coll) to beat it; (coll) to kick the bucket || *ref* to join together, to be associated; to have a liaison; (coll) to become embroiled, become involved; **liárselos** (coll) to roll one's own (*i.e.*, *cigarettes*)

libación *f* libation; (*acción de beber vino u otro licor*) libation

liba·nés -nesa *adj* & *mf* Lebanese

Líbano, el Lebanon

libar *tr* to suck; to taste, to sip || *intr* to pour out a libation; to imbibe

libelo *m* lampoon, libel; (law) petition

libélula *f* dragonfly

liberación *f* liberation; (*cancelación de la carga que grava un inmueble*) redemption; (*de una cuenta*) settlement, closing; quittance

liberal *adj* liberal; (*expedito*) quick, ready; (pol) liberal; (*de amplias miras*) (Arg) liberal-minded || *mf* (pol) liberal

liberalidad *f* liberality

liberar *tr* to free

libertad *f* liberty, freedom; **libertad de cátedra** academic freedom; **libertad de cultos** freedom of worship; **libertad de empresa** free enterprise; **libertad de enseñanza** academic freedom; **libertad de imprenta** freedom of the press; **libertad de los mares** freedom of the seas; **libertad de palabra** freedom of speech, free speech; **libertad de reunión** freedom of assembly; **libertad vigilada** probation; **plena libertad** free hand; **tomarse la libertad de** to take the liberty of

liberta·do -da *adj* bold, daring; free, brash, unrestrained

liberta·dor -dora *mf* liberator

libertar *tr* to liberate, to set free; (*de un peligro, la muerte, etc.*) to save

liberta·rio -ria *adj* anarchistic

libertinaje *m* licentiousness, profligacy; impiety, ungodliness

liberti·no -na *adj* & *mf* libertine

liber·to -ta *mf* (law) probationer || *m* freedman || *m* freedwoman

libídine *f* lewdness, lust; (*impulso a las actividades sexuales*) libido

libidino·so -sa *adj* libidinous

libido *f* libido

libra *f* pound; **libra esterlina** pound sterling

libraco or **libracho** *m* (coll) trashy book

libra·do -da *mf* (com) drawee

libra·dor -dora *mf* (com) drawer

libranza *f* (com) draft; **libranza postal** money order

librar *tr* to free; to save, to spare; (*la esperanza*) to place; (*batalla*) to give, to join; (com) to draw || *intr* to be delivered, to give birth; (*una religiosa*) to receive a visitor in the locutory; (com) to draw; **librar bien** to come off well, to succeed; **librar mal** to come off badly, to fail || *ref* to free oneself; to escape

libre *adj* free; free, brash, outspoken; free, unmarried; free, loose, licentious; innocent, guiltless; **libre de porte** postage prepaid

librea *f* livery

librecambio *m* free trade

librecambista *mf* freetrader

librepensa·dor -dora *adj* freethinking || *mf* freethinker

librería *f* bookstore, bookshop; book business; (*mueble*) bookshelf; **librería de viejo** second-hand bookshop

libreril *adj* book

librero *m* bookseller; (*encuadernador*) bookbinder; (Cuba, Mex) bookshelf

libres·co -ca *adj* bookish

libreta *f* notebook; **libreta de banco** bankbook

libreto *m* (mus) libretto

librillo *m* earthen washtub; (*de papel de fumar, de sellos, etc.*) book

libro *m* book; **ahorcar los libros** (coll) to become a dropout; **a libro abierto** at sight; **hacer libro nuevo** (coll) to turn over a new leaf; **libro a la rústica** paperbound book; **libro de caballerías** romance of chivalry; **libro de cocina** cookbook; **libro de cheques** checkbook; **libro de chistes** joke book; **libro de lance** second-hand book; **libro de mayor venta** best seller; **libro de memoria** memo book; **libro de oro** guest book; **libro de recuerdos** scrapbook; **libro de teléfonos** telephone book; **libro de texto** textbook; **libro diario** day book; **libro en rústica** paperbound book; **libro mayor** (com) ledger; **libro talonario** checkbook, stub book

libro-registro *m* (com) book

licencia *f* license; leave of absence; (mil) furlough; **licencia absoluta** (mil) discharge; **licencia por enfermedad** sick leave

licencia·do -da *adj* pedantic ‖ *mf* licenciate ‖ *m* lawyer; (mil) discharged soldier; (coll) university student (*wearing the long student gown*)

licenciar *tr* to license; to allow, permit; to confer the degree of licenciate or master on; (mil) to discharge ‖ *ref* to receive the degree of licenciate or master; to become dissolute; (mil) to be discharged

licenciatura *f* licenciate, master's degree; graduation with a licenciate or master's degree; work leading to a licenciate or master's degree

licencio·so -sa *adj* licentious

liceo *m* (*sociedad literaria, establecimiento de enseñanza popular*) lyceum; (*instituto de segunda enseñanza*) (Chile) lycée; (Mex) primary school

licitación *f* bidding

licita·dor -dora *mf* bidder

licitar *tr* to bid on; (Arg) to buy at auction, to sell at auction ‖ *intr* to bid

lici·to -ta *adj* fair, just; licit, legal

licor *m* (*bebida espiritosa; cuerpo líquido*) liquor; (*bebida espiritosa preparada por mezcla de azúcar y substancias aromáticas*) liqueur

licorera *f* cellaret

licorista *mf* distiller; liquor dealer

licoro·so -sa *adj* spirituous, alcoholic; (*vino*) rich, generous

licuar §21 & regular *tr* to liquefy

lid *f* fight, combat; dispute, argument; **en buena lid** by fair means

líder *m* leader

lidia *f* fight; bullfight

lidiadera *f* (Ecuad) quarreling, bickering

lidia·dor -dora *mf* fighter ‖ *m* bullfighter

lidiar *tr* (*un toro*) to fight ‖ *intr* to fight; **lidiar con** to fight with; to have to put up with

liebre *f* hare; (*hombre cobarde*) (coll) coward

liendre *f* nit

lien·to -ta *adj* damp, dank

lienza *f* strip of cloth

lienzo *m* linen, linen cloth; linen handkerchief; (*de edificio o pared*) face, front; (*pintura sobre lienzo*) canvas; **lienzo de la Verónica** veronica (*representing face of Christ*)

liga *f* (*cinta elástica para asegurar las medias*) garter; (*aleación*) alloy; (*materia pegajosa para cazar pájaros*) birdlime; (*confederación, alianza*) league; (*muérdago*) mistletoe; band; **liga de goma** rubber band

ligado *m* (mus & typ) ligature

ligadura *f* tie, bond; (mus) ligature, glide; (surg) ligature

ligamento *m* ligament

ligar §44 *tr* to tie, bind; to join, combine; to alloy; (*bebidas*) to mix; (surg) to ligate ‖ *ref* to league together; to be committed; to be bound or attached (*e.g., in friendship*)

ligereza *f* lightness; speed, rapidity; fickleness, inconstancy; tactlessness

lige·ro -ra *adj* light; (*té*) weak; (*tejido*) light, thin; quick; slight; **a la ligera** lightly; quickly; unceremoniously; **de ligero** thoughtlessly, rashly; **ligero de cascos** light-headed, scatterbrained; **ligero de lengua** loose-tongued; **ligero de pies** light-footed; **ligero de ropa** scantily clad ‖ **ligero** *adv* (Am) fast, rapidly

lignito *m* lignite

ligustro *m* privet

lija *f* (*pez*) dogfish; (*papel que sirve para pulir*) sandpaper; **darse lija** (W-I) to boast, brag, pat oneself on the back

lijar *tr* to sand, to sandpaper

lila *adj* (coll) silly, simple ‖ *m* lilac (*color*) ‖ *f* lilac (*plant and flower*)

li·lac *f* (*pl* **-laques**) lilac

liliputiense *adj* & *mf* Lilliputian

lima *f* (*herramienta*) file; sweet lime; sweet-lime tree; (*del tejado*) hip; hip rafter; correcting, polishing; **lima de uñas** nail file; **lima hoya** valley (*of roof*)

limadura *f* filing; (*partecillas*) filings

limalla *f* filings

limar *tr* to file; to file down; to polish, touch up; to smooth, smooth over; (*cercenar*) to curtail

limaza *f* (*babosa*) slug; (Ven) large file

limazo *m* slime, sliminess

limbo *m* (*borde*) edge; (theol) limbo; **estar en el limbo** (coll) to be quite distraught

limen *m* (physiol, psychol & fig) threshold

limensón *m* (Chile) honeydew melon

lime·ño -ña *adj* & *mf* Limean

limero *m* sweet-lime tree

limita·do -da *adj* limited; dull-witted

limitador m — **limitador de corriente** clock meter; slot meter
limitar tr to limit; to cut down, reduce || intr — **limitar con** to border on
límite m limit; boundary, border
limítrofe adj bordering
limo m slime, mud
limón m lemon; lemon tree; (de un coche o carro) shaft
limonada f lemonade
limoncillo m citronella
limonera f shaft
limonero m lemon tree
limosna f alms
limosnear intr to beg
limosne·ro -ra adj almsgiving, charitable || mf almsgiver; (Am) beggar || m alms box
limo·so -sa adj slimy, muddy
limpia f cleaning
limpiabo·rros m (pl -rros) scraper, foot scraper
limpiabo·tas m (pl -tas) bootblack
limpiacrista·les m (pl -les) windshield washer
limpiachimene·as m (pl -as) chimney sweep
limpiadien·tes m (pl -tes) toothpick
limpia·dor -dora adj cleaning || mf cleaner
limpiadura f cleaning; **limpiaduras** cleanings, dirt
limpiama·nos m (pl -nos) (Guat, Hond) towel
limpiamente adv in a clean manner; with ease, skillfully; simply, sincerely; unselfishly
limpiameta·les m (pl -les) metal polish
limpianieve m snowplow
limpiaparabri·sas m (pl -sas) windshield wiper
limpia·piés m (pl -piés) (Mex) door mat
limpiapi·pas m (pl -pas) pipe cleaner
limpiaplu·mas m (pl -mas) penwiper
limpiar tr to clean; (purificar) to cleanse; (de culpas) to exonerate; (un árbol) to clean out, to prune; (zapatos) to shine; (hurtar) (coll) to snitch; (a una persona en el juego) (coll) to clean out; (dinero en el juego) (coll) to clean up; (mil) to mop up; **limpiarle a uno de** to clean someone out of || ref to clean, to clean oneself
limpiaú·ñas m (pl -ñas) nail cleaner, orange stick
limpiaví·as m (pl -as) track cleaner
limpieza f (acción de limpiar) cleaning; (calidad de limpio) cleanness; (hábito del aseo) cleanliness; neatness, tidiness; honesty; chastity; ease, skill; (observancia de las reglas en los juegos) fair play; **limpieza de bolsa** (coll) emptiness of the pocketbook; **limpieza de la casa** house cleaning; **limpieza en seco** dry cleaning
lim·pio -pia adj clean; (que tiene el hábito del aseo) cleanly; neat, tidy; honest; chaste; clear, free; **dejar limpio** (coll) to clean out; **en limpio** (com) net; **limpio de polvo y paja** (coll) free, for nothing; (coll) net, after deducting expenses; **poner en**

limpio to make a clear or fair copy of; **quedar limpio** (coll) to be cleaned out; **sacar en limpio** to make a clear or clean copy of; to deduce, to understand || f see **limpia** || **limpio** adv fair; cleanly; **jugar limpio** to play fair
limpión m (limpiadura ligera) lick; (coll) cleaner; (Col) scolding; (Col, Ven) dustcloth; (Ecuad) dishcloth
limusina f limousine
lín. abbr **línea**
lina f (Chile) coarse wool
linaje m lineage; class, description; **linaje humano** mankind
linaju·do -da adj highborn || mf highborn person
linaza f flaxseed, linseed
lince adj keen, shrewd, discerning; (ojos) keen || m lynx; (fig) keen person
lincear tr (coll) to see into
linchamiento m lynching
linchar tr to lynch
lindante adj bordering, adjoining
lindar intr to border, be contiguous; **lindar con** to border on
linde m & f limit, boundary
linde·ro -ra adj bordering, adjoining || m edge; (Am) boundary stone, landmark || f limit, boundary; (bot) picebush
lindeza f prettiness, niceness; elegance; witticism, funny remark; (coll) flirting; **lindezas** (coll) insults
lin·do -da adj pretty, nice; fine, perfect; **de lo lindo** (coll) a lot, a great deal; wonderfully || m (coll) dude, sissy
lindura f prettiness, niceness
línea f line; (contorno de una figura, un vestido) lines; figure, waistline; **conservar la línea** to keep one's figure; **leer entre líneas** to read between the lines; **línea de agua** water line; **línea de batalla** line of battle; **línea de empalme** (rr) branch line; **línea de flotación** water line; **línea de fuego** firing line; **línea de fuerza** (elec) power line; (phys) line of force; **línea del partido** party line; **línea de mira** line of sight; **línea de montaje** assembly line; **línea de puntos** dotted line; **línea de tiro** (mil) line of fire; **línea férrea** railway; **línea internacional de cambio de fecha** international date line; **línea suplementaria** (mus) added line, ledger line
lineal adj linear
lineamentos mpl lineaments
linfa f lymph; (poet) water
linfáti·co -ca adj lymphatic
lingote m ingot, slug; (naut) ballast bar
lingual adj & f lingual
lingüista mf linguist
lingüísti·co -ca adj linguistic || f linguistics
linimento m liniment
lino m flax; (tela) linen; (poet) sail
linóleo m linoleum
linón m lawn
linotipia f linotype

linotípi·co -ca *adj* linotype
linotipista *mf* linotype operator
linotipo *m* linotype
linterna *f* lantern; **linterna eléctrica** flashlight
lío *m* bundle; *(de papeles)* batch; (coll) muddle, mess; (coll) liaison, affair; **armar un lío** (coll) to raise a row; **hacerse un lío** (coll) to get into a jam
lionesa — a la lionesa (culin) lyonnaise
liorna *f* (coll) hubbub, uproar ‖ **Liorna** *f* Leghorn
lio·so -sa *adj* (coll) trouble-making; (coll) knotty, troublesome
liq.ⁿ *abbr* **liquidación**
liq.° *abbr* **líquido**
liquen *m* lichen
liquidar *tr* to liquefy; (com) to liquidate ‖ *intr* (com) to liquidate ‖ *ref* to liquefy
liquidez *f* liquidity
líqui·do -da *adj* & *m* liquid; (com) net ‖ *f* (phonet) liquid
lira *f* (mus) lyre; *(numen de un poeta)* inspiration; poems, poetry
lírica *f* lyric poetry
líri·co -ca *adj* lyric(al); *(músico, operístico)* lyric; (Am) fantastic, utopian ‖ *m* lyric poet; (Arg, Ven) visionary ‖ *f* see **lírica**
lirio *m* (bot) iris; **lirio blanco** *(azucena)* Madonna lily; **lirio de agua** (bot) calla, calla lily; **lirio de los valles** (bot) lily of the valley
lirismo *m* lyricism; spellbinding; (Am) fancy, illusion
lirón *m* (bot) water plantain; (zool) dormouse; (coll) sleepyhead
lis *m* (bot) lily ‖ *f* (bot) iris; (heral) fleur-de-lis
Lisboa *f* Lisbon
lisia·do -da *adj* hurt, injured; crippled; *(muy deseoso)* eager ‖ *mf* cripple
lisiar *tr* to hurt, injure; to cripple ‖ *ref* to become crippled
lisimaquia *f* loosestrife
li·so -sa *adj* even, smooth; *(vestido)* plain, unadorned; *(franco, sincero)* simple, plain-dealing; (Am) brash, insolent; **liso y llano** (coll) simple, easy
lisonja *f* flattery
lisonjear *tr* to flatter; to please ‖ *intr* to flatter
lisonje·ro -ra *adj* flattering; pleasing ‖ *mf* flatterer
lista *f* list; *(tira)* strip; *(en un tejido)* colored stripe; *(recuento en alta voz de las personas que deben estar en un lugar)* roll call; **lista de bajas** casualty list; **lista de comidas** bill of fare; **lista de correos** general delivery; **lista de espera** waiting list; **lista de frecuencia** frequency list; **lista de pagos** pay roll; **pasar lista** to call the roll
listar *tr* to list
listero *m* roll keeper, timekeeper
lis·to -ta *adj* ready; quick, prompt; alert, wide-awake; **estar listo** to be ready; to be finished; **listo de manos** (coll) light-fingered; **pasarse de listo** to be shrewd, to be clever ‖ *f* see **lista**
listón *m* *(cinta)* ribbon, tape; *(pedazo*

de tabla angosta) lath, strip of wood
listonado *m* lath, lathing
lisura *f* evenness, smoothness; plainness; simpleness, candor; (Am) brashness, insolence
lit. *abbr* **literalmente**
lite *f* lawsuit
litera *f* *(vehículo llevado por hombres o por animales)* litter; *(cama fija en los camarotes)* berth; **litera alta** upper berth; **litera baja** lower berth
literal *adj* literal
litera·rio -ria *adj* literary
litera·to -ta *adj* literary ‖ *mf* literary person; **literatos** literati
literatura *f* literature; **literatura de escape** or **de evasión** escape literature
litigación *s* litigation
litigante *adj* & *mf* litigant
litigar §44 *tr* & *intr* to litigate
litigio *m* litigation, lawsuit; argument, dispute
litigio·so -sa *adj* litigious
litina *s* (chem) lithia
litio *m* (chem) lithium
litisexpensas *fpl* (law) costs
litografía *f* *(arte de grabar en piedra para la reproducción en estampa)* lithography; *(estampa)* lithograph
litografiar §77 *tr* to lithograph
litógra·fo -fa *mf* lithographer
litoral *adj* coastal, littoral ‖ *m* coast, shore
litro *m* liter
liturgia *f* liturgy
litúrgi·co -ca *adj* liturgic(al)
liviandad *f* lightness; inconstancy, fickleness; lewdness
livia·no -na *adj* light; inconstant, fickle; lewd ‖ *m* leading donkey; **livianos** lights, lungs
liví·do -da *adj* livid
liza *f* combat, fight; *(campo para lidiar)* lists; **entrar en liza** to enter the lists
lo *art def neut* (used with *masc sg* form of *adj*) the, e.g., **lo bueno** the good; what is, e.g., **lo útil** what is useful; **lo mío** what is mine; (used with *adv* or inflected *adj*) the + noun, e.g., **lo aprisa que habla** the speed with which he speaks; **lo tacaños que son** the stinginess of them; how, e.g., **Vd.**, no sabe **lo felices que son** you do not know how happy they are; **lo más** as . . . as, e.g., **lo más temprano posible** as early as possible ‖ *pron pers masc* him, it; you; (with *estar, ser, parecer*, and the like, it stands for an adjective or noun understood and is either not translated or is translated by 'so'), e.g., **Vd. está preparado pero ella no lo está** you are ready but she is not ‖ *pron dem* that; **de lo que** + *verb* than + *verb*, e.g., **ese libro ha costado más dinero de lo que vale** that book cost more money than it is worth; **lo de** the matter of, the question of, e.g., **lo de sus deudas** the matter of your debts; **lo de que** the fact that, the statement that; **lo de siempre** the same old story; **lo que** what, that which; **todo lo que** all

(that), e.g., **me dió todo lo que tenía** he gave me all he had

loa *f* praise; (*del teatro antiguo*) prologue; short dramatic poem

loable *adj* laudable, praiseworthy

loar *tr* to praise

loba *f* she-wolf; ridge

lobagante *m* lobster (*Homarus*)

lobanillo *m* wen, cyst

lobato *m* wolf cub

lo·bo -ba *adj & mf* (Mex) half-breed ‖ *m* wolf; **coger** or **pillar un lobo** (coll) to go on a jag; **desollar** or **dormir un lobo** (coll) to sleep off a drunk; **lobo de mar** (ichth) sea wolf; (coll) old salt, sea dog; **lobo solitario** (fig) lone wolf ‖ *f* see **loba**

lóbre·go -ga *adj* dark, dismal; gloomy

lobreguez *f* darkness; gloominess

lobu·no -na *adj* wolf, wolfish

locación *f* lease

local *adj* local ‖ *m* quarters, place

localidad *f* (*lugar, sitio*) location, locality; (*plaza en un tren*) accommodations; (theat) seat

localización *f* localization; location; **localización de averías** trouble shooting

localizar §60 *tr* (*limitar a un punto determinado*) to localize; (*determinar el lugar de*) to locate

locería *f* (Am) pottery

loción *f* wash; (pharm) lotion

lo·co -ca *adj* crazy, insane, mad; terrific, wonderful; **estar loco por** (coll) to be crazy about, to be mad about; **loco de amor** madly in love; **loco de atar** (coll) raving mad; **loco perenne** insane, demented; (coll) full of fun; **loco rematado** (coll) stark-mad; **volver loco** to drive crazy ‖ *mf* crazy person, lunatic ‖ *m* (*bufón*) fool

locomotora *f* engine, locomotive; **locomotora de maniobras** shifting engine

locro *m* (SAm) meat and vegetable stew

lo·cuaz *adj* (*pl* **-cuaces**) loquacious

locución *f* expression, locution; idiomatic phrase, idiom

locuela *f* speech, way of speaking

locue·lo -la *adj* (coll) wild, frisky ‖ *f* see **locuela**

locura *f* insanity, madness; folly, madness

locu·tor -tora *mf* announcer, commentator

locutorio *m* (*en un convento de monjas*) parlor, locutory; telephone booth

lodazal *m* mudhole

lodo *m* mud, mire; (*substancia que sirve para cerrar junturas, tapar grietas, etc.*) (chem) lute

lodo·so -sa *adj* muddy

logaritmo *m* logarithm

logia *f* (*p.ej., de francmasones*) lodge; (archit) loggia

lógi·co -ca *adj* logical ‖ *mf* logician ‖ *f* logic

logísti·co -ca *adj* logistic(al) ‖ *f* logistics

logrado -da *adj* successful

lograr *tr* to get, to obtain; to achieve, attain; **lograr** + *inf* to succeed in + *ger* ‖ *ref* to be successful

logrear *intr* to be a moneylender; to profiteer

logre·ro -ra *adj* moneylending; profiteering ‖ *mf* moneylender; profiteer; (Chile) sponger

logro *m* attainment, success; gain, profit; usury; **dar** or **prestar a logro** to lend at usurious rates

loma *f* low hill, elevation

Lombardía *f* Lombardy

lombar·do -da *adj & mf* Lombard

lombriguera *f* wormhole in the ground; (bot) tansy

lom·briz *f* (*pl* **-brices**) worm, earthworm; (pathol) worm; (*persona muy alta y delgada*) (coll) beanpole; **lombriz de tierra** earthworm; **lombriz solitaria** tapeworm

lona *f* canvas; sailcloth; (Mex) burlap

loncha *f* slab, flagstone; slice, strip

londinense *adj* London ‖ *mf* Londoner

Londres *m* London; **el Gran Londres** Greater London

longáni·mo -ma *adj* long-suffering

longaniza *f* pork sausage

longevidad *f* longevity

longe·vo -va *adj* long-lived

longitud *f* length; (astr & geog) longitude

lonja *f* exchange, commodity exchange; grocery store; wool warehouse; (*de carne*) slice; (*de cuero*) strip; (*a la entrada de un edificio*) elevated parvis; (Arg) rawhide

lonjeta *f* bower, summerhouse

lonjista *mf* grocer

lontananza *f* (*de una pintura*) background; **en lontananza** in the distance, on the horizon

loor *m* praise

loquear *intr* to talk nonsense, to play the fool; to carry on, to have a high time

loquería *f* (Chile) madhouse, insane asylum

loque·ro -ra *mf* guard in a mental hospital ‖ *m* (Arg) confusion, pandemonium; (Arg) insane asylum

loques·co -ca *adj* crazy; funny, jolly

lord *m* (*pl* **-lores**) lord

lo·ro -ra *adj* dark-brown ‖ *m* parrot; cherry laurel; (Chile) spy; (Chile) glass bedpan; (Chile) third degree

losa *f* slab, flagstone; tomb

losange *m* lozenge; (baseball) diamond

lote *m* lot, share, portion; lottery prize; (Cuba, Mex) remnant; (Arg) dunce, simpleton; (Col) swallow, swig; (*de terreno*) (Cuba, Mex) lot

lotear *tr* (Chile) to divide up, divide into lots

lotería *f* lottery; (*juego casero*) lotto; (*cosa insegura, riesgo*) gamble

lote·ro -ra *mf* vendor of lottery tickets

lotizar §60 *tr* (Peru) to divide into lots

loto m lotus

loza f (barro cocido y barnizado) porcelain; crockery, earthenware; **loza fina** china, chinaware

lozanear intr to be luxuriant; to be full of life || ref (deleitarse) to luxuriate

lozanía f luxuriance, verdure; exuberance, vigor; pride, haughtiness

loza·no -na adj luxuriant, verdant; exuberant, vigorous; proud, haughty

lubricante adj & m lubricant

lubricar §73 tr to lubricate

lúbri·co -ca adj (resbaladizo; lascivo) lubricous (slippery; lewd)

lubrificar §73 tr to lubricate

lucera f skylight

lucerna f large chandelier; (abertura, tronera) loophole

lucero m bright star; (planeta) Venus; (ventanillo en un muro) light; **lucero del alba** or **de la mañana** morning star; **lucero de la tarde** evening star; **luceros** (poet) eyes

luci·do -da adj generous, magnificent; brilliant, successful; sumptuous; (Arg) striking, dashing

lúci·do -da adj lucid

luciente adj bright, shining

luciérnaga f glowworm, firefly

lucifer m overbearing fellow || **Lucifer** m Lucifer

lucífe·ro -ra adj (poet) bright, dazzling || m morning star; (Col) match

lucimiento m brilliance, luster; show, dash; success; **quedar** or **salir con lucimiento** to come off with flying colors

lu·cio -cia adj shiny || m salt pool; (pez) pike, luce

lucir §45 tr to light, light up; to show, display; (p.ej., un traje nuevo) to sport; to help; to plaster || intr to shine || ref to dress up; to come off with great success; (sobresalir, distinguirse) to shine; (coll) to flop, e.g., **lucido me quedé** I was a flop

lucrar tr to get, obtain || intr & ref to profit, make money

lucrati·vo -va adj lucrative

lucro m gain, profit; **lucros y daños** profit and loss

lucro·so -sa adj lucrative

luctuo·so -sa adj sad, mournful, gloomy

lucha f fight; (disputa) quarrel; (actividad forzada) struggle; (combate cuerpo a cuerpo) wrestling; **lucha de la cuerda** (sport) tug of war; **lucha por la vida** struggle for existence

lucha·dor -dora mf fighter; wrestler

luchar intr (combatir) to fight; (disputar) to quarrel; (esforzarse) to struggle; (pelear cuerpo a cuerpo) to wrestle

ludibrio m derision, mockery, scorn

ludir tr, intr & ref to rub, rub together

luego adv next, then; therefore; soon; desde luego right away; of course; hasta luego good-bye, so long; luego como as soon as; luego de after, right after; luego que as soon as

luen·go -ga adj long

lúes f pestilence; **lúes canina** distemper; **lúes venérea** syphilis

lugano m (orn) siskin

lugar m place; site, spot; job, position; (espacio) room, space; (asiento) seat; village, hamlet; (geom) locus; **dar lugar** to make room; **dar lugar a** to give cause for; to give rise to; **en lugar de** instead of, in place of; **hacer lugar** to make room; **lugar común** (expresión trivial) commonplace; (retrete) toilet, water closet; **lugar de cita** tryst; **lugares estrechos** close quarters; **lugar geométrico** locus; **lugar religioso** place of burial

lugarejo m hamlet

lugare·ño -ña adj village || mf villager

lugarteniente m lieutenant

luge f sled

lúgubre adj dismal, gloomy, lugubrious

luir §20 tr (naut) to gall, to wear; (Chile) to muss, to rumple; (vasijas de barro) (Chile) to polish || ref (Chile) to rub, wear away

luisa f (bot) lemon verbena

lujo m luxury; **de lujo** de luxe; **gastar mucho lujo** to live in high style; **lujo de** abundance of, excess of

lujo·so -sa adj luxurious

lujuria f lust, lechery

lujuriante adj (lozano) luxuriant, lush; (libidinoso) lustful

lujuriar intr to lust, be lustful; (los animales) to copulate

lujurio·so -sa adj lustful, lecherous || m lecher

lu·lo -la adj (Chile) lank, slender || m (Chile) bundle

lu·lú m (pl -lúes) spitz dog

lumbago m lumbago

lumbre f light; fire; (para encender el cigarrillo) light; (hueco en un muro por donde entra la luz) light; brightness, brilliance; knowledge, learning; **echar lumbre** (coll) to blow one's top; **lumbre del agua** surface of the water; **lumbres** tinderbox; **ni por lumbre** (coll) not for love or money; **ser la lumbre de los ojos de** to be the light of the eyes of

lumbrera f light, source of light; light, lamp; (abertura por donde entran el aire y la luz) louver; sky light; dormer window; air duct, ventilating shaft; (persona insigne) light, luminary; (mach) port; **lumbreras** eyes

luminar m luminary

luminiscente adj luminescent

lumino·so -sa adj luminous; (idea) bright

luminotecnia f lighting engineering

lun. abbr **lunes**

luna f moon; moonlight; (tabla de cristal) plate glass; (espejo) mirror; (de los anteojos) lens, glass; (coll) caprice, whim; **estar de buena luna** to be in a good mood; **estar de mala luna** to be in a bad mood; **luna de miel** honeymoon; **luna llena** full moon; **luna menguante** waning moon; **luna nueva** new moon; **media luna** half moon; (figura de cuarto de luna creciente o menguante) crescent; **quedarse a la luna de Valencia** (coll) to be disappointed

lunar *adj* lunar ‖ *m* (*mancha de la piel*) mole; (*punto en un diseño de puntos*) polka dot; (fig) stain, blot, stigma; **lunar postizo** beauty spot

lunáti·co -ca *adj* & *mf* lunatic

lu·nes *m* (*pl* **-nes**) Monday; **hacer San Lunes** (Am) to knock off on Monday

luneta *f* (*de los anteojos*) lens, glass; orchestra seat; (aut) rear window

lunfardo *m* (Arg) thief; (Am) underworld slang

lupa *m* magnifying glass

lupanar *m* brothel, bawdyhouse

lupia *mf* (Hond) quack, healer ‖ *f* wen, cyst; **lupias** (Col) small amount of money, small change

lúpulo (*vid*) hop; (*flores desecadas de la vid*) hops

luquete *m* slice of orange or lemon used to flavor wine; (Chile) bald spot; (*en la ropa*) (Chile) spot, hole

lu·rio -ria *adj* (Mex) mad, crazy

lusitanismo *m* Lusitanism

lusitano -na *adj* & *mf* Lusitanian, Portuguese

lustrabo·tas *m* (*pl* **-tas**) (Am) bootblack

lustrar *tr* to shine, to polish ‖ *intr* to wander, roam

lustre *m* shine, polish; luster, gloss; (*fama, gloria*) (fig) luster

lustrina *f* (Chile) shoe polish

lustro *m* five years; chandelier

lustro·so -sa *adj* shining, bright, lustrous

lutera·no -na *adj* & *mf* Lutheran

luto *m* (*señal exterior de duelo*) mourning; (*duelo, aflicción*) sorrow, bereavement; **estar de luto** to be in mourning; **lutos** crape; **luto riguroso** deep mourning

lutocar *m* (Chile) trash cart

luz *f* (*pl* **luces**) light; window, light; guiding light; (*dinero*) (coll) money, cash; **a primera luz** at dawn; **a toda luz** or **a todas luces** everywhere; by all means; **dar a luz** to have a child; to give birth to; to bring out, to publish; **entre dos luces** at twilight; (coll) half-seas over; **luces de carretera** (aut) bright lights; **luces de cruce** (aut) dimmers; **luz de balizaje** (aer) marker light; **luz de magnesio** magnesium light; (phot) flash bulb, flashlight; **luz de matrícula** license-plate light; **luz de parada** stop light; **luz trasera** tail light; **sacar a luz** to bring to light; **salir a luz** to come to light; to come out, be published; to take place; **ver la luz** to see the light, see the light of day

Luzbel *m* Lucifer

Ll

Ll, ll (elle) *f* fourteenth letter of the Spanish alphabet

llaga *f* sore, ulcer; sorrow, grief; (*entre dos ladrillos*) (mas) seam, joint; (fig) ulcer

llagar §44 *tr* to make sore; to hurt

llama *f* flame, blaze; marsh, swamp; (zool) llama; (fig) fire, passion; **saltar de las llamas y caer en las brasas** to jump out of the frying pan into the fire

llamada *f* call; (*movimiento con que se llama la atención de uno*) sign, signal; knock, ring; reference, reference mark; (mil) call, call to arms; **batir** or **tocar a llamada** (mil) to sound the call to arms; **llamada a filas** (mil) call to the colors; **llamada a quintas** draft call

llamadera *f* goad

llama·do -da *adj* so-called ‖ *f* see **llamada**

llama·dor -dora *mf* caller ‖ *m* messenger; door knocker; push button

llamamiento *m* call; calling, vocation

llamar *tr* to call; (*dar nombre a*) to name, to call; to summon; to invoke, call upon; (*la atención*) to attract ‖ *intr* to call; (*golpear en la puerta*) to knock; (*hacer sonar la campanilla*) to ring; (*el viento*) (naut) to veer ‖ *ref* to be called, to be named; se **llama Juan** his name is John

llamarada *f* blaze, flare-up; (*encendimiento repentino del rostro*) flush; (fig) flare-up, outburst

llamarón *m* (Am) flare-up

llamati·vo -va *adj* showy, loud, flashy, gaudy; (*manjar*) thirst-raising

llamazar *m* swamp, marsh

llame *m* (Chile) bird net, bird trap

llamear *intr* to blaze, flame, flash

llampo *m* (Chile) ore

llana *f* trowel, float; plain; **dar de llana** to smooth with the trowel

llanada *f* plain

llanero *m* (Am) ranger, plainsman

llaneza *f* plainness, simplicity; familiarity; sincerity

lla·no -na *adj* even, level, smooth; (*parecido a un plano geométrico*) plane; (*sencillo*) plain, simple; clear, evident; (*palabras*) frank; accented on the next to last syllable ‖ *m* plain; (*de la escalera*) landing ‖ *f* see **llana**

llanque *m* (Peru) rawhide sandal

llanta *f* (*cerco exterior de la rueda*) tire (*of iron or rubber*); (*borde exterior de la rueda*) rim; (*pieza de hierro más ancha que gruesa*) iron flat; **llanta de goma** rubber tire; **llanta de oruga** (*de un tractor de oruga*) track

llanto *m* weeping, crying; **en llanto** in tears

llanura *f* evenness, level, smoothness; (*terreno extenso y llano*) plain

llapan·go -ga *adj* (Ecuad) barefooted

llares *m* pothanger

llave *adj* key ‖ *f* (*pieza para abrir y cerrar las cerraduras*) key; (*herramienta*) wrench; (*grifo*) faucet, spigot, cock; (*de arma de fuego*) cock; (*elec*) switch; (*de un instrumento de viento*) (mus) key; (*de un enigma, secreto, traducción, cifra; lugar estratégico más propicio*) key; **bajo llave** under lock and key; **echar la llave a** to lock; **llave de caja** socket wrench; **llave de caño** pipe wrench; **llave de cubo** socket wrench; **llave de chispa** flintlock; **llave de estufa** damper; **llave de mandíbulas dentadas** alligator wrench; **llave de paso** stopcock; passkey; **llave de purga** drain cock; **llave espacial** space key; **llave inglesa** monkey wrench; **llave maestra** master key, skeleton key; **llave para tubos** pipe wrench

llave-ro -ra *mf* keeper of the keys; (*carcelero*) turnkey ‖ *m* key ring

llavín *m* latchkey

llegada *f* arrival

llegar §44 *tr* to bring up, bring close ‖ *intr* to arrive; to happen; **llegar a** to arrive at; to reach; to amount to; to be equal to; **llegar a** + *inf* to come to + *inf*; to succeed in + *ger*; **llegar a ser** to become ‖ *ref* to come close

llena *f* flood

llenado *m* filling

llena·dor -dora *adj* (*alimento*) (Chile) filling

llenar *tr* to fill; (*un formulario*) to fill out; (*ciertas condiciones*) to fulfill; to satisfy; (*colmar*) to overwhelm ‖ *intr* (*la luna*) to be full ‖ *ref* to fill, fill up; (coll) to stuff oneself; **llenarse a rebosar** to be filled to overflowing

llene *m* filling; full tank

lle·no -na *adj* full; **lleno a rebosar** full to overflowing; **lleno de goteras** (coll) full of aches and pains ‖ *m* fill, plenty; fulness, full enjoyment; completeness; full moon; (*en el teatro*) full house ‖ *f* see **llena**

lleva or **llevada** *f* carrying, conveying; ride; **lleva gratuita** free ride

llevade·ro -ra *adj* bearable, tolerable

llevar *tr* (*transportar*) to carry; (*traer consigo*) to take; (*conducir*) to lead; to carry away, to take away; (*cuentas, libros; la anotación en los naipes*) to keep; (*la correspondencia con una persona*) to carry on; (*un drama a la pantalla*) to put on; (*buena o mala vida*) to lead; (*aguantar*) to bear, to stand for; (*castigo*) to suffer; to get, obtain; to win; (*cierto precio*) to charge; (*traje, vestido*) to wear; (*armas*) to bear; (*cierto tiempo*) to have been, e.g., **llevo ocho días en cama** I have been in bed for a week; (*ropa*) **a todo llevar** for all kinds of wear; **llevar** (*cierto tiempo*) **a** (*uno*) to be older than (*someone*) by (*a certain age*); (*cierta distancia*) **a** (*uno*) to be ahead of (*someone*) by (*a certain distance*); (*cierto peso*) **a** (*uno*) to be heavier than (*someone*) by (*a certain weight*); **llevarla hecha** (coll) to have it all figured out; **llevar puesto** to wear, to have on; **llevar** + *pp* to have + *pp*, e.g., **lleva conseguidas muchas victorias** he has won many victories ‖ *ref* to carry away; to take, take away; to carry off; to win; to get along; **llevarse algo a alguien** to take something away from someone

lloradue·los *mf* (*pl* -**los**) crybaby, sniveler

lloralásti·mas *mf* (*pl* -**mas**) (coll) poverty-crying skinflint

llorar *tr* to weep over; to mourn, lament ‖ *intr* to weep, to cry; (*los ojos*) to water, to run

lloriquear *intr* to whine, to whimper

lloriqueo *m* whining, whimpering

lloro *m* weeping, crying; tears

llo·rón -rona *adj* weeping, crying ‖ *mf* weeper, crybaby ‖ *m* weeping willow; pendulous plume ‖ *f* hired mourner

lloro·so -sa *adj* weepy; sad, tearful

llovedi·zo -za *adj* (*agua*) rain; (*techo*) leaky

llover §47 *tr* (*enviar como lluvia*) to rain ‖ *intr* to rain; **como llovido** unexpectedly; **llueva o no** rain or shine; **llueve** it is raining ‖ *ref* (*el techo*) to leak

llovido *m* stowaway

llovizna *f* drizzle

lloviznar *intr* to drizzle

llovizno·so -sa *adj* moist, damp (*from drizzle*); (Am) drizzly

lluvia *f* rain; rain water; (*copia, muchedumbre*) (fig) shower, downpour; **lluvia radiactiva** fallout, radioactive fallout

lluvio·so -sa *adj* rainy

M

M, m (eme) *f* fifteenth letter of the Spanish alphabet

m. *abbr* **mañana, masculino, meridiano, metro, minuto, muerto**

maca *f* flaw, blemish; bruise (*on fruit*); spot, stain; hammock

maca·co -ca *adj* (Am) ugly, misshapen ‖ *m* — **macaco de la India** rhesus

macadamizar §60 *tr* to macadamize

macadán *m* macadam

macana *f* cudgel, club; drug on the market; (Am) nonsense; (Arg) botch; (Arg) lie, trick

macanu·do -da *adj* terrific, swell, grand; (Col, Ecuad) strong, husky

macarrón *m* macaroon; **macarrones** macaroni

macear *tr* to mace, hammer ‖ *intr* to pester, to bore

macelo *m* slaughterhouse

macero *m* macebearer

maceta *f* stone hammer; flowerpot; flower vase; (*de herramienta*) handle; (*de cantero*) hammer; (Mex) head

macfarlán *m* inverness cape

macilen·to -ta *adj* pale, wan, gaunt

macillo *m* hammer (*of piano*)

macis *m* mace (*spice*)

macizar §60 *tr* to fill in, fill up

maci·zo -za *adj* solid; massive ‖ *m* solid; flower bed; bulk, mass; massif; wall space

macu·co -ca *adj* (Chile) sly, cunning; (Arg, Chile, Ven) important, notable; (Ecuad) old, worthless; (Arg, Chile, Peru) strong, husky ‖ *m* (Arg, Bol, Col) overgrown boy

mácula *f* spot; stain; blemish; (coll) trick, deception

macha *f* (Bol) drunkenness; (Arg) joke; (Bol) mannish woman

machaca *mf* (coll) pest, bore ‖ *f* crusher

machacar §73 *tr* to crush, mash, pound ‖ *intr* to pester, bore

macha·cón -cona *adj* boring, tiresome, importunate ‖ *mf* bore

machada *f* flock of billy goats; (coll) stupidity

machado *m* hatchet

machamartillo — a machamartillo (coll) solidly, firmly, lastingly

machaque·ro -ra *adj* (coll) tiresome, boring ‖ *mf* (coll) bore

machar *tr* to crush, grind, pound ‖ *ref* (Bol, Ecuad) to get drunk

machete *m* machete, cane knife

machi *mf* (Chile) quack, healer

machihembrar *tr* (*ensamblar a ranura y lengüeta*) to feather; (*ensamblar a caja y espiga*) to mortise

machina *f* derrick, crane; pile driver; (P-R) merry-go-round

macho *adj invar* (*animal, planta, herramienta*) male; strong, robust; dull, stupid ‖ *m* sledge hammer; abutment, pillar; male; he-mule; dullard; (*del corchete*) hook; (mach) male piece; (coll) he-man; (C-R) blond foreigner; **macho cabrío** he-goat, billy goat; **macho de aterrajar** or **macho de terraja** (mach) tap, screw tap

machona *f* (Arg, Bol, Ecuad, Guat) mannish woman

macho·rro -rra *adj* barren, sterile ‖ *f* barren woman; (Mex) mannish woman

machucar §73 *tr* to beat, pound, bruise

machu·cho -cha *adj* sedate, judicious, elderly

madamita *m* (coll) sissy

madeja *f* hank, skein; tangle of hair; (*hombre flojo*) (coll) jellyfish; **madeja sin cuenda** (coll) hopeless tangle

madera *m* Madeira wine ‖ *f* wood; piece of wood; (coll) knack, flair; (coll) makings; **madera aserradiza** lumber; **madera contrachapada** plywood; **madera de sierra** lumber; **madera laminada** plywood

maderada *f* raft, float

maderaje *m* or **maderamen** *m* woodwork

maderería *f* lumberyard

madere·ro -ra *adj* lumber ‖ *m* lumberman; carpenter; log driver

madero *m* log, beam; ship, vessel; (coll) blockhead

madrastra *f* stepmother; bother

madraza *f* (coll) doting mother

madre *adj* mother ‖ *f* mother; matron; womb; main sewer; river bed; dregs, sediment; **madre adoptiva** foster mother; **madre de leche** wet nurse; **madre patria** mother country, old country; **madre política** mother-in-law; stepmother; **sacar de madre** (coll) to annoy, to upset

madreperla *f* (*molusco*) pearl oyster; (*nácar*) mother-of-pearl

madreselva *f* honeysuckle

madriga·do -da *adj* twice-married; (*toro*) that has sired; (coll) worldly-wise

madriguera *f* burrow, lair, den

madrile·ño -ña *adj* Madrid ‖ *mf* native or inhabitant of Madrid

madrina *f* godmother; patroness, protectress; prop, shore, brace; joke; leading mare; **madrina de boda** bridesmaid; **madrina de guerra** war mother

madrugada *f* early morning, dawn; early rising

madruga·dor -dora *adj* early-rising ‖ *mf* early riser

madrugar §44 *intr* to get up early; to be out in front

madurar *tr* to ripen; to mature; to think out ‖ *intr* to ripen; to mature

madurez *f* ripeness; maturity

madu·ro -ra ripe; mature

maestra *f* teacher; elementary girls' school; **maestra de escuela** schoolmistress

maestranza *f* arsenal, armory; navy yard; order of equestrian knights

maestría *f* mastery; mastership

maes·tro -tra *adj* master; masterly; chief, main; (*perro*) trained ‖ *m* master; teacher; (*en la música y la pintura*) maestro; **maestro de capilla** choirmaster; **maestro de ceremonias** master of ceremonies; **maestro de equitación** riding master; **maestro de escuela** elementary schoolteacher; **maestro de esgrima** fencing master; **maestro de obras** master builder ‖ *f* see **maestra**

Magallanes *m* Magellan

magancear *intr* (Col, Chile) to loaf around

magan·to -ta *adj* dull, spiritless

magia *f* magic

magiar *adj* & *mf* Magyar

mági·co -ca *adj* magic ‖ *mf* magician, wizard ‖ *f* magic

magín *m* (coll) fancy, imagination

magisterio *m* teaching; teachers

magistrado *m* magistrate

magistral *adj* masterly

magnáni·mo -ma *adj* magnanimous

magnesio *m* magnesium; (phot) flashlight

magnetismo *m* magnetism

magnetizar §60 *tr* magnetize

magneto *m* & *f* magneto

magnetofón *m* or **magnetófono** *m* tape recorder, wire recorder
magnificar §73 *tr* to magnify; to exalt
magnífi·co -ca *adj* magnificent
magnitud *f* magnitude
mag·no -na *adj* great, e.g., **Alejandro Magno** Alexander the Great
mago *m* magician; soothsayer; (fig) wizard, expert; **Magos de Oriente** Wise Men of the East
ma·gro -gra *adj* lean, thin || *m* (coll) loin of pork || *f* slice of ham
maguar §10 *ref* (Ven, W-I) to be dis-appointed
magüeta *f* heifer
magüeto *m* young bull
maguey *m* century plant
magullar *tr* to bruise || *ref* to get bruised
mahometa·no -na *adj & mf* Mohammedan
mahometismo *m* Mohammedanism
mahonesa *f* mayonnaise
maído *m* meow
maitines *mpl* matins
maíz *m* maize, Indian corn; **maíz en la mazorca** corn on the cob
maizal *m* cornfield
maja *f* flashy dame
majada *f* sheepfold; dung, manure
majadería *f* piece of folly, nonsensical remark
majade·ro -ra *adj* pestiferous, stupid || *mf* bore, dunce || *m* pestle
majar *tr* to crush, mash, grind, pound; (coll) to annoy, bother
majestad *f* majesty
majestuo·so -sa *adj* majestic
ma·jo -ja *adj* sporty; handsome, dashing; pretty, nice; (coll) all dressed up || *mf* sport || *m* bully || *f* see **maja**
mal *adj* apocopated form of **malo**, used only before nouns in masculine singular || *adv* badly, poorly; wrong; hardly, scarcely; **mal** de short of; **mal que le pese** in spite of him || *m* evil; damage, harm; wrong; sickness; misfortune; **mal de altura** mountain sickness; **mal de la tierra** homesickness; **mal de mar** seasickness; **mal de piedra** (pathol) stone; **mal de rayos** radiation sickness; **mal de vuelo** airsickness; **por mal de mis pecados** to my sorrow; **tener a mal** to object to; **¡mal haya . . .!** curses on . . .!
mala *f* mail; mailbag; mailboat
malabarista *mf* juggler; (Am) sneak thief
malacate *m* whim; (*hoisting machine*) (Mex, Hond) spindle
malaconseja·do -da *adj* ill-advised
malagradecí·do -da *adj* (Am) ungrateful
malandante *adj* unlucky, unfortunate
malandanza *f* bad luck, misfortune
malan·drín -drina *adj* evil, wicked || *mf* scoundrel, rascal
malaria *f* malaria
malaventura *f* misfortune
mala·yo -ya *adj & mf* Malay
malbaratar *tr* to undersell; to squander
malcasa·do -da *adj* mismated; undutiful
malcasar *tr* to mismate || *intr & ref* to be mismated
malcaso *m* treachery

malconten·to -ta *adj & mf* malcontent
malcria·do -da *adj* ill-bred
malcriar §77 *tr* to spoil, pamper
maldad *f* evil, wickedness
maldecir §11 *tr* to curse || *intr* to curse, to damn; **maldecir de** to slander, to vilify
maldición *f* malediction, curse; (coll) oath, curse
maldispues·to -ta *adj* ill, indisposed; unwilling, ill-disposed
maldi·to -ta *adj* damned, accursed; wicked; (Mex) coarse, crude, indecent; **no saber maldita la cosa de** (coll) to not know a single thing about || **el Maldito** the Evil One || *f* (coll) tongue; **soltar la maldita** (coll) to talk too much
maleante *adj* wicked, evil || *mf* crook, hoodlum, rowdy
malear *tr* to spoil; to corrupt || *ref* to spoil, get spoiled; to be corrupted
malecón *m* levee, dike, mole, jetty
maledicencia *f* calumny, slander
maleficiar *tr* to damage, harm; to curse, bewitch, cast a spell on
maleficio *m* curse, spell; witchcraft
malentender §51 *tr* to misunderstand
malentendido *m* misunderstanding, misapprehension
malestar *m* malaise, indisposition
maleta *m* (coll) bungler; (coll) ham bullfighter || *f* valise; **hacer la maleta** to pack up
maletín *m* satchel
malevolencia *f* malice, malevolence
malévo·lo -la *adj* malevolent
maleza *f* thicket, underbrush; weeds
malgasta·do -da *adj* ill-spent
malgastar *tr* to waste, squander
malgenio·so -sa *adj* (Am) ill-tempered, irritable
malhabla·do -da *adj* foul-mouthed
malhada·do -da *adj* ill-starred
malhe·cho -cha *adj* deformed || *m* misdeed
malhe·chor -chora *mf* malefactor || *f* malefactress
malherir §68 *tr* to injure badly
malhumora·do -da *adj* ill-humored
malicia *f* (*maldad*) evil; (*bellaquería, malevolencia*) malice; insidiousness, trickiness; (coll) suspicion
malicio·so -sa *adj* evil; malicious; insidious, tricky
malignar *tr* to corrupt, vitiate; to spoil
malignidad *f* malignity
malig·no -na *adj* (*malévolo; pernicioso*) malign; (*malicioso; perjudicial*) malignant; (pathol) malignant
malintenciona·do -da *adj* ill-disposed, evil-minded
malmaridada *f* (coll) faithless wife
malmeter *tr* to lead astray, misguide; to alienate, estrange
ma·lo -la *adj* bad, poor, evil; (*travieso*) naughty, mischievous; (*enfermo*) sick, ill; (*que no es como debiera ser*) wrong; (*inflamado, dolorido*) sore; **estar de malas** to be out of luck; **lo malo es que** the trouble is that; **malo con** or **para con** mean to; **por malas o por buenas** willingly or unwillingly;

ser **malo de engañar** to be hard to trick || el **Malo** the Evil One || *f* see **mala**

malogra·do -da *adj* late, ill-fated

malograr *tr* to miss || *ref* to fail; to come to an untimely end

malogro *m* failure; disappointment

maloliente *adj* malodorous, foul-smelling

malón *m* mean trick; (SAm) Indian incursion; (Chile) surprise party

malpara·do -da *adj* hurt; **salir malparado (de)** to fail (in), to come out worsted (in)

malparar *tr* to mistreat

malparir *intr* to miscarry, have a miscarriage

malparto *m* miscarriage

malquerencia *f* dislike

malquerer §55 *tr* to dislike

malquistar *tr* to alienate, estrange || *ref* to become alienated

malquis·to -ta *adj* disliked, unpopular

malrotar *tr* to squander

malsa·no -na *adj* unhealthy

malsín *m* mischief-maker

malsonante *adj* obnoxious, odious

malsufri·do -da *adj* impatient

malta *m* malt || *f* asphalt, tar; (Am) dark beer; (Chile) premium beer

maltraer §75 *tr* to abuse, ill-treat; to call down, scold

maltratar *tr* to abuse, ill-treat, maltreat; to damage, spoil

maltre·cho -cha *adj* battered, damaged

malu·co -ca or **malu·cho -cha** *adj* (coll) sickish, upset

malva *f* mallow; **malva arbórea** hollyhock, rose mallow; **ser como una malva** (coll) to be meek and mild

malvado -da *adj* evil, wicked || *mf* evildoer

malvarrosa *f* hollyhock, rose mallow

malvavisco *m* marsh mallow

malvender *tr* to sell at a loss

malversación *f* graft, embezzlement, misappropriation

malversar *tr & intr* to graft, embezzle

malvezar §60 *tr* to give bad habits to || *ref* to acquire bad habits

malla *f* mesh, meshing; (de la armadura) mail; (traje) tights; bathing suit

mallete *m* mallet

Mallorca *f* Majorca

mallor·quín -quina *adj & mf* Majorcan

mama *f* mamma

ma·má *f* (pl **-más**) mamma

mamada *f* suck; sucking; (Am) cinch

mama·lón -lona *adj* (Ven, W-I) loafing || *mf* (Cuba) sponger

mamama *f* (Hond) granny

mamamama *f* (Peru) granny

mamar *tr* to suck; to learn as a child; (coll) to swallow; (coll) to wangle; **mamóla** (coll) he was taken in || *intr* to suck || *ref* (coll) to swallow; (obtener sin mérito) (coll) to wangle; (SAm) to get drunk; **mamarse a uno** (coll) to get the best of someone; (coll) to take someone in; (Col, Chile, Peru) to do away with someone

mamarracho *m* (coll) mess, sight; (hombre ridículo) milksop

mamelón *m* knoll, mound

mamífe·ro -ra *adj* mammalian || *m* mammal, mammalian

mamola *f* chuck (under the chin); **hacer la mamola a** to chuck under the chin; (coll) to take in, make a fool of

ma·món -mona *adj* sucking; fond of sucking || *mf* suckling || *m* shoot, sucker; (Guat, Hond) club; (Mex) soft cake || *f* chuck (under chin)

mamonear *tr* (Guat, Hond) to beat, cudgel; (S-D) to put off, delay; (el tiempo) (S-D) to waste

mamotreto *m* memo book; (coll) batch of papers; (coll) hulk, bulk

mampara *f* screen; folding screen; (Peru) glass door

mamparo *m* bulkhead

mampostería *f* rubble, rubblework; masonry, stone masonry

ma·mut *m* (pl **-muts**) mammoth

manada *f* (de ganado vacuno) herd, drove; (de ganado lanar) flock; (de lobos) pack; (de gente) gang, troop; (de hierba, trigo, etc.) handful

manade·ro -ra *adj* flowing || *m* spring, source; shepherd

manantial *adj* flowing, running || *m* spring, source; (fig) source

manar *tr* to run with || *intr* to pour forth, to run; to abound

manaza *f* big hand

mancar §73 *tr* to maim, cripple || *intr* (el viento) (naut) to abate, subside

manca·rrón -rrona *adj* (caballería) skinny, worn-out; (Chile) tired out, exhausted || *m* old nag; (Chile, Peru) dam, dike

manceba *f* mistress, concubine

mancebía *f* bawdyhouse, brothel; wild oats; youth

mance·bo -ba *adj* youthful || *m* youngster; youth, young man; (en una farmacia, barbería, etc.) helper || *f* see **manceba**

mancerina *f* saucer with hook to hold chocolate cup

mancilla *f* spot, blemish

mancillar *tr* to spot, blemish

man·co -ca *adj* armless, one-armed; one-handed; defective, faulty || *mf* cripple || *m* (Chile) old nag

mancomún — de mancomún jointly, in common

mancomunar *tr* to unite, combine; (fuerzas, caudales, etc.) to pool || *ref* to unite, combine

mancomunidad *f* association, union; (asociación de provincias) commonwealth

mancornar §61 *tr* (un novillo) to throw and hold on the ground; (una res vacuna) to tie a horn and front leg of; (dos reses) to tie together by the horns; (coll) to join, bring together

mancuernas *fpl* (Mex) cuff links

mancuernillas *fpl* (Guat, Hond) cuff links

mancha *f* spot, stain; (de vegetación) patch; speckle; (fig) stain, blot; **mancha solar** sunspot

manchar *tr* to spot, stain; to speckle;

(fig) to stain, disgrace || intr to spot; ¡mancha! wet paint!

manda f gift, offer; bequest, legacy

mandade•ro -ra mf messenger || m errand boy

mandado m order, command; errand; **hacer un mandado** to run an errand

manda•más m (pl **-mases**) (slang) big shot; (jefe político) (slang) boss

mandamiento m order, command; (Bib) commandment; (law) writ; **los cinco mandamientos** (coll) the five fingers of the hand

mandar tr to order, command; (legar) to bequeath; (enviar) to send; **mandar + inf** to have + inf, e.g., **la mandé leer en voz alta** I had her read aloud || intr to be in command, be the boss; **mandar llamar** to send for; **mandar por** to send for; **mande Vd.** I beg your pardon || ref (un enfermo) to manage to get around; (dos piezas) to be communicating; **mandarse con** (otra pieza) to communicate with; (Am) to be rude to

mandarina f tangerine

mandatario m agent, proxy; (Am) chief executive

mandato m mandate; (Am) term (of office)

mandíbula f jaw, jawbone; **reír a mandíbula batiente** (coll) to roar with laughter

mandil m apron

mando m command; control, drive; **alto mando** (mil) high command; **mando a distancia** remote control; **mando a punta de dedo** finger-tip control; **mando de las válvulas** timing gears; **mando por botón** push-button control; **tener el mando y el palo** (coll) to be the boss, rule the roost

mandolina f mandolin

man•dón -dona adj bossy || mf domineering person || m (en las minas) (Am) boss, foreman; (en las carreras de caballos) (Chile) starter

mandrágora f mandrake

mandril m (mach) chuck

mandrilar tr to bore

manea f hobble

manear tr to hobble

manecilla f (de reloj) hand; clasp, book clasp; (bot) tendril; (typ) fist, index

manejable adj manageable

manejar tr to manage; to handle, wield; (un automóvil) (Am) to drive || ref to behave; to get around, move about

manejo m management; handling; intrigue, scheming; horsemanship; (Am) driving; **manejo a distancia** remote control; **manejo doméstico** housekeeping

manera f manner, way; **a la manera de** in the manner of; like; **de manera que** so that; **en gran manera** to a great extent; extremely; **sobre manera** exceedingly

manga f (parte del vestido) sleeve; (tubo de caucho) hose; waterspout; (bridge) game; **en mangas de camisa** in shirt sleeves; **ir de manga** (coll) to be in cahoots; **manga de agua** waterspout; cloudburst; **manga de camisa** shirt sleeve; **manga de riego** watering hose; **manga de viento** whirlwind; **manga marina** waterspout; **mangas** extras, profits

mangana f lasso

manganear tr to lasso; (Peru) to annoy, bother

manganeso m manganese

mango m handle; **mango de escoba** broomstick; (aer) stick, control stick

mangonear tr (Am) to plunder || intr (coll) to loaf around; (coll) to meddle; (coll) to dabble

mangosta f mongoose

mangote m sleeve protector

manguera f hose; (tubo de ventilación) funnel

mangueta f fountain syringe; door jamb

manguitero m furrier

manguito m muff; sleeve guard; coffee cake; (mach) sleeve

ma•ní m (pl **-níes** or **-nises**) peanut

manía f mania; craze, whim; (coll) grudge; **tener manía a** (coll) to dislike

maniabier•to -ta adj open-handed

maní•co -ca adj maniac(al) || mf maniac

maniatar tr to tie the hands of

maniáti•co -ca adj stubborn; queer, eccentric; (entusiasta) crazy || mf crank, eccentric

manicomio m madhouse, insane asylum

manicor•to -ta adj closefisted, tight

manicu•ro -ra mf manicure, manicurist || f manicure, manicuring

maní•do -da adj shabby, worn; hackneyed; (culin) high || f haunt, hangout

manifestación f manifestation; (reunión pública para dar a conocer un sentimiento u opinión) demonstration

manifestante mf demonstrator

manifestar §2 tr to manifest; (el Santísimo Sacramento) to expose || intr to demonstrate || ref to become manifest

manifies•to -ta adj manifest || m manifesto; (eccl) exposition of the Host; (naut) manifest

manigua f (Mex, W-I) thicket, jungle; **irse a la manigua** (W-I) to revolt

manija f handle; clamp; crank

manilar•go -ga adj ready-fisted; generous

manilla f bracelet; handcuff, manacle

manillar m handle bar

maniobra f handling; lever; maneuver; (naut) gear, tackle

maniobrar intr to work with the hands; to maneuver; (rr) to shift

maniota f hobble

manipula•dor -dora mf manipulator || m (telg) key

manipular tr to manipulate

maní•quí m (pl **-quíes**) m manikin, mannequin; (para exponer prendas de ropa) dress form; (de pintores y escultores) lay figure; (fig) puppet; **ir hecho un maniquí** to be a fashion plate || f (mujer joven que luce los trajes de última moda) mannequin, model

manirro•to -ta adj lavish, prodigal

manivací•o -a *adj* empty-handed

manivela *f* crank; **manivela de arranque** starting crank

manjar *m* dish, food, tidbit, delicacy; lift, recreation

mano *m* first to play, e.g., **soy mano** I'm first || *f* hand; (*de cuadrúpedo*) forefoot; (*de pintura*) coat; (*de papel*) quire; (*saetilla de reloj u otro instrumento*) hand; (*lance en un juego*) round, hand; (*del elefante*) trunk; pestle, masher; **a la mano** at hand, on hand; within reach; understandable; **a mano airada** violently; **asidos de la mano** hand in hand; **bajo mano** underhandedly; **caer en manos de** to fall into the hands of; **¡dame esa mano!** put it here!; **dar la mano** to lend a hand; **darse las manos** to join hands; to shake hands; **de las manos** hand in hand; **de primera mano** at first hand; first-hand; **de segunda mano** second-hand; **echar mano de** to resort to; **echar una mano** to lend a hand; to play a game; **en buena mano está** (coll) after you, you drink first; **escribir a la mano** to take dictation; **escribir a manos de** to write in care of; **estrecharse la mano** to shake hands; **ganarle a uno por la mano** to steal a march on someone; **lavarse las manos de** to wash one's hands of; **llegar a las manos** to come to blows; **malas manos** awkwardness; **mano de gato** cat's-paw; master hand, master touch; **mano de obra** labor; **mano derecha** right-hand man; **mano de santo** (coll) sure cure; **¡manos a la obra!** let's get to work!; **manos libres** outside work; **manos limpias** extras, perquisites; (coll) clean hands; **manos puercas** (coll) graft; **probar la mano** to try one's hand; **tener mano con** to have a pull with; **tener mano izquierda** (coll) to be on one's toes; **untar la mano a** (coll) to grease the palm of; **venir a las manos** to come to blows; **vivir de la mano a la boca** to live from hand to mouth

manojo *m* bunch, bundle, handful; **a manojos** in abundance

manopla *f* gauntlet; postilion's whip; (Chile) knuckles, brass knuckles

manosear *tr* to finger, to paw; to muss, to rumple; to fiddle with; (Am) to pet || *ref* (Am) to spoon, to neck

manotada *f* slap

manotear *tr* to slap, to smack || *intr* to gesticulate

manquedad *f* lack of one or both hands or arms; disability; deficiency

mansalva — **a mansalva** without risk; without warning; **a mansalva de** safe from

mansarda *f* mansard, mansard roof

mansedumbre *f* gentleness, mildness, meekness; tameness

mansión *f* mansion, sojourn; abode, dwelling; **hacer mansión** to stop, stay

man•so -sa *adj* gentle, mild, meek; tame || *m* bellwether; farm

manta *f* blanket; heavy shawl; (coll) beating, thrashing; (Chile, Ecuad) poncho; (Col, Mex, Ven) coarse cotton cloth; **a manta de Dios** copiously; **dar una manta a** to toss in a blanket; **manta de coche** lap robe; **manta de viaje** steamer rug; **tirar de la manta** (coll) to let the cat out of the bag

mantear *tr* to toss in a blanket; (Am) to abuse, mistreat

manteca *f* (*grasa de los animales, esp. la del cerdo*) lard; butter; pomade; (*dinero*) (slang) dough; **como manteca** smooth as butter; **manteca de puerco** lard; **manteca de vaca** butter

mantecado *m* custard ice cream, French ice cream

mantecón *m* (coll) mollycoddle, milksop

mantel *m* tablecloth; altar cloth

mantelería *f* table linen

mantelillo *m* embroidered centerpiece

mantelito *m* lunch cloth

mantener §71 *tr* to maintain; to keep; to keep up; to sustain, defend || *ref* to keep, remain, continue

mantenida *f* (Am) kept woman

mantenido *m* (*hombre que vive a expensas de su mujer*) (Guat, Mex, W-I) gigolo; (Guat, Mex, W-I) sponger

mantenimiento *m* maintenance; food, support, living

manteo *m* mantle, cloak

mantequera *f* churn, butter churn; butter dish

mantequería *f* creamery; delicatessen

mantequilla *f* butter; **mantequilla azucarada** hard sauce; **mantequilla derretida** drawn butter

mantilla *f* mantilla (*silk or lace head scarf*); **mantillas** swaddling clothes

mantillo *m* humus, mold

manto *m* mantle, cloak; (*de chimenea*) mantel; (*ropa talar de algunos religiosos, catedráticos, alumnos*) robe, gown; (fig) cloak

mantón *m* shawl, kerchief

manuable *adj* handy

manual *adj* (*que se hace con las manos*) hand; (*fácil de manejar*) handy; easy; easy to understand; easy-going; manual || *m* manual, handbook; notebook

manubrio *m* handle; crank, winch

manuela *f* open hack (*in Madrid*)

manufactura *f* (*fábrica*) factory; (*obra fabricada*) manufacture

manufacturar *tr* to manufacture

manuscribir §83 *tr* to write by hand

manuscri•to -ta *adj & m* manuscript

manutención *f* maintenance; care, upkeep; shelter, protection

manutener §71 *tr* (law) to maintain, support

manzana *f* apple; (*conjunto aislado de varias casas contiguas*) block, city block; (*remate en un mueble*) knob, finial; **manzana de Adán** (Chile) Adam's apple

manzanar *m* apple orchard

manzanilla *f* camomile; (*aceituna pequeña; vino blanco*) manzanilla (*small olive; white wine*); (*remate en un mueble*) knob, finial

manzano *m* apple tree

maña *f* skill, dexterity; cunning, craftiness; bad habit, vice; (*de lino, cáñamo, etc.*) bunch; (Am) sister; **darse maña** to manage, contrive; **hacer maña** (Col) to fool around

mañana *adv* tomorrow; **¡hasta mañana!** see you tomorrow!; **pasado mañana** the day after tomorrow || *m* tomorrow; (*tiempo venidero*) morrow || *f* morning; **de mañana** in the morning; **muy de mañana** very early in the morning; **por la mañana** in the morning; **tomar la mañana** to get up early; (coll) to have a shot of liquor before breakfast

mañanear *intr* to be in the habit of getting up early

mañane·ro -ra *adj* morning; early-rising

mañanica *f* early morning, break of day

mañanita *f* woman's bed jacket

mañear *tr* to manage craftily || *intr* to act with cunning

mañerear *intr* (Arg) to dawdle, dilly-dally

mañería *f* sterility

mañe·ro -ra *adj* clever, shrewd; simple, easy; (Am) skittish

ma·ño -ña *mf* (coll) Aragonese || *m* (Am) brother || *f* see **maña**

maño·so -sa *adj* skillful, clever; crafty, tricky; vicious

mañuela *f* craftiness, trickiness

mañue·las *mf* (*pl* **-las**) (coll) tricky person

mapa *m* map; **mapa itinerario** road map || *f* — **llevarse la mapa** (coll) to take the prize

mapache *m* coon, raccoon

mapamundi *m* map of the world; (coll) buttocks, behind

mapurite *m* (CAm) skunk

maque *m* lacquer

maquear *tr* to lacquer; (Mex) to varnish

maqueta *f* (*en tamaño reducido*) maquette; (*en tamaño natural*) mock-up; (*de un libro*) dummy

maquillador *m* (theat) make-up man

maquillaje *m* (theat) make-up

maquillar *tr* & *ref* to make up

máquina *f* machine; (*motor*) engine; locomotive; plan, project; (fig) machinery; (coll) heap, pile, lot; (Cuba) auto; (Chile) ganging up; **escribir a máquina** to typewrite; **máquina de afeitar** safety razor; **máquina de apostar** gambling machine; **máquina de componer** typesetter; **máquina de coser** sewing machine; **máquina de escribir** typewriter; **máquina de lavar** washing machine; **máquina de sumar** adding machine; **máquina de volar** flying machine; **máquina fotográfica** camera; **máquina parlante** talking machine; **máquina sacaperras** slot machine

maquinación *f* machination, scheming

máquina-herramienta *f* (*pl* **máquinas-herramientas**) machine tool

maquinal *adj* mechanical

maquinar *tr* to plot, to scheme

maquinaria *f* machinery; applied mechanics

maquinilla *f* windlass, winch; clippers; **maquinilla cortapelos** clippers, hair clippers; **maquinilla de afeitar** safety razor; **maquinilla de rizar** curling iron

maquinista *mf* (*persona que fabrica máquinas*) machinist; (*persona que dirige una máquina o locomotora*) engineer; **segundo maquinista** (naut) machinist

mar *m* & *f* sea; tide, flood; **alta mar** high seas; **a mares** abundantly, copiously; **arrojarse a la mar** to plunge, take great risks; **baja mar** low tide; **correr los mares** to follow the sea; **hablar de la mar** (coll) to talk wildly, to talk on and on; **hacerse a la mar** to put to sea; **la mar de** (fig) oceans of, large numbers of; **mar alta** rough sea; **mar ancha** high seas; **mar bonanza** calm sea; **mar Caribe** Caribbean Sea, Caribbean; **mar de las Antillas** Caribbean Sea; **mar de las Indias** Indian Ocean; **mar de nubes** cloud bank; **mar Latino** Mediterranean Sea; **mar llena** high tide; **meter la mar en un pozo** to attempt the impossible; **meterse mar adentro** (fig) to go beyond one's depth

maraña *f* undergrowth, thicket; silk waste; (*de hilo, pelo, etc.*) tangle; trick, scheme; puzzle

marañón *m* cashew

maraño·so -sa *adj* scheming || *mf* schemer

maravilla *f* wonder, marvel; (bot) marigold, calendula; **a las maravillas** or **a las mil maravillas** magnificently; **a maravilla** wonderfully well; **por maravilla** rarely, occasionally

maravillar *tr* to astonish || *ref* to wonder, to marvel; **maravillarse con** or **de** to marvel at, to wonder at

maravillo·so -sa *adj* wonderful, marvelous

marbete *m* label, tag; baggage check; edge, border; **marbete engomado** sticker

marca *f* mark; (*tipo de producto*) make, brand; (*de tamaño*) standard; score; record; height-measuring device; **de marca** outstanding; **marca de agua** watermark; **marca de fábrica** trademark; **marca de reconocimiento** (naut) landmark, seamark; **marca de taquilla** box-office record; **marca registrada** registered trademark

marca·do -da *adj* marked, pronounced

marcaje *m* (sport) scoring; (sport) interfering; (telp) dialing

marcapaso *m* pacemaker

marcar §73 *tr* to mark; to brand; to embroider; (*p.ej., un pañuelo*) to initial; (*la hora un reloj*) to show; (*un tanto*) to make, to score; (*el número telefónico*) to dial || *ref* (*un buque*) to take bearings

marcear *tr* to shear || *ref* to be March-like

marcial *adj* martial; gallant, noble

marco *m* frame; framework; *(de pesas y medidas)* standard

marcha *f* march; *(funcionamiento)* running, operation; *(p.ej., de los astros)* course, path; *(desenvolvimiento de un asunto)* course, march, progress; *(grado de velocidad)* rate of speed; *(de los engranajes)* (aut) speed; **cambiar de marcha** to shift gears; **en marcha** on the march; underway; in motion; **marcha atrás** reverse; **marcha del hambre** hunger march; **marcha directa** high gear; **marcha forzada** (mil) forced march

marchamo *m* customhouse mark; (Arg, Bol) tax on slaughtered cattle

marchante *adj* commercial ‖ *m* dealer, merchant; (Am) customer

marchapié *m* running board

marchar *intr* to march; to run, work, go; to leave, go away; to come along, proceed; **marchar en vacío** to idle ‖ *ref* to leave, go away

marchitar *tr* to wilt, wither ‖ *ref* to wilt, wither; to languish

marchi·to -ta *adj* withered, faded; (fig) languid

marea *f* tide; tideland; gentle sea breeze; dew; drizzle; **marea alta** high tide; **marea baja** low tide; **marea creciente** or **entrante** flood tide; **marea menguante** ebb tide; **marea muerta** neap tide; **marea viva** spring tide; **rendir la marea** to stem the tide

marea·do -da *adj* nauseated, sick, light-headed; seasick

mareaje *m* navigation, seamanship; *(de un buque)* course

marear *tr* to sail; (coll) to annoy, pester ‖ *intr* (coll) to be annoying ‖ *ref* to get sick, to get giddy; to get seasick; to be damaged at sea; (Am) to fade

marejada *f* heavy sea; *(de desorden)* stirring, undercurrent; **marejada de fondo** ground swell

maremagno or **maremágnum** *m* (coll) big mess

mareo *m* nausea, dizziness, sickness; seasickness; (coll) annoyance

marfil *m* ivory

marfile·ño -ña *adj* ivory

mar·fuz -fuza *adj* *(pl* -fuces -fuzas) cast aside, rejected; deceptive

marga *f* marl

margar §44 *tr* to marl

margarita *f* pearl; (bot) daisy; **margarita de los prados** English daisy

margen *m & f* margin; border, edge; marginal note; **al margen de** aloof from; outside of; independent of; aside from; **dar margen para** to give occasion for; **dejar al margen** to leave out; **quedar al margen de** to be left out of

marginal *adj* marginal

mariache *m* Mexican band and singers

marica *m* (coll) sissy, milksop ‖ *f* magpie

maricón *m* (coll) sissy

maridable *adj* marital

maridaje *m* married life; (fig) union

maridar *tr* to combine, unite ‖ *intr* to get married; to live as man and wife

marido *m* husband

mariguana *f* marihuana

mariguanza *f* (Chile) hocus-pocus; (Chile) pirouette; **mariguanzas** (Chile) clowning; (Chile) powwowing

marimacho *m* (coll) mannish woman

marimandona *f* (coll) queen bee, bossy woman

marimarica *m* (coll) sissy

marimorena *f* (coll) fight, row

marina *f* navy; *(conjunto de buques)* marine, fleet; *(cuadro o pintura)* seascape; shore, seaside; sailing, navigation; **marina de guerra** navy; **marina mercante** merchant marine

marinar *tr* to marinate, to salt; *(un buque)* to man ‖ *intr* to be a sailor

marinera *f* sailor blouse; *(blusa de niño)* middy, middy blouse

marinería *f* sailoring; sailors

marine·ro -ra *adj* sea, marine; seaworthy; seafaring ‖ *m* mariner, seaman, sailor; **marinero de agua dulce** *(el que ha navegado poco)* landlubber *(person unacquainted with the sea)*; **marinero matalote** *(hombre de mar, rudo y torpe)* landlubber *(awkward and unskilled seaman)* ‖ *f* see **marinera**

marines·co -ca *adj* sailor; sailorly

mari·no -na *adj* marine, sea ‖ *m* mariner, seaman, sailor ‖ *f* see **marina**

marioneta *f* marionette

mariposa *f* butterfly; butterfly valve; wing nut; rushlight; (Col) blindman's buff; **mariposa nocturna** moth

mariposear *intr* to flit about; to be fickle

mariposón *m* (Cuba, Guat, Mex) fickle flirt

mariquita *m* (coll) sissy, milksop, popinjay ‖ *f* (ent) ladybird

marisabidilla *f* (coll) bluestocking

mariscal *m* blacksmith; (mil) marshal; **mariscal de campo** (mil) field marshal

marisco *m* shellfish; **mariscos** seafood

marisma *f* swamp, marsh, salt marsh

marisquería *f* seafood store, seafood restaurant

maríti·mo -ma *adj* maritime; marine, sea

maritor·nes *f* *(pl* -nes) (coll) mannish maidservant, wench

marmita *f* pot, boiler, kettle

marmitón *m* kitchen scullion

mármol *m* marble

marmóre·o -a *adj* marble

marmosete *m* vignette

marmota *f* marmot; sleepyhead; worsted cap; **marmota de Alemania** hamster; **marmota de América** ground hog, woodchuck

maroma *f* hemp rope, esparto rope; (Am) acrobatic stunt

maromear *intr* (Am) to perform acrobatic stunts, to walk the tight rope; (Am) to wobble, to sway from side to side *(e.g., in politics)*; (Am) to hesitate

marome·ro -ra *mf* (Am) acrobat, tightrope walker; (Am) weaseler

marqués *m* marquis; **los marqueses** the marquis and marchioness

marquesa *f* marchioness, marquise; (*sobre la puerta de un hotel*) marquee

marquesina *f* cover over field tent; (*sobre la puerta de un hotel*) marquee; locomotive cab

marquetería *f* cabinetwork, woodwork; (*taracea*) marquetry

marra·jo -ja *adj* sly, tricky; (*toro*) vicious

marrana *f* sow; (coll) slattern, slut

marranada *f* (coll) piggishness, filth

marranalla *f* (coll) rabble, riffraff

marra·no -na *adj* base, vile; (coll) dirty, sloppy ‖ *mf* hog ‖ *m* male hog, boar; filthy person, hog; cad, cur ‖ *f* see **marrana**

marrar *intr* to miss, fail; to go astray

marras *adv* (coll) long ago; **hacer marras que** (Bol, Ecuad) to be a long time since

marro *m* game resembling quoits and played with a stone; (*juego de muchachos*) tag; (*ladeo*) dodge, duck; slip, miss

marrón *adj invar* maroon (*dark-red*); tan (*shoes*) ‖ *m* maroon; candied chestnut; stone (*used as a sort of quoit*)

marro·quí (*pl* **-quíes**) *adj & mf* Moroccan ‖ *m* morocco, morocco leather

marro·quín -quina *adj & mf* var of **marroquí**

marrubio *m* horehound

marrue·co -ca *adj & mf* Moroccan

Marruecos *m* Morocco

marrulle·ro -ra *adj* cajoling, wheedling ‖ *mf* cajoler, wheedler

Marsella *f* Marseille

marsopa or **marsopla** *f* porpoise

mart. *abbr* **martes**

marta *f* pine marten; **marta cebellina** sable, Siberian sable; **marta del Canadá** fisher

Marte *m* Mars

mar·tes *m* (*pl* **-tes**) Tuesday; **martes de carnaval** or **carnestolendas** Shrove Tuesday

martillar *tr* to hammer; to pester, worry ‖ *intr* to hammer

martillazo *m* blow with a hammer

martillear *tr & intr* var of **martillar**

martillero *m* (Chile) auctioneer

martillo *m* hammer; auction house; (*persona*) scourge; (mus) tuning hammer; (*de arma de fuego*) cock

martín *m* — **martín pescador** (*pl* **martín pescadores**) kingfisher

martinete *m* drop hammer; pile driver; (*del piano*) hammer

martínico *m* (coll) ghost, goblin

mártir *mf* martyr

martirio *m* martyrdom

márts. *abbr* **mártires**

marullo *m* surge, swell

marxista *adj & mf* Marxist or Marxian

marzo *m* March

mas *conj* but

más *adv* more; most; **a lo más** at most, at the most; **a más de** besides, in addition to; **como el que más** the next one, as well as anybody; **cuando**

más at the most; **de más** extra; too much, too many; **estar de más** to be in the way; to be unnecessary; to be superfluous; **los más de** most of, the majority of; **más bien** rather; **más de** + *número* more than; **más de lo que** + *verbo* more than; **más que** more than; better than; **no . . . más** no longer; **no . . . más nada** nothing more; **no . . . más que** only ‖ *prep* plus ‖ *m* more; (*signo de adición*) plus

masa *f* mass; (*pasta que se forma con agua y harina*) dough; (*masa aplastada*) mash; nature, disposition; (Chile, Ecuad) puff paste; (*p.ej., de un automóvil*) (elec) ground; **las masas** the masses

masada *f* farm

masadero *m* farmer

masaje *m* massage; **masaje facial** facial

masajear *tr* to massage

masajista *m* masseur ‖ *f* masseuse

masar *tr* to knead; to massage

mascar §73 *tr* to chew; (coll) to mumble, mutter ‖ *ref* (*un cabo*) (naut) to gall

máscara *mf* (*persona*) mask, mummer ‖ *f* mask; (*traje, disfraz*) masquerade; **máscara antigás** gas mask

mascarada *f* masquerade

mascarilla *f* half mask; false face; death mask

mascarón *m* false face; (*persona fea*) fright; (archit) mask; **mascarón de proa** (naut) figurehead

mascota *f* mascot

mascujar *tr & intr* (coll) to chew with difficulty; (coll) to mumble

masculi·no -na *adj* masculine; (*sexo*) male; (*traje*) men's ‖ *m* masculine

mascullar *tr & intr* (coll) to mumble, mutter; (coll) to chew with difficulty

masera *f* kneading trough

masilla *f* putty

masita *f* (mil) money withheld for clothing; (Arg, Bol) cake

masón *m* Mason

masonería *f* Masonry

mastelero *m* (naut) topmast

masticar §73 *tr* to chew, masticate; to meditate on; to mumble

mástil *m* (*de una embarcación*) mast; (*de un violín o guitarra*) neck; stalk; (*de pluma*) shaft, stem; upright

mas·tín -tina *mf* mastiff; **mastín danés** Great Dane

mastodonte *m* mastodon

mastuerzo *m* (bot) cress; (coll) dolt

masturbar *ref* to masturbate

mat. *abbr* **matemática**

mata *f* bush, shrub; blade, sprig; brush, underbrush; **mata de pelo** crop of hair, head of hair; **mata parda** chaparro (*oak*); **saltar de la mata** (coll) to come out of hiding

mataca·bras *m* (*pl* **-bras**) cold blast from the north

matacán *m* dog poison

matacande·las *m* (*pl* **-las**) candle snuffer

matadero *m* abattoir, slaughterhouse; (coll) drudgery

mata·dor -dora *mf* killer || *m* matador; **matador de mujeres** lady-killer

matadura *f* sore, gall

matafue·gos *m* (*pl* **-gos**) fire extinguisher; (*oficial*) fireman

matalo·bos *m* (*pl* **-bos**) wolf's-bane

mata·lón -lona *mf* (coll) skinny old nag

matalotaje *m* (naut) ship stores; (coll) mess, hodgepodge

matamale·zas *m* (*pl* **-zas**) weed killer

matamari·dos *f* (*pl* **-dos**) (coll) many times a widow

matamo·ros *m* (*pl* **-ros**) (coll) bully

matamos·cas *m* (*pl* **-cas**) fly swatter; flypaper

matanza *f* slaughter, massacre; butchering; pork products; (CAm) butcher shop; (Ven) slaughterhouse

matape·rros *m* (*pl* **-rros**) (coll) harum-scarum, street urchin

matar *tr* to kill; to butcher; (*el fuego, la luz*) to put out; (*la cal*) to slack; (*el metal*) to mat; (*un color*) to tone down; (*un naipe*) to spot; to play a card higher than; (*a un caballo*) to gall; to bore to death; (*el tiempo, el hambre, etc.*) (fig) to kill || *intr* to kill || *ref* to kill oneself; to drudge, overwork; to be disappointed; **matarse con** to quarrel with; **matarse por** to struggle for; to struggle to

matarratas *m* rat poison; (*aguardiente de mala calidad*) (coll) rotgut

matarro·tos *m* (*pl* **-tos**) (Chile) pawnshop

matasa·nos *m* (*pl* **-nos**) quack doctor

matasellar *tr* to cancel, to postmark

matase·llos *m* (*pl* **-llos**) postmark

matasie·te *m* (*pl* **-te**) (coll) bully, swashbuckler

matatí·as *m* (*pl* **-as**) moneylender, pawnbroker

matazar·zas *m* (*pl* **-zas**) weed killer

mate *adj* dull, flat || *m* checkmate; (SAm) maté; (SAm) maté gourd; **dar mate a** to checkmate; to make fun of; **dar mate ahogado a** to stalemate; **mate ahogado** stalemate

matear *tr* to plant at regular intervals; to make dull; (Chile) to checkmate || *ref* (*el trigo*) to sprout; (*un perro de caza*) to hunt through the bushes

matemáti·co -ca *adj* mathematical || *mf* mathematician || *f* mathematics; **matemáticas** mathematics

materia *f* matter; material, stuff; **materia colorante** dyestuff; **materia prima** or **primera materia** raw material

material *adj* material; (*grosero*) crude || *m* material; (*conjunto de objetos necesario para un servicio*) matériel; (typ) matter, copy; **material de guerra** matériel; **material fijo** (rr) permanent way; **material móvil** or **rodante** (rr) rolling stock; **ser material** (coll) to be immaterial

materialismo *m* materialism

materializar §60 *tr* (*beneficios*) to realize

maternal *adj* maternal, mother; (*afectos, cuidados, etc.*) motherly

maternidad *f* maternity; motherhood

mater·no -na *adj* maternal, mother

matinal *adj* morning

matinée *f* matinée; dressing gown, wrapper

ma·tiz *m* (*pl* **-tices**) shade, hue, nuance

matizar §60 *tr* (*diversos colores*) to blend; (*un color, un sonido*) to shade; (*en cuanto al color*) to match

matón *m* (coll) bully, browbeater

matorral *m* thicket, underbrush

matraca *f* rattle, noisemaker; taunting, bantering; bore, pest; **dar matraca a** (coll) to taunt, to tease

matraquear *intr* (coll) to make a racket; (coll) to taunt, to tease

ma·traz *m* (*pl* **-traces**) flask

matre·ro -ra *adj* cunning, shrewd || *m* (SAm) cheat, swindler

matriarca *f* matriarch

matricida *adj* matricidal || *mf* matricide

matricidio *m* matricide

matrícula *f* register, roster, roll; licence; registry

matricular *tr* & *ref* to matriculate

matrimonialmente *adv* as husband and wife

matrimoniar *intr* to marry, get married

matrimonio *m* marriage, matrimony; (*marido y mujer*) (coll) married couple; **matrimonio consensual** common-law marriage

ma·triz (*pl* **-trices**) *adj* main, first, mother || *f* matrix; (*del libro talonario*) stub; screw nut; first draft

matrona *f* matron; (coll) matronly lady

matronal *adj* matronly

matun·go -ga *adj* (Am) skinny, full of sores || *m* (Am) old nag

maturran·go -ga *adj* (SAm) poor, clumsy || *m* (SAm) stranger; (SAm) old nag || *f* (coll) trickery

Matusalén *m* Methuselah; **vivir más años que Matusalén** to be as old as Methuselah

matute *m* smuggling; smuggled goods; gambling den

matutear *intr* to smuggle

matute·ro -ra *mf* smuggler

matutinal or **matuti·no -na** *adj* morning

maula *mf* (coll) lazy loafer; (coll) poor pay; (coll) tricky person, cheat || *f* junk, trash; remnant; trickery

maulería *f* remnant shop; trickiness

maullar §8 *intr* to meow

maullido or **maúllo** *m* meow

mausoleo *m* mausoleum

máxima *f* maxim; principle

máxime *adv* chiefly, mainly, especially

máxi·mo -ma *adj* maximum; top; superlative || *m* maximum || *f* see **máxima**

may. *abbr* **mayúscula**

maya *f* May queen; English daisy

mayal *m* flail

mayear *intr* to be Maylike

mayestáti·co -ca *adj* royal

mayido *m* meow

mayo *m* May; Maypole

mayonesa *f* mayonnaise

mayor *adj* greater; larger; older, elder; greatest; largest; oldest, eldest; major; elderly; (*calle*) main; (*altar, misa*) high; **hacerse mayor de edad**

to come of age; **ser mayor de edad** to be of age || *m* chief, head, superior; **al por mayor** wholesale; **mayor de edad** (*persona de edad legal*) major; **mayores** elders; ancestors, forefathers; **mayor general** staff officer

mayoral *m* boss, foreman; head shepherd; stagecoach driver; (Arg) streetcar conductor

mayorazgo *m* primogeniture; entailed estate descending by primogeniture; first-born son

mayordoma *f* stewardess, housekeeper

mayordomo *m* steward, butler, majordomo

mayoreo *m* (Am) wholesale

mayoría *f* (*mayor edad; el mayor número, la mayor parte*) majority; superiority; **alcanzar su mayoría de edad** to come of age; **mayoría de edad** majority

mayoridad *f* majority

mayorista *adj* (Arg, Chile) wholesale || *mf* (Arg, Chile) wholesaler

mayorita-rio -ria *adj* majority

mayormente *adv* chiefly, mainly, mostly

mayúscu-lo -la *adj* (*letra*) capital; (coll) awful, tremendous || *f* capital, capital letter

maza *f* mace; heavy drumstick; (coll) bore, pedant; **la maza y la mona** constant companions; **maza de gimnasia** Indian club

mazacote *m* barilla; concrete, cement; botched job; (coll) tough, doughy food; (coll) bore

mazar §60 *tr* to churn

mazmorra *f* dungeon

mazo *m* mallet, maul; bunch; (*de la campana*) clapper; (*hombre fastidioso*) bore, pest

mazonería *f* stone masonry; (*obra de relieve*) relief; gold or silver embroidery

mazorca *f* ear of corn; cocoa bean; (*husada*) spindleful; (*de un balustre*) spindle; **comer maíz de or en la mazorca** to eat corn on the cob

mazorral *adj* coarse, crude

m/c *abbr* **mi cargo, mi cuenta, moneda corriente**

m/cta *abbr* **mi cuenta**

m/cte *abbr* **moneda corriente**

me (used as object of verb) *pron pers* me, to me; || *pron reflex* myself, to myself

meada *f* urination, water; urine stain

meadero *m* urinal

meados *mpl* urine

meaja *f* crumb; **meaja de huevo** tread

meandro *m* meander; wandering speech, wandering writing

mear *tr* to urinate on || *intr & ref* to urinate

Meca, La Mecca

mecáni-co -ca *adj* mechanical; (coll) low, mean || *m* (*obrero perito en el arreglo de las máquinas*) mechanic; (*obrero que fabrica y compone máquinas*) machinist; workman, repairman; driver, chauffeur || *f* mechanics; (*aparato que da movimiento a un artefacto*) machinery, works; (coll)

meanness; **mecánicas** (coll) household chores

mecanismo *m* mechanism, machinery

mecanizar §60 *tr* to mechanize; to motorize

mecanografía *f* typewriting; **mecanografía al tacto** touch typewriting

mecanografiar §77 *tr & intr* to typewrite

mecanógra-fo -fa *mf* typist, typewriter

mecapale-ro -ra *m* (Mex) messenger, porter

mece-dor -dora *adj* swinging, rocking || *m* stirrer; (*columpio*) swing || *f* rocker, rocking chair

mecer §46 *tr* (*un líquido*) to stir; (*la cuna*) to rock || *ref* to rock, swing

mecha *f* (*de vela o bujía*) wick; (*tubo de pólvora*) fuse; lock of hair; (*para mechar carne*) slice of bacon; bundle of thread; (Col, Ecuad, Ven) joke

mechar *tr* (*la carne*) to lard, interlard

mechera *f* (coll) shoplifter

mechero *m* (*p.ej., de cigarrillos*) lighter, pocket lighter; (*de aparato de alumbrado*) burner; (*de candelero*) socket; **mechero encendedor** pilot, pilot light

mechón *m* cowlick; (Guat) torch

medalla *f* medal; medallion

medallón *m* medallion; (*joya en que se colocan retratos, etc.*) locket

médano *m* dune, sandbank

media *f* stocking; (math) mean; **media corta** (Arg) sock; **media media** (Arg, Ecuad, Ven) sock; **y media** half past, e.g., **las dos y media** half past two

mediación *f* mediation

media-do -da *adj* half over; half-full; **a mediados de** about the middle of; **mediada la tarde** in the middle of the afternoon

media-dor -dora *mf* mediator

mediana *f* long billiard cue

medianería *f* party wall; party fence

mediane-ro -ra *adj* middle; mediating || *mf* mediator; partner; owner of a row house

medianía *f* average; (*persona que carece de dotes relevantes*) mediocrity

media-no -na *adj* middling, medium; average, fair; (coll) mediocre || *f* see **mediana**

medianoche *f* midnight; small meat pie

mediante *adj* interceding || *prep* by means of, by virtue of

mediar *intr* to be half over; to be in the middle; to intercede, mediate; to elapse; to take place

mediatinta *f* half-tone

medible *adj* measurable

medical *adj* medical

medicamento *m* medicine

medicamento-so -sa *adj* medicinal

medicastro *m* quack

medicina *f* medicine

medicinar *tr* to treat || *ref* to take medicine

medición *f* measurement; metering

médi-co -ca *adj* medical || *mf* doctor, physician; **médico de cabecera** family physician

medida *f* measurement; measure; caution, moderation; **a medida de** in proportion to; according to; **a medida que** in proportion as; **en la medida que** to the extent that; **hecho a la medida** custom-made; **medida para áridos** dry measure; **medida para líquidos** liquid measure; **tomarle a uno las medidas** to take someone's measure, to size up someone

medidamente *adv* with moderation

medidor *m* measurer; (Mex, SAm) meter

medie·ro -ra *mf* hosier; partner

medieval *adj* medieval

medievalista *mf* medievalist

medievo *m* Middle Ages

me·dio -dia *adj* middle; medium; medieval; half; a half, e.g., **media libra** a half pound; half a, e.g., **media naranja** half an orange; average, mean; mid, in the middle of, e.g., **a media tarde** in mid afternoon, in the middle of the afternoon; **a medias** half; half-and-half; **ir a medias (con)** to go halves (with), to go fifty-fifty (with) ‖ *m* middle; medium; environment; step, measure; means; (en el espiritismo) medium; (baseball) shortstop; (arith) half; (del ruedo) (taur) center; **a medio** half; **en medio de** in the middle of; in the midst of; **justo medio** happy medium, golden mean; **por medio de** by means of; **quitarse de en medio** (coll) to get out of the way ‖ *f* see **media** ‖ **medio** *adv* half

mediocre *adj* mediocre

mediocridad *f* mediocrity

mediodía *m* noon, midday; south; **en pleno mediodía** at high noon; **hacer mediodía** to stop for the noon meal

mediquillo *m* quack

medir §50 *tr* to measure ‖ *intr* to measure ‖ *ref* to act with moderation

meditabun·do -da *adj* meditative

meditar *tr* to meditate; to plan, contemplate ‖ *intr* to meditate

mediterráne·o -na *adj* inland ‖ **Mediterráne·o -na** *adj & m* Mediterranean

mé·dium *m* (*pl* **-dium** or **-diums**) medium

medra *f* growth, prosperity

medrana *f* fear

medrar *intr* to thrive, prosper, improve

medro *m* growth, prosperity; **medros** progress

medro·so -sa *adj* fearful, scared; frightful, terrible

médula or **medula** *f* marrow, medulla; (bot) pith; (fig) pith, gist, essence; **médula espinal** spinal cord

medular *adj* pithy

medusa *f* jellyfish

mefistoféli·co -ca *adj* Mephistophelian

megaciclo *m* megacycle

megáfono *m* megaphone

me·go -ga *adj* meek, gentle, mild

megohmio *m* megohm

Méj. *abbr* **Méjico**

mejica·no -na *adj & mf* Mexican

Méjico *m* Mexico; **Nuevo Méjico** New Mexico

meji·do -da *adj* beaten with sugar and milk

mejilla *f* cheek

mejor *adj* better; best; (licitador) highest; **a lo mejor** (coll) unexpectedly; (coll) worse luck; (coll) perhaps, maybe; **el mejor día** some fine day ‖ *adv* better; best; **mejor dicho** rather

mejora *f* growth, improvement; higher bid; alteration

mejoramiento *m* improvement

mejorana *f* sweet marjoram

mejorar *tr* to improve; (los licitadores el precio de una cosa) to raise; **mejorando lo presente** present company excepted ‖ *intr & ref* to improve, get better, recover; to make progress; (el tiempo) to clear up

mejoría *f* improvement; (en una enfermedad) betterment, recovery

mejunje *m* brew, potion, mixture

mela·do -da *adj* honey-colored ‖ *m* (Am) thick cane syrup

melancolía *f* (tristeza vaga) melancholy; (depresión moral) melancholia

melancóli·co -ca *adj* melancholy

melaza *f* molasses

melcocha *f* taffy, molasses candy

melchor *m* German silver

melena *f* hair falling over the eyes; long hair, loose hair; (del león) mane; (del caballo) forelock; **andar a la melena** (coll) to pull each other's hair; (coll) to get into a fight; **estar en melena** (coll) to have one's hair down

melga *f* (Am) ridge made by plow; (Col, Chile) plot of ground to be sown; (Hond) small piece of work to be finished

melindre *m* honey fritter; (dulce de pasta de mazapán) ladyfinger; narrow ribbon; prudery, finickiness

melindrear *intr* to be prudish, be finicky

melindro·so -sa *adj* prudish, finicky

melocotón *m* peach tree; peach

melocotonero *m* peach tree

melodía *f* melody

melodio·so -sa *adj* melodious

melodramáti·co -ca *adj* melodramatic

melón *m* melon; (Cucumis melo) muskmelon; (coll) blockhead; (coll) bald head; **melón de agua** watermelon

melo·so -sa *adj* sweet, honeyed; gentle, mild, mellow

mella *f* dent, nick, notch; gap, hollow; harm, injury; **hacer mella a** to have an effect on; **hacer mella en** to harm

mellar *tr* to dent, nick, notch; to harm

melli·zo -za *adj & mf* twin

membrana *f* membrane; (del teléfono, micrófono) diaphragm

membrete *m* note, memo; letterhead; heading; written invitation

membrillero *m* quince tree

membrillo *m* quince; quince tree

membru·do -da *adj* brawny, burly

memeches — a memeches (CAm) on horseback

memela *f* (CAm, Mex) cornmeal pancake

me·mo -ma *adj* foolish, simple ‖ *mf* fool, simpleton

memorán·dum *m* (*pl* **-dum**) memorandum book, notebook; (sección en los periódicos) professional services; (papel con membrete) letterhead

memorar tr & ref to remember

memoria f memory; (exposición de ciertos hechos) memoir; account, record; **de memoria** by heart; **encomendar a la memoria** to commit to memory; **hablar de memoria** (coll) to say the first thing that comes to one's mind; **hacer memoria de** to bring up; **memorias** memoirs; regards

memorial m memorandum book; memorial, petition; (law) brief

memorizar §60 tr to memorize

mena f ore

menaje m household furniture; school supplies

mención f mention

mencionar tr to mention

men·daz (pl -daces) adj mendacious || mf liar

mendicante adj & mf mendicant

mendigante adj begging, mendicant || mf beggar, mendicant

mendigar §44 tr to beg for || intr to beg, go begging

mendi·go -ga mf beggar

mendiguez f begging

mendo·so -sa adj false, wrong

mendrugo m crumb, crust

menear tr to stir, to shake; to wiggle; (la cola) to wag; (un negocio) to manage; **peor es meneallo** (i.e., menearlo) better keep hands off || ref to shake; to wiggle; to wag; (coll) to hustle, bestir oneself

meneo m stirring, shaking; wagging; hustling; (coll) drubbing, thrashing

menester m need; want, lack; job, occupation; **haber menester** to be necessary, to be need for; **menesteres** bodily needs; property; (coll) implements, tools; **ser menester** to be necessary

menestero·so -sa adj needy || mf needy person

menestra f vegetable soup

menes·tral -trala mf mechanic

meng. abbr **menguante**

mengua f want, lack; poverty; decline; decrease, diminution; **en mengua de** to the discredit of

mengua·do -da adj timid, cowardly; simple, silly; mean, stingy; wretched, miserable; poor, needy; fatal

menguante adj decreasing; declining; waning || f decrease; decline; low water; ebb tide; **menguante de la luna** wane, waning of the moon

menguar §10 tr to diminish, lessen; to discredit || intr to diminish, lessen; to decline; to decrease; (la luna) to wane; (la marea) to fall

mengue m (coll) devil

menina f young lady in waiting

menino m noble page of the royal family

menor adj less, lesser; smaller; younger; least; smallest; youngest; slightest; minor || m minor; **al por menor** retail; **menor de edad** minor; **por menor** retail; in detail, minutely || f minor premise

Menorca f Minorca

menoría f inferiority, subordination; (tiempo de menor edad) minority

menorista adj (Arg, Chile) retail || mf (Arg, Chile) retailer

menor·quín -quina adj & mf Minorcan

menos adv less; fewer; least; fewest; **al menos** at least; **a lo menos** at least; **a menos que** unless; **echar de menos** to miss; **¡menos mal!** lucky break!; **menos mal que** it is a good thing that; **no poder menos de** + inf to not be able to help + ger; **por lo menos** at least; **tener en menos** to think little of; **venir a menos** to decline; to become poor || prep less, minus; (al decir la hora) of, to, e.g., **las tres menos diez** ten minutes of (or to) three || m less; (signo de resta o sustracción) minus, minus sign

menoscabar tr to lessen, diminish, reduce; to damage; to discredit

menoscabo m lessening, reduction; damage; discredit; **con menoscabo de** to the detriment of

menoscuenta f part payment

menospreciable adj despicable, contemptible

menospreciar tr to underestimate, underrate; to scorn, despise

menosprecio m underestimation; scorn

mensaje m message

mensajería f public conveyance; **mensajerías** transportation company; shipping line

mensaje·ro -ra mf messenger || m harbinger

men·so -sa adj (Mex) foolish, stupid

menstruar §21 intr to menstruate

menstruo m menses

mensual adj monthly

mensualidad f monthly pay, monthly instalment

ménsula f bracket; elbow rest

mensurar tr to measure

menta f mint; **menta piperita** peppermint; **menta romana** or **verde** spearmint

menta·do -da adj famous, renowned

mentar §2 tr to mention

mente f mind

mentecatería or **mentecatez** f simpleness, folly

menteca·to -ta adj simple, foolish || mf simpleton, fool

mentidero m (coll) hangout; (coll) gossip column

mentir §68 tr to disappoint || intr to lie; to be misleading; (un color) to clash; **¡miento!** my mistake!

mentira f lie; error, mistake; **mentira inocente** or **oficiosa** white lie; **parece mentira** it's hard to believe

mentirilla f fib, white lie; **de mentirillas** for fun

mentirón m whopper

mentiro·so -sa adj lying; false, deceptive; full of errors || mf liar

men·tís m (pl -tís) insulting contradiction; **dar un mentís a** to give the lie to

mentón m chin

me·nú m (pl -nús) menu

menudamente *adv* in detail; at retail

menudear *tr* to make frequently; to tell in detail; (Col) to sell at retail || *intr* to happen frequently, to be frequent; to go into detail; (Arg) to grow, increase

menudencia *f* smallness; trifle; meticulousness; **menudencias** pork products; (Col, Mex) giblets

menudeo *m* constant repetition; detailed accounting; **al menudeo** at retail

menudillos *mpl* giblets

menu·do -da *adj* small, slight, minute; futile, worthless; meticulous; common, vulgar; petty || *m* innards (*of fowl and other animals*); rice coal; **al menudo** at retail; **a menudo** often; **menudos** small change; **por menudo** in detail; at retail

meñique *adj* little, tiny; (*dedo*) little || *m* little finger

meollo *m* marrow; pith; (*seso*) brain; brains, intelligence; gist, marrow, essence

me·ón -ona *adj* (*niño*) piddling; (*niebla*) dripping

mequetrefe *m* (coll) whippersnapper, jackanapes

mercachifle *m* peddler; small dealer

mercadear *intr* to deal, to trade

merca·der -dera *mf* merchant; **mercader de grueso** wholesale merchant

mercadería *f* merchandise, commodity; **mercaderías** goods, merchandise

mercado *m* market; **lanzar al mercado** to put on the market; **mercado de valores** stock market; **mercado negro** black market

mercaduría *f* commodity

mercancía *f* trade, commerce; merchandise; piece of merchandise; merchandise || **mercancías** goods, merchandise || **mercancías** *msg* (*pl -as*) freight train

mercante *adj* & *m* merchant

mercantil *adj* mercantile

mercar §73 *tr* to buy || *intr* to trade, deal

merced *f* pay, wages; favor, grace; a **merced de** at the mercy of; **merced a** thanks to; **merced de agua** distribution of irrigating water; **vuestra merced** your grace

mercena·rio -ria *adj* mercenary || *m* mercenary; day laborer, hireling

mercería *f* haberdashery, notions store; (Am) dry-goods store; (Chile) hardware store

mercología *f* marketing

mercurio *m* mercury

merecer §22 *tr* to deserve, merit; (*lo que se desea*) to attain; (*alabanza*) to win; (*cierta suma*) to be worth; **merecer la pena** to be worth while || *intr* to be deserving; **merecer bien de** to deserve the gratitude of

mereci·do -da *adj* deserved || *m* just deserts; **llevar su merecido** to get what's coming to one

mereciente *adj* deserving

merecimiento *m* desert, merit

merendar §2 *tr* to lunch on, have for lunch; to keep an eye on, to peep at

|| *intr* to lunch || *ref* to manage to get; (*en el juego*) (Chile) to clean out

merendero *m* lunchroom; picnic grounds

merendona *f* fine spread

merengar §44 *tr* to whip (*cream*)

merengue *m* meringue

mere·triz *f* (*pl* -trices) harlot

meridiana *f* lounge, couch; afternoon nap; meridian line; **a la meridiana** at noon

meridia·no -na *adj* meridian; bright, dazzling || *m* meridian || *f* see **meridiana**

meridional *adj* southern || *mf* southerner

merienda *f* lunch, snack; (coll) hunchback

meri·no -na *adj* merino; (*cabello*) thick and curly || *mf* merino || *m* merino shepherd; merino wool

mérito *m* merit, desert; value, worth; **hacer mérito de** to make mention of; **hacer méritos** to try to please, to put one's best foot forward

merito·rio -ria *adj* meritorious || *m* volunteer worker; unpaid learner, apprentice

merluza *f* (*pez*) hake; (coll) drunk, spree

merma *f* decrease, reduction; leakage, shrinkage

mermar *tr* to decrease, reduce || *intr* to decrease, shrink, dwindle

mermelada *f* marmalade

me·ro -ra *adj* mere, pure; (Col, Ven) alone || *m* grouper, jewfish || **mero** *adv* (CAm) almost, soon

merodea·dor -dora *adj* marauding || *m* marauder

merodear *intr* to maraud

mes *m* month; monthly pay; menses; **caer en el mes del obispo** (coll) to come at the right time

mesa *f* table; (*mostrador*) counter; (*escritorio*) desk; (*de arma blanca o herramienta*) flat side; (*de escalera*) landing; (*comida*) fare, food; (*conjunto de dirigentes*) board; **alzar la mesa** to clear the table; **hacer mesa limpia** to clean up (*in gambling*); **levantar la mesa** to clear the table; **mesa de batalla** sorting table; **mesa de extensión** extension table; **mesa de juego** gambling table; **mesa de milanos** (coll) scanty fare; **mesa de trucos** pool table; **mesa perezosa** drop table; **poner la mesa** to set or lay the table; **tener a mesa y mantel** to feed, to support; **tener mesa** to keep open house

mesana *f* (naut) mizzen

mesar *tr* (*los cabellos*) to tear, pull out || *ref* **mesarse los cabellos** to pull out one's hair; to pull out each other's hair

mescolanza *f* (coll) jumble, hodge-podge, medley

mesegueria *f* harvest watch

mesera *f* (Am) waitress

mesero *m* journeyman on monthly pay; (Am) waiter

meseta *f* plateau, tableland; (*de escalera*) landing

Mesías *m* Messiah

mesilla *f* mantel, mantelpiece; *(de escalera)* landing; window sill

mesita *f* stand, small table; **mesita portatieléfono** telephone table

mesnada *f* armed retinue; band, company

mesón *m* inn, tavern; (Chile) bar; (Chile) counter

mesone·ro -ra *adj* inn, tavern ‖ *mf* innkeeper, tavern keeper

mester *m* (archaic) craft, trade; (archaic) literary genre; **mester de clerecía** clerical verse of the Middle Ages; **mester de juglaría** popular minstrelsy of the Middle Ages

mesti·zo -za *adj & mf* half-breed; *(perro)* mongrel

mesura *f* dignity, gravity; calm, restraint; courtesy, civility

mesura·do -da *adj* dignified, sedate; calm, restrained; polite; moderate, temperate

mesurar *tr* to temper, moderate ‖ *ref* to act with restraint

meta *f* goal

metafonía *f* umlaut

metáfora *f* metaphore

metafóri·co -ca *adj* metaphorical

metal *m* metal; money; *(de la voz)* timbre; condition, quality; (mus) brass; **el vil metal** (coll) filthy lucre; **metal blanco** nickel silver; **metal de imprenta** type metal

metale·ro -ra *adj* (Bol, Chile, Peru) metal ‖ *m* (Bol, Chile, Peru) metalworker

metáli·co -ca *adj* metallic ‖ *m* metalworker; cash, coin

metalistería *f* metalwork

metalizar §60 *tr* to make metallic; to put a metal coating on; to turn into cash ‖ *ref* to become mercenary

metaloide *m* nonmetal

metalurgia *f* metallurgy

metamorfo·sis *f* *(pl* **-sis)** metamorphosis

metano *m* methane

metate *m* (CAm, Mex) flat stone on which corn is ground

metáte·sis *f* *(pl* **-sis)** metathesis

mete·dor -dora *mf* smuggler

meteduría *f* smuggling

metemuer·tos *m* *(pl* **-tos)** stagehand; busybody, meddler

meteo *f* weather bureau, weather report

meteóri·co -ca *adj* meteoric

meteoro or **metéoro** *m* meteor; atmospheric phenomenon

meteorología *f* meteorology

meter *tr* to put, to place; to insert; *(un ruido)* to make; *(miedo)* to cause; *(mentiras)* to tell; *(chismes, enredos)* to start; *(dinero en el juego)* to stake; to smuggle; *(un golpe)* (Am) to strike ‖ *ref* to project; to meddle, butt in; **meterse a** to set oneself up as; to take it upon oneself to; **meterse con** to pick a quarrel with; **meterse en** to get into; to plunge into; to empty into

meticulo·so -sa *adj* meticulous; shy, timid

meti·do -da *adj* close, tight; rich, abundant; (Am) meddlesome; **muy metido con** on close terms with; **muy metido en** deeply involved in ‖ *m* push; punch; strong lye; loose leaf; *(tela sobrante en las costuras de una prenda)* seam

metódi·co -ca *adj* methodic(al)

metodista *adj & mf* Methodist

método *m* method

metraje *m* distance or length in meters; *(cine)* **de corto metraje** short; *(cine)* **de largo metraje** full-length

metralla *f* scrap iron; grapeshot; shrapnel

métri·co -ca *adj* metric(al) ‖ *f* prosody

metro *m* meter; ruler; tape measure; subway; **metro plegadizo** folding rule

metrónomo *m* metronome

metrópoli *f* metropolis; mother country

metropolita·no -na *adj* metropolitan ‖ *m* subway; (eccl) metropolitan

Méx. *abbr* **México**

mexica·no -na *adj & mf* (Am) Mexican

México *m* (Am) Mexico; **Nuevo México** New Mexico

mezcla *f* mixture; *(argamasa)* mortar; *(tejido)* tweed

mezclar *tr* to mix; to blend ‖ *ref* to mix; *(introducirse uno entre otros)* to mingle; to intermarry; to meddle

mezclilla *f* light tweed

mezcolanza *f* jumble, hodgepodge, medley

mezquinar *tr* (Am) to be stingy with ‖ *intr* (Am) to be stingy

mezquindad *f* meanness, stinginess; need, poverty; smallness, tininess; wretchedness

mezqui·no -na *adj* mean, stingy; needy, poor; small, tiny; wretched

mezquita *f* mosque

mi *adj poss* my

mí *pron pers* me ‖ *pron reflex* myself (used as object of a preposition)

miar §77 *intr* to meow

miau *m* meow

mica *f* mica; (Guat) flirt; **ponerse una mica** (CAm) to go on a jag

mico *m* long-tailed monkey; libertine; (coll) hoodlum; **dar mico** (coll) to not keep a date

microbio *m* microbe

microbiología *f* microbiology

microbús *m* (Chile) jitney

microfaradio *m* microfarad

microficha *f* microcard

micro·film *m* *(pl* **-films** o **-filmes)** microfilm

microfilmar *tr* to microfilm

micrófono *m* microphone

microonda *f* microwave

micropelícula *f* microfilm

microscópi·co -ca *adj* microscopic

microscopio *m* microscope

microsurco *adj invar* microgroove ‖ *m* microgroove

microteléfono *m* handset, French telephone

mi·cho -cha *mf* (coll) pussy cat

miedo *m* fear, dread; **miedo cerval**

great fear; **por miedo de** for fear of; **por miedo (de) que** for fear that; **tener miedo (a)** to be afraid (of); **tener miedo de** to be in fear of, be afraid of; to be afraid to

miedo·so -sa adj (coll) fearful, afraid

miel f honey; (jarabe saturado) molasses; **dejar con la miel en los labios** to spoil the fun for; **hacerse de miel** to be peaches and cream

mielga f lucerne

miembro m member; (extremidad del hombre y los animales) member, limb

mientes fpl mind, thought; wish, desire; **caer en las mientes** or **en mientes** to come to mind; **parar** or **poner mientes en** to reflect on; **venírsele a uno a las mientes** to come to one's mind

mientras conj while; whereas; **mientras que** while; whereas; **mientras tanto** meanwhile

miérco·les m (pl -les) Wednesday; **miércoles de ceniza** Ash Wednesday

mies f cereal, grain; harvest time; **mieses** grain fields

miga f (porción pequeña) bit; (parte más blanda del pan) crumb; (fig) substance; **hacer buenas migas con** to get along well with; **migas** fried crumbs

migaja f bit, piece; (de inteligencia) smattering; **migajas** crumbs; leavings

migajón m crumb; (coll) substance

migar §44 tr (el pan) to crumb; (p.ej., la leche) to put crumbs in

migrato·rio -ria adj migratory

miguelear tr (CAm) to make love to

migüele·ño -ña adj (Hond) impolite, discourteous

mijo m millet

mil adj & m thousand, a thousand, one thousand; **a las mil quinientas** (coll) at an unearthly hour

milagre·ro -ra adj superstitious; miracle-working

milagro m (hecho sobrenatural) miracle; (cosa rara) wonder; votive offering; **colgar el milagro a** (coll) to put the blame on; **vivir de milagro** to have a hard time getting along; to have had a narrow escape

milagrón m (coll) fuss, excitement

milagro·so -sa adj miraculous; marvelous, wonderful

milano m burr, down; (orn) kite

mil·deu m (pl -deus) mildew

milena·rio -ria adj millennial || m millennium

milenio m millennium

milenrama f yarrow

milési·mo -ma adj & m thousandth

miliamperio m milliampere

milicia f militia; soldiery; warfare; military service

milicia·no -na adj military || m militiaman

miligramo m milligram

milímetro m millimeter

militante adj militant

militar adj military; army || m soldier, military man || intr to fight, go to

war; to struggle; to serve in the army; (surtir efecto) to militate

militarismo m militarism

militarista adj & mf militarist

militarizar §60 tr to militarize

milite m soldier

milpa f (CAm, Mex) cornfield

milla f mile

millar m thousand

millarada f about a thousand; **echar millaradas** to boast about one's wealth

millo m millet

millón m million

millona·rio -ria adj of a million or more inhabitants || mf millionaire

mimar tr to fondle, to pet; to pamper, indulge, spoil

mimbre m & f (bot) osier; osier, wicker, withe

mimbrear intr & ref to sway

mimbre·ño -ña adj willowy

mimbrera f (bot) osier, osier willow

mimbro·so -sa adj osier; (hecho de mimbre) wicker

mimeografiar §77 tr to mimeograph

mimeógrafo m mimeograph

mímica f mimicry; sign language

mimo m (entre los griegos y romanos) mime; fondling, petting; pampering

mimo·so -sa adj delicate, tender; finicky, fussy

mina f mine; (de lápiz) lead; (fig) mine, gold mine, storehouse; underground passage; (SAm) moll; **beneficiar una mina** to work a mine; **mina de carbón** or **mina hullera** coal mine; **voló la mina** the truth is out

minado m mine work; (nav) mining

mina·dor -dora adj (nav) mine-laying || m (mil) miner; (nav) mine layer

minar tr to mine; to undermine; to consume; to plug away at || intr to mine

minarete m minaret

mineraje m mining; **mineraje a tajo abierto** strip mining

mineral adj & m mineral

mineralogía f mineralogy

minería f mining; mine operators

mine·ro -ra adj mining || m miner; mine operator; (fig) source, origin

mingitorio m street urinal

min·gón -gona adj (Ven) spoiled, pampered

miniar tr to paint in miniature; (un manuscrito) to illuminate

miniatura f miniature

miniaturización f miniaturization

míni·mo -ma adj minimum; tiny, small, minute; least, smallest || m minimum || f tiny bit

mini·no -na mf (coll) kitty, pussy

ministerial adj ministerial

ministerio m ministry, cabinet, government; **formar ministerio** to form a government; **ministerio de Hacienda** Treasury Department (U.S.A.); Treasury (Brit); **ministerio de la Gobernación** Department of the Interior (U.S.A.); Home Office (Brit); **ministerio del Ejército** Department of the Army (U.S.A.); War Office (Brit); **ministerio de Marina** Department of the Navy (U.S.A.); Board of Admiralty (Brit)

ministrar *tr* to administer; to furnish

ministro *m* minister; bailiff, constable; **ministro de asuntos exteriores** foreign minister; **ministro de Gobernación** Home Secretary (Brit); **ministro de Hacienda** Secretary of the Treasury (U.S.A.); Chancellor of the Exchequer (Brit); **ministro de Justicia** Attorney General (U.S.A.); **primer ministro** prime minister, premier

minorar *tr* to diminish, reduce; to weaken

minorati·vo -va *adj & m* laxative

minoría *f* minority

minoridad *f* minority

minorí·rio -ria *adj* minority

minucia *f* trifle; **minucias** minutiae

minucio·so -sa *adj* minute, meticulous

minué *m* or **minuete** *m* minuet

minúscu·lo -la *adj* (*letra*) small; (coll) small, tiny ‖ *f* small letter

minuta *f* first draft, rough draft; memorandum; menu, bill of fare; roll, list

minutero *m* minute hand

minu·to -ta *adj* minute ‖ *m* minute ‖ *f* see **minuta**

mí·o -a *adj poss* mine; of mine, e.g., **un amigo mío** a friend of mine ‖ *pron poss* mine

miope *adj* near-sighted ‖ *mf* near-sighted person

miopía *f* near-sightedness

mira *f* (*de arma de fuego, telescopio, etc.*) sight; aim, object, purpose; target; watchtower; **estar a la mira** to be on the lookout; **poner la mira en** to have designs on

mirada *f* glance, look; **apuñalar con la mirada** to look daggers at; **mirada de soslayo** side glance

miradero *m* (*lugar desde donde se mira*) lookout; (*persona o cosa que es objeto de la atención pública*) cynosure

mira·do -da *adj* cautious, circumspect; **bien mirado** highly regarded ‖ *f* see **mirada**

mirador *m* belvedere; bay window, oriel

miramiento *m* considerateness, courtesy, regard; look; **miramientos** (coll) fuss, bother

miranda *f* eminence, vantage point

mirar *tr* to look at, to watch; to consider, contemplate; **mirar bien** to look with favor on; **mirar por encima** to glance at ‖ *intr* to look, to glance; ¡**mira!** look out!; **mirar a** to look at, glance at; to face, overlook; to aim at; to aim to; **mirar por** to look after ‖ *ref* to look at oneself; to look at each other; **mirarse en ello** to watch one's step; **mirarse en una persona** to be all wrapped up in a person

mirasol *m* sunflower

miríada *f* myriad

mirilla *f* peephole; (*para dirigir visuales*) target; (phot) finder

miriñaque *m* hoop skirt, crinoline; bauble, trinket; (Arg) cowcatcher

mirística *f* nutmeg tree

mirlar *ref* (coll) to try to look important

mirlo *m* blackbird; (coll) solemn look; **mirlo blanco** (coll) rare bird; **soltar el mirlo** (coll) to start to jabber

mirmidón *m* tiny fellow, nincompoop

mi·rón -rona *adj* onlooking; nosy ‖ *mf* onlooker; (*de una partida de juego*) kibitzer; busybody

mirra *f* myrrh

mirto *m* myrtle

misa *f* mass; **cantar misa** to say mass; **como en misa** in dead silence; **misa cantada** High Mass; **misa de prima** early mass; **misa mayor** High Mass; **misa rezada** Low Mass

misal *m* missal

misantropía *f* misanthropy

misántropo *m* misanthrope

misar *intr* (coll) to say mass; (coll) to hear mass

misario *m* acolyte

miscelá·neo -na *adj* miscellaneous ‖ *f* miscellany

miserable *adj* miserable, wretched; mean, stingy; despicable, vile ‖ *mf* cur, cad; wretch; miser

miseran·do -da *adj* pitiful

miserear *intr* (coll) to be stingy

miseria *f* misery, wretchedness; poverty; stinginess; (coll) trifle, pittance; **comerse de miseria** (coll) to live in great poverty

misericordia *f* compassion, mercy, pity

misericordio·so -sa *adj* merciful

mise·ro -ra *adj* miserable, wretched ‖ *mf* wretch

misión *f* mission; ration for harvesters; **ir a misiones** to go away as a missionary

misional *adj* missionary

misionario *m* missionary; envoy, messenger

misionero *m* missionary

misi·vo -va *adj & f* missive

mismísi·mo -ma *adj* very same, self-same

mis·mo -ma *adj & pron indef* same; own, very; -self, e.g., **ella misma** herself; myself, e.g., **yo mismo** I myself; yourself, himself, herself, itself; **así mismo** likewise, also; **casi lo mismo** much the same; **lo mismo** just the same; **lo mismo me da** (coll) it's all the same to me; **mismo . . . que** same . . . as; **por lo mismo** for that very reason ‖ **mismo** *adv* right, e.g., **ahora mismo** right now; **aquí mismo** right here

mistela *f* flavored brandy; needled must, spiked must

misterio *m* mystery; **hablar de misterio** to talk mysteriously

misterio·so -sa *adj* mysterious

misticismo *m* mysticism

místi·co -ca *adj* mystic(al) ‖ *mf* mystic

mistificación *f* hoax, mystification

mistificar §73 *tr* to hoax, to mystify

mistifori *m* (coll) hodgepodge

misturera *f* (Peru) flower girl

mita *f* mite, cheese mite; (SAm) Indian slave labor; (*turno en el trabajo*) (Arg, Chile) shift, turn

mitad f half; middle; **a (la) mitad de** halfway through; **cara mitad** (coll) better half; **en la mitad de** in the middle of; **la mitad de** half the; **mitad y mitad** half-and-half; **por la mitad** in half, in the middle

míti·co -ca adj mythical

mitigar §44 tr to mitigate, appease, allay

mitin m (pl **mitins** or **mítines**) meeting, rally

mito m myth

mitología f mythology

mitológi·co -ca adj mythological

mitón m mitten

mitra f chimney pot; (eccl) miter

mixtificación f hoax, mystification

mixtificar §73 tr to hoax, to mystify

mixtifori m (coll) hodgepodge

mixtión f mixture

mix·to -ta adj mixed || m compound number; sulphur match; explosive compound

mixtura f mixture

mixturar tr to mix

mixturera f (Peru) flower girl

miz interj here, pussy!; here, kitty!

mízcalo m edible milk mushroom

m/l abbr **mi letra**

m/n abbr **moneda nacional**

mobilia·rio -ria adj personal (property) || m furniture, suit of furniture

moblaje m furniture, suit of furniture

moblar §61 tr to furnish

moca m Mocha coffee || f (Ecuad) mudhole; (Mex) wineglass

mocador m handkerchief

mocar §73 tr to blow the nose of || ref to blow one's nose

mocarro m (coll) snot

mocasín m moccasin

mocear intr to act young; to sow one's wild oats

mocedad f youth; wild oats

mocerío m young people

mocero adj masc woman-crazy

mocetón m strapping young fellow

mocetona f buxom young woman

mocil adj youthful

moción f motion, movement; (en junta deliberante) motion; **hacer** or **presentar una moción** to make a motion

mocionante mf (Am) mover

mocionar tr & intr (Am) to move

moci·to -ta adj young || mf youngster

moco m (humor segregado por una membrana mucosa) mucus; (mocarro) snot; (extremo del pabilo de una vela) snuff; **a moco de candil** by candle light; **llorar a moco tendido** (coll) to cry like a baby; **moco de pavo** crest of a turkey; (bot) cockscomb; (col) trifle

moco·so -sa adj snotty, snively; rude, ill-bred; flip, saucy; mean, worthless || mf brat

mochar tr to butt; (Arg) to rob; (Am) to chop off; (Col) to fire

mochil m errand boy for farmers in the field

mochila f knapsack, haversack; tool bag; (mil) ration

mochín m (slang) executioner

mo·cho -cha adj blunt, stub, flat; (árbol) topped; stub-horned || m butt end

mochuelo m (orn) little owl; (de una o más palabras) omission; **cargar con el mochuelo** or **tocarle a (uno) el mochuelo** (coll) to get the worst of a deal

moda f fashion, mode, style; **a la moda de** after the fashion of, in the style of; **alta moda** haute couture; **de moda** in fashion; **fuera de moda** out of fashion; **pasar de moda** to go out of fashion

modales mpl manners

modalidad f manner, way, nature, kind

modelar tr to model; to form, shape; to mold || ref to model; **modelarse sobre** to pattern oneself after

modelo adj invar model, e.g., **ciudad modelo** model city || mf model, mannequin, fashion model || m model, pattern; form, blank; equal, peer; style

modera·do -da adj moderate

moderador m regulator; (para retardar el efecto de los neutrones) moderator

moderar tr to moderate, control, restrain || ref to moderate, control oneself, restrain oneself

modernizar §60 tr to modernize

moder·no -na adj modern

modestia f modesty

modes·to -ta adj modest

modicidad f moderateness, reasonableness

módi·co -ca adj moderate, reasonable

modificante adj modifying || m (gram) modifier

modificar §73 tr to modify

modismo m idiom

modista f dressmaker; **modista de sombreros** milliner

modistería f dressmaking; (Am) ladies' dress shop

modistilla f (coll) dressmaker's helper; (coll) unskilled dressmaker

modisto m ladies' tailor

modo m manner, mode, way; (gram) mood, mode; **al** or **a modo de** like, on the order of; **de buen modo** politely; **de ese modo** at that rate; **de tal modo que** with the result that; **de modo que** so that; and so; **de ningún modo** by no means; **de todos modos** anyhow, at any rate; **en cierto modo** after a fashion; **modo de ser** nature, disposition; **por modo de** as, by way of; **sobre modo** extremely; **uno a modo de** a sort of, a kind of

modorra f drowsiness, heaviness

modorrar tr to make drowsy || ref to get drowsy, fall asleep; (la fruta) to get squashy

modo·rro -rra adj drowsy, heavy; dull, stupid; (fruta) squashy || f see **modorra**

modo·so -sa adj quiet, well-behaved

modrego m (coll) boor, awkward fellow

modulación f modulation; **modulación de altura** or **de amplitud** amplitude modulation; **modulación de frecuencia** frequency modulation

modular tr & intr to modulate

modulo·to -sa adj harmonious

mofa f jeering, scoffing, mockery

mofeta f skunk; (gas pernicioso que se desprende de las minas) blackdamp, firedamp

moflete m (coll) fat cheek, jowl

mofletu·do -da adj fat-cheeked

mo·gol -gola adj & mf Mongol, Mongolian

mogollón m — **comer de mogollón** (coll) to sponge

mo·gón -gona adj one-horned, broken-horned

mogote m knoll, hillock; stack of sheaves; budding antler

mohatra f fake sale; cheating

mohien·to -ta adj moldy, musty; (hierro) rusty

mohín m face, grimace

mohína f annoyance, displeasure

mohi·no -na adj sad, melancholy, moody; (caballo, buey, vaca) black, black-nosed || mf hinny || m blue magpie || f see **mohína**

moho m mold, must; (del hierro) rust; sloth, laziness; **no dejar criar moho** (coll) to keep in constant use, to use up quickly

moho·so -sa adj moldy, musty; (hierro) rusty; (chiste) stale

Moisés m Moses

moja·do -da adj wet; (p.ej., por la lluvia) drenched, soaked; (húmedo) moist; (phonet) liquid || m (Mex) wetback

mojar tr to wet; (la lluvia a una persona) to drench, soak; (humedecer) to dampen, to moisten; (ensopar) to dunk; (coll) to stab || intr — **mojar en** to get mixed up in || ref to get wet; to get drenched, get soaked

mojarrilla mf (coll) jolly person

moje m sauce, gravy

mojicón m muffin, bun; (coll) slap in the face

mojiganga f masquerade, mummery; clowning

mojigatería or **mojigatez** f hypocrisy; prudery, sanctimoniousness

mojiga·to -ta adj hypocritical; prudish, sanctimonious || mf hypocrite; prude, sanctimonious person

mojinete m (de un muro) coping; (de un tejado) ridge; (Arg) gable; (Chile) gable end

mojón m boundary stone, landmark; (montón sin orden) pile, heap; (guía en desplobado) road mark; (porción de excremento humano) turd

moldar tr to mold; to put molding on

molde m mold; pattern; cast, stamp, matrix; (persona) model, ideal; (letra) **de molde** printed; **venir de molde** to be just right

moldear tr to mold; (vaciar) to cast; to put molding on

moldura f molding

moldurar tr to put molding on

mole adj soft || m (Mex) stew seasoned with chili sauce || f bulk, mass

molécula f molecule

molende·ro -ra mf miller, grinder || m chocolate grinder; (CAm) grinding table

moler §47 tr (granos) to grind, to mill; to annoy, harass, weary; to tire out, fatigue; (coll) to chew; **moler a palos** (coll) to beat up

molesquina f moleskin

molestar tr to disturb, molest; to bother, annoy; to tire, weary || ref to bother; to be annoyed; **molestarse en** to take the trouble to

molestia f disturbance, discomfort; annoyance, bother, nuisance

moles·to -ta adj bothersome, troublesome; boring, tedious; bored, tired

molesto·so -sa adj (Am) bothersome

moleteado m knurl

moletear tr to knurl

molibdeno m molybdenum

molicie f softness; effeminacy, voluptuous living

moli·do -da adj exhausted, worn out

molienda f grinding, milling; (cantidad que se muele de una vez) grist; (molino) mill; (coll) bore, annoyance; (coll) fatigue, weariness

molimiento m grinding; weariness

moline·ro -ra adj mill || m miller || f miller's wife

molinete m little mill; ventilating fan; (juguete de papel) windmill; (movimiento que se hace con el bastón) twirl; (con la espada) flourish; (naut) windlass; (rueda de cohetes) (Mex) pinwheel

molinillo m hand mill; **molinillo de café** coffee grinder

molino m mill; **luchar con los molinos de viento** to tilt at windmills; **molino de sangre** animal-driven mill; **molino de viento** windmill; **molino harinero** gristmill, flour mill

moloc m (Ecuad) mashed potatoes

molondrón m (coll) lazy bum; (Ven) large inheritance, large amount of money

molusco m mollusk

mollar adj soft, tender; mushy, squashy; (carne) lean; profitable; (coll) gullible, easily taken in

mollear intr to give, to yield; to bend

molleja f gizzard; **criar molleja** (coll) to get lazy; **mollejas** sweetbread

mollejón m grindstone; (coll) big fat loafer; (coll) good-natured fellow

mollera f crown (of the head); (coll) brains, sense; **cerrado de mollera** (coll) stupid; **duro de mollera** (coll) stubborn

mollete m muffin

molli·no -na adj drizzly || f drizzle

mollizna f drizzle

momentáne·o -a adj momentary

momento m moment; **al momento** at once; **de un momento a otro** at any moment

momería f clowning

mome·ro -ra adj clowning || mf clown

momia f mummy

momificar §73 tr to mummify

mo·mio -mia *adj* lean, skinny ‖ *m* extra; (*ganga*) bargain; sinecure ‖ *f* see **momia**

momo *m* face, grimace; (coll) caress

mona *f* female monkey; Barbary ape; (coll) ape, copycat; (coll) drunkenness; (*persona*) (coll) drunk; (taur) guard for right leg; **dormir la mona** (coll) to sleep off a drunk; **pillar una mona** (coll) to go on a jag; **pintar la mona** (coll) to put on airs

monacal *adj* monachal

monacato *m* monkhood

monacillo *m* altar boy, acolyte

monada *f* monkeyshine; (*gesto*) face, grimace, monkey face; darling; cuteness; flattery; folly, childishness

monaguillo *m* altar boy, acolyte

monaquismo *m* monasticism

monarca *m* monarch

monarquía *f* monarchy

monárqui·co -ca *adj* monarchic(al) ‖ *mf* monarchist

monasterio *m* monastery

monásti·co -ca *adj* monastic

monda *f* pruning, trimming; parings, peelings; (Am) beating, whipping

mondadien·tes *m* (*pl* -tes) toothpick

mondadura *f* pruning, trimming; **mondaduras** peelings

mondar *tr* to clean; to prune, to trim; to peel, pare, hull, husk; (*quitar con engaño los bienes a*) to fleece; (Am) to beat, whip

mon·do -da *adj* clean; pure; **mondo y lirondo** (coll) pure, unadulterated ‖ *f* see **monda**

mondonga *f* (coll) kitchen wench

mondongo *m* intestines, insides; (*del hombre*) (coll) guts

monear *intr* (coll) to act like a monkey; (Am) to boast ‖ *ref* (Hond) to plug away; (Hond) to punch each other

moneda *f* coin; (coll) money; **la Moneda** the government of Chile; **moneda corriente** currency; (coll) common knowledge; **moneda falsa** counterfeit; **moneda menuda** change; **moneda metálica** or **sonante** specie; **moneda suelta** change; **pagar en la misma moneda** to pay back in one's own coin

monedar *tr* to coin, to mint

monedero *m* moneybag; **monedero falso** counterfeiter

monería *f* monkeyshine; cuteness; childishness

mones·co -ca *adj* (coll) apish

moneta·rio -ria *adj* monetary

mon·gol -gola *adj* & *mf* Mongol, Mongolian

monigote *m* lay brother; rag figure, stuffed form; botched painting, botched statue; (coll) sap, boob

monipodio *m* (coll) collusion, deal, plot

monís *m* trinket; **monises** (coll) money, dough

mónita *f* (coll) cunning, smoothness, slickness

monitor *m* monitor

monja *f* nun; **monjas** lingering sparks in burning paper

monje *m* monk

monjía *f* monkhood

monjil *adj* nunnish ‖ *m* nun's dress

mono -na *adj* (coll) cute, nice; (Am) blond; (*cabello*) (Am) red ‖ *m* monkey, ape; (*traje de faena*) coveralls; whippersnapper, squirt; (taur) attendant of picador; (Chile) pyramid of fruit or vegetables; **estar de monos** (coll) to be on the outs; **mono de Gibraltar** Barbary ape ‖ *f* see **mona**

monóculo *m* monocle

monogamia *f* monogamy

monografía *f* monograph

monograma *m* monogram

monolíti·co -ca *adj* monolithic

monologar §44 *intr* to soliloquize

monólogo *m* monologue

monomanía *f* monomania

monomio *m* monomial

mono·no -na *adj* (coll) cute, sweet

monopatín *m* scooter

monoplano *m* monoplane

monopolio *m* monopoly

monopolizar §60 *tr* to monopolize

monorriel *m* monorail

monosabio *m* (taur) attendant of picador

monosílabo *m* monosyllable

monoteísta *adj* monotheistic ‖ *mf* monotheist

monotipia *f* monotype

monotipista *mf* monotype operator

monotipo *m* monotype

monotonía *f* monotony

monóto·no -na *adj* monotonous

monóxido *m* monoxide

monseñor *m* monseigneur; (eccl) monsignor

monserga *f* (coll) gibberish

monstruo *m* monster

monstruosidad *f* monstrosity

monstruo·so -sa *adj* monstrous

monta *f* sum, total; **de poca monta** of little account

montacar·gas *m* (*pl* -gas) hoist, freight elevator

montadero *m* horse block

montadura *f* mounting; (*de una caballería de silla*) harness; (*engaste*) setting, mount

montaje *m* montage; setting up; (mach) assembly; (rad) hookup

montanero *m* forest ranger

montante *m* post, upright; (*suma*) amount; (*hueco cuadrilongo sobre una puerta*) transom; (*espadón*) broadsword ‖ *f* flood tide

montaña *f* mountain; mountain country; **la Montaña** the Province of Santander, Spain; **montaña de hielo** iceberg; **montaña rusa** roller coaster

monta·ñés -ñesa *adj* mountain ‖ *mf* mountaineer, highlander

montaño·so -sa *adj* mountainous

montapla·tos *m* (*pl* -tos) dumbwaiter

montar *tr* to mount, to get on; (*un caballo, una bicicleta, los hombros de una persona*) to ride; (*un servicio*) to set up, establish; (*un fusil*) to cock; (*una piedra preciosa*) to set, to mount; (*el caballo a la yegua*) to cover; (*un reloj*) to wind; (elec) to hook up; (mach) to assemble, to mount; (*la guardia*) (mil) to mount; (*un cabo*) (naut) to round; (*un buque*) (naut) to command; (*importar*) to amount to ‖ *intr* to mount; to get on top; to weigh, to be important; **tanto monta** it's all the same ‖ *ref* to mount; to get on top; **montarse en cólera** to fly into a rage

monta·raz (*pl* -**races**) *adj* backwoods; wild, untamed ‖ *m* forester, warden

monte *m* mountain, mount; woods, woodland; obstruction, interference; backwoods, wilds; bank, kitty; (coll) dirty head of hair; **andar al monte** (coll) to take to the woods; **monte alto** forest; **monte bajo** thicket, brushwood; **monte de piedad** pawnshop; **monte pío** pension fund for widows and orphans; mutual benefit society; **monte tallar** tree farm

montear *tr* to hunt, to track down; to make a working drawing of; to arch, to vault

montecillo *m* mound, hillock

montepío *m* pension fund for widows and orphans; mutual benefit society

montera *f* cloth cap; glass roof; wife of hunter; bullfighter's black bicorne; (Hond) drunk, jag

montería *f* hunting, big-game hunting; hunting party; (Bol, Ecuad) canoe to shoot the rapids; (Mex) lumbermen's camp

monterilla *f* (naut) moonsail

montero *m* hunter, huntsman

montés or **montesi·no -na** *adj* wild (*e.g.*, goat)

montículo *m* mound, hillock

montilla *f* montilla (*a pale dry sherry*)

monto *m* sum, total

montón *m* pile, heap; (*de gente*) crowd; (coll) lot, great deal, great many; **a, de,** or **en montón** (coll) taken together; **a montones** (coll) in abundance; **ser del montón** (coll) to be quite ordinary

montonera *f* (Am) heap, pile; (Am) band of mounted rebels

montu·no -na *adj* wooded; (Am) wild, untamed, rustic

montuo·so -sa *adj* wooded, woody, rugged, hilly

montura *f* (*cabalgadura*) mount; (*de una cabalgadura*) harness; seat, saddle; (*de una piedra preciosa, de un instrumento astronómico*) mounting; (*de gafas*) frame

monumento *m* monument

monzón *m* monsoon

moña *f* doll; mannequin; ribbon, hair ribbon; (coll) drunk, jag

moño *m* topknot; crest, top; (Col) caprice, whim; (*de caballo*) (Chile) forelock; **moños** frippery

moquear *intr* to snivel

moqueo *m* snivel, sniveling

moquero *m* handkerchief

moquete *m* punch in the nose

moquillo *m* runny nose; (vet) distemper

moquita *f* mucus, snivel

mor *m* — **por mor de** for love of; because of

mora *f* black mulberry; blackberry; brambleberry; white mulberry

morada *f* dwelling; stay, sojourn

mora·do -da *adj* purple, mulberry ‖ *f* see **morada**

moral *adj* moral ‖ *m* black mulberry tree ‖ *f* (*ciencia de la conducta; conducta*) morals; (*espíritu, confianza*) morale; (*p.ej.*, *de una fábula*) (coll) moral

moraleja *f* moral

moralidad *f* morality; (*de una fábula*) moral

morar *intr* to live, dwell

moratoria *f* moratorium

mórbi·do -da *adj* (*perteneciente a la enfermedad*) morbid; soft, delicate, mellow

morbo *m* sickness, illness; **morbo gálico** syphilis; **morbo regio** jaundice

morbo·so -sa *adj* morbid, diseased

morcilla *f* blood pudding, black pudding; (*añadidura que mete un actor en su papel*) gag

mor·daz *adj* (*pl* -**daces**) mordant, mordacious, sharp, caustic

mordaza *f* (*pañuelo o instrumento que se pone en la boca para impedir el hablar*) gag; (*aparato que sirve para apretar*) clamp, jaw; pipe vise; **poner la mordaza a** to gag

mordedura *f* bite

morder §47 *tr* to bite; to nibble at; to wear away; to gossip about, ridicule; (Mex, Ven, W-I) to cheat ‖ *intr* to bite; to take hold

mordicar §73 *tr & intr* to bite, sting

mordida *f* (Am) bite; (*para eludir una multa*) (Mex) payoff

mordiente *m* mordant

mordiscar §73 *tr* to nibble at ‖ *intr* to nibble, gnaw away; to champ

mordisco *m* nibble, bite; champ

more·no -na *adj* brown, dark-brown; dark, dark-complexioned; (*de la raza negra*) (coll) colored; (Am) mulato ‖ *mf* (coll) colored person; (Am) mulato ‖ *m* brunet ‖ *f* brunette; loaf of brown bread; rick of new-mown hay

morería *f* Moorish quarter; Moorish land

moretón *m* (coll) black-and-blue mark

morfina *f* morphine

morfinomanía *f* morphine habit, drug habit

morfinóma·no -na *adj* addicted to morphine, addicted to drugs ‖ *mf* morphine addict, drug addict

morfología *f* morphology

moribun·do -da *adj* moribund, dying ‖ *mf* dying person

morillo *m* andiron, firedog

morir §30 & §83 *intr* to die; (*el fuego, la luz, etc.*) to die away; **morir ahogado** to drown; **morir de risa** to die laughing; **morir de viejo** to die of old age; **morir helado** to freeze to death; **morir quemado** to burn to death; **morir vestido** (coll) to die a violent death ‖ *ref* to die; to be dying; to die away, die out; (*una pierna, un brazo*) to go to sleep; **morirse por** to be crazy about; to be dying to

moris·co -ca *adj* Morisco, Moorish ‖ *mf* Moor converted to Christianity (*after the Reconquest*); (*descendiente de mulato y española o de mulata y español*) (Mex) Morisco

mo·ro -ra *adj* Moorish; (*vino*) (coll) unwatered ‖ *mf* Moor; **hay moros en la costa** (coll) there's trouble brewing; **moro de paz** man of peace ‖ *f* see **mora**

moro·cho -cha *adj* (Am) strong, robust; (SAm) dark

morón *m* mound, knoll; moron

moron·do -da *adj* bare, stripped

moro·so -sa *adj* slow, tardy; (*retrasado en el pago de deudas*) delinquent

morra *f* (*de la cabeza*) top, crown; (*de gato*) purr; **andar a la morra** to come to blows

morrada *f* slap, punch; (*golpe dado con la cabeza*) butt

morral *m* nose bag; (*saco de cazador*) game bag; (*de soldado, viandante, etc.*) knapsack; (coll) boor, lout

morralla *f* small fish; (*gente de escaso valor*) rabble, trash; (*mezcla de cosas inútiles*) junk, trash; (Mex) change, small change

morriña *f* (coll) blues, melancholy; **morriña de la tierra** (coll) homesickness

morri·ño·so -sa *adj* sickly; (coll) blue, melancholy

morrión *m* helmet; (mil) bearskin

morro *m* (*cosa redonda*) knob; (*monte redondo*) knoll; (*guijarro*) pebble; (*saliente que forman los labios*) snout; **beber a morro** (slang) to drink out of the bottle; **estar de morro** or **de morros** (coll) to be on the outs; **poner morro** to make a snout

morrocotu·do -da *adj* (coll) strong, thick, heavy; (*asunto, negocio*) (coll) weighty; (Am) big, enormous; (Col) rich, wealthy; (Chile) graceless, monotonous

morsa *f* walrus

mortaja *f* shroud, winding sheet; (carp) mortise; (Am) cigarette paper

mortal *adj* mortal; deadly; mortally ill; deathly pale; sure, conclusive ‖ *m* mortal

mortalidad *f* mortality; death rate

mortandad *f* massacre, mortality, butchery

morteci·no -na *adj* dead; dying; failing, weak; **hacer la mortecina** (coll) to play dead, to play possum

mortero *m* (*vaso que sirve para machacar; argamasa*) mortar; (*en los molinos de aceite*) nether stone; (arti) mortar

mortífe·ro -ra *adj* deadly

mortificar §73 *tr* to vex, annoy, bother; to mortify ‖ *ref* (Mex) to be mortified, be embarrassed

mortuo·rio -ria *adj* mortuary, funeral; (*casa*) of the deceased ‖ *m* (archaic) funeral

morueco *m* ram

moru·no -na *adj* Moorish

mosai·co -ca *adj* Mosaic ‖ *m* tile, pav-

ing tile; mosaic; **mosaico de madera** marquetry

mosca *f* fly; (*barba*) imperial; (coll) cash, dough; (coll) disappointment; (coll) bore, nuisance; **aflojar la mosca** (coll) to shell out, to fork out; **mosca borriquera** horsefly; **mosca de las frutas** fruit fly; **mosca del vinagre** fruit fly; **mosca muerta** (coll) hypocrite; **moscas** sparks; **moscas volantes** spots before the eyes; **papar moscas** (coll) to gape, gawk

moscareta *f* (orn) flycatcher

moscona *f* hussy, brazen woman

Moscú Moscow

mosquear *tr* (*moscas*) to shoo; to beat, to whip; to answer sharply ‖ *intr* (Mex) to sneak a ride ‖ *ref* to shake off annoyances; to take offense

mosquero *m* flytrap; fly swatter

mosquete *m* musket

mosquetear *intr* (Arg, Bol) to snoop

mosquete·ro -ra *adj* idle ‖ *mf* (Arg, Bol) bystander, snooper ‖ *m* musketeer ‖ *f* wallflower

mosquetón *m* snap hook

mosquitera *f* or **mosquitero** *m* mosquito net; fly net

mosquito *m* (*Culex pungens*) mosquito; (*insecto parecido al anterior*) gnat; (coll) tippler

mostacera *f* mustard jar

mostacho *m* mustache; (coll) spot on the face

mostachón *m* macaroon

mostaza *f* mustard; (*semilla; munición*) mustard seed; **subírsele a** (*uno*) **la mostaza a las narices** (coll) to fly into a rage

mosto *m* must; **mosto de cerveza** wort

mostrador *m* (*en las tiendas*) counter; (*en las tabernas*) bar; (*de reloj*) dial

mostrar §61 *tr* to show ‖ *ref* to show; to show oneself to be

mostrear *tr* to spot, to splash

mostren·co -ca *adj* ownerless, unclaimed; (*que no tiene casa ni hogar*) (coll) homeless; (*animal*) (coll) stray; (coll) slow, dull; (coll) fat, heavy ‖ *mf* (coll) dolt, dullard

mota *f* mote, speck; (*en el paño*) burl, knot; hill, rise; defect, fault; (Mex, W-I) powder puff

mote *m* device, emblem, riddle; (*apodo*) nickname; (Chile) mistake; (SAm) stewed corn

motear *tr* to speck, speckle; to dapple, mottle ‖ *intr* (Peru) to eat stewed corn

motejar *tr* to call names; to scoff at, make fun of; **motejar de** to brand as

motín *m* mutiny, riot

motinista *mf* (Peru) rioter

motivar *tr* to explain, account for; to rationalize

moti·vo -va *adj* motive ‖ *m* motive, reason; (mus) motif; **con motivo de** because of; on the occasion of; **de su motivo propio** on his own accord; **motivo conductor** (mus) leitmotif; **motivos** grounds, reasons; (Chile) finickiness, prudery

moto *m* guidepost, landmark ‖ *f* (coll) motorcycle

motobomba *f* fire truck, fire engine

motocarro *m* three-wheel delivery truck

motocicleta *f* motorcycle

motogrúa *f* truck crane

motoli•to **-ta** *adj* simple, stupid; **vivir de motolito** to be a sponger, to live on other people ‖ *f* (orn) wagtail; (Ven) decent woman

motón *m* (naut) block, pulley

motonáuti•co **-ca** *adj* motorboat ‖ *f* motorboating

motonautismo *m* (sport) motorboating

motonave *f* motor launch; motor ship

motoneta *f* motor scooter; light three-wheel delivery truck

mo•tor **-tora** *adj* motor, motive ‖ *m* motor, engine; **motor a chorro** jet engine; **motor de arranque** (aut) starter, starting motor; **motor de cuatro tiempos** four-cycle engine; **motor de dos tiempos** two-cycle engine; **motor de explosión** internal-combustion engine; **motor fuera de borda** outboard motor; **motor térmico** heat engine ‖ *f* small motor boat

motorista *mf* motorist; motorcyclist; motorcycle racer ‖ *m* motorcycle policeman; (Am) motorman

motorizar §60 *tr* to motorize

motosegadora *f* power mower

motovelero *m* (naut) motor sailer

motriz *adj fem* (*fuerza*) motive

movedi•**zo** **-za** *adj* shaky, unsteady; fickle, inconstant; (*arena*) quick, shifting

mover §47 *tr* to move; (*la cola el perro*) to wag; (*discordia*) to stir up ‖ *intr* to move; to abort, miscarry; to bud, sprout ‖ *ref* to move; to be moved

movible *adj* movable; fickle, inconstant, changeable

móvil *adj* movable, mobile; fickle, changeable; moving ‖ *m* moving body; cause, motive

movilizar §60 *tr* to mobilize

movimiento *m* movement, motion

moza *f* girl, lass; mistress, concubine; maid, kitchen maid; (*en algunos juegos de naipes*) last hand; wash bat; **buena moza** or **real moza** good-looking girl or woman; **moza de fortuna** or **del partido** prostitute; **moza de taberna** barmaid

mozalbete *m* lad, young fellow

mozárabe *adj* Mozarabic ‖ *mf* Mozarab

mo•zo **-za** *adj* young, youthful; single, unmarried ‖ *m* youth, lad; (*camarero*) waiter; (*criado*) servant; porter; (*cuelgacapas*) cloak hanger; **buen mozo** or **real mozo** handsome fellow; **mozo de caballerías** hostler, stable boy; **mozo de café** waiter; **mozo de cámara** (naut) cabin boy; **mozo de ciego** blind man's guide; **mozo de cordel** street porter, public errand boy; **mozo de cuadra** stable boy; **mozo de cuerda** public errand boy; **mozo de espuelas** groom who walks in front of master's horse; **mozo de esquina** street porter, public errand boy; **mozo de estación** station porter;

mozo de estoques (taur) sword handler; **mozo de hotel** bellboy, bellhop; **mozo de paja y cebada** hostler (*at an inn*); **mozo de restaurante** waiter ‖ *f* see **moza**

mozue•lo **-la** *mf* youngster ‖ *m* lad, young fellow ‖ *f* lass, young girl

m/p *abbr* **mi pagaré**

m/r *abbr* **mi remesa**

Mro. *abbr* **Maestro**

M.S. *abbr* **manuscrito**

mtd. *abbr* **mitad**

mu *m* moo ‖ *f* bye-bye; **ir a la mu** to go bye-bye

muaré *adj invar* & *m* moiré

muca•mo **-ma** *mf* (Arg, Urug) house servant ‖ *f* (Arg, Chile, Urug) servant girl

muceta *f* (*de los doctores en los actos universitarios*) hood; (eccl) mozzetta

muco•so **-sa** *adj* mucous ‖ *f* mucous membrane

múcura *f* (Bol, Col, Ven, W-I) water pitcher; (Col) thickhead

muchacha *f* girl; maid, servant girl

muchachada *f* youthful prank

muchachez *f* boyishness, girlishness

mucha•cho **-cha** *adj* young, youthful ‖ *mf* youth, young person; servant ‖ *m* boy ‖ *f* see **muchacha**

muchedumbre *f* crowd, multitude, flock

mu•cho **-cha** *adj* much, a lot of, a great deal of; (*tiempo*) a long ‖ *pron* much, a lot, a great deal ‖ **mu•chos** **-chas** *adj* & *pron* many ‖ **mucho** *adv* much; (*más de lo regular*) hard; often; a long time; **con mucho** by far; **ni con mucho** or **ni mucho menos** not by a long shot; **por mucho que** however much; **sentir mucho** to be very sorry; **tener mucho de** to take after

muda *f* change; change of voice; change of clothes; (*cambio de plumas o de piel*) molt, molting; molting season; **estar de muda** to be changing one's voice; **estar en muda** (coll) to keep too quiet; **hacer la muda** to molt; **muda de ropa** change of clothing

mudable *adj* fickle, inconstant

mudada *f* (Am) change of clothing; (Am) move, change of residence

mudadi•zo **-za** *adj* fickle, inconstant

mudanza *f* change; (*cambio de domicilio*) moving; fickleness, inconstancy; (*en el baile*) figure

mudar *tr* to change ‖ *intr* to change; **mudar de** to change ‖ *ref* to change; to change clothing; to move; to move away; to have a movement of the bowels; **mudarse de** to change

mudez *f* muteness, dumbness; continued silence

mu•do **-da** *adj* dumb, mute; (phonet) voiceless, surd ‖ *mf* mute ‖ *f* see **muda**

mueblaje *m* furniture, suit of furniture

mueble *adj* movable ‖ *m* piece of furniture; (*p.ej., de un aparato de radio*) cabinet; **muebles** furniture

mueblería *f* furniture shop

mueblista *mf* furniture dealer

mueca *f* face, grimace

muela f grindstone; knoll, mound; back tooth, grinder; **muela cordal** wisdom tooth; **muela de esmeril** emery wheel; **muela del juicio** wisdom tooth; **muela de molino** millstone

muellaje m dockage, wharfage

muelle adj soft; voluptuous ‖ m (pieza elástica de metal) spring; (obra en la orilla del mar o de un río) dock, wharf, pier; (rr) freight platform; **muelle real** mainspring

muérdago m mistletoe

muérgano m (Col, Ven) piece of junk, drug on the market; (Col, Ecuad, Ven) boor, nobody

muermo m (vet) glanders

muerte f death; **cada muerte de obispo** once in a blue moon; **dar la muerte a** to put to death; **de mala muerte** (coll) crummy, not much of a; **estar a la muerte** to be at death's door; **muerte chiquita** (coll) nervous shudder

muer·to -ta adj dead; (apagado, marchito) flat, dull; (cal, yeso) slaked; **muerto de dying of; muerto por** crazy about ‖ mf corpse, dead person ‖ m (en los naipes) dummy; **hacerse el muerto** to play possum; to play deaf; **tocar a muerto** to toll

muesca f nick, notch; (carp) mortise

muestra f (porción de un producto que sirve para conocer su calidad) sample; model, specimen; (rótulo sobre una tienda u hotel) sign; show, exhibition, indication; (esfera de reloj) dial, face; (parada del perro para levantar la caza) set; (ademán, porte) bearing; **dar muestras de** to show signs of

mugido m moo, low; bellow, roar

mugir §27 intr (la res vacuna) to moo, to low; (con ira) to bellow; (el viento, el mar) to roar

mugre f dirt, filth, grime

mugrien·to -ta adj dirty, filthy, grimy

muguete m lily of the valley

mujer f woman; (esposa) wife; **mujer de gobierno** housekeeper; **mujer de su casa** good manager; **mujer fatal** vamp; **ser mujer** to be a grown woman

mujeren·go -ga adj (Arg, Urug, CAm) effeminate

mujerie·go -ga adj feminine, womanly; effeminate, womanish; fond of women; **a mujeriegas** sidesaddle ‖ m flock of women

mujeril adj womanly; womanish

mújol m mullet, striped mullet

mula f mule, she-mule; junk, trash; (Arg) ingrate, traitor; (Arg) hoax; (C-R) jag, drunk; (Guat, Hond) anger, rage; (Mex) drug on the market; (Ven) flask; **devolver la mula** (CAm) to pay back in one's own coin; **echar la mula a** (Mex) to rake over the coals; **en mula de San Francisco** on shank's mare

mulada f drove of mules

muladar m dungheap, dunghill; dump, trash heap; filth

mula·to -ta adj & mf mulatto

muleta f (palo para apoyarse al andar) crutch; muleta (cloth attached to a stick, used by matador); support, prop; snack

muletilla f cross-handle cane; pet word, pet phrase; (taur) muleta

mulo m mule

multa f fine

multar tr to fine

multicopista m duplicating machine, copying machine

multigrafiar §77 tr to multigraph

multígrafo m multigraph

multilateral adj multilateral

multiláte·ro -ra adj multilateral

múltiple adj multiple, manifold ‖ m manifold; **múltiple de admisión** intake manifold; **múltiple de escape** exhaust manifold

multiplicar §73 tr, intr, & ref to multiply

multiplicidad f multiplicity

múlti·plo -pla adj multiple, manifold ‖ m (math) multiple

multitud f multitude

mulli·do -da adj soft, fluffy ‖ m stuffing (for cushions, pillows, etc.) ‖ f bedding, litter (for animals)

mullir §13 tr to soften, fluff up; (la cama) to beat up, shake up; (la tierra) to loosen around a stalk ‖ ref to get fluffy

munda·no -na adj mundane, worldly; (mujer) loose

mundial adj world-wide, world

mundillo m arched clotheshorse; cushion for making lace; warming pan; guelder-rose, cranberry tree; world (of artists, scholars, etc.)

mundo m world; **así va el mundo** so it goes; **desde que el mundo es mundo** (coll) since the world began; **echar al mundo** to bring into the world; to bring forth; **el otro mundo** the other world; **gran mundo** high society; **medio mundo** (mucha gente) (coll) half the world; **tener mucho mundo** (coll) to know one's way around; **todo el mundo** everybody; **ver mundo** to see the world, to travel

mundonuevo m peep show

munición f munition, ammunition; **de munición** (mil) government issue; (coll) donar hurriedly

municionar tr to supply with munition

municipal adj municipal ‖ m policeman

múnícipe m citizen

municipio m municipality; town council

munidad f susceptibility to infection

munífi·co -ca adj munificent

muñeca f (figurilla infantil con que juegan las niñas) doll; (parte del cuerpo humano en donde se articula la mano con el brazo) wrist; manikin, dress form; tea bag; (mujer linda; mozuela frívola) (coll) doll; **muñeca de trapo** rag doll, rag baby; **muñeca parlante** talking doll

muñeco m doll (representing a male child or animal); dummy, manikin; fop, effeminate fellow; (fig) puppet; (coll) lad, little fellow

muñequera *f* strap for wrist watch

muñequilla *f* (mach) chuck; (Arg, Chile) young ear of corn

muñidor *m* heeler, henchman

muñir §12 *tr* to convoke, summon; (pol) to fix, to rig

muñón *m* (*p.ej., de un brazo cortado*) stump; (mach) journal, gudgeon; **muñón de cola** dock

mural *adj* mural

muralla *f* wall, rampart

murar *tr* to surround with a wall

murciélago *m* bat

murga *f* (coll) tin-pan band

muriente *adj* dying, faint

murmujear *tr & intr* (coll) to mumble

murmullar *intr* to murmur

murmullo *m* murmur; whisper; (*de aguas corrientes*) ripple; (*del viento*) rustle

murmurar *tr* to murmur, to mutter; to murmur at ‖ *intr* to murmur, to mutter; to whisper; (*las aguas corrientes*) to ripple, to purl; (*el viento*) to rustle; (coll) to gossip

muro *m* wall

murria *f* (coll) blues, dejection

musa *f* muse; **las Musas** the Muses; **soplarle a uno la musa** (coll) to be inspired to write poetry; (coll) to be lucky at games of chance

musaraña *f* shrew, shrewmouse; bug, worm; **mirar a las musarañas** (coll) to stare vacantly

músculo *m* muscle

musculo·so -sa *adj* muscular

muselina *f* muslin

museo *m* museum; **museo de cera** waxworks

muserola *f* noseband

mus·go -ga *adj* dark-brown ‖ *m* moss

musgo·so -sa *adj* mossy, moss-covered

música *f* music; (*músicos que tocan juntos*) band; (coll) noise, racket; **con**

la música a otra parte (coll) don't bother me, get out; **música celestial** (coll) nonsense, piffle; **música de fondo** background music; **poner en música** to set to music

musical *adj* musical

musicalidad *f* musicianship

music-hall *s* vaudeville theater, burlesque show

músi·co -ca *adj* musical ‖ *mf* musician; **músico mayor** bandmaster ‖ *f* see **música**

musicología *f* musicology

musicólo·go -ga *mf* musicologist

musiquero *m* music cabinet

musitar *tr & intr* to mutter, mumble

muslime *adj & mf* Moslem

muslo *m* thigh; (*de ave cocida*) (coll) leg, drumstick

mustiar *ref* to wither

mus·tio -tia *adj* sad, gloomy; (*marchito*) withered; (Mex) hypocritical; (Mex) stand-offish

musul·mán -mana *adj & mf* Mussulman

mutación *f* mutation; unsettled weather, change of weather; (biol) mutation, sport; (theat) change of scene

mutila·do -da *adj* crippled ‖ *mf* cripple

mutilar *tr* to mutilate; to cripple

múti·lo -la *adj* mutilated; crippled

mutis *m* (theat) exit; **hacer mutis** (theat) to exit; to keep quiet

mutual *adj* mutual

mutualidad *f* mutuality; mutual benefit; mutual benefit association

mutualista *mf* member of a mutual benefit association

mu·tuo -tua *adj* mutual, reciprocal

muy *adv* very; very much; too, e.g., **es muy tarde para dar un paseo tan largo** it is too late to take such a long walk; **muy de noche** late at night; **Muy señor mío** Dear Sir

N

N, n (ene) *f* sixteenth letter of the Spanish alphabet

n/ *abbr* **nuestro**

N. *abbr* **Norte**

nabo *m* turnip; (naut) mast

Nabucodonosor *m* Nebuchadnezzar

nácar *m* mother-of-pearl

nacara·do -da *adj* mother-of-pearl

nacatamal *m* (CAm, Mex) meat-filled tamale

nacela *f* nacelle

nacencia *f* birth; growth, tumor

nacer §22 *intr* to be born; to bud, take rise, originate, appear; to dawn ‖ *ref* to bud, to shoot, to sprout; (*abrirse la ropa por las costuras*) to split

naci·do -da *adj* natural, innate; apt, proper, fit; **nacida** née or nee ‖ *m* human being; growth, boil

naciente *adj* incipient; resurgent; (*sol*) rising ‖ *m* east

nacimiento *m* birth; origin, beginning, fountainhead; descent, lineage; (*de agua*) spring, fountainhead; crèche

nación *f* nation

nacional *adj* national; domestic ‖ *mf* national ‖ *m* militiaman

nacionalidad *f* nationality

nacionalismo *m* nationalism

nacionalista *adj & mf* nationalist

nacionalizar §60 *tr* to nationalize ‖ *ref* to be naturalized; to become a citizen

nacista *adj & mf* Nazi

naco *m* (Arg, Bol, Urug) black rolled leaf of chewing tobacco; (Arg) fear, scare; (Col) stewed corn; (Col) mashed potatoes

nada *pron indef* nothing, not . . . anything; **de nada** don't mention it, you're welcome ‖ *adv* not at all

nadaderas *fpl* water wings

nada·dor -dora *adj* swimming, floating

‖ *mf* swimmer ‖ *m* (Chile) fishnet float

nadar *intr* to swim; to float; to fit loosely or too loosely; **nadar en** (*riqueza*) to be rolling in; (*suspiros*) to be full of; (*sangre*) to be bathed in

nadear *tr* to destroy, wipe out

nadería *f* trifle

nadie *pron indef* nobody, not . . . anybody; **nadie más** nobody else; **nadie más que** nobody but ‖ *m* nobody; **un don nadie** a nonentity

nado — a nado swimming, floating; **echarse a nado** to dive in; **pasar a nado** to swim across

nafta *f* naphtha

nagual *m* (Guat, Hond) (*dícese de un animal*) inseparable companion; (Mex) sorcerer, wizard; (Mex) lie

nagualear *intr* (Mex) to lie; (Mex) to be out looking for trouble all night

naguas *fpl* petticoat

naipe *m* playing card; deck of cards; **naipe de figura** face card; **tener buen naipe** to be lucky

naire *m* mahout

nalgada *f* shoulder, ham; blow on or with the buttocks

nalgas *fpl* buttocks, rump

nana *f* grandma; lullaby, cradlesong; (CAm, Mex, W-I) child's nurse; (Arg, Chile, Urug) child's complaint

nao *f* ship, vessel

napoleóni·co -ca *adj* Napoleonic

Napoles *f* Naples

napolita·no -na *adj* & *mf* Neapolitan

naranja *f* orange; **media naranja** (coll) sidekick, better half; **naranja cajel** Seville orange, sour orange; ¡**naranjas!** nonsense!

naranjada *f* orangeade; orange juice; orange marmalade

naranjal *m* orange grove

naranjo *m* orange tree; (coll) boob, simpleton

narciso *m* narcissus; fop, dandy; **narciso trompón** daffodil ‖ **Narciso** *m* Narcissus

narcóti·co -ca *adj* & *m* narcotic

narcotizar §60 *tr* to dope, to drug

narguile *m* hookah

narigada *f* (SAm) pinch of snuff

nari·gón -gona *adj* big-nosed ‖ *m* big nose

narigu·do -da *adj* big-nosed; noseshaped

nariguera *f* nose ring

na·riz (*pl* -**rices**) *f* nose; nostril; sense of smell; (*del vino*) bouquet; **nariz de pico de loro** hooknose; **sonarse las narices** to blow one's nose; **tabicarse las narices** to hold one's nose; **tener agarrado por las narices** to lead by the nose

narración *f* narration

narra·dor -dora *adj* narrating ‖ *mf* narrator

narrar *tr* to narrate

narrati·vo -va *adj* narrative ‖ *f* (*relato; habilidad en narrar*) narrative

narria *f* sled, sledge, drag

nasal *adj* & *f* nasal

nasalizar §60 *tr* to nasalize

nata *f* cream; whipped cream; élite, choice; skim, scum

natación *f* swimming

natal *adj* natal; native ‖ *m* birth; birthday

natali·cio -cia *adj* birth ‖ *m* birthday

natalidad *f* birth rate

naterón *m* cottage cheese

natillas *fpl* custard

natividad *f* birth; Christmas; (*día; festividad; pintura*) Nativity

nati·vo -va *adj* native; natural; natural-born; innate

na·to -ta *adj* born, e.g., **criminal nato** born criminal ‖ *f* see **nata**

natural *adj* natural; native; (mus) natural ‖ *mf* native ‖ *m* temper, disposition, nature; **al natural** au naturel; rough, unfinished; live; **del natural** from life, from nature

naturaleza *f* nature; disposition, temperament; nationality; **naturaleza muerta** still life

naturalidad *f* naturalness; nationality

naturalismo *m* naturalism

naturalista *mf* naturalist

naturalización *f* naturalization

naturalizar §60 *tr* to naturalize; to acclimatize ‖ *ref* to become naturalized; to go native

naturalmente *adv* naturally; easily, readily

naufragar §44 *intr* to be shipwrecked; to fail

naufragio *m* shipwreck; failure, ruin

náufra·go -ga *adj* shipwrecked ‖ *mf* shipwrecked person ‖ *m* shark

náusea *f* nausea; **dar náuseas a** to nauseate; to sicken, disgust; **tener náuseas** to be nauseated, to be sick at one's stomach

nauseabun·do -da *adj* nauseating, nauseous, loathsome, sickening

nauta *m* mariner, sailor

náuti·co -ca *adj* nautical ‖ *f* sailing, navigation

nava *f* hollow plain between mountains

navaja *f* folding knife; razor; penknife; tusk of wild boar; razor clam; (coll) evil tongue; **navaja barbera** straight razor

navajada *f* or **navajazo** *m* slash, gash

navajero *m* razor case; razor cloth

naval *adj* naval; nautical; **naval militar** naval

nava·rro -rra *adj* & *mf* Navarrese ‖ **Navarra** *f* Navarre

navazo *m* garden in sandy marshland

nave *f* ship, vessel; (*de un taller, fábrica, tienda, iglesia, etc.*) aisle; commercial ground floor; hall, shed, bay, building; **nave central** or **principal** (archit) nave; **nave lateral** (archit) aisle

navegable *adj* navigable

navegación *f* navigation; sailing; sea voyage; **navegación a vela** sailing

navega·dor -dora or **navegante** *adj* navigating ‖ *mf* navigator

navegar §44 *tr* to sail ‖ *intr* to navigate, to sail; to move around

navel *f* (*pl* -**vels**) navel orange

Navidad *f* Christmas; Christmas time;

¡Felices Navidades! Merry Christmas!; **contar** or **tener muchas Navidades** to be pretty old

navidal m Christmas card

navide·ño -ña adj Christmas

navie·ro -ra adj ship, shipping || m shipowner; outfitter

navío m ship, vessel; **navío de guerra** warship

náyade f naiad

nazare·no -na adj & mf Nazarene || m penitent in Passion Week procession || **nazarenas** fpl (SAm) large gaucho spurs

nazi adj & mf Nazi

N.B. abbr **nota bene** (Lat) note well

nébeda f catnip

neblina f fog, mist

neblino·so -sa adj foggy, misty

nebulo·so -sa adj nebulous, cloudy, misty, hazy, vague; gloomy, sullen || f nebula

necedad f foolishness, stupidity, nonsense

necesa·rio -ria adj necessary || f water closet, privy

neceser m toilet case; sewing kit; **neceser de belleza** vanity case; **neceser de costura** workbasket

necesidad f necessity; need, want; starvation; **de necesidad** from weakness; of necessity; **necesidad mayor** bowel movement; **necesidad menor** urination

necesita·do -da adj necessitous, poor, needy; **estar necesitado de** to be in need of || mf needy person

necesitar tr to necessitate; to need; **necesitar** + inf to have to, to need to + inf || intr to be in need; **necesitar de** to be in need of, to need || ref to be needed, to be necessary

ne·cio -cia adj foolish, stupid; imprudent; stubborn; (Am) touchy || mf fool

necrología f necrology

necromancia f necromancy

néctar m nectar

neerlan·dés -desa adj Netherlandish, Dutch || mf Netherlander || m Dutchman; (idioma) Netherlandish or Dutch || f Dutchwoman

nefalista mf teetotaler

nefan·do -da adj base, infamous

nefas·to -ta adj ominous, fatal, tragic

negable adj deniable

negación f negation; denial; refusal

nega·do -da adj unfit, incompetent; dull, indifferent

negar §66 tr to deny; to refuse; to prohibit; to disown; to conceal || intr to deny || ref to avoid; to refuse; to deny oneself to callers; **negarse a** to refuse; **negarse a** + inf to refuse to + inf

negati·vo -va adj negative || f negative; denial; refusal

negligencia f negligence

negligente adj negligent

negociable adj negotiable

negociación f negotiation; deal, matter

negociado m department, bureau; affair, business; (SAm) illegal dealing; (Chile) store

negociante m dealer, trader

negociar tr to negotiate || intr to negotiate; to deal, to trade

negocio m business; affair, deal, transaction; profit; (SAm) store

negocio·so -sa adj businesslike

negrear intr to turn black; to look black

negre·ro -ra adj slave-trading; (fig) slave-driving || mf slave trader; (fig) slave driver

negrilla f (typ) boldface

ne·gro -gra adj black; dark; gloomy; dismal; fatal, evil, wicked; Negro; (coll) broke || mf Negro; (Am) dear, darling || m black; **negro de humo** lampblack

negror m or **negrura** f blackness

negruz·co -ca adj blackish

néme·sis f (pl -sis) (justo castigo; castigador) nemesis || **Némesis** f Nemesis

nemoro·so -sa adj (poet) woody, sylvan

ne·ne -na mf baby; dear, darling || m rascal, villain

nenúfar m white water lily

neo m neon

neocelan·dés -desa adj New Zealand || mf New Zealander

neoesco·cés -cesa adj & mf Nova Scotian

neófi·to -ta mf neophyte

neologismo m neologism

neomejica·no -na adj & mf New Mexican

neomicina f neomycin

neón m neon

neoyorki·no -na adj New York || mf New Yorker

Nepal, el Nepal

nepa·lés -lesa adj & mf Nepalese

nepente m nepenthe

nepote m relative and favorite of the Pope || **Nepote** m Nepos

neptunio m neptunium

Neptuno m Neptune

nereida f Nereid

Nerón m Nero

nervio m nerve; (del ala del insecto) rib; strength, vigor

nerviosidad f nervousness

nervio·so -sa adj nervous; energetic, vigorous, sinewy; (célula; centro; tónico) nerve; (sistema; enfermedad; postración, colapso) nervous

nervosidad f nervosity; ductility, flexibility; (de un argumento) force, cogency

nervo·so -sa adj var of **nervioso**

nervu·do -da adj vigorous, sinewy

nervura f backbone (of book)

nesga f gore

nesgar §44 tr to gore

ne·to -ta adj net

neumáti·co -ca adj pneumatic; air || m tire

neumonía f pneumonia

neuralgia f neuralgia

neurología f neurology

neuro·sis f (pl -sis) neurosis; **neurosis de guerra** shell shock

neuróti·co -ca adj & mf neurotic

neutral adj & mf neutral

neutralidad f neutrality

neutralismo m neutralism

neutralista *adj* & *mf* neutralist
neutralizar §60 *tr* to neutralize
neu‧tro **-tra** *adj* neuter; (*que no es de un color ni de otro*) neutral; (bot, chem, elec, phonet, zool) neutral; (*verbo*) intransitive
neutrón *m* neutron
neva‧do **-da** *adj* snow-covered; snow-white || *f* snowfall
nevar §2 *tr* to make snow-white || *intr* to snow
nevasca *f* snowfall; snowstorm, blizzard
nevazón *f* (SAm) snowfall
nevera *f* icebox, refrigerator; icehouse; (P-R) jail
nevería *f* ice-cream parlor
neve‧ro **-ra** *mf* ice-cream dealer || *m* place of perpetual snow; perpetual snow || *f* see **nevera**
nevisca *f* snow flurry
neviscar §73 *intr* to snow lightly
nevo *m* mole; **nevo materno** birth mark
nevo‧so **-sa** *adj* snowy
ni *conj* neither, nor; **ni . . . ni** neither . . . nor; **ni . . . siquiera** not even
niacina *f* niacin
nicaragüense or **nicaragüe‧ño** **-ña** *adj* & *mf* Nicaraguan
Nicolás *m* Nicholas
nicotina *f* nicotine
nicho *m* niche
nidada *f* (*huevos en el nido*) nestful of eggs; (*pajarillos en el nido*) nest, brood, hatch
nidal *m* (*donde la gallina pone sus huevos*) nest; nest egg; haunt; source; basis, foundation
nido *m* nest; haunt; home; source; (*de ladrones*) nest, den
niebla *f* fog, mist, haze; mildew; fog, confusion; **hay niebla** it is foggy; **niebla artificial** smoke screen
nie‧to **-ta** *mf* grandchild || *m* grandson; **nietos** grandchildren || *f* granddaughter
nieve *f* snow; (Am) water ice
nigromancia *f* necromancy
nihilismo *m* nihilism
nihilista *mf* nihilist
Nilo *m* Nile; **Nilo Azul** Blue Nile
nilón *m* nylon
nimbo *m* nimbus; halo
nimiedad *f* excess; fussiness, fastidiousness; (coll) timidity
ni‧mio **-mia** *adj* excessive; fussy, fastidious; (Am) tiny
ninfa *f* nymph; **ninfa marina** mermaid
ninfea *f* white water lily
ningún *adj indef* apocopated form of **ninguno**, used only before masculine singular nouns and adjectives
ningu‧no **-na** *adj indef* no, not any || *pron indef* none, not any; neither, neither one; **ninguno de los dos** neither one || **ninguno** *pron indef* nobody, no one
niña *f* child, girl; (*del ojo*) pupil; **niña del ojo** (coll) apple of one's eye; **niña exploradora** girl scout
niñada *f* childishness
niñera *f* nursemaid
niñería *f* childishness; trifle

niñero **-ra** *adj* fond of children || *f* see **niñera**
niñez *f* childhood; childishness; (fig) infancy
ni‧ño **-ña** *adj* childlike, childish; young, inexperienced || *mf* child; (*persona joven e inexperta*) babe; **desde niño** from childhood; **niño expósito** foundling; **niño travieso** imp || *m* child, boy; **niño bonito** playboy; **niño de coro** choirboy; **niño de la bola** child Jesus; (coll) lucky fellow; **niño explorador** boy scout; **niño gótico** playboy || *f* see **niña**
ni‧pón **-pona** *adj* & *mf* Nipponese
níquel *m* nickel
niquelar *tr* to nickel-plate
nirvana, el nirvana
níspero *m* medlar (*tree and fruit*)
níspola *f* medlar (*fruit*)
nitidez *f* brightness, clearness; sharpness
níti‧do **-da** *adj* bright, clear; sharp
nitrato *m* nitrate
nítri‧co **-ca** *adj* nitric
nitro *m* niter; **nitro de Chile** saltpeter
nitrógeno *m* nitrogen
nitro‧so **-sa** *adj* nitrous
nitruro *m* nitride
nivel *m* level; **nivel de burbuja** spirit level; **nivel de vida** standard of living
nivelar *tr* to level; to even, make even; to grade; to survey
no *adv* not; no; **¿cómo no?** why not?; of course, certainly; **creer que no** to think not, to believe not; **¿no?** is it not so?; **no bien** no sooner; **no más que** not more than; only; no sea que lest; **no . . . sino** only; **ya no** no longer
nobabia *f* (aer) dope
noble *adj* noble || *m* noble, nobleman
nobleza *f* nobility
noción *f* notion, idea; rudiment
noci‧vo **-va** *adj* noxious, harmful
noctur‧no **-na** *adj* nocturnal; lonely, sad, melancholy; night, nighttime
noche *f* night, nighttime; darkness; **buenas noches** good evening; good night; **de la noche a la mañana** overnight; unexpectedly, suddenly; **de noche** at night, in the nighttime; **esta noche** tonight; **hacer noche en** to spend the night in; **hacerse de noche** to grow dark; **muy de noche** late at night; **por la noche** at night, in the nighttime; **noche buena** Christmas Eve; **noche de estreno** (theat) first night; **noche de uvas** New Year's Eve; **noche vieja** New Year's Eve; watch night
nochebuena *f* Christmas Eve
nochebueno *m* Christmas cake; Yule log
nodo *m* (astr, med, phys) node
No-Do *m* (acronym for **Noticiario y Documentales**) newsreel; newsreel theater
nodriza *f* wet nurse; vacuum tank
Noé *m* Noah
nogal *m* walnut; **nogal de la brujería** witch hazel
nómada or **nómade** *adj* & *mf* nomad

nomádi·co -ca *adj* nomadic

nombradía *f* fame, renown, reputation

nombra·do -da *adj* famous

nombramiento *m* naming; appointment

nombrar *tr* to name; to appoint

nombre *m* name; fame, reputation; nickname; watchword; noun; **del mismo nombre** (elec) like; **de nombres contrarios** (elec) unlike; **nombre comercial** firm name; **nombre de lugar** place name; **nombre de pila** first name, Christian name; **nombre de soltera** maiden name; **nombre substantivo** noun; **nombre supuesto** alias

nomeolvi·des *f* (*pl* **-des**) forget-me-not; German madwort

nómina *f* list, roll; pay roll

nominal *adj* nominal; noun

nominar *tr* to name; to appoint

nominati·vo -va *adj & m* nominative

non *adj* odd, uneven ǁ *m* odd number

nonada *f* trifle, nothing

no·na -na *adj & m* ninth

nopal *m* prickly pear

norcorea·no -na *adj & mf* North Korean

nordestada *f* or **nordeste** *m* (*viento*) northeaster (*wind*)

noria *f* chain pump; (*pozo*) draw well; Ferris wheel; (coll) treadmill, drudgery

norma *f* norm, standard; rule, method; (carp) square

normal *adj* normal; standard; perpendicular

Normandía *f* Normandy

norman·do -da *adj & mf* Norman ǁ *m* Norseman

norte *m* north; north wind; (*guía*) (fig) polestar, lodestar

Norteamérica *f* North America; America, the United States

norteamerica·no -na *adj & mf* North American; (*estadunidense*) American

norte·ño -ña *adj* northern

norue·go -ga *adj & mf* Norwegian ǁ Noruega *f* Norway

nos (used as object of verb) *pron pers* us; to us ǁ *pron reflex* ourselves, to ourselves; each other, to each other

noso·tros -tras *pron pers* we; us; ourselves

nostalgia *f* nostalgia

nota *f* note; (*en la escuela*) mark, grade; (*en el restaurante*) check; (mus) note; **nota de adorno** grace note; **nota tónica** keynote

notar *tr* to note; to dictate; to annotate; to criticize; to discredit

notario *m* notary, notary public

noticia *f* news; notice, information; notion, rudiment; knowledge; **noticias de actualidad** news of the day; **noticias de última hora** late news; **una noticia** a piece of news, a news item

noticiar *tr* to notify; to give notice of

noticia·rio -ria *adj* news ǁ *m* up-to-the-minute news; newsreel; newscast; **noticiario gráfico** picture page; **noticiario teatral** theater page

noticie·ro -ra *adj* news ǁ *m* newsman, reporter; late news

noticio·so -sa *adj* informed; learned; well-informed; (Am) newsy ǁ *m* (Am) news item

notificar §73 *tr* to notify; to report on

no·to -ta *adj* known, well-known ǁ *m* south wind ǁ *f* see **nota**

notoriedad *f* general knowledge; fame

noto·rio -ria *adj* manifest, well-known

nov. *abbr* **noviembre**

novatada *f* hazing; beginner's blunder

nova·to -ta *adj* beginning ǁ *mf* beginner; freshman

novecien·tos -tas *adj & pron* nine hundred ǁ **novecientos** *m* nine hundred

novedad *f* newness, novelty; news; fashion; happening; change; failing health; **sin novedad** as usual; safe; well; without anything happening

novel *adj* new, inexperienced, beginning ǁ *m* beginner

novela *f* novel; story, lie; **novela caballista** novel of western life; **novela policíaca** or **policial** detective story; **novela por entregas** serial

novele·ro -ra *adj* fond of novelty; fond of fiction; gossipy; fickle

noveles·co -ca *adj* novelistic, fictional; romantic, fantastic

novelista *mf* novelist

novelísti·co -ca *adj* fictional ǁ *f* fiction

novelizar §60 *tr* to fictionalize

nove·no -na *adj & m* ninth

noventa *adj, pron & m* ninety

noventa·vo -va *adj & m* ninetieth

novia *f* fiancée; bride; **novia de guerra** war bride

noviazgo *m* engagement, courtship

novi·cio -cia *adj & mf* novice

noviembre *m* November

novilunio *m* new moon

novilla *f* heifer

novillada *f* drove of young bulls; (taur) fight with young bulls by aspiring bullfighters

novillero *m* herdsman of young cattle; (taur) aspiring fighter, untrained fighter; (coll) truant

novillo *m* young bull; (coll) cuckold; **hacer novillos** (coll) to play truant

novio *m* suitor; fiancé; bridegroom; **novios** engaged couple; bride and groom, newlyweds

novocaína *f* novocaine

nro. *abbr* **nuestro**

N.S. *abbr* **Nuestro Señor**

ntro. *abbr* **nuestro**

nubada *f* local shower; abundance

nubarrón *m* storm cloud

nube *f* cloud; andar (*los precios*) **por las nubes** to be sky-high; **bajar de las nubes** to come back to or down to earth; **poner en** or **sobre las nubes** to praise to the skies

nube-hongo *f* mushroom cloud

nubla·do -da *adj* cloudy ǁ *m* storm cloud; impending danger; abundance; **aguantar el nublado** to suffer resignedly

nublar *tr* to cloud, cloud over ǁ *ref* to become cloudy

nu·blo -bla *adj* cloudy ǁ *m* storm cloud

nublo·so -sa *adj* cloudy; adverse, unfortunate

nubo·so -sa *adj* cloudy

nuca *f* nape

nuclear *adj* nuclear

núcleo *m* nucleus; core; *(de nuez)* kernel; *(de la fruta)* stone; *(de un electroimán)* core

nudillo *m* knuckle; stocking stitch; plug *(in wall)*

nudo *m* knot; bond, tie, union; crux; tangle, plot; difficulty; *(en el drama)* crisis; center, juncture; *(bot)* node; *(naut)* knot; **cortar el nudo gordiano** to cut the Gordian knot; **hacérsele a (uno) un nudo en la garganta** to get a lump in one's throat

nudo·so -sa *adj* knotted, knotty

nuera *f* daughter-in-law

nues·tro -tra *adj poss* our ‖ *pron poss* ours

nueva *f* news; piece of news; **nuevas** *fpl* news

Nueva York *m & f* New York; **el Gran Nueva York** Greater New York

Nueva Zelanda New Zealand

nueve *adj & pron* nine; **las nueve** nine o'clock ‖ *m* nine; *(en las fechas)* ninth

nue·vo -va *adj* new; **de nuevo** again, anew; **nuevo flamante** brand-new; **¿qué hay de nuevo?** what's new? ‖ *mf* novice; freshman ‖ *f* see **nueva**

nuevomejica·no -na *adj & mf* New Mexican

Nuevo Méjico *m* New Mexico

nuez *f* (*pl* **nueces**) nut; walnut; Adam's apple; **nuez dura** *(árbol)* hickory; hickory nut; **nuez moscada** nutmeg

nulidad *f* nullity; incapacity; (coll) nobody

nu·lo -la *adj* null, void, worthless

núm. *abbr* **número**

numen *m* deity; inspiration

numeral *adj* numeral

numerar *tr* to number; to count; to numerate

numerario *m* cash, coin, specie

numéri·co -ca *adj* numerical

número *m* number; *(de un periódico)* copy, issue; *(de zapatos)* size; lottery ticket; **cargar** or **cobrar al número llamado** (telp) to reverse the charges; **de número** *(dícese de los individuos de una sociedad)* regular; **mirar por el número uno** to look out for number one; **número de serie** series number; **número equivocado** (telp) wrong number

numero·so -sa *adj* numerous

nunca *adv* never; **no ... nunca** not ... ever, never **nunca jamás** never more

nupcial *adj* nuptial

nupcialidad *f* marriage rate

nupcias *fpl* nuptials, marriage; **casarse en segundas nupcias** to marry the second time

nutria *f* otter

nutrición *f* nutrition

nutri·do -da *adj* great, intense, robust, vigorous, steady; full, abounding, rich, heavy; *(carácter, letra)* thick; *(cañoneo)* heavy, sustained

nutrimento or **nutrimiento** *m* nourishment, nutriment

nutrir *tr* to nourish, to feed; to supply, to stock; to support, back up; to fill to overflowing

nu·triz *f* (*pl* **-trices**) wet nurse

Ñ

Ñ, ñ (eñe) *f* seventeenth letter of the Spanish alphabet

ñadí *m* (Chile) broad, shallow swamp

ñajú *m* (Am) okra, gumbo

ñámbar *m* Jamaica rosewood

ñame *m* yam; (W-I) blockhead, dunce

ñan·dú *m* (*pl* **-dúes**) nandu, American ostrich

ñaño -ña *adj* (Am) close, intimate; (Am) spoiled, overindulged ‖ *m* (Am) elder brother ‖ *f* (Am) elder sister; (Am) nursemaid; (Am) dear

ñapa *f* (Am) something thrown in; **de ñapa** (Am) in the bargain

ñaque *m* junk, pile of junk

ña·to -ta *adj* (Am) pug-nosed; (Arg) ugly, deformed

ñeque *adj* (Am) strong, vigorous; *(dícese de los ojos)* (Am) drooping ‖ *m* (Am) slap, blow; (Am) pep

ñiqueñaque *m* (coll) trash

ñisca *f* (Am) bit, fragment; (Am) excrement

ñoclo *m* macaroon

ñolombre *m* (Am) old peasant; **¡viene ñolombre!** (Am) here comes the bogeyman

ñon·go -ga *adj* (Am) slow, lazy; (Am) foolish, stupid; (Am) tricky; (Am) suspicious

ñoñería or **ñoñez** *f* timidity; inanity; dotage

ño·ño -ña *adj* timid; inane; doting

O

O, o (o) *f* eighteenth letter of the Spanish alphabet

o *conj* or; **o ... o** either ... or

oa·sis *m* (*pl* **-sis**) oasis

ob. *abbr* **obispo**

obduración *f* obduracy

obedecer §22 *tr* (with personal **a**) to obey ‖ *intr* to obey; **obedecer a** to yield to, be due to, be in keeping with, arise from

obediencia *f* obedience
obediente *adj* obedient
obelisco *m* obelisk; (typ) dagger
obertura *f* (mus) overture
obesidad *f* obesity
obe·so -sa *adj* obese
obispo *m* bishop
óbito *m* decease, demise
obituario *m* (Am) obituary
objeción *f* objection
objetable *adj* objectionable (*open to objection*)
objetar *tr* to object; (*dudas*) to raise; (*una razón contraria*) to set up, offer, present; to object to
objeti·vo -va *adj & m* objective
objeto *m* object; subject matter; **objetos de cotillón** favors
oblea *f* wafer; pill, tablet; **hecho una oblea** (coll) nothing but skin and bones
obli·cuo -cua *adj* oblique
obligación *f* obligation, duty; bond, debenture; **obligaciones** *fpl* family responsibilities
obligacionista *mf* bondholder
obliga·do -da *adj* obliged, grateful; submissive; (mus) obbligato ǁ *m* (mus) obbligato
obligar §44 *tr* to obligate; to oblige
obliterar *tr* to cancel
oblon·go -ga *adj* oblong
oboe *m* oboe; oboist
oboísta *mf* oboist
óbolo *m* mite
obra *f* work; **obra de** a matter of; **obra de consulta** reference work; **obra maestra** masterpiece; **obra pía** charity; (coll) useful effort; **obra prima** shoemaking; **obras** construction, repairs, alterations; **obra segunda** shoe repairing; **poner por obra** to undertake, set to work on
obra·dor -dora *mf* worker ǁ *m* workman; shop, workshop ǁ *f* workingwoman
obrajero *m* foreman; (Arg) lumberman; (Bol) artisan
obrar *tr* to build; to perform; to work ǁ *intr* to work; to act, operate, proceed; to have a movement of the bowels; **obra en mi poder** I have at hand, I have in my possession
obrera *f* workingwoman
obrerismo *m* labor; labor movement
obre·ro -ra *adj* working; labor ǁ *m* workman; **los obreros** labor ǁ *f* see **obrera**
obrero-patronal *adj* labor-management
obscenidad *f* obscenity
obsce·no -na *adj* obscene
obscurecer §22 *tr* to darken; to dim; to discredit; to cloud, confuse ǁ *intr* to grow dark ǁ *ref* to cloud over; to become dimmed; (coll) to fade away
obscuridad *f* obscurity; darkness
obscu·ro -ra *adj* obscure; dark; gloomy; uncertain, dangerous; **a obscuras** in the dark ǁ *m* dark; (paint) shading
obsequia·do -da *mf* recipient; guest of honor
obsequiar *tr* to fawn over, flatter; to present, to give; to court, to woo

obsequio *m* flattery; gift; attention, courtesy; **en obsequio de** in honor of
obsequio·so -sa *adj* obsequious; obliging, courteous
observación *f* observation
observa·dor -dora *adj* observant ǁ *mf* observer
observancia *f* observance; deference, respectfulness
observar *tr* to observe
observatorio *m* observatory
obsesión *f* obsession
obsesionar *tr* to obsess
obstaculizar §60 *tr* to prevent; to obstruct
obstáculo *m* obstacle
obstante *adj* standing in the way; **no obstante** however, nevertheless; in spite of
obstar *intr* to stand in the way; **obstar a** or **para** to hinder, check, oppose
obstetricia *f* obstetrics
obstétri·co -ca *adj* obstetrical ǁ *mf* obstetrician
obstinación *f* obstinacy
obstina·do -da *adj* obstinate
obstinar *ref* to be obstinate
obstrucción *f* obstruction
obstruir §20 *tr* to obstruct; to block; to stop up
obtención *f* obtaining
obtener §71 *tr* to obtain; to keep
obtenible *adj* obtainable
obturador *m* stopper, plug; (aut) choke; (aut) throttle; (phot) shutter; **obturador de guillotina** drop shutter
obtu·so -sa *adj* obtuse
obús *m* howitzer; shell; (*de válvula de neumático*) plunger
obvención *f* extra, bonus, incidental
obvencional *adj* incidental
obviar §77 & *regular tr* to obviate, prevent ǁ *intr* to stand in the way
ob·vio -via *adj* obvious; unnecessary
oca *f* goose
ocasión *f* occasion; opportunity; chance; danger, risk; **aprovechar la ocasión** to improve the occasion; **aprovechar la ocasión de** to avail oneself of the opportunity to; **asir la ocasión por la melena** to take time by the forelock; **de ocasión** secondhand
ocasiona·do -da *adj* dangerous, risky; exposed, subject, liable; annoying
ocasionar *tr* to occasion, to cause; to stir up; to endanger
ocasional *adj* occasional; causal; causing; (*causa*) responsible; accidental
ocaso *m* west; (*de un cuerpo celeste*) setting; sunset; decline; end, death
occidental *adj* western; occidental
occidente *m* occident
oceáni·co -ca *adj* oceanic
océano *m* ocean
ocio *m* idleness, leisure; distraction, pastime; spare time
ocio·so -sa *adj* idle; useless, needless
oclusión *f* occlusion
oclusi·vo -va *adj & f* occlusive
ocote *m* (Mex) torch pine
octava *f* octave
octavilla *f* handbill; eight-syllable verse

octavín *m* piccolo

octa·vo -va *adj* eighth || *mf* octoroon || *m* eighth || *f* see **octava**

oct.ᵉ *abbr* octubre

octogési·mo -ma *adj & m* eightieth

octubre *m* October

ocular *adj* ocular, eye || *m* eyepiece, eyeglass, ocular

oculista *mf* oculist; (Am) fawner, flatterer

ocultar *tr & ref* to hide

ocul·to -ta *adj* hidden, concealed; (*misterioso, sobrenatural*) occult

ocupación *f* occupation; occupancy; employment

ocupa·do -da *adj* busy; occupied; **ocupada** pregnant

ocupante *adj* occupying || *mf* occupant || **ocupantes** *mpl* occupying forces

ocupar *tr* to occupy; to busy, keep busy; to employ; to bother, annoy; to attract the attention of || *ref* to be occupied; to be busy; to be preoccupied; to bother

ocurrencia *f* occurrence; witticism; bright idea

ocurrente *adj* witty

ocurrir *intr* to occur, happen; to come; (*venir a la mente*) to occur

ocha·vo -va *adj* eighth; octagonal || *m* eighth; octagon

ochenta *adj, pron & m* eighty

ochenta·vo -va *adj & m* eightieth

ocho *adj & pron* eight; **las ocho** eight o'clock || *m* eight; (*en las fechas*) eighth

ochocien·tos -tas *adj & pron* eight hundred || **ochocientos** *m* eight hundred

oda *f* ode

odiar *tr* to hate

odio *m* hate, hatred

odio·so -sa *adj* odious, hateful

Odisea *f* Odyssey

Odiseo *m* Odysseus

odontología *f* odontology, dentistry

odontólo·go -ga *mf* odontologist, dentist

odre *m* goatskin wine bag; (coll) toper

OEA *f* OAS

oeste *m* west; west wind

ofender *tr & intr* to offend || *ref* to take offense

ofensa *f* offense

ofensi·vo -va *adj & f* offensive

ofen·sor -sora *adj* offending || *mf* offender

oferta *f* offer; gift, present; **oferta y demanda** supply and demand

oficial *adj* official || *m* official, officer; skilled workman; clerk, office worker; journeyman; commissioned officer; **oficial de derrota** navigator

oficiar *tr* to announce officially in writing; (*la misa*) to celebrate; to officiate at || *intr* to officiate; **oficiar de** (coll) to act as

oficina *f* office; shop; pharmacist's laboratory; **oficina de objetos perdidos** lost-and-found department

oficines·co -ca *adj* office, clerical; bureaucratic

oficinista *mf* clerk, office worker

oficio *m* office, occupation; function,

rôle; craft, trade; memo, official note; (eccl) office, service; **de oficio** officially; professionally; **hacer oficios de** to function as; **tomar por oficio** (coll) to take to, to keep at

oficio·so -sa *adj* diligent; obliging; officious, meddlesome; profitable; unofficial

ofrecer *tr & intr* to offer; (*una recepción*) to give || *ref* to offer; to offer oneself; to happen

ofrecimiento *m* offer, offering; **ofrecimiento de presentación** introductory offer

ofrenda *f* offering; gift

ofrendar *tr* to make offerings of; to contribute

oftalmología *f* ophthalmology

oftalmólo·go -ga *mf* ophthalmologist

ofuscar §73 *tr* to obfuscate; to dazzle

ogro *m* ogre

Oh *interj* O!, Oh!

ohmio *m* ohm

oíble *adj* audible

oída *f* hearing; **de** or **por oídas** by hearsay

oído *m* hearing; ear; **abrir tanto oído** to be all ears; **al oído** by listening; confidentially; **decir al oído** to whisper; **hacer** or **tener oídos de mercader** to turn a deaf ear

oír §48 *tr* to hear; to listen to; (*una conferencia*) to attend; **oír + inf** to hear + *inf*, e.g., **oí entrar a mi hermano** I heard my brother come in; to hear + *ger*, e.g., **oí cantar a la muchacha** I heard the girl singing; to hear + *pp*, e.g., **oí tocar la campana** I heard the bell rung; **oír decir que** to hear that; **oír hablar de** to hear about || *intr* to hear; to listen; **¡oiga!** say!, listen!; **the idea!**, the very idea!

ojada *f* (Col) skylight

ojal *m* buttonhole; eyelet; grommet

ojalá *interj* God grant . . . !, would to God . . . !; **¡ojalá que . . . !** I would that . . . !, I hope that . . . !

ojeada *f* glimpse, glance; **buena ojeada** eyeful

ojear *tr* to eye, stare at; to hoodoo, to cast the evil eye on; (*la caza*) to start, to rouse; to frighten, to startle

ojera *f* eyecup, eyeglass; **ojeras** (*bajo los párpados inferiores*) rings, circles

ojeriza *f* grudge, ill will

ojero·so -sa *adj* with rings or circles under the eyes

ojete *m* eyelet, eyehole

ojienju·to -ta *adj* dry-eyed, tearless

ojituer·to -ta *adj* cross-eyed

ojiva *f* ogive, pointed arch

ojo *m* eye; (*de la escalera*) opening, well; (*del puente*) bay, span; (*de agua*) spring; **a ojos vistas** visibly, openly; **costar un ojo de la cara** to cost a mint, to cost a fortune; **dar los ojos de la cara por** to give one's eyeteeth for; **hasta los ojos** up to one's ears; **mirar con ojos de carnero degollado** to make sheep's eyes at; **no pegar el ojo** to not sleep a wink; **ojo de buey** (archit, meteor, naut) bull's-eye; (bot) oxeye; **ojo de la cerradura**

keyhole; **poner los ojos en blanco** to roll one's eyes; **saltar a los ojos** to be self-evident; **valer un ojo de la cara** to be worth a mint || *interj* beware!; look out!; attention!; **¡mucho ojo!** be careful!, watch out!; **¡ojo con . . . !** look out for . . . !; **¡ojo, mancha!** fresh paint!

ojota *f* (SAm) sandal; (SAm) tanned llama hide

ola *f* wave; (*de gente apiñada*) surge

ole *m* or **olé** *m* bravo || *interj* bravo!

oleada *f* big wave; (*de gente apiñada*) surge, swell

oleaje *m* surge, rush of waves

óleo *m* oil; holy oil; oil painting; **los santos óleos** extreme unction

oleoducto *m* pipe line

oler §49 *tr* to smell; to pry into; to sniff out || *intr* to smell, to smell fragrant, to smell bad; **no oler bien** (coll) to look suspicious; **oler a** to smell of, to smell like; to smack of

olfatear *tr* to smell, scent, sniff; (coll) (*p.ej., un buen negocio*) to scent, to sniff out

olfato *m* smell, sense of smell; scent; keen insight

olíbano *m* frankincense

oliente *adj* smelling, odorous

oligarquía *f* oligarchy

Olimpíada *f* Olympiad

olímpi·co -ca *adj* Olympian; Olympic; haughty

oliscar §73 *tr* to smell, scent, sniff; to investigate || *intr* to smell bad

oliva *f* olive; olive tree; barn owl; olive branch, peace

olivar *m* olive grove

olivillo *m* mock privet

olivo *m* olive tree; **tomar el olivo** (taur) to duck behind the barrier; (coll) to beat it

olmeda *f* or **olmedo** *m* elm grove

olmo *m* elm tree

olor *m* odor; promise, hope; trace, suspicion; **olores** (Chile, Mex) spice, condiment

oloro·so -sa *adj* odorous, fragrant

olote *m* (CAm & Mex) cob, corncob

olvidadi·zo -za *adj* forgetful; ungrateful

olvida·do -da *adj* forgetful; ungrateful

olvidar *tr & intr* to forget; **olvidar +** *inf* to forget to + *inf* || *ref* to forget oneself; **olvidarse de** to forget; **olvidarse de +** *inf* to forget to + *inf*; **olvidársele a uno** to forget, e.g., **se me olvidó mi pasaporte** I forgot my passport; **olvidársele a uno +** *inf* to forget to + *inf*, e.g., **se me olvidó cerrar la ventana** I forgot to close the window

olvido *m* forgetfulness; oblivion

olla *f* pot; kettle; stew; eddy, whirlpool; **olla a** or **de presión** pressure cooker

ombligo *m* navel; (*centro, punto medio*) (fig) navel

omino·so -sa *adj* ominous

omisión *f* omission; oversight, neglect

omi·so -sa *adj* neglectful, remiss

omitir *tr* to omit; to overlook, neglect

ómni·bus *adj* (*tren*) accommodation || *m* (*pl* **-bus**) bus, omnibus; **ómnibus de dos pisos** double-decker

omnímo·do -da *adj* all-inclusive

omnipotente *adj* omnipotent

omnisciente or **omnis·cio -cia** *adj* omniscient

omnívo·ro -ra *adj* omnivorous

omóplato *m* shoulder blade

once *adj & pron* eleven; **las once** eleven o'clock || *m* eleven; (*en las fechas*) eleventh

oncea·vo -va *adj & m* eleventh

once·no -na *adj & m* eleventh

onda *f* wave; flicker; (*en el pelo*) wave; **onda portadora** (rad) carrier wave; **ondas entretenidas** (rad) continuous waves

ondear *tr* (*el pelo*) to wave || *intr* to wave; to ripple; to flow; to flicker; to be wavy || *ref* to wave, sway, swing

ondo·so -sa *adj* wavy

ondulación *f* undulation; wave; wave motion

ondula·do -da *adj* wavy, ripply; rolling; corrugated || *m* (*en el pelo*) wave

ondular *tr* (*el pelo*) to wave || *intr* to undulate; (*una bandera*) to wave, flutter; (*las ondas del mar*) to billow; (*una culebra*) to wriggle

onero·so -sa *adj* onerous, burdensome

ónice *m*, **ónique** *m* or **ónix** *m* onyx

onomásti·co -ca *adj* of proper names || *m* name day || *f* study of proper names

ONU *f* UN

onza *f* ounce; (zool) snow leopard

onza·vo -va *adj & m* eleventh

opa·co -ca *adj* opaque; sad, gloomy

ópalo *m* opal

opción *f* option, choice

ópera *f* opera; **ópera semiseria** light opera; **ópera seria** grand opera

operación *f* operation; transaction

operar *tr* to operate on || *intr* to operate; to work || *ref* to occur, come about; to be operated on

opera·rio -ria *mf* worker || *m* workman || *f* working woman

opereta *f* operetta

operista *mf* opera singer

operísti·co -ca *adj* operatic

opia·to -ta *adj, m & f* opiate

opinable *adj* moot

opinar *intr* to opine; to think; to pass judgment

opinión *f* opinion, view; reputation, public image

opio *m* opium

opípa·ro -ra *adj* sumptuous, lavish

oponer §54 *tr* to oppose; (*resistencia*) to offer, put up || *ref* to oppose each other; to face each other; **oponerse a** to oppose, be opposed to; to be against, to resist; to compete for

oporto *m* port, port wine

oportunidad *f* opportunity; opportuneness; **oportunidades** *fpl* witticisms

oportunista *adj* opportunistic || *mf* opportunist

oportu·no -na *adj* opportune, timely; proper; witty

oposición *f* opposition; competitive examination

oposi•tor -tora *adj* rivaling, competing || *mf* opponent; competitor

opresión *f* oppression

opresi•vo -va *adj* oppressive

opre•sor -sora *adj* oppressive || *mf* oppressor

oprimir *tr* to oppress; to squeeze, to press

oprobiar *tr* to defame, to revile

oprobio *m* opprobrium

oprobio•so -sa *adj* opprobrious

optar *tr* to choose, to select; *intr* — **optar entre** to choose between; **optar por** to choose to

ópti•co -ca *adj* optical || *mf* optician || *f* optics

óptimamente *adv* to perfection

optimismo *m* optimism

optimista *adj* optimistic || *mf* optimist

ópti•mo -ma *adj* fine, excellent

optometrista *mf* optometrist

opues•to -ta *adj* opposite, contrary

opugnar *tr* to attack; to lay siege to; to contradict

opulen•to -ta *adj* oppulent

opúsculo *m* short work, opuscule

oquedad *f* hollow; hollowness

ora *conj* — **ora . . . ora** now . . . now, now . . . then

oración *f* oration, speech; prayer; sentence; **oración dominical** Lord's prayer; **ponerse en oración** to get down on one's knees

oráculo *m* oracle

ora•dor -dora *mf* orator, speaker; **orador de plazuela** soapbox orator; **orador de sobremesa** after-dinner speaker

oraje *m* rough weather, storm

oral *adj* oral

orangután *m* orang-outang

orar *intr* to pray; to make a speech

orato•rio -ria *adj* oratorical || *m* oratorio; (*capilla privada*) oratory || *f* (*arte de la elocuencia*) oratory

orbe *m* orb; world

órbita *f* orbit

orca *f* killer whale

Órcadas *fpl* Orkney Islands

órdago — **de órdago** (coll) swell, real

orden *m & f* order; **hasta nueva orden** until further notice; **orden** *f* **de allanamiento** search warrant; **orden** *m* **de colocación** word order

ordenancista *adj* strict, severe || *mf* taskmaster, disciplinarian, martinet

ordenanza *m* errand boy; (mil) orderly || *f* ordinance; order, system; command; **ser de ordenanza** (coll) to be the rule

ordenar *tr* to order; to put in order; to ordain || *ref* to be ordained, to take orders

ordeñadero *m* milk pail

ordeñar *tr* to milk

ordeño *m* milking

ordinal *adj* orderly; ordinal || *m* ordinal

ordinariez *f* (coll) coarseness, crudeness

ordina•rio -ria *adj* ordinary || *m* daily household expenses; delivery man

orear *tr* to air || *ref* to be aired; to dry in the air; to take an airing

orégano *m* pot or wild marjoram, winter sweet

oreja *f* ear; (*del zapato*) flap; (*de martillo*) claw; lug, flange, ear; **aguzar las orejas** to prick up one's ears; **con las orejas caídas** crestfallen; **con las orejas tan largas** all ears; **descubrir** or **enseñar las orejas** (coll) to give oneself away

oreja•no -na *adj* (*res*) unbranded; (*animal*) (Am) skittish; (Am) shy; (Am) cautious

orejera *f* earflap, earmuff

orejeta *f* lug

ore•jón -jona *adj* (Am) coarse, uncouth; (Mex) skinny || *m* strip of dried peach; pull on the ear; (*de la hoja de un libro*) dog's-ear

oreju•do -da *adj* big-eared

oreo *m* breeze

orfanato *m* orphanage

orfandad *f* orphanage, orphanhood

orfebre *m* goldsmith; silversmith

Orfeo *m* Orpheus

orfeón *m* glee club, choral society

organ•dí *m* (*pl* **-díes**) organdy

orgáni•co -ca *adj* organic

organillero -ra *mf* organ-grinder

organillo *m* barrel organ, hand organ, hurdy-gurdy

organismo *m* organism; organization

organista *mf* organist

organizar §60 *tr* to organize

órgano *m* organ; (*de una máquina*) part; (*medio, conducto*) organ; (mus) organ

orgía *f* orgy

orgullo *m* haughtiness; pride

orgullo•so -sa *adj* haughty; proud

oriental *adj* eastern; oriental

orientar *tr* to orient; to guide, direct; (*una vela*) to trim || *ref* to orient oneself; to find one's bearings

oriente *m* east; source, origin; east wind; youth || **Oriente** *m* Orient; **el Cercano Oriente** the Near East; **el Extremo Oriente** the Far East; **el Lejano Oriente** the Far East; **el Oriente Medio** the Middle East; **el Próximo Oriente** the Near East; **gran oriente** (*logia masónica central*) grand lodge

orificar §73 *tr* to fill with gold

orífice *m* goldsmith

orificio *m* orifice, aperture, hole

origen *m* origin; source

original *adj* original; queer, odd, quaint || *m* original; character, queer duck; **de buen original** on good authority; **original de imprenta** copy

originar *tr & ref* to originate, to start

orilla *f* border, edge; margin; bank, shore; sidewalk; breeze; **orillas** (Arg, Mex) outskirts; **salir a la orilla** to manage to get through

orillar *tr* to put a border or edge on; to trim || *intr* to come up to the shore

orillo *m* selvage, list

orín *m* rust; **orines** urine; **tomarse de orines** to get rusty

orina *f* urine

orinal *m* chamber pot

orinar tr to pass, to urinate || intr & ref to urinate

oriun•do -da adj & mf native; **ser oriundo de** to come from, to hail from

orla f border, edge; trimming, fringe

orlar tr to border, to put an edge on; to trim, to trim with a fringe

orn. abbr **orden**

ornamentar tr to ornament, adorn

ornamento m ornament, adornment

ornar tr to adorn

ornato m adornment, show

oro m gold; playing card (representing a gold coin) equivalent to diamond; **de oro y azul** (coll) all dressed up; **oro batido** gold leaf; **oro de ley** standard gold; **poner de oro y azul** (coll) to rake over the coals; **ponerle colores al oro** to gild the lily

oron•do -da adj big-bellied; (coll) hollow, spongy, puffed up; (coll) pompous, self-satisfied

oropel m tinsel; **gastar mucho oropel** (coll) to put up a big front

oropéndola f golden oriole

orozuz m licorice

orquesta f orchestra; **orquesta típica** regional orchestra

orquestar tr to orchestrate

órquide f or **orquídea** f orchid

ortiga f nettle; **ser como unas ortigas** (coll) to be a grouch

orto m rise (of sun or star)

ortodo•xo -xa adj orthodox

ortografía f orthography; spelling

ortografiar §77 tr & intr to spell

oruga f caterpillar

orujo m bagasse of grapes or olives

orzuelo m sty

os pron pers & reflex (used as object of verb and corresponding to **vos** and **vosotros**) you, to you; yourself, to yourself; yourselves, to yourselves; each other, to each other

osa f she-bear; **Osa mayor** Great Bear; **Osa menor** Little Bear

osadía f boldness, daring

osa•do -da adj bold, daring

osamenta f skeleton; bones

osar intr to dare

osario m ossuary, charnel house

oscilar intr to oscillate; to fluctuate; to waver, hesitate

ósculo m kiss

oscurecer §22 tr, intr & ref var of **obscurecer**

oscuridad f var of **obscuridad**

oscu•ro -ra adj & m var of **obscuro**

osera f bear's den

osificar §73 tr & ref to ossify

oso m bear; **hacer el oso** (coll) to make a fool of oneself; (coll) to make love in the open; **oso blanco** polar bear; **oso hormiguero** ant bear, anteater; **oso lavador** raccoon

ostensorio m (eccl) monstrance

ostentar tr to show; to make a show of || ref to show off; to boast

ostentati•vo -va adj ostentatious

ostento m portent, prodigy

ostento•so -sa adj magnificent, showy

osteópata mf osteopath

osteopatía f osteopathy

ostión m large oyster

ostra f oyster; **ostras en su concha** oyster cocktail, oysters on the half shell

ostracismo m ostracism

ostral m oyster bed, oyster farm

ostrería f oysterhouse

ostre•ro -ra adj oyster || m oysterman; oyster bed, oyster farm

osu•do -da adj bony

osu•no -na adj bearish, bearlike

O.T.A.N., la Nato

O.T.A.S.E., la Seato

otate m Mexican giant grass (Guadua amplexifolia); otate stick

otero m hillock, knoll

otomán m ottoman

otoma•no -na adj & mf Ottoman || f ottoman

otoñal adj autumnal

otoño m autumn, fall

otorgar §44 tr to agree to; to grant, to confer; (law) to execute

o•tro -tra adj indef other, another || pron indef other one, another one; **como dijo el otro** as someone said

ovación f ovation

ovacionar tr to give an ovation to

oval adj oval

óvalo m oval

ovante adj victorious, triumphant

ovario m ovary

oveja f ewe, female sheep; **oveja negra** (fig) black sheep; **oveja perdida** (fig) lost sheep

oveje•ro -ra adj sheep || mf sheep raiser

oveju•no -na adj sheep, of sheep

ove•ro -ra adj blossom-colored; egg-colored

Ovidio m Ovid

ovillar tr to wind up; to sum up || intr to form into a ball || ref to curl up into a ball

ovillo m ball of yarn; ball, heap; tangled ball; **hacerse un ovillo** (coll) to cower, to recoil; (hablando) (coll) to get all tangled up

oxear tr & intr to shoo

oxiacanta f hawthorn

oxidar tr to oxidize || ref to oxidize; to get rusty

óxido m oxide; **óxido de carbono** carbon monoxide; **óxido de mercurio** mercuric oxide

oxígeno m oxygen

oxíto•no -na adj oxytone

oxte interj get out!, beat it!; **sin decir oxte ni moxte** (coll) without opening one's mouth

oyente mf hearer; (a la radio) listener; (en la escuela) auditor

ozono m ozone

P

P, p (pe) *f* nineteenth letter of the Spanish alphabet

P. *abbr* **Padre, Papa, Pregunta**

pabellón *m* pavilion; bell tent; flag, banner; (*de fusiles*) stack; canopy; summerhouse; (*de instrumento de viento*) bell

pabilo *or* **pábilo** *m* wick

Pablo *m* Paul

pábulo *m* food; support, encouragement, fuel

pacana *f* pecan

paca·to -ta *adj* mild, gentle

pacer §22 *tr* to pasture, graze; to gnaw, eat away ‖ *intr* to pasture, graze

paciencia *f* patience

paciente *adj & mf* patient

pacien·do -da *adj* long-suffering

pacificar §73 *tr* to pacify ‖ *intr* to sue for peace ‖ *ref* to calm down

pacífi·co -ca *adj* pacific

pacifismo *m* pacifism

pacifista *adj & mf* pacifist

pa·co -ca *adj* (Chile) bay, reddish ‖ *m* paco, alpaca; Moorish sniper; sniper ‖ **Paco** *m* Frank

pacotilla *f* trash, junk; (Chile) rabble, mob; **hacer su pacotilla** (coll) to make a cleanup; **ser de pacotilla** to be shoddy, to be poorly made

pacotille·ro -ra *mf* (Chile, Ven) peddler

pactar *tr* to agree upon ‖ *intr* to come to an agreement

pacto *m* pact, covenant

pacha·cho -cha *adj* (Chile) short-legged; (Chile) lax, lazy; (Chile) chubby

pa·chón -chona *adj* (CAm) shaggy, hairy, wooly ‖ *m* (*perro*) pointer; (*hombre flemático*) sluggard

pachorra *f* (coll) sluggishness, indolence

padecer §22 *tr* to suffer; to be victim of ‖ *intr* to suffer

padrastro *m* stepfather; hangnail

padre *adj* (Am) huge; (Peru) terrific ‖ *m* father; stallion, sire; **padres** parents; ancestors; **tener el padre alcalde** to have pull, to have a friend at court

padrina *f* godmother

padrinazgo *m* godfathership; sponsorship, patronage

padrino *m* godfather; sponsor; (*en un desafío*) second; **padrino de boda** best man; **padrinos** godparents

padrón *m* poll, census; pattern, model; memorial column; (coll) indulgent father; (Am) stallion; (Col) stock bull

padrote *m* (Am) stock animal; (Mex) pimp, procurer

paella *f* saffron-flavored stew of chicken, seafood, and rice with vegetables

paf *interj* bang!

pág. *abbr* **página**

paga *f* pay, payment; wages; fine

paga-alquiler *f* rent, rent money

pagadero -ra *adj* payable

paga·do -da *adj* pleased, cheerful; **estamos pagados** we are quits; **pagado de sí mismo** self-satisfied, conceited

paga·dor -dora *adj* paying ‖ *mf* payer ‖ *m* paymaster

paganismo *m* paganism

paga·no -na *adj & mf* pagan ‖ *m* (coll) easy mark

pagar §44 *tr* to pay; to pay for; (*una bondad, una visita*) to return ‖ *intr* to pay ‖ *ref* to become fond; to be flattered; to boast; to be satisfied

pagaré *m* promissory note, I.O.U.

página *f* page

paginar *tr* to page

pago *m* payment; (*de viñas u olivares*) district, region

pagote *m* (coll) easy mark

paila *f* large pan

pairar *intr* (naut) to lie to

país *m* country, land; landscape; **el país de Gales** Wales; **los Países Bajos** (*Bélgica, Holanda y Luxemburgo*) the Low Countries; (*Holanda*) The Netherlands

paisaje *m* landscape

paisajista *mf* landscape painter

paisa·no -na *adj* of the same country ‖ *mf* peasant; civilian; (Mex) Spaniard ‖ *m* fellow countryman; **de paisano** in civies

paja *f* straw; chaff; trash, rubbish; **no dormirse en las pajas** to not let the grass grow under one's feet; **no levantar paja del suelo** to not lift a hand, to not do a stroke of work

pájara *f* paper kite; paper rooster; bird; crafty female

pajarera *f* aviary; large bird cage

pajarería *f* flock of birds; bird store; pet shop

pajare·ro -ra *adj* (coll) bright, cheerful; (coll) bright-colored, gaudy ‖ *m* bird dealer; bird fancier ‖ *f* see **pajarera**

pajarita *f* paper kite; bow tie; wing collar, piccadilly

pájaro *m* bird; crafty fellow; expert; **pájaro bobo** penguin; (Am) motmot; **pájaro carpintero** woodpecker; **pájaro de cuenta** (coll) big shot; **pájaro mosca** hummingbird

pajarota *or* **pajarotada** *f* hoax, canard

paje *m* page; valet; dressing table; (naut) cabin boy

pajilla *f* cornhusk cigarette; **pajilla de madera** excelsior

paji·zo -za *adj* straw; straw-colored; straw-thatched

pajuela *f* short straw; sulfur match or fuse; (Am) toothpick; (Bol) match

Pakistán *m* var of **Paquistán**

pakista·ní (*pl* -níes) *adj & mf* var of **paquistaní**

pala *f* shovel; (*de remo, de la azada, etc.*) blade; (*del panadero*) peel; scoop; racket; (*del calzado*) upper; (*de excavadora*) bucket; shoulder strap; (coll) cunning, craftiness

palabra *f* word; speech; (*de una canción*) words; (*derecho para hablar en asambleas*) floor; **palabras mayores**

words, angry words; **remojar la palabra** (coll) to wet one's whistle; **usar
de la palabra** to speak, make a speech
palabre·ro -ra *adj* wordy, windy || *mf*
windbag
palabrota *f* vulgarity, obscenity
palacie·go -ga *adj* palace, court || *m*
courtier
palacio *m* palace; mansion; **palacio
municipal** city hall
palada *f* shovelful; *(de remo)* stroke
paladar *m* palate; taste; gourmet
paladear *tr* to taste, to relish
paladín *m* champion, hero
palafrén *m* palfrey
palanca *f* lever; pole; crowbar; **palanca
de mando** (aer) control stick; **palanca
de mayúsculas** shift key
palancada *f* leverage
palangana *f* washbowl, basin
palanganero *m* washstand
palangre *m* trawl, trawl line
palanqueta *f* jimmy; **palanquetas** (Arg)
dumbbell
palatal *adj* & *f* palatal
palco *m* (theat) box
palear *tr* to beat, to pound; (Am) to
shovel
palenque *m* paling, palisade; (SAm)
hitching post; (C-R) Indian ranch;
(Chile) pandemonium
paleta *f* palette; small shovel; trowel;
(de una rueda) paddle; blade, bucket,
vane; shoulder blade; *(dulce con un
palito que sirve de mango)* lollipop
paletilla *f* shoulder blade
paleto *m* fallow deer; rustic, yokel
palia *f* altar cloth; (eccl) pall
paliacate *m* (Mex) bandanna
paliar §77 & regular *tr* to palliate
palidecer §22 *intr* to pale, to turn pale
palidez *f* paleness, pallor
páli·do -da *adj* pale, pallid
palillo *m* toothpick; drumstick; bobbin; **palillos** chopsticks; castanets;
(coll) rudiments; (coll) trifles
palinodia *f* backdown; **cantar la palinodia** to eat crow, eat humble pie
palique *m* (coll) chit-chat, small talk
paliquear *intr* (coll) to chat, to gossip
paliza *f* beating, thrashing
palizada *f* fenced-in enclosure; stockade; embankment
palma *f* *(de la mano)* palm; *(árbol y
hoja)* palm; **batir palmas** to clap, to
applaud; **llevarse la palma** to carry
off the palm
palmada *f* slap; hand, applause, clapping; **dar palmadas** to clap hands
palma·rio -ria *adj* clear, evident
palmatoria *f* candlestick
palmera *f* date palm
palmito *m* palmetto; (coll) woman's
face; (coll) slender figure
palmo *m* span, palm; **dejar con un
palmo de narices** (coll) to disappoint
palmotear *tr* to pat; to clap, applaud ||
intr to clap, applaud
palo *m* stick; pole; staff; handle;
(golpe) whack; *(madera)* wood; *(grupo de naipes de la baraja)* suit;
(naut) mast; (Am) tree; **dar palos de
ciego** to lay about, to swing wildly;

de tal palo tal astilla like father like
son; **palo de escoba** broomstick; **palo
en alto** (fig) big stick; **palo mayor**
(naut) mainmast; **servir del palo** to
follow suit
paloma *f* pigeon, dove; prostitute; (fig)
dove, meek person; **paloma mensajera** carrier pigeon; **palomas** whitecaps
palomar *m* pigeon house, dovecot
palomilla *f* doveling; small butterfly;
white horse; *(del caballo)* back; pillow block, journal bearing; **palomi-
llas** whitecaps
palomita *f* doveling; (baseball) fly;
palomitas (Am) popcorn
palpable *adj* palpable
palpar *tr* to touch, to feel; to grope
through || *intr* to grope
palpitante *adj* throbbing; thrilling;
(cuestión) burning
palpitar *intr* to palpitate, to throb; *(un
afecto)* to flash, break forth
pálpito *m* (SAm) hunch
palta *f* (SAm) alligator pear, avocado
(fruit)
palto *m* (SAm) alligator pear, avocado
(tree)
palúdi·co -ca *adj* marshy; malarial
paludismo *m* malaria
palur·do -da *adj* rustic, boorish || *mf*
rustic, boor
pallador *m* (SAm) Gaucho minstrel
pampa *f* pampa; **La Pampa** the Pampas
pámpana *f* vine leaf
pámpano *m* tendril; vine leaf
pan *m* bread; loaf; loaf of bread;
wheat; food; livelihood; pie dough;
(de jabón, cera, etc.) cake; gold foil
or leaf; silver foil or leaf; **como el
pan bendito** (coll) as easy as pie; **de
pan llevar** arable, tillable; **llamar al
pan pan y al vino vino** to call a
spade a spade; **panes** grain, bread-
stuff; **venderse como pan bendito** to
sell like hot cakes || **Pan** *m* Pan
pana *f* corduroy; (aut) breakdown
panacea *f* panacea
panadería *f* bakery; baking business
panade·ro -ra *mf* baker; (Chile) flatterer
panadizo *m* felon; (coll) sickly person
panal *m* honeycomb
pana·má *m* (*pl* -maes) Panama hat
paname·ño -ña *adj* & *mf* Panamanian
panamerica·no -na *adj* Pan-American
pancarta *f* placard, poster
pancista *adj* weaseling || *mf* weaseler
páncre·as *m* (*pl* -as) pancreas
pancho *m* (coll) paunch, belly
pandear *intr* & *ref* to warp, to bulge, to
buckle, to sag, to bend
pandereta *f* tambourine
pandilla *f* party, faction; gang, band;
picnic, excursion
pan·do -da *adj* bulging; slow-moving;
slow, deliberate
pandorga *f* kite; (coll) fat, lazy woman
panecillo *m* roll, crescent
panfleto *m* pamphlet
paniaguado *m* servant, minion; protégé,
favorite

pá·ni·co -ca *adj* panic, panicky ‖ *m* panic

panizo *m* Italian millet; (Chile) gangue; (Chile) abundance

panocha *f* ear of grain; ear of corn; (Am) pancake made of corn and cheese; (Mex) panocha (*brown sugar*)

panoja *f* ear of grain; ear of corn

panorama *m* panorama

pano·so -sa *adj* mealy

panqué *m* or **panqueque** *m* pancake

pantalán *m* pier, wooden pier

pantalón *m* trousers; **calzarse los pantalones** to wear the pants; **pantalones** trousers, pants

pantalla *f* lamp shade; fire screen; motion-picture screen; television screen; (*persona que encubre a otra*) blind; (*cine, arte del cine*) screen; (Am) fan; **llevar a la pantalla** to put on the screen; **pantalla de plata** silver screen; **servir de pantalla a** to be a blind for

pantano *m* bog, marsh, swamp; dam, reservoir; trouble, obstacle

pantano·so -sa *adj* marshy, swampy; muddy; knotty, difficult

panteísmo *m* pantheism

panteón *m* pantheon; cemetery

pantera *f* panther

pantomima *f* pantomime

pantoque *m* (naut) bilge

pantorrilla *f* calf (*of leg*)

pantufla *f* or **pantuflo** *m* house slipper

panza *f* paunch, belly

panzu·do -da *adj* paunchy, big-bellied

pañal *m* diaper; shirttail; **pañales** swaddling clothes; infancy; early stages

pañe·ro -ra *adj* dry-goods, cloth ‖ *mf* dry-goods dealer, clothier

paño *m* cloth; rag; (*de agujas*) paper; (*ancho de la tela*) breadth; (*mancha en el rostro*) spot; (*en, p.ej., un espejo*) blur; sailcloth, canvas; al **paño** off-stage; **conocer el paño** (coll) to know one's business, to know the ropes; **paño de adorno** doily; **paño de cocina** washrag, dishcloth; **paño de lágrimas** helping hand, stand-by; **paño de mesa** tablecloth; **paño de tumba** crape; **paño mortuorio** pall; **paños menores** underclothing

pañuelo *m* handkerchief; shawl; **pañuelo de hierbas** bandanna

papa *m* pope ‖ *f* potato; (coll) fake, hoax; (coll) food, grub; (Am) snap, cinch; **ni papa** (Am) nothing

pa·pá *m* (*pl* -**pás**) papa, daddy

papada *f* double chin; (*de animal*) dewlap; (Guat) stupidity

papado *m* papacy

papagayo *m* parrot

papalina *f* sunbonnet; (coll) drunk

papana·tas *m* (*pl* -**tas**) (coll) simpleton, gawk

paparrucha *f* (coll) hoax; (coll) trifle

papel *m* paper; piece of paper; rôle, part; character, figure; **desempeñar** or **hacer un papel** to play a rôle; **papel alquitranado** tar paper; **papel cebolla** onionskin; **papel de empapelar** wallpaper; **papel de esmeril** emery paper; **papel de estaño** tin foil;

papel de excusado toilet paper; **papel de fumar** cigarette paper; **papel de lija** sandpaper; **papel de oficio** foolscap; **papel de seda** tissue paper; **papel de segundón** (fig) second fiddle; **papel de tornasol** litmus paper; **papel filtrante** filter paper; **papel higiénico** toilet paper; **papel moneda** paper money; **papel pintado** wallpaper; **papel secante** blotting paper; **papel viejo** waste paper; **papel volante** handbill, printed leaflet

papeleo *m* red tape

papelera *f* paper case; writing desk; wastebasket; paper factory

papelería *f* stationery store; mess of papers, litter

papele·ro -ra *adj* paper; boastful, showy ‖ *mf* stationer; paper manufacturer; (Mex) paperboy ‖ *f see* **papelera**

papeleta *f* slip of paper; card, file card; ticket; **papeleta de empeño** pawn ticket

papelista *m* paper maker, paper manufacturer; stationer; paper hanger

pape·lón -lona *adj* (coll) bluffing, four-flushing ‖ *mf* (coll) bluffer, four-flusher ‖ *m* thin cardboard

papelonear *intr* (coll) to bluff, to four-flush

papelote *m* worthless piece of paper; (Am) paper kite

papel-prensa *m* newsprint

papera *f* goiter; mumps

papilla *f* pap; guile, deceit

papiro *m* papyrus

papirote *m* fillip, flick; (coll) nincompoop

paq. *abbr* **paquete**

paquear *tr* to snipe at ‖ *intr* to snipe

paque·te -ta *adj* (Arg) chic, dolled-up; (Am) self-important, pompous ‖ *m* package, parcel, bundle, bale; (coll) sport, dandy; **darse paquete** (Guat, Mex) to put on airs; **en paquete aparte** under separate cover, in a separate package; **paquetes postales** parcel post

Paquistán, el Pakistan

paquista·ní (*pl* -**níes**) or **paquistano -na** *adj & mf* Pakistani

Paquita *f* Fanny

par *adj* like, similar, equal; (math) even ‖ *m* pair, couple; peer; (elec, mech) couple; (math) even number; **a pares** in twos; **de par en par** wide-open; completely; overtly; **¿pares o nones?** odd or even? ‖ *f* par; **a la par** equally; jointly; at the same time; at par; **bajo la par** below par, under par; **sobre la par** above par

para *prep* to, for; towards; compared to; (*antes de*) by; **para** + *inf* in order to + *inf*; about to + *inf*; **para con** towards; **para que** in order that, so that

parabién *m* congratulation

parábola *f* parable

parabri·sa *m* or **parabri·sas** *m* (*pl* -**sas**) windshield

paracaí·das *m* (*pl* -**das**) parachute; **lanzarse en paracaídas** to parachute; **sal-**

varse en paracaídas to parachute to safety

paracaidismo m parachute jumping; (sport) sky diving

paracaidista mf parachutist || m paratrooper

parachis·pas m (pl -pas) spark arrester

paracho·ques m (pl -ques) bumper

parada f stop; end; stay; shutdown; (en el juego) stake; dam; (para el ganado) stall; stud farm; (en la esgrima) parry; (tiro de caballerías de reemplazo) relay; (mil) parade, dress parade, review; **parada de taxi** taxi stand

paradero m end; whereabouts; stopping place; (Am) wayside station

para·do -da adj slow, spiritless, witless; idle, unemployed; closed; (Am) proud, stiff || f see **parada**

paradoja f paradox

paradóji·co -ca adj paradoxical

parador m inn, wayside inn; motel

parafina f paraffin

paragol·pes m (pl -pes) buffer, bumper

para·guas m (pl -guas) umbrella

Paraguay, el Paraguay

paraguaya·no -na or **paragua·yo -ya** adj & mf Paraguayan

paragüero m umbrella man; umbrella stand

paraíso m paradise

paraje m place, spot; state, condition

paralela f parallel, parallel line; **paralelas** parallel bars

paralelizar §60 tr to parallel, compare

parale·lo -la adj parallel || m (geog) parallel || f see **paralela**

parál·sis f (pl -sis) paralysis

paralíti·co -ca adj & mf paralytic

paralizar §60 tr to paralyze || ref to become paralyzed

páramo m high barren plain; bleak windy spot; (Bol, Col, Ecuad) cold drizzle

parani·ves m (pl -ves) snow fence

paraninfo m assembly hall, auditorium

paranoi·co -ca adj & mf paranoiac

parapeto m parapet

parar tr to stop; to check; to change; to prepare; to put up, to stake; to parry; to order; to get, acquire; (la atención) to fix; (la caza) to point; (typ) to set || intr to stop; (en un hotel) to put up; **parar en** to become; to run to, to run as far as || ref to stop; to stop work; to turn, to become; (el perro de muestra) to point; (el pelo) to stand on end; (Am) to stand; **pararse en** to pay attention to

pararra·yo or **pararra·yos** m (pl -yos) (barra metálica que sirve para preservar los edificios del rayo) lightning rod; (dispositivo que sirve para preservar una instalación eléctrica de la electricidad atmosférica o de las chispas que produce) lightning arrester

parasíti·co -ca adj parasitic

parási·to -ta adj parasitic; (elec) stray || m parasite; **parásitos atmosféricos** atmospherics, static

parasol m parasol

parato·pes m (pl -pes) bumper

Parcas fpl Fates

parcela f particle; plot of ground

parcelar tr to parcel, to divide into lots

parcial adj partial; partisan || mf partisan

par·co -ca adj frugal, sparing; moderate

parchar tr (Am) to mend, patch

parche m plaster, sticking plaster; patch; drum; drumhead; daub, botch, splotch; **parche poroso** porous plaster

pardal m linnet; (coll) sly fellow

pardiez interj (coll) by Jove!

pardillo m linnet

par·do -da adj brown, drab; dark; cloudy; (voz) dull, flat; (cerveza) dark; (Am) mulatto || mf (Am) mulatto || m brown, drab; leopard

pardus·co -ca adj dark-brown, drabbish

parea·do -da adj rhymed || m couplet

parear tr to pair; to match || ref to pair off

parecer m opinion; look, mien, countenance || v §22 intr to appear; to show up; to look, to seem; **me parece que . . . I** think that . . . || ref to look alike, to resemble each other; **parecerse a** to look like

pareci·do -da adj like, similar; **bien parecido** good-looking; **parecido a** like, e.g., **esta casa es parecida a la otra** this house is like the other one; **parecidos** alike, e.g., **estas casas son parecidas** these houses are alike || m similarity, resemblance, likeness; **tener un gran parecido** to be a good likeness

pared f wall; **dejar pegado a la pared** to nonplus; **paredes** house

pareja f pair, couple; dancing partner; **correr parejas** or **a las parejas** to be abreast, arrive together; to go together, match, be equal; **correr parejas con** to keep up with, to keep abreast of; **parejas** (de naipes) pair

pareje·ro -ra adj even, equal; (Am) servile, fawning; (Am) forward, overfamiliar || m (Am) race horse

pare·jo -ja adj equal, like; even, smooth || m (CAm) dancing partner || f see **pareja**

parentela f kinsfolk, relations

parentesco m relationship; bond, tie

parénte·sis m (pl -sis) parenthesis; break, interval

parhilera f ridgepole

paria mf pariah, outcast

paridad f par, parity; comparison

parien·te -ta adj related || mf relative; (coll) spouse

parihuela f handbarrow; (camilla) stretcher

parir tr to bear, give birth to, bring forth || intr to give birth; to come forth, to come to light; to talk well

parisiense adj & mf Parisian

parlamentar intr to talk, chat; to parley

parlamento m parliament; parley; speech; (theat) speech

parlan·chín -china adj (coll) jabbering || mf (coll) chatterbox

parlar intr to speak with facility; to

chatter, talk too much; (*el loro*) to talk

parle-ro -ra *adj* loquacious, garrulous; gossipy; (*ave*) singing, song; (*ojos*) expressive; (*arroyo, fuente*) babbling

parlotear *intr* (coll) to prattle, jabber, chin

parloteo *m* (coll) jabber, prattle

parnaso *m* (*colección de poesías*) Parnassus; **el Parnaso** Parnassus, Mount Parnassus

paro *m* shutdown, work stoppage; lockout; titmouse; (*de dados*) (SAm) throw; **paro forzoso** layoff

parodia *f* parody, travesty

parodiar *tr* to parody, to travesty, to burlesque

paroxíto-no -na *adj & m* paroxytone

parpadear *intr* to blink, wink; to flicker

parpadeo *m* blinking, winking; flicker

párpado *m* eyelid

parque *m* park; parking; parking lot; **parque de atracciones** amusement park

parqué *m* floor, inlaid floor

parqueadero *m* (Col) parking lot

parquear *tr* to park

parquímetro *m* parking meter

parra *f* grapevine; earthen jug

párrafo *m* paragraph; (coll) chat

parral *m* grape arbor

parranda *f* (coll) spree, party; (Col) large number; **andar de parranda** (coll) to go out on a spree, go out to celebrate

parricida *mf* patricide, parricide

parricidio *m* patricide, parricide

parrilla *f* grill, gridiron, broiler; grate, grating; grillroom, grill; **asar a la parrilla** to broil

párroco *m* parish priest

parroquia *f* parish; parish church; customers, clientele

parroquial *adj* parochial

parroquia-no -na *mf* parishioner; customer

parte *m* dispatch, communiqué; **parte meteorológico** weather report ‖ *f* part; share; party; side; direction; (*papel de un actor*) role; (law) party; **de un mes a esta parte** for about a month past; **en ninguna otra parte** nowhere else; **en ninguna parte** nowhere; **ir a la parte** to go shares; **la mayor parte** most, the majority; **parte del león** lion's share; **parte de por medio** (theat) bit part, walk-on; **partes** parts, gifts, talent; faction; parts, genitals; **por otra parte** in another direction; elsewhere; on the other hand; **por todas partes** everywhere; **salva sea la parte** excuse me for not mentioning where

partea-guas *m* (*pl* **-guas**) divide, ridge

partear *tr* to deliver

parte-luz *m* (*pl* **-luces**) mullion, sash bar

Partenón *m* Parthenon

partera *f* midwife

partición *f* partition, division

participar *tr* to notify, to inform; to give notice of ‖ *intr* to participate; to partake

participio *m* participle

partícula *f* particle

particular *adj* particular; peculiar; private, personal ‖ *m* particular; matter, subject; individual

particulizar §60 *tr* to itemize ‖ *ref* to stand out; to specialize

partida *f* departure; entry, item; certificate; party, group, band; band of guerrillas; game; (*de cartas*) hand; (*de tenis*) set; lot, shipment; (coll) behavior; **mala partida** (coll) mean trick; **partida de campo** picnic; **partida doble** (com) double entry; **partida sencilla** (com) single entry

partida-rio -ria or **partidista** *adj & mf* partisan

parti-do -da *adj* generous, open-handed ‖ *m* (pol) party; decision; profit; advantage; step, measure; deal, agreement; protection, support; (*casamiento que elegir*) match; district, county; (sport) team; (sport) game, match; **partido de desempate** play-off; **tomar partido** to take a stand, to take sides ‖ *f see* **partida**

partir *tr* to divide; to distribute; to share; to split, split open; to break, crack; (coll) to upset, disconcert ‖ *intr* to start, depart, leave, set out; **a partir de** beginning with ‖ *ref* to become divided; to crack, to split

partisa-no -na *mf* (mil) partisan

partitura *f* (mus) score

parto *m* childbirth, confinement; newborn child; offspring; **estar de parto** to be in labor, to be confined; **parto del ingenio** brain child

parva *f* light breakfast (*on fast days*); heap of unthreshed grain; heap, pile

parvulista *mf* kindergarten teacher

párvu-lo -la *adj* small, tiny; simple, innocent; humble ‖ *mf* child, tot; (*niño*) kindergartner

pasa *f* raisin; (*del pelo de los negros*) kink; **pasa de Corinto** currant

pasada *f* passage; passing; **de pasada** in passing, hastily; **mala pasada** (coll) mean trick

pasade-ro -ra *adj* passable ‖ *f* stepping stone; walkway, catwalk

pasadizo *m* passage, corridor, hallway, alley; catwalk

pasa-do -da *adj* past; gone by; overripe, spoiled; overdone; stale; burned out; antiquated; faded ‖ *m* past; **pasados** ancestors ‖ *f see* **pasada**

pasa-dor -dora *mf* smuggler ‖ *m* door bolt; bolt, pin; hatpin; brooch; stickpin; safety pin; strainer

pasaje *m* passage; fare; fares; passengers; **cobrar el pasaje** to collect fares

pasaje-ro -ra *adj* passing, fleeting; (*camino, calle*) common, traveled ‖ *mf* passenger; **pasajero colgado** straphanger; **pasajero no presentado** no-show

pasamano *m* lace trimming; (*baranda*) handrail; (naut) gangway

pasamonta-ña *m* or **pasamonta-ñas** *m* (*pl* **-ñas**) ski mask, storm hood

pasaporte *m* passport

pasar *m* livelihood ‖ *tr* to pass; to

cross; to take across; to send, transfer, transmit; (*contrabando*) to slip in; to spend; to swallow; to excel; to overlook, stand for; to undergo, suffer; (*un libro*) to go through; (*una película*) to show; to dry in the sun; to tutor; to study with or under; **pasarlo** to get along; to live; (*dícese de la salud*) to be; **pasar por alto** to disregard; to omit, leave out, skip ‖ *intr* to pass; to go; to pass away; to pass over; to happen; to last; to spread; to get along; to yield; to come in, e.g., **pase Vd.** come in; **pasar de** to go beyond, to exceed; to go above; to be more than; **pasar por** to pass by, down, through, over, etc.; to pass as, pass for; to stop or call at; **pasar sin** to do without ‖ *ref* to pass; to go; to excel; to pass over; to get along; to pass away; to take an examination; to leak; to go too far; to become overripe, become overcooked; to rot; to melt; to burn out; (*una llave, un tornillo*) to not fit, to be loose; to forget; **pasarse por** to stop or call at; **pasarse sin** to do without

pasarela *f* footbridge; catwalk, gangplank

pasatiempo *m* pastime

pascua *f* Passover; Easter; Twelfth-night; Pentecost; Christmas; **dar las pascuas** to wish a Happy New Year; **estar como una pascua** or **unas pascuas** (coll) to be bubbling over with joy; **¡Felices Pascuas!** Merry Christmas!; **Pascua de flores** Easter; **Pascua del Espíritu Santo** Pentecost; **Pascua de Navidad** Christmas; **Pascua de Resurrección** or **Pascua florida** Easter; **Pascuas navideñas** Christmas

pase *m* (*permiso; billete gratuito; movimiento de las manos del mesmerista, el torero*) pass; (*en la esgrima*) feint; **pase de cortesía** complimentary ticket

paseante *adj* strolling ‖ *mf* stroller

pasear *tr* to walk; to promenade, show off ‖ *intr* to take a walk; to go for a ride ‖ *ref* to take a walk; to go for a ride; to wander, ramble; to take it easy

pasillo *m* processional entrance of bullfighters

paseo *m* walk, stroll, promenade; ride; drive; avenue; **dar un paseo** to take a walk; to take a ride; **enviar a paseo** (coll) to send on his way, to dismiss without ceremony; **paseo de caballos** bridle path; **paseo de la cuadrilla** processional entrance of the bullfighters

pasillo *m* short step; passage, corridor; (theat) short piece, sketch

pasión *f* passion

pasi•vo -va *adj* passive; (*pensión*) retirement ‖ *m* liabilities; debit side

pasmar *tr* to chill; to frostbite; to stun, benumb; to dumbfound, astound ‖ *ref* to chill; to become frostbitten; to be astounded; to get lockjaw; (*los colores*) to become dull or flat

pasmo *m* cold; lockjaw, tetanus; astonishment; wonder, prodigy

pasmo•so -sa *adj* astounding; awesome

paso *m* step; pace; (*de la escalera*) step; gait; walk; passing; passage; step, measure, démarche; pass, permit; strait; footstep, footprint; incident, happening; (*de hélice, tornillo*) pitch; (elec) pitch; (rad) stage; (theat) short piece, sketch, skit; **al paso** in passing, on the way; **al paso que** at the rate that; (*a la vez que, mientras*) while, whereas; **ceder el paso** to make way; to keep clear; **de paso** in passing; at the same time; **paso a nivel** grade crossing; **paso de ganado** cattle crossing; **paso de ganso** goose step

paspa *f* (SAm) crack in the lips

pasquín *m* lampoon

pasquinar *tr* to lampoon

pasta *f* paste, dough, pie crust, soup paste; mash; (*para hacer papel*) pulp; cardboard; board binding; (*de un diente*) filling; (*dinero*) (coll) dough; **pasta dentífrica** tooth paste; **pasta española** marbled leather binding, tree calf; **pastas** noodles, macaroni, spaghetti, etc.; **pasta seca** cookie

pastar *tr* & *intr* to graze

pastel *m* pie; pastry roll; pastel; settlement, pacification; cheat, trick; (typ) pi; (typ) smear; (coll) plot, deal; **pastel de cumpleaños** birthday cake

pastelería *f* pastry; pastry shop

pastele•ro -ra *mf* pastry cook

pastelillo *m* tart, cake; (*de mantequilla*) pat

pasterizar §60 *tr* to pasteurize

pastilla *f* tablet, lozenge, drop; (*pequeña masa pastosa*) dab; (*de jabón, chocolate, etc.*) cake

pasto *m* pasture; grass; food, nourishment; **a pasto** to excess; in abundance; **a todo pasto** freely, without restriction; **de pasto** ordinary, everyday

pastor *m* shepherd; pastor

pastora *f* shepherdess

pastoral *adj* & *f* pastoral

pastorear *tr* (*a las ovejas o los fieles*) to shepherd; (Am) to lie in ambush for; (Am) to spoil, pamper; (Arg, Urug) to court

pasto•so -sa *adj* pasty, doughy; (*voz*) mellow; (Arg, Chile) grassy

pastura *f* pasture; fodder

pasu•do -da *adj* (Am) kinky

pata *f* paw, foot, leg; (*de un mueble*) leg; duck; **a cuatro patas** (coll) on all fours; **estirar la pata** (coll) to kick the bucket; **meter la pata** (coll) to butt in, to put one's foot in it; **pata de gallo** crow's-foot; (coll) blunder; (coll) piece of nonsense; **pata de palo** peg leg, wooden leg; **pata galana** (coll) game leg; (coll) lame person; **patas arriba** (coll) on one's back, upside down; (coll) topsy-turvy

patada *f* kick; stamp, stamping; (coll) step; (coll) footstep, track; **en dos patadas** (Am) in a jiffy

patalear *intr* to kick; to stamp the feet

pataleta *f* (coll) fit; (coll) feigned fit or convulsion; (dial) tantrum

patán *m* (coll) churl, boor, lout; (coll) peasant

pataplún *interj* kerplunk!

patata *f* potato

patear *tr* (coll) to kick; (coll) to trample on ‖ *intr* (coll) to stamp one's foot; (coll) to bustle around; (Am) to kick

patentar *tr* to patent

patente *adj* patent, clear, evident ‖ *f* grant, privilege, warrant; patent; **de patente** (Chile) excellent, first-class; **patente de circulación** owner's license; **patente de invención** patent; **patente de sanidad** bill of health

paternal *adj* paternal, fatherly

paternidad *f* paternity, fatherhood; **paternidad literaria** authorship

pater·no -na *adj* paternal

pateta *m* (coll) the devil; (coll) cripple

patéti·co -ca *adj* pathetic

patetismo *m* pathos

patíbula·rio -ria *adj* hair-raising

patíbulo *m* scaffold

patiesteva·do -da *adj* bowlegged

patilla *f* small paw or foot; pocket flap; (naut) compass; (Am) watermelon; **patillas** sideburns, side whiskers

patín *m* small patio; skate; skid, slide, runner; (*ave marina*) petrel; **patín de cuchilla** or **de hielo** ice skate; **patín de ruedas** roller skate

patinadero *m* skating rink

patina·dor -dora *mf* skater

patinaje *m* skating; skidding; **patinaje artístico** figure skating; **patinaje de fantasía** fancy skating; **patinaje de figura** figure skating

patinar *intr* to skate; to skid; to slip

patinazo *m* skid; slip; (coll) slip, blunder

patinete *m* scooter

patio *m* patio, court, yard; campus; (rr) yard, switchyard; **patio de recreo** playground

patituer·to -ta *adj* crooked-legged; (coll) crooked, lopsided

patizam·bo -ba *adj* knock-kneed

pato *m* duck, drake; **pagar el pato** (coll) to be the goat; **pato de flojel** eider duck

patochada *f* (coll) blunder, stupidity

patología *f* pathology

patota *f* (Arg, Urug) teen-age gang

patraña *f* fake, humbug, hoax

patria *f* country; mother country, fatherland, native land; birthplace; (*p.ej., de las artes*) home; **patria chica** native heath

patriarca *m* patriarch

patri·cio -cia *adj & mf* patrician

patrimonio *m* patrimony

pa·trio -tria *adj* native, home; paternal ‖ *f* see **patria**

patriota *mf* patriot

patrióti·co -ca *adj* patriotic

patriotismo *m* patriotism

patrocinar *tr* to sponsor, patronize

patrocinio *m* sponsorship

patrón *m* sponsor, protector; patron saint; patron; landlord; owner, master; boss, foreman; host; (*de un barco*) skipper; pattern; standard; **patrón oro** gold standard; **patrón picado** stencil

patrona *f* patroness; landlady; owner, mistress; hostess

patronal *adj* management, employers'

patronato *m* employers' association; foundation; board of trustees; patronage

patronear *tr* to skipper

patro·no -na *mf* sponsor, protector; employer ‖ *m* patron; landlord; boss, foreman; lord of the manor; **los patronos** the management ‖ *f* see **patrona**

patrulla *f* patrol; gang, band

patrullar *tr & intr* to patrol

paulati·no -na *adj* slow, gradual

Paulo *m* Paul

pausa *f* pause; slowness, delay; (mus) rest

pausa·do -da *adj* slow, calm, deliberate ‖ **pausado** *adv* slowly, calmly

pausar *tr & intr* to slow down

pauta *f* ruler; guide lines; guideline, rule, guide, standard, model

pava *f* turkey hen; **pelar la pava** (coll) to make love at a window

pavesa *f* ember, cinder, spark

pavimentar *tr* to pave

pavimento *m* pavement

pavo *m* turkey; turkey cock; **comer pavo** (coll) to be a wallflower; **pavo real** peacock

pavón *m* bluing; peacock

pavonar *tr* to blue

pavonear *intr & ref* to strut, swagger

pavor *m* fear, terror, dread

pavoro·so -sa *adj* frightful, dreadful

payador *m* (SAm) gaucho minstrel

payasada *f* clownishness, clownish remark

payaso *m* clown; laughingstock

paz *f* (*pl* **paces**) peace; peacefulness; **dejar en paz** to leave alone, stop pestering; **estar en paz** to be even; to be quits; **hacer las paces con** to make peace with, to come to terms with; **salir en paz** to break even

pazgua·to -ta *adj* simple, doltish ‖ *mf* simpleton, dolt

pazpuerca *f* (coll) slut, slattern

P.D. *abbr* posdata

peaje *m* toll

peatón *m* pedestrian; rural postman

pebete *m* punk, joss stick; fuse; (*cosa hedionda*) (coll) stinker

peca *f* freckle

pecado *m* sin

peca·dor -dora *adj* sinning, sinful ‖ *mf* sinner

pecamino·so -sa *adj* sinful

pecar §73 *intr* to sin; **pecar de** to be too, e.g., **pecar de confiado** to be too trusting

pecera *f* fish globe, fish bowl

pecino·so -sa *adj* slimy

pecio *m* flotsam

pecíolo *m* leafstalk

pécora *f* head of sheep; **buena pécora** or **mala pécora** (coll) schemer, scheming woman

peco·so -sa *adj* freckly, freckle-faced

peculado *m* embezzlement, peculation

peculiar *adj* peculiar

pecunia·rio -ria *adj* pecuniary

pechada *f* (Am) bump or push with the chest; (Am) tossing an animal (*with a bump of horse's chest*); (Am) bumping contest between two horsemen

pechar *tr* to pay as a tax; to fulfill; to take on; (Am) to drive one's horse against; (Am) to bump with the chest; (Am) to strike for a loan ‖ *ref* (*dos jinetes*) (Am) to vie in a bumping contest

pechera *f* shirt front, shirt bosom; chest protector; (*del delantal*) bib; breast strap; (coll) bosom; **pechera postiza** dickey

pecho *m* chest; breast, bosom; heart, courage; **dar el pecho** to nurse, to suckle; (coll) to face it out; **de dos pechos** double-breasted; **de un solo pecho** single-breasted; **echar el pecho al agua** (coll) to put one's shoulder to the wheel; (coll) to speak out; **en pechos de camisa** (Am) in shirt sleeves; **tomar a pecho** to take to heart; **¡pecho al agua!** take heart!, put your shoulder to the wheel!

pechuga *f* (*del ave*) breast; (coll) breast, bosom; (coll) slope, hill; (Am) brass, cheek; (Am) treachery, perfidy

pechu·gón -gona *adj* (coll) big-chested; (Am) brazen ‖ *mf* (Am) sponger ‖ *m* slap or blow on the chest; fall on the chest

pedagogía *f* pedagogy

pedal *m* pedal, treadle

pedalear *intr* to pedal

pedante *adj* pedantic ‖ *mf* pedant

pedantería *f* pedantry

pedantes·co -ca *adj* pedantic

pedantismo *m* pedantry

pedazo *m* piece; **hacer pedazos** (coll) to break to pieces; **hacerse pedazos** (coll) to fall to pieces; (coll) to strain, to wear oneself out; **pedazo de alcornoque, de animal or de bruto** (coll) dolt, imbecile, good-for-nothing; **pedazo del alma, de las entrañas** or **del corazón** (*niño*) (coll) darling, apple of one's eye; **pedazo de pan** (*pequeña cantidad*) crumb; (*precio bajo*) (coll) song

pedernal *m* flint; flintiness; flint-hearted person

pedestal *m* pedestal

pedestre *adj* pedestrian

pedestrismo *m* pedestrianism; walking; foot racing; cross-country racing

pediatría *f* pediatrics

pedido *m* request; (*encargo de mercancías*) order

pedigüe·ño -ña *adj* insistent, demanding, bothersome

pedir §50 *tr* to ask, to ask for; to request; to demand, require; to need; to ask for the hand of; (*mercancías*) to order; (gram) to govern; **pedir prestado a** to borrow from ‖ *intr* to ask; to beg; to bring suit; **a pedir de boca** opportunely; as desired

pedorre·ro -ra *adj* flatulent ‖ *f* flatulence; (orn) tody; **pedorreras** tights

pedrada *f* stoning; hit or blow with a stone; (coll) hint, taunt

pedregal *m* rocky ground; pile of rocks

pedrego·so -sa *adj* stony, rocky; suffering from gallstones ‖ *mf* sufferer from gallstones

pedrejón *m* boulder

pedrera *f* quarry, stone quarry

pedrería *f* precious stones, jewelry

Pedro *m* Peter

pedrusco *m* boulder

pedúnculo *m* stem, stalk

peer §43 *intr* & *ref* to break wind

pega *f* sticking; pitch varnish; drubbing; (*en un examen*) catch question; (coll) trick, joke; (W-I) work, jobs; **de pega** (coll) fake

pegadi·zo -za *adj* sticky; catching, contagious; sponging; fake, imitation

pegajo·so -sa *adj* sticky; contagious; tempting; (coll) soft, gentle; (coll) mushy

pegar §44 *tr* to stick, to paste; to fasten, attach, tie; (*carteles*) to post; (*fuego*) to set; (*una enfermedad*) to transmit; (*un botón*) to sew on; (*un grito*) to let out; (*un salto*) to take; (*un golpe, una bofetada*) to let go; to beat; **no pegar el ojo** to not sleep a wink ‖ *intr* to stick, to catch; to take root, take hold; to cling; to join; to fit, to match; to be fitting; to pass, be accepted; to beat; to knock ‖ *ref* to stick, to catch; to take root, take hold; to hang on, stick around; (*una enfermedad*) to be catching; **pegársela a uno** (coll) to make a fool of someone

pegotear *intr* (coll) to hang around, to sponge

peina·do -da *adj* groomed; effeminate ‖ *m* hairdo, coiffure; (*manera de componer el pelo*) hairstyle; **peinado al agua** finger wave

peina·dor -dora *mf* hairdresser ‖ *m* wrapper, dressing gown

peinar *tr* to comb ‖ *ref* to comb oneself, comb one's hair

peine *m* comb; (coll) sly fellow

peineta *f* back comb

pelada *f* pelt, sheepskin

peladilla *f* sugar almond; small pebble

peladillo *m* clingstone peach

pela·do -da *adj* bare; bald; barren; penniless; (*decena, centena, etc.*) even ‖ *m* raggedy fellow; (W-I) haircut ‖ *f* see **pelada**

pelafus·tán -tana *mf* (coll) derelict, good-for-nothing

pelaga·tos *m* (*pl* -tos) (coll) wretch, ragamuffin

pelaje *m* coat, fur; (*especie, calidad*) (coll) sort, stripe

pelar *tr* (*pelo*) to cut; (*pelo, plumas*) to pluck, pull out; to peel, skin, husk, hull, shell; (*los dientes*) to show; (*en el juego*) (coll) to clean out; (Am) to beat, thrash ‖ *ref* to peel off; to lose one's hair; to get a haircut; (Am) to clear out, make a getaway; **pelárselas por** (coll) to crave; (coll) to crave to

peldaño *m* step

pelea *f* fight; quarrel; struggle; **pelea de gallos** cockfight

pelear *intr* to fight; to quarrel; to struggle || *ref* to fight, fight each other

pele·ón -ona *adj* (coll) pugnacious, quarrelsome; (*vino*) (coll) cheap, ordinary || *mf* (coll) quarrelsome person || *m* (coll) cheap wine || *f* row, scuffle, fracas

peletería *f* furriery; fur shop; (Cuba) shoe store

pelete·ro -ra *mf* furrier; (Cuba) shoe dealer

peliagu·do -da *adj* furry, long-haired; (coll) arduous, ticklish

película *f* film; motion picture; **película de dibujos** animated cartoon; **película del Oeste** western; **película sonora** sound film

pelicule·ro -ra *adj* moving-picture || *mf* scenario writer || *m* movie actor || *f* movie actress

peligrar *intr* to be in danger

peligro *m* danger, peril, risk; **ponerse en peligro de paz** to be alerted for war

peligro·so -sa *adj* dangerous

pelillo *m* (coll) trifle; **echar pelillos a la mar** (coll) to bury the hatchet; **no pararse en pelillos** (coll) to not bother about trifles, to pay no attention to small matters; **no tener pelillos en la lengua** (coll) to speak right out

pelirro·jo -ja *adj* red-haired, redheaded || *mf* redhead

pelo *m* hair; (*en las frutas y el cuerpo humano*) down; (*del paño*) nap; (*de la madera*) grain; (*de un animal*) coat; (*en las piedras preciosas*) flaw; (*del caballo*) color; (*en el billar*) kiss; (*del reloj*) hairspring; hair trigger; fiber, filament; raw silk; **al pelo** with the hair, with the nap; (coll) perfectly, to the point; **con todos sus pelos y señales** chapter and verse; **en pelo** bareback; **escapar por un pelo** to escape by a hairbreadth, to have a narrow escape; **no tener pelos en la lengua** (coll) to be outspoken, to not mince words; **ponerle a uno los pelos de punta** to make one's hair stand on end; **tomar el pelo a** (coll) to make fun of, make a fool of; **venir a pelo** to come in handy

pe·lón -lona *adj* bald, hairless; (coll) dull, stupid; (coll) penniless

Pélope *m* Pelops

peloponense *adj* & *mf* Peloponnesian

Peloponeso *m* Peloponnesus

pelo·so -sa *adj* hairy

pelota *f* ball; ball game; handball; **en pelota** stripped; stark-naked; **pelota acuática** water polo; **pelota rodada** (baseball) grounder; **pelota vasca** pelota, jai alai

pelotari *mf* pelota player

pelotear *intr* to knock a ball around; to wrangle, to argue

pelotera *f* (coll) row, brawl

pelotón *m* large ball; gang; crowd; platoon; **pelotón de fusilamiento** firing squad; **pelotón de los torpes** awkward squad

peltre *m* pewter

peluca *f* wig

pelu·do -da *adj* hairy, furry; bushy

peluquería *f* hairdresser's, barbershop

peluque·ro -ra *mf* hairdresser, barber; wigmaker

pelusa *f* down; lint, fuzz; nap; (coll) jealousy, envy

pellejo *m* skin; pelt, rawhide; peel, rind; wineskin; (*la vida de uno*) (coll) hide, skin; (coll) sot, drunkard; **dar, dejar or perder el pellejo** (coll) to die

pellizcar §73 to pinch; to nip; to take a pinch of || *ref* (coll) to long, to pine

pellizco *m* pinch; nip; bit, pinch

pena *f* punishment; penalty; pain, hardship, toil; sorrow, grief; effort, trouble; **a duras penas** hardly, with great difficulty; **de pena** of a broken heart; **¡qué pena!** what a pity!; **so pena de** on pain of, under penalty of; **valer la pena** to be worth while (to)

penacho *m* crest; tuft, plume; arrogance; (bot) tassel

pena·do -da *adj* afflicted, grieved; difficult || *mf* convict

penalidad *f* trouble, hardship; (law) penalty

penar *tr* to penalize; to punish || *intr* to suffer; to linger; **penar por** to pine for, long for || *ref* to grieve

penca *f* pulpy leaf; cowhide; **coger una penca** (Am) to get a jag on

penco *m* nag, jade; (Am) boor

pendejo *m* pubes; (coll) coward

pendencia *f* dispute, quarrel, fight; pending litigation

pendencie·ro -ra *adj* quarrelsome || *mf* wrangler

pender *intr* to hang, dangle; to depend; to be pending

pendiente *adj* pendent, hanging, dangling; pending; under way; expecting; **estar pendiente de** (*las palabras de una persona*) to hang on; to depend on; to be in the process of || *m* earring, pendant; watch chain || *f* slope, grade; dip, pitch

péndola *f* feather; pendulum; clock; pen, quill; queen post

pendolón *m* king post

pendón *m* banner, standard, pennon

péndulo *m* pendulum; clock

penetrar *tr* to penetrate; to pierce; to grasp, fathom || *intr* to penetrate || *ref* to grasp, fathom; to realize; to become convinced

penicilina *f* penicillin

península *f* peninsula

peninsular *adj* & *mf* peninsular; (íbero) Peninsular

penique *m* penny

penitencia *f* penitence; penance; **hacer penitencia** to do penance; to eat sparingly; to take potluck

penitente *adj* & *mf* penitent

penol *m* (naut) yardarm

peno·so -sa *adj* arduous, difficult; suffering; (coll) conceited; (Am) shy

pensa·dor -dora *adj* thinking ‖ *mf* thinker

pensamiento *m* thought; (*planta y flor*) pansy

pensar §2 *tr* to think; to think over; (*un naipe, un número, etc.*) to think of; to intend to; **pensar de** to think of, e.g., **¿qué piensa Vd. de este libro?** what do you think of this book? ‖ *intr* to think; **pensar en** (*dirigir sus pensamientos a*) to think of (*to turn one's thoughts to*)

pensati·vo -va *adj* pensive, thoughtful

pensión *f* pension; annuity; allowance; boardinghouse; (*para ampliar estudios*) fellowship; **pensión completa** board and lodging

pensionar *tr* to pension

pensionista *mf* pensioner; boarder; boarding-school pupil; **medio pensionista** day boarder

pentagrama *m* staff, musical staff

Pentecostés, el Pentecost

penúlti·mo -ma *adj* penultimate; next to last ‖ *f* penult

penumbra *f* penumbra; semidarkness, half-light

penuria *f* shortage

peña *f* rock, boulder; cliff; club, group, circle

peñasco *m* pinnacle; crag

peñasco·so -sa *adj* rocky, craggy

peñón *m* rock, spire; **peñón de Gibraltar** rock of Gibraltar

peón *m* laborer; pedestrian; foot soldier; (*en el ajedrez*) pawn; (*en las damas*) man; top, peg top; spindle, axle; (*taur*) attendant; (*Am*) farm hand; **peón de albañil** or **de mano** hod carrier

peor *adj & adv* worse; worst

pepa *f* (*de la manzana*) (Col) seed; (*del durazno*) (Arg) stone; (*canica*) (Arg) marble; (Col) lie, cheat, trick

Pepe *m* Joe

pepinillo *m* gherkin

pepino *m* cucumber

pepita *f* seed, pip; nugget; (*vet*) pip

peque *m* tot

pequén *m* (Chile) burrowing owl

pequeñez *f* (*pl* **-ñeces**) smallness; infancy; trifle

peque·ño -ña *adj* little, small; young; low, humble

Pequín *m* Peking

pequi·nés -nesa *adj & mf* Pekinese

pera *f* pear; goatee; cinch, sinecure; pear-shaped bulb; pear-shaped switch

peral *m* pear tree

perca *f* (*ichth*) perch

percance *m* mischance, misfortune; **percances** perquisites

percatar *ref* — **percatarse de** to be aware of; to beware of, guard against

percebe *m* barnacle; (coll) fool, sap

percepción *f* perception; collection

percibir *tr* to perceive; to collect

percudir *tr* to tarnish, to dull; to spread through

percha *f* perch, pole, roost; clothes tree; coat hanger; coat hook; barber pole

perchero *m* rack, clothes rack, clothes hanger

perde·dor -dora *adj* losing ‖ *mf* loser

perder §51 *tr* to lose; to waste, squander; (*un tren, una ocasión*) to miss; (*una asignatura*) to flunk; to ruin; to spoil ‖ *intr* to lose; to fade ‖ *ref* to get lost; to miscarry; to sink; to become ruined; to spoil; to go to the dogs

perdición *f* perdition; loss; outrage; ruination

pérdida *f* loss; waste; ruination; **no tener pérdida** (coll) to be easy to find

perdi·do -da *adj* (*bala*) stray, wild; (*manga*) wide, loose; fruitless; (*horas*) off, spare, idle; distracted; inveterate; madly in love ‖ *m* profligate, rake

perdido·so -sa *adj* unlucky; easily lost

perdigón *m* young partridge; (coll) profligate; (coll) heavy loser; (*alumno*) (coll) failure; **perdigones** (*granos de plomo*) shot; **perdigón zorrero** buckshot

per·diz *f* (*pl* **-dices**) partridge

perdón *m* pardon, forgiveness; **con perdón** by your leave

perdonable *adj* pardonable

perdonar *tr* to pardon, forgive, excuse; **no perdonar** to not miss, to not omit

perdula·rio -ria *adj* careless, sloppy; incorrigible, vicious ‖ *mf* good-for-nothing, profligate

perdurable *adj* long-lasting; everlasting

perdurar *intr* to last, last a long time, survive

perecede·ro -ra *adj* perishable; mortal ‖ *m* (coll) extreme want

perecer §22 *intr* to perish; to suffer; to be in great want ‖ *ref* to pine; **perecerse por** to be dying for; (*una mujer*) to be mad about

peregrinación *f* peregrination; pilgrimage

peregri·no -na *adj* wandering, traveling; foreign; rare, strange; beautiful; mortal; (*ave*) migratory ‖ *mf* pilgrim

perejil *m* parsley; (coll) frippery

perenne *adj* perennial

pereza *f* laziness; slowness

perezo·so -sa *adj* lazy; slow, dull, heavy ‖ *mf* lazybones; sleepyhead ‖ *m* (zool) sloth

perfección *f* perfection

perfeccionar *tr* to perfect, to improve

perfec·to -ta *adj & m* perfect

perfidia *f* perfidy

pérfi·do -da *adj* perfidious

perfil *m* profile; side view; cross section; thin stroke; outline, sketch; **perfil aerodinámico** streamlining; **perfiles** finishing touches; courtesies

perfila·do -da *adj* (*cara*) long and thin; (*nariz*) well-formed; (*facciones*) delicate; streamlined

perfilar *tr* to profile, outline; to perfect, polish, finish ‖ *ref* to be outlined; to show one's profile, to stand sidewise; to stand out; (coll) to dress up

perfora·dor -dora *adj* perforating; drilling ‖ *f* pneumatic drill, rock drill

perforar *tr* to perforate; to drill, to bore; to puncture; (*una tarjeta*) to punch

perfumar *tr* to perfume

perfume *m* perfume

pergamino *m* parchment

pericia *f* skill, expertness

periclitar *intr* to be in jeopardy, to be shaky

perico *m* (*pelo postizo*) periwig; parakeet; (slang) chamber pot; **perico entre ellas** (coll) lady's man

periferia *f* periphery; surroundings

perifollos *mpl* finery, frippery, chiffons

perilla *f* pear-shaped ornament; goatee; knob, doorknob; (*del arzón*) pommel; (*de la oreja*) lobe; **de perilla** (coll) apropos, to the point

periodísti·co -ca *adj* newspaper, journalistic

periódi·co -ca *adj* periodic ‖ *m* newspaper; periodical

periodismo *m* journalism

periodista *mf* journalist ‖ *m* newspaperman ‖ *f* newspaperwoman

período *m* period; compound sentence; (phys) cycle; **período lectivo** (*en la escuela*) term

peripues·to -ta *adj* (coll) dudish, all spruced up, sporty

periquete *m* (coll) jiffy; **en un periquete** (coll) in a jiffy

periquito *m* parakeet; **periquito de Australia** budgerigar

periscopio *m* periscope

peri·to -ta *adj* skilled, skillful; expert ‖ *m* expert

perjudicar §73 *tr* to damage, impair, hurt, prejudice

perjudicial *adj* harmful, injurious, detrimental, prejudicial

perjuicio *m* harm, injury, damage, prejudice; **en perjuicio de** to the detriment of

perjurar *intr* to commit perjury; to swear, be profane ‖ *ref* to commit perjury; to perjure oneself

perjurio *m* perjury

perla *f* pearl; **de perlas** perfectly

perlesía *f* palsy

permanecer §22 *intr* to stay, to remain

permanencia *f* permanence; stay, sojourn

permanente *adj* permanent ‖ *f* permanent wave

permiso *m* permission; permit; time off; (*en el monedaje*) tolerance; leave; **con permiso** excuse me; **permiso de circulación** owner's license; **permiso de conducir** driver's license

permitir *tr* to permit, to allow ‖ *ref* to be permitted; **no se permite fumar** no smoking

permutar *tr* to interchange; to barter; to permute

pernear *intr* to kick; (coll) to hustle; (coll) to fuss, fret

pernera *f* trouser leg

pernicio·so -sa *adj* pernicious

pernil *m* trouser leg; (*anca y muslo*) ham

perno *m* bolt; **perno con anillo** ringbolt; **perno roscado** screw bolt

pernoctar *intr* to spend the night

pero *conj* but, yet ‖ *m* (coll) but; (coll) fault, defect; **poner pero a** (coll) to find fault with

perogrullada *f* (coll) platitude, inanity

peroración *f* peroration; (coll) harangue

perorar *intr* to perorate; (coll) to orate

peróxido *m* peroxide; **peróxido de hidrógeno** hydrogen peroxide

perpendicular *adj* & *f* perpendicular

perpetrar *tr* to perpetrate

perpetuar §21 *tr* to perpetuate

perpe·tuo -tua *adj* perpetual; life

perplejidad *f* perplexity; worry, anxiety

perple·jo -ja *adj* perplexed; worried, anxious; baffling, perplexing

perra *f* bitch; tantrum; drunkenness

perrada *f* pack of dogs; (coll) dirty trick

perrera *f* kennel, doghouse; tantrum; toil, drudgery

perro *m* dog; **el perro del hortelano** dog in the manger; **perro caliente** (slang) hot dog; **perro cobrador** retriever; **perro de aguas** spaniel; **perro de lanas** poodle; **perro de muestra** pointer; **perro faldero** lap dog; **perro marino** dogfish, shark; **perro raposero** foxhound; **perro viejo** (coll) wise old owl

perro-lazarillo *m* (*pl* **perros-lazarillos**) Seeing Eye dog

persa *adj* & *mf* Persian

persecución *f* persecution; pursuit; annoyance, harassment

perseguir §67 *tr* to persecute; to pursue; to annoy, harass

perseverar *intr* to persevere

persiana *f* slatted shutter; flowered silk; louver; Venetian blind; **persiana del radiador** (aut) louver

persistir *intr* to persist

persona *f* person; personage; **persona desplazada** displaced person; **personas** people; **por persona** per capita

personaje *m* personage; (theat) character; person of importance

personal *adj* personal ‖ *m* personnel, staff, force

personalidad *f* personality

personificar §73 *tr* to personify

perspectiva *f* perspective; outlook, prospect; appearance

perspi·caz *adj* (*pl* **-caces**) perspicacious, discerning; keen-sighted

persuadir *tr* to persuade

persuasión *f* persuasion

pertenecer §22 *intr* to belong; to pertain ‖ *ref* to be independent, be free

perteneciente *adj* pertaining

pértiga *f* pole, rod, staff

perti·naz *adj* (*pl* **-naces**) pertinacious; (*dolor de cabeza*) persistent

pertinente *adj* pertinent, relevant

pertrechos *mpl* supplies, provisions, equipment; tools; **pertrechos de guerra** ordnance

perturbar *tr* to perturb; to disturb; to upset, disconcert; to confuse, interrupt

Perú, el Peru

perua·no -na *adj* & *mf* Peruvian

perversidad *f* perversity

perversión f perversion

perver·so -sa adj perverse; wicked, depraved || mf profligate

perverti·do -da mf pervert

pervertir §68 tr to pervert || ref to become perverted; to go to the bad

pesa f weight

pesacar·tas m (pl -tas) letter scales

pesadez f heaviness; slowness; tiresomeness; harshness; (phys) gravity

pesadilla f nightmare

pesa·do -da adj heavy; slow; tiresome; harsh; boring

pesadumbre f sorrow, grief; trouble; weight, heaviness

pesaje m weighing; (sport) weigh-in

pésame m condolence; **dar el pésame a** to extend one's sympathy to

pesantez f (phys) gravity

pesar m sorrow, regret; **a pesar de** in spite of || tr to weigh; to make sorry || intr to weigh; to be heavy; to cause regret, cause sorrow

pesaro·so -sa adj sorrowful, regretful

pesca f fishing; catch; **ir de pesca** to go fishing; **pesca de bajura** off-shore fishing; **pesca de gran altura** deep-sea fishing

pescadería f fish market; fish store; fish stand

pescade·ro -ra mf fish dealer, fishmonger

pescado m fish (that has been caught)

pesca·dor -dora adj fishing || m fisherman || f fisherwoman, fishwife

pescante m coach box; (de una grúa) jib; (aut) front seat; (naut) davit; (theat) trap door

pescar §73 tr to fish; to fish for; to fish out; (peces) to catch; (coll) to manage to get || intr to fish

pescozón m slap on the neck or head

pescuezo m neck

pesebre m crib, rack, manger; (Am) crèche

pesimismo m pessimism

pesimista adj pessimistic || mf pessimist

pési·mo -ma adj very bad, abominable

peso m weight; scale, balance; burden, load; judgment, good sense; (unidad monetaria) (Am) peso; **caerse de su peso** to be self-evident; **llevar el peso de la batalla** to bear the brunt of the battle

pespuntar tr & intr to backstitch

pespunte m backstitch

pesquera f fishery; fishing grounds; (presa para detener los peces) weir

pesquería f fishing; fishery

pesque·ro -ra adj fishing || m fishing boat || f see **pesquera**

pesquis m acumen, keenness

pesquisa m (Arg) detective || f inquiry, investigation

pesquisar tr to investigate, inquire into

pestaña f eyelash; flange; fringe, edging; index tab

pestañear intr to wink, blink; **sin pestañear** without batting an eye

peste f pest, plague; epidemic; stink, stench; (coll) abundance; (Col, Peru) head cold; (Chile) smallpox; **pestes** (coll) insults

pesticida m pesticide

pestífe·ro -ra adj pestiferous; stinking

pestilencia f pestilence

pestillo m bolt; doorlatch

petaca f cigar case; cigarette case; tobacco pouch; leather-covered hamper

pétalo m petal

petardear tr to swindle || intr (aut) to backfire

petardeo m swindling; (aut) backfire

petardo m petard; bomb; swindle, cheat

petate m sleeping bag; bedding; (coll) luggage; (coll) cheat; (coll) poor soul; **liar el petate** (coll) to pack up and get out; (coll) to kick the bucket

petición f petition; request; plea; (law) claim, bill; **a petición de** at the request of; **petición de mano** formal betrothal

petimetre m dude, sport, dandy

petirrojo m redbreast, robin

Petrarca m Petrarch

petrificar §73 tr & ref to petrify

petróleo m petroleum; **petróleo combustible** fuel oil

petrole·ro -ra adj oil, petroleum || mf oil dealer || m oil tanker

petulancia f flippancy, pertness

petulante adj flippant, pert

pez m (pl **peces**) fish; (coll) reward, just desert; **como un pez en el agua** (coll) snug as bug in a rug; **pez de plata** (ent) silverfish **salga pez o salga rana** (coll) blindly, hit or miss || f pitch, tar

pezón m stem; nipple, teat

pezonera f linchpin

pezuña f hoof

piado·so -sa adj merciful; pitiful; pious

piafar intr (el caballo) to paw, to stamp

piano m piano; **piano de cola** grand piano; **piano de media cola** baby grand

piar §77 intr to peep, to chirp

pica f pike; pikeman; picador's goad; (Col) pique, resentment

picada f peck; bite; (Bol) knock at the door; (Arg, Bol, Urug) narrow ford; (SAm) path, trail

picadillo m (carne, verduras, ajos, etc. reducidos a pequeños trozos) hash; (carne picada) mincemeat

pica·do -da adj perforated; pitted; (tabaco) cut; (hielo) cracked; (mar) choppy; piqued || m mincemeat; (aer) dive; **picado con motor** (aer) power dive || f see **picada**

picador m horsebreaker; (torero de a caballo) picador (mounted bullfighter); chopping block

picadura f bite, prick, sting; nick; puncture; cut tobacco; (en un diente) cavity

picaflor m hummingbird

picahie·los m (pl -los) ice pick

picamade·ros m (pl -ros) green woodpecker

picante adj biting, pricking, stinging; piquant, juicy, racy; (SAm) highly seasoned || m mordancy; piquancy

picapedrero m stonecutter

picaplei·tos m (pl -tos) (coll) troublemaker; (coll) shyster, pettifogger

picaporte *m* latch; latchkey; door knocker

picar §73 *tr* to prick, pierce, puncture; to sting; to bite; to burn; to peck; to nibble; to pit, to pock; to mince, chop up, cut up; to stick, poke; to spur; to goad; to perforate; (*hielo*) to crack; to harass, pursue; to tame; to pique, annoy || *intr* to itch; (*el sol*) to burn; to nibble; to have a smattering; to be catching; (*los negocios*) to pick up; (aer) to dive; (*caer en el lazo*) (coll) to bite; **picar en** to nibble at; to dabble in; **picar muy alto** (coll) to aim high, expect too much || *ref* to rot; (*la ropa*) to be moth-eaten; (*el vino*) to turn sour; (*un diente*) to be decayed; (*el mar*) to get rough; to be offended; (Am) to get drunk; **picarse de** to boast of being

picardía *f* roguishness, knavery; crudeness, coarseness; mischief

picares·co -ca *adj* roguish, rascally; picaresque; rough, coarse, crude; (coll) witty, humorous, gay

píca·ro -ra *adj* roguish; scheming, tricky; low, vile; mischievous || *mf* rogue; schemer

picaza *f* magpie

picazón *f* itch, itching; (coll) annoyance

picea *f* spruce tree

pick-up *m* pickup; phonograph

pico *m* beak, bill; (*de jarra*) spout; (*del yunque*) beak; (*del pañuelo*) corner; nib, tip; (*de la pluma de escribir*) point; peak; (*herramienta*) pick; (*de dinero*) pile, lot; talkativeness; (elec) peak; (naut) bow, prow; **callar el pico** (coll) to shut up; **darse el pico** (*las palomas*) to bill; **pico de oro** silver-tongue; **tener mucho pico** (coll) to talk too much; **y pico** odd, e.g., trescientos y pico three hundred odd; a little after, e.g., **a las tres y pico** a little after three o'clock

picor *m* (*del paladar*) smarting, itch, itching, burning

pico·so -sa *adj* pock-marked

picota *f* pillory; peak, point, spire

picotazo *m* peck

picotear *tr* to peck || *intr* (*el caballo*) to toss the head; (coll) to chatter, jabber, gab; (*las mujeres*) (coll) to wrangle

pichel *m* pewter tankard

pi·chón -chona *mf* (coll) darling || *m* young pigeon; **pichón de barro** clay pigeon

pie *m* foot; footing; foothold; base, stand; (*de copa*) stem; (*de la cama*) footboard; cause, origin, reason; (*de la página*) foot, bottom; (theat) cue; (Chile) down payment; **a cuatro pies** on all fours; **al pie de fábrica** (coll) at the factory; **al pie de la letra** literally; **al pie de la obra** (com) delivered; **a pie** on foot, walking; **buscar cisco** (or **tres**) **pies al gato** (coll) to be looking for trouble; **de pie** standing; up and about; firm, steady; firmly, steadily; **en pie de guerra** on a war footing; **ir a pie** to go on foot, to walk; **morir al pie del cañón** to

die in the harness, to die with one's boots on; **nacer de pie** or **de pies** to be born with a silver spoon in one's mouth; **pie de atleta** athlete's foot; **pie de cabra** crowbar; **pie de imprenta** imprint, printer's mark; **pie derecho** upright, stanchion; **pie marino** sea legs; **pie quebrado** (*de verso*) short line; **vestirse por los pies** (coll) to be a man

piedad *f* (*devoción a las cosas santas*) piety; (*misericordia*) pity, mercy

piedra *f* stone; rock; (*pedernal*) flint; heavy hailstone; (pathol) stone; **piedra angular** cornerstone; (fig) cornerstone, keystone; **piedra arenisca** sandstone; **piedra azul** (chem) bluestone; **piedra de albardilla** copestone; **piedra de amolar** grindstone; **piedra de chispa** flint; **piedra de pipas** meerschaum; **piedra imán** loadstone; **piedra miliar** or **miliaria** milestone; **piedra movediza** rolling stone; **piedra pómez** pumice, pumice stone

piel *f* skin; hide, pelt; fur; leather; (*de las frutas*) peel, skin; **piel de cabra** goatskin; **piel de foca** sealskin; **piel de gallina** goose flesh; **piel roja** *m* (*pl* **pieles rojas**) (*indio norteamericano*) redskin

pienso *m* feed, feeding; **ni por pienso** by no means, don't think of it

pierna *f* leg; post, upright; **dormir a pierna suelta** or **tendida** (coll) to sleep like a log; **estirar la pierna** (coll) to lie down on the job; (coll) to kick the bucket; **estirar** or **extender las piernas** (coll) to stretch one's legs, go for a walk; **ser buena pierna** (Arg, Urug) to be a good-natured fellow

pieza *f* (*órgano de una máquina o artefacto; obra dramática; composición suelta de música; cañón; figura que sirve para jugar a las damas, al ajedrez, etc.; moneda*) piece; (*objeto; mueble; porción de tela*) piece or article; (*habitación, cuarto*) room; **buena pieza** hussy; sly fox; **pieza de recambio** or **de repuesto** spare part; **quedarse en una pieza** or **hecho una pieza** to be dumbfounded, to stand motionless

pífano *m* fife; fifer

pifia *f* (billiards) miscue; (coll) miscue, slip

pifiar *intr* to miscue

pigmentar *tr* & *ref* to pigment

pigmento *m* pigment

pigme·o -a *adj* & *mf* pygmy

pijama *m* pajamas

pila *f* basin; trough; sink; font; pile, heap; (elec) battery, cell; (elec & phys) pile; **pila de linterna** flashlight battery

pilar *m* (*de una fuente*) basin, bowl; pillar; stone post, milestone; (*persona*) (fig) pillar || *tr* (*el grano*) to crush, to pound

Pilatos *m* Pilate

píldora *f* pill; (coll) bad news; **píldora para dormir** sleeping pill

pileta *f* sink; basin, bowl; font; swimming pool

pilón *m* pylon; drinking trough; loaf of sugar; counterpoise; drop hammer

pilotar *tr* to pilot

pilote *m* pile

piloto *m* pilot; first mate; (Chile) hail fellow well met

pillar *tr* to pillage, plunder; to catch

pi·llo -lla *adj* (coll) roguish, rascally; (coll) sly, crafty || *m* (coll) rogue, rascal; (coll) crafty fellow

pilluelo *m* (coll) scamp, little scamp

pimentero *m* pepper, black pepper; pepperbox

pimentón *m* cayenne pepper, red pepper; (*condimento preparado moliendo pimientos encarnados secos*) paprika

pimienta *f* pepper, black pepper; allspice, pimento; allspice tree

pimiento *m* (*planta*) pepper, black pepper; Guinea pepper

pimpante *adj* smart, spruce

pimpollo *m* sucker, shoot, sprout; rosebud; (*árbol nuevo*) sapling; (coll) handsome child; (coll) handsome young person

pina *f* felloe

pinacoteca *f* picture gallery

pináculo *m* pinnacle

pincel *m* brush; painter; painting; (*de luz*) pencil, beam

pincelada *f* brush stroke; touch, finish, flourish

pincelar *tr* to paint; to picture; (med) to pencil

pincia·no -na *adj* Valladolid || *mf* native or inhabitant of Valladolid

pincha *f* kitchenmaid

pinchar *tr* to prick, jab, pierce, puncture; to stir up, prod, provoke || *intr* to have a puncture; **no pinchar ni cortar** to have no say

pinchazo *m* prick, jab, puncture; provocation; **a prueba de pinchazos** puncture-proof

pinche *m* scullion, kitchen boy; helper

pincho *m* thorn, prick; snack; spike

Píndaro *m* Pindar

pingajo *m* (coll) rag, tatter

pingo *m* (coll) rag, tatter; (coll) ragamuffin; (coll) horse; **andar** or **ir de pingo** (*una mujer*) (coll) to gad about

pingüe *adj* oily, greasy, fat; abundant, rich; fertile; profitable

pingüino *m* penguin

pinito *m* first step, little step; **hacer pinitos** to begin to walk; (fig) to take the first steps

pino *m* pine tree; first step; **hacer pinos** to begin to walk; (fig) to take the first steps

pinocha *f* pine needle

pinta *m* (coll) scoundrel || *f* spot, mark, sign; dot; pint

pintacilgo *m* goldfinch

pintada *f* Guinea hen

pinta·do -da *adj* spotted, mottled; tipsy; accented; **el más pintado** (coll) the aptest one; (coll) the shrewdest one; (coll) the best one; **venir como pintado** to be just the thing || *m* (*acto de pintar*) painting || *f* see **pintada**

pintar *tr* to paint; (*una letra, un acento,*

etc.) to draw; to picture, depict; to put an accent mark on; **pintarla** (coll) to put it on, to put on airs || *intr* to paint; to begin to turn red, begin to ripen; (coll) to show, to turn out || *ref* to paint, put on make-up; to begin to turn red, begin to ripen

pintarrajear *tr* to daub, to smear

pin·to -ta *adj* (Am) speckled, spotted || *f* see **pinta**

pin·tor -tora *mf* painter; **pintor de brocha gorda** painter, house painter; (coll) dauber

pintores·co -ca *adj* picturesque

pintura *f* (*color preparado para pintar*) paint; (*arte; obra pintada*) painting; **hacer pinturas** (coll) to prance; **no poder ver ni en pintura** to not be able to stand the sight of

pinture·ro -ra *adj* (coll) showy, conceited || *mf* (coll) show-off

pinza *f* clothespin; (*de langosta, cangrejo, etc.*) claw; **pinzas** pliers; pincers; tweezers; forceps

pinzón *m* pump handle; (orn) finch

piña *f* fir cone, pine cone; knob; plug; cluster, knot; pineapple

piñonear *intr* (*un arma de fuego*) to click; (coll) to reach the age of puberty; (coll) to be an old goat

piñoneo *m* click (*of a firearm*)

pi·o -a *adj* pious; merciful, compassionate; (*caballo*) pied, dappled || *m* peeping, chirping; (coll) keen desire

piocha *f* jeweled head adornment; artificial flower made of feathers; pick

piojo *m* louse

piojo·so -sa *adj* lousy; mean, stingy

pione·ro -ra *adj & mf* pioneer

pipa *f* (*para fumar tabaco*) pipe; (*medida para vinos*) butt; wine cask; (*simiente*) pip; (mus) pipe, reed; **pipa de espuma de mar** meerschaum pipe; **pipa de riego** watering cart; **pipa de tierra** clay pipe

pique *m* pique, resentment; eagerness; (*insecto*) chigger; (*naipe*) spade; **a pique** steep; **a pique de** in danger of; on the verge of; **echar a pique** to sink; to ruin; **irse a pique** to sink; to go to ruin, be ruined

piquera *f* bung, bunghole; (Mex) dive, joint

piquete *m* sharp jab; small hole; stake, picket; (*de soldados, de huelguistas*) picket; **piquete de ejecución** firing squad; **piquete de salvas** firing squad

pira *f* pyre

piragua *f* pirogue; (sport) single shell

piragüista *m* (sport) crewman

pirámide *f* pyramid

pirata *m* pirate

piratear *intr* to pirate, be a pirate

pirca *f* (SAm) dry stone wall

pirco *m* (Chile) succotash

Pireo, el Piraeus

pirine·o -a *adj* Pyrenean || **Pirineos** *mpl* Pyrenees

pirita *f* pyrites

pirófa·go -ga *adj* fire-eating || *mf* fire-eater

piropear *tr* (coll) to flatter, flirt with

piropo *m* garnet, carbuncle; (coll) flattery, compliment, flirtatious remark

piróscafo *m* steamship

pirotecnia *f* pyrotechnics

pirotécni•co -ca *adj* pyrotechnical ‖ *m* powder maker, fireworks manufacturer

pirueta *f* pirouette; somersault; caper

piruetear *intr* to pirouette

pisada *f* tread; footstep; footprint; trampling

pisapape•les *m* (*pl* **-les**) paperweight

pisar *tr* to trample, tread on, step on; to tamp, pack down; (*p.ej.*, *uvas*) to tread; to cover part of; to ram; (*una tecla*) to strike; (*mus*) to pluck; (coll) to abuse, tread all over; **pisar algo a alguien** (coll) to snitch something from someone ‖ *intr* to be right above; to step ‖ *ref* (Arg) to guess wrong, come out wrong

pisaverde *m* (coll) fop, dandy

piscina *f* swimming pool; fishpond

pisco *m* Peruvian brandy

pisicorre *f* (W-I) station wagon

piso *m* tread; floor; flooring; (*de una carretera*) surface; flat, apartment; **buscar piso** to be looking for a place to live; **piso alto** top floor; **piso bajo** street floor, ground floor; **piso principal** main floor, second floor

pisón *m* ram, tamper

pisotear *tr* to trample, to tread on, to tread under foot; (coll) to abuse, tread all over

pisotón *m* stamp, tread

pista *f* track; trace, trail; clew; race track; (*de bolera*) alley; (*de cabaret*) floor; (aer) runway; **pista de esquí** ski run; **pista de patinar** skating rink

pisto *m* (*para los enfermos*) chicken broth; vegetable cutlet; jumbled speech or writing; mess

pistola *f* pistol; sprayer; rock drill; **pistola de arzón** horse pistol; **pistola engrasadora** grease gun

pistolera *f* holster

pistolerismo *m* gangsterism

pistolero *m* gangster, gunman

pistón *m* piston

pistonear *intr* to knock

pistoneo *m* knock

pistonu•do -da *adj* (coll) stunning, swank

pita *f* century plant; hiss, hissing; glass marble

pitar *tr* to pay, pay off; (*a un torero*) to whistle disapproval of ‖ *intr* to blow a whistle, to whistle; to blow the horn, to honk; (coll) to talk nonsense; **no pitar** (coll) to not be popular; **salir pitando** to run away, dash away

pitazo *m* blast, toot, honk

pitillera *f* cigarette maker; cigarette case

pitillo *m* cigarette

pito *m* whistle; horn; fife; fifer; cigarette; jackstone; (*insecto*) tick; woodpecker; (coll) continental, straw, tinker's dam

pitón *m* lump, sprig; tenderling; (*del cuerno*) tip; nozzle, spout; python

pitonisa *f* witch, siren; pythoness

pitu•so -sa *adj* tiny, cute ‖ *mf* tot

piular *intr* to peep, to chirp

pivotar *intr* to pivot

pivote *m* pivot; **pivote de dirección** (aut) kingpin

píxide *f* pyx

pizarra *f* slate; blackboard

pizarrero *m* roofer, slater

pizarrín *m* slate pencil

pizca *f* (coll) mite, whit, jot

placa *f* plaque, tablet; badge; plate; slab, sheet; (anat, elec, electron, phot, zool) plate; (Am) scab; **placa de matrícula** license plate; **placa giratoria** (*de ferrocarril*; *de gramófono*) turntable

placaminero *m* persimmon

placebo *m* placebo

pláceme *m* congratulation

placente•ro -ra *adj* pleasant, agreeable

placer *m* pleasure; sandbank, reef; **a placer** at one's convenience ‖ *v* §52 *tr* to please

place•ro -ra *adj* public ‖ *mf* market vendor; loafer, town gossip

pláci•do -da *adj* placid; pleasing

plaga *f* plague; pest; scourge; abundance; sore; clime, region

plagar §44 *tr* to plague, infest; (*de minas*) to sow

plagiar *tr* to plagiarize

plagio *m* plagiarism; (Am) abduction, kidnaping

plan *m* plan; level, height; **plan de estudios** or **plan escolar** curriculum

plana *f* plain, flat country; trowel; cooper's plane; page

plancha *f* plate, sheet; iron, flatiron; gangplank; (coll) blunder; **a la plancha** grilled; (*huevo*) fried; **plancha de blindaje** armor plate

planchado *m* ironing; pressing

planchar *tr* (*la ropa interior blanca*) to iron; (*un traje de hombre*) to press ‖ *intr* (Am) to be a wallflower

planchear *tr* to plate

planear *tr* to plan, to outline; (*una tabla*) to plane ‖ *intr* to hover; (aer) to volplane, to glide

planeta *m* planet

planicie *f* plain

planificar §73 *tr* to plan

planilla *f* (Am) list, roll, schedule; (*de candidatos para un puesto público*) (Mex) panel; (Mex) ballot; (Mex) commutation ticket

pla•no -na *adj* plane; level, smooth, even; flat ‖ *m* plan; map; (*superficie*) plane; (aer) plane; **de plano** clearly, plainly, flatly; flat; **levantar un plano** to make a survey; **primer plano** foreground ‖ *f* see **plana**

planta *f* (*del pie*) sole; foot; plan; project; floor plan; (*del personal de una oficina*) roster; plant, factory; (bot) plant; (sport) stance; **de planta** from the ground up; **echar plantas** to swagger, to bully; **planta baja** ground floor; **planta del sortilegio** (bot) witch hazel; **tener buena planta** (coll) to make a fine appearance

plantar *tr* to plant; to establish, to

found; (*un golpe*) (coll) to plant; (coll) to jilt; (*en la calle, en la cárcel*) (coll) to throw ‖ *ref* to take a stand; to gang together; (*un animal*) (coll) to balk; (coll) to land, to arrive

plantear *tr* to plan, to outline; to establish, execute, carry out; to state, set up, expound, pose

plantel *m* nursery garden; educational establishment

plantificar §73 *tr* to plan, to outline; (*un golpe*) (coll) to plant; (*en la calle, la cárcel*) (coll) to throw ‖ *ref* (coll) to land, to arrive

plantilla *f* plantlet, young plant; insole; reinforced sole; model, pattern, template; (*de empleados*) staff; (*del personal de una oficina*) roster; plan, design; (*bizcocho*) (Am) ladyfinger

plantío *m* planting; garden patch; tree nursery

plantón *m* (*que ha de ser transplantado*) shoot; graft; guard, watchman; waiting, standing around

plañide·ro -ra *adj* mournful, plaintive ‖ *f* hired mourner

plañir §12 *tr* to lament, grieve over ‖ *intr* to lament, grieve, bewail

plasmar *tr* to mold, shape

plasta *f* paste, soft mass; flattened object; (coll) poor job, bungle

plástica *f* (*arte de plasmar*) plastic; plastic arts

plásti·co -ca *adj* plastic ‖ *m* (*substancia*) plastic ‖ *f* see **plástica**

plata *f* silver; (*moneda o monedas*) silver; wealth; money; **en plata** (coll) briefly, to the point; (coll) plainly; **plata de ley** sterling silver

plataforma *f* platform; platform car; (*del ferrocarril*) roadbed; (*programa político*) platform; (*de lanzamiento de cohete*) pad; **plataforma giratoria** (rr) turntable

platanal *m* or **platanar** *m* banana plantation

plátano *m* banana; banana tree; plane tree; **plátano de occidente** buttonwood tree

platea *f* (theat) orchestra, parquet

platear *tr* to silver, coat or plate with silver

platero *m* silversmith; jeweler

plática *f* talk, chat; talk, informal lecture; sermon

platicar §73 *tr* to talk over, to discuss ‖ *intr* to talk, to chat; to discuss; to preach

platillo *m* plate; saucer; (*de la balanza*) pan; (mus) cymbal; **platillo volador** or **volante** flying saucer

platino *m* platinum

plato *m* dish; plate; (*de una comida*) course; daily fare; **plato fuerte** main course; **plato giratorio** (*del gramófono*) turntable

pla·tó *m* (*pl* **-tós**) (mov) set

Platón *m* Plato

plausible *adj* praiseworthy; acceptable

playa *f* beach, shore, strand; **playa infantil** sand pile

playera *f* fishwoman; beach shoe

plaza *f* plaza, square; market place; town, city; fortified town; space, room; yard; office, employment; character, reputation; seat; **sentar plaza** to enlist; **plaza de armas** parade ground; (Am) public square; **plaza de gallos** cockpit; **plaza de toros** bullring; **plaza mayor** main square

plazo *m* term; time; time limit; date of payment; instalment; **a plazo** on credit, on time; **en plazos** in instalments

pleamar *f* high tide, high water

plebe *f* common people

plebe·yo -ya *adj* & *mf* plebeian

plegadi·zo -za *adj* folding; pliable

plegar §66 *tr* to fold; to crease; to pleat ‖ *ref* to yield, to give in

plegaria *f* prayer; noon call to prayer

pleito *m* litigation, lawsuit; dispute, quarrel; fight; **pleito de acreedores** bankruptcy proceedings; **pleito homenaje** (feud) homage; **pleito viciado** mistrial

plenilunio *m* full moon

plenitud *f* fullness, abundance

ple·no -na *adj* full; **en plena marcha** in full swing; **en pleno rostro** right in the face

pleuresía *f* pleurisy

pliego *m* (*de papel*) sheet; folder; cover, envelope; bid, specification; sealed letter; printer's proof

pliegue *m* fold, crease, pleat; **pliegue de tabla** box pleat

plisar *tr* to pleat

plomada *f* carpenter's lead pencil; plummet; plumb bob; sinker, sinkers; scourge tipped with lead balls

plomar *tr* to seal with lead

plomazo *m* (Guat, Mex, W-I) gunshot

plomería *f* lead roofing; leadwork, plumbing

plomero *m* lead worker; plumber

plomi·zo -za *adj* lead, leaden

plomo *m* lead; (*pedazo de plomo; bala*) lead; (elec) fuse; (coll) bore; **a plomo** plumb, perpendicularly; straight down; (coll) just right

pluma *f* feather; quill; plume; pen; (Am) faucet; (CAm) hoax; (Chile) crane, derrick; **pluma esferográfica** (Am) ball-point pen; **pluma estilográfica** or **pluma fuente** fountain pen

plumaje *m* plumage

plúmbe·o -a *adj* lead

plumero *m* (*caja o vaso para las plumas*) penholder; feather duster

plumífe·ro -ra *adj* (*escritor*) (coll) hack, second-rate; (poet) feathered ‖ *m* padded or quilted jacket, ski jacket; (coll) hack writer; (coll) newshound

plumilla *f* small feather; (*de la pluma fuente*) point, tip

plumón *m* down; feather bed

plumo·so -sa *adj* downy, feathery

plural *adj* & *m* plural

pluriempleo *m* moonlighting

plus *m* extra, bonus

plusmarca *f* (sport) record

plusmarquista *mf* (sport) record breaker

plusvalía f appreciation (*in value*)

Plutarco m Plutarch

plutonio m plutonium

población f population; village, town, city

poblada f (SAm) riot, mob

pobla·do -da adj thick, bushy ‖ m town, community ‖ f see **poblada**

poblar §61 tr to people, to populate; to found, settle, colonize; (*un estanque, una colmena*) to stock; (*con árboles*) to plant ‖ intr to settle, colonize; to multiply, be prolific ‖ ref to become full, covered, or crowded

pobre adj poor ‖ mf pauper; beggar

pobreza f poverty, want; poorness

pociga f pigpen

poción f potion, dose

po·co -ca adj & pron (*comp & super* **menos**) little; few, e.g., **poca gente** few people; **pocos** few; **unos pocos** a few ‖ **poco** adv little; **a poco** shortly afterwards; **a poco de** shortly after; **dentro de poco** shortly; **por poco** almost, nearly; **tener en poco** to hold in low esteem, to think little of; **un poco (de)** a little

po·cho -cha adj faded, discolored; over-ripe; rotten; (Chile) chubby

podar tr to prune, to trim

podenco m hound

poder m power; power of attorney, proxy; **el cuarto poder** the fourth estate; **obra en mi poder** I have at hand, I have in my possession; **poder adquisitivo** purchasing power ‖ v §53 intr to be possible; to be able, to have power or strength; **a más no poder** as hard as possible; **no poder con** to not be able to stand, to not be able to manage; **no poder más** to be exhausted, to be all in; **no poder menos de** to not be able to keep from, to not be able to help ‖ v aux to be able to, may, can, might, could; **no poder ver** to not be able to stand

poderhabiente mf attorney, proxy

poderío m power, might; wealth, riches; sway, dominion

podero·so -sa adj powerful, mighty; wealthy, rich

podre f pus

podredumbre f corruption, putrefaction; pus; deep grief

poema m poem

poesía f poetry; poem; **bella poesía** (fig) fairy tale

poeta m poet

poéti·co -ca adj poetic(al) ‖ f poetics

poetisa f poetess

pola·co -ca adj Polish ‖ mf Pole ‖ m (*idioma*) Polish

polaina f legging

polar adj pole; polar ‖ f polestar

polarizar §60 tr to polarize

polea f pulley

poleame m (naut) tackle

polen m pollen

policía m policeman ‖ f police; policing; politeness; cleanliness, neatness; **policía urbana** street cleaning

policía·co -ca or **policial** adj police; (*novela*) detective

polifacéti·co -ca adj many-sided

políga·mo -ma adj polygamous ‖ mf polygamist

poliglo·to -ta adj polyglot ‖ mf polyglot, linguist

polígono m polygon

polígrafo m prolific writer; copying machine; ball-point pen; lie detector

polilla f moth

Polimnia f Polyhymnia

polinizar §60 tr to pollinate

polinomio m polynomial

polio f (path) polio

pólipo m polyp

polisón m bustle

polista mf poloist, polo player

politeísta adj polytheistic ‖ mf polytheist

política f politics; policy; manners, politeness, courtesy; **política de café** parlor politics; **política del buen vecino** Good Neighbor Policy

políti·co -ca adj political; politic, tactful; polite, courteous; -in-law, e.g., **padre político** father-in-law ‖ mf politician ‖ f see **política**

póliza f policy, contract; draft, check; customhouse permit; **póliza de seguro** insurance policy

polizón m bum, tramp; stowaway

polizonte m (coll) cop, policeman

polo m pole; popsicle; (*juego*) polo; **polo de agua** water polo; **polo de atracción popular** drawing card

Polonia f Poland

pol·trón -trona adj idle, lazy, comfort-loving ‖ f easy chair

polvareda f cloud of dust; rumpus

polvera f compact, powder case

polvo m dust; powder; pinch of snuff; **polvo dentífrico** tooth powder; **polvos** dust; powder; **polvos de la madre Celestina** (coll) hocus-pocus; **polvos de talco** talcum powder

pólvora f powder, gunpowder; fireworks; (*persona avispada*) (coll) live wire; **correr como pólvora en reguero** to spread like wildfire

polvorear tr to dust, sprinkle with dust or powder

polvorien·to -ta adj dusty; powdery

polvorín m powder magazine; powder flask; (*insecto*) (Am) tick; (Chile) spitfire

polvoro·so -sa adj dusty; **poner pies en polvorosa** (coll) to take to one's heels

polla f pullet; (*puesta en juegos de naipes*) stake, kitty; (coll) lassie

pollera f poultry woman; chicken coop; poultry yard; gocart; (Arg, Chile) skirt

pollero m poulterer; poultry yard

polli·no -na mf donkey, ass

polli·to -ta mf chick; (*persona joven*) (coll) chick, chicken

pollo m chicken; (*persona joven*) chicken

pomada f pomade

pómez f pumice stone

pomo m pome; (*de la guarnición de la espada*) pommel; (*bola aromática*) pomander; (*frasco para perfume*) flacon; **pomo de puerta** doorknob

pompa *f* pomp; soap bubble; swell, bulge; (*de la ropa*) billowing, ballooning; (*de las alas del pavo real*) spread; (naut) pump; **pompa fúnebre** funeral

pompo·so -sa *adj* pompous; high-flown, highfalutin

pómulo *m* cheekbone

ponche *m* (*bebida*) punch; **ponche de huevo** eggnog

ponchera *f* punch bowl

pon·cho -cha *adj* lazy, careless, easygoing; (Col) chubby || *m* poncho; greatcoat

ponderar *tr* to weigh; to ponder, ponder over; to exaggerate; to praise to the skies; to balance; to weight

ponencia *f* paper, report

poner §54 *tr* to put, place, lay, set; to arrange, dispose; (*una observación*) to put in; (*una pieza dramática*) to put on; (*la mesa*) to set; to assume, suppose; (*una ley, un impuesto*) to impose; to wager, to stake; (*huevos*) to lay; (*por escrito*) to set down, put down; (*tiempo*) to take; (*p.ej., miedo*) to cause; to make, to turn; (*la luz, la radio*) to turn on; (*marcha directa*) (aut) to go in; **poner en limpio** to make a clean copy of; **poner por encima** to prefer, to put ahead || *ref* to put or place oneself; to become, to get, to turn; (*el sol, los astros*) to set; (*sombrero, saco, etc.*) to put on; to dress, dress up; to get spotted; to get, reach, arrive; **ponerse a** to set out to, to begin to; **ponerse tan alto** to take offense, to become hoity-toity

poniente *m* west; west wind

ponqué *m* (Am) poundcake

pontífice *m* pontiff

pontón *m* pontoon; pontoon bridge; (*buque viejo*) hulk

ponzoña *f* poison

ponzoño·so -sa *adj* poisonous

popa *f* poop, stern

popote *m* (Mex) straw for brooms; (*para tomar refrescos*) (Mex) straw

populache·ro -ra *adj* popular; cheap, vulgar; rabble-rousing || *mf* rabble rouser

populacho *m* populace, mob, rabble

popular *adj* popular

popularizar §60 *tr* to popularize

populo·so -sa *adj* populous

popu·rrí *m* (*pl* -rríes) medley

poquedad *f* paucity, scantiness, scarcity; timidity; trifle

poqui·to -ta *adj* very little; (Am) timid, shy, backward

por *prep* by; through, over; via, by way of; in, e.g., **por la mañana** in the morning; for; because of; for the sake of; on account of; in exchange for; in order to; as; about, e.g., **por Navidad** about Christmastime; out of, e.g., **por ignorancia** out of ignorance; times, e.g., **tres por cuatro** four times three; **estar por** to be on the point of, to be ready to; to be still to be, e.g., **la carta está por escribir** the letter is still to be written; **ir por**

to go for, to go after; to follow; **por ciento** per cent; **por entre** among, between; **por que** because; in order that; **por qué** why; **por** + *adj* or *adv* + **que** however

porcelana *f* porcelain, chinaware; (*usado por los plateros*) enamel; (Mex) washbowl

porcentaje *m* percentage

porción *f* portion

porche *m* porch, portico

pordiosear *intr* to beg, to go begging

pordiose·ro -ra *mf* beggar

porfía *f* persistence, stubbornness, obstinacy; **a porfía** in emulation; insistently

porfia·do -da *adj* persistent, stubborn, obstinate; opinionated

porfiar §77 *intr* to persist; to argue stubbornly

pórfido *m* porphyry

pormenor *m* detail, particular

pormenorizar §60 *tr* to detail, tell in detail; to itemize

poro *m* pore

poro·so -sa *adj* porous

poroto *m* (SAm) bean, string bean; (Chile) little runt

porque *conj* because; in order that

porqué *m* (coll) why; (coll) quantity, share; (coll) wherewithal, money

porquería *f* (coll) dirt, filth; (coll) trifle; (coll) crudity; (*alimento dañoso a la salud*) (coll) junk

porra *f* club, bludgeon; (coll) bore, nuisance; (coll) boasting; (*pelos enredados*) (Arg, Bol) knot, tangle; (Mex) claque

porrazo *m* clubbing; blow, bump, thump

porta *f* porthole

portaavio·nes *m* (*pl* -nes) aircraft carrier, flattop

portacandado *m* hasp

portada *f* front, façade; portal; title page; (*de una revista*) cover; **falsa portada** half title

portadis·cos *m* (*pl* -cos) turntable

porta·dor -dora *adj* (onda) (rad) carrier || *mf* bearer; carrier || *m* waiter's tray

portaequipaje *m* (aut) trunk

portaequipa·jes *m* (*pl* -jes) baggage rack

portaguan·tes *m* (*pl* -tes) (aut) glove compartment

portal *m* vestibule, entrance hall; porch, portico; arcade; city gate; (*de un túnel*) portal *m*; (Am) crèche

portalámpa·ras *m* (*pl* -ras) (elec) socket

portalón *m* gate, portal; (*en el costado del buque*) gangway

portamira *m* (surv) rodman

portamone·das *m* (*pl* -das) pocketbook

portanue·vas *mf* (*pl* -vas) newsmonger

portañuela *f* (*de los pantalones*) fly; (Col, Mex) carriage door

portapape·les *m* (*pl* -les) brief case

portaplu·mas *m* (*pl* -mas) penholder

portar *tr* (Am) to carry, to bear; (hunt) to retrieve || *ref* to behave, conduct oneself

portase·nos *m* (*pl* -nos) brassière

portátil *adj* portable

portatinte·ro m inkstand
portavian·das m (pl -das) dinner pail
porta·voz m (pl -voces) megaphone; mouthpiece, spokesman
portazgo m toll, road toll
portazo m bang, slam
porte m portage; carrying charge, freight; postage; behavior, conduct; dress, bearing; size, capacity; (Chile) birthday present; **porte concertado** mailing permit; **porte pagado** postage prepaid, freight prepaid
portear tr to carry, transport || intr to slam || ref (las aves) to migrate
portento m prodigy, wonder
portento·so -sa adj portentous, extraordinary
porte·ño -ña adj Buenos Aires; Valparaiso; pertaining to any large South American city with a port || mf native or inhabitant of Buenos Aires, Valparaiso or any large South American city with a port
porte·ro -ra mf doorkeeper; gatekeeper; (sport) goalkeeper || m porter, janitor; doorman || f portress, janitress
portezuela f small door; (de un coche o automóvil) door; pocket flap
pórtico m portico, porch; little gate
portilla f porthole; private cart road, private cattle pass
portillo m gap, opening; nick, notch; (puerta chica en otra mayor) wicket; gate; narrow pass; side entrance
portorrique·ño -ña adj & mf Puerto Rican
portua·rio -ria adj port, harbor, dock || m dock hand, dock worker
Portugal m Portugal
portu·gués -guesa adj & mf Portuguese
porvenir m future
pos — en pos de after, behind; in pursuit of
posa f knell, toll
posada f inn, wayside inn; lodging; boarding house; home, dwelling; camp; **posadas** (Mex) pre-Christmas celebration
posadero -ra mf innkeeper; **posaderas** buttocks
posar tr to put down || intr to put up, lodge; to alight, to perch; to pose || ref to alight, to perch; to settle; to rest
posbéli·co -ca adj postwar
posdata f postscript
pose f pose; (phot) exposure
poseer §43 tr to own, possess, hold; to have a mastery of || ref to control oneself
posesión f possession; **tomar posesión de** (un cargo) to take up
posesionar tr to give possession to || ref to take possession
posfecha f postdate
posguerra f postwar period
posible adj possible; **hacer todo lo posible** to do one's best || **posibles** mpl means, income, property
posición f position; standing
positi·vo -va adj positive || f (phot) print, positive

poso m sediment, dregs; grounds; rest, quiet; **poso del café** coffee grounds
posponer §54 tr to subordinate; to think less of
posta f (de caballos) relay; posthouse; stage; stake, wager; slice; **a posta** (coll) on purpose; **por la posta** (coll) posthaste; **postas** buckshot
postal adj postal || f post card; **postal ilustrada** picture post card
poste m post, pilar, pole; **poste de alumbrado** or **de farol** lamppost; **poste de telégrafo** telegraph pole; (persona muy alta y delgada) beanpole; **poste indicador** road sign
postergar §44 tr to delay, postpone; to pass over
posteridad f posterity; posthumous fame
posterior adj back, rear; later, subsequent
postigo m (puerta chica en otra mayor) wicket; (puertecilla en una ventana) peep window; (puerta excusada) postern; shutter
posti·zo -za adj false, artificial; (cuello) detachable || m switch, false hair, rat
postóni·co -ca adj posttonic
postor m bidder; **el mejor postor** the highest bidder
postración f prostration
postrar tr to prostrate; to weaken, exhaust || ref to collapse, be prostrated; to prostrate oneself
postre adj last, final; **a la postre** at last; afterwards || m dessert; **postres** dessert
postulación f postulation; nomination
postulante mf applicant, candidate
póstu·mo -ma adj posthumous
postura f posture; attitude, stand; stake, wager; agreement, pact; egg, eggs; (de huevos) laying; **postura del sol** sunset
potabilizar §60 tr to make drinkable
potable adj drinkable
potaje m pottage; jumble; (bebida) mixture; (Am) scheme; **potajes** vegetables
potasa f potash
potasio m potassium
pote m pot, jug; flowerpot; **a pote** (coll) in abundance
potencia f potency; power; **potencia de choque** striking power
potenciación f (math) involution
potencial adj & m potential
potenciar tr (las aguas de un río; el entusiasmo de una persona) to harness; (elevar a una potencia) (math) to raise
potentado m potentate
potente adj powerful; (coll) big, huge
potestad f power
potista mf (coll) toper, soak
potosí m great wealth, gold mine
potra f filly; (coll) hernia, rupture
potranca f young mare
potro m colt; pest, annoyance
pozal m bucket, pail
pozo m well; pit; whirlpool; (min) shaft; (naut) hold; (Chile, Col) pool, puddle; (Ecuad) spring, fountain;

pozo de ciencia fountain of knowledge; **pozo de lanzamiento** launching silo; **pozo de lobo** (mil) foxhole; **pozo negro** cesspool

P.P. *abbr* **porte pagado, por poder**

p.p.ᵈᵒ *abbr* **próximo pasado**

práctica *f* practice; method; skill; **prácticas** studies, training

prácticamente *adv* through practice, by experience

practicar §73 *tr* to practice; to bring about; (*un agujero*) to make, to cut

prácti·co -ca *adj* practical; skillful, practiced; practicing ǁ *m* medical practitioner; (naut) pilot ǁ *f* see **práctica**

pradera *f* meadowland; prairie

prado *m* meadow, pasture; promenade

Praga *f* Prague

pral. *abbr* **principal**

pralte. *abbr* **principalmente**

prángana — estar en la prángana (Mex, W-I) to be broke; (P-R) to be naked

preámbulo *m* preamble; evasion; **no andarse en preámbulos** (coll) to come to the point

prebéli·co -ca *adj* prewar

prebenda *f* prebend; (coll) sinecure

preca·rio -ria *adj* precarious

precaución *f* precaution

precaver *tr* to stave off, head off ǁ *intr* & *ref* to be on one's guard; **precaverse contra** or **de** to guard against

precavido -da *adj* cautious

precedente *adj* preceding ǁ *m* precedent

preceder *tr* & *intr* to precede

precepto *m* precept; order, injunction; **los preceptos** the Ten Commandments

preces *fpl* devotions; supplications

precia·do -da *adj* esteemed, valued; precious, valuable; boastful, proud

preciar *tr* to appraise, estimate ǁ *ref* to boast

precintar *tr* to bind, strap; to seal

precio *m* price; value, worth; esteem, credit; **a precio de quemazón** (coll) at a giveaway price; **precios de cierre** closing prices; **precio tope** ceiling price

preciosidad *f* preciousness; beauty, gem, jewel

precio·so -sa *adj* precious; valuable; witty; (coll) beautiful

precipicio *m* precipice; destruction

precipitación *f* precipitation; **precipitación acuosa** rainfall; **precipitación radiactiva** fallout

precipitar *tr* to precipitate; to rush, hurl, throw headlong ǁ *ref* to rush, throw oneself headlong

precipito·so -sa *adj* precipitous, rash, reckless; risky, dangerous

precisar *tr* to state precisely, to specify; to fix; to need; to oblige, to force ǁ *intr* to be necessary; to be important; to be urgent; **precisar de** to need

precisión *f* precision; necessity, obligation; (Chile) haste; **precisiones** data

preci·so -sa *adj* necessary; precise; (Ven) haughty

precita·do -da *adj* above-mentioned

precla·ro -ra *adj* illustrious, famous

preconizar §60 *tr* to proclaim, commend publicly

pre·coz *adj* (*pl* **-coces**) precocious

predato·rio -ria *adj* predatory

predecir §24 *tr* to predict, foretell

prédica *f* protestant sermon; harangue

predicar §73 *tr* to preach; to praise to the skies; to scold, preach to

predicción *f* prediction; **predicción del tiempo** weather forecasting

predilec·to -ta *adj* favorite, preferred

predio *m* property, estate

predisponer §54 *tr* to predispose

predominante *adj* predominant

preeminente *adj* preëminent

preestreno *m* (mov) preview

prefabricar §73 *tr* to prefabricate

prefacio *m* preface

preferencia *f* preference; **de preferencia** preferably

preferente *adj* preferable; favored; (*acciones*) preferred

preferible *adj* preferable

preferir §68 *tr* to prefer

prefigurar *tr* to foreshadow

prefijar *tr* to prefix; to prearrange

prefijo *m* prefix

pregón *m* proclamation, public announcement (*by town crier*)

pregonar *tr* to proclaim, announce publicly; to hawk; to reveal; to outlaw; to praise openly

pregonero *m* auctioneer; town crier

preguerra *f* prewar period

pregunta *f* question; **hacer una pregunta** to ask a question

preguntar *tr* to ask; to question ǁ *intr* to ask, to inquire; **preguntar por** to ask after or for ǁ *ref* to ask oneself; to wonder

pregun·tón -tona *adj* (coll) inquisitive ǁ *mf* (coll) inquisitive person

prejudicio or **prejuicio** *m* prejudgment; prejudice

prelado *m* prelate

preliminar *adj* & *m* preliminary; **preliminares** (*de un libro*) front matter

preludio *m* prelude

premeditar *tr* to premeditate

premiar *tr* to reward; to give an award to

premio *m* reward, prize; premium; **a premio** at a premium; **premio de enganche** (mil) bounty; **premio gordo** first prize

premio·so -sa *adj* tight, close; bothersome; strict, rigid; slow, dull

premisa *f* premise; mark, token, clue

premura *f* pressure, haste, urgency

premuro·so -sa *adj* pressing, urgent

prenda *f* pledge; security; pawn; jewel, household article; garment, article of clothing; gift, talent; darling, loved one; **en prenda** in pawn; **en prenda de** as a pledge of; **prenda perdida** forfeit; **prendas** (*juego*) forfeits

prendar *tr* to pawn; to pledge; to charm, captivate ǁ *ref* — **prendarse de** to take a liking for, fall in love with

prendedero *m* fillet, brooch; stickpin

prender *tr* to seize, grasp; to catch; to imprison; to dress up; to pin; to fasten ‖ *intr* to catch; to catch fire; to take root; to turn out well ‖ *ref* to dress up; to be fastened; to catch hold

prendería *f* second-hand shop

prende•ro -ra *mf* second-hand dealer

prensa *f* press; printing press; vise; press, newspapers; press, frame; **entrar en prensa** to go to press; **meter en prensa** (coll) to put the squeeze on; **prensa taladradora** drill press

prensado *m* pressing; (*lustre de los tejidos prensados*) sheen

prensar *tr* to press; to squeeze

preña•do -da *adj* pregnant; sagging, bulging; full, charged

preñez *f* pregnancy; fullness; impending danger; inherent confusion

preocupación *f* (*posesión anticipada; cuidado, desvelo*) preoccupation; (*posesión anticipada*) preoccupancy; bias, prejudice

preocupar *tr* to preoccupy, to worry ‖ *ref* to become preoccupied, to be worried

preparación *f* preparation

prepara•do -da *adj* ready, prepared ‖ *m* (pharm) preparation

preparar *tr* to prepare ‖ *ref* to prepare, to get ready

preparati•vo -va *adj* preparatory ‖ *m* preparation, readiness

preponderante *adj* preponderant

preposición *f* preposition

prepóste•ro -ra *adj* reversed, upset, out of order, inopportune

prerrogativa *f* prerogative

presa *f* capture, seizure; catch, prey; booty, spoils; dam; trench, ditch, flume; bit, morsel; fang, tusk, claw; fishweir; (sport) hold; **hacer presa** to seize; **ser presa de** to be a victim of; to be prey to

presagiar *tr* to presage, forebode

presagio *m* presage, omen, token

présbita or **présbite** *adj* far-sighted ‖ *mf* presbyte

presbiteria•no -na *adj* & *mf* Presbyterian

prescindir *intr* — **prescindir de** to leave aside, leave out, disregard; to do without, dispense with; to avoid

prescribir §83 *tr* & *intr* to prescribe

presencia *f* presence; show, display; **presencia de ánimo** presence of mind

presenciar *tr* to witness, be present at

presentación *f* presentation; (*de una persona en el trato de otra u otras*) introduction; (*de un nuevo automóvil, libro, etc.*) appearance

presentar *tr* to present; to introduce ‖ *ref* to present oneself; to appear, show up; to introduce oneself

presente *adj* present; **hacer presente** to notify of, to remind of; **tener presente** to bear or keep in mind ‖ *interj* here!, present! ‖ *m* present, gift; person present

presentimiento *m* presentiment, premonition

presentir §68 *tr* to have a presentiment of

preservar *tr* to preserve, protect

preservati•vo -va *adj* & *m* preventive; preservative

presidencia *f* presidency; chairmanship

presidente *m* president; chairman; presiding judge

presidiario *m* convict

presidio *m* garrison; fortress; citadel; penitentiary; imprisonment; hard labor; aid, help

presidir *tr* to preside over; to dominate ‖ *intr* to preside

presilla *f* loop, fastener; clip; shoulder strap

presión *f* pressure; (*cerveza*) **a presión** on draught; **presión de inflado** tire pressure

presionar *tr* to press; to put pressure on ‖ *intr* to press; **presionar sobre** to put pressure on

pre•so -sa *adj* seized; imprisoned ‖ *mf* prisoner; convict; *f* see presa

presta•do -da *adj* lent, loaned; **dar prestado** to lend; **pedir** or **tomar prestado** to borrow

prestamista *mf* moneylender; pawnbroker

préstamo *m* loan; **préstamo lingüístico** loan word, borrowing

prestar *tr* to lend, to loan; (*oído; ayuda; noticias*) to give; (*atención*) to pay; (*un favor*) to do; (*un servicio*) to render; (*juramento*) to take; (*silencio*) to keep; (*paciencia*) to show ‖ *intr* (*un paño, la ropa*) to give, to yield; to be useful ‖ *ref* to lend oneself, to lend itself

prestatar•rio -ria *mf* borrower

presteza *f* speed, promptness, readiness

prestidigitación *f* sleight of hand

prestidigita•dor -dora *adj* captivating ‖ *mf* magician; faker, impostor

prestigio *m* prestige; good standing; spell; illusion

prestigio•so -sa *adj* captivating, spellbinding; famous, renowned; illusory

pres•to -ta *adj* quick, prompt, ready; nimble ‖ *presto adv* right away

presumi•do -da *adj* conceited, vain ‖ *mf* would-be

presumir *tr* to presume ‖ *intr* to boast, be conceited

presunción *f* presumption; conceit

presuntuo•so -sa *adj* conceited, vain

presuponer §54 *tr* to presuppose; to budget

presupuestar *tr* to budget; (*el coste de una obra*) to estimate

presupuesto *m* budget; reason, motive; supposition; estimate

presuro•so -sa *adj* speedy, quick, hasty; zealous, persistent

pretencio•so -sa *adj* pretentious, showy; conceited, vain

pretender *tr* to claim, to pretend to; to try for, to try to do; to be a suitor for ‖ *intr* to insist; **pretender + inf** to try to + *inf*

pretendiente *mf* pretender, claimant; office seeker ‖ *m* suitor

pretensión *f* pretension; claim; pretense; presumption; effort, pursuit

pretéri•to -ta *adj* & *m* past

pretil *m* parapet, railing; walk along a parapet

pretina *f* girdle, belt; waistband

pretóni•co -ca *adj* pretonic

prevalecer §22 *intr* to prevail; to take root; to thrive

prevaler §76 *ref* — **prevalerse de** to avail oneself of, take advantage of

prevaricar §73 *intr* to collude, connive; to play false; to transgress; (coll) to rave, be delirious

prevención *f* preparation; prevention; foresight; warning; prejudice; stock, supply; jail, lockup; guardhouse; a or **de prevención** spare, emergency

preveni•do -da *adj* prepared, ready; foresighted, forewarned; stocked, full

prevenir §79 *tr* to prepare, make ready; to forestall, prevent, anticipate; to overcome; to warn; to prejudice || *intr* (*una tempestad*) to come up || *ref* to get ready; to come to mind

prever §80 *tr* to foresee

pre•vio -via *adj* previous; preliminary; after, with previous, subject to, e.g., **previo acuerdo** subject to agreement

previsión *f* prevision, foresight; foresightedness; forecast; **previsión del tiempo** weather forecasting

prie•to -ta *adj* dark, blackish, stingy, mean; tight, compact; (Am) dark-complexioned || *mf* (W-I) darling

prima *f* early morning; bonus, bounty; (ins) premium; (mil) first quarter of the night; (*cuerda*) (mus) treble

pri•mal -mala *adj & mf* yearling

prima•rio -ria *adj* primary || *m* (elec) primary

primavera *f* spring, springtime; cowslip, primrose; robin

primer *adj* apocopated form of **primero**, used only before masculine singular nouns and adjectives

prime•ro -ra *adj* first; former; early; primary; prime; (*materia*) raw || *m* first; **a primeros de** around the beginning of || **primero** *adv* first

primicia *f* first fruits

primige•nio -nia *adj* original, primitive

primiti•vo -va *adj* primitive

pri•mo -ma *adj* first; prime, excellent; skillful; (*materia*) raw || *mf* cousin; (coll) sucker, dupe; **primo carnal** or **primo hermano** first cousin, cousin-german || *f* see **prima** || **primo** *adv* in the first place

primogéni•to -ta *adj & mf* first-born

primor *m* care, skill, elegance; beauty

primoro•so -sa *adj* careful, skillful, elegant; fine, exquisite

princesa *f* princess; **princesa viuda** dowager princess

principal *adj* principal, main, chief; first, foremost; essential, important; famous, illustrious; (*piso*) second || *m* principal, head, chief

príncipe *m* prince; **portarse como un príncipe** to live like a prince; **príncipe de Asturias** heir apparent of the King of Spain; **príncipe de Gales** prince of Wales; **príncipes** prince and princess

principiante *adj* beginning || *mf* beginner, apprentice, novice

principiar *tr, intr & ref* to begin

principio *m* start, beginning; principle; origin, source; (culin) entree; **a principios de** around the beginning of; **en un principio** at the beginning; **principio de admiración** inverted exclamation point; **principio de interrogación** inverted question mark

pringar §44 *tr* to dip or soak in grease or fat; to spot or stain with grease; (coll) to make bleed; (coll) to slander, run down; (Am) to splash || *intr* (coll) to meddle; (CAm, Mex) to drizzle || *ref* to peculate

pringo•so -sa *adj* greasy, fatty

prioridad *f* priority; **de máxima prioridad** of the highest priority

prisa *f* hurry, haste; urgency; crush, crowd; **darse prisa** to hurry, make haste; **estar de prisa** or **tener prisa** to be in a hurry

prisión *f* seizure, capture; imprisonment; prison; **prisión celular** cell house; **prisiones** shackles, fetters

prisione•ro -ra *mf* prisoner; (*cautivo de una pasión o afecto*) captive || *m* setscrew; studbolt

prisma *m* prism

prismáticos *mpl* binoculars

priva•do -da *adj* private || *m* (*de un alto personaje*) favorite || *f* cesspool

privar *tr* to deprive; to forbid, prohibit || *intr* to be in vogue; to prevail; to be in favor || *ref* to deprive oneself; **privarse de** to give up

privilegiar *tr* to grant a privilege to

privilegio *m* privilege

pro *m & f* profit, advantage; ¡**buena pro**! good appetite!; **de pro** of note, of worth; **el pro y el contra** the pros and the cons; **en pro de** on behalf of

proa *f* (aer) nose; (naut) prow

probable *adj* probable, likely

probar §61 *tr* to prove; to test; to try; (*clothing*) to try on; to try out; to sample; to fit; to suit; (*vino*) to touch || *intr* to taste; **probar de** to take a taste of || *ref* to try on

probidad *f* probity, integrity, honesty

problema *m* problem

pro•caz *adj* (*pl* -**caces**) impudent, insolent, bold

procedencia *f* origin, source; point of departure

procedente *adj* coming, originating; proper

proceder *m* conduct, behavior || *intr* to proceed; to originate; to behave; to be proper

procedimiento *m* procedure; proceeding; process

procelo•so -sa *adj* tempestuous, stormy

prócer *adj* high, lofty || *m* hero, leader

procesar *tr* to sue, prosecute; to indict; to try

procesión *f* procession; origin, emergence

proceso *m* process; progress; suit, lawsuit; **proceso verbal** (Am) minutes

proclama *f* proclamation; marriage banns

proclamar *tr* to proclaim; to acclaim
proclíti•co -ca *adj & m* proclitic
procurador *m* attorney, solicitor; proxy
procurar *tr* to strive for; to manage as attorney; to yield, produce; to try to
prodigar §44 *tr* to lavish; to squander; to waste || *ref* to be a show-off
prodigio *m* prodigy
prodigio•so -sa *adj* prodigious, marvelous; fine, excellent
pródigo -ga *adj* prodigal; lavish || *mf* prodigal
producción *f* production; crop, yield, produce; **producción en masa** or **en serie** mass production
producir §19 *tr* to produce; to yield, to bear; to cause, bring about || *ref* to explain oneself; to come about; to take place
producto *m* product; produce; proceeds
proeza *f* prowess; feat, stunt
prof. *abbr* **profeta**
profanar *tr* to profane
profa•no -na *adj* profane; indecent, immodest; worldly; lay || *mf* profane; worldly person; layman
profecía *f* prophecy || **las Profecías** (Bib) the Prophets
proferir §68 *tr* to utter
profesar *tr & intr* to profess
profesión *f* profession; **profesión de fe** confession of faith
profe•sor -sora *mf* teacher; professor
profeta *m* prophet
profetisa *f* prophetess
profetizar §60 *tr* to prophesy
profilácti•co -ca *adj & m* prophylactic; preventive || *f* hygiene
prófu•go -ga *adj & mf* fugitive || *m* slacker, draft dodger
profundidad *f* profundity; depth
profundizar §60 *tr* to deepen; to fathom, get to the bottom of
profun•do -da *adj* profound; deep
progenie *f* descent, lineage, parentage
progno•sis *f* (*pl* **-sis**) prognosis; (*del tiempo*) forecast
programa *m* program; **programa continuo** (mov) continuous showing; **programa de estudios** curriculum
programar *tr* to program
progresar *intr* to progress
progresista *adj & mf* (pol) progressive
progreso *m* progress; **hacer progresos** to make progress
prohibir *tr* to prohibit, forbid || *ref se* **prohibe fijar carteles** post no bills
prohijar *tr* to adopt
prohombre *m* (*en los gremios de los artesanos*) master; leader, head; (coll) big shot
prójimo *m* fellow man, fellow creature, neighbor; (coll) fellow
pról. *abbr* **prólogo**
prole *f* progeny, offspring
proletariado *m* proletariat
proleta•rio -ria *adj & m* proletarian
proliferar *intr* to proliferate
prolífi•co -ca *adj* prolific
proli•jo -ja *adj* tedious, too long; fussy, fastidious; long-winded; tiresome

prologar §44 *tr* to preface, write a preface for
prólogo *m* prologue; preface
prolongar §44 *tr* to prolong, extend; (geom) to produce
promediar *tr* to divide into two equal parts; to average || *intr* to mediate; to be half over
promedio *m* average, mean; middle
promesa *f* promise
promete•dor -dora *adj* promising
prometer *tr & intr* to promise || *ref* to become engaged
prometi•do -da *adj* engaged, betrothed || *m* promise; fiancé || *f* fiancée
prominente *adj* prominent
promiso•rio -ria *adj* promissory
promoción *f* promotion; advancement; (*conjunto de individuos que obtienen un grado en un mismo año*) class, year, crop
promontorio *m* promontory, headland; unwieldy thing
promover §47 *tr* to promote; to advance, to further
promulgar §44 *tr* to promulgate
pronombre *m* pronoun
pronosticar §73 *tr* to prognosticate, to foretell
pronóstico *m* prognostic, forecast; almanac; (med) prognosis
pron•to -ta *adj* quick, speedy; prompt; ready || *m* jerk; (coll) sudden impulse, fit of anger || **pronto** *adv* right away, soon; early; promptly; **lo más pronto posible** as soon as possible; **tan pronto como** as soon as
pronunciación *f* pronunciation
pronuncia•do -da *adj* marked; (*curva*) sharp; (*pendiente*) steep; bulky
pronunciamiento *m* insurrection, uprising; (*golpe de estado militar*) pronunciamento; (law) decree
pronunciar *tr* to pronounce; to utter; (*un discurso*) to make; to deliver; to decide on || *ref* to rebel; to declare oneself
propaganda *f* propaganda; advertising
propagar §44 *tr* to propagate; to spread; to broadcast
propalar *tr* to divulge, to spread
proparoxíto•no -na *adj & m* proparoxytone
propasar *ref* to go too far, to take undue liberty
propender *intr* to tend, to incline, to be inclined
propensión *f* propensity; predisposition
propen•so -sa *adj* inclined, disposed, prone
propiciar *tr* to propitiate; (Am) to support, favor, sponsor
propi•cio -cia *adj* propitious, favorable
propiedad *f* property; ownership; naturalness, likeness; **es propiedad** copyrighted; **propiedad horizontal** one-floor ownership in an apartment house; **propiedad literaria** copyright
propieta•rio -ria *mf* owner || *m* proprietor || *f* proprietress
propina *f* tip, fee, gratuity
propinar *tr* (*algo a beber*) to offer; (*medicamentos*) to prescribe or ad-

minister; (*palos, golpes, etc.*) (coll) to give ‖ *ref* (*una bebida*) to treat oneself to

propin•cuo -cua *adj* near, close at hand

pro•pio -pia *adj* proper, suitable; peculiar, characteristic; natural; same; himself, herself, etc.; own ‖ *m* messenger; native; **propios** public lands

proponer §54 *tr* to propose; to propound; (*a una persona para un empleo*) to name, to present ‖ *ref* to plan; to propose

proporción *f* proportion; opportunity

proporciona•do -da *adj* proportionate; fit, suitable

proporcionar *tr* to furnish, provide, supply, give; to proportion; to adapt, adjust

proposición *f* proposition; **proposición dominante** main clause

propósito *m* aim, purpose, intention; subject matter; **a propósito** by the way; apropos, fitting; in place; **a propósito de** apropos of; **de propósito** on purpose; **fuera de propósito** irrelevant, beside the point

propuesta *f* proposal, proposition

propulsar *tr* to propel, to drive

propulsión *f* propulsion; **propulsión a chorro** jet propulsion; **propulsión a cohete** rocket propulsion

pror. *abbr* procurador

prorratear *tr* to prorate

prórroga *f* extension, renewal

prorrogar §44 *tr* to defer, postpone, extend

prorrumpir *intr* to spurt, shoot forth; to break forth, burst out

prosa *f* prose; (coll) chatter, idle talk

prosai•co -ca *adj* prose; prosaic, dull

proscribir §83 *tr* to outlaw, to proscribe

proscrip•to -ta *mf* exile, outlaw

prosecución *f* continuation, prosecution; pursuit

proseguir §67 *tr* to continue, carry on ‖ *intr* to continue

prosélito *m* proselyte

prosista *mf* prose writer; (coll) chatterbox

prosódi•co -ca *adj* (*acento*) stress

prospectar *tr* & *intr* to prospect

prosperar *tr* to make prosper ‖ *intr* to prosper, to thrive

prosperidad *f* prosperity

próspe•ro -ra *adj* prosperous, thriving, successful

prosternar *ref* to prostrate oneself

prostituir §20 *tr* to prostitute ‖ *ref* to prostitute oneself; to become a prostitute

prostituta *f* prostitute

prosu•do -da *adj* (Chile, Ecuad, Peru) pompous, solemn

protagonista *mf* protagonist

protagonizar §60 *tr* to play the leading rôle of

protección *f* protection; **protección aduanera** protective tariff; **protección a la infancia** child welfare

proteger §17 *tr* to protect

protegida *f* protégée

protegido *m* protégé

proteína *f* protein

proter•vo -va *adj* perverse

protesta *f* protest; pledge, promise

protestante *adj* & *mf* protestant; Protestant

protestar *tr* to protest, asseverate; (*la fe*) to profess ‖ *intr* to protest; **protestar de** (*aseverar con ahinco*) to protest (*to state positively*); **protestar contra** (*negar la validez de*) to protest (*to deny forcibly*)

protocolo *m* protocol

protoplasma *m* protoplasm

prototipo *m* prototype

protozoario or **protozoo** *m* protozoön

provec•to -ta *adj* old, ripe

provecho *m* advantage, benefit; profit, gain; advance, progress; **¡buen provecho!** good luck!; good appetite!; **de provecho** useful; **provechos** perquisites

provecho•so -sa *adj* advantageous, beneficial; profitable; useful

proveedor -dora *mf* supplier, provider, purveyor; steward

proveer §43 & §83 *tr* to provide, furnish; to supply; to resolve, settle ‖ *intr* to provide; **proveer a** to provide for ‖ *ref* to supply oneself; to have a movement of the bowels

provenir §79 *intr* to come, arise

Provenza, la Provence

provenzal *adj* & *mf* Provençal

proverbio *m* proverb

providencia *f* providence, foresight; step, measure

providencial *adj* providential

provincia *f* province

provisión *f* provision; supply, stock; **provisiones de boca** foodstuffs

proviso•rio -ria *adj* provisory, provisional

provocar §73 *tr* to provoke; to promote, bring about; to incite, to tempt, to move ‖ *intr* to provoke; (coll) to vomit

proxeneta *mf* go-between

proximidad *f* proximity; **proximidades** neighborhood

próxi•mo -ma *adj* next; near; neighboring, close; early; **próximo pasado** last

proyección *f* projection; influence

proyectar *tr* to project; to cast; to design ‖ *ref* to project, stick out; (*una sombra*) to be projected, to fall

proyectil *m* projectile; **proyectil buscador del blanco** homing missile; **proyectil dirigido** or **teleguiado** guided missile

proyecto *m* project; **proyecto de ley** bill

proyector *m* projector, searchlight; projection machine

prudencia *f* prudence

prudente *adj* prudent

prueba *f* proof; trial, test; examination; (*de un traje*) fitting; (*de un alimento o una bebida*) sample, sampling; evidence; (sport) event; (Am) acrobatics; (Am) sleight of hand; **a prueba** on approval, on trial; **a prueba de** proof against, -proof, e.g., **a prueba de escaladores** burglarproof;

pruebas de planas page proof; **pruebas de primeras** first proof (*for proofreader*); **pruebas de segundas** galley proof (*for author*)
pruebista *mf* (Am) acrobat
prurito *m* itching; eagerness, itch
psicoanálisis *m* psychoanalysis
psicoanalizar §60 *tr* to psychoanalyze
psicología *f* psychology
psicológi•co -ca *adj* psychologic(al)
psicólo•go -ga *mf* psychologist
psicópata *mf* psychopath
psico•sis *f* (*pl* -sis) psychosis; **psicosis de guerra** war psychosis, war scare
psicóti•co -ca *adj* & *mf* psychotic
psique *f* cheval glass || **Psique** *f* Psyche
psiquiatra *mf* psychiatrist
psiquiatría *f* psychiatry
psíqui•co -ca *adj* psychic
P.S.M. *abbr* por su mandato
pte. *abbr* parte, presente
púa *f* point; prick, barb; tine, prong; (*del fonógrafo*) needle; (*del peine*) tooth; thorn; (*del puerco espín*) spine, quill; sting; graft; plectrum; (coll) tricky person
pubertad *f* puberty
publicación *f* publication
publicar §73 *tr* to publish; to publicize
publicidad *f* publicity; advertising; **publicidad de lanzamiento** advance publicity
publicita•rio -ria *adj* publicity; advertising
públi•co -ca *adj* & *m* public
pucha *f* (W-I) small bouquet; (Mex) crescent roll
puchero *m* pot, kettle; stew; (coll) daily bread; (coll) pouting; **hacer pucheros** to pout, screw up one's face
pucho *m* (Am) fag end, remnant; (*de cigarro*) (Am) stump; (Am) trifle, trinket; (*el hijo menor*) (Am) baby
puden•do -da *adj* ugly, shameful; obscene; (*partes*) private
pudiente *adj* powerful; well-off, well-to-do
pudín *m* pudding
pudor *m* modesty, shyness; chastity
pudoro•so -sa *adj* modest, shy; chaste
pudrición *f* rot, rotting
pudrir §83 *tr* to rot; to worry || *intr* to be dead and buried || *ref* to rot; to be worried; (*en la cárcel*) to languish
pueblo *m* people; common people; town, village; **pueblo de Dios** or **de Israel** children of Israel
puente *m* bridge; (dent, mus) bridge; (aut) axle, rear axle; **hacer puente** to take the intervening day off; **puente aéreo** airlift, air bridge; **puente colgante** suspension bridge; **puente de engrase** grease lift; **puente levadizo** drawbridge, lift bridge
puer•co -ca *adj* piggish, hoggish; dirty, filthy; slovenly; coarse, mean; lewd || *m* hog; **puerco espín** or **espino** porcupine || *f* sow; slattern, slut
puericia *f* childhood
pueril *adj* puerile, childish
puerilidad *f* puerility, childishness
puerro *m* leek

puerta *f* door, doorway; gate, gateway; **a puerta cerrada** or **a puertas cerradas** behind closed doors
puerto *m* harbor, port; haven; mountain pass; **puerto aéreo** airport; **puerto brigantino** Corunna; **puerto de arribada** port of call; **puerto de mar** seaport; **puerto franco** free port; **puerto marítimo** dock, port; **puerto seco** frontier customhouse
puertorrique•ño -ña *adj* & *mf* Puerto Rican
pues *adv* then, well; yes, certainly; why; anyhow; **pues bien** well then; **pues que** since || *conj* for, since, because, inasmuch as || *interj* well!, then!
puesta *f* setting; laying; putting; (*dinero apostado*) stake; **a puesta del sol** or **a puestas del sol** at sunset; **puesta a punto** adjustment; carrying out, completion; **puesta a tierra** (elec) grounding; **puesta de largo** coming out, social debut
pues•to -ta *adj* dressed; **puesto que** since, inasmuch as || *m* place; booth, stand; office; station; barracks; (*para cazadores*) blind; **puesto de socorros** first-aid station || *f* see **puesta**
púgil *m* pugilist
pugilato *m* boxing; fist fight
pugilismo *m* pugilism
pugna *f* fight, battle; struggle, conflict; **en pugna** at issue; **en pugna con** at odds with
pugnar *intr* to fight; to struggle; to strive, persist
pug•naz *adj* (*pl* -naces) pugnacious
pujante *adj* powerful, mighty, vigorous
pujar *tr* (*un proyecto*) to push; (*un precio*) to raise; to push up || *intr* to struggle, strain; to falter; (*por decir una cosa*) to grope; (coll) to snivel; **pujar para adentro** (CAm, W-I) to keep silent, say nothing
pul•cro -cra *adj* neat, tidy, trim; circumspect
pulga *f* flea; **de malas pulgas** peppery, hot-tempered; **hacer de una pulga un camello** or **un elefante** (coll) to make a mountain out of a molehill; **no aguantar pulgas** (coll) to stand for no nonsense
pulgada *f* inch
pulgar *m* thumb
puli•do -da *adj* pretty; neat; polished; clean, spotless
pulimentar *tr* to polish
pulimento *m* polish
pulir *tr* to polish; to finish; to give a polish to
pulmón *m* lung; **pulmón de acero** or **de hierro** iron lung
pulmonía *f* pneumonia
púlpito *m* pulpit
pulpo *m* octopus
pulsación *f* pulsation, throb; beat; strike, striking; (*del pianista, el mecanógrafo*) touch
pulsar *tr* (*un botón*) to push; (*un piano, arpa, guitarra*) to play; (*una tecla*) to strike; to feel or take the pulse

of; to sound out, examine ‖ *intr* to pulsate, throb, beat

pulsear *intr* to hand-wrestle

pulsera *f* bracelet; wristlet, watch strap; **pulsera de pedida** engagement bracelet

pulso *m* pulse; steadiness, steady hand; tact, care, caution; (Am) bracelet; (Am) wrist watch; **a pulso** with hand and wrist; by main strength; (dibujo) freehand; **sacar a pulso** (coll) to carry out against odds; **tomar el pulso a** to feel or take the pulse of

pulular *intr* to swarm; to bud, to sprout

pulverizar §60 *tr* to pulverize; to atomize; to spray

pulla *f* dig, cutting remark; filthy remark; witticism

pum *interj* bang!

puma *m* cougar

puna *f* (SAm) bleak tableland in the Andes; (SAm) mountain sickness

pundonor *m* point of honor; face

pundonoro·so -sa *adj* punctilious, scrupulous; haughty, dignified

pungir §27 *tr* to prick; to sting

punta *f* (extremo agudo) point; tip, end; (del cigarro) butt; nail; point, cape, headland; (del toro) horn; (del asta del ciervo) tine, prong; style, graver; touch, tinge, trace; (del vino) souring; (elec) point; **de punta** on end; on tiptoe; **de punta en blanco** in full armor; (coll) in full regalia; **estar de punta (con)** to be at odds (with); **punta de combate** (del torpedo) warhead; **punta de lanza** spearhead; **punta de París** wire nail; **sacar punta a** to put a point on, to sharpen; **tener en la punta de la lengua** (coll) to have on the tip of one's tongue

puntada *f* hint; (sew) stitch; (dolor agudo) (Am) stitch, sharp pain

puntal *m* prop, support; stay, stanchion; (naut) depth of hold; backing, support; (Am) bite, snack

puntapié *m* kick; **echar a puntapiés** (coll) to kick out

puntear *tr* to dot, mark with dots; (guitarra) to pluck; to stipple; to stitch ‖ *intr* (naut) to tack

puntera *f* toe, toe patch; leather tip; (coll) kick

puntería *f* aim, aiming; marksmanship

puntero *m* pointer; (del reloj) hand; stonecutter's chisel; punch; (Am) leading animal

puntiagu·do -da *adj* sharp-pointed

puntilla *f* brad; narrow lace edging; (de la pluma fuente) point; (carp) tracing point; dagger; **de puntillas** on tiptoe; **puntilla francesa** finishing nail

puntillero *m* bullfighter who delivers coup de grace with dagger

puntillo·so -sa *adj* punctilious

punto *m* (señal de dimensiones poco perceptibles) point, dot; stitch, loop; mesh; (rotura en un tejido de punto) break; jot; cabstand, hackstand; (gram) period; (math, typ, sport, fig) point; **a buen punto** opportunely; **al punto** at once; **a punto de** on the point of; **a punto fijo** for certain; **de punto** knitted; **dos puntos** (gram) colon; **en punto** sharp, on the dot; **poner punto final a** to wind up, to bring to an end; **punto de admiración** exclamation mark or point; **punto de aguja** knitting; **punto de Hungría** herringbone; **punto de media** knitwork; **punto de mira** aim; center of attraction; **¡punto en boca!** mum's the word!; **punto interrogante** question mark; **punto menos** almost; **puntos y rayas** dots and dashes; **punto y coma** *msg* semicolon

puntuación *f* punctuation; mark, grade; scoring

puntual *adj* punctual; certain, sure; exact, accurate

puntualizar §60 *tr* to fix in the memory; to give a detailed account of; to finish; to draw up

puntuar §21 *tr & intr* to punctuate; to score

puntura *f* puncture, prick

punzada *f* prick; shooting pain; (del remordimiento) pang

punzante *adj* sharp, pricking; barbed, biting, caustic

punzar §60 *tr* to prick, puncture, punch; to sting; to grieve ‖ *intr* to sting

punzón *m* punch; pick; burin, graver; budding horn, tenderling; **punzón de marcar** center punch

puñada *f* punch

puñado *m* handful, bunch

puñal *m* dagger, poniard

puñalada *f* stab; blow, sudden sorrow; **puñalada de misericordia** coup de grâce; **puñalada trapera** stab in the back

puñetazo *m* punch; bang with the fist

puño *m* fist; cuff; wristband; grasp; fistful, handful; hilt; (p.ej., del paraguas) handle; (del bastón) head; punch; **como un puño** (coll) whopping big; (coll) tiny, microscopic; (coll) close-fisted; **de su propio puño** or **de su puño y letra** in his own hand, in his own writing

pupa *f* pimple; fever blister

pupila *f* (del ojo) pupil

pupi·lo -la *mf* boarder; orphan, ward; pupil ‖ *f* see **pupila**

pupitre *m* writing desk

puquio *m* (SAm) spring or pool of fresh, clear water

puré *m* purée; **puré de patatas** mashed potatoes; **puré de tomates** stewed tomatoes

pureza *f* purity

purga *f* purge; purgative; drain valve

purgante *adj & m* purgative

purgar §44 *tr* to purge; to physic; to drain; to purify, refine; to expiate; (pasiones) to control, to check; (sospechas) to clear away ‖ *ref* to take a physic; to unburden oneself

puridad *f* purity

purificar §73 *tr* to purify

purita·no -na *adj* & *mf* puritan; Puritan
pu·ro -ra *adj* pure; sheer; (*cielo*) clear; out-and-out, outright; **de puro** completely, totally; because of being ‖ *m* cigar
púrpura *f* purple
purpura·do -da *adj* purple ‖ *m* (eccl) cardinal
purpúre·o -a *adj* purple

pusilánime *adj* pusillanimous
pústula *f* pustule
puta *f* whore
putañear or **putear** *intr* (coll) to whore around, to chase after lewd women
putati·vo -va *adj* spurious
putrefac·to -ta *adj* rotten, putrid
pútri·do -da *adj* putrid, rotten
puya *f* steel point; (*del gallo*) spur

Q

Q, q (cu) *f* twentieth letter of the Spanish alphabet
q.b.s.m. *abbr* que besa su mano
q.b.s.p. *abbr* que besa sus pies
q.e.p.d. *abbr* que en paz descanse
q.e.s.m. *abbr* que estrecha su mano
quántum *m* (*pl* **quanta**) quantum
que *pron rel* that, which; who, whom; **el que** he who; which, the one which; who, the one who ‖ *adv* than ‖ *conj* that; for, because; let, e.g., **que entre** let him come in; **a que** (coll) I'll bet that
qué *adj* & *pron interr* what, which; **¿qué tal?** how?; hello, how's everything? ‖ *interj* what!; what a!; how!
quebrada *f* gorge, ravine, gap; failure, bankruptcy; (Am) brook
quebradi·zo -za *adj* brittle, fragile; frail
quebra·do -da *adj* weakened; bankrupt; ruptured; rough; winding; fractional ‖ *m* (math) fraction; (Am) tobacco leaf full of holes ‖ *f* see **quebrada**
quebrantable *adj* breakable
quebrantar *tr* to break; to break open; to break out of; to grind, crush; to soften, mollify; (*un contrato; la ley; un hábito; un testamento; el corazón de una persona*) to break ‖ *ref* to break; to become broken
quebrantaterro·nes *m* (*pl* **-nes**) (coll) clodhopper
quebranto *m* break, breaking; heavy loss; great sorrow; discouragement
quebrar §2 *tr* to bend, twist; to crush; to overcome; to temper, soften ‖ *intr* to break; to fail; to weaken, give in ‖ *ref* to break; to weaken; to become ruptured
queda *f* curfew
quedar *intr* to remain; to stay; to be left; to be left over; to stop, leave off; to turn out; to be; to be found, be located; **quedar en** to agree on; to agree to; **quedar por** + *inf* or **sin** + *inf* to remain to be + *pp* ‖ *ref* to remain; to stay; to stop; to be; to be left; to put up; **quedarse con** to keep, to take; **quedarse tan fresco** (coll) to show no offense
que·do -da *adj* quiet, still; gentle ‖ *f* see **queda** ‖ **quedo** *adv* softly, in a low voice; gropingly
quehacer *m* work, task, chore
queja *f* complaint, lament; whine, moan

quejar *ref* to complain, lament; to whine, moan
quejido *m* complaint, whine, moan
quejumbre *f* complaining, whine, moan
quejumbro·so -sa *adj* complaining; whining, whiny
quema *f* fire; burning; **a quema ropa** point-blank; **de quema** distilled; **hacer quema** (Arg, Bol) to hit the mark
quemada *f* burnt brush; (Mex) fire
quemadero *m* incinerator; (*poste destinado para quemar a los condenados a la pena de fuego*) stake
quema·do -da *adj* burned; burnt out; (Am) angry ‖ *m* burnt brush; **oler a quemado** (coll) to smell of fire; **saber a quemado** (coll) to taste burned ‖ *f* see **quemada**
quema·dor -dora *adj* burning; incendiary ‖ *m* burner
quemadura *f* burn; (agr) smut
quemar *tr* to burn; to scald; to set on fire; to scorch; to frostbite; to sell too cheap ‖ *intr* to burn, be hot ‖ *ref* to burn; to be burning up; (coll) to fret; (*estar cercano a lo que se busca*) (coll) to be warm, to be hot; **quemarse las cejas** (coll) to burn the midnight oil
quemarropa — a quemarropa point-blank
quemazón *f* burn; burning; intense heat; (*de un fusible*) blowout; (coll) itch; (coll) cutting remark; (coll) pique, anger; (hum) bargain sale; (Arg, Bol, Chile) mirage on the pampas
que·pis *m* (*pl* **-pis**) kepi
querella *f* complaint; dispute, quarrel
querellar *ref* to complain; to whine
querencia *f* liking, affection; attraction; love of home; (*de animales*) haunt; favorite spot
querencio·so -sa *adj* homing; (*sitio*) favorite
querer *m* love, affection; liking, fondness ‖ *v* §55 *tr* to wish, want, desire; to like; to love; **como quiera** anyhow; anyway; **como quiera que** whereas; inasmuch as; no matter how; **cuando quiera** any time; **donde quiera** anywhere; **querer bien** to love; **sin querer** unwillingly; unintentionally ‖ *v aux* to wish to, to want to, to desire to; will; to be about to, to be trying to,

e.g., **quiere llover** it is trying to rain; **querer decir** to mean; **querer más** to prefer to, would rather

queri·do -da *adj* dear ‖ *mf* lover; paramour; (coll) dearie ‖ *f* mistress

quermés *f* or **quermese** *f* bazaar; village or country fair

queroseno *m* var of **keroseno**

querubín *m* cherub

quesadilla *f* cheesecake; sweet pastry

quese·ro -ra *adj* cheesy ‖ *mf* cheesemonger; cheesemaker ‖ *f* cheese board; cheese mold; cheese dish

queso *m* cheese; **queso de cerdo** headcheese; **queso helado** brick ice cream

quevedos *mpl* nose glasses

quiá *interj* oh, no!

quicio *m* pivot hole (*of hinge*); **fuera de quicio** out of order; **sacar de quicio** to put out of order; to unhinge

quiebra *f* crack; damage, loss; bankruptcy

quien *pron rel* who, whom; he who, she who; someone who, anyone who

quién *pron interr* who, whom

quienquiera *pron indef* anyone, anybody; **quienquiera que** whoever; **a quienquiera que** whomever

quie·to -ta *adj* quiet, calm; virtuous

quietud *f* quiet, calm, stillness

quijada *f* jaw, jawbone

quijotes·co -ca *adj* quixotic

quilate *m* carat

quilo *m* kilogram; **sudar el quilo** (coll) to slave, be a drudge

quilla *f* keel; (*de ave*) breastbone; **dar de quilla** (naut) to keel over

quimera *f* chimera; dispute, quarrel

química *f* chemistry

quími·co -ca *adj* chemical ‖ *mf* chemist ‖ *f* see **química**

quimicultura *f* tank farming

quimono *m* kimono

quina *f* cinchona, Peruvian bark

quincalla *f* hardware

quincallería *f* hardware store; hardware business; hardware factory

quincalle·ro -ra *mf* hardware merchant

quince *adj* & *pron* fifteen ‖ *m* fifteen; (*en las fechas*) fifteenth

quincea·vo -va *adj* & *m* fifteenth

quince·no -na *adj* & *m* fifteenth ‖ *f* fortnight, two weeks; two weeks' pay

quincuagési·mo -ma *adj* & *m* fiftieth

quiniela *f* pelota game of five; soccer lottery; daily double; (Arg, Urug) numbers game

quinien·tos -tas *adj* & *pron* five hundred ‖ **quinientos** *m* five hundred

quinina *f* quinine

quinqué *m* student lamp, oil lamp

quinquenal *adj* five-year

quinta *f* villa, country house; draft, induction; **ir a quintas** to be drafted; **redimirse de las quintas** to be exempted from the draft

quintacolumnista *mf* fifth columnist

quintal *m* quintal, hundredweight

quintar *tr* to draft

quinteto *m* quintet

quintilla *f* five-line stanza of eight syllables and two rhymes; any five-line stanza with two rhymes

quintilli·zo -za *mf* quint, quintuplet

Quintín — **armar la de San Quintín** to raise a rumpus, raise a row

quin·to -ta *adj* fifth ‖ *m* fifth; lot; pasture; draftee ‖ *f* see **quinta**

quinza·vo -va *adj* & *m* fifteenth

quiosco *m* kiosk, summerhouse; stand; **quiosco de música** bandstand; **quiosco de necesidad** comfort station; **quiosco de periódicos** newsstand

quiquiri·quí *m* (*pl* -quíes) cock-a-doodle-doo; (coll) cock of the walk

quirófano *m* operating room

quiromancia or **quiromancía** *f* palmistry

quiropodista *mf* chiropodist

quiroprácti·co -ca *adj* chiropractic ‖ *mf* chiropractor

quirúrgi·co -ca *adj* surgical

quirurgo *m* surgeon

quiscal *m* grackle

quisicosa *f* puzzler

quisqui·do -da *adj* (Arg) constipated

quisquilla *f* trifle, triviality; **pararse en quisquillas** to bicker, to make a fuss over trifles; **quisquillas** hairsplitting, quibbling

quisquillo·so -sa *adj* trifling; touchy; fastidious; hairsplitting

quiste *m* cyst

quis·to -ta *adj* — **bien quisto** well-liked, welcome; **mal quisto** disliked, unwelcome

quitaesmalte *m* nail-polish remover

quitaman·chas (*pl* -chas) *mf* (*persona*) clothes cleaner, spot remover ‖ *m* (*substancia*) clothes cleaner, spot remover

quitamo·tas *mf* (*pl* -tas) (coll) bootlicker, apple polisher

quitanie·ve *m* or **quitanie·ves** *m* (*pl* -ves) snowplow

quitaple·dras *m* (*pl* -dras) cowcatcher

quitapintura *m* paint remover

quitapón *m* pompon for draft mules; **de quitapón** detachable, removable

quitar *tr* to remove; to take away; (*la mesa*) to clear; (*esfuerzo, trabajo*) to save; (*tiempo*) to take; to free; to parry; **quitar algo a algo** to take something off something, to remove something from something; **quitar algo a uno** to remove something from someone; to take something away from someone ‖ *intr* — **de quita y pon** detachable, removable ‖ *ref* (*el sombrero, una prenda de vestir*) to take off; (*el sombrero en señal de cortesía*) to tip; (*una mancha*) to come out, to come off; (*un vicio*) to give up; to withdraw

quitasol *m* parasol

quite *m* removal; hindrance; dodge; (*en la esgrima*) parry; (taur) passes made with the cape to draw the bull away from the man in danger

quizá or **quizás** *adv* maybe, perhaps

quó·rum *m* (*pl* -rum) quorum

R

R, r (ere) *f* twenty-first letter of the Spanish alphabet

R. *abbr* respuesta, Reverencia, Reverendo

rabada *f* hind quarter, rump

rabadilla *f* base of the spine

rábano *m* radish; **rábano picante** or **rusticano** horseradish; **tomar el rábano por las hojas** (coll) to be on the wrong track

ra·bí *m* (*pl* **-bíes**) rabbi

rabia *f* anger, rage; (*hidrofobia*) rabies; **tener rabia a** (coll) to have a grudge against

rabiar *intr* to rage, to rave; to get mad; to go mad, to have rabies; **que rabia** like the deuce; **rabiar por** to be dying for; to be dying to

rabieta *f* (coll) tantrum

rabillo *m* leafstalk; flower stalk; (*en los cereales*) mildew spot; (*del ojo*) corner

rabio·so -sa *adj* mad, rabid

rabo *m* tail; (*del ojo*) corner; (fig) tail, train; **rabo verde** (CAm) old rake

ra·bón -bona *adj* bobtail; (Chile) bare, naked; (Mex) mean, wretched ‖ *f* (Am) camp follower; **hacer rabona** (coll) to play hooky

rabotada *f* swish of the tail; (coll) coarse remark

rabu·do -da *adj* long-tailed

racial *adj* racial

racimar *ref* to cluster, to gather together

racimo *m* bunch; cluster; (*de perlas*) string

raciocinio *m* reasoning

ración *f* ration; allowance; **ración de hambre** starvation wages

racional *adj* rational

racionar *tr* to ration

racha *f* split, crack; chip; squall, gust of wind; streak of luck

rada *f* (naut) road, roadstead

radar *m* radar

radiación *f* radiation

radiacti·vo -va *adj* radioactive

radia·dor -dora *adj* radiating ‖ *m* radiator

radiante *adj* radiant; (*alegre, sonriente*) radiant

radiar *tr* to radiate; to radio; to broadcast; to cross out, erase ‖ *intr* to radiate

radicación *f* taking root; (math) evolution

radical *adj & m* radical

radicar §73 *intr* to take root; to be located ‖ *ref* to take root; to settle; (*un negocio*) to be based

radio *m* edge, outskirts; (*de una rueda*) spoke, rung; (*de acción*) radius; (chem) radium; (math) radius ‖ *m & f* radio

radioaficiona·do -da *mf* radio amateur, radio fan

radiodifundir *tr & intr* to broadcast

radiodifusión *f* broadcasting

radioemisora *f* broadcasting station

radioescucha *mf* radio listener; radio monitor

radiofrecuencia *f* radio frequency

radiografiar §77 *tr* to X-ray; to radio, to wireless

radiograma *m* X ray (*photograph*)

radioperturbación *f* jamming

radioyente *mf* radio listener

raer §56 *tr* to scrape, scrape off; to smooth, to level; to wipe ‖ *ref* to become frayed, to wear away

ráfaga *f* gust, puff; gust of wind; flash of light; (*de ametralladora*) burst

raí·do -da *adj* threadbare; barefaced

ra·íz *f* (*pl* **-íces**) root; **a raíz de** close to the root of; even with; right after, hard upon; **de raíz** by the root; completely; **echar raíces** to take root

raja *f* crack, split; splinter, chip; slice

rajar *tr* to crack, to split; to splinter, chip; to slice ‖ *intr* (coll) to boast; (coll) to chatter ‖ *ref* to crack, to split; to splinter, chip; (Mex, CAm, W-I) to back down, to break one's promise

rajatabla — a rajatabla (coll) desperately, ruthlessly

ralea *f* kind, quality; breed, ilk

ralear *intr* to thin out; to be true to form

ra·lo -la *adj* sparse, thin

rallador *m* grater

rallar *tr* to grate; (coll) to grate on, annoy

rallo *m* grater; scraper; rasp; (*de la regadera*) spout, nozzle; unglazed porous jug (*for cooling water by evaporation*)

rama *f* branch, bough; **andarse por las ramas** (coll) to beat about the bush; **en rama** raw; unbound, in sheets; **in the grain**

ramaje *m* branches, foliage

ramal *m* (*de una cuerda*) strand; halter; branch; (rr) branch line

ramalazo *m* lash; (*señal en el cutis por un golpe o enfermedad*) spot, pock; sharp pain; blow, sudden sorrow

rambla *f* dry ravine; avenue, boulevard

ramera *f* whore, harlot

ramificar §73 *tr & ref* to ramify

ramillete *m* bouquet; centerpiece, epergne; (bot) cluster

ramo *m* branch, limb; bouquet, cluster; (*de géneros, negocios, etc.*) line; (*p.ej., de una ciencia*) branch; (*de una enfermedad*) touch, slight attack

ramojo *m* brushwood, dead wood

ramonear *intr* to trim twigs; to browse

rampa *f* ramp; cramp; (aer) apron; (Bol) litter, stretcher

ram·plón -plona *adj* (*zapato*) heavy, coarse; common, vulgar

ramplonería *f* coarseness, vulgarity

rana *f* frog; **no ser rana** (coll) to be a past master; **rana toro** bullfrog

ran·cio -cia *adj* rank, rancid, stale;

(*vino*) old; old, ancient; old, old-fashioned

ranchar *ref* (Col, Ven) to balk

ranchear *tr* (Am) to sack, pillage ‖ *intr* & *ref* to build huts, form a settlement

ranchero *m* messman; (Am) rancher, ranchman

rancho *m* mess; meeting, gathering; camp; thatched hut; (naut) stock of provisions; (Am) ranch; (Arg) straw hat; **hacer rancho** (coll) to make room; **hacer rancho aparte** (coll) to be a lone wolf, to go one's own way

randa *m* (coll) pickpocket ‖ *f* lace trimming

rango *m* rank; class, nature; (Am) pomp, splendor; .(*elevada condición social*) (Am) status, standing

ranura *f* groove; slot

rapagón *m* stripling

rapar *tr* to shave; to crop; to scrape; (coll) to snatch, filch ‖ *ref* to shave; (*una vida regalada*) to lead

ra·paz (*pl* -paces) *adj* thievish; rapacious ‖ *m* young boy, lad

rapaza *f* young girl, lass

rapé *m* snuff

rápi·do -da *adj* rapid ‖ *m* (rr) express; **rápidos** (*de un río*) rapids

raposa *f* fox; female fox; (*persona*) (coll) fox

raposo *m* male fox; (coll) foxy fellow; (coll) slipshod fellow

raptar *tr* to abduct; to kidnap

rapto *m* abduction; kidnaping; rapture; faint, swoon

raque *m* beachcombing; **andar al raque** to go beachcombing

raquear *intr* to beachcomb

raquero *m* pirate; beachcomber

raqueta *f* racket; battledore; badminton; snowshoe; **raqueta y volante** battledore and shuttlecock

raquíti·co -ca *adj* (*que padece raquitis*) rickety; flimsy, weak, miserable

raquitis *f* rickets

raramente *adv* rarely, seldom; oddly

rareza *f* rareness; rarity; oddness, strangeness; peculiarity

ra·ro -ra *adj* rare; odd, strange; thin, sparse

ras *m* evenness; **a ras** close, even, flush; **a ras de** even with, flush with; **ras con ras** flush, at the same level; grazing

rasar *tr* to graze, to skim ‖ *ref* to clear up

rascacie·los *m* (*pl* -los) skyscraper ·

rascamoño *m* fancy hairpin; (bot) zinnia

rascar §73 *tr* to scrape; to scuff; to scratch; to scrape clean ‖ *ref* (*una cicatriz, un grano*) to pick; (Am) to get drunk

rasete *m* satinet

rasga·do -da *adj* (*boca; ventana*) wide-open; (*ojos*) large; (Am) outspoken; (Col) generous ‖ *m* tear, rip, rent

rasgar §44 *tr* to tear, to rip ‖ *ref* to become torn

rasgo *m* (*de una pluma de escribir*) flourish, stroke; trait, characteristic;

feat, deed; flash of wit, bright remark; **a grandes rasgos** in bold strokes; **rasgos** (*de la cara*) features

rasguear *tr* to thrum on ‖ *intr* to make a flourish

rasgón *m* tear, rip, rent

rasguñar *tr* to scratch; to sketch, outline

rasguño *m* scratch; sketch, outline

ra·so -sa *adj* smooth, flat, level, even; common, plain; clear, cloudless; (coll) brazen, shameless ‖ *m* flat country; satin; **al raso** in the open

raspa *f* stalk, stem; (*de mazorca de maíz*) beard; (*de pez*) spine, backbone; shell, rind

raspadura *f* scraping; erasure; (Am) pan sugar

raspar *tr* to scrape, scrape off; to scratch, scratch out; to graze; (*el vino*) to bite; to take, to steal; (W-I) to. dismiss, fire; (W-I) to scold ‖ *intr* (Ven) to go away; (Ven) to die

raspear *tr* (SAm) to scold ‖ *intr* (*una pluma*) to scratch

rastra *f* rake; harrow; drag; track, trail; (*p.ej., de cebollas*) string; (naut) drag; **pescar a la rastra** to trawl

rastracuero *m* (Am) show-off; (Am) upstart; (Am) sharper, adventurer

rastreador *m* dredge; (nav) mine sweeper

rastrear *tr* to trail, track, trace; to drag; to dredge; to check into ‖ *intr* to rake; to skim the ground, fly low

rastre·ro -ra *adj* dragging, trailing; creeping; low-flying; groveling, cringing; low, vile

rastrillar *tr* to rake; (*cáñamo, lino*) to hatchel, to comb; (Arg, Col) to shoot, to fire; (*un fósforo*) (Arg, Col) to strike (*a match*)

rastrillo *m* rake; hackle, hatchel, flax comb; (*de cerradura o llave*) ward; grating, iron grate; (rr) cowcatcher

rastro *m* rake; harrow; track, trail; scent; trace, vestige; slaughterhouse; wholesale meat market; rag fair; **rastro de condensación** (aer) contrail ·

rastrojo *m* stubble

rasura *f* shaving; scraping

rasurar *tr* & *ref* to shave

rata *f* rat; female rat; **rata del trigo** hamster

ratear *tr* to apportion; to snitch

ratería *f* baseness, meanness, vileness; petty thievery; petty theft

rate·ro -ra *adj* thievish; trailing, dragging; base, vile ‖ *mf* sneak thief

ratificar §73 *tr* to ratify

rato *m* time, while, little while; **a ratos** from time to time; **a ratos perdidos** in spare time, in one's leisure hours; **buen rato** pleasant time; (coll) large amount; **pasar el rato** (coll) to waste one's time; **un rato** awhile

ratón *m* mouse; (Ven) hangover; **ratón de biblioteca** (coll) bookworm

ratonera *f* (*trampa*) mousetrap; (*agujero*) mousehole; nest of mice; (Am) hut, shop

raudal *m* stream, torrent; abundance

rau·do -da *adj* rapid, swift, impetuous

raya f stripe; (*línea fina; pez*) ray; (*en la imprenta, la escritura y la telegrafía*) dash; (*de los pantalones*) crease; (*en los cabellos*) part; boundary line, limit; (*para impedir la comunicación del incendio en los campos*) firebreak; (*del espectro*) (phys) line; (Mex) pay, wages; **a rayas** striped; **hacerse la raya** to part one's hair; **pasar de la raya** to go too far; **tener a raya** to keep within bounds

raya·no -na adj bordering; borderline

rayar tr (*papel*) to rule, to line; to stripe; to scratch, score, mark; to cross out; to underscore ‖ intr to border; to stand out; (*el alba, el día, la luz, el sol*) to begin, arise, come forth; **rayar en** to verge on, to border on ‖ ref (Col) to get rich

rayo m (*de luz*) ray; (*de rueda*) spoke; lightning, flash of lightning, stroke of lightning, thunderbolt; (*persona*) (fig) live wire; **echar rayos** (coll) to blow up, hit the ceiling; **rayo mortífero** death ray; **rayos X X** rays

rayón m rayon

raza f race; breed, stock; crack, slit; quality; ray of light (*coming through a crack*)

razón f reason; right, justice; account, story; (*cantidad o grado medidos por otra cosa tomada como unidad*) rate; (math) ratio; **a razón de** at the rate of; **con razón o sin ella** right or wrong; **hacer la razón** to return a toast; to join at table; **meterse en razón** to listen to reason; **no tener razón** to be wrong; **razón social** firm name, trade name; **tener razón** to be right; to be in the right

razonable adj reasonable

razonar tr to reason, reason out; to itemize ‖ intr to reason

reabrir §83 tr & ref to reopen

reacción f reaction; **reacción en cadena** chain reaction

reaccionar intr to react

reacciona·rio -ria adj & mf reactionary

rea·cio -cia adj stubborn, obstinate

reactivo m reagent

real adj real; royal; fine, splendid ‖ m army camp; fairground; real (*old Spanish coin; Spanish money of account equal to a quarter of a peseta*)

realce m embossment, raised work; enhancement, lustre; emphasis; **bordar de realce** to embroider in relief; (fig) to embroider, to exaggerate

realeza f royalty

realidad f reality; truth; **hecho realidad** come true, e.g., **un sueño hecho realidad** a dream come true

realismo m realism

realista mf (*persona que tiende a ver las cosas como son*) realist; (*partidario de la monarquía*) royalist

realización f realization, fulfillment; achievement; sale; **realización de beneficios** profit taking

realizar §60 tr to fulfill; to carry out; to turn into cash ‖ ref to become fulfilled; to be carried out

realquilar tr to sublet

realzar §60 tr to raise, elevate; to emboss; to enhance, set off; to emphasize

reanimar tr to revive, restore; to cheer, encourage ‖ ref to revive, recover one's spirits

reanudar tr to renew, to resume

reaparecer §22 intr to reappear

reata f rope to keep animals in single file; single file; **de reata** in single file; (coll) in blind submission; (coll) next, following

rebaba f burr, fin

rebaja f rebate; diminution

rebajar tr to lower; to diminish, reduce; to rebate; (*precios*) to mark down; (*a una persona*) to deflate; (carp) to rabbet ‖ ref to stoop; to humble oneself

rebajo m rabbet, groove; offset, recess

rebalsar tr to dam ‖ ref to become dammed up; to be checked; to pile up, accumulate

rebanada f slice

rebanar tr to slice; to cut through

rebañadera f grapnel

rebaño m flock

rebarbati·vo -va adj crabbed, surly

rebasar tr to exceed; to overflow; to sail past

rebatiña f grabbing, scramble; **andar a la rebatiña** (coll) to scramble

rebatir tr to repel, drive back; to check; to resist; to strengthen; to rebut, refute; to deduct, rebate; to beat hard

rebato m alarm, call to arms; alarm, excitement; (mil) surprise attack

rebeca f cardigan

rebelar ref to revolt, rebel; to resist; to break away

rebelde adj rebellious; stubborn ‖ mf rebel

rebeldía f rebelliousness; defiance, stubbornness

rebelión f rebellion, revolt

rebe·lón -lona adj balky, restive

reborde m flange, rim, collar

rebosar tr to cause to overflow ‖ intr to overflow, run over; to be in abundance; **rebosar de** or **en** to overflow with, to burst with; to be rich in; to have an abundance of ‖ ref to overflow, run over

rebotar tr to bend back; to repel; (coll) to annoy, worry ‖ intr to bounce; to bounce back, rebound ‖ ref (coll) to become annoyed, become worried

rebote m bounce; rebound

rebozar §60 tr (*la cara*) to muffle up; to cover with batter ‖ ref to muffle up, to muffle oneself up

rebozo m muffling; muffler; shawl; **de rebozo** secretly; **sin rebozo** frankly, openly

rebulta·do -da adj bulky, massive

rebullicio m hubbub, loud uproar

rebullir §13 intr to stir, begin to move; to give signs of life ‖ ref to stir, begin to move

rebusca f seeking, searching; gleaning; leavings, refuse

rebusca·do -da *adj* affected, unnatural, recherché

rebuscar §73 *tr* to seek after; to search into; to glean

rebuznar *intr* to bray; (coll) to talk nonsense

rebuzno *m* braying; (coll) nonsense

recade·ro -ra *mf* messenger ‖ *m* errand boy

recado *m* errand; message; gift, present; daily marketing; compliments, regards; safety, security; equipment, outfit; **mandar recado** to send word; **recado de escribir** writing materials

recaer §15 *intr* to fall again; to fall back; to relapse; **recaer en** to fall to; **recaer sobre** to fall upon, devolve upon

recaída *f* relapse; backsliding

recalar *tr* to soak, saturate ‖ *intr* to sight land

recalcar §73 *tr* to press, squeeze; to cram, pack, stuff; (*sus palabras*) to stress ‖ *intr* (naut) to list, to heel; **recalcar en** to lay stress on ‖ *ref* (coll) to harp on the same string; (coll) to sprawl; (*p.ej.*, *la muñeca*) (coll) to sprain

recalentar §2 *tr* to overheat; (*la comida*) to warm over

recalmón *m* (naut) lull

recamado *m* embroidery

recamar *tr* to embroider

recámara *f* dressing room; (*de un arma de fuego*) breech, chamber; (coll) reserve, caution; (Mex) bedroom

recamarera *f* (Mex) chambermaid

recambio *m* spare part; (*parte, rueda, etc.*) **de recambio** spare

recapacitar *tr* to run over in one's mind ‖ *intr* to refresh one's memory; to reflect

recargar §44 *tr* to reload; to overload; to recharge; to overcharge; to over-adorn; (*una cuota de impuesto*) to increase; (elec) to recharge ‖ *ref* to become more feverish

recargo *m* new burden; extra charge; new charge; (*que paga el contribuyente moroso*) penalty; (pathol) rise in temperature; **recargo de tarifa** extra fare

recata·do -da *adj* cautious, circumspect; modest; shy

recatar *tr* to hide, conceal ‖ *ref* to hide; to be afraid to take a stand

recato *m* caution, reserve; modesty

recauchutaje *m* recapping, retreading

recauchutar *tr* to recap, to retread

recaudar *tr* (*impuestos, tributos*) to gather, collect; to guard, watch over

recaudo *m* tax collecting; care, precaution; bail, surety; **a buen recaudo** under guard, in safety

recelar *tr* to fear, distrust ‖ *intr* & *ref* to fear, be afraid

recelo *m* fear, distrust

recelo·so -sa *adj* fearful, distrustful

recensión *f* review, book review

recepción *f* reception; reception desk

recepcionista *m* room clerk. ‖ *f* receptionist

receptáculo *m* receptacle; shelter, refuge

receptar *tr* to receive, welcome; (*delincuentes*) to hide, conceal; (*cosas robadas*) to receive

recepti·vo -va *adj* receptive; susceptible

receptor *m* receiver; **receptor de cabeza** headpiece; **receptor telefónico** receiver

receta *f* recipe; (pharm) prescription

recetar *tr* (*un medicamento*) to prescribe; (coll) to request

recibí *m* receipt; received payment

recibi·dor -dora *mf* receiver; receiving teller; ticket collector ‖ *m* reception room

recibimiento *m* reception; welcome; reception room; (*visita en que una persona recibe a sus amistades*) at-home

recibir *tr* to receive; (*visitas*) to entertain ‖ *intr* to receive; to entertain ‖ *ref* to be received, be admitted; **recibirse de** to be admitted to practice as; to be graduated as

recibo *m* reception; receipt; hall; parlor; at-home; **acusar recibo de** to acknowledge receipt of; **estar de recibo** to be at home; **ser de recibo** to be acceptable

recién *adv* (used before past participles) recently, just, newly, e.g., **recién llegado** newly arrived; (Am) just now, recently

reciente *adv* recently

recinto *m* area, inclosure, place

re·cio -cia *adj* strong; thick, coarse, heavy; harsh; hard, bitter, arduous; (*tiempo*) severe; swift, impetuous ‖ **recio** *adv* strongly; swiftly; hard; loud

reciprocidad *f* reciprocity

recípro·co -ca *adj* reciprocal

recital *m* (*de música o poesía*) recital

recitar *tr* to recite; (*un discurso*) to deliver

reclamación *f* claim, demand; objection; protest, complaint

reclamar *tr* to claim, demand; (*un ave*) to decoy, lure ‖ *intr* to cry out, protest, complain

reclamo *m* bird call; decoy bird; (*para aves*) lure; allurement, attraction; advertisement; blurb, puff; reference; (typ) catchword

reclinar *tr* (*p.ej.*, *la cabeza*) to lean, to bend ‖ *ref* to recline

reclinatorio *m* prie-dieu; couch, lounge

recluir §20 *tr* to seclude, shut in; to imprison ‖ *ref* to go into seclusion

reclusión *f* seclusion; imprisonment

reclu·so -sa *adj* secluded; imprisoned ‖ *mf* prisoner; inmate

recluta *m* recruit ‖ *f* recruiting; (*del ganado disperso*) (Arg) roundup

reclutar *tr* to recruit; (Arg) to round up

recobrar *tr* to recover ‖ *ref* to recover; to come to

recobro *m* recovery; (*de un motor*) pickup

recodar *intr* to lean; to bend, twist, turn, wind

recodo *m* bend, twist, turn

recoger §17 *tr* to pick up; to gather,

collect; to harvest; to shorten, draw in; to keep; to welcome; to lock up || *ref* to take shelter, take refuge; to withdraw; (*echarse en la cama*) to retire; to go home; to cut down expenses

recogida *f* collection; withdrawal; suspension

recogimiento *m* gathering, collecting; harvesting; seclusion, retreat; concentration; self-communion

recolectar *tr* to gather, gather in; (*el algodón*) to pick

recomendable *adj* commendable

recomendar §2 *tr* to recommend; to commend

recompensa *f* recompense, reward

recompensar *tr* to recompense, reward

recomprar *tr* to buy back, to repurchase

reconcentrar *tr* to bring together; (*un sentimiento o afecto*) to conceal, disguise || *ref* to come together; to be absorbed in thought

reconciliar *tr* to reconcile || *ref* to become reconciled

recóndi•to -ta *adj* hidden, concealed

reconfortar *tr* to comfort, to cheer

reconocer §22 *tr* to recognize; to admit, to acknowledge; to examine; (mil) to reconnoiter || *intr* (mil) to reconnoiter || *ref* to be clear

reconoci•do -da *adj* grateful

reconocimiento *m* recognition; admission, acknowledgment; gratitude; reconnaissance; **reconocimiento médico** inquest

reconquista *f* reconquest

reconsiderar *tr* to reconsider

reconstruir §20 *tr* to reconstruct, to rebuild, to recast

recontar §61 *tr* (*volver a contar; narrar*) to recount (*to count again; to narrate*)

reconvenir §79 *tr* to expostulate with, to remonstrate with

reconversión *f* reconversion

recopilar *tr* to compile

re•cord *m* (*pl* -**cords**) (sport) record; **batir un record** to break a record; **establecer un record** to make a record

recordar §61 *tr* to remember; to remind || *intr* to remember; to get awake; to come to; **si mal no recuerdo** (coll) if I remember correctly

recordati•vo -va *adj* reminding, reminiscent || *m* reminder

recordatorio *m* reminder; memento

record•man (*pl* -**men**) record holder

recorrer *tr* to go over, to go through; to look over, look through; (*un libro*) to run through; to overhaul

recorrido *m* trip, run, route; (*del émbolo*) stroke; repair

recortado *m* cutout

recortar *tr* to trim, to cut off; (*figuras en una tela, en un papel*) to cut out; to outline || *ref* to stand out

recorte *m* cutting; (*de un periódico*) clipping; dodge, duck; **recortes** cuttings, trimmings

recostar §61 *tr* to lean || *ref* to lean, lean back, sit back

recova *f* poultry business; poultry stand; (Arg) portico; (SAm) food market

recoveco *m* bend, turn, twist; subterfuge, trick

recreación *f* recreation

recreo *m* recreation; place of amusement

recrudecer §22 *intr* & *ref* to flare up, get worse

rectángu•lo -la *adj* right-angled || *m* rectangle

rectificar §73 *tr* to rectify; (*un cilindro de motor*) to rebore

rec•to -ta *adj* straight; (*ángulo*) right; right, just, righteous || *m* rectum

rec•tor -tora *adj* governing, managing || *mf* principal, superior || *m* rector; (*de una universidad*) rector, president

recua *f* drove; (*de personas o cosas*) (coll) string, line

recuadro *m* panel, square; (*sección de un impreso encerrada dentro de un marco*) box

recubrir §83 *tr* to cover, cap, coat

recuento *m* count; recount; inventory

recuerdo *m* memory, remembrance; keepsake, souvenir

recuero *m* muleteer

recular *intr* to back up; (*un arma de fuego*) to recoil; (coll) to back down

reculón *m* (Am) backing; **a reculones** (coll) backing away, recoiling

recuperar *tr* & *ref* to recuperate, to recover

recurrir *intr* to resort, have recourse; to revert

recurso *m* recourse; resource; resort; appeal, petition

recusar *tr* to refuse, reject; (law) to challenge

rechazar §60 *tr* to refuse, to reject; to repel, drive back

rechazo *m* rejection; rebound, recoil

rechifla *f* catcall

rechiflar *tr* & *intr* to catcall, to hiss || *ref* to make fun

rechinar *intr* to creak, grate, squeak; to act with bad grace

rechon•cho -cha *adj* (coll) chubby, tubby, plump

rechupete — de rechupete (coll) fine, wonderful

red *f* net; netting; network; system; baggage netting; (fig) net, snare, trap; **a red barredera** with a clean sweep; **red barredera** dragnet

redacción *f* writing; editing; editorial staff; newspaper office, city room

redactar *tr* to write up; to edit

redac•tor -tora *mf* writer; editor, newspaper editor; **redactor publicitario** copy writer

redada *f* (*de peces*) catch, netful; (*p.ej., de criminales*) (coll) haul, roundup

redecilla *f* hair net

rededor *m* surroundings; **al rededor** (**de**) around

redención *f* redemption; help, recourse

reden•tor -tora *mf* redeemer

redición *f* constant repetition

redi•cho -cha *adj* (coll) overprecise

redil *m* sheepfold

redimir tr to redeem; to ransom; to buy back

rédito m income, revenue, yield

redituar §21 tr to yield, produce

redobla·do -da adj stocky, heavy-built, heavy, strong; (mil) double-quick

redoblar tr to double; to clinch; to repeat || intr (un tambor) to roll

redoble m doubling; clinching; repeating; roll of a drum

redoma f phial, flask

redoma·do -da adj sly, crafty

redonda f district, neighborhood; (mus) semibreve; **a la redonda** around, roundabout

redondear tr to round, make round; to round off; to round out || ref to be well-off; to be out of debt

redondel m circle; round cloak; (espacio destinado a la lidia) (taur) ring

redondilla f eight-syllable quatrain with rhyme abba or abab

redon·do -da adj round; straightforward; (terreno) pasture; (Am) honest; (Am) stupid || m ring, circle; (coll) cash || f see **redonda**

redopelo m (coll) row, scuffle; **al redopelo** against the grain, the wrong way; (coll) roughly, violently

reducir §19 tr & ref to reduce; **reducirse a** to come to, to amount to; to be obliged to

reducto m (fort) redoubt

redundante adj redundant

redundar intr to redound; to overflow; **redundar en** to redound to

reelección f reëlection

reembarcar §73 tr, intr & ref to reship, to reëmbark

reembarco m reshipment (of persons); reëmbarkation

reembarque m reshipment (of goods)

reembolsar tr to reimburse; to refund || ref to collect a debt, to be reimbursed

reembolso m reimbursement; refund; **contra reembolso** collect on delivery; cash on delivery

reemplazar §60 tr to replace

reemplazo m replacement; (mil) replacements; (hombre que sirve en lugar de otro) (mil) replacement

reencuadernar tr (bb) to rebind

reencuentro m collision; (de tropas) clash

reenganchar tr & ref to reënlist

reentrada f reëntry

reestrenar tr (theat) to revive

reestreno m (theat) revival

reexamen m or **reexaminación** f reëxamination

reexpedición f forwarding, reshipment

reexpedir §50 tr to forward, reship

refacción f refreshment; allowance; repair, repairs; (coll) extra, bonus; (Am) spare part

refajo m underskirt, slip

referencia f reference; account, report

referi·do -da adj above-mentioned

referir §68 tr to refer; to tell, report || ref to refer

refinamiento m refinement

refinar tr to refine; to polish, perfect

refinería f refinery

reflejar tr to reflect; to reflect on; to show, reveal || intr to reflect

reflejo m glare; reflection; reflex; **reflejo patelar** or **rotuliano** knee jerk

reflexión f reflection

reflexionar tr to reflect on or upon || intr to reflect

reflujo m ebb

refocilar tr to cheer; to strengthen || intr (Arg, Urug) to lighten || ref to be cheered; to take it easy

reforma f reform; reformation; alteration, renovation || **la Reforma** the Reformation

reformación f reformation

reformar tr to reform; to mend, repair; to alter, renovate; to revise; to reorganize || ref to reform; to hold oneself in check

reforzar §35 tr to reinforce; to strengthen; to encourage

refracción f refraction

refracta·rio -ria adj rebellious, unruly, stubborn

refrán m proverb, saying

refregar §66 tr to rub; (coll) to upbraid

refrenar tr to curb, to rein; to check, restrain

refrendar tr to countersign; to authenticate; to visé; (coll) to repeat

refrescar §73 tr to refresh; to cool, to refrigerate || intr & ref to refresh; to refresh oneself; to cool off; to go out for fresh air; (el viento) (naut) to blow up

refresco m refreshment; cold drink, soft drink

refriega f fray, scuffle

refrigerador m refrigerator; ice bucket

refrigerio m coolness; relief; pick-me-up, light lunch

refuerzo m reinforcement

refugia·do -da mf refugee

refugiar tr to shelter || ref to take refuge

refugio m refuge; hospice; shelter; haunt; (para peatones en medio de la calle) safety zone; **refugio antiaéreo** air-raid shelter; **refugio antiatómico** fallout shelter

refundición f recast; revision; (de una pieza dramática) adaptation

refundir tr to recast; to revise; (una pieza dramática) to adapt || intr to redound

refunfuñar intr to grumble, to growl

refutar tr to refute

regadera f watering can; street sprinkler

regadí·o -a or **regadi·zo -za** adj irrigable || m irrigated land

regala f gunwale

regala·do -da adj dainty, delicate; pleasing, pleasant; (vida) of ease

regalar tr to give; to regale, entertain; to treat; to caress, fondle; to indulge

regalía f privilege, perquisite; bonus; (Arg, Chile) muff; (Am) royalty

regaliz m licorice

regalo m gift, present; treat; joy, pleasure; **regalos de fiesta** favors

rega·lón -lona adj (coll) comfort-loving, pampered; (vida) (coll) soft, easy

regañar tr (coll) to scold || intr to

growl, snarl; to grumble; to quarrel; (coll) to scold

regaño *m* (coll) scolding; growl, snarl; grumble

regar §66 *tr* to water, sprinkle; to irrigate; to spread, sprinkle, strew

regate *m* dodge, duck; (fig) dodge, subterfuge

regatear *tr* to haggle over; to sell at retail; (coll) to avoid, to shun || *intr* to haggle, to bargain; (naut) to race; (coll) to duck, to dodge

regazo *m* lap

regenerar *tr* & *ref* to regenerate

regente *m* director, manager; registered pharmacist; (typ) foreman

regicida *mf* regicide

regicidio *m* regicide

regi·dor -dora *adj* ruling, governing || *m* alderman, councilman

régimen *m* (*pl* **regímenes**) regime; diet; rate; management; (gram) government; **régimen de hambre** starvation diet; **régimen de justicia** rule of law

regimental *adj* regimental

regimentar §2 *tr* to regiment

regimiento *m* regiment; rule, government; city council

re·gio -gia *adj* regal, royal; magnificent

región *f* region

regir §57 *tr* to rule, govern; to control, manage; to guide, steer; (gram) to govern || *intr* to prevail, be in force

registra·dor -dora *adj* registering; recording || *m* registrar, recorder; inspector || *f* cash register

registrar *tr* to register; to record; to examine, inspect || *ref* to register; to be recorded; to take place

registro *m* registration, registry; recording; examination, inspection; entry, record; bookmark; manhole; (*de chimenea*) damper; (*de reloj*) regulator; (*de órgano*) (mus) stop; (*de piano*) (mus) pedal

regla *f* rule; (*para trazar líneas*) ruler; measure, moderation; order; menstruation; **regla de cálculo** slide rule; **reglas** monthlies, menses

reglamenta·rio -ria *adj* prescribed, statutory

reglamento *m* rules, regulations

reglar *tr* to regulate; (*papel*) to rule || *ref* to guide oneself, be guided

regleta *f* (typ) lead

regletear *tr* (typ) to lead, to space

regocijar *tr* to cheer, delight || *ref* to rejoice

regocijo *m* cheer, delight, rejoicing

regoldar §3 *intr* to belch

regolfar *intr* & *ref* to surge back, flow back, back up

regorde·te -ta *adj* dumpy, plump

regresar *intr* to return

regreso *m* return; **estar de regreso** to be back

regüeldo *m* belch, belching

reguero *m* drip, trickle; (*señal que deja una cosa que se va vertiendo*) track; irrigating ditch; **ser un reguero de pólvora** to spread like wildfire

regulador *m* regulator; (*de locomotora*) throttle; (mach) governor

regular *adj* regular; fair, moderate, medium; **por lo regular** as a rule || *tr* to regulate; to put in order; to throttle

rehacer §39 *tr* to remake, make over, do over; to mend, repair, renovate || *ref* to recover, to rally

rehén *m* hostage; **llevarse en rehenes** to carry off as a hostage

rehilandera *f* pinwheel

rehilar *intr* to quiver; to whiz by

rehilete *m* shuttlecock; (*que se lanza por diversión*) dart; dig, cutting remark; (taur) banderilla

rehuir §20 *tr* to avoid, shun; to shrink from; to refuse; to dislike || *intr* & *ref* to flee

rehusar *tr* to refuse, turn down

reimpresión *f* reprint

reimprimir §83 *tr* to reprint

reina *f* queen; **reina Margarita** aster, China aster; **reina viuda** queen dowager

reinado *m* reign

reinar *intr* to reign; to prevail

reincidir *intr* to backslide; to repeat an offense

reingreso *m* reëntry

reino *m* kingdom; **Reino Unido** United Kingdom

reinstalar *tr* to reinstate, reinstall

reintegrar *tr* to refund, pay back

reintegro *m* refund, payment

reír §58 *tr* to laugh at || *intr* & *ref* to laugh; **reír de** or **reírse de** to laugh at

reja *f* grate, grating, grille; plowshare, colter; **entre rejas** behind bars

rejilla *f* screen; grating; lattice, latticework; cane, cane upholstery; foot brasier; fire grate; (electron) grid; (*de acumulador*) (elec) grid; (rr) baggage rack

rejón *m* spear; dagger; (taur) lance

rejonear *tr* (*el jinete al toro*) (taur) to jab with a lance made to break off in the bull's neck

rejuvenecimiento *m* rejuvenation

relación *f* relation; account; list; (*en un drama*) speech; **relación de ciego** blind man's ballad; **relaciones** betrothal, engagement

relacionar *tr* to relate || *ref* to be related

relajación *f* or **relajamiento** *m* relaxation; slackening; laxity; rupture, hernia

relajar *tr* to relax; to slacken; to debauch || *intr* to relax || *ref* to relax, become relaxed; to become debauched; to be ruptured

relamer *ref* to lick one's lips; to gloat; to relish; to boast; to slick oneself up

relami·do -da *adj* prim, overnice

relámpago *m* flash of lightning; flash of wit; **relámpago fotogénico** flash bulb, flashlight; **relámpagos** lightning

relampaguear *intr* to lighten; to flash

relatar *tr* to relate, report

relati·vo -va *adj* relative

relato *m* story; statement, report

relé *m* (elec) relay

releer §43 *tr* to reread

relegar §44 *tr* to relegate; to banish, exile; to shelve, lay aside

relente *m* night dew, light drizzle

relevador *m* (elec) relay

relevante *adj* outstanding

relevar *tr* to emboss; to make stand out; to relieve; to release; to absolve; to replace ǁ *intr* to stand out in relief

relevo *m* (elec) relay; (mil) relief; **relevos** (sport) relay race

relicario *m* shrine; (*medallón*) (Am) locket

relieve *m* relief; merit, distinction; **en relieve** in relief; **poner de relieve** to point out; to make stand out; **relieves** scraps, leftovers

religión *f* religion

religio·so -sa *adj* religious

relinchar *intr* to neigh

relincho *m* neigh, neighing; cry of joy

reliquia *f* relic; trace, vestige; **reliquia de familia** heirloom

reloj *m* watch; clock; meter; **como un reloj** like clockwork; **conocer el reloj** to know how to tell time; **reloj de caja** grandfather's clock; **reloj de carillón** chime clock; **reloj de cuclillo** cuckoo clock; **reloj de ocho días cuerda** eight-day clock; **reloj de pulsera** wrist watch; **reloj de sol** sundial; **reloj despertador** alarm clock; **reloj registrador** time clock; **reloj registrador de tarjetas** punch clock

relojera *f* watch case; watch pocket

relojería *f* watchmaking, clockmaking; watchmaker's shop

reloje·ro -ra *mf* watchmaker, clockmaker ǁ *f* see **relojera**

reluciente *adj* shining, brilliant, flashing

relucir §45 *intr* to shine

relumbrar *intr* to shine, dazzle, glare

relumbre *m* beam, sparkle; flash; dazzle, glare

relumbrón *m* flash, glare; tinsel; **de relumbrón** showy, tawdry

rellano *m* (*en la pendiente de un terreno*) level stretch; (*de escalera*) landing

rellenar *tr* to refill; to fill up; to stuff; to pad; to fill out; (coll) to cram, to stuff ǁ *ref* to fill up; (coll) to cram, stuff oneself

relle·no -na *adj* full, packed; stuffed ǁ *m* refill; filling, stuffing; padding, wadding; (*en un escrito*) filler

remachar *tr* (*un clavo ya clavado*) to clinch; (*un roblón*) to rivet; to stress, emphasize ǁ *ref* (Col) to maintain strict silence

remache *m* clinching; riveting; rivet

remanso *m* dead water, backwater

remar *intr* to row; to toil, struggle

remata·do -da *adj* hopeless; **loco rematado** (coll) raving mad

rematar *tr* to finish, put an end to; to finish off, kill off; (*en una subasta*) to knock down ǁ *intr* to end ǁ *ref* to come to ruin

remate *m* end; crest, top, finial; closing; highest bid; (*en una subasta*) sale; **de remate** hopelessly

remecer §46 *tr & ref* to shake, swing, rock

remedar *tr* to copy, imitate; to ape, mimic; to mock

remediar *tr* to remedy; to help; to prevent; (*del peligro*) to free, to save

remediava·gos *m* (*pl* -gos) short cut

remedio *m* remedy; help; recourse; **no hay remedio or no hay más remedio** it can't be helped; **no tener remedio** to be unavoidable

remedión *m* (theat) substitute performance

remedo *m* copy, imitation; poor imitation

remendar §2 *tr* to patch, mend, repair; to darn; to emend, correct; to touch up

remen·dón -dona *mf* mender, repairer; shoe mender; tailor (*who does mending*)

reme·ro -ra *mf* rower ǁ *m* oarsman

remesa *f* remittance; shipment

remesar *tr* to remit; to ship

remezón *m* (Am) hard shake; (Am) tremor

remiendo *m* patch; mending, repair; retouching; emendation, correction; job printing, job work; **a remiendos** (coll) piecemeal

remilga·do -da *adj* prim and finicky; affected, smirking

remilgar §44 *intr* to be prim and finicky, to smirk

remilgo *m* primness, affectation

remira·do -da *adj* circumspect, discreet

remisión *f* remission; reference

remitente *mf* sender, shipper

remitido *m* (*noticia de un particular a un periódico*) personal; letter to the editor

remitir *tr* to remit; to forward, send, ship; to refer; to defer, postpone; to pardon, forgive ǁ *intr* to remit, let up; to refer ǁ *ref* to remit, let up; to defer, yield

remo *m* oar; leg, arm, wing; toil, labor; (sport) rowing; **aguantar los remos** to lie or rest on one's oars

remoción *f* discharge, dismissal; removal

remojar *tr* to soak, to steep, to dip; to celebrate with a drink; **remojar la palabra** (coll) to wet one's whistle

remojo *m* soaking, steeping; **poner en remojo** (coll) to put off to a more suitable time

remolacha *f* beet; **remolacha azucarera** sugar beet

remolcador *m* tug, tugboat; towboat; tow car

remolcar §73 *tr* to tow; to take in tow

remoler §47 *tr* to grind up; (coll) to bore

remolinear *tr, intr & ref* to eddy, whirl about

remolino *m* eddy, whirlpool; swirl, whirl; disturbance, commotion; throng, crowd; cowlick

remo·lón -lona *adj* lazy, indolent ǁ *mf* shirker, quitter

remolonear *intr* to refuse to budge

remolque *m* tow; towing; trailer; **a remolque** in tow

remontar *tr* to mend, repair; to frighten

away; to elevate, raise up; (*p.ej., un río*) to go up ‖ *intr* (*en el tiempo*) to go back ‖ *ref* to rise, rise up; to soar; (*en el tiempo*) to go back

remontuar *m* stem-winder

remoquete *m* punch; nickname; sarcasm; (coll) flirting

rémora *f* hindrance, obstacle

remordimiento *m* remorse

remo·to -ta *adj* remote; unlikely; **estar remoto** to be rusty

remover §47 *tr* to remove; to shake; to stir; to disturb, upset; to dismiss, to discharge ‖ *ref* to move away

remozar §60 *tr* to rejuvenate ‖ *ref* to become rejuvenated

rempujar *tr* (coll) to push, jostle

rempujón *m* (coll) push, jostle

remuda *f* change, replacement; change of clothes

remudar *tr* to change, replace; to move around

remuneración *f* remuneration; **remuneración por rendimiento** piece wage

renacer §22 *intr* to be reborn, to be born again; to recover

renacimiento *m* rebirth; renaissance

renacuajo *m* tadpole; (coll) shrimp, little squirt

Renania *f* Rhineland

ren·co -ca *adj* lame

rencor *m* rancor; **guardar rencor** to bear malice

rendición *f* surrender; submission; fatigue, exhaustion; yield

rendi·do -da *adj* tired, worn-out; submissive

rendija *f* crack, split, slit

rendimiento *m* submission; exhaustion; yield; output; (mech) efficiency

rendir §50 *tr* to conquer; to subdue; to surrender; to exhaust, wear out; to return, give back; to yield, produce; (*gracias, obsequios, homenaje*) to render ‖ *intr* to yield ‖ *ref* to surrender; to yield, give in; to be exhausted, to be worn out

renegar §66 *tr* to deny vigorously; to abhor, detest ‖ *intr* to curse; (coll) to be insulting; **renegar de** to deny; to curse; to abhor, detest

renegociación *f* renegotiation

Renfe, la acronym for **la Red Nacional de los Ferrocarriles Españoles** the Spanish National Railroad System

renglón *m* line; **a renglón seguido** right below; **leer entre renglones** to read between the lines

reniego *m* curse

reno *m* reindeer

renombra·do -da *adj* renowned, famous

renombre *m* renown, fame

renovar §61 *tr* to renew; to renovate; to transform, restore; to remodel

renquear *intr* to limp

renta *f* income; private income; annuity; public debt; rent; **renta nacional** gross national product

rentar *tr* to produce, yield

rentista *mf* bondholder; financier; person of independent means

renuente *adj* reluctant, unwilling

renuevo *m* sprout, shoot; renewal

renuncia *f* renunciation; resignation; (law) waiver

renunciar *tr* to renounce; to resign ‖ *intr* to renounce; (*no servir al palo que se juega*) to renege; **renunciar a** to give up, to renounce, to waive

renuncio *m* slip, mistake; (*en juegos de naipes*) renege; (coll) lie

reñi·do -da *adj* on bad terms; bitter, hard-fought

reñir §72 *tr* (*regañar*) to scold; (*una batalla, un desafío*) to fight ‖ *intr* to fight; to be at odds, to fall out

re·o -a *adj* guilty, criminal ‖ **reo** *mf* offender, criminal; (law) defendant

reojo — de reojo askance, out of the corner of one's eye; hostilely

reorganizar §60 *tr* & *ref* to reorganize

reóstato *m* rheostat

repanchigar or **repantigar** §44 *ref* to sprawl, to loll

reparar *tr* to repair, to mend; to make amends for; to notice, observe; (*un golpe*) to parry ‖ *intr* to stop; **reparar en** to notice, pay attention to ‖ *ref* to stop; to refrain

reparo *m* repairing, repairs; notice, observation; doubt, objection; shelter; bashfulness

repa·rón -rona *adj* (coll) faultfinding ‖ *mf* (coll) faultfinder

repartir *tr* to distribute; (*naipes*) to deal

reparto *m* distribution; (*de naipes*) deal; (theat) cast; **reparto de acciones gratis** stock dividend

repasar *tr* to repass; to retrace; to review; to revise; (*la ropa*) to mend

repasata *f* (coll) scolding, reprimand

repaso *m* revision; (*de una lección*) review; mending; (coll) reprimand

repatriar §77 *tr* to repatriate; to send home ‖ *intr* & *ref* to be repatriated; to go or come home

repeler *tr* to repel, to repulse

repente *m* start, sudden movement; **de repente** suddenly

repenti·no -na *adj* sudden, unexpected

repentista *mf* (mus) improviser; (mus) sight reader

repentizar §60 *intr* to improvise; (mus) to sight-read, perform at sight

repercutir *intr* to rebound; to reëcho, reverberate

repertorio *m* repertory

repetición *f* repetition; (mus) repeat

repetir §50 *tr* & *intr* to repeat

repicar §73 *tr* to mince, to chop up; to ring, to sound; to sting again ‖ *intr* to peal, ring out, resound ‖ *ref* to boast, be conceited

repique *m* chopping, mincing; peal, ringing; (coll) squabble, quarrel

repiqueteo *m* pealing, ringing; beating, rapping

repisa *f* shelf, ledge; bracket; **repisa de chimenea** mantelpiece; **repisa de ventana** window sill

replantear *tr* to lay out again; to reaffirm, to reimplement

replegar §66 *tr* to fold over and over ‖ *ref* to fold, fold up; (mil) to fall back

reple·to -ta *adj* replete, full, loaded; fat, chubby

réplica *f* answer, retort; replica

replicar §73 *tr* to argue against ‖ *intr* to answer back, retort

repli·cón ·cona *adj* (coll) saucy, flip

repliegue *m* fold, crease; (mil) falling back

repollo *m* cabbage; (*p.ej., de lechuga, col*) head

reponer §54 *tr* to replace, put back; to restore; (*una pieza dramática*) to revive; **repuso** he replied ‖ *ref* to recover; to calm down

reportaje *m* reporting; news coverage; report

reportar *tr* to check, restrain; to get, obtain; to bring, carry; to report ‖ *ref* to restrain or control oneself

reporte *m* report, news report; gossip

repórter *m* reporter

reporte·ro ·ra *mf* reporter

reposar *intr & ref* to rest, repose; to take a nap; (*en la sepultura*) to lie, be at rest; (*poso, sedimento*) to settle

reposición *f* replacement; (*de la salud*) recovery; (theat) revival

reposo *m* rest, repose

repostar *tr, intr & ref* to stock up; to refuel

repostería *f* pastry shop, confectionery; pantry

reposte·ro ·ra *mf* pastry cook, confectioner

repregunta *f* (law) cross-examination

repreguntar *tr* (law) to cross-examine

reprender *tr* to reprehend, to scold

represa *f* dam; damming; repression, check; (*de un buque*) recapture

represalia *f* reprisal; retaliation

represar *tr* to dam; to repress, to check; (*un buque*) to recapture

representación *f* representation; dignity, standing; performance; **en representación de** representing

representante *adj* representing ‖ *mf* representative; actor, player; (com) agent, representative

representar *tr* to represent; to show, express; to state, declare; to act, perform, play; (*determinada edad*) to appear to be ‖ *ref* to imagine

representati·vo ·va *adj* representative

reprimenda *f* reprimand

reprimir *tr* to repress

reprobación *f* reproof; flunk, failure

reprobar §61 *tr* to reprove; to flunk, to fail

reprochar *tr* to reproach

reproche *m* reproach

reproducción *f* reproduction; breeding

reproducir §19 *tr & ref* to reproduce

repro·pio ·pia *adj* balky

reptar *intr* to crawl; to cringe

reptil *m* reptile

república *f* republic

republica·no ·na *adj & mf* republican ‖ *m* patriot

repudiar *tr* to repudiate, to disown, to disavow

repues·to ·ta *adj* secluded; spare, extra ‖ *m* stock, supply; serving table; pantry; **de repuesto** spare, extra

repugnante *adj* repugnant, disgusting

repugnar *tr* to conflict with; to contra-

dict; to object to, to avoid; to revolt, be repugnant to ‖ *intr* to be repugnant

repujar *tr* to emboss

repulgar §44 *tr* to hem, to border

repulgo *m* hem, border

repuli·do ·da *adj* highly polished; all dolled up

repulsar *tr* to reject, refuse

repulsi·vo ·va *adj* repulsive

repuntar *tr* (*animales dispersos*) (Arg, Chile, Urug) to round up ‖ *intr* to begin to appear; (naut) to begin to rise; (naut) to begin to ebb ‖ *ref* to begin to turn sour; (coll) to fall out

repuso see **reponer**

reputación *f* reputation, repute

reputar *tr* to repute; to esteem

requebra·dor ·dora *adj* flirtatious ‖ *mf* flirt

requebrar §2 *tr* to break into smaller pieces; to flatter, to flirt with

requemar *tr* to burn again; to parch; to overcook; to inflame; to bite, sting ‖ *ref* to become tanned or sunburned; to smolder, burn within

requerir §68 *tr* to notify; to summon; to request; to urge; to check, examine; to require; to seek, look for; to reach for; to court, make love to

requesón *m* cottage cheese

requiebro *m* fine crushing; flattery, flattering remarks, flirtation

requisi·to ·ta *adj* requisite ‖ *m* requisite, requirement; accomplishment; **requisito previo** prerequisite

res *f* head of cattle; beast; **reses** cattle

resabio *m* unpleasant aftertaste; bad habit, vice

resabio·so ·sa *adj* (Am) sly, crafty; (*caballo*) (Am) vicious

resaca *f* surge, surf; undertow; (com) redraft; (slang) hangover

resalir §65 *intr* to jut out, project

resaltar *tr* to emphasize ‖ *intr* to bounce, rebound; to jut out, project; to stand out

resanar *tr* to retouch, patch, repair

resarcir §36 *tr* to indemnify, to make amends to; (*un daño, un agravio*) to repay; (*una pérdida*) to make good; to mend, repair ‖ *ref* — **resarcirse de** to make up for

resbaladi·zo ·za *adj* slippery; skiddy; risky; (*memoria*) shaky

resbalar *intr* to slide; to skid; to slip ‖ *ref* to slide; to slip; (fig) to slip, to misstep

rescatar *tr* to ransom, redeem; to rescue; (*el tiempo perdido*) to make up for; to relieve; to atone for

rescate *m* ransom, redemption; rescue; salvage; ransom money

rescindir *tr* to rescind

rescoldera *f* heartburn

rescoldo *m* embers; smoldering; doubt, scruple; **arder en rescoldo** to smolder

resenti·do ·da *adj* resentful

resentimiento *m* resentment; sorrow, disappointment

resentir §68 *ref* to be resentful; **resentirse de** to feel the bad effects of; to resent; to suffer from

reseña f outline; book review; newspaper account; (mil) review

reseñar tr to outline; (un libro) to review; (mil) to review

reserva f reserve; reservation; **con or bajo la mayor reserva** in strictest confidence; **reserva de caza** game preserve

reservar tr to reserve; to put aside; to postpone; to exempt; to keep secret || ref to save oneself, to bide one's time; to beware, be distrustful

resfriado m cold

resfriar §77 tr to cool, chill || intr to turn cold || ref to catch cold; to cool off, grow cold

resguardar tr to defend; to protect, shield || ref to take shelter; to protect oneself

resguardo m defense; protection; check, voucher; collateral; (naut) wide berth, sea room

residencia f residence; impeachment

residenciar tr to call to account; to impeach

residir intr to reside

residuo m residue, remains; remainder

resignación f resignation

resignar tr to resign || ref to resign, become resigned; **resignarse con** (p.ej., su suerte) to be resigned to

resina f resin

resistencia f resistance; strength; **resistencia de rejilla** (electron) grid leak

resistente adj resistant; strong; (hort) hardy

resistir tr to bear, to stand; (la tentación) to resist || intr to resist; to hold out; **resistir a** (la violencia; la risa) to resist; to refuse to || ref to resist; to struggle; **resistirse a** to refuse to

resma f ream

resobrina f grandniece, greatniece

resobrino m grandnephew, greatnephew

resolución f resolution; **en resolución** in brief, in a word

resolver §47 & §83 tr to resolve; to solve; to decide on; to dissolve; || ref to resolve; to make up one's mind

resollar §61 intr to breathe; to breathe hard, pant; to stop for a rest

resonar §61 intr to resound, to echo

resoplar intr to puff; to snort

resoplido m puffing; snort

resorte m spring; springiness; means; province, scope; (Am) rubber band; **resorte espiral** coil spring; **tocar resortes** to pull wires, to pull strings

respailar intr — **ir respailando** (coll) to scurry along

respaldar m back || tr to back; to indorse || ref to lean back; to sprawl

respaldo m back; backing; indorsement

respectar tr (with personal a) to concern; **por lo que respecta a . . .** as far as . . . is concerned

respecti·vo -va adj respective

respecto m respect, reference, relation; **al respecto** in the matter; **respecto a or de** with respect to, in or with regard to

respetable adj respectable

respetar tr to respect

respeto m respect; consideration; **campar por sus respetos** (coll) to be inconsiderate, to go one's (his, her, etc.) own way; **de respeto** spare, extra

respetuo·so -sa adj respectful; awesome, impressive; humble, obedient

respigón m hangnail

respingar §44 intr to balk, to shy; (elevarse el borde, p.ej., de la falda) to curl up; (coll) to give in unwillingly

respin·gón -gona adj (nariz) snubby, upturned; (Am) surly, churlish

respirar tr to breathe || intr to breathe; to breath freely; to breathe a sigh of relief; to catch one's breath, to stop for a rest; **no respirar** (coll) to not breathe a word; **sin respirar** without respite, without letup

respiro m breathing; respite, breather, breathing spell; (para el pago de una deuda) extension of time

resplandecer §22 intr to shine; to flash, glitter

resplandeciente adj brilliant; resplendent

resplandor m brilliance, radiance; resplendence; glare

responder tr to answer || intr to answer, respond; to correspond; to answer back; **responder de** (una cosa) to answer for; **responder por** (una persona) to answer for

respon·dón -dona adj (coll) saucy

responsable adj responsible; **responsable de** responsible for

respuesta f answer, response

resquebrajar tr & ref to crack, to split

resquemar tr & intr to bite, to sting || ref to be parched; (resentirse sin manifestarlo) to smolder

resquemo m bite, sting

resquicio m crack, chink; chance, opportunity

restablecer §22 tr to reëstablish, to restore || ref to recover

restañar tr to retin; (sangre) to stanch, stop the flow of

restar tr to deduct; to reduce; to take away; (una pelota) to return; to subtract || intr to remain, be left

restaurante m restaurant; **restaurante automático** automat

restaurar tr to restore; to recover

restitución f restitution, return

restituir §20 tr to return, give back; to restore || ref to return, come back

resto m rest, remainder, residue; (en juegos de naipes) stakes; (de una pelota) return, **a resto abierto** (coll) without limit; **echar el resto** to stake all, to shoot the works; **restos** remains, mortal remains; **restos de serie** remnants

restregar §66 tr to rub hard; to scrub hard

restringir §27 tr to restrict; to constrict, to contract

resucitar tr & intr to resuscitate; to resurrect; (coll) to revive

resuel·to -ta adj resolute, resolved, determined; prompt, quick

resuello m breathing; hard breathing, panting

resulta f result; outcome; vacancy; **de resultas de** as a result of

resultado m result

resultar intr to result; to prove to be, to turn out to be; to be, to become

resumen m summary, résumé; **en resumen** in brief, in a word

resumir tr to summarize, to sum up ‖ ref to be reduced, be transformed

resurrección f resurrection

retaguardia f rearguard

retal m piece, remnant

retama f Spanish broom; **retama de escoba** furze

retar tr to challenge, to dare; (coll) to blame, find fault with

retardar tr to retard, slow down

retardo m retard, delay

retazo m piece, remnant; scrap, fragment

retén m store, stock, reserve; catch, pawl; (mil) reserve

retener §71 tr to retain, keep, withhold; to detain, arrest; (el pago de un haber) to stop

reticente adj deceptive, misleading; noncommittal

retintín m jingle, tinkling; (en el oído) ringing; (coll) tone of reproach, sarcasm, mockery

retiñir §12 intr to jingle, to tinkle; (los oídos) to ring

retirada f retirement, withdrawal; place of refuge; (mil) retreat, retirement; (toque) (mil) retreat; **batirse en retirada** to beat a retreat

retirar tr to retire, to withdraw; to take away; to pull back ‖ ref to retire, to withdraw; (mil) to retire

reto m challenge, dare; threat

retocar §73 tr to retouch; to touch up; (un disco de fonógrafo) to play back

retoño m sprout, shoot, sucker

retorcer §74 tr to twist; to twist together; (las manos) to wring; (fig) to twist, misconstrue ‖ ref to twist; to writhe

retórico -ca adj rhetorical ‖ f rhetoric

retornar tr to return, give back; to back, back up ‖ intr & ref to return, go back

retorno m return; barter, exchange; reward, requital; **retorno terrestre** (elec) ground

retorta f (chem) retort

retozar §60 intr to frolic, gambol, romp

retozo m frolic, gambol, romping; **retozo de la risa** giggle, titter

retozón -zona adj frolicsome, frisky

retractar tr & ref to retract

retraer §75 tr to bring again, to bring back; to dissuade ‖ ref to withdraw, retire; to take refuge

retraído -da adj solitary; reserved, shy

retransmisión f rebroadcasting

retransmitir tr to rebroadcast

retrasar tr to delay, retard; to put off; (un reloj) to set or turn back ‖ intr to be too slow; (en los estudios) to be or fall behind ‖ ref to delay, be late, be slow, be behind time; (un reloj) to go or be slow

retraso m delay; **tener retraso** to be late

retratar tr to portray; to photograph; to imitate ‖ ref to sit for a portrait; to have one's picture taken

retrato m portrait; photograph; copy, imitation; description; **el vivo retrato de** the living image of

retrepar ref to lean back, to lean back in the chair

retreta f (mil) retreat, tattoo; (Am) outdoor band concert

retrete m toilet, lavatory

retribuir §20 tr to repay, to pay back

retroactivo -va adj retroactive

retroceder intr to retrogress; to back away; to back down, back out

retroceso m retrogression; (de un arma de fuego) recoil; (de una enfermedad) flare-up

retrocohete m retrorocket

retrodisparo m retrofiring

retropropulsión f (aer) jet propulsion

retrospectivo -va adj retrospective ‖ f (mov) flashback

retrovisor m rear-view mirror

retrucar §73 intr to answer, reply; (billiards) to kiss

retruco m (billiards) kiss

retruécano m pun

retumbar intr to resound, to rumble

retumbo m resounding, rumble, echo

reumático -ca adj & mf rheumatic

reumatismo m rheumatism

reunificación f reunification

reunión f reunion, gathering, meeting; assemblage

reunir §59 tr to join, unite; to assemble, gather together, bring together; to reunite; (dinero) to raise ‖ ref to unite; to assemble, gather together, come together, meet; to reunite

reválida f final examination (for a higher degree)

revejecer §22 intr & ref to grow old before one's time

revelación f revelation

revelado m (phot) development

revelador m (phot) developer

revelar tr to reveal; (phot) to develop

revender tr to resell; to retail

reventa f resale

reventar §2 tr to smash, crush; to burst, blow out, explode; to ruin; to annoy, bore; (a una persona) to work to death; (a un caballo) to run to death ‖ intr to burst, blow out, explode; (las olas) to break; (morir) (coll) to croak; (de ira) (coll) to blow up, hit the ceiling; **reventar por** to be dying to ‖ ref to burst, blow out, explode; to be worked to death; (un caballo) to be run to death

reventón m burst; (aut) blowout

rever §80 tr to revise, to review; (un caso legal) to retry

reverberar intr to reverberate

reverbero m reflector; street lamp; (Am) chafing dish

reverencia f reverence; bow, curtsy

reverenciar tr to revere, to reverence ‖ intr to bow, to curtsy

reveren·do -da *adj & m* reverend

reverso *m* back; wrong side; reverse

revertir §68 *intr* to revert

revés *m* back, reverse; wrong side; backhand; (*desgracia, contratiempo*) reverse, setback; **al revés** wrong side out; inside out; upside down; backwards

revestir §50 *tr* to put on, to don; to cover, coat, face, line, surface; to assume, take on; to disguise; (*un cuento*) to adorn; to invest || *ref* to put on vestments; to be haughty; to gird oneself

revirar *tr* to turn, twist; to turn over

revisar *tr* to revise, review, check; to audit

revisión *f* revision, review, check

revisionismo *m* revisionism

revisionista *adj & mf* revisionist

revisor *m* inspector, examiner; (rr) conductor, ticket collector

revista *f* review; (mil) review; (theat) review, revue; (law) new trial

revistar *tr* (mil) to review

revivir *tr & intr* to revive

revocar §73 *tr* to revoke; to dissuade; to drive back, drive away; to plaster, to stucco

revolar §61 *intr & ref* to flutter, to flutter around

revolcar §81 *tr* to knock down; (*a un adversario*) (coll) to floor; (*a un alumno en un examen*) (coll) to flunk, to fail || *ref* to wallow, roll around; to be stubborn

revolotear *tr* to fling up || *intr* to flutter, flutter around, flit

revoltijo or **revoltillo** *m* mess, jumble; (Am) stew

revolto·so -sa *adj* rebellious, riotous; (*niño*) unruly, mischievous; complicated; winding || *mf* troublemaker, rioter

revolución *f* revolution

revoluciona·rio -ria *adj & mf* revolutionary

revolver §47 & §83 *tr* to shake; to stir; to turn around; to turn upside down; to wrap up; to mess up; to disturb; (*sus pasos*) to retrace; to alienate, estrange || *intr* to retrace one's steps || *ref* to retrace one's steps; to turn around; to toss and turn; (*un astro en su órbita*) to revolve; (*el mar*) to get rough

revólver *m* revolver

revuelco *m* upset, tumble; wallowing

revuelo *m* whirl, flying around; stir, commotion

revuelta *f* revolution, revolt; disturbance; turning point; fight, row

rey *m* king; (coll) swineherd; **los Reyes Católicos** Ferdinand and Isabella; **los Reyes Magos** the Three Wise Men; **ni rey ni roque** (coll) nobody; **rey de zarza** wren; **reyes** king and queen; **Reyes** Twelfth-night

reyerta *f* quarrel, wrangle

reyezuelo *m* (orn) kinglet; **reyezuelo moñudo** goldcrest

rezaga·do -da *mf* straggler, laggard

rezagar §44 *tr* to outstrip, leave behind; to postpone || *ref* to fall behind

rezar §60 *tr* (*una oración*) to pray; (*una oración; la misa*) to say; (coll) to say, to read; (*anunciar*) (coll) to call for || *intr* to pray; (coll) to grumble; (coll) to say, to read; **rezar con** (coll) to concern

rezo *m* prayer; devotions

rezón *m* grapnel

rezongar §44 *tr* (CAm) to scold || *intr* to grumble, growl

rezumar *intr* to ooze, seep || *ref* to ooze, seep; to leak; (*una especie*) (coll) to leak out

ría *f* estuary, fiord

riachuelo *m* rivulet, streamlet

riada *f* flood, freshet

ribazo *m* slope, embankment

ribera *f* bank, shore; riverside

ribe·reño -ña *adj* riverside

ribero *m* levee, dike

ribete *m* edge, trimming, border; (*a un cuento*) embellishment

ribetear *tr* to edge, trim, border, bind

ri·co -ca *adj* rich; dear, darling

ridiculizar §60 *tr* to ridicule

ridícu·lo -la *adj* ridiculous; touchy || *m* ridiculous situation; **poner en ridículo** to ridicule, to expose to ridicule

riego *m* irrigation; watering

riel *m* ingot; curtain rod; rail

rielar *intr* to shimmer, gleam; (poet) to twinkle

rienda *f* rein; **a rienda suelta** swiftly, violently; with free rein

riente *adj* laughing; bright, cheerful

riesgo *m* risk, danger; **correr riesgo** to run or take a risk

rifa *f* raffle; fight, quarrel

rifar *tr* to raffle, to raffle off || *intr* to raffle; to fight, quarrel

rígi·do -da *adj* rigid, stiff; strict, severe

riguro·so -sa *adj* rigorous; severe

rima *f* rhyme; **rimas** poems, poetry

rimar *tr & intr* to rhyme

rimbombante *adj* resounding; flashy

rimero *m* heap, pile

Rin *m* Rhine

rincón *m* corner; nook; piece of land; (coll) home

rinconera *f* corner piece of furniture; corner table; corner cupboard

ringla *f*, **ringle** *m* or **ringlera** *f* row, tier

ringorrango *m* (coll) curlicue; (coll) frill, frippery

rinoceronte *m* rhinoceros

riña *f* fight, scuffle

riñón *m* kidney; (fig) heart, center, interior; **tener bien cubierto el riñón** (coll) to be well-heeled

río *m* river; **pescar en río revuelto** to fish in troubled waters

riostra *f* brace, stay; guy wire

riostrar *tr* to brace, stay

ripia *f* shingle

ripio *m* debris; rubble; (*palabras inútiles empleadas para completar el verso*) padding; **no perder ripio** (coll) to not miss a trick

riqueza *f* riches, wealth; richness

risa *f* laugh, laughter

risco *m* cliff, crag; honey fritter

risible *adj* laughable

risotada *f* guffaw, horse laugh

ristra *f* string of onions, string of garlic; (coll) string, row, file

ristre *m* lance rest

risue·ño -ña *adj* smiling

rítmi·co -ca *adj* rhythmic(al)

ritmo *m* rhythm; **a gran ritmo** at great speed

rito *m* rite

rival *mf* rival

rivalidad *f* rivalry; enmity

rivalizar §60 *intr* to vie, compete; **rivalizar con** to rival

riza·do -da *adj* curly; ripply || *m* curl, curling; rippling

rizador *m* curling iron, hair curler

rizar §60 *tr & ref* to curl; (*la superficie del agua*) to ripple

ri·zo -za *adj* curly || *m* curl, ringlet; ripple; (aer) loop; **rizar el rizo** (aer) to loop the loop

ro *interj* — ¡ro ro! hushaby!, bye-bye!

roba·dor -dora *mf* robber, thief

róbalo or **robalo** *m* (*Labrax lupus*) bass; (*Centropomus undecimalis*) snook

robar *tr* to rob, steal; (*un naipe o ficha de dominó*) to draw || *intr & ref* to steal

robinete *m* faucet, spigot, cock

roblar *tr* to clinch, to rivet

roble *m* oak; (*Quercus robur*) British oak tree; (coll) husky fellow

roblón *m* rivet

robo *m* robbery, theft; (*naipe tomado del monte*) draw; **robo con escalamiento** burglary

ro·bot *m* (*pl* -bots) robot

robus·to -ta *adj* robust

roca *f* rock

rocalla *f* pebbles; stone chips; large glass bead

rocallo·so -sa *adj* stony, pebbly

roce *m* rubbing; close contact

rociada *f* sprinkling; dew; (*de balas, piedras, etc.*) shower; (*de invectivas*) volley

rociadera *f* sprinkling can

rociar §77 *tr* to sprinkle; to spray; to bedew; to scatter || *intr* to drizzle; **rocía** there is dew

rocín *m* hack, nag; work horse, draft horse; (coll) rough fellow; (Am) riding horse

rocío *m* dew; drizzle; sprinkling

roco·so -sa *adj* rocky

rodada *f* rut, track

roda·do -da *adj* (*fácil, fluído*) rounded, fluent; (*tránsito*) vehicular || *f* see **rodada**

rodadura *f* rolling; rut; (*de neumático*) tread

rodaja *f* disk, caster; round slice

rodaje *m* wheels; (*de una película cinematográfica*) shooting, filming; **en rodaje** (aut) being run in; (mov) being filmed

rodamiento *m* bearing; (*de un neumático*) tread; **rodamientos** running gear

Ródano *m* Rhone

rodante *adj* rolling; on wheels; (Chile) wandering

rodapié *m* baseboard, washboard

rodar §61 *tr* to roll; (*una película cinematográfica*) to shoot, to film, to take; to screen, to project; to drag along; (*una llave*) to turn; (*la escalera*) to roll down; (*un nuevo coche*) to run in; (*válvulas de un motor*) to grind || *intr* to roll, roll along; to roll down; to rotate, revolve; to tumble; to roam, wander about; (*por medio de ruedas*) to run; to prowl

Rodas *f* Rhodes

rodear *tr* to surround; (Am) to round up || *intr* to go around; to go by a roundabout way; to beat about the bush || *ref* to turn, twist, toss about

rodela *f* buckler, target; padded ring

rodeo *m* detour, roundabout way; dodge, duck; rodeo, roundup; **andar con rodeos** to beat about the bush; **dar un rodeo** to go a roundabout way

rodilla *f* knee; floor rag, mop; padded ring; **de rodillas** kneeling, on one's knees

rodillera *f* kneepad; baggy knee; (*de prenda de vestir*) knee; (*del órgano*) (mus) knee swell

rodillo *m* roller; rolling pin; road roller; inking roller; (*de la máquina de escribir*) platen

rodrigar §44 *tr* to prop, prop up, stake

rodrigón *m* prop, stake

roer §62 *tr* to gnaw, to gnaw away at; (*un hueso*) to pick; to wear down

rogar §63 *tr & intr* to beg; to pray; **hacerse de rogar** to like to be coaxed

roi·do -da *adj* (coll) miserly, stingy

ro·jo -ja *adj* red; ruddy; red-haired; Red || *mf* (*comunista*) Red || *m* red; **al rojo** to a red heat

rollar *tr* to roll, roll up

rolli·zo -za *adj* round, cylindrical; plump, stocky || *m* round log

rollo *m* roll, coil; roller, rolling pin; round log; yoke pad; rôle; (*de tela*) bolt

romadizo *m* cold in the head

romance *adj* (*neolatino*) Romance || *m* Romance language; Spanish language; romance of chivalry; octosyllabic verse with alternate lines in assonance; narrative poem in octosyllabic verse; ballad; **romance heroico** hendecasyllabic verse with alternate lines in assonance

romancero *m* collection of Old Spanish romances

romancillo *m* verse of less than eight syllables with alternate lines in assonance

románi·co -ca *adj* (*neolatino*) Romance, Romanic; (*arquitectura*) Romanesque || *m* Romanesque

roma·no -na *adj & mf* Roman

romanticismo *m* romanticism

románti·co -ca *adj* romantic

romanza *f* (mus) romance, romanza

romería *f* pilgrimage; crowd, gathering

rome·ro -ra *mf* pilgrim || *m* rosemary

ro·mo -ma *adj* blunt, dull; flat-nosed

rompeáto·mos *m* (*pl* -mos) atom smasher

rompecabe·zas *m* (*pl* -zas) riddle, puzzle; (*figura que ha sido cortada en trozos menudos y que hay que recomponer*) jigsaw puzzle

rompehie·los *m* (*pl* -los) iceboat, icebreaker

rompehuel·gas *m* (*pl* -gas) strikebreaker

rompeo·las *m* (*pl* -las) mole, breakwater

romper §83 *tr* to break; to break through; to break up; to tear ‖ *intr* to break; (*las flores*) to break open, to burst open; to break down; **romper a** to start to, to burst out

rompiente *m* reef, shoal; (*oleaje que choca contra las rocas*) breaker

rompope *m* (Am) eggnog

ron *m* rum; **ron de laurel** or **de malagueta** bay rum

ronca *f* (*época del celo*) rut; cry of buck in rutting season; (coll) bullying

roncar §73 *intr* to snore; (*el viento, el mar*) to roar; to cry in rutting season; (coll) to bully

ronce·ro -ra *adj* slow, poky; grouchy

ron·co -ca *adj* hoarse; harsh ‖ *f* see **ronca**

roncha *f* weal, welt; black-and-blue mark

ronchar *tr* to crunch

ronda *f* (*de un policía; de visitas; de cigarros o bebidas*) round; (*juego del corro*) (Chile) ring-around-a-rosy

rondar *tr* to go around; to fly around; to patrol; (coll) to hang around; (coll) to court ‖ *intr* to patrol by night; to gad about at nighttime; to go serenading; to prowl; (mil) to make the rounds

ronquedad *f* hoarseness; harshness

ronquera *f* hoarseness

ronquido *m* snore; rasping sound

ronronear *intr* to purr

ronroneo *m* purr, purring

ronzal *m* halter

ronzar §60 *tr* to crunch, to munch

roña *f* scab, mange; sticky dirt; pine bark; stinginess; (Col) malingering; (Am) spite, ill will; **jugar a roña** (Peru) to play for fun

roño·so -sa *adj* scabby, mangy; dirty, filthy; stingy; (Am) spiteful

ropa *f* clothing, clothes; dry goods; a **quema ropa** point-blank; **ropa blanca** linen; **ropa de cama** bed linen; bedclothes; **ropa dominguera** Sunday best; **ropa hecha** ready-made clothes; **ropa interior** underwear; **ropa sucia** laundry

ropaje *m* clothes, clothing; gown, robe; drapery

ropaveje·ro -ra *mf* old-clothes dealer

rope·ro -ra *mf* ready-made clothier; wardrobe keeper ‖ *m* wardrobe, clothes closet

roque *m* rook, castle

roque·ño -ña *adj* rocky; hard, flinty

rorro *m* baby; (Mex) doll

rosa *f* rose; **rosa de los vientos** or **rosa náutica** (naut) compass card; **rosas** popcorn; **verlo todo de color de rosa** to see everything through rose-colored glasses

rosa·do -da *adj* rose-colored, rosy; pink; flushed ‖ *f* frost

rosaleda or **rosalera** *f* rose garden

rosario *m* rosary; (*de sucesos*) string; chain pump

ros·bif *m* (*pl* -bifs) roast beef

rosca *f* coil, spiral; (*de una espiral*) turn; twisted roll; (*de un tornillo*) thread; (Chile) padded ring

roscar §73 *tr* to thread

roseta *f* sprinkling spout or nozzle; red spot on cheek; **rosetas** popcorn

rosetón *m* rose window

rosita *f* little rose; (Chile) earring; **rositas** popcorn

rosquilla *f* coffeecake, doughnut, cruller

rostro *m* face; snout; beak; (*retrato*) de **rostro entero** full-faced

rostropáli·do -da *mf* paleface

rota *f* rout, defeat; (naut) route, course

rotograbado *m* rotogravure

rótula *f* lozenge; kneecap; knuckle

rotular *tr* to label, title, letter

rótulo *m* label, title; poster, show bill

rotun·do -da *adj* round; rotund, sonorous, full; peremptory

rotura *f* break, breaking; breach, opening; tear, tearing

roya *f* (agr) blight, rust

rozamiento *m* rubbing; friction; (*desavenencia*) (fig) friction

rozar §60 *tr* to graze; to scrape; to border on; to grub, to stub; (*las tierras*) to clear; (*la hierba*) to nibble; (*leña menuda*) to cut and gather ‖ *intr* to graze by ‖ *ref* to be on close terms, to rub elbows, to hobnob; to falter, stammer; to be alike

rozuar *tr* to crunch ‖ *intr* to bray

roznido *m* crunch, crunching noise; bray, braying

Rte. *abbr* **Remite**

ru·bí *m* (*pl* -bíes) ruby; (*de un reloj*) ruby, jewel

rubia *f* blonde; station wagon; (coll) peseta; **rubia oxigenada** peroxide blonde; **rubia platino** platinum blonde

rubia·les *mf* (*pl* -les) (coll) goldilocks

ru·bio -bia *adj* blond, fair; golden ‖ *m* blond ‖ *f* see **rubia**

rubor *m* bright red; blush, flush; bashfulness

ruborizar §60 *tr* to make blush ‖ *ref* to blush

rúbrica *f* title, heading; (*rasgo después de la firma de uno*) flourish

ru·bro -bra *adj* red ‖ *m* (Am) title, heading; (Chile) (com) entry

rudimento *m* rudiment

ru·do -da *adj* coarse, rough; rude, crude; dull, stupid; hard, severe

rueca *f* distaff

rueda *f* wheel; caster, roller; (*de gente*) ring, circle; round slice; pinwheel; (*de la cola del pavo*) spread; sunfish; **hacer la rueda** (*el pavo*) to spread its tail; **hacer la rueda a** (coll) to play up to; **rueda de andar** treadmill; **rueda de cadena** sprocket, sprocket wheel; **rueda de escape** escapement wheel; **rueda de fuego** pinwheel; **rueda dentada** gearwheel; **rueda de paletas** paddle wheel; **rueda de pre-**

sos line-up; **rueda de recambio** spare wheel; **rueda de tornillo sin fin** worm wheel; **rueda motriz** drive wheel

ruedo *m* turn, rotation; round mat; selvage; hemline; (taur) ring; **a todo ruedo** at all events

ruego *m* request, entreaty; prayer

ru·fián -fiana *mf* bawd, go-between ‖ *m* cur, cad

ru·fo -fa *adj* sandy, sandy-haired; curly-haired

rugido *m* roar; (*de las tripas*) rumble

rugir §27 *intr* to roar; to rumble

rugo·so -sa *adj* rugged, wrinkled

ruibarbo *m* rhubarb

ruido *m* noise; rumor; row, rumpus

ruido·so -sa *adj* noisy; loud; sensational

ruin *adj* base, mean, vile; stingy; (*animal*) vicious

ruina *f* ruin

ruindad *f* baseness, meanness, vileness; stinginess; viciousness

ruino·so -sa *adj* tottery, run-down

ruiseñor *m* nightingale

ruleta *f* roulette; (CAm, Arg) tape measure

ruletero *m* (Mex) cruising taxi driver (*in search of fares*)

ruma·no -na *adj* & *mf* Rumanian

rumbo *m* bearing, course, direction; (coll) pomp, show; (coll) generosity; **por aquellos rumbos** in those parts; **rumbo a** bound for

rumbo·so -sa *adj* pompous, magnificent; (coll) generous

rumiar *tr* & *intr* to ruminate

rumor *m* rumor; (*de voces*) murmur, buzz; rumble

rumorear *tr* to rumor, to circulate by a rumor ‖ *intr* to murmur, buzz, rumble ‖ *ref* to be rumored; **se rumorea que** it is rumored that

rumoro·so -sa *adj* noisy, loud, rumbling

runfla or **runflada** *f* (coll) string, row; (*en los naipes*) (coll) sequence

ruptor *m* (elec) contact breaker

ruptura *f* rupture, break; crack, split; (*cesación de relaciones*) rupture

Rusia *f* Russia; **la Rusia Soviética** Soviet Russia

ru·so -sa *adj* & *mf* Russian

rúst. *abbr* **rústica**

rústi·co -ca *adj* rustic; coarse, crude, clumsy; (*latín*) Vulgar; **en rústica** paper-bound ‖ *m* rustic, peasant

ruta *f* route; **ruta aérea** air lane

rutilante *adj* shining, sparkling

rutina *f* routine

rutina·rio -ria *adj* routine

S

S, s (ese) *f* twenty-second letter of the Spanish alphabet

S. *abbr* **San, Santo, sobresaliente, sur**

sábado *m* (*de los cristianos*) Saturday; (*de los judíos*) Sabbath

sábalo *m* shad

sabana *f* (Am) savanna, pampa; **ponerse en la sabana** (Ven) to get rich overnight

sábana *f* sheet; altar cloth

sabandija *f* insect, bug, worm; (*persona*) vermin; **sabandijas** (*animales o personas*) vermin

sabanilla *f* kerchief; altar cloth

sabañón *m* chilblain

sabe·dor -dora *adj* aware, informed

sabelotodo *m* (*pl* **sabelotodo**) know-it-all, wise guy

saber *m* knowledge, learning ‖ *v* §64 *tr* & *intr* to know; to find out; to taste; **a saber** namely, to wit; **no saber dónde meterse** to not know which way to turn; **que yo sepa** as far as I know; **saber a** to taste of; to smack of; **saber a poco** to be just a taste, to taste like more; **saber de** to be aware of; to hear from ‖ *ref* to know; to be or become known

sabidi·llo -lla *adj* & *mf* (coll) know-it-all

sabi·do -da *adj* well-informed; learned; **de sabido** certainly, surely

sabiduría *f* wisdom; knowledge, learning

sabiendas — **a sabiendas** knowingly, consciously; **a sabiendas de que** knowing that, aware that

sabihon·do -da *adj* & *mf* (coll) know-it-all

sa·bio -bia *adj* wise; learned; (*animal*) trained ‖ *mf* wise person, scholar, scientist ‖ *m* wise man, sage

sablazo *m* stroke with a saber, wound made by a saber; (coll) sponging; **dar un sablazo a** (coll) to hit for a loan

sable *m* saber, cutlass; (coll) sponging

sablear *tr* (coll) to hit for a loan, to sponge on ‖ *intr* (coll) to go around sponging

sablista *mf* (coll) sponger

sabor *m* taste, flavor

saborcillo *m* slight taste, touch

saborear *tr* to flavor; to taste; to savor; to entice ‖ *ref* to smack one's lips; **saborearse de** to taste; to savor

sabotaje *m* sabotage

sabotear *tr* & *intr* to sabotage

sabro·so -sa *adj* tasty, savory, delicious

sabueso *m* bloodhound; sleuth

saburro·so -sa *adj* (*boca*) foul; (*lengua*) coated

sacaboca·do or **sacaboca·dos** *m* (*pl* -dos) ticket punch; (coll) sure thing

sacabotas *m* (*pl* -tas) bootjack

sacacor·chos *m* (*pl* -chos) corkscrew

sacaman·chas *mf* (*pl* -chas) clothes cleaner, spot remover; dry cleaner; dyer

sacamue•las *mf* (*pl* **-las**) (coll) tooth puller; (coll) quack, cheat

sacamuer•tos *m* (*pl* **-tos**) stagehand

sacapintura *m* paint remover

sacapun•tas *m* (*pl* **-tas**) pencil sharpener

sacar §73 *tr* (*un clavo, una espada, agua, una conclusión*) to draw; to pull out; to pull up; to take out; to extract, remove; to show; to bring out, publish; to find out, to solve; (*un secreto*) to elicit, draw out; to copy; (*una fotografía*) to take; to except, exclude; to get; obtain; to produce, invent, imitate; (*un premio*) to win; (*una pelota*) to serve; (*el pecho*) to stick out; **sacar a bailar** (coll) to drag in; **sacar a relucir** (coll) to bring up unexpectedly; **sacar en claro** or **en limpio** to recopy clearly; to deduce, to clear up

sacarina *f* saccharin

sacasi•llas *m* (*pl* **-llas**) stagehand

sacerdocio *m* priesthood

sacerdote *m* priest

saciar *tr* to satiate

saco *m* bag, sack; coat, jacket; sack, plunder, pillage; (*de mentiras*) pack; **saco de dormir** sleeping bag; **saco de noche** overnight bag

sacramento *m* sacrament

sacrificar §73 *tr* to sacrifice; to slaughter || *intr* to sacrifice || *ref* to sacrifice; to sacrifice onself

sacrificio *m* sacrifice; **sacrificio del altar** Sacrifice of the Mass

sacrilegio *m* sacrilege

sacríle•go -ga *adj* sacrilegious

sacristán *m* sacristan; sexton; **sacristán de amén** yes man

sacristía *f* sacristy, vestry

sa•cro -cra *adj* sacred

sacudida *f* shake, jar, jolt, jerk, bump; (elec) shock

sacudi•do -da *adj* intractable; determined || *f* see **sacudida**

sacudir *tr* to shake; to beat; to jar, jolt; to rock; to shake off || *ref* to shake, to shake oneself; to rock; **sacudirse bien** (coll) to wangle one's way out

sádi•co -ca *adj* sadistic || *mf* sadist

saeta *f* arrow, dart; (*del reloj*) hand; magnetic needle

saetilla *f* small arrow; (*del reloj*) hand; magnetic needle; (bot) arrowhead

saetín *m* flume, millrace

sa•gaz *adj* (*pl* **-gaces**) sagacious; keen-scented

sagra•do -da *adj* sacred || *m* asylum, haven, sanctuary; **acogerse a sagrado** to take sanctuary

sagrario *m* sanctuary, shrine; ciborium

sahariana *f* tight-fitting military jacket

sahornar *ref* to skin oneself

sahumar *tr* to perfume with smoke or incense; (Chile) to gold-plate, to silver-plate

sainete *m* one-act farce; flavor, relish, spice, zest; sauce, seasoning; tidbit

sa•jón -jona *adj & mf* Saxon

sal *f* salt; grace, charm; wit; (CAm) misfortune; **sal de sosa** washing soda;

sales aromáticas smelling salts; **sal gema** rock salt

sala *f* hall; drawing room, living room, sitting room; **sala de batalla** sorting room; **sala de calderas** boiler room; **sala de enfermos** infirmary; **sala de espera** waiting room; **sala de estar** living room, sitting room; **sala de fiestas** night club; **sala del cine** moving-picture house; **sala de máquinas** engine room

saladillo *m* salted peanut

Salamina *f* Salamis

salar *tr* to salt; (Am) to spoil, ruin; (Am) to bring bad luck to

salario *m* wages, pay; **salario de hambre** starvation wages

salcochar *tr* to boil in salt water

salcocho *m* (Am) food boiled in salt water

salchicha *f* sausage

salchiche•ro -ra *mf* pork butcher

saldar *tr* to settle, liquidate; to sell out

saldo *m* settlement; balance; remnant; bargain; **saldo de mercancías** job lot; **saldo deudor** debit balance

salero *m* saltshaker, saltcellar; salt lick; (coll) grace, charm, wit

salero•so -sa *adj* (coll) charming, winsome, lively; (coll) salty, witty

salgar §44 *tr* (*el ganado*) to salt

salida *f* start; departure; exit; outcome, result; subterfuge; pretext; outlay, expenditure; projection; outlying fields; (elec) output; (sport) start; (mil) sally, sortie; (coll) witticism, sally; **salida de baño** bathrobe; **salida del sol** sunrise; **salida de teatro** evening wrap; **salida de teatros** after-theater party; **salida de tono** (coll) irrelevancy, impropriety; **salida lanzada** (sport) running start; **tener salida** to sell well; (*una muchacha*) to be popular with the boys

saliente *adj* projecting; (*p.ej., tren*) outbound; (*sol*) rising || *m* east || *f* projection; (*de la carretera*) shoulder

salir §65 *intr* to go out, come out; to leave, to go away, depart; to sail; to run out, come to an end; to appear, show up; (*una mancha*) to come out, come off; (*p.ej., el sol*) to rise; to shoot, spring, come up; to project, stick out; to make the first move; to result, turn out; to be elected; **salga lo que saliere** (coll) come what may; **salir a** to amount to; to open into; to resemble, look like; **salir al encuentro a** to go to meet; to take a stand against; to get ahead of; **salir bien en un examen** to pass an examination; **salir con bien** to be successful; **salir de** to depart from; to cease being; to get rid of; (*p.ej., su juicio, sentido*) to lose; **salir disparado** to start like a shot; **salir pitando** (coll) to start off on a mad run; (coll) to blow up, hit the ceiling; **salir reprobado** (*en un examen*) to fail || *ref* to slip out, escape; to slip off, run off; to leak; to boil over; **salirse con la suya** to have one's own way; to carry one's point

salitre *m* saltpeter

saliva *f* saliva; **gastar saliva** (coll) to rattle along; (coll) to waste one's breath

salmo *m* psalm

salmón *m* salmon

salmuera *f* brine, pickle; salty food or drink

salobre *adj* brackish, saltish

salón *m* salon, drawing room; (*de un buque*) saloon; meeting room; **salón de actos** auditorium; **salón de baile** ballroom; **salón de belleza** beauty parlor; **salón del automóvil** automobile show; **salón de refrescos** ice-cream parlor; **salón de tertulia** or **salón social** lounge

saloncillo *m* (*p.ej., de un teatro*) rest room

salpicar §73 *tr* to splash; to sprinkle

salpimentar §2 *tr* to salt and pepper, season with salt and pepper; (fig) to sweeten

salpullido *m* rash, eruption

salpullir §13 *tr* to cause a rash in; to splotch || *ref* to break out

salsa *f* sauce, dressing, gravy; **salsa de ají** chili sauce; **salsa de tomate** catsup, ketchup; **salsa inglesa** Worcestershire sauce

salsera *f* gravy dish; small saucer (*to mix paints*)

saltaban·co or **saltaban·cos** *m* (*pl* -cos) quack, mountebank; prestidigitator; (coll) nuisance

saltamon·tes *m* (*pl* -tes) grasshopper

saltar *tr* to jump, jump over; to skip, skip over || *intr* to jump, leap, hop, skip; to bounce; to shoot up, spurt; to come loose, come off; to crack, break, burst; to chip; to project, stick out; **saltar a la vista** or **los ojos** to be self-evident; **saltar por** to jump over, to jump out of || *ref* to skip; to come off

saltatum·bas *m* (*pl* -bas) (coll) burying parson

salteador *m* highwayman, holdup man

saltear *tr* to attack, hold up, waylay; to take by surprise

saltimbanco *m* var of **saltabanco**

salto *m* jump, leap, bound; skip; dive; fall, waterfall; leapfrog; **salto de altura** high jump; **salto de ángel** swan dive; **salto de cama** morning wrap, dressing gown; **salto de carpa** jackknife; **salto de esquí** ski jump; **salto de viento** (naut) sudden shift in the wind; **salto mortal** somersault; **salto ornamental** fancy dive

salubre *adj* healthful, salubrious

salud *f* health; welfare; salvation; greeting; **gastar, vender** or **verter salud** (coll) to radiate health || *interj* greetings!; **¡salud y pesetas!** health and wealth!

saludar *tr* to greet, salute, hail, bow to; to give regards to || *intr* to salute; to bow

saludo *m* greeting, salute, bow; salutation; **saludo final** conclusion

salutación *f* salutation, greeting, bow

salva *f* greeting, welcome; salvo; oath; tray; (*de aplausos; de una batería de artillería*) round

salvado *m* bran

salva·dor **-dora** *mf* savior, saver, rescuer || **el Salvador** the Saviour; (*país de la América Central*) El Salvador

salvadore·ño **-ña** *adj & mf* Salvadoran

salvaguardar *tr* to safeguard

salvaguardia *m* bodyguard, escort || *f* safeguard, safe-conduct; protection, shelter

salvaje *adj* wild, uncultivated; savage; stupid || *mf* savage; dolt

salvaji·no **-na** *adj* wild; (*de la carne de los animales monteses*) gamy || *f* wild animal; wild animals

salvamante·les *m* (*pl* -les) coaster

salvamento *m* salvation; lifesaving; rescue; salvage; place of safety

salvar *tr* to save, rescue; to salvage; (*una dificultad*) to avoid, overcome; (*un obstáculo*) to clear, get around; (*una distancia*) to cover, get over; to rise above; to jump over; to make an exception of; **salvar apariencias** to save face || *ref* to save onself, escape danger; to be saved; **sálvese el que pueda** every man for himself

salvavi·das *m* (*pl* -das) life preserver; lifeboat; (*empleado de una estación de salvamento*) lifeguard

salvedad *f* reservation, exception

salvia *f* (bot) sage

sal·vo **-va** *adj* safe; omitted; **a salvo** safe, out of danger; **a salvo de** safe from || **salvo** *prep* save, except for; **salvo error u omisión** barring error or omission; **salvo que** unless || *f* see **salva**

salvoconducto *m* safe-conduct

sámara *f* (bot) key, key fruit

san *adj* apocopated and unstressed form of **santo**

sanaloto·do *m* (*pl* -do) cure-all

sanar *tr* to cure, heal || *intr* to heal; to recover

sanción *f* (*aprobación*) sanction; (*castigo, pena*) penalty

sancionar *tr* (*aprobar*) to sanction; (*imponer pena a*) to penalize

sancochar *tr* to parboil

sandalia *f* sandal

sándalo *m* (yellow) sandalwood

san·dez *f* (*pl* -deces) folly, nonsense; piece of folly

sandía *f* watermelon

san·dio **-dia** *adj* foolish, nonsensical

saneamiento *m* sanitation, drainage; guarantee

sanear *tr* to guarantee; to indemnify; to make sanitary, to drain, dry up

sangrar *tr* to bleed; to drain; to tap; (typ) to indent; (coll) to rob || *intr* to bleed; **estar sangrando** to be new or recent; to be plain or obvious || *ref* to have oneself bled; (*los colores*) to run

sangre *f* blood; **a sangre** by horsepower; **a sangre fría** in cold blood; **pura sangre** *m* thoroughbred; **sangre torera** bullfighting in the blood

sangría *f* bleeding; outlet, draining;

ditch, trench; (*bebida*) sangaree; tap; tapping; (typ) indentation

sangrien·to -ta *adj* bloody; bleeding; cruel, sanguinary

sangüesa *f* raspberry

sangüeso *m* raspberry bush

sanguijuela *f* leech

sanguina·rio -ria *adj* sanguinary, bloodthirsty

sanidad *f* healthiness; healthfulness; health; sanitation; **sanidad pública** health department

sanita·rio -ria *adj* sanitary

sa·no -na *adj* hale, healthy; healthful; sound; sane; earnest, sincere; safe, sure; (coll) whole, untouched, unharmed; **sano y salvo** safe and sound

santiague·ro -ra *adj* Santiago de Cuba ‖ *mf* native or inhabitant of Santiago de Cuba

santia·gués -guesa *adj* Santiago de Compostela ‖ *mf* native or inhabitant of Santiago de Compostela

santagul·no -na *adj* Santiago de Chile ‖ *mf* native or inhabitant of Santiago de Chile

santiamén *m* (coll) jiffy; **en un santiamén** (coll) in the twinkling of an eye

santidad *f* holiness, sanctity, saintliness; **su Santidad** his Holiness

santificar §73 *tr* to sanctify, to hallow, to consecrate; (*las fiestas*) to keep; (coll) to excuse, justify

santiguar §10 *tr* to bless, make the sign of the cross over; (coll) to punish, slap, abuse ‖ *ref* to cross oneself, make the sign of the cross

san·to -ta *adj* holy, saintly, blessed; (*día*) live-long; (coll) artless, simple; **santo y bueno** well and good ‖ *mf* saint ‖ *m* name day; image of a saint; **a santo de** because of; **desnudar a un santo para vestir a otro** to rob Peter to pay Paul; **írsele a uno el santo al cielo** (coll) to forget what one was up to; **santo y seña** password, watchword

Santo Domingo Hispaniola

santuario *m* sanctuary, shrine; (Col) buried treasure; (Col, Ven) Indian idol

santu·rrón -rrona *adj* sanctimonious ‖ *mf* sanctimonious person

saña *f* fury, rage; cruelty

sañu·do -da *adj* furious, enraged; cruel

sapiente *adj* wise, intelligent

sapo *m* toad; (coll) stuffed shirt; (Chile) little runt

saque *m* (*en el tenis*) serve, service; server; service line; (Col) distillery; **tener buen saque** (coll) to be a heavy eater and drinker

saquear *tr* to sack, plunder, pillage, loot

sarampión *m* measles

sarao *m* soirée, evening party

sarape *m* (Guat, Mex) bright-colored woolen poncho

sarcásti·co -ca *adj* sarcastic

sardina *f* sardine; **como sardinas en banasta** or **en lata** (coll) packed in like sardines

sar·do -da *adj & mf* Sardinian

sarga *f* serge

sargento *m* sergeant

sarmiento *m* vine shoot, running stem

sarna *f* itch, mange

sarno·so -sa *adj* itchy, mangy

sarrace·no -na *adj & mf* Saracen

sarracina *f* scuffle, free fight; bloody brawl

sarro *m* crust; (*p.ej., en la lengua*) fur; (*en los dientes*) tartar

sarta *f* string; line, file, series

sartén *f* frying pan; **saltar de la sartén y dar en las brasas** (coll) to jump from the frying pan into the fire

sastre *m* tailor

satélite *m* satellite

satelizar §60 *tr* to put into orbit; (pol) to make a satellite of ‖ *ref* to go into orbit

satén *m* sateen

satíri·co -ca *adj* satiric(al) ‖ *mf* satirist

satirizar §60 *tr & intr* to satirize

satisfacción *f* satisfaction

satisfacer §39 *tr & intr* to satisfy ‖ *ref* to satisfy oneself, be satisfied, take satisfaction

satisfacto·rio -ria *adj* satisfactory

saturar *tr* to saturate; to satiate

sauce *m* willow tree; **sauce de Babilonia** or **sauce llorón** weeping willow

saúco *m* elder, elderberry

savia *f* sap

saxofón *m* or **saxófono** *m* saxophone

saya *f* skirt; petticoat

sayo *m* smock frock, tunic; (coll) garment

sazón *f* ripeness; season; time, occasion; taste, seasoning; **a la sazón** at that time; **en sazón** in season, ripe; on time, opportunely

sazonar *tr* to ripen; to season ‖ *ref* to ripen, mature

s/c *abbr* **su cuenta**

S.E. *abbr* **Su Excelencia**

se *pron reflex* himself, to himself; herself, to herself; itself, to itself; themselves, to themselves; yourself, to yourself; yourselves, to yourselves; oneself, to oneself; each other, to each other ‖ *pron pers* (used before the pronouns **lo, la, le,** etc.) to him, to her, to it, to them, to you

sebo *m* tallow; fat, suet

seca *f* drought; dry season

secador *m* drier, hair drier

secadora *f* clothes dryer

secafir·mas *m* (*pl* -**mas**) blotter

secano *m* dry land, unwatered land

secansa *f* sequence

secante *m* blotting paper

secar §73 *tr* to dry, wipe dry; to annoy, bore ‖ *ref* to dry, get dry; to dry oneself; to wither; to be dry, be thirsty; (*un pozo*) to run dry

secarropa *f* clothes dryer; **secarropa de travesaños** clotheshorse

sección *f* section; cross section; **sección de fondo** editorial section

secesión *f* secession

se·co -ca *adj* dry; dried up, withered; lank, lean; harsh, sharp; (*bebida*) straight; indifferent; plain, unadorned ‖ *f* see **seca**

secreta·rio -ria *adj* confidential, trusted || *mf* secretary
secreter *m* secretary (*writing desk*)
secre·to -ta *adj* secret || *m* secret; secrecy; hiding place, secret drawer; (*mecanismo oculto para abrir una cerradura*) key; **en el secreto de las cosas** on the inside
secta *f* sect
secta·rio -ria *adj* & *mf* sectarian
sector *m* sector; **sector de distribución** house current, power line
se·cuaz (*pl* **-cuaces**) *adj* partisan || *mf* partisan, follower
secuela *f* sequel, result
secuencia *f* sequence
secuestrar *tr* to kidnap; (law) to sequester
secular *adj* secular
secundar *tr* to second, to back
secunda·rio -ria *adj* secondary || *m* (elec) secondary
sed *f* thirst; drought; **tener sed** to be thirsty
seda *f* silk; **como una seda** smooth as silk; easy as pie; sweet-natured; **seda encerada** dental floss
sedal *m* fish line
sedán *m* sedan; **sedán de reparto** delivery truck
sede *f* (*p.ej., del gobierno*) seat; (eccl) see; **Santa Sede** Holy See
sedenta·rio -ria *adj* sedentary
sede·ño -ña *adj* silk, silken
sedición *f* sedition
sedicio·so -sa *adj* seditious
sedien·to -ta *adj* thirsty; (*terreno*) dry; anxious, eager
sedimento *m* sediment
sedo·so -sa *adj* silky
seducción *f* seduction; charm, captivation
seducir §19 *tr* to seduce; to tempt, lead astray; to charm, captivate
seducti·vo -va *adj* seductive; tempting; charming, captivating
seduc·tor -tora *adj* seductive; tempting; charming || *mf* seducer; tempter; charmer
sefar·dí (*pl* **-fíes**) *adj* Sephardic || *mf* Sephardi
sega·dor -dora *adj* harvesting || *m* harvestman || *f* harvester; mowing machine; **segadora de césped** lawn mower; **segadora trilladora** combine
segar §66 *tr* to reap, harvest, mow; to mow down || *intr* to reap, harvest, mow
segazón *f* harvest; harvest time
seglar *adj* secular, lay || *m* layman || *f* laywoman
segmento *m* segment; **segmento de émbolo** piston ring
segregacionista *mf* segregationist
segregar §44 *tr* to segregate
seguida *f* series, succession; **de seguida** without interruption, continuously; at once; in a row; **en seguida** at once, immediately
seguidilla *f* Spanish stanza made up of a quatrain and a tercet; **seguidillas** seguidilla (*Spanish dance and music*)

segui·do -da *adj* continued, successive; straight, direct; running, in a row; **todo seguido** straight ahead || *f* see **seguida**
seguimiento *m* chase, hunt, pursuit; continuation; (*de vehículos espaciales*) tracking
seguir §67 *tr* to follow; to pursue; to continue; to dog, to hound || *intr* to go on, to continue; to still be, to be now; to keep + *ger* || *ref* to follow, ensue; to issue, to spring
según *prep* according to, as per; **según que** according as || *conj* as, according as
segunda *f* double meaning; (aut & mus) second
segundero *m* second hand; **segundero central** sweep-second, center-second
segun·do -da *adj* second || *m* second; **ser sin segundo** to be second to none || *f* see **segunda**
segur *f* axe; sickle
segurador *s* security, bondsman
seguridad *f* security; safety; surety; certainty; assurance; confidence
segu·ro -ra *adj* sure, certain; secure, safe; reliable; constant; steady, unfailing || *m* assurance, certainty; safety; confidence; insurance; **a buen seguro** surely, truly; **seguro contra accidentes** accident insurance; **seguro de desempleo** or **desocupación** unemployment insurance; **seguro de enfermedad** health insurance; **seguro de incendios** fire insurance; **seguro sobre la vida** life insurance; **sobre seguro** without risk || **seguro** *adv* surely
seis *adj* & *pron* six; **las seis** six o'clock || *m* six; (*en las fechas*) sixth
seiscien·tos -tas *adj* & *pron* six hundred || **seiscientos** *m* six hundred
selección *f* selection
seleccionar *tr* to select, to choose
selec·to -ta *adj* select, choice
selva *f* forest, woods; jungle
selváti·co -ca *adj* woodsy; rustic, wild
sellar *tr* to seal; to stamp; to close; to finish up
sello *m* seal; stamp; signet; wafer; **sello aéreo** air-mail stamp; **sello de correo** postage stamp; **sello de urgencia** special-delivery stamp; **sello fiscal** revenue stamp
semáforo *m* semaphore; traffic light
semana *f* week; week's pay; **semana inglesa** working week of five and a half days
semanal *adj* weekly
semanalmente *adv* weekly
semana·rio -ria *adj* & *m* weekly
semánti·co -ca *adj* semantic || *f* semantics
semblante *m* face, mien, countenance; appearance, expression, look
semblanza *f* biographical sketch, portrait
sembrado *m* sown ground, grain field
sembrar §2 *tr* to seed, to sow; to scatter, to spread; to sprinkle
semejante *adj* like, similar; such; **semejante a** like; **semejantes** alike, e.g., **estas sillas son semejantes** these

chairs are alike || *m* resemblance, likeness; fellow, fellow man

semejanza *f* similarity, resemblance; simile; **a semejanza de** like

semejar *tr* to resemble, to be like || *intr & ref* to be alike; **semejar a** or **semejarse a** to resemble, to be like

semen *m* semen

semental *adj* (*animal*) stud, breeding || *m* sire; stallion; stock bull

semestral *adj* semester

semestre *m* semester

semibola *f* little slam

semibreve *f* (mus) whole note

semiconductor *m* semiconductor

semiconsciente *adj* semiconscious

semicul·to -ta *adj* semilearned

semidifun·to -ta *adj* half-dead

semidormi·do -da *adj* half-asleep

semifinal *adj & f* (sport) semifinal

semilla *f* seed; **semilla de césped** grass seed

semillero *m* seedbed

seminario *m* seminary; seminar; nursery

semi-remolque *m* semitrailer

semita *mf* Semite || *n* (*idioma*) Semitic

semíti·co -ca *adj* Semitic

semivi·vo -va *adj* half-alive

semovientes *mpl* stock, livestock

sempiter·no -na *adj* everlasting

Sena *m* Seine

senado *m* senate

senador *m* senator

senaduría *f* senatorship

sencillez *f* simplicity, plainness, candor

senci·llo -lla *adj* simple, plain, candid; single || *m* change, loose change

senda *f* path, footpath

sendero *m* path, footpath, byway

sen·dos -das *adj pl* one each, one to each, e.g., **les dio sendos libros** he gave one book to each of them, he gave each of them a book

senectud *f* age, old age

senil *adj* senile

senilidad *f* senility

senilismo *m* (pathol) senility

seno *m* bosom, breast; lap; heart; womb; bay, gulf; cavity, hollow, recess; asylum, refuge

sensación *f* sensation

sensatez *f* good sense

sensa·to -ta *adj* sensible

sensibilizar §60 *tr* to sensitize

sensible *adj* appreciable, perceptible, noticeable, sensible; considerable; sensitive; deplorable, regrettable

sensiblería *f* mawkishness

sensible·ro -ra *adj* mawkish

sensiti·vo -va *adj* (*de los sentidos*) sense, sensitive; sentient; stimulating

senso·rio -ria *adj* sensory

sensual *adj* sensual, sensuous

sentada *f* sitting; **de una sentada** at one sitting

senta·do -da *adj* seated; settled; stable, permanent; sedate; **dar por sentado** to take for granted || *f* see **sentada**

sentar §2 *tr* to seat; to settle; to fit, to suit; to agree with || *ref* to sit, to sit down; to settle, settle down

sentencia *f* maxim; (law) sentence

sentenciar *tr* to sentence; (*una cuestión*) to decide; (*p.ej., un libro a la hoguera*) (coll) to consign

senti·do -da *adj* felt; deep-felt; sensitive; eloquent; **darse por sentido** to take offense || *m* sense, meaning; direction; consciousness; **sentido común** common sense

sentimiento *m* sentiment; feeling; sorrow, regret

sentir *m* feeling; opinion; judgment || §68 *tr* to feel; to hear; to be or feel sorry for; to sense || *intr* to feel; to be sorry, to feel sorry || *ref* to feel; to feel oneself to be; to be resentful; to crack, be cracked; **sentirse de** to feel; to have a pain in; to resent

seña *f* sign, mark, token; password, watchword; **por las señas** (coll) to all appearances; **por más señas** or **por señas** (coll) as a greater proof; **señas** address; description

señal *f* sign, mark, token; landmark; bookmark; trace, vestige; scar; signal; traffic light; representation; reminder; pledge; brand; down payment; **señal de ocupado** (telp) busy signal; **señal de tramo** (rr) block signal; **señal de vídeo** video signal; **señal digital** fingerprint; **señal para marcar** (telp) dial tone

señala *f* (Chile) earmark (*on livestock*)

señala·do -da *adj* noted, distinguished

señalar *tr* to mark; to show, indicate; to point at, point out; to signal; to brand; to determine, fix; to appoint; to sign and seal; to scar; to threaten || *ref* to distinguish oneself, to excel

señalizar §60 *tr* to signal

señor *m* sir, mister; lord, master, owner; **muy señor mío** Dear Sir; **señores** Mr. and Mrs.; ladies and gentlemen

señora *f* madam, missus; mistress, owner; wife; **muy señora mía** Dear Madam; **Nuestra Señora** our Lady; **señora de compañía** chaperon

señorear *tr* to dominate, to rule; to master, to control; to seize, take control of; to tower over; to excel || *intr* to strut, to swagger || *ref* to strut, to swagger; to control oneself; **señorearse de** to seize, take control of

señoría *f* lordship; ladyship; rule, sway

señoril *adj* lordly; haughty; majestic

señorío *m* dominion, sway, rule; mastery; arrogance, lordliness, majesty; gentry, nobility

señorita *f* young lady; miss

señorito *m* master; young gentleman; (coll) playboy

señuelo *m* decoy, lure; bait; enticement

separa·do -da *adj* separate; separated; apart; **por separado** separately; under separate cover

separar *tr* to separate; to dismiss, discharge || *ref* to separate; to resign

separata *f* reprint, offprint

sept.e *abbr* **septiembre**

septeto *m* septet

sépti·co -ca *adj* septic

septiembre *m* September

sépti·mo -ma *adj & m* seventh

sepulcro *m* sepulcher, tomb, grave; **santo sepulcro** Holy Sepulcher

sepultar *tr* to bury; to hide away

sepultura *f* burial; grave; **estar con un pie en la sepultura** to have one foot in the grave

sepulturero *m* gravedigger

sequedad *f* dryness, drought; gruffness, surliness

sequía *f* drought

séquito *m* retinue, suite; following, popularity

ser *m* being; essence; life || *v* §69 *v aux* (to form passive voice) to be, e.g., **el discurso fue aplaudido por todos** the speech was applauded by everybody || *intr* to be; **a no ser por** if it were not for; **a no ser que** unless; **érase que se era** (coll) once upon a time there was; **es decir** that is to say; **sea lo que fuere** be that as it may; **ser de** to belong to; to become of; to be, e.g., **el reloj es de oro** the watch is gold; **ser de ver** to be worth seeing; **soy yo** it is I

serafín *m* seraph; great beauty (*person*)

serena *f* night love song; (coll) night dew, night air

serenar *tr* to calm; to pacify; to cool; to settle

serenata *f* serenade

serenidad *f* serenity; **serenidad del espíritu** peace of mind

sere•no -na *adj* serene, calm; clear, cloudless || *m* night watchman; night dew, night air || *f* see **serena**

serial *adj* serial || *m* (rad) serial; **serial lacrimógeno** soap opera; **serial radiado** (rad) serial

serie *f* series; **de serie** stock, e.g., **coche de serie** stock car; **en serie** mass; **fuera de serie** custom-built, special; outsize

seriedad *f* seriousness; reliability; sternness, severity; solemnity

se•rio -ria *adj* serious; reliable; stern; solemn

sermón *m* sermon

sermonear *tr* & *intr* to sermonize

serpear or **serpentear** *intr* to wind, meander; to wriggle, squirm

serpentín *m* coil

serpiente *f* serpent, snake; **serpiente de cascabel** rattlesnake

serranía *f* range of mountains, mountainous country

serra•no -na *adj* highland, mountain || *mf* highlander, mountaineer

serrar §2 *tr* to saw

serrería *f* sawmill

serrín *m* sawdust

serrucho *m* handsaw

Servia *f* Serbia

servicial *adj* accommodating, obliging

servicio *m* service; (tennis) service, serve; (Am) toilet; **libre servicio** self-service; **servicio de grúa** (aut) towing service

servi•dor -dora *mf* servant; humble servant; (tennis) server; **servidor de Vd.** your servant, at your service || *m* waiter; suitor || *f* waitress

servidumbre *f* servitude; servants, help;

compulsion; (law) easement; **servidumbre de la gleba** serfdom; **servidumbre de paso** (law) right of way; **servidumbre de vía** (rr) right of way

servil *adj* servile

servilleta *f* napkin

servilletero *m* napkin ring

ser•vio -via *adj* & *mf* Serbian || *f* see **Servia**

servir §50 *tr* to serve; to help, wait on; (*un pedido*) to fill; (tennis) to serve; **para servir a Vd.** at your service || *intr* to serve; (*en los naipes*) to follow suit; **servir de** to serve as; to be used as; **servir para** to be good for, to be used for || *ref* to help oneself, to serve oneself; to have the kindness to, to deign to; **servirse de** to use, to make use of; **sírvase** please

serv.° *abbr* **servicio**

servocroata *adj* & *mf* Serbo-Croatian

servodirección *f* (aut) power steering

servoembrague *m* (aut) automatic clutch

sésamo *m* sesame; **sésamo ábrete** open sesame

sesenta *adj*, *pron* & *m* sixty

sesenta•vo -va *adj* & *m* sixtieth

sesgar §44 *tr* (*el paño*) to cut on the bias; to bevel, slant, slope

ses•go -ga *adj* beveled, slanting, sloped; oblique; stern; calm || *m* bevel; bias; slant, slope; turn; compromise; **al sesgo** obliquely; on the bias

sesión *f* session; sitting; meeting; (*cada representación de un drama o película*) show; **sesión continua** (mov) continuous showing; **sesión de espiritistas** séance, spiritualistic séance

sesionar *intr* to be in session

seso *m* brain; brains, intelligence; **calentarse** or **devanarse los sesos** to rack one's brain

sestear *intr* to take a siesta; (*el ganado*) to rest in the shade

sesu•do -da *adj* brainy; (Chile) stubborn

seta *f* bristle; toadstool

setecien•tos -tas *adj* & *pron* seven hundred || **setecientos** *m* seven hundred

setenta *adj*, *pron* & *m* seventy

setenta•vo -va *adj* & *m* seventieth

seto *m* fence; **seto vivo** hedge, quickset

seudónimo *m* pseudonym, pen name

s.e.u.o. *abbr* **salvo error u omisión**

seve•ro -ra *adj* severe; stern; strict

sevicia *f* ferocity, cruelty

sexo *m* sex; **el bello sexo** the fair sex; **el sexo feo** the sterner sex

sextante *m* sextant

sex•to -ta *adj* & *m* sixth

sexual *adj* sexual, sex

si *conj* if; whether; I wonder if; **por si acaso** just in case; **si acaso** if by chance; **si no** otherwise

sí *adv* yes; indeed; (gives emphasis to verb and is often equivalent to English auxiliary verb) **él sí habla español** he does speak Spanish || *pron reflex* himself, herself, itself, themselves; yourself, yourselves; oneself; each other || *m* (*pl* síes) yes; **dar el sí** to say yes

sia·més -mesa *adj & mf* Siamese

siberia·no -na *adj & mf* Siberian

sibila *f* sibyl

sicalipsis *f* spiciness, suggestiveness

sicalípti·co -ca *adj* spicy, suggestive, sexy

Sicilia *f* Sicily

sicilia·no -na *adj & mf* Sicilian

sicoanálisis *m* var of **psicoanálisis**

sicoanalizar §60 *tr* var of **psicoanalizar**

sicología *f* var of **psicología**

sicológi·co -ca *adj* var of **psicológico**

sicólo·go -ga *mf* var of **psicólogo**

sicópata *mf* var of **psicópata**

sico·sis *f* (*pl* **-sis**) *(afección de la piel)* sycosis

sicóti·co -ca *adj* var of **psicótico**

sideral or **sidére·o -a** *adj* sidereal

siderurgia *f* iron and steel industry

sidra *f* cider; **sidra achampañada** hard cider

siega *f* reaping, mowing; harvest; crop

siembra *f* sowing; seeding; seedtime; sown field

siempre *adv* always; **de siempre** usual; **para siempre** or **por siempre** forever; **por siempre jamás** forever and ever; **siempre que** whenever; provided

siempreviva *f* everlasting flower

sien *f* temple

sierpe *f* serpent, snake

sierra *f* saw; sierra, mountain range; **sierra circular** buzz saw; **sierra continua** band saw; **sierra de armero** hacksaw; **sierra de bastidor** bucksaw; **sierra de hilar** ripsaw; **sierra de vaivén** jig saw; **sierra sin fin** band saw

sier·vo -va *mf* slave; servant; **siervo de la gleba** serf

siesta *f* siesta; hot time of day; **siesta del carnero** nap before lunch

siete *adj & pron* seven; **las siete** seven o'clock ‖ *m* seven; *(en las fechas)* seventh; (coll) V-shaped tear or rip

sífilis *f* syphilis

sifón *m* siphon; siphon bottle; *(tubo doblemente acodado)* trap

sig.ᵉ *abbr* **siguiente**

sigilar *tr* to seal, to stamp; to conceal, keep silent

sigilo *m* seal; concealment, reserve; **sigilo sacramental** inviolable secrecy of the confessional

sigilo·so -sa *adj* tight-lipped; reserved

sigla *f* initial; abbreviation, symbol

siglo *m* (*cien años*) century; *(comercio de los hombres)* world; *(largo tiempo)* age; **siglo de la ilustración** or **de las luces** Age of Enlightenment

signar *tr* to mark; to sign; to make the sign of the cross over

signatura *f* library number; (mus & typ) signature

significado *m* meaning

significar §73 *tr* to signify, to mean; to point out, make known ‖ *intr* to be important

signo *m* sign; mark; sign of the cross; fate, destiny; **signo de admiración** exclamation mark; **signo de interrogación** question mark

siguiente *adj* following; next

sílaba *f* syllable; **última sílaba** ultima

silbar *tr* (*p.ej.*, *una canción*) to whistle; (*un silbato*) to blow; (*a un actor*) to hiss ‖ *intr* to whistle; (*ir zumbando por el aire*) to whiz, to whiz by

silbato *m* whistle

silbido *m* whistle, whistling, hiss; (rad) howling, squealing; **silbido de oídos** ringing in the ears

silbo *m* whistle, hiss

silenciador *m* silencer; (aut) muffler

silencio *m* silence; (*toque que manda que cada cual se acueste*) (mil) taps; (mus) rest

silencio·so -sa *adj* silent, noiseless, quiet, still ‖ *m* (aut) muffler

sílfide *f* sylph

silo *m* silo; cave, dark place

silogismo *m* syllogism

silueta *f* silhouette

siluetear *tr* to silhouette

silva *f* (*materias escritas sin orden*) miscellany; verse of iambic hendecasyllables intermingled with seven-syllable lines

silvestre *adj* wild; rustic, uncultivated

silvicultura *f* forestry

silla *f* chair; **silla alta** high chair; **silla de balanza** (Am) rocking chair; **silla de cubierta** deck chair; **silla de junco** rush-bottomed chair; **silla de manos** sedan chair; **silla de montar** saddle, riding saddle; **silla de ruedas** wheel chair; **silla de tijera** folding chair; **silla giratoria** swivel chair; **silla hamaca** (Arg) rocking chair; **silla plegadiza** folding chair; **silla poltrona** armchair, easy chair

sillar *m* ashlar

silleta *f* bedpan

sillico *m* chamber pot, commode

sillín *m* saddle (*of bicycle*)

sillón *m* armchair, easy chair; **sillón de orejas** wing chair

sima *f* chasm, abyss

simbóli·co -ca *adj* symbolic(al)

simbolizar §60 *tr* to symbolize

símbolo *m* symbol; **Símbolo de la fe** or **de los Apóstoles** Apostles' Creed

simetría *f* symmetry

simétri·co -ca *adj* symmetric(al)

simiente *f* seed

símil *adj* like, similar ‖ *m* similarity; (rhet) simile

similar *adj* similar

similigrabado *m* (typ) half-tone

similor *m* ormolu, similor; **de similor** fake, sham

simón *m* cab, hack (*in old Madrid*); hackman

simpatía *f* affection, attachment, fondness, liking; friendliness; congeniality; **tomar simpatía a** to take a liking for

simpáti·co -ca *adj* agreeable, pleasant, likeable, congenial

simpatizar §60 *intr* to be congenial, to get on well together; **simpatizar con** to get on well with

simple *adj* simple; single ‖ *mf* simpleton ‖ *m* (*planta medicinal*) simple

simpleza *f* simpleness; stupidity

simulacro *m* phantom, vision; idol,

image; semblance, show; pretense; sham battle; **simulacro de ataque aéreo** air-raid drill; **simulacro de combate** sham battle

simula·do -da adj fake; (com) pro forma

simular tr to simulate, feign, fake || intr to malinger; to pretend

simultáne·o -a adj simultaneous

simún m simoon

sin prep without; **sin embargo** nevertheless, however; **sin que** + subj without + ger

sinagoga f synagogue

sinapismo m mustard plaster; (coll) bore, nuisance

sincerar tr to vindicate, justify

sinceridad f sincerity

since·ro -ra adj sincere

síncopa f (phonet) syncope

síncope m fainting spell

sincróni·co -ca adj synchronous

sincronizar §60 tr & intr to synchronize

sindicar §73 tr & ref to syndicate

sindicato m syndicate; labor union

síndico m trustee; (en una quiebra) receiver

sin·diós (pl **-diós**) adj godless || mf atheist

sinecura f sinecure

sinfín m endless amount, number

sinfonía f symphony

sinfóni·co -ca adj symphonic

singladura f (naut) day's run; (de mediodía a mediodía) (naut) day

singular adj singular; special; single || m singular; **en singular** in particular

singularizar §60 tr to distinguish, to single out || ref to distinguish oneself, to stand out

sinhueso f (coll) tongue

sinies·tro -tra adj evil, perverse; calamitous, disastrous || m calamity, disaster || f left hand, left-hand side

sinnúmero m great amount, great number

sino conj but, except; **no . . . sino** only; **no . . . sino que** only; **no solo . . . sino que** not only . . . but also || m fate, destiny

sinóni·mo -ma adj synonymous || m synonym

sinop·sis f (pl **-sis**) synopsis

sinrazón f wrong, injustice

sinsabor m displeasure; anxiety, trouble, worry

sinsonte m mockingbird

sintaxis f syntax

sínte·sis f (pl **-sis**) synthesis

sintéti·co -ca adj synthetic(al)

sintetizar §60 tr to synthesize

síntoma m symptom

sintonía f (rad) tuning; (rad) theme song

sintonizar §60 tr (el aparato receptor) to tune; (la estación emisora) to tune in

sinuo·so -sa adj sinuous, winding; wavy; evasive

sinvergüenza adj (coll) brazen, shameless || mf (coll) scoundrel, rascal

sionismo m Zionism

siquiatra mf var of **psiquiatra**

siquiatría f var of **psiquiatría**

síqui·co -ca adj var of **psíquico**

siquiera adv even; at least || conj although, even though

sirena f siren; mermaid; **sirena de la playa** bathing beauty; **sirena de niebla** foghorn

sirga f towrope, towline

sirgar §44 tr to tow

Siria f Syria

si·rio -ria adj & mf Syrian || **Sirio** m (astr) Sirius || f see **Siria**

sirvienta f maid, servant girl

sirviente m servant; waiter

sisa f petty theft; (para fijar los panes de oro) sizing

sisar tr to filch, to snitch; (lo que se ha de dorar) to size

sisear tr to hiss || intr to hiss; to sizzle

siseo m hiss, hissing; sizzle, sizzling

Sísifo m Sisyphus

sismógrafo m seismograph

sismología f seismology

sistema m system

sistematizar §60 tr to systematize

sístole f systole

sitiar tr to surround, hem in; to siege, besiege

sitio m place, spot, room; location, site; country place; seat; (mil) siege; (Am) cattle ranch; (Am) taxi stand

si·to -ta adj situated, located

situación f situation, position; **pedir situación** (aer) to ask for bearings

situar §21 tr to situate, locate, place; (dinero) to place, invest; (un pedido) to place || ref to take a position; to settle; (aer) to get one's bearings

s.l. abbr **sin lugar**

S.M. abbr **Su majestad**

smo·king m (pl **-kings**) tuxedo, dinner coat

so prep under, e.g., **so pena de** under penalty of || interj whoal; (coll) you . . . !, e.g., **¡so animal!** you beast!

sobaco m armpit

sobajar tr to crush, to rumple; (Am) to humiliate

sobaquera f (en el vestido) armhole; (para resguardar del sudor la parte del vestido correspondiente al sobaco) shield

sobar tr to knead; to massage; to beat, slap; to paw, pet, feel; to annoy, be fresh to; (Am) to flatter; (un hueso dislocado) (CAm) to set; (la caballadura) (Arg) to tire out; (Col) to flay, to skin; (P-R) to bribe

sobarba f noseband

soberanía f sovereignty

sobera·no -na adj sovereign; superb || mf sovereign || m (moneda) sovereign

sober·bio -bia adj proud, haughty; arrogant; magnificent, superb || f pride, haughtiness; arrogance; magnificence

so·bón -bona adj (coll) malingering; (coll) fresh, mushy, spoony

sobornar tr to bribe

soborno m bribery; (SAm) extra load; **de soborno** (Bol) in addition; **soborno de testigo** (law) subornation of perjury

sobra *f* extra, surplus; **sobras** leftovers, leavings; trash
sobradillo *m* penthouse
sobra·do -da *adj* excessive, superfluous; bold, daring; rich, wealthy || *m* attic, garret || **sobrado** *adv* too
sobrante *adj* remaining, leftover, surplus || *m* leftover, surplus
sobrar *tr* to exceed, surpass || *intr* to be more than enough; to be in the way; to be left, to remain
sobre *prep* on, upon; over; above; about; near; after; in addition to; out of, e.g., **en nueve casos sobre diez** in nine out of ten cases || *m* envelope; **sobre de ventanilla** window envelope
sobrealimentar *tr* to overfeed; to supercharge
sobrecama *f* bedspread
sobrecarga *f* overload, extra load; overcharge; surcharge
sobrecargar §44 *tr* to overload, to overburden; to overcharge; to surcharge
sobrecargo *m* (naut) supercargo; (Am) purser || *f* (Am) air hostess, stewardess
sobrecejo *m* frown
sobreceño *m* frown
sobrecoger §17 *tr* to surprise, catch; to scare, terrify || *ref* to be surprised; to be scared; **sobrecogerse de** to be seized with
sobrecubierta *f* extra cover; (*de un libro*) jacket, dust jacket
sobredi·cho -cha *adj* above-mentioned
sobreexcitar *tr* to overexcite || *ref* to become overexcited
sobreexponer §54 *tr* to overexpose
sobreexposición *f* overexposure
sobregirar *tr* & *intr* to overdraw
sobregiro *m* overdraft
sobrehombre *m* superman
sobrehuma·no -na *adj* superhuman
sobrellevar *tr* to bear, carry; (*la carga de otra persona*) to ease; (*los trabajos o molestias de la vida*) to share; (*molestias*) to suffer with patience
sobremanera *adv* exceedingly, beyond measure
sobremesa *f* tablecloth, table cover; **de sobremesa** desk, e.g., **reloj de sobremesa** desk clock; after-dinner, e.g., **discurso de sobremesa** after-dinner speech
sobremodo *adv* var of **sobremanera**
sobrenadar *intr* to float
sobrenatural *adj* supernatural
sobrenombrar *tr* to surname; to nickname
sobrenombre *m* surname; nickname
sobrentender §51 *tr* to understand || *ref* to be understood, be implied
sobrepasar *tr* to excel, surpass, outdo; to exceed; to overtake || *ref* to outdo each other; to go too far
sobrepe·lliz *f* (*pl* -llices) surplice
sobreponer §54 *tr* to superpose, put on top; to superimpose || *ref* to control oneself; to triumph over adversity; **sobreponerse a** to overcome
sobreprecio *m* extra charge, surcharge
sobreproducción *f* overproduction
sobrepujar *tr* to excel, surpass

sobresaliente *adj* projecting; conspicuous, outstanding; (*en un examen*) distinguished || *mf* substitute; understudy
sobresalir §65 *intr* to project, jut out; to stand out, excel
sobresaltar *tr* to assail, to rush upon; to startle, frighten || *intr* to stand out clearly || *ref* to be startled, be frightened; to start, to wince
sobresalto *m* fright, scare; start, shock, wince; **de sobresalto** suddenly, unexpectedly
sobrescribir §83 *tr* to address
sobrescrito *m* address
sobrestante *m* boss, foreman
sobresueldo *m* extra wages, extra pay
sobretiro *m* offprint
sobretodo *adv* especially || *m* overcoat, topcoat
sobrevenir §79 *intr* to happen, take place; to supervene, to set in; **sobrevenir a** to overtake
sobrevidriera *f* window screen; window grill; storm window
sobrevivencia *f* (Ecuad) survival
sobreviviente *adj* surviving || *mf* survivor
sobrevivir *intr* to survive; **sobrevivir a** to survive, to outlive
sobrevolar §61 *tr* to overfly
sobriedad *f* sobriety, moderation
sobrina *f* niece
sobrino *m* nephew
so·brio -bria *adj* sober, moderate, temperate
socaire *m* (naut) lee; **al socaire de** (naut) under the lee of; (coll) under the shelter of; **estar al socaire** (coll) to shirk
socapa *f* subterfuge; **a socapa** clandestinely
socarrén *m* eaves
socarrar *tr* to singe, scorch
soca·rrón -rrona *adj* crafty, cunning, sly; sneering; roguish
socavar *tr* to undermine, to dig under
socavón *m* cave-in; cave; (min) gallery
sociable *adj* sociable
social *adj* social; company, e.g., **edificio social** company building
socialismo *m* socialism
socialista *mf* socialist
sociedad *f* society; company, firm; **buena sociedad** (*mundo elegante*) society; **sociedad anónima** stock company; **sociedad de control** holding company; **Sociedad de las Naciones** League of Nations
so·cio -cia *mf* partner; companion; member || *m* fellow; (scornful) fellow, guy
sociología *f* sociology
socorrer *tr* to aid, help, succor
socorri·do -da *adj* ready; handy, useful; hackneyed, trite, worn; well stocked
socorro *m* aid, help, succor
socoyote *m* (Mex) baby, youngest son
soda *f* soda; soda water
sodio *m* sodium
so·ez *adj* (*pl* -eces) base, mean, vile
so·fá *m* (*pl* -fás) sofa; **sofá cama** day bed

soflama _f_ glow, flicker; blush; deceit; cheating

soflamar _tr_ to flimflam; to make blush || _ref_ to become scorched

sofocar §73 _tr_ to choke, suffocate, stifle, smother; to quench, extinguish; to make blush; (coll) to bother, harass || _ref_ to choke, suffocate; to blush; to get excited; to get out of breath

sofoco _m_ blush, embarrassment

sofrenar _tr_ (_un caballo_) to check suddenly; (_una pasión_) to control; to chide, reprimand

soga _m_ sly fellow || _f_ rope, cord; **dar soga a** (coll) to make fun of; **hacer soga** (coll) to lag behind

soja _f_ soy, soy bean

sojuzgar §44 _tr_ to subjugate, subdue

sol _m_ sun; sunlight; sunny side; **de sol a sol** from sunrise to sunset; **hacer sol** to be sunny; **soles** (poet) eyes

solamente _adv_ only

solana _f_ sunny spot; sun porch

solapa _f_ lapel; pretext, pretense; flap

solapa·do -da _adj_ overlapping; cunning, underhanded, sneaky

solapar _tr_ to put lapels on; to overlap; to conceal, cover up || _intr_ to overlap

solapo _m_ lapel; flap; (coll) chuck under chin

solar _adj_ solar; ancestral || _m_ ground, plot; manor house, ancestral mansion; noble lineage; (Cuba) tenement || _v_ §61 _tr_ to pave, to floor; (_zapatos_) to sole

solarie·go -ga _adj_ ancestral; manorial

so·laz _m_ (_pl_ **-laces**) solace, consolation; recreation; **a solaz** with pleasure

soldada _f_ wages, pay

soldadera _f_ (Mex) camp follower

soldadesca _f_ soldiery; undisciplined troops

soldado _m_ soldier; **soldado de a pie** foot soldier; **soldado de juguete** toy soldier; **soldado de marina** marine; **soldado de plomo** tin soldier; **soldado de primera** private first class; **soldado raso** buck private

soldadura _f_ solder; soldering; weld; welding; **soldadura al arco** arc welding; **soldadura autógena** welding; **soldadura a tope** butt welding; **soldadura por puntos** spot welding

soldar §61 _tr_ to solder; (_sin materia extraña_) to weld || _ref_ (_los huesos_) to knit

solear _tr_ to sun || _ref_ to sun, sun oneself

soledad _f_ solitude, loneliness; longing, grieving; lonely spot

soledo·so -sa _adj_ solitary, lonely; longing, grieving

solemne _adj_ solemn; (_error, mentira, etc._) (coll) downright

soler §47 _intr_ to be accustomed to

solera _f_ crossbeam; lumber, timber; mother liquor, mother of the wine; blend of sherry; old vintage sherry; tradition, standing; (Chile) curb; (Mex) brick, tile, stone; **de solera** or **de rancia solera** of the good old school, of the good old times

solevantar _tr_ to raise up; to rouse, stir up, incite || _ref_ to rise up; to revolt

solevar _tr_ to raise up; to incite to rebellion || _ref_ to rise up; to revolt

solicitante _mf_ petitioner; applicant

solicitar _tr_ to solicit, ask for; to apply for; to woo, to court; to drive, to pull; (_la atención_) to attract; (phys) to attract

solíci·to -ta _adj_ solicitous; careful, diligent; obliging; (coll) fond, affectionate

solicitud _f_ solicitude; petition, request; application

solidar _tr_ to harden; to establish, to prove

solida·rio -ria _adj_ jointly liable; jointly binding; **solidario con** or **de** integral with

solidez _f_ solidity; strength, soundness; constancy

sóli·do -da _adj_ solid; strong, sound || _m_ solid

soliloquio _m_ soliloquy

solista _adj_ (_p.ej., instrumento_) (mus) solo || _mf_ (mus) soloist

solita·rio -ria _adj_ solitary; lonely || _mf_ hermit, recluse, solitary || _m_ (_juego y diamante_) solitaire || _f_ tapeworm

sóli·to -ta _adj_ accustomed, customary

solivantar _tr_ to rouse, stir up, incite

soliviar _tr_ to lift, lift up

so·lo -la _adj_ only, sole; alone; lonely; (_p.ej., whisky_) straight; (_café_) black; **a mis solas** alone, all by myself; **a solas** alone, unaided || _pron_ only one || _m_ (mus) solo

sólo _adv_ only, solely

solomillo _m_ sirloin

solomo _m_ sirloin; loin of pork

solsticio _m_ solstice

soltador _m_ release; **soltador del margen** margin release

soltar §61 _tr_ to untie, unfasten, loosen; to let go; to let go of; (_una observación_) to drop, to let slip; (_el agua_) to turn on || _ref_ to get loose or free; to come loose, come off; to loosen up; to burst out; to thaw out, let oneself go

solte·ro -ra _adj_ single, unmarried || _m_ bachelor || _f_ spinster, maiden lady

solterona _f_ (coll) old maid

soltura _f_ looseness; agility, ease, freedom; fluency; dissoluteness; release

solución _f_ solution

solucionar _tr_ to solve, to resolve

solventar _tr_ (_lo que uno debe_) to settle, to pay up; (_una dificultad_) to solve

solvente _adj_ & _m_ solvent

sollastre _m_ scullion

sollozar §60 _intr_ to sob

sollozo _m_ sob

sombra _f_ (_falta de luz brillante_) shade; (_imagen obscura que proyecta un cuerpo opaco_) shadow; shady side; darkness; parasol; ignorance; ghost, spirit; grace, charm, wit; favor, protection; (coll) luck; **a la sombra** in the shade; (coll) in jail; **a sombra de tejado** (coll) stealthily, sneakingly; **ni por sombra** by no means; without any notice; **no ser su sombra** to be but a shadow of one's former self; **tener buena sombra** (coll) to be likeable; (coll) to bring good luck

sombrear *tr* to shade; (*un dibujo*) to hatch

sombrerera *f* bandbox, hatbox

sombrerería *f* hat store, hat factory; millinery shop

sombrere•ro -ra *mf* hatter, hat maker || *f* see sombrerera

sombrero *m* hat; sombrero de copa high hat, top hat; sombrero de muelles opera hat; sombrero de paja straw hat; sombrero de pelo (Am) high hat; sombrero de tres picos three-cornered hat; sombrero gacho slouch hat; sombrero hongo derby; sombrero jarano (Am) sombrero

sombrilla *f* parasol, sunshade; sombrilla de playa beach umbrella; sombrilla protectora (mil) umbrella

sombrí•o -a *adj* shady; somber; gloomy

sombro•so -sa *adj* shadowy, full of shadows; shady

some•ro -ra *adj* brief, summary; slight; superficial, shallow

someter *tr* to subdue, to subject; (*razones, reflexiones; un negocio*) to submit || *ref* to yield, submit, surrender

someti•do -da *adj* humble, submissive

sometimiento *m* subjection

somier *m* bedspring, spring mattress

somorgujar *tr* to plunge, to submerge || *intr* to dive || *ref* to plunge

son *m* sound; news, rumor; pretext, motive; manner, mode; en son de in the manner of, by way of; as

sona•do -da *adj* talked-about; famous, noted

sonaja *f* jingle

sonajero *m* rattle, child's rattle

sonámbu•lo -la *mf* sleepwalker, somnambulist

sonar §61 *tr* to sound, to ring; (*un instrumento de viento, un silbato*) to blow; (*un instrumento de viento*) to play || *intr* to sound, to ring; (*un reloj*) to strike; to seem; (coll) to sound familiar; sonar a to sound like, have the appearance of || *ref* to be rumored; (*las narices*) to blow

sonda *f* sounding; plummet, lead; drill; (surg) probe, sound

sondar or sondear *tr & intr* to sound, to probe

sonetizar §60 *intr* to sonneteer

soneto *m* sonnet

sóni•co -ca *adj* sonic

sonido *m* sound; report, rumor

sonoridad *f* sonority

sonorizar §60 *tr* (*una película cinematográfica*) to record sound effects on; (*una consonante sorda*) to voice || *ref* to voice

sono•ro -ra *adj* sound; clear, loud, resounding

sonreír §58 *intr & ref* to smile

sonriente *adj* smiling

sonrisa *f* smile

sonrojar or sonrojear *tr* to make blush || *ref* to blush

sonrojo *m* blush; word that causes blushing

sonrosar or sonrosear *tr* to rose-color; to make blush || *ref* to become rose-colored; to blush

sonsacar §73 *tr* to pilfer; to entice away; to elicit, draw out

sonsonete *m* rhythmical tapping; sing-song

soña•dor -dora *adj* dreamy || *mf* dreamer

soñar §61 *tr* to dream; ni soñarlo (coll) not even in a dream, by no means || *intr* to dream; soñar con to dream of; soñar despierto to daydream

sofiolien•to -ta *adj* sleepy, dozy, drowsy, somnolent; lazy

sopa *f* (*pan u otra cosa empapada en un líquido*) sop; soup; hecho una sopa (coll) soaked to the skin, sopping wet; sopa de pastas noodle soup

sopapo *m* chuck under the chin; (coll) blow, slap

sopetear *tr* to dip, to dunk; to abuse

sopetón *m* slap, box; de sopetón suddenly

sopista *mf* beggar

soplar *tr* to blow; to blow away; to blow up, inflate; to snitch, swipe; to inspire; to prompt; to tip off; (*la dama a un rival*) to cut out; (coll) to squeal on || *intr* to blow; (coll) to squeal || *ref* to be puffed up, be conceited; (coll) to swill, gulp, gobble

soplete *m* blowpipe

soplillo *m* blower, fan; chiffon, silk gauze; light sponge cake

soplo *m* blowing, blast; breath; gust of wind; instant, moment; (*informe dado en secreto*) tip; (coll) squealing; (coll) squealer

so•plón -plona *adj* (coll) tattletale || *mf* (coll) tattletale, squealer

sopor *m* sleepiness, drowsiness; stupor

soportal *m* porch, portico, arcade

soportar *tr* to support, hold up, bear; to endure, suffer

soporte *m* support, bearing, rest, standard; base, stand

soprano *mf* (*persona*) soprano || *m* (*voz*) soprano

sor *f* (used before names of nuns) Sister

sorber *tr* to sip; to absorb, soak up

sorbete *m* sherbet, water ice

sorbetera *f* ice-cream freezer; (coll) high hat

sorbo *m* sip; gulp

sordera *f* deafness

sórdi•do -da *adj* sordid

sordina *f* silencer; (mus) mute; (mus) damper; a la sordina silently, on the quiet

sor•do -da *adj* deaf; silent, mute; muffled, dull; (*dolor, ruido*) dull || *mf* deaf person; hacerse el sordo to pretend to be deaf; to turn a deaf ear

sordomu•do -da *adj* deaf and dumb || *mf* deaf-mute

sorgo *m* sorghum, broomcorn

sorna *f* slowness; sluggishness; cunning

sorochar *ref* (SAm) to become mountain-sick; (Am) to blush

soroche *m* (SAm) mountain sickness; (Am) flush, blush; (Bol, Chile) silver-bearing galena

sorprendente *adj* surprising

sorprender *tr* to surprise; to catch; (*un secreto*) to discover

sorpresa *f* surprise; surprise package

sortear *tr* to draw or cast lots for; to choose by lot; to dodge; to duck through || *intr* to draw or cast lots

sorteo *m* drawing, casting of lots; choosing by lot; dodging; (taur) workout, performance

sortija *f* ring; curl; hoop; **sortija de sello** signet ring

sortilegio *m* sorcery, witchery

sortíle·go -ga *mf* fortuneteller || *m* sorcerer || *f* sorceress

sosa *f* soda

sosega·do -da *adj* calm, quiet, peaceful

sosegar §66 *tr* to calm, quiet, allay || *intr* to become calm, to rest || *ref* to calm down, to quiet down

sosiega *f* nightcap

sosiego *m* calm, quiet, serenity

sosla·yo -ya *adj* slanting, oblique; **al soslayo** or **de soslayo** slantingly; askance

so·so -sa *adj* insipid; tasteless; dull, inane || *f see* **sosa**

sospecha *f* suspicion

sospechar *tr* to suspect

sospecho·so -sa *adj* suspicious; suspect || *m* suspect

sostén *m* support; (*de un buque*) steadiness; brassiere

sostener §71 *tr* to support, hold up; to sustain; to maintain; to bear, to stand || *ref* to remain

sosteni·do -da *adj & m* (mus) sharp

sota *f* (Chile) boss, foreman || *f* (*en los naipes*) jack; jade, hussy

sotana *f* soutane, cassock

sótano *m* basement, cellar

sotavento *m* (naut) leeward

soterrar §2 *tr* to bury; to hide away

soto *m* grove; brush, thicket, copse

so·viet *m* (*pl* **-viets**) soviet

soviéti·co -ca *adj* soviet, sovietic

sovietizar §60 *tr* to sovietize

sovoz — **a sovoz** sotto voce, in a low tone

Sr. *abbr* **Señor**

Sra. *abbr* **Señora**

Srta. *abbr* **Señorita**

S.S.S. *abbr* **su seguro servidor**

ss. ss. *abbr* **seguros servidores**

su *adj poss* his, her, its, their, your, one's

suave *adj* suave, smooth, soft; gentle, mild, meek

suavizador *m* razor strop

suavizar §60 *tr* to smooth, ease, sweeten, soften, mollify; (*una navaja de afeitar*) to strop

subalter·no -na *adj & mf* subaltern, subordinate

subasta *f* auction, auction sale; **sacar a pública subasta** to sell at auction

subastar *tr* to auction, sell at auction

subcampe·ón -ona *mf* (sport) runner-up

subcentral *f* (elec) substation

subconsciencia *f* subconscious, subconsciousness

subconsciente *adj* subconscious

subdesarrolla·do -da *adj* underdeveloped

súbdi·to -ta *adj & mf* subject

subentender §51 *tr* to understand || *ref* to be understood, be implied

subestimar *tr* to underestimate

subfusil *m* submachine gun

subli·do -da *adj* high, fine, superior; strong, intense; (*color*) bright; high, high-priced || *f* rise; ascent; (*p.ej., al trono*) accession

subir *tr* to raise; to lift; to carry up; (*p.ej., una escalera*) to go up; (mus) to raise the pitch of || *intr* to go up, to come up; to rise; to get worse; to spread; **subir a** to climb; to climb on; to get in or into; to get on, to mount || *ref* to rise

súbi·to -ta *adj* sudden, unexpected; hurried; hasty, impetuous || **súbito** *adv* suddenly

subjeti·vo -va *adj* subjective

subjunti·vo -va *adj & m* subjunctive

sublevación *f* uprising, revolt

sublevado *m* rebel, insurrectionist

sublevar *tr* to incite to rebellion || *ref* to revolt

submarinista *mf* (sport) skin diver || *m* (nav) submariner

submari·no -na *adj & m* submarine

suboficial *m* sergeant major; noncommissioned officer

subordina·do -da *adj & mf* subordinate

subordinar *tr* to subordinate

subproducto *m* by-product

subrayar *tr* to underline; to emphasize

subrepti·cio -cia *adj* surreptitious

subsanar *tr* to excuse, overlook; to correct, repair

subscribir §83 *tr* to subscribe; to subscribe to, to endorse; to subscribe to or for; to sign; to sign up || *ref* to subscribe

subseguir §67 *intr & ref* to follow next

subsidiar *tr* to subsidize

subsidio *m* subsidy; aid, help

subsiguiente *adj* subsequent

subsistencia *f* subsistence, sustenance

subsistir *intr* to subsist

substancia *f* substance

substanciar *tr* to abstract, to abridge

substanti·vo -va *adj & m* substantive

substitución *f* replacement; (chem, law, math) substitution

substitui·dor -dora *adj & mf* substitute

substituir §20 *tr* to replace; to substitute for, take the place of || *intr* to take someone's place || *ref* to be replaced; to relieve each other

substituti·vo -va *adj & m* substitutive

substitu·to -ta *mf* substitute

substraer §75 *tr* to remove; to deduct; to rob, steal; to subtract || *ref* to withdraw; **substraerse a** to evade, avoid, slip away from

subte *m* (Arg, Urug) subway

subteniente *m* second lieutenant

subterrá·neo -a *adj* subterranean, underground || *m* subterranean; (Arg) subway

subtitular *tr* to subtitle

subtítulo *m* subtitle, subheading

suburbio *m* suburb; outlying slum

subvención *f* subvention, subsidy

subvencionar *tr* to subvention, to subsidize

subvenir §79 *intr* to provide; **subvenir a** to provide for; (*gastos*) to defray

subvertir §68 *tr* to subvert

subyugar §44 *tr* to subjugate, to subdue

sucedáne·o -a *adj & m* substitute

suceder *tr* to succeed, follow ‖ *intr* to happen; **suceder a** (*p.ej., el trono*) to succeed to ‖ *ref* to follow one another

sucesi·vo -va *adj* successive; **en lo sucesivo** in the future

suceso *m* event, happening; issue, outcome; **sucesos de actualidad** current events

suciedad *f* dirt, filth; dirtiness, filthiness

su·cio -cia *adj* dirty, filthy; base, low; tainted; blurred; (sport) foul ‖ **sucio** *adv* (sport) foully, unfairly

sucumbir *intr* to succumb

sucursal *f* branch, branch office

Sudamérica *f* South America

sudamerica·no -na *adj & mf* South American

sudar *tr* to sweat; (coll) to cough up ‖ *intr* to sweat; (*trabajar mucho*) (coll) to sweat

sudario *m* shroud, winding sheet

sudcorea·no -na *adj & mf* South Korean

sudor *m* sweat; (fig) sweat, toil; **chorrear de sudor** to swelter

sudoro·so -sa *adj* sweaty

Suecia *f* Sweden

sue·co -ca *adj* Swedish ‖ *mf* Swede ‖ *m* (*idioma*) Swedish

suegra *f* mother-in-law

suegro *m* father-in-law

suela *f* sole; sole leather; (*fish*) sole

sueldacostilla *f* grape hyacinth

sueldo *m* salary, pay

suelo *m* ground, soil, land; floor, flooring; pavement; (*p.ej., de una botella*) bottom; **no pisar en el suelo** to walk on air; **suelo franco** loam; **suelo natal** home country

suel·to -ta *adj* loose; free; easy; swift, agile, nimble; fluent; bold, daring; (*ejemplar*) single; (*verso*) blank; odd, separate; spare; bulk; **suelto de lengua** loose-tongued ‖ *m* small change; news item

sueñecillo *m* nap; **descabezar un sueñecillo** to take a nap

sueño *m* sleep; dream; (*cosa de gran belleza*) (fig) dream; **conciliar el sueño** to manage to go to sleep; **ni por sueños** by no means; **no dormir sueño** to not sleep a wink; **tener sueño** to be sleepy; **último sueño** (*muerte*) last sleep; **sueño hecho realidad** dream come true; **sueños dorados** daydreams

suero *m* serum

suerte *f* fortune, luck; piece of luck; fate, lot; kind, sort; way, manner; feat, trick; (taur) play, suerte; (Peru) lottery ticket; **de esta suerte** in this way; **de suerte que** so that, with the result that; **la suerte está echada** the die is cast; **suerte de capa** (taur) capework

suerte·ro -ra *adj* (Am) fortunate, lucky

sué·ter *m* (*pl* -ters) sweater

suficiente *adj* sufficient; adequate; fit, competent

sufijo *m* suffix

sufragar §44 *tr* to help, support, favor; to defray ‖ *intr* (SAm) to vote

sufragio *m* help, succor; benefit; (*voto*) suffrage

sufragismo *m* woman suffrage

sufragista *mf* woman-suffragist ‖ *f* suffragette

sufri·do -da *adj* long-suffering; (*color*) serviceable; (*marido*) complaisant

sufrir *tr* to suffer; to undergo, experience; to support, hold up; to tolerate; (*un examen*) to take ‖ *intr* to suffer

sugerencia *f* suggestion

sugerir §68 *tr* to suggest

sugestión *f* suggestion

sugestionar *tr* to influence by suggestion

sugesti·vo -va *adj* suggestive; stimulating, striking, conspicuous

suicida *adj* suicidal ‖ *mf* suicide

suicidar *ref* to commit suicide

suicidio *m* suicide

Suiza *f* Switzerland

sui·zo -za *adj & mf* Swiss ‖ *f* see **Suiza**

sujeción *f* subjection; surrender; fastening; fastener

sujetahilo *m* (elec) binding post

sujetapape·les *m* (*pl* -les) paper clip

sujetar *tr* to subject; to subdue; to fasten, tighten ‖ *ref* to subject oneself, to submit, to stick, adhere

suje·to -ta *adj* subject, liable; (Am) able, capable ‖ *m* subject; fellow, individual; **buen sujeto** good egg

sulfato *m* sulfate

sulfito *m* sulfite

sulfúri·co -ca *adj* sulfuric

sulfuro *m* sulfide; **sulfuro de hidrógeno** hydrogen sulfide

sulfuro·so -sa *adj* sulfurous

sultán *m* sultan; (*galanteador*) (coll) sheik

suma *f* sum, addition; summary; sum and substance; **en suma** in short, in a word

sumadora *f* adding machine

sumamente *adv* extremely, exceedingly

sumar *tr* to add; to sum up; to amount to ‖ *intr* to add; to amount; **suma y sigue** add and carry ‖ *ref* to add up; to adhere

suma·rio -ria *adj & m* summary

sumergir §27 *tr* to submerge ‖ *ref* to submerge; (*un submarino*) to dive

sumersión *f* submersion; (*de un submarino*) dive

sumidad *f* top, apex, summit

sumidero *m* drain, sewer; sink

suministrar *tr* to provide, to supply

suministro *m* provision, supply; **suministros** supplies

sumir *tr* to sink; to press down; to overwhelm ‖ *ref* to sink; (*p.ej., los carrillos, el pecho*) to be sunken; (Am) to shrink, to shrivel; (Am) to cower; (*p.ej., el sombrero*) (Am) to pull down

sumisión *f* submission; (*sometimiento*) subjection

sumi·so -sa *adj* submissive

su·mo -ma *adj* high, great, extreme;

supreme; **a lo sumo** at most, at the most || *f* sce **suma**

suncho *m* hoop

suntuo·so -sa *adj* sumptuous

supeditar *tr* to hold down, oppress

superar *tr* to surpass, excel; to conquer

superávit *m* (com) surplus

supercarburante *m* high-test fuel

superchería *f* fraud, deceit

superficial *adj* superficial; surface

superficie *f* surface; exterior, outside; area; **superficie de sustentación** (aer) airfoil

super·fluo -flua *adj* superfluous

superhombre *m* superman

superintendente *mf* superintendent, supervisor; **superintendente de patio** (rr) yardmaster

superior *adj* superior; upper; higher; **superior a** superior to; higher than; more than; larger than || *m* superior

superiora *f* mother superior

superioridad *f* superiority; authorities

superlati·vo -va *adj & m* superlative

supermercado *m* supermarket

super·no -na *adj* highest, supreme

superpoblar §61 *tr* to overpopulate

superponer §54 *tr* to superpose

superproducción *f* overproduction

supersóni·co -ca *adj* supersonic || *f* supersonics

superstición *f* superstition

supersticio·so -sa *adj* superstitious

supervisar *tr* to supervise

supervivencia *f* survival; (law) survivorship

súpi·to -ta *adj* sudden; (coll) impatient; (Col) dumbfounded

suplantar *tr* to supplant by treachery; (*un documento*) to alter fraudulently

suplefal·tas *mf* (*pl* -tas) substitute, fill-in

suplemento *m* supplement; excess fare

súplica *f* entreaty, supplication; request

suplicante *adj & mf* suppliant

suplicar §73 *tr & intr* to entreat, implore; (law) to petition

suplicio *m* torture; punishment, execution; anguish

suplir *tr* to supplement, make up for; to replace, take the place of; (*un defecto de otra persona*) to cover up; (gram) to understand

suponer §54 *tr* to suppose; to presuppose, imply; to entail || *intr* to have weight, have authority

suposición *f* supposition; distinction; falsehood, imposture

supositorio *m* suppository

supradi·cho -cha *adj* above-mentioned

supre·mo -ma *adj* supreme

supresión *f* suppression, elimination, omission; cancellation; deletion

suprimir *tr* to suppress, eliminate, do away with; to cancel; to delete

supues·to -ta *adj* supposed, assumed, hypothetical; **supuesto que** since, inasmuch as || *m* assumption, hypothesis; **dar por supuesto** to take for

granted; **por supuesto** of course, naturally

supurar *intr* suppurate, discharge pus

sur *m* south; south wind

Suramérica *f* South America

surcar §73 *tr* to furrow; to plough; to cut through; to streak through

surco *m* furrow; wrinkle, rut, cut; (*del disco gramofónico*) groove; **echarse en el surco** (coll) to lie down on the job

surcorea·no -na *adj & mf* South Korean

sure·ño -ña *adj* (Am) southern || *mf* (Am) southerner

surestada *f* (Arg) southeaster

surgir §27 *intr* to spout, spurt; to come forth, spring up; to arise, appear

suripanta *f* (hum) chorine; (scornful) slut, jade

surti·do -da *adj* assorted || *m* assortment; supply, stock

surtidor *m* jet, spout, fountain; **surtidor de gasolina** gasoline pump

surtir *tr* to furnish, provide, supply || *intr* to spout, spurt, shoot up

susceptible *adj* susceptible; touchy

suscitar *tr* to stir up, provoke; (*dudas, una cuestión*) to raise

susodi·cho -cha *adj* above-mentioned

suspender *tr* to hang; to suspend; to astonish; to postpone; to fail, to flunk || *ref* to be suspended

suspensión *f* suspension; astonishment; **suspensión de fuegos** cease fire

suspen·so -sa *adj* suspended, hanging; baffled, bewildered; (theat) closed || *m* flunk, condition

suspensores *mpl* (Am) suspenders

suspensorio *m* jockstrap, supporter

suspi·caz *adj* (*pl* -caces) suspicious, distrustful

suspirar *intr* to sigh

suspiro *m* sigh; ladyfinger; (mus) quarter rest

sustentación *f* support, prop; (aer) lift

sustentar *tr* to sustain, support, feed; to maintain; (*una tesis*) to defend

sustento *m* sustenance, support, food; maintenance

susto *m* scare, fright

susurrar *tr* to whisper || *intr* to whisper; to murmur, rustle, purl, hum; to be bruited about || *ref* to be bruited about

susurro *m* whisper; murmur, rustle, purling, hum

susu·rrón -rrona *adj* (coll) whispering || *mf* (coll) whisperer

sutil *adj* subtle; keen, observant; thin, delicate

su·yo -ya *adj poss* of his, of hers, of yours, of theirs, e.g., **un amigo suyo** a friend of his; *pron poss* his, hers, yours, theirs, its, one's; **hacer de las suyas** (coll) to be up to one's old tricks; **salirse con la suya** to have one's way; to carry one's point

T

T, t (te) *f* twenty-third letter of the Spanish alphabet
t. *abbr* tarde
taba *f* anklebone; (*del carnero*) knucklebones; (*juego*) knucklebones
tabaco *m* tobacco; cigar; snuff; (Cuba, CAm, Mex) punch; **tabaco en rama** leaf tobacco
tabalada *f* (coll) bump, thump, heavy fall; (coll) slap
tabalear *tr* to rock, to sway ǁ *intr* to drum with the fingers
tabanazo *m* (coll) slap; (coll) slap in the face
tabanco *m* stand, stall, booth
tábano *m* horsefly, gadfly
tabanque *m* treadle wheel
tabaola *f* noise, hubbub
tabaquera *f* snuffbox; (*de la pipa de fumar*) bowl; (Arg, Chile) tobacco pouch
tabaquería *f* tobacco store, cigar store
tabaque·ro -ra *adj* tobacco ǁ *mf* tobacconist; cigar maker ǁ *m* (Bol) pocket handkerchief ǁ *f* see **tabaquera**
tabardete *m* or **tabardillo** *m* (coll) sunstroke; (coll) harum-scarum
tabarra *f* (coll) bore, tiresome talk
taberna *f* tavern, saloon, barroom, pub
tabernáculo *m* tabernacle
tabernera *f* barmaid
tabernero *m* tavern keeper; bartender
tabica *f* (*para cubrir un hueco*) board; (*del frente de un escalón*) riser
tabicar §73 *tr* to close up, to shut up; to wall up
tabique *m* thin wall; partition wall, partition
tabla *f* (*de madera*) board; (*de metal*) sheet; (*de piedra*) slab; (*de tierra*) strip; (*cuadro pintado en una tabla*) panel; (*lista, catálogo; índice de materias*) table; **escapar** or **salvarse en una tabla** to have a narrow escape; **tabla de lavar** washboard; **tabla de planchar** ironing board; **tabla de salvación** lifesaver, helping hand; **tablas** draw, tie; (*escenario del teatro*) stage; (*de la plaza de toros*) barrier; **tener tablas** to have stage presence
tablado *m* flooring; scaffold; (*escenario del teatro*) stage
tablear *tr* to cut into boards; to divide into plots or patches; to level, to grade
tablero *m* boarding; timber; table top; gambling table; cutting board; checkerboard, chessboard; counter; blackboard; **poner al tablero** to risk; **tablero de instrumentos** (aer) control panel; (aut) dashboard
tableta *f* small board; (*taco de papel; comprimido, pastilla*) tablet
tabletear *intr* to rattle
tablilla *f* tablet; splint; bulletin board
tablón *m* plank; beam
tabloncillo *m* (taur) seat in last row
ta·bú *m* (*pl* -búes) taboo
tabuco *m* hovel

tabulador *m* tabulator
tabular *tr* to tabulate
taburete *m* stool
tac *m* tick
tacada *f* stroke (*of a billiard cue*)
taca·ño -ña *adj* stingy
táci·to -ta *adj* tacit; silent
taciturno *-na* *adj* taciturn; melancholy
taco *m* bung, plug; wad, wadding; billiard cue; pad, tablet; drumstick; (coll) snack, bite; (coll) drink; (coll) oath, curse; (Am) heel; (Am) muddle, mess
tacón *m* heel
taconear *tr* (Chile) to fill, to stuff ǁ *intr* to click the heels; to strut
taconeo *m* click, clicking (*of heels*)
tácti·co -ca *adj* tactical ǁ *m* tactician ǁ *f* tactics
tacto *m* (sense of) touch; (*del dactilógrafo, el pianista, el instrumento*) touch; skill; tact
tacha *f* defect, fault, flaw
tachar *tr* to erase; to strike out; to blame, find fault with
tacho *m* (Arg) garbage can; (Arg) watch; (Arg, Chile) boiler; (Cuba) sugar pan; (Am) tin sheet
tachón *m* scratch, erasure; ornamental tack or nail; trimming
tachonar *tr* to adorn with ornamental tacks; to trim with ribbon; to spangle, to stud
tachuela *f* tack; hobnail; (Chile, Mex) runt, half pint; (SAm) drinking cup
Tadeo *m* Thaddeus
tafetán *m* taffeta; (coll) finery; **tafetán inglés** court plaster
tafilete *m* morocco leather; (Am) sweatband
tagarote *m* sparrow hawk; scrivener; (coll) lout; (coll) gentleman sponger
tagua *f* (Chile) mud hen; (*arbusto*) (SAm) ivory palm; (*fruto*) (SAm) ivory nut
taha·lí *m* (*pl* -líes) baldric
tahona *f* horse-driven flour mill; bakery
ta·hur -hura *adj* gambling; cheating ǁ *mf* gambler, cheat; cardsharp
tailan·dés -desa *adj* & *mf* Thai
Tailandia *f* Thailand
taima·do -da *adj* sly, crafty; (Arg, Ecuad) lazy; (Chile) gruff, sullen
tajada *f* cut; slice; (coll) hoarseness; (coll) drunk
tajadero *m* chopping block
tajalá·piz *m* (*pl* -pices) pencil sharpener
tajamar *m* cutwater; (Am) dike, dam
tajar *tr* to cut; to slice; (*un lápiz*) to sharpen
tajo *m* cut; cutting edge; chopping block; execution block; steep cliff ǁ **Tajo** *m* Tagus
tal *adj indef* such; such a ǁ *pron indef* so-and-so; such a thing; someone ǁ *adv* so; in such a way; **con tal (de) que** provided (that); **¿qué tal?** how?; hello!, how's everything?

talabarte *m* sword belt
talabartero *m* saddler, harness maker
talache *m* or **talacho** *m* (Mex) mattock
taladrar *tr* to bore, drill, pierce, perforate; *(un billete)* to punch; *(un problema)* to get to the bottom of
taladro *m* drill; auger; drill hole; drill press
tálamo *m* bridal bed
talán *m* ding-dong
talante *m* countenance, mien; desire, will, pleasure; way, manner
talar *adj (traje, vestidura)* long ‖ *tr (árboles)* to fell; to destroy, lay waste
talco *m* tinsel; talc; **talco en polvo** talcum powder
talega *f* bag, sack; **talegas** (coll) money, wealth
talego *m* big bag, sack; (coll) slob; **tener talego** (coll) to have money tucked away
taleguilla *f* small bag; bullfighter's breeches
talento *m* talent
talento·so -sa *adj* talented
Tales *m* Thales
Talía *f* Thalia
talismán *m* talisman
talón *m* heel; (aut) lug, flange; check, voucher, coupon; *(de un cheque)* stub
talona·rio -ria *adj* stub ‖ *m* stub book, checkbook
talonear *intr* (coll) to dash along
talud *m* slope
talla *f* cut; carving; height, stature; size; ransom; reward; (Arg) chatting, prattle; (CAm) fraud, lie; (Col) beating, thrashing
tallar *tr* to carve; *(una piedra preciosa)* to cut; *(naipes)* to deal; to appraise; to engrave; to grind; to size up; (Col) to beat, to thrash ‖ *intr* (Arg) to chat, converse; (Chile) to make love
tallarín *m* noodle
talle *m* shape, figure, stature; waist; fit; appearance, outline; (Am) bodice
taller *m* shop, workshop; factory, mill; atelier, studio; laboratory; **taller agremiado** closed shop; **taller franco** open shop; **taller penitenciario** workhouse
tallo *m* stem, stalk; shoot, sprout; (Col) cabbage
tamal *m* (CAm, Mex) tamale; (Am) intrigue; (Chile) bundle
tamañi·to -ta *adj* so small; very small; confused, disconcerted
tama·ño -ña *adj* so big; such a big; very big, very large; so small; **abrir tamaños ojos** to open one's eyes wide ‖ *m* size
tambaleante *adj* staggering
tambalear *intr & ref* to stagger, reel, totter
también *adv* also, too
tambo *m* (Arg, Chile) brothel; (SAm) roadside inn; (Arg, Urug) dairy
tambor *m* drum; *(persona que toca el tambor)* drummer; sieve, screen; eardrum; coffee roaster; **a tambor batiente** with drums beating; in triumph; **tambor mayor** drum major

tamborilear *tr* to praise to the skies ‖ *intr* to drum
Támesis *m* Thames
ta·miz *m* (*pl* -**mices**) sieve
tamizar §60 *tr* to sift, to sieve
tamo *m* fuzz, fluff
tampoco *adv* neither, not either; **ni yo tampoco** nor I either
tampón *m* stamp pad
tan *adv* so; **tan . . . como** or **cuan** as . . . as; **tan siquiera** at least; **un tan + adj** such a + *adj* ‖ *m* boom *(of a drum)*
tanda *f* turn; shift, relay; task; coat, layer; game, match; flock, lot, pack; (Am) show; (Am) habit, bad habit
tangente *adj & f* tangent; **escaparse, irse or salir por la tangente** (coll) to evade the issue
Tánger *f* Tangier
tanguista *f* hostess *(in a night club)*
ta·no -na *adj & mf* (Arg) Neapolitan, Italian
tanque *m* tank; (dial) dipper, drinking cup
tantán *m* tom-tom; clanging; boom
tantear *tr* to compare; to size up; to probe, test, feel out; to sketch, outline; to keep the score of ‖ *intr* to keep score; (Am) to grope; **¡tantee Vd.!** (Am) just imagine!, fancy that!
tanteo *m* comparison; careful consideration; test, probe, trial; trial and error; score
tan·to -ta *adj & pron indef* so much; as much; **tanto . . . como** as much . . . as; both . . . and; **tan·tos -tas** so many; as many; **tantos . . . como** as many . . . as; **y tantos** odd, or more, e.g., **veinte y tantos** twenty odd, twenty or more ‖ *m* copy; counter, chip; point; (Am) portion, part; **apuntar los tantos** to keep score; **entre tanto** in the meantime; **estar al tanto de** to be aware of, to be or keep informed about; **poner al tanto de** to make aware of, to keep informed of; **por lo tanto** or **por tanto** therefore ‖ **tanto** *adv* so much; so hard; so often; so long; as much
tañer §70 *tr* *(un instrumento músico)* to play; *(una campana)* to ring ‖ *intr* to drum with the fingers
tañido *m* sound, tone; twang; ring, tang
tapa *f* lid, cover, top, cap; *(de un cilindro, un barril)* head; *(de una compuerta)* gate; *(de un libro)* board cover; shirt front; (aut) valve cap; **levantarse** or **saltarse la tapa de los sesos** to blow one's brains out; **tapas** appetizer, free lunch
tapabalazo *m* (Am) fly *(of trousers)*
tapabarro *m* (Chile) mudguard
tapaboca *f* slap in the mouth; muffler; (coll) squelch, squelcher
tapacu·bo or **tapacu·bos** *m* (*pl* -**bos**) (aut) hubcap
tapadera *f* lid, cover, cap
tapagote·ras *m* (*pl* -**ras**) (Arg) roofing cement; (Col) roofer
tapaguje·ros *m* (*pl* -**ros**) (coll) bungling mason; (coll) substitute, replacement
tapar *tr* to cover; to cover up, to hide;

to plug, stop, stop up; to conceal; to obstruct; to wrap up; (un diente) (Chile) to fill

tapara f (Ven) gourd; vaciarse como una tapara (Ven) to spill all one knows

taparrabo m loincloth; bathing trunks

tapera f (SAm) ruins; (SAm) shack

tapete m rug; runner; table scarf; estar sobre el tapete to be on the carpet, be under discussion; tapete verde card table, gambling table

tapia f mud wall, adobe wall

tapiar tr to wall up, wall in; to close up

tapicería f tapestries; upholstery; tapestry shop; upholstery shop

tapicero m tapestry maker; upholsterer; carpet maker; carpet layer

ta·piz m (pl -pices) tapestry

tapizar §60 tr to tapestry; to upholster; to carpet; to cover

tapón m stopper, cork; cap; bottle cap; bung, plug; (elec) fuse; (surg) tampon; tapón de algodón (surg) swab; tapón de cubo (aut) hubcap; tapón de desagüe drain plug; tapón de tráfico traffic jam; tapón de vaciado (aut) drain plug

taponar tr to plug, stop up; (surg) to tampon

taponazo m pop

taque m click; knock, rap

taqué m (aut) tappet

taquigrafía f shorthand, stenography

taquigrafiar §77 tr to take down in shorthand || intr to take shorthand

taquígra·fo -fa mf stenographer

taquilla f ticket rack; ticket window; ticket office; box office; gate, take; file; (C-R) inn, tavern

taquille·ro -ra adj box-office || mf ticket agent

taquimeca mf (coll) shorthand-typist

taquimecanógra·fo -fa mf shorthand-typist

tarabilla f millclapper; catch; turn-buckle; (de la hebilla de la correa) tongue; (coll) chatterbox; (coll) jabber; soltar la tarabilla (coll) to talk a blue streak

tarabita f (clavillo de la hebilla) tongue; (SAm) rope of rope bridge

taracea f marquetry, inlaid work

tarambana adj & mf (coll) crackpot

tararear tr & intr to hum

tarasca f dragon (in Corpus Christi procession); (mujer fea) (coll) hag

tarascada f bite; (coll) tart reply

tardanza f slowness, delay, tardiness

tardar intr to be long, to be slow; to be late; a más tardar at the latest; tardar en + inf to be late in + ger || ref to be long, to be slow; to be late

tarde adv late; too late; hacerse tarde to grow late; tarde o temprano sooner or later || f afternoon; evening; de la tarde a la mañana overnight; suddenly, in no time; unexpectedly

tardecer §22 intr to grow dark, to grow late

tardí·o -a adj late, delayed; dilatory; tardy; slow

tar·do -da adj slow; late; slow, dull, dense

tar·dón -dona mf (coll) poke, slow poke

tarea f task, job; care, worry

tarifa f tariff; price list; rate; fare; (telp) toll; tarifa recargada extra fare

tarima f platform; stand; stool; low bench; (entablado para dormir) bunk

tarjeta f card; tarjeta de buen deseo or de felicitación greeting card; tarjeta de visita calling card, visiting card; tarjeta navideña Christmas card; tarjeta perforada punch card; tarjeta postal post card, postal card

tarjetero m card case; card index

tarquín m mire, slime, mud

tarro m jar; milk pail; (Am) horn; (SAm) top hat

tarta f tart, cake; pan

tartajear intr to stutter

tartalear intr (coll) to stagger, to sway; (coll) to be speechless

tartamudear intr to stutter, to stammer

tartamudeo m stuttering, stammering

tartamu·do -da mf stutterer, stammerer

tartán m Scotch plaid

tartana f tartana (two-wheeled round-top carriage of Valencia)

tarugo m wooden plug; wooden paving block; (Guat, Mex) dolt, blockhead

tasa f appraisal; measure, standard; rate; ceiling price

tasación f appraisal; regulation

tasajo m jerked beef

tasar tr to appraise; to regulate; to hold down, keep within bounds; to grudge

tasca f dive, joint; tavern; (Peru) surf, breakers

tata m (coll) daddy || f (coll) nurse-maid; (Am) little sister

tato m (Am) little brother

tatuaje m tattoo, tattooing

tatuar §21 tr & ref to tattoo

taurino -na adj bullfighting

taurófi·lo -la mf bullfight fan

tauromaquia f bullfighting

taxear intr (aer) to taxi

taxi m taxi, taxicab || f taxi dancer

taxista mf taxi driver

taza f cup; (de la fuente) basin; (del inodoro) bowl

te pron pers & reflex thee, to thee; you, to you; thyself, to thyself; yourself, to yourself

té m tea; té bailable tea dance

tea f torch, firebrand

teatral adj theatrical

teatre·ro -ra mf (Am) theater-goer

teatro m theater; dar teatro a to bally-hoo; teatro de estreno first-run house; teatro de repertorio stock company

teatrólo·go -ga mf theater critic || m actor || f actress

Tebas f Thebes

tebe·o -a adj & mf Theban || m comic book, funny paper

teca f teak

tecla f (de piano, máquina de escribir, etc.) key; touchy subject; dar en la tecla (coll) to get the knack of it; tecla de cambio shift key; tecla de escape margin release; tecla de espa-

cios space bar; **tecla de retroceso** backspacer

teclado *m* keyboard; **teclado manual** (mus) manual

teclear *tr* (coll) to feel out ‖ *intr* to run over the keys; to drum, to thrum; (Chile) to be at death's door; (*un jugador*) (Chile) to be losing one's last cent

tecleo *m* fingering; touch; (*de la máquina de escribir*) click

técni·co -ca *adj* technical ‖ *m* technician; expert ‖ *f* technique; technics

tecolote *m* eagle owl (*of Central America*); (Mex) night policeman

techado *m* roof; **bajo techado** indoors

techar *tr* to roof

techo *m* ceiling; roof; (*sombrero*) (coll) hat; **techo de paja** thatched roof

techumbre *f* ceiling; roof

tedio *m* ennui, boredom

tedio·so -sa *adj* tedious, boresome

teja *f* roofing tile; shovel hat; yew tree; linden tree; **a toca teja** (coll) for cash; **teja de madera** shingle

tejadillo *m* cover, top; (*de coche*) roof

tejado *m* tile roof; roof; **tejado de vidrio** (fig) glass house

tejama·ní *m* (*pl* -**níes**) (Am) shake (*long shingle*)

tejar *m* tile works ‖ *tr* to tile, roof with tiles

teja·roz *m* (*pl* -**roces**) eaves

teje·dor -dora *adj* weaving; (coll) scheming ‖ *mf* weaver; (coll) schemer

tejer *tr* & *intr* to weave

tejido *m* weave, texture; web; fabric, textile; tissue; (biol & fig) tissue; **tejido adhesivo** friction tape; **tejido de saco** (Mex) burlap; **tejido de punto** knitted fabric, jersey

tejo *m* disk; quoit; yew tree

tejón *m* badger

tela *f* cloth, fabric; (*de cebolla*) skin; (*del insecto*) web; film; (bb) cloth; (paint) canvas; (*dinero*) (slang) dough; **poner en tela de juicio** to question, to doubt; **tela de alambre** wire screen; **tela de araña** spider web, cobweb; **tela emplástica** court plaster; **tela metálica** chicken wire; wire screen

telar *m* loom; frame; embroidery frame; (bb) sewing press

telaraña *f* spider web, cobweb

telecontrol *m* remote control

teledifundir *tr* & *intr* to telecast

teledifusión *f* telecasting; telecast

telefonar *tr* & *intr* (Am) to telephone

telefonazo *m* (coll) telephone call

telefonear *tr* & *intr* to telephone

telefonema *m* telephone message

telefonista *mf* telephone operator

teléfono *m* telephone; **teléfono automático** dial telephone; **teléfono público** pay station

teleg. *abbr* **telégrafo, telegrama**

telegrafiar §77 *tr* & *intr* to telegraph

telegrafista *mf* telegrapher

telégrafo *m* telegraph; **telégrafo de banderas** wigwagging; **telégrafo de máquinas** (naut) engine-room tele-

graph; **telégrafo sin hilos** wireless telegraph

telegrama *m* telegram

teleimpresor *m* teletype, teleprinter

Telémaco *m* Telemachus

telemando *m* remote control

telemetrar *tr* to telemeter

telemetría *f* telemetry

telémetro *m* telemeter; (mil) range finder

telen·do -da *adj* sprightly, lively

telerreceptor *m* television set

telescopar *tr* & *ref* to telescope

telescopio *m* telescope

telesilla *f* chair lift

telespecta·dor -dora *mf* viewer, televiewer

telesquí *m* ski lift, ski tow

teleta *f* blotter, blotting paper

teletipo *m* teletype

teletubo *m* (telv) picture tube

televidente *mf* viewer, televiewer

televisar *tr* to televise

televisión *f* television; **televisión en circuito cerrado** closed-circuit television; **televisión en colores** color television

televi·sor -sora *adj* televising; television ‖ *m* television set ‖ *f* television transmitter

telón *m* drop curtain; **telón de acero** (fig) iron curtain; **telón de boca** (theat) front curtain; **telón de fondo** or **foro** (theat) backdrop

tema *m* theme, subject; exercise; (gram) stem; (mus) theme ‖ *f* fixed idea; persistence; grudge; **a tema** in emulation

temario *m* agenda

temblar §2 *intr* to tremble, shake, quiver, shiver; **estar temblando** to teeter

tem·blón -blona *adj* (coll) shaking, tremulous ‖ *m* aspen tree

temblor *m* tremor, shaking, trembling; **temblor de tierra** earthquake

embloro·so -sa *adj* trembling, shaking, tremulous

tem·bo -ba *adj* (Col) silly, stupid

temer *tr* & *intr* to fear

temera·rio -ria *adj* rash, reckless, foolhardy

temeridad *f* rashness, recklessness, foolhardiness, temerity

temero·so -sa *adj* frightful, dread; timid; fearful

temible *adj* dreadful, terrible, fearful

temor *m* fear, dread

témpano *m* small drum; drumhead; (*de barril*) head; (*de tocino*) flitch; (*de hielo*) iceberg, floe; (archit) tympan; (mus) kettledrum

temperamental *adj* temperamental

temperamento *m* temperament; conciliation, compromise; weather

temperar *tr* to temper, soften, moderate, calm; to tune ‖ *intr* (Am) to go to a warmer climate

temperatura *f* temperature; weather

temperie *f* weather, state of the weather

tempestad *f* storm, tempest; **tempestad de arena** sandstorm; **tempestades de risas** gales of laughter

tempesti·vo -va *adj* opportune, timely

tempestuo·so -sa *adj* stormy, tempestuous

templa·do -da *adj* temperate; moderate; lukewarm, medium; (coll) brave, courageous; (SAm) in love; (Am) drunk, tipsy; (CAm, Mex) clever

templanza *f* temperance; mildness

templar *tr* to temper; to soften; to ease; to dilute; (*colores*) to blend; (*velas*) to trim || *intr* (*el tiempo*) to warm up || *ref* to temper; to moderate; (Am) to fall in love; (Am) to die

temple *m* weather, state of the weather; temper, disposition; humor; average; dash, boldness; (*del acero, el vidrio, etc.*) temper

templo *m* temple

témpora *f* Ember days

temporada *f* season; period; (*p.ej., de buen tiempo*) spell; **de temporada** temporarily; vacationing

temporal *adj* temporal; temporary || *m* weather; storm, tempest; spell of rainy weather

temporáne·o -a or **tempora·rio -ria** *adj* temporary

temporizar §60 *intr* to temporize; to putter around

temprane·ro -ra *adj* early

tempra·no -na *adj* early || **temprano** *adv* early

tenacidad *f* tenacity; persistence

tenacillas *fpl* sugar tongs; hair curler; tweezers; snuffers

te·naz *adj* (*pl* **-naces**) tenacious; persistent

tenazas *fpl* pincers, pliers; tongs

tenazón — **a** or **de tenazón** without taking aim; offhand

tenazuelas *fpl* tweezers

tendedera *f* (Am) clothesline; (Am) litter

tendedero *m* drier, frame for drying clothes; drying ground

tendencia *f* tendency

tender §51 *tr* to spread; to stretch out; to extend; to reach out; to offer, to tender; (*la ropa*) to hang out; (*con una capa de cal o yeso*) to coat; (*un puente*) to throw, build; (*una trampa*) to set; (*conductores eléctricos, vías de ferrocarril, cañerías*) to lay; (*la cama*) (Am) to make; (*un cadáver*) (Am) to lay out || *intr* to tend || *ref* to stretch out; to throw one's cards on the table; to run at full gallop

ténder *m* tender

tenderete *m* stand, booth

tende·ro -ra *mf* shopkeeper, storekeeper || *m* tent maker

tendido *m* (*p.ej., de un cable*) laying; (*de una cortina de humo*) spreading; (*de alambres*) hanging, stretching; wires; (*trecho de ferrocarril*) stretch; (*ropa que tiende la lavandera*) wash; (*de cal o yeso*) coat; (*del tejado*) slope; (*de panes*) batch; (taur) uncovered stand; (Col) bedclothes

tendón *m* tendon

tenducha *f* or **tenducho** *m* miserable old store

tenebro·so -sa *adj* dark, gloomy; (*negocio*) dark, shady; (*estilo*) obscure

tenedor *m* holder, bearer; fork, table fork; **tenedor de acciones** stockholder; **tenedor de bonos** bondholder; **tenedor de libros** bookkeeper

teneduría *f* bookkeeping

tenencia *f* tenure, tenancy; (mil & nav) lieutenancy

tener §71 *tr* to have; to hold; to keep; to own, possess; to consider; (*recibir*) to get; to esteem; to stop; **no tenerlas todas consigo** (coll) to be alarmed, dismayed; **no tener nada que ver con** to have nothing to do with; **no tener sobre qué caerse muerto** (coll) to not have a cent to one's name; **tener que** to have to; for expressions like **tener hambre** to be hungry, see the noun || *ref* to stop; to catch oneself, to keep from falling; to consider oneself; to fit, to go

tenería *f* tannery

tenida *f* (Am) meeting, session

teniente *adj* holding, owning; unripe; mean, miserly; (coll) hard of hearing || *m* lieutenant; **teniente coronel** lieutenant colonel; **teniente de navío** (nav) lieutenant

tenis *m* tennis

tenista *mf* tennis player

tenor *m* tenor, character, import, drift; (mus) tenor; **a tenor de** in accordance with

tenorio *m* lady-killer

tensión *f* tension, stress; (elec) tension, voltage; (mech) stress; **tensión arterial** or **sanguínea** blood pressure

ten·so -sa *adj* tense, tight, taut

tentación *f* temptation

tentáculo *m* tentacle, feeler

tenta·dor -dora *adj* tempting || *m* tempter

tentar §2 *tr* to touch; (*el camino*) to feel; to try, to attempt; to examine; to try out, to test; to tempt; to probe

tentati·vo -va *adj* tentative || *f* attempt; trial, feeler

tentempié *m* (coll) snack, bite, pick-me-up; (*juguete*) (coll) tumbler

tenue *adj* tenuous; light, soft; faint, subdued; (*estilo*) simple

teñir §72 *tr* to dye; to stain; to tinge, shade, color

teología *f* theology; **no meterse en teologías** (coll) to keep out of deep water

teorema *m* theorem

teoría *f* theory

tepe *m* turf, sod

tequila *m* (Mex) tequila (*distilled liquor*)

terapéuti·co -ca *adj* therapeutic(al) || *f* therapeutics

terapia *f* therapy

tercena *f* government tobacco warehouse; (Ecuad) butcher shop

terce·ro -ra *adj* third || *mf* third; mediator; go-between || *m* procurer, bawd; referee, umpire

terceto *m* tercet; trio

terciar *tr* to place diagonally; to divide into three parts; (*p.ej., la capa, el* *fusil*) to swing over one's shoulder; (*licor*) (Am) to water ‖ *intr* to intercede, mediate ‖ *ref* to happen; to be opportune

tercia·rio -ria *adj* tertiary

ter·cio -cia *adj* third ‖ *m* third; (mil) corps; **hacer buen tercio a** to do a good turn

terciopelo *m* velvet

ter·co -ca *adj* stubborn; hard, resistant

Teresa *f* Theresa

tergiversar *tr* to slant, to twist, to distort

terliz *m* ticking

termal *adj* thermal; steam

termas *fpl* hot baths

térmi·co -ca *adj* temperature; steam; steam-generated

terminación *f* termination

terminal *adj* terminal ‖ *m* (elec) terminal

terminante *adj* final, definitive, peremptory

terminar *tr* to end, terminate; to finish ‖ *intr* to end, terminate

término *m* end, limit; boundary; bearing, manner; term; **medio término** subterfuge, evasion; compromise; **primer término** foreground; (mov) close-up; **segundo término** middle distance; **término medio** average; **último término** no background

termistor *m* (elec) thermistor

termite *m* termite

termodinámi·co -ca *adj* thermodynamic ‖ *f* thermodynamics

termómetro *m* thermometer; **termómetro clínico** clinical thermometer

termonuclear *adj* thermonuclear

termopar *m* (elec) thermocouple

Termópilas, las Thermopylae

ter·mos *m* (pl **-mos**) thermos bottle; hot-water heater; **termos de acumulación** (elec) off-peak heater

termosifón *m* hot-water boiler

termóstato *m* thermostat

terna *f* trio

terne·jo -ja *adj* (Ecuad, Peru) peppy, energetic

ternera *f* calf; (*carne*) veal

terneza *f* tenderness; fondness, love; **ternezas** flirting, flirtation

ternilla *f* gristle

terno *m* suit of clothes; oath, curse; trio; (coll) piece of luck; (Col) cup and saucer; (W-I) set of jewelry

ternura *f* tenderness; fondness, love

terquedad *f* stubbornness; hardness, resistance

terraja *f* diestock

terral *adj* (*viento*) land ‖ *m* land breeze

Terranova *m* (*perro*) Newfoundland (dog) ‖ *f* (*isla y provincia*) Newfoundland (*island and province*)

terraplén *m* fill; embankment; terrace, platform; earthwork, rampart

terrateniente *mf* landholder, landowner

terraza *f* terrace; veranda; flat roof; (*de jardín*) border, edge; sidewalk cafe; glazed jar with two handles

terremoto *m* earthquake

terrenal *adj* earthly, mundane, worldly

terre·no -na *adj* terrestrial; mundane, worldly ‖ *m* land, ground, terrain; lot, plot; (sport) field; (fig) field, sphere; **sobre el terreno** on the spot; with data in hand; **terreno echadizo** refuse dump

terre·ro -ra *adj* earthly; of earth; humble ‖ *m* pile, heap; mark, target; terrace; public square; (min) dump

terrestre *adj* terrestrial; ground, land

terrible *adj* terrible; gruff, surly, ill-tempered

territorio *m* territory

terromontero *m* hill, butte

terrón *m* clod; lump, cake

terror *m* terror

terrorismo *m* terrorism, frightfulness

terro·so -sa *adj* earthly; dirty

terruño *m* piece of ground; soil; country, native soil

ter·so -sa *adj* smooth, glossy, polished; smooth, limpid, flowing

tertulia *f* party, social gathering; literary gathering; game room; **estar de tertulia** to sit around and talk

tertulia·no -na *mf* party-goer; regular member

Tesalia, la Thessaly

te·sis *f* (pl **-sis**) thesis

te·so -sa *adj* taut, tight, tense ‖ *m* top of hill; (*en superficie lisa*) rough spot

tesón *m* grit, pluck, tenacity

tesone·ro -ra *adj* (Am) obstinate, stubborn, tenacious

tesorería *f* treasury

tesore·ro -ra *mf* treasurer

tesoro *m* treasure; treasury; treasure house; thesaurus

Tespis *m* Thespis

testa *f* head; front; (coll) head, brains; **testa coronada** crowned head

testaferro *m* (coll) dummy, figurehead, straw man

testamento *m* testament, will; **Antiguo Testamento** Old Testament; **Nuevo Testamento** New Testament; **Viejo Testamento** Old Testament

testar *tr* (Ecuad) to cross out ‖ *intr* to make a will

testaru·do -da *adj* stubborn, pig-headed

testera *f* front; (*de animal*) forehead; (*de coche*) back seat

testículo *m* testicle

testificar §73 *tr* & *intr* to testify

testigo *mf* witness; **testigo de vista, testigo ocular,** or **testigo presencial** eyewitness ‖ *m* (*evidencia*) witness; (*en un experimento*) control

testimoniar *tr* to attest, to testify to, to bear witness to

testimonio *m* testimony; affidavit; false witness

tes·tuz *m* (pl **-tuces**) (p.ej., *de caballo*) face; nape

teta *f* teat; breast

tetera *f* teapot, teakettle

tetilla *f* nipple

tétri·co -ca *adj* dark, gloomy; sad, sullen, gloomy

textil *adj* & *m* textile

texto *m* text; **fuera de texto** tipped-in

textura *f* texture

tez *f* complexion

ti *pron pers* thee; you

tía *f* aunt; old lady, old woman; (coll) bawd; **no hay tu tía** (coll) there's no chance; **tía abuela** grandaunt

tiara *f* tiara

tibante *adj* (Col) haughty, proud

tibia *f* shinbone; pipe, flute

ti·bio -bia *adj* tepid, lukewarm; (SAm) angry ‖ *f* see **tibia**

tibor *m* large porcelain vase; (Am) chamber pot

tiburón *m* shark

Ticiano, El Titian

tictac *m* tick-tock

tiemblo *m* aspen tree

tiempo *m* time; weather; (gram) tense; (*de un motor de combustión interna*) cycle; (*de una sinfonía*) (mus) movement; (mus) tempo; **darse buen tiempo** to have a good time; **de cuatro tiempos** (mach) four-cycle; **de dos tiempos** (mach) two-cycle; **de un tiempo a esta parte** for some time now; **el Tiempo** Father Time; **fuera de tiempo** untimely, at the wrong time; **hacer buen tiempo** to be clear; **mucho tiempo** a long time; **tomarse tiempo** to bide one's time

tienda *f* store, shop; tent; **ir de tiendas** to go shopping; **tienda de campaña** army tent; camping tent; **tienda de modas** ladies' dress shop; **tienda de objetos de regalo** gift shop; **tienda de raya** (Mex) company store

tienta *f* cleverness; probe; (taur) testing the mettle of a young bull; **andar a tientas** to grope in the dark; to feel one's way

tiento *m* touch; blind man's stick; rope-walker's pole; steady hand; care, caution; mahlstick; (coll) blow, hit; (coll) swig; **andarse con tiento** to watch one's step; **perder el tiento** to lose one's touch

tier·no -na *adj* tender; loving; tearful; soft

tierra *f* earth; ground; land; dirt; (elec) ground; **dar en tierra con** to upset, overthrow, ruin; **echar tierra a** to hush up; **en tierra, mar y aire** on land, on sea, and in the air; **irse a tierra** to topple, to collapse; **la tierra de nadie** (mil) no man's land; **tierra adentro** inland; **tierra de pan llevar** wheat land, cereal-growing land; **tierra firme** mainland; land, terra firma; **Tierra Firme** Spanish Main; **Tierra Santa** Holy Land; **tomar tierra** to land; to find one's way around; **venir** or **venirse a tierra** to topple, to collapse; **ver tierras** to see the world, to go traveling

tierral *m* (Am) cloud of dust

tie·so -sa *adj* stiff; tight, taut, tense; stubborn; bold, enterprising; strong, well; stiff, stuck-up; **tenérselas tiesas a** or **con** to stand up to ‖ **tieso** *adv* hard

ties·to -ta *adj* stiff; tight, taut, tense; stubborn ‖ *m* flowerpot; (*pedazo roto*) potsherd ‖ **tiesto** *adv* hard

tiesura *f* stiffness

ti·fo -fa *adj* (coll) full, satiated ‖ *m*

typhus; **tifo de América** yellow fever; **tifo de Oriente** bubonic plague

tifón *m* waterspout; typhoon

tigra *f* tigress; (Am) female jaguar

tigre *m* tiger; (Am) jaguar

tijera *f* scissors, shears; sawbuck; **buena tijera** (coll) good cutter; (coll) good eater; (coll) gossip; **tijeras** scissors, shears

tijeretear *tr* to snip, clip, cut; (coll) to meddle with ‖ *intr* (Am) to gossip

tila *f* linden tree; linden-blossom tea

tildar *tr* to put a tilde or dash over; to erase, strike out; **tildar de** to brand as

tilde *m* & *f* tilde; accent mark; superior dash; blemish, flaw; censure ‖ *f* jot, tittle

tiliche *m* (CAm, Mex) trinket

tiliche·ro -ra *mf* (CAm) peddler

tilín *m* ting-a-ling

tilo *m* linden tree; (Am) linden-blossom tea

tilo·so -sa *adj* (CAm) dirty, filthy

timar *tr* to snitch; to swindle ‖ *ref* (coll) to make eyes at each other

timba *f* (coll) game of chance; (coll) gambling den; (CAm, Mex) belly

timbal *m* kettledrum; (*pastel relleno*) casserole

timbrar *tr* to stamp

timbre *m* stamp, seal; tax stamp; stamp tax; deed of glory; (phonet & phys) timbre; **timbre nasal** twang; **timbres** glockenspiel

timi·do -da *adj* timid, bashful

timo *m* (coll) theft, swindle; (coll) lie; (coll) catch phrase

timón *m* (*del arado*) beam; rudder; (fig) helm; **timón de dirección** (aer) vertical rudder; **timón de profundidad** (aer) elevator

timonel *m* helmsman, steersman

timonera *f* (naut) pilot house, wheelhouse

timora·to -ta *adj* God-fearing; chicken-hearted

tímpano *m* eardrum; kettledrum

tina *f* large earthen jar; wooden vat; bathtub

tinaja *f* large earthen jar

tincazo *m* (Arg, Ecuad) fillip

tinglado *m* shed; intrigue, trick; (zool) leatherback

tinieblas *fpl* darkness

tino *m* feel (*for things*); good aim; knack; insight, wisdom; **coger el tino** to get the knack of it

tinta *f* ink; tint, hue; dyeing; **de buena tinta** (coll) on good authority; **tinta china** India ink; **tinta simpática** invisible ink

tinte *m* dye; dyeing; dyer's shop; (fig) coloring, false appearance

tinterillo *m* (coll) clerk, lawyer's clerk; (Am) pettifogger

tintero *m* inkstand, inkwell

tintín *m* clink; jingle

tintinear *intr* to clink; to jingle

tin·to -ta *adj* red ‖ *m* red table wine ‖ *f* see **tinta**

tintorería *f* dyeing; dyeing establishment; dry-cleaning establishment

tintore·ro -ra *mf* dyer; dry cleaner

tintura *f* dye; dyeing; rouge; tincture; (fig) smattering; **tintura de tornasol** litmus, litmus solution; **tintura de yodo** iodine

tiña *f* ringworm; (coll) stinginess

tiño·so -sa *adj* scabby, mangy; (coll) stingy

tío *m* uncle; old man; (coll) guy, fellow; **tío abuelo** granduncle; **tíos** uncle and aunt

tiovivo *m* merry-go-round, carrousel

tipiadora *f* (*máquina*) typewriter; (*mujer*) typist

tipiar *tr & intr* to type, to typewrite

tipicista *adj* regional, local

típi·co -ca *adj* typical; regional; quaint

tipismo *m* quaintness

tipista *mf* typist, typewriter

tiple *mf* soprano (*person*); treble-guitar player ‖ *m* soprano (*voice*); treble guitar

tipo *m* type; (*de descuento, de interés, de cambio*) rate; shape, figure, build; (coll) fellow, guy, specimen; **tener buen tipo** to have a good figure; **tipo de ensayo** or **prueba** eye-test chart; **tipo de impuesto** tax rate; **tipo de letra** typeface; **tipo menudo** small print

tipografía *f* typography

típula *f* (ent) daddy-longlegs

tira *m* (Arg, Chile, Col) detective ‖ *f* strip, **hecho tiras** (Chile) in rags; **tira emplástica** (Arg) court plaster; **tira proyectable** film strip; **tiras cómicas** comics, funnies

tirabala *f* popgun

tirabuzón *m* corkscrew; corkscrew curl

tirada *f* throw; distance, stretch; time, period; printing; edition; shooting party, hunting party; tirade; **de** or **en una tirada** at one stroke; **tirada aparte** reprint

tira·do -da *adj* dirt-cheap; (*letra*) cursive ‖ *f* see **tirada**

tira·dor -dora *mf* shot, good shot ‖ *m* knob; doorknob; pull chain; **tirador certero** sharpshooter; **tirador emboscado** sniper

tirafondo *m* wood screw

tiraje *m* draft; printing, edition

tiramira *f* long, narrow mountain range; (*de personas o cosas*) string; distance, stretch

tiranía *f* tyranny

tiráni·co -ca *adj* tyrannic(al)

tira·no -na *adj* tyrannous ‖ *mf* tyrant

tirante *adj* tense, taut, tight; (fig) tense, strained ‖ *m* (*de los arreos de una caballería*) trace; **tirantes** suspenders

tirantez *f* tenseness, tautness, tightness; strain

tirar *tr* to throw, cast, fling; to throw away; to shoot, fire; (*alambre*) to draw, pull, stretch; (*una línea*) to draw; (*una coz, un pellizco*) to give; to print; to attract; to tear down, knock down; (phot) to print ‖ *intr* to pull; to last; to appeal, have an appeal; (*una chimenea*) to draw; (*a la derecha, a la izquierda*) to bear, to turn; **ir tirando** (coll) to get along; **tirar a** to shoot at; (*la espada*) to

handle; to shade into; to tend to; to aspire to; **tirar de** to pull, pull on; (*una espada*) to draw; to attract; to boast of being; **tira y afloja** (coll) give and take; (coll) hot and cold ‖ *ref* to rush, throw oneself; to give oneself over; to lie down

tirilla *f* neckband; **tirilla de bota** bootstrap; **tirilla de camisa** collarband

tiritar *intr* to shiver

tiro *m* throw; shot; charge, load; (*estampido*) report; rifle range; (*p.ej., de chimenea*) draft; (*de caballos*) team; (*de escalera*) flight; (*de las guarniciones*) trace; (*de un paño*) length; pull cord, pull chain; reach; hurt, damage; trick; theft; (min) shaft; (sport) drive, shot; (*alusión desfavorable*) shot; (fig) shot, marksman; **a tiro de fusil** within gunshot; **a tiro de piedra** within a stone's throw; **matar a tiros** to shoot to death; **ni a tiros** not for love nor money; **poner el tiro muy alto** to hitch one's wagon to a star; **tiro al blanco** target practice; **tiro al vuelo** trapshooting; **tiro de la pesa** (sport) shot-put

tirón *m* tyro, novice; jerk; tug, pull; **de un tirón** all at once; at a stretch

tirotear *tr* to snipe at, to blaze away at ‖ *ref* to fire at each other; to bicker

tirria *f* (coll) dislike, grudge; **tener tirria a** (coll) to have it in for

tisana *f* tea, infusion

tisis *f* consumption, tuberculosis

titanio *m* titanium

tít. *abbr* **título**

títere *m* marionette, puppet; fixed idea; (coll) whipper-snapper, nincompoop; **no dejar títere con cabeza** or **cara** (coll) to upset the applecart; **títeres** puppet show

titilar *tr* to titillate ‖ *intr* to flutter, quiver; to twinkle

titubear *intr* to stagger, totter; to stammer, stutter; to waver, hesitate

titular *m* bearer, holder; incumbent; headline ‖ *f* capital letter ‖ *tr* to title, entitle ‖ *intr* to receive a title ‖ *ref* to be called; to call oneself

titulillo *m* running head

título *m* title; titled person; regulation; bond; certificate; degree; diploma; headline; **a título de** as a, by way of, on the score of; **títulos** credentials

tiza *f* chalk

tiznar *tr* to soil with soot; to spot, stain; to defame ‖ *ref* to become soiled; to get spotted or stained; (Arg, Chile, CAm) to get drunk

tizne *m & f* soot ‖ *m* firebrand

tiznón *m* smudge, spot of soot

tizón *m* brand, firebrand; wheat smut; brand, dishonor

tizonear *intr* to stir up the fire

tlapalería *f* (Mex) paint store

toalla *f* towel; **toalla rusa** Turkish towel; **toalla sin fin** roller towel

toallero *m* towel rack

toar *tr* (naut) to tow

tobar *tr* (Col) to tow

tobillera *f* anklet; (sport) ankle support; (coll) subdeb; (coll) flapper

tobillo *m* ankle

tobo *m* (Ven) bucket

tobogán *m* toboggan; chute, slide

toca *f* toque; headdress

tocadis•cos *m* (*pl* -cos) record player; **tocadiscos automático** record changer

toca•do -da *adj* (*echado a perder; medio loco*) touched; **tocado de la cabeza** (coll) touched in the head || *m* hairdo, coiffure; headdress

toca•dor -dora *mf* performer, player || *m* boudoir; dressing table; dressing case, toilet case

tocante *adj* touching; **tocante a** concerning, with reference to

tocar §73 *tr* to touch; to touch on; to feel; to ring; to toll; to strike; to come to know, to suffer, to feel; (*el cabello*) to do; (*un tambor*) to beat; (mus) to play; (paint) to touch up || *intr* to touch; **tocar a** to knock at; to pertain to, to concern; to fall to the lot of; to be the turn of; (*el fin*) to approach; **tocar en** (*un puerto*) to touch at; (*tierra*) to touch; to touch on; to approach, border on || *ref* to put one's hat on, to cover one's head; to touch each other; to be related; to make one's toilet; to become mentally unbalanced; (*el sombrero*) to tip; **tocárselas** (coll) to beat it

toca•yo -ya *mf* namesake

tocino *m* bacon; salt pork

tocón *m* stump

tocuyo *m* (SAm) coarse cotton cloth

tochimbo *m* (Peru) smelting furnace

to•cho -cha *adj* rough, coarse, crude

todavía *adv* still, yet; **todavía no** not yet

to•do -da *adj* all, whole, every; any || *m* whole; everything; **con todo** still, however; **del todo** wholly, entirely; **jugar el todo por el todo** to stake everything, to shoot the works; **sobre todo** above all, especially; **todo el que** everybody who; **todo lo que** all that; **todos** all, everybody; **todos cuantos** all those who

todopodero•so -sa *adj* all-powerful, almighty

toga *f* (academic) gown

toldilla *f* poop, poop deck

toldería *f* (SAm) Indian camp, Indian village

toldo *m* awning; pride, haughtiness; (SAm) Indian hut

tole *m* hubbub, uproar; **tole tole** gossip, talk; **tomar el tole** (coll) to run away

tolerancia *f* tolerance; **por tolerancia** on sufferance

tolerar *tr* to tolerate

tolete *m* (Am) club, cudgel; (Am) raft; (Cuba) dunce

toletole *m* (Col) persistence, obstinacy; (Ven) merry life of a wanderer

tolon•dro -dra *adj* scatterbrained || *mf* scatterbrain || *m* bump, lump

tolva *f* hopper; chute

tolvanera *f* dust storm

tolla *f* quagmire; (Cuba) watering trough

tom. *abbr* tomo

toma *f* taking; seizure, capture; tap; in-

take, inlet; (elec) tap, outlet; (elec) plug; (elec) terminal; (*de rapé*) pinch; **toma de posesión** installation, induction; inauguration; **toma de tierra** (aer) landing; (rad) ground connection; **toma directa** high gear

toma-corrien•te *m* or **toma-corrien•tes** *m* (*pl* -tes) (elec) current collector; (elec) tap, outlet; (elec) plug

tomadero *m* handle; intake, inlet

toma•dor -dora *mf* (com) drawee; (coll) thief; (Am) drinker, toper

tomar *tr* to take; to get; to seize; to take on; (*un resfriado*) to catch; (*p.ej., el desayuno*) to have, to eat; (*el café, un trago*) to take, to drink; **tomar a bien** to take in the right spirit; **tomar a mal** to take offense at; **tomarla con** to pick a quarrel with; to have a grudge against; **tomar prestado** to borrow; **tomar sobre sí** to take upon oneself || *intr* to take, to turn || *ref* to take; (*p.ej., el desayuno*) to have, to eat; (*el café*) to take, to drink; to get rusty

tomate *m* tomato; (*en medias, calcetines, etc.*) (coll) tear, run

tomavis•tas *m* (*pl* -tas) motion-picture camera; cameraman

tómbola *f* raffle, charity raffle

tomillo *m* thyme

tomo *m* volume; bulk; importance, consequence; **de tomo y lomo** of consequence; (coll) bulky and heavy

ton. *abbr* tonelada

ton *m* — **sin ton ni son** without rhyme or reason

tonada *f* air, melody, song; (Cuba) hoax; (*pronunciación particular*) (Arg, Chile) accent; (Am) singsong

tonel *m* cask, barrel

tonelada *f* (*unidad de peso; unidad de volumen; unidad de desplazamiento*) ton; (*medida de capacidad para el vino*) tun

tonelaje *m* tonnage

tonele•ro -ra *mf* barrelmaker, cooper

tonga *f* coat, layer; (Arg, Col) task; (Col) sleep; (Cuba) heap, pile

tongonear *ref* (Am) to strut, swagger

tóni•co -ca *adj* & *m* tonic || *f* (mus) keynote

tonillo *m* singsong; (*pronunciación particular*) accent

tono *m* tone; tune; (mus) pitch; (mus) key; (*de un instrumento de bronce*) (mus) slide; **dar el tono** to set the standard; **darse tono** (coll) to put on airs; **de buen tono** stylish, elegant; **estar a tono** (coll) to be in style; **poner a tono** (*un motor de automóvil*) to tune up; **tono mayor** (mus) major key; **tono menor** (mus) minor key

tonsila *f* tonsil

tonsilitis *f* tonsilitis

tonsurar *tr* to shear, to clip

tontear *intr* to talk nonsense, to act foolishly

tontería *f* foolishness, nonsense

ton•to -ta *adj* foolish, stupid, silly; **a tontas y a locas** wildly, recklessly; in disorder, haphazardly || *mf* fool, dolt; **tonto de capirote** (coll) blatant fool

tonu·do -da *adj* (Arg) magnificent, showy, conceited

topacio *m* topaz

topar *tr* to butt; to bump; to run into, encounter || *intr* to butt; to succeed; to lie, be found; **topar con** or **en** to run into, encounter

tope *adj* (*precio*) top; (*fecha*) last || *m* butt; bumper; bump, collision; rub, difficulty; scuffle; masthead; **al tope** or **a tope** end to end; flush; **estar hasta el tope** or **los topes** to be loaded to the gunwales; (coll) to be fed up; **tope de puerta** doorstop

topera *f* molehill

topetada *f* butt

topetar *tr* to butt || *intr* to butt; **topetar con** (coll) to bump, bump into; (coll) to run across

topetón *m* butt; bump, collision

tópi·co -ca *adj* local || *m* topic; (med) external application

topinera *f* molehill; **beber como una topinera** to drink like a fish

topo *m* mole; (coll) blunderer; (coll) stumbler, awkward person

topografía *f* topography

toque *m* touch; (*de una campana*) ringing; (*del tambor*) beat; sound; knock; stroke; check, test; (*punto esencial*) gist; (paint) touch; (coll) blow; **dar un toque a** (coll) to put to the test; (coll) to feel out; to sound out; **toque a muerto** knell, toll; **toque de diana** reveille; **toque de queda** curfew; **toque de retreta** (mil) tattoo; **toque de tambor** drumbeat

torada *f* drove of bulls

tó·rax *m* (*pl* **-rax**) thorax

torbellino *m* whirlwind; (*persona bulliciosa*) (coll) harum-scarum

torcecuello *m* (orn) wryneck

torcedura *f* twist; sprain; dislocation

torcer §74 *tr* to twist; to bend; to turn; to sprain; (*la cara*) to screw up; (*el tobillo*) to wrench; to turn; (*interpretar mal*) to distort, to misconstrue || *intr* to turn || *ref* to twist; to bend; to sprain, dislocate; to turn sour; to go crooked; to fail

torci·do -da *adj* twisted; crooked; bent; (*ojos*) cross; (*persona o conducta*) crooked; (Guat) unlucky || *f* wick, lampwick; curlpaper

tor·do -da *adj* dapple-gray || *mf* dapple-gray horse || *m* thrush; (Am) starling

torear *tr* (*toros*) to fight; to banter, tease, string along || *intr* to fight bulls, be a bullfighter

toreo *m* bullfighting; (taur) performance

tore·ro -ra *adj* (coll) bullfighting || *mf* bullfighter

toril *m* (taur) bull pen

tormenta *f* storm; adversity, misfortune

tormento *m* torment, torture; anguish

tormento·so -sa *adj* stormy; (*barco*) storm-ridden

torna *f* return; dam; tap; **se han vuelto las tornas** the luck has changed; **volver las tornas** to give tit for tat

tornar *tr* to return, give back; to turn; to make || *intr* to return; to turn; **tornar a** + *inf* verb + again, e.g., **tornó a abrir la puerta** he opened the door again || *ref* to turn, to become

tornasol *m* sunflower; litmus; iridescence

tornasola·do -da *adj* changeable, iridescent

tornavía *m* (rr) turntable

torna·voz *m* (*pl* **-voces**) sounding board; **hacer tornavoz** to cup one's hands to one's mouth

tornear *tr* to turn, turn up || *intr* to go around; to tourney; to muse, meditate

torneo *m* tourney; match, tournament; **torneo radiofónico** quiz program

tornillo *m* (*cilindro que entra en la tuerca*) screw; (*clavo con resalto helicoidal*) bolt; (*instrumento con dos mandíbulas*) vise; (mil) desertion; (CAm, Ven) screw tree; **apretar los tornillos a** (coll) to put the screws on; **tener flojos los tornillos** (coll) to have a screw loose; **tornillo de mariposa** or **de orejas** thumbscrew; **tornillo de presión** setscrew; **tornillo para metales** machine screw

torniquete *m* (*para contener hemorragias*) tourniquet; (*torno para cerrar un paso*) turnstile; **dar torniquete a** to twist the meaning of

torno *m* turn, revolution; (*máquina simple que consiste en un cilindro que gira sobre su eje*) winch, windlass; (*de alfarero*) potter's wheel; (*instrumento con dos mandíbulas*) vise; (*máquina herramienta que sirve para labrar metal o madera*) lathe; (*de coche*) brake; (*de un río*) bend, turn; revolving server; **en torno a** or **de** around; **torno de alfarero** potter's wheel, **torno de banco** bench vise; **torno de hilar** spinning wheel

toro *m* bull; **toro corrido** (coll) smart fellow; **toros** bullfight

torón *m* strand

toronja *f* grapefruit

toronjo *m* grapefruit (tree)

torpe *adj* slow, heavy; clumsy, awkward; stupid; lewd; crude, ugly

torpedear *tr* to torpedo

torpedo *m* torpedo; touring car

torpeza *f* torpidity, slowness; clumsiness, awkwardness; stupidity; lewdness; turpitude; crudeness, ugliness

torrar *tr* to toast

torre *f* tower; watchtower; (*en el ajedrez*) castle, rook; **torre del homenaje** donjon, keep; **torre de lanzamiento** launching tower; **torre de marfil** (fig) ivory tower; **torre de vigía** (naut) crow's-nest; **torre maestra** donjon, keep; **torre reloj** clock tower

torreja *f* (dial, Am) French toast

torrentada *f* flash flood

torrente *m* torrent

torreón *m* (archit) turret

torreta *f* (nav) turret

tórri·do -da *adj* torrid

torrija *f* French toast

torta *f* cake; (typ) font; (coll) slap; **ser tortas y pan pintado** (coll) to be a cinch; **torta a la plancha** hot cake, griddle cake

torticolis *m* or **torticolis** *m* wryneck, stiff neck

tortilla *f* omelet; (CAm, Mex) tortilla (*corn-meal cake*); **tortilla a la española** potato omelet; **tortilla a la francesa** plain omelet; **tortilla de tomate** Spanish omelet

tórtola *f* turtledove

tortuga *f* tortoise, turtle

tortuo·so -sa *adj* winding; (fig) devious

tortura *f* torture

torturar *tr* to torture

tor·vo -va *adj* grim, stern

tos *f* cough; **tos ferina** whooping cough

tosca·no -na *adj* Tuscan ǁ **la Toscana** Tuscany

tos·co -ca *adj* coarse, rough; uncouth

toser *intr* to cough

tósigo *m* poison; sorrow

tosiguero *m* poison ivy

tosquedad *f* coarseness, roughness; uncouthness

tostada *f* piece of toast; toast; **dar** or **pegar la tostada** or **una tostada a** (coll) to cheat, to trick; **tostadas** toast

tosta·do -da *adj* brown; tan, sunburned ǁ *m* toasting; roasting ǁ *f* see **tostada**

tostador *m* toaster, roaster

tostar §61 *tr* & *ref* to toast; to roast; to tan, to burn

tostón *m* roasted chickpea; toast dipped in olive oil; roast pig; scorched food

total *adj* & *m* total ǁ *adv* (coll) in a word

totalidad *f* totality; entirety; **en su totalidad** in its entirety

tóxi·co -ca *adj* & *m* toxic

toxicomanía *f* drug addiction

toxicóma·no -na *adj* drug-addicted ǁ *mf* drug addict

tozu·do -da *adj* stubborn

tpo. *abbr* **tiempo**

traba *f* bond, tie; clasp, lock; hobble, clog; obstacle, hindrance

traba·do -da *adj* tied, fastened; joined, connected, robust, sinewy; (*sílaba*) checked, (Am) tongue-tied; (*ojos*) (Col) cross

trabaja·do -da *adj* overworked, worn-out; strained, forced, labored; busy

trabaja·dor -dora *adj* working; industrious, hard-working ǁ *mf* worker, toiler ǁ *m* workman, workingman ǁ *f* workingwoman

trabajar *tr* to work; to till; to bother, disturb; (*a una persona*) to work, to drive ǁ *intr* to work; to strain; to warp; **trabajar en** or **por** to strive to ǁ *ref* to strive, to exert oneself

trabajo *m* work; trouble; (*en contraposición de capital*) labor; **costar trabajo** + *inf* to be hard to + *inf*; **trabajo a destajo** piecework; **trabajo a domicilio** homework; **trabajo a jornal** timework; **trabajo de menores** child labor; **trabajo de oficina** clerical work; **trabajo de taller** shopwork; **trabajos** hardships, tribulations; **trabajos forzados** or **forzosos** hard labor, penal labor

trabajo·so -sa *adj* arduous, laborious; (*maganto*) wan, languid; (*falto de espontaneidad*) labored; (Am) unpleasant, annoying

trabalen·guas *m* (*pl* -**guas**) tongue twister, jawbreaker

trabar *tr* to join, unite; to catch, seize; to fasten; to fetter; to lock; to begin; (*una batalla*) to join; (*una conversación, amistad*) to strike up ǁ *intr* to take hold ǁ *ref* to become entangled; to jam; to foul; **trabársele a uno la lengua** to become tongue-tied

trabe *f* beam

trabilla *f* gaiter strap; belt loop; end stitch, loose stitch

trabuco *m* blunderbuss; popgun

trac *m* stage fright

tracale·ro -ra *adj* (CAm, Mex, W-I) cheating, tricky ǁ *mf* (CAm, Mex, W-I) cheat, trickster

tracción *f* traction; **tracción delantera** front drive; **tracción trasera** rear drive

tractor *m* tractor; **tractor de oruga** caterpillar tractor

tradición *f* tradition

tradicionista *mf* folklorist

traducción *f* translation; **traducción automática** machine translation

traducir §19 *tr* to translate; to change

traduc·tor -tora *mf* translator

traer §75 *tr* to bring; to bring on; to draw, pull; to make, keep; to wear; to have, carry; **traer a mal traer** (coll) to abuse, mistreat ǁ *intr* — **traer y llevar** to gossip ǁ *ref* to dress; to behave; **traérselas** (coll) to get worse and worse, to cause a lot of trouble

tráfago *m* traffic, trade; toil, drudgery

trafa·gón -gona *adj* (coll) hustling, lively; (coll) slick, tricky ǁ *mf* hustler, live wire

traficante *mf* dealer, merchant

traficar §73 *intr* to deal, trade, traffic; to travel about

tráfico *m* trade, traffic

tragaderas *fpl* (coll) gullibility; (coll) tolerance, **tener buenas tragaderas** (coll) to be too gullible

tragalda·bas *mf* (*pl* -**bas**) (coll) glutton; (coll) easy mark

tragale·guas *mf* (*pl* -**guas**) (coll) great walker

traga·luz *m* (*pl* -**luces**) skylight, bull's-eye; cellar window

tragamone·das *m* (*pl* -**das**) or **tragaperras** *m* (*pl* -**rras**) (coll) slot machine

tragar §44 *tr* to swallow; to swallow up; to gulp down; (*creer fácilmente*) to swallow; to overlook; **no poder tragar** (coll) to not be able to stomach ǁ *intr* & *ref* to swallow

tragasable *m* sword swallower

tragavenado *f* (SAm) anaconda

tragaviro·tes *m* (*pl* -**tes**) (coll) stuffed shirt

tragedia *f* tragedy

trági·co -ca *adj* tragic(al) ǁ *m* tragedian

trago *m* swallow; swig; (coll) misfortune; **a tragos** (coll) slowly

tra·gón -gona *adj* (coll) gluttonous ǁ *mf* (coll) glutton

traición *f* treachery, betrayal; (*delito contra la patria*) treason; treacherous act; **alta traición** high treason; **a traición** treacherously; **hacer traición a** to betray

traicionar *tr* to betray

traicione·ro -ra *adj* treacherous; treasonable || *mf* traitor

traída *f* conveyance, transfer; (Guat) sweetheart; **traída de aguas** water supply

traí·do -da *adj* worn, threadbare || *f see* traída

trai·dor -dora *adj* treacherous; treasonable || *mf* traitor; betrayer || *m* villain || *f* traitress

tralla *f* leash; road scraper

traje *m* suit; clothes; dress; gown; **cortar un traje a** (coll) to gossip about; **traje a la medida** suit made to order; **traje de baño** bathing suit; **traje de calle** street clothes; **traje de ceremonia** or **de etiqueta** dress suit; full dress; evening clothes; **traje de faena** (mil) fatigue clothes; **traje de luces** bullfighter's costume; **traje de malla** tights; **traje de montar** riding habit; **traje de paisano** civilian clothes; **traje hecho** ready-made suit; **traje sastre** lady's tailor-made suit; **traje serio** formal dress; **vestir su primer traje largo** to come out, to make one's debut

trajear *tr* to dress, clothe

trajín *m* carrying, transfer, conveyance; going and coming; bustle, commotion

trajinar *tr* to carry, convey; (Arg, Chile) to poke into; (Arg, Chile) to deceive; (Pan) to annoy || *intr* to bustle around

tralla *f* lash, whiplash; whipcord

trama *f* weft, woof; plot, scheme, machination; (*de un drama o novela*) plot

tramar *tr* to weave; to plot, to scheme; (*un enredo*) to hatch (*a plot*)

trambucar §73 *intr* (Col, Ven) to be shipwrecked; (Col, Ven) to go out of one's mind

tramitación *f* transaction, negotiation; procedure, steps; **tramitación automática de datos** data processing

tramitar *tr* to transact, to negotiate

trámite *m* step, procedure; proceeding; transaction

tramo *m* tract; stretch; (*de una escalera*) flight; (*de un puente*) span; (*de un canal entre dos esclusas*) level

tramontana *f* north; north wind; pride, haughtiness

tramoya *f* stage machinery; scheme

tramoyista *adj* scheming, tricky || *mf* schemer, impostor || *m* stagehand

trampa *f* trap; trap door; (*de un mostrador*) flap; (*de los pantalones*) fly; **armar una trampa a** (coll) to lay a trap for; **trampa explosiva** (mil) booby trap

trampear *tr* (coll) to trick, to swindle || *intr* (coll) to cheat; (coll) to manage to get along

trampilla *f* peephole in the floor; (*de los pantalones*) fly; (*de un secreter*) top, lid; (*de una mesa*) leaf, hinged leaf

trampolín *m* diving board; springboard; ski jump

trampo·so -sa *adj* tricky, crooked || *mf* cheat, swindler

tranca *f* beam, pole; crossbar; (Arg, Chile) drunk, spree; (P-R) dollar; **a trancas y barrancas** (coll) through fire and water

trancar §73 *tr* to bar || *intr* (coll) to stride along

trance *m* crisis; peril; trance; **a todo trance** at any cost; **último trance** (*de la vida*) last stage, end

tranco *m* long stride; threshold

tranquera *f* palisade, fence

tranquilidad *f* tranquillity

tranquilizante *m* tranquilizer

tranquilizar §60 *tr, intr & ref* to tranquilize, to calm down

tranqui·lo -la *adj* tranquil, calm

tranquilla *f* feeler

tranquillo *m* knack

transacción *f* settlement, compromise; transaction

transaéreo *m* air liner

transar *tr* (Am) to settle || *intr* (Am) to yield, give in, compromise

transatlánti·co -ca *adj & m* transatlantic

transbordador *m* ferry

transbordar *tr* to tranship; to transfer || *intr* to transfer, to change trains

transbordo *m* transshipment; transfer

transcribir §83 *tr* to transcribe

transcripción *f* transcription

transcurrir *intr* to pass, elapse

transcurso *m* course (*of time*)

transepto *m* transept

transeúnte *adj* transient || *mf* transient; passer-by

transferencia *f* transfer

transferir §68 *tr* to transfer; to postpone

transformador *m* transformer

transformar *tr* to transform || *ref* to transform, be transformed

tránsfuga *mf* turncoat; fugitive

transfusión *f* transfusion; **transfusión de sangre** transfusion, blood transfusion

transgredir §1 *tr* to transgress

transgresión *f* transgression

transi·do -da *adj* overcome, paralyzed; mean, cheap, stingy

transigencia *f* compromise; compromising

transigente *adj* compromising

transigir §27 *tr* to settle, to compromise || *intr* to settle, to compromise; to agree

transistor *m* transistor

transitable *adj* passable, practicable

transitar *intr* to go, walk; to travel

transiti·vo -va *adj* transitive

tránsito *m* transit; traffic; stop; passage; transfer

transito·rio -ria *adj* transitory

translúci·do -da *adj* translucent

transmisión *f* transmission; **transmisión del pensamiento** thought transference

transmisor *m* transmitter; **transmisor de órdenes** (naut) engine-room telegraph

transmitir *tr & intr* to transmit

transmudar *tr* to transfer; to persuade, convince

transmutar *tr, intr & ref* to transmute

transparecer §22 *intr* to show through
transparencia *f* transparency; slide
transparentar *ref* to show through
transparente *adj* transparent || *m* curtain, window curtain; **transparente de resorte** window blind or shade
transpirar *intr* to transpire; (*dejarse conocer una cosa secreta*) to transpire
transplantar *tr* to transplant
transponer §54 *tr* to transpose; to disappear behind || *ref* (*ocultarse detrás del horizonte*) to set; to get sleepy
transportar *tr* to transport; (mus) to transpose
transporte *m* transport; transportation; (aer & naut) transport
transportista *mf* transport worker
tranvía *m* trolley, trolley car, streetcar; **tranvía de sangre** horsecar
tranzar §60 *tr* to cut off, rip off; to plait, braid
trapacear *tr* to cheat, swindle
trapacería *f* cheating, swindling
trapace•ro -ra *adj* cheating, swindling || *mf* cheat, swindler
trapajo *m* rag, tatter
trápala *adj* (coll) chattering; (coll) cheating || *mf* (coll) chatterbox; (coll) cheat || *m* loquacity || *f* noise, uproar; (*del trote de un caballo*) clatter; (coll) cheating
trapear *tr* (Am) to mop
trapecio *m* (geom) trapezoid; (sport) trapeze
trapecista *mf* trapeze performer
trape•ro -ra *mf* ragpicker; junk dealer
trapiche *m* sugar mill; olive press; ore crusher
trapien•to -ta *adj* raggedy, in rags
trapío *m* (coll) flipness, pertness; (*del toro de lidia*) spirit
trapisonda *f* (coll) brawl, row; (coll) scheming
trapisondista *mf* (coll) schemer
trapo *m* rag; (naut) canvas, sails; bullfighter's bright-colored cape; (*de la muleta*) cloth; **a todo trapo** full sail; **poner como un trapo** (coll) to rake over the coals; **sacar los trapos a la colada, a relucir** or **al sol** (coll) to wash one's dirty linen in public; **soltar el trapo** (coll) to burst out crying, to burst out laughing; **trapos** (coll) rags, duds; **trapos de cristianar** (coll) Sunday best
trapo•so -sa *adj* (Am) raggedy, in rags
tráquea *f* trachea, windpipe
traquea•do -da *adj* (*sendero*) (Arg) beaten
traquear *tr* to shake, to rattle; (coll) to fool with || *intr* to crackle; to rattle, to chatter
traqueo *m* shake, rattle, chatter
traquetear *tr* & *intr* to rattle; to jerk
tras *prep* after; behind; **tras de** behind; in addition to
trasatlánti•co -ca *adj* & *m* var of **transatlántico**
trasbordador *m* var of **transbordador**
trasbordar *tr* & *intr* var of **trasbordar**
trasbordo *m* var of **transbordo**
trascendencia *f* penetration, keenness; importance

trascendente *adj* penetrating; important
trascender §51 *tr* to go into, dig up || *intr* to smell; to come to be known, to leak out
trascendi•do -da *adj* keen, perspicacious
trascocina *f* scullery
trascorral *m* back yard; (coll) backside
trascribir §83 *tr* var of **transcribir**
trascripción *f* var of **transcripción**
trascuarto *m* back room
trascurrir *intr* var of **transcurrir**
trascurso *m* var of **transcurso**
trasegar §66 *tr* to upset, turn topsy-turvy; to decant, to draw off
trase•ro -ra *adj* back, rear || *m* buttock, rump
trasferir §68 *tr* var of **transferir**
trasformador *m* var of **transformador**
trasformar *tr* & *intr* var of **transformar**
trásfuga *mf* var of **tránsfuga**
trasfusión *f* var of **transfusión**
trasgo *m* goblin, hobgoblin; imp
trashojar *tr* to leaf through
trasiego *m* upset, disorder; decantation
trasladar *tr* to transfer; to postpone; to copy, transcribe; to transmit; to move || *intr* to go; to move
traslado *m* transfer; copy, transcript; moving
traslapar *tr*, *intr* & *ref* to overlap
traslapo *m* lap, overlap
traslúci•do -da *adj* var of **translúcido**
traslucir §45 *tr* to guess || *intr* to leak out || *ref* to be translucent; to leak out
traslumbrar *tr* to dazzle || *ref* to be dazzled; to vanish
trasluz *m* diffused light; glint, gleam; **al trasluz** against the light
trasmisión *f* var of **transmisión**
trasmisor *m* var of **transmisor**
trasmitir *tr* & *intr* var of **transmitir**
trasmóvil *m* (Col) mobile unit, radio pickup
trasmudar *tr* var of **transmudar**
trasmundo *m* afterlife, future life
trasmutar *tr*, *intr* & *ref* var of **transmutar**
trasnocha•do -da *adj* stale; haggard, run-down; hackneyed || *f* last night; sleepless night; (mil) night attack
trasnocha•dor -dora *mf* night owl
trasnochar *tr* (*un problema*) to sleep over || *intr* to spend the night; to spend a sleepless night; to stay up late
trasoír §48 *tr* to hear wrong
traspapelar *tr* to mislay || *ref* to become mislaid
trasparecer §22 *intr* var of **transparecer**
trasparencia *f* var of **transparencia**
trasparente *adj* & *m* var of **transparente**
traspasar *tr* to cross, cross over; to send; to transfer; to move; to pierce, to transfix; to pain, grieve || *ref* to go too far
traspié *m* slip, stumble; trip
traspirar *intr* var of **transpirar**
trasplantar *tr* var of **transplantar**
trasponer §54 *tr* & *ref* var of **transponer**
trasportar *tr* var of **transportar**
trasporte *m* var of **transporte**
trasportista *mf* var of **transportista**

traspunte *m* (theat) callboy

traspuntín *m* flap seat, folding seat, jump seat

trasquilar *tr* to crop, to lop; (*las ovejas*) to shear; (coll) to curtail

trastazo *m* (coll) whack, blow

traste *m* fret; **dar al traste con** to throw away, ruin, spoil

trastera *f* attic, junk room

trastienda *f* back room

trasto *m* piece of furniture; piece of junk; (coll) good-for-nothing; **trastos** tools, implements, utensils; arms, weapons; junk; muleta and sword

trastornar *tr* to upset, overturn; to disturb; to perplex; to daze, to make dizzy; to persuade

trastorno *m* upset; disturbance

trastrocar §81 *tr* to turn around, to reverse, to change

trasudor *m* cold sweat

trasueño *m* blurred dream, vague recollection

trasuntar *tr* to copy; to abstract, to sum up

trasunto *m* copy; record; likeness

trasverter §51 *intr* to run over, to overflow

trasvolar §61 *tr* to fly over

trata *f* traffic, trade, slave trade; **trata de blancas** white slavery; **trata de esclavos** slave trade

tratado *m* (*escrito, libro*) treatise; (*convenio entre gobiernos*) treaty; agreement

tratamiento *m* treatment; title; **apear el tratamiento** to leave off the title

tratante *mf* dealer, retailer

tratar *tr* to handle; to deal with; to treat; **tratar a uno de** to address someone as; to charge someone with being ‖ *intr* to deal; to treat; to try; **tratar de** to deal with; to treat of; to come in contact with; to try to ‖ *ref* to deal; to behave; (*bien o mal*) to live; **tratarse de** to deal with; to be a question of

trate·ro -ra *mf* (Chile) pieceworker

trato *m* treatment; deal, agreement; manner; business; title; friendly relations; **tener buen trato** to be very nice, to be very pleasant; **trato colectivo** collective bargaining; **trato doble** double-dealing; **¡trato hecho!** it's a deal!

través *m* bend, bias, turn; reverse, misfortune; (naut) beam; **al** or **a través de** through, across; **dar al través con** to do away with; **mirar de través** to squint; to look at out of the corner of one's eye

travesaño *m* crosspiece; (*de cama*) bolster; (*p.ej., de una silla*) rung

travesear *intr* to romp, carry on; to sparkle, be witty; to lead a wild life

travesía *f* crossing, voyage; crossroad; distance, passage; cross wind; (Arg, Bol) wasteland; (Chile) west wind

travesura *f* prank, antic, caper; mischief; sparkle, wit; slick trick

traviesa *f* crossing, voyage; rafter; side bet; (rr) tie

travie·so -sa *adj* cross; keen, shrewd; restless, fidgety; naughty, mischievous; debauched ‖ *f* see **traviesa**

trayecto *m* journey, passage, course; stretch, run

trayectoria *f* trajectory; path

traza *f* plan, design; scheme; means; appearance; mark, trace; footprint; streak, trait; **tener trazas de** to show signs of; to look like

trazar §60 *tr* to plan, design; to outline; to trace; (*una línea*) to draw; to lay out, to plot

trazo *m* line, stroke; trace; outline

trebejo *m* implement; chessman

trébol *m* clover; (*naipe que corresponde al basto*) club

trece *adj* & *pron* thirteen ‖ *m* thirteen; (*en las fechas*) thirteenth; **estarse, mantenerse** or **seguir en sus trece** (coll) to stand firm

trecea·vo -va *adj* & *m* thirteenth

trecho *m* stretch; while; **a trechos** at intervals

tregua *f* truce; respite, letup

treinta *adj* & *pron* thirty ‖ *m* thirty; (*en las fechas*) thirtieth

treinta·vo -va *adj* & *m* thirtieth

tremar *intr* to tremble, to shake

tremen·do -da *adj* frightful, terrible, tremendous; (*muy grande*) (coll) tremendous

trementina *f* turpentine

tremer *intr* to tremble, shake

tremolar *tr* & *intr* to wave

tren *m* (*de coches o vagones; de ondas*) train; outfit, equipment; following, retinue; show, pomp; (*de la vida*) way; **tren aerodinámico de lujo** (rr) streamliner; **tren ascendente** (rr) up train; **tren correo** (rr) mail train; **tren de aterrizaje** (aer) landing gear; **tren de laminadores** rolling mill; **tren de lavado** (Am) laundry; **tren de mercancías** freight train; **tren de mudadas** (Am) moving company; **tren descendente** (rr) down train; **tren de viajeros** passenger train; **tren ómnibus** (rr) accommodation train; **tren rápido** (rr) flyer

treno *m* dirge

trenza *f* braid, plait; tress; (*p.ej., de ajos*) (Am) string; **en trenzas** with her hair down

trenzar §60 *tr* to braid, plait ‖ *intr* to caper; to prance

trepa·dor -dora *adj* climbing ‖ *mf* climber ‖ *f* (bot) climber

trepar *tr* to climb; to drill, bore ‖ *intr* to climb; **trepar por** to climb up ‖ *ref* to lean back

trepidar *intr* to shake, vibrate; (Chile) to hesitate, waver

tres *adj* & *pron* three; **las tres** three o'clock ‖ *m* three; (*en las fechas*) third

trescien·tos -tas *adj* & *pron* three hundred ‖ **trescientos** *m* three hundred

tresillo *m* ombre; three-piece living-room suit; (mus) triplet

tresnal *m* (agr) shock

treta *f* trick, scheme; (*del esgrimidor*) feint

treza·vo -va *adj* & *m* thirteenth

triángulo *m* triangle
triar §77 *tr* to sort
tribu *f* tribe
tribuna *f* tribune, rostrum, platform; grandstand; (*en la iglesia*) gallery; **tribuna de la prensa** press box; **tribuna del órgano** (mus) organ loft; **tribuna de los acusados** (law) dock
tribunal *m* tribunal, court; **tribunal tutelar de menores** juvenile court
tributar *tr* (*contribuciones, impuestos, etc.*) to pay; (*admiración, gratitud, etc.*) to render
tributa·rio -ria *adj* tributary; tax; **ser tributario de** to be indebted to || *m* tributary
tributo *m* tribute; tax
tricornio *m* tricorn, three-cornered hat
trifocal *adj* trifocal
trifulca *f* (coll) wrangle, squabble
trigési·mo -ma *adj* & *m* thirtieth
trigo *m* wheat; (slang) dough, money; **trigo sarraceno** buckwheat
trigonometría *f* trigonometry
trigue·ño -ña *adj* swarthy, olive-skinned
trilogía *f* trilogy
trilla *f* threshing
trilla·do -da *adj* (*sendero*) beaten; trite, commonplace
trilladora *f* threshing machine
trillar *tr* to thresh; to mistreat; (coll) to frequent
trilli·zo -za *mf* triplet
trillón *m* British trillion; quintillion (*in U.S.A.*)
trimestral *adj* quarterly
trimestre *m* quarter
trinado *m* trill, warble
trinar *intr* to trill, warble, quaver; (coll) to get angry
trinca *f* trinity
trincar §73 *tr* to bind, to lash, to tie fast; to crush; (slang) to kill || *intr* to take a drink
trinchar *tr* to carve, to slice
trinchera *f* cut; trench; trench coat
trineo *m* sleigh, sled
Trinidad *f* Trinity
trino *m* trill
trinquete *m* pawl, ratchet; (naut) foresail
trin·quis *m* (*pl* -quis) drink, swig
trío *m* sorting; trio; (mus) trio
tripa *f* gut, intestine; belly; (*del cigarro*) filler; **hacer de tripas corazón** (coll) to pluck up courage
triple *adj* & *m* triple
triplica·do -da *adj* & *m* triplicate; **por triplicado** in triplicate
triplicar §73 *tr* to triplicate || *intr* to treble
trípode *m* tripod
tríptico *m* triptych
tripu·do -da *adj* big-bellied, potbellied
tripulación *f* crew
tripulante *m* crew member
tripular *tr* to man; to fit out, equip
trique *m* crack, swish; **a cada trique** (coll) at every turn; **triques** (Mex) tools, implements
triquiñuela *f* (coll) chicanery, subterfuge
triquitraque *m* clatter; firecracker

tris *m* crackle; (coll) shave, inch; (coll) trice
trisar *tr* (Chile) to crack, to chip || *intr* to chirp
triscar §73 *tr* to mix; (*una sierra*) to set || *intr* to stamp the feet; to romp, frisk around; (Col) to gossip
trismo *m* lockjaw
triste *adj* sad; dismal, gloomy; (*despreciable, ridículo*) sorry
tristeza *f* sadness; gloominess
tris·tón -tona *adj* wistful, melancholy
tritón *m* eft, newt, triton; (*hombre experto en la natación*) merman
trituradora *f* crushing machine
triturar *tr* to grind, crush; to abuse
triunfal *adj* triumphal
triunfante *adj* triumphant
triunfar *intr* to triumph; to trump; **triunfar de** to triumph over; to trump
triunfo *m* triumph; trump; **sin triunfo** no trump
trivial *adj* trivial; trite, commonplace; (*sendero*) beaten
trivialidad *f* triviality; triteness
triza *f* shred; **hacer trizas** to tear to pieces
trizar §60 *tr* to tear to pieces
trocar §81 *tr* to exchange, to swap; to barter; to confuse, to twist, to distort || *intr* to swap || *ref* to change; to change seats
trocha *f* trail, narrow path; (Am) gauge
trofeo *m* trophy; victory
troj *f* or **troje** *f* granary; olive bin
trole *m* trolley pole
trolebús *m* trolley bus, trackless trolley
tromba *f* (*de polvo, agua, etc.*) whirl, column; **tromba marina** waterspout; **tromba terrestre** tornado
trombón *m* trombone
trompa *f* (*del elefante*) trunk; waterspout; top; nozzle; (anat) duct, tube; (mus) horn; (Col, Chile) cowcatcher; **trompa de armonía** French horn; **trompa de Eustaquio** Eustachian tube
trompada *f* (coll) bump, collision; (coll) punch
trompar *intr* to spin a top
trompeta *f* trumpet; bugle, clarion; (coll) good-for-nothing; (Am) drunkenness
trompetear *intr* (coll) to trumpet, to sound the trumpet
trompetilla *f* ear trumpet; (Am) Bronx cheer
trompicar §44 *tr* to trip, make stumble || *intr* to stumble
trompicón *m* stumble
trompiza *f* (Am) fist fight
trompo *m* (*juguete*) top; (*en el ajedrez*) man; (*buque malo y pesado*) tub
tronada *f* thunderstorm
tronar §61 *tr* (Mex) to shoot || *intr* to thunder; (coll) to fail, collapse; **por lo que pueda tronar** (coll) just in case
troncar §44 *tr* to cut off the head of; (*un escrito*) to cut, shorten
tronco *m* (*del cuerpo, del árbol, de una familia, del ferrocarril*) trunk; (*leño*) log; (*de caballerías*) team; (coll) sap, fathead; **estar hecho un tronco** (coll)

to be knocked out; (coll) to be sound asleep

troncha *f* (Am) slice; (Am) cinch

tronchar *tr* to smash, split; to chop off

tronera *m* madcap, roisterer || *f* embrasure, loophole; louver; (*de la mesa de billar*) pocket

tronido *m* thunderclap

trono *m* throne

tronquista *m* driver, teamster

tronzar §60 *tr* to shatter, break to pieces; to pleat; to wear out

tropa *f* troop; (Am) herd, drove; **en tropa** straggling, without formation; **tropas de asalto** shock troops, storm troops

tropel *m* crowd, throng; rush, hurry; jumble; **de** or **en tropel** in a mad rush

tropelía *f* mad rush; outrage

tropero *m* (Arg) cowboy

tropezar §18 *tr* to strike || *intr* to stumble; to slip, to blunder; **tropezar con** or **en** to stumble over, to trip over; to run into; to come upon

trope-zón -zona *adj* stumbly || *m* stumble; stumbling place; a **tropezones** by fits and starts; falteringly; **dar un tropezón** to stumble, to trip

tropical *adj* tropic(al)

trópico *m* tropic

tropiezo *m* stumble; stumbling block; slip, blunder, fault; obstacle; quarrel

tropilla *f* (Arg, Urug) drove of horses following a leading mare

troposfera *f* troposphere

troquel *m* die

trotaconven-tos *f* (*pl* -**tos**) (coll) procuress, bawd

trotamun-dos *m* (*pl* -**dos**) globetrotter

trotar *intr* to trot; (coll) to hustle

trote *m* trot; (coll) chore; **al trote** (coll) right away; **para todo trote** (coll) for everyday wear; **trote de perro** jog trot

trotona *f* chaperone

trovador *m* troubadour

trovadores-co -ca *adj* troubadour

trovero *m* trouvère

Troya *f* Troy; **ahí fué Troya** (coll) it's a shambles; **¡arda Troya!** (coll) come what may!

troya-no -na *adj & mf* Trojan

troza *f* log

trozar §60 *tr* to break to pieces; (*un tronco*) to cut into logs

trozo *m* piece, fragment; block; excerpt, selection

truco *m* contrivance, device; trick; pocketing of ball; **truco de naipes** card trick; **trucos** pool

truculen-to -ta *adj* truculent

trucha *f* trout

trueno *m* thunder, thunderclap; shot, report; (coll) rake, roué; **trueno gordo** finale (*of fireworks*); big scandal; **truenos** (Ven) heavy shoes

trueque *m* barter; exchange, swap; trade-in; **a trueque de** in exchange for; **trueques** (Col) change

trufa *f* truffle; fib, lie

tru-hán -hana *adj* crooked; clownish || *mf* crook; clown

trujal *m* wine press; oil press

trulla *f* noise, bustle; crowd; trowel

truncar §73 *tr* to cut off the head of; (*palabras o frases*) to cut, slash; to cut off, interrupt

trusas *fpl* trunk hose; (Am) trunks

tu *adj poss* thy, your

tú *pron pers* thou, you

tubérculo *m* (*rizoma engrosado, p.ej., de la patata*) tuber; (*protuberancia*) tubercle

tuberculosis *f* tuberculosis

tubería *f* tubing; piping

tubo *m* tube, pipe; **tubo de desagüe** drainpipe; **tubo de ensayo** test tube; **tubo de humo** flue, **tubo de imagen** picture tube **tubo de vacío** vacuum tube; **tubo digestivo** alimentary canal; **tubo sonoro** chime

tuerca *f* nut; **tuerca de aletas** wing nut

tuer-to -ta *adj* crooked, bent, one-eyed; **a tuertas** upside down; crosswise; **a tuertas o a derechas** rightly or wrongly, thoughtlessly || *mf* one-eyed person || *m* wrong, harm, injustice; **tuertos** afterpains

tuétano *m* marrow; pith; **hasta los tuétanos** (coll) through and through; (coll) head over heels

tufi-llas *mf* (*pl* -**llas**) (coll) touchy person

tufillo *m* whiff, smell

tufo *m* fume, vapor; sidelock; foul odor, foul breath; **tufos** (coll) airs, conceit

tugurio *m* shepherd's hut; hovel

tuición *f* protection, custody

tulipán *m* tulip

tullecer §22 *tr* to abuse, mistreat || *intr* to be crippled

tulli-do -da *adj* paralyzed, crippled || *mf* paralytic, cripple

tullir §13 *tr* to cripple, to paralyze; to abuse, mistreat || *ref* to become crippled or paralyzed

tumba *f* grave, tomb; tombstone; arched top; (Am) felling of trees

tumbacuarti-llos *mf* (*pl* -**llos**) (coll) old toper, rounder

tumbar *tr* to knock down; to catch; to trick; (coll) to stun || *intr* to tumble; to capsize || *ref* (coll) to lie down

tumbo *m* fall, tumble; boom, rumble; crisis; rise and fall of sea; rough surf

tumbona *f* hammock

tumor *m* tumor

túmulo *m* catafalque

tumulto *m* tumult

tuna *f* loafing, bumming

tunante *adj* bumming, loafing; crooked, tricky || *mf* bum, loafer; crook

tundidora *f* lawn mower

tuneci-no -na *adj & mf* Tunisian

túnel *m* tunnel

tunes *mpl* (Col) little steps, first steps

Túnez (*ciudad*) Tunis; (*país*) Tunisia

tungsteno *m* tungsten

túnica *f* tunic

tu-no -na *adj* crooked, tricky || *mf* crook || *f* see **tuna**

tupé *m* toupee; (coll) nerve, cheek, brass

tupi-do -da *adj* thick, dense, compact; dull, stupid; (Am) clogged up

tupir *tr* to pack tight ‖ *ref* to stuff, stuff oneself

turba *f* crowd, mob; peat

turbamulta *f* (coll) mob, rabble

turbar *tr* to disturb, trouble; to stir up ‖ *ref* to be confused

turbiedad *f* muddiness; confusion

turbina *f* turbine

tur·bio -bia *adj* turbid, muddy, cloudy; confused; obscure

turbión *m* squall, thunderstorm; (*p.ej., de balas*) (fig) hail

turbopropulsor *m* turboprop (*engine*)

turborreactor *m* turbojet (*engine*)

turbulen·to -ta *adj* turbulent

tur·co -ca *adj* Turkish ‖ *mf* Turk ‖ *m* (*idioma*) Turkish

turfista *adj* horsy ‖ *m* turfman

turismo *m* touring; touring car

turista *mf* tourist

turísti·co -ca *adj* tourist; touring

turnar *intr* to alternate, take turns

tur·nio -nia *adj* (*ojos*) cross; cross-eyed; (*que mira con ceño*) cross-looking

turno *m* turn, shift; **aguardar turno** to wait one's turn; **por turno** in turn; **turno diurno** day shift

turón *m* polecat

turquesa *s* turquoise

Turquía *s* Turkey

turrón *m* nougat; (coll) plum

tusa *f* (Am) corncob; (Am) corn silk; (Chile) mane; (Col) pockmark; (CAm, W-I) trollop

tusar *tr* to shear, clip, cut

tutear *tr* to thou, to address familiarly ‖ *ref* to thou each other, to address each other familiarly

tutela *f* guardianship; protection

tutelar *adj* guardian; protecting ‖ *tr* to protect, shelter, guide

tu·tor -tora *or* **-triz** (*pl* **-trices**) *mf* guardian, tutor

tu·yo -ya *adj poss* of thee ‖ *pron poss* thine, yours

tuza *f* gopher

U

U, u (u) *f* twenty-fourth letter of the Spanish alphabet

u *conj* (used before words beginning with *o* or *ho*) or

U. *abbr* usted

ubicar §73 *tr* (Am) to locate, place ‖ *intr & ref* to be situated

ubi·cuo -cua *adj* ubiquitous

ubre *f* udder

Ucrania *f* Ukraine

ucrania·no -na *adj & mf* Ukrainian

ucra·nio -nia *adj & mf* Ukrainian ‖ *f* see **Ucrania**

Ud. *abbr* usted

Uds. *abbr* ustedes

ufanar *ref* — **ufanarse con** or **de** to boast of, be proud of

ufanía *f* pride, conceit; cheer, satisfaction; ease, smoothness

ufa·no -na *adj* proud, conceited; cheerful, satisfied; easy, smooth

ujier *m* doorman, usher

úlcera *f* ulcer, fester, sore; **úlcera de decúbito** bedsore

ulcerar *tr & ref* to ulcerate, to fester

ulterior *adj* ulterior; subsequent

ulteriormente *adv* subsequently, later

últimamente *adv* finally; lately, recently

ultimar *tr* to finish, end, conclude, wind up; (Am) to kill, finish off

ultimátum *m* (*pl* **-tums**) ultimatum; (coll) definite decision

últi·mo -ma *adj* last, latest; final; excellent, superior; (*precio*) lowest, final; most remote; (*piso*) top; (*hora*) late; **a la última** in the latest fashion; **a última hora** at the eleventh hour; **a últimos de** toward the end of, in the latter part of; **de última hora** last-minute; **estar a lo último** or **en las últimas** to be up to date, to be well-informed; to be on one's last legs; **por último** at last, finally; **último suplicio** capital punishment

ultraatmosféri·co -ca *adj* outer (*space*)

ultraeleva·do -da *adj* (rad) ultrahigh

ultrajar *tr* to outrage, to offend

ultraje *m* outrage, offense

ultrajo·so -sa *adj* outrageous, offensive

ultramar *m* country overseas

ultramari·no -na *adj* overseas ‖ **ultramarinos** *mpl* groceries, delicatessen

ultranza — **a ultranza** to the death; unflinchingly

ultrarro·jo -ja *adj & m* infrared

ultratumba *adv* beyond the grave

ultraviola·do -da or **ultravioleta** *adj & m* ultraviolet

ululación *f* howl; whoop; (*del buho*) hoot; (*del disco del fonógrafo*) wow

ulular *intr* to howl; to whoop; (*el buho*) to hoot

ululato *m* howl; (*del buho*) hoot

umbilical *adj* umbilical

umbral *m* threshold, doorsill; (*madero que sostiene el muro encima de un vano*) lintel; (physiol, psychol & fig) threshold; **atravesar** or **pisar los umbrales** to cross the threshold; **estar en los umbrales de** to be on the threshold of

umbralada *f* (Col) threshold

umbrí·o -a *adj* shady ‖ *f* shady side

umbro·so -sa *adj* shady

un, una (the apocopated form **un** is used before masculine singular nouns and adjectives and before feminine singular nouns beginning with stressed *a* or *ha*) *art indef* a ‖ *adj* one

unánime *adj* unanimous

unanimidad *f* unanimity

unción *f* unction

uncir §36 *tr* (*bueyes*) to yoke, to hitch
undéci·mo -ma *adj & m* eleventh
undo·so -sa *adj* wavy
ungir §27 *tr* to smear with ointment or with oil; to anoint
ungüento *m* unguent, ointment, salve
únicamente *adv* only, solely
úni·co -ca *adj* only, sole; (*sin otro de su especie*) unique; one, e.g., **precio único** one price
unicornio *m* unicorn
unidad *f* (*concepto de una sola cosa o persona; cantidad que se toma como medida común de todas las demás de su clase; el número entero más pequeño*) unit; (*indivisión; armonía de conjunto; el número uno*) unity
uni·do -da *adj* united; smooth, even; close-knit
unificar §73 *tr* to unify
uniformar *tr* to make uniform; to provide with a uniform
uniforme *adj* uniform ‖ *m* uniform; **uniforme de gala** (mil) full dress
uniformidad *f* uniformity
unilateral *adj* unilateral
unión *f* union; double ring
unir *tr & ref* to unite
unisonancia *f* (mus) unison; (*de un orador*) monotony
unísono — **al unísono** in unison; unanimously; **al unísono de** in unison with
unita·rio -ria *adj* unit
universal *adj* universal; (*teclado de máquina de escribir*) standard
universidad *f* university
universita·rio -ria *adj* university ‖ *mf* (Am) university student, college student ‖ *m* university professor
universo *m* universe
u·no -na *pron* one, someone; a una of one accord; **la una** one o'clock; **somos uno** we are one; **uno a otro, unos a otros** each other, one another; **uno que otro** one or more, a few; **u·nos -nas** some; a pair of, e.g., **unas gafas** a pair of glasses; **unas tijeras** a pair of scissors; **unos cuantos** some; **uno y otro** both ‖ *pron indef* one, e.g., **uno no sabe qué hacer aquí** one does not know what to do here ‖ *m* (*unidad y signo que la representa*) one
untar *tr* to smear, to grease; to anoint; (coll) to bribe ‖ *ref* to get smeared; to grease oneself; (coll) to peculate
unto *m* grease; (*gordura del cuerpo del animal*) fat; (Chile) shoe polish; **unto de Méjico** or **de rana** (coll) bribe money
untuo·so -sa *adj* unctuous, greasy, sticky
uña *f* nail, fingernail, toenail; (*pezuña*) hoof; (*del ancla*) fluke, bill; (mach) claw, gripper; **enseñar** or **mostrar las uñas** to show one's teeth; **ser largo de uñas** to have long fingers; **ser uña y carne** (coll) to be hand in glove; **tener en la uña** to have on the tip of one's fingers
uñada *f* scratch, nail scratch; (*impulso dado con la uña*) flip
uñero *m* ingrowing nail; (*inflamación*

del dedo en la raíz de la uña) whitlow
ural *adj* Ural ‖ **Urales** *mpl* Urals
uranio *m* uranium
urbanidad *f* urbanity
urbanismo *m* city planning
urbanista *mf* city planner
urbanísti·co -ca *adj* city-planning ‖ *f* city planning
urbanizar §60 *tr* (*convertir en poblado*) to urbanize; to refine, polish
urba·no -na *adj* urban, city; (*atento, cortés*) urbane ‖ *m* policeman
urbe *f* metropolis
urdemb·las *mf* (*pl* -las) (coll) schemer
urdimbre *f* warp; scheme, scheming; **estar en la urdimbre** (Chile) to be thin, be emaciated
urdir *tr* (*los hilos*) to beam; (*una conspiración*) to hatch
urente *adj* burning, smarting
uretra *f* urethra
urgencia *f* urgency; **de urgencia** special-delivery
urgente *adj* urgent; (*correo*) special-delivery
urgir §27 *intr* to be urgent
urina·rio -ria *adj* urinary ‖ *m* urinal
urna *f* glass case; ballot box; (*para guardar las cenizas de los cadáveres*) urn; **acudir** or **ir a las urnas** to go to the polls
urología *f* urology
urraca *f* magpie
U.R.S.S. *abbr* Unión de Repúblicas Socialistas Soviéticas
urticaria *f* hives
Uruguay, el Uruguay
urugua·yo -ya *adj & mf* Uruguayan
usa·do -da *adj* (*empleado; gastado por el uso; acostumbrado*) used; skilled, experienced; (*vocablo*) **poco usado** rare
usanza *f* use, usage, custom
usar *tr* to use, make use of; (*un cargo, un oficio*) to follow ‖ *intr* — **usar + inf** to be accustomed to + *inf*; **usar de** to use, to have recourse to; **usar de la palabra** to speak, make a speech ‖ *ref* to be the custom
usina *f* (Am) factory, plant; (Am) powerhouse; (*estación de tranvía*) (Arg) carbarn
uso *m* use; custom, usage; wear, wear and tear; habit, practice; **al uso** according to custom; **en buen uso** (coll) in good condition; **hacer uso de la palabra** to speak, make a speech
usted *pron pers* you
usual *adj* (*de uso común*) usual; (*que se usa con facilidad*) usable; sociable
usualmente *adv* usually
usua·rio -ria *mf* user
usufructo *m* use, enjoyment
usufructuar §21 *tr* to enjoy the use of
usura *f* usury; profit; **pagar con usura** to pay back a thousandfold
usurero *m* loan shark; profiteer
usurpar *tr* to usurp
utensilio *m* utensil
útero *m* uterus, womb
útil *adj* useful ‖ **útiles** *mpl* utensils, tools, equipment

utilería f (Arg) properties, stage equipment

utilero m (Arg) property man

utilidad f utility, usefulness; profit, earnings

utilita·rio -ra adj utilitarian

utilizable adj usable

utilizar §60 tr to utilize, to use ‖ ref — **utilizarse con,** de or en to make use of; **utilizarse para** to be good for

utopía f utopia

utopista adj & mf utopian

UU. abbr ustedes

uva f grape; wart on eyelid; (baya) berry; **estar hecho una uva** (coll) to have a load on; **uva crespa** gooseberry; **uva de Corinto** currant; **uva de raposa** nightshade; **uva espín** or **espina** gooseberry; **uva pasa** raisin; **uvas verdes** (de la fábula de Esopo) sour grapes

uve f (letra del alfabeto) V

uxoricida m uxoricide (husband)

uxoricidio m uxoricide (act)

uxo·rio -ria adj uxorious

V

V, v (ve or uve) f twenty-fifth letter of the Spanish alphabet

V. abbr usted, véase, venerable

V.A. abbr Vuestra Alteza

vaca f cow; (cuero) cowhide; (carne de vaca o de buey) beef; gambling pool; **hacer vaca** (Peru) to play truant; **vaca de la boda** (coll) goat, laughingstock; (coll) friend in need; **vaca de leche** milch cow; **vaca de San Antón** (ent) ladybird

vacación f (cargo que está sin proveer) vacancy; **de vacaciones** on vacation; **vacaciones** vacation; **vacaciones retribuídas** vacation with pay

vacacionista mf vacationist

vacancia f vacancy

vacante adj f vacancy

vacar §73 intr (un empleo, un cargo) to be vacant, be unfilled; to take off, take a vacation; **vacar a** to attend to; **vacar de** to lack, be devoid of

vacia·do -da adj hollow-ground ‖ m cast, casting; plaster cast

vaciante f ebb tide

vaciar §77 & regular tr to empty, to drain; to cast, to mold; (formar un hueco en) to hollow out; to sharpen on a grindstone; to copy, transcribe; to explain in detail ‖ intr to empty; to flow; (el agua en el río) to fall, go down ‖ ref (coll) to blab

vacilación f vacillation; flickering; hesitancy, hesitation

vacilada f (Mex) spree, high time; (Mex) drunk

vacilante adj vacillating; (luz) flickering; (irresoluto) hesitant

vacilar intr to vacillate; (la luz) to flicker; to shake, wobble; (estar irresoluto) to hesitate, to waver

vací·o -a adj empty; (hueco) hollow; idle, useless, unsuccessful; (vaca) barren; presumptuous ‖ m emptiness; (laguna, abertura, vacante) vacancy; (espacio que no contiene ninguna materia) void; (espacio de que se ha extraído el aire) vacuum; (ijada) side, flank; **de vacío** light, unloaded; **hacer el vacío a** to isolate

vacuidad f vacuity, emptiness

vacuna f (enfermedad de las vacas) cowpox; (virus cuya inoculación preserva de una enfermedad determinada) vaccine

vacunación f vaccination

vacunar tr to vaccinate

vacu·no -na adj bovine; cowhide ‖ f see vacuna

va·cuo -cua adj vacant ‖ m cavity, hollow

vadear tr (un río) to ford; to wade through; to overcome; to sound out ‖ ref to behave; to manage

vado m ford; expedient, resource; **al vado o a la puente** (coll) one way or another; **no hallar vado** to see no way out; **tentar el vado** to feel one's way

vagabundaje m vagrancy

vagabundear intr to wander, to roam; to loaf around

vagabun·do -da adj vagabond ‖ mf vagabond, tramp; wanderer

vagancia f loafing, vagrancy

vagar m leisure; **con vagar** slowly; **estar de vagar** to have nothing to do ‖ §44 intr to wander, to roam; to be idle; to have plenty of leisure; (una cosa) to lie around; (p.ej., una sonrisa por los labios) to play

vagido m cry of a newborn baby

vagneria·no -na adj & mf Wagnerian

va·go -ga adj wandering, roaming; idle, loafing; lax, loose; hesitating, wavering; (indefinido, indeciso) vague; (mirada) blank ‖ m vagabond; idler, loafer; **en vago** shakily; in vain; in the air; **poner en vago** to tilt

vagón m car, railroad car; **vagón cama** sleeping car; **vagón carbonero** coal car; **vagón cerrado** boxcar; **vagón cisterna** tank car; **vagón de carga** freight car; **vagón de cola** caboose; **vagón de mercancías** freight car; **vagón de plataforma** flatcar; **vagón frigorífico** refrigerator car; **vagón salón** chair car; **vagón tolva** hopperbottom car; **vagón volquete** dump car

vagoneta f tip car; station wagon

vaguear intr to wander around

vaguedad f vagueness; vague remark

vaguido m faintness, fainting spell

vaharada f breath, exhalation

vahear *intr* to emit odors, to give forth an aroma

vahido *f* faintness, fainting spell

vaho *m* odor, aroma, vapor, fume

vaina *f* sheath; scabbard; knife case; *(de ciertas semillas)* pod, husk; (Am) annoyance, bother; (Col) luck, stroke of luck

vainica *f* hemstitch

vainilla *f* vanilla

vainita *f* (Ven) string bean

valvén *m* swing, seesaw, backward and forward motion; unsteadiness, inconstancy; risk, chance

vajilla *f* dishes, set of dishes; **lavar la vajilla** to wash the dishes; **vajilla de oro** gold plate; **vajilla de plata** silver plate, silverware; **vajilla de porcelana** chinaware

vale *m* promissory note; voucher; farewell; (Ven) chum, pal; **vale respuesta** reply coupon

valede•ro -ra *adj* valid, effective

vale•dor -dora *mf* defender, protector; (Mex) friend, companion

valedura *f* (Mex) favor, protection

valencia *f* (chem) valence

valentía *f* bravery, valor; feat, exploit; dash, boldness; boast; **pisar de valentía** to strut, swagger

valen•tón -tona *adj* arrogant, boastful || *mf* braggart, boaster || *f* bragging

valer *m* worth, merit, value || **§76** *tr* to defend, protect; to favor, patronize; to avail; to yield; to be worth, be valued at; to be equal to; to suit; **valer la pena** to be worth while (to); **valerle a uno** + *inf* to help someone to + *inf*, to get someone to + *inf*; **valer lo que pesa** (coll) to be worth its (his, her, etc.) weight in gold; **valga lo que valiere** come what may; **¡válgame Dios!** bless my soul!, so help me God! || *intr* to have worth; to be worthy; to be valuable; to be valid; to prevail; to hold, to count; to have influence; **hacer valer** *(sus derechos)* to assert; to make felt; to make good; to turn to account; **más vale** it is better (to); **vale O.K.**; **valer para** to be useful for; **valer por** to be equal to || *ref* to help oneself, to defend oneself; **valerse de** to make use of, to avail oneself of

valero•so -sa *adj* valorous, brave; strong, active, effective

va•let *m* (*pl* -**lets**) (cards) jack

valía *f* value, worth; favor, influence; **mayor valía** or **plus valía** appreciation, increased value; **unearned increment**

validación *f* validation

validar *tr* to validate

validez *f* validity; strength, vigor

vali•do -da *adj* highly esteemed, influential || *m* court favorite; prime minister

váli•do -da *adj* valid; strong, robust

valiente *adj* valiant; strong, robust; fine, excellent; *(grande y excesivo)* terrific || *m* brave fellow; bully

valija *f* satchel, brief case; mailbag;

mailpouch; mail; **valija diplomática** diplomatic pouch

valimiento *m* favor, protection; favor at court, favoritism

vallo•so -sa *adj* valuable; influential; wealthy

va•lón -lona *adj* & *mf* Walloon

valor *m* value, worth; valor, courage; meaning, import; efficacy; equivalence; *(rédito)* income, return; effrontery; *(persona, cosa o cualidad dignas de ser poseídas)* (fig) asset; **¿cómo va ese valor?** (coll) how are you?; **valor de rescate** (ins) surrender value; **valores** securities

valoración *f* valuation, appraisal

valorar or **valorear** *tr* (*poner precio a*) to value, to appraise; to enhance the value of

valorizar **§60** *tr* to value; to enhance the value of; (Am) to sell off (*for quick realization*)

vals *m* waltz

valsar *intr* to waltz

valuación *f* valuation, appraisal

valuar **§21** *tr* to estimate

válvula *f* valve; **válvula corrediza** slide valve; **válvula de admisión** intake valve; **válvula de escape** exhaust valve; **válvula de escape libre** cutout; **válvula de seguridad** safety valve; **válvula en cabeza** valve in the head, overhead valve

valla *f* fence, railing; barricade; hindrance, obstacle; (sport) hurdle; (W-I) cockpit; **valla paranieves** snow fence

vallado *m* barricade, stockade

valle *m* valley; river bed; valley dwellings; **valle de lágrimas** vale of tears

vampiresa *f* vampire

vampíri•co -ca *adj* vampire; ghoulish

vampiro *m* vampire; *(persona que se deleita con cosas horribles)* ghoul

vanadio *m* vanadium

vanagloriar **§77** & *regular ref* to boast

vanaglorio•so -sa *adj* vainglorious, conceited, boastful

vanamente *adv* vainly

vandalismo *m* vandalism

vánda•lo -la *adj* & *mf* Vandal; (fig) vandal

vanguardia *f* (mil & fig) vanguard, van; **a vanguardia** in the vanguard

vanguardismo *m* avant-garde

vanguardista *adj* avant-garde || *mf* avant-gardist

vanidad *f* vanity; *(fausto)* pomp, show; **ajar la vanidad de** (coll) to take down a peg; **hacer vanidad de** to boast of

vanido•so -sa *adj* vain, conceited

va•no -na *adj* vain; hollow, empty; **en vano** in vain || *m* opening in a wall

vapor *m* steam: *(el visible: exhalación, vaho, niebla, etc.)* vapor; steamer, steamboat; **al vapor** at full speed; **vapores** gas *(belched)*; blues; **vapor volandero** tramp steamer

vaporar *tr* & *ref* to evaporate

vaporizador *m* atomizer, sprayer

vaporizar **§60** *tr* to vaporize; to spray || *ref* to vaporize

vaporo•so -sa *adj* vaporous

vapular or **vapulear** tr whip, to flog

vaquería f drove of cattle; dairy; (Mex) party

vaqueri-zo -za adj milk || f winter stable for cattle

vaque-ro -ra adj cattle || mf cattle tender; (Peru) truant || m cow hand; cowboy

vaqueta f leather; (P-R) strop; **zurrarle a uno la vaqueta** (Am) to tan someone's hide

vaquillona f (Arg, Chile) heifer

vara f pole, rod, staff; (de carruaje) shaft; (bastón de mando) wand; measuring stick; (taur) thrust with goad; **tener vara alta** to have the upper hand; **vara alcándara** shaft; vara alta upper hand; **vara buscadora** divining rod (ostensibly to discover water or metals); **vara de adivinar** divining rod; **vara de oro** goldenrod; **vara de pescar** fishing rod; **vara de San José** goldenrod

vara-alta m (coll) boss

varada f beaching; running aground

varadero m repair dock

varapalo m long pole; (coll) setback, disappointment, reverse

varar tr (una embarcación) to beach || intr to run aground; (un negocio) to come to a standstill

varear tr (los frutos de los árboles) to beat down, knock down; to beat, strike; (taur) to goad; (los caballos de carreras) (SAm) to exercise, to train || ref to lose weight, get thin

varec m (bot) wrack

varenga f (naut) floor, floor timber

vareta f twig, stick; lime twig for catching birds; colored stripe; (coll) cutting remark; (coll) hint; **irse de vareta** (coll) to have diarrhea

variable adj & f variable

variación f variation

varia-do -da adj varied; variegated

variante adj & f variant

variar §77 to vary, to change || intr to vary, to change; to be different; **variar de** or **en opinión** to change one's mind

varice f or **várice** f varicose veins

varicela f chicken pox

varico-so -sa adj varicose

variedad f variety; **variedades** variety show, vaudeville

varilla f rod, stem, twig; (bastón de mando) wand; (de paraguas, abanico, etc.) rib; (del corsé) stay; (de rueda) wire spoke; (coll) jawbone; (Mex) peddler's wares; **varilla de nivel** dipstick; **varilla de virtudes** wand, magician's wand

varillaje m ribs, ribbing; (de máquina de escribir) type bars

varille-ro -ra adj (caballo) (Ven) race || m (Mex) peddler

va-rio -ria adj (de diversos colores; que tiene variedad) various, varied; fickle, inconstant; **varios** various; several

varón adj male, e.g., **hijo varón** male child || m man, male; grown man, adult male; man of standing; **santo varón** (coll) plain artless fellow

varonía f male issue

varonil adj manly, virile; courageous

Varsovia f Warsaw

vasa-llo -lla adj & mf vassal

vas-co -ca adj & mf Basque (of Spain and France) || m Basque (language)

vas-cón -cona adj & mf Basque (of old Spain)

vasconga-do -da adj & mf Basque (of Spain) || m Basque (language) || **las Vascongadas** the Basque Provinces

vascuence adj & m Basque (language) || m (coll) gibberish

vaselina f vaseline

vasera f kitchen shelf; bottle rack, tumbler rack

vasija f container, vessel

vaso m tumbler, glass; vase, flower jar; (anat) duct, vessel; **vaso de engrase** (mach) grease cup; **vaso de noche** pot, chamber pot; **vaso graduado** measuring glass; **vaso sanguíneo** blood vessel

vástago m shoot, sapling; scion, offspring; rod, stem; **vástago de émbolo** piston rod; **vástago de válvula** valve stem

vastedad f vastness

vas-to -ta adj vast

vate m bard, seer, poet

váter m (coll) toilet, water closet

vatiaje m wattage

vaticinar tr to prophesy, predict

vaticinio m prophecy, prediction

vatídi-co -ca adj prophetical || mf prophet

vatímetro m wattmeter

vatio m watt

vatio-hora m (pl vatios-hora) watt-hour

vaya f jest, jeer

Vd. abbr **usted**

Vds. abbr **ustedes**

V.E. abbr **Vuestra Excelencia**

vece-ro -ra adj alternating; yielding in alternate years || mf person waiting his turn

vecinamente adv nearby

vecindad f neighborhood, vicinity; residency; residents; **hacer mala vecindad** to be a bad neighbor

vecindario m neighborhood, community; people, population

veci-no -na adj neighboring; like, similar || mf neighbor; resident, citizen

veda f prohibition; (de la caza y la pesca) closed season

vedado m game preserve

vedar tr to forbid, prohibit; to hinder, stop; to veto

vedija f fleece, tuft of wool; mat of hair; matted hair

vee-dor -dora adj curious, spying || mf busybody || m supervisor, overseer

vega f fertile plain; (Cuba) tobacco plantation

vegetación f vegetation; **vegetaciones adenoideas** adenoids

vegetal adj & m vegetable

vegetaria-no -na adj & mf vegetarian

vego-so -sa adj (Chile) damp, wet

vehemencia f vehemence

vehemente adj vehement

vehículo *m* vehicle; **vehículo espacial** space vehicle

veintavo -va *adj & m* twentieth

veinte *adj & pron* twenty; **a las veinte** (coll) late, untimely || *m* twenty; (*en las fechas*) twentieth

veintena *f* score, twenty

veintiún *adj* this apocopated form of **veintiuno** is used before masculine singular nouns and adjectives

veintiu-no -na *adj & pron* twenty-one || *m* twenty-one; (*en las fechas*) twenty-first || *f* (*juego de naipes*) twenty-one

vejación *f* vexation, annoyance

vejamen *m* vexation, annoyance; bantering, taunting

vejar *tr* to vex, annoy; to taunt

vejestorio *m* (coll) old dodo

vejete *m* (coll) little old fellow

vejez *f* old age; oldness; dotage; platitude, old story; **a la vejez, viruelas** there's no fool like an old fool

vejiga *f* (*órgano que recibe la orina de los riñones*) bladder; (*ampolla*) blister; (*saco hecho de piel, goma, etc.*) bag, pouch, bladder; **vejiga de la bilis** or **de la hiel** gall bladder

vela *f* wakefulness; pilgrimage; evening; work in the evening; sail; sailboat; (*cilindro con una torcida que sirve para alumbrar*) candle; vigil (*before Eucharist*); awning; (Mex) scolding; **a toda vela** full sail; **a vela** under sail; **a vela llena** under full sail; **en vela** awake; **estar entre dos velas** to be half-seas over, to have a sheet in the wind; **hacerse a la vela** to set sail; **vela latina** lateen sail; **vela mayor** mainsail; **vela romana** Roman candle

velada *f* evening party, soirée; vigil, watch

vela-do -da *adj* veiled, hidden; (phot) light-struck || *f* see **velada**

velador *m* pedestal table, gueridon; wooden candlestick; watchman; (SAm) night table; (Mex) lamp globe

velaje *m* or **velamen** *m* (naut) canvas, sails

velar *adj & f* velar || *tr* to watch over; to guard; (*la guardia*) to keep; to hold a wake over; (*cubrir con un velo*) to veil; (phot) to fog; (fig) to veil, hide, conceal || *intr* to stay awake; to stay awake working; to keep vigil; (*el viento*) to keep up all night; (*un escollo, un peñasco*) to stick up out of the water; **velar por** or **sobre** to watch over || *ref* (phot) to fog, to be light-struck

velatorio *m* wake

veleidad *f* whim, caprice; fickleness, flightiness

veleido-so -sa *adj* whimsical, capricious; fickle, flighty

vele-ro -ra *adj* swift-sailing || *m* sailboat

veleta *mf* (*persona inconstante*) (coll) weathercock || *f* vane, weathervane, weathercock; (*de un molino*) rudder vane; (*de la caña de pescar*) bob; streamer, pennant; **veleta de manga** (aer) air sleeve, air sock

velís *m* (Mex) valise

velita *f* little candle

velo *m* veil; taking the veil; confusion, perplexity; (*disfraz*) veil; (*de lágrimas*) mist; (phot) fog; **correr el velo** to pull aside the curtain, to dispel the mystery; **tomar el velo** to take the veil; **velo del paladar** soft palate

velocidad *f* (*rapidez*) speed, velocity; (mech) velocity; **en gran velocidad** (rr) by express; **en pequeña velocidad** (rr) by freight; **primera velocidad** (aut) low gear; **segunda velocidad** (aut) second; **tercera velocidad** (aut) high gear; **velocidad con respecto al suelo** (aer) ground speed; **velocidad permitida** speed limit

velocímetro *m* speedometer

velón *m* brass olive-oil lamp

velorio *m* evening party or bee; wake; wake for a dead child; (Am) dull party; (Am) come-on

ve-loz *adj* (pl -loces) swift, speedy; agile, quick

vello *m* down, fuzz

vellocino *m* fleece; **vellocino de oro** Golden Fleece

vellón *m* fleece; unsheared sheepskin; lock of wool; copper coin; copper-silver alloy

vello-so -sa *adj* downy, hairy, fuzzy

velludillo *m* velveteen

vellu-do -da *adj* shaggy, hairy, fuzzy || *m* (*felpa*) plush; (*terciopelo*) velvet

vena *f* vein; (*en piedras*) grain; (fig) poetical inspiration; **estar en vena** (coll) to be all set, to be inspired; (coll) to sparkle with wit; **vena de loco** fickle disposition

venablo *m* dart, javelin; **echar venablos** to burst forth in anger

venado *m* deer, stag; **pintar el venado** (Mex) to play hooky

venáti-co -ca *adj* (coll) fickle, unsteady; (coll) daffy, nutty

vence-dor -dora *adj* conquering, victorious || *mf* conqueror, victor

venceju *m* band, string; (orn) European swift, black martin

vencer §78 *tr* to vanquish, conquer; to excel, outdo; to overcome, to surmount || *intr* to conquer, be victorious; (*un plazo*) to be up; (*un contrato*) to expire; (*una letra*) to mature, fall due || *ref* to control oneself; (*un camino*) to bend, turn; (Chile) to wear out, become useless

vencetósigo *m* milkweed, tame poison

venci-do -da *adj* conquered; (com) due, mature, payable

vencimiento *m* (*acción de vencer*) victory; (*hecho de ser vencido*) defeat; (com) expiration, maturity

venda *f* (*para ligar un miembro herido*) bandage; (*para tapar los ojos*) blindfold

vendaje *m* bandage, dressing; **vendaje enyesado** plaster cast

vendar *tr* (*un miembro, una herida*) to bandage; (*los ojos*) to blindfold; (*cegar*) (fig) to blind; (*engañar*) (fig) to hoodwink

vendaval *m* strong southeasterly wind from the sea; strong wind, gale

vendedera *f* saleswoman, saleslady

vende·dor -dora *adj* selling || *m* salesman || *f* saleslady, sales girl

vendehu·mos *mf* (*pl* -mos) (coll) influence peddler

vendeja *f* public sale

vender *tr* to sell; to betray, sell out; vender salud to be the picture of health || *intr* to sell; ¡vendo, vendo, vendí! going, going, gone! || *ref* to sell oneself; to sell, be for sale; to betray oneself, to give oneself away; venderse caro to be hard to see; to be quite a stranger; venderse en (*p.ej.*, cien pesetas) to sell for; venderse por to pass oneself off as

ven·dí *m* (*pl* -díes) certificate of sale

vendible *adj* salable, marketable

vendimia *f* vintage; (fig) big profit

vendimia·dor -dora *mf* vintager

vendimiar *tr* (*la uva*) to gather, to harvest; (*las viñas*) to gather the grapes of; to make off with; (coll) to kill

venduta *f* (Am) public sale; (W-I) greengrocery

Venecia *f* (*ciudad*) Venice; (*provincia*) Venetia

venecia·no -na *adj* & *mf* Venetian

veneno *m* poison, venom

veneno·so -sa *adj* poisonous, venomous

venera *f* scallop shell; (*manantial de agua*) spring; empeñar la venera (coll) to go all out, spare no expense

venerable *adj* venerable

venerar *tr* to venerate, revere; to worship

venére·o -a *adj* venereal || *m* venereal disease

venero *m* (*de agua*) spring; (*filón de mineral*) lode, vein; (fig) source

venezola·no -na *adj* & *mf* Venezuelan

Venezuela *f* Venezuela

venga·dor -dora *adj* avenging || *mf* avenger

venganza *f* vengeance, revenge

vengar §44 *tr* to avenge || *ref* to take revenge; vengarse de to take revenge on

vengati·vo -va *adj* vengeful, vindictive

venia *f* forgiveness, pardon; leave, permission; bow, greeting

venida *f* coming; return; flood, freshet

venide·ro -ra *adj* coming, future || venideros *mpl* successors, posterity

venir §79 *intr* to come; que viene coming, next; venga lo que viniere come what may; venir + ger to be + ger; venir a + inf to come to + inf; to amount to + ger; to happen to + inf; to finally + inf, e.g., después de una larga enfermedad, vino a morir after a long illness he finally died; venir a ser to turn out to be || *ref* to ferment; venirse abajo to collapse

veno·so -sa *adj* venous

venta *f* sale; roadside inn; (Chile) refreshment stand; (S-D) grocery store; de venta or en venta on sale, for sale; ser una venta (coll) to be an expensive place; venta al descubierto short sale

ventaja *f* advantage; (*en juegos o apuestas*) odds; extra pay

ventajo·so -sa *adj* advantageous

---

ventalla *f* valve

ventana *f* window; (*de la nariz*) nostril; echar la casa por la ventana (coll) to go to a lot of expense; ventana batiente casement; ventana de guillotina sash window; ventana salediza bay window

ventanal *m* church window; picture window

ventanear *intr* (coll) to be at the window all the time

ventanilla *f* (*de coche, de banco, de sobre*) window; ticket window; (*de la nariz*) nostril

ventanillo *m* (*postigo de puerta o ventana*) wicket; (*mirilla*) peephole

ventar §2 *tr* to sniff || *impers* — vienta it is windy

ventarrón *m* gale, windstorm

ventear *tr* to sniff; to dry in the wind; to snoop into || *intr* to snoop, pry around || *impers* — ventea it is windy || *ref* (*henderse*) to split; (coll) to break wind; (Am) to spend a lot of time in the open

vente·ro -ra *mf* innkeeper

ventilador *m* ventilator; fan; (naut) funnel; ventilador aspirador exhaust fan

ventilar *tr* to ventilate; (fig) to air, ventilate

ventisca *f* drift, snowdrift; (*borrasca*) blizzard

ventiscar §73 *intr* to snow and blow; (*la nieve*) to drift

ventisquero *m* snowdrift; blizzard; snow-capped mountain; glacier

ventolera *f* blast of wind; (*molinete*) pinwheel; vanity, pride; (coll) wild idea; (Mex) wind

ventosa *f* vent, air hole; pegar una ventosa a (coll) to swindle

ventosear *intr* to break wind

vento·so -sa *adj* windy || *f* see ventosa

ventregada *f* brood, litter; outpouring, abundance

ventrículo *m* ventricle

ventrílo·cuo -cua *mf* ventriloquist

ventriloquia *f* or ventriloquismo *m* ventriloquism

ventura *f* happiness; luck, chance; danger, risk; a la ventura at random; at a risk; por ventura perhaps, perchance; probar ventura to try one's luck

venture·ro -ra *adj* adventurous; fortunate, lucky || *mf* adventurer

ventu·ro -ra *adj* future, coming || *f* see ventura

venturón *m* stroke of luck

venturo·so -sa *adj* fortunate, lucky

Venus *m* (astr) Venus || *f* (myth) Venus; (*mujer de gran belleza*) Venus

venus·to -ta *adj* beautiful, graceful

venza *f* goldbeater's skin

ver *m* (*vista*) sight; (*apariencia*) appearance; opinion; a mi ver in my opinion || §80 *tr* to see; to look at; (law) to hear, to try; no poder ver to not be able to bear; no tener nada que ver con to have nothing to do with; ver + inf to see + inf, e.g., vi entrar a mi hermano I saw my brother come in; **to see** + **ger**, e.g., **vi bailar a la muchacha** I saw the girl dancing; **to see** + **pp**, e.g., **vi ahorcar al criminal** I saw the criminal hanged; **ver venir a uno** to see what someone is up to || *intr* to see; **a más ver** so long; **a ver** let's see; **hasta más ver** good-bye, so long; **ver de** to try to; **ver y creer** seeing is believing || *ref* to be seen; to be obvious; to see oneself; to see each other; to meet; (*encontrarse*) to be, to find oneself; **verse con** to see, have a talk with; **ya se ve** of course, certainly

vera *f* edge, border; **a la vera de** near, beside; **de veras** in truth; **jugar de veras** to play for keeps; **veras** truth, reality; earnestness

veracidad *f* veracity, truthfulness

veranda *f* verandah; bay window, closed porch

veraneante *mf* summer vacationist, summer resident

veranear *intr* to summer

veranie·go -ga *adj* summer; unimportant, insignificant

veranillo *m* Indian summer; **veranillo de San Martín** Indian summer

ve·raz *adj* (*pl* -**races**) veracious, truthful

verbena *f* fair, country fair, night festival; (bot) verbena

verbigracia *adv* for example

verbo *m* verb || **Verbo** *m* (theol) Word

verbo·so -sa *adj* verbose, wordy

verdacho *m* green earth

verdad *f* truth; **a la verdad** in truth, as a matter of fact; **de verdad** really; **la verdad desnuda** the plain truth; **¿no es verdad?** or **¿verdad?** isn't that so? La traducción al inglés de esta pregunta depende generalmente de la aseveración que la precede. Si la aseveración es afirmativa, la pregunta es negativa, p.ej., **Vd. vivió aquí. ¿No es verdad?** You lived here. Did you not?; Si la aseveración es negativa, la pregunta es afirmativa, p.ej., **Vd. no vivió aquí. ¿No es verdad?** You did not live here? Did you? Si el sujeto de la aseveración es un nombre sustantivo, va representado en la pregunta con un pronombre personal, p.ej., **Juan no estuvo aquí anoche. ¿No es verdad?** John was not here last evening. Was he?; **ser verdad** to be true; **verdad trillada** truism

verdade·ro -ra *adj* true; real; (*que dice siempre la verdad*) truthful

verde *adj* green; young, youthful; (*viuda*) merry; (*viejo*) gay; (*cuento*) shady, off-color; **están verdes** (coll) they're hard to reach || *m* green; foliage, verdure

verdear *intr* to turn green, to look green

verdecer §22 *intr* to turn green, to grow green again

verdecillo *m* (orn) greenfinch

verdemar *m* sea green

verdete *m* verdigris

verdín *m* fresh green; (*capa verde de*

aguas estancadas) mold, pond scum; (*cardenillo*) verdigris

verdise·co -ca *adj* half-dry

verdor *m* verdure; youth

verdo·so -sa *adj* greenish

verdugado *m* hoop skirt

verdugo *m* shoot, sucker; (*estoque*) rapier; (*azote*) scourge; (*roncha*) welt; executioner, hangman; torment; butcher bird, shrike

verdugón *m* wale, weal

verdulería *f* greengrocery

verdule·ro -ra *mf* greengrocer || *f* fishwife

verdura *f* greenness; (*color verde de las plantas*) verdure; (*obscenidad*) smuttiness; **verduras** vegetables, greens

verecundia *f* bashfulness, shyness

verecun·do -da *adj* bashful, shy

vereda *f* path, lane; (Am) sidewalk

veredicto *m* verdict

verga *f* (naut) yard

vergel *m* flower and fruit garden

vergonzo·so -sa *adj* (*que causa vergüenza*) shameful; (*que tiene vergüenza*) ashamed; (*que se avergüenza con facilidad*) bashful, shy; (*que causa humillación*) embarrassing; shabby, wretched || *mf* bashful person || *m* armadillo

vergüenza *f* (*arrepentimiento*) shame; (*oprobio*) shamefulness; (*pudor, timidez*) bashfulness, shyness; (*desconcierto, humillación*) embarrassment; (*pundonor*) dignity, face; public punishment; **¡qué vergüenza!** shame on you!; **tener vergüenza** to be ashamed; **vergüenzas** privates, genitals

vericueto *m* rough, rocky ground

verídi·co -ca *adj* truthful

verificación *f* verification; checking, testing, inspection

verifica·dor -dora *adj* verifying || *m* meter inspector

verificar §73 *tr* to verify, to check; (*llevar a cabo*) to carry out; (*los contadores de agua, gas y electricidad*) to inspect || *ref* to prove true; to take place

verja *f* iron gate, iron fence, grating

ver·mú *m* (*pl* -**mús**) vermouth; (Am) matinée

vernácu·lo -la *adj* vernacular

verónica *f* (bot) veronica; (taur) veronica (*graceful pass in which the bullfighter waits for the bull with open cape*)

veroniquear *intr* (taur) to perform veronicas

verosímil *adj* likely, probable

verraco *m* male hog, boar

verraquear *intr* (coll) to grunt, grumble; (coll) to cry hard

verruga *f* wart; (coll) bore, nuisance

verrugo *m* (coll) miser

versal *adj* & *f* capital

versalilla or **versalita** *f* small capital

Versalles Versailles

versar *intr* — **versar acerca de** or **sobre** to deal with, to treat of || *ref* — **versarse en** to be or become versed in

versátil *adj* fickle

versículo *m* verse (*in the Bible*)
versificación *f* versification
versificar §73 *tr & intr* to versify
versión *f* version; translation
verso *m* verse; (*typ*) verso; **versos pareados** rhymed couplet
vertebra·do -da *adj & m* vertebrate
vertedero *m* dump; weir, spillway
verter §51 *tr* (*un líquido, un polvo*) to pour; (*un recipiente*) to empty; (*lágrimas; luz; sangre*) to shed; (*descargar*) to dump; to translate || *intr* to flow || *ref* to run, to empty
vertical *adj & f* vertical
vértice *m* vertex
vertiente *m & f* (*declive*) slope; (*colina por donde corre el agua*) shed || *f* (Arg, Col, Chile) spring, fountain
vertigino·so -sa *adj* dizzy
vértigo *m* vertigo, dizziness; fit of insanity
vesícula *f* vesicle; **vesícula biliar** gall bladder
veso *m* polecat
Véspero *m* Vesper
vesperti·no -na *adj* evening || *m* evening sermon
vestíbulo *m* vestibule; (*theat*) foyer, lobby
vestido *m* clothing, dress; (*de mujer*) gown, dress; (*de hombre*) suit; costume; **vestido de ceremonia** dress suit; **vestido de etiqueta** evening clothes; **vestido de etiqueta de mujer** or **vestido de noche** evening gown; **vestido de gala** (*mil*) full dress; **vestido de serio** evening clothes; **vestido de tarde-noche** cocktail dress
vestidura *f* clothing; (*del sacerdote*) vestment
vestigio *m* vestige, trace; track, footprint
vestir §50 *tr* to dress, to clothe; to adorn; to cover up; to disguise; (*tal o cual vestido*) to wear; to put on; **vestir el cargo** to look the part || *intr* to dress; (*una prenda o la materia*) to be dressy; **vestir de** (*p.ej., blanco*) to dress in; **vestir de etiqueta** to dress in evening clothes, **vestir de paisano** to dress in civilian clothes || *ref* to dress, to get dressed; to dress oneself; (*de una enfermedad*) to be up, to be about; **vestirse de** (*nubes, flores, hierba, etc.*) to be covered with; (*importancia, humildad, etc.*) to assume
vestuario *m* (*las prendas de uno*) wardrobe; dressing room; bathhouse; checkroom, cloakroom; (*mil*) uniform; (*theat*) dressing room
Vesubio *m* el Vesuvius
veta *f* vein; streak, stripe; **descubrir la veta de** (*coll*) to be on to
vetar *tr* to veto
vetea·do -da *adj* veined, striped || *m* graining || *f* (Ecuad) whipping
vetear *tr* to grain, to stripe; (Ecuad) to whip, to flog
veteranía *f* experience, know-how
vetera·no -na *adj & mf* veteran
veterina·rio -ria *adj* veterinary || *mf* veterinarian || *f* veterinary medicine

vetus·to -ta *adj* old, ancient
vez *f* (*pl* veces) time; (*tiempo de hacer una cosa por turno*) turn; **a la vez** at the same time; **a la vez que** while; **alguna vez** sometimes; ever; **a su vez** in turn; on his part; **a veces** at times, sometimes; **cada vez** every time; **cada vez más** more and more; **cuántas veces** how often; **de una vez** at one time; once and for all; **de vez en cuando** once in a while; **dos veces** twice; **en vez de** instead of; **esperar vez** to wait one's turn; **hacer las veces de** to take the place of; **las más veces** most of the time; **muchas veces** often; **otra vez** again; **raras veces** or **rara vez** seldom, rarely; **repetidas veces** over and over again; **tal vez** perhaps; **tomar la vez a** (coll) to get ahead of; **una que otra vez** once in a while; **una vez** once
veza *f* vetch, spring vetch
v.g. or **v.gr.** *abbr* **verbigracia**
vía *f* road, route, way; (*par de rieles y el suelo en que se asientan*) (rr) track; (*el mismo carril*) (rr) rail, track; (*anat*) passage, tract; (*fig*) way; **por la vía de vía**; **por vía aérea** by air; **por vía bucal** by mouth; **vía aérea** airway; **vía ancha** (rr) broad gauge; **vía de agua** waterway; (naut) leak; **vía estrecha** (rr) narrow gauge; **vía férrea** railway; **vía fluvial** waterway; **Vía Láctea** Milky Way; **vía muerta** (rr) siding; **vía normal** (rr) standard gauge; **vía pública** thoroughfare; **vías de hecho** (law) assault and battery || *prep* via
viable *adj* feasible
viaducto *m* viaduct
viajante *adj* traveling || *mf* traveler || *m* drummer, traveling salesman
viajar *tr* to sell on the road; (*ciertas comarcas*) to cover as salesman || *intr* to travel, to journey
viaje *m* trip, journey; travel book; water supply; **¡buen viaje!** bon voyage!; **viaje de ida y vuelta** or **viaje redondo** round trip
viaje·ro -ra *adj* traveling || *mf* traveler; passenger
vial *adj* road, highway || *m* tree-lined road
vianda *f* food, viand; meal
viandante *mf* traveler; itinerant
viático *m* travel allowance; (eccl) viaticum
víbora *f* viper
vibración *f* vibration
vibrar *tr* to vibrate; (*la voz; la r*) to roll; (*una lanza*) to hurl || *intr* to vibrate || *ref* to be thrilled
vicaría *f* vicarage
vicario *m* vicar
vicealmirante *m* vice-admiral
vicepresiden·te -ta *mf* vice-president
viceversa *adv* vice versa
viciar *tr* to vitiate; (*una proposición*) to slant || *ref* to become vitiated; to give oneself up to vice; to become addicted; (*una tabla*) to warp
vicio *m* vice; pampering, spoiling; luxuriance, overgrowth; **hablar de**

vicio (coll) to talk all the time, to talk too much; **quejarse de vicio** (coll) to be a chronic complainer

vicio·so -sa adj vicious; faulty, defective; strong, robust; luxuriant, overgrown; dissolute; (niño) (coll) spoiled

victima f victim, **victima propiciatoria** scapegoat

victimar tr (Am) to kill, murder

victoria f victory

victorio·so -sa adj victorious

vid f vine, grapevine

vida f life; living, livelihood; **darse buena vida** to live high; to live in comfort; **de por vida** for life; **en mi vida** never; **escapar con vida** to have a narrow escape; **ganar** or **ganarse la vida** to earn one's livelihood, to make a living; **hacer por la vida** (coll) to get a bite to eat; **mudar de vida** to mend one's ways; **¡por vida mía!** upon my soul!; **vida airada** licentious living; **vida ancha** loose living; **vida de familia** or **de hogar** home life; **vida mía** my darling

vidalita f (Arg, Chile, Urug) mournful love song

vidente mf clairvoyant || m prophet, seer || f seeress

videograbación f video-tape recording

videoseñal f picture signal

vidria·do -da adj glazed; brittle || m glaze, glazing; glazed pottery; dishes

vidriar §77 & regular tr to glaze || ref (los ojos) to become glassy

vidriera f glass window, glass door; (Am) shopwindow, store window; **vidriera de colores** or **vidriera pintada** stained-glass window

vidriería f glassworks; glass store

vidriero m glass blower, glassworker; glazier; glass dealer

vidrio m glass; piece of glass; windowpane; **pagar los vidrios rotos** (coll) to take the blame, to be the goat; **vidrio cilindrado** plate glass; **vidrio de aumento** magnifying glass; **vidrio de color** stained glass; **vidrio deshustrado** ground glass; **vidrio tallado** cut glass

vidrio·so -sa adj glassy, vitreous; (quebradizo) brittle; (resbaladizo) slippery; (que se resiente fácilmente) (coll) touchy; (mirada, ojos) (fig) glassy

vie·jo -ja adj old || m old man; **viejo verde** old goat, old rake || f old woman

vie·nés -nesa adj & mf Viennese

viento m wind; course, direction; (cuerda que mantiene una cosa derecha) guy; (gases intestinales) (coll) wind; **ceñir el viento** (naut) to sail close to the wind; **viento de cola** (aer) tail wind; **viento en popa** (naut) tail wind; **vientos alisios** trade winds

vientre m belly; (parte de la ondulación entre dos nodos) (phys) loop; **evacuar** or **exonerar el vientre** to have a bowel movement; **vientre flojo** loose bowels

vier·nes m (pl -nes) Friday; **Viernes santo** Good Friday

vertea·guas m (pl -guas) m flashing

vietna·més -mesa adj & mf Vietnamese

viga f beam, girder, rafter; **estar contando las vigas** (coll) to gaze blankly at the ceiling; **viga de celosía** lattice girder

vigencia f force, operation; (de una póliza de seguro) life; **en vigencia** in force, in effect

vigente adj effective, in force

vigési·mo -ma adj & m twentieth

vigía m lookout, watch; **vigía de incendios** firewarden || f watch; watchtower; (naut) rock, reef

vigiar §77 tr to watch over

vigilancia f vigilance, watchfulness; **bajo vigilancia médica** under the care of a physician

vigilante adj vigilant, watchful || m guard, watchman; **vigilante nocturno** night watchman

vigilar tr to watch over; to look out for || intr to watch, keep guard

vigilia f vigil; wakefulness; night work, night study; (víspera) eve; (mil) guard, watch; **comer de vigilia** to fast, to abstain from meat

vigor m vigor; **en vigor** in force; **into effect**

vigoriza·dor -dora adj invigorating || m tonic; **vigorizador del cabello** hair tonic

vigorizante adj invigorating

vigorizar §60 tr to invigorate; to encourage

vigoro·so -sa adj vigorous

vigueta f small beam, small girder

vihuela f Spanish lute

vil adj vile, base, mean || mf scoundrel

vilano m bur, down

vileza f vileness, baseness

vilipendiar tr to scorn, despise

vilipendio·so -sa adj contemptible

vilo — **en vilo** in the air; (fig) up in the air

vilorta f reed hoop; (arandela) washer

villa f town; (casa de recreo en el campo) villa; **la Villa** the city (Madrid)

villancico m carol, Christmas carol

villanes·co -ca adj boorish, crude, rustic

villanía f humbleness, humble birth; vileness, meanness; foul remark

villa·no -na adj base, vile; rude, impolite || mf peasant; knave, scoundrel

villorrio m small country town

vinagre m vinegar; (persona de genio áspero) (coll) grouch

vinagrera f vinaigrette; (bot) sorrel; (SAm) heartburn; **vinagreras** cruet stand

vinagreta f French dressing, vinaigrette sauce

vinagro·so -sa adj vinegary

vinariego m vineyardist

vinatería f wine business; wine shop

vinate·ro -ra adj wine || m wine dealer, vintner

vincular tr to bind, to tie, to unite; to continue, to perpetuate; (esperanzas) to found, to base; (law) entail

vínculo m bond, tie; (law) entail

vindicar §73 tr (vengar) to avenge; (exculpar) to vindicate

vindicta f revenge

vinicul·tor -tora *mf* winegrower

vinicultura *f* winegrowing

vinilo *m* vinyl

vino *m* wine; sherry reception, wine party; **tener mal vino** to be a quarrelsome drunk; **vino cubierto** dark-red wine; **vino de Jerez** sherry; **vino del terruño** local wine; **vino de mesa** table wine; **vino de Oporto** port wine; **vino de pasto** table wine; **vino de postre** after-dinner wine; **vino de segunda** second-run wine; **vino de solera** solera sherry; **vino tinto** red table wine

vinolen·to -ta *adj* too fond of wine

viña *f* vineyard; **ser una viña** (coll) to be a mine; **tener una viña** (coll) to have a sinecure

viña·dor -dora *mf* vineyardist, vine-dresser ‖ *m* guard of a vineyard

viñedo *m* vineyard

viñeta *f* vignette, headpiece

viola·do -da *adj & m* violet (*color*)

violar *m* bed of violets ‖ *tr* to violate; to ravish, rape; to profane, desecrate; to tamper with

violencia *f* violence

violentar *tr* to do violence to; (*p.ej.*, *una casa*) to break into ‖ *ref* to force oneself

violen·to -ta *adj* violent

violeta *m* (*color; colorante*) violet ‖ *f* (bot) violet

violín *m* violin; (billiards) bridge, cue rest; **embolsar el violín** (Arg, Ven) to cower, to slink away

violinista *mf* violinist

violón *m* (mus) bass viol; **tocar el violón** (coll) to talk nonsense

violoncelista *mf* cellist, violoncellist

violoncelo *m* (mus) cello, violoncello

violonchelista *mf* cellist, violoncellist

violonchelo *m* (mus) cello, violoncello

vira *f* welt; (*saetilla*) dart

virada *f* turn, change of direction; (naut) tack

virago *f* mannish woman

viraje *m* turn, swerve; (phot) toning

virar *tr* (naut) to wind; (naut) to tack, to veer; (phot) to tone ‖ *intr* to turn, to swerve; (naut) to tack, to veer

virgen *adj* virgin ‖ *f* virgin, maiden

virginidad *f* virginity

vírgula *f* rod, thin line, light dash

virgulilla *f* fine line; diacritic mark

virilidad *f* virility

virin·go -ga *adj* (Col) naked

virolen·to -ta *adj* pock-marked; having smallpox

virología *f* virology

virote *m* (*saeta*) bolt; (coll) sporty young fellow; (coll) stuffed shirt

virrey *m* viceroy

virtual *adj* virtual

virtud *f* virtue

virtuosismo *m* virtuosity

virtuo·so -sa *adj* virtuous ‖ *m* virtuoso

viruela *f* smallpox; pock mark; **viruelas locas** chicken pox

virulencia *f* virulence

virulen·to -ta *adj* virulent

vi·rus *m* (*pl* -rus) virus

viruta *f* shaving

virutilla *f* thin shaving; **virutillas de acero** steel wool

visado *m* visa

visaje *m* face, grimace

visar *tr* to visa; to O.K.; (arti & surv) to sight

vísceras *fpl* viscera

visco *m* birdlime

viscosa *f* viscose

viscosilla *f* rayon thread

visco·so -sa *adj* viscous ‖ *f* see **viscosa**

visera *f* (*del yelmo, de las gorras, del parabrisas del automóvil, etc.*) visor; (*pequeña pantalla que se pone en la frente para resguardar la vista*) eyeshade; (W-I) blinder, blinker

visible *adj* visible (*manifiesto*) evident; (*que llama la atención*) conspicuous

visigo·do -da *adj* Visigothic ‖ *mf* Visigoth

visillo *m* window curtain, window shade

visión *f* vision; view; (*persona fea y ridícula*) (coll) sight, scarecrow; **ver visiones** (coll) to be seeing things; **visión negra** (*del aviador*) blackout

visionar *tr* to contemplate, to look at

visiona·rio -ria *adj & mf* visionary

visir *m* vizier; **gran visir** grand vizier

visita *f* visit; visitor, caller; inspection; **ir de visitas** to go calling; **pagar la visita a** to return the call of; **tener visita** to have callers; **visita de cumplido** formal call; **visita de médico** (coll) short call

visita·dor -dora *mf* frequent caller ‖ *m* inspector ‖ *f* (Hond, Ven) enema

visitante *adj* visiting ‖ *mf* visitor

visitar *tr* to visit; to inspect

visite·ro -ra *adj* (coll) visiting; (*médico*) (coll) fond of making calls ‖ *mf* (coll) visitor

vislumbrar *tr* to descry, to glimpse; to surmise, suspect ‖ *ref* (*verse confusamente por la distancia*) to glimmer; (*aparecer en la distancia*) to loom

vislumbre *f* glimpse, glimmer; **vislumbres** inkling, notion

viso *m* sheen, gleam, (*de ciertas telas*) luster; streak, strain; appearance, thin veneer; elevation, height; colored material worn under transparent outer garment; **a dos visos** with a double purpose; **de viso** conspicuous; **hacer visos** to be iridescent

visón *m* mink

visor *m* (aer) bombsight; (phot) finder

víspera *f* eve, day before; **en vísperas de** on the eve of; **víspera de año nuevo** New Year's Eve; **víspera de Navidad** Christmas Eve; **vísperas** (eccl) vespers, evensong

vista *m* custom-house inspector ‖ *f* (*sentido del ver*) vision, sight; (*paisaje que se ve desde un punto; estampa que representa un lugar*) view; (*panorama, perspectiva*) vista; comparison; purpose, design; (*ojeada*) glance, look; interview; eye; eyes; (law) hearing, trial; **a la vista** (com) at sight; **a vista de** in view of; compared with; **con vistas a** with a view to; **de vista** by sight; **doble vista** second sight; **hacer la vista gorda**

ante to shut one's eyes to; **hasta la vista** good-bye, so long; **medir con la vista** to size up; **saltar a la vista** to be self-evident; **tener a la vista** to keep one's eyes on; (*p.ej., una carta*) to have at hand; **torcer la vista** to squint; **vista a ojo de pájaro** bird's-eye view; **vistas** (*aberturas de un edificio*) lights, openings; view, outlook; visible parts, parts that show

vistazo *m* look, glance

vistillas *fpl* eminence, height; **irse a las vistillas** (coll) to try to get a look at one's opponent's cards

vis·to -ta *adj* evident, obvious; in view of; **bien visto** looked upon with approval; **mal visto** looked upon with disapproval; **no visto** or **nunca visto** unheard-of; **por lo visto** apparently, judging from the facts; **visto bueno** approved, O.K.; **visto que** whereas, inasmuch as ‖ *m* whereas ‖ *f* see **vista**

visto·so -sa *adj* showy, flashy, loud

visual *adj* visual ‖ *f* line of sight

vital *adj* vital

vitali·cio -cia *adj* life, lifetime ‖ *m* life-insurance policy; life annuity

vitalidad *f* vitality

vitalizar §60 *tr* to vitalize

vitamina *f* vitamin

vitan·do -da *adj* hateful, odious; to be shunned

vitela *f* vellum

viticul·tor -tora *mf* grape grower, vineyardist

viticultura *f* grape growing

vitola *f* cigar size; mien, appearance; (Cuba) cigar band

vítor *interj* hurray! ‖ *m* panegyric tablet; triumphal pageant

vitorear *tr* to cheer, to acclaim

vitral *m* stained-glass window

vítre·o -a *adj* vitreous, glassy

vitrina *f* showcase, glass cabinet; (Am) shopwindow

vitrióli·co -ca *adj* (chem) vitriolic

vituallas *fpl* victuals

vituperable *adj* vituperable

vituperar *tr* to vituperate

viuda *f* widow; **viuda de marido vivo** or **viuda de paja** grass widow

viudedad *f* widowhood; dower, widow's pension

viudez *f* (*estado de viuda*) widowhood; (*estado de viudo*) widowerhood

viu·do -da *adj* left a widow; left a widower ‖ *m* widower ‖ *f* see **viuda**

viva *interj* viva!, long live! ‖ *m* viva

vivacidad *f* longevity; vivacity, liveliness; brightness, brilliance

vivande·ro -ra *mf* (mil) sutler, camp follower

vivaque *m* bivouac; guardhouse; (Am) police headquarters; **estar al vivaque** to bivouac

vivaquear *intr* to bivouac

vivar *m* warren, burrow; aquarium ‖ *tr* (Am) to cheer, acclaim

vivara·cho -cha *adj* (coll) vivacious, lively

vi·vaz *adj* (*pl* **-vaces**) long-lived; viva-

cious, lively; keen, perceptive; (bot) perennial

víveres *mpl* food, provisions, victuals

vivero *m* tree nursery; fishpond; (*origen de cosas perjudiciales*) (fig) hotbed

viveza *f* agility, briskness; ardor, vehemence; sharpness, keenness; perception; brightness, brilliance; witticism; (*de los ojos*) sparkle; (*acción o palabra poco consideradas*) thoughtlessness

vivide·ro -ra *adj* livable

vivi·do -da *adj* quick, perceptive; lively

vivienda *f* dwelling; life, way of life

viviente *adj* living, alive

vivificar §73 *tr* to vivify, to enliven

vivir *m* life, living ‖ *tr* (*una experiencia o ventura*) to live; (*toda la vida; la vejez*) to live out; (*habitar*) to live in ‖ *intr* to live; ¿**quién vive?** who goes there?; **vivir de** (*p.ej., carne*) to live on; **vivir para ver** to live and learn; **vivir y dejar vivir** to live and let live

vivisección *f* vivisection

vi·vo -va *adj* living, alive, live; (*lleno de vida; intenso*) live; (*sutil, agudo*) sharp, keen; (*dolor*) acute; (*carne*) raw; active, effective; (*luz*) bright, intense; (*pronto y ágil*) quick; (*idioma*) living, modern; **de viva voz** viva voce, by word of mouth; **herir en lo vivo** to cut or to sting to the quick ‖ *mf* living person; **los vivos y los muertos** the quick and the dead ‖ *m* edging, border; (vet) mange

Vizcaya *f* Biscay; **llevar hierro a Vizcaya** to carry coals to Newcastle

vizconde *m* viscount

vizcondesa *f* viscountess

V.M. *abbr* **Vuestra Majestad**

V.°B.° *abbr* **visto bueno**

vocablista *mf* punster

vocablo *m* word; **jugar del vocablo** to pun

vocabulario *m* vocabulary

vocación *f* vocation, calling

vocal *adj* vocal ‖ *mf* director ‖ *f* vowel

vocalista *mf* singer, vocalist

vocativo *m* vocative

voceador *m* town crier; (Col, Ecuad) paper boy

vocear *tr* to cry, shout; to cheer, acclaim; to call, to page; (coll) to boast about publicly ‖ *intr* to shout

vocería *f* shouting, outcry; spokesmanship

vocerío *m* shouting, outcry

vocero *m* spokesman, mouthpiece

vociferar *tr* (*injurias*) to shout; to boast loudly about ‖ *intr* to vociferate, to shout

vocingle·ro -ra *adj* loudmouthed; loud, talkative

vo·dú *m* (*pl* **-dúes**) voodoo

voduísta *adj* & *mf* voodoo

vol. *abbr* **volumen, voluntad**

volada *f* short flight; (*del jugador de billar*) (Arg) stroke; (Col, Ecuad) trick; (*noticia inventada*) (Mex) hoax

voladi·zo -za *adj* projecting ‖ *m* projection

vola·do -da *adj* (typ) superior ‖ *f* see volada

vola·dor -dora *adj* flying; hanging, dangling; swift, fast ‖ *m* rocket; flying fish

voladura *f* blast, explosion

volandas — en volandas in the air; fast

volante *adj* flying; unsettled ‖ *m* shuttlecock; battledore and shuttlecock; *(rueda que regula el movimiento de una máquina)* flywheel; *(rueda de mano para la dirección del automóvil)* steering wheel; *(pieza del reloj movida por la espiral)* balance wheel; flunkey, lackey; *(criado que iba a pie delante del coche o caballo)* outrunner; *(de papel)* slip, leaflet; (sew) flounce, ruffle; **un buen volante** a good driver

volan·tín -tina *adj* unsettled ‖ *m* fish line; (Am) kite

volantista *m* (coll) driver, man at the wheel

volan·tón -tona *mf* fledgling ‖ *f* (Ven) loose woman

volapié *m* (taur) stroke in which the matador moves in for the kill; **a volapié** half running, half flying; half walking, half swimming

volar §61 *tr (llevar en un aparato de aviación)* to fly; to blow up, to explode; to irritate; *(una letra, tipo o signo)* (typ) to raise ‖ *intr* to fly; to fly away; to disappear; to jut out, project; *(una especie)* to spread rapidly; *(p.ej., una especie)* to rise in the air; **volar sin motor** (aer) to glide ‖ *ref* to fly away; (Am) to fly off the handle

volatería *f* fowling with decoys; **de volatería** offhand

volátil *adj* volatile

volatilizar *tr & ref* to volatilize

volatín *m* ropewalker, acrobat, tumbler

volatine·ro -ra *mf* ropewalker, acrobat, tumbler

volcán *m* volcano

volcar §81 *tr* to upset, overturn, dump; to tip, to tilt; *(a una persona un olor fuerte)* to make dizzy; to change the mind of; to irritate, tease ‖ *intr* to upset ‖ *ref* to turn upside down

volear *tr* (tennis) to volley

voleo *m* (tennis) volley; reeling punch; **del primer voleo** or **de un voleo** (coll) with a smash, all at once; **sembrar al voleo** to sow broadcast

volframio *m* wolfram

volibol *m* volleyball

volquete *m* dumpcart, dump truck

voltai·co -ca *adj* voltaic

voltaje *m* voltage

volta·rio -ria *adj* fickle, inconstant; (Chile) willful; (Chile) sporty

voltea·do -da *mf* (Col) turncoat, deserter

voltear *tr* to upset, turn over; to turn around; to move, to transform ‖ *intr* to roll over, to tumble

volteo *m* upset, overturning; tumbling; (P-R) scolding

voltereta *f* tumble; turning up card to determine trump

voltímetro *m* voltmeter

voltio *m* volt

volti·zo -za *adj* curled, twisted; fickle

voluble *adj* easily turned; fickle, inconstant

volumen *m* volume; **volumen sonoro** volume; (geom) volume

volumino·so -sa *adj* voluminous

voluntad *f* will; *(amor, cariño)* fondness, love; **a voluntad** at will; **buena voluntad** willingness; **de buena voluntad** willingly; **de mala voluntad** unwillingly; **de su propia voluntad** of one's own volition; **última voluntad** last will and testament; last wish; **voluntad de hierro** iron will

voluntariedad *f* willfulness

volunta·rio -ria *adj (que se hace por espontánea voluntad)* voluntary; *(que tiene voluntad obstinada)* willful; *(que se presta voluntariamente a hacer algo)* voluntary ‖ *mf* volunteer

voluntario·so -sa *adj* willful

voluptuo·so -sa *adj (que inspira complacencia en los placeres sensuales)* voluptuous; *(dado a los placeres sensuales)* voluptuary ‖ *mf* voluptuary

voluta *f* (archit) scroll, volute; *(p.ej., de humo)* ring

volvedor *m* screwdriver; (Col) extra, something thrown in; **volvedor de machos** tap wrench

volver §47 & §83 *tr* to turn; to turn upside down; to turn inside out; to return, send back, give back; *(una puerta)* to push to, to pull to; to translate; to vomit ‖ *intr* to turn; to return, come back; **volver a** + *inf* verb + again, e.g., **volvió a abrir la puerta** he opened the door again; **volver en sí** to come to; **volver por** to defend, to stand up for ‖ *ref* to become; to turn around; to return, come back; to change one's mind; to turn, turn sour; **volverse atrás** to back out; **volverse contra** to turn on

vomitar *tr* to vomit, throw up; *(fuego los cañones)* to belch forth; *(maldiciones)* to utter; *(un secreto)* to let out; *(lo que uno retiene indebidamente)* (coll) to cough up ‖ *intr* to vomit, throw up; (coll) to come across, disgorge

vómito *m* vomit, vomiting; **provocar a vómito** (coll) to nauseate; **vómitos del embarazo** morning sickness

voracidad *f* voracity

vorágine *f* whirlpool, vortex

vo·raz *adj (pl -races)* voracious

vormela *f* polecat

vórtice *m* vortex

vos *pron pers* (subject of verb and object of preposition; takes plural form of verb but is singular in meaning; used in addressing the Deity, the Virgin, etc., and distinguished persons; in Spanish America is much used instead of **tú**) you

voso·tros -tras *pron pers* (plural of **tú**) you

votación *f* vote, voting

votante *adj* voting ‖ *mf* voter

votar *tr* to vote for; *(sí, no)* to vote; *(p.ej., un cirto a la Virgen)* to vow ‖ *intr* to vote; to vow; to swear, curse

voti·vo -va *adj* votive

voto *m (sufragio; derecho de votar; persona que da su voto)* vow; *(promesa solemne)* vow; *(exvoto)* votive offering; *(blasfemia)* oath, curse; wish, desire; **echar votos** to swear, to curse; **regular los votos** to tally the votes; **voto de amén** (coll) vote of a yes man; (coll) yes man; **voto de calidad** casting vote; **voto informativo** straw vote; **votos** good wishes; **¡voto va!** come now!

voz *f (pl* **voces)** *(vocablo)* voice; *(vocablo)* word; **aclarar la voz** to clear one's throat; **a una voz** with one voice; **a voces** shouting; **a voz en cuello** or **en grito** at the top of one's voice; **correr la voz que** to be rumored that; **dar voces** to shout, to cry out; **de viva voz** viva voce, by word of mouth; **en alta voz** aloud, in a loud voice; **en voz baja** in a low voice; **llevar la voz cantante** (coll) to have the say, to be the boss; **voces** outcry

vro. *abbr* **vuestro**

V.S. *abbr* **Vueseñoría**

vuelco *m* upset, overturn; **darle a uno un vuelco el corazón** (coll) to have a presentiment

vuelo *m* flight; flying; *(de una falda)* flare, fullness; projection; lace cuff trimming; **al vuelo** at once; on the wing; scattered at random; (chess) *en passant*; **alzar el vuelo** to take flight; (coll) to dash away; **echar a vuelo las campanas** to ring a full peal; **tirar al vuelo** to shoot on the wing; **tocar a vuelo las campanas** to ring a full peal; **vuelo a ciegas** (aer) blind flying; **vuelo de distancia** (aer) long-distance flight; **vuelo de ensayo** or **de prueba** (aer) test flight; **vuelo espacial tripulado** manned space flight; **vuelo planeado** (aer) volplane; **vuelo rasante** (aer) hedgehopping; **vuelo sin escala** (aer) nonstop flight; **vuelo sin motor** (aer) glide, gliding

vuelta *f* turn; *(regreso; devolución)* return; *(dinero sobrante de un pago)* change; *(de un camino)* bend, turn; *(del pantalón)* cuff; cuff trimming; *(paseo corto)* stroll; *(revés)* other side; *(paliza)* beating, whipping; *(en un cabo)* loop; *(en la media)* clock; *(mudanza)* change; **a la vuelta** on returning; please turn the page; **a la vuelta de** at the end of; at the turn of; *(la esquina)* around; **a vuelta de** about; **a vuelta de correo** by return mail; **dar cien vueltas a** to run rings around, be away ahead of; **dar la vuelta de campana** to turn somersault; **darse una vuelta a la redonda** (coll) to tend to one's own business; **dar una vuelta** to take a stroll, take a walk; to take a look; to change one's ways; **dar vuelta** to turn around; *(el vino)* to turn sour; **dar vuelta a** to reverse, to turn around; **estar de vuelta** to be back; **quedarse con la vuelta** to keep the change; **vuelta de campana** somersault; **vuelta del mundo** trip around the world

vuelto *m* (Am) change

vues·tro -tra (corresponds to **vos** and **vosotros)** *adj poss* your ‖ *pron poss* yours

vulcanizar §60 *tr* to vulcanize

vulgacho *m* (coll) populace, mob

vulgar *adj* vulgar, popular, common, vernacular

vulgarismo *m* popular expression; (philol) popular word, popular form

vulgarizar §60 *tr* to popularize; to translate into the vernacular ‖ *ref* to associate with the people

Vulgata *f* Vulgate

vulgo *adv* commonly ‖ *m* common people; *(personas que en una materia sólo conocen la parte superficial)* laity

vulnerable *adj* vulnerable

vulnerar *tr* to hurt, injure; *(la reputación de una persona)* to damage; *(una ley, un precepto)* to break

vulpeja *f* she-fox, vixen

V.V. or **VV** *abbr* **ustedes**

X

X, x (equis) *f* twenty-sixth letter of the Spanish alphabet

xenia *f* xenia

xenofobia *f* xenophobia

xenófo·bo -ba *mf* xenophobe

xenón *m* xenon

xilófono *m* (mus) xylophone

xilografía *f (arte)* xylography; *(grabado)* xylograph

xpiano *abbr* **cristiano**

Xpo *abbr* **Cristo**

xptiano *abbr* **cristiano**

Xpto *abbr* **Cristo**

xunde *m* (Mex) reed basket, palm basket

Y

Y, y (ye) *f* twenty-seventh letter of the Spanish alphabet

y *conj* and

ya *adv* already; right away; now; no

ya not only; **ya no** no longer; **ya que** since, inasmuch as

yac *m (bandera de proa)* (naut) jack; *(bóvido del Tibet)* yak

yacer §82 *intr* to lie

yacija *f* bed, couch; (*sepultura*) grave

yacimiento *m* bed, field, deposit

yámbi·co -ca *adj* iambic

yambo *m* iamb, iambus

yanqui *adj & mf* Yankee

Yanquilandia *f* Yankeedom

yapa *f* (Am) bonus, extra, allowance; **de yapa** (Am) in the bargain, extra

yarda *f* yard; yardstick

yate *m* yacht

yedra *f* ivy

yegua *f* mare; (CAm) cigar butt

yeguada *f* stud

yelmo *m* helmet

yema *f* (*de huevo*) yolk; candied yolk; (*del invierno*) dead; (*renuevo*) bud; (fig) cream; **dar en la yema** (coll) to put one's finger on the spot; **yema del dedo** finger tip; **yema mejida** eggnog

yente — yentes y vinientes *mpl* habitués, frequenters

yerba *f* var of hierba

yer·mo -ma *adj* deserted, uninhabited; (*suelo*) unsown; (*mujer*) not pregnant ‖ *m* desert, wilderness

yerno *m* son-in-law

yerro *m* error, mistake; **yerro de cuenta** miscalculation; **yerro de imprenta** printer's error

yer·to -ta *adj* stiff, rigid

yesca *f* punk, tinder; (*cosa que excita una pasión*) fuel; **echar una yesca** to strike a light

yeso *m* gypsum; plaster cast

yo *pron pers* I; **soy yo** it is I

yodhídri·co -ca *adj* hydriodic

yodo *m* iodine

yoduro *m* iodide

yola *f* (sport) shell

yugo *m* yoke; **sacudir el yugo** to throw off the yoke

Yugoeslavia *f* Yugoslavia

yugoesla·vo -va *adj & mf* Yugoslav

yugular *adj & f* jugular ‖ *tr* to cut off, to nip in the bud

yunque *m* anvil; (fig) drudge, work horse

yunta *f* yoke, team

yute *m* jute

yuxtaponer §54 *tr* to juxtapose

yuyo *m* (Arg, Chile) weed; **yuyos** (Col, Ecuad, Peru) greens

Z

Z, z (zeda or zeta) *f* twenty-eighth letter of the Spanish alphabet

zabordar *intr* (naut) to run aground

zabullir §13 *tr* (*p.ej., a un perro*) to duck, give a ducking to; (coll) to throw, to hurl ‖ *ref* (*meterse debajo del agua con ímpetu*) to dive; (*esconderse rápidamente*) to duck

zacapela or **zacapella** *f* row, rumpus

zacate *m* (CAm, Mex) hay, fodder; **zacate de empaque** (Am) excelsior

zacateca *m* (Cuba) undertaker, gravedigger

zacatín *m* old-clothes market

zacear *tr* (*al perro*) to chase away ‖ *intr* to lisp

zafaduría *f* (Arg) brazenness, effrontery

zafar *tr* to adorn, bedeck; to loosen, untie; to clear, to free; (*un buque*) to lighten ‖ *ref* to slip away; to slip off, come off; **zafarse** to get out of

zafarrancho *m* (naut) clearing the decks; (coll) havoc, ravage; (coll) scuffle, row; **zafarrancho de combate** (naut) clearing the deck for action

za·fio -fia *adj* rough, uncouth, boorish

zafiro *m* sapphire

za·fo -fa *adj* unhurt, intact; (naut) free, clear ‖ **zafo** *prep* (Col) except

zafra *f* olive-oil can; drip jar; sugar crop; sugar making; sugar-making season; (min) rubbish, muck

zaga *f* rear; load carried in the rear; (mil) rearguard; **a la zaga, a zaga** or **en zaga** behind, in the rear; **no ir en zaga a** (coll) to not be behind, to be as good as

zagal *m* young fellow; strapping young fellow; shepherd boy; footboy

zagala *f* lass, maiden; young shepherdess

zaguán *m* vestibule, hall, entry

zague·ro -ra *adj* back, rear ‖ *m* (sport) back, backstop

zaherir §68 *tr* to upbraid, reproach; to scold shamefully

zahones *mpl* chaps, hunting breeches

zaho·rí *m* (*pl* -ríes) keen observer; seer, clairvoyant

zahurda *f* pigpen

zai·no -na *adj* treacherous, false; (*caballo*) vicious; (*caballo*) dark-chestnut; **mirar a lo zaino** or **de zaino** to look askance at

za·lá *f* (*pl* -laes) Mohammedan prayer; **hacer la zalá a** (coll) to fawn on

zalagarda *f* ambush; skirmish; (*trampa para cazar animales*) trap; (coll) trick; (coll) row, rumpus; (coll) mock fight

zalamería *f* flattery, cajolery

zalame·ro -ra *adj* flattering, fawning ‖ *mf* flatterer, fawner

zalea *f* unsheared sheepskin

zalear *tr* to drag around, to shake; (*al perro*) to chase away

zalema *f* salaam

zamacuco *m* (coll) blockhead; (coll) sullen fellow; (coll) drunkenness

zamacueca *f* cueca (*Chilean courtship dance*)

zamarra *f* undressed sheepskin; sheepskin jacket

zam·bo -ba *adj* knock-kneed

zambra *f* merrymaking, celebration; Moorish boat

zambucar §73 *tr* (coll) to slip away, hide away

zambullida f dive, plunge; (fencing) thrust to the breast

zambulli·dor -dora adj diving, plunging || mf diver, plunger || m (orn) diver, loon

zambullir §13 tr (p.ej., a un perro) to duck, to give a ducking to; (coll) to throw, to hurl || ref (meterse debajo del agua con ímpetu) to dive; (esconderse rápidamente) to duck

zampa f pile, bearing pile

zampacuarti·llos mf (pl -llos) (coll) toper, soak

zampalimos·nas mf (pl -nas) (coll) bum, ordinary bum

zampar tr to slip away, hide away; to gobble down || ref to slip away, hide away

zampator·tas mf (pl -tas) (coll) glutton; (coll) boor

zampear tr (el terreno) to strengthen with piles and rubble

zampoña f shepherd's pipe, rustic flute; (coll) nonsense, folly

zampuzar §60 tr to duck, give a ducking to; (coll) to slip away, hide away

zanahoria f carrot

zanca f long leg; (de la escalera) horse

zancada f long stride; **en dos zancadas** (coll) in a flash, in a jiffy

zancadilla f (coll) booby trap; **echar la zancadilla a** to stick out one's foot and trip

zancajo m heel; **no llegar a los zancajos a** (coll) to not come up to, to not be equal to

zancajo·so -sa adj duck-toed; down-at-the-heel

zancarrón m (coll) dirty old fellow

zanco m stilt; **en zancos** (coll) from a vantage point

zancu·do -da adj long-legged; (orn) wading || m mosquito || f wading bird

zanfonía f hurdy-gurdy

zangala f buckram

zangamanga f (coll) trick

zanganada f (coll) impertinence, impudence

zanganear intr (coll) to loaf around

zángano m (ent) drone; (fig) drone, loafer; (CAm) scoundrel

zangarrear intr (coll) to thrum a guitar

zangolotear tr (coll) to jiggle || intr (coll) to fuss around || ref (coll) to jiggle, to flop around, to rattle

zangoloteo m (coll) jiggle, jiggling, rattle; (coll) fuss, bother

zanguanga f (coll) malingering; (coll) flattery; **hacer la zanguanga** (coll) to malinger

zanguan·go -ga adj (coll) slow, lazy || mf (coll) loafer || f see zanguanga

zanja f ditch, trench; (SAm) gully; **abrir las zanjas** to lay the foundations

zanquear intr to waddle; to rush around

zanquilar·go -ga adj leggy, long-legged

zanquituer·to -ta adj bandy-legged

zapa f spade; sharkskin, shagreen; (mil) sap

zapapico m mattock, pickax

zapar tr (mil) to sap, mine, excavate

zaparrastrar intr — **ir zaparrastrando** (coll) to go along trailing one's clothes on the ground

zapateado m clog dance, tap dance

zapatear tr to hit with the shoe; to tap with the feet; (coll) to abuse, ill-treat || intr to tap-dance; (las velas) to flap || ref — **zapatearse con** to hold out against

zapatería f shoemaking; shoemaker's shop; (tienda) shoe store

zapate·ro -ra adj poorly cooked || mf shoemaker; shoe dealer; **quedarse zapatero** (coll) to not take a trick; **¡zapatero, a tus zapatos!** stick to your last!; **zapatero de viejo** or **zapatero remendón** cobbler, shoemaker

zapatilla f slipper; (escarpín) pump; (del grifo) washer; (del florete) leather tip or button; cloven hoof

zapato m shoe, low shoe; **andar con zapatos de fieltro** to gumshoe; **como tres en un zapato** (coll) hard up; (coll) like sardines: **zapato de goma** overshoe; **zapato inglés** low shoe

zapatón m (Guat, SAm) overshoe

zapear tr (al gato) to scare away, chase away

zaque m wineskin; (coll) tippler, drunk

zaquiza·mí m (pl -míes) attic, garret; hovel, pigpen

zar m czar

zarabanda f (mus) saraband; (coll) noise, confusion, uproar; (Mex) beating, thrashing

zaragata f (coll) scuffle, row; **zaragatas** (W-I) flattery

Zaragoza f Saragossa

zaranda f sieve, screen; colander; (Ven) horn; (Ven) top

zarandajas fpl (coll) odds and ends, trinkets

zarandar tr to sift, to screen; to winnow, pick out, select; (coll) to jiggle || ref (coll) to jiggle; (Am) to swagger, strut

zaraza f chintz, printed cotton

zarcillo m eardrop; (bot) tendril

zarigüeya f opossum

zarina f czarina

zarpa f claw, paw; (naut) weighing anchor

zarpar tr (el ancla) (naut) to weigh (anchor) || intr (naut) to weigh anchor, to set sail

zarpo·so -sa adj mud-splashed

zarracatería f (coll) cajolery, insincere flattery

zarracatín m (coll) sharp trader

zarramplín m (coll) botcher, bungler

zarrien·to -ta adj mud-splashed

zarza f blackberry, bramble (bush)

zarzamora f blackberry (fruit)

zarzaparrilla f sarsaparilla

zarzo m hurdle, wattle

zarzo·so -sa adj brambly

zarzuela f small bramble; (theat) zarzuela (Spanish musical comedy); **zarzuela grande** three-act zarzuela

zas interj bang!; **¡zas, zas!** bing, bang!

zascandilear intr (coll) to meddle, to scheme

zepelín m zeppelin

Zeus m Zeus

zigzag *m* zigzag
zigzaguear *intr* to zigzag
zinc *m* (*pl* **zinces**) zinc
zipizape *m* (coll) scuffle, row, rumpus
ziszás *m* zigzag
zoca *f* public square
zócalo *m* (archit) socle; (*de una pared*) dado; (rad) socket; (Mex) public square, center square
zoca·to -ta *adj* (*fruto*) corky, pithy; (coll) left; (coll) left-handed || *mf* (coll) left-handed person
zoclo *m* clog, wooden shoe
zo·co -ca *adj* (coll) left; (coll) left-handed || *mf* (coll) left-handed person || *m* clog, wooden shoe; Moroccan market place; (archit) socle; **andar de zocos en colodros** (coll) to jump from the frying pan into the fire || *f* see **zoca**
zodíaco *m* zodiac
zofra *f* Moorish carpet, Moorish rug
zolo·cho -cha *adj* (coll) stupid, simple || *mf* (coll) simpleton
zollipar *intr* (coll) to sob
zollipo *m* (coll) sob
zona *m* (pathol) shingles || *f* zone; (*banda, faja*) belt, girdle; **zona a batir** target area
zon·zo -za *adj* tasteless, insipid; dull, inane || *mf* dolt, dimwit
zoófito *m* zoöphyte
zoología *f* zoölogy
zooógi·co -ca *adj* zoölogic(al)
zoólo·go -ga *mf* zoölogist
zopen·co -ca *adj* (coll) dull, stupid || *mf* (coll) dullard, blockhead
zopilote *m* (Mex, CAm) turkey buzzard, turkey vulture
zo·po -pa *adj* crippled; awkward, gauche || *mf* cripple
zoquete *m* (*de madera*) block, chunk, end; (*de pan*) bit, crust; (coll) chump, lout
zoquetu·do -da *adj* coarse, crude
zorra *f* fox; female fox; (coll) foxy person; (coll) prostitute; (coll) drunkenness; dray, truck; **pillar una zorra** (coll) to get drunk
zorrera *f* (*cueva de zorros*) foxhole; smoke-filled room; (coll) worry, confusion
zorrería *f* (coll) foxiness
zorre·ro -ra *adj* (coll) sly, foxy; (coll) slow, heavy, tardy || *f* see **zorrera**
zorrillo *m* (Am) skunk
zorro *m* male fox; (*piel*) fox; (*hombre taimado*) (coll) fox; **estar hecho un zorro** (coll) to be overwhelmed with sleep; (coll) to be dull and sullen; **zorros** duster
zorzal *m* (orn) fieldfare; sly fellow; (Chile) simpleton
zozobra *f* capsizing, sinking; anxiety
zozobrar *tr* (*un buque*) to sink; (*un negocio*) to wreck || *intr* to capsize, sink; (*la embarcación en la tempestad*) to wallow; (*un negocio*) to be in great danger; to be greatly worried || *ref* to capsize, sink
zueco *m* clog, wooden shoe, sabot
zulacar §73 *tr* to waterproof
zulaque *m* waterproofing

zulú (*pl* **-lús** o **-líes**) *adj* & *mf* Zulu
zullar *ref* (coll) to have a movement of the bowels; (coll) to break wind
zullen·co -ca *adj* (coll) windy, flatulent
zumaque *m* sumach; (coll) wine
zumaya *f* (*autillo*) tawny owl; (*chotacabras*) goatsucker
zumba *f* bell worn by leading mule; (Mex) drunkenness; **hacer zumba a** to make fun of; **sin zumba** (Mex) in a rush, in a hurry
zumbador *m* buzzer; (Mex) pauraque; (Mex, CAm, W-I) hummingbird
zumbar *tr* to make fun of; (*un golpe, una bofetada*) to let have || *intr* to buzz; to zoom; (*los oídos*) to ring; **zumbar a** (*frisar con*) to be close to, to border on || *ref* (Cuba) to go too far, to forget oneself; (P-R) to rush ahead; **zumbarse de** to make fun of
zumbido *m* buzz; zoom; (coll) blow, smack; **zumbido de ocupación** (telp) busy signal; **zumbido de oídos** ringing in the ears
zum·bón -bona *adj* waggish, playful || *mf* wag, jester
zumien·to -ta *adj* juicy
zumo *m* juice; advantage, profit; **zumo de cepas** or **de parras** (coll) fruit of the vine
zumo·so -sa *adj* juicy
zunchar *tr* to band, to hoop
zuncho *m* band, hoop
zupia *f* (*del vino*) dregs; slop, wine full of dregs; (fig) junk, trash
zurcido *m* darning; darn; invisible mending
zurcir §36 *tr* to darn; (*una mentira*) (coll) to hatch, concoct; (*unas mentiras*) (coll) to weave (*a tissue of lies*)
zurdazo *m* (box) left, blow with the left
zur·do -da *adj* left; left-handed; **a zurdas** with the left hand; the wrong way || *mf* left-handed person
zurear *intr* to coo
zuro *m* stripped corncob
zurra *f* dressing, currying; scuffle, quarrel; drubbing, thrashing; (*trabajo o estudio continuados*) grind
zurrapa *f* thread, filament; (coll) trash, rubbish; **con zurrapas** (coll) in a sloppy manner
zurrar *tr* (*el cuero*) to dress, to curry; to get the best of; (*censurar con dureza*) to dress down; (*castigar con azotes*) to drub, to thrash || *ref* (*hacer sus necesidades involuntariamente*) to have an accident; (coll) to be scared to death; (Arg) to break wind noiselessly
zurriagar §44 *tr* to whip, to horsewhip
zurriago *m* whip, lash
zurribanda *f* (coll) rain of blows; (coll) rumpus, scuffle
zurrir *intr* to buzz, to grate
zurrón *m* shepherd's leather bag; leather bag; (*cáscara*) husk
zurrona *f* (coll) loose, evil woman
zurullo *m* (coll) soft roll; (coll) turd
zurupeto *m* (coll) unregistered broker; (coll) shyster notary
zuta·no -na *mf* (coll) so-and-so

MODEL VERBS

ORDER OF TENSES

(a) gerund
(b) past participle
(c) imperative
(d) present indicative

(e) present subjunctive
(f) imperfect indicative
(g) future indicative
(h) preterit indicative

All simple tenses are shown in these tables if they contain one irregular form or more, except the conditional (which can always be derived from the stem of the future indicative) and the imperfect and future subjunctive (which can always be derived from the third plural preterit indicative minus the last syllable -ron). The tenses are identified with the letters (a) to (h) as shown above.

---

§1 **abolir:** defective verb used only in forms whose endings contain the vowel **i**

§2 **acertar**
   (c) **acierta,** acertad
   (d) **acierto, aciertas, acierta,** acertamos, acertáis, **aciertan**
   (e) **acierte, aciertes, acierte,** acertemos, acertéis, **acierten**

§3 **agorar:** like §61 but with diaeresis on the **u** of **ue**
   (c) **agüera,** agorad
   (d) **agüero, agüeras, agüera,** agoramos, agoráis, **agüeran**
   (e) **agüere, agüeres, agüere,** agoremos, agoréis, **agüeren**

§4 **airar**
   (c) **aíra,** airad
   (d) **aíro, aíras, aíra,** airamos, airáis, **aíran**
   (e) **aíre, aíres, aíre,** airemos, airéis, **aíren**

§5 **andar**
   (h) **anduve, anduviste, anduvo, anduvimos, anduvisteis, anduvieron**

§6 **argüir:** like §20 but with diaeresis on **u** in forms with accented **i** in the ending
   (a) **arguyendo**
   (b) **argüido**
   (c) **arguye,** argüid
   (d) **arguyo, arguyes, arguye,** argüimos, argüís, **arguyen**
   (e) **arguya, arguyas, arguya, arguyamos, arguyáis, arguyan**
   (h) **argüí,** argüiste, **arguyó,** argüimos, argüisteis, **arguyeron**

§7 **asir**
   (d) **asgo,** ases, ase, asimos, asís, asen
   (e) **asga, asgas, asga, asgamos, asgáis, asgan**

§8 **aunar**
   (c) **aúna,** aunad
   (d) **aúno, aúnas, aúna,** aunamos, aunáis, **aúnan**
   (e) **aúne, aúnes, aúne,** aunemos, aunéis, **aúnen**

§9 **avergonzar:** combination of §3 and §60
   (c) **avergüenza,** avergonzad

(d) **avergüenzo, avergüenzas, avergüenza,** avergonzamos, avergonzáis, **avergüenzan**

(e) **avergüence, avergüences, avergüence, avergoncemos, avergoncéis, avergüencen**

(h) **avergoncé,** avergonzaste, avergonzó, avergonzamos, avergonzasteis, avergonzaron

§10 **averiguar**

(e) **averigüe, averigües, averigüe, averigüemos, averigüéis, averigüen**

(h) **averigüé,** averiguaste, averiguó, averiguamos, averiguasteis, averiguaron

§11 **bendecir**

(a) **bendiciendo**

(c) **bendice,** bendecid

(d) **bendigo, bendices, bendice,** bendecimos, bendecís, **bendicen**

(e) **bendiga, bendigas, bendiga, bendigamos, bendigáis, bendigan**

(h) **bendije, bendijiste, bendijo, bendijimos, bendijisteis, bendijeron**

§12 **bruñir**

(a) **bruñendo**

(h) bruñí, bruñiste, **bruñó,** bruñimos, bruñisteis, **bruñeron**

§13 **bullir**

(a) **bullendo**

(h) bullí, bulliste, **bulló,** bullimos, bullisteis, **bulleron**

§14 **caber**

(d) **quepo,** cabes, cabe, cabemos, cabéis, caben

(e) **quepa, quepas, quepa, quepamos, quepáis, quepan**

(g) **cabré, cabrás, cabrá, cabremos, cabréis, cabrán**

(h) **cupe, cupiste, cupo, cupimos, cupisteis, cupieron**

§15 **caer**

(a) **cayendo**

(b) **caído**

(d) **caigo,** caes, cae, caemos, caéis, caen

(e) **caiga, caigas, caiga, caigamos, caigáis, caigan**

(h) caí, **caíste, cayó, caímos, caísteis, cayeron**

§16 **cocer:** combination of §47 and §78

(c) **cuece,** coced

(d) **cuezo, cueces, cuece,** cocemos, cocéis, **cuecen**

(e) **cueza, cuezas, cueza, cozamos, cozáis, cuezan**

§17 **coger**

(d) **cojo,** coges, coge, cogemos, cogéis, cogen

(e) **coja, cojas, coja, cojamos, cojáis, cojan**

§18 **comenzar:** combination of §2 and §60

(c) **comienza,** comenzad

(d) **comienzo, comienzas, comienza,** comenzamos, comenzáis, **comienzan**

(e) **comience, comiences, comience, comencemos, comencéis, comiencen**

(h) **comencé,** comenzaste, comenzó, comenzamos, comenzasteis, comenzaron

§19 conducir
 (d) **conduzco,** conduces, conduce, conducimos, conducís, con-
    ducen
 (e) **conduzca, conduzcas, conduzca, conduzcamos, conduzcáis,**
    conduzcan
 (h) **conduje, condujiste, condujo, condujimos, condujisteis,**
    condujeron

§20 construir
 (a) **construyendo**
 (b) **construído**
 (c) **construye,** construid
 (d) **construyo, construyes, construye,** construimos, construís,
    construyen
 (e) **construya, construyas, construya, construyamos, constru-**
    yáis, construyan
 (h) construí, construiste, **construyó,** construimos, construisteis,
    construyeron

§21 continuar
 (c) **continúa,** continuad
 (d) **continúo, continúas, continúa,** continuamos, continuáis,
    continúan
 (e) **continúe, continúes, continúe,** continuemos, continuéis,
    continúen

§22 crecer
 (d) **crezco,** creces, crece, crecemos, crecéis, crecen
 (e) **crezca, crezcas, crezca, crezcamos, crezcáis, crezcan**

§23 dar
 (d) **doy,** das, da, damos, dais, dan
 (e) **dé,** des, **dé,** demos, deis, den
 (h) **dí, diste, dio, dimos, disteis, dieron**

§24 decir
 (a) **diciendo**
 (b) **dicho**
 (c) **di,** decid
 (d) **digo, dices, dice,** decimos, decís, **dicen**
 (e) **diga, digas, diga, digamos, digáis, digan**
 (g) **diré, dirás, dirá, diremos, diréis, dirán**
 (h) **dije, dijiste, dijo, dijimos, dijisteis, dijeron**

§25 delinquir
 (d) **delinco,** delinques, delinque, delinquimos, delinquís, delin-
    quen
 (e) **delinca, delincas, delinca, delincamos, delincáis, delincan**

§26 desosar: like **§61** but with **h** before **ue**
 (c) **deshuesa,** desosad
 (d) **deshueso, deshuesas, deshuesa,** desosamos, desosáis, **des-**
    huesan
 (e) **deshuese, deshueses, deshuese,** desosemos, desoséis, **des-**
    huesen

§27 dirigir
 (d) **dirijo,** diriges, dirige, dirigimos, dirigís, dirigen
 (e) **dirija, dirijas, dirija, dirijamos, dirijáis, dirijan**

347

§28 **discernir**
- (c) **discierne,** discernid
- (d) **discierno, disciernes, discierne,** discernimos, discernís, **disciernen** .
- (e) **discierna, disciernas, discierna,** discernamos, discernáis, **disciernan**

§29 **distinguir**
- (d) **distingo,** distingues, distingue, distinguimos, distinguís, distinguen
- (e) **distinga, distingas, distinga, distingamos, distingáis, distingan**

§30 **dormir**
- (a) **durmiendo**
- (c) **duerme,** dormid
- (d) **duermo, duermes, duerme,** dormimos, dormís, **duermen**
- (e) **duerma, duermas, duerma, durmamos, durmáis, duerman**
- (h) dormí, dormiste, **durmió,** dormimos, dormisteis, **durmieron**

§31 **empeller**
- (a) **empellendo**
- (h) empellí, empelliste, **empelló,** empellimos, empellisteis, **empelleron**

§32 **enraizar:** combination of §4 and §60
- (c) **enraíza,** enraizad
- (d) **enraízo, enraízas, enraíza,** enraizamos, enraizáis, **enraízan**
- (e) **enraíce, enraíces, enraíce, enraicemos, enraicéis, enraícen**
- (h) **enraicé,** enraizaste, enraizó, enraizamos, enraizasteis, enraizaron

§33 **erguir:** combination of §29 and §50 or §68
- (a) **irguiendo**
- (c) **irgue** or **yergue,** erguid
- (d) **irgo, irgues, irgue,** / **irguen**
  yergo, yergues, yergue, } erguimos, erguís, { **yerguen**
- (e) **irga, irgas, irga,** / **irgan**
  yerga, yergas, yerga, } **irgamos, irgáis,** { **yergan**
- (h) erguí, erguiste, **irguió,** erguimos, erguisteis, **irguieron**

§34 **errar:** like §2 but with initial **ye** for **ie**
- (c) **yerra,** errad
- (d) **yerro, yerras, yerra,** erramos, erráis, **yerran**
- (e) **yerre, yerres, yerre,** erremos, erréis, **yerren**

§35 **esforzar:** combination of §60 and §61
- (c) **esfuerza,** esforzad
- (d) **esfuerzo, esfuerzas, esfuerza,** esforzamos, esforzáis, **esfuerzan**
- (e) **esfuerce, esfuerces, esfuerce, esforcemos, esforcéis, esfuercen**
- (h) **esforcé,** esforzaste, esforzó, esforzamos, esforzasteis, esforzaron

§36 **esparcir**
- (d) **esparzo,** esparces, esparce, esparcimos, esparcís, esparcen
- (e) **esparza, esparzas, esparza, esparzamos, esparzáis, esparzan**

§37 estar
- (c) **está, estad**
- (d) **estoy, estás, está,** estamos, estáis, **están**
- (e) **esté, estés, esté,** estemos, estéis, **estén**
- (h) **estuve, estuviste, estuvo, estuvimos, estuvisteis, estuvieron**

§38 haber
- (c) **hé,** habed
- (d) **he, has, ha, hemos,** habéis, **han** (*v impers*) hay
- (e) **haya, hayas, haya, hayamos, hayáis, hayan**
- (g) **habré, habrás, habrá, habremos, habréis, habrán**
- (h) **hube, hubiste, hubo, hubimos, hubisteis, hubieron**

§39 hacer
- (b) **hecho**
- (c) **haz,** haced
- (d) **hago, haces, hace, hacemos,** hacéis, **hacen**
- (e) **haga, hagas, haga, hagamos, hagáis, hagan**
- (g) **haré, harás, hará, haremos, haréis, harán**
- (h) **hice, hiciste, hizo, hicimos, hicisteis, hicieron**

§40 inquirir
- (c) **inquiere,** inquirid
- (d) **inquiero, inquieres, inquiere,** inquirimos, inquirís, **inquieren**
- (e) **inquiera, inquieras, inquiera,** inquiramos, inquiráis, **inquieran**

§41 ir
- (a) **yendo**
- (c) **vé, vamos,** id
- (d) **voy, vas, va, vamos, vais, van**
- (e) **vaya, vayas, vaya, vayamos, vayáis, vayan**
- (f) **iba, ibas, iba, íbamos, ibais, iban**
- (h) **fui, fuiste, fue, fuimos, fuisteis, fueron**

§42 jugar: like §63 but with radical **u**
- (c) **juega,** jugad
- (d) **juego, juegas, juega,** jugamos, jugáis, **juegan**
- (e) **juegue, juegues, juegue, juguemos, juguéis, jueguen**
- (h) **jugué,** jugaste, jugó, jugamos, jugasteis, jugaron

§43 leer
- (a) **leyendo**
- (b) **leído**
- (h) **leí, leíste, leyó, leímos, leísteis, leyeron**

§44 ligar
- (e) **ligue, ligues, ligue, liguemos, liguéis, liguen**
- (h) **ligué,** ligaste, ligó, ligamos, ligasteis, ligaron

§45 lucir
- (d) **luzco,** luces, luce, lucimos, lucís, lucen
- (e) **luzca, luzcas, luzca, luzcamos, luzcáis, luzcan**

§46 mecer
- (d) **mezo,** meces, mece, mecemos, mecéis, mecen
- (e) **meza, mezas, meza, mezamos, mezáis, mezan**

§47 mover
- (c) **mueve**, moved
- (d) **muevo, mueves, mueve**, movemos, movéis, **mueven**
- (e) **mueva, muevas, mueva**, movamos, továis, **muevan**

§48 oír
- (a) **oyendo**
- (b) **oído**
- (c) **oye, oíd**
- (d) **oigo, oyes, oye**, oímos, oís, **oyen**
- (e) **oiga, oigas, oiga, oigamos, oigáis, oigan**
- (h) **oí, oíste, oyó, oímos, oísteis, oyeron**

§49 oler: like §47 but with h before ue
- (c) **huele**, oled
- (d) **huelo, hueles, huele**, olemos, oléis, **huelen**
- (e) **huela, huelas, huela**, olamos, oláis, **huelan**

§50 pedir
- (a) **pidiendo**
- (c) **pide**, pedid
- (d) **pido, pides, pide**, pedimos, pedís, **piden**
- (e) **pida, pidas, pida, pidamos, pidáis, pidan**
- (h) pedí, pediste, **pidió**, pedimos, pedisteis, **pidieron**

§51 perder
- (c) **pierde**, perded
- (d) **pierdo, pierdes, pierde**, perdemos, perdéis, **pierden**
- (e) **pierda, pierdas, pierda**, perdamos, perdáis, **pierdan**

§52 placer
- (d) **plazco**, places, place, placemos, placéis, placen
- (e) **plazca, plazcas, plazca, plazcamos, plazcáis, plazcan**
- (h) plací, placiste, plació (or **plugo**), placimos, placisteis, placieron

§53 poder
- (a) **pudiendo**
- (c) (**puede**, poded)
- (d) **puedo, puedes, puede**, podemos, podéis, **pueden**
- (e) **pueda, puedas, pueda**, podamos, podáis, **puedan**
- (g) **podré, podrás, podrá, podremos, podréis, podrán**
- (h) **pude, pudiste, pudo, pudimos, pudisteis, pudieron**

§54 poner
- (b) **puesto**
- (c) **pon**, poned
- (d) **pongo**, pones, pone, ponemos, ponéis, ponen
- (e) **ponga, pongas, ponga, pongamos, pongáis, pongan**
- (g) **pondré, pondrás, pondrá, pondremos, pondréis, pondrán**
- (h) **puse, pusiste, puso, pusimos, pusisteis, pusieron**

§55 querer
- (c) **quiere**, quered
- (d) **quiero, quieres, quiere**, queremos, queréis, **quieren**
- (e) **quiera, quieras, quiera**, queramos, queráis, **quieran**
- (g) **querré, querrás, querrá, querremos, querréis, querrán**
- (h) **quise, quisiste, quiso, quisimos, quisisteis, quisieron**

350

§56 raer
  (a) **rayendo**
  (b) **raído**
  (d) **raigo** (or **rayo**), raes, rae, raemos, raéis, raen
  (e) **raiga** (or **raya**), **raigas, raiga, raigamos, raigáis, raigan**
  (h) raí, **raíste, rayó, raímos, raísteis, rayeron**

§57 regir: combination of §27 and §50
  (a) **rigiendo**
  (c) **rige,** regid
  (d) **rijo, riges, rige,** regimos, regís, **rigen**
  (e) **rija, rijas, rija, rijamos, rijáis, rijan**
  (h) regí, registe, **rigió,** regimos, registeis, **rigieron**

§58 reír
  (a) **riendo**
  (b) **reído**
  (c) **ríe,** reíd
  (d) **río, ríes, ríe, reímos,** reís, **ríen**
  (e) **ría, rías, ría, riamos, riáis, rían**
  (h) reí, **reíste, rió, reímos, reísteis, rieron**

§59 reunir
  (c) **reúne,** reunid
  (d) **reúno, reúnes, reúne,** reunimos, reunís, **reúnen**
  (e) **reúna, reúnas, reúna,** reunamos, reunáis, **reúnan**

§60 rezar
  (e) **rece, reces, rece, recemos, recéis, recen**
  (h) **recé,** rezaste, rezó, rezamos, rezasteis, rezaron

§61 rodar
  (c) **rueda,** rodad
  (d) **ruedo, ruedas, rueda,** rodamos, rodáis, **ruedan**
  (e) **ruede, ruedes, ruede,** rodemos, rodéis, **rueden**

§62 roer
  (a) **royendo**
  (b) **roído**
  (d) roo (**roigo,** or **royo**), roes, roe, roemos, roéis, roen
  (e) roa (**roiga,** or **roya**), roas, roa, roamos, roáis, roan
  (h) roí, **roíste, royó, roímos, roísteis, royeron**

§63 rogar: combination of §44 and §61
  (c) **ruega,** rogad
  (d) **ruego, ruegas, ruega,** rogamos, rogáis, **ruegan**
  (e) **ruegue, ruegues, ruegue, roguemos, roguéis, rueguen**
  (h) **rogué,** rogaste, rogó, rogamos, rogasteis, rogaron

§64 saber
  (d) **sé,** sabes, sabe, sabemos, sabéis, saben
  (e) **sepa, sepas, sepa, sepamos, sepáis, sepan**
  (g) **sabré, sabrás, sabrá, sabremos, sabréis, sabrán**
  (h) **supe, supiste, supo, supimos, supisteis, supieron**

§65 salir
  (c) **sal,** salid
  (d) **salgo,** sales, sale, salimos, salís, salen
  (e) **salga, salgas, salga, salgamos, salgáis, salgan**
  (g) **saldré, saldrás, saldrá, saldremos, saldréis, saldrán**

§66 segar: combination of §2 and §44
- (c) siega, segad
- (d) siego, siegas, siega, segamos, segáis, siegan
- (e) siegue, siegues, siegue, seguemos, seguéis, sieguen
- (h) segué, segaste, segó, segamos, segasteis, segaron

§67 seguir: combination of §29 and §50
- (a) siguiendo
- (c) sigue, seguid
- (d) sigo, sigues, sigue, seguimos, seguís, siguen
- (e) siga, sigas, siga, sigamos, sigáis, sigan
- (h) seguí, seguiste, siguió, seguimos, seguisteis, siguieron

§68 sentir
- (a) sintiendo
- (c) siente, sentid
- (d) siento, sientes, siente, sentimos, sentís, sienten
- (e) sienta, sientas, sienta, sintamos, sintáis, sientan
- (h) sentí, sentiste, sintió, sentimos, sentisteis, sintieron

§69 ser
- (c) sé, sed
- (d) soy, eres, es, somos, sois, son
- (e) sea, seas, sea, seamos, seáis, sean
- (f) era, eras, era, éramos, erais, eran
- (h) fui, fuiste, fue, fuimos, fuisteis, fueron

§70 tañer
- (a) tañendo
- (h) tañí, tañiste, tañó, tañimos, tañisteis, tañeron

§71 tener
- (c) ten, tened
- (d) tengo, tienes, tiene, tenemos, tenéis, tienen
- (e) tenga, tengas, tenga, tengamos, tengáis, tengan
- (g) tendré, tendrás, tendrá, tendremos, tendréis, tendrán
- (h) tuve, tuviste, tuvo, tuvimos, tuvisteis, tuvieron

§72 teñir: combination of §12 and §50
- (a) tiñendo
- (c) tiñe, teñid
- (d) tiño, tiñes, tiñe, teñimos, teñís, tiñen
- (e) tiña, tiñas, tiña, tiñamos, tiñáis, tiñan
- (h) teñí, teñiste, tiñó, teñimos, teñisteis, tiñeron

§73 tocar
- (e) toque, toques, toque, toquemos, toquéis, toquen
- (h) toqué, tocaste, tocó, tocamos, tocasteis, tocaron

§74 torcer: combination of §47 and §78
- (c) tuerce, torced
- (d) tuerzo, tuerces, tuerce, torcemos, torcéis, tuercen
- (e) tuerza, tuerzas, tuerza, torzamos, torzáis, tuerzan

§75 traer
- (a) trayendo
- (b) traído
- (d) traigo, traes, trae, traemos, traéis, traen
- (e) traiga, traigas, traiga, traigamos, traigáis, traigan
- (h) traje, trajiste, trajo, trajimos, trajisteis, trajeron

§76 valer
- (d) valgo, vales, vale, valemos, valéis, valen
- (e) valga, valgas, valga, valgamos, valgáis, valgan
- (g) valdré, valdrás, valdrá, valdremos, valdréis, valdrán

§77 variar
- (c) varía, variad
- (d) varío, varías, varía, variamos, variáis, varían
- (e) varíe, varíes, varíe, variemos, variéis, varíen

§78 vencer
- (d) venzo, vences, vence, vencemos, vencéis, vencen
- (e) venza, venzas, venza, venzamos, venzáis, venzan

§79 venir
- (a) viniendo
- (c) ven, venid
- (d) vengo, vienes, viene, venimos, venís, vienen
- (e) venga, vengas, venga, vengamos, vengáis, vengan
- (g) vendré, vendrás, vendrá, vendremos, vendréis, vendrán
- (h) vine, viniste, vino, vinimos, vinisteis, vinieron

§80 ver
- (b) visto
- (d) veo, ves, ve, vemos, veis, ven
- (e) vea, veas, vea, veamos, veáis, vean
- (f) veía, veías, veía, veíamos, veíais, veían

§81 volcar: combination of §61 and §73
- (c) vuelca, volcad
- (d) vuelco, vuelcas, vuelca, volcamos, volcáis, vuelcan
- (e) vuelque, vuelques, vuelque, volquemos, volquéis, vuelquen
- (h) volqué, volcaste, volcó, volcamos, volcasteis, volcaron

§82 yacer
- (c) yaz (or yace), yaced
- (d) yazco (yazgo, or yago), yaces, yace, yacemos, yacéis, yacen
- (e) yazca (yazga, or yaga), yazcas, yazca, yazcamos, yazcáis, yazcan

§83 The following verbs, some of which are included in the foregoing table, and their compounds have irregular past participles:

abrir	abierto	morir	muerto
cubrir	cubierto	poner	puesto
decir	dicho	proveer	provisto
escribir	escrito	pudrir	podrido
freír	frito	romper	roto
hacer	hecho	solver	suelto
imprimir	impreso	ver	visto
		volver	vuelto

353

PART TWO

Inglés-Español

La pronunciación del inglés

Los símbolos siguientes representan aproximadamente todos los sonidos del idioma inglés.

VOCALES

SÍMBOLO	SONIDO	EJEMPLO
[æ]	Más cerrado que la a de caro.	hat [hæt]
[ɑ]	Como la a de bajo.	father ['fɑðər] proper ['prɑpər]
[ɛ]	Como la e de perro.	met [mɛt]
[e]	Más cerrado que la e de canté. Suena como si fuese seguido de [ɪ].	fate [fet] they [ðe]
[ə]	Como la e de la palabra francesa le.	heaven ['hevən] pardon ['pardən]
[i]	Como la i de nido.	she [ʃi] machine [mə'ʃin]
[ɪ]	Como la i de tilde.	fit [fɪt] beer [bɪr]
[o]	Más cerrado que la o de habló. Suena como si fuese seguido de [ʊ].	nose [noz] road [rod]
[ɔ]	Menos cerrado que la o de torre.	bought [bɔt] law [lɔ]
[ʌ]	Más o menos como eu en la palabra francesa peur.	cup [kʌp] come [kʌm] mother ['mʌðər]
[ʊ]	Menos cerrado que la u de bulto.	pull [pʊl] book [bʊk] wolf [wʊlf]
[u]	Como la u de agudo.	rude [rud] move [muv] tomb [tum]

DIPTONGOS

SÍMBOLO	SONIDO	EJEMPLO
[aɪ]	Como ai de amáis.	night [naɪt] eye [aɪ]
[aʊ]	Como au de causa.	found [faʊnd] cow [kaʊ]
[ɔɪ]	Como oy de estoy.	voice [vɔɪs] oil [ɔɪl]

CONSONANTES

SÍMBOLO	SONIDO	EJEMPLO
[b]	Como la b de hombre. Sonido bilabial oclusivo sonoro.	bed [bɛd] robber ['rɑbər]
[d]	Como la d de conde. Sonido dental oclusivo sonoro.	dead [dɛd] add [æd]
[dʒ]	Como la y de cónyuge. Sonido palatal africado sonoro.	gem [dʒɛm] jail [dʒel]
[ð]	Como la d de nada. Sonido interdental fricativo sonoro.	this [ðɪs] father ['fɑðər]
[f]	Como la f de fecha. Sonido labiodental sordo.	face [fes] phone [fon]
[g]	Como la g de gato. Sonido velar oclusivo sonoro.	go [go] get [gɛt]

SÍMBOLO	SONIDO	EJEMPLO
[h]	Sonido más aspirado pero menos áspero que el sonido velar fricativo sordo de la **j** de **junto**.	hot [hɑt] alcohol ['ælkə ˌhɔl]
[j]	Como la **y** de **cuyo**. Sonido palatal semi-consonantal sonoro.	yes [jes] unit ['junɪt]
[k]	Como la **c** de **cama**. Sonido velar oclusivo sordo.	cat [kæt] chord [kɔrd] kill [kɪl]
[l]	Como la **l** de **lado**. Sonido alveolar fricativo lateral sonoro.	late [let] allow [ə'laʊ]
[m]	Como la **m** de **madre**. Sonido bilabial nasal sonoro.	more [mor] command [kə'mænd]
[n]	Como la **n** de **carne**. Sonido alveolar nasal sonoro.	nest [nest] manner ['mænər]
[ŋ]	Como la **n** de **banco**. Sonido velar nasal sonoro.	king [kiŋ] conquer ['kɑŋkər]
[p]	Como la **p** de **tapar**. Sonido bilabial oclusivo sordo.	pen [pen] cap [kæp]
[r]	La **r** más común en muchas partes de Inglaterra y en la mayor parte de los Estados Unidos y el Canadá es un sonido semivocal que se articula con la punta de la lengua elevada más hacia el paladar duro que en la **r** fricativa española y aun doblada hacia atrás. Intervocálica y al final de sílaba, es muy débil y casi no se puede oír. La **r**, precedida de los sonidos [ʌ] o [ə], da colorido propio a estos sonidos y desaparece completamente como sonido consonantal.	run [rʌn] far [fɑr] art [ɑrt] carry ['kæri] burn [bʌrn] learn [lʌrn] weather ['weðər]
[s]	Como la **s** de **clase**. Sonido alveolar fricativo sordo.	send [send] cellar ['selər]
[ʃ]	Como **ch** de la palabra francesa **chose**. Sonido palatal fricativo sordo.	shall [ʃæl] machine [mə'ʃin] nation ['neʃən]
[t]	Como la **t** de **arte**. Sonido dental oclusivo sordo.	ten [ten] dropped [drɑpt]
[tʃ]	Como la **ch** de **mucho**. Sonido palatal africado sordo.	child [tʃaɪld] much [mʌtʃ] nature ['netʃər]
[θ]	Como la **z** de **zapato** en la pronunciación de Castilla. Sonido interdental fricativo sordo.	think [θɪŋk] truth [truθ]
[v]	Como la **v** de la palabra francesa **avant**. Sonido labiodental fricativo sonoro.	vest [vest] over ['ovər] of [ɑv]
[w]	Como la **u** de **hueso**. Sonido labiovelar fricativo sonoro.	work [wʌrk] tweed [twid] queen [kwin]
[z]	Como la **s** de **mismo**. Sonido alveolar fricativo sonoro.	zeal [zil] busy ['bɪzi] his [hɪz]
[ʒ]	Como la **j** de la palabra francesa **jardin**. Sonido palatal fricativo sonoro.	azure ['ɔʒər] measure ['meʒər]

4

INGLÉS-ESPAÑOL

A

A, a [e] primera letra del alfabeto inglés

a [e] *art indef* un

aback [ə'bæk] *adv* atrás; **to be taken aback** quedar desconcertado; **to take aback** desconcertar

abaft [ə'bæft] o [ə'bɑft] *adv* a popa, en popa; *prep* detrás de

abandon [ə'bændən] *s* abandono ‖ *tr* abandonar

abase [ə'bes] *tr* degradar, humillar

abash [ə'bæʃ] *tr* avergonzar

abate [ə'bet] *tr* disminuir, reducir; deducir ‖ *intr* disminuir, moderarse

aba·tis ['æbətɪs] *s* (*pl* -tis) abatida

abattoir ['æbə,twɑr] *s* matadero

abba·cy ['æbəsɪ] *s* (*pl* -cies) abadía

abbess ['æbɪs] *s* abadesa

abbey ['æbɪ] *s* abadía

abbot ['æbət] *s* abad *m*

abbreviate [ə'brivɪ,et] *tr* abreviar

abbreviation [ə,brivɪ'eʃən] *s* (*shortening*) abreviación; (*shortened form*) abreviatura

A B C [,e,bi'si] *s* abecé *m*; **A B C's** abecedario

abdicate ['æbdɪ,ket] *tr & intr* abdicar

abdomen ['æbdəmən] o [æb'domən] *s* abdomen *m*

abduct [æb'dʌkt] *tr* raptar, secuestrar

abed [ə'bed] *adv* en cama, acostado

abet [ə'bet] *v* (*pret & pp* abetted; *ger* abetting) *tr* incitar (*a una persona, esp. al mal*); fomentar (*el crimen*)

abeyance [ə'be·əns] *s* suspensión; **in abeyance** en suspenso

ab·hor [æb'hɔr] *v* (*pret & pp* -horred; *ger* -horring) *tr* aborrecer, detestar

abhorrent [æb'hɔrənt] o [æb'hɔrənt] *adj* aborrecible, detestable

abide [ə'baɪd] *v* (*pret & pp* abode o abided) *tr* esperar; tolerar ‖ *intr* permanecer; **to abide by** cumplir con; atenerse a

abili·ty [ə'brlɪtɪ] *s* (*pl* -ties) habilidad, capacidad; talento

abject [æb'dʒɛkt] *adj* abyecto, servil

ablative ['æblətɪv] *s* ablativo

ablaut ['æblaʊt] *s* apofonía

ablaze [ə'blez] *adj* brillante; ardiente; encolerizado ‖ *adv* en llamas, ardiendo

able ['ebəl] *adj* hábil, capaz; **to be able to** poder

able-bodied ['ebəl'bɑdɪd] *adj* sano; fornido; experto

abloom [ə'blum] *adj* floreciente ‖ *adv* en flor

abnormal [æb'nɔrməl] *adj* anormal

aboard [ə'bord] *adv* a bordo; al bordo; **all aboard!** ¡señores viajeros al tren!; **to go aboard** ir a bordo; **to take aboard** embarcar ‖ *prep* a bordo de; (*a train*) en

abode [ə'bod] *s* domicilio, residencia

abolish [ə'bɑlɪʃ] *tr* eliminar, suprimir

A-bomb ['e,bɑm] *s* bomba atómica

abomination [ə,bɑmɪ'neʃən] *s* abominación

aborigines [,æbə'rɪdʒɪ,niz] *spl* aborígenes *mf*

abort [ə'bɔrt] *tr & intr* abortar

abortion [ə'bɔrʃən] *s* aborto

abound [ə'baʊnd] *intr* abundar

about [ə'baʊt] *adv* casi; aquí; **to be about** to estar a punto de, estar para ‖ *prep* acerca de; con respecto a; cerca de; hacia, a eso de; **to be about** tratar de

above [ə'bʌv] *adj* antedicho ‖ *adv* arriba, encima ‖ *prep* sobre, encima de, más alto que; superior a; **above all** sobre todo

above-mentioned [ə'bʌv'menʃənd] *adj* sobredicho, antedicho, susodicho

abrasive [ə'bresɪv] o [ə'brezɪv] *adj & s* abrasivo

abreast [ə'brest] *adj & adv* de frente; **to be abreast of** correr parejas con; estar al corriente de

abridge [ə'brɪdʒ] *tr* abreviar; disminuir; condensar, resumir

abroad [ə'brɔd] *adv* al extranjero; en el extranjero; fuera de casa

abrupt [ə'brʌpt] *adj* brusco; repentino; áspero; abrupto, escarpado

abscess ['æbsɛs] *s* absceso

abscond [æb'skɑnd] *intr* irse a hurtadillas; **to abscond with** alzarse con

absence ['æbsəns] *s* ausencia

absent ['æbsənt] *adj* ausente ‖ [æb'sent] *tr*—**to absent oneself** ausentarse

absentee [,æbsən'ti] *s* ausente *mf*

absent-minded ['æbsənt'maɪndɪd] *adj* distraído, absorto

absinth ['æbsɪnθ] *s* (*plant*) absintio, ajenjo; (*drink*) absenta, ajenjo

absolute ['æbsə,lut] *adj & s* absoluto

absolutely ['æbsə,lutlɪ] *adv* absolutamente ‖ [,æbsə'lutlɪ] *adv* (coll) positivamente

absolve [æb'sɑlv] *tr* absolver

absorb [æb'sɔrb] *tr* absorber; **to be o become absorbed** ensimismarse

absorbent [æb'sɔrbənt] *adj* absorbente; (*cotton*) hidrófilo

absorbing [æb'sɔrbɪŋ] *adj* absorbente

abstain [æb'sten] *intr* abstenerse

abstemious [æb'stimɪ·əs] *adj* abstemio, sobrio

abstinent ['æbstɪnənt] *adj* abstinente

abstract ['æbstrækt] *adj* abstracto || *s* resumen *m*, sumario, extracto || *tr* resumir, compendiar, extractar || [æb'strækt] *tr* abstraer; quitar

abstruse [æb'strus] *adj* abstruso

absurd [æb'sʌrd] o [æb'zʌrd] *adj* absurdo

absurdi·ty [æb'sʌrdɪti] o [æb'zʌrdɪti] *s* (*pl* -ties) absurdidad, absurdo

abundant [ə'bʌndənt] *adj* abundante

abuse [ə'bjus] *s* maltrato; injuria, insulto; (*bad practice; injustice*) abuso || [ə'bjuz] *tr* maltratar; injuriar, insultar; (*to misapply, take unfair advantage of*) abusar de

abusive [ə'bjusɪv] *adj* injurioso, insultante; abusivo

abut [ə'bʌt] *v* (*pret & pp* abutted; *ger* abutting) *intr*—to abut on confinar con, terminar en

abutment [ə'bʌtmənt] *s* confinamiento; estribo, contrafuerte *m*

abyss [ə'bɪs] *s* abismo

academic [ˌækə'dɛmɪk] *adj* académico

academic costume *s* toga, traje *m* de catedrático

academic freedom *s* libertad de cátedra, libertad de enseñanza

academician [ə,kædə'mɪʃən] *s* académico

academic subjects *spl* materias no profesionales

academic year *s* año escolar

acade·my [ə'kædəmi] *s* (*pl* -mies) academia

accede [æk'sid] *intr* acceder; **to accede to** acceder a, condescender a; (*e.g., the throne*) ascender a, subir a

accelerate [æk'sɛlə,ret] *tr* acelerar || *intr* acelerarse

accelerator [æk'sɛlə,retər] *s* acelerador *m*

accent ['æksɛnt] *s* acento || ['æksɛnt] o [æk'sɛnt] *tr* acentuar

accent mark *s* acento ortográfico

accentuate [æk'sɛntʃu,et] *tr* acentuar

accept [æk'sɛpt] *tr* aceptar

acceptable [æk'sɛptəbəl] *adj* aceptable

acceptance [æk'sɛptəns] *s* aceptación

access ['æksɛs] *s* acceso

accessible [æk'sɛsɪbəl] *adj* accesible

accession [æk'sɛʃən] *s* accesión; (*to a dignity*) ascenso; (*of books in a library*) adquisición

accesso·ry [æk'sɛsəri] *adj* accesorio || *s* (*pl* -ries) accesorio; (*to a crime*) cómplice *mf*

accident ['æksɪdənt] *s* accidente *m*; **by accident** por casualidad

accidental [ˌæksɪ'dɛntəl] *adj* accidental

acclaim [ə'klem] *s* aclamación || *tr & intr* aclamar

acclimate ['æklɪ,met] *tr* aclimatar || *intr* aclimatarse

accolade [ˌækə'led] *s* acolada; elogio, premio

accommodate [ə'kɑmə,det] *tr* acomodar; alojar

accommodating [ə'kɑmə,detɪŋ] *adj* acomodadizo, servicial

accommodation [ə,kɑmə'deʃən] *s* acomodación; **accommodations** facilidades, comodidades; (*in a train*) localidad; (*in a hotel*) alojamiento

accommodation train *s* tren *m* ómnibus

accompaniment [ə'kʌmpənɪmənt] *s* acompañamiento

accompanist [ə'kʌmpənɪst] *s* acompañante *m*

accompa·ny [ə'kʌmpəni] *v* (*pret & pp* -nied) *tr* acompañar

accomplice [ə'kɑmplɪs] *s* cómplice *mf*, codelincuente *mf*

accomplish [ə'kɑmplɪʃ] *tr* realizar, llevar a cabo

accomplished [ə'kɑmplɪʃt] *adj* realizado; culto, talentoso; (*fact*) consumado

accomplishment [ə'kɑmplɪʃmənt] *s* realización; **accomplishments** prendas, talentos

accord [ə'kɔrd] *s* acuerdo; **in accord with** de acuerdo con: **of one's own accord** de buen grado, voluntariamente; **with one accord** de común acuerdo || *tr* conceder, otorgar || *intr* concordar, avenirse

accordance [ə'kɔrdəns] *s* conformidad; **in accordance with** de acuerdo con

according [ə'kɔrdɪŋ] *adj* — **according as** según que; **according to** según

accordingly [ə'kɔrdɪŋli] *adv* en conformidad; por consiguiente

accordion [ə'kɔrdɪ·ən] *s* acordeón *m*

accost [ə'kɔst] o [ə'kɑst] *tr* abordar, acercarse a

accouchement [ə'kuʃmənt] *s* alumbramiento, parto

account [ə'kaunt] *s* informe *m*, relato; cuenta; estado de cuenta; importancia; **by all accounts** según el decir general; **of no account** de poca importancia; **on account of** a causa de; **to bring to account** pedir cuentas a; **to buy on account** comprar a plazos; **to turn to account** sacar provecho de, hacer valer || *intr*—**to account for** explicar; responder de

accountable [ə'kauntəbəl] *adj* responsable; explicable

accountant [ə'kauntənt] *s* contador *m*, contable *m*

accounting [ə'kauntɪŋ] *s* arreglo de cuentas; contabilidad

accouterments [ə'kutərmənts] *spl* equipo, avíos

accredit [ə'krɛdɪt] *tr* acreditar

accrue [ə'kru] *intr* acumularse; resultar

acct. *abbr* **account**

accumulate [ə'kjumjə,let] *tr* acumular || *intr* acumularse

accuracy ['ækjərəsi] *s* exactitud, precisión

accurate ['ækjərɪt] *adj* exacto

accusation [ˌækjə'zeʃən] *s* acusación

accusative [ə'kjuzətɪv] *adj & s* acusativo

accuse [ə'kjuz] *tr* acusar

accustom [ə'kʌstəm] *tr* acostumbrar

ace [es] *s* as *m*; **to be within an ace of** estar a dos dedos de

acetate ['æsɪ‚tet] s acetato

acetic acid [ə'sitɪk] s ácido acético

aceti·fy [ə'setɪ‚faɪ] v (pret & pp -fied) tr acetificar || intr acetificarse

acetone ['æsɪ‚ton] s acetona

acetylene [ə'setɪ‚lin] s acetileno

acetylene torch s soplete oxiacetilénico

ache [ek] s achaque m, dolor m || intr doler

achieve [ə'tʃiv] tr llevar a cabo; alcanzar, ganar, lograr

achievement [ə'tʃivmənt] s realización; (feat) hazaña

Achilles' heel [ə'kɪliz] s talón m de Aquiles

acid ['æsɪd] adj ácido; agrio, mordaz || s ácido

acidi·fy [ə'sɪdɪ‚faɪ] v (pret & pp -fied) tr acidificar || intr acidificarse

acidi·ty [ə'sɪdɪti] s (pl -ties) acidez f

acid test s prueba decisiva

ack-ack ['æk‚æk] s (slang) artillería antiaérea; (slang) fuego antiaéreo

acknowledge [æk'nɑlɪdʒ] tr reconocer; acusar (recibo de una carta); agradecer (p. ej., un favor)

acknowledgment [æk'nɑlɪdʒmənt] s reconocimiento; (of receipt of a letter) acuse m; (of a favor) agradecimiento

acme ['ækmi] s auge m, colmo

acolyte ['ækə‚laɪt] s acólito

acorn ['ekɔrn] o ['ekɔrn] s bellota

acoustic [ə'kustɪk] adj acústico || acoustics ssg acústica

acquaint [ə'kwent] tr informar, poner al corriente; to be acquainted conocerse; to be acquainted with conocer; estar al corriente de

acquaintance [ə'kwentəns] s conocimiento; (person) conocido

acquiesce [‚ækwɪ'ɛs] intr consentir, condescender, asentir

acquiescence [‚ækwɪ'ɛsəns] s consentimiento, condescendencia, aquiescencia

acquire [ə'kwaɪr] tr adquirir

acquisition [‚ækwɪ'zɪʃən] s adquisición

acquit [ə'kwɪt] v (pret & pp acquitted; ger acquitting) tr absolver, exculpar; to acquit oneself conducirse, portarse

acquittal [ə'kwɪtəl] s absolución, exculpación

acrid ['ækrɪd] adj acre, acrimonioso

acrobat ['ækrə‚bæt] s acróbata mf

acrobatic [‚ækrə'bætɪk] adj acrobático || acrobatics ssg (profession) acrobatismo; spl (stunts) acrobacia

acronym ['ækrənɪm] s acrónimo

acropolis [ə'krɑpəlɪs] s acrópolis f

across [ə'krɔs] o [ə'krɑs] prep al través de; al otro lado de; to come across encontrarse con; to go across atravesar

across'-the-board' adj comprensivo, general

acrostic [ə'krɔstɪk] o [ə'krɑstɪk] s acróstico

act [ækt] s acto; (law) decreto; in the act en flagrante || tr representar;

desempeñar (un papel); to act the fool hacer el bufón; to act the part of hacer o desempeñar el papel de || intr actuar; funcionar, obrar; conducirse; to act as if hacer como que; to act for representar; to act up travesear; to act up to hacer fiestas a

acting ['æktɪŋ] adj interino || s actuación

action ['ækʃən] s acción; to take action tomar medidas

activate ['æktɪ‚vet] tr activar

active ['æktɪv] adj activo

activi·ty [æk'tɪvɪti] s (pl -ties) actividad

act of God s fuerza mayor

actor ['æktər] s actor m

actress ['æktrɪs] s actriz f

actual ['æktʃʊəl] adj real, efectivo

actually ['æktʃʊ‚əli] adv en realidad

actuar·y ['æktʃʊ‚ɛri] s (pl -ies) actuario (de seguros)

actuate ['æktʃʊ‚et] tr actuar; estimular, mover

acuity [ə'kjuˌɪti] s agudeza

acumen [ə'kjumən] s cacumen m, perspicacia

acute [ə'kjut] adj agudo

A.D. abbr anno Domini (Lat) in the year of our Lord

ad [æd] s (coll) anuncio

adage ['ædɪdʒ] s adagio, refrán m

Adam ['ædəm] s Adán m; the old Adam la inclinación al pecado

adamant ['ædəmənt] adj firme, inexorable

Adam's apple s nuez f

adapt [ə'dæpt] tr adaptar; refundir (un drama)

adaptation [‚ædæp'teʃən] s adaptación; (of a play) refundición

add [æd] tr agregar, añadir; sumar || intr sumar; to add up to subir a; (coll) querer decir

added line s (mus) línea suplementaria

adder ['ædər] s víbora; serpiente f

addict ['ædɪkt] s enviciado; adicto, partidario || [ə'dɪkt] tr enviciar; entregar; to addict oneself to enviciarse con o en; entregarse a

addiction [ə'dɪkʃən] s enviciamiento; adhesividad

adding machine s sumadora, máquina de sumar

addition [ə'dɪʃən] s adición; in addition to además de

additive ['ædɪtɪv] adj & s aditivo

address [ə'drɛs] o ['ædrɛs] s dirección; consignación || [ə'drɛs] s alocución, discurso; to deliver an address hacer uso de la palabra || tr dirigirse a; dirigir (p. ej., una alocución, una carta); consignar

addressee [‚ædrɛ'si] s destinatario; (com) consignatario

addressing machine s máquina para dirigir sobres

adduce [ə'djus] o [ə'dus] tr aducir

adenoids ['ædə‚nɔɪdz] spl vegetaciones adenoides

adept [ə'dɛpt] adj & s experto, perito

adequate ['ædɪkwɪt] adj suficiente

adhere [æd'hɪr] *intr* adherir, adherirse; conformarse

adherence [æd'hɪrəns] *s* adhesión

adherent [æd'hɪrənt] *adj & s* adherente *m*

adhesion [æd'hiʒən] *s* (*sticking*) adherencia; (*support, loyalty*) adhesión; (pathol) adherencia; (phys) adherencia o adhesión

adhesive [æd'hisɪv] o [æd'hizɪv] *adj* adhesivo

adhesive tape *s* tafetán adhesivo

adieu [ə'dju] o [ə'du] *interj* ¡adiós! ‖ *s* (*pl* **adieus** o **adieux**) adiós *m*; **to bid adieu to** despedirse de

adjacent [ə'dʒesənt] *adj* adyacente

adjective ['ædʒɪktɪv] *adj & s* adjetivo

adjoin [ə'dʒɔɪn] *tr* lindar con ‖ *intr* colindar

adjoining [ə'dʒɔɪnɪŋ] *adj* colindante, contiguo

adjourn [ə'dʒʌrn] *tr* prorrogar, suspender ‖ *intr* prorrogarse, suspenderse; (coll) ir

adjournment [ə'dʒʌrnmənt] *s* prorrogación, suspensión

adjust [ə'dʒʌst] *tr* ajustar, arreglar; corregir, verificar; (ins) liquidar

adjustable [ə'dʒʌstəbəl] *adj* ajustable, arreglable

adjustment [ə'dʒʌstmənt] *s* ajuste *m*, arreglo; (ins) liquidación de la avería

adjutant ['ædʒətənt] *s* ayudante *m*

ad-lib [ˌæd'lɪb] *v* (*pret & pp* **-libbed**; *ger* **-libbing**) *tr & intr* improvisar

Adm. *abbr* **Admiral**

administer [æd'mɪnɪstər] *tr* administrar; **to administer an oath** tomar juramento ‖ *intr* — **to administer to** cuidar de

administrator [æd'mɪnɪs,tretər] *s* administrador *m*

admiral ['ædmɪrəl] *s* almirante *m*; buque *m* almirante

admiralty ['ædmɪrəltɪ] *s* (*pl.* **-ties**) almirantazgo

admire [æd'maɪr] *tr* admirar

admirer [æd'maɪrər] *s* admirador *m*; enamorado

admissible [æd'mɪsɪbəl] *adj* admisible

admission [æd'mɪʃən] *s* admisión; (*in a school*) ingreso; precio de entrada; **to gain admission** lograr entrar

admit [æd'mɪt] *v* (*pret & pp* **-mitted**; *ger* **-mitting**) *tr* admitir ‖ *intr* dar entrada; **to admit of** admitir, permitir

admittance [æd'mɪtəns] *s* admisión; derecho de entrar; **no admittance** acceso prohibido, se prohíbe la entrada

admonish [æd'mɑnɪʃ] *tr* amonestar

ado [ə'du] *s* bulla, excitación

adobe [ə'dobɪ] *s* adobe *m*; casa de adobe

adolescence [ˌædə'lɛsəns] *s* adolescencia

adolescent [ˌædə'lɛsənt] *adj & s* adolescente *mf*

adopt [ə'dɑpt] *tr* adoptar

adoption [ə'dɑpʃən] *s* adopción

adorable [ə'dorəbəl] *adj* adorable

adore [ə'dor] *tr* adorar

adorn [ə'dorn] *tr* adornar

adornment [ə'dornmənt] *s* adorno

adrenal gland [æd'rinəl] *s* glándula suprarrenal

Adriatic [ˌedrɪ'ætɪk] o [ˌædrɪ'ætɪk] *adj & s* Adriático

adrift [ə'drɪft] *adj & adv* al garete, a la deriva

adroit [ə'drɔɪt] *adj* diestro

adult [ə'dʌlt] o ['ædʌlt] *adj & s* adulto

adulterate [ə'dʌltə,ret] *tr* adulterar

adulterer [ə'dʌltərər] *s* adúltero

adulteress [ə'dʌltərɪs] *s* adúltera

adultery [ə'dʌltərɪ] *s* (*pl* **-ies**) adulterio

advance [æd'væns] o [æd'vɑns] *adj* adelantado; anticipado ‖ *s* adelanto, avance *m*; aumento, subida; **advances** propuestas; requerimiento amoroso; propuesta indecente; préstamo; **in advance** de antemano, por anticipado ‖ *tr* adelantar ‖ *intr* adelantar; adelantarse

advanced [æd'vænst] o [æd'vɑnst] *adj* avanzado; **advanced in years** avanzado de edad, entrado en años

advanced standing *s* traspaso de matrículas, traspaso de crédito académico

advanced studies *spl* altos estudios

advancement [æd'vænsmənt] o [æd'vɑnsmənt] *s* adelanto, avance *m*; subida; promoción

advance publicity *s* publicidad de lanzamiento

advantage [æd'væntɪdʒ] o [æd'vɑntɪdʒ] *s* ventaja; **to take advantage of** aprovecharse de; abusar de, engañar

advantageous [ˌædvən'tedʒəs] *adj* ventajoso

advent ['ædvɛnt] *s* advenimiento ‖ **Advent** *s* (eccl) Adviento

adventure [æd'vɛntʃər] *s* aventura ‖ *tr* aventurar ‖ *intr* aventurarse

adventurer [æd'vɛntʃərər] *s* aventurero

adventuresome [æd'vɛntʃərsəm] *adj* aventurero

adventuress [æd'vɛntʃərɪs] *s* aventurera

adventurous [æd'vɛntʃərəs] *adj* aventurero

adverb ['ædvʌrb] *s* adverbio

adversary ['ædvər,sɛrɪ] *s* (*pl* **-ies**) adversario

adversity [æd'vʌrsɪtɪ] *s* (*pl* **-ties**) adversidad

advertise ['ædvər,taɪz] o [ˌædvər'taɪz] *tr & intr* anunciar

advertisement [ˌædvər'taɪzmənt] o [æd'vʌrtɪzmənt] *s* anuncio

advertiser ['ædvər,taɪzər] o [ˌædvər'taɪzər] *s* anunciante *mf*

advertising ['ædvər,taɪzɪŋ] *s* propaganda, publicidad, anuncios

advertising agency *s* empresa anunciadora

advertising campaign *s* campaña de publicidad

advertising man *s* empresario de publicidad

advertising manager *s* gerente *m* de publicidad

advice [æd'vais] *s* consejo; aviso, noticia; a piece of advice un consejo

advisable [æd'vaizǝbǝl] *adj* aconsejable

advise [æd'vaiz] *tr* aconsejar, asesorar; advertir, avisar

advisement [æd'vaizmǝnt] *s* consideración; to take under advisement someter a consideración

advisory [æd'vaizǝri] *adj* consultivo

advocate ['ædvǝ,ket] *s* defensor *m*; abogado || *tr* abogar por

Aegean Sea [i'dʒiǝn] *s* Archipiélago; (*of the ancients*) mar Egeo

aegis ['idʒis] *s* égida

aerate ['eret] o ['eǝ,ret] *tr* airear

aerial ['eri·ǝl] *adj* aéreo || *s* antena

aerialist ['eri·ǝlist] *s* volatinero

aerodrome ['erǝ,drom] *s* aeródromo

aerodynamic [,erodai'næmik] *adj* aerodinámico || **aerodynamics** *ssg* aerodinámica

aeronaut ['erǝ,nɔt] *s* aeronauta *mf*

aeronautic [,erǝ'nɔtik] *adj* aeronáutico || **aeronautics** *ssg* aeronáutica

aerosol ['erǝ,sɔl] *s* aerosol *m*

aerospace ['ero,spes] *adj* aeroespacial

aesthete ['esθit] *s* esteta *mf*

aesthetic [es'θetik] *adj* estético || **aesthetics** *sg* estética

afar [ǝ'far] *adv* lejos

affable ['æfǝbǝl] *adj* afable

affair [ǝ'fer] *s* asunto, negocio; lance *m*; amorío; encuentro, combate *m*; **affairs** negocios

affect [ǝ'fekt] *tr* influir en; impresionar, enternecer; (*to assume; to pretend*) afectar; aficionarse a

affectation [,æfek'teʃǝn] *s* afectación

affected [ǝ'fektid] *adj* afectado

affection [ǝ'fekʃǝn] *s* afecto, cariño, afección; (*pathol*) afección

affectionate [ǝ'fekʃǝnit] *adj* afectuoso, cariñoso

affidavit [,æfi'devit] *s* declaración jurada, acta notarial

affiliate [ǝ'fili,et] *adj* afiliado || *s* afiliado; filial *f* || *tr* afiliar || *intr* afiliarse

affinity [ǝ'finiti] *s* (*pl* -ties) afinidad

affirm [ǝ'fʌrm] *tr* & *intr* afirmar

affirmative [ǝ'fʌrmǝtiv] *adj* afirmativo || *s* afirmativa

affix ['æfiks] *s* añadidura; (*gram*) afijo || [ǝ'fiks] *tr* añadir; atribuir (*p.ej., culpa*); poner (*una firma, sello, etc.*)

afflict [ǝ'flikt] *tr* afligir; to be afflicted with sufrir de, adolecer de

affliction [ǝ'flikʃǝn] *s* aflicción, desgracia; achaque *m*

affluence ['æflu·ǝns] *s* (*abundance*) afluencia; (*wealth*) opulencia

afford [ǝ'fɔrd] *tr* proporcionar; to be able to afford (*to*) poder darse el lujo de, poder permitirse

affray [ǝ'fre] *s* pendencia, riña

affront [ǝ'frʌnt] *s* afrenta || *tr* afrentar

Afghan ['æfgǝn] o ['æfgæn] *adj* & *s* afgano

Afghanistan [æf'gæni,stæn] *s* el Afganistán

afire [ǝ'fair] *adj* & *adv* ardiendo

aflame [ǝ'flem] *adj* & *adv* en llamas

afloat [ǝ'flot] *adj* & *adv* a flote; a bordo; inundado; sin rumbo; (*rumor*) en circulación

afoot [ǝ'fut] *adj* & *adv* a pie; en marcha

afoul [ǝ'faul] *adj* & *adv* enredado; en colisión; to run afoul of enredarse con

afraid [ǝ'fred] *adj* asustado; to be afraid tener miedo

Africa ['æfrikǝ] *s* África

African ['æfrikǝn] *adj* & *s* africano

aft [æft] o [aft] *adj* & *adv* en popa

after ['æftǝr] o ['aftǝr] *adj* siguiente || *adv* después || *prep* después de; según; after all al fin y al cabo || *conj* después de que

after-dinner speaker *s* orador *m* de sobremesa

after-dinner speech *s* discurso de sobremesa

af'ter-hours' *adv* después del trabajo

af'ter-life' *s* vida venidera; resto de la vida

aftermath ['æftǝr,mæθ] o ['aftǝr,mæθ] *s* segunda siega; consecuencias, consecuencias desastrosas

af'ter-noon' *s* tarde *f*

af'ter-taste' *s* dejo, gustillo, resabio

af'ter-thought' *s* idea tardía, expediente tardío

afterward ['æftǝrwǝrd] o ['aftǝrwǝrd] *adv* después, luego

af'ter-while' *adv* dentro de poco

again [ǝ'gen] *adv* otra vez, de nuevo; además; to + *inf* + again volver a + *inf*, p.ej., he will come again volverá a venir

against [ǝ'genst] *prep* contra; cerca de; en contraste con; por; para

agape [ǝ'gep] *adj* abierto de par en par || *adv* con la boca abierta

age [edʒ] *s* edad; (*old age*) vejez *f*; (*one hundred years; a long time*) siglo; edad mental; of age mayor de edad; to come of age alcanzar su mayoría de edad, llegar a mayor edad; under age menor de edad || *tr* envejecer || *intr* envejecer, envejecerse

aged [edʒd] *adj* de la edad de || ['edʒid] *adj* anciano, viejo

ageless ['edʒlis] *adj* eternamente joven

agency ['edʒǝnsi] *s* (*pl* -cies) agencia; mediación

agenda [ǝ'dʒendǝ] *s* agenda, temario

agent ['edʒǝnt] *s* agente *m*

Age of Enlightenment *s* siglo de las luces

agglomeration [ǝ,glamǝ'reʃǝn] *s* aglomeración

aggrandizement [ǝ'grændizmǝnt] *s* engrandecimiento

aggravate ['ægrǝ,vet] *tr* agravar; (*coll*) exasperar, irritar

aggregate ['ægri,get] *adj* & *s* agregado || *tr* agregar, juntar; ascender a

aggression [ǝ'greʃǝn] *s* agresión

aggressive [ə'grɛsɪv] *adj* agresivo

aggressor [ə'grɛsər] *s* agresor *m*

aghast [ə'gæst] o [ə'gɑst] *adj* horrorizado

agile ['ædʒɪl] *adj* ágil

agitate ['ædʒɪˌtet] *tr & intr* agitar

aglow [ə'glo] *adj & adv* fulgurante

agnostic [æg'nɑstɪk] *adj & s* agnóstico

ago [ə'go] *adv* hace, p.ej., **two days ago** hace dos días

ago·ny ['ægənɪ] *s* (*pl* **-nies**) angustia, congoja; (*anguish; death struggle*) agonía

agrarian [ə'grɛrɪ·ən] *adj* agrario || *s* agrariense *mf*

agree [ə'gri] *intr* estar de acuerdo, ponerse de acuerdo; sentar bien; (*gram*) concordar

agreeable [ə'grɪ·əbəl] *adj* (*to one's liking*) agradable; (*willing to consent*) acorde, conforme

agreement [ə'grimənt] *s* acuerdo, convenio; concordancia; **in agreement** de acuerdo

agric. *abbr* **agriculture**

agriculture ['ægrɪˌkʌltʃər] *s* agricultura

agronomy [ə'grɑnəmɪ] *s* agronomía

aground [ə'graund] *adv* encallado, varado; **to run aground** encallar, varar

agt. *abbr* **agent**

ague ['egju] *s* escalofrío; fiebre *f* intermitente

ahead [ə'hɛd] *adj & adv* delante, al frente; **ahead of** antes de; delante de; al frente de; **to get ahead (of)** adelantarse (a)

ahoy [ə'hɔɪ] *interj* — **ship ahoy!** ¡ah del barco!

aid [ed] *s* ayuda, auxilio; (*mil*) ayudante *m* || *tr* ayudar, auxiliar; **to aid and abet** auxiliar e incitar, ser cómplice de || *intr* ayudar

aide-de-camp ['eddə'kæmp] *s* (*pl* **aides-de-camp**) ayudante *m* de campo, edecán *m*

ail [el] *tr* inquietar; **what ails you?** ¿qué tiene Vd.? || *intr* sufrir, estar enfermo

aileron ['elə·rɑn] *s* alerón *m*

ailing ['elɪŋ] *adj* enfermo, achacoso

ailment ['elmənt] *s* enfermedad, achaque *m*

aim [em] *s* puntería; intento; punto de mira || *tr* apuntar, encarar; dirigir (*p.ej., una observación*) || *intr* apuntar

air [ɛr] *s* aire *m*; **by air** por vía aérea; **in the open air** al aire libre; **on the air** en antena, en la radio; **to let the air out of** desinflar; **to put on airs** darse aires; **to put on the air** llevar a las antenas; **to walk on air** no pisar en el suelo || *tr* airear, ventilar; radiodifundir; (*fig*) ventilar

air'-a·tom'ic *adj* aeroatómico

air'-borne' *adj* aerotransportado

air brake *s* freno de aire comprimido

air castle *s* castillo en el aire

air'-condi'tion *tr* climatizar

air conditioner *s* acondicionador *m* de aire

air conditioning *s* acondicionamiento del aire, clima *m* artificial

air corps *s* cuerpo de aviación

air'craft' *ssg* máquina de volar; *spl* máquinas de volar

aircraft carrier *s* portaaviones *m*

airdrome ['ɛrˌdrom] *s* aeródromo

air'drop' *s* lanzamiento || *tr* lanzar

air field *s* campo de aviación

air'foil' *s* superficie *f* de sustentación

air force *s* fuerza aérea, ejército del aire

air gap *s* (*phys*) entrehierro

air'-ground' *adj* aeroterrestre

air hostess *s* aeromoza, azafata

air lane *s* ruta aérea

air'lift' *s* puente aéreo

air liner *s* transaéreo, avión *m* de travesía

air mail *s* correo aéreo, aeroposta

air'-mail' letter *s* carta aérea, carta por avión

air-mail pilot *s* aviador *m* postal

air-mail stamp *s* sello aéreo

air·man ['ɛrmən] o ['ɛrˌmæn] *s* (*pl* **-men** ['mɛn] o [ˌmɛn]) aviador *m*

air'plane' *s* avión *m*

airplane carrier *s* portaaviones *m*

air pocket *s* bache aéreo

air pollution *s* contaminación atmosférica

air'port' *s* aeropuerto

air raid *s* ataque aéreo

air'-raid' drill *s* simulacro de ataque aéreo

air-raid shelter *s* abrigo antiaéreo

air-raid warning *s* alarma aérea

air rifle *s* escopeta de viento, escopeta de aire comprimido

air'ship' *s* aeronave *f*

air'sick' *adj* mareado en el aire

air sleeve o **sock** *s* veleta de manga

air'strip' *s* pista de despegue, pista de aterrizaje

air'tight' *adj* herméticamente cerrado, estanco al aire

air'waves' *spl* ondas de radio

air'way' *s* aerovía, vía aérea

airway lighting *s* balizaje *m*

air·y ['ɛrɪ] *adj* (*comp* **-ier**; *super* **-iest**) airoso; aireado; alegre; impertinente; (*coll*) afectado

aisle [aɪl] *s* (*in theater, movie, etc.*) pasillo; (*in a store, factory, etc.*) nave *f*; (*archit*) nave *f* lateral; (*any of the long passageways of a church*) (*archit*) nave *f*

ajar [ə'dʒɑr] *adj* entreabierto, entornado

akimbo [ə'kɪmbo] *adj & adv* — **with arms akimbo** en jarras

akin [ə'kɪn] *adj* emparentado; semejante

alabaster ['ælə·ˌbæstər] o ['ælə·ˌbɑstər] *s* alabastro

alarm [ə'lɑrm] *s* alarma || *tr* alarmar

alarm clock *s* reloj *m* despertador

alarmist [ə'lɑrmɪst] *s* alarmista *mf*

alas [ə'læs] o [ə'lɑs] *interj* ¡ay!, ¡ay de mí!

Albanian [æl'benɪ·ən] *adj & s* albanés *m*

albatross ['ælbə‚trɔs] o ['ælbə‚trɑs] s albatros m

album ['ælbəm] s álbum m

albumen [æl'bjumən] s albumen m; albúmina

alchemy ['ælkɪmɪ] s alquimia

alcohol ['ælkə‚hɔl] o ['ælkə‚hɑl] s alcohol m

alcoholic [‚ælkə'hɔlɪk] o [‚ælkə'hɑlɪk] adj & s alcohólico

alcove ['ælkov] s gabinete m, rincón m; (in a bedroom) trasalcoba; (in a garden) cenador m

alder ['ɔldər] s aliso

alder-man ['ɔldərmən] s (pl -men [mən]) concejal m

ale [el] s ale f (cerveza inglesa, obscura, espesa y amarga)

alembic [ə'lɛmbɪk] s alambique m

alert [ə'lʌrt] adj listo, vivo; vigilante || s (aer) alarma; (mil) alerta m; to be on the alert estar sobre aviso, estar alerta || tr alertar

Aleutian Islands [ə'luʃən] spl islas Aleutas, islas Aleutianas

Alexandrine [‚ælɪg'zændrɪn] adj & s alejandrino

alg. abbr **algebra**

algae ['ældʒɪ] spl algas

algebra ['ældʒɪbrə] s álgebra

algebraic [‚ældʒɪ'bre‧ɪk] adj algebraico

Algeria [æl'dʒɪrɪ‧ə] s Argelia

Algerian [æl'dʒɪrɪ‧ən] adj & s argelino

Algiers [æl'dʒɪrz] s Argel f

alias ['elɪ‧əs] adv alias || s alias m, nombre supuesto

ali-bi ['ælɪ‚baɪ] s (pl -bis) coartada, (coll) excusa

alien ['eljən] o ['elɪ‧ən] adj & s extranjero

alienate ['eljə‚net] o ['elɪ‧ə‚net] tr enajenar, alienar

alight [ə'laɪt] v (pret & pp alighted o alit [ə'lɪt]) intr bajar, apearse; posarse (un ave)

align [ə'laɪn] tr alinear || intr alinearse

alike [ə'laɪk] adj semejantes; to look alike parecerse || adv igualmente

alimentary canal [‚ælɪ'mɛntərɪ] s canal alimenticio, tubo digestivo

alimony ['ælɪ‚monɪ] s alimentos

alive [ə'laɪv] adj vivo, viviente; animado; alive to despierto para, sensible a; alive with hormigueante en

alka-li ['ælkə‚laɪ] s (pl -lis o -lies) álcali m

alkaline ['ælkə‚laɪn] o ['ælkəlɪn] adj alcalino

all [ɔl] adj indef todo, todos; todo el, todos los || pron indef todo; todos, todo el mundo; after all sin embargo; all of todo el, todos los; all that todo lo que, todos los que; for all I know que yo sepa; a lo mejor; not at all nada; no hay de qué || adv enteramente; all along desde el principio; a lo largo de; all at once de golpe; all right bueno, corriente; all too excesivamente

Allah ['ælə] s Alá m

allay [ə'le] tr aliviar, calmar

all-clear ['ɔl'klɪr] s cese m de alarma

allege [ə'lɛdʒ] tr alegar

allegiance [ə'lidʒəns] s fidelidad, lealtad; homenaje m; to swear allegiance to jurar fidelidad a; rendir homenaje a

allegoric(al) [‚ælɪ'gɑrɪk(əl)] o [‚ælɪ'gɔrɪk(əl)] adj alegórico

allego-ry ['ælɪ‚gorɪ] s (pl -ries) alegoría

aller-gy ['ælərdʒɪ] s (pl -gies) alergia

alleviate [ə'livɪ‚et] tr aliviar

alley ['ælɪ] s callejuela; paseo arbolado, paseo de jardín; (bowling) pista; (tennis) espacio lateral

All Fools' Day s var of **April Fools' Day**

Allhallows [‚ɔl'hæloz] s día m de todos los santos

alliance [ə'laɪ‧əns] s alianza

alligator ['ælɪ‚getər] s caimán m

alligator pear s aguacate m

alligator wrench s llave f de mandíbulas dentadas

alliteration [ə‚lɪtə'reʃən] s aliteración

all-knowing ['ɔl'no‧ɪŋ] adj omnisciente

allocate ['ælə‚ket] tr asignar, distribuir

allot [ə'lɑt] v (pret & pp allotted; ger allotting) tr asignar, distribuir

all'-out' adj acérrimo

allow [ə'lau] tr dejar, permitir; admitir; conceder || intr — to allow for tener en cuenta; to allow of permitir; admitir

allowance [ə'lau‧əns] s permiso; concesión; ración; descuento, rebaja; tolerancia; to make allowance for tener en cuenta

alloy ['ælɔɪ] o [ə'lɔɪ] s aleación, liga || [ə'lɔɪ] tr alear, ligar

all-powerful ['ɔl'pau‧ərfəl] adj todopoderoso

All Saints' Day s día m de todos los santos

All Souls' Day s día m de los difuntos

allspice ['ɔl‚spaɪs] s pimienta inglesa

all'-star' game s (sport) juego de estrellas

allude [ə'lud] intr aludir

allure [ə'lur] s tentación, encanto, fascinación || tr tentar, encantar

alluring [ə'urɪŋ] adj tentador, encantador, fascinante

allusion [ə'luʒən] s alusión

al-ly ['ælaɪ] o ['ə'laɪ] s (pl -lies) aliado || [ə'laɪ] v (pret & pp -lied) tr aliar || intr aliarse

almanac ['ɔlmə‚næk] s almanaque m

almighty [ɔl'maɪtɪ] adj todopoderoso, omnipotente

almond ['ɑmənd] o ['æmənd] s almendra

almond brittle s crocante m

almond tree s almendro

almost ['ɔlmost] o [ɔl'most] adv casi

alms [ɑmz] s limosna

alms'house' s casa de beneficencia

aloe ['ælo] s áloe m

aloft [ə'lɔft] o [ə'lɑft] adv arriba; (aer) en vuelo; (naut) en la arboladura

alone [ə'lon] adj solo; let alone sin

mencionar; y mucho menos; **to let alone** no molestar; no mezclarse en || *adv* solamente

along [ə'lɔŋ] o [ə'lɑŋ] *adv* conmigo, consigo, etc.; **all along** desde el principio; **along with** junto con || *prep* a lo largo de

along·side' *adv* a lo largo; (naut) al costado; **to bring alongside** acostar || *prep* a lo largo de; (naut) al costado de

aloof [ə'luf] *adj* apartado; reservado || *adv* lejos, a distancia

aloud [ə'laud] *adv* alto, en voz alta

alphabet ['ælfə,bet] *s* alfabeto

alpine ['ælpaɪn] *adj* alpestre, alpino

Alps [ælps] *spl* Alpes *mpl*

already [ɔl'redi] *adv* ya

Alsace [æl'ses] o ['ælsæs] *s* Alsacia

Alsatian [æl'seʃən] *adj* & *s* alsaciano

also ['ɔlso] *adv* también

alt. *abbr* **alternate, altitude**

altar ['ɔltər] *s* altar *m*; **to lead to the altar** conducir al altar

altar boy *s* acólito, monaguillo

altar cloth *s* sabanilla, palia

al'tar-piece' *s* retablo

altar rail *s* comulgatorio

alter ['ɔltər] *tr* alterar || *intr* alterarse

alteration [,ɔltə'reʃən] *s* alteración; (*in a building*) reforma; (*in clothing*) arreglo

alternate ['ɔltərnɪt] o ['æltərnɪt] *adj* alterno || ['ɔltər,net] o ['æltər,net] *tr* & *intr* alternar

alternating current *s* corriente alterna o alternativa

although [ɔl'ðo] *conj* aunque

altimetry [æl'tɪmɪtri] *s* altimetría

altitude ['æltɪ,tjud] o ['æltɪ,tud] *s* altitud, altura

al·to ['ælto] *s* (*pl* -**tos**) contralto

altogether [,ɔltə'geðər] *adv* enteramente, en conjunto

altruist ['æltru·ɪst] *s* altruísta *mf*

altruistic [,æltru'ɪstɪk] *adj* altruísta

alum ['æləm] *s* alumbre *m*

aluminum [ə'lumɪnəm] *s* aluminio

alum·na [ə'lʌmnə] *s* (*pl* -**nae** [ni]) graduada

alum·nus [ə'lʌmnəs] *s* (*pl* -**ni** [naɪ]) graduado

alveo·lus [æl'vi·ələs] *s* (*pl* -**li** [,laɪ]) alvéolo

always ['ɔlwɪz] o ['ɔlwez] *adv* siempre

A.M. *abbr* **ante meridiem,** i.e., **before noon; amplitude modulation**

Am. *abbr* **America, American**

amalgam [ə'mælgəm] *s* amalgama *f*

amalgamate [ə'mælgə,met] *tr* amalgamar || *intr* amalgamarse

amass [ə'mæs] *tr* amontonar; amasar (*dinero*)

amateur ['æmət/ər] *adj* & *s* chapucero, principiante *mf*; aficionado

amateur performance *s* función de aficionados

amaze [ə'mez] *tr* asombrar, maravillar

amazing [ə'mezɪŋ] *adj* asombroso, maravilloso

Amazon ['æmə,zɑn] o ['æməzən] *s* Amazonas *m*

ambassador [æm'bæsədər] *s* embajador *m*

ambassadress [æm'bæsədrɪs] *s* embajadora

amber ['æmbər] *adj* ambarino || *s* ámbar *m*

ambigui·ty [,æmbɪ'gju·ɪti] *s* (*pl* -**ties**) ambigüidad

ambiguous [æm'bɪgju·əs] *adj* ambiguo

ambition [æm'bɪʃən] *s* ambición

ambitious [æm'bɪʃəs] *adj* ambicioso

amble ['æmbəl] *s* ambladura || *intr* amblar

ambulance ['æmbjələns] *s* ambulancia

ambush ['æmbuʃ] *s* emboscada; **to lie in ambush** estar emboscado || *tr* (*to station in ambush*) emboscar; (*to lie in wait for and attack*) insidiar || *intr* emboscarse

amelioration [ə,miljə'reʃən] *s* mejoramiento

amen ['e'men] o ['ɑ'men] *interj* ¡amén! || *s* amén *m*

amenable [ə'minəbəl] o [ə'menəbəl] *adj* dócil; responsable

amend [ə'mend] *tr* enmendar || *intr* enmendarse || **amends** *spl* enmienda; **to make amends for** enmendar

amendment [ə'mendmənt] *s* enmienda

ameni·ty [ə'minɪti] o [ə'menɪti] *s* (*pl* -**ties**) amenidad

America [ə'merɪkə] *s* América

American [ə'merɪkən] *adj* & *s* americano; norteamericano, estadounidense

Americanize [ə'merɪkə,naɪz] *tr* americanizar

amethyst ['æmɪθɪst] *s* amatista

amiable ['emɪ·əbəl] *adj* amable, bonachón

amicable ['æmɪkəbəl] *adj* amigable

amid [ə'mɪd] *prep* en medio de

amidship [ə'mɪd/ɪp] *adv* en medio del navío

amiss [ə'mɪs] *adj* inoportuno; malo || *adv* inoportunamente; mal; **to take amiss** llevar a mal, tomar en mala parte

ami·ty ['æmɪti] *s* (*pl* -**ties**) amistad

ammeter ['æm,mitər] *s* anmetro, amperímetro

ammonia [ə'monɪ·ə] *s* amoníaco; agua amoniacal

ammunition [,æmjə'nɪʃən] *s* munición

amnes·ty ['æmnɪsti] *s* (*pl* -**ties**) amnistía || *v* (*pret* & *pp* -**tied**) *tr* amnistiar

amoeba [ə'mibə] *s* amiba

among [ə'mʌŋ] *prep* entre, en medio de, en el número de

amorous ['æmərəs] *adj* amoroso; erótico, sensual, voluptuoso

amortize ['æmər,taɪz] *tr* amortizar

amount [ə'maunt] *s* cantidad, importe *m* || *intr* — **to amount to** ascender a; significar

amp. *abbr* **ampere, amperage**

ampere ['æmpɪr] *s* amperio

am'pere-hour' *s* amperio-hora *m*

amphibious [æm'fɪbɪ·əs] *adj* anfibio

amphitheater ['æmfɪ,θi·ətər] *s* anfiteatro

ample ['æmpəl] amplio; bastante, suficiente; abundante

amplifier ['æmplɪ ,faɪ·ər] s amplificador m

ampli·fy ['æmplɪ ,faɪ] v (pret & pp -fied) tr amplificar ǁ intr espaciarse

amplitude ['æmplɪ ,tjud] o ['æmplɪ ,tud] s amplitud

amplitude modulation s modulación de amplitud

amputate ['æmpjə ,tet] tr amputar

amt. abbr **amount**

amuck [ə'mʌk] adv frenéticamente; **to run amuck** atacar a ciegas

amulet ['æmjəlɪt] s amuleto

amuse [ə'mjuz] tr divertir, entretener

amusement [ə'mjuzmənt] s diversión, entretenimiento; pasatiempo, recreación; (in a park or circus) atracción

amusement park s parque m de atracciones

amusing [ə'mjuzɪŋ] adj divertido, gracioso

an [æn] o [ən] art indef (antes de sonido vocal) un

anachronism [ə'nækrə ,nɪzəm] s anacronismo

anaemia [ə'nimɪ·ə] s anemia

anaemic [ə'nimɪk] adj anémico

anaesthesia [,ænɪs'θiʒə] s anestesia

anaesthetic [,ænɪs'θetɪk] adj & s anestésico

anaesthetize [æ'nesθɪ ,taɪz] tr anestesiar

analogous [ə'næləgəs] adj análogo

analo·gy [ə'nælədʒɪ] s (pl -gies) analogía

analyse ['ænə ,laɪz] tr analizar

analy·sis [ə'nælɪsɪs] s (pl -ses [,siz]) análisis m & f

analyst ['ænəlɪst] s analista mf

analytic(al) [,ænə'lɪtɪk(əl)] adj analítico

analyze ['ænə ,laɪz] tr analizar

anarchist ['ænərkɪst] s anarquista mf

anarchy ['ænərkɪ] s anarquía

anathema [ə'næθɪmə] s anatema m & f

anatomic(al) [,ænə'tɑmɪk(əl)] adj anatómico

anato·my [ə'nætəmɪ] s (pl -mies) anatomía

ancestor ['ænsestər] s antecesor m, antepasado

ances·try ['ænsestrɪ] s (pl -tries) abolengo, alcurnia

anchor ['æŋkər] s ancla, áncora; (fig) áncora; **to cast anchor** echar anclas; **to weigh anchor** levar anclas ǁ tr sujetar con el ancla ǁ intr anclar, ancorar

ancho·vy ['æntʃovɪ] s (pl -vies) anchoa

ancient ['enʃənt] adj antiguo

and [ænd] o [ənd] conj y; **and so forth** y así sucesivamente

Andalusia [,ændə'luʒə] s Andalucía

Andalusian [,ændə'luʒən] adj & s andaluz m

Andean [æn'di·ən] o ['ændɪ·ən] adj & s andino

Andes ['ændiz] spl Andes mpl

andirons ['ænd ,aɪ·ərnz] spl morillos

anecdote ['ænɪk ,dot] s anécdota

anemia [ə'nimɪ·ə] s anemia

anemic [ə'nimɪk] adj anémico

aneroid barometer ['ænə ,rɔɪd] s barómetro aneroide

anesthesia [,ænɪs'θiʒə] s anestesia

anesthetic [,ænɪs'θetɪk] adj & s anestésico

anesthetize [æ'nesθɪ ,taɪz] tr anestesiar

aneurysm ['ænjə ,rɪzəm] s aneurisma m

anew [ə'nju] o [ə'nu] adv de nuevo, nuevamente

angel ['endʒəl] s ángel m; (financial backer) caballo blanco

angelic(al) [æn'dʒelɪk(əl)] adj angélico, angelical

anger ['æŋgər] s cólera, ira ǁ tr encolerizar, airar

angina pectoris [æn'dʒaɪnə 'pektərɪs] s angina de pecho

angle ['æŋgəl] s ángulo; punto de vista ǁ intr pescar con caña; intrigar

angle iron s ángulo de hierro, hierro angular

angler ['æŋglər] s pescador m de caña; intrigante mf

Anglo-Saxon [,æŋglo'sæksən] adj & s anglosajón m

an·gry ['æŋgri] adj (comp -grier; super -griest) encolerizado, airado; (pathol) inflamado, irritado; **to become angry at** enojarse de; **to become angry with** enojarse con o contra

anguish ['æŋgwɪʃ] s angustia, congoja

angular ['æŋgjələr] adj angular; (features) anguloso

anhydrous [æn'haɪdrəs] adj anhidro

aniline dyes ['ænɪlɪn] o ['ænɪ ,laɪn] s colores mpl de anilina

animal ['ænɪməl] adj & s animal m

animal spirits spl ardor m, vigor m, vivacidad

animated cartoon ['ænɪ ,metɪd] s película de dibujos, dibujo animado

animation [,ænɪ'meʃən] s animación

animosi·ty [,ænɪ'mɑsɪtɪ] s (pl -ties) animosidad

anion ['æn ,aɪ·ən] s anión m

anise ['ænɪs] s anís m

aniseed ['ænɪ ,sid] s grano de anís

anisette [,ænɪ'zet] s anisete m

ankle ['æŋkəl] s tobillo

an'kle-bone s hueso del tobillo

ankle support s tobillera

anklet ['æŋklɪt] s ajorca; (sock) tobillera

annals ['ænəlz] spl anales mpl

anneal [ə'nil] tr recocer

annex ['æneks] s anexo; (of a building) pabellón m ǁ [ə'neks] tr anexar

annihilate [ə'naɪ·ɪ ,let] tr aniquilar

anniversa·ry [,ænɪ'vʌrsərɪ] adj aniversario ǁ s (pl -ries) aniversario

annotate ['ænə ,tet] tr anotar

announce [ə'nauns] tr anunciar

announcement [ə'naunsmənt] s anuncio

announcer [ə'naunsər] s anunciador m; (rad) locutor m

annoy [ə'nɔɪ] tr fastidiar, molestar

annoyance [ə'nɔɪ·əns] s fastidio, molestia

annoying [ə'nɔɪ·ɪŋ] adj fastidioso, molesto

annual ['ænju·əl] adj anual ǁ s publicación anual; planta anual

annui·ty [ə'nju·ɪtɪ] o [ə'nu·ɪtɪ] s (pl -ties) anualidad; renta vitalicia

an·nul [ə'nʌl] v (pret & pp -nulled; ger -nulling) tr anular, invalidar

anode ['ænod] s ánodo

anoint [ə'nɔɪnt] tr ungir, untar

anomalous [ə'nɑmələs] adj anómalo

anoma·ly [ə'nɑmɛlɪ] s (pl -lies) anomalía

anon. abbr anonymous

anonymity [,ænə'nɪmɪtɪ] s anónimo; to preserve one's anonymity guardar o conservar el anónimo

anonymous [ə'nɑnɪməs] adj anónimo

another [ə'nʌðər] adj & pron indef otro

ans. abbr answer

answer ['ænsər] o ['ɑnsər] s contestación, respuesta; (to a problem or puzzle) solución || tr contestar, responder; resolver (un problema o un enigma) || intr contestar, responder; to answer for responder de (una cosa); responder por (una persona)

ant [ænt] s hormiga

antagonism [æn'tægə,nɪzəm] s antagonismo

antagonize [æn'tægə,naɪz] tr oponerse a; enemistar, enajenar

antarctic [ænt'ɑrktɪk] adj antártico || the Antarctic las Tierras Antárticas

antecedent [,æntɪ'sidənt] adj antecedente || s antecedente m; antecedents antecedentes mpl; antepasados

antechamber ['æntɪ,tʃembər] s antecámara

antedate ['æntɪ,det] tr antedatar; preceder

antelope ['æntɪ,lop] s antílope m

anten·na [æn'tɛnə] s (pl -nae [ni]) (ent) antena || s (pl -nas) (rad) antena

antepenult [,æntɪ'pinʌlt] s antepenúltima

anteroom ['æntɪ,rum] o ['æntɪ,rʊm] s antecámara

anthem ['ænθəm] s himno; antífona

ant'hill' s hormiguero

antholo·gy [æn'θɑlədʒɪ] s (pl -gies) antología

anthracite ['ænθrə,saɪt] s antracita

anthrax ['ænθræks] s ántrax m

anthropology [,ænθrə'pɑlədʒɪ] s antropología

anti-aircraft [,æntɪ'ɛr,kræft] o [,æntɪ'ɛr,krɑft] adj antiaéreo

antibiotic [,æntɪbaɪ'atɪk] adj & s antibiótico

antibod·y ['æntɪ,badɪ] s (pl -ies) anticuerpo

anticipate [æn'tɪsɪ,pet] tr esperar, prever; anticipar; (to get ahead of) anticiparse a; impedir; prometerse (p. ej., un placer); temerse (algo desagradable)

antics ['æntɪks] spl cabriolas, gracias, travesuras

antidote ['æntɪ,dot] s antídoto

antifreeze [,æntɪ'friz] s anticongelante m

antiglare [,æntɪ'glɛr] adj antideslumbrante

antiknock [,æntɪ'nɑk] adj & s antidetonante m

antilabor [,æntɪ'lebər] adj antiobrero

Antilles [æn'tɪlɪz] spl Antillas

antimissile [,æntɪ'mɪsɪl] adj antiproyectil

antimony ['æntɪ,monɪ] s antimonio

antipas·to [,ɑntɪ'pɑsto] s (pl -tos) aperitivo, entremés m

antipa·thy [æn'tɪpəθɪ] s (pl -thies) antipatía

antiquar·y ['æntɪ,kwɛrɪ] s (pl -ies) anticuario

antiquated ['æntɪ,kwetɪd] adj anticuado

antique [æn'tik] adj antiguo || s antigüedad

antique dealer s anticuario

antique store s tienda de antigüedades

antiqui·ty [æn'tɪkwɪtɪ] s (pl -ties) antigüedad

anti-Semitic [,æntɪsɪ'mɪtɪk] adj antisemítico

antiseptic [,æntɪ'sɛptɪk] adj & s antiséptico

antislavery [,æntɪ'slevərɪ] adj antiesclavista

anti-Soviet [,æntɪ'sovɪ,ɛt] adj antisoviético

antitank [,æntɪ'tæŋk] adj antitanque

antithe·sis [æn'tɪθɪsɪs] s (pl -ses [,siz]) antítesis f

antitoxin [,æntɪ'taksɪn] s antitoxina

antitrust [,æntɪ'trʌst] adj anticartel

antiwar [,æntɪ'wɔr] adj antibélico

antler ['æntlər] s cuerna

antonym ['æntənɪm] s antónimo

Antwerp ['æntwərp] s Amberes f

anvil ['ænvɪl] s yunque m

anxie·ty [æŋ'zaɪ·ətɪ] s (pl -ties) ansiedad, inquietud; ansia, anhelo

anxious ['æŋk/əs] adj ansioso, inquieto; anhelante; to be anxious to tener ganas de

any ['ɛnɪ] adj indef algún, cualquier; todo; any place dondequiera; any time cuando quiera; alguna vez || pron indef alguno, cualquiera || adv algo

an'y·bod'y pron indef alguno, alguien, cualquiera, quienquiera; todo el mundo; not anybody nadie

an'y·how' adv de cualquier modo; de todos modos; sin embargo

an'y·one' pron indef alguno, alguien, cualquiera

an'y·thing' pron indef algo, alguna cosa; cualquier cosa; todo cuanto; anything at all cualquier cosa que sea; anything else cualquier otra cosa; anything else? ¿algo más?; not anything nada

an'y·way' adv de cualquier modo; de todos modos; sin embargo; sin esmero, sin orden ni concierto

an'y·where' adv dondequiera; adondequiera; not anywhere en ninguna parte

apace [ə'pes] adv aprisa

apart [ə'part] adv aparte; en pedazos; to fall apart caerse a pedazos; desunirse; ir al desastre; to live apart vivir separados; vivir aislado; to stand apart mantenerse apartado; to take apart descomponer, desarmar, desmontar; to tell apart distinguir

apartment [ə'pɑrtmənt] s apartamento

apartment house s casa de pisos

apathetic [ˌæpə'θεtɪk] adj apático

apa·thy ['æpəθɪ] s (pl -ties) apatía

ape [ep] s mono || tr imitar, remedar

aperture ['æpərtʃər] s abertura, orificio

apex ['epɛks] s (pl apexes o apices ['æpɪ,siz]) ápex m, ápice m

aphorism ['æfə,rɪzəm] s aforismo

aphrodisiac [ˌæfrə'dɪzɪˌæk] adj & s afrodisíaco

apiar·y ['epɪ,ɛrɪ] s (pl -ies) abejar m, colmenar m

apiece [ə'pis] adv cada uno; por persona

apish ['epɪʃ] adj monesco; tonto

aplomb [ə'plɑm] s aplomo, sangre fría

apogee ['æpə,dʒi] s apogeo

apologetic [əˌpɑlə'dʒɛtɪk] adj lleno de excusas

apologize [ə'pɑlə,dʒaɪz] intr excusarse, disculparse; to apologize for disculparse de; to apologize to disculparse con

apolo·gy [ə'pɑlədʒɪ] s (pl -gies) excusa; (makeshift) expediente m

apoplectic [ˌæpə'plɛktɪk] adj & s apoplético

apoplexy ['æpə,plɛksɪ] s apoplejía

apostle [ə'pɑsəl] s apóstol m

apostrophe [ə'pɑstrəfɪ] s (written sign) apóstrofo; (words addressed to absent person) apóstrofe m & f

apothecar·y [ə'pɑθɪ,kɛrɪ] s (pl -ies) boticario

apothecary's jar s bote m de porcelana

apothecary's shop s botica

appall [ə'pɔl] tr espantar, pasmar

appalling [ə'pɔlɪŋ] adj aterrador, espantoso, pasmoso

appara·tus [ˌæpə'rɛtəs] o [ˌæpə'rætəs] s (pl -tus o -tuses) aparato

apparel [ə'pærəl] s indumentaria, vestido

apparent [ə'pærənt] o [ə'pɛrənt] adj aparente

apparition [ˌæpə'rɪʃən] s aparición

appeal [ə'pil] s súplica, instancia, solicitud; atracción, interés m; (law) apelación || intr ser atrayente; to appeal to (to make an entreaty to) suplicar; (to be attractive to) atraer, interesar; (law) apelar a

appear [ə'pɪr] intr (to come into sight; to be in sight; to be published) aparecer; (to come into sight; to be in sight; to look; to seem) parecer; (to come before the public) presentarse; (to come before a court) comparecer

appearance [ə'pɪrəns] s (act of appearing) aparición; (outward look) apariencia, aspecto; (law) comparecencia

appease [ə'piz] tr apaciguar

appeasement [ə'pizmənt] s apaciguamiento

appendage [ə'pɛndɪdʒ] s apéndice m

appendicitis [əˌpɛndɪ'saɪtɪs] s apendicitis f

appen·dix [ə'pɛndɪks] s (pl -dixes o -dices [dɪˌsiz]) apéndice m

appertain [ˌæpər'ten] intr relacionarse

appetite ['æpɪˌtaɪt] s apetito

appetizer ['æpɪˌtaɪzər] s aperitivo, apetite m

appetizing ['æpɪˌtaɪzɪŋ] adj apetitoso

applaud [ə'plɔd] tr & intr aplaudir

applause [ə'plɔz] s aplauso, aplausos

apple ['æpəl] s manzana

ap'ple·jack' s aguardiente m de manzana

apple of the eye s niña del ojo

apple pie s pastel m de manzana

apple polisher s (slang) quitamotas mf

ap'ple·sauce' s compota de manzanas; (slang) música celestial

apple tree s manzano

appliance [ə'plaɪ·əns] s artificio, dispositivo, aparato; aplicación

applicant ['æplɪkənt] s aspirante mf, pretendiente mf, solicitante mf

ap·ply [ə'plaɪ] v (pret & pp -plied) tr aplicar || intr aplicarse; dirigirse; to apply for pedir, solicitar

appoint [ə'pɔɪnt] tr designar, nombrar; señalar; amueblar

appointment [ə'pɔɪntmənt] s designación, nombramiento; empleo, puesto; cita; appointments instalación, accesorios, adornos; by appointment cita previa

apportion [ə'pɔrʃən] tr prorratear

appraisal [ə'prezəl] s tasación, valoración, apreciación

appraise [ə'prez] tr tasar, valorar, apreciar

appreciable [ə'priʃɪ·əbəl] adj apreciable; sensible

appreciate [ə'priʃɪ,et] tr apreciar; aprobar; comprender; estar agradecido por || intr subir de valor

appreciation [əˌpriʃɪ'eʃən] s aprecio; agradecimiento; plusvalía, aumento de valor

appreciative [ə'priʃɪ,etɪv] adj apreciador; agradecido

apprehend [ˌæprɪ'hɛnd] tr aprehender, prender; comprender; temer

apprehension [ˌæprɪ'hɛnʃən] s aprehensión; (fear, worry) aprensión; comprensión

apprehensive [ˌæprɪ'hɛnsɪv] adj (fearful, worried) aprehensivo, aprensivo

apprentice [ə'prɛntɪs] s aprendiz m, meritorio || tr poner de aprendiz

apprenticeship [ə'prɛntɪs,ʃɪp] s aprendizaje m

apprise o **apprize** [ə'praɪz] tr informar; apreciar, tasar

approach [ə'protʃ] s acercamiento; vía de entrada; proposición; (to a problem) enfoque m || tr abordar, acercarse a; (to bring closer) acercar || intr acercarse, aproximarse

approbation [ˌæprə'beʃən] s aprobación

appropriate [ə'propri·ɪt] adj apropiado, a propósito || [ə'propri,et] tr apropiarse; asignar, destinar (*el parlamento determinada suma a un determinada fin*)

approval [ə'pruvəl] *s* aprobación; **on approval** a prueba

approve [ə'pruv] *tr & intr* aprobar

approximate [ə'prɑksımıt] *adj* aproximado || [ə'prɑksı‚met] *tr* aproximar || *intr* aproximarse

apricot l'epri‚kɑt] o ['æpri‚kɑt] *s* albaricoque *m*

apricot tree *s* albaricoquero

April ['epril] *s* abril *m*

April fool *s* — **to make an April fool of** coger por inocente

April Fools' Day *s* día *m* de engañabobos, primer día de abril, en que se coge por inocente a la gente

apron ['eprən] *s* delantal *m*; (*of a workman*) mandil *m*; **tied to the apron strings of** cosido a las faldas de

apropos [‚æprə'po] *adj* oportuno || *adv* a propósito; **apropos of** a propósito de

apse [æps] *s* ábside *m*

apt [æpt] *adj* apto; a propósito; dispuesto, inclinado

aptitude ['æpti‚tjud] o ['æpti‚tud] *s* aptitud

aquamarine [‚ækwəmə'rin] *s* aguamarina

aquaplane ['ækwə‚plen] *s* acuaplano || *intr* correr en acuaplano

aquari•um [ə'kwerı‚əm] *s* (*pl* -**ums** o -**a** [ə]) acuario

aquatic [ə'kwætık] o [ə'kwɑtık] *adj* acuático || **aquatics** *spl* deportes acuáticos

aqueduct ['ækwə‚dʌkt] *s* acueducto

aquiline nose ['ækwı‚laın] *s* nariz aguileña

Arab ['ærəb] *adj* árabe || *s* árabe *mf*; caballo árabe

Arabia [ə'rebı‚ə] *s* la Arabia

Arabian [ə'rebı‚ən] *adj* árabe; arábigo || *s* árabe *mf*

Arabic l'ærəbık] *adj* arábigo || *s* árabe *m*, arábigo

Aragon ['ærə‚gɑn] *s* Aragón *m*

Arago•nese [‚ærəgə'niz] *adj* aragonés || *s* (*pl* -**nese**) aragonés *m*

arbiter ['ɑrbıtər] *s* árbitro

arbitrary ['ɑrbı‚treri] *adj* arbitrario

arbitrate ['ɑrbı‚tret] *tr & intr* arbitrar

arbitration [‚ɑrbı'treʃən] *s* arbitraje *m*

arbor ['ɑrbər] *s* emparrado, glorieta

arbore•tum [‚ɑrbə'ritəm] *s* (*pl* -**tums** o -**ta** [tə]) jardín botánico de árboles

arbor vitae ['ɑrbər 'vaıti] *s* árbol *m* de la vida

arbutus [ɑr'bjutəs] *s* madroño

arc [ɑrk] *s* arco

arcade [ɑr'ked] *s* arcada, galería

arch. *abbr* **archaic, archaism, archipelago, architect**

arch [ɑrtʃ] *adj* astuto; travieso; principal || *s* arco || *tr* arquear, enarcar; atravesar

archaeology [‚ɑrkı'ɑlədʒı] *s* arqueología

archaic [ɑr'ke‚ık] *adj* arcaico

archaism ['ɑrke‚ızəm] o ['ɑrkı‚ızəm] *s* arcaísmo

archangel ['ɑrk‚endʒəl] *s* arcángel *m*

archbishop ['ɑrtʃ'bı‚əp] *s* arzobispo

archduke l'ɑrtʃ'djuk] o ['ɑrtʃ'duk] *s* archiduque *m*

archene•my ['ɑrtʃ‚ænımı] *s* (*pl* -**mies**) archienemigo

archeology [‚ɑrkı'ɑlədʒı] *s* arqueología

archer l'ɑrtʃər] *s* arquero, flechero

archery l'ɑrtʃərı] *s* tiro de flechas

archipela•go [‚ɑrkı'peləgo] *s* (*pl* -**gos** o -**goes**) archipiélago

architect l'ɑrkı‚tekt] *s* arquitecto

architectural [‚ɑrkı'tektʃərəl] *adj* arquitectónico, arquitectural

architecture ['ɑrkı‚tektʃər] *s* arquitectura

archives l'ɑrkaıvz] *spl* archivo

arch'way' *s* arcada

arc lamp *s* lámpara de arco

arctic ['ɑrktık] *adj* ártico || **the Arctic** las Tierras Árticas

arc welding *s* soldadura de arco

ardent l'ɑrdənt] *adj* ardiente

ardor l'ɑrdər] *s* ardor *m*

arduous ['ɑrdʒu‚əs] o ['ɑrdju‚əs] *adj* arduo, difícil; enérgico; (*steep*) escarpado

area ['eri‚ə] *s* área, superficie *f*; comarca, región; zona; patio

ar'ea‚way' *s* entrada baja de un sótano

Argentina [‚ɑrdʒən'tinə] *s* la Argentina

Argentine ['ɑrdʒən‚tin] o ['ɑrdʒən‚taın] *adj & s* argentino || **the Argentine** la Argentina

Argentinean [‚ɑrdʒən'tinı‚ən] *adj & s* argentino

Argonaut ['ɑrgə‚nɔt] *s* argonauta *m*

argue ['ɑrgju] *tr* argüir; **to argue into** persuadir a + *inf*; **to argue out of** disuadir de + *inf* || *intr* argüir

argument l'ɑrgjəmənt] *s* argumento; disputa

argumentative [‚ɑrgjə'mentatıv] *adj* argumentador

aria ['ɑrı‚ə] o ['erı‚ə] *s* (mus) aria

arid l'ærıd] *adj* árido

aridity [ə'rıdıtı] *s* aridez *f*

aright [ə'raıt] *adv* acertadamente; **to set aright** rectificar

arise [ə'raız] *v* (*pret* **arose** [ə'roz]; *pp* **arisen** [ə'rızən]) *intr* levantarse; subir; aparecer; **to arise from** provenir de

aristocra•cy [‚ærıs'tɑkrəsı] *s* (*pl* -**cies**) aristocracia

aristocrat [ə'rıstə‚kræt] *s* aristócrata *mf*

aristocratic [ə‚rıstə'krætık] *adj* aristocrático

Aristotelian [‚ærıstə'tilı‚ən] *adj & s* aristotélico

Aristotle l'ærı‚tɑtəl] *s* Aristóteles *m*

arith. *abbr* **arithmetic**

arithmetic [ə'rıθmətık] *s* aritmética

arithmetical [‚ærıθ'metıkəl] *adj* aritmético

arithmetician [ə‚rıθmə'tıʃən] *s* aritmético

ark [ɑrk] *s* arca de Noé

ark of the covenant *s* arca de la alianza
arm [ɑrm] *s* brazo; (*weapon*) arma; **arm in arm** de bracero, asidos del brazo; **in arms** de pecho, de teta; **the three arms of the service** los tres ejércitos; **to be up in arms** estar en armas; **to keep at arm's length** mantener a distancia; mantenerse a distancia; **to lay down one's arms** rendir las armas; **to rise up in arms** alzarse en armas; **under arms** sobre las armas || *tr* armar || *intr* armarse
armament ['ɑrməmənt] *s* armamento
armature ['ɑrmə,tʃər] *s* armadura; (*of a dynamo or motor*) (elec) inducido
arm'chair' *adj* de gabinete || *s* butaca, sillón *m*, silla de brazos
Armenian [ɑr'minɪ·ən] *adj* & *s* armenio
armful ['ɑrm,ful] *s* brazado
arm'hole' *s* (*in clothing*) sobaquera
armistice ['ɑrmɪstɪs] *s* armisticio
armor ['ɑrmər] *s* armadura; coraza, blindaje *m* || *tr* acorazar, blindar
armored car *s* carro blindado
armorial bearings [ɑr'morɪ·əl] *spl* blasón *m*, escudo de armas
armor plate *s* plancha de blindaje
ar'mor-plate' *tr* acorazar, blindar
armor·y ['ɑrməri] *s* (*pl* -ies) arsenal *m*; (*arms factory*) armería
arm'pit' *s* sobaco, hueco de la axila
arm'rest' *s* apoyabrazos *m*
ar·my ['ɑrmi] *adj* militar, castrense || *s* (*pl* -mies) ejército
army corps *s* cuerpo de ejército
aroma [ə'romə] *s* aroma *m*, fragancia
aromatic [,ærə'mætɪk] *adj* aromático
around [ə'raund] *adv* alrededor, a la redonda; en la dirección opuesta || *prep* alrededor de, en torno a o de; cerca de; (*the corner*) a la vuelta de
arouse [ə'rauz] *tr* despertar; excitar, incitar
arpeg·gio [ɑr'pedʒo] *s* (*pl* -glos) arpegio
arraign [ə'ren] *tr* acusar; presentar al tribunal
arrange [ə'rendʒ] *tr* arreglar, disponer; (mus) adaptar, refundir
array [ə're] *s* orden *m*; orden *m* de batalla; adorno, atavío || *tr* poner en orden; poner en orden de batalla; adornar, ataviar
arrears [ə'rɪrz] *spl* atrasos; **in arrears** atrasado en pagos
arrest [ə'rest] *s* arresto, prisión; detención; **under arrest** bajo arresto || *tr* arrestar; detener; atraer (*la atención*)
arresting [ə'restɪŋ] *adj* impresionante
arrival [ə'raɪvəl] *s* llegada; (*person*) llegado
arrive [ə'raɪv] *intr* llegar; tener éxito
arrogance ['ærəgəns] *s* arrogancia
arrogant ['ærəgənt] *adj* arrogante
arrogate ['ærə,get] *tr* — **to arrogate to oneself** arrogarse
arrow ['æro] *s* flecha
ar'row-head' *s* punta de flecha; (bot) saetilla
arsenal ['ɑrsənəl] *s* arsenal *m*

arsenic ['ɑrsɪnɪk] *s* arsénico
arson ['ɑrsən] *s* incendio premeditado, delito de incendio
art [ɑrt] *s* arte *m* & *f*
arter·y ['ɑrtəri] *s* (*pl* -ies) arteria
artful ['ɑrtfəl] *adj* astuto, mañoso; diestro, ingenioso
arthritic [ɑr'θrɪtɪk] *adj* & *s* artrítico
arthritis [ɑr'θraɪtɪs] *s* artritis *f*
artichoke ['ɑrtɪ,tʃok] *s* alcachofa
article ['ɑrtɪkəl] *s* artículo; **an article of clothing** una prenda de vestir
articulate [ɑr'tɪkjəlɪt] *adj* claro, distinto; capaz de hablar || [ɑr'tɪkjə,let] *tr* articular
artifact ['ɑrtɪ,fækt] *s* artefacto
artifice ['ɑrtɪfɪs] *s* artificio
artificial [,ɑrtɪ'fɪʃəl] *adj* artificial
artillery [ɑr'tɪləri] *s* artillería
artillery-man [ɑr'tɪlərimən] *s* (*pl* -men [mən]) artillero
artisan ['ɑrtɪzən] *s* artesano
artist ['ɑrtɪst] *s* artista *mf*
artistic [ɑr'tɪstɪk] *adj* artístico
artistry ['ɑrtɪstri] *s* habilidad artística
artless ['ɑrtlɪs] *adj* sencillo, natural; ingenuo, inocente; (*crude, clumsy*) chabacano
arts and crafts *spl* artes y oficios
art·y ['ɑrti] *adj* (*comp* -ier; *super* -iest) (coll) ostentosamente artístico
Aryan ['ɛrɪ·ən] o ['ɑrjən] *adj* & *s* ario
as [æz] o [əz] *pron rel* que; **the same as** el mismo que || *adv* tan; **as . . . as** tan . . . como; **as for** en cuanto a; **as long as** mientras que; ya que; **as many as** tantos como; **as much as** tanto como; **as regards** en cuanto a; **as soon as** tan pronto como; **as soon as possible** cuanto antes, lo más pronto posible; **as though** como si; **as to** en cuanto a; **as well** también; **as yet** hasta ahora || *conj* como; que; ya que; a medida que; **as it seems** por lo visto, según parece || *prep* por, como; **as a rule** por regla general
asbestos [æs'bɛstəs] *s* asbesto, amianto
ascend [ə'sɛnd] *tr* subir a (*p.ej., el trono*) || *intr* ascender
ascendancy [ə'sɛndənsi] *s* ascendiente *m*
ascension [ə'sɛnʃən] *s* ascensión
Ascension Day *s* fiesta de la Ascensión
ascent [ə'sɛnt] *s* ascensión, subida; ascenso, promoción
ascertain [,æsər'ten] *tr* averiguar
ascertainable [,æsər'tenəbəl] *adj* averiguable
ascetic [ə'sɛtɪk] *adj* ascético || *s* asceta *mf*
ascorbic acid [ə'skɔrbɪk] *s* ácido ascórbico
ascribe [ə'skraɪb] *tr* atribuir
aseptic [ə'sɛptɪk] o [e'sɛptɪk] *adj* aséptico
ash [æʃ] *s* ceniza; (*tree; wood*) fresno; **ashes** ceniza, cenizas; (*mortal remains*) cenizas
ashamed [ə'ʃemd] *adj* avergonzado; **to be ashamed** tener vergüenza
ashlar ['æʃlər] *s* sillar *m*
ashore [ə'ʃor] *adv* en tierra, a tierra

ash tray s cenicero
Ash Wednesday s miércoles m de ceniza
Asia ['eʒə] o ['eʃə] s Asia
Asia Minor s el Asia Menor
Asian ['eʒən] o ['eʃən] o **Asiatic** [,eʒɪ'ætɪk] o [,eʃɪ'ætɪk] adj & s asiático
aside [ə'saɪd] adv aparte; **aside from** además de; **to step aside** hacerse a un lado ‖ s (theat) aparte m
asinine ['æsɪ,naɪn] adj tonto, necio
ask [æsk] o [ɑsk] tr (to request) pedir; (to inquire of) preguntar; hacer (una pregunta); invitar; **to ask in** invitar a entrar ‖ intr — **to ask about, after,** or **for** preguntar por; **to ask for** pedir
askance [ə'skæns] adv al sesgo, de soslayo; con desdén, sospechosamente
asleep [ə'slip] adj dormido; **to fall asleep** dormirse
asp [æsp] s áspid m
asparagus [ə'spærəgəs] s espárrago
aspect ['æspekt] s aspecto
aspen ['æspən] s tiemblo, álamo temblón
aspersion [ə'spʌrʒən] o [ə'spʌrʃən] s calumnia, difamación
asphalt ['æsfɔlt] o ['æsfælt] s asfalto ‖ tr asfaltar
asphyxiate [æs'fɪksɪ,et] tr asfixiar
aspirant [ə'spaɪrənt] o ['æspɪrənt] s pretendiente mf, candidato
aspire [ə'spaɪr] intr aspirar
aspirin ['æspɪrɪn] s aspirina
ass [æs] s asno
assail [ə'sel] tr asaltar, acometer
assassin [ə'sæsɪn] s asesino
assassinate [ə'sæsɪ,net] tr asesinar
assassination [ə,sæsɪ'neʃən] s asesinato
assault [ə'sɔlt] s asalto ‖ tr asaltar
assault and battery s vías de hecho, violencias
assay [ə'se] o ['æse] s ensaye m; muestra de ensaye ‖ [ə'se] tr ensayar; apreciar
assemble [ə'sembəl] tr reunir; (mach) armar, montar ‖ intr reunirse
assem-bly [ə'semblɪ] s (pl -blies) asamblea; reunión; (mach) armadura, montaje m
assembly hall s aula magna, paraninfo; salón m de sesiones
assembly line s línea de montaje
assembly plant s fábrica de montaje
assembly room s sala de reunión; (mach) taller m de montaje
assent [ə'sent] s asentimiento, asenso ‖ intr asentir
assert [ə'sʌrt] tr afirmar, aseverar, declarar; **to assert oneself** imponerse, hacer valer sus derechos
assertion [ə'sʌrʃən] s aserción, aseveración
assess [ə'ses] tr amillarar, gravar; fijar (daños y perjuicios); apreciar, estimar
assessment [ə'sesmənt] s amillaramiento, gravamen m; fijación; apreciación, estimación

asset ['æset] s posesión, ventaja; (person, thing, or quality worth having) (fig) valor m; **assets** (com) activo
assiduous [ə'sɪdʒu·əs] o [ə'sɪdju·əs] adj asiduo
assign [ə'saɪn] tr asignar
assignment [ə'saɪnmənt] s asignación, cometido; lección
assimilate [ə'sɪmɪ,let] tr asimilarse (los alimentos, el conocimiento) ‖ intr asimilarse
assist [ə'sɪst] tr ayudar, asistir, auxiliar
assistant [ə'sɪstənt] adj & s auxiliar mf, ayudante mf
assn. abbr **association**
associate [ə'soʃɪ,ɪt] o [ə'soʃɪ,et] adj asociado ‖ s asociado, socio ‖ [ə'soʃɪ,et] tr asociar ‖ intr asociarse
association [ə,soʃɪ'eʃən] s asociación
assort [ə'sɔrt] tr clasificar, ordenar
assortment [ə'sɔrtmənt] s surtido; clase f, grupo
asst. abbr **assistant**
assume [ə'sum] o [ə'sjum] tr asumir (p.ej., responsabilidades); arrogarse; suponer, dar por sentado
assumption [ə'sʌmpʃən] s asunción; suposición
assurance [ə'ʃurəns] s aseguramiento; seguridad, confianza; (com) seguro
assure [ə'ʃur] tr asegurar; (com) asegurar
Assyria [ə'sɪrɪ·ə] s Asiria
Assyrian [ə'sɪrɪ·ən] adj & s asirio
astatine ['æstə,tin] s ástato
aster ['æstər] s (bot) aster m; (China aster) reina Margarita
asterisk ['æstə,rɪsk] s asterisco
astern [ə'stʌrn] adv por la popa
asthma ['æzmə] o ['æsmə] s asma f
astonish [ə'stanɪʃ] tr asombrar
astonishing [ə'stanɪʃɪŋ] adj asombroso
astound [ə'staund] tr pasmar
astounding [ə'staundɪŋ] adj pasmoso
astraddle [ə'strædəl] adv a horcajadas
astray [ə'stre] adv por mal camino; **to go astray** extraviarse; **to lead astray** extraviar
astride [ə'straɪd] adv a horcajadas ‖ prep a horcajadas de
astrology [ə'stralədʒɪ] s astrología
astronaut ['æstrə,nɔt] s astronauta m
astronautic [,æstrə'nɔtɪk] adj astronáutico ‖ **astronautics** s astronáutica
astronomer [ə'stranəmər] s astrónomo
astronomic(al) [,æstrə'namɪk(əl)] adj astronómico
astronomy [ə'stranəmɪ] s astronomía
Asturian [æs'sturɪ·ən] adj & s asturiano
astute [ə'stjut] o [ə'stut] adj astuto, sagaz
asunder [ə'sʌndər] adv a pedazos, en dos
asylum [ə'saɪləm] s asilo
asymmetry [ə'sɪmɪtrɪ] s asimetría
at [æt] o [ət] prep en, p.ej., **I saw her at the library** la ví en la biblioteca; a, p.ej., **at five o'clock** a las cinco; de, p.ej., **to be surprised at** estar sorprendido de; **to laugh at** reírse de; en casa de, p.ej., **at John's** en casa de Juan

atheism ['eθɪ,ɪzəm] s ateísmo
atheist ['eθɪ.ɪst] s ateísta mf, ateo
Athenian [ə'θinɪ.ən] adj & s ateniense mf
Athens ['æθɪnz] s Atenas f
athirst [ə'θʌrst] adj sediento
athlete ['æθlit] s atleta mf
athlete's foot s pie m de atleta
athletic [æθ'lɛtɪk] adj atlético || **athletics** s atletismo
Atlantic [æt'læntɪk] adj & s Atlántico
atlas ['ætləs] s atlas m
atmosphere ['ætməs,fɪr] s atmósfera
atmospheric [,ætməs'fɛrɪk] adj atmosférico || **atmospherics** spl parásitos atmosféricos
atom ['ætəm] s átomo
atom bomb s bomba atómica
atomic [ə'tɑmɪk] adj atómico
atomic bomb s bomba atómica
atomize ['ætə,maɪz] tr atomizar
atomizer ['ætə,maɪzər] s pulverizador m, vaporizador m
atom smasher s rompeátomos m
atone [ə'ton] intr dar reparación; to **atone for** dar reparación por, expiar
atonement [ə'tonmənt] s reparación, expiación
atop [ə'tɑp] adv encima || prep encima de
atrocious [ə'troʃəs] adj atroz; (coll) abominable, muy malo
atroci·ty [ə'trɑsɪti] s (pl -ties) atrocidad
atro·phy ['ætrəfi] s atrofia || v (pret & pp -phied) tr atrofiar || intr atrofiarse
attach [ə'tætʃ] tr atar, ligar; atribuir (p.ej., importancia); (law) embargar; **to be attached to** aficionarse a; (to be officially associated with) depender de
attaché [,ætə'ʃe] o [ə'tæʃe] s agregado
attachment [ə'tætʃmənt] s atadura, enlace m; atribución; apego, cariño; accesorio; (law) embargo
attack [ə'tæk] s ataque m || tr & intr atacar
attain [ə'ten] tr alcanzar, lograr
attainment [ə'tenmənt] s consecución, logro; **attainments** dotes fpl, prendas
attempt [ə'tɛmpt] s tentativa; (assault) atentado, conato || tr procurar, intentar; (e.g., the life of a person) atentar a o contra
attend [ə'tɛnd] tr atender, asistir; asistir a (p.ej., la escuela); auxiliar (a un moribundo) || intr atender; **to attend to** atender a
attendance [ə'tɛndəns] s asistencia, concurrencia; **to dance attendance** hacer antesala
attendant [ə'tɛndənt] adj & s asistente mf; concomitante m
attention [ə'tɛnʃən] s atención; **to attract attention** llamar la atención; **to call attention to** hacer presente; **to pay attention to** hacer caso de
attentive [ə'tɛntɪv] adj atento
attenuate [ə'tɛnju,et] tr adelgazar; debilitar || intr debilitarse; desaparecer

attest [ə'tɛst] tr atestiguar; juramentar || intr dar fe; **to attest to** dar fe de
attic ['ætɪk] s buharda, guardilla, desván m
attire [ə'taɪr] s atavío, traje m || tr ataviar, vestir
attitude ['ætɪ,tjud] o ['ætɪ,tud] s actitud, además m
attorney [ə'tʌrni] s abogado; procurador m
attract [ə'trækt] tr atraer; llamar (la atención)
attraction [ə'trækʃən] s atracción; (personal charm) atractivo
attractive [ə'træktɪv] adj atractivo; (agreeable, interesting) atrayente
attribute ['ætrɪ,bjut] s atributo || [ə'trɪbjut] tr atribuir
atty. abbr **attorney**
auburn ['ɔbərn] adj & s castaño rojizo
auction ['ɔkʃən] s almoneda, remate m, subasta || tr rematar, subastar
auctioneer [,ɔkʃən'ɪr] s subastador m || tr & intr rematar, subastar
auction house s martillo
audacious [ɔ'deʃəs] adj audaz
audaci·ty [ɔ'dæsɪti] s (pl -ties) audacia
audience ['ɔdɪ.əns] s (hearing; formal interview) audiencia; público, auditorio
audio frequency ['ɔdɪ,o] s audiofrecuencia
audiometer [,ɔdɪ'ɑmɪtər] s audiómetro
audit ['ɔdɪt] s intervención || tr intervenir
audition [ɔ'dɪʃən] s audición || tr dar audición a
auditor ['ɔdɪtər] s oyente mf; (com) interventor m
auditorium [,ɔdɪ'torɪ.əm] s auditorio, anfiteatro, paraninfo
auger ['ɔgər] s barrena
augment [ɔg'mɛnt] tr & intr aumentar
augur ['ɔgər] s augur m || tr & intr augurar; **to augur well** ser de buen agüero
augu·ry ['ɔgəri] s (pl -ries) augurio
august [ə'gʌst] adj augusto || **August** ['ɔgəst] s agosto
aunt [ænt] o [ɑnt] s tía
aurora [ə'rorə] s aurora
auspice ['ɔspɪs] s auspicio; **under the auspices of** bajo los auspicios de
austere [ɔs'tɪr] adj austero
Australia [ɔ'streljə] s Australia
Australian [ɔ'streljən] adj & s australiano
Austria ['ɔstrɪ.ə] s Austria
Austrian ['ɔstrɪ.ən] adj & s austríaco
authentic [ɔ'θɛntɪk] adj auténtico
authenticate [ɔ'θɛntɪ,ket] tr autenticar
author ['ɔθər] s autor m
authoress ['ɔθərɪs] s autora
authoritarian [ɑ,θɔrɪ'tɛrɪ.ən] o [ə-,θɔrɪ'tɛrɪ.ən] adj & s autoritario
authoritative [ə'θɔrɪ,tetɪv] o [ə'θɔrɪ-,tetɪv] adj autorizado; (dictatorial) autoritario
authori·ty [ə'θɔrɪti] o [ə'θɑrɪti] s (pl -ties) autoridad; **on good authority** de buena tinta, de fuente fidedigna
authorize ['ɔθə,raɪz] tr autorizar

authorship ['ɔθər ˌʃɪp] s paternidad literaria

au·to ['ɔto] s (pl -tos) (coll) auto, coche m

autobiogra·phy [ˌɔtobaɪ'agrəfi] u [ˌɔtobɪ'agrəfi] s (pl -phies) autobiografía

autobus ['ɔto ˌbʌs] s autobús m

autocratic(al) [ˌɔtə'krætɪk(əl)] adj autocrático

autograph ['ɔtə ˌgræf] u ['ɔtə ˌgrɑf] adj & s autógrafo || tr autografiar

autograph seeker s cazaautógrafos m

automat ['ɔtə ˌmæt] s restaurante automático

automatic [ˌɔtə'mætɪk] adj automático

automatic clutch s servoembrague m

automation [ˌɔtə'meʃən] s automación, automatización

automa·ton [ɔ'tɑmə ˌtɑn] s (pl -tons o -ta [tə]) autómata

automobile [ˌɔtəmo'bil] u [ˌɔtə'mobil] s automóvil m

automobile show s salón m del automóvil

autonomous [ɔ'tɑnəməs] adj autónomo

autonomy [ɔ'tɑnəmi] s autonomía

autop·sy [ˈɔtɑpsi] s (pl -sies) autopsia

autumn ['ɔtəm] s otoño

autumnal [ə'tʌmnəl] adj otoñal

auxilia·ry [ɔg'zɪljəri] adj auxiliar || s (pl -ries) auxiliar mf; **auxiliaries** tropas auxiliares

av. abbr avenue, average, avoirdupois

avail [ə'vel] s provecho, utilidad || tr beneficiar; to avail oneself of aprovecharse de, valerse de || intr aprovechar

available [ə'veləbəl] adj disponible; to make available to poner a la disposición de

avalanche ['ævə ˌlæntʃ] o ['ævə ˌlɑntʃ] s alud m, avalancha

avant-garde [avã'gɑrd] adj vanguardista || s vanguardismo

avant-guardist [avã'gɑrdɪst] s vanguardista mf

avarice [ˈævərɪs] s avaricia

avaricious [ˌævə'rɪʃəs] adj avaricioso, avariento

Ave. abbr Avenue

avenge [ə'vendʒ] tr vengar; to avenge oneself on vengarse en

avenue ['ævə ˌnju] o ['ævə ˌnu] s avenida

aver [ə'vʌr] v (pret & pp averred; ger averring) tr afirmar, declarar

average [ˈævərɪdʒ] adj común, mediano, ordinario || s promedio, término medio; (naut) avería || tr calcular el término medio de; prorratear; ser de un promedio de

averse [ə'vʌrs] adj renuente, contrario

aversion [ə'vʌrʒən] s aversión, antipatía; cosa aborrecida

avert [ə'vʌrt] tr apartar, desviar; impedir

aviar·y ['evɪ ˌeri] s (pl -ies) avería, pajarera

aviation [ˌevɪ'eʃən] s aviación

aviation medicine s aeromedicina

aviator ['evɪ ˌetər] s aviador m

avid ['ævɪd] adj ávido

avidity [ə'vɪdɪti] s avidez f

avocation [ˌævə'keʃən] s distracción, diversión

avoid [ə'vɔɪd] tr evitar

avoidable [ə'vɔɪdəbəl] adj evitable

avoidance [ə'vɔɪdəns] s evitación

avow [ə'vau] tr admitir, confesar

avowal [ə'vau·əl] s admisión, confesión

await [ə'wet] tr aguardar, esperar

awake [ə'wek] adj despierto || v (pret & pp awoke [ə'wok] o awaked) tr & intr despertar

awaken [ə'wekən] tr & intr despertar

awakening [ə'wekənɪŋ] s despertamiento; desilusión

award [ə'wɔrd] s premio; condecoración; adjudicación || tr conceder; adjudicar

aware [ə'wer] adj enterado; to become aware of enterarse de, darse cuenta de

awareness [ə'wernɪs] s conciencia

away [ə'we] adj ausente; distante || adv lejos; a lo lejos; **away from** lejos de; **to do away with** deshacerse de; **to get away** escapar; **to go away** irse; **to make away with** robar, hurtar; **to run away** fugarse; **to send away** enviar; despedir; **to take away** llevarse; quitar

awe [ɔ] s temor m reverencial || tr infundir temor reverencial a

awesome ['ɔsəm] adj imponente

awestruck ['ɔ ˌstrʌk] adj espantado

awful [ˈɔfəl] adj atroz, horrible; impresionante; (coll) muy malo, muy feo, enorme

awfully [ˈɔfəli] adv atrozmente, horriblemente; (coll) muy, excesivamente

awhile [ə'hwaɪl] adv un rato, algún tiempo

awkward [ˈɔkwərd] adj desmañado, torpe, lerdo; embarazoso, delicado

awkward squad s pelotón m de los torpes

awl [ɔl] s alesna, lezna

awning ['ɔnɪŋ] s toldo

ax [æks] s hacha

axiom ['æksɪ·əm] s axioma m

axiomatic [ˌæksɪ·ə'mætɪk] adj axiomático

axis ['æksɪs] s (pl axes ['æksiz]) s eje m

axle ['æksəl] s eje m, árbol m

ax'le·tree' s eje m de carretón

ay [aɪ] adv & s sí || [e] adv siempre; **for ay** por siempre || [e] interj ¡ay!

aye [aɪ] adv & s sí || [e] adv siempre; **for aye** por siempre

azimuth ['æzɪməθ] s acimut m

Azores [ə'zorz] o ['ezorz] spl Azores fpl

Aztec ['æztek] adj & s azteca mf

azure ['æʒər] o ['eʒər] adj & s azul m

B

B, b [bi] segunda letra del alfabeto inglés

b. *abbr* **bass, bay, born, brother**

baa [bɑ] *s* be *m*, balido ‖ *intr* balar

babble [ˈbæbəl] *s* barboteo; charla; (*of a brook*) murmullo ‖ *tr* barbotar; decir indiscretamente ‖ *intr* barbotar; murmurar (*un arroyo*)

babe [beb] *s* rorro, criatura; (*innocent, gullible person*) niño; (slang) chica, chica hermosa

baboon [bæˈbun] *s* babuíno

ba·by [ˈbebi] *s* (*pl* -bies) rorro, criatura, bebé *m*; (*the youngest child*) benjamín *m* ‖ *v* (*pret* & *pp* -bied) *tr* mimar; tratar como niño

baby carriage *s* cochecillo para niños

baby grand *s* piano de media cola

babyhood [ˈbebiˌhud] *s* primera infancia, niñez *f*

babyish [ˈbebi·ɪʃ] *adj* aniñado, infantil

Babylon [ˈbæbɪlən] o [ˈbæbɪˌlɑn] *s* Babilonia (*ciudad*)

Babylonia [ˌbæbɪˈlonɪ·ə] *s* Babilonia (*imperio*)

Babylonian [ˌbæbɪˈlonɪ·ən] *adj* & *s* babilonio

baby sitter *s* niñera tomada por horas

baccalaureate [ˌbækəˈlɔrɪ·ɪt] *s* bachillerato

bachelor [ˈbætʃələr] *s* (*unmarried man*) soltero; (*holder of bachelor's degree*) bachiller *mf*; (*apprentice knight*) doncel *m*

bachelorhood [ˈbætʃələrˌhud] *s* celibato, soltería (*del hombre*)

bacil·lus [bəˈsɪləs] *s* (*pl* -li [laɪ]) bacilo

back [bæk] *adj* trasero, posterior; atrasado ‖ *adv* atrás, detrás; de vuelta; (*ago*) hace; **back of** detrás de; **to go back** to remontarse a; **to send back** devolver ‖ *s* espalda; dorso; (*of a coin*) reverso; (*of a chair*) espaldar *m*, respaldo; (*of an animal, of a book*) lomo; (*of a writing, a book*) final *m*; **behind one's back** a espaldas de uno; **on one's back** postrado, en cama; **a cuestas** ‖ *tr* mover hacia atrás; apoyar, respaldar ‖ *intr* moverse hacia atrás; **to back down** u **out** volverse atrás, echarse atrás; **to back up** retroceder; regolfar (*el agua*)

back'ache' *s* dolor *m* de espalda

back'bone' *s* espinazo; (*of a book*) nervura; firmeza, resistencia

back'break'ing *adj* deslomador

back'down' *s* palinodia, retractación

back'drop' *s* telón *m* de fondo o de foro

backer [ˈbækər] *s* sostenedor *m*, defensor *m*; (*of a business venture*) impulsador *m*

back'fire' *s* (aut) petardeo ‖ *intr* (aut) petardear

back'ground' *s* fondo; antecedentes *mpl*; conocimientos, educación; (*of a painting*) lontananza

background music *s* música de fondo

backing [ˈbækɪŋ] *s* apoyo, sostén *m*; garantía, respaldo; (bb) lomera

back'lash' *s* (mach) contragolpe *m*; (mach) juego; (fig) reacción violenta

back'log' *s* (com) reserva de pedidos pendientes; (*e.g., of work*) acumulación

back number *s* número atrasado; (coll) persona anticuada

back pay *s* sueldo retrasado

back seat *s* puesto secundario; **to take a back seat** perder influencia

back'side' *s* espalda; trasero

back'slide' *v* (*pret* & *pp* -slid [ˌslɪd]) *intr* reincidir

backspacer [ˈbækˌspesər] *s* tecla de retroceso

back'stage' *adv* detrás del telón; entre bastidores

back'stairs' *adj* indirecto, secreto

back stairs *spl* escalera trasera; medios indirectos

back'stitch' *s* pespunte *m* ‖ *tr* & *intr* pespuntar

back'stop' *s* reja o red *f* para detener la pelota

back'swept' wing *s* (aer) ala en flecha

back talk *s* respuesta insolente

backward [ˈbækwərd] *adj* atrasado, tardío; tímido ‖ *adv* de atrás; de espaldas; al revés; cada vez peor; para atrás, hacia atrás

back'wa'ter *s* remanso; (fig) atraso, yermo

back'woods' *spl* monte *m*, región alejada de los centros de población

back yard *s* patio trasero, corral trasero

bacon [ˈbekən] *s* tocino

bacteria [bækˈtɪrɪ·ə] *pl de* **bacterium**

bacterial [bækˈtɪrɪ·əl] *adj* bacteriano

bacteriologist [bækˌtɪrɪ·ˈɑlədʒɪst] *s* bacteriólogo

bacteriology [bækˌtɪrɪ·ˈɑlədʒi] *s* bacteriología

bacteri·um [bækˈtɪrɪ·əm] *s* (*pl* -a [ə]) bacteria

bad [bæd] *adj* (*comp* **worse** [wʌrs]; *super* **worst** [wʌrst]) malo; (*money*) falso; (*debt*) incobrable; **from bad to worse** de mal en peor; **to be bad** (coll) caer en desgracia; **to be too bad** ser lástima; **to go to the bad** (coll) ir por mal camino; (coll) arruinarse; **to look bad** tener mala cara

bad breath *s* mal aliento

badge [bædʒ] *s* divisa, insignia

badger [ˈbædʒər] *s* tejón *m*

badly [ˈbædli] *adv* mal; con urgencia; gravemente

badly off *adj* malparado; muy enfermo

badminton [ˈbædmɪntən] *s* juego del volante

baffle [ˈbæfəl] *s* deflector *m*; (rad)

pantalla acústica ‖ *tr* confundir; burlar, frustrar

baffling ['bæflɪŋ] *adj* perplejo, desconcertador

bag [bæg] *s* saco; saquito de mano; (*in clothing*) bolsa; (*purse*) bolso; (*take of game*) caza; to be in the bag (*slang*) ser cosa segura ‖ *v* (*pret & pp* bagged; *ger* bagging) *tr* ensacar; coger, cazar ‖ *intr* hacer bolsa (*un vestido*)

baggage ['bægɪdʒ] *s* equipaje *m*; (*mil*) bagaje *m*

baggage car *s* furgón *m* de equipajes

baggage check *s* contraseña de equipajes

baggage rack *s* red *f* de equipajes

baggage room *s* sala de equipajes

bag'pipe' *s* gaita, cornamusa

bag'pi'per *s* gaitero

bail [bel] *s* caución, fianza; to go bail for salir fiador por ‖ *tr* caucionar, afianzar; achicar (*la embarcación; el agua*); to bail out salir fiador por; achicar ‖ *intr* achicar; to bail out lanzarse en paracaídas

bailiff ['belɪf] *s* alguacil *m*, corchete *m*

bailiwick ['belɪwɪk] *s* alguacilazgo; to be in the bailiwick of ser de la pertenencia de

bait [bet] *s* carnada, cebo; señuelo; to swallow the bait tragar el anzuelo ‖ *tr* cebar, encarnar (*el anzuelo*); tentar, seducir; (*to pester*) hostigar

baize [bez] *s* bayeta

bake [bek] *tr* cocer al horno; cocer (*loza, gres, etc.*)

bakelite ['bekə,laɪt] *s* baquelita

baker ['bekər] *s* panadero, hornero

baker's dozen *s* docena del fraile

baker·y ['bekəri] *s* (*pl* -ies) panadería

baking powder ['bekɪŋ] *s* levadura en polvo

baking soda *s* bicarbonato de sosa

bal. *abbr* **balance**

balance ['bæləns] *s* (*instrument for weighing*) balanza; (*state of equilibrium*) equilibrio; (*amount left over*) resto; (*amount still owed*) saldo; (*statement of debits and credits*) balance *m*; to lose one's balance perder el equilibrio; to strike a balance hacer o pasar balance ‖ *tr* balancear; equilibrar; equilibrar, nivelar (*el presupuesto*) ‖ *intr* equilibrarse; (*to waver*) balancear

balance of payments *s* balanza de pagos

balance of power *s* equilibrio político

balance sheet *s* balance *m*, avanzo

balco·ny ['bælkəni] *s* (*pl* -nies) balcón *m*; (*in a theater*) galería, paraíso

bald [bɔld] *adj* calvo; franco, directo

baldness ['bɔldnɪs] *s* calvicie *f*

baldric ['bɔldrɪk] *s* tahalí *m*

bale [bel] *s* bala ‖ *tr* embalar

Balearic [,bælɪ'ærɪk] *adj* balear

Balearic Islands *spl* islas Baleares

baleful ['belfəl] *adj* funesto, maligno

balk [bɔk] *tr* burlar, frustrar ‖ *intr* emperrarse, resistirse

Balkan ['bɔlkən] *adj* balcánico ‖ the Balkans los Balcanes

balk·y ['bɔki] *adj* (*comp* -ier; *super* -iest) rebelón, repropio

ball [bɔl] *s* bola, pelota; (*of wool, yarn*) ovillo; (*of finger*) yema; (*projectile*) bala; (*dance*) baile *m*

ballad ['bæləd] *s* balada

ballade [bə'lɑd] *s* (*mus*) balada

ballast ['bæləst] *s* (*aer, naut*) lastre *m*; (*rr*) balasto ‖ *tr* lastrar; balastar

ball bearing *s* cojinete *m* de bolas

ballerina [,bælə'rinə] *s* bailarina

ballet ['bæle] *s* ballet *m*, baile *m*

ballistic [bə'lɪstɪk] *adj* balístico

balloon [bə'lun] *s* globo

ballot ['bælət] *s* balota; sufragio ‖ *intr* balotar

ballot box *s* urna electoral

ball'play'er *s* pelotari *m*; beisbolero

ball'-point' pen *s* polígrafo, bolígrafo, pluma esferográfica

ball'room' *s* salón *m* de baile

ballyhoo ['bælɪ,hu] *s* alharaca, bombo ‖ *tr* dar teatro a, dar bombo a

balm [bɑm] *s* bálsamo

balm·y ['bɑmi] *adj* (*comp* -ier; *super* -iest) bonancible, suave

balsam ['bɔlsəm] *s* bálsamo

Baltic ['bɔltɪk] *adj* báltico

Baltimore oriole ['bɔltɪ,mor] *s* cacique veranero

baluster ['bæləstər] *s* balaustre *m*

bamboo [bæm'bu] *s* bambú *m*

bamboozle [bæm'buzəl] *tr* (*coll*) embaucar, engañar

bamboozler [bæm'buzlər] *s* (*coll*) embaucador *m*, engañabobos *mf*

ban [bæn] *s* prohibición; excomunión, entredicho; (*of marriage*) amonestación ‖ *v* (*pret & pp* banned; *ger* banning) *tr* prohibir; excomulgar

banana [bə'nænə] *s* banana, plátano; (*tree*) banano, bananero, plátano

banana oil *s* esencia de pera

band [bænd] *s* banda; (*of people*) cuadrilla; (*of a hat*) cintillo; (*of a cigar*) anillo; liga de goma; (*mus*) banda, música, charanga ‖ *intr* abanderizarse

bandage ['bændɪdʒ] *s* venda ‖ *tr* vendar

bandanna [bæn'dænə] *s* pañuelo de hierbas

band'box' *s* sombrerera

bandit ['bændɪt] *s* bandido

band'mas'ter *s* músico mayor

bandoleer [,bændə'lɪr] *s* bandolera

band saw *s* sierra continua, sierra sin fin

band'stand' *s* quiosco de música

baneful ['benfəl] *adj* nocivo, venenoso; (*e.g., influence*) funesto

bang [bæŋ] *adv* de golpe ‖ *interj* ¡pum! *s* golpazo; (*of a door*) portazo; bangs flequillo ‖ *tr* golpear con ruido; cerrar (*p.ej., una puerta*) de golpe ‖ *intr* hacer estrépito

banish ['bænɪʃ] *tr* desterrar; despedir (*p.ej., miedo*)

banishment ['bænɪʃmənt] *s* destierro

banister ['bænɪstər] *s* balaustre *m*

bank [bæŋk] *s* banco; (*in certain games*) banca; (*small container for* coins) alcancía; (of a river) ribera, orilla; (of earth, snow, clouds) montón m || tr depositar o guardar (dinero) en un banco; amontonar; cubrir (un fuego) con cenizas || intr depositar dinero; **to bank on** (coll) contar con

bank account s cuenta de banco

bank'book' s libreta de banco

banker ['bæŋkər] s banquero

banking ['bæŋkɪŋ] adj bancario || s banca

bank note s billete m de banco

bank roll s lío de papel moneda

bankrupt ['bæŋkrʌpt] adj & s bancarrotero; **to go bankrupt** hacer bancarrota || tr hacer quebrar; arruinar

bankrupt·cy ['bæŋkrʌptsi] s (pl -cies) bancarrota

banner ['bænər] s bandera, estandarte m

banner cry s grito de combate

banquet ['bæŋkwɪt] s banquete m || tr & intr banquetear

banter ['bæntər] s burla, chanza || intr burlar, chancear

baptism ['bæptɪzəm] s bautismo, bautizo; (fig) bautismo

Baptist ['bæptɪst] adj & s baptista mf, bautista mf

baptister·y ['bæptɪstəri] s (pl -ies) baptisterio, bautisterio

baptize [bæp'taɪz] o ['bæptaɪz] tr bautizar

bar. abbr barometer, barrel, barrister

bar [bɑr] s barra; (of door or window) tranca; (of jail) reja; barrera; (legal profession) abogacía; (members of legal profession) curia; (of public opinion) tribunal m; (mus) barra; (unit between two bars) (mus) compás m; **behind bars** entre rejas || prep salvo; **bar none** sin excepción || v (pret & pp **barred;** ger **barring**) tr barrear, atrancar; impedir; prohibir; excluir

bar association s colegio de abogados

barb [bɑrb] s púa, lengüeta; (of a pen) barbilla

Barbados [bɑr'bedoz] s la Barbada

barbarian [bɑr'berɪ-ən] s bárbaro

barbaric [bɑr'bærɪk] adj bárbaro

barbarism ['bɑrbə,rɪzəm] s barbaridad f; (gram) barbarismo

barbari·ty [bɑr'bærɪti] s (pl -ties) barbarie f

barbarous ['bɑrbərəs] adj bárbaro

Barbary ape ['bɑrbəri] s mono de Gibraltar

barbed [bɑrbd] adj armado de púas; mordaz, punzante

barbed wire s alambre m de espino, alambre de púas

barber ['bɑrbər] adj barberil || s barbero, peluquero

barber pole s percha de barbero

bar'ber-shop' s barbería, peluquería

bard [bɑrd] s bardo; (horse armor) barda || tr bardar

bare [ber] adj desnudo; (head) descubierto; (unfurnished) desamueblado; (wire) sin aislar; mero, sencillo, puro || tr desnudar; descubrir

bare'back' adj & adv en pelo, sin silla

barefaced ['ber,fest] adj desvergonzado

bare'foot' adj descalzo || adv con los pies desnudos

bareheaded ['ber,hedɪd] adj descubierto || adv con la cabeza descubierta

barelegged ['ber,legɪd] o ['ber,legd] adj con las piernas desnudas

barely ['berli] adv apenas

bargain ['bɑrgɪn] s (deal) convenio, trato; (cheap purchase) ganga; **in the bargain** de añadidura || tr — to bargain away vender regalado || intr negociar; (to haggle) regatear

bargain counter s baratillo

bargain sale s venta de saldos

barge [bɑrdʒ] s gabarra, lanchón m || intr moverse pesadamente; **to barge in** entrar sin pedir permiso, entrar sin llamar a la puerta

barium ['berɪ-əm] s bario

bark [bɑrk] s (of tree) corteza; (of dog) ladrido; (boat) barca || tr ladrar (p.ej., injurias) || intr ladrar

barley ['bɑrli] s cebada

barley water s hordiate m

bar magnet s barra imantada

bar'maid' s moza de taberna

barn [bɑrn] s granero, troje m; caballeriza, establo; cochera

barnacle ['bɑrnəkəl] s cirrópodo

barn owl s lechuza, oliva

barn'yard' s corral m

barnyard fowl spl aves fpl de corral

barometer [bə'rɑmɪtər] s barómetro

baron ['bærən] s barón m

baroness ['bærənɪs] s baronesa

baroque [bə'rok] adj & s barroco

barracks ['bærəks] spl cuartel m

barrage [bə'rɑʒ] s (dam) presa; (mil) barrera de fuego

barrel ['bærəl] s barril m, tonel m; (of a gun, pen, etc.) cañón m

barrel organ s organillo

barren ['bærən] adj árido, estéril

barricade [,bærɪ'ked] s barrera || tr barrear

barrier ['bærɪ-ər] s barrera

barrier reef s barrera de arrecifes

barrister ['bærɪstər] s (Brit) abogado

bar'room' s bar m, cantina

bar'tend'er s cantinero, tabernero

barter ['bɑrtər] s trueque m || tr trocar

base [bes] adj bajo, humilde; infame, vil; (metal) bajo de ley || s base f; (of electric light or vacuum tube; of projectile) culote m; (mus) bajo || tr basar

base'ball' s béisbol m; pelota de béisbol

base'board' s rodapié m

Basel ['bɑzəl] s Basilea

baseless ['beslɪs] adj infundado

basement ['besmənt] s sótano

bashful ['bæʃfəl] adj encogido, tímido

basic ['besɪk] adj básico

basic commodities spl artículos de primera necesidad

basilica [bə'sɪlɪkə] s basílica

basin ['besɪn] s jofaina, palangana;

(*of a fountain*) tazón *m*; (*of a river*) cuenca; (*of a harbor*) dársena

ba·sis ['besɪs] *s* (*pl* -ses [siz]) base *f*; **on the basis of** a base de

bask [bæsk] o [bɑsk] *intr* asolearse, calentarse

basket ['bæskɪt] o ['bɑskɪt] *s* cesta; (*large basket*) cesto; (*with two handles*) canasta; (*with lid*) excusabaraja; (*sport*) cesto, red *f*

bas'ket-ball' *s* baloncesto, basquetbol *m*

Basle [bɑl] *s* Basilea

Basque [bæsk] *adj* & *s* (*of Spain*) vascongado; (*of Spain and France*) vasco; (*of old Spain*) vascón *m*

bas-relief [,bɑrɪ'lif] o [,bærɪ'lif] *s* bajo relieve

bass [bes] *adj* & *s* (mus) bajo ‖ [bæs] *s* (ichth) róbalo; (ichth) micróptero

bass drum *s* bombo

bass horn *s* tuba

bas·so ['bæso] o ['bɑso] *s* (*pl* -sos o -si [si]) (mus) bajo

bassoon [bə'sun] *s* bajón *m*

bass viol ['vaɪ·əl] *s* violón *m*, contrabajo

bastard ['bæstərd] *adj* & *s* bastardo

bastard title *s* anteportada

baste [best] *tr* (*to sew slightly*) hilvanar; (*to moisten with drippings while roasting*) enlardar; (*to thrash*) azotar; (*to scold*) regañar

bat. *abbr* battalion, battery

bat [bæt] *s* palo; (coll) golpe *m*; (zool) murciélago ‖ *v* (*pret* & *pp* batted; *ger* batting) *tr* golpear; batear (*una pelota*); **without batting an eye** sin inmutarse, sin pestañear ‖ *intr* golpear

batch [bætʃ] *s* (*of bread*) hornada; (*of papers*) lío

bath [bæθ] o [bɑθ] *s* baño

bathe [beð] *tr* bañar ‖ *intr* bañarse; **to go bathing** ir a bañarse

bather ['beðər] *s* bañista *mf*

bath'house' *s* casa de baños; caseta de baños

bathing beach *s* playa de baños

bathing beauty *s* sirena de la playa

bathing resort *s* estación balnearia

bathing suit *s* traje *m* de baño, bañador *m*

bathing trunks *spl* taparrabo

bath'robe' *s* albornoz *m*, bata de baño; bata, peinador *m*

bath'room' *s* baño, cuarto de baño

bathroom fixtures *spl* aparatos sanitarios

bath'tub' *s* bañera, baño

baton [bæ'tɑn] o ['bætən] *s* bastón *m*; (mus) batuta

battalion [bə'tæljən] *s* batallón *m*

batter ['bætər] *s* pasta, batido; (baseball) bateador *m* ‖ *tr* magullar, estropear

battering ram *s* ariete *m*

batter·y ['bætərɪ] *s* (*pl* -ies) batería; (*primary*) (elec) pila; (*secondary*) (elec) acumulador *m*; (law) violencia

battle ['bætəl] *s* batalla; **to do battle** librar batalla ‖ *tr* batallar

battle array *s* orden *m* de batalla

battle cry *s* grito de combate

battledore ['bætəl,dor] *s* raqueta; **battledore and shuttlecock** raqueta y volante

bat'tlefield' *s* campo de batalla

battle front *s* frente *m* de combate

battlement ['bætəlmənt] *s* almenaje *m*

battle piece *s* (paint) batalla

bat'tle-ship' *s* acorazado

battue [bæ'tu] o [bæ'tju] *s* batida

bauble ['bɔbəl] *s* chuchería; cetro de bufón

Bavaria [bə'verɪ·ə] *s* Baviera

Bavarian [bə'verɪ·ən] *adj* & *mf* bávaro

bawd [bɔd] *s* alcahuete *m*, alcahueta

bawd·y ['bɔdɪ] *adj* (*comp* -ier; *super* -iest) indecente, obsceno

bawd'y-house' *s* mancebía, lupanar *m*

bawl [bɔl] *s* voces *fpl*, gritos ‖ *tr* — **to bawl out** (slang) regañar ‖ *intr* vocear, gritar; llorar ruidosamente

bay [be] *adj* bayo ‖ *s* bahía; aullido, ladrido; caballo bayo; (bot) laurel *m*; **to keep at bay** tener a raya ‖ *intr* aullar, ladrar

Bay of Biscay *s* golfo de Vizcaya

bayonet ['be·ənɪt] *s* bayoneta ‖ *tr* herir o matar con bayoneta

bay rum *s* ron *m* de laurel, ron de malagueta

bay window *s* ventana saledíza, mirador *m*

bazooka [bə'zukə] *s* bazuca

bbl. *abbr* barrel, barrels

B.C. *abbr* before Christ

bd. *abbr* board

be [bi] *v* (*pres* am [æm], is [ɪz], are [ɑr]; *pret* was [wɑz] o [wʌz], were [wʌr]; *pp* been [bɪn]) *intr* estar; ser; tener, p.ej., **to be cold** tener frío; **to be wrong** no tener razón; tener la culpa; **here is** o **here are** aquí tiene Vd.; **there is** o **there are** hay ‖ *v aux* estar, p.ej., **he is studying** está estudiando; ser, p.ej., **she was hit by a car** fué atropellada por un coche; deber, p.ej., **what am I to do?** ¿qué debo hacer? ‖ *v impers* ser, p.ej., **it is necessary to get up early** es necesario levantarse temprano; haber, p.ej., **it is sunny** hay sol; hacer, p.ej., **it is cold** hace frío

beach [bitʃ] *s* playa

beach'comb' *intr* raquear; **to go beach-combing** andar al raque

beach'comb'er *s* raquero; vago de playa

beach'head' *s* cabeza de playa

beach robe *s* albornoz *m*

beach shoe *s* playera

beach umbrella *s* sombrilla de playa

beach wagon *s* rubia, coche *m* rural

beacon ['bikən] *s* señal luminosa; (*lighthouse*) faro; (*hill overlooking sea*) hacho; radiofaro; (*guide*) faro ‖ *tr* iluminar, guiar ‖ *intr* brillar

bead [bid] *s* cuenta; (*of glass*) abalorio; (*of sweat*) gota; (*moulding on corner of wall*) guardavivo; **to say** o **tell one's beads** rezar el rosario

beadle ['bidəl] *s* bedel *m*

beagle ['bigəl] *s* sabueso

beak [bik] *s* pico; cabo, promontorio

beam [bim] s (of wood) viga; (of light, heat, etc.) rayo; (naut) bao; (direction perpendicular to the keel) (naut) través m; (of hope) (fig) rayo; **on the beam** siguiendo el haz del radiofaro; (coll) siguiendo el buen camino ‖ tr emitir (luz, ondas) ‖ intr brillar; sonreír alegremente

bean [bin] s haba (Vicia faba); alubia, judía (Phaseolus vulgaris); (of coffee, cocoa) haba; (slang) cabeza

bean'pole' s rodrigón m para frijoles; (tall, skinny person) (coll) poste m de telégrafo

bear [ber] s oso; (in stock market) bajista mf ‖ v (pret **bore** [bor]; pp **borne** [born]) tr cargar; traer; llevar (armas); apoyar; aguantar; sentir, experimentar; producir, rendir (frutos; interés); (to give birth to) parir; tener (amor, odio); **to bear out** confirmar ‖ intr dirigirse, volver; **to bear on** referirse a; **to bear up** no perder la esperanza; **to bear with** ser indulgente para con

beard [bird] s barba; (of wheat) arista

beard'less ['birdlıs] adj imberbe

bearer ['berər] s portador m

bearing ['berıŋ] s porte m, presencia; referencia, relación; (mach) cojinete m; **bearings** orientación; **to lose one's bearings** desorientarse

bearish ['berıʃ] adj bajista

bear'skin' s piel f de oso; (military cap) morrión m

beast [bist] s bestia

beast·ly ['bistli] adj (comp **-lier**; super **-liest**) bestial; (coll) muy malo ‖ adv (coll) muy mal

beast of burden s bestia de carga, acémila

beat [bit] s golpe m; (of heart) latido; (of rhythm) compás m; (mus) tiempo; (phys) batimiento; (rad) batido; (of a policeman) ronda; (sponger) (slang) embestidor m ‖ v (pret **beat**; pp **beat** o **beaten**) tr azotar, pegar; batir; sacudir (una alfombra); aventajar; llevar (el compás); tocar (un tambor); ganar (a una persona en una contienda); **to beat it** (slang) largarse; **to beat up** batir (p.ej., huevos); (slang) aporrear ‖ intr batir; latir (el corazón); **to beat against** azotar

beaten path ['bitən] s camino trillado

beater ['bitər] s batidor m; (mixer) batidora

beati·fy [bı'ætı,faı] v (pret & pp **-fied**) tr beatificar

beating ['bitıŋ] s golpeo; (of wings) aleteo; (with a whip) paliza; (defeat) derrota

beau [bo] s (pl **beaus** o **beaux** [boz]) galán m, cortejo; novio; elegante m

beautician [bju'tıʃən] s embellecedora, esteta mf, esteticista mf

beautiful ['bjutıfəl] adj bello, hermoso

beauti·fy ['bjutı,faı] v (pret & pp **-fied**) tr hermosear, embellecer

beau·ty ['bjuti] s (pl **-ties**) beldad f, belleza

beauty contest s concurso de belleza

beauty parlor s salón m de belleza

beauty queen s reina de la belleza

beauty sleep s primer sueño (antes de medianoche)

beauty spot s lunar postizo; sitio pintoresco

beaver ['bivər] s castor m; piel f de castor

becalm [bı'kam] tr calmar, serenar

because [bı'kɔz] conj porque; **because of** por, por causa de

beck [bek] s seña (con la cabeza o la mano); **at the beck and call of** a la disposición de

beckon ['bekən] tr seña (con la cabeza o la mano) ‖ tr llamar por señas; atraer, tentar ‖ intr hacer señas

be·come [bı'kʌm] v (pret **-came**; pp **-come**) tr convenir, sentar bien ‖ intr hacerse; llegar a ser; ponerse, volverse; convertirse en; **to become of** ser de, p.ej., **what will become of the soldier?** ¿qué será del soldado?; hacerse, p.ej., **what became of his pencil?** ¿qué se ha hecho su lápiz?

becoming [bı'kʌmıŋ] adj conveniente, decente; que sienta bien

bed [bed] s cama; (of a river) cauce m; (of flower garden) macizo; **to go to bed** acostarse; **to take to bed** encamarse

bed and board s pensión completa, casa y comida

bed'bug' s chinche f

bed'cham'ber s alcoba, cuarto de dormir

bed'clothes' spl ropa de cama

bed'cov'er s cubrecama, cobertor m

bedding ['bedıŋ] s ropa de cama; (for animals) cama

bedev·il [bı'devəl] v (pret & pp **-iled** o **-illed**; ger **-iling** o **-illing**) tr atormentar, confundir

bed'fast' adj postrado en cama

bed'fel'low s compañero o compañera de cama

bedlam ['bedləm] s confusión, desorden m, tumulto

bed linen s ropa de cama

bed'pan' s silleta

bed'post' s pilar m de cama

bedridden ['bed,rıdən] adj postrado en cama

bed'room' s alcoba, cuarto de dormir

bed'side' s cabecera

bed'sore' s úlcera de decúbito; **to get bedsores** decentarse

bed'spread' s sobrecama, cobertor m

bed'spring' s colchón m de muelles, somier m

bed'stead' s cuja

bed'straw' s paja de jergón

bed'tick' s cutí m

bed'time' s hora de acostarse

bed warmer s calientacamas m

bee [bi] s abeja

beech [bitʃ] s haya

beech'nut' s hayuco

beef [bif] s carne f de vaca; ganado vacuno de engorde; (coll) fuerza muscular; (slang) queja ‖ tr — **to**

beef up (coll) reforzar || *intr* (slang) quejarse; (slang) soplar

beef cattle *s* ganado vacuno de engorde

beef'steak' *s* biftec *m*

bee'hive' *s* colmena

bee'line' *s* — **to make a beeline for** ir en línea recta hacia, ir derecho a

beer [bɪr] *s* cerveza; **dark beer** cerveza parda, cerveza negra; **light beer** cerveza clara

beeswax ['biz,wæks] *s* cera de abejas || *tr* encerar

beet [bit] *s* remolacha

beetle ['bitəl] *s* escarabajo

beetle-browed ['bitəl,braud] *adj* cejijunto; (*sullen*) ceñudo

beet sugar *s* azúcar *m* de remolacha

be·fall [bɪ'fɔl] *v* (*pret* **-fell** ['fɛl]; *pp* **-fallen** ['fɔlən]) *tr* acontecer a || *intr* acontecer

befitting [bɪ'fɪtɪŋ] *adj* conveniente; decoroso

before [bɪ'fɔr] *adv* antes; delante, enfrente || *prep* (*in time*) antes de; (*in place*) delante de; (*in the presence of*) ante || *conj* antes (de) que

before'hand' *adv* de antemano, con anticipación

befriend [bɪ'frɛnd] *tr* ofrecer amistad a, amparar, proteger

befuddle [bɪ'fʌdəl] *tr* aturdir, confundir

beg [bɛg] *v* (*pret* & *pp* **begged**; *ger* **begging**) *tr* pedir, rogar, solicitar; mendigar || *intr* mendigar; **to beg off** excusarse

be·get [bɪ'gɛt] *v* (*pret* **-got** ['gɑt]; *pp* **-gotten** o **-got**; *ger* **-getting**) *tr* engendrar

beggar ['bɛgər] *s* mendigo; pobre *mf*; pícaro, bribón *m*; sujeto, tipo

be·gin [bɪ'gɪn] *v* (*pret* **-gan** ['gæn]; *pp* **-gun** ['gʌn]; *ger* **-ginning**) *tr* & *intr* comenzar, empezar; **beginning with** a partir de

beginner [bɪ'gɪnər] *s* principiante *mf*; iniciador *m*

beginning [bɪ'gɪnɪŋ] *s* comienzo, principio

begrudge [bɪ'grʌdʒ] *tr* dar de mala gana; envidiar

beguile [bɪ'gaɪl] *tr* engañar; divertir, entretener, engañar (*el tiempo*)

behalf [bɪ'hæf] o [bɪ'hɑf] *s* — **on behalf of** en nombre de; a favor de

behave [bɪ'hev] *intr* conducirse, comportarse; portarse bien, funcionar

behavior [bɪ'hevjər] *s* conducta, comportamiento; funcionamiento

behead [bɪ'hɛd] *tr* decapitar, descabezar

behind [bɪ'haɪnd] *adv* detrás; hacia atrás; con retraso; **to stay behind** quedarse atrás || *prep* detrás de; **behind the back of** a espaldas de; **behind the times** atrasado de noticias; **behind time** tarde || *s* (slang) trasero

behold [bɪ'hold] *v* (*pret* & *pp* **-held** ['hɛld]) *tr* contemplar || *interj* ¡he aquí!

behoove [bɪ'huv] *tr* convenir, tocar

being ['bi·ɪŋ] *adj* existente; **for the**

time being por ahora, por el momento || *s* ser, ente *m*

belch [bɛltʃ] *s* eructo, regüeldo || *tr* vomitar (*p.ej., llamas, injurias*) || *intr* eructar, regoldar

beleaguer [bɪ'ligər] *tr* sitiar, cercar

bel·fry ['bɛlfri] *s* (*pl* **-fries**) campanario

Belgian ['bɛldʒən] *adj* & *s* belga *mf*

Belgium ['bɛldʒəm] *s* Bélgica

be·lie [bɪ'laɪ] *v* (*pret* & *pp* **-lied** ['laɪd]; *ger* **-lying** ['laɪ·ɪŋ]) *tr* desmentir

belief [bɪ'lif] *s* creencia

believable [bɪ'livəbəl] *adj* creíble

believe [bɪ'liv] *tr* & *intr* creer

believer [bɪ'livər] *s* creyente *mf*

belittle [bɪ'lɪtəl] *tr* empequeñecer, despreciar

bell [bɛl] *s* campana; (*electric bell*) timbre *m*, campanilla; (*ring of bell*) campanada || *intr* bramar, berrear

bell'boy' *s* botones *m*

belle [bɛl] *s* beldad *f*, belleza

belles-lettres [,bɛl'lɛtrə] *spl* bellas letras

bell gable *s* espadaña

bell glass *s* fanal *m*

bell'hop' *s* (slang) botones *m*

bellicose ['bɛlɪ,kos] *adj* belicoso

belligerent [bə'lɪdʒərənt] *adj* & *s* beligerante *mf*

bellow ['bɛlo] *s* bramido; **bellows** fuelle *m*, barquín *m* || *tr* gritar || *intr* bramar

bell ringer *s* campanero

bellwether ['bɛl,wɛðər] *s* manso

bel·ly ['bɛli] *s* (*pl* **-lies**) barriga, vientre *m*; estómago || *v* (*pret* & *pp* **-lied**) *intr* hacer barriga; hacer bolso (*las velas*)

bel'ly·ache' *s* (slang) dolor *m* de barriga || *intr* (slang) quejarse

belly button *s* (coll) ombligo

belly dance *s* (coll) danza del vientre

bellyful ['bɛlɪ,ful] *s* (slang) panzada

bel'ly·land' *intr* (aer) aterrizar de panza

belong [bɪ'lɔŋ] o [bɪ'lɑŋ] *intr* pertenecer; deber estar

belongings [bɪ'lɔŋɪŋz] o [bɪ'lɑŋɪŋz] *spl* pertenencias, efectos

beloved [bɪ'lʌvɪd] o [bɪ'lʌvd] *adj* & *s* querido, amado

below [bɪ'lo] *adv* abajo; (*in a text*) más abajo; bajo cero, p.ej., **ten below** diez grados bajo cero || *prep* debajo de; inferior a

belt [bɛlt] *s* cinturón *m*; (aer, mach) correa; (geog) faja, zona; **to tighten one's belt** ceñirse

bemoan [bɪ'mon] *tr* deplorar, lamentar

bench [bɛntʃ] *s* banco; (law) tribunal

bend [bɛnd] *s* curva; (*in a road, river, etc.*) recodo, vuelta || *v* (*pret* & *pp* **bent** [bɛnt]) *tr* encorvar; doblar (*un tubo; la rodilla*); inclinar (*la cabeza*); dirigir (*sus esfuerzos*) || *intr* encorvarse; doblarse; inclinarse

beneath [bɪ'niθ] *adv* abajo || *prep* debajo de; inferior a

benediction [‚benɪ'dɪkʃən] s bendición f

benefaction [‚benɪ'fækʃən] s beneficio

benefactor ['benɪ‚fæktər] o [‚benɪ-'fæktər] s bienhechor m

benefactress ['benɪ‚fæktrɪs] o [‚benɪ-'fæktrɪs] s bienhechora

beneficence [bɪ'nɛfɪsəns] s beneficencia

beneficent [bɪ'nefɪsənt] adj bienhechor

beneficial [‚benɪ'fɪʃəl] adj beneficioso

beneficiar·y [‚benɪ'fɪʃɪ‚erɪ] s (pl -ies) beneficiario

benefit ['benɪfɪt] s beneficio; for the benefit of a beneficio de || tr beneficiar

benefit performance s beneficio

benevolence [bɪ'nevələns] s benevolencia

benevolent [bɪ'nevələnt] adj benévolo; (e.g., institution) benéfico

benign [bɪ'naɪn] adj benigno

benigni·ty [bɪ'nɪgnɪti] s (pl -ties) benignidad

bent [bent] adj encorvado, doblado, torcido; bent on resuelto a, empeñado en; bent over cargado de espaldas || s encorvadura; inclinación f, propensión f

benzine [ben'zin] s bencina

bequeath [bɪ'kwið] o [bɪ'kwiθ] tr legar

bequest [bɪ'kwest] s manda, legado

berate [bɪ'ret] tr regañar, reñir

be·reave [bɪ'riv] v (pret & pp -reaved o -reft ['reft]) tr despojar, privar; desconsolar

bereavement [bɪ'rivmənt] s despojo, privación f; desconsuelo

berkelium [bər'kilɪəm] s berkelio

Berliner [bər'lɪnər] s berlinés m

ber·ry ['berɪ] s (pl -ries) baya; (of coffee plant) grano, haba

berserk ['bʌrsʌrk] adj frenético || adv frenéticamente

berth [bʌrθ] s (bed) litera; (room) camarote m; (for a ship) amarradero; (coll) empleo, puesto

beryllium [bə'rɪlɪəm] s berilio

be·seech [bɪ'sitʃ] v (pret & pp -sought ['sɔt] o -seeched) tr suplicar

be·set [bɪ'set] v (pret & pp -set; ger -setting) tr acometer, acosar; cercar, sitiar

beside [bɪ'saɪd] adv además, también || prep cerca de, junto a; en comparación de; excepto; beside oneself fuera de sí; beside the point incongruente

besiege [bɪ'sidʒ] tr asediar, sitiar

besmirch [bɪ'smʌrtʃ] tr ensuciar, manchar

bespatter [bɪ'spætər] tr salpicar

be·speak [bɪ'spik] v (pret -spoke ['spok]; pp -spoken) tr apalabrar, pedir de antemano

best [best] adj super mejor; óptimo || adv super mejor; had best debería || s (lo) mejor; (lo) más; at best a lo más; to do one's best hacer lo mejor posible; to get the best of aventajar,

sobresalir; to make the best of sacar el mejor partido de

best girl s (coll) amiga preferida, novia

be·stir [bɪ'stʌr] v (pret & pp -stirred; ger -stirring) tr excitar, incitar; to bestir oneself esforzarse, afanarse

best man s padrino de boda

bestow [bɪ'sto] tr otorgar, conferir; dedicar

best seller s éxito de venta, campeón m de venta; éxito de librería

bet. abbr between

bet [bet] s apuesta || v (pret & pp bet o betted; ger betting) tr & intr apostar; I bet a que, apuesto a que; to bet on apostar por; you bet (slang) ya lo creo

be·take [bɪ'tek] v (pret -took ['tʊk]; pp -taken) tr — to betake oneself dirigirse; darse, entregarse

be·think [bɪ'θɪŋk] v (pret & pp -thought ['θɔt]) tr — to bethink oneself of considerar, acordarse de

Bethlehem ['beθlɪ‚əm] o ['beθlɪ‚hem] s Belén m

betide [bɪ'taɪd] tr presagiar; acontecer a || intr acontecer

betoken [bɪ'tokən] tr anunciar, indicar, presagiar

betray [bɪ'tre] tr traicionar; descubrir, revelar

betrayal [bɪ'tre·əl] s traición; descubrimiento, revelación

betroth [bɪ'troð] o [bɪ'trɔθ] tr prometer en matrimonio; to become betrothed desposarse

betrothal [bɪ'troðəl] o [bɪ'trɔθəl] s desposorios, esponsales mpl

betrothed [bɪ'troðd] o [bɪ'trɔθt] s prometido, novio

better ['betər] adj comp mejor; it is better to más vale; to grow better mejorarse; to make better mejorar || adv comp mejor; más; had better debería; to like better preferir || s superior; ventaja; to get the better of llevar la ventaja a || tr aventajar; mejorar; to better oneself mejorar su posición

better half s (coll) cara mitad

betterment [‚betərmənt] s mejoramiento; (in an illness) mejoría

between [bɪ'twin] adv en medio, entremedias || prep entre; between you and me entre Vd. y yo; acá para los dos

be·tween'-decks' s entrecubiertas, entrepuentes mpl

between decks adv entrecubiertas

bev·el ['bevəl] adj biselado || s (instrument) cartabón m; (sloping part) bisel m || v (pret & pp -eled o -elled; ger -eling o -elling) tr biselar

beverage ['bevərɪdʒ] s bebida

bev·y ['bevɪ] s (pl -ies) (of birds) bandada; (of girls) grupo

bewail [bɪ'wel] tr & intr lamentar

beware [bɪ'wer] tr guardarse de || intr tener cuidado; beware of ...! ¡ojo con ...!, ¡cuidado con ...!; to beware of guardarse de

bewilder [bɪ'wɪldər] *tr* aturdir, dejar perplejo, desatinar

bewilderment [bɪ'wɪldərmənt] *s* aturdimiento, perplejidad

beyond [bɪ'jɑnd] *adv* más allá, más lejos || *prep* más allá de; además de; no capaz de; **beyond a doubt** fuera de duda; **beyond the reach of** fuera del alcance de || *s* — **the great beyond** el más allá, el otro mundo

bg. *abbr* **bag**

bias ['baɪəs] *s* sesgo, diagonal *f;* prejuicio; (electron) polarización de rejilla || *tr* predisponer, prevenir

Bib. *abbr* **Bible, Biblical**

bib [bɪb] *s* babero; (*of apron*) pechera

Bible ['baɪbəl] *s* Biblia

Biblical ['bɪblɪkəl] *adj* bíblico

bibliographer [,bɪblɪ'ɑgrəfər] *s* bibliógrafo

bibliogra·phy [,bɪblɪ'ɑgrəfi] *s* (*pl* -**phies**) bibliografía

bibliophile ['bɪblɪ-ə,faɪl] *s* bibliófilo

bicameral [baɪ'kæmərəl] *adj* bicameral

bicarbonate [baɪ'kɑrbə,net] *s* bicarbonato

bicker ['bɪkər] *s* discusión ociosa || *intr* discutir ociosamente

bicycle ['baɪsɪkəl] *s* bicicleta

bid [bɪd] *s* oferta, postura; (*in bridge*) declaración || *v* (*pret* **bade** [bæd] o **bid;** *ger* **bidden** ['bɪdən]) *tr & intr* ofrecer, pujar, licitar; (*in bridge*) declarar

bidder ['bɪdər] *s* postor *m;* (*in bridge*) declarante *mf;* **the highest bidder** el mejor postor

bidding ['bɪdɪŋ] *s* mandato, orden *f;* postura; (*in bridge*) declaración

bide [baɪd] *tr* — **to bide one's time** esperar la hora propicia

biennial [baɪ'enɪ-əl] *adj* bienal

bier [bɪr] *s* féretro, andas

bifocal [baɪ'fokəl] *adj* bifocal || **bifocals** *spl* anteojos bifocales

big [bɪg] *adj* (*comp* **bigger;** *super* **biggest**) grande; (*considerable*) importante; (*grown-up*) adulto; **big with child** preñada || *adv* (coll) con jactancia; **to talk big** (coll) hablar gordo

bigamist ['bɪgəmɪst] *s* bígamo

bigamous ['bɪgəməs] *adj* bígamo

bigamy ['bɪgəmi] *s* bigamia

big-bellied ['bɪg,belɪd] *adj* panzudo

Big Dipper *s* Carro mayor

big game *s* caza mayor

big-hearted ['bɪg,hɑrtɪd] *adj* magnánimo, generoso

bigot ['bɪgət] *s* intolerante *mf,* fanático

bigoted ['bɪgətɪd] *adj* intolerante, fanático

bigot·ry ['bɪgətri] *s* (*pl* -**ries**) intolerancia, fanatismo

big shot *s* (slang) pájaro de cuenta, señorón *m*

big stick *s* palo en alto

big toe *s* dedo gordo o grande (*del pie*)

bile [baɪl] *s* bilis *f*

bilge [bɪldʒ] *s* pantoque *m* || *tr* desfondar

bilge pump *s* bomba de sentina

bilge water *s* agua de pantoque

bilge ways *spl* anguilas

bilingual [baɪ'lɪŋgwəl] *adj* bilingüe

bilious ['bɪljəs] *adj* bilioso

bilk [bɪlk] *tr* estafar, trampear

bill [bɪl] *s* (*statement of charges for goods or service*) cuenta, factura; (*paper money*) billete *m;* (*poster*) cartel *m,* aviso; cartel de teatro; (*draft of law*) proyecto de ley; (*handbill*) hoja suelta; (*of bird*) pico; (com) giro, letra de cambio || *tr* facturar; cargar en cuenta a; anunciar por carteles || *intr* darse el pico (*las palomas*); acariciarse (*los enamorados*); **to bill and coo** acariciarse y arrullarse

bill'board' *s* cartelera

billet ['bɪlɪt] *s* (mil) boleta; (mil) alojamiento || *tr* (mil) alojar

billet-doux ['bɪle'du] *s* (*pl* **billets-doux** ['bɪle'duz]) esquela amorosa

bill'fold' *s* cartera de bolsillo, billetero

bill'head' *s* encabezamiento de factura

billiards ['bɪljərdz] *s* billar *m*

billion ['bɪljən] *s* (U.S.A.) mil millones; (Brit) billón *m*

bill of exchange *s* letra de cambio

bill of fare *s* lista de comidas, menú *m*

bill of lading *s* conocimiento de embarque

bill of sale *s* escritura de venta

billow ['bɪlo] *s* oleada, ondulación || *intr* ondular, hincharse

bill'post'er *s* fijacarteles *m,* fijador *m* de carteles

bil·ly ['bɪlɪ] *s* (*pl* -**lies**) cachiporra

billy goat *s* macho cabrío

bin [bɪn] *s* arcón *m,* hucha

bind [baɪnd] *v* (*pret & pp* **bound** [baʊnd]) *tr* ligar, atar; juntar, unir; (*with a garland*) enguirlandar; ribetear (*la orilla del vestido*); agavillar (*las mieses*); vendar (*una herida*); encuadernar (*un libro*); estreñir (*el vientre*)

binder·y ['baɪndəri] *s* (*pl* -**ies**) taller *m* de encuadernación

binding ['baɪndɪŋ] *s* atadura; (*of a book*) encuadernación

binding post *s* borne *m,* sujetahilo

binge [bɪndʒ] *s* (slang) borrachera; **to go on a binge** (slang) pegarse una mona

binnacle ['bɪnəkəl] *s* bitácora

binoculars [bɪ'nɑkjələrz] o [baɪ'nɑkjələrz] *spl* gemelos, prismáticos

biochemical [,baɪ-ə'kemɪkəl] *adj* bioquímico

biochemist [,baɪ-ə'kemɪst] *s* bioquímico

biochemistry [,baɪ-ə'kemɪstri] *s* bioquímica

biog. *abbr* **biographical, biography**

biographer [baɪ'ɑgrəfər] *s* biógrafo

biographic(al) [,baɪ-ə'græfɪk(əl)] *adj* biográfico

biogra·phy [baɪ'ɑgrəfi] *s* (*pl* -**phies**) biografía

biologist [baɪˈɑlədʒɪst] s biólogo

biology [baɪˈɑlədʒɪ] s biología

biophysical [ˌbaɪ-əˈfɪzɪkəl] adj bioffsico

biophysics [ˌbaɪ-əˈfɪzɪks] s biofísica

birch [bɑrtʃ] s abedul m || tr azotar, varear

bird [bʌrd] s ave f, pájaro

bird cage s jaula

bird call s reclamo

bird'lime' s liga

bird of passage s ave f de paso

bird of prey s ave f de rapiña

bird'seed' s alpiste m, cañamones mpl

bird's'-eye' view s vista a ojo de pájaro

bird shot s perdigones mpl

birth [bʌrθ] s nacimiento; (childbirth) parto; origen m

birth certificate s partida de nacimiento

birth control s limitación de la natalidad

birth'day' s cumpleaños m, natal m; (of any event) aniversario; to have a birthday cumplir años

birthday cake s pastel m de cumpleaños

birthday present s regalo de cumpleaños

birth'mark' s antojo, nevo materno

birth'place' s suelo natal, patria, lugar m de nacimiento

birth rate s natalidad

birth'right' s derechos de nacimiento; primogenitura

Biscay [ˈbɪske] s Vizcaya

biscuit [ˈbɪskɪt] s panecillo redondo; bizcocho

bisect [baɪˈsekt] tr bisecar || intr empalmar (dos caminos)

bishop [ˈbɪʃəp] s obispo; (in chess) alfil m

bismuth [ˈbɪzməθ] s bismuto

bison [ˈbaɪsən] o [ˈbaɪzən] s bisonte m

bit [bɪt] s poquito, pedacito; (of food) bocado; (of time) ratito; (part of bridle) bocado, freno; (for drilling) barrena; a good bit una buena cantidad

bitch [bɪtʃ] s (dog) perra; (fox) zorra; (wolf) loba; (vulg) mujer f de mal genio

bite [baɪt] s mordedura; (of bird or insect) picadura; (burning sensation on tongue) resquemo; (of food) bocado; (snack) (coll) tentempié m, refrigerio || v (pret bit [bɪt]; pp bit o bitten [ˈbɪtən]) tr morder, picar (los peces, los insectos); resquemar (la lengua los alimentos); comerse (las uñas) || intr morder, picar; resquemar; (to be caught by a trick) (slang) picar

biting [ˈbaɪtɪŋ] adj penetrante; mordaz, picante

bitter [ˈbɪtər] adj amargo; (e.g., struggle) encarnizado; to the bitter end hasta el extremo; hasta la muerte

bitter almond s almendra amarga

bitterness [ˈbɪtərnɪs] s amargura

bitumen [bɪˈtjumən] o [bɪˈtumən] s betún m

bivouac [ˈbɪvʊ-æk] o [ˈbɪvwæk] s vivaque m || v (pret & pp -acked; ger -acking) intr vivaquear

bizarre [bɪˈzɑr] adj original, rato

bk. abbr bank, block, book

bkg. abbr banking

bl. abbr barrel

b.l. abbr bill of lading

blabber [ˈblæbər] tr & intr barbullar

black [blæk] adj negro || s negro; luto; to wear black ir de luto

black'-and-blue' adj encardenalado, amoratado

black'-and-white' adj en blanco y negro

black'ber'ry s (pl -ries) (bush) zarza; (fruit) zarzamora

black'bird' s mirlo

black'board' s encerado, pizarra

black'damp' s mofeta

blacken [ˈblækən] tr ennegrecer; (to defame) desacreditar, denigrar

blackguard [ˈblægɑrd] s bribón m, canalla m || tr injuriar, vilipendiar

black'head' s espinilla, comedón m

blackish [ˈblækɪʃ] adj negruzco

black'jack' s (club) cachiporra; (flag) bandera negra (de pirata) || tr aporrear

black'mail' s chantaje m || tr amenazar con chantaje

blackmailer [ˈblæk,melər] s chantajista mf

Black Maria [məˈraɪ-ə] s (coll) coche m celular

black market s estraperlo, mercado negro

blackness [ˈblæknɪs] s negror m, negrura

black'out' s (in wartime) apagón m; (in theater) apagamiento de luces; (of aviators) visión negra; pérdida de la memoria

black sheep s (fig) oveja negra, garbanzo negro

black'smith' s (man who works with iron) herrero, (man who shoes horses) herrador m

black'thorn' s espino negro, endrino

black tie s corbata de smoking; smoking m

bladder [ˈblædər] s vejiga

blade [bled] s (of a knife, sword) hoja; (of a propeller) aleta; (of a fan) paleta; (of an oar) pala; (of an electric switch) cuchilla; (sword) espada; tallo de hierba; (coll) gallardo joven

blame [blem] s culpa || tr culpar

blameless [ˈblemlɪs] adj inculpable, irreprochable

blanch [blæntʃ] o [blɑntʃ] tr blanquear || intr palidecer

bland [blænd] adj apacible; suave; (character; weather) blando

blandish [ˈblændɪʃ] tr engatusar, lisonjear

blank [blæŋk] adj en blanco; blanco, vacío; (stare, look) vago || s blanco; papel blanco; formulario

blank check s firma en blanco; (fig) carta blanca

blanket ['blæŋkɪt] *adj* general, comprensivo || *s* manta, frazada; (fig) capa, manto || *tr* cubrir con manta; cubrir, obscurecer

blasé [bla'ze] *adj* hastiado

blaspheme [blæs'fim] *tr* blasfemar contra || *intr* blasfemar

blasphemous ['blæsfɪməs] *adj* blasfemo

blasphe·my ['blæsfɪmi] *s* (*pl* -mies) blasfemia

blast [blæst] o [blɑst] *s* (*of wind*) ráfaga; (*of air, sand, water*) chorro; (*of bellows*) soplo; (*of a horn*) toque *m*; carga de pólvora; voladura, explosión; **full blast** en plena marcha || *tr* (*to blow up*) volar; arruinar; infamar, maldecir

blast furnace *s* alto horno

blast'off' *s* lanzamiento de cohete

blatant ['bletənt] *adj* ruidoso; vocinglero, intruso; chillón, cursi

blaze [blez] *s* llamarada; (*fire*) incendio; (*bonfire*) hoguera; luz *f* brillante || *tr* encender, inflamar; **to blaze a trail** abrir una senda || *intr* encenderse; resplandecer

bldg. *abbr* building

bleach [blitʃ] *s* blanqueo || *tr* blanquear; colar (*la ropa*)

bleachers ['blitʃərz] *spl* gradas al aire libre

bleak [blik] *adj* desierto, yermo, frío, triste

bleat [blit] *s* balido || *intr* balar

bleed [blid] *v* (*pret & pp* **bled** [blɛd]) *tr & intr* sangrar

blemish ['blɛmɪʃ] *s* mancha || *tr* manchar

blend [blɛnd] *s* mezcla; armonía || *v* (*pret & pp* **blended** o **blent** [blɛnt]) *tr* mezclar; armonizar; fusionar || *intr* mezclarse; armonizar; fusionarse

bless [blɛs] *tr* bendecir; **to be blessed with** estar dotado de

blessed [ˈblɛsɪd] *adj* bendito, santo

blessedness [ˈblɛsɪdnɪs] *s* bienaventuranza

blessing ['blɛsɪŋ] *s* bendición

blight [blaɪt] *s* niebla, roya; ruina || *tr* anublar; arruinar

blimp [blɪmp] *s* dirigible pequeño

blind [blaɪnd] *adj* ciego || *s* (*window shade*) estor *m*, transparente *m* de resorte; (*Venetian blind*) persiana; pretexto, subterfugio || *tr* cegar; (*to dazzle*) deslumbrar; (*to deceive*) cegar, vendar

blind alley *s* callejón *m* sin salida

blind date *s* cita a ciegas

blinder [ˈblaɪndər] *s* anteojera

blind flying *s* (aer) vuelo a ciegas

blind'fold' *adj* vendado de ojos || *s* venda || *tr* vendar los ojos a

blind landing *s* aterrizaje *m* a ciegas

blind man *s* ciego

blind'man's' buff *s* gallina ciega

blindness ['blaɪndnɪs] *s* ceguedad

blink [blɪŋk] *s* guiñada, parpadeo || *tr* guiñar (*el ojo*) || *intr* guiñar, parpadear, pestañear; oscilar (*la luz*)

blip [blɪp] *s* bache *m*

bliss [blɪs] *s* bienaventuranza, felicidad

blissful ['blɪsfəl] *adj* bienaventurado, feliz

blister ['blɪstər] *s* ampolla, vejiga || *tr* ampollar || *intr* ampollarse

blithe [blaɪð] *adj* alegre, animado

blitzkrieg ['blɪts ˌkrig] *s* guerra relámpago

blizzard ['blɪzərd] *s* ventisca, chubasco de nieve

bloat [blot] *tr* hinchar || *intr* hincharse, abotagarse

block [blɑk] *s* bloque *m*; (*of hatter*) horma; (*of houses*) manzana; (*for chopping meat*) tajo; estorbo, obstáculo || *tr* cerrar, obstruir; conformar (*un sombrero*)

blockade [blɑ'ked] *s* bloqueo || *tr* bloquear

blockade runner *s* forzador *m* de bloqueo

block and tackle *s* aparejo de poleas

block'bust'er *s* (coll) bomba rompedora

block'head' *s* tonto, zoquete *m*

block signal *s* (rr) señal *f* de tramo

blond [blɑnd] *adj* rubio, blondo || *s* rubio (*hombre rubio*)

blonde [blɑnd] *s* rubia (*mujer rubia*)

blood [blʌd] *s* sangre *f*; **in cold blood** a sangre fría

bloodcurdling ['blʌd ˌkɑrdlɪŋ] *adj* horripilante

blood'hound' *s* sabueso

blood poisoning *s* envenenamiento de la sangre

blood pressure *s* presión arterial

blood pudding *s* morcilla

blood relation *s* pariente consanguíneo

blood'shed' *s* efusión de sangre

blood'shot' *adj* inyectado en sangre, encarnizado

blood test *s* análisis *m* de sangre

blood'thirst'y *adj* sanguinario

blood transfusion *s* transfusión de sangre

blood vessel *s* vaso sanguíneo

blood·y ['blʌdi] *adj* (*comp* -ier; *super* -lest) sangriento || *v* (*pret & pp* -ied) *tr* ensangrentar

bloom [blum] *s* florecimiento; flor *f* || *intr* florecer

blossom ['blɑsəm] *s* brote *m*, flor *f*; **in blossom** en cierne || *intr* cerner, florecer

blot [blɑt] *s* borrón *m* || *v* (*pret & pp* **blotted**; *ger* **blotting**) *tr* (*to smear*) borrar; secar con papel secante; **to blot out** borrar || *intr* borrarse; echar borrones (*una pluma*)

blotch [blɑtʃ] *s* manchón *m*; (*in the skin*) erupción

blotter [ˈblɑtər] *s* teleta, secafirmas *m*

blotting paper *s* papel *m* secante

blouse [blaus] *s* blusa

blow [blo] *s* (*hit, stroke*) golpe; (*blast of air*) soplo, soplido; (*blast of wind*) ventarrón *m*; (*of horn*) toque *m*, trompetazo; (*sudden sorrow*) estocada, ramalazo; (*boaster*) (slang) fanfarrón *m*; **to come to blows** venir a las manos || *v* (*pret* **blew** [blu]; *pp*

blown || *tr* soplar; sonar, tocar (*un instrumento de viento*); silbar (*un silbato*); sonarse (*las narices*); quemar (*un fusible*); (slang) malgastar (*dinero*); to blow out apagar soplando; quemar (*un fusible*); to blow up (*with air*) inflar (*e.g., with dynamite*) volar, hace saltar, ampliar (*una foto*) || *intr* soplar; (*to pant*) jadear, resoplar; fundirse (*un fusible*); (slang) fanfarronear; to blow out apagarse con el aire; quemarse, fundirse (*un fusible*) reventar (*un neumático*); to blow up volarse; (*to fail*) fracasar; (*with anger*) (slang) estallar, reventar

blow'out' *s* (aut) reventón *m*; (*of a fuse*) quemazón *f*; (slang) tertulia concurrida, festín *m*

blowout patch *s* parche *m* para neumático

blow'pipe' *s* (*torch*) soplete *m*; (*peashooter*) cerbatana

blow'torch' *s* antorcha a soplete, lámpara de soldar

blubber ['blʌbər] *s* grasa de ballena; lloro ruidoso || *intr* llorar ruidosamente

bludgeon ['blʌdʒən] *s* cachiporra || *tr* aporrear; intimidar

blue [blu] *adj* azul; abatido, triste || *s* azul *m*; the blues la murria, la morriña || *tr* azular, añilar (*la ropa blanca*) || *intr* azularse

blue'ber'ry *s* (*pl* -ries) mirtilo

blue chip *s* valor *m* de primera fila

blue'jay' *s* cianocita

blue moon *s* cosa muy rara; once in a blue moon cada muerte de obispo, de Pascuas a Ramos

Blue Nile *s* Nilo Azul

blue'-pen'cil *tr* marcar o corregir con lápiz azul

blue'print' *s* cianotipo || *tr* copiar a la cianotipia

blue'stock'ing *s* (coll) marisabidilla

blue streak *s* (coll) rayo; to talk a blue streak (coll) soltar la tarabilla

bluff [blʌf] *adj* escarpado || *s* risco, peñasco escarpado; (*deception*) farol *m*; to call someone's bluff cogerle la palabra a uno || *intr* farolear, papelonear

blunder ['blʌndər] *s* disparate *m*, desatino || *intr* disparatar, desatinar

blunt [blʌnt] *adj* despuntado, embotado; brusco, franco, directo || *tr* despuntar, embotar

bluntness ['blʌntnɪs] *s* embotadura; brusquedad, franqueza

blur [blʌr] *s* borrón *m*, mancha || *v* (*pret & pp* blurred; *ger* blurring) *tr* empañar; obscurecer (*la vista*) || *intr* empañarse

blurb [blʌrb] *s* anuncio efusivo

blurt [blʌrt] *tr* — to blurt out soltar abrupta e impulsivamente

blush [blʌʃ] *s* rubor *m*, sonrojo || *intr* ruborizarse, sonrojarse

bluster ['blʌstər] *s* tumulto, gritos; jactancia || *intr* soplar con furia (*el viento*); bravear, fanfarronear

blustery ['blʌstərɪ] *adj* tempestuoso; (*wind*) violento; (*swaggering*) fanfarrón

blvd. *abbr* boulevard

boar [bor] *s* (*male swine*) verraco; (*wild hog*) jabalí *m*

board [bord] *s* tabla; (*to post announcements*) tablillo; (*table with meal*) mesa (*daily meals*) pensión; (*organized group*) junta, consejo; (naut) bordo; in boards (bb) en cartoné, on board en el tren; (naut) a bordo || *tr* entablar; subir a (*un tren*); embarcarse en (*un buque*) || *intr* hospedarse; estar de pupilo

board and lodging *s* mesa y habitación, pensión completa

boarder ['bordər] *s* pensionista *mf*, pupilo

boarding house *s* pensión, casa de huéspedes

boarding school *s* escuela de internos

board of health *s* junta de sanidad

board of trade *s* junta de comercio

board of trustees *s* consejo de administración

board'walk' *s* paseo entablado a la orilla del mar

boast [bost] *s* jactancia, baladronada || *intr* jactarse, baladronear

boastful ['bostfəl] *adj* jactancioso

boat [bot] *s* barco, buque *m*, nave *f*; (*small boat*) bote *m*; to be in the same boat correr el mismo riesgo

boat hook *s* bichero

boat'house' *s* casilla para botes

boating ['botɪŋ] *s* paseo en barco

boat-man ['botmən] *s* (*pl* -men [mən]) barquero, lanchero

boat race *s* regata

boatswain *s* ['bosən] o ['bot,swen] *s* contramaestre *m*

boatswain's chair *s* guindola

boatswain's mate *s* segundo contramaestre

bob [bab] *s* (*of pendulum of clock*) lenteja; (*of plumb line*) plomo; (*of a fishing line*) corcho; (*of a horse*) cola cortada; (*of a girl*) pelo cortado corto (*jerk, motion*) sacudida || *v* (*pret & pp* bobbed; *ger* bobbing) *tr* cortar corto || *intr* agitarse, menearse; to bob up and down subir y bajar con sacudidas cortas

bobbin ['babɪn] *s* broca, canilla, bobina

bobby pin ['babɪ] *s* horquillita para el pelo

bob'by-socks' *spl* (coll) tobilleras (*de jovencita*)

bobbysoxer ['babɪ,saksər] *s* (coll) tobillera

bobolink ['babə,lɪŋk] *s* chambergo

bob'sled *s* doble trineo articulado

bob'tail' *s* animal *m* rabón; cola corta; cola cortada

bob'white' *s* colín *m* de Virginia

bock beer [bak] *s* cerveza de marzo

bode [bod] *tr & intr* anunciar, presagiar; to bode ill ser un mal presagio; to bode well ser un buen presagio

bodice ['badɪs] s jubón m, corpiño
bodily ['badɪlɪ] adj corporal, corpóreo || adv en persona; en conjunto
bodkin ['badkɪn] s (needle) aguja roma; (for lady's hair) espadilla; (to make holes in cloth) punzón m
bod·y ['badɪ] s (pl -ies) cuerpo; (of a carriage or auto) caja, carrocería
bod'y-guard' s (mil) guardia de corps; guardaespaldas m
Boer [bor] o [bur] s bóer mf
Boer War s guerra del Transvaal
bog [bag] s pantano || v (pret & pp bogged; ger bogging) intr — **to bog down** atascarse, hundirse
bogey ['bogɪ] s duende m, coco
bo'gey-man' s (pl -men [ˌmɛn]) duende m, espantajo
bogus ['bogəs] adj (coll) fingido, falso
bo·gy ['bogɪ] s (pl -gies) duende m, demonio, coco
Bohemian [bo'himɪ·ən] adj & s bohemio
boil [bɔɪl] s hervor m, ebullición; (pathol) divieso, furúnculo || tr hacer hervir, herventar || intr hervir, bullir; **to boil over** salirse (un líquido) al hervir
boiler ['bɔɪlər] s caldera; (for cooking) marmita, olla
boil'er-mak'er s calderero
boiler room s sala de calderas
boiling ['bɔɪlɪŋ] adj hirviente, hirviendo || s hervor m, ebullición
boiling point s punto de ebullición
boisterous ['bɔɪstərəs] adj bullicioso, ruidoso, estrepitoso
bold [bold] adj audaz, arrojado, osado; descarado, impudente; temerario
bold'face' s negrilla
boldness ['boldnɪs] s audacia, arrojo, osadía; descaro, impudencia; temeridad
Bolivia [bo'lɪvɪ·ə] s Bolivia
Bolivian [bo'lɪvɪ·ən] adj & s boliviano
boll weevil [bol] s gorgojo del algodón
Bologna [bə'lonjə] s Bolonia
Bolshevik ['bulʃəvɪk] o ['bɔlʃəvɪk] adj & s bolchevique mf
Bolshevism ['bulʃəˌvɪzəm] o ['bɔlʃəˌvɪzəm] s bolchevismo
bolster ['bolstər] s (of bed) larguero, travesaño; refuerzo, soporte m || tr apoyar, sostener; animar, alentar
bolt [bolt] s perno; (to fasten a door) cerrojo, pasador m; (arrow) cuadrillo; (of lightning) rayo; (of cloth or paper) rollo || tr empernar; acerrojar; deglutir de una vez; cribar, tamizar; disidir de (un partido político) || intr salir de repente; disidir; desbocarse (un caballo)
bolter ['boltər] s disidente mf; (sieve) criba, tamiz m
bolt from the blue s rayo en cielo sin nubes; suceso inesperado
bomb [bam] s bomba || tr bombear, bombardear
bombard [bam'bard] tr bombardear; (e.g., with questions) asediar
bombardment [bam'bardmənt] s bombardeo

bombast ['bambæst] s ampulosidad
bombastic [bam'bæstɪk] adj ampuloso
bomb crater s (mil) embudo de bomba
bomber ['bamər] s bombardero
bomb'proof' adj a prueba de bombas
bomb release s lanzabombas m
bomb'shell' s bomba; **to fall like a bombshell** caer como una bomba
bomb shelter s refugio antiaéreo
bomb'sight' s mira de bombardeo, visor m
bona fide ['bonəˌfaɪdə] adj & adv de buena fe
bonbon ['banˌban] s bombón m, confite m
bond [band] s (tie, union) enlace m, vínculo, lazo de unión; (interest-bearing certificate) bono, obligación; (surety) fianza; (mas) aparejo; **bonds** cadenas, grillos; **in bond** en depósito bajo fianza
bondage ['bandɪdʒ] s cautiverio, servidumbre
bonded warehouse s depósito comercial
bond'hold'er s obligacionista mf, tenedor m de bonos
bonds-man ['bandzmən] s (pl -men [ˌmən]) fiador m
bone [bon] s hueso; (of fish) espina; **bones** esqueleto; (mortal remains) huesos; castañuelas; (dice) (coll) dados; **to have a bone to pick with** tener una queja con; **to make no bones about** no andarse con rodeos en || tr desosar; quitar la espina a; emballenar (un corsé) || intr — **to bone up on** (coll) empollar, estudiar con ahinco
bone'head' s (coll) mentecato, zopenco
boneless ['bonlɪs] adj mollar, desosado; (fish) sin espinas
boner ['bonər] s (coll) patochada, plancha, gazapo
bonfire ['banˌfaɪr] s hoguera
bonnet ['banɪt] s gorra; (sunbonnet) papalina, (of auto) cubierta, capó m
bonus ['bonəs] s prima, plus m; dividendo extraordinario
bon·y ['bonɪ] adj (comp -ier; super -iest) osudo; descarnado; (fish) espinoso
boo [bu] s rechifla; **not to say boo** no decir ni chus ni mus || tr & intr abuchear, rechiflar
boo·by ['bubɪ] s (pl -bies) bobalicón m, zopenco; el peor jugador
booby prize s premio al peor jugador
booby trap s (mine) trampa explosiva; (trick) zancadilla
boogie-woogie ['bugɪ'wugɪ] s buguibugui m
book [buk] s libro; (bankbook) libreta; (book containing records of business transactions) libro-registro; (of cigaret paper, stamps, etc.) librillo; **to keep books** llevar libros || tr reservar (un pasaje); escriturar (a un actor)
bookbinder ['bukˌbaɪndər] s encuadernador m

book′bind′er·y *s* (*pl* **-ies**) encuadernación (*taller*)

book′bind′ing *s* encuadernación (*acción, arte*)

book′case′ *s* armario para libros, estante *m* para libros

book end *s* apoyalibros *m*

bookie [′bukɪ] *s* (coll) corredor *m* de apuestas

booking [′bukɪŋ] *s* (*of passage*) reservación; (*of an actor*) escritura

booking clerk *s* taquillero (*que despacha pasajes o localidades*)

bookish [′bukɪʃ] *adj* libresco

book′keep′er *s* tenedor *m* de libros

book′keep′ing *s* teneduría de libros, contabilidad

book′mak′er *s* corredor *m* de apuestas

book′mark′ *s* registro

book′plate′ *s* ex libris *m*

book review *s* reseña

book′sell′er *s* librero

book′shelf′ *s* (*pl* **-shelves** [ˌʃɛlvz]) estante *m* para libros

book′stand′ *s* (*rack*) atril *m*; mostrador *m* para libros; puesto de venta para libros

book′store′ *s* librería

hook′worm′ *s* polilla que roe los libros; (fig) ratón *m* de biblioteca

boom [bum] *s* (*sudden prosperity*) auge *m*; (*noise*) estampido, trueno; (*of a crane*) aguilón *m*; (naut) botalón *m* || *intr* hacer estampido, tronar; estar en auge

boomerang [′bumə‚ræŋ] *s* bumerán *m*

boom town *s* pueblo en bonanza

boon [bun] *s* bendición, dicha

boon companion *s* buen compañero

boor [bur] *s* patán *m*, rústico

boorish [′burɪʃ] *adj* rústico, zafio

boost [bust] *s* empujón *m* hacia arriba; (*in price*) alza; alabanza; ayuda || *tr* empujar hacia arriba; alzar (*el precio*); alabar; ayudar

booster [′bustər] *s* cohete *m* lanzador; primera etapa de un cohete lanzador; (*enthusiastic backer*) bombista *mf*; (med) inyección secundaria

boot [but] *s* bota; **to boot** de añadidura, además; **to die with one's boots on** morir al pie del cañón || *tr* dar un puntapié a; **to boot out** (slang) poner en la calle

boot′black′ *s* limpiabotas *m*

booth [buθ] *s* casilla, quiosco; (*to telephone, to vote, etc.*) cabina; (*at a fair or market*) puesto

boot′jack′ *s* sacabotas *m*

boot′leg′ *adj* contrabandista; de contrabando || *s* contrabando de licores || *v* (*pret & pp* **-legged**; *ger* **-legging**) *tr* pasar de contrabando || *intr* contrabandear en bebidas alcohólicas

bootlegger [′but‚lɛgər] *s* destilador *m* clandestino, contrabandista

boot′leg′ging *s* contrabando en bebidas alcohólicas

bootlicker [′but‚lɪkər] *s* (slang) quitamotas *mf*, lavacaras *mf*

boot′strap′ *s* tirilla de bota

boo·ty [′butɪ] *s* (*pl* **-ties**) botín *m*, presa

booze [buz] *s* (coll) bebida alcohólica || *intr* borrachear

bor. *abbr* **borough**

borax [′boræks] *s* bórax *m*

Bordeaux [bɔr′do] *s* Burdeos

border [′bɔrdər] *adj* frontero, fronterizo || *s* borde *m*, margen *m & f*; frontera; **borders** bambalinas || *tr* bordear; deslindar || *intr* confinar

border clash *s* encuentro fronterizo

bor′der·line′ *adj* incierto, indefinido || *s* frontera

bore [bor] *s* (*drill hole*) barreno; (*size of hole*) calibre *m*; (*of firearm*) alma, ánima; (*of cylinder*) alesaje *m*; (*wearisome person*) latoso, machaca *mf*; fastidio || *tr* aburrir, fastidiar; barrenar, hacer (*un agujero*)

boredom [′bordəm] *s* aburrimiento, fastidio

boring [′borɪŋ] *adj* aburrido, pesado

born [bɔrn] *adj* nacido; (*natural, by birth*) nato, innato; **to be born** nacer

borough [′bʌro] *s* (*town*) villa; distrito electoral de municipio

borrow [′bɔro] o [′baro] *tr* pedir o tomar prestado; apropiarse (*p.ej., una idea*); incorporar (*un elemento lingüístico extranjero*); **to borrow trouble** tomarse una molestia sin motivo alguno

borrower [′baro·ər] o [′bɔro·ər] *s* prestatario

borrowing [′baro·ɪŋ] o [′bɔro·ɪŋ] *s* préstamo; préstamo lingüístico, extranjerismo

bosom [′buzəm] *s* seno; (*of shirt*) pechera; corazón *m*, pecho

bosom friend *s* amigo de la mayor confianza

Bosporus [′baspərəs] *s* Bósforo

boss [bɔs] o [bas] *s* (coll) amo, capataz *m*, mandamás, *m*, jefe *m*; (*in politics*) (coll) cacique *m*; protuberancia || *tr* (coll) mandar, dominar

boss·y [′bɔsɪ] o [′basɪ] *adj* (*comp* **-ier**; *super* **-iest**) mandón

botanical [bə′tænɪkəl] *adj* botánico

botanist [′butənɪst] *s* botánico

botany [′butənɪ] *s* botánica

botch [batʃ] *s* remiendo chapucero || *tr* remendar chapuceramente

both [boθ] *adj & pron* ambos || *adv* igualmente || *conj* a la vez; **both . . . and** tanto . . . como, así . . . como

bother [′baðər] *s* incomodidad, molestia || *tr* incomodar, molestar || *intr* molestarse

bothersome [′baðərsəm] *adj* incómodo, molesto, fastidioso

bottle [′batəl] *s* botella, frasco || *tr* embotellar; **to bottle up** (nav) embotellar

bot′tle·neck′ *s* gollete *m*; (*in traffic*) embotellado

bottle opener [′opənər] *s* abrebotellas

bottom [′batəm] *adj* (*price*) (el) más bajo; (*e.g., dollar*) último || *s* fondo; (*of a chair*) asiento; (*of jar*) culo;

(coll) trasero; **at bottom** en el fondo; **to go to the bottom** irse a pique

bottomless ['batəmlɪs] *adj* sin fondo, insondable

boudoir [bu'dwar] *s* tocador *m*

bough [bau] *s* rama

bouillon ['buljan] *s* caldo

boulder ['boldər] *s* pedrejón *m*

boulevard ['bulə,vard] *s* bulevar *m*

bounce [bauns] *s* rebote *m* || *tr* hacer botar; (slang) despedir || *intr* botar, rebotar; saltar; **to bounce along** dar saltos al andar

bouncer ['baunsər] *s* cosa grande; (slang) apagabroncas *m*

bouncing ['baunsɪŋ] *adj* frescachón, vigoroso; (baby) gordinflón

bound [baund] *adj* atado, ligado; (book) encuadernado; dispuesto, propenso; puesto en aprendizaje; **bound for** con destino a, con rumbo a; **bound in boards** (bb) encartonado, en cartoné; **bound up in** entregado a, muy adicto a; absorto en || *s* salto; (of a ball) bote *m*; límite *m*, confín *m*; **bounds** región, comarca; **out of bounds** fuera de los límites; **within bounds** a raya

bounda·ry ['baundəri] *s* (*pl* **-ries**) límite *m*, frontera

boundary stone *s* mojón *m*

bounder ['baundər] *s* persona vulgar y malcriada

boundless ['baundlɪs] *adj* ilimitado, inmenso, infinito

bountiful ['bauntɪfəl] *adj* generoso, liberal; abundante

boun·ty ['baunti] *s* (*pl* **-ties**) generosidad, liberalidad, don *m*, favor *m*; galardón *m*, premio; (bonus) prima; (mil) premio de enganche

bouquet [bu'ke] o [bo'ke] *s* ramillete *m*; (aroma of a wine) nariz *f*

bourgeois ['burʒwa] *adj* & *s* burgués *m*

bourgeoisie [,burʒwa'zi] *s* burguesía

bout [baut] *s* encuentro; rato; (of an illness) ataque *m*

bow [bau] *s* inclinación, reverencia; (of a ship) proa || *tr* inclinar (la cabeza) || *intr* inclinarse; **to bow and scrape** hacer reverencias obsequiosas; **to bow to** saludar inclinarse delante || [bo] *s* (for shooting an arrow) arco; lazo, nudo; (mus) arco; (stroke of bow) (mus) arqueada || *tr* (mus) tocar con arco || *intr* arquearse

bowdlerize ['baudlə,raɪz] *tr* expurgar

bowel ['bau·əl] *s* intestino; **bowels** intestinos, (inner part) entrañas

bowel movement *s* evacuación del vientre; **to have a bowel movement** evacuar el vientre

bower ['bau·ər] *s* emparrado, glorieta

bower·y ['bau·əri] *adj* frondoso, sombreado || *s* (*pl* **-ies**) finca, granja

bowknot ['bo,nat] *s* lazada

bowl [bol] *s* (for soup or broth) escudilla, cuenco; (for washing hands) jofaina, palangana; (of toilet) cubeta, taza; (of fountain) tazón *m*; (of spoon) paleta; (of pipe) hornillo;

(hollow place) concavidad, cuenco || *tr* — **to bowl over** tumbar || *intr* jugar a los bolos; **to bowl along** rodar

bowlegged ['bo,legd] o ['bo,legɪd] *adj* patiestevado

bowler ['bolər] *s* jugador *m* de bolos; (Brit) sombrero hongo

bowling ['bolɪŋ] *s* juego de bolos, boliche *m*

bowling alley *s* bolera, boliche *m*

bowling green *s* bolera encespada

bowshot ['bo,ʃat] *s* tiro de flecha

bowsprit ['bausprɪt] o ['bosprɪt] *s* bauprés *m*

bow tie [bo] *s* corbata de mariposa, pajarita

bowwow ['bau,wau] *interj* ¡guau! || *s* guau guau *m*

box [baks] *s* caja; (slap) bofetada; (plant) boj *m*; (in newspaper) recuadro; (theat) palco || *tr* encajonar; (to slap) abofetear; (naut) cuartear (la aguja) || *intr* boxear

box'car' *s* vagón *m* de carga cerrado

boxer ['baksər] *s* embalador *m*; (sport) boxeador *m*

boxing ['baksɪŋ] *s* embalaje *m*; (sport) boxeo

boxing gloves *spl* guantes *mpl* de boxeo

box office *s* taquilla, despacho de localidades; boletería (Am)

box'-of'fice hit *s* éxito de taquilla

box-office record *s* marca de taquilla

box-office sale *s* venta de localidades en taquilla

box pleat *s* pliegue *m* de tabla

box seat *s* asiento de palco

box'wood' *s* boj *m*

boy [bɔɪ] *s* muchacho; (servant) mozo; (coll) compadre *m*

boycott ['bɔɪkat] *s* boicoteo || *tr* boicotear

boyhood ['bɔɪhud] *s* muchachez *f*; muchachería

boyish ['bɔɪ·ɪʃ] *adj* amuchachado, muchachil

boy scout *s* niño explorador

Bp. *abbr* bishop

b.p. *abbr* bills payable, boiling point

br. *abbr* brand, brother

b.r. *abbr* bills receivable

bra [bra] *s* (coll) portasenos *m*, sostén *m*

brace [bres] *s* riostra; berbiquí *m*; **braces** (Brit) tirantes *mpl* || *tr* arriostrar; asegurar; vigorizar; **to brace oneself** (coll) cobrar ánimo || *intr* — **to brace up** (coll) cobrar ánimo

brace and bit *s* berbiquí y barrena

bracelet ['breslɪt] *s* brazalete *m*, pulsera

bracer ['bresər] *s* (coll) trago de licor

bracing ['bresɪŋ] *adj* fortificante, tónico

bracket ['brækɪt] *s* puntal *m*, soporte *m*; ménsula, repisa; (mark used in printing) corchete *m*; clase *f*, categoría || *tr* acorchetar, agrupar

brackish ['brækɪʃ] *adj* salobre

brad [bræd] *s* clavito, estaquilla

brag [bræg] *s* jactancia || *v* (pret & pp **bragged**; ger **bragging**) *intr* jactarse

braggart ['brægərt] s fanfarrón m
braid [bred] s (flat strip of cotton, silk, etc.) cinta, galón m; (something braided) trenza || tr encintar, galonear; trenzar
brain [bren] s cerebro; **brains** cerebro, inteligencia; **to rack one's brains** devanarse los sesos || tr descerebrar
brain child s parto del ingenio
brain drain s (coll) éxodo de técnicos
brainless ['brenlɪs] adj tonto, sin seso
brain power s capacidad mental
brain'storm' s acceso de locura; (coll) confusión mental; (coll) buena idea, hallazgo
brain trust s grupo de peritos
brain'wash'ing s lavado cerebral
brain wave s onda encefálica; (coll) buena idea, hallazgo
brain'work' s trabajo intelectual
brain-y ['breni] adj (comp -ier; super -iest) (coll) inteligente, sesudo
braise [brez] tr soasar y cocer (la carne) a fuego lento en vasija bien tapada
brake [brek] s freno; (for dressing flax) agramadera; (thicket) matorral m; (fern) helecho común || tr frenar; agramar (el lino o el cáñamo)
brake band s cinta de freno
brake drum s tambor m de freno
brake lining s forro o cinta de freno
brake-man ['brekmən] s (pl -men [mən]) guardafrenos m
brake shoe s zapata de freno
bramble ['bræmbəl] s frambueso, zarza
bram-bly ['bræmbli] adj (comp -blier; super -bliest) zarzoso
bran [bræn] s afrecho, salvado
branch [bræntʃ] s (of tree) rama; (smaller branch; branch cut from tree; of a science, etc.) ramo; (of vine) sarmiento; (of road, railroad) ramal m; (of candlestick, river, etc.) brazo; (of a store, bank) sucursal f || intr ramificarse; **to branch out** extender sus actividades
branch line s ramal m, línea de empalme
branch office s sucursal f
brand [brænd] s (kind, make) marca; (trademark) marca de fábrica; (branding iron) hierro de marcar; (mark stamped with hot iron) hierro; (dishonor) tizón m || tr poner marca de fábrica en; herrar con hierro candente; tiznar (la reputación de una persona); **to brand as** tildar de
brandied ['brændid] adj macerado en aguardiente
branding iron s hierro de marcar
brandish ['brændiʃ] tr blandear
brand'-new' adj nuevecito, flamante
bran-dy ['brændi] s (pl -dies) aguardiente m
brash [bræʃ] adj atrevido, impetuoso; descarado, respondón || s acceso, ataque m
brass [bræs] o [brɑs] s latón m; (in army and navy) (slang) los mandamases; (coll) descaro; **brasses** (mus) cobres mpl

brass band s banda, charanga
brass hat s (slang) espadón m, mandamás m
brassière [brə'zɪr] s portasenos m, sostén m
brass knuckles s llave inglesa, bóxer m
brass tack s clavito dorado de tapicería; **to get down to brass tacks** (coll) entrar en materia
brass winds spl (mus) cobres mpl, instrumentos músicos de metal
brass-y ['bræsi] o ['brɑsi] adj (comp -ier; super -iest) hecho de latón; metálico; descarado
brat [bræt] s rapaz m, mocoso, braguillas m
brava-do [brə'vɑdo] s (pl -does o -dos) bravata
brave [brev] adj bravo, valiente || s valiente m; guerrero indio norteamericano || tr hacer frente a, arrostrar; desafiar, retar
bravery ['brevəri] s bravura, valor m
bra-vo ['brɑvo] interj ¡bravo! || s (pl -vos) bravo
brawl [brɔl] s pendencia, reyerta; alboroto || intr armar pendencia; alborotar
brawler ['brɔlər] s pendenciero; alborotador m
brawn [brɔn] s fuerza musculosa
brawn-y ['brɔni] adj (comp -ier; super -iest) fornido, musculoso
bray [bre] s rebuzno || intr rebuznar
braze [brez] tr soldadura de latón || tr soldar con latón; cubrir de latón; adornar con latón
brazen ['brezən] adj de latón; descarado || tr — **to brazen through** llevar a cabo descaradamente
brazier ['breʒər] s brasero
Brazil [brə'zɪl] s el Brasil
Brazilian [brə'zɪljən] adj & s brasileño
Brazil nut s castaña de Pará
breach [britʃ] s (opening) abertura; (in a wall) brecha; abuso, violación || tr abrir brecha en
breach of faith s falta de fidelidad
breach of peace s perturbación del orden público
breach of promise s incumplimiento de la palabra de matrimonio
breach of trust s abuso de confianza
bread [bred] s pan m || tr empanar
bread and butter s pan m con mantequilla; (coll) pan de cada día
bread crumbs spl pan rallado
breaded ['bredid] adj empanado
bread line s cola del pan
breadth [bredθ] s anchura; alcance m, extensión; (e.g., of judgment) amplitud f
bread'win'ner s sostén m de la familia
break [brek] s rompimiento; interrupción; intervalo, pausa; (split) hendidura, grieta; (in prices) baja; (in clouds) claro; (from jail) evasión, huída; (among friends) ruptura; (luck, good or bad) (slang) suerte f; (slang) disparate m; **to give someone a break** abrirle a uno la puerta || v (pret **broke** [brok]; pp **broken**) tr

romper, quebrar; cambiar (un billete); comunicar (una mala noticia); suspender (relaciones); faltar a (la palabra); batir (un récord); cortar (un circuito); quebrantar (un testamento; un hábito); romper (una ley); levantar (el campo); (mil) degradar; **to break in** forzar (una puerta); **to break open** abrir por la fuerza ‖ intr romperse, quebrarse; reventar, aclarar (el tiempo); bajar (los precios); quebrantarse (la salud), **to break down** perder la salud; prorrumpir en llanto; **to break even** salir sin ganar ni perder; **to break in** entrar por fuerza; irrumpir en, **to break loose** desprenderse; escaparse desbocarse (un caballo); desencadenarse (una tempestad); **to break out** estallar, declararse; (in laughter weeping) romper; (on the skin) brotar granos; **to break through** abrirse paso; abrir paso por entre; **to break up** desmenuzarse; levantarse (una reunión); **to break with** romper con

breakable ['brekəbəl] adj rompible

breakage ['brekɪdʒ] s estropicio; indemnización por objetos rotos

break'down' s mal éxito; avería, pana; (in health) colapso; (in negotiations) ruptura; análisis m

breaker ['brekər] s cachón m, rompiente m

breakfast ['brekfəst] s desayuno ‖ intr desayunar

breakfast food s cereal m para el desayuno

break'neck' adj vertiginoso; **at breakneck speed** a mata caballo

break of day s alba, amanecer m

break'through' s (mil) brecha, ruptura; (fig) descubrimiento sensacional

break'up' s disolución, dispersión; desplome m; (in health) postración

break'wa'ter s rompeolas m, escollera

breast [brest] s pecho, seno; (of fowl) pechuga; (of garment) pechera; **to make a clean breast of it** confesarlo todo

breast'bone' s esternón m; (of fowl) quilla

breast drill s berbiquí m de pecho

breast'pin' s alfiler m de pecho

breast stroke s brazada de pecho

breath [brɛθ] s aliento, respiración; **out of breath** sin aliento; **short of breath** corto de resuello; **to gasp for breath** respirar anhelosamente; **under one's breath** por lo bajo, en voz baja

breathe [brið] tr respirar; **to breathe one's last** dar el último suspiro ‖ intr respirar; **to breathe freely** cobrar aliento; **to breathe in** aspirar; **to breathe out** espirar

breathing spell s respiro, rato de descanso

breathless ['brɛθlɪs] adj falto de aliento, jadeante; intenso, vivo; sin aliento

breath'tak'ing adj conmovedor, imponente

breech [britʃ] s culata, recámara; **breeches** ['brɪtʃɪz] calzones mpl; (coll) pantalones mpl; **to wear the breeches** (coll) calzarse los pantalones

breed [brid] s casta, raza; clase f, especie f ‖ v (pret & pp bred [bred]) tr criar ‖ intr criar; criarse

breeder ['bridər] s (of animals) criador m; (animal) reproductor m

breeding ['bridɪŋ] s cría, crianza, modales mpl; **bad breeding** mala crianza; **good breeding** buena crianza

breeze [briz] s brisa

breez•y ['brizi] adj (comp -ier; super -iest) airoso, animado, vivo; (coll) desenvuelto, vivaracho

brevi•ty ['brevɪti] s (pl -ties) brevedad

brew [bru] s calderada de cerveza; mezcla ‖ tr fabricar (cerveza); preparar (té); (fig) tramar, urdir ‖ intr amenazar (una tormenta)

brewer ['bruər] s cervecero

brewer's yeast s levadura de cerveza

brewer•y ['bruəri] s (pl -ies) cervecería, fábrica de cerveza

bribe [braɪb] s soborno ‖ tr sobornar

briber•y ['braɪbəri] s (pl -ies) soborno

bric-a-brac ['brɪkə,bræk] s chucherías, curiosidades fpl

brick [brɪk] s ladrillo; (coll) buen sujeto ‖ tr enladrillar

brick'bat' s pedazo de ladrillo; (coll) palabra hiriente

brick ice cream s queso helado, helado al corte

brickkiln ['brɪk,kɪl] s horno de ladrillero

bricklayer ['brɪk,le•ər] s ladrillador m

brick'yard' s ladrillal m

bridal ['braɪdəl] adj nupcial; de novia

bridal wreath s corona nupcial

bride [braɪd] s desposada, novia

bride'groom' s desposado, novio

bridesmaid ['braɪdz,med] s madrina de boda

bridge [brɪdʒ] s puente m; (of nose) caballete m; (card game) bridge m ‖ tr tender un puente sobre; salvar (un obstáculo); colmar, llenar (un vacío)

bridge'head' s (mil) cabeza de puente

bridle ['braɪdəl] s brida ‖ tr embridar ‖ intr engallarse, erguirse

bridle path s camino de herradura

brief [brif] adj breve, corto, conciso ‖ s resumen m; (law) escrito; **in brief** en resumen ‖ tr resumir; dar consejos anticipados a; dar informes a

brief case s cartera

brier ['braɪ•ər] s zarza; brezo blanco

brig [brɪg] s (naut) bergantín m; prisión en buque de guerra

brigade [brɪ'ged] s brigada

brigadier [,brɪgə'dɪr] s general m de brigada

brigand ['brɪgənd] s bandolero

brigantine ['brɪgən,tin] o ['brɪgən,taɪn] s (naut) bergantín m goleta

bright [braɪt] adj brillante; (e.g., day) claro; (color) subido; listo, inteligente, despierto; (idea, thought) luminoso; (disposition) alegre, vivo

brighten ['braɪtən] *tr* abrillantar; alegrar, avivar ‖ *intr* avivarse; alegrarse; despejarse (*el cielo*)
bright lights *spl* luces *fpl* brillantes; (aut) faros o luces de carretera
brilliance ['brɪljəns] o **brilliancy** ['brɪljənsi] *s* brillantez *f*, brillo
brilliant ['brɪljənt] *adj* brillante
brim [brɪm] *s* borde *m*; (*of hat*) ala
brim'stone' *s* azufre *m*
brine [braɪn] *s* salmuera, agua salobre
bring [brɪŋ] *v* (*pret & pp* **brought** [brɔt]) *tr* traer; llevar; **to bring about** efectuar; **to bring back** devolver; **to bring down** abatir; **to bring forth** sacar a luz; **to bring in** traer a colación; servir (*una comida*); introducir, presentar; **to bring into play** poner en juego; **to bring on** causar, producir; **to bring out** sacar; presentar al público; **to bring suit** poner pleito; **to bring to** sacar de un desmayo; **to bring together** reunir; confrontar; reconciliar; **to bring to pass** efectuar, llevar a cabo; **to bring up** arrimar (*p.ej., una silla*); educar, criar; traer a colación; **to bring upon oneself** atraerse (*un infortunio*)
bringing-up ['brɪŋɪŋ'ʌp] *s* educación, crianza
brink [brɪŋk] *s* borde *m*, margen *m*; **on the brink of** al borde de
brisk [brɪsk] *adj* animado, vivo, vivaz
bristle ['brɪsəl] *s* cerda ‖ *intr* erizarse, encresparse; (*to be visibly annoyed*) encresparse
bris-tly ['brɪsli] *adj* (*comp* **-tlier**; *super* **-tliest**) cerdoso, erizado
Britannic [brɪ'tænɪk] *adj* británico
British ['brɪtɪʃ] *adj* británico ‖ **the British** los britanos
Britisher ['brɪtɪʃər] *s* britano
Briton ['brɪtən] *s* britano
Brittany ['brɪtəni] *s* Bretaña
brittle ['brɪtəl] *adj* quebradizo, frágil
bro. *abbr* **brother**
broach [brotʃ] *s* (*skewer*) asador *m*, espetón *m*; (*ornamental pin*) broche *m*, prendedero ‖ *tr* sacar a colación
broad [brɔd] *adj* ancho; liberal, tolerante; (*day, noon, etc.*) pleno
broad'cast' *s* radiodifusión; audición, programa radiotelefónico ‖ *v* (*pret & pp* **-cast** o **-casted**) *tr* difundir, esparcir ‖ (*pret & pp* **-cast** o **-casted**) *tr* radiodifundir, radiar, emitir
broadcasting station *s* emisora, estación de radiodifusión
broad'cloth' *s* paño fino
broaden ['brɔdən] *tr* ensanchar ‖ *intr* ensancharse
broad'loom' *adj* tejido en telar ancho y en color sólido
broad-minded ['brɔd'maɪndɪd] *adj* tolerante, de amplias miras
broad-shouldered ['brɔd'ʃoldərd] *adj* ancho de espaldas
broad'side' *s* (naut) costado; (naut) andanada; (coll) torrente *m* de injurias
broad'sword' *s* espada ancha
brocade [bro'ked] *s* brocado

broccoli ['brɑkəli] *s* brécol *m*, brécoles *mpl*
brochure [bro'ʃur] *s* folleto
brogue [brog] *s* acento irlandés
broil [brɔɪl] *tr* asar a la parrilla ‖ *intr* asarse
broiler ['brɔɪlər] *s* parrilla; pollo para asar a la parrilla
broken ['brokən] *adj* roto, quebrado; agotado; amansado; (*accent*) chapurrado; suelto
bro'ken-down' *adj* abatido; descompuesto; destartalado
broken-hearted ['brokən'hɑrtɪd] *adj* abrumado por el dolor
broker ['brokər] *s* corredor *m*
brokerage ['brokərɪdʒ] *s* corretaje *m*
bromide ['bromaɪd] *s* bromuro; (slang) trivialidad
bromine ['bromin] *s* bromo
bronchitis [brɑŋ'kaɪtɪs] *s* bronquitis *f*
bron·co ['brɑŋko] *s* (*pl* **-cos**) potro cerril
bron'co-bust'er *s* domador *m* de potros; vaquero
bronze [brɑnz] *adj* bronceado ‖ *s* bronce *m* ‖ *tr* broncear ‖ *intr* broncearse
brooch [brotʃ] o [brutʃ] *s* alfiler *m* de pecho, prendedero, pasador *m*
brood [brud] *s* cría; nidada; casta, raza ‖ *tr* empollar ‖ *intr* enclocar; **to brood on** meditar con preocupación
brook [bruk] *s* arroyo ‖ *tr* — **to brook no** no tolerar, no aguantar
broom [brum] o [brum] *s* escoba; (bot) hiniesta
broom'corn' *s* sorgo
broom'stick' *s* palo de escoba
bros. *abbr* **brothers**
broth [brɔθ] *s* caldo
brothel ['brɑθəl] o ['brɑðəl] *s* burdel *m*
brother ['brʌðər] *s* hermano
brotherhood ['brʌðər‚hud] *s* hermandad
broth'er-in-law' *s* (*pl* **brothers-in-law**) cuñado, hermano político; (*husband of one's wife's or husband's sister*) concuñado
brotherly ['brʌðərli] *adj* fraternal
brow [brau] *s* (*forehead*) frente *f*; (*eyebrow*) ceja; **to knit one's brow** fruncir las cejas
brow'beat' *v* (*pret* **-beat**; *pp* **beaten**) *tr* intimidar con mirada ceñuda
brown [braun] *adj* pardo, castaño, moreno; (*race*) cobrizo; tostado del sol ‖ *s* castaño, moreno ‖ *tr* poner moreno; tostar, quemar, broncear; (culin) dorar
brownish ['braunɪʃ] *adj* que tira a moreno
brown study *s* absorción, pensamiento profundo, ensimismamiento
brown sugar *s* azúcar *m* terciado
browse [brauz] *intr* (*to nibble at twigs*) ramonear; (*to graze*) pacer; hojear un libro ociosamente; **to browse about** o **around** curiosear
bruise [bruz] *s* contusión, magulladura

|| *tr* contundir, magullar || *intr* contundirse, magullarse

brunet [bru'net] *adj* moreno || *s* moreno (*hombre moreno*)

brunette [bru'net] *s* morena (*mujer morena*)

brunt [brʌnt] *s* fuerza, choque *m*, empuje *m*; (*e.g., of a battle*) peso, (lo) más reñido

brush [brʌʃ] *s* brocha, cepillo, escobilla; (*stroke*) brochada; (*light touch*) roce *m*; (*brief encounter*) encuentro, escaramuza; (*growth of bushes*) maleza; (elec) escobilla || *tr* acepillar; (*to graze*) rozar; **to brush aside** echar a un lado || *intr* pasar ligeramente; **to brush up on** repasar

brush'-off' *s* (slang) desaire *m*; **to give the brush-off to** (slang) despedir noramala

brush'wood' *s* broza, ramojo

brusque [brʌsk] *adj* brusco, rudo

brusqueness ['brʌsknɪs] *s* brusquedad

Brussels ['brʌsəlz] *s* Bruselas

Brussels sprouts *spl* bretones *mpl*, col *f* de Bruselas

brutal ['brutəl] *adj* brutal, bestial

brutality [bru'tælɪtɪ] *s* (*pl* -ties) brutalidad, crueldad

brute [brut] *adj* bruto; (*force*) inconsciente, ciego || *s* bruto

brutish ['brutɪʃ] *adj* abrutado, estúpido

bu. *abbr* **bushel**

bubble ['bʌbəl] *s* burbuja; ampolla; ilusión, quimera || *intr* burbujear; **to bubble over** desbordar, rebosar

buck [bʌk] *s* (*goat*) cabrón *m*; (*deer*) gamo; (*rabbit*) conejo, piel *f* de; corveta, encorvada; (*youth*) pisaverde *m*; (slang) dólar *m*; **to pass the buck** (coll) echar la carga a otro || *tr* hacer frente a, resistir a; (*to butt*) acornear, topetar; colar (*la ropa*); **to buck up** (coll) alentar, animar || *intr* botarse, encorvarse; **to buck against** embestir contra

bucket ['bʌkɪt] *s* balde *m*, cubo; (*of a well*) pozal *m*; **to kick the bucket** (slang) estirar la pata, liar el petate

bucket seat *s* baquet *m*

buckle ['bʌkəl] *s* hebilla; (*bend, bulge*) alabeo, pandeo || *tr* abrochar con hebilla || *intr* (*to bend, bulge*) alabearse, pandear; **to buckle down to** (coll) dedicarse con empeño a

buck private *s* (slang) soldado raso

buckram ['bʌkrəm] *s* zangala; (bb) bocací *m*, bucarán *m*

buck'saw' *s* sierra de bastidor

buck'shot' *s* postas

buck'tooth' *s* (*pl* -teeth) diente *m* saliente

buck'wheat' *s* alforfón *m*, trigo sarraceno

bud [bʌd] *s* botón *m*, brote *m*; **to nip in the bud** cortar de raíz || *v* (*pret & pp* budded*) ger* **budding** *intr* abotonar, brotar

buddy ['bʌdɪ] *s* (*pl* -dies) (coll) camarada *m*; (coll) muchachito

budge [bʌdʒ] *tr* mover || *intr* moverse

budget ['bʌdʒɪt] *s* presupuesto || *tr* presuponer, presupuestar

budgetary ['bʌdʒɪˌterɪ] *adj* presupuestario

buff [bʌf] *adj* de ante || *s* (*leather*) ante *m*; color *m* de ante; chaqueta de ante; rueda pulidora; (coll) piel desnuda; aficionado || *tr* dar color de ante a; pulimentar

buffa·lo ['bʌfəˌlo] *s* (*pl* -loes o -los) búfalo || *tr* (slang) intimidar

buffer ['bʌfər] *s* amortiguador *m* de choques; tope *m*, paragolpes *m*; pulidor *m*

buffer state *s* estado tapón

buffet [bu'fe] *s* (*piece of furniture*) aparador *m*; restaurante *m* de estación || ['bʌfɪt] *tr* abofetear, golpear, pegar

buffet car [bu'fe] *s* coche *m* bar

buffet lunch [bu'fe] *s* servicio de bufet

buffet supper [bu'fe] *s* ambigú *m*, bufet *m*

buffoon [bə'fun] *s* bufón *m*, payaso

buffoner·y [bə'funərɪ] *s* (*pl* -ies) bufonada, chocarrería

bug [bʌg] *s* insecto, bicho, sabandija; microbio; (*bedbug*) (Brit) chinche *f*; (coll) defecto; (slang) micrófono escondido; (slang) loco; (slang) entusiasta *mf* || *v* (*pret & pp* bugged*) ger* **bugging** *tr* (slang) esconder un micrófono en

bug'bear' *s* espantajo; aversión

buggy ['bʌgɪ] *adj* (*comp* -gier; *super* -giest) infestado de bichos; (slang) loco || *s* (*pl* -gies) calesa

bug'house' *adj* (slang) loco || *s* (slang) manicomio, casa de locos

bugle ['bjugəl] *s* corneta

bugle call *s* toque *m* de corneta

bugler ['bjuglər] *s* corneta *m*

build [bɪld] *s* forma, hechura, figura; (*of human being*) talle *m* || *v* (*pret & pp* built [bɪlt]) *tr* construir, edificar; componer; establecer, fundar; crearse (*p.ej., una clientela*)

builder ['bɪldər] *s* constructor *m*; aparejador *m*, maestro de obras

building ['bɪldɪŋ] *s* construcción; edificio; (*one of several in a group*) pabellón *m*

building and loan association *s* sociedad *f* de crédito para la construcción

building lot *s* solar *m*

building site *s* terreno para construir

building trades *spl* oficios de edificación

build'-up' *s* acumulación, formación; (coll) propaganda anticipada

built'-in' *adj* integrante, incorporado, empotrado

built'-up' *adj* armado, montado; (*land*) aglomerado

bulb [bʌlb] *s* (*of plant*) bulbo; (*of thermometer*) bola, cubeta; (*of syringe*) pera; (*of electric light*) ampolla, bombilla

Bulgaria [bʌl'gerɪə] *s* Bulgaria

Bulgarian [bʌl'gerɪən] *adj & s* búlgaro

bulge [bʌldʒ] *s* protuberancia, bulto, bombeo; **to get the bulge on** (coll) llevar la ventaja a || *intr* hacer bulto, bombearse

bulk [bʌlk] *s* bulto, volumen *m*; (*main mass*) grueso; **in bulk** a granel || *intr* abultar, hacer bulto; tener importancia

bulk'head' *s* mamparo; tabique hermético

bulk·y ['bʌlki] *adj* (*comp* -ier; *super* -iest) abultado, voluminoso, grueso

bull [bul] *s* toro; (*in stockmarket*) alcista *m*; (*papal document*) bula; disparate *m*; **to take the bull by the horns** asir al toro por las astas || *tr* — **to bull the market** jugar al alza

bull'dog' *s* dogo

bulldoze [bul,doz] *tr* coaccionar, intimidar con amenazas

bulldozer ['bul,dozər] *s* explanadora de empuje, empujatierra

bullet ['bulɪt] *s* bala

bulletin ['bulətɪn] *s* boletín *m*; comunicado; (*of a school*) anuario

bulletin board *s* tablilla

bul'let-proof' *adj* a prueba de balas, blindado

bull'fight' *s* corrida de toros

bull'fight'er *s* torero

bull'fight'ing *adj* torero || *s* toreo

bull'finch' *s* (*orn*) camachuelo

bull'frog' *s* rana toro

bull-headed ['bul,hɛdɪd] *adj* obstinado, terco

bullion ['buljən] *s* oro en barras, plata en barras; (*twisted fringe*) entorchado

bullish ['bulɪʃ] *adj* obstinado; (*market*) en alza; (*speculator*) alcista; optimista

bullock ['bulək] *s* buey *m*

bull'pen' *s* (taur) toril *m*; (*jail*) (coll) prevención

bull'ring' *s* plaza de toros

bull's-eye ['bulz,aɪ] *s* (*of a target*) diana; (archit, meteor, naut) ojo de buey; **to hit the bull's-eye** hacer diana

bul·ly ['buli] *adj* (coll) excelente, magnífico || *s* (*pl* -lies) matón *m*, valentón *m* || *v* (*pret & pp* -lied) *tr* intimidar, maltratar

bulrush ['bul,rʌʃ] *s* junco; junco de laguna; (*Typha*) anea, espadaña; (Bib) papiro

bulwark ['bulwərk] *s* baluarte *m* || *tr* abaluartar; defender, proteger

bum [bʌm] *s* (slang) holgazán *m*; (slang) vagabundo; (slang) mendigo || *v* (*pret & pp* **bummed**; *ger* **bumming**) *tr* (slang) mendigar || *intr* holgazanear; (slang) vagabundear; (slang) mendigar

bumblebee ['bʌmbəl,bi] *s* abejorro

bump [bʌmp] *s* (*collision*) topetón *m*; (*shake*) sacudida; (*on falling*) batacazo; (*of plane in rough air*) rebote *m*; (*swelling*) hinchazón *f*, chichón *m*; protuberancia || *tr* dar contra, topar; (*to bruise*) abollar || *intr* chocar; dar sacudidas; **to bump into** tropezar con; encontrarse con

bumper ['bʌmpər] *adj* (coll) abun-

dante, grande || *s* tope *m*, paratopes *m*; (aut) amortiguador *m*, parachoques *m*; vaso lleno

bumpkin ['bʌmpkɪn] *s* patán *m*, palurdo

bumptious ['bʌmpʃəs] *adj* engreído, presuntuoso

bump·y ['bʌmpi] *adj* (*comp* -ier; *super* -iest) (*ground*) desigual, áspero; (*air*) agitado

bun [bʌn] *s* buñuelo, bollo; (*of hair*) castaña

bunch [bʌntʃ] *s* manojo, puñado; (*of grapes, bananas, etc.*) racimo; (*of flowers*) ramillete *m*; (*of people*) grupo || *tr* agrupar, juntar || *intr* agruparse; arracimarse

bundle ['bʌndəl] *s* atado, bulto, lío, paquete *m*; (*of papers*) legajo; (*of wood*) haz *m* || *tr* atar, liar, empaquetar, envolver; **to bundle off** despedir precipitadamente; **to bundle up** arropar || *intr* — **to bundle up** arroparse

bung [bʌŋ] *s* bitoque *m*, tapón *m*

bungalow ['bʌŋgə,lo] *s* bungalow *m*, casa de una sola planta

bung'hole' *s* piquera, boca de tonel

bungle ['bʌŋgəl] *s* chapucería || *tr & intr* chapucear

bungler ['bʌŋglər] *s* chapucero

bungling ['bʌŋglɪŋ] *adj* chapucero || *s* chapucería

bunion ['bʌnjən] *s* juanete *m*

bunk [bʌŋk] *s* tarima; (slang) palabrería vana, música celestial

bunker ['bʌŋkər] *s* carbonera; (mil) fortín *m*

bun·ny ['bʌni] *s* (*pl* -nies) conejito

bunting ['bʌntɪŋ] *s* banderas colgadas como adorno; (*of a ship*) empavesado; (orn) gorrión triguero

buoy [bɔɪ] o ['bu·i] *s* boya, boya salvavidas, guindola || *tr* — **to buoy up** mantener a flote, animar, alentar

buoyancy ['bɔɪ·ənsi] o ['bujənsi] *s* flotación; alegría, animación

buoyant ['bɔɪ·ənt] o ['bujənt] *adj* boyante; alegre, animado

bur [bʌr] *s* erizo, vilano

burble ['bʌrbəl] *s* burbujeo || *intr* burbujear

burden ['bʌrdən] *s* carga; (*of a speech*) tema *m*; (*of a poem*) estribillo || *tr* cargar; agobiar, gravar

burden of proof *s* peso de la prueba

burdensome ['bʌrdənsəm] *adj* gravoso, oneroso

burdock ['bʌrdɑk] *s* bardana, cadillo

bureau ['bjuro] *s* cómoda; despacho, oficina; departamento, negociado

bureaucra·cy [bju'rɑkrəsi] *s* (*pl* -cies) burocracia

bureaucrat ['bjurə,kræt] *s* burócrata *mf*

bureaucratic [,bjurə'krætɪk] *adj* burocrático

burgess ['bʌrdʒɪs] *s* burgués *m*, ciudadano; alcalde *m* de un pueblo o villa

burglar ['bʌrglər] *s* escalador *m*

burglar alarm *s* alarma de ladrones

bur'glar·proof' adj a prueba de escaladores

burglar·y ['bʌrglərɪ] s (pl -ies) robo con escalamiento

Burgundian [bər'gʌndɪ·ən] adj & s borgoñón m

Burgundy ['bʌrgəndi] s la Borgoña; (wine) borgoña m

burial ['berɪ·əl] s entierro

burial ground s cementerio

burlap ['bʌrlæp] s arpillera

burlesque [bər'lesk] adj burlesco, festivo || s parodia || tr parodiar

burlesque show s espectáculo de bailes y cantos groseros, music-hall m

bur·ly ['bʌrli] adj (comp -lier; super -liest) fornido, corpulento, membrudo

Burma ['bʌrmə] s Birmania

Bur·mese [bər'miz] adj birmano || s (pl -mese) birmano

burn [bʌrn] s quemadura, quemazón f || v (pret & pp burned o burnt [bʌrnt]) tr quemar || intr quemar, quemarse; estar encendido (p.ej., un faro); **to burn out** quemarse (un fusible); fundirse (una bombilla); **to burn within** requemarse

burner ['bʌrnər] s (of furnace) quemador m; (of gas fixture or lamp) mechero

burning ['bʌrnɪŋ] adj ardiente || s quema, incendio

burning question s cuestión palpitante

burnish ['bʌrnɪʃ] s bruñido || tr bruñir || intr bruñirse

burnoose [bər'nus] s albornoz m

burnt almond [bʌrnt] s almendra tostada

burr [bʌr] s (of plant) erizo; (of cut in metal) rebaba

burrow ['bʌro] s madriguera, conejera || tr hacer madrigueras en; socavar || intr amadrigarse; esconderse

bursar ['bʌrsər] s tesorero universitario

burst [bʌrst] s explosión, reventón m, estallido; (of machine gun) ráfaga; salida brusca || v (pret & pp burst) tr reventar || intr reventar, reventarse; partirse (el corazón); **to burst into** irrumpir en (un cuarto); desatarse en (amenazas); prorrumpir en (lágrimas); **to burst out crying** deshacerse en lágrimas; **to burst with laughter** reventar de risa

bur·y ['beri] v (pret & pp -ied) tr enterrar; **to be buried in thought** estar absorto en meditación; **to bury the hatchet** hacer la paz; echar pelillos a la mar

burying ground s cementerio

bus. abbr business

bus [bʌs] s (pl busses o buses) autobús m || tr llevar en un autobús

bus boy s ayudante m de camarero

bus·by ['bʌzbi] s (pl -bies) morrión m de húsar, colbac m

bush [buʃ] s arbusto; (scrubby growth) matorral m, monte m; **to beat about the bush** andar con rodeos

bushel ['buʃəl] s medida para áridos (35,23 litros en E.U.A. y 36,35 litros en Inglaterra)

bushing ['buʃɪŋ] s buje m, forro

bush·y ['buʃi] adj (comp -ier; super -iest) arbustivo; peludo, lanudo; espeso

business ['bɪznɪs] adj comercial, de negocios || s negocio, comercio; (company, concern) empresa; (job, employment) empleo, oficio; (matter) asunto, cuestión; (duty) obligación; (right) derecho; **on business** por negocios; **to have no business to** no tener derecho a; **to make it one's business to** proponerse; **to mean business** (coll) obrar en serio, hablar en serio; **to mind one's own business** no meterse en lo que no le importa a uno; **to send about one's business** mandar a paseo

business district s barrio comercial

businesslike ['bɪznɪs,laɪk] adj práctico, sistemático, serio

business·man ['bɪznɪs,mæn] s (pl -men [,mɛn]) comerciante m, hombre m de negocios

business suit s traje m de calle

bus·man ['bʌsmən] s (pl -men [mən]) conductor m de autobús

buss [bʌs] s (coll) beso sonado || tr (coll) dar besos sonados a || intr (coll) dar besos sonados; (coll) darse besos sonados

bust [bʌst] s busto; (of woman) pecho; (slang) fracaso; (slang) borrachera || tr (slang) reventar, romper; (slang) arruinar; (slang) golpear, pegar || intr (slang) reventar; (slang) fracasar

buster ['bʌstər] s muchachito

bustle ['bʌsəl] s (of woman's dress) polisón m; alboroto, bullicio || intr ajetrearse, menearse

bus·y ['bɪzi] adj (comp -ier; super -iest) ocupado; (e.g., street) concurrido; (meddling) intruso, entremetido || v (pret & pp -ied) tr ocupar; **to busy oneself with** ocuparse de

busybod·y ['bɪzi,badi] s (pl -ies) entremetido, fisgón m

busy signal s (telp) señal f de ocupado

but [bʌt] adv sólo, solamente, no . . . más que; **but for** a no ser por; **but little** muy poco || prep excepto, salvo; **all but** casi || conj pero; sino, p.ej., **nobody came but John** no vino sino Juan

butcher ['butʃər] s carnicero || tr matar (reses para el consumo); dar muerte a; (to bungle) chapucear

butcher knife s cuchilla de carnicero

butcher shop s carnicería

butcher·y ['butʃəri] s (pl -ies) (slaughterhouse) matadero; (wanton slaughter) matanza, carnicería

butler ['bʌtlər] s despensero, mayordomo

butt [bʌt] s (of gun) culata; (of cigaret) colilla, punta; (of horned animal) cabezada, topetada, topetón m; (target) blanco; hazmerreír m; (large

cask) pipa ‖ *tr* topar, topetar; acornear ‖ *intr* dar cabezadas; **to butt against** confinar con; **to butt in** (slang) entremeterse
butter ['bʌtər] *s* mantequilla ‖ *tr* untar con mantequilla; **to butter up** (coll) adular, lisonjear
but'ter-cup' *s* botón *m* de oro
butter dish *s* mantequillera
but'ter-fly' *s* (*pl* -**flies**) mariposa
butter knife *s* cuchillo mantequillero
but'ter-milk' *s* leche *f* de manteca
butter sauce *s* mantequilla fundida
but'ter-scotch' *s* bombón *m* escocés, bombón hecho con azúcar terciado y mantequilla
buttocks ['bʌtəks] *spl* nalgas
button ['bʌtən] *s* botón *m* ‖ *tr* abotonar, abrocharse
but'ton-hole' *s* ojal *m* ‖ *tr* detener con conversación
but'ton-hook' *s* abotonador *m*
but'ton-wood' tree *s* plátano de occidente
buttress ['bʌtrɪs] *s* contrafuerte *m*; (fig) apoyo, sostén *m* ‖ *tr* estribar; (fig) apoyar, sostener
butt weld *s* soldadura a tope
buxom ['bʌksəm] *adj* rolliza, frescachona
buy [baɪ] *s* (coll) compra; (*bargain*) (coll) ganga ‖ *v* (*pret & pp* **bought** [bɔt]) *tr* comprar; **to buy back** recomprar; **to buy off** comprar, sobornar; **to buy out** comprar la parte de (*un socio*); **to buy up** acaparar

buyer ['baɪər] *s* comprador *m*
buzz [bʌz] *s* zumbido ‖ *intr* zumbar; **to buzz about** ajetrearse, cazcalear
buzzard ['bʌzərd] *s* alfaneque *m*
buzz bomb *s* bomba volante
buzzer ['bʌzər] *s* zumbador *m*
buzz saw *s* sierra circular
bx. *abbr* **box**
by [baɪ] *adv* cerca; a un lado; **by and by** luego ‖ *prep* por; cerca de, al lado de; (*not later than*) para; **by far** con mucho; **by the way** de paso; a propósito
by-and-by ['baɪ-ənd'baɪ] *s* porvenir *m*
bye-bye ['baɪ'baɪ] *s* mu *f*; **to go bye-bye** ir a la mu ‖ *interj* (coll) ¡adiosito!; (*to a child*) ¡ro ro!
bygone ['baɪ,gɑn] o ['baɪ,gɑn] *adj* pasado ‖ *s* pasado, **let bygones be bygones** olvidemos lo pasado
bylaw ['baɪ,lɔ] *s* reglamento, estatuto
bypass ['baɪ,pæs] o ['baɪ,pɑs] *s* desviación; tubo de paso ‖ *tr* desviar; (*a difficulty*) eludir
by'-prod'uct *s* subproducto, derivado
bystander ['baɪ,stændər] *s* asistente *mf*, circunstante *mf*
byway ['baɪ,we] *s* camino apartado
byword ['baɪ,wɑrd] *s* objeto de oprobio; refrán *m*, muletilla; apodo
Byzantine ['bɪzən,tin] o [bɪ'zæntin] *adj & s* bizantino
Byzantium [bɪ'zænʃɪ-əm] o [bɪ'zæntɪ-əm] *s* Bizancio

C

C, c [si] tercera letra del alfabeto inglés
c. *abbr* **cent, center, centimeter**
C. *abbr* **centigrade, Congress, Court**
cab [kæb] *s* coche *m* de plaza o de punto; taxi *m*; (*of a truck*) casilla
cabaret [,kæbə're] *s* cabaret *m*
cabbage ['kæbɪdʒ] *s* col *f*, berza
cab driver *s* cochero de plaza; taxista *m*
cabin ['kæbɪn] *s* (*hut, cottage*) cabaña; (aer) cabina; (naut) camarote *m*
cabin boy *s* mozo de cámara
cabinet ['kæbɪnɪt] *s* (*piece of furniture for displaying objects*) escaparate *m*, vitrina; (*for a radio*) caja, mueble *m*; (*closet*) armario; (*private room; ministry of a government*) gabinete *m*
cab'inet-ma'ker *s* ebanista *m*
cab'inet-ma'king *s* ebanistería
cable ['kebəl] *adj* cablegráfico ‖ *s* cable *m*; cablegrama *m* ‖ *tr & intr* cablegrafiar
cable address *s* dirección cablegráfica
cable car *s* tranvía *m* de tracción por cable

cablegram ['kebəl,græm] *s* cablegrama *m*
caboose [kə'bus] *s* (rr) furgón de cola
cab'stand' *s* punto de coches, punto de taxis
cache [kæʃ] *s* escondrijo; víveres escondidos ‖ *tr* depositar en un escondrijo; ocultar
cachet [kæ'ʃe] *s* sello
cackle ['kækəl] *s* (*of a hen*) cacareo; (*idle talk*) charla ‖ *intr* cacarear; charlar
cac-tus ['kæktəs] *s* (*pl* -**tuses** o -**ti** [taɪ]) cacto
cad [kæd] *s* sinvergüenza *mf*
cadaver [kə'dævər] *s* cadáver *m*
cadaverous [kə'dævərəs] *adj* cadavérico
caddie ['kædi] *s* caddie *m* (*muchacho que lleva los utensilios en el juego de golf*) ‖ *intr* servir de caddie
cadence ['kedəns] *s* cadencia
cadet [kə'det] *s* hermano menor, hijo menor; (*student at military school*) cadete *m*
cadmium ['kædmɪ-əm] *s* cadmio
cadre ['kædri] *s* (mil) cuadro
Caesar ['sizər] *s* César *m*

café [kæ'fe] *s* bar *m*, cabaret *m; restaurante m*
café society *s* gente *f* del mundo elegante que frecuenta los cabarets de moda
cafetería [ˌkæfə'tɪrɪ.ə] *s* cafetería
cage [kedʒ] *s* jaula ‖ *tr* enjaular
cageling ['kedʒlɪŋ] *s* pájaro enjaulado
ca·gey ['kedʒi] *adj* (*comp* **-gier;** *super* **-giest**) (coll) astuto
cahoots [kə'huts] *s* — **to be in cahoots** (slang) confabularse (*dos o más personas*); **to go cahoots** (slang) entrar por partes iguales
Cain [ken] *s* Caín *m;* **to raise Cain** (slang) armar camorra
Cairo ['kaɪro] *s* El Cairo
caisson ['kesən] *s* cajón *m* de aire comprimido, esclusa de aire
cajole [kə'dʒol] *tr* adular, lisonjear, halagar
cajoler·y [kə'dʒoləri] *s* (*pl* **-ies**) adulación, lisonja, halago
cake [kek] *s* pastel *m*, bollo; (*small cake*) pastelillo; (*sponge cake*) bizcocho; (*of fish*) fritada; (*of earth*) terrón *m;* (*of soap*) pan *m*, pastilla; (*of ice*) témpano *m;* **to take the cake** (coll) ser el colmo ‖ *intr* apelmazarse, aterronarse
calabash ['kælə,bæʃ] *s* calabacera; (*fruit*) calabaza
calamitous [kə'læmɪtəs] *adj* calamitoso
calami·ty [kə'læmɪti] *s* (*pl* **-ties**) calamidad
calci·fy ['kælsɪ,faɪ] *v* (*pret & pp* **-fied**) calcificar ‖ *intr* calcificarse
calcium ['kælsɪ·əm] *s* calcio
calculate ['kælkjə,let] *tr* calcular; (*to reckon*) (coll) calcular ‖ *intr* calcular; **to calculate on** contar con
calculating ['kælkjə,letɪŋ] *adj* de calcular; astuto, intrigante
calculating machine *s* calculadora, máquina de calcular
calcu·lus ['kælkjələs] *s* (*pl* **-luses** o **-li** [ˌlaɪ]) (math, pathol) cálculo
caldron ['kɔldrən] *s* calderón *m*
calendar ['kæləndər] *s* calendario, almanaque *m*
calf [kæf] o [kɑf] *s* (*pl* **calves** [kævz] o [kɑvz]) ternero; (*of the leg*) pantorrilla
calf'skin' *s* becerro, becerrillo
caliber ['kælɪbər] *s* calibre *m*
calibrate ['kælɪ,bret] *tr* calibrar
cali·co ['kælɪ,ko] *s* (*pl* **-coes** o **-cos**) calicó *m*, indiana
California [ˌkælɪ'fɔrnɪ·ə] *s* California
calipers ['kælɪpərz] *spl* calibrador *m*, compás *m* de calibres
caliph ['kelɪf] o ['kælɪf] *s* califa *m*
caliphate ['kælɪ,fet] *s* califato
calisthenic [ˌkælɪs'θenɪk] *adj* calisténico ‖ **calisthenics** *spl* calistenia
calk [kɔk] *tr* calafatear
calking ['kɔkɪŋ] *s* calafateo
call [kɔl] *s* llamada; (*of a boat or airplane*) escala; visita; vocación; **within call** al alcance de la voz ‖ *tr* llamar; convocar (*p.ej., una huelga*); **to call back** mandar volver; **to call down**

(coll) reprender, regañar; **to call in** hacer entrar; (*from circulation*) retirar; **to call off** aplazar, suspender; **to call out** llamar (*a uno*) que salga; **to call together** convocar, reunir; **to call up** llamar por teléfono; evocar, recordar ‖ *intr* llamar, gritar; hacer una visita; (naut) hacer escala; **to call on** acudir a; visitar; **to call out** gritar; **to go calling** ir de visitas
calla lily ['kælə] *s* cala, lirio de agua
call bell *s* timbre *m* de llamada
call'boy' *s* (*in a hotel*) botones *m;* (theat) traspunte *m*
caller ['kɔlər] *s* visitante *mf*
call girl *s* chica de cita
calling ['kɔlɪŋ] *s* profesión, vocación
calling card *s* tarjeta de visita
calliope [kə'laɪ·əpi] o ['kælɪ,op] *s* (mus) órgano de vapor ‖ **Calliope** [kə'laɪ·əpi] *s* Calíope *f*
call number *s* número de teléfono; (*of a book*) número de clasificación
callous ['kæləs] *adj* calloso; (fig) duro, insensible
call to arms *s* — **to sound the call to arms** (mil) batir o tocar a llamada
call to the colors *s* (mil) llamada a filas
callus ['kæləs] *s* callo
calm [kɑm] *adj* tranquilo, quieto; (*sea*) bonancible ‖ *s* tranquilidad, calma ‖ *tr* tranquilizar, calmar ‖ *intr* — **to calm down** tranquilizarse, calmarse; abonanzar, calmar (*el viento, el tiempo*)
calmness ['kɑmnɪs] *s* tranquilidad, calma
calorie ['kæləri] *s* caloría
calum·ny ['kæləmni] *s* (*pl* **-nies**) calumnia
calva·ry ['kælvəri] *s* (*pl* **-ries**) (*at the entrance to a town*) humilladero ‖ **Calvary** *s* Calvario
calyp·so [kə'lɪpso] *s* (*pl* **-sos**) calipso ‖ **Calypso** *s* Calipso *f*
cam [kæm] *s* leva
cambric ['kembrɪk] *s* batista
camel ['kæməl] *s* camello
came·o ['kæmɪ·o] *s* (*pl* **-os**) camafeo
camera ['kæmərə] *s* cámara fotográfica, máquina fotográfica
camera·man ['kæmərə,mæn] *s* (*pl* **-men** [ˌmen]) camarógrafo, tomavistas *m*
camomile ['kæmə,maɪl] *s* manzanilla
camouflage ['kæmə,flɑʒ] *s* camuflaje *m* ‖ *tr* camuflar
camp [kæmp] *s* campamento ‖ *intr* acampar
campaign [kæm'pen] *s* campaña ‖ *intr* hacer campaña
campaigner [kæm'penər] *s* propagandista *mf;* veterano
camp'fire' *s* hoguera de campamento
camphor ['kæmfər] *s* alcanfor *m*
camp'stool' *s* silla de tijera, catrecillo
campus ['kæmpəs] *s* terrenos, recinto (*de la universidad*)
cam'shaft' *s* árbol *m* de levas
can [kæn] *s* bote *m*, envase *m*, lata ‖ *v* (*pret & pp* **canned;** *ger* **canning**) *tr* envasar, enlatar ‖ *v* (*pret & cond*

could) *v aux* he can come tomorrow puede venir mañana; **can you swim?** ¿sabe Vd. nadar?

Canada ['kænədə] *s* el Canadá

Canadian [kə'nedɪ-ən] *adj & s* canadiense

canal [kə'næl] *s* canal *m*

canar·y [kə'nerɪ] *s (pl -ies)* canario **|| Canaries** *spl* Canarias

can·cel ['kænsəl] *(pret & pp -celed* o *-celled; ger -celing* o *-celling) tr* cancelar, eliminar, suprimir; matasellar, obliterar (*sellos de correo*)

canceler ['kænsələr] *s* matasellos *m*

cancellation [,kænsə'leʃən] *s* cancelación, eliminación, supresión; (*of stamps*) obliteración

cancer ['kænsər] *s* cáncer *m*

cancerous ['kænsərəs] *adj* canceroso

candela·brum [,kændə'lebrəm] *s (pl -bra* [brə] o *-brums*) candelabro

candid ['kændɪd] *adj* franco, sincero; imparcial

candida·cy ['kændɪdəsi] *s (pl -cies)* candidatura

candidate ['kændɪ,det] *s* candidato; (*for a degree*) graduando

candid camera *s* cámara indiscreta

candle ['kændəl] *s* bujía, candela, vela

can·dle·hold·er *s* candelero

can·dle·light· *s* luz *f* de vela; crepúsculo

candle power *s* bujía

can·dle·stick· *s* palmatoria

candor ['kændər] *s* franqueza, sinceridad; imparcialidad

can·dy ['kændɪ] *s (pl -dies)* bombón *m*, confite *m*, dulce *m*; dulces *mpl* **||** *v (pret & pp -died) tr* almibarar, confitar, garapiñar **||** *intr* almibararse

candy box *s* bombonera, confitera

candy store *s* confitería, dulcería

cane [ken] *s (plant; stem)* caña; (*walking stick*) bastón *m;* (*for chair seats*) junco, mimbre *m*, rejilla

cane seat *s* asiento de rejilla

cane sugar *s* azúcar *m* de caña

canine ['kenaɪn] *adj* canino **||** *s (tooth)* canino; perro

canned goods *spl* conservas alimenticias

canner·y ['kænərɪ] *s (pl -ies)* conservera, fábrica de conservas

cannibal ['kænɪbəl] *adj & s* caníbal *mf*

canning ['kænɪŋ] *adj* conservero **||** *s* conservería

cannon ['kænən] *s* cañón *m;* cañones

cannonade [,kænə'ned] *s* cañoneo **||** *tr* cañonear

cannon ball *s* bala de cañón

cannon fodder *s* carne *f* de cañón

can·ny ['kænɪ] *adj (comp -nier; super -niest)* cauteloso, cuerdo; astuto

canoe [kə'nu] *s* canoa

canoeist [kə'nu·ɪst] *s* canoero

canon ['kænən] *s* canon *m;* (*priest*) canónigo

canonical [kə'nɑnɪkəl] *adj* canónico; aceptado, auténtico, establecido **|**

canonicals *spl* vestiduras sacerdotales

canonize ['kænə,naɪz] *tr* canonizar

canon law *s* cánones *mpl*, derecho canónico

canon·ry ['kænənrɪ] *s (pl -ries)* canonjía

can opener ['opənər] *s* abrelatas *m*

cano·py ['kænəpi] *s (pl -pies)* dosel *m*, pabellón *m;* (*over an entrance*) marquesina; (*for electrical fixtures*) campana

canopy of heaven *s* bóveda celeste

cant [kænt] *s* hipocresía; jerga, jerigonza

cantaloupe ['kæntə,lop] *s* cantalupo

cantankerous [kæn'tæŋkərəs] *adj* de mal genio, pendenciero

canteen [kæn'tin] *s (shop)* cantina; (*water flask*) cantimplora; (*mil*) centro de recreo

canter ['kæntər] *s* medio galope **||** *intr* ir a medio galope

canticle ['kæntɪkəl] *s* cántico

cantilever ['kæntɪ,livər] *adj* voladizo **||** *s* viga voladiza

cantle ['kæntəl] *s* arzón trasero

canton [kæn'tɑn] *tr* acantonar

cantonment [kæn'tɑnmənt] *s* acantonamiento

cantor ['kæntər] o ['kæntɔr] *s* chantre *m;* (*in a synagogue*) cantor *m* principal

canvas ['kænvəs] *s* cañamazo, lona; (*naut*) vela, lona; (*painting*) lienzo; **under canvas** (*mil*) en tiendas; (*naut*) con las velas izadas

canvass ['kænvəs] *s* pesquisa, escrutinio; (*of votes*) solicitación **||** *tr* escrutar, solicitar; discutir detenidamente

canyon ['kænjən] *s* cañón *m*

cap. *abbr* capital, capitalize

cap [kæp] *s* gorra, gorra de visera; (*of academic costume*) birrete *m;* (*of bottle*) cápsula, (*e.g., of a fountain pen*) capuchón *m* **||** *v (pret & pp capped; ger capping) tr* cubrir con gorra; capsular (*una botella*); **to cap the climax** ser el colmo

capabili·ty [,kepə'bɪlɪtɪ] *s (pl -ties)* habilidad, capacidad

capable ['kepəbəl] *adj* hábil, capaz

capacious [kə'peʃəs] *adj* espacioso, capaz

capaci·ty [kə'pæsɪtɪ] *s (pl -ties)* (*room, space; ability, aptitude*) capacidad; (*status, function*) calidad; **in the capacity of** en calidad de

cap and bells *spl* caperuza de bufón; cetro de la locura

cap and gown *s* birrete y toga

caparison [kə'pærɪsən] *s* caparazón *m* **||** *tr* engualdrapar

cape [kep] *s* cabo, promontorio; (*garment*) capa, esclavina

Cape Colony *s* la Colonia del Cabo

Cape Horn *s* el Cabo de Hornos

Cape of Good Hope *s* Cabo de Buena Esperanza

caper ['kepər] *s (gay jump)* cabriola; (*prank*) travesura; **to cut capers** dar cabriolas; hacer travesuras || *intr* cabriolear; retozar

Cape'town' o **Cape Town** *s* El Cabo, la Ciudad del Cabo

cape'work' *s* (taur) suerte *f* de capa, lance *m*

capital ['kæpɪtəl] *adj* capital || *s* (*money*) capital *m*; (*city*) capital *f*; (*top of a column*) capitel *m*; **to make capital out of** sacar beneficio de

capitalism ['kæpɪtə,lɪzəm] *s* capitalismo

capitalize ['kæpɪtə,laɪz] *tr* escribir con mayúscula; capitalizar || *intr —* **to capitalize on** aprovecharse de

capital letter *s* letra mayúscula

capitol ['kæpɪtəl] *s* capitolio

capitulate [kə'pɪtʃə,let] *intr* capitular

capon ['kepɑn] *s* capón *m*

caprice [kə'pris] *s* capricho, antojo; veleidad

capricious [kə'prɪʃəs] *adj* caprichoso, antojadizo

Capricorn ['kæprɪ,kɔrn] *s* Capricornio

capsize ['kæpsaɪz] *tr* volcar || *intr* volcar; tumbar, zozobrar (*un barco*)

capstan ['kæpstən] *s* cabrestante *m*

cap'stone' *s* coronamiento

capsule ['kæpsəl] *s* cápsula

Capt. *abbr* **Captain**

captain ['kæptən] *s* capitán *m* || *tr* capitanear

captain·cy ['kæptənsi] *s* (*pl* **-cies**) capitanía

caption ['kæpʃən] *s* título; (*in a movie*) subtítulo

captivate ['kæptɪ,vet] *tr* cautivar, encantar

captive ['kæptɪv] *adj* & *s* cautivo

captivi·ty [kæp'tɪvɪti] *s* (*pl* **-ties**) cautividad, cautiverio

captor ['kæptər] *s* aprehensor *m*

capture ['kæptʃər] *s* apresamiento, captura; (*of a stronghold*) toma || *tr* apresar, capturar; tomar (*una plaza*); captar (*p.ej., la atención de una persona*)

Capuchin nun ['kæpjutʃɪn] o ['kæpjʊ/ɪn] *s* capuchina

car [kɑr] *s* coche *m*; (*of an elevator*) caja, carro

carafe [kə'ræf] *s* garrafa

caramel ['kærəməl] o ['kɑrməl] *s* (*burnt sugar*) caramelo; bombón *m* de caramelo

carat ['kærət] *s* quilate *m*

caravan ['kærə,væn] *s* caravana

caravansa·ry [,kærə'vænsəri] *s* (*pl* **-ries**) caravanera

caraway ['kærə,we] *s* alcaravea

car'barn' *s* cochera de tranvías

carbide ['kɑrbaɪd] *s* carburo

carbine ['kɑrbaɪn] *s* carabina

carbolic acid [kɑr'bɑlɪk] *s* ácido carbólico

carbon ['kɑrbən] *s* (*chemical element*) carbono; (*pole of arc light or battery*) carbón *m*; papel *m* carbón; (*in auto cylinders*) carbonilla

carbon copy *s* copia al carbón

carbon dioxide *s* dióxido de carbono

carbon monoxide *s* óxido de carbono, monóxido de carbono

carbon paper *s* papel *m* carbón

car'boy' *s* bombona, garrafón *m*

carbuncle ['kɑrbʌŋkəl] *s* (*stone*) carbunclo, carbúnculo; (*pathol*) carbunclo, carbunco

carburetor ['kɑrbə,retər] o ['kɑrbjə,retər] *s* carburador *m*

car caller *s* avisacoches *m*

carcass ['kɑrkəs] *s* res muerta, cadáver *m*

card [kɑrd] *s* tarjeta; (*for playing games*) naipe *m*, carta; (*for filing*) ficha; (*person*) (coll) sujeto, tipo

card'board' *s* cartón *m*

cardboard binding *s* encuadernación en pasta

card case *s* tarjetero

card catalogue *s* catálogo de fichas

cardiac ['kɑrdɪ,æk] *adj* cardíaco || *s* (*medicine; sufferer*) cardíaco

cardigan ['kɑrdɪgən] *s* albornoz *m*, rebeca

cardinal ['kɑrdɪnəl] *adj* cardinal; purpurado || *s* (*prelate; bird*) cardenal *m*; número cardinal

card index *s* fichero, tarjetero

card party *s* tertulia de baraja

card'sharp' *s* fullero, tahur *m*

card trick *s* truco de naipes

care [ker] *s* (*worry*) inquietud, ansiedad; (*watchful attention*) esmero; (*charge*) cargo, custodia; **care of** suplicada en casa de; **to take care of oneself** cuidarse || *intr* inquietarse, preocuparse; **to care for** cuidar de; amar, querer; **to care to** tener ganas de

careen [kə'rin] *intr* inclinarse; mecerse precipitadamente

career [kə'rɪr] *adj* de carrera || *s* carrera

care'free' *adj* despreocupado, libre de cuidados

careful ['kerfəl] *adj* (*acting with care*) cuidadoso; (*done with care*) esmerado; **to be careful to** cuidarse de

careless ['kerlɪs] *adj* descuidado, negligente

carelessness ['kerlɪsnɪs] *s* descuido, negligencia

caress [kə'res] *s* caricia || *tr* acariciar || *intr* acariciarse

caretaker ['ker,tekər] *s* curador *m*, guardián *m*, custodio

care'worn' *adj* fatigado, rendido

car'fare' *s* pasaje *m* de tranvía o autobús

car·go ['kɑrgo] *s* (*pl* **-goes** o **-gos**) carga, cargamento

cargo boat *s* barco de carga

Caribbean [,kærɪ'bi·ən] o [kə'rɪbiən] *adj* caribe || *s* mar *m* Caribe

caricature ['kærɪkətʃər] *s* caricatura || *tr* caricaturizar

caricaturist ['kærɪkətʃərɪst] *s* caricaturista *mf*

carillon ['kærɪ,lɑn] o [kə'rɪljən] *s* carillón *m*

car'load' *s* furgonada, vagonada

carnage ['kɑrnɪdʒ] *s* carnicería, matanza

carnation [kɑr'neʃən] *adj* encarnado || *s* clavel *m*, clavel reventón

carnival ['kɑrnɪvəl] *adj* carnavalesco || *s* (*period before Lent*) carnaval *m*; verbena, espectáculo de atracciones

car·ol ['kærəl] *s* canción alegre, villancico || *v* (*pret & pp* -oled o -olled; *ger* -oling o -olling); *tr* celebrar con villancicos || *intr* cantar con alegría

carom ['kærəm] *s* carambola || *intr* carambolear

carousal [kə'rauzəl] *s* juerga, borrachera, jarana

carouse [kə'rauz] *intr* emborracharse, jaranear

carp [kɑrp] *s* carpa || *intr* quejarse

carpenter ['kɑrpəntər] *s* carpintero

carpentry ['kɑrpəntri] *s* carpintería

carpet ['kɑrpɪt] *s* alfombra; **to be on the carpet** estar sobre el tapete || *tr* alfombrar

carpet sweeper *s* barredora de alfombras

car'-rent'al service *s* alquiler *m* de coches

carriage ['kærɪdʒ] *s* carruaje *m*; (*cost of carrying*) porte *m*, transporte *m*; (*bearing*) porte *m*, continente *m*; (*mach*) carro

carrier ['kærɪ·ər] *s* portador *m*, transportador *m*; portador de gérmenes; empresa de transportes; (*mailman*) cartero; vendedor *m* de periódicos; portaaviones *m*; (*rad*) onda portadora

carrier pigeon *s* paloma mensajera

carrier wave *s* (rad) onda portadora

carrion ['kærɪ·ən] *adj* carroño; inmundo || *s* carroña; inmundicia

carrot ['kærət] *s* zanahoria

carrousel [,kærə'zel] *s* caballitos, tiovivo

car·ry ['kæri] *v* (*pret & pp* -ried) *tr* llevar, portar, traer; transportar; sostener (*una carga*); **to carry away** llevarse; encantar, entusiasmar; **to carry into effect** llevar a cabo; **to carry one's point** salirse con la suya; **to carry out** llevar a cabo; **to carry the day** quedar victorioso, ganar la palma; **to carry weight** ser de peso || *intr* tener alcance; **to carry on** continuar, perseverar; (coll) travesear; (coll) comportarse de un modo escandaloso; (coll) hacer locuras

cart [kɑrt] *s* carreta, carro || *tr* carretear

carte blanche ['kɑrt'blɑnʃ] *s* carta blanca

cartel [kɑr'tel] *s* cartel *m*

Carthage ['kɑrθɪdʒ] *s* Cartago

Carthaginian [,kɑrθə'dʒɪnɪ·ən] *adj & s* cartaginés *m*

cart horse *s* caballo de tiro

cartilage ['kɑrtɪlɪdʒ] *s* cartílago

cartoon [kɑr'tun] *s* caricatura; (*comic strip*) tira cómica; (*film*) película de dibujos || *tr* caricaturizar

cartoonist [kɑr'tunɪst] *s* caricaturista *mf*

cartridge ['kɑrtrɪdʒ] *s* cartucho

cartridge belt *s* canana

carve [kɑrv] *tr* trinchar (*carne*); esculpir, tallar

carving knife ['kɑrvɪŋ] *s* cuchillo de trinchar

car washer *s* lavacoches *m*

caryatid [,kæri'ætɪd] *s* cariátide *f*

cascade [kæs'ked] *s* cascada

case [kes] *s* (*instance; form of a word*) caso; (*box*) caja; (*small container*) estuche *m*; (*for cigarettes*) pitillera; (*sheath*) vaina, funda; (law) causa, pleito; **in case** caso que; **in no case** de ninguna manera || *tr* encajonar, enfundar

casement ['kesmənt] *s* ventana batiente; bastidor *m* (*de la ventana*)

cash [kæʃ] *s* dinero contante; pago al contado; **cash on delivery** contra reembolso, pago contra entrega; **to pay cash** pagar al contado || *tr* cobrar (*un cheque al portador*); abonar, pagar (*un cheque al banco*) || *intr* — **to cash in on** (coll) sacar provecho de

cash and carry *s* pago al contado con transporte a cargo del comprador

cash'box' *s* caja

cashew ['kæʃu] *s* anacardo, marañón

cashew nut *s* anacardo, nuez *f* de marañón

cashier [kæ'ʃɪr] *s* cajero || *tr* destruir; (*in the army*) degradar

cashier's check *s* cheque *m* de caja

cashier's desk *s* caja

cashmere [,kæʃ'mɪr] *s* casimir *m*, cachemir *m*

cash on hand *s* efectivo en caja

cash payment *s* pago al contado

cash purchase *s* compra al contado

cash register *s* caja registradora

casing ['kesɪŋ] *s* caja, cubierta, envoltura; (*of door or window*) marco, cerco; (*of tire*) cubierta; (sew) jareta

cask [kæsk] o [kɑsk] *s* casco, pipa, tonel *m*

casket ['kæskɪt] o ['kɑskɪt] *s* (*box for valuables*) cajita, joyero; (*coffin*) caja, ataúd *m*

casserole ['kæsə,rol] *s* cacerola; (*dish cooked in a casserole*) timbal *m*

cassock ['kæsək] *s* balandrán *m*, sotana

cast [kæst] o [kɑst] *s* echada, tiro; forma, molde *m*; aire *m*, semblante *m*; matiz *m*, tinte *m*; (*of actors*) reparto || *v* (*pret & pp* cast) *tr* echar, tirar; volver (*los ojos*); proyectar (*una sombra*); colar, fundir (*metales*); depositar (*votos*); echar (*suertes*); (theat) repartir (*papeles*); **to cast aside** desechar; **to cast loose** soltar; **to cast out** arrojar, echar fuera; despedir, desterrar || *intr* echar los dados; arrojar el sedal o el anzuelo; **to cast about** revolver proyectos; **to cast off** (naut) soltar las amarras

castanet [ˌkæstə'net] s castañuela, castañeta

cast'a·way' adj & s proscrito, réprobo; náufrago

caste [kæst] o [kɑst] s casta; **to lose caste** desprestigiarse

caster ['kæstər] o ['kɑstər] s ruedecilla de mueble; (cruet stand) angarillas, vinagreras; frasco

Castile [kæs'til] s Castilla

Castile soap s jabón m de Castilla

Castilian [kæs'tɪljən] adj & s castellano

casting ['kæstɪŋ] o ['kɑstɪŋ] s fundición, pieza fundida; (theat) reparto

casting vote s voto de calidad

cast iron s hierro colado, hierro fundido

cast'-i'ron adj de hierro colado; fuerte, endurecido; duro, inflexible

castle ['kæsəl] o ['kɑsəl] s castillo; (chess) roque m, torre f ǁ tr & intr (chess) enrocar

castle in Spain, castle in the air s castillo en el aire

cast'off' adj abandonado, desechado; (clothing) de desecho ǁ s desecho

castor oil ['kæstər] o ['kɑstər] s aceite m de ricino

castrate ['kæstret] tr capar, castrar

casual ['kæʒʊ·əl] adj casual, fortuito; descuidado, indiferente

casual·ty ['kæʒʊ·əltɪ] s (pl -ties) desgracia, accidente m; accidentado, víctima; (in war) baja

casualty list s lista de bajas

cat. abbr **catalogue, catechism**

cat [kæt] s gato, mujer maligna; **to bell the cat** ponerle cascabel al gato; **to let the cat out of the bag** revelar el secreto

catacomb ['kætə.kom] s catacumba

Catalan ['kætə.læn] adj & s catalán m

catalogue ['kætə.lɔg] o ['kætə.lɑg] s catálogo ǁ tr catalogar

Catalonia [.kætə'lonɪ·ə] s Cataluña

Catalonian [.kætə'lonɪ·ən] adj & s catalán m

catapult ['kætə.pʌlt] s catapulta ǁ tr catapultar

cataract ['kætə.rækt] s catarata; (pathol) catarata

catarrh [kə'tɑr] s catarro

catastrophe [kə'tæstrəfɪ] s catástrofe f

cat'call' s rechifla ǁ tr & intr rechiflar

catch [kætʃ] s (of a ball) cogida; (of fish) pesca; (of a lock) cerradura, pestillo; (booty) botín m, presa; (fastener) broche m; (good match) buen partido ǁ v (pret & pp caught [kɔt]) tr asir, coger, atrapar; llegar a oír; coger (un resfriado); **to come upon suddenly** sorprender; comprender; capturar (al delincuente); **to catch fire** encenderse; **to catch hold of** agarrar, coger, apoderarse de; **to catch it** (coll) merecerse un regaño; **to catch oneself** contenerse; recobrar el equilibrio; **to catch sight of** alcanzar a ver; **to**

catch up arrebatar; coger al vuelo; (in a mistake) cazar ǁ intr pegarse (una enfermedad); encenderse; **to catch at** agarrarse a, tratar de asir; **to catch on** prender en (p.ej., un gancho); comprender, coger el tino; **to catch up** salir del atraso; (in one's debts) ponerse al día; **to catch up with** emparejar con

catcher ['kætʃər] s (baseball) receptor, parador m

catching ['kætʃɪŋ] adj pegajoso, contagioso; atrayente, cautivador

catch question s pega

catchup ['kætʃəp] o ['ketʃəp] s salsa de tomate condimentada

catch'word' s lema m, palabra de efecto; (actor's cue) pie m; (typ) reclamo

catch·y ['kætʃɪ] adj (comp -ier; super -iest) (tune) animado, vivo; (title of a book) impresionante, llamativo; (question) intrincado; (breathing) espasmódico

catechism ['kætɪ.kɪzəm] s catecismo

catego·ry ['kætɪ.gorɪ] s (pl -ries) categoría

cater ['ketər] tr & intr abastecer, proveer; **to cater to** proveer a

cater-cornered ['kætər.kɔrnərd] adj diagonal ǁ adv diagonalmente

caterer ['ketərər] s abastecedor m, proveedor m de alimentos (esp. para fiestas caseras)

caterpillar ['kætər.pɪlər] s oruga

caterpillar tractor s tractor m de oruga

cat'fish' s bagre m

cat'gut' s (mus) cuerda de tripa; (surg) catgut m

Cath. abbr **Catholic**

cathartic [kə'θɑrtɪk] adj & s catártico

cathedral [kə'θidrəl] s catedral f

catheter ['kæθɪtər] s catéter m

catheterize ['kæθɪtə.raɪz] tr cateterizar

cathode ['kæθod] s cátodo

catholic ['kæθəlɪk] adj católico ǁ **Catholic** adj & s católico

catkin ['kætkɪn] s candelilla, amento

cat nap s sueñecito

catnip ['kætnɪp] s hierba gatera, nébeda

cat-o'-nine-tails [.kætə'naɪn.telz] s azote m con nueve ramales

cat's cradle s juego de la cuna

cat's-paw o **catspaw** ['kæts.pɔ] s mano f de gato, instrumento

catsup ['kætsəp] o ['ketʃəp] s salsa de tomate condimentada

cat'tail' s anea, espadaña; amento

cattle ['kætəl] s ganado vacuno

cattle crossing s paso de ganado

cattle·man ['kætəlmən] s (pl -men [mən]) s ganadero

cattle raising s ganadería

cattle ranch s hacienda de ganado

cat·ty ['kætɪ] adj (comp -tier; super -tiest) (like a cat) felino, gatuno; (spiteful) malicioso; (gossipy) chismoso

cat'walk' s pasadero, pasarela

Caucasian [kɔ'keʒən] o [kɔ'keʃən] *adj* & *s* caucasiano, caucásico

Caucasus ['kɔkəsəs] *s* Cáucaso

caucus | 'kɔkəs] *s* junta de políticos

cauliflower ['kɔlɪ ,flau·ər] *s* coliflor *f*

cause |kɔz] *s* causa; (*person*) causante *mf* || *tr* causar

cause'way' *s* (*highway*) calzada; calzada elevada

caustic ['kɔstɪk] *adj* cáustico

cauterize ['kɔtə ,raɪz] *tr* cauterizar

caution ['kɔʃən] *s* (*carefulness*) cautela; (*warning*) advertencia, amonestación || *tr* advertir, amonestar

cautious ['kɔʃəs] *adj* cauteloso, cauto

Cav. *abbr* **Cavalry**

cavalcade [,kævəl'ked] o ['kævəl,ked] *s* cabalgata

cavalier [,kævə'lɪr] *adj* (*haughty*) altivo, desdeñoso; (*offhand*) alegre, desenvuelto, inceremonioso || *s* (*horseman*) caballero; (*lady's escort*) galán *m*

caval·ry ['kævəlrɪ] *s* (*pl* **-ries**) caballería

cavalry·man ['kævəlrɪmən] *s* (*pl* **-men** [mən]) soldado de caballería

cave [kev] *s* cueva, caverna || *intr* — **to cave in** hundirse; (*to give in, yield*) (coll) ceder, rendirse

cave'-in' *s* hundimiento, derrumbe *m*, socavón *m*

cave man *s* hombre grosero

cavern ['kævərn] *s* caverna

cav·il ['kævɪl] *v* (*pret* & *pp* **-iled** o **-illed**; *ger* **-iling** o **-illing**) *intr* buscar quisquillas

cavi·ty ['kævɪtɪ] *s* (*pl* **-ties**) cavidad; (*in a tooth*) picadura

cavort [kə'vɔrt] *intr* (coll) cabriolar

caw [kɔ] *s* graznido || *intr* graznar

cc. *abbr* **cubic centimeter**

cease [sɪs] *tr* parar, suspender || *intr* cesar; cesar de, dejar de + *inf*

cease'fire' *s* cese *m* de fuego || *intr* suspender hostilidades

ceaseless ['sɪslɪs] *adj* incesante, continuo

cedar ['sidər] *s* cedro

cede [sid] *tr* ceder, traspasar

ceiling ['silɪŋ] *s* techo, cielo raso; (aer) techo, cielo máximo

ceiling price *s* precio tope

celebrant ['sɛlɪbrənt] *s* celebrante *m*

celebrate ['sɛlɪ ,bret] *tr* celebrar || *intr* (*to say mass*) celebrar; divertirse, festejarse

celebrated ['sɛlɪ ,bretɪd] *adj* célebre, renombrado

celebration [,sɛlɪ'breʃən] *s* celebración; diversión, festividad

celebri·ty [sɪ'lebrɪtɪ] *s* (*pl* **-ties**) (*fame, famous person*) celebridad

celery ['sɛlərɪ] *s* apio

celestial [sɪ'lestʃəl] *adj* celeste, celestial

celiba·cy ['sɛlɪbəsɪ] *s* (*pl* **-cies**) celibato

celibate ['sɛlɪ ,bet] o ['sɛlɪbɪt] *adj* & *s* célibe *mf*

cell [sɛl] *s* (*of convent or jail*) celda; (*of honeycomb*) celdilla; (*of elec-*

tric battery) elemento; (*of plant or animal; of photoelectric device; of political group*) célula

cellar ['sɛlər] *s* sótano; (*for wine*) bodega

cellaret [,sɛlə'ret] *s* licorera

cell house *s* prisión celular

cellist o **'cellist** ['tʃɛlɪst] *s* violoncelista *mf*

cel·lo o **'cel·lo** ['tʃɛlo] *s* (*pl* **-los**) violoncelo

cellophane ['sɛlə ,fen] *s* celofán *m*

celluloid ['sɛljə ,lɔɪd] *s* celuloide *m*

Celt [sɛlt] o [kɛlt] *s* celta *mf*

Celtic ['sɛltɪk] o ['keltɪk] *adj* céltico || *s* (*language*) celta *m*

cement [sɪ'ment] *s* cemento || *tr* revestir con cemento; (*la amistad*) consolidar

cemeter·y ['sɛmɪ ,terɪ] *s* (*pl* **-ies**) cementerio

cen. *abbr* **central**

censer ['sensər] *s* incensario

censor ['sensər] *s* censor *m* || *tr* censurar

censure ['senʃər] *s* censura || *tr* censurar

census ['sensəs] *s* censo; **to take the census** levantar el censo

cent. *abbr* **centigrade, central, century**

cent [sɛnt] *s* centavo

centaur ['sɛntɔr] *s* centauro

centennial [sɛn'tɛnɪ·əl] *adj* & *s* centenario

center ['sentər] *adj* centrista || *s* centro || *tr* centrar

cen'ter·piece' *s* centro de mesa

center punch *s* granete *m*, punzón *m* de marcar

centigrade ['sentɪ ,gred] *adj* centígrado

centimeter ['sentɪ ,mitər] *s* centímetro

centipede ['sentɪ ,pid] *s* ciempiés *m*

central ['sentrəl] *adj* central || *s* (telp) central *f*, central de teléfonos; (*operator*) telefonista *mf*

Central America *s* Centro América, la América Central

Central American *adj* & *mf* centroamericano

centralize ['sentrə ,laɪz] *tr* centralizar || *intr* centralizarse

centu·ry ['sentʃərɪ] *s* (*pl* **-ries**) siglo

century plant *s* pita, maguey *m*

ceramic [sɪ'ræmɪk] *adj* cerámico

cereal ['sɪrɪ·əl] *adj* & *s* cereal *m*

ceremonious [,sɛrɪ'monɪ·əs] *adj* ceremonioso, etiquetero

ceremo·ny ['sɛrɪ ,monɪ] *s* (*pl* **-nies**) ceremonia; **to stand on ceremony** hacer ceremonias, ser etiquetero

certain ['sʌrtən] *adj* cierto; **a certain** cierto; **for certain** por cierto

certainly ['sɜrtənlɪ] *adj* ciertamente; (*gladly*) con mucho gusto

certain·ty ['sʌrtəntɪ] *s* (*pl* **-ties**) certeza; **with certainty** a ciencia cierta

certificate [sər'tɪfɪkɪt] *s* certificación, certificado; (*of birth, death, etc.*) partida, fe *f*; (*document representing financial assets*) título || [sər'tɪfɪ ,ket] *tr* certificar

certified public accountant [ˈsʌrtɪ-ˌfaɪd] s censor jurado de cuentas

certi‧fy [ˈsʌrtɪˌfaɪ] v (pret & pp -fied) tr certificar

cervix [ˈsɑrvɪks] s (pl cervices [sər-ˈvaɪsiz]) cerviz f

cessation [seˈseʃən] s cesación

cessation of hostilities s suspensión de hostilidades

cesspool [ˈsesˌpul] s pozo negro; (fig) sitio inmundo

Ceylon [sɪˈlɑn] s Ceilán

Ceylo‧nese [ˌsiləˈniz] adj ceilanés || (pl -nese) ceilanés m

cf. abbr confer, i.e., compare

C.F.I., c.f.i. abbr cost, freight, and insurance

cg. abbr centigram

ch. abbr chapter, church

chafe [tʃef] s fricción, roce m; desgaste m; irritación || tr (to rub) frotar; (to rub and make sore) escocer; (to wear) desgastar; irritar || intr escocerse; desgastarse; irritarse

chaff [tʃæf] o [tʃɑf] s barcia; paja menuda; broza, desperdicio

chafing dish [ˈtʃefɪŋ] s cocinilla, infernillo

chagrin [ʃəˈgrɪn] s desazón f, disgusto || tr desazonar, disgustar

chain [tʃen] s cadena || tr encadenar

chain gang s cadena de presidiarios, collera, cuerda de presos

chain reaction s reacción en cadena

chain‧smoke′ intr fumar un pitillo tras otro

chain store s empresa con una cadena de tiendas; tienda de una cadena de tiendas

chair [tʃer] s silla; (de catedrático) cátedra; presidencia; to take the chair presidir la reunión; abrir la sesión || tr presidir (una reunión)

chair lift s telesilla

chair‧man [ˈtʃermən] s (pl -men [mən]) presidente m

chairmanship [ˈtʃermənˌʃɪp] s presidencia

chair rail s guardasilla

chalice [ˈtʃælɪs] s cáliz m

chalk [tʃɔk] s (soft white limestone) creta; (piece used for writing) tiza || tr marcar o escribir con tiza; to chalk up apuntar; marcar (un tanto)

challenge [ˈtʃælɪndʒ] s desafío; (law) recusación || tr desafiar; (law) recusar

chamber [ˈtʃembər] s cámara; (of a gun) recámara; dormitorio; chambers oficina de juez

chamberlain [ˈtʃembərlɪn] s chambelán m

cham′ber‧maid′ s camarera

chamber pot s orinal m

chameleon [kəˈmiliən] s camaleón m

chamfer [ˈtʃæmfər] s chaflán m || tr chaflanar

cham‧ois [ˈʃæmi] s (pl -ois) gamuza

champ [tʃæmp] s mordisco; (slang) campeón m || tr & intr mordiscar; (el freno) morder

champagne [ʃæmˈpen] s champaña m

champion [ˈtʃæmpɪ‧ən] s campeón m || tr defender

championess [ˈtʃæmpɪ‧ənɪs] s campeona

championship [ˈtʃæmpɪ‧ənˌʃɪp] s campeonato

chance [tʃæns] o [tʃɑns] adj casual, imprevisto || s oportunidad, ocasión; casualidad, suerte f; probabilidad; peligro, riesgo; by chance por casualidad; to not stand a chance no tener probabilidad de éxito; to take a chance probar fortuna; comprar un billete de lotería; to take chances probar fortuna; to wait for a chance esperar la oportunidad || intr acontecer; to chance on o upon tropezar con; to chance to acertar a

chancel [ˈtʃænsəl] o [ˈtʃɑnsəl] s entrecoro

chancellery [ˈtʃænsələri] o [ˈtʃɑnsəl-əri] s (pl -ies) cancillería

chancellor [ˈtʃænsələr] o [ˈtʃɑnsələr] s canciller m

chandelier [ˌʃændəˈlɪr] s araña de luces

change [tʃendʒ] s cambio, mudanza; suelto, moneda suelta; (surplus money returned with a purchase) vuelta; (of clothing) muda; for a change por variedad; to keep the change quedarse con la vuelta; || tr cambiar, mudar, cambiar de, mudar de; reemplazar; to change clothes cambiar de ropa; to change gears cambiar de velocidades; to change hands cambiar de dueño; to change money cambiar moneda; to change one's mind cambiar de parecer; to change trains cambiar de tren, transbordar || intr cambiar, mudar; corregirse

changeable [ˈtʃendʒəbəl] adj cambiable, inconstante, cambiante, mudable

change of clothing s muda de ropa

change of heart s arrepentimiento, conversión

change of life s cesación natural de las reglas

change of voice s muda

chan‧nel [ˈtʃænəl] s (body of water joining two others) canal m; (bed of river) álveo, cauce m; (means of communication) vía; (passage) conducto; (groove) ranura, surco; (telv) canal m; the Channel el Canal de la Mancha || v (pret & pp -neled o -nelled; ger -neling o -nelling) tr acanalar; canalizar (esfuerzos, dinero, etc.)

chant [tʃænt] o [tʃɑnt] s (song) canción; (song sung in a monotone) canto || tr & intr cantar

chanter [ˈtʃæntər] o [ˈtʃɑntər] s cantor m; (priest) chantre m

chanticleer [ˈtʃæntɪˌklɪr] s el gallo

chaos [ˈke‧ɑs] s caos m

chaotic [keˈɑtɪk] adj caótico

chap. abbr chaplain, chapter

chap [tʃæp] s (jaw) mandíbula; (cheek) mejilla; (crack in the skin) grieta; chico, tipo; **chaps** zahones *mpl* || *v* (*pret & pp* **chapped;** *ger* **chapping**) *tr* agrietar, rajar || *intr* agrietarse, rajarse

chapel ['t∫æpəl] *s* capilla

chaperon o **chaperone** ['∫æpə‚ron] *s* carabina, señora de compañía || *tr* acompañar (*una señora a una o más señoritas*)

chaplain ['t∫æplɪn] *s* capellán *m*

chaplet ['t∫æplɪt] *s* (*wreath for head*) guirnalda; rosario

chapter ['t∫æptər] *s* capítulo; (*of the Scriptures*) capítula; (*of a cathedral*) cabildo

chapter and verse *adv* con todos sus pelos y señales

char [t∫ɑr] *v* (*pret & pp* **charred;** *ger* **charring**) *tr* carbonizar; (*to scorch*) socarrar

character ['kærɪktər] *s* carácter *m;* (*conspicuous person; person in a play or novel*) personaje *m;* (*part or role in a play*) papel *m;* (*fellow*) (coll) tipo, sujeto

characteristic [‚kærɪktə'rɪstɪk] *adj* característico || *s* característica

characterize ['kærɪktə‚raɪz] *tr* caracterizar

char'coal' *s* carbón *m* de leña; (*for sketching*) carboncillo; (*sketch*) dibujo al carbón

charcoal burner *s* (*person*) carbonero; horno para hacer carbón de leña

charge [t∫ɑrdʒ] *s* (*of an explosive, of electricity, of soldiers against the enemy; responsibility*) carga; (*accusation; amount owed; recording of amount owed*) cargo; (*heral*) blasón *m;* (*attack*) embestida; **in charge of** a cargo de; **to reverse the charges** (telp) cargar al número llamado; **to take charge of** hacerse cargo de || *tr* cargar; cobrar (*cierto precio*); (*to order*) encargar, mandar; cargar (*un acumulador; al enemigo*); **to charge to the account of someone** cargarle a uno en cuenta; **to charge with** cargar de || *intr* embestir

charge account *s* cuenta corriente

chargé d'affaires [∫ɑr'ʒe də'fer] *s* (*pl* **chargés d'affaires**) encargado de negocios

charger ['t∫ɑrdʒər] *s* caballo de guerra; (*of a battery*) cargador *m*

chariot ['t∫ærɪ-ət] *s* carro romano

charioteer [‚t∫ærɪ-ə'tɪr] *s* carretero, auriga *m*

charitable ['t∫ærɪtəbəl] *adj* caritativo

chari•ty ['t∫ærɪti] *s* (*pl* **-ties**) caridad; asociación de beneficencia, obra pía; **charity begins at home** la caridad bien ordenada empieza por uno mismo

charity performance *s* función benéfica

charlatan ['∫ɑrlətən] *s* charlatán *m*

charlatanism ['∫ɑrlətən‚ɪzəm] *s* charlatanismo

Charlemagne ['∫ɑrlə‚men] *s* Carlomagno

Charles [t∫ɑrlz] *s* Carlos *m*

charlotte ['∫ɑrlət] *s* carlota || **Charlotte** *s* Carlota

charlotte russe ['∫ɑrlət 'rus] *s* carlota rusa

charm [t∫ɑrm] *s* encanto, hechizo; (*trinket*) amuleto, dije *m* || *tr* encantar, hechizar

charming ['t∫ɑrmɪŋ] *adj* encantador

charnel ['t∫ɑrnəl] *adj* cadavérico, horrible || *s* carnero, osario

charnel house *s* carnero, osario

chart [t∫ɑrt] *s* mapa geográfico; (naut) carta de marear; cuadro, diagrama *m* || *tr* bosquejar; **to chart a course** trazar una ruta

charter ['t∫ɑrtər] *s* carta (de privilegio) || *tr* alquilar (*un autobús*); fletar (*un barco*)

charter member *s* socio fundador

char•woman ['t∫ɑr‚wumən] *s* (*pl* **-women** [‚wɪmɪn]) alquilona, asistenta

Charybdis [kə'rɪbdɪs] *s* Caribdis *f*

chase [t∫es] *s* caza, persecución || *tr* cazar, perseguir; **to chase away** ahuyentar

chasm ['kæzəm] *s* abismo

chas•sis ['t∫æsi] *s* (*pl* **-sis** [siz]) chasis *m*

chaste [t∫est] *adj* casto; (*style*) castizo

chasten ['t∫esən] *tr* castigar, corregir

chastise [t∫æs'taɪz] *tr* castigar

chastity ['t∫æstɪti] *s* castidad

chasuble ['t∫æzjəbəl] *s* casulla

chat [t∫æt] *s* charla, plática || *v* (*pret & pp* **chatted;** *ger* **chatting**) *intr* charlar, platicar

chatelaine ['∫ætə‚len] *s* castellana

chattels ['t∫ætəlz] *spl* bienes *mpl* muebles, enseres *mpl*

chatter ['t∫ætər] *s* (*talk*) cháchara; (*rattling*) traqueo; (*of teeth*) castañeteo; (*of birds*) chirrido || *intr* chacharear; traquear; castañetear, dentellar (*los dientes*)

chat'ter•box' *s* charlador *m*, tarabilla

chauffeur ['∫ofər] o [∫o'fʌr] *s* chófer *m*

cheap [t∫ip] *adj* barato; (*charging low prices*) no carero, baratero; (*flashy*) cursi; **to feel cheap** sentirse avergonzado || *adv* barato

cheapen ['t∫ipən] *tr* abaratar

cheapness ['t∫ipnɪs] *s* baratura; (*flashiness*) cursilería

cheat [t∫it] *s* trampa, fraude *m;* (*person*) trampista *mf*, defraudador *m* || *tr* trampear, defraudar

check [t∫ek] *s* (*of bank*) cheque *m;* (*for baggage*) talón *m*, contraseña; (*in a restaurant*) cuenta; (*in theater or movie*) contraseña, billete *m* de salida; (*restraint*) freno; (*to hold a door*) amortiguador *m;* (*in chess*) jaque *m;* inspección; comprobación, verificación; (*cloth*) paño a cuadros; **in check** en jaque; **to hold in check** contener, refrenar || *interj* ¡jaque! || *tr* parar súbitamente; contener, refrenar; amortiguar; facturar (*equipajes*); inspeccionar; comprobar, verificar; marcar, señalar; (*in chess*) jaquear, dar jaque a; **to check up** comprobar, verificar || *intr* pararse súbitamente; corresponder punto por punto; **to check in** (*at a hotel*) llegar e inscribirse; **to check out** pagar la cuenta y despedirse. (slang) morir

check'book' *s* talonario (de cheques)

checker ['tʃɛkər] *s* inspector *m*; cuadro; dibujo a cuadros. (*in game of checkers*) ficha. pieza. **checkers** damas, juego de damas || *tr* marcar con cuadros, diversificar. variar

check'er·board' *s* damero. tablero

check girl *s* moza de guardarropa

checking account *s* cuenta corriente

check'mate' *s* mate *m*. jaque *m* mate || *tr* dar mate a, dar jaque mate a; (fig) derrotar completamente

check'out' *s* (*from a hotel*) salida; hora de salida; (*in a self-service retail store*) revisión y pago

checkout counter *s* mostrador *m* de revisión

check'point' *s* punto de inspección

check'rein' *s* engallador *m*

check'room' *s* guardarropa *m*; (rr) consigna, depósito de equipajes

check'up' *s* verificación rigurosa; (*of an automobile*) revisión. (med) reconocimiento general

cheek [tʃik] *s* mejilla, carrillo; (coll) descaro, frescura

cheek'bone' *s* pómulo

cheek by jowl *adv* cara a cara, en estrecha intimidad

cheek·y ['tʃiki] *adj* (*comp* -ier; *super* -iest) (coll) descarado. fresco

cheer [tʃɪr] *s* alegría. regocijo. (*shout*) viva *m*, aplauso. **what cheer?** ¿qué tal? || *tr* alegrar. animar. aplaudir. vitorear. dar la bienvenida a. con vivas y aplausos || *intr* alegrarse, animarse; **cheer up!** ¡ánimo!

cheerful ['tʃɪrfəl] *adj* alegre

cheerio ['tʃɪri,o] *interj* (coll) ¡hola!, ¡qué tal!; (coll) ¡adiós!, ¡hasta la vista!

cheerless ['tʃɪrlɪs] *adj* sombrío, triste

cheese [tʃiz] *s* queso

cheese'cloth' *s* estopilla

chef [ʃɛf] *s* primer cocinero, jefe *m* de cocina

chem. *abbr* **chemical, chemist, chemistry**

chemical ['kɛmɪkəl] *adj* químico || *s* producto químico, substancia química

chemise [ʃə'miz] *s* camisa (de mujer)

chemist ['kɛmɪst] *s* químico

chemistry ['kɛmɪstri] *s* química

cherish ['tʃɛrɪʃ] *tr* acariciar; (*a hope*) abrigar, acariciar

cher·ry ['tʃɛri] *s* (*pl* -ries) (*fruit; color*) cereza; (*tree*) cerezo

cher·ub ['tʃɛrəb] *s* (*pl* -ubim [əbɪm]) querubín *m* || *s* (*pl* -ubs) niño angelical

chess [tʃɛs] *s* ajedrez *m*

chess'board' *s* tablero de ajedrez

chess·man ['tʃɛs,mæn] *s* (*pl* -men [,mɛn]) pieza de ajedrez, trebejo

chess player *s* ajedrecista *mf*

chess set *s* ajedrez *m*

chest [tʃɛst] *s* (*part of body*) pecho; (*receptacle*) cajón *m*, cofre *m*; (*piece of furniture*) cómoda

chestnut ['tʃɛsnət] *s* (*tree, wood, color*) castaño; (*fruit*) castaña

chest of drawers *s* cómoda

cheval glass [ʃə'væl] *s* psique *f*

chevalier [,ʃɛvə'lɪr] *s* caballero

chevron ['ʃɛvrən] *s* galón *m* en forma de V invertida

chew [tʃu] *s* mascadura || *tr* mascar; **to chew the rag** (slang) dar la lengua || *intr* mascar

chewing gum *s* goma de mascar, chicle *m*

chg. *abbr* **charge**

chic [ʃik] *adj* & *s* chic *m*

chicaner·y [ʃɪ'kenəri] *s* (*pl* -ies) triquiñuela

chick [tʃɪk] *s* pollito; (slang) polla

chicken ['tʃɪkən] *s* pollo; (*young person*) pollo. (*young girl*) polla

chicken coop *s* pollera

chicken feed *s* (coll) calderilla

chickenhearted ['tʃɪkən,hɑrtɪd] *adj* gallina

chicken pox *s* viruelas locas

chicken wire *s* alambrada, tela metálica

chick'pea' *s* garbanzo

chico·ry ['tʃɪkəri] *s* (*pl* -ries) achicoria

chide [tʃaɪd] *s* (*pret* chided o chid [tʃɪd]. *pp* chided. chid o chidden ['tʃɪdən]) *tr* reprender, regañar

chief [tʃif] *adj* principal || *s* jefe *m*; (*of American Indians*) cacique *m*

chief executive *s* jefe *m* del gobierno

chief justice *s* presidente *m* de sala; presidente del tribunal supremo

chiefly ['tʃifli] *adv* principalmente, mayormente

chief of staff *s* jefe *m* de estado mayor

chief of state *s* jefe *m* del estado

chieftain ['tʃiftən] *s* (*of a clan or tribe*) jefe *m*, adalid *m*, caudillo

chiffon [ʃɪ'fɑn] *s* gasa, soplillo; **chiffons** atavíos, perifollos

chiffonier [,ʃɪfə'nɪr] *s* cómoda alta

chignon ['ʃɪnjɑn] *s* castaña, moño

chilblain ['tʃɪl,blen] *s* sabañón *m*

child [tʃaɪld] *s* (*pl* children ['tʃɪldrən]) *s* (*infant. youngster*) niño; (*one's offspring*) hijo. descendiente *mf*; **with child** encinta. embarazada

child'birth' *s* alumbramiento, parto

childhood ['tʃaɪldhʊd] *s* niñez *f*, puericia. **from childhood** desde niño

childish ['tʃaɪldɪʃ] *adj* aniñado, pueril

childishness ['tʃaɪldɪnɪs] *s* puerilidad

child labor *s* trabajo de menores

childless ['tʃaɪldlɪs] *adj* sin hijos

child'like' *adj* aniñado

child's play *s* juego de niños

child welfare *s* protección a la infancia

Chile ['tʃɪli] *s* Chile *m*

Chilean ['tʃɪliən] *adj* & *s* chileno

chili sauce ['tʃɪli] *s* ají *m*, salsa de ají

chill [tʃɪl] *adj* frío || *s* frío desapacible; *(sensation of cold)* escalofrío; *(lack of cordiality)* frialdad ‖ *tr* enfriar ‖ *intr* calofriarse

chill·y [ˈtʃɪlɪ] *adj (comp* -ier; *super* -iest) *(causing shivering)* frío; *(sensitive to cold)* escalofriado, friolero; *(indifferent)* (fig) frío

chime [tʃaɪm] *s* campaneo, repique *m;* tubo sonoro; **chimes** juego de campanas ‖ *tr & intr* campanear, repicar

chime clock *s* reloj *m* de carillón

chimera [kaɪˈmɪrə] o [kɪˈmɪrə] *s* quimera

chimney [ˈtʃɪmnɪ] *s* chimenea; *(for a lamp)* tubo

chimney cap *s* caperuza

chimney flue *s* cañón *m* de chimenea

chimney pot *s* mitra, guardavientos *m*

chimney sweep *s* limpiachimeneas *m,* deshollinador *m*

chimpanzee [ˌtʃɪmˈpænzi] o [ˌtʃɪmpænˈzi] *s* chimpancé *m*

chin [tʃɪn] *s* barba, mentón *m;* **to keep one's chin up** (coll) no desanimarse ‖ *v (pret & pp* chinned; *ger* chinning) *intr* (coll) charlar

china [ˈtʃaɪnə] *s* china, porcelana ‖ **China** *s* China

china closet *s* chinero

China·man [ˈtʃaɪnəmən] *s (pl* -men [mən]) *(offensive)* chino

chi'na·ware' *s* porcelana, vajilla de porcelana

Chi·nese [tʃaɪˈniz] *adj* chino ‖ *s (pl* -nese) chino

Chinese gong *s* batintín *m*

Chinese lantern *s* farolillo veneciano

Chinese puzzle *s* problema embrollado

chink [tʃɪŋk] *s* grieta, hendidura; sonido metálico

chin strap *s* barboquejo, carrillera

chintz [tʃɪnts] *s* zaraza

chip [tʃɪp] *s* astilla, brizna; *(in china)* desconchado; *(in poker)* ficha; **chip off the old block** hijo de su padre ‖ *v (pret & pp* chipped; *ger* chipping) *tr* astillar *(la madera)*; desconchar *(la porcelana)*; **to chip in** contribuir con su cuota ‖ *intr* astillarse; desconcharse

chipmunk [ˈtʃɪpˌmʌŋk] *s* ardilla listada

chipper [ˈtʃɪpər] *adj* (coll) alegre, jovial, vivo

chiropodist [kaɪˈrapədɪst] o [kɪˈrapədɪst] *s* quiropodista *mf*

chiropractor [ˈkaɪrəˌpræktər] *s* quiropráctico

chirp [tʃɪrp] *s* chirrido, gorjeo ‖ *intr* chirriar, gorjear; hablar alegremente

chis·el [ˈtʃɪzəl] *s (for wood)* escoplo, formón *m; (for stone and metal)* cincel *m* ‖ *v (pret & pp* -eled o -elled) *ger* -eling o -elling) *tr* escoplear; cincelar; (slang) estafar

chit-chat [ˈtʃɪtˌtʃæt] *s* charla, palique *m;* hablilla, chismes *mpl*

chivalric [ˈʃɪvəlrɪk] o [ʃɪˈvælrɪk] *adj* caballeresco

chivalrous [ˈʃɪvəlrəs] *adj* caballeroso

chivalry [ˈʃɪvəlrɪ] *s (knighthood)* caballería; *(gallantry, gentlemanliness)* caballerosidad

chloride [ˈklɔraɪd] *s* cloruro

chlorine [ˈklɔrin] *s* cloro

chloroform [ˈklɔrəˌfɔrm] *s* cloroformo ‖ *tr* cloroformizar

chlorophyll [ˈklɔrəfɪl] *s* clorofila

chock-full [ˈtʃakˈful] *adj* de bote en bote, colmado

chocolate [ˈtʃɔkəlɪt] o [ˈtʃakəlɪt] *s* chocolate *m*

choice [tʃɔɪs] *adj* escogido, selecto, superior ‖ *s* elección, selección; lo más escogido; **to have no choice** no tener alternativa

choir [kwaɪr] *s* coro

choir'boy' *s* niño de coro, infante *m* de coro

choir desk *s* facistol *m*

choir loft *s* coro

choir'mas'ter *s* jefe *m* de coro, maestro de capilla

choke [tʃok] *s* estrangulación; *(of carburetor)* cierre *m,* obturador *m;* (elec) choque *m* ‖ *tr* ahogar, sofocar, estrangular; obstruir, tapar; (aut) obturar; **to choke down** atragantar ‖ *intr* sofocarse; atragantarse; **to choke on** atragantarse con

choke coil *s* (elec) bobina de reacción, choque *m*

cholera [ˈkalərə] *s* cólera *m*

choleric [ˈkalərɪk] *adj* colérico

cholesterol [kəˈlestəˌrol] o [kəˈlestəˌral] *s* colesterol *m*

choose [tʃuz] *v (pret* chose [tʃoz]; *pp* chosen [ˈtʃozən]) *tr* escoger, elegir ‖ *intr* — **to choose between** optar entre; **to choose to** optar por

chop [tʃap] *s* golpe *m* cortante; *(of meat)* chuleta; **chops** boca, labios ‖ *v (pret & pp* chopped; *ger* chopping) *tr* cortar, tajar; picar *(la carne)*; **to chop off** tronchar; **to chop up** desmenuzar

chop'house' *s* restaurante *m,* figón *m,* colmado

chopper [ˈtʃapər] *s (person)* tajador *m; (tool)* hacha; *(of butcher)* cortante *m;* (slang) helicóptero

chopping block *s* tajo

chop·py [ˈtʃapɪ] *adj (comp* -pier; *super* -piest) *(sea)* agitado, picado; *(wind)* variable; *(style)* cortado, inciso

chop'sticks' *spl* palillos

choral [ˈkɔrəl] *adj* coral

chorale [koˈral] *s* coral *m*

choral society *s* orfeón *m*

chord [kɔrd] *s (harmonious combination of tones)* (mus) acorde *m;* (aer, anat, geom) cuerda

chore [tʃor] *s* tarea, quehacer *m*

choreography [ˌkorɪˈagrəfɪ] *s* coreografía

chorine [koˈrin] *s* (slang) corista, suripanta

chorus [ˈkorəs] *s* coro; *(refrain of a song)* estribillo

chorus girl *s* corista, conjuntista

chorus man *s* corista *m,* conjuntista *m*

chowder ['tʃaʊdər] s estofado de almejas o pescado

Chr. abbr **Christian**

Christ [kraɪst] s Cristo

christen ['krɪsən] tr bautizar

Christendom ['krɪsəndəm] s cristiandad

christening ['krɪsənɪŋ] s bautismo, bautizo

Christian ['krɪstʃən] adj & s cristiano

Christianity [ˌkrɪstʃɪˈænɪti] s cristianismo

Christianize ['krɪstʃəˌnaɪz] tr cristianizar

Christian name s nombre m de pila

Christmas ['krɪsməs] adj navideño || s Navidad, Pascua de Navidad

Christmas card s aleluya navideña

Christmas carol s villancico

Christmas Eve s nochebuena

Christmas gift s aguinaldo, regalo de Navidad

Christmas tree s árbol m de Navidad

Christopher ['krɪstəfər] s Cristóbal m

chrome [krom] adj cromado || s cromo || tr cromar

chromium ['kromɪ·ən] s cromo

chro·mo ['kromo] s (pl -mos) (colored picture) cromo; (piece of junk) (slang) trasto

chromosome ['kroməˌsom] s cromosoma m

chron. abbr **chronological, chronology**

chronic ['krɑnɪk] adj crónico

chronicle ['krɑnɪkəl] s crónica || tr narrar en una crónica; narrar, contar

chronicler ['krɑnɪklər] s cronista mf

chronolo·gy [krəˈnɑlədʒi] s (pl -gies) cronología

chronometer [krəˈnɑmɪtər] s cronómetro

chrysanthemum [krɪˈsænθɪməm] s crisantemo

chub·by ['tʃʌbi] adj (comp -bier; super -biest) rechoncho, regordete

chuck [tʃʌk] s (throw) echada, tirada; (under the chin) mamola; (of a lathe) mandril m || tr arrojar; **to chuck under the chin** hacer la mamola a

chuckle ['tʃʌkəl] s risa ahogada || intr reírse con risa ahogada

chug [tʃʌg] s ruido explosivo sordo; (of a locomotive) resoplido || v (pret & pp **chugged**; ger **chugging**) intr hacer ruidos explosivos sordos, moverse con ruidos explosivos sordos

chum [tʃʌm] s (coll) compinche mf; compañero de cuarto || v (pret & pp **chummed**; ger **chumming**) intr (coll) ser compinche, ser compinches; (coll) compartir un cuarto

chum·my ['tʃʌmi] adj (comp -mier; super -miest) muy amigable, íntimo

chump [tʃʌmp] s tarugo, zoquete m; (coll) estúpido, tonto

chunk [tʃʌŋk] s trozo, pedazo grueso

church [tʃʌrtʃ] s iglesia

churchgoer ['tʃʌrtʃˌgo·ər] s persona que frecuenta la iglesia

church·man ['tʃʌrtʃmən] s (pl -men

[mən]) sacerdote m, eclesiástico; feligrés m

church member s feligrés m

Church of England s Iglesia Anglicana

church'ward'en s capiller m

church'yard' s patio de iglesia; cementerio

churl [tʃʌrl] s palurdo, patán m

churlish ['tʃʌrlɪʃ] adj palurdo, insolente

churn [tʃʌrn] s mantequera || tr mazar (leche); hacer (mantequilla) en una mantequera; agitar, revolver || intr revolverse

chute [ʃut] s cascada, salto de agua; rápidos; conducto inclinado; (e.g., into a swimming pool) tobogán m; (e.g., for grain) tolva; paracaídas m

ciborium [sɪˈborɪ·əm] s (pl -a [ə]) (canopy) ciborio, baldaquín m; (cup) copón m

Cicero ['sɪsəˌro] s Cicerón m

cider ['saɪdər] s sidra

C.I.F., c.i.f. abbr **cost, insurance, and freight**

cigar [sɪˈgɑr] s cigarro, puro

cigar band s anillo de cigarro

cigar case s cigarrera, petaca

cigar cutter s cortacigarros m

cigaret o **cigarette** [ˌsɪgəˈret] s cigarrillo, pitillo

cigarette case s pitillera

cigarette holder s boquilla

cigarette lighter s mechero, encendedor m de bolsillo

cigarette paper s papel m de fumar

cigar holder s boquilla

cigar store s estanco, tabaquería

cinch [sɪntʃ] s (of saddle) cincha; (sure grip) (coll) agarro; (something easy) (slang) breva || tr cinchar; (coll) agarrar

cinder ['sɪndər] s ceniza; (coal burning without flame) pavesa

cinder bank s escorial m

Cinderella [ˌsɪndəˈrelə] s la Cenicienta

cinder track s pista de cenizas

cinema ['sɪnəmə] s cine m

cinematograph [ˌsɪnəˈmætəˌgræf] o [ˌsɪnəˈmætəˌgrɑf] s cinematógrafo || tr & intr cinematografiar

cinnabar ['sɪnəˌbɑr] s cinabrio

cinnamon ['sɪnəmən] s canela

cipher ['saɪfər] s cifra; cero; (nonentity) cero a la izquierda; (key to a cipher) clave f || tr cifrar; calcular

circle ['sʌrkəl] s círculo || tr circundar; dar la vuelta a; girar alrededor de

circuit ['sʌrkɪt] s circuito

circuit breaker s disyuntor m

circuitous [sərˈkjuˑɪtəs] adj indirecto, tortuoso

circular ['sʌrkjələr] adj tortuoso || s circular f, carta circular

circularize ['sʌrkjələˌraɪz] tr anunciar por circular; enviar circulares a

circulate ['sʌrkjəˌlet] tr & intr circular

circumcise ['sʌrkəmˌsaɪz] tr circuncidar

circumference [sər'kʌmfərəns] s circunferencia

circumflex ['sʌrkəm,flɛks] adj circunflejo

circumlocution [,sʌrkəmlo'kjuʃən] s circunlocución, circunloquio

circumnavigate [,sʌrkəm'nævɪ,get] tr circunnavegar

circumnavigation [,sʌrkəm,nævɪ'geʃən] s circunnavegación

circumscribe [,sʌrkəm'skraɪb] tr circunscribir

circumspect ['sʌrkəm,spɛkt] adj circunspecto

circumstance ['sʌrkəm,stæns] s circunstancia; ceremonia, ostentación; **in easy circumstances** acomodado; **under no circumstances** de ninguna manera

circumstantial [,sʌrkəm'stænʃəl] adj (derived from circumstances) circunstancial; (detailed) circunstanciado

circumstantial evidence s (law) indicios vehementes

circumstantiate [,sʌrkəm'stænʃɪ,et] tr apoyar con pruebas y detalles; (to describe in detail) circunstanciar

circumvent [,sʌrkəm'vɛnt] tr (to catch by a trick) entrampar, embaucar; (to outwit) burlar; (to keep away from, get around) evitar

circus ['sʌrkəs] s circo

cistern ['sɪstərn] s cisterna, aljibe m

citadel ['sɪtədəl] s ciudadela

citation [saɪ'teʃən] s (of a text) cita; (before a court of law) citación; (for gallantry) mención

cite [saɪt] tr (to quote; to summon) citar; (for gallantry) mencionar

citizen ['sɪtɪzən] s ciudadano; (civilian) paisano

citizen·ry ['sɪtɪzənri] s (pl -ries) conjunto de ciudadanos

citizenship ['sɪtɪzən,ʃɪp] s ciudadanía

citron ['sɪtrən] s (fruit) cidra; (tree) cidro; (candied rind) cidrada

citronella [,sɪtrə'nɛlə] s limoncillo (Andropogon nardus); aceite m de limoncillo

citrus fruit ['sɪtrəs] s agrios, frutas cítricas

cit·y ['sɪti] s (pl -ies) ciudad

city clerk s archivero

city council s ayuntamiento

city editor s redactor de periódico encargado de noticias locales

city fathers s concejales mpl

city hall s casa consistorial

city plan s plano de la ciudad

city planner s urbanista mf

city planning s urbanismo

city room s redacción

cit'y-state' s ciudad-estado f

civic ['sɪvɪk] adj cívico || **civics** s estudio de los deberes y derechos del ciudadano

civies ['sɪvɪz] spl (coll) traje m de paisano; **in civies** (coll) de paisano

civil ['sɪvɪl] adj civil

civilian [sɪ'vɪljən] adj civil || s civil mf, paisano

civilian clothes spl traje m de paisano

civili·ty [sɪ'vɪlɪti] s (pl -ties) civilidad

civilization [,sɪvɪlɪ'zeʃən] s civilización

civilize ['sɪvɪ,laɪz] tr civilizar

civil servant s funcionario del estado

claim [klem] s demanda, pretensión, reclamación || tr demandar, pretender, reclamar; afirmar, declarar; **to claim to** + inf pretender + inf

claim check s comprobante m

clairvoyance [klɛr'vɔɪ·əns] s clarividencia

clairvoyant [klɛr'vɔɪ·ənt] adj & s clarividente mf

clam [klæm] s almeja; (tight-lipped person) (coll) chiticalla m || intr — **to clam up** (coll) callarse la boca

clamber ['klæmər] intr — **to clamber up** subir gateando

clamor ['klæmər] s clamor m, clamoreo || intr clamorear

clamorous ['klæmərəs] adj clamoroso

clamp [klæmp] s abrazadera, grapa; (vise-like device) mordaza || tr agarrar, afianzar con abrazadera; sujetar en una mordaza || intr — **to clamp down on** (coll) apretar los tornillos a

clan [klæn] s clan m

clandestine [klæn'dɛstɪn] adj clandestino

clang [klæŋ] s tantán m, sonido metálico resonante || tr hacer sonar fuertemente || intr sonar fuertemente

clank [klæŋk] s sonido metálico seco || tr hacer sonar secamente || intr sonar secamente

clannish ['klænɪʃ] adj exclusivista

clap [klæp] s golpe seco; (of the hands) palmada; (of thunder) estampido || v (pret & pp **clapped**; ger **clapping**) tr batir (palmas); palmotear, aplaudir; **to clap shut** cerrar de golpe || intr palmotear, dar palmadas

clap of thunder s estampido de trueno

clapper ['klæpər] s palmoteador m; (of a bell) badajo; (to cause grain to slide) tarabilla

clap'trap' s faramalla; (of an actor) latiguillo

claque [klæk] s (paid clappers) claque f; (crush hat) clac m

claret ['klærɪt] s clarete m

clari·fy ['klærɪ,faɪ] v (pret & pp **-fied**) tr clarificar; encolar (el vino)

clarinet [,klærɪ'nɛt] s clarinete m

clarion ['klærɪ·ən] adj claro, brillante || s clarín m

clarity ['klærɪti] s claridad

clash [klæʃ] s choque m, encontrón m; estruendo, ruido || intr chocar, entrechocarse

clasp [klæsp] o [klɑsp] s (fastener) abrazadera, cierre m; (for, e.g., a necktie) broche m; (buckle) hebilla; (embrace) abrazo; (grip) agarro || tr abrochar; abrazar; agarrar, apretar (*la mano*); apretarse (*la mano*)

class. *abbr* **classical**

class [klæs] o [klɑs] *s* clase *f;* (slang) elegancia, buen tono || *tr* clasificar || *intr* clasificarse

class consciousness *s* sentimiento de clase

classic ['klæsɪk] *adj* & *s* clásico; **the classics** las obras clásicas

classical ['klæsɪkəl] *adj* clásico

classical scholar *s* erudito en las lenguas clásicas

classicist ['klæsɪsɪst] *s* clasicista *mf*

classified ['klæsɪ ˌfaɪd] *adj* clasificado; clasificado como secreto

classified ads *spl* anuncios clasificados en secciones

classi·fy ['klæsɪ ˌfaɪ] *v* (*pret* & *pp* **-fied**) *tr* clasificar

class'mate' *s* compañero de clase

class'room' *s* aula, sala de clase

class struggle *s* lucha de clases

class·y ['klæsi] *adj* (*comp* **-ier;** *super* **-lest**) (slang) elegante

clatter ['klætər] *s* estruendo confuso; algazara, gresca; (*of hoofs*) trápala || *intr* caer o moverse con estruendo confuso; hablar rápida y ruidosamente; **to clatter down the stairs** bajar la escalera ruidosamente

clause [klɔz] *s* (*article in a legal document*) cláusula; (gram) oración dependiente

clavichord ['klævɪ ˌkɔrd] *s* clavicordio

clavicle ['klævɪkəl] *s* clavícula

clavier ['klævɪ-ər] o [klə'vɪr] *s* teclado || [klə'vɪr] *s* instrumento musical con teclado

claw [klɔ] *s* garra, uña; (*of lobster, crab, etc.*) pinza; (*of hammer, wrench, etc.*) oreja; (coll) dedos, mano *f* || *tr* (*to clutch*) agarrar; (*to scratch*) arañar; (*to tear*) desgarrar

clay [kle] *adj* arcilloso || *s* arcilla

clay pigeon *s* pichón *m* de barro

clay pipe *s* pipa de tierra

clean [klin] *adj* limpio; distinto, neto, nítido; completo || *adv* completamente; **to come clean** (slang) confesarlo todo || *tr* limpiar; (*to tidy up*) asear; **to be cleaned out** (*of money*) (slang) quedar limpio; **to clean out** limpiar; (slang) dejar limpio || *intr* limpiarse; asearse; **to clean up** limpiarse; (coll) llevárselo todo; (*in gambling*) (slang) hacer mesa limpia; **to clean up after someone** limpiar lo que alguno ha ensuciado

clean bill of health *s* patente limpia de sanidad

cleaner ['klinər] *s* limpiador *m;* (*dry cleaner*) tintorero; (*preparation*) quitamanchas *m;* **to send to the cleaners** (slang) dejar limpio

cleaning ['klinɪŋ] *s* limpieza

cleaning fluid *s* quitamanchas *m*

cleaning woman *s* criada que hace la limpieza, alquilona

cleanliness ['klɛnlɪnɪs] *s* limpieza

clean·ly ['klɛnli] *adj* (*comp* **-lier;** *super* **-liest**) limpio (*que tiene el hábito del aseo*)

cleanse [klɛnz] *tr* limpiar, lavar, depurar

clean-shaven ['klin'ʃevən] *adj* lisamente afeitado

clean'up' *s* limpieza general; **to make a cleanup** (slang) hacer su pacotilla

clear [klɪr] *adj* claro; (*cloudless*) despejado; (*of guilt, debts, annoyances*) libre || *adv* claro, claramente; **clear through** de parte a parte || *tr* despejar (*un bosque*); clarificar (*lo que estaba turbio*); (*to make less dark*) aclarar; saltar por encima de; (*to prove the innocence of*) absolver; sacar (*una ganancia neta*); abonar, acreditar; liquidar (*una cuenta*); (*in the customhouse*) despachar; salvar (*un obstáculo*); levantar (*la mesa*); desmontar (*un terreno*); **to clear the way** abrir camino || *intr* clarificarse; aclararse; **to clear away** (coll) irse, desaparecer; **to clear up** abonanzarse (*el tiempo*); despejarse (*el cielo, el tiempo*)

clearance ['klɪrəns] *s* aclaración, abono, acreditación; (*between two objects*) espacio libre; (*in a cylinder*) espacio muerto; (com) compensación

clearance sale *s* venta de liquidación

clearing ['klɪrɪŋ] *s* (*in a woods*) claro; (com) compensación

clearing house *s* cámara de compensación

clear-sighted ['klɪr'saɪtɪd] *adj* clarividente, perspicaz

clear'sto'ry *s* (*of* **-ries**) var of **clerestory**

cleat [klit] *s* abrazadera, listón *m*

cleavage ['klivɪdʒ] *s* división, hendidura; (fig) desunión

cleave [kliv] *v* (*pret* & *pp* **cleft** [klɛft] o **cleaved**) *tr* rajar, partir; hender (*las aguas un buque, los aires una flecha*) || *intr* adherirse, pegarse; apegarse, ser fiel

cleaver ['klivər] *s* cortante *m*, cuchilla de carnicero

clef [klɛf] *s* (mus) clave *f*

cleft palate [klɛft] *s* fisura del paladar

clematis ['klɛmətɪs] *s* clemátide *f*

clemen·cy ['klɛmənsi] *s* (*pl* **-cies**) clemencia; (*of the weather*) benignidad

clement ['klɛmənt] *adj* clemente; (*weather*) benigno

clench [klɛntʃ] *s* agarro || *tr* agarrar; apretar, cerrar (*el puño, los dientes*)

cleresto·ry ['klɪr ˌstori] *s* (*pl* **-ries**) ciaraboya

cler·gy ['klɜrdʒi] *s* (*pl* **-gies**) clerecía, clero

clergy·man ['klɜrdʒimən] *s* (*pl* **-men** [mən]) clérigo, pastor *m*

cleric ['klɛrɪk] *s* clérigo

clerical ['klɛrɪkəl] *adj* (*of clergy*) clerical; (*of office work*) oficinesco || *s* clérigo, eclesiástico; (*supporter of power of clergy*) clerical *m;* **clericals** (coll) hábitos clericales

clerical error *s* error *m* de pluma

clerical work *s* trabajo de oficina

clerk [klʌrk] s (in a store) dependiente mf; (in an office) oficinista mf; (in a city hall) archivero; (in a church) lego, seglar m; (in law office, in court) escribano

clever ['klevər] adj hábil, diestro, mañoso; inteligente

cleverness ['klevərnɪs] s habilidad, destreza, maña; inteligencia

clew [klu] s indicio, pista

cliché [kli'ʃe] s (printing plate) clisé m; (trite expression) cliché m

click [klɪk] s golpecito; (of typewriter) tecleo; (of firearm) piñoneo; (of heels) taconeo; (of tongue) claqueo, chasquido || tr hacer sonar con un golpecito seco; chascar (la lengua); **to click the heels** taconear; cuadrarse (un soldado) || intr sonar con un golpecito seco; piñonear (el gatillo de un arma de fuego); claquear (la lengua)

client ['klaɪ·ənt] s cliente mf; cliente de abogado

clientele [ˌklaɪ·ən'tel] s clientela

cliff [klɪf] s acantilado, escarpa, risco

climate ['klaɪmɪt] s clima m

climax ['klaɪmæks] s colmo; **to cap the climax** ser el colmo

climb [klaɪm] s subida, trepa || tr & intr escalar, subir, trepar

climber ['klaɪmər] s trepador m; ambicioso de figurar; (bot) enredadera, trepadora

clinch [klɪntʃ] s agarro, abrazo; (of a nail) remache m || tr afianzar, sujetar; agarrar, abrazar; apretar (el puño); remachar (un clavo ya clavado); resolver decisivamente

cling [klɪŋ] v (pret & pp **clung** [klʌŋ]) intr adherirse, pegarse; **to cling to** agarrarse a, asirse de

cling'stone' peach s albérchigo, peladillo

clinic ['klɪnɪk] s clínica

clinical ['klɪnɪkəl] adj clínico

clinical chart s hoja clínica

clinician [klɪ'nɪʃən] s clínico

clink [klɪŋk] s tintín m || tr hacer tintinear; chocar (vasos, copas) || intr tintinear

clinker ['klɪŋkər] s escoria de hulla

clip [klɪp] s tijereteo, esquileo; grapa, pinza; (to fasten papers) sujetapapeles m, presilla de alambre; **at a good clip** a buen paso || v (pret & pp **clipped**; ger **clipping**) tr tijeretear, esquilar; (to fasten with a clip) afianzar, sujetar; recortar (p.ej., un cupón) || intr moverse con rapidez

clipper ['klɪpər] s tijera, cizalla; **clippers** maquinilla cortapelos; tijeras podadoras

clipping ['klɪpɪŋ] s tijereteo, esquileo; (from a newspaper) recorte m

clique [klik] s pandilla, corrillo || intr — **to clique together** apandillarse

cliquish ['klikɪʃ] adj exclusivista

clk. abbr **clerk, clock**

cloak [klok] s capote m; (disguise, excuse) capa || tr encapotar; disimular, encubrir

cloak-and-dagger ['klokən'dægər] adj de capa y espada (dícese de duelos, espionaje, etc.)

cloak-and-sword ['klokən'sord] adj de capa y espada (dícese, p.ej., de las costumbres caballerescas)

cloak hanger s cuelgacapas m

cloak'room' s guardarropa m; (Brit) excusado

clock [klɑk] s reloj m (de pared o de mesa); (in a stocking) cuadrado || tr registrar; (sport) cronometrar

clock'mak'er s relojero

clock tower s torre f reloj

clock'wise' adj & adv en el sentido de las agujas del reloj

clock'work' s mecanismo de relojería; **like clockwork** como un reloj

clod [klɑd] s terrón m

clod'hop'per s destripaterrones m, quebrantaterrones m; **clodhoppers** zapatos fuertes de trabajo

clog [klɑg] s estorbo, obstáculo; (wooden shoe) zueco; (dance) zapateado; (hobble on animal) traba || v (pret & pp **clogged**; ger **clogging**) tr atascar || intr atascarse; bailar el zapateado

clog dance s zapateado

cloister ['klɔɪstər] s claustro || tr enclaustrar

cloistral ['klɔɪstrəl] adj claustral

close [klos] adj cercano, próximo; casi igual; (translation) fiel, exacto; (fabric) compacto; (weather, atmosphere) pesado, sofocante; (stingy) tacaño; (battle, race, election) reñido; (friend) íntimo; (shut in, enclosed) cerrado; (narrow) estrecho || adv cerca; **close to** cerca de || [kloz] s fin m, terminación; (of business, of stock market) cierre m; **at the close of day** a la caída de la tarde; **to bring to a close** poner término a; **to come to a close** tocar a su fin || tr cerrar; (to cover) tapar; (to finish) concluir; saldar (una cuenta); cerrar (un trato); **to close in** cerrar, encerrar; **to close ranks** cerrar las filas || intr cerrar, cerrarse; **to close in on** cerrar con (el enemigo)

close call [klos] s (coll) escape m por un pelo

closed car [klozd] s coche cerrado, conducción interior

closed chapter s asunto concluido

closed season s veda

closed shop s taller agremiado

closefisted ['klos'fɪstɪd] adj cicatero, tacaño, manicorto

close-fitting ['klos'fɪtɪŋ] adj ajustado, ceñido al cuerpo

close-lipped ['klos'lɪpt] adj callado, reservado

closely ['klosli] adv de cerca; estrechamente; fielmente; atentamente

close quarters [klos] spl lugar muy estrecho, lugares estrechos

close shave [klos] s afeitado a ras; (coll) escape m por un pelo

closet ['klɑzɪt] s alacena; (wardrobe) armario; (small private room) aposento, gabinete *m;* (*for keeping clothing*) guardarropa *m;* (*toilet*) retrete *m* || *tr* — **to be closeted with** encerrarse con

close-up ['klos,ʌp] *s* (*moving picture*) vista de cerca; fotografía de cerca

closing ['kloziŋ] *s* cerradura, cierre *m*

closing prices *spl* precios de cierre

clot [klɑt] *s* grumo, coágulo || *v* (*pret & pp* **clotted;** *ger* **clotting**) *intr* engrumecerse, coagularse

cloth [klɔθ] o [klɑθ] *s* paño, tela; ropa clerical; (*canvas, sails*) lona, trapo, vela; (*for binding books*) tela; **the cloth** la clerecía

clothe [kloð] *v* (*pret & pp* **clothed** o **clad** [klæd]) *tr* trajear, vestir; cubrir; (*e.g., with authority*) investir

clothes [kloz] o [kloðz] *spl* ropa, vestidos; ropa de cama

clothes'bas'ket *s* cesto de la ropa, cesto de la colada

clothes'brush' *s* cepillo de ropa

clothes closet *s* ropero

clothes dryer *s* secadora de ropa, secarropa

clothes hanger *s* colgador *m,* perchero

clothes'horse' *s* enjugador *m,* secarropa de travesaños

clothes'line' *s* cordel *m* para tender la ropa, tendedera

clothes'pin' *s* pinza, alfiler *m* de madera

clothes tree *s* percha

clothes wringer *s* exprimidor *m* de ropa

clothier ['kloðjər] *s* (*person who sells ready-made clothes*) ropero; (*dealer in cloth*) pañero

clothing ['kloðiŋ] *s* ropa, vestidos, ropaje *m*

cloud [klaud] *s* nube *f* || *tr* anublar || *intr* — **to cloud over** anublarse

cloud bank *s* mar *m* de nubes

cloud'burst' *s* aguacero, chaparrón *m*

cloud-capped ['klaud,kæpt] *adj* coronado de nubes

cloudless ['klaudlɪs] *adj* despejado, sin nubes

cloud of dust *s* polvareda, nube *f* de polvo

cloud-y ['klaudi] *adj* (*comp* **-ier;** *super* **-iest**) nuboso, nublado; (*muddy, turbid*) turbio; confuso, obscuro; melancólico, sombrío

clove [klov] *s* (*flower*) clavo de especia; (*spice*) clavo

clover ['klovər] *s* trébol *m;* **to be in clover** vivir en el lujo

clo'ver-leaf' *s* (*pl* **-leaves** [,livz]) *s* cruce *m* en trébol

clove tree *s* clavero

clown [klaun] *s* bufón *m,* payaso; (*rustic*) patán *m* || *intr* hacer el payaso

clownish ['klaunɪʃ] *adj* bufonesco; rústico

cloy [klɔɪ] *tr* hastiar, empalagar

club [klʌb] *s* porra, clava; (*playing card*) basto, trébol *m;* club *m,* casino || *v* (*pret & pp* **clubbed;** *ger*

clubbing) *tr* aporrear || *intr* — **to club together** unirse; formar club

club car *s* coche *m* club, coche bar

club'house' *s* casino, club *m*

club-man ['klʌbmən] *s* (*pl* **-men** [mən]) clubista *m*

club-woman ['klʌb,wumən] *s* (*pl* **-women** [,wimin]) clubista *f*

cluck [klʌk] *s* cloqueo, clo clo || *intr* cloquear, hacer clo clo

clue [klu] *s* indicio, pista

clump [klʌmp] *s* (*of earth*) terrón *m;* (*of trees or shrubs*) grupo; pisada fuerte || *intr* — **to clump along** andar pesadamente

clum-sy ['klʌmzi] *adj* (*comp* **-sier;** *super* **-siest**) (*worker*) chapucero, desmañado, torpe; (*work*) chapucero, tosco, grosero

cluster ['klʌstər] *s* grupo; (*of grapes or other things growing or joined together*) racimo || *intr* arracimarse; **to cluster around** reunirse en torno a; **to cluster together** agruparse

clutch [klʌtʃ] *s* (*grasp, grip*) agarro, apretón *m* fuerte; (aut) embrague *m;* (aut) pedal *m* de embrague; **to fall into the clutches of** caer en las garras de; **to throw the clutch in** embragar; **to throw the clutch out** desembragar || *tr* agarrar, empuñar

clutter ['klʌtər] *tr* — **to clutter up** cubrir o llenar desordenadamente

cm. *abbr* **centimeter**

cml. *abbr* **commercial**

Co. *abbr* **Company, County**

coach [kotʃ] *s* coche *m,* diligencia; (aut) coche cerrado; (rr) coche de viajeros, coche ordinario *m;* (sport) entrenador *m* || *tr* aleccionar; (sport) entrenar || *intr* entrenarse

coach house *s* cochera

coaching ['kotʃɪŋ] *s* lecciones *fpl* particulares; (sport) entrenamiento

coach-man ['kotʃmən] *s* (*pl* **-men** [mən]) *s* cochero

coagulate [ko'ægjə,let] *tr* coagular || *intr* coagularse

coal [kol] *s* carbón *m,* hulla || *tr* proveer de carbón || *intr* proveerse de carbón

coal'bin' *s* carbonera

coal bunker *s* carbonera

coal car *s* vagón carbonero

coal'deal'er *s* carbonero

coaling ['kolɪŋ] *adj* carbonero || *s* toma de carbón

coalition [,ko.ə'lɪʃən] *s* unión; (*alliance between states or factions*) coalición

coal mine *s* mina de carbón

coal oil *s* aceite *m* mineral

coal scuttle *s* cubo para carbón

coal tar *s* alquitrán *m* de hulla

coal'yard' *s* carbonería

coarse [kors] *adj* (*of inferior quality*) basto, burdo; (*composed of large particles*) grueso; (*crude in manners*) grosero, rudo, vulgar

coast [kost] *s* costa; **the coast is clear** ya no hay peligro || *tr* costear || *intr*

deslizarse cuesta abajo; **to coast along** avanzar sin esfuerzo
coastal ['kostəl] *adj* costero
coaster ['kostər] *s* salvamanteles *m*
coaster brake *s* freno de contrapedal
coast guard *s* guardacostas *mpl;* guardia *m* de los guardacostas
coast guard cutter *s* escampavía de los guardacostas
coasting trade *s* cabotaje *m*
coast'land' *s* litoral *m*
coast'line' *s* línea de la costa
coast'wise' *adj* costanero || *adv* a lo largo de la costa
coat [kot] *s (jacket)* americana, saco; *(topcoat)* abrigo, sobretodo; *(of an animal)* lana, pelo; *(of paint)* capa, mano *f* || *tr* cubrir, revestir; dar una capa de pintura a
coated ['kotɪd] *adj* revestido; *(tongue)* saburroso
coat hanger *s* colgador *m*
coating ['kotɪŋ] *s* revestimiento; *(of paint)* capa; *(of plaster)* enlucido
coat of arms *s* escudo de armas
coat'room' *s* guardarropa *m*
coat'tail' *s* faldón *m*
coax [koks] *tr* engatusar
cob [kab] *s* zuro; **to eat corn on the cob** comer maíz en la mazorca
cobalt ['kobəlt] *s* cobalto
cobbler ['kablər] *s* remendón *m*, zapatero de viejo
cob'ble-stone' *s* guijarro
cob'web' *s* telaraña
cocaine [ko'ken] *s* cocaína
cock [kak] *s (rooster)* gallo; *(faucet, valve)* espita, grifo; *(of firearm)* martillo; *(weathervane)* veleta; caudillo, jefe *m* || *tr* amartillar *(un arma de fuego)*; ladear *(la cabeza)*; enderezar, levantar
cockade [ka'ked] *s* cucarda, escarapela
cock-a-doodle-doo ['kakə,dudəl'du] *s* quiquiriquí *m*
cock-and-bull story ['kakənd'bʊl] *s* cuento absurdo, cuento increíble
cocked hat [kakt] *s* sombrero de candil, sombrero de tres picos; **to knock into a cocked hat** (slang) apabullar
cockeyed ['kak,aɪd] *adj* bisojo, bizco; (coll) encorvado, torcido; (slang) disparatado, extravagante
cock'fight' *s* pelea de gallos
cockney ['kakni] *s* londinense *mf* de la clase pobre que habla un dialecto característico; dialecto de la clase pobre de Londres
cock of the walk *s* quiquiriquí *m*, gallito del lugar
cock'pit' *s* gallera; (aer) carlinga
cock'roach' *s* cucaracha
cockscomb ['kaks,kom] *s* cresta de gallo; gorro de bufón; (bot) cresta de gallo, moco de pavo
cock'sure' *adj* muy seguro de sí mismo
cock'tail' *s* coctel *m;* *(of fruit, oysters, etc.)* aperitivo
cocktail party *s* coctel *m*
cocktail shaker ['ʃekər] *s* coctelera

cock·y ['kaki] *adj (comp* **-ier;** *super* **-iest)** (coll) arrogante, hinchado; **to be cocky** (coll) tener mucho gallo
cocoa ['koko] *s* cacao; *(drink)* chocolate *m*
cocoanut o coconut ['kokə,nʌt] *s* coco
cocoanut palm o tree *s* cocotero
cocoon [kə'kun] *s* capullo
C.O.D., c.o.d. *abbr* **collect on delivery;** (Brit) **cash on delivery**
cod [kad] *s* abadejo, bacalao
coddle ['kadəl] *tr* consentir, mimar
code [kod] *s (of laws; of manners; of signals)* código; *(of telegraphy)* alfabeto; *(secret system of writing)* cifra, clave *f;* (com) cifrario; **in code** en cifra || *tr (to put in code)* cifrar
code word *s* clave telegráfica
codex ['kodeks] *s (pl* **codices** ['kodɪ,siz] o ['kadɪ,siz] *s* códice *m*
cod'fish' *s* abadejo, bacalao
codger ['kadʒər] *s* — **old codger** (coll) anciano, tío *m*
codicil ['kadɪsɪl] *s* codicilo; apéndice *m*
codi·fy ['kadɪ,faɪ] o ['kodɪ,faɪ] *v (pret & pp* **-fied)** *tr* codificar
cod'-liv'er oil *s* aceite *m* de hígado de bacalao
coed o co-ed ['ko,ed] *s* alumna de una escuela coeducativa
coeducation [,ko,edʒə'ke/ən] *s* coeducación
coefficient [,ko·ɪ'fɪ/ənt] *adj & s* coeficiente *m*
coerce [ko'ʌrs] *tr* forzar, coactar
coercion [ko'ʌrʃən] *s* compulsión, coacción
coeval [ko'ivəl] *adj & s* coetáneo
coexist [,ko·ɪg'zɪst] *intr* coexistir
coexistence [,ko·ɪg'zɪstəns] *s* coexistencia
coffee ['kɔfi] o ['kafi] *s* café *m;* *(plant)* cafeto; **black coffee** café solo
coffee bean *s* grano de café
cof'fee-cake' *s* rosquilla (que se come con el café)
coffee grinder *s* molinillo de café
coffee grounds *spl* poso del café
coffee mill *s* molinillo de café
coffee plantation *s* cafetal *m*
coffee pot *s* cafetera
coffee tree *s* cafeto
coffer ['kɔfər] o ['kafər] *s* arca, cofre *m;* **coffers** tesoro, fondos
cof'fer-dam' *s* ataguía, encajonado
coffin ['kɔfɪn] o ['kafɪn] *s* ataúd *m*
C. of S. *abbr* **Chief of Staff**
cog [kag] *s* diente *m (de rueda dentada);* rueda dentada; **to slip a cog** equivocarse
cogency ['kodʒənsi] *s* fuerza (de un argumento)
cogent ['kodʒənt] *adj* fuerte, convincente
cogitate ['kadʒɪ,tet] *tr & intr* cogitar, meditar
cognac ['konjæk] o ['kanjæk] *s* coñac *m*
cognizance ['kagnɪzəns] o ['kanɪzəns]

s conocimiento; **to take cognizance of** enterarse de

cognizant ['kagnɪzənt] o ['kɑnɪzənt] *adj* sabedor, enterado

cog′wheel′ s rueda dentada

cohabit [ko'hæbɪt] *intr* cohabitar

coheir [ko'er] s coheredero

cohere [ko'hɪr] *intr* adherirse, pegarse; conformarse, corresponder

coherent [ko'hɪrənt] *adj* coherente

cohesion [ko'hiʒən] s cohesión

coiffeur [kwɑ'fʌr] s peluquero

coiffure [kwɑ'fjur] s peinado, tocado

coil [kɔɪl] s (*something wound in a spiral*) rollo; (*single turn of spiral*) vuelta; (*of a still*) serpentín m; (*of hair*) rizo; (*of a spring*) espiral f; (elec) carrete m || tr arrollar, enrollar; (naut) adujar || intr arrollarse, enrollarse; (*like a snake*) serpentear

coil spring s resorte m espiral

coin [kɔɪn] s moneda; (*wedge*) cuña; **to pay back in one's own coin** pagar en la misma moneda; **to toss a coin** echar a cara o cruz || tr acuñar; forjar, inventar (*palabras o frases*); **to coin money** (coll) ganar mucho dinero

coincide [,ko·ɪn'saɪd] *intr* coincidir

coincidence [ko'ɪnsɪdəns] s coincidencia

coition [ko'ɪʃən] o **coitus** ['ko·ɪtəs] s coito

coke [kok] s coque m, cok m

col. *abbr* colored, colony, column

colander ['kʌləndər] o ['kɑləndər] s colador m, escurridor m

cold [kold] *adj* frío; **to be cold** (*said of a person*) tener frío; (*said of the weather*) hacer frío || s frío; (*indisposition*) resfriado; **to catch cold** resfriarse, coger un resfriado

cold blood s — **in cold blood** a sangre fría

cold chisel s cortafrío

cold comfort s poca consolación

cold cream s colcrén m

cold cuts *spl* fiambres *mpl*

cold feet *spl* (coll) desánimo, miedo

cold′heart′ed *adj* duro, insensible

cold meat s carne f fiambre

coldness ['koldnɪs] s frialdad

cold shoulder s — **to turn a cold shoulder on** (coll) tratar con suma frialdad

cold snap s corto rato de frío agudo

cold storage s conservación en cámara frigorífica

cold war s guerra fría

coleslaw ['kol,slɔ] s ensalada de col

colic ['kalɪk] *adj & s* cólico

coliseum [,kalɪ'si·əm] s coliseo

coll. *abbr* colleague, collection, college, colloquial

collaborate [kə'læbə,ret] *intr* colaborar

collaborationist [kə,læbə'reʃənɪst] s colaboracionista *mf*

collaborator [kə'læbə,retər] s colaborador m

collapse [kə'læps] s desplome m; (*in business*) fracaso; (pathol) colapso || *intr* desplomarse; fracasar; postrarse, sufrir colapso

collapsible [kə'læpsɪbəl] *adj* abatible, plegable, desmontable

collar ['kalər] s cuello; (*of dog, horse*) collar m; (mach) collar

col′lar·band′ s tirilla de camisa

col′lar·bone′ s clavícula

collate [kə'let] o ['kɑlet] *tr* colacionar, cotejar

collateral [kə'lætərəl] *adj* colateral || s (*relative*) colateral *mf;* (com) colateral m

collation [kə'leʃən] s (*act of comparing; light meal*) colación

colleague ['kalig] s colega *mf*

collect ['kalekt] s (eccl) colecta || [kə'lekt] *tr* acumular, reunir; colectar, recaudar (*impuestos*); coleccionar (*sellos de correo, antiguallas*); recolectar (*cosechas*); cobrar (*pasajes*); recoger (*billetes; el correo*); **to collect onself** reponerse || *intr* acumularse; **collect on delivery** contra reembolso, cobro contra entrega

collected [kə'lektɪd] *adj* sosegado, dueño de sí mismo

collection [kə'lekʃən] s colección; (*of taxes*) recaudación; (*of mail*) recogida

collection agency s agencia de cobros de cuentas

collective [kə'lektɪv] *adj* colectivo

collector [kə'lektər] s (*of stamps, antiques*) coleccionista *mf;* (*of taxes*) recaudador m; (*of tickets*) cobrador m

college ['kalɪdʒ] s colegio universitario; (*of cardinals, electors, etc.*) colegio

collide [kə'laɪd] *intr* chocar; **to collide with** chocar con

collie ['kali] s perro pastoril escocés

collier ['kaljer] s barco carbonero; minero de carbón

collier·y ['kaljeri] s (*pl* -ies) mina de carbón

collision [kə'lɪʒən] s colisión

colloid ['kalɔɪd] *adj & s* coloide m

colloquial [kə'lokwɪ·əl] *adj* coloquial, familiar

colloquialism [kə'lokwɪ·ə,lɪzəm] s coloquialismo

collo·quy ['kaləkwi] s (*pl* -quies) coloquio

collusion [kə'luʒən] s colusión, confabulación; **to be in collusion with** estar en inteligencia con

cologne [kə'lon] s agua de colonia, colonia || **Cologne** o Colonia

colon ['kolən] s (anat) colon m; (gram) dos puntos

colonel ['kʌrnəl] s coronel m

colonel·cy ['kʌrnəlsi] s (*pl* -cies) coronelía

colonial [kə'lonɪ·əl] *adj* colonial || s colono

colonize ['kalə,naɪz] *tr & intr* colonizar

colonnade [,kalə'ned] s columnata

colo·ny ['kaləni] s (*pl* -nies) colonia

colophon ['kalə,fan] s colofón m

color [ˈkʌlər] s color; **the colors** los colores, la bandera; **to call to the colors** llamar a filas; **to give** o **to lend color to** dar visos de probabilidad a; **under color of** so color de, bajo pretexto de; **with flying colors** con banderas desplegadas || *tr* colorar, colorear; (*to excuse, palliate*) colorear; (*to dye*) teñir || *intr* sonrojarse, ponerse colorado, demudarse

col'or-blind' *adj* ciego para los colores

colored [ˈkʌlərd] *adj* de color; (*specious*) colorado

colorful [ˈkʌlərfəl] *adj* colorido; pintoresco

coloring [ˈkʌlərɪŋ] *adj* & *s* colorante *m*

colorless [ˈkʌlərlɪs] *adj* incoloro; (fig) insulso

color photography s fotografía en colores

color salute s (mil) saludo con la bandera

color sargent s sargento abanderado

color screen s (phot) pantalla de color

color television s telivisión en colores

colossal [kəˈlɑsəl] *adj* colosal

colossus [kəˈlɑsəs] s coloso

colt [kolt] s potro

Columbus [kəˈlʌmbəs] s Colón *m*

Columbus Day s día *m* de la raza, fiesta de la hispanidad

column [ˈkɑləm] s columna

columnist [ˈkɑləmɪst] s columnista *mf*

com. *abbr* **comedy, commerce, common**

Com. *abbr* **Commander, Commissioner, Committee**

coma [ˈkomə] s (pathol) coma *m*

comb [kom] s peine *m*; (*currycomb*) almohaza; (*of rooster*) cresta; cresta de ola || *tr* peinar; explorar con minuciosidad

com·bat [ˈkʌmbæt] s combate *m* || [ˈkʌmbæt] o [kəmˈbæt] *v* (*pret* & *pp* **-bated** o **-batted**; *ger* **-bating** o **-batting**) *tr* & *intr* combatir

combatant [ˈkʌmkətənt] *adj* & *s* combatiente *m*

combat duty s servicio de frente

combination [ˌkɑmbɪˈneʃən] s combinación

combine [ˈkɑmbaɪn] s monopolio; segadora trilladora; (coll) combinación || [kəmˈbaɪn] *tr* combinar || *intr* combinarse

combining form s (gram) elemento de compuestos

combustible [kəmˈbʌstɪbəl] *adj* combustible; (fig) ardiente, impetuoso || *s* combustible *m*

combustion [kəmˈbʌstʃən] s combustión

come [kʌm] *v* (*pret* **came** [kem]; *pp* **come**) *intr* venir; **to come about** suceder; **to come across** encontrarse con; **to come after** venir detrás de; venir después de; venir por, venir en busca de; **to come again** volver; **to come apart** desunirse, desprenderse; **to come around** restablecerse; volver

en sí; rendirse; ponerse de acuerdo; cambiar de dirección; **to come at** alcanzar; **to come back** volver; (coll) rehabilitarse; **to come before** anteponerse; **to come between** interponerse; desunir, separar; **to come by** conseguir; **to come down** bajar; (*in social position, financial status, etc.*) descender; (*from one person to another*) ser transmitido; **to come downstairs** bajar (*de un piso a otro*); **to come down with** enfermarse de; **to come for** venir por, venir en busca de; **to come forth** salir; aparecer; **to come forward** avanzar; presentarse; **to come from** venir de; provenir de; **to come in** entrar; entrar en; empezar; ponerse en uso; **to come in for** conseguir, recibir; **to come into one's own** ser reconocido; **to come off** desprenderse; acontecer; **to come out** salir; salir a luz; ponerse de largo (*una joven*); divulgarse (*una noticia*); **to come out for** anunciar su apoyo de; **to come out with** descolgarse con; **to come over** dejarse persuadir; pasar, p.ej., what's come over him? ¿qué le ha pasado?; **to come through** salir bien, tener éxito; ganar; **to come to** volver en sí; **to come together** juntarse, reunirse; **to come true** hacerse realidad; **to come up** subir; presentarse; **to come upstairs** subir (*de un piso a otro*); **to come up to** acercarse a; subir a; estar a la altura de; **to come up with** proponer

come'back' s (coll) rehabilitación; (slang) respuesta aguda; **to stage a comeback** (coll) rehabilitarse

comedian [kəˈmidɪ·ən] s cómico, comediante *m*; autor *m* de comedias

comedienne [kəˌmidɪˈɛn] s cómica, comedianta

come'down' s (coll) humillación, revés *m*

come·dy [ˈkɑmədi] s (*pl* **-dies**) comedia cómica; (*comicalness*) comicidad

come·ly [ˈkʌmli] *adj* (*comp* **-lier**; *super* **-liest**) (*attractive*) donairoso, gracioso; (*decorous*) conveniente, decente

comet [ˈkɑmɪt] s cometa *m*

comfort [ˈkʌmfərt] s comodidad, confort *m*; (*encouragement, consolation*) confortación; (*person*) confortador *m*; (*bed cover*) colcha, cobertor *m* || *tr* confortar

comfortable [ˈkʌmfərtəbəl] *adj* cómodo, confortable; (*fairly well off*) holgado; (*salary*) (coll) suficiente || *s* colcha, cobertor *m*

comforter [ˈkʌmfərtər] s confortador *m*, consolador *m*; colcha, cobertor *m*; bufanda de lana

comforting [ˈkʌmfərtɪŋ] *adj* confortante

comfort station s quiosco de necesidad

comfrey [ˈkʌmfri] s consuelda

comic [ˈkɑmɪk] *adj* cómico || s cómico; (coll) periódico cómico; **comics** (coll) tiras cómicas

comical ['kɑmɪkəl] *adj* cómico

comic book *s* tebeo

comic opera *s* ópera cómica

comic strip *s* tira cómica

coming ['kʌmɪŋ] *adj* que viene, venidero; (coll) prometedor ‖ *s* venida

coming out *s* (*of stocks, bonds, etc.*) emisión; (*of a young girl*) puesta de largo, entrada en sociedad

comma ['kɑmə] *s* coma

command [kə'mænd] o [kə'mɑnd] *s* (*commanding*) dominio, mando; (*order, direction*) mandato, orden *f*; (*e.g., of a foreign language*) dominio; (mil) comando; **to be in command** of estar al mando de; **to take command** tomar el mando ‖ *tr* mandar, ordenar; dominar (*un idioma extranjero*); merecer (*p.ej., respeto*); (mil) comandar ‖ *intr* mandar

commandant [,kɑmən'dænt] o [,kɑmən'dɑnt] *s* comandante *m*

commandeer [,kɑmən'dɪr] *tr* reclutar forzosamente; expropiar; (coll) apoderarse de

commander [kə'mændər] o [kə'mɑndər] *s* comandante *m*; (*of a military order*) comendador *m*

commandment [kə'mændmənt] o [kə'mɑndmənt] *s* (Bib) mandamiento

commemorate [kə'memə,ret] *tr* conmemorar

commence [kə'mɛns] *tr & intr* comenzar, empezar

commencement [kə'mɛnsmənt] *s* comienzo, principio; día *m* de graduación; ceremonia de graduación

commend [kə'mɛnd] *tr* (*to entrust*) encargar, encomendar; (*to recommend*) recomendar; (*to praise*) alabar, elogiar

commendable [kə'mɛnəbəl] *adj* recomendable

commendation [,kɑmən'deʃən] *s* encargo, encomienda; recomendación; alabanza, elogio

comment ['kɑmɛnt] *s* comentario, comento ‖ *intr* comentar; **to comment on** comentar

commentar·y ['kɑmən,teri] *s* (*pl* **-ies**) comentario

commentator ['kɑmən,tetər] *s* comentarista *mf*

commerce ['kɑmərs] *s* comercio

commercial [kə'mɑrʃəl] *adj* comercial ‖ *s* anuncio publicitario radiofónico o televisivo; (rad & telv) programa publicitario

commercial traveler *s* agente viajero

commiserate [kə'mɪzə,ret] *intr* — **to commiserate with** condolerse de

commiseration [kə,mɪzə'reʃən] *s* conmiseración

commissar [,kɑmɪ'sɑr] *s* comisario (*en Rusia*)

commissar·y ['kɑmɪ,seri] *s* (*pl* **-ies**) (*deputy*) comisario; (*store*) economato

commission [kə'mɪʃən] *s* comisión; (mil) nombramiento; **to put in commission** poner en uso; poner (*un buque*) en servicio activo; **to put out of commission** inutilizar, descomponer; retirar (*un buque*) del servicio activo ‖ *tr* comisionar; poner en uso; poner (*un buque*) en servicio activo; (mil) nombrar

commissioned officer *s* oficial *m*

commissioner [kə'mɪʃənər] *s* comisario; (*person authorized by a commission*) comisionado

com·mit [kə'mɪt] *v* (*pret & pp* **-mitted**; *ger* **-mitting**) *tr* cometer (*un crimen, una falta*; *un negocio a una persona*); (*to hand over*) confiar, entregar; dar, empeñar (*la palabra*); (*to bind, pledge*) comprometer; internar (*a un demente*); (*to memory*) encomendar; **to commit oneself** comprometerse, empeñarse; **to commit to writing** poner por escrito

commitment [kə'mɪtmənt] *s* (*act of committing*) comisión; (*to an asylum*) internación; (*written order*) auto de prisión; compromiso, cometido, empeño

committee [kə'mɪti] *s* comité *m*, comisión

commode [kə'mod] *s* (*chest of drawers*) cómoda; (*washstand*) lavabo; (*chamber pot*) sillico

commodious [kə'modɪ·əs] *adj* espacioso, holgado

commodi·ty [kə'mɑdɪti] *s* (*pl* **-ties**) artículo de consumo, mercancía

commodity exchange *s* lonja, bolsa mercantil

common ['kɑmən] *adj* común ‖ *s* campo común, ejido; **commons** estado llano; (*of a school*) refectorio; **the Commons** (Brit) los Comunes

common carrier *s* empresa de transportes públicos

commoner ['kɑmənər] *s* plebeyo; (Brit) miembro de la Cámara de los Comunes

common law *s* derecho consuetudinario

com'mon-law' marriage *s* matrimonio consensual

com'mon·place' *adj* común, trivial, ordinario ‖ *s* lugar *m* común, trivialidad

common sense *s* sentido común

com'mon-sense' *adj* cuerdo, razonable

common stock *s* acción ordinaria; acciones ordinarias

commonweal ['kɑmən,wil] *s* bien público

com'mon·wealth' *s* estado, nación; república; (*state of U.S.A.*) estado; (*self-governing associated country*) estado libre asociado; (*association of states*) mancomunidad

commotion [kə'moʃən] *s* conmoción

commune [kə'mjun] *intr* conversar; (eccl) comulgar

communicant [kə'mjunɪkənt] *s* comunicante *mf*; (eccl) comulgante *mf*

communicate [kə'mjunɪ ,ket] *tr* comunicar || *intr* comunicarse
communicating [kə'mjunɪ ,ketɪŋ] *adj* comunicador
communicative [kə'mjunɪ ,ketɪv] *adj* comunicativo
communion [kə'mjunjən] *s* comunión; **to take communion** comulgar
communion rail *s* comulgatorio
communiqué [kə ,mjunɪ'ke] o [kə-'mjunɪ ,ke] *s* comunicado, parte *m*
communism ['kɑmjə ,nɪzəm] *s* comunismo
communist ['kɑmjənɪst] *s* comunista *mf*
communi-ty [kə'mjunɪti] *s* (*pl* -ties) vecindario; (*group of people living together*) comunidad
communize ['kɑmjə ,naɪz] *tr* comunizar
commutation ticket [,kɑmjə'teʃən] *s* billete *m* de abono
commutator ['kɑmjə ,tetər] *s* (elec) colector *m*
commute [kə'mjut] *tr* conmutar || *intr* viajar con billete de abono
commuter [kə'mjutər] *s* abonado al ferrocarril
comp. *abbr* **compare, comparative, composer, composition, compound**
compact [kəm'pækt] *adj* compacto; breve, preciso || ['kɑmpækt] *s* convenio, pacto; estuche *m* de afeites
companion [kəm'pænjən] *s* compañero
companionable [kəm'pænjənəbəl] *adj* afable, sociable, simpático
companionship [kəm'pænjən ,ʃɪp] *s* compañerismo
companionway [kəm'pænjən ,we] *s* (naut) escalera de cámara
compa-ny ['kʌmpəni] *s* (*pl* -nies) compañía; visita, visitas, invitado, invitados; (naut) tripulación; **to be good company** ser compañero alegre; **to keep company** ir juntos (*un hombre y una mujer*); **to keep someone company** hacerle compañía a una persona; **to part company** separarse; enemistarse
company building *s* edificio social
company office *s* domicilio social
comparative [kəm'pærətɪv] *adj* & *s* comparativo
compare [kəm'per] *s* — **beyond compare** sin comparación, sin par || *tr* comparar
comparison [kəm'pærɪsən] *s* comparación
compartment [kəm'pɑrtmənt] *s* compartimiento; (rr) departamento
compass ['kʌmpəs] *s* brújula, compás *m*; ámbito, recinto; alcance *m*, extensión; **compass o compasses** (*for drawing circles*) compás *m*
compass card *s* (naut) rosa náutica, rosa de los vientos
compassion [kəm'pæʃən] *s* compasión
compassionate [kəm'pæʃənɪt] *adj* compasivo
com-pel [kəm'pel] *v* (*pret* & *pp* -pelled; *ger* -pelling) *tr* forzar, obli-

gar, compeler; imponer (*respeto, silencio*)
compendious [kəm'pendɪ-əs] *adj* compendioso
compendi-um [kəm'pendɪ-əm] *s* (*pl* -ums o -a [ə]) compendio
compensate ['kɑmpən ,set] *tr* & *intr* compensar; **to compensate for** compensar
compensation [,kɑmpən'seʃən] *s* compensación
compete [kəm'pit] *intr* competir
competence ['kɑmpɪtəns] o **competency** ['kɑmpɪtənsi] *s* (*aptitude; legal capacity*) competencia; (*sufficient means to live comfortably*) buen pasar *m*
competent ['kɑmpɪtənt] *adj* competente
competition [,kɑmpɪ'tɪʃən] *s* (*rivalry*) competencia; (*in a match, examination, etc.*) certamen *m*, concurso; (*in business*) concurrencia
competitive examination [kəm'petɪtɪv] *s* oposición
competitive prices *spl* precios de competencia
competitor [kəm'petɪtər] *s* competidor *m*
compilation [,kɑmpɪ'leʃən] *s* compilación, recopilación
compile [kəm'paɪl] *tr* compilar, recopilar
complacence [kəm'plesəns] o **complacency** [kəm'plesənsi] *s* (*quiet satisfaction*) complacencia; satisfacción de sí mismo
complacent [kəm'plesənt] *adj* (*willing to please*) complaciente; satisfecho de sí mismo
complain [kəm'plen] *intr* quejarse
complainant [kəm'plenənt] *s* (law) demandante *mf*
complaint [kəm'plent] *s* queja; (*grievance*) agravio; (*illness*) enfermedad, mal *m*; (law) demanda, querella
complaisance [kəm'plezəns] o ['kɑmplɪ ,zæns] *s* amabilidad, cortesía
complaisant [kəm'plezənt] o ['kɑmplɪ ,zænt] *adj* amable, cortés
complement ['kɑmplɪmənt] *s* complemento; (nav) dotación || ['kɑmplɪ ,ment] *tr* complementar
complete [kəm'plit] *adj* completo || *tr* completar, terminar, realizar
completion [kəm'pliʃən] *s* terminación, realización
complex [kəm'pleks] o ['kɑmpleks] *adj* (*not simple*) complexo; (*composite*) complejo; (*intricate*) complicado || ['kɑmpleks] *s* complejo; (psychol) complejo; (coll) obsesión
complexion [kəm'plekʃən] *s* (*constitution*) complexión; (*texture of skin, esp. of face*) tez *f*; aspecto general, índole *f*
compliance [kəm'plaɪ-əns] *s* condescendencia; sumisión, rendimiento; **in compliance with** de acuerdo con, en conformidad con
complicate ['kʌmplɪ ,ket] *tr* complicar

complicated ['kamplɪˌketɪd] *adj* complicado

complici·ty [kəm'plɪsɪti] *s* (*pl* -ties) complicidad, codelincuencia

compliment ['kamplɪmənt] *s* (*show of courtesy*) cumplimiento; (*praise*) alabanza, halago; **compliments** saludos, recuerdos || ['kamplɪˌment] *tr* cumplimentar; alabar, halagar

complimentary copy [ˌkamplɪ'mentəri] *s* ejemplar *m* de cortesía

complimentary ticket *s* billete *m* de regalo, pase *m* de cortesía

com·ply [kəm'plaɪ] *v* (*pret & pp* -plied) *intr* conformarse; **to comply with** conformarse con, obrar de acuerdo con

component [kəm'ponənt] *adj* componente || *m* componente *m*; (*mech*) componente *f*

compose [kəm'poz] *tr* componer; **to be composed of** estar compuesto de

composed [kəm'pozd] *adj* sosegado, tranquilo

composer [kəm'pozer] *s* componedor *m*; (*mus*) compositor *m*; autor *m*

composing stick *s* componedor *m*

composite [kəm'pazɪt] *adj & s* compuesto

composition [ˌkampə'zɪʃən] *s* composición

compositor [kəm'pazɪtər] *s* cajista *mf*, componedor *m*

composure [kəm'pozər] *s* serenidad, sosiego

compote ['kampot] *s* (*stewed fruit*) compota; (*dish*) compotera

compound ['kampaund] *adj* compuesto || *s* compuesto; (*gram*) vocablo compuesto || [kəm'paund] *tr* componer, combinar; (*interest*) capitalizar

comprehend [ˌkamprɪ'hend] *tr* comprender

comprehensible [ˌkamprɪ'hensɪbəl] *adj* comprensible

comprehension [ˌkamprɪ'henʃən] *s* comprensión

comprehensive [ˌkamprɪ'hensɪv] *adj* comprensivo, inclusivo, completo

compress ['kampres] *s* (*med*) compresa || [kəm'pres] *tr* comprimir

compression [kəm'preʃən] *s* compresión

comprise o **comprize** [kəm'praɪz] *tr* abarcar, comprender, incluir

compromise ['kamprəˌmaɪz] *s* (*adjustment*) componenda, transigencia, transacción; (*endangering*) comprometimiento || *tr* (*by mutual concessions*) componer, transigir; (*to endanger*) comprometer, exponer || *intr* transigir, avenirse

comptroller [kən'trolər] *s* contralor *m*, interventor *m*

compulsory [kəm'pʌlsəri] *adj* obligatorio

compute [kəm'pjut] *tr & intr* computar, calcular

computer [kəm'pjutər] *s* computador *m*

comrade ['kamræd] o ['kamrɪd] *s* camarada *m*

con. *abbr* **conclusion, consolidated, contra**

con [kan] *s* (*opposite opinion*) contra *m* || *v* (*pret & pp* **conned**; *ger* **conning**) *tr* leer con atención, aprender de memoria

concave ['kankev] o [kan'kev] *adj* cóncavo

conceal [kən'sil] *tr* encubrir, ocultar

concealment [kən'silmənt] *s* encubrimiento, ocultación; (*place*) escondite *m*

concede [kən'sid] *tr* conceder

conceit [kən'sit] *s* (*vanity*) orgullo, engreimiento; (*witty expression*) concepto, dicho ingenioso

conceited [kən'sitɪd] *adj* orgulloso, engreído

conceivable [kən'sivəbəl] *adj* concebible

conceive [kən'siv] *tr & intr* concebir

concentrate ['kansənˌtret] *tr* concentrar || *intr* concentrarse; **to concentrate on** o **upon** reconcentrarse en

concentric [kən'sentrɪk] *adj* concéntrico

concept ['kansept] *s* concepto

conception [kən'sepʃən] *s* concepción

concern [kən'sʌrn] *s* (*business establishment*) empresa, casa comercial, razón *f* social; (*worry*) inquietud, preocupación; (*relation, reference*) concernencia; (*matter*) asunto, negocio || *tr* atañer, concernir; interesar; **as concerns** respecto de; **to whom it may concern** a quien pueda interesar, a quien corresponda

concerning [kən'sʌrnɪŋ] *prep* respecto de, tocante a

concert ['kansərt] *s* concierto || [kən'sʌrt] *tr & intr* concertar

con'cert·mas'ter *s* concertino

concer·to [kən'tʃerto] *s* (*pl* -tos o -ti [ti]) concierto

concession [kən'seʃən] *s* concesión

concessive [kən'sesɪv] *adj* concesivo

concierge [ˌkansɪ'ɑrʒ] *s* conserje *m*

conciliate [kən'sɪlɪˌet] *tr* conciliar; conciliarse (*el respeto, la estima*)

conciliatory [kən'sɪlɪəˌtori] *adj* conciliador

concise [kən'saɪs] *adj* conciso

conclude [kən'klud] *tr & intr* concluir

conclusion [kən'kluʒən] *s* conclusión; (*of a letter*) despedida

conclusive [kən'klusɪv] *adj* concluyente

concoct [kən'kakt] *tr* confeccionar; (*a story*) forjar, inventar

concomitant [kan'kamɪtənt] *adj & s* concomitante *m*

concord ['kaŋkord] *s* concordia; (*gram, mus*) concordancia

concordance [kən'kordəns] *s* concordancia

concourse ['kaŋkors] *s* (*of people*) concurso; (*of streams*) confluencia; bulevar *m*, gran vía; (*of railroad station*) gran salón *m*

concrete [ˈkɑnkrit] o [kɑnˈkrit] *adj* concreto; de hormigón ‖ *s* hormigón *m*

concrete block *s* bloque *m* de hormigón

concrete mixer *s* hormigonera, mezcladora de hormigón

concubine [ˈkɑŋkjəˌbaɪn] *s* concubina

con·cur [kənˈkʌr] *v* (*pret* & *pp* -curred; *ger* -curring) *intr* concurrir

concurrence [kənˈkʌrəns] *s* (*happening together*) concurrencia; (*agreement*) acuerdo

concussion [kənˈkʌʃən] *s* concusión

condemn [kənˈdɛm] *tr* condenar

condemnation [ˌkɑndɛmˈneʃən] *s* condenación

condense [kənˈdɛns] *tr* condensar ‖ *intr* condensarse

condescend [ˌkɑndɪˈsɛnd] *intr* dignarse

condescending [ˌkɑndɪˈsɛndɪŋ] *adj* condescendiente con inferiores

condescension [ˌkɑndɪˈsɛnʃən] *s* dignación, aire *m* protector

condiment [ˈkɑndɪmənt] *s* condimento

condition [kənˈdɪʃən] *s* condición; **on condition that** a condición (de) que ‖ *tr* acondicionar

conditional [kənˈdɪʃənəl] *adj* condicional

condole [kənˈdol] *intr* condolerse

condolence [kənˈdoləns] *s* condolencia

condone [kənˈdon] *tr* condonar

conduce [kənˈdjus] o [kənˈdus] *intr* conducir

conducive [kənˈdjusɪv] o [kənˈdusɪv] *adj* conducente, contribuyente

conduct [ˈkɑndʌkt] *s* conducta ‖ [kənˈdʌkt] *tr* conducir; **to conduct oneself** conducirse, comportarse

conductor [kənˈdʌktər] *s* conductor *m*, guía *mf*; (elec & phys) conductor *m*, conductora *f*; (rr) revisor *m*; (*on trolley or bus*) cobrador *m*

conduit [ˈkɑndɪt] o [ˈkɑnduˌɪt] *s* canal *f* para alambres o cables

cone [kon] *s* cono; (*of pastry*) barquillo; (*of paper*) cucurucho

confectioner·y [kənˈfɛkʃəˌnɛri] *s* (*pl* -ies) (*shop*) confitería; (*sweetmeats*) dulces *mpl*, confites *mpl*, confituras

confedera·cy [kənˈfɛdərəsi] (*pl* -cies) confederación; (*for unlawful purpose*) conjuración

confederate [kənˈfɛdərɪt] *s* confederado; cómplice *mf* ‖ [kənˈfɛdəˌret] *tr* confederar ‖ *intr* confederarse

con·fer [kənˈfʌr] *v* (*pret* & *pp* -ferred; *ger* -ferring) *tr* conferir ‖ *intr* conferenciar, consultar

conference [ˈkɑnfərəns] *s* conferencia, coloquio

confess [kənˈfɛs] *tr* confesar ‖ *intr* confesar, confesarse

confession [kənˈfɛʃən] *s* confesión

confessional [kənˈfɛʃənəl] *s* confesonario

confession of faith *s* profesión de fe

confessor [kənˈfɛsər] *s* (*person who confesses*) confesante *mf*; (*Christian, esp. in spite of persecution; priest*) confesor *m*

confide [kənˈfaɪd] *tr* confiar ‖ *intr* confiar, confiarse; **to confide in** confiarse en

confidence [ˈkɑnfɪdəns] *s* confianza; (*secret*) confidencia; **in strictest confidence** bajo la mayor reserva

confident [ˈkɑnfɪdənt] *adj* seguro ‖ *s* confidente *m*, confidenta

confidential [ˌkɑnfɪˈdɛnʃəl] *adj* confidencial

confine [ˈkɑnfaɪn] *s* confín *m*; **the confines** los confines ‖ [kənˈfaɪn] *tr* (*to keep within limits*) limitar, restringir; (*to keep shut in*) encerrar; **to be confined** estar de parto; **to be confined to bed** tener que guardar cama

confinement [kənˈfaɪnmənt] *s* limitación; encierro; parto, sobreparto

confirm [kənˈfʌrm] *tr* confirmar

confirmed [kənˈfʌrmd] *adj* confirmado; empedernido, inveterado

confiscate [ˈkɑnfɪsˌket] *tr* confiscar

conflagration [ˌkɑnfləˈgreʃən] *s* conflagración

conflict [ˈkɑnflɪkt] *s* conflicto; (*of interests, class hours, etc.*) incompatibilidad ‖ [kənˈflɪkt] *intr* chocar, desavenirse

conflicting [kənˈflɪktɪŋ] *adj* contradictorio; (*events, appointments, class hours, etc.*) incompatible

confluence [ˈkɑnfluˌəns] *s* confluencia

conform [kənˈfɔrm] *intr* conformar, conformarse

conformance [kənˈfɔrməns] *s* conformidad

conformi·ty [kənˈfɔrmɪti] *s* (*pl* -ties) conformidad

confound [kɑnˈfaʊnd] *tr* confundir ‖ [ˈkɑnˈfaʊnd] *tr* maldecir; **confound it!** ¡maldito sea!

confounded [kɑnˈfaʊndɪd] o [ˈkɑnˈfaʊndɪd] *adj* confundido; aborrecible; maldito

confrere [ˈkɑnfrer] *s* colega *m*

confront [kənˈfrʌnt] *tr* (*to face boldly*) confrontarse con, hacer frente a; (*to meet face to face*) encontrar cara a cara; (*to bring face to face; to compare*) confrontar

confuse [kənˈfjuz] *tr* confundir

confusion [kənˈfuʒən] *s* confusión

confute [kənˈfjut] *tr* confutar

Cong. *abbr* **Congregation, Congressional**

congeal [kənˈdʒil] *tr* congelar ‖ *intr* congelarse

congenial [kənˈdʒinjəl] *adj* simpático; agradable; compatible; (*having the same nature*) congenial

congenital [kənˈdʒɛnɪtəl] *adj* congénito

conger eel [ˈkɑŋgər] *s* congrio

congest [kənˈdʒɛst] *tr* congestionar ‖ *intr* congestionarse

congestion [kənˈdʒɛstʃən] *s* congestión

congratulate [kənˈgrætʃəˌlet] *tr* congratular, felicitar

congratulation [kən ‚græt∫ə'le∫ən] *s* congratulación, felicitación

congregate ['kaŋgrɪ ‚get] *intr* congregarse

congregation [‚kaŋgrɪ'ge∫ən] *s* congregación; feligresía, fieles *mf* (*de una iglesia*)

congress ['kaŋgrɪs] *s* congreso

congress·man ['kaŋgrɪsmən] *s* (*pl* -men [mən]) congresista *m*

conical ['kanɪkəl] *adj* cónico

conj. *abbr* **conjugation, conjunction**

conjecture [kən'dʒektʃər] *s* conjetura || *tr & intr* conjeturar

conjugal ['kandʒəgəl] *adj* conyugal

conjugate ['kandʒə ‚get] *tr* conjugar

conjugation [‚kandʒə'ge∫ən] *s* conjugación

conjunction [kən'dʒʌŋk∫ən] *s* conjunción

conjuration [‚kandʒə're∫ən] *s* (*superstitious invocation*) conjuro; (*magic spell*) hechizo

conjure [kən'dʒur] *tr* (*to appeal to solemnly*) conjurar || ['kʌndʒər] o ['kandʒər] *tr* (*to exorcise, drive away*) conjurar; **to conjure away** conjurar; **to conjure up** evocar; crear, suscitar (*dificultades*)

connect [kə'nekt] *tr* conectar; asociar, relacionar || *intr* enlazarse; asociarse, relacionarse; empalmar, enlazar (*dos trenes*)

connecting rod *s* biela

connection [kə'nek∫ən] *s* conexión; (*relative*) pariente *mf;* (*of trains*) combinación, enlace *m,* empalme *m;* (*in subway*) correspondencia; **in connection with** con respecto a; juntamente con

conning tower ['kanɪŋ] *s* torreta de mando

conniption [kə'nɪp∫ən] *s* pataleta, berrinche *m*

connive [kə'naɪv] *intr* confabularse, estar en connivencia

conquer ['kaŋkər] *tr* vencer; (*by force of arms*) conquistar || *intr* triunfar

conqueror ['kaŋkərər] *s* conquistador *m,* vencedor *m*

conquest ['kaŋkwest] *s* conquista

conscience ['kan∫əns] *s* conciencia; **in all conscience** en conciencia

conscientious [‚kan∫ɪ'en∫əs] *adj* concienzudo

conscientious objector [ab'dʒektər] *s* objetante *m* de conciencia

conscious ['kan∫əs] *adj* (*aware of one's own existence*) consciente; (*deliberate*) intencional; (*self-conscious*) encogido, tímido; **to become conscious** volver en sí

consciousness ['kan∫əsnɪs] *s* conciencia, conocimiento

conscript ['kanskrɪpt] *s* conscripto || [kən'skrɪpt] *tr* reclutar

conscription [kən'skrɪp∫ən] *s* conscripción

consecrate ['kansɪ ‚kret] *tr* consagrar

consecutive [kən'sekjətɪv] *adj* (*successive*) consecutivo; (*continuous*) consecuente

consensus [kən'sɛnsəs] *s* consenso; **the consensus of opinion** la opinión general

consent [kən'sɛnt] *s* consentimiento; **by common consent** de común acuerdo || *intr* consentir; **to consent to** consentir en

consequence ['kansɪ ‚kwens] *s* consecuencia; aires *mpl* de importancia

consequential [‚kansɪ'kwen∫əl] *adj* consiguiente; importante; altivo, pomposo

consequently ['kansɪ ‚kwentli] *adv* por consiguiente

conservation [‚kansər've∫ən] *s* conservación

conservatism [kən'sʌrvə ‚tɪzəm] *s* conservadurismo

conservative [kən'sʌrvətɪv] *adj* (*preservative*) conservativo; (*disposed to maintain existing views and institutions*) conservador; cauteloso, moderado || *s* preservativo; conservador *m*

conservato·ry [kən'sʌrvə ‚tori] *s* (*pl* -ries) (*school of music*) conservatorio; (*greenhouse*) invernadero

consider [kən'sɪdər] *tr* considerar

considerable [kən'sɪdərəbəl] *adj* considerable

considerate [kən'sɪdərɪt] *adj* considerado

consideration [kən ‚sɪdə're∫ən] *s* consideración; **for a consideration** por un precio; **in consideration of** en consideración de; en cambio de; **on no consideration** bajo ningún concepto; **out of consideration for** por respeto a; **without due consideration** sin reflexión

considering [kən'sɪdərɪŋ] *adv* (coll) teniendo en cuentas las circunstancias || *prep* en vista de, en razón de || *conj* en vista de que

consign [kən'saɪn] *tr* consignar

consignee [‚kansaɪ'ni] *s* consignatario

consignment [kən'saɪnmənt] *s* consignación

consist [kən'sɪst] *intr* — **to consist in** consistir en; **to consist of** consistir en, constar de

consisten·cy [kən'sɪstənsi] *s* (*pl* -cies) (*firmness, amount of firmness*) consistencia; (*logical connection*) consecuencia

consistent [kən'sɪstənt] *adj* (*holding firmly together*) consistente; (*agreeing with itself or oneself*) consecuente; **consistent with** (*in accord with*) compatible con

consisto·ry [kən'sɪstəri] *s* (*pl* -ries) consistorio

consolation [‚kansə'le∫ən] *s* consolación, consuelo

console ['kansol] *s* consola; mesa de consola || [kən'sol] *tr* consolar

consommé ['kansə ‚me] *s* consumado, consommé *m*

consonant ['kansənənt] *adj & s* consonante *f*

consort ['kansərt] *s* consorte *mf;* embarcación que acompaña a otra ||

[kən'sɔrt] *tr* asociar ‖ *intr* asociarse; armonizar, concordar

consorti•um [kən'sɔrʃɪ•əm] *s* (*pl* -a [ə]) consorcio

conspicuous [kən'spɪkju•əs] *adj* manifiesto, claro, evidente; llamativo, vistoso, sugestivo; conspicuo, notable

conspira•cy [kən'spɪrəsɪ] *s* (*pl* -cies) conspiración, conjuración

conspire [kən'spaɪr] *intr* conspirar, conjurar

constable ['kʌnstəbəl] o ['kʌnstəbəl] *s* policía *m*, guardia *m*, alguacil *m*

constancy ['kʌnstənsɪ] *s* constancia; fidelidad

constant ['kʌnstənt] *adj* constante; incesante; fiel ‖ *s* constante *f*

constellation [,kʌnstə'leʃən] *s* constelación

constipate ['kʌnstɪ,pet] *tr* estreñir

constipation [,kʌnstɪ'peʃən] *s* estreñimiento

constituen•cy [kən'stɪtʃu•ənsɪ] *s* (*pl* -cies) votantes *mpl*; clientela; comitentes *mpl*; distrito electoral

constituent [kən'stɪtʃu•ənt] *adj* constitutivo, componente; (*having power to create or revise a constitution*) constituyente ‖ *s* constitutivo, componente *m*; (*person who appoints another to act for him*) comitente *m*

constitute ['kʌnstɪ,tjut] o ['kʌnstɪ,tut] *tr* constituir

constitution [,kʌnstɪ'tjuʃən] o [,kʌnstɪ'tuʃən] *s* constitución

constrain [kən'stren] *tr* constreñir; detener, encerrar; restringir

construct [kən'strʌkt] *tr* construir

construction [kən'strʌkʃən] *s* construcción; interpretación

construe [kən'stru] *tr* interpretar; deducir, inferir; traducir; (*to combine syntactically*) construir; (*to explain the syntax of*) analizar

consul ['kʌnsəl] *s* cónsul *m*

consular ['kʌnsələr] o ['kʌnsjələr] *adj* consular

consulate ['kʌnsəlɪt] o ['kʌnsjəlɪt] *s* consulado

consulship ['kʌnsəl,ʃɪp] *s* consulado

consult [kən'sʌlt] *tr & intr* consultar

consultant [kən'sʌltənt] *s* consultor *m*

consultation [,kʌnsəl'teʃən] *s* (*consulting*) consulta; (*meeting*) consulta, consultación

consume [kən'sum] o [kən'sjum] *tr* consumir; (*to absorb the interest of*) preocupar; ‖ *intr* consumirse

consumer [kən'sumər] o [kən'sjumər] *s* consumidor *m*; (*of gas, electricity, etc.*) abonado

consumer credit *s* crédito consuntivo

consumer goods *spl* bienes *mpl* de consumo

consummate [kən'sʌmɪt] *adj* consumado ‖ ['kʌnsə,met] *tr* consumar

consumption [kən'sʌmpʃən] *s* consunción, consumo; (*pathol*) consunción, tisis *f*

consumptive [kən'sʌmptɪv] *adj* consuntivo; (*path*) tísico ‖ *s* tísico *m*

cont. *abbr* **contents, continental, continued**

contact ['kʌntækt] *s* contacto; (elec) contacto; (elec) toma de corriente ‖ *tr* (coll) ponerse en contacto con ‖ *intr* contactar

contact breaker *s* (elec) ruptor *m*

contact lens *s* lente *m* de contacto, lente invisible

contagion [kən'tedʒən] *s* contagio

contagious [kən'tedʒəs] *adj* contagioso

contain [kən'ten] *tr* contener; to contain oneself contenerse, refrenarse

container [kən'tenər] *s* continente *m*, recipiente *m*, vaso, caja, envase *m*

containment [kən'tenmənt] *s* contención, refrenamiento

contaminate [kən'tæmɪ,net] *tr* contaminar

contamination [kən,tæmɪ'neʃən] *s* contaminación

contd. *abbr* **continued**

contemplate ['kʌntəm,plet] *tr & intr* contemplar; pensar, proyectar

contemplation [,kʌntəm'pleʃən] *s* contemplación; intención, propósito

contemporaneous [kən,tempə'renɪ•əs] *adj* contemporáneo

contemporar•y [kən'tempə,rerɪ] *adj* contemporáneo, coetáneo ‖ *s* (*pl* -ies) contemporáneo, coetáneo

contempt [kən'tempt] *s* desprecio; (law) contumacia

contemptible [kən'temptɪbəl] *adj* despreciable

contemptuous [kən'temptʃu•əs] *adj* despreciativo, desdeñoso

contend [kən'tend] *tr* sostener, mantener ‖ *intr* contender

contender [kən'tendər] *s* contendiente *mf*, concurrente *mf*

content [kən'tent] *adj & s* contento ‖ ['kʌntent] *s* contenido; contents contenido ‖ [kən'tent] *tr* contentar

contented [kən'tentɪd] *adj* contento, satisfecho

contentedness [kən'tentɪdnɪs] *s* contentamiento, satisfacción

contention [kən'tenʃən] *s* (*strife; dispute*) contención; (*point argued for*) argumento

contentious [kən'tenʃəs] *adj* contencioso

contentment [kən'tentmənt] *s* contentamiento, contento

contest ['kʌntest] *s* (*struggle, fight*) contienda; (*competition*) competencia, concurso ‖ [kən'test] *tr* disputar; tratar de conseguir ‖ *intr* contender

contestant [kən'testənt] *s* contendiente

context ['kʌntekst] *s* contexto

contiguous [kən'tɪgju•əs] *adj* contiguo

continence ['kʌntɪnəns] *s* continencia

continent ['kʌntɪnənt] *adj & s* continente *m*; the Continent la Europa continental

continental [,kʌntɪ'nentəl] *adj* continental ‖ Continental *s* habitante *mf* del continente europeo

contingen·cy [kən'tɪndʒənsi] s (pl -cies) contingencia

contingent [kən'tɪndʒənt] adj & s contingente m

continual [kən'tɪnju·əl] adj continuo

continue [kən'tɪnju] tr & intr continuar; **to be continued** continuará

continui·ty [,kɑntɪ'nju·ɪti] o [,kɑntɪ'nu·ɪti] s (pl -ties) continuidad; (mov, rad, telv) guión m; (rad, telv) comentarios o anuncios entre las partes de un programa

continuous [kən'tɪnju·əs] adj continuo

continuous showing s (mov) sesión continua

continuous waves spl (rad) ondas entretenidas

contortion [kən'tɔrʃən] s contorsión

contour ['kɑntur] s contorno

contr. abbr **contracted, contraction**

contraband ['kɑntrə,bænd] adj contrabandista || s contrabando

contrabass ['kɑntrə,bes] s contrabajo

contraceptive [,kɑntrə'septɪv] adj & s anticonceptivo, contraceptivo

contract ['kɑntrækt] s contrato || ['kɑntrækt] o [kən'trækt] tr contraer (p.ej., matrimonio) || intr (to shrink) contraerse; (to enter into an agreement) comprometerse; **to contract for** contratar

contraction [kən'trækʃən] s contracción

contractor [kən'træktər] s contratista mf

contradict [,kɑntrə'dɪkt] tr contradecir

contradiction [,kɑntrə'dɪkʃən] s contradicción

contradictory [,kɑntrə'dɪktəri] adj (involving contradiction) contradictorio; (inclined to contradict) contradictor

contrail ['kɑn,trel] s (aer) estela de vapor, rastro de condensación

contral·to [kən'trælto] s (pl -tos) (person) contralto mf; (voice) contralto m

contraption [kən'træpʃən] s (coll) artilugio, dispositivo

contra·ry ['kɑntreri] adv contrariamente || adj contrario || [kən'treri] adj obstinado, terco || ['kɑntreri] s (pl -ries) contrario; **on the contrary** al contrario

contrast ['kɑntræst] s contraste m || [kən'træst] tr comparar; poner en contraste || intr contrastar

contravene [,kɑntrə'vin] tr contradecir; contravenir a (una ley)

contribute [kən'trɪbjut] tr contribuir || intr contribuir; (to a newspaper, conference, etc.) colaborar

contribution [,kɑntrɪ'bjuʃən] s contribución; (to a newspaper, conference, etc.) colaboración

contributor [kən'trɪbjutər] s contribuidor m, contribuyente mf; colaborador m

contrite [kən'traɪt] adj contrito

contrition [kən'trɪʃən] s contrición

contrivance [kən'traɪvəns] s aparato, dispositivio; idea, plan m, designio

contrive [kən'traɪv] tr (to devise) idear, inventar; (to scheme up) maquinar, tramar; (to bring about) efectuar || intr maquinar; **to contrive to** + inf ingeniarse a + inf

con·trol [kən'trol] s gobierno, mando; (of a scientific experiment) contrarregistro, control m; controls mandos; **to get under control** conseguir dominar (un incendio) || v (pret & pp -trolled) ger -trolling) tr gobernar, mandar; comprobar, controlar; **to control oneself** dominarse

controlling interest s (el) mayor porcentaje de acciones

control panel s (aer) tablero de instrumentos

control stick s (aer) mango de escoba, palanca de mando

controversial [,kɑntrə'vʌrʃəl] adj controvertible, disputable; disputador

controver·sy ['kɑntrə,vʌrsi] s (pl -sies) controversia, polémica

controvert ['kɑntrə,vʌrt] o [,kɑntrə'vʌrt] tr (to argue against) contradecir; (to argue about) controvertir

contumacious [,kɑntju'meʃəs] o [,kɑntu'meʃəs] adj contumaz

contuma·cy [kɑntjuməsi] o ['kɑntuməsi] s (pl -cies) contumacia

contume·ly ['kɑntjumɪli] o ['kɑntumɪli] s (pl -lies) contumelia

contusion [kən'tjuʒən] o [kən'tuʒən] s contusión

conundrum [kə'nʌndrəm] s acertijo, adivinanza; problema complicado

convalesce [,kɑnvə'les] intr convalecer

convalescence [,kɑnvə'lesəns] s convalecencia

convalescent [,kɑnvə'lesənt] adj & s convaleciente mf

convalescent home s clínica de reposo

convene [kən'vin] tr convocar || intr convenir, reunirse

convenience [kən'vinjəns] s comodidad, conveniencia; **at your earliest convenience** a la primera oportunidad que Vd. tenga

convenient [kən'vinjənt] adj cómodo, conveniente; próximo

convent ['kɑnvent] s convento; convento de religiosas

convention [kən'venʃən] s (agreement) convención, conveniencia; (accepted usage) costumbre f, conveniencia social, convención; (meeting) congreso, convención

conventional [kən'venʃənəl] adj convencional

conventionali·ty [kən,venʃə'næliti] s (pl -ties) precedente m convencional

converge [kən'vʌrd] intr convergir

conversant [kən'vʌrsənt] adj familiarizado, versado

conversation [,kɑnvər'seʃən] s conversación

conversational [,kɑnvər'seʃənəl] adj conversacional

converse ['kɑnvʌrs] adj & s contrario || [kən'vʌrs] intr conversar

conversion [kən'vʌrʒən] s conversión;

(unlawful appropriation) malversación

convert [ˈkɑnvʌrt] *s* convertido, converso ‖ [kənˈvʌrt] *tr* convertir ‖ *intr* convertirse

convertible [kənˈvʌrtɪbəl] *adj* convertible ‖ *s* (aut) convertible *m*, descapotable *m*

convex [ˈkɑnveks] o [kɑnˈveks] *adj* convexo

convey [kənˈve] *tr* llevar, transportar; comunicar, participar *(informes)*; transferir, traspasar *(bienes de una persona a otra)*

conveyance [kənˈve-əns] *s* transporte *m*; comunicación, participación; vehículo; *(transfer of property)* traspaso; escritura de traspaso

convict [ˈkɑnvɪkt] *s* reo convicto, presidiario ‖ [kənˈvɪkt] *tr* probar la culpabilidad de; declarar convicto *(a un acusado)*

conviction [kənˈvɪkʃən] *s* convencimiento; condena, fallo de culpabilidad

convince [kənˈvɪns] *tr* convencer

convincing [kənˈvɪnsɪŋ] *adj* convincente

convivial [kənˈvɪvɪ-əl] *adj* jovial

convocation [ˌkɑnvəˈkeʃən] *s* asamblea

convoke [kənˈvok] *tr* convocar

convoy [ˈkɑnvɔɪ] *s* convoy *m*, conserva ‖ *tr* convoyar

convulse [kənˈvʌls] *tr* convulsionar; agitar; **to convulse with laughter** mover a risas convulsivas

coo [ku] *intr* arrullar

cook [kʊk] *s* cocinero ‖ *tr* cocer, cocinar, guisar; **to cook up** (coll) falsificar; (coll) maquinar, tramar ‖ *intr* cocer, cocinar

cook′book′ *s* libro de cocina

cookie [ˈkʊki] *s* var de **cooky**

cooking [ˈkʊkɪŋ] *s* cocina, arte *m* de cocinar

cook′stove′ *s* cocina económica

cook·y [ˈkʊki] *s (pl -ies)* pasta seca, pastelito dulce

cool [kul] *adj* fresco; frío, indiferente ‖ *s* fresco ‖ *tr* refrescar; moderar ‖ *intr* refrescarse; moderarse; **to cool off** refrescarse; serenarse

cooler [ˈkulər] *s* heladera, refrigerador *m*; refrigerante *m*; (coll) cárcel *f*

cool′-head′ed *adj* sereno, tranquilo, juicioso

coolie [ˈkuli] *s* culí *m*

coolish [ˈkulɪʃ] *adj* fresquito

coolness [ˈkulnɪs] *s* fresco, frescura; (fig) frialdad

coon [kun] *s* mapache *m*, oso lavandero

coop [kup] *s* gallinero; *(for fattening capons)* caponera; jaula, redil *m*; *(jail)* (slang) caponera; **to fly the coop** (slang) escabullirse ‖ *tr* encerrar en un gallinero; enjaular; **to coop up** emparedar

coöp. *abbr* **cooperative**

cooper [ˈkupər] *s* barrilero, tonelero

coöperate [koˈɑpəˌret] *intr* cooperar

coöperation [koˌɑpəˈreʃən] *s* cooperación

coöperative [koˈɑpəˌretɪv] *adj* cooperativo

coördinate [koˈɔrdɪnɪt] *adj* coordenado; (gram) coordinante ‖ *s* (math) coordenada ‖ [koˈɔrdɪˌnet] *tr & intr* coordinar

cootie [ˈkuti] *s* (slang) piojo

cop [kɑp] *s* (slang) polizonte *m* ‖ *v (pret & pp* copped; *ger* copping) *tr* (slang) hurtar

copartner [koˈpɑrtnər] *s* consocio, copartícipe *mf*

cope [kop] *intr* — **to cope with** hacer frente a, enfrentarse con

cope′stone′ *s* piedra de albardilla

copier [ˈkɑpɪ-ər] *s (person who copies)* copiante *mf*, copista *mf*; imitador *m*; *(apparatus)* copiador *m*

copilot [ˈkoˌpaɪlət] *s* copiloto

coping [ˈkopɪŋ] *s* albardilla

copious [ˈkopɪ-əs] *adj* copioso

copper [ˈkɑpər] *adj* cobreño; *(in color)* cobrizo ‖ *s* cobre *m*; *(coin)* calderilla, vellón *m*; (slang) polizonte *m*

cop′per·head′ *s* víbora de cabeza de cobre

cop′per·smith′ *s* cobrero

coppery [ˈkɑpəri] *adj* cobreño; *(in color)* cobrizo

coppice [ˈkɑpɪs] o **copse** [kɑps] *s* soto, monte bajo

copulate [ˈkɑpjəˌlet] *intr* copularse

cop·y [ˈkɑpi] *s (pl -ies)* copia; *(of a book)* ejemplar *m*; *(of a magazine)* número; *(document to be reproduced in print)* original *m*, manuscrito ‖ *v (pret & pp -led) tr* copiar

cop′y·book′ *s* cuaderno de escritura

copyist [ˈkɑpɪ-ɪst] *s* copiante *mf*, copista *mf*; imitador *m*

cop′y·right′ *s* (derechos de) propiedad literaria ‖ *tr* registrar en el registro de la propiedad literaria

copy writer *s* escritor publicitario

co·quet [koˈket] *v (pret & pp -quetted; ger -quetting) intr* coquetear; burlarse

coquet·ry [ˈkokətri] o [koˈketri] *s (pl -ries)* coquetería; burla

coquette [koˈket] *s* coqueta

coquettish [koˈketɪʃ] *adj* coqueta

cor. *abbr* **corner, coroner, correction, corresponding**

coral [ˈkɑrəl] o [ˈkɔrəl] *adj* coralino ‖ *s* coral *m*

coral reef *s* arrecife *m* de coral

cord [kɔrd] *s* cordón *m* ‖ *tr* acordonar

cordial [ˈkɔrdʒəl] *adj* cordial ‖ *s* licor tónico; *(stimulating medicine)* cordial *m*

cordiali·ty [kɔrˈdʒælɪti] *s (pl -ties)* cordialidad

corduroy [ˈkɔrdəˌrɔɪ] *s* pana; **corduroys** pantalones *mpl* de pana

core [kor] *s* corazón *m*; *(of an electromagnet)* núcleo

corespondent [ˌkorɪsˈpɑndənt] *s* cómplice *mf* del demandado en juicio de divorcio

Corinth ['karɪnθ] o ['kɔrɪnθ] *s* Corinto *f*

cork [kɔrk] *s* corcho; corcho, tapón *m* de corcho; tapón (*de cualquier materia*) || *tr* encorchar, tapar con corcho

corking ['kɔrkɪŋ] *adj* (slang) brutal, extraordinario

cork oak *s* alcornoque *m*

cork'screw' *s* sacacorchos *m*, tirabuzón *m*

cormorant ['kɔrmərənt] *s* cormorán *m*, cuervo marino

corn [kɔrn] *s* (*in U.S.A.*) maíz *m*; (*in England*) trigo; (*in Scotland*) avena; grano (*de maíz, trigo*); (*on the foot*) callo; (coll) aguardiente *m*; (slang) trivialidad

corn bread *s* pan *m* de maíz

corn'cake' *s* tortilla de maíz

corn'cob' *s* mazorca de maíz, carozo

corncob pipe *s* pipa de fumar hecha de una mazorca de maíz

corn'crib' *s* granero para maíz

corn cure *s* callicida *m*

cornea ['kɔrnɪə] *s* córnea

corner ['kɔrnər] *s* ángulo; (*esp. where two streets meet*) esquina; (*inside angle formed by two or more surfaces; secluded place; region, quarter*) rincón *m*; (*of eye*) comisura, rabillo; (*of lips*) comisura; (*awkward position*) apuro, aprieto; monopolio; **around the corner** a la vuelta de la esquina; **to turn the corner** doblar la esquina; pasar el punto más peligroso || *tr* arrinconar; monopolizar

corner cupboard *s* rinconera

corner room *s* habitación de esquina

cor'ner·stone' *s* piedra angular; (*of a new building*) primera piedra

cornet [kɔr'nɛt] *s* corneta

corn exchange *s* bolsa de granos

corn'field' *s* (*in U.S.A.*) maizal *m*; (*in England*) trigal *m*; (*in Scotland*) avenal *m*

corn flour *s* harina de maíz

corn'flow'er *s* cabezuela

corn'husk' *s* perfolla

cornice ['kɔrnɪs] *s* cornisa

Cornish ['kɔrnɪʃ] *adj & s* córnico

corn liquor *s* chicha

corn meal *s* harina de maíz

corn on the cob *s* maíz *m* en la mazorca

corn plaster *s* emplasto para los callos

corn silk *s* cabellos, barbas del maíz

corn'stalk' *s* tallo de maíz

corn'starch' *s* almidón *m* de maíz

cornucopia [,kɔrnə'kopɪ·ə] *s* cornucopia

Cornwall ['kɔrn,wɔl] o ['kɔrnwəl] *s* Cornualles

corn·y ['kɔrni] *adj* (*comp* -**ier**; *super* -**iest**) de maíz; (coll) gastado, trivial, pesado

corollar·y ['kɑrə,lɛri] o ['kɔrə,lɛri] *s* (*pl* -**ies**) corolario

coronation [,kɑrə'neʃən] o [,kɔrə'neʃən] *s* coronación

coroner ['kɑrənər] o ['kɔrənər] *s* juez *m* de guardia

coroner's inquest *s* pesquisa dirigida por el juez de guardia

coronet ['kɑrə,nɛt] o ['kɔrə,nɛt] *s* (*worn by members of nobility*) corona; (*ornamental band of jewels worn on head*) diadema *f*

Corp. *abbr* **Corporation**

corporal ['kɔrpərəl] *adj* corporal || *s* (mil) cabo

corporation [,kɔrpə'reʃən] *s* (*provincial, municipal, or service entity*) corporación; sociedad anónima por acciones

corps [kɔr] *s* (*pl* **corps** [kɔrz]) cuerpo; (mil) cuerpo

corps de ballet [kɔr də bæ'le] *s* cuerpo de baile

corpse [kɔrps] *s* cadáver *m*

corpulent ['kɔrpjələnt] *adj* corpulento

corpuscle ['kɔrpəsəl] *s* corpúsculo, partícula; (physiol) glóbulo

corr. *abbr* **correspondence, corresponding**

cor·ral [kə'ræl] *s* corral *m* || *v* (*pret & pp* -**ralled**; *ger* -**ralling**) *tr* acorralar

correct [kə'rɛkt] *adj* correcto; (*proper*) cumplido || *tr* corregir

correction [kə'rɛkʃən] *s* corrección

corrective [kə'rɛktɪv] *adj & s* correctivo

correctness [kə'rɛktnɪs] *s* corrección; cumplimiento, cumplido

correlate ['kɑrə,let] o ['kɔrə,let] *tr* correlacionar || *intr* correlacionarse

correlation [,kɑrə'leʃən] o [,kɔrə'leʃən] *s* correlación

correlative [kə'rɛlətɪv] *adj & s* correlativo

correspond [,kɑrɪ'spand] o [,kɔrɪ'spand] *intr* corresponder; (*to communicate by writing*) corresponderse

correspondence [,kɑrɪ'spandəns] o [,kɔrɪ'spandəns] *s* correspondencia

correspondence school *s* escuela por correspondencia

correspondent [,kɑrɪ'spandənt] o [,kɔrɪ'spandənt] *adj* correspondiente || *s* correspondiente *mf*; (*for a newspaper*) corresponsal *mf*

corresponding [,kɑrɪ'spandɪŋ] o [,kɔrɪ'spandɪŋ] *adj* correspondiente

corridor ['kɑrɪdər] o ['kɔrɪdər] *s* corredor *m*, pasillo

corroborate [kə'rabə,ret] *tr* corroborar

corrode [kə'rod] *tr* corroer || *intr* corroerse

corrosion [kə'roʒən] *s* corrosión

corrosive [kə'rosɪv] *adj & s* corrosivo

corrugated ['kɑrə,getɪd] o ['kɔrə,getɪd] *adj* acanalado, ondulado

corrupt [kə'rʌpt] *adj* corrompido || *tr* corromper || *intr* corromperse

corruption [kə'rʌpʃən] *s* corrupción

corsage [kɔr'saʒ] *s* (*bodice*) corpiño, jubón *m*; (*bouquet*) ramillete *m* que se lleva en el pecho o la cintura

corsair ['kɔr,sɛr] *s* corsario

corset ['kɔrsɪt] *s* corsé *m*

corset cover *s* cubrecorsé *m*

Corsica ['korsikə] s Córcega

Corsican ['korsıkən] adj & s corso

cortege [kor'teʒ] s procesión; (retinue) cortejo, séquito

cor·tex ['kor‚teks] s (pl -tices [tı‚siz]) corteza; corteza cerebral

cortisone ['kortı‚son] s cortisona

corvette [kor'vet] s corbeta

cosmetic [kaz'metık] adj & s cosmético

cosmic ['kazmık] adj cósmico

cosmonaut ['kazmə‚nɔt] s cosmonauta mf

cosmopolitan [‚kazmə'palıtən] adj & s cosmopolita mf

cosmos ['kazməs] s cosmos m; (bot) cosmos

Cossack ['ka‚sæk] adj & s cosaco

cost [kɔst] o [kast] s coste m, costo; **at cost** a coste y costas; **at all costs** a toda costa; **costs** (law) costas || v (pret & pp cost) intr costar; cost; **cost what it may** cueste lo que cueste

cost accounting s escandallo

Costa Rican ['kastə 'rikən] o ['kɔste 'rikən] adj & s costarricense mf, costarriqueño

cost, insurance, and freight costo, seguro y flete

cost·ly ['kɔstli] o ['kastli] adj (comp -lier; super -liest) costoso, (dispendioso; (lavish) pródigo; (magnificent) suntuoso

cost of living s costo de la vida, carestía de la vida

costume ['kastjum] o ['kastum] s traje m; (garb worn on stage, at balls, etc.) disfraz m, traje de época

costume ball s baile m de trajes

costume jewelry s joyas de fantasía, bisutería

cot [kat] s catre m

coterie ['kotəri] s círculo, grupo; (clique) corrillo

cottage ['katıdʒ] s cabaña; casita de campo

cottage cheese s naterón m, requesón m

cotter pin ['katər] s chaveta

cotton ['katən] s algodón m || intr — **to cotton up to** (coll) aficionarse a

cotton field s algodonal m

cotton gin s desmotadera de algodón

cotton picker ['pıkər] s recogedor m de algodón; máquina para recolectar el algodón

cot'ton·seed' s semilla de algodón

cottonseed oil s aceite m de algodón

cotton waste s hilacha de algodón, estopa de algodón

cot'ton·wood' s chopo del Canadá, chopo de Virginia

cottony ['katəni] adj algodonoso

couch [kautʃ] s canapé m, sofá m || tr expresar

cougar ['kugər] s puma m

cough [kɔf] o [kaf] s tos f || tr — **to cough up** arrojar por la boca; (slang) sudar, entregar || intr toser; (artificially, to attract attention) destoserse

cough drop s pastilla para la tos

cough syrup s jarabe m para la tos

could [kud] v aux pude, podía; podría

council ['kaunsəl] s (deliberative or legislative assembly) consejo; (of a municipality) concejo; (eccl) concilio

council·man ['kaunsəlmən] s (pl -men [mən]) concejal m

councilor ['kaunsələr] s consejero

coun·sel ['kaunsəl] s consejo; (advisor) consejero; (consultant) consultor m; (lawyer) abogado consultor; **to keep one's own counsel** no revelar sus intenciones || v (pret & pp -seled o -selled; ger -seling o -selling) tr aconsejar || intr aconsejarse

counselor ['kaunsələr] s consejero; abogado

count [kaunt] s (act of counting) cuenta, recuento; (result of counting) suma, total m; (nobleman) conde m; (charge) (law) cargo; **to take the count** (box) dejarse contar diez || tr contar; **to count off** separar contando; **to count out** no incluir; (sport) declarar vencido || intr contar; (to be worth consideration) valer; **to count for** valer; **to count on** contar con

countable ['kauntəbəl] adj contable

count'-down' s cuenta a cero

countenance ['kauntınəns] s cara, rostro, semblante m; (composure) compostura, serenidad; **to keep one's countenance** contenerse; **to lose countenance** conturbarse; **to put out of countenance** avergonzar, confundir || tr aprobar, apoyar, favorecer

counter ['kauntər] adj contrario || adv en el sentido opuesto; **counter to** a contrapelo de || s contador m; (piece of wood or metal for keeping score); (board in shop over which business is transacted) mostrador m; (box) contragolpe m || tr oponerse a; contradecir || intr (box) dar un contragolpe; **to counter with** replicar con

coun'ter·act' tr contrarrestar, contrariar

coun'ter·attack' s contraataque m || coun'ter·attack' tr & intr contraatacar

coun'ter·bal'ance s contrabalanza, contrapeso || coun'ter·bal'ance tr contrabalancear, contrapesar

coun'ter·clock'wise' adj & adv en el sentido contrario al de las agujas del reloj

coun'ter·es'pionage s contraespionaje m

counterfeit ['kauntərfıt] adj contrahecho, falsificado || s contrahechura, falsificación; **counterfeit money** moneda falsa || tr contrahacer, falsificar

counterfeiter ['kauntər‚fıtər] s contrahacedor m, falsificador m; monedero falso

counterfeit money s moneda falsa

countermand ['kaundər‚mænd] o ['kauntər‚mand] s contramandato || tr contramandar; hacer volver

coun'ter·march' s contramarcha ‖ intr contramarchar

coun'ter·offen'sive s contraofensiva

coun'ter·pane' s cubrecama

coun'ter·part' s contraparte f; copia, duplicado

coun'ter·plot' s contratreta ‖ v (pret & pp -plotted; ger -plotting) tr complotar contra (la treta de otro u otros)

coun'ter·point' s contrapunto

Counter Reformation s Contrarreforma

coun'ter·rev'olu'sion s contrarrevolución

coun'ter·sign' s contraseña ‖ tr refrendar

coun'ter·sink' v (pret & pp -sunk) tr avellanar

coun'ter·spy' s (pl -spies) contraespía mf

coun'ter·stroke' s contragolpe m

coun'ter·weight' s contrapeso

countess ['kɑuntɪs] s condesa

countless ['kɑuntlɪs] adj incontable, innumerable

countrified ['kʌntrɪ‚faɪd] adj campesino, rústico

coun·try ['kʌntri] s (pl -tries) (territory of a nation) país m; (land of one's birth) patria; (not the city) campo

country club s club m campestre

country cousin s isidro

country estate s heredad, hacienda de campo

coun'try·folk' s gente f del campo, campesinos

country gentleman s propietario acomodado de finca rural

country house s casa de campo, quinta

country jake [dʒek] s (coll) patán m

country life s vida rural

coun·try·man ['kʌntrimən] s (pl -men [mən]) compatriota m; campesino

country people s gente f del campo, gente de capa parda

coun'try·side' s campiña

coun'try·wide' adj nacional

country·woman ['kʌntrɪ‚wumən] s (pl -women [‚wimin]) compatriota f: campesina

coun·ty ['kɑunti] s (pl -ties) (small political unit) partido; (domain of a count) condado

county seat s cabeza de partido

coup [ku] s golpe m

coup de grâce [ku də 'grɑs] s puñalada de misericordia, golpe m de gracia

coup d'état [ku de'tɑ] s golpe m de estado

coupé [ku'pe] s cupé m

couple ['kʌpəl] s par m; (man and wife) matrimonio; (two people dancing together) pareja; (elec, mech) par m; (two more or less) (coll) par m ‖ tr acoplar, juntar, unir ‖ intr juntarse, unirse

coupler ['kʌplər] s (rr) enganche m

couplet ['kʌplɪt] s copla, pareado

coupon [ku'pɑn] o [kju'pɑn] s (of a bond) cupón m; (piece detached from larger piece) talón m

courage ['kʌrɪdʒ] s valor m, ánimo; firmeza, resolución; to have the courage of one's convictions ajustarse abiertamente con su conciencia; to pluck up courage hacer de tripas corazón

courageous [kə'redʒəs] adj valiente, animoso

courier ['kʌrɪ·ər] o ['kurɪ·ər] s estafeta, mensajero; guía m

course [kors] s (onward movement) curso; (of a ship) derrota, rumbo; (of time) transcurso; (of events) marcha; (in school) asignatura, curso; (of a meal) plato; campo de golf; (mas) hilada; in the course of en el decurso de; of course por supuesto, naturalmente

court [kort] s (of justice) tribunal m; (of a king) corte f; (open space enclosed by a building) atrio, patio; (for tennis) cancha, pista; to pay court to hacer la corte a ‖ tr cortejar; buscar, solicitar

courteous ['kʌrtɪ·əs] adj cortés

courtesan ['kʌrtɪzən] o ['kortɪzən] s cortesana

courte·sy ['kʌrtɪsi] s (pl -sies) cortesía

court'house' s palacio de justicia

courtier ['kortɪ·ər] s cortesano, palaciego

court jester s bufón m

court·ly ['kortli] adj (comp -lier; super -liest) cortés, cortesano; (pertaining to the court) cortesano

court'-mar'tial s (pl courts-martial) consejo de guerra ‖ v (pret & pp -tialed o -tialled; ger -tialing o -tialling) tr someter a consejo de guerra

court plaster s tafetán m inglés

court'room' s sala de justicia, tribunal m

courtship ['kortʃɪp] s cortejo, galanteo; noviazgo

court'yard' s atrio, patio

cousin ['kʌzɪn] s primo

cove [kov] s cala, ensenada

covenant ['kʌvənənt] s convenio, pacto; contrato; (Bib) alianza ‖ tr & intr pactar

cover ['kʌvər] s cubierta; (of a magazine) portada; (place for one person at table) cubierto; (for a bed) cobertor m; to take cover ocultarse; under cover bajo cubierto, bajo techado; oculto; disfrazado; under cover of (e.g., the night) a cubierto de; so capa de; under separate cover bajo cubierta separada, por separado ‖ tr cubrir; (to line, to coat) recubrir, revestir; recorrer (cierta distancia); cubrirse (la cabeza); tapar (una olla) ‖ intr cubrirse

coverage ['kʌvərɪdʒ] s (amount or space covered) alcance m; (of news) reportaje m; (funds to meet liabilities) cobertura

coveralls ['kʌvər‚ɔlz] s mono

cover charge s precio del cubierto

covered ['kʌvərd] adj cubierto; (wire) forrado; (bridge) cubierto

covered wagon s carromato

cover girl s (coll) muchacha hermosa en la portada de una revista

covering ['kʌvəriŋ] s cubierta, envoltura

covert ['kʌvərt] adj disimulado, secreto

cov'er-up' s efugio, subterfugio

covet ['kʌvit] tr codiciar

covetous ['kʌvitəs] adj codicioso

covetousness ['kʌvitəsnis] s codicia

covey ['kʌvi] s (brood) nidada; (in flight) bandada; corro, grupo

cow [kau] s vaca || tr acobardar, intimidar

coward ['kau·ərd] s cobarde mf

cowardice ['kau·ərdis] s cobardía

cowardly ['kau·ərdli] adj cobarde || adv cobardemente

cow'bell' s cencerro

cow'boy' s vaquero; gaucho (Arg)

cowcatcher ['kau,kætʃər] s quitapiedras m, rastrillo; trompa (Col, Chile)

cower ['kau·ər] intr agacharse

cow'herd' s vaquero, pastor m de ganado vacuno

cow'hide' s cuero; (whip) zurriago || tr zurriagar

cowl [kaul] s capucha, cogulla; (aer) cubierta del motor; (aut) cubretablero, bóveda

cow'lick' s mechón m, remolino (pelos que se levantan sobre la frente)

cowpox ['kau ,pɑks] s vacuna

coxcomb ['kɑks,kom] s petimetre m, mequetrefe m

coxswain ['kɑksən] o ['kɑk,swen] s timonel m; contramaestre m

coy [kɔɪ] adj recatado, modesto; coquetón

co-zy ['kozi] adj (comp -zier; super -ziest) cómodo || s (pl -zies) cubretetera

cp. abbr compare

c.p. abbr candle power

C.P.A. abbr certified public accountant

cpd. abbr compound

cr. abbr credit, creditor

crab [kræb] s cangrejo; (grouch) cascarrabias mf

crab apple s manzana silvestre

crabbed ['kræbid] adj avinagrado, ceñudo

crab grass s garranchuelo

crab louse s ladilla

crack [kræk] adj (coll) de primera clase; (shot) (coll) certero || s grieta, hendidura; (noise) crujido, estallido; (coll) instante m, momento; (joke) (slang) chiste m; at the crack of dawn al romper el alba || tr agrietar, hender; chasquear (un látigo); abrir (una caja fuerte) por la fuerza; cascar (nueces); descifrar (un código); (slang) decir (un chiste); (slang) descubrir (un secreto); to crack a smile (slang) sonreír; to crack up

(coll) alabar, elogiar || intr agrietarse; crujir; cascarse (la voz de una persona); enloquecerse; ceder, someterse; to crack up fracasar; perder la salud; estrellarse (un avión)

cracked [krækt] adj agrietado; (ice) picado; (coll) mentecato, loco

cracker ['krækər] s galleta

crack'le-ware' s grietado

crack'pot' adj & s (slang) excéntrico, tarambana mf

crack'-up' s fracaso; colisión; derrota; (aer) aterrizaje violento; (coll) colapso

cradle ['kredəl] s cuna; (of handset) horquilla || tr acunar

cra'dle-song' s canción de cuna, arrullo

craft [kræft] o [krɑft] s arte m, arte manual; astucia, maña; nave f || spl naves

craftiness ['kræftinis] o ['krɑftinis] s astucia

crafts·man ['kræftsmən] o ['krɑftsmən] s (pl -men [mən]) artesano; artista m

craftsmanship ['kræftsmən,ʃip] o ['krɑftsmən,ʃip] s artesanía

craft·y ['kræfti] o ['krɑfti] adj (comp -ier; super -iest) astuto, mañoso

crag [kræg] s peñasco, despeñadero

cram [kræm] v (pret & pp crammed; ger cramming) tr atascar, atracar, embutir; (coll) aprender apresuradamente || intr atracarse; (to study hard) (coll) empollar

cramp [kræmp] s (metal bar) grapa, laña; (clamp) abrazadera; (painful contraction of muscle) calambre m; cramps retortijón m de tripas || tr engrapar, lañar; apretar; dar calambre a

cranber·ry ['kræn ,beri] s (pl -ries) arándano agrio

crane [kren] s (bird) grulla; (derrick) grúa || tr estirar (el cuello) || intr estirar el cuello

crani·um ['kreni·əm] s (pl -a [ə]) cráneo

crank [kræŋk] s manivela, manubrio; (coll) estrafalario || tr hacer girar (el motor) con la manivela

crank'case' s caja de cigüeñal, cárter m del cigüeñal

crank'shaft' s cigüeñal m

crank·y ['kræŋki] adj (comp -ier; super -iest) malhumorado; (queer) estrafalario

cran·ny ['kræni] s (pl -nies) hendidura, grieta, rendija

crape [krep] s crespón m; crespón fúnebre, crespón negro

crape'hang'er s (slang) aguafiestas mf

craps [kræps] s juego de dados; to shoot craps jugar a los dados

crash [kræʃ] s caída, desplome m; colisión, choque m; estallido, estrépito; fracaso; crac financiero; lienzo grueso; (aer) aterrizaje violento || tr romper con estrépito, estrellar; to crash a party (slang) asistir a una fiesta sin invitación; to crash the gate

(slang) colarse de gorra || *intr* caer, desplomarse; romperse con estrépito, estallar; (*in business*) quebrar; aterrizar violentamente, estrellarse (*un avión*); **to crash into** chocar con
crash dive *s* sumersión instantánea (*de submarino*)
crash landing *s* aterrizaje violento
crash program *s* programa intensivo
crass [kræs] *adj* espeso, tosco; (*ignorance, mistake*) craso
crate [kret] *s* (*box made of slats*) jaula; (*basket*) banasta, cuévano || *tr* embalar en jaula, embalar con listones
crater ['kretər] *s* cráter *m*
cravat [krə'væt] *s* corbata
crave [krev] *tr* anhelar, ansiar; pedir (*indulgencia*) || *intr* — **to crave for** anhelar, ansiar; pedir con insistencia
craven ['krevən] *adj & s* cobarde *mf*
craving ['krevɪŋ] *s* anhelo, ansia, deseo ardiente
craw [krɔ] *s* buche *m*
crawl [krɔl] *s* arrastre *m*; gateado || *intr* reptar, arrastrarse, gatear; (*to have a feeling of insects on skin*) hormiguear; **to crawl along** andar paso a paso; **to crawl up** trepar
crayon ['kre‧ən] *s* creyón *m*
craze [krez] *s* boga, moda; locura, manía || *tr* enloquecer
cra‧zy ['krezi] *adj* (*comp* **-zier**; *super* **-ziest**) loco; (*rickety*) desvencijado; achacoso, débil; **crazy as a bedbug** (slang) loco de atar; **to be crazy about** (coll) estar loco por; **to drive crazy** volver loco
crazy bone *s* hueso de la alegría
creak [krik] *s* crujido, rechinamiento || *intr* crujir, rechinar
creak‧y ['kriki] *adj* (*comp* **-ier**; *super* **-iest**) crujidero, rechinador
cream [krim] *s* crema; (*e.g., of society*) crema, nata y flor || *tr* desnatar (*la leche*)
creamer‧y ['krimɛri] *s* (*pl* **-ies**) mantequería, quesería, lechería
cream puff *s* bollo de crema
cream separator *s* desnatadora
cream‧y ['krimi] *adj* (*comp* **-ier**; *super* **-iest**) cremoso
crease [kris] *s* arruga, pliegue *m*; (*in trousers*) raya || *tr* arrugar, plegar
create [kri'et] *tr* crear
creation [kri'eʃən] *s* creación
creative [kri'etɪv] *adj* creativo
creator [kri'etər] *s* creador *m*
creature ['kritʃər] *s* criatura; (*being, strange being*) ente *m*; animal *m*
credence ['kridəns] *s* creencia; **to give credence to** dar fe a
credentials [krɪ'denʃəlz] *spl* credenciales *fpl*
credible ['kredɪbəl] *adj* creíble
credit ['kredɪt] *s* crédito; **to take credit for** atribuirse el mérito de || *tr* acreditar; **to credit a person with** atribuirle a una persona el mérito de
creditable ['kredɪtəbəl] *adj* honorable, estimable
credit card *s* tarjeta de crédito

creditor ['kredɪtər] *s* acreedor *m*
cre‧do ['krido] o ['kredo] *s* (*pl* **-dos**) credo
credulous ['kredʒələs] *adj* crédulo
creed [krid] *s* credo
creek [krik] *s* arroyo, riachuelo
creep [krip] *v* (*pret & pp* **crept** [krept]) *intr* arrastrarse; (*on all fours*) gatear; (*to climb*) trepar; (*with a sensation of insects*) hormiguear; **to creep up on** acercarse insensiblemente a
creeper ['kripər] *s* planta rastrera, planta trepadora
creeping ['kripɪŋ] *adj* lento, progresivo; (*plant*) rastrero || *s* arrastramiento
cremate ['krimet] *tr* incinerar
cremation [krɪ'meʃən] *s* cremación, incineración
cremato‧ry ['krimə‚tori] *adj* crematorio || *s* (*pl* **-ries**) crematorio
crème de menthe [krɛm də 'mãt] *s* crema de menta
Creole ['kri‧ol] *adj & s* criollo
crescent ['kresənt] *s* (*moon in first or last quarter*) creciente *f* de la luna; (*shape of moon in either of these phases*) media luna; panecillo (*en forma de media luna*)
cress [kres] *s* mastuerzo
crest [krest] *s* cresta
crestfallen ['krest‚fɔlən] *adj* cabizbajo
Cretan ['kritən] *adj & s* cretense *mf*
Crete [krit] *s* Creta
cretonne [krɪ'tɑn] *s* cretona
crevice ['krevɪs] *s* grieta
crew [kru] *s* equipo; (*of a ship*) dotación, tripulación; (*group, esp. of armed men*) banda, cuadrilla
crew cut *s* corte *m* de pelo a cepillo
crib [krɪb] *s* pesebre *m*; camita de niño; (*coll*) plagio; (*student's pony*) (coll) chuleta || *v* (*pret & pp* **cribbed**; *ger* **cribbing**) *tr & intr* (coll) hurtar
cricket ['krɪkɪt] *s* (ent) grillo; (sport) cricquet *m*; (coll) juego limpio
crier ['kraɪ‧ər] *s* pregonero
crime [kraɪm] *s* crimen *m*, delito
criminal ['krɪmɪnəl] *adj & s* criminal *mf*
criminal code *s* código penal
criminal law *s* derecho penal
criminal negligence *s* imprudencia temeraria
crimp [krɪmp] *s* rizado, rizo; **to put a crimp in** (coll) estorbar, impedir || *tr* rizar
crimple ['krɪmpəl] *tr* arrugar, rizar || *intr* arrugarse, rizarse
crimson ['krɪmzən] *adj & s* carmesí *m* || *intr* enrojecerse
cringe [krɪndʒ] *intr* arrastrarse, reptar, encogerse
crinkle ['krɪŋkəl] *s* arruga, pliegue *m*; (*in the water*) rizo u onda || *tr* arrugar, plegar || *intr* arrugarse
cripple ['krɪpəl] *s* zopo, lisiado || *tr* lisiar, estropear; dañar, perjudicar
cri‧sis ['kraɪsɪs] *s* (*pl* **-ses** [siz]) crisis *f*

crisp [krɪsp] *adj* frágil, quebradizo; (*air, weather*) refrescante; decisivo
criteri·on [kraɪˈtɪrɪ·ən] *s* (*pl* -a [ə]) u -ons) criterio
critic [ˈkrɪtɪk] *s* crítico; (*faultfinder*) criticón *m*
critical [ˈkrɪtɪkəl] *adj* crítico; (*faultfinding*) crítico
criticism [ˈkrɪtɪ͵sɪzəm] *s* crítica
criticize [ˈkrɪtɪ͵saɪz] *tr & intr* criticar
critique [krɪˈtik] *s* (*art of criticism*) crítica; ensayo crítico
croak [krok] *s* (*of raven*) graznido; canto de ranas ‖ *intr* graznar (*el cuervo*); croar (*la rana*); (*morir*) (slang) reventar
Croat [krot] *s* (*native or inhabitant*) croata *mf*; (*language*) croata *m*
Croatian [kroˈeʃən] *adj & mf* croata *mf*
cro·chet [kroˈʃe] *s* croché *m* ‖ *v* (*pret & pp* -cheted [ˈʃed]); *ger* -cheting [ˈʃe·ɪŋ]) *tr* trabajar con aguja de gancho ‖ *intr* hacer croché
crocheting [kroˈʃe·ɪŋ] *s* labor *f* de ganchillo
crochet needle *s* aguja de gancho
crock [krak] *s* cacharro, vasija de barro cocido
crockery [ˈkrakərɪ] *s* loza
crocodile [ˈkrakə͵daɪl] *s* cocodrilo
crocodile tears *spl* lágrimas de cocodrilo
crocus [ˈkrokəs] *s* azafrán *m*, croco
crone [kron] *s* vieja acartonada, vieja arrugada
cro·ny [ˈkronɪ] *s* (*pl* -nies) compinche *mf*
crook [kruk] *s* gancho, garfio; curva; (*of shepherd*) cayado; (coll) fullero, ladrón *m* ‖ *tr* encorvar; (slang) empinar (*el codo*) ‖ *intr* encorvarse
crooked [ˈkrukɪd] *adj* encorvado, torcido; (*person or his conduct*) torcido; **to go crooked** (coll) torcerse
croon [krun] *intr* cantar con voz suave, cantar con melancolía exagerada
crooner [ˈkrunər] *s* cantor de voz suave, cantor melancólico
crop [krap] *s* cosecha; (*head of hair*) cabellera; cabello corto; (*of a bird*) buche *m*; (*whip*) látigo; (*of appointments, promotions, heroes, etc.*) hornada ‖ *v* (*pret & pp* **cropped**; *ger* **cropping**) *tr* desmochar (*un árbol*); desorejar (*a un animal*); esquilar, trasquilar ‖ *intr* — **to crop out** u up aflorar; asomar, dejarse ver, manifestarse inesperadamente
crop dusting *s* aerofumigación, fumigación aérea
croquet [kroˈke] *s* crocquet *m*
croquette [kroˈket] *s* croqueta
crosier [ˈkroʒər] *s* báculo pastoral, cayado
cross [krɔs] o [krɑs] *adj* transversal, travieso; (*breed*) cruzado; malhumorado, enfadado ‖ *s* cruz *f*; (*of races; of two roads*) cruce *m*; **to take the cross** (*to join a crusade*) cruzarse ‖ *tr* cruzar; (*to oppose*)

contrariar, frustrar; **to cross off** u **out** borrar; **to cross oneself** hacerse la señal de la cruz; **to cross one's mind** ocurrírsele a uno; **to cross one's t's** poner travesaño a las tes, poner el palo a las tes ‖ *intr* cruzar; cruzarse; **to cross over** atravesar de un lado a otro
cross'bones' *spl* huesos cruzados (*símbolo de la muerte*)
cross'bow' *s* ballesta
cross'breed' *v* (*pret & pp* -bred [͵bred]) *tr* cruzar (*animales o plantas*)
cross'coun'try *a* campo traviesa; a través del país
cross'cur'rent *s* contracorriente *f*; (fig) tendencia encontrada
cross'-exam'i·na'tion *s* interrogatorio riguroso; (law) interrogatorio
cross'-ex·am'ine *tr* interrogar rigurosamente; (law) repreguntar
cross-eyed [ˈkrɔs͵aɪd] o [ˈkrɑs͵aɪd] *adj* bisojo, bizco, ojituerto
crossing [ˈkrɔsɪŋ] o [ˈkrɑsɪŋ] *s* (*of lines, streets, etc.*) cruce *m*; (*of the ocean*) travesía; (*of a river*) vado; (rr) crucero, paso a nivel
crossing gate *s* barrera, barrera de paso a nivel
crossing point *s* punto de cruce
cross'patch' *s* (coll) gruñón *m*
cross'piece' *s* travesaño
cross reference *s* contrarreferencia, remisión
cross'road' *s* vía transversal; **crossroads** encrucijada, cruce *m*; **at the crossroads** en el momento crítico
cross section *s* corte *m* transversal; (fig) sección representativa
cross street *s* calle traviesa, calle de travesía
cross'word' puzzle *s* crucigrama *m*
crotch [krɑtʃ] *s* (*forked piece*) horcajadura, bifurcación; (*between legs*) entrepierna, bragadura, horcajadura
crotchety [ˈkrɑtʃtɪ] *adj* caprichoso, estrambótico, de mal genio
crouch [krautʃ] *s* posición agachada ‖ *intr* agacharse, acuclillarse
croup [krup] *s* garrotillo, crup *m*; (*of horse*) anca, grupa
croupier [ˈkrupɪ·ər] *s* crupié *m*
crouton [ˈkrutɑn] *s* corteza de pan
crow [kro] *s* corneja, grajo, chova; (*cry of the cock*) quiquiriquí *m*; (*crowbar*) alzaprima; **as the crow flies** a vuelo de pájaro; **to eat crow** (coll) cantar la palinodia; **to have a crow to pick with** (coll) tener que habérselas con ‖ *intr* cantar (*el gallo*); jactarse; **to crow over** jactarse de
crow'bar' *s* alzaprima, pie *m* de cabra
crowd [kraud] *s* gentío, multitud; (*flock of people*) caterva, tropel *m*; (*mob, common people*) populacho, vulgo; (*clique, set*) corrillo, grupo ‖ *tr* apiñar, apretar, atestar; (*to push*) empujar ‖ *intr* apiñarse, apretarse, atestarse; (*to mill around*) arremolinarse

crowded ['kraudɪd] *adj* atestado, concurrido

crown [kraun] *s* corona; (*of hat*) copa ‖ *tr* coronar; (*checkers*) coronar; (*slang*) golpear en la cabeza

crowned head *s* testa coronada

crown prince *s* príncipe heredero

crown princess *s* princesa heredera

crow's'-foot' *s* (*pl* -feet') pata de gallo

crow's'-nest' *s* (naut) cofa de vigía, torre *f* de vigía

crucial ['kruʃəl] *adj* crucial; difícil, penoso

crucible ['krusɪbəl] *s* crisol *m*

crucifix ['krusɪfɪks] *s* crucifijo

crucifixion [,krusɪ'fɪkʃən] *s* crucifixión

cruci‧fy ['krusɪ,faɪ] *v* (*pret* & *pp* -fied) *tr* crucificar

crude [krud] *adj* (*raw, unrefined*) crudo; (*lacking culture*) grosero, tosco; (*unfinished*) basto, sin labrar

crudi‧ty ['krudɪti] *s* (*pl* -ties) crudeza; grosería, tosquedad; bastedad

cruel ['kru‧əl] *adj* cruel

cruel‧ty ['kru‧əlti] *s* (*pl* -ties) crueldad

cruet ['kru‧ɪt] *s* ampolleta

cruet stand *s* angarillas, vinagreras

cruise [kruz] *s* viaje *m* por mar; (aer, naut) crucero ‖ *tr* (naut) cruzar ‖ *intr* cruzar; (coll) andar de un lado a otro

cruiser ['kruzər] *s* (nav) crucero

cruising ['kruzɪŋ] *adj* de crucero ‖ *s* (aer, naut) crucero

cruising radius *s* autonomía

cruller ['krʌlər] *s* buñuelo

crumb [krʌm] *s* migaja; (*soft part of bread*) miga; (*given to a beggar*) mendrugo ‖ *tr* desmigar (*el pan*); (culin) empanar, cubrir con pan rallado; limpiar (*la mesa*) de migajas ‖ *intr* desmigarse, desmenuzarse

crumble ['krʌmbəl] *tr* desmenuzar ‖ *intr* desmenuzarse; (*to fall to pieces gradually*) desmoronarse

crum‧my ['krʌmi] *adj* (*comp* -mier; *super* -miest) (slang) desaseado, sucio; (slang) de mal gusto, de mala muerte

crumple ['krʌmpəl] *tr* arrugar, ajar, chafar ‖ *intr* arrugarse, ajarse

crunch [krʌntʃ] *tr* ronchar, ronzar ‖ *intr* crujir

crusade [kru'sed] *s* cruzada ‖ *intr* hacer una cruzada

crusader [kru'sedər] *s* cruzado

crush [krʌʃ] *s* aplastamiento; (*of people*) aglomeración, bullaje *m;* **to have a crush on** (slang) estar perdido por ‖ *tr* aplastar, machacar, magullar; (*to grind*) moler; bocartear (*el mineral*); (*to oppress, grieve*) abrumar

crush hat *s* clac *m*

crust [krʌst] *s* corteza; corteza de pan; (*scab*) costra

crustacean [krʌs'teʃən] *s* crustáceo

crustaceous [krʌs'teʃəs] *adj* crustáceo

crust‧y ['krʌsti] *adj* (*comp* -ier; *super* -iest) (*scabby*) costroso; áspero, grosero, rudo

crutch [krʌtʃ] *s* muleta

crux [krʌks] *s* punto capital; enigma *m*

cry [kraɪ] *s* (*pl* cries) grito; (*weeping*) lloro; (*of peddler*) pregón *m;* (*of wolf*) aullido; (*of bull*) bramido; **in full cry** en plena persecución; **to have a good cry** desahogarse en lágrimas abundantes ‖ *v* (*pret* & *pp* cried) *tr* decir a gritos; (*to announce publicly*) pregonar; **to cry one's eyes o heart out** llorar amargamente; **to cry out** decir a gritos; pregonar ‖ *intr* gritar; (*to weep*) llorar; aullar (*el lobo*); bramar (*el toro*); **to cry for** clamar por; **to cry for joy** llorar de alegría; **to cry out** clamar; **to cry out against** clamar contra; **to cry out for** clamar, clamar por

cry'ba'by *s* (*pl* -bies) llorón *m*, llorona, lloraduelos *mf*

crypt [krɪpt] *s* cripta

cryptic(al) ['krɪptɪk(əl)] *adj* enigmático, misterioso

crystal ['krɪstəl] *s* cristal *m*

crystal ball *s* bola de cristal

crystalline ['krɪstəlɪn] o ['krɪstə,laɪn] *adj* cristalino

crystallize ['krɪstə,laɪz] *tr* cristalizar ‖ *intr* cristalizarse

C.S. *abbr* **Christian Science, Civil Service**

ct. *abbr* **cent**

cu. *abbr* **cubic**

cub [kʌb] *s* cachorro

Cuban ['kjubən] *adj* & *s* cubano

cubbyhole ['kʌbɪ,hol] *s* chiribitil *m*

cube [kjub] *adj* (*root*) cúbico ‖ *s* cubo; (*of ice*) cubito ‖ *tr* cubicar

cubic ['kjubɪk] *adj* cúbico

cub reporter *s* (coll) reportero novato

cuckold ['kʌkəld] *adj* & *s* cornudo ‖ *tr* encornudar

cuckoo ['kuku] *adj* (slang) mentecato, loco ‖ *s* cuclillo, cuco; (*call of cuckoo*) cucú *m*

cuckoo clock *s* reloj *m* de cuclillo

cucumber ['kjukəmbər] *s* pepino

cud [kʌd] *s* bolo alimenticio; **to chew the cud** rumiar

cuddle ['kʌdəl] *s* abrazo cariñoso ‖ *tr* abrazar con cariño ‖ *intr* estar abrazados, arrimarse cariñosamente

cudg‧el ['kʌdʒəl] *s* garrote *m*, porra; **to take up the cudgels for** salir a la defensa de ‖ *v* (*pret* & *pp* -eled o -elled; *ger* -eling o -elling) *tr* apalear, aporrear

cue [kju] *s* señal *f*, indicación; (*hint*) indirecta; (*rôle*) papel *m;* (*rod used in billiards*) taco; (*of hair*) coleta; (*of people in line*) cola; (theat) apunte *m*

cuff [kʌf] *s* (*of shirt*) puño; (*of trousers*) doblez *f*, vuelta; (*blow*) bofetada ‖ *tr* abofetear

cuff links *spl* gemelos

cuirass [kwɪ'ræs] *s* coraza

cuisine [kwɪ'zin] *s* cocina (*arte culinario*)

culinary ['kjulɪ,neri] *adj* culinario

cull [kʌl] *tr* (*to choose, pick*) entresacar, escoger; (*to gather, pluck*) coger, recoger

culm [kʌlm] *s* (*coal dust*) cisco; (*stalk of grasses*) caña, tallo

culminate ['kʌlmɪ,net] *intr* culminar; **to culminate in** conducir a, terminar en

culpable ['kʌlpəbəl] *adj* culpable

culprit ['kʌlprɪt] *s* acusado; reo

cult [kʌlt] *s* culto; secta

cultivate ['kʌltɪ,vet] *tr* cultivar

cultivated ['kʌltɪ,vetɪd] *adj* culto, cultivado

cultivation [,kʌltɪ'veʃən] *s* (*of the land, the arts, one's memory, etc.*) cultivo; (*refinement*) cultura

culture ['kʌltʃər] *s* cultura

cultured ['kʌltʃərd] *adj* culto

culvert ['kʌlvərt] *s* alcantarilla

cumbersome ['kʌmbərsəm] *adj* incómodo, molesto; (*clumsy*) pesado, inmanejable

cunning ['kʌnɪŋ] *adj* (*sly*) astuto; (*clever*) hábil; (*attractive*) gracioso, mono || *s* astucia; habilidad, destreza

cup [kʌp] *s* taza; (*of thermometer*) cubeta; (*mach*) vaso de engrase; (*sport*) copa; (*of sorrow*) (fig) copa; **in one's cups** borracho || *v* (*pret & pp* **cupped**; *ger* **cupping**) *tr* ahuecar dando forma de taza o copa a; poner ventosa a

cupboard ['kʌbərd] *s* alacena, aparador *m*, armario

cupidity [kju'pɪdɪti] *s* codicia

cupola ['kjupələ] *s* cúpula

cur [kʌr] *s* perro mestizo, perro de mala raza; (*despicable fellow*) canalla *m*

curate ['kjurɪt] *s* cura *m*

curative ['kjurətɪv] *adj* curativo || *s* curativa

curator [kju'retər] *s* conservador *m*

curb [kʌrb] *s* (*of sidewalk*) encintado; (*of well*) brocal *m*; (*of bit*) barbada; (*market*) bolsín *m*; (*check, restraint*) freno; (vet) corva || *tr* contener, refrenar

curb'stone' *s* piedra de encintado; brocal *m* de pozo

curd [kʌrd] *s* cuajada || *tr* cuajar || *intr* cuajarse

curdle ['kʌrdəl] *tr* cuajar; **to curdle the blood** horrorizar || *intr* cuajar

cure [kjur] *s* cura, curación || *tr* curar || *intr* curar; curarse

cure'-all' *s* sanalotodo

curfew ['kʌrfju] *s* queda, cubrefuego; toque *m* de queda

curi·o ['kjurɪ,o] *s* (*pl* **-os**) curiosidad

curiosi·ty [,kjurɪ'ɑsɪti] *s* (*pl* **-ties**) curiosidad

curious ['kjurɪ·əs] *adj* curioso

curl [kʌrl] *s* bucle *m*, rizo; (*spiral-shaped curl*) tirabuzón *m*; (*of smoke*) espiral *f*; (*curling*) rizado || *tr* encrespar, ensortijar, rizar; (*to coil, to roll up*) arrollar; fruncir (*los labios*) || *intr* encresparse, ensortijarse, rizarse; arrollarse; **to curl up** arrollarse; (*in bed*) encogerse; (*to break up, collapse*) (coll) desplomarse

curlicue ['kʌrlɪ,kju] *s* ringorrango

curling iron *s* rizador *m*, maquinilla de rizar

curl'pa'per *s* torcida, papelito para rizar el pelo

curl·y ['kʌrli] *adj* (*comp* **-ier;** *super* **-iest**) crespo, rizo

curmudgeon [kər'mʌdʒən] *s* cicatero, tacaño, erizo

currant ['kʌrənt] *s* pasa de Corinto; (*Ribes alpinum*) calderilla

curren·cy ['kʌrənsi] *s* (*pl* **-cies**) moneda corriente, dinero en circulación; uso corriente

current ['kʌrənt] *adj* corriente || *s* corriente *f*; (elec) corriente *f*

current account *s* cuenta corriente

current events *spl* actualidades, sucesos de actualidad

curricu·lum [kə'rɪkjələm] *s* (*pl* **-lums** o **-la** [lə]) plan *m* de estudios

cur·ry ['kʌri] *s* (*pl* **-ries**) cari *m* || *v* (*pret & pp* **-ried**) *tr* curtir (*las pieles*); almohazar (*el caballo*); **to curry favor** procurar complacer

cur'ry·comb' *s* almohaza || *tr* almohazar

curse [kʌrs] *s* maldición; (*profane oath*) reniego, voto; (*evil, misfortune*) calamidad || *tr* maldecir || *intr* jurar, echar votos

cursed ['kʌrsɪd] o [kʌrst] *adj* maldito, aborrecible

cursive ['kʌrsɪv] *adj* cursivo || *s* cursiva

cursory ['kʌrsəri] *adj* apresurado, rápido, superficial, de paso

curt [kʌrt] *adj* áspero, brusco; corto, conciso

curtail [kər'tel] *tr* acortar, abreviar, cercenar

curtain ['kʌrtən] *s* cortina; (theat) telón *m*; **to draw the curtain** correr la cortina; **to drop the curtain** (theat) bajar el telón || *tr* encortinar; separar con cortina; cubrir, ocultar

curtain call *s* llamada a la escena para recibir aplausos

curtain raiser ['rezər] *s* (theat) pieza preliminar

curtain ring *s* anilla

curtain rod *s* riel *m*

curt·sy ['kʌrtsi] *s* (*pl* **-sies**) cortesía, reverencia || *v* (*pret & pp* **-sied**) *intr* hacer una cortesía

curve [kʌrv] *s* curva || *tr* encorvar || *intr* encorvarse; volver, virar

curved [kʌrvd] *adj* curvo, encorvado; (*crooked*) combo

cushion ['kuʃən] *s* cojín *m*, almohada; (*of billiard table*) baranda || *tr* amortiguar

cusp [kʌsp] *s* cúspide *f*

cuspidor ['kʌspɪ,dɔr] *s* escupidera

custard ['kʌstərd] *s* flan *m*, natillas

custodian [kəs'todɪ·ən] *s* custodio; (*of a house or building*) casero

custo·dy ['kʌstədi] *s* (*pl* **-dies**) custodia; **in custody** en prisión; **to take into custody** prender

custom ['kʌstəm] *s* costumbre; (*cus-*

tomers) parroquia, clientela; **customs** aduana; derechos de aduana

customary [ˈkʌstəˌmɛri] *adj* acostumbrado, de costumbre

cus'tom-built' *adj* hecho por encargo, fuera de serie

customer [ˈkʌstəmər] *s* parroquiano, cliente *mf*; (*of a café or restaurant*) consumidor *m*; (coll) individuo, sujeto, tipo

cus'tom-house' *adj* aduanero ‖ *s* aduana

cus'tom-made' *adj* hecho a la medida

customs clearance *s* despacho de aduana

customs officer *s* aduanero

custom tailor *s* sastre *m* a la medida

custom work *s* trabajo hecho a la medida

cut [kʌt] *s* corte *m*; (*piece cut off*) tajada; (*wound*) cuchillada; (*for a canal, highway, etc.*) desmonte *m*; (*shortest way*) atajo; (*in prices, wages, etc.*) reducción; (*of a garment*) corte *m*, hechura; (*in winnings, earnings, etc.*) parte *f*; (typ) estampa, grabado; (tennis) golpe *m* cortante; (*absence from school*) (coll) falta de asistencia; (snub) (coll) desaire *m*; (coll) palabra hiriente ‖ *v* (*pret & pp* cut; *ger* cutting) *tr* cortar; practicar (*un agujero*); reducir (*gastos*); capar, castrar; desleír, diluir; (coll) ausentarse de, faltar a (*la clase*); (coll) desairar; (coll) herir; **to cut down** cortar; derribar cortando; castigar (*gastos*); **cut off** cortar; desheredar; amputar (*una pierna*); (elec) cortar (*la corriente, la ignición*); cerrar (*el carburador*); **to cut open** abrir cortando; **to cut out** cortar; sacar cortando; labrar; suprimir, omitir; **to take the place of**) desbancar; soplar (*la dama a un rival*); (slang) dejarse de (*disparates*); **to cut short** terminar de repente; interrumpir, chafar; **to cut teeth** endentecer; **to cut up** desmenuzar, despedazar; criticar severamente; (coll) afligir ‖ *intr* cortar; cortarse; salir (*los dientes*); (coll) fumarse la clase; **to cut in** entrar de repente; interrumpir; (*in a dance*) cortar o separar la pareja; **to cut under** vender a menor precio que; **to cut up** (slang) travesear, hacer travesuras; (slang) jaranear

cut-and-dried [ˈkʌtənˈdraɪd] *adj* dispuesto de antemano; monótono, poco interesante

cutaway coat [ˈkʌtəˌwe] *s* chaqué *m*

cut'back' *s* reducción; discontinuación, incumplimiento; (mov) retorno a una época anterior

cute [kjut] *adj* (coll) mono, monono; (coll) astuto, listo

cut glass *s* cristal tallado

cuticle [ˈkjutɪkəl] *s* cutícula

cutlass [ˈkʌtləs] *s* alfanje *m*

cutler [ˈkʌtlər] *s* cuchillero

cutlery [ˈkʌtləri] *s* cuchillería; (*knives, forks, and spoons*) cubierto

cutlet [ˈkʌtlɪt] *s* chuleta; croqueta

cut'out' *s* (*design to be cut out*) recortado; (aut) escape *m* libre, válvula de escape libre

cut'-rate' *adj* de precio reducido

cutter [ˈkʌtər] *s* cortador *m*; (*machine*) cortadora; (naut) escampavía

cut'throat' *adj* asesino; implacable ‖ *s* asesino

cutting [ˈkʌtɪŋ] *adj* cortante; hiriente, mordaz ‖ *s* corte *m*; (*from a newspaper*) recorte *m*; (hort) esqueje *m*

cutting edge *s* canto de corte

cuttlefish [ˈkʌtəlˌfɪʃ] *s* jibia

cut'wa'ter *s* espolón *m*, tajamar *m*

cwt. *abbr* **hundredweight**

cyanamide [saɪˈænəˌmaɪd] *s* cianamida; cianamida de calcio

cyanide [ˈsaɪˌə̯naɪd] *s* cianuro

cycle [ˈsaɪkəl] *s* ciclo; bicicleta; (*of an internal-combustion engine*) tiempo; (phys) período ‖ *intr* montar en bicicleta

cyclic(al) [ˈsaɪklɪk(əl)] o [ˈsɪklɪk(əl)] *adj* cíclico

cyclone [ˈsaɪklon] *s* ciclón *m*

cyl. *abbr* **cylinder, cylindrical**

cylinder [ˈsɪlɪndər] *s* cilindro

cylinder block *s* bloque *m* de cilindros

cylinder bore *s* alesaje *m*

cylinder head *s* (*of steam engine*) tapa del cilindro; (*of gas engine*) culata del cilindro

cylindric(al) [sɪˈlɪndrɪk(əl)] *adj* cilíndrico

cymbal [ˈsɪmbəl] *s* címbalo, platillo

cynic [ˈsɪnɪk] *adj & s* cínico

cynical [ˈsɪnɪkəl] *adj* cínico

cynicism [ˈsɪnɪˌsɪzəm] *s* cinismo

cynosure [ˈsaɪnəˌʃʊr] o [ˈsɪnəˌʃʊr] *s* blanco de las miradas; guía, norte *m*

cypress [ˈsaɪprəs] *s* ciprés *m*

Cyprus [ˈsaɪprəs] *s* Chipre *f*

Cyrillic [sɪˈrɪlɪk] *adj* cirílico

Cyrus [ˈsaɪrəs] *s* Ciro

cyst [sɪst] *s* quiste *m*

czar [zar] *s* zar *m*; (fig) autócrata *m*

czarina [zɑˈrinə] *s* zarina

Czech [tʃɛk] *adj & s* checo

Czecho-Slovak [ˈtʃɛkoˈslovæk] *adj & s* checoeslovaco o checoslovaco

Czecho-Slovakia [ˌtʃɛkoslovˈvækɪə] *s* Checoeslovaquia o Checoslovaquia

D

D, d [di] cuarta letra del alfabeto inglés

d. *abbr* **date, day, dead, degree, delete, diameter, died, dollar, denarius** (penny)

D. *abbr* **December, Democrat, Duchess, Duke, Dutch**

D.A. *abbr* **District Attorney**

dab [dæb] *s* toque ligero; masa pastosa || *v* (*pret & pp* **dabbed**; *ger* **dabbing**) *tr* tocar ligeramente, frotar suavemente

dabble ['dæbəl] *tr* salpicar || *intr* chapotear; **to dabble in** meterse en; jugar a (*la Bolsa*); especular en (*granos*)

dad [dæd] *s* (coll) papá *m*

dad·dy ['dædi] *s* (*pl* -**dies**) (coll) papá *m*

daffodil ['dæfədɪl] *s* narciso trompón

daff·y ['dæfi] *adj* (*comp* -**ier**; *super* -**iest**) (coll) chiflado

dagger ['dægər] *s* daga, puñal *m*; (typ) cruz *f*, obelisco; **to look daggers at** apuñalar con la mirada

dahlia ['dæljə] *s* dalia

dai·ly ['deli] *adj* cotidiano, diario || *adv* diariamente || *s* (*pl* -**lies**) diario

dain·ty ['denti] *adj* (*comp* -**tier**; *super* -**tiest**) delicado || *s* (*pl* -**ties**) golosina

dair·y ['deri] *s* (*pl* -**ies**) lechería, vaquería

dais ['de·ɪs] *s* estrado

dai·sy ['dezi] *s* (*pl* -**sies**) margarita

dal·ly ['dæli] *v* (*pret & pp* -**lied**) *intr* juguetear, retozar; tardar, malgastar el tiempo

dam [dæm] *s* represa, embalse *m*; (*female quadruped*) madre *f*; (dent) dique *m* || *v* (*pret & pp* **dammed**; *ger* **damming**) *tr* represar, embalsar; cerrar, tapar, obstruir

damage ['dæmɪdʒ] *s* daño, perjuicio; (*to one's reputation*) desdoro; (com) avería; **damages** daños y perjuicios || *tr* dañar, perjudicar; averiar

damascene ['dæmə,sin] o [,dæmə'sin] *adj* damasquino || *s* ataujía, damasquinado || *tr* ataujiar, damasquinar

dame [dem] *s* dama, señora; (coll) mujer *f*

damn [dæm] *s* terno; **I don't give a damn** (slang) maldito lo que me importa; **that's not worth a damn** (slang) eso no vale un pito || *tr* condenar (a pena eterna); condenar; maldecir || *intr* maldecir, echar ternos

damnation [dæm'neʃən] *s* damnación; (theol) condenación

damned [dæmd] *adj* condenado (a pena eterna); abominable, detestable || **the damned** los malditos, los condenados (a pena eterna)

damp [dæmp] *adj* húmedo, mojado || *s* humedad; (*firedamp*) grisú *m* || *tr* humedecer, mojar; (*to deaden, muffle*) amortecer, amortiguar; (*to dis-*

courage) abatir, desalentar; (elec) amortiguar (*ondas electromagnéticas*)

dampen ['dæmpən] *tr* humedecer, mojar; amortecer, amortiguar; abatir, desalentar

damper ['dæmpər] *s* (*of chimney*) registro; (*of piano*) apagador *m*, sordina

damsel ['dæmzəl] *s* señorita, muchacha

dance [dæns] o [dɑns] *s* baile *m*, danza || *tr & intr* bailar, danzar

dance band *s* orquesta de jazz

dance floor *s* pista de baile

dance hall *s* salón *m* de baile

dancer ['dænsər] o ['dɑnsər] *s* bailador *m*, danzador *m*; (*professional*) bailarín *m*

dancing partner *s* pareja (de baile)

dandelion ['dændɪ,laɪ·ən] *s* diente *m* de león

dandruff ['dændrəf] *s* caspa

dan·dy ['dændi] *adj* (*comp* -**dier**; *super* -**diest**) (coll) excelente, magnífico || *s* (*pl* -**dies**) currutaco, petimetre *m*

Dane [den] *s* danés *m*, dinamarqués *m*

danger ['dendʒər] *s* peligro

dangerous ['dendʒərəs] *adj* peligroso

dangle ['dæŋgəl] *tr & intr* colgar flojamente, colgar en el aire

Danish ['denɪʃ] *adj & s* danés *m*, dinamarqués *m*

dank [dæŋk] *adj* húmedo, liento

Danube ['dænjub] *s* Danubio

dapper ['dæpər] *adj* aseado, apuesto

dapple ['dæpəl] *adj* habado, rodado || *tr* motear

dare [der] *s* desafío, reto || *tr* retar; **to dare to** (*to challenge to*) desafiar a || *intr* osar, atreverse; **I dare say** talvez; **to dare to** (*to have the courage to*) atreverse a

dare'dev'il *s* calavera *m*, temerario

daring ['derɪŋ] *adj* atrevido, osado || *s* atrevimiento, osadía

dark [dɑrk] *adj* obscuro; (*in complexion*) moreno; secreto, oculto; (*gloomy*) lóbrego; (*beer*) pardo || *s* obscuridad, tinieblas; noche *f*; **in the dark** a obscuras

Dark Ages *spl* edad media; principios de la edad media

dark-complexioned ['dɑrkkəm'plekʃənd] *adj* moreno

darken ['dɑrkən] *tr* obscurecer; entristecer; cegar || *intr* obscurecerse

dark horse *s* caballo desconocido; candidato nombrado inesperadamente

darkly ['dɑrkli] *adv* obscuramente; secretamente, misteriosamente

dark meat *s* carne *f* del ave que no es la pechuga

darkness ['dɑrknɪs] *s* obscuridad

dark'room' *s* (phot) cuarto obscuro

darling ['dɑrlɪŋ] *adj & s* querido, amado; predilecto

darn [dɑrn] *tr & intr* zurcir; (coll) maldecir

darnel ['dɑrnəl] s cizaña
darning ['dɑrnɪŋ] s zurcido
darning needle s aguja de zurcir
dart [dɑrt] s dardo; (small missile used in a game) rehilete m || intr lanzarse, precipitarse; volar como dardo
dash [dæʃ] s arranque m; (splash) rociada; carrera corta; (spirit) brío; pequeña cantidad; (in printing, writing, telegraphy) raya || tr lanzar; estrellar, romper; frustrar (las esperanzas de uno); rociar, salpicar; **to dash off** escribir de prisa; **to dash to pieces** hacer añicos || intr estrellarse (las olas del mar); lanzarse, precipitarse; **to dash by** pasar corriendo; **to dash in** entrar como un rayo
dash′board′ s tablero de instrumentos; (on front or side of vehicle) guardabarros m
dashing ['dæʃɪŋ] adj brioso; ostentoso, vistoso || s (of waves) embate m
dastard ['dæstərd] adj & s vil mf, miserable mf, cobarde mf
data processing ['detə] s tramitación automática de datos
date [det] s (time) fecha, data; (palm) datilera; (fruit) dátil m; (appointment) (coll) cita; **out of date** anticuado, fuera de moda; **to date** hasta la fecha; **under date of** con fecha de || tr fechar, datar; (coll) tener cita con || intr — **to date from** datar de
date line s línea de cambio de fecha
date palm s palmera (datilera)
dative ['detɪv] adj & s dativo
datum ['detəm] o ['dætəm] s (pl **data** ['detə] o ['dætə]) dato
dau. abbr **daughter**
daub [dɔb] s embadurnamiento || tr embadurnar
daughter ['dɔtər] s hija
daughter-in-law ['dɔtərɪn‚lɔ] s (pl **daughters-in-law**) nuera, hija política
daunt [dɔnt] tr asustar, espantar; desanimar, acobardar
dauntless ['dɔntlɪs] adj atrevido, intrépido, impávido
dauphin ['dɔfɪn] s delfín m
davenport ['dævən‚pɔrt] s sofá m cama
davit ['dævɪt] s (naut) pescante m, grúa de bote
daw [dɔ] s corneja
dawdle ['dɔdəl] intr malgastar el tiempo, haronear
dawn [dɔn] s amanecer m, alba || intr amanecer; despuntar (el día, la mañana); empezar a mostrarse; **to dawn on** empezar a hacerse patente a
day [de] adj diurno || s día m; (of travel, work, worry, etc.) jornada; (from noon to noon) (naut) singladura; **any day now** de un día para otro; **by day** de día; **the day after** el día siguiente; **the day after tomorrow** pasado mañana; **the day before** la víspera; la víspera de; **the day before yesterday** anteayer; **to call it a day** (coll) dejar de trabajar; **to win the day** ganar la jornada

day bed s sofá m cama
day′break′ s amanecer m
day coach s (rr) coche m de viajeros
day′dream′ s ensueño || intr soñar despierto
day laborer s jornalero
day′light′ s luz f del día; amanecer m; **in broad daylight** en pleno día; **to see daylight** comprender; ver el fin de una tarea difícil
day′light′-sav′ing time s hora de verano
day nursery s guardería infantil
day off s asueto
day of reckoning s día m de ajustar cuentas
day shift s turno diurno
day′time′ adj diurno || día m
daze [dez] s aturdimiento; **in a daze** aturdido || tr aturdir
dazzle ['dæzəl] s deslumbramiento || tr deslumbrar
dazzling ['dæzlɪŋ] adj deslumbrante
deacon ['dikən] s diácono
deaconess ['dikənɪs] s diaconisa
dead [dɛd] adj muerto; (coll) cansado || adv (coll) completamente, muy || s — **in the dead of night** en plena noche; **the dead** los muertos; **the dead of winter** lo más frío del invierno
dead beat s (slang) gorrón m; (slang) holgazán m
dead bolt s cerrojo dormido
dead calm s calma chicha, calmazo
dead center s punto muerto
dead′drunk′ adj difunto de taberna
deaden ['dɛdən] tr amortiguar, amortecer
dead end s callejón m sin salida
dead′latch′ s aldaba dormida
dead′-let′ter office s departamento de cartas no reclamadas
dead′line′ s línea vedada; fin m del plazo
dead′lock′ s cerradura dormida; desacuerdo insuperable || tr entrabar
dead-ly ['dɛdli] adj (comp **-lier**; super **-liest**) mortal; (sin) capital; abrumador
dead pan s (slang) semblante m sin expresión
dead reckoning s (naut) estima
dead ringer ['rɪŋər] s segunda edición
dead′wood′ s leña seca; cosa inútil, gente f inútil
deaf [dɛf] adj sordo; **to turn a deaf ear** hacerse el sordo, hacer oídos de mercader
deaf and dumb adj sordomudo
deafen ['dɛfən] tr asordar, ensordecer
deafening ['dɛfənɪŋ] adj ensordecedor
deaf′-mute′ s sordomudo
deafness ['dɛfnɪs] s sordera
deal [dil] s negocio, trato; (of cards) mano f; turno de dar; (share) parte f, porción; (coll) convenio secreto; **a good deal (of)** o **a great deal (of)** mucho; **to make a great deal of** hacer fiestas a || v (pret & pp **dealt** [dɛlt]) tr asestar (un golpe); repartir (la baraja) || intr negociar, comerciar; intervenir; (in card games) ser

mano; **to deal with** entender en; tratar de; tratar con

dealer ['dilər] s comerciante mf, concesionario; (of cards) repartidor m

dean [din] s decano; (eccl) deán m

deanship ['din/ɪp] s decanato

dear [dɪr] adj (beloved) caro; (expensive) caro; (charging high prices) carero; **dear me!** ¡Dios mío! || s querido

dearie ['dɪri] s (coll) queridito

dearth [dʌrθ] s carestía

death [deθ] s muerte f; **to bleed to death** morir desangrado; **to bore to death** matar de aburrimiento; **to burn to death** morir quemado; **to choke to death** morir atragantado; **to die a violent death** morir vestido; **to freeze to death** morir helado; **to put to death** dar la muerte a; **to shoot to death** matar a tiros; **to stab to death** escabechar; **to starve to death** matar de hambre; morir de hambre

death'bed' s lecho de muerte

death'blow' s golpe m mortal

death certificate s fe f de óbito, partida de defunción

death house s capilla (de los reos de muerte)

deathless ['deθlɪs] adj inmortal, eterno

deathly ['deθli] adj mortal, de muerte || adv mortalmente; excesivamente

death penalty s pena de muerte

death rate s mortalidad

death rattle s estertor agónico

death ray s rayo mortífero

death warrant s sentencia de muerte; fin m de toda esperanza

death'watch' s vela de un difunto; guardia de un reo de muerte

debacle [de'bakəl] s desastre m, ruina, derrota; (in a river) deshielo

de·bar [dɪ'bar] v (pret & pp **-barred;** ger **-barring**) tr excluir; prohibir

debark [dɪ'bark] tr & intr desembarcar

debarkation [ˌdibar'keʃən] s (of passengers) desembarco; (of freight) desembarque m

debase [dɪ'bes] tr degradar; falsificar

debatable [dɪ'betəbəl] adj disputable

debate [dɪ'bet] s debate m || tr debatir || intr debatir; deliberar

debauchee [ˌdebɔ'ʃi] o [ˌdebɔ't/i] s libertino, disoluto

debaucher·y [dɪ'bɔt/əri] s (pl **-ies**) libertinaje m, crápula

debenture [dɪ'bent/ər] s (bond) obligación; (voucher) vale m

debilitate [dɪ'bɪlɪˌtet] tr debilitar

debili·ty [dɪ'bɪlɪti] s (pl **-ties**) debilidad

debit ['debɪt] s debe m; (entry on debit side) cargo || tr adeudar, cargar

debit balance s saldo deudor

debonair [ˌdebə'ner] adj alegre; cortés

debris [de'bri] s despojos, ruinas

debt [det] s deuda; **to run into debt** endeudarse, entramparse

debtor ['detər] s deudor m

debut [de'bju] o ['debju] s estreno,

debut m; **to make one's debut** estrenarse, debutar; ponerse de largo, entrar en sociedad (una joven)

debutante [ˌdebju'tant] o ['debjəˌtænt] s joven f que se pone de largo

dec. abbr **deceased**

decade ['deked] s decenio

decadence [dɪ'kedəns] s decadencia

decadent [dɪ'kedənt] adj & s decadente mf

decanter [dɪ'kæntər] s garrafa

decapitate [dɪ'kæpɪˌtet] tr decapitar

decay [dɪ'ke] s (decline) decaimiento, descaecimiento; (rotting) podredumbre; (of teeth) caries f || tr pudrir || intr pudrirse; decaer; cariarse (los dientes)

decease [dɪ'sis] s fallecimiento || intr fallecer

deceased [dɪ'sist] adj & s difunto

deceit [dɪ'sit] s engaño, fraude m

deceitful [dɪ'sitfəl] adj engañoso, fraudulento

deceive [dɪ'siv] tr & intr engañar

decelerate [dɪ'seləˌret] tr desacelerar || intr desacelerarse

December [dɪ'sembər] s diciembre m

decen·cy ['disənsi] s (pl **-cies**) decencia, honestidad; (propriety) conveniencia

decent ['disənt] adj decente, honesto; (proper) conveniente

decentralize [dɪ'sentrəˌlaɪz] tr descentralizar

deception [dɪ'sepʃən] s engaño

deceptive [dɪ'septɪv] adj engañoso

decide [dɪ'saɪd] tr & intr decidir

decimal ['desɪməl] adj & s decimal m

decimal point s (in Spanish the comma is used to separate the decimal fraction from the integer) coma

decimate ['desɪˌmet] tr diezmar

decipher [dɪ'saɪfər] tr descifrar

decision [dɪ'sɪʒən] s decisión

decisive [dɪ'saɪsɪv] adj decisivo; determinado, resuelto

deck [dek] s (of cards) baraja; (of ship) cubierta; **between decks** (naut) entre cubiertas || tr — **to deck out** adornar, engalanar

deck chair s silla de cubierta

deck hand s marinero de cubierta

deck'-land' intr apontizar

deck'-land'ing s apontizaje m

deckle edge ['dekəl] s barba

declaim [dɪ'klem] tr & intr declamar

declaration [ˌdeklə'reʃən] s declaración

declarative [dɪ'klærətɪv] adj declarativo; (gram) enunciativo

declare [dɪ'kler] tr & intr declarar

declension [dɪ'klenʃən] s declinación

declination [ˌdeklɪ'neʃən] s declinación

decline [dɪ'klaɪn] s bajada, declinación; (in prices) baja; (in health, wealth, etc.) bajón m; (of sun) ocaso || tr & intr declinar; rehusar

decliv·i·ty [dɪ'klɪvɪti] s (pl **-ties**) declividad, declive m

decode [di'kod] tr descifrar

décolleté [ˌdekɑl'te] adj escotado

decompose [ˌdikəmˈpoz] *tr* descomponer || *intr* descomponerse

decomposition [ˌdikɑmpəˈzɪʃən] *s* descomposición

decompression [ˌdikəmˈpreʃən] *s* descompresión

decontamination [ˌdikəmˌtæmɪˈneʃən] *s* descontaminación

décor [deˈkor] *s* decoración; (theat) decorado

decorate [ˈdekəˌret] *tr* decorar; (with medal, badge) condecorar

decoration [ˌdekəˈreʃən] *s* decoración; (medal, badge) condecoración

decorator [ˈdekəˌretər] *s* decorador *m*; (of interiors) adornista *mf*

decorous [ˈdekərəs] o [dɪˈkorəs] *adj* decoroso

decorum [dɪˈkorəm] *s* decoro

decoy [dɪˈkoɪ] o [ˈdikoɪ] *s* añagaza, señuelo; (person) entruchón *m* || [dɪˈkoɪ] *tr* atraer con señuelo; entruchar

decoy pigeon *s* cimbel *m*

decrease [ˈdikris] o [dɪˈkris] *s* disminución || [dɪˈkris] *tr* disminuir || *intr* disminuir, disminuirse

decree [dɪˈkri] *s* decreto || *tr* decretar

decrepit [dɪˈkrepɪt] *adj* decrépito

de-cry [dɪˈkraɪ] *v* (pret & pp -cried) *tr* censurar, denigrar

dedicate [ˈdedɪˌket] *tr* dedicar

dedication [ˌdedɪˈkeʃən] *s* dedicación; (inscription in a book) dedicatoria

deduce [dɪˈdjus] o [dɪˈdus] *tr* deducir (inferir, concluir; derivar)

deduct [dɪˈdʌkt] *tr* deducir (rebajar, substraer)

deduction [dɪˈdʌkʃən] *s* deducción

deed [did] *s* acto, hecho; (feat, exploit) hazaña; (law) escritura || *tr* traspasar por escritura

deem [dim] *tr & intr* creer, juzgar

deep [dip] *adj* profundo; (sound) grave; (color) subido; de hondo, p.ej., two meters deep dos metros de hondo; deep in debt cargado de deudas; deep in thought absorto en la meditación || *adv* hondo; deep into the night muy entrada la noche

deepen [ˈdipən] *tr* profundizar || *intr* profundizarse

deep-laid [ˈdipˌled] *adj* concebido con astucia

deep mourning *s* luto riguroso

deep-rooted [ˈdipˌrutɪd] *adj* profundamente arraigado

deep'-sea' fishing *s* pesca de gran altura

deep-seated [ˈdipˌsitɪd] *adj* profundamente arraigado

deer [dɪr] *s* ciervo, venado

deer'skin' *s* piel *f* de ciervo

def. *abbr* defendant, deferred, definite

deface [dɪˈfes] *tr* desfigurar

de facto [diˈfækto] *adv* de hecho

defamation [ˌdefəˈmeʃən] o [ˌdifəˈmeʃən] *s* difamación

defame [dɪˈfem] *tr* difamar

default [dɪˈfolt] *s* falta, incumplimiento; by default (sport) por no

presentarse; in default of por falta de || *tr* dejar de cumplir; no pagar || *intr* faltar; (sport) perder por no presentarse

defeat [dɪˈfit] *s* derrota || *tr* derrotar, vencer

defeatism [dɪˈfitɪzəm] *s* derrotismo

defeatist [dɪˈfitɪst] *adj & s* derrotista *mf*

defecate [ˈdefɪˌket] *intr* defecar

defect [dɪˈfekt] o [ˈdifekt] *s* defecto, imperfección || [dɪˈfekt] *intr* desertar

defection [dɪˈfekʃən] *s* defección; (lack, failure) falta

defective [dɪˈfektɪv] *adj* defectivo, defectuoso

defend [dɪˈfend] *tr* defender

defendant [dɪˈfendənt] *s* (law) demandado, acusado

defender [dɪˈfendər] *s* defensor *m*

defense [dɪˈfens] *s* defensa

defenseless [dɪˈfenslɪs] *adj* indefenso

defensive [dɪˈfensɪv] *adj* defensivo || *s* defensiva

de·fer [dɪˈfʌr] *v* (pret & pp -ferred; ger -ferring) *tr* aplazar, diferir || *intr* deferir

deference [ˈdefərəns] *s* deferencia

deferential [ˌdefəˈrenʃəl] *adj* deferente

deferment [dɪˈfʌrmənt] *s* aplazamiento, dilación

defiance [dɪˈfaɪəns] *s* oposición; desafío, provocación; in defiance of sin mirar a, a despecho de

defiant [dɪˈfaɪənt] *adj* provocante, hostil

deficien·cy [dɪˈfɪʃənsi] *s* (pl -cies) carencia, deficiencia; (com) descubierto

deficient [dɪˈfɪʃənt] *adj* deficiente, defectuoso

deficit [ˈdefɪsɪt] *adj* deficitario || *s* déficit *m*

defile [dɪˈfaɪl] o [ˈdifaɪl] *s* desfiladero || [dɪˈfaɪl] *tr* corromper, manchar || *intr* desfilar

define [dɪˈfaɪn] *tr* definir

definite [ˈdefɪnɪt] *adj* definido

definition [ˌdefɪˈnɪʃən] *s* definición

definitive [dɪˈfɪnɪtɪv] *adj* definitivo

deflate [dɪˈflet] *tr* desinflar

deflation [dɪˈfleʃən] *s* desinflación; (of prices) deflación

deflect [dɪˈflekt] *tr* desviar || *intr* desviarse

deflower [diˈflauˌər] *tr* desflorar

deforest [diˈfɑrest] o [diˈforest] *tr* desforestar, despoblar

deform [dɪˈform] *tr* deformar

deformed [dɪˈformd] *adj* deforme

deformi·ty [dɪˈformɪti] *s* (pl -ties) deformidad

defraud [dɪˈfrod] *tr* defraudar

defray [dɪˈfre] *tr* sufragar, subvenir a

defrost [diˈfrost] o [diˈfrɑst] *tr* descongelar, deshelar

deft [deft] *adj* diestro, hábil

defunct [dɪˈfʌŋkt] *adj* difunto

de·fy [dɪˈfaɪ] *v* (pret & pp -fied) *tr* desafiar, provocar

deg. *abbr* degree

degeneracy [dɪ'dʒenərəsi] s degeneración

degenerate [dɪ'dʒenərɪt] adj & s degenerado ‖ [dɪ'dʒenə,ret] intr degenerar

degrade [dɪ'gred] tr degradar

degrading [dɪ'gredɪŋ] adj degradante

degree [dɪ'gri] s grado; **by degrees** de grado en grado; **to take a degree** graduarse, recibir un grado o título

dehumidifier [,dɪhju'mɪdɪ,faɪ·ər] s deshumedecedor m

dehydrate [di'haɪdret] tr deshidratar

deice [di'aɪs] tr deshelar

dei·fy ['di·ɪ,faɪ] v (pret & pp -fied) tr deificar

deign [den] intr dignarse

dei·ty ['di·ɪti] s (pl -ties) deidad; **the Deity** Dios m

dejected [dɪ'dʒektɪd] adj abatido

dejection [dɪ'dʒek/ən] s abatimiento

del. abbr **delegate, delete**

delay [dɪ'le] s retraso, tardanza ‖ tr retrasar ‖ intr demorarse

delectable [dɪ'lektəbəl] adj deleitable

delegate ['delɪ,get] o ['delɪgɪt] s diputado, delegado; (to a convention) congresista mf ‖ ['delɪ,get] tr delegar

delete [dɪ'lit] tr borrar, suprimir

deletion [dɪ'li/ən] s supresión

deliberate [dɪ'lɪbərɪt] adj pensado, reflexionado; (slow in deciding) cauto, circunspecto; (slow in moving) espacioso, lento ‖ [dɪ'lɪbə,ret] tr & intr deliberar

delica·cy ['delɪkəsi] s (pl -cies) delicadeza; (choice food) golosina

delicatessen [,delɪkə'tesən] s colmado, tienda de ultramarinos ‖ spl ultramarinos

delicious [dɪ'lɪ/əs] adj delicioso, sabroso

delight [dɪ'laɪt] s deleite m, delicia ‖ tr deleitar ‖ intr deleitarse

delightful [dɪ'laɪtfəl] adj deleitoso, ameno, exquisito

delinquen·cy [dɪ'lɪŋkwənsi] s (pl -cies) culpa; (in payment of debt) morosidad; (debt in arrears) atrasos

delinquent [dɪ'lɪŋkwənt] adj culpado; (in payment) moroso, atrasado; no pagado ‖ s culpado; deudor moroso

delirious [dɪ'lɪrɪ·əs] adj delirante

deliri·um [dɪ'lɪrɪ·əm] s (pl -ums o -a [ə]) delirio

deliver [dɪ'lɪvər] tr entregar; asestar (un golpe); pronunciar, recitar (un discurso); transmitir, rendir (energía); partear (a la mujer que está de parto)

deliver·y [dɪ'lɪvəri] s (pl -ies) entrega; (of mail) distribución, reparto; (of a speech) declamación; (childbirth) alumbramiento, parto

delivery·man [dɪ'lɪvərimən] s (pl -men [mən]) mozo de reparto

delivery room s sala de alumbramiento

delivery truck s sedán m de reparto

dell [del] s vallecito

delouse [di'laus] o [di'lauz] tr despiojar

delphinium [del'fɪnɪ·əm] s (Delphinium ajacis) espuela de caballero; (Delphinium consolida) consuelda real

delude [dɪ'lud] tr deludir, engañar

deluge ['deljudʒ] s diluvio ‖ tr inundar

delusion [dɪ'luʒən] s engaño, decepción

de luxe [dɪ'lʊks] o [dɪ'lʌks] adj & adv de lujo

delve [delv] intr cavar; **to delve into** cavar en

demagnetize [di'mægnɪ,taɪz] tr desimantar

demagogue ['demə,gag] s demagogo

demand [dɪ'mænd] o [dɪ'mand] s demanda; **to be in demand** tener demanda ‖ tr demandar perentoriamente

demanding [dɪ'mændɪŋ] o [dɪ'mandɪŋ] adj exigente

demarcate [dɪ'market] o ['dimar,ket] tr demarcar

démarche ['demar/] s diligencia, gestión, paso

demeanor [dɪ'minər] s conducta, porte m

demented [dɪ'mentɪd] adj demente

demigod ['demɪ,gad] s semidiós m

demijohn ['demɪ,dʒan] s damajuana

demilitarize [di'mɪlɪtə,raɪz] tr desmilitarizar

demimonde ['demɪ,mand] s mujeres de vida alegre

demise [dɪ'maɪz] s fallecimiento

demisemiquaver [,demɪ'semɪ,kwevər] s (mus) fusa

demitasse ['demɪ,tæs] o ['demɪ,tas] s taza pequeña

demobilize [di'mobɪ,laɪz] tr desmovilizar

democra·cy [dɪ'makrəsi] s (pl -cies) democracia

democrat ['demə,kræt] s demócrata mf

democratic [,demə'krætɪk] adj democrático

demodulate [di'madʒə,let] tr desmodular

demolish [dɪ'malɪ/] tr demoler

demolition [,demə'lɪ/ən] o [,dimə'lɪ/ən] s demolición

demon ['dimən] s demonio

demoniacal [,dimə'naɪ·əkəl] adj demoníaco

demonstrate ['demən,stret] tr demostrar ‖ intr demostrar; (to show feelings in public gatherings) manifestar

demonstration [,demən'stre/ən] s demostración; (public show of feeling) manifestación

demonstrative [dɪ'manstrətɪv] adj demostrativo; (giving open exhibition of emotion) extremoso

demonstrator ['demən,stretər] s demostrador m; manifestante mf

demoralize [dɪ'marə,laɪz] o [dɪ'mɔrə,laɪz] tr desmoralizar

demote [dɪ'mot] *tr* degradar
demotion [dɪ'moʃən] *s* degradación
de·mur [dɪ'mʌr] *v* (*pret & pp* **-murred;** *ger* **-murring**) *intr* poner reparos
demure [dɪ'mjur] *adj* modesto, recatado; grave, serio
demurrage [dɪ'mʌrɪdʒ] *s* (com) estadía
den [dɛn] *s* (*of animals, thieves*) madriguera; (*dirty little room*) cuchitril *m*; lugar *m* de retiro; cuarto de estudio; (*of lions*) (Bib) fosa
denaturalize [di'nætʃərə,laɪz] *tr* desnaturalizar
denatured alcohol [di'netʃərd] *s* alcohol desnaturalizado
denial [dɪ'naɪ·əl] *s* denegación; negación, desmentida
denim ['dɛnɪm] *s* dril *m* de algodón
denizen ['dɛnɪzən] *s* habitante *mf*, vecino
Denmark ['dɛnmɑrk] *s* Dinamarca
denomination [dɪ,nɑmɪ'neʃən] *s* denominación; categoría, clase *f*; secta, confesión, comunión
denote [dɪ'not] *tr* denotar
dénoument [denu'mɑ̃] *s* desenlace *m*
denounce [dɪ'nauns] *tr* denunciar
dense [dɛns] *adj* denso; estúpido
densi·ty ['dɛnsɪti] *s* (*pl* **-ties**) densidad
dent [dɛnt] *s* abolladura, mella ‖ *tr* abollar, mellar ‖ *intr* abollarse, mellarse
dental ['dɛntəl] *adj & s* dental *f*
dental floss *s* hilo dental, seda encerada
dentifrice ['dɛntɪfrɪs] *s* dentífrico
dentist ['dɛntɪst] *s* dentista *mf*
dentistry ['dɛntɪstri] *s* odontología
denture ['dɛntʃər] *s* dentadura artificial
denunciation [dɪ,nʌnsɪ'eʃən] o [dɪ,nʌnʃɪ'eʃən] *s* denuncia
de·ny [dɪ'naɪ] *v* (*pret & pp* **-nied**) *tr* (*to declare not to be true*) negar; (*to refuse*) denegar; **to deny oneself to callers** negarse ‖ *intr* negar; denegar
deodorant [di'odərənt] *adj & s* desodorante *m*
deodorize [di'odə,raɪz] *tr* desodorizar
deoxidize [di'ɑksɪ,daɪz] *tr* desoxidar
dep. *abbr* department, departs, deputy
depart [dɪ'pɑrt] *intr* partir, salir, irse; desviarse
department [dɪ'pɑrtmənt] *s* departamento; (*of government*) ministerio
department store *s* grandes almacenes *mpl*
departure [dɪ'pɑrtʃər] *s* partida, salida; desviación
depend [dɪ'pɛnd] *intr* depender; **to depend on** depender de
dependable [dɪ'pɛndəbəl] *adj* confiable, fidedigno
dependence [dɪ'pɛndəns] *s* dependencia
dependen·cy [dɪ'pɛndənsi] *s* (*pl* **-cies**) dependencia; (*country, territory*) posesión
dependent [dɪ'pɛndənt] *adj* dependiente ‖ *s* carga de familia, familiar *m* dependiente

depict [dɪ'pɪkt] *tr* describir, representar, pintar
deplete [dɪ'plit] *tr* agotar, depauperar
deplorable [dɪ'plorəbəl] *adj* deplorable
deplore [dɪ'plor] *tr* deplorar
deploy [dɪ'plɔɪ] *tr* (mil) desplegar ‖ *intr* (mil) desplegarse
deployment [dɪ'plɔɪmənt] *s* (mil) despliegue *m*
depolarize [di'polə,raɪz] *tr* despolarizar
depopulate [di'pɑpjə,let] *tr* despoblar
deport [dɪ'port] *tr* deportar; **to deport oneself** conducirse, portarse
deportation [,dipor'teʃən] *s* deportación
deportee [,dipor'ti] *s* deportado
deportment [dɪ'portmənt] *s* conducta, comportamiento
depose [dɪ'poz] *tr & intr* deponer
deposit [dɪ'pɑzɪt] *s* depósito; (*down payment*) señal *f*, pago anticipado; (min) yacimiento ‖ *tr* depositar ‖ *intr* depositarse
deposit account *s* cuenta corriente
depositor [dɪ'pɑzɪtər] *s* cuentacorrentista *mf*, imponente *mf*
depot ['dipo] o ['depo] *s* almacén *m*, depósito; (mil) depósito; (rr) estación
depraved [dɪ'prevd] *adj* depravado
depravi·ty [dɪ'prævɪti] *s* (*pl* **-ties**) depravación
deprecate ['dɛprɪ,ket] *tr* desaprobar
depreciate [dɪ'priʃɪ,et] *tr* (*to lower value or price of*) depreciar; (*to disparage*) desapreciar ‖ *intr* depreciarse
depreciation [dɪ,priʃɪ'eʃən] *s* (*drop in value*) depreciación; (*disparagement*) desaprecio
depress [dɪ'prɛs] *tr* deprimir; desanimar, desalentar; bajar (*los precios*)
depression [dɪ'prɛʃən] *s* depresión; desaliento; (*slump*) crisis *f*
deprive [dɪ'praɪv] *tr* privar
dept. *abbr* department
depth [dɛpθ] *s* profundidad; (*of a house, of a room*) fondo; **in the depth of night** en mitad de la noche; **in the depth of winter** en pleno invierno; **to go beyond one's depth** meterse en agua demasiado profunda; (fig) meterse en honduras
depth of hold *s* (naut) puntal *m*
depu·ty ['dɛpjəti] *s* (*pl* **-ties**) diputado
derail [dɪ'rel] *tr* hacer descarrilar ‖ *intr* descarrilar
derailment [dɪ'relmənt] *s* descarrilamiento
derange [dɪ'rendʒ] *tr* desarreglar, descomponer; trastornar el juicio a
derangement [dɪ'rendʒmənt] *s* desarreglo, descompostura; locura
der·by ['dʌrbi] *s* (*pl* **-bies**) sombrero hongo
derelict ['dɛrɪlɪkt] *adj* abandonado; negligente ‖ *s* pelafustán *m*; (naut) derrelicto
deride [dɪ'raɪd] *tr* burlarse de, ridiculizar

derision [dɪ'rɪʒən] s burla, irrisión
derive [dɪ'raɪv] tr & intr derivar
derogatory [dɪ'rɑgə,tori] adj despreciativo
derrick ['derɪk] s grúa
dervish ['dʌrvɪʃ] s derviche m
desalinization [dɪ,selɪnɪ'zeʃən] s desalinización
desalt [dɪ'sɔlt] tr desalar
descend [dɪ'send] tr bajar, descender (la escalera) || intr bajar, descender; **to descend on** caer sobre, invadir
descendant [dɪ'sendənt] adj descendente || s descendiente mf
descendent [dɪ'sendənt] adj descendente
descent [dɪ'sent] s (passing from higher to lower state) descenso; (extraction; lineage) descendencia; cuesta, bajada; invasión
describe [dɪ'skraɪb] tr describir
description [dɪ'skrɪpʃən] s descripción
descriptive [dɪ'skrɪptɪv] adj descriptivo
de·scry [dɪ'skraɪ] v (pret & pp -scried) tr avistar, divisar; descubrir
desecrate ['desɪ,kret] tr profanar
desegregation [di,segrɪ'geʃən] s desegregación
desert ['dezərt] adj & s desierto, yermo || [dɪ'zʌrt] s mérito; **he received his just deserts** llevó su merecido || tr desertar de || intr desertar
deserter [dɪ'zʌrtər] s desertor m
desertion [dɪ'zʌrʃən] s deserción; abandono de cónyuge
deserve [dɪ'zʌrv] tr & intr merecer
deservedly [dɪ'zʌrvɪdlɪ] adv merecidamente
design [dɪ'zaɪn] s diseño; (combination of details; art of designing) dibujo; (plan, scheme) designio; **to have designs on** poner la mira en || tr diseñar, dibujar; idear, proyectar || intr diseñar, dibujar
designate ['dezɪg,net] tr designar
designing [dɪ'zaɪnɪŋ] adj intrigante, maquinador
desirable [dɪ'zaɪrəbəl] adj deseable
desire [dɪ'zaɪr] s deseo || tr desear
desirous [dɪ'zaɪrəs] adj deseoso
desist [dɪ'zɪst] intr desistir
desk [desk] s bufete m, escritorio; (lectern) atril m; (clerk's counter in a hotel) caja
desk clerk s cajero, recepcionista m
desk set s juego de escritorio
desolate ['desəlɪt] adj (hopeless) desolado; despoblado, yermo, desierto; solitario; (dismal) lúgubre || ['desə,let] tr desconsolar; (to lay waste) desolar, devastar; despoblar
desolation [,desə'leʃən] s (devastation; great affliction) desolación; (dreariness) lobreguez f
despair [dɪ'sper] s desesperación || intr desesperar, desesperarse
despairing [dɪ'sperɪŋ] adj desesperado
despera·do [,despə'redo] o [,despə'rɑdo] s (pl -does o -dos) criminal dispuesto a todo

desperate ['despərɪt] adj dispuesto a todo; (bitter, excessive) encarnizado; (hopeless) desesperado; (remedy) heroico
despicable ['despɪkəbəl] adj despreciable, ruin
despise [dɪ'spaɪz] tr despreciar, desdeñar
despite [dɪ'spaɪt] prep a despecho de
desponden·cy [dɪ'spɑndənsi] s (pl -cies) abatimiento, desaliento
despondent [dɪ'spɑndənt] adj abatido, desalentado
despot ['despɑt] s déspota m
despotic [des'pɑtɪk] adj despótico
despotism ['despə,tɪzəm] s despotismo
dessert [dɪ'zʌrt] s postre m
destination [,destɪ'neʃən] s (end of a journey or shipment) destino; (purpose) destinación
destine ['destɪn] tr destinar
desti·ny ['destɪni] s (pl -nies) destino
destitute ['destɪ,tjut] o ['destɪ,tut] adj (being in complete poverty) indigente; (lacking, deprived) desprovisto
destitution [,destɪ'tjuʃən] o [,destɪ'tuʃən] s indigencia
destroy [dɪ'strɔɪ] tr destruir
destroyer [dɪ'strɔɪ·ər] s (nav) destructor m
destruction [dɪ'strʌkʃən] s destrucción
destructive [dɪ'strʌktɪv] adj destructivo
desultory ['desəl,tori] adj deshilvanado, descosido
detach [dɪ'tætʃ] tr desprender, separar; (mil) destacar
detachable [dɪ'tætʃəbəl] adj desprendible, separable; (collar) postizo
detached [dɪ'tætʃt] adj separado, suelto; imparcial, desinteresado
detachment [dɪ'tætʃmənt] s desprendimiento, separación; imparcialidad, desinterés m; (mil) destacamento
detail [dɪ'tel] o ['ditel] s detalle m, pormenor m; (mil) destacamento || [dɪ'tel] tr detallar; (mil) destacar
detain [dɪ'ten] tr detener; tener preso
detect [dɪ'tekt] tr detectar
detection [dɪ'tekʃən] s detección
detective [dɪ'tektɪv] s detective m
detective story s novela policíaca o policial
detector [dɪ'tektər] s detector m
detention [dɪ'tenʃən] s detención
de·ter [dɪ'tʌr] v (pret & pp -terred; ger -terring) tr impedir, refrenar
detergent [dɪ'tʌrdʒənt] adj & s detergente m
deteriorate [dɪ'tɪri·ə,ret] tr deteriorar || intr deteriorarse
determine [dɪ'tʌrmɪn] tr determinar
deterrent [dɪ'tʌrənt] s impedimento, refrenamiento
detest [dɪ'test] tr detestar, aborrecer
dethrone [dɪ'θron] tr destronar
detonate ['detə,net] o ['dɪtə,net] tr hacer estallar || intr detonar
detour ['ditur] o [dɪ'tur] s desvío;

rodeo, vuelta; manera indirecta ‖ *tr* desviar (*el tráfico*) ‖ *intr* desviarse

detract [dɪ'trækt] *tr* detraer ‖ *intr* — **to detract from** disminuir, rebajar

detriment ['detrɪmənt] *s* perjuicio, detrimento; **to the detriment of** en perjuicio de

detrimental [ˌdetrɪ'mentəl] *adj* perjudicial

deuce [djus] o [dus] *s* (*in cards*) dos *m*; **the deuce!** ¡demonio!

devaluation [diˌvælju'eʃən] *s* desvalorización, devaluación

devastate ['devəsˌtet] *tr* devastar

devastation [ˌdevəs'teʃən] *s* devastación

develop [dɪ'veləp] *tr* desarrollar, desenvolver; (*phot*) revelar; explotar (*una mina*) ‖ *intr* desarrollarse, desenvolverse; evolucionar, manifestarse

developer [dɪ'veləpər] *s* fomentador *m*; (*phot*) revelador *m*

development [dɪ'veləpmənt] *s* desarrollo, desenvolvimiento; (*phot*) revelado; (*of a mine*) explotación; acontecimiento nuevo

deviate ['divɪˌet] *tr* desviar ‖ *intr* desviarse

deviation [ˌdivɪ'eʃən] *s* desviación

deviationism [ˌdivɪ'eʃəˌnɪzəm] *s* desviacionismo

deviationist [ˌdivɪ'eʃənɪst] *s* desviacionista *mf*

device [dɪ'vaɪs] *s* dispositivo, aparato; (*trick*) ardid *m*, treta; (*motto*) lema *m*, divisa; **to leave someone to his own devices** dejarle a uno que haga lo que se le antoje

dev·il ['devəl] *s* diablo; **between the devil and the deep blue sea** entre la espada y la pared; (*slang*) armar un alboroto ‖ *v* (*pret & pp* **-iled** o **-illed**; *ger* **-iling** o **-illing**) *tr* condimentar con picantes; (*coll*) acosar, molestar

devilish ['devəlɪʃ] *adj* diabólico

devilment ['devəlmənt] *s* (*mischief*) diablura; (*evil*) maldad

devil·try ['devəltri] *s* (*pl* **-tries**) maldad, crueldad; (*mischief*) diablura

devious ['divɪ·əs] *adj* (*straying*) desviado, extraviado; (*roundabout; shifty*) tortuoso

devise [dɪ'vaɪz] *tr* idear, inventar; (*law*) legar

devoid [dɪ'vɔɪd] *adj* desprovisto

devote [dɪ'vot] *tr* dedicar

devoted [dɪ'votɪd] *adj* (*zealous, ardent*) devoto; dedicado

devotee [ˌdevə'ti] *s* devoto

devotion [dɪ'voʃən] *s* devoción; (*to study, work, etc.*) dedicación; **devotions** oraciones, preces *fpl*

devour [dɪ'vaur] *tr* devorar

devout [dɪ'vaut] *adj* devoto; cordial, sincero

dew [dju] o [du] *s* rocío

dew'drop *s* gota de rocío

dew'lap *s* papada

dew·y ['dju·i] o ['du·i] *adj* rociado

dexterity [deks'terɪti] *s* destreza

D.F. *abbr* **Defender of the Faith**

diabetes [ˌdaɪ·ə'bitɪs] o [ˌdaɪ·ə'bitiz] *s* diabetes *f*

diabetic [ˌdaɪ·ə'betɪk] o [ˌdaɪ·ə'bitɪk] *adj & s* diabético

diabolic(al) [ˌdaɪ·ə'bɑlɪk(əl)] *adj* diabólico

diacritical [ˌdaɪ·ə'krɪtɪkəl] *adj* diacrítico

diadem ['daɪ·əˌdem] *s* diadema *f*

diaere·sis [daɪ'erɪsɪs] *s* (*pl* **-ses** [ˌsiz]) diéresis *f*

diagnose [ˌdaɪ·əg'nos] o [ˌdaɪ·əg'noz] *tr* diagnosticar

diagno·sis [ˌdaɪ·əg'nosɪs] *s* (*pl* **-ses** [siz]) diagnosis *f*, diagnóstico

diagonal [daɪ'ægənəl] *adj & s* diagonal *f*

diagram ['daɪ·əˌgræm] *s* diagrama *m*

dial. *abbr* **dialect**

dial ['daɪ·əl] *s* (*of radio*) cuadrante *m*; (*of watch*) cuadrante *m*, esfera, muestra; (*of telephone*) disco selector ‖ *tr* sintonizar (*el radiorreceptor*); marcar (*el número telefónico*); llamar (*a una persona*) por teléfono automático ‖ *intr* (telp) marcar

dialect ['daɪ·əˌlekt] *s* dialecto

dialing ['daɪ·əlɪŋ] *s* (telp) marcaje *m*

dialogue ['daɪ·əˌlɔg] o ['daɪ·əˌlɑg] *s* diálogo

dial telephone *s* teléfono automático

dial tone *s* (telp) señal *f* para marcar

diam. *abbr* **diameter**

diameter [daɪ'æmɪtər] *s* diámetro

diametric(al) [ˌdaɪ·ə'metrɪk(əl)] *adj* diamétrico

diamond ['daɪmənd] *s* diamante *m*; (*figure of a rhombus*) losange *m*; (*playing card*) carró *m*, diamante *m*; (*baseball*) losange *m*

diaper ['daɪ·pər] *s* pañal *m*

diaphanous [daɪ'æfənəs] *adj* diáfano

diaphragm ['daɪ·əˌfræm] *s* diafragma *m*

diarrhea [ˌdaɪ·ə'ri·ə] *s* diarrea

dia·ry ['daɪ·əri] *s* (*pl* **-ries**) diario

diastole [daɪ'æstəli] *s* diástole *f*

diathermy ['daɪ·əˌθʌrmi] *s* diatermia

dice [daɪs] *spl* dados; (*small cubes*) cubitos; **to load the dice** cargar los dados ‖ *tr* cortar en cubos

dice'box *s* cubilete *m*

dichloride [daɪ'klorɑɪd] *s* dicloruro

dichoto·my [daɪ'kɑtəmi] *s* (*pl* **-mies**) dicotomía

dickey ['dɪki] *s* camisolín *m*, pechera postiza; babero de niño

dict. *abbr* **dictionary**

dictaphone ['dɪktəˌfon] *s* dictáfono

dictate ['dɪktet] *s* mandato ‖ ['dɪktet] o [dɪk'tet] *tr* dictar; mandar

dictation [dɪk'teʃən] *s* dictado; (*orders; giving orders*) mandato; **to take dictation** escribir al dictado

dictator ['dɪktetər] o [dɪk'tetər] *s* dictador *m*

dictatorship ['dɪktetərˌʃɪp] o [dɪk'tetərˌʃɪp] *s* dictadura

diction ['dɪkʃən] *s* dicción

dictionar·y ['dɪkʃənˌeri] *s* (*pl* **-ies**) diccionario

dic·tum ['dɪktəm] *s* (*pl* **-ta** [tə]) dictamen *m*; aforismo, sentencia

didactic(al) [daɪ'dæktɪk(əl)] o [dɪ'dæktɪk(əl)] *adj* didáctico

die [daɪ] *s* (*pl* **dice** [daɪs]) dado; **the die is cast** la suerte está echada ‖ *s* (*pl* **dies**) (*for stamping coins, medals, etc.*) troquel *m*; (*for cutting threads*) hembra de terraja ‖ *v* (*pret & pp* **died**; *ger* **dying**) *intr* morir; **to be dying** estar agonizando; **to die laughing** morir de risa

die′-hard *adj & s* intransigente *mf*

diesel oil ['dizəl] *s* gas-oil *m*

die′stock′ *s* terraja

diet ['daɪ·ət] *s* dieta, régimen alimenticio ‖ *intr* estar a dieta

dietitian [ˌdaɪ·ə'tɪʃən] *s* dietista *mf*

diff. *abbr* difference, different

differ ['dɪfər] *intr* (*to be different*) diferir, diferenciarse; (*to dissent*) diferenciar; **to differ with** desavenirse con

difference ['dɪfərəns] *s* diferencia; **to make no difference** no importar; **to split the difference** partir la diferencia

different ['dɪfərənt] *adj* diferente

differentiate [ˌdɪfə'rɛnʃɪˌet] *tr* diferenciar ‖ *intr* diferenciarse

difficult ['dɪfɪˌkʌlt] *adj* difícil

difficul·ty ['dɪfɪˌkʌltɪ] *s* (*pl* **-ties**) dificultad

diffident ['dɪfɪdənt] *adj* apocado, tímido

diffuse [dɪ'fjus] *adj* difuso ‖ [dɪ'fjuz] *tr* difundir ‖ *intr* difundirse

dig [dɪg] *s* (*poke*) empuje *m*; (*jibe*) pulla, palabra hiriente ‖ *v* (*pret & pp* **dug** [dʌg] o **digged**; *ger* **digging**) *tr* cavar, excavar; **to dig up** desenterrar ‖ *intr* cavar, excavar; **to dig in** (coll) poner manos a la obra; (mil) atrincherarse; **to dig under** socavar

digest ['daɪdʒɛst] *s* compendio, resumen *m*; (law) digesto ‖ [dɪ'dʒɛst] o [daɪ'dʒɛst] *tr & intr* digerir

digestible [dɪ'dʒɛstɪbəl] o [daɪ'dʒɛstɪbəl] *adj* digerible, digestible

digestion [dɪ'dʒɛstʃən] o [daɪ'dʒɛstʃən] *s* digestión

digestive [dɪ'dʒɛstɪv] o [daɪ'dʒɛstɪv] *adj & s* digestivo

digit ['dɪdʒɪt] *s* dígito

dignified ['dɪgnɪˌfaɪd] *adj* digno, grave, decoroso

digni·fy ['dɪgnɪˌfaɪ] *v* (*pret & pp* **-fied**) *tr* dignificar; engrandecer el mérito de

dignitar·y ['dɪgnɪˌtɛrɪ] *s* (*pl* **-ies**) dignatario

digni·ty ['dɪgnɪtɪ] *s* (*pl* **-ties**) dignidad; **to stand upon one's dignity** ponerse tan alto

digress [dɪ'grɛs] o [daɪ'grɛs] *intr* divagar

digression [dɪ'grɛʃən] o [daɪ'grɛʃən] *s* digresión, divagación

dike [daɪk] *s* dique *m*; (*bank of earth thrown up in digging*) montón *m*; (*causeway*) arrecife *m*, malecón *m*

dilapidated [dɪ'læpɪˌdetɪd] *adj* destartalado, desvencijado

dilate [daɪ'let] *tr* dilatar ‖ *intr* dilatarse

dilatory ['dɪlə-torɪ] *adj* tardío

dilemma [dɪ'lɛmə] *s* dilema *m*, disyuntiva

dilettan·te [ˌdɪlə'tænti] *adj* diletante ‖ *s* (*pl* **-tes** o **-ti** [ti]) diletante *mf*

diligence ['dɪlɪdʒəns] *s* diligencia

diligent ['dɪlɪdʒənt] *adj* diligente

dill [dɪl] *s* eneldo

dillydal·ly ['dɪlɪˌdælɪ] *v* (*pret & pp* **-lied**) *intr* malgastar el tiempo, haraganear

dilute [dɪ'lut] o [daɪ'lut] *adj* diluído ‖ [dɪ'lut] *tr* diluir ‖ *intr* diluirse

dilution [dɪ'luʃən] *s* dilución

dim. *abbr* diminutive

dim [dɪm] *adj* (*comp* **dimmer**; *super* **dimmest**) débil, indistinto, confuso; obscuro, poco claro; (*chance*) escaso; (*not clearly understanding*) torpe, lerdo; **to take a dim view of** mirar escépticamente ‖ *v* (*pret & pp* **dimmed**; *ger* **dimming**) *tr* desaguar (*la luz*); poner (*un faro*) a media luz; disminuir ‖ *intr* obscurecerse

dime [daɪm] *s* moneda de diez centavos

dimension [dɪ'mɛnʃən] *s* dimensión

diminish [dɪ'mɪnɪʃ] *tr* disminuir ‖ *intr* disminuir, disminuirse

diminutive [dɪ'mɪnjətɪv] *adj* (*tiny*) diminuto; (gram) diminutivo ‖ *s* diminutivo

dimi·ty ['dɪmɪtɪ] *s* (*pl* **-ties**) cotonía

dimly ['dɪmlɪ] *adv* indistintamente

dimmer ['dɪmər] *s* amortiguador *m* de luz; (aut) lámpara de cruce, luz *f* de cruce

dimple ['dɪmpəl] *s* hoyuelo

dimwit ['dɪmˌwɪt] *s* (slang) mentecato, bobo

dim-witted ['dɪmˌwɪtɪd] *adj* (slang) mentecato, bobo

din [dɪn] *s* estruendo, ruido ensordecedor ‖ *v* (*pret & pp* **dinned**; *ger* **dinning**) *tr* ensordecer con mucho ruido; repetir insistentemente; impresionar con repetición ruidosa ‖ *intr* sonar estrepitosamente

dine [daɪn] *tr* dar de comer a; obsequiar con una cena o comida ‖ *intr* cenar, comer; **to dine out** cenar fuera de casa

diner ['daɪnər] *s* invitado a una cena, convidado a una comida; coche-comedor *m*

ding-dong ['dɪŋˌdɔŋ] o ['dɪŋˌdɑŋ] *s* dindán *m*

din·gy ['dɪndʒɪ] *adj* (*comp* **-gier**; *super* **-giest**) deslustrado, sucio

dining car *s* coche-comedor *m*

dining room *s* comedor *m*

din′ing-room′ suit *s* juego de comedor

dinner ['dɪnər] *s* cena, comida; (*formal meal*) banquete *m*

dinner coat o **jacket** *s* smoking *m*

dinner pail *s* fiambrera, portaviandas *m*

dinner set *s* vajilla

dinner time *s* hora de la cena o comida

dint [dɪnt] *s* abolladura; **by dint of** a fuerza de ‖ *tr* abollar

diocese ['daɪ·ə‚sɪs] o ['daɪ·əsɪs] *s* diócesis *f* o diócesis *f*

diode ['daɪ·od] *s* diodo

dioxide [daɪ'aksaɪd] *s* dióxido

dip [dɪp] *s* zambullida, inmersión; baño corto; (*in a road*) depresión; (*of magnetic needle*) inclinación ‖ *v* (*pret & pp* **dipped**; *ger* **dipping**) *tr* sumergir; sacar con cuchara; (*bread*) sopetear; **to dip the colors** saludar con la bandera ‖ *intr* sumergirse; inclinarse hacia abajo; desaparecer súbitamente; **to dip into** hojear (*un libro*); meterse en (*un comercio*); **to dip into one's purse** gastar dinero

diphtheria [dɪf'θɪrɪ·ə] *s* difteria

diphthong ['dɪfθɔŋ] o ['dɪfθaŋ] *s* diptongo

diphthongize ['dɪfθɔŋ‚gaɪz] o ['dɪfθaŋ‚gaɪz] *tr* diptongar ‖ *intr* diptongarse

diploma [dɪ'plomə] *s* diploma *m*

diploma·cy [dɪ'ploməsi] *s* (*pl* **-cies**) diplomacia

diplomat ['dɪplə‚mæt] *s* diplomático

diplomatic [‚dɪplə'mætɪk] *adj* diplomático

diplomatic pouch *s* valija diplomática

dipper ['dɪpər] *s* cazo, cucharón *m*

dip'stick' *s* varilla de nivel

dire [daɪr] *adj* horrendo, espantoso

direct [dɪ'rɛkt] o [daɪ'rɛkt] *adj* directo; franco, sincero ‖ *tr* dirigir; mandar, ordenar

direct current *s* corriente continua

direct discourse *s* (*gram*) estilo directo

direct hit *s* blanco directo, impacto directo

direction [dɪ'rɛkʃən] o [daɪ'rɛkʃən] *s* dirección; instrucción

direct object *s* (*gram*) complemento directo

director [dɪ'rɛktər] o [daɪ'rɛktər] *s* director *m*, administrador *m*; (*member of a governing body*) vocal *m*

directorship [dɪ'rɛktər‚ʃɪp] o [daɪ'rɛktər‚ʃɪp] *s* dirección, directorio

directo·ry [dɪ'rɛktəri] o [daɪ'rɛktəri] *s* (*pl* **-ries**) (*list of names and addresses; board of directors*) directorio; anuario telefónico, guía telefónica

dirge [dʌrdʒ] *s* endecha, canto fúnebre, treno; (*eccl*) misa de réquiem

dirigible ['dɪrɪdʒɪbəl] *adj & s* dirigible *m*

dirt [dʌrt] *s* (*soil*) tierra, suelo; (*dust*) polvo; (*mud*) barro, lodo; (*accumulation of dirt*) suciedad; (*moral filth*) suciedad, porquería, obscenidad; (*gossip*) chismes *mpl*

dirt'cheap' *adj* tirado, muy barato

dirt road *s* camino de tierra

dirt·y ['dʌrti] *adj* (*comp* **-ier**; *super* **-iest**) puerco, sucio; barroso, enlodado; polvoriento; (*obscene*) hediondo; bajo, vil ‖ *v* (*pret & pp* **-tied**) *tr* ensuciar

dirty linen *s* ropa sucia; **to air one's**

dirty linen in public sacar los trapos sucios a relucir

dirty trick *s* (slang) perrada, mala partida

disabili·ty [‚dɪsə'bɪlɪti] *s* (*pl* **-ties**) incapacidad, inhabilidad

disable [dɪs'ebəl] *tr* incapacitar, inhabilitar, lisiar; (law) descalificar

disabuse [‚dɪsə'bjuz] *tr* desengañar

disadvantage [‚dɪsəd'væntɪdʒ] o [‚dɪsəd'vantɪdʒ] *s* desventaja

disadvantageous [‚dɪs‚ædvən'tdʒəs] *adj* desventajoso

disagree [‚dɪsə'gri] *intr* desavenirse, desconvenirse; (*to quarrel*) altercar, contender; **to disagree with** no estar de acuerdo con; no sentar bien

disagreeable [‚dɪsə'gri·əbəl] *adj* desagradable

disagreement [‚dɪsə'grimənt] *s* desavenencia, desacuerdo; disensión

disappear [‚dɪsə'pɪr] *intr* desaparecer, desaparecerse

disappearance [‚dɪsə'pɪrəns] *s* desaparecimiento, desaparición

disappoint [‚dɪsə'pɔɪnt] *tr* decepcionar, desilusionar, chasquear; **to be disappointed** chasquearse, llevarse chasco

disappointment [‚dɪsə'pɔɪntmənt] *s* decepción, desilusión, chasco

disapproval [‚dɪsə'pruvəl] *s* desaprobación

disapprove [‚dɪsə'pruv] *tr & intr* desaprobar

disarm [dɪs'arm] *tr* desarmar ‖ *intr* desarmar, desarmarse

disarmament [dɪs'arməmənt] *s* desarme *m*

disarming [dɪs'armɪŋ] *adj* congraciador, simpático

disarray [‚dɪsə're] *s* desorden *m*; (*in apparel*) desatavío ‖ *tr* desordenar; desataviar

disaster [dɪ'zæstər] o [dɪ'zɑstər] *s* desastre *m*, siniestro

disastrous [dɪ'zæstrəs] o [dɪ'zɑstrəs] *adj* desastroso, desastrado

disavow [‚dɪsə'vau] *tr* desconocer, negar, repudiar

disband [dɪs'bænd] *tr* disolver (*una asamblea*); licenciar (*tropas*) ‖ *intr* desbandarse

dis·bar [dɪs'bar] *v* (*pret & pp* **-barred**; *ger* **-barring**) *tr* (law) expulsar del foro

disbelief [‚dɪsbɪ'lif] *s* incredulidad

disbelieve [‚dɪsbɪ'liv] *tr & intr* descreer

disburse [dɪs'bʌrs] *tr* desembolsar

disbursement [dɪs'bʌrsmənt] *s* desembolso

disc. *abbr* **discount, discoverer**

disc [dɪsk] *s* disco

discard [dɪs'kard] *s* descarte *m*; **to put into the discard** desechar ‖ *tr* descartar; desechar

discern [dɪ'zʌrn] o [dɪ'sʌrn] *tr* discernir, percibir

discerning [dɪ'zʌrnɪŋ] o [dɪ'sʌrnɪŋ] *adj* discerniente, perspicaz

discharge [dɪs'tʃardʒ] *s* (*of a gun, of*

a battery) descarga; (*of a prisoner*) liberación; (*of a duty*) desempeño; (*of a debt, of an obligation*) descargo; (*from a job*) despedida, remoción; (mil) certificado de licencia; (pathol) derrame *m* || *tr* descargar; desempeñar (*un deber*); libertar (*a un preso*); despedir, remover (*a un empleado*); (*from the hospital*) dar de alta; (mil) licenciar || *intr* descargar (*un tubo, río, etc.*); descargarse (*un arma de fuego*)

disciple [dɪ'saɪpəl] *s* discípulo
disciplinarian [ˌdɪsɪplɪ'nɛrɪ·ən] *s* ordenancista *mf*
discipline ['dɪsɪplɪn] *s* disciplina; castigo || *tr* disciplinar; castigar
disclaim [dɪs'klem] *tr* desconocer, negar
disclose [dɪs'kloz] *tr* divulgar, revelar; descubrir
disclosure [dɪs'kloʒər] *s* divulgación, revelación; descubrimiento
discolor [dɪs'kʌlər] *tr* descolorar || *intr* descolorarse
discomfiture [dɪs'kʌmfɪt/ər] *s* desconcierto; frustración
discomfort [dɪs'kʌmfərt] *s* incomodidad || *tr* incomodar
disconcert [ˌdɪskən'sʌrt] *tr* desconcertar, confundir
disconnect [ˌdɪskə'nɛkt] *tr* desunir, separar; desconectar
disconsolate [dɪs'kɑnsəlɪt] *adj* desconsolado, desolado
discontent [ˌdɪskən'tɛnt] *adj* & *s* descontento || *tr* descontentar
discontented [ˌdɪskən'tɛntɪd] *adj* descontento
discontinue [ˌdɪskən'tɪnju] *tr* descontinuar
discord ['dɪskɔrd] *s* desacuerdo, discordia; discordancia
discordance [dɪs'kɔrdəns] *s* discordancia
discotheque [ˌdɪsko'tɛk] *s* discoteca
discount ['dɪskaʊnt] *s* descuento || ['dɪskaʊnt] o [dɪs'kaʊnt] *tr* descontar; descontar por exagerado
discount rate *s* tipo de descuento; tipo de redescuento
discourage [dɪs'kʌrɪdʒ] *tr* desalentar, desanimar; desaprobar; disuadir
discouragement [dɪs'kʌrɪdʒmənt] *s* desaliento; desaprobación; disuasión
discourse ['dɪskors] o [dɪs'kors] *s* discurso || [dɪs'kors] *intr* discurrir
discourteous [dɪs'kʌrtɪ·əs] *adj* descortés
discourte·sy [dɪs'kʌrtəsi] *s* (*pl* -sies) descortesía
discover [dɪs'kʌvər] *tr* descubrir
discover·y [dɪs'kʌvəri] *s* (*pl* -ies) descubrimiento
discredit [dɪs'krɛdɪt] *s* descrédito || *tr* desacreditar
discreditable [dɪs'krɛdɪtəbəl] *adj* deshonroso
discreet [dɪs'krit] *adj* discreto
discrepan·cy [dɪs'krɛpənsi] *s* (*pl* -cies) discrepancia
discrete [dɪs'krit] *adj* discreto

discretion [dɪs'krɛʃən] *s* discreción; **at discretion** a discreción
discriminate [dɪs'krɪmɪˌnet] *intr* discriminar; **to discriminate against** discriminar
discrimination [dɪsˌkrɪmɪ'neʃən] *s* discriminación
discriminatory [dɪs'krɪmɪnəˌtori] *adj* discriminatorio
discus ['dɪskəs] *s* (sport) disco
discuss [dɪs'kʌs] *tr* & *intr* discutir
discussion [dɪs'kʌʃən] *s* discusión
discus thrower ['θroˌər] *s* discóbolo
disdain [dɪs'den] *s* desdén *m* || *tr* desdeñar
disdainful [dɪs'denfəl] *adj* desdeñoso
disease [dɪ'ziz] *s* enfermedad
diseased [dɪ'zizd] *adj* morboso
disembark [ˌdɪsɛm'bɑrk] *tr* & *intr* desembarcar
disembarkation [dɪsˌɛmbɑr'keʃən] *s* (*of passengers*) desembarco; (*of freight*) desembarque *m*
disembowel [ˌdɪsɛm'baʊ·əl] *tr* desentrañar
disenchant [ˌdɪsɛn't/ænt] o [ˌdɪsɛn't/ɑnt] *tr* desencantar
disenchantment [ˌdɪsɛn't/æntmənt] o [ˌdɪsɛn't/ɑntmənt] *s* desencanto
disengage [ˌdɪsɛn'gedʒ] *tr* (*from a pledge*) desempeñar; (*to disconnect*) desenganchar; desembragar (*el motor*)
disengagement [ˌdɪsɛn'gedʒmənt] *s* desempeño; desenganche *m;* desembrague *m*
disentangle [ˌdɪsɛn'tæŋgəl] *tr* desenredar
disentanglement [ˌdɪsɛn'tæŋgəlmənt] *s* desenredo
disestablish [ˌdɪsɛs'tæblɪʃ] *tr* separar (*la Iglesia*) del Estado
disfavor [dɪs'fevər] *s* disfavor *m*
disfigure [dɪs'fɪgjər] *tr* desfigurar
disfranchise [dɪs'fræntʃaɪz] *tr* privar de los derechos de ciudadanía
disgorge [dɪs'gɔrdʒ] *tr* & *intr* vomitar
disgrace [dɪs'gres] *s* deshonra, vergüenza; disfavor *m* || *tr* deshonrar, avergonzar; despedir con ignominia
disgraceful [dɪs'gresfəl] *adj* deshonroso, vergonzoso
disgruntle [dɪs-grʌntəl] *tr* disgustar, enfadar
disguise [dɪs'gaɪz] *s* disfraz *m* || *tr* disfrazar
disgust [dɪs'gʌst] *s* asco, repugnancia || *tr* dar asco a, repugnar
disgusting [dɪs'gʌstɪŋ] *adj* asqueroso, repugnante
dish [dɪʃ] *s* (*any container used at table*) vasija; (*shallow, circular dish; its contents*) plato; **to wash the dishes** lavar la vajilla || *tr* servir en un plato; (slang) arruinar
dish'cloth' *s* albero
dishearten [dɪs'hɑrtən] *tr* descorazonar, desalentar, desanimar
dishev·el [dɪ'ʃɛvəl] *v* (*pret* & *pp* -eled o -elled; *ger* -eling o -elling) desgreñar, desmelenar

dishonest [dɪs'ɑnɪst] *adj* no honrado, ímprobo

dishones·ty [dɪs'ɑnɪsti] *s* (*pl* -**ties**) falta de honradez, improbidad

dishonor [dɪs'ɑnər] *s* deshonra, deshonor *m* ‖ *tr* deshonrar, deshonorar; (com) no aceptar, no pagar

dishonorable [dɪs'ɑnərəbəl] *adj* ignominioso, deshonroso

dish'pan' *s* paila de lavar la vajilla

dish rack *s* escurreplatos *m*

dish'rag' *s* albero

dish'tow'el *s* paño para secar platos

dish'wash'er *s* (*person*) fregona; (*machine*) lavaplatos *m*

dish'wa'ter *s* agua de lavar platos, agua sucia

disillusion [ˌdɪsɪ'luʒən] *s* desilusión ‖ *tr* desilusionar

disillusionment [ˌdɪsɪ'luʒənmənt] *s* desilusión

disinclination [dɪsˌɪnklɪ'neʃən] *s* aversión, desafición

disinclined [ˌdɪsɪn'klaɪnd] *adj* desinclinado

disinfect [ˌdɪsɪn'fɛkt] *tr* desinfectar, desinficionar

disinfectant [ˌdɪsɪn'fɛktənt] *adj* & *s* desinfectante *m*

disingenuous [ˌdɪsɪn'dʒɛnju·əs] *adj* insincero, poco ingenuo

disinherit [ˌdɪsɪn'hɛrɪt] *tr* desheredar

disintegrate [dɪs'ɪntɪˌgret] *tr* desagregar, desintegrar ‖ *intr* desagregarse, desintegrarse

disintegration [dɪsˌɪntɪ'greʃən] *s* desagregación, desintegración

disin·ter [ˌdɪsɪn'tʌr] *v* (*pret & pp* -**terred**; *ger* -**terring**) *tr* desenterrar

disinterested [dɪs'ɪntəˌrɛstɪd] o [dɪs'ɪntrɪstɪd] *adj* desinteresado

disinterestedness [dɪs'ɪntəˌrɛstɪdnɪs] o [dɪs'ɪntrɪstɪdnɪs] *s* desinterés *m*

disjunctive [dɪs'dʒʌŋktɪv] *adj* disyuntivo

disk [dɪsk] *s* disco

disk jockey *s* (rad) locutor *m* de un programa de discos

dislike [dɪs'laɪk] *s* aversión, antipatía; **to take a dislike for** cobrar aversión a ‖ *tr* desamar

dislocate ['dɪslo·ˌket] *tr* dislocar, dislocarse (*un hueso*)

dislodge [dɪs'lɑdʒ] *tr* desalojar

disloyal [dɪs'lɔɪ·əl] *adj* desleal

disloyal·ty [dɪs'lɔɪ·əlti] *s* (*pl* -**ties**) deslealtad

dismal ['dɪzməl] *adj* lúgubre, tenebroso; terrible, espantoso

dismantle [dɪs'mæntəl] *tr* desarmar, desmontar

dismay [dɪs'me] *s* consternación ‖ *tr* consternar

dismember [dɪs'mɛmbər] *tr* desmembrar

dismiss [dɪs'mɪs] *tr* despedir, destituir; desechar; alejar del pensamiento, echar en olvido

dismissal [dɪs'mɪsəl] *s* despedida, destitución

dismount [dɪs'maunt] *tr* desmontar ‖ *intr* desmontarse

disobedience [ˌdɪsə'bidɪ·əns] *s* desobediencia

disobedient [ˌdɪsə'bidɪ·ənt] *adj* desobediente

disobey [ˌdɪsə'be] *tr & intr* desobedecer

disorder [dɪs'ɔrdər] *s* desorden *m* ‖ *tr* desordenar

disorderly [dɪs'ɔrdərli] *adj* desordenado; alborotador, revoltoso

disorderly conduct *s* conducta contra el orden público

disorderly house *s* burdel *m*, lupanar *m*

disorganize [dɪs'ɔrgəˌnaɪz] *tr* desorganizar

disown [dɪs'on] *tr* desconocer, repudiar

disparage [dɪs'pærɪdʒ] *tr* desacreditar, desdorar

disparagement [dɪs'pærɪdʒmənt] *s* descrédito, desdoro

disparate ['dɪspərɪt] *adj* disparejo

dispari·ty [dɪs'pærɪti] *s* (*pl* -**ties**) disparidad

dispassionate [dɪs'pæʃənɪt] *adj* desapasionado

dispatch [dɪs'pætʃ] *s* despacho ‖ *tr* despachar; (coll) despabilar (*una comida*)

dis·pel [dɪs'pɛl] *v* (*pret & pp* -**pelled**; *ger* -**pelling**) *tr* desvanecer, disipar

dispensa·ry [dɪs'pɛnsəri] *s* (*pl* -**ries**) dispensario

dispense [dɪs'pɛns] *tr* dispensar (*medicamentos*); administrar (*justicia*); expender (*p.ej.*, gasolina); (*to exempt*) eximir ‖ *intr* — **to dispense with** deshacerse de; pasar sin, prescindir de

disperse [dɪs'pʌrs] *tr* dispersar ‖ *intr* dispersarse

displace [dɪs'ples] *tr* remover, trasladar; despedir, deponer; reemplazar; desplazar (*un volumen de agua*)

displaced person *s* persona desplazada

display [dɪs'ple] *s* despliegue *m*; exhibición, exposición; ostentación ‖ *tr* (*to unfold; to reveal*) desplegar; (*to exhibit, show*) exhibir, exponer; (*to show ostentatiously*) ostentar

display cabinet *s* vitrina, escaparate *m*

display window *s* escaparate *m* de tienda

displease [dɪs'pliz] *tr* desagradar, disgustar, desplacer

displeasing [dɪs'plizɪŋ] *adj* desagradable

displeasure [dɪs'plɛʒər] *s* desagrado, disgusto, desplacer *m*

disposable [dɪs'pozəbəl] *adj* (*available for any use*) disponible; (*made to be thrown away after serving its purpose*) desechable, descartable

disposal [dɪs'pozəl] *s* disposición; donación, liquidación, venta; **at the disposal of** a la disposición de; **to have at one's disposal** disponer de

dispose [dɪs'poz] *tr* disponer; inducir, mover ‖ *intr* disponer; **to dispose of** disponer de; deshacerse de; dar, vender; acabar con

disposition [ˌdɪspəˈzɪʃən] *s* disposición; índole *f*, genio, natural *m;* ajuste *m*, arreglo; venta

dispossess [ˌdɪspəˈzes] *tr* desposeer; *(to evict, oust)* desahuciar

disproof [dɪsˈpruf] *s* confutación, refutación

disproportionate [ˌdɪsprəˈpɔrʃənɪt] *adj* desproporcionado

disprove [dɪsˈpruv] *tr* confutar, refutar

dispute [dɪsˈpjut] *s* disputa; **beyond dispute** sin disputa; **in dispute** disputado || *tr & intr* disputar

disquali•fy [dɪsˈkwɑlɪˌfaɪ] *v (pret & pp -fied)* descalificar, desclasificar

disquiet [dɪsˈkwaɪ•ət] *s* desasosiego, inquietud || *tr* desasosegar, inquietar

disregard [ˌdɪsrɪˈgɑrd] *s* desatención, desaire *m* || *tr* desatender, desairar, pasar por alto

disrepair [ˌdɪsrɪˈpɛr] *s* desconcierto, descompostura

disreputable [dɪsˈrɛpjətəbəl] *adj* desacreditado, de mala fama; raído, usado, desaliñado

disrepute [ˌdɪsrɪˈpjut] *s* descrédito, mala fama; **to bring into disrepute** desacreditar, dar mala fama a

disrespect [ˌdɪsrɪˈspɛkt] *s* desacato || *tr* desacatar

disrespectful [ˌdɪsrɪˈspɛktfəl] *adj* irrespetuoso

disrobe [dɪsˈrob] *tr* desnudar || *intr* desnudarse

disrupt [dɪsˈrʌpt] *tr* romper; *(to throw into disorder)* desbaratar

dissatisfaction [ˌdɪssætɪsˈfækʃən] *s* desagrado, descontento

dissatisfied [dɪsˈsætɪsˌfaɪd] *adj* descontento

dissatis•fy [dɪsˈsætɪsˌfaɪ] *v (pret & pp -fied)* tr descontentar

dissect [dɪˈsɛkt] *tr* disecar

dissemble [dɪˈsɛmbəl] *tr* disimular || *intr* disimular; obrar hipócritamente

disseminate [dɪˈsɛmɪˌnet] *tr* diseminar, difundir

dissension [dɪˈsɛnʃən] *s* disensión

dissent [dɪˈsɛnt] *s* disensión; *(nonconformity)* disidencia || *intr* disentir; *(from doctrine or authority)* disidir

dissenter [dɪˈsɛntər] *s* disidente *mf*

disservice [dɪsˈsʌrvɪs] *s* desservicio

dissidence [ˈdɪsɪdəns] *s* disidencia

dissident [ˈdɪsɪdənt] *adj & s* disidente *mf*

dissimilar [dɪˈsɪmɪlər] *adj* disímil, desemejante

dissimilate [dɪˈsɪmɪˌlet] *tr* disimilar || *intr* disimilarse

dissimulate [dɪˈsɪmjəˌlet] *tr & intr* disimular

dissipate [ˈdɪsɪˌpet] *tr* disipar || *intr* disiparse; entregarse a la disipación

dissipated [ˈdɪsɪˌpetɪd] *adj* disipado, disoluto

dissipation [ˌdɪsɪˈpeʃən] *s* disipación

dissociate [dɪˈsoʃɪˌet] *tr* disociar

dissolute [ˈdɪsəˌlut] *adj* disoluto

dissolution [ˌdɪsəˈluʃən] *s* disolución

dissolve [dɪˈzɑlv] *tr* disolver || *intr (to*

have *the power of dissolving)* disolver; *(to pass into a liquid)* disolverse

dissonance [ˈdɪsənəns] *s* disonancia

dissuade [dɪˈswed] *tr* disuadir

dissyllabic [ˌdɪsɪˈlæbɪk] *adj* disílabo, disilábico

dissyllable [dɪˈsɪləbəl] *s* disílabo

dist. *abbr* distance, distinguish, district

distaff [ˈdɪstæf] o [ˈdɪstɑf] *s* rueca

distaff side *s* rama femenina de la familia

distance [ˈdɪstəns] *s* distancia; **at a distance** a distancia; **in the distance** a lo lejos; **to keep at a distance** no permitir familiaridades; **to keep one's distance** mantenerse a distancia

distant [ˈdɪstənt] *adj* distante; *(relative)* lejano; *(not familiar)* frío, indiferente

distaste [dɪsˈtest] *s* aversión, repugnancia

distasteful [dɪsˈtestfəl] *adj* desagradable, repugnante

distemper [dɪsˈtɛmpər] *s* enfermedad; *(of dogs)* moquillo

distend [dɪsˈtɛnd] *tr* ensanchar, distender || *intr* ensancharse, distender

distension [dɪsˈtɛnʃən] *s* ensanche *m*, distensión

distill [dɪsˈtɪl] *tr* destilar

distillation [ˌdɪstɪˈleʃən] *s* destilación

distiller•y [dɪsˈtɪlərɪ] *s (pl -ies)* destilería, destilatorio

distinct [dɪsˈtɪŋkt] *adj* distinto; cierto, indudable; *(not blurred)* nítido, bien definido

distinction [dɪsˈtɪŋkʃən] *s* distinción; *(distinguishing characteristic)* distintivo

distinctive [dɪsˈtɪŋktɪv] *adj* distintivo

distinguish [dɪsˈtɪŋgwɪʃ] *tr* distinguir

distinguished [dɪsˈtɪŋgwɪʃt] *adj* distinguido

distort [dɪsˈtɔrt] *tr* deformar, torcer; *(the truth)* falsear

distortion [dɪsˈtɔrʃən] *s* deformación, torcimiento; *(of the truth)* falseamiento; *(rad)* deformación, distorsión

distract [dɪsˈtrækt] *tr* distraer

distraction [dɪsˈtrækʃən] *s* distracción

distraught [dɪsˈtrɔt] *adj* trastornado, perplejo, aturdido

distress [dɪsˈtres] *s* pena, aflicción, angustia; infortunio, peligro || *tr* apenar, afligir, angustiar

distressing [dɪsˈtresɪŋ] *adj* penoso, angustioso

distress signal *s* señal *f* de socorro

distribute [dɪsˈtrɪbjut] *tr* distribuir, repartir

distribution [ˌdɪstrɪˈbjuʃən] *s* distribución, repartimiento

distributor [dɪsˈtrɪbjətər] *s* distribuidor *m;* (aut) distribuidor

district [ˈdɪstrɪkt] *s* comarca, región; *(of a city)* barrio; *(administrative division)* distrito || *tr* dividir en distritos

district attorney *s* fiscal *m*

distrust [dɪs'trʌst] *s* desconfianza ‖ *tr* desconfiar de
distrustful [dɪs'trʌstfəl] *adj* desconfiado
disturb [dɪs'tʌrb] *tr* disturbar, incomodar, molestar; desordenar, revolver; inquietar, dejar perplejo; perturbar (*el orden público*)
disturbance [dɪs'tʌrbəns] *s* disturbio, molestia; desorden *m;* inquietud; tumulto, trastorno
disuse [dɪs'jus] *s* desuso
ditch [dɪtʃ] *s* zanja ‖ *tr* zanjar; echar en una zanja; (slang) deshacerse de ‖ *intr* amarar forzosamente
ditch reed *s* carrizo
dither ['dɪðər] *s* agitación, temblor; **to be in a dither** (coll) estar muy agitado
dit·to ['dɪto] *s* (*pl* -tos) ídem *m; (ditto symbol)* íd.; copia, duplicado ‖ *tr* copiar, duplicar
ditto mark *s* la sigla " (*es decir:* íd.)
dit·ty ['dɪti] *s* (*pl* -ties) cancioneta
div. *abbr* **dividend, division**
diva ['divə] *s* (mus) diva
divan ['daɪvæn] o [dɪ'væn] *s* diván *m*
dive [daɪv] *s* zambullida; (*of a submarine*) sumersión; (aer) picado; (coll) leonera, tasca ‖ *v* (*pret & pp* **dived** o **dove** [dov]) *intr* zambullirse; (*to work as a diver*) bucear; sumergirse (*un submarino*); (aer) picar
dive'-bomb' *tr & intr* bombardear en picado
dive bombing *s* bombardeo en picado
diver ['daɪvər] *s* zambullidor *m; (person who works under water)* escafandrista *mf*, buzo; (orn) zambullidor *m*
diverge [dɪ'vʌrdʒ] o [daɪ'vʌrdʒ] *intr* divergir
divers ['daɪvərz] *adj* diversos, varios
diverse [daɪ'vʌrs], [daɪ'vʌrs] o ['daɪvʌrs] *adj* (*different*) diverso; (*of various kinds*) variado
diversification [dɪ‚vʌrsɪfɪ'keʃən] o [daɪ‚vʌrsɪfɪ'keʃən] *s* diversificación
diversi·fy [dɪ'vʌrsɪ‚faɪ] o [daɪ'vʌrsɪ‚faɪ] *v* (*pret & pp* -fied) *tr* diversificar ‖ *intr* diversificarse
diversion [dɪ'vʌrʒən] o [daɪ'vʌrʒən] *s* diversión
diversi·ty [dɪ'vʌrsɪti] o [daɪ'vʌrsɪti] *s* (*pl* -ties) diversidad
divert [dɪ'vʌrt] o [daɪ'vʌrt] *tr* apartar, divertir; (*to entertain*) divertir, entretener; (mil) divertir
diverting [dɪ'vʌrtɪŋ] o [daɪ'vʌrtɪŋ] *adj* divertido
divest [dɪ'vɛst] o [daɪ'vɛst] *tr* desnudar; despojar, desposeer; **to divest oneself of** desposeerse de
divide [dɪ'vaɪd] *s* (geog) divisoria ‖ *tr* dividir ‖ *intr* dividirse
dividend ['dɪvɪ‚dɛnd] *s* dividendo
dividers [dɪ'vaɪdərz] *spl* compás *m* de división
divination [‚dɪvɪ'neʃən] *s* adivinación
divine [dɪ'vaɪn] *adj* divino ‖ *s* sacerdote *m*, clérigo ‖ *tr* adivinar

diving ['daɪvɪŋ] *s* zambullida; buceo
diving bell *s* campana de buzo
diving board *s* trampolín *m*
diving suit *s* escafandra
divining rod [dɪ'vaɪnɪŋ] *s* vara de adivinar; (*ostensibly to discover water or metals*) vara buscadora
divini·ty [dɪ'vɪnɪti] *s* (*pl* -ties) divinidad; teología; **the Divinity** Dios *m*
division [dɪ'vɪʒən] *s* división
divisor [dɪ'vaɪzər] *s* (math) divisor *m*
divorce [dɪ'vors] *s* divorcio; **to get a divorce** divorciarse ‖ *tr* divorciar (*los cónyuges*); divorciarse de (*la mujer o el marido*) ‖ *intr* divorciarse
divorcee [dɪvor'si] *s* persona divorciada; mujer divorciada
divulge [dɪ'vʌldʒ] *tr* divulgar, revelar
dizziness ['dɪzɪnɪs] *s* vértigo; confusión, perplejidad
diz·zy ['dɪzi] *adj* (*comp* -zier; *super* -ziest) (*suffering or causing dizziness*) vertiginoso; confuso, perplejo; aturdido, incauto; (coll) tonto
do. *abbr* **ditto**
do [du] *v* (*tercera persona* **does** [dʌz]; *pret* **did** [dɪd]; *pp* **done** [dʌn]) *tr* hacer; resolver (*un problema*); recorrer (*cierta distancia*); cumplir con (*un deber*); aprender (*una lección*); componer (*la cama*); tocar (*el cabello*); rendir (*homenaje*); **to do one's best** hacer todo lo posible; **to do over** volver a hacer; repetir; renovar; **to do right by** tratar bien; **to do someone out of something** (coll) defraudar algo a alguien; **to do to death** despachar, matar; **to do up** empaquetar; poner en orden; almidonar y planchar (*una camisa*) ‖ *intr* actuar, obrar; conducirse; servir, ser suficiente; estar, hallarse; **how do you do?** ¿cómo está Vd.?; **that will do** eso sirve, eso es bastante; no digas más; **to have done** haber terminado; **to have done with** no tener más que ver con; **to have nothing to do with** no tener nada que ver con; **to have to do with** tratar de; **to do away with** suprimir; matar; **to do for** servir para; **to do well** salir bien; **to do without** pasar sin ‖ *v aux* úsase 1) en oraciones interrogativas: **Do you speak Spanish?** ¿Habla Vd. español?; 2) en oraciones negativas: **I do not speak Spanish** No hablo español; 3) para substituir a otro verbo en oraciones elípticas: **Did you go to church this morning? Yes, I did** ¿Fué Vd. a la iglesia esta mañana? Sí, fuí; 4) para dar más energía a la oración: **I do believe what you told me** Yo sí creo lo que me dijo Vd.; 5) en inversiones después de ciertos adverbios: **Seldom does he come to see me** él rara vez viene a verme; 6) en tono suplicante con el imperativo: **Do come in** pase Vd., por favor
docile ['dɑsɪl] *adj* dócil
dock [dak] *s* (*wharf*) muelle *m; (wa-*

terway between two piers) dársena; (*area including piers and waterways*) puerto de mar; muñón *m* de cola; (law) tribuna de los acusados || *tr* (naut) atracar en el muelle; derrabar, descolar (*a un animal*); reducir o suprimir (*el salario*) || *intr* (naut) atracar

dockage ['dɑkɪdʒ] *s* entrada en un puerto; (*charges*) muellaje *m*

docket ['dɑkɪt] *s* actas, orden *m* del día; lista de causas pendientes; **on the docket** (coll) pendiente, entre manos

dock hand *s* portuario

dock'yard' *s* arsenal *m*, astillero

doctor ['dɑktər] *s* doctor *m*; (*physician*) médico || *tr* medicinar; (coll) componer, reparar || *intr* (coll) ejercer la medicina; (coll) tomar medicinas

doctorate ['dɑktərɪt] *s* doctorado

doctrine ['dɑktrɪn] *s* doctrina

document ['dɑkjəmənt] *s* documento || ['dɑkjə,ment] *tr* documentar

documenta‧ry [,dɑkjə'mentəri] *adj* documental || *s* (*pl* -ries) documental *m*

documentation [,dɑkəmən'teʃən] *s* documentación

doddering ['dɑdərɪŋ] *adj* chocho, temblón

dodge [dɑdʒ] *s* esguince *m*, regate *m*; (fig) regate || *tr* evitar (*un golpe*); (fig) evitar mañosamente || *intr* regatear, hurtar el cuerpo; **to dodge around the corner** voltear la esquina

do‧do ['dodo] *s* (*pl* -dos o -does) (coll) inocente *m* de ideas anticuadas

doe [do] *s* cierva, gama, coneja

doeskin ['do,skɪn] *s* ante *m*, piel *f* de ante; tejido fino de lana

doff [dɑf] o [dɔf] *tr* quitarse (*el sombrero, la ropa*)

dog [dɔg] o [dɑg] *s* perro; **to go to the dogs** darse al abandono; **to put on the dog** (coll) darse ínfulas || *v* (*pret & pp* dogged; *ger* dogging) *tr* acosar, perseguir

dog'catch'er *s* lacero

dog days *spl* canícula, caniculares *mpl*

doge [dodʒ] *s* dux *m*

dogged ['dɔgɪd] o ['dɑgɪd] *adj* tenaz, terco

doggerel ['dɔgərəl] o ['dɑgərəl] *s* coplas de ciego

dog‧gy ['dɔgi] o ['dɑgi] *adj* (*comp* -gier; *super* -giest) emperejilado || *s* (*pl* -gies) perrito

dog'house' *s* perrera

dog in the manger *s* el perro del hortelano

dog Latin *s* latinajo, latín *m* de cocina

dogmatic [dɔg'mætɪk] o [dɑg'mætɪk] *adj* dogmático

dog racing *s* carreras de galgos

dog's-ear ['dɔgz,ɪr] o ['dɑgz,ɪr] *s* orejón *m*

dog show *s* exposición canina

dog's life *s* vida miserable

Dog Star *s* Canícula

dog'-tired' *adj* cansadísimo

dog'tooth' *s* (*pl* -teeth [,tiθ]) colmillo

dog track *s* galgódromo

dog'watch' *s* (naut) guardia de cuartillo

dog'wood' *s* cornejo

doi‧ly ['dɔɪli] *s* (*pl* -lies) pañito de adorno

doings ['du‧ɪŋz] *spl* acciones, obras, actividad

doldrums ['dɑldrəmz] *spl* (naut) calmas ecuatoriales; desanimación, inactividad

dole [dol] *s* limosna; subsidio a los desocupados || *tr* — **to dole out** distribuir en pequeñas porciones

doleful ['dolfəl] *adj* triste, lúgubre

doll [dɑl] *s* muñeca || *intr* — **to doll up** (slang) emperejilarse

dollar ['dɑlər] *s* dólar *m*

dollar mark *s* signo del dólar

dol‧ly ['dɑli] *s* (*pl* -lies) muñequita; (*low, wheeled frame for moving heavy loads*) gato rodante

dolphin ['dɑlfɪn] *s* delfín *m*

dolt [dolt] *s* bobalicón *m*

doltish ['doltɪʃ] *adj* bobalicón

dom. *abbr* **domestic, dominion**

domain [do'men] *s* dominio; heredad, propiedad; (*of learning*) campo

dome [dom] *s* cúpula, domo

dome light *s* (aut) lámpara de techo

domestic [də'mestɪk] *adj & s* doméstico

domesticate [də'mestɪ,ket] *tr* domesticar

domicile ['dɑmɪsɪl] o ['dɑmɪ,saɪl] *s* domicilio || *tr* domiciliar

dominance ['dɑmɪnəns] *s* dominación

dominant ['dɑmɪnənt] *adj & s* dominante *f*

dominate ['dɑmɪ,net] *tr & intr* dominar

domination [,dɑmɪ'neʃən] *s* dominación

domineer [,dɑmɪ'nɪr] *intr* dominar

domineering [,dɑmɪ'nɪrɪŋ] *adj* dominante, mandón

Dominican [də'mɪnɪkən] *adj & s* dominicano

dominion [də'mɪnjən] *s* dominio

domi‧no ['dɑmɪ,no] *s* (*pl* -noes o -nos) (*costume*) dominó *m*; antifaz *m*; persona que lleva dominó; ficha (*del juego de dominó*); **dominoes** *ssg* dominó (*juego*)

don [dɑn] *s* caballero, señor *m*, personaje *m* de alta categoría; (coll) preceptor *m*, socio de uno de los colegios de las Universidades de Oxford y Cambridge || *v* (*pret & pp* donned; *ger* donning) *tr* ponerse (*el sombrero, la ropa*)

donate ['donet] *tr* dar, donar

donation [do'neʃən] *s* donación

done [dʌn] *adj* hecho, terminado; cansado, rendido; bien asado

done for *adj* (coll) cansado, rendido, agotado; (coll) arruinado, destruído; (coll) fuera de combate; (coll) muerto

donjon ['dʌndʒən] o ['dɑndʒən] *s* torre *f* del homenaje

donkey ['daŋki] s asno, burro
donnish ['danɪʃ] adj magistral, pedantesco
donor ['donər] s donador m
doodle ['dudəl] tr & intr borrajear
doom [dum] s ruina, perdición, muerte f; condena, juicio; juicio final; hado, destino || tr condenar; sentenciar a muerte; predestinar a la ruina, a la muerte
doomsday ['dumz,de] s día m del juicio final; día del juicio
door [dor] s puerta; (of a carriage or automobile) portezuela; (one part of a double door) hoja, batiente m; behind closed doors a puertas cerradas; to see to the door acompañar a la puerta
door'bell' s campanilla de puerta, timbre m de puerta
door check s amortiguador m, cierre m de puerta
door'frame' s bastidor m de puerta, marco de puerta
door'head' s dintel m
door'jamb' s jamba de puerta
door'knob' s botón m de puerta, pomo de puerta
door knocker s aldaba
door latch s pestillo
door·man ['dormən] s (pl -men [mən]) portero; (one who helps people in and out of cars) abrecoches m
door'mat' s felpudo de puerta
door'nail' s clavo de adorno para puertas; **dead as a doornail** (coll) muerto sin duda alguna
door'post' s jamba de puerta
door scraper s limpiabarros m
door'sill' s umbral m
door'step' s escalón m delante de la puerta; escalera exterior
door'stop' s tope m de puerta
door'way' s puerta, portal m
dope [dop] s grasa lubricante; (aer) barniz m, nobabia; (slang) bobo, tonto; (slang) informes mpl; (slang) narcótico || tr (slang) narcotizar, drogar; **to dope out** (slang) descifrar
dope fiend s (slang) toxicómano
dope sheet s (slang) hoja confidencial sobre los caballos de carreras
dormant ['dormənt] adj durmiente, latente
dormer window ['dormər] s buharda, buhardilla
dormi·to·ry ['dormɪ,tori] s (pl -ries) dormitorio común
dor·mouse ['dor,maus] s (pl -mice [,maɪs]) lirón m
dosage ['dosɪdʒ] s dosificación
dose [dos] s dosis f; (coll) mal trago ‖ tr medicinar; dosificar (un medicamento)
dossier ['dasɪ,e] s expediente m
dot [dat] s punto; **on the dot** (coll) en punto ‖ v (pret & pp **dotted**; ger **dotting**) tr (to make with dots) puntear; poner punto a; **to dot one's i's** poner los puntos sobre las íes
dotage ['dotɪdʒ] s chochera, chochez f; **to be in one's dotage** chochear

dotard ['dotərd] s viejo chocho
dote [dot] intr chochear; **to dote on** estar chocho por
doting ['dotɪŋ] adj chocho
dots and dashes spl (telg) puntos y rayas
dotted line ['datɪd] s línea de puntos; **to sign on the dotted line** firmar ciegamente
double ['dʌbəl] adj doble ‖ adv doble; dos juntos ‖ s doble m, duplo (m); (mov, theat) doble mf; **doubles** (tennis) juego de dobles ‖ tr doblar; ser el doble de; (bridge) doblar ‖ intr doblarse; (mov, theat, bridge) doblar; **to double up** doblarse en dos; ocupar una misma habitación, dormir en una misma cama (dos personas)
double-barreled ['dʌbəl'bærəld] adj de dos cañones; (fig) para dos fines
double bass [bes] s contrabajo
double bassoon s contrabajón m
double bed s cama de matrimonio
double-breasted ['dʌbəl'brestɪd] adj cruzado, de dos pechos
double chin s papada
dou'ble-cross' tr traicionar (a un cómplice)
double date s cita de dos parejas
doub'le-deal'er s persona doble
double-edged ['dʌbəl'ɛdʒd] adj de dos filos
double entry s (com) partida. doble
double feature s (mov) programa m doble, programa de dos películas de largo metraje
double-header ['dʌbəl'hedər] s tren m con dos locomotoras; (baseball) dos partidos jugados sucesivamente
double-jointed ['dʌbəl'dʒɔɪntɪd] adj de articulaciones dobles
dou'ble-park' tr & intr aparcar en doble fila
dou'ble-quick' adj & adv a paso ligero ‖ s paso ligero ‖ intr marchar a paso ligero
doublet ['dʌblɪt] s (close-fitting jacket) jubón m; (counterfeit stone; each of two words having the same origin) doblete m
double talk s (coll) galimatías m; (coll) habla ambigua para engañar
double time s pago doble por horas extraordinarias de trabajo; (mil) paso redoblado
doubleton ['dʌbəltən] s doblete m
double track s doble vía
doubt [daut] s duda; **beyond doubt** sin duda; **if in doubt** en caso de duda; **no doubt** sin duda ‖ tr dudar, dudar de ‖ intr dudar
doubter ['dautər] s incrédulo
doubtful ['dautfəl] adj dudoso
doubtless ['dautlɪs] adj indudable ‖ adv sin duda; probablemente
douche [duʃ] s ducha; (instrument) jeringa ‖ tr duchar ‖ intr ducharse
dough [do] s masa, pasta; (money) (slang) pasta
dough'boy' s (coll) soldado norteamericano de infantería

dough'nut' s rosquilla, buñuelo

dough·ty ['dauti] adj (comp -tier; super -tiest) (hum) fuerte, valiente

dough·y ['do·i] adj (comp -ier; super -iest) pastoso

dour [daur] o [dur] adj triste, melancólico, austero

douse [daus] tr empapar, mojar, salpicar; (slang) apagar (la luz)

dove [dʌv] s paloma

dovecote ['dʌv,kot] s palomar m

dove'tail' s cola de milano, cola de pato || tr ensamblar a cola de milano, ensamblar a cola de pato; (to make fit) encajar || intr (to fit) encajar; concordar, corresponder

dowager ['dau·ədʒər] s viuda con título o bienes que proceden del marido, p.ej., **dowager duchess** duquesa viuda; (coll) matrona, señora anciana respetable

dow·dy ['daudi] adj (comp -dier; super -diest) desaliñado

dow·el ['dau·əl] s clavija || v (pret & pp -eled o -elled; ger -eling o -elling) tr enclavijar

dower ['dau·ər] s (widow's portion) viudedad; (marriage portion) dote m & f; (natural gift) prenda || tr señalar viudedad a; dotar

down [daun] adj descendente; abatido, triste; enfermo, malo; acostado, echado; (money, payment) anticipado; (storage battery) agotado || adv abajo; hacia abajo; en tierra; al sur; por escrito; al contado; **down and out** arruinado; sin blanca; **down from** desde; **down on one's knees** de rodillas; **down to** hasta; **down under** entre los antípodas; **down with . . . !** ¡abajo . . . !; **to get down to work** aplicarse resueltamente al trabajo; **to go down** bajar; **to lie down** acostarse; **to sit down** sentarse || prep bajando; **down the river** río abajo; **down the street** calle abajo || s (of fruit and human body) vello; (of birds) plumón m; descenso; revés m de fortuna; (sand hill) duna || tr derribar; (coll) tragar

down'cast' adj cariacontecido

down'fall' s caída, ruina; chaparrón m; nevazo

down'grade' adj (coll) pendiente, en declive || adv (coll) cuesta abajo || s bajada, declive m; **to be on the downgrade** decaer, declinar || tr disminuir la categoría de

downhearted ['daun,hartɪd] adj abatido, desanimado

down'hill' adj pendiente || adv cuesta abajo; **to go downhill** ir cabeza abajo

down'pour' s aguacero, chaparrón m

down'right' adj absoluto, categórico; franco; claro || adv absolutamente

down'stairs' adj de abajo || adv abajo || s piso inferior, pisos inferiores; (the help) la servidumbre

down'stream' adv aguas abajo, río abajo

down'stroke' s carrera descendente

down'town' adj céntrico || adv al centro de la ciudad, en el centro de la ciudad || s barrios céntricos, calles céntricas

down train s tren m descendente

down'trend' s tendencia a la baja

downtrodden ['daun,tradən] adj pisoteado, oprimido

downward ['daunwərd] adj descendente || adv hacia abajo; hacia una época posterior

down·y ['dauni] adj (comp -ier; super -iest) plumoso, felpudo, velloso; suave, blando

dow·ry ['dauri] s (pl -ries) dote m & f

doz. abbr **dozen**

doze [doz] s duermevela, sueño ligero || intr dormitar

dozen ['dʌzən] s docena

doz·y ['dozi] adj soñoliento

D.P. abbr **displaced person**

dpt. abbr **department**

dr. abbr **debtor, drawer, dram**

Dr. abbr **debtor, Doctor**

drab [dræb] adj (comp **drabber**; super **drabbest**) gris amarillento; monótono || s gris amarillento; ramera; mujer desaliñada

drach·ma ['drækmə] s (pl -mas o -mae [mi]) dracma

draft [dræft] o [draft] s corriente f de aire; (pulling; current of air in a chimney) tiro; (sketch, outline) bosquejo; (first form of a writing) borrador m; (drink) bebida, trago; (com) giro, letra de cambio, libranza; aire inspirado; (naut) calado; (mil) conscripción, quinta; **drafts** damas, juego de damas; **on draft** a presión; **to be exempted from the draft** redimirse de las quintas || tr dibujar; bosquejar; hacer un borrador de; redactar (un documento); (mil) quintar; **to be drafted** (mil) ir a quintas

draft age s edad f de quintas

draft beer s cerveza a presión

draft board s (mil) junta de reclutamiento

draft call s llamada a quintas

draft dodger ['dadʒər] s emboscado

draftee [,dræf'ti] o [,draf'ti] s conscripto, quinto

draft horse s caballo de tiro

drafting room s sala de dibujo

drafts·man ['dræftsmən] o ['draftsmən] s (pl -men [mən]) dibujante m; (man who draws up documents) redactor m; (in checkers) peón m

draft treaty s proyecto de convenio

draft·y ['dræfti] o ['drafti] adj (comp -ier; super -iest) airoso, con corrientes de aire

drag [dræg] s (sledge for conveying heavy bodies) narria; (on a cigarette) chupada; fumada; (naut) rastra; (aer) resistencia al avance; (fig) estorbo, impedimento; **to have a drag** (slang) tener buenas aldabas, tener enchufe || v (pret & pp **dragged**; ger **dragging**) tr arrastrar; (naut) rastrear || intr arrastrarse por el suelo; avanzar muy lentamente; decaer (el *interés*); **to drag on** ser interminable, prolongarse interminablemente

drag'net' *s* red barredera

dragon ['drægən] *s* dragón *m*

drag'on-fly' *s* (*pl* **-flies**) caballito del diablo, libélula

dragoon [drə'gun] *s* (*soldier*) dragón *m* ‖ *tr* tiranizar; forzar, constreñir

drain [dren] *s* dren *m*, desaguadero, desagüe *m*; (*surg*) dren *m*; (*source of continual expense*) (fig) desaguadero ‖ *tr* drenar, desaguar; avenar (*terrenos húmedos*); escurrir (*una vasija; un liquido*) ‖ *intr* desaguarse; escurrirse

drainage ['drenɪdʒ] *s* drenaje *m*, desagüe *m*

drain'board' *s* escurridero

drain cock *s* llave *f* de purga

drain'pipe' *s* tubo de desagüe, escurridero

drain plug *s* tapón *m* de desagüe; (aut) tapón de vaciado

drake [drek] *s* pato

dram [dræm] *s* dracma; trago de aguardiente

drama ['dramə] o ['dræmə] *s* drama *m*; (*art and genre*) dramática

dramatic [drə'mætɪk] *adj* dramático ‖ **dramatics** *ssg* representación de aficionados; *spl* obras representadas por aficionados

dramatist ['dræmətɪst] *s* dramático

dramatize ['dræmə,taɪz] *tr* dramatizar

dram'shop' *s* bar *m*, taberna

drape [drep] *s* cortina, colgadura; (*hang of a curtain, skirt, etc.*) caída ‖ *tr* cubrir con colgaduras; adornar con colgaduras; disponer los pliegues de (*una colgadura, una prenda de vestir*)

draper·y ['drepəri] *s* (*pl* **-ies**) colgaduras, ropaje *m*

drastic ['dræstɪk] *adj* drástico

draught [dræft] o [draft] *s* & *tr* var de **draft**

draught beer *s* cerveza a presión

draw [drɔ] *s* (*in a game or other contest*) empate *m*; (*in chess or checkers*) tablas; (*in a lottery*) sorteo; (*card drawn from the bank*) robo; (*of a drawbridge*) compuerta; (*of a chimney*) tiro ‖ *v* (*pret* **drew** [dru]; *pp* **drawn** [drɔn]) *tr* tirar (*una línea; alambre*); (*to attract*) tirar; (*to pull*) tirar de; derretir (*la mantequilla*); sacar (*un clavo, una espada, agua, una conclusión*); atraerse (*aplausos*); atraer (*a la gente*); aspirar (*el aire*); llamar (*la atención*); dar (*un suspiro*); correr (*una cortina*); cobrar (*un salario*); sacarse (*un premio*); empatar (*una partida*); robar (*fichas, naipes*); levantar (*un puente levadizo*); calar (*un buque cierta profundidad*); hacer (*una comparación*); consumir (*amperios*); (*to sketch in lines*) dibujar; (*to sketch in words*) redactar; (com) girar, librar; (com) devengar (*interés*); **to draw forth** hacer salir; **to draw off** sacar, extraer; trasegar (*un líquido*);

to draw on ocasionar, provocar; ponerse (*p.ej., los zapatos*); (com) girar a cargo de; **to draw oneself up** enderezarse con dignidad; **to draw out** (*to persuade to talk*) sonsacar, tirar de la lengua a; **to draw up** redactar (*un documento*); (mil) ordenar para el combate ‖ *intr* tirar, tirar bien (*una chimenea*); empatar; echar suertes; atraer mucha gente; dibujar; **to draw aside** apartarse; **to draw back** retroceder, retirarse; **to draw near** acercarse; acercarse a; **to draw to a close** estar para terminar; **to draw together** juntarse, unirse

draw'back' *s* desventaja, inconveniente *m*

draw'bridge' *s* puente levadizo

drawee [,drɔ'i] *s* girado, librado

drawer ['drɔ·ər] *s* dibujante *mf*; (com) girador *m*, librador *m* ‖ [drɔr] *s* cajón *m*, gaveta; **drawers** calzoncillos

drawing ['drɔ·ɪŋ] *s* dibujo; (*in a lottery*) sorteo

drawing board *s* tablero de dibujo

drawing card *s* polo de atracción popular

drawing room *s* sala, salón *m*

draw'knife' *s* (*pl* **-knives** [,naɪvz]) cuchilla de dos mangos

drawl [drɔl] *s* habla lenta y prolongada ‖ *tr* decir lenta y prolongadamente ‖ *intr* hablar lenta y prolongadamente

drawn butter [drɔn] *s* mantequilla derretida

drawn work *s* calado, deshilado

dray [dre] *s* carro fuerte, camión *m*; (*sledge*) narria

drayage ['dre·ɪdʒ] *s* acarreo

dread [drɛd] *adj* espantoso, terrible ‖ *s* pavor *m*, terror *m* ‖ *tr* & *intr* temer

dreadful ['drɛdfəl] *adj* espantoso, terrible; (coll) feo, desagradable

dread'naught' *s* (nav) gran buque acorazado

dream [drim] *s* sueño, ensueño; (*thing of great beauty*) sueño; (*fancy, illusion*) ensueño; **dream come true** sueño hecho realidad ‖ *v* (*pret* & *pp* **dreamed** o **dreamt** [drɛmt]) *tr* soñar; **to dream up** (coll) imaginar, inventar; ‖ *intr* soñar; **to dream of** soñar con

dreamer ['drimər] *s* soñador *m*

dream'land' *s* reino del ensueño

dream world *s* tierra de la fantasía

dream·y ['drimi] *adj* (*comp* **-ier**; *super* **-iest**) soñador; visionario; vago

drear·y ['drɪri] *adj* (*comp* **-ier**; *super* **-iest**) sombrío, triste; monótono, pesado

dredge [drɛdʒ] *s* draga ‖ *tr* dragar, rastrear; (culin) enharinar

dredger ['drɛdʒər] *s* draga (*barco*)

dredging ['drɛdʒɪŋ] *s* dragado

dregs [drɛgz] *spl* heces *fpl*; (*of society*) hez *f*

drench [drɛntʃ] *tr* mojar, empapar

dress [drɛs] *s* ropa, vestidos; vestido de mujer; (*skirt*) falda; traje *m* de

etiqueta; (of a bird) plumaje m ‖ tr
vestir; (to provide with clothing) trajear; peinar (el pelo); curar (una
herida); zurrar (el cuero); empavesar
(un barco); adornar, ataviar; adere-
zar, aliñar (los manjares); **to dress
down** (coll) reprender; **to get dressed**
vestirse ‖ intr (to put one's clothing
on) vestirse; (to wear clothes) vestir;
(mil) alinearse; **to dress up** vestirse
de etiqueta; ponerse de veinticinco
alfileres; disfrazarse

dress ball s baile m de etiqueta

dress coat s frac m

dresser ['dresər] s tocador m; cómoda
con espejo; (sideboard) aparador m;
to be a good dresser vestir con elegancia

dress form s maniquí m

dress goods spl géneros para vestidos

dressing ['dresɪŋ] s adorno; (for food)
aliño, salsa; (stuffing for fowl) relleno; (fertilizer) abono; (for a
wound) vendaje m

dress'ing-down' s (coll) repasata, regaño

dressing gown s bata, peinador m

dressing room s cuarto de vestir;
(theat) camarín m

dressing station s (mil) puesto de socorro

dressing table s tocador m

dress'mak'er s costurera, modista

dress'mak'ing s costura, modistería

dress rehearsal s ensayo general

dress shirt s camisa de pechera almido-
nada, camisa de pechera de encaje

dress shop s casa de modas

dress suit s traje m de etiqueta

dress tie s corbata de smoking, corbata
de frac

dress•y ['dresi] adj (comp **-ier;** super
-iest) (coll) elegante; (showy) acica-
lado, vistoso, peripuesto

dribble ['drɪbəl] s goteo; (coll) llovizna
‖ tr (sport) driblar ‖ intr gotear; (at
the mouth) babear; (sport) driblar

driblet ['drɪblɪt] s gotita; pedacito

dried beef s cecina

dried fig s higo paso

dried peach s orejón m

drier ['draɪ-ər] s enjugador m; (for
hair) secador m; (for clothes) secadora; (rack for drying clothes) tendedero (de ropa)

drift [drɪft] s movimiento; (of sand,
snow) montón m; (movement of
snow) ventisca; tendencia, dirección;
intención, sentido; (aer, naut) deriva; (rad, telv) desviación ‖ intr
flotar a la deriva; amontonarse (la
nieve); ventiscar; (aer, naut) derivar, ir a la deriva; (fig) vivir sin
rumbo

drift ice s hielo flotante

drift'wood' s madera flotante; madera
llevada por el agua; madera arro-
jada a la playa por el agua; (people)
vagos

drill [drɪl] s taladro; instrucción;
(fabric) dril m; (mil) ejercicio ‖ tr
taladrar; instruir; (mil) enseñar el

ejercicio a ‖ intr adiestrarse; (mil)
hacer el ejercicio

drill'mas'ter s amaestrador m; (mil)
instructor m

drill press s prensa taladradora

drink [drɪŋk] s bebida; **the drinks are
on the house!** ¡convida la casa! ‖ v
(pret **drank** [dræŋk]; pp **drunk**
[drʌŋk]) tr beber; beberse (su sueldo); **to drink down** beber de una
vez; **to drink in** beber (las palabras
de una persona); beberse (un libro);
aspirar (el aire) ‖ intr beber; **to
drink out of** beber de o en; **to drink
to the health of** beber a o por la
salud de

drinkable ['drɪŋkəbəl] adj bebedizo,
potable

drinker ['drɪŋkər] s bebedor m

drinking ['drɪŋkɪŋ] s (el) beber

drinking cup s taza para beber

drinking fountain s fuente f para beber

drinking song s canción báquica, canción de taberna

drinking trough s abrevadero

drinking water s agua para beber

drip [drɪp] s goteo; gotas ‖ v (pret &
pp **dripped;** ger **dripping**) intr caer
gota a gota, gotear

drip coffee s café m de maquinilla

drip'-dry' adj de lava y pon

drip pan s colector m de aceite

drive [draɪv] s paseo en coche; calzada; fuerza, vigor m; urgencia;
campaña vigorosa; venta a bajo precio; (aut) tracción (delantera o trasera); (mach) transmisión, mando ‖
v (pret **drove** [drov]; pp **driven**
['drɪvən]) tr conducir, guiar, manejar (un automóvil); clavar, hincar
(un clavo); arrear (a las bestias); (in
a carriage or auto) llevar (a una
persona); empujar, impeler; estimular; forzar, compeler; obligar a trabajar mucho; (sport) golpear con
gran fuerza; **to drive away** ahuyentar; **to drive back** rechazar; **to drive
mad** volver loco ‖ intr ir en coche;
to drive at aspirar a; querer decir; **to
drive hard** trabajar mucho; **to drive
in** entrar en coche; entrar en (un
sitio) en coche; **to drive on the right**
circular por la derecha; **to drive out**
salir en coche; **to drive up** llegar en
coche

drive-in movie theater ['draɪv‚ɪn] s
auto-teatro

drive-in restaurant s restaurante m
donde los clientes no necesitan dejar sus coches

driv•el ['drɪvəl] s (slobber) baba;
(nonsense) bobería ‖ v (pret **-eled** o
-elled; ger **-eling** o **-elling**) intr babear; (to talk nonsense) bobear

driver ['draɪvər] s conductor m; (of a
carriage) cochero; (of a locomotive)
maquinista m; (of pack animals)
arriero

driver's license s carnet m de chófer,
permiso de conducir

drive shaft s árbol m de mando, eje m
motor

drive'way' s calzada; camino de entrada para coches

drive wheel s rueda motriz

drive'-your-self' service s alquiler m sin chófer

driving school s auto-escuela

drizzle ['drɪzəl] s llovizna ‖ intr lloviznar

droll [drol] adj chusco, gracioso

dromedar-y ['dramə‚deri] s (pl -ies) dromedario

drone [dron] s zángano; (buzz, hum) zumbido; (of bagpipe) bordón m, roncón m; avión radiodirigido ‖ tr decir monótonamente ‖ intr hablar monótonamente; (to live in idleness) zanganear; (to buzz, hum) zumbar

drool [drul] s (slobber) baba; (slang) bobería ‖ intr babear; (slang) bobear

droop [drup] s inclinación ‖ intr caer, colgar; inclinarse; marchitarse; abatirse; encamarse (el grano)

drooping ['drupɪŋ] adj (eyelid, shoulder) caído

drop [drap] s gota; (slope) pendiente f; (earring) pendiente m; (in temperature) descenso; (of supplies from an airplane) lanzamiento; (trap door) escotillón m; (gallows) horca; (lozenge) pastilla; (small amount) chispa; (slit for letters) buzón m; (curtain) telón m; a drop in the bucket una gota en el mar ‖ v (pret & pp dropped; ger dropping) tr dejar caer; echar (una carta) al buzón; bajar (una cortina); soltar (una indirecta); escribir (una esquela); omitir, suprimir; abandonar, dejar; echar (el ancla); borrar de la lista (a un alumno); lanzar (bombas o suministros de un avión) ‖ intr caer; bajar; cesar, terminar; to drop dead caer muerto; to drop in entrar al pasar, visitar de paso; to drop off desaparecer; quedarse dormido; morir de repente; to drop out desaparecer; retirarse; darse de baja

drop curtain s telón m

drop hammer s martinete m

drop'-leaf' table s mesa de hoja plegadiza

drop'light' s lámpara colgante

drop'out' s fracasado, desertor m escolar; to become a dropout ahorcar los libros

dropper ['drapər] s cuentagotas m

drop shutter s obturador m de guillotina

dropsical ['drapsɪkəl] adj hidrópico

dropsy ['drapsi] s hidropesía

drop table s mesa perezosa

dross [drɔs] o [dras] s (of metals) escoria; (fig) escoria, hez f

drought [draut] s (long period of dry weather) sequía; (dryness) sequedad

drove [drov] s manada, rebaño, hato; gentío, multitud

drover ['drovər] s ganadero

drown [draun] tr anegar, ahogar ‖ intr anegarse, ahogarse

drowse [drauz] intr adormecerse, amodorrarse

drow·sy ['drauzi] adj (comp -sier; super -siest) soñoliento, modorro

drub [drʌb] v (pret & pp drubbed; ger -drubbing) tr apalear, pegar, tundir; derrotar completamente

drudge [drʌdʒ] s yunque m, esclavo del trabajo ‖ intr afanarse

drudger·y ['drʌdʒəri] s (pl -ies) trabajo penoso

drug [drʌg] s droga, medicamento; narcótico; drug on the market macana, artículo invendible ‖ v (pret & pp drugged; ger drugging) tr narcotizar; mezclar con drogas

drug addict s toxicómano

drug addiction s toxicomanía

druggist ['drʌgɪst] s boticario, farmacéutico; (dealer in drugs, chemicals, dyes, etc.) droguero

drug habit s vicio de los narcóticos

drug store s farmacia, botica, droguería

drug traffic s contrabando de narcóticos

druid ['dru·ɪd] s druida m

drum [drʌm] s (cylinder; instrument of percussion) tambor m; (container for oil, gasoline, etc.) bidón m ‖ v (pret & pp drummed; ger drumming) tr reunir a toque de tambor; to drum up trade fomentar ventas ‖ intr tocar el tambor; (with the fingers) teclear

drum'beat' s toque m de tambor

drum corps s banda de tambores

drum'fire' s fuego graneado, fuego nutrido

drum'head' s parche m de tambor

drum major s tambor m mayor

drummer ['drʌmər] s tambor m, tamborilero; agente viajero

drum'stick' s baqueta, palillo; (coll) muslo (de ave cocida)

drunk [drʌŋk] adj borracho; to get drunk emborracharse ‖ s (coll) borracho; (spree) (coll) borrachera

drunkard ['drʌŋkərd] s borrachín m

drunken ['drʌŋkən] adj borracho

drunken driving s — to be arrested for drunken driving ser arrestado por conducir en estado de embriaguez

drunkenness ['drʌŋkənnɪs] s embriaguez f

dry [draɪ] adj (comp drier; super driest) seco; (thirsty) sediento; (dull, boring) árido ‖ s (pl drys) (prohibitionist) (coll) seco ‖ v (pret & pp dried) tr secar; (to wipe dry) enjugar ‖ intr secarse; to dry up secarse completamente; (slang) callar, dejar de hablar

dry battery s pila seca; (group of dry cells) batería seca

dry cell s pila seca

dry'-clean' tr lavar en seco, limpiar en seco

dry cleaner s tintorero

dry cleaning s lavado a seco, limpieza en seco

dry'-clean'ing establishment s tintorería

dry dock s dique seco

dryer ['draɪ·ər] s var de drier

dry'-eyed' *adj* ojienjuto
dry farming *s* cultivo de secano
dry goods *spl* mercancías generales (*tejidos, lencería, pañería, sedería*)
dry ice *s* carbohielo, hielo seco
dry law *s* ley seca
dry measure *s* medida para áridos
dryness ['draɪnɪs] *s* sequedad; (*e.g., of a speaker*) aridez *f*
dry nurse *s* ama seca
dry season *s* estación de la seca
dry wash *s* ropa lavada y secada pero no planchada
d.s. *abbr* days after sight, daylight saving
D.S.T. *abbr* **Daylight Saving Time**
dual ['djuəl] o ['duəl] *adj & s* dual *m*
duali·ty [dju'ælɪti] o [du'ælɪti] *s* (*pl* -ties) dualidad
dub [dʌb] *s* (*slang*) jugador *m* torpe ‖ *v* (*pret & pp* **dubbed**; *ger* **dubbing**) *tr* apellidar; armar caballero; (*mov*) doblar
dubbing ['dʌbɪŋ] *s* doblado, doblaje *m*
dubious ['djubɪ·əs] o ['dubɪ·əs] *adj* dudoso
ducat ['dʌkət] *s* ducado
duchess ['dʌtʃɪs] *s* duquesa
duch·y ['dʌtʃi] *s* (*pl* -ies) ducado
duck [dʌk] *s* pato; (*female*) pata; agachada rápida; (*in the water*) zambullida; **ducks** (*coll*) pantalones *mpl* de dril ‖ *tr* bajar rápidamente (*la cabeza*); (*in water*) chapuzar; (*coll*) esquivar, evitar (*un golpe*) ‖ *intr* chapuzar; **to duck out** (*coll*) escabullirse
duck'-toed' *adj* zancajoso
duct [dʌkt] *s* conducto, canal *m*
ductile ['dʌktɪl] *adj* dúctil
ductless gland ['dʌktlɪs] *s* glándula cerrada
duct'work' *s* canalización
dud [dʌd] *s* (*slang*) bomba que no estalla; (*slang*) fracaso; **duds** (*coll*) trapos, prendas de vestir
dude [djud] o [dud] *s* caballerete *m*
due [dju] o [du] *adj* debido; aguardado, esperado; pagadero; **due to** debido a; **to fall due** vencer; **when is the train due?** ¿a qué hora debe llegar el tren? ‖ *adv* directamente, derecho ‖ *s* deuda; **dues** derechos; (*of a member*) cuota; **to get one's due** llevar su merecido; **to give the devil his due** ser justo hasta con el diablo
duel ['djuəl] o ['duəl] *s* duelo; **to fight a duel** batirse en duelo ‖ *v* (*pret & pp* **dueled** o **duelled**; *ger* **dueling** o **duelling**) *intr* batirse en duelo
duelist o **duellist** ['djuəlɪst] o ['duəlɪst] *s* duelista *m*
dues-paying ['djuz‚pe·ɪŋ] o ['duz‚pe·ɪŋ] *adj* cotizante
duet [dju'et] o [du'et] *s* dúo
duke [djuk] o [duk] *s* duque *m*
dukedom ['djukdəm] o ['dukdəm] *s* ducado
dull [dʌl] *adj* (*not sharp*) embotado, romo; (*color*) apagado; (*sound;*

pain) sordo; (*stupid*) lerdo, torpe; (*business*) inactivo, muerto; (*boring*) aburrido, tedioso; (*flat*) deslucido, deslustrado ‖ *tr* embotar, enromar; deslucir, deslustrar; enfriar (*el entusiasmo*) ‖ *intr* embotarse, enromarse; deslucirse, deslustrarse
dullard ['dʌlərd] *s* estúpido
duly ['djuli] o ['duli] *adv* debidamente
dumb [dʌm] *adj* (*lacking the power to speak*) mudo; (*coll*) estúpido, torpe
dumb'bell' *s* halterio; (*slang*) estúpido, tonto
dumb creature *s* animal *m*, bruto
dumb show *s* pantomima
dumb'wait'er *s* montaplatos *m*
dumfound [‚dʌm'faund] *tr* pasmar, dejar sin habla
dum·my ['dʌmi] *adj* falso, fingido, simulado ‖ *s* (*pl* -mies) (*dress form*) maniquí *m*; cabeza para pelucas; (*in card games*) muerto; cartas del muerto; (*figurehead, straw man*) testaferro; (*skeleton copy of a book*) maqueta; imitación, copia; (*slang*) estúpido
dump [dʌmp] *s* basurero, vertedero; montón *m* de basuras; (*mil*) depósito de municiones; (*min*) terrero; **to be down in the dumps** (*coll*) tener murria ‖ *tr* descargar, verter; vaciar de golpe; vender en grandes cantidades y a precios inferiores a los corrientes
dumping ['dʌmpɪŋ] *s* descarga; venta en grandes cantidades y a precios inferiores a los corrientes
dumpling ['dʌmplɪŋ] *s* bola de pasta rellena de fruta o carne
dump truck *s* camión *m* volquete
dump·y ['dʌmpi] *adj* (*comp* -ier; *super* -iest) regordete, rollizo
dun [dʌn] *adj* bruno, pardo, castaño ‖ *s* acreedor importuno; (*demand for payment*) apremio ‖ *v* (*pret & pp* **dunned**; *ger* **dunning**) *tr* importunar para el pago, apremiar (*a un deudor*)
dunce [dʌns] *s* zopenco, bodoque *m*
dunce cap *s* capirote *m* que se le pone al alumno torpe
dune [djun] o [dun] *s* duna, médano
dung [dʌŋ] *s* estiércol *m* ‖ *tr* estercolar
dungarees [‚dʌŋgə'riz] *spl* pantalones *mpl* de trabajo de tela basta de algodón
dungeon ['dʌndʒən] *s* calabozo, mazmorra; (*fortified tower of medieval castle*) torre *f* del homenaje
dung'hill' *s* estercolar *m*; lugar inmundo
dunk [dʌŋk] *tr* sopetear, ensopar
duo ['dju·o] o ['du·o] *s* dúo
duode·num [‚dju·ə'dinəm] o [‚du·ə'dinəm] *s* (*pl* -na [nə]) duodeno
dupe [djup] o [dup] *s* víctima, primo, inocentón *m* ‖ *tr* embaucar, engañar
duplex house ['djupleks] o ['dupleks] *s* casa para dos familias
duplicate ['djuplɪkɪt] o ['duplɪkɪt] *adj & s* duplicado; **in duplicate** por

duplicado || ['djuplɪ ˌket] o ['duplɪ- ˌket] *tr* duplicar

duplici•ty [dju'plɪsɪti] o [du'plɪsɪti] *s* (*pl* -ties) duplicidad

durable ['djurəbəl] o ['durəbəl] *adj* durable, duradero

durable goods *spl* artículos duraderos

duration [djʊ'reʃən] o [du'reʃən] *s* duración

during ['djurɪŋ] o ['durɪŋ] *prep* durante

dusk [dʌsk] *s* crepúsculo

dust [dʌst] *s* polvo || *tr* (*to free of dust*) desempolvar; (*to sprinkle with dust*) polvorear; to dust off desempolvar

dust bowl *s* cuenca de polvo

dust'cloth' *s* trapo para quitar el polvo

dust cloud *s* nube *f* de polvo, polvareda

duster ['dʌstər] *s* paño, plumero; (*light overgarment*) guardapolvo

dust jacket *s* sobrecubierta

dust'pan' *s* pala para recoger la basura

dust rag *s* trapo para quitar el polvo

dust storm *s* tolvanera

dust•y ['dʌsti] *adj* (*comp* -ler; *super* -lest) polvoriento; (*grayish*) grisáceo

Dutch [dʌtʃ] *adj* holandés; (slang) alemán || *s* (*language*) holandés *m*; (*language*) (slang) alemán *m*; in Dutch (slang) en la desgracia, (slang) en un apuro; the Dutch los holandeses; (slang) los alemanes; to go Dutch (coll) pagar a escote

Dutch•man ['dʌtʃmən] *s* (*pl* -men [mən]) holandés *m*; (slang) alemán *m*

Dutch treat *s* (coll) convite *m* a escote

dutiable ['djutɪ-əbəl] o ['dutɪ-əbəl] *adj* sujeto a derechos de aduana

dutiful ['djutɪfəl] o ['dutɪfəl] *adj* obediente, sumiso, solícito

du•ty ['djuti] o ['duti] *s* (*pl* -ties) deber *m*; (*task*) faena, quehacer *m*; derechos de aduana; off duty libre; on duty de servicio, de guardia; to do one's duty cumplir con su deber; to take up one's duties entrar en funciones

du'ty-free' *adj* libre de derechos

D.V. *abbr* Deo volente, i.e., God willing

dwarf [dwɔrf] *adj* & *s* enano || *tr* achicar, empequeñecer || *intr* achicarse, empequeñecerse

dwarfish ['dwɔrfɪʃ] *adj* enano, diminuto

dwell [dwel] *v* (*pret* & *pp* dwelled o dwelt [dwelt]) *intr* vivir, morar; to dwell on o upon hacer hincapié en

dwelling ['dwelɪŋ] *s* morada, vivienda

dwelling house *s* casa, domicilio

dwindle ['dwɪndəl] *intr* disminuir; decaer, consumirse

dwt. *abbr* pennyweight

dye [daɪ] *s* tinte *m*, tintura, color *m* || *v* (*pret* & *pp* dyed; *ger* dyeing) *tr* teñir

dyed-in-the-wool ['daɪdɪnðə ˌwul] *adj* intransigente

dyeing ['daɪ-ɪŋ] *s* tinte *m*, tintura

dyer ['daɪ-ər] *s* tintorero

dye'stuff' *s* materia colorante

dying ['daɪ-ɪŋ] *adj* moribundo

dynamic [daɪ'næmɪk] o [dɪ'næmɪk] *adj* dinámico

dynamite ['daɪnə ˌmaɪt] *s* dinamita || *tr* dinamitar

dyna•mo ['daɪnə ˌmo] *s* (*pl* -mos) dínamo *f*

dynast ['daɪnæst] *s* dinasta *m*

dynas•ty ['daɪnəsti] *s* (*pl* -ties) dinastía

dysentery ['dɪsən ˌteri] *s* disentería

dyspepsia [dɪs'pepsɪ-ə] o [dɪs'pep/ə] *s* dispepsia

dz. *abbr* dozen

E

E, e [i] quinta letra del alfabeto inglés

ea. *abbr* each

each [itʃ] *adj indef* cada || *pron indef* cada uno; each other nos, se; uno a otro, unos a otros || *adv* cada uno; por persona

eager ['igər] *adj* (*enthusiastic*) ardiente, celoso; eager for muy deseoso de; eager to | *inf* muy deseoso de | *inf*

eagerness ['igərnɪs] *s* ardor *m*, celo; deseo ardiente, empeño

eagle ['igəl] *s* águila

eagle owl *s* buho

ear [ɪr] *s* (*organ and sense of hearing*) oído; (*external part*) oreja; (*of corn*) mazorca; (*of wheat*) espiga; all ears con las orejas tan largas; to be all ears ser todo oídos, abrir tanto oído; to prick up one's ears aguzar las orejas; to turn a deaf ear hacer o tener oídos de mercader

ear'ache' *s* dolor *m* de oído

ear'drop' *s* arete *m*

ear'drum' *s* tímpano

ear'flap' *s* orejera

earl [ɑrl] *s* conde *m*

earldom ['ɑrldəm] *s* condado

ear•ly ['ʌili] (*comp* -ller; *super* -llest) *adj* (*occurring before customary time*) temprano; (*first in a series*) primero; (*far back in time*) primero, remoto, antiguo; (*occurring in near future*) cercano, próximo || *adv* temprano; al principio; en los primeros tiempos; as early as (*a certain time of day*) ya a; (*a certain time or date*) ya en; as early as possible lo más pronto posible; early in (*e.g., the month of December*) ya en; early in the morning muy de mañana; **early in the year** a principios del año; **to rise early** madrugar

early bird s (coll) madrugador m

early mass s misa de prima

early riser s madrugador m

ear'mark' s señal f, distintivo ‖ tr destinar, poner aparte (para un fin determinado)

ear'muff' s orejera

earn [ʌrn] tr ganar, ganarse; (to get as one's due) merecerse; (com) devengar (intereses) ‖ intr ganar; rendir

earnest ['ʌrnɪst] adj serio, grave; **in earnest** en serio, de buena fe ‖ s arras

earnest money s arras

earnings ['ʌrnɪŋz] s ganancia; salario

ear'phone' s audífono

ear'piece' s auricular m

ear'ring' s arete m

ear'shot' s alcance m del oído; **within earshot** al alcance del oído

ear'split'ting adj ensordecedor

earth [ʌrθ] s tierra; **to come back to** o **down to earth** bajar de las nubes

earthen ['ʌrθən] adj de tierra; de barro

ear'then-ware' s loza, vasijas de barro

earthly ['ʌrθli] adj terrenal; concebible, posible; **to be of no earthly use** no servir para nada

earth'quake' s terremoto, temblor m de tierra

earth'work' s terraplén m

earth'worm' s lombriz f de tierra

earth•y ['ʌrθi] adj (comp -ier; super -iest) terroso; (worldly) mundanal; (unrefined) grosero; franco, sincero

ear trumpet s trompetilla

ear'wax' s cera de los oídos

ease [iz] s facilidad; (readiness, naturalness) desenvoltura, soltura; (comfort, wellbeing) comodidad, bienestar m; **with ease** con facilidad ‖ tr facilitar; aligerar (un peso); (to let up on) aflojar, soltar; aliviar, mitigar ‖ intr aliviarse, mitigarse, disminuir; moderar la marcha

easel ['izəl] s caballete m

easement ['izmənt] s alivio; (law) servidumbre

easily ['izɪli] adj fácilmente; suavemente; sin duda; probablemente

easiness ['izɪnɪs] s facilidad; desenvoltura, soltura; (e.g., of motion of a machine) suavidad; indiferencia

east [ist] adj oriental, del este ‖ adv al este, hacia el este ‖ s este m

Easter ['istər] s Pascua de flores, Pascua de Resurrección, Pascua florida

Easter egg s huevo duro decorado o huevo de imitación que se da como regalo en el día de Pascua de Resurrección

Easter Monday s lunes m de Pascua de Resurrección

eastern ['istərn] adj oriental

East'er-tide' s aleluya m, tiempo de Pascua

eastward ['istwərd] adv hacia el este

eas•y ['izi] adj (comp -ier; super -iest) fácil; (conducive to ease) cómodo; (not tight) holgado; (amenable) manejable; (not forced or hurried) lento, pausado, moderado ‖ adv (coll) fácilmente; (coll) despacio; **to take it easy** (coll) descansar, holgar; (coll) ir despacio

easy chair s poltrona, silla poltrona

eas'y•go'ing adj despacioso, comodón

easy mark s (coll) víctima, inocentón m

easy money s dinero ganado sin pena; (com) dinero abundante

easy payments spl facilidades de pago

eat [it] v (pret **ate** [et]; pp **eaten** ['itən]) tr comer; **to eat away** corroer; **to eat up** comerse ‖ intr comer

eatable ['itəbəl] adj comestible ‖ **eatables** spl comestibles mpl

eaves [ivz] spl alero, socarrén m, tejaroz m

eaves'drop' v (pret & pp **-dropped**; ger **-dropping**) intr escuchar a escondidas, estar de escucha

ebb [eb] s reflujo; decadencia ‖ intr bajar (la marea); decaer

ebb and flow s flujo y reflujo

ebb tide s marea menguante

ebon•y ['ebəni] s (pl -ies) ébano

ebullient [ɪ'bʌljənt] adj hirviente; entusiasta

eccentric [ɛk'sɛntrɪk] adj excéntrico ‖ m (odd person) excéntrico; (device) excéntrica

eccentrici•ty [,ɛksɛn'trɪsɪti] s (pl -ties) excentricidad

ecclesiastic [ɪ,klizi'æstɪk] adj & s eclesiástico

echelon ['ɛʃə,lɑn] s escalón m; (mil) escalón ‖ tr (mil) escalonar

ech•o ['ɛko] s (pl -oes) eco ‖ tr repetir (un sonido); imitar ‖ intr hacer eco

éclair [e'klɛr] s bollo de crema

eclectic [ɛk'lɛktɪk] adj & s ecléctico

eclipse [ɪ'klɪps] s eclipse m ‖ tr eclipsar

eclogue ['ɛklɔg] o ['ɛklɑg] s égloga

economic [,ikə'nɑmɪk] o [,ɛkə'nɑmɪk] adj económico (perteneciente a la economía)

economical [,ikə'nɑmɪkəl] o [,ɛkə'nɑmɪkəl] adj económico (ahorrador; poco costoso)

economics [,ikə'nɑmɪks] o [,ɛkə'nɑmɪks] s economía política

economist [ɪ'kɑnəmɪst] s economista mf

economize [ɪ'kɑnə,maɪz] tr & intr economizar

econo•my [ɪ'kɑnəmi] s (pl -mies) economía

ecsta•sy ['ɛkstəsi] s (pl -sies) éxtasis m

ecstatic [ɛk'stætɪk] adj extático

Ecuador ['ɛkwə,dɔr] s el Ecuador

Ecuadoran [,ɛkwə'dɔrən] o **Ecuadorian** [,ɛkwə'dɔri•ən] adj & s ecuatoriano

ecumenic(al) [,ɛkjə'mɛnɪk(əl)] adj ecuménico

eczema ['ɛksɪmə] o [ɛg'zimə] s eczema m & f, eccema m & f

ed. abbr **edited, edition, editor**

ed·dy ['ɛdɪ] s (pl **-dies**) remolino || v (pret & pp **-died**) tr & intr remolinear

edelweiss ['edəl,vaɪs] s estrella de los Alpes

edge [edʒ] s (of a knife, sword, etc.) filo, corte m; (of a cup, glass, piece of paper, piece of cloth, an abyss, etc.) borde m; (of a piece of cloth; of a body of water) orilla; (of a table) canto; (of a book) corte m; (of clothing) ribete m; (slang) ventaja; **on edge** de canto; (fig) nervioso; **to have the edge on** (coll) llevar ventaja a; **to set the teeth on edge** dar dentera || tr afilar, aguzar; bordear; ribetear (un vestido) || intr avanzar de lado; **to edge in** lograr entrar

edgeways ['edʒ,wez] adv de filo, de canto; **to not let a person get a word in edgeways** no dejarle a una persona decir ni una palabra

edging ['edʒɪŋ] s orla, pestaña

edgy ['edʒɪ] adj agudo, angular; nervioso, irritable

edible ['edɪbəl] adj & s comestible m

edict ['idɪkt] s edicto

edification [,edɪfɪ'keʃən] s edificación

edifice ['edɪfɪs] s edificio

edi·fy ['edɪ,faɪ] v (pret & pp **-fied**) tr edificar

edifying ['edɪ,faɪɪŋ] adj edificante

edit. abbr **edited, edition, editor**

edit ['edɪt] tr preparar para la publicación; dirigir, redactar (un periódico)

edition [ɪ'dɪʃən] s edición

editor ['edɪtər] s (of a newspaper or magazine) director m, redactor m; (of a manuscript) revisor m; (of an editorial) cronista mf

editorial [,edɪ'torɪ·əl] adj editorial || editorial m, artículo de fondo

editorial staff s redacción, cuerpo de redacción

editor in chief s jefe m de redacción

educate ['edʒʊ,ket] tr educar, instruir

education [,edʒʊ'keʃən] s educación, instrucción

educational [,edʒʊ'keʃənəl] adj educativo, educacional

educational institution s centro docente

educator ['edʒʊ,ketər] s educador m

eel [il] s anguila; **to be as slippery as an eel** escurrirse como una anguila

ee·rie o **ee·ry** ['ɪrɪ] adj (comp **-rier**; super **-riest**) espectral, misterioso

efface [ɪ'fes] tr destruir; borrar; **to efface oneself** retirarse, no dejarse ver

effect [ɪ'fɛkt] s efecto; **in effect** vigente; en efecto, en realidad; **to feel the effects of** resentirse de; **to go into effect** o **to take effect** hacerse vigente, entrar en vigor; **to put into effect** poner en vigor || tr efectuar

effective [ɪ'fɛktɪv] adj eficaz; (actually in effect) efectivo; (striking) impresionante; **to become effective** hacerse efectivo, entrar en vigencia

effectual [ɪ'fɛktʃʊ·əl] adj eficaz

effectuate [ɪ'fɛktʃʊ,et] tr efectuar

effeminacy [ɪ'fɛmɪnəsɪ] s afeminación

effeminate [ɪ'fɛmɪnɪt] adj afeminado

effervesce [,efər'vɛs] intr estar en efervescencia

effervescence [,efər'vɛsəns] s efervescencia

effervescent [,efər'vɛsənt] adj efervescente

effete [ɪ'fit] adj estéril, infructuoso

efficacious [,efɪ'keʃəs] adj eficaz

effica·cy ['efɪkəsɪ] s (pl **-cies**) eficacia

efficien·cy [ɪ'fɪʃənsɪ] s (pl **-cies**) eficiencia; (mech) rendimiento, efecto útil

efficient [ɪ'fɪʃənt] adj eficiente, eficaz; (person) competente; (mech) de buen rendimiento

effi·gy ['efɪdʒɪ] s (pl **-gies**) efigie f

effort ['efort] s esfuerzo, empeño

effronter·y [ɪ'frʌntərɪ] s (pl **-ies**) desfachatez f, descaro

effusion [ɪ'fjuʒən] s efusión

effusive [ɪ'fjusɪv] adj efusivo, expansivo

e.g. abbr **exempli gratia, i.e., for example**

egg [eg] s huevo; (slang) buen sujeto || tr — **to egg on** incitar, instigar

egg beater s batidor m de huevos

egg′cup′ s huevera

egg′head′ s intelectual mf, erudito

eggnog ['eg,nɑg] s caldo de la reina, yema mejida

egg′plant′ s berenjena

egg′shell′ s cascarón m, cáscara de huevo

egoism ['ego,ɪzəm] o ['igo,ɪzəm] s egoísmo

egoist ['ego·ɪst] o ['igo·ɪst] s egoísta mf

egotism ['ego,tɪzəm] o ['igo,tɪzəm] s egotismo

egotist ['egotɪst] o ['igotɪst] s egotista mf

egregious [ɪ'gridʒəs] adj enorme, escandaloso

egress ['igres] s salida

Egypt ['idʒɪpt] s Egipto

Egyptian [ɪ'dʒɪpʃən] adj & s egipcio

eider ['aɪdər] s pato de flojel

eider down s edredón m

eight [et] adj & pron ocho || s ocho; **eight o'clock** las ocho

eight′-day′ clock s reloj m de ocho días cuerda

eighteen ['et'tin] adj, pron & s dieciocho, diez y ocho

eighteenth ['et'tinθ] adj & s (in a series) decimoctavo; (part) diec iochavo || s (in dates) dieciocho, diez y ocho

eighth [etθ] adj & s octavo, ochavo || s (in dates) ocho

eight hundred adj & pron ochocientos || s ochocientos m

eightieth ['etɪ·ɪθ] adj & s (in a series) octogésimo; (part) ochentavo

eigh·ty ['etɪ] adj & pron ochenta || s (pl **-ties**) ochenta m

either ['iðər] o ['aɪðər] adj uno u otro, cada . . . (de los dos), cual-

quier . . . de los dos; ambos || *pron*
uno u otro, cualquiera de los dos ||
adv — not either tampoco, no . . .
tampoco || *conj* — either . . . or o
. . . o

ejaculate [ɪ'dʒækjə,let] *tr & intr* exclamar; (physiol) eyacular

eject [ɪ'dʒɛkt] *tr* arrojar, expulsar,
echar; (to evict) desahuciar

ejection [ɪ'dʒɛkʃən] *s* expulsión; (of a
tenant) desahucio

ejection seat *s* (aer) asiento lanzable

eke [ik] *tr* — to eke out ganarse (la
vida) con dificultad

elaborate [ɪ'læbərɪt] *adj* (done with
great care) elaborado; (detailed,
ornate) primoroso, recargado ||
[ɪ'læbə,ret] *tr* elaborar || *intr* — to
elaborate on o upon explicar con
más detalles

elapse [ɪ'læps] *intr* pasar, transcurrir

elastic [ɪ'læstɪk] *adj & s* elástico

elasticity [ɪ,læs'tɪsɪti] o [,ilæs'tɪsɪti]
s elasticidad

elated [ɪ'letɪd] *adj* alborozado, regocijado

elation [ɪ'leʃən] *s* alborozo, regocijo

elbow ['ɛlbo] *s* codo; (in a river) recodo; (of a chair) brazo; at one's
elbow a la mano; out at the elbows
andrajoso, enseñando los codos; to
crook the elbow empinar el codo; to
rub elbows codearse, rozarse; up to
the elbows hasta los codos || *tr* —
to elbow one's way abrirse paso a
codazos || *intr* codear

elbow grease *s* (coll) muñeca, jugo de
muñeca

elbow patch *s* codera

elbow rest *s* ménsula

el'bow·room' *s* espacio suficiente; libertad de acción

elder ['ɛldər] *adj* mayor, más antiguo
|| *s* mayor, señor *m* mayor; (eccl)
anciano; (plant) saúco

el'der·ber'ry *s* (pl -ries) saúco; baya
del saúco

elderly ['ɛldərli] *adj* viejo, anciano

elder statesman *s* veterano de la política

eldest ['ɛldɪst] *adj* (el) mayor, (el)
más antiguo

elec. *abbr* electrical, electricity

elect [ɪ'lɛkt] *adj* (chosen) escogido;
(selected but not yet installed) electo
|| *s* elegido; the elect los elegidos ||
tr elegir

election [ɪ'lɛkʃən] *s* elección

electioneer [ɪ,lɛkʃə'nɪr] *intr* solicitar
votos

elective [ɪ'lɛktɪv] *adj* electivo || *s*
asignatura electiva

electorate [ɪ'lɛktərɪt] *s* electorado

electric(al) [ɪ'lɛktrɪk(əl)] *adj* eléctrico

electric fan *s* ventilador eléctrico

electrician [ɪ,lɛk'trɪʃən] o [,ɛlɛk-
'trɪʃən] *s* electricista *mf*

electricity [ɪ,lɛk'trɪsɪti] o [,ɛlɛk-
'trɪsɪti] *s* electricidad

electric percolator *s* cafetera eléctrica

electric shaver *s* electroafeitadora

electric tape *s* cinta aislante

electri·fy [ɪ'lɛktrɪ,faɪ] *v* (pret & pp
-fied) *tr* (to provide with electric
power) electrificar; (to communicate
electricity to; to thrill) electrizar

electrocute [ɪ'lɛktrə,kjut] *tr* electrocutar

electrode [ɪ'lɛktrod] *s* electrodo

electrolysis [ɪ,lɛk'trɑlɪsɪs] o [,elɛk-
'trɑlɪsɪs] *s* electrolisis *f*

electrolyte [ɪ'lɛktrə,laɪt] *s* electrólito

electromagnet [ɪ,lɛktrə'mægnɪt] *s*
electro, electroimán *m*

electromagnetic [ɪ,lɛktrəmæg'nɛtɪk]
adj electromagnético

electromotive [ɪ,lɛktrə'motɪv] *adj*
electromotor

electron [ɪ'lɛktrɑn] *s* electrón *m*

electronic [ɪ,lɛk'trɑnɪk] o [,elɛk-
'trɑnɪk] *adj* electrónico || **elec-
tronics** *s* electrónica

electroplating [ɪ'lɛktrə,pletɪŋ] *s* galvanoplastia

electrostatic [ɪ,lɛktrə'stætɪk] *adj* elec-
trostático

electrotype [ɪ'lɛktrə,taɪp] *s* electro-
tipo || *tr* electrotipar

eleemosynary [,elɪ'mɑsɪ,neri] *adj*
limosnero

elegance ['ɛlɪgəns] *s* elegancia

elegant ['ɛlɪgənt] *adj* elegante

elegiac [ɛlɪ'dʒaɪ·æk] o [ɪ'lidʒɪ,æk]
adj elegiaco

ele·gy ['ɛlɪdʒɪ] *s* (pl -gies) elegía

element ['ɛlɪmənt] *s* elemento; to be in
one's element estar en su elemento

elementary [,ɛlɪ'mɛntəri] *adj* elemental

elephant ['ɛlɪfənt] *s* elefante *m*

elevate ['ɛlɪ,vet] *tr* elevar

elevated ['ɛlɪ,vetɪd] *adj* elevado || *s*
(coll) ferrocarril aéreo o elevado

elevation [,ɛlɪ've ʃən] *s* elevación

elevator [ɪ'lɛ,vetər] *s* ascensor *m*;
elevador *m* (Am); (for freight) mon-
tacargas *m*; (for hoisting grain) elevador de granos; (warehouse for
storing grain) depósito de cereales;
(aer) timón *m* de profundidad

eleven [ɪ'lɛvən] *adj & pron* once || *s*
once *m*; eleven o'clock las once

eleventh [ɪ'lɛvənθ] *adj & s* (in a series)
undécimo, onceno; (part) onzavo ||
s (in dates) once *m*

eleventh hour *s* último momento

elf [ɛlf] *s* (pl elves [ɛlvz]) elfo, trasgo;
enano

elicit [ɪ'lɪsɪt] *tr* sacar, sonsacar

elide [ɪ'laɪd] *tr* elidir

eligible ['ɛlɪdʒɪbəl] *adj* elegible; deseable, aceptable

eliminate [ɪ'lɪmɪ,net] *tr* eliminar

elision [ɪ'lɪʒən] *s* elisión

elite [e'lit] *adj* selecto || *s* — the elite
la élite

elk [ɛlk] *s* alce *m*

ellipse [ɪ'lɪps] *s* (geom) elipse *f*

ellip·sis [ɪ'lɪpsɪs] *s* (pl -ses [siz])
(gram) elipsis *f*

elliptic(al) [ɪ'lɪptɪk(əl)] *adj* (geom &
gram) elíptico

elm tree [ɛlm] *s* olmo

elope [ɪ'lop] *intr* fugarse con un amante

elopement [ɪ'lopmənt] *s* fuga con un amante

eloquence ['ɛləkwəns] *s* elocuencia

eloquent ['ɛləkwənt] *adj* elocuente

else [ɛls] *adj* — nobody else ningún otro, nadie más; nothing else nada más; somebody else algún otro, otra persona; something else otra cosa; what else qué más, qué otra cosa; who else quién más; whose else de qué otra persona || *adv* de otro modo; how else de qué otro modo; or else si no, o bien; when else en qué otro tiempo; a qué otra hora; where else en qué otra parte

else'where' *adv* en otra parte, a otra parte

elucidate [ɪ'lusɪ,det] *tr* elucidar

elude [ɪ'lud] *tr* eludir

elusive [ɪ'lusɪv] *adj* fugaz, efímero; evasivo; (*baffling*) deslumbrador

emaciated [ɪ'meʃɪ,etɪd] *adj* enflaquecido, macilento

emancipate [ɪ'mænsɪ,pet] *tr* emancipar

embalm [ɛm'bɑm] *tr* embalsamar

embankment [ɛm'bæŋkmənt] *s* terraplén *m*

embar·go [ɛm'bɑrgo] *s* (*pl* -goes) embargo || *tr* embargar

embark [ɛm'bɑrk] *intr* embarcarse

embarkation [,ɛmbɑr'keʃən] *s* (*of passengers*) embarco; (*of freight*) embarque *m*

embarrass [ɛm'bærəs] *tr* (*to make feel self-conscious*) avergonzar; (*to put obstacles in the way of*) embarazar; poner en apuros de dinero

embarrassing [ɛm'bærəsɪŋ] *adj* desconcertante, vergonzoso; embarazoso

embarrassment [ɛm'bærəsmənt] *s* desconcierto, vergüenza; (*interference*; *perplexity*) embarazo; (*financial difficulties*) apuros

embas·sy ['ɛmbəsɪ] *s* (*pl* -sies) embajada

em·bed [ɛm'bɛd] *s* (*pret & pp* -bedded; *ger* -bedding) *tr* empotrar, encajar

embellish [ɛm'bɛlɪʃ] *tr* embellecer

embellishment [ɛm'bɛlɪʃmənt] *s* embellecimiento

ember ['ɛmbər] *s* ascua, pavesa; embers rescoldo

Ember days *spl* témpora

embezzle [ɛm'bɛzəl] *tr & intr* desfalcar, malversar

embezzlement [ɛm'bɛzəlmənt] *s* desfalco, malversación

embezzler [ɛm'bɛzlər] *s* malversador *m*

embitter [ɛm'bɪtər] *tr* amargar

emblazon [ɛm'blezən] *tr* blasonar; (*fig*) blasonar

emblem ['ɛmbləm] *s* emblema *m*

emblematic(al) [,ɛmblə'mætɪk(əl)] *adj* emblemático

embodiment [ɛm'bɑdɪmənt] *s* incorporación; personificación, encarnación

embod·y [ɛm'bɑdɪ] *v* (*pret & pp* -ied) *tr* incorporar; personificar, encarnar

embolden [ɛm'boldən] *tr* envalentonar

embolism ['ɛmbə,lɪzəm] *s* embolia

emboss [ɛm'bɔs] o [ɛm'bɑs] *tr* (*to raise in relief*) realzar; abollonar (*metal*); repujar (*cuero*)

embrace [ɛm'bres] *s* abrazo || *tr* abrazar || *intr* abrazarse

embrasure [ɛm'breʒər] *s* alféizar *m*

embroider [ɛm'brɔɪdər] *tr* bordar, recamar

embroider·y [ɛm'brɔɪdərɪ] *s* (*pl* -ies) bordado, recamado

embroil [ɛm'brɔɪl] *tr* embrollar; (*to involve in contention*) envolver

embroilment [ɛm'brɔɪlmənt] *s* embrollo; (*in contention*) envolvimiento

embry·o ['ɛmbrɪ,o] *s* (*pl* -os) embrión *m*

embryology [,ɛmbrɪ'ɑlədʒɪ] *s* embriología

emend [ɪ'mɛnd] *tr* enmendar

emendation [,imɛn'deʃən] *s* enmienda

emerald ['ɛmərəld] *s* esmeralda

emerge [ɪ'mʌrdʒ] *intr* emerger

emergence [ɪ'mʌrdʒəns] *s* emergencia (*acción de emerger*)

emergen·cy [ɪ'mʌrdʒənsɪ] *s* (*pl* -cies) emergencia (*caso urgente*)

emergency exit *s* salida de auxilio

emergency landing *s* aterrizaje forzoso

emergency landing field *s* aeródromo de urgencia

emersion [ɪ'mʌrʒən] o [ɪ'mʌrʃən] *s* emersión

emery ['ɛmərɪ] *s* esmeril *m*

emery cloth *s* tela de esmeril

emery wheel *s* esmeriladora, rueda de esmeril, muela de esmeril

emetic [ɪ'mɛtɪk] *adj & s* emético

emigrant ['ɛmɪgrənt] *adj & s* emigrante *mf*

emigrate ['ɛmɪ,gret] *intr* emigrar

émigré [emɪ'gre] o ['ɛmɪ,gre] *s* emigrado

eminence ['ɛmɪnəns] *s* eminencia

eminent ['ɛmɪnənt] *adj* eminente

emissar·y ['ɛmɪ,sɛrɪ] *s* (*pl* -ies) emisario

emission [ɪ'mɪʃən] *s* emisión

emit [ɪ'mɪt] *v* (*pret & pp* emitted; *ger* emitting) *tr* emitir

emotion [ɪ'moʃən] *s* emoción

emotional [ɪ'moʃənəl] *adj* emocional, emotivo

emperor ['ɛmpərər] *s* emperador *m*

empha·sis ['ɛmfəsɪs] *s* (*pl* -ses [,siz]) énfasis *m*

emphasize ['ɛmfə,saɪz] *tr* acentuar, hacer hincapié en

emphatic [ɛm'fætɪk] *adj* enfático

emphysema [,ɛmfɪ'simə] *s* enfisema *m*

empire ['ɛmpaɪr] *s* imperio

empiric(al) [ɛm'pɪrɪk(əl)] *adj* empírico

empiricist [ɛm'pɪrɪsɪst] *s* empírico

emplacement [ɛm'plesmənt] *s* emplazamiento

employ [ɛm'plɔɪ] *s* empleo || *tr* emplear

employee [ɛm'plɔɪ·i] o [,ɛmplɔɪ'i] *s* empleado

employer [ɛm'plɔɪ·ər] *s* patrono

employment [ɛmˈplɔɪmənt] *s* empleo, colocación

employment agency *s* agencia de colocaciones

empower [ɛmˈpaʊ.ər] *tr* autorizar, facultar; habilitar, permitir

empress [ˈɛmprɪs] *s* emperatriz *f*

emptiness [ˈɛmptɪnɪs] *s* vaciedad, vacuidad

emp·ty [ˈɛmptɪ] *adj (comp* **-tier;** *super* **-tiest)** vacío; (coll) hambriento ‖ *v (pret & pp* **-tied)** *tr & intr* vaciar

empty-handed [ˈɛmptɪˈhændɪd] *adj* manivacío

empty-headed [ˈɛmptɪˈhɛdɪd] *adj* tonto, ignorante

empye·ma [ˌɛmpɪˈimə] *s (pl* **-mata** [mətə]) empiema *m*

empyrean [ˌɛmpɪˈri·ən] *adj & s* empíreo

emulate [ˈɛmjəˌlet] *tr & intr* emular

emulator [ˈɛmjəˌletər] *s* émulo

emulous [ˈɛmjələs] *adj* émulo

emulsi·fy [ɪˈmʌlsɪˌfaɪ] *v (pret & pp* **-fied)** *tr* emulsionar

emulsion [ɪˈmʌlʃən] *s* emulsión

enable [ɛnˈebəl] *tr* habilitar, facilitar

enact [ɛnˈækt] *tr* decretar, promulgar; hacer el papel de

enactment [ɛnˈæktmənt] *s* ley *f; (of a law)* promulgación; *(of a play)* representación

enam·el [ɛnˈæməl] *s* esmalte *m* ‖ *v (pret & pp* **-eled** o **-elled;** *ger* **-eling** o **-elling)** *tr* esmaltar

enam'el·ware' *s* utensilios de cocina de hierro esmaltado

enamor [ɛnˈæmər] *tr* enamorar

encamp [ɛnˈkæmp] *tr* acampar ‖ *intr* acampar, acamparse

encampment [ɛnˈkæmpmənt] *s* acampamiento

enchant [ɛnˈtʃænt] o [ɛnˈtʃɑnt] *tr* encantar

enchanting [ɛnˈtʃæntɪŋ] o [ɛnˈtʃɑntɪŋ] *adj* encantador

enchantment [ɛnˈtʃæntmənt] o [ɛnˈtʃɑntmənt] *s* encanto

enchantress [ɛnˈtʃæntrɪs] o [ɛnˈtʃɑntrɪs] *s* encantadora

enchase [ɛnˈtʃes] *tr* engastar

encircle [ɛnˈsʌrkəl] *tr* encerrar, rodear; (mil) envolver

enclitic [ɛnˈklɪtɪk] *adj & s* enclítico

enclose [ɛnˈkloz] *tr* encerrar; *(in a letter)* adjuntar, incluir; **to enclose herewith** remitir adjunto

enclosure [ɛnˈkloʒər] *s* recinto; cosa inclusa, carta inclusa

encomi·um [ɛnˈkomɪ·əm] *s (pl* **-ums** o **-a** [ə]) encomio

encompass [ɛnˈkʌmpəs] *tr* encuadrar, abarcar

encore [ˈɑnkor] *s* bis *m* ‖ *interj* ¡bis!, ¡que se repita! ‖ *tr* pedir la repetición de *(p.ej., de una pieza o canción);* pedir la repetición a *(un actor)*

encounter [ɛnˈkaʊntər] *s* encuentro ‖ *tr* encontrar, encontrarse con ‖ *intr* batirse, combatirse

encourage [ɛnˈkʌrɪdʒ] *tr* animar, alentar; *(to foster)* fomentar

encouragement [ɛnˈkʌrɪdʒmənt] *s* ánimo, aliento; fomento

encroach [ɛnˈkrotʃ] *intr* — **to encroach on** o **upon** pasar los límites de; abusar de; invadir, entremeterse en

encumber [ɛnˈkʌmbər] *tr* embarazar, estorbar, impedir; *(to load with debts, etc.)* gravar

encumbrance [ɛnˈkʌmbrəns] *s* embarazo; estorbo; gravamen *m*

ency. o **encyc.** *abbr* encyclopedia

encyclical [ɛnˈsɪklɪkəl] o [ɛnˈsaɪklɪkəl] *s* encíclica

encyclopedia [ɛnˌsaɪkləˈpidɪ·ə] *s* enciclopedia

encyclopedic [ɛnˌsaɪkləˈpidɪk] *adj* enciclopédico

end [ɛnd] *s (in time)* fin *m; (in space)* extremo, remate *m; (e.g., of the month)* fines *mpl; (small piece)* cabo, pieza, fragmento; *(purpose)* intento, objeto, fin, mira; **at the end of** al cabo de; a fines de; **in the end** al fin; **no end of** (coll) un sin fin de; **to make both ends meet** pasar con lo que se tiene; **to no end** sin efecto; **to stand on end** poner de punta; ponerse de punta; crizarse, encresparse *(el pelo);* **to the end that** a fin de que ‖ *tr* acabar, terminar ‖ *intr* acabar, terminar; desembocar *(p.ej., una calle);* **to end up** acabar, morir; **to end up as** acabar siendo, parar en *(p.ej., ladrón)*

endanger [ɛnˈdendʒər] *tr* poner en peligro

endear [ɛnˈdɪr] *tr* hacer querer; **to endear oneself to** hacerse querer por

endeavor [ɛnˈdevər] *s* esfuerzo, empeño ‖ *intr* esforzarse, empeñarse

endemic [ɛnˈdɛmɪk] *adj* endémico ‖ *s* endemia

ending [ˈɛndɪŋ] *s* fin *m*, terminación; (gram) desinencia, terminación

endive [ˈɛndaɪv] *s* escarola

endless [ˈɛndlɪs] *adj* interminable; *(chain, screw, etc.)* sin fin

end'most' *adj* último, extremo

endorse [ɛnˈdɔrs] *tr* endosar; (fig) apoyar, aprobar

endorsee [ˌɛndɔrˈsi] *s* endosatario

endorsement [ɛnˈdɔrsmənt] *s* endoso; (fig) apoyo, aprobación

endorser [ɛnˈdɔrsər] *s* endosante *mf*

endow [ɛnˈdaʊ] *tr* dotar

endowment [ɛnˈdaʊmənt] *adj* dotal ‖ *s (of an institution)* dotación; *(gift, talent)* dote *f*, prenda

endurance [ɛnˈdjʊrəns] o [ɛnˈdʊrəns] *s* aguante *m*, paciencia; *(ability to hold out)* resistencia, fortaleza; *(lasting time)* duración

endure [ɛnˈdjʊr] o [ɛnˈdʊr] *tr* aguantar, tolerar, sufrir ‖ *intr* durar; sufrir con paciencia

enduring [ɛnˈdjʊrɪŋ] o [ɛnˈdʊrɪŋ] *adj* duradero, permanente, resistente

enema [ˈɛnəmə] *s* enema, ayuda; *(liquid and apparatus)* lavativa

ene·my [ˈɛnəmɪ] *adj* enemigo ‖ *s (pl* **-mies)** enemigo

enemy alien s extranjero enemigo

energetic [ˌenərˈdʒetɪk] adj enérgico, vigoroso

ener·gy [ˈenərdʒi] s (pl -gies) energía

enervate [ˈenərˌvet] tr enervar

enfeeble [enˈfibəl] tr debilitar

enfold [enˈfold] tr arrollar, envolver

enforce [enˈfors] tr hacer cumplir, poner en vigor; obtener por fuerza; (e.g., obedience) imponer; (an argument) hacer valer

enforcement [enˈforsmənt] s compulsión; (e.g., of a law) ejecución

enfranchise [enˈfræntʃaɪz] tr franquear, libertar; conceder el derecho de sufragio a

eng. abbr **engineer, engraving**

engage [enˈgedʒ] tr ocupar, emplear; alquilar, reservar; atraer (p.ej., la atención de una persona); engranar con; trabar batalla con; to be engaged; to be engaged to be married estar prometido, estar comprometido para casarse; to engage someone in conversation entablar conversación con una persona ‖ intr empeñarse, comprometerse; empotrar, encajar; engranar; to engage in ocuparse en

engaged [enˈgedʒd] adj comprometido, prometido; (column) embebido, entregado

engagement [enˈgedʒmənt] s ajuste m, contrato, empeño; esponsales mpl, palabra de casamiento; (duration of betrothal) noviazgo; (appointment) cita; (mil) acción, batalla

engagement ring s anillo de compromiso, anillo de pedida

engaging [enˈgedʒɪŋ] adj agraciado, simpático

engender [enˈdʒendər] tr engendrar

engine [ˈendʒɪn] s máquina; (of automobile) motor m; (rr) máquina, locomotora

engine driver s maquinista m

engineer [ˌendʒəˈnɪr] s ingeniero; (engine driver) maquinista m ‖ tr dirigir o construir como ingeniero; llevar a cabo con acierto

engineering [ˌendʒəˈnɪrɪŋ] s ingeniería

engine house s cuartel m de bomberos

engine-man [ˈendʒɪnmən] s (pl -men [mən]) maquinista m, conductor m de locomotora

engine room s sala de máquinas; (naut) cámara de las máquinas

en'gine-room' telegraph s (naut) transmisor m de órdenes, telégrafo de máquinas

England [ˈɪŋglənd] s Inglaterra

Englander [ˈɪŋgləndər] s natural m inglés

English [ˈɪŋglɪʃ] adj inglés ‖ s inglés m; (in billiards) efecto m; **the English** los ingleses

English Channel s Canal m de la Mancha

English daisy s margarita de los prados

English horn s (mus) corno inglés, cuerno inglés

English·man [ˈɪŋglɪʃmən] s (pl -men [mən]) inglés m

Eng'lish-speak'ing adj de habla inglesa

Eng'lish·wom'an s (pl -wom'en) inglesa

engraft [enˈgræft] o [enˈgraft] tr (hort & surg) injertar; (fig) implantar

engrave [enˈgrev] tr grabar; (in the memory) grabar

engraver [enˈgrevər] s grabador m

engraving [enˈgrevɪŋ] s grabado

engross [enˈgros] tr absorber; poner en limpio; copiar caligráficamente

engrossing [enˈgrosɪŋ] adj acaparador, absorbente

engulf [enˈgʌlf] tr hundir, inundar

enhance [enˈhæns] o [enˈhans] tr realzar

enhancement [enˈhænsmənt] o [enˈhansmənt] s realce m

enigma [ɪˈnɪgmə] s enigma m

enigmatic(al) [ˌɪnɪgˈmætɪk(əl)] adj enigmático

enjambment [enˈdʒæmmənt] o [enˈdʒæmbmənt] s encabalgamiento

enjoin [enˈdʒɔɪn] tr encargar, ordenar

enjoy [enˈdʒɔɪ] tr gozar; **to enjoy +** ger gozarse en + inf; **to enjoy oneself** divertirse

enjoyable [enˈdʒɔɪ·əbəl] adj agradable, deleitable

enjoyment [enˈdʒɔɪmənt] s (pleasure) placer m; (pleasurable use) goce m

enkindle [enˈkɪndəl] tr encender

enlarge [enˈlardʒ] tr agrandar, aumentar; (phot) ampliar ‖ intr agrandarse, aumentar; (to talk at length) explayarse; exagerar; **to enlarge on** o **upon** tratar con más extensión; exagerar

enlargement [enˈlardʒmənt] s agrandamiento, aumento; (phot) ampliación

enlighten [enˈlaɪtən] tr ilustrar, instruir

enlightenment [enˈlaɪtənmənt] s ilustración, instrucción

enlist [enˈlɪst] tr alistar; ganar (a una persona; el favor, los servicios de una persona) ‖ intr alistarse; **to enlist in** (a cause) poner empeño en

enliven [enˈlaɪvən] tr avivar, animar

enmesh [enˈmeʃ] tr enredar

enmi·ty [ˈenmɪti] s (pl -ties) enemistad

ennoble [enˈnobəl] tr ennoblecer

ennui [ˈɑnwi] s aburrimiento, tedio

enormous [ɪˈnɔrməs] adj enorme

enough [ɪˈnʌf] adj, adv & s bastante m ‖ interj ¡basta!, ¡no más!

enounce [ɪˈnauns] tr enunciar; pronunciar

en passant [ˌɑn pæˈsant] adv (chess) al vuelo

enrage [enˈredʒ] tr enrabiar, encolerizar

enrapture [enˈræptʃər] tr embelesar, transportar, arrebatar

enrich [enˈrɪtʃ] tr enriquecer

enroll [enˈrol] tr alistar, inscribir; (to wrap up) envolver, enrollar ‖ intr alistarse, inscribirse

en route [ɑn ˈrut] adv en camino; **en route to** camino de, rumbo a

ensconce [enˈskɑns] tr esconder, abrigar; **to ensconce oneself** instalarse cómodamente

ensemble [ɑnˈsɑmbəl] s conjunto;

grupo de músicos que tocan o cantan juntos; traje armonioso

ensign ['ensaɪn] s (*standard*) enseña, bandera; (*badge*) divisa, insignia ‖ ['ensən] o ['ensaɪn] s (nav) alférez *m* de fragata

enslave [en'slev] tr esclavizar

enslavement [ɛn'slevmənt] s esclavización

ensnare [ɛn'sner] tr entrampar

ensue [ɛn'su] o [ɛn'sju] intr seguirse; resultar

ensuing [ɛn'su·ɪŋ] o [ɛn'sju·ɪŋ] adj siguiente; resultante

ensure [ɛn'ʃur] tr asegurar, garantizar

entail [ɛn'tel] s (law) vínculo ‖ tr acarrear, ocasionar; (law) vincular

entangle [ɛn'tæŋgəl] tr enmarañar, enredar

entanglement [ɛn'tæŋgəlmənt] s enmarañamiento, enredo

enter ['ɛntər] tr entrar en (*una habitación*); entrar por (*una puerta*); (*in the customhouse*) declarar; (*to make a record of*) registrar, asentar; matricular (*a un alumno*); matricularse en; hacer miembro a; hacerse miembro de; (*to undertake*) emprender; asentar (*un pedido*); **to enter one's head** metérsele a uno en la cabeza ‖ intr entrar; (theat) entrar en escena, salir; **to enter into** entrar en; celebrar (*p.ej., un contrato*); **to enter on** o **upon** emprender

enterprise ['ɛntər,praɪz] s (*undertaking*) empresa; (*spirit, push*) empuje *m*

enterprising ['ɛntər,praɪzɪŋ] adj emprendedor

entertain [,ɛntər'ten] tr entretener, divertir; (*to show hospitality to*) recibir; considerar, abrigar (*esperanzas, ideas, etc.*) ‖ intr recibir

entertainer [,ɛntər'tenər] s (*host*) anfitrión *m*; (*in public*) actor *m*, bailador *m*, músico, vocalista *mf* (*esp. en un café cantante*)

entertaining [,ɛntər'tenɪŋ] adj entretenido

entertainment [,ɛntər'tenmənt] s entretenimiento, diversión; atracción, espectáculo; buen recibimiento; (*of hopes, ideas, etc.*) consideración, abrigo

enthrall [ɛn'θrɔl] tr cautivar, encantar; esclavizar, sojuzgar

enthrone [ɛn'θron] tr entronizar

enthuse [ɛn'θuz] o [ɛn'θjuz] tr (coll) entusiasmar ‖ intr (coll) entusiasmarse

enthusiasm [ɛn'θuzɪ,æzəm] o [ɛn'θjuzɪ,æzəm] s entusiasmo

enthusiast [ɛn'θuzɪ,æst] o [ɛn'θjuzɪ,æst] s entusiasta *mf*

enthusiastic [ɛn,θuzɪ'æstɪk] o [ɛn,θjuzɪ'æstɪk] adj entusiástico

entice [ɛn'taɪs] tr atraer, tentar; inducir al mal, extraviar

enticement [ɛn'taɪsmənt] s atracción, tentación; extravío

entire [ɛn'taɪr] adj entero

entirely [ɛn'taɪrlɪ] adv enteramente, (*exclusively*) solamente

entire·ty [ɛn'taɪrtɪ] s (*pl* -ties) entereza; conjunto, totalidad

entitle [ɛn'taɪtəl] tr dar derecho a; (*to give a name to*; *to honor with a title*) intitular

enti·ty ['ɛntɪtɪ] s (*pl* -ties) entidad

entomb [ɛn'tum] tr sepultar

entombment [ɛn'tummənt] s sepultura

entomology [,ɛntə'mɑlədʒɪ] s entomología

entourage [,ɑntu'rɑʒ] s cortejo, séquito

entrails ['ɛntrelz] o ['ɛntrəlz] spl entrañas

entrain [ɛn'tren] tr despachar en el tren ‖ intr embarcar, salir en el tren

entrance ['ɛntrəns] s entrada, ingreso; (theat) entrada en escena ‖ [ɛn-'træns] o [ɛn'trans] tr arrebatar, encantar

entrance examination s examen *m* de ingreso; **to take entrance examinations** examinarse de ingreso

entrancing [ɛn'trænsɪŋ] o [ɛn'transɪŋ] adj arrebatador, encantador

entrant ['ɛntrənt] s entrante *mf*; (sport) concurrente *mf*

en·trap [ɛn'træp] v (*pret* & *pp* -trapped; *ger* -trapping) tr entrampar

entreat [ɛn'trit] tr rogar, suplicar

entreat·y [ɛn'tritɪ] s (*pl* -ies) ruego, súplica

entree ['ɑntre] s entrada, ingreso; (culin) entrada, principio

entrench [ɛn'trɛntʃ] tr atrincherar ‖ intr — **to entrench on** o **upon** infringir, violar

entrust [ɛn'trʌst] tr confiar

en·try ['ɛntrɪ] s (*pl* -tries) entrada; (*item*) partida, entrada; (*in a dictionary*) artículo; (sport) concurrente *mf*

entwine [ɛn'twaɪn] tr entretejer, entrelazar

enumerate [ɪ'njumə,ret] o [ɪ'numə,ret] tr enumerar

enunciate [ɪ'nʌnsɪ,et] o [ɪ'nʌnʃɪ,et] tr enunciar; pronunciar

envelop [ɛn'vɛləp] tr envolver

envelope ['ɛnvə,lop] o ['ɑnvə,lop] s (*for a letter*) sobre *m*; (*wrapper*) envoltura

envenom [ɛn'vɛnəm] tr envenenar

enviable ['ɛnvɪ·əbəl] adj envidiable

envious ['ɛnvɪ·əs] adj envidioso

environment [ɛn'vaɪrənmənt] s medio ambiente; (*surroundings*) inmediaciones

environs [ɛn'vaɪrənz] spl inmediaciones, alrededores *mf*

envisage [ɛn'vɪzɪdʒ] tr (*to look in the face of*) encarar; considerar, representarse

envoi ['ɛnvɔɪ] s despedida (*copla al fin de una composición poética*)

envoy ['ɛnvɔɪ] s (*diplomatic agent*) enviado; (*short concluding stanza*) despedida

en·vy ['ɛnvɪ] s (*pl* -vies) envidia ‖ v (*pret* & *pp* -vied) tr envidiar

enzyme ['ɛnzaɪm] o ['ɛnzɪm] s enzima *f*

epaulet o **epaulette** ['epə‚let] s charretera

epenthe·sis [e'penθɪsɪs] s (pl -ses [‚siz]) epéntesis f

epergne [ɪ'pʌrn] o [e'pern] s ramillete m, centro de mesa

ephemeral [ɪ'femərəl] adj efímero

epic ['epɪk] adj épico || s epopeya

epicure ['epɪ‚kjur] s epicúreo

epicurean [‚epɪkju'ri·ən] adj & s epicúreo

epidemic [‚epɪ'demɪk] adj epidémico || s epidemia

epidemiology [‚epɪ‚dimɪ'ɑlədʒɪ] s epidemiología

epidermis [‚epɪ'dʌrmɪs] s epidermis f

epigram ['epɪ‚græm] s epigrama m

epilepsy ['epɪ‚lepsɪ] s epilepsia

epileptic [‚epɪ'leptɪk] adj & s epiléptico

Epiphany [ɪ'pɪfənɪ] s Epifanía

Episcopalian [ɪ‚pɪskə'pelɪ·ən] adj & s episcopalista mf

episode ['epɪ‚sod] s episodio

epistemology [ɪ‚pɪstɪ'mɑlədʒɪ] s epistemología

epistle [ɪ'pɪsəl] s epístola

epitaph ['epɪ‚tæf] s epitafio

epithet ['epɪ‚θet] s epíteto

epitome [ɪ'pɪtəmɪ] s epítome m; (fig) esencia, personificación

epitomize [ɪ'pɪtə‚maɪz] tr epitomar; (fig) encarnar, personificar

epoch ['epək] o ['ipɑk] s época

epochal ['epəkəl] adj memorable, trascendental

ep'och-mak'ing adj que hace época

equable ['ekwəbəl] o ['ikwəbəl] adj constante, uniforme; sereno

equal ['ikwəl] adj igual; equal to a la altura de || s igual mf || v (pret & pp equaled o equalled; ger equaling o equalling) tr (to be equal to) igualarse a o con; (to make equal) igualar

equali·ty [ɪ'kwɑlɪtɪ] s (pl -ties) igualdad

equalize ['ikwə‚laɪz] tr igualar; (to make uniform) equilibrar

equally ['ikwəlɪ] adv igualmente

equanimity [‚ikwə'nɪmɪtɪ] s ecuanimidad, igualdad de ánimo

equate [i'kwet] tr poner en ecuación; considerar equivalente(s)

equation [i'kweʒən] o [i'kweʃən] s ecuación

equator [i'kwetər] s ecuador m

equer·ry ['ekwərɪ] o [ɪ'kwerɪ] s (pl -ries) caballerizo

equestrian [ɪ'kwestrɪ·ən] adj ecuestre || m jinete m, caballista m

equilateral [‚ikwɪ'lætərəl] adj equilátero

equilibrium [‚ikwɪ'lɪbrɪ·əm] s equilibrio

equinoctial [‚ikwɪ'nɑkʃəl] adj equinoccial

equinox ['ikwɪ‚nɑks] s equinoccio

equip [ɪ'kwɪp] v (pret & pp equipped; ger equipping) tr equipar

equipment [ɪ'kwɪpmənt] s equipo, avíos, pertrechos; aptitud, capacidad

equipoise ['ikwɪ‚pɔɪz] o ['ekwɪ‚pɔɪz]

s equilibrio; contrapeso || tr equilibrar; equipesar

equitable ['ekwɪtəbəl] adj equitativo

equi·ty ['ekwɪtɪ] s (pl -ties) (fairness) equidad; valor líquido

equivalent [ɪ'kwɪvələnt] adj & s equivalente m

equivocal [ɪ'kwɪvəkəl] adj equívoco

equivocate [ɪ'kwɪvə‚ket] intr usar de equívocos para engañar, mentir

equivocation [ɪ‚kwɪvə'keʃən] s equívoco

era ['ɪrə] o ['irə] s era

eradicate [ɪ'rædɪ‚ket] tr erradicar

erase [ɪ'res] tr borrar

eraser [ɪ'resər] s goma de borrar; (for blackboard) cepillo

erasure [ɪ'reʃər] o [ɪ'reʒər] s borradura, tachón m

ere [er] prep antes de || conj antes de que; más bien que

erect [ɪ'rekt] adj derecho, enhiesto, erguido; (hair) erizado || tr (to set in upright position) erguir, enhestar; erigir (un edificio); armar, montar (una máquina)

erection [ɪ'rekʃən] s erección

erg [ʌrg] s ergio

ermine ['ʌrmɪn] s armiño; (fig) toga, judicatura

erode [ɪ'rod] tr erosionar || intr erosionarse

erosion [ɪ'roʒən] s erosión

err [ʌr] intr errar, equivocarse, marrar; pecar, marrar

errand ['erənd] s mandado, recado, comisión; to run an errand hacer un mandado

errand boy s recadero, mandadero

erratic [ɪ'rætɪk] adj irregular, inconstante, variable; excéntrico

erra·tum [ɪ'retəm] o [ɪ'rɑtəm] s (pl -ta [tə]) errata

erroneous [ɪ'ronɪ·əs] adj erróneo

error ['erər] s error m

erudite ['eru‚daɪt] o ['erju‚daɪt] adj erudito

erudition [‚eru'dɪʃən] o [‚erju'dɪʃən] s erudición

erupt [ɪ'rʌpt] intr hacer erupción (la piel, los dientes de un niño); erumpir (un volcán)

eruption [ɪ'rʌpʃən] s erupción

escalate ['eskə‚let] intr escalarse

escalation [‚eskə'leʃən] s escalada, escalación

escalator ['eskə‚letər] s escalera mecánica, móvil o rodante

escallop [es'kæləp] s concha de peregrino; (on edge of cloth) festón m || tr hornear a la crema y con migajas de pan; cocer (p.ej., ostras) en su concha; festonear

escapade [‚eskə'ped] s calaverada, aventura atolondrada; (flight) escapada

escape [es'kep] s (getaway) escape m, escapatoria; (from responsibilities, duties, etc.) escapatoria || tr evitar, eludir; to escape someone escapársele a uno; olvidársele a uno || intr escapar, escaparse; to escape from

escaparse a (*una persona*); escaparse de (*la cárcel*)
escapee [ˌeskəˈpi] *s* evadido
escape literature *s* literatura de escape o de evasión
escapement [esˈkepmənt] *s* escape *m*
escapement wheel *s* rueda de escape
escarpment [esˈkɑrpmənt] *s* escarpa
eschew [esˈtʃu] *tr* evitar, rehuir
escort [ˈeskɔrt] *s* escolta; (*man or boy who accompanies a woman or girl in public*) acompañante *m*, caballero, galán *m* ‖ [esˈkɔrt] *tr* escoltar
escutcheon [esˈkʌtʃən] *s* escudo de armas; (*plate in front of lock on door*) escudo, escudete *m*
Eski·mo [ˈeskɪˌmo] *adj* esquimal ‖ *s* (*pl -mos o -mo*) esquimal *mf*
esopha·gus [iˈsɑfəgəs] *s* (*pl -gi* [ˌdʒaɪ]) esófago
esp. *abbr* **especially**
espalier [esˈpæljər] *s* espaldar *m*, espalera
especial [esˈpeʃəl] *adj* especial
espionage [ˈespɪ·ənɪdʒ] o [ˌespɪ·əˈnɑʒ] *s* espionaje *m*
esplanade [ˌespləˈned] o [ˌespləˈnɑd] *s* explanada
espousal [esˈpaʊzəl] *s* desposorios; (*of a cause*) adhesión
espouse [esˈpaʊz] *tr* casarse con; (*to advocate, adopt*) abogar por, adherirse a
Esq. *abbr* **Esquire**
esquire [esˈkwaɪr] o [ˈeskwaɪr] *s* escudero ‖ **Esquire** *s* título de cortesía que se escribe después del apellido y que se usa en vez de **Mr.**
essay [ˈese] *s* ensayo
essayist [ˈese·ɪst] *s* ensayista *mf*
essence [ˈesəns] *s* esencia
essential [esˈsenʃəl] *adj & s* esencial *m*
est. *abbr* **established, estate, estimated**
establish [esˈtæblɪʃ] *tr* establecer
establishment [esˈtæblɪʃmənt] *s* establecimiento
estate [esˈtet] *s* estado; situación social; (*landed property*) finca, hacienda, heredad; (*a person's possessions*) bienes *mpl*, propiedad; (*left by a decedent*) herencia, bienes relictos
esteem [esˈtim] *s* estima ‖ *tr* estimar
esthete [ˈesθit] *s* esteta *mf*
esthetic [esˈθetɪk] *adj* estético ‖ **esthetics** *ssg* estética
estimable [ˈestɪməbəl] *adj* estimable
estimate [ˈestɪˌmet] o [ˈestɪmɪt] *s* (*calculation of value, judgment of worth*) estimación; (*statement of cost of work to be done*) presupuesto ‖ [ˈestɪˌmet] *tr* (*to judge, deem*) estimar; presupuestar (*el coste de una obra*)
estimation [ˌestɪˈmeʃən] *s* estimación
estrangement [esˈtrendʒmənt] *s* extrañeza
estuar·y [ˈestʃʊˌeri] *s* (*pl -ies*) estero
etc. *abbr* **et cetera**
etch [etʃ] *tr & intr* grabar al agua fuerte
etcher [ˈetʃər] *s* aguafortista *mf*
etching [ˈetʃɪŋ] *s* aguafuerte *f*

eternal [ɪˈtʌrnəl] *adj* eterno
eterni·ty [ɪˈtʌrnɪti] *s* (*pl -ties*) eternidad
ether [ˈiθər] *s* éter *m*
ethereal [ɪˈθɪrɪ·əl] *adj* etéreo
ethical [ˈeθɪkəl] *adj* ético
ethics [ˈeθɪks] *ssg* ética
Ethiopian [ˌiθɪˈopɪ·ən] *adj & s* etíope *mf*
Ethiopic [ˌiθɪˈopɪk] *adj & s* etiópico
ethnic(al) [ˈeθnɪk(əl)] *adj* étnico
ethnography [eθˈnɑgrəfi] *s* etnografía
ethnology [eθˈnɑlədʒi] *s* etnología
ethyl [ˈeθɪl] *s* etilo
ethylene [ˈeθɪˌlin] *s* etileno
etiquette [ˈetɪˌket] *s* etiqueta
et seq. *abbr* **et sequens, et sequentes, et sequentia** (Lat) **and the following**
étude [eˈtjud] *s* (mus) estudio
etymology [ˌetɪˈmalədʒi] *s* etimología
ety·mon [ˈetɪˌman] *s* (*pl -mons o -ma* [mə]) étimo
eucalyp·tus [ˌjukəˈlɪptəs] *s* (*pl -tuses o -ti* [taɪ]) eucalipto
Eucharist [ˈjukərɪst] *s* Eucaristía
euchre [ˈjukər] *s* juego de naipes ‖ *tr* (coll) ser más listo que
eugenics [juˈdʒenɪks] *s* eugenesia
eulogistic [ˌjuləˈdʒɪstɪk] *adj* elogiador
eulogize [ˈjuləˌdʒaɪz] *tr* elogiar
eulo·gy [ˈjulədʒi] *s* (*pl -gies*) elogio
eunuch [ˈjunək] *s* eunuco
euphemism [ˈjufɪˌmɪzəm] *s* eufemismo
euphemistic [ˌjufɪˈmɪstɪk] *adj* eufemístico
euphonic [juˈfanɪk] *adj* eufónico
eupho·ny [ˈjufəni] *s* (*pl -nies*) eufonía
euphoria [juˈfɔrɪ·ə] *s* euforia
euphuism [ˈjufjuˌɪzəm] *s* eufuísmo
euphuistic [ˌjufjuˈɪstɪk] *adj* eufuístico
Europe [ˈjurəp] *s* Europa
European [ˌjurəˈpi·ən] *adj & s* europeo
euthanasia [ˌjuθəˈneʒə] *s* eutanasia
evacuate [ɪˈvækjuˌet] *tr & intr* evacuar
evacuation [ɪˌvækjuˈeʃən] *s* evacuación
evade [ɪˈved] *tr* evadir ‖ *intr* evadirse
evaluate [ɪˈvæljuˌet] *tr* evaluar
Evangel [ɪˈvændʒəl] *s* Evangelio
evangelic(al) [ˌivænˈdʒelɪk(əl)] o [ˌevənˈdʒelɪk(əl)] *adj* evangélico
Evangelist [ɪˈvændʒəlɪst] *s* Evangelista *m*
evaporate [ɪˈvæpəˌret] *tr* evaporar ‖ *intr* evaporarse
evasion [ɪˈveʒən] *s* evasión, evasiva
evasive [ɪˈvesɪv] *adj* evasivo
eve [iv] *s* víspera; **on the eve of** en vísperas de
even [ˈivən] *adj* (*smooth*) parejo, llano, liso; (*number*) par; constante, uniforme, invariable; (*temperament*) apacible, sereno; exacto, igual; **even with** al nivel de; **to be even** estar en paz; no deber nada a nadie; **to get even** desquitarse ‖ *adv* aun, hasta; sin embargo; también; exactamente, igualmente; **even as** así como; **even if** aunque, aun cuando; **even so** aun así; **even though** aunque, aun cuando; **even when** aun cuando; **not even** ni . . . siquiera; **to break even** salir

sin ganar ni perder; (*in gambling*) salir en paz ‖ *tr* allanar, igualar

evening ['ivnɪŋ] *adj* vespertino ‖ *s* tarde *f*

evening clothes *spl* traje *m* de etiqueta

evening gown *s* vestido de noche (*de mujer*)

evening primrose *s* hierba del asno

evening star *s* estrella vespertina, lucero de la tarde

evening wrap *s* salida de teatro

e'ven·song' *s* canción de la tarde; (*eccl*) vísperas

event [ɪ'vɛnt] *s* acontecimiento, suceso; (*outcome*) resultado; (*public function*) acto; (*sport*) prueba; **at all events** o **in any event** en todo caso; **in the event that** en caso que

eventful [ɪ'vɛntfəl] *adj* lleno de acontecimientos; importante, memorable

eventual [ɪ'vɛntʃʊ·əl] *adj* final

eventuali·ty [ɪ,vɛntʃʊ'ælɪti] *s* (*pl* **-ties**) eventualidad

eventually [ɪ'vɛntʃʊ·əli] *adv* finalmente, con el tiempo

eventuate [ɪ'vɛntʃʊ,et] *intr* concluir, resultar

ever ['ɛvər] *adv* (*at all times*) siempre; (*at any time*) jamás, nunca, alguna vez; **as ever** como siempre; **as much as ever** tanto como antes; **ever since** (*since that time*) desde entonces; después de que; **ever so** muy; **ever so much** muchísimo; **hardly ever** o **scarcely ever** casi nunca; **not . . . ever** no . . . nunca

ev'er·glade' *s* tierra pantanosa cubierta de hierbas altas

ev'er·green' *adj* siempre verde ‖ *s* planta siempre verde; **evergreens** ramas colgadas como adorno

ev'er·last'ing *adj* sempiterno; (*lasting indefinitely*) duradero; (*wearisome*) aburrido, cansado ‖ *s* eternidad; (*bot*) siemprepreviva

ev'er·more' *adv* eternamente; **for evermore** para siempre jamás

every ['ɛvri] *adj* todos los; (*each*) cada, todo; (*being each in a series*) cada, p.ej., **every three days** cada tres días; **every bit** (coll) todo, p.ej., **every bit a man** todo un hombre; **every now and then** de vez en cuando; **every once in a while** una que otra vez; **every other day** cada dos días, un día sí y otro no; **every which way** (coll) por todas partes; (coll) en desarreglo

ev'ery·bod'y *pron indef* todo el mundo

ev'ery·day' *adj* de todos los días; cotidiano, diario; común, ordinario

every man Jack o **every mother's son** *s* cada hijo de vecino

ev'ery·one' o **every one** *pron indef* cada uno, todos, todo el mundo

ev'ery·thing' *pron indef* todo

ev'ery·where' *adv* en o por todas partes; a todas partes

evict [ɪ'vɪkt] *tr* desahuciar

eviction [ɪ'vɪkʃən] *s* desahucio

evidence ['ɛvɪdəns] *s* evidencia; (law) prueba

evident ['ɛvɪdənt] *adj* evidente

evil ['ivəl] *adj* malo, malvado ‖ *s* mal *m*, maldad

e'vil·do'er *s* malhechor *m*, malvado

e'vil·do'ing *s* malhecho, maldad

evil eye *s* mal *m* de ojo

evil-minded ['ivəl'maɪndɪd] *adj* mal pensado, malintencionado

Evil One, the el enemigo malo

evince [ɪ'vɪns] *tr* manifestar, mostrar

evoke [ɪ'vok] *tr* evocar

evolution [,ɛvə'luʃən] *s* evolución; (math) extracción de raíces, radicación

evolve [ɪ'vɑlv] *tr* desarrollar; desprender (*olores, gases, calor*) ‖ *intr* evolucionar

ewe [ju] *s* oveja

ewer ['ju·ər] *s* aguamanil *m*

ex. *abbr* **examination, example, except, exchange, express**

ex [ɛks] *prep* sin incluir, sin participación en

exact [ɛg'zækt] *adj* exacto ‖ *tr* exigir

exacting [ɛg'zæktɪŋ] *adj* exigente

exaction [ɛg'zækʃən] *s* exacción

exactly [ɛg'zæktli] *adv* exactamente; (*sharp, on the dot*) en punto

exactness [ɛg'zæktnɪs] *s* exactitud

exaggerate [ɛg'zædʒə,ret] *tr* exagerar

exalt [ɛg'zɔlt] *tr* exaltar, ensalzar

exam [ɛg'zæm] *s* (coll) examen *m*

examination [ɛg,zæmɪ'neʃən] *s* examen *m*; **to take an examination** sufrir un examen, examinarse

examine [ɛg'zæmɪn] *tr* examinar

example [ɛg'zæmpəl] o [ɛg'zɑmpəl] *s* ejemplo; (*case serving as a warning to others*) ejemplar *m*; (*of mathematics*) problema *m*; **for example** por ejemplo

exasperate [ɛg'zæspə,ret] *tr* exasperar

excavate ['ɛkskə,vet] *tr* excavar

exceed [ɛk'sid] *tr* exceder; sobrepasar (*p.ej., el límite de velocidad*)

exceedingly [ɛk'sidɪŋli] *adv* sumamente, sobremanera

ex·cel [ɛk'sɛl] *v* (*pret & pp* **-celled**; *ger* **-celling**) *tr* aventajar ‖ *intr* sobresalir

excellence ['ɛksələns] *s* excelencia

excellen·cy ['ɛksələnsi] *s* (*pl* **-cies**) excelencia; **Your Excellency** Su Excelencia

excelsior [ɛk'sɛlsɪ·ər] *s* pajilla de madera, virutas de madera

except [ɛk'sɛpt] *prep* excepto; **except for** sin; **except that** a menos que ‖ *tr* exceptuar

exception [ɛk'sɛpʃən] *s* excepción; **to take exception** poner reparos, objetar; otenderse; **with the exception of** a excepción de

exceptional [ɛk'sɛpʃənəl] *adj* excepcional

excerpt ['ɛksʌrpt] o [ɛk'sʌrpt] *s* excerta, selección ‖ [ɛk'sʌrpt] *tr* escoger

excess ['ɛksɛs] o [ɛk'sɛs] *adj* excedente, sobrante ‖ [ɛk'sɛs] *s* (*amount or degree by which one thing exceeds another*) exceso, excedente *m*; (*excessive amount; immoderate indulgence, unlawful conduct*) exceso; **in excess of** más que, superior a

excess baggage *s* exceso de equipaje

excess fare *s* suplemento

excessive [ɛk'sɛsɪv] *adj* excesivo

ex'cess-prof'its tax *s* impuesto sobre beneficios extraordinarios

excess weight *s* exceso de peso

exchange [ɛks't∫endʒ] *s* (*of greetings, compliments, blows, etc.*) cambio; (*of prisoners, merchandise, newspapers, credentials, etc.*) canje *m*; (*periódico de canje*; (*place for buying and selling*) bolsa, lonja; estación telefónica, central *f* de teléfonos; **in exchange for** en cambio de, a trueque de ‖ *tr* cambiar; canjear (*prisioneros, mercancías, etc.*); darse, hacerse (*cortesías*); **to exchange greetings** saludarse; **to exchange shots** cambiar disparos

exchequer [ɛks't∫ɛkər] o ['ɛkst∫ɛkər] *s* tesorería; fondos nacionales

excise tax [ɛk'saɪz] o ['ɛksaɪz] *m* impuesto sobre ciertas mercancías de comercio interior

excitable [ɛk'saɪtəbəl] *adj* excitable

excite [ɛk'saɪt] *tr* excitar

excitement [ɛk'saɪtmənt] *s* excitación

exciting [ɛk'saɪtɪŋ] *adj* emocionante, conmovedor; (*stimulating*) excitante

exclaim [ɛks'klem] *tr & intr* exclamar

exclamation [ˌɛksklə'me∫ən] *s* exclamación

exclamation mark o **point** *s* punto de admiración

exclude [ɛks'klud] *tr* excluir

exclusion [ɛks'kluʒən] *s* exclusión; **to the exclusion of** con exclusión de

exclusive [ɛks'klusɪv] *adj* exclusivo; (*clannish*) exclusivista; (*expensive*) (coll) carero; (*fashionable*) (coll) muy de moda; **exclusive of** con exclusión de

excommunicate [ˌɛkskə'mjunɪˌket] *tr* excomulgar

excommunication [ˌɛkskəˌmjunɪ'ke∫ən] *s* excomunión

excoriate [ɛks'korɪˌet] *tr* (fig) desollar, vituperar

excrement ['ɛkskrəmənt] *s* excremento

excruciating [ɛks'kruʃɪˌetɪŋ] *adj* atroz, agudísimo, vivísimo

exculpate ['ɛkskʌlˌpet] o [ɛks'kʌlpet] *tr* exculpar

excursion [ɛks'kʌrʒən] o [ɛks'kʌr∫ən] *s* excursión

excursionist [ɛks'kʌrʒənɪst] o [ɛks'kʌr∫ənɪst] *s* excursionista *mf*

excusable [ɛks'kjusəbəl] *adj* excusable

excuse [ɛks'kjus] *s* excusa ‖ [ɛks'kjuz] *tr* excusar, disculpar; dispensar, perdonar

execute ['ɛksɪˌkjut] *tr* ejecutar; (law) celebrar, finalizar (*una escritura*)

execution [ˌɛksɪ'kju∫ən] *s* ejecución

executioner [ˌɛksɪ'kju∫ənər] *s* ejecutor *m* de la justicia, verdugo

executive [ɛg'zɛkjətɪv] *adj* ejecutivo ‖ *m* poder ejecutivo; (*of a school, business, etc.*) dirigente *mf*

Executive Mansion *s* (U.S.A.) palacio presidencial

executor [ɛg'zɛkjətər] *s* albacea *m*, ejecutor testamentario

executrix [ɛg'zɛkjətrɪks] *s* albacea *f*, ejecutora testamentaria

exemplary [ɛg'zɛmplərɪ] o ['ɛgzəmˌplɛrɪ] *adj* ejemplar

exempli-fy [ɛg'zɛmplɪˌfaɪ] *v* (*pret & pp* **-fied**) *tr* ejemplificar

exempt [ɛg'zɛmpt] *adj* exento ‖ *tr* eximir, exentar

exemption [ɛg'zɛmp∫ən] *s* exención

exercise ['ɛksərˌsaɪz] *s* ejercicio; ceremonia; **to take exercise** hacer ejercicio ‖ *tr* ejercer (*p.ej., caridad, influencia*); ejercitar (*un arte, profesión, etc.; adiestrar con el ejercicio*); inquietar, preocupar; poner (*cuidado*) ‖ *ref* ejercitarse

exert [ɛg'zʌrt] *tr* ejercer (*una fuerza*); **to exert oneself** esforzarse

exertion [ɛg'zʌr∫ən] *s* esfuerzo, empeño; (*active use*) ejercicio

exhalation [ˌɛks-hə'le∫ən] *s* (*of gas, vapors, etc.*) exhalación; (*of air from lungs*) espiración

exhale [ɛks'hel] o [ɛg'zel] *tr* exhalar (*gases, vapores*); espirar (*el aire aspirado*) ‖ *intr* exhalarse; espirar

exhaust [ɛg'zɔst] *s* escape *m*; tubo de escape ‖ *tr* (*to wear out; fatigue; to use up*) agotar; hacer el vacío en; apurar (*todos los medios*)

exhaust fan *s* ventilador *m* aspirador

exhaustion [ɛg'zɔst∫ən] *s* agotamiento

exhaustive [ɛg'zɔstɪv] *adj* exhaustivo; comprensivo

exhaust manifold *s* múltiple *m* de escape

exhaust pipe *s* tubo de escape

exhaust valve *s* válvula de escape

exhibit [ɛg'zɪbɪt] *s* exhibición; (law) documento de prueba ‖ *tr* exhibir

exhibition [ˌɛksɪ'bɪ∫ən] *s* exhibición

exhibitor [ɛg'zɪbɪtər] *s* expositor *m*

exhilarating [ɛg'zɪləˌretɪŋ] *adj* alegrador, regocijador, alborozador

exhort [ɛg'zɔrt] *tr* exhortar

exhume [ɛks'hjum] o [ɛg'zjum] *tr* exhumar

exigen-cy ['ɛksɪdʒənsɪ] *s* (*pl* **-cies**) exigencia

exigent ['ɛksɪdʒənt] *adj* exigente

exile ['ɛgzaɪl] o ['ɛksaɪl] *s* destierro; (*person*) desterrado ‖ *tr* desterrar

exist [ɛg'zɪst] *intr* existir

existence [ɛg'zɪstəns] *s* existencia

existing [ɛg'zɪstɪŋ] *adj* existente

exit ['ɛgzɪt] o ['ɛksɪt] *s* salida ‖ *intr* salir

exodus ['ɛksədəs] *s* éxodo

exonerate [ɛg'zɑnəˌret] *tr* (*to free from blame*) exculpar; (*to free from an obligation*) exonerar

exorbitant [ɛg'zɔrbɪtənt] *adj* exorbitante

exorcise ['ɛksɔrˌsaɪz] *tr* exorcizar

exotic [ɛg'zɑtɪk] *adj* exótico

exp. *abbr* **expenses, expired, export, express**

expand [ɛks'pænd] *tr* dilatar (*un gas, el metal*); (*to enlarge, develop*) ampliar, ensanchar; (*to unfold, stretch out*) desplegar, extender; (math) desarrollar (*una ecuación*) ‖ *intr* dilatarse; ampliarse, ensancharse; desplegarse, extenderse

expanse [ɛks'pæns] s extensión

expansion [ɛks'pænʃən] s expansión

expansive [ɛks'pænsɪv] *adj* expansivo

expatiate [ɛks'peʃɪ,et] *intr* espaciarse, explayarse

expatriate [ɛks'petrɪ·ɪt] *adj* & s expatriado

expect [ɛks'pɛkt] *tr* esperar; (coll) creer, suponer

expectan·cy [ɛks'pɛktənsi] s (*pl* -cies) expectación

expectant mother [ɛks'pɛktənt] s futura madre

expectation [,ɛkspɛk'teʃən] s expectativa

expectorate [ɛks'pɛktə,ret] *tr* & *intr* expectorar

expedien·cy [ɛks'pidɪ·ənsi] s (*pl* -cies) conveniencia, oportunidad; ventaja personal

expedient [ɛks'pidɪ·ənt] *adj* conveniente, oportuno; egoísta, ventajoso; (*acting with self-interest*) ventajista || s expediente *m*

expedite ['ɛkspɪ,daɪt] *tr* apresurar, despachar; dar curso a (*un documento*)

expedition [,ɛkspɪ'dɪʃən] s expedición

expeditious [,ɛkspɪ'dɪʃəs] *adj* expeditivo

expeditiously [,ɛkspɪ'dɪʃəsli] *adv* ejecutivamente

ex·pel [ɛks'pɛl] *v* (*pret* & *pp* -pelled; *ger* -pelling) *tr* expeler, expulsar

expend [ɛks'pɛnd] *tr* gastar, consumir

expendable [ɛks'pɛndəbəl] *adj* gastable; (*to be thrown away after use*) desechable; (*soldier*) sacrificable

expenditure [ɛks'pɛndɪtʃər] s gasto, consumo

expense [ɛks'pɛns] s gasto; **expenses** gastos, expensas; **to go to the expense of** meterse en gastos con; **to meet expenses** hacer frente a los gastos

expense account s cuenta de gastos

expensive [ɛks'pɛnsɪv] *adj* caro, costoso, dispendioso; (*charging high prices*) carero

experience [ɛks'pɪrɪ·əns] s experiencia || *tr* experimentar

experienced [ɛks'pɪrɪ·ənst] *adj* experimentado

experiment [ɛks'pɛrɪmənt] s experiencia, experimento || [ɛks'pɛrɪ,mɛnt] *intr* experimentar

expert ['ɛkspərt] *adj* & s experto

expiate ['ɛkspɪ,et] *tr* expiar

expiation [,ɛkspɪ'eʃən] s expiación

expire [ɛks'paɪr] *tr* expeler (*el aire de los pulmones*) || *intr* expirar (*expeler el aire de los pulmones; acabarse, p.ej., un plazo; fallecer*)

explain [ɛks'plen] *tr* explicar; **to explain away** descartar con explicaciones; (*to make excuse for*) explicar || *intr* explicar, explicarse

explanation [,ɛksplə'neʃən] s explicación

explanatory [ɛks'plænə,tori] *adj* explicativo

explicit [ɛks'plɪsɪt] *adj* explícito

explode [ɛks'plod] *tr* volar, hacer saltar; desacreditar (*una teoría*) || *intr* explotar, estallar, reventar

exploit [ɛks'plɔɪt] o ['ɛksplɔɪt] s hazaña, proeza || [ɛks'plɔɪt] *tr* explotar

exploitation [,ɛksplɔɪ'teʃən] s explotación

exploration [,ɛksplə'reʃən] s exploración

explore [ɛks'plor] *tr* explorar

explorer [ɛks'plorər] s explorador *m*

explosion [ɛks'ploʒən] s explosión; (*of a theory*) refutación

explosive [ɛks'plosɪv] *adj* explosivo || s explosivo; (phonet) explosiva

exponent [ɛks'ponənt] s exponente *m*, expositor *m*; (math) exponente *m*

export ['ɛksport] *adj* de exportación || s exportación; **exports** (*articles exported*) exportación || [ɛks'port] o ['ɛksport] *tr* & *intr* exportar

exportation [,ɛkspor'teʃən] s exportación

exporter ['ɛksportər] o [ɛks'portər] s exportador *m*

expose [ɛks'poz] *tr* exponer; (*to unmask*) desenmascarar; (*the Host*) manifestar, exponer; (phot) impresionar

exposé [,ɛkspo'ze] s desenmascaramiento

exposition [,ɛkspə'zɪʃən] s exposición; (rhet) exposición

expostulate [ɛks'pɑstʃə,let] *intr* protestar; **to expostulate with** reconvenir

exposure [ɛks'poʒər] s (*to a danger; position with respect to points of compass*) exposición; (*unmasking*) desenmascaramiento; (phot) exposición

expound [ɛks'paund] *tr* exponer

express [ɛks'prɛs] *adj* expreso || *adv* (*for a special purpose*) expresamente; por expreso || s expreso; **by express** (rr) en gran velocidad || *tr* expresar; (*to squeeze out*) exprimir; enviar por expreso; **to express oneself** expresarse

express company s compañía de transportes rápidos

expression [ɛks'prɛʃən] s expresión

expressive [ɛks'prɛsɪv] *adj* expresivo

expressly [ɛks'prɛsli] *adv* expresamente

express·man [ɛks'prɛsmən] s (*pl* -men [mən]) (U.S.A.) empleado del servicio de transportes rápidos

express train s tren expreso

express'way s carretera de vía libre

expropriate [ɛks'proprɪ,et] *tr* expropiar

expulsion [ɛks'pʌlʃən] s expulsión

expunge [ɛks'pʌndʒ] *tr* borrar, cancelar, arrasar

expurgate ['ɛkspər,get] *tr* expurgar

exquisite [ɛks'kwɪzɪt] o [ɛks'kwɪzɪt] *adj* exquisito; agudo, vivo; sensible

ex-service·man [,ɛks'sɑrvɪs,mæn] s (*pl* -men [,mɛn]) ex militar *m*, ex combatiente *m*

extant [′ɛkstənt] o [ɛks′tænt] *adj* existente

extemporaneous [ɛks‚tɛmpə′rɛnɪ-əs] *adj* sin preparación; (*made for the occasion*) provisional

extempore [ɛks′tɛmpəri] *adj* improvisado || *adv* improvisadamente

extemporize [ɛks′tɛmpə‚raɪz] *tr* & *intr* improvisar

extend [ɛks′tɛnd] *tr* extender; dar, ofrecer; hacer extensivos (*p.ej., vivos deseos*); prorrogar (*un plazo*) || *intr* extenderse

extended [ɛks′tɛndɪd] *adj* extenso; prolongado

extension [ɛks′tɛnʃən] *s* extensión; prolongación

extension ladder *s* escalera extensible

extension table *s* mesa de extensión

extensive [ɛks′tɛnsɪv] *adj* (*having great extent*) extenso; (*characterized by extension*) extensivo

extent [ɛks′tɛnt] *s* extensión; **to a certain extent** hasta cierto punto; **to a great extent** en sumo grado; **to the full extent** en toda su extensión

extenuate [ɛks′tɛnju‚et] *tr* (*to make seem less serious*) atenuar; (*to underrate*) menospreciar, no dar importancia a

exterior [ɛks′tɪrɪ-ər] *adj* & *s* exterior *m*

exterminate [ɛks′tɑrmɪ‚net] *tr* exterminar

external [ɛks′tɑrnəl] *adj* externo || **externals** *spl* exterioridad

extinct [ɛks′tɪŋkt] *adj* desaparecido; (*volcano*) extinto

extinguish [ɛks′tɪŋgwɪʃ] *tr* extinguir

extinguisher [ɛks′tɪŋgwɪʃər] *s* apagador *m*, extintor *m*

extirpate [′ɛkstər‚pet] o [ɛks′tɑrpet] *tr* extirpar

ex-tol [ɛks′tol] o [ɛks′tal] *v* (*pret* & *pp* **-tolled;** *ger* **-tolling**) *tr* ensalzar

extort [ɛks′tɔrt] *tr* obtener por amenazas, fuerza o engaño

extortion [ɛks′tɔrʃən] *s* extorción

extra [′ɛkstrə] *adj* extra; (*spare*) de repuesto || *adv* extraordinariamente || *s* (*of a newspaper*) extra *m*; pieza de repuesto; (*something additional*) extra *m*; (*theat*) extra *mf*

extract [′ɛkstrækt] *s* selección; (*pharm*) extracto || [ɛks′trækt] *tr* (*to pull out, remove*) extraer; seleccionar (*pasajes de un libro*); (*math*) extraer

extraction [ɛks′trækʃən] *s* extracción

extracurricular [‚ɛkstrəkə′rɪkjələr] *adj* extracurricular

extradition [‚ɛkstrə′dɪʃən] *s* extradición

extra fare *s* recargo de tarifa, tarifa recargada

ex′tra-flat′ *adj* extraplano

extramural [‚ɛkstrə′mjurəl] *adj* extramural

extraneous [ɛks′trɛnɪ-əs] *adj* ajeno, extraño

extraordinary [ɛks′trɔrdɪ‚nɛri] o [ɛks′trɔrdɪ‚nɛri] *adj* extraordinario

extrapolate [ɛks′træpə‚let] *tr* & *intr* extrapolar

extrasensory [‚ɛkstrə′sɛnsəri] *adj* extrasensorio

extravagance [ɛks′trævəgəns] *s* derroche *m*, prodigalidad, gasto excesivo; (*wildness, folly*) extravagancia

extravagant [ɛks′trævəgənt] *adj* derrochador, pródigo, gastador; (*wild, foolish*) extravagante

extreme [ɛks′trim] *adj* & *s* extremo; **in the extreme** en sumo grado; **to go to extremes** excederse, propasarse

extremely [ɛks′trimli] *adv* extremadamente, sumamente

extreme unction *s* extremaunción

extremi-ty [ɛks′trɛmɪti] *s* (*pl* **-ties**) extremidad; (*great want*) extrema necesidad; **extremities** medidas extremas; (*hands and feet*) extremidades

extricate [′ɛkstrɪ‚ket] *tr* desembarazar, desenredar

extrinsic [ɛks′trɪnsɪk] *adj* extrínseco

extrovert [′ɛkstrə‚vʌrt] *s* extrovertido

extrude [ɛks′trud] *intr* resaltar, sobresalir

exuberant [ɛg′zubərənt] o [ɛg′zjubərənt] *adj* exuberante

exude [ɛg′zud] o [ɛk′sud] *tr* & *intr* exudar

exult [ɛg′zʌlt] *intr* exultar, gloriarse

exultant [ɛg′zʌltənt] *adj* exultante

eye [aɪ] *s* ojo; (*of hook and eye*) hembra, corcheta; **to catch one's eye** llamar la atención a uno; **to feast one's eyes on** delicitar la vista en; **to lay eyes on** alcanzar a ver; **to make eyes at** hacer guiños a; **to roll one's eyes** poner los ojos en blanco; **to see eye to eye** estar completamente de acuerdo; **to shut one's eyes to** hacer la vista gorda ante; **without batting an eye** sin pestañear, sin inmutarse || *v* (*pret* & *pp* **eyed;** *ger* **eying**) *tr* ojear; **to eye up and down** mirar de hito en hito

eye′ball′ *s* globo del ojo

eye′bolt′ *s* armella, cáncamo

eye′brow′ *s* ceja; **to raise one's eyebrows** arquear las cejas

eye′cup′ *s* ojera, lavaojos *m*

eyeful [′aɪful] *s* (coll) buena ojeada

eye′glass′ *s* (*of optical instrument*) ocular *m*; (*eyecup*) ojera, lavaojos *m*; **eyeglasses** gafas, anteojos

eye′lash′ *s* pestaña

eyelet [′aɪlɪt] *s* ojete *m*, ojal *m*; (*hole to look through*) mirilla

eye′lid′ *s* párpado

eye of the morning *s* sol *m*

eye opener [′opənər] *s* noticia asombrosa o inesperada; (coll) trago de licor

eye′piece′ *s* ocular *m*

eye′-shade′ *s* visera

eye shadow *s* crema para los párpados

eye′shot′ *s* alcance *m* de la vista

eye′sight′ *s* vista; (*range*) alcance *m* de la vista

eye socket *s* cuenca del ojo

eye′sore′ *s* cosa que ofende la vista

eye′strain′ *s* vista fatigada

eye′-test′ chart *s* escala tipográfica oftalmométrica, tipo de ensayo, tipo de prueba

eye'tooth' *s* (*pl* **teeth'**) colmillo, diente canino; **to cut one's eyeteeth** (coll) tener el colmillo retorcido; **to give one's eyeteeth for** (coll) dar los ojos de la cara por

eye'wash' *s* colirio; (slang) halago para engañar

eye'wit'ness *s* testigo ocular, testigo presencial

ey·rie o **ey·ry** [ˈerɪ] *s* (*pl* **-ries**) nido de águilas, nido de aves de rapiña; (fig) altura, morada elevada

F

F, f [ef] sexta letra del alfabeto inglés

f. *abbr* **feminine, folio**

F. *abbr* **Fahrenheit, Friday**

fable [ˈfebəl] *s* fábula

fabric [ˈfæbrɪk] *s* tejido; textura; (*structure*) fábrica

fabricate [ˈfæbrɪˌket] *tr* fabricar

fabrication [ˌfæbrɪˈkeʃən] *s* fabricación; mentira

fabulous [ˈfæbjələs] *adj* fabuloso

façade [fəˈsɑd] *s* fachada

face [fes] *s* cara, rostro; (*of cloth*) haz *f*; (*of earth*) faz *f*; (*grimace*) mueca; (*of watch*) esfera, muestra; (*impudence*) descaro; **in the face of** en presencia de; **to keep a straight face** contener la risa; **to lose face** desprestigiarse; **to save face** salvar las apariencias; **to show one's face** dejarse ver ‖ *tr* volver la cara hacia; arrostrar; revestir (*un muro*); forrar (*un vestido*); **facing** cara a ‖ *intr* — **to face about** volver la mirada; dar media vuelta; cambiar de opinión; **to face on** dar a o sobre; **to face up to** encararse con

face card *s* figura, naipe *m* de figura

face lifting *s* cirugía estética

face powder *s* polvos de tocador

facet [ˈfæsɪt] *s* faceta

facial [ˈfeʃəl] *adj* facial ‖ *s* masaje *m* facial

facilitate [fəˈsɪlɪˌtet] *tr* facilitar

facili·ty [fəˈsɪlɪti] *s* (*pl* **-ties**) facilidad

facing [ˈfesɪŋ] *s* revestimiento, paramento

facsimile [fækˈsɪmɪli] *s* facsímile *m*

fact [fækt] *s* hecho; **in fact** en realidad; **the fact is that** ello es que

faction [ˈfækʃən] *s* facción; discordia

factional [ˈfækʃənəl] *adj* faccionario

factionalism [ˈfækʃənəˌlɪzəm] *s* parcialidad, partidismo

factor [ˈfæktər] *s* factor *m* ‖ *tr* descomponer en factores

facto·ry [ˈfæktəri] *s* (*pl* **-ries**) fábrica

factual [ˈfæktʊˌəl] *adj* verdadero, objetivo

facul·ty [ˈfækəlti] *s* (*pl* **-ties**) facultad

fad [fæd] *s* afición pasajera, moda pasajera

fade [fed] *tr* desteñir ‖ *intr* desteñir, desteñirse; apagarse (*un sonido*); (rad) desvanecerse

fade'out' *s* desaparición gradual; (rad) desvanecimiento

fag [fæg] *s* (*drudge*) yunque *m*; (coll) cigarrillo ‖ *tr* — **to fag out** cansar

fagot [ˈfægət] *s* haz *m* de leña

fail [fel] *s* — **without fail** sin falta ‖ *tr* faltar a; reprobar, suspender (*a un alumno*); salir mal en (*un examen*) ‖ *intr* malograrse, fracasar; salir mal (*un alumno*); fallar (*un motor*); (com) quebrar, hacer bancarrota; **to fail to** dejar de

failure [ˈfeljər] *s* malogro, fracaso, mal éxito; (*student*) perdigón *m*; (com) quiebra

faint [fent] *adj* débil; **to feel faint** sentirse desfallecido ‖ *s* desmayo ‖ *intr* desmayarse

faint-hearted [ˈfentˈhɑrtɪd] *adj* cobarde, tímido, apocado

fair [fer] *adj* justo, imparcial; regular, ordinario; favorable, propicio; (*hair*) rubio; (*complexion*) blanco; (*sky*) despejado; (*weather*) bueno, bonancible ‖ *adv* imparcialmente; **to play fair** jugar limpio ‖ *s* (*exhibition*) feria; (*carnival*) quermese *m*, verbena

fair'ground' *s* real *m*, campo de una feria

fairly [ˈferli] *adv* justamente; bastante

fair-minded [ˈferˈmaɪndɪd] *adj* justo, imparcial

fairness [ˈfernɪs] *s* justicia, imparcialidad; (*of weather*) serenidad; (*of complexion*) blancura

fair play *s* juego limpio, limpieza

fair sex *s* bello sexo

fair to middling *adj* bastante bueno, mediano

fair'weath'er *adj* — **a fair-weather friend** amigo del buen viento

fair·y [ˈferi] *adj* feérico ‖ *s* (*pl* **-ies**) hada

fairy godmother *s* hada madrina

fair'y·land' *s* tierra de las hadas

fairy ring *s* corro de brujas

fairy tale *s* cuento de hadas; (fig) bella poesía

faith [feθ] *s* fe *f*; **to break faith with** faltar a la palabra dada a; **to keep faith with** cumplir la palabra dada a; **to pin one's faith on** tener puesta su esperanza en; **upon my faith!** ¡a fe mía!

faithful [ˈfeθfəl] *adj* fiel, leal ‖ **the faithful** los fieles

faithless [ˈfeθlɪs] *adj* infiel, desleal

fake [fek] *adj* (coll) falso, fingido ‖ *s* impostura, patraña; (*person*) farsante *mf* ‖ *tr* & *intr* falsificar, fingir

faker [ˈfekər] *s* (coll) impostor *m*, patrañero; (*peddler*) (coll) buhonero

falcon [ˈfɔkən] o [ˈfɔlkən] *s* halcón *m*

falconer [ˈfɔkənər] o [ˈfɔlkənər] s cetrero, halconero

falconry [ˈfɔkənrɪ] o [ˈfɔlkənrɪ] s cetrería, halconería

fall [fɔl] adj otoñal ‖ s caída; (of water) catarata, salto de agua; (of prices) baja; (autumn) otoño; falls catarata, caída de agua ‖ v (pret fell [fel]; pp fallen [ˈfɔlən]) intr caer, caerse; **to fall apart** caerse a pedazos; **to fall back** (mil) replegarse; **to fall behind** quedarse atrás; **to fall down** caerse; **to fall due** vencer (una letra); **to fall flat** caer tendido; no tener éxito; **to fall for** (slang) ser engañado por; (slang) enamorarse de; **to fall in** desplomarse (un techo); ponerse de acuerdo; **to fall in with** trabar amistades con; ponerse de acuerdo con; **to fall off** caer de; disminuir; **to fall out** desavenirse; **to fall out of** caerse de; **to fall out with** esquinarse con; **to fall over** caerse; (coll) adular, halagar; **to fall through** fracasar, malograrse; **to fall to recaer** (la herencia, la elección) en; **to fall under** estar comprendido en

fallacious [fəˈleʃəs] adj erróneo, engañoso

falla·cy [ˈfæləsɪ] s (pl -cies) error m, equivocación

fall guy s (slang) cabeza de turco

fallible [ˈfælɪbəl] adj falible

falling star s estrella fugaz

fall'out' s caída radiactiva, precipitación radiactiva

fallout shelter s refugio antiatómico

fallow [ˈfælo] adj barbechado; **to lie fallow** estar en barbecho (tierra labrantía); (fig) quedar sin emplear, quedar sin ejecutar (una cosa provechosa) ‖ s barbecho ‖ tr barbechar

false [fɔls] adj falso; (hair, teeth, etc.) postizo ‖ adv falsamente; **to play false** traicionar

false colors spl pretextos falsos

false face s mascarilla; (ugly false face) carantamaula

false-hearted [ˈfɔlsˈhɑrtɪd] adj pérfido

falsehood [ˈfɔlsˈhʊd] s falsedad

false pretenses spl impostura, falsas apariencias

false return s declaración falsa

falset·to [fɔlˈsɛto] s (pl -tos) (voice) falsete m; (person) falsetista m

falsi·fy [ˈfɔlsɪˌfaɪ] v (pret & pp -fied) tr falsificar; (to disprove) refutar ‖ intr falsificar; mentir

falsi·ty [ˈfɔlsɪtɪ] s (pl -ties) falsedad

falter [ˈfɔltər] s vacilación; (in speech) balbuceo ‖ intr vacilar; balbucear

fame [fem] s fama

famed [femd] adj afamado

familiar [fəˈmɪljər] adj familiar; conocido; común; **familiar with** familiarizado con

familiari·ty [fəˌmɪlɪˈærɪtɪ] s (pl -ties) familiaridad; conocimiento

familiarize [fəˈmɪljəˌraɪz] tr familiarizar

fami·ly [ˈfæmɪlɪ] adj familiar; **in the family way** (coll) en estado de buena esperanza ‖ s (pl -lies) familia

family man s padre m de familia; hombre casero

family name s apellido

family physician s médico de cabecera

family tree s árbol genealógico

famish [ˈfæmɪʃ] tr & intr hambrear

famished [ˈfæmɪʃt] adj famélico

famous [ˈfeməs] adj famoso; (notable, excellent) (coll) famoso

fan [fæn] s abanico; ventilador m; (slang) hincha mf, aficionado ‖ v (pret & pp fanned) ger fanning) tr abanicar; (to winnow) aventar; ahuyentar con abanico; avivar (el fuego); excitar (las pasiones); (slang) azotar ‖ intr abanicarse; **to fan out** salir (un camino) en todas direcciones

fanatic [fəˈnætɪk] adj & s fanático

fanatical [fəˈnætɪkəl] adj fanático

fanaticism [fəˈnætɪˌsɪzəm] s fanatismo

fancied [ˈfænsɪd] adj imaginario

fancier [ˈfænsɪ·ər] s aficionado; visionario; (of animals) criador aficionado

fanciful [ˈfænsɪfəl] adj fantástico, extravagante; imaginativo

fan·cy [ˈfænsɪ] adj (comp -cier; super -ciest) de fantasía, de imitación; fino, de lujo, precioso; ornamental; primoroso; fantástico, extravagante ‖ s (pl -cies) fantasía; afición, gusto; **to take a fancy to** aficionarse a, prendarse de ‖ v (pret & pp -cied) tr imaginar

fancy ball s baile m de trajes

fancy dive s salto ornamental

fancy dress s traje m de fantasía

fancy foods spl comestibles mpl de lujo

fan'cy-free' adj libre del poder del amor

fancy jewelry s joyas de fantasía

fancy skating s patinaje m de fantasía

fan'cy·work' s (sew) labor f

fanfare [ˈfænfer] s fanfarria

fang [fæŋ] s colmillo; (of reptile) diente m

fan'light' s abanico

fantastic(al) [fænˈtæstɪk(əl)] adj fantástico

fanta·sy [ˈfæntəzɪ] o [ˈfæntəsɪ] s (pl -sies) fantasía

far [fɑr] adj lejano; **on the far side of** del otro lado de ‖ adv lejos; as far as hasta; en cuanto; **as far as I am concerned** por lo que a mí me toca; **as far as I know** que yo sepa; **by far** con mucho; **far and near** por todas partes; **far away** muy lejos; **far be it from me** no lo permita Dios; **far better** mucho mejor; **far different** muy diferente; **far from** lejos de; **far from it** ni con mucho; **far into** hasta muy adentro de; hasta muy tarde de; **far more** mucho más; **far off** a gran distancia; **far how** far cuán lejos; **how far is it?** ¿cuánto hay de aquí?; **in so far as** en cuanto; **thus far** hasta ahora; **thus far this year** en lo que va del año; **to go far towards** contribuir mucho a

faraway [ˈfɑrəˌwe] adj lejano, distante; abstraído, preocupado

farce [fɑrs] s farsa
farcical ['fɑrsɪkəl] adj ridículo
fare [fer] s pasaje m; pasajero; alimento; comida; **to collect fares** cobrar el pasaje || intr pasarlo, p.ej., **how did you fare?** ¿cómo lo pasó Vd.?
Far East s Extremo Oriente, Lejano Oriente
fare'well' s despedida; **to bid farewell to** o **to take farewell of** despedirse de || interj ¡adiós!
far-fetched ['fɑr'fɛtʃt] adj traído por los pelos
far-flung ['fɑr'flʌŋ] adj de gran alcance, vasto
farm [fɑrm] adj agrícola; agropecuario || s granja; terreno agrícola || tr cultivar, labrar (la tierra) || intr cultivar la tierra y criar animales
farmer ['fɑrmər] s granjero; agricultor m, labrador m
farm hand s peón m, mozo de granja
farm'house' s alquería, cortijo
farming ['fɑrmɪŋ] s agricultura, labranza
farm'yard' s corral m de granja
far'-off' adj lejano, distante
far-reaching ['fɑr'ritʃɪŋ] adj de mucho alcance
far-sighted ['fɑr'saɪtɪd] adj longividente; precavido; présbita
farther ['fɑrðər] adj más lejano; adicional || adv más lejos, más allá; además, también; **farther on** más adelante
farthest ['fɑrðɪst] adj (el) más lejano; último || adv más lejos; más
farthing ['fɑrðɪŋ] s (Brit) cuarto de penique
Far West s (U.S.A.) Lejano Oeste
fascinate ['fæsɪ,net] tr fascinar
fascinating ['fæsɪ,netɪŋ] adj fascinante, cautivador
fascism ['fæsɪzəm] s fascismo
fascist ['fæsɪst] adj & s fascista mf
fashion ['fæʃən] s moda, boga; estilo, manera; alta sociedad; **after a fashion** en cierto modo; **in fashion** de moda; **out of fashion** fuera de moda; **to go out of fashion** pasar de moda || tr labrar, forjar
fashion designing s alta costura
fashion plate s figurín m; (person) (coll) figurín m, elegante mf; **to be a fashion plate** (coll) ir hecho un maniquí
fashion show s desfile m de modas
fast [fæst] o [fast] adj rápido, veloz; (clock) adelantado; fijado; disipado; (friend) fiel || adv aprisa, rápidamente; firmemente; (asleep) profundamente; **to hold fast** mantenerse firme; **to live fast** vivir de una manera disipada || s ayuno; **to break one's fast** romper el ayuno || intr ayunar
fast day s día m de ayuno
fasten ['fæsən] o ['fasən] tr fijar; atar; abrochar; cerrar con llave; (one's belt) ajustarse; (blame) aplicar || intr fijarse

fastener ['fæsənər] o ['fasənər] s asilla; (snap, clasp) cierre m; (for papers) sujetapapeles m
fastidious [fæs'tɪdɪ·əs] adj esquilmoso, quisquilloso, descontentadizo
fasting ['fæstɪŋ] o ['fastɪŋ] s ayuno
fat [fæt] adj (comp fatter; super fattest) gordo; poderoso; opulento; (profitable) pingüe; (spark) caliente; **to get fat** engordar || s grasa; (suet) gordo, sebo
fatal ['fetəl] adj fatal
fatalism ['fetə,lɪzəm] s fatalismo
fatalist ['fetəlɪst] s fatalista mf
fatali·ty [fə'tælɪti] s (pl -ties) fatalidad; (in accidents, war, etc.) muerte f
fate [fet] s sino, hado; **the Fates** las Parcas || tr condenar, predestinar
fated ['fetɪd] adj hadado, predestinado
fateful ['fetfəl] adj fatídico; fatal
fat'head' s (coll) tronco, estúpido
father ['fɑðər] s padre m; (an elderly man) (coll) tío || tr servir de padre a; engendrar; inventar
fatherhood ['fɑðər,hʊd] s paternidad
fa'ther-in-law' s (pl fathers-in-law) suegro
fa'ther·land' s patria
fatherless ['fɑðərlɪs] adj huérfano de padre, sin padre
fatherly ['fɑðərli] adj paternal
Father's Day s día m del padre
Father Time s el Tiempo
fathom ['fæðəm] s braza || tr sondear; profundizar
fathomless ['fæðəmlɪs] adj insondable
fatigue [fə'tig] s fatiga; (mil) faena || tr fatigar, cansar
fatigue clothes spl (mil) traje m de faena
fatigue duty s faena
fatten ['fætən] tr & intr engordar
fat·ty ['fæti] adj (comp -tier; super -tiest) graso; (pathol) grasoso; (chubby) (coll) gordiflón || s (pl -ties) (coll) gordiflón m
fatuous ['fætʃu·əs] adj fatuo; irreal, ilusivo
faucet ['fɔsɪt] s grifo
fault [fɔlt] s (misdeed, blame) culpa; (defect) falta; (geol) falla; (sport) falta; **it's your fault** Vd. tiene la culpa; **to a fault** excesivamente; **to find fault with** culpar, echar la culpa a; hallar defecto en
fault'find'er s criticón m, reparón m
fault'find'ing adj criticón, reparón || s manía de criticar
faultless ['fɔltlɪs] adj perfecto, impecable
fault·y ['fɔlti] adj (comp -ier; super -iest) defectuoso, imperfecto
faun [fɔn] s fauno
fauna ['fɔnə] s fauna
favor ['fevər] s favor m; (letter) atenta, grata; **do me the favor to** hágame Vd. el favor de; **by your favor** con permiso de Vd.; **favors** regalos de fiesta, objetos de cotillón; **to be in favor with** disfrutar del favor de; **to be out of favor** caer en desgracia || tr favorecer; (coll) parecerse a

favorable ['fevərəbəl] *adj* favorable
favorite ['fevərɪt] *adj* & *s* favorito
favoritism ['fevərɪ,tɪzəm] *s* favoritismo
fawn [fɔn] *s* cervato || *intr* — **to fawn on** adular servilmente; hacer fiestas a
faze [fez] *tr* (coll) molestar, desanimar
FBI [,ɛf,bi'aɪ] *s* (letterword) Federal Bureau of Investigation
fear [fɪr] *s* miedo; **for fear of** por miedo de, por temor de; **for fear that** por miedo (de) que; **no fear** no hay peligro; **to be in fear of** tener miedo de || *tr* & *intr* temer
fearful ['fɪrfəl] *adj* medroso; (coll) enorme, muy malo
fearless ['fɪrlɪs] *adj* arrojado, intrépido
feasible [fisɪbəl] *adj* factible, viable
feast [fist] *s* fiesta; (*sumptuous meal*) festín *m*, banquete *m* || *tr* & *intr* banquetear; **to feast on** regalarse con
feat [fit] *s* hazaña, proeza
feather ['fɛðər] *s* pluma; (*plume; arrogance*) penacho; clase *f*, género; **in fine feather** de buen humor; en buena salud || *tr* emplumar; (carp) machihembrar; **to feather one's nest** hacer todo para enriquecerse
feather bed *s* colchón *m* de plumas; (*comfortable situation*) lecho de plumas
feath'er-bed'ding *s* empleo de más obreros de lo necesario (*exigido por los sindicatos*)
feath'er-brain' *s* cascabelero
feath'er-edge' *s* (*of board*) bisel *m*; (*of sharpened tool*) filván *m*
feathery ['fɛðəri] *adj* plumoso
feature ['fit/ər] *s* facción; característica, rasgo distintivo; película principal; artículo principal; **features** facciones || *tr* delinear; ofrecer como cosa principal; (coll) destacar, hacer resaltar
feature writer *s* articulista *mf*
February ['fɛbru,ɛri] *s* febrero
feces [fisiz] *spl* heces *fpl*
feckless ['fɛklɪs] *adj* abatido, sin valor; débil
federal ['fɛdərəl] *adj* & *s* federal *mf*
federate ['fɛdə,ret] *adj* federado || *tr* federar || *intr* federarse
federation [,fɛdə'reʃən] *s* federación
fedora [fɪ'dorə] *s* sombrero de fieltro suave con ala vuelta
fed up [fɛd] *adj* harto
fee [fi] *s* honorarios; (*for admission, tuition, etc.*) cuota, precio; (*tip*) propina || *tr* pagar; dar propina a
feeble ['fibəl] *adj* débil
feeble-minded ['fibəl'maɪndɪd] *adj* imbécil; irresoluto, vacilante
feed [fid] *s* alimento, comida; (mach) dispositivo de alimentación || *v* (*pret* & *pp* fed [fɛd]) *tr* alimentar || *intr* alimentarse
feed'back' *s* regeneración, realimentación
feed bag *s* cebadera, morral *m*
feed pump *s* bomba de alimentación
feed trough *s* comedero

feed wire *s* (elec) conductor *m* de alimentación
feel [fil] *s* sensación; (*sense of what is right*) tino || *v* (*pret* & *pp* felt [fɛlt]) *tr* sentir; (*e.g., with the hands*) palpar, tentar; tomar (*el pulso*); tantear (*el camino*) || *intr* (*sick, tired, etc.*) sentirse; palpar; **to feel bad** sentirse mal; condolerse; **to feel cheap** avergonzarse; **to feel comfortable** sentirse a gusto; **to feel for** buscar tentando; condolerse de; **to feel like** tener ganas de; **to feel safe** sentirse a salvo; **to feel sorry** sentir; arrepentirse; **to feel sorry for** compadecer; arrepentirse de
feeler ['filər] *s* (*something said to draw someone out*) buscapié *m*, tranquilla; **feelers** (*of insect*) anténulas, palpos; (*of mollusk*) tentáculos
feeling ['filɪŋ] *s* (*with senses*) sensación; (*impression, emotion*) sentimiento; presentimiento; parecer *m*
feign [fen] *tr* aparentar, fingir || *intr* fingir; **to feign to be** fingirse
feint [fent] *s* (*threat*) finta; (*of fencer*) pase *m*, treta || *intr* hacer una finta
feldspar ['fɛld,spɑr] *s* feldespato
felicitate [fə'lɪsɪ,tet] *tr* felicitar
felicitous [fə'lɪsɪtəs] *adj* (*opportune*) feliz; elocuente
fell [fɛl] *adj* cruel, feroz, mortal || *tr* talar (*árboles*)
felloe ['fɛlo] *s* aro de la rueda; (*part of this*) pina
fellow ['fɛlo] *s* (coll) mozo, tipo, sujeto; (coll) pretendiente *m*; prójimo; (*of a society*) socio, miembro; (*holder of fellowship*) pensionista *mf*
fellow being *s* prójimo
fellow citizen *s* conciudadano
fellow countryman *s* compatriota *mf*
fellow man *s* prójimo
fellow member *s* consocio
fellowship ['fɛlo,ʃɪp] *s* compañerismo; (*for study*) pensión
fellow traveler *s* compañero de viaje
felon ['fɛlən] *s* delincuente *mf* de mayor cuantía; (pathol) panadizo
felo-ny ['fɛləni] *s* (*pl* -nies) delito de mayor cuantía; **to compound a felony** aceptar dinero para no procesar
felt [fɛlt] *s* fieltro
female ['fimel] *adj* (*sex*) femenino; (*animal, plant, piece of a device*) hembra || *s* hembra
feminine ['fɛmɪnɪn] *adj* & *s* femenino
feminism ['fɛmɪ,nɪzəm] *s* feminismo
fen [fɛn] *s* pantano
fence [fɛns] *s* cerca, cercado; (*for stolen goods*) alcahuete *m*; (*of a saw*) guía; **on the fence** (coll) indeciso || *tr* cercar || *intr* esgrimir
fencing ['fɛnsɪŋ] *s* (*art*) esgrima; (*act*) esgrimidura
fencing academy *s* escuela de esgrima
fend [fɛnd] *tr* — **to fend off** apartar, resguardarse de || *intr* — **to fend for oneself** (coll) tirar por su lado
fender ['fɛndər] *s* (*mudguard*) guardafango, guardabarros *m*; (*of locomotive*) quitapiedras *m*; (*of trolley car*)

salvavidas *m;* (*of ¶replace*) guarda-fuego

fennel ['fɛnəl] *s* hinojo

ferment ['fɑrment] *s* fermento; fermentación || [fər'ment] *tr & intr* fermentar

fern [fʌrn] *s* helecho

ferocious [fə'roʃəs] *adj* feroz

feroci-ty [fə'rɑsɪti] *s* (*pl* **-ties**) ferocidad

ferret ['ferɪt] *s* hurón *m* || *tr* — to ferret out huronear || *intr* huronear

Ferris wheel ['ferɪs] *s* rueda de feria, noria

fer-ry ['feri] *s* (*pl* **-ries**) bote *m* de paso, ferry-boat *m* || *v* (*pret & pp* **-ried**) *tr* pasar (*viajeros, mercancías*) a través del río || *intr* cruzar el río en barco

fer'ry-boat' *s* bote *m* de paso, ferry-boat *m*

fertile ['fʌrtɪl] *adj* fértil

fertilize ['fʌrtɪ,laɪz] *tr* abonar, fertilizar; (*to impregnate*) fecundar

fervid ['fʌrvɪd] *adj* férvido, vehemente

fervor ['fʌrvər] *s* fervor *m*

fervent ['fʌrvənt] *adj* ferviente, fervoroso

fester ['festər] *s* úlcera || *tr* enconar || *intr* enconarse (*una herida; el ánimo de uno*)

festival ['festɪvəl] *adj* festivo || *s* fiesta; (*of music*) festival *m*

festive ['festɪv] *adj* festivo

festivi-ty [fes'tɪvɪti] *s* (*pl* **-ties**) festividad

festoon [fes'tun] *s* festón *m* || *tr* festonear

fetch [fetʃ] *tr* ir por, hacer venir, traer; venderse a, venderse por

fetching ['fetʃɪŋ] *adj* (coll) encantador, atractivo

fete [fet] *s* fiesta || *tr* festejar

fetid ['fetɪd] o ['fitɪd] *adj* fétido

fetish ['fitɪʃ] o ['fetɪʃ] *s* fetiche *m*

fetlock ['fetlɑk] *s* espolón *m;* (*tuft of hair*) cerneja

fetter ['fetər] *s* grillete *m,* grillo || *tr* engrillar; impedir

fettle ['fetəl] *s* estado, condición; **in fine fettle** en buena condición

fetus ['fitəs] *s* feto

feud [fjud] *s* odio hereditario, enemistad de larga duración

feudal ['fjudəl] *adj* feudal

feudalism ['fjudə,lɪzəm] *s* feudalismo

fever ['fivər] *s* fiebre *f,* calentura

fever blister *s* escupidura, fuegos en los labios

feverish ['fivərɪʃ] *adj* febril, calenturiento

few [fju] *adj & pron* pocos, no muchos; **a few** unos pocos, unos cuantos; **quite a few** muchos

fiancé [,fi.ɑn'se] *s* novio, prometido

fiancée [,fi.ɑn'se] *s* novia, prometida

fias-co [fɪ'æsko] *s* (*pl* **-cos** o **-coes**) fiasco

fib [fɪb] *s* mentirilla || *v* (*pret & pp* **fibbed;** *ger* **fibbing**) *intr* decir mentirillas

fiber ['faɪbər] *s* fibra; carácter *m,* índole *f*

fibrous ['faɪbrəs] *adj* fibroso

fickle ['fɪkəl] *adj* inconstante, veleidoso

fiction ['fɪkʃən] *s* (*invention*) ficción; (*branch of literature*) novelística; **pure fiction!** ¡puro cuento!

fictional ['fɪkʃənəl] *adj* novelesco

fictionalize ['fɪkʃənə,laɪz] *tr* novelizar

fictitious [fɪk'tɪʃəs] *adj* ficticio

fiddle ['fɪdəl] *s* violín *m* || *tr* tocar (*un aire*) con el violín; **to fiddle away** (coll) malgastar || *intr* tocar el violín; **to fiddle with** manosear

fiddler ['fɪdlər] *s* (coll) violinista *m*

fiddling ['fɪdlɪŋ] *adj* (coll) despreciable, insignificante

fideli-ty [faɪ'delɪti] o [fɪ'delɪti] *s* (*pl* **-ties**) fidelidad

fidget ['fɪdʒɪt] *intr* agitarse, menearse; **to fidget with** manosear

fidgety ['fɪdʒɪti] *adj* inquieto, nervioso

fiduciar-y [fɪ'djuʃɪ,eri] o [fɪ'duʃɪ,eri] *adj* fiduciario || *s* (*pl* **-ies**) fiduciario

fie [faɪ] *interj* ¡qué vergüenza!

fief [fif] *s* feudo

field [fild] *adj* (mil) de campaña || *s* campo; (*sown with grain*) sembrado; (baseball) jardín *m;* (elec) campo magnético; (*of motor or dynamo*) (elec) inductor *m*

fielder ['fildər] *s* (baseball) jardinero

field glasses *spl* gemelos de campo

field hockey *s* hockey *m* sobre hierba

field magnet *s* imán *m* inductor

field marshal *s* (mil) mariscal *m* de campo

field'piece' *s* cañón *m* de campaña

fiend [find] *s* diablo; (*person*) fiera; **to be a fiend for** ser una fiera pues

fiendish ['findɪʃ] *adj* diabólico

fierce [fɪrs] *adj* feroz, fiero; (*wind*) furioso; (coll) muy malo

fierceness ['fɪrsnɪs] *s* ferocidad, fiereza; furia

fier-y ['faɪri] o ['faɪ.əri] *adj* (*comp* **-ier;** *super* **-iest**) ardiente, caliente; brioso

fife [faɪf] *s* pífano

fifteen ['fɪf'tin] *adj, pron & s* quince *m*

fifteenth ['fɪf'tinθ] *adj & s* (*in a series*) decimoquinto; (*part*) quinzavo || *s* (*in dates*) quince *m*

fifth [fɪfθ] *adj & s* quinto || *s* (*in dates*) cinco

fifth column *s* quinta columna

fifth columnist *s* quintacolumnista *mf*

fiftieth ['fɪftɪ.ɪθ] *adj & s* (*in a series*) quincuagésimo; (*part*) cincuentavo || *s* (*in dates*) cincuenta *m*

fif-ty ['fɪfti] *adj & pron* cincuenta || *s* (*pl* **-ties**) cincuenta *m*

fif'ty-fif'ty *adv* — **to go fifty-fifty** (coll) ir a medias

fig. *abbr* **figure, figuratively**

fig [fɪg] *s* higo, breva; (*tree*) higuera; (*merest trifle*) bledo

fight [faɪt] *s* lucha, pelea; ánimo, brío; **to pick a fight with** meterse con, buscar la lengua a || *tr* luchar con; dar (*batalla*); lidiar (*al toro*) || *intr* luchar, pelear; **to fight shy of** tratar de evitar

fighter ['faɪtər] s luchador m, peleador m; (warrior) combatiente m; (game person) porfiador m; (aer) avión m de combate, caza m

fig leaf s hoja de higuera; (on statues) hoja de parra

figment ['fɪgmənt] s ficción, invención

figurative ['fɪgjərətɪv] adj figurado; (representing by a likeness) figurativo

figure ['fɪgjər] s figura; (bodily form) talle m; precio; to be good at figures ser listo en aritmética; to cut a figure hacer figura; to have a good figure tener buen tipo; to keep one's figure conservar la línea || tr adornar con figuras; figurarse, imaginar; suponer, calcular; to figure out descifrar || intr figurar; to figure on contar con

fig'ure-head' s (naut) figurón m de proa, mascarón de proa; (straw man) testaferro

figure of speech s figura retórica

figure skating s patinaje artístico

figurine [ˌfɪgjə'rin] s figurilla, figurina

filament ['fɪləmənt] s filamento

filch [fɪltʃ] tr birlar, ratear

file [faɪl] s fila, hilera; (tool) lima; (collection of papers) archivo; (cabinet) archivador m, fichero || tr poner en fila; limar, archivar, clasificar; anotar || intr desfilar; to file for solicitar

file case s fichero

file clerk s fichador m

filet [fɪ'le] o ['fɪle] s filete m || tr cortar en filetes

filial ['fɪlɪəl] o ['fɪljəl] adj filial

filiation [ˌfɪlɪ'eʃən] s filiación

filibuster ['fɪlɪˌbʌstər] s obstrucción (de la aprobación de una ley); obstruccionista mf; (buccaneer) filibustero || tr obstruir (la aprobación de una ley)

filigree ['fɪlɪˌgri] adj afiligranado || s filigrana || tr afiligranar

filing ['faɪlɪŋ] s (of documents) clasificación; limadura; **filings** limadura, limalla

filing cabinet s archivador m, clasificador m

filing card s ficha

Filipi·no [ˌfɪlɪ'pino] adj filipino s (pl -nos) filipino

fill [fɪl] s (sufficiency) hartazgo; (place filled with earth) terraplén m; to have o get one's fill of darse un hartazgo de || tr llenar; rellenar; despachar (un pedido); tapar (un agujero); empastar (un diente); inflar (un neumático); llenar, ocupar (un puesto); colmar (lagunas); to fill out llenar (un formulario) || intr llenarse; rellenarse; to fill in hacer de suplente; to fill up ahogarse de emoción

filler ['fɪlər] s relleno; (of cigar) tripa; (sizing) aparejo; (in a writing) relleno

fillet ['fɪlɪt] s cinta, tira; (for hair) prendedero; (archit, bb) filete m || tr filetear || ['fɪle] o ['fɪlɪt] s (of

meat or fish) filete m || tr cortar en filetes

filling ['fɪlɪŋ] s (of a tooth) empaste m; (e.g., of a turkey) relleno; (of cigar) tripa

filling station s estación gasolinera

fillip ['fɪlɪp] s aguijón m, estímulo; (with finger) capirotazo

fil·ly ['fɪli] s (pl -lies) potra; (coll) muchacha retozona

film [fɪlm] s película; (mov) película, film m; (phot) película || tr filmar

film star s estrella de la pantalla

film strip s tira proyectable

film·y ['fɪlmi] adj (comp -ier; super -iest) delgadísimo, diáfano, sutil

filter ['fɪltər] s filtro || tr filtrar || intr filtrarse

filtering ['fɪltərɪŋ] s filtración

filter paper s papel m filtrante

filter tip s embocadura de filtro

filth [fɪlθ] s suciedad, porquería

filth·y ['fɪlθi] adj (comp -ier; super -iest) sucio, puerco

filthy lucre ['lukər] s (coll) el vil metal (dinero, raíz de muchos males)

filtrate ['fɪltret] s filtrado || tr filtrar || intr filtrarse

fin [fɪn] s aleta

final ['faɪnəl] adj final; (last in a series) último; decisivo, terminante || s examen m final; **finals** (sport) final f

finale [fɪ'nɑli] s (mus) final m

finalist ['faɪnəlɪst] s finalista mf

finally ['faɪnəli] adv finalmente, por último

finance [fɪ'næns] o ['faɪnæns] s financiación; **finances** finanzas || tr financiar

financial [fɪ'nænʃəl] o [faɪ'nænʃəl] adj financiero

financier [ˌfɪnən'sɪr] o [ˌfaɪnən'sɪr] s financiero

financing [fɪ'nænsɪŋ] o ['faɪnænsɪŋ] s financiación

finch [fɪntʃ] s pinzón m

find [faɪnd] s hallazgo || v (pret & pp found [faʊnd]) tr hallar, encontrar; to find out averiguar, darse cuenta de || intr (law) pronunciar fallo; to find out about informarse de

finder ['faɪndər] s (of camera) visor m; (of microscope) portaobjeto cuadriculado

finding ['faɪndɪŋ] s descubrimiento; (law) laudo, fallo

fine [faɪn] adj fino; (weather) bueno; divertido || adv (coll) muy bien; to feel fine (coll) sentirse muy bien de salud || s multa || tr multar

fine arts spl bellas artes

fineness s fineza; (of metal) ley f

fine print s letra menuda, tipo menudo

finer·y ['faɪnəri] s (pl -ies) adorno, galas, atavíos

fine-spun ['faɪn,spʌn] adj estirado en hilo finísimo; (fig) alambicado

finesse [fɪ'nɛs] s sutileza; (in bridge) impás m || tr hacer el impás con || intr hacer un impás

fine-toothed comb ['faɪn,tuθt] s len-

drera, peine *m* de púas finas; **to go
over with a fine-toothed comb** escudriñar minuciosamente
finger ['fɪŋgər] *s* dedo; **to burn one's
fingers** cogerse los dedos; **to put
one's finger on the spot** poner el
dedo en la llaga; **to slip between
the fingers** irse de entre los dedos;
to snap one's fingers at tratar con
desprecio; **to twist around one's
little finger** manejar a su gusto ‖ *tr*
manosear; (slang) acechar, espiar;
(slang) identificar
finger board *s* (*of guitar*) diapasón *m*;
(*of piano*) teclado
finger bowl *s* lavadedos *m*, lavafrutas
m
finger dexterity *s* (mus) dedeo
fingering ['fɪŋgərɪŋ] *s* manoseo; (mus)
digitación
fin'ger-nail' *s* uña
fingernail polish *s* esmalte *m* para las
uñas
fin'ger-print' *s* huella digital, dactilograma *m* ‖ *tr* tomar las huellas digi-
tales de
finger tip *s* punta del dedo; **to have at
one's finger tips** tener en la punta
de los dedos, saber al dedillo
finial ['fɪnɪ·əl] *s* florón *m*
finical ['fɪnɪkəl] o **finicky** ['fɪnɪki] *adj*
delicado, melindroso
finish ['fɪnɪʃ] *s* acabado; fin *m*, conclusión ‖ *tr* acabar; **to be finished**
estar listo ‖ *intr* acabar; **to finish** +
ger acabar de + *inf*; **to finish by** +
ger acabar por + *inf*
finishing nail *s* puntilla francesa
finishing school *s* escuela particular de
educación social para señoritas
finishing touch *s* toque *m* final, última
mano
finite ['faɪnaɪt] *adj* finito
finite verb *s* forma verbal flexional
Finland ['fɪnlənd] *s* Finlandia
Finlander ['fɪnləndər] *s* finlandés *m*
Finn [fɪn] *s* (*member of a Finnish-
speaking group of people*) finés *m*;
(*native or inhabitant of Finland*)
finlandés *m*
Finnish ['fɪnɪʃ] *adj* finlandés ‖ *s* (*language*) finlandés *m*
fir [fʌr] *s* abeto
fire [faɪr] *s* fuego; (*destructive burning*) incendio; **through fire and water** a trancos y barrancos; **to be on
fire** estar ardiendo; **to be under
enemy fire** estar expuesto al fuego
del enemigo; **to catch fire** encenderse; **to hang fire** estar en suspensión; **to open fire** abrir fuego, romper el fuego; **to set on fire, to set
fire to** pegar fuego a; **under fire** bajo
el fuego del enemigo; acusado, in-
culpado ‖ *interj* (mil) ¡fuego! ‖ *tr*
encender; calentar (*el horno*); cocer
(*ladrillos*); disparar (*un arma de
fuego*); pegar (*un tiro*); excitar (*la
imaginación*); (coll) despedir (*a un
empleado*) ‖ *intr* encenderse; **to fire
on** hacer fuego sobre; **to fire up**
cargar el horno; calentar el horno
fire alarm *s* alarma de incendios, avi-

sador *m* de incendios; **to sound the
fire alarm** tocar a fuego
fire'arm' *s* arma de fuego
fire'ball' *s* bola de fuego; (*lightning*)
rayo en bola
fire'bird' *s* cacique veranero
fire'boat' *s* buque *m* con mangueras
para incendios
fire'box' *s* caja de fuego, fogón *m*
fire'brand' *s* tizón *m*; (*hothead*) botafuego
fire'break' *s* raya
fire'brick' *s* ladrillo refractario
fire brigade *s* cuerpo de bomberos
fire'bug' *s* (coll) incendiario
fire company *s* cuerpo de bomberos;
compañía de seguros
fire'crack'er *s* triquitraque *m*
fire'damp' *s* grisú *m*, mofeta
fire department *s* servicio de bomberos
fire'dog' *s* morillo
fire drill *s* ejercicio para caso de incendio
fire engine *s* coche *m* bomba, bomba
de incendios, motobomba
fire escape *s* escalera de salvamento
fire extinguisher *s* extintor *m*, apaga-
fuegos *m*
fire'fly' *s* (*pl* **-flies**) luciérnaga
fire'guard' *s* guardafuego
fire hose *s* manguera para incendios
fire'house' *s* cuartel *m* de bomberos,
estación de bomberos
fire hydrant *s* boca de incendio
fire insurance *s* seguro contra incendios
fire irons *spl* badil *m* y tenazas
fireless cooker ['faɪrlɪs] *s* cocinilla sin
fuego
fire·man ['faɪrmən] *s* (*pl* **-men** [mən])
(*man who stokes fires*) fogonero;
(*man who extinguishes fires*) bombero
fire'place' *s* chimenea, chimenea francesa
fire plug *s* boca de agua
fire power *s* (mil) potencia de fuego
fire'proof' *adj* incombustible ‖ *tr* hacer
incombustible
fire sale *s* venta de mercancías ave-
riadas en un incendio
fire screen *s* pantalla de chimenea
fire ship *s* brulote *m*
fire shovel *s* badil *m*
fire'side' *s* hogar *m*
fire'trap' *s* edificio sin medios ade-
cuados de escape en caso de incendio
fire wall *s* cortafuego
fire'ward'en *s* vigía *m* de incendios
fire'wa'ter *s* aguardiente *m*
fire'wood' *s* leña
fire'works' *spl* fuegos artificiales
firing ['faɪrɪŋ] *s* encendimiento; (*of
bricks*) cocción; (*of a gun*) disparo;
(*of soldiers*) tiroteo; (*of an internal-
combustion engine*) encendido; (*of
an employee*) (coll) despedida
firing line *s* línea de fuego, frente *m*
de batalla
firing order *s* (aut) orden *m* del encendido
firing squad *s* (*for saluting at a burial*)

piquete *m* de salvas; (*for executing*) pelotón *m* de fusilamiento, piquete *m* de ejecución

firm [fʌrm] *adj* firme ‖ *s* empresa, casa comercial

firmament ['fʌrməmənt] *s* firmamento

firm name *s* razón *f* social

firmness ['fʌrmnɪs] *s* firmeza

first [fʌrst] *adj* primero ‖ *adv* primero; **first of all** ante todo ‖ *s* primero; (aut) primera (velocidad); (mus) voz *f* principal; **at first** al principio; en primer lugar; **from the first** desde el principio

first aid *s* cura de urgencia, primeros auxilios

first'-aid' kit *s* botiquín *m*, equipo de urgencia

first-aid station *s* puesto de socorro, puesto de primera intención

first'-born' *adj & s* primogénito

first'-class' *adj* de primera, de primera clase ‖ *adv* en primera clase

first cousin *s* primo hermano

first draft *s* borrador *m*

first finger *s* dedo índice, dedo mostrador

first floor *s* piso bajo

first fruits *spl* primicia

first lieutenant *s* teniente

firstly ['fʌrstli] *adv* en primer lugar

first mate *s* (naut) piloto

first name *s* nombre *m* de pila

first night *s* (theat) noche *f* de estreno

first'-night'er *s* (theat) estrenista *mf*

first officer *s* (naut) piloto

first quarter *s* cuarto creciente (*de la luna*)

first'-rate' *adj* de primer orden; (coll) excelente ‖ *adv* (coll) muy bien

first'-run' house *s* teatro de estreno

fiscal ['fɪskəl] *adj* (*pertaining to public treasury*) fiscal; económico ‖ *s* (*public prosecutor*) fiscal *m*

fiscal year *s* año económico, ejercicio

fish [fɪʃ] *s* pez *m*; (*that has been caught, that is ready to eat*) pescado; **to be like a fish out of water** estar como gallina en corral ajeno; **to be neither fish nor fowl** no ser carne ni pescado; **to drink like a fish** beber como una topinera, beber como una esponja ‖ *tr* pescar ‖ *intr* pescar; **to fish for compliments** buscar alabanzas; **to go fishing** ir de pesca; **to take fishing** llevar de pesca

fish'bone' *s* espina de pez

fish bowl *s* pecera

fisher ['fɪʃər] *s* pescador *m*; embarcación de pesca; (zool) marta del Canadá

fisher·man ['fɪʃərmən] *s* (*pl* -men [mən]) pescador *m*; barco pesquero

fisher·y ['fɪʃəri] *s* (*pl* -les) (*activity*) pesca; (*business*) pesquería; (*grounds*) pesquera

fish glue *s* cola de pescado

fish hawk *s* halieto

fish'hook' *s* anzuelo

fishing ['fɪʃɪŋ] *adj* pesquero ‖ *s* pesca

fishing ground *s* pesquería, pesquera

fishing reel *s* carrete *m*

fishing rod *s* caña de pescar

fishing tackle *s* aparejo de pescar, avíos de pescar

fishing torch *s* candelero

fish line *s* sedal *m*

fish market *s* pescadería

fish'plate' *s* (rr) eclisa

fish'pool' *s* piscina

fish spear *s* fisga

fish story *s* (coll) andaluzada, patraña; **to tell fish stories** (coll) mentir por la barba

fish'tail' *s* (aer) coleadura ‖ *intr* (aer) colear

fish'wife' *s* (*pl* -wives [,waɪvz]) pescadera; (*foul-mouthed woman*) verdulera

fish'worm' *s* lombriz *f* de tierra (*cebo para pescar*)

fish·y ['fɪʃi] *adj* (*comp* -ier; *super* -iest) que huele o sabe a pescado; (coll) dudoso, inverosímil

fission ['fɪʃən] *s* (biol) escisión; (phys) fisión

fissionable ['fɪʃənəbəl] *adj* fisionable

fissure ['fɪʃər] *s* hendidura, grieta; (anat, min) fisura

fist [fɪst] *s* puño; (typ) manecilla; **to shake one's fist at** amenazar con el puño

fist fight *s* pelea con los puños

fisticuff ['fɪstɪ,kʌf] *s* puñetazo; **fisticuffs** pelea a puñetazos

fit [fɪt] *adj* (*comp* -fitter; *super* -fittest) apropiado, conveniente; apto; sano; **fit to be tied** (coll) impaciente, encolerizado; **fit to eat** bueno de comer; **to feel fit** gozar de buena salud; **to see fit** juzgar conveniente ‖ *s* ajuste *m*, talle *m*; (*of one piece with another*) encaje *m*; (*of coughing*) acceso, ataque *m*; (*of anger*) arranque *m*; **by fits and starts** intermitentemente ‖ *v* (*pret & pp* -fitted; *ger* fitting) *tr* ajustar, entallar; cuadrar, sentar; encajar; cuadrar con (*p.ej., las señas de una persona*); equipar, preparar; servir para; estar de acuerdo con (*p.ej., los hechos*); **to fit out** o **up** pertrechar ‖ *intr* ajustar; encajar; sentar; **to fit in** caber en; encajar en

fitful ['fɪtfəl] *adj* caprichoso; intermitente, vacilante

fitness ['fɪtnɪs] *s* conveniencia; aptitud; tempestividad; buena salud

fitter ['fɪtər] *s* ajustador *m*; (*of machinery*) montador *m*; (*of clothing*) probador *m*

fitting ['fɪtɪŋ] *adj* apropiado, conveniente, justo ‖ *s* ajuste *m*; encaje *m*; (*of a garment*) prueba; tubo de ajuste; **fittings** accesorios, avíos; (*iron trimmings*) herraje *m*

five [faɪv] *adj & pron* cinco ‖ *s* cinco; **five o'clock** las cinco

five hundred *adj & pron* quinientos ‖ *s* quinientos *m*

five'-year' plan *s* plan *m* quinquenal

fix [fɪks] *s* — **in a tight fix** (coll) en calzas prietas; **to be in a fix** (coll) hallarse en un aprieto ‖ *tr* arreglar, componer, reparar; fijar (*una fecha;*

los cabellos; una imagen fotográfica; los precios; la atención; una hora, una cita); calar (la bayoneta); (coll) desquitarse con; (pol) muñir ‖ intr fijarse; **to fix** on decidir, escoger

fixed [fɪkst] adj fijo

fixing ['fɪksɪŋ] adj fijador ‖ s (fastening) fijación; (phot) fijado

fixing bath s fijador m

fixture ['fɪkstʃər] s accesorio, artefacto; (of a lamp) guarnición; **fixtures** (e.g., of a store) instalaciones

fizz [fɪz] s ruido sibilante; bebida gaseosa; (Brit) champaña ‖ intr hacer un ruido sibilante

fizzle ['fɪzəl] s (coll) fracaso ‖ intr chisporrotear débilmente; (coll) fracasar

fl. abbr **flourished, fluid**

flabbergast ['flæbər,gæst] tr (coll) dejar sin habla, dejar estupefacto

flab-by ['flæbi] adj (comp **-bier**; super **-biest**) flojo, lacio

flag [flæg] s bandera ‖ v (pret & pp **flagged**; ger **flagging**) tr hacer señal a (una persona) con una bandera; hacer señal de parada a (un tren) ‖ intr aflojar, flaquear

flag captain s (nav) capitán m de bandera

flageolet [,flædʒə'lɛt] s chirimía, dulzaina

flag-man ['flægmən] s (pl **-men** [mən]) (rr) guardafrenos m; (rr) guardavía m

flag of truce s bandera de parlamento

flag'pole' s asta de bandera; (surv) jalón m

flagrant ['flegrənt] adj enorme, escandaloso

flag'ship' s (nav) capitana

flag'staff' s asta de bandera

flag'stone' s losa

flag stop s (rr) apeadero

flail [flel] s mayal m ‖ tr golpear con mayal; golpear, azotar

flair [fler] s instinto, perspicacia

flak [flæk] s fuego antiaéreo

flake [flek] s (thin piece) hojuela; (of snow) copo ‖ intr desprenderse en hojuelas; caer en copos pequeños

flak-y ['fleki] adj (comp **-ier**; super **-lest**) escamoso, laminoso

flamboyant [flæm'bɔɪ·ənt] adj flameante; llamativo; rimbombante; (archit) flameante, flamígero

flame [flem] s llama ‖ tr (to sterilize with a flame) llamear ‖ intr flamear

flame thrower ['θro·ər] s lanzallamas m

flaming ['flemɪŋ] adj llameante; flamante, resplandeciente; apasionado

flamin-go [flə'mɪŋgo] s (pl **-gos** o **-goes**) flamenco

flammable ['flæməbəl] adj inflamable

Flanders ['flændərz] s Flandes f

flange [flændʒ] s pestaña

flank [flæŋk] s flanco; tr flanquear

flannel ['flænəl] s franela

flap [flæp] s (fold in clothing; of a hat) falda; (of a pocket) cartera; (of a table) hoja plegadiza; (of shoe) oreja; (of an envelope) tapa; (of

wings) aletazo; (of the counter in a store) trampa ‖ v (pret & pp **flapped**; ger **flapping**) tr golpear con ruido seco; batir, sacudir (las alas) ‖ intr aletear; flamear con ruido

flare [fler] s llamarada, destello; cohete m de señales; (aer) bengala; (outward curvature) abocinamiento; (of a dress) vuelo ‖ tr abocinar ‖ intr arder con gran llamarada, destellar; (to spread outward) abocinarse; **to flare up** inflamarse; recrudecer (una enfermedad); encolerizarse

flare star s (astr) estrella fulgurante

flare'-up' s llamarada; (of an illness) retroceso; (coll) llamarada, arrebato de cólera

flash [flæʃ] s (of light) relumbrón m, ráfaga; (of lightning) relámpago; (of hope) rayo; (of joy) acceso; (of insight) rasgo; mensaje m urgente ‖ tr quemar (pólvora); enviar (un mensaje) como un rayo ‖ intr destellar, centellear; relampaguear (los ojos); **to flash by** pasar como un rayo

flash'back' s (mov) retrospectiva

flash bulb s luz f de magnesio; bombilla de destello

flash flood s torrentada, avenida repentina

flashing ['flæʃɪŋ] s despidiente m de agua, vierteaguas m

flash'light' s linterna eléctrica, lámpara eléctrica de bolsillo; (of a lighthouse) luz f intermitente, fanal m de destellos; (for taking photographs) flash m, relámpago

flashlight battery s pila de linterna

flashlight bulb s bombilla de linterna

flashlight photography s fotografía instantánea de relámpago

flash sign s anuncio intermitente

flash-y ['flæʃi] adj (comp **-ier**; super **-iest**) chillón, llamativo

flask [flæsk] o [flɑsk] s frasco; frasco de bolsillo; (for laboratory use) matraz m, redoma

flat [flæt] adj (comp **flatter**; super **flattest**) plano; (nose; boat) chato; (surface) mate, deslustrado; (beer) muerto; (tire) desinflado; (e.g., denial) terminante; (mus) bemol ‖ adv — **to fall flat** caer de plano; (fig) no surtir efecto, no tener éxito ‖ s banco, bajío; (apartment) piso; (mus) bemol m; (coll) neumático desinflado

flat'boat' s chalana

flat'car' s vagón m de plataforma

flat-footed ['flæt,futɪd] adj de pies planos; (coll) inflexible

flat'head' s (of a bolt) cabeza chata; clavo, tornillo o perno de cabeza chata; (coll) tonto, mentecato

flat'i'ron s plancha

flatten ['flætən] tr allanar, aplanar; chafar, aplastar; achatar ‖ intr allanarse, aplanarse; aplastarse; achatarse; **to flatten out** ponerse horizontal, enderezarse

flatter ['flætər] tr lisonjear; (to make more attractive than is) favorecer ‖ intr lisonjear

flatterer ['flætərər] s lisonjero
flattering ['flætərɪŋ] adj lisonjero
flatter·y ['flætəri] s (pl -ies) lisonja
flat'top' s portaaviones m
flatulence ['flætʃələns] s flatulencia
flat'ware' s vajilla de plata; vajilla de porcelana
flaunt [flɔnt] o [flɑnt] tr ostentar, hacer gala de
flautist ['flɔtɪst] s flautista mf
flavor ['flevər] s sabor m, gusto; condimento, sazón f; (of ice cream) clase f ‖ tr saborear; condimentar, sazonar; aromatizar, perfumar
flavoring ['flevərɪŋ] s condimento, sainete m
flaw [flɔ] s defecto, imperfección; (crack) grieta
flawless ['flɔlɪs] adj perfecto, entero
flax [flæks] s lino
flaxen ['flæksən] adj blondo, rubio
flax'seed' s linaza
flay [fle] tr desollar
flea [fli] s pulga
flea'bite' s picadura de pulga; molestia insignificante
fleck [flɛk] s pinta, punto; partícula, pizca ‖ tr puntear
fledgling ['flɛdʒlɪŋ] s pajarito, volantón m; (fig) novato, novel m
flee [fli] v (pret & pp fled [flɛd]) tr & intr huir
fleece [flis] s (coat of wool) lana; (wool shorn at one time; tuft of wool or hair) vellón m ‖ tr esquilar; (to strip of money) desplumar
fleec·y ['flisi] adj (comp -ier; super -iest) lanudo; (clouds) aborregado
fleet' [flit] adj veloz ‖ s armada; (of merchant vessels, airplanes, automobiles) flota
fleeting ['flitɪŋ] adj fugaz, efímero; transitorio
Fleming ['flɛmɪŋ] s flamenco
Flemish ['flɛmɪʃ] adj & s flamenco
flesh [flɛʃ] s carne f; in the flesh en persona; to lose flesh perder carnes; to put on flesh cobrar carnes
flesh and blood s (relatives) carne y sangre; el cuerpo humano
flesh-colored ['flɛʃ‚kʌlərd] adj encarnado, de color de carne
fleshiness ['flɛʃɪnɪs] s carnosidad
fleshless ['flɛʃlɪs] adj descarnado
flesh'pot' s olla, marmita; fleshpots vida regalona; suntuosos nidos de vicios
flesh wound s herida superficial
flesh·y ['flɛʃi] adj (comp -ier; super -iest) carnoso
flex [flɛks] tr doblar ‖ intr doblarse
flexible ['flɛksɪbəl] adj flexible
flexible cord s (elec) flexible m
flick [flɪk] s (with finger) papirote m; (with whip) latigazo; ruido seco ‖ tr golpear rápida y ligeramente
flicker ['flɪkər] s llama trémula; (of eyelids) parpadeo; (of emotion) temblor momentáneo ‖ intr flamear con llama trémula; aletear
flier ['flaɪ-ər] s aviador m; tren rápido; (coll) negocio arriesgado; (coll) hoja volante

flight [flaɪt] s fuga, huída; (of an airplane) vuelo; (of birds) bandada; (of stairs) tramo; (of fancy) arranque m; to put to flight poner en fuga; to take flight darse a la fuga
flight deck s (nav) cubierta de vuelo
flight·y ['flaɪti] adj (comp -ier; super -iest) veleidoso; casquivano
film·flam ['flɪm‚flæm] s (coll) engaño, trampa; (coll) tontería ‖ v (pret & pp -flammed; ger -flamming) tr (coll) engañar, trampear
film·sy ['flɪmzi] adj (comp -sier; super -siest) débil, endeble, flojo
flinch [flɪntʃ] intr encogerse de miedo
fling [flɪŋ] s echada, tiro; baile escocés muy vivo; to go on a fling echar una cana al aire; to have a fling at ensayar, probar; to have one's fling correrla, mocear ‖ v (pret & pp flung [flʌŋ]) tr arrojar; (e.g., on the floor, out the window, in jail) echar; to fling open abrir de golpe; to fling shut cerrar de golpe
flint [flɪnt] s pedernal m
flint'lock' s llave f de chispa; trabuco de chispa
flint·y ['flɪnti] adj (comp -ier; super -iest) pedernalino; (fig) empedernido
flip [flɪp] adj (comp flipper; super flippest) (coll) petulante ‖ s capirotazo ‖ v (pret & pp flipped; ger flipping) tr echar de un capirotazo, mover de un tirón; to flip a coin echar a cara o cruz; to flip shut cerrar de golpe (p.ej., un abanico)
flippancy ['flɪpənsi] s petulancia
flippant ['flɪpənt] adj petulante
flirt [flɜrt] s (woman) coqueta; (man) galanteador m ‖ intr coquetear (una mujer); galantear (un hombre); to flirt with flirtear con; acariciar (una idea); jugar con (la muerte)
flit [flɪt] v (pret & pp flitted; ger flitting) intr revolotear, volar; pasar rápidamente
flitch [flɪtʃ] s hoja de tocino
float [flot] s (raft) balsa; (of fishing line) flotador m; (of mason) llana; carroza alegórica, carro alegórico ‖ tr poner a flote; lanzar (una empresa); emitir (acciones, bonos, etc.) ‖ intr flotar
floating ['flotɪŋ] adj flotante
flock [flɑk] s (of birds) bandada; (of sheep) grey f, rebaño, manada; (of people) muchedumbre; (e.g., of nonsense) hatajo, (of faithful) grey f, rebaño ‖ intr congregarse, reunirse; llegar en tropel
floe [flo] s banquisa, témpano
flog [flɑg] v (pret & pp flogged; ger flogging) tr azotar, fustigar
flood [flʌd] s inundación; (caused by heavy rain) diluvio; (sudden rise of river) crecida; (of tide) pleamar f; (of words, etc.) diluvio, torrente m ‖ tr inundar; (to overwhelm) abrumar ‖ intr desbordar, rebosar; entrar a raudales
flood'gate' s (of a dam) compuerta; (of a canal) esclusa

flood'light' s faro de inundación || tr iluminar con faro de inundación

flood tide s pleamar f, marea montante

floor [flor] s (inside bottom surface of room) piso, suelo; (story of a building) piso, alto; (of the sea, a swimming pool, etc.) fondo; (of an assembly hall) hemiciclo; (naut) varenga; **to ask for the floor** pedir la palabra; **to have the floor** tener la palabra; **to take the floor** tomar la palabra || tr entarimar; derribar, echar al suelo; (coll) confundir, envolver, revolcar (al adversario en controversia); (coll) vencer

floor lamp s lámpara de pie

floor mop s fregasuelos m, estropajo

floor plan s planta

floor show s espectáculo de cabaret

floor timber s (naut) varenga

floor'walk'er s jefe m de sección

floor wax s cera de pisos

flop [flɑp] s (coll) fracaso, caída; **to take a flop** (coll) caerse || v (pret & pp **flopped**) ger **flopping**) intr agitarse; caerse; venirse abajo; fracasar; **to flop over** volcarse; cambiar de partido

flora ['florə] s flora

floral ['florəl] adj floral

Florentine ['florən,tin] o ['florən,tin] adj & s florentino

florescence [flo'resəns] s florescencia

florid ['florɪd] o ['flɑrɪd] adj (complexion) encarnado; (showy, ornate) florido

Florida Keys ['florɪdə] o ['flɑrɪdə] s Cayos m de la Florida

florist ['florɪst] s florero, florista mf

floss [flos] o [flɑs] s cadarzo; (of corn) cabellos

floss silk s seda floja sin torcer

floss·y ['flosi] o ['flɑsi] adj (comp -ler; super -lest) ligero, velloso; (slang) cursi, vistoso

flotsam ['flɑtsəm] s pecio

flotsam and jetsam s pecios, despojos; (trifles) baratijas; gente f trashumante, gente perdida

flounce [flauns] s faralá m, volante m || tr adornar con faralaes o volantes || intr moverse airadamente

flounder ['flaundər] s platija || intr forcejear, obrar torpemente, andar tropezando

flour [flaur] adj harinero || s harina

flourish ['flʌrɪʃ] s (with the sword) molinete m; (with the pen) plumada, rasgo; (as part of signature) rúbrica; (mus) floreo || tr blandir (la espada) || intr florecer, prosperar

flourishing ['flʌrɪʃɪŋ] adj floreciente, próspero

flour mill s molino de harina

floury ['flauri] adj harinoso

flout [flaut] tr mofarse de, burlarse de || intr mofarse, burlarse

flow [flo] s flujo || intr fluir; subir (la marea); ondear (el pelo en el aire); **to flow into** desaguar en, desembocar en; **to flow over** rebosar; **to flow with** nadar en, abundar en

flower ['flau·ər] s flor f || tr florear || intr florecer

flower bed s macizo, parterre m

flower garden s jardín m

flower girl s florera; (at a wedding) damita de honor

flower piece s ramillete m; (painting) florero

flow'er·pot' s tiesto, maceta

flower shop s floristería

flower show s exposición de flores

flower stand s florero

flowery ['flau·əri] adj florido, cubierto de flores

flu [flu] s (coll) gripe f, influenza

fluctuate ['flʌktʃu,et] intr fluctuar

flue [flu] s cañón m de chimenea; tubo de humo

fluency ['flu·ənsi] s afluencia, facundia

fluent ['flu·ənt] adj (flowing) fluente; afluente, facundo, fluido

fluently ['flu·əntli] adv corrientemente

fluff [flʌf] s pelusa, tamo; vello, pelusilla; (of an actor) gazapo || tr esponjar, mullir || intr esponjarse

fluff·y ['flʌfi] adj (comp -ler; super -lest) fofo, esponjoso, mullido; velloso

fluid ['flu·ɪd] adj & s fluido

fluidity [flu'ɪdɪti] s fluidez f

fluke [fluk] s (of anchor) uña; (in billiards) chiripa

flume [flum] s caz m, saetín m

flunk [flʌŋk] s (coll) reprobación || tr (coll) reprobar, dar calabazas a; perder (un examen o asignatura) || intr (coll) fracasar, salir mal; **to flunk out** (coll) tener que abandonar los estudios por no poder aprobar

flunk·y ['flʌŋki] s (pl -ies) lacayo; adulador m

fluor ['flu·ər] s fluorita

fluorescence [,flu·ə'resəns] s fluorescencia

fluorescent [,flu·ə'resənt] adj fluorescente

fluoridate ['flu·ərɪ,det] tr fluorizar

fluoridation [,flu·ərɪ'deʃən] s fluorización

fluoride ['flu·ə,raɪd] s fluoruro

fluorine ['flu·ə,rin] s flúor m

fluorite ['flu·ə,raɪt] s fluorita

fluoroscope ['flu·ərə,skop] s fluoroscopio

fluor spar s espato flúor

flur·ry ['flʌri] s (pl -ries) agitación; (of wind) racha, ráfaga; (of rain) chaparrón m; (of snow) nevisca || v (pret & pp -ried) tr agitar

flush [flʌʃ] adj rasante, nivelado; (set in, in order to be flush) embutido; abundante; robusto, vigoroso; próspero, bien provisto; coloradote; (in printing) justificado; **flush with** a ras de || adv ras con ras, al mismo nivel || s (of water) flujo repentino; (in the cheeks) rubor m; sonrojo; (in the springtime) floración repentina; (of joy) acceso; (of youth) vigor m; chorro del inodoro; (in poker) flux m || tr (to cause to blush) abochornar; limpiar con un chorro de agua; hacer saltar (una liebre) || intr abochornarse, estar encendido (*el rostro*); (*to gush*) brotar

Flushing [ˈflʌʃɪŋ] *s* Flesinga

flush outlet *s* (elec) caja de enchufe embutida

flush switch *s* (elec) llave embutida

flush tank *s* depósito de limpia

flush toilet *s* inodoro con chorro de agua

fluster [ˈflʌstər] *s* confusión, aturdimiento ‖ *tr* confundir, aturdir

flute [flut] *s* (*of a column*) estría; (mus) flauta ‖ *tr* estriar, acanalar

flutist [ˈflutɪst] *s* flautista *mf*

flutter [ˈflʌtər] *s* aleteo, revoloteo; confusión, turbación ‖ *intr* aletear, revolotear; flamear, ondear; agitarse; alterarse (*el pulso*); palpitar (*el corazón*)

flux [flʌks] *s* (*flow; flowing of tide*) flujo; (*for fusing metals*) flujo, fundente *m*

fly [flaɪ] *s* (*pl* **flies**) mosca; (*of trousers*) portañuela, bragueta; (*for fishing*) mosca artificial; **flies** (theat) bambalinas; **to die like flies** morir como chinches ‖ *v* (*pret* **flew** [flu]; *pp* **flown** [flon]) *tr* hacer volar (*una cometa*); dirigir (*un avión*); (*to carry in an airship*) volar; atravesar en avión; desplegar, llevar (*una bandera*) ‖ *intr* volar; huir; ondear (*una bandera*); **to fly off** salir volando; desprenderse; **to fly open** abrirse de repente; **to fly over** trasvolar; **to fly shut** cerrarse de repente

fly ball *s* (baseball) palomita

fly'blow' *s* cresa

fly'-by-night' *adj* indigno de confianza

fly'catch'er *s* moscareta, papamoscas *m*

fly chaser *s* espantamoscas *m*

flyer [ˈflaɪ‑ər] *s* var de **flier**

fly'-fish' *tr & intr* pescar con moscas artificiales

flying [ˈflaɪ‑ɪŋ] *adj* volante; rápido, veloz ‖ *s* aviación

flying boat *s* hidroavión *m*

flying buttress *s* arbotante *m*

flying colors *spl* gran éxito

flying field *s* campo de aviación

flying saucer *s* platillo volante

flying sickness *s* mal *m* de altura

flying time *s* horas de vuelo

fly in the ointment *s* mosca muerta que malea el perfume

fly'leaf' *s* (*pl* **-leaves'**) guarda, hoja de guarda

fly net *s* (*for a bed*) mosquitero; (*for a horse*) espantamoscas *m*

fly'pa'per *s* papel *m* matamoscas

fly'speck' *s* mancha de mosca

fly swatter [ˈswɑtər] *s* matamoscas *m*

fly'trap' *s* atrapamoscas *m*

fly'wheel' *s* volante *m*

fm. *abbr* fathom

F.M. *abbr* frequency modulation

foal [fol] *s* potro ‖ *intr* parir (*la yegua*)

foam [fom] *s* espuma ‖ *intr* espumar

foam extinguisher *s* lanzaespumas *m*, extintor *m* de espuma

foam rubber *s* caucho esponjoso, espuma de caucho

foam·y [ˈfomɪ] *adj* (*comp* **-ier**; *super* **-iest**) espumoso, espumajoso

fob [fɑb] *s* faltriquera de reloj; (*chain*) leopoldina; (*ornament*) dije *m*

F.O.B. *abbr* free on board

focal [ˈfokəl] *adj* focal

fo·cus [ˈfokəs] *s* (*pl* **-cuses** o **-ci** [saɪ]) foco; **in focus** enfocado; **out of focus** desenfocado ‖ *v* (*pret & pp* **-cused** o **-cussed**; *ger* **-cusing** o **-cussing**) *tr* enfocar; fijar (*la atención*) ‖ *intr* enfocarse

fodder [ˈfɑdər] *s* forraje *m*

foe [fo] *s* enemigo

fog [fɑg] o [fɔg] *s* niebla; (phot) velo ‖ *v* (*pret & pp* **fogged**; *ger* **fogging**) *tr* envolver en niebla; (*to blur*) empañar; (phot) velar ‖ *intr* empañarse; (phot) velarse

fog bank *s* banco de nieblas

fog bell *s* campana de nieblas

fog'bound' *adj* atascado en la niebla, envuelto en la niebla

fog·gy [ˈfɑgɪ] o [ˈfɔgɪ] *adj* (*comp* **-gier**; *super* **-giest**) neblinoso, brumoso; confuso; (phot) velado; **it is foggy** hay neblina

fog'horn' *s* sirena de niebla

foible [ˈfɔɪbəl] *s* flaqueza, lado flaco

foil [fɔɪl] *s* (*thin sheet of metal*) hojuela, laminilla; (*of mirror*) azogado, plateado; contraste *m*, realce *m*; (*sword*) florete *m* ‖ *tr* frustrar; azogar, platear (*un espejo*)

foist [fɔɪst] *tr* — **to foist something on someone** encajar una cosa a uno

fol. *abbr* folio, following

fold [fold] *s* pliegue *m*, doblez *m*; arruga; (*for sheep*) aprisco, redil *m*; (*of the faithful*) rebaño ‖ *tr* plegar, doblar; cruzar (*los brazos*); **to fold up** doblar (*p.ej., un mapa*) ‖ *intr* plegarse, doblarse

folder [ˈfoldər] *s* (*covers for holding papers*) carpeta; (*pamphlet*) folleto

folderol [ˈfɑldə‑ˌrɑl] *s* tontería, necedad; bagatela

folding [ˈfoldɪŋ] *adj* plegadizo, plegable; plegador

folding camera *s* cámara de fuelle

folding chair *s* silla de tijera, silla plegadiza; (*of canvas*) catrecillo

folding cot *s* catre *m* de tijera

folding door *s* puerta plegadiza

folding rule *s* metro plegador

foliage [ˈfolɪ‑ɪdʒ] *s* follaje *m*

foli·o [ˈfolɪ‑o] *adj* en folio ‖ *s* (*pl* **-os**) (*sheet*) folio; infolio, libro en folio ‖ *tr* foliar

folk [fok] *adj* popular, tradicional, del pueblo ‖ *s* (*pl* **folk** o **folks**) gente *f*; **folks** (coll) gente (*familia*)

folk'lore' *s* folklore *m*

folk music *s* música folklórica

folk song *s* canción típica, canción tradicional

folk·sy [ˈfoksɪ] *adj* (*comp* **-sier**; *super* **-siest**) (coll) sociable, tratable; (*like common people*) (coll) plebeyo

folk'way' *s* costumbre tradicional

follicle [ˈfɑlɪkəl] *s* folículo

follow [ˈfɑlo] *tr* seguir; seguir el hilo de; interesarse en (*las noticias del* día) ‖ *intr* seguir; resultar; **as follows** como sigue; **it follows** síguese

follower ['fɑlo-ər] *s* seguidor *m*; secuaz *mf*; partidario; imitador *m*; discípulo

following ['fɑlo-ɪŋ] *adj* siguiente ‖ *s* séquito; partidarios

fol'low-up' *adj* consecutivo; recordativo ‖ *s* carta recordativa, circular recordativa

fol·ly ['fɑli] *s* (*pl* **-lies**) desatino, locura; empresa temeraria; **follies** revista teatral

foment [fo'ment] *tr* fomentar

fond [fɑnd] *adj* afectuoso, cariñoso; **to become fond of** encariñarse con, aficionarse a o de

fondle ['fɑndəl] *tr* acariciar, mimar

fondness ['fɑndnɪs] *s* afición, cariño

font [fɑnt] *s* (*source; source of water*) fuente *f*; (*for holy water*) pila; (*of type*) fundición

food [fud] *adj* alimenticio ‖ *s* comida, alimento; **food for thought** cosa en qué pensar

food store *s* tienda de comestibles, colmado

food'stuffs' *spl* comestibles *mpl*, víveres *mpl*

fool [ful] *s* tonto, necio; (*jester*) bufón *m*; (*person imposed on*) inocente *mf*, víctima; **to make a fool of** poner en ridículo; **to play the fool** hacer el tonto ‖ *tr* embaucar, engañar; **to fool away** malgastar (*tiempo, dinero*) ‖ *intr* tontear; **to fool around** (coll) malgastar el tiempo; **to fool with** (coll) ajar, manosear

fooler·y ['fuləri] *s* (*pl* **-ies**) locura, tontería

fool'har'dy *adj* (*comp* **-dier**; *super* **-diest**) temerario

fooling ['fulɪŋ] *s* broma; engaño; **no fooling** hablando en serio

foolish ['fulɪʃ] *adj* tonto; ridículo

fool'proof' *adj* (coll) a prueba de mal trato; (coll) infalible

fools'cap' *s* gorro de bufón; papel *m* de oficio

fool's errand *s* caza de grillos

fool's scepter *s* cetro de locura

foot [fut] *s* (*pl* **feet** [fit]) pie *m*; **to drag one's feet** ir a paso de caracol; **to have one foot in the grave** estar con un pie en la sepultura; **to put one's best foot forward** (coll) hacer méritos; **to put one's foot in it** (coll) meter la pata; (coll) tirarse una plancha; **to stand on one's own feet** volar con sus propias alas; **to tread under foot** hollar ‖ *tr* pagar (*la cuenta*); **to foot it** andar a pie; bailar

footage ['futɪdʒ] *s* distancia o largura en pies

foot'ball' *s* (*game*) balompié *m*, fútbol *m*; (*ball*) balón *m*

foot'board' *s* (*support for foot*) estribo; (*of bed*) pie *m*

foot'bridge' *s* pasarela, puente *m* para peatones

foot'fall' *s* paso

foot'hill' *s* colina al pie de una montaña

foot'hold' *s* arraigo, pie *m*; **to gain a foothold** ganar pie

footing ['futɪŋ] *s* pie *m*, p.ej., **he lost his footing** perdió el pie; **on a friendly footing** en relaciones amistosas; **on an equal footing** en pie de igualdad; **on a war footing** en pie de guerra

foot'lights' *spl* candilejas, batería; (fig) tablas, escena

foot'loose' *adj* libre, no comprometido

foot·man ['futmən] *s* (*pl* **-men** [mən]) lacayo, criado de librea

foot'mark' *s* huella

foot'note' *s* nota al pie de la página

foot'path' *s* senda para peatones

foot'print' *s* huella

foot race *s* carrera a pie

foot'rest' *s* apoyapié *m*, descansapié *m*

foot rule *s* regla de un pie

foot soldier *s* soldado de a pie

foot'sore' *adj* despeado

foot'step' *s* paso; **to follow in the footsteps of** seguir los pasos de

foot'stone' *s* lápida al pie de una sepultura

foot'stool' *s* escabel *m*, escañuelo

foot warmer *s* calientapiés *m*

foot'wear' *s* calzado

foot'work' *s* juego de piernas

foot'worn' *adj* (*road*) trillado; (*person*) despeado

foozle ['fuzəl] *s* chambonada; (coll) chambón *m*, torpe *m* ‖ *tr* chafallar; errar (*un golpe*) de manera torpe ‖ *intr* chambonear

fop [fɑp] *s* currutaco, petimetre *m*

for [fɔr] *prep* para; por; como, p.ej., **he uses his living room for an office** usa la sala como oficina; de, p.ej., **time for bed** hora de acostarse; desde hace, p.ej., **he has been here for a week** está aquí desde hace una semana; en honor de; a pesar de ‖ *conj* pues, porque

for. *abbr* **foreign**

forage ['fɑrɪdʒ] o ['fɔrɪdʒ] *adj* forrajero ‖ *s* forraje *m* ‖ *tr* & *intr* forrajear; saquear

foray ['fɑre] o ['fɔre] *s* correría; saqueo ‖ *intr* hacer correrías

for·bear [fɔr'bɛr] *v* (*pret* **-bore** ['bor]; *pp* **-borne** ['born]) *tr* abstenerse de ‖ *intr* contenerse

forbearance [fɔr'bɛrəns] *s* abstención; paciencia

for·bid [fɔr'bɪd] *v* (*pret* **-bade** ['bæd] o **-bad** ['bæd]; *pp* **-bidden** ['bɪdən]; *ger* **-bidding**) *tr* prohibir

forbidding [fɔr'bɪdɪŋ] *adj* repugnante, repulsivo

force [fɔrs] *s* fuerza; (*staff of workers*) personal *m*; (*of soldiers, police, etc.*) cuerpo; (phys) fuerza; **by force of** a fuerza de; **by main force** con todas sus fuerzas; **in force** vigente, en vigor; en gran número; **to join forces** juntar diestra con diestra ‖ *tr* forzar; obligar; **to force back** hacer retroceder; **to force open** abrir por fuerza; **to force through** llevar a cabo por fuerza

forced [forst] *adj* forzado

forced air *s* aire *m* a presión

forced landing *s* aterrizaje forzado o forzoso

forced march *s* marcha forzada

forceful ['forsfəl] *adj* enérgico, eficaz

for-ceps ['forsəps] *s* (*pl* -ceps o -cipes [sɪ,piz]) (dent, surg) pinzas; (obstet) fórceps *m*

force pump *s* bomba impelente

forcible ['forsɪbəl] *adj* eficaz, convincente; forzado

ford [ford] *s* vado ‖ *tr* vadear

fore [for] *adj* anterior; (naut) de proa ‖ *adv* antes, anteriormente; delante; (naut) avante ‖ *interj* ¡ojo!, ¡cuidado! ‖ *s* delantera; **to the fore** destacado; a mano; vivo

fore and aft *adv* de popa a proa

fore'arm' *s* antebrazo ‖ **fore-arm'** *tr* armar de antemano; prevenir

fore'bear' *s* antepasado

forebode [for'bod] *tr* (*to portend*) presagiar; (*to have a presentiment of*) presentir, prever

foreboding [for'bodɪŋ] *s* presagio; presentimiento

fore'cast' *s* pronóstico ‖ *v* (*pret & pp* -cast o -casted) *tr* pronosticar

forecastle ['foksəl], ['for,kæsəl] o ['for,kɑsəl] *s* castillo de proa

fore-close' *tr* excluir; extinguir el derecho de redimir (*una hipoteca*); privar del derecho de redimir una hipoteca

fore-doom' *tr* condenar de antemano, predestinar al fracaso

fore edge *s* canal *f*

fore'fa'ther *s* antepasado

fore'fin'ger *s* dedo índice, dedo mostrador

fore'front' *s* puesto delantero; sitio de actividad más intensa; **in the forefront** a vanguardia

fore-go' *v* (*pret* -went; *pp* -gone') *tr & intr* preceder

foregoing ['for,go·ɪŋ] o [for'go·ɪŋ] *adj* anterior, precedente

fore'gone' conclusion *s* resultado inevitable; decisión adoptada de antemano

fore'ground' *s* primer plano, primer término

forehanded ['for,hændɪd] *adj* (*thrifty*) ahorrado; hecho de antemano

forehead ['forɪd] o ['forɪd] *s* frente *f*

foreign ['farɪn] o ['forɪn] *adj* extranjero, exterior; **foreign to** (*not belonging to or connected with*) ajeno a

foreign affairs *spl* asuntos exteriores

for'eign-born' *adj* nacido en el extranjero

foreigner ['farɪnər] o ['forɪnər] *s* extranjero

foreign exchange *s* cambio extranjero; (*currency*) divisa

foreign minister *s* ministro de asuntos exteriores

foreign office *s* ministerio de asuntos exteriores

foreign service *s* servicio diplomático y consular; servicio militar extranjero

foreign trade *s* comercio extranjero

fore'leg' *s* brazo, pata delantera

fore'lock' *s* mechón *m* de pelo sobre la frente; (*of a horse*) copete *m*; **to take time by the forelock** asir la ocasión por la melena

fore-man ['formən] *s* (*pl* -men [mən]) capataz *m*, mayoral *m*, sobrestante *m*; (*in a machine shop*) contramaestre *m*; presidente *m* de jurado

foremast ['forməst], ['for,mæst] o ['for,mɑst] *s* palo de trinquete

foremost ['for,most] *adj* primero, principal, más eminente

fore'noon' *adj* matinal ‖ *s* mañana

fore'part' *s* parte delantera; primera parte

fore'paw' *s* pata delantera

fore'quar'ter *s* cuarto delantero

fore'run'ner *s* precursor *m*; predecesor *m*; antepasado; anuncio, presagio

fore-sail ['forsəl] o ['for,sel] *s* trinquete *m*

fore-see' *v* (*pret* -saw'; *pp* -seen') *tr* prever

foreseeable [for'si·əbəl] *adj* previsible

fore-shad'ow *tr* presagiar, prefigurar

fore-short'en *tr* escorzar

fore-short'ening *s* escorzo

fore'sight' *s* previsión, presciencia

fore'sight'ed *adj* previsor, presciente

fore'skin' *s* prepucio

forest ['farɪst] o ['forɪst] *adj* forestal ‖ *s* bosque *m*

fore-stall' *tr* impedir, prevenir; anticipar; acaparar

forest ranger *s* guarda *m* forestal, montanero

forestry ['farɪstri] o ['forɪstri] *s* silvicultura, ciencia forestal

fore'taste' *s* goce anticipado, conocimiento anticipado

fore-tell' *v* (*pret & pp* -told') *tr* predecir; presagiar

fore'thought' *s* premeditación; providencia, previsión

forever [for'evər] *adv* por siempre; siempre

fore-warn' *tr* prevenir, poner sobre aviso

fore'word' *s* advertencia, prefacio

forfeit ['forfɪt] *adj* perdido ‖ *s* multa, pena; prenda perdida; **forfeits** (*game*) prendas ‖ *tr* perder el derecho a

forfeiture ['forfɪtʃər] *s* multa, pena; prenda perdida

forgather [for'gæðər] *intr* reunirse; encontrarse; **to forgather with** asociarse con

forge [fordʒ] *s* fragua; (*blacksmith shop*) herrería; ‖ *tr* fraguar, forjar; falsificar (*la firma de otra persona*); fraguar, forjar (*mentiras*) ‖ *intr* fraguar, forjar; **to forge ahead** avanzar despacio y con esfuerzo

forger-y ['fordʒəri] *s* (*pl* -ies) falsifica-

for-get [for'get] *v* (*pret* -got ['gat]; *pp* -got o -gotten; *ger* -getting) *tr* olvidar, olvidarse de, olvidársele a uno, p.ej., **he forgot his overcoat** se le olvidó su abrigo; **forget it!** ¡no se preocupe!; **to forget oneself** no pensar en sí mismo; ser distraído; propasarse

forgetful [fɔr'gɛtfəl] *adj* olvidado, olvidadizo; descuidado

forgetfulness [fɔr'gɛtfəlnɪs] *s* olvido; descuido

for·get'-me-not' *s* nomeolvides *m*

forgivable [fɔr'gɪvəbəl] *adj* perdonable

for·give [fɔr'gɪv] *v* (*pret* **-gave';** *pp* **-giv'en**) *tr* perdonar

forgiveness [fɔr'gɪvnɪs] *s* perdón *m*; misericordia

forgiving [fɔr'gɪvɪŋ] *adj* perdonador, misericordioso, clemente

for·go [fɔr'go] *v* (*pret* **-went';** *pp* **-gone'**) *tr* privarse de

fork [fɔrk] *s* horca; (*of a gardener; of bicycle*) horquilla; (*of two rivers*) horcajo; (*of railroad*) ramal *m*; (*of a tree*) horqueta; (*for eating*) tenedor *m* ‖ *tr* ahorquillar; cargar con horquilla; (*in chess*) amenazar (*dos piezas*); **to fork out** (slang) entregar, sudar ‖ *intr* bifurcarse

forked [fɔrkt] *adj* ahorquillado

forked lightning *s* relámpago en zigzag

fork'lift' truck *s* carretilla elevadora de horquilla

forlorn [fɔr'lɔrn] *adj* desamparado; desesperado; miserable

forlorn hope *s* empresa desesperada

form [fɔrm] *s* forma; (*paper to be filled out*) formulario; (*construction to give shape to cement*) encofrado; (*type in a frame*) molde *m* ‖ *tr* formar ‖ *intr* formarse

formal ['fɔrməl] *adj* formal, ceremonioso; etiquetero

formal attire *s* vestido de etiqueta

formal call *s* visita de cumplido

formali·ty [fɔr'mælɪti] *s* (*pl* **-ties**) (*standard procedure*) formalidad; ceremonia, etiqueta

formal party *s* reunión de etiqueta

formal speech *s* discurso de aparato

format ['fɔrmæt] *s* formato

formation [fɔr'meʃən] *s* formación

former ['fɔrmər] *adj* (*preceding*) anterior; (*long past*) antiguo; primero (*de dos*); **the former** aquél

formerly ['fɔrmərli] *adv* antes, en tiempos pasados

form'-fit'ting *adj* ceñido al cuerpo

formidable ['fɔrmɪdəbəl] *adj* formidable

formless ['fɔrmlɪs] *adj* informe

form letter *s* carta general

formu·la ['fɔrmjələ] *s* (*pl* **-las** o **-lae** [ˌli]) fórmula

formulate ['fɔrmjəˌlet] *tr* formular

for·sake [fɔr'sek] *v* (*pret* **-sook** ['sʊk]; *pp* **-saken** ['sekən]) *tr* abandonar, desamparar; dejar

fort [fɔrt] *s* fuerte *m*, fortaleza

forte [fɔrt] *s* (*strong point*) fuerte *m*, caballo de batalla

forth [forθ] *adv* adelante; **and so forth** y así sucesivamente; **from this day**

forth de hoy en adelante; **to go forth** salir

forth'com'ing *adj* próximo, venidero

forth'right' *adj* directo, franco, sincero ‖ *adv* derecho; sinceramente, francamente; en seguida

forth'with' *adv* inmediatamente

fortieth ['fɔrtɪɪθ] *adj* & *s* (*in a series*) cuadragésimo; (*part*) cuarentavo

fortification [ˌfɔrtɪfɪ'keʃən] *s* fortificación

forti·fy ['fɔrtɪˌfaɪ] *v* (*pret* & *pp* **-fied**) *tr* fortificar; encabezar (*vinos*)

fortitude ['fɔrtɪˌtjud] o ['fɔrtɪˌtud] *s* fortaleza, firmeza

fortnight ['fɔrtnaɪt] o ['fɔrtnɪt] *s* quincena, dos semanas

fortress ['fɔrtrɪs] *s* fortaleza

fortuitous [fɔr'tju·ɪtəs] o [fɔr'tu·ɪtəs] *adj* fortuito

fortunate ['fɔrtʃənɪt] *adj* afortunado

fortune ['fɔrtʃən] *s* fortuna; **to make a fortune** enriquecerse; **to tell someone his fortune** decirle a uno la buenaventura

fortune hunter *s* cazador *m* de dotes

for'tune-tel'ler *s* adivino, agorero

for·ty ['fɔrti] *adj* & *pron* cuarenta ‖ *s* (*pl* **-ties**) cuarenta *m*

fo·rum ['forəm] *s* (*pl* **-rums** o **-ra** [rə]) foro; (*e.g., of public opinion*) tribunal *m*

forward ['fɔrwərd] *adj* delantero; precoz; atrevido, impertinente ‖ *adv* hacia adelante; **to bring forward** pasar a cuenta nueva; **to come forward** adelantarse; **to look forward to** esperar con placer anticipado ‖ *tr* cursar, hacer seguir, reexpedir; fomentar, patrocinar

fossil ['fɑsɪl] *adj* & *s* fósil *m*

foster ['fʌstər] o ['fɔstər] *adj* adoptivo, de leche, de crianza ‖ *tr* fomentar

foster home *s* hogar *m* de adopción

foul [faʊl] *adj* sucio, puerco; (*air*) viciado; (*wind*) contrario; (*weather*) malo; obsceno; pérfido; (*breath*) fétido; (*baseball*) fuera del cuadro

foul-mouthed ['faʊl'maʊðd] o ['faʊl'maʊθt] *adj* deslenguado

foul play *s* mal encuentro; (*sport*) juego sucio

foul'spo'ken *adj* malhablado

found [faʊnd] *tr* fundar; (*to melt, to cast*) fundir

foundation [faʊn'deʃən] *s* fundación; (*endowment*) dotación; (*basis*) fundamento; (*masonry support*) cimiento

founder ['faʊndər] *s* fundador *m*; (*of metals*) fundidor *m* ‖ *intr* despearse (*un caballo*); hundirse, irse a pique (*un buque*); (*to fail*) fracasar

foundling ['faʊndlɪŋ] *s* niño expósito

foundling hospital *s* casa de expósitos

found·ry ['faʊndri] *s* (*pl* **-ries**) fundición

foundry·man ['faʊndrɪmən] *s* (*pl* **-men** [mən]) fundidor *m*

fount [faʊnt] *s* fuente *f*

fountain ['faʊntən] *s* fuente *f*, manantial *m*

foun'tain·head' s nacimiento

fountain pen s pluma estilográfica, pluma fuente

fountain syringe s mangueta

four [for] adj & pron cuatro ‖ s cuatro; **four o'clock** las cuatro; **on all fours** a gatas

four'-cy'cle adj (mach) de cuatro tiempos

four'-cyl'inder adj (mach) de cuatro cilindros

four'-flush' intr (coll) bravear, papelonear

fourflusher ['for ˌflʌʃər] s (coll) bravucón m

four-footed ['for'futɪd] adj cuadrúpedo

four hundred adj & pron cuatrocientos ‖ s cuatrocientos m; **the four hundred** la alta sociedad

four'-in-hand' s corbata de nudo corredizo; coche tirado por cuatro caballos

four'-lane' adj cuadriviario

four'-leaf' adj cuadrifoliado

four-legged ['for'legɪd] o ['for'legd] adj de cuatro patas; (schooner) de cuatro mástiles

four'-let'ter word s palabra impúdica de cuatro letras

four'-mo'tor plane s cuadrimotor m

four'-o'clock' s dondiego

four'-post'er s cama imperial

four'score' adj cuatro veintenas

foursome ['forsəm] s cuatrinca; cuatro jugadores; juego de cuatro

fourteen ['for'tin] adj, pron & s catorce m

fourteenth ['for'tinθ] adj & s (in a series) decimocuarto; (part) catorzavo ‖ s (in dates) catorce m

fourth [forθ] adj & s cuarto ‖ s (in dates) cuatro

fourth estate s cuarto poder

four'-way' adj de cuatro direcciones; (elec) de cuatro terminales

fowl [faul] s ave f; aves; gallina; gallo; carne f de ave

fowling piece s escopeta de caza

fox [faks] s zorra; (fur) zorro; (cunning person) (fig) zorro ‖ tr (coll) engañar con astucia

fox'glove' s dedalera

fox'hole' s zorrera; (mil) pozo de lobo

fox'hound' s perro raposero, perro zorrero

fox hunt s caza de zorras

fox terrier s fox-terrier m (casta de perro de talla pequeña)

fox trot s trote corto (de caballo); foxtrot m (baile de compás cuaternario)

fox·y ['faksɪ] adj (comp -ier; super -iest) zorrero, astuto, taimado

foyer ['fɔɪ·ər] s (of a private house) vestíbulo; (theat) salón m de entrada, vestíbulo

fr. abbr **fragment, franc, from**

Fr. abbr **Father, French, Friday**

Fra [frɑ] s fray m

fracas ['frekəs] s alboroto, riña

fraction ['frækʃən] s fracción; porción muy pequeña

fractional ['frækʃənəl] adj fraccionario; insignificante

fractious ['frækʃəs] adj reacio, rebelón; quisquilloso, regañón

fracture ['fræktʃər] s fractura ‖ tr fracturar; (e.g., an arm) fracturarse; intr fracturarse

fragile ['frædʒɪl] adj frágil

fragment ['frægmənt] s fragmento

fragrance ['fregrəns] s fragancia

fragrant ['fregrənt] adj fragante

frail [frel] adj (not robust) débil; (easily broken; morally weak) frágil ‖ s cesto de junco

frail·ty ['frelti] s (pl -ties) debilidad; (moral weakness) fragilidad

frame [frem] s (of a picture, mirror) marco; (of glasses) montura, armadura; (structure) armazón f, esqueleto; (for embroidering) bastidor m; (of government) sistema m; (mov, telv) encuadre m; (naut) cuaderna ‖ tr (to put in a frame) enmarcar; formar, forjar; construir; redactar, formular; (slang) incriminar (a un inocente)

frame house s casa de madera

frame of mind s manera de pensar

frame'-up' s (slang) treta, trama para incriminar a un inocente

frame'work' s armazón f, esqueleto, entramado

franc [fræŋk] s franco

France [fræns] o [frɑns] s Francia

Frances ['frænsɪs] o ['frɑnsɪs] s Francisca

franchise ['fræntʃaɪz] s franquicia, privilegio; (right to vote) sufragio

Francis ['frænsɪs] o ['frɑnsɪs] s Francisco

Franciscan [fræn'sɪskən] adj & s franciscano

frank [fræŋk] adj franco, sincero ‖ s carta franca, envío franco; franquicia postal; sello de franquicia ‖ tr franquear ‖ **Frank** s (member of a Frankish tribe) franco; (masculine name) Paco

frankfurter ['fræŋkfərtər] s salchicha de carne de vaca y de cerdo

frankincense ['fræŋkɪnˌsens] s olíbano

Frankish ['fræŋkɪʃ] adj & s franco

frankness ['fræŋknɪs] s franqueza, abertura, sinceridad

frantic ['fræntɪk] adj frenético

frappé [fræ'pe] adj helado ‖ s refresco helado de zumo de frutas

frat [fræt] s (slang) club m de estudiantes

fraternal [frə'tʌrnəl] adj fraternal

fraterni·ty [frə'tʌrnɪti] s (pl -ties) (brotherliness) fraternidad; cofradía; asociación secreta; (U.S.A.) club m de estudiantes

fraternize ['frætərˌnaɪz] intr fraternizar

fraud [frɔd] s fraude m; (person) (coll) impostor m

fraudulent ['frɔdjələnt] adj fraudulento

fraught [frɔt] adj — **fraught with** cargado de, lleno de

fray [fre] *s* combate *m*, riña, batalla || *intr* deshilacharse, raerse

freak [frik] *s* (*sudden fancy*) capricho, antojo; (*person, animal*) fenómeno

freakish ['frikɪʃ] *adj* caprichoso, antojadizo; raro, fantástico

freckle ['frekəl] *s* peca

freckle-faced ['frekəl‚fest] *adj* pecoso

freckly ['frekli] *adj* pecoso

Frederick ['fredərɪk] *s* Federico

free [fri] *adj* (*comp* **freer** ['fri·ər]; *super* **freest** ['fri·ɪst]) libre; gratis, franco; liberal, generoso; **to be free with** dar abundantemente; **to set free** libertar || *adv* libremente; en libertad; de balde, gratis || *v* (*pret* & *pp* **freed** [frid]; *ger* **freeing** ['fri·ɪŋ]) *tr* libertar, poner en libertad; soltar; exentar, eximir

free and easy *adj* despreocupado

freebooter ['fri‚butər] *s* forbante *m*, filibustero, pirata *m*

free'born' *adj* nacido libre; propio de un pueblo libre

freedom ['fridəm] *s* libertad

freedom of speech *s* libertad de palabra

freedom of the press *s* libertad de imprenta

freedom of the seas *s* libertad de los mares

freedom of worship *s* libertad de cultos

free enterprise *s* libertad de empresa

free fight *s* sarracina, riña tumultuaria

free'-for-all' *s* concurso abierto a todo el mundo; sarracina, riña tumultuaria

free hand *s* plena libertad, carta blanca

free'hand' drawing *s* dibujo a pulso

freehanded ['fri‚hændɪd] *adj* dadivoso, generoso

free'hold' *s* (law) feudo franco

free lance *s* soldado mercenario; periodista *mf* sin empleo fijo; (*writer not on regular salary*) destajista *mf*

free lunch *s* tapas, enjutos

free·man ['frimən] *s* (*pl* **-men** [mən]) hombre *m* libre; ciudadano

Free'ma'son *s* francmasón *m*

Free'ma'sonry *s* francmasonería

free of charge *adj* gratis, de balde

free on board *adj* franco a bordo

free port *s* puerto franco

free ride *s* llevada gratuita

free service *s* servicio post-venta

free'-spo'ken *adj* franco, sin reserva

free'stone' *adj* & *s* abridero

free'think'er *s* librepensador *m*

free thought *s* librepensamiento

free trade *s* librecambio

free'trad'er *s* librecambista *mf*

free'way' *s* autopista

free will *s* libre albedrío

freeze [friz] *s* helada || *v* (*pret* **froze** [froz]; *pp* **frozen**) *tr* helar; congelar (*créditos, fondos, etc.*) || *intr* helarse; congelarse; helársele a uno la sangre (*p.ej., de miedo*)

freezer ['frizər] *s* heladora, sorbetera

freight [fret] *s* carga; (naut) flete *m*; **by freight** como carga; (rr) en pequeña velocidad || *tr* enviar por carga

freight car *s* vagón *m* de carga, vagón de mercancías

freighter ['fretər] *s* buque *m* de carga, carguero

freight platform *s* (rr) muelle *m*

freight station *s* (rr) estación de carga

freight train *s* mercancías *msg*, tren *m* de mercancías

freight yard *s* (rr) patio de carga

French [frentʃ] *adj* & *s* francés *m*; **the French** los franceses

French chalk *s* jaboncillo de sastre

French doors *spl* puertas vidrieras dobles

French dressing *s* salsa francesa, vinagreta

French fried potatoes *spl* patatas fritas en trocitos

French horn *s* (mus) trompa de armonía

French horsepower *s* caballo de fuerza, caballo de vapor

French leave *s* despedida a la francesa; **to take French leave** despedirse a la francesa

French·man ['frentʃmən] *s* (*pl* **-men** [mən]) francés *m*

French telephone *s* microteléfono

French toast *s* torrija

French window *s* puerta ventana

French'wom'an *s* (*pl* **-wom'en**) francesa

frenzied ['frenzid] *adj* frenético

fren·zy ['frenzi] *s* (*pl* **-zies**) frenesí *m*

frequen·cy ['frikwənsi] *s* (*pl* **-cies**) frecuencia

frequency list *s* lista de frecuencia

frequency modulation *s* modulación de frecuencia

frequent ['frikwənt] *adj* frecuente || [frɪ'kwent] o ['frikwənt] *tr* frecuentar

frequently ['frikwəntli] *adv* con frecuencia, frecuentemente

fres·co ['fresko] *s* (*pl* **-coes** o **-cos**) fresco || *tr* pintar al fresco

fresh [freʃ] *adj* fresco; (*water*) dulce; (*wind*) fresquito; novicio, inexperto; (*cheeky*) (slang) fresco; (*toward women*) (slang) atrevido; **fresh paint!** ¡ojo manchal || *adv* recientemente, recién; **fresh in** (coll) recién llegado, acabado de llegar; **fresh out** (coll) recién agotado

freshen ['freʃən] *tr* refrescar || *intr* refrescarse

freshet ['freʃɪt] *s* avenida, crecida

fresh·man ['freʃmən] *s* (*pl* **-men** [mən]) novato; estudiante *mf* de primer año

freshness ['freʃnɪs] *s* frescura; (*cheek*) (slang) frescura

fresh'-wa'ter *adj* de agua dulce; no acostumbrado a navegar; de poca monta

fret [fret] *s* (*interlaced design*) calado; (mus) ceja, traste *m*; queja || *v* (*pret* & *pp* **fretted**; *ger* **fretting**) *tr* adornar con calados || *intr* irritarse, quejarse, agitarse

fretful ['fretfəl] *adj* irritable, enojadizo, displicente

fret'work' *s* calado

Freudianism ['frɔɪdɪ·ə‚nɪzəm] s freudismo

friar ['fraɪ·ər] s fraile m

friar·y ['fraɪ·ərɪ] s (pl -ies) convento de frailes

fricassee [‚frɪkə'si] s fricasé m

friction ['frɪkʃən] s fricción, rozamiento; (fig) desavenencia, rozamiento

friction tape s cinta aislante

Friday ['fraɪdɪ] s viernes m

fried [fraɪd] adj frito

fried egg s huevo a la plancha, huevo frito o estrellado

friend [frend] s amigo; (in answer to "Who is there?") gente f de paz; to be friends with ser amigo de; to make friends trabar amistades; to make friends with hacerse amigo de

friend·ly ['frendlɪ] adj (comp -lier; super -liest) amigo, amistoso, amigable

friendship ['frendʃɪp] s amistad

frieze [friz] s (archit) friso

frigate ['frɪgɪt] s fragata

fright [fraɪt] s susto, espanto; (grotesque or ridiculous person) (coll) espantajo; to take fright at asustarse de

frighten ['fraɪtən] tr asustar, espantar; to frighten away espantar, ahuyentar || intr asustarse

frightful ['fraɪtfəl] adj espantoso, horroroso; (coll) feúcho, repugnante; (coll) enorme, tremendo

frightfulness ['fraɪtfəlnɪs] s espanto, horror m; terrorismo

frigid ['frɪdʒɪd] adj frío; (fig) frío; (zone) glacial

frigidity [frɪ'dʒɪdɪtɪ] s frialdad; (pathol) frialdad; (fig) frialdad, frigidez f

frill [frɪl] s lechuga; (of birds and other animals) collarín m; (frippery) (coll) ringorrango; (in dress, speech, etc.) (coll) afectación

fringe [frɪndʒ] s franja, orla; (opt) franja || tr franjar, orlar

fringe benefits spl beneficios accesorios

fripper·y ['frɪpərɪ] s (pl -ies) (flashiness) cursilería; (flashy clothes) perejil m, perifollos

frisk [frɪsk] tr (slang) cachear; (slang) registrar y robar || intr retozar

frisk·y ['frɪskɪ] adj (comp -ier; super -iest) juguetón, retozón; (horse) fogoso

fritter ['frɪtər] s fruta de sartén; fragmento || tr — to fritter away desperdiciar, malgastar poco a poco

frivolous ['frɪvələs] adj frívolo

friz [frɪz] s (pl frizzes) rizo, pelo rizado apretadamente || v (pret & pp frizzed; ger frizzing) tr rizar, rizar apretadamente

frizzle ['frɪzəl] s rizo apretado; chirrido, siseo || tr rizar apretadamente; asar o freír en parrilla || intr chirriar, sisear

friz·zly ['frɪzlɪ] adj (comp -zlier; super -zliest) muy ensortijado

fro [fro] adv — to and fro de acá para allá; to go to and fro ir y venir

frock [frɑk] s vestido; bata, blusa; (of priest) vestido talar

frock coat s levita

frog [frɑg] o [frɔg] s rana; (button and loop on a garment) alamar m; (in throat) ronquera, gallo

frog'man' s (pl -men') hombre-rana m

frol·ic ['frɑlɪk] s juego alegre, travesura; fiesta, holgorio || v (pret & pp -icked; ger -icking) intr juguetear, travesear, jaranear

frolicsome ['frɑlɪksəm] adj juguetón, travieso

from [frʌm], [frɑm] o [frəm] prep de; desde; de parte de; según; a, p.ej., to take something away from someone quitarle algo a alguien

front [frʌnt] adj delantero; anterior || s frente m & f; (of a shirt) pechera; (of a book) principio; apariencia falsa (p.ej., de riqueza); además estudiado; (mil) frente m; in front of delante de, frente a, en frente de; to put on a front (coll) gastar mucho oropel; to put up a bold front (coll) hacer de tripas corazón || tr (to face) dar a; (to confront) afrontar, arrostrar; (to supply with a front) poner frente o fachada a || intr — to front on dar a; to front towards mirar hacia

frontage ['frʌntɪdʒ] s fachada, frontera; terreno frontero

front door s puerta de entrada

front drive s (aut) tracción delantera

frontier [frʌn'tɪr] adj fronterizo || s frontera

frontiers·man [frʌn'tɪrzmən] s (pl -men [mən]) hombre m de la frontera, explorador m

frontispiece ['frʌntɪs‚pis] s (of book) portada; (archit) frontispicio

front matter s preliminares mpl (de un libro)

front page s primera plana

front porch s soportal m

front room s cuarto que da a la calle

front row s primera fila

front seat s asiento delantero

front steps spl escalones mpl de acceso a la puerta de entrada

front view s vista de frente

frost [frɔst] o [frɑst] s (freezing) helada; (frozen dew) escarcha; (slang) fracaso || tr cubrir de escarcha, escarchar (confituras); helar (el frío las plantas); deslustrar (el vidrio)

frost'bit'ten adj dañado por la helada; quemado por la helada o la escarcha

frosted glass s vidrio deslustrado

frosting ['frɔstɪŋ] o ['frɑstɪŋ] s garapiña; (of glass) deslustre m

frost·y ['frɔstɪ] o ['frɑstɪ] adj (comp -ier; super -iest) cubierto de escarcha; escarchado; frío, poco amistoso; canoso, gris

froth [frɔθ] o [frɑθ] s espuma; frivolidad, vanidad || intr espumar, echar espuma; (at the mouth) espumajear

froth·y ['frɔθɪ] o ['frɑθɪ] adj (comp -ier; super -iest) espumoso; frívolo, vano

froward ['frowərd] *adj* díscolo, indócil

frown [fraun] *s* ceño, entrecejo ‖ *intr* fruncir el entrecejo; **to frown at u on** mirar con ceño, desaprobar

frows·y o **frowz·y** ['frauzi] *adj* (*comp* **-ier;** *super* **-iest**) desaseado, desaliñado; maloliente; mal peinado

frozen foods ['frozən] *spl* viandas congeladas

F.R.S. *abbr* **Fellow of the Royal Society**

frt. *abbr* **freight**

frugal ['frugəl] *adj* (*moderate in the use of things*) parco; (*not very abundant*) frugal

fruit [frut] *adj* (*tree*) frutal; (*boat, dish*) frutero ‖ *s* (*such as apple, pear, strawberry*) fruta; frutas, p.ej., **I like fruit** me gustan las frutas; (*part containing seed*) fruto; (*effect, result*) (fig) fruto

fruit cake *s* torta de frutas

fruit cup *s* compota de frutas picadas

fruit fly *s* mosca del vinagre; mosca de las frutas

fruitful ['frutfəl] *adj* fructuoso

fruition [fru'ɪʃən] *s* buen resultado, cumplimiento; **to come to fruition** lograrse cumplidamente

fruit jar *s* tarro para frutas

fruit juice *s* jugo de frutas

fruitless ['frutlɪs] *adj* infructuoso

fruit of the vine *s* zumo de cepas o de parras

fruit salad *s* ensalada de frutas, macedonia de frutas

fruit stand *s* puesto de frutas

fruit store *s* frutería

frumpish ['frʌmpɪʃ] *adj* basto, desgarbado, desaliñado

frustrate ['frʌstret] *tr* frustrar

fry [fraɪ] *s* (*pl* **fries**) fritada ‖ *v* (*pret & pp* **fried**) *tr & intr* freír

frying pan ['fraɪ·ɪŋ] *s* sartén *f;* **to jump from the frying pan into the fire** saltar de la sartén y dar en las brasas

ft. *abbr* **foot, feet**

fudge [fʌdʒ] *s* dulce *m* de chocolate

fuel ['fju·əl] *s* combustible *m;* (fig) pábulo ‖ *v* (*pret & pp* **fueled** o **fuelled;** *ger* **fueling** o **fuelling**) *tr* aprovisionar de combustible ‖ *intr* aprovisionarse de combustible

fuel cell *s* cámara de combustión, célula electrógena

fuel oil *s* aceite *m* combustible

fuel tank *s* depósito de combustible

fugitive ['fjudʒɪtɪv] *adj & s* fugitivo

fugue [fjug] *s* (mus) fuga

ful·crum ['fʌlkrəm] *s* (*pl* **-crums** o **-cra** [krə]) fulcro

fulfill [ful'fɪl] *tr* (*to carry out*) cumplir, realizar; cumplir con (*una obligación*); llenar (*una condición*)

fulfillment [ful'fɪlmənt] *s* cumplimiento, realización

full [ful] *adj* lleno; (*dress, garment*) amplio, holgado; (*formal dress*) de etiqueta; (*voice*) sonoro, fuerte; (*of food*) harto; **full of aches and pains** lleno de goteras; **full of fun** muy divertido, muy chistoso; **full of play** muy juguetón; **full to overflowing** lleno a rebosar ‖ *adv* completamente; **full many** (a) muchísimos; **full well** muy bien, perfectamente ‖ *s* colmo; **in full** por completo; sin abreviar; **to the full** completamente ‖ *tr* abatanar

full-blooded ['ful'blʌdɪd] *adj* vigoroso; completo, pletórico; de raza

full-blown ['ful'blon] *adj* (*flower, blossom*) abierto; desarrollado, maduro

full-bodied ['ful'badɪd] *adj* fuerte, espeso, consistente; aromático

full dress *s* traje *m* de etiqueta; (mil) uniforme *m* de gala

full'-dress' coat *s* frac *m*

full-faced ['ful'fest] *adj* carilleno; (*view*) de cuadrado; (*portrait*) de rostro entero

full-fledged ['ful'fledʒd] *adj* hecho y derecho, nada menos que

full-grown ['ful'gron] *adj* crecido, completamente desarrollado

full house *s* lleno, entrada llena; (poker) fulján *m*

full'-length' mirror *s* espejo de cuerpo entero, espejo de vestir

full-length movie *s* largometraje *m,* cinta de largo metraje

full load *s* plena carga; (aer) peso total

full moon *s* luna llena, plenilunio

full name *s* nombre *m* y apellidos

full'-page' adj a página entera

full powers *spl* plenos poderes, amplias facultades

full sail *adv* a todo trapo

full'-scale' adj de tamaño natural; total, completo; pleno

full-sized ['ful'saɪzd] *adj* de tamaño natural

full speed *adv* a toda velocidad

full stop *s* parada completa; (gram) punto

full swing *s* plena actividad

full tilt *adv* a toda velocidad

full'-time' adj a tiempo completo

full'-view' adj de vista completa

full volume *s* (rad) máximo de volumen

fully ['fuli] o ['fʊli] *adv* completamente; cabalmente; por lo menos

fulsome ['fulsəm] o ['fʌlsəm] *adj* bajo, craso, de mal gusto

fumble ['fʌmbl] *tr* no coger (*la pelota*), dejar caer (*la pelota*) desmañadamente; manosear desmañadamente ‖ *intr* revolver papeles; titubear; andar a tientas; (*in one's pockets*) buscar con las manos

fume [fjum] *s* humo, vapor *m,* gas *m,* vaho ‖ *tr* (*to treat with fumes*) ahumar ‖ *intr* (*to give off fumes*) humear; (*to show anger*) echar pestes; **to fume at** echar pestes contra

fumigate ['fjumɪˌget] *tr* fumigar

fumigation [ˌfjumɪ'geʃən] *s* fumigación

fun [fʌn] *s* divertimiento; broma, chacota; **to be fun** ser divertido; **to have fun** divertirse; **to make fun of** reírse de, burlarse de

function ['fʌŋkʃən] s función ‖ *intr* funcionar

functional ['fʌŋkʃənəl] *adj* funcional

functionar·y ['fʌŋkʃə‚nerɪ] s (*pl* -ies) funcionario

fund [fʌnd] s fondo; **funds** fondos ‖ *tr* consolidar (*una deuda*)

fundamental [‚fʌndə'mentəl] *adj* fundamental ‖ s fundamento

funeral ['fjunərəl] *adj* funeral; (*march, procession*) fúnebre; (*expense*) funerario ‖ s funeral *m*, funerales *mpl*, pompa fúnebre (*de cuerpo presente*); **it's not my funeral** (slang) no corre a mi cuidado

funeral director s empresario de pompas fúnebres

funeral home o **parlor** s funeraria

funeral service s oficio de difuntos, misa de cuerpo presente

funereal [fju'nɪrɪ·əl] *adj* fúnebre

fungous ['fʌŋgəs] *adj* fungoso

fungus ['fʌŋgəs] s (*pl* **funguses** o **fungi** ['fʌndʒaɪ]) hongo; (pathol) fungo

funicular [fju'nɪkjələr] *adj & s* funicular *m*

funk [fʌŋk] s (coll) miedo, cobardía; (coll) cobarde *mf*; **in a funk** (coll) asustado

fun·nel ['fʌnəl] s embudo; (*smokestack*) chimenea; (*tube for ventilation*) manguera, ventilador *m* ‖ *v* (*pret & pp* -neled o -nelled; *ger* -neling o -nelling) *tr* verter por medio de un embudo

funnies ['fʌnɪz] *spl* páginas cómicas, tiras cómicas, tebeo

fun·ny ['fʌnɪ] *adj* (*comp* -nier; *super -niest*) cómico; divertido, chistoso; (coll) extraño, raro; **to strike someone as funny** hacerle a uno gracia

funny bone s hueso de la alegría

funny paper s páginas cómicas

fur. *abbr* **furlong, furnished**

fur [fʌr] s piel *f*; abrigo de pieles; (*on the tongue*) sarro

furbelow ['fʌrbə‚lo] s (*ruffle*) faralá *m*; (*frippery*) ringorrango

furbish ['fʌrbɪʃ] *tr* acicalar, limpiar; **to furbish up** renovar

furious ['fjurɪ·əs] *adj* furioso

furl [fʌrl] *tr* enrollar; (naut) aferrar

fur-lined ['fʌr‚laɪnd] *adj* forrado con pieles

furlong ['fʌrlɔŋ] o ['fʌrlɑŋ] s estadio *m*

furlough ['fʌrlo] s licencia ‖ *tr* dar licencia a

furnace ['fʌrnɪs] s horno; (*to heat a house*) calorífero

furnish ['fʌrnɪʃ] *tr* amueblar; proporcionar, suministrar

furnishings ['fʌrnɪʃɪŋz] *spl* muebles *mpl*; (*things to wear*) artículos

furniture ['fʌrnɪtʃər] s muebles *mpl*, mobiliario; (naut) aparejo; **a piece of furniture** un mueble

furniture dealer s mueblista *mf*

furniture store s mueblería

furrier ['fʌrɪ·ər] s peletero

furrier·y ['fʌrɪ·ərɪ] s (*pl* -ies) peletería

furrow ['fʌro] s surco ‖ *tr* surcar

further ['fʌrðər] *adj* adicional; nuevo; más lejano ‖ *adv* además; más lejos ‖ *tr* adelantar, promover, fomentar

furtherance ['fʌrðərəns] s adelantamiento, promoción, fomento

furthermore ['fʌrðər‚mor] *adv* además

furthest ['fʌrðɪst] *adj* (el) más lejano ‖ *adv* más lejos

furtive ['fʌrtɪv] *adj* furtivo

fu·ry ['fjurɪ] s (*pl* -ries) furia

furze [fʌrz] s aulaga; retama de escoba

fuse [fjuz] s (*tube or wick filled with explosive material*) mecha; (*device for detonating an explosive charge*) espoleta; (elec) fusible *m*, cortacircuitos *m*, tapón *m*; **to burn out a fuse** quemar un fusible ‖ *tr* fundir; (*to unite*) fusionar ‖ *intr* fundirse; fusionarse

fuse box s caja de fusibles

fuselage ['fjuzəlɪdʒ] o [‚fjuzə'lɑʒ] s fuselaje *m*

fusible ['fjuzɪbəl] *adj* fundible, fusible

fusillade [‚fjuzɪ'led] s fusilería; (*e.g., of questions*) andanada ‖ atacar o matar con una descarga de fusilería, fusilar

fusion ['fjuʒən] s fusión

fuss [fʌs] s alharaca, hazañería; (coll) disputa por ligero motivo; **to make a fuss** hacer alharacas; **to make a fuss over** hacer fiestas a; disputar sobre ‖ *tr* atolondrar, inquietar, confundir ‖ *intr* hacer alharacas, inquietarse por bagatelas

fuss·y ['fʌsɪ] *adj* (*comp* -ier; *super -iest*) alharaquiento, alborotado; descontentadizo, quisquilloso, melindroso; funcionero, hazañero; muy adornado

fustian ['fʌstʃən] s (*coarse cloth*) fustán *m*; (*sort of velveteen*) pana; (*bombast*) cultedad, follaje *m*

fust·y ['fʌstɪ] *adj* (*comp* -ier; *super -iest*) mohoso, rancio; que huele a cerrado; pasado de moda

futile ['fjutɪl] *adj* (*unproductive*) estéril; (*unimportant*) fútil

futili·ty [fju'tɪlɪtɪ] s (*pl* -ties) esterilidad; futilidad

future ['fjutʃər] *adj* futuro ‖ s futuro, porvenir *m*; (gram) futuro; **futures** (com) futuros; **in the future** en el futuro; **in the near future** en un futuro próximo

fuze [fjuz] s (*tube or wick filled with explosive material*) mecha; (*device for detonating an explosive charge*) espoleta; (elec) fusible *m* ‖ *tr* poner la espoleta a

fuzz [fʌz] s (*as on a peach*) pelusa, vello; (*in pockets and corners*) borra, tamo

fuzz·y ['fʌzɪ] *adj* (*comp* -ier; *super -iest*) cubierto de pelusa, velloso; polvoriento; (*indistinct*) borroso

G

G, g [dʒi] *s* séptima letra del alfabeto inglés

G. *abbr* **German, Gulf**

g. *abbr* **gender, genitive, gram**

gab [gæb] *s* (coll) cotorreo ‖ (*pret & pp* **gabbed;** *ger* **gabbing**) *intr* (coll) cotorrear

gabardine ['gæbər,din] *s* gabardina

gabble ['gæbəl] *s* cotorreo, parloteo ‖ *intr* cotorrear, parlotear

gable ['gebəl] *s* (*of roof*) aguilón *m*; (*over a door or window*) gablete *m*, frontón *m*

gable end *s* hastial *m*

gable roof *s* tejado de dos aguas

gad [gæd] *v* (*pret & pp* **gadded;** *ger* **gadding**) *intr* callejear, andar de acá para allá; **to gad about** pindonguear (*una mujer*)

gad·a·bout ['gæd·ə·baʊt] *adj* callejero ‖ *s* cirigallo; (*woman*) pindonga

gad'fly' *s* (*pl* **-flies**) tábano

gadget ['gædʒɪt] *s* adminículo, chisme *m*, artilugio

Gael [gel] *s* gaélico

Gaelic ['gelɪk] *adj & s* gaélico

gaff [gæf] *s* garfio, arpón *m*; **to stand the gaff** (slang) tener aguante

gag [gæg] *s* mordaza; (*interpolation by an actor*) morcilla; (*joke*) chiste *m*, payasada ‖ *v* (*pret & pp* **gagged;** *ger* **gagging**) *tr* amordazar; dar bascas a ‖ *intr* sentir bascas, arquear

gage [gedʒ] *s* (*pledge*) prenda; (*challenge*) desafío

gaie·ty ['ge·ɪti] *s* (*pl* **-ties**) alegría, algazara, diversión; (*of colors*) viveza

gaily ['geli] *adv* alegremente

gain [gen] *s* ganancia; (*increase*) aumento ‖ *tr* ganar; (*to reach*) alcanzar ‖ *intr* ganar terreno; mejorar (*un enfermo*); adelantarse (*un reloj*); **to gain on** ir alcanzando

gainful ['genfəl] *adj* ganancioso, provechoso

gain'say' *v* (*pret & pp* **-said** ['sed] o ['sed]) *tr* negar; contradecir; prohibir

gait [get] *s* paso, manera de andar

gaiter ['getər] *s* polaina corta

gal. *abbr* **gallon**

gala ['gælə] o ['gelə] *adj* de gala ‖ *s* fiesta

galax·y ['gæləksi] *s* (*pl* **-ies**) galaxia

gale [gel] *s* ventarrón *m*; **gales of laughter** tempestades de risas; **to weather the gale** correr el temporal; (fig) ir tirando

Galician [gə'lɪʃən] *adj & s* gallego

gall [gɔl] *s* bilis *f*, hiel *f*; vejiga de la bilis; (*something bitter*) (fig) hiel *f*; rencor *m*, odio; (*gallnut*) agalla; (*audacity*) (coll) descaro ‖ *tr* lastimar rozando; irritar ‖ *intr* raerse; (naut) mascarse (*un cabo*)

gallant ['gælənt] o [gə'lænt] *adj* (*attentive to women*) galante; (*pertaining to love*) amoroso ‖ ['gælənt]

adj (*stately, grand*) gallardo; (*spirited, daring*) hazañoso; (*showy, gay*) vistoso, festivo ‖ *s* hombre *m* valiente; (*man attentive to women*) galán *m*

gallant·ry ['gæləntri] *s* (*pl* **-ries**) galantería; gallardía

gall bladder *s* vejiga de la bilis, vesícula biliar

gall duct *s* conducto biliar

galleon ['gælɪ·ən] *s* (naut) galeón *m*

galler·y ['gæləri] *s* (*pl* **-ies**) galería; (*in church, theater, etc.*) tribuna; (*cheapest seats in theater*) gallinero; **to play to the gallery** (coll) hablar para la galería

galley ['gæli] *s* (naut & typ) galera; (naut) cocina

galley proof *s* (typ) galerada, pruebas de segundas

galley slave *s* galeote *m*; (*drudge*) esclavo del trabajo

Gallic ['gælɪk] *adj* gálico

galling ['gɔlɪŋ] *adj* irritante, ofensivo

gallivant ['gælɪ,vænt] *intr* andar a placer

gall'nut' *s* agalla

gallon ['gælən] *s* galón *m* (*medida*)

galloon [gə'lun] *s* galón *m* (*cinta*)

gallop ['gæləp] *s* galope *m*; **at a gallop** a galope ‖ *tr* hacer galopar ‖ *intr* galopar; **to gallop through** (fig) hacer muy aprisa

gal·lows ['gæloz] *s* (*pl* **-lows** o **-lowses**) horca

gallows bird *s* (coll) carne *f* de horca

gall'stone' *s* cálculo biliar

galore [gə'lor] *adv* en abundancia

galosh [gə'lɑʃ] *s* chanclo alto

galvanize ['gælvə,naɪz] *tr* galvanizar

galvanized iron *s* hierro galvanizado

gambit ['gæmbɪt] *s* gambito

gamble ['gæmbəl] *s* (coll) empresa arriesgada ‖ *tr* aventurar en el juego; **to gamble away** perder en el juego ‖ *intr* jugar; (*in the stock market*) especular, aventurarse

gambler ['gæmblər] *s* jugador *m*; especulador *m*

gambling ['gæmblɪŋ] *s* juego

gambling den *s* garito

gambling house *s* casa de juego, juego público

gambling table *s* mesa de juego

gam·bol ['gæmbəl] *s* cabriola, retozo, salto ‖ *v* (*pret & pp* **-boled** o **-bolled;** *gen* **-boling** o **-bolling**) *intr* cabriolar, retozar, saltar

gambrel ['gæmbrəl] *s* corvejón *m*

gambrel roof *s* techo a la holandesa

game [gem] *adj* bravo, peleón; dispuesto, resuelto; (*leg*) cojo; de caza ‖ *s* (*form of play*) juego; (*single contest*) partida; (*score*) tantos; (*in bridge*) manga; (*any sport*) deporte *m*; (*animal or bird hunted for sport or food*) caza; (*any pursuit*) actividad; (*pursuit of diplomacy*) juego;

the game is up estamos frescos; **to make game of** burlarse de; **to play the game** jugar limpio

game bag s morral m

game bird s ave f de caza

game'cock' s gallo de pelea

game'keep'er s guardabosque m

game of chance s juego de azar

game preserve s vedado

game warden s guardabosque m

gamut ['gæmət] s (mus & fig) gama

gam·y ['gemɪ] adj (comp **-ier;** super **-iest**) (having flavor of uncooked game) salvajino; bravo, peleón

gander ['gændər] s ganso

gang [gæŋ] adj múltiple || s (of workmen) brigada, cuadrilla; (of thugs) pandilla || intr — **to gang up** acuadrillarse; **to gang up against** u **on** atacar juntos; conspirar contra

gangling ['gæŋglɪŋ] adj larguirucho

gangli·on ['gæŋglɪ·ən] s (pl **-ons** o **-a** [ə]) ganglio

gang'plank' s plancha, pasarela

gangrene ['gæŋgrin] s gangrena || tr gangrenar || intr gangrenarse

gangster ['gæŋstər] s (coll) gángster m, pistolero

gang'way' s (passageway) pasillo; (gangplank) plancha, pasarela; (in ship's side) portalón m || interj ¡abran paso!, ¡paso libre!

gantlet ['gɑntlɪt] o ['gɔntlɪt] s (rr) vía traslapada

gan·try ['gæntrɪ] s (pl **-tries**) caballete m, poino; (rr) puente m transversal de señales

gantry crane s grúa de caballete

gap [gæp] s (break, open space) laguna; (in a wall) boquete m; (between mountains) garganta, quebrada; (between two points of view) sima

gape [gep] o [gæp] s abertura, brecha; (yawn) bostezo; mirada de asombro; **the gapes** ganas de bostezar || intr estar abierto de par en par; bostezar; embobarse; **to gape at** mirar embobado; **to stand gaping** embobarse

G.A.R. abbr **Grand Army of the Republic**

garage [gə'rɑz] s garage m

garb [gɑrb] s vestidura || tr vestir

garbage ['gɑrbɪdʒ] s basuras, desperdicios, bazofia

garbage can s cubo para bazofia, latón m de la basura

garbage disposal s evacuación de basuras

garble ['gɑrbəl] tr mutilar (un texto)

garden ['gɑrdən] s (of vegetables) huerto; (of flowers) jardín m

gardener ['gɑrdənər] s (of vegetables) hortelano; (of flowers) jardinero

gardenia [gɑr'dinɪ·ə] s gardenia, jazmín m de la India

gardening ['gɑrdənɪŋ] s horticultura; jardinería

garden party s fiesta que se da en un jardín o parque

gargle ['gɑrgəl] s gargarismo || intr gargarizar

gargoyle ['gɑrgɔɪl] s gárgola

garish ['gerɪʃ] o ['gærɪʃ] adj charro, chillón, cursi

garland ['gɑrlənd] s guirnalda

garlic ['gɑrlɪk] s ajo

garment ['gɑrmənt] s prenda de vestir

garner ['gɑrnər] tr (to gather, collect) acopiar; adquirir; (cereales) entrojar

garnet ['gɑrnɪt] adj & s granate m

garnish ['gɑrnɪʃ] s adorno; (culin) aderezo, condimento de adorno || tr adornar; (culin) aderezar; (law) embargar

garret ['gærɪt] s buhardilla, desván m

garrison ['gærɪsən] s plaza fuerte; (troops) guarnición || tr guarnecer, guarnicionar (una plaza fuerte); guarnecer una plaza fuerte de (tropas)

garrote [gə'rɑt] o [gə'rot] s estrangulación para robar; (method of execution; iron collar used for such execution) garrote m || tr estrangular; estrangular para robar; agarrotar, dar garrote a

garrulous ['gærələs] o ['gærjələs] adj gárrulo, locuaz

garter ['gɑrtər] s liga, jarretera

garth [gɑrθ] s patio de claustro

gas [gæs] s gas m; (coll) gasolina; (coll) palabrería || v (pret & pp **gassed;** ger **gassing**) tr abastecer de gas; (to attack, asphyxiate, or poison with gas) gasear; (coll) abastecer de gasolina || intr despedir gas; (slang) charlar

gas'bag' s (aer) cámara de gas; (slang) charlatán m

gas burner s mechero de gas

Gascony ['gæskənɪ] s Gascuña

gas engine s motor m a gas

gaseous ['gæsɪ·əs] adj gaseoso

gas fitter s gasista m

gas generator s gasógeno

gash [gæʃ] s cuchillada, chirlo || tr acuchillar

gas heat s calefacción por gas

gas'hold'er s gasómetro

gasi·fy ['gæsɪ‚faɪ] v (pret & pp **-fied**) tr gasificar || intr gasificarse

gas jet s mechero de gas; llama de gas

gasket ['gæskɪt] s empaquetadura

gas'light' s luz f de gas

gas main s cañería de gas

gas mask s careta antigás

gas meter s contador m de gas

gasoline ['gæsə‚lin] o [‚gæsə'lin] s gasolina

gasoline pump s poste m distribuidor m de gasolina, surtidor m de gasolina

gasp [gæsp] o [gɑsp] s respiración entrecortada; (of death) boqueada || tr decir con voz entrecortada || intr boquear

gas producer s gasógeno

gas range s cocina a gas

gas station s estación gasolinera

gas stove s cocina a gas

gas tank s gasómetro; (aut) depósito de gasolina

gastric ['gæstrɪk] adj gástrico

gastronomy [gæs'trɑnəmi] s gastronomía

gas'works' s fábrica de gas

gate [get] s puerta; (in fence or wall; of bird cage) portillo; (of sluice or lock) compuerta; (number of people paying admission; amount they pay) entrada, taquilla; (rr) barrera; (fig) entrada, camino; **to crash the gate** (coll) colarse de gorra

gate'keep'er s portero; (rr) guardabarrera mf

gate'post' s poste m de una puerta de cercado

gate'way' s entrada, paso, camino

gather ['gæðər] tr recoger, reunir; recolectar (la cosecha); coger (leña, flores, etc.); cubrirse de (polvo), recoger (una persona sus pensamientos); (bb) alzar; (sew) fruncir; (to deduce) (fig) calcular, deducir; **to gather oneself together** componerse ‖ intr reunirse; amontonarse; saltar (lágrimas)

gathering ['gæðərɪŋ] s reunión; recolección; (bb) alzado; (sew) frunce m

gaud·y ['gɔdi] adj (comp -ier; super -iest) cursi, chillón, llamativo

gauge [gedʒ] s medida, norma; calibre m; (of liquid in a container) nivel m; (of carpenter) gramil m; (of gasoline) medidor m; (rr) ancho de vía, entrevía ‖ tr medir; calibrar; graduar; aforar (la cantidad de agua de una corriente); arquear (una nave)

gauge glass s tubo indicador, vidrio de nivel

Gaul [gɔl] s la Galia; (native) galo

Gaulish ['gɔlɪʃ] adj & s galo

gaunt [gɔnt] o [gɑnt] adj desvaído, macilento; hosco, tétrico

gauntlet ['gɔntlɪt] o ['gɑntlɪt] s guantelete m; guante con puño abocinado; carrera de baquetas; (rr) vía traslapada; **to run the gauntlet** correr baquetas, pasar por baquetas; **to take up the gauntlet** recoger el guante; **to throw down the gauntlet** arrojar el guante

gauze [gɔz] s gasa, cendal m

gavel ['gævəl] s mazo, martillo

gavotte [gə'vɑt] s gavota

gawk [gɔk] s (coll) palurdo, papanatas m ‖ intr (coll) mirar de modo impertinente; papar moscas, mirar embobado

gawk·y ['gɔki] adj (comp -ier; super -iest) desgarbado, torpe, bobo

gay [ge] adj alegre, festivo; (brilliant) vistoso; amigo de los placeres

gaye·ty ['ge·ɪti] s var de gaiety

gaze [gez] s mirada fija ‖ intr mirar fijamente

gazelle [gə'zɛl] s gacela

gazette [gə'zɛt] s periódico; anuncio oficial

gazetteer [ˌgæzə'tɪr] s diccionario geográfico

gear [gɪr] s pertrechos, utensilios; (of transmission, steering, etc.) mecanismo, aparato; rueda dentada; (two or more toothed wheels meshed to-

gether) engranaje m; **out of gear** desengranado; (fig) descompuesto; **to throw into gear** engranar; **to throw out of gear** desengranar; (fig) descomponer ‖ tr & intr engranar

gear'box' s caja de engranajes; (aut) caja de velocidades

gear case s caja de engranajes

gear'shift' s cambio de marchas, cambio de velocidades

gearshift lever s palanca de cambio de marchas

gear'wheel' s rueda dentada

gee [dʒi] interj ¡caramba!; **gee up!** (get up!, said to a horse) ¡arre!

Gehenna [gɪ'hɛnə] s gehena m

gel [dʒɛl] s gel m ‖ v (pret & pp gelled; ger gelling) intr cuajarse en forma de gel

gelatine ['dʒɛlətɪn] s gelatina

geld [gɛld] v (pret & pp gelded o gelt [gɛlt]) tr castrar

gem [dʒɛm] s gema, piedra preciosa; (fig) joya, preciosidad

Gemini ['dʒɛmɪˌnaɪ] s (constellation) Géminis m o Gemelos; (sign of zodiac) Géminis m

gen. abbr gender, general, genitive, genus

gender ['dʒɛndər] s (gram) género; (coll) sexo

genealo·gy [ˌdʒɛnɪ'ælədʒi] o [ˌdʒini-'ælədʒi] s (pl -gies) genealogía

general ['dʒɛnərəl] adj & s general m; **in general** en general o por lo general

general delivery s lista de correos

generalissi·mo [ˌdʒɛnərə'lɪsɪmo] s (pl -mos) generalísimo

generali·ty [ˌdʒɛnə'rælɪti] s (pl -ties) generalidad

generalize ['dʒɛnərəˌlaɪz] tr & intr generalizar

generally ['dʒɛnərəli] adv por lo general

general practitioner s médico general

generalship ['dʒɛnərəlˌʃɪp] s generalato; don m de mando

general staff s estado mayor general

generate ['dʒɛnəˌret] tr (to beget) engendrar; generar (electricidad); (geom) engendrar

generating station s central f

generation [ˌdʒɛnə're(ə)n] s generación

generator ['dʒɛnəˌretər] s generador m

generic [dʒɪ'nɛrɪk] adj genérico

generous ['dʒɛnərəs] adj generoso; abundante, grande

gene·sis ['dʒɛnɪsɪs] s (pl -ses [ˌsiz]) génesis f ‖ **Genesis** s (Bib) el Génesis

genetic [dʒɪ'nɛtɪk] adj genético ‖ **genetics** s genética

Geneva [dʒɪ'nivə] s Ginebra

Genevan [dʒɪ'nivən] adj & s ginebrino

genial ['dʒinɪəl] adj afable, complaciente

genie ['dʒini] s genio

genital ['dʒɛnɪtəl] adj genital ‖ **genitals** spl genitales mpl, órganos genitales

genitive ['dʒɛnɪtɪv] adj & s genitivo

genius ['dʒinjəs] o ['dʒinɪ·əs] s (pl geniuses) (great inventive gift; person possessing it) genio ‖ s (pl genii ['dʒɪnɪ,aɪ]) (*guardian spirit; pagan deity*) genio

Genoa ['dʒɛno·ə] s Génova

genocidal [,dʒɛnə'saɪdəl] *adj* genocida

genocide ['dʒɛnə,saɪd] s (*act*) genocidio; (*person*) genocida *mf*

Geno·ese [,dʒɛno'iz] *adj* genovés ‖ s (*pl* -ese) genovés *m*

genre ['ʒɑnrə] *adj* de género

gent. o **Gent.** *abbr* **gentleman, gentlemen**

genteel [dʒɛn'til] *adj* gentil, elegante; cortés, urbano

gentian ['dʒɛnʃən] s genciana

gentile ['dʒɛntɪl] o ['dʒɛntaɪl] *adj* gentilicio; (gram) gentilicio ‖ ['dʒɛn-taɪl] *adj* & s no judío; cristiano; (*pagan*) gentil *mf*

gentili·ty [dʒɛn'tɪlɪti] s (*pl* -ties) gentileza

gentle ['dʒɛntəl] *adj* apacible, benévolo; dulce, manso, suave; cortés, fino; (*e.g., tap on the shoulder*) ligero

gen'tle·folk' s gente bien nacida

gentle·man ['dʒɛntəlmən] s (*pl* -men [mən]) s caballero; (*attendant to a person of high rank*) gentilhombre *m*

gentleman in waiting s gentilhombre *m* de cámara

gentlemanly ['dʒɛntəlmənli] *adj* caballeroso

gentleman of leisure s señor *m* que vive sin trabajar, caballero de vida holgada

gentleman of the road s salteador *m* de caminos

gentleman's agreement s acuerdo verbal

gentle sex s bello sexo, sexo débil

gentry ['dʒɛntri] s gente bien nacida

genuine ['dʒɛnju·ɪn] *adj* genuino; sincero, franco

genus ['dʒinəs] s (*pl* **genera** ['dʒɛnərə] o **genuses**) (biol, log) género

geog. *abbr* **geography**

geographer [dʒɪ'ɑgrəfər] s geógrafo

geographic(al) [,dʒɪ·ə'græfɪk(əl)] *adj* geográfico

geogra·phy [dʒɪ'ɑgrəfi] s (*pl* -phies) geografía

geol. *abbr* **geology**

geologic(al) [,dʒɪ·ə'lɑdʒɪk(əl)] *adj* geológico

geologist [dʒɪ'ɑlədʒɪst] s geólogo

geolo·gy [dʒɪ'ɑlədʒi] s (*pl* -gies) geología

geom. *abbr* **geometry**

geometric(al) [,dʒɪ·ə'mɛtrɪk(əl)] *adj* geométrico

geometrician [dʒɪ,ɑmɪ'trɪʃən] s geómetra *mf*

geome·try [dʒɪ'ɑmɪtri] s (*pl* -tries) geometría

geophysics [,dʒɪ·ə'fɪzɪks] s geofísica

geopolitics [,dʒɪ·ə'pɑlɪtɪks] s geopolítica

George [dʒɔrdʒ] s Jorje *m*

geranium [dʒɪ'renɪ·əm] s geranio

geriatrical [,dʒɛrɪ'ætrɪkəl] *adj* geriátrico

geriatrician [,dʒɛrɪ·ə'trɪʃən] s geriatra *mf*

geriatrics [,dʒɛrɪ'ætrɪks] s geriatría

germ [dʒɜrm] s germen *m*

German ['dʒɜrmən] *adj* & s alemán *m*

germane [dʒər'men] *adj* pertinente, relacionado

Germanize ['dʒɜrmə,naɪz] *tr* germanizar

German measles s rubéola

German silver s melchor *m*, alpaca

Germany ['dʒɜrməni] s Alemania

germ cell s célula germen

germ carrier s portador *m* de gérmenes

germicidal [,dʒɜrmɪ'saɪdəl] *adj* germicida

germicide ['dʒɜrmɪ,saɪd] s germicida *m*

germinate ['dʒɜrmɪ,net] *intr* germinar

germ plasm s germen *m* plasma

germ theory s teoría germinal

germ warfare s guerra bacteriana

gerontology [,dʒɛrɑn'tɑlədʒi] s gerontología

gerund ['dʒɛrənd] s gerundio

gerundive [dʒɪ'rʌndɪv] s gerundio adjetivo

gestation [dʒɛs'teʃən] s gestación

gesticulate [dʒɛs'tɪkjə,let] *intr* accionar, manotear

gesticulation [dʒɛs,tɪkjə'leʃən] s ademán *m*, manoteo

gesture ['dʒɛstʃər] s ademán *m*, gesto; demostración, muestra ‖ *intr* hacer ademanes, hacer gestos

get [gɛt] *v* (*pret* **got** [gɑt]; *pp* **got** o **gotten** ['gɑtən]; *ger* **getting**) *tr* conseguir, obtener; recibir; ir por, buscar; tomar (*p.ej., un billete*); alcanzar; encontrar, hallar; hacer (*p.ej., la comida*); resolver (*un problema*); aprender de memoria; captar (*una estación emisora*); **to get across** hacer aceptar; hacer comprender; **to get back** recobrar; **to get down** descolgar; (*to swallow*) tragar; **to get off** quitar (*p.ej., una mancha*); **to get someone to** + *inf* lograr que alguien + *subj*; **to get** + *pp* hacer + *inf*; **to have got** + *inf* tener; **to have got to** + *inf* (coll) tener que + *inf* ‖ *intr* (*to become*) hacerse, ponerse, volverse; (*to arrive*) llegar; **get up!** (*to an animal*) ¡arre!; **to get about** estar levantado (*un convaleciente*); **to get along** seguir andando; irse; ir tirando; tener éxito; llevarse bien; **to get along in years** ponerse viejo; **to get along with** congeniar con; **to get angry** enfadarse, **to get around** divulgarse; salir mucho, ir a todas partes; eludir; manejar (*a una persona*); **to get away** conseguir marcharse; evadirse; **to get away with** llevarse, escaparse con; (coll) hacer impunemente; **to get back** volver, regresar; **to get back at** (coll) desquitarse con; **to get behind** quedarse atrás; apoyar, abogar por; **to get by** lograr pasar; (*to manage to shift*) (coll) arreglárselas; **to get going** ponerse en marcha; **to get in** entrar; volver a casa; llegar (*un tren*); **to get in with**

llegar a ser amigo de; **to get married** casarse; **to get off** apearse; marcharse; **to get old** envejecer; **to get on** subir; llevarse bien; **to get out** salir; marcharse; divulgarse; **to get out of** bajar de (*un coche*); librarse de; perder (*la paciencia*); **to get out of the way** quitarse de en medio; **to get run over** ser atropellado; **to get through** pasar por entre; terminar; **to get to be** llegar a ser; **to get under way** ponerse en camino; **to get up** levantarse; **to not get over it** (coll) no volver de su asombro

get'a•way' s escapatoria, escape m; (*of an automobile*) arranque m

get'-to•geth'er s reunión, tertulia

get'-up' s (coll) disposición, presentación; (coll) atavío, traje m

gewgaw ['gjugɔ] adj cursi, charro, chillón ‖ s fruslería, chuchería; adorno charro

geyser ['gaizər] s géiser m ‖ ['gizər] s (Brit) calentador m de agua

ghast•ly ['gæstli] o ['gɑstli] adj (*comp* -**lier;** *super* -**liest**) cadavérico, espectral; espantoso, horrible

Ghent [gent] s Gante

gherkin ['gɑrkɪn] s pepinillo

ghet•to ['geto] s (*pl* -**tos**) ghetto

ghost [gost] s espectro, fantasma m; (telv) fantasma m; **not a ghost of a** ni sombra de; **to give up the ghost** entregar el alma, rendir el alma

ghost•ly ['gostli] adj (*comp* -**lier;** *super* -**liest**) espectral

ghost story s cuento de fantasmas

ghost writer s colaborador anónimo, escritor anónimo de obras firmadas por otra persona

ghoul [gul] s demonio que se alimenta de cadáveres; ladrón m de tumbas; (*person who revels in horrible things*) vampiro

ghoulish ['gulɪʃ] adj vampírico, horrible

G.H.Q. abbr **General Headquarters**

GI ['dʒi'aɪ] s (*pl* GI's) (coll) soldado raso (*del ejército norteamericano*)

giant ['dʒaɪ•ənt] adj & s gigante m

giantess ['dʒaɪ•əntɪs] s giganta

gibberish ['dʒɪbərɪʃ] o ['gɪbərɪʃ] s guirigay m

gibbet ['dʒɪbɪt] s horca ‖ tr ahorcar; poner a la vergüenza

gibe [dʒaɪb] s remoque m, mofa ‖ intr mofarse; **to gibe at** mofarse de

giblets ['dʒɪblɪts] spl menudillos

giddiness ['gɪdɪnɪs] s vértigo, vahído; falta de juicio

gid•dy ['gɪdi] adj (*comp* -**dier;** *super* -**diest**) vertiginoso; mareado; casquivano, ligero de cascos

Gideon ['gɪdɪ•ən] s (Bib) Gedeón m

gift [gɪft] s regalo m; (*natural ability*) don m, dote f, prenda

gifted ['gɪftɪd] adj talentoso; muy inteligente

gift horse s — **never look a gift horse in the mouth** a caballo regalado no se le mira el diente

gift of gab s (coll) facundia, labia

gift shop s comercio de objetos de regalo, tienda de regalos

gift'-wrap' v (*pret & pp* -**wrapped;** *ger* **wrapping**) tr envolver en paquete regalo

gigantic [dʒaɪ'gæntɪk] adj gigantesco

giggle ['gɪgəl] s risita, risa ahogada, retozo de la risa ‖ intr reírse bobamente

gigo•lo ['dʒɪgə‚lo] s (*pl* -**los**) acompañante m profesional de mujeres; (*man supported by a woman*) mantenido

gild [gɪld] v (*pret & pp* **gilded** o **gilt** [gɪlt]) tr dorar

gilding ['gɪldɪŋ] s dorado

gill [gɪl] s (*of fish*) agalla; (*of cock*) barba ‖ [dʒɪl] s cuarta parte de una pinta

gillyflower ['dʒɪlɪ‚flaʊ•ər] s alhelí m

gilt [gɪlt] adj & s dorado

gilt-edged ['gɪlt‚edʒd] adj de toda confianza, de lo mejor que hay

gilt'head' s dorada

gimcrack ['dʒɪm‚kræk] adj de oropel ‖ s chuchería

gimlet ['gɪmlɪt] s barrena de mano

gimmick ['gɪmɪk] s (slang) adminículo; (slang) adminículo mágico

gin [dʒɪn] s (*alcoholic liquor*) ginebra; desmotadera de algodón; trampa; (*fish trap*) garlito; torno de izar ‖ v (*pret & pp* **ginned;** *ger* **ginning**) tr desmotar

gin fizz s ginebra con gaseosa

ginger ['dʒɪndʒər] s jenjibre m; (coll) energía, viveza

ginger ale s cerveza de jengibre gaseosa

gin'ger•bread' s pan m de jengibre; adorno charro

gingerly ['dʒɪndʒərli] adj cauteloso, cuidadoso ‖ adv cautelosamente

gin'ger•snap' s galletita de jengibre

gingham ['gɪŋəm] s guinga

giraffe [dʒɪ'ræf] o [dʒɪ'rɑf] s jirafa

girandole ['dʒɪrən‚dol] s girándula

gird [gʌrd] v (*pret & pp* **girt** [gʌrt] o **girded**) tr ceñir; (*to equip*) dotar; (*to prepare*) aprestar; (*to surround, hem in*) rodear, encerrar

girder ['gʌrdər] s viga, trabe f

girdle ['gʌrdəl] s faja; corsé pequeño ‖ tr ceñir; circundar, rodear

girl [gʌrl] s muchacha, niña, chica; (*servant*) moza

girl friend s (coll) amiguita

girlhood ['gʌrlhʊd] s muchachez f; juventud femenina

girlish ['gʌrlɪʃ] adj de muchacha, juvenil

girl scout s niña exploradora

girth [gʌrθ] s (*band*) cincha; (*waistband*) pretina; circunferencia

gist [dʒɪst] s esencia

give [gɪv] s elasticidad ‖ v (*pret* **gave** [gev]; *pp* **given** ['gɪvən]) tr dar; ocasionar (*molestia, trabajo, etc.*); representar (*una obra dramática*); pronunciar (*un discurso*); **to give away** dar de balde; revelar; llevar (*a la novia*); (coll) traicionar; **to give back** devolver; **to give forth** despedir (*p.ej., olores*); **to give oneself up**

entregarse; **to give up** abandonar, dejar (*un empleo*); renunciar ‖ *intr* dar; dar de sí; romperse (*p.ej., una cuerda*); **to give in** ceder, rendirse; **to give out** agotarse; no poder más; **to give up** darse por vencido

give'-and-take' *s* concesiones mutuas; conversación sazonada de burlas

give'a·way' *s* (coll) revelación involuntaria; (coll) traición; (*e.g., in checkers*) (coll) ganapierde *m & f*

given ['gɪvən] *adj* dado; (math) conocido; **given that** dado que, suponiendo que

given name *s* nombre *m* de pila

giver ['gɪvər] *s* dador *m*, donador *m*

gizzard ['gɪzərd] *s* molleja

glacial ['gleʃəl] *adj* glacial

glacier ['gleʃər] *s* glaciar *m*, helero

glad [glæd] *adj* (*comp* **gladder;** *super* **gladdest**) alegre, contento; **to be glad (to)** alegrarse (de)

gladden ['glædən] *tr* alegrar

glade [gled] *s* claro, claro herboso (*en un bosque*)

glad hand *s* (coll) acogida efusiva

gladiola [ˌglædɪ'olə] o [glə'daɪ·ələ] *s* estoque *m*

gladly ['glædlɪ] *adv* alegremente; de buena gana, con mucho gusto

gladness ['glædnɪs] *s* alegría, regocijo

glad rags *spl* (slang) trapitos de cristianar; (slang) vestido de etiqueta

glamorous ['glæmərəs] *adj* fascinador, elegante

glamour ['glæmər] *s* fascinación, elegancia, hechizo

glamour girl *s* belleza exótica

glance [glæns] o [glɑns] *s* ojeada, vistazo, golpe *m* de vista; **at a glance** de un vistazo; **at first glance** a primera vista ‖ *intr* lanzar una mirada; **to glance at** lanzar una mirada a; examinar de paso; **to glance off** desviarse de soslayo; desviarse de, al chocar; **to glance over** mirar por encima

gland [glænd] *s* glándula

glanders ['glændərz] *spl* muermo

glare [gler] *s* fulgor *m* deslumbrante, luz intensa; mirada feroz, mirada de indignación ‖ *intr* relumbrar; lanzar miradas feroces; **to glare at** echar una mirada feroz a

glaring ['glerɪŋ] *adj* deslumbrante, relumbrante, (*look*) feroz, penetrante; manifiesto, que salta a la vista

glass [glæs] o [glɑs] *s* vidrio, cristal *m*; (*tumbler*) vaso, copa; (*mirror*) espejo, (*glassware*) vajilla de cristal; **glasses** anteojos

glass blower ['blo·ər] *s* soplador *m* de vidrio, vidriero

glass case *s* vitrina

glass cutter *s* cortavidrios *m*

glass door *s* puerta vidriera

glassful ['glæsful] o ['glɑsful] *s* vaso

glass'house' *s* invernadero; (fig) tejado de vidrio

glassine [glæ'sin] *s* papel *m* cristal

glass'ware' *s* cristalería, vajilla de vidrio

glass wool *s* cristal hilado

glass'works' *s* cristalería, vidriería

glass'work'er *s* vidriero

glass·y ['glæsɪ] o ['glɑsɪ] *adj* (*comp* -ier; *super* -lest) vidrioso

glaze [glez] *s* vidriado, esmalte *m*; (*of ice*) capa resbaladiza ‖ *tr* vidriar, esmaltar; garapiñar (*golosinas*)

glazier ['gleʒər] *s* vidriero

gleam [glim] *s* destello, rayo de luz; luz *f* tenue; (*of hope*) rayo ‖ *intr* destellar; brillar con luz tenue

glean [glin] *tr* espigar; (*to gather bit by bit, e.g., out of books*) espigar

glee [gli] *s* alegría, regocijo

glee club *s* orfeón *m*

glib [glɪb] *adj* (*comp* **glibber;** *super* **glibbest**) locuaz; (*tongue*) suelto; fácil e insincero

glide [glaɪd] *s* deslizamiento; (aer) vuelo sin motor, planeo; (mus) ligadura ‖ *intr* deslizarse; (aer) volar sin motor, planear; **to glide along** pasar suavemente

glider ['glaɪdər] *s* (aer) planeador *m*, deslizador *m*

glimmer ['glɪmər] *s* luz *f* tenue; (*faint perception*) vislumbre *f* ‖ *intr* brillar con luz tenue; (*to appear faintly*) vislumbrarse

glimmering ['glɪmərɪŋ] *adj* tenue, trémulo ‖ *s* luz *f* tenue; vislumbre *f*

glimpse [glɪmps] *s* vislumbre *f*; **to catch a glimpse of** entrever, vislumbrar ‖ *tr* vislumbrar

glint [glɪnt] *s* destello, rayo ‖ *intr* destellar

glisten ['glɪsən] *s* centelleo ‖ *intr* centellear

glitter ['glɪtər] *s* resplandor *m*, brillo ‖ *intr* resplandecer, brillar

gloaming ['glomɪŋ] *s* crepúsculo vespertino

gloat [glot] *intr* relamerse; **to gloat over** mirar con satisfacción maligna

globe [glob] *s* globo

globetrotter ['glob ˌtrɑtər] *s* trotamundos *m*

globule ['glɑbjul] *s* glóbulo

glockenspiel ['glɑkən ˌspil] *s* juego de timbres, órgano de campanas

gloom [glum] *s* lobreguez *f*, tinieblas, obscuridad; abatimiento, tristeza; aspecto abatido

gloom·y ['glumɪ] *adj* (*comp* -ier; *super* -lest) (*dark; sad*) lóbrego; pesimista

glori·fy ['glorɪˌfaɪ] *v* (*pret & pp* -fied) *tr* glorificar; (*to enhance*) realzar

glorious ['glorɪ·əs] *adj* glorioso; espléndido, magnífico, (coll) alegre

glo·ry ['glorɪ] *s* (*pl* -ries) gloria; **to go to glory** ganar la gloria; (slang) fracasar ‖ *v* (*pret & pp* -ried) *intr* gloriarse

gloss [glɔs] o [glɑs] *s* brillo, lustre *m*; (*note, commentary*) glosa; glosario ‖ *tr* (*to annotate*) glosar; lustrar, satinar; **to gloss over** disculpar, paliar

glossa·ry ['glɑsərɪ] *s* (*pl* -ries) glosario

gloss·y ['glɔsɪ] o ['glɑsɪ] *adj* (*comp* -ier; *super* -lest) brillante, lustroso; (*silk*) joyante

glottal ['glɑtəl] *adj* glótico
glove [glʌv] *s* guante *m*
glove compartment *s* portaguantes *m*
glove stretcher *s* ensanchador *m*, juanas
glow [glo] *s* (*light of incandescence*) resplandor *m*; (*e.g., of sunset*) brillo, esplendor *m*; sensación de calor; color *m* en las mejillas ‖ *intr* brillar sin llama; estar encendido (*el rostro, el cielo*); estar muy animado
glower ['glɑu·ər] *s* ceño, mirada ceñuda ‖ *intr* mirar con ceño
glowing ['glo·ɪŋ] *adj* ardiente, encendido; radiante; entusiasta, elogioso
glow'worm' *s* gusano de luz, luciérnaga
glucose ['glukos] *s* glucosa
glue [glu] *s* cola ‖ *tr* encolar; pegar fuertemente
glue pot *s* cazo de cola
gluey ['glu·i] *adj* (*comp* **gluier**; *super* **gluiest**) pegajoso; (*smeared with glue*) encolado
glug [glʌg] *s* gluglú *m* ‖ *v* (*pret & pp* **glugged**; *ger* **glugging**) *intr* hacer gluglú (*el agua*)
glum [glʌm] *adj* (*comp* **glummer**; *super* **glummest**) hosco
glut [glʌt] *s* abundancia, gran acopio; exceso; **to be a glut on the market** abarrotar ‖ *v* (*pret & pp* **glutted**; *ger* **glutting**) *tr* hartar, saciar; inundar (*el mercado*); obstruir
glutton ['glʌtən] *adj & s* glotón *m*
gluttonous ['glʌtənəs] *adj* glotón
glutton·y ['glʌtəni] *s* (*pl* **-ies**) glotonería, gula
glycerine ['glɪsərɪn] *s* glicerina
G.M. *abbr* **general manager**, **Grand Master**
G-man ['dʒi͡‚mæn] *s* (*pl* **-men** [‚mɛn]) (coll) agente *m* de la policía federal
G.M.T. *abbr* **Greenwich mean time**
gnarl [nɑrl] *s* nudo ‖ *tr* torcer ‖ *intr* gruñir
gnarled [nɑrld] *adj* nudoso, retorcido
gnash [næʃ] *tr* hacer rechinar (*los dientes*) ‖ *intr* hacer rechinar los dientes
gnat [næt] *s* jején *m*
gnaw [nɔ] *tr* roer; practicar (*un agujero*) royendo
gnome [nom] *s* gnomo
go [go] *s* (*pl* **goes**) ida; (coll) energía, ímpetu *m*; (coll) boga; (coll) ensayo; (*for traffic*) paso libre; **it's a go** (coll) es un trato hecho; **it's all the go** (coll) hace furor; **it's no go** (coll) es imposible; **on the go** (coll) en continuo movimiento; **to make a go of** (coll) lograr éxito en ‖ *v* (*pret* **went** [wɛnt]; *pp* **gone** [gɔn] o [gɑn]) *tr* (coll) soportar, tolerar; **to go it alone** obrar sin ayuda ‖ *intr* ir; (*to work, operate*) funcionar, marchar; andar (*p.ej., desnudo*); volverse (*p.ej., loco*); **going, going, gone!** ¡vendo, vendo, vendi!; **so it goes así va el mundo**; **to be going to** + *inf* ir a + *inf*; **to be gone** haber ido; haberse agotado; haber dejado de ser; **to go against** ir en contra de; **to go ahead** seguir adelante; **to go away** irse,

marcharse; **to go back** volver; **to go by** pasar por; guiarse por; atenerse a; **to go down** bajar; hundirse (*un buque*); **to go fishing** ir de pesca; **to go for** ir por; **to go get** ir por, ir a buscar; **to go house hunting** ir a buscar casa; **to go hunting** ir de caza; **to go in** entrar; entrar en; (*to fit in*) caber en; **to go in for** dedicarse a, interesarse por; **to go into** entrar en; investigar; (aut) poner (*p.ej., primera*); **to go in with** asociarse con; **to go off** irse, marcharse; llevarse a cabo; estallar (*p.ej., una bomba*); dispararse (*un fusil*); **to go on** seguir adelante; ir tirando; **to go on** + *ger* seguir + *ger*; **to go on with** continuar; **to go out** salir; pasar de moda; apagarse (*un fuego, una luz*); declararse en huelga; (*for entertainment, etc.*) salir; **to go over** tener éxito; releer; examinar, revisar; pasar por encima de; **to go over to** pasarse a las filas de; **to go through** pasar por; llegar al fin de; agotar (*una fortuna*); **to go with** ir con, acompañar; salir con (*una muchacha*); hacer juego con; **to go without** andarse sin, pasarse sin
goad [god] *s* aguijada, aguijón *m* ‖ *tr* aguijonear
go'-a-head' *adj* (coll) emprendedor ‖ *s* (coll) señal *f* para seguir adelante, luz *f* verde
goal [gol] *s* meta; (*in football*) gol *m*
goal'keep'er *s* guardameta *m*, portero
goal line *s* raya de la meta
goal post *s* poste *m* de la meta
goat [got] *s* cabra; (*male goat*) macho cabrío; (coll) víctima inocente; **to be the goat** (slang) pagar el pato; **to get the goat of** (slang) tomar el pelo a; **to ride the goat** (coll) ser iniciado en una sociedad secreta
goatee [go'ti] *s* perilla
goat'herd' *s* cabrero
goat'skin' *s* piel *f* de cabra
goat'suck'er *s* chotacabras *m*
gob [gɑb] *s* (coll) masa informe y pequeña; (coll) marinero de guerra
gobble ['gɑbəl] *s* gluglú *m* ‖ *tr* engullir; **to gobble up** engullirse ávidamente; (coll) asir de repente, apoderarse ávidamente de ‖ *intr* engullir; gluglutear, gorgonear (*el pavo*)
gobbledegook ['gɑbəldɪ‚guk] *s* (coll) lenguaje obscuro e incomprensible, galimatías *m*
go'-be-tween' *s* (*intermediary*) medianero; (*in promoting marriages*) casamentero; (*in shady love affairs*) alcahuete *m*, alcahueta *f*
goblet ['gɑblɪt] *s* copa
goblin ['gɑblɪn] *s* duende *m*, trasgo
go'-by' *s* (coll) desaire *m*; **to give someone the go-by** (coll) negarse al trato de alguien
go'cart' *s* andaderas; cochecito para niños; carruaje ligero
god [gɑd] *s* dios *m*; **God forbid** no lo quiera Dios; **God grant** permita Dios; **God willing** Dios mediante

god'child' s (pl **chil'dren**) ahijado, ahijada
god'daugh'ter s ahijada
goddess ['gɑdɪs] s diosa
god'fa'ther s padrino
God'-fear'ing adj timorato; devoto, pío
God'for•sak'en adj dejado de la mano de Dios; (coll) desolado, desierto
god'head' s divinidad || **Godhead** s Dios m
godless ['gɑdlɪs] adj infiel, impío; desalmado, malvado
god•ly ['gɑdli] adj (comp **-lier;** super **-liest**) devoto, pío
god'moth'er s madrina
God's acre s campo santo
god'send' s cosa llovida del cielo, bendición
god'son' s ahijado
God'speed' s bienandanza, buena suerte, buen viaje m
go'-get'ter s (slang) buscavidas mf, persona emprendedora
goggle ['gɑgəl] intr volver los ojos; abrir los ojos desmesuradamente
goggle-eyed ['gɑgəl,aɪd] adj de ojos saltones
goggles ['gɑgəlz] spl anteojos de camino, gafas contra el polvo
going ['go•ɪŋ] adj en marcha, funcionando; **going on** casi, p.ej., **it is going on nine o'clock** son casi las nueve || s ida, partida
going concern s empresa que marcha
goings on spl actividades; bulla, jarana
goiter ['gɔɪtər] s bocio
gold [gold] adj áureo, de oro; dorado || s oro
gold'beat'er s batidor m de oro, batihoja m
goldbeater's skin s venza
gold brick s — **to sell a gold brick** (coll) vender gato por liebre
gold'crest' s reyezuelo moñudo
gold digger ['dɪgər] s (slang) extractora de oro
golden ['goldən] adj áureo, de oro; (gilt) dorado; (hair) rubio; excelente, favorable, floreciente
golden age s edad de oro, siglo de oro
golden calf s becerro de oro
Golden Fleece s vellocino de oro
golden mean s justo medio
golden plover s chorlito
gold'en•rod' s vara de oro, vara de San José
golden rule s regla de la caridad cristiana
golden wedding s bodas de oro
gold-filled ['gold,fɪld] adj empastado en oro
gold'finch' s jilguero, pintacilgo
gold'fish' s carpa dorada, pez m de color
goldilocks ['goldɪ,lɑks] s rubiales mf
gold leaf s pan m de oro
gold mine s mina de oro; **to strike a gold mine** (fig) encontrar una mina
gold plate s vajilla de oro
gold'-plate' tr dorar
gold'smith' s orfebre m
gold standard s patrón m oro

golf [gɑlf] s golf m || intr jugar al golf
golf club s palo de golf; asociación de jugadores de golf
golfer ['gɑlfər] s golfista mf
golf links spl campo de golf
Golgotha ['gɑlgəθə] s el Gólgota
gondola ['gɑndələ] s góndola
gondolier [,gɑndə'lɪr] s gondolero
gone [gɔn] o [gɑn] adj agotado; arruinado; desaparecido; muerto; **gone on** (coll) enamorado de
gong [gɔŋ] o [gɑŋ] s batintín m
gonorrhea [,gɑnə'ri•ə] s gonorrea
goo [gu] s (slang) substancia pegajosa
good [gud] adj (comp **better;** super **best**) bueno; **good and ...** (coll) muy, p.ej., **good and cheap** muy barato; **good for** bueno para; capaz de hacer; capaz de pagar; capaz de vivir (cierto tiempo); **to be good at** tener talento para; **to be no good** (coll) no servir para nada; (coll) ser un perdido; **to make good** tener éxito; cumplir (sus promesas); pagar (una deuda); responder de (los daños) || s bien m, provecho, utilidad; **for good** para siempre; **for good and all** de una vez para siempre; **goods** efectos; géneros, mercancías; **the good** lo bueno; los buenos; **to catch with the goods** (slang) coger en flagrante; **to deliver the goods** (slang) cumplir lo prometido; **to do good** hacer el bien; dar salud o fuerzas a; **to the good** de sobra, en el haber; **what is the good of ... ?** ¿para qué sirve ... ?
good afternoon s buenas tardes
good'-by' o **good'-bye'** s adiós m || interj ¡adiós!
good day s buenos días
good evening s buenas noches, buenas tardes
good fellow s (coll) buen chico, buen sujeto
good fellowship s compañerismo
good'-for-noth'ing adj inútil, sin valor || s pelafustán m, perdido
Good Friday s Viernes santo
good graces spl favor m, estimación
good-hearted ['gud'hɑrtɪd] adj de buen corazón
good-humored ['gud'hjumərd] o ['gud'jumərd] adj de buen humor; afable
good-looking ['gud'lukɪŋ] adj guapo, bien parecido
good looks spl hermosura, guapeza
good•ly ['gudli] adj (comp **-lier;** super **-liest**) considerable; bien parecido, hermoso; bueno, excelente
good morning s buenos días
good-natured ['gud'netʃərd] adj bonachón, afable
Good Neighbor Policy s política del buen vecino
goodness ['gudnɪs] s bondad; **for goodness' sake!** ¡por Dios!; **goodness knows!** ¡quién sabe! || interj ¡válgame Dios!
good night s buenas noches
good sense s buen sentido, sensatez f

good-sized ['gud'saɪzd] *adj* bastante grande, de buen tamaño

good speed *s* adiós *m* y buena suerte

good-tempered ['gud'tempərd] *adj* de natural apacible

good time *s* rato agradable; **to have a good time** divertirse; **to make good time** ir a buen paso; llegar en poco tiempo

good turn *s* favor *m*, servicio

good way *s* buen trecho

good will *s* buena voluntad; (com) buen nombre *m*, clientela

good·y ['gudi] *adj* (coll) beatuco, santurrón || *s* (pl -ies) (coll) golosina || *interj* (coll) ¡qué bien!, ¡qué alegría!

gooey ['gu·i] *adj* (comp **gooier;** super **gooiest**) (slang) pegajoso, fangoso

goof [guf] *s* (slang) tonto || *tr & intr* (slang) chapucear

goof·y ['gufi] *adj* (comp **-ier;** super **-iest**) (slang) tonto, mentecato

goon [gun] *s* (roughneck) (coll) gamberro, canalla *m*; (coll) terrorista *m* de alquiler; (slang) estúpido

goose [gus] *s* (pl **geese** [gis]) *s* ánsar *m*, ganso, oca; **the goose hangs high** todo va a pedir de boca; **to cook one's goose** malbaratarle a uno los planes; **to kill the goose that lays the golden eggs** matar la gallina de los huevos de oro || *s* (pl **gooses**) plancha de sastre

goose'ber'ry *s* (pl **-ries**) (plant) grosellero silvestre; (fruit) grosella silvestre

goose egg *s* huevo de oca; (slang) cero

goose flesh *s* carne *f* de gallina

goose'neck' *s* cuello de cisne; (naut) gancho de botalones

goose pimples *spl* carne *f* de gallina

goose step *s* (mil) paso de ganso

G.O.P. *abbr* Grand Old Party

gopher ['gofər] *s* ardilla de tierra, ardillón *m*; (Geomys) tuza

Gordian knot ['gɔrdɪ·ən] *s* nudo gordiano; **to cut the Gordian knot** cortar el nudo gordiano

gore [gor] *s* sangre derramada, sangre cuajada; (insert in a piece of cloth) cuchillo, nesga || *tr* (to pierce with a horn) acornar; poner cuchillo o nesga a; nesgar

gorge [gɔrdʒ] *s* garganta, desfiladero; (in a river) atasco de hielo || *tr* atiborrar || *intr* atiborrarse

gorgeous ['gɔrdʒəs] *adj* primoroso, brillante, magnífico, suntuoso

gorilla [gə'rɪlə] *s* gorila

gorse [gɔrs] *s* aulaga

gor·y ['gori] *adj* (comp **-ier;** super **-iest**) ensangrentado, sangriento

gosh [gɑʃ] *interj* ¡caramba!

goshawk ['gɑs,hɔk] *s* azor *m*

gospel ['gɑspəl] *s* evangelio || **Gospel** *s* Evangelio

gospel truth *s* evangelio, pura verdad

gossamer ['gɑsəmər] *s* telaraña flotante; gasa sutilísima; tela impermeable muy delgada; impermeable *m* de tela muy delgada

gossip ['gɑsɪp] *s* chismes *m*; (person) chismoso; **piece of gossip** chisme *m* || *intr* chismear

gossip column *s* mentidero

gossip columnist *s* gacetillero, cronista *mf* social

gossipy ['gɑsɪpi] *adj* chismoso

Goth [gɑθ] *s* godo; (fig) bárbaro

Gothic ['gɑθɪk] *adj & s* gótico

gouge [gaudʒ] *s* gubia; (cut made with a gouge) muesca; (coll) estafa || *tr* excavar con gubia; (coll) estafar

goulash ['gulɑʃ] *s* puchero húngaro

gourd [gord] *o* [gurd] *s* calabaza

gourmand ['gurmənd] *s* gastrónomo; glotón *m*, goloso

gourmet ['gurme] *s* gastrónomo delicado

gout [gaut] *s* gota

gout·y ['gauti] *adj* (comp **-ier;** super **-iest**) gotoso

gov. *abbr* governor, government

govern ['gʌvərn] *tr* gobernar; (gram) regir || *intr* gobernar

governess ['gʌvərnɪs] *s* aya, institutriz *f*

government ['gʌvərnmənt] *s* gobierno; (gram) régimen *m*

governmental [,gʌvərn'mentəl] *adj* gubernamental, gubernativo

government in exile *s* gobierno exilado

governor ['gʌvərnər] *s* gobernador *m*; (of a jail, castle, etc.) alcaide *m*; (mach) regulador *m*

governorship ['gʌvərnər,ʃɪp] *s* gobierno

govt. *abbr* government

gown [gaun] *s* (of a woman) vestido; (of a professor, judge, etc.) toga; (of a priest) traje *m* talar; (dressing gown) bata, peinador *m*; (nightgown) camisa de dormir

G.P.O. *abbr* General Post Office, Government Printing Office

gr. *abbr* gram, grams, grain, grains, gross

grab [græb] *s* asimiento, presa; (coll) robo || *v* (pret & pp **grabbed;** ger **grabbing**) *tr* asir, agarrar; arrebatar || *intr* — **to grab at** tratar de asir

grace [gres] *s* (charm; favor; pardon) gracia; (prayer at table) benedícite *m*; (extension of time) demora; **to be in the good graces of** gozar del favor de; **to say grace** rezar el benedícite; **with good grace** de buen talante || *tr* adornar, engalanar; favorecer

graceful ['gresfəl] *adj* agraciado, gracioso

grace note *s* apoyatura, nota de adorno

gracious ['greʃəs] *adj* graciable, gracioso; misericordioso || *interj* ¡válgame Dios!

grackle ['grækəl] *s* (myna) estornino de los pastores; (purple grackle) quiscal *m*

grad. *abbr* graduate

gradation [gre'deʃən] *s* (gradual change) paso gradual; (arrangement in grades) graduación; (step in a series) paso, grado

grade [gred] *s* grado; (slope) pendiente *f*; (mark for work in class) calificación, nota; **to make the grade**

lograr subir la cuesta; vencer los obstáculos || tr graduar, calificar; dar nota a (un alumno); explanar, nivelar

grade crossing s (rr) paso a nivel, cruce m a nivel

grade school s escuela elemental

gradient ['gredɪ·ənt] adj pendiente || s pendiente f; (phys) gradiente m

gradual ['grædʒʊ·əl] adj paulatino

gradually ['grædʒʊ·əli] adv paulatinamente, gradualmente, poco a poco

graduate ['grædʒʊ·ɪt] adj graduado || s graduado; (candidate for a degree) graduando; vasija graduada || ['grædʒʊ‚et] tr graduar || intr graduarse

graduate school s facultad de altos estudios

graduate student s estudiante graduado

graduate work s altos estudios

graduation [‚grædʒʊ'eʃən] s graduación; ceremonia de graduación

graft [græft] o [graft] s (hort & surg) injerto; (coll) soborno político, ganancia ilegal || tr & intr (hort & surg) injertar; (coll) malversar

graham bread ['gre·əm] s pan m integral

graham flour s harina de trigo sin cerner

grain [gren] s (small seed; tiny particle of sand, etc.; small unit of weight) grano; (cereal seeds) granos; (in stone) vena; (in wood) fibra; **against the grain** a contrapelo || tr granear (la pólvora; una piedra litográfica); crispir, vetear (la madera); granular (una piel)

grain elevator s elevador m de granos; (tall building where grain is stored) depósito de cereales

grain'field' s sembrado

graining ['grenɪŋ] s veteado

gram [græm] s gramo

grammar ['græmər] s gramática

grammarian [grə'mɛrɪ·ən] s gramático

grammar school s escuela pública elemental

grammatical [grə'mætɪkəl] adj gramático

gramophone ['græmə‚fon] s (trademark) gramófono

grana·ry ['grænəri] s (pl -ries) granero

grand [grænd] adj espléndido, grandioso; importante, principal

grand'aunt' s tía abuela

grand'child' s (pl -chil'dren) nieto, nieta

grand'daugh'ter s nieta

grand duchess s gran duquesa

grand duchy s gran ducado

grand duke s gran duque m

grandee [græn'di] s grande m de España

grandeur ['grændʒər] o ['grændʒʊr] s grandeza, magnificencia

grand'fa'ther s abuelo; (forefather) antepasado

grandfather's clock s reloj m de caja

grandiose ['grændɪ‚os] adj grandioso; hinchado, pomposo

grand jury s jurado de acusación

grand larceny s hurto mayor

grand lodge s gran oriente m

grandma ['grænd‚ma], ['græm‚ma] o ['græmə] s (coll) abuela, abuelita

grand'moth'er s abuela

grand'neph'ew s resobrino

grand'niece s resobrina

grand opera s ópera seria

grandpa ['grænd‚pa], ['græn‚pa] o ['græmpə] s (coll) abuelo, abuelito

grand'par'ent s abuelo, abuela

grand piano s piano de cola

grand slam s bola

grand'son' s nieto

grand'stand' s gradería cubierta, tribuna

grand strategy s alta estrategia

grand total s gran total m, suma de totales

grand'un'cle s tío abuelo

grand vizier s gran visir m

grange [grendʒ] s (farm with barns, etc.) granja; (organization of farmers) cámara agrícola

granite ['grænɪt] s granito

grant [grænt] o [grant] s concesión; donación, subvención; traspaso de propiedad || tr conceder; dar (permiso, perdón); transferir (bienes inmuebles); **to take for granted** dar por sentado; tratar con indiferencia

grantee [græn'ti] o [gran'ti] s cesionario

grant'-in-aid' s (pl grants-in-aid) subvención concedida por el gobierno para obras de utilidad pública; pensión para estimular conocimientos científicos, literarios, artísticos

grantor [græn'tɔr] o [gran'tɔr] s cesionista mf, otorgante mf

granular ['grænjələr] adj granular

granulate ['grænjə‚let] tr granular || intr granularse

granule ['grænjul] s gránulo

grape [grep] s (fruit) uva; (vine) vid f

grape arbor s parral m

grape'fruit' s (fruit) toronja; (tree) toronjo

grape hyacinth s sueldacostilla

grape juice s zumo de uva

grape'shot' s metralla

grape'vine' s vid f, parra; **by the grapevine** por vías secretas, por vías misteriosas

graph [græf] o [graf] s (diagram) gráfica; (gram) grafía

graphic(al) ['græfɪk(əl)] adj gráfico

graphite ['græfaɪt] s grafito

graph paper s papel m cuadriculado

grapnel ['græpnəl] s rebañadera; (anchor) rezón m

grapple ['græpəl] s asimiento, presa; lucha cuerpo a cuerpo || tr asir, agarrar || intr agarrarse; luchar a brazo partido; **to grapple with** luchar a brazo partido con; tratar de resolver

grappling iron s arpeo

grasp [græsp] o [grasp] s asimiento; (power, reach) poder m, alcance m; (fig) comprensión; **to have a good grasp of** saber a fondo; **within the grasp of** al alcance de || tr (with hand) empuñar; (to get control of) apoderarse de; (fig) comprender ‖ *intr* — **to grasp at** tratar de asir; aceptar con avidez

grasping ['græspɪŋ] o ['grɑspɪŋ] *adj* avaro, codicioso

grass [græs] o [grɑs] *s* hierba; (*pasture land*) pasto; (*lawn*) césped *m;* **to go to grass** ir a pacer; disfrutar de una temporada de descanso; gastarse, arruinarse; morir; **to not let the grass grow under one's feet** no dormirse en las pajas

grass court *s* cancha de césped

grass'hop'per *s* saltamontes *m*

grass pea *s* almorta, guija

grass'-roots' *adj* (coll) de la gente común

grass seed *s* semilla de césped

grass widow *s* viuda de paja, viuda de marido vivo

grass·y ['græsi] o ['grɑsi] *adj* (*comp* **-ier;** *super* **-iest**) herboso

grate [gret] *s* (*at a window*) reja; (*for cooking*) parrilla ‖ *tr* (*to put a grate on*) enrejar; rallar (*p.ej., queso*) ‖ *intr* crujir, rechinar; **to grate on** (fig) rallar

grateful ['gretfəl] *adj* agradecido; (*pleasing*) agradable

grater ['gretər] *s* rallador *m*

grati·fy ['grætɪ‚faɪ] *v* (*pret & pp* **-fied**) *tr* complacer, gratificar

gratifying ['grætɪ‚faɪ‚ɪŋ] *adj* grato, satisfactorio

grating ['gretɪŋ] *adj* áspero, irritante; (*sound*) chirriante ‖ *s* enrejado

gratis ['gretɪs] o ['grætɪs] *adj* gracioso, gratuito ‖ *adv* gratis, de balde

gratitude ['grætɪ‚tjud] o ['grætɪ‚tud] *s* gratitud, reconocimiento

gratuitous [grə'tju·ɪtəs] o [grə'tu·ɪtəs] *adj* gratuito

gratu·ity [grə'tju·ɪti] o [grə'tu·ɪti] *s* (*pl* **-ties**) propina

grave [grev] *adj* (*serious, dangerous, important*) grave; solemne; (*sound; accent*) grave ‖ *s* sepulcro, sepultura; **to have one foot in the grave** estar con un pie en la sepultura

gravedigger ['grev‚dɪgər] *s* enterrador *m,* sepulturero

gravel ['grævəl] *s* grava, cascajo

graven image ['grevən] *s* ídolo

grave'stone' *s* lápida sepulcral

grave'yard' *s* camposanto

gravitate ['grævɪ‚tet] *intr* gravitar; ser atraído

gravitation [‚grævɪ'teʃən] *s* gravitación

gravi·ty ['grævɪti] *s* (*pl* **-ties**) gravedad

gravure [grə'vjur] o ['grevjur] *s* fotograbado

gra·vy ['grevi] *s* (*pl* **-vies**) (*juice from cooking meat*) jugo; (*sauce made with this juice*) salsa; (slang) ganga, breva

gravy dish *s* salsera

gray [gre] *adj* gris; (*gray-haired*) cano, canoso ‖ *s* gris *m;* traje *m* gris ‖ *intr* encanecer

gray'beard' *s* anciano, viejo

gray-haired ['gre‚herd] *adj* canoso

gray'hound' *s* galgo

grayish ['gre·ɪʃ] *adj* grisáceo; (*person; hair*) entrecano

gray matter *s* substancia gris; (*intelligence*) (coll) materia gris

graze [grez] *tr* (*to touch lightly*) rozar; (*to scratch lightly in passing*) raspar; pacer (*la hierba*); apacentar (*el ganado*); (*to lead to the pasture*) pastar ‖ *intr* pacer, pastar

grease [gris] *s* grasa ‖ [gris] o [griz] *tr* engrasar; (slang) sobornar

grease cup [gris] *s* vaso de engrase

grease gun [gris] *s* engrasador *m* de pistón, jeringa de engrase

grease lift [gris] *s* puente *m* de engrase

grease paint [gris] *s* maquillaje *m*

grease pit [gris] *s* fosa de engrase

grease spot [gris] *s* lámpara, mancha de grasa

greas·y ['grisi] o ['grizi] *adj* (*comp* **-ier;** *super* **-iest**) grasiento, pringoso

great [gret] *adj* grande; (coll) excelente ‖ **the great** los grandes

great'-aunt' *s* tía abuela

Great Bear *s* Osa Mayor

Great Britain ['brɪtən] *s* la Gran Bretaña

great'coat' *s* gabán *m* de mucho abrigo

Great Dane *s* mastín *m* danés

Greater London *s* el Gran Londres

Greater New York *s* el Gran Nueva York

great'-grand'child' *s* (*pl* **-chil'dren**) bisnieto, bisnieta

great'-grand'daugh'ter *s* bisnieta

great'-grand'fa'ther *s* bisabuelo

great'-grand'moth'er *s* bisabuela

great'-grand'par'ent *s* bisabuelo, bisabuela

great'-grand'son' *s* bisnieto

greatly ['gretli] *adj* grandemente

great'-neph'ew *s* resobrino

greatness ['gretnɪs] *s* grandeza

great'-niece' *s* resobrina

great'-un'cle *s* tío abuelo

Great War *s* Gran guerra

Grecian ['griʃən] *adj & s* griego

Greece [gris] *s* Grecia

greed [grid] *s* codicia, avaricia; (*in eating and drinking*) glotonería

greed·y ['gridi] *adj* (*comp* **-ier;** *super* **-iest**) codicioso, avaro; glotón

Greek [grik] *adj & s* griego

green [grin] *adj* verde; inexperto ‖ *s* verde *m;* (*lawn*) césped *m; greens* verduras

green'back' *s* (U.S.A.) billete *m* de banco (*de dorso verde*)

green corn *s* maíz tierno

green earth *s* verdacho

greener·y ['grinəri] *s* (*pl* **-ies**) (*foliage*) verdura; (*hothouse*) invernáculo

green-eyed ['grin‚aɪd] *adj* de ojos verdes; celoso

green'gage' *s* ciruela claudia

green grasshopper *s* langostón *m*

green'gro'cer *s* verdulero

green'gro'cer·y *s* (*pl* **-ies**) verdulería

green'horn' *s* novato; (*dupe*) primo, inocentón *m;* (coll) papanatas *m,* isidro

green'house' *s* invernáculo

greenish ['grinɪʃ] *adj* verdoso
Greenland ['grinlənd] *s* Groenlandia
greenness ['grinnɪs] *s* verdura, verdor *m*; falta de experiencia
green'room' *s* saloncillo; chismería de teatro
greensward ['grin‚swɔrd] *s* césped *m*
green thumb *s* pulgares *mpl* verdes (don de criar plantas)
green vegetables *spl* verduras
green'wood' *s* bosque *m* verde, bosque frondoso
greet [grit] *tr* saludar; acoger, recibir; presentarse a (los ojos u los oídos de uno)
greeting ['gritɪŋ] *s* saludo; acogida, recibimiento ‖ **greetings** *interj* ¡salud!
greeting card *s* tarjeta de buen deseo
gregarious [grɪ'gɛrɪ·əs] *adj* (living in the midst of others) gregario; (fond of the company of others) sociable
Gregorian [grɪ'gorɪ·ən] *adj* gregoriano
grenade [grɪ'ned] *s* granada; (to put out fires) granada extintora
grenadier [‚grɛnə'dɪr] *s* granadero
grenadine [‚grɛnə'din] *s* granadina
grey [gre] *adj*, *s* & *intr* var de gray
grid [grɪd] *s* parrilla, rejilla; (electron) rejilla; (of a storage battery) (elec) rejilla
griddle ['grɪdəl] *s* plancha
grid'dle-cake' *s* tortada (de harina) a la plancha
grid'i'ron *s* parrilla; campo de fútbol
grid leak *s* (electron) resistencia de rejilla, escape *m* de rejilla
grief [grif] *s* aflicción, pesar *m*; (coll) desgracia, disgusto; **to come to grief** fracasar, arruinarse
grievance ['grivəns] *s* agravio, injusticia; despecho, disgusto; motivo de queja
grieve [griv] *tr* afligir, penar ‖ *intr* afligirse, apenarse; **to grieve over** añorar
grievous ['grivəs] *adj* doloroso, penoso; atroz, cruel; (deplorable) lastimoso
griffin ['grɪfɪn] *s* (myth) grifo
grill [grɪl] *s* parrilla ‖ *tr* emparrillar; someter (a un acusado) a un interrogatorio muy apremiante
grille [grɪl] *s* reja, verja; (of an automobile) parrilla, rejilla
grill'room' *s* parrilla
grim [grɪm] *adj* (comp **grimmer**; super **grimmest**) (fierce) cruel, feroz; (repellent) horrible, siniestro; (unyielding) formidable, implacable; (stern-looking) ceñudo
grimace ['grɪməs] o [grɪ'mes] *s* mueca, gesto ‖ *intr* hacer muecas, gestear
grime [graɪm] *s* mugre *f*; (soot) tizne *m* & *f*
grim•y ['graɪmi] *adj* (comp -ier; super -iest) mugriento; tiznado
grin [grɪn] *s* sonrisa bonachona; mueca (mostrando los dientes) ‖ *v* (pret & pp **grinned**; ger **grinning**) *intr*

sonreírse bonachonamente; hacer una mueca (mostrando los dientes)
grind [graɪnd] *s* molienda; (long hard work or study) (coll) zurra; (student) (coll) empollón *m* ‖ *v* (pret & pp **ground** [graʊnd]) *tr* moler; (to sharpen) afilar, amolar; tallar (lentes); pulverizar; picar (carne); rodar (las válvulas de un motor); dar vueltas a (un manubrio) ‖ *intr* hacer molienda; molerse; rechinar; (coll) echar los bofes
grinder ['graɪndər] *s* (to sharpen tools) muela, esmoladera; (to grind coffee, pepper, etc.) molinillo; (back tooth) muela
grind'stone' *s* esmoladera, piedra de amolar; **to keep one's nose to the grindstone** trabajar con ahinco
grin•go ['grɪŋgo] *s* (pl -gos) (disparaging) gringo
grip [grɪp] *s* (grasp) asimiento; (with hand) apretón *m*; (handle) asidero; saco de mano; **to come to grips (with)** luchar cuerpo a cuerpo (con); arrostrarse (con) ‖ *v* (pret & pp **gripped**; ger **gripping**) *tr* asir, agarrar; tener asido; absorber (la atención); absorber la atención a (una persona)
gripe [graɪp] *s* (coll) queja; **gripes** retortijón *m* de tripas ‖ *intr* (coll) quejarse, refunfuñar
grippe [grɪp] *s* gripe *f*
gripping ['grɪpɪŋ] *adj* conmovedor, impresionante
gris•ly ['grɪzli] *adj* (comp -lier; super -liest) espantoso, espeluznante
grist [grɪst] *s* (batch of grain for one grinding) molienda; (grain that has been ground) harina; (coll) acopio, acervo; **to be grist to one's mill** (coll) serle a uno de mucho provecho
gristle ['grɪsəl] *s* cartílago, ternilla
gris•tly ['grɪsli] *adj* (comp -tlier; super -tliest) cartilaginoso, ternilloso
grist'mill' *s* molino harinero
grit [grɪt] *s* arena, guijo fino; (fig) ánimo, valentía; **grits** farro, sémola ‖ *v* (pret & pp **gritted**; ger **gritting**) *tr* hacer rechinar (los dientes); cerrar fuertemente (los dientes)
grit•ty ['grɪti] *adj* (comp -tier; super -tiest) arenoso; (fig) valiente, resuelto
griz•zly ['grɪzli] *adj* (comp -zlier; super -zliest) grisáceo; canoso ‖ *s* (pl -zlies) oso gris
grizzly bear *s* oso gris
groan [gron] *s* gemido, quejido ‖ *intr* gemir, quejarse; estar muy cargado, crujir por exceso de peso
grocer ['grosər] *s* abacero, tendero de ultramarinos
grocer•y ['grosəri] *s* (pl -ies) abacería, tienda de ultramarinos, colmado; **groceries** víveres *mpl*, ultramarinos
grocery store *s* abacería, tienda de ultramarinos, colmado
grog [grag] *s* grog *m*
grog•gy ['grɑgi] *adj* (comp -gier; super -giest) (coll) inseguro, vacilante;

(shaky, e.g., from a blow) (coll) atontado; (coll) borracho

groin [grɔɪn] *s* (anat) ingle *f*; (archit) arista de encuentro

groom [grum] *s (bridegroom)* novio; mozo de caballos || *tr* asear, acicalar; almohazar *(caballos)*; enseñar *(a un político)* para presentarse como candidato

grooms·man ['grumzmən] *s (pl* -men [mən]) padrino de boda

groove [gruv] *s* ranura; *(of a pulley)* garganta; *(of a phonograph record)* surco; *(mark left by a wheel)* rodada; (coll) rutina, hábito arraigado || *tr* ranurar, acanalar

grope [grop] *intr* andar a tientas; *(for words)* pujar; **to grope for** buscar a tientas, buscar tentando; **to grope through** palpar *(p.ej., la obscuridad)*

gropingly ['grɔpɪŋli] *adv* a tientas

grosbeak ['gros,bik] *s* pico duro

gross [gros] *adj (dense, thick)* denso, espeso; *(coarse; vulgar)* grosero; *(fat, burly)* grueso; *(with no deductions)* bruto || *s* conjunto, totalidad; *(twelve dozen)* gruesa; **in gross** en grueso || *tr* obtener un ingreso bruto de

grossly ['grosli] *adv* aproximadamente

gross national product *s* renta nacional

grotesque [gro'tɛsk] *adj (ridiculous, extravagant)* grotesco; (f.a.) grotesco || *s* (f.a.) grutesco

grot·to ['grato] *s (pl* -toes o -tos) gruta

grouch [grautʃ] *s* (coll) mal humor *m*; *(person)* (coll) cascarrabias *mf*, vinagre *m* || *intr* (coll) refunfuñar

grouch·y ['grautʃi] *adj (comp* -ier; *super* -iest) (coll) gruñón, malhumorado

ground [graund] *s (earth, soil, land)* tierra; *(piece of land)* terreno; *(basis, foundation)* causa, fundamento; motivo, razón *f*; (elec) tierra; *(body of automobile corresponding to ground)* (elec) masa; (elec) borne *m* de tierra; **ground for complaint** motivo de queja; **grounds** terreno; jardines *mpl*; causa, fundamento; *(of coffee)* posos; **on the ground of** con motivo de; **to break ground** empezar la excavación; **to fall to the ground** fracasar, abandonarse, **to gain ground** ganar terreno; **to give ground** ceder terreno; **to lose ground** perder terreno; **to stand one's ground** mantenerse firme; **to yield ground** ceder terreno || *tr* establecer, fundar; (elec) poner a tierra; **to be grounded** estar sin volar *(un avión)*; **to be well grounded** ser muy versado || *intr* (naut) encallar, varar

ground connection *s* (rad) toma de tierra

ground crew *s* (aer) personal *m* de tierra

grounder ['graundər] *s* (baseball) pelota rodada

ground floor *s* piso bajo

ground glass *s* vidrio deslustrado

ground hog *s* marmota de América

ground lead [lid] *s* (elec) conductor *m* a tierra

groundless ['graundlɪs] *adj* infundado

ground plan *s* primer proyecto; *(of a building)* planta

ground speed *s* (aer) velocidad con respecto al suelo

ground swell *s* marejada de fondo

ground troops *spl* (mil) tropas terrestres

ground wire *s* (rad) alambre *m* de tierra; (aut) hilo de masa

ground'work' *s* infraestructura

group [grup] *adj* grupal; colectivo || *s* grupo || *tr* agrupar || *intr* agruparse

grouse [graus] *s* perdiz blanca, bonasa americana, gallo de bosque; (slang) refunfuño || *intr* (slang) refunfuñar

grout [graut] *s* lechada || *tr* enlechar

grove [grov] *s* arboleda, bosquecillo

grov·el ['grɑvəl] o ['grʌvəl] *v (pret & pp* -eled o -elled; *ger* -eling o -elling) *intr* arrastrarse servilmente; rebajarse servilmente; deleitarse en vilezas

grow [gro] *v (pret* grew [gru]; *pp* grown [gron]) *tr* cultivar *(plantas)*; criar *(animales)*; dejarse *(la barba)* || *intr* crecer; cultivarse; criarse; brotar, nacer; *(to become)* hacerse, ponerse, volverse; **to grow angry** enfadarse; **to grow old** envejecerse; **to grow out of** tener su origen en; perder *(p.ej., la costumbre)*; **to grow together** adherirse el uno al otro; **to grow up** crecer, desarrollar

growing child ['gro·ɪŋ] *s* muchacho de creces

growl [graul] *s* gruñido; refunfuño || *intr* gruñir *(el perro)*; refunfuñar

grown'-up' *adj* adulto; juicioso || *s (pl* grown-ups) adulto; **grown-ups** personas mayores

growth [groθ] *s* crecimiento; desarrollo; aumento; *(of trees, grass, etc.)* cobertura; (pathol) tumor *m*

growth stock *s* acción crecedera

grub [grʌb] *s (drudge)* esclavo del trabajo; *(larva)* gorgojo; (coll) comida, alimento || *v (pret & pp* grubbed; *ger* grubbing) *tr* arrancar *(tocones)*; desmalezar *(un terreno)* || *intr* cavar; trabajar como esclavo

grub·by ['grʌbi] *adj (comp* -bier; *super* -biest) gorgojoso; sucio, roñoso

grudge [grʌdʒ] *s* rencor *m*, inquina; **to have a grudge against** guardar rencor a, tener inquina a || *tr* dar de mala gana; envidiar

grudgingly ['grʌdʒɪŋli] *adv* de mala gana

gru·el ['gru·əl] *s* avenate *m* || *v (pret & pp* -eled o -elled; *ger* -eling o -elling) *tr* agotar, castigar cruelmente

gruesome ['grusəm] *adj* espantoso, horripilante

gruff [grʌf] *adj* áspero, brusco, rudo; *(voice, tone)* ronco

grumble ['grʌmbəl] *s* gruñido, refunfuño; ruido sordo y prolongado || *intr* gruñir, refunfuñar; retumbar

grump·y ['grʌmpi] *adj* (*comp* **-ier;** *super* **-iest**) gruñón, malhumorado

grunt [grʌnt] *s* gruñido ‖ *intr* gruñir

G-string ['dʒi,strɪŋ] *s* (*loincloth*) taparrabo; (*worn by women entertainers*) cubresexo

gt. *abbr* **great; gutta** (Lat) **drop**

g.u. *abbr* **genitourinary**

Guadeloupe [,gwɑdə'lup] *s* Guadalupe *f*

guarantee [,gærən'ti] *s* garantía; (*guarantor*) garante *mf;* persona de quien otra sale fiadora ‖ *tr* garantizar

guarantor ['gærən,tɔr] *s* garante *mf*

guaran·ty ['gærənti] *s* (*pl* **-ties**) garantía ‖ *v* (*pret & pp* **-tied**) *tr* garantizar

guard [gɑrd] *s* (*act of guarding; part of handle of sword*) guarda; (*person who guards or takes care of something*) guarda *mf;* (*group of armed men; posture in fencing*) guardia; (*member of group of armed men*) guardia *m;* (*in front of trolley car*) salvavidas *m;* (*sport*) coraza; (rr) guardabarrera *mf;* (rr) guardafrenos *m;* **off guard** desprevenido; **on guard** alerta, prevenido; de centinela; **to mount guard** montar la guardia; **under guard** a buen recaudo ‖ *tr* guardar ‖ *intr* estar de centinela; **to guard against** guardarse de, precaverse contra o de

guard'house' *s* cuartel *m* de la guardia; prisión militar

guardian ['gɑrdɪ·ən] *adj* tutelar ‖ *s* guardián *m;* (*law*) curador *m,* tutor *m*

guardian angel *s* ángel *m* custodio, ángel de la guarda

guardianship ['gɑrdɪ·ən,ʃɪp] *s* amparo, protección; (*law*) curaduría, tutela

guard'rail' *s* baranda; (naut) barandilla; (rr) contracarril *m*

guard'room' *s* cuarto de guardia; cárcel *f* militar

guards·man ['gɑrdzmən] *s* (*pl* **-men** [mən]) guardia *m,* soldado de guardia

Guatemalan [,gwɑtɪ'mɑlən] *adj & s* guatemalteco

guerrilla [gə'rɪlə] *s* guerrillero

guerrilla warfare *s* guerra de guerrillas

guess [ges] *s* conjetura, suposición; adivinación ‖ *tr & intr* conjeturar, suponer; (*to judge correctly*) acertar, adivinar; (coll) creer, suponer; **I guess so** (coll) creo que sí, me parece que sí

guess'work' *s* conjetura; **by guesswork** por conjeturas

guest [gest] *s* convidado; (*lodger*) huésped *m;* (*of a boarding house*) pensionista *mf;* (*of a hotel*) cliente *mf;* (*caller*) visita

guest book *s* libro de oro

guest room *s* cuarto de reserva

guffaw [gə'fɔ] *s* risotada, carcajada ‖ *intr* risotear, reír a carcajadas

Guiana [gɪ'ɑnə] o [gɪ'ænə] *s* Guayana

guidance ['gaɪdəns] *s* guía, gobierno,

dirección; **for your guidance** para su gobierno

guide [gaɪd] *s* (*person*) guía *mf;* (*book*) guía; (*guidance*) guía; dirección; poste *m* indicador; (mach) guía, guiadera; (mil) guía *m* ‖ *tr* guiar

guide'board' *s* señal *f* de carretera

guide'book' *s* guía *m,* guía del viajero

guided missile ['gaɪdɪd] *s* proyectil dirigido o teleguiado

guide dog *s* perro-lazarillo

guide'line' *s* cuerda de guía; norma, pauta, directorio

guide'post' *s* poste *m* indicador

guidon ['gaɪdən] *s* (mil) guión *m;* (mil) portaguión *m*

guild [gɪld] *s* (*medieval association of craftsmen*) gremio; asociación benéfica

guild'hall' *s* casa consistorial

guile [gaɪl] *s* astucia, dolo, maña

guileful ['gaɪlfəl] *adj* astuto, doloso, mañoso

guileless ['gaɪllɪs] *adj* cándido, inocente, sencillo

guillotine ['gɪlə,tin] *s* guillotina ‖ [,gɪlə'tin] *tr* guillotinar

guilt [gɪlt] *s* culpa

guiltless ['gɪltlɪs] *adj* inocente, libre de culpa

guilt·y ['gɪlti] *adj* (*comp* **-ier;** *super* **-iest**) culpable; (*charged with guilt*) culpado; (*found guilty*) reo

guimpe [gɪmp] o [gæmp] *s* canesú *m*

guinea ['gɪni] *s* (*monetary unit*) guinea; gallina de Guinea

guinea fowl *s* pintada, gallina de Guinea

guinea hen *s* pintada, gallina de Guinea (*hembra*)

guinea pig *s* conejillo de Indias

guise [gaɪz] *s* traje *m;* aspecto, semejanza; **under the guise of** so capa de

guitar [gɪ'tɑr] *s* guitarra

guitarist [gɪ'tɑrɪst] *s* guitarrista *mf*

gulch [gʌltʃ] *s* barranco, quebrada

gulf [gʌlf] *s* golfo

Gulf of Mexico *s* golfo de Méjico

Gulf Stream *s* Corriente *f* del Golfo

gull [gʌl] *s* gaviota; (coll) bobo ‖ *tr* estafar, engañar

gullet ['gʌlɪt] *s* gaznate *m,* garguero; esófago

gullible ['gʌlɪbəl] *adj* crédulo; **to be too gullible** tener buenas tragaderas

gul·ly ['gʌli] *s* (*pl* **-lies**) barranca, arroyada; (*channel made by rain water*) badén *m*

gulp [gʌlp] *s* trago ‖ *tr* — **to gulp down** engullir; reprimir (*p.ej., sollozos*) ‖ *intr* respirar entrecortadamente

gum [gʌm] *s* goma; chanclo de goma; (*firm flesh around base of teeth*) encía; (*mucous on edge of eyelid*) legaña ‖ *v* (*pret & pp* **gummed**) *ger* **gumming**) *tr* engomar ‖ *intr* exudar goma

gum arabic *s* goma arábiga

gum'boil' *s* flemón *m*

gum boot *s* bota de agua

gum'drop' *s* frutilla
gum-my ['gʌmi] *adj* (*comp* -mier; *super* -miest) gomoso; (*eyelid*) lega-ñoso
gumption ['gʌmpʃən] *s* (coll) ánimo, iniciativa, empuje *m*, fuerza; (coll) juicio, seso
gum'shoe' *s* chanclo de goma; (coll) detective *m* ‖ *v* (*pret & pp* -shoed; *ger* -shoeing) *intr* (slang) andar con zapatos de fieltro
gun [gʌn] *s* escopeta, fusil *m*; cañón *m*; (*for injections*) jeringa; (coll) revólver *m*; to stick to one's guns mantenerse en sus trece ‖ *v* (*pret & pp* gunned; *ger* gunning) *tr* hacer fuego sobre; (slang) acelerar rápidamente (*un motor, un avión*) ‖ *intr* andar a caza; disparar; to gun for ir en busca de; buscar para matar
gun'boat' *s* cañonero
gun carriage *s* cureña, encabalgamiento
gun'cot'ton *s* fulmicotón *m*, algodón *m* pólvora
gun'fire' *s* fuego (*de armas de fuego*); cañoneo
gun-man ['gʌnmən] *s* (*pl* -men [mən]) bandido armado, pistolero
gun metal *s* bronce *m* de cañón; metal pavonado
gunnel ['gʌnəl] *s* (naut) borda, regala
gunner ['gʌnər] *s* artillero; cazador *m*
gunnery ['gʌnəri] *s* artillería
gunny sack ['gʌni] *s* saco de yute
gun'pow'der *s* pólvora
gun'run'ner *s* contrabandista *m* de armas de fuego
gun'run'ning *s* contrabando de armas de fuego
gun'shot' *s* escopetazo, tiro de fusil; alcance *m* de un fusil; within gunshot a tiro de fusil
gunshot wound *s* escopetazo
gun'smith' *s* armero
gun'stock' *s* caja de fusil
gunwale ['gʌnəl] *s* (naut) borda, regala
gup-py ['gʌpi] *s* (*pl* -pies) lebistes *m*
gurgle ['gʌrgəl] *s* gorgoteo, gluglú *m*; (*of a child*) gorjeo ‖ *intr* gorgotear, hacer gluglú; gorjearse (*el niño*)
gush [gʌʃ] *s* borbollón *m*, chorro ‖ *intr* surgir, salir a borbollones; (coll) hacer extremos, ser extremoso
gusher ['gʌʃər] *s* pozo de chorro de petróleo; (coll) persona extremosa
gushing ['gʌʃɪŋ] *adj* surgente; (coll) extremoso ‖ *s* borbollón *m*, chorro; (coll) efusión, extremos

gush-y ['gʌʃi] *adj* (*comp* -ier; *super* -iest) (coll) efusivo, extremoso
gusset ['gʌsɪt] *s* escudete *m*
gust [gʌst] *s* (*of wind*) ráfaga; (*of rain*) aguacero; (*of smoke*) bocanada; (*of noise*) explosión; (*of anger or enthusiasm*) arrebato
gusto ['gʌsto] *s* deleite *m*, entusiasmo; with gusto con sumo placer
gust-y ['gʌsti] *adj* (*comp* -ier; *super* -iest) tempestuoso, borrascoso
gut [gʌt] *s* tripa; cuerda de tripa; guts tripas; (slang) agallas ‖ *v* (*pret & pp* gutted; *ger* gutting) *tr* destripar; destruir lo interior de
gutta-percha ['gʌtə'pʌrtʃə] *s* gutapercha
gutter ['gʌtər] *s* (*on side of road*) cuneta; (*in street*) arroyo; (*of roof*) canal *f*; (*ditch formed by rain water*) badén *m*; barrios bajos
gut'ter-snipe' *s* pilluelo, hijo de la miseria; gamberro
guttural ['gʌtərəl] *adj* gutural ‖ *s* sonido gutural
guy [gaɪ] *s* viento, cable *m* de retén; (coll) tipo, tío, sujeto ‖ *tr* (coll) burlarse de
guy wire *s* cable *m* de retén
guzzle ['gʌzəl] *tr & intr* beber con exceso
guzzler ['gʌzlər] *s* borrachín *m*
gym [dʒɪm] *s* (coll) gimnasio
gymnasi-um [dʒɪm'nezi-əm] *s* (*pl* -ums o -a [ə]) gimnasio
gymnast ['dʒɪmnæst] *s* gimnasta *mf*
gymnastic [dʒɪm'næstɪk] *adj* gimnástico ‖ **gymnastics** *spl* gimnasia, gimnástica
gynecologist [ˌgaɪnə'kɑlədʒɪst], [ˌdʒaɪnə'kɑlədʒɪst] *s* ginecólogo
gynecology [ˌgaɪnə'kɑlədʒi] o [ˌdʒaɪnə'kɑlədʒi] *s* ginecología
gyp [dʒɪp] *s* (slang) estafa, timo; (*person*) (slang) estafador *m*, timador *m* ‖ *v* (*pret & pp* gypped; *ger* gypping) *tr* (slang) estafar, timar
gypsum ['dʒɪpsəm] *s* yeso, aljez *m*
gyp-sy ['dʒɪpsi] *adj* gitano ‖ *s* (*pl* -sies) gitano ‖ **Gypsy** *s* gitano (*idioma*)
gypsyish ['dʒɪpsɪ-ɪʃ] *adj* gitanesco
gypsy moth *s* lagarta
gyrate ['dʒaɪret] *intr* girar
gyroscope ['dʒaɪrəˌskop] *s* giroscopio

H

H, h [etʃ] octava letra del alfabeto inglés
h. *abbr* harbor, high, hour, husband
haberdasher ['hæbərˌdæʃər] *s* camisero; (*dealer in notions*) mercero
haberdasher-y ['hæbərˌdæʃəri] *s* (*pl*

-ies) camisería, tienda de artículos para hombres; artículos para hombres
habit ['hæbɪt] *s* costumbre *f*, hábito; (*costume*) traje *m*; to be in the habit of acostumbrar

habitat ['hæbɪ,tæt] s habitación
habitation [,hæbɪ'teʃən] s habitación
habit-forming ['hæbɪt,fɔrmɪŋ] adj enviciador
habitual [hə'bɪtʃu·əl] adj habitual
habitué [hə,bɪtʃu'e] s habituado
hack [hæk] s (cut) corte m; (notch) mella; (cough) tos seca; coche m de alquiler; caballo de alquiler; caballo de silla; (old nag) rocín m; escritor m a sueldo || tr cortar, machetear
hack-man ['hækmən] s (pl -men [mən]) cochero de punto
hackney ['hæknɪ] s caballo de silla; coche m de alquiler; esclavo del trabajo
hackneyed ['hæknɪd] adj trillado, gastado
hack'saw' s sierra de armero, sierra de cortar metales
haddock ['hædək] s eglefino
haft [hæft] o [hɑft] s mango, puño
hag [hæg] s (ugly old woman) tarasca; (witch) bruja
haggard ['hægərd] adj ojeroso, maciento, trasnochado
haggle ['hægəl] intr regatear
Hague, The [heg] La Haya
hail [hel] s (frozen rain) granizo; (greeting) saludo; **within hail** al alcance de la voz || interj ¡salud!, ¡salve! || tr saludar; dar vivas a, acoger con vivas; aclamar; granizar (p.ej., golpes) || intr granizar; **to hail from** venir de, ser oriundo de
hail'-fel'low well met s compañero muy afable y simpático
Hail Mary s avemaría
hail'stone' s piedra de granizo
hail'storm' s granizada
hair [her] s pelo, cabellos; **to a hair** con la mayor exactitud; **to get in one's hair** (slang) enojarle a uno; **to have one's hair down** estar en melena; **to let one's hair down** (slang) hablar con mucha desenvoltura; **to make one's hair stand on end** ponerle a uno los pelos de punta; **to not turn a hair** no inmutarse; **to split hairs** pararse en quisquillas
hair'breadth' s (el) grueso de un pelo, casi nada; **to escape by a hairbreadth** escapar por un pelo
hair'brush' s cepillo de cabeza
hair'cloth' s tela de crin; (worn as a penance) cilicio
hair curler ['kʌrlər] s rizador m, tenacillas
hair'cut' s corte m de pelo; **to get a haircut** cortarse el pelo
hair'do' s (pl -dos) peinado, tocado
hair'dress'er s peinador m, peluquero
hair dryer s secador m
hair dye s tinte m para el pelo
hairless ['herlɪs] adj pelón
hair net s redecilla
hair'pin' s horquilla
hair-raising ['her,rezɪŋ] adj (coll) espeluznante, horripilante
hair restorer [rɪ'storər] s crecepelo
hair ribbon s cinta para el cabello
hair set s fijapeinados m

hair shirt s cilicio
hairsplitting ['her,splɪtɪŋ] adj quisquilloso || s quisquillas
hair'spring' s espiral f
hair'style' s peinado
hair tonic s vigorizador m del cabello
hair-y ['herɪ] adj (comp -ier; super -iest) peludo, cabelludo
hake [hek] s merluza; (genus: Urophycis) fice m
halberd ['hælbərd] s alabarda
halberdier [,hælbər'dɪr] s alabardero
halcyon days ['hælsɪ·ən] s días tranquilos, época de paz
hale [hel] adj sano, robusto; **hale and hearty** sano y fuerte || tr llevar a la fuerza
half [hæf] o [hɑf] adj medio; **a half** o **half a** medio; **half the** la mitad de || adv medio, p.ej., **half asleep** medio dormido; a medio, p.ej., **half finished** a medio acabar; a medias, p.ej., **half owner** dueño a medias; **half past** y media, p.ej., **half past three** las tres y media; **half ... half** medio ... medio || s (pl **halves** [hævz] o [hɑvz]) mitad; (arith) medio; **in half** por la mitad; **to go halves** ir a medias
half'-and-half' adj mitad y mitad; indeterminado || adv a medias, en partes iguales || s mezcla de leche y crema; mezcla de dos cervezas inglesas
half'back' s (football) medio
half-baked ['hæf,bekt] o ['hɑf,bekt] adj a medio cocer; incompleto; poco juicioso, inexperto
half binding s (bb) encuadernación a la holandesa, media pasta
half'-blood' s mestizo; medio hermano
half boot s bota de media caña
half'-bound' adj (bb) a la holandesa
half'-breed' s mestizo
half brother s medio hermano
half-cocked ['hæf'kɑkt] o ['hɑf'kɑkt] adv (coll) con precipitación
half fare s medio billete
half'-full' adj mediado
half-hearted ['hæf,hɑrtɪd] o ['hɑf,hɑrtɪd] adj indiferente, frío
half holiday s mañana o tarde f de asueto
half hose spl calcetines mpl
half'-hour' s media hora; **on the half-hour** a la media en punto cada media hora
half leather s (bb) encuadernación a la holandesa, media pasta
half'-length' adj de medio cuerpo
half'-mast' s — **at half-mast** a media asta
half moon s media luna
half mourning s medio luto
half note s (mus) nota blanca
half pay s media paga; medio sueldo
halfpen-ny ['hepənɪ] o ['hepnɪ] s (pl -nies) medio penique
half pint s media pinta; (little runt) (slang) gorgojo, mirmidón m
half'-seas' over adj — **to be half-seas over** (slang) estar entre dos velas, estar entre dos luces

half shell s (*either half of a bivalve*) concha; (*oysters*) **on the half shell** en su concha

half sister s media hermana

half sole s media suela

half'-sole' tr poner media suela a

half'-staff' s — **at half-staff** a media asta

half-timbered ['hæf,tımbərd] o ['hɑf-,tımbərd] adj entramado

half title s anteportada, falsa portada

half'-tone' s (phot & paint) mediatinta; (typ) similigrabado

half'-track' s media oruga, semitractor m

half'truth' s verdad a medias

half'way' adj a medio camino; incompleto, hecho a medias || adv a medio camino; **halfway through** a la mitad de; **to meet halfway** partir el camino con; partir la diferencia con; hacer concesiones mutuas (*dos personas*)

half-witted ['hæf,wıtıd] o ['hɑf-,wıtıd] adj imbécil; necio, tonto

halibut ['hælıbət] s halibut m

halide ['hælaıd] o ['helaıd] s (chem) haluro

halitosis [,hælı'tosıs] s halitosis f, aliento fétido

hall [hɔl] s (*passageway*) corredor m; (*entranceway*) vestíbulo, zaguán m; (*large meeting room*) sala, salón m; (*assembly room of a university*) paraninfo; (*building, e.g., of a university*) edificio

hallelujah o **hallelujah** [,hælı'lujə] s aleluya m & f || interj ¡aleluya!

hall'mark' s marca de contraste; (*distinguishing feature*) (fig) sello

hal·lo [hə'lo] s (pl -los) grito || interj ¡hola!; (*to incite dogs in hunting*) ¡sus! || intr gritar

hallow ['hælo] tr santificar

hallowed ['hælod] adj santo, sagrado

Halloween o **Hallowe'en** [,hælo'in] s víspera de Todos los Santos

hallucination [hə,lusı'neʃən] s alucinación

hall'way' s corredor m; vestíbulo, zaguán m

ha·lo ['helo] s (pl -los o -loes) halo

halogen ['hælədʒən] s halógeno

halt [hɔlt] adj cojo, renco || s alto, parada; **to call a halt** mandar hacer alto; **to come to a halt** pararse, detenerse, interrumpirse || tr parar, detener || intr hacer alto

halter ['hɔltər] s (*for leading or fastening horse*) cabestro, ronzal m, dogal m; (*noose*) dogal m, cuerda de ahorcar; muerte f en la horca

halting ['hɔltıŋ] adj cojo, renco; vacilante

halve [hæv] o [hɑv] tr partir en dos, partir por la mitad

halyard ['hæljərd] s (naut) driza

ham [hæm] s (*part of leg behind knee*) corva; (*thigh and buttock*) pernil m; (*cured meat from hog's hind leg*) jamón m; (slang) comicastro; (slang) aficionado (*a la radio*); **hams** nalgas

ham and eggs spl huevos con jamón

hamburger ['hæm,bʌrgər] s hamburguesa

hamlet ['hæmlıt] s aldehuela, caserío

hammer ['hæmər] s martillo; (*of piano*) macillo, martinete m; **to go under the hammer** venderse en pública subasta || tr martillar; **to hammer out** formar a martillazos; sacar en limpio a fuerza de mucho esfuerzo || intr martillar; **to hammer away** trabajar asiduamente

hammock ['hæmək] s hamaca

hamper ['hæmpər] s canasto, cesto grande con tapa || tr estorbar, impedir

hamster ['hæmstər] s marmota de Alemania, rata del trigo

ham-string ['hæm,strıŋ] v (pret & pp -strung) tr desjarretar; (fig) estropear, incapacitar

hand [hænd] adj (*done or operated with the hands*) manual || s mano f; (*workman*) obrero, peón m; (*way of writing*) escritura, puño y letra; (*signature*) firma; (*clapping of hands*) salva de aplausos; (*of clock or watch*) mano f, manecilla; (*all the cards in one's hand*) juego; (*a round of play*) mano f; (*player*) jugador m; (*source, origin*) fuente f; (*skill*) destreza; **all hands** (naut) toda la tripulación; (coll) todos; **at first hand** de primera mano; directamente, de buena tinta; **at hand** disponible; **hand in glove** uña y carne; **hand in hand** asidos de la mano; juntos; **hands up!** ¡arriba las manos!; **hand to hand** cuerpo a cuerpo; **in hand** entre manos; **in his own hand** de su propio puño; **on hand** entre manos; disponible; **on hands and knees** (*crawling*) a gatas; (*beseeching*) de rodillas; **on the one hand** por una parte; **on the other hand** por otra parte; **out of hand** luego, en seguida; desmandado; **to be at hand** obrar en mi (nuestro) poder (*una carta*); **to change hands** mudar de manos; **to clap hands** batir palmas; **to eat out of one's hand** aceptar dócilmente la autoridad de uno; **to fall into the hands of** caer en manos de; **to have a hand in** tomar parte en; **to have one's hands full** estar ocupadísimo; **to hold hands** tomarse de las manos; **to hold up one's hands** (*as a sign of surrender*) alzar las manos; **to join hands** darse las manos; casarse; **to keep one's hands off** no tocar, no meterse en; **to lend a hand** echar una mano; **to live from hand to mouth** vivir al día, vivir de la mano a la boca; **to not lift a hand** no levantar paja del suelo; **to play into the hands of** hacer el caldo gordo a; **to raise one's hand** (*in taking an oath*) alzar el dedo; **to shake hands** estrecharse la mano; **to show one's hand** descubrir su juego; **to take in hand** hacerse cargo de; tratar, estudiar (*una cuestión*); **to throw up one's hands** darse por vencido; **to try one's hand** probar la mano; **to turn one's hand**

to dedicarse a, ocuparse en; **to wash one's hands of** lavarse las manos de; **under my hand** con mi firma, bajo mi firma, de mi puño y letra; **under the hand and seal of** firmado y sellado por ‖ *tr* dar, entregar; **to hand in** entregar; **to hand on** transmitir; **to hand out** repartir

hand'bag' *s* saco de noche; bolso *m* de señora

hand baggage *s* equipaje *m* de mano

hand'ball' *s* pelota; juego de pelota a mano

hand'bill' *s* hoja volante

hand'book' *s* manual *m*; guía de turistas; registro para apuestas

hand'breadth' *s* palmo menor

hand'car' *s* (rr) carrito de mano

hand'cart' *s* carretilla de mano

hand control *s* mando a mano

hand'cuff' *s* manilla; **handcuffs** manillas, esposas ‖ *tr* poner esposas a

handful ['hænd,fʊl] *s* puñado, manojo

hand glass *s* espejo de mano; lupa

hand grenade *s* granada de mano

handi-cap ['hændɪ,kæp] *s* desventaja, obstáculo; (sport) handicap *m* ‖ *v* (pret & pp **-capped**; ger **-capping**) *tr* poner trabas a; (sport) handicapar

handicraft ['hændɪ,kræft] o ['hændɪ,krɑft] *s* destreza manual; arte mecánica

handiwork ['hændɪ,wʌrk] *s* hechura, trabajo; obra manual

handkerchief ['hæŋkərtʃɪf] o ['hæŋkər,tʃif] *s* pañuelo

handle ['hændəl] *s* (of a basket, crock, pitcher) asa; (of a shovel, rake, etc.) mango; (of an umbrella, sword) puño; (of a door, drawer) tirador *m*; (of a hand organ) manubrio; (of a water pump) guimbalete *m*; (opportunity, pretext) asidero; **to fly off the handle** (slang) salirse de sus casillas ‖ *tr* manosear, manipular; dirigir, manejar, gobernar; comerciar en ‖ *intr* manejarse

handle bar *s* manillar *m*, guía

handler ['hændlər] *s* (sport) entrenador *m*

hand'made' *adj* hecho a mano

hand'maid' o **hand'maid'en** *s* criada, sirvienta

hand'-me-down' *s* (coll) prenda de vestir de segunda mano

hand organ *s* organillo

hand'out' *s* comida que se da de limosna; comunicado de prensa

hand-picked ['hænd,pɪkt] *adj* escogido a mano; escogido escrupulosamente; escogido con motivos ocultos

hand'rail' *s* barandilla, pasamano

hand'saw' *s* serrucho, sierra de mano

hand'set' *s* microteléfono

hand'shake' *s* apretón *m* de manos

handsome ['hænsəm] *adj* hermoso, elegante, guapo; considerable

hand'spring' *s* voltereta sobre las manos

hand'-to-hand' *adj* cuerpo a cuerpo

hand'-to-mouth' *adj* inseguro, precario; impróvido

hand'work' *s* trabajo a mano

hand'-wres'tle *intr* pulsear

hand'-writ'ing *s* escritura; (writing by hand which characterizes a particular person) letra

hand·y ['hændɪ] *adj* (comp **-ier**; super **-iest**) (easy to handle) manuable; (within easy reach) próximo, a la mano; (skillful) diestro, hábil; **to come in handy** venir a pelo

handy man *s* dije *m*, factótum *m*

hang [hæŋ] *s* (of a dress, curtain, etc.) caída; (skill; insight) tino; **I don't care a hang** (coll) no me importa un bledo; **to get the hang of it** (coll) coger el tino ‖ *v* (pret & pp **hung** [hʌŋ]) *tr* colgar; tender (la ropa mojada); pegar (el papel pintado); fijar (un cartel, un letrero); enquiciar (una puerta, una ventana); bajar (la cabeza); **hang it!** (coll) ¡caramba!; **to hang up** colgar (el sombrero); impedir los progresos de ‖ *intr* colgar, pender; estar agarrado; vacilar, **to hang around** esperar sin hacer nada; haraganear; rondar; **to hang on** colgar de; depender de; estar pendiente de (las palabras de una persona); estar sin acabar de morir; agarrarse; **to hang out** asomarse; (slang) recogerse, alojarse; **to hang over** (to threaten) cernerse sobre; **to hang together** mantenerse unidos; **to hang up** (telp) colgar ‖ *v* (pret **hanged** o **hung**) *tr* ahorcar ‖ *intr* ahorcarse

hangar ['hæŋər] o ['hæŋgɑr] *s* cobertizo; (aer) hangar *m*

hang'bird' *s* pájaro de nido colgante; (Baltimore oriole) cacique veranero

hanger ['hæŋər] *s* colgador *m*, suspensión; (hook) colgadero

hang'er-on' *s* (pl **hangers-on**) secuaz *mf*; parásito; (sponger) pegote *m*

hanging ['hæŋɪŋ] *adj* colgante, pendiente ‖ *s* ahorcadura, muerte *f* en la horca; **hangings** colgaduras

hang·man ['hæŋmən] *s* (pl **-men** [mən]) verdugo

hang'nail' *s* padrastro, respigón *m*

hang'out' *s* guarida, querencia; (place to loaf and gossip) mentidero

hang'o'ver *s* (slang) resaca

hank [hæŋk] *s* madeja

hanker ['hæŋkər] *intr* sentir anhelo

Hannibal ['hænɪbəl] *s* Aníbal *m*

haphazard [,hæp'hæzərd] *adj* casual, fortuito, impensado ‖ *adv* al acaso, a la ventura

hapless ['hæplɪs] *adj* desgraciado, desventurado

happen ['hæpən] *intr* acontecer, suceder; (to turn out) resultar; (to be the case by chance) dar la casualidad; **to happen in** entrar por casualidad; **to happen on** encontrarse con; **to happen to** hacerse de; **to happen to** + *inf* por casualidad + *ind*, p.ej., **I happened to see her at the theater** por casualidad la vi en el teatro

happening ['hæpənɪŋ] *s* acontecimiento, suceso

happily ['hæpɪlɪ] *adv* felizmente

happiness ['hæpɪnɪs] *s* felicidad

hap·py ['hæpi] *adj* (*comp* **-pier;** *super* **-piest**) feliz; (*pleased*) contento; **to be happy to** alegrarse de, tener gusto en

hap'py-go-luck'y *adj* irresponsable, impróvido ‖ *adv* a la buenaventura

happy medium *s* justo medio

Happy New Year *interj* ¡Feliz Año Nuevo!

harangue [hə'ræŋ] *s* arenga ‖ *tr* & *intr* arengar

harass ['hærəs] o [hə'ræs] *tr* acosar, hostigar; molestar, vejar

harbinger ['hɑrbɪndʒər] *s* precursor *m*; anuncio, presagio ‖ *tr* anunciar, presagiar

harbor ['hɑrbər] *adj* portuario ‖ *s* puerto ‖ *tr* albergar; alcahuetar, encubrir (*delincuentes u objetos robados*); guardar (*sentimientos de odio*)

harbor master *s* capitán *m* de puerto

hard [hɑrd] *adj* duro; (*difficult*) difícil; (*water*) crudo, duro; (*solder*) fuerte; (*work*) asiduo; (*drinker*) empedernido; espiritoso, fuertemente alcohólico; **to be hard on** (*to treat severely*) ser muy duro con; (*to wear out fast*) gastar, echar a perder ‖ *adv* duro; fuerte; mucho; **hard upon** a raíz de; **to drink hard** beber de firme; **to rain hard** llover de firme

hard and fast *adj* inflexible, riguroso ‖ *adv* firmemente

hard-bitten ['hɑrd'bɪtən] *adj* terco, tenaz, inflexible

hard-boiled ['hɑrd'bɔɪld] *adj* (*egg*) duro, muy cocido; (*coll*) duro, inflexible

hard candy *s* caramelos

hard cash *s* dinero contante y sonante

hard cider *s* sidra muy fermentada

hard coal *s* antracita

hard-earned ['hɑrd'ʌrnd] *adj* ganado a pulso

harden ['hɑrdən] *tr* endurecer ‖ *intr* endurecerse

hardening ['hɑrdənɪŋ] *s* endurecimiento

hard facts *spl* realidades

hard-fought ['hɑrd'fɔt] *adj* reñido

hard-headed ['hɑrd'hedɪd] *adj* astuto, sagaz; terco, tozudo

hard-hearted ['hɑrd'hɑrtɪd] *adj* duro de corazón

hardihood ['hɑrdɪ,hʊd] *s* audacia, resolución; descaro, insolencia

hardiness ['hɑrdɪnɪs] *s* fuerza, robustez; audacia, resolución

hard labor *s* trabajos forzados

hard luck *s* mala suerte

hard'-luck' story *s* (coll) cuento de penas; **to tell a hard-luck story** (coll) contar lástimas

hardly ['hɑrdli] *adv* apenas; casi no; (*with great difficulty*) a duras penas; (*grievously*) penosamente; **hardly ever** casi nunca

hardness ['hɑrdnɪs] *s* dureza; (*of water*) crudeza

hard of hearing *adj* duro de oído, teniente

hard-pressed ['hɑrd'prest] *adj* acosado; (*for money*) apurado, alcanzado

hard rubber *s* vulcanita

hard sauce *s* mantequilla azucarada

hard'-shell' clam *s* almeja redonda

hard-shell crab *s* cangrejo de cáscara dura

hardship ['hɑrd/ɪp] *s* penalidad, infortunio, apuro

hard'tack' *s* galleta, sequete *m*

hard times *spl* período de miseria, apuros

hard to please *adj* difícil de contentar

hard up *adj* (coll) apurado, alcanzado

hard'ware' *s* ferretería, quincalla; (*metal trimmings*) herraje *m*

hardware·man ['hɑrd,wermən] *s* (*pl* **-men** [mən]) ferretero, quincallero

hardware store *s* ferretería, quincallería

hard-won ['hɑrd,wʌn] *adj* ganado a pulso

hard'wood' *s* madera dura; árbol *m* de madera dura

hardwood floor *s* entarimado

har·dy ['hɑrdi] *adj* (*comp* **-dier;** *super* **-diest**) fuerte, robusto; audaz, resuelto; (*rash*) temerario; (hort) resistente

hare [her] *s* liebre *f*

harebrained ['her,brend] *adj* atolondrado

hare'lip' *s* labio leporino

harelipped ['her,lɪpt] *adj* labiohendido

harem ['herəm] *s* harén *m*

hark [hɑrk] *intr* escuchar; **to hark back** volver (*la jauría*) sobre la pista; **to hark back to** volver a, recordar

harken ['hɑrkən] *intr* escuchar, atender

harlequin ['hɑrləkwɪn] *s* arlequín *m*

harlot ['hɑrlət] *s* meretriz *f*

harm [hɑrm] *s* daño, perjuicio ‖ *tr* dañar, perjudicar, hacer daño a

harmful ['hɑrmfəl] *adj* dañoso, perjudicial; (*e.g., pests*) dañino

harmless ['hɑrmlɪs] *adj* innocuo, inofensivo

harmonic [hɑr'mɑnɪk] *adj* & *s* armónico

harmonica [hɑr'mɑnɪkə] *s* armónica

harmonious [hɑr'monɪ·əs] *adj* armonioso

harmonize ['hɑrmə,naɪz] *tr* & *intr* armonizar

harmo·ny ['hɑrməni] *s* (*pl* **-nies**) armonía

harness ['hɑrnɪs] *s* arreos, guarniciones; **to get back in the harness** volver a la rutina; **to die in the harness** morir al pie del cañón ‖ *tr* enjaezar, poner las guarniciones a; enganchar; captar (*las aguas de un río*)

harness maker *s* guarnicionero

harness race *s* carrera con sulky

harp [hɑrp] *s* arpa ‖ *intr* — **to harp on** repetir porfiadamente

harpist ['hɑrpɪst] *s* arpista *mf*

harpoon [hɑr'pun] *s* arpón *m* ‖ *tr* & *intr* arponear

harpsichord ['hɑrpsɪ,kɔrd] *s* clave *m*

har·py ['hɑrpɪ] *s* (*pl* -**pies**) arpía

harrow ['hæro] *s* (*agr*) grada ‖ *tr* (*agr*) gradar; atormentar

harrowing ['hæro·ɪŋ] *adj* horripilante, espantoso

har·ry ['hærɪ] *v* (*pret* & *pp* -**ried**) *tr* acosar, hostilizar, hostigar; atormentar, molestar

harsh [hɑrʃ] *adj* (*to touch, taste, eyes, hearing*) áspero; duro, cruel

harshness ['hɑrʃnɪs] *s* aspereza; dureza, crueldad

hart [hɑrt] *s* ciervo

harum-scarum ['herəm'skerəm] *adj* atolondrado ‖ *adv* atolondradamente ‖ *s* mataperros *m*

harvest ['hɑrvɪst] *s* cosecha ‖ *tr* & *intr* cosechar

harvester ['hɑrvɪstər] *s* cosechero; (*helper*) agostero; (*machine*) segadora

harvest home *s* entrada de los frutos; fiesta de segadores; canción de segadores

harvest moon *s* luna de la cosecha

has-been ['hæz,bɪn] *s* (coll) antigualla

hash [hæʃ] *s* picadillo ‖ *tr* picar

hash house *s* bodegón *m*

hashish ['hæʃɪʃ] *s* hachich *m*

hasp [hæsp] o [hɑsp] *s* portacandado; (*of book covers*) broche *m*

hassle ['hæsəl] *s* (coll) riña, disputa

hassock ['hæsək] *s* cojín *m* (*para los pies o las rodillas*)

haste [hest] *s* prisa; **in haste** de prisa; **to make haste** darse prisa

hasten ['hesən] *tr* apresurar; apretar (*el paso*) ‖ *intr* apresurarse

hast·y ['hestɪ] *adj* (*comp* -**ier**; *super* -**iest**) apresurado; inconsiderado, impulsivo, colérico

hat [hæt] *s* sombrero; **to keep under one's hat** (coll) callar, no divulgar; **to throw one's hat in the ring** (coll) decidirse a bajar a la arena

hat'band' *s* cintillo; (*worn to show mourning*) gasa

hat block *s* horma, conformador *m*

hat'box' *s* sombrerera

hatch [hætʃ] *s* (*brood*) cría, nidada; (*trap door*) escotillón *m*; (*lower half of door*) media puerta; (*opening in ship's deck*) escotilla; (*lid for opening in ship's deck*) cuartel *m* ‖ *tr* empollar (*huevos*); sombrear (*un dibujo*); maquinar, tramar ‖ *intr* empollarse; salir del huevo

hat'-check' girl *s* guardarropa

hatchet ['hætʃɪt] *s* destral *m*, hacha pequeña; **to bury the hatchet** envainar la espada

hatch'way' *s* (*trap door*) escotillón *m*; (*opening in ship's deck*) escotilla

hate [het] *s* odio, aborrecimiento ‖ *tr* & *intr* odiar, aborrecer, detestar

hateful ['hetfəl] *adj* odioso, aborrecible

hat'pin' *s* aguja de sombrero, pasador *m*

hat'rack' *s* percha

hatred ['hetrɪd] *s* odio, aborrecimiento

hatter ['hætər] *s* sombrerero

haughtiness ['hɔtɪnɪs] *s* altanería, altivez *f*

haugh·ty ['hɔtɪ] *adj* (*comp* -**tier**; *super* -**tiest**) altanero, altivo

haul [hɔl] *s* (*pull, tug*) tirón *m*; (*amount caught*) redada; (*distance transported*) trayecto, recorrido; (*roundup, e.g., of thieves*) redada ‖ *tr* acarrear, transportar; (naut) halar

haunch [hɔntʃ] o [hɑntʃ] *s* (*hip*) cadera; (*hind quarter of an animal*) anca; (*leg of animal used for food*) pierna

haunt [hɔnt] o [hɑnt] *s* guarida, nidal *m*, querencia ‖ *tr* andar por, vagar por; frecuentar; inquietar, molestar; perseguir (*las memorias a una persona*)

haunted house *s* casa de fantasmas

haute couture [ot ku'tyr] *s* alta moda

Havana [hə'vænə] *s* La Habana

have [hæv] *v* (*pret* & *pp* **had** [hæd]) *tr* tener; (*to get, to take*) tomar; **to have and to hold** (úsase sólo en el infinitivo) para ser poseído en propiedad; **to have got** (coll) tener, poseer; **to have got to** + *inf* (coll) tener que + *inf*; **to have it in for** (coll) tener tirria a; **to have it out with** (coll) habérselas con, emprenderla con; **to have on** llevar puesto; **to have** (*something*) **to do with** tener que ver con; **to have** + *inf* hacer, mandar + *inf*, p.ej., **I had him go out that door** le hice salir por esa puerta; **to have** + *pp* hacer, mandar + *inf*, p.ej., **I had my watch repaired** hice componer mi reloj ‖ *intr* — **to have at** atacar, embestir; **to have to** + *inf* tener que + *inf*; **to have to do with** (*to be concerned with*) tratar de; (*to have connections with*) tener relaciones con ‖ *v aux* haber, p.ej., **he has studied his lesson** ha estudiado su lección

havelock ['hævlɑk] *s* cogotera

haven ['hevən] *s* puerto; abrigo, asilo, buen puerto

have-not ['hæv,nɑt] *s* — **the haves and the have-nots** (coll) los ricos y los desposeídos

haversack ['hævər,sæk] *s* barjuleta; (*of soldier*) mochila

havoc ['hævək] *s* estrago, estragos; **to play havoc with** hacer grandes estragos en

haw [hɔ] *s* (*of hawthorn*) baya, simiente *f*; (*in speech*) vacilación ‖ *interj* ¡a la izquierda! ‖ *tr* & *intr* volver a la izquierda

haw'-haw' *s* carcajada

hawk [hɔk] *s* halcón *m*, gavilán *m*, cernícalo; (*mortarboard*) esparavel *m*; (*sharper*) (coll) fullero ‖ *tr* pregonar; **to hawk up** arrojar tosiendo ‖ *intr* carraspear, gargajear

hawker ['hɔkər] *s* buhonero

hawksbill turtle ['hɔks,bɪl] *s* carey *m*

hawse [hɔz] *s* (naut) muz *m*; (*hole*) (naut) escobén *m*; (naut) longitud de cadenas

hawse'hole' *s* (naut) escobén *m*

hawser ['hɔzər] s (naut) guindaleza

haw'thorn' s espino, oxiacanta

hay [he] s heno; to hit the hay (slang) acostarse; to make hay while the sun shines hacer su agosto

hay fever s fiebre f del heno

hay'field' s henar m

hay'fork' s horca; (machine) elevador m de heno

hay'loft' s henil m, henal m

hay'mak'er s (box) golpe m que pone fuera de combate

haymow ['he‚mau] s henil m; acopio de heno

hay'rack' s pesebre m

hayrick ['he‚rɪk] s almiar m

hay ride s paseo de placer en carro de heno

hay'seed' s simiente f de heno; (coll) patán m, campesino

hay'stack' s almiar m

hay'wire' adj (slang) descompuesto; (slang) destornillado, loco ‖ s alambre m para embalar el heno

hazard ['hæzərd] s peligro, riesgo; (chance) acaso, azar m; (golf) obstáculo; at all hazards por grande que sea el riesgo ‖ tr arriesgar; aventurar (una opinión)

hazardous ['hæzərdəs] adj peligroso, arriesgado

haze [hez] s calina, bruma; (fig) confusión, vaguedad ‖ tr dar novatada a

hazel ['hezəl] adj castaño claro ‖ s avellano

ha'zel·nut' s avellana

hazing ['hezɪŋ] s novatada

ha·zy ['hezi] adj (comp -zier; super -ziest) calinoso, brumoso; confuso, vago

H-bomb ['etʃ‚bɑm] s bomba de hidrógeno

H.C. abbr House of Commons

hd. abbr head

hdqrs. abbr headquarters

H.E. abbr His Eminence, His Excellency

he [hi] pron pers (pl they) él ‖ s (pl hes) macho, varón m

head [hed] s cabeza; (of a bed) cabecera; (caption) encabezamiento; (of a boil) centro; (on a glass of beer) espuma; (of a drum) parche m; (of a cane) puño; (of a barrel, cylinder, etc.) fondo, tapa; (of cylinder of automobile engine) culata; crisis f, punto decisivo; at the head of al frente de; from head to foot de pies a cabeza; head over heels en un salto mortal; hasta los tuétanos; precipitadamente; heads (of a coin) cara; heads or tails a cara o cruz; over one's head fuera del alcance de uno; (going to a higher authority) por encima de uno; to be out of one's head (coll) delirar; to come into one's head pasarle a uno por la cabeza; to go to one's head subírsele a uno a la cabeza; to keep one's head no perder la cabeza; to keep one's head above water no dejarse vencer; to put heads together con-

sultarse entre sí; to not make head or tail of no ver pies ni cabeza a ‖ tr acaudillar, dirigir, mandar; estar a la cabeza de (p.ej., la clase); venir primero en (una lista) ‖ intr — to head towards dirigirse hacia

head'ache' s dolor m de cabeza

head'band' s cinta para la cabeza; (of a book) cabezada

head'board' s cabecera de cama

head'cheese' s queso de cerdo

head'dress' s (style of hair) tocado; prenda para la cabeza

header ['hedər] s — to take a header (coll) caerse de cabeza

head'first' adv de cabeza; precipitadamente

head'gear' s sombrero; (for protection) casco

head'hunt'er s cazador m de cabezas

heading ['hedɪŋ] s encabezamiento; (of a letter) membrete m; (of a chapter of a book) cabecera

headland ['hedlənd] s promontorio

headless ['hedlɪs] adj sin cabeza; sin jefe; estúpido

head'light' s (aut) faro; (naut) farol m de tope; (rr) farol m

head'line' s (of newspaper) cabecera; (of a page of a book) titulillo, título de página ‖ tr poner cabecera a; (slang) destacar, dar cartel a (un actor)

head'lin'er s (slang) atracción principal

head'long' adj de cabeza; precipitado ‖ adv de cabeza; precipitadamente

head·man ['hed‚mæn] s (pl -men [‚men]) caudillo, jefe m

head'mas'ter s director m de un colegio

head'most' adj delantero, primero

head office s oficina central

head of hair s cabellera

head'-on' adj & adv de frente; head-on collision colisión de frente

head'phone' s auricular m de casco, receptor m de cabeza

head'piece' s (any covering for head) casco, yelmo, morrión m; (brains, judgment) cabeza, juicio; cabecera de cama; (headset) auricular m de casco, receptor m de cabeza; (typ) cabecera, viñeta

head'quar'ters s centro de dirección; (of police) jefatura; (mil) cuartel m general

head'rest' s apoyo para la cabeza

head'set' s auricular m de casco, receptor m de cabeza

head'ship' s jefatura, dirección

head'stone' s (cornerstone) piedra angular; (on a grave) lápida sepulcral

head'stream' s afluente m principal

head'strong' adj cabezudo, terco

head'wait'er s jefe m de camareros, encargado de comedor

head'wa'ters spl cabecera

head'way' s avance m, progreso; espacio libre; to make headway avanzar, progresar

head'wear' s prendas de cabeza

head wind s viento de frente, viento por la proa

head'work' s trabajo intelectual

head·y ['hedi] adj (comp -ier; super -iest) excitante, emocionante; impetuoso, violento; (intoxicating) cabezudo; (clever) sesudo

heal [hil] tr curar, sanar; cicatrizar; remediar (un daño) || intr curar, sanar; cicatrizarse; remediarse

healer ['hilər] s curador m, sanador m

health [hɛlθ] s salud f; **to be in good health** estar bien de salud; **to be in poor health** estar mal de salud; **to drink to the health of** beber a la salud de; **to radiate health** verter salud; **to your health!** ¡a su salud!

healthful ['hɛlθfəl] adj saludable; sano

health·y ['hɛlθi] adj (comp -ier; super -iest) sano; saludable

heap [hip] s montón m || tr amontonar, apilar; (to supply with, e.g., favors) colmar; (to bestow in great quantity) dar generosamente || intr amontonarse, apilarse

hear [hɪr] v (pret & pp **heard** [hʌrd]) tr oír; **to hear it said** oírlo decir || intr oír; **hear! hear!** ¡bravo!; **to hear about** oír hablar de; **to hear from** tener noticias de; **to hear of** oír hablar de; **to hear tell of** oír hablar de; **to hear that** oír decir que

hearer ['hɪrər] s oyente mf

hearing ['hɪrɪŋ] s (sense) oído; (act) oída; audiencia; **in the hearing of** en presencia de; **within hearing** al alcance del oído

hearing aid s aparato auditivo

hear'say' s rumor m; **by hearsay** de o por oídas

hearse [hʌrs] s coche m fúnebre, carroza fúnebre

heart [hɑrt] s corazón m; (e.g., of lettuce) cogollo; **after one's heart** enteramente del gusto de uno; **by heart** de memoria; **heart and soul de todo corazón; to break the heart of** partir el corazón de; **to die of a broken heart** morir de pena; **to eat one's heart out** sufrir en silencio; **to get to the heart of** llegar al fondo de; **to have one's heart in one's work** trabajar con entusiasmo; **to have one's heart in the right place** tener buenas intenciones; **to lose heart** descorazonarse; **to open one's heart to** descubrirse con; **to take heart** cobrar aliento; **to take to heart** tomar a pecho; **to wear one's heart on one's sleeve** llevar el corazón en la mano; **with all one's heart** con toda el alma de uno; **with one's heart in one's mouth** con el credo en la boca

heart'ache' s angustia, congoja

heart attack s ataque m de corazón, ataque cardíaco

heart'beat' s latido del corazón

heart'break' s angustia, dolor m abrumador

heart'break'er s ladrón m de corazones

heartbroken ['hɑrt,brokən] adj transido de dolor, muerto de pena

heart'burn' s acedía, rescoldera; (jealousy) celos

heart disease s enfermedad del corazón

hearten ['hɑrtən] tr alentar, animar

heart failure s debilidad coronaria; (death) paro del corazón; (faintness) desfallecimiento, desmayo

heartfelt ['hɑrt,fɛlt] adj cordial, sentido, sincero

hearth [hɑrθ] s hogar m

hearth'stone' s solera del hogar; (home) hogar m

heartily ['hɑrtɪli] adv cordialmente; con buen apetito; de buena gana; bien, mucho

heartless ['hɑrtlɪs] adj cruel, inhumano

heart-rending ['hɑrt,rɛndɪŋ] adj angustioso, que parte el corazón

heart'seed' s farolillo

heart'sick' adj afligido, desconsolado

heart'strings' spl fibras del corazón, entretelas

heart'-to-heart' adj franco, sincero

heart trouble s — **to have heart trouble** enfermar del corazón

heart'wood' s madera de corazón

heart·y ['hɑrti] adj (comp -ier; super -iest) cordial, sincero; sano, fuerte; (meal) abundante; (laugh) bueno; (eater) grande

heat [hit] adj térmico || s calor m; (warming of a room, house, etc.) calefacción; (rut of animals) celo; (in horse racing) carrera de prueba; (fig) ardor m, ímpetu m; **in heat** en celo || tr calentar; calefaccionar (p.ej., una casa); (fig) acalorar, excitar || intr calentarse; (fig) acalorarse, excitarse

heated ['hitɪd] adj acalorado

heater ['hitər] s calentador m; (for central heating) calorífero; (electron) calefactor m

heater man s calefactor m

heath [hiθ] s (shrub) brezo; (tract of land) brezal m

hea·then ['hiðən] adj gentil, pagano; irreligioso || s (pl -then o -thens) gentil mf, pagano

heathendom ['hiðəndəm] s gentilidad

heather ['hɛðər] s brezo

heating ['hitɪŋ] adj calentador || s calefacción

heat lightning s fucilazo, relámpago de calor

heat shield s blindaje térmico, escudo térmico

heat'stroke' s insolación

heat wave s (phys) onda calorífica; (coll) ola de calor

heave [hiv] s esfuerzo para levantar; esfuerzo para levantarse; heaves (vet) huélfago || v (pret & pp **heaved** o **hov** [hov]) tr alzar, levantar; arrojar, lanzar; exhalar (un suspiro) || intr levantarse y bajar alternativamente; palpitar (el pecho); elevarse; hacer esfuerzos por vomitar

heaven ['hɛvən] s cielo; **for heaven's sake!** ¡o good heavens! ¡válgame Dios!; **heavens** (firmament) cielo ||

Heaven s cielo (*mansión de los bienaventurados*)
heavenly ['hɛvənlɪ] adj (*body*) celeste; (*life, home*) celestial; (fig) celestial
heavenly body s astro, cuerpo celeste
heav·y ['hɛvɪ] adj (*comp* -ier; *super* -iest) (*of great weight*) pesado; (*liquid*) espeso, denso; (*cloth, paper, sea, line*) grueso; (*traffic*) denso; (*crop, harvest*) abundante, copioso; (*expense*) fuerte; (*rain*) recio; (*features*) basto; (*eyes*) agravado; (*gunfire*) fragoroso; (*heart*) abatido, triste; (*drinker*) grande; (*stock market*) postrado; (*clothing*) de mucho abrigo ‖ adv pesadamente; **to hang heavy** pasar (*el tiempo*) con gran lentitud
heav·y·du·ty adj extrafuerte
heavy-hearted ['hɛvɪ'hɑrtɪd] adj afligido, acongojado
heav·y·set' adj costilludo, espaldudo
heav·y·weight' s (box) peso pesado
Hebrew ['hibru] adj & s hebreo
hecatomb ['hɛkə,tom] o ['hɛkə,tum] s hecatombe f
heckle ['hɛkəl] tr interrumpir (*a un orador*) con preguntas impertinentes
hectic ['hɛktɪk] adj (coll) agitado, turbulento
hedge [hɛdʒ] s cercado, vallado; (*of bushes*) seto vivo; apuesta compensatoria; (*in stock market*) operación compensatoria ‖ tr cercar con vallado; cercar con seto vivo; **to hedge in** encerrar, rodear ‖ intr no querer comprometerse; hacer apuestas compensatorias; hacer operaciones compensatorias
hedge·hog' s erizo; (*porcupine*) puerco espín m
hedge·hop' v (pret & pp -hopped; ger -hopping) intr (aer) volar rasando el suelo
hedgehopping ['hɛdʒ,hɑpɪŋ] s (aer) vuelo rasante
hedge·row' s cercado de arbustos, seto vivo
heed [hid] s atención, cuidado; **to take heed** ir con cuidado ‖ tr atender a, hacer caso de ‖ intr atender, hacer caso
heedless ['hidlɪs] adj desatento, descuidado
heehaw ['hi,hɔ] s (*of donkey*) rebuzno; risotada ‖ intr rebuznar; reír groseramente
heel [hil] s (*of foot*) calcañar m, talón m; (*of stocking or shoe*) talón m; (*raised part of shoe below heel*) tacón m; (slang) sinvergüenza mf; **down at the heel** desaliñado, mal vestido; **to cool one's heels** (coll) hacer antesala; **to kick up one's heels** (slang) mostrarse alegre; **to show a clean pair of heels** o **to take to one's heels** poner pies en polvorosa
heeler ['hilər] s (slang) muñidor m
heft·y ['hɛftɪ] adj (comp -ier; super -iest) (*heavy*) pesado; (*strong*) fuerte, fornido
hegemo·ny [hɪ'dʒɛmənɪ] o ['hɛdʒɪ,monɪ] s (pl -nies) hegemonía

hegira [hɪ'dʒaɪrə] o ['hɛdʒɪrə] s fuga, huída
heifer ['hɛfər] s novilla, vaquilla
height [haɪt] s altura; (*e.g., of folly*) colmo
heighten ['haɪtən] tr hacer más alto; (*to increase the amount of*) aumentar; (*to set off, bring out*) realzar ‖ intr aumentarse
heinous ['henəs] adj atroz, nefando
heir [ɛr] s heredero
heir apparent s (pl **heirs apparent**) heredero forzoso
heirdom ['ɛrdəm] s herencia
heiress ['ɛrɪs] s heredera
heirloom ['ɛr,lum] s joya de familia, reliquia de familia
helicopter ['hɛlɪ,kɑptər] s helicóptero
heliotrope ['hilɪ-ə,trop] s heliotropo
heliport ['hɛlɪ,port] s helipuerto
helium ['hilɪ-əm] s helio
helix ['hilɪks] s (pl **helixes** o **helices** ['hɛlɪ,siz]) hélice f
hell [hɛl] s infierno
hell-bent ['hɛl'bɛnt] adj (slang) muy resuelto; **hell-bent on** (slang) empeñado en
hell'cat' s (*bad-tempered woman*) arpía, mujer perversa; (*witch*) bruja
hellebore ['hɛlɪ,bor] s eléboro
Hellene ['hɛlin] s heleno
Hellenic [hɛ'lɛnɪk] o [hɛ'linɪk] adj helénico
hell'fire' s fuego del infierno
hellish ['hɛlɪʃ] adj infernal
hel·lo [hɛ'lo] s saludo ‖ interj ¡qué tal!; (*on telephone*) ¡diga!
hello girl s (coll) chica telefonista
helm [hɛlm] s barra del timón; rueda del timón; (fig) timón m ‖ tr dirigir, gobernar
helmet ['hɛlmɪt] s casco; (*of ancient armor*) yelmo
helms·man ['hɛlmzmən] s (pl -men [mən]) timonel m
help [hɛlp] s ayuda, socorro; (*of food*) ración; (*relief*) remedio, p.ej., **there's no help for it** no hay remedio; criados; empleados; obreros; **to come to the help of** acudir en socorro de ‖ interj ¡socorro! ‖ tr ayudar, socorrer; aliviar, mitigar; (*to wait on*) servir; **it can't be helped** no hay remedio; **so help me God!** ¡así Dios me salve!; **to help down** ayudar a bajar; **to help a person with his coat** ayudarle a una persona a ponerse el abrigo; **to help oneself** valerse por sí mismo; servirse; **to help up** ayudar a subir; ayudar a levantarse; **to not be able to help** + ger no poder menos de + inf, p.ej., **he can't help laughing** no puede menos de reír ‖ intr ayudar
helper ['hɛlpər] s ayudante mf; (*in a drug store, barbershop, etc.*) mancebo
helpful ['hɛlpfəl] adj útil, provechoso; servicial
helping ['hɛlpɪŋ] s ración (*de alimento*)
helpless ['hɛlplɪs] adj (*weak*) débil; (*powerless*) impotente; (*penniless*)

desvalido; (*confused*) perplejo; (*situation*) irremediable

help'meet' *s* compañero; (*wife*) compañera

helter-skelter ['heltər'skeltər] *adj, adv & s* cochite hervite *m*

hem [hem] *s* tos fingida; (*of a garment*) bastilla, dobladillo || *interj* ¡ejem! || *v* (*pret & pp* **hemmed**) *ger* **hemming**) *tr* bastillar, dobladillar; **to hem in** encerrar, rodear || *intr* destoserse; vacilar; **to hem and haw** vacilar al hablar; ser evasivo

hemisphere ['hemɪ,sfɪr] *s* hemisferio

hemistich ['hemɪ,stɪk] *s* hemistiquio

hem'line' *s* ruedo de la falda, borde *m* de la falda

hem'lock' *s* (*Tsuga canadensis*) abeto del Canadá; (*herb and poison*) cicuta

hemoglobin [,hemə'globɪn] o [,himə'globɪn] *s* hemoglobina

hemophilia [,hemə'fɪlɪ·ə] o [,himə'fɪlɪ·ə] *s* hemofilia

hemorrhage ['hemərɪdʒ] *s* hemorragia

hemorrhoids ['hemə,rɔɪdz] *spl* hemorroides *fpl*

hemostat ['hemə,stæt] o ['himə,stæt] *s* hemóstato

hemp [hemp] *s* cáñamo

hemstitch ['hem,stɪtʃ] *s* vainica || *tr* hacer vainica en || *intr* hacer vainica

hen [hen] *s* gallina

hence [hens] *adv* de aquí; desde ahora; por lo tanto, por consiguiente; de aquí a, p.ej., **three weeks hence** de aquí a tres semanas

hence'forth' *adv* de aquí en adelante

hench·man ['hentʃmən] *s* (*pl* **-men** [mən]) secuaz *m*, servidor *m*; (*political schemer*) muñidor *m*

hen'coop' *s* gallinero

hen'house' *s* gallinero

henna ['henə] *s* alcana, alheña; (*dye*) henna *f* || *tr* alheñarse (*el pelo*)

hen'peck' *tr* dominar (*la mujer al marido*)

henpecked husband *s* calzonazos *m*, gurrumino

hep [hep] *adj* (slang) enterado; **to be hep to** (slang) estar al corriente de

her [hʌr] *adj poss* su; el . . . de ella || *pron pers* la; ella; **to her** le; **a ella**

herald ['herəld] *s* heraldo; anunciador *m* || *tr* anunciar; ser precursor de

heraldic [he'rældɪk] *adj* heráldico

herald·ry ['herəldrɪ] *s* (*pl* **-ries**) (*office or duty of herald*) heraldía; (*science of armorial bearings*) blasón *m*, heráldica; (*heraldic device; coat of arms*) blasón; pompa heráldica

herb [ʌrb] o [hʌrb] *s* hierba; hierba aromática; hierba medicinal

herbaceous [hʌr'be/əs] *adj* herbáceo

herbage ['ʌrbɪdʒ] o ['hʌrbɪdʒ] *s* herbaje *m*

herbal ['ʌrbəl] o ['hʌrbəl] *adj & s* herbario

herbalist ['hʌrbəlɪst] o ['ʌrbəlɪst] *s* herbolario

herbari·um [hʌr'berɪ·əm] *s* (*pl* **-ums** o **-a** [ə]) herbario

herb doctor *s* herbolario

herculean [hʌr'kjulɪ·ən] o [,hʌrkju-ˈli·ən] *adj* (*hard to perform*) penoso, laborioso; (*strong, big*) hercúleo

herd [hʌrd] *s* manada, rebaño, hato; (*of people*) chusma, multitud || *tr* reunir en manada; reunir || *intr* reunirse en manada; reunirse, ir juntos

herds·man ['hʌrdzmən] *s* (*pl* **-men** [mən]) manadero; (*of sheep*) pastor *m*; (*of cattle*) vaquero

here [hɪr] *adj* presente || *adv* aquí; **here and there** acá y allá; **here is** o **here are** aquí tiene Vd.; **that's neither here nor there** eso no viene al caso || *s* — **the here and the hereafter** esta vida y la futura || *interj* ¡presente!

hereabouts ['hɪrə,bauts] *adv* por aquí, cerca de aquí

here·af'ter *adv* de aquí en adelante; en lo sucesivo; en la vida futura || *s* **the hereafter** la otra vida, el más allá

here·by' *adv* por esto; por la presente

hereditary [hɪ'redɪ,terɪ] *adj* hereditario

heredi·ty [hɪ'redɪtɪ] *s* (*pl* **-ties**) herencia

here·in' *adv* aquí dentro; en este asunto

here·of' *adv* de esto

here·on' *adv* en esto, sobre esto

here·sy ['herəsɪ] *s* (*pl* **-sies**) herejía

heretic ['herətɪk] *adj* herético || *s* hereje *mf*

heretical [hɪ'retɪkəl] *adj* herético

heretofore [,hɪrtu'for] *adv* antes, hasta ahora

here·u·pon' *adv* en esto, sobre esto; en seguida

here·with' *adv* adjunto, con la presente; de este modo

heritage ['herɪtɪdʒ] *s* herencia

hermetic(al) [hʌr'metɪk(əl)] *adj* hermético

hermit ['hʌrmɪt] *s* eremita *m*, ermitaño

hermitage ['hʌrmɪtɪdʒ] *s* ermita

herni·a ['hʌrnɪ·ə] *s* (*pl* **-as** o **-ae** [,i]) hernia

he·ro ['hɪro] *s* (*pl* **-roes**) héroe *m*

heroic [hɪ'ro·ɪk] *adj* heroico || **heroics** *spl* verso heroico; lenguaje rimbombante

heroin ['hero·ɪn] *s* heroína (*polvo cristalino*)

heroine ['hero·ɪn] *s* heroína (*mujer*)

heroism ['hero,ɪzəm] *s* heroísmo

heron ['herən] *s* garza; (*Ardea cinerea*) airón *m*, garza real

herring ['herɪŋ] *s* arenque *m*

her'ring·bone' *s* (*in fabrics*) espina de pescado; (*in hardwood floors*) espinapez *m*, punto de Hungría

hers [hʌrz] *pron poss* el suyo, el de ella; suyo

herself [hʌr'self] *pron pers* ella misma; sí, sí misma; se, p.ej., **she enjoyed herself** se divirtió; **with herself** consigo

hesitan·cy ['hezɪtənsɪ] *s* (*pl* **-cies**) vacilación

hesitant ['hezɪtənt] *adj* vacilante

hesitate ['hɛzɪ,tet] *intr* vacilar, titubear; (*to stutter*) titubear
hesitation [,hɛzɪ'teʃən] *s* vacilación
heterodox ['hɛtərə,dɑks] *adj* heterodoxo
heterodyne ['hɛtərə,daɪn] *adj* heterodino || *tr* heterodinar
heterogenei·ty [,hɛtərədʒɪ'ni·ɪti] *s* (*pl* -ties) heterogeneidad
heterogeneous [,hɛtərə'dʒɪnɪ·əs] *adj* heterogéneo
hew [hju] *v* (*pret* hewed; *pp* hewed o hewn) *tr* cortar, tajar; (*with an ax*) hachear; labrar (*madera*); picar (*piedra*); **to hew down** derribar a hachazos || *intr* — **to hew close to the line** (coll) hilar delgado
hex [hɛks] *s* (coll) bruja; (coll) hechizo || *tr* (coll) embrujar
hexameter [hɛks'æmɪtər] *s* hexámetro
hey [he] *interj* ¡oye!, ¡oiga!
hey'day' *s* época de mayor prosperidad
hf. *abbr* half
H.H. *abbr* His Highness, Her Highness; His Holiness
hia·tus [haɪ'etəs] *s* (*pl* -tuses o -tus) (*gap*) abertura, laguna; (*in a text; in verse*) hiato
hibernate ['haɪbər,net] *intr* invernar; estar inactivo
hibiscus [hɪ'bɪskəs] o [haɪ'bɪskəs] *s* hibisco
hiccough o **hiccup** ['hɪkəp] *s* hipo || *intr* hipar
hick [hɪk] *adj* & *s* (coll) campesino, palurdo
hicko·ry ['hɪkəri] *s* (*pl* -ries) nuez encarcelada, nuez dura (*árbol*)
hickory nut *s* nuez encarcelada, nuez dura (*fruto*)
hidden ['hɪdən] *adj* escondido, oculto; obscuro
hide [haɪd] *s* cuero, piel *f*; hides corambre *f*; **neither hide nor hair** ni un vestigio; **to tan someone's hide** (coll) zurrarle a uno la badana || *v* (*pret* hid [hɪd]; *pp* hid o hidden ['hɪdən]) *tr* esconder, ocultar || *intr* esconderse, ocultarse; **to hide out** (coll) recatarse
hide'-and-seek' *s* escondite *m*; **to play hide-and-seek** jugar al escondite
hide'bound' *adj* fanático, obstinado, dogmático
hideous ['hɪdɪ·əs] *adj* (*very ugly*) feote; (*heinous*) atroz, nefando; (*distressingly large*) brutal, enorme
hide'-out' *s* (coll) guarida, refugio, escondrijo
hiding ['haɪdɪŋ] *s* ocultación; (*place of concealment*) escondite *m*, escondrijo; **in hiding** escondido, oculto; (*in ambush*) emboscado
hiding place *s* escondite *m*, escondrijo
hie [haɪ] *v* (*pret* & *pp* hied; *ger* hieing o hying) *tr* — **hie thee home** apresúrate a volver a casa || *intr* apresurarse, ir volando
hierar·chy ['haɪə,rɑrkɪ] *s* (*pl* -chies) jerarquía
hieroglyphic [,haɪərə'glɪfɪk] *adj* & *s* jeroglífico

hi-fi ['haɪ'faɪ] *adj* (coll) de alta fidelidad || *s* (coll) alta fidelidad
hi-fi fan *s* (coll) aficionado a la alta fidelidad
higgledy-piggledy ['hɪgəldɪ'pɪgəldɪ] *adj* confuso, revuelto || *adv* confusamente, revueltamente
high [haɪ] *adj* alto; (*river*) crecido; (*sound*) agudo; (*wind*) fuerte; (coll) borracho; (culin) manido; **high and dry** abandonado, desamparado; **high and mighty** (coll) muy arrogante || *adv* en sumo grado; a gran precio; **to aim high** poner el tiro muy alto; **to come high** venderse caro || *s* (aut) marcha directa; **on high** en el cielo
high altar *s* altar *m* mayor
high'ball' *s* highball *m*
high blood pressure *s* hipertensión arterial
high'born' *adj* linajudo, de ilustre cuna
high'boy' *s* cómoda alta con patas altas
high'brow' *adj* & *s* (slang) erudito
high chair *s* silla alta
high command *s* alto mando
high cost of living *s* carestía de la vida
higher education *s* enseñanza superior
higher-up [,haɪ·ər'ʌp] *s* (coll) superior jerárquico
high explosive *s* explosivo rompedor
highfalutin [,haɪfə'lutən] *adj* (coll) pomposo, presuntuoso
high fidelity *s* alta fidelidad
high'-fre'quency *adj* de alta frecuencia
high gear *s* marcha directa, toma directa
high'-grade' *adj* de calidad superior
high-handed ['haɪ'hændɪd] *adj* arbitrario
high hat *s* sombrero de copa
high'-hat' *adj* (coll) copetudo, esnob; **to be high-hat** (coll) tener mucho copete || **high'-hat'** *v* (*pret* & *pp* -hatted; *ger* -hatting) *tr* (coll) desairar
high-heeled shoe ['haɪ,hild] *s* zapato de tacón alto
high horse *s* ademán *m* arrogante
high'jack' *tr* var de hijack
high jinks [dʒɪŋks] *s* (slang) jarana, payasada
high jump *s* salto de altura
highland ['haɪlənd] *s* región montañosa; **highlands** montañas, tierras altas
high life *s* alta sociedad, gran mundo
high'light' *s* elemento sobresaliente || *tr* destacar
highly ['haɪlɪ] *adv* altamente; en sumo grado; a gran precio; con aplauso general; **to speak highly of** decir mil bienes de
High Mass *s* misa cantada, misa mayor
high-minded ['haɪ'maɪndɪd] *adj* noble, magnánimo
highness ['haɪnɪs] *s* altura || **Highness** *s* Alteza
high noon *s* pleno mediodía
high-pitched ['haɪ'pɪtʃt] *adj* agudo; tenso, impresionable
high-powered ['haɪ'pau·ərd] *adj* de alta potencia
high'-pres'sure *adj* de alta presión;

(fig) emprendedor, enérgico ‖ *tr* (coll) apremiar

high-priced ['haɪ'praɪst] *adj* de precio elevado

high priest *s* sumo sacerdote

high rise *s* edificio de muchos pisos

high'road' *s* camino real

high school *s* escuela de segunda enseñanza

high sea *s* mar gruesa; **high seas** alta mar

high society *s* alta sociedad, gran mundo

high'-speed' *adj* de alta velocidad

high-spirited ['haɪ'spɪrɪtɪd] *adj* animoso; vivaz; (*horse*) fogoso

high spirits *spl* alegría, buen humor *m*, animación

high-strung ['haɪ'strʌŋ] *adj* tenso, impresionable

high'-test' fuel *s* supercarburante *m*

high tide *s* pleamar *f*, marea alta; (fig) punto culminante

high time *s* hora, p.ej., **it is high time for you to go** ya es hora de que Vd. se marche; (slang) jarana, parranda

high treason *s* alta traición

high water *s* aguas altas; pleamar *f*, marea alta

high'way' *s* carretera

highway-man ['haɪ‚wemən] *s* (*pl* **-men** [mən]) salteador *m* de caminos

hijack ['haɪ‚dʒæk] *tr* (coll) robar (*a un contrabandista de licores*); (coll) robar (*el licor a un contrabandista*)

hike [haɪk] *s* caminata, marcha; (*increase, rise*) aumento ‖ *tr* elevar de un tirón; aumentar ‖ *intr* dar una caminata

hiker ['haɪkər] *s* caminador *m*, aficionado a las caminatas

hilarious [hɪ'lerɪ‚əs] o [haɪ'lerɪ‚əs] *adj* jubiloso, regocijado

hill [hɪl] *s* colina, collado ‖ *tr* aporcar (*las hortalizas*)

hillbill-ly ['hɪl‚bɪlɪ] *s* (*pl* **-lies**) (coll) rústico montañés (*del sur de los EE.UU.*)

hillock ['hɪlək] *s* altozano, montecillo

hill'side' *s* ladera

hill'top' *s* cumbre *f*, cima

hill·y ['hɪlɪ] *adj* (*comp* **-ier;** *super* **-iest**) colinoso; (*steep*) empinado

hilt [hɪlt] *s* empuñadura, puño; **up to the hilt** completamente

him [hɪm] *pron pers* le, lo; él; **to him** le; a él

himself [hɪm'self] *pron pers* él mismo; sí, sí mismo; se, p.ej., **he enjoyed himself** se divirtió; **with himself** consigo

hind [haɪnd] *adj* posterior, trasero ‖ *s* cierva

hinder ['hɪndər] *tr* estorbar, impedir

hindmost ['haɪnd‚most] *adj* postrero, último

Hindoo ['hɪndu] *adj* & *s* hindú *m*

hind'quar'ter *s* cuarto trasero

hindrance ['hɪndrəns] *s* estorbo, impedimento, obstáculo

hind'sight' *s* (*of a firearm*) mira posterior; percepción tardía, sabiduría tardía

Hindu ['hɪndu] *adj* & *s* hindú *m*

hinge [hɪndʒ] *s* (*of a door*) charnela, gozne *m*, bisagra; (*of a mollusk*) charnela; (bb) cartivana; punto capital ‖ *tr* engoznar ‖ *intr* — **to hinge on** depender de

hin·ny ['hɪnɪ] *s* (*pl* **-nies**) burdégano, mohino

hint [hɪnt] *s* indirecta, insinuación; **to take the hint** darse por aludido ‖ *tr* & *intr* insinuar; indicar; **to hint at** aludir indirectamente a

hinterland ['hɪntər‚lænd] *s* región interior

hip [hɪp] *s* cadera; (*of a roof*) caballete *m*, lima

hip'bone' *s* cía, hueso de la cadera

hipped [hɪpt] *adj* (*livestock*) renco; (*roof*) a cuatro aguas; **hipped on** (coll) obsesionado por

hippety-hop ['hɪpɪtɪ'hɑp] *adv* (coll) a coxcojita

hip·po ['hɪpo] *s* (*pl* **-pos**) (coll) hipopótamo

hippodrome ['hɪpə‚drom] *s* hipódromo

hippopota·mus [‚hɪpə'pɑtəməs] *s* (*pl* **-muses** o **-mi** [‚maɪ]) hipopótamo

hip roof *s* tejado a cuatro aguas

hire [haɪr] *s* alquiler *m*; precio; salario; **for hire** de alquiler ‖ *tr* alquilar (*p.ej., un coche*); ajustar (*p.ej., a un criado*) ‖ *intr* — **to hire out** ajustarse

hired girl *s* criada

hired man *s* (coll) mozo de campo

hireling ['haɪrlɪŋ] *adj* & *s* alquiladizo

his [hɪz] *adj poss* su; el . . . de él ‖ *pron poss* el suyo, el de él; suyo

Hispanic [hɪs'pænɪk] *adj* hispánico

Hispaniola [‚hɪspən'jolə] *s* Santo Domingo

hispanist ['hɪspənɪst] *s* hispanista *mf*

hiss [hɪs] *s* siseo, silbido ‖ *tr* sisear, silbar (*p.ej., una escena, a un actor por malo*) ‖ *intr* sisear, silbar

hist. *abbr* **historian, history**

histology [hɪs'tɑlədʒɪ] *s* histología

historian [hɪs'torɪ‚ən] *s* historiador *m*

historic(al) [hɪs'tɑrɪk(əl)] o [hɪs'tɔrɪk(əl)] *adj* histórico

histo·ry ['hɪstərɪ] *s* (*pl* **-ries**) historia

histrionic [‚hɪstrɪ'ɑnɪk] *adj* histriónico; teatral ‖ **histrionics** *s* actitud teatral, modales *mpl* teatrales

hit [hɪt] *s* golpe *m*; (*of a bullet*) impacto; (*blow that hits its mark*) tiro certero; (*sarcastic remark*) censura acerba; (*baseball*) batazo; (coll) éxito; **to make a hit** (coll) dar golpe; **to make a hit with** caer en la gracia de (*una persona*) ‖ *v* (*pret* & *pp* **hit;** *ger* **hitting**) *tr* golpear, pegar; dar con, dar contra, chocar con; dar en (*p.ej., el blanco*); censurar acerbamente; (*to run over in a car*) atropellar; afectar mucho (*un acontecimiento a una persona*) ‖ *intr* chocar; **to hit against** dar contra; **to hit on** dar con (*lo que se busca*)

hit'-and-run' *adj* que atropella y se da a la huída

hitch [hɪtʃ] *s* (*jerk*) tirón *m*; dificultad; obstáculo; **without a hitch** a pedir de boca, sin tropiezo || *tr* (*to tie*) atar, sujetar; enganchar (*un caballo*); uncir (*bueyes*); (slang) casar

hitch'hike' *intr* (coll) hacer autostop, viajar en autostop

hitch'hik'er *s* autostopista *mf*

hitching post *s* poste *m* para atar a las cabalgaduras

hither ['hɪðər] *adv* acá, hacia acá; **hither and thither** acá y allá

hith'er·to' *adv* hasta ahora, hasta aquí

hit'-or-miss' *adj* descuidado, casual

hit parade *s* (rad) canciones que gozan de más popularidad en la actualidad

hit record *s* (coll) disco de mucho éxito

hit'-run' *adj* que atropella y se da a la huída

hive [haɪv] *s* (*box for bees*) colmena; (*swarm*) enjambre *m*; **hives** urticaria || *tr* encorchar (*abejas*)

H.M. *abbr* **Her Majesty, His Majesty**

H.M.S. *abbr* **Her Majesty's Ship, His Majesty's Ship**

hoard [hord] *s* (*of money, provisions, etc.*) cúmulo; tesoro escondido || *tr* acumular secretamente; atesorar (*dinero*) || *intr* guardar víveres; atesorar dinero

hoarding ['hordɪŋ] *s* acumulación secreta; atesoramiento

hoar'frost' *s* helada blanca, escarcha

hoarse [hors] *adj* ronco

hoarseness ['horsnɪs] *s* ronquedad; (*from a cold*) ronquera

hoar·y ['hori] *adj* (*comp* -ler; *super* -iest) cano, canoso; (*old*) vetusto

hoax [hoks] *s* pajarota, mistificación || *tr* mistificar

hob [hab] *s* repisa interior del hogar; **to play hob with** (coll) trastornar

hobble ['habəl] *s* (*limp*) cojera; (*rope used to tie legs of animal*) manea, traba || *tr* dejar cojo; manear, trabar; dificultar || *intr* cojear; tambalear

hobble skirt *s* falda de medio paso

hob·by ['habi] *s* (*pl* -bies) comidilla, afición favorita, trabajo preferido; **to ride a hobby** entregarse demasiado al tema favorito

hob'by·horse' *s* (*stick with horse's head*) caballito; (*rocking horse*) caballo mecedor

hob'gob'lin *s* duende *m*, trasgo; (*bogy*) bu *m*, coco

hob'nail' *s* tachuela || *tr* clavetear con tachuelas; (fig) atropellar

hob·nob ['hab,nab] *v* (*pret & pp* -nobbed; *ger* -nobbing) *intr* codearse, rozarse; beber juntos

ho·bo ['hobo] *s* (*pl* -bos o -boes) vagabundo

Hobson's choice ['habsənz] *s* alternativa entre la cosa ofrecida o ninguna

hock [hak] *s* jarrete *m*, corvejón *m* || *tr* (*to hamstring*) desjarretar; (coll) empeñar

hockey ['haki] *s* hockey *m*, chueca

hock'shop' *s* (slang) casa de empeños, monte *m* de piedad

hocus-pocus ['hokəs'pokəs] *s* (*mean-ingless formula*) abracadabra *m;* burla, engaño; juego de manos

hod [had] *s* capacho, cuezo; cubo para carbón

hod carrier *s* peón *m* de albañil, peón de mano

hodgepodge ['hadʒ,padʒ] *s* baturrillo

hoe [ho] *s* azada, azadón *m* || *tr & intr* azadonar

hog [hag] o [hɔg] *s* cerdo, puerco || *v* (*pret & pp* **hogged;** *ger* **hogging**) *tr* (slang) tragarse lo mejor de

hog'back' *s* cuchilla

hoggish ['hagɪʃ] o ['hɔgɪʃ] *adj* comilón; glotón; egoísta

hog Latin *s* latín *m* de cocina

hogs'head' *s* pipa de 63 galones o más; medida de capacidad de 63 galones

hog'wash' *s* bazofia

hoist [hɔɪst] *s* (*apparatus for lifting*) montacargas *m*, torno izador, grúa; empujón *m* hacia arriba || *tr* alzar, levantar; enarbolar (*p.ej., una bandera*); (naut) izar

hoity-toity ['hɔɪti'tɔɪti] *adj* frívolo, veleidoso; arrogante, altanero; **to be hoity-toity** ponerse tan alto

hokum ['hokəm] *s* (coll) música celestial, tonterías

hold [hold] *s* (*grip*) agarro; (*handle*) asa, mango; autoridad, dominio; (*in wrestling*) presa; (aer) cabina de carga; (mus) calderón *m*; (naut) bodega; **to take hold of** agarrar, coger; apoderarse de || *v* (*pret & pp* **held** [held]) *tr* tener, retener; (*to hold up, support*) apoyar, sostener; (*e.g., with a pin*) sujetar; contener, tener cabida para; ocupar (*un cargo, puesto, etc.*); celebrar (*una reunión*); sostener (*una opinión*); (mus) sostener (*una nota*); **to hold back** detener; retener; contener; **to hold in** refrenar; **to hold one's own** mantenerse firme, no perder terreno; **to hold over** aplazar, diferir; **to hold up** apoyar, sostener; (*to rob*) (coll) atracar || *intr* ser valedero, seguir vigente; pegarse; **hold on!** ¡un momento!; **to hold back** refrenarse; **to hold forth** poner cátedra; **to hold off** esperar; mantenerse a distancia; **to hold on** agarrarse bien; **to hold on** to asirse de; **to hold out** no cejar; ir tirando; **to hold out for** insistir en

holder ['holdər] *s* tenedor *m*, posesor *m;* (*for a cigar or cigaret*) boquilla; (*to hold, e.g., a hot plate*) cojinillo; (*e.g., of a passport*) titular *m;* asa, mango

holding ['holdɪŋ] *s* tenencia, posesión; **holdings** valores habidos

holding company *s* sociedad de control, compañía tenedora

hold'up' *s* (*stop, delay*) detención; (coll) atraco, asalto; (coll) precio excesivo

holdup man *s* (coll) atracador *m*, salteador *m*

hole [hol] *s* agujero; (*in cheese, bread, etc.*) ojo; (*in a road*) bache *m;* (*den of animals; den of vice*) guarida; (*dirty, disorderly dwelling*) cochitril *m;* **in the hole** adeudado, perdidoso; **to burn a hole in one's pocket** írsele a uno (*el dinero*) de entre las manos; **to pick holes in** (coll) poner reparos a || *intr* — **to hole up** encovarse; buscar un rincón cómodo

holiday ['halɪ‚de] *s* día festivo; vacación

holiday attire *s* trapos de cristianar

holiness ['holɪnɪs] *s* santidad; **his Holiness** su Santidad

Holland ['halənd] *s* Holanda

Hollander ['haləndər] *s* holandés *m*

hollow ['halo] *adj* hueco; (*voice*) ahuecado, sepulcral; (*eyes, cheeks*) hundido; falso, engañoso || *adv* — **to beat all hollow** (coll) derrotar completamente || *s* hueco, cavidad; (*small valley*) vallecito || *tr* ahuecar, excavar

hol·ly ['halɪ] *s* (*pl* **-lies**) acebo

hol'ly·hock' *s* malva arbórea

holm oak [hom] *s* encina

holocaust ['halə‚kɔst] *s* holocausto

holster ['holstər] *s* pistolera

ho·ly ['holɪ] *adj* (*comp* **-lier**; *super* **-liest**) santo; (*e.g., writing*) sagrado; (*e.g., water*) bendito

Holy Ghost *s* Espíritu Santo

holy orders *spl* órdenes sagradas; **to take holy orders** recibir las órdenes sagradas, ordenarse

holy rood [rud] *s* crucifijo || **Holy Rood** *s* Santa Cruz

Holy Scripture *s* Sagrada Escritura

Holy See *s* Santa Sede

Holy Sepulcher *s* santo sepulcro

holy water *s* agua bendita

Holy Writ *s* Sagrada Escritura

homage ['hamɪdʒ] *o* ['amɪdʒ] *s* homenaje *m;* (*feud*) homenaje, pleito homenaje

home [hom] *adj* casero, doméstico; nacional || *s* casa, domicilio, hogar *m;* (*native heath*) patria chica; (*of the arts, etc.*) patria; (*for the sick, poor, etc.*) asilo; (*sport*) meta; **at home** en casa; en su propio país; (*ready to receive callers*) de recibo; (*at ease, comfortable*) a gusto; (*sport*) en campo propio; **away from home** fuera de casa; **make yourself at home** está Vd. en su casa || *adv* en casa; a casa; **to see home** acompañar a casa; **to strike home** dar en lo vivo

home'bod'y *s* (*pl* **-ies**) hogareño

homebred ['hom‚bred] *adj* doméstico; sencillo, inculto, tosco

home'-brew' *s* cerveza o vino caseros

home-coming ['hom‚kʌmɪŋ] *s* regreso al hogar

home country *s* suelo natal

home delivery *s* distribución a domicilio

home front *s* frente doméstico

home'land' *s* tierra natal, patria

homeless ['homlɪs] *adj* sin casa, sin hogar

home life *s* vida de familia

home-loving ['hom‚lʌvɪŋ] *adj* casero, hogareño

home·ly ['homlɪ] *adj* (*comp* **-lier**; *su-*

per **-liest**) (*not attractive or good-looking*) feo; (*plain, not elegant*) sencillo, llano

homemade ['hom'med] *adj* casero, hecho en casa

homemaker ['hom‚mekər] *s* ama de casa

home office *s* domicilio social, oficina central || **Home Office** *s* (Brit) ministerio de la Gobernación

homeopath ['homɪ·ə‚pæθ] *o* ['hamɪ·ə‚pæθ] *s* homeópata *mf*

homeopathy [‚homɪ'apəθɪ] *o* [‚hamɪ'apəθɪ] *s* homeopatía

home plate *s* (baseball) puesto meta

home port *s* puerto de origen

home rule *s* autonomía, gobierno autónomo

home run *s* (baseball) jonrón *m,* cuadrangular *m*

home'sick' *adj* nostálgico; **to be homesick (for)** sentir nostalgia (de)

home'sick'ness *s* nostalgia, mal *m* de la tierra

homespun ['hom‚spʌn] *adj* hilado en casa; sencillo, llano

home'stead' *s* casa y terrenos, heredad

home stretch *s* esfuerzo final, último trecho

home town *s* ciudad natal

homeward ['homwərd] *adj* de regreso || *adv* hacia casa; hacia su país

home'work' *s* trabajo a domicilio; (*of a student*) deber *m,* trabajo escolar

homey ['homɪ] *adj* (*comp* **homier**; *super* **homiest**) (coll) íntimo, cómodo

homicidal [‚hamɪ'saɪdəl] *adj* homicida

homicide ['hamɪ‚saɪd] *s* (*act*) homicidio; (*person*) homicida *mf*

homi·ly ['hamɪlɪ] *s* (*pl* **-lies**) homilía

homing ['homɪŋ] *adj* (*animal*) querencioso; (*weapon*) buscador del blanco

homing pigeon *s* paloma mensajera

hominy ['hamɪnɪ] *s* maíz molido

homogenei·ty [‚homədʒɪ'ni·ɪtɪ] *o* [‚hamədʒɪ'ni·ɪtɪ] *s* (*pl* **-ties**) homogeneidad

homogeneous [‚homə'dʒɪnɪ·əs] *o* [‚hamə'dʒɪnɪ·əs] *adj* homogéneo

homogenize [hə'madʒə‚naɪz] *tr* homogeneizar

homonym ['hamənɪm] *s* homónimo

homonymous [hə'manɪməs] *adj* homónimo

homosexual [‚homə'sɛkʃu·əl] *adj & s* homosexual *mf*

hon. *abbr* **honorary**

Hon. *abbr* **Honorable**

Honduran [han'durən] *adj & s* hondureño

hone [hon] *s* piedra de afilar || *tr* afilar, aguzar, asentar

honest ['anɪst] *adj* honrado, probo, recto; (*money*) bien adquirido; sincero; genuino

honesty ['anɪstɪ] *s* honradez *f,* probidad, rectitud; (bot) hierba de la plata

hon·ey ['hʌnɪ] *adj* meloso, dulce; (coll) querido || *s* miel *f;* (coll) vida mía; **it's a honey** (slang) es una preciosidad || *v* (*pret & pp* **-eyed** *o* **-ied**) *tr* enmelar, endulzar con miel; adular, lisonjear

hon'ey·bee' *s* abeja doméstica, abeja de miel

hon'ey·comb' *s* panal *m* ‖ *tr* (*to riddle*) acribillar; llenar, penetrar

hon'ey·dew' *melon s* melón muy dulce, blanco y terso

honeyed ['hʌnɪd] *adj* dulce, enmelado; melodioso; adulador

honey locust *s* acacia de tres espinas

hon'ey·moon' *s* luna de miel; viaje *m* de bodas ‖ *intr* pasar la luna de miel

honeysuckle ['hʌnɪ,sʌkəl] *s* madreselva

honk [haŋk] o [hɔŋk] *s* (*of wild goose*) graznido; (*of automobile horn*) bocinazo ‖ *tr* tocar (*la bocina*) ‖ *intr* graznar (*el ganso silvestre*); tocar la bocina

honkytonk ['haŋkɪ,taŋk] o ['hɔŋkɪ,tɔŋk] *s* (*slang*) sala de fiestas de mala muerte

honor ['anər] *s* (*distinction; award for distinction; integrity*) honor *m*; (*good reputation; chastity*) honor, honra ‖ *tr* honrar; hacer honor a (*su firma*); aceptar y pagar (*una letra*)

honorable ['anərəbəl] *adj* (*behaving with honor; performed with honor*) honrado; (*bringing honor; associated with honor*) honroso; (*worthy, of honor*) honorable

honorary ['anə,rerɪ] *adj* honorario

honorific [,anə'rɪfɪk] *adj* honorífico ‖ *s* antenombre *m*

honor system *s* acatamiento voluntario del reglamento

hood [hʊd] *s* capilla; (*one with a point*) caperuza; (*one which covers the face*) capirote *m*; (*worn with academic gown*) muceta, capirote *m*; (*of a chimney*) sombrerete *m*; (*aut*) capó *m*, cubierta; (*slang*) gambero ‖ *tr* encapirotar; ocultar

hoodlum ['hudləm] *s* (*coll*) gambero, maleante *m*

hoodoo ['hudu] *s* (*body of primitive rites*) vudú *m*; (*coll*) mala suerte ‖ *tr* traer mala suerte a

hood'wink' *tr* burlar, engañar, vendar

hooey ['hu·i] *s* (*slang*) música celestial

hoof [huf] o [hʊf] *s* casco, pezuña; **on the hoof** (*cattle*) vivo, en pie ‖ *tr & intr* (*coll*) caminar; **to hoof it** (*coll*) caminar, ir a pie; (*coll*) bailar

hoof'beat' *s* pisada, ruido de la pisada (*de animal ungulado*)

hook [hʊk] *s* gancho; (*for fishing*) anzuelo; (*to join two things*) enganche *m*; (*bend, curve*) ángulo, recodo; (*box*) crochet *m*, golpe *m* de gancho; (*of hook and eye*) corchete *m*, macho; **by hook or by crook** por fas o por nefas; **to swallow the hook** tragar el anzuelo ‖ *tr* enganchar; (*to bend*) encorvar, doblar; coger, pescar (*un pez*); (*to wound with the horns*) acornar ‖ *intr* engancharse; encorvarse, doblarse

hookah ['hukə] *s* narguile *m*

hook and eye *s* broche *m*, corchete *m* (*macho y hembra*)

hook and ladder *s* carro de escaleras de incendio

hooked rug *s* tapete *m* de crochet

hook'nose' *s* nariz *f* de pico de loro

hook'up' *s* montaje *m*

hook'worm' *s* anquilostoma *m*

hooky ['hukɪ] *s* — **to play hooky** hacer novillos

hooligan ['hulɪgən] *s* gamberro

hooliganism ['hulɪgən,ɪzəm] *s* gamberrismo

hoop [hup] o [hʊp] *s* aro ‖ *tr* herrar, enarcar, enzunchar

hoop skirt *s* miriñaque *m*

hoot [hut] *s* resoplido, ululato; grito ‖ *tr* reprobar a gritos; echar a gritos (*p.ej., a un cómico*) ‖ *intr* resoplar, ulular; **to hoot at** dar grita a

hoot owl *s* autillo, cárabo

hop [hap] *s* saltito; (*coll*) vuelo en avión; (*coll*) sarao; (*coll*) baile *m*; lúpulo, hombrecillo; **hops** (*dried flowers of hop vine*) lúpulo ‖ *v* (*pret & pp* **hopped**; *ger* **hopping**) *tr* cruzar de un salto; (*coll*) atravesar (*p.ej., el mar*) en avión; (*coll*) subir a (*un tren, taxi, etc.*) ‖ *intr* saltar, brincar; (*on one foot*) saltar a la pata coja

hope [hop] *s* esperanza ‖ *tr & intr* esperar; **to hope for** esperar

hope chest *s* ajuar *m* de novia

hopeful ['hopfəl] *adj* (*feeling hope*) esperanzado; (*giving hope*) esperanzador

hopeless ['hoplɪs] *adj* desesperanzado; (*situation*) desesperado

hopper ['hapər] *s* (*funnel-shaped container*) tolva; (*of blast furnace*) tragante *m*

hopper car *s* (rr) vagón *m* tolva

hop'scotch' *s* infernáculo

horde [hord] *s* horda

horehound ['hor,haʊnd] *s* marrubio; extracto de marrubio

horizon [hə'raɪzən] *s* horizonte *m*

horizontal [,harɪ'zantəl] o [,hɔrɪ'zantəl] *adj & s* horizontal *f*

hormone ['hɔrmon] *s* hormón *m* u hormona

horn [hɔrn] *s* (*bony projection on head of certain animals*) cuerno; (*of bull*) asta, cuerno; (*of moon, anvil, etc.*) cuerno; (*of automobile*) bocina; (*mus*) cuerno; (*French horn*) (*mus*) trompa de armonía; **to blow one's own horn** cantar sus propias alabanzas; **to pull in one's horns** contenerse, volverse atrás ‖ *intr* — **to horn in** (*slang*) entrometerse (en)

hornet ['hɔrnɪt] *s* crabrón *m*, avispón *m*

hornet's nest *s* panal *m* del avispón; **to stir up a hornet's nest** (*coll*) armar camorra, armar cisco

horn of plenty *s* cuerno de la abundancia

horn'pipe' *s* chirimía

horn-rimmed glasses ['hɔrn'rɪmd] *spl* anteojos de concha

horn·y ['hɔrnɪ] *adj* (*comp* **-ier;** *super*

-**iest**) córneo; (*callous*) calloso; (*having hornlike projections*) cornudo

horoscope ['harə,skop] o ['hɔrə,skɔp] s horóscopo; **to cast a horoscope** sacar un horóscopo

horrible ['harɪbəl] o ['hɔrɪbəl] *adj* horrible; (coll) muy desagradable

horrid ['harɪd] o ['hɔrɪd] *adj* horroroso; (coll) muy desagradable

horri-fy ['harɪ,faɪ] o ['hɔrɪ,faɪ] *v* (*pret & pp* -**fied**) *tr* horrorizar

horror ['harər] o ['hɔrər] s horror *m*; **to have a horror of** tener horror a

hors d'oeuvre [ɔr 'dʌrv] s (*pl* **hors d'oeuvres** [ɔr 'dʌrvz]) s entremés *m*

horse [hɔrs] s caballo; (*of carpenter*) caballete *m*; **hold your horses** (coll) pare Vd. el carro; **to back the wrong horse** (coll) jugar a la carta mala; **to be a horse of another color** (coll) ser harina de otro costal

horse'back' s — **on horseback** o a caballo ‖ *adv* — **to ride horseback** montar a caballo

horse blanket s manta para caballo

horse block s montadero

horse'break'er s domador *m* de caballos

horse'car' s tranvía *m* de sangre

horse chestnut s (*tree*) castaño de Indias; (*nut*) castaña de Indias

horse collar s collera

horse dealer s chalán *m*

horse doctor s veterinario

horse'fly' s (*pl* -**flies**) mosca borriquera, tábano

horse'hair' s crines *fpl* de caballo; (*fabric*) tela de crin

horse'hide' s cuero de caballo

horse laugh s risotada

horse-man ['hɔrsmən] s (*pl* -**men** [mən]) jinete *m*, caballista *m*

horsemanship ['hɔrsmən,ʃɪp] s equitación, manejo

horse meat s carne *f* de caballo

horse opera s (U.S.A.) melodrama *m* del Oeste

horse pistol s pistola de arzón

horse'play' s chanza pesada, payasada

horse'pow'er s caballo de vapor inglés

horse race s carrera de caballos

horse'rad'ish s (*plant*) rábano picante o rusticano; (*condiment*) mostaza de los alemanes

horse sense s (coll) sentido común

horse'shoe' s herradura

horseshoe magnet s imán *m* de herradura

horseshoe nail s clavo de herrar

horse show s concurso hípico

horse'tail' s cola de caballo

horse thief s abigeo, cuatrero

horse'-trade' *intr* chalanear

horse trading s chalanería

horse'-trad'ing *adj* chalanesco

horse'whip' s látigo ‖ *v* (*pret & pp* -**whipped**; *ger* -**whipping**) *tr* dar latigazos a

horse-woman ['hɔrs,wumən] s (*pl* -**women** [,wɪmɪn]) amazona, caballista *f*

hors-y ['hɔrsi] *adj* (*comp* -**ier**; *super* -**iest**) caballar, hípico; (*interested in horses and horse racing*) carrerista, turfista; (coll) desmañado

horticultural [,hɔrtɪ'kʌltərəl] *adj* hortícola

horticulture ['hɔrtɪ,kʌltʃər] s horticultura

horticulturist [,hɔrtɪ'kʌltʃərɪst] s horticultor *m*

hose [hoz] s (*stocking*) media; (*sock*) calcetín *m*; (*flexible tube*) manguera ‖ **hose** *spl* calzas

hosier ['hoʒər] s mediero, calcetero

hosiery ['hoʒəri] s calcetas; calcetería

hospice ['haspɪs] s hospicio

hospitable ['haspɪtəbəl] o [has'pɪtəbəl] *adj* hospitalario

hospital ['haspɪtəl] s hospital *m*

hospitali-ty [,haspɪ'tælɪti] s (*pl* -**ties**) hospitalidad

hospitalize ['haspɪtə,laɪz] *tr* hospitalizar

host [host] s anfitrión *m*; (*at an inn*) huésped *m*, mesonero; (*army*) hueste *f*; multitud, sinnúmero ‖ **Host** s (eccl) hostia

hostage ['hastɪdʒ] s rehén *m*; **to be held a hostage** quedar en rehenes

hostel-ry ['hastəlri] s (*pl* -**ries**) parador *m*, hostería

hostess ['hostɪs] s anfitriona; dueña, patrona; (*in a night club*) tanguista; (ñer) azafata, aeromoza; (*e.g., on a bus*) jefa de ruta

hostile ['hastɪl] *adj* hostil

hostili-ty [has'tɪlɪti] s (*pl* -**ties**) hostilidad

hostler ['haslər] o ['aslər] s mozo de cuadra, mozo de paja y cebada

hot [hat] *adj* (*comp* **hotter**; *super* **hottest**) (*water, air, coffee, etc.*) caliente; (*climate, country, taste*) cálido; (*fiery, excitable*) caluroso; (*pursuit*) enérgico; (*in rut*) caliente; (coll) muy radiactivo; **to be hot** (*said of a person*) tener calor; (*said of the weather*) hacer calor; **to make it hot for** (coll) hostilizar

hot air s (slang) palabrería, música celestial

hot'-air' furnace s calorífero de aire

hot and cold running water s circulación de agua fría y caliente

hot baths *spl* caldas, termas

hot'bed' s (hort) almajara; (*e.g., of vice*) sementera, semillero

hot-blooded ['hat'blʌdɪd] *adj* apasionado; temerario, irreflexivo

hot cake s torta a la plancha; **to sell like hot cakes** (coll) venderse como pan bendito

hot dog s (slang) perro caliente

hotel [ho'tɛl] *adj* hotelero ‖ s hotel *m*

ho-tel'-keep'er s hotelero

hot'head' s botafuego

hot-headed ['hat'hɛdɪd] *adj* caliente de cascos

hot'house' s estufa, invernáculo

hot plate s hornillo, calientaplatos *m*

hot springs *spl* fuentes *fpl* termales

hot-tempered ['hɑt'tempərd] *adj* irascible

hot water *s* — **to be in hot water** (coll) estar en calzas prietas

hot'-wa'ter boiler *s* termosifón *m*

hot-water bottle *s* bolsa de agua caliente

hot-water heater *s* calentador *m* de acumulación

hot-water heating *s* calefacción por agua caliente

hot-water tank *s* depósito de agua caliente

hound [haund] *s* podenco, perro de caza; **to follow the hounds** o **to ride to hounds** cazar a caballo con jauría || *tr* acosar, hostigar

hour [aur] *s* hora; **by the hour** por horas; **in an evil hour** en hora mala; **on the hour** a la hora en punto cada hora; **to keep late hours** acostarse tarde; **to work long hours** trabajar muchas horas cada día

hour'glass' *s* reloj *m* de arena

hour hand *s* horario

hourly ['aurlɪ] *adj* de cada hora; por hora || *adv* cada hora; muy a menudo

house [haus] *s* (*pl* **houses** ['hauzɪz]) casa; (*legislative body*) cámara; teatro; (*size of audience*) entrada, p.ej., **a good house** mucha entrada; **to keep house** tener casa puesta; hacer los quehaceres domésticos; **to put one's house in order** arreglar sus asuntos || [hauz] *tr* domiciliar, alojar, hospedar

house arrest *s* arresto domiciliario

house'boat' *s* barco vivienda

house'break'er *s* escalador *m*

housebreaking ['haus,brekɪŋ] *s* escalo, allanamiento de morada

housebroken ['haus,brokən] *adj* (*perro* o *gato*) enseñado (*a hábitos de limpieza*)

house cleaning *s* limpieza de la casa

house coat *s* bata

house current *s* sector *m* de distribución, canalización de consumo

house'fly' *s* (*pl* **-flies**) mosca doméstica

houseful ['haus,ful] *s* casa llena

house'fur'nishings *spl* menaje *m*, enseres domésticos

house'hold' *adj* casero, doméstico || *s* casa, familia

house'hold'er *s* dueño de la casa; jefe *m* de familia

house'-hunt' *intr* — **to go house-hunting** ir a buscar casa

house'keep'er *s* ama de llaves, mujer *f* de gobierno

house'keep'ing *s* manejo doméstico, gobierno doméstico; **to set up housekeeping** poner casa

housekeeping apartment *s* apartamento con cocina

house'maid' *s* criada de casa

house meter *s* contador *m* de abonado

house'moth'er *s* mujer encargada de una residencia de estudiantes

house of cards *s* castillo de naipes

house of ill fame *s* lupanar *m*, casa de prostitución

house painter *s* pintor *m* de brocha gorda

house physician *s* médico residente

house'top' *s* tejado; **to shout from the housetops** pregonar a los cuatro vientos

housewarming ['haus,wɔrmɪŋ] *s* fiesta para celebrar el estreno de una casa; **to have a housewarming** estrenar la casa

house'wife' *s* (*pl* **-wives**) ama de casa, madre *f* de familia

house'work' *s* quehaceres domésticos

housing ['hauzɪŋ] *s* (*of a horse*) gualdrapa; (aut) cárter *m*; (mach) caja, bastidor *m*

housing shortage *s* crisis *f* de viviendas

hovel ['hʌvəl] o ['hɑvəl] *s* casucha, choza; (*shed for cattle, tools, etc.*) cobertizo

hover ['hʌvər] o ['hɑvər] *intr* cernerse (*un ave*); (*to hesitate; to be in danger*) fluctuar; asomar (*p.ej., una sonrisa en los labios de uno*)

how [hau] *adv* cómo; (*at what price*) a cómo; **how early** cuándo, a qué hora; **how else** de qué otra manera; **how far** hasta dónde; cuánto, p.ej., **how far is it to the airport?** ¿cuánto hay de aquí al aeropuerto?; **how long** cuánto tiempo; **how many** cuántos; **how much** cuánto; lo mucho que; **how often** cuántas veces; **how old are you?** ¿cuántos años tiene Vd.?; **how soon** cuándo, a qué hora; **how** + *adj* qué + *adj*, p.ej., **how beautiful she is!** ¡qué hermosa es!; lo + *adj*, p.ej., **you know how intelligent he is** Vd. sabe lo inteligente que es; **to know how to** + *inf* saber + *inf*

howdah ['haudə] *s* castillo

how·ev'er *adv* no obstante, sin embargo; por muy . . . que, por mucho . . . que

howitzer ['hau·ɪtsər] *s* cañón *m* obús

howl [haul] *s* aullido; chillido; risa muy aguda; (*of wind*) bramido || *tr* decir a gritos; **to howl down** imponerse a gritos a (*una persona*) || *intr* aullar; chillar; reír a más no poder; bramar (*el viento*)

howler ['haulər] *s* aullador *m*; (coll) plancha, desacierto

hoyden ['hɔɪdən] *s* muchacha traviesa, tunantuela

H.P. *abbr* **horsepower**

hr. *abbr* **hour**

H.R.H. *abbr* **Her** (o **His**) **Royal Highness**

ht. *abbr* **height**

hub [hʌb] *s* cubo; (fig) centro, eje *m*

hubbub ['hʌbʌb] *s* gritería, alboroto

hub'cap' *s* tapacubo, embellecedor *m*

huckster ['hʌkstər] *s* (*peddler*) buhonero; vendedor *m* ambulante de hortalizas; vil traficante *m*, sujeto ruin

huddle ['hʌdəl] *s* (coll) reunión secreta; **to go into a huddle** (coll) conferenciar en secreto || *intr* acurrucarse, arrimarse

hue [hju] *s* matiz *m*; gritería; **hue and cry** vocería de indignación

huff [hʌf] *s* arrebato de cólera; **in a huff** encolerizado, ofendido

hug [hʌg] *s* abrazo ‖ *v* (*pret & pp* **hugged;** *ger* **hugging**) *tr* abrazar, apretar con los brazos; ahogar entre los brazos; navegar muy cerca de (*la costa*); ceñirse a (*p.ej., un muro*) ‖ *intr* abrazarse

huge [hjudʒ] *adj* enorme, descomunal

huh [hʌ] *interj* ¡eh!

hulk [hʌlk] *s* (*body of an old ship*) casco; (*clumsy old ship*) carcamán *m*, carraca; (*old ship tied up at a wharf and used as a warehouse, prison, etc.*) pontón *m*; (*shell of an old building, piece of furniture, machine, etc.; heavy, unwieldy person*) armatoste *m*

hulking [hʌlkɪŋ] *adj* grueso, pesado

hull [hʌl] *s* (*of ship or hydroplane*) casco; (*of a dirigible*) armazón *f*; (*of certain vegetables*) hollejo, vaina ‖ *tr* deshollejar, desvainar; mondar, pelar

hullabaloo [ˌhʌləbəˌlu] o [ˌhʌləbəˈlu] *s* alboroto, gritería, tumulto

hum [hʌm] *s* canturreo, tarareo; (*of a bee, machine, etc.*) zumbido ‖ *interj* ¡ejem! ‖ *v* (*pret & pp* **hummed;** *ger* **humming**) *tr* canturrear, tararear; *intr* canturrear, tararear; (*to buzz*) zumbar; (coll) estar muy activo

human [ˈhjumən] *adj* humano (*perteneciente al hombre*)

human being *s* ser humano

humane [hjuˈmen] *adj* humano (*compasivo*)

humanist [ˈhjumənɪst] *adj & s* humanista *mf*

humanitarian [hjuˌmænɪˈteri·ən] *adj & s* humanitario

humani-ty [hjuˈmænɪti] *s* (*pl* **-ties**) humanidad

hu'man-kind' *s* género humano

humble [ˈhʌmbəl] o [ˈʌmbəl] *adj* humilde ‖ *tr* humillar

humble pie *s* — **to eat humble pie** cantar la palinodia

hum'bug' *s* patraña; (*person*) patrañero ‖ *v* (*pret & pp* **-bugged;** *ger* **-bugging**) *tr* embaucar, engaitar

hum'drum' *adj* monótono, tedioso

humer·us [ˈhjumərəs] *s* (*pl* **-i** [ˌaɪ]) húmero

humid [ˈhjumɪd] *adj* húmedo

humidifier [hjuˈmɪdɪˌfaɪ·ər] *s* humectador *m*

humidi-fy [hjuˈmɪdɪˌfaɪ] *v* (*pret & pp* **-fied**) *tr* humedecer

humidity [hjuˈmɪdɪti] *s* humedad

humiliate [hjuˈmɪli·et] *tr* humillar

humiliating [hjuˈmɪli·etɪŋ] *adj* humillante

humili-ty [hjuˈmɪlɪti] *s* (*pl* **-ties**) humildad

hummingbird [ˈhʌmɪŋˌbʌrd] *s* colibrí *m*, pájaro mosca

humor [ˈhjumər] o [ˈjumər] *s* humor *m*; **out of humor** de mal humor; **to be in the humor for** estar de humor para ‖ *tr* seguir el humor a; manejar con delicadeza

humorist [ˈhjumərɪst] o [ˈjumərɪst] *s* humorista *mf*

humorous [ˈhjumərəs] o [ˈjumərəs] *adj* humorístico

hump [hʌmp] *s* corcova, joroba; (*in the ground*) montecillo

hump'back' *s* corcova, joroba; (*person*) corcovado, jorobado

humus [ˈhjuməs] *s* mantillo

hunch [hʌntʃ] *s* corcova, joroba; (*premonition*) (coll) corazonada ‖ *tr* encorvar ‖ *intr* encorvarse

hunch'back' *s* corcova, joroba; (*person*) corcovado, jorobado

hundred [ˈhʌndrəd] *adj* cien ‖ *s* ciento, cien; **a hundred u one hundred** ciento, cien; **by the hundreds** a centenares

hundredth [ˈhʌndrədθ] *adj & s* centésimo

hun'dred·weight' *s* quintal *m*

Hundred Years' War *s* guerra de los Cien Años

Hungarian [hʌŋˈgeri·ən] *adj & s* húngaro

Hungary [ˈhʌŋgəri] *s* Hungría

hunger [ˈhʌŋgər] *s* hambre *f* ‖ *intr* hambrear; **to hunger for** tener hambre de

hunger march *s* marcha del hambre

hunger strike *s* huelga de hambre

hun-gry [ˈhʌŋgri] *adj* (*comp* **-grier;** *super* **-griest**) hambriento; **to be hungry** tener hambre; **to go hungry** pasar hambre

hunk [hʌŋk] *s* (coll) buen pedazo, pedazo grande

hunt [hʌnt] *s* (*act of hunting*) caza; (*hunting party*) cacería; (*a search*) busca; **on the hunt for** a caza de ‖ *tr* cazar; (*to seek, look for*) buscar ‖ *intr* cazar; buscar; **to go hunting** ir de caza; **to hunt for** buscar; **to take hunting** llevar de caza

hunter [ˈhʌntər] *s* cazador *m*; perro de caza

hunting [ˈhʌntɪŋ] *adj* de caza ‖ *s* (*act*) caza; (*art*) cacería, montería

hunting dog *s* perro de caza

hunting ground *s* cazadero

hunt'ing-horn' *s* cuerno de caza

hunting jacket *s* cazadora

hunting lodge *s* casa de montería

hunting season *s* época de caza

huntress [ˈhʌntrɪs] *s* cazadora

hunts·man [ˈhʌntsmən] *s* (*pl* **-men** [mən]) cazador *m*, montero

hurdle [ˈhʌrdəl] *s* (*hedge over which horses must jump*) zarzo; (*wooden frame over which runners and horses must jump*) valla; (fig) obstáculo; **hurdles** carrera de vallas ‖ *tr* saltar por encima de

hurdle race *s* carrera de vallas

hurdy-gur-dy [ˈhʌrdiˌgʌrdi] *s* (*pl* **-dies**) organillo

hurl [hʌrl] *s* lanzamiento ‖ *tr* lanzar

hurrah [huˈrɑ] o **hurray** [huˈre] *s* viva *m* ‖ *interj* ¡viva! **hurrah for . . . !** ¡viva . . . ! ‖ *tr* aplaudir, vitorear ‖ *intr* dar vivas

hurricane [ˈhʌrɪˌken] *s* huracán *m*

hurried ['hʌrɪd] *adj* apresurado; hecho de prisa

hur·ry ['hʌri] *s* (*pl* **-ries**) prisa; **to be in a hurry** tener prisa, estar de prisa ‖ *v* (*pret* & *pp* **-ried**) *tr* apresurar, dar prisa a ‖ *intr* apresurarse, darse prisa; **to hurry after** correr en pos de; **to hurry away** marcharse de prisa; **to hurry back** volver de prisa; **to hurry up** darse prisa

hurt [hʌrt] *adj* (*injured*) lastimado, herido; (*offended*) resentido, herido ‖ *s* (*harm*) daño; (*injury*) herida; (*pain*) dolor *m* ‖ *v* (*pret* & *pp* **hurt**) *tr* (*to harm*) dañar, perjudicar; (*to injure*) lastimar, herir; (*to offend*) ofender, herir; (*to pain*) doler ‖ *intr* doler

hurtle ['hʌrtəl] *intr* lanzarse con violencia, pasar con gran estruendo

husband ['hʌzbənd] *s* marido, esposo ‖ *tr* manejar con economía

husband-man ['hʌzbəndmən] *s* (*pl* **-men** [mən]) agricultor *m*, granjero

husbandry ['hʌzbəndri] *s* agricultura, labranza; buena dirección, buen gobierno (*de la hacienda de uno*)

hush [hʌʃ] *s* silencio ‖ *interj* ¡chito! ‖ *tr* callar; **to hush up** echar tierra a (*un escándalo*) ‖ *intr* callarse

hushaby ['hʌʃə,baɪ] *interj* ¡ro ro!

hush'-hush' *adj* muy secreto

hush money *s* precio del silencio

husk [hʌsk] *s* cáscara, hollejo, vaina; (*of corn*) perfolla ‖ *tr* descascarar, deshollejar, desvainar; espinochar (*el maíz*)

husk·y ['hʌski] *adj* (*comp* **-ier**; *super* **-iest**) fortachón, fornido; (*voice*) ronco

hus·sy ['hʌzi] o ['hʌsi] *s* (*pl* **-sies**) buena pieza, moza descarada; mujer desvergonzada

hustle ['hʌsəl] *s* (coll) energía, vigor *m* ‖ *tr* apresurar; echar a empellones ‖ *intr* apresurarse; (coll) menearse, trabajar con gran ahinco

hustler ['hʌslər] *s* trafagón *m*, buscavidas *m*

hut [hʌt] *s* casucha, choza

hyacinth ['haɪəsɪnθ] *s* jacinto

hybrid ['haɪbrɪd] *adj* & *s* híbrido

hybridization [,haɪbrɪdɪ'zeʃən] *s* hibridación

hybridize ['haɪbrɪ,daɪz] *tr* & *intr* hibridar

hy·dra ['haɪdrə] *s* (*pl* **-dras** o **-drae** [dri]) hidra

hydrant ['haɪdrənt] *s* boca de agua, boca de riego; (*water faucet*) grifo

hydrate ['haɪdret] *s* hidrato ‖ *tr* hidratar ‖ *intr* hidratarse

hydraulic [haɪ'drɔlɪk] *adj* hidráulico ‖ **hydraulics** *s* hidráulica

hydraulic ram *s* ariete hidráulico

hydriodic [,haɪdrɪ'ɑdɪk] *adj* yodhídrico

hydrobromic [,haɪdrə'bromɪk] *adj* bromhídrico

hydrocarbon [,haɪdrə'kɑrbən] *s* hidrocarburo

hydrochloric [,haɪdrə'klorɪk] *adj* clorhídrico

hydroelectric [,haɪdro·ɪ'lɛktrɪk] *adj* hidroeléctrico

hydrofluoric [,haɪdrəflu'ɑrɪk] o [,haɪdrəflu'ɔrɪk] *adj* fluorhídrico

hydrofoil ['haɪdrə,fɔɪl] *s* superficie hidrodinámica; (*wing designed to lift vessel*) hidroaleta; (*vessel*) hidroala *m*

hydrogen ['haɪdrədʒən] *s* hidrógeno

hydrogen bomb *s* bomba de hidrógeno

hydrogen peroxide *s* peróxido de hidrógeno

hydrogen sulfide *s* sulfuro de hidrógeno

hydrometer [haɪ'drɑmɪtər] *s* areómetro

hydrophobia [,haɪdrə'fobɪ·ə] *s* hidrofobia

hydroplane ['haɪdrə,plen] *s* hidroavión *m*

hydroxide [haɪ'drɑksaɪd] *s* hidróxido

hyena [haɪ'inə] *s* hiena

hygiene ['haɪdʒin] o ['haɪdʒɪ,in] *s* higiene *f*

hygienic [,haɪdʒɪ'ɛnɪk] o [haɪ'dʒinɪk] *adj* higiénico

hymn [hɪm] *s* himno

hymnal ['hɪmnəl] *s* himnario

hyp. *abbr* **hypotenuse**, **hypothesis**

hyperacidity [,haɪpərə'sɪdɪti] *s* hiperacidez *f*

hyperbola [haɪ'pʌrbələ] *s* (geom) hipérbola

hyperbole [haɪ'pʌrbəli] *s* (rhet) hipérbole *f*

hyperbolic [,haɪpər'bɑlɪk] *adj* (geom & rhet) hiperbólico

hypersensitive [,haɪpər'sɛnsɪtɪv] *adj* extremadamente sensible; (*allergic*) hipersensible

hypertension [,haɪpər'tɛnʃən] *s* hipertensión

hyphen ['haɪfən] *s* guión *m*

hyphenate ['haɪfə,net] *tr* unir con guión; escribir con guión

hypno·sis [hɪp'nosɪs] *s* (*pl* **-ses** [siz]) hipnosis *f*

hypnotic [hɪp'nɑtɪk] *adj* hipnótico ‖ *s* (*person; sedative*) hipnótico

hypnotism ['hɪpnə,tɪzəm] *s* hipnotismo

hypnotist ['hɪpnətɪst] *s* hipnotista *mf*

hypnotize ['hɪpnə,taɪz] *tr* hipnotizar

hypochondriac [,haɪpə'kɑndrɪ,æk] o [,haɪpə'kɑndrɪ,æk] *s* hipocondríaco

hypocri·sy [hɪ'pɑkrəsi] *s* (*pl* **-sies**) hipocresía

hypocrite ['hɪpəkrɪt] *s* hipócrita *mf*

hypocritical [,haɪpə'krɪtɪkəl] *adj* hipócrita

hypodermic [,haɪpə'dʌrmɪk] *adj* hipodérmico

hyposulfite [,haɪpə'sʌlfaɪt] *m* hiposulfito

hypotenuse [haɪ'pɑtɪ,nus] o [haɪ'pɑtɪ,njus] *s* hipotenusa

hypothe·sis [haɪ'pɑθɪsɪs] *s* (*pl* **-ses** [,siz]) hipótesis *f*

hypothetic(al) [,haɪpə'θɛtɪk(əl)] *adj* hipotético

hyssop ['hɪsəp] s (bot) hisopo
hysteria [hɪs'tɪrɪ-ə] s histerismo, histeria

hysteric [hɪs'terɪk] adj histérico ‖
hysterics s paroxismo histérico
hysterical [hɪs'terɪkəl] adj histérico

I

I, i [aɪ] novena letra del alfabeto inglés
I. abbr Island
I [aɪ] pron pers (pl we [wi]) yo; it is I soy yo
iambic [aɪ'æmbɪk] adj yámbico
iam-bus [aɪ'æmbəs] s (pl -bi [baɪ]) yambo
ib. abbr ibidem
Iberian [aɪ'bɪrɪ-ən] adj ibérico ‖ s ibero
ibex ['aɪbeks] s (pl ibexes o ibices ['ɪbɪ,siz]) íbice m, cabra montés
ibid. abbr ibidem
ice [aɪs] s hielo; to break the ice (to overcome reserve) romper el hielo; to cut no ice (coll) no importar nada; to skate on thin ice (coll) buscar el peligro ‖ tr helar; enfriar con hielo; (to cover with icing) garapiñar ‖ intr helarse
ice age s época glacial
ice bag s bolsa para hielo
iceberg ['aɪs,bʌrg] s banquisa, iceberg m
ice'boat' s cortahielos m, rompehielos m; trineo con vela para deslizarse sobre el hielo
ice'bound' adj rodeado de hielo; detenido por el hielo
ice'box' s nevera, fresquera
ice'break'er s cortahielos m, rompehielos m
ice'cap' s bolsa para hielo; manto de hielo
ice cream s helado
ice'-cream' cone s cucurucho de helado, barquillo de helado
ice-cream freezer s heladora, garapiñera
ice-cream parlor s salón m de refrescos, tienda de helados
ice-cream soda s agua gaseosa con helado
ice cube s cubito de hielo
ice hockey s hockey m sobre patines
Iceland ['aɪslənd] s Islandia
Icelander ['aɪs,lændər] o ['aɪsləndər] s islandés m
Icelandic [aɪs'lændɪk] adj islandés ‖ s islandés m (idioma)
ice·man ['aɪs,mæn] s (pl -men [,men]) vendedor m de hielo, repartidor m de hielo
ice pack s hielo flotante; bolsa de hielo
ice pail s enfriadera
ice pick s picahielos m
ice skate s patín m de cuchilla, patín de hielo
ice tray s bandejita de hielo
ice water s agua helada

ichthyology [,ɪkθɪ'ɑlədʒɪ] s ictiología
icicle ['aɪsɪkəl] s carámbano
icing ['aɪsɪŋ] s garapiña, capa de azúcar; (aer) formación de hielo
iconoclasm [aɪ'kɑnə,klæzəm] s iconoclasia, iconoclasmo
iconoclast [aɪ'kɑnə,klæst] s iconoclasta mf
iconoscope [aɪ'kɑnə,skop] s (trademark) iconoscopio
icy ['aɪsɪ] adj (comp icier; super iciest) cubierto de hielo; (slippery) resbaladizo; (fig) frío
id. abbr idem
id [ɪd] s (psychoanalysis) ello
idea [aɪ'di-ə] s idea
ideal [aɪ'di-əl] adj & s ideal m
idealist [aɪ'di-əlɪst] adj & s idealista mf
idealize [aɪ'di-ə,laɪz] tr idealizar
identic(al) [aɪ'dentɪk(əl)] adj idéntico
identification [aɪ,dentɪfɪ'keʃən] s identificación
identification tag s disco de identificación
identify [aɪ'dentɪ,faɪ] v (pret & pp -fied) tr identificar
identi-ty [aɪ'dentɪtɪ] s (pl -ties) identidad
ideolo·gy [,aɪdɪ'ɑlədʒɪ] o [,ɪdɪ'ɑlədʒɪ] s (pl -gies) ideología
ides [aɪdz] spl idus mpl
idio·cy ['ɪdɪ-əsɪ] s (pl -cies) idiotez f
idiom ['ɪdɪ-əm] s (expression that is contrary to the usual patterns of the language) modismo; (style of language) idioma m, lenguaje m; (style of an author) estilo; (character of a language) índole f
idiomatic [,ɪdɪ-ə'mætɪk] adj idiomático
idiosyncra·sy [,ɪdɪ-ə'sɪnkrəsɪ] s (pl -sies) idiosincrasia
idiot ['ɪdɪ-ət] s idiota mf
idiotic [,ɪdɪ-'ɑtɪk] adj idiota
idle ['aɪdəl] adj desocupado, ocioso; at idle moments a ratos perdidos; to run idle marchar en ralentí ‖ tr — to idle away gastar ociosamente (el tiempo) ‖ intr estar ocioso, holgar; marchar (un motor) en ralentí
idleness ['aɪdəlnɪs] s desocupación, ociosidad
idler ['aɪdlər] s haragán m, ocioso
idol ['aɪdəl] s ídolo
idola·try [aɪ'dɑlətrɪ] s (pl -tries) idolatría
idolize ['aɪdə,laɪz] tr idolatrar
idyll ['aɪdəl] s idilio
idyllic [aɪ'dɪlɪk] adj idílico
if [ɪf] conj si; as if como si; even if

aunque; **if so** si es así; **if true** si es cierto

ignis fatuus ['ɪgnɪs'fætʃʊ·əs] s (pl **ignes fatui** ['ɪgniz'fætʃʊ‚aɪ]) fuego fatuo

ignite [ɪg'naɪt] tr encender ‖ intr encenderse

ignition [ɪg'nɪʃən] s inflamación; (aut) encendido

ignition switch s (aut) interruptor m de encendido

ignoble [ɪg'nobəl] adj innoble

ignominious [‚ɪgnə'mɪnɪ·əs] adj ignominioso

ignoramus [‚ɪgnə'reməs] s ignorante mf

ignorance ['ɪgnərəns] s ignorancia

ignorant ['ɪgnərənt] adj ignorante

ignore [ɪg'nor] tr no hacer caso de, pasar por alto

ilk [ɪlk] s especie f, jaez m

ill. abbr **Illustrated, illustration**

ill [ɪl] adj (comp **worse** [wʌrs]; super **worst** [wʌrst]) enfermo, malo ‖ adv mal; **to take ill** tomar a mal; caer enfermo

ill-advised ['ɪləd'vaɪzd] adj desaconsejado, malaconsejado

ill at ease adj inquieto, incómodo

ill-bred ['ɪl'bred] adj malcriado

ill-considered ['ɪlkən'sɪdərd] adj desconsiderado, mal considerado

ill-disposed ['ɪldɪs'pozd] adj malintencionado, maldispuesto

illegal [ɪ'ligəl] adj ilegal

illegible [ɪ'ledʒɪbəl] adj ilegible

illegitimate [‚ɪlɪ'dʒɪtɪmɪt] adj ilegítimo

ill fame s mala fama, reputación de inmoral

ill-fated ['ɪl'fetɪd] adj aciago, funesto

ill-gotten ['ɪl'gatən] adj mal ganado

ill health s mala salud

ill-humored ['ɪl'hjumərd] adj malhumorado

illicit [ɪ'lɪsɪt] adj ilícito

illiteracy [ɪ'lɪtərəsɪ] s (pl -cies) ignorancia; analfabetismo

illiterate [ɪ'lɪtərɪt] adj (uneducated) iliterato; (unable to read or write) analfabeto ‖ s analfabeto

ill-mannered ['ɪl'mænərd] adj de malos modales

illness ['ɪlnɪs] s enfermedad

illogical [ɪ'ladʒɪkəl] adj ilógico

ill-spent ['ɪl'spent] adj malgastado

ill-starred ['ɪl'stard] adj malhadado

ill-tempered ['ɪl'tempərd] adj de mal genio

ill-timed ['ɪl'taɪmd] adj inoportuno, intempestivo

ill'-treat' tr maltratar

illuminate [ɪ'lumɪ‚net] tr alumbrar, iluminar; **miniar** (un manuscrito)

illuminating gas s gas m de alumbrado

illumination [ɪ‚lumɪ'neʃən] s iluminación

illusion [ɪ'luʒən] s ilusión

illusive [ɪ'lusɪv] adj ilusivo

illusory [ɪ'lusərɪ] adj ilusorio

illustrate ['ɪləs‚tret] o [ɪ'lʌstret] tr ilustrar

illustration [‚ɪləs'treʃən] s ilustración

illustrious [ɪ'lʌstrɪ·əs] adj ilustre

ill will s mala voluntad

image ['ɪmɪdʒ] s imagen f; **the very image of** la propia estampa de

imagery ['ɪmɪdʒrɪ] o ['ɪmɪdʒərɪ] s (pl -ries) (formation of mental images; product of the imagination) fantasía; (images collectively) imágenes fpl

imaginary [ɪ'mædʒɪ‚nerɪ] adj imaginario

imagination [ɪ‚mædʒɪ'neʃən] s imaginación

imagine [ɪ'mædʒɪn] tr & intr imaginar; (to conjecture) imaginarse

imbecile ['ɪmbɪsɪl] adj & s imbécil mf

imbecility [‚ɪmbɪ'sɪlɪtɪ] s (pl -ties) imbecilidad

imbibe [ɪm'baɪb] tr (to drink) beber; (to absorb) embeber; (to become absorbed in) embeberse de o en ‖ intr beber, empinar el codo

imbue [ɪm'bju] tr imbuir

imitate ['ɪmɪ‚tet] tr imitar

imitation [‚ɪmɪ'teʃən] adj (e.g., jewelry) imitado, imitación, de imitación ‖ s imitación; **in imitation of** a imitación de

immaculate [ɪ'mækjəlɪt] adj inmaculado

immaterial [‚ɪmə'tɪrɪ·əl] adj inmaterial; poco importante

immature [‚ɪmə'tjur] o [‚ɪmə'tur] adj inmaturo

immeasurable [ɪ'meʒərəbəl] adj inmensurable

immediacy [ɪ'midɪ·əsɪ] s inmediación

immediate [ɪ'midɪ·ɪt] adj inmediato

immediately [ɪ'midɪ·ɪtlɪ] adv inmediatamente

immemorial [‚ɪmɪ'morɪ·əl] adj inmemorial

immense [ɪ'mens] adj inmenso; (coll) excelente

immerge [ɪ'mʌrdʒ] intr sumergirse

immerse [ɪ'mʌrs] tr sumergir, inmergir

immersion [ɪ'mʌrʃən] o [ɪ'mʌrʒən] s sumersión, inmersión

immigrant ['ɪmɪgrənt] adj & s inmigrante mf

immigrate ['ɪmɪ‚gret] intr inmigrar

immigration [‚ɪmɪ'greʃən] s inmigración

imminent ['ɪmɪnənt] adj inminente

immobile [ɪ'mobɪl] o [ɪ'mobɪl] adj inmoble, inmóvil

immobilize [ɪ'mobɪ‚laɪz] tr inmovilizar

immoderate [ɪ'madərɪt] adj inmoderado

immodest [ɪ'madɪst] adj inmodesto

immoral [ɪ'marəl] o [ɪ'mɔrəl] adj inmoral

immortal [ɪ'mɔrtəl] adj & s inmortal mf

immortalize [ɪ'mɔrtə‚laɪz] tr inmortalizar

immune [ɪ'mjun] adj inmune

immunize ['ɪmjə‚naɪz] o [ɪ'mjunaɪz] tr inmunizar

imp [ɪmp] s diablillo; (child) niño travieso

impact ['ɪmpækt] s impacto

impair [ɪm'per] tr empeorar, deteriorar

impan•el [ɪm'pænəl] v (pret & pp -eled o -elled; ger -eling o -elling) tr inscribir en la lista de los jurados; elegir (un jurado)

impart [ɪm'part] tr (to make known) dar a conocer, hacer saber; (to transmit, communicate) imprimir

impartial [ɪm'parʃəl] adj imparcial

impassable [ɪm'pæsəbəl] o [ɪm'pasə-bəl] adj intransitable, impracticable

impasse [ɪm'pæs] o ['ɪmpæs] s callejón m sin salida

impassible [ɪm'pæsɪbəl] adj impasible

impassioned [ɪm'pæʃənd] adj ardiente, vehemente

impassive [ɪm'pæsɪv] adj impasible

impatience [ɪm'peʃəns] s impaciencia

impatient [ɪm'peʃənt] adj impaciente

impeach [ɪm'pitʃ] tr residenciar

impeachment [ɪm'pitʃmənt] s residencia

impeccable [ɪm'pɛkəbəl] adj impecable

impecunious [ˌɪmpɪ'kjunɪ•əs] adj inope

impedance [ɪm'pidəns] s impedancia

impede [ɪm'pid] tr estorbar, dificultar

impediment [ɪm'pedɪmənt] s impedimento; (e.g., in speech) defecto

im•pel [ɪm'pɛl] v (pret & pp -pelled; ger -pelling) tr impeler, impulsar

impending [ɪm'pendɪŋ] adj inminente

impenetrable [ɪm'penətrəbəl] adj impenetrable

impenitent [ɪm'penɪtənt] adj & s impenitente mf

imperative [ɪm'perɪtɪv] adj (commanding) imperativo; (urgent, absolutely necessary) imperioso || s imperativo

imperceptible [ˌɪmpər'septɪbəl] adj imperceptible, inapreciable

imperfect [ɪm'pʌrfɪkt] adj & s imperfecto

imperfection [ˌɪmpər'fɛkʃən] s imperfección

imperial [ɪm'pɪrɪ•əl] adj imperial; majestuoso || s (goatee) perilla; (top of coach) imperial f

imperialist [ɪm'pɪrɪ•əlɪst] adj & s imperialista mf

imper•il [ɪm'perɪl] v (pret & pp -iled o -illed; ger -iling o -illing) tr poner en peligro

imperious [ɪm'pɪrɪ•əs] adj imperioso

imperishable [ɪm'perɪʃəbəl] adj imperecedero

impersonal [ɪm'pʌrsənəl] adj impersonal

impersonate [ɪm'pʌrsə‚net] tr personificar; hacer el papel de

impertinence [ɪm'pʌrtɪnəns] s impertinencia

impertinent [ɪm'pʌrtɪnənt] adj & s impertinente mf

impetuous [ɪm'petʃu•əs] adj impetuoso

impetus ['ɪmpɪtəs] s ímpetu m

imple•ty [ɪm'par•əti] s (pl -ties) impiedad

impinge [ɪm'pɪndʒ] intr — to impinge on o upon incidir en o sobre, herir; infringir, violar

impious ['ɪmpɪ•əs] adj impío

impish ['ɪmpɪʃ] adj endiablado, travieso

implant [ɪm'plænt] tr implantar

implement ['ɪmplɪmənt] s instrumento, utensilio, herramienta || ['ɪm-plɪ‚ment] tr poner por obra, llevar a cabo; (to provide with implements) pertrechar

implicate ['ɪmplɪ‚ket] tr implicar, comprometer, enredar

implicit [ɪm'plɪsɪt] adj implícito; (unquestioning) absoluto, ciego

implied [ɪm'plaɪd] adj implícito, sobrentendido

implore [ɪm'plor] tr implorar, suplicar

im•ply [ɪm'plaɪ] v (pret & pp -plied) tr dar a entender; implicar, incluir en esencia

impolite [ˌɪmpə'laɪt] s descortés

import ['ɪmport] s importación; artículo importado; importancia, significación || [ɪm'port] o ['ɪmport] tr importar; significar || intr importar

importance [ɪm'portəns] s importancia

important [ɪm'portənt] adj importante

importation [ˌɪmpor'teʃən] s importación

importer [ɪm'portər] s importador m

importunate [ɪm'portʃənɪt] adj importuno

importune [ˌɪmpor'tjun] o [ɪmpor-'tun] tr importunar

impose [ɪm'poz] tr imponer || intr — to impose on o upon abusar de

imposing [ɪm'pozɪŋ] adj imponente

imposition [ˌɪmpə'zɪʃən] s (of someone's will) imposición; abuso, engaño

impossible [ɪm'pasɪbəl] adj imposible

impostor [ɪm'pastər] s impostor m

imposture [ɪm'pastʃər] s impostura

impotence ['ɪmpətəns] s impotencia

impotent ['ɪmpətənt] adj impotente

impound [ɪm'paʊnd] tr acorralar, encerrar; rebalsar (agua); (law) embargar, secuestrar

impoverish [ɪm'pavərɪʃ] tr empobrecer

impracticable [ɪm'præktɪkəbəl] adj impracticable; (intractable) intratable

impractical [ɪm'præktɪkəl] adj impracticable; soñador, utópico

impregnable [ɪm'pregnəbəl] adj inexpugnable

impregnate [ɪm'pregnet] tr (to make pregnant) empreñar; (to soak) empapar; (to fill the interstices of) impregnar; (to infuse, infect) imbuir

impresari•o [ˌɪmprɪ'sarɪ‚o] s (pl -os) empresario, empresario de teatro

impress [ɪm'pres] tr (to have an effect on the mind or emotions of) impresionar; (to mark by using pres-

sure) imprimir; (*on the memory*) grabar; (mil) enganchar

impression [ɪmˈpreʃən] *s* impresión

impressionable [ɪmˈpreʃənəbəl] *adj* impresionable

impressive [ɪmˈpresɪv] *adj* impresionante

imprint [ˈɪmprɪnt] *s* impresión; (typ) pie *m* de imprenta || [ɪmˈprɪnt] *tr* imprimir

imprison [ɪmˈprɪzən] *tr* encarcelar

imprisonment [ɪmˈprɪzənmənt] *s* encarcelamiento

improbable [ɪmˈprabəbəl] *adj* improbable

impromptu [ɪmˈpramptju] o [ɪmˈpramptu] *adj* improvisado || *adv* de improviso || *s* improvisación; (mus) impromptu *m*

improper [ɪmˈprapər] *adj* impropio; (*contrary to good taste or decency*) indecoroso

improve [ɪmˈpruv] *tr* perfeccionar, mejorar; aprovechar (*la oportunidad*) || *intr* perfeccionarse, mejorar; **to improve on** o **upon** mejorar

improvement [ɪmˈpruvmənt] *s* perfeccionamiento, mejoramiento; (*e.g., in health*) mejoría; (*useful employment, e.g., of time*) aprovechamiento

improvident [ɪmˈpravɪdənt] *adj* improvisor

improvise [ˈɪmprəˌvaɪz] *tr & intr* improvisar

imprudent [ɪmˈprudənt] *adj* imprudente

impudence [ˈɪmpjədəns] *s* insolencia, descaro, impertinencia

impudent [ˈɪmpjədənt] *adj* insolente, descarado, impertinente

impugn [ɪmˈpjun] *tr* poner en tela de juicio

impulse [ˈɪmpʌls] *s* impulso

impulsive [ɪmˈpʌlsɪv] *adj* impulsivo

impunity [ɪmˈpjunɪti] *s* impunidad

impure [ɪmˈpjur] *adj* impuro

impuri·ty [ɪmˈpjurɪti] *s* (*pl* **-ties**) impureza, impuridad

impute [ɪmˈpjut] *tr* imputar

in [ɪn] *adj* interior || *adv* dentro; en casa, en la oficina; **in here** aquí dentro; **in there** allí dentro; **to be in** estar en casa; **to be in for** estar expuesto a; **to be in with** gozar del favor de || *prep* en; (*within*) dentro de; (*over, through*) por; (*a period of the day*) en o por; **dressed in** . . . vestido de . . . ; **in so far as** en tanto que; **in that** en que, por cuanto || *s* — **ins and outs** recovecos, pormenores minuciosos

inability [ˌɪnəˈbɪlɪti] *s* inhabilidad, incapacidad

inaccessible [ˌɪnækˈsesɪbəl] *adj* inaccesible

inaccura·cy [ɪnˈækjərəsi] *s* (*pl* **-cies**) inexactitud, incorrección

inaccurate [ɪnˈækjərɪt] *adj* inexacto, incorrecto

inaction [ɪnˈækʃən] *s* inacción

inactive [ɪnˈæktɪv] *adj* inactivo

inactivity [ˌɪnækˈtɪvɪti] *s* inactividad

inadequate [ɪnˈædɪkwɪt] *adj* insuficiente, inadecuado

inadvertent [ˌɪnədˈvʌrtənt] *adj* inadvertido

inadvisable [ˌɪnədˈvaɪzəbəl] *adj* poco aconsejable, imprudente

inane [ɪnˈen] *adj* inane

inanimate [ɪnˈænɪmɪt] *adj* inanimado

inappreciable [ˌɪnəˈpriʃɪ·əbəl] *adj* inapreciable

inappropriate [ˌɪnəˈproprɪ·ɪt] *adj* no apropiado, no a propósito

inarticulate [ˌɪnɑrˈtɪkjəlɪt] *adj* (*sounds, words*) inarticulado; (*person*) incapaz de expresarse

inartistic [ˌɪnɑrˈtɪstɪk] *adj* antiartístico, inartístico

inasmuch as [ˌɪnəzˈmʌtʃˌæz] *conj* ya que, puesto que; en cuanto, hasta donde

inattentive [ˌɪnəˈtentɪv] *adj* desatento

inaugural [ɪnˈɔgjərəl] *adj* inaugural || *s* discurso inaugural

inaugurate [ɪnˈɔgjəˌret] *tr* inaugurar

inauguration [ɪnˌɔgjəˈreʃən] *s* (*formal initiation or opening*) inauguración; (*investiture of a head of government*) toma de posesión

inborn [ˈɪnˈbɔrn] *adj* innato, ingénito

inbreeding [ˈɪnˈbridɪŋ] *s* intracruzamiento

inc. *abbr* **inclosure, included, including, incorporated, increase**

Inca [ˈɪŋkə] *adj* incaico || *s* inca *mf*

incandescent [ˌɪnkənˈdesənt] *adj* incandescente

incapable [ɪnˈkepəbəl] *adj* incapaz

incapacitate [ˌɪnkəˈpæsɪˌtet] *tr* incapacitar, inhabilitar

incapaci·ty [ˌɪnkəˈpæsɪti] *s* (*pl* **-ties**) incapacidad

incarcerate [ɪnˈkɑrsəˌret] *tr* encarcelar

incarnate [ɪnˈkɑrnɪt] o [ɪnˈkɑrnet] *adj* encarnado || [ɪnˈkɑrnet] *tr* encarnar

incarnation [ˌɪnkɑrˈneʃən] *s* encarnación

incendiarism [ɪnˈsendɪ·əˌrɪzəm] *s* incendio intencionado; incitación al desorden

incendiar·y [ɪnˈsendɪˌeri] *adj* incendiario || *s* (*pl* **-ies**) incendiario

incense [ˈɪnsens] *s* incienso || *tr* (*to burn incense before*) incensar || [ɪnˈsens] *tr* exasperar, encolerizar

incense burner *s* incensario

incentive [ɪnˈsentɪv] *adj & s* incentivo

inception [ɪnˈsepʃən] *s* principio, comienzo

incertitude [ɪnˈsʌrtɪˌtjud] o [ɪnˈsʌrtɪˌtud] *s* incertidumbre

incessant [ɪnˈsesənt] *adj* incesante

incest [ˈɪnsest] *s* incesto

incestuous [ɪnˈsestʃu·əs] *adj* incestuoso

inch [ɪntʃ] *s* pulgada; **to be within an inch of** estar a dos dedos de || *intr* — **to inch ahead** avanzar poco a poco

incidence [ˈɪnsɪdəns] *s* incidencia; (*range of occurrence*) extensión

incident [ˈɪnsɪdənt] *adj & s* incidente *m*

incidental [ˌɪnsɪˈdentəl] *adj* incidente; (*incurred in addition to the regular amount*) obvencional ‖ *s* elemento incidental; **incidentals** gastos menudos

incidentally [ˌɪnsɪˈdentəli] *adv* incidentemente; a propósito

incipient [ɪnˈsɪpɪənt] *adj* incipiente

incision [ɪnˈsɪʒən] *s* incisión

incisive [ɪnˈsaɪsɪv] *adj* incisivo

incite [ɪnˈsaɪt] *tr* incitar

incl. *abbr* **inclosure, inclusive**

inclemen·cy [ɪnˈklemənsi] *s* (*pl* -cies) inclemencia

inclement [ɪnˈklemənt] *adj* inclemente

inclination [ˌɪnklɪˈneʃən] *s* inclinación

incline [ˈɪnklaɪn] o [ɪnˈklaɪn] *s* declive *m*, pendiente *f* ‖ [ɪnˈklaɪn] *tr* inclinar ‖ *intr* inclinarse

inclose [ɪnˈkloz] *tr* encerrar; (*in a letter*) adjuntar, incluir; **to inclose herewith** remitir adjunto

inclosure [ɪnˈkloʒər] *s* recinto; cosa inclusa, carta inclusa

include [ɪnˈklud] *tr* incluir, comprender

including [ɪnˈkludɪŋ] *prep* incluso, inclusive

inclusive [ɪnˈklusɪv] *adj* inclusivo; **inclusive of** comprensivo de ‖ *adv* inclusive

incogni·to [ɪnˈkɑgnɪˌto] *adj* incógnito ‖ *adv* de incógnito ‖ *s* (*pl* -tos) incógnito

incoherent [ˌɪnkoˈhɪrənt] *adj* incoherente

incombustible [ˌɪnkəmˈbʌstɪbəl] *adj* incombustible

income [ˈɪnkʌm] *s* renta, ingreso, utilidad

income tax *s* impuesto sobre rentas

in′come-tax′ return *s* declaración de impuesto sobre rentas

in′com′ing *adj* de entrada, entrante; (*tide*) ascendente ‖ *s* entrada

incomparable [ɪnˈkɑmpərəbəl] *adj* incomparable

incompatible [ˌɪnkəmˈpætɪbəl] *adj* incompatible

incompetent [ɪnˈkɑmpɪtənt] *adj* incompetente

incomplete [ˌɪnkəmˈplit] *adj* incompleto

incomprehensible [ˌɪnkɑmprɪˈhensɪbəl] *adj* incomprensible

inconceivable [ˌɪnkənˈsivəbəl] *adj* inconcebible

inconclusive [ˌɪnkənˈklusɪv] *adj* inconcluyente

incongruous [ɪnˈkɑŋgruˈəs] *adj* incongruo

inconsequential [ɪnˌkɑnsɪˈkwenʃəl] *adj* (*lacking proper sequence of thought or speech*) inconsecuente; (*trivial*) de poca importancia

inconsiderate [ˌɪnkənˈsɪdərɪt] *adj* desconsiderado, inconsiderado

inconsisten·cy [ˌɪnkənˈsɪstənsi] *s* (*pl* -cies) (*lack of coherence*) inconsistencia; (*lack of logical connection or uniformity*) inconsecuencia

inconsistent [ˌɪnkənˈsɪstənt] *adj* (*lacking coherence of parts*) inconsistente; (*not agreeing with itself or oneself*) inconsecuente

inconsolable [ˌɪnkənˈsoləbəl] *adj* inconsolable

inconspicuous [ˌɪnkənˈspɪkjuˈəs] *adj* poco impresionante, poco aparente

inconstant [ɪnˈkɑnstənt] *adj* inconstante

incontinent [ɪnˈkɑntɪnənt] *adj* incontinente

incontrovertible [ˌɪnkɑntrəˈvʌrtɪbəl] *adj* incontrovertible

inconvenience [ˌɪnkənˈvinɪˈəns] *s* incomodidad, inconveniencia, molestia ‖ *tr* incomodar, molestar

inconvenient [ˌɪnkənˈvinɪˈənt] *adj* incómodo, inconveniente, molesto

incorporate [ɪnˈkɔrpəˌret] *tr* incorporar; constituir en sociedad anónima ‖ *intr* incorporarse; constituirse en sociedad anónima

incorporation [ɪnˌkɔrpəˈreʃən] *s* incorporación; constitución en sociedad anónima

incorrect [ˌɪnkəˈrekt] *adj* incorrecto

increase [ˈɪnkris] *s* aumento; ganancia, interés *m*; **to be on the increase** ir en aumento ‖ [ɪnˈkris] *tr* aumentar; (*by propagation*) multiplicar ‖ *intr* aumentar; multiplicarse

increasingly [ɪnˈkrisɪŋli] *adv* cada vez más

incredible [ɪnˈkredɪbəl] *adj* increíble

incredulous [ɪnˈkredʒələs] *adj* incrédulo

increment [ˈɪnkrɪmənt] *s* incremento

incriminate [ɪnˈkrɪmɪˌnet] *tr* acriminar, incriminar

incrust [ɪnˈkrʌst] *tr* incrustar

incubate [ˈɪnkjəˌbet] *tr* & *intr* incubar

incubator [ˈɪnkjəˌbetər] *s* incubadora

inculcate [ɪnˈkʌlket] o [ˈɪnkʌlˌket] *tr* inculcar

incumben·cy [ɪnˈkʌmbənsi] *s* (*pl* -cies) incumbencia

incumbent [ɪnˈkʌmbənt] *adj* — **to be incumbent on** incumbir a ‖ *s* titular *m*

incunabula [ˌɪnkjuˈnæbjələ] *spl* (*beginnings*) orígenes *mpl*; (*early printed books*) incunables *mpl*

in·cur [ɪnˈkʌr] *v* (*pret* & *pp* -curred; *ger* -curring) *tr* incurrir en; (*a debt*) contraer

incurable [ɪnˈkjurəbəl] *adj* & *s* incurable *mf*

incursion [ɪnˈkʌrʒən] o [ɪnˈkʌrʃən] *s* incursión, correría

ind. *abbr* **independent, industrial**

indebted [ɪnˈdetɪd] *adj* adeudado; obligado

indecen·cy [ɪnˈdisənsi] *s* (*pl* -cies) indecencia, deshonestidad

indecent [ɪnˈdisənt] *adj* indecente, deshonesto

indecisive [ˌɪndɪˈsaɪsɪv] *adj* indeciso

indeclinable [ˌɪndɪˈklaɪnəbəl] *adj* (*gram*) indeclinable

indeed [ɪnˈdid] *adv* verdaderamente, claro ‖ *interj* ¡de veras!

indefatigable [ˌɪndɪˈfætɪgəbəl] *adj* incansable, infatigable

indefensible [‚ɪndɪ'fensɪbəl] *adj* indefendible

indefinable [‚ɪndɪ'faɪnəbəl] *adj* indefinible

indefinite [ɪn'defɪnɪt] *adj* indefinido

indelible [ɪn'delɪbəl] *adj* indeleble

indelicate [ɪn'delɪkɪt] *adj* indelicado

indemnification [ɪn‚demnɪfɪ'keʃən] *s* indemnización

indemni·fy [ɪn'demnɪ‚faɪ] *v* (*pret & pp* **-fied**) *tr* indemnizar

indemni·ty [ɪn'demnɪtɪ] *s* (*pl* **-ties**) (*security against loss*) indemnidad; (*compensation*) indemnización

indent [ɪn'dent] *tr* dentar, mellar; (typ) sangrar

indentation [‚ɪnden'teʃən] *s* mella, muesca; (typ) sangría

indenture [ɪn'dentʃər] *s* escritura, contrato; contrato de aprendizaje || *tr* obligar por contrato

independence [‚ɪndɪ'pendəns] *s* independencia

independen·cy [‚ɪndɪ'pendənsɪ] *s* (*pl* **-cies**) independencia; país *m* independiente

independent [‚ɪndɪ'pendənt] *adj & s* independiente *mf*

indescribable [‚ɪndɪ'skraɪbəbəl] *adj* indescriptible

indestructible [‚ɪndɪ'strʌktɪbəl] *adj* indestructible

indeterminate [‚ɪndɪ'tʌrmɪnɪt] *adj* indeterminado

index ['ɪndeks] *s* (*pl* **indexes** o **indices** ['ɪndɪ‚siz]) *s* índice *m*; (typ) manecilla || *tr* poner índice a; poner en un índice || **Index** *s* Índice de los libros prohibidos

index card *s* ficha catalográfica

index finger *s* dedo índice

index tab *s* pestaña

India ['ɪndɪ‚ə] *s* la India

India ink *s* tinta china

Indian ['ɪndɪ‚ən] *adj & s* indio

Indian club *s* maza de gimnasia

Indian corn *s* maíz *m*, panizo

Indian file *s* fila india || *adv* en fila india

Indian Ocean *s* mar *m* de las Indias, océano Índico

Indian summer *s* veranillo de San Martín

India paper *s* papel *m* de China

India rubber *s* caucho

indicate ['ɪndɪ‚ket] *tr* indicar

indication [‚ɪndɪ'keʃən] *s* indicación

indicative [ɪn'dɪkətɪv] *adj & s* indicativo

indicator ['ɪndɪ‚ketər] *s* indicador *m*

indict [ɪn'daɪt] *tr* (law) acusar, procesar

indictment [ɪn'daɪtmənt] *s* acusación, procesamiento; auto de acusación formulado por el gran jurado

indifferent [ɪn'dɪfərənt] *adj* indiferente; (*not particularly good*) pasadero, mediano

indigenous [ɪn'dɪdʒɪnəs] *adj* indígena

indigent ['ɪndɪdʒənt] *adj* indigente

indigestible [‚ɪndɪ'dʒestɪbəl] *adj* indigestible

indigestion [‚ɪndɪ'dʒestʃən] *s* indigestión

indignant [ɪn'dɪgnənt] *adj* indignado

indignation [‚ɪndɪg'neʃən] *s* indignación

indigni·ty [ɪn'dɪgnɪtɪ] *s* (*pl* **-ties**) indignidad

indi·go ['ɪndɪ‚go] *adj* azul de añil || *s* (*pl* **-gos** o **-goes**) índigo

indirect [‚ɪndɪ'rekt] o [‚ɪndaɪ'rekt] *adj* indirecto

indirect discourse *s* estilo indirecto

indiscernible [‚ɪndɪ'zʌrnɪbəl] o [‚ɪndɪ'sʌrnɪbəl] *adj* indiscernible

indiscreet [‚ɪndɪs'krit] *adj* indiscreto

indispensable [‚ɪndɪs'pensəbəl] *adj* indispensable, imprescindible

indispose [‚ɪndɪs'poz] *tr* indisponer

indisposed [‚ɪndɪs'pozd] *adj* (*disinclined*) maldispuesto; (*somewhat ill*) indispuesto

indissoluble [‚ɪndɪ'saljəbəl] *adj* indisoluble

indistinct [‚ɪndɪs'stɪŋkt] *adj* indistinto

indite [ɪn'daɪt] *tr* redactar, poner por escrito

individual [‚ɪndɪ'vɪdʒu‚əl] *adj* individual || *s* individuo

individuali·ty [‚ɪndɪ‚vɪdʒu'ælɪtɪ] *s* (*pl* **-ties**) individualidad; (*person of distinctive character*) personaje *m*

Indochina ['ɪndo'tʃaɪnə] *s* la Indochina

Indo-Chinese ['ɪndotʃaɪ'niz] *adj* indochino || *s* (*pl* **-nese**) indochino

indoctrinate [ɪn'daktrɪ‚net] *tr* adoctrinar

Indo-European ['ɪndo‚jurə'pi‚ən] *adj & s* indoeuropeo

indolent ['ɪndələnt] *adj* indolente

Indonesia [‚ɪndo'niʃə] o [‚ɪndo'niʒə] *s* la Indonesia

Indonesian [‚ɪndo'niʃən] o [‚ɪndo'niʒən] *adj & s* indonesio

indoor ['ɪn‚dor] *adj* interior, de puertas adentro; (*inclined to stay in the house*) casero

indoors ['ɪn'dorz] *adv* dentro, en casa, bajo techado, bajo cubierto

indorse [ɪn'dors] *tr* endosar; (fig) apoyar, aprobar

indorsee [‚ɪndor'si] *s* endosatario

indorsement [ɪn'dorsmənt] *s* endoso; (fig) apoyo, aprobación

indorser [ɪn'dorsər] *s* endosante *mf*

induce [ɪn'djus] o [ɪn'dus] *tr* inducir; causar, ocasionar

inducement [ɪn'djusmənt] o [ɪn'dusmənt] *s* aliciente *m*, estímulo, incentivo

induct [ɪn'dʌkt] *tr* instalar; introducir, iniciar; (mil) quintar

induction [ɪn'dʌkʃən] *s* instalación; introducción; (elec & log) inducción; (mil) quinta

indulge [ɪn'dʌldʒ] *tr* gratificar (*p.ej., los deseos de uno*); mimar (*a un niño*) || *intr* abandonar; **to indulge in** entregarse a, permitirse el placer de

indulgence [ɪn'dʌldʒəns] *s* gusto, inclinación; intemperancia, desenfreno; (*leniency*) indulgencia

indulgent [ɪn'dʌldʒənt] *adj* indulgente
industrial [ɪn'dʌstrɪ·əl] *adj* industrial
industrialist [ɪn'dʌstrɪ·əlɪst] *s* industrial *m*
industrialize [ɪn'dʌstrɪ·ə‚laɪz] *tr* industrializar
industrious [ɪn'dʌstrɪ·əs] *adj* industrioso, aplicado
indus·try ['ɪndəstrɪ] *s* (*pl* -tries) industria
inebriation [ɪn‚ibrɪ'eʃən] *s* embriaguez *f*
inedible [ɪn'ɛdɪbəl] *adj* incomible
ineffable [ɪn'ɛfəbəl] *adj* inefable
ineffective [‚ɪnɪ'fɛktɪv] *adj* ineficaz; (*person*) incapaz
ineffectual [‚ɪnɪ'fɛktʃʊ·əl] *adj* ineficaz, fútil
inefficacy [ɪn'ɛfɪkəsɪ] *s* ineficacia
inefficient [‚ɪnɪ'fɪʃənt] *adj* de mal rendimiento
ineligible [ɪn'ɛlɪdʒɪbəl] *adj* inelegible
inequali·ty [‚ɪnɪ'kwɑlɪtɪ] *s* (*pl* -ties) desigualdad
inequi·ty [ɪn'ɛkwɪtɪ] *s* (*pl* -ties) inequidad
ineradicable [‚ɪnɪ'rædɪkəbəl] *adj* inextirpable
inertia [ɪn'ʌrʃə] *s* inercia
inescapable [‚ɪnɛs'kepəbəl] *adj* ineludible
inevitable [ɪn'ɛvɪtəbəl] *adj* inevitable
inexact [‚ɪnɛg'zækt] *adj* inexacto
inexcusable [‚ɪnɛks'kjuzəbəl] *adj* indisculpable, inexcusable
inexhaustible [‚ɪnɛg'zɔstɪbəl] *adj* inagotable
inexorable [ɪn'ɛksərəbəl] *adj* inexorable
inexpedient [‚ɪnɛk'spidɪ·ənt] *adj* malaconsejado, inoportuno
inexpensive [‚ɪnɛk'spɛnsɪv] *adj* barato, poco costoso
inexperience [‚ɪnɛk'spɪrɪ·əns] *s* inexperiencia
inexplicable [ɪn'ɛksplɪkəbəl] *adj* inexplicable
inexpressible [‚ɪnɛk'sprɛsɪbəl] *adj* inexpresable
Inf. *abbr* **Infantry**
infallible [ɪn'fælɪbəl] *adj* infalible
infamous ['ɪnfəməs] *adj* infame
infa·my ['ɪnfəmɪ] *s* (*pl* -mies) infamia
infan·cy ['ɪnfənsɪ] *s* (*pl* -cies) infancia
infant ['ɪnfənt] *adj* infantil; (*in the earliest stage*) (fig) naciente || *s* criatura, nene *m*
infantile ['ɪnfən‚taɪl] o ['ɪnfəntɪl] *adj* infantil; (*childish*) aniñado
infan·try ['ɪnfəntrɪ] *s* (*pl* -tries) infantería
infantry·man ['ɪnfəntrɪmən] *s* (*pl* -men [mən]) infante *m*, soldado de infantería
infatuated [ɪn'fætʃʊ‚etɪd] *adj* apasionado, locamente enamorado
infect [ɪn'fɛkt] *tr* inficionar, infectar; influir sobre
infection [ɪn'fɛkʃən] *s* infección
infectious [ɪn'fɛkʃəs] *adj* infeccioso
in·fer [ɪn'fʌr] *v* (*pret & pp* -ferred; *ger* -ferring) *tr* inferir; (coll) conjeturar, suponer

inferior [ɪn'fɪrɪ·ər] *adj & s* inferior *m*
inferiority [ɪn‚fɪrɪ'ɑrɪtɪ] *s* inferioridad
inferiority complex *s* complejo de inferioridad
infernal [ɪn'fʌrnəl] *adj* infernal
infest [ɪn'fɛst] *tr* infestar
infidel ['ɪnfɪdəl] *adj & s* infiel *mf*
infideli·ty [‚ɪnfɪ'dɛlɪtɪ] *s* (*pl* -ties) infidelidad
in'field' *s* (baseball) cuadro interior
infiltrate [ɪn'fɪltret] o ['ɪnfɪl‚tret] *tr* infiltrar; infiltrarse en || *intr* infiltrarse
infinite ['ɪnfɪnɪt] *adj & s* infinito
infinitive [ɪn'fɪnɪtɪv] *adj & s* infinitivo
infini·ty [ɪn'fɪnɪtɪ] *s* (*pl* -ties) infinidad; (math) infinito
infirm [ɪn'fʌrm] *adj* infirme, achacoso; (*unsteady*) inestable, inseguro; poco firme, poco sólido
infirma·ry [ɪn'fʌrmərɪ] *s* (*pl* -ries) enfermería
infirmi·ty [ɪn'fʌrmɪtɪ] *s* (*pl* -ties) achaque *m*; inestabilidad
in'fix' *s* (gram) infijo
inflame [ɪn'flem] *tr* inflamar
inflammable [ɪn'flæməbəl] *adj* inflamable
inflammation [‚ɪnflə'meʃən] *s* inflamación
inflate [ɪn'flet] *tr* inflar || *intr* inflarse
inflation [ɪn'fleʃən] *s* inflación; (*of a tire*) inflado
inflect [ɪn'flɛkt] *tr* doblar, torcer; modular (*la voz*); (gram) modificar por inflexión
inflection [ɪn'flɛkʃən] *s* inflexión
inflexible [ɪn'flɛksɪbəl] *adj* inflexible
inflict [ɪn'flɪkt] *tr* infligir
influence ['ɪnflu·əns] *s* influencia || *tr* influir sobre, influenciar
influential [‚ɪnflu'ɛnʃəl] *adj* influyente
influenza [‚ɪnflu'ɛnzə] *s* influenza
inform [ɪn'fɔrm] *tr* informar, avisar, enterar || *intr* informar
informal [ɪn'fɔrməl] *adj* (*not according to established rules*) informal; (*unceremonious; colloquial*) familiar
information [‚ɪnfər'meʃən] *s* información, informes *mpl*
informational [‚ɪnfər'meʃənəl] *adj* informativo
informed sources *spl* los entendidos
infraction [ɪn'frækʃən] *s* infracción
infrared [‚ɪnfrə'rɛd] *adj & s* infrarrojo
infrequent [ɪn'frikwənt] *adj* infrecuente
infringe [ɪn'frɪndʒ] *tr* infringir || *intr* — **to infringe on** o **upon** invadir, abusar de
infringement [ɪn'frɪndʒmənt] *s* infracción
infuriate [ɪn'fjurɪ‚et] *tr* enfurecer
infuse [ɪn'fjuz] *tr* infundir
infusion [ɪn'fjuʒən] *s* infusión
ingenious [ɪn'dʒinjəs] *adj* ingenioso
ingenui·ty [‚ɪndʒɪ'nju·ɪtɪ] o [‚ɪndʒɪ'nu·ɪtɪ] *s* (*pl* -ties) ingeniosidad
ingenuous [ɪn'dʒɛnju·əs] *adj* ingenuo
ingenuousness [ɪn'dʒɛnju·əsnɪs] *s* ingenuidad
ingest [ɪn'dʒɛst] *tr* injerir
in'go'ing *adj* entrante

ingot ['ɪŋgət] s lingote m
ingraft [ɪn'græft] o [ɪn'grɑft] tr (hort & surg) injertar; (fig) implantar
ingrate ['ɪŋgret] s ingrato
ingratiate [ɪn'greʃɪ͵et] tr — to ingratiate oneself with congraciarse con
ingratiating [ɪn'greʃɪ͵etɪŋ] adj atrayente, obsequioso
ingratitude [ɪn'grætɪ͵tjud] o [ɪn'grætɪ͵tud] s ingratitud, desagradecimiento
ingredient [ɪn'gridɪ.ənt] s ingrediente m
in'grow'ing nail s uñero
ingulf [ɪn'gʌlf] tr hundir, inundar
inhabit [ɪn'hæbɪt] tr habitar, poblar
inhabitant [ɪn'hæbɪtənt] s habitante mf
inhale [ɪn'hel] tr aspirar, inspirar || intr aspirar, inspirar; tragar el humo
inherent [ɪn'hɪrənt] adj inherente
inherit [ɪn'herɪt] tr & intr heredar
inheritance [ɪn'herɪtəns] s herencia
inheritor [ɪn'herɪtər] s heredero
inhibit [ɪn'hɪbɪt] tr inhibir, prohibir
inhospitable [ɪn'hɑspɪtəbəl] o [͵ɪnhɑs'pɪtəbəl] adj inhospitalario; (affording no shelter or protection) inhóspito
inhuman [ɪn'hjumən] adj inhumano
inhumane [͵ɪnhju'men] adj inhumano
inhumani·ty [͵ɪnhju'mænɪti] s (pl -ties) inhumanidad
inimical [ɪ'nɪmɪkəl] adj enemigo
iniqui·ty [ɪ'nɪkwɪti] s (pl -ties) iniquidad
ini·tial [ɪ'nɪʃəl] adj & s inicial f || v (pret -tialed o -tialled; ger -tialing o -tialling) tr firmar con sus iniciales; marcar (p.ej., un pañuelo)
initiate [ɪ'nɪʃɪ͵et] tr iniciar
initiation [ɪ͵nɪʃɪ'eʃən] s iniciación
initiative [ɪ'nɪʃɪ.ətɪv] o [ɪ'nɪʃ/ətɪv] s iniciativa
inject [ɪn'dʒekt] tr inyectar; introducir (una especie, una advertencia) || **injection** [ɪn'dʒekʃən] s inyección
injudicious [͵ɪndʒu'dɪʃəs] adj imprudente
injunction [ɪn'dʒʌŋkʃən] s admonición, mandato; (law) entredicho
injure ['ɪndʒər] tr (to harm) dañar, hacer daño a; (to wound) herir, lisiar, lastimar; (to offend) agraviar
injurious [ɪn'dʒʊrɪ.əs] adj dañoso, perjudicial; (offensive) agravioso
inju·ry ['ɪndʒəri] s (pl -ries) (harm) daño; (wound) herida, lesión; (offense) agravio
injustice [ɪn'dʒʌstɪs] s injusticia
ink [ɪŋk] s tinta || tr entintar
inkling ['ɪŋklɪŋ] s sospecha, indicio, noción vaga, vislumbre f
ink'stand' s (cuplike container) tintero; (stand for ink, pens, etc.) portatintero
ink'well' s tintero
ink·y ['ɪŋki] adj (comp -ier; super -iest) entintado; negro
inlaid ['ɪn͵led] o [͵ɪn'led] adj embutido, taraceado
inland ['ɪnlənd] adj & s interior m || adv tierra adentro

in'-law' s (coll) pariente político
in·lay ['ɪn͵le] s embutido || [ɪn'le] o ['ɪn͵le] v (pret & pp -laid) tr embutir, taracear
in'let s ensenada, cala, caleta
in'mate' s (in a hospital or home) asilado, recluso, acogido; (in a jail) presidiario, preso
inn [ɪn] s mesón m, posada
innate [ɪ'net] o ['ɪnet] adj ingénito, innato
inner ['ɪnər] adj interior; secreto
in'ner-spring' mattress s colchón m de muelles interiores
inner tube s cámara (de neumático)
inning ['ɪnɪŋ] s mano f, entrada, turno
inn'keep'er s mesonero, posadero
innocence ['ɪnəsəns] s inocencia
innocent ['ɪnəsənt] adj & s inocente mf
innovate ['ɪnə͵vet] tr innovar
innovation [͵ɪnə've ʃən] s innovación
innuen·do [͵ɪnju'endo] s (pl -does) indirecta, insinuación
innumerable [ɪ'njumərəbəl] o [ɪ'numərəbəl] adj innumerable, incontable
inoculate [ɪn'ɑkjə͵let] tr inocular; (fig) imbuir
inoculation [ɪn͵ɑkjə'leʃən] s inoculación
inoffensive [͵ɪnə'fensɪv] adj inofensivo
inopportune [ɪn͵ɑpər'tjun] o [ɪn͵ɑpər'tun] adj inoportuno
inordinate [ɪn'ɔrdɪnɪt] adj excesivo; (unrestrained) desenfrenado
inorganic [͵ɪnɔr'gænɪk] adj inorgánico
in'put' s gasto, consumo; (elec) entrada; (mech) potencia consumida
inquest ['ɪnkwest] s encuesta; (of coroner) pesquisa judicial, levantamiento del cadáver
inquire [ɪn'kwaɪr] tr averiguar, inquirir || intr preguntar; **to inquire about, after** o **for** preguntar por; **to inquire into** averiguar, inquirir
inquir·y [ɪn'kwaɪri] o ['ɪnkwɪri] s (pl -ies) averiguación, encuesta; pregunta
inquisition [͵ɪnkwɪ'zɪʃən] s inquisición
inquisitive [ɪn'kwɪzɪtɪv] adj curioso, preguntón
in'road' s incursión
ins. abbr **insulated, insurance**
insane [ɪn'sen] adj loco, insano
insane asylum s manicomio, casa de locos
insani·ty [ɪn'sænɪti] s (pl -ties) demencia, locura, insania
insatiable [ɪn'seʃəbəl] adj insaciable
inscribe [ɪn'skraɪb] tr inscribir; dedicar (una obra literaria)
inscription [ɪn'skrɪpʃən] s inscripción; (of a book) dedicatoria
inscrutable [ɪn'skrutəbəl] adj inescrutable
insect ['ɪnsekt] s insecto
insecticide [ɪn'sektɪ͵saɪd] s insecticida m
insecure [͵ɪnsɪ'kjʊr] adj inseguro

inseparable [ɪn'sepərəbəl] *adj* inseparable

insert ['ɪnsʌrt] *s* inserción || [ɪn'sʌrt] *tr* insertar

insertion [ɪn'sʌrʃən] *s* inserción; (*strip of lace*) entredós *m*

in·set ['ɪn,set] *s* intercalación || [ɪn-'set] o ['ɪn,set] *v* (*pret & pp* -set; *ger* -setting) *tr* intercalar, encastrar

in'shore' *adj* cercano a la orilla || *adv* cerca de la orilla; hacia la orilla

in'side' *adj* interior; interno; secreto || *adv* dentro, adentro; **inside of** dentro de; **to turn inside out** volver al revés; volverse al revés || *prep* dentro de || *s* interior *m*; **insides** (coll) entrañas; **on the inside** (coll) en el secreto de las cosas

inside information *s* informes *mpl* confidenciales

insider [,ɪn'saɪdər] *s* persona enterada

insidious [ɪn'sɪdɪ·əs] *adj* insidioso

in'sight' *s* penetración

insigni·a [ɪn'sɪgnɪ·ə] *s* (*pl* -a o -as) insignia

insignificant [,ɪnsɪg'nɪfɪkənt] *adj* insignificante

insincere [,ɪnsɪn'sɪr] *adj* insincero

insinuate [ɪn'sɪnju,et] *tr* insinuar

insipid [ɪn'sɪpɪd] *adj* insípido

insist [ɪn'sɪst] *intr* insistir

insofar as [,ɪnso'far,æz] *conj* en cuanto

insolence ['ɪnsələns] *s* insolencia

insolent ['ɪnsələnt] *adj* insolente

insoluble [ɪn'saljəbəl] *adj* insoluble

insolven·cy [ɪn'salvənsɪ] *s* (*pl* -cies) insolvencia

insomnia [ɪn'samnɪ·ə] *s* insomnio

insomuch [,ɪnso'mʌt] *adv* hasta tal punto; **insomuch as** ya que, puesto que; **insomuch that** hasta el punto que

inspect [ɪn'spekt] *tr* inspeccionar

inspection [ɪn'spekʃən] *s* inspección

inspiration [,ɪnspɪ're ʃən] *s* inspiración

inspire [ɪn'spaɪr] *tr & intr* inspirar

inspiring [ɪn'spaɪrɪŋ] *adj* inspirante

inst. *abbr* instant (*i.e.*, present month)

Inst. *abbr* Institute, Institution

install [ɪn'stɔl] *tr* instalar

installment [ɪn'stɔlmənt] *s* instalación; entrega; **in installments** por entregas; a plazos

installment buying *s* compra a plazos

installment plan *s* pago a plazos, compra a plazos; **on the installment plan** con facilidades de pago

instance ['ɪnstəns] *s* caso, ejemplo; **for instance** por ejemplo

instant ['ɪnstənt] *adj* instantáneo || *s* instante *m*, momento; mes *m* corriente

instantaneous [,ɪnstən'tenɪ·əs] *adj* instantáneo

instantly ['ɪnstəntlɪ] *adv* al instante

instead [ɪn'sted] *adv* preferiblemente; en su lugar; **instead of** en vez de, en lugar de

in'step' *s* empeine *m*

instigate ['ɪnstɪ,get] *tr* instigar

in·still' *tr* instilar

instinct ['ɪnstɪŋkt] *s* instinto

instinctive [ɪn'stɪŋktɪv] *adj* instintivo

institute ['ɪnstɪ,tjut] o ['ɪnstɪ,tut] *s* instituto || *tr* instituir

institution [,ɪnstɪ'tjuʃən] o [,ɪnstɪ-'tuʃən] *s* institución

instruct [ɪn'strʌkt] *tr* instruir

instruction [ɪn'strʌkʃən] *s* instrucción

instructive [ɪn'strʌktɪv] *adj* instructivo

instructor [ɪn'strʌktər] *s* instructor *m*

instrument ['ɪnstrəmənt] *s* instrumento || ['ɪnstrə,ment] *tr* instrumentar

instrumentalist [,ɪnstrə'mentəlɪst] *s* instrumentista *mf*

instrumentali·ty [,ɪnstrəmən'tælɪtɪ] *s* (*pl* -ties) agencia, mediación

insubordinate [,ɪnsə'bɔrdɪnɪt] *adj* insubordinado

insufferable [ɪn'sʌfərəbəl] *adj* insufrible

insufficient [,ɪnsə'fɪʃənt] *adj* insuficiente

insular ['ɪnsələr] o ['ɪnsjulər] *adj* insular; (fig) de miras estrechas

insulate ['ɪnsə,let] *tr* aislar

insulation [,ɪnsə'leʃən] *s* aislación

insulator ['ɪnsə,letər] *s* aislador *m*

insulin ['ɪnsəlɪn] *s* insulina

insult ['ɪnsʌlt] *s* insulto || [ɪn'sʌlt] *tr* insultar

insurance [ɪn'ʃurəns] *s* seguro

insure [ɪn'ʃur] *tr* asegurar

insurer [ɪn'ʃurər] *s* asegurador *m*

insurgent [ɪn'sʌrdʒənt] *adj & s* insurgente *mf*

insurmountable [,ɪnsər'mauntəbəl] *adj* insuperable

insurrection [,ɪnsə'rekʃən] *s* insurrección

insusceptible [,ɪnsə'septɪbəl] *adj* insusceptible

int. *abbr* **interest, interior, internal, international**

intact [ɪn'tækt] *adj* intacto, ileso

in'take' *s* (*place of taking in*) entrada; (*act or amount*) toma; (mach) admisión

intake manifold *s* múltiple *m* de admisión, colector *m* de admisión

intake valve *s* válvula de admisión

intangible [ɪn'tændʒɪbəl] *adj* intangible; vago, indefinido

integer ['ɪntɪdʒər] *s* (arith) entero

integral ['ɪntɪgrəl] *adj* íntegro; **integral with** solidario de || *s* conjunto

integration [,ɪntɪ'greʃən] *s* integración

integrity [ɪn'tegrɪtɪ] *s* integridad

intellect ['ɪntɪ,lekt] *s* intelecto; (*person*) intelectual *mf*

intellectual [,ɪntə'lektʃu·əl] *adj & s* intelectual *mf*

intellectuali·ty [,ɪntə,lektʃu'ælɪtɪ] *s* (*pl* -ties) intelectualidad

intelligence [ɪn'telɪdʒəns] *s* inteligencia; información

intelligence bureau *s* departamento de inteligencia

intelligence quotient *s* cociente *m* intelectual

intelligent [ɪn'telɪdʒənt] *adj* inteligente

intelligentsia [ɪn,telɪ'dʒentsɪ·ə] o [ɪn-,telɪ'gentsɪ·ə] *s* intelectualidad (*con-*

junto de los intelectuales de un país o región)

intelligible [ɪn'telɪdʒɪbəl] *adj* inteligible

intemperance [ɪn'tempərəns] *s* intemperancia

intemperate [ɪn'tempərɪt] *adj* intemperante; *(climate)* riguroso

intend [ɪn'tend] *tr* pensar, proponerse, intentar; *(to mean for a particular purpose)* destinar; *(to signify)* querer decir

intendance [ɪn'tendəns] *s* intendencia

intendant [ɪn'tendənt] *s* intendente *m*

intended [ɪn'tendɪd] *adj & s* (coll) prometido, prometida

intense [ɪn'tens] *adj* intenso

intensi-fy [ɪn'tensɪ,faɪ] *v (pret & pp -fied) tr* intensificar, intensar; (phot) reforzar ‖ *intr* intensificarse, intensarse

intensi-ty [ɪn'tensɪti] *s (pl -ties)* intensidad

intensive [ɪn'tensɪv] *adj* intensivo

intent [ɪn'tent] *adj* atento; resuelto; intenso; **intent on** resuelto a ‖ *s (purpose)* intento; *(meaning)* acepción, sentido; **to all intents and purposes** en realidad de verdad

intention [ɪn'tenʃən] *s* intención

intentional [ɪn'tenʃənəl] *adj* intencional, deliberado

in•ter [ɪn'tʌr] *v (pret & pp -terred; ger -terring) tr* enterrar

interact ['ɪntər,ækt] *s* (theat) entreacto ‖ [,ɪntər'ækt] *intr* obrar recíprocamente

interaction [,ɪntər'ækʃən] *s* interacción

inter-American [,ɪntərə'merɪkən] *adj* interamericano

inter-breed [,ɪntər'brid] *v (pret & pp -bred* ['bred]) *tr* entrecruzar ‖ *intr* entrecruzarse

intercalate [ɪn'tʌrkə,let] *tr* intercalar

intercede [,ɪntər'sid] *intr* interceder

intercept [,ɪntər'sept] *tr* interceptar

interceptor [,ɪntər'septər] *s* interceptor *m*

interchange ['ɪntər,tʃendʒ] *s* intercambio; *(on a highway)* correspondencia ‖ [,ɪntər'tʃendʒ] *tr* intercambiar ‖ *intr* intercambiarse

intercollegiate [,ɪntərkə'lidʒɪ-ɪt] *adj* interescolar

intercom ['ɪntər,kɑm] *s* interfono

intercourse ['ɪntər,kors] *s* comunicación, trato; *(interchange of products, ideas, etc.)* intercambio; *(copulation)* cópula, comercio; **to have intercourse** juntarse

intercross [,ɪntər'krɔs] *o* [,ɪntər'krɑs] *tr* entrecruzar ‖ *intr* entrecruzarse

interdict [,ɪntər'dɪkt] *s* entredicho ‖ [,ɪntər'dɪkt] *tr* interdecir

interest ['ɪntərɪst] *o* ['ɪntrɪst] *s* interés *m*; **the interests** las grandes empresas, el grupo influyente; **to put out at interest** poner a interés ‖ ['ɪntərɪst], ['ɪntrɪst] *o* ['ɪntə,rest] *tr* interesar

interested ['ɪntrɪstɪd] *o* ['ɪntə,restɪd] *adj* interesado

interesting ['ɪntrɪstɪŋ] *o* ['ɪntə,restɪŋ] *adj* interesante

interfere [,ɪntər'fɪr] *intr* inmiscuirse, injerirse, interferir; (sport) parar una jugada; **to interfere with** dificultar, impedir, interferir

interference [,ɪntər'fɪrəns] *s* injerencia, interferencia

interim ['ɪntərɪm] *adj* interino ‖ *s* intermedio, intervalo; **in the interim** entretanto

interior [ɪn'tɪrɪ-ər] *adj & s* interior *m*

interject [,ɪntər'dʒekt] *tr* interponer ‖ *intr* interponerse

interjection [,ɪntər'dʒekʃən] *s* interposición; exclamación; (gram) interjección

interlard [,ɪntər'lɑrd] *tr* interpolar; mechar *(la carne)*

interline [,ɪntər'laɪn] *tr* interlinear; entretelar *(una prenda de vestir)*

interlining ['ɪntər,laɪnɪŋ] *s (of a garment)* entretela

interlink [,ɪntər'lɪŋk] *tr* eslabonar

interlock [,ɪntər'lɑk] *tr* trabar ‖ *intr* trabarse

interlope [,ɪntər'lop] *intr* entremeterse; traficar sin derecho

interloper [,ɪntər'lopər] *s* intruso

interlude ['ɪntər,lud] *s* intervalo; (mus) interludio; (theat) intermedio

intermarriage [,ɪntər'mærɪdʒ] *s* casamiento entre parientes; casamiento entre personas de distintas razas, castas, etc.

intermediar•y [,ɪntər'midɪ,eri] *adj* intermediario ‖ *s (pl -ies)* intermediario

intermediate [,ɪntər'midɪ-ɪt] *adj* intermedio

interment [ɪn'tʌrmənt] *s* entierro

intermez•zo [,ɪntər'metso] *o* [,ɪntər'medzo] *s (pl -zos o -zi* [tsi] *o* [dzi]) (mus) intermedio, intermezzo

intermingle [,ɪntər'mɪŋgəl] *tr* entremezclar ‖ *intr* entremezclarse

intermittent [,ɪntər'mɪtənt] *adj* intermitente

intermix [,ɪntər'mɪks] *tr* entremezclar ‖ *intr* entremezclarse

intern ['ɪntʌrn] *s* interno de hospital ‖ [ɪn'tʌrn] *tr* internar, recluir

internal [ɪn'tʌrnəl] *adj* interno

inter'nal-combus'tion engine *s* motor *m* de explosión

internal revenue *s* rentas internas

international [,ɪntər'næʃənəl] *adj* internacional

international date line *s* línea internacional de cambio de fecha

internationalize [,ɪntər'næʃənə,laɪz] *tr* internacionalizar

internecine [,ɪntər'nisɪn] *adj* sanguinario

internee [,ɪntʌr'ni] *s* (mil) internado

internist [ɪn'tʌrnɪst] *s* internista *mf*

internment [ɪn'tʌrnmənt] *s* internamiento

internship ['ɪntʌrn,ʃɪp] *s* residencia de un médico en un hospital

interpellate [ˌɪntərˈpɛlet] o [ɪnˈtɑrpɪˌlet] *tr* interpelar
interplay [ˈɪntərˌple] *s* interacción
interpolate [ɪnˈtɑrpəˌlet] *tr* interpolar
interpose [ˌɪntərˈpoz] *tr* interponer
interpret [ɪnˈtɑrprɪt] *tr* interpretar
interpreter [ɪnˈtɑrprɪtər] *s* intérprete *mf*
interrogate [ɪnˈterəˌget] *tr & intr* interrogar
interrogation [ɪnˌterəˈgeʃən] *s* interrogación
interrogation mark o **point** *s* signo de interrogación
interrupt [ˌɪntəˈrʌpt] *tr* interrumpir
interscholastic [ˌɪntərskəˈlæstɪk] *adj* interescolar
intersection [ˌɪntərˈsekʃən] *s* (*of streets, roads, etc.*) cruce *m*; (geom) intersección
intersperse [ˌɪntərˈspʌrs] *tr* entremezclar, esparcir
interstice [ɪnˈtʌrstɪs] *s* intersticio
intertwine [ˌɪntərˈtwaɪn] *tr* entrelazar ‖ *intr* entrelazarse
interval [ˈɪntərvəl] *s* intervalo; **at intervals** (*now and then*) de vez en cuando; (*here and there*) de trecho en trecho
intervene [ˌɪntərˈwiv] *intr* intervenir
intervening [ˌɪntərˈvinɪŋ] *adj* intermedio
intervention [ˌɪntərˈvenʃən] *s* intervención
interview [ˈɪntərˌvju] *s* entrevista, interview *m* ‖ *tr* entrevistarse con
inter·weave [ˌɪntərˈwiv] *v* (*pret* -wove [ˈwov] o -weaved; *pp* -wove, woven o weaved*) *tr* entretejer
intestate [ɪnˈtestet] o [ɪnˈtestɪt] *adj & s* intestado
intestine [ɪnˈtestɪn] *s* intestino
inthrall [ɪnˈθrɔl] *tr* cautivar, encantar; esclavizar, sojuzgar
inthrone [ɪnˈθron] *tr* entronizar
intima·cy [ˈɪntɪməsi] *s* (*pl* -cies) intimidad
intimate [ˈɪntɪmɪt] *adj* íntimo ‖ *s* amigo íntimo ‖ [ˈɪntɪˌmet] *tr* insinuar, intimar
intimation [ˌɪntɪˈmeʃən] *s* insinuación
intimidate [ɪnˈtɪmɪˌdet] *tr* intimidar
intitle [ɪnˈtaɪtəl] *tr* dar derecho a; (*to give a name to; to honor with a title*) intitular
into [ˈɪntu] o [ˈɪntu] *prep* en; hacia; hacia el interior de
intolerant [ɪnˈtɑlərənt] *adj & s* intolerante *mf*
intomb [ɪnˈtum] *tr* sepultar
intombment [ɪnˈtummənt] *s* sepultura
intonation [ˌɪntoˈneʃən] *s* entonación
intone [ɪnˈton] *tr* entonar
intoxicant [ɪnˈtɑksɪkənt] *s* bebida alcohólica
intoxicate [ɪnˈtɑksɪˌket] *tr* embriagar, emborrachar; (*to exhilarate*) alegrar, excitar; (*to poison*) envenenar, intoxicar
intoxication [ɪnˌtɑksɪˈkeʃən] *s* embriaguez *f*; alegría, excitación; (*poi-*

soning) envenenamiento, intoxicación
intractable [ɪnˈtræktəbəl] *adj* intratable
intransigent [ɪnˈtrænsɪdʒənt] *adj & s* intransigente *mf*
intransitive [ɪnˈtrænsɪtɪv] *adj* intransitivo
intrench [ɪnˈtrentʃ] *tr* atrincherar ‖ *intr* — **to intrench on** o **upon** infringir, violar
intrepid [ɪnˈtrepɪd] *adj* intrépido
intrepidity [ˌɪntrɪˈpɪdɪti] *s* intrepidez *f*
intricate [ˈɪntrɪkɪt] *adj* intrincado
intrigue [ɪnˈtrig] o [ˈɪntrig] *s* intriga; intriga amorosa, enredo amoroso ‖ [ɪnˈtrig] *tr* (*to arouse the curiosity of*) intrigar ‖ *intr* intrigar; tener intrigas amorosas
intrinsic(al) [ɪnˈtrɪnsɪk(əl)] *adj* intrínseco
introd. *abbr* **introduction**
introduce [ˌɪntrəˈdjus] o [ˌɪntrəˈdus] *tr* introducir; (*to make acquainted*) presentar
introduction [ˌɪntrəˈdʌkʃən] *s* introducción; (*of one person to another or others*) presentación
introductory offer [ˌɪntrəˈdʌktəri] *s* ofrecimiento de presentación, oferta preliminar
introit [ˈɪntroˌɪt] *s* (eccl) introito
introspective [ˌɪntrəˈspektɪv] *adj* introspectivo
introvert [ˈɪntrəˌvʌrt] *s* introvertido
intrude [ɪnˈtrud] *intr* injerirse, entremeterse
intruder [ɪnˈtrudər] *s* intruso, entremetido
intrusive [ɪnˈtrusɪv] *adj* intruso
intrust [ɪnˈtrʌst] *tr* confiar
intuition [ˌɪntuˈɪʃən] o [ˌɪntjuˈɪʃən] *s* intuición
inundate [ˈɪnənˌdet] *tr* inundar
inundation [ˌɪnənˈdeʃən] *s* inundación
inure [ɪnˈjur] *tr* acostumbrar, endurecer, aguerrir ‖ *intr* ponerse en efecto; **to inure to** redundar en
inv. *abbr* **inventor, invoice**
invade [ɪnˈved] *tr* invadir
invader [ɪnˈvedər] *s* invasor *m*
invalid [ɪnˈvælɪd] *adj* inválido (*nulo, de ningún valor*) ‖ [ˈɪnvəlɪd] *adj* inválido (*por viejo o por enfermo*) ‖ [ˈɪnvəlɪd] *s* inválido
invalidate [ɪnˈvælɪˌdet] *tr* invalidar
invalidity [ˌɪnvəˈlɪdɪti] *s* invalidez *f*
invaluable [ɪnˈvælju·əbəl] *adj* inestimable, inapreciable
invariable [ɪnˈveri·əbəl] *adj* invariable
invasion [ɪnˈveʒən] *s* invasión
invective [ɪnˈvektɪv] *s* invectiva
inveigh [ɪnˈve] *intr* — **to inveigh against** lanzar invectivas contra
inveigle [ɪnˈvegəl] o [ɪnˈvigəl] *tr* engatusar
invent [ɪnˈvent] *tr* inventar
invention [ɪnˈvenʃən] *s* invención, invento
inventive [ɪnˈventɪv] *adj* inventivo
inventiveness [ɪnˈventɪvnɪs] *s* inventiva

inventor [ɪn'vɛntər] s inventor m

invento·ry ['ɪnvən,tori] s (pl -ries) inventario ‖ v (pret & pp -ried) tr inventariar

inverse [ɪn'vʌrs] adj inverso

inversion [ɪn'vʌrʒən] o [ɪn'vʌrʃən] s inversión

invert ['ɪnvʌrt] s invertido ‖ [ɪn'vʌrt] tr invertir

invertebrate [ɪn'vʌrtɪ,bret] o [ɪn-'vʌrtɪbrɪt] adj & s invertebrado

inverted exclamation point s principio de admiración

inverted question mark s principio de interrogación

invest [ɪn'vɛst] tr (to vest, to install) investir; invertir (dinero); (to besiege) cercar, sitiar; (to surround, envelop) cubrir, envolver

investigate [ɪn'vɛstɪ,get] tr investigar

investigation [ɪn,vɛstɪ'geʃən] s investigación

investment [ɪn'vɛstmənt] s (of money) inversión; (with an office or dignity) investidura; (siege) cerco, sitio

investor [ɪn'vɛstər] s inversionista mf

inveterate [ɪn'vɛtərɪt] adj inveterado, empedernido

invidious [ɪn'vɪdɪ·əs] adj irritante, odioso, injusto

invigorate [ɪn'vɪgə,ret] tr vigorizar

invigorating [ɪn'vɪgə,retɪŋ] adj vigorizador, vigorizante

invincible [ɪn'vɪnsɪbəl] adj invencible

invisible [ɪn'vɪzɪbəl] adj invisible

invisible ink s tinta simpática

invitation [,ɪnvɪ'teʃən] s invitación, convite m

invite [ɪn'vaɪt] tr invitar, convidar

inviting [ɪn'vaɪtɪŋ] adj atractivo, seductor; (e.g., food) apetitoso

invoice ['ɪnvɔɪs] s factura; as per invoice según factura ‖ tr facturar

invoke [ɪn'vok] tr invocar; evocar, conjurar (p.ej., los demonios)

involuntary [ɪn'vɑlən,tɛri] adj involuntario

involution [,ɪnvə'luʃən] s (math) elevación a potencias, potenciación

involve [ɪn'vɑlv] tr envolver, comprometer

invulnerable [ɪn'vʌlnərəbəl] adj invulnerable

inward ['ɪnwərd] adj interior ‖ adv interiormente, hacia dentro

iodide ['aɪ·ə,daɪd] s yoduro

iodine ['aɪ·ə,daɪn] s yodo ‖ ['aɪ·ə,daɪn] s tintura de yodo

ion ['aɪ·ən] o ['aɪ·ɑn] s ion m

ionize ['aɪ·ə,naɪz] tr ionizar

IOU ['aɪ,o'ju] s (letterword) pagaré m

I.Q. ['aɪ'kju] abbr & s (letterword) **intelligence quotient**

Iran [ɪ'rɑn] o [aɪ'ræn] s el Irán

Iranian [aɪ'renɪ·ən] adj & s iranés m o iranio

Iraq [ɪ'rɑk] s el Irak

Ira·qi [ɪ'rɑki] adj iraqués o iraquiano ‖ s (pl -qis) iraqués m o iraquiano

irate ['aɪret] o [aɪ'ret] adj airado

ire [aɪr] s ira, cólera

Ireland ['aɪrlənd] s Irlanda

iris ['aɪrɪs] s (of the eye) iris m; (rainbow) iris, arco iris; (bot) lirio

Irish ['aɪrɪʃ] adj irlandés ‖ s (language) irlandés m; whisky m de Irlanda; **the Irish** los irlandeses

Irish·man ['aɪrɪʃmən] s (pl -men [mən]) irlandés m

Irish stew s guisado de carne con patatas y cebollas

I'rish·wom'an s (pl -wom'en) irlandesa

irk [ʌrk] tr fastidiar, molestar

irksome ['ʌrksəm] adj fastidioso, molesto

iron ['aɪ·ərn] adj férreo ‖ s hierro; (implement used to press or smooth clothes) plancha; **irons** (fetters) hierros, grilletes mpl; **strike while the iron is hot** a hierro caliente batir de repente ‖ tr planchar (la ropa); **to iron out** allanar (una dificultad)

i'ron·bound' adj zunchado con hierro; (unyielding) férreo, duro, inflexible; (rock-bound) escabroso, rocoso

ironclad ['aɪ·ərn,klæd] adj acorazado, blindado; inflexible, exigente

iron curtain s (fig) telón m de hierro, cortina de hierro

iron digestion s estómago de avestruz

iron horse s (coll) locomotora

ironic(al) [aɪ'rɑnɪk(əl)] adj irónico

ironing ['aɪ·ərnɪŋ] s planchado; ropa planchada; ropa por planchar

ironing board s tabla de planchar

iron lung s pulmón m de acero o de hierro

i'ron·ware' s ferretería

iron will s voluntad de hierro

i'ron·work' s herraje m; **ironworks** ferrería, herrería

i'ron·work'er s herrero de grueso; (metalworker) cerrajero

iro·ny ['aɪrəni] s (pl -nies) ironía

irradiate [ɪ'redɪ,et] tr irradiar; (med) someter a radiación ‖ intr irradiar

irrational [ɪ'ræʃənəl] adj irracional

irrecoverable [,ɪrɪ'kʌvərəbəl] adj incobrable, irrecuperable

irredeemable [,ɪrɪ'diməbəl] adj irredimible

irrefutable [,ɪrɪ'fjutəbəl] o [ɪ'refjutəbəl] adj irrebatible

irregular [ɪ'rɛgjələr] adj irregular ‖ s (mil) irregular m

irrelevance [ɪ'rɛləvəns] s impertinencia, inaplicabilidad

irrelevant [ɪ'rɛləvənt] adj impertinente, inaplicable

irreligious [,ɪrɪ'lɪdʒəs] adj irreligioso

irremediable [,ɪrɪ'midɪ·əbəl] adj irremediable

irremovable [,ɪrɪ'muvəbəl] adj inamovible

irreparable [ɪ'rɛpərəbəl] adj irreparable

irreplaceable [,ɪrɪ'plesəbəl] adj insubstituible, irreemplazable

irrepressible [,ɪrɪ'prɛsɪbəl] adj irreprimible, incontenible

irreproachable [,ɪrɪ'protʃəbəl] adj irreprochable

irresistible [,ɪrɪ'zɪstɪbəl] adj irresistible

irrespective [,ɪrɪ'spɛktɪv] adj — irre-

spective of sin hacer caso de, independiente de

irresponsible [,ırı'spɑnsıbəl] *adj* irresponsable

irretrievable [,ırı'trivəbəl] *adj* irrecuperable

irreverent [ı'revərənt] *adj* irreverente

irrevocable [ı'revəkəbəl] *adj* irrevocable

irrigate ['ırı ,get] *tr* irrigar

irrigation [,ırı'geʃən] *s* irrigación

irritant ['ırıtənt] *adj & s* irritante *m*

irritate ['ırı ,tet] *tr* irritar

irruption [ı'rʌpʃən] *s* irrupción

is. *abbr* **island**

isinglass ['aızıŋ ,glæs] o ['aızıŋ ,glɑs] *s (form of gelatine)* cola de pescado, colapez *f;* mica

isl. *abbr* **island**

Islam ['ısləm] o [ıs'lɑm] *s* el Islam

island ['aılənd] *adj* isleño ‖ *s* isla

islander ['aıləndər] *s* isleño

isle [aıl] *s* isleta

isolate ['aısə ,let] o ['ısə ,let] *tr* aislar

isolation [,aısə'leʃən] o [,ısə'leʃən] *s* aislamiento

isolationist [,aısə'leʃənıst] o [,ısə'leʃənıst] *s* aislacionista *mf*

isosceles [aı'sɑsə ,liz] *adj* isosceles

isotope ['aısə ,top] *s* isótopo

Israe-li [ız'reli] *adj* israelí ‖ *s (pl* **-lis** [liz]) israelí *mf*

Israelite ['ızrı-ə ,laıt] *adj & s* israelita *mf*

issuance ['ıʃu-əns] *s* emisión, expedición

issue ['ıʃu] *s (outgoing; outlet)* salida; *(result)* consecuencia, resultado; *(offspring)* descendencia, sucesión; *(of a magazine)* edición, impresión, tirada, número; *(e.g., of a bond)* emisión; *(yield, profit)* beneficios, producto; punto en disputa; *(pathol)* flujo; **at issue** en disputa; **to face the issue** afrontar la situación; **to force the issue** forzar la solución; **to take issue with** llevar la contraria a ‖ *tr* publicar, dar a luz *(un nuevo libro, una*

revista, etc.); emitir, expedir *(títulos, obligaciones, etc.)*; distribuir *(ropa, alimento)* ‖ *intr* salir; **to issue from** provenir de

isthmus ['ısməs] *s* istmo

it [ıt] *pron pers* (aplícase a cosas inanimadas, a niños de teta, a animales cuyo sexo no se conoce; y muchas veces no se traduce) él, ella; lo, la; **it is I** soy yo; **it is snowing** nieva; **it is three o'clock** son las tres

ital. *abbr* **italics**

Ital. *abbr* **Italian, Italy**

Italian [ı'tæljən] *adj & s* italiano

italic [ı'tælık] *adj (typ)* itálico ‖ **italics** *s (typ)* itálica, bastardilla ‖ **Italic** *adj* itálico

italicize [ı'tælı ,saız] *tr* imprimir en bastardilla; subrayar

Italy ['ıtəli] *s* Italia

itch [ıtʃ] *s* comezón *f;* (pathol) sarna; *(eagerness)* (fig) comezón, prurito ‖ *tr* dar comezón a ‖ *intr* picar; **to itch to** tener prurito por

itch-y ['ıtʃi] *adj (comp* **-ier;** *super* **-iest)** picante, hormigoso; (pathol) sarnoso

item ['aıtəm] *s* artículo; noticia, suelto; *(in an account)* partida

itemize ['aıtə ,maız] *tr* particularizar, especificar, pormenorizar

itinerant [aı'tınərənt] o [ı'tınərənt] *adj* ambulante, errante ‖ *s* viandante *mf*

itinerar-y [aı'tınə ,reri] o [ı'tınə ,reri] *adj* itinerario ‖ *s (pl* **-ies)** itinerario

its [ıts] *adj poss* su ‖ *pron poss* el suyo; suyo

itself [ıt'sɛlf] *pron pers* mismo; sí, sí mismo; se

ivied ['aıvıd] *adj* cubierto de hiedra

ivo-ry ['aıvəri] *adj* marfileño ‖ *s (pl* **-ries)** marfil *m;* **ivories** (slang) teclas del piano; (slang) bolas de billar; *(dice)* (slang) dados; (slang) dientes *mpl*

ivory tower *s* (fig) torre *f* de marfil

ivy ['aıvi] *s (pl* **ivies)** hiedra

J

J, j [dʒe] décima letra del alfabeto inglés

J. *abbr* **Judge, Justice**

jab [dʒæb] *s* hurgonazo; *(prick)* pinchazo; *(with elbow)* codazo ‖ *v (pret & pp* **jabbed;** *ger* **jabbing)** *tr* hurgonear; dar un codazo a ‖ *intr* hurgonear

jabber ['dʒæbər] *s* chapurreo ‖ *tr & intr* chapurrear

jabot [dʒæ'bo] o ['dʒæbo] *s* chorrera

jack [dʒæk] *s (for lifting heavy objects)* gato, cric *m;* (fellow) mozo, sujeto; *(jackass)* asno, burro; *(in card games)* sota, valet *m;* (small ball for bowling) boliche *m;* (jackstone) cantillo; *(device for turning a*

spit) torno de asador; *(figure which strikes a clock bell)* jaquemar *m;* (to remove a boot) sacabotas *m;* marinero; *(flag at the bow)* (naut) yac *m;* (rad & telv) jack *m;* (elec) caja de enchufe; (slang) dinero; **every man Jack** cada hijo de vecino; **jacks** cantillos, juego de los cantillos ‖ *tr —* **to jack up** alzar con el gato; (coll) subir *(sueldos, precios, etc.)*; (coll) recordar su obligación a

jackal ['dʒækɔl] *s* chacal *m*

jackanapes ['dʒækə ,neps] *s* mequetrefe *m*

jack'ass' *s* asno, burro

jack'daw' *s* corneja

jacket ['dʒækıt] *s* chaqueta; *(folded*

paper) cubierta, envoltura; *(paper cover of a book)* sobrecubierta; *(metal casing)* camisa

jack'ham'mer *s* martillo perforador

jack'-in-the-box' *s* caja de sorpresa, jugete-sorpresa *m*, muñeco en una caja de resorte

jack'knife' *s* (*pl* **-knives'**) navaja de bolsillo; *(fancy dive)* salto de carpa

jack of all trades *s* hombre que hace toda clase de oficios, dije *m*

jack-o'-lantern ['dʒækə‚læntərn] *s* fuego fatuo; linterna hecha con una calabaza cortada de modo que remede una cabeza humana

jack pot *s* — **to hit the jack pot** (slang) ponerse las botas

jack rabbit *s* liebre grande norteamericana

jack'screw' *s* cric *m* o gato de tornillo

jack'stone' *s* cantillo; **jackstones** cantillos, juego de los cantillos

jack'-tar' *s* (coll) marinero

jade [dʒed] *adj* verdoso como el jade ‖ *s* *(ornamental stone)* jade *m*; verde *m* de jade; *(worn-out horse)* jamelgo; picarona, mujerzuela ‖ *tr* cansar, ahitar, saciar

jaded ['dʒedɪd] *adj* ahito, saciado

jag [dʒæg] *s* diente *m*, púa; **to have a jag on** (slang) estar borracho

jagged ['dʒægɪd] *adj* dentado, mellado; rasgado en sietes

jaguar ['dʒægwər] *s* jaguar *m*

jail [dʒel] *s* cárcel *f*; **to break jail** escaparse de la cárcel ‖ *tr* encarcelar

jail'bird' *s* (coll) preso, encarcelado; (coll) infractor *m* habitual

jail delivery *s* evasión de la cárcel

jailer ['dʒelər] *s* carcelero

jalop·y [dʒə'lɑpɪ] *s* (*pl* **-ies**) automóvil viejo y ruinoso

jamb [dʒæm] *s* apiñadura, apretura; *(e.g., in traffic)* embotellamiento, bloqueo; *(preserve)* compota, conserva; *(difficult situation)* (coll) aprieto, apuros ‖ *v* (*pret & pp* **jammed**; *ger* **jamming**) *tr* apiñar, apretujar; machucarse *(p.ej., un dedo)*; (rad) perturbar, sabotear; **to jam on the brakes** frenar de golpe

Jamaican [dʒə'mekən] *adj & s* jamaicano; jamaiquino (Am)

jamb [dʒæm] *s* jamba

jamboree [‚dʒæmbə'ri] *s* (coll) francachela, holgorio; reunión de niños exploradores

jamming ['dʒæmɪŋ] *s* radioperturbación

jam nut *s* contratuerca

jam-packed ['dʒæm'pækt] *adj* (coll) apiñado, apretujado, atestado

jam session *s* reunión de músicos de jazz para tocar improvisaciones

jangle ['dʒæŋgəl] *s* cencerreo; altercado, riña ‖ *tr* hacer sonar con ruido discordante ‖ *intr* cencerrear; reñir

janitor ['dʒænɪtər] *s* portero, conserje *m*

janitress ['dʒænɪtrɪs] *s* portera

January ['dʒænju‚erɪ] *s* enero

Ja·pan [dʒə'pæn] *s* laca japonesa; obra japonesa laqueada; aceite *m* secante

(paper); v (*pret & pp* **-panned**; *ger* **-panning**) *tr* barnizar, charolar, laquear con laca japonesa ‖ **Japan** *s* el Japón

Japa·nese [‚dʒæpə'niz] *adj* japonés ‖ *s* (*pl* **-nese**) japonés *m*

Japanese beetle *s* escarabajo japonés

Japanese lantern *s* farolillo veneciano

Japanese persimmon *s* caqui *m*

jar [dʒɑr] *s* tarro; *(e.g., of olives)* frasco; *(of a storage battery)* recipiente *m*; *(jolt)* sacudida; ruido desapacible; sorpresa desagradable; **on the jar** *(said of a door)* entreabierto, entornado ‖ *v* (*pret & pp* **jarred**; *ger* **jarring**) *tr* sacudir; chocar; *(with a noise)* traquetear ‖ *intr* sacudirse; traquetear; disputar; **to jar on** irritar

jardiniere [‚dʒɑrdɪ'nɪr] *s* (*stand*) jardinera; *(pot, bowl)* florero

jargon ['dʒɑrgən] *s* jerga, jerigonza

jasmine ['dʒæsmɪn] o ['dʒæzmɪn] *s* jazmín *m*

jasper ['dʒæspər] *s* jaspe *m*

jaundice ['dʒɔndɪs] o ['dʒɑndɪs] *s* ictericia; (fig) envidia, celos, negro humor

jaundiced ['dʒɔndɪst] o ['dʒɑndɪst] *adj* ictericiado; (fig) avinagrado

jaunt [dʒɔnt] o [dʒɑnt] *s* caminata, excursión, paseo

jaun·ty ['dʒɔntɪ] o ['dʒɑntɪ] *adj* (*comp* **-tier**; *super* **-tiest**) airoso, gallardo, vivo; elegante, de buen gusto

Java·nese [‚dʒævə'niz] *adj* javanés ‖ *s* (*pl* **-nese**) javanés *m*

javelin ['dʒævlɪn] o ['dʒævəlɪn] *s* jabalina

jaw [dʒɔ] *s* mandíbula, quijada; **into the jaws of death** a las garras de la muerte; **jaws** boca, garganta ‖ *tr* (slang) regañar ‖ *intr* (slang) regañar; (slang) chacharear, chismear

jaw'bone' *s* mandíbula, quijada

jaw'break'er *s* *(word)* (coll) trabalenguas *m*; *(candy)* (coll) hinchabocas *m*; (mach) trituradora de quijadas

jay [dʒe] *s* (orn) arrendajo; (coll) tonto, necio

jay'walk' *intr* (coll) cruzar la calle descuidadamente

jay'walk'er *s* (coll) peatón descuidado

jazz [dʒæz] *s* (mus) jazz *m*; (coll) animación, viveza ‖ *tr* — **to jazz up** (coll) animar, dar viveza a

jazz band *s* orquesta de jazz

J.C. *abbr* **Jesus Christ, Julius Caesar**

jct. *abbr* **junction**

jealous ['dʒeləs] *adj* celoso; envidioso; *(watchful in keeping or guarding something)* solícito, vigilante

jealous·y ['dʒeləsɪ] *s* (*pl* **-ies**) celosía, celos; envidia; solicitud, vigilancia

jean [dʒin] *s* dril *m*; **jeans** pantalones *mpl* de dril

Jeanne d'Arc [‚ʒɑn'dɑrk] *s* Juana de Arco

jeep [dʒip] *s* jip *m*, pequeño automóvil de propulsión total

jeer [dʒɪr] *s* befa, mofa, vaya ‖ *tr*

befar || *intr* mofarse; **to jeer at** befar, mofarse de

jelab [dʒə'lɑb] *s* chilaba

jell [dʒɛl] *s* jalea || *intr* (*to become jellylike*) cuajarse; (*to take hold, catch on*) (fig) cuajar

jel·ly ['dʒɛli] *s* (*pl* **-lies**) jalea || *v* (*pret & pp*) *tr* convertir en jalea || *intr* convertirse en jalea

jel'ly-fish' *s* aguamala, medusa; (*weak person*) (coll) calzonazos *m*

jeopardize ['dʒɛpər,daɪz] *tr* arriesgar, exponer, poner en peligro

jeopardy ['dʒɛpərdi] *s* riesgo, peligro

jeremiad [,dʒɛrɪ'maɪæd] *s* jeremiada

Jericho ['dʒɛrɪ,ko] *s* Jericó

jerk [dʒʌrk] *s* arranque *m*, estirón *m*, tirón *m*; tic *m*, espasmo muscular; **by jerks** a sacudidas || *tr* mover de un tirón; arrojar de un tirón; atasajar (*carne*) || *intr* avanzar a tirones

jerked beef *s* tasajo

jerkin ['dʒʌrkɪn] *s* jubón *m*, justillo

jerk'wa'ter train *s* (coll) tren de ferrocarril económico

jerk·y ['dʒʌrki] *adj* (*comp* **-ier**; *super* **-iest**) (*road; style*) desigual; que va dando tumbos, que anda a tirones

Jerome [dʒə'rom] *s* Jerónimo

jersey ['dʒʌrzi] *s* jersey *m*, chaqueta de punto

Jerusalem [dʒɪ'rusələm] *s* Jerusalén

jest [dʒɛst] *s* broma, chanza, chiste *m*; cosa de risa; **in jest** en broma || *intr* bromear

jester ['dʒɛstər] *s* bromista *mf*, burlón *m*; (*professional fool of medieval rulers*) bufón *m*

Jesuit ['dʒɛʒʊ·ɪt] *o* ['dʒɛzjʊ·ɪt] *adj & s* jesuíta *m*

Jesuitic(al) [,dʒɛʒʊ'ɪtɪk(əl)] *o* [,dʒɛzjʊ'ɪtɪk(əl)] *adj* jesuítico

Jesus ['dʒizəs] *s* Jesús *m*

Jesus Christ *s* Jesucristo

jet [dʒɛt] *adj* de azabache; azabachado || *s* (*of a fountain*) surtidor *m*; (*of gas*) mechero; (*stream shooting forth from nozzle, etc.*) chorro; avión *m* a reacción, avión de chorro; (*hard black mineral; lustrous black*) azabache *m* || *v* (*pret & pp* **jetted**) *ger* **jetting**) *tr* arrojar en chorro || *intr* chorrear, salir en chorro; volar en avión de chorro

jet age *s* era de los aviones de chorro

jet'-black' *adj* azabachado

jet bomber *s* bombardero de reacción a chorro

jet coal *s* carbón *m* de bujía, carbón de llama larga

jet engine *s* motor *m* a chorro, motor de reacción

jet fighter *s* caza *m* de reacción, cazareactor *m*

jet'lin'er *s* avión *m* de travesía con propulsión a chorro

jet plane *s* avión *m* de chorro

jet propulsion *s* propulsión a chorro, propulsión de escape

jetsam ['dʒɛtsəm] *s* (naut) echazón *f*; cosas desechadas

jet stream *s* escape *m* de un motor cohete; (meteor) chorros de viento

(*que soplan de oeste a este a la altura de 10 kilómetros*)

jettison ['dʒɛtɪsən] *s* (naut) echazón *f* || *tr* (naut) echar al mar; desechar, rechazar

jettison gear *s* (aer) lanzador *m*

jet·ty ['dʒɛti] *s* (*pl* **-ties**) (*structure projecting into sea to protect harbor*) escollera, malecón *m*; (*wharf*) muelle *m*, desembarcadero

Jew [dʒu] *s* judío

jewel ['dʒu·əl] *s* piedra preciosa; (*valuable personal ornament*) alhaja, joya; (*of a watch*) rubí *m*; (*article of costume jewelry*) joya de imitación; (*highly prized person or thing*) alhaja, joya

jewel case *s* guardajoyas *m*, estuche *m*, joyero

jeweler *o* **jeweller** ['dʒu·ələr] *s* joyero; relojero

jewelry ['dʒu·əlri] *s* joyería, joyas

jewelry shop *s* joyería; relojería

Jewess ['dʒu·ɪs] *s* judía

jew'fish' *s* mero

Jewish ['dʒu·ɪʃ] *adj* judío

Jew·ry ['dʒu·ri] *s* (*pl* **-ries**) judería

jews'-harp *o* **jew's-harp** ['dʒuz,harp] *s* birimbao

jib [dʒɪb] *s* (*of a crane*) aguilón *m*, pescante *m*; (naut) foque *m*

jib boom *s* (naut) botalón *m* de foque

jibe [dʒaɪb] *s* remoque *m*, mofa || *intr* mofarse; (coll) concordar (*dos cosas*); **to jibe at** mofarse de

jif·fy ['dʒɪfi] *s* (*pl* **-fies**) — **in a jiffy** (coll) en un santiamén

jig [dʒɪg] *s* (*dance and music*) giga; **the jig is up** (slang) ya se acabó todo, estamos perdidos

jigger ['dʒɪgər] *s* (*for fishing*) anzuelo de cuchara; (*for separating ore*) criba de vaivén; (*flea*) nigua; (*gadget*) cosilla, chisme *m*, dispositivo; vasito para medir el licor de un coctel (*onza y media*)

jiggle ['dʒɪgəl] *s* zangoloteo || *tr* zangolotear || *intr* zangolotearse

jig saw *s* sierra de vaivén

jig'saw' puzzle *s* rompecabezas *m* (*figura que ha sido cortada caprichosamente en trozos menudos y que hay que recomponer*)

jilt [dʒɪlt] *tr* dar calabazas a (*un novio*)

jim·my ['dʒɪmi] *s* (*pl* **-mies**) palanqueta || *v* (*pret & pp* **-mied**) *tr* forzar con palanqueta; **to jimmy open** abrir con palanqueta

jingle ['dʒɪŋgəl] *s* (*small bell*) cascabel *m*; (*of tambourine*) sonaja; (*sound*) cascabeleo; rima infantil; (rad) anuncio rimado y cantado || *tr* hacer sonar || *intr* cascabelear

jin·go ['dʒɪŋgo] *adj* jingoísta || *s* (*pl* **-goes**) jingoísta *mf*; **by jingo!** (coll) ¡caramba!

jingoism ['dʒɪŋgo,ɪzəm] *s* jingoísmo

jinx [dʒɪŋks] *s* gafe *m* || *tr* (coll) traer mala suerte a

jitters ['dʒɪtərz] *spl* (coll) inquietud, nerviosidad; **to give the jitters to**

(coll) poner nervioso; **to have the jitters** (coll) ponerse nervioso

jittery ['dʒɪtəri] *adj* (coll) nervioso

Joan of Arc ['dʒɔn əv 'ɑrk] *s* Juana de Arco

job [dʒɑb] *s* (*piece of work*) trabajo; (*task, chore*) quehacer *m*, tarea; (*work done by contract*) destajo; (*employment*) empleo, oficio; (coll) robo; **by the job** a destajo; **on the job** trabajando de aprendiz; (slang) vigilante, atento a sus obligaciones; **to be out of a job** estar desocupado, estar sin trabajo; **to lie down on the job** (slang) echarse en el surco, estirar la pierna

job analysis *s* análisis *m* ocupacional

jobber ['dʒɑbər] *s* comerciante medianero; (*pieceworker*) destajero; (*dishonest official*) agiotista *m*

job'hold'er *s* empleado; (*in the government*) burócrata *mf*

jobless ['jɑblɪs] *adj* desocupado, sin empleo

job lot *s* saldo de mercancías

job printer *s* impresor *m* de remiendos

job printing *s* remiendo

jockey ['dʒɑki] *s* jockey *m* ‖ *tr* montar (*un caballo*) en la pista; maniobrar; embaucar

jockstrap ['dʒɑk ˌstræp] *s* suspensorio (*para sostener el escroto*)

jocose [dʒo'kos] *adj* jocoso

jocular ['dʒɑkjələr] *adj* jocoso, festivo

jog [dʒɑg] *s* golpecito; (*to the memory*) estímulo; trote corto ‖ *v* (*pret & pp* **jogged;** *ger* **jogging**) *tr* empujar levemente; estimular (*la memoria*) ‖ *intr* — **to jog along** avanzar al trote corto

jog trot *s* trote *m* de perro; (fig) rutina

John [dʒɑn] *s* Juan *m*

John Bull *s* el inglés típico, el pueblo inglés

John Hancock ['hænkɑk] *s* (coll) la firma de uno

johnnycake ['dʒɑni ˌkek] *s* pan *m* de maíz

John'ny-come'-late'ly *s* (coll) recién llegado

John'ny-jump'-up' *s* (*pansy*) pensamiento, trinitaria; violeta

John'ny-on-the-spot' *s* (coll) el que está siempre presente y listo

John the Baptist *s* San Juan Bautista

join [dʒɔɪn] *tr* juntar, unir, ensamblar; asociarse a, unirse a; incorporarse a, ingresar en; abrazar (*un partido*); hacerse socio de (*una asociación*); alistarse en (*el ejército*); trabar (*batalla*); desaguar en (*el océano*) ‖ *intr* juntarse, unirse; confluir (*p.ej., dos ríos*)

joiner ['dʒɔɪnər] *s* carpintero; (coll) el que tiene la manía de incorporarse a muchas asociaciones

joint [dʒɔɪnt] *s* (*in a pipe*) empalme *m*, juntura; (*of bones*) articulación, juntura, coyuntura; (*backbone of book*) nervura; (*hinge of book*) cartivana; (*in woodwork*) emsambladura; (*of meat*) tajada; (elec) empalme *m*; (*gambling den*) (slang)

garito; (slang) restaurante *m* de mala muerte; **out of joint** desencajado, descoyuntado; (fig) en desorden, desbarajustado; **to throw out of joint** descoyuntarse (*p.ej., el brazo*)

joint account *s* cuenta en común

Joint Chiefs of Staff *spl* (U.S.A.) Estado mayor conjunto

jointly ['dʒɔɪntli] *adv* juntamente, en común

joint owner *s* condueño

joint session *s* sesión conjunta

joint'-stock' company *s* sociedad anónima, compañía por acciones

joist [dʒɔɪst] *s* viga

joke [dʒok] *s* broma, chiste *m*; (*trifling matter*) cosa de reír; (*person laughed at*) bufón *m*, hazmerreír *m*; **no joke** cosa seria; **to tell a joke** contar un chiste; **to play a joke on** gastar una broma a ‖ *tr* — **to joke one's way into** conseguir (*p.ej., un empleo*) burla burlando ‖ *intr* bromear, hablar en broma; **joking aside** o **no joking** burlas aparte

joke book *s* libro de chistes

joker ['dʒokər] *s* bromista *mf*; (*wise guy*) sábelotodo; (*playing card*) comodín *m*; (*hidden provision*) cláusula engañadora

jol·ly ['dʒɑli] *adj* (*comp* **-lier;** *super* **-liest**) alegre, festivo ‖ *adv* (coll) muy, harto ‖ *v* (*pret & pp* **-lied**) *tr* (coll) candonguear

jolt [dʒolt] *s* sacudida ‖ *tr* sacudir ‖ *intr* dar tumbos

Jonah ['dʒonə] *s* Jonás *m*; (fig) ave *f* de mal agüero

jongleur ['dʒɑŋglər] *s* juglar *m*, trovador *m*

jonquil ['dʒɑŋkwɪl] *s* junquillo

Jordan ['dʒɔrdən] *s* (*country*) Jordania; (*river*) Jordán *m*

Jordan almond *s* almendra de Málaga

Jordanian [dʒɔr'denɪən] *adj & s* jordano

josh [dʒɑʃ] *tr* (coll) dar broma a ‖ *intr* dar broma

jostle ['dʒɑsəl] *s* empellón *m*, empujón *m* ‖ *tr* empellar, empujar ‖ *intr* chocar, encontrarse; avanzar a fuerza de empujones o codazos

jot [dʒɑt] *s* — **I don't care a jot for** no se me da un bledo de ‖ *v* (*pret & pp* **jotted;** *ger* **jotting**) *tr* — **to jot down** apuntar, anotar

jounce [dʒaʊns] *s* sacudida ‖ *tr* sacudir ‖ *intr* dar tumbos

journal ['dʒʌrnəl] *s* (*newspaper*) periódico; (*magazine*) revista; (*daily record*) diario; (com) libro diario; (naut) cuaderno de bitácora; (mach) gorrón *m*, muñón *m*

journalese [ˌdʒʌrnə'liz] *s* lenguaje periodístico

journalism ['dʒʌrnə ˌlɪzəm] *s* periodismo

journalist ['dʒʌrnəlɪst] *s* periodista *mf*

journalistic [ˌdʒʌrnə'lɪstɪk] *adj* periodístico

journey ['dʒʌrni] *s* viaje *m* ‖ *intr* viajar

journey·man ['dʒʌrnimən] s (pl **-men** [mən]) oficial m

joust [dʒʌst] o [dʒust] o [dʒaust] s justa || *intr* justar

jovial ['dʒovɪ·əl] *adj* jovial

joviality [ˌdʒovɪˈælɪti] s jovialidad

jowl [dʒaul] s (*cheek*) moflete m; (*jawbone*) quijada; (*of cattle*) papada; (*of fowl*) barba

joy [dʒɔɪ] s alegría, regocijo; **to leap with joy** saltar de gozo

joyful ['dʒɔɪfəl] *adj* alegre; **joyful over** gozoso con o de

joyless ['dʒɔɪlɪs] *adj* triste, sin alegría

joyous ['dʒɔɪ·əs] *adj* alegre

joy ride s (coll) paseo de recreo en coche; (coll) paseo alocado en coche

J.P. *abbr* **Justice of the Peace**

Jr. *abbr* **junior**

jubilant ['dʒubɪlənt] *adj* jubiloso

jubilation [ˌdʒubɪˈleʃən] s júbilo, viva alegría

jubilee ['dʒubɪˌli] s (*jubilation*) júbilo; aniversario; quincuagésimo aniversario; (eccl) jubileo

Judaism ['dʒude ˌɪzəm] s judaísmo

judge [dʒʌdʒ] s juez m; **to be a good judge of** ser buen juez de o en || *tr* & *intr* juzgar; **judging by** a juzgar por

judge advocate s (*in the army*) auditor m de guerra; (*in the navy*) auditor de marina

judgeship ['dʒʌdʒʃɪp] s judicatura

judgment ['dʒʌdʒmənt] s juicio; (*legal decision*) sentencia, fallo

judgment day s día m del juicio

judgment seat s tribunal m

judicature ['dʒudɪkətʃər] s judicatura

judicial [dʒuˈdɪʃəl] *adj* judicial; (*becoming a judge*) crítico, juicioso

judiciar·y [dʒuˈdɪʃɪˌɛri] *adj* judicial || s (pl **-ies**) (*judges of a city, country, etc.*) judicatura; (*branch of government that administers justice*) poder m judicial

judicious [dʒuˈdɪʃəs] *adj* juicioso

jug [dʒʌg] s botija, jarra, cántaro; (*jail*) (slang) chirona

juggle ['dʒʌgəl] s juego de manos; (*trick, deception*) trampa || *tr* hacer suertes con (p.ej., *bolas*); alterar fraudulentamente, falsear (*cuentas, documentos, etc.*); **to juggle away** escamotear || *intr* hacer suertes; hacer trampas

juggler ['dʒʌglər] s malabarista mf; impostor m

juggling ['dʒʌglɪŋ] s juegos malabares

Jugoslav ['jugo'slɑv] *adj* & s yugoeslavo

Jugoslavia ['jugo'slɑvɪ·ə] s Yugoeslavia

jugular ['dʒʌgjələr] o ['dʒugjələr] *adj* & s yugular f

juice [dʒus] s jugo, zumo; (*natural fluid of an animal body*) jugo; (slang) electricidad; (slang) gasolina; **to stew in one's own juice** (coll) freír en su aceite

juic·y ['dʒusi] *adj* (*comp* **-ier;** *super* **-lest**) jugoso, zumoso; (*interesting, spicy*) picante

jukebox ['dʒuk ˌbɑks] s tocadiscos m tragamonedas

julep ['dʒulɪp] s julepe m

julienne [ˌdʒulɪ'ɛn] s sopa juliana

July [dʒu'laɪ] s julio

jumble ['dʒʌmbəl] s revoltijo, masa confusa || *tr* emburujar, revolver

jum·bo ['dʒʌmbo] *adj* (coll) enorme, colosal || s (pl **-bos**) (*large clumsy person*) (coll) elefante m; (coll) objeto enorme

jump [dʒʌmp] s salto; (*in a parachute*) lanzamiento; (*of prices*) alza repentina; **to be always on the jump** (coll) andar siempre de aquí para allí; **to get o to have the jump on** (slang) ganar la ventaja a || *tr* saltar; hacer saltar (*a un caballo*); (*in checkers*) comer; salir (*un tren*) fuera de (*el carril*) || *intr* saltar; (*in a parachute from an airplane*) lanzarse; pasar del tope (*el carro de la máquina de escribir*); **to jump at** apresurarse a aceptar (*un convite*); apresurarse a aprovechar (*la oportunidad*); **to jump on** saltar a (*un tren*); (slang) regañar, criticar; **to jump over** saltar por, pasar de un salto; saltar (*la página de un libro*); **to jump to a conclusion** sacar una conclusión precipitadamente

jumper ['dʒʌmpər] s saltador m; blusa de obrero; **jumpers** traje holgado de juego para niños

jumping jack ['dʒʌmpɪŋ] s títere m

jump'ing-off' place s fin m del camino

jump seat s estrapontín m, traspuntín m

jump spark s (elec) chispa de entrehierro

jump wire s (elec) alambre m de cierre

jump·y ['dʒʌmpi] *adj* (*comp* **-ier;** *super* **-lest**) saltón; asustadizo, nervioso

junc. *abbr* **junction**

junction ['dʒʌŋk[ən] s juntura, unión; (*of pieces of wood*) ensambladura; (*of two rivers*) confluencia; (*rail connection*) empalme m; (rr) estación de empalme

juncture ['dʒʌŋktʃər] s juntura, unión; (*time, occasion*) coyuntura; **at this juncture** a esta sazón, a estas alturas

June [dʒun] s junio

jungle ['dʒʌŋgəl] s jungla, selva; revoltijo, maraña

junior ['dʒunjər] *adj* menor, de menor edad; joven; del penúltimo año; hijo, p.ej., **John Jones, Junior** Juan Jones, hijo || s menor m; socio menor; alumno del penúltimo año

junior college s escuela de estudios universitarios de primero y segundo años

junior high school s escuela intermedia entre la primaria y la secundaria

juniper ['dʒunɪpər] s enebro; (*red cedar*) cedro de Virginia

juniper berry s enebrina

junk [dʒʌŋk] s chatarra, hierro viejo; ropa vieja; (*useless stuff*) (coll) trastos viejos, baratijas viejas; (*old cable*) jarcia trozada; (*Chinese ship*) junco; (naut) carne salada || *tr* (slang) echar a la basura; reducir a hierro viejo

junk dealer s chatarrero, chapucero

junket ['dʒʌŋkɪt] s manjar m de leche, cuajo y azúcar; (*outing*) viaje m de recreo; (*trip paid out of public funds*) jira || *intr* hacer un viaje de recreo; ir de jira

junk·man ['dʒʌŋk ,mæn] s (pl -**men** [,men]) chatarrero, chapucero; ropavejero; tripulante m de junco

junk room s leonera, trastera

junk shop s tienda de trastos viejos

junk yard s chatarrería

juridical [dʒʊ'rɪdɪkəl] adj jurídico

jurisdiction [,dʒʊrɪs'dɪkʃən] s jurisdicción

jurisprudence [,dʒʊrɪs'prudəns] s jurisprudencia

jurist ['dʒʊrɪst] s jurista mf

juror ['dʒʊrər] s (*individual*) jurado

ju·ry ['dʒʊri] s (pl -**ries**) (*group*) jurado

jury box s tribuna del jurado

jury·man ['dʒʊrimən] s (pl -**men** [mən]) (*individual*) jurado

Jus. P. *abbr* **justice of the peace**

just [dʒʌst] adj justo || adv justamente, justo; hace poco, apenas; sólo; (coll) absolutamente; **just** + *pp* acabado de + *inf*, p.ej., **just received** acabado de recibir; **recién** + *pp*, p.ej., **just arrived** recién llegado; **just as** como; en el momento en que; tal como, lo mismo que; **just beyond** un poco más allá (de); **just now** hace poco; ahora mismo; **just out** acabado de

aparecer, recién publicado; **to have just** + *pp* acabar de + *inf*, p.ej., I **have just arrived** acabo de llegar; I **had just arrived** acababa de llegar

justice ['dʒʌstɪs] s justicia; (*judge*) juez m; (*just deserts*) premio merecido; **to bring to justice** aprehender y condenar por justicia; **to do justice to** hacer justicia a; apreciar debidamente

justice of the peace s juez m de paz

justifiable ['dʒʌstɪ ,faɪ·əbəl] adj justificable

justi·fy ['dʒʌstɪ ,faɪ] v (pret & pp -**fied**) *tr* justificar; (typ) justificar

justly ['dʒʌstli] adj justamente, debidamente

jut [dʒʌt] v (pret & pp **jutted**; ger **jutting**) intr — **to jut out** resaltar, proyectarse

jute [dʒut] s yute m || **Jute** m juto

Jutland ['dʒʌtlənd] s Jutlandia

juvenile ['dʒuvənɪl] o ['dʒuvə ,naɪl] adj juvenil; para jóvenes || s joven mf, mocito; libro para niños; (theat) galán m, galancete m

juvenile court s tribunal m tutelar de menores

juvenile delinquency s delincuencia de menores

juvenile lead [lid] s (theat) papel m de galancete; (theat) galancete m

juvenilia [,dʒuvə'nɪlɪ·ə] spl obras de juventud

juxtapose [,dʒʌkstə'poz] *tr* yuxtaponer

K

K, k [ke] undécima letra del alfabeto inglés

k. *abbr* **karat, kilogram**

K. *abbr* **King, Knight**

kale [kel] s col f, berza; (slang) dinero, pasta

kaleidoscope [kə'laɪdə ,skop] s calidoscopio

kangaroo [,kæŋgə'ru] s canguro

kapok ['kepɑk] s capoc m, lana de ceiba

katydid ['ketidɪd] s saltamontes m cuyo macho emite un sonido chillón

kc. *abbr* **kilocycle**

kedge [kedʒ] s (naut) anclote m

keel [kil] s quilla || *intr* — **to keel over** (naut) dar de quilla; volcarse; (coll) desmayarse

keelson ['kelsən] o ['kɪlsən] s (naut) sobrequilla

keen [kin] adj (*having a sharp edge*) agudo, afilado; (*sharp, cutting*) mordaz, penetrante; (*sharp-witted*) sutil, astuto, perspicaz; (*eager, much interested*) entusiasta; intenso, vivo; (slang) maravilloso; **to be keen on** ser muy aficionado a

keep [kip] s manutención, subsisten-

cia; (*of medieval castle*) torre f del homenaje; **for keeps** (coll) de veras; (coll) para siempre; **to earn one's keep** (coll) ganarse la vida || v (pret & pp **kept** [kept]) *tr* guardar, conservar; (*deciding to make a purchase*) quedarse con; cumplir, guardar (*su palabra, su promesa*); llevar (*cuentas*); apuntar (*los tantos*); tener (*criados, caballos, huéspedes*); cultivar (*una huerta*); dirigir (*un hotel, una escuela*); celebrar (*una fiesta*); hacer tardar (*a una persona*); **to keep away** tener alejado; **to keep back** retener; beberse (*las lágrimas*); reservar, no divulgar; **to keep down** reprimir; reducir (*los gastos*) al mínimo; **to keep** (*a person*) **from** + *ger* no 'dejarle (*a una persona*) + *inf*; **to keep in** no dejar salir; **to keep off** tener a distancia; no dejar penetrar (*p.ej., la lluvia*); evitar (*p.ej., el polvo*); **to keep out** no dejar entrar; no dejar penetrar; **to keep someone informed** (about) ponerle a uno al corriente (de); **to keep someone waiting** hacerle a uno esperar; **to keep up** mantener, conservar || intr permanecer, quedarse; conservarse, no echarse a perder; **to keep +** ger seguir + ger; **to keep away** mantenerse a distancia; no dejarse ver; **to keep from** + ger abstenerse de + inf; **to keep informed (about)** ponerse al corriente (de); **to keep in with** (coll) congraciarse con, no perder el favor de; **to keep off** no acercarse a; no pisar (el césped); **to keep on** + ger seguir + ger; **to keep on with** continuar con; **to keep out** mantenerse fuera, no entrar; **to keep out of** no entrar en; no meterse en; evitar (el peligro); **to keep quiet** estarse quieto; **to keep to** seguir por, llevar (la derecha, la izquierda); **to keep to oneself** quedarse a solas; **to keep up** continuar; no rezagarse; **to keep up with** correr parejas con; llevar adelante, proseguir

keeper ['kipər] s guardián m, custodio; (of a game preserve) guardabosque m; (of a magnet) armadura, culata

keeping ['kipɪŋ] s custodia, cuidado; (of a holiday) celebración; **in keeping with** de acuerdo con, en armonía con; **in safe keeping** en lugar seguro, a buen recaudo; **out of keeping with** en desacuerdo con

keep'sake' s recuerdo

keg [kɛg] s cuñete m, cubeto

ken [kɛn] s alcance m de la vista, alcance del saber; **beyond the ken of** fuera del alcance de

kennel ['kɛnəl] s perrera

kep·i ['kepi] o ['kɛpi] s (pl -is) quepis m

kept woman [kɛpt] s entretenida, manceba

kerchief ['kʌrtʃɪf] s pañuelo, mantón m

kerchoo [kər'tʃu] interj ¡ah-chís!

kernel ['kʌrnəl] s (inner part of a nut or fruit stone) almendra, núcleo; (of wheat or corn) grano; (fig) medula

kerosene ['kɛrəˌsin] o [ˌkɛrə'sin] s keroseno

kerosene lamp s lámpara de petróleo

kerplunk [kər'plʌŋk] interj ¡pataplún!

ketchup ['kɛtʃəp] s salsa de tomate condimentada

kettle ['kɛtəl] s caldera, marmita; (teakettle) tetera

ket'tle-drum' s timbal m, tímpano

key [ki] adj clave || s (of door, trunk, etc.) llave f; (of piano, typewriter, etc.) tecla; (wedge or cotter used to lock parts together) clavija, cuña, chaveta; (reef or low island) cayo; (bot) sámara; (tone of voice) tono; (mus) clave f o llave f; (telg) manipulador m; (to a puzzle, secret, translation, code) (fig) clave o llave; (place giving control to a region) (fig) llave f; (fig) persona principal; **off key** desafinado; desafinadamente || tr acuñar, enchavetar; **to key up** alentar, excitar

key'board' s teclado

key fruit s sámara

key'hole' s ojo de la cerradura; (of a clock) agujero de cuerda

key'note' s (mus) tónica, nota tónica; (fig) idea fundamental

keynote speech s discurso de apertura (en que se expone el programa de un partido político)

key ring s llavero

key'stone' s clave f, espinazo; (fig) piedra angular

Key West s Cayo Hueso

key word s palabra clave

kg. abbr **kilogram**

K.G. abbr **Knight of the Garter**

kha·ki ['kɑki] o ['kæki] adj caqui || s (pl -kis) caqui m

khedive [kə'div] s jedive m

kibitz ['kɪbɪts] intr (coll) dar consejos molestos a los jugadores

kibitzer ['kɪbɪtsər] s (coll) mirón molesto (de una partida de juego); (coll) entremetido

kiblah ['kɪblə] s alquibla

kibosh ['kaɪbɑʃ] o [kɪ'bɑʃ] s (coll) música celestial; **to put the kibosh on** (coll) desbaratar, imposibilitar

kick [kɪk] s puntapié m; (of an animal) coz f; (of a gun) coz, culatazo; (complaint) (slang) queja, protesta; (of liquor) (slang) fuerza, estímulo; (thrill) gusto, placer intenso; **to get a kick out of** (slang) hallar mucho placer en || tr acerca, dar de puntapiés a; sacudir (los pies); **to kick out** (coll) echar a puntapiés a la calle; (coll) echar, despedir; **to kick up a row** (slang) armar un bochinche || intr cocear; dar culetazos (un arma de fuego); (coll) quejarse; **to kick about** (coll) quejarse de; **to kick against the pricks** dar coces contra el aguijón; **to kick off** (football) dar el golpe de salida

kick'back' s (coll) contragolpe m; (slang) devolución a un cómplice de una parte de lo robado

kick'off' s (football) golpe m de salida, puntapié m inicial

kid [kɪd] s (young goat) cabrito; (leather) cabritilla; (coll) chiquillo, chico; **kids** guantes mpl o zapatos de cabritilla || v (pret & pp **kidded;** ger **kidding**) tr (slang) embromar, tomar el pelo a; **to kid oneself** (slang) forjarse ilusiones || intr (slang) decirlo en broma

kidder ['kɪdər] s (slang) bromista mf

kid gloves spl guantes mpl de cabritilla; **to handle with kid gloves** tratar con suma discreción o cautela

kid'nap' s (pret & pp **-naped** o **-napped;** ger **-naping** o **-napping**) tr secuestrar

kidnaper o **kidnapper** ['kɪdˌnæpər] s secuestrador m, ladrón m de niños

kidney ['kɪdni] s riñón m; (coll) clase f, especie f; (coll) carácter m

kidney bean s judía

kidney stone s cálculo renal

kill [kɪl] s matanza; (of a wild beast, an army, a pack of hounds) ataque m final; (creek) arroyo, riachuelo; **for the kill** para el golpe final || tr matar; ahogar (*un proyecto de ley*); quitar (*el sabor*); producir una impresión irresistible en

killer ['kɪlər] *s* matador *m*

killer whale *s* orca

killing ['kɪlɪŋ] *adj* matador; (*exhausting*) abrumador; (coll) muy divertido, de lo más ridículo ‖ *s* matanza; (*game killed on a hunt*) cacería, piezas; (coll) gran ganancia; **to make a killing** (coll) enriquecerse de golpe

kill'-joy' *s* aguafiestas *mf*

kiln [kɪl] o [kɪln] *s* horno

kil·o ['kɪlo] o ['kilo] *s* (*pl* -os) kilo, kilogramo; kilómetro

kilocycle ['kɪlə,saɪkəl] *s* kilociclo

kilogram ['kɪlə,græm] *s* kilogramo

kilometer ['kɪlə,mitər] o [kɪ'lɑmɪtər] *s* kilómetro

kilometric [,kɪlə'metrɪk] *adj* kilométrico

kilowatt ['kɪlə,wɑt] *s* kilovatio

kilowatt-hour ['kɪlə,wɑt'aʊr] *s* (*pl* **kilowatt-hours**) kilovatio-hora

kilt [kɪlt] *s* enagüillas, falda corta

kilter ['kɪltər] *s* — **to be out of kilter** (coll) estar descompuesto

kimo·no [kɪ'monə] o [kɪ'mono] *s* (*pl* -nos) quimono

kin [kɪn] *s* (*family relationship*) parentesco; (*relatives*) deudos; **near of kin** muy allegado; **of kin** allegado; **the next of kin** el pariente más próximo, los parientes próximos

kind [kaɪnd] *adj* bueno, bondadoso; (*greeting*) afectuoso; **kind to** bueno para con ‖ *s* clase *f*, especie *f*, suerte *f*, género; **a kind of** uno a modo de; **all kinds of** (coll) gran cantidad de; **in kind** en especie; en la misma moneda; **kind of** (coll) algo, más bien; **of a kind** de una misma clase; (*poor, mediocre*) de poco valor, de mala muerte; **of the kind** por el estilo

kindergarten ['kɪndər,gɑrtən] *s* escuela de párvulos, jardín *m* de la infancia

kindergartner ['kɪndər,gɑrtnər] *s* (*child*) párvulo; (*teacher*) parvulista *mf*

kind-hearted ['kaɪnd'hɑrtɪd] *adj* bondadoso, de buen corazón

kindle ['kɪndəl] *tr* encender ‖ *intr* encenderse

kindling ['kɪndlɪŋ] *s* encendajas

kindling wood *s* leña

kind·ly ['kaɪndli] *adj* (*comp* -lier; *super* -liest) (*kind-hearted*) bondadoso; apacible, benigno; favorable ‖ *adv* bondadosamente; cordialmente; con gusto; por favor; **to not take kindly to** no aceptar de buen grado

kindness ['kaɪndnɪs] *s* bondad; **have the kindness to** tenga Vd. la bondad de

kindred ['kɪndrɪd] *adj* emparentado; afín, semejante ‖ *s* parentela; semejanza, afinidad

kinescope ['kɪnɪ,skop] *s* (trademark) cinescopio, kinescopio

kinetic [kɪ'netɪk] o [kaɪ'netɪk] *adj* cinético ‖ **kinetics** *s* cinética

kinetic energy *s* fuerza viva, energía cinética

king [kɪŋ] *s* rey *m*; (cards, chess, & fig) rey; (checkers) dama

king'bolt' *s* pivote *m* central

kingdom ['kɪŋdəm] *s* reino

king'fish'er *s* martín *m* pescador

king·ly ['kɪŋli] *adj* (*comp* -lier; *super* -liest) real, regio; (*stately*) majestuoso ‖ *adv* regiamente

king'pin' *s* (bowling) bolo delantero; pivote *m* central; (aut) pivote de dirección; (coll) persona principal

king post *s* pendolón *m*

king's evil *s* escrófula

kingship ['kɪŋʃɪp] *s* dignidad real

king'-size' *adj* de tamaño largo

king's ransom *s* riquezas de Creso

kink [kɪŋk] *s* (*twist, e.g., in a rope*) enroscadura, coca; (*e.g., in Negro's hair*) pasa; (*soreness in neck*) tortícolis *m*; (*flaw, difficulty*) estorbo, traba; (*mental twist*) chifladura, manía ‖ *tr* enroscar ‖ *intr* enroscarse

kink·y ['kɪŋki] *adj* (*comp* -ier; *super* -iest) encarrujado, ensortijado

kinsfolk ['kɪnz,fok] *s* parentela, familia, deudos

kinship ['kɪnʃɪp] *s* parentesco; semejanza, afinidad

kins·man ['kɪnzmən] *s* (*pl* -men [mən]) pariente *m*

kins·woman ['kɪnz,wumən] *s* (*pl* -women [,wɪmɪn]) *s* parienta

kipper ['kɪpər] *s* arenque acecinado, salmón acecinado ‖ *tr* acecinar (*el arenque o el salmón*)

kiss [kɪs] *s* beso; (billiards) retruco; (*confection*) dulce *m*, merengue *m* ‖ *tr* besar; **to kiss away** borrar con besos (*las penas de una persona*) ‖ *intr* besar; besarse; (billiards) retrucar

kit [kɪt] *s* cartera de herramientas; (*case and its contents for various purposes*) estuche *m*; (*of a soldier*) equipo, pertrechos; (*of a traveler*) equipaje *m*; (pail, tub) balde *m*

kitchen ['kɪtʃən] *s* cocina

kitchenette [,kɪtʃə'net] *s* cocinilla

kitchen garden *s* huerto

kitch'en-maid' *s* ayudanta de cocina, pincha

kitchen police *s* (mil) trabajo de cocina; soldados que están de cocina

kitchen range *s* cocina económica

kitchen sink *s* fregadero

kitch'en-ware' *s* utensilios de cocina

kite [kaɪt] *s* cometa; (orn) milano; **to fly a kite** hacer volar una cometa

kith and kin [kɪθ] *spl* parientes *mpl*; parientes y amigos

kitten ['kɪtən] *s* gatito, minino

kittenish ['kɪtənɪʃ] *adj* juguetón, retozón; (*coy, flirtatious*) coquetón

kit·ty ['kɪti] *s* (*pl* -ties) gatito, minino; (*in card games*) polla, puesta ‖ *interj* ¡miz!

kleptomaniac [,kleptə'menɪ,æk] *s* cleptómano

km. *abbr* **kilometer**

knack [næk] *s* tino, tranquillo, maña

knapsack ['næp,sæk] *s* mochila

knave [nev] *s* bribón *m*, pícaro; (cards) sota

knaver·y ['nevəri] *s* (*pl* -ies) bribonería, picardía

knead [nid] *tr* amasar, sobar

knee [ni] *s* rodilla; (*of animal*) codillo; (*e.g., of trousers*) rodillera; (mach) ángulo, codo; **to bring** (*someone*) **to his knees** rendir, vencer; **to go down on one's knees** hincarse de rodillas, caer de rodillas; **to go down on one's kness to** implorar de rodillas

knee breeches ['brɪtʃɪz] *spl* pantalones cortos

knee'cap' *s* rótula; (*protective covering*) rodillera

knee'-deep' *adj* metido hasta las rodillas

knee'-high' *adj* que llega hasta la rodilla

knee'hole' *s* hueco para acomodar las rodillas

knee jerk *s* reflejo rotuliano

kneel [nil] *v* (*pret & pp* **knelt** [nelt] o **kneeled**) *intr* arrodillarse; estar de rodillas

knee'pad' *s* rodillera

knee'pan' *s* rótula

knee swell *s* (*of organ*) (mus) rodillera

knell [nel] *s* doble *m*, toque *m* de difuntos; mal agüero; **to toll the knell of** anunciar la muerte de, anunciar el fin de ‖ *intr* doblar, tocar a muerto; sonar tristemente

knickers ['nɪkərz] *spl* pantalones *mpl* de media pierna

knickknack ['nɪk‚næk] *s* chuchería, bujería, baratija

knife [naɪf] *s* (*pl* **knives** [naɪvz]) cuchillo; (*of a paper cutter or other instrument*) cuchilla; **to go under the knife** (coll) hacerse operar ‖ *tr* acuchillar; (slang) traicionar

knife sharpener *s* afilador *m*, afilón *m*

knife switch *s* (elec) interruptor *m* de cuchilla

knight [naɪt] *s* caballero; (chess) caballo ‖ *tr* armar caballero

knight-errant ['naɪt'erənt] *s* (*pl* **knights-errant**) caballero andante

knight-errant·ry ['naɪt'erəntri] *s* (*pl* -ries) caballería andante; (*quixotic behavior*) quijotada

knighthood ['naɪt‚hʊd] *s* caballería

knightly ['naɪtli] *adj* caballeroso, caballeresco

Knight of the Rueful Countenance *s* Caballero de la triste figura (*Don Quijote*)

knit [nɪt] *v* (*pret & pp* **knitted** o **knit**; *ger* **knitting**) *tr* tejer a punto de aguja; enlazar, unir; fruncir (*las cejas*), arrugar (*la frente*) ‖ *intr* hacer calceta, hacer malla; trabarse, unirse; soldarse (*un hueso*)

knit goods *spl* géneros de punto

knitting ['nɪtɪŋ] *s* punto de media, trabajo de punto

knitting machine *s* máquina de hacer tejidos de punto

knitting needle *s* aguja de hacer media

knit'wear' *s* géneros de punto

knob [nɑb] *s* (*lump*) bulto, protuberancia; (*of a door*) botón *m*, tirador *m*; (*of a radio set*) botón, perilla; (*ornament on furniture*) manzana; colina o montaña redondeada

knock [nɑk] *s* golpe *m*; (*e.g., on a door*) toque *m*, llamada; (*with a door knocker*) aldabazo; (*of an internal-combustion engine*) pistoneo; (slang) censura, crítica ‖ *tr* golpear; (*repeatedly*) golpetear; (slang) censurar, criticar; **to knock down** (*with a blow, punch, etc.*) derribar; (*to the highest bidder*) rematar; desarmar, desmontar (*un aparato o máquina*); **to knock off** hacer saltar con un golpe; suspender (*el trabajo*); poner fin a; (slang) matar; **to knock out** agotar; (box) poner fuera de combate ‖ *intr* tocar, llamar; golpear, pistonear (*el motor de combustión interna*); (slang) censurar, criticar; **to knock about** andar vagando; **to knock against** dar contra, tropezar con; **to knock at** tocar a, llamar a (*la puerta*); **to knock off** dejar de trabajar

knocker ['nɑkər] *s* (*on a door*) aldaba; (coll) criticón *m*

knock-kneed ['nɑk‚nid] *adj* patizambo, zambo

knock'out' *s* golpe decisivo, puñetazo decisivo; (box) (el) fuera de combate; (elec) destapadero; (coll) real moza

knockout drops *spl* (slang) gotas narcóticas

knoll [nol] *s* loma, otero

knot [nɑt] *s* nudo; (*worn as ornament*) lazo; corrillo, grupo; (*difficult matter; bond or tie*) nudo; nudo o lazo de matrimonio; (*protuberance in a fabric*) envoltorio; (naut) nudo; **to tie the knot** (coll) casarse ‖ *v* (*pret & pp* **knotted;** *ger* **knotting**) *tr* anudar; fruncir (*las cejas*) ‖ *intr* anudarse

knot'hole' *s* agujero en la madera (*que deja un nudo al desprenderse*)

knot·ty ['nɑti] *adj* (*comp* -tier; *super* -tiest) nudoso; (fig) espinoso, difícil

know [no] *s* — **to be in the know** estar enterado, tener informes secretos ‖ *v* (*pret* **knew** [nju] o [nu]; *pp* **known**) *tr & intr* (*by reasoning or learning*) saber; (*by the senses or by perception; through acquaintance or recognition*) conocer; **as far as I know** que yo sepa; **to know about** saber de; **to know best** ser el mejor juez, saber lo que más conviene; **to know how to** + *inf* saber + *inf*; **to know it all** (coll) sabérselo todo; **to know what one is doing** obrar con conocimiento de causa; **to know what's what** (coll) saber cuántas son cinco; **you ought to know better** deberías tener vergüenza

knowable ['no·əbəl] *adj* conocible

know'-how' *s* conocimiento, destreza, habilidad

knowingly ['no·ɪŋli] *adv* a sabiendas,

con conocimiento de causa; (*on purpose*) adrede

know'-it-all' *adj & s* (coll) sabidillo

knowledge ['nɑlɪdʒ] *s* (*faculty*) ciencia, conocimientos, el saber; (*awareness, acquaintance, familiarity*) conocimiento; **to have a thorough knowledge of** conocer a fondo; **to my knowledge** que yo sepa; **to the best of my knowledge** según mi leal saber y entender; **with full knowledge** con conocimiento de causa; **without my knowledge** sin saberlo yo

knowledgeable ['nɑlɪdʒəbəl] *adj* (coll) conocedor, inteligente

know'-noth'ing *s* ignorante *mf*

knuckle ['nʌkəl] *s* nudillo; (*of a quadruped*) jarrete *m*; (mach) junta de charnela; **knuckles** bóxer *m* ǁ *intr* — **to knuckle down** someterse, darse por vencido; aplicarse con empeño al trabajo

knurl [nʌrl] *s* moleteado ǁ *tr* moletear, cerrillar (*p.ej., las piezas de moneda*)

k.o. *abbr* **knockout**

Koran [ko'rɑn] o [ko'ræn] *s* Corán *m*

Korea [ko'ri.ə] *s* Corea

Korean [ko'ri.ən] *adj & s* coreano

kosher ['koʃər] *adj* autorizado por la ley judía; (coll) genuino

kowtow ['kau'tau] o ['ko'tau] *intr* arrodillarse y tocar el suelo con la frente; doblegarse servilmente, mostrarse servilmente obsequioso

Kt. *abbr* **Knight**

kudos ['kjudɑs] o ['kudɑs] *s* (coll) gloria, renombre *m*, fama

kw. *abbr* **kilowatt**

K.W.H. *abbr* **kilowatt-hour**

L

L, l [εl] duodécima letra del alfabeto inglés

l. *abbr* **liter, line, league, length**

L. *abbr* **Latin, Low**

la·bel ['lebəl] *s* etiqueta, marbete *m*, rótulo; (*descriptive word*) calificación ǁ *v* (*pret & pp* -beled o -belled; *ger* -beling o -belling) *tr* poner etiqueta o marbete a, rotular; calificar

labial ['lebɪ·əl] *adj & s* labial *f*

labor ['lebər] *adj* obrero ǁ *s* trabajo, labor *f*; (*job, task*) tarea, faena; (*manual work involved in an undertaking; the wages for such work*) mano *f* de obra; (*wage-earning workers as contrasted with capital and management*) los obreros; (*childbirth*) parto; **labors** esfuerzos; **to be in labor** estar de parto ǁ *intr* trabajar; (*to exert oneself*) forcejar; estar de parto; moverse penosamente; cabecear y balancear (*un buque*); **to labor under** ser víctima de

labor and management *spl* los obreros y los patronos

laborato·ry ['læbərə,tori] *s* (*pl* -ries) laboratorio

labored ['lebərd] *adj* penoso, dificultoso; artificial, forzado

laborer ['lebərər] *s* trabajador *m*, obrero; (*unskilled worker*) bracero, jornalero, peón *m*

laborious [lə'borɪ·əs] *adj* laborioso

la'bor-man'agement *adj* obrero-patronal

labor union *s* gremio obrero, sindicato

Labourite ['lebə,raɪt] *s* laborista *mf*

Labrador ['læbrə,dɔr] *s* el Labrador

labyrinth ['læbɪrɪnθ] *s* laberinto

lace [les] *s* encaje *m*; (*string to tie shoe, corset, etc.*) cordón *m*, lazo; (*braid*) galón *m* de oro o plata ǁ *tr* adornar con encaje; atar (*los zapatos, el corsé*); (coll) dar una paliza a

lace trimming *s* randa

lace'work' *s* encaje *m*, obra de encaje

lachrymose ['lækrɪ,mos] *adj* lacrimoso

lacing ['lesɪŋ] *s* cordón *m*; lazo; galón *m*; (coll) paliza

lack [læk] *s* carencia, falta; (*complete lack*) defecto ǁ *tr* carecer de, necesitar ǁ *intr* (*to be lacking*) faltar

lackadaisical [,lækə'dezɪkəl] *adj* desaprovechado, indiferente

lackey ['lækɪ] *s* lacayo; secuaz *m* servil

lacking ['lækɪŋ] *prep* sin, carente de

lack'lus'ter *adj* deslustrado, deslucido

laconic [lə'kɑnɪk] *adj* lacónico

lacquer ['lækər] *s* laca ǁ *tr* laquear

lacquer ware *s* lacas, objetos de laca

lacu·na [lə'kjunə] *s* (*pl* -nas o -nae [ni]) laguna

lac·y ['lesɪ] *adj* (*comp* -ier; *super* -iest) de encaje; (fig) diáfano

lad [læd] *s* muchacho, chico

ladder ['lædər] *s* escalera; (*stepladder*) escala, escalera de mano; (*two ladders fastened together at the top with hinges*) escalera de tijera; (*stepping stone*) (fig) escalón *m*

ladder truck *s* carro de escaleras de incendio

ladies' room *s* cuarto tocador

ladle ['ledəl] *s* cazo; (*for soup*) cucharón *m*; (*of tinsmith*) cucharilla ǁ *tr* servir con cucharón; sacar con cucharón

la·dy ['ledɪ] *s* (*pl* -dies) señora, dama

la'dy-bird' o **la'dy-bug'** *s* mariquita, vaca de San Antón

la'dy-fin'ger *s* melindre *m*

lady in waiting *s* camarera de la reina

la'dy-kil'ler *s* ladrón *m* de corazones

la'dy-like' *adj* elegante; **to be ladylike** ser muy dama

la'dy-love' s amada, amiga querida

lady of the house s ama de casa

ladyship ['ledi‚ʃɪp] s señoría

lady's maid s doncella

lady's man s perico entre ellas

lag [læg] s retraso || v (pret & pp **lagged;** ger **lagging**) intr retrasarse; **to lag behind** quedarse atrás, rezagarse

lager beer ['lɑgər] s cerveza reposada

laggard ['lægərd] s perezoso, rezagado

lagoon [lə'gun] s laguna

laid paper [led] s papel vergueteado

laid up adj almacenado, ahorrado; (naut) inactivo; (coll) encamado por estar enfermo

lair [ler] s cubil m

lai·ty ['le·ɪti] s legos

lake [lek] adj lacustre || s lago

lamb [læm] s cordero; carne f de cordero; piel f de cordero; (meek person) (fig) cordero

lambaste [læm'best] tr (to thrash) (coll) dar una paliza a; (to reprimand harshly) (coll) dar una jabonadura a

lamb chop s chuleta de cordero

lambkin ['læmkɪn] s corderito; (fig) nenito

lamb's-skin' s piel f de cordero, corderina; (dressed with its wool) corderillo

lame [lem] adj cojo; (sore) dolorido; (e.g., excuse) débil, pobre || tr encojar

lament [lə'ment] s lamento; (dirge) elegía || tr lamentar || intr lamentarse

lamentable ['læməntəbəl] adj lamentable

lamentation [‚læmən'teʃən] s lamentación

laminate ['læmɪ‚net] tr laminar

lamp [læmp] s lámpara

lamp'black' s negro de humo

lamp chimney s tubo de lámpara

lamp'light' s luz f de lámpara

lamp'light'er s farolero

lampoon [læm'pun] s pasquín m, libelo || tr pasquinar

lamp'post' s poste m de farol

lamp shade s pantalla de lámpara

lamp'wick' s mecha de lámpara, torcida

lance [læns] o [lɑns] s lanza; (surg) lanceta || tr alancear; (surg) abrir con lanceta

lance rest s ristre m

lancet ['lænsɪt] o ['lɑnsɪt] s (surg) lanceta

land [lænd] adj terrestre; (wind) terral || s tierra; **on land, on sea, and in the air** en tierra, mar y aire; **to make land** atracar a tierra; **to see how the land lies** medir el terreno, ver el cariz que van tomando las cosas || tr desembarcar; conducir (un avión) a tierra; coger (un pez); (coll) conseguir || intr desembarcar; (to reach land) arribar, aterrar; aterrizar (un avión); (to arrive or come to rest) ir a dar, ir a parar; **to land on one's**

feet caer de pies; **to land on one's head** caer de cabeza

landau ['lændɔ] o ['lændau] s landó m

land breeze s terral m

landed ['lændɪd] adj (owning land) hacendado; (real-estate) inmobiliario; **landed property** bienes mpl raíces

land'fall' s (sighting land) aterrada; (landing of ship or plane) aterraje m; tierra vista desde el mar; (landslide) derrumbe m

land grant s donación de tierras

land'hold'er s terrateniente mf, hacendado

landing ['lændɪŋ] s (of ship or plane) aterraje m; (of passengers) desembarco; (place where passengers and goods are landed) desembarcadero; (of stairway) desembarco, descanso

landing beacon s (aer) radiofaro de aterrizaje

landing craft s (nav) lancha de desembarco

landing field s (aer) pista de aterrizaje

landing force s (nav) compañía de desembarco

landing gear s (aer) tren m de aterrizaje

landing stage s embarcadero flotante

landing strip s (aer) faja de aterrizaje

land'la'dy s (pl -dies) (e.g., of an apartment) casera, dueña; (of a lodging house) ama, patrona; (of an inn) mesonera, posadera

landlocked ['lænd‚lɑkt] adj rodeado de tierra

land'lord' s (e.g., of an apartment) casero, dueño; (of a lodging house) amo, patrón m; (of an inn) mesonero, posadero

land'lub'ber s (person unacquainted with the sea) marinero de agua dulce; (awkward and unskilled seaman) marinero matalote

land'mark' s (boundary stone) mojón m; (feature of landscape that marks a location) guía; suceso que hace época; (naut) marca de reconocimiento

land office s oficina del catastro

land'-of'fice business s (coll) negocio de mucho movimiento

land'own'er s terrateniente mf, hacendado

landscape ['lænd‚skep] s paisaje m || tr ajardinar

landscape architect s arquitecto paisajista

landscape gardener s jardinero adornista, jardinista mf

landscape painter s paisajista mf

landscapist ['lænd‚skepɪst] s paisajista mf

land'slide' s derrumbe m, derrumbamiento de tierra, corrimiento; (fig) mayoría de votos abrumadora; (fig) victoria arrolladora

landward ['lændwərd] adv hacia tierra, hacia la costa

land wind s terral m

lane [len] s (narrow street or passage) callejuela; (path) carril m; (of an *automobile highway*) faja; (*of an air or ocean route*) derrotero, vía

langsyne ['læŋ'saɪn] *adv* (Scotch) hace mucho tiempo || *s* (Scotch) tiempo de antaño

language ['læŋgwɪdʒ] *s* idioma *m*, lengua; (*way of speaking or writing, style; figurative or poetic expression; communication of meaning said to be employed by flowers, birds, art, etc.*) lenguaje *m*; (*of a special group of people*) jerga

languid ['læŋgwɪd] *adj* lánguido

languish ['læŋgwɪʃ] *intr* languidecer; afectar languidez

languor ['læŋgər] *s* languidez *f*

languorous ['læŋgərəs] *adj* lánguido; (*causing languor*) enervante

lank [læŋk] *adj* descarnado, larguirucho; (*hair*) lacio

lank·y ['læŋkɪ] *adj* (*comp* **-ier;** *super* **-iest**) descarnado, larguirucho

lantern ['læntərn] *s* linterna

lantern slide *s* diapositiva, tira de vidrio

lanyard ['lænjərd] *s* (naut) acollador *m*

lap [læp] *s* (*of human body or clothing*) regazo; (*loose fold*) caída, doblez *f*; (*overlap of garment*) traslapo; (*with the tongue*) lametada; (*of the waves*) chapaleteo; (*in a race*) (sport) etapa, vuelta; **to live in the lap of luxury** llevar una vida regalada || *v* (*pret & pp* **lapped;** *ger* **lapping**) *tr* beber con la lengua; lamer (*las olas la playa*); (*to overlap*) traslapar; juntar a traslapo; **to lap up** tragar a lengüetadas; (coll) aceptar con entusiasmo || *intr* traslapar; traslaparse (*dos o más cosas*); **to lap against** lamer (*las olas la playa*); **to lap over** salir fuera, rebosar

lap'board' *s* tabla faldera

lap dog *s* perro de falda

lapel [lə'pɛl] *s* solapa

Lap'land' *s* Laponia

Laplander ['læp,lændər] *s* lapón *m* (*habitante*)

Lapp [læp] *s* lapón *m* (*habitante; idioma*)

lap robe *s* manta de coche

lapse [læps] *s* (*passing of time; slipping into guilt or error*) lapso; (*fall, decline*) caída; caída en desuso; (*e.g., of an insurance policy*) invalidación || *intr* caer en culpa o error; decaer, pasar (*p.ej., el entusiasmo*); caducar (*p.ej., una póliza de seguro*)

lap'wing' *s* ave fría

larce·ny ['larsənɪ] *s* (*pl* **-nies**) hurto, robo

larch [lartʃ] *s* alerce *m*, lárice *m*

lard [lard] *s* cochevira, manteca de puerco || *tr* (culin) mechar

larder ['lardər] *s* despensa

large ['lardʒ] *adj* grande; **at large** en libertad

large intestine *s* intestino grueso

largely ['lardʒlɪ] *adv* por la mayor parte

largeness ['lardʒnɪs] *s* grandeza

large'-scale' *adj* en grande escala, grande escala

lariat ['lærɪ·ət] *s* (*for catching animals*) lazo; (*for tying grazing animals*) cuerda, soga

lark [lark] *s* alondra; (coll) parranda; **to go on a lark** (coll) andar de parranda, echar una cana al aire

lark'spur' *s* (*rocket larkspur*) espuela de caballero; (*field larkspur*) consuelda real

lar·va ['larvə] *s* (*pl* **-vae** [vi]) larva

laryngeal [lə'rɪndʒɪ·əl] o [,lærɪn'dʒɪ·əl] *adj* laríngeo

laryngitis [,lærɪn'dʒaɪtɪs] *s* laringitis *f*

laryngoscope [lə'rɪŋgə,skop] *s* laringoscopio

larynx ['lærɪŋks] *s* (*pl* **larynxes** o **larynges** [lə'rɪndʒiz]) laringe *f*

lascivious [lə'sɪvɪ·əs] *adj* lascivo

lasciviousness [lə'sɪvɪ·əsnɪs] *s* lascivia

lash [læʃ] *s* (*cord on end of whip*) tralla; (*blow with whip; scolding*) latigazo; (*e.g., of animal's tail*) coletazo; (*of waves*) embate *m*; (*eyelash*) pestaña || *tr* (*to beat, whip*) azotar; (*to bind, tie*) atar; (*to shake, to switch*) agitar, sacudir; (*to attack with words*) increpar, reñir || *intr* lanzarse, pasar rápidamente; **to lash out at** azotar; embestir; vituperar

lashing ['læʃɪŋ] *s* atadura; paliza, zurra; (*severe scolding*) latigazo

lass [læs] *s* muchacha, chica; amada

las·so ['læso] o [læ'su] *s* (*pl* **-sos** o **-soes**) lazo || *tr* lazar

last [læst] o [last] *adj* (*after all others; the only remaining; utmost, extreme*) último; (*most recent*) pasado; **before last** antepasado; **every last one** todos sin excepción; **last but one** penúltimo || *adv* después de todos; por último; por última vez || *s* última persona; última cosa; fin *m*; (*for holding shoe*) horma; **at last** por fin; **at long last** al fin y al cabo; **stick to your last!** ¡zapatero, a tus zapatos!; **the last of the month** a fines del mes; **to breathe one's last** dar el último suspiro; **to see the last of** no volver a ver; **to the last** hasta el fin || *intr* durar; resistir; dar buen resultado (*p.ej., una prenda de vestir*); seguir así

lasting ['læstɪŋ] o ['lastɪŋ] *adj* perdurable, duradero

lastly ['læstlɪ] o ['lastlɪ] *adv* finalmente, por último

last'-min'ute news *s* noticias de última hora

last name *s* apellido

last night *adv* anoche

last quarter *s* cuarto menguante

last sleep *s* último sueño

last straw *s* acabóse *m*, colmo

Last Supper *s*, **the** la Cena

last will and testament *s* última disposición, última voluntad

last word *s* última palabra; (*latest style*) (coll) última palabra

lat. *abbr* **latitude**

Lat. *abbr* **Latin**

latch [lætʃ] s picaporte m || tr cerrar con picaporte

latch'key' s llavín m

latch'string' s cordón m de aldaba; the latchstring is out ya sabe Vd. que ésta es su casa

late [let] adj (happening after the usual time) tardío; (person) atrasado; (hour of the night) avanzado; (news) de última hora; (party, meeting, etc.) que termina tarde; (coming toward the end of a period of time) de fines de; (incumbent of an office) anterior; (deceased) difunto, fallecido; of late recientemente, últimamente; to be late ser tarde; tardar (p.ej., el tren); to be late in + ger tardar en + inf; to grow late hacerse tarde || adv tarde; late in (the week, the month, etc.) a fines de, hacia fines de; late in life a una edad avanzada

late-comer ['let,kʌmər] s recién llegado; (one who arrives late) rezagado

lateen sail [læ'tin] s vela latina

lateen yard s entena

lately ['letli] adv recientemente, últimamente

latent ['letənt] adj latente

lateral ['lætərəl] adj lateral

lath [læθ] o [lɑθ] s lata, listón; enlistonado || tr enlistonar

lathe [leð] s torno (máquina que sirve para labrar madera, hierro, etc. con un movimiento circular)

lather ['læðər] s espuma de jabón; espuma de sudor || tr enjabonar; (coll) tundir, zurrar || intr espumar

lathery ['læðəri] adj espumoso, jabonoso

lathing ['læθɪŋ] o ['lɑθɪŋ] s enlistonado

Latin ['lætɪn] o ['lætən] adj latino || s (language) latín m; (person) latino

Latin America s Latinoamérica, la América Latina

Latin American s latinoamericano

Lat'in-Amer'ican adj latinoamericano

latitude ['lætɪ,tjud] o ['lætɪ,tud] s latitud

latrine [lə'trin] s letrina

latter ['lætər] adj (more recent) posterior; segundo (de dos); the latter éste; the latter part of fines mpl de (p.ej., el siglo)

lattice ['lætɪs] s enrejado || tr enrejar

lattice girder s viga de celosía

lat'tice-work' s enrejado

Latvia ['lætvɪ-ə] s Letonia, Latvia

laudable ['lɔdəbəl] adj laudable

laudanum ['lɔdənəm] o ['lɔdnəm] s láudano

laudatory ['lɔdə,tori] adj laudatorio

laugh [læf] o [lɑf] s risa || tr — to laugh away ahogar en risas; to laugh off tomar a risa || intr reír, reírse

laughable ['læfəbəl] o ['lɑfəbəl] adj risible

laughing ['læfɪŋ] o ['lɑfɪŋ] adj reidor; to be no laughing matter no ser cosa de risa || s risa, (el) reír

laughing gas s gas m hilarante

laugh'ing-stock' s hazmerreír m

laughter ['læftər] o ['lɑftər] s risa, risas

launch [lɔntʃ] o [lɑntʃ] s (of a ship) botadura; (of a rocket) lanzamiento; (open motorboat) lancha automóvil; (nav) lancha || tr botar, lanzar (un buque); (to throw; to start, set going, send forth) lanzar || intr lanzarse

launching ['lɔntʃɪŋ] o ['lɑntʃɪŋ] s lanzamiento

launching pad s plataforma de lanzamiento

launder ['lɔndər] o ['lɑndər] tr lavar y planchar || intr resistir el lavado

launderer ['lɔndərər] o ['lɑndərər] s lavandero

laundress ['lɔndrɪs] o ['lɑndrɪs] s lavandera

laun-dry ['lɔndri] o ['lɑndri] s (pl -dries) lavadero; lavado de la ropa; ropa lavada o para lavar

laundry-man ['lɔndrimən] o ['lɑndrimən] s (pl -men [mən]) lavandero

laun'dry-wom'an s (pl -wom'en) lavandera

laureate ['lɔri-it] adj laureado || s laureado; poeta laureado

lau-rel ['lɔrəl] o ['lɑrəl] s laurel m; laurels laurel (de la victoria); to rest o sleep on one's laurels dormirse sobre sus laureles || v (pret & pp -reled o -relled; ger -reling o -relling) tr laurear, coronar de laurel

lava ['lɑvə] o ['lævə] s lava

lavato-ry ['lævə,tori] s (pl -ries) (room equipped for washing hands and face) lavabo; (bowl with running water) lavamanos m; (toilet) excusado

lavender ['lævəndər] s alhucema, espliego, lavanda

lavender water s agua de alhucema, agua de lavanda

lavish ['lævɪʃ] adj pródigo || tr prodigar

law [lɔ] s (of man, of nature, of science) ley f; (branch of knowledge concerned with law; body of laws; study of law, profession of law) derecho; to enter the law hacerse abogado; to go to law recurrir a la ley; to lay down the law dar órdenes terminantes; to maintain law and order mantener la paz; to practice law ejercer la profesión de abogado; to read law estudiar derecho

law-abiding ['lɔ-ə,baɪdɪŋ] adj observante de la ley

law'break'er s infractor m de la ley

law court s tribunal m de justicia

lawful ['lɔfəl] adj legal, legítimo

lawless ['lɔlɪs] adj ilegal; (unbridled) desenfrenado, licencioso

law'mak'er s legislador m

lawn [lɔn] s césped m; (fabric) linón m

lawn mower s cortacésped m, tundidora de césped

law office s bufete m, despacho de abogado

law of nations s derecho de gentes

law of the jungle s ley f de la selva

law student s estudiante mf de derecho

law'suit' s pleito, proceso, litigio
lawyer ['lɔjər] s abogado
lax [læks] adj (in morals, discipline, etc.) laxo, relajado; vago, indeterminado; (loose, not tense) laxo, flojo, suelto
laxative ['læksətɪv] adj & s laxante m
lay [le] adj (not belonging to clergy) lego, seglar; (not having special training) lego, profano || s situación, orientación || v (pret & pp laid [led]) tr poner, colocar; dejar en el suelo; tender (un cable); echar (los cimientos; la culpa); situar (la acción de un drama); asentar (el polvo); poner (huevos la gallina; la mesa una criada); formar (planes); hacer (una apuesta); **to be laid in** ser (la escena) en; **to lay aside** echar a un lado; ahorrar; **to lay down** afirmar, declarar; dar (la vida); deponer (las armas); **to lay low** abatir, derribar; obligar a guardar cama; matar; **to lay off** despedir (a obreros); (to mark off the boundaries of) marcar, trazar; **to lay open** descubrir, revelar; (to a risk or danger) exponer; **to lay out** extender, tender; marcar (una tarea, un trabajo); gastar (dinero); amortajar (a un difunto); **to lay up** obligar a guardar cama; ahorrar; (naut) desarmar || intr poner (las gallinas); **to lay about** dar palos de ciego; **to lay for** acechar; **to lay off** (coll) dejar de trabajar; (coll) dejar de molestar; **to lay over** detenerse durante un viaje; **to lay to** (naut) capear
lay brother s donado, lego
lay day s (naut) día m de estadía
layer ['le·ər] s (e.g., of paint) capa; (e.g., of bricks) camada; (e.g., of coal, rocks) estrato, capa; (hort) codadura || tr (hort) acodar
layer cake s bizcocho de varias camadas
layette [le'et] s canastilla
lay figure s maniquí m
laying ['le·ɪŋ] s colocación; (of eggs) postura; (of a cable) tendido
lay·man ['lemən] s (pl -men [mən]) (person who is not a clergyman) lego, seglar m; (person who has no special training) lego, profano
lay'off' s (dismissal of workmen) despido; (period of unemployment) paro forzoso
lay of the land s cariz m que van tomando las cosas
lay'out' s plan m; (of tools) equipo; disposición, organización; (coll) banquete m, festín m
lay'o'ver s parada en un viaje
lay sister s donada
laziness ['lezɪnɪs] s pereza
la·zy ['lezi] adj (comp -zier; super -ziest) perezoso
la'zy·bones' s (coll) perezoso
lb. abbr pound
l.c. abbr lower case; loco citato (Lat) in the place cited
Ld. abbr Lord
lea [li] s prado

lead [led] adj plomizo || s plomo; (of lead pencil) mina; (for sounding depth) (naut) escandallo; (typ) interlínea, regleta || [lid] v (pret & pp leaded; ger leading) tr emplomar; (typ) interlinear, regletear || s [lid] s (foremost place) primacía; (guidance) conducta, guía, dirección; indicación; ejemplo; (cards) salida; (leash) trailla; (of a newspaper article) primer párrafo; (elec) conductor m; (elec & mach) avance m; (min) filón m; (rad) alambre m de entrada; (theat) papel m principal; (theat) galán m; (theat) dama; **to take the lead** tomar la delantera || [lid] v (pret & pp led [led]) tr conducir, llevar; (to command) acaudillar, mandar; estar a la cabeza de; dirigir (p.ej., una orquesta); llevar (buena o mala vida); salir con (cierto naipe); (elec & mach) avanzar; **to lead someone to** + inf llevar a alguien a + inf || intr ir delante, enseñar el camino; ser el primero; tener el mando; (cards) salir, ser mano; (mus) llevar la batuta; **to lead up to** conducir a, llevar a; llevar la conversación a
leaden ['ledən] adj (of lead; like lead) plomizo; (heavy as lead) plúmbeo; (sluggish) tardo, indolente; (with sleep) cargado; triste, lóbrego
leader ['lidər] s caudillo, jefe m, líder m; (ringleader) cabecilla m; (of an orchestra) director m; (in a dance; among animals) guión m; (horse) guía; (in a newspaper) artículo de fondo
leader dog s perro-lazarillo
leadership ['lidər,ʃɪp] s caudillaje m, jefatura; dotes fpl de mando
leading ['lidɪŋ] adj primero, principal; preeminente; delantero
leading article s artículo de fondo
leading edge s (aer) borde m de ataque
leading lady s primera actriz, dama
leading man s primer actor m, primer galán m
leading question s pregunta tendenciosa
leading strings spl andadores mpl
lead-in wire ['lid ,ɪn] s (rad) bajada de antena, alambre m de entrada
lead pencil [led] s lápiz m
leaf [lif] s (pl leaves [livz]) hoja; (of vine) pámpano; (hinged leaf of table) trampilla; **to shake like a leaf** temblar como un azogado; **to turn over a new leaf** hacer libro nuevo || intr echar hojas; **to leaf through** hojear, trashojar
leafless ['liflɪs] adj deshojado
leaflet ['liflɪt] s hoja suelta, hoja volante; (blade of compound leaf) hojuela
leaf'stalk' s pecíolo
leaf·y ['lifi] adj (comp -ier; super -iest) hojoso, frondoso
league [lig] s (unit of distance) legua; (association, alliance) liga || tr asociar || intr asociarse, ligarse

League of Nations s Sociedad de las Naciones

leak [lik] s (in a roof) gotera; (in a ship) agua, vía de agua; (of water, gas, electricity, steam) escape m, fuga, salida; agujero, grieta, raja (por donde se escapa el agua, etc.); (of money, news, etc.) filtración; **to spring a leak** tener un escape; (naut) empezar a hacer agua ǁ tr dejar escapar, dejar salir (el agua, gas, etc.); dejar filtrar (una noticia) ǁ intr rezumarse (un barril); escaparse, salirse (el agua, gas, etc.); (naut) hacer agua; filtrarse (el dinero); **to leak away** rezumarse (una especie); trascender (un hecho que estaba oculto)

leakage ['likɪdʒ] s escape m, fuga, salida; (com) merma

leak·y ['liki] adj (comp -ier; super -iest) agujereado, roto; (roof) llovedizo; (naut) que hace agua; (coll) indiscreto

lean [lin] adj magro, mollar; (thin) flaco; (gasoline mixture) pobre; **lean years** años de carestía ǁ v (pret & pp leaned o leant [lent]) tr inclinar, ladear, arrimar ǁ intr inclinarse, ladearse, arrimarse; (fig) inclinarse, tender; **to lean against** arrimarse a, estar arrimado a; **to lean back** retreparse, recostarse; **to lean on** apoyarse en; (with the elbows) acodarse sobre; **to lean out (of)** asomarse (a); **to lean over backwards** (coll) extremar la imparcialidad; **to lean toward** (fig) inclinarse a, ladearse a

leaning ['linɪŋ] adj inclinado ǁ s inclinación; (fig) inclinación, tendencia

lean'-to' s (pl -tos) colgadizo

leap [lip] s salto; **by leaps and bounds** a pasos agigantados; **leap in the dark** salto a ciegas, salto en vago ǁ v (pret & pp leaped o leapt [lept]) tr saltar ǁ intr saltar; dar un salto (el corazón de uno)

leap day s día m intercalar

leap'frog' s fil derecho, juego del salto; **to play leapfrog** jugar a la una la mula

leap year s año bisiesto

learn [lʌrn] v (pret & pp learned o learnt [lʌrnt]) tr aprender; oír decir; saber (una noticia) ǁ intr aprender

learned ['lʌrnɪd] adj docto, erudito; (e.g., word) culto

learned journal s revista científica

learned society s sociedad de eruditos

learned word s cultismo, voz culta

learned world s mundo de la erudición

learner ['lʌrnər] s principiante mf, aprendiz m, estudiante mf

learning ['lʌrnɪŋ] s (act and time devoted) aprendizaje m; (scholarship) erudición

lease [lis] s arrendamiento, locación; **to give a new lease on life to** renovar completamente; volver a hacer feliz ǁ tr arrendar ǁ intr arrendarse

lease'hold' adj arrendado ǁ s arrendamiento; bienes raíces arrendados

leash [liʃ] s traílla; **to strain at the leash** sufrir la sujeción con impaciencia ǁ tr atraillar

least [list] adj (el) menor, mínimo, más pequeño ǁ adv menos ǁ s (el) menor; (lo) menos; **at least** o **at the least** al menos, a lo menos, por lo menos; **not in the least** de ninguna manera

leather ['lɛðər] s cuero

leath'er·back' turtle s laúd m

leath'er·neck' s (slang) soldado de infantería de marina de los EE.UU.

leathery ['lɛðəri] adj correoso, coriáceo

leave [liv] s (permission) permiso; (permission to be absent) licencia; (farewell) despedida; **on leave** con licencia; **to give leave to dar** licencia a; **to take leave (of)** despedirse (de) ǁ v (pret & pp left [left]) tr (to let stay; to stop, give up; to disregard) dejar; (to go away from) salir de; (to bequeath) legar; **leave it to me!** ¡déjemelo a mí!; **to be left** quedar p.ej., **the letter was left unanswered** la carta quedó sin contestar; **to leave alone** dejar en paz, dejar tranquilo; **to leave no stone unturned** no dejar piedra por mover; **to leave off** dejar; no ponerse (una prenda de vestir); **to leave out** omitir; **to leave things as they are** dejarlo como está ǁ intr irse, marcharse; salir (un avión, un tren, un vapor)

leaven ['lɛvən] s levadura; (fig) influencia ǁ tr leudar; (fig) transformar

leavening ['lɛvənɪŋ] s levadura

leave of absence s licencia

leave'-tak'ing s despedida

leavings ['livɪŋz] spl desperdicios, sobras

Leb·a·nese [ˌlɛbə'niz] adj libanés ǁ s (pl -nese) libanés m

Lebanon ['lɛbənən] s el Líbano

Lebanon Mountains spl cordillera del Líbano

lecher ['lɛtʃər] s libertino, lujurioso

lecherous ['lɛtʃərəs] adj lascivo, lujurioso

lechery ['lɛtʃəri] s lascivia, lujuria

lectern ['lɛktərn] s atril m

lecture ['lɛktʃər] s conferencia; (tedious reprimand) sermoneo ǁ tr instruir por medio de una conferencia; sermonear ǁ intr dar una conferencia, dar conferencias

lecturer ['lɛktʃərər] s conferenciante mf

ledge [lɛdʒ] s (projection in a wall) retallo; cama de roca; arrecife m

ledger ['lɛdʒər] s (com) libro mayor

ledger line s (mus) línea suplementaria

lee [li] s (shelter) (naut) socaire m; (quarter sheltered from the wind) sotavento; **lees** heces fpl

leech [litʃ] s sanguijuela; **to stick like a leech** pegarse como ladilla

leek [lik] s puerro

leer [lɪr] s mirada de soslayo, mirada lujuriosa ǁ intr — **to leer at** mirar de soslayo, mirar lujuriosamente

leery ['lɪri] *adj* (coll) receloso, suspicaz

leeward ['liwərd] o ['lu·ərd] *adj* (naut) de sotavento || *adv* (naut) a sotavento || *s* (naut) sotavento

Leeward Islands ['liwərd] *spl* islas de Sotavento

lee'way' *s* (aer & naut) deriva; (coll) tiempo de sobra, espacio de sobra, dinero de sobra; (coll) libertad de acción

left [lɛft] *adj* izquierdo || *adv* hacia la izquierda || *s* (*left hand*) izquierda; (box) zurdazo; (pol) izquierda; **on the left** a la izquierda

left field *s* (baseball) jardín izquierdo

left'-hand' drive *s* conducción o dirección a la izquierda

left-handed ['lɛft'hændɪd] *adj* (*individual*) zurdo; (*clumsy*) desmañado, torpe; insincero; contrario a las agujas del reloj

leftish ['lɛftɪʃ] *adj* izquierdizante

leftist ['lɛftɪst] *adj* & *s* izquierdista *mf*

left'o'ver *adj* & *s* sobrante *m*; **leftovers** *spl* sobras

left'-wing' *adj* izquierdista

left-winger ['lɛft'wɪŋər] *s* (coll) izquierdista *mf*

leg. *abbr* **legal, legislature**

leg [lɛg] *s* (*of man or animal*) pierna; (*of animal, table, chair, etc.*) pata; (*of boot or stocking*) caña; (*of trousers*) pernera; (*of a cooked fowl*) muslo; (*of a journey*) etapa, trecho; **to be on one's last legs** estar sin recursos; estar en las últimas; **to not have a leg to stand on** (coll) no tener justificación alguna, no tener disculpa alguna; **to pull the leg of** (coll) tomar el pelo a; **to shake a leg** (coll) darse prisa; (*to dance*) (coll) bailar; **to stretch one's legs** estirar las piernas, dar un paseíto

lega·cy ['lɛgəsi] *s* (*pl* **-cies**) legado

legal ['ligəl] *adj* legal

legali·ty [lɪ'gælɪti] *s* (*pl* **-ties**) legalidad

legalize ['ligə,laɪz] *tr* legalizar

legal tender *s* curso legal

legate ['lɛgɪt] *s* legado

legatee [,lɛgə'ti] *s* legatario

legation [lɪ'geʃən] *s* legación

legend ['lɛdʒənd] *s* leyenda

legendary ['lɛdʒən,dɛri] *adj* legendario

legerdemain [,lɛdʒərdɪ'men] *s* juego de manos, prestidigitación; (*cheating, trickery*) trapacería

legging ['lɛgɪŋ] *s* polaina

leg·gy ['lɛgi] *adj* (*comp* **-gier**; *super* **-giest**) zanquilargo; de piernas largas y elegantes

leg'horn' *s* sombrero de paja de Italia || **Leghorn** *s* Liorna

legible ['lɛdʒɪbəl] *adj* legible

legion ['lidʒən] *s* legión

legislate ['lɛdʒɪs,let] *tr* imponer mediante legislación || *intr* legislar

legislation [,lɛdʒɪs'leʃən] *s* legislación

legislative ['lɛdʒɪs,letɪv] *adj* legislativo

legislator ['lɛdʒɪs,letər] *s* legislador *m*

legislature ['lɛdʒɪs,letʃər] *s* asamblea legislativa, cuerpo legislativo

legitimacy [lɪ'dʒɪtɪməsi] *s* legitimidad

legitimate [lɪ'dʒɪtɪmɪt] *adj* legítimo || [lɪ'dʒɪtɪ,met] *tr* legitimar

legitimate drama *s* drama serio (*a distinción del cine o el melodrama*)

legitimize [lɪ'dʒɪtɪ,maɪz] *tr* legitimar

leg'work' *s* (coll) el mucho caminar

leisure ['liʒər] o ['lɛʒər] *s* desocupación, ocio; **at leisure** desocupado, libre; **at one's leisure** a la comodidad de uno, cuando uno pueda

leisure class *s* gente acomodada

leisure hours *spl* horas de ocio, ratos perdidos

leisurely ['liʒərli] o ['lɛʒərli] *adj* lento, pausado || *adv* lentamente, despacio, sin prisa

lemon ['lɛmən] *s* limón *m*

lemonade [,lɛmə'ned] *s* limonada

lemon squeezer *s* exprimidera de limón

lemon verbena *s* luisa

lend [lɛnd] *s* (*pret* & *pp* **lent** [lɛnt]) *tr* prestar

lending library *s* biblioteca de préstamo

length [lɛŋθ] *s* largura, largo; (*of time*) extensión; (naut) eslora; **at length** por fin; largamente; **to go to any length** hacer cuanto esté de su parte; **to keep at arm's length** mantener a distancia; mantenerse a distancia

lengthen ['lɛŋθən] *tr* alargar || *intr* alargarse

length'wise' *adj* longitudinal || *adv* longitudinalmente

length·y ['lɛŋθi] *adj* (*comp* **-ier**; *super* **-iest**) muy largo, prolongado

leniency ['linɪ·ənsi] *s* clemencia, indulgencia, lenidad

lenient ['linɪ·ənt] *adj* clemente, indulgente

lens [lɛnz] *s* lente *m* & *f*; (*of the eye*) cristalino

Lent [lɛnt] *s* cuaresma *f*

Lenten ['lɛntən] *adj* cuaresmal

lentil ['lɛntəl] *s* lenteja

leopard ['lɛpərd] *s* leopardo

leotard ['li·ə,tɑrd] *s* leotardo

leper ['lɛpər] *s* leproso

leper house *s* leprosería

leprosy ['lɛprəsi] *s* lepra

leprous ['lɛprəs] *adj* leproso; (*covered with scales*) escamoso

Lesbian ['lɛzbɪ·ən] *adj* lesbio || *s* lesbio; (*female homosexual*) lesbia

lesbianism ['lɛzbɪ·ə,nɪzəm] *s* lesbianismo

lese majesty ['liz'mædʒɪsti] *s* delito de lesa majestad

lesion ['liʒən] *s* lesión

less [lɛs] *adj* menor || *adv* menos; **less and less** cada vez menos; **less than** menos que; (*followed by numeral*) menos de; (*followed by verb*) menos de lo que || *s* menos *m*

lessee ['lɛs'i] *s* arrendatario

lessen ['lɛsən] *tr* disminuir, reducir a menos; quitar importancia a || *intr*

disminuirse, reducirse; amainar (*el viento*)
lesser ['lesər] *adj* menor, más pequeño
lesson ['lesən] *s* lección
lessor ['lesər] *s* arrendador *m*
lest [lest] *conj* no sea que, de miedo que
let [let] *v* (*pret & pp* let; *ger* letting) *tr* dejar, permitir; alquilar, arrendar; **let + *inf*** que + *subj*, p.ej., **let him come in** que entre; **let alone** y mucho menos; **let good enough alone** bueno está lo bueno; **let us + *inf*** vamos a + *inf*, p.ej., **let us eat** vamos a comer, comamos; **to let se** alquila; **to let alone** dejar en paz, dejar tranquilo; **to let be** no tocar; dejar en paz; **to let by** dejar pasar; **to let down** dejar bajar; desilusionar, traicionar; dejar plantado; **to let fly** disparar; (fig) disparar, soltar (*palabras injuriosas*); **to let go** soltar, desasirse de; vender; **to let in** dejar entrar, dejar entrar en; **to let it go at that** no hacer o decir nada más; **to let know** hacer saber; **to let loose** soltar; **to let on** (coll) dar a entender; **to let out** dejar salir; revelar, publicar; dar, soltar (*p.ej., más cuerda*); dar (*un grito*); ensanchar (*un vestido que aprieta*); dar en arrendamiento; (coll) despedir; **to let through** dejar pasar, dejar pasar por; **to let up** dejar subir; dejar levantarse ‖ *intr* alquilarse, arrendarse; **to let down** (coll) ir más despacio; **to let go** desasirse; **to let go of** desasirse de; **to let on** (coll) fingir; **to let out** (coll) despedirse, cerrarse (*p.ej., la escuela*); **to let up** (coll) desistir; (coll) aflojar, amainar
let'down' *s* disminución; aflojamiento; desilusión, decepción; humillación
lethal ['liθəl] *adj* letal
lethargic [lɪ'θɑrdʒɪk] *adj* (*affected with lethargy*) letárgico; (*producing lethargy*) letargoso
lethar·gy ['lεθərdʒi] *s* (*pl* -gies) letargo
Lett [let] *s* letón *m*
letter ['letər] *s* (*written message*) carta; (*of the alphabet*) letra; (*literal meaning*) (fig) letra; **letters** (*literature*) letras; **to the letter** al pie de la letra ‖ *tr* estampar o marcar con letras
letter box *s* buzón *m* (*caja*)
letter carrier *s* cartero
letter drop *s* buzón *m* (*agujero*)
letter file *s* guardacartas *m*
let'ter·head' *s* membrete *m*; (*paper with printed heading*) memorándum *m*
lettering ['letərɪŋ] *s* inscripción; letras
letter of credit *s* carta de crédito
letter opener *s* ['opənər] *s* abrecartas *m*
letter paper *s* papel *m* de cartas
let'ter·per'fect *adj* que tiene bien aprendido su papel; correcto, exacto
let'ter·press' *s* impresión tipográfica; texto (*a distinción de los grabados*)
letter scales *spl* pesacartas *m*
Lettish ['letɪʃ] *adj* letón ‖ *s* letón *m*

lettuce ['letɪs] *s* lechuga
let'up' *s* (coll) calma, interrupción; **without letup** (coll) sin cesar
leucorrhea [,lukə'riə] *s* leucorrea
leukemia [lu'kimɪə] *s* leucemia
Levant [lɪ'vænt] *s* Levante *m* (*países de la parte oriental del Mediterráneo*)
Levantine ['levən,tin] o [lɪ'væntin] *adj & s* levantino
levee ['levi] *s* (*embankment to hold back water*) ribero; (*reception at court*) besamanos *m*
lev·el ['levəl] *adj* raso, llano; nivelado; (coll) sensato, juicioso; **level with** al nivel de, a flor de, a ras de ‖ *s* (*device for determining horizontal position; degree of elevation*) nivel *m*; (*flat and even area of land*) terreno llano, llanura; (*part of a canal between two locks*) tramo; **to be on the level** obrar sin engaño, decir la pura verdad; **to find one's level** hallar su propio nivel ‖ *v* (*pret & pp* -eled o -elled; *ger* -eling o -elling) *tr* nivelar; (*to smooth, flatten out*) arrasar, allanar; (*to bring down*) derribar, echar por tierra; apuntar (*un arma de fuego*); (fig) allanar (*dificultades*) ‖ *intr* — **to level off** (aer) enderezarse para aterrizar
level-headed ['levəl'hedɪd] *adj* sensato, juicioso
leveling rod *s* (surv) jalón *m* de mira
lever ['livər] o ['levər] *s* palanca ‖ *tr* apalancar
leverage ['livərɪdʒ] o ['levərɪdʒ] *s* palancada; poder *m* de una palanca; (fig) influencia, poder *m*
leviathan [lɪ'vaɪəθən] *s* (Bib & fig) leviatán *m*; buque *m* muy grande
levitation [,levɪ'teʃən] *s* levitación
levi·ty ['levɪti] *s* (*pl* -ties) frivolidad; (*fickleness*) ligereza
lev·y ['levi] *s* (*pl* -ies) (*of taxes*) exacción, recaudación; dinero recaudado; (mil) leva, enganche *m*, recluta ‖ *v* (*pret & pp* -ied) *tr* exigir, recaudar (*impuestos*); (mil) enganchar, reclutar; hacer (*la guerra*)
lewd [lud] *adj* lascivo, lujurioso; obsceno
lewdness ['ludnɪs] *s* lascivia, lujuria; obscenidad
lexical ['leksɪkəl] *adj* léxico
lexicographer [,leksɪ'kɑgrəfər] *s* lexicógrafo
lexicographic(al) [,leksɪkə'græfɪk(əl)] *adj* lexicográfico
lexicography [,leksɪ'kɑgrəfi] *s* lexicografía
lexicology [,leksɪ'kɑlədʒi] *s* lexicología
lexicon ['leksɪkən] *s* léxico, lexicón *m*
liabili·ty [,laɪə'bɪlɪti] *s* (*pl* -ties) (*e.g., to disease*) propensión; responsabilidad, obligación; desventaja; **liabilities** deudas; (*as detailed in balance sheet*) pasivo
liability insurance *s* seguro de responsabilidad civil
liable ['laɪəbəl] *adj* (*e.g., to disease*) propenso, expuesto; responsable; **to**

be liable to + *inf* (coll) amenazar + *inf*

liaison ['li·ə,zɑn] o [li'ezən] *s* enlace *m*, unión; (*illicit relationship between a man and woman*) amancebamiento, enredo, lío; (mil, nav & phonet) enlace *m*

liaison officer *s* (mil) oficial *m* de enlace

liar ['laɪ·ər] *s* mentiroso

lb. *abbr* **librarian, library**

libation [laɪ'beʃən] *s* libación; (*drink*) libación

li·bel ['laɪbəl] *s* calumnia, difamación; (*defamatory writing*) libelo || *v* (*pret & pp* **-beled** o **-belled**; *ger* **-beling** o **-belling**) *tr* calumniar, difamar

libelous ['laɪbələs] *adj* calumniador

liberal ['lɪbərəl] *adj* (*generous; done or given generously*) (*open-minded*) tolerante, de amplias miras; (*translation*) libre; (pol) liberal || liberal *mf*

liberali·ty [,lɪbə'rælɪti] *s* (*pl* **-ties**) liberalidad

liberal-minded ['lɪbərəl'maɪndɪd] *adj* tolerante, de amplias miras

liberate ['lɪbə,ret] *tr* libertar; (*to disengage from a combination*) (chem) desprender

liberation [,lɪbə'reʃən] *s* liberación; (chem) desprendimiento

liberator ['lɪbə,retər] *s* libertador *m*

libertine ['lɪbər,tin] *adj & s* libertino

liber·ty ['lɪbərti] *s* (*pl* **-ties**) libertad; **to take the liberty to** tomarse la libertad de

liberty-loving ['lɪbərti'lʌvɪŋ] *adj* amante de la libertad

libidinous [lɪ'bɪdɪnəs] *adj* libidinoso

libido [lɪ'bido] o [lɪ'bɑrdo] *s* libídine *f*, libido *f*

librarian [laɪ'brɛrɪ·ən] *s* bibliotecario

librar·y ['laɪ,brɛri] o ['laɪbrəri] *s* (*pl* **-ies**) biblioteca

library number *s* signatura

library school *s* escuela de bibliotecarios

library science *s* bibliotecnia

libret·to [lɪ'breto] *s* (*pl* **-tos**) (mus) libreto

license ['laɪsəns] *s* licencia || *tr* licenciar

license number *s* número de matrícula

license plate o **tag** *s* chapa de circulación, placa de matrícula

licentious [laɪ'sɛnʃəs] *adj* licencioso, disoluto

lichen ['laɪkən] *s* liquen *m*

lick [lɪk] *s* lamedura; (*place where animals go to lick*) lamedero; (*blow*) (coll) bofetón *m*; (*speed*) (coll) velocidad; (*beating*) (coll) zurra; (*quick cleaning*) (coll) limpión *m*; **to give a lick and a promise to** (coll) hacer rápida y superficialmente || *tr* lamer; lamerse (*p.ej., los dedos*); lamer (*las llamas un tejado*); (*to beat, thrash*) (coll) zurrar; (*to conquer*) (coll) vencer

licorice ['lɪkərɪs] *s* regaliz *m*, orozuz *m*; dulce *m* de regaliz

lid [lɪd] *s* (*of a box, trunk, chest, etc.*) tapa, tapadera; (*of a dish, pot, etc.*) cobertera; (*eyelid*) párpado; (*hat*) (slang) techo

lie [laɪ] *s* mentira; **to catch in a lie** coger en una mentira; **to give the lie to** dar un mentís a || *v* (*pret & pp* **lied**; *ger* **lying**) *tr* — **to lie oneself out of** o **to lie one's way out of** librarse de un aprieto mintiendo || *intr* mentir || *v* (*pret* **lay** [le]; *pp* **lain** [len]; *ger* **lying**) *intr* estar echado; hallarse, estar situado; (*e.g., in the grave*) yacer, estar enterrado; **to lie down** echarse, acostarse

lie detector *s* detector *m* de mentiras

lien [lin] o ['li·ən] *s* gravamen *m*, derecho de retención

lieu [lu] *s* — **in lieu of** en lugar de, en vez de

lieutenant [lu'tɛnənt] *s* lugarteniente *m*; (mil) teniente *m*; (nav) teniente de navío

lieutenant colonel *s* (mil) teniente coronel *m*

lieutenant commander *s* (nav) capitán *m* de corbeta

lieutenant governor *s* (U.S.A.) vicegobernador *m* (*de un Estado*)

lieutenant junior grade *s* (nav) alférez *m* de navío

life [laɪf] *adj* (*animate*) vital; (*lifelong*) perpetuo; (*annuity, income*) vitalicio; (*working from nature*) (fa) del natural || *s* (*pl* **lives** [laɪvz]) vida; (*of an insurance policy*) vigencia; **for life** de por vida; **for the life of me** así me matan; **the life and soul of** (*e.g., a party*) la alegría de; **to come to life** volver a la vida; **to depart this life** partir de esta vida; **to run for one's life** salvarse por los pies

life annuity *s* renta vitalicia

life belt *s* cinturón *m* salvavidas

life′boat′ *s* bote *m* de salvamento, bote salvavidas; (*for shore-based rescue services*) lancha de auxilio

life buoy *s* boya salvavidas, guindola

life float *s* balsa salvavidas

life′guard′ *s* salvavidas *m*, guardavida *m*

life imprisonment *s* cadena perpetua

life insurance *s* seguro sobre la vida

life jacket *s* chaleco salvavidas

lifeless ['laɪflɪs] *adj* muerto, sin vida; (*in a faint*) desmayado, exánime; (*dull, colorless*) deslucido

life′like′ *adj* natural, vivo

life line *s* cuerda salvavidas; cuerda de buzo

life′long′ *adj* perpetuo, de toda la vida

life of leisure *s* vida de ocio

life of Riley ['raɪli] *s* (slang) vida regalada

life of the party *s* (coll) alegría de la fiesta, alma de la fiesta

life preserver [prɪ'zʌrvər] *s* chaleco salvavidas

lifer ['laɪfər] *s* (slang) presidiario de por vida

life′sav′er *s* salvador *m* (*de vidas*); (*something that saves a person from* *a predicament)* (coll) tabla de salvación

lifesaving ['laif,seviŋ] *adj* de salvamento ‖ *s* salvamento *(de vidas)*

life sentence *s* condena a cadena perpetua

life'-size' *adj* de tamaño natural

life'time' *adj* vitalicio ‖ *s* vida, curso de la vida, jornada

life'work' *s* obra principal de la vida de uno

lift [lift] *s* elevación, levantamiento; ayuda *(para levantar una carga)*; (aer) sustentación; **to give a lift to** invitar *(a un peatón)* a subir a un coche; llevar en un coche; (fig) reanimar ‖ *tr* elevar, levantar; quitarse *(el sombrero)*; (naut) izar *(velas, vergas, etc.)*; (fig) reanimar, exaltar; (coll) robar; (coll) plagiar ‖ *intr* elevarse, levantarse; disiparse *(las nubes, las nieblas, la obscuridad, etc.)*

lift bridge *s* puente levadizo

lift'-off' *s* despegue *m* vertical

lift truck *s* carretilla elevadora

ligament ['ligəmənt] *s* ligamento

ligature ['ligətʃər] *s* (mus & surg) ligadura; (mus & typ) ligado

light [lait] *adj (in weight)* ligero, leve, liviano; *(having illumination; whitish)* claro; *(hair)* blondo, rubio; *(complexion)* blanco; *(oil)* flúido; *(beer)* claro; *(reading)* poco serio; *(heart)* alegre, despreocupado; *(carrying a small cargo or none at all)* (naut) boyante; **light in the head** *(dizzy)* aturdido, mareado; *(simple, silly)* tonto, necio; **to make light of** no dar importancia a, no tomar en serio ‖ *adv* sin carga; sin equipaje ‖ *s* luz *f*; *(to light a cigarette)* lumbre *f*, fuego; *(to control traffic)* luz, señal *f*; *(window or other opening in a wall)* luz, claro, hueco; *(example, shining figure)* lumbrera; **according to one's lights** según Dios le da a uno a entender; **against the light** al trasluz; **in this light** desde este punto de vista; **lights** noticias; *(of sheep, etc.)* bofes *mpl*; **to come to light** salir a luz, descubrirse; **to shed o throw light on** echar luz sobre; **to strike a light** echar una yesca; encender un fósforo ‖ *v (pret & pp lighted o lit* [lit]*) tr (to furnish with illumination)* alumbrar, iluminar; *(to set afire, ignite)* encender; **to light up** iluminar ‖ *intr* alumbrarse; encenderse; posar *(un ave)*; *(from an auto)* bajar; **to light into** *(to attack)* (slang) arremeter contra; *(to scold, berate)* (slang) poner de oro y azul; **to light out** (slang) poner pies en polvorosa; **to light upon** tropezar con, hallar por casualidad

light bulb *s* (elec) bombilla

light complexion *s* tez blanca

lighten ['laitən] *tr (to make lighter in weight)* aligerar; iluminar; *(to cheer up)* alegrar, regocijar ‖ *intr (to become less dark)* iluminarse;

(to give off flashes of lightning) relampaguear; (fig) iluminarse *(los ojos, la cara de una persona)*

lighter ['laitər] *s (to light a cigarette)* encendedor *m*; *(flat-bottomed barge)* alijador *m*

light-fingered ['lait'fingərd] *adj* largo de uñas, listo de manos

light-footed ['lait'futid] *adj* ligero de pies

light-headed ['lait'hedid] *adj (dizzy)* aturdido, mareado; *(simple, silly)* tonto, necio, ligero de cascos

light-hearted ['lait'hartid] *adj* alegre, libre de cuidados

light'house' *s* faro

lighting ['laitiŋ] *s* alumbrado, iluminación

lighting fixtures *spl* artefactos de alumbrado

lightly ['laitli] *adv* ligeramente

light meter *s* exposímetro

lightness ['laitnis] *s (in weight)* ligereza; *(in illumination)* claridad

lightning ['laitniŋ] *s* relámpagos, relampagueo ‖ *intr* relampaguear

lightning arrester [ə'restər] *s* pararrayos *m*

lightning bug *s* luciérnaga

lightning rod *s* pararrayos *m*

light opera *s* opereta

light'ship' *s* buque *m* fanal, buque faro

light-struck ['lait,strʌk] *adj* velado

light'weight' *adj* ligero; de entretiempo, p.ej., **lightweight coat** abrigo de entretiempo

light'-year' *s* año luz

lignite ['lignait] *s* lignito

lignum vitae ['lignəm'vaiti] *s* guayaco, palo santo

likable ['laikəbəl] *adj* simpático

like [laik] *adj* parecido, semejante; parecido a, semejante a, p.ej., **this hat is like mine** este sombrero es parecido al mío; (elec) del mismo nombre; **like father like son** de tal palo tal astilla; **to feel like** + *ger* tener ganas de + *inf*; **to look like** parecerse a; parecer que, p.ej., **it looks like rain** parece que va a llover ‖ *adv* como; **like enough** (coll) probablemente; **nothing like** ni con mucho ‖ *prep* a semejanza de ‖ *conj* (coll) del mismo modo que; (coll) que, p.ej., **it seems like he is right** parece que tiene razón ‖ *s (liking)* gusto, preferencia; *(fellow, fellow man)* prójimo, semejante *m*; **and the like** y cosas por el estilo; **to give like for like** pagar en la misma moneda ‖ *tr* gustar de, p.ej., **I like music** gusto de la música; gustar, p.ej., **Mary likes peaches** a María le gustan los melocotones; **to like best o better** preferir; **to like it in** encontrarse a gusto en *(p.ej., el campo)*; **to like to** + *inf* gustarle a uno + *inf*, p.ej., **I like to travel me** gusta viajar; gustarle a uno que + *subj*, p.ej., **I should like him to come to see me** me gustaría que él viniese a verme ‖

intr querer, p.ej., **as you like** como Vd. quiera; **if you like** si Vd. quiere

likelihood ['laɪklɪ,hud] *s* probabilidad

like·ly ['laɪklɪ] *adj (comp* **-lier;** *super* **-liest)** probable; a propósito; prometedor; **to be likely to** + *inf* ser probable que + *ind,* p.ej., **Mary is likely to come to see us tomorrow** es probable que María vendrá a vernos mañana || *adv* probablemente

like-minded ['laɪk'maɪndɪd] *adj* del mismo parecer; de natural semejante

liken ['laɪkən] *tr* asemejar, comparar

likeness ['laɪknɪs] *s (picture or image)* retrato; *(similarity)* semejanza, parecido; forma, aspecto, apariencia

like'wise' *adv* igualmente, asimismo; **to do likewise** hacer lo mismo

liking ['laɪkɪŋ] *s* gusto, afición, simpatía; **to be to the liking of** ser del gusto de; **to have a liking for** aficionarse a

lilac ['laɪlək] *adj* de color lila || *s* lilac *m,* lila

Lilliputian [,lɪlɪ'pjuʃən] *adj & s* liliputiense *mf*

lilt [lɪlt] *s* paso airoso, movimiento airoso; canción cadenciosa, música alegre

lil·y ['lɪlɪ] *s (pl* **-ies)** *(Lilium candidum)* azucena, lirio blanco; cala, lirio de agua; *(fleur-de-lis, the royal arms of France)* flor *f* de lis; **to gild the lily** ponerle colores al oro

lily of the valley *s* lirio de los valles, muguete *m*

lily pad *s* hoja de nenúfar

Lima bean ['laɪmə] *s* judía de la peladilla, frijol *m* de media luna

limb [lɪm] *s (arm or leg)* miembro; *(of a tree)* rama; *(of a cross; of the sea)* brazo; **to be out on a limb** (coll) estar en un aprieto

limber ['lɪmbər] *adj* ágil; flexible || *intr* — **to limber up** agilitarse

lim·bo ['lɪmbo] *s (pl* **-bos)** lugar *m* de olvido; (theol) limbo

lime [laɪm] *s (calcium oxide)* cal *f;* *(Citrus aurantifolia)* limero agrio; *(its fruit)* lima agria; *(linden tree)* tila o tilo

lime'kiln' *s* calera, horno de cal

lime'light' *s* — **to be in the limelight** estar a la vista del público

limerick ['lɪmərɪk] *s* quintilla jocosa

lime'stone' *adj* calizo || *s* caliza, piedra caliza

limit ['lɪmɪt] *s* límite *m;* **to be the limit** (slang) ser el colmo; **to go the limit** no dejar piedra por mover || *tr* limitar

lim'ited-ac'cess high'way *s* carretera de vía libre

limited monarchy *s* monarquía constitucional

limitless ['lɪmɪtlɪs] *adj* ilimitado

limousine ['lɪmə,zin] o [,lɪmə'zin] *s* (aut) limusina

limp [lɪmp] *adj* flojo, débil, flexible || *s* cojera || *intr* cojear

limpid ['lɪmpɪd] *adj* diáfano, cristalino

linage ['laɪnɪdʒ] *s* (typ) número de líneas

linchpin ['lɪntʃ,pɪn] *s* pezonera

linden ['lɪndən] *s* tila, tilo

line [laɪn] *s* línea; *(of people, houses, etc.)* hilera; *(rope, string)* cuerda, cordel *m;* *(wrinkle)* arruga; *(for fishing)* sedal *m;* *(written or printed line; line of goods)* renglón *m;* manera *(de pensar);* *(of the spectrum)* (phys) raya; **all along the line** por todas partes; desde cualquier punto de vista; **in line** alineado; dispuesto, preparado; **in line with** de acuerdo con; **out of line** desalineado; en desacuerdo; **to bring into line** poner de acuerdo; **to draw the line at** no ir más allá de; **to fall in line** conformarse; formar cola; alinearse; **to have a line on** (coll) estar enterado de; **to read between the lines** leer entre líneas; **to stand in line** hacer cola; **to toe the line** obrar como se debe; **to wait in line** hacer cola, esperar vez || *tr* alinear, rayar; arrugar *(p.ej., la cara);* formar hilera a lo largo de *(la acera, la calle);* forrar *(un vestido);* guarnecer *(un freno)* || *intr* — **to line up** ponerse en fila; hacer cola

lineage ['lɪnɪ·ɪdʒ] *s* linaje *m*

lineaments ['lɪnɪ·əmənts] *spl* lineamentos

linear ['lɪnɪ·ər] *adj* lineal

line-man ['laɪnmən] *s (pl* **-men** [mən]) (elec) celador *m,* recorredor *m* de la línea; (rr) guardavía *m;* (surv) cadenero

linen ['lɪnən] *adj* de lino || *s (fabric)* lienzo, lino; *(yarn)* hilo de lino; ropa blanca, ropa de cama

linen closet *s* armario para la ropa blanca

line of battle *s* línea de batalla

line of fire *s* (mil) línea de tiro

line of least resistance *s* ley *f* del menor esfuerzo; **to follow the line of least resistance** seguir la corriente, no oponer resistencia

line of sight *s* visual *f;* *(of firearm)* línea de mira

liner ['laɪnər] *s* vapor *m* de travesía; (baseball) pelota rasa, lineazo

line'-up' *s* agrupación, formación; *(of prisoners)* rueda

linger ['lɪŋgər] *intr* estarse, quedarse; *(to be tardy)* demorar, tardar; tardar en marcharse; tardar en morirse; pasearse con paso lento; **to linger over** contemplar, reflexionar

lingerie [,lænʒə'ri] *s* ropa interior de mujer

lingering ['lɪŋgərɪŋ] *adj* prolongado

lingual ['lɪŋgwəl] *adj & s* lingual *f*

linguist ['lɪŋgwɪst] *s (person skilled in several languages)* poligloto; *(specialist in linguistics)* lingüista *mf*

linguistic [lɪŋ'gwɪstɪk] *adj* lingüístico || **linguistics** *s* lingüística

liniment ['lɪnɪmənt] *s* linimento

lining ['laɪnɪŋ] *s (of a coat)* forro; *(of auto brake)* guarnición; *(of a fur-*

nace) camisa; (*of a wall*) revestimiento

link [lɪŋk] s eslabón m; **links** campo de golf || tr eslabonar || intr eslabonarse

linnet ['lɪnɪt] s pardillo

linoleum [lɪ'nolɪ·əm] s linóleo

linotype ['laɪnə‚taɪp] (trademark) adj linotípico || s (machine) linotipia; (matter produced by machine) linotipo || tr componer con linotipia

linotype operator s linotipista mf

linseed ['lɪn‚sid] s linaza

linseed oil s aceite m de linaza

lint [lɪnt] s borra, pelusa, hilaza; (used to dress wounds) hilas

lintel ['lɪntəl] s dintel m, umbral m

lion ['laɪ·ən] s león m; (man of strength and courage) (fig) león; (fig) celebridad muy solicitada; **to beard the lion in his den** ir a desafiar la cólera de un jefe; **to put one's head in the lion's mouth** meterse en la boca del lobo

lioness ['laɪ·ənɪs] s leona

lion-hearted ['laɪ·ən‚hɑrtɪd] adj valiente

lionize ['laɪ·ə‚naɪz] tr agasajar

lions' den s (Bib) fosa de los leones

lion's share s (la) parte f del león

lip [lɪp] s labio; (slang) lenguaje m insolente; **to hang on the lips of** estar pendiente de las palabras de; **to smack one's lips** chuparse los labios

lip'-read' v (pret & pp **-read** [‚rɛd]) tr & intr leer en los labios

lip reading s labiolectura

lip service s homenaje m de boca, jarabe m de pico

lip'stick' s lápiz m de labios, lápiz labial

liq. abbr **liquid**, **liquor**

lique·fy ['lɪkwɪ‚faɪ] v (pret & pp -fied) tr liquidar || intr liquidarse

liqueur [lɪ'kʌr] s licor m

liquid ['lɪkwɪd] adj líquido || s líquido; (phonet) líquida

liquidate ['lɪkwɪ‚det] tr & intr liquidar

liquidity [lɪ'kwɪdɪti] s liquidez f

liquid measure s medida para líquidos

liquor ['lɪkər] s licor m

Lisbon ['lɪzbən] s Lisboa

lisle [laɪl] s hilo fino de algodón, muy retorcido, sedalina

lisp [lɪsp] s ceceo || intr cecear

lissome ['lɪsəm] adj flexible, elástico; ágil, ligero

list [lɪst] s lista; (strip) lista, tira; (border) orilla; (selvage) orillo; (naut) ladeo; **lists** liza; **to enter the lists** entrar en liza; **to have a list** (naut) irse a la banda || tr alistar, listar; registrar || intr (naut) irse a la banda

listen ['lɪsən] intr escuchar; obedecer; **to listen in** escuchar a hurtadillas; escuchar por radio; **to listen to** escuchar; obedecer; **to listen to reason** meterse en razón

listener ['lɪsənər] s oyente mf; radioescucha mf, radioyente mf

listening post ['lɪsənɪŋ] s puesto de escucha

listless ['lɪstlɪs] adj distraído, desatento, indiferente

list price s precio de catálogo, precio de tarifa

lit. abbr **liter**, **literal**, **literature**

lita·ny ['lɪtəni] s (pl -nies) letanía; (repeated series) (fig) letanía

liter ['litər] s litro

literacy ['lɪtərəsi] s capacidad de leer y escribir; instrucción

literal ['lɪtərəl] adj literal

literary ['lɪtə‚rɛri] adj literario; (individual) literato

literate ['lɪtərɪt] adj que sabe leer y escribir; (well-read) literato, muy leído; (educated) instruído || s persona que sabe leer y escribir; literato, erudito

literati [‚lɪtə'rɑti] spl literatos

literature ['lɪtərətʃər] s literatura; impresos, escritos de publicidad

lithe [laɪð] adj flexible, cimbreño

lithia ['lɪθɪ·ə] s (chem) litina

lithium ['lɪθɪ·əm] s (chem) litio

lithograph ['lɪθə‚græf] o ['lɪθə‚grɑf] s litografía || tr litografiar

lithographer [lɪ'θɑgrəfər] s litógrafo

lithography [lɪ'θɑgrəfi] s litografía

litigant ['lɪtɪgənt] adj & s litigante mf

litigate ['lɪtɪ‚get] tr & intr litigar

litigation [‚lɪtɪ'geʃən] s litigación; (lawsuit) litigio

litigious [lɪ'tɪdʒəs] adj litigioso

litmus ['lɪtməs] s tornasol m

litmus paper s papel m de tornasol

litter ['lɪtər] s desorden m; (scattered rubbish) basura, papelería; (young brought forth at one birth) camada, ventregada; (bedding for animals) cama, paja; (vehicle carried by men or animals) litera; (stretcher) camilla, parihuela || tr esparcir papeles por; esparcir (desechos, papeles, etc.); cubrir (el suelo) con paja || intr parir

lit'ter·bug' s persona que ensucia las calles tirando papeles rotos

littering ['lɪtərɪŋ] s — **no littering** se prohíbe tirar papeles rotos

little ['lɪtəl] adj (in size) pequeño; (in amount) poco, p.ej., **little money** poco dinero; **a little** un poco de, p.ej., **a little money** un poco de dinero || adv poco; **little by little** poco a poco || s poco; **a little** un poco; (somewhat) algo; **to make little of** no dar importancia a, no tomar en serio; **to think little of** tener en poco; no vacilar en

Little Bear s Osa menor

Little Dipper s Carro menor

little finger s dedo auricular, dedo meñique; **to twist around one's little finger** manejar con suma facilidad

lit'tle·neck' s almeja redonda (Venus mercenaria)

little owl s mochuelo (Athene noctua)

little people spl hadas; gente menuda

Little Red Ridinghood ['raɪdɪŋ‚hʊd] s Caperucita Roja

little slam s (bridge) semibola

liturgic(al) [lɪ'tʌrdʒɪk(əl)] *adj* litúrgico

litur·gy ['lɪtərdʒi] *s* (*pl* -gies) liturgia

livable ['lɪvəbəl] *adj* habitable, vividero; llevadero, tolerable

live [laɪv] *adj* (*living; full of life; intense*) vivo; (*coals; flame*) ardiente; de actualidad; (elec) cargado || [lɪv] *tr* llevar (*tal o cual vida*); vivir (*una experiencia, una aventura; un actor sus personajes*); **to live down** borrar (*una falta*); **to live out** vivir (*toda la vida*); salir con vida de (*un desastre, una guerra*) || *intr* vivir; **to live and learn** vivir para ver; **to live and let live** vivir y dejar vivir; **to live high** darse buena vida; **to live on** seguir viviendo; vivir de (*p.ej., carne*); vivir a expensas de; **to live up to** cumplir (*lo prometido*); gastar (*todas sus rentas*)

live coal *s* ascua

livelihood ['laɪvlɪ,hʊd] *s* vida; **to earn one's livelihood** ganarse la vida

livelong ['lɪv,lɔŋ] o ['lɪv,lɑŋ] *adj*— **all the livelong day** todo el santo día

live·ly ['laɪvli] *adj* (*comp* -lier; *super* -liest) animado, vivaz; alegre, festivo; (*active, keen*) vivo; (*resilient*) elástico

liven ['laɪvən] *tr* animar, regocijar || *intr* animarse, regocijarse

liver ['lɪvər] *s* vividor *m*; habitante *mf*; (anat) hígado

liver·y ['lɪvəri] *s* (*pl* -ies) librea

livery·man ['lɪvərimən] *s* (*pl* -men [mən]) dueño de una cochera; mozo de cuadra

livery stable *s* cochera de carruajes de alquiler

live'stock' *adj* ganadero || *s* ganadería

live wire *s* (elec) alambre cargado; (slang) trafagón *m*

livid ['lɪvɪd] *adj* lívido, amoratado; encolerizado; pálido

living ['lɪvɪŋ] *adj* vivo, viviente || *s* vida; **to earn** o **to make a living** ganarse la vida

living quarters *spl* aposentos, habitaciones

living room *s* sala, sala de estar

living wage *s* jornal *m* suficiente para vivir

lizard ['lɪzərd] *s* lagarto; (slang) holgón *m*

load [lod] *s* carga; loads (coll) muchísimo; **loads of** (coll) gran cantidad de; **to get a load of** (slang) escuchar, oír; (slang) mirar; **to have a load on** (slang) estar borracho || *tr* cargar || *intr* cargar; cargarse

loaded ['lodɪd] *adj* cargado; (slang) muy borracho; (slang) muy rico

loaded dice *spl* dados cargados

load'stone' *s* piedra imán; (fig) imán *m*

loaf [lof] *s* (*pl* loaves [lovz]) pan *m*; (*of sugar*) pilón *m* || *intr* haraganear

loafer ['lofər] *s* haragán *m*

loam [lom] *s* suelo franco; (*mixture used in making molds*) tierra de moldeo

loamy ['lomi] *adj* franco

loan [lon] *s* (*among individuals*) préstamo; (*between companies or governments*) empréstito; **to hit for a loan** (coll) dar un sablazo a || *tr* prestar

loan shark *s* (coll) usurero

loan word *s* préstamo lingüístico

loath [loθ] *adj* poco dispuesto; **nothing loath** de buena gana

loathe [loð] *tr* abominar, detestar

loathing ['loðɪŋ] *s* abominación, detestación

loathsome ['loðsəm] *adj* abominable, asqueroso

lob [lɑb] *v* (*pret & pp* lobbed; *ger* lobbing) *tr* (tennis) volear desde muy ⸜ alto

lob·by ['lɑbi] *s* (*pl* -bies) salón *m* de entrada, vestíbulo; cabilderos || *v* (*pret & pp* -bied) *intr* cabildear

lobbying ['lɑbɪ·ɪŋ] *s* cabildeo

lobbyist ['lɑbɪ·ɪst] *s* cabildero

lobster ['lɑbstər] *s* (*spiny lobster*) langosta; (*Homarus*) bogavante *m*

lobster pot *s* langostera

local ['lokəl] *adj* local || *s* tren suburbano; (*branch of a union*) junta local; noticia de interés local

locale [lo'kæl] *s* localidad

locali·ty [lo'kælɪti] *s* (*pl* -ties) localidad

localize ['lokə,laɪz] *tr* localizar

local option *s* derecho local de legislar sobre la venta de bebidas alcohólicas

locate [lo'ket] o ['loket] *tr* (*to discover the location of*) localizar; (*to place, to settle*) colocar, establecer; (*to ascribe a particular location to*) situar || *intr* establecerse

location [lo'keʃən] *s* (*place, position*) localidad; (*act of placing*) colocación; (*act of finding*) localización; **on location** (mov) en exteriores

loc. cit. *abbr* loco citato (Lat) **in the place cited**

lock [lɑk] *s* cerradura; (*of a canal*) esclusa; (*of hair*) bucle *m*; (*of a firearm*) llave *f*; **lock, stock, and barrel** (coll) del todo, por completo; **under lock and key** bajo llave || *tr* echar la llave a, cerrar con llave; (*to key*) acuñar; hacer pasar (*un buque*) por la esclusa; abrazar, enlazar; **to lock in** encerrar, poner debajo de llave; **to lock out** cerrar la puerta a, dejar en la calle; dejar sin trabajo (*a los obreros*); **to lock up** encerrar, poner debajo de llave; encarcelar

locker ['lɑkər] *s* armario cerrado con llave

locket ['lɑkɪt] *s* guardapelo, medallón *m*

lock'jaw' *s* trismo, oclusión forzosa de la boca

lock nut *s* contratuerca

lock'out' *s* huelga patronal

lock'smith' *s* cerrajero

lock step *s* marcha en fila apretada

lock stitch *s* punto encadenado

lock tender *s* esclusero

lock'up' *s* cárcel *f*

lock washer *s* arandela de seguridad

locomotive [,lokə'motɪv] s locomotora

lo·cus ['lokəs] s (pl **-ci** [saɪ]) sitio, lugar m; lugar (geométrico)

locust ['lokəst] s (ent) langosta (*Pachytylus*); (ent) cigarra (*Cicada*); (bot) acacia falsa

lode [lod] s filón m, venero, veta

lode'star' s (astr) estrella polar; estrella de guía; (guide, direction) guía, norte m

lodge [ladʒ] s casa de guarda; casa de campo; (*e.g., of Masons*) logia || tr alojar, hospedar; depositar, colocar; presentar (*una queja*) || alojarse, hospedarse; quedar colgado, ir a parar

lodger ['ladʒər] s inquilino (*en parte de una casa*)

lodging ['ladʒɪŋ] s alojamiento, hospedaje m; (*without meals*) cobijo

loft [lɔft] o [laft] s (attic) desván m, sobrado; (*hayloft*) henal m, pajar m; (*in theater or church*) galería; (*in a store or office building*) piso alto

loft·y ['lɔftɪ] o ['laftɪ] adj (comp **-ier**; super **-iest**) (*towering; sublime*) encumbrado; (*haughty*) altivo, orgulloso

log. abbr logarithm

log [lɔg] o [lag] s leño, tronco; (*log chip*) (naut) barquilla; (*chip and line*) (naut) corredera; (aer) diario de vuelo; **to sleep like a log** dormir como un leño || v (pret & pp **logged**; ger **logging**) tr registrar; recorrer (*cierta distancia*)

logarithm ['lɔgə,rɪðəm] o ['lɑgə,rɪðəm] s logaritmo

log'book' s (aer) libro de vuelo; (naut) cuaderno de bitácora

log cabin s cabaña de troncos

log chip s (naut) barquilla

log driver s ganchero, maderero

log driving s flotaje m

logger ['lɔgər] o ['lɑgər] s leñador m, maderero; grúa de troncos; tractor m

log'ger·head' s mentecato; **at loggerheads** reñidos

loggia ['lɔdʒə] s (archit) logia

logic ['lɑdʒɪk] s lógica

logical ['lɑdʒɪkəl] adj lógico

logician [lo'dʒɪʃən] s lógico

logistic(al) [lo'dʒɪstɪk(əl)] adj logístico

logistics [lo'dʒɪstɪks] s logística

log'jam' s atasco de rollizos; (fig) estancación

log line s (naut) corredera

log'roll' intr trocar favores políticos

log'wood' s campeche m

loin [lɔɪn] s lomo; **to gird up one's loins** apercibirse para la acción

loin'cloth' s taparrabo

loiter ['lɔɪtər] tr — **to loiter away** malgastar (*el tiempo*) || intr holgazanear, rezagarse

loiterer ['lɔɪtərər] s holgazán m, rezagado

loll [lɑl] intr colgar flojamente; arrellanarse, repantigarse

lollipop ['lɑli,pɑp] s paleta (*dulce en el extremo de un palito*)

Lombard ['lɑmbɑrd] o ['lɑmbərd] adj & s lombardo

Lombardy ['lɑmbərdɪ] s Lombardía

Lombardy poplar s álamo de Italia, chopo lombardo

lon. abbr longitude

London ['lʌndən] adj londinense || s Londres m

Londoner ['lʌndənər] s londinense mf

lone [lon] adj solo, solitario; (*sole, single*) único

loneliness ['lonlinɪs] s soledad

lone·ly ['lonli] adj (comp **-lier**; super **-liest**) soledoso

lonesome ['lonsəm] adj soledoso; (*spot, atmosphere*) solitario

lone wolf s (fig) lobo solitario

long. abbr longitude

long [lɔŋ] o [laŋ] (comp **longer** ['lɔŋgər] o ['laŋgər]; super **longest** ['lɔŋgɪst] o ['laŋgɪst]) adj largo; de largo, p.ej., **two meters long** dos metros de largo || adv mucho tiempo, largo tiempo; **as long as** mientras; (*provided*) con tal de que; (*inasmuch as*) puesto que; **before long** dentro de poco; **how long** cuánto tiempo; **long ago** hace mucho tiempo; **long before** mucho antes; **longer** más tiempo; **long since** desde hace mucho tiempo; **no longer** ya no; **so long!** (coll) ¡hasta luego!; **so long as** con tal de que || intr anhelar, suspirar; **to long for** anhelar por, ansiar

long'boat' s (naut) lancha

long'-dis'tance call s (telp) llamada a larga distancia

long-distance flight s (aer) vuelo a distancia

long'-drawn'-out' adj prolongado, pesado

longeron ['lɑndʒərən] s larguero

longevity [lɑn'dʒevɪtɪ] s longevidad

long face s (coll) cara triste

long'hair' adj & s intelectual mf; aficionado a la música clásica

long'hand' s escritura a mano

longing ['lɔŋɪŋ] o ['laŋɪŋ] adj anhelante || s anhelo, ansia

longitude ['lɑndʒɪ,tjud] o ['lɑndʒɪ,tud] s longitud

long-lived ['lɔŋ 'laɪvd], ['lɔŋ 'lɪvd], ['laŋ 'laɪvd] o ['laŋ 'lɪvd] adj longevo, de larga vida

long-playing record ['lɔŋ 'ple·ɪŋ] o ['laŋ 'ple·ɪŋ] s disco de larga duración

long primer ['prɪmər] s (typ) entredós m

long'-range' adj de largo alcance

longshore·man ['lɔŋ ,ʃormən] o ['laŋ ,ʃormən] s (pl **-men** [mən]) s estibador m, portuario

long'-stand'ing adj que existe desde hace mucho tiempo

long'-suf'fering adj longánimo, sufrido

long suit s (cards) palo fuerte; (fig) fuerte m

long'-term' adj a largo plazo

long'-wind'ed adj difuso, palabrero

look [lʊk] s (*appearance*) aspecto, apariencia; (*glance*) mirada; (*search*) búsqueda; **looks** aspecto, apariencia; **to take a look at** echar una mirada a ‖ *tr* expresar con la mirada; representar (*la edad que uno tiene*); **to look daggers at** apuñalar con la mirada; **to look the part** vestir el cargo; **to look up** (*e.g., in a dictionary*) buscar; ir a visitar, venir a ver ‖ *intr* mirar; buscar; parecer; **look out!** ¡cuidado!, ¡ojo!; **to look after** mirar por; ocuparse en; **to look at** mirar; **to look back** mirar hacia atrás; (fig) mirar el pasado; **to look down on** mirar por encima del hombro; **to look for** buscar; creer, p.ej., **I look for rain** creo que va a llover; **to look forward to** esperar con placer anticipado; **to look ill** tener mala cara; **to look in on** pasar por la casa o la oficina de; **to look into** averiguar, estudiar; **to look like** parecerse a; amenazar, p.ej., **it looks like rain** amenaza lluvia, parece que va a llover; **to look oneself** parecer el mismo; tener buena cara; **to look out** tener cuidado; mirar por (*p.ej., la ventana*); **to look out for** mirar por, cuidar de; guardarse de; **to look out on** dar a; **to look through** mirar por; hojear (*un libro*); **to look toward** dar a; **to look up to** admirar, mirar con respeto; **to look well** tener buena cara

looker-on [ˌlʊkərˈɑn] o [ˌlʊkərˈɔn] *s* (*pl* **lookers-on**) mirón *m*, espectador *m*

looking glass [ˈlʊkɪŋ] *s* espejo

look'out' *s* vigilancia; (*tower*) atalaya; (*person keeping watch*) vigilante *mf*; (*man watching from lookout tower*) atalaya *m*; (*care, concern*) (coll) cuidado; **to be on the lookout for** estar a la mira de

loom [lum] *s* telar *m* ‖ *intr* (*to appear indistinctly*) vislumbrarse; amenazar, parecer inevitable

loon [lun] *s* tonto, bobo; (orn) zambullidor *m*

loon·y [ˈluni] *adj* (*comp* **-ier;** *super* **-iest**) (slang) loco ‖ *s* (*pl* **-ies**) (slang) loco

loop [lup] *s* lazo; (*in a cable or rope*) vuelta; (*of a river*) meandro; (*of a road*) recoveco; (*for fastening a button*) presilla; (aer) rizo; (elec) circuito cerrado; (*part of vibrating body between two nodes*) vientre *m*; **to loop the loop** (aer) rizar el rizo ‖ *tr* hacer lazos en; enlazar ‖ *intr* hacer lazo; (aer) hacer el rizo

loop'hole' *s* (*narrow opening in wall*) lucerna; (*means of evasion*) efugio, escapatoria

loose [lus] *adj* (*dress, tooth, screw, bowels*) flojo; (*fitting, thread, wire, rivet, tongue, bowels*) suelto; (*sleeve*) perdido; (*earth, soil*) desmenuzado; (*unpackaged*) a granel, sin envase; (*unbound papers*) sin encuadernar; (*pulley*) loco; (*translation*) libre; (*life, morals*) relajado; (*woman*) fácil, frágil; **to become loose** desatarse, aflojarse; **to break loose** ponerse en libertad; **to turn loose** sol-

tar ‖ *s* — **to be on the loose** (coll) ser libre, estar sin trabas; (coll) estar de juerga ‖ *tr* soltar; desatar, desencadenar

loose end *s* cabo suelto; **at loose ends** desarreglado, indeciso

loose'-leaf' notebook *s* cuaderno de hojas cambiables, cuaderno de hojas sueltas

loosen [ˈlusən] *tr* desatar, aflojar, desapretar; aflojar, laxar (*el vientre*) ‖ *intr* desatarse, aflojarse, desapretarse

looseness [ˈlusnɪs] *s* flojedad, soltura; (*in morals*) relajamiento

loose'strife' *s* lisimaquia; salicaria

loose-tongued [ˈlusˈtʌŋd] *adj* largo de lengua, ligero de lengua

loot [lut] *s* botín *m*, presa ‖ *tr* saquear, pillar

lop [lɑp] *v* (*pret & pp* **lopped;** *ger* **lopping**) *tr* dejar caer (*p.ej., los brazos*); **to lop off** cortar; podar (*un árbol, una vid*) ‖ *intr* colgar

lopsided [ˈlɑpˈsaɪdɪd] *adj* ladeado, sesgado; desproporcionado, asimétrico, patituerto

loquacious [loˈkweʃəs] *adj* locuaz

lord [lɔrd] *s* señor *m*; (Brit) lord *m*; (hum & poet) marido ‖ *tr* — **to lord it over** dominar despóticamente, imponerse a

lord·ly [ˈlɔrdli] *adj* (*comp* **-lier;** *super* **-liest**) señoril; magnífico; despótico, imperioso; altivo, arrogante

Lord's Day, the *el* domingo

lordship [ˈlɔrdʃɪp] *s* señoría, excelencia

Lord's Prayer *s* oración dominical, padrenuestro

Lord's Supper *s* sagrada comunión; Cena del Señor

lore [lɔr] *s* ciencia, saber *m*; ciencia popular, saber *m* popular

lorgnette [lɔrnˈjɛt] *s* (*eyeglasses*) impertinentes *mpl*; (*opera glasses*) gemelos de teatro con manija

lor·ry [ˈlɑri] o [ˈlɔri] *s* (*pl* **-ries**) carro de plataforma; (Brit) autocamión *m*; (Brit) vagoneta

lose [luz] *v* (*pret & pp* **lost** [lɔst] o [lɑst]) *tr* perder; no lograr salvar (*el médico al enfermo*); **to lose heart** desalentarse; **to lose oneself** perderse, errar el camino; ensimismarse ‖ *intr* perder; quedar vencido; retrasarse (*el reloj*)

loser [ˈluzər] *s* perdedor *m*

losing [ˈluzɪŋ] *adj* perdedor ‖ **losings** *spl* pérdidas, dinero perdido

loss [lɔs] o [lɑs] *s* pérdida; **to be at a loss** estar perplejo, no saber qué hacer; **to be at a loss to** + *inf* no saber como + *inf*; **to sell at a loss** vender con pérdida

loss of face *s* pérdida de prestigio, desprestigio

lost [lɔst] o [lɑst] *adj* perdido; **lost in thought** ensimismado, abismado; **lost to** perdido para; insensible a

lost'-and-found' department *s* oficina de objetos perdidos

lost sheep *s* oveja perdida

lot [lɑt] s (*for building*) solar m, parcela; (*fate, destiny*) suerte f; (*portion, parcel*) lote m; (*of people*) grupo; (coll) gran cantidad, gran número; (coll) sujeto, tipo; **a lot (of)** o **lots of** (coll) mucho, muchos; **to cast** o **to throw in one's lot with** compartir la suerte de; **to draw** o **to cast lots** echar suertes

lotion ['loʃən] s loción

lotter·y ['lɑtəri] s (pl **-ies**) lotería

lotto ['lɑto] s lotería

lotus ['lotəs] s loto

loud [laud] adj alto; (*noisy*) ruidoso; (*voice*) fuerte; (*garish*) chillón, llamativo; (*conspicuously vulgar*) charro, cursi; (*foul-smelling*) apestoso, maloliente || adv alto, en voz alta; ruidosamente

loudmouthed ['laud,mauθt] o ['laud,mauðd] adj vocinglero

loud'speak'er s altavoz m

lounge [laundʒ] s diván m, sofá m cama; salón m de descanso, salón social || intr repantigarse a su sabor, recostarse cómodamente; **to lounge around** estar arrimado a la pared, pasearse perezosamente

lounge lizard s (slang) holgón m

louse [laus] s (pl **lice** [lais]) piojo

lous·y ['lauzi] adj (comp **-ier**; super **-iest**) piojoso; (*mean*) (coll) vil, ruin; (*filthy*) (coll) asqueroso, sucio; (*bungling*) (coll) chapucero; **lousy with** (slang) colmado de (*p.ej.,* dinero)

lout [laut] s patán m

louver ['luvər] s (*opening to let in air and light*) lumbrera; tablilla de persiana; (aut) persiana del radiador

lovable ['lʌvəbəl] adj amable

love [lʌv] s amor m; (*tennis*) cero, nada; **not for love nor money** ni a tiros; **to be in love (with)** estar enamorado (de); **to fall in love (with)** enamorarse (de); **to make love to** cortejar, galantear || tr amar, querer; gustar de, tener afición a

love affair s amores mpl, amorío

love'bird' s inseparable m; **lovebirds** recién casados muy enamorados

love child s hijo del amor

love feast s ágape m

loveless ['lʌvlɪs] adj abandonado, sin amor; (*feeling no love*) desamado

lovelorn ['lʌv,lɔrn] adj abandonado por su amor, herido de amor

love·ly ['lʌvli] adj (comp **-lier**; super **-liest**) bello, hermoso; adorable, precioso; (coll) encantador, gracioso

love match s matrimonio de amor

love potion s filtro, filtro de amor

lover ['lʌvər] s amante mf; (*e.g., of hunting, sports*) aficionado; (*e.g., of work*) amigo

love seat s confidente m

love'sick' adj enfermo de amor

love'sick'ness s mal m de amor

love song s canción de amor

loving ['lʌvɪŋ] adj amoroso, afectuoso

lov'ing-kind'ness s bondad infinita, misericordia

low [lo] adj bajo; (*diet; visibility; opinion*) malo; (*dress, waist*) escotado; (*depressed*) abatido; gravemente enfermo; (*fire*) lento; **to lay low** dejar tendido, derribar; matar; **to lie low** no dejarse ver || adv bajo || s punto bajo; precio bajo, precio mínimo; (*moo of cow*) mugido; (aut) primera marcha, primera velocidad; (meteor) depresión || intr mugir (*la vaca*)

low'born' adj de humilde cuna

low'boy' s cómoda baja con patas cortas

low'brow' adj & s (slang) ignorante mf

low'-cost' housing s casas baratas

Low Countries, the los Países Bajos

low'-down' adj (coll) bajo, vil, ruin || **low'-down'** s (slang) informes mf confidenciales, hechos verdaderos

lower ['lo·ər] adj bajo, inferior || tr & intr bajar || ['lau·ər] intr poner mala cara, fruncir el entrecejo; encapotarse (*el cielo*)

lower berth ['lo·ər] s litera baja, cama baja

Lower California ['lo·ər] s la Baja California

lower case ['lo·ər] s (typ) caja baja

lower middle class ['lo·ər] s pequeña burguesía

lowermost ['lo·ər,most] adj (el) más bajo

low'-fre'quency adj de baja frecuencia

low gear s primera marcha, primera velocidad

lowland ['loland] s tierra baja || **Lowlands** spl Tierra Baja (*de Escocia*)

low·ly ['loli] adj (comp **-lier**; super **-liest**) humilde; (*in growth or position*) bajo

Low Mass s misa rezada

low-minded ['lo'maindɪd] adj vil, ruin

low neck s escote m, escotado

low-necked ['lo'nekt] adj escotado

low-pitched ['lo'pɪtʃt] adj (*sound*) grave; (*roof*) poco declive

low'-pres'sure adj de baja presión

low-priced ['lo'praist] adj barato, de precio bajo

low shoe s zapato inglés

low'-speed' adj de baja velocidad

low-spirited ['lo'spɪrɪtɪd] adj abatido

low spirits spl abatimiento

low tide s bajamar f, marea baja; (fig) punto mas bajo

low visibility s (aer) poca visibilidad

low water s (*of a river*) nivel mínimo; (*because of drought*) estiaje m; bajamar f, marea baja

loyal ['lɔɪ·əl] adj leal

loyalist ['lɔɪ·əlɪst] s leal m

loyal·ty ['lɔɪ·əlti] s (pl **-ties**) lealtad

lozenge ['lɑzɪndʒ] s losange m; (*candy cough drop*) pastilla, tableta

LP ['ɛl'pi] s (letterword) (trademark) disco de larga duración

Ltd. abbr **limited**

lubricant ['lubrɪkənt] adj & s lubricante m

lubricate ['lubrɪ,ket] tr lubricar

lubricous ['lubrɪkəs] adj (*slippery; lewd*) lúbrico (*resbaladizo; lascivo*); incierto, inconstante

lucerne [lu'sʌrn] *s* mielga

lucid ['lusɪd] *adj* claro, inteligible; (*rational, sane*) lúcido; (*bright, shining*) luciente; (*clear, transparent*) cristalino

Lucifer ['lusɪfər] *s* Lucifer *m*

luck [lʌk] *s* (*good or bad*) suerte *f;* (*good*) suerte, buena suerte; **down on one's luck** de mala suerte, de malas; **in luck** de buena suerte, de buenas; **out of luck** de mala suerte, de malas; **to bring luck** traer buena suerte; **to try one's luck** probar fortuna; **worse luck** desgraciadamente

luckily ['lʌkɪli] *adv* afortunadamente

luckless ['lʌklɪs] *adj* desgraciado

luck·y ['lʌki] *adj* (*comp* **-ier;** *super* **-iest**) afortunado; (*supposed to bring luck*) de buen agüero; **to be lucky** tener suerte

lucky hit *s* (coll) golpe *m* de fortuna

lucrative ['lukrətɪv] *adj* lucrativo

ludicrous ['ludɪkrəs] *adj* absurdo, ridículo

lug [lʌg] *s* orejeta; (*pull, tug*) estirón *m*, esfuerzo ‖ *v* (*pret & pp* **lugged;** *ger* **lugging**) *tr* tirar con fuerza de; (*to bring up irrelevantly*) (coll) traer a colación

luggage ['lʌgɪdʒ] *s* equipaje *m*

lugubrious [lu'gubrɪ·əs] o [lu'gjubrɪ·əs] *adj* lúgubre

lukewarm ['luk,wɔrm] *adj* tibio, templado

lull [lʌl] *s* momento de calma, momento de silencio; (naut) recalmón *m* ‖ *tr* adormecer; calmar, aquietar; apaciguar

lulla·by ['lʌlə,baɪ] *s* (*pl* **-bies**) arrullo, canción de cuna

lumbago [lʌm'bego] *s* lumbago

lumber ['lʌmbər] *s* madera aserrada, madera aserradiza, madera de sierra; trastos viejos ‖ *intr* andar pesadamente

lum'ber-jack' *s* leñador *m*, hachero

lumber-man ['lʌmbərmən] *s* (*pl* **-men** [mən]) (*dealer*) maderero; (*man who cuts down lumber*) leñador *m*, hachero

lumber room *s* leonera, trastera

lum'ber-yard' *s* maderería, depósito de maderas

luminar·y ['lumɪ,neri] *s* (*pl* **-ies**) luminar *m*, lumbrera

luminescent [,lumɪ'nesənt] *adj* luminiscente

luminous ['lumɪnəs] *adj* luminoso

lummox ['lʌməks] *s* (coll) jergón *m*

lump [lʌmp] *s* terrón *m;* (*swelling*) chichón *m*, bulto, hinchazón *m;* (*stupid person*) (coll) bodoque *m;* **in the lump** en grueso, por junto; **to get a lump in one's throat** hacérsele a (*uno*) un nudo en la garganta ‖ *tr* juntar, mezclar; (*to make into lumps*) aterronar; (coll) aguantar, tragar (*cosa repulsiva*)

lumpish ['lʌmpɪʃ] *adj* hobachón, torpe, pesado

lump sum *s* suma global, suma total

lump·y ['lʌmpi] *adj* (*comp* **-ier;** *super*

-iest) aterronado, borujoso; torpe, pesado; (*sea*) agitado

luna·cy ['lunəsi] *s* (*pl* **-cies**) demencia, locura

lunar ['lunər] *adj* lunar

lunar landing *s* alunizaje *m*

lunatic ['lunətɪk] *adj & s* lunático, loco

lunatic asylum *s* manicomio

lunatic fringe *s* minoría fanática

lunch [lʌntʃ] *s* (*regular midday meal*) almuerzo; (*light meal*) colación, merienda ‖ *intr* almorzar; merendar, tomar una colación

lunch basket *s* fiambrera

lunch cloth *s* mantelito

luncheon ['lʌntʃən] *s* almuerzo; almuerzo de ceremonia

lunch'room' *s* cantina, merendero

lung [lʌŋ] *s* pulmón *m*

lunge [lʌndʒ] *s* arremetida, embestida; (*with a sword*) estocada ‖ *intr* arremeter, lanzarse; **to lunge at** arremeter contra

lurch [lʌrtʃ] *s* sacudida, tumbo; (naut) bandazo; **to leave in the lurch** dejar en la estacada, dejar colgado ‖ *intr* dar una sacudida, dar un tumbo; (naut) dar un bandazo

lure [lur] *s* (*decoy*) cebo, señuelo; (fig) aliciente *m*, señuelo ‖ *tr* atraer con cebo, atraer con señuelo; (fig) atraer, tentar, seducir; **to lure away** llevarse con señuelo; (*from one's obligations*) desviar

lurid ['lurɪd] *adj* sensacional; (*gruesome*) espeluznante; (*fiery*) ardiente, encendido

lurk [lʌrk] *intr* acechar, andar furtivamente

luscious ['lʌʃəs] *adj* delicioso; lujoso; voluptuoso

lush [lʌʃ] *adj* jugoso, lozano; lujuriante; lujoso

Lusitanian [,lusɪ'tenɪ·ən] *adj & s* lusitano

lust [lʌst] *s* deseo vehemente; (*greed*) codicia; (*strong sexual appetite*) lujuria; entusiasmo ‖ *intr* lujuriar; **to lust after** o **for** codiciar; desear con lujuria

luster ['lʌstər] *s* (*gloss*) lustre *m;* (*of certain fabrics*) viso; (*fame, glory*) (fig) lustre

lus'ter-ware' *s* loza con visos metálicos

lustful ['lʌstfəl] *adj* lujurioso

lustrous ['lʌstrəs] *adj* lustroso

lust·y ['lʌsti] *adj* (*comp* **-ier;** *super* **-iest**) fuerte, robusto, lozano

lute [lut] *s* (mus) laúd *m;* (*substance used to close or seal a joint*) (chem) lodo

Lutheran ['luθərən] *adj & s* luterano

luxuriance [lʌg'ʒurɪ·əns] *s* lozanía

luxuriant [lʌg'ʒurɪ·ənt] *adj* lozano, lujuriante; (*overornamented*) recargado

luxuriate [lʌg'ʒurɪ,et] o [lʌk'ʃurɪ,et] *intr* crecer con lozanía; entregarse al lujo; (*to find keen pleasure*) lozanearse

luxurious [lʌg'ʒurɪ·əs] o [lʌk'ʃurɪ·əs] *adj* lujoso

luxu‧ry [ˈlʌkʃəri] o [ˈlʌgʒəri] s (pl -ries) lujo
lye [laɪ] s lejía
lying [ˈlaɪ‧ɪŋ] adj mentiroso ‖ s el mentir
ly'ing-in' hospital s casa de maternidad, clínica de parturientas
lymph [lɪmf] s linfa
lymphatic [lɪmˈfætɪk] adj linfático
lynch [lɪntʃ] tr linchar
lynching [ˈlɪntʃɪŋ] s linchamiento
lynch law s justicia de la soga

lynx [lɪŋks] s lince m
lynx-eyed [ˈlɪŋks͵aɪd] adj de ojos linces
lyonnaise [͵laɪ‧əˈnez] adj (culin) a la lionesa
lyre [laɪr] s (mus) lira
lyric [ˈlɪrɪk] adj lírico ‖ s poema lírico; (words of a song) (coll) letra
lyrical [ˈlɪrɪkəl] adj lírico
lyricism [ˈlɪrɪ͵sɪzəm] s lirismo
lyricist [ˈlɪrɪsɪst] s (writer of words for songs) letrista mf; (poet) poeta lírico

M

M, m [ɛm] decimotercera letra del alfabeto inglés
m. abbr **married, masculine, meter, midnight, mile, minute, month**
ma'am [mæm] o [mɑm] s (coll) señora
macadam [məˈkædəm] s macadán m
macadamize [məˈkædə͵maɪz] tr macadamizar
macaro‧ni [͵mækəˈroni] s (pl -nis o -nies) macarrones mpl
macaroon [͵mækəˈrun] s mostachón m, almendrado
macaw [məˈkɔ] s aracanga, guacamayo
mace [mes] s maza; (spice) macis m
mace'bear'er s macero
machination [͵mækɪˈneʃən] s maquinación
machine [məˈʃin] s máquina; automóvil m, coche m; (of a political party) camarilla ‖ tr trabajar a máquina
machine gun s ametralladora
ma‧chine'-gun' tr ametrallar
ma‧chine'-made' adj hecho a máquina
machiner‧y [məˈʃinəri] s (pl -ies) maquinaria
machine screw s tornillo para metales
machine shop s taller mecánico
machine tool s máquina-herramienta
machine translation s traducción automática
machinist [məˈʃinɪst] s (person who makes machines) maquinista mf; (person who operates machines) mecánico; (naut) segundo maquinista; (theat) maquinista mf, tramoyista mf
mackerel [ˈmækərəl] s caballa, escombro
mackerel sky s cielo aborregado
mackintosh [ˈmækɪn͵taʃ] s impermeable m
mad [mæd] adj (comp **madder;** super **maddest**) (angry) enojado, furioso; (crazy) loco; (foolish) tonto, necio; (rabid) rabioso; **to be mad about** (coll) estar loco por; **to drive mad** volver loco; **to go mad** volverse loco; rabiar (un perro)
madam [ˈmædəm] s señora
mad'cap' s alocado, tarambana mf
madden [ˈmædən] tr (to make angry) enojar, enfurecer; (to make insane) enloquecer

made-to-order [ˈmedtəˈɔrdər] adj hecho de encargo; (clothing) hecho a la medida
made'-up' adj inventado, ficticio; (artificial) postizo; (face) pintado
mad'house' s casa de locos, manicomio
madman [ˈmæd͵mæn] s (pl -men [͵men]) loco
madness [ˈmædnɪs] s furia, rabia; locura; (of a dog) rabia
Madonna lily [məˈdɑnə] s azucena
maelstrom [ˈmelstrəm] s remolino
mag. abbr **magazine**
magazine [ˈmægə͵zin] o [͵mægəˈzin] s (periodical) revista, magazine m; (warehouse) almacén m; (for cartridges) cámara; (for powder) polvorín m; (naut) santabárbara; (phot) almacén m
Magellan [məˈdʒɛlən] s Magallanes m
maggot [ˈmægət] s cresa
Magi [ˈmedʒaɪ] spl magos de Oriente, Reyes Magos
magic [ˈmædʒɪk] adj mágico ‖ s magia; ilusionismo, prestidigitación; **as if by magic** como por encanto
magician [məˈdʒɪʃən] s (entertainer with sleight of hand) ilusionista mf, prestidigitador m; (sorcerer) mágico
magistrate [ˈmædʒɪs͵tret] s magistrado
magnanimous [mægˈnænɪməs] adj magnánimo
magnesium [mægˈniʃɪ‧əm] o [mægˈnɪʒɪ‧əm] s magnesio
magnet [ˈmægnɪt] s imán m
magnetic [mægˈnɛtɪk] adj magnético; (fig) atrayente, cautivador
magnetic curves spl fantasma magnético
magnetism [ˈmægnɪ͵tɪzəm] s magnetismo
magnetize [ˈmægnɪ͵taɪz] tr magnetizar, imanar
magne‧to [mægˈnito] s (pl -tos) magneto m & f
magnificent [mægˈnɪfɪsənt] adj magnífico
magni‧fy [ˈmægnɪ͵faɪ] v (pret & pp -fied) tr magnificar; exagerar
magnifying glass s lupa, vidrio de aumento
magnitude [ˈmægnɪ͵tjud] o [ˈmægnɪ͵tud] s magnitud
magpie [ˈmæg͵paɪ] s picaza, urraca

Magyar ['mægjər] *adj & s* magiar *mf*

mahlstick ['mɑl,stɪk] o ['mɔl,stɪk] *s* tiento

mahoga·ny [mə'hagəni] *s* (*pl* -**nies**) caoba

Mahomet [mə'hɑmɪt] *s* Mahoma *m*

mahout [mə'haut] *s* naire *m*, cornaca *m*

maid [med] *s* (*female servant*) criada, moza; (*young girl; housemaid*) doncella; (*spinster*) soltera

maiden ['medən] *s* doncella

maid'en·hair' *s* (bot) cabello de Venus

maid'en·head' *s* himen *m*

maidenhood ['medən,hud] *s* doncellez *f*

maiden lady *s* soltera

maiden name *s* apellido de soltera

maiden voyage *s* primera travesía

maid'-in-wait'ing *s* (*pl* maids-in-waiting) dama

maid of honor *s* (*at a wedding*) primera madrina de boda; (*attendant on a princess*) doncella de honor; (*attendant on a queen*) dama de honor

maid'serv'ant *s* criada, doméstica

mail [mel] *s* correspondencia, correo; (*of armor*) malla; **by return mail** a vuelta de correo ‖ *tr* echar al correo

mail'bag' *s* valija

mail'boat' *s* vapor *m* correo

mail'box' *s* buzón *m*

mail car *s* carro correo, coche-correo, ambulancia de correos

mail carrier *s* cartero

mailing list *s* lista de envío

mailing permit *s* porte concertado

mail·man ['mel,mæn] *s* (*pl* -**men** [,men]) cartero

mail order *s* pedido postal

mail'-or'der house *s* casa de ventas por correo

mail'plane' *s* avión-correo

mail train *s* tren *m* correo

maim [mem] *tr* estropear, mutilar

main [men] *adj* principal, primero, maestro, mayor ‖ *s* cañería maestra; **in the main** mayormente

main clause *s* proposición dominante

main course *s* plato principal, plato fuerte

main deck *s* cubierta principal

mainland ['men,lænd] o ['menlənd] *s* continente *m*, tierra firme

main line *s* (rr) tronco, línea principal

mainly ['menli] *adv* principalmente, en su mayor parte

mainmast ['menməst], ['men,mæst] o ['men,mɑst] *s* palo mayor

mainsail ['mensəl] o ['men,sel] *s* vela mayor

main'spring' *s* (*of watch*) muelle *m* real; (fig) móvil *m*, origen *m*

main'stay' *s* (naut) estay *m* mayor; (fig) soporte *m* principal

main street *s* calle *f* mayor

maintain [men'ten] *tr* mantener; (*to support*) (law) manutener

maintenance ['mentɪnəns] *s* mantenimiento; (*upkeep*) conservación; gastos de conservación

maître d'hôtel [,metər do'tel] *s* (*but-*

ler) mayordomo; (*headwaiter*) jefe *m* de comedor

maize [mez] *s* maíz *m*

majestic [mə'dʒestɪk] *adj* majestuoso

majes·ty ['mædʒɪsti] *s* (*pl* -**ties**) majestad

major ['medʒər] *adj* (*greater*) mayor; (*elder*) mayor de edad; (mus) mayor ‖ *s* (educ) especialización; (mil) comandante *m* ‖ *intr* (educ) especializarse

Majorca [mə'dʒɔrkə] *s* Mallorca

Majorcan [mə'dʒɔrkən] *adj & s* mallorquín *m*

major·do·mo [,medʒər'domo] *s* (*pl* -**mos**) mayordomo

major general *s* general *m* de división

majori·ty [mə'dʒɑrɪti] o [mə'dʒɔrɪti] *adj* mayoritario ‖ *s* (*pl* -**ties**) (*being of full age; larger number or part*) mayoría; (*full age*) mayoridad; (mil) comandancia

make [mek] *s* (*brand*) marca; (*form, build*) hechura; carácter *m*, natural *m*; **on the make** (slang) buscando provecho ‖ *v* (*pret & pp* made [med]) *tr* hacer; cometer (*un error*); efectuar (*un pago*); ganar (*dinero; una baza*); coger (*un tren*); dar (*dinero una empresa*); pronunciar (*un discurso*); cerrar (*un circuito*); poner (*a uno, p.ej., nervioso*); ser, p.ej., **she will make a good wife** será una buena esposa; **to make + *inf*** hacer + *inf*, p.ej., **she made him study** le hizo estudiar; **to make into** convertir en; **to make known** declarar; dar a conocer; **to make of** pensar de; **to make oneself known** darse a conocer; **to make out** distinguir, vislumbrar; descifrar; escribir (*una receta*); llenar (*un cheque*); **to make over** convertir; rehacer (*un traje*); (com) transferir; **to make up** preparar, confeccionar; inventar (*un cuento*); recobrar (*el tiempo perdido*); (theat) maquillar ‖ *intr* estar (*p.ej., seguro*); **to make away with** llevarse; deshacerse de; matar; **to make believe** fingir, p.ej., **he made believe he knew me** fingió conocerme; **to make for** ir hacia; embestir contra; contribuir a (*p.ej., mejores relaciones*); **to make much of** (coll) hacer fiestas a, mostrar cariño a; **to make off** largarse; **to make off with** llevarse, hacerse con; **to make out** arreglárselas; **to make toward** encaminarse a; **to make up** maquilarse, pintarse; componerse, hacer las paces; **to make up for** suplir; compensar por (*una pérdida*); **to make up to** (coll) tratar de congraciarse con

make'-be·lieve' *adj* simulado ‖ *s* pretexto, simulación, fantasía

maker ['mekər] *s* constructor *m*, fabricante *mf*

make'shift' *adj* de fortuna, provisional ‖ *s* expediente *m*; (*person*) tapagujeros *m*

make'-up' *s* composición, constitución;

afeite *m*, maquillaje *m*; (typ) imposición

make-up man *s* (theat) maquillador *m*

make'weight' *s* contrapeso; suplente *mf*

making ['mekɪŋ] *s* fabricación; material necesario; causa del éxito; **makings** elementos, materiales *mpl*; (*personal qualities necessary for some purpose*) madera

malachite ['mælə,kaɪt] *s* malaquita

maladjustment [,mælə'dʒʌstmənt] *s* desadaptación

mala·dy ['mælədi] *s* (*pl* **-dies**) dolencia, enfermedad

malaise [mæ'lez] *s* indisposición, malestar *m*

malapropos [,mæləprə'po] *adj* impropio || *adv* fuera de propósito

malaria [mə'lɛrɪ·ə] *s* malaria, paludismo

Malay ['mele] o [mə'le] *adj* & *s* malayo

malcontent ['mælkən,tɛnt] *adj* & *s* malcontento

male [mel] *adj* (*sex*) masculino; (*animal, plant, piece of a device*) macho; (*human being*) varón, p.ej., **male child** hijo varón || *s* macho; varón *m*

malediction [,mælɪ'dɪkʃən] *s* maldición

malefactor ['mælɪ,fæktər] *s* malhechor *m*

male nurse *s* enfermero

malevolent [mə'lɛvələnt] *adj* malévolo

malice ['mælɪs] *s* malicia, malevolencia; **to bear malice** guardar rencor; **with malice prepense** [prɪ'pɛns] (law) con malicia y premeditación

malicious [mə'lɪʃəs] *adj* malicioso, malévolo

malign [mə'laɪn] *adj* maligno || *tr* calumniar

malignant [mə'lɪgnənt] *adj* maligno

maligni·ty [mə'lɪgnɪti] *s* (*pl* **-ties**) malignidad

malinger [mə'lɪŋgər] *intr* hacer la zanguanga, fingirse enfermo

mall [mɔl] o [mæl] *s* alameda, paseo de árboles

mallet ['mælɪt] *s* (*wooden hammer*) mazo; (*for croquet and polo*) mallete *m*

mallow ['mælo] *s* malva

malnutrition [,mælnju'trɪʃən] o [,mælnu'trɪʃən] *s* desnutrición

malodorous [mæl'odərəs] *adj* maloliente

malt [mɔlt] *s* malta *m*; (coll) cerveza

maltreat [mæl'trit] *tr* maltratar

mamma ['mɔmə] o [mə'mɑ] *s* mama o mamá *f*

mammal ['mæməl] *s* mamífero

mammalian [mæ'melɪ·ən] *adj* & *s* mamífero

mammoth ['mæməθ] *adj* gigantesco, enorme || *s* mamut *m*

man [mæn] *s* (*pl* **men** [mɛn]) *s* hombre *m*; (*in chess*) pieza; (*in checkers*) pieza, peón *m*; **a man** uno, p.ej., **man can't get work in this town** uno no puede obtener empleo en este pueblo; **as one man** unánimemente; **man alive!** ¡hombre!; **man and wife** marido y mujer; **to be one's own man** no depender de nadie || *v* (*pret* & *pp* **manned**; *ger* **manning**) *tr* dotar, tripular (*un buque*); guarnecer (*una fortaleza*); servir (*los cañones*)

man about town *s* bulevardero, hombre *m* de mucho mundo

manacle ['mænəkəl] *s* manilla; **manacles** esposas || *tr* poner esposas a

manage ['mænɪdʒ] *tr* manejar || *intr* arreglárselas; **to manage to** ingeniarse a o para; **to manage to get along** ingeniarse para ir viviendo

manageable ['mænɪdʒəbəl] *adj* manejable

management ['mænɪdʒmənt] *s* manejo, dirección, gerencia; (*group who manage a business*) la empresa, la parte patronal, los patronos

manager ['mænədʒər] *s* director *m*, administrador *m*, gerente *mf*; empresario; (sport) manager *m*

managerial [,mænə'dʒɪrɪ·əl] *adj* empresarial

mandate ['mændet] *s* mandato || *tr* asignar por mandato

mandolin ['mændəlɪn] *s* mandolina

mandrake ['mændrek] *s* mandrágora

mane [men] *s* (*of horse*) crines *fpl*; (*of lion; of person*) melena

maneuver [mə'nuvər] *s* maniobra || *tr* hacer maniobrar || *intr* maniobrar

manful ['mænfəl] *adj* varonil, resuelto

manganese ['mæŋgə,nis] o ['mæŋgə,niz] *s* manganeso

mange [mendʒ] *s* sarna

manger ['mendʒər] *s* pesebre *m*

mangle ['mæŋgəl] *tr* lacerar, aplastar

man·gy ['mendʒi] *adj* (*comp* **-gier**; *super* **-giest**) sarnoso; (*dirty, squalid*) roñoso

man'han'dle *tr* maltratar

man'hole' *s* caja de registro, pozo de inspección

manhood ['mænhud] *s* virilidad; hombres *mpl*

man hunt *s* caza al hombre

mania ['menɪ·ə] *s* manía

maniac ['menɪ,æk] *adj* & *s* maníaco

manicure ['mænɪ,kjur] *s* (*care of hands*) manicura; (*person*) manicuro, manicura || *tr* hacer la manicura a (*una persona*); hacer (*las manos y las uñas*)

manicurist ['mænɪ,kjurɪst] *s* manicuro, manicura

manifest ['mænɪ,fɛst] *adj* manifiesto || *s* (naut) manifiesto || *tr* manifestar

manifes·to [,mænɪ'fɛsto] *s* (*pl* **-toes**) manifiesto

manifold ['mænɪ,fold] *adj* múltiple, vario || *s* copia, ejemplar *m*; (*pipe with outlets or inlets*) colector *m*, múltiple *m*

manikin ['mænɪkɪn] *s* maniquí *m*; (*dwarf*) enano

man in the moon *s* cara o cuerpo de hombre imaginarios en la luna llena

manipulate [mə'nɪpjə,let] *tr* manipular

man'kind' *s* el género humano ‖ **man'kind'** *s* el sexo masculino, los hombres

manliness ['mænlınıs] *s* masculinidad, virilidad

man·ly ['mænli] *adj* (*comp* **-lier;** *super* **-liest**) masculino, varonil

manned spaceship [mænd] *s* astronave tripulada

mannequin ['mænıkın] *s* maniquí *m*; (*young woman employed to exhibit clothing*) maniquí *f*

manner ['mænər] *s* manera; **by all manner of means** de todos modos; **in a manner of speaking** como si dijéramos; **in the manner of** a la manera de; **manners** modales *mpl*, crianza; **to the manner born** avezado desde la cuna

mannish ['mænıʃ] *adj* hombruno

man of letters *s* hombre *m* de letras

man of means *s* hombre *m* de dinero

man of parts *s* hombre *m* de buenas prendas

man of straw *s* hombre *m* de suposición

man of the world *s* hombre *m* de mundo

man-of-war [ˌmænəv'wɔr] *s* (*pl* **men-of-war** [ˌmenəv'wɔr]) *s* buque *m* de guerra

manor ['mænər] *s* señorío

manor house *s* casa solariega

man overboard *interj* ¡hombre al agua!

man'pow'er *s* número de hombres; personal *m* competente; (*mil*) fuerzas nacionales

mansard ['mænsɑrd] *s* mansarda; piso de mansarda

man'serv'ant *s* (*pl* **men'serv'ants**) criado

mansion ['mænʃən] *s* hotel *m*, palacio; (*manor house*) casa solariega

man'slaugh'ter *s* (*law*) homicidio sin premeditación

mantel ['mæntəl] *s* manto (*de chimenea*); (*shelf above it*) mesilla, repisa de chimenea

man'tel·piece' *s* mesilla, repisa de chimenea

mantle ['mæntəl] *s* capa, manto ‖ *tr* vestir con manto; cubrir, tapar; ocultar ‖ *intr* encenderse (*el rostro*)

manual ['mænjʊ·əl] *adj* manual ‖ *s* (*book*) manual *m*; (*mil*) ejercicio; (*mus*) teclado manual

manual training *s* enseñanza de los artes y oficios

manufacture [ˌmænjə'fæktʃər] *s* fabricación; (*thing manufactured*) manufactura ‖ *tr* fabricar, manufacturar

manufacturer [ˌmænjə'fæktʃərər] *s* fabricante *mf*

manure [mə'njʊr] o [mə'nʊr] *s* estiércol *m* ‖ *tr* estercolar

manuscript ['mænjə.skrıpt] *adj* & *s* manuscrito

many ['meni] *adj* & *pron* muchos; **a good many** o a great many un buen número; **as many as** tantos como; hasta, p.ej., **as many as twenty** hasta veinte; **how many** cuántos; **many a** muchos, p.ej., **many a person** muchas

personas; **many another** muchos otros; **many more** muchos más; **so many** tantos; **too many** demasiados; **twice as many as** dos veces más que

many-sided ['meni,saɪdɪd] *adj* multilátero; (*having many interests or capabilities*) polifacético

map [mæp] *s* mapa *m*; (*of a city*) plano ‖ *v* (*pret* & *pp* **mapped;** *ger* **mapping**) *tr* trazar el mapa de; indicar en el mapa; **to map out** trazar el plan de

maple ['mepəl] *s* arce *m*

maquette [ma'ket] *s* maqueta

Mar. *abbr* **March**

mar [mɑr] *v* (*pret* & *pp* **marred;** *ger* **marring**) *tr* desfigurar, estropear; frustrar

maraud [mə'rɔd] *tr* saquear ‖ *intr* merodear

marauder [mə'rɔdər] *s* merodeador *m*

marble ['mɑrbəl] *adj* marmóreo ‖ *s* mármol *m*; (*little ball of glass, etc.*) canica; **marbles** (*game*) canica ‖ *tr* crispir, jaspear

march [mɑrtʃ] *s* marcha; (*frontier, territory*) marca; **to steal a march on someone** ganarle a uno por la mano ‖ *tr* hacer marchar ‖ *intr* marchar ‖ **March** *s* marzo

marchioness ['mɑrʃənıs] *s* marquesa

mare [mer] *s* (*female horse*) yegua; (*female donkey*) asna

margarine ['mɑrdʒərın] *s* margarina

margin ['mɑrdʒın] *s* margen *m* & *f*; (*collateral deposited with a broker*) doble *m*

marginal ['mɑrdʒınəl] *adj* marginal

margin release *s* tecla de escape

margin stop *s* fijamárgenes *m*, cierrarrenglón *m*, cortarrenglón *m*

marigold ['mærı,gold] *s* clavelón *m*; (*Calendula*) maravilla, flamenquilla

marihuana o **marijuana** [ˌmɑrı'hwɑnə] *s* mariguana

marinate ['mærı,net] *tr* escabechar, marinar

marine [mə'rin] *adj* marino, marítimo ‖ *s* marina; soldado de infantería de marina; **marines** infantería de marina; **tell that to the marines** (coll) cuénteselo a su abuela, a otro perro con ese hueso

mariner ['mærınər] *s* marino

marionette [ˌmærı·ə'net] *s* marioneta, títere *m*

marital status ['mærıtəl] *s* estado civil

maritime ['mærı,taım] *adj* marítimo

marjoram ['mɑrdʒərəm] *s* orégano; mejorana

mark [mɑrk] *s* marca, señal *f*; (*label*) marbete *m*; (*of punctuation*) punto; (*in an examination*) calificación, nota; (*used instead of signature by an illiterate person*) cruz *f*, signo; (*spot, stain*) mancha; (*coin*) marco; (*starting point in a race*) raya; (*target to shoot at*) blanco; **to be beside the mark** no venir al caso; **to hit the mark** dar en el blanco; **to leave one's mark** dejar memoria de sí; **to make one's mark** llegar a ser célebre; **miss the mark** errar el tiro; **to toe**

the mark ponerse en la raya; obedecer rigurosamente || *tr* marcar, señalar; dar nota a (*un alumno*); calificar (*un examen*); advertir, notar; **to mark down** poner por escrito; rebajar el precio de

mark'down' *s* reducción de precio

market ['markɪt] *s* mercado; **to bear the market** jugar a la baja; **to bull the market** jugar al alza; **to play the market** jugar a la bolsa; **to put on the market** lanzar al mercado || *tr* llevar al mercado; vender

marketable ['markɪtəbəl] *adj* comerciable, vendible

market basket *s* cesta para compras

marketing ['markɪtɪŋ] *s* mercología, mercadotecnia

market place *s* plaza del mercado

market price *s* precio corriente

marking gauge ['markɪŋ] *s* gramil *m*

marks·man ['marksmən] *s* (*pl* -men [mən]) tirador *m*; **a good marksman** un buen tiro

marksmanship ['marksmən,ʃɪp] *s* puntería

mark'up' *s* aumento de precio

marl [marl] *s* marga || *tr* margar

marmalade ['marmə,led] *s* mermelada

marmot ['marmət] *s* marmota

maroon [mə'run] *adj* & *s* marrón *m*, castaño obscuro || *tr* dejar abandonado (*en una isla desierta*)

marquee [mar'ki] *s* marquesina

marquess ['markwɪs] *s* marqués *m*

marque·try ['markətri] *s* (*pl* -tries) marquetería (*taracea*)

marquis ['markwɪs] *s* marqués *m*

marquise [mar'kiz] *s* marquesa; (*over the entrance to a hotel*) marquesina

marriage ['mærɪdʒ] *s* casamiento, matrimonio; (*married life; intimate union*) maridaje *m*

marriageable ['mærɪdʒəbəl] *adj* casadero

marriage portion *s* dote *m* & *f*

marriage rate *s* nupcialidad

married life ['mærɪd] *s* vida conyugal

marrow ['mæro] *s* médula, tuétano

mar·ry ['mæri] *v* (*pret* & *pp* -ried) *tr* casar (*el sacerdote o el juez a un hombre y una mujer*); (*to take in marriage*) casar con, casarse con; (*to unite intimately*) maridar; **to get married** casar con, casarse con || *intr* casar, casarse; **to marry into** emparentar con (*p.ej., una familia rica*); **to marry the second time** casarse en segundas nupcias

Mars [marz] *s* Marte *m*

Marseille [mar'se:j] *s* Marsella

marsh [marʃ] *s* ciénaga, pantano

mar·shal ['marʃəl] *s* cursor *m* de procesiones, maestro de ceremonias; (mil) mariscal *m*; (U.S.A.) oficial *m* de justicia || *v* (*pret* & *pp* -shaled o -shalled; *ger* -shaling o -shalling) *tr* conducir con ceremonia; ordenar, reunir (*los hechos de una argumentación*)

marsh mallow *s* (bot) malvavisco

marsh'mal'low *s* bombón *m* de meren-

gue y gelatina; bombón de malvavisco

marsh·y ['marʃi] *adj* (*comp* -ier; *super* -iest) pantanoso, palúdico

marten ['martən] *s* (*pine marten*) marta; (*beech marten*) garduña

martial ['marʃəl] *adj* marcial

martial law *s* ley *f* marcial; **to be under martial law** estar en estado de guerra

martin ['martɪn] *s* (orn) avión *m*

martinet [,martɪ'nɛt] o ['martɪ,nɛt] *s* ordenancista *mf*

martyr ['martər] *s* mártir *mf*

martyrdom ['martərdəm] *s* martirio

mar·vel ['marvəl] *s* maravilla || *v* (*pret* & *pp* -veled o -velled; *ger* -veling o -velling) *intr* maravillarse; **to marvel at** maravillarse con o de

marvelous ['marvələs] *adj* maravilloso

Marxist ['marksɪst] *adj* & *s* marxista *mf*

masc. *abbr* **masculine**

mascara [mæs'kærə] *s* tinte *m* para las pestañas

mascot ['mæskət] *s* mascota

masculine ['mæskjəlɪn] *adj* & *s* masculino

mash [mæʃ] *s* (*crushed mass*) masa; (*to form wort*) masa de cebada || *tr* machacar, majar

mashed potatoes [mæʃt] *spl* puré *m* de patatas

masher ['mæʃər] *s* (*device*) mano *f*; (slang) galanteador atrevido

mask [mæsk] o [mask] *s* máscara; (*of beekeeper*) carilla; (*made from a corpse*) mascarilla; (*person*) máscara *mf*; (phot) desvanecedor *m* || *tr* enmascarar; (phot) desvanecer || *intr* enmascararse

masked ball [mæskt] *s* baile *m* de máscaras

mason ['mesən] *s* albañil *m* || **Mason** *s* masón *m*

mason·ry ['mesənri] *s* (*pl* -ries) albañilería || **Masonry** *s* masonería

masquerade [,mæskə'red] o [,maskə'red] *s* mascarada; (*costume, disguise*) máscara; (*false show*) farsa || *intr* enmascararse; **to masquerade as** disfrazarse de

masquerade ball *s* baile *m* de máscaras

mass [mæs] *s* masa; gran cantidad; (*bulk, heap*) mole *f*; (*something glimpsed, e.g., in the fog*) bulto informe; (*big splotch in a painting*) gran mancha; (*celebration of the Eucharist*) misa; **the masses** las masas || *tr* juntar, reunir; enmasar (*tropas*) || *intr* juntarse, reunirse

massacre ['mæsəkər] *s* carnicería, matanza || *tr* degollar, matar

massage [mə'saʒ] *s* masaje *m* || *tr* masar, masajear

masseur [mæ'sœr] *s* masajista *m*

masseuse [mæ'sœz] *s* masajista *f*

massive ['mæsɪv] *adj* macizo; sólido, imponente

mass meeting *s* mitin *m* popular

mass production *s* fabricación en serie

mast [mæst] o [mast] *s* (*for a flag*) palo; (*of a ship*) palo, mástil *m*;

(*food for swine*) bellotas, hayucos; **before the mast** como simple marinero

master ['mæstər] o ['mɑstər] s (*employer*) dueño, patrón m; (*male head of household*) amo; (*man who possesses some special skill; teacher*) maestro; (*commander of merchant vessel*) capitán m; (*title of respect for a boy*) señorito || tr dominar

master bedroom s alcoba de respeto

master blade s hoja maestra (*de una ballesta*)

master builder s maestro de obras

masterful ['mæstərfəl] o ['mɑstərfəl] adj hábil, experto; dominante, imperioso

master key s llave maestra

masterly ['mæstərli] o ['mɑstərli] adj magistral || adv magistralmente

master mechanic s maestro mecánico

mas'ter-mind' s mente directora || tr dirigir con gran acierto

master of ceremonies s maestro de ceremonias; (*in a night club, radio, etc.*) animador m

mas'ter-piece' s obra maestra

master stroke s golpe maestro

mas'ter-work' s obra maestra

master-y ['mæstəri] o ['mɑstəri] s (pl -ies) (*command, as of a subject*) dominio; ventaja, superioridad; (*skill*) maestría

mast'head' s (*of a newspaper*) cabecera editorial; (naut) tope m

masticate ['mæstɪ‚ket] tr masticar

mastiff ['mæstɪf] o ['mɑstɪf] s mastín m

masturbate ['mæstər‚bet] intr masturbarse

mat [mæt] s (*for floor*) estera; (*for a cup, vase, etc.*) esterilla, ruedo; (*before a door*) felpudo; (*around a picture*) borde m de cartón || v (pret & pp matted; ger matting) tr (*to cover with matting*) esterar; enmarañar || intr enmarañarse

match [mætʃ] s fósforo; (*wick*) mecha; (*counterpart*) compañero; (*suitable partner in marriage*) partido; (*suitably associated pair*) pareja; (*game, contest*) match m, partido; to be a match for poder con, poder vencer; to meet one's match hallar la horma de su zapato || tr igualar; aparear, emparejar; hacer juego con; to match someone for the drinks jugarle a uno las bebidas || intr hacer juego, correr parejas; to match a juego, p.ej., a chair to match una silla a juego

match'box' s fosforera; (*of wax matches*) cerillera

matchless ['mætʃlɪs] adj incomparable, sin par

matchmaker ['mætʃ‚mekər] s casamentero

mate [met] s compañero; (*e.g., of a shoe*) compañero, hermano; (*husband or wife*) cónyuge mf; (*to a female*) macho; (*to a male*) hembra; (*in chess*) mate m; (naut) piloto || tr aparear, casar; (*in chess*) dar jaque

mate a; **to be well mated** hacer una buena pareja || intr aparearse, casarse

material [mə'tɪrɪ‑əl] adj material; importante || s material m; (*what a thing is made of*) materia; (*cloth, fabric*) tela, género

materialism [mə'tɪrɪ‑ə‚lɪzəm] s materialismo

materialize [mə'tɪrɪ‑ə‚laɪz] intr realizarse

matériel [mə‚tɪrɪ'el] s material m; material de guerra

maternal [mə'tʌrnəl] adj materno; (*motherly*) maternal

maternity [mə'tʌrnɪti] s maternidad

maternity hospital s casa de maternidad

math. abbr **mathematics**

mathematical [‚mæθɪ'mætɪkəl] adj matemático

mathematician [‚mæθɪmə'tɪʃən] s matemático

mathematics [‚mæθɪ'mætɪks] s matemática, matemáticas

matinée [‚mætɪ'ne] s matinée f, función de tarde

mating season s época de celo

matins ['mætɪnz] spl maitines mpl

matriarch ['metrɪ‚ɑrk] s matriarca

matricidal [‚metrɪ'saɪdəl] o [‚mætrɪ'saɪdəl] adj matricida

matricide ['metrɪ‚saɪd] o [‚mætrɪ‚saɪd] s (*act*) matricidio; (*person*) matricida mf

matriculate [mə'trɪkjə‚let] tr matricular || intr matricularse

matrimo-ny ['mætrɪ‚moni] s (pl -nies) matrimonio

matron ['metrən] s matrona

matronly ['metrənli] adj matronal

matter ['mætər] s (*physical substance; pus*) materia; (*subject talked or written about*) asunto; (*reason, ground*) motivo; (*copy for printer*) material m; (*printed material*) impresos; a matter of cosa de, obra de; for that matter en cuanto a eso; in the matter al respecto; no matter no importa; no matter when cuando quiera; no matter where dondequiera; what is the matter? ¿qué hay?; what is the matter with you? ¿qué tiene Vd.? || intr importar

matter of course s cosa de cajón; as a matter of course por rutina

matter of fact s — **as a matter of fact** en realidad, en honor a la verdad

matter-of-fact ['mætərəv‚fækt] adj prosaico, práctico, de poca imaginación

mattock ['mætək] s zapapico

mattress ['mætrɪs] s colchón m

mature [mə'tʃur] o [mə'tur] adj maduro; (*due*) pagadero, vencido || tr madurar || intr madurar; (*to become due*) (com) vencer

maturity [mə'tʃurɪti] o [mə'turɪti] s madurez f; (com) vencimiento

maudlin ['mɔdlɪn] adj lacrimoso, sensiblero; chispo y lloroso

maul [mɔl] tr aporrear, maltratar

maulstick ['mɔl‚stɪk] s tiento

maundy ['mɔndɪ] s lavatorio
Maundy Thursday s Jueves Santo
mausole·um [,mɔsə'lɪi·əm] s (pl -ums o -a [ə]) mausoleo
maw [mɔ] s (of fowl) buche m; (of fish) vejiga de aire
mawkish ['mɔkɪʃ] adj (sickening) empalagoso; (sentimental) sensiblero
max. abbr maximum
maxim ['mæksɪm] s máxima
maximum ['mæksɪməm] adj & s máximo
may v aux it may be puede ser; **may I come in?** ¿puedo entrar? **may you be happy!** ¡que seas feliz! || **May** s mayo
maybe ['mebɪ] o ['mebɪ] adv acaso, quizá, tal vez
May Day s primero de mayo; fiesta del primero de mayo
mayhem ['mehem] o ['me·əm] s (law) mutilación criminal
mayonnaise [,me·ə'nez] s mayonesa
mayor ['me·ər] o [mer] s alcalde m
mayoress ['me·ərɪs] o ['merɪs] s alcaldesa
May'pole' s mayo
Maypole dance s danza de cintas
May queen s maya
maze [mez] s laberinto
M.C. abbr Master of Ceremonies, Member of Congress
mdse. abbr merchandise
me [mi] pron pers me; mí; to me me; a mí; **with me** conmigo
meadow ['mɛdo] s prado, vega
mead'ow·land' s pradera
meager ['migər] adj escaso, pobre; flaco, magro
meal [mil] s (regular repast) comida; (edible grain coarsely ground) harina
meal'time' s hora de comer
mean [min] adj (intermediate) medio; (low in station or rank) humilde, obscuro; (shabby) andrajoso, raído; (stingy) mezquino, tacaño; (of poor quality) inferior, pobre; (small-minded) vil, ruin, innoble; insignificante; (vicious, as a horse) arisco, mal intencionado; (coll) indispuesto; (coll) avergonzado; (coll) de mal genio; **no mean** famoso, excelente || s promedio, término medio; **by all means** sí, por cierto, sin falta; **by means of** por medio de; **by no means** de ningún modo, en ningún caso; **means** bienes mpl de fortuna; (agency) medio, medios; **means** to an end paso para lograr un fin; to **live on one's means** vivir de sus rentas || v (pret & pp **meant** [ment]) tr significar, querer decir; to **mean** to pensar || intr — **to mean well** tener buenas intenciones
meander [mɪ'ændər] s meandro || intr serpentear; vagar
meaning ['minɪŋ] s sentido, significado
meaningful ['minɪŋfəl] adj significativo
meaningless ['minɪŋlɪs] adj sin sentido
meanness ['minnɪs] s bajeza, vileza, ruindad; (stinginess) mezquindad; (lowliness) humildad, pobreza

mean'time' adv entretanto, mientras tanto || s medio tiempo; **in the meantime** entretanto, mientras tanto
mean'while' adv & s var de meantime
measles ['mizəlz] s sarampión m; (German measles) rubéola
mea·sly ['mizlɪ] adj (comp -slier; super -sliest) sarampioso; (slang) despreciable, mezquino
measurable ['mɛʒərəbəl] adj medible
measure ['mɛʒər] s medida; (step, procedure) paso, gestión; (legislative bill) proyecto de ley; (of verse) pie m; (mus) compás m; **beyond measure** con exceso; **in a measure** hasta cierto punto; **in great measure** en gran parte; (suit) to measure hecho a la medida; **to take measures** tomar las medidas necesarias; **to take someone's measure** tomarle a uno las medidas || tr medir; recorrer (cierta distancia); **to measure out** medir; distribuir || intr medir
measurement ['mɛʒərmənt] s (act of measuring) medición; (measuring; dimension) medida
measuring glass s vaso graduado
meat [mit] s carne f; (food in general) manjar m, vianda; (substance, gist) meollo
meat ball s albóndiga
meat'hook' s garabato de carnicero
meat market s carnicería
meat·y ['mitɪ] adj (comp -ier; super -iest) carnoso; (fig) jugoso, substancioso
Mecca ['mɛkə] s La Meca
mechanic [mɪ'kænɪk] s mecánico
mechanical [mɪ'kænɪkəl] adj mecánico, maquinal; (machinelike) (fig) maquinal
mechanical toy s juguete m de movimiento
mechanics [mɪ'kænɪks] ssg mecánica
mechanism ['mɛkə,nɪzəm] s mecanismo
mechanize ['mɛkə,naɪz] tr mecanizar
med. abbr medicine, medieval
medal ['mɛdəl] s medalla
medallion [mɪ'dæljən] s medallón m
meddle ['mɛdəl] intr meterse, entremeterse
meddler ['mɛdlər] s entremetido
meddlesome ['mɛdəlsəm] adj entremetido
median ['midɪ·ən] adj intermedio, medio || s punto medio, número medio
median strip s faja central o divisoria
mediate ['midɪ,et] tr dirimir (una controversia); reconciliar || intr (to be in the middle) mediar; (to intervene to settle a dispute) intervenir
mediation [,midɪ'eʃən] s mediación
mediator ['midɪ,etər] s mediador m
medical ['mɛdɪkəl] adj médico
medical student s estudiante mf de medicina
medicine ['mɛdɪsɪn] s (science and art) medicina; (remedy, treatment) medicina, medicamento
medicine cabinet s armario botiquín
medicine kit s botiquín m

medicine man s curandero, hechicero (*entre los pieles rojas*)

medieval [,midɪ'ivəl] o [,medɪ'ivəl] *adj* medieval

medievalist [,midɪ'ivəlɪst] o [,medɪ-'ivəlɪst] s medievalista *mf*

mediocre ['midɪ,okər] o [,midɪ'okər] *adj* mediocre

mediocri•ty [,midɪ'ɑkrɪti] s (*pl* **-ties**) mediocridad

meditate ['medɪ ,tet] *tr & intr* meditar

Mediterranean [,medɪtə'reni•ən] *adj & s* Mediterráneo

medi•um ['midɪ•əm] *adj* intermedio; a medio asar ‖ s (*pl* **-ums** o **-a** [ə]) medio; (*in spiritualism*) medio, médium *m*; (*publication*) órgano; **through the medium of** por medio de

me'dium-range *adj* de alcance medio

medlar ['medlər] s (*tree and fruit*) níspero; (*fruit*) níspola

medley ['medlɪ] s mescolanza; (*mus*) popurrí *m*

medul•la [mɪ'dʌlə] s (*pl* **-lae** [li]) médula

meek [mik] *adj* dócil, manso

meekness ['miknɪs] s docilidad, mansedumbre

meerschaum ['mɪr/əm] s ['mɪr/əm] s espuma de mar; pipa de espuma de mar

meet [mit] *adj* conveniente, a propósito ‖ s concurso deportivo ‖ v (*pret & pp* **met** [met]) *tr* encontrar, encontrarse con; (*to make the acquaintance of*) conocer; empalmar con (*otro tren o autobús*); ir a esperar; honrar, pagar (*una letra*); hacer frente a (*gastos*); cumplir (*sus obligaciones*); batirse con; hallar (*la muerte*); tener (*mala suerte*); aparecer a (*la vista*) ‖ *intr* encontrarse; reunirse; conocerse; **till we meet again** hasta la vista; **to meet with** encontrarse con; reunirse con; empalmar (*un tren*) con (*otro tren*); tener (*un accidente*)

meeting ['mitɪŋ] s junta, sesión; reunión; encuentro; (*of two rivers or roads*) confluencia; desafío, duelo

meeting of the minds s concierto de voluntades

meeting place s lugar *m* de reunión

megacycle ['mega ,saɪkəl] s megaciclo

megaphone ['megə ,fon] s megáfono

megohm ['meg ,om] s megohmio

melancholia [,melən'kolɪ•ə] s melancolía

melanchol•y ['melən,kɑli] *adj* melancólico ‖ s (*pl* **-ies**) melancolía

melee ['mele] o ['mele] s refriega, reyerta

mellow ['melo] *adj* maduro, jugoso; suave, meloso; melodioso ‖ *tr* suavizar ‖ *intr* suavizarse

melodious [mɪ'lodɪ•əs] *adj* melodioso

melodramatic [,melədrə'mætɪk] *adj* melodramático

melo•dy ['melədi] s (*pl* **-dies**) melodía

melon ['melən] s melón *m*

melt [melt] *tr* derretir; fundir (*metales*); ablandar, aplacar ‖ *intr* derretirse; fundirse; ablandarse, apla-

carse; **to melt away** desvanecerse; **to melt into** convertirse en; deshacerse en (*lágrimas*)

melting pot s crisol *m*; (fig) caldero de razas

member ['membər] s miembro

membership ['membər ,/ɪp] s asociación; (*e.g., of a club*) personal *m*; número de miembros

membrane ['membren] s membrana

memen•to [mɪ'mento] s (*pl* **-tos** o **-toes**) recordatorio, prenda de recuerdo

mem•o ['memo] s (*pl* **-os**) (coll) apunte *m*, membrete *m*

memoir ['memwɑr] s memoria; biografía; **memoirs** memorias

memoran•dum [,memə'rændəm] s (*pl* **-dums** o **-da** [də]) apunte *m*, membrete *m*

memorial [mɪ'morɪ•əl] *adj* conmemorativo ‖ s monumento conmemorativo; (*petition*) memorial *m*

memorial arch s arco triunfal

Memorial Day s día *m* de los caídos

memorialize [mɪ'morɪ•ə ,laɪz] *tr* conmemorar

memorize ['memə ,raɪz] *tr* aprender de memoria

memo•ry ['meməri] s (*pl* **-ries**) memoria; **to commit to memory** encomendar a la memoria

menace ['menɪs] s amenaza ‖ *tr & intr* amenazar

ménage [me'nɑʒ] s casa, hogar *m*; economía doméstica

menagerie [mə'næʒərɪ] o [mə'nædʒərɪ] s casa de fieras; colección de fieras

mend [mend] s remiendo; **to be on the mend** ir mejorando ‖ *tr* (*to repair*) componer, reparar; (*to patch*) remendar; (*to improve*) reformar, mejorar ‖ *intr* mejorar

mendacious [men'de/əs] *adj* mendaz

mendicant ['mendɪkənt] *adj & s* mendicante *mf*

mending ['mendɪŋ] s remiendo, zurcido

menfolk ['men ,fok] spl hombres *mpl*

menial ['minɪ•əl] *adj* bajo, servil ‖ s criado, doméstico

menses ['mensiz] spl menstruo

men's furnishings spl artículos para caballeros

men's room s lavabo para caballeros

menstruate ['menstru ,et] *intr* menstruar

mental illness ['mentəl] s enfermedad mental

mental reservation s reserva mental

mental test s prueba de inteligencia

mention ['men/ən] s mención ‖ *tr* mencionar; **don't mention it** no hay de qué; **not to mention** sin contar

menu ['menju] o ['menju] s menú *m*, lista de comidas; comida

meow [mɪ'au] s maullido ‖ *intr* maullar

Mephistophelian [,mefɪstə'fili•ən] *adj* mefistofélico

mercantile ['mʌrkən ,til] o ['mʌrkən ,taɪl] *adj* mercantil

mercenar·y ['mʌrsə‚neri] *adj* merce-nario || *s* (*pl* -ies) mercenario

merchandise ['mʌrtʃən‚daɪz] *s* mer-cancías, mercaderías

merchant ['mʌrtʃənt] *adj* mercante || *s* mercante *m*, mercader *m*

merchant·man ['mʌrtʃəntmən] *s* (*pl* -men [mən]) buque *m* mercante

merchant marine *s* marina mercante

merchant vessel *s* buque *m* mercante

merciful ['mʌrsɪfəl] *adj* misericordioso

merciless ['mʌrsɪlɪs] *adj* despiadado, cruel, implacable

mercu·ry ['mʌrkjəri] *s* (*pl* -ries) mer-curio, azogue *m;* columna de mercu-rio

mer·cy ['mʌrsi] *s* (*pl* -cies) miseri-cordia; (*discretionary power*) mer-ced *f;* **at the mercy of** a merced de

mere [mɪr] *adj* mero, puro; nada más que

meretricious [‚merɪ'trɪʃəs] *adj* postizo, de oropel; cursi, llamativo

merge [mʌrdʒ] *tr* enchufar, fusionar || *intr* enchufarse, fusionarse; conver-gir (*p.ej., dos caminos*); **to merge into** convertirse gradualmente en

merger ['mʌrdʒər] *s* fusión de em-presas

meridian [mə'rɪdɪən] *adj* meridiano; (el) más elevado || *s* meridiano; (fig) auge *m*, apogeo

meringue [mə'ræŋ] *s* merengue *m*

meri·no [mə'rino] *adj* merino || *s* (*pl* -nos) merino

merit ['merɪt] *s* mérito || *tr* merecer

merlon ['mʌrlən] *s* almena, merlón *m*

mermaid ['mʌr‚med] *s* sirena; (*girl who swims well*) ninfa marina

mer·man ['mʌr‚mæn] *s* (*pl* -men [‚men]) tritón *m;* (*good swimmer*) tritón

merriment ['merɪmənt] *s* alegría, regocijo

mer·ry ['meri] *adj* (*comp* -rier; *super* -riest) alegre, regocijado; **to make merry** divertirse

Merry Christmas *interj* ¡Felices Pas-cuas!, ¡Felices Navidades!

mer'ry-go-round' *s* tiovivo, caballito; serie ininterrumpida (de fiestas, ter-tulias, etc.)

mer'ry·mak'er *s* fiestero, jaranero

mesh [meʃ] *s* (*net, network*) red *f;* (*each open space of net*) malla; (*en-gagement of gears*) engrane *m;* **meshes** celada, red *f* || *tr* enredar; (mach) engranar || *intr* enredarse; (mach) engranar

mess [mes] *s* (*dirty condition*) cochi-nería; fregado, lío, embrollo; (*meal for a group of people; such a group*) rancho; (*refuse*) bazofia; **to get into a mess** meterse en un lío; **to make a mess of** ensuciar, echar a perder || *tr* ensuciar; desarreglar; estropear, echar a perder || *intr* comer; **to mess around** (coll) ocuparse en fruslerías

message ['mesɪdʒ] *s* mensaje *m;* re-cado

messenger ['mesəndʒər] *s* mensajero; (*one who goes on errands*) manda-dero; precursor *m*

mess hall *s* sala de rancho; comedor *m* de militares

Messiah [mə'saɪ-ə] *s* Mesías *m*

mess kit *s* utensilios de rancho

mess'mate' *s* comensal *mf*, compañero de rancho

mess of pottage ['pɑtɪdʒ] *s* (Bib) pla-to de lentejas; cosa de ningún valor

Messrs. ['mesərz] *pl* de **Mr.**

mess·y ['mesi] *adj* (*comp* -ier; *super* -iest) desaliñado, desarreglado; sucio

met. *abbr* **metropolitan**

metal ['metəl] *adj* metálico || *s* metal *m;* (fig) brío, ánimo

metallic [mɪ'tælɪk] *adj* metálico

metallurgy ['metə‚lʌrdʒi] *s* metalurgia

metal polish *s* limpiametales *m*

met'al·work' *s* metalistería

metamorpho·sis [‚metə'mɔrfəsɪs] *s* (*pl* -ses [‚siz]) metamorfosis *f*

metaphore ['metəfər] o ['metə‚fɔr] *s* metáfora

metaphorical [‚metə'fɑrɪkəl] o [‚metə-'fɔrɪkəl] *adj* metafórico

metathe·sis [mɪ'tæθɪsɪs] *s* (*pl* -ses [‚siz]) metátesis *f*

mete [mit] *tr* — **to mete out** repartir

meteor ['mitɪ-ər] *s* estrella fugaz; (*atmospheric phenomenon*) meteoro

meteorology [‚mitɪ-ə'rɑlədʒi] *s* meteo-rología

meter ['mitər] *s* (*unit of measurement; verse*) metro; (*instrument for meas-uring gas, electricity, water*) con-tador *m;* (mus) compás *m*, tiempo || *tr* medir (con contador)

metering ['mitərɪŋ] *s* medición

meter reader *s* lector *m* (del contador)

methane ['meθen] *s* metano

method ['meθəd] *s* método

methodic(al) [mɪ'θɑdɪk(əl)] *adj* metó-dico

Methodist ['meθədɪst] *adj* & *s* meto-dista *mf*

Methuselah [mɪ'θuzələ] *s* Matusalén *m;* **to be as old as Methuselah** vivir más años que Matusalén

meticulous [mɪ'tɪkjələs] *adj* meticu-loso, minucioso

metric(al) ['metrɪk(əl)] *adj* métrico

metronome ['metrə‚nom] *s* metró-nomo

metropolis [mɪ'trapəlɪs] *s* metrópoli *f*

metropolitan [‚metrə'pɑlɪtən] *adj* me-tropolitano || *s* (eccl) metropolitano

mettle ['metəl] *s* ánimo, brío; **on one's mettle** dispuesto a hacer todo el es-fuerzo posible

mettlesome ['metəlsəm] *adj* animoso, brioso

mew [mju] *s* maullido; (orn) gaviota; **mews** (Brit) caballerizas alrededor de un corral

Mexican ['meksɪkən] *adj* & *s* mejicano

Mexico ['meksɪ‚ko] *s* Méjico

mezzanine ['mezə‚nin] *s* entresuelo

mfr. *abbr* **manufacturer**

mi. *abbr* **mile**

mica ['maɪkə] *s* mica

microbe ['maɪkrob] *s* microbio

microbiology [‚maɪkrəbaɪ'alədʒi] *s* microbiología

microcard ['maɪkrə‚kɑrd] *s* microficha

microfarad [ˌmaɪkrəˈfæræd] s microfaradio

microfilm [ˈmaɪkrəˌfɪlm] s microfilm m, micropelícula || tr microfilmar

microgroove [ˈmaɪkrəˌgruv] adj microsurco || s microsurco; disco microsurco

microphone [ˈmaɪkrəˌfon] s micrófono

microscope [ˈmaɪkrəˌskop] s microscopio

microscopic [ˌmaɪkrəˈskɑpɪk] adj microscópico

microwave [ˈmaɪkrəˌwev] s microonda

mid [mɪd] adj medio, p.ej., **in mid course** a medio camino

mid'day' adj del mediodía || s mediodía m

middle [ˈmɪdəl] adj medio || s centro, medio; (of the human body) cintura; **about the middle of** a mediados de; **in the middle of** en medio de

middle age s mediana edad || **Middle Ages** spl Edad Media

middle class s burguesía, clase media

Middle East s Oriente Medio

Middle English s el inglés medio

middle finger s dedo cordial, de en medio o del corazón

mid'dle-man' s (pl **-men** [ˌmen]) intermediario

middling [ˈmɪdlɪŋ] adj mediano, regular, pasadero || adv (coll) medianamente; **fairly middling** (coll) así, así || s (coarsely ground wheat) cabezuela; **middlings** artículos de calidad o precio medianos

mid·dy [ˈmɪdi] s (pl **-dies**) (coll) aspirante m de marina; (child's blouse) marinera

middy blouse s marinera

midget [ˈmɪdʒɪt] s enano, liliputiense mf

midland [ˈmɪdlənd] adj de tierra adentro || s región central

mid'night' adj de medianoche; **to burn the midnight oil** quemarse las cejas || s medianoche f

midriff [ˈmɪdrɪf] s (anat) diafragma m; talle m

midship-man [ˈmɪdˌʃɪpmən] s (pl **-men** [mən]) guardia marina m, aspirante m de marina

midst [mɪdst] s centro; **in the midst of** en medio de; en lo más recio de

mid'stream' s — **in midstream** en pleno río

mid'sum'mer s pleno verano

mid'way' adj situado a mitad del camino || adv a mitad del camino || s mitad del camino; (of a fair or exposition) avenida central

mid'week' s mediados de la semana

mid'wife' s (pl **-wives**) partera, comadrona

mid'win'ter s pleno invierno

mid'year' adj de mediados del año || s mediados del año; **midyears** (coll) examen m de mediados del año escolar

mien [min] s aspecto, semblante m, porte m

miff [mɪf] s (coll) desavenencia || tr (coll) ofender

might [maɪt] s fuerza, poder m; **with might and main** con todas sus fuerzas, a más no poder || v aux se emplea para formar el modo potencial, p.ej., **she might not come** es posible que no venga

might·y [ˈmaɪti] adj (comp **-ier;** super **-iest**) potente, poderoso; (of great size) grandísimo || adv (coll) muy

migrate [ˈmaɪgret] intr emigrar

migratory [ˈmaɪgrəˌtori] adj migratorio

mil. abbr **military, militia**

milch [mɪltʃ] adj lechero

mild [maɪld] adj blando, suave; dócil, manso; leve, ligero; (climate) templado

mildew [ˈmɪlˌdju] o [ˈmɪlˌdu] s (mold) moho; (plant disease) mildeu m

mile [maɪl] s milla inglesa

mileage [ˈmaɪlɪdʒ] s recorrido en millas

mileage ticket s billete contado por millas, semejante al billete kilométrico

mile'post' s poste miliario

mile'stone' s piedra miliaria; **to be a milestone** hacer época

milieu [mɪlˈju] s ambiente m, medio

militancy [ˈmɪlɪtənsi] s belicosidad

militant [ˈmɪlɪtənt] adj militante, belicoso

militarism [ˈmɪlɪtəˌrɪzəm] s militarismo

militarist [ˈmɪlɪtərɪst] adj & s militarista mf

militarize [ˈmɪlɪtəˌraɪz] tr militarizar

military [ˈmɪlɪˌteri] adj militar || s (los) militares

Military Academy s (U.S.A.) Academia General Militar

military police s policía militar

militate [ˈmɪlɪˌtet] intr militar

militia [mɪˈlɪʃə] s milicia

militia·man [mɪˈlɪʃəmən] s (pl **-men** [mən]) miliciano

milk [mɪlk] adj lechero, de leche || s leche f || tr ordeñar; chupar (los bienes de uno); abusar de, explotar || intr dar leche

milk can s lechera

milk diet s régimen lácteo

milking [ˈmɪlkɪŋ] s ordeño

milk'maid' s lechera

milk·man [ˈmɪlkˌmæn] s (pl **-men** [ˌmen]) lechero

milk of human kindness s compasión, humanidad

milk pail s ordeñadero

milk shake s batido de leche

milk'sop' s calzonazos m, marica m

milk'weed' s algodoncillo, vencetósigo

milk·y [ˈmɪlki] adj (comp **-ier;** super **-iest**) lechoso, lácteo

Milky Way s Vía Láctea

mill [mɪl] s (for grinding grain) molino; (for making fabrics) hilandería; (for cutting wood) aserradero; (for refining sugar) ingenio; (for produc-

ing steel) fábrica; *(to grind coffee)* molinillo; *(part of a dollar)* milésima; **to put through the mill** (coll) poner a prueba, someter a un entrenamiento riguroso || *tr* moler *(granos)*; acordonar, cerrillar *(monedas)*; laminar *(el acero)*; triturar *(mena)*; *(with a milling cutter)* fresar; batir *(chocolate)* || *intr* — **to mill about** o **around** arremolinarse

mill end *s* retal *m* de hilandería

millennial [mɪ'lɛnɪ·əl] *adj* milenario

millenni·um [mɪ'lɛnɪ·əm] *s (pl* -**ums** o -**a** [ə]) milenario, milenio

miller ['mɪlər] *s* molinero; (ent) polilla blanca

millet ['mɪlɪt] *s* mijo, millo

milliampere [‚mɪlɪ'æmpɪr] *s* miliamperio

milligram ['mɪlɪ‚græm] *s* miligramo

millimeter ['mɪlɪ‚mitər] *s* milímetro

milliner ['mɪlɪnər] *s* modista *mf* de sombreros

millinery ['mɪlɪ‚nɛrɪ] o ['mɪlɪnərɪ] *s* artículos para sombreros de señora; confección de sombreros de señora; venta de sombreros de señora

millinery shop *s* sombrerería

milling ['mɪlɪŋ] *s (of grain)* molienda; *(of coins)* acordonamiento, cordoncillo; fresado

milling machine *s* fresadora

million ['mɪljən] *adj* millón de, millones de || *s* millón *m*

millionaire [‚mɪljən'ɛr] *s* millonario

millionth ['mɪljənθ] *adj & s* millonésimo

millivolt ['mɪlɪ‚volt] *s* milivoltio

mill'pond' *s* represa de molino

mill'race' *s* caz *m*

mill'stone' *s* muela de molino; (fig) carga pesada

mill wheel *s* rueda de molino

mill'work' *s* carpintería de taller

mime [maɪm] *s* mimo || *tr* remedar

mimeograph ['mɪmɪ·ə‚græf] o ['mɪmɪ·ə‚grɑf] *s* (trademark) mimeógrafo || *tr* mimeografiar

mim·ic ['mɪmɪk] *s* imitador *m*, remedador *m* || *v (pret & pp* -**icked;** *ger* -**icking)** *tr* imitar, remedar

mimic·ry ['mɪmɪkrɪ] *s (pl* -**ries**) mímica, remedo

min. *abbr* **minimum, minute**

minaret [‚mɪnə'rɛt] o ['mɪnə‚rɛt] *s* alminar *m*, minarete *m*

mince [mɪns] *tr* desmenuzar; picar *(carne)* || *intr* andar remilgadamente; hablar remilgadamente

mince'meat' *s* cuajado, picadillo

mince pie *s* pastel relleno de carne picada con frutas

mind [maɪnd] *s* mente *f*, espíritu *m*; **to bear in mind** tener presente; **to be not in one's right mind** no estar en sus cabales; **to be of one mind** estar de acuerdo; **to be out of one's mind** estar fuera de juicio; **to change one's mind** mudar de parecer; **to go out of one's mind** volverse loco; **to have a mind to** tener ganas de; **to have in mind to** pensar en; **to have on one's**

mind preocuparse con; **to lose one's mind** perder el juicio; **to make up one's mind** resolverse; **to my mind a** mi parecer; **to say whatever comes into one's mind** decir lo que se le viene a la boca; **to set one's mind on** resolverse a; **to slip one's mind** escaparse de la memoria; **to speak one's mind** decir su parecer; **with one mind** unánimamente || *tr (to take care of)* cuidar, estar al cuidado de; obedecer; fijarse en; sentir molestia por; **do you mind the smoke?** ¿le molesta el humo?; **mind your own business** no se meta Vd. en lo que no le toca || *intr* tener inconveniente; tener cuidado; **never mind** no se preocupe, no se moleste

mindful ['maɪndfəl] *adj* atento; **mindful of** atento a, cuidadoso de

mind reader *s* adivinador *m* del pensamiento ajeno, lector *m* mental

mind reading *s* adivinación del pensamiento ajeno, lectura de la mente

mine [maɪn] *pron poss* el mío; mío || *s* mina; **to work a mine** beneficiar una mina || *tr* minar; beneficiar *(un terreno)*; extraer *(mineral, carbón, etc.)* || *intr* minar; abrir minas

mine field *s* campo de minas

mine layer *s* buque *m* portaminas, lanzaminas *m*

miner ['maɪnər] *s* minero; (mil, nav) minador *m*

mineral ['mɪnərəl] *adj & s* mineral *m*

mineralogy [‚mɪnə'rælədʒɪ] *s* mineralogía

mineral wool *s* lana de escorias

mine sweeper *s* dragaminas *m*

mingle ['mɪŋgəl] *tr* mezclar, confundir || *intr* mezclarse, confundirse; asociarse

miniature ['mɪnɪ·ətər] o ['mɪnɪt/ər] *s* miniatura; **to paint in miniature** miniar, pintar de miniatura

miniaturization [‚mɪnɪ·ətʃərɪ'zeʃən] o [‚mɪnɪtʃərɪ'zeʃən] *s* miniaturización

minimal ['mɪnɪməl] *adj* mínimo

minimize ['mɪnɪ‚maɪz] *tr* empequeñecer

minimum ['mɪnɪməm] *adj & s* mínimo

minimum wage *s* jornal mínimo

mining ['maɪnɪŋ] *adj* minero || *s* mineraje *m*, minería; (nav) minado

minion ['mɪnjən] *s* paniaguado *m*

minion of the law *s* esbirro, polizonte *m*

minister ['mɪnɪstər] *s* ministro; pastor *m* prostestante || *tr & intr* ministrar

ministerial [‚mɪnɪs'tɪrɪ·əl] *adj* ministerial

minis·try ['mɪnɪstrɪ] *s (pl* -**tries**) ministerio

mink [mɪŋk] *s* visón *m*

minnow ['mɪno] *s* pececillo; (ichth) foxino

minor ['maɪnər] *adj (smaller)* menor; de menor importancia; *(younger)* menor de edad; (mus) menor || *s* menor *m* de edad; (educ) asignatura secundaria

Minorca [mɪ'nɔrkə] *s* Menorca

Minorcan [mɪ'nɔrkən] *adj & s* menorquín *m*

minori·ty [mɪ'nɔrɪtɪ] o [mɪ'nɔrɪtɪ] *adj* minoritario ‖ *s* (*pl* **-ties**) (*being under age; smaller number or part*) minoría; (*less than full age*) minoridad

minstrel ['mɪnstrəl] *s* (*retainer who sang and played for his lord*) ministril *m*; (*medieval musician and poet*) juglar *m*, trovador *m*; (*U.S.A.*) cantor cómico disfrazado de negro

minstrel·sy ['mɪnstrəlsɪ] *s* (*pl* **-sies**) juglaría; compañía de juglares; poesía trovadoresca

mint [mɪnt] *s* casa de moneda; (*plant*) menta, hierbabuena; montón *m* de dinero; fuente *f* inagotable ‖ *tr* acuñar; (fig) inventar

minuet ['mɪnju'ɛt] *s* minué *m*, minuete *m*

minus ['maɪnəs] *adj* menos ‖ *prep* menos; falto de, sin ‖ *s* menos *m*

minute [maɪ'njut] o [maɪ'nut] *adj* diminuto, menudo ‖ ['mɪnɪt] *s* minuto; (*short space of time*) momento; **minutes** acta; **to write up the minutes** levantar acta; **up to the minute** al corriente; de última hora

minute hand ['mɪnɪt] *s* minutero

minutiae [mɪ'nju/ɪ,i] o [mɪ'nu/ɪ,i] *spl* minucias

minx [mɪŋks] *s* moza descarada

miracle ['mɪrəkəl] *s* milagro

miracle play *s* auto

miraculous [mɪ'rækjələs] *adj* milagroso

mirage [mɪ'rɑʒ] *s* espejismo

mire [maɪr] *s* fango, lodo

mirror ['mɪrər] *s* espejo; (aut) retrovisor *m* ‖ *tr* reflejar

mirth [mʌrθ] *s* alegría, regocijo

miry ['maɪrɪ] *adj* (*comp* **-ier**; *super* **-iest**) fangoso, lodoso; sucio

misadventure [,mɪsəd'ventʃər] *s* desgracia, contratiempo

misanthrope ['mɪsən,θrop] *s* misántropo

misanthropy [mɪs'ænθrəpɪ] *s* misantropía

misapprehension [,mɪsæprɪ'henʃən] *s* malentendido

misappropriation [,mɪsə,proprɪ'eʃən] *s* malversación

misbehave [,mɪsbɪ'hev] *intr* conducirse mal, portarse mal

misbehavior [,mɪsbɪ'hevɪ·ər] *s* mala conducta, mal comportamiento

misc. *abbr* **miscellaneous, miscellany**

miscalculation [,mɪskælkjə'leʃən] *s* mal cálculo

miscarriage [mɪs'kærɪdʒ] *s* aborto, malparto; fracaso, malogro; (*of a letter*) extravío

miscar·ry [mɪs'kærɪ] *v* (*pret & pp* **-ried**) *intr* abortar, malparir; malograrse; extraviarse (*una carta*)

miscellaneous [,mɪsə'lenɪ·əs] *adj* misceláneo

miscella·ny ['mɪsə,lenɪ] *s* (*pl* **-nies**) miscelánea

mischief ['mɪstʃɪf] *s* (*harm*) daño,

mal *m*; (*disposition to annoy*) malicia; (*prankishness*) travesura

mis'chief-mak'er *s* malsín *m*, cizañero

mischievous ['mɪstʃɪvəs] *adj* dañoso, malo; malicioso; travieso

misconception [,mɪskən'sepʃən] *s* concepto erróneo, mala interpretación

misconduct [mɪs'kɑndəkt] *s* mala conducta

misconstrue [,mɪskən'stru] o [mɪs'kɑnstru] *tr* interpretar mal

miscount [mɪs'kaunt] *s* cuenta errónea ‖ *tr & intr* contar mal

miscue [mɪs'kju] *s* (*in billiards*) pifia; (*slip*) pifia ‖ *intr* pifiar; (theat) equivocarse de apunte

mis·deal [mɪs,dil] *s* repartición errónea ‖ [mɪs'dil] *v* (*pret & pp* **-dealt** ['delt]) *tr & intr* repartir mal

misdeed [mɪs'did] o ['mɪs,did] *s* malhecho, fechoría

misdemeanor [,mɪsdɪ'minər] *s* mala conducta; (law) delito de menor cuantía

misdirect [,mɪsdɪ'rekt] o [,mɪsdaɪ'rekt] *tr* dirigir erradamente; hacer perder el camino

misdoing [mɪs'du·ɪŋ] *s* mala acción

miser ['maɪzər] *s* avaro, verrugo

miserable ['mɪzərəbəl] *adj* miserable; (coll) achacoso, indispuesto

miserly ['maɪzərlɪ] *adj* avariento, mezquino

miser·y ['mɪzərɪ] *s* (*pl* **-ies**) miseria

misfeasance [mɪs'fizəns] *s* (law) fraude *m*

misfire [mɪs'faɪr] *s* falla de tiro; (*of internal-combustion engine*) falla de encendido ‖ *intr* fallar (*un arma de fuego, el encendido de un motor*)

mis·fit ['mɪs,fɪt] *s* vestido mal cortado; cosa que no encaja bien; persona mal adaptada a su ambiente ‖ [mɪs'fɪt] *v* (*pret & pp* **-fitted**; *ger* **-fitting**) *tr & intr* encajar mal, sentar mal

misfortune [mɪs'fortʃən] *s* desgracia

misgiving [mɪs'gɪvɪŋ] *s* mal presentimiento, rescoldo

misgovern [mɪs'gʌvərn] *tr* desgobernar

misguidance [mɪs'gaɪdəns] *s* error *m*, extravío

misguided [mɪs'gaɪdɪd] *adj* descarriado, malaconsejado

mishap ['mɪshæp] o [mɪs'hæp] *s* accidente *m*, percance *m*

misinform [,mɪsɪn'fɔrm] *tr* dar informes erróneos a

misinterpret [,mɪsɪn'terprɪt] *tr* interpretar mal

misjudge [mɪs'dʒʌdʒ] *tr & intr* juzgar mal

mis·lay [mɪs'le] *v* (*pret & pp* **-laid** [,led]) *tr* extraviar, perder; (*among one's papers*) traspapelar

mis·lead [mɪs'lid] *v* (*pret & pp* **-led** [,led]) *tr* (*to lead astray*) extraviar, descaminar; (*to lead into wrongdoing*) seducir, inducir al mal; (*to deceive*) engañar

misleading [mɪs'lidɪŋ] *adj* engañoso

mismanagement [mɪs'mænɪdʒmənt] *s* mala administración, desgobierno

misnomer [mɪs'noməɾ] s nombre impropio, mal nombre

misplace [mɪs'ples] tr colocar fuera de su lugar; colocar mal; (to mislay) (coll) extraviar, perder

misprint ['mɪs,prɪnt] s errata de imprenta || [mɪs'prɪnt] tr imprimir con erratas

mispronounce [,mɪsprə'nauns] tr pronunciar mal

mispronunciation [,mɪsprə,nʌnsɪ'eʃən] o [,mɪsprə,nʌnʃɪ'eʃən] s pronunciación incorrecta

misquote [mɪs'kwot] tr citar equivocadamente

misrepresent [,mɪsreprɪ'zent] tr tergiversar

miss [mɪs] s falta, error m; fracaso, malogro; tiro errado; jovencita, muchacha || tr echar de menos; perder (el tren, la función, la oportunidad); errar (el blanco; la vocación); no entender, no comprender; omitir; no ver; no dar con, no encontrar; librarse de (p.ej., la muerte); escapársele a uno, p.ej., **I missed what you said** se me escapó lo que dijo Vd.; por poco, p.ej., **the car missed hitting me** el coche por poco me atropella || intr fallar; errar el blanco; malograrse || **Miss** s señorita

missal ['mɪsəl] s misal m

misshapen [mɪs'ʃepən] adj deforme, contrahecho

missile ['mɪsɪl] adj arrojadizo || s arma arrojadiza; proyectil m; proyectil dirigido

missing ['mɪsɪŋ] adj extraviado, perdido; desaparecido; ausente; **to be missing** hacer falta; haber desaparecido

missing link s hombre m mono

missing persons spl desaparecidos

mission ['mɪʃən] s misión; casa de misión

missionary ['mɪʃən,eri] adj misional || s (pl -ies) (one sent to work to propagate his faith) misionario, misionero; (on a political or diplomatic mission) misionario

missive ['mɪsɪv] adj misivo || s misiva

mis-spell [mɪs'spel] v (pret & pp -spelled o -spelt ['spelt]) tr & intr deletrear mal, escribir mal

misspelling [mɪs'spelɪŋ] s falta de ortografía

misspent [mɪs'spent] adj malgastado

misstatement [mɪs'stetmənt] s relación equivocada, relación falsa

misstep [mɪs'step] s paso falso; (slip in conduct) resbalón m

missy ['mɪsi] s (pl -ies) (coll) señorita

mist [mɪst] s neblina; (of tears) velo; (fine spray) vapor m

mistake [mɪs'tek] s error m, equivocación; **and no mistake** sin duda alguna; **by mistake** por descuido; **to make a mistake** equivocarse || v (pret -took ['tuk]; pp -taken ['tekən]) tr tomar (por otro; por lo que no es); entender mal; **to be mistaken for** equivocarse con

mistaken [mɪs'tekən] adj (person)

equivocado; (idea) erróneo; (act) desacertado

mistakenly [mɪs'tekənli] adv equivocadamente, por error

mistletoe ['mɪsəl,to] s (Viscum album) muérdago; (Phoradendron flavescens, used in Christmas decorations in the U.S.A.) cabellera

mistreat [mɪs'trit] tr maltratar

mistreatment [mɪs'tritmənt] s maltratamiento

mistress ['mɪstrɪs] s (of a household) ama, dueña; moza, querida, manceba; (Brit) maestra de escuela

mistrial [mɪs'traɪ·əl] s pleito viciado de nulidad

mistrust [mɪs'trʌst] s desconfianza || tr desconfiar de || intr desconfiar

mistrustful [mɪs'trʌstfəl] adj desconfiado

misty ['mɪsti] adj (comp -ier; super -iest) brumoso, neblinoso; indistinto

misunderstand [,mɪsʌndəɾ'stænd] v (pret & pp -stood ['stud]) tr no comprender, entender mal

misunderstanding [,mɪsʌndəɾ'stændɪŋ] s malentendido; (disagreement) desavenencia

misuse [mɪs'jus] s abuso, mal uso; (of funds) malversación || [mɪs'juz] tr abusar de, emplear mal; malversar (fondos)

misword [mɪs'wʌɾd] tr redactar mal

mite [maɪt] s (small contribution) óbolo; (small amount) pizca; (ent) ácaro

miter ['maɪtəɾ] s mitra; (carp) inglete m || tr cortar ingletes en; juntar con junta a inglete

miter box s caja de ingletes

mitigate ['mɪtɪ,get] tr mitigar, atenuar, paliar

mitten ['mɪtən] s confortante m, mitón m

mix [mɪks] tr mezclar; amasar (una torta); aderezar (ensalada); **to mix up** equivocar, confundir || intr mezclarse; asociarse

mixed [mɪkst] adj mixto, mezclado; (e.g., candy) variados, (coll) confundido

mixed company s reunión de personas de ambos sexos

mixed drink s bebida mezclada

mixed feeling s concepto vacilante

mixer ['mɪksəɾ] s (of concrete) mezcladora, hormigonera; **to be a good mixer** (coll) tener don de gentes

mixture ['mɪkstʃəɾ] s mezcla, mixtura

mix'-up s confusión; enredo, lío; (of people) equivocación

mizzen ['mɪzən] s mesana

mo. abbr **month**

M.O. abbr **money order**

moan [mon] s gemido || intr gemir

moat [mot] s foso

mob [mab] s chusma, populacho; (crowd bent on violence) muchedumbre airada || v (pret & pp mobbed; ger mobbing) tr asaltar, atropellar

mobile ['mobɪl] o ['mobɪl] adj móvil

mobility [mo'bɪlɪti] s movilidad

mobilization [,mobɪlɪ'zeʃən] s movilización

mobilize ['mobɪ,laɪz] tr movilizar || intr movilizar, movilizarse

mob rule s gobierno del populacho

mobster ['mabstər] s (slang) gamberro, pandillero

moccasin ['makəsɪn] s mocasín m

Mocha coffee ['mokə] s moca m, café m de moca

mock [mak] adj simulado, fingido || s burla, mofa || tr burlarse de, mofarse de; despreciar; engañar || intr mofarse; **to mock at** mofarse de

mocker·y ['makəri] s (pl -ies) burla, mofa, escarnio; (subject of derision) hazmerreír m; (poor imitation) mal remedo; (e.g., of justice) negación

mock'ing-bird' s burlón m, sinsonte m

mock orange s jeringuilla, celinda

mock privet s olivillo

mock turtle soup s sopa de cabeza de ternera

mock'-up' s maqueta

mode [mod] s modo, manera; (fashion) moda; (gram) modo

mod·el ['madəl] adj modelo, p.ej., **model city** ciudad modelo || s modelo || v (pret & pp -eled o -elled; ger -eling o -elling) tr (to fashion in clay, wax, etc.) modelar || intr modelarse; servir de modelo

model airplane s aeromodelo

mod'el-air'plane builder s aeromodelista mf

model-airplane building s aeromodelismo

model sailing s navegación de modelos a vela

moderate ['madərɪt] adj moderado; (tiempo) templado; (precio) módico || ['madə,ret] tr moderar; presidir (una asamblea) || intr moderarse

moderator ['madə,retər] s (over an assembly) presidente m; (mediator) árbitro; (for slowing down neutrons) moderador m

modern ['madərn] adj moderno

modernize ['madər,naɪz] tr modernizar

modest ['madɪst] adj modesto

modes·ty ['madɪsti] s (pl -ties) modestia

modicum ['madɪkəm] s pequeña cantidad

modifier ['madɪ,faɪ·ər] s (gram) modificador m

modi·fy ['madɪ,faɪ] v (pret & pp -fied) tr modificar

modish ['modɪʃ] adj de moda, elegante

modulate ['madʒə,let] tr & intr modular

modulation [,madʒə'leʃən] s modulación

mohair ['mo,her] s mohair m (pelo de cabra de Angora)

Mohammedan [mo'hæmɪdən] adj & s mahometano

Mohammedanism [mo'hæmɪdə,nɪzəm] s mahometismo

moist [mɔɪst] adj húmedo, mojado; (weather) lluvioso; (eyes) lagrimoso

moisten ['mɔɪsən] tr humedecer || intr humedecerse

moisture ['mɔɪstʃər] s humedad

molar ['molər] s diente m molar

molasses [mə'læsɪz] s melaza

molasses candy s melcocha

mold [mold] s molde m; cosa moldeada; (shape) forma; (fungus) moho; (humus) mantillo; (fig) carácter m, índole f || tr amoldar, moldear; (to make moldy) enmohecer || intr enmohecerse

molder ['moldər] s moldeador m || intr convertirse en polvo, consumirse

molding ['moldɪŋ] s moldeado; (cornice, shaped strip of wood, etc.) moldura

mold·y ['moldi] adj (comp -ier; super -iest) (overgrown with mold) mohoso; (stale) rancio, pasado

mole [mol] s (breakwater) rompeolas m; (inner harbor) dársena; (spot on skin) lunar m; (small mammal) topo

molecule ['malɪ,kjul] s molécula

mole'hill' s topinera

mole'skin' s piel f de topo, molesquina

molest [mə'lest] tr molestar; faltar al respeto a (una mujer)

moll [mal] s (slang) mujer f del hampa; (slang) ramera

molli·fy ['malɪ,faɪ] v (pret & pp -fied) tr apaciguar, aplacar

mollusk ['maləsk] s molusco

mollycoddle ['malɪ,kadəl] s mantecón m, marica m || tr consentir, mimar

molt [molt] s muda || intr hacer la muda

molten ['moltən] adj fundido, derretido; fundido, vaciado

molybdenum [mə'lɪbdɪnəm] o [,malɪb'dinəm] s molibdeno

moment ['momənt] s momento; **at any moment** de un momento a otro

momentary ['momən,teri] adj momentáneo

momentous [mo'mentəs] adj importante, grave

momen·tum [mo'mentəm] s (pl -tums o -ta [tə]) ímpetu m; (mech) cantidad de movimiento

monarch ['manərk] s monarca m

monarchic(al) [mə'narkɪk(əl)] adj monárquico

monarchist ['manərkɪst] adj & s monárquico, monarquista mf

monar·chy ['manərki] s (pl -chies) monarquía

monaster·y ['manəs,teri] s (pl -ies) monasterio

monastic [mə'næstɪk] adj monástico

monasticism [mə'næstɪ,sɪzəm] s monaquismo

Monday ['mʌndi] s lunes m

monetary ['manɪ,teri] adj monetario; pecuniario

money ['mʌni] s dinero; **to make money** ganar dinero; dar dinero (una empresa)

mon'ey·bag' s monedero, talega; **moneybags** (wealth) (coll) talegas; (wealthy person) (coll) ricacho

moneychanger ['mʌni,tʃendʒər] s cambista *mf*

moneyed ['mʌnid] *adj* adinerado

moneylender ['mʌni,lɛndər] s prestamista *mf*

mon'ey•mak'er s acaudalador *m;* (fig) manantial *m* de beneficios

money order s giro postal

Mongol ['maŋgəl] o ['maŋgal] *adj* & *s* mogol *mf*

Mongolian [maŋ'golɪ•ən] *adj* & *s* mogol *mf*

mon•goose ['maŋgus] s (*pl* -gooses) mangosta

mongrel ['mʌŋgrəl] o ['maŋgrəl] *adj* & *s* mestizo

monitor ['manɪtər] s monitor *m* || *tr* controlar (*la señal*); escuchar (*radiotransmisiones*); superentender

monk [mʌŋk] s monje *m*

monkey ['mʌŋki] s mono; **to make a monkey of** tomar el pelo a || *intr* — **to monkey around** haraganear; **to monkey with** ajar, manosear

mon'key•shine s (slang) monería, monada, payasada

monkey wrench s llave inglesa

monkhood ['mʌŋkhud] s monacato; los monjes

monkshood ['mʌŋks•hud] s cogulla de fraile

monocle ['manəkəl] s monóculo

monogamy [mə'nagəmi] s monogamia

monogram ['manə,græm] s monograma *m*

monograph ['manə,græf] o ['manə,graf] s monografía

monolithic [,manə'lɪθɪk] *adj* monolítico

monologue ['manə,ləg] o ['manə,lag] s monólogo

monomania [,manə'meni•ə] s monomanía

monomial [mə'nomi•əl] s monomio

monopolize [mə'napə,laɪz] *tr* monopolizar; acaparar (*p.ej., la conversación*)

monopo•ly [mə'napəli] s (*pl* -lies) monopolio

monorail ['manə,rel] s monorriel *m*

monosyllable ['manə,sɪləbəl] s monosílabo

monotheist ['manə,θi•ɪst] *adj* & *s* monoteísta *mf*

monotonous [mə'natənəs] *adj* monótono

monotony [mə'natəni] s monotonía

monotype ['manə,taɪp] s (*machine; method*) monotipia; (*machine*) monotipo

monotype operator s monotipista *mf*

monoxide [mə'naksaɪd] s monóxido *m*

monseigneur [,mansen'jœr] s monseñor *m*

monsignor [man'sinjər] s (*pl* **monsignors** o **monsignori** [,monsi'njori]) (eccl) monseñoɪ *m*

monsoon [man'sun] s monsón *m*

monster ['manstər] *adj* monstruoso || s monstruo

monstrance ['manstrəns] s custodia, ostensorio

monstrosi•ty [man'strasɪti] s (*pl* -ties) monstruosidad

monstrous ['manstrəs] *adj* monstruoso

month [mʌnθ] s mes *m*

month•ly ['mʌnθli] *adj* mensual || *adv* mensualmente || s (*pl* -lies) revista mensual **monthlies** (coll) reglas

monument ['manjəmənt] s monumento

moo [mu] s mugido || *intr* mugir

mood [mud] s humor *m*, genio; (gram) modo: **moods** accesos de mal humor

mood•y ['mudi] *adj* (*comp* -ier; *super* -iest) triste, hosco, melancólico; caprichoso, veleidoso

moon [mun] s luna

moon'beam s rayo lunar

moon'light' s claror *m* de luna, luz *f* de la luna

moon'light'ing s multiempleo, pluriempleo

moon'sail' s (naut) monterilla

moon'shine' s luz *f* de la luna; (*idle talk*) cháchara, música celestial; (coll) whisky destilado ilegalmente

moon shot s lanzamiento a la Luna

moor [mur] s brezal *m*, páramo || *tr* (naut) amarrar || *intr* (naut) echar las amarras || **Moor** s moro

Moorish ['murɪʃ] *adj* moro

moor'land' s brezal *m*

moose [mus] s (*pl* **moose**) alce *m* de América

moot [mut] *adj* discutible, dudoso

mop [map] s aljofifa, fregasuelos *m*, estropajo, (*of hair*) espesura || *v* (*pret* & *pp* **mopped;** *ger* **mopping**) *tr* aljofifar, enjugarse (*la frente con un pañuelo*); **to mop up** limpiar de enemigos

mope [mop] *intr* andar abatido, entregarse a la melancolía

mopish ['mopɪʃ] *adj* abatido, melancólico

moral ['marəl] o ['mɔrəl] *adj* moral || s (*of a fable*) moraleja, moral *f;* **morals** (*ethics; conduct*) moral *f*

moral certainty s evidencia moral

morale [mə'ræl] o [ma'ral] s moral *f* (*estado de ánimo, confianza en sí mismo*)

morali•ty [mə'rælɪti] s (*pl* -ties) moralidad

morals charge s acusación por delito sexual

morass [mə'ræs] s pantano

moratori•um [,mɔrə'tori•əm] o [,marə'tori•əm] s (*pl* -ums o -a [ə]) s moratoria

morbid ['mɔrbid] *adj* (*feelings, curiosity* malsano; (*gruesome*) horripilante (*pertaining to disease; pathologic*) morboso

mordacious [mɔr'deʃəs] *adj* mordaz

mordant ['mɔrdənt] *adj* mordaz || s mordiente *m*

more [mor] *adj* & *adv* más; **more and more** cada vez más; **more than** más que; (*followed by numeral*) más de; (*followed by verb*) más de lo que || s más *m*

more•o'ver *adv* además, por otra parte

Moresque [mo'resk] *adj* moro; (archit) árabe || *s* estilo árabe

morgue [mɔrg] *s* depósito de cadáveres

moribund ['mɔrɪ,bʌnd] o ['mɑrɪ,bʌnd] *adj* moribundo

Moris·co [mə'rɪsko] *adj* morisco, moro || *s* (*pl* -cos o -coes) moro; moro de España; (*offspring of mulatto and Spaniard, in Mexico*) morisco

morning ['mɔrnɪŋ] *adj* matinal || *s* mañana; (*time between midnight and dawn*) madrugada; **in the morning** de mañana, por la mañana

morning coat *s* chaqué *m*

morn'ing-glo'ry *s* (*pl* -ries) dondiego de día

morning sickness *s* vómitos del embarazo

morning star *s* lucero del alba

Moroccan [mə'rɑkən] *adj* & *s* marroquí *mf* o marroquín *m*

morocco [mə'rɑko] *s* (*leather*) marroquí *m* o marroquín *m* || **Morocco** *s* Marruecos *m*

moron ['mɔrɑn] *s* (*person of arrested intelligence*) morón *m*; (coll) imbécil *mf*

morose [mə'ros] *adj* adusto, hosco, malhumorado

morphine ['mɔrfin] *s* morfina

morphology [mɔr'fɑlədʒɪ] *s* morfología

Morris chair ['mɑrɪs] o ['mɔrɪs] *s* poltrona extensible

morrow ['mɑro] o ['mɔro] *s* (*future time*) mañana *m*; (*time following some event*) día *m* siguiente; **on the morrow** en el día de mañana; el día siguiente

morsel ['mɔrsəl] *s* bocadito; pedacito

mortal ['mɔrtəl] *adj* & *s* mortal *m*

mortality [mɔr'tælrtɪ] *s* mortalidad; (*death or destruction on a large scale*) mortandad

mortar ['mɔrtər] *s* (*bowl used for crushing; mixture of lime, etc.*) mortero; (arti) mortero

mor'tar-board' *s* esparavel *m*; gorro académico cuadrado

mortgage ['mɔrgɪdʒ] *s* hipoteca || *tr* hipotecar

mortgagee [,mɔrgɪ'dʒi] *s* acreedor hipotecario

mortgagor ['mɔrgɪdʒər] *s* deudor hipotecario

mortician [mɔr'tɪ/ən] *s* empresario de pompas fúnebres

morti·fy ['mɔrtɪ,faɪ] *v* (*pret & pp* -fied*) tr* humillar; mortificar (*el cuerpo, las pasiones*); **to be mortified** avergonzarse

mortise ['mɔrtɪs] *s* mortaja, muesca || *tr* amortajar, enmuescar

mortise lock *s* cerradura embutida

mortuar·y ['mɔrt/u,erɪ] *adj* mortuorio || *s* (*pl* -ies) depósito de cadáveres; funeraria

mosaic [mo'ze·ɪk] *m* mosaico

Moscow ['mɑskau] o ['mɑsko] *s* Moscú

Moses ['moziz] o ['mozɪs] *s* Moisés *m*

Mos·lem ['mɑzləm] o ['mɑsləm] *adj* muslime, musulmán || *s* (*pl* -lems o -lem) muslime *mf*, musulmán *m*

mosque [mɑsk] *s* mezquita

mosqui·to [məs'kito] *s* (*pl* -toes o -tos) mosquito

mosquito net *s* mosquitero

moss [mɔs] o [mɑs] *s* musgo

moss'back' *s* (coll) reaccionario; (*old-fashioned person*) (coll) fósil *m*

moss·y ['mɔsi] o ['mɑsi] *adj* (*comp* -ier; *super* -iest) musgoso

most [most] *adj* más; la mayor parte de, los más de || *adv* más; muy, sumamente; (coll) casi || *s* la mayor parte, el mayor número, los más; **to make the most of** sacar el mejor partido de

most of la mayor parte de, el mayor número de; **to make the most of** sacar el mejor partido de

mostly ['mostlɪ] *adv* por la mayor parte, mayormente; casi

moth [mɔθ] o [mɑθ] *s* mariposa nocturna; (*clothes moth*) polilla

moth ball *s* bola de alcanfor, bola de naftalina

moth'-ball' fleet *s* (nav) flota en conserva

moth'-eat'en *adj* apolillado; (fig) anticuado

mother ['mʌðər] *adj* (*love*) maternal; (*tongue*) materno; (*country*) madre; (*church*) metropolitano || *s* madre *f*; (*an elderly woman*) (coll) tía || *tr* servir de madre a

mother country *s* madre patria

Mother Goose *s* supuesta autora o narradora de una colección de cuentos infantiles (in Spain: *Cuentos de Calleja*)

motherhood ['mʌðər,hud] *s* maternidad

moth'er-in-law' *s* (*pl* mothers-in-law) suegra

moth'er·land' *s* patria

motherless ['mʌðərlɪs] *adj* huérfano de madre, sin madre

motherly ['mʌðərli] *adj* maternal

mother-of-pearl ['mʌðərəv'pʌrl] *adj* nacarado || *s* nácar *m*

Mother's Day *s* día *m* de la madre

mother superior *s* superiora

mother tongue *s* (*language naturally acquired by reason of nationality*) lengua materna; (*language from which another language is derived*) lengua madre, lengua matriz

mother wit *s* gracia natural, chispa

moth hole *s* apolilladura

moth·y ['mɔθɪ] o ['mɑθɪ] *adj* (*comp* -ier; *super* -iest) apolillado

motif [mo'tif] *s* motivo

motion ['mo/ən] *s* movimiento; (*signal, gesture*) seña, indicación; (*in a deliberating assembly*) moción || *intr* hacer señas con la mano o la cabeza

motionless ['mo/ənlɪs] *adj* inmoble

motion picture *s* película cinematográfica

mo'tion-pic'ture *adj* cinematográfico

motivate ['motɪ,vet] *tr* animar, incitar, mover

motive ['motɪv] *adj* (*promoting action*) motivo; (*producing motion*) motor || *s* motivo

motive power *s* fuerza motriz, potencia

motora o motriz; (rr) conjunto de locomotoras de un ferrocarril

motley ['matli] *adj* abigarrado; mezclado, variado

motor ['motər] *s* motor m; motor eléctrico; automóvil m || *intr* viajar en automóvil

mo'tor·boat' *s* gasolinera, canoa automóvil

mo'tor·bus' *s* autobús m

motorcade ['motər,ked] *s* caravana de automóviles

mo'tor·car' *s* automóvil m

mo'tor·cy'cle *s* motocicleta

motorist ['motərɪst] *s* motorista mf, automovilista mf

motorize ['motə,raɪz] *tr* motorizar

motor launch *s* lancha automóvil

motor·man ['motərmən] *s* (pl -men [mən]) conductor m de tranvía, conductor de locomotora eléctrica

motor sailer ['selər] *s* motovelero

motor scooter *s* motoneta

motor ship *s* motonave f

motor truck *s* autocamión m

motor vehicle *s* vehículo motor, autovehículo

mottle ['matəl] *tr* abigarrar, jaspear, motear

mot·to ['mato] *s* (pl -toes o -tos) lema m, divisa

mould [mold] *s, tr, & intr* var de mold

moulder ['moldər] *s & intr* var de molder

moulding ['moldɪŋ] *s* var de molding

mouldy ['moldi] *adj* var de moldy

mound [maund] *s* montón m de tierra; montecillo

mount [maunt] *s* (hill, mountain) monte m; (horse for riding) montura; (setting for a jewel) montadura; soporte m; cartón m, tela (en que está pegada una fotografía); (mach) montaje m || *tr* subir (una escalera, una cuesta); subir a (una plataforma); escalar (una muralla); montar (un servicio; una piedra preciosa); poner a caballo; pegar (vistas, pruebas); (mil) montar (la guardia) || *intr* montar, montarse; aumentar, subir (los precios)

mountain ['mauntən] *s* montaña; to make a mountain out of a molehill hacer de una pulga un camello

mountain climbing *s* alpinismo, montañismo

mountaineer [,mauntə'nɪr] *s* montañés m

mountainous ['mauntənəs] *adj* montañoso

mountain railroad *s* ferrocarril m de cremallera

mountain range *s* cordillera, sierra

mountain sickness *s* mal m de las montañas

mountebank ['maunti,bæŋk] *s* saltabanco

mounting ['mauntɪŋ] *s* (of a precious stone, of an astronomical instrument) montura; papel m de soporte; papel o tela (en que está pegada una fotografía); (mach) montaje m

mourn [morn] *tr* llorar (p.ej., la muerte

de una persona); lamentar (una desgracia) || *intr* lamentarse; vestir de luto

mourner ['mornər] *s* doliente mf; (person who makes a public profession of penitence) penitente mf; (person hired to attend a funeral) plañidera; **mourners** duelo

mourners' bench *s* banco de los penitentes

mournful ['mornfəl] *adj* (sorrowful) doloroso; (gloomy) lúgubre

mourning ['mornɪŋ] *s* luto; to be in mourning estar de luto

mourning band *s* crespón m fúnebre, brazal m de luto

mouse [maus] *s* (pl mice [maɪs]) ratón m

mouse'hole' *s* ratonera

mouser ['mauzər] *s* desmurador m

mouse'trap' *s* ratonera

moustache [məs'tæʃ] o [məs'taʃ] *s* bigote m, mostacho

mouth [mauθ] *s* (pl mouths [mauðz]) boca; (of a river) desembocadura, embocadura; by mouth por vía bucal; to be born with a silver spoon in one's mouth nacer de pie; to make one's mouth water hacérsele a uno la boca agua; to not open one's mouth no decir esta boca es mía

mouthful ['mauθ,ful] *s* bocado

mouth organ *s* armónica de boca

mouth'piece' *s* (of wind instrument) boquilla; (of bridle) embocadura; (spokesman) portavoz m

mouth'wash' *s* enjuague m, enjuagadientes m

movable ['muvəbəl] *adj* movible, móvil

move [muv] *s* movimiento; (démarche) acción, gestión, paso; (from one house to another) mudanza; on the move en marcha, en movimiento; to get a move on (slang) menearse, darse prisa; to make a move dar un paso; hacer una jugada || *tr* mover; evacuar (el vientre); (to stir, excite the feelings of) conmover, enternecer; to move up adelantar (una fecha) || *intr* moverse; desplazarse (un viajante; un planeta); mudarse, mudar de casa; (e.g., to another store, to another city) trasladarse; hacer una jugada; hacer una moción; venderse, tener salida (una mercancía); evacuarse, moverse (el vientre); to move away apartarse; marcharse; mudarse de casa; to move in instalarse; alternar con, frecuentar (la buena sociedad); to move off alejarse

movement ['muvmənt] *s* movimiento; aparato de relojería; (of the bowels) evacuación; (e.g., of a symphony) tiempo

movie ['muvi] *s* (coll) película, cinta

movie·goer ['muvi,go·ər] *s* (coll) aficionado al cine

movie house *s* (coll) cineteatro

mov'ie·land' *s* (coll) cinelandia

moving ['muvɪŋ] *adj* conmovedor, impresionante || *s* movimiento; (from one house to another) mudanza

moving picture s película cinematográfica

moving spirit s alma (de una empresa)

moving stairway s escalera mecánica, móvil o rodante

mow [mo] v (pret **mowed**; pp **mowed** o **mown**) tr segar; **to mow down** matar (soldados) con fuego graneado ‖ intr segar

mower ['mo·ər] s segador m; segadora mecánica

mowing machine s segadora mecánica

Mozarab [mo'zærəb] s mozárabe mf

Mozarabic [mo'zærəbɪk] adj mozárabe

M.P. abbr **Member of Parliament, Military Police**

m.p.h. abbr **miles per hour**

Mr. ['mɪstər] s (pl **Messrs.** ['mesərz]) señor m (tratamiento)

Mrs. ['mɪsɪz] s señora (tratamiento)

MS. o **ms.** abbr **manuscript**

Mt. abbr **Mount**

much [mʌt/] adj & pron mucho; **too much** demasiado ‖ adv mucho; **however much** por mucho que; **how much** cuánto; **too much** demasiado; **very much** muchísimo

mucilage ['mjusɪlɪdʒ] s goma para pegar; (gummy secretion in plants) mucílago

muck [mʌk] s estiércol húmedo; suciedad, porquería; (min) zafra

muck'rake' intr (coll) exponer ruindades

mucous ['mjukəs] adj mucoso

mucus ['mjukəs] s moco

mud [mʌd] s barro, fango, lodo; **to sling mud at** llenar de fango

muddle ['mʌdəl] s confusión, embrollo ‖ tr confundir, embrollar; atontar, aturdir ‖ intr obrar torpemente; **to muddle through** salir del paso a pesar suyo

mud'dle-head' s farraguista mf, cajón m de sastre

mud-dy ['mʌdɪ] adj (comp **-dier**; super **-diest**) barroso, fangoso, lodoso; (obscure) turbio ‖ v (pret & pp **-died**) tr embarrar, enturbiar

mud'guard' s guardabarros m

mud'hole' s atolladero, ciénaga

mudslinger ['mʌd,slɪŋər] s (fig) lanzador m de lodo

muezzin [mju'ezɪn] s almuecín m, almuédano

muff [mʌf] s manguito ‖ tr & intr chapucear

muffin ['mʌfɪn] s mollete m

muffle ['mʌfəl] tr arropar; (about the face) embozar, amortiguar (un ruido); enfundar (un tambor)

muffler ['mʌflər] s bufanda, tapaboca; (aut) silenciador m, silencioso

mufti ['mʌftɪ] s traje m de paisano

mug [mʌg] s pichel m; (slang) jeta, hocico ‖ v (pret & pp **mugged**; ger **mugging**) tr (slang) fotografiar; (slang) atacar ‖ intr (slang) hacer muecas

mug·gy ['mʌgɪ] adj (comp **-gier**; super **-giest**) bochornoso, sofocante

mulat·to [mju'læto] o [mə'læto] s (pl **-toes**) mulato

mulber·ry ['mʌl,berɪ] s (pl **-ries**) (tree) moral m; (fruit) mora

mulct [mʌlkt] tr defraudar

mule [mjul] s mulo, macho; (slipper) babucha

mule chair s artolas, jamugas

muleteer [,mjulə'tɪr] s mulatero

mulish ['mjulɪʃ] adj terco, obstinado

mull [mʌl] tr calentar (vino) con especias ‖ intr — **to mull over** reflexionar sobre

mullion ['mʌljən] s parteluz m

multigraph ['mʌltɪ,græf] o ['mʌltɪ,grɑf] s (trademark) multígrafo ‖ tr multigrafiar

multilateral [,mʌltɪ'lætərəl] adj (having many sides) multilátero; (participated in by more than two nations) multilateral

multiple ['mʌltɪpəl] adj múltiple, múltiplo ‖ s (math) múltiplo

multiplici·ty [,mʌltɪ'plɪsɪtɪ] s (pl **-ties**) multiplicidad

multi·ply ['mʌltɪ,plaɪ] v (pret & pp **-plied**) tr multiplicar ‖ intr multiplicar, multiplicarse

multitude ['mʌltɪ,tjud] o ['mʌltɪ,tud] s multitud

mum [mʌm] adj callado; **mum's the word!** ¡punto en boca!; **to keep mum about** callar ‖ interj ¡chitón!

mumble ['mʌmbəl] tr & intr mascullar, mascujar

mummer·y ['mʌmərɪ] s (pl **-ies**) mojiganga

mum·my ['mʌmɪ] s (pl **-mies**) momia

mumps [mʌmps] s papera

munch [mʌnt/] tr ronzar

mundane ['mʌnden] adj mundano

municipal [mju'nɪsɪpəl] adj municipal

municipali·ty [mju,nɪsɪ'pælɪtɪ] s (pl **-ties**) municipio

munificent [mju'nɪfɪsənt] adj munífico

munition [mju'nɪʃən] s munición ‖ tr municionar

munition dump s depósito de municiones

mural ['mjurəl] adj mural ‖ s pintura mural; decoración mural

murder ['mʌrdər] s asesinato, homicidio ‖ tr asesinar; (to spoil, mar) (coll) estropear

murderer ['mʌrdərər] s asesino

murderess ['mʌrdərɪs] s asesina

murderous ['mʌrdərəs] adj asesino; cruel, sanguinario

murk·y ['mʌrkɪ] adj (comp **-ier**; super **-iest**) (hazy) calinoso; (gloomy) lóbrego

murmur ['mʌrmər] s murmullo ‖ tr & intr murmurar

mus. abbr **museum, music**

muscle ['mʌsəl] s músculo; (fig) fuerza muscular

muscular ['mʌskjələr] adj musculoso

muse [mjuz] s musa; **the Muses** las Musas ‖ intr meditar, reflexionar; **to muse on** contemplar

museum [mju'zɪəm] s museo

mush [mʌʃ] s gachas; (coll) sentimentalismo exagerado, sensiblería

mush'room' s hongo, seta ‖ intr aparecer de la noche a la mañana; **to**

mushroom into convertirse rápidamente en

mushroom cloud s nube-hongo f

mush·y ['mʌʃi] adj (comp -ier; super -iest) mollar, pulposo; (coll) sensiblero, sobón; (with women) (coll) baboso; **to be mushy** (coll) hacerse unas gachas

music ['mjuzɪk] s música; **to face the music** (coll) afrontar las consecuencias; **to set to music** poner en música

musical ['mjuzɪkəl] adj musical, músico

musical comedy s comedia musical

musicale [,mjuzi'kæl] s velada musical, concierto casero

music box s caja de música

music cabinet s musiquero

music hall s salón m de conciertos; (Brit) teatro de variedades

musician [mju'zɪʃən] s músico

musicianship [mju'zɪʃən,ʃɪp] s musicalidad

musicologist [,mjuzi'kɑlədʒɪst] s musicólogo

musicology [,mjuzi'kɑlədʒi] s musicología

music rack o **music stand** s atril m

musk [mʌsk] s almizcle m; olor m de almizcle

musk deer s almizclero

musket ['mʌskɪt] s mosquete m

musketeer [,mʌskɪ'tɪr] s mosquetero

musk·mel·on s melón m

musk·rat s almizclera

muslin ['mʌzlɪn] s muselina

muss [mʌs] tr (the hair) (coll) descabellar, desarreglar; (clothing) (coll) chafar, arrugar

Mussulman ['mʌsəlmən] adj & s musulmán m

muss·y ['mʌsi] adj (comp -ier; super -iest) desaliñado, desgreñado

must [mʌst] s mosto; (mold) moho; cosa que debe hacerse ‖ v aux **I must study my lesson** debo estudiar mi lección; **he must work tomorrow** tiene que trabajar mañana; **she must be ill** estará enferma

mustache [məs'tæʃ], [məs'tɑʃ] o ['mʌstæʃ] s bigote m, mostacho

mustard ['mʌstərd] s mostaza

mustard plaster s sinapismo, cataplasma f

muster ['mʌstər] s asamblea; matrícula de revista; **to pass muster** pasar revista; ser aceptable ‖ tr llamar a asamblea; reunir para pasar revista; reunir, acumular; **to muster in** alistar; **to muster out** dar de baja a; **to muster up courage** cobrar ánimo

muster roll s lista de revista

mus·ty ['mʌsti] adj (comp -tier; super -tiest) (moldy) mohoso; (stale) trasnochado; anticuado, pasado de moda

mutation [mju'teʃən] s mutación

mute [mjut] adj & s mudo ‖ tr poner sordina a

mutilate ['mjutɪ,let] tr mutilar

mutineer [,mjutɪ'nɪr] s amotinado

mutinous ['mjutɪnəs] adj amotinado

muti·ny ['mjutɪni] s (pl -nies) motín m ‖ v (pret & pp -nied) intr amotinarse

mutt [mʌt] s (slang) perro cruzado; (slang) bobo, tonto

mutter ['mʌtər] tr & intr murmurar

mutton ['mʌtən] s carnero, carne f de carnero

mutton chop s chuleta de carnero

mutual ['mut∫u·əl] adj mutual, mutuo

mutual aid s apoyo mutuo

mutual benefit association s mutualidad

muzzle ['mʌzəl] s (projecting part of head of animal) hocico; (device to keep animal from biting) bozal m; (of firearm) boca ‖ tr abozalar; (to keep from speaking) amordazar

my [maɪ] adj poss mi

myriad ['mɪrɪ·əd] s miríada

myrrh [mʌr] s mirra

myrtle ['mʌrtəl] s arrayán m, mirto

myself [maɪ'self] pron pers yo mismo; mí, mí mismo; me, p.ej., **I enjoyed myself** me divertí; **with myself** conmigo

mysterious [mɪs'tɪrɪ·əs] adj misterioso

myster·y ['mɪstəri] s (pl -ies) misterio

mystic ['mɪstɪk] adj & s místico

mystical ['mɪstɪkəl] adj místico

mysticism ['mɪstɪ,sɪzəm] s misticismo

mystification [,mɪstɪfɪ'keʃən] s confusión, mistificación

mysti·fy ['mɪstɪ,faɪ] v (pret & pp -fied) tr rodear de misterio; (to hoax) confundir, mistificar

myth [mɪθ] s mito

mythical ['mɪθɪkəl] adj mítico

mythological [,mɪθə'lɑdʒɪkəl] adj mitológico

mytholo·gy [mɪ'θɑlədʒi] s (pl -gies) mitología

N

N, n [ɛn] decimocuarta letra del alfabeto inglés

n. abbr **neuter, nominative, noon, north, noun, number**

N. abbr **Nationalist, Navy, Noon, North, November**

N.A. abbr **National Academy, National Army, North America**

nab [næb] v (pret & pp **nabbed**; ger **nabbing**) tr (slang) agarrar, coger; (slang) poner preso, prender

nag [næg] s caballejo, jaco; pequeño caballo de silla ‖ v (pret & pp **nagged**; ger **nagging**) tr importunar regañando ‖ intr regañar

naiad ['ne·æd] o ['naɪ·æd] s náyade f; (fig) nadadora

nail [nel] s (of finger) uña; (to fasten

wood, etc.) clavo; **to hit the nail on the head** dar en el clavo || *tr* clavar
nail brush *s* cepillo de uñas
nail file *s* lima para las uñas
nail polish *s* esmalte *m* para las uñas, laca de uñas
nailset ['nel,set] *s* contrapunzón *m*
naïve [nɑ'iv] *adj* cándido, ingenuo
naked ['nekɪd] *adj* desnudo; **to go naked** ir desnudo, andar a la cordobana; **to strip naked** desnudar; desnudarse; **with the naked eye** a simple vista
name [nem] *s* nombre *m*; (*first name*) nombre de pila; (*last name*) apellido; fama, reputación, renombre *m*; linaje. *m*, raza; **to call someone names** maltratar a uno de palabra; **to go by the name of** ser conocido por el nombre de; **to make a name for oneself** darse a conocer, hacerse un nombre; **what is your name?** ¿cómo se llama Vd.? || *tr* nombrar; fijar (*un precio*)
name day *s* santo
nameless ['nemlɪs] *adj* sin nombre, anónimo
namely ['nemli] *adv* a saber, es decir
namesake ['nem,sek] *s* homónimo, tocayo
nanny goat ['næni] *s* (coll) cabra
nap [næp] *s* lanilla, flojel *m*; sueñecillo; **to take a nap** descabezar un sueñecillo || *v* (*pret & pp* **napped;** *ger* **napping**) *intr* echar un sueñecillo; estar desprevenido; **to catch napping** coger desprevenido
napalm ['nepɑm] *s* (mil) gelatina incendiaria
nape [nep] *s* cogote *m*, nuca
naphtha ['næfθə] *s* nafta
napkin ['næpkɪn] *s* servilleta; (*of a baby*) (Brit) pañal *m*
napkin ring *s* servilletero
Naples ['nepəlz] *s* Nápoles
Napoleonic [nə,poli'ɑnɪk] *adj* napoleónico
narcissus [nɑr'sɪsəs] *s* (bot) narciso || **Narcissus** *s* Narciso
narcotic [nɑr'kɑtɪk] *adj & s* narcótico
narrate [næ'ret] *tr* narrar
narration [næ'reʃən] *s* narración
narrative ['nærətɪv] *adj* narrativo || *s* (*story, tale; art of telling stories*) narrativa
narrator [næ'retər] *s* narrador *m*
narrow ['næro] *adj* angosto, estrecho; intolerante; minucioso; (*sense of a word*) estricto || **narrows** *spl* angostura, paso estrecho || *tr* enangostar, estrechar; reducir, limitar || *intr* enangostarse, estrecharse; reducirse, limitarse
narrow escape *s* trance *m* difícil; **to have a narrow escape** escapar por un pelo, salvarse en una tabla
narrow gauge *s* trocha angosta, vía estrecha
narrow-minded ['næro'maɪndɪd] *adj* intolerante, de miras estrechas, poco liberal
nasal ['nezəl] *adj & s* nasal *f*
nasalize ['nezə,laɪz] *tr* nasalizar || *intr* ganguear

nasturtium [nə'stʌrʃəm] *s* capuchina, espuela de galán
nas·ty ['næsti] o ['nɑsti] *adj* (*comp* **-tier;** *super* **-tiest**) asqueroso, sucio; desagradable; desvergonzado; amenazador; horrible
natatorium [,netə'tori·əm] *s* piscina de natación
nation ['neʃən] *s* nación
national ['næʃənəl] *adj & s* nacional *mf*
national anthem *s* himno nacional
national hero *s* benemérito de la patria
national holiday *s* fiesta nacional
nationalism ['næʃənə,lɪzəm] *s* nacionalismo
nationalist ['næʃənəlɪst] *adj & s* nacionalista *mf*
nationali·ty [,næʃən'ælɪti] *s* (*pl* **-ties**) nacionalidad, naturalidad
nationalize ['næʃənə,laɪz] *tr* nacionalizar
na'tion-wide' *adj* de toda la nación
native ['netɪv] *adj* nativo, natural; indígena; (*language*) materno; **to go native** vivir como los indígenas || *s* natural *mf*; indígena *mf*
native land *s* patria
nativi·ty [nə'tɪvɪti] *s* (*pl* **-ties**) nacimiento || **Nativity** *s* (*day; festival; painting*) natividad
Nato ['neto] *s* (acronym) la O.T.A.N.
nat·ty ['næti] *adj* (*comp* **-tier;** *super* **-tiest**) elegante, garboso
natural ['nætʃərəl] *adj* natural; (mus) natural || *s* imbécil *mf*; (mus) tono natural, nota natural; (*sign*) (mus) becuadro; (mus) tecla blanca; (coll) cosa de éxito certero
naturalism ['nætʃərə,lɪzəm] *s* naturalismo
naturalist ['nætʃərəlɪst] *s* naturalista *mf*
naturalization [,nætʃərəlɪ'zeʃən] *s* naturalización
naturalization papers *spl* carta de naturaleza
naturalize ['nætʃərə,laɪz] *tr* naturalizar
naturally ['nætʃərəli] *adv* naturalmente; claro, desde luego, por supuesto
nature ['netʃər] *s* naturaleza; **from nature** del natural
naught [nɔt] *s* nada; cero; **to bring to naught** anular, invalidar, destruir; **to come to naught** reducirse a nada, frustrarse
naugh·ty ['nɔti] *adj* (*comp* **-tier;** *super* **-tiest**) desobediente, pícaro; desvergonzado; (*story, tale*) verde
nausea ['nɔʃɪ·ə] o ['nɔsɪ·ə] *s* náusea
nauseate ['nɔʃɪ,et] o ['nɔsɪ,et] *tr* dar náuseas a || *intr* nausear, marearse
nauseating ['nɔʃɪ,etɪŋ] o ['nɔsɪ,etɪŋ] *adj* nauseabundo, asqueroso
nauseous ['nɔʃɪ·əs] o ['nɔsɪ·əs] *adj* nauseabundo
nautical ['nɔtɪkəl] *adj* náutico, marino, naval
nav. *abbr* naval, navigation
naval ['nevəl] *adj* naval, naval militar

Naval Academy s (U.S.A.) Escuela Naval Militar
naval officer s oficial m de marina
naval station s apostadero
nave [nev] s (of a church) nave f central, nave principal; (of a wheel) cubo
navel ['nevəl] s ombligo; (center point, middle) (fig) ombligo
navel orange s navel f, naranja de ombligo
navigability [ˌnævɪgə'bɪlɪti] s (of a river) navegabilidad; (of a ship) buen gobierno
navigable ['nævɪgəbəl] adj (river, canal, etc.) navegable; (ship) marinero, de buen gobierno
navigate ['nævɪˌget] tr & intr navegar
navigation [ˌnævɪ'geʃən] s navegación
navigator ['nævɪˌgetər] s navegador m, navegante m; (he who is in charge of course of ship or plane) oficial m de derrota; (Brit) peón m
nav·vy ['nævi] s (pl -vies) (Brit) bracero, peón m
na·vy ['nevi] adj azul oscuro || s (pl -vies) marina de guerra; (personnel) marina; azul oscuro
navy bean s frijol blanco común
navy blue s azul marino, azul oscuro
navy yard s arsenal m de puerto
Nazarene [ˌnæzə'rin] adj & s nazareno
Nazi ['nɑtsi] o ['nætsi] adj & s nazi mf, nacista mf
n.b. abbr **nota bene** (Lat) note well
N-bomb ['ɛnˌbɑm] s bomba de neutrones
Neapolitan [ˌni·ə'pɑlɪtən] adj & s napolitano
neap tide [nip] s marea muerta
near [nɪr] adj cercano, próximo; íntimo; imitado || adv cerca; íntimamente || prep cerca de; hacia, por || tr acercarse a || intr acercarse
nearby ['nɪrˌbaɪ] adj cercano, próximo || adv cerca
Near East s Cercano Oriente, Próximo Oriente
nearly ['nɪrli] adv casi; de cerca; íntimamente; por poco, p.ej., **he nearly fell** por poco se cae
near-sighted ['nɪr'saɪtɪd] adj miope
near-sightedness s miopía
neat [nit] adj aseado, pulcro; pulido; diestro, primoroso; puro, sin mezcla || ssg res vacuna || spl ganado vacuno
neat's'-foot' oil s aceite m de pie de buey
Nebuchadnezzar [ˌnɛbjəkəd'nɛzər] s Nabucodonosor m
nebu·la ['nɛbjələ] s (pl -lae [ˌli] o -las) nebulosa
nebular ['nɛbjələr] adj nebular
nebulous ['nɛbjələs] adj nebuloso
necessary ['nɛsɪˌsɛri] adj necesario
necessitate [nɪ'sɛsɪˌtet] tr necesitar, exigir
necessitous [nɪ'sɛsɪtəs] adj necesitado
necessi·ty [nɪ'sɛsɪti] s (pl -ties) necesidad
neck [nɛk] s cuello; (of a bottle) go-

llete m; (of violin or guitar) mástil m; istmo, península; estrecho; **neck and neck** parejos; **to break one's neck** (coll) matarse trabajando; **to stick one's neck out** (coll) descubrir el cuerpo || intr (slang) acariciarse (dos enamorados)
neck'band' s tirilla de camisa
necklace ['nɛklɪs] s gargantilla, collar m
necktie ['nɛkˌtaɪ] s corbata
necktie pin s alfiler m de corbata
necrology [nɛ'krɑlədʒi] s necrología
necromancy ['nɛkrəˌmænsi] s necromancia, nigromancia
nectarine [ˌnɛktə'rin] s griñón m
née o **nee** [ne] adj nacida o de soltera, p.ej., **Mary Wilson, née Miller** María Wilson, nacida Miller o María Wilson, de soltera Miller
need [nid] s necesidad; pobreza; **in need** necesitado || tr necesitar || intr estar necesitado; ser necesario || v aux — **if need be** si fuere necesario; **to need** + inf deber, tener que + inf
needful ['nidfəl] adj necesario || **the needful** lo necesario; (slang) el dinero
needle ['nidəl] s aguja; **to look for a needle in a haystack** buscar una aguja en un pajar || tr coser con aguja; (coll) aguijonear, incitar; (coll) añadir alcohol a (la cerveza o el vino)
needle bath s ducha en alfileres
needle'case' s alfiletero
needle point s bordado al pasado; encaje m de mano
needless ['nidlɪs] adj innecesario, inútil
needle'work' s costura, labor f
needs [nidz] adv necesariamente, forzosamente
need·y ['nidi] adj (comp -ier; super -iest) necesitado, indigente || **the needy** los necesitados
ne'er-do-well ['nɛrduˌwɛl] adj & s holgazán, perdido
negation [nɪ'geʃən] s negación
negative ['nɛgətɪv] adj negativo || s negativa; electricidad negativa, borne negativo; (gram) negación; (math) término negativo; (phot) prueba negativa || tr desaprobar; anular
neglect [nɪ'glɛkt] s negligencia, descuido || tr descuidar; **to neglect to** dejar de, olvidarse de
neglectful [nɪ'glɛktfəl] adj negligente, descuidado
négligée o **negligee** [ˌnɛgli'ʒe] s bata de mujer, traje m de casa
negligence ['nɛglɪdʒəns] s negligencia, descuido
negligent ['nɛglɪdʒənt] adj negligente, descuidado
negligible ['nɛglɪdʒɪbəl] adj insignificante, imperceptible
negotiable [nɪ'goʃɪəbəl] adj negociable; transitable
negotiate [nɪ'goʃɪˌet] tr negociar; (coll) salvar, vencer || intr negociar
negotiation [nɪˌgoʃɪ'eʃən] s negociación; trámite m

Ne·gro ['nigro] *adj* negro ‖ *s* (*pl* -groes) negro

neigh [ne] *s* relincho ‖ *intr* relinchar

neighbor ['nebər] *adj* vecino ‖ *s* vecino; (*fellow man*) prójimo ‖ *tr* ser vecino de; ser amigo de ‖ *intr* estar cercano; tener relaciones amistosas

neighborhood ['nebər,hud] *s* vecindad, vecindario, cercanías; **in the neighborhood of** en las inmediaciones de; (coll) cerca de, aproximadamente

neighboring ['nebərɪŋ] *adj* vecino, colindante

neighborly ['nebərli] *adj* buen vecino, amable, sociable

neither ['niðər] o ['naɪðər] *adj indef* ninguno . . . (de los dos); **neither one** ninguno de los dos ‖ *pron indef* ninguno (de los dos); ni uno ni otro, ni lo uno ni lo otro ‖ *conj* ni; tampoco, ni . . . tampoco, p.ej., **neither do I** yo tampoco, ni yo tampoco; **neither . . . nor** ni . . . ni

neme·sis ['nemɪsɪs] *s* (*pl* -ses [,siz]) (*someone or something that punishes*) némesis *f* ‖ **Nemesis** *s* Némesis *f*

neologism [nɪ'alə,dʒɪzəm] *s* neologismo

neomycin [,ni·ə'maɪsɪn] *s* neomicina

neon ['ni·an] *s* neo, neón *m*

neophyte ['ni·ə,faɪt] *s* neófito

Nepal [nɪ'pɔl] *s* el Nepal

Nepa·lese [,nepə'liz] *adj* nepalés ‖ *s* (*pl* -lese) nepalés *m*

nepenthe [nɪ'penθɪ] *s* nepente *m*

nephew ['nefju] o ['nevju] *s* sobrino

Nepos ['nipas] o ['nepas] *s* Nepote *m*

Neptune ['neptʃun] o ['neptjun] *s* Neptuno

neptunium [nep'tʃunɪ·əm] o [nep'tjunɪ·əm] *s* neptunio

Nereid ['nɪrɪ·ɪd] *s* nereida

Nero ['nɪro] *s* Nerón *m*

nerve [nʌrv] *adj* (*center; system; tonic; disease; prostration; breakdown*) nervioso ‖ *s* nervio; ánimo, valor *m*; audacia; (coll) descaro; **nerves** excitabilidad nerviosa; **to get on one's nerves** irritar los nervios a uno; **to strain every nerve** esforzarse al máximo

nerve-racking ['nʌrv,rækɪŋ] *adj* irritante, exasperante

nervous ['nʌrvəs] *adj* nervioso

nervous breakdown *s* colapso nervioso

nervousness ['nʌrvəsnɪs] *s* nerviosidad

nervous shudder *s* muerte chiquita

nerv·y ['nʌrvi] *adj* (*comp* -ier; *super* -iest) (*strong, vigorous*) nervioso; atrevido, audaz; (coll) descarado

nest [nest] *s* nido; (*where hen lays eggs*) nidal *m*; (*birds in a nest*) nidada; (*set of things fitting within each other*) juego; (*of, e.g., thieves*) nido; **to feather one's nest** hacer todo para enriquecerse ‖ *tr* colocar en un nido ‖ *intr* anidar

nest egg *s* (*eggs left in a nest to induce hen to lay more*) nidal *m*; ahorros, hucha

nestle ['nesəl] *tr* poner en un nido;

arrimar afectuosamente ‖ *intr* anidar; arrimarse cómodamente; **to nestle up to** arrimarse a

net [net] *adj* neto, líquido ‖ *s* red *f*; precio neto, peso neto, ganancia líquida ‖ *v* (*pret & pp* netted; *super* netting) *tr* enredar, tejer; coger con red; producir (*cierta ganancia líquida*)

nether ['neðər] *adj* inferior, más bajo

Netherlander ['neðər,lændər] o ['neðərləndər] *s* neerlandés *m*

Netherlandish ['neðər,lændɪʃ] o ['neðərləndɪʃ] *adj* neerlandés ‖ *s* neerlandés *m*

Netherlands, The ['neðərləndz] los Países Bajos (*Holanda*)

netting ['netɪŋ] *s* red *f*

nettle ['netəl] *s* ortiga ‖ *tr* irritar, provocar

net'work' *s* red *f*; (rad & telv) cadena

neuralgia [nju'rældʒə] o [nu'rældʒə] *s* neuralgia

neurology [nju'ralədʒi] o [nu'ralədʒi] *s* neurología

neuro·sis [nju'rosɪs] o [nu'rosɪs] *s* (*pl* -ses [sɪz]) neurosis *f*

neurotic [nju'ratɪk] o [nu'ratɪk] *adj & s* neurótico

neut. *abbr* neuter

neuter ['njutər] o ['nutər] *adj* neutro ‖ *s* género neutro

neutral ['njutrəl] o ['nutrəl] *adj* (*on neither side in a quarrel or war*) neutral; (*having little or no color*) neutro; (bot, chem, elec, phonet, zool) neutro ‖ *s* neutral *mf*; (aut) punto neutral, punto muerto

neutralism ['njutrə,lɪzəm] o ['nutrə,lɪzəm] *s* neutralismo

neutralist ['njutrəlɪst] o ['nutrəlɪst] *adj & s* neutralista *mf*

neutrality [nju'trælɪti] o [nu'trælɪti] *s* neutralidad

neutralize ['njutrə,laɪz] o ['nutrə,laɪz] *tr* neutralizar

neutron ['njutran] o ['nutran] *s* neutrón *m*

neutron bomb *s* bomba de neutrones, bomba neutrónica

never ['nevər] *adv* nunca; en mi vida; de ningún modo; **never fear** no hay cuidado; **never mind** no importa

nev'er-more' *adv* nunca más

nevertheless [,nevərðə'les] *adv* no obstante, sin embargo

new [nju] o [nu] *adj* nuevo; **what's new?** ¿qué hay de nuevo?

new arrival *s* recién llegado; recién nacido

new'born' *adj* recién nacido; renacido

New Castile *s* Castilla la Nueva

New'cas'tle *s* — **to carry coals to Newcastle** echar agua al mar, llevar hierro a Vizcaya, llevar leña al monte

newcomer ['nju,kʌmər] o ['nu,kʌmər] *s* recién llegado, recién venido

New England *s* la Nueva Inglaterra

newfangled ['nju,fæŋgəld] o ['nu,fæŋgəld] *adj* de última moda, recién inventado

Newfoundland ['njufənd,lænd] o

['nufənd,lænd] s (island and province) Terranova ‖ [nju'faundlənd] o [nu'faundlənd] s (dog) Terranova m

newly ['njuli] o ['nuli] adv nuevamente; **newly** + pp recién + pp

new'ly·wed' s recién casado

New Mexican adj & s neomejicano, nuevomejicano

New Mexico s Nuevo Méjico

new moon s luna nueva, novilunio

news [njuz] o [nuz] s noticias; periódico; **a news item** una noticia; **a piece of news** una noticia

news agency s agencia de noticias

news beat s exclusiva, anticipación de una noticia por un periódico

news'boy' s vendedor m de periódicos

news'cast' s noticiario radiofónico ‖ tr radiodifundir (noticias) ‖ intr radiodifundir noticias

news'cast'er s cronista mf de radio

news conference s var de **press conference**

news coverage s reportaje m

news·man ['njuzmən] o ['nuzmən] s (pl -men [mən]) noticiero

New South Wales s la Nueva Gales del Sur

news'pa'per adj periodístico ‖ s periódico

newspaper·man ['njuz,pepər,mæn] o ['nuz,pepər,mæn] s (pl -men [,men]) periodista m

news'print' s papel-prensa m

news'reel' s actualidades, noticiario cinematográfico

news'stand' s quiosco de periódicos, puesto de periódicos

news'week'ly s (pl -lies) semanario de noticias

news'wor'thy adj de gran actualidad, de interés periodístico

news·y ['njuzi] o ['nuzi] adj (comp -ier; super -iest) (coll) informativo

new'-world' adj del Nuevo Mundo

New Year's card s tarjeta de felicitación de Año Nuevo

New Year's Day s el Día de Año Nuevo

New Year's Eve s la noche vieja, la víspera de año nuevo

New York [jɔrk] adj neoyorkino ‖ s Nueva York

New Yorker ['jɔrkər] s neoyorkino

New Zealand ['zilənd] adj neocelandés ‖ s Nueva Zelanda

New Zealander ['ziləndər] s neocelandés m

next [nekst] adj próximo, siguiente; de al lado; venidero, que viene ‖ adv luego, después; la próxima vez; **next to** junto a; después de; **next to nothing** casi nada; **the next best** lo mejor después de eso; **to come next** venir después, ser el que sigue

next door s la casa de al lado; **next door to** en la casa siguiente de; (coll) casi

next'door' adj siguiente, de al lado

next of kin s (pl next of kin) pariente más cercano

niacin ['naɪ·əsɪn] s niacina

Niagara Falls [naɪ'ægərə] spl las Cataratas del Niágara

nibble ['nɪbəl] s mordisco ‖ tr & intr mordiscar; picar (un pez); **to nibble at** picar de o en

Nicaraguan [,nɪkə'rɑgwən] adj & s nicaragüense, nicaragüeño

nice [naɪs] adj delicado, fino, sutil; primoroso, pulido, refinado; dengoso, melindroso; atento, cortés, culto; escrupuloso, esmerado; agradable, simpático; decoroso, conveniente; complaciente; preciso; satisfactorio; (weather) bueno; (attractive) bonito; **nice and . . .** (coll) muy, mucho; **not nice** (coll) feo

nice-looking ['naɪs'lukɪŋ] adj hermoso, guapo, bien parecido

nicely ['naɪsli] adv con precisión; escrupulosamente; satisfactoriamente; (coll) muy bien

nice·ty ['naɪsəti] s (pl -ties) precisión; sutileza; finura; **to a nicety** con la mayor precisión

niche [nɪtʃ] s hornacina, nicho; colocación conveniente

Nicholas ['nɪkələs] s Nicolás m

nick [nɪk] s mella, muesca; **in the nick of time** en el momento crítico ‖ tr mellar, hacer muescas en; cortar

nickel ['nɪkəl] s níquel m; (U.S.A.) moneda de cinco centavos ‖ tr niquelar

nick'el-plate' tr niquelar

nicknack ['nɪk,næk] s chuchería, friolera

nick'name' s apodo, mote m ‖ tr apodar

nicotine ['nɪkə,tin] s nicotina

niece [nis] s sobrina

nif·ty ['nɪfti] adj (comp -tier; super -tiest) (slang) elegante; (slang) excelente

niggard ['nɪgərd] adj & s tacaño

night [naɪt] adj nocturno ‖ s noche f; **at o by night** de noche o por la noche; **night before last** anteanoche; **to make a night of it** (coll) divertirse hasta muy entrada la noche

night'cap' s gorro de dormir; trago antes de acostarse, sosiega

night club s cabaret m, café m cantante, sala de fiestas

night driving s conducción de noche

night'fall' s anochecer m, caída de la noche

night'gown' s camisa de dormir

nightingale ['naɪtən,gel] s ruiseñor m

night latch s cerradura de resorte

night letter s carta telegráfica nocturna

night'long' adj de toda la noche ‖ adv durante toda la noche

nightly ['naɪtli] adj nocturno; de cada noche ‖ adv de noche, por la noche; cada noche

night'mare' s pesadilla

nightmarish ['naɪt,merɪʃ] adj espeluznante, horroroso

night owl s buho nocturno; (coll) anochecedor m, trasnochador m

night'shirt' s camisa de dormir

night'time' adj nocturno ‖ s noche f

night'walk'er s vagabundo nocturno; ladrón nocturno; ramera callejera nocturna; sonámbulo

night watch s guardia de noche, ronda de noche; sereno; (mil) vigilia

night watchman s vigilante nocturno

nihilism ['naɪ‧ɪ‚lɪzəm] s nihilismo

nihilist ['naɪ‧ɪlɪst] s nihilista mf

nil [nɪl] s nada

Nile [naɪl] s Nilo

nimble ['nɪmbəl] adj ágil, ligero; listo, vivo

nim‧bus ['nɪmbəs] s (pl -buses o -bi [baɪ]) nimbo

Nimrod ['nɪmrɑd] s Nemrod m

nincompoop ['nɪnkəm‚pup] s badulaque m, papirote m

nine [naɪn] adj & pron nueve || s nueve m; equipo de béisbol; **nine o'clock** las nueve; **the Nine** las nueve musas

nine hundred adj & pron novecientos || s novecientos m

nineteen ['naɪn'tin] adj, pron & s diecinueve m, diez y nueve m

nineteenth ['naɪn'tinθ] adj & s (in a series) decimonono; (part) diecinueveavo || s (in dates) diecinueve m

ninetieth ['naɪntɪ‧ɪθ] adj & s (in a series) nonagésimo; (part) noventavo

nine‧ty ['naɪntɪ] adj & pron noventa || s (pl -ties) noventa m

ninth [naɪnθ] adj & s nono, noveno || s (in dates) nueve m

nip [nɪp] s mordisco, pellizco; helada, escarcha; traguito; **nip and tuck** a quién ganará || v (pret & pp nipped; ger nipping) tr mordiscar, pellizcar; helar, escarchar; (slang) asir, coger; **to nip in the bud** atajar en el principio || intr beborrotear

nipple ['nɪpəl] s (of female) pezón m; (of male; of nursing bottle) tetilla; (mach) tubo roscado de unión, entrerrosca

Nippon [nɪ'pɑn] o ['nɪpɑn] s el Japón

Nippon‧ese [‚nɪpə'niz] adj nipón || s (pl -ese) nipón m

nip‧py ['nɪpɪ] adj (comp -pier; super -piest) mordaz, picante; frío, helado; (Brit) ágil, ligero

nirvana [nɪr'vɑnə] s el nirvana

nit [nɪt] s piojito; (egg of insect) liendre f

niter ['naɪtər] s nitro; (agr) nitro de Chile

nitrate ['naɪtret] s nitrato; (agr) nitrato de potasio, nitrato de sodio

nitric acid ['naɪtrɪk] s ácido nítrico

nitride ['naɪtraɪd] s nitruro

nitrogen ['naɪtrədʒən] s nitrógeno

nitroglycerin [‚naɪtrə'glɪsərɪn] s nitroglicerina

nitrous oxide ['naɪtrəs] s óxido nitroso

nitwit ['nɪt‚wɪt] s (slang) bobalicón m

no [no] adj indef ninguno; **no admittance** no se permite la entrada; **no matter** no importa; **no parking** se prohibe estacionarse; **no smoking** se prohibe fumar; **no thoroughfare** prohibido el paso; **no use** inútil; **with**

no sin || adv no; **no good** de ningún valor; ruin, vil; **no longer** ya no; **no sooner** no bien

Noah ['no‧ə] s Noé m

nob‧by ['nɑbɪ] adj (comp -bier; super -biest) (slang) elegante; (slang) excelente

nobili‧ty [no'bɪlɪtɪ] s (pl -ties) nobleza; (of sentiments, character, etc.) nobleza, ennoblecimiento

noble ['nobəl] adj & s noble m

noble‧man ['nobəlmən] s (pl -men [mən]) noble m, hidalgo

nobod‧y ['no‚bɑdɪ] o ['nobədɪ] pron indef nadie, ninguno; **nobody but** nadie más que; **nobody else** nadie más, ningún otro || s (pl -ies) nadie m, don nadie

nocturnal [nɑk'tʌrnəl] adj nocturno

nod [nɑd] s inclinación de cabeza; seña con la cabeza; (of a person going to sleep) cabezada || v (pret & pp nodded; ger nodding) tr inclinar (la cabeza); indicar con una inclinación de cabeza || intr inclinar la cabeza; (in going to sleep) cabecear

node [nod] s bulto, protuberancia; nudo, enredo; (astr, med & phys) nodo; (bot) nudo

nohow ['no‚haʊ] adv (coll) de ninguna manera

noise [nɔɪz] s ruido || tr divulgar

noiseless ['nɔɪzlɪs] adj silencioso, sin ruido

nois‧y ['nɔɪzɪ] adj (comp -ier; super -iest) ruidoso; (boisterous) estrepitoso

nom. abbr nominative

nomad ['nomæd] adj & s nómada mf

nomadic [no'mædɪk] adj nomádico

no man's land s terreno sin reclamar; (mil) la tierra de nadie

nominal ['nɑmɪnəl] adj nominal; (price) módico

nominate ['nɑmɪ‚net] tr postular como candidato; (to appoint) nombrar, designar

nomination [‚nɑmɪ'neʃən] s postulación

nominative ['nɑmɪnətɪv] adj & s nominativo

nominee [‚nɑmɪ'ni] s propuesto, candidato

nonbelligerent [‚nɑnbə'lɪdʒərənt] adj & s no beligerante m

nonbreakable [nɑn'brekəbəl] adj irrompible

nonchalance ['nɑnʃələns] o [‚nɑnʃə'lɑns] s indiferencia, desenvoltura

nonchalant ['nɑnʃələnt] o [‚nɑnʃə'lɑnt] adj indiferente, desenvuelto

noncom ['nɑn‚kɑm] s (coll) clase, suboficial m

noncombatant [nɑn'kɑmbətənt] adj & s no combatiente m

noncommissioned officer [‚nɑnkə'mɪʃənd] s clase, suboficial m

noncommittal [‚nɑnkə'mɪtəl] adj evasivo, reticente

noncommitted [‚nɑnkə'mɪtɪd] adj no empeñado

non compos mentis ['nɑn'kɑmpəs-'mentɪs] *adj* falto de juicio, loco

nonconformist [,nɑnkən'fɔrmɪst] *s* disidente *mf*

nondelivery [,nɑndɪ'lɪvəri] *s* falta de entrega

nondescript ['nɑndɪ,skrɪpt] *adj* inclasificable, indefinido

none [nʌn] *pron indef* nadie, ninguno, ningunos; **none of** ninguno de; nada de; **none other** ningún otro || *adv* nada, de ninguna manera; **none the less** sin embargo, no obstante

nonentity [nɑn'entɪtɪ] *s* (*pl* -ties) cosa inexistente; (*person*) nulidad

nonfiction [nɑn'fɪkʃən] *s* literatura no novelesca

nonfulfillment [,nɑnful'fɪlmənt] *s* incumplimiento

nonintervention [,nɑnɪntər'venʃən] *s* no intervención

nonmetal ['nɑn,metəl] *s* metaloide *m*

nonpayment [nɑn'pemənt] *s* falta de pago

non-plus ['nɑnplʌs] o [nɑn'plʌs] *s* estupefacción || *v* (*pret & pp* -plused o -plussed; *ger* -plusing o -plussing) *tr* dejar estupefacto, dejar pegado a la pared

nonprofit [nɑn'prɑfɪt] *adj* sin fin lucrativo

nonrefillable [,nɑnrɪ'fɪləbəl] *adj* irrellenable

nonresident [nɑn'rezɪdənt] *s* transeúnte *mf*

nonresidential [nɑn,rezɪ'denʃəl] *adj* comercial

nonscientific [nɑn,saɪ·ən'tɪfɪk] *adj* anticientífico

nonsectarian [,nɑnsek'terɪ·ən] *adj* no sectario

nonsense ['nɑnsens] *s* disparate *m*, tontería

nonsensical [nɑn'sensɪkəl] *adj* disparatado, tonto

nonskid ['nɑn'skɪd] *adj* antideslizante

nonstop ['nɑn'stɑp] *adj & adv* sin parar, sin escala

nonsupport [,nɑnsə'pɔrt] *s* falta de manutención

noodle ['nudəl] *s* tallarín *m*; (slang) mentecato, tonto; (slang) cabeza

noodle soup *s* sopa de pastas, sopa de fideos

nook [nʊk] *s* rinconcito

noon [nun] *s* mediodía *m*; **at high noon** en pleno mediodía

no one o **no-one** ['no,wʌn] *pron indef* nadie, ninguno; **no one else** nadie más, ningún otro

noontime ['nun,taɪm] *s* mediodía *m*

noose [nus] *s* lazo corredizo; (*to hang a criminal*) dogal *m*; trampa || *tr* lazar; hacer un lazo corredizo en

nor [nɔr] *conj* ni

Nordic ['nɔrdɪk] *adj & s* nórdico

norm [nɔrm] *s* norma

normal ['nɔrməl] *adj* normal

Norman ['nɔrmən] *adj & s* normando

Normandy ['nɔrməndɪ] *s* Normandía

Norse [nɔrs] *adj* nórdico; noruego || *s* (*ancient Scandanavian language*) nórdico; (*language of Norway*) no-

ruego; **the Norse** los nórdicos; los noruegos

Norse-man ['nɔrsmən] *s* (*pl* -men [mən]) normando

north [nɔrθ] *adj* septentrional, del norte || *adv* al norte, hacia el norte || *s* norte *m*

North America *s* Norteamérica, la América del Norte

North American *adj & s* norteamericano

north'east'er *s* (*wind*) nordestada, nordeste *m* (*viento*)

northern ['nɔrðərn] *adj* septentrional; (*Hemisphere*) boreal

North Korea *s* la Corea del Norte

North Korean *adj & s* norcoreano

northward ['nɔrθwərd] *adv* hacia el norte

north wind *s* norte *m*, aquilón *m*

Norway ['nɔrwe] *s* Noruega

Norwegian [nɔr'widʒən] *adj & s* noruego

nos. *abbr* **numbers**

nose [noz] *s* nariz *f*; (aer) proa; **to blow one's nose** sonarse las narices; **to count noses** averiguar cuántas personas hay; **to follow one's nose** seguir todo derecho; avanzar guiándose por el instinto; **to hold one's nose** tabicarse las narices; **to lead by the nose** llevar por la barba, tener agarrado por las narices; **to look down one's nose at** mirar por encima del hombro; **to pay through the nose** pagar un precio escandaloso; **to pick one's nose** hurgarse las narices; **to poke one's nose into** meter las narices en; **to speak through the nose** ganguear; **to thumb one's nose at** señalar (*a una persona*) poniendo el pulgar sobre la nariz en son de burla; tratar con sumo desprecio; **to turn up one's nose at** mirar con desprecio; **under the nose of** en las narices de, en las barbas de || *tr* olfatear || *intr* ventear; **to nose about** curiosear; **to nose over** capotar (*un avión*); **to nose up** encabritarse (*un buque, un avión*)

nose bag *s* cebadera, morral *m*

nose'band' *s* muserola, sobarba

nose'bleed' *s* hemorragia nasal

nose cone *s* cono de proa

nose dive *s* (aer) descenso de picado; (fig) descenso precipitado

nose'-dive' *intr* (aer) picar; (fig) descender precipitadamente

nosegay ['noz,ge] *s* ramillete *m*

nose ring *s* nariguera

no'-show' *s* pasajero no presentado

nostalgia [nɑ'stældʒə] *s* nostalgia

nostril ['nɑstrɪl] *s* nariz *f*, ventana

nos·y ['nozi] *adj* (*comp* -ier; *super* -iest) (coll) curioso, husmeador

not [nɑt] *adv* no; **not at all** nada, de ningún modo; **not yet** todavía no; **to think not** creer que no; **why not?** ¿cómo no?

notable ['notəbəl] *adj & s* notable *m*

notarize ['notə,raɪz] *tr* abonar con fe notarial

nota·ry ['notəri] *s* (*pl* -ries) notario

notch [nɑtʃ] s muesca, mella, corte m; (U.S.A.) desfiladero, paso; (coll) grado ‖ tr hacer muescas en, mellar

note [not] s nota; apunte m; esquela, cartita; marca, señal f; (com) pagaré m, vale m; canto, melodía; acento, voz f; (mus) nota ‖ tr notar, apuntar; marcar, señalar

note'book' s cuaderno, libro de apuntes

noted ['notɪd] adj afamado, conocido

note paper s papel m de cartas

note'wor'thy adj notable, digno de notarse

nothing ['nʌθɪŋ] pron indef nada; **for nothing** inútilmente; de balde, gratis; **nothing doing** (slang) ni por pienso; **nothing else** nada más; **that's nothing to me** eso nada me importa; **to make nothing** of no hacer caso de; no aprovecharse de; no entender; despreciar; **to think nothing of** no hacer caso de; tener por fácil; despreciar ‖ adv nada, de ninguna manera; **nothing daunted** sin temor alguno ‖ s nada; nadería, friolera

notice ['notɪs] s atención, reparo, advertencia; aviso, noticia; letrero; mención, reseña; llamada; notificación; **on short notice** con poco tiempo de aviso; **to escape one's notice** pasarle inadvertido a uno; **to serve notice** dar noticia, hacer saber ‖ tr notar, observar, reparar, reparar en; mencionar

noticeable ['notɪsəbəl] adj sensible, perceptible; notable

noti•fy ['notɪ‚faɪ] v (pret & pp **-fied**) tr notificar, avisar, hacer saber

motion ['noʃən] s noción; capricho; **motions** mercería, artículos menudos; **to have a notion to** + inf pensar + inf, tener ganas de + inf

notorie•ty [‚notə'raɪɪti] s (pl **-ties**) mala reputación; (condition of being well known) notoriedad; (person) notable mf

notorious [no'torɪəs] adj reputado, mal reputado; bien conocido

no'-trump' adj & s sin triunfo; **a no-trump hand** un sin triunfo

notwithstanding [‚nɑtwɪð'stændɪŋ] o [‚nɑtwɪθ'stændɪŋ] adv no obstante ‖ prep a pesar de ‖ conj a pesar de que

nougat ['nugət] s turrón m

noun [naun] s nombre, nombre sustantivo

nourish ['nʌrɪʃ] tr alimentar, nutrir; abrigar (p.ej., esperanzas)

nourishing ['nʌrɪʃɪŋ] adj alimenticio, nutritivo

nourishment ['nʌrɪʃmənt] s alimento, nutrimento

Nov. abbr November

Nova Scotia ['novə'skoʃə] s la Nueva Escocia

Nova Scotian ['novə'skoʃən] adj & s neoescocés m

novel ['nɑvəl] adj nuevo; insólito, extraño, original ‖ s novela

novelist ['nɑvəlɪst] s novelista mf

novel•ty ['nɑvəlti] s (pl **-ties**) novedad,

innovación; **novelties** bisutería, baratijas

November [no'vɛmbər] s noviembre m

novice ['nɑvɪs] s novicio

novocaine ['novə‚ken] s novocaína

now [nau] adv ahora; ya; entonces; **from now on** de ahora en adelante; **how now?** ¿cómo?; **just now** hace un momento; **now and again** o **now and then** de vez en cuando; **now . . . now** ora . . . ora, ya . . . ya; **now that** ya que; **now then** ahora bien ‖ interj ¡vamos! ‖ s actualidad

nowadays ['nau‚ə‚dez] adv hoy en día, hoy día

no'way' o **no'ways'** adv de ningún modo

no'where' adv en ninguna parte, a ninguna parte; **nowhere else** en ninguna otra parte

noxious ['nɑkʃəs] adj nocivo

nozzle ['nɑzəl] s (of hose) lanza; (of sprinkling can) rallo, roseta; (of candlestick) cubo; (slang) nariz f

N.T. abbr New Testament

nth [ɛnθ] adj nᵐᵒ (enésimo); **to the nth degree** elevado a la potencia n; a más no poder

nuance [nju'ɑns] o ['nju‚ɑns] s matiz m

nub [nʌb] s protuberancia; pedazo; (coll) meollo

nuclear ['njuklɪ‚ər] o ['nuklɪ‚ər] adj nuclear

nuclear test ban s proscripción de las pruebas nucleares

nucle•us ['njuklɪ‚əs] o ['nuklɪ‚əs] s (pl **-i** [‚aɪ] o **-uses**) núcleo

nude [njud] o [nud] adj desnudo ‖ s — **in the nude** desnudo; **the nude** el desnudo

nudge [nʌdʒ] s codazo suave ‖ tr dar un codazo suave a, empujar suavemente

nugget ['nʌgɪt] s pedazo; (of, e.g., gold) pepita; preciosidad

nuisance ['njusəns] o ['nusəns] s molestia, estorbo; persona o cosa fastidiosas

null [nʌl] adj nulo; **null and void** nulo, írrito, nulo y sin valor

nulli•fy ['nʌlɪ‚faɪ] v (pret & pp **-fied**) tr anular, invalidar

nulli•ty ['nʌlɪti] s (pl **-ties**) nulidad

numb [nʌm] adj entumecido ‖ tr entumecer

number ['nʌmbər] s número; **a number of** varios ‖ tr numerar; ascender a (cierto número); **his days are numbered** tiene sus días contados o sus horas contadas; **to be numbered among** hallarse entre; **to number among** contar entre

numberless ['nʌmbərlɪs] adj innumerable

numeral ['njumərəl] o ['numərəl] adj numeral ‖ s número

numerical [nju'mɛrɪkəl] o [nu'mɛrɪkəl] adj numérico

numerous ['njumərəs] o ['numərəs] adj numeroso

numskull ['nʌm‚skʌl] s (coll) bodoque m, mentecato

nun [nʌn] s monja, religiosa

nuptial ['nʌpʃəl] adj nupcial || **nuptials** spl nupcias, bodas

nurse [nʌrs] s enfermera; (to suckle a child) ama de cría, nodriza; (to take care of a child) niñera || tr cuidar (a una persona enferma); amamantar; alimentar; criar; tratar de curarse de (p.ej., un resfriado); abrigar (p.ej., odio) || intr ser enfermera

nurser·y ['nʌrsəri] s (pl -ies) cuarto de los niños; (of plants) criadero, plantel m, semillero; (fig) semillero

nursery·man ['nʌrsərimən] s (pl -men [mən]) cultivador m de semillero

nursery rhymes spl versos para niños

nursery tales spl cuentos para niños

nursing bottle s biberón m

nursing home s clínica de reposo

nurture ['nʌrtʃər] s alimentación, nutrimento; crianza, educación || tr alimentar, nutrir; criar, educar; acariciar (p.ej., una esperanza)

nut [nʌt] s nuez f; (to screw on a bolt)

tuerca; (slang) estrafalario; **a hard nut to crack** (coll) hueso duro de roer

nut'crack'er s cascanueces m

nutmeg ['nʌt,meg] s nuez moscada; (tree) mirística

nutriment ['njutrimənt] o ['nutrimənt] s nutrimento

nutrition [nju'trɪʃən] o [nu'trɪʃən] s nutrición

nutritious [nju'trɪʃəs] o [nu'trɪʃəs] adj nutricioso, nutritivo

nut'shell' s cáscara de nuez; **in a nutshell** en pocas palabras

nut·ty ['nʌti] adj (comp -tier; super -tiest) abundante en nueces; que sabe a nueces; (slang) chiflado, loco; **nutty about** (slang) loco por

nuzzle ['nʌzəl] tr hocicar, hozar || intr hocicar; arrimarse cómodamente; arroparse bien

nylon ['naɪlɑn] s nilón m; **nylons** medias de nilón

nymph [nɪmf] s ninfa

O

O, o [o] decimoquinta letra del alfabeto inglés

O interj ¡oh!; ¡ay!, p.ej., **O, how pretty she is!** ¡Ay qué linda!; **O that . . . !** ¡Ojalá que . . . !

oaf [of] s zoquete m, zamacuco; niño contrahecho

oak [ok] s roble m

oaken ['okən] adj hecho de roble

oakum ['okəm] s estopa, estopa de calafatear

oar [or] s remo; **to lie o rest on one's oars** aguantar los remos; aflojar en el trabajo || tr conducir a remo || intr remar, bogar

oars·man ['orzmən] s (pl -men [mən]) remero

OAS ['o'e'es] s (letterword) OEA f

oa·sis [o'esɪs] s (pl -ses [siz]) oasis m

oat [ot] s avena; **oats** (edible grain) avena; **to feel one's oats** (slang) estar fogoso y brioso; (slang) estar muy pagado de sí mismo; **to sow one's wild oats** correrla, pasar las mocedades

oath [oθ] s juramento; **on oath** bajo juramento; **to take an oath** prestar juramento

oat'meal' s harina de avena; gachas de avena

ob. abbr **obiit** (Lat) died

obbligato [,ɑblɪ'gɑto] adj & s obligado

obduracy ['ɑbdjərəsi] s obduración

obdurate ['ɑbdjərɪt] adj obstinado, terco; empedernido

obedience [o'bidɪ·əns] s obediencia

obedient [o'bidɪ·ənt] adj obediente

obeisance [o'besəns] u [o'bisəns] s saludo respetuoso; homenaje m, respeto

obelisk ['ɑbəlɪsk] s obelisco

obese [o'bis] adj obeso

obesity [o'bisɪti] s obesidad

obey [o'be] tr & intr obedecer

obfuscate [ɑb'fʌsket] o ['ɑbfəs,ket] tr ofuscar

obituar·y [o'bɪtʃʊ,eri] adj necrológico || s (pl -ies) necrología

obj. abbr **object, objection, objective**

object ['ɑbdʒɪkt] s objeto || [əb'dʒekt] tr objetar || intr hacer objeciones

objection [əb'dʒekʃən] s reparo, objeción; **to have no objections to make** no tener nada que objetar

objectionable [əb'dʒekʃənəbəl] adj desagradable, reprensible; (causing disapproval) objetable

objective [əb'dʒektɪv] adj & s objetivo

obl. abbr **oblique, oblong**

obligate ['ɑblɪ,get] tr obligar

obligation [,ɑblɪ'geʃən] s obligación

oblige [ə'blaɪdʒ] tr obligar; complacer; **much obliged** muchas gracias

obliging [ə'blaɪdʒɪŋ] adj complaciente, condescendiente, servicial

oblique [ə'blik] adj oblicuo; indirecto, evasivo

obliterate [ə'blɪtə,ret] tr borrar; arrasar, destruir

oblivion [ə'blɪvɪ·ən] s olvido

oblivious [ə'blɪvɪ·əs] adj olvidadizo

oblong ['ɑblɔŋ] o ['ɑblɑŋ] adj oblongo

obnoxious [əb'nɑkʃəs] adj detestable, ofensivo

oboe ['obo] s oboe m

oboist ['obo·ɪst] s oboísta mf

obs. abbr **obsolete**

obscene [əb'sin] adj obsceno

obsceni·ty [ɑbˈsenɪtɪ] o [ɑbˈsinɪtɪ] s (pl -ties) obscenidad

obscure [əbˈskjur] adj obscuro; (vowel) relajado, neutro

obscuri·ty [əbˈskjurɪtɪ] s (pl -ties) obscuridad

obsequies [ˈɑbsɪkwɪz] spl exequias

obsequious [əbˈsikwɪ·əs] adj obsequioso, servil, rastrero

observance [əbˈzʌrvəns] s observancia; ceremonia, rito

observant [əbˈzʌrvənt] adj observador

observation [ˌɑbzərˈveʃən] s observación; observancia

observato·ry [əbˈzʌrvəˌtorɪ] s (pl -ries) observatorio

observe [əbˈzʌrv] tr observar; (a holiday; silence) guardar

observer [əbˈzʌrvər] s observador m

obsess [əbˈses] tr obsesionar

obsession [əbˈseʃən] s obsesión

obsolescent [ˌɑbsəˈlesənt] adj arcaizante

obsolete [ˈɑbsəˌlit] adj desusado, caído en desuso

obstacle [ˈɑbstəkəl] s obstáculo

obstetrical [ɑbˈstetrɪkəl] adj obstétrico

obstetrics [ɑbˈstetrɪks] ssg obstetricia

obstina·cy [ˈɑbstɪnəsɪ] s (pl -cies) obstinación

obstinate [ˈɑbstɪnɪt] adj obstinado

obstruct [əbˈstrʌkt] tr obstruir

obstruction [əbˈstrʌkʃən] s obstrucción

obtain [əbˈten] tr obtener ‖ intr existir, prevalecer

obtrusive [əbˈtrusɪv] adj entremetido, intruso

obtuse [əbˈtjus] o [əbˈtus] adj obtuso

obviate [ˈɑbvɪˌet] tr obviar

obvious [ˈɑbvɪ·əs] adj obvio

occasion [əˈkeʒən] s ocasión; to improve the occasion aprovechar la ocasión

occasional [əˈkeʒənəl] adj raro, poco frecuente; alguno que otro; de circunstancia

occasionally [əˈkeʒənəlɪ] adv ocasionalmente, de vez en cuando

occident [ˈɑksɪdənt] s occidente m

occidental [ˌɑksɪˈdentəl] adj occidental

occlusive [əˈklusɪv] adj oclusivo ‖ s oclusiva

occult [əˈkʌlt] o [ɑkˈʌlt] adj oculto

occupancy [ˈɑkjəpənsɪ] s ocupación

occupant [ˈɑkjəpənt] s ocupante mf; inquilino

occupation [ˌɑkjəˈpeʃən] s ocupación

occu·py [ˈɑkjəˌpaɪ] v (pret & pp -pied) tr ocupar; habitar

oc·cur [əˈkʌr] v (pret & pp -curred; ger -curring) intr ocurrir, acontecer, suceder; encontrarse; (to come to mind) ocurrir

occurrence [əˈkʌrəns] s acontecimiento; caso, aparición

ocean [ˈoʃən] s océano

oceanic [ˌoʃɪˈænɪk] adj oceánico

ocean liner s buque transoceánico

o'clock [əˈklɑk] adv por el reloj; it is one o'clock es la una; it is two

o'clock son las dos; what o'clock is it? ¿qué hora es?

Oct. abbr October

octave [ˈɑktɪv] o [ˈɑktev] s octava

October [ɑkˈtobər] s octubre m

octo·pus [ˈɑktəpəs] s (pl -puses o -pi [ˌpaɪ]) pulpo

octoroon [ˌɑktəˈrun] s octavo

ocular [ˈɑkjələr] adj & s ocular m

oculist [ˈɑkjəlɪst] s oculista mf

O.D. abbr officer of the day, olive drab

odd [ɑd] adj suelto; (number) impar; (that doesn't match) dispar; libre, de ocio; sobrante; extraño, raro, singular; y pico, y tantos, p.ej., two hundred odd doscientos y pico ‖ odds ssg o spl (in betting) ventaja; apuesta desigual; puntos de ventaja; at odds de monos, riñendo; by all odds muy probablemente, sin duda alguna; it makes no odds lo mismo da; the odds are lo probable es; la ventaja es de; to be at odds estar de punta, estar encontrados; to set at odds enemistar, malquistar

oddi·ty [ˈɑdɪtɪ] s (pl -ties) rareza, cosa rara

odd jobs spl pequeñas tareas

odd lot s lote m inferior al centenar

odds and ends spl pedacitos varios, cajón m de sastre

ode [od] s oda

odious [ˈodɪ·əs] adj odioso, abominable

odor [ˈodər] s olor m; to be in bad odor tener mala fama

odorless [ˈodərlɪs] adj inodoro

odorous [ˈodərəs] adj oloroso

Odysseus [oˈdɪsjus] o [oˈdɪsɪ·əs] s Odiseo

Odyssey [ˈɑdɪsɪ] s Odisea

Oedipus [ˈedɪpəs] o [ˈidɪpəs] s Edipo

of [ʌv] o [əv] prep de, p.ej., the top of the mountain la cima de la montaña; a: to smell of oler a; con: to dream of soñar con; en: to think of pensar en; menos: a quarter of two las dos menos un cuarto

off. abbr office, officer, official

off [ɔf] o [ɑf] adj malo, p.ej., off day día malo; (account, sum) errado; más distante; libre; sin trabajo; quitado; apagado; (electric current) cortado; de descuento, de rebaja; de la parte del mar; (season) muerto ‖ adv fuera, a distancia, lejos; allá; off of (coll) de; (coll) a expensas de; to be off ponerse en marcha ‖ prep de, desde; al lado de, a nivel de; fuera de; libre de; (naut) a la altura de

offal [ˈɑfəl] u [ˈɔfəl] s (of butchered meat) carniza; basura, desperdicios

off and on adv unas veces sí y otras no

off'beat' adj (slang) insólito, chocante, original

off'chance' s posibilidad poco probable

off'-col'or adj descolorido; indispuesto; (indecent, risqué) colorado, subido de color

offend [əˈfend] tr & intr ofender

offender [əˈfendər] s ofensor m

offense [ə'fɛns] *s* ofensa; **to take offense (at)** ofenderse (de)

offensive [ə'fɛnsɪv] *adj* ofensivo || *f* ofensiva

offer ['ɔfər] o ['ɑfər] *s* ofrecimiento, oferta || *tr* ofrecer; rezar (*oraciones*); oponer (*resistencia*)

offering ['ɔfərɪŋ] o ['ɑfərɪŋ] *s* ofrecimiento; (*gift, present*) oferta; (*presentation in worship*) ofrenda

off'hand' *adj* hecho de improviso; brusco, desenvuelto || *adv* de improviso, súbitamente; bruscamente

office ['ɔfɪs] o ['ɑfɪs] *s* oficina, despacho; función, oficio; cargo, ministerio; (*of a lawyer*) bufete *m*; (*of a doctor*) consultorio

office boy *s* mandadero

office desk *s* escritorio ministro

of'fice-hold'er *s* funcionario, burócrata *m*

office hours *spl* horas de oficina; (*of a doctor*) horas de consultorio

officer ['ɔfɪsər] o ['ɑfɪsər] *s* jefe *m*, director *m*; (*of army, an order, a society, etc.*) oficial *m*; agente *m* de policía

office seeker ['sikər] *s* aspirante *m*, pretendiente *m*

office supplies *spl* suministros para oficinas

official [ə'fɪʃəl] *adj* oficial || *s* jefe *m*, director *m*; (*of a society*) dignatario

officiate [ə'fɪʃɪˌet] *intr* oficiar

officious [ə'fɪʃəs] *adj* oficioso

off'-peak' heater *s* (elec) termos *m* de acumulación

off-peak load *s* (elec) carga de las horas de valle

off'print' *s* sobretiro

off'set' *s* compensación; (typ) offset *m* || **off'set'** *v* (*pret* & *pp* -set; *ger* -setting) *tr* compensar; imprimir por offset

off'shoot' *s* (*of plant*) retoño, renuevo; (*of a family or race*) descendiente *mf*; (*branch*) ramal *m*; consecuencia

off'shore' *adj* (*wind*) terral; (*fishing*) de bajura; (*said of islands*) costero || *adv* a lo largo

off'spring' *s* descendencia, sucesión; hijo, hijos

off'-stage' *adj* de entre bastidores

off'-the-rec'ord *adj* extraoficial, confidencial

often ['ɔfən] o ['ɑfən] *adv* a menudo, muchas veces; **how often?** ¿cuántas veces?; **not often** pocas veces

ogive ['odʒaɪv] u [o'dʒaɪv] *s* ojiva

ogle ['ogəl] *tr* & *intr* ojear; mirar amorosamente

ogre ['ogər] *s* ogro

ohm [om] *s* ohmio

oil [ɔɪl] *adj* (*burner; field; well*) de petróleo; (*pump; stove*) de aceite; (*company; tanker*) petrolero; (*land*) petrolífero || *s* aceite *m*; (*consecrated oil; painting*) óleo; **to burn the midnight oil** quemarse las cejas; **to pour oil on troubled waters** mojar la pólvora; **to strike oil** encontrar una capa de petróleo; (fig) enriquecerse de súbito || *tr* aceitar; lubricar; li-

sonjear; (*to bribe*) untar || *intr* proveerse de petróleo (*un buque*)

oil'can' *s* aceitera

oil'cloth' *s* encerado, hule *m*

oil gauge indicador *m* del nivel de aceite

oil pan *s* colector *m* de aceite

oil tanker *s* petrolero

oil·y ['ɔɪli] *adj* (*comp* -ier; *super* -iest) aceitoso; liso, resbaladizo; zalamero

ointment ['ɔɪntmənt] *s* ungüento

O.K. ['o'ke] *adj* (coll) aprobado, conforme || *adv* (coll) muy bien, está bien || *s* (coll) aprobación || *v* (*pret* & *pp* **O.K.'d**; *ger* **O.K.'ing**) *tr* (coll) aprobar

okra ['okrə] *s* quingombó *m*

old [old] *adj* viejo; antiguo; (*wine*) añejo; **how old is . . . ?** ¿cuántos años tiene . . . ?; **of old** de antaño, antiguamente; **to be . . . years old** tener . . . años

old age *s* ancianidad, vejez *f*; **to die of old age** morir de viejo

old boy *s* viejo; graduado; **the Old Boy** (slang) el diablo

Old Castile *s* Castilla la Vieja

old-clothes·man ['old'kloðzˌmæn] *s* (*pl* -men [ˌmen]) ropavejero

old country *s* madre patria

old-fashioned ['old'fæʃənd] *adj* chapado a la antigua; anticuado, fuera de moda

old fo·gey u **old fo·gy** ['fogi] *s* (*pl* -gies) persona un poco ridícula por sus ideas o costumbres atrasadas

Old Glory *s* la bandera de los Estados Unidos

Old Guard *s* (U.S.A.) bando conservador del partido republicano

old hand *s* práctico *m*, veterano

old maid *s* solterona

old master *s* (paint) gran maestro; obra de un gran maestro

old moon *s* luna menguante

old salt *s* lobo de mar

old school *s* gente chapada a la antigua

old'-time' *adj* del tiempo viejo

old-timer ['old'taɪmər] *s* (coll) antiguo residente, veterano; (coll) persona chapada a la antigua

old wives' tale *s* cuento de viejas

old'-world' *adj* del Viejo Mundo

oleander [ˌolɪ'ændər] *s* adelfa

oligar·chy ['ɑlɪˌgɑrki] *s* (*pl* -chies) oligarquía

olive ['ɑlɪv] *adj* aceitunado || *s* aceituna

olive branch *s* ramo de olivo; (*peace*) oliva; hijo, vástago

olive grove *s* olivar *m*

olive oil *s* aceite *m*, aceite de oliva

olive tree *s* aceituno, olivo

Olympiad [o'lɪmpɪˌæd] *s* Olimpíada

Olympian [o'lɪmpɪˌən] *adj* olímpico || *s* dios griego

Olympic [o'lɪmpɪk] *adj* olímpico

omelet u **omelette** ['aməlɪt] o ['amlɪt] *s* tortilla (de huevos)

omen ['omən] *s* agüero

ominous ['amɪnəs] *adj* ominoso

omission [o'mɪʃən] *s* omisión

omit [o'mɪt] v (pret & pp **omitted;** ger **omitting**) tr omitir

omnibus ['ɑmnɪ,bʌs] o ['ɑmnɪbəs] adj general; (volume) colecticio ‖ s ómnibus m

omnipotent [am'nɪpətənt] adj omnipotente

omniscient [am'nɪʃənt] adj omnisciente

omnivorous [am'nɪvərəs] adj omnívoro

on [ɑn] u [ɔn] adj puesto, p.ej., **with his hat on** con el sombrero puesto; principiando; en funcionamiento; encendido; conectado; **the deal is on** ya está concertado el trato; **the game is on** ya están jugando; **the race is on** allá van los corredores; **what is on at the theater this evening?** ¿qué representan esta noche? ‖ adv adelante; encima; **and so on** y así sucesivamente; **come on!** ¡anda, anda!; **farther on** más allá, más adelante; **later on** más tarde, después; **to be on to a person** (coll) conocerle a uno el juego; **to have on** tener puesto; **to . . . on** seguir + ger, **he played on** siguió tocando ‖ prep en, sobre, encima de; a, p.ej., **on foot** a pie; **on my arrival** a mi llegada; bajo, p.ej., **on my responsibility** bajo mi responsabilidad; contra, p.ej., **an attack on liberty** un ataque contra la libertad; de, p.ej., **on good authority** de buena tinta; **on a journey of viaje**; hacia, p.ej., **to march on the capital** marchar hacia la capital; por, p.ej., **on all sides** por todos lados; tras, p.ej., **defeat on defeat** derrota tras derrota; **on** + ger al + inf, p.ej., **on arriving** al llegar

on and on adv continuamente, sin cesar, sin parar

once [wʌns] adv una vez; antes, p.ej., **once so happy** antes tan feliz; alguna vez, p.ej., **if this once becomes known** si esto llega a saberse alguna vez; **all at once** de súbito, de repente; **at once** en seguida; a la vez, en el mismo momento; **for once** una vez por lo menos; **once and again** repetidas veces; **once in a blue moon** cada muerte de obispo; **once in a while** de vez en cuando; **once more** otra vez; una vez más; **once upon a time there was** érase una vez, érase que se era ‖ conj una vez que ‖ s una vez; vez, p.ej., **this once** esta vez

once'-o'ver s (slang) examen rápido; **to give a thing the once-over** (coll) examinar una cosa superficialmente

one [wʌn] adj un, uno; un tal, p.ej., **one Smith** un tal Smith; único, p.ej., **one price** precio único ‖ pron uno, p.ej., **one does not know what to do here** uno no sabe qué hacer aquí; se, p.ej., **how does one go to the station?** ¿cómo se va a la estación?; **I for one** yo por lo menos; **it's all one and the same to me** me es igual; **my little one** mi chiquito; **of one another** el uno del otro, los unos de otros,

p.ej., **we took leave of one another** nos despedimos el uno del otro; **one and all** todos; **one another se**, p.ej., **they greeted one another** se saludaron; uno a otro, unos a otros, p.ej., **they looked at one another** se miraron uno a otro; **one by one** uno a uno; **one o'clock** la una; **one or two** unos pocos; **one's** su, el . . . de uno; **the blue book and the red one** el libro azul y el rojo; **the one and only** el único; **the one that** el que, la que; **this one** éste; **that one** ése, aquél; **to make one** unir; casar ‖ s uno

one'-horse' adj de un solo caballo, tirado por un solo caballo; (coll) insignificante, de poca monta

onerous ['ɑnərəs] adj oneroso

one'self' pron uno mismo; sí, sí mismo; se; **to be oneself** tener dominio de sí mismo; **conducirse** con naturalidad

one-sided ['wʌn'saɪdɪd] adj de un solo lado; injusto, parcial; desigual; unilateral

one'-track' adj de carril único; (coll) con un solo interés

one'-way' adj de una sola dirección, de dirección única; (ticket) sencillo, de ida

onion ['ʌnjən] s cebolla

on'ion-skin' s papel m de seda, papel cebolla

on'look'er s mirón m, espectador m

only ['onlɪ] adj solo, único ‖ adv solamente, sólo, únicamente; no . . . más que; **not only . . . but also** no sólo . . . sino también ‖ conj sólo que, pero

on'set' s arremetida, embestida; (of an illness) principio

onward ['ɑnwərd] u **onwards** ['ɑnwərdz] adv adelante, hacia adelante

onyx ['ɑnɪks] s ónice m u ónix m

ooze [uz] s chorro suave; cieno, limo, lama ‖ tr rezumar ‖ intr rezumar, rezumarse; manar suavemente (p.ej., **la sangre de una herida**); agotarse poco a poco

op. abbr **opera, operation, opus, opposite**

opal ['opəl] s ópalo

opaque [o'pek] adj opaco; (writer's style) obscuro; estúpido

open ['opən] adj abierto; descubierto; destapado; sin tejado; vacante; (hour) libre; discutible, pendiente; (hand) liberal; (hunting season) legal; **to break o to crack open** abrir con violencia, abrir por la fuerza; **to throw open** abrir de par en par ‖ s abertura; (in the woods) claro; **in the open** al aire libre; a campo raso; en alta mar; abiertamente ‖ tr abrir; desbullar (una ostra) ‖ intr abrir; abrirse; estrenarse (un drama); **to open into** desembocar en; **to open on** dar a; **to open up** descubrirse; descubrir el pecho

o'pen-air' adj al aire libre, a cielo abierto

open-eyed ['opən ,aɪd] adj alerta, vigilante; con ojos asombrados; hecho con los ojos abiertos

open-handed [ˈopənˈhændɪd] *adj* maniabierto, liberal

open-hearted [ˈopənˈhɑrtɪd] *adj* franco, sincero

open house *s* coliche *m*; **to keep open house** recibir a todos, gustar de tener siempre convidados en casa

opening [ˈopənɪŋ] *s* abertura; (*of, e.g., school*) apertura; (*in the woods*) claro; (*vacancy*) hueco, vacante *f*; (*chance to say something*) ocasión

opening night *s* noche *f* de estreno

opening number *s* primer número

opening price *s* primer curso, precio de apertura

open-minded [ˈopənˈmaɪndɪd] *adj* receptivo, razonable, imparcial

open secret *s* secreto a voces

open shop *s* taller franco

o'pen·work *s* calado

opera [ˈɑpərə] *s* ópera

opera glasses *spl* gemelos de teatro

opera hat *s* clac *m*, sombrero de muelles

opera house *s* teatro de la ópera

operate [ˈɑpəˌret] *tr* hacer funcionar; dirigir, manejar; explotar ‖ *intr* funcionar; operar; **to operate on** operar (*p.ej., una hernia; a un niño*)

operatic [ˌɑpəˈrætɪk] *adj* operístico

operating expenses *spl* gastos de explotación

operating room *s* quirófano

operating table *s* mesa operatoria

operation [ˌɑpəˈreʃən] *s* operación; funcionamiento; explotación

operator [ˈɑpəˌretər] *s* operador *m*, maquinista *m*; (com) empresario; (coll) corredor *m* de bolsa; (surg, telp) operador *m*

operetta [ˌɑpəˈretə] *s* opereta

opiate [ˈopɪ·ɪt] u [ˈopɪˌet] *adj & s* opiato

opinion [əˈpɪnjən] *s* opinión; **in my opinion** a mi parecer; **to have a high opinion of** tener buen concepto de

opinionated [əˈpɪnjəˌnetɪd] *adj* porfiado en su parecer, dogmático

opium [ˈopɪ·əm] *s* opio

opium den *s* fumadero de opio

opossum [əˈpɑsəm] *s* zarigüeya

opponent [əˈponənt] *s* contrario

opportune [ˌɑpərˈtjun] o [ˌɑpərˈtun] *adj* oportuno

opportunist [ˌɑpərˈtjunɪst] o [ˌɑpərˈtunɪst] *s* oportunista

opportuni·ty [ˌɑpərˈtjunɪti] o [ˌɑpərˈtunɪti] *s* (*pl* **-ties**) oportunidad, ocasión

oppose [əˈpoz] *tr* oponerse a

opposite [ˈɑpəsɪt] *adj* opuesto; de enfrente, p.ej., **the house opposite** la casa de enfrente ‖ *prep* enfrente de ‖ *s* contrario

opposite number *s* igual *mf*, doble *mf*

opposition [ˌɑpəˈzɪʃən] *s* oposición

oppress [əˈpres] *tr* oprimir

oppression [əˈpreʃən] *s* opresión

oppressive [əˈpresɪv] *adj* opresivo; sofocante, bochornoso

opprobrious [əˈprobrɪ·əs] *adj* oprobioso

opprobrium [əˈprobrɪ·əm] *s* oprobio

optic [ˈɑptɪk] *adj* óptico ‖ *s* (coll) ojo; **optics** *ssg* óptica

optical [ˈɑptɪkəl] *adj* óptico

optician [ɑpˈtɪʃən] *s* óptico

optimism [ˈɑptɪˌmɪzəm] *s* optimismo

optimist [ˈɑptɪmɪst] *s* optimista *mf*

optimistic [ˌɑptɪˈmɪstɪk] *adj* optimístico

option [ˈɑpʃən] *s* opción

optional [ˈɑpʃənəl] *adj* facultativo, potestativo

optometrist [ɑpˈtɑmɪtrɪst] *s* optometrista *mf*

opulent [ˈɑpjələnt] *adj* opulento

or [ɔr] *conj* o, u

oracle [ˈɑrəkəl] o [ˈɔrəkəl] *s* oráculo

oracular [oˈrækjələr] *adj* sentencioso; ambiguo, misterioso; fatídico; sabio

oral [ˈorəl] *adj* oral

orange [ˈɑrɪndʒ] u [ˈɔrɪndʒ] *adj* anaranjado ‖ *s* naranja

orangeade [ˌɑrɪndʒˈed] u [ˌɔrɪndʒˈed] *s* naranjada

orange blossom *s* azahar *m*

orange grove *s* naranjal *m*

orange juice *s* zumo de naranja

orange squeezer *s* exprimidera de naranjas

orange tree *s* naranjo

orang-outang [oˈræŋuˌtæŋ] *s* orangután *m*

oration [oˈreʃən] *s* oración, discurso

orator [ˈɑrətər] u [ˈɔrətər] *s* orador *m*

oratorical [ˌɑrəˈtɑrɪkəl] u [ˌɔrəˈtɔrɪkəl] *adj* oratorio

oratori·o [ˌɑrəˈtorɪˌo] u [ˌɔrəˈtorɪˌo] *s* (*pl* **-os**) oratorio

orato·ry [ˈɑrəˌtori] u [ˈɔrəˌtori] *s* (*pl* **-ries**) (*art of public speaking*) oratoria; (*small chapel*) oratorio

orb [ɔrb] *s* orbe *m*

orbit [ˈɔrbɪt] *s* órbita; **to go into orbit** entrar en órbita ‖ *tr* poner en órbita; moverse en órbita alrededor de ‖ *intr* moverse en órbita

orchard [ˈɔrtʃərd] *s* huerto

orchestra [ˈɔrkɪstrə] *s* orquesta; (*parquet*) platea

orchestrate [ˈɔrkɪsˌtret] *tr* orquestar

orchid [ˈɔrkɪd] *s* orquídea

ordain [ɔrˈden] *tr* (eccl) ordenar; destinar; mandar

ordeal [ɔrˈdil] u [ɔrˈdi·əl] *s* prueba rigurosa o penosa; (hist) juicio de Dios

order [ˈɔrdər] *s* (*way one thing follows another; formal or methodical arrangement; peace, quiet; class, category*) orden *m*; (*command; honor society; monastic brotherhood; fraternal organization*) orden *f*; tarea, p.ej., **a big order** una tarea peliaguda; (com) pedido; (com) giro, libranza; (*formation*) (mil) orden *m*; (*command*) (mil) orden *f*; **in order that** para que, a fin de que; **in order to** + *inf* para + *inf*, a fin de + *inf*; **to get out of order** descomponerse; **to give an order** dar una orden; (com) hacer un pedido ‖ *tr* ordenar;

mandar; encargar, pedir; mandar hacer; **to order around** ser muy mandón con; **to order someone away** mandar a uno que se marche

order blank s hoja de pedidos

order·ly ['ɔrdɜrli] adj ordenado, gobernoso; tranquilo, obediente ‖ s (pl -lies) asistente m en un hospital; (mil) ordenanza m

ordinal ['ɔrdɪnəl] adj & s ordinal m

ordinance ['ɔrdɪnəns] s ordenanza

ordinary ['ɔrdɪ,nɛri] adj ordinario

ordnance ['ɔrdnəns] s artillería, cañones mpl; pertrechos de guerra

ore [ɔr] s mena, mineral metalífero

organ ['ɔrgən] s órgano

organ·dy ['ɔrgəndi] s (pl -dies) organdí m

or'gan-grind'er s organillero

organic [ɔr'gænɪk] adj orgánico

organism ['ɔrgə,nɪzəm] s organismo

organist ['ɔrgənɪst] s organista mf

organize ['ɔrgə,naɪz] tr organizar

organ loft s tribuna del órgano

or·gy ['ɔrdʒi] s (pl -gies) orgía

orient ['ɔrɪ·ənt] s oriente m ‖ **Orient** s oriente m ‖ **orient** ['ɔrɪ,ɛnt] tr orientar

oriental [,ɔrɪ'ɛntəl] adj oriental

orifice ['ɑrɪfɪs] u ['ɔrɪfɪs] s orificio

origin ['ɑrɪdʒɪn] u ['ɔrɪdʒɪn] s origen m

original [ə'rɪdʒɪnəl] adj & s original m

originate [ə'rɪdʒɪ,net] tr originar ‖ intr originarse

oriole ['ɔrɪ,ol] s oropéndola

Orkney Islands ['ɔrkni] spl Órcadas

ormolu ['ɔrmə,lu] s (gold powder used in gilding) oro molido; (alloy of zinc and copper) similor m; bronce dorado

ornament ['ɔrnəmənt] s ornamento ‖ ['ɔrnə,mɛnt] tr ornamentar

ornate [ɔr'net] u ['ɔrnet] adj muy ornado; (style) florido

orphan ['ɔrfən] adj & s huérfano ‖ tr dejar huérfano

orphanage ['ɔrfənɪdʒ] s (institution) orfanato; (state, condition) orfandad

orphan asylum s asilo de huérfanos

Orpheus ['ɔrfjus] u ['ɔrfɪ·əs] s Orfeo

orthodox ['ɔrθə,dɑks] adj ortodoxo

orthogra·phy [ɔr'θɑgrəfi] s (pl -phies) ortografía

oscillate ['ɑsɪ,let] intr oscilar

osier ['oʒər] s mimbre m & f; sauce mimbreo

ossi·fy ['ɑsɪ,faɪ] v (pret & pp -fied) tr osificar ‖ intr osificarse

ostensible [ɑs'tɛnsɪbəl] adj aparente, pretendido, supuesto

ostentatious [,ɑstɛn'teʃəs] adj (pretentious) ostentativo; (showy) ostentoso

osteopath ['ɑstɪ·ə,pæθ] s osteópata m

osteopathy [,ɑstɪ'ɑpəθi] s osteopatía

ostracism ['ɑstrə,sɪzəm] s ostracismo

ostrich ['ɑstrɪtʃ] s avestruz m

O.T. abbr **Old Testament**

other ['ʌðər] adj & pron indef otro ‖ adv — **other than** de otra manera que

otherwise ['ʌðər,waɪz] adv otramente,

de otra manera; en otras circunstancias; fuera de eso; si no, de otro modo

otter ['ɑtər] s nutria

ottoman ['ɑtəmən] s (corded fabric) otomán m; (sofa) otomana; escabuelo con cojín ‖ **Ottoman** adj & s otomano

ouch [autʃ] interj ¡ax!

ought [ɔt] s alguna cosa; cero; **for ought I know** por lo que yo sepa ‖ v aux se emplea para formar el modo potencial, p.ej., **he ought to go at once** debiera salir en seguida

ounce [auns] s onza

our [aur] adj poss nuestro

ours [aurz] pron poss el nuestro; nuestro

ourselves [aur'sɛlvz] pron pers nosotros mismos; nos, p.ej., **we enjoyed ourselves** nos divertimos

oust [aust] tr echar fuera, desposeer; desahuciar (al inquilino)

out [aut] adj ausente; apagado; exterior; divulgado; publicado; (size) poco común ‖ adv afuera, fuera; al aire libre; hasta el fin; **out for** buscando; **out of** de; entre; de entre; fuera de; más allá de; (kindness, fear, etc.) por; (money) sin; (a suit of cards) fallo a, sin de, p.ej., **in nine out of ten cases** en nueve casos sobre diez; **out to** + inf esforzándose por + inf ‖ prep por; allá en ‖ interj ¡fuera de aquí! ‖ s cesante mf; **to be at outs** u **on the outs** estar de monos

out and away adv con mucho

out'-and-out' adj perfecto, verdadero, rematado ‖ adv completamente

out'-and-out'er s intransigente mf; extremista mf

out·bid' v (pret -bid; pp -bid o -bidden; ger -bidding) tr pujar más que (otra persona); (bridge) sobrepasar

out'board' motor s motor m fuera de borda

out'break' s tumulto, motín m; (of anger) arranque m; (of war) estallido; (of an epidemic) brote m

out'build'ing s dependencia, edificio accesorio

out'burst' s explosión, arranque m; **outburst of laughter** carcajada

out'cast' s proscripto, paria mf; vagabundo

out'come' s resultado

out'cry' s (pl -cries) grito; gritería, clamoreo

out·dat'ed adj fuera de moda, anticuado

out·do' v (pret -did; pp -done) tr exceder; **to outdo oneself** excederse a sí mismo

out'door' adj al aire libre

out'doors' adv al aire libre, fuera de casa ‖ s aire m libre, campo raso

outer space ['autər] s espacio exterior

out'field' s (baseball) jardín m

out'field'er s (baseball) jardinero

out'fit' s equipo; traje m; juego de herramientas; (of soldiers) cuerpo; (of a bride) ajuar m; (com) compañía ‖

v (*pret* & *pp* **-fitted;** *ger* **-fitting**) *tr* equipar

out'go'ing *adj* de salida; cesante; (*tide*) descendente; (*nature, character*) exteriorista ‖ *s* salida

out-grow' *v* (*pret* **-grew;** *pp* **-grown**) *tr* crecer más que; ser ya grande para; ser ya viejo para; ser ya más apto que; dejar (*las cosas de los niños; a los niños de la niñez, etc.*) ‖ *intr* extenderse

out'growth' *s* excrecencia, bulto; (*of leaves in springtime*) nacimiento; consecuencia, resultado

outing [ˈautɪŋ] *s* jira, excursión al campo

outlandish [autˈlændɪʃ] *adj* estrafalario; de aspecto extranjero; de acento extranjero

out-last' *tr* durar más que; sobrevivir a

out'law' *s* forajido, bandido; prófugo, proscrito ‖ *tr* proscribir; declarar ilegal

out'lay' *s* desembolso ‖ **out·lay'** *v* (*pret* & *pp* **-laid**) *tr* desembolsar

out'let' *s* salida; desaguadero; orificio de salida; (*elec*) caja de enchufe; (*tap*) (elec) toma-corriente *m*

out'line' *s* contorno; trazado; esquema *m*; esbozo, bosquejo; compendio ‖ *tr* contornar; trazar; trazar el esquema de; esbozar, bosquejar; compendiar

out-live' *tr* sobrevivir a; durar más que

out'look' *s* perspectiva; expectativa; concepto de la vida, punto de vista; atalaya

out'ly'ing *adj* remoto, circundante, de las afueras

out·mod'ed *adj* fuera de moda

out·num'ber *tr* exceder en número, ser más numeroso que

out'-of-date' *adj* fuera de moda, anticuado

out'-of-door' *adj* al aire libre

out'-of-doors' *adj* al aire libre ‖ *adv* al aire libre, fuera de casa ‖ *s* aire *m* libre, campo raso

out'-of-print' *adj* agotado

out'-of-the-way' *adj* apartado, remoto; poco usual, poco común

out of tune *adj* desafinado ‖ *adv* desafinadamente

out of work *adj* desempleado, sin trabajo

out'pa'tient *s* paciente *mf* de consulta externa

out'post' *s* avanzada

out'put' *s* rendimiento; (elec) salida; (mech) rendimiento de trabajo, efecto útil

out'rage *s* atrocidad; ultraje *m* ‖ *tr* maltratar; ultrajar; escandalizar

outrageous [autˈredʒəs] *adj* (*grossly offensive*) ultrajoso; (*shocking, fierce*) atroz; (*extreme*) extravagante

out-rank' *tr* exceder en rango o grado

out'rid'er *s* carrerista *m;* (Brit) viajante *m* de comercio

out'right' *adj* cabal, completo; franco, sincero ‖ *adv* enteramente; de una vez; sin rodeos; en seguida

out'run'ner *s* volante *m* (*criado*)

out'set' *s* principio

out'side' *adj* exterior; superficial; ajeno; (*price*) (el) máximo ‖ *s* fuera, afuera; **outside of** fuera de ‖ *prep* fuera de; más allá de; (coll) a excepción de ‖ *s* exterior *m;* superficie *f;* apariencia

outsider [ˌautˈsaɪdər] *s* forastero; intruso

out'skirts' *spl* afueras

out'spo'ken *adj* boquifresco, franco

out·stand'ing *adj* sobresaliente; prominente; sin pagar, sin cobrar

outward [ˈautwərd] *adj* exterior; superficial ‖ *adv* exteriormente, hacia fuera

out·weigh' *tr* pesar más que; contrapesar, compensar

out·wit' *v* (*pret* & *pp* **-witted;** *ger* **-witting**) *tr* burlar, ser más listo que; despistar (*al perseguidor*)

oval [ˈovəl] *adj* oval ‖ *s* óvalo

ova·ry [ˈovəri] *s* (pl **-ries**) ovario

ovation [oˈveʃən] *s* ovación

oven [ˈʌvən] *s* horno

over [ˈovər] *adj* acabado, concluído; superior; adicional; excesivo ‖ *adv* encima; al otro lado, a la otra orilla; hacia abajo; al revés; patas arriba; otra vez, de nuevo; de añadidura; (*at the bottom of a page*) a la vuelta; acá, p.ej., **hand over the money** déme acá el dinero; **over again** una vez más; **over against** enfrente de; a distinción de; en contraste con; **over and over** repetidas veces; **over here** acá; **over in** allá en; **over there** allá ‖ *prep* sobre, encima de, por encima de; por; de un extremo a otro de; al otro lado de; más allá de; desde; (*a certain number*) más de; acerca de; por causa de; durante; **over and above** además de, en exceso de

o'ver·all' *adj* cabal, completo; extremo, total ‖ **overalls** *spl* pantalones *mf* de trabajo

o'ver·bear'ing *adj* altanero, imperioso

o'ver·board' *adv* al agua; **man overboard!** ¡hombre al agua!; **to throw overboard** arrojar, echar o tirar por la borda

o'ver·cast' *adj* encapotado, nublado ‖ *s* cielo encapotado ‖ *v* (*pret* & *pp* **-cast**) *tr* nublar

o'ver·charge' *s* cargo excesivo; recargo de precio; sobrecarga; (elec) carga excesiva ‖ **o'ver·charge'** *tr* hacer pagar más del valor, cobrar demasiado a; cargar (*p.ej., 50 pesetas*) de más; (elec) poner una carga excesiva a

o'ver·coat' *s* abrigo, gabán *m,* sobretodo

o'ver·come' *v* (*pret* **-came;** *pp* **-come**) *tr* vencer; rendir; superar (*dificultades*)

o'ver·crowd' *tr* atestar, apiñar; poblar con exceso

o'ver·do' *v* (*pret* **-did;** *pp* **-done**) *tr* exagerar; agobiar; asurar, requemar ‖ *intr* cansarse mucho, excederse en el trabajo

o'ver·dose' *s* dosis excesiva

o'ver·draft' *s* sobregiro, giro en descubierto

o'ver·draw' *v* (*pret* -drew; *pp* -drawn) *tr & intr* sobregirar

o'ver·due' *adj* atrasado; vencido y no pagado

o'ver·eat' *v* (*pret* -ate; *pp* -eaten) *tr & intr* comer con exceso

o'ver·exer'tion *s* esfuerzo excesivo

o'ver·expose' *tr* sobreexponer

o'ver·expo'sure *s* sobreexposición

o'ver·flow' *s* desbordamiento, rebosamiento, derrame *m*; caño de reboso ‖ o'ver·flow' *intr* desbordar, rebosar

o'ver·fly' *v* (*pret* -flew; *pp* -flown) *tr* sobrevolar

o'ver·grown' *adj* demasiado grande para su edad; denso, frondoso

o'ver·hang' *v* (*pret & pp* -hung) *tr* sobresalir por encima de, estar pendiente o colgando sobre; salir fuera del nivel de; amenazar ‖ *intr* estar pendiente, estar colgando

o'ver·haul' *tr* examinar, registrar, revisar; ir alcanzando, alcanzar; componer, rehabilitar, reacondicionar

o'ver·head' *adj* de arriba; aéreo, elevado; general, de conjunto ‖ o'ver·head' *adv* por encima de la cabeza; arriba, en lo alto ‖ o'ver·head' *s* gastos generales

o'ver·hear' *v* (*pret & pp* -heard) *tr* oír por casualidad; acertar a oír, alcanzar a oír

o'ver·heat' *tr* recalentar ‖ *intr* recalentarse

overjoyed [,ovər'dʒɔɪd] *adj* lleno de alegría; to be overjoyed no caber de contento

overland ['ovər,lænd] u [,'ovərlənd] *adj & adv* por tierra, por vía terrestre

o'ver·lap' *v* (*pret & pp* -lapped; *ger* -lapping) *tr* solapar, traslapar ‖ *intr* solapar, traslapar; traslaparse (*dos o más cosas*); suceder (*dos hechos*) en parte al mismo tiempo

o'ver·load' *s* sobrecarga ‖ o'ver·load' *tr* sobrecargar

o'ver·look' *tr* dominar con la vista; pasar por alto, no hacer caso de; perdonar, tolerar; espiar, vigilar; cuidar de, dirigir; dar a, p.ej., **the window overlooks the garden** la ventana da al jardín

o'ver·lord' *s* jefe supremo ‖ o'ver·lord' *tr* dominar despóticamente, imponerse a

overly ['ovərli] *adv* (coll) excesivamente, demasiado

o'ver·night' *adv* toda la noche; de la tarde a la mañana; to stay overnight pasar la noche

overnight bag *s* saco de noche

o'ver·pass' *s* viaducto

o'ver·pop'u·late' *tr* superpoblar

o'verpow'er *tr* dominar, supeditar, subyugar, colmar, dejar estupefacto

overpowering *adj* abrumador, arrollador, irresistible

o'ver·produc'tion *s* superproducción, sobreproducción

o'ver·rate' *tr* exagerar el valor de

o'ver·run' *v* (*pret* -ran; *pp* -run; *ger* -running) *tr* cubrir enteramente; infestar; exceder; to overrun one's time quedarse más de lo justo; hablar más de lo justo

o'ver·sea' u o'ver·seas' *adj* de ultramar ‖ o'ver·sea' u o'ver·seas' *adv* allende los mares, en ultramar

o'ver·seer' *s* director *m*, superintendente *mf*

o'ver·shad'ow *tr* sombrear; (fig) eclipsar

o'ver·shoe' *s* chanclo, zapato de goma

o'ver·shoot' *v* (*pret & pp* -shot) *tr* tirar por encima de o más allá de; to overshoot oneself pasarse de listo, excederse

o'ver·sight' *s* inadvertencia, descuido

o'ver·sleep' *v* (*pret & pp* -slept) *intr* dormir demasiado tarde

o'ver·step' *v* (*pret & pp* -stepped; *ger* -stepping) *tr* exceder, traspasar

o'ver·stock' *tr* abarrotar

o'ver·sup'ply *s* (*pl* -plies) provisión excesiva ‖ o'ver·sup·ply' *v* (*pret* -plied) *tr* proveer en exceso

overt ['ovərt] u [o'vərt] *adj* abierto, manifiesto; premeditado

o'ver·take' *v* (*pret* -took; *pp* -taken) *tr* alcanzar; sobrepasar; sorprender; sobrevenir a

o'ver-the-count'er *adj* vendido directamente al comprador; vendido en tienda al por mayor

o'ver·throw' *s* derrocamiento; trastorno ‖ o'ver·throw' *v* (*pret* -threw; *pp* -thrown) *tr* derrocar; trastornar

o'ver·time' *s* contrafallo ‖ o'ver·time' *tr & intr* contrafallar

overture ['ovərtʃər] *s* insinuación, proposición; (mus) obertura

o'ver·turn' *s* vuelco; movimiento de mercancías ‖ o'ver·turn' *tr* volcar; trastornar; derrocar ‖ *intr* volcar; trastornarse

overweening [,ovər'winɪŋ] *adj* arrogante, presuntuoso

o'ver·weight' *adj* excesivamente gordo o grueso ‖ *s* sobrepeso; exceso de peso; peso de añadidura

overwhelm [,ovər'hwelm] *tr* abrumar; inundar; anonadar; (with favors, gifts, etc.) colmar

o'ver·work' *s* trabajo excesivo, exceso de trabajo; trabajo fuera de las horas regulares ‖ o'ver·work' *tr* hacer trabajar demasiado; oprimir con el trabajo ‖ *intr* trabajar demasiado

Ovid ['ovɪd] *s* Ovidio

ow [au] *interj* ¡ax!

owe [o] *tr* deber, adeudar ‖ *intr* tener deudas

owing ['o·ɪŋ] *adj* adeudado; debido, pagadero; owing to debido a, por causa de

owl [aul] *s* buho, lechuza, mochuelo

own [on] *adj* propio, p.ej., **my own brother** mi propio hermano ‖ *s* suyo, lo suyo; on one's own (coll) por su propia cuenta; (without tak-

ing advice from anyone) por su cabeza; (*without help from anyone*) de su cabeza; **to come into one's own** entrar en posesión de lo suyo; tener el éxito merecido, recibir el honor merecido; **to hold one's own** no aflojar, no cejar, mantenerse firme ‖ *tr* poseer; reconocer ‖ *intr* confesar; **to own up to** (coll) confesar de plano (*una culpa, un delito, etc.*)

owner ['onər] *s* amo, dueño, poseedor *m*, propietario

ownership ['onər,ʃɪp] *s* posesión, propiedad

owner's license *s* permiso de circulación, patente *f* de circulación

ox [ɑks] *s* (*pl* **oxen** ['ɑksən]) buey *m*

ox'cart' *s* carreta de bueyes

oxide ['ɑksaɪd] *s* óxido

oxidize ['ɑksɪ,daɪz] *tr* oxidar ‖ *intr* oxidarse

oxygen ['ɑksɪdʒən] *s* oxígeno

oxygen tent *s* cámara o tienda de oxígeno

oxytone ['ɑksɪ,ton] *adj & s* oxítono

oyster ['ɔɪstər] *s* ostrero ‖ *s* ostra

oyster bed *s* ostrero

oyster cocktail *s* ostras en su concha

oyster fork *s* desbullador *m*

oys'ter-house' *s* ostrería

oys'ter-knife' *s* abreostras *m*

oyster-man ['ɔɪstərmən] *s* (*pl* **-men** [mən]) ostrero

oyster opener ['opənər] *s* desbullador *m*

oyster shell *s* desbulla, concha de ostra

oyster stew *s* sopa de ostras

oz. *abbr* **ounce, ounces**

ozone ['ozon] *s* ozono; (coll) aire fresco

ozs. *abbr* **ounces**

P

P, p [pi] decimosexta letra del alfabeto inglés

p. *abbr* **page, participle**

P.A. *abbr* **Passenger Agent, power of attorney, Purchasing Agent**

pace [pes] *s* paso; **to keep pace with** ir, andar o avanzar al mismo paso que; **to put through one's paces** poner (*a uno*) a prueba; dar a (*uno*) ocasión de lucirse; **to set the pace** establecer el paso; dar el ejemplo ‖ *tr* establecer el paso para; medir a pasos; recorrer a pasos; **to pace the floor** pasearse desesperadamente por la habitación ‖ *intr* andar a pasos regulares

pace'mak'er *s* (med) marcapaso

pacific [pə'sɪfɪk] *adj* pacífico ‖ **Pacific** *adj & s* Pacífico

pacifier ['pæsɪ,faɪ-ər] *s* pacificador *m*; (*teething ring*) chupador *m*

pacifism ['pæsɪ,fɪzəm] *s* pacifismo

pacifist ['pæsɪfɪst] *adj & s* pacifista *mf*

paci-fy ['pæsɪ,faɪ] *v* (*pret & pp* **-fied**) *tr* pacificar

pack [pæk] *s* lío, fardo; paquete *m*; (*of hounds*) jauría; (*of cattle*) manada; (*of evildoers*) pandilla; (*of lies*) sarta, montón *m*; (*of playing cards*) baraja; (*of cigarettes*) cajetilla; (*of floating ice*) témpano; (med) compresa ‖ *tr* empaquetar; embaular; encajonar; hacer (*el baúl, la maleta*); conservar en latas; apretar, atestar, cargar (*una acémila*); escoger de modo fraudulento (*un jurado*); **to be packed in** (coll) estar como sardinas en banasta ‖ *intr* empaquetarse; hacer el baúl, hacer la maleta; consolidarse, formar masa compacta

package ['pækɪdʒ] *s* paquete *m* ‖ *tr* empaquetar

pack animal *s* acémila, animal *m* de carga

packing box o **case** *s* caja de embalaje

packing house *s* frigorífico

packing slip *s* hoja de embalaje

pack'sad'dle *s* albarda

pack'thread' *s* bramante *m*

pack train *s* recua

pact [pækt] *s* pacto

pad [pæd] *s* cojincillo, almohadilla; (*of writing paper*) bloc *m*; (*for inking*) tampón *m*; (*of an aquatic plant*) hoja; (*for launching a rocket*) plataforma *f*; (*sound of footsteps*) pisada ‖ *v* (*pret & pp* **padded;** *ger* **padding**) *tr* acolchar, rellenar; meter mucho ripio en (*un escrito*) ‖ *intr* andar, caminar; caminar despacio y pesadamente

paddle ['pædəl] *s* (*of a canoe*) canalete *m*; (*of a wheel*) pala, paleta; (*for spanking*) palo ‖ *tr* impulsar con canalete; (*to spank*) apalear ‖ *intr* remar con canalete; remar suavemente; (*to splash*) chapotear

paddle wheel *s* rueda de paletas

paddock ['pædək] *s* dehesa; (*at race-course*) paddock *m*

pad'lock' *s* candado ‖ *tr* cerrar con candado; (*to lock up officially*) condenar (*una habitación, un teatro*)

pagan ['pegən] *adj & s* pagano

paganism ['pegə,nɪzəm] *s* paganismo

page [pedʒ] *s* (*of a book*) página; (*boy attendant*) paje *m*; (*in a hotel or club*) botones *m* ‖ *tr* paginar; buscar llamando

pageant ['pædʒənt] *s* espectáculo público

pageant-ry ['pædʒəntri] *s* (*pl* **-ries**) pompa, fausto; (*empty display*) bambolla

pail [pel] *s* balde *m*, cubo

pain [pen] *s* dolor *m*; **on pain of** so pena de; **pains** esmero, trabajo; dolores de parto; **to take pains** esmerarse ‖ *tr & intr* doler

painful ['penfəl] *adj* doloroso; penoso

pain'kill'er *s* (coll) remedio contra el dolor

painless ['penlıs] *adj* sin dolor, indoloro; fácil, sin trabajo

pains'tak'ing *adj* esmerado

paint [pent] *s* pintura; (*rouge*) afeite *m*, colorete *m* || *tr* pintar || *intr* pintar; pintarse, repintarse

paint'box' *s* caja de colores

paint'brush' *s* brocha, pincel *m*

painter ['pentər] *s* pintor *m*

painting ['pentıŋ] *s* pintura

paint remover [rɪ'muvər] *s* sacapintura *m*, quitapintura *f*

pair [per] *s* par *m*; (*of people*) pareja; (*of cards*) parejas || *tr* aparear || *intr* aparearse

pair of scissors *s* tijeras

pair of trousers *s* pantalones *mpl*

pajamas [pə'dʒaməz] o [pə'dʒæməz] *spl* pijama

Pakistan [,pakı'stan] *s* el Paquistán

Pakistani [,pakı'stanı] *adj* & *s* paquistano, paquistaní *mf*

pal [pæl] *s* (coll) compañero || *v* (*pret* & *pp* **palled**; *ger* **palling**) *intr* (coll) ser compañeros

palace ['pælıs] *s* palacio

palatable ['pælətəbəl] *adj* sabroso, apetitoso

palatal ['pælətəl] *adj* & *s* palatal *f*

palate ['pælɪt] *s* paladar *m*

pale [pel] *adj* pálido; (*color*) claro || *s* estaca; palizada; límite *m*, término || *intr* palidecer

pale'face' *s* rostropálido

palette ['pælɪt] *s* paleta

palfrey ['pɔlfrɪ] *s* palafrén *m*

palisade [,pælɪ'sed] *s* estaca; estacada; (*line of cliffs*) acantilado

pall [pɔl] *s* paño de ataúd, paño mortuorio; (eccl) palia || *tr* hartar, saciar; quitar el sabor a || *intr* perder el sabor; **to pall on** hartar, saciar

pall'bear'er *s* acompañante *m* de un cadáver; portador *m* del féretro

palliate ['pælɪ,et] *tr* paliar

pallid ['pælɪd] *adj* pálido

pallor ['pælər] *s* palidez *f*, palor *m*

palm [pɑm] *s* (*of the hand*) palma; (*measure*) palmo; (*tree and leaf*) palma; **to carry off the palm** llevarse la palma; **to grease the palm of** (slang) untar la mano a; **to yield the palm to** reconocer por vencedor || *tr* esconder en la mano; escamotear (*una carta*); **to palm off something on someone** encajarle una cosa a uno

palmet-to [pæl'meto] *s* (*pl* -tos o -toes) palmito

palmist ['pamıst] *s* quiromántico

palmistry ['pamıstrı] *s* quiromancia

palm leaf *s* palma, hoja de la palmera

palm oil *s* aceite *m* de palma; (slang) propina; (slang) soborno

Palm Sunday *s* domingo de ramos

palpable ['pælpəbəl] *adj* palpable

palpitate ['pælpɪ,tet] *intr* palpitar

pal-sy ['pɔlzı] *s* (*pl* -sies) perlesía || *v* (*pret* & *pp* -sied) *tr* paralizar

pal-try ['pɔltrı] *adj* (*comp* -trier; *super* -triest) vil, ruin, mezquino

pamper ['pæmpər] *tr* mimar, consentir

pamphlet ['pæmflıt] *s* folleto, panfleto

pan [pæn] *s* cacerola, cazuela, sartén *f*; caldera, perol *m* || *v* (*pret* & *pp* **panned**; *ger* **panning**) *tr* cocer, freír; separar (*el oro*) en la gamella; (coll) criticar ásperamente || *intr* separar el oro en la gamella; dar oro; **to pan out well** (coll) tener éxito, dar buen resultado || **Pan** *s* Pan

panacea [,pænə'si-ə] *s* panacea

Panama Canal ['pænə,ma] *s* canal *m* de Panamá

Panama Canal Zone *s* Zona del Canal

Panama hat *s* panamá *m*

Panamanian [,pænə'menı-ən] o [,pænə'manı-ən] *adj* & *s* panameño

Pan-American [,pænə'merıkən] *adj* panamericano

pan'cake' *s* hojuela, panqueque *m* || *intr* (aer) desplomarse

pancake landing *s* aterrizaje aplastado, aterrizaje en desplome

pancreas ['pænkrı-əs] *s* páncreas *m*

pander ['pændər] *s* alcahuete *m* || *intr* alcahuetear; **to pander to** gratificar

pane [pen] *s* cristal *m*, vidrio, hoja de vidrio

pan-el ['pænəl] *s* panel *m*, entrepaño, cuarterón *m*; grupo de personas en discusión cara al público; (aut, elec) tablero, panel *m*; (law) lista de personas que pueden servir como jurados || *v* (*pret* & *pp* -eled o -elled; *ger* -eling o -elling) *tr* adornar con cuarterones, labrar en cuarterones; artesonar (*un techo o bóveda*)

panel discussion *s* coloquio cara al público

panelist ['pænəlıst] *s* coloquiante *mf* cara al público

panel lights *spl* luces *fpl* del tablero

pang [pæŋ] *s* dolor agudo; (*of remorse*) punzada; (*of death*) agonía

pan'han'dle *s* mango de sartén || *intr* (slang) mendigar, pedir limosna

pan-ic ['pænık] *adj* & *s* pánico || *v* (*pret* & *pp* -icked; *ger* -icking) *tr* sobrecoger de pánico || *intr* sobrecogerse de pánico

pan'ic-strick'en *adj* muerto de miedo, sobrecogido de terror

pano-ply ['pænəplı] *s* (*pl* -plies) panoplia; traje *m* ceremonial

panorama [,pænə'ræmə] o [,pænə'ramə] *s* panorama *m*

pan-sy ['pænzı] *s* (*pl* -sies) pensamiento

pant [pænt] *s* jadeo; palpitación; **pants** pantalones *mpl*; **to wear the pants** (coll) calzarse los pantalones || *intr* jadear; palpitar

pantheism ['pænθı,ızəm] *s* panteísmo

pantheon ['pænθı,an] o ['pænθı-ən] *s* panteón *m*

panther ['pænθər] *s* pantera; puma

panties ['pæntız] *spl* pantaloncillos de mujer

pantomime ['pæntə,maım] *s* pantomima

pan·try ['pæntri] s (pl -tries) despensa
pap [pæp] s papilla, papas
papa·cy ['pepəsɪ] s (pl -cies) papado
paper ['pepər] s papel m; (newspaper) periódico; (of needles) paño || tr empapelar
pa'per·back' s libro en rústica
pa'per·boy' s vendedor m de periódicos
paper clip s sujetapapeles m
paper cone s cucurucho
paper cutter s cortapapeles m, guillotina
paper doll s muñeca de papel
paper hanger s empapelador m, papelista mf
paper knife s cortapapeles m
paper mill s fábrica de papel
paper money s papel m moneda
paper profits spl ganancias no realizadas sobre valores no vendidos
paper tape s cinta perforada
pa'per·weight' s pisapapeles m
paper work s preparación o comprobación de escritos
paprika [pæ'prikə] o ['pæprɪkə] s pimentón m
papy·rus [pə'paɪrəs] s (pl -ri [raɪ]) papiro
par. abbr **paragraph, parallel, parenthesis, parish**
par [par] adj a la par; nominal; normal || s paridad; valor m nominal; **above par** sobre la par; **con beneficio, con premio; below par** o **under par** bajo la par; con pérdida; (coll) indispuesto; **to be on a par with** correr parejas con
parable ['pærəbəl] s parábola
parachute ['pærə.ʃut] s paracaídas m || intr lanzarse en paracaídas; **to parachute to safety** salvarse en paracaídas
parachute jump s salto en paracaídas
parachutist ['pærə.ʃutɪst] s paracaidista mf
parade [pə'red] s desfile m; paseo; ostentación || tr ostentar, pasear || intr desfilar, pasar por las calles; (mil) formar en parada
paradise ['pærə.daɪs] s paraíso
paradox ['pærə.dɑks] s paradoja; persona o cosa incomprensibles
paradoxical [.pærə'dɑksɪkəl] adj paradójico
paraffin ['pærəfɪn] s parafina
paragon ['pærə.gɑn] s dechado
paragraph ['pærə.græf] o ['pærə.grɑf] s párrafo
Paraguay ['pærə.gwe] o ['pærə.gwaɪ] s el Paraguay
Paraguayan [.pærə'gwe.ən] o [.pærə'gwaɪ.ən] adj & s paraguayano, paraguayo
parakeet ['pærə.kit] s perico, periquito
paral·lel ['pærə.lɛl] adj paralelo || s (línea) paralela; (plano) paralelo; (geog) paralelo; **parallels** (typ) doble raya vertical || v (pret & pp -leled o -lelled; ger -leling o -lelling) tr ser paralelo a; poner en dirección paralela; correr parejas con; (to compare) paralelizar

parallel bars spl paralelas, barras paralelas
paraly·sis [pə'rælɪsɪs] s (pl -ses [.siz]) parálisis f
paralytic [.pærə'lɪtɪk] adj & s paralítico
paralyze ['pærə.laɪz] tr paralizar
paramount ['pærə.maunt] adj capital, supremo, principalísimo
paranoiac [.pærə'nɔɪ.æk] adj & s paranoico
parapet ['pærə.pet] s parapeto
paraphernalia [.pærəfər'nelɪ.ə] spl trastos, atavíos
parasite ['pærə.saɪt] s parásito
parasitic(al) [.pærə'sɪtɪk(əl)] adj parasítico, parasitario
parasol ['pærə.sɔl] o ['pærə.sɑl] s quitasol m, parasol m
pa'ra·troop'er s paracaidista m
pa'ra·troops' spl tropas paracaidistas
parboil ['par.bɔɪl] tr sancochar; calentar con exceso
par·cel ['parsəl] s paquete m, atado, bulto || v (pret & pp -celed o -celled; ger -celing o -celling) tr empaquetar; parcelar (el terreno); **to parcel out** repartir
parcel post s paquetes mpl postales
parch [partʃ] tr abrasar, tostar; **to be parched** tener mucha sed
parchment ['partʃmənt] s pergamino
pardon ['pardən] s perdón m; (remission of penalty by the state) indulto; **I beg your pardon** dispense Vd. || tr perdonar, dispensar; indultar
pardonable ['pardənəbəl] adj perdonable
pardon board s junta de perdones
pare [per] tr mondar (fruta); pelar (patatas); cortar (callos, uñas); desplamar (la pluma córnea de los animales); adelgazar; reducir (gastos)
parent ['perənt] adj madre, matriz, principal || s padre o madre; autor m, fuente f, origen m; **parents** padres mpl
parentage ['perəntɪdʒ] s paternidad o maternidad; abolengo, linaje m
parenthe·sis [pə'renθɪsɪs] s (pl -ses [.siz]) paréntesis m
parenthood ['perənt.hud] s paternidad o maternidad
pariah [pə'raɪ.ə] o ['parɪ.ə] s paria mf
paring knife ['perɪŋ] s cuchillo para mondar
parish ['pærɪʃ] s parroquia, feligresía
parishioner [pə'rɪ/ənər] s parroquiano, feligrés m
Parisian [pə'rɪʒən] adj & s parisiense mf
parity ['pærɪtɪ] s paridad
park [park] s parque m || tr estacionar, parquear; (coll) colocar, dejar || intr estacionar, parquear
parking ['parkɪŋ] s aparcamiento, estacionamiento; **no parking** se prohíbe estacionarse
parking lights spl (aut) faros de situación
parking lot s parque m de estacionamiento

parking meter *s* reloj *m* de estacionamiento, parquímetro

parking ticket *s* aviso de multa

park'way' *s* gran vía adornada con árboles

parley ['parli] *s* parlamento || *intr* parlamentar

parliament ['parlmənt] *s* parlamento

parlor ['parlər] *s* sala; parlatorio, locutorio

parlor car *s* coche-salón *m*

parlor politics *spl* política de café

Parnassus [par'næsəs] *s* (*collection of poems*) parnaso; el Parnaso; **to try to climb Parnassus** hacer pinos en poesía

parochial [pə'roki·əl] *adj* parroquial; estrecho, limitado

paro·dy ['pærədi] *s* (*pl* **-dies**) parodia || *v* (*pret & pp* **-died**) *tr* parodiar

parole [pə'rol] *s* palabra de honor; libertad bajo palabra || *tr* dejar libre bajo palabra

paroxytone [pær'aksı,ton] *adj & s* paroxítono

par·quet [par'ke] *s* entarimado; (*theat*) platea || *v* (*pret & pp* **-queted** ['ked]; *ger* **-queting** ['ke·ıŋ]) *tr* entarimar

parricide ['pærı,saıd] *s* (*act*) parricidio; (*person*) parricida *mf*

parrot ['pærət] *s* papagayo, loro; (*fig*) papagayo || *tr* repetir o imitar como loro

par·ry ['pæri] *s* (*pl* **-ries**) parada, quite *m* || *v* (*pret & pp* **-ried**) *tr* parar; defenderse de

parse [pars] *tr* analizar (*una oración*) gramaticalmente; describir (*una palabra*) gramaticalmente

parsley ['parsli] *s* perejil *m*

parsnip ['parsnıp] *s* chirivía

parson ['parsən] *s* cura *m*, párroco; clérigo; pastor *m* protestante

part [part] *s* parte *f*; (*of a machine*) pieza; (*of the hair*) raya; (*theat*) parte *f*, papel *m*; **part and parcel** parte esencial, parte inseparable, elemento esencial; **parts** partes *fpl*; prendas, dotes *fpl*; **to do one's part** cumplir con su obligación; **to look the part** vestir el cargo; **to take the part of** tomar el partido de, defender; desempeñar el papel de || *tr* dividir, partir, separar; **to part the hair** hacerse la raya || *intr* separarse; **to part with** deshacerse de, abandonar; despedirse de

par·take [par'tek] *v* (*pret* **-took** ['tʊk]; *pp* **-taken**) *tr* compartir; comer; beber || *intr* participar

Parthenon ['parθı,nan] *s* Partenón *m*

partial ['parʃəl] *adj* parcial; aficionado

participate [par'tısı,pet] *intr* participar

participle ['partı,sıpəl] *s* participio

particle ['partıkəl] *s* partícula, corpúsculo

particular [pər'tıkjələr] *adj* particular; difícil, exigente, quisquilloso; esmerado; minucioso; **a particular ... cierto ...** || *s* particular *m*

partisan ['partızən] *adj & s* partidario, partidista *mf*; (*mil*) partisano

partition [par'tıʃən] *s* partición, distribución; división; porción; tabique *m* || *tr* repartir; dividir en cuartos, aposentos; tabicar

partner ['partnər] *s* compañero; (*wife or husband*) cónyuge *mf*; (*in a dance*) pareja *f*; (*in business*) socio

partnership ['partnər,ıp] *s* asociación; consorcio, vida en común; (com) sociedad, asociación comercial

partridge ['partrıdʒ] *s* perdiz *f*

part'-time' *adj* por horas, parcial

par·ty ['parti] *adj* de partido; de gala || *s* (*pl* **-ties**) convite *m*, reunión, fiesta, tertulia, recepción; (*for fishing, hunting, etc.*; *of armed men*) partida; cómplice *mf*, interesado; (pol) partido; (coll) persona, individuo

party girl *s* chica de vida alegre

party-goer ['parti,go·ər] *s* tertuliano; fiestero

party line *s* (*between two properties*) linde *m*, lindero; (*of communist party*) línea del partido; (telp) línea compartida

party politics *s* política de partido

pass. *abbr* **passenger, passive**

pass [pæs] o [pas] *s* paso; (*permit; free ticket; movement of hands of mesmerist, of bullfighter*) pase *m*; (*in an examination*) aprobación; nota de aprobación || *tr* pasar; pasar de largo (*una luz roja*); aprobar (*un proyecto de ley; un examen; a un alumno*); ser aprobado en (*un examen*); dejar atrás; cruzarse con; expresar (*una opinión*); pronunciar (*una sentencia*); dar (*la palabra*); dejar sin protestar; no pagar (*un dividendo*); **to pass off** colar, pasar, hacer aceptar (*una moneda falsa*); disimular (*p.ej., una ofensa con una risa*); **to pass over** omitir, pasar por alto; excusar; desdeñar; dejar sin protestar; postergar (*a un empleado*) || *intr* pasar; pasarse (*introducirse*); aprobar; **to bring to pass** llevar a cabo; **to come to pass** suceder; **to pass as** pasar por; **to pass away** pasar, pasar a mejor vida; **to pass off** pasar (*una enfermedad, una tempestad, etc.*); tener lugar; **to pass out** salir; (slang) desmayarse; **to pass over** to pasarse a (*p.ej., el enemigo*)

passable ['pæsəbəl] o ['pasəbəl] *adj* pasadero; (*law*) promulgable

passage ['pæsıdʒ] *s* pasaje *m*; paso; pasillo; (*of time*) transcurso; (*of bowels*) evacuación

pass'book' *s* cartilla, libreta de banco

passenger ['pæsəndʒər] *adj* de viajeros || *s* pasajero, viajero

passer-by ['pæsər'baı] o ['pasər'baı] *s* (*pl* **passers-by**) transeúnte *mf*

passing ['pæsıŋ] o ['pasıŋ] *adj* pasajero; corriente; de aprobado || *s* (*act of passing; death*) paso; (*in an examination*) aprobación

passion ['pæʃən] *s* pasión

passionate ['pæʃənıt] *adj* apasionado

passive ['pæsɪv] *adj* pasivo || *s* voz pasiva, verbo pasivo

pass'key' *s* llave *f* de paso

Pass'o'ver *s* pascua (*de los hebreos*)

pass'port' *s* pasaporte *m*

pass'word' *s* santo y seña

past [pæst] o [pɑst] *adj* pasado; último; que fué, p.ej., **past president** presidente que fué; acabado, concluído || *adv* más allá; por delante || *prep* más allá de; más de; por delante de; fuera de; después de, p.ej., **past two o'clock** después de las dos; **past belief** increíble; **past cure** incurable; **past hope** sin esperanza || *s* pasado

paste [pest] *s* (*dough; spaghetti, etc.*) pasta; (*for sticking things together*) engrudo || *tr* engrudar, pegar con engrudo

paste'board' *s* cartón *m*

pasteurize ['pæstə,raɪz] *tr* pasterizar

pastime ['pæs,taɪm] o ['pɑs,taɪm] *s* pasatiempo

pastor ['pæstər] o ['pɑstər] *s* pastor *m*, clérigo, cura *m*

pastoral ['pæstərəl] o ['pɑstərəl] *adj* & *s* pastoral *f*

pas·try ['pestri] *s* (*pl* **-tries**) pastelería

pastry cook *s* pastelero, pastelera

pastry shop *s* pastelería, repostería

pasture ['pæstʃər] o ['pɑstʃər] *s* pasto, pastura, dehesa || *tr* apacentar, pacer || *intr* apacentarse, pacer

past·y ['pesti] *adj* (*comp* **-ler;** *super* **-lest**) pastoso; flojo, fofo, pálido

pat [pæt] *s* golpecito, palmadita; ruido de pasos ligeros; (*of butter*) pastelillo || *v* (*pret* & *pp* **patted;** *ger* **patting**) *tr* dar golpecitos a, golpear ligeramente; palmotear, acariciar con la mano; **to pat on the back** elogiar, cumplimentar

patch [pætʃ] *s* remiendo, parche *m*; terreno, pedazo de terreno; mancha; lunar postizo || *tr* remendar; **to patch up** componer (*una desavenencia*); componer lo mejor posible (*una cosa descompuesta*); hacer aprisa y mal

patent ['petənt] *adj* patente; abierto || ['pætənt] *adj* de patentes || *s* patente *f*, patente de invención; propiedad industrial; **patent applied for** se ha solicitado patente || *tr* patentar

patent leather ['pætənt] *s* charol *m*

patent medicine ['pætənt] *s* medicamento de patente

patent rights ['pætənt] *spl* derechos de patente

paternal [pə'tʌrnəl] *adj* paterno; (*affection*) paternal

paternity [pə'tʌrnɪti] *s* paternidad

path [pæθ] o [pɑθ] *s* senda, sendero, trayectoria

pathetic [pə'θɛtɪk] *adj* patético

path'find'er *s* baquiano; explorador *m*

patholo·gy [pə'θɑlədʒi] *s* patología

pathos ['peθɑs] *s* patetismo

path'way' *s* senda, sendero

patience ['peʃəns] *s* paciencia

patient ['peʃənt] *adj* paciente || *s* paciente *mf*, enfermo

patriarch ['petri,ɑrk] *s* patriarca *m*

patrician [pə'trɪʃən] *adj* & *s* patricio

patricide [,petri,saɪd] *s* (*act*) parricidio; (*person*) parricida *mf*

Patrick ['pætrɪk] *s* Patricio

patrimo·ny ['pætri,moni] *s* (*pl* **-nies**) patrimonio

patriot ['petri·ət] o ['pætri·ət] *s* patriota *mf*

patriotic [,petri'ɑtɪk] o [,pætri'ɑtɪk] *adj* patriótico

patriotism ['petri·ə,tɪzəm] o ['pætri·ə,tɪzəm] *s* patriotismo

pa·trol [pə'trol] *s* patrulla || *v* (*pret* & *pp* **-troled** o **-trolled;** *ger* **-troling** o **-trolling**) *tr* & *intr* patrullar

patrol·man [pə'trolmən] *s* (*pl* **-men** [mən]) guardia *m* municipal, vigilante *m* de policía

patrol wagon *s* camión *m* de policía

patron ['petrən] o ['pætrən] *adj* tutelar || *s* parroquiano; patrocinador *m*

patronize ['petrə,naɪz] o ['pætrə,naɪz] *tr* ser parroquiano de (*un tendero*); comprar de costumbre en; patrocinar; tratar con aire protector

patron saint *s* patrón *m*, santo titular

patter ['pætər] *s* golpeteo; (*of rain*) chapaleteo; charla, parloteo || *intr* golpetear; charlar, parlotear

pattern ['pætərn] *s* patrón *m*; modelo

P.A.U. *abbr* Pan American Union

paucity ['pɔsɪti] *s* corto número; falta, escasez *f*, insuficiencia

Paul [pɔl] *s* Pablo; (*name of popes*) Paulo

paunch [pɔntʃ] *s* panza

paunchy ['pɔntʃi] *adj* panzudo

pauper ['pɔpər] *s* pobre *mf*, indigente *mf*

pause [pɔz] *s* pausa; (*mus*) calderón *m*; **to give pause (to)** dar que pensar (a) || *intr* hacer pausa, detenerse brevemente; vacilar

pave [pev] *tr* pavimentar; (*with flagstones*) enlosar; (*with bricks*) enladrillar; (*with pebbles*) enchinar; **to pave the way (for)** preparar el terreno (para), abrir el camino (a)

pavement ['pevmənt] *s* pavimento; (*of brick*) enladrillado; (*of flagstone*) enlosado; (*sidewalk*) acera

pavilion [pə'vɪljən] *s* pabellón *m*

paw [pɔ] *s* pata; garra, zarpa; (*coll*) mano *f* || *tr* dar zarpazos a, restregar con las uñas; golpear, patear (*el suelo los caballos*); (*coll*) manosear; (*to handle overfamiliarly*) (*coll*) sobar || *intr* piafar (*el caballo*)

pawn [pɔn] *s* (*in chess*) peón *m*; (*security, pledge*) prenda; (*tool of another person*) instrumento; víctima || *tr* empeñar, dar en prenda

pawn'bro'ker *s* prestamista *mf*

pawn'shop' *s* casa de empeños, monte *m* de piedad

pawn ticket *s* papeleta de empeño

pay [pe] *s* paga; recompensa; castigo merecido || *v* (*pret* & *pp* **paid** [ped]) *tr* pagar; prestar o poner (*atención*);

dar (*cumplidos*); dar (*dinero una actividad comercial*); dar dinero a, ser provechoso a; pagar en la misma moneda; pagar con creces; sufrir (*el castigo de una ofensa*); hacer (*una visita*); cubrir (*los gastos*); **to pay back** devolver; pagar en la misma moneda; **to pay off** pagar y despedir (*a un empleado*); pagar todo lo adeudado a; vengarse de; redimir (*una hipoteca*) ‖ *intr* pagar; ser provechoso, valer la pena; **pay as you enter** pague a la entrada; **pay as you go** pagar el impuesto de utilidades con descuentos anticipados; **pay as you leave** pague a la salida

payable ['pe.əbəl] *adj* pagadero
pay boost *s* aumento de salario
pay'check' *s* cheque *m* en pago del sueldo; sueldo
pay'day' *s* día *m* de pago
payee [pe'i] *s* portador *m* o tenedor *m* (*de un giro*)
pay envelope *s* sobre *m* con el jornal; jornal *m*, salario
payer ['pe.ər] *s* pagador *m*
pay load *s* carga útil
pay'mas'ter *s* pagador *m*
payment ['pemənt] *s* pago; castigo
pay roll *s* nómina, hoja de paga
pay station *s* teléfono público
pd. *abbr* **paid**
p.d. *abbr* **per diem, potential difference**
pea [pi] *s* guisante *m*, chícharo
peace [pis] *s* paz *f*; **to make peace with** hacer las paces con
peaceable ['pisəbəl] *adj* pacífico
peaceful ['pisfəl] *adj* tranquilo, pacífico, sosegado
peace'mak'er *s* iris *m* de paz
peace of mind *s* serenidad del espíritu
peace pipe *s* pipa ceremonial (*de los pieles rojas*)
peach [pitʃ] *s* melocotón *m*; (slang) persona o cosa admirables
peach tree *s* melocotonero
peach·y ['pitʃi] *adj* (*comp* **-ier**; *super* **-iest**) (slang) estupendo, magnífico
pea'cock' *s* pavo real, pavón *m*; (fig) pinturero
peak [pik] *s* pico, cima, cumbre *f*; punta, extremo; máximo; (*of a cap*) visera; (*of a curve*) cresta; (elec) pico
peak hour *s* hora punta
peak load *s* (elec) carga de punta
peal [pil] *s* fragor *m*; estruendo; (*of bells*) repique *m*; juego de campanas ‖ *intr* repicar; resonar
peal of laughter *s* carcajada
peal of thunder *s* trueno
pea'nut' *s* cacahuete *m*, aráquida
pear [per] *s* pera
pearl [pʌrl] *s* margarita, perla; (*of running water*) murmullo ‖ *tr* aljofarar
pearl oyster *s* madreperla
pear tree *s* peral *m*
peasant ['pezənt] *adj* & *s* campesino, rústico
pea'shoot'er *s* cerbatana, bodoquera
pea soup *s* sopa de guisantes; (coll) neblina espesa y amarillenta

peat [pit] *s* turba
pebble ['pebəl] *s* china, guija ‖ *tr* agranelar (*el cuero*)
peck [pek] *s* medida de áridos (*nueve litros*); montón *m*; picotazo; beso dado de mala gana ‖ *tr* picotear ‖ *intr* picotear; (coll) comer melindrosamente; **to peck at** querer picar; regañar constantemente; (coll) comer melindrosamente
peculate ['pekjə,let] *tr* & *intr* malversar
peculiar [pɪ'kjuljər] *adj* peculiar; singular, raro; excéntrico
pedagogue ['pedə,gɑg] *s* pedagogo; dómine *m*, pedante *m*
pedagogy ['pedə,godʒi] o ['pedə,gɑdʒi] *s* pedagogía
ped·al ['pedəl] *s* pedal *m* ‖ *v* (*pret* & *pp* **-aled** o **-alled**; *ger* **-aling** o **-alling**) *tr* impulsar pedaleando ‖ *intr* pedalear
pedant ['pedənt] *s* pedante *mf*
pedantic [pɪ'dæntɪk] *adj* pedantesco
pedant·ry ['pedəntri] *s* (*pl* **-ries**) pedantería
peddle ['pedəl] *tr* ir vendiendo de puerta en puerta; traer y llevar (*chismes*); vender (*favores*) ‖ *intr* ser buhonero
peddler ['pedlər] *s* buhonero
pedestal ['pedɪstəl] *s* pedestal *m*
pedestrian [pɪ'destrɪ·ən] *adj* pedestre ‖ *s* peatón *m*
pediatrics [,pidɪ'ætrɪks] o [,pedɪ'ætrɪks] *ssg* pediatría
pedigree ['pedɪ,gri] *s* árbol genealógico; ascendencia; fuente *f*, origen *m*
pediment ['pedɪmənt] *s* frontón *m*
peek [pik] *s* mirada rápida y furtiva ‖ *intr* mirar a hurtadillas
peel [pil] *s* cáscara, pellejo ‖ *tr* pelar ‖ *intr* pelarse
peep [pip] *s* mirada a hurtadillas; (*of chickens*) pío ‖ *intr* mirar a hurtadillas; piar (*los pollos*)
peep'hole' *s* atisbadero; (*in a door*) mirilla, ventanillo
peep show *s* mundonuevo; (slang) vistas sicalípticas
peer [pɪr] *s* par *m* ‖ *intr* mirar fijando la vista de cerca; **to peer at** mirar con ojos de miope; **to peer into** mirar hacia lo interior de, escudriñar
peerless ['pɪrlɪs] *adj* sin par
peeve [piv] *s* (coll) cojijo ‖ *tr* (coll) enojar, irritar
peevish ['pivɪʃ] *adj* cojijoso, displicente
peg [peg] *s* clavija, claveta, estaquilla; **to take down a peg** (coll) bajar los humos a ‖ *v* (*pret* & *pp* **pegged**; *ger* **pegging**) *tr* enclavijar; señalar con clavijas; fijar (*precios*) ‖ *intr* trabajar con ahinco; **to peg away at** afanarse en
peg leg *s* pata de palo
peg top *s* peonza; **peg tops** pantalones anchos de caderas y perniles ajustados
Peking ['pi'kɪŋ] *s* Pequín

Peking·ese [ˌpikɪˈniz] adj pequinés || s (pl -ese) pequinés m

pelf [pɛlf] s dinero mal ganado

pell-mell [ˈpɛlˈmɛl] adj tumultuoso || adv atropelladamente

Peloponnesian [ˌpɛləpəˈniʃən] adj & s peloponense mf

Peloponnesus [ˌpɛləpəˈnisəs] s Peloponeso

Pelops [ˈpilɑps] s Pélope m

pelota [pɛˈlotə] s pelota vasca

pelt [pɛlt] s pellejo; golpe violento; (of a person) (hum) pellejo || tr golpear violentamente; apedrear || intr golpear violentamente; caer con fuerza (el granizo, la lluvia, etc.); apresurarse

pen. abbr **peninsula**

pen [pɛn] s pluma; corral m, redil m; **the pen and the sword** las letras y las armas || v (pret & pp **penned**; ger **penning**) tr escribir (con pluma), redactar || v (pret & pp **penned** o **pent** [pɛnt]) tr acorralar, encerrar

penalize [ˈpinəˌlaɪz] tr penar; (sport) sancionar

penal·ty [ˈpɛnəlti] s (pl -ties) pena; (for late payment) recargo; (sport) sanción; **under penalty of** so pena de

penance [ˈpɛnəns] s penitencia; **to do penance** hacer penitencia

penchant [ˈpɛnʃənt] s afición, inclinación, tendencia

pen·cil [ˈpɛnsəl] s lápiz m; (of light) pincel m, haz m || v (pret & pp **-ciled** o **-cilled**; ger **-ciling** o **-cilling**) tr marcar con lápiz; (med) pincelar

pencil sharpener s afilalápices m, cortalápices m

pendent [ˈpɛndənt] adj pendiente; sobresaliente || s medallón m; (earring) pendiente m

pending [ˈpɛndɪŋ] adj pendiente || prep hasta; durante

pendulum [ˈpɛndʒələm] s péndulo; (of a clock) péndola

pendulum bob s lenteja

penetrate [ˈpɛnɪˌtret] tr & intr penetrar

penguin [ˈpɛŋgwɪn] s pingüino, pájaro bobo

pen'hold'er s (handle) portaplumas m; (box) plumero

penicillin [ˌpɛnɪˈsɪlɪn] s penicilina

peninsula [pəˈnɪnsələ] s península

peninsular [pəˈnɪnsələr] adj & s peninsular mf || **Peninsular** adj & s (Iberian) peninsular mf

penitence [ˈpɛnɪtəns] s penitencia

penitent [ˈpɛnɪtənt] adj & s penitente mf

pen'knife' s (pl -knives) navaja, cortaplumas m

penmanship [ˈpɛnmənˌʃɪp] s caligrafía; (hand of a person) letra

pen name s seudónimo

pennant [ˈpɛnənt] s gallardete m

penniless [ˈpɛnɪlɪs] adj pelón, sin dinero

pennon [ˈpɛnən] s pendón m

pen·ny [ˈpɛni] s (pl -nies) (U.S.A.)

centavo || s (pl **pence** [pɛns]) (Brit) penique m

pen'ny-weight' s peso de 24 granos

pen pal s (coll) amigo por correspondencia

pen point s punta de la pluma; puntilla de la pluma fuente

pension [ˈpɛnʃən] s pensión, jubilación || tr pensionar, jubilar

pensioner [ˈpɛnʃənər] s pensionista mf; **pensioners** clases pasivas

pensive [ˈpɛnsɪv] adj pensativo; melancólico

Pentecost [ˈpɛntɪˌkɑst] o [ˈpɛntɪˌkɑst] s el Pentecostés

penthouse [ˈpɛntˌhaus] s alpende m, colgadizo; casa de azotea

pent-up [ˈpɛntˌʌp] adj contenido, reprimido

penult [ˈpinʌlt] s penúltima

penum·bra [pɪˈnʌmbrə] s (pl **-brae** [bri] o **-bras**) penumbra

penurious [pɪˈnurɪəs] adj (stingy) tacaño, mezquino; (poor) pobre, indigente

penury [ˈpɛnjəri] s tacañería, mezquindad; pobreza, miseria

pen'wip'er s limpiaplumas m

people [ˈpipəl] spl gente f; personas; gente del pueblo; se, p.ej., **people say** se dice || ssg (pl **peoples**) pueblo, nación || tr poblar

pep [pɛp] s (slang) ánimo, brío, vigor m || v (pret & pp **pepped**; ger **pepping**) tr — **to pep up** (slang) animar, dar vigor a

pepper [ˈpɛpər] s (spice) pimienta; (plant and fruit) pimiento || tr sazonar con pimienta; (with bullets) acribillar; salpicar

pep'per·box' s pimentero

pep'per·mint' s (plant) menta piperita; esencia de menta; pastilla de menta

per [pʌr] prep por; as **per** según

perambulator [pərˈæmbjəˌletər] s cochecillo de niño

per capita [pər ˈkæpɪtə] por cabeza, por persona

perceive [pərˈsiv] tr percibir

per cent o **percent** [pərˈsɛnt] por ciento

percentage [pərˈsɛntɪdʒ] s porcentaje m; (slang) provecho, ventaja

perception [pərˈsɛpʃən] s percepción; comprensión, penetración

perch [pʌrtʃ] s percha, rama, varilla; sitio o posición elevada; (fish) perca || tr colocar en un sitio algo elevado || intr sentarse en un sitio algo elevado; posar (un ave)

percolator [ˈpʌrkəˌletər] s cafetera filtradora

per diem [pər ˈdaɪəm] por día

perdition [pərˈdɪʃən] s perdición

perennial [pəˈrɛnɪəl] adj perenne; (bot) vivaz || s planta vivaz

perfect [ˈpʌrfɪkt] adj & s perfecto || [pərˈfɛkt] tr perfeccionar

perfidious [pərˈfɪdɪəs] adj pérfido

perfi·dy [ˈpʌrfɪdi] s (pl -dies) perfidia

perforate [ˈpʌrfəˌret] tr perforar

perforce [pərˈfors] adv por fuerza, necesariamente

perform [pər'fɔrm] *tr* ejecutar; (theat) representar ‖ *intr* ejecutar; funcionar (*p.ej., una máquina*)

performance [pər'fɔrməns] *s* ejecución; representación; funcionamiento; (theat) función

performer [pər'fɔrmər] *s* ejecutante *mf*; actor *m*; acróbata *mf*

perfume ['pʌrfjum] *s* perfume *m* ‖ [pər'fjum] *tr* perfumar

perfunctory [pər'fʌŋktəri] *adj* hecho sin cuidado, hecho a la ligera; indiferente, negligente

perhaps [pər'hæps] *adv* acaso, tal vez, quizá

per·il ['pɛrəl] *s* peligro ‖ *v* (*pret & pp* -iled o -illed; *ger* -iling o -illing) *tr* poner en peligro

perilous ['pɛrɪləs] *adj* peligroso

period ['pɪrɪ·əd] *s* período; (*in school*) hora; (gram) punto; (sport) división

period costume *s* traje *m* de época

periodic [,pɪrɪ'ɑdɪk] *adj* periódico

periodical [,pɪrɪ'ɑdɪkəl] *adj* periódico ‖ *s* periódico, revista periódica

peripher·y [pə'rɪfəri] *s* (*pl* -ies) periferia

periscope ['pɛrɪ,skop] *s* periscopio

perish ['pɛrɪʃ] *intr* perecer

perishable ['pɛrɪʃəbəl] *adj* perecedero; (*merchandise*) corruptible

periwig ['pɛrɪ,wɪg] *s* perico

perjure ['pʌrdʒər] *tr* hacer (*a una persona*) quebrantar el juramento; **to perjure oneself** perjurarse

perju·ry ['pʌrdʒəri] *s* (*pl* -ries) perjurio

perk [pʌrk] *tr* alzar (*la cabeza*); aguzar (*las orejas*) ‖ *intr* pavonearse; engalanarse; **to perk up** reanimarse, sentirse mejor

permanence ['pʌrmənəns] *s* permanencia

permanen·cy ['pʌrmənənsi] *s* (*pl* -cies) permanencia; persona, cosa o posición permanentes

permanent ['pʌrmənənt] *adj* permanente ‖ *s* permanente *f*, ondulación permanente

permanent tenure *s* inamovilidad

permanent way *s* (rr) material fijo

permeate ['pʌrmɪ,et] *tr & intr* penetrar

permission [pər'mɪʃən] *s* permisión

per·mit ['pʌrmɪt] *s* permiso; cédula de aduana ‖ [pər'mɪt] *v* (*pret & pp* -mitted; *ger* -mitting) *tr* permitir

permute [pər'mjut] *tr* permutar

pernicious [pər'nɪʃəs] *adj* pernicioso

pernickety [pər'nɪkɪti] *adj* (coll) descontentadizo, quisquilloso

perorate ['pɛrə,ret] *intr* perorar

peroration [,pɛrə'reʃən] *s* peroración

peroxide [pər'ɑksaɪd] *s* peróxido; peróxido de hidrógeno

peroxide blonde *s* rubia oxigenada

perpendicular [,pʌrpən'dɪkjələr] *adj & s* perpendicular *f*

perpetrate ['pʌrpɪ,tret] *tr* perpetrar

perpetual [pər'pet/u·əl] *adj* perpetuo

perpetuate [pər'pet/u,et] *tr* perpetuar

perplex [pər'plɛks] *tr* dejar perplejo

perplexed [pər'plɛkst] *adj* perplejo

perplexi·ty [pər'plɛksiti] *s* (*pl* -ties) perplejidad; problema *m*

per se [pər 'si] por sí mismo, en sí mismo, esencialmente

persecute ['pʌrsɪ,kjut] *tr* perseguir

persecution [,pʌrsɪ'kju/ən] *s* persecución

persevere [,pʌrsɪ'vɪr] *intr* perseverar

Persian ['pʌrʒən] *adj & s* persa *mf*

persimmon [pər'sɪmən] *s* placaminero

persist [pər'sɪst] o [pər'zɪst] *intr* persistir

persistent [pər'sɪstənt] o [pər'zɪstənt] *adj* persistente; (*insistent*) porfiado; (*e.g., headache*) pertinaz

person ['pʌrsən] *s* persona; **no person** nadie

personage ['pʌrsənɪdʒ] *s* personaje *m*; persona

personal ['pʌrsənəl] *adj* personal; de uso personal ‖ *s* nota de sociedad; (*in a newspaper*) remitido

personali·ty [,pʌrsə'næliti] *s* (*pl* -ties) personalidad

personality cult *s* culto a la personalidad

personal property *s* bienes *mpl* muebles

personi·fy [pər'sɑnɪ,faɪ] *v* (*pret & pp* -fied) *tr* personificar

personnel [,pʌrsə'nɛl] *s* personal *m*

perspective [pər'spɛktɪv] *s* perspectiva

perspicacious [,pʌrspɪ'ke/əs] *adj* perspicaz

perspire [pər'spaɪr] *intr* sudar, transpirar

persuade [pər'swed] *tr* persuadir

persuasion [pər'sweʒən] *s* persuasión; creencia religiosa; creencia fuerte

pert [pʌrt] *adj* atrevido, descarado; (coll) animado, vivo

pertain [pər'ten] *intr* pertenecer; **pertaining to** perteneciente a

pertinacious [,pʌrtɪ'ne/əs] *adj* pertinaz

pertinent ['pʌrtɪnənt] *adj* pertinente

perturb [pər'tʌrb] *tr* perturbar

Peru [pə'ru] *s* el Perú

perusal [pə'ruzəl] *s* lectura cuidadosa

peruse [pə'ruz] *tr* leer con atención

Peruvian [pə'ruvɪ·ən] *adj & s* peruano

pervade [pər'ved] *tr* penetrar, esparcirse por, extenderse por

perverse [pər'vʌrs] *adj* perverso; avieso, díscolo; contumaz

perversion [pər'vʌrʒən] *s* perversión

perversi·ty [pər'vʌrsiti] *s* (*pl* -ties) perversidad; indocilidad; contumacia

pervert ['pʌrvərt] *s* renegado, apóstata; pervertido ‖ [pər'vʌrt] *tr* pervertir; emplear mal (*p.ej., los talentos que uno tiene*)

pes·ky ['pɛski] *adj* (*comp* -kier; *super* -kiest) (coll) cargante, molesto

pessimism ['pɛsɪ,mɪzəm] *s* pesimismo

pessimist ['pɛsɪmɪst] *s* pesimista *mf*

pessimistic [,pɛsɪ'mɪstɪk] *adj* pesimista

pest [pɛst] *s* peste *f*; insecto nocivo; (*misfortune*) plaga; (*annoying person, bore*) machaca *mf*

pester ['pɛstər] *tr* molestar, importunar

pest'house' s lazareto, hospital m de contagiosos
pesticide ['pestɪˌsaɪd] s pesticida m
pestiferous [pɛs'tɪfərəs] adj pestífero; (coll) engorroso, molesto
pestilence ['pestɪləns] s pestilencia
pestle ['pesəl] s mano f de almirez
pet [pet] s animal mimado, animal casero; niño mimado; favorito; enojo pasajero || v (pret & pp **petted**; ger **petting**) tr acariciar, mimar || intr (slang) besuquearse
petal ['petəl] s pétalo
petard [pɪ'tard] s petardo
pet'cock' s llave f de desagüe, llave de purga
Peter ['pitər] s Pedro; **to rob Peter to pay Paul** desnudar a un santo para vestir a otro
petition [pɪ'tɪʃən] s petición; (formal request signed by a number of people) memorial m, instancia, solicitud || tr suplicar; dirigir una instancia a, solicitar
pet name s nombre m de cariño
Petrarch ['pitrark] s Petrarca m
petri·fy ['petrɪˌfaɪ] v (pret & pp **-fied**) tr petrificar || intr petrificarse
petrol ['petrəl] s (Brit) gasolina
petroleum [pɪ'trolɪ·əm] s petróleo
pet shop s pajarería
petticoat ['petɪˌkot] s enaguas; (woman, girl) (slang) falda
pet·ty ['petɪ] adj (comp **-tier**; super **-tiest**) insignificante, pequeño; mezquino; intolerante
petty cash s caja de menores, efectivo para gastos menores
petty larceny s ratería, hurto
petty officer s (naut) suboficial m
petulant ['petʃələnt] adj malhumorado, enojadizo
pew [pju] s banco de iglesia
pewter ['pjutər] s peltre m; vajilla de peltre
pfd. abbr **preferred**
Phaëthon ['fe·ɪθən] s Faetón m
phalanx ['felæŋks] o ['fælæŋks] s falange f
phantasm ['fæntæzəm] s fantasma m
phantom ['fæntəm] s fantasma m
Pharaoh ['fero] s Faraón m
pharisee ['færɪˌsi] s fariseo || **Pharisee** s fariseo
pharmaceutical [ˌfarmə'sutɪkəl] adj farmacéutico
pharmacist ['farməsɪst] s farmacéutico
pharma·cy ['farməsi] s (pl **-cies**) farmacia
pharynx ['færɪŋks] s faringe f
phase [fez] s fase f || tr poner en fase; llevar a cabo a etapas uniformes; (coll) inquietar, molestar; **to phase out** deshacer paulatinamente
pheasant ['fezənt] s faisán m
phenobarbital [ˌfino'barbɪˌtæl] s fenobarbital m
phenomenal [fɪ'namɪnəl] adj fenomenal
phenome·non [fɪ'namɪˌnan] s (pl **-na** [nə]) fenómeno
phial ['faɪ·əl] s frasco pequeño
Phidias ['fɪdɪ·əs] s Fidias m

philanderer [fɪ'lændərər] s galanteador m, tenorio
philanthropist [fɪ'lænθrəpɪst] s filántropo
philanthro·py [fɪ'lænθrəpi] s (pl **-pies**) filantropía
philatelist [fɪ'lætəlɪst] s filatelista mf
philately [fɪ'lætəli] s filatelia
Philip ['fɪlɪp] s Felipe m; (of Macedon) Filipo
Philippine ['fɪlɪˌpin] adj filipino || **Philippines** spl Islas Filipinas
Philistine [fɪ'lɪstin], ['fɪlɪˌstin] o ['fɪlɪˌstaɪn] adj & s filisteo
philologist [fɪ'lalədʒɪst] s filólogo
philology [fɪ'lalədʒi] s filología
philosopher [fɪ'lasəfər] s filósofo
philosophic(al) [ˌfɪlə'safɪk(əl)] adj filosófico
philoso·phy [fɪ'lasəfi] s (pl **-phies**) filosofía
philter ['fɪltər] s filtro
phlebitis [flɪ'baɪtɪs] s flebitis f
phlegm [flem] s flema f, gargajo; **to cough up phlegm** gargajear
phlegmatic(al) [fleg'mætɪk(əl)] adj flemático
Phoebe ['fibi] s Febe f
Phoebus ['fibəs] s Febo
Phoenicia [fɪ'nɪʃə] o [fɪ'niʃə] s Fenicia
Phoenician [fɪ'nɪʃən] o [fɪ'niʃən] adj & s fenicio
phoenix ['finɪks] s fénix m
phone [fon] s (coll) teléfono; **to come o to go to the phone** acudir al teléfono, ponerse al aparato || tr & intr (coll) telefonear
phone call s llamada telefónica
phonetic [fo'netɪk] adj fonético
phonograph ['fonəˌgræf] o ['fonəˌgraf] s fonógrafo
phonology [fə'nalədʒi] s fonología
pho·ny ['foni] adj (comp **-nier**; super **-niest**) falso, contrahecho || s (pl **-nies**) (slang) farsa; (coll) farsante m
phosphate ['fasfet] s fosfato
phosphorescent [ˌfasfə'resənt] adj fosforescente
phospho·rus ['fasfərəs] s (pl **-ri** [ˌraɪ]) fósforo
pho·to ['foto] s (pl **-tos**) foto f
photoengraving [ˌfoto·ɛn'grevɪŋ] s fotograbado
photo finish s (sport) llegada a la meta, determinada mediante el fotofija
pho'to-fin'ish camera s fotofija m
photogenic [ˌfoto'dʒenɪk] adj fotogénico
photograph ['fotəˌgræf] o ['fotəˌgraf] s fotografía || tr & intr fotografiar
photographer [fə'tagrəfər] s fotógrafo
photography [fə'tagrəfi] s fotografía
photojournalism [ˌfoto'dʒɜrnəˌlɪzəm] s fotoperiodismo
pho'to-play' s fotodrama m
photostat ['fotəˌstæt] s (trademark) fotóstato || tr & intr fotostatar
phototube ['fotəˌtjub] o ['fotəˌtub] s fototubo
phrase [frez] s frase f || tr frasear
phrenology [frɪ'nalədʒi] s frenología

Phyllis ['fɪlɪs] s Filis f

phys. abbr **physical, physician, physics, physiology**

phys·ic ['fɪzɪk] s medicamento; purgante m || v (pret & pp **-icked;** ger **-icking**) tr curar; purgar

physical ['fɪzɪkəl] adj físico

physician [fɪ'zɪʃən] s médico

physicist ['fɪzɪsɪst] s físico

physics ['fɪzɪks] s física

physiognomy [,fɪzɪ'ɑgnəmɪ] o [,fɪzɪ'ɑnəmɪ] s fisonomía

physiological [,fɪzɪə'lɑdʒɪkəl] adj fisiológico

physiology [,fɪzɪ'ɑlədʒɪ] s fisiología

physique [fɪ'zɪk] s físico, talle m, exterior m

pi [paɪ] s (math) pi f; (typ) pastel m || v (pret & pp **pied;** ger **piing**) tr (typ) empastelar

pian·o [pɪ'æno] s (pl **-os**) piano

picaresque [,pɪkə'resk] adj picaresco

picayune [,pɪkə'jun] adj de poca monta, mezquino

piccadil·ly [,pɪkə'dɪlɪ] s (pl **-lies**) cuello de pajarita

piccol·o ['pɪkə,lo] s (pl **-los**) flautín m

pick [pɪk] s (tool) pico; (choice) selección; (choicest) flor f || tr escoger; recoger (p.ej., flores); recolectar (p.ej., algodón); romper (el hielo) con un picahielos; escarbarse (los dientes); descañonar, desplumar (un ave); hurgarse (la nariz); rascarse (una cicatriz, un grano); roer (un hueso); mondar (las frutas); falsear, forzar (una cerradura); armar (una pendencia); herir (las cuerdas de un instrumento); buscar (defectos); hurtar de (los bolsillos); **to pick out** entresacar; **to pick someone to pieces** (coll) no dejarle a uno un hueso sano; **to pick up** recoger; recobrar (ánimo; velocidad); descolgar (el receptor); hallar por casualidad; aprender con la práctica; aprender de oídas; invitar a subir a un coche; entablar conservación con (sin presentación previa); captar (una señal de radio) || intr comer melindrosamente; escoger esmeradamente; **to pick at** comer melindrosamente; tomarla con, regañar; **to pick on** escoger; (coll) regañar; (coll) molestar; **to pick over** ir revolviendo y examinando; **to pick up** (coll) ir mejor, sentirse mejor; recobrar velocidad

pick'ax' s zapapico

picket ['pɪkɪt] s (stake, pale) piquete m; (of strikers; of soldiers) piquete m || tr poner un cordón de piquetes a || intr servir de piquete

picket fence s cerca de estacas

picket line s línea de piquetes

pickle ['pɪkəl] s encurtido; escabeche m, salmuera; (coll) apuro, aprieto || tr encurtir; escabechar

pick-me-up ['pɪkmɪ,ʌp] s (coll) tentempié m; (coll) trago fortificante

pick'pock'et s carterista m, ratero

pick'up' s recolección; (of a motor) recobro; (of an automobile) aceleración; (elec) pick-up, fonocaptor m

pic·nic ['pɪknɪk] s jira, partida de campo || v (pret & pp **-nicked;** ger **-nicking**) intr hacer una jira al campo, merendar en el campo

pictorial [pɪk'torɪəl] adj gráfico; ilustrado || s revista ilustrada

picture ['pɪktʃər] s cuadro; retrato; imagen f; lámina, grabado; fotografía; película; pintura || tr dibujar; pintar; describir; **to picture to oneself** representarse

picture gallery s galería de pinturas

picture post card s postal ilustrada

picture show s exhibición de pinturas; cine m

picture signal s videoseñal f

picturesque [,pɪktʃə'resk] adj pintoresco

picture tube s tubo de imagen, tubo de televisión

picture window s ventana panorámica

piddling ['pɪdlɪŋ] adj de poca monta, insignificante

pie [paɪ] s pastel m; (bird) picaza; (typ) pastel m || v (pret & pp **pied;** ger **pieing**) tr (typ) empastelar

piece [pis] s (fragment; section of cloth) pedazo; (part of a machine; drama; single composition of music; coin; figure or block used in checkers, chess, etc.) pieza; (of land) lote m, parcela; **a piece of advice** un consejo; **a piece of baggage** un bulto; **a piece of furniture** un mueble; **to break to pieces** despedazar, hacer pedazos; despedazarse; **to fall to pieces** desbaratarse, caer en ruina; **to give someone a piece of one's mind** decirle a uno su parecer con toda franqueza; **to go to pieces** desvencijarse; darse a la desesperación; ir al desastre (un negocio); sufrir un ataque de nervios; perder por completo la salud; **to pick someone to pieces** (coll) no dejarle a uno un hueso sano || tr formar juntando piezas; remendar || intr (coll) comer a deshora

piece'work' s destajo, trabajo a destajo

piece'work'er s destajero, destajista mf

pier [pɪr] s muelle m; (of a bridge) estribo, sostén m; (of a harbor) rompeolas m; (wall between two openings) (archit) entrepaño

pierce [pɪrs] tr agujerear, horadar, taladrar; atravesar, traspasar; picar, pinchar, punzar; (fig) traspasar (de dolor) || intr penetrar, entrar a la fuerza

piercing ['pɪrsɪŋ] adj agudo, penetrante, desgarrador; (pain) lancinante

pier glass s espejo de cuerpo entero

pie·ty ['paɪətɪ] s (pl **-ties**) piedad, devoción

piffle ['pɪfəl] s (coll) disparates mpl, música celestial

pig [pɪg] s cerdo; (young hog) lechón m; (domestic hog) puerco, cochino; carne f de puerco; (metal) lingote m; (person who acts like a pig) (coll) marrano, cochino

pigeon ['pɪdʒən] s paloma

pi'geon·hole' s hornilla, casilla de paloma; casilla || tr encasillar

pigeon house s palomar m

piggish ['pɪgɪʃ] adj glotón, voraz

pig'gy·back' adv a cuestas, en hombros

pig'-head'ed adj terco, cabezudo

pig iron s arrabio, hierro en lingotes

pigment ['pɪgmənt] s pigmento || tr pigmentar || intr pigmentarse

pig'pen' s pocilga; (fig) pocilga, corral m de vacas

pig'skin' s piel f de cerdo; (coll) balón m (con que se juega al fútbol)

pig'sty' s (pl -sties) pocilga

pig'tail' s coleta, trenza; (of tobacco) andullo

pike [paɪk] s pica; (of an arrow) punta; carretera; camino de barrera; (fish) lucio

piker ['paɪkər] s (slang) persona de poco fuste

Pilate ['paɪlət] s Pilatos m

pile [paɪl] s pila, montón m; (stake) pilote m; lanilla, pelusa; pira; (elec, phys) pila; (coll) caudal m; **piles** almorranas || tr apilar, amontonar || intr apilarse, amontonarse **to pile in** o **into** entrar atropelladamente en; entrar todos en; subir todos a (p.ej., un coche)

pile driver s martinete m

pilfer ['pɪlfər] tr & intr ratear

pilgrim ['pɪlgrɪm] s peregrino, romero

pilgrimage ['pɪlgrɪmɪdʒ] s peregrinación, romería

pill [pɪl] s píldora; mal trago, sinsabor m; (coll) persona molesta

pillage ['pɪlɪdʒ] s pillaje m, saqueo || tr & intr pillar, saquear

pillar ['pɪlər] s pilar m; **from pillar to post** de acá para allá sin objeto determinado

pillo·ry ['pɪləri] s (pl -ries) picota || v (pret & pp -ried) tr empicotar; (fig) motejar, poner en ridículo

pillow ['pɪlo] s almohada

pil'low·case' o **pil'low·slip'** s funda de almohada

pilot ['paɪlət] s piloto; (of a harbor) práctico; (of a gas range) mechero encendedor; (rr) trompa, delantera || tr pilotar; conducir

pimp [pɪmp] s alcahuete m

pimple ['pɪmpəl] s barro, grano

pim·ply ['pɪmpli] adj (comp -plier; super -pliest) granujoso

pin [pɪn] s alfiler m; (e.g., for a necktie) prendedero; (peg) clavija; (e.g., to hold scissors together) clavillo, clavito; (bowling) bolo; **to be on pins and needles** estar en espinas || v (pret & pp pinned; ger pinning) tr alfilerar; clavar, fijar, sujetar; **to pin something on someone** (coll) acusarle a uno de una cosa; **to pin up** recoger y apuntar con alfileres; fijar en la pared con alfileres

pinafore ['pɪnə,for] s delantal m de niño

pin'ball' s billar romano, bagatela

pince-nez ['pæns,ne] s lentes mpl de nariz, lentes de pinzas

pincers ['pɪnsərz] ssg o spl pinzas

pinch [pɪntʃ] s pellizco; (of hunger) tormento; (slang) arresto; (slang) hurto, robo; **in a pinch** en un aprieto; en caso necesario || tr pellizcar; coger (los dedos, p.ej., en una puerta); apretar (p.ej., el zapato a una persona); contraer (el frío la cara de uno); limitar los gastos de; (slang) arrestar, prender; (slang) hurtar, robar || intr apretar; economizar, privarse de lo necesario

pinchers ['pɪntʃərz] ssg o spl var of **pincers**

pin'cush'ion s acerico

Pindar ['pɪndər] s Píndaro

pine [paɪn] s pino || intr languidecer; **to pine away** consumirse; **to pine for** penar por

pine'ap'ple s ananás m, piña

pine cone s piña

pine needle s pinocha

ping [pɪŋ] s silbido de bala || intr silbar (una bala); silbar como una bala

pin'head' s cabecilla de alfiler; cosa muy pequeña o insignificante; (coll) bobalicón m

pink [pɪŋk] adj rosado, sonrosado || s estado perfecto; comunistoide mf; (bot) clavel m, clavellina

pin money s alfileres mpl

pinnacle ['pɪnəkəl] s pináculo

pin'point' adj exacto, preciso || s punta de alfiler || tr & intr señalar con precisión

pin'prick' s alfilerazo

pinup girl ['pɪn,ʌp] s guapa

pin'wheel' s rueda de fuego, rueda giratoria de fuegos artificiales; (child's toy) rehilandera, ventolera

pioneer [,paɪə'nɪr] s pionero; (mil) zapador m || intr abrir nuevos caminos, explorar

pious ['paɪəs] adj pío, piadoso; mojigato; respetuoso

pip [pɪp] s (seed) pepita; (on a card, dice, etc.) punto; (vet) pepita

pipe [paɪp] s caño, conducto, tubo; (to smoke tobacco) pipa; (mus) pipa, caramillo, zampoña; (of an organ) cañón m || tr conducir por medio de tubos o cañerías; proveer de tuberías o cañerías || intr tocar el caramillo; **to pipe down** (slang) callarse

pipe cleaner s limpiapipas m

pipe dream s esperanza imposible, castillo en el aire

pipe line s cañería, tubería; oleoducto; fuente f de informes confidenciales

pipe organ s (mus) órgano

piper ['paɪpər] s flautista m; gaitero; **to pay the piper** pagar los vidrios rotos

pipe wrench s llave f para tubos

pippin ['pɪpɪn] s (apple) camuesa; (tree) camueso, (slang) real moza

piquancy ['pikənsi] s picante m

piquant ['pikənt] adj picante

pique [pik] s pique m, resentimiento || tr picar, enojar; despertar, excitar

Piraeus [paɪ'riəs] s el Pireo

pirate ['paɪrɪt] s pirata m || tr pillar,

robar; publicar fraudulentamente ‖ *intr* piratear

pirouette [‚pɪru'et] *s* pirueta ‖ *intr* piruetear

pistol ['pɪstəl] *s* pistola

piston ['pɪstən] *s* (mach) émbolo, pistón *m*; (mus) pistón *m*

piston displacement *s* cilindrada

piston ring *s* anillo de émbolo, aro de émbolo, segmento de émbolo

piston rod *s* vástago de émbolo

piston stroke *s* carrera de émbolo

pit [pɪt] *s* hoyo; (*in the skin*) cacaraña; (*of certain fruit*) hueso; (*for cockfights, etc.*) cancha, reñidero; (*of the stomach*) boca; abismo, infierno; (min) pozo; (theat) foso ‖ *v* (*pret & pp* **pitted**; *ger* **pitting**) *tr* marcar con hoyos; dejar hoyoso (*el rostro*); deshuesar (*p.ej., una ciruela*)

pitch [pɪtʃ] *s* (*black sticky substance*) pez *f*; echada, lanzamiento; cosa lanzada; pelota lanzada; (*of a boat*) arfada, cabezada; (*of a roof*) pendiente *f*; (*of, e.g., a screw*) paso; (*of a winding*) (elec) paso; (mus) tono, altura; (fig) grado, extremo; (coll) bombo, elogio ‖ *tr* echar, lanzar; elevar (*el heno*) con la horquilla; armar o plantar (*una tienda de campaña*); embrear; (mus) graduar el tono de ‖ *intr* caerse, caer de cabeza; bajar en declive, inclinarse; arfar, cabecear (*un buque*); **to pitch in** (coll) poner manos a la obra; (coll) comenzar a comer

pitch accent *s* acento de altura

pitcher ['pɪtʃər] *s* jarro; (*in baseball*) lanzador *m*

pitch'fork' *s* horca, horquilla; **to rain pitchforks** (coll) llover a cántaros

pitch pipe *s* (mus) diapasón *m*

pit'fall' *s* callejo, trampa; (*danger for the unwary*) escollo, atascadero

pith [pɪθ] *s* médula; (*essential part*) (fig) médula; (fig) fuerza, vigor *m*

pith·y ['pɪθi] ! ['pɪθi] *adj* (*comp* **-ier**; *super* **-lest**) medular; enérgico, expresivo

pitiful ['pɪtɪfəl] *adj* lastimoso; compasivo; despreciable

pitiless ['pɪtɪlɪs] *adj* despiadado, empedernido, incompasivo

pit·y ['pɪti] *s* (*pl* **-ies**) piedad, compasión, lástima; **for pity's sake!** ¡por piedad!; **to have o to take pity on** tener piedad de, apiadarse de; **what a pity!** ¡qué lástima!, ¡qué pena! ‖ *v* (*pret & pp* **-ied**) *tr* apiadarse de, compadecer

pivot ['pɪvət] *s* pivote *m*, gorrón *m*, eje *m* de rotación; (fig) eje *m* ‖ *intr* pivotar; **to pivot on** girar sobre; depender de

placard ['plækard] *s* cartel *m* ‖ *tr* fijar carteles en; fijar (*un anuncio*) en sitio público; publicar por medio de carteles

place [ples] *s* sitio, lugar *m*; (*of business*) local *m*; (*job*) puesto; grado, rango; **in no place** en ninguna parte; **in place of** en lugar de; **out of place** fuera de su lugar; fuera de propósito; **to be looking for a place to live**

buscar piso; **to take place** tener lugar ‖ *tr* poner, colocar; acordarse bien de; dar empleo a; prestar (*dinero*) a interés ‖ *intr* colocarse (*un caballo en las carreras*)

place·bo [plə'sibo] *s* (*pl* **-bos o -boes**) placebo

place card *s* tarjetita con el nombre (*que indica la colocación de uno en la mesa*)

placement ['plesmənt] *s* colocación

place name *s* nombre *m* de lugar, topónimo

placid ['plæsɪd] *adj* plácido, tranquilo

plagiarism ['pledʒə‚rɪzəm] *s* plagio

plagiarize ['pledʒə‚raɪz] *tr* plagiar

plague [pleg] *s* peste *f*, plaga; (*great public calamity*) plaga ‖ *tr* apestar, plagar; atormentar, molestar

plaid [plæd] *s* (*cloth*) tartán *m*; cuadros a la escocesa

plain [plen] *adj* llano, claro, evidente; abierto, franco; ordinario; feo; humilde; solo, natural; **in plain English** sin rodeos; **in plain sight o view** en plena vista ‖ *s* llano, llanura

plain clothes *spl* traje *m* de calle, traje de paisano

plainclothesman ['plen'kloðz‚mæn] *s* (*pl* **-men** [‚mɛn]) policía *m* que lleva traje de paisano

plain omelet *s* tortilla a la francesa

plains·man ['plenzmən] *s* (*pl* **-men** [mən]) llanero

plaintiff ['plentɪf] *s* (law) demandante *mf*

plaintive ['plentɪv] *adj* quejumbroso

plan [plæn] *s* plan *m*, intento, proyecto; (*drawing, diagram*) plan *m*, plano; **to change one's plans** cambiar de proyecto ‖ *v* (*pret & pp* **planned**; *ger* **planning**) *tr* planear, planificar; **to plan to** proponerse ‖ *intr* hacer proyectos

plane [plen] *adj* plano ‖ *s* (*surface*) plano; aeroplano, avión *m*; (*of an airplane*) plano; (carp) cepillo; (*tree*) plátano ‖ *tr* cepillar ‖ *intr* viajar en aeroplano

plane sickness *s* mareo del aire, mal *m* de vuelo

planet ['plænɪt] *s* planeta *m*

plane tree *s* plátano

planing mill ['plenɪŋ] *s* taller *m* de cepillado

plank [plæŋk] *s* tabla gruesa, tablón *m*; artículo de un programa político ‖ *tr* entablar, entarimar

plant [plænt] o [plɑnt] *s* fábrica, taller *m*; (*of an automobile*) grupo motor; (*educational establishment*) plantel *m*; (bot) planta ‖ *tr* plantar; sembrar (*semillas*); inculcar (*doctrinas*); (slang) ocultar (*géneros robados*)

plantation [plæn'teʃən] *s* plantación, campo de plantas; (*estate cultivated by workers living on it*) hacienda

planter ['plæntər] *s* plantador *m*, cultivador *m*

plaster ['plæstər] o ['plɑstər] *s* (*gypsum*) yeso; (*mixture of lime, sand,* *water, etc.*) argamasa; (*coating*) enlucido; (*poultice*) emplasto || *tr* enyesar; argamasar; enlucir; emplastar; embadurnar; pegar (*anuncios*)

plas′ter·board′ *s* cartón *m* de yeso y fieltro

plaster cast *s* (surg) vendaje enyesado; (*sculp*) yeso

plaster of Paris *s* estuco de París

plastic [′plæstɪk] *adj* plástico || *s* (*substance*) plástico; (*art of modeling*) plástica

plate [plet] *s* (*dish*) plato; (*sheet of metal, etc.*), chapa, placa; vajilla de oro, vajilla de plata; (dentadura postiza, base *f* de la dentadura postiza; (baseball) puesto meta, puesto del batter; (anat, elec, electron, phot, zool) placa; (typ) clisé *m* || *tr* chapear, planchear; blindar; platear, dorar, niquelar (*por la galvanoplastia*); (typ) clisar

plateau [plæ′to] *s* meseta

plate glass *s* vidrio o cristal cilindrado

platen [′plætən] *s* rodillo

platform [′plæt ˌfɔrm] *s* plataforma *f*; (*of passenger station*) andén *m*; (*of freight station*) cargadero; (*of a speaker*) tribuna; (*political program*) plataforma

platform car *s* plataforma *f*

platinum [′plætɪnəm] *s* platino

platinum blonde *s* rubia platino

platitude [′plætɪˌtjud] o [′plætɪˌtud] *s* perogrullada, trivialidad

Plato [′pleto] *s* Platón *m*

platoon [plə′tun] *s* pelotón *m*

platter [′plætər] *s* fuente *f*; (slang) disco de fonógrafo

plausible [′plɔzɪbəl] *adj* aparente, especioso; bien hablado; (coll) creíble

play [ple] *s* juego; (*act or move in a game*) jugada; (*drama*) pieza; (*of water, colors, lights*) juego; (mach) huelgo, juego; **to give full play to** dar rienda suelta a || *tr* jugar (*p.ej., un naipe, una partida de juego*); jugar a (*p.ej., los naipes*); jugar con (*un contrario*); dar (*un chasco*); gastar (*una broma*); hacer (*una mala jugada*); dirigir (*agua, una manguera*); desempeñar (*un papel*); desempeñar el papel de; representar (*una obra dramática, un film*); apostar por (*un caballo*); tocar (*un instrumento, una pieza, un disco de fonógrafo*) || *intr* jugar; desempeñar un papel, representar; correr (*una fuente*); rielar (*la luz en la superficie del agua*); vagar (*p.ej., una sonrisa por los labios*); **to play out** rendirse; agotarse; acabarse; **to play safe** tomar sus precauciones; **to play sick** hacerse el enfermo; **to play up to** hacer la rueda a

play′back′ *s* lectura; aparato de lectura

play′bill′ *s* (*poster*) cartel *m*; (*of a play*) programa *m*

player piano [′ple·ər] *s* autopiano

playful [′plefəl] *adj* juguetón, retozón; dicho en broma

playgoer [′ple ˌgo·ər] *s* aficionado al teatro

play′ground′ *s* campo de juego; patio de recreo

play′house′ *s* casita de muñecas; teatro

playing card [′ple·ɪŋ] *s* naipe *m*

playing field *s* campo de deportes

play′mate′ *s* compañero de juego

play′-off′ *s* partido de desempate

play′pen′ *s* parque *m*, corral *m* (*para bebés*)

play′thing′ *s* juguete *m*

play′time′ *s* hora de recreo, hora de juego

playwright [′ple ˌraɪt] *s* dramaturgo, autor dramático

play′writ′ing *s* dramaturgia, dramática

plea [pli] *s* ruego, súplica; disculpa, excusa; (law) contestación a la demanda

plead [plid] *v* (*pret & pp* **pleaded** o **pled** [pled]) *tr* defender (*una causa*) || *intr* suplicar; abogar; **to plead guilty** confesarse culpable; **to plead not guilty** negar la acusación, declararse inocente

pleasant [′plezənt] *adj* agradable; simpático

pleasant·ry [′plezəntri] *s* (*pl* **-ries**) broma, chiste *m*, dicho gracioso

please [pliz] *tr & intr* gustar; **as you please** como Vd. quiera; **if you please** si me hace el favor; **please** + *inf* hágame Vd. el favor de + *inf*; **to be pleased to** alegrarse de, complacerse en; **to be pleased with** estar satisfecho de o con

pleasing [′plizɪŋ] *adj* agradable, grato

pleasure [′plezər] *s* placer *m*, gusto; **what is your pleasure?** ¿en qué puedo servirle?, ¿qué es lo que Vd. desea?; **with pleasure** con mucho gusto

pleasure seeker [′sikər] *s* amigo de los placeres

pleat [plit] *s* pliegue *m*, plisado || *tr* plegar, plisar

plebeian [plɪ′bi·ən] *adj & s* plebeyo

pledge [pledʒ] *s* empeño, prenda; (*vow*) voto, promesa; (*toast*) brindis *m*; **as a pledge of** en prenda de; **to take the pledge** comprometerse a no tomar bebidas alcohólicas || *tr* empeñar, prendar; dar (*la palabra*); brindar por

plentiful [′plentɪfəl] *adj* abundante, copioso

plenty [′plenti] *adv* (coll) completamente || *s* abundancia, copia; suficiencia

pleurisy [′plurɪsi] *s* pleuresía

pliable [′plaɪ·əbəl] *adj* flexible, plegable; dócil

pliers [′plaɪ·ərz] *ssg* o *spl* alicates *mpl*

plight [plaɪt] *s* estado, situación; apuro, aprieto; compromiso solemne || *tr* dar o empeñar (*su palabra*); **to plight one's troth** prometer fidelidad; dar palabra de casamiento

plod [plɑd] *v* (*pret & pp* **plodded**; *ger* **plodding**) *tr* recorrer (*un camino*) pausada y pesadamente || *intr* caminar pausada y pesadamente; trabajar laboriosamente

plot [plɑt] *s* complot *m*, conspiración; (*of a play or novel*) argumento, trama; parcela, solar *m;* cuadro de flores; cuadro de hortalizas; plano, mapa *m* ‖ *v* (*pret & pp* **plotted;** *ger* **plotting**) *tr* fraguar, tramar, urdir, maquinar; dividir en parcelas o solares; trazar el plano de; trazar, tirar (*líneas*) ‖ *intr* conspirar

plough [plaʊ] *s, tr & intr* var de plow

plover ['plʌvər] o ['plovər] *s* chorlito

plow [plaʊ] *s* arado; quitanieve *m* ‖ *tr* arar; surcar; quitar o barrer (*la nieve*); **to plow back** reinvertir (*ganancias*) ‖ *intr* arar; avanzar como un arado

plow-man ['plaʊmən] *s* (*pl* -**men** [mən]) arador *m*, yuguero

plow'share' *s* reja de arado

pluck [plʌk] *s* ánimo, coraje *m*, valor *m;* tirón *m* ‖ *tr* arrancar; coger (*flores*); desplumar (*un ave*); puntear (*p.ej., una guitarra*) ‖ *intr* dar un tirón; **to pluck up** recobrar ánimo

pluck·y ['plʌki] *adj* (*comp* -**ier;** *super* -**iest**) animoso, valiente

plug [plʌg] *s* taco, tarugo; boca de agua; tableta de tabaco; (*hat*) (slang) chistera; (elec) clavija, toma, ficha; (aut) bujía; (coll) rocín; (slang) elogio incidental ‖ *v* (*pret & pp* **plugged;** *ger* **plugging**) *tr* atarugar; calar (*un melón*); **to plug in** (elec) enchufar ‖ *intr* (coll) trabajar con ahinco

plum [plʌm] *s* (*tree*) ciruelo; (*fruit*) ciruela; (slang) turrón *m*, pingüe destino

plumage ['plumɪdʒ] *s* plumaje *m*

plumb [plʌm] *adj* vertical; (coll) completo ‖ *adv* a plomo; (coll) verticalmente; (coll) directamente ‖ *tr* aplomar; sondear

plumb bob *s* plomada

plumber ['plʌmər] *s* fontanero; (*worker in lead*) plomero

plumbing ['plʌmɪŋ] *s* instalación sanitaria; conjunto de cañerías; (*working in lead*) plomería; sondeo

plumbing fixtures *spl* artefactos sanitarios

plumb line *s* cuerda de plomada

plum cake *s* pastel aderezado con pasas de Corinto y ron

plume [plum] *s* (*of a bird*) pluma; (*tuft of feathers worn as ornament*) penacho *m* ‖ *tr* emplumar; componerse (*las plumas*); **to plume oneself on** enorgullecerse de

plummet ['plʌmɪt] *s* plomada ‖ *intr* caer a plomo, precipitarse

plump [plʌmp] *adj* rechoncho, regordete; brusco, franco ‖ *adv* de golpe; francamente ‖ *s* (coll) caída pesada; (coll) ruido sordo ‖ *intr* caer a plomo

plum pudding *s* pudín *m* inglés con pasas de Corinto, corteza de limón, huevos y ron

plum tree *s* ciruelo

plunder ['plʌndər] *s* pillaje *m;* botín *m* ‖ *tr* pillar, saquear

plunge [plʌndʒ] *s* zambullida; caída a plomo; sacudida violenta; salto; baño de agua fría; (*of a boat*) cabeceo ‖ *tr* zambullir; sumergir; hun-

dir (*p.ej., un puñal*) ‖ *intr* zambullirse; sumergirse; hundirse (*p.ej., en la tristeza*); caer a plomo; arrojarse, precipitarse; cabecear (*un buque*); (slang) entregarse al juego, entregarse a las especulaciones

plunger ['plʌndʒər] *s* zambullidor *m;* émbolo buzo; (*of a tire valve*) obús *m;* (slang) jugador o especulador desenfrenado

plunk [plʌŋk] *adv* (coll) con un golpe seco, con un ruido de golpe seco ‖ *tr* (coll) arrojar, empujar o dejar caer pesadamente ‖ *intr* sonar o caer con un ruido de golpe seco

plural ['plʊrəl] *adj & s* plural *m*

plus [plʌs] *adj* más; y pico; **to be plus** (coll) tener por añadidura ‖ *prep* más ‖ *s* (*sign*) más *m;* añadidura

plush [plʌʃ] *adj* afelpado; (coll) lujoso, suntuoso ‖ *s* felpa

Plutarch ['plutɑrk] *s* Plutarco

plutonium [plu'tonɪ·əm] *s* plutonio

ply [plaɪ] *s* (*pl* **plies**) (*e.g., of a cloth*) capa, doblez *m;* (*of a cable*) cordón *m* ‖ *v* (*pret & pp* **plied**) *tr* manejar (*la aguja, etc.*); ejercer (*un oficio*); batir (*el agua con los remos*); importunar; navegar por (*p.ej., un río*) ‖ *intr* avanzar; **to ply between** hacer (*un barco*) el servicio entre

ply'wood' *s* chapeado, madera laminada

P.M. *abbr* **Postmaster, post meridiem** (Lat) **afternoon**

pneumatic [nju'mætɪk] o [nu'mætɪk] *adj* neumático

pneumatic drill *s* perforadora de aire comprimido

pneumonia [nju'monɪ·ə] o [nu-'monɪ·ə] *s* neumonía o pulmonía

P.O. *abbr* **post office**

poach [potʃ] *tr* escalfar (*huevos*) ‖ *intr* cazar o pescar en vedado

poacher ['potʃər] *s* cazador furtivo, pescador furtivo

pock [pɑk] *s* cacaraña, hoyuelo

pocket ['pɑkɪt] *s* bolsillo, faltriquera; (*in billiards*) tronera; (aer) bolsa de aire; (mil) bolsón *m* ‖ *tr* embolsar; entronerar (*una bola de billar*); tragarse (*injurias*)

pock'et·book' *s* portamonedas *m;* (*of a woman*) bolsa

pocket handkerchief *s* pañuelo de bolsillo o de mano

pock'et·knife' *s* (*pl* -**knives**) navaja, cortaplumas *m*

pocket money *s* alfileres *mpl,* dinero de bolsillo

pock'mark' *s* cacaraña, hoyuelo

pod [pɑd] *s* vaina

poem ['po·ɪm] *s* poema *m,* poesía

poet ['po·ɪt] *s* poeta *m*

poetess ['po·ɪtɪs] *s* poetisa

poetic [po'etɪk] *adj* poético ‖ **poetics** *ssg* poética

poetry ['po·ɪtri] *s* poesía

pogrom ['pogrəm] *s* levantamiento contra los judíos

poignancy ['pɔɪnənsi] *s* picante *m,* viveza, intensidad

poignant ['pɔɪnənt] *adj* picante, vivo, intenso

point [pɔɪnt] *s* (*of a sword, pencil; of land*) punta; (*of pen*) pico; (*of fountain pen*) puntilla; (*mark of imperceptible dimensions*) punto; (*of a joke*) gracia; (elec) punta; (math, typ, sport, fig) punto; (coll) indirecta, insinuación; **beside the point** fuera de propósito; **on the point of** a punto de; **to carry one's point** salirse con la suya; **to come to the point** venir al caso o al grano; **to get the point** caer en la cuenta ‖ *tr* aguzar, sacar punta a; apuntar (*p.ej., un arma de fuego*); resanar (*una pared*); **to point one's finger at** señalar con el dedo; **to point out** señalar, indicar, hacer notar ‖ *intr* apuntar; pararse (*el perro de muestra*); **to point at** señalar con el dedo

point'blank' *adj* & *adv* a quemarropa

pointed ['pɔɪntɪd] *adj* puntiagudo; picante; acentuado, directo

pointer ['pɔɪntər] *s* puntero; indicador *m;* (*of a clock*) manecilla; perro de muestra; (mas) fijador *m;* (coll) indicación, dirección

poise [pɔɪz] *s* aplomo, equilibrio ‖ *tr* equilibrar; considerar ‖ *intr* equilibrarse; estar suspendido

poison ['pɔɪzən] *s* veneno, ponzoña ‖ *tr* envenenar

poison ivy *s* tosiguero

poisonous ['pɔɪzənəs] *adj* venenoso

poke [pok] *s* (*push*) empuje *m,* empujón *m;* (*thrust*) hurgonazo; (*with elbow*) codazo; (*slow person*) tardón *m* ‖ *tr* empujar; hacer (*un agujero*) a empujones; abrirse (*paso*) a empujones; atizar, hurgar (*el fuego*); **to poke fun at** burlarse de; **to poke one's nose into** entremeterse en ‖ *intr* fisgar, husmear; andar perezosamente

poker ['pokər] *s* hurgón *m;* (*card game*) póker *m,* pócar *m*

poker face *s* (coll) cara de jugador de póker; **to keep a poker face** (coll) disfrazar la expresión del rostro, mantener una expresión imperturbable

pok·y ['poki] *adj* (*comp* **-ier;** *super* **-iest**) (coll) tardo, roncero

Poland ['polənd] *s* Polonia

polar bear ['polər] *s* oso blanco

polarize ['polə‚raɪz] *tr* polarizar

pole [pol] *s* (*long rod or staff*) pértiga; (*of a flag*) asta; (*upright support*) poste *m;* (*to push a boat*) botador *m;* (astr, biol, elec, geog, math) polo ‖ *tr* impeler (*un barco*) con botador ‖ **Pole** *s* polaco

pole'cat' *s* turón *m,* veso

pole'star' *s* estrella polar; (*guide*) norte *m;* (*center of interest*) miradero

pole vault *s* salto con garrocha o con pértiga

police [pə'lis] *s* policía ‖ *tr* poner o mantener servicio de policía en; (mil) limpiar

police·man [pə'lismən] *s* (*pl* **-men** [mən]) policía *m,* guardia urbano

police state *s* estado-policía *m*

police station *s* cuartel *m* o estación de policía

pol·i·cy ['palɪsi] *s* (*pl* **-cies**) política; (ins) póliza

polio ['polɪ‚o] *s* (coll) polio *f*

polish ['palɪʃ] *s* pulimento; cera de lustrar; (*for shoes*) bola, betún *m,* lustre *m;* elegancia; cultura, urbanidad ‖ *tr* pulimentar, pulir; embolar, dar betún a (*los zapatos*); **to polish off** (coll) terminar de prisa; (slang) engullir (*la comida, un trago*) ‖ **Polish** ['polɪʃ] *adj* & *s* polaco

polisher ['palɪʃər] *s* pulidor *m;* (*machine*) pulidora; (*for floors, tables, etc.*) enceradora

polite [pə'laɪt] *adj* cortés, fino, urbano; culto

politeness [pə'laɪtnɪs] *s* cortesía, fineza, urbanidad; cultura

politic ['palɪtɪk] *adj* prudente, sagaz; astuto; juicioso

political [pə'lɪtɪkəl] *adj* político

politician [‚palɪ'tɪʃən] *s* político; (*politician seeking personal or partisan gain*) politiquero

politics ['palɪtɪks] *ssg* o *spl* política

poll [pol] *s* (*questionnaire to determine opinion*) encuesta; votación; lista electoral; cabeza; **polls** urnas electorales; **to go to the polls** acudir a las urnas; **to take a poll** hacer una encuesta ‖ *tr* dar (*un voto*); recibir (*votos*)

pollen ['palən] *s* polen *m*

pollinate ['palɪ‚net] *tr* polinizar

polling booth ['polɪŋ] *s* cabina o caseta de votar

polliwog ['palɪ‚wɑg] *s* renacuajo; (slang) persona que atraviesa el ecuador en un barco por primera vez

poll tax *s* capitación, impuesto por cabeza

pollute [pə'lut] *tr* contaminar, corromper, ensuciar

pollution [pə'luʃən] *s* contaminación

polo ['polo] *s* polo

polo player *s* polista *mf,* jugador *m* de polo

polygamist [pə'lɪgəmɪst] *s* polígamo

polygamous [pə'lɪgəməs] *adj* polígamo

polyglot ['palɪ‚glat] *adj* & *s* poligloto

polygon ['palɪ‚gan] *s* polígono

Polyhymnia [‚palɪ'hɪmnɪ‚ə] *s* Polimnia

polynomial [‚palɪ'nomɪ‚əl] *s* polinomio

polyp ['palɪp] *s* pólipo

polytheist ['palɪ‚θi‚ɪst] *s* politeísta *mf*

polytheistic [‚palɪθi'ɪstɪk] *adj* politeísta

pomade [pə'med] o [pə'mad] *s* pomada

pomegranate ['pam‚grænɪt] *s* (*shrub*) granado; (*fruit*) granada

pom·mel ['pʌməl] o ['paməl] *s* (*on hilt of sword*) pomo; (*on saddle*) perilla ‖ *v* (*pret* & *pp* **-meled** o

-melled; *ger* **-meling** o **-melling**) *tr* apuñear, aporrear

pomp [pɑmp] *s* pompa, fausto

pompadour [ˈpɑmpəˌdor] o [ˈpɑmpəˌdur] *s* copete *m*

pompous [ˈpɑmpəs] *adj* pomposo, fastuoso

pon•cho [ˈpɑntʃo] *s* (*pl* **-chos**) capote *m* de monte, poncho

pond [pɑnd] *s* estanque *m*, charca

ponder [ˈpɑndər] *tr* ponderar ‖ *intr* meditar; **to ponder over** ponderar, considerar con cuidado

ponderous [ˈpɑndərəs] *adj* pesado, inmanejable; tedioso, fastidioso

pond scum *s* lama, verdín *m*

poniard [ˈpɑnjərd] *s* puñal *m*

pontiff [ˈpɑntɪf] *s* pontífice *m*

pontoon [pɑnˈtun] *s* pontón *m*

po•ny [ˈponi] *s* (*pl* **-nies**) jaca, caballito; (*for drinking liquor*) (coll) pequeño vaso; (*translation used dishonestly in school*) (coll) chuleta

poodle [ˈpudəl] *s* perro de lanas

pool [pul] *s* (*small puddle*) charco; (*for swimming*) piscina; (*game*) trucos; (*in certain games*) polla, puesta; combinación de intereses; caudales unidos para un fin ‖ *tr* mancomunar

pool'room' *s* sala de trucos

pool table *s* mesa de trucos

poop [pup] *s* popa; (*deck*) toldilla

poor [pur] *adj* (*having few possessions; arousing pity*) pobre; (*not good, inferior*) malo

poor box *s* cepillo, caja de limosnas

poor'house' *s* asilo de pobres, casa de caridad

poorly [ˈpurli] *adv* mal

poor white *s* pobre *mf* de la raza blanca (*en el sur de los EE.UU.*)

pop. *abbr* **popular, population**

pop [pɑp] *s* estallido, taponazo; bebida gaseosa ‖ *v* (*pret & pp* **popped;** *ger* **popping**) *tr* hacer estallar; **to pop the question** (coll) hacer una declaración de amor ‖ *intr* estallar

pop'corn' *s* rosetas, palomitas (de maíz)

pope [pop] *s* papa *m*

popeyed [ˈpɑpˌaɪd] *adj* de ojos saltones; (*with fear, surprise, etc.*) desorbitado

pop'gun' *s* tirabala

poplar [ˈpɑplər] *s* álamo, chopo

pop•py [ˈpɑpi] *s* (*pl* **-ples**) amapola

pop'py•cock' *s* (coll) necedad, tontería

popsicle [ˈpɑpsɪkəl] *s* polo

populace [ˈpɑpjələs] *s* populacho

popular [ˈpɑpjələr] *adj* popular

popularize [ˈpɑpjələˌraɪz] *tr* popularizar, vulgarizar

populous [ˈpɑpjələs] *adj* populoso

porcelain [ˈpɔrsəlɪn] o [ˈpɔrslɪn] *s* porcelana

porch [pɔrtʃ] *s* porche *m*, pórtico

porcupine [ˈpɔrkjəˌpaɪn] *s* puerco espín

pore [por] *s* poro ‖ *intr* — **to pore over** estudiar larga y detenidamente

pork [pork] *s* carne *f* de cerdo

pork chop *s* chuleta de cerdo

porous [ˈporəs] *adj* poroso

porous plaster *s* parche poroso

porphy•ry [ˈpɔrfri] *s* (*pl* **-ries**) pórfido

porpoise [ˈpɔrpəs] *s* marsopa, puerco de mar; (*dolphin*) delfín *m*

porridge [ˈpʌrɪdʒ] o [ˈpɔrɪdʒ] *s* gachas

port [port] *adj* portuario ‖ *s* puerto; (*opening in ship's side*) portilla; (*left side of ship or airplane*) babor *m;* oporto, vino de Oporto; (mach) lumbrera

portable [ˈportəbəl] *adj* portátil

portal [ˈportəl] *s* portal *m*

portend [porˈtend] *tr* anunciar de antemano, presagiar

portent [ˈportent] *s* augurio, presagio

portentous [porˈtentəs] *adj* portentoso, extraordinario; amenazante, ominoso

porter [ˈportər] *s* (*doorkeeper*) portero, conserje *m;* (*in hotels and trains*) mozo de servicio; pórter *m* (*cerveza de Inglaterra de color obscuro*)

portfoli•o [portˈfoliˌo] *s* (*pl* **-os**) cartera

port'hole' *s* porta, portilla

porti•co [ˈportɪˌko] *s* (*pl* **-coes** o **-cos**) pórtico

portion [ˈporʃən] *s* porción; (*dowry*) dote *m & f*

port•ly [ˈportli] *adj* (*comp* **-lier;** *super* **-liest**) corpulento; grave, majestuoso

port of call *s* escala

portrait [ˈportret] o [ˈportrɪt] *s* retrato; **to sit for a portrait** retratarse

portray [porˈtre] *tr* retratar

portrayal [porˈtre-əl] *s* representación gráfica; retrato, descripción acertada

Portugal [ˈportʃəgəl] *s* Portugal *m*

Portu•guese [ˈportʃəˌgiz] *adj* portugués ‖ *s* (*pl* **-guese**) portugués *m*

port wine *s* vino de Oporto

pose [poz] *s* pose *f* ‖ *tr* plantear (*una pregunta, cuestión, etc.*) ‖ *intr* posar (*para retratarse; como modelo*); tomar una postura afectada; **to pose as** hacerse pasar por

posh [pɑʃ] *adj* (slang) elegante; (slang) lujoso, suntuoso

position [pəˈzɪʃən] *s* posición; empleo, puesto; opinión, **to be in a position to** estar en condiciones de

positive [ˈpɑzɪtɪv] *adj* positivo ‖ *s* positiva

possess [pəˈzes] *tr* poseer

possession [pəˈzeʃən] *s* posesión

possible [ˈpɑsɪbəl] *adj* posible

possum [ˈpɑsəm] *s* zarigüeya; **to play possum** hacer la mortecina

post [post] *s* (*piece of wood, metal, etc. set upright*) poste *m;* (*position*) puesto; (*job*) puesto, cargo; casa de correos ‖ *tr* fijar (*carteles*); echar al correo; apostar, situar; tener al corriente; **post no bills** se prohíbe fijar carteles

postage [ˈpostɪdʒ] *s* porte *m*, franqueo; **postage will be paid by addressee** a franquear en destino

postage meter *s* franqueadora

postage stamp *s* sello de correo; estampilla, timbre *m* (Am)

postal ['postəl] adj postal || s postal f
postal card s tarjeta postal
postal permit s franqueo concertado
postal savings bank s caja postal de ahorros
post card s tarjeta postal
post'date' s posfecha || post'date' tr posfechar
poster ['postər] s cartel m, cartelón m, letrero
posterity [pɑs'tɛrɪti] s posteridad
postern ['postərn] s postigo, portillo
post'haste' adv por la posta, a toda prisa
posthumous ['pɑstʃuməs] adj póstumo
post-man ['postmən] s (pl -men [mən]) cartero
post'mark' s matasellos m, timbre m de correos || tr matasellar, timbrar
post'mas'ter s administrador m de correos
post-mortem [,post'mɔrtəm] adj posterior a la muerte || s examen m de un cadáver
post office s casa de correos
post'-of'fice box s apartado de correos, casilla postal
postpaid ['post,ped] adj con porte pagado, franco de porte
postpone [post'pon] tr aplazar
postscript ['post,skrɪpt] s posdata
posttonic [post'tɑnɪk] adj postónico
posture [ˈpɑstʃər] s postura || intr adoptar una postura
post'war' adj de la posguerra
po-sy ['pozi] s (pl -sies) flor f, ramillete m
pot [pɑt] s pote m; (for flowers) tiesto; (for the kitchen) caldera, olla, puchero; vaso de noche, orinal m; (in gambling) puesta; (slang) mariguana
potash [ˈpɑt,æʃ] s potasa
potassium [pə'tæsɪəm] s potasio
pota-to [pə'teto] s (pl -toes) patata, papa; (sweet potato) batata, buniato
potato omelet s tortilla a la española
potbellied ['pɑt,belid] adj barrigón, panzudo
poten-cy ['potənsi] s (pl -cies) potencia
potent ['potənt] adj potente
potentate ['potən,tet] s potentado
potential [pə'tɛnʃəl] adj & s potencial m
pot'hang'er s llares fpl
pot'hook' s garabato
potion ['poʃən] s poción
pot'luck' s lo que hay de comer; to take potluck hacer penitencia
pot shot s tiro a corta distancia
potter ['pɑtər] s alfarero || intr ocuparse en fruslerías
potter's clay s arcilla figulina
potter's field s cementerio de los pobres, hoyanca
potter's wheel s torno de alfarero
potter-y ['pɑtəri] s (pl -ies) alfarería; cacharros (de alfarería)
pouch [pautʃ] s bolsa, saquillo; (of kangaroo) bolsa; (for tobacco) petaca; valija
poulterer ['poltərər] s pollero

poultice ['poltɪs] s cataplasma f
poultry ['poltri] s aves fpl de corral
pounce [pauns] intr — to pounce on saltar sobre, precipitarse sobre
pound [paund] s (weight) libra; (for stray animals) corral m de concejo || tr golpear; machacar, moler; encerrar en el corral de concejo; bombardear incesantemente; (to keep walking over) desempedrar || intr golpear
pound'cake' s pastel m en que entra una libra de cada ingrediente; ponqué m (Am)
pound sterling s libra esterlina
pour [por] tr vaciar, verter, derramar; echar, servir (p.ej., té); escanciar (vino) || intr fluir rápidamente; llover a torrentes; to pour out of salir a montones de (p.ej., el teatro)
pout [paut] s mala cara, puchero || intr poner mala cara, hacer pucheros
poverty ['pɑvərti] s pobreza
POW abbr prisoner of war
powder ['paudər] s polvo; (for face) polvos; (explosive) pólvora || tr pulverizar; (to sprinkle with powder) empolvar, polvorear
powder puff s borla para empolvarse
powder room s cuarto tocador, cuarto de aseo
powdery ['paudəri] adj (like powder) polvoriento; (sprinkled with powder) empolvado; (crumbly) quebradizo
power ['pau·ər] s (ability to act or do something; possession) poder m; (control, influence; wealth) poderío; (influential nation; energy, force, strength) potencia; the powers that be las autoridades, los que mandan || tr accionar, impulsar
power dive s (aer) picado con motor
powerful ['pau·ərfəl] adj poderoso
pow'er·house' s central eléctrica
powerless ['pau·ərlɪs] adj impotente
power line s (elec) sector m de distribución
power mower s motosegadora
power of attorney s poder m
power plant s (aer) grupo motopropulsor; (aut) grupo motor; (elec) central eléctrica, estación generadora
power steering s (aut) servodirección
power tool s herramienta motriz
pp. abbr pages
p.p. abbr parcel post, postpaid
pr. abbr pair, present, price
practical ['præktɪkəl] adj práctico
practically ['præktɪkəli] adv poco más o menos
practice ['præktɪs] s práctica; uso, costumbre; ensayo; (of a profession) ejercicio; (of a doctor) clientela || tr practicar; ejercitar (p.ej., la caridad); ejercer (una profesión); estudiar (p.ej., el piano); tener por costumbre || intr ejercitarse; practicar la medicina; ejercer; entrenarse, adiestrarse; to practice as ejercer de (p.ej., abogado)
practitioner [præk'tɪʃənər] s (medical doctor) práctico
Prague [prɑg] o [preg] s Praga

prairie ['preri] s pradera, llanura, pampa

prairie dog s ardilla ladradora

prairie wolf s coyote m

praise [prez] s alabanza, elogio || tr alabar, elogiar

praise'wor'thy adj laudable, plausible

pram |præm| s cochecillo de niño

prance [præns] o [prans] s cabriola, trenzado || intr cabriolar, trenzar

prank [præŋk] s travesura

prate [pret] intr charlar, parlotear

prattle ['prætəl] s charla, parloteo || intr charlar, parlotear; balbucear (un niño)

pray [pre] tr implorar, rogar, suplicar; rezar (una oración) || intr orar, rezar; **pray tell me** sírvase decirme

prayer [prer] s ruego, súplica; oración, rezo

prayer book s devocionario

preach [prit∫] tr predicar; aconsejar (p.ej., la paciencia) || intr predicar

preacher |'prit∫ər| s predicador m

preamble |'pri,æmbəl| s preámbulo

prebend | 'prebənd| s prebenda

precarious |pri'keri-əs| adj precario

precaution [pri'kɔ∫ən] s precaución

precede [pri'sid] tr & intr preceder

precedent |'presidənt| s precedente m

precept ['prisept] s precepto

precinct ['prisiŋkt] s barriada; distrito electoral

precious ['pre∫əs] adj precioso; caro, amado; (coll) considerable || adv (coll) muy, p.ej., **precious little** muy poco

precipice ['presipis] s precipicio

precipitate [pri'sipi,tet] adj & s precipitado || tr precipitar || intr precipitarse

precipitous [pri'sipitəs] adj empinado, escarpado; (hurried, reckless) precipitoso

precise [pri'sais] adj preciso; meticuloso

precision [pri'siʒən] s precisión

preclude [pri'klud] tr excluir, imposibilitar

precocious [pri'ko∫əs] adj precoz

predatory ['predə,tori] adj predatorio

predicament [pri'dikəmənt] s apuro, situación difícil

predict [pri'dikt] tr predecir

prediction [pri'dik∫ən] s predicción

predispose [,pridis'poz] tr predisponer

predominant [pri'dɑminənt] adj predominante

preëminent [pri'eminənt] adj preeminente

preëmpt [pri'empt] tr apropiarse o apropiarse de

preen [prin] tr arreglarse (las plumas) con el pico; **to preen oneself** componerse, vestirse cuidadosamente

pref. abbr **preface, preferred, prefix**

prefabricate [pri'fæbri,ket] tr prefabricar

preface ['prefis] s prefacio, advertencia || tr introducir, empezar

pre-fer [pri'fʌr] v (pret & pp -ferred; ger -ferring) tr preferir; presentar; promover

preferable ['prefərəbəl] adj preferible

preference ['prefərəns] s preferencia

prefix ['prifiks] s prefijo || tr prefijar

pregnan-cy ['pregnənsi| s (pl -cies) preñez f, embarazo

pregnant ['pregnənt| adj preñado

prejudice ['predʒədis| s prejuicio; (detriment) perjuicio; **to the prejudice of** con perjuicio de; **without prejudice** (law) sin detrimento de sus propios derechos || tr predisponer, prevenir; (to harm) perjudicar

prejudicial [,predʒə'diʃəl] adj perjudicial

prelate ['prelit] s prelado

pre-Lenten [pri'lentən] adj carnavalesco

preliminar-y [pri'limi,neri] adj preliminar || s (pl -ies) preliminar m

prelude ['preljud] o ['priljud] s preludio || tr preludiar

premeditate [pri'medi,tet] tr premeditar

premier [pri'mir] o ['primi-ər] s primer ministro, presidente m del consejo

première [prə'mjer] o [pri'mir] s estreno; actriz f principal

premise ['premis] s premisa; **on the premises** en el local mismo; **premises** predio, local m

premium |'primi-əm| s premio; (ins) prima

premonition [,primə'niʃən] s presagio; presentimiento

preoccupancy [pri'ɑkjəpənsi] s preocupación

preoccupation [pri,ɑkjə'peʃən] s preocupación

preoccu-py [pri'ɑkjə,pai] v (pret & pp -pied) tr preocupar

prepaid [pri'ped] adj pagado por adelantado; con porte pagado

preparation [,prepə're∫ən] s preparación; (e.g., for a trip) preparativo; (pharm) preparado

preparatory [pri'pærə,tori] adj preparativo, preparatorio

prepare [pri'per] tr preparar || intr prepararse

preparedness [pri'peridnis] o [pri'perdnis] s preparación; preparación militar

pre-pay [pri'pe] v (pret & pp -paid) tr pagar por adelantado

preponderant [pri'pɑndərənt] adj preponderante

preposition [,prepə'ziʃən] s preposición

prepossessing [,pripə'zesiŋ] adj atractivo, simpático

preposterous [pri'pɑstərəs] adj absurdo, ridículo

prep school [prep] s (coll) escuela preparatoria

prerecorded [,priri'kɔrdid] adj (rad & telv) grabado de antemano

prerequisite [pri'rekwizit] s requisito previo

prerogative [pri'rɑgətiv] s prerrogativa

Pres. abbr **Presbyterian, President**

presage ['prɛsɪdʒ] s presagio ‖ [prɪ-'sedʒ] tr presagiar

Presbyterian [,prɛzbɪ'tɪrɪ·ən] adj & s presbiteriano

prescribe [prɪ'skraɪb] tr & intr prescribir

prescription [prɪ'skrɪpʃən] s prescripción; (pharm) receta

presence ['prɛzəns] s presencia

present ['prɛzənt] adj presente ‖ s presente m, regalo ‖ [prɪ'zɛnt] tr presentar, obsequiar

presentable [prɪ'zɛntəbəl] adj bien apersonado

presentation [,prɛzən'teʃən] o [,prɪ-zən'teʃən] s presentación

presentation copy s ejemplar m de cortesía con dedicatoria del autor

presentiment [prɪ'zɛntɪmənt] s presentimiento

presently ['prɛzəntli] adv luego, dentro de poco

preserve [prɪ'zʌrv] s conserva, compota; (for game) vedado m ‖ tr conservar; preservar, proteger

preserved fruit s dulce m de almíbar

preside [prɪ'zaɪd] intr presidir; to preside over presidir

presiden·cy ['prɛzɪdənsi] s (pl -cies) presidencia

president ['prɛzɪdənt] s presidente m; (of a university) rector m

press [prɛs] s apretón o apretón m; (e.g., of business) urgencia; muchedumbre; (machine for printing, for making wine; newspapers and newspapermen) prensa; (printing) imprenta; (closet) armario; to go to press entrar en prensa ‖ tr apretar (p.ej., un botón); (in a press) prensar; planchar (la ropa); imprimir (discos de fonógrafo); oprimir (una tecla); apresurar; abrumar; apremiar, instar; insistir en

press agent s agente m de publicidad

press conference s conferencia de prensa

pressing ['prɛsɪŋ] adj apremiante, urgente ‖ s planchado

press release s comunicado de prensa

pressure ['prɛʃər] s presión; premura, urgencia

pressure cooker ['kukər] s olla de presión, cocina de presión

prestige [prɛs'tiʒ] o ['prɛstɪdʒ] s prestigio

presumably [prɪ'zuməbli] o [prɪ-'zjuməbli] adv probablemente, verosímilmente

presume [prɪ'zum] o [prɪ'zjum] tr presumir; suponer; to presume to tomar la libertad de ‖ intr suponer; to presume on o upon abusar de

presumption [prɪ'zʌmpʃən] s presunción; pretensión

presumptuous [prɪ'zʌmptʃu·əs] adj confianzudo, desenvuelto

presuppose [,prisə'poz] tr presuponer

pretend [prɪ'tɛnd] tr aparentar, fingir ‖ intr fingir; to pretend to pretender (p.ej., el trono)

pretender [prɪ'tɛndər] s pretendiente mf

pretense [prɪ'tɛns] o ['pritɛns] s pre-

tensión; fingimiento; under false pretenses con apariencias fingidas; under pretense of so pretexto de

pretentious [prɪ'tɛnʃəs] adj pretencioso, aparatoso; ambicioso, vasto

pretonic [pri'tanɪk] adj pretónico

pret·ty ['priti] adj (comp -tier; super -tiest) bonito, lindo; (coll) bastante, considerable ‖ adv algo; bastante; muy

prevail [prɪ'vel] intr prevalecer, reinar; to prevail on o upon persuadir

prevailing [prɪ'velɪŋ] adj prevaleciente, reinante; común, corriente

prevalent ['prɛvələnt] adj común, corriente, en boga

prevaricate [prɪ'værɪ,ket] intr mentir

prevent [prɪ'vɛnt] tr impedir ‖ intr obstar

prevention [prɪ'vɛnʃən] s (el) impedir; medidas de precaución

preventive [prɪ'vɛntɪv] adj & s preservativo

preview ['pri,vju] s vista anticipada; (private showing) (mov) preestreno; (showing of brief scenes for advertising) (mov) avance m

previous ['privɪ·əs] adj previo, anterior ‖ adv previamente; previous to con anterioridad a, antes de

prewar ['pri,wɔr] adj prebélico, de preguerra

prey [pre] s presa; víctima; to be prey to ser presa de ‖ intr cazar; to prey on o upon apresar y devorar; pillar, robar; tener preocupado

price [praɪs] s precio ‖ tr apreciar, estimar; fijar el precio de, poner precio a; pedir el precio de

price control s intervención de precios

price cutting s reducción de precios

price fixing s fijación de precios

price freezing s congelación de precios

priceless ['praɪslɪs] adj inapreciable, sin precio; (coll) absurdo, divertido

price war s guerra de precios

prick [prɪk] s (pointed weapon or instrument) espiche m; (sharp point) púa; (small hole made with sharp point) agujerillo; (spur) aguijón m; (jab; sharp pain) pinchazo, punzada; to kick against the pricks dar coces contra el aguijón ‖ tr pinchar; marcar con agujerillos; dar una punzada a; (to sting) punzar; to prick up aguzar (las orejas)

prick·ly ['prɪkli] adj (comp -lier; super -liest) espinoso, puado, punzante

prickly heat s salpullido causado por el calor

prickly pear s (plant) chumbera; (fruit) higo chumbo

pride [praɪd] s orgullo; arrogancia; the pride of la flor y nata de ‖ tr — to pride oneself on o upon enorgullecerse de

priest [prist] s sacerdote m

priesthood ['prist·hud] s sacerdocio

priest·ly ['pristli] adj (comp -lier; super -liest) sacerdotal

prig [prɪg] s gazmoño, pedante mf

prim [prɪm] adj (comp primmer; super primmest) estirado, relamido

prima·ry ['praɪˌmeri] o ['praɪməri] *adj* primario || *s* (*pl* -ries) elección preliminar; (elec) primario

prime [praim] *adj* primero, principal; (*of the best quality*) primo || *s* flor *f*, juventud, primavera; alba, aurora; (la) flor y nata; (*of a degree*) (phys) minuto; (typ) virgulilla; **prime of life** edad viril, flor *f* de edad || *tr* informar de antemano; cebar (*un arma de fuego, una bomba, un carburador*); (*for painting*) imprimar; poner la primera capa o la primera mano a; poner virgulilla a

prime minister *s* primer ministro

primer ['praɪmər] *s* cartilla || ['praɪmər] *s* (*for paint*) aprestado *m*; (mach) cebador *m*

primitive ['prɪmɪtɪv] *adj* primitivo

primp [prɪmp] *tr* acicalar, engalanar || *intr* acicalarse, engalanarse

prim'rose' *s* primavera

primrose path *s* vida dada a los placeres de los sentidos

prin. *abbr* **principal**

prince [prɪns] *s* príncipe *m*; **to live like a prince** portarse como un príncipe

Prince of Wales *s* príncipe *m* de Gales

princess ['prɪnsɪs] *s* princesa

principal ['prɪnsɪpəl] *adj* principal || *s* principal *m*, jefe *m*; (*of a school*) director *m*; criminal *mf*; (*main sum, not interest*) capital *m*

principle ['prɪnsɪpəl] *s* principio

print [prɪnt] *s* marca, impresión; (*printed cloth*) estampado; (*design in printed cloth*) diseño; grabado, lámina; letras de molde; (*act of printing*) impresión; edición, tirada; (phot) impresión; **in print** impreso, publicado; **out of print** agotado || *tr* imprimir; estampar; hacer imprimir; publicar; escribir en caracteres de imprenta; (phot) tirar, imprimir; (fig) imprimir o grabar (*en la memoria*)

printed matter *s* impresos

printer ['prɪntər] *s* impresor *m*

printer's devil *s* aprendiz *m* de imprenta

printer's ink *s* tinta de imprenta

printer's mark *s* pie *m* de imprenta

printing ['prɪntɪŋ] *s* impresión; caracteres impresos; edición, tirada; letras de mano imitación de las impresas; (phot) tiraje *m*

prior ['praɪər] *adj* anterior || *adv* anteriormente; **prior to** antes de

prior·i·ty [praɪˈɑrɪti] o [praɪˈɔrɪti] *s* (*pl* -ties) prioridad; **of the highest priority** de máxima prioridad

prism ['prɪzəm] *s* prisma *m*

prison ['prɪzən] *s* cárcel *f*, prisión || *tr* encarcelar

prison van *s* coche *m* celular

prisoner ['prɪzənər] o ['prɪznər] *s* preso; (mil) prisionero

pris·sy ['prɪsi] *adj* (*comp* -sier; *super* -siest*) (coll) remilgado, melindroso

priva·cy ['praɪvəsi] *s* (*pl* -cies) aislamiento, retiro; secreto, reserva

private ['praɪvɪt] *adj* particular, privado; confidencial; || *s* soldado raso; **in private** privadamente; en secreto; **privates** partes pudendas

private first class *s* soldado de primera, aspirante *m* a cabo

private hospital *s* clínica, casa de salud

private property *s* bienes *mpl* particulares

private view *s* día *m* de inauguración

privet ['prɪvɪt] *s* aligustre *m*

privilege ['prɪvɪlɪdʒ] *s* privilegio

priv·y ['prɪvi] *adj* privado; **privy to** enterado secretamente de || *s* (*pl* -ies) letrina

prize [praɪz] *s* premio; (*something captured*) presa || *tr* apreciar, estimar

prize fight *s* partido de boxeo profesional

prize fighter *s* boxeador *m* profesional

prize ring *s* cuadrilátero de boxeo

pro [pro] *prep* en pro de || *s* (*pl* pros) voto afirmativo; (coll) deportista *mf* profesional; **the pros and the cons** el pro y el contra

probabili·ty [ˌprabəˈbɪlɪti] *s* (*pl* -ties) probabilidad, acontecimiento probable; tiempo probable

probable ['prabəbəl] *adj* probable

probation [proˈbeʃən] *s* libertad vigilada; período de prueba

probe [prob] *s* encuesta, indagación; (*instrument*) sonda || *tr* indagar; sondar

problem ['prabləm] *s* problema *m*

procedure [proˈsidʒər] *s* procedimiento

proceed [proˈsid] *intr* proceder || **proceeds** ['prosidz] *spl* producto, ganancia

proceeding [proˈsidɪŋ] *s* procedimiento; **proceedings** actas; diligencias

process ['prasɛs] *s* procedimiento; proceso, progreso; **in the process of time** con el tiempo || *tr* elaborar

process server *s* entregador *m* de la citación

proclaim [proˈklem] *tr* proclamar

proclitic [proˈklɪtɪk] *adj* & *s* proclítico

procommunist [proˈkamjənɪst] *adj* & *s* filocomunista *mf*

procrastinate [proˈkræstɪˌnet] *tr* diferir de un día para otro || *intr* tardar, no decidirse

procure [proˈkjur] *tr* conseguir, obtener || *intr* alcahuetear

prod [prad] *s* aguijada; empuje *m* || *v* (*pret* & *pp* **prodded**; *ger* **prodding**) *tr* aguijar, pinchar; aguijonear, estimular

prodigal ['pradɪgəl] *adj* & *s* pródigo

prodigious [prəˈdɪdʒəs] *adj* prodigioso, maravilloso; enorme, inmenso

prodi·gy ['pradɪdʒi] *s* (*pl* -gies) prodigio

produce ['prodjus] o ['produs] *s* producto; productos agrícolas || [proˈdjus] o [proˈdus] *tr* producir; presentar (*p.ej., un drama*) al público; (geom) prolongar

product ['pradəkt] *s* producto

production [proˈdʌkʃən] *s* producción

profane [proˈfen] *adj* profano; (*lan-*

guage) injurioso, blasfemo ‖ *s* profano ‖ *tr* profanar

profani-ty [proˈfæniti] *s* (*pl* -ties) blasfemia

profess [proˈfes] *tr & intr* profesar

profession [proˈfeʃən] *s* profesión

professor [proˈfesər] *s* profesor *m*, catedrático; (coll) profesor, maestro

proffer [ˈprafər] *s* oferta, propuesta ‖ *tr* ofrecer, proponer

proficient [proˈfiʃənt] *adj* perito, diestro, hábil

profile [ˈprofail] *s* perfil *m* ‖ *tr* perfilar

profit [ˈprafit] *s* provecho, beneficio, utilidad, ganancia; **at a profit** con ganancia ‖ *tr* servir, ser de utilidad a ‖ *intr* sacar provecho, ganar; **to profit by** aprovechar, sacar provecho de

profitable [ˈprafitəbəl] *adj* provechoso

profit and loss *s* ganancias y pérdidas

profiteer [ˌprafiˈtir] *s* logrero, explotador *m* ‖ *intr* logrear, explotar

profit taking *s* realización de beneficios

profligate [ˈprafligit] *adj & s* libertino; pródigo

pro forma invoice [pro ˈfɔrmə] *s* factura simulada

profound [proˈfaund] *adj* profundo

profuse [proˈfjus] *adj* (*extravagant*) pródigo; (*abundant*) profuso

progeny [ˈpradʒəni] *s* (*pl* -nies) prole *f*

progno-sis [pragˈnosis] *s* (*pl* -ses [siz]) pronóstico

prognostic [pragˈnastik] *s* pronóstico

program [ˈprogræm] *s* programa *m* ‖ *tr* programar

progress [ˈpragres] *s* progreso; progresos; **to make progress** hacer progresos ‖ [prəˈgres] *intr* progresar

progressive [prəˈgresiv] *adj* progresivo; (pol) progresista ‖ *s* (pol) progresista *mf*

prohibit [proˈhibit] *tr* prohibir

project [ˈpradʒekt] *s* proyecto ‖ [prəˈdʒekt] *tr* proyectar ‖ *intr* proyectarse

projectile [prəˈdʒektil] *s* proyectil *m*

projection [prəˈdʒekʃən] *s* proyección

projector [prəˈdʒektər] *s* proyector *m*

proletarian [ˌproliˈteriən] *adj & s* proletario

proletariat [ˌproliˈteriət] *s* proletariado

proliferate [prəˈlifəˌret] *intr* proliferar

prolific [prəˈlifik] *adj* prolífico

prolix [ˈproliks] o [proˈliks] *adj* difuso, verboso

prologue [ˈprolɔg] o [ˈprolag] *s* prólogo

prolong [proˈlɔŋ] o [proˈlaŋ] *tr* prolongar

promenade [ˌpramiˈned] o [ˌpramiˈnad] *s* paseo; baile *m* de gala ‖ *intr* pasear o pasearse

promenade deck *s* (naut) cubierta de paseo

prominent [ˈpramInənt] *adj* prominente

promise [ˈpramis] *s* promesa ‖ *tr & intr* prometer

promising young man *s* joven *m* de esperanzas

promissory [ˈpramiˌsori] *adj* promisorio

promissory note *s* pagaré *m*

promonto-ry [ˈpramənˌtori] *s* (*pl* -ries) promontorio

promote [prəˈmot] *tr* promover; fomentar

promotion [prəˈmoʃən] *s* promoción; fomento

prompt [prampt] *adj* pronto, puntual; listo, dispuesto ‖ *tr* incitar, mover; inspirar, sugerir; (theat) apuntar

prompter [ˈpramptər] *s* (theat) apuntador *m*

prompter's box *s* (theat) concha

promulgate [ˈpraməlˌget] o [proˈmʌlget] *tr* promulgar

prone [pron] *adj* postrado boca abajo; extendido sobre el suelo; dispuesto, propenso

prong [prɔŋ] o [praŋ] *s* punta (*de un tenedor, horquilla, etc.*)

pronoun [ˈpronaun] *s* pronombre *m*

pronounce [prəˈnauns] *tr* pronunciar

pronouncement [prəˈnaunsmənt] *s* declaración; decisión, opinión

pronunciamen-to [prəˌnʌnsiəˈmento] *s* (*pl* -tos) pronunciamiento

pronunciation [prəˌnʌnsiˈeʃən] o [prəˌnʌnʃiˈeʃən] *s* pronunciación

proof [pruf] *adj* de prueba; **proof against** a prueba de ‖ *s* prueba

proof'read'er *s* corrector *m* de pruebas

prop [prap] *s* apoyo, puntal *m*; (*to hold up a plant*) rodrigón *m*; **props** (theat) accesorios ‖ *v* (*pret & pp* **propped;** *ger* **propping**) *tr* apoyar, apuntalar; poner un rodrigón a

propaganda [ˌprapəˈgændə] *s* propaganda

propagate [ˈprapəˌget] *tr* propagar

proparoxytone [ˌprapærˈaksiˌton] *adj & s* proparoxítono

pro-pel [prəˈpel] *v* (*pret & pp* **-pelled;** *ger* **-pelling**) *tr* propulsar, impeler

propeller [prəˈpelər] *s* hélice *f*

propensi-ty [prəˈpensiti] *s* (*pl* -ties) propensión

proper [ˈprapər] *adj* propio, conveniente; decente, decoroso; exacto, justo

proper-ty [ˈprapərti] *s* (*pl* -ties) propiedad; **properties** (theat) accesorios

property owner *s* propietario de bienes raíces

prophe-cy [ˈprafisi] *s* (*pl* -cies) profecía

prophe-sy [ˈprafiˌsai] *v* (*pret & pp* -sied) *tr* profetizar

prophet [ˈprafit] *s* profeta *m*

prophetess [ˈprafitis] *s* profetisa

prophylactic [ˌprofiˈlæktik] *adj & s* profiláctico

propitiate [prəˈpiʃiˌet] *tr* propiciar

propitious [prəˈpiʃəs] *adj* propicio

prop'jet' *s* turbohélice *m*

proportion [prəˈporʃən] *s* proporción; **in proportion as** a medida que; **out of proportion** desproporcionado ‖ *tr* proporcionar

proportionate [prə'porʃənɪt] *adj* proporcionado

proposal [prə'pozəl] *s* propuesta; oferta de matrimonio

propose [prə'poz] *tr* proponer || *intr* proponer matrimonio; **to propose to** pedir la mano a; proponerse a + *inf*

proposition [‚prapə'zıʃən] *s* proposición, propuesta

propound [prə'paund] *tr* proponer

proprietor [prə'praɪ·ətər] *s* propietario

proprietress [prə'praɪ·ətrıs] *s* propietaria

proprie·ty [prə'praɪ·əti] *s* (*pl* **-ties**) corrección, conducta decorosa, conveniencia; **proprieties** cánones *mpl* sociales, convenciones

propulsion [prə'pʌlʃən] *s* propulsión

prorate [pro'ret] *tr* prorratear

prosaic [pro'ze·ɪk] *adj* prosaico

proscribe [pro'skraɪb] *tr* proscribir

prose [proz] *adj* prosaico || *s* prosa

prosecute ['prası‚kjut] *tr* llevar a cabo; (*law*) procesar

prosecutor ['prası‚kjutər] *s* acusador *m*, demandante *mf*; (*lawyer*) fiscal *m*

proselyte ['prası‚laıt] *s* prosélito *m*

prose writer *s* prosista *mf*

prosody ['prasədɪ] *s* métrica

prospect ['praspɛkt] *s* vista; esperanza; probabilidad de éxito; cliente *mf* o comprador *m* probable || *tr & intr* prospectar; **to prospect for** buscar (*p.ej.*, *oro*, *petróleo*)

prosper ['praspər] *tr & intr* prosperar

prosperi·ty [pras'pɛrıti] *s* (*pl* **-ties**) prosperidad

prosperous ['praspərəs] *adj* próspero

prostitute ['prastı‚tjut] o ['prastı‚tut] *s* prostituta || *tr* prostituir

prostrate ['prastret] *adj* postrado, prosternado || *tr* postrar

prostration [pras'treʃən] *s* postración

Prot. *abbr* **Protestant**

protagonist [pro'tægənıst] *s* protagonista *mf*

protect [prə'tɛkt] *tr* proteger

protection [prə'tɛkʃən] *s* protección

protégé ['protə‚ʒe] *s* protegido

protégée ['protə‚ʒe] *s* protegida

protein ['proti·ın] o ['protin] *s* proteína

pro-tempore [pro'tɛmpəri] *adj* interino

protest ['protɛst] *s* protesta || [pro'tɛst] *tr & intr* protestar

protestant ['pratıstənt] *adj & s* protestante *mf* || **Protestant** *adj & s* protestante *mf*

prothonotar·y [pro'θanə‚tɛri] *s* (*pl* **-ies**) escribano principal (*de un tribunal*)

protocol ['protə‚kal] *s* protocolo

protoplasm ['protə‚plæzəm] *s* protoplasma *m*

prototype ['protə‚taıp] *s* prototipo

protozoön [‚protə'zo·an] *s* protozoo

protract [pro'trækt] *tr* prolongar

protrude [pro'trud] *intr* resaltar

proud [praud] *adj* orgulloso; soberbio; glorioso

proud flesh *s* carnosidad, bezo

prov. *abbr* **provincialism**

prove [pruv] *v* (*pret* **proved**; *pp* **proved** o **proven**) *tr* probar || *intr* resultar; **to prove to be** venir a ser, resultar

proverb ['pravərb] *s* proverbio

provide [prə'vaɪd] *tr* proporcionar, suministrar || *intr* — **to provide for** proveer a; asegurarse (*el porvenir*)

provided [prə'vaɪdɪd] *conj* a condición (de) que, con tal (de) que

providence ['pravɪdəns] *s* providencia

providential [‚pravɪ'dɛnʃəl] *adj* providencial

providing [prə'vaɪdıŋ] *conj* var de **provided**

province ['pravıns] *s* provincia; (*sphere of activity or knowledge*) competencia

provision [prə'vɪʒən] *s* provisión; condición, estipulación

provi·so [prə'vaɪzo] *s* (*pl* **-sos** o **-soes**) condición, estipulación, salvedad

provoke [prə'vok] *tr* provocar

provoking [prə'vokıŋ] *adj* provocador, irritante

prow [prau] *s* proa

prowess ['prau·ıs] *s* proeza; destreza

prowl [praul] *intr* cazar al acecho, rodar, vagabundear

prowler ['praulər] *s* rondador *m*; ladrón *m*

proximity [prak'sımıtı] *s* proximidad

prox·y ['praksı] *s* (*pl* **-ies**) poder *m*, poderhabiente *mf*

prude [prud] *s* mojigato, gazmoño

prudence ['prudəns] *s* prudencia

prudent ['prudənt] *adj* prudente

pruder·y ['prudərı] *s* (*pl* **-ies**) mojigatería, gazmoñería

prudish ['prudıʃ] *adj* mojigato, gazmoño

prune [prun] *s* ciruela pasa || *tr* podar, escamondar

pry [praɪ] *v* (*pret & pp* **pried**) *tr* — **to pry open** forzar con la alzaprima o palanca; **to pry out of** arrancar (*p.ej.*, *un secreto*) a (*una persona*) || *intr* entremeterse; **to pry into** entremeterse en

P.S. *abbr* **postscript, Privy Seal**

psalm [sɑm] *s* salmo

Psalter ['sɔltər] *s* Salterio

pseudo ['sudo] o ['sjudo] *adj* supuesto, falso, fingido

pseudonym ['sudənım] o ['sjudənım] *s* seudónimo

Psyche ['saɪkı] *s* Psique *f*

psychiatrist [saɪ'kaɪ·ətrıst] *s* psiquiatra *mf*

psychiatry [saɪ'kaɪ·ətrı] *s* psiquiatría

psychic ['saɪkık] *adj* psíquico; mediúmnico || *s* médium *mf*

psychoanalysis [‚saɪko·ə'nælısıs] *s* psicoanálisis *m*

psychoanalyze [‚saɪko'ænə‚laɪz] *tr* psicoanalizar

psychologic(al) [‚saɪko'ladʒık(əl)] *adj* psicológico

psychologist [saɪ'kalədʒıst] *s* psicólogo

psychology [saɪ'kalədʒı] *s* psicología

psychopath ['saɪkə‚pæθ] *s* psicópata *mf*

psycho·sis [saɪ'kosɪs] *s* (*pl* -ses [siz]) psicosis *f*; estado mental
psychotic [saɪ'katɪk] *adj & s* psicótico
pt. *abbr* part, pint, point
pub [pʌb] *s* (Brit) taberna
puberty ['pjubɚti] *s* pubertad
public ['pʌblɪk] *adj & s* público
publication [,pʌblɪ'keʃən] *s* publicación
public conveyance *s* vehículo de servicio público
publicity [pʌb'lɪsɪti] *s* publicidad
publicize ['pʌblɪ,saɪz] *tr* publicar
public library *s* biblioteca municipal
public school *s* (U.S.A.) escuela pública, (Brit) internado privado con dote
public speaking *s* elocución, oratoria
public spirit *s* celo patriótico del buen ciudadano
public toilet *s* quiosco de necesidad
public utility *s* empresa de servicio público; **public utilities** acciones emitidas por empresas de servicio público
publish ['pʌblɪʃ] *tr* publicar
publisher ['pʌblɪʃɚ] *s* editor *m*
publishing house *s* casa editorial
pucker ['pʌkɚ] *s* (*small fold*) frunce *m*; pliego mal hecho || *tr* fruncir (*una tela*; *la frente*); plegar mal || *intr* plegarse mal
pudding ['pudɪŋ] *s* budín *m*, pudín *m*
puddle ['pʌdəl] *s* aguazal *m*, charco
pudg·y ['pʌdʒi] *adj* (*comp* -ier; *super* -iest) gordinflón, rechoncho
puerile ['pjuərɪl] *adj* pueril
puerili·ty [,pjuə'rɪlɪti] *s* (*pl* -ties) puerilidad
Puerto Rican ['pwerto 'rikən] *adj & s* puertorriqueño
puff [pʌf] *s* soplo vivo; (*of smoke*) bocanada; (*in clothing*) bullón *m*; borla de polvos; pastelillo de crema o jalea; alabanza exagerada; ráfaga, ventolera || *tr* soplar; hinchar; alabar exageradamente || *intr* soplar; hincharse; enorgullecerse exageradamente
puff paste *s* hojaldre *m & f*
pugilism ['pjudʒɪ,lɪzəm] *s* pugilismo
pugilist ['pjudʒɪlɪst] *s* pugilista *m*
pug-nosed ['pʌg,nozd] *adj* braco
puke [pjuk] *s* (slang) vómito || *tr & intr* (slang) vomitar
pull [pul] *s* estirón *m*, tirón *m*; (*on a cigar*) chupada; (*of a door*) tirador *m*; (slang) enchufe *m*, buenas aldabas || *tr* tirar de; torcer (*un ligamento*); (typ) sacar (*una impresión o prueba*); **to pull down** demoler, derribar; bajar (*p.ej., la cortinilla*); abatir, degradar; **to pull oneself together** componerse, recobrar la calma || *intr* tirar; moverse despacio, moverse con esfuerzo, **to pull at** tirar de (*p.ej., la corbata*); chupar (*p.ej., un cigarro*); **to pull for** (slang) abogar por, ayudar; **to pull for oneself** tirar por su lado, **to pull in** llegar (*un tren*) a la estación; **to pull out** partir (*un tren*) de la estación; **to pull through** salir a flote; recobrar la salud

pullet ['pulɪt] *s* polla
pulley ['puli] *s* polea
pulp [pʌlp] *s* pulpa; (*to make paper*) pasta; (*of tooth*) bulbo
pulpit ['pulpɪt] *s* púlpito
pulsate ['pʌlset] *intr* pulsar; vibrar
pulsation [pʌl'seʃən] *s* pulsación; vibración
pulse [pʌls] *s* pulso; **to feel o take the pulse of** tomar el pulso a
pulverize ['pʌlvə,raɪz] *tr* pulverizar
pumice stone ['pʌmɪs] *s* pómez *f*, piedra pómez
pum·mel ['pʌməl] *v* (*pret & pp* -meled o -melled; *ger* -meling o -melling) *tr* apuñear, aporrear
pump [pʌmp] *s* bomba; (*slipperlike shoe*) escarpín *m*, zapatilla || *tr* elevar o sacar (*agua*) por medio de una bomba; (coll) tirar de la lengua a (*una persona*); **to pump up** hinchar, inflar (*un neumático*)
pump handle *s* guimbalete *m*
pumpkin ['pʌmpkɪn] o ['pʌŋkɪn] *s* calabaza común; **some pumpkins** (coll) persona de muchas campanillas
pump-priming ['pʌmp,praɪmɪŋ] *s* inyección económica (*por parte del gobierno*)
pun [pʌn] *s* equívoco, retruécano || *v* (*pret & pp* punned; *ger* punning) *intr* decir equívocos, jugar del vocablo
punch [pʌntʃ] *s* puñetazo; (*tool*) punzón *m*; (*for tickets*) sacabocado; (*drink*) ponche *m* || *tr* dar un puñetazo a; taladrar, perforar (*un billete, una tarjeta*)
punch bowl *s* ponchera
punch card *s* tarjeta perforada
punch clock *s* reloj *m* registrador de tarjetas
punch'-drunk' *adj* atontado (*p.ej., por una tunda de golpes*); completamente aturdido
punched tape *s* cinta perforada
punching bag *s* punching *m*, boxibalón *m*
punch line *s* broche *m* de oro, colofón *m* del artículo
punctilious [pʌŋk'tɪlɪ·əs] *adj* puntilloso, pundonoroso
punctual ['pʌŋktʃu·əl] *adj* puntual
punctuate ['pʌŋktʃu,et] *tr* puntuar; acentuar, destacar; interrumpir || *intr* puntuar
punctuation [,pʌŋktʃu'eʃən] *s* puntuación
punctuation mark *s* signo de puntuación
puncture ['pʌŋktʃɚ] *s* puntura; (*of a tire*) picadura, pinchazo || *tr* pinchar, picar, perforar
punc'ture-proof' *adj* a prueba de pinchazos
pundit ['pʌndɪt] *s* erudito, sabio
pungent ['pʌndʒənt] *adj* picante; estimulante
punish ['pʌnɪʃ] *tr* castigar; (coll) maltratar
punishment ['pʌnɪʃmənt] *s* castigo; (coll) maltrato

punk [pʌŋk] *adj* (slang) malo, de mala calidad ‖ *s* yesca, pebete *m;* (*decayed wood*) hupe *m;* (slang) pillo, gamberro

punster [ˈpʌnstər] *s* equivoquista *mf,* vocablista *mf*

pu·ny [ˈpjuni] *adj* (*comp* -nier; *super* -niest) encanijado, débil; insignificante, mezquino

pup [pʌp] *s* cachorro

pupil [ˈpjupəl] *s* alumno; (*of the eye*) pupila

puppet [ˈpʌpɪt] *s* títere *m;* (*doll*) muñeca; (*person controlled by another*) maniquí *m*

puppet government *s* gobierno de monigotes

puppet show *s* función de títeres

puppy love [ˈpʌpi] *s* (coll) primeros amores

purchase [ˈpʌrtʃəs] *s* compra; agarre *m* firme ‖ *tr* comprar

purchasing power *s* poder adquisitivo

pure [pjur] *adj* puro

purgative [ˈpʌrgətɪv] *adj & s* purgante *m*

purge [pʌrdʒ] *s* purga ‖ *tr* purgar

puri·fy [ˈpjurɪ‚faɪ] *v* (*pret & pp* -fied) *tr* purificar

puritan [ˈpjurɪtən] *adj & s* puritano ‖ **Puritan** *adj & s* puritano

purity [ˈpjurɪti] *s* pureza

purloin [pərˈlɔɪn] *tr & intr* robar, hurtar

purple [ˈpʌrpəl] *adj* purpurado, rojo morado ‖ *m* púrpura, rojo morado

purport [ˈpʌrport] *s* significado, idea principal ‖ [pərˈport] *tr* significar, querer decir

purpose [ˈpʌrpəs] *s* intención, propósito; fin *m,* objeto; **for the purpose al efecto; for what purpose?** ¿con qué fin?; **on purpose** adrede, de propósito; **to good purpose** con buenos resultados; **to no purpose** sin resultado; **to serve one's purpose** servir para el caso

purposely [ˈpʌrpəsli] *adv* adrede, de propósito

purr [pʌr] *s* ronroneo ‖ *intr* ronronear

purse [pʌrs] *s* bolsa; (*money collected for charity*) colecta ‖ *tr* fruncir

purser [ˈpʌrsər] *s* contador *m* de navío, comisario de a bordo

purse snatcher [ˈsnætʃər] *s* carterista *mf*

purse strings *spl* cordones *mpl* de la bolsa; **to hold the purse strings** tener las llaves de la caja

pursue [pərˈsu] o [pərˈsju] *tr* perseguir (*al que huye*), proseguir (*lo empezado*); seguir (*una carrera*); dedicarse a

pursuit [pərˈsut] o [pərˈsjut] *s* persecución; prosecución; (*e.g., of happiness*) busca o búsqueda; empleo

pursuit plane *s* caza *m,* avión *m* de caza

purvey [pərˈve] *tr* proveer, suministrar

pus [pʌs] *s* pus *m*

push [puʃ] *s* empuje *m,* empujón *m* ‖ *tr* empujar; pulsar (*un botón*); extender (*p.ej., conquistas*); **to push around** (coll) tratar a empujones; **to**

push aside hacer a un lado; **to push through** forzar (*p.ej., una resolución*) ‖ *intr* empujar; **to push off** (coll) irse, salir; (naut) desatracarse

push button *s* botón *m* de llamada, botón interruptor

push'-but'ton control *s* mando por botón

push'cart' *s* carretilla de mano

pushing [ˈpuʃɪŋ] *adj* emprendedor; entremetido, agresivo

pusillanimous [‚pjusɪˈlænɪməs] *adj* pusilánime

puss [pus] *interj* ¡miz! ‖ *s* micho; chica, muchacha; (slang) cara, boca

puss in the corner *s* las cuatro esquinas

puss·y [ˈpusi] *s* (*pl* -ies) michito

pussy willow *s* sauce norteamericano de amentos muy sedosos

pustule [ˈpʌstʃul] *s* pústula

put [put] *v* (*pret & pp* put; *ger* putting) *tr* poner, colocar; arrojar, echar, lanzar; hacer (*una pregunta*); **to put across** llevar a cabo; hacer aceptar; **to put aside** poner aparte; rechazar; ahorrar (*dinero*); **to put down** anotar, apuntar; sofocar (*una insurrección*); rebajar (*los precios*); **to put off** posponer; deshacerse de; **to put on** ponerse (*la ropa*); poner en escena; llevar (*p.ej., un drama a la pantalla*); accionar (*un freno*); cargar (*impuestos*); fingir; atribuir; **to put oneself out** incomodarse, molestarse; afanarse, desvivirse; **to put out** extender (*la mano*); apagar (*el fuego, la luz*); poner en la calle; dar a luz, publicar; decepcionar; (sport) sacar fuera de la partida; **to put over o through** (coll) llevar a cabo; **to put up** construir, edificar; abrir (*un paraguas*); conservar (*fruta, legumbres*); (coll) incitar ‖ *intr* dirigirse; **to put on** fingir; **to put up** parar, hospedarse; **to put up with** aguantar, tolerar

put'-out' *adj* contrariado, enojado

putrid [ˈpjutrɪd] *adj* pútrido; corrompido, perverso

Putsch [putʃ] *s* intentona de sublevación; sublevación

putter [ˈpʌtər] *intr* trabajar sin orden ni sistema; **to putter around** ocuparse en fruslerías, temporizar

put·ty [ˈpʌti] *s* (*pl* -ties) masilla ‖ *v* (*pret & pp* -tied) *tr* enmasillar

putty knife *s* cuchillo de vidriero, espátula

put'-up' *adj* (coll) premeditado con malicia

puzzle [ˈpʌzəl] *s* enigma *m;* acertijo, rompecabezas *m* ‖ *tr* confundir, poner perplejo; **to puzzle out** descifrar ‖ *intr* estar perplejo; **to puzzle over** tratar de descifrar

puzzler [ˈpʌzlər] *s* quisicosa

PW *abbr* prisoner of war

pyg·my [ˈpɪgmi] *adj* pigmeo ‖ *s* (*pl* -mies) pigmeo

pylon [ˈpaɪlɑn] *s* pilón *m*

pyramid [ˈpɪrəmɪd] *s* pirámide *f* ‖ aumentar (*su dinero*) comprando o vendiendo al crédito y empleando las ganancias para comprar o vender más

pyre [paɪr] *s* pira
Pyrenean [,pɪrɪ'ni-ən] *adj* pirineo
Pyrenees ['pɪrɪ,niz] *spl* Pirineos
pyrites [paɪ'raɪtiz] o ['paɪraɪts] *s* pirita

pyrotechnical [,paɪrə'teknɪkəl] *adj* pirotécnico
pyrotechnics [,paɪrə'teknɪks] *spl* pirotecnia
python ['paɪθən] o ['paɪθən] *s* pitón *m*
pythoness ['paɪθənɪs] *s* pitonisa
pyx [pɪks] *s* píxide *f*, copón *m*

Q

Q, q [kju] decimoséptima letra del alfabeto inglés
Q. *abbr* quarto, queen, question, quire
Q.M. *abbr* quartermaster
qr. *abbr* quarter, quire
qt. *abbr* quantity, quart
qu. *abbr* quart, quarter, quarterly, queen, query, question
quack [kwæk] *adj* falso ‖ *s* graznido del pato; charlatán *m*; medicastro, curandero ‖ *intr* parpar (*el pato*)
quacker•y ['kwækəri] *s* (*pl* -ies) charlatanismo
quadrangle ['kwad,ræŋgəl] *s* cuadrángulo; patio cuadrangular
quadrant ['kwadrənt] *s* cuadrante *m*
quadroon [kwad'run] *s* cuarterón *m*
quadruped ['kwadru,ped] *adj* & *s* cuadrúpedo
quadruple ['kwadrupəl] o [kwad'rupəl] *adj* & *s* cuádruple *m* ‖ *tr* cuadruplicar ‖ *intr* cuadruplicarse
quadruplet ['kwadru,plet] o [kwad'ruplet] *s* cuatrillizo
quaff [kwaf] o [kwæf] *s* trago grande ‖ *tr* & *intr* beber en gran cantidad
quail [kwel] *s* codorniz *f* ‖ *intr* acobardarse
quaint [kwent] *adj* curioso, raro; afectado, rebuscado; fantástico, singular
quake [kwek] *s* temblor *m*, terremoto ‖ *intr* temblar
Quaker ['kwekər] *adj* & *s* cuáquero
Quaker meeting *s* reunión de cuáqueros; reunión en que hay poca conversación
quali•fy ['kwalɪ,faɪ] *v* (*pret* & *pp* -fied) *tr* calificar; capacitar, habilitar ‖ *intr* capacitarse, habilitarse
quali•ty ['kwalɪti] *s* (*pl* -ties) (*characteristic; virtue*) calidad; (*property, attribute*) cualidad; (*of a sound*) timbre *m*
qualm [kwam] *s* escrúpulo de conciencia; duda, inquietud; (*nausea*) basca
quanda•ry ['kwandəri] *s* (*pl* -ries) incertidumbre, perplejidad
quanti•ty ['kwantɪti] *s* (*pl* -ties) cantidad
quan•tum ['kwantəm] *adj* cuántico ‖ *s* (*pl* -ta [tə]) cuanto, quántum *m*
quantum theory *s* teoría cuántica
quarantine ['kwarən,tin] o ['kwɔrən,tin] *s* cuarentena; estación de cuarentena ‖ *tr* poner en cuarentena
quar•rel ['kwarəl] o ['kwɔrəl] *s* disputa, riña, pelea; **to have no quarrel with** no estar en desacuerdo con; **to pick a quarrel with** tomarse con ‖ *v*

(*pret* & *pp* -reled o -relled; *ger* -reling o -relling) *intr* disputar, reñir, pelear
quarrelsome ['kwarəlsəm] o ['kwɔrəlsəm] *adj* pendenciero
quar•ry ['kwari] o ['kwɔri] *s* (*pl* -ries) cantera, pedrera; caza, presa *f* ‖ *v* (*pret* & *pp* -ried) *tr* sacar de una cantera; extraer, sacar
quart [kwɔrt] *s* cuarto de galón
quarter ['kwɔrtər] *adj* cuarto ‖ *s* cuarto, cuarta parte; (*three months*) trimestre *m*; moneda de 25 centavos; cuarto de luna; barrio; región, lugar *m*; (*clemency*) (mil) cuartel *m*; **quarters** morada, vivienda; local *m*; (mil) cuarteles *mpl*; **to take up quarters** alojarse ‖ *tr* descuartizar
quar'ter•deck *s* alcázar *m*
quar'ter-hour *s* cuarto de hora; **on the quarter-hour** al cuarto en punto cada cuarto de hora
quarter•ly ['kwɔrtərli] *adj* trimestral ‖ *adv* trimestralmente ‖ *s* (*pl* -lies) publicación o revista trimestral
quar'ter•mas'ter *s* (mil) comisario; (nav) cabo de brigadas
quartet [kwɔr'tet] *s* cuarteto
quartz [kwɔrts] *s* cuarzo
quasar ['kwesar] *s* (astr) objeto del espacio, fuente *f* cuasiestelar de radio
quash [kwaʃ] *tr* sofocar, reprimir; anular, invalidar
quaver ['kwevər] *s* temblor *m*, estremecimiento; (mus) trémolo ‖ *intr* temblar, estremecerse
quay [ki] *s* muelle *m*, desembarcadero
queen [kwin] *s* reina; (*in chess*) dama o reina; (*in cards*) dama (*que corresponde al caballo*); abeja reina
queen bee *s* abeja reina, abeja maestra; (slang) marimandona, la que lleva la voz cantante
queen dowager *s* reina viuda
queen•ly ['kwinli] *adj* (*comp* -lier; *super* -liest) de reina; como reina; regio
queen mother *s* reina madre
queen olive *s* aceituna de la reina, aceituna gordal
queen post *s* péndola
queen's English *s* inglés castizo
queer [kwɪr] *adj* curioso, raro; estrambótico, estrafalario; aturdido, indispuesto; (coll) sospechoso, misterioso ‖ *tr* (slang) echar a perder; (slang) comprometer
quell [kwel] *tr* sofocar, reprimir; mitigar (*una pena o dolor*)

quench [kwentʃ] *tr* apagar (*el fuego; la sed*); sofocar, reprimir; (electron) amortiguar

que·ry [ˈkwɪri] *s* (*pl* -ries) pregunta; signo de interrogación; duda ‖ *v* (*pret & pp* -ried) *tr* interrogar; marcar con signo de interrogación; dudar

ques. *abbr* **question**

quest [kwest] *s* búsqueda; (*of the Holy Grail*) demanda; **in quest of** en busca de

question [ˈkwestʃən] *s* pregunta; (*problem for discussion*) cuestión; asunto, proposición; **beside the question** que no viene al caso; **beyond question** fuera de duda; **out of the question** imposible, indiscutible; **to ask a question** hacer una pregunta; **to be a question of** tratarse de, ser cuestión de; **to call in question** poner en duda; **without question** sin duda ‖ *tr* interrogar; cuestionar (*poner en tela de juicio*)

questionable [ˈkwestʃənəbəl] *adj* cuestionable

question mark *s* punto interrogante, signo de interrogación

questionnaire [ˌkwestʃənˈer] *s* cuestionario

queue [kju] *s* (*of hair*) coleta; (*of people*) cola ‖ *intr* hacer cola

quibble [ˈkwɪbəl] *intr* sutilizar

quick [kwɪk] *adj* rápido, veloz; ágil, vivo; despierto, listo; **the quick and the dead** los vivos y los muertos; **to cut** o **to sting to the quick** herir en lo vivo, tocar en la herida

quicken [ˈkwɪkən] *tr* acelerar, avivar; animar ‖ *intr* acelerarse; animarse

quick'lime' *s* cal viva

quick lunch *s* servicio de la barra, servicio rápido

quick'sand' *s* arena movediza

quick'sil'ver *s* azogue *m*

quiet [ˈkwaɪ·ət] *adj* (*still*) quieto; silencioso; (*market*) (com) encalmado; **to keep quiet** callarse ‖ *s* quietud; silencio; **on the quiet** a las calladas ‖ *tr* aquietar; acallar ‖ *intr* aquietarse; callarse; **to quiet down** calmarse

quill [kwɪl] *s* pluma de ave; cañón *m* de pluma; (*of hedgehog, porcupine*) púa

quilt [kwɪlt] *s* edredón *m*, colcha ‖ *tr* acolchar

quince [kwɪns] *s* membrillo

quinine [ˈkwaɪnaɪn] *s* quinina

quinsy [ˈkwɪnzi] *s* cinanquia, esquinencia

quintessence [kwɪnˈtesəns] *s* quintaesencia

quintet [kwɪnˈtet] *s* quinteto

quintuplet [kwɪnˈtjuplet] o [kwɪnˈtuplet] *s* quintillizo

quip [kwɪp] *s* chufleta, pulla ‖ *v* (*pret & pp* **quipped**; *ger* **quipping**) *tr* decir en son de burla ‖ *intr* echar pullas

quire [kwaɪr] *s* mano *f* de papel; (bb) alzado

quirk [kwʌrk] *s* excentricidad, rareza; sutileza; vuelta repentina

quit [kwɪt] *adj* libre, descargado; **to be quits** estar desquitados; **to cry quits** pedir treguas ‖ *v* (*pret & pp* **quit** o **quitted**; *ger* **quitting**) *tr* dejar ‖ *intr* irse; (coll) dejar de trabajar

quite [kwaɪt] *adv* enteramente; verdaderamente; (coll) bastante, muy

quitter [ˈkwɪtər] *s* remolón *m*; (*of a cause*) desertor *m*

quiver [ˈkwɪvər] *s* temblor *m*; (*to hold arrows*) aljaba, carcaj *m* ‖ *intr* temblar

quixotic [kwɪksˈɑtɪk] *adj* quijotesco

quiz [kwɪz] *s* (*pl* **quizzes**) examen *m*; interrogatorio ‖ *v* (*pret & pp* **quizzed**; *ger* **quizzing**) *tr* examinar; interrogar

quiz game *s* torneo de preguntas y respuestas

quiz program *s* programa *m* de preguntas y respuestas, torneo radiofónico

quiz section *s* grupo de práctica

quizzical [ˈkwɪzɪkəl] *adj* curioso; cómico; burlón

quoin [kɔɪn] o [kwɔɪn] *s* esquina; piedra angular; (*wedge*) cuña ‖ *tr* (typ) acuñar

quoit [kwɔɪt] o [kɔɪt] *s* herrón *m*, tejo; **quoits** *ssg* hito

quondam [ˈkwɑndæm] *adj* antiguo, de otro tiempo

quorum [ˈkworəm] *s* quórum *m*

quota [ˈkwotə] *s* cuota

quotation [kwoˈteʃən] *s* (*from a book*) cita; (*of prices*) cotización

quotation marks *spl* comillas

quote [kwot] *s* (coll) cita; (coll) cotización; **close quote** fin de la cita; **quotes** (coll) comillas ‖ *tr & intr* citar; cotizar; **quote cito**

quotient [ˈkwoʃənt] *s* cociente *m*

q.v. *abbr* **quod vide** (Lat) **which see**

R

R, r [ɑr] decimoctava letra del alfabeto inglés

r. *abbr* **railroad, railway, road, rod, ruble, rupee**

R. *abbr* **railroad, railway, Regina** (Lat) **Queen; Republican, response, Rex** (Lat) **King; River, Royal**

rabbet [ˈræbɪt] *s* barbilla, rebajo ‖ *tr* embarbillar, rebajar

rab·bi [ˈræbaɪ] *s* (*pl* -bis o -bies) rabino

rabbit [ˈræbɪt] *s* conejo

rabble [ˈræbəl] *s* canalla, gentuza

rabble rouser [ˈrauzər] *s* populachero, alborotapueblos *mf*

rabies [ˈrebiz] o [ˈrebɪ ˌiz] *s* rabia

raccoon [ræˈkun] *s* mapache *m*, oso lavador

race [res] *s* (*people of same stock*) raza; (*contest in speed, etc.*) carrera; (*channel to lead water*) caz *m* ‖ *tr* competir con, en una carrera; hacer correr de prisa; hacer funcionar (*un motor*) a velocidad excesiva ‖ *intr* correr de prisa; correr en una carrera; competir en una carrera; embalarse (*un motor*); (naut) regatear

race horse *s* caballo de carreras

race riot *s* disturbio racista

race track *s* pista de carreras

racial ['reʃəl] *adj* racial

racing car *s* coche *m* de carreras

rack [ræk] *s* (*sort of shelf*) estante *m*; (*to hang clothes*) percha; (*for fodder for cattle*) pesebre *m*; (*for baggage*) red *f* de equipaje; (*for guns*) armero; (*bar made to gear with a pinion*) cremallera; **to go to rack and ruin** desvencijarse; ir al desastre ‖ *tr* estirar, forzar; atormentar; despedazar; oprimir, agobiar; **to rack off** trasegar (*el vino*); **to rack one's brains** calentarse la cabeza, devanarse los sesos

racket ['rækɪt] *s* raqueta; (*noise*) baraúnda, alboroto; (slang) trapisonda, trapacería; **to raise a racket** armar un alboroto

racketeer [,rækɪ'tɪr] *s* trapisondista *mf*, trapacista *mf* ‖ *intr* trapacear

rack railway *s* ferrocarril *m* de cremallera

rac·y ['resɪ] *adj* (*comp* **-ler;** *super* **-lest**) espirituoso, chispeante; perfumado; (*somewhat indecent*) picante

radar ['redɑr] *s* radar *m*

radiant ['redɪənt] *adj* radiante, resplandeciente; (*cheerful, smiling*) radiante

radiate ['redɪ,et] *tr* radiar; difundir (*p.ej., felicidad*) ‖ *intr* radiar, irradiar

radiation [,redɪ'eʃən] *s* radiación

radiation sickness *s* enfermedad de radiación, mal *m* de rayos

radiator ['redɪ,etər] *s* radiador *m*

radiator cap *s* tapón *m* de radiador

radical ['rædɪkəl] *adj* & *s* radical *m*

radi·o ['redɪ,o] *s* (*pl* **-os**) radio *f*; radiograma *m* ‖ *tr* radiodifundir

radioactive [,redɪ·o'æktɪv] *adj* radiactivo

radio amateur *s* radioaficionado

radio announcer *s* locutor *m* de radio

ra'dio-broad'cast'ing *s* radiodifusión

radio frequency *s* radiofrecuencia

radio listener *s* radioescucha *mf*, radioyente *mf*

radiology [,redɪ'ɑlədʒɪ] *s* radiología

radio network *s* red *f* de emisoras

radio newscaster *s* cronista *mf* de radio

radio receiver *s* radiorreceptor *m*

radio set *s* aparato de radio

radish ['rædɪʃ] *s* rábano

radium ['redɪəm] *s* radio

radi·us ['redɪ·əs] *s* (*pl* **-i** [,aɪ] o **-uses**) radio; (*range of operation*) radio; **within a radius of** en . . . a la redonda

raffle ['ræfəl] *s* rifa ‖ *tr* & *intr* rifar

raft [ræft] o [rɑft] *s* armadía, balsa; (coll) gran número

rafter ['ræftər] o ['rɑftər] *s* cabrio, contrapar *m*, traviesa

rag [ræg] *s* trapo; **to chew the rag** (slang) dar la lengua

ragamuffin ['rægə,mʌfɪn] *s* pelagatos *m*; golfo, chiquillo haraposo

rag baby o **rag doll** *s* muñeca de trapo

rage [redʒ] *s* rabia; **to be all the rage** estar en boga, hacer furor; **to fly into a rage** montar en cólera

ragged ['rægɪd] *adj* andrajoso; (*edge*) cortado en dientes

ragpicker ['ræg,pɪkər] *s* andrajero, trapero

rag'weed' *s* ambrosía

raid [red] *s* incursión, invasión; ataque de sorpresa; ataque aéreo ‖ *tr* invadir; atacar inesperadamente; capturar (*p.ej., la policía un garito*)

rail [rel] *s* carril *m*, riel *m*; (*railing*) barandilla; (*of a bridge*) guardalado; (*at a bar*) apoyo para los pies; palo; **by rail** por ferrocarril; **rails** títulos o valores de ferrocarril ‖ *tr* poner barandilla a ‖ *intr* quejarse amargamente; **to rail at** injuriar, ultrajar

rail fence *s* cerca hecha de palos horizontales

rail'head' *s* (rr) cabeza de línea

railing ['relɪŋ] *s* barandilla, pasamano

rail'road' *adj* ferroviario ‖ *s* ferrocarril *m* ‖ *tr* (coll) llevar a cabo con demasiada precipitación; (slang) encarcelar falsamente ‖ *intr* trabajar en el ferrocarril

railroad crossing *s* paso a nivel

rail'way' *adj* ferroviario ‖ *s* ferrocarril *m*

raiment ['remənt] *s* prendas de vestir, indumentaria

rain [ren] *s* lluvia; **rain or shine** llueva o no, con buen o mal tiempo ‖ *tr* & *intr* llover

rain'bow' *s* arco iris

rain'coat' *s* impermeable *m*

rain'fall' *s* lluvia repentina; precipitación acuosa

rain·y ['renɪ] *adj* (*comp* **-ler;** *super* **-lest**) lluvioso

rainy day *s* día lluvioso; tiempo futuro de posible necesidad

raise [rez] *s* aumento ‖ *tr* levantar; aumentar; criar (*a niños, animales*); cultivar (*plantas*); reunir (*dinero*); suscitar (*una duda*); resucitar (*a los muertos*); abrasar (*barba, bigote*); poner (*una objeción*), plantear (*una pregunta*); levantar (*tropas; un sitio*); (math) elevar; (*to come in sight of*) (naut) avistar

raisin ['rezən] *s* pasa, uva seca

rake [rek] *s* rastro, rastrillo; (*person*) calavera *m*, libertino ‖ *tr* rastrillar; **to rake together** acumular (*dinero*)

rake'-off' *s* (slang) dinero obtenido ilícitamente

rakish ['rekɪʃ] *adj* airoso, gallardo; listo, vivo; libertino

ral·ly ['rælɪ] *s* (*pl* **-lies**) reunión popular, reunión política; recuperación, recobro ‖ *v* (*pret* & *pp* **-lied**) *tr* reunir; reanimar; recobrar (*la fuerza, la salud, el ánimo*) || *intr* reunirse; recobrarse (*p.ej., los precios en la Bolsa*); recobrar la fuerza, la salud, el ánimo; **to rally to the side of** acudir a, ir en socorro de

ram [ræm] *s* (*male sheep*) morueco, carnero padre; (*device for battering, crushing, etc.*) pisón *m* || *v* (*pret & pp* **rammed**; *ger* **ramming**) *tr* dar contra, chocar en; atestar, rellenar || *intr* chocar; **to ram into** chocar en

ramble ['ræmbəl] *s* paseo || *intr* pasear; serpentear (*p.ej., un río*); extenderse serpenteando (*las enredaderas*); (*to wander aimlessly; to talk in an aimless way*) divagar

rami•fy ['ræmɪ͵faɪ] *v* (*pret & pp* **-fied**) *tr* ramificar || *intr* ramificarse

ramp [ræmp] *s* rampa

rampage ['ræmpedʒ] *s* alboroto; **to go on a rampage** alborotar, comportarse como un loco

rampart ['ræmpɑrt] *s* muralla, terraplén *m*; amparo, defensa

ram'rod' *s* atacador *m*, baqueta

ram'shack'le *adj* desvencijado, destartalado

ranch [ræntʃ] *s* granja, hacienda

rancid ['rænsɪd] *adj* rancio

rancor ['ræŋkər] *s* rencor *m*

random ['rændəm] *adj* casual, fortuito; **at random** al azar, a la ventura

range [rendʒ] *s* (*row, line*) fila, hilera; (*scope, reach*) alcance *m*; (*of speeds, prices, etc.*) escala; campo de tiro; terreno de pasto; (*of a boat or airplane*) autonomía; (*of the voice*) extensión; (*of colors*) gama, serie *f*; (*stove*) cocina económica; **within range of** al alcance de || *tr* alinear; recorrer (*un terreno*); ir a lo largo de (*la costa*); arreglar, ordenar || *intr* fluctuar, variar (*entre ciertos límites*); extenderse; divagar, errar; **to range over** recorrer

range finder *s* telémetro

rank [ræŋk] *adj* exuberante, lozano; denso, espeso; grosero; maloliente; excesivo; incorregible, rematado; indecente, vulgar || *s* categoría, rango; condición, posición; distinción; (*line of soldiers standing abreast*) fila; (*mil*) empleo, grado || *tr* alinear; ordenar; tener grado o posición más alta que || *intr* ocupar el último grado; **to rank high** ocupar alta posición; ser tenido en alta estima; sobresalir; **to rank low** ocupar baja posición; **to rank with** estar al nivel de; tener el mismo grado que

rank and file *s* soldados de fila; pueblo, gente *f* común

rankle ['ræŋkəl] *tr* enconar, irritar || *intr* enconarse

ransack ['rænsæk] *tr* registrar, escudriñar; robar, saquear

ransom ['rænsəm] *s* rescate *m* || *tr* rescatar

rant [rænt] *intr* desvariar, despotricar

rap [ræp] *s* golpe corto y seco; (*noise*) taque *m*; (*coll*) ardite *m*, bledo; (*slang*) crítica mordaz; **to take the**

rap (slang) pagar la multa; sufrir las consecuencias || *v* (*pret & pp* **rapped**; *ger* **rapping**) *tr* golpear con golpe corto y seco; decir vivamente; (slang) criticar mordazmente || *intr* golpear con golpe corto y seco; **to rap at the door** tocar a la puerta

rapacious [rə'peʃəs] *adj* rapaz

rape [rep] *s* rapto; (*of a woman*) estupro, violación || *tr* raptar; estuprar, violar

rapid ['ræpɪd] *adj* rápido || **rapids** *spl* (*of a river*) rápidos

rap'id-fire' *adj* de tiro rápido; hecho vivamente

rapier ['repɪ•ər] *s* estoque *m*, espadín *m*

rapt [ræpt] *adj* arrebatado, extático, transportado; absorto

rapture ['ræptʃər] *s* embeleso, éxtasis *f*, rapto

rare [rer] *adj* raro; (*word*) poco usado; (*meat*) poco asado; (*gem*) precioso

rare bird *s* mirlo blanco

rare•fy ['rerɪ͵faɪ] *v* (*pret & pp* **-fied**) *tr* enrarecer || *intr* enrarecerse

rarely ['rerlɪ] *adv* rara vez

rascal ['ræskəl] *s* bellaco, bribón *m*, pícaro

rash [ræʃ] *adj* temerario || *s* brote *m*, salpullido, erupción

rasp [ræsp] *o* [rɑsp] *s* escofina; (*sound of a rasp*) sonido áspero || *tr* escofinar; irritar, molestar; decir con voz ronca || *intr* hacer sonido áspero

raspber•ry ['ræz͵berɪ] *o* ['rɑz͵berɪ] *s* (*pl* **-ries**) frambuesa, sangüesa

raspberry bush *s* frambueso, sangüeso

rat [ræt] *s* rata; (*false hair*) (coll) postizo; **to smell a rat** (coll) olerse una trama, sospechar una intriga

ratchet ['rætʃɪt] *s* trinquete *m*

rate [ret] *s* (*amount or degree measured in proportion to something else*) razón *f*; (*of interest*) tipo; velocidad; precio; **at any rate** de todos modos; **at the rate of** a razón de || *tr* valuar; estimar, juzgar; clasificar || *intr* ser considerado, ser tenido; estar clasificado

rate of exchange *s* tipo de cambio

rather ['ræðər] *o* ['rɑðər] *adv* algo, un poco; bastante; antes, más bien; mejor dicho; por el contrario; muy, mucho; **rather than** antes que, más bien que || *interj* ¡ya lo creo!

rati•fy ['rætɪ͵faɪ] *v* (*pret & pp* **-fied**) *tr* ratificar

ra•tio ['reʃo] *o* ['reʃɪ͵o] *s* (*pl* **-tios**) (math) razón *f*; (math) cociente *m*

ration ['reʃən] *o* ['ræʃən] *s* ración || *tr* racionar

ration book *s* cartilla de racionamiento

rational ['ræʃənəl] *adj* racional

rat poison *s* matarratas *m*

rattle ['rætəl] *s* (*number of short, sharp sounds*) traqueteo; (*noise-making device*) carraca, matraca; (*child's toy*) sonajero; barahúnda; (*in the throat*) estertor *m* || *tr* tabletear, traquetear; (*to confuse*) (coll) atortolar, desconcertar; **to rattle off**

deeir rápidamente || *intr* tabletear, traquetear

rat'tle•snake' *s* serpiente *f* de cascabel

rat'trap' *s* ratonera; trance apurado, atolladero

raucous ['rɔkəs] *adj* ronco

ravage ['rævɪdʒ] *s* destrucción, estrago, ruina || *tr* destruir, estragar, arruinar

rave [rev] *intr* desvariar, delirar; bramar, enfurecerse; **to rave about** hacerse lenguas de, deshacerse en elogios de

raven ['revən] *s* cuervo

ravenous ['rævənəs] *adj* famélico, hambriento, voraz, rapaz

ravine [rə'vin] *s* cañón *m*, hondonada

ravish ['rævɪʃ] *tr* encantar, entusiasmar; raptar, viola (*a una mujer*)

ravishing ['rævɪʃɪŋ] *adj* encantador

raw [rɔ] *adj* crudo (*cotton silk*) en rama; inexperto, principiante; ulceroso; (*weather, day*) crudo

raw deal *s* (slang) mala pasada

raw'hide' *s* cuero en verde; látigo hecho de cuero en verde

raw material *s* primera materia, materia prima

ray [re] *s* (*of light*) rayo; (*fine line; fish*) raya

rayon ['re‑ɑn] *s* rayón *m*

raze [rez] *tr* arrasar, asolar

razor ['rezər] *s* navaja de afeitar

razor blade *s* hoja u hojita de afeitar

razor strop *s* asentador *m*, suavizador *m*

razz [ræz] *s* (slang) irrisión || *tr* (slang) mofarse de

R.C. *abbr* Red Cross, Reserve Corps, Roman Catholic

R.D. *abbr* Rural Delivery

reach [ritʃ] *s* alcance *m*; extensión; **out of reach (of)** fuera del alcance (de); **within reach of** al alcance de || *tr* alcanzar; extender; entregar con la mano; llegar a; ponerse en contacto con; influenciar; cumplir (*cierto número de años*) || *intr* alcanzar; extender la mano o el brazo; **to reach after o for** esforzarse por coger

react [rɪ'ækt] *intr* reaccionar

reaction [rɪ'ækʃən] *s* reacción

reactionary [rɪ'ækʃən‚erɪ] *adj* reaccionario || *s* (*pl* -ies) reaccionario

read [rid] *v* (*pret & pp* read [red]) *tr* leer; recitar (*poesía*), estudiar (*derecho*); leer en, adivinar (*el pensamiento ajeno*); **to read over** recorrer, repasar || *intr* leer, rezar, p.ej., **this page reads thus** esta página reza así; leerse, p.ej., **this book reads easily** este libro se lee con facilidad; **to read on** seguir leyendo

reader ['ridər] *s* lector *m*; libro de lectura

readily ['redɪlɪ] *adv* de buena gana; fácilmente

reading ['ridɪŋ] *s* lectura; recitación

reading desk *s* atril *m*

reading glass *s* lente *f* para leer, vidrio de aumento; **reading glasses** anteojos para la lectura

reading lamp *s* lámpara de sobremesa

reading room *s* gabinete *m* de lectura; sala de lectura

ready ['redɪ] *adj* (*comp* -ier; *super* -iest) listo, preparado, pronto; ágil, diestro; vivo; disponible; **to make ready** preparar; prepararse || *v* (*pret & pp* -ied) *tr* preparar || *intr* prepararse

ready cash *s* dinero a la mano, dinero contante y sonante

ready-made clothing *s* ropa hecha

ready-made suit *s* traje hecho

reagent [rɪ'edʒənt] *s* reactivo

real ['ri‑əl] *adj* real, verdadero

real estate *s* bienes *mpl* raíces, bienes inmuebles

re'al•es•tate' *adj* inmobiliario

realism ['ri‑ə‚lɪzəm] *s* realismo

realist ['ri‑əlɪst] *s* realista *mf*

reality [rɪ'ælɪtɪ] *s* (*pl* -ties) realidad

realize ['ri‑ə‚laɪz] *tr* darse cuenta de; realizar, llevar a cabo; adquirir (*ganancias*); reportar (*ganancias*) || *intr* (*to sell property for ready money*) realizar

realm [relm] *s* reino

Realtor ['ri‑əl‚tər] o ['ri‑əltər] *s* corredor *m* de bienes raíces

realty ['ri‑əltɪ] *s* bienes *mpl* raíces, bienes inmuebles

ream [rim] *s* resma; **reams** (coll) montones *mpl* || *tr* escariar

reap [rip] *tr & intr* (*to cut*) segar; (*to gather*) cosechar

reaper ['ripər] *s* (*person*) segador *m*; máquina segadora

reappear [‚ri‑ə'pɪr] *intr* reaparecer

reapportionment [‚ri‑ə'pɔrʃənmənt] *s* nuevo prorrateo

rear [rɪr] *adj* posterior, trasero; de atrás || *s* espalda; (*of a room*) fondo; (*of a row; of an automobile*) cola; retaguardia; (slang) culo, trasero || *tr* levantar; edificar, criar, educar || *intr* encabritarse (*un caballo*)

rear admiral *s* contraalmirante *m*

rear drive *s* tracción trasera

rearmament [rɪ'ɑrməmənt] *s* rearme *m*

rear'-view' mirror *s* retrovisor *m*, espejo de retrovisión

rear window *s* (aut) luneta, luneta posterior

reason ['rizən] *s* razón *f*; **by reason of** con motivo de, a causa de; **to listen to reason** meterse en razón; **to stand to reason** ser razonable || *tr & intr* razonar

reasonable ['rizənəbəl] *adj* razonable

reassessment [‚ri‑ə'sɛsmənt] *s* nuevo amillaramiento; nueva estimación

reassure [‚ri‑ə'ʃur] *tr* volver a asegurar; tranquilizar

reawaken [‚ri‑ə'wekən] *tr* volver a despertar || *intr* volver a despertarse

rebate ['ribet] o [rɪ'bet] *s* rebaja || *tr* rebajar

rebel ['rebəl] *adj & s* rebelde *mf* || **re•bel** [rɪ'bel] *v* (*pret & pp* -belled; *ger* -belling) *intr* rebelarse

rebellion [rɪ'beljən] *s* rebelión

rebellious [rɪ'beljəs] *adj* rebelde

re•bind [rɪ'baɪnd] *v* (*pret & pp* -bound

['baund]) *tr* reatar; (*to edge, to border*) ribetear; (bb) reencuadernar
rebirth ['ri,bʌrθ] o [ri'bʌrθ] *s* renacimiento
rebore [ri'bor] *tr* rectificar
rebound ['ri,baund] o [ri'baund] *s* rebote *m* || [ri'baund] *intr* rebotar
rebroad-cast [ri'brɔd,kæst] o [ri'brɔd,kɑst] *s* retransmisión || *v* (*pret & pp* -cast o -casted) *tr* retransmitir
rebuff [ri'bʌf] *s* desaire *m*, rechazo || *tr* desairar, rechazar
re-build [ri'bɪld] *v* (*pret & pp* -built ['bɪlt]) *tr* reconstruir, reedificar
rebuke [ri'bjuk] *s* reprensión || *tr* reprender
re-but [ri'bʌt] *v* (*pret & pp* -butted; *ger* -butting) *tr* rebatir, refutar
rebuttal [ri'bʌtəl] *s* rebatimiento, refutación
rec. *abbr* receipt, recipe, record, recorder
recall [ri'kɔl] o ['rikɔl] *s* llamada; recordación; revocación; (*of a diplomat*) retirada || [ri'kɔl] *tr* hacer volver, mandar volver; recordar; revocar; retirar (*a un diplomático*)
recant [ri'kænt] *tr* retractar || *intr* retractarse
re-cap ['ri,kæp] o [ri'kæp] *v* (*pret & pp* -capped; *ger* -capping) *tr* recauchutar
recapitalization [ri,kæpɪtəlɪ'zeʃən] *s* recapitalización
recapitulation [,rikə,pɪtʃə'leʃən] *s* recapitulación
re-cast ['ri,kæst] o ['ri,kɑst] *s* refundición; (*of a sentence*) reconstrucción || [ri'kæst] o [ri'kɑst] *v* (*pret & pp* -cast) *tr* refundir; reconstruir (*p.ej., una frase*)
recd. o **rec'd.** *abbr* **received**
recede [ri'sid] *intr* (*to move back*) retroceder; (*to move away*) alejarse, retirarse; deprimirse (*p.ej., la frente de una persona*)
receipt [ri'sit] *s* recepción; (*acknowledgment*) recibo; (*acknowledgment of payment*) recibí *m*; (*recipe*) receta; **receipt in full** finiquito; **receipts** entradas, ingresos || *tr* poner el recibí a
receive [ri'siv] *tr* recibir; receptar (*cosas que son materia de delito*); **received payment** recibí || *intr* recibir
receiver [ri'sivər] *s* receptor *m*; (*in bankruptcy*) contador *m*, síndico; receptor telefónico
receiving set *s* aparato receptor
receiving teller *s* recibidor *m* (*de un banco*)
recent ['risənt] *adj* reciente
recently ['risəntli] *adv* recientemente; recién, p.ej., **recently arrived** recién llegado
receptacle [ri'septəkəl] *s* receptáculo
reception [ri'sepʃən] *s* recepción; (*welcome*) recibimiento
reception desk *s* recepción
receptionist [ri'sepʃənɪst] *s* recepcionista *f*
receptive [ri'septɪv] *adj* receptivo
recess [ri'ses] o ['rises] *s* intermisión;

descanso; hora de recreo; (*in a surface*) depresión; (*in a wall*) hueco, nicho; escondrijo || [ri'ses] *tr* ahuecar; empotrar; deprimir || *intr* prorrogarse, suspenderse
recession [ri'seʃən] *s* retroceso, retirada; (*e.g., in a wall*) depresión; procesión de vuelta; contracción económica
recipe ['resɪ,pi] *s* receta (de cocina)
reciprocal [ri'sɪprəkəl] *adj* recíproco
reciprocity [,resɪ'prasɪti] *s* reciprocidad
recital [ri'saɪtəl] *s* narración; (*of music or poetry*) recital *m*
recite [ri'saɪt] *tr* narrar; (*formally*) recitar
reckless ['reklɪs] *adj* atolondrado, temerario
reckon ['rekən] *tr* calcular; considerar; (coll) calcular, conjeturar || *intr* calcular; **to reckon on** contar con; **to reckon with** tener en cuenta
reclaim [ri'klem] *tr* hacer utilizable; hacer labrantío (*un terreno*); ganar (*terreno*) a la mar; recuperar (*materiales usados*); conducir, guiar (*a los que hacen mala vida*)
recline [ri'klaɪn] *intr* reclinarse
recluse [ri'klus] o ['reklus] *s* solitario, ermitaño
recognize ['rekəg,naɪz] *tr* reconocer
recoil [ri'kɔɪl] *s* reculada; (*of a firearm*) reculada, culetazo || *intr* recular, apartarse; recular (*un arma de fuego*)
recollect [,rekə'lekt] *tr & intr* recordar
recommend [,rekə'mend] *tr* recomendar
recompense ['rekəm,pens] *s* recompensa || *tr* recompensar
reconcile ['rekən,saɪl] *tr* reconciliar; **to reconcile oneself** resignarse
reconnaissance [ri'kanɪsəns] *s* reconocimiento
reconnoiter [,rekə'nɔɪtər] o [,rikə'nɔɪtər] *tr & intr* reconocer
reconquest [ri'kaŋkwest] *s* reconquista
reconsider [,rikən'sɪdər] *tr* reconsiderar
reconstruct [,rikən'strʌkt] *tr* reconstruir
reconversion [,rikən'vʌrʒən] o [,rikən'vʌrʃən] *s* reconversión
record ['rekərd] *s* anotación; ficha, historial *m*, historia personal; (*of a notary*) protocolo; (*of a phonograph*) disco; (educ) expediente académico; (sport) record *m*, plusmarca; **off the record** confidencialmente; **records** anales *mpl*, memorias; archivo; **to break a record** batir un record; **to make a record** establecer un record; grabar un disco || [ri'kɔrd] *tr* asentar; registrar; inscribir; grabar (*un sonido, una canción, un disco fonográfico, etc.*)
record breaker *s* plusmarquista *mf*
record changer ['tʃendʒər] *s* cambiadiscos *m*, tocadiscos automático
record holder *s* (sport) recordman *m*
recording [ri'kɔrdɪŋ] *adj* registrador;

(*wire or tape*) magnetofónico || *s* registro; (*of phonograph records*) grabación o grabado

recording secretary *s* secretario escribiente, secretario de actas

record player *s* tocadiscos *m*

recount ['ri,kaunt] *s* recuento || [ri-'kaunt] *tr* (*to count again*) recontar || [ri'kaunt] *tr* (*to narrate*) recontar

recourse [ri'kors] o ['rikors] *s* recurso; (*helping hand*) paño de lágrimas; **to have recourse to** recurrir a

recover [ri'kʌvər] *tr* recobrar; rescatar; **to recover consciousness** recobrar el conocimiento, volver en sí || *intr* recobrarse; recobrar la salud; ganar un pleito

recover·y [ri'kʌvəri] *s* (*pl* -**ies**) recobro, recuperación; **past recovery** sin remedio

recreant ['rekri·ənt] *adj & s* cobarde *mf*, traidor *m*

recreation [,rekri'eʃən] *s* recreación

recruit [ri'krut] *tr* recluta *m* || *tr* reclutar || *intr* alistar reclutas; ganar reclutas; restablecerse, reponerse

rect. *abbr* **receipt, rector, rectory**

rectangle ['rek,tæŋgəl] *s* rectángulo

recti·fy ['rekti,fai] *v* (*pret & pp* -**fied**) *tr* rectificar

rec·tum ['rektəm] *s* (*pl* -**ta** [tə]) recto

recumbent [ri'kʌmbənt] *adj* reclinado, recostado

recuperate [ri'kjupə,ret] *tr* recuperar; restablecer, reponer || *intr* recuperarse, recobrarse

re·cur [ri'kʌr] *v* (*pret & pp* -**curred;** *ger* -**curring**) *intr* volver a ocurrir; volver a presentarse (*a la memoria*); volver (*a un asunto*)

recurrent [ri'kʌrənt] *adj* repetido; periódico; (*illness*) recurrente

red [red] *adj* (*comp* **redder;** *super* **reddest**) rojo, colorado; (*wine*) tinto; enrojecido, inflamado || *s* rojo; **in the red** (*coll*) endeudado; **to see red** (*coll*) enfurecerse || **Red** *adj & s* (*communist*) rojo

red'bait' *tr* motejar (*a uno*) de rojo o comunista

red'bird' *s* cardenal *m;* piranga

red-blooded ['red,blʌdid] *adj* fuerte, valiente, vigoroso

red'breast' *s* petirrojo

red'bud' *s* ciclamor *m* del Canadá

red'cap' *s* (Brit) policía militar; (U.S.A.) mozo de estación

red cell *s* glóbulo rojo, hematíe *m*

red'coat' *s* (hist) soldado inglés

redden ['redən] *tr* enrojecer || *intr* enrojecerse

redeem [ri'dim] *tr* redimir; cumplir (*una promesa*)

redeemer [ri'dimər] *s* redentor *m*

redemption [ri'dempʃən] *s* redención

red-haired ['red,herd] *adj* pelirrojo

red'head' *s* pelirrojo

red herring *s* artificio para distraer la atención del asunto de que se trata

red'-hot' *adj* candente, calentado al rojo; ardiente, entusiasta; fresco, nuevo

rediscount rate [ri'diskaunt] *s* tipo de redescuento

rediscover [,ridis'kʌvər] *tr* redescubrir

red'-let'ter day *s* día *m* memorable

red'-light' district *s* barrio de los lupanares, barrio de mala vida

red man *s* piel roja *m*

re·do ['ri'du] *v* (*pret* -**did** ['did]; *pp* -**done** ['dʌn]) *tr* rehacer, repetir; refundir; reformar

redolent ['redələnt] *adj* fragante, perfumado; **redolent of** que huele a

redoubt [ri'daut] *s* (fort) reducto

redound [ri'daund] *intr* redundar; **to redound to** redundar en

red pepper *s* pimentón *m*

redress [ri'dres] o ['ridres] *s* reparación; remedio || [ri'dres] *tr* reparar; remediar

Red Ridinghood ['raidiŋ,hud] *s* Caperucita Roja

red'skin' *s* piel roja *m*

red tape *s* expedienteo, papeleo

reduce [ri'djus] o [ri'dus] *tr* reducir; (mil) degradar || *intr* reducirse; reducir peso

reducing exercises *spl* ejercicios físicos para reducir peso

redundant [ri'dʌndənt] *adj* redundante

red'wood' *s* secoya

reed [rid] *adj* (*organ, musical instrument*) de lengüeta || *s* (*stalk*) caña; (*plant*) carrizo, caña; (mus) instrumento de lengüeta; (*of instrument*) lengüeta

reëdit [ri'edit] *tr* refundir

reef [rif] *s* arrecife *m*, escollo; (min) filón *m*, veta || *tr* (naut) arrizar

reefer ['rifər] *s* chaquetón *m;* (slang) pitillo de mariguana

reek [rik] *intr* vahear, humear; estar bañado en sudor; estar mojado con sangre; **to reek of** o **with** oler a

reel [ril] *s* (*spool*) carrete *m;* (*of a shuttle*) broca; (*of motion pictures*) cinta; (*sway, staggering*) tambaleo; **off the reel** (coll) fácil y prestamente || *tr* aspar, devanar; **to reel off** (coll) narrar fácil y prestamente || *intr* tambalear; cejar (*p.ej., el enemigo*)

reëlection [,ri·i'lekʃən] *s* reelección

reënlist [,ri·en'list] *tr* reenganchar || *intr* reengancharse

reën·try [ri'entri] *s* (*pl* -**tries**) reingreso, nueva entrada; (*return to earth's atmosphere*) reentrada

reëxamination [,ri·eg,zæmi'neʃən] *s* reexaminación

ref. *abbr* **referee, reference, reformation**

re·fer [ri'fʌr] *v* (*pret & pp* -**ferred;** *ger* -**ferring**) *tr* referir || *intr* referirse

referee [,refə'ri] *s* árbitro || *tr & intr* arbitrar

reference ['refərəns] *adj* (*library, book, work*) de consulta || *s* referencia

referen·dum [,refə'rendəm] *s* (*pl* -**da** [də]) *s* referéndum *m*

refill ['rifil] *s* relleno || [ri'fil] *tr* rellenar

refine [ri'fain] *tr* refinar

refinement [rɪ'faɪnmənt] s refinamiento; buena crianza, cultura

refiner·y [rɪ'faɪnərɪ] s (pl -ies) refinería

reflect [rɪ'flekt] tr reflejar || intr reflejar; (to meditate) reflexionar; **to reflect on** o **upon** reflexionar en o sobre; perjudicar

reflection [rɪ'flekʃən] s (thinking) reflexión; (reflected light; image) reflejo

reforestation [ˌrifɑrɪs'teʃən] o [ˌriˌfɔrɪs'teʃən] s reforestación

reform [rɪ'form] s reforma || tr reformar || intr reformarse

reformation [ˌrefər'meʃən] s reformación || **the Reformation** la Reforma

reformato·ry [rɪ'formə,torɪ] s (pl -ries) reformatorio

reform school s casa de corrección

refraction [rɪ'frækʃən] s refracción

refrain [rɪ'fren] s estribillo || intr abstenerse

refresh [rɪ'freʃ] tr refrescar || intr refrescarse

refreshing [rɪ'freʃɪŋ] adj confortante, restaurante

refreshment [rɪ'freʃmənt] s refresco

refrigerator [rɪ'frɪdʒə,retər] s heladera, nevera, refrigerador m

refrigerator car s carro o vagón frigorífico

refuel [rɪ'fjul] tr & intr repostar

refuge ['refjudʒ] s refugio; expediente m, subterfugio; **to take refuge (in)** refugiarse (en)

refugee [ˌrefju'dʒi] s refugiado

refund ['rifʌnd] s reembolso || [rɪ-'fʌnd] tr reembolsar || [rɪ'fʌnd] tr consolidar

refurnish [rɪ'fʌrnɪʃ] tr amueblar de nuevo

refusal [rɪ'fjuzəl] s negativa

refuse ['refjus] s basura, desecho, desperdicios || [rɪ'fjuz] tr rehusar; rechazar, no querer aceptar; **to refuse to** negarse a

refute [rɪ'fjut] tr refutar

reg. abbr **register, registrar, registry, regular**

regain [rɪ'gen] tr recobrar, recuperar; volver a alcanzar; **to regain consciousness** recobrar el conocimiento, volver en sí

regal ['rigəl] adj regio

regale [rɪ'gel] tr regalar, agasajar

regalia [rɪ'gelɪ·ə] spl (of an office or order) distintivos; galas, trajes mpl de lujo

regard [rɪ'gɑrd] s consideración, miramiento; (esteem) respeto; (particular matter) respecto; (look) mirada; **in regard to** respecto a o de; **regards** recuerdos; **without regard to** sin hacer caso de; **with regard to** respecto a o de || tr considerar; mirar; tocar a, referirse a; **as regards** en cuanto a

regarding [rɪ'gɑrdɪŋ] prep tocante a, respecto a o de

regardless [rɪ'gɑrdlɪs] adj desatento, indiferente || adv (coll) pese a quien pese, cueste lo que cueste; **regardless of** sin hacer caso de; a pesar de

regenerate [rɪ'dʒenə,ret] tr regenerar || intr regenerarse

regent ['ridʒənt] s regente mf

regicide ['redʒɪˌsaɪd] s (act) regicidio; (person) regicida mf

regime o **régime** [re'ʒim] s régimen m

regiment ['redʒɪmənt] s regimiento || ['redʒɪˌment] tr regimentar

regimental [ˌredʒɪ'mentəl] adj regimental || **regimentals** spl uniforme m militar

region ['ridʒən] s región, comarca

register ['redʒɪstər] s (record; book for keeping such a record) registro; reja regulable de calefacción; (of the voice or an instrument) extensión || tr (to indicate by a record; to show, as on a scale) registrar; empadronar (los vecinos en el padrón); manifestar, dar a conocer; certificar (envíos por correo); inscribir || intr registrarse; empadronarse; inscribirse

registered letter s carta certificada

registrar ['redʒɪsˌtrɑr] s registrador m, archivero

registration fee [ˌredʒɪs'treʃən] s derechos de matrícula

re·gret [rɪ'gret] s pesar m, sentimiento; pesadumbre, remordimiento; **regrets** excusas || v (pret & pp -gretted; ger -gretting) tr sentir, lamentar; lamentar la pérdida de; arrepentirse de; **to regret to** sentir

regrettable [rɪ'gretəbəl] adj lamentable

regular ['regjələr] adj regular; (coll) cabal, completo, verdadero || s obrero permanente; parroquiano regular; **regulars** tropas regulares

regulate ['regjə,let] tr regular

rehabilitate [ˌrihə'bɪlɪ,tet] tr rehabilitar

rehearsal [rɪ'hʌrsəl] s ensayo

rehearse [rɪ'hʌrs] tr ensayar || intr ensayarse

reign [ren] s reinado || intr reinar

reimburse [ˌriɪm'bʌrs] tr reembolsar

rein [ren] s rienda; **to give free rein to** dar rienda suelta a || tr dirigir por medio de riendas; contener, refrenar, gobernar

reincarnation [ˌri·ɪnkɑr'neʃən] s reencarnación

reindeer ['ren,dɪr] s reno

reinforce [ˌri·ɪn'fors] tr reforzar; armar (el hormigón)

reinforcement [ˌri·ɪn'forsmənt] s refuerzo

reinstate [ˌri·ɪn'stet] tr reinstalar

reiterate [ri'ɪtə,ret] tr reiterar

reject [rɪ'dʒekt] tr rechazar

rejection [rɪ'dʒekʃən] s rechazamiento

rejoice [rɪ'dʒɔɪs] intr regocijarse

rejoinder [rɪ'dʒɔɪndər] s contestación; (law) contrarréplica

rejuvenation [rɪˌdʒuvɪ'neʃən] s rejuvenecimiento

rel. abbr **relating, relative, religion, religious**

relapse [rɪ'læps] s recaída || intr recaer

relate [rɪ'let] tr (to establish relationship between) relacionar; (to narrate) contar, relatar

relation [rɪ'leʃən] *s* (*connection; narration*) relación; (*narration*) relato; (*relative*) pariente *mf*; (*kinship*) parentesco; **in relation to** o **with** tocante a, respecto a o de

relationship [rɪ'leʃən‿ʃɪp] *s* (*connection*) relación; (*kinship*) parentesco

relative ['rɛlətɪv] *adj* relativo ‖ *s* deudo, pariente *mf*

relax [rɪ'læks] *tr & intr* relajar

relaxation [‚rilæks'eʃən] *s* relajación; despreocupación

relaxation of tension *s* disminución de tensión; disminución de la tirantez internacional

relaxing [rɪ'læksɪŋ] *adj* relajador; despreocupante, tranquilizador

relay ['rile] o [rɪ'le] *s* (elec) relais *m*, relevador *m*, relevo; (mil & sport) relevo; (sport) carrera de relevos ‖ *v* (*pret & pp* -**layed**) *tr* transmitir relevándose; transmitir con un relais; retransmitir (*una emisión*); reexpedir (*un radiotelegrama*) ‖ [rɪ'le] *v* (*pret & pp* -**laid**) *tr* volver a colocar, volver a tender

relay race *s* carrera de relevos

release [rɪ'lis] *s* liberación; (*from jail*) excarcelación; alivio; permiso de publicación, venta, etc.; obra o pieza lista para la publicación, venta, etc.; (aer) lanzamiento; (mach) escape *m*, disparador *m* ‖ *tr* soltar; libertar, excarcelar (*a un preso*); permitir la publicación, venta, etc. de; (aer.) lanzar (*una bomba*)

relent [rɪ'lɛnt] *intr* ablandarse, aplacarse

relentless [rɪ'lɛntlɪs] *adj* implacable

relevant ['rɛlɪvənt] *adj* pertinente

reliable [rɪ'laɪ‿əbəl] *adj* confiable, fidedigno

reliance [rɪ'laɪ‿əns] *s* confianza

relic ['rɛlɪk] *s* reliquia

relief [rɪ'lif] *s* alivio; caridad; (*projection of figures; elevation*) relieve *m*; (mil) relevo; **in relief** en relieve; **on relief** viviendo de socorro, recibiendo auxilio social

relieve [rɪ'liv] *tr* (*to release from a post*) relevar; aliviar; auxiliar (*a los necesitados*); (mil) relevar

religion [rɪ'lɪdʒən] *s* religión

religious [rɪ'lɪdʒəs] *adj* religioso

relinquish [rɪ'lɪŋkwɪʃ] *tr* abandonar, dejar

relish ['rɛlɪʃ] *s* buen sabor, gusto; condimento, sazón *f*; entremés *m*; buen apetito ‖ *tr* gustar de; comer o beber con placer

reluctance [rɪ'lʌktəns] *s* renuencia, aversión

reluctant [rɪ'lʌktənt] *adj* renuente, maldispuesto

re‧ly [rɪ'laɪ] *v* (*pret & pp* -**lied**) *intr* depender, confiar; **to rely on** depender de, confiar en

remain [rɪ'men] *intr* permanecer, quedarse ‖ **remains** *spl* desechos, restos; restos mortales; obra póstuma

remainder [rɪ'mendər] *s* resto, residuo; libro casi invendible ‖ *tr* saldar (*libros que ya no se venden*)

re‧make [rɪ'mek] *v* (*pret & pp* -**made** ['med]) *tr* rehacer

remark [rɪ'mɑrk] *s* observación ‖ *tr & intr* observar; **to remark on** aludir a, comentar

remarkable [rɪ'mɑrkəbəl] *adj* notable, extraordinario

remar‧ry [rɪ'mæri] *v* (*pret & pp* -**ried**) *intr* volver a casarse

reme‧dy ['rɛmɪdɪ] *s* (*pl* -**dies**) remedio ‖ *v* (*pret & pp* -**died**) *tr* remediar

remember [rɪ'mɛmbər] *tr* acordarse de, recordar; dar recuerdos de parte de, p.ej., **remember me to your brother** déle Vd. a su hermano recuerdos de mi parte ‖ *intr* acordarse, recordar; **if I remember correctly** si mal no me acuerdo

remembrance [rɪ'mɛmbrəns] *s* recuerdo

remind [rɪ'maɪnd] *tr* recordar

reminder [rɪ'maɪndər] *s* recordatorio, recordativo

reminisce [‚rɛmɪ'nɪs] *intr* entregarse a los recuerdos, contar sus recuerdos

remiss [rɪ'mɪs] *adj* descuidado, negligente

re‧mit [rɪ'mɪt] *v* (*pret & pp* -**mitted**; *ger* -**mitting**) *tr* (*to send, to ship; to pardon*) remitir

remittance [rɪ'mɪtəns] *s* remesa

remnant ['rɛmnənt] *s* (*something left over*) remanente *m*; (*of cloth*) retal *m*, retazo; (*piece of cloth to be sold at reduced price*) saldo; vestigio

remod‧el [rɪ'mɑdəl] *v* (*pret & pp* -**eled** o -**elled**; *ger* -**eling** o -**elling**) *tr* modelar de nuevo; rehacer, reconstruir; convertir, transformar

remonstrate [rɪ'mɑnstret] *intr* protestar; **to remonstrate with** reconvenir

remorse [rɪ'mɔrs] *s* remordimiento

remorseful [rɪ'mɔrsfəl] *adj* compungido, arrepentido

remote [rɪ'mot] *adj* remoto

remote control *s* comando a distancia, telecontrol *m*

removable [rɪ'muvəbəl] *adj* amovible

removal [rɪ'muvəl] *s* remoción; mudanza, traslado; (*dismissal*) deposición

remove [rɪ'muv] *tr* remover; quitar de en medio, apartar matando ‖ *intr* removerse

remuneration [rɪ‚mjunə're ʃən] *s* remuneración

renaissance [‚rɛnə'sɑns] o [rɪ'nesəns] *s* renacimiento

rend [rɛnd] *v* (*pret & pp* rent [rɛnt]) *tr* (*to tear*) desgarrar; (*to split*) hender, rajar; estremecer (*un ruido el aire*)

render ['rɛndər] *tr* rendir (*gracias, obsequios, homenaje*); prestar, suministrar (*ayuda*); pagar (*tributo*); desempeñar (*un papel*); traducir (*sentimientos*); (*from one language to another*) verter; hacer (*justicia*); ejecutar (*una pieza de música*); derretir (*cera, manteca*); extraer la grasa o el sebo de; poner, volver

rendezvous ['rɑndə‚vu] *s* (*pl* -**vous** [‚vuz]) cita; (*in space*) encuentro,

reunión || *v* (*pret & pp* -voused
[,vud]; *ger* -vousing [,vu·ɪŋ]) *intr*
reunirse en una cita

rendition [ren'dɪʃən] *s* rendición; traducción; (mus) ejecución

renege [rɪ'nɪg] *s* renuncio || *intr* renunciar; (coll) volverse atrás

renegotiation [,rini,goʃɪ'eʃən] *s* renegociación

renew [rɪ'nju] o [rɪ'nu] *tr* renovar ||
intr renovarse

renewable [rɪ'nju·əbəl] o [rɪ'nu·əbəl]
adj renovable

renewal [rɪ'nju·əl] o [rɪ'nu·əl] *s* renovación

renounce [rɪ'nauns] *tr* renunciar; renunciar a (*p.ej., el mundo*) || *intr* renunciar

renovate ['renə,vet] *tr* renovar; reformar (*p.ej., una tienda, una casa*)

renown [rɪ'naun] *s* renombre *m*

renowned [rɪ'naund] *adj* renombrado

rent [rent] *adj* desgarrado || *s* alquiler
m, arriendo; (*tear, slit*) desgarro ||
tr alquilar, arrendar || *intr* alquilarse, arrendarse

rental ['rentəl] *s* alquiler *m*, arriendo

renunciation [rɪ,nʌnsɪ'eʃən] o [rɪ
,nʌnʃɪ'eʃən] *s* renunciación

reopen [rɪ'opən] *tr* reabrir || *intr* reabrirse

reorganize [rɪ'ɔrgə,naɪz] *tr* reorganizar || *intr* reorganizarse

rep. *abbr* report, reporter, representative, republic

repair [rɪ'pɛr] *s* reparación; in repair
en buen estado || *tr* reparar || *intr*
dirigirse; volver

repaper [rɪ'pepər] *tr* empapelar de
nuevo

reparation [,repə'reʃən] *s* reparación

repartee [,rɪpɑr'ti] *s* respuesta viva;
agudeza y gracia en responder

repast [rɪ'pæst] o [rɪ'pɑst] *s* comida,
comilona

repatriate [ri'petrɪ,et] *tr* repatriar

re·pay [rɪ'pe] *v* (*pret & pp* -paid
['ped]) *tr* reembolsar; resarcir (*un
daño, una injuria*); compensar

repayment [rɪ'pemənt] *s* reembolso;
resarcimiento; compensación

repeal [rɪ'pil] *s* abrogación, revocación || *tr* abrogar, revocar

repeat [rɪ'pit] *s* repetición || *tr & intr*
repetir

re·pel [rɪ'pel] *v* (*pret & pp* -pelled; *ger*
-pelling) *tr* rechazar, repeler; repugnar

repent [rɪ'pent] *tr* arrepentirse de ||
intr arrepentirse

repentance [rɪ'pentəns] *s* arrepentimiento

repentant [rɪ'pentənt] *adj* arrepentido

repertory theater ['repər,tori] *s* teatro
de repertorio

repetition [,repɪ'tɪʃən] *s* repetición

repine [rɪ'paɪn] *intr* afligirse, quejarse

replace [rɪ'ples] *tr* (*to put back*) reponer; (*to take the place of*) reemplazar

replacement [rɪ'plesmənt] *s* reposición; reemplazo; pieza de repuesto;
soldado reemplazante

replenish [rɪ'plenɪʃ] *tr* rellenar; reaprovisionar

replete [rɪ'plit] *adj* repleto

replica ['replɪkə] *s* réplica

re·ply [rɪ'plaɪ] *s* (*pl* -plies) contestación, respuesta || *v* (*pret & pp* -plied)
tr & intr contestar, responder

reply coupon *s* vale *m* respuesta

report [rɪ'port] *s* relato, informe *m*;
voz *f*, rumor *m*; (*e.g., of a firearm*)
detonación, tiro; denuncia || *tr* relatar, informar acerca de; denunciar
|| *intr* hacer un relato; redactar un
informe; ser repórter; presentarse; to
report on dar cuenta de, notificar

report card *s* certificado escolar

reportedly [rɪ'portɪdli] *adv* según se
informa

reporter [rɪ'portər] *s* repórter *m*

reporting [rɪ'portɪŋ] *s* reportaje *m*

repose [rɪ'poz] *s* descanso || *tr* descansar; poner (*confianza*) || *intr* descansar

reprehend [,reprɪ'hend] *tr* reprender

represent [,reprɪ'zent] *tr* representar

representative [,reprɪ'zentətɪv] *adj* representativo || *s* representante *mf*

repress [rɪ'pres] *tr* reprimir

reprieve [rɪ'priv] *s* suspensión temporal de un castigo, suspensión temporal de la pena de muerte; respiro,
alivio temporal || *tr* suspender temporalmente el castigo de o la pena de
muerte de; aliviar temporalmente

reprimand ['reprɪ,mænd] o ['reprɪ
,mɑnd] *s* reprimenda || *tr* reconvenir, reprender

reprint ['ri,prɪnt] *s* reimpresión; tirada aparte || [ri'prɪnt] *tr* reimprimir

reprisal [rɪ'praɪzəl] *s* represalia

reproach [rɪ'protʃ] *s* reproche *m*;
oprobio || *tr* reprochar; oprobiar

reproduce [,riprə'djus] o [,riprə'dus]
tr reproducir || *intr* reproducirse

reproduction [,riprə'dʌkʃən] *s* reproducción

reproof [rɪ'pruf] *s* reprobación

reprove [rɪ'pruv] *tr* reprobar

reptile ['reptɪl] *s* reptil *m*

republic [rɪ'pʌblɪk] *s* república

republican [rɪ'pʌblɪkən] *adj & s* republicano

repudiate [rɪ'pjudɪ,et] *tr* repudiar; no
reconocer (*p.ej., una deuda*)

repugnant [rɪ'pʌgnənt] *adj* repugnante

repulse [rɪ'pʌls] *s* repulsión, rechazo ||
tr repeler, rechazar

repulsive [rɪ'pʌlsɪv] *adj* repulsivo

reputation [,repjə'teʃən] *s* reputación;
buena reputación

repute [rɪ'pjut] *s* reputación; buena
reputación || *tr* reputar

reputedly [rɪ'pjutɪdli] *adv* según la
opinión común

request [rɪ'kwest] *s* petición, solicitud;
at the request of a petición de || *tr*
pedir

require [rɪ'kwaɪr] *tr* exigir, requerir

requirement [rɪ'kwaɪrmənt] *s* requisito; necesidad

requisite ['rekwɪzɪt] *adj & s* requisito

requital [rɪ'kwaɪtəl] *s* compensación,
retorno

requite [rɪ'kwaɪt] *tr* corresponder a (*los beneficios, el amor, etc.*); corresponder con (*el bienhechor*)

re·read [ri'rid] *v* (*pret & pp* **-read** ['red]) *tr* releer

resale ['ri,sel] o [ri'sel] *s* reventa

rescind [rɪ'sɪnd] *tr* rescindir

rescue ['reskju] *s* salvación, rescate *m*, liberación; **to go to the rescue of** acudir al socorro de || *tr* salvar, rescatar, libertar

rescue party *s* pelotón *m* de salvamento

research [rɪ'sʌrtʃ] o ['risʌrtʃ] *s* investigación || *intr* investigar

re·sell [ri'sel] *v* (*pret & pp* **-sold** ['sold]) *tr* revender

resemblance [rɪ'zembləns] *s* parecido, semejanza

resemble [rɪ'zembəl] *tr* parecerse a, asemejarse a

resent [rɪ'zent] *tr* resentirse de o por

resentful [rɪ'zentfəl] *adj* resentido

resentment [rɪ'zentmənt] *s* resentimiento

reservation [,rezər've∫ən] *s* reserva

reserve [rɪ'zʌrv] *s* reserva || *tr* reservar

reservoir ['rezər,vwar] *s* depósito; (*where water is dammed back*) embalse *m*, pantano; (*of wisdom*) fondo

re·ship [ri'∫ɪp] *v* (*pret & pp* **-shipped**; *ger* **-shipping**) *tr* reenviar, reexpedir; (*on a ship*) reembarcar || *intr* reembarcarse

reshipment [ri'∫ɪpmənt] *s* reenvío, reexpedición; (*of persons*) reembarco; (*of goods*) reembarque *m*

reside [rɪ'zaɪd] *intr* residir

residence ['rezɪdəns] *s* residencia

resident ['rezɪdənt] *adj & s* residente *mf*, vecino

residue ['rezɪ,dju] o ['rezɪ,du] *s* residuo

resign [rɪ'zaɪn] *tr* dimitir, resignar, renunciar || *intr* dimitir; (*to yield, submit*) resignarse; **to resign to** resignarse con (*p.ej., su suerte*)

resignation [,rezɪg'ne∫ən] *s* (*from a job, etc.*) dimisión; (*state of being submissive*) resignación

resin ['rezɪn] *s* resina

resist [rɪ'zɪst] *tr* resistir (*la tentación*); resistir a (*la violencia; la risa*) || *intr* resistirse

resistance [rɪ'zɪstəns] *s* resistencia

resole [ri'sol] *tr* sobresolar

resolute ['rezə,lut] *adj* resuelto

resolution [,rezə'lu∫ən] *s* resolución; **good resolutions** buenos propósitos

resolve [rɪ'zɑlv] *s* resolución || *tr* resolver || *intr* resolverse

resort [rɪ'zɔrt] *s* lugar muy frecuentado; (*e.g., for vacations*) estación; (*for help or support*) recurso; **as a last resort** como último recurso || *intr* recurrir

resound [rɪ'zaund] *intr* resonar

resource [rɪ'sors] o ['risors] *s* recurso

resourceful [rɪ'sorsfəl] *adj* ingenioso

respect [rɪ'spekt] *s* (*deference, esteem*) respeto; (*reference, relation; detail*) respecto; **respects** recuerdos, saludos; **to pay one's respects (to)** ofre-

cer sus respetos (a); **with respect to** respecto a o de || *tr* respetar

respectable [rɪ'spektəbəl] *adj* respetable; decente, presentable

respectful [rɪ'spektfəl] *adj* respetuoso

respectfully [rɪ'spektfəli] *adj* respetuosamente; **respectfully yours** de Vd. atento y seguro servidor

respecting [rɪ'spektɪŋ] *prep* con respecto a, respecto de

respective [rɪ'spektɪv] *adj* respectivo

respire [rɪ'spaɪr] *tr & intr* respirar

respite ['respɪt] *s* (*temporary relief*) respiro; (*postponement, especially of death sentence*) suspensión; **without respite** sin respirar

resplendent [rɪ'splendənt] *adj* resplandeciente

respond [rɪ'spand] *intr* responder

response [rɪ'spans] *s* respuesta

responsible [rɪ'spansɪbəl] *adj* responsable; (*job, position*) de confianza; **responsible for** responsable de

rest [rest] *s* (*after exertion or work; sleep*) descanso; (*lack of motion*) reposo; (*of the dead*) paz *f*; (*what remains*) resto; (*mus*) pausa; **at rest** (*not moving*) en reposo; tranquilo; dormido; (*dead*) muerto; **the rest** lo demás; los demás; **to come to rest** venir a parar; **to lay to rest** enterrar || *tr* descansar; parar; poner (*p.ej., confianza*) || *intr* descansar; estar, hallarse; **to rest assured (that)** estar seguro, tener la seguridad (de que); **to rest on** descansar en o sobre, estribar en

restaurant ['restərənt] o ['restə,rant] *s* restaurante *m*

rest cure *s* cura de reposo

restful ['restfəl] *adj* descansado, tranquilo, reposado

resting place *s* lugar *m* de descanso; (*of a staircase*) descansadero; (*of the dead*) última morada

restitution [,restɪ'tju∫ən] o [,restɪ'tu∫ən] *s* restitución

restless ['restlɪs] *adj* intranquilo; (*sleepless*) insomne

restock [ri'stak] *tr* reaprovisionar; repoblar (*p.ej., un acuario*)

restore [rɪ'stor] *tr* restaurar; (*to give back*) devolver

restrain [rɪ'stren] *tr* contener, refrenar; aprisionar

restraint [rɪ'strent] *s* restricción; comedimiento, moderación

restrict [rɪ'strɪkt] *tr* restringir

rest room *s* sala de descanso; excusado, retrete *m*; (*of a theater*) saloncillo

result [rɪ'zʌlt] *s* resultado; **as a result of** de resultas de || *intr* resultar; **to result in** dar por resultado, parar en

resume [rɪ'zum] o [rɪ'zjum] *tr* reasumir; reanudar (*el viaje, el vuelo, etc.*); volver a tomar (*su asiento*) || *intr* continuar; recomenzar; reanudar el hilo del discurso

résumé [,rezu'me] o [,rezju'me] *s* resumen *m*

resurface [rɪ'sʌrfɪs] *tr* dar nueva superficie a || *intr* volver a emerger (*un submarino*)

resurrect [,rezə'rekt] *tr* & *intr* resucitar

resurrection [,rezə'rek/ən] *s* resurrección

resuscitate [rɪ'sʌsɪ,tet] *tr* & *intr* resucitar

retail ['ritel] *adj* & *adv* al por menor ‖ *s* venta al por menor ‖ *tr* detallar, vender al por menor ‖ *intr* vender al por menor; venderse al por menor

retailer ['ritelər] *s* detallista *mf*, comerciante *mf* al por menor

retain [rɪ'ten] *tr* retener; contratar (*a un abogado*)

retaliate [rɪ'tælɪ,et] *intr* desquitarse, vengarse

retaliation [rɪ,tælɪ'e/ən] *s* desquite *m*, venganza

retard [rɪ'tɑrd] *s* retardo ‖ *tr* retardar

retch [ret/] *tr* vomitar ‖ *intr* arquear, esforzarse por vomitar

retching ['ret/ɪŋ] *s* arcadas

ret'd. *abbr* **returned**

reticence ['retɪsəns] *s* reserva, circunspección, sigilo

reticent ['retɪsənt] *adj* reservado, circunspecto

retinue ['retɪ,nju] o ['retɪ,nu] *s* comitiva, séquito

retire [rɪ'taɪr] *tr* retirar; jubilar (*a un empleado*) ‖ *intr* retirarse; jubilarse; (*to go to bed*) recogerse; (mil) retirarse

retirement [rɪ'taɪrmənt] *s* retiro; (*of an employee with pension*) jubilación; (mil) retirada

retirement annuity *s* jubilación

retort [rɪ'tɔrt] *s* respuesta pronta y aguda, réplica; (chem) retorta ‖ *intr* replicar

retouch [ri'tʌt/] *tr* retocar

retrace [rɪ'tres] *tr* repasar; **to retrace one's steps** volver sobre sus pasos

retract [rɪ'trækt] *tr* retractarse de, desdecirse de (*lo que se ha dicho*) ‖ *intr* retractarse, desdecirse

re-tread ['ri,tred] *s* neumático recauchutado; neumático ranurado ‖ [ri-'tred] *v* (*pret* & *pp* **-treaded**) *tr* recauchutar; volver a ranurar ‖ *v* (*pret* **-trod** ['trɑd]; *pp* **-trod** o **-trodden**) *tr* desandar ‖ *intr* volverse atrás

retreat [rɪ'trit] *s* (*act of withdrawing; place of seclusion*) retiro; (eccl) retiro; (mil) retreta, retirada; (*signal*) (mil) retreta; **to beat a retreat** retirarse; (mil) batirse en retirada ‖ *intr* retirarse

retrench [rɪ'trent/] *tr* cercenar ‖ *intr* recogerse

retribution [,retrɪ'bju/ən] *s* justo castigo; (theol) juicio final

retrieve [rɪ'triv] *tr* cobrar; reparar (*p.ej., un daño*); desquitarse de (*una pérdida, una derrota*); (hunt) cobrar, portar ‖ *intr* (hunt) cobrar, portar

retriever [rɪ'trivər] *s* perro cobrador, perro traedor

retroactive [,retro'æktɪv] *adj* retroactivo

retrofiring [,retro'faɪrɪŋ] *s* retrodisparo

retrogress ['retrə,gres] *intr* retroceder; empeorar

retrorocket [,retro'rɑkɪt] *s* retrocohete *m*

retrospect ['retrə,spekt] *s* retrospección; **in retrospect** retrospectivamente

retrospective [,retro'spektɪv] *adj* retrospectivo

re-try [ri'traɪ] *v* (*pret* & *pp* **-tried**) *tr* reensayar; rever (*un caso legal*); procesar de nuevo (*a una persona*)

return [rɪ'tʌrn] *adj* repetido; de vuelta; **by return mail** a vuelta de correo ‖ *s* vuelta; devolución; recompensa; respuesta; informe *m*, noticia; ganancia, beneficio, rédito; (*of an election*) resultado; (*of income tax*) declaración; **in return (for)** en cambio (de); **many happy returns of the day!** ¡que cumpla muchos más! ‖ *tr* devolver; dar en cambio; corresponder a (*un favor*); dar (*una respuesta, las gracias*) ‖ *intr* volver; responder

return address *s* dirección del remitente

return bout o engagement *s* (box) combate *m* revancha

return game *s* desquite *m*

return ticket *s* billete *m* de vuelta; billete de ida y vuelta

return trip *s* viaje *m* de vuelta

reunification [ri,junɪfɪ'ke/ən] *s* reunificación

reunion [ri'junjən] *s* reunión

reunite [,riju'naɪt] *tr* reunir ‖ *intr* reunirse

rev. *abbr* **revenue, reverse, review, revised, revision, revolution**

Rev. *abbr* **Revelation, Reverend**

rev [rev] *s* revolución ‖ *v* (*pret* & *pp* **revved**; *ger* **revving**) *tr* cambiar la velocidad de; **to rev up** acelerar ‖ *intr* acelerarse

revamp [ri'væmp] *tr* componer, renovar, remendar

reveal [rɪ'vil] *tr* revelar

reveille ['revəli] *s* diana, toque *m* de diana

rev-el ['revəl] *s* jarana, regocijo tumultuoso ‖ *v* (*pret* & *pp* **-eled** o **-elled**; *ger* **-eling** o **-elling**) *intr* jaranear; deleitarse

revelation [,revə'le/ən] *s* revelación

revel-ry ['revəlri] *s* (*pl* **-ries**) jarana, diversión tumultuosa

revenge [rɪ'vendʒ] *s* venganza ‖ *tr* vengar

revengeful [rɪ'vendʒfəl] *adj* vengativo

revenue ['revə,nju] o ['revə,nu] *s* renta, rédito, rentas públicas

revenue cutter *s* escampavía

revenue stamp *s* sello fiscal, timbre *m* del estado

reverberate [rɪ'vʌrbə,ret] *intr* reverberar

revere [rɪ'vɪr] *tr* reverenciar, venerar

reverence ['revərəns] *s* reverencia ‖ *tr* reverenciar

reverend ['revərənd] *adj* & *s* reverendo

reverie ['revəri] *s* ensueño

reversal [rɪ'vʌrsəl] *s* inversión; (*e.g., of opinion*) cambio

reverse [rɪ'vʌrs] *adj* invertido; contrario; de marcha atrás ‖ *s (opposite or rear)* revés *m;* contrario; contramarcha, marcha atrás; *(check, defeat)* revés *m,* contratiempo ‖ *tr* invertir; dar vuelta a; poner en marcha atrás; **to reverse oneself** cambiar de opinión; **to reverse the charges** cobrar al destinatario; (telp) cobrar al número llamado ‖ *intr* invertirse

reverse lever *s* palanca de marcha atrás

revert [rɪ'vʌrt] *intr* revertir; saltar atrás; **to revert to one's old tricks** volver a las andadas

review [rɪ'vju] *s (reëxamination; survey; magazine; musical show)* revista; *(of a book)* reseña, revista; *(of a lesson)* repaso; (mil) reseña, revista ‖ *tr* rever, revisar; reseñar *(un libro)*; repasar *(una lección)*; (mil) revistar

revile [rɪ'vaɪl] *tr* ultrajar, vilipendiar

revise [rɪ'vaɪz] *s* revisión; refundición; (typ) segunda prueba ‖ *tr* rever, revisar; refundir *(un libro)*; enmendar

revision [rɪ'vɪʒən] *s* revisión; *(of a book)* refundición; enmienda

revisionism [rɪ'vɪʒə,nɪzəm] *s* revisionismo

revisionist [rɪ'vɪʒənɪst] *adj & s* revisionista

revival [rɪ'vaɪvəl] *s* resucitación; reanimación; *(e.g., of learning)* renacimiento; despertamiento religioso; (theat) reestreno, reposición

revive [rɪ'vaɪv] *tr* revivir; (theat) reestrenar, reponer ‖ *intr* revivir; volver en sí, recordar

revoke [rɪ'vok] *tr* revocar

revolt [rɪ'volt] *s* rebelión, sublevación ‖ *tr* dar asco a, repugnar ‖ *intr* rebelarse, sublevarse

revolting [rɪ'voltɪŋ] *adj* asqueroso, repugnante; rebelde

revolution [,revə'luʃən] *s* revolución

revolutionary [,revə'luʃə,neri] *adj* revolucionario ‖ *s (pl -ies)* revolucionario

revolve [rɪ'valv] *tr* hacer girar; *(in one's mind)* revolver ‖ *intr* girar; revolverse *(un astro en su órbita)*

revolver [rɪ'valvər] *s* revólver *m*

revolving bookcase *s* giratoria

revolving door *s* puerta giratoria

revolving fund *s* fondo rotativo

revue [rɪ'vju] *s* (theat) revista

revulsion [rɪ'vʌlʃən] *s* aversión, repugnancia; reacción fuerte

reward [rɪ'wɔrd] *s* premio, recompensa; *(money used to recapture or recover)* rescate *m;* hallazgo, p.ej., **five dollars reward** cinco dólares de hallazgo ‖ *tr* premiar, recompensar

rewarding [rɪ'wɔrdɪŋ] *adj* remunerador, provechoso, agradecido

re-write [ri'raɪt] *v (pret* -wrote ['rot]; *pp* -written ['rɪtən]) *tr* escribir de nuevo; refundir *(un escrito)*; redactar *(un escrito de otra persona)*

R.F. *abbr* radio frequency

R.F.D. *abbr* Rural Free Delivery

R.H. *abbr* Royal Highness

rhapsody ['ræpsədi] *s (pl* -dies) rapsodia

rheostat ['ri·ə,stæt] *s* reóstato

rhesus ['risəs] *s* macaco de la India

rhetoric ['retərɪk] *s* retórica

rhetorical [rɪ'tɑrɪkəl] o [rɪ'tɔrɪkəl] *adj* retórico

rheumatic [ru'mætɪk] *adj & s* reumático

rheumatism ['rumə,tɪzəm] *s* reumatismo

Rhine [raɪn] *s* Rin *m*

Rhineland ['raɪn,lænd] *s* Renania

rhinestone *s* diamante de imitación hecho de vidrio

rhinoceros [raɪ'nɑsərəs] *s* rinoceronte *m*

Rhodes [rodz] *s* Rodas *f*

Rhone [ron] *s* Ródano

rhubarb ['rubɑrb] *s* ruibarbo

rhyme [raɪm] *s* rima; **without rhyme or reason** sin ton ni son ‖ *tr & intr* rimar

rhythm ['rɪðəm] *s* ritmo

rhythmic(al) ['rɪðmɪk(əl)] *adj* rítmico

Rialto [rɪ'ælto] *s (pl* -tos) mercado; **the Rialto** el puente del Rialto; el centro teatral de Nueva York

rib [rɪb] *s* costilla; *(of a fan or umbrella)* varilla; *(of a tire)* cuerda; *(in cloth)* canilla; *(of the wing of an insect)* nervio ‖ *v (pret & pp* ribbed; *ger* ribbing) *tr* proveer de costillas; hacer canillas en; (slang) tomar el pelo a

ribald ['rɪbəld] *adj* grosero y obsceno

ribbon ['rɪbən] *s* cinta

rice [raɪs] *s* arroz *m*

rich [rɪtʃ] *adj* rico; *(color)* vivo; *(voice)* sonoro; *(wine)* generoso; azucarado, condimentado; (coll) divertido; (coll) ridículo; **to strike it rich** descubrir un buen filón ‖ **riches** *spl* riquezas; **the rich** los ricos

rickets ['rɪkɪts] *s* raquitis *f*

rickety ['rɪkɪti] *adj (object)* destartalado, desvencijado; *(person)* tambaleante, vacilante; *(suffering from rickets)* raquítico

rid [rɪd] *v (pret & pp* rid; *ger* ridding) *tr* desembarazar; **to get rid of** desembarazarse de, deshacerse de; matar

riddance ['rɪdəns] *s* supresión, libramiento; **good riddance!** ¡adiós, gracias!, ¡de buena me he librado!

riddle ['rɪdəl] *s* acertijo, adivinanza; *(person or thing hard to understand)* enigma *m;* criba gruesa ‖ *tr* acribillar; destruir *(un argumento;* la reputación *de una persona)*; **to riddle with bullets** acribillar a balazos; **to riddle with questions** acribillar a preguntas

ride [raɪd] *s* paseo ‖ *v (pret* rode [rod]; *pp* ridden ['rɪdən]) *tr* montar *(un caballo)*; montar sobre *(los hombros de una persona)*; recorrer a caballo; flotar sobre *(las olas)*; dominar, tiranizar; (coll) burlarse de; **to ride down** atropellar; vencer; **to ride out** luchar felizmente con *(una tempestad)*; aguantar con buen éxito *(una desgracia)* ‖ *intr* montar; pasear en coche o carruaje; **to let ride** (slang) dejar correr; **to take riding** llevar de paseo

rider ['raɪdər] s jinete m; pasajero

ridge [rɪdʒ] s (of a roof; of earth between two furrows) caballete m; (of a fabric) cordoncillo; (of mountains) cordillera; (of two plane surfaces) arista

ridge'pole' s parhilera

ridicule ['rɪdɪ‚kjul] s irrisión; **to expose to ridicule** poner en ridículo ‖ tr ridiculizar

ridiculous [rɪ'dɪkjələs] adj ridículo

riding academy s escuela de equitación

riding boot s bota de montar

riding habit s amazona, traje m de montar

rife [raɪf] adj común, corriente, general; abundante, lleno; **rife with** abundante en, lleno de

riffraff ['rɪf‚ræf] s bahorrina, canalla

rifle ['raɪfəl] s rifle m, fusil m ‖ tr hurtar, robar; escudriñar y robar; desnudar, despojar

rift [rɪft] s abertura, raja; desacuerdo, desavenencia

rig [rɪg] s equipaje m; carruaje m con caballo o caballos; traje extraño; (naut) aparejo ‖ v (pret & pp rigged; ger rigging) tr equipar; aprestar, disponer; improvisar; vestir de una manera extraña; arreglar de una manera fraudulenta; (naut) aparejar

rigging ['rɪgɪŋ] s avíos, instrumentos, equipo; (naut) aparejo, cordaje m

right [raɪt] adj derecho, verdadero; exacto; conveniente; favorable; sano, normal; bien; correcto; señalado; correspondiente. que se busca, p.ej., **this is the right house** ésta es la casa que se busca, que se necesita, p.ej., **this is the right train** éste es el tren que se necesita; que debe, p.ej., **he is going the right way** sigue el camino que debe; **right or wrong** con razón o sin ella, bueno o malo; **to be all right** estar bien; estar bien de salud; **to be right** tener razón ‖ adv derechamente; directamente; correctamente; exactamente. favorablemente; en orden, en buen estado; hacia la derecha; completamente; (coll) muy; mismo, p.ej., **right here** aquí mismo; **all right** muy bien ‖ interj ¡bien! ‖ s (justice, reason) derecho; (right hand) derecha; (box) derechazo; (com) derecho, (pol) derecha; **by right** según derecho; **on the right** a la derecha. **to be in the right** tener razón ‖ tr enderezar; corregir, rectificar; hacer justicia a; deshacer (un entuerto) ‖ intr enderezarse

righteous ['raɪtʃəs] adj recto, justo; virtuoso

right field s (baseball) jardín derecho

rightful ['raɪtfəl] adj justo; legítimo

right'-hand' drive s conducción o dirección a la derecha

right-hand man s mano derecha, brazo derecho

rightist ['raɪtɪst] adj & s derechista mf

rightly ['raɪtli] adv derechamente; correctamente; con razón; convenientemente; **rightly or wrongly** con razón o sin ella; **rightly so** a justo título

right mind s entero juicio

right of way s derecho de tránsito o de paso; (law) servidumbre de paso; (rr) servidumbre de vía; **to yield the right of way** ceder el paso

rights of man spl derechos del hombre

right'-wing' adj derechista

right-winger ['raɪt'wɪŋər] s (coll) derechista mf

rigid ['rɪdʒɪd] adj rígido

rigmarole ['rɪgmə‚rol] s galimatías m

rigorous ['rɪgərəs] adj riguroso

rile [raɪl] tr (coll) exasperar

rill [rɪl] s arroyuelo

rim [rɪm] s canto, borde m; (of a wheel) llanta; (of a tire) aro

rime [raɪm] s (in verse) rima; (frost) escarcha; **without rime or reason** sin ton ni son ‖ tr & intr rimar

rind [raɪnd] s cáscara, corteza

ring [rɪŋ] s (circular band, line, or mark) anillo; (for the finger) sortija; (for curtains; for gymnastics) anilla; (for nose of animal) argolla; (for fruit jars) círculo de goma; (for some sport or exhibition) circo; (for boxing) cuadrilátero, ruedo; (for bullfight) redondel m, ruedo; boxeo; (of a group of people) corro; (of evildoers) pandilla; (under the eyes) ojera; (of the anchor) arganeo; (sound of a bell, of a clock) campanada; (of a small bell; of the glass of glassware) tintineo; (to summon a person) llamada; (character, nature, spirit) tono; **to be in the ring (for)** ser candidato a (a); **to run rings around** dar cien vueltas a ‖ v (pret & pp ringed) tr cercar, rodear; (to put a ring on) anillar ‖ intr formar círculo o corro ‖ v (pret rang [ræŋ]; pp rung [rʌŋ]) tr tañer, tocar; (to peal, ring out) repicar; llamar al timbre; dar (las horas la campana del reloj); llamar por teléfono; **to ring up** llamar por teléfono; marcar (una compra) con el timbre ‖ intr sonar (una campana, un timbre, el teléfono); tintinear (el choque de copas, una campanilla); resonar, retumbar; llamar; zumbar (los oídos); **to ring for** llamar, llamar al timbre; **to ring off** terminar una llamada por teléfono; **to ring up** llamar por teléfono

ring-around-a-rosy ['rɪŋə‚raundə'rozi] s juego del corro

ringing ['rɪŋɪŋ] adj resonante, retumbante ‖ s anillamiento; campaneo, repique m; (of the glass of glassware) tintineo; (in the ears) retintín m, silbido

ring'lead'er s cabecilla m

ring'mas'ter s hombre encargado de los ejercicios ecuestres y acrobáticos de un circo

ring'side' s lugar junto al cuadrilátero; lugar desde el cual se puede ver de cerca

ring'worm' s tiña

rink [rɪŋk] s patinadero

rinse [rɪns] s aclaración, enjuague m ‖ tr aclarar, enjuagar

riot ['raɪ·ət] s alboroto, tumulto; regocijos ruidosos; (of colors) exhibición brillante; **to run riot** desenfrenarse; crecer lozanamente (las plantas) ‖ intr alborotarse, amotinarse

rioter ['raɪ·ətər] s alborotador m, amotinado

rip [rɪp] s rasgón m, siete m; (open seam) descosido ‖ v (pret & pp **ripped;** ger **ripping**) tr desgarrar, rasgar; descoser (lo que estaba cosido) ‖ intr desgarrarse, rasgarse; (coll) adelantar o moverse de prisa o con violencia; **to rip out with** (coll) decir con violencia

ripe [raɪp] adj maduro; acabado, hecho; dispuesto, preparado; (boil, tumor) madurado; (olive) negro

ripen ['raɪpən] tr & intr madurar

ripple ['rɪpəl] s temblor m, rizo; (sound) murmullo, susurro ‖ tr rizar ‖ intr rizarse; murmurar, susurrar

rise [raɪz] s (of temperature, prices, a road) subida; (of ground, of the voice) elevación; (of a heavenly body) salida; (of a step) altura; (in one's employment) ascenso; (of water) crecida; (of a source of water) nacimiento; (of a valve) levantamiento; **to get a rise out of** (slang) sacar una réplica mordaz a; **to give rise to** dar origen a ‖ v (pret **rose** [roz]; pp **risen** ['rɪzən]) intr subir; levantarse; salir (un astro); asomar (un peligro); brotar (un manantial, una planta); (in someone's esteem) ganar; resucitar; **to rise above** alzarse por encima de; mostrarse superior a; **to rise early** madrugar; **to rise to** ponerse a la altura de

riser ['raɪzər] s contraescalón m, contrahuella; **early riser** madrugador m; **late riser** dormilón m

risk [rɪsk] s riesgo; **to run** o **take a risk** correr riesgo, correr peligro ‖ tr arriesgar; arriesgarse en (una empresa dudosa)

risk·y ['rɪskɪ] adj (comp **-ier;** super -iest) arriesgado; escabroso

risqué [rɪs'ke] adj escabroso

rite [raɪt] s rito; **last rites** honras fúnebres

ritual ['rɪtʃʊ·əl] adj & s ritual m

riv. abbr **river**

ri·val ['raɪvəl] s rival mf ‖ v (pret & pp **-valed** o **-valled;** ger **-valing** o **-valling**) tr rivalizar con

rival·ry ['raɪvəlrɪ] s (pl **-ries**) rivalidad

river ['rɪvər] s río; **down the river** río abajo; **up the river** río arriba

river basin s cuenca de río

river bed s cauce m

river front s orilla del río

riv'er·side' adj ribereño ‖ s ribera

rivet ['rɪvɪt] s roblón m, remache m; (e.g., to hold scissors together) clavillo ‖ tr remachar; clavar (p.ej., los ojos en una persona)

rm. abbr **ream, room**

R.N. abbr **registered nurse, Royal Navy**

roach [rotʃ] s cucaracha

road [rod] adj itinerario, caminero ‖ s camino; (naut) rada; **to be in the road** estorbar el paso; incomodar; **to get out of the road** quitarse de en medio

road'bed' s (of a highway) firme m; (rr) infraestructura

road'block' s (mil) barricada; (fig) obstáculo

road'house' s posada en el camino

road laborer s peón caminero

road map s mapa itinerario

road service s auxilio en carretera

road'side' s borde m del camino, borde de la carretera

roadside inn s posada en el camino

road sign s señal f de carretera, poste m indicador

road'stead' s rada

road'way' s camino, vía

roam [rom] s vagabundeo ‖ tr vagar por, recorrer a la ventura ‖ intr vagar, andar errante

roar [ror] s bramido, rugido ‖ intr bramar, rugir; reírse a carcajadas

roast [rost] s asado; café tostado ‖ tr asar; tostar (café); (coll) despellejar ‖ intr asarse; tostarse

roast beef s rosbif m

roast of beef s carne de vaca asada o para asar

roast pork s carne de cerdo asada

rob [rɑb] v (pret & pp **robbed;** ger **robbing**) tr & intr robar

robber ['rɑbər] s robador m, ladrón m

robber·y ['rɑbərɪ] s (pl **-ies**) robo

robe [rob] s manto; abrigo; (of a woman) traje m, vestido; (of a professor, judge, etc.) toga, túnica; (of a priest) traje m talar; (dressing gown) bata; (for lap in a carriage) manta ‖ tr vestir ‖ intr vestirse

robin ['rɑbɪn] s (in Europe) petirrojo; (in North America) primavera

robot ['robɑt] s robot m

robust [ro'bʌst] adj robusto; vigoroso

rock [rɑk] s roca; (sticking out of water) escollo; (one that is thrown) piedra; (slang) diamante m, piedra preciosa; **on the rocks** arruinado, en pobreza extrema; (said of hard liquor) (coll) sobre hielo ‖ tr acunar, mecer; (to sleep) arrullar; sacudir; **to rock to sleep** adormecer meciendo ‖ intr mecerse; sacudirse

rock'-bot'tom adj (el) mínimo, (el) más bajo

rock candy s azúcar m cande

rock crystal s cristal m de roca

rocker ['rɑkər] s (chair) mecedora; (curved piece at bottom of rocking chair or cradle) arco; (mach) balancín m; (mach) eje m de balancín

rocket ['rɑkɪt] s cohete m ‖ intr subir como un cohete

rocket bomb s bomba cohete

rocket launcher ['lɔntʃər] o ['lɑntʃər] s lanzacohetes m

rocket ship s aeronave f cohete

rock garden s jardín m entre rocas

rocking chair s mecedora, sillón m de hamaca

rocking horse s caballo mecedor

Rock of Gibraltar [dʒɪ'brɒltər] s peñón m de Gibraltar

rock salt s sal f de compás, sal gema

rock wool s lana mineral

rock·y ['rɑki] adj (comp -ier; super -iest) rocoso, roqueño; (slang) débil, poco firme

rod [rɑd] s vara; varilla; barra; (authority) vara alta; opresión, tiranía; (of the retina) bastoncillo; (elongated microörganism) bastoncito; (mach) vástago; (surv) jalón m; (Bib) linaje m, raza, vástago; (slang) revólver m, pistola; **to spare the rod** excusar la vara

rodent ['rodənt] adj & s roedor m

rod·man ['rɑdmən] s (pl -men [mən]) jalonero, portamira m

roe [ro] s (deer) corzo; (of fish) hueva

rogue [rog] s bribón m, pícaro

rogues' gallery s colección de retratos de malhechores para uso de la policía

roguish ['rogɪʃ] adj bribón, pícaro; travieso, retozón

rôle o **role** [rol] s papel m; **to play a rôle** desempeñar un papel

roll [rol] s (of cloth, film, paper, fat, etc.) rollo; (roller) rodillo; (cake of bread) panecillo; (of dice) echada; (of a boat) balance m; (of a drum) redoble m; (of thunder) retumbo; bamboleo; ondulación; rol m; lista; (of paper money) fajo; **to call the roll** pasar lista ‖ tr hacer rodar; empujar hacia adelante; cilindrar, laminar; (to wrap up with rolling motion) arrollar; alisar con rodillo; liar (un cigarrillo); mover de un lado a otro; poner (los ojos) en blanco; tocar redobles con (el tambor); vibrar (la voz; la r); **to roll one's own** liárselos; **to roll up** arremangar (p.ej., las mangas); amontonar (p.ej., una fortuna) ‖ intr rodar; bambolear; balancear (un barco); girar; retumbar (el trueno); redoblar (un tambor); **to roll around** revolcarse

roll call s lista, (el) pasar lista

roller ['rolər] s rodillo; (of a piece of furniture) ruedecilla; (of a skate) rueda; ola larga y creciente

roller bearing s cojinete m de rodillos

roller coaster s montaña rusa

roller skate s patín m de ruedas

roller towel s toalla sin fin

rolling mill ['rolɪŋ] s taller m de laminación; tren m de laminadores

rolling pin s rodillo, hataca

rolling stock s (rr) material m móvil, material rodante

rolling stone s piedra movediza

roll'-top' desk s escritorio norteamericano, escritorio de cortina corrediza

roly-poly ['roli'poli] adj regordete, rechoncho

Rom. abbr **Roman, Romance**

roman ['romən] adj (typ) redondo ‖ s

(typ) letra redonda ‖ **Roman** adj & s romano

Roman candle s vela romana

Roman Catholic adj & s católico romano

romance [ro'mæns] o ['romæns] s (tale of chivalry) romance m; cuento de aventuras; cuento de amor; intriga amorosa; novela sentimental; (mus) romanza ‖ [ro'mæns] intr contar o escribir romances, cuentos de aventuras o cuentos de amor; pensar o hablar de un modo romántico; exagerar, mentir ‖ **Romance** ['romæns] o [ro'mæns] adj (Neo-Latin) romance o románico

romance of chivalry s libro de caballerías

Roman Empire s Imperio romano

Romanesque [,romən'ɛsk] adj & s románico

Roman nose s nariz aguileña

romantic [ro'mæntɪk] adj romántico; (spot, place) encantador

romanticism [ro'mæntɪ,sɪzəm] s romanticismo

romp [rɑmp] intr corretear, triscar

rompers ['rɑmpərz] spl traje holgado de juego

roof [ruf] o [rʊf] s (top outer covering of a house) tejado; (of a car or bus) imperial f, tejadillo; (of the mouth) paladar m; (of heaven) bóveda; (home, dwelling) (fig) techo; **to raise the roof** (slang) poner el grito en el cielo ‖ tr techar

roofer ['rufər] o ['rʊfər] s techador m, pizarrero

roof garden s (garden on the roof) pérgola; azotea de baile y diversión

rook [rʊk] s (bird) grajo; (in chess) roque m ‖ tr trampear

rookie ['rʊki] s (slang) bisoño, novato

room [rum] o [rʊm] s aposento, cuarto, habitación, pieza; espacio, sitio, lugar m; ocasión; **to make room** abrir paso, hacer lugar ‖ intr alojarse

room and board s pensión completa

room clerk s empleado en la recepción, encargado de las reservas

roomer ['rumər] o ['rʊmər] s inquilino

rooming house s casa donde se alquilan cuartos

room'mate' s compañero de cuarto

room·y ['rumi] o ['rʊmi] adj (comp -ier; super -iest) amplio, espacioso

roost [rust] s percha de gallinero; gallinero; lugar m de descanso; **to rule the roost** ser el amo del cotarro, tener el mando y el palo ‖ intr descansar (las aves) en la percha; estar alojado; pasar la noche

rooster ['rustər] s gallo

root [rut] o [rʊt] s raíz f; **to get to the root of** profundizar; **to take root** echar raíces ‖ tr hocicar, hozar ‖ intr arraigar; **to root for** (slang) gritar alentando

rooter ['rutər] o ['rʊtər] s (slang) hincha mf

rope [rop] s cuerda; (of a hangman)

dogal *m;* (*to catch an animal*) lazo;
to jump rope saltar a la comba; **to
know the ropes** (slang) saber todas
las tretas || *tr* atar con una cuerda;
coger con lazo; **to rope in** (slang)
embaucar, engañar
rope'walk'er *s* funámbulo, volatinero
rosa·ry ['rozəri] *s* (*pl* **-ries**) rosario
rose [roz] *adj* de color de rosa || *s*
rosa
rose'bud' *s* pimpollo, capullo de rosa
rose'bush' *s* rosal *m*
rose'-col'ored *adj* rosado; **to see everything through rose-colored glasses**
verlo todo de color de rosa
rose garden *s* rosaleda, rosalera
rosemar·y ['roz,meri] *s* (*pl* **-ies**) romero
rose of Sharon ['ʃɛrən] *s* granado
blanco, rosa de Siria
rose window *s* rosetón *m*
rose'wood' *s* palisandro
rosin ['razɪn] *s* colofonia, brea seca
roster ['rastər] *s* catálogo, lista; horario escolar, horas de clase
rostrum ['rastrəm] *s* tribuna
ros·y ['rozi] *adj* (*comp* **-ier;** *super*
-iest) rosado, sonrosado; alegre
rot [rɑt] *s* podredumbre; (slang) ton-
tería || *v* (*pret* & *pp* **rotted;** *ger* **rot-
ting**) *tr* pudrir || *intr* pudrirse
rotate ['rotet] o [ro'tet] *tr* hacer girar;
alternar || *intr* girar; alternar
rote [rot] *s* rutina, repetición maquinal; **by rote** de memoria, maquinal-
mente
rot'gut' *s* (slang) matarratas *m*
rotogravure [,rotəgrə'vjur] o [,rotə-
'grevjur] *s* rotograbado
rotten ['rɑtən] *adj* putrefacto, pútrido;
corrompido
rotund [ro'tʌnd] *adj* redondo de
cuerpo; (*language*) redondo
rouge [ruʒ] *s* arrebol *m*, colorete *m* ||
tr arrebolar, pintar || *intr* arrebo-
larse, pintarse
rough [rʌf] *adj* áspero; (*sea*) agitado,
picado; (*crude, unwrought*) tosco,
grosero; aproximado || *tr* — **to
rough it** vivir sin comodidades, hacer
vida campestre
rough'cast' *s* modelo tosco; mezcla
gruesa || *v* (*pret* & *pp* **-cast**) *tr* (*to
prepare in rough form*) bosquejar;
dar a (*la pared*) una capa de mezcla
gruesa
rough copy *s* borrador *m*
roughly ['rʌfli] *adv* asperamente;
brutalmente; aproximadamente
roulette [ru'let] *s* ruleta
round [raund] *adj* redondo || *adv* re-
dondamente; alrededor; de boca en
boca; por todas partes || *prep* alre-
dedor de; (*e.g., the corner*) a la
vuelta de; cerca de; acá y allá en ||
s camino, circuito; (*of a policeman;
of visits; of drinks or cigars*) ronda;
(*of applause; discharge of guns*)
salva; (*discharge of a single gun*)
disparo, tiro; (*of people*) corro, círculo; (*of golf*) partido; rutina, serie
f, sucesión; redondez *f;* revolución;
(box) asalto; **to go the rounds** ir de

boca en boca; ir de mano en mano ||
tr (*to make round*) redondear; cercar, rodear; doblar (*una esquina, un
promontorio*); **to round off** u **out** redondear; acabar, completar, perfeccionar; **to round up** juntar, recoger;
rodear (*el ganado*)
roundabout ['raundə,baut] *adj* indi-
recto || *s* curso indirecto; (Brit) tío
vivo; (Brit) glorieta de tráfico
rounder ['raundər] *s* (coll) pródigo;
(coll) catavinos *m,* borrachín habitual
round'house' *s* cocherón *m*, casa de
máquinas, depósito de locomotoras
round-shouldered ['raund'ʃoldərd] *adj*
cargado de espaldas
Round Table *s* Tabla Redonda
round'-trip' ticket *s* billete *m* de ida y
vuelta
round'up' *s* (*of cattle*) rodeo; (*of
criminals*) redada; (*of old friends*)
reunión
rouse [rauz] *tr* despertar; excitar, pro-
vocar; levantar (*la caza*) || *intr* des-
pertarse, despabilarse
rout [raut] *s* derrota, fuga desorde-
nada || *tr* derrotar; poner en fuga
desordenada; arrancar hozando ||
intr hozar
route [rut] o [raut] *s* ruta; itinerario
|| *tr* encaminar
routine [ru'tin] *adj* rutinario || *s* rutina
rove [rov] *intr* andar errante, vagar
row [rau] *s* (coll) camorra, pendencia,
riña; (coll) alboroto, bullicio; **to
raise a row** (coll) armar camorra ||
[ro] *s* fila, hilera; (*of houses*) crujía;
in a row seguidos, p.ej., **five hours
in a row** cinco horas seguidas || *intr*
remar
rowboat ['ro,bot] *s* bote *m*, bote de
remos
row·dy ['raudi] *adj* (*comp* **-dier;** *super*
-diest) gamberro || *s* (*pl* **-dies**) gam-
berro
rower ['ro·ər] *s* remero
royal ['rɔɪ·əl] *adj* real; (*magnificent,
splendid*) regio
royalist ['rɔɪ·əlɪst] *s* realista *mf*
royal·ty ['rɔɪ·əlti] *s* (*pl* **-ties**) realeza;
personaje *m* real, personajes reales;
derechos de autor; derechos de inventor
r.p.m. *abbr* **revolutions per minute**
R.R. *abbr* **railroad, Right Reverend**
rub [rʌb] *s* frotación, roce *m;* **there's
the rub** ahí está el busilis || *v* (*pret* &
pp **rubbed;** *ger* **rubbing**) *tr* frotar;
to rub elbows with rozarse mucho
con; **to rub out** borrar; (slang) asesi-
nar || *intr* frotar; **to rub off** quitarse
frotando; borrarse
rubber ['rʌbər] *s* caucho, goma; goma
de borrar; chanclo, zapato de goma;
(*in bridge*) robre *m* || *intr* (slang)
estirar el cuello o volver la cabeza
para ver
rubber band *s* liga de goma
rubber plant *s* árbol *m* del caucho
rubber plantation *s* cauchal *m*
rubber stamp *s* cajetín *m*, sello de
goma; (*with a person's signature*)

estampilla; (coll) persona que aprueba sin reflexionar

rub'ber-stamp' *tr* estampar con un sello de goma; (*with a person's signature*) estampillar; (coll) aprobar sin reflexionar

rubbish ['rʌbɪʃ] *s* basura, desecho, desperdicios; (coll) disparate *m*, tontería

rubble ['rʌbəl] *s* (*broken stone*) ripio; (*masonry*) mampostería

rub'down' *s* masaje *m*, fricción

rube [rub] *s* (slang) isidro, rústico

ru-by ['rubi] *s* (*pl* -bies) rubí *m*

rudder ['rʌdər] *s* timón *m*, gobernalle *m*

rud-dy ['rʌdi] *adj* (*comp* -dier; *super* -diest) coloradote, rubicundo

rude [rud] *adj* rudo

rudiment ['rudɪmənt] *s* rudimento

rue [ru] *tr* lamentar, arrepentirse de

rueful ['rufəl] *adj* lamentable; triste

ruffian ['rʌfɪ-ən] *s* hombre grosero y brutal

ruffle ['rʌfəl] *s* arruga; (*of drum*) redoble *m*; (sew) volante *m* || *tr* arrugar; agitar, descomponer; enojar, molestar; confundir; redoblar (*el tambor*); (sew) fruncir un volante en, adornar o guarnecer con volante

rug [rʌg] *s* alfombra; alfombrilla; (*lap robe*) manta

rugged ['rʌgɪd] *adj* áspero, rugoso; recio, vigoroso; tempestuoso

ruin ['ru·ɪn] *s* ruina || *tr* arruinar; estropear; echar a perder

rule [rul] *s* regla; autoridad, mando; regla de imprenta; (*reign*) reinado; (*of a court of law*) decisión, fallo; **as a rule** por regla general; **to be the rule** ser lo que se hace || *tr* gobernar, regir; dirigir, guiar; contener, reprimir; (*to mark with lines*) reglar; (law) decidir, determinar; **to rule out** excluir, rechazar || *intr* gobernar, regir; prevalecer; **to rule over** gobernar, regir

rule of law *s* régimen *m* de justicia

ruler ['rulər] *s* gobernante *mf*; soberano; (*for ruling lines*) regla

ruling ['rulɪŋ] *adj* gobernante, dirigente, imperante || *s* (*of a court or judge*) decisión, fallo; (*of paper*) rayado

rum [rʌm] *s* ron *m*; (*any alcoholic drink*) (U.S.A.) aguardiente *m*

Rumanian [ru'menɪ-ən] *adj* & *s* rumano

rumble ['rʌmbəl] *s* retumbo; (*of the intestines*) rugido; (slang) riña entre pandillas || *intr* retumbar; avanzar retumbando

ruminate ['rumɪ‚net] *tr* & *intr* rumiar

rummage ['rʌmɪdʒ] *tr* & *intr* buscar revolviéndolo todo

rummage sale *s* venta de prendas usadas

rumor ['rumər] *s* rumor *m* || *tr* rumorear; **it is rumored that** se rumorea que

rump [rʌmp] *s* anca, nalga; (*cut of beef*) cuarto trasero

rumple ['rʌmpəl] *s* arruga || *tr* arrugar, ajar, chafar || *intr* arrugarse

rumpus ['rʌmpəs] *s* (coll) batahola, alboroto; **to raise a rumpus** (coll) armar la de San Quintín

run [rʌn] *s* carrera; clase *f*, tipo; arroyo; (*e.g., in a stocking*) carrera; (*on a bank by depositors*) asedio; (*of consecutive performances of a play*) serie *f*; (baseball & mus) carrera; **in the long run** a la larga; **on the run** a escape; en fuga desordenada; **the common run of people** el común de las gentes; **the general run** of la generalidad de; **to have a long run** permanecer en cartel durante mucho tiempo; **to have the run of** hallar el secreto de; tener libertad de ir y venir por || *v* (*pret ran* [ræn]; *pp* run; *ger* running) *tr* hacer funcionar; dirigir, manejar; trazar, tirar (*una línea*); exhibir (*un cine*); hacer (*mandados*); tener como candidato; burlar, violar (*un bloqueo*); tener (*calentura*); correr (*un caballo; un riesgo*); **to run down** cazar y matar; derribar; atropellar (*a un peatón*); (coll) denigrar, desacreditar; **to run in** rodar (*un nuevo coche*); **to run off** tocar (*una pieza de música*); tirar, imprimir; **to run up** (coll) aumentar (*gastos*) || *intr* correr; (*on wheels*) rodar; darse prisa; trepar (*la vid*); ir y venir (*un vapor*); supurar (*una llaga*); colar (*un líquido*); correrse (*un color o tinte*); presentar su candidatura; andar, funcionar, marchar; deshilarse (*las medias*); migrar (*los peces*); estar en fuerza; (*to be worded or written*) rezar; **to run across** dar con, tropezar con; **to run away** correr, huir; desbocarse (*un caballo*); **to run down** escurrir, gotear (*un líquido*); descargarse (*un acumulador*); distenderse (*el muelle de un reloj*); acabarse la cuerda, p.ej., **the watch ran down** se acabó la cuerda; **to run for** presentar su candidatura a; **to run in the family** venir de familia; **to run into** tropezar con; chocar con, topar con; **to run off the track** descarrilar (*un tren*); **to run out** salir; expirar, terminar; acabarse; agotarse; **to run out of** acabársele a uno, e.g., **I have run out of money** se me ha acabado el dinero; **to run over** atropellar (*a un peatón*); registrar a la ligera; pasar por encima; leer rápidamente; rebosar (*un líquido*); **to run through** disipar rápidamente (*una fortuna*); registrar a la ligera; estar difundido en

run'a·way' *adj* fugitivo; (*horse*) desbocado || *s* fugitivo; caballo desbocado; fuga

run'-down' *adj* desmedrado; desmantelado; inculto; (*clock spring*) sin cuerda, distendido; (*storage battery*) descargado

rung [rʌŋ] *s* (*of ladder or chair*) travesaño; (*of wheel*) radio, rayo

runner ['rʌnər] *s* corredor *m*; caballo

de carreras; mensajero; (*of an ice skate*) cuchilla; (*of a sleigh*) patín *m*; (*long narrow rug*) pasacaminos *m*; (*strip of cloth for table top*) tapete *m*; (*in stockings*) carrera

run'ner-up' *s* (*pl* **runners-up**) subcampeón *m*

running ['rʌnɪŋ] *adj* corredor; (*expenses; water*) corriente; (*knot*) corredizo; (*sore*) supurante; (*writing*) cursivo; continuo; consecutivo; en marcha; (*start*) (*sport*) lanzado || *s* carrera, corrida; administración, dirección; marcha funcionamiento; **to be in the running** tener esperanzas o posibilidades de ganar

running board *s* estribo

running head *s* titulillo

running start *s* (sport) salida lanzada

run-of-mine coal ['rʌnəv'main] *s* carbón *m* tal como sale

run'proof' *adj* indesmallable

runt [rʌnt] *s* enano, hombrecillo; (*little child*) redrojo; animal achaparrado

run'way' *s* (*of a stream*) cauce *m*; senda trillada; (aer) pista de aterrizaje

rupture ['rʌptʃər] *s* ruptura; (pathol) quebradura; (*break in relations*) ruptura || *tr* romper; causar una hernia en || *intr* romperse; padecer hernia

rural free delivery ['rurəl] *s* distribución gratuita del correo en el campo

rural police *s* guardia civil

rural policeman *s* guardiacivil *m*

ruse [ruz] *s* astucia, artimaña

rush [rʌʃ] *adj* urgente || *s* prisa grande, precipitación; agolpamiento de gente; (bot) junco; **in a rush** de prisa || *tr* empujar con violencia o prisa; despachar con prontitud; (slang) cortejar insistentemente (*a una mujer*); **to rush through** ejecutar de prisa, despachar rápidamente || *intr* lanzarse, precipitarse; venir de prisa, ir de prisa; actuar con prontitud; **to rush through** lanzarse a través de, lanzarse por entre

rush-bottomed chair ['rʌʃ'batəmd] *s* silla de junco

rush hour *s* hora de aglomeración, horas de punta

rush'light' *s* mariposa, lamparilla

rush order *s* pedido urgente

russet ['rʌsɪt] *adj* canelo

Russia ['rʌʃə] *s* Rusia

Russian ['rʌʃən] *adj & s* ruso

rust [rʌst] *s* orín *m*, moho, herrumbre; (agr) roña, roya; color rojizo o anaranjado || *tr* aherrumbrar || *intr* aherrumbrarse

rustic ['rʌstɪk] *adj* rústico; sencillo, sin artificio || *s* rústico

rustle ['rʌsəl] *s* susurro, crujido || *tr* hacer susurrar, hacer crujir; hurtar (*ganado*) || *intr* susurrar, crujir; (slang) trabajar con ahinco

rust•y ['rʌstɪ] *adj* (*comp* **-ier**; *super* **-iest**) herrumbroso, mohoso; rojizo; (*out of practice*) empolvado, desusado, remoto

rut [rʌt] *s* (*track, groove in road*) rodada, bache *m*; hábito arraigado; (*sexual excitement in animals*) celo; (*period of this excitement*) brama

ruthless ['ruθlɪs] *adj* despiadado, cruel

Ry. *abbr* railway

rye [rai] *s* centeno; whisky de centeno

S

S, s [es] decimonona letra del alfabeto inglés

s *abbr* **second, shilling, singular**

Sabbath ['sæbəθ] *s* (*of Jews*) sábado; (*of Christians*) dominica; **to keep the Sabbath** observar el descanso dominical, guardar el domingo

saber ['sebər] *s* sable *m*

sable ['sebəl] *adj* negro || *s* marta cebellina, **sables** vestidos de luto

sabotage ['sæbə,taʒ] *s* sabotaje *m* || *tr & intr* sabotear

saccharin ['sækərɪn] *s* sacarina

sachet ['sæʃe] o [sɑ'ʃe] *s* polvo oloroso; saquito de perfumes

sack [sæk] *s* saco, vino blanco generoso; (mil) saqueo, saco; (*of an employee*) (slang) despedida || *tr* ensacar; saquear, pillar; (slang) despedir (*a un empleado*)

sack'cloth' *s* harpillera; (*worn for penitence*) cilicio

sacrament ['sækrəmənt] *s* sacramento

sacred ['sekrəd] *adj* sagrado

sacrifice ['sækrɪ,fais] *s* sacrificio; **at a sacrifice** con pérdida || *tr* sacrificar; (*to sell at a loss*) malvender || *intr* sacrificar; sacrificarse

Sacrifice of the Mass *s* sacrificio del altar

sacrilege ['sækrɪlɪdʒ] *s* sacrilegio

sacrilegious [,sækrɪ'lɪdʒəs] o [,sækrɪ'lidʒəs] *adj* sacrílego

sacristan ['sækrɪstən] *s* sacristán *m*

sacris•ty ['sækrɪstɪ] *s* (*pl* **-ties**) sacristía

sad [sæd] *adj* (*comp* **sadder**; *super* **saddest**) triste; (slang) malo

sadden ['sædən] *tr* entristecer || *intr* entristecerse

saddle ['sædəl] *s* silla de montar; (*of a bicycle*) sillín *m* || *tr* ensillar; **to saddle with** echar a cuestas a

sad'dle-bags' *spl* alforjas

sad'dle-bow' [,bo] *s* arzón delantero

sad'dle-tree' *s* arzón *m*

sadist ['sædɪst] o ['sedɪst] *s* sádico

sadistic [sæ'dɪstɪk] o [se'dɪstɪk] *adj* sádico

sadness ['sædnɪs] *s* tristeza

safe [sef] *adj* seguro, ileso, salvo;

cierto, digno de confianza; **sin peligro, a salvo; safe and sound** sano y salvo; **safe from** a salvo de ‖ s caja fuerte, caja de caudales

safe′-con′duct s salvoconducto

safe′-depos′it box s caja de seguridad

safe′guard′ s salvaguardia, medida de seguridad ‖ tr salvaguardar

safe·ty [′seftɪ] adj de seguridad ‖ s (pl **-ties**) seguridad; **to parachute to safety** lanzarse en paracaídas; **to reach safety** ponerse a salvo, llegar a lugar seguro

safety belt s (aer, aut) correa de seguridad; (naut) cinturón m salvavidas

safety match s fósforo de seguridad

safety pin s imperdible m, alfiler m de seguridad

safety rail s guardarriel m

safety razor s maquinilla de seguridad

safety valve s válvula de seguridad

saffron [′sæfrən] adj azafranado ‖ s azafrán m ‖ tr azafranar

sag [sæg] s comba, combadura; (e.g., of a cable) flecha ‖ v (pret & pp **sagged**; ger **sagging**) intr combarse; (to slacken, yield) aflojar, ceder, doblegarse; bajar (los precios)

sagacious [sə′geʃəs] adj sagaz

sage [sedʒ] adj sabio, cuerdo ‖ s sabio; (bot) salvia; (bot) artemisa

sage′brush′ s (bot) artemisa

sail [sel] s vela; barco de vela; **to set sail** hacerse a la vela; **under full sail** a vela llena ‖ v gobernar (un barco de vela); navegar (un mar, río, etc.) ‖ intr navegar, navegar a la vela; salir, salir de viaje; deslizarse, flotar, volar; **to sail into** (slang) atacar, regañar, reñir

sail′boat′ s barco de vela, buque m de vela, velero

sail′cloth′ s lona, paño

sailing [′selɪŋ] adj de salida ‖ s paseo en barco de vela; navegación; salida

sailing vessel s buque velero

sailor [′selər] s (one who makes a living sailing) marinero; (an enlisted man in the navy) marino

saint [sent] adj & s santo ‖ tr (coll) canonizar

saintliness [′sentlɪnɪs] s santidad

Saint Vitus's dance [′vaɪtəsəs] s (pathol) baile m de San Vito

sake [sek] s respeto, bien, amor m; **for his sake** por su bien; **for the sake of** por, por motivo de, por amor a; **for your own sake** por su propio bien

salaam [sə′lɑm] s zalema ‖ tr saludar con zalemas, hacer zalemas a

salable [′seləbəl] adj vendible

salad [′sæləd] s ensalada

salad bowl s ensaladera

salad oil s aceite m de comer

Salamis [′sæləmɪs] s Salamina

sala·ry [′sæləri] s (pl **-ries**) sueldo

sale [sel] s venta; (auction) almoneda, subasta; **for sale** de venta; **se vende(n)**

sales′clerk′ s dependiente mf de tienda

sales′la′dy s (pl **-dies**) vendedora

sales·man [′selzmən] s (pl **-men**

-men]) vendedor m, dependiente m de tienda

sales manager s gerente m de ventas

sales′man·ship′ s arte de vender

sales′room′ s salón m de ventas; salón de exhibición

sales talk s argumento para inducir a comprar

sales tax s impuesto sobre ventas

saliva [sə′laɪvə] s saliva

sallow [′sælo] adj cetrino

sal·ly [′sæli] s (pl **-lies**) paseo, viaje m; ímpetu m, arranque m; salida, ocurrencia; (mil) salida, surtida ‖ v (pret & pp **-lied**) intr salir, hacer una salida; ir de paseo; **to sally forth** salir, avanzar con denuedo

salmon [′sæmən] s salmón m

salon [sæ′lɑn] s salón m

saloon [sə′lun] s cantina, taberna; (on a steamer) salón m

saloon′keep′er s tabernero

salt [sɔlt] s sal f; **to be not worth one's salt** no valer (uno) el pan que come ‖ tr salar; (to preserve with salt) salpresar; marinar (el pescado); salgar (al ganado); **to salt away** (slang) ahorrar, guardar para uso futuro

salt′cel′lar s salero

salted peanuts spl saladillos

saltine [sɔl′tin] s galletita salada

saltish [′sɔltɪʃ] adj salobre

salt lick s salero, lamedero

salt of the earth, the lo mejor del mundo

salt′pe′ter s (potassium nitrate) salitre m; (sodium nitrate) nitro de Chile

salt′sha′ker s salero

salt·y [′sɔlti] adj (comp **-ier**; super **-iest**) salado

salubrious [sə′lubrɪ·əs] adj salubre

salutation [,sæljə′teʃən] s salutación

salute [sə′lut] s saludo ‖ tr saludar

Salvadoran [,sælvə′dorən] o **Salvadorian** [,sælvə′dorɪ·ən] adj & s salvadoreño

salvage [′sælvɪdʒ] s salvamento ‖ tr salvar; recobrar

Salvation Army [sæl′veʃən] s ejército de Salvación

salve [sæv] o [sɑv] s ungüento ‖ tr curar con ungüento; preservar; aliviar

sal·vo [′sælvo] s (pl **-vos** o **-voes**) salva

Samaritan [sə′mærɪtən] adj & s samaritano

same [sem] adj & pron indef mismo; **it's all the same to me** lo mismo me da; **just the same** lo mismo, sin embargo; **same . . . as** mismo . . . que

samite [′sæmaɪt] o [′semaɪt] s jamete m

sample [′sæmpəl] s muestra ‖ tr catar, probar

sample copy s ejemplar m muestra

sancti·fy [′sæŋktɪ,faɪ] v (pret & pp **-fied**) tr santificar

sanctimonious [,sæŋktɪ′monɪ·əs] adj santurrón

sanction [′sæŋkʃən] s sanción ‖ tr sancionar

sanctuar·y [′sæŋktʃu,eri] s (pl **-ies**)

santuario; asilo, refugio; **to take sanctuary** acogerse a sagrado

sand [sænd] *s* arena || *tr* enarenar; lijar con papel de lija

sandal ['sændəl] *s* sandalia

san'dal-wood' *s* (bot) sándalo

sand'bag' *s* saco de arena

sand'bank' *s* banco de arena

sand bar *s* barra de arena

sand'blast' *s* chorro de arena || *tr* limpiar con chorro de arena

sand'box' *s* (rr) arenero

sand dune *s* duna, médano

sand'glass' *s* reloj *m* de arena, ampolleta

sand'pa'per *s* papel *m* de lija || *tr* lijar

sand'stone' *s* piedra arenisca

sand'storm' *s* tempestad de arena

sandwich ['sændwɪtʃ] *s* emparedado, sandwich *m* || *tr* intercalar

sandwich man *s* hombre-anuncio

sand-y ['sændɪ] *adj* (*comp* **-ier**; *super* **-iest**) arenoso; (*hair*) rufo; cambiante, movible

sane [sen] *adj* cuerdo, sensato; (*principles*) sano

sanguinary ['sæŋgwɪn‚ɛri] *adj* sanguinario

sanguine ['sæŋgwɪn] *adj* confiado, esperanzado; (*countenance*) coloradote

sanitary ['sænɪ‚tɛri] *adj* sanitario

sanitary napkin *s* compresa higiénica

sanitation [‚sænɪ'teʃən] *s* (*sanitary measures*) sanidad; (*drainage*) saneamiento

sanity ['sænɪti] *s* cordura, sensatez *f*

Santa Claus ['sæntə‚klɔz] *s* el Papá Noel, San Nicolás

sap [sæp] *s* savia; (mil) zapa; (coll) necio, tonto || *v* (*pret* & *pp* **sapped**; *ger* **sapping**) *tr* agotar, debilitar; zapar, socavar

sap'head' *s* (coll) cabeza de chorlito

sapling ['sæplɪŋ] *s* árbol *m* muy joven, pimpollo; jovenzuelo, mozuelo

sapphire ['sæfaɪr] *s* zafiro

saraband ['særə‚bænd] *s* zarabanda

Saracen ['særəsən] *adj* & *s* sarraceno

Saragossa [‚særə'gɑsə] *s* Zaragoza

sardine [sɑr'din] *s* sardina; **packed in like sardines** como sardinas en banasta o en lata

Sardinia [sɑr'dɪnɪ‚ə] *s* Cerdeña

Sardinian [sɑr'dɪnɪ‚ən] *adj* & *s* sardo

sarsaparilla [‚sɑrsəpə'rɪlə] *s* zarzaparrilla

sash [sæʃ] *s* banda, faja; (*of a window*) marco

sash window *s* ventana de guillotina

satchel ['sætʃəl] *s* maletín *m*; (*of a schoolboy*) cartapacio

sateen [sæ'tin] *s* satén *m*

satellite ['sætə‚laɪt] *s* satélite *m*

satellite country *s* país *m* satélite

satiate ['seʃɪ‚et] *adj* ahíto, harto || *tr* saciar

satin ['sætən] *s* raso

satinet [‚sætɪ'nɛt] *s* rasete *m*

satiric(al) [sə'tɪrɪk(əl)] *adj* satírico

satirist ['sætɪrɪst] *s* satírico

satirize ['sætɪ‚raɪz] *tr* & *intr* satirizar

satisfaction [‚sætɪs'fækʃən] *s* satisfacción

satisfactory [‚sætɪs'fæktəri] *adj* satisfactorio

satis·fy ['sætɪs‚faɪ] *v* (*pret* & *pp* **-fied**) *tr* & *intr* satisfacer

saturate ['sætʃə‚ret] *tr* saturar

Saturday ['sætərdɪ] *s* sábado

sauce [sɔs] *s* salsa; (*of fruit*) compota; (*of chocolate*) crema; gracia, viveza; (coll) insolencia, lenguaje descomedido || *tr* condimentar; [sɔs] o [sæs] *tr* (coll) ser respondón con

sauce'pan' *s* cacerola

saucer ['sɔsər] *s* platillo

sau·cy ['sɔsi] *adj* (*comp* **-cier**; *super* **-ciest**) descarado, insolente; gracioso, vivo

sauerkraut ['saur‚kraut] *s* chucruta

saunter ['sɔntər] *s* paseo tranquilo y alegre || *intr* dar un paseo tranquilo y alegre; pasear tranquila y alegremente

sausage ['sɔsɪdʒ] *s* salchicha, embutido

savage ['sævɪdʒ] *adj* & *s* salvaje *mf*

savant ['sævənt] *s* sabio, erudito

save [sev] *prep* salvo, excepto, menos || *tr* salvar (p.ej., *una vida, un alma*); ahorrar (*dinero*); conservar, guardar; proteger, amparar; **God save the Queen!** ¡Dios guarde a la Reina!; **to save face** salvar las apariencias

saving ['sevɪŋ] *prep* salvo, excepto; con el debido respeto a || *adj* económico || **savings** *spl* ahorros, economías

savings account *s* cuenta de ahorros

savings bank *s* banco de ahorros, caja de ahorros

savior ['sevjər] *s* salvador *m*

Saviour ['sevjər] *s* Salvador *m*

savor ['sevər] *s* sabor *m* || *tr* saborear || *intr* oler; **to savor of** oler a, saber a

savor·y ['sevəri] *adj* (*comp* **-ier**; *super* **-iest**) sabroso; picante; fragante || *s* (*pl* **-ies**) (bot) ajedrea

saw [sɔ] *s* (*tool*) sierra; proverbio, refrán *m* || *tr* aserrar, serrar

saw'buck' *s* cabrilla, caballete *m*

saw'dust' *s* aserrín *m*, serrín *m*

saw'horse' *s* cabrilla, caballete *m*

saw'mill' *s* aserradero, serrería

Saxon ['sæksən] *adj* & *s* sajón *m*

saxophone ['sæksə‚fon] *s* saxofón *m*

say [se] *s* decir *m*; **to have one's say** decir su parecer || *v* (*pret* & *pp* **said** [sed]) *tr* decir; **I should say so!** ¡ya lo creo!; **it is said** se dice, **no sooner said than done** dicho y hecho; **that is to say** es decir, esto es, **to go without saying** caerse de su peso

saying ['se‚ɪŋ] *s* dicho; proverbio, refrán *m*

sc. *abbr* **scene, science, scruple, scilicet** (Lat) **namely**

scab [skæb] *s* costra; (*strikebreaker*) esquirol *m*; (slang) bribón *m*, golfo

scabbard ['skæbərd] *s* funda, vaina

scab·by ['skæbi] *adj* (*comp* **-bier**; *super* **-biest**) costroso; (coll) ruin, vil

scabrous ['skæbrəs] *adj* escabroso

scads [skædz] *spl* (slang) montones *mpl*

scaffold ['skæfəld] *s* andamio; *(to ex-ecute a criminal)* cadalso, patíbulo

scaffolding ['skæfəldɪŋ] *s* andamiaje *m*

scald [skɔld] *tr* escaldar

scale [skel] *s* escama; balanza; platillo de balanza; *(e.g., of a map)* escala; *(mus)* escala; **on a scale of** en escala de; **on a large scale** en grande escala; **scales** balanza; **to tip the scales** inclinar la balanza || *tr* escamar; descortezar, descostrar; escalar, subir, trepar; graduar || *intr* descamarse; descortezarse, descostrarse; subir, trepar

scallop ['skɑləp] o ['skæləp] *s* concha de peregrino; *(shell or dish for serving fish)* concha; *(thin slice of meat)* escalope *m*; *(on edge of cloth)* festón *m* || *tr* cocer *(p.ej., ostras)* en su concha; festonear

scalp [skælp] *s* cuero cabelludo || *tr* escalpar; comprar y revender *(billetes de teatro)* a precios extraoficiales

scalpel ['skælpəl] *s* escalpelo

scal·y ['skelɪ] *adj (comp* -ier; *super* -iest) escamoso

scamp [skæmp] *s* bribón *m*, golfo

scamper ['skæmpər] *intr* escaparse precipitadamente; **to scamper away** escaparse precipitadamente

scan [skæn] *v (pret & pp* scanned; *ger* scanning) *tr* escudriñar; escandir *(versos)*; (telv) explorar; (coll) dar un vistazo a

scandal ['skændəl] *s* escándalo

scandalize ['skændə,laɪz] *tr* escandalizar

scandalous ['skændələs] *adj* escandaloso

Scandinavian [,skændɪ'nevɪ·ən] *adj & s* escandinavo

scanning ['skænɪŋ] *s* (telv) escansión, exploración

scansion ['skænʃən] *s* escansión

scant [skænt] *adj* escaso, insuficiente; solo, apenas suficiente || *tr* escatimar

scant·y ['skæntɪ] *adj (comp* -ier; *super* -iest) escaso, insuficiente, poco suficiente; *(clothing)* ligero

scape'goat' *s* cabeza de turco, víctima propiciatoria

scar [skɑr] *s* cicatriz *f*, señal *f* || *v (pret & pp* scarred; *ger* scarring) *tr* señalar, marcar || *intr* cicatrizarse

scarce [skɛrs] *adj* escaso, raro; **to make oneself scarce** (coll) no dejarse ver

scarcely ['skɛrslɪ] *adv* apenas; probablemente no; ciertamente no; **scarcely ever** raramente

scarci·ty ['skɛrsɪtɪ] *s (pl* -ties) escasez *f*, carestía

scare [skɛr] *s* susto, alarma || *tr* asustar, espantar; **to scare away** espantar, ahuyentar; **to scare up** (coll) juntar, recoger *(dinero)*

scare'crow' *s* espantajo, espantapájaros *m*

scarf [skɑrf] *s (pl* scarfs o scarves [skɑrvz]) bufanda; pañuelo para el cuello; *(cover for a table, bureau, etc.)* tapete *m*; corbata

scarf'pin' *s* alfiler *m* de corbata

scarlet ['skɑrlɪt] *adj* escarlata

scarlet fever *s* escarlata

scar·y ['skɛrɪ] *adj (comp* -ier; *super* -iest) *(easily frightened)* (coll) asustadizo, espantadizo; *(causing fright)* (coll) espantoso

scathing ['skeðɪŋ] *adj* acerbo, duro

scatter ['skætər] *tr* esparcir, dispersar || *intr* esparcirse, dispersarse

scatterbrained ['skætər,brend] *adj* (coll) alegre de cascos, casquivano

scattered showers *spl* lluvias aisladas

scenari·o [sɪ'nɛrɪ,o] o [sɪ'nɑrɪ,o] *s (pl* -os) guión *m*, escenario

scenarist [sɪ'nɛrɪst] o [sɪ'nɑrɪst] *s* guionista *mf*, escenarista *mf*

scene [sin] *s (view)* paisaje *m*; *(in literature, art, the theater, the movie)* escena; escándalo, demostración de pasión; **behind the scenes** entre bastidores; **to make a scene** causar escándalo

scener·y ['sinərɪ] *s (pl* -ies) paisaje *m*; (theat) decoraciones

scene shifter ['ʃɪftər] *s* tramoyista *m*

scenic ['sinɪk] o ['sɛnɪk] *adj* pintoresco; *(representing an action graphically)* gráfico; *(pertaining to the stage)* escénico

scent [sɛnt] *s* olor *m*; perfume *m*; *(sense of smell)* olfato; *(trail)* rastro, pista || *tr* oler; perfumar; olfatear, ventear; sospechar

scepter ['sɛptər] *s* cetro

sceptic ['skɛptɪk] *adj & s* escéptico

sceptical ['skɛptɪkəl] *adj* escéptico

schedule ['skɛdjʊl] *s* catálogo, cuadro, lista; plan *m*, programa *m*; *(of trains, planes, etc.)* horario || *tr* catalogar; proyectar; fijar la hora de

scheme [skim] *s* esquema *m*; plan *m*, proyecto; *(trick)* ardid *m*, treta; *(plot)* intriga, trama || *tr & intr* proyectar; tramar

schemer ['skimər] *s* proyectista *mf*; intrigante *mf*

scheming ['skimɪŋ] *adj* astuto, mañoso, intrigante || *s* intriga

schism ['sɪzəm] *s* cisma *m*; facción cismática

schist [ʃɪst] *s* esquisto

scholar ['skɑlər] *s (pupil)* alumno; *(scholarship holder)* becario; *(learned person)* sabio, erudito

scholarly ['skɑlərlɪ] *adj* sabio, erudito

scholarship ['skɑlər,ʃɪp] *s* erudición; *(grant to study)* beca

school [skul] *s* escuela; *(of a university)* facultad; *(of fish)* banco, cardume *m* || *tr* enseñar, instruir, disciplinar

school age *s* edad escolar

school attendance *s* escolaridad

school board *s* junta de instrucción pública

school'boy' *s* alumno de escuela

school day *s* día lectivo

school'girl' *s* alumna de escuela

school'house' *s* escuela

schooling ['skulɪŋ] *s* instrucción, enseñanza; experiencia

school'mate' *s* compañero de escuela

school'room' *s* aula, sala de clase

school'teach'er s maestro de escuela

school year s año lectivo

schooner ['skunər] s go'eta

sci. *abbr* **science, scientific**

science ['saɪ·əns] s ciencia

scientific [‚saɪ·ən'tɪfɪk] *adj* científico

scientist ['saɪ·əntɪst] s científico, sabio, hombre *m* de ciencia

scil. *abbr* **scilicet** (Lat) **namely**

scimitar ['sɪmɪtər] s cimitarra

scintillate ['sɪntɪ‚let] *intr* chispear, centellear

scion ['saɪ·ən] s vástago

Scipio ['sɪpɪ‚o] s Escipión *m*

scissors ['sɪzərz] *ssg* o *spl* tijeras

scoff [skɔf] o [skaf] s burla, mofa || *intr* burlarse, mofarse; **to scoff at** burlarse de, mofarse de

scold [skold] s regañón *m*, regañona || *tr & intr* regañar

scoop [skup] s (*instrument like a spoon*) cuchara, cucharón *m*; (*tool like a shovel*) pala; (*kitchen utensil*) paleta; (*for water*) achicador *m*; cucharada, palada, paletada; (*hollow made by a scoop*) hueco; (*big haul*) (coll) buena ganancia || *tr* sacar con cuchara, pala, paleta; achicar (*agua*); **to scoop out** ahuecar, vaciar

scoot [skut] s (coll) carrera precipitada || *intr* (coll) correr precipitadamente

scooter ['skutər] s monopatín *m*, patinete *m*

scope [skop] s alcance *m*, extensión; campo, espacio; **to give free scope to** dar campo libre a

scorch [skɔrtʃ] s chamusco || *tr* chamuscar; (*to dry, wither*) abrasar; criticar acerbamente || *intr* chamuscarse; abrasarse

scorching ['skɔrtʃɪŋ] *adj* abrasador; acerbo, duro, mordaz

score [skor] s (*in a game*) cuenta, tantos; (*in an examination*) nota; entalladura, muesca; línea, raya; (*twenty*) veintena; (mus) partitura; **on the score of** a título de; **to keep score** apuntar los tantos || *tr* anotar (*los tantos*); ganar, tantear (*tantos*); rayar, señalar; regañar acerbamente; (mus) instrumentar || *intr* ganar tantos; marcar los tantos

score board s marcador *m*, cuadro indicador

scorn [skɔrn] s desdén *m*, desprecio || *tr & intr* desdeñar, despreciar; **to scorn to** no dignarse

scornful ['skɔrnfəl] *adj* desdeñoso

scorpion ['skɔrpɪ·ən] s alacrán *m*, escorpión *m*

Scot [skat] s escocés *m*

Scotch [skatʃ] *adj* escocés || s (*dialect*) escocés *m*; whisky *m* escocés; **the Scotch** los escoceses

Scotch•man ['skatʃmən] s (*pl* -men [mən]) escocés *m*

Scotland ['skatlənd] s Escocia

Scottish ['skatɪʃ] *adj* escocés || s (*dialect*) escocés *m*; **the Scottish** los escoceses

scoundrel ['skaundrəl] s bribón *m*, pícaro

scour [skaur] *tr* fregar, estregar; recorrer, explorar detenidamente

scourge [skʌrdʒ] s azote *m* || *tr* azotar

scout [skaut] s (mil) escucha, explorador *m*; niño explorador, niña exploradora; exploración, reconocimiento; (slang) individuo, sujeto, tipo || *tr* explorar, reconocer (*un territorio*); observar (*al enemigo*); negarse a creer

scout'mas'ter s jefe *m* de tropa de niños exploradores

scowl [skaul] s ceño, semblante ceñudo || *intr* mirar con ceño, poner mal gesto, poner mala cara

scramble ['skræmbəl] s arrebatiña || *tr* arrebatar; recoger de prisa; revolver; hacer un revoltillo de (*huevos*); trepar || *intr* luchar; trepar

scrambled eggs *spl* revoltillo, huevos revueltos

scrap [skræp] s fragmento, pedacito; desecho; chatarra; (slang) riña, contienda; scraps desperdicios, desechos; (*from the table*) sobras || *v* (*pret & pp* **scrapped**; *ger* **scrapping**) *tr* desechar, descartar, echar a la basura; reducir a hierro viejo || *intr* (slang) reñir, pelear

scrap'book' s álbum *m* de recortes, libro de recuerdos

scrape [skrep] s raspadura; (*place scratched*) raspazo; aprieto, enredo; || *tr* raspar; (*to gather together with much difficulty*) arañar || *intr* raspar; **to scrape along** ir tirando; **to scrape through** aprobar justo

scrap heap s montón *m* de cachivaches

scrap iron s chatarra, desecho de hierro

scrap paper s papel *m* para apuntes, papel de desecho

scratch [skrætʃ] s arañazo, rasguño; marca, raya, garrapato; (billiards) chiripa; (sport) línea de partida; **to start from scratch** empezar desde el principio; **up to scratch** en buena condición || *tr* arañar, rasguñar; borrar, rasgar (*lo escrito*); garrapatear; (sport) borrar (*a un corredor o caballo*) || *intr* arañar, rasguñar; garrapatear; raspear (*una pluma*)

scratch pad s cuadernillo de apuntes

scratch paper s papel *m* para apuntes

scrawl [skrɔl] s garrapatos || *tr & intr* garrapatear

scraw•ny ['skrɔnɪ] *adj* (*comp* -nier; *super* -niest) huesudo, flaco

scream [skrim] s chillido, grito || *tr* vociferar || *intr* chillar, gritar; reírse a gritos

screech [skritʃ] s chillido || *intr* chillar

screech owl s buharro; (*barn owl*) lechuza

screen [skrin] s mampara, biombo; (*in front of chimney*) pantalla; (*to keep flies out*) alambrera; (*to sift sand*) tamiz *m*; (mov, phys, telv) pantalla; **to put on the screen** llevar a la pantalla, llevar al celuloide || *tr* defender, proteger; cubrir, ocultar; cinematografiar; rodar, proyectar (*una película*); adaptar para el cine; tamizar (*p.ej., arena*)

screen grid *s* (electron) rejilla blindada

screen'play' *s* cinedrama *m*

screw [skru] *s* tornillo; (*internal or female screw*) rosca, tuerca; (*of a boat*) hélice *f*; **to have a screw loose** (slang) tener flojos los tornillos; **to put the screws on** apretar los tornillos a || *tr* atornillar; (*to twist, twist in*) enroscar; **to screw up** torcer (*el rostro*); || *intr* atornillarse

screw'ball' *s* (slang) estrafalario, excéntrico

screw'driv'er *s* destornillador *m*

screw eye *s* armella

screw jack *s* gato de tornillo

screw propeller *s* hélice *f*

scribal error ['skraɪbəl] *s* error *m* de escribiente

scribble ['skrɪbəl] *s* garrapatos || *tr* & *intr* garrapatear

scribe [skraɪb] *s* (*teacher of Jewish law*) escriba *m*; escribiente *mf*; copista *mf*; autor *m*, escritor *m* || *tr* arañar, rayar; trazar con punzón

scrimp [skrɪmp] *tr* & *intr* escatimar

script [skrɪpt] *s* escritura, letra cursiva; manuscrito, texto; (*of a play, movie, etc.*) palabras; (rad, telv) guión *m*; (typ) plumilla inglesa

scripture ['skrɪptʃər] *s* escrito sagrado || **Scripture** *s* Escritura

script'writ'er *s* guionista *mf*, cinematurgo

scrofula ['skrɑfjələ] *s* escrófula

scroll [skrol] *s* rollo de papel, rollo de pergamino; (archit) voluta

scroll'work' *s* obra de volutas, adornos de voluta

scrub [skrʌb] *s* chaparral *m*, monte bajo; animal achaparrado; persona de poca monta; (*act of scrubbing*) fregado; (sport) jugador *m* no oficial || *v* (*pret* & *pp* **scrubbed**); *ger* **scrubbing**) *tr* fregar, restregar

scrub oak *s* chaparro

scrub woman *s* fregona

scruff [skrʌf] *s* nuca; piel *f* que cubre la nuca; capa, superficie *f*; espuma

scruple ['skrupəl] *s* escrúpulo

scrupulous ['skrupjələs] *adj* escrupuloso

scrutinize ['skrutɪ‚naɪz] *tr* escudriñar, escrutar

scruti·ny ['skrutɪnɪ] *s* (*pl* **-nies**) escudriñamiento, escrutinio

scuff [skʌf] *s* rascadura, desgaste *m* || *tr* rascar, desgastar

scuffle ['skʌfəl] *s* lucha, sarracina || *intr* forcejear, luchar

scull [skʌl] *s* espadilla || *tr* impulsar con espadilla || *intr* remar con espadilla

sculler·y ['skʌlərɪ] *s* (*pl* **-ies**) trascocina

scullery maid *s* fregona

scullion ['skʌljən] *s* pinche *m*

sculptor ['skʌlptər] *s* escultor *m*

sculptress ['skʌlptrɪs] *s* escultora

sculpture ['skʌlptʃər] *s* escultura || *tr* & *intr* esculpir

scum [skʌm] *s* espuma, nata; (*on metals*) escoria; (fig) escoria, canalla, gente baja || *v* (*pret* & *pp*

scummed; *ger* **scumming**) *tr* & *intr* espumar

scum·my ['skʌmɪ] *adj* (*comp* **-mier**; *super* **-miest**) espumoso; (fig) vil, ruin

scurf [skʌrf] *s* (*shed by the skin*) caspa; (*shed by any surface*) costra

scurrilous ['skʌrɪləs] *adj* chocarrero, grosero, insolente, difamatorio

scur·ry ['skʌrɪ] *v* (*pret* & *pp* **-ried**) *intr* echar a correr, escabullirse; **to scurry around** menearse; **to scurry away** ir respaldando

scur·vy ['skʌrvɪ] *adj* (*comp* **-vier**; *super* **-viest**) despreciable, ruin, vil || *s* escorbuto

scuttle ['skʌtəl] *s* (*bucket for coal*) cubo, balde *m*; (*trap door*) escotillón *m*; fuga, paso acelerado; (naut) escotilla || *tr* barrenar, dar barreno a || *intr* echar a correr

Scylla ['sɪlə] *s* Escila; **between Scylla and Charybdis** entre Escila y Caribdis

scythe [saɪð] *s* dalle *m*, guadaña

sea [si] *s* mar *m* & *f*; **at sea** en el mar; confuso, perplejo; **by the sea** a la orilla del mar; **to follow the sea** correr los mares, ser marinero; **to put to sea** hacerse a la mar

sea'board' *adj* costanero, costero || *s* costa del mar, litoral *m*

sea breeze *s* brisa de mar

sea'coast' *s* costa marítima, litoral *m*

sea dog *s* (seal) foca; (coll) marinero viejo, lobo de mar

seafarer ['si‚ferər] *s* marinero; viajero por mar

sea'food' *s* mariscos

seagoing ['si‚goɪŋ] *adj* de alta mar

sea gull *s* gaviota

seal [sil] *s* (*raised design; stamp; mark*) sello; (*sea animal*) foca || *tr* sellar; cerrar herméticamente; decidir irrevocablemente; (*with sealing wax*) lacrar

sea legs *spl* pie marino

sea level *s* nivel *m* del mar

sealing wax *s* lacre *m*

seal'skin' *s* piel *f* de foca

seam [sim] *s* costura; (*edges left after making a seam*) metido; (*mark, line*) arruga; (*scar*) costurón *m*; grieta, juntura; (min) filón *m*, veta

sea·man ['simən] *s* (*pl* **-men** [mən]) marinero; (nav) marino

sea mile *s* milla náutica

seamless ['simlɪs] *adj* inconsútil, sin costura

seamstress ['simstrɪs] *s* costurera; (*dressmaker's helper*) modistilla

seam·y ['simɪ] *adj* (*comp* **-ier**; *super* **-iest**) lleno de costuras; tosco, burdo; vil, soez; miserable

séance ['se‚ɑns] *s* sesión de espiritistas

sea'plane' *s* hidroavión *m*, hidroplano

sea'port' *s* puerto de mar

sea power *s* potencia naval

sear [sɪr] *adj* seco, marchito; gastado, raído || *s* chamusco, socarra || *tr* chamuscar, socarrar; quemar; marchitar; cauterizar

search [sʌrtʃ] *s* busca; pesquisa, indagación; (*frisking a person*) cacheo; **in search of** en busca de ‖ *tr* averiguar, explorar; registrar ‖ *intr* buscar; **to search for** buscar; **to search into** indagar, investigar

search'light' *s* reflector *m*, proyector *m*

search warrant *s* auto de registro domiciliario, orden *f* de allanamiento

sea'scape' *s* vista del mar; (*painting*) marina

sea shell *s* concha marina

sea'shore' *s* costa, playa, ribera del mar

sea'sick' *adj* mareado

sea'sick'ness *s* mareo

sea'side' *s* orilla del mar, ribera del mar, playa

season ['sizən] *s* (*one of four parts of year*) estación; (*period of the year; period marked by certain activities*) temporada; (*opportune time; time of maturity, of ripening*) sazón *f*; **in season** en sazón; **in season and out of season** en tiempo y a destiempo; **out of season** fuera de sazón ‖ *tr* condimentar, sazonar; curar (*la madera*); moderar, templar

seasonal ['sizənəl] *adj* estacional

seasoning ['sizənɪŋ] *s* aderezo, aliño, condimento; (*of wood*) cura; (fig) sal *f*, chiste *m*

season ticket *s* billete *m* de abono

seat [sit] *s* asiento; (*of trousers*) fondillos; morada; sitio, lugar *m*; (e.g., *of government*) sede *f*; (in *parliament*) escaño; (e.g., *of a war*) teatro; (e.g., *of learning*) centro; (*of a saddle*) batalla; (*of human body*) nalgas; (theat) localidad ‖ *tr* sentar; tener asientos para; poner asiento a (*una silla*); echar fondillos a (*pantalones*); arraigar, establecer; **to be seated** estar sentado; **to seat oneself** sentarse

seat belt *s* cinturón *m* de asiento

seat cover *s* funda de asiento, cubreasiento

SEATO ['sito] *s* (acronym) la O.T.A.S.E.

sea wall *s* dique marítimo

sea'way' *s* ruta marítima; avance *m* de un buque por mar; vía de agua interior para buques de alta mar; mar gruesa

sea'weed' *s* alga marina; plantas marinas

sea wind *s* viento que sopla del mar

sea'wor'thy *adj* marinero, en condiciones de navegar

sec. *abbr* **secant, second, secondary, secretary, section, sector**

secede [sɪ'sid] *intr* separarse, retirarse

secession [sɪ'sɛʃən] *s* secesión

seclude [sɪ'klud] *tr* recluir

secluded [sɪ'kludɪd] *adj* aislado, apartado, solitario

seclusion [sɪ'kluʒən] *s* reclusión, soledad

second ['sɛkənd] *adj* segundo; **to be second to none** ser tan bueno como el que más, no tener segundo ‖ *adv* en segundo lugar ‖ *s* segundo; artículo de segunda calidad; (*in dates*)

dos *m*; (*in a challenge*) padrino; (aut) segunda (velocidad); (mus) semoción ‖ *tr* secundar; apoyar (*una moción*)

secondar·y ['sɛkən,dɛri] *adj* secundario ‖ *s* (*pl* -ies) (elec) secundario

sec'ond-best' *adj* (el) mejor después del primero

sec'ond-class' *adj* de segunda clase

second hand *s* segundero

sec'ond-hand' *adj* de segunda mano, de ocasión

second-hand bookshop *s* librería de viejo

second lieutenant *s* alférez *m*, subteniente *m*

sec'ond-rate' *adj* de segundo orden; de calidad inferior

second sight *s* doble vista

second wind *s* nuevo aliento

secre·cy ['sikrəsi] *s* (*pl* -cies) secreto; **in secrecy** en secreto

secret ['sikrɪt] *adj* & *s* secreto; **in secret** en secreto

secretar·y ['sɛkrɪ,tɛri] *s* (*pl* -ies) secretario; (*desk*) secreter *m*, escritorio

secrete [sɪ'krit] *tr* encubrir, esconder; (physiol) secretar

secretive [sɪ'kritɪv] *adj* callado, reservado

sect [sɛkt] *s* secta, comunión

sectarian [sɛk'tɛrɪən] *adj* & *s* sectario

section ['sɛkʃən] *s* sección; (*of a country*) región; (*of a city*) barrio; (*of a law*) artículo; (*department, bureau*) negociado; (rr) tramo

secular ['sɛkjələr] *adj* secular, seglar ‖ *s* clérigo secular

secularism ['sɛkjələ,rɪzəm] *s* laicismo

secure [sɪ'kjur] *adj* seguro ‖ *tr* asegurar; conseguir, obtener

securi·ty [sɪ'kjurɪti] *s* (*pl* -ties) seguridad; (*person*) segurador *m*; **securities** valores *mpl*, obligaciones, títulos

secy. o **sec'y.** *abbr* **secretary**

sedan [sɪ'dæn] *s* silla de manos; (aut) sedán *m*

sedate [sɪ'det] *adj* sentado, sosegado

sedative ['sɛdətɪv] *adj* & *s* sedativo

sedentary ['sɛdən,tɛri] *adj* sedentario

sedge [sɛdʒ] *s* juncia

sediment ['sɛdɪmənt] *s* sedimento

sedition [sɪ'dɪʃən] *s* sedición

seditious [sɪ'dɪʃəs] *adj* sedicioso

seduce [sɪ'djus] o [sɪ'dus] *tr* seducir

seducer [sɪ'djusər] o [sɪ'dusər] *s* seductor *m*

seduction [sɪ'dʌkʃən] *s* seducción

seductive [sɪ'dʌktɪv] *adj* seductivo

sedulous ['sɛdʒələs] *adj* cuidadoso, diligente

see [si] *s* (eccl) sede *f* ‖ *v* (*pret* **saw** [so]; *pp* **seen** [sin]) *tr* ver; **to see off** ir a despedir; **to see through** llevar a cabo; seguir en un trance difícil ‖ *intr* ver; **see here!** ¡mire Vd.!; **to see into** o **to see through** conocer el juego de

seed [sid] *s* semilla, simiente *f*; **to go to seed** dar semilla; echarse a perder ‖ *tr* sembrar; (*to remove the seeds from*) despepitar ‖ *intr* sembrar; dejar caer semillas

seed'bed' *s* semillero

seedling ['sidlɪŋ] s planta de semilla; árbol m de pie

seed·y ['sidi] adj (comp -ier; super -iest) lleno de granos; (coll) andrajoso, raído

seeing ['si·ɪŋ] adj vidente ‖ s vista, visión ‖ conj visto que

Seeing Eye dog s perro-lazarillo

seek [sik] v (pret & pp sought [sɔt]) tr buscar; recorrer buscando; dirigirse a ‖ intr buscar; **to seek after** tratar de obtener; **to seek to** esforzarse por

seem [sim] intr parecer

seemingly ['simɪŋli] adv aparentemente, al parecer

seem·ly ['simli] adj (comp -lier; super -liest) decente, decoroso, correcto; bien parecido

seep [sip] intr escurrirse, rezumarse

seer [sɪr] s profeta m, vidente m

see'saw' s balancín m, columpio de tabla; (motion) vaivén m ‖ intr columpiarse; alternar; vacilar

seethe [sið] intr hervir

segment ['sɛgmənt] s segmento

segregate ['sɛgrɪ ˌget] tr segregar

segregationist [ˌsɛgrɪ'geʃənɪst] s segregacionista mf

Seine [sen] s Sena m

seismograph ['saɪzmə ˌgræf] o ['saɪzme ˌgraf] s sismógrafo

seismology [saɪz'malədʒi] s sismología

seize [siz] tr agarrar, asir, coger; atar, prender, sujetar; apoderarse de; comprender; (law) embargar, secuestrar; aprovecharse de (una oportunidad)

seizure ['siʒər] s prendimiento, prisión; captura, toma; (of an illness) ataque m; (law) embargo, secuestro

seldom ['sɛldəm] adv raramente, rara vez

select [sɪ'lɛkt] adj escogido, selecto ‖ tr seleccionar

selectee [sɪ ˌlɛk'ti] s (mil) quinto

selection [sɪ'lɛkʃən] s selección; trozo escogido; (of goods for sale) surtido

self [sɛlf] adj mismo ‖ s (pl selves [sɛlvz]) uno mismo; ser m; yo; **all by one's self** sin ayuda de nadie

self'-abuse' s abuso de sí mismo; masturbación

self'-addressed' envelope s sobre m con el nombre y dirección del remitente

self'-cen'tered adj egocéntrico

self'-con'scious adj cohibido, apocado, tímido

self'-con·trol' s dominio de sí mismo

self'-de·fense' s autodefensa; **in self-defense** en defensa propia

self'-de·ni'al s abnegación

self'-de·ter'mi·na'tion s autodeterminación

self'-dis'cipline s autodisciplina

self'-ed'u·cat'ed adj autodidacto

self'-em·ployed' adj que trabaja por su propia cuenta

self'-ev'i·dent adj patente, manifiesto

self'-ex·plan'a·tor'y adj que se explica por sí mismo

self'-gov'ernment s autogobierno, autonomía; dominio sobre sí mismo

self'-im·por'tant adj altivo, arrogante

self'-in·dul'gence s intemperancia, desenfreno

self'-in'terest s egoísmo, interés m personal

selfish ['sɛlfɪʃ] adj egoísta

selfishness ['sɛlfɪ/nɪs] s egoísmo

selfless ['sɛlflɪs] adj desinteresado

self'-liq'ui·dat'ing adj autoamortizable

self'-love' s amor propio, egoísmo

self'-made' man s hijo de sus propias obras

self'-por'trait s autorretrato

self'-pos·sessed' adj dueño de sí mismo

self'-pres'er·va'tion s propia conservación

self'-re·li'ant adj confiado en sí mismo

self'-re·spect'ing adj lleno de dignidad, decoroso

self'-right'eous adj santurrón

self'-sac'ri·fice' s sacrificio de sí mismo

self'same' adj mismísimo

self'-sat'is·fied' adj pagado de sí mismo

self'-seek'ing adj egoísta ‖ s egoísmo

self'-ser'vice restaurant s restaurante m de libre servicio, restaurante de autoservicio

self'-start'er s arranque automático

self'-sup·port' s mantenimiento económico propio

self'-taught' adj autodidacto

self'-willed' adj obstinado, terco

self'-wind'ing clock s reloj m de cuerda automática, reloj de autocuerda

sell [sɛl] v (pret & pp sold [sold]) tr vender; **to sell out** realizar, saldar; (to betray) vender ‖ intr venderse, estar de venta; **to sell for** venderse a o en (p.ej., cien pesetas); **to sell off** bajar (el mercado de valores); **to sell out** venderlo todo, realizar

seller ['sɛlər] s vendedor m

sell'out' s (slang) realización; saldo; (slang) traición

Seltzer water ['sɛltsər] s agua de seltz

selvage ['sɛlvɪdʒ] s orillo, vendo

semantic [sɪ'mæntɪk] adj semántico ‖ **semantics** s semántica

semaphore ['sɛmə ˌfor] s semáforo; (rr) disco de señales

semblance ['sɛmbləns] s apariencia, imagen f, simulacro

semen ['simen] s semen m

semester [sɪ'mɛstər] adj semestral ‖ s semestre m

semester hour s hora semestral

sem'ico'lon s punto y coma

sem'iconduc'tor s semiconductor m

sem'icon'scious adj semiconsciente

sem'ifi'nal adj & s (sport) semifinal f

sem'illearn'ed adj semiculto

sem'imonth'ly adj quincenal ‖ s (pl -lies) periódico quincenal

seminar ['sɛmɪ ˌnar] o [ˌsɛmɪ'nar] s seminario

seminar·y ['sɛmɪ ˌneri] s (pl -ies) seminario

sem'ipre'cious adj semiprecioso, fino

Semite ['sɛmaɪt] o ['simaɪt] s semita mf

Semitic [sɪ'mɪtɪk] *adj* semítico ‖ *s* semita *mf; (language)* semita *m*

sem'itrail'er *s* semi-remolque *m*

sem'iweek'ly *adj* bisemanal ‖ *s (pl -lies)* periódico bisemanal

sem'iyear'ly *adj* semestral

Sen. o **sen.** *abbr* **Senate, Senator, Senior**

senate ['sɛnɪt] *s* senado

senator ['sɛnətər] *s* senador *m*

senatorship ['sɛnətər‚ʃɪp] *s* senaduría

send [sɛnd] *v (pret & pp sent* [sɛnt]) *tr* enviar, mandar; expedir, remitir; lanzar *(una bola, flecha, etc.);* **to send back** devolver; **to send packing** despedir con cajas destempladas ‖ *intr* (rad) transmitir; **to send for** enviar por, enviar a buscar

sender ['sɛndər] *s* remitente *mf;* (telg) transmisor *m*

send'-off' *s* (coll) despedida afectuosa

senile ['sinaɪl] o ['sɪnɪl] *adj* senil

senility [sɪ'nɪlɪtɪ] *s* senilidad; (pathol) senilismo

senior ['sinjər] *adj* mayor, de mayor edad; viejo; del último año; padre, p.ej., **John Jones, Senior** Juan Jones, padre ‖ *s* mayor *m;* socio más antiguo; alumno del último año

senior citizens *spl* gente *f* de edad

seniority [sin'jɔrɪtɪ] o [sin'jɑrɪtɪ] *s* antigüedad; precedencia, prioridad

sensation [sɛn'seʃən] *s* sensación

sense [sɛns] *s* sentido; **to make sense out of** comprender, explicarse ‖ *tr* intuir, sentir, sospechar; (coll) comprender

senseless ['sɛnslɪs] *adj* falto de sentido; desmayado; insensato, necio

sense of guilt *s* cargo de conciencia

sense organ *s* órgano sensorio

sensibili-ty [‚sɛnsɪ'bɪlɪtɪ] *s (pl -ties)* sensibilidad; **sensibilities** sentimientos delicados

sensible ['sɛnsɪbəl] *adj* cuerdo, sensato; perceptible, sensible

sensitive ['sɛnsɪtɪv] *adj* sensible; *(of the senses)* sensorio, sensitivo

sensitize ['sɛnsɪ‚taɪz] *tr* sensibilizar

sensory ['sɛnsəri] *adj* sensorio

sensual ['sɛnʃʊ-əl] *adj* sensual, voluptuoso

sensuous ['sɛnʃʊ-əs] *adj* sensual

sentence ['sɛntəns] *s* (gram) frase *f,* oración; (law) sentencia ‖ *tr* sentenciar, condenar

sentiment ['sɛntɪmənt] *s* sentimiento

sentimentali-ty [‚sɛntɪmɛn'tælɪtɪ] *s (pl -ties)* sentimentalismo

sentinel ['sɛntɪnəl] *s* centinela *m* or *f;* **to stand sentinel** estar de centinela, hacer centinela

sen-try ['sɛntri] *s (pl -tries)* centinela *m* or *f*

sentry box *s* garita de centinela

separate ['sɛpərɪt] *adj* separado; suelto ‖ ['sɛpə‚ret] *tr* separar ‖ *intr* separarse

Sephardic [sɪ'fɑrdɪk] *adj* sefardí, sefardita

Sephardim [sɪ'fɑrdɪm] *spl* sefardíes *mpl*

September [sɛp'tɛmbər] *s* septiembre *m*

septet [sɛp'tɛt] *s* septeto

septic ['sɛptɪk] *adj* séptico

sepulcher ['sɛpəlkər] *s* sepulcro

seq. *abbr* **sequentia** (Lat) **the following**

sequel ['sikwəl] *s* resultado, secuela; continuación

sequence ['sikwəns] *s* serie *f,* sucesión; (cards) secansa, escalera, runfla; (gram, mov & mus) secuencia

sequester [sɪ'kwɛstər] *tr* apartar, separar; (law) secuestrar

sequin ['sikwɪn] *s* lentejuela

ser-aph ['sɛrəf] *s (pl -aphs* o **-aphim** [əfɪm]) serafín *m*

Serb [sɑrb] *adj & s* servio

Serbia ['sɑrbɪ-ə] *s* Servia

Serbian ['sɑrbɪ-ən] *adj & s* servio

Serbo-Croatian [‚sɑrbokro'eʃən] *adj & s* servocroata *mf*

sere [sɪr] *adj* seco, marchito

serenade [‚sɛrə'ned] *s* serenata ‖ *tr* dar serenata a ‖ *intr* dar serenatas

serene [sɪ'rin] *adj* sereno

serenity [sɪ'rɛnɪtɪ] *s* serenidad

serf [sɑrf] *s* siervo de la gleba

serfdom ['sɑrfdəm] *s* servidumbre de la gleba

serge [sɑrdʒ] *s* sarga

sergeant ['sɑrdʒənt] *s* sargento

ser'geant-at-arms' *s (pl* **sergeants-at-arms**) oficial *m* de orden

sergeant major *s (pl* **sergeant majors**) sargento mayor

serial ['sɪrɪ-əl] *adj* serial; publicado por entregas ‖ *s* cuento o novela por entregas; (rad) serial *m,* serial radiado, emisión seriada

serially ['sɪrɪ-əli] *adv* en serie, por series; por entregas

serial number *s* número de serie

se-ries ['sɪrɪz] *s (pl -ries)* serie *f*

serious ['sɪrɪ-əs] *adj (e.g., person, face, matter)* serio; *(e.g., condition, illness)* grave

sermon ['sɑrmən] *s* sermón *m*

sermonize ['sɑrmə‚naɪz] *tr & intr* sermonear

serpent ['sɑrpənt] *s* serpiente *f*

se-rum ['sɪrəm] *s (pl -rums* o **-ra** [rə]) suero

servant ['sɑrvənt] *s* criado, sirviente *m*

servant girl *s* criada, sirvienta

servant problem *s* crisis *f* del servicio doméstico

serve [sɑrv] *s (in tennis)* saque *m,* servicio ‖ *tr* servir; *(to supply)* abastecer, proporcionar; cumplir *(una condena);* (in tennis) servir; **it serves me right** bien me lo merezco ‖ *intr* servir; **to serve as** servir de

service ['sɑrvɪs] *s* servicio; **at your service** para servir a Vd.; **the services** las fuerzas armadas ‖ *tr* instalar; mantener, reparar

serviceable ['sɑrvɪsəbəl] *adj* útil; duradero; cómodo

service-man ['sɑrvɪs‚mæn] *s (pl -men* [‚mɛn]) reparador *m,* mecánico; militar *m*

service record *s* hoja de servicios

service station *s* estación de servicio, taller *m* de reparaciones

service stripe *s* galón *m* de servicio

servile ['sʌrvɪl] *adj* servil

servitude ['sʌrvɪ‚tjud] o ['sʌrvɪ‚tud] *s* servidumbre; trabajos forzados

sesame ['sesəmi] *s* sésamo; **open sesame** sésamo ábrete

session ['seʃən] *s* sesión; **to be in session** sesionar

set [set] *adj* determinado, resuelto; inflexible, obstinado; fijo, firme; estudiado, meditado ‖ *s* (*of books, chairs, etc.*) juego; (*of gears*) tren *m;* (*of horses*) pareja; (*of diamonds*) aderezo; (*of tennis*) partida; (*of dishes*) servicio; (*of kitchen utensils*) batería; clase *f*, grupo; equipo; porte *m*, postura; (*of a garment*) caída, ajuste *m;* (*of glue*) endurecimiento; (*of cement*) fraguado; (*of artificial teeth*) caja; (*mov*) plató *m;* (*rad*) aparato; (*theat*) decoración ‖ *v* (*pret & pp* **set;** *ger* **setting**) *tr* asentar; colocar; poner; establecer, instalar; arreglar, preparar; adornar; apostar; poner (*un reloj*) en hora; (*in bridge*) reenvidar; poner, meter, pegar (*fuego*); fijar (*el precio*); engastar, montar (*una piedra preciosa*); encasar (*un hueso dislocado*); disponer (*los tipos*); triscar (*una sierra*); armar, colocar (*una trampa*); fijar (*el peinado*); poner (*la mesa*); dar (*un ejemplo*); to **set back** parar; poner obstáculos a; hacer retroceder; atrasar, retrasar (*el reloj*); **to set forth** exponer, dar a conocer; **to set one's heart on** tener la esperanza puesta en; **to set store by** dar mucha importancia a; **to set up shop** poner tienda; **to set up the drinks** (coll) convidar a beber ‖ *intr* ponerse (*el Sol, la Luna, etc.*); cuajarse (*un líquido*); endurecerse (*la cola*); fraguar (*el cemento, el yeso*); empollar (*una gallina*); caer, sentar (*una prenda de vestir*); **to set about** ponerse a; **to set out** ponerse en camino; emprender un negocio; **to set out to** ponerse a; **to set to work** poner manos a la obra; **to set upon** acometer, atacar

set'back' *s* revés *m*, contrariedad

set'screw' *s* tornillo de presión

settee [se'ti] *s* sofá *m*, canapé *m*

setting ['setɪŋ] *s* (*environment*) ambiente *m;* (*of a gem*) engaste *m*, montadura; (*of cement*) fraguado; (*e.g., of the sun*) puesta, ocaso; (*theat*) escena; (*theat*) puesta en escena, decoración

set'ting-up' exercises *spl* ejercicios sin aparatos, gimnasia sueca

settle ['setəl] *tr* asentar, colocar; asegurar, fijar; componer, conciliar; calmar, moderar; matar (*el polvo*); casar; poblar, colonizar; ajustar, arreglar (*cuentas*) ‖ *intr* asentarse (*un líquido, un edificio*); establecerse; componerse; calmarse, moderarse; solidificarse; **to settle down to work** ponerse seriamente a trabajar;

to settle on escoger; fijar (*p.ej., una fecha*)

settlement ['setəlmənt] *s* establecimiento; colonia, caserío; decisión; (*of accounts*) arreglo, ajuste *m;* traspaso; casa de beneficencia

settler ['setlər] *s* fundador *m;* poblador *m;* colono; árbitro, conciliador *m*

set'up' *s* porte *m*, postura; (*e.g., of the parts of a machine*) disposición; (coll) organización; (slang) invitación a beber

seven ['sevən] *adj & pron* siete ‖ *s* siete *m;* **seven o'clock** las siete

seven hundred *adj & pron* setecientos ‖ *s* setecientos *m*

seventeen ['sevən'tin] *adj, pron & s* diecisiete *m*, diez y siete

seventeenth ['sevən'tinθ] *adj & s* (*in a series*) decimoséptimo; (*part*) diecisieteavo ‖ *s* (*in dates*) diecisiete *m*

seventh ['sevənθ] *adj & s* séptimo ‖ *s* (*in dates*) siete *m*

seventieth ['sevəntɪ‚ɪθ] *adj & s* (*in a series*) septuagésimo; (*part*) setentavo

seven-ty ['sevənti] *adj & pron* setenta ‖ *s* (*pl* **-ties**) setenta *m*

sever ['sevər] *tr* desunir, separar; romper (*relaciones*) ‖ *intr* desunirse, separarse

several ['sevərəl] *adj* diversos, varios; distintos, respectivos ‖ *spl* varios; algunos

severance pay ['sevərəns] *s* indemnización por despido

severe [sɪ'vɪr] *adj* severo; (*weather*) riguroso; recio, violento; (*look*) adusto; (*pain*) agudo; (*illness*) grave

sew [so] *v* (*pret* **sewed;** *pp* **sewed** o **sewn**) *tr & intr* coser

sewage ['su‚ɪdʒ] o ['sju‚ɪdʒ] *s* agua de albañal, aguas cloacales

sewer ['su‚ər] *s* albañal *m*, cloaca, alcantarilla ‖ *tr* alcantarillar

sewerage ['su‚ərɪdʒ] o ['sju‚ərɪdʒ] *s* desagüe *m;* (*system*) alcantarillado; aguas de albañal

sewing basket ['so‚ɪŋ] *s* cesta de costura

sewing machine *s* máquina de coser

sex [seks] *s* sexo; **the fair sex** el bello sexo; **the sterner sex** el sexo feo

sex appeal *s* atracción sexual; encanto femenino

sextant ['sekstənt] *s* sextante *m*

sextet [seks'tet] *s* sexteto

sexton ['sekstən] *s* sacristán *m*

sexual ['sekʃu‚əl] *adj* sexual

sex-y ['seksi] *adj* (*comp* **-ier;** *super* **-iest**) (slang) sicalíptico, erótico

shab-by ['ʃæbi] *adj* (*comp* **-bier;** *super* **-biest**) gastado, raído, usado; andrajoso, desaseado; ruin, vil

shack [ʃæk] *s* casucha, choza

shackle ['ʃækəl] *s* grillete *m;* (*to tie an animal*) maniota; (fig) impedimento, traba; **shackles** cadenas, esposas, grillos ‖ *tr* poner grilletes a, poner esposas a; encadenar; (fig) trabar

shad [ʃæd] *s* sábalo, alosa

shade [ʃed] *s* sombra; (*of a lamp*)

pantalla; (of a window) cortina, estor m, visillo, cortina de resorte; (for the eyes) visera; (hue; slight difference) matiz m; **the shades** las tinieblas; (of the dead) las sombras || tr sombrear; obscurecer; rebajar ligeramente (el precio)

shadow ['ʃædo] s sombra || tr sombrear; simbolizar; acechar, espiar (a una persona); **to shadow forth** representar vagamente, representar de un modo profético

shadowy ['ʃædo-i] adj sombroso; ligero, vago; imaginario; simbólico

shad·y ['ʃedi] adj (comp -ier; super -iest) sombrío, umbroso; (coll) sospechoso; (coll) de mala fama; (story) (coll) verde; **to keep shady** (slang) no dejarse ver

shaft [ʃæft] o [ʃɑft] s dardo, flecha, saeta; (of an arrow; of a feather) astil m; (of light) rayo; (of a wagon) vara alcándara, limonera; (of a mine; of an elevator) pozo; (of a column) fuste m, caña; (of a flag) asta; (of a motor) árbol m; (to make fun of someone) dardo

shag·gy ['ʃægi] adj (comp -gier; super -giest) hirsuto, peludo, veludo; lanudo; áspero

shake [ʃek] s sacudida; (coll) apretón m de manos; (slang) instante m, momento || v (pret **shook** [ʃʊk]; pp **shaken**) tr sacudir; agitar; apretar, estrechar (la mano a uno); inquietar, perturbar; (to get rid of) (slang) dar esquinazo a, zafarse de || intr sacudirse; agitarse; temblar; inquietarse, perturbarse; (from cold) tiritar; **shake!** (coll) ¡choque Vd. esos cinco!, ¡vengan esos cinco!

shake'down' s (slang) exacción, concusión

shake'-up' s profunda conmoción; cambio de personal, reorganización completa

shak·y ['ʃeki] adj (comp -ier; super -iest) trémulo, vacilante, movedizo; indigno de confianza

shall [ʃæl] v (cond **should** [ʃʊd]) v aux empléase para formar (1) el fut de ind, p.ej., **I shall do it lo haré**; (2) el fut perf de ind, p.ej., **I shall have done it lo habré hecho**; (3) el modo potencial, p.ej., **what shall I do?** ¿qué he de hacer?, ¿qué debo hacer?

shallow ['ʃælo] adj bajo, poco profundo; (fig) frívolo, superficial

sham [ʃæm] adj falso, fingido; postizo || s fingimiento, falsificación, engaño; (person) (coll) farsante mf || v (pret & pp **shammed**; ger **shamming**) tr & intr fingir

sham battle s simulacro de combate

shambles ['ʃæmbəlz] s destrucción, ruina; (confusion, mess) lío, revoltijo

shame [ʃem] s vergüenza; deshonra; **shame on you!** ¡qué vergüenza!; **what a shame!** ¡qué lástima! || tr avergonzar; deshonrar

shameful ['ʃemfəl] adj vergonzoso

shameless ['ʃemlɪs] adj descarado, desvergonzado

shampoo [ʃæm'pu] s champú m || tr lavar (la cabeza); lavar la cabeza a

shamrock ['ʃæmrɑk] s trébol m irlandés

shanghai ['ʃæŋhaɪ] o [ʃæŋ'haɪ] tr embarcar emborrachando, embarcar narcotizando; llevarse con violencia, llevarse con engaño

shank [ʃæŋk] s (of the leg) caña, canilla; (of an animal) pierna; (of a bird) zanca; (of an anchor) caña; (of the sole of a shoe) enfranque m; astil m, caña, fuste m; extremidad, remate m; **to go o to ride on shank's mare** caminar en coche de San Francisco

shan·ty ['ʃænti] s (pl -ties) chabola, choza

shape [ʃep] s forma; **in bad shape** (coll) arruinado; (coll) muy enfermo; **out of shape** deformado; descompuesto || tr formar, dar forma a; amoldar || intr formarse; **to shape up** tomar forma; desarrollarse bien

shapeless ['ʃeplɪs] adj informe

shape·ly ['ʃepli] adj (comp -lier; super -liest) bien formado, esbelto

share [ʃer] s parte f, porción; (of stock in a company) acción; **to go shares** ir a la parte || tr (to enjoy jointly) compartir; (to apportion) repartir || intr participar, tener parte

share'hold'er s accionista mf

shark [ʃɑrk] s tiburón m; (swindler) estafador m; (slang) experto, perito

sharp [ʃɑrp] adj afilado, agudo; anguloso; (curve, slope, etc.) fuerte, pronunciado; (photograph) nítido; (hearing) fino; (step, gait) rápido; atento, despierto; picante, mordaz; listo, vivo; (mus) sostenido; (slang) elegante; **sharp features** facciones bien marcadas || adv agudamente; en punto, p.ej., **at four o'clock sharp** a las cuatro en punto || s (mus) sostenido

sharpen ['ʃɑrpən] tr aguzar; sacar punta a (un lápiz) || intr afilarse

sharper ['ʃɑrpər] s fullero, jugador m de ventaja

sharp'shoot'er s tirador certero; (mil) tirador distinguido

shatter ['ʃætər] tr hacer astillas, romper de un golpe; quebrantar (la salud); destruir, destrozar; agitar, perturbar || intr hacerse pedazos, romperse

shat'ter·proof' adj inastillable

shave [ʃev] s afeitado; rebanada delgada; **to have a close shave** (coll) escapar en una tabla || tr afeitar (la cara); raer, raspar; (to graze; to cut close) rozar; (to slice thin) rebanar; (carp) cepillar || intr afeitarse

shaving ['ʃevɪŋ] adj de afeitar, para afeitar, p.ej., **shaving soap** jabón m de o para afeitar || s afeitado; **shavings** acepilladuras, virutas

shawl [ʃɔl] s chal m, mantón m

she [ʃi] pron pers (pl **they**) ella || s (pl **shes**) hembra

sheaf [ʃif] s (pl **sheaves** [ʃivz]) gavilla; (of paper) atado

shear [ʃɪr] *s* hoja de la tijera; **shears** tijeras grandes; (*to cut metal*) cizallas || *v* (*pret* sheared; *pp* sheared o **shorn** [ʃɔrn]) *tr* esquilar, trasquilar (*las ovejas*); cizallar; quitar cortando; tundir (*paño*)

sheath [ʃiθ] *s* (**sheaths** [ʃiðz]) envoltura, estuche *m*, funda; (*for a sword*) funda, vaina

sheathe [ʃið] *tr* enfundar, envainar

shed [ʃed] *s* cobertizo; (*line from which water flows in two directions*) vertiente *m* & *f* || *v* (*pret* & *pp* shed; *ger* shedding) *tr* derramar, verter (*p.ej., sangre*); dar, echar, esparcir (*luz*); mudar (*la pluma, el pellejo*)

sheen [ʃin] *s* brillo, lustre *m*; (*of pressed cloth*) prensado

sheep [ʃip] *s* (*pl* sheep) carnero; (*female*) oveja; tonto; **to make sheep's eyes** (**at**) mirar con ojos de carnero degollado

sheep dog *s* perro ovejero, perro de pastor

sheep'fold' *s* aprisco, redil *m*

sheepish [ˈʃipɪʃ] *adj* avergonzado, corrido; tímido, tonto

sheep'skin' *s* (*undressed*) zalea; (*dressed*) badana; (coll) diploma *m*

sheer [ʃɪr] *adj* delgado, fino, ligero; casi transparente; escarpado; puro, sin mezcla completa || *intr* desviarse

sheet [ʃit] *s* (*e.g., for the bed*) sábana; (*of paper*) hoja; (*of metal*) hoja, lámina; (*of water*) extensión; hoja impresa; periódico; (naut) escota

sheet lightning *s* fucilazo

sheet metal *s* metal laminado

sheet music *s* música en hojas sueltas

sheik [ʃik] *s* jeque *m*; (*great lover*) (slang) sultán *m*

shelf [ʃelf] *s* (*pl* shelves [ʃelvz]) estante *m*, anaquel *m*; bajío, banco de arena; **on the shelf** arrinconado, desechado, olvidado

shell [ʃel] *s* (*of an egg, nut, etc.*) cáscara; (*of a crustacean*) caparazón *m*, concha; (*of a vegetable*) vaina; (*of a cartridge*) cápsula; (*of a boiler*) cuerpo; armazón *f*, esqueleto; bomba, proyectil *m*; (*long, narrow racing boat*) (sport) yola || *tr* descascarar; desgranar, desvainar (*legumbres*); bombardear, cañonear; **to shell out** (coll) entregar (*dinero*)

shel·lac [ʃəˈlæk] *s* laca, goma laca || *v* (*pret* & *pp* -lacked; *ger* -lacking) *tr* barnizar con goma laca, (slang) azotar, zurrar; (slang) derrotar

shell'fish' *s* marisco, mariscos

shell hole *s* (mil) embudo

shell shock *s* neurosis *f* de guerra

shelter [ˈʃeltər] *s* abrigo, asilo, amparo, refugio; **to take shelter** abrigarse, refugiarse || *tr* abrigar, amparar, proteger

shelve [ʃelv] *tr* poner sobre un estante; proveer de estantes; arrinconar, dejar a un lado; diferir indefinidamente

shepherd [ˈʃepərd] *s* pastor *m* || *tr* pastorear (*a las ovejas o los fieles*)

shepherd dog *s* perro ovejero, perro de pastor

shepherdess [ˈʃepərdɪs] *s* pastora

sherbet [ˈʃɑrbət] *s* sorbete *m*

shereef [ʃeˈrif] *s* jerife *m*

sheriff [ˈʃerɪf] *s* alguacil *m* mayor

sher·ry [ˈʃeri] *s* (*pl* -ries) jerez *m*, vino de Jerez

shield [ʃild] *s* escudo; (*for armpit*) sobaquera; (elec) blindaje *m* || *tr* amparar, defender, escudar; (elec) blindar

shift [ʃɪft] *s* cambio; (*order of work or other activity*) turno; (*group of workmen*) tanda; maña, subterfugio || *tr* cambiar; deshacerse de; echar (*la culpa*); (aut) cambiar de (*marcha*) || *intr* cambiar, cambiar de puesto; mañear; (naut) correrse (*el lastre*); (rr) maniobrar; **to shift for oneself** ayudarse, ingeniarse

shift key *s* tecla de cambio, palanca de mayúsculas

shiftless [ˈʃɪftlɪs] *adj* desidioso, perezoso

shift·y [ˈʃɪfti] *adj* (*comp* -ier; *super* -iest) ingenioso, mañoso; evasivo, tramoyista; (*glance*) huyente

shilling [ˈʃɪlɪŋ] *s* chelín *m*

shimmer [ˈʃɪmər] *s* luz trémula || *intr* rielar

shin [ʃɪn] *s* espinilla || *v* (*pret* & *pp* shinned; *ger* shinning) *tr* & *intr* trepar

shin'bone' *s* espinilla

shine [ʃaɪn] *s* brillo, luz *f*; bruñido, lustre *m*; buen tiempo; (*on shoes*) (coll) lustre *m*; **to take a shine to** (slang) tomar simpatía a || *v* (*pret* & *pp* shined) *tr* pulir, lustrar; (coll) embolar, limpiar (*el calzado*) || *v* (*pret* & *pp* shone [ʃon]) *intr* brillar, lucir, resplandecer; hacer sol, hacer buen tiempo; (*to be distinguished, to stand out*) (fig) brillar, lucir

shingle [ˈʃɪŋɡəl] *s* ripia, teja de madera; tejamaní *m* (Am); pelo a la garçonne; (coll) letrero de oficina; **shingles** (pathol) zona; **to hang out one's shingle** (coll) abrir una oficina; (coll) abrir un consultorio médico || *tr* cubrir con ripias; cortar (*el pelo*) a la garçonne

shining [ˈʃaɪnɪŋ] *adj* brillante, luciente

shin·y [ˈʃaɪni] *adj* (*comp* -ier; *super* -iest) brillante, lustroso, (*paper*) glaseado; (*from much wear*) brilloso

ship [ʃɪp] *s* nave *f*, buque *m*, barco, navío; (*steamer*) vapor *m*; aeronave *f* || *v* (*pret* & *pp* shipped; *ger* shipping) *tr* embarcar, enviar, remitir, remesar; armar (*los remos*); embarcar (*agua*) || *intr* embarcarse

ship'board' *s* bordo; **on shipboard** a bordo

ship'build'er *s* arquitecto naval, constructor *m* de buques

ship'build'ing *s* arquitectura naval, construcción de buques

ship'mate' *s* camarada *m* de a bordo

shipment [ˈʃɪpmənt] *s* embarque *m* (*por agua*); envío, expedición, remesa

shipper ['ʃɪpər] s embarcador m; expedidor m, remitente mf

shipping memo ['ʃɪpɪŋ] s nota de remisión

ship'shape' adj & adv en buen orden

ship'side' adj & adv al costado del buque ‖ s zona de embarque y desembarque; muelle m

ship's papers spl documentación del buque

ship's time s hora local del buque

ship'wreck' s naufragio; barco náufrago ‖ tr hacer naufragar ‖ intr naufragar

ship'yard' s astillero, varadero

shirk [ʃʌrk] tr evitar (el trabajo); faltar a (un deber) ‖ intr escurrir el hombro

shirred eggs [ʃʌrd] spl huevos al plato

shirt [ʃʌrt] s camisa; **to keep one's shirt on** (slang) quedarse sereno; **to lose one's shirt** (slang) perder hasta la camisa

shirt'band' s cuello de camisa

shirt front s pechera de camisa, camisolín m

shirt sleeve s manga de camisa; **in shirt sleeves** en mangas de camisa

shirt'tail' s faldón m, pañal m

shirt'waist' s blusa (de mujer)

shiver ['ʃɪvər] s estremecimiento, tiritón m ‖ intr estremecerse, tiritar

shoal [ʃol] s bajío, banco de arena

shock [ʃɑk] s (sudden and violent blow or encounter) choque m; (sudden agitation of mind or emotions) sobresalto; temblor m de tierra; (of hair) greña; (agr) tresnal m; (elec) sacudida; (med) choque m; (profound depression) (pathol) choque m; (coll) parálisis f ‖ tr chocar; sobresaltar; dar una sacudida eléctrica a; chocar, escandalizar

shock absorber [æb'sorbər] s amortiguador m

shocking ['ʃɑkɪŋ] adj chocante, escandalizador

shock troops spl tropas de asalto

shod·dy ['ʃɑdi] adj (comp -dier; super -diest) falso, de imitación

shoe [ʃu] s (which goes above the ankle) bota, botina; (which does not go above the ankle) zapato; (of a tire) cubierta; **to put on one's shoes** calzarse ‖ v (pret & pp shod [ʃɑd]) tr calzar; herrar (un caballo)

shoe'black' s limpiabotas m

shoe'horn' s calzador m

shoe'lace' s cordón m de zapato, lazo de zapato

shoe'mak'er s zapatero; zapatero remendón

shoe mender ['mendər] s zapatero remendón

shoe polish s betún m, bola

shoe'shine' s brillo, lustre m; limpiabotas m

shoe store s zapatería

shoe'string' s cordón m de zapato, lazo de zapato; **on a shoestring** con muy poco dinero

shoe tree s horma

shoo [ʃu] tr & intr oxear

shoot [ʃut] s (sprout, twig) renuevo, vástago; conducto inclinado; (for grain, sand, etc.) tolva; tiro al blanco, certamen m de tiradores; (hunting party) partida de caza ‖ v (pret & pp shot [ʃɑt]) tr tirar, disparar (un arma); herir o matar con arma; (to execute with a discharge of rifles) fusilar; fotografiar; (to take a moving picture of) rodar; echar (los dados); medir la altura de (p.ej., el Sol); **to shoot down** derribar (un avión); **to shoot up** (slang) destrozar echando balas a diestra y siniestra ‖ intr tirar; nacer, brotar; lanzarse, precipitarse, moverse rápidamente; punzar (un dolor, una llaga); **to shoot at** tirar a; (to strive for) (coll) poner el tiro en

shooting gallery s galería de tiro al blanco

shooting match s certamen m de tiro al blanco; (slang) conjunto, totalidad

shooting star s estrella fugaz, estrella filante

shop [ʃɑp] s (store) tienda; (workshop) taller m; **to talk shop** hablar de su oficio, hablar del propio trabajo (fuera de tiempo) ‖ v (pret & pp shopped; ger shopping) intr ir de compras, ir de tiendas, **to go shopping** ir de compras, ir de tiendas; **to send shopping** mandar a la compra; **to shop around** ir de tienda en tienda buscando gangas

shop'girl' s muchacha de tienda

shop'keep'er s tendero

shoplifter ['ʃɑp,lɪftər] s mechera, ratero de tiendas

shopper ['ʃɑpər] s comprador m

shopping center s centro comercial (grupo de establecimientos minoristas, con aparcamiento)

shopping district s barrio comercial

shop'win'dow s escaparate m

shop'work' s trabajo de taller

shop'worn' adj desgastado con el trajín de la tienda

shore [ʃor] s orilla, ribera; costa, playa; **shores** (poet) clima m, región ‖ tr acodalar, apuntalar

shore dinner s comida de pescado y mariscos

shore leave s (nav) permiso para ir a tierra

shore line s línea de la playa; línea de buques costeros

shore patrol s (nav) patrulla en tierra

short [ʃort] adj (in space, time, and quantity) corto; (in time) breve; (in stature) bajo, (fig) corto, sucinto, (fig) brusco, seco; **in a short time** dentro de poco; **in short** en fin; **on short notice** con poco tiempo de aviso; **to be short of** estar escaso de; **short of breath** corto de resuello ‖ adv brevemente, bruscamente; (without possessing the stock sold) al descubierto, p.ej., **to sell short** vender al descubierto; **to run short of** acabársele a uno, p.ej., **I am running short of gasoline** se me acaba la gasolina; **to stop short** parar de repente ‖ *s* (elec) cortocircuito; (mov) cortometraje *m*; **shorts** calzones cortos, calzoncillos ‖ *tr* (elec) poner en cortocircuito ‖ *intr* (elec) ponerse en cortocircuito

shortage [ˈʃɔrtɪdʒ] *s* carestía, escasez *f*, falta; déficit *m*; *(from pilfering)* substracción

short'cake' *s* torta de frutas; torta quebradiza

short'change' *tr* (coll) no devolver la vuelta debida a

short circuit *s* (elec) cortocircuito

short'cir'cuit *tr* (elec) cortocircuitar ‖ *intr* (elec) cortocircuitarse

short'com'ing *s* falta, defecto, desperfecto

short cut *s* atajo; *(method)* remediavagos *m*

shorten [ˈʃɔrtən] *tr* acortar, abreviar ‖ *intr* acortarse, abreviarse

short'hand' *adj* taquigráfico ‖ *s* taquigrafía; **to take shorthand** taquigrafiar

short-lived [ˈʃɔrtˈlaɪvd] o [ˈʃɔrtˈlɪvd] *adj* de breve vida, de breve duración

shortly [ˈʃɔrtli] *adv* en breve, luego; descortésmente; **shortly after** poco tiempo después (de)

short'-range' *adj* de poco alcance

short sale *s* (coll) venta al descubierto

short-sighted [ˈʃɔrtˈsaɪtɪd] *adj* miope; (fig) falto de perspicacia

short'stop' *s* (baseball) medio; guardabosque *m*, torpedero (Am)

short story *s* cuento

short-tempered [ˈʃɔrtˈtempərd] *adj* de mal genio

short'-term' *adj* a corto plazo

shot [ʃɑt] *s* tiro, disparo; *(hit or wound made with a bullet)* balazo; *(distance)* alcance *m*; *(in certain games)* jugada, tirada, golpe *m*; *(of a rocket into space)* lanzamiento; conjetura, tentativa; fotografía, instantánea; *(small pellets of lead)* perdigones *mpl*; munición; *(marksman)* tiro; *(heavy metal ball)* (sport) pesa; *(hypodermic injection)* (slang) jeringazo; *(drink of liquor)* (slang) trago; **not by a long shot** ni con mucho, ni por pienso; **to start like a shot** salir disparado

shot'gun' *s* escopeta

shot'-put' *s* (sport) tiro de la pesa

should [ʃud] *v aux* empléase para formar (1) el pres de cond, p.ej., **if I should wait for him, I should miss the train** si yo le esperase, perdería el tren; (2) el perf de cond, p.ej., **if I had waited for him, I should have missed the train** si yo le hubiese esperado, habría perdido el tren; y (3) el modo potencial, p.ej., **he should go at once** debiera salir en seguida; **he should have gone at once** debiera haber salido en seguida

shoulder [ˈʃoldər] *s* hombro; *(of slaughtered animal)* brazuelo; *(of a garment)* hombrera; **across the shoulder** en bandolera; **to put one's shoulders to the wheel** arrimar el hombro, echar el pecho al agua; **to turn a cold shoulder to** volver las espaldas a ‖ *tr* cargar sobre las espaldas; tomar sobre sí, hacerse responsable de; empujar con el hombro para abrirse paso

shoulder blade *s* escápula, omóplato

shoulder strap *s* *(of underwear)* presilla; (mil) charretera

shout [ʃaʊt] *s* grito, voz *f* ‖ *tr* gritar, vocear; **to shout down** hacer callar a gritos ‖ *intr* gritar, dar voces

shove [ʃʌv] *s* empujón *m* ‖ *tr* empujar ‖ *intr* dar empujones, avanzar a empujones; **to shove off** alejarse de la costa; (slang) ponerse en marcha, salir

shov·el [ˈʃʌvəl] *s* pala ‖ *v* (*pret & pp* -eled o -elled; *ger* -eling o -elling) *tr* traspalar; espalar (*p.ej., la nieve*) ‖ *intr* trabajar con pala

show [ʃo] *s* exhibición, exposición, muestra; espectáculo; *(in the theater)* función; *(each performance of a play or movie)* sesión; demostración, prueba; indicación, señal *f*, signo; apariencia; *(e.g., of confidence)* alarde *m*; (coll) ocasión, oportunidad; ostentación; espectáculo ridículo, hazmerreír *m*; **to make a show of** hacer gala de; **to steal the show from** robar la obra a *(otro actor)* ‖ *tr* mostrar, enseñar; demostrar, probar; poner, proyectar *(un film)*; *(e.g., to the door)* acompañar; **to show up** (coll) desenmascarar ‖ *intr* mostrarse, aparecer, asomar; salir *(p.ej., las enaguas)*; **to show off** fachendear; **to show through** clarearse, transparentarse; **to show up** (coll) presentarse, dejarse ver

show bill *s* cartel *m*

show business *s* comercio de los espectáculos

show'case' *s* vitrina (de exposición)

show'down' *s* cartas boca arriba; (coll) revelación forzosa, arreglo terminante

shower [ˈʃaʊ·ər] *s* *(sudden fall of rain)* aguacero, chaparrón *m*; *(shower bath)* ducha; *(e.g., of bullets)* rociada; despedida de soltera ‖ *tr* regar; **to shower with** colmar de ‖ *intr* llover

shower bath *s* ducha, baño de ducha

show girl *s* (theat) corista *f*, conjuntista *f*

show·man [ˈʃomən] *s* (*pl* -men [mən]) empresario de teatro, empresario de circo

show'-off' *s* (coll) pinturero

show'piece' *s* objeto de arte sobresaliente

show'place' *s* sitio o edificio que se exhibe por su belleza o lujo

show'room' *s* sala de muestras, sala de exhibición

show window *s* escaparate *m* de tienda

show·y [ˈʃo·ɪ] *adj* (*comp* -ier; *super* -iest) aparatoso, cursi, ostentoso

shrapnel [ˈʃræpnəl] *s* granada de metralla

shred [ʃred] *s* jirón *m*, tira, triza; fragmento, pizca; **to tear to shreds** hacer trizas || v (pret & pp **shredded** o **shred;** ger **shredding**) tr desmenuzar, hacer trizas; deshilar (carne)

shrew [ʃru] s (nagging woman) arpía, fierecilla; (animal) musaraña

shrewd [ʃrud] adj astuto; despierto; listo

shriek [ʃrik] s chillido, grito agudo; risotada chillona || intr chillar

shrill [ʃrɪl] adj agudo, chillón

shrimp [ʃrɪmp] s camarón m; (little insignificant person) renacuajo

shrine [ʃraɪn] s relicario; sepulcro de santo; lugar sagrado

shrink [ʃrɪŋk] v (pret **shrank** [ʃræŋk] o **shrunk** [ʃrʌŋk]; pp **shrunk** o **shrunken**) tr contraer, encoger || intr contraerse, encogerse; moverse hacia atrás; rehuirse, retirarse

shrinkage [ˈʃrɪŋkɪdʒ] s contracción, encogimiento; disminución, reducción; merma, pérdida

shrivel [ˈʃrɪvəl] v (pret & pp **-eled** o **-elled;** ger **-eling** o **-elling**) tr arrugar, marchitar, fruncir || intr arrugarse, marchitarse, fruncirse; **to shrivel up** avellanarse

shroud [ʃraud] s mortaja, sudario; cubierta, velo || tr amortajar; cubrir, velar

Shrove Tuesday [ʃrov] s martes m de carnaval

shrub [ʃrʌb] s arbusto

shrubber·y [ˈʃrʌbəri] s (pl **-ies**) arbustos; plantío de arbustos

shrug [ʃrʌg] s encogimiento de hombros || v (pret & pp **shrugged;** ger **shrugging**) tr contraer; **to shrug one's shoulders** encogerse de hombros || intr encogerse de hombros

shudder [ˈʃʌdər] s estremecimiento || intr estremecerse

shuffle [ˈʃʌfəl] s (of cards) barajadura; turno de barajar; (of feet) arrastramiento; evasiva; recomposición || tr barajar (naipes); arrastrar (los pies); mezclar, revolver || intr barajar; caminar arrastrando los pies; bailar arrastrando los pies; moverse rápidamente de un lado a otro; **to shuffle along** ir arrastrando los pies; ir tirando; **to shuffle off** irse arrastrando los pies

shuf'fle-board' s juego de tejo

shun [ʃʌn] v (pret & pp **shunned;** ger **shunning**) tr esquivar, evitar, rehuir

shunt [ʃʌnt] tr apartar, desviar; (elec) poner en derivación; (rr) desviar

shut [ʃʌt] adj cerrado || v (pret & pp **shut;** ger **shutting**) tr cerrar, **to shut in** encerrar; **to shut off** cortar (electricidad, gas, etc.); **to shut up** cerrar bien; aprisionar; (coll) hacer callar || intr cerrarse; **to shut up** (coll) callarse la boca

shut'down' s cierre m, paro

shutter [ˈʃʌtər] s celosía, persiana; (outside a window) contraventana; (outside a show window) cierre metálico; (phot) obturador m

shuttle [ˈʃʌtəl] s (used in sewing) lan-

zadera || intr hacer viajes cortos de ida y vuelta

shuttle train s tren m lanzadera

shy [ʃaɪ] adj (comp **shyer** o **shier;** super **shyest** o **shiest**) arisco, recatado, tímido, (fearful) asustadizo; escaso, pobre; **I am shy a dollar** me falta un dólar || v (pret & pp **shied**) intr esquivarse, hacerse a un lado; espantarse, respingar; **to shy away** alejarse asustado

shyster [ˈʃaɪstər] s (coll) abogado trampista

Sia·mese [ˌsaɪəˈmiz] adj siamés || s (pl **-mese**) siamés m

Siamese twins spl hermanos siameses

Siberian [saɪˈbɪrɪən] adj & s siberiano

sibilant [ˈsɪbɪlənt] adj & s sibilante f

sibyl [ˈsɪbɪl] s sibila

Sicilian [sɪˈsɪljən] adj & s siciliano

Sicily [ˈsɪsɪli] s Sicilia

sick [sɪk] adj enfermo, malo; nauseado; **sick and tired of** (coll) harto y cansado de; **sick at heart** afligido de corazón; **to be sick at one's stomach** tener náuseas; **to take sick** caer enfermo || tr azuzar (a un perro)

sick'bed' s lecho de enfermo

sicken [ˈsɪkən] tr & intr enfermar

sickening [ˈsɪkənɪŋ] adj repelente, repugnante, nauseabundo

sick headache s jaqueca con náuseas

sickle [ˈsɪkəl] s hoz f

sick leave s licencia por enfermedad

sick·ly [ˈsɪkli] adj (comp **-lier;** super **-liest**) enfermizo

sickness [ˈsɪknɪs] s enfermedad; náusea

side [saɪd] adj lateral || s lado; (of a solid; of a phonograph record) cara; (of a hill) falda; (of human body, of a ship) costado; facción, partido || intr tomar partido; **to side with** tomar el partido de

side arms spl armas de cinto

side'board' s aparador m

side'burns' spl patillas

side dish s plato de entrada

side door s puerta lateral; puerta excusada

side effect s efecto secundario perjudicial (de ciertos medicamentos)

side glance s mirada de soslayo

side issue s cuestión secundaria

side line s negocio accesorio; **on the side lines** sin tomar parte

sidereal [saɪˈdɪrɪəl] adj sidéreo

side'sad'dle adv a asentadillas, a mujeriegas

side show s función secundaria, espectáculo de atracciones

side'split'ting adj desternillante

side'track' s apartadero, desviadero, vía muerta || tr desviar (un tren); echar a un lado

side view s perfil m, vista de lado

side'walk' s acera; banqueta (Guat, Mex); vereda (Arg, Cuba, Peru)

sidewalk café s terraza, café m en la acera

sideward [ˈsaɪdwərd] adj oblicuo, sesgado || adv de lado, hacia un lado

side'ways' adj oblicuo, sesgado || adv de lado, hacia un lado; al través

side whiskers spl patillas

side'wise' adj oblicuo, sesgado || adv de lado, hacia un lado; al través

siding ['saɪdɪŋ] s (rr) apartadero, desviadero, vía muerta

sidle ['saɪdəl] intr ir de lado; **to sidle up to** acercarse de lado a (una persona) para no ser visto

siege [sidʒ] s sitio, cerco; **to lay siege to** poner sitio o cerco a; (fig) asediar (p.ej., el corazón de una mujer)

sieve [sɪv] s cedazo, tamiz m || tr cerner, tamizar

sift [sɪft] tr cerner, cribar; escudriñar, examinar; (to screen, separate) entresacar; (to scatter with or as with a sieve) empolvar

sigh [saɪ] s suspiro; **to breathe a sigh of relief** respirar || tr decir con suspiros || intr suspirar; **to sigh for** suspirar por

sight [saɪt] s vista; cosa digna de verse; (of a firearm, telescope, etc.) mira; (coll) gran cantidad, montón m; (coll) horror m, atrocidad; **at first sight** a primera vista; **at sight** a primera vista; (translation) a libro abierto; (com) a la vista; **out of sight** fuera del alcance de la vista; (prices) por las nubes; **to catch sight of** alcanzar a ver; **to know by sight** conocer de vista; **to not be able to stand the sight of** no poder ver ni en pintura; **to see the sights** visitar los puntos de interés || tr avistar, alcanzar con la vista || intr apuntar con una mira; (arti & surv) visar

sight draft s (com) giro a la vista, letra a la vista

sight'-read' v (pret & pp -read [ˌred]) tr leer a libro abierto; (mus) ejecutar a la primera lectura || intr leer a libro abierto; (mus) repentizar

sight reader s lector m a libro abierto; (mus) repentista mf

sight'see'ing s turismo, visita de puntos de interés; **to go sightseeing** ir a ver los puntos de interés

sightseer ['saɪtˌsiˑər] s turista mf, excursionista mf

sign [saɪn] s signo; señal f, marca; huella, vestigio; letrero, muestra; **to show signs of** dar muestras de, tener trazas de; **to make the sign of the cross** hacerse la señal de la cruz || tr firmar; contratar; ceder, traspasar || intr firmar; **to sign off** (rad) terminar la transmisión; **to sign up** (coll) firmar el contrato

sig·nal ['sɪgnəl] adj señalado, notable || s señal f || v (pret & pp -naled o -nalled; ger -naling o -nalling) tr señalar || intr hacer señales

signal tower s (rr) garita de señales

signato·ry ['sɪgnɪˌtori] s (pl -ries) firmante mf

signature ['sɪgnətʃər] s firma; (mus & typ) signatura

sign'board' s cartelón m, letrero

signer ['saɪnər] s firmante mf

signet ring ['sɪgnɪt] s anillo sigilar, sortija de sello

signi·fy ['sɪgnɪˌfaɪ] v (pret & pp -fied) tr significar

sign'post' s hito, poste m de guía

silence ['saɪləns] s silencio || tr acallar; (mil) apagar el fuego de; (mil) apagar (el fuego del enemigo)

silent ['saɪlənt] adj silencioso

silent movie s cine mudo

silhouette [ˌsɪluˈet] s silueta || tr siluetear

silk [sɪlk] adj sedeño || s seda; **to hit the silk** (slang) lanzarse en paracaídas

silken ['sɪlkən] adj sedeño

silk hat s sombrero de copa

silk'-stock'ing adj aristocrático || s aristócrata mf

silk'worm' s gusano de seda

silk·y ['sɪlki] adj (comp -ier; super -iest) sedoso, asedado

sill [sɪl] s travesaño; (of a door) umbral m; (of a window) antepecho

sil·ly ['sɪli] adj (comp -lier; super -liest) necio, tonto

si·lo ['saɪlo] s (pl -los) silo || tr asilar

silt [sɪlt] s cieno, sedimento

silver ['sɪlvər] adj de plata; (voice) argentino; elocuente || s plata || tr platear; azogar (un espejo)

sil'ver·fish' s (ent) pez m de plata

silver foil s hoja de plata

silver lining s aspecto agradable de una condición desgraciada o triste

silver plate s vajilla de plata

silver screen s pantalla de plata

sil'ver·smith' s platero, orfebre m

silver spoon s riqueza heredada; **to be born with a silver spoon in one's mouth** nacer de pie

sil'ver·tongue' s (coll) pico de oro

sil'ver·ware' s plata, vajilla de plata

similar ['sɪmɪlər] adj similar, semejante, análogo

simile ['sɪmɪli] s (rhet) símil m

simmer ['sɪmər] tr cocer a fuego lento || intr cocer a fuego lento; (coll) estar a punto de estallar; **to simmer down** (coll) tranquilizarse lentamente

simoon [sɪˈmun] s simún m

simper ['sɪmpər] s sonrisa boba || intr sonreír bobamente

simple ['sɪmpəl] adj simple, sencillo || s (medicinal plant) simple m

simple-minded ['sɪmpəlˈmaɪndɪd] adj candoroso, ingenuo; idiota, mentecato; estúpido, ignorante

simple substance s (chem) cuerpo simple

simpleton ['sɪmpəltən] s simple mf, bobo, mentecato

simulate ['sɪmjəˌlet] tr simular

simultaneous [ˌsaɪməlˈteni·əs] o [ˌsɪməlˈteni·əs] adj simultáneo

sin [sɪn] s pecado || v (pret & pp sinned; ger sinning) intr pecar

since [sɪns] adv desde entonces, después || prep desde; después de || conj desde que; después (de) que; ya que, puesto que

sincere [sɪnˈsɪr] adj sincero

sincerity [sɪnˈserɪti] s sinceridad

sinecure ['saɪnɪ,kjʊr] o ['sɪnɪ,kjʊr] s sinecura

sinew ['sɪnju] s tendón m; (fig) fibra, nervio, vigor m

sinful ['sɪnfəl] adj (person) pecador; (act, intention, etc.) pecaminoso

sing [sɪŋ] v (pret **sang** [sæŋ] o **sung** [sʌŋ]; pp **sung**) tr cantar; **to sing to sleep** arrullar || intr cantar

singe [sɪndʒ] v (ger **singeing**) tr chamuscar, socarrar

singer ['sɪŋər] s cantante mf; (in a night club) vocalista mf

single ['sɪŋgəl] adj solo, único; simple, sencillo; particular; (e.g., room in a hotel) individual; (copy) suelto; (unmarried) soltero; solteril, de soltero || tr escoger, elegir; **to single out** singularizar

single blessedness s el bendito celibato

single-breasted ['sɪŋgəl'brestɪd] adj sin cruzar, de un solo pecho

single entry s (com) partida simple

single file s fila india; **in single file** de reata

single-handed ['sɪŋgəl'hændɪd] adj solo, sin ayuda

single life s vida de soltero

sin'gle-track' adj de vía única; (coll) de cortos alcances

sing'song' adj monótono || s sonsonete m

singular ['sɪŋgjələr] adj & s singular m

sinister ['sɪnɪstər] adj amenazante, ominoso, funesto

sink [sɪŋk] s fregadero, pila || v (pret **sank** [sæŋk] o **sunk** [sʌŋk]; pp **sunk**) tr hundir, sumergir; echar a pique; abrir, cavar (un pozo); hincar (los dientes); invertir (mucho dinero) perdiéndolo todo || intr hundirse; irse a pique; hundirse (p.ej., el Sol en el horizonte); descender, desaparecer; decaer (un enfermo; una llama); (e.g., in a chair) dejarse caer

sinking fund s fondo de amortización

sinless ['sɪnlɪs] adj impecable

sinner ['sɪnər] s pecador m

sinuous ['sɪnju·əs] adj sinuoso

sinus ['saɪnəs] s seno

sip [sɪp] s sorbo, trago || v (pret & pp **sipped**; ger **sipping**) tr sorber, beber a tragos

siphon ['saɪfən] s sifón m || tr sacar con sifón, trasegar con sifón

siphon bottle s sifón m

sir [sʌr] s señor m; (British title) sir m; **Dear Sir** Muy señor mío, Estimado señor

sire [saɪr] s padre m, semental m; caballo padre || tr engendrar

siren ['saɪrən] s sirena

Sirius ['sɪrɪ·əs] s (astr) Sirio

sirloin ['sʌrlɔɪn] s solomillo

sirup ['sɪrəp] o ['sʌrəp] s var de syrup

sissi·fy ['sɪsɪ,faɪ] v (pret & pp **-fied**) tr (coll) afeminar

sis·sy ['sɪsɪ] s (pl **-sies**) (coll) hermanita; (coll) maricón m, santito

sister ['sɪstər] adj (ship) gemelo; (language) hermano || s hermana

sis'ter-in-law' s (pl **sisters-in-law**) cu-

ñada, hermana política; (wife of one's husband's or wife's brother) concuñada

Sisyphus ['sɪsɪfəs] s Sísifo

sit [sɪt] v (pret & pp **sat** [sæt]; ger **sitting**) intr estar sentado; sentarse; echarse (un ave sobre los huevos); reunirse, celebrar junta; descansar; **to sit down** sentarse; **to sit still** estarse quieto; **to sit up** incorporarse (el que estaba echado)

sit'-down' strike s huelga de sentados, huelga de brazos caídos

site [saɪt] s sitio, paraje m

sitting ['sɪtɪŋ] s (period one remains seated) sentada; (of a painter) estadía; (of a court or legislature) sesión; **at one sitting** de una sentada

sitting duck s pato sentado en el agua (fácil de matar a tiro de escopeta); (coll) blanco de fácil alcance

sitting room s sala de estar

situate ['sɪtʃʊ,et] tr situar

situation [,sɪtʃʊ'eʃən] s situación; colocación, puesto

sitz bath [sɪts] s baño de asiento

six [sɪks] adj & pron seis || s seis m; **at sixes and sevens** en confusión, en desacuerdo; **six o'clock** las seis

six hundred adj & pron seiscientos || s seiscientos m

sixteen ['sɪks'tin] adj, pron & s dieciséis m, diez y seis

sixteenth ['sɪks'tinθ] adj & s (in a series) decimosexto; (part) diecisei-savo || s (in dates) dieciséis m

sixth [sɪksθ] adj & s sexto || s (in dates) seis m

sixtieth ['sɪkstɪ·ɪθ] adj & s (in a series) sexagésimo; (part) sesentavo

six·ty ['sɪkstɪ] adj & pron sesenta || s (pl **-ties**) sesenta m

sizable ['saɪzəbəl] adj considerable, bastante grande

size [saɪz] s tamaño; (of a person or garment) talla; (of a pipe, a wire) diámetro; (for gilding) sisa, cola de retazo; (coll) verdadera situación || tr clasificar según tamaño; sisar, encolar; **to size up** enfocar (un problema); medir con la vista

sizzle ['sɪzəl] s siseo || intr sisear

S.J. abbr **Society of Jesus**

skate [sket] s patín m; (slang) adefesio, tipo || intr patinar; **to skate on thin ice** buscar el peligro

skating rink s patinadero, pista de patinar

skein [sken] s madeja; enredo, maraña

skeleton ['skelɪtən] adj esquelético || s esqueleto

skeleton key s llave maestra

skeptic ['skeptɪk] adj & s escéptico

skeptical ['skeptɪkəl] adj escéptico

sketch [sketʃ] s boceto, dibujo; bosquejo, esbozo; drama corto, pieza corta || tr dibujar; bosquejar, esbozar

sketch'book' s libro de bocetos; libro de esbozos literarios

skewer ['skju·ər] s broqueta || tr espetar; traspasar con aguja

ski [ski] *s* (*pl* **skis** o **ski**) esquí *m* || *intr* esquiar

skid [skɪd] *s* (*of an auto*) resbalón *m;* (*of a wheel*) patinaje *m,* patinazo; calzo || *v* (*pret & pp* **skidded;** *ger* **skidding**) *tr* calzar || *intr* resbalar (*un coche*); patinar (*una rueda*)

skier [ˈski·ər] *s* esquiador *m*

skiff [skɪf] *s* esquife *m*

skiing [ˈski·ɪŋ] *s* esquiísmo

ski jacket *s* plumífero

skijoring [skiˈdʒorɪŋ] *s* esquí remolcado

ski jump *s* salto de esquí; cancha de esquiar; trampolín *m*

ski lift *s* telesquí *m*

skill [skɪl] *s* destreza, habilidad, pericia

skilled [skɪld] *adj* hábil, experimentado, experto

skillet [ˈskɪlɪt] *s* cacerola de mango largo; sartén *f*

skillful [ˈskɪlfəl] *adj* diestro, hábil

skim [skɪm] *v* (*pret & pp* **skimmed;** *ger* **skimming**) *tr* desnatar (*la leche*); espumar (*el caldo, el almíbar*); (*to graze*) rasar, rozar; examinar ligeramente || *intr* rozar; **to skim over** pasar rozando; examinar a la ligera

ski mask *s* pasamontaña *m*

skimmer [ˈskɪmər] *s* (*utensil*) espumadera; (*straw hat*) canotié *m*

skim milk *s* leche desnatada

skimp [skɪmp] *tr* escatimar; chapucear || *intr* economizar, apretarse; chapucear

skimp·y [ˈskɪmpi] *adj* (*comp* **-ier;** *super* **-iest**) escaso; tacaño, mezquino

skin [skɪn] *s* piel *f;* (*of an animal, of fruit*) pellejo; **to be nothing but skin and bones** estar hecho un costal de huesos, estar en los huesos; **to get soaked to the skin** calarse hasta los huesos; **to save one's skin** salvar el pellejo || *v* (*pret & pp* **skinned;** *ger* **skinning**) *tr* pelar, desollar; escoriarse (*p.ej., el codo*); (*coll*) timar; **to skin alive** (*coll*) desollar vivo; (*coll*) vencer completamente

skin'-deep' *adj* superficial

skin diver *s* submarinista *mf*

skin'flint' *s* escasero, avaro

skin game *s* (*slang*) fullería

skin-ny [ˈskɪni] *adj* (*comp* **-nier;** *super* **-niest**) flaco, enjuto, magro, seco

skip [skɪp] *s* salto || *v* (*pret & pp* **skipped;** *ger* **skipping**) *tr* saltar || *intr* saltar; saltar espacios (*la máquina de escribir*); moverse saltando; irse precipitadamente

skip bombing *s* (aer) bombardeo de rebote

ski pole *s* bastón *m* de esquiar

skipper [ˈskɪpər] *s* caudillo, jefe *m;* (*of a boat*) patrón *m;* gusano del queso || *tr* patronear

skirmish [ˈskʌrmɪʃ] *s* escaramuza || *intr* escaramuzar

skirt [skʌrt] *s* falda; borde *m,* orilla; (*woman*) (*slang*) falda || *tr* seguir el borde de; moverse a lo largo de

ski run *s* pista de esquí

ski stick *s* bastón *m* de esquiar

skit [skɪt] *s* boceto burlesco, paso cómico

skittish [ˈskɪtɪʃ] *adj* caprichoso; asustadizo; tímido; (*bull*) abanto

skulduggery [skʌlˈdʌgəri] *s* (coll) trampa, embuste *m*

skull [skʌl] *s* cráneo, calavera

skull'cap' *s* casquete *m*

skunk [skʌŋk] *s* mofeta; (*person*) (coll) canalla *m*

sky [skaɪ] *s* (*pl* **skies**) cielo; **to praise to the skies** poner por las nubes, poner en el cielo

sky'lark' *s* alondra || *intr* jaranear

sky'light' *s* tragaluz *m,* claraboya

sky'line' *s* línea del horizonte, línea de los edificios contra el cielo

sky'rock'et *s* cohete *m* || *intr* subir como un cohete

sky'scrap'er *s* rascacielos *m*

sky'writ'ing *s* escritura aérea

slab [slæb] *s* losa; plancha, tabla

slack [slæk] *adj* flojo; perezoso; negligente; inactivo || *s* flojedad; inactividad; estación muerta, temporada inactiva; **slacks** pantalones flojos || *tr* aflojar; apagar (*la cal*) || *intr* atrasarse; descuidarse; **to slack up** aflojar el paso

slacker [ˈslækər] *s* perezoso; (mil) prófugo

slag [slæg] *s* escoria

slake [slek] *tr* aplacar, calmar; apagar (*la cal*)

slalom [ˈslaləm] *s* eslálom *m*

slam [slæm] *s* golpe *m;* (*of a door*) portazo; (coll) crítica acerba || *v* (*pret & pp* **slammed;** *ger* **slamming**) *tr* cerrar de golpe; golpear o empujar estrepitosamente; (coll) criticar acerbamente || *intr* cerrarse de golpe

slam'-bang' *adv* (coll) de golpe y porrazo

slander [ˈslændər] *s* calumnia, difamación || *tr* calumniar, difamar

slanderous [ˈslændərəs] *adj* calumnioso, difamatorio

slang [slæŋ] *s* caló *m,* jerigonza

slant [slænt] *s* inclinación; parecer *m,* punto de vista || *tr* inclinar, sesgar; deformar, tergiversar (*un informe*) || *intr* inclinarse, sesgarse

slap [slæp] *s* manazo, palmada; (*in the face*) bofetada; (*in the back*) espaldarazo; desaire *m,* insulto || *v* (*pret & pp* **slapped;** *ger* **slapping**) *tr* dar una palmada a; abofetear

slash [slæʃ] *s* cuchillada || *tr* acuchillar; hacer fuerte rebaja de (*precios, sueldos, etc.*)

slat [slæt] *s* lámina, tablilla

slate [slet] *s* pizarra; candidatura, lista de candidatos || *tr* empizarrar; designar, destinar; poner en la lista de candidatos

slate pencil *s* pizarrín *m*

slate roof *s* empizarrado

slattern [ˈslætərn] *s* mujer desaliñada, pazpuerca

slaughter [ˈslɔtər] *s* carnicería, matanza || *tr* matar

slaughter house *s* matadero

Slav [slɑv] o [slæv] *adj & s* eslavo

slave [slev] *adj & s* esclavo || *intr* trabajar como esclavo
slave driver *s* negrero; (fig) negrero
slave'hold'er *s* dueño de esclavos
slavery ['slevəri] *s* esclavitud
slave trade *s* trata de esclavos
slave trader *s* negrero
Slavic ['slɑvɪk] o ['slævɪk] *adj & s* eslavo
slay [sle] *v (pret* slew [slu]; *pp* slain [slen]) *tr* matar
slayer ['sle·ər] *s* matador *m*
sled [sled] *s* luge *m* || *v (pret & pp* **sledded;** *ger* **sledding)** *intr* deslizarse en luge o trineo
sledge hammer [sledʒ] *s* acotillo
sleek [slik] *adj* liso y brillante || *tr* alisar y pulir; suavizar
sleep [slip] *s* sueño; **to be overcome with sleep** caerse de sueño; **to go to sleep** dormirse; dormirse. morirse *(un miembro)*; **to put to sleep** adormecer; matar por anestesia || *v (pret & pp* slept [slept]) *tr* pasar durmiendo; **to sleep it off** dormir la mona; **to sleep it over** consultar con la almohada; **to sleep off** dormir *(p.ej., una borrachera)* || *intr* dormir
sleeper ['slipər] *s (person)* durmiente *mf; (girder)* durmiente *m*
sleeping bag *s* saco de dormir
sleeping car *s* coche-cama *m*
sleeping pill *s* píldora para dormir
sleepless ['sliplɪs] *adj* insomne, desvelado; pasado en vela
sleep'walk'er *s* sonámbulo
sleep·y ['slipi] *adj (comp* -ier; *super* -iest) soñoliento; **to be sleepy** tener sueño
sleep'y·head' *s* dormilón *m*
sleet [slit] *s* cellisca || *intr* cellisquear
sleeve [sliv] *s* manga; (mach) manguito; **to laugh in** o **up one's sleeve** reírse para sí
sleigh [sle] *s* trineo || *intr* pasearse en trineo
sleigh bell *s* cascabel *m*
sleigh ride *s* paseo en trineo
sleight of hand [slaɪt] *s* juego de manos, prestidigitación
slender ['slendər] *adj* esbelto, flaco, delgado; escaso, insuficiente
sleuth [sluθ] *s* sabueso
slew [slu] *s (coll)* montón *m*
slice [slaɪs] *s* rebanada, tajada; *(of an orange)* gajo || *tr* rebanar, tajar; dividir; cortar
slick [slɪk] *adj* liso y brillante; meloso, suave; (coll) astuto, mañoso || *s* lugar aceitoso y lustroso *(en el agua)*
slicker ['slɪkər] *s* impermeable *m* de hule; (coll) embaucador *m*
slide [slaɪd] *s* resbalón *m; (slippery place)* resbaladero; *(slippery surface)* desliz *m;* derrumbamiento de tierra; *(image for projection)* diapositiva, transparencia; *(of a microscope)* plaquilla de vidrio; *(piece of a device that slides)* cursor *m; (of a trombone)* corredera (tubular) || *v (pret & pp* slid [slɪd]) *tr* deslizar || *intr* deslizar, resbalar; **to let slide** dejar pasar, no hacer caso de

slide fastener *s* cierre *m* cremallera, cierre relámpago
slide rule *s* regla de cálculo
slide valve *s* corredera, válvula corrediza
sliding contact *s* cursor *m*
sliding door *s* puerta de corredera
sliding scale *s* regla de cálculo; *(of salaries)* escala móvil
slight [slaɪt] *adj* delgado; leve; pequeño; escaso || *s* desatención, descuido; desaire *m,* menosprecio || *tr* desatender, descuidar; desairar
slim [slɪm] *adj (comp* **slimmer;** *super* **slimmest)** delgado, esbelto; débil, leve, pequeño, escaso
slime [slaɪm] *s* légamo; *(of snakes, fish, etc.)* baba
slim·y ['slaɪmi] *adj (comp* -ier; *super* -iest) legamoso; baboso, viscoso; puerco, sucio
sling [slɪŋ] *s (to shoot stones)* honda; *(to hold up a broken arm)* cabestrillo || *v (pret & pp* slung [slʌŋ]) *tr* lanzar con una honda; lanzar, tirar; poner en cabestrillo; colgar flojamente
sling'shot' *s* honda
slink [slɪŋk] *v (pret & pp* slunk [slʌŋk]) *intr* andar furtivamente; **to slink away** escabullirse, salir con el rabo entre piernas
slip [slɪp] *s* resbalón *m,* desliz *m;* falta, error *m,* desliz *m;* lapso; embarcadero; *(cover for a pillow, for furniture)* funda; *(piece of paper)* papeleta; *(cutting from a plant)* sarmiento; *(piece of underclothing)* combinación; *(of a dog)* traílla; huída, evasión; mozuelo, mozuela; **to give the slip to** burlar la vigilancia de || *v (pret & pp* slipped; *ger* slipping) *tr* poner rápidamente; quitar rápidamente; pasar por alto; eludir, evadir; **to slip off** (coll) quitarse de prisa; **to slip on** (coll) ponerse de prisa; **to slip one's mind** olvidársele a uno || *intr* deslizarse; patinar *(el embrague),* errar, equivocarse; (coll) declinar, deteriorarse; **to let slip** dejar pasar; decir inadvertidamente; **to slip away** escurrirse; **to slip by** pasar inadvertido; pasar rápidamente *(el tiempo);* **to slip out of one's hands** escurrirse de entre las manos; **to slip up** (coll) errar, equivocarse
slip cover *s* funda
slip of the pen *s* error *m* de pluma
slip of the tongue *s* error *m* de lengua
slipper ['slɪpər] *s* zapatilla, babucha
slippery ['slɪpəri] *adj* deslizadizo, resbaladizo; astuto, zorro, evasivo
slip'-up' *s* (coll) error *m,* equivocación
slit [slɪt] *s* hendidura, raja; cortada, incisión || *v (pret & pp* slit; *ger* slitting) *tr* hender, rajar; cortar
slob [slɑb] *s* (slang) sujeto desaseado, puerco
slobber ['slɑbər] *s* baba; sensiblería || *intr* babear; hablar con sensiblería
sloe [slo] *s (shrub)* endrino; *(fruit)* endrina

slogan ['sloɡən] *s* lema *m*, mote *m*; grito de combate; *(striking phrase used in advertising)* eslogan *m*

sloop [slup] *s* balandra

slop [slɑp] *s* gacha, zupia, agua sucia ‖ *v* (*pret & pp* **slopped**; *ger* **slopping**) *tr* salpicar, ensuciar ‖ *intr* derramarse; chapotear

slope [slop] *s* cuesta, pendiente *f; (of a continent or a roof)* vertiente *m* & *f* ‖ *tr* inclinar ‖ *intr* inclinarse

slop·py ['slɑpi] *adj* (*comp* **-pier**; *super* **-piest**) mojado y sucio; *(in one's dress)* desgalichado; *(in one's work)* chapucero

slot [slɑt] *s* ranura; *(for letters)* buzón *m*

sloth [sloθ] o [slɔθ] *s* pereza; (zool) perezoso

slot machine *s* tragamonedas *m*, máquina sacaperras

slot meter *s* contador automático

slouch [slautʃ] *s* postura relajada; persona torpe de movimientos ‖ *intr* agacharse, andar caído de hombros; **to slouch in a chair** repanchigarse

slouch hat *s* sombrero gacho

slough [slau] *s* cenagal *m*, fangal *m;* estado de abandono moral ‖ [slʌf] *s* (*of a snake*) camisa; (pathol) escara ‖ *tr* mudar, echar de sí ‖ *intr* caerse, desprenderse

Slovak ['slovæk] o [slo'væk] *adj & s* eslovaco

sloven·ly ['slʌvənli] *adj* (*comp* **-lier**; *super* **-liest**) desaseado, desaliñado

slow [slo] *adj* lento; *(sluggish)* cachazudo, despacioso; *(clock, watch)* atrasado; *(in understanding)* lerdo, tardo, torpe ‖ *adv* despacio ‖ *tr* retrasar; atrasar *(un reloj)* ‖ *intr* retardarse, ir más despacio; atrasarse *(un reloj)*

slow′down′ *s* huelga de brazos caídos

slow′-mo′tion *adj* a cámara lenta

slow′poke′ *s* tardón *m*

slug [slʌɡ] *s* (*heavy piece of metal*) lingote *m; (metal disk used as a coin)* ficha; (zool) limaza, babosa; (coll) porrazo, puñetazo ‖ *v* (*pret & pp* **slugged**; *ger* **slugging**) *tr* (coll) aporrear, apuñear

sluggard ['slʌɡərd] *s* pachón *m*, perezoso

sluggish ['slʌɡɪʃ] *adj* inactivo, indolente, tardo; pachorrudo, perezoso

sluice [slus] *s* canal *m; (floodgate)* compuerta; *(dam; flume)* presa

sluice gate *s* compuerta de presa

slum [slʌm] *s* barrio bajo ‖ *v* (*pret & pp* **slummed**; *ger* **slumming**) *intr* visitar los barrios bajos

slumber ['slʌmbər] *s* sueño ligero, sueño tranquilo ‖ *intr* dormir; dormitar

slump [slʌmp] *s* depresión, crisis económica; *(in prices, stocks, etc.)* baja repentina ‖ *intr* hundirse, desplomarse; bajar repentinamente *(los precios, valores, etc.)*

slur [slʌr] *s* pronunciación indistinta; reparo crítico; (mus) ligado ‖ *v* (*pret & pp* **slurred**; *ger* **slurring**) *tr* co-

merse (*sonidos, sílabas*); despreciar, insultar; (mus) ligar

slush [slʌʃ] *s* fango muy blando, agua nieve fangosa, nieve *f* a medio derretir; sentimentalismo tonto

slut [slʌt] *s* perra; *(slovenly woman)* pazpuerca; ramera, mala mujer

sly [slaɪ] *adj* (*comp* **slyer** o **slier**; *super* **slyest** o **sliest**) furtivo, secreto; astuto, socarrón; travieso; **on the sly** a hurtadillas

smack [smæk] *adv* (coll) de golpe, de sopetón ‖ *s* dejo, gustillo; palmada, manotada; golpe *m;* beso sonado; *(of a whip)* chasquido ‖ *tr* dar una manotada a; golpear; hacer chasquidos con *(un látigo);* besar sonoramente; **to smack one's lips** chuparse los labios ‖ *intr* — **to smack of** saber a, oler a

small [smɔl] *adj* pequeño, chico; *(short in stature)* bajo; pobre, obscuro; humilde; (typ) minúsculo

small arms *spl* armas ligeras

small beer *s* cerveza floja; bagatela; persona de poca monta

small business *s* pequeña empresa

small capital *s* versalilla o versalita

small change *s* suelto, dinero menudo

small fry *s* gente menuda; gente de poca monta

small′-fry′ *adj* de niños, para niños; de poca monta

small hours *spl* primeras horas (*de la mañana*)

small intestine *s* intestino delgado

small-minded ['smɔl'maɪndɪd] *adj* tacaño, mezquino; intolerante

smallpox ['smɔl,pɑks] *s* viruela

small print *s* tipo menudo

small talk *s* palique *m*, charlas frívolas

small′-time′ *adj* de poca monta

small′-town′ *adj* lugareño, apegado a cosas lugareñas

smart [smɑrt] *adj* listo, vivo, inteligente; agudo, penetrante; astuto; elegante, majo; picante, punzante; (coll) grande, considerable ‖ *s* escozor *m;* dolor vivo ‖ *intr* escocer, picar; padecer, sufrir

smart aleck ['ælɪk] *s* (coll) fatuo, sabihondo

smart set *s* gente *f* chic, gente de buen tono

smash [smæʃ] *s* rotura violenta; fracaso, ruina; quiebra, bancarrota; (coll) choque violento, tope violento ‖ *tr* romper con fuerza; arruinar, destrozar; aplastar ‖ *intr* romperse con fuerza; arruinarse, destrozarse; aplastarse; **to smash into** chocar con, topar con

smash hit *s* (coll) éxito rotundo

smash′-up′ *s* colisión violenta; ruina, desastre *m;* quiebra, bancarrota

smattering ['smætərɪŋ] *s* barniz *m*, tintura, migaja

smear [smɪr] *s* embarradura; calumnia; (bact) frotis *m* ‖ *tr* embarrar; calumniar ‖ *intr* embarrarse

smear campaign *s* campaña de calumnias

smell [smɛl] *s* olor *m; (sense)* olfato;

fragancia, perfume *m* ‖ *v* (*pret* & *pp* **smelled** o **smelt** [smelt]) *tr* oler, olfatear ‖ *intr* oler; heder, oler mal; **to smell of** oler a

smelling salts *spl* sales aromáticas

smell·y ['smɛli] *adj* (*comp* -ier; *super* -iest) hediondo, maloliente

smelt [smelt] *s* (*fish*) eperlano, esperinque *m* ‖ *tr* & *intr* fundir

smile [smaɪl] *s* sonrisa ‖ *intr* sonreír, sonreírse

smiling ['smaɪlɪŋ] *adj* risueño

smirk [smʌrk] *s* sonrisa fatua y afectada ‖ *intr* sonreír fatua y afectadamente

smite [smaɪt] *v* (*pret* **smote** [smot]; *pp* **smitten** ['smɪtən] o **smit** [smɪt]) *tr* golpear o herir súbitamente y con fuerza; caer con fuerza sobre; apenar, afligir; castigar

smith [smɪθ] *s* forjador *m*, herrero

smith·y ['smɪθi] *s* (*pl* -ies) herrería

smitten ['smɪtən] *adj* afligido; (coll) muy enamorado

smock [smɑk] *s* bata

smock frock *s* blusa de obrero

smog [smɑg] *s* (coll) mezcla de humo y niebla

smoke [smok] *s* humo; **to go up in smoke** irse todo en humo ‖ *s* (*to cure o treat with smoke*) ahumar; fumar (*tabaco*); **to smoke out** ahuyentar con humo, dar humazo a; descubrir ‖ *intr* humear; fumar; hacer humo (*una chimenea dentro de la habitación*)

smoked glasses *spl* gafas ahumadas

smokeless powder ['smoklɪs] *s* pólvora sin humo

smoker ['smokər] *s* fumador *m*; (*room*) fumadero; (rr) coche-fumador *m*; reunión de fumadores

smoke rings *spl* anillos de humo; **to blow smoke rings** sacar humo formando anillos

smoke screen *s* cortina de humo

smoke′stack′ *s* chimenea

smoking ['smokɪŋ] *s* el fumar; **no smoking** se prohibe fumar

smoking car *s* coche-fumador *m*, vagón *m* de fumar

smoking jacket *s* batín *m*

smoking room *s* fumadero, saloncito para fumadores

smok·y ['smoki] *adj* (*comp* -ier; *super* -iest) humoso; (*emitting smoke*) humeante

smolder ['smoldər] *s* fuego lento sin llama y con mucho humo ‖ *intr* arder en rescoldo, arder sin llamas; (fig) estar latente; (*to burn within*) (fig) requemarse; (fig) expresar (*p.ej., los ojos*) una ira latente

smooth [smuð] *adj* liso, terso, suave; plano, llano; igual; acaramelado, afable, blando, meloso; (*water*) tranquilo; (*style*) fluido; **smooth as butter** como manteca ‖ *tr* alisar, suavizar; allanar; facilitar; **to smooth away** quitar (*p.ej. obstáculos*) suavemente; **to smooth down** ablandar, calmar

smooth-faced ['smuð,fest] *adj* barbilampiño

smooth-spoken ['smuθ,spokən] *adj* meloso, lisonjero

smooth·y ['smuði] *s* (*pl* -ies) (coll) galante *m*; (coll) elegante *m*; (coll) adulador *m*

smother ['smʌðər] *tr* ahogar, sofocar; suprimir; reprimir

smudge [smʌdʒ] *s* tiznón *m*; mancha ‖ *tr* tiznar; manchar; ahumar, fumigar (*una huerta*)

smug [smʌg] *adj* (*comp* **smugger**; *super* **smuggest**) pagado de sí mismo; compuesto, pulcro; relamido

smuggle ['smʌgəl] *tr* meter de contrabando ‖ *intr* contrabandear

smuggler ['smʌglər] *s* contrabandista *m*

smuggling ['smʌglɪŋ] *s* contrabando

smut [smʌt] *s* tiznón *m*; obscenidad; (agr) carbón *m*, tizón *m*

smut·ty ['smʌti] *adj* (*comp* -tier; *super* -tiest) tiznado, manchado; obsceno; (agr) atizonado

snack [snæk] *s* parte *f*, porción; bocadillo, tentempié *m*

snag [snæg] *s* (*of a tree*) tocón *m*; (*of a tooth*) raigón *m*; obstáculo, tropiezo; **to strike** o **to hit a snag** tropezar con un obstáculo

snail [snel] *s* caracol *m*; (*slow person*) pachón *m*; **at a snail's pace** a paso de caracol, a paso de tortuga

snake [snek] *s* culebra, serpiente *f*

snake in the grass *s* traidor *m*, amigo pérfido

snap [snæp] *s* (*crackling sound*) chasquido, estallido; (*of the fingers*) castañetazo; (*bite*) mordisco; (*cracker*) galletita; (*of cold weather*) corto período; (*catch or fastener*) broche *m* de presión; (phot) instantánea; (coll) brío, vigor *m*; (slang) breva, cosa fácil ‖ *v* (*pret* & *pp* **snapped**) *ger* **snapping**) *tr* asir, cerrar, etc. de golpe; castañetear (*los dedos*); chasquear (*el látigo*); fotografiar instantáneamente; tomar (*una instantánea*); **to snap one's fingers at** tratar con desprecio; **to snap up** aceptar con avidez, comprar con avidez; cortar la palabra a ‖ *intr* chasquear, estallar; (*to crack*) saltar; (*from fatigue*) estallar; **to snap at** querer morder; asir (*una oportunidad*); **to snap out of it** (slang) cambiarse repentinamente; **to snap shut** cerrarse de golpe

snap′drag′on *s* (bot) boca de dragón

snap fastener *s* corchete *m* de presión

snap judgment *s* decisión atolondrada

snap·py ['snæpi] *adj* (*comp* -pier; *super* -piest) mordaz; (coll) elegante, garboso; (coll) enérgico, vivo; (*food*) acre, picante

snap′shot′ *s* instantánea

snap switch *s* (elec) interruptor *m* de resorte

snare [sner] *s* lazo, trampa; (*of a drum*) bordón *m*, tirante *m*

snare drum *s* caja clara

snarl [snɑrl] *s* gruñido; regaño; maraña, enredo ‖ *tr* decir con un grufiido; enmarañar, enredar ‖ *intr* gruñir; regañar; enmarañarse, enredarse

snatch [snætʃ] *s* arrebatamiento; pedacito, trocito; ratito ‖ *tr* & *intr* arrebatar; **to snatch at** tratar de asir o agarrar; **to snatch from** arrebatar a

sneak [snik] *adj* furtivo ‖ *s* sujeto solapado ‖ *tr* mover a hurtadillas ‖ *intr* andar furtivamente, moverse a hurtadillas

sneaker ['snikər] *s* sujeto solapado; (coll) zapato blando, zapato de lona

sneak thief *s* ratero, descuidero

sneak·y ['sniki] *adj* (*comp* **-ier;** *super* **-iest**) solapado, furtivo

sneer [snir] *s* expresión de desprecio ‖ *intr* hablar con desprecio, echar una mirada de desprecio; **to sneer at** mofarse de

sneeze [sniz] *s* estornudo ‖ *intr* estornudar; **not to be sneezed at** (coll) no ser despreciable

snicker ['snikər] *s* risa tonta ‖ *intr* reírse tontamente

sniff [snif] *s* husmeo, venteo; sorbo por las narices ‖ *tr* husmear, ventear; sorber por las narices; (fig) husmear, averiguar; (fig) sospechar ‖ *intr* ventear; **to sniff at** husmear; menospreciar

sniffle ['snifəl] *s* resuello fuerte y repetido; **the sniffles** ataque *m* de resfriados ‖ *intr* resollar fuerte y repetidamente

snip [snip] *s* tijeretada; recorte *m,* pedacito; (coll) persona pequeña e insignificante ‖ *v* (*pret* & *pp* **snipped;** *ger* **snipping**) *tr* tijeretear

snipe [snaip] *s* agachadiza, becacín *m* ‖ *intr* paquear, tirar desde un escondite

sniper ['snaipər] *s* paco, tirador emboscado

snippet ['snipit] *s* recorte *m;* (coll) persona pequeña e insignificante

snip·py ['snipi] *adj* (*comp* **-pier;** *super* **-piest**) (coll) arrogante, desdeñoso; (coll) acre, brusco

snitch [snitʃ] *tr* & *intr* (slang) escamotear, ratear

sniv·el ['snivəl] *s* gimoteo, lloriqueo; moqueo ‖ *v* (*pret* & *pp* **-eled** o **-elled;** *ger* **-eling** o **-elling**) *intr* gimotear, lloriquear; (*to have a runny nose*) moquear

snob [snɑb] *s* esnob *mf*

snobbery ['snɑbəri] *s* esnobismo

snobbish ['snɑbiʃ] *adj* esnob, esnobista

snoop [snup] *s* (coll) buscavidas *mf,* curioso ‖ *intr* (coll) curiosear, ventear

snoopy ['snupi] *adj* (coll) curioso, entremetido

snoot [snut] *s* (slang) cara, narices *fpl*

snoot·y ['snuti] *adj* (*comp* **-ier;** *super* **-iest**) (slang) esnob

snooze [snuz] *s* (coll) sueñecito ‖ *intr* echar un sueñecito

snore [snor] *s* ronquido ‖ *intr* roncar

snort [snort] *s* bufido ‖ *intr* bufar

snot [snɑt] *s* (slang) mocarro

snot·ty ['snɑti] *adj* (*comp* **-tier;** *super*

-tiest) (coll) mocoso; (coll) asqueroso, sucio; (slang) engreído

snout [snaut] *s* hocico; (*something shaped like the snout of an animal*) morro; (*of a person*) (coll) hocico

snow [sno] *s* nieve *f* ‖ *intr* nevar

snow'ball' *s* bola de nieve ‖ *tr* lanzar bolas de nieve a ‖ *intr* aumentar rápidamente

snow'-blind' *adj* cegado por reflejos de la nieve

snow-capped ['sno,kæpt] *adj* coronado de nieve

snow'drift' *s* ventisquero, masa de nieve

snow'fall' *s* nevada

snow fence *s* valla paranieves

snow'flake' *s* copo de nieve, ampo

snow flurry *s* nevisca

snow line o **limit** *s* límite *m* de las nieves perpetuas

snow man *s* figura de nieve

snow'plow' *s* expulsanieves *m,* quitanieves *m*

snow'shoe' *s* raqueta de nieve

snow'storm' *s* nevasca, fuerte nevada

snow'-white' *adj* blanco como la nieve

snow·y ['sno-i] *adj* (*comp* **-ier;** *super* **-iest**) nevoso

snowy owl *s* lechuza blanca

snub [snʌb] *s* desaire *m* ‖ *v* (*pret* & *pp* **snubbed;** *ger* **snubbing**) *tr* desairar

snub·by ['snʌbi] *adj* (*comp* **-bier;** *super* **-biest**) (*nose*) respingona

snuff [snʌf] *s* rapé; (*of a candlewick*) moco; **up to snuff** (slang) en buena condición; (slang) difícil de engañar ‖ *tr* husmear, olfatear; sorber por la nariz; despabilar (*una candela*); **to snuff out** apagar, extinguir

snuff'box' *s* tabaquera

snuffers ['snʌfərz] *spl* despabiladeras

snug [snʌg] *adj* (*comp* **snugger;** *super* **snuggest**) cómodo; (*garment*) ajustado, ceñido; (*well-off*) acomodado; (*in hiding*) escondido

snuggle ['snʌgəl] *intr* apretarse, arrimarse; dormir bien abrigado; **to snuggle up to** arrimarse a

so [so] *adv* así; tan + *adj* o *adv;* por tanto; también; **and so** así pues; también, lo mismo; **and so on** y así sucesivamente; **or so** más o menos; **to think so** creer que sí; **so as to** + *inf* para + *inf;* **so far** hasta aquí; hasta ahora; **so long** hasta la vista; **so many** tantos, **so much** tanto; **so so** tal cual, así así, **so that** de modo que, de suerte que, así que; para que; con tal de que; **so to speak** por decirlo así ‖ *conj* así que ‖ *interj* ¡bien!; ¡verdad!

soak [sok] *s* mojada; (*toper*) (coll) potista *mf* ‖ *tr* empapar, remojar; embeber; (slang) aporrear; (slang) hacer pagar un precio exorbitante; **to soak up** absorber, embeber; (fig) entender; **soaked to the skin** calado hasta los huesos ‖ *intr* empaparse, remojarse

so'-and-so' *s* (*pl* **-sos**) fulano, fulano de tal; tal cosa

soap [sop] *s* jabón *m* ‖ *tr* jabonar

soap'box' *s* caja de jabón; tribuna callejera

soapbox orator *s* orador *m* de plazuela

soap bubble *s* burbuja de jabón, pompa de jabón

soap dish *s* jabonera

soap flakes *spl* copos de jabón

soap'mak'er *s* jabonero

soap opera *s* (coll) serial lacrimógeno

soap powder *s* jabón *m* en polvo, polvo de jabón

soap'stone' *s* jaboncillo de sastre

soap'suds' *spl* jabonaduras

soap·y ['sopi] *adj* (*comp* **-ier;** *super* **-iest**) jabonoso

soar [sor] *intr* encumbrarse, subir muy alto, volar a gran altura; aspirar, pretender; (aer) planear

sob [sɑb] *s* sollozo ‖ *v* (*pret* & *pp* **sobbed;** *ger* **sobbing**) *tr* decir o expresar sollozando ‖ *intr* sollozar

sober ['sobər] *adj* sobrio; no embriagado; grave, serio; cuerdo, sensato; sereno, tranquilo; (*color*) apagado ‖ *tr* poner sobrio; desemborrachar ‖ *intr* volverse sobrio; desemborracharse; **to sober down** calmarse, sosegarse; **to sober up** desemborracharse

sobriety [so'braɪ·əti] *s* sobriedad, moderación; gravedad, seriedad; cordura, sensatez; serenidad

sobriquet ['sobrɪ·ke] *s* apodo

sob sister *s* (slang) periodista llorona

sob story *s* (slang) historia de lagrimitas

soc. o Soc. *abbr* **society**

so'-called' *adj* llamado, así llamado; supuesto

soccer ['sɑkər] *s* fútbol *m* asociación

sociable ['soʃəbəl] *adj* sociable

social ['soʃəl] *adj* social ‖ *s* reunión social

social climber ['klaɪmər] *s* ambicioso de figurar

socialism ['soʃə·lɪzəm] *s* socialismo

socialist ['soʃəlɪst] *s* socialista *mf*

socialite ['soʃə·laɪt] *s* (coll) personaje *m* de la buena sociedad

social register *s* guía *m* social, registro de la buena sociedad

soci·e·ty [sə'saɪ·əti] *s* (*pl* **-ties**) sociedad; (*companionship or company*) compañía; buena sociedad, mundo elegante

society editor *s* cronista *mf* de la vida social

sociology [,sosɪ'ɑlədʒi] o [,soʃɪ·'ɑlədʒi] *s* sociología

sock [sɑk] *s* calcetín *m;* (slang) golpe *m* fuerte ‖ *tr* (slang) golpear con fuerza

socket ['sɑkɪt] *s* (*of the eyes*) cuenca; (*of a tooth*) alvéolo; (*of a candlestick*) cañón *m;* (*of a socket wrench*) cubo; (elec) portalámparas; (rad) zócalo

socket wrench *s* llave *f* de caja, llave de cubo

sod [sɑd] *s* césped *m;* terrón *m* de césped ‖ *v* (*pret* & *pp* **sodded;** *ger* **sodding**) *tr* encespedar

soda ['sodə] *s* soda, sosa; (*drink*) soda

soda fountain *s* fuente *f* de sodas

soda water *s* agua gaseosa

sodium ['sodɪ·əm] *adj* sódico, de sodio ‖ *s* sodio

sofa ['sofə] *s* sofá *m*

soft [sɔft] o [sɑft] *adj* blando, muelle; (*skin*) suave; (*iron*) dulce; (*hat*) flexible; (*solder*) tierno; (coll) fácil

soft-boiled egg ['sɔft'bɔɪld] o ['sɑft-'bɔɪld] *s* huevo pasado por agua

soft coal *s* hulla grasa

soft drink *s* bebida no alcohólica, refresco

soften ['sɔfən] o ['sɑfən] *tr* ablandar; **to soften up** (*by bombardment*) ablandar ‖ *intr* ablandarse

soft'-ped'al *tr* (mus) disminuir la intensidad de, por medio del pedal suave; (slang) moderar

soft soap *s* jabón blando o graso; (coll) adulación

soft'-soap' *tr* (coll) enjabonar, dar jabón a

sog·gy ['sɑgi] *adj* (*comp* **-gier;** *super* **-giest**) remojado, ensopado

soil [sɔɪl] *s* suelo; país *m,* región; (*spot, stain*) mancha; (fig) mancha, deshonra ‖ *tr* manchar, ensuciar; manchar, deshonrar; viciar, corromper ‖ *intr* mancharse, ensuciarse

soil pipe *s* tubo de desagüe sanitario

soiree o soirée [swɑ're] *s* sarao, velada

sojourn ['sodʒʌrn] *s* estancia, permanencia ‖ ['sodʒʌrn] o [so'dʒʌrn] *intr* estarse, permanecer

sol. *abbr* **soluble, solution**

solace ['sɑlɪs] *s* solaz *m,* consuelo ‖ *tr* solazar, consolar

solar ['solər] *adj* solar

solar battery *s* fotopila

solder ['sɑdər] *s* soldadura ‖ *tr* soldar

soldering iron *s* cautín *m,* soldador *m*

soldier ['soldʒər] *s* (*enlisted man as distinguished from an officer*) soldado; (*man in military service*) militar *m* ‖ *intr* servir como soldado

soldier of fortune *s* aventurero militar

soldier·y ['soldʒəri] *s* (*pl* **-ies**) soldadesca

sold out [sold] *adj* agotado; **the theater is sold out** todas las localidades están vendidas; **we are sold out of those neckties** se nos han agotado esas corbatas

sole [sol] *adj* solo, único; exclusivo ‖ *s* (*of foot*) planta; (*of shoe*) suela; (*fish*) lenguado ‖ *tr* solar

solely ['solli] *adv* solamente, únicamente

solemn ['sɑləm] *adj* solemne

solicit [sə'lɪsɪt] *tr* solicitar; intentar seducir

solicitor [sə'lɪsɪtər] *s* solicitador *m,* agente *m;* (law) procurador *m*

solicitous [sə'lɪsɪtəs] *adj* solícito

solicitude [sə'lɪsɪ·tjud] o [sə'lɪsɪ·tud] *s* solicitud

solid ['sɑlɪd] *adj* sólido; unánime; (*sound, good*) sólido, macizo; (*e.g., clouds*) denso; (*without pause or interruption*) entero; (*e.g., gold*) puro ‖ *s* sólido

solid geometry *s* geometría del espacio

solidity [sə'lɪdɪti] *s* (*pl* **-ties**) solidez *f*

solid tire s (aut) macizo
solilo·quy [sə'lɪləkwɪ] s (pl -quies) soliloquio
solitaire ['salɪ,ter] s (game and diamond) solitario; sortija solitario
solitar·y ['salɪ,terɪ] adj solitario ‖ s (pl -ies) solitario
solitary confinement s incomunicación, aislamiento penal
solitude ['salɪ,tjud] o ['salɪ,tud] s soledad
so·lo ['solo] adj (instrument) solista; a solas, hecho a solas ‖ s (pl -los) (mus) solo
soloist ['solo·ɪst] s solista mf
solstice ['salstɪs] s solsticio
solution [sə'luʃən] s solución
solve [salv] tr resolver, solucionar; adivinar (un enigma)
solvent ['salvənt] adj & s solvente m
somber ['sambər] adj sombrío
some [sʌm] adj indef algún; un poco de; unos; (coll) grande, bueno, famoso ‖ pron indef pl algunos, unos
some'body pron indef alguien; **somebody else** algún otro, otra persona ‖ s (pl -ies) (coll) personaje m
some'day' adv algún día
some'how' adv de algún modo, de alguna manera; **somehow or other** de un modo u otro
some'one pron indef alguien; **someone else** algún otro, otra persona
somersault ['sʌmər,səlt] s salto mortal ‖ intr dar un salto mortal
something ['sʌmθɪŋ] adv algo, un poco; (coll) muy, excesivamente ‖ pron indef alguna cosa, algo; **something else** otra cosa
some'time' adj antiguo, de otro tiempo ‖ adv alguna vez; antiguamente
some'times' adv a veces; algunas veces
some'way' adv de algún modo
some'what' adv algo, un poco ‖ s alguna cosa, algo
some'where adv en alguna parte, a alguna parte, en algún tiempo; **somewhere else** en otra parte, a otra parte
somnambulist [sam'næmbjəlɪst] s sonámbulo
somnolent ['samnələnt] adj soñoliento
son [sʌn] s hijo
song [səŋ] o [saŋ] s canción, canto; **for a song** muy barato; **to sing the same old song** volver a la misma canción
song'bird' s ave canora
Song of Songs s Cantar m de los Cantares
sonic ['sanɪk] adj sónico
sonic boom s (aer) estampido sónico
son'-in-law' s (pl sons-in-law) yerno, hijo político
sonnet ['sanɪt] s soneto
sonneteer [,sanɪ'tɪr] s sonetista mf; poetastro ‖ intr sonetizar
son·ny ['sʌnɪ] s (pl -nies) hijito
sonori·ty [sə'narɪtɪ] s (pl -ties) sonoridad
soon [sun] adv pronto, en breve; temprano; de buena gana; **as soon as** así que, en cuanto, luego que, tan

pronto como; **as soon as possible** cuanto antes, lo más pronto posible; **had sooner** preferiría; **how soon?** ¿cuándo?; **soon after** poco después, poco después de; **sooner or later** tarde o temprano
soot [sut] o [sut] s hollín m
soothe [suð] tr aliviar, calmar, sosegar
soothsayer ['suθ,se·ər] s adivino
soot·y ['sutɪ] o ['sutɪ] adj (comp -ier; super -iest) holliniento, tiznado
sop [sap] s (food soaked in milk, etc.) sopa; regalo (para acallar, apaciguar o sobornar) ‖ v (pret & pp sopped; ger sopping) tr empapar, ensopar; **to sop up** absorber
sophisticated [sə'fɪstɪ,ketɪd] adj mundano, falto de simplicidad, corrido
sophomore ['safə,mor] s estudiante mf de segundo año
sopran·o [sə'præno] o [sə'prano] adj de soprano; para soprano ‖ s (pl -os) soprano mf
sorcerer ['sɔrsərər] s brujo, hechicero
sorceress ['sɔrsərɪs] s bruja, hechicera
sorcer·y ['sɔrsərɪ] s (pl -ies) brujería, hechicería, sortilegio
sordid ['sɔrdɪd] adj sórdido
sore [sor] adj enrojecido, inflamado; (coll) resentido, picado; **to be sore at** (coll) estar enojado con ‖ s llaga, úlcera; pena, dolor m, aflicción; **to open an old sore** renovar la herida
sorely ['sorlɪ] adv penosamente; con urgencia
sore throat s dolor m de garganta
sorori·ty [sə'rarɪtɪ] o [sə'rɔrɪtɪ] s (pl -ties) hermandad de estudiantas
sorrel ['sarəl] o ['sɔrəl] adj alazán
sorrow ['saro] o ['sɔro] s dolor m, pena pesar m; arrepentimiento ‖ intr dolerse, apenarse, sentir pena; arrepentirse; **to sorrow for** añorar
sorrowful ['sarəfəl] o ['sɔrəfəl] adj doloroso, pesaroso, acongojado
sor·ry ['sarɪ] o ['sɔrɪ] adj (comp -rier; super -riest) afligido, apenado, pesaroso; arrepentido; malo, pésimo; despreciable, ridículo; **to be o feel sorry** sentir; arrepentirse; **to be o feel sorry for** compadecer; arrepentirse de
sort [sɔrt] s clase f, especie f; modo, manera, **a sort of** uno a modo de; **out of sorts** de mal humor; **sort of** (coll) algo, en cierta medida ‖ tr clasificar, separar; escoger, entresacar
so'-so' adj mediano, regular, talcualillo ‖ adv así así, tal cual
sot [sat] s borracho
sotto voce ['sato 'votʃe] adv a sovoz, en voz baja
soubrette [su'bret] s (theat) confidenta de comedia; (theat) doncella coquetona
soul [sol] s alma; **upon my soul!** ¡por vida mía!
sound [saund] adj sano; sólido, firme; solvente; sonoro; (sleep) profundo;

prudente; legal, válido || *adv* profundamente || *s* sonido; ruido; (*passage of water*) estrecho, brazo de mar; (surg) sonda, tienta; **within sound of** al alcance de || *tr* sonar; tocar (*p.ej.*, *campanas*); tantear, sondear; auscultar (*p.ej.*, *los pulmones*); entonar (*p.ej.*, *alabanzas*) || *intr* sonar, resonar; sondar; parecer; **to sound like** sonar a, sonar como

sound film *s* película sonora

soundly ['saʊndli] *adv* sanamente; profundamente; a fondo, completamente

sound'proof' *adj* antisonoro || *tr* insonorizar

soup [sup] *s* sopa

soup kitchen *s* comedor *m* de beneficencia, dispensario de alimentos

soup spoon *s* cuchara de sopa

sour [saʊr] *adj* agrio || *tr* agriar || *intr* agriarse

source [sors] *s* fuente *f*, manantial *m*

source material *s* fuentes *fpl* originales

sour cherry *s* (*tree*) guindo; (*fruit*) guinda

sour grapes *interj* ¡están verdes las uvas!

south [saʊθ] *adj* meridional, del sur || *adv* al sur, hacia el sur || *s* sur *m*, mediodía *m*

South America *s* Sudamérica, la América del Sur

South American *adj* & *s* sudamericano

southern ['sʌðərn] *adj* meridional

Southern Cross *s* Cruz *f* del Sur

southerner ['sʌðərnər] *s* meridional *mf*; sureño (Am)

South Korea *s* la Corea del Sur

South Korean *adj* & *s* surcoreano

south'paw' *adj* & *s* (slang in sport) zurdo

southward ['saʊθwərd] *adv* hacia el sur

south wind *s* austro, noto

souvenir [,suvə'nɪr] o ['suvə,nɪr] *s* recuerdo, memoria

sovereign ['sɑvrɪn] o ['sʌvrɪn] *adj* soberano || *s* (*king; coin*) soberano; (*queen*) soberana

sovereign·ty ['sɑvrɪnti] o ['sʌvrɪnti] *s* (*pl* -ties) soberanía

soviet ['sovɪ,et] o [,sovɪ'et] *adj* soviético || *s* soviet *m*

sovietize ['sovɪ·ɛ,taɪz] *tr* sovietizar

Soviet Russia *s* la Rusia Soviética

Soviet Union *s* Unión Soviética

sow [saʊ] *s* puerca || [so] *v* (*pret* **sowed**; *pp* **sown** o **sowed**) *tr* sembrar; (*with mines*) plagar

soybean ['sɔɪ,bin] *s* soja; semilla de soja

sp. *abbr* **special, species, specific, specimen, spelling**

spa [spɑ] *s* caldas, balneario

space [spes] *adj* espacial, del espacio || *s* espacio; **in the space of** por espacio de || *tr* espaciar

space bar *s* espaciador *m*, tecla de espacios

space'craft' *s* astronave *f*

space flight *s* vuelo espacial

space key *s* llave *f* espacial.

space·man ['spes,mæn] *s* (*pl* -men [,men]) navegador *m* del espacio; visitante *m* a la Tierra del espacio exterior

space'ship' *s* nave *f* del espacio

space suit *s* escafandra espacial

space vehicle *s* vehículo espacial

spacious ['speʃəs] *adj* espacioso

spade [sped] *s* laya; (*playing card*) pique *m*; **to call a spade a spade** llamar al pan pan y al vino vino

spade'work' *s* trabajo preliminar

Spain [spen] *s* España

span [spæn] *s* palmo, cuarta, llave *f* de la mano; espacio, lapso, trecho; (*of horses*) pareja; (*of a bridge*) ojo; (aer) envergadura || *v* (*pret* & *pp* **spanned**; *ger* **spanning**) *tr* medir a palmos; atravesar, extenderse sobre

spangle ['spæŋɡəl] *s* lentejuela || *tr* adornar con lentejuelas; (*to stud with bright objects*) estrellar || *intr* brillar

Spaniard ['spænjərd] *s* español *m*

spaniel ['spænjəl] *s* perro de aguas

Spanish ['spænɪʃ] *adj* & *s* español *m*; **the Spanish** los españoles

Spanish America *s* la América Española, Hispanoamérica

Spanish broom *s* retama

Spanish fly *s* abadejo, cantárida

Spanish Main *s* Costa Firme, Tierra Firme; mar *m* Caribe

Spanish moss *s* barba española

Spanish omelet *s* tortilla de tomate

Span'ish-speak'ing *adj* de habla española, hispanohablante

spank [spæŋk] *tr* azotar, zurrar

spanking ['spæŋkɪŋ] *adj* rápido; fuerte; (coll) muy grande, muy hermoso, extraordinario || *s* azote *m*

spar *s* (mineral) espato; (naut) mástil *m*, palo, verga || *v* (*pret* & *pp* **sparred**; *ger* **sparring**) *intr* pelear, reñir; boxear

spare [sper] *adj* sobrante; libre, disponible; de repuesto; delgado, enjuto, flaco; parco, sobrio || *tr* pasar sin; perdonar; guardar, salvar; ahorrar; **to have** ... **to spare** tener de sobra; **to spare oneself** ahorrarse esfuerzos

spare bed *s* cama de sobra

spare parts *spl* piezas de repuesto o de recambio

spare room *s* cuarto de reserva

sparing ['sperɪŋ] *adj* económico; (*scanty*) escaso

spark [spɑrk] *s* chispa; (*e.g., of truth*) centellita || *tr* (coll) cortejar, galantear (*a una mujer*) || *intr* chispear

spark coil *s* bobina de chispas, bobina de encendido

spark gap *s* (*of induction coil*) entrehierro; (*of spark plug*) espacio de chispa

sparkle ['spɑrkəl] *s* chispita, destello; (*wit*) travesura; alegría, viveza || *intr* chispear; ser alegre; espumar, ser efervescente

sparkling ['spɑrklɪŋ] *adj* centelleante, chispeante; (*wine*) espumante, espumoso; (*water*) gaseoso

spark plug s bujía

sparrow ['spæro] s gorrión m

sparse [spɑrs] adj (population) poco denso; (hair) ralo

Spartan ['spɑrtən] adj & s espartano

spasm ['spæzəm] s espasmo; esfuerzo súbito y de breve duración

spasmodic [spæz'mɑdɪk] adj espasmódico; intermitente; caprichoso

spastic ['spæstɪk] adj espástico

spat [spæt] s disputa, riña; botín m, polaina corta

spatial ['speʃəl] adj espacial

spatter ['spætər] tr salpicar; manchar || intr chorrear; chapotear

spatula ['spætʃələ] s espátula

spavin ['spævɪn] s esparaván m

spawn [spɔn] s freza; prole f; producto, resultado || tr engendrar || intr desovar, frezar (los peces)

speak [spik] v (pret spoke [spok]; pp spoken) tr hablar (un idioma); decir (la verdad) || intr hablar; so to speak por decirlo así; speaking! ¡al habla!; to speak out o up osar hablar, elevar la voz

speak'-eas'y s (pl -ies) (slang) taberna clandestina

speaker ['spikər] s hablante mf; orador m; (of a legislative assembly) presidente m; (rad) altavoz m

speaking ['spikɪŋ] adj hablante; to be on speaking terms hablarse || s habla; elocuencia

speaking tube s tubo acústico

spear [spɪr] s lanza; (for fishing) arpón m; (of grass) hoja || tr alancear, herir con lanza

spear'head' s punta de lanza || tr dirigir, conducir; encabezar; dar impulso a

spear'mint' s menta verde, menta romana

spec. abbr special

special ['speʃəl] adj especial || s tren m especial

spe'cial-deliv'ery adj urgente, de urgencia

specialist ['speʃəlɪst] s especialista mf

speciali-ty [,speʃɪ'ælɪti] s (pl -ties) especialidad

specialize ['speʃə,laɪz] tr especializar || intr especializar o especializarse

special-ty ['speʃəlti] s (pl -ties) especialidad

spe-cies ['spisiz] s (pl -cies) especie f

specific [spɪ'sɪfɪk] adj & s específico

speci-fy ['spesɪ,faɪ] v (pret & pp -fied) tr especificar

specimen ['spesɪmən] s espécimen m; (coll) tipo, sujeto

specious ['spiʃəs] adj especioso, engañoso

speck [spek] s mota, manchita || tr motear, manchar, salpicar de manchas

speckle ['spekəl] s mota, punto || tr motear, puntear

spectacle ['spektəkəl] s espectáculo; spectacles anteojos, gafas

spectator ['spektetər] o [spek'tetər] s espectador m

specter ['spektər] s espectro

spec-trum ['spektrəm] s (pl -tra [trə] o -trums) espectro

speculate ['spekjə,let] intr especular

speech [spitʃ] s habla; (of an actor) parlamento; (talk before an audience) conferencia, discurso

speech clinic s clínica de la palabra

speech correction s rehabilitación del habla

speechless ['spitʃlɪs] adj sin habla; estupefacto

speed [spid] s velocidad; (aut) marcha, velocidad || v (pret & pp sped [sped]) tr apresurar; despedir; ayudar || intr apresurarse; adelantar, progresar; ir con exceso de velocidad

speeding ['spidɪŋ] s exceso de velocidad

speed king s as m del volante

speed limit s velocidad permitida

speedometer [spi'dɑmɪtər] s (to indicate speed) velocímetro; velocímetro y cuentakilómetros unidos

speed record s marca de velocidad

speed-y ['spidi] adj (comp -ier; super -iest) rápido, veloz

spell [spel] s encanto, hechizo; tanda, turno; rato, poco tiempo; (e.g., of good weather) temporada; to cast a spell on encantar, hechizar || v (pret & pp spelled o spelt [spelt]) tr deletrear; indicar, significar; to spell out (coll) explicar detalladamente || intr deletrear || v (pret & pp spelled) tr reemplazar, relevar

spell'bind'er s (coll) orador m fascinante, orador persuasivo

spelling ['spelɪŋ] adj ortográfico || s (act) deletreo; (subject or study) ortografía; (way a word is spelled) grafía

spelunker [spɪ'lʌŋkər] s espeleólogo de afición

spend [spend] v (pret & pp spent [spent]) tr gastar; pasar (nna hora, un día, etc.)

spender ['spendər] s gastador m

spending money s dinero para gastos menudos

spend'thrift' s derrochador m, pródigo

sperm [spɑrm] s esperma f

sperm whale s cachalote m

spew [spju] tr & intr vomitar

sp. gr. abbr specific gravity

sphere [sfɪr] s esfera; astro, cuerpo celeste

spherical ['sferɪkəl] adj esférico

sphinx [sfɪŋks] s (pl sphinxes o sphinges ['sfɪndʒiz]) esfinge f

spice [spaɪs] s especia; (zest, piquancy) sainete m; fragancia || tr especiar; dar gusto o picante a

spice box s especiero

spick-and-span ['spɪkənd'spæn] adj flamante; limpio, pulcro

spic-y ['spaɪsi] adj (comp -ier; super -iest) especiado; picante; aromático; sicalíptico

spider ['spaɪdər] s araña

spider web s tela de araña, telaraña

spiff·y ['spɪfi] *adj* (*comp* **-ier;** *super* **-iest**) (slang) guapo, elegante

spigot ['spɪgət] *s* grifo; (*plug to stop a vent*) espiche *m*

spike [spaɪk] *s* (*long, heavy nail*) estaca, escarpia; (*sharp projection or part*) punta, pico, púa; (bot) espiga || *tr* empernar; acabar, poner fin a

spill [spɪl] *s* derrame *m;* líquido derramado; (coll) caída, vuelco || *v* (*pret & pp* **spilled** o **spilt** [spɪlt]) *tr* derramar, verter; (coll) hacer caer, volcar || *intr* derramarse, verterse; (coll) caer, volcarse

spill'way' *s* bocacaz *m*, canal *m* de desagüe

spin [spɪn] *s* vuelta, giro muy rápido; (coll) paseo en coche, etc.; **to go into a spin** (aer) entrar en barrena || *v* (*pret & pp* **spun** [spʌn]) *ger* **spinning**) *tr* hacer girar; hilar (*p.ej., lino*); bailar (*un trompo*); **to spin out** extender, prolongar; **to spin yarns** contar cuentos increíbles || *intr* dar vueltas, girar; hilar; bailar (*un trompo*); (aer) entrar en barrena

spinach ['spɪnɪtʃ] o ['spɪnɪdʒ] *s* espinaca; (*leaves used as food*) espinacas

spinal ['spaɪnəl] *adj* espinal

spinal column *s* espina dorsal, columna vertebral

spinal cord *s* médula espinal

spindle ['spɪndəl] *s* (*rounded rod tapering toward each end*) huso; (*small shaft, axle*) eje *m;* (*turned ornament in a baluster*) mazorca

spine [spaɪn] *s* espina, púa; (*rib, ridge*) cordoncillo; loma, cerro; (anat) espina; (bb) lomo; (fig) ánimo, valor *m*

spineless ['spaɪnlɪs] *adj* sin espinas, sin espinazo; sin firmeza de carácter

spinet ['spɪnɪt] *s* espineta

spinner ['spɪnər] *s* hilandero; máquina de hilar

spinning ['spɪnɪŋ] *adj* hilador || *s* (*act*) hila; (*art*) hilandería

spinning wheel *s* torno de hilar

spinster ['spɪnstər] *s* solterona

spi·ral ['spaɪrəl] *adj & s* espiral *f* || *v* (*pret & pp* **-raled** o **-ralled;** *ger* **-raling** o **-ralling**) *intr* dar vueltas como una espiral; (aer) volar en espiral

spiral staircase *s* escalera de caracol

spire [spaɪr] *s* cima, ápice *m;* (*of a steeple*) aguja, chapitel *m;* (*e.g., of grass*) tallo

spirit ['spɪrɪt] *s* espíritu *m;* humor *m*, temple *m;* personaje *m;* licor *m* || *tr* — **to spirit away** llevarse misteriosamente

spirited ['spɪrɪtɪd] *adj* fogoso, espiritoso

spirit lamp *s* lámpara de alcohol

spiritless ['spɪrɪtlɪs] *adj* apocado, tímido, sin ánimo

spirit level *s* nivel *m* de burbuja

spiritual ['spɪrɪtʃu·əl] *adj* espiritual

spiritualism ['spɪrɪtʃu·ə‚lɪzəm] *s* espiritismo; (*belief that all reality is spiritual*) espiritualismo

spirituous liquors ['spɪrɪtʃu·əs] *spl* licores espirituosos

spit [spɪt] *s* esputo, saliva; (*for roasting*) asador *m*, espetón *m;* punta o lengua de tierra; **the spit and image of** la segunda edición de, el retrato de || *v* (*pret & pp* **spat** [spæt] o **spit;** *ger* **spitting**) *tr* escupir || *intr* escupir; lloviznar; neviscar; fufar (*el gato*)

spite [spaɪt] *s* despecho, rencor *m*, inquina; **in spite of** a pesar de, a despecho de; **out of spite** por despecho || *tr* despechar, molestar, picar

spiteful ['spaɪtfəl] *adj* despechado, rencoroso

spit'fire' *s* fierabrás *m;* mujer *f* de mal genio

spittoon [spɪ'tun] *s* escupidera

splash [splæʃ] *s* rociada, salpicadura; (*e.g., with the hands*) chapaleo, chapoteo; **to make a splash** (coll) hacer impresión, llamar la atención || *tr & intr* salpicar; chapotear

splash'down' *s* acuatizaje *m*

spleen [splin] *s* mal humor *m;* (anat) bazo; **to vent one's spleen** descargar la bilis

splendid ['splɛndɪd] *adj* espléndido; (coll) magnífico, maravilloso

splendor ['splɛndər] *s* esplendor *m*

splice [splaɪs] *s* empalme *m*, junta || *tr* empalmar, juntar

splint [splɪnt] *s* (*splinter*) astilla, tablilla; (surg) tablilla || *tr* entablillar (*un hueso roto*)

splinter ['splɪntər] *s* astilla; (*of stone, glass, bone*) esquirla || *tr* astillar || *intr* astillarse, hacerse astillas

splinter group *s* grupo disidente

split [splɪt] *adj* hendido, partido; dividido || *s* división, fractura; (slang) porción || *v* (*pret & pp* **split;** *ger* **splitting**) *tr* dividir, partir; **to split one's sides with laughter** desternillarse de risa || *intr* dividirse a lo largo; **to split away (from)** separarse (de)

split fee *s* dicotomía (*entre médicos*)

split personality *s* personalidad desdoblada

splitting ['splɪtɪŋ] *adj* partidor; fuerte, violento; (*headache*) enloquecedor

splotch [splɑtʃ] *s* borrón *m*, mancha grande || *tr* salpicar, manchar

splurge [splʌrdʒ] *s* (coll) fachenda, ostentación || *intr* (coll) fachendear

splutter ['splʌtər] *s* chisporroteo; (*manner of speaking*) farfulla || *tr* farfullar || *intr* chisporrotear; farfullar

spoil [spɔɪl] *s* botín *m*, presa; **spoils** (*taken from an enemy*) botín, despojos; (*of political victory*) enchufes *mpl* || *v* (*pret & pp* **spoiled** o **spoilt** [spɔɪlt]) *tr* echar a perder, estropear; mimar (*a un niño*); amargar (*una tertulia*) || *intr* echarse a perder

spoiled [spɔɪld] *adj* (*child*) consentido, mimado; (*food*) pasado, podrido

spoils·man ['spɔɪlzmən] *s* (*pl* **-men** [mən]) enchufista *m*

spoils system *s* enchufismo

spoke [spok] *s* (*of a wheel*) radio, rayo; (*of a ladder*) escalón *m*

spokes·man ['spoksmən] s (pl -men [mən]) portavoz m, vocero
sponge [spʌndʒ] s esponja; **to throw in** (o up) **the sponge** (coll) tirar la esponja || tr limpiar con esponja; borrar; absorber || intr ser absorbente; **to sponge on** (coll) vivir a costa de
sponge cake s bizcocho muy ligero
sponger ['spʌndʒər] s esponja (gorrón, parásito)
sponge rubber s caucho esponjoso
spon·gy ['spʌndʒi] adj (comp -gier; super -giest) esponjoso
sponsor ['spʌnsər] s patrocinador m; (godfather) padrino; (godmother) madrina || tr patrocinar
sponsorship ['spʌnsər‚ʃɪp] s patrocinio
spontaneous [spɑn'teni·əs] adj espontáneo
spoof [spuf] s (slang) mistificación, engaño; (slang) broma || tr (slang) mistificar, engañar || intr (slang) bromear, burlar; (slang) parodiar
spook [spuk] s (coll) aparecido, espectro
spook·y ['spuki] adj (comp -ier; super -iest) (coll) espectral, espeluznante; (horse) (coll) asustadizo
spool [spul] s carrete m, bobina
spoon [spun] s cuchara || tr cucharear || intr (slang) besuquearse (los enamorados)
spoonful ['spun‚ful] s cucharada
spoon·y ['spuni] adj (comp -ier; super -iest) (coll) baboso, sobón
sporadic(al) [spə'rædɪk(əl)] adj esporádico
spore [spor] s espora
sport [sport] adj deportivo, de deporte || s deporte m; deportista mf; (person or thing controlled by some power or passion) juguete m; (laughingstock) hazmerreír m; (gambler) (coll) tahur m, jugador m; (in gambling or playing games) (coll) buen perdedor; (flashy fellow) (coll) guapo, majo; (biol) mutación; **to make sport of** burlarse de, reírse de || tr (coll) lucir (p.ej., un traje nuevo) || intr divertirse; estar de burla; juguetear
sport clothes spl trajes mpl de sport
sport fan s (slang) aficionado al deporte, deportista mf
sporting chance s (coll) riesgo de buen perdedor
sporting goods spl artículos de deporte
sporting house s (coll) casa de juego; (coll) casa de rameras
sports'cast'er s locutor deportivo
sports·man ['sportsmən] s (pl -men [mən]) deportista m; jugador honrado
sports news s noticiario deportivo
sports'wear' s trajes deportivos
sports writer s cronista deportivo
sport·y ['sporti] adj (comp -ier; super -iest) (coll) elegante, guapo; (coll) alegre, brillante; (coll) magnánimo; (coll) disipado, libertino
spot [spɑt] s mancha; sitio, lugar m; (coll) poquito; **on the spot** allí mismo; al punto; (slang) en dificultad; (slang) en peligro de muerte; **to hit the spot** tener razón; (coll) dar completa satisfacción || v (pret & pp spotted; ger spotting) tr manchar; (coll) descubrir, reconocer || intr mancharse, tener manchas
spot cash s dinero contante
spotless ['spɑtlɪs] adj inmaculado, sin manchas
spot'light' s proyector m orientable; luz concentrada; (aut) faro piloto, faro giratorio; (fig) atención del público
spot remover [rɪ'muvər] s (person) quitamanchas mf; (material) quitamanchas m
spot welding s soldadura por puntos
spouse [spauz] o [spaus] s cónyuge mf, consorte mf
spout [spaut] s (to carry off water from roof) canalón m; (of a jar, pitcher, etc.) pico; (of a sprinkling can) rallo, roseta; (jet) chorro; **up the spout** (slang) acabado, arruinado || tr echar en chorro; (coll) declamar || intr chorrear; (coll) declamar
sprain [spren] s torcedura, esguince m || tr torcer, torcerse
sprawl [sprɔl] intr arrellanarse
spray [spre] s rociada; (of the sea) espuma; (device) pulverizador m; (twig) ramita || tr & intr rociar
sprayer ['spre·ər] s rociador m, pulverizador m, vaporizador m
spread [spred] s extensión; amplitud, anchura; difusión; diferencia; cubrecama, sobrecama; mantel m, tapete m; (of the wings of a bird; of the wings of an airplane) envergadura; (coll) festín m, comilona || v (pret & pp spread) tr extender; difundir, propagar; esparcir; escalonar; abrir, separar; poner (la mesa) || intr extenderse; difundirse; esparcirse; abrirse, separarse
spree [spri] s juerga, parranda, borrachera; **to go on a spree** ir de juerga; pillar una mona
sprig [sprɪg] s ramita
spright·ly ['spraɪtli] adj (comp -lier; super -liest) alegre, animado, vivo
spring [sprɪŋ] adj primaveral; de manantial; de muelle, de resorte || s (season of the year) primavera; (issue of water from earth) fuente f, manantial m; (elastic device) muelle m, resorte m; (of an automobile or wagon) ballesta; (leap, jump) brinco, salto; abertura, grieta; tensión, tirantez f || v (pret sprang [spræŋ] o sprung [sprʌŋ]; pp sprung) tr soltar (un muelle o resorte); torcer, combar, encorvar; hacer saltar (una trampa, una mina) || intr saltar; saltar de golpe; brotar, nacer, proceder; torcerse, combarse, encorvarse; **to spring at** abalanzarse sobre; **to spring forth** precipitarse; brotar; **to spring up** levantarse de un salto; brotar, nacer; presentarse a la vista
spring'board' s trampolín m

spring chicken *s* polluelo; (*young person*) (coll) pollita

spring fever *s* (hum) ataque *m* primaveral, galbana

spring mattress *s* colchón *m* de muelles, somier *m*

spring'time' *s* primavera

sprinkle |'sprɪŋkəl| *s* rociada; llovizna; pizca || *tr* regar, rociar; salpicar, sembrar; espolvorear (*p.ej.*, *azucar*) || *intr* rociar; lloviznar, gotear

sprinkling can *s* regadera, rociadera

sprint [sprɪnt] *s* (sport) embalaje *m* || *intr* (sport) embalarse, lanzarse

sprite [spraɪt] *s* duende *m*, trasgo

sprocket ['sprɑkɪt] *s* diente *m* de rueda de cadena; rueda de cadena

sprout [spraʊt] *s* brote *m*, renuevo, retoño || *intr* brotar, germinar, echar renuevos; crecer rápidamente

spruce [sprus] *adj* apuesto, elegante, garboso || *s* abeto del Norte, abeto falso, pícea || *tr* ataviar, componer || *intr* ataviarse, componerse; **to spruce up** emperifollarse

spry [spraɪ] *adj* (*comp* **spryer** *o* **sprier;** *super* **spryest** *o* **spriest**) activo, ágil

spud [spʌd] *s* (*chisel*) escoplo; (agr) escoda; (coll) patata

spun glass [spʌn] *s* vidrio hilado, cristal hilado

spunk [spʌŋk] *s* (coll) ánimo, coraje *m*, corazón *m*, valor *m*

spun silk *s* seda cardada o hilada

spur [spʌr] *s* espuela; (*central point of an auger*) gusanillo; (*of a cock, mountain, warship*) espolón *m*; (rr) ramal corto; (*goad, stimulus*) (fig) espuela; **on the spur of the moment** impulsivamente, sin la reflexión debida || *v* (*pret & pp* **spurred;** *ger* **spurring**) *tr* espolear; **to spur on** espolear, aguijonear

spurious ['spjʊrɪ-əs] *adj* espurio

spurn [spʌrn] *s* desdén *m*, menosprecio || *tr* desdeñar, menospreciar; rechazar con desdén

spurt [spʌrt] *s* chorro repentino; esfuerzo repentino; arranque *m* || *intr* salir en chorro, salir a borbotones

sputter |'spʌtər| *s* (*manner of speaking*) farfulla; (*sizzling*) chisporroteo || *tr* farfullar || *intr* farfullar; chisporrotear

spy [spaɪ] *s* (*pl* **spies**) espía *mf* || *v* (*pret & pp* **spied**) *tr* columbrar, divisar || *intr* espiar; **to spy on** espiar

spy'glass' *s* catalejo, anteojo

sq. *abbr* **square**

squabble ['skwɑbəl] *s* reyerta, riña || *intr* reñir, disputar

squad [skwɑd] *s* escuadra

squadron ['skwɑdrən] *s* (aer) escuadrilla; (*of cavalry*) (mil) escuadrón *m*; (nav) escuadra

squalid ['skwɑlɪd] *adj* escuálido

squall [skwɔl] *s* grupada, turbión *m*; (*quarrel*) (coll) riña; (*upset, commotion*) (coll) chubasco

squalor ['skwɑlər] *s* escualidez *f*

squander ['skwɑndər] *tr* despilfarrar, malgastar

square [skwɛr] *adj* cuadrado, p.ej., **eight square inches** ocho pulgadas cuadradas; en cuadro, de lado, p.ej., **eight inches square** ocho pulgadas en cuadro, ocho pulgadas de lado; rectangular; justo, recto; honrado, leal; saldado; fuerte, sólido; (coll) abundante, completo; **to get square with** (coll) hacérselas pagar a || *adv* en cuadro; en ángulo recto; honradamente, lealmente || *s* cuadrado; (*of checkerboard or chessboard*) casilla, escaque *m*; (*city block*) manzana; (*open area in town or city*) plaza; (*carpenter's tool*) escuadra; **to be on the square** (coll) obrar de buena fe || *tr* cuadrar; dividir en cuadros; ajustar, nivelar, conformar; saldar (*una cuenta*); (carp) escuadrar || *intr* cuadrarse; **to square off** (coll) colocarse en posición de defensa

square dance *s* danza de figuras

square deal *s* (coll) trato equitativo

square meal *s* (coll) comida abundante

square shooter ['ʃutər] *s* (coll) persona leal y honrada

squash [skwɑʃ] *s* aplastamiento; (bot) calabaza; (sport) frontón *m* con raqueta; || *tr* aplastar, despachurrar; confutar (*un argumento*); acallar con un argumento, respuesta, etc || *intr* aplastarse

squash·y ['skwɑʃɪ] *adj* (*comp* **-ier;** *super* **-iest**) mojado y blando; (*muddy*) lodoso; (*fruit*) modorro

squat [skwɑt] *adj* en cuclillas; rechoncho || *v* (*pret & pp* **squatted;** *ger* **squatting**) *intr* acuclillarse, agacharse; sentarse en el suelo; establecerse en terreno ajeno sin derecho; establecerse en terreno público para crear un derecho

squatter ['skwɑtər] *s* advenedizo, intruso, colono usurpador

squaw [skwɔ] *s* india norteamericana; mujer, esposa, muchacha

squawk [skwɔk] *s* graznido; (slang) queja chillona || *intr* graznar; (slang) quejarse chillando

squaw man *s* blanco casado con india

squeak [skwik] *s* chillido; chirrido || *intr* dar chillidos; chirriar

squeal [skwil] *s* chillido || *intr* dar chillidos; (slang) delatar, soplar; **to squeal on** (slang) delatar, soplar (*a una persona*)

squealer |'skwilər| *s* (coll) soplón *m*

squeamish ['skwimɪʃ] *adj* escrupuloso, remilgado; excesivamente modesto; (*easily nauseated*) asqueroso

squeeze [skwiz] *s* apretón *m*; **to put the squeeze on someone** (coll) hacer a uno la forzosa, meter en prensa a uno || *tr* apretar; agobiar, oprimir; exprimir || *intr* apretar; **to squeeze through** abrirse paso a estrujones por entre; salir de un aprieto a duras penas

squeezer ['skwizər] *s* exprimidera

squelch [skwɛltʃ] *s* (coll) tapaboca || *tr* apabullar, despachurrar

squid [skwɪd] *s* calamar *m*

squint [skwɪnt] s mirada bizca; mirada furtiva; (*strabismus*) bizquera || *tr* achicar, entornar (*los ojos*) || *intr* bizquear: torcer la vista; tener los ojos medio cerrados

squint-eyed [ˈskwɪnt͵aɪd] *adj* bisojo, bizco; malévolo, sospechoso

squire [skwaɪr] s acompañante m (*de una señora*); (Brit) terrateniente m de antigua heredad; (U.S.A.) juez m de paz, juez local || *tr* acompañar (*a una señora*)

squirm [skwʌrm] s retorcimiento || *intr* retorcerse; **to squirm out of** escaparse de (*p.ej., un aprieto*) haciendo mucho esfuerzo

squirrel [ˈskwʌrəl] s ardilla

squirt [skwʌrt] s chorro; jeringazo; (coll) mono, presuntuoso || *tr* arrojar a chorros || *intr* salir a chorros

Sr. *abbr* señor, Sir

S.S. *abbr* **Secretary of State, steamship, Sunday school**

St. *abbr* **Saint, Strait, Street**

stab [stæb] s puñalada; (coll) tentativa; **to make a stab at** (slang) esforzarse por hacer || *v* (*pret & pp* **stabbed**; *ger* **stabbing**) *tr* apuñalar; traspasar || *intr* apuñalar

stab in the back s puñalada trapera

stable [ˈstebəl] *adj* estable || s establo, cuadra, caballeriza

stack [stæk] s montón m, pila; (*of rifles*) pabellón m; (*of books in a library*) estantería, depósito; (*of a chimney*) cañón m; (*of straw*) niara; (*of firewood*) hacina; (coll) montón m, gran número || *tr* amontonar, apilar; florear (*el naipe*); hacinar (*leña*)

stadi·um [ˈstedɪ·əm] s (*pl* **-ums** o **-a** [ə]) estadio

staff [stæf] o [staf] s bastón m, apoyo, sostén m; personal m; (mil) estado mayor; (mus) pentagrama m || *tr* dotar, proveer de personal, nombrar personal para

stag [stæg] *adj* exclusivo para hombres, de hombres solos || s (*male deer*) ciervo; varón m; varón solo (*no acompañado de mujeres*)

stage [stedʒ] s escena; etapa, jornada; (*coach*) diligencia; (*scene of an event*) teatro; (*of a microscope*) portaobjeto; (rad) etapa; **by easy stages** a pequeñas etapas; lentamente; **to go on the stage** hacerse actor || *tr* poner en escena, representar; preparar, organizar

stage'coach' s diligencia

stage'craft' s arte f teatral

stage door s (theat) entrada de los artistas

stage fright s trac m, miedo al público

stage'hand' s tramoyista m, metemuertos m, metesillas m

stage manager s director m de escena

stage'-struck' *adj* loco por el teatro

stage whisper s susurro en voz alta

stagger [ˈstægər] *tr* sorprender; asustar; escalonar (*las horas de trabajo*) || *intr* tambalear, hacer eses al andar

staggering *adj* tambaleante; sorprendente

stagnant [ˈstægnənt] *adj* estancado; (fig) estancado, inactivo, paralizado

staid [sted] *adj* grave, serio, formal

stain [sten] s mancha; tinte m, tintura; materia colorante || *tr* manchar; teñir; colorar || *intr* mancharse; hacer manchas

stained glass s vidrio de color

stained'glass' window s vidriera de colores, vidriera pintada, vitral m

stainless [ˈstenlɪs] *adj* inmanchable; (*steel*) inoxidable; inmaculado

stair [ster] s escalera; (*step of a series*) escalón m; **stairs** escalera

stair'case' s escalera

stair'way' s escalera

stair well s hueco de escalera

stake [stek] s estaca; (*of a cart or truck*) telero; (*to hold up a plant*) rodrigón m; (*in gambling*) puesta; premio del vencedor; **at stake** en juego; en gran peligro; **to die at the stake** morir en la hoguera; **to pull up stakes** (coll) irse; (coll) mudarse de casa || *tr* estacar; atar a una estaca; rodrigar (*plantas*); apostar; arriesgar, aventurar; **to stake all** jugarse el todo por el todo; **to stake off** o **to stake out** estacar, señalar con estacas

stale [stel] *adj* añejo, rancio, viejo; (*air*) viciado; (*joke*) mohoso; anticuado

stale'mate' s mate ahogado; **to reach a stalemate** llegar a un punto muerto || *tr* dar mate ahogado a; estancar, paralizar

stalk [stɔk] s tallo || *tr* cazar al acecho; acechar, espiar || *intr* cazar al acecho; andar con paso majestuoso; andar con paso altivo; **to stalk out** salir con paso airado

stall [stɔl] s cuadra, establo; pesebre m; (*booth in a market*) puesto; (*at a fair*) caseta; (Brit) butaca; (slang) pretexto || *tr* encerrar en un establo; poner trabas a; parar (*un motor*); **to stall off** (coll) eludir, evitar || *intr* atascarse, atollarse; pararse (*un motor*); (slang) eludir para engañar o demorar; **to stall for time** (slang) tardar para ganar tiempo

stallion [ˈstæljən] s caballo padre, caballo semental

stalwart [ˈstɔlwərt] *adj* fornido, forzudo; valiente; leal, constante || s persona fornida; partidario leal

stamen [ˈstemən] s estambre m

stamina [ˈstæmɪnə] s fuerza, nervio, vigor m, resistencia

stammer [ˈstæmər] s balbuceo, tartamudeo || *tr* balbucear (*p.ej., excusas*) || *intr* balbucear, tartamudear

stamp [stæmp] s (*device used for making an impression; mark made with it; piece of paper or mark used to show payment of postage*) sello; (*tool used for crushing or marking*) pisón m; (*tool for stamping coins and medals*) cuño, troquel m; marca, impresión; clase f, tipo || *tr* sellar; troquelar; estampar, imprimir; hollar, pisotear; indicar, señalar; poner el sello a; bocartear (*el mineral*); **to stamp out** apagar pateando, extinguir por la fuerza; suprimir; **to stamp the feet** dar patadas || *intr* patalear

stampede [stæm'pid] *s* fuga precipitada; estampida (Am) || *tr* hacer huir en desorden; provocar a pánico || *intr* huir en tropel; obrar por común impulso

stamping grounds *spl* (slang) guarida (*sitio frecuentado por una persona*)

stamp pad *s* tampón *m*

stamp'-vend'ing machine *s* máquina expendedora de sellos

stance [stæns] *s* (sport) postura, planta

stanch [stɑntʃ] *adj* firme, fuerte; constante, leal; (*watertight*) estanco || *tr* estancar; restañar (*la sangre de una herida*)

stand [stænd] *s* parada; alto para defenderse; postura, posición, resistencia; estrado, tribuna; sostén *m*, soporte *m*, pie *m*; puesto, quiosco || *v* (*pret & pp* **stood** [stud]) *tr* poner, colocar; poner derecho, soportar, tolerar, resistir; (coll) aguantar (*una persona*); (coll) sufragar (*un gasto*); **to stand off** tener a raya; **to stand one's ground** mantenerse firme || *intr* estar, estar situado; estar parado; estacionarse; estar de pie, estar derecho; ponerse de pie, levantarse; resultar; persistir; mantenerse; **to stand aloof, apart** o **aside** mantenerse apartado; **to stand back of** respaldar; **to stand for** significar, representar; apoyar, defender; apadrinar; mantener (*p.ej., una opinión*); presentarse como candidato de; navegar hacia; (coll) tolerar; **to stand in line** hacer cola; **to stand out** sobresalir; destacarse, resaltar; **to stand up** ponerse de pie, levantarse; durar; **to stand up to** hacer resueltamente frente a

standard ['stændərd] *adj* normal; (*typewriter keyboard*) universal; corriente, regular; legal; clásico || *s* patrón *m*; norma, regla establecida; bandera, estandarte *m*; emblema *m*, símbolo; soporte *m*, pilar *m*

standardize ['stændər‚daɪz] *tr* normalizar, estandardizar

standard of living *s* nivel *m* de vida

standard time *s* hora legal, hora oficial

standee [stæn'di] *s* (coll) espectador *m* que asiste de pie; (coll) pasajero de pie

stand'-in' *s* (theat & mov) doble *mf*; (coll) buenas aldabas

standing ['stændɪŋ] *adj* derecho, en pie; de pie; parado, inmóvil; (*water*) encharcado, estancado; (*army: committee*) permanente, vigente || *s* condición, posición; reputación; parada; **in good standing** en posición acreditada; **of long standing** de mucho tiempo, de antigua fecha

standing army *s* ejército permanente

standing room *s* sitio para estar de pie

stand'point' *s* punto de vista

stand'still' *s* detención, parada; alto;

descanso, inactividad; **to come to a standstill** cesar, pararse

stanza ['stænzə] *s* estancia, estrofa

staple ['stepl] *adj* primero, principal; corriente, establecido || *s* (*to fasten papers*) grapa, artículo o producto de primera necesidad; materia prima; fibra textil || *tr* sujetar con grapas

stapler ['steplər] *s* engrapador *m*, cosepapeles *m*

star [stɑr] *s* (*heavenly body*) astro; (*heavenly body except sun and moon; figure that represents a star*) estrella; (mov & theat) estrella; (*of football*) as *m*; (typ) estrella o asterisco; (*fate, destiny*) (fig) estrella; **to see stars** (coll) ver las estrellas; **to thank one's lucky stars** estar agradecido por su buena suerte || *v* (*pret & pp* **starred**) *tr* estrellar, adornar o señalar con estrellas; marcar con asterisco; presentar como estrella (*a un actor*) || *intr* ser la estrella; lucirse; sobresalir

starboard ['stɑrbərd] o ['stɑr‚bord] *adj* de estribor || *adv* a estribor || *s* estribor *m*

starch [stɑrtʃ] *s* almidón *m*, fécula; arrogancia, entono; (slang) fuerza, vigor *m* || *tr* almidonar

stare [stɛr] *s* mirada fija || *intr* mirar fijamente; **to stare at** clavar la vista en, mirar con fijeza

star'fish' *s* estrella de mar, estrellamar *m*

star'gaze' *intr* mirar las estrellas; ser distraído, soñar despierto

stark [stɑrk] *adj* cabal, completo, puro; rígido tieso; duro, severo || *adv* completamente, enteramente; rígidamente, severamente

stark'-na'ked *adj* en pelota, en cueros

star'light' *s* luz *f* de las estrellas

starling ['stɑrlɪŋ] *s* estornino

Star'-Span'gled Ban'ner *s* bandera estrellada (*bandera de los EE.UU.*)

start [stɑrt] *s* comienzo, principio; salida, partida; lugar *m* de partida; (*scare*) sobresalto (*sudden start*) arranque *m*; (*advantage*) ventaja || *tr* empezar, principiar; poner en marcha; hacer arrancar; dar la señal de partida a; entablar (*una conversación*); levantar (*la caza*) || *intr* empezar, principiar; ponerse en marcha; arrancar; (*to be startled*) sobresaltar; nacer, provenir; **starting from** o **with** a partir de; **to start after** salir en busca de

starter ['stɑrtər] *s* iniciador *m*; (*of a series*) primero; (aut) arranque *m*, motor *m* de arranque; (sport) juez *m* de salida

starting ['stɑrtɪŋ] *adj* de salida; de arranque || *s* puesta en marcha

starting crank *s* manivela de arranque

starting point *s* punto de partida, arrancadero

startle ['stɑrtl] *tr* asustar, sorprender, sobrecoger || *intr* asustarse, sorprenderse, sobrecogerse

startling ['stɑrtlɪŋ] *adj* alarmante, asombroso

starvation [star'veʃən] s hambre f, inanición

starvation diet s régimen m de hambre, cura de hambre

starvation wages spl salario de hambre

starve [starv] tr hambrear; hacer morir de hambre; **to starve out** hacer rendirse por hambre ‖ intr hambrear; morir de hambre; (coll) tener hambre

starving ['starvɪŋ] adj hambriento, famélico

stat. abbr **statuary, statute, statue**

state [stet] adj de estado; del estado; estatal; público; de gala, de lujo ‖ s estado; fausto, ceremonia, pompa; **to lie in state** estar expuesto en capilla ardiente, estar de cuerpo presente; **to live in state** gastar mucho lujo; **to ride in state** pasear en carruaje de lujo ‖ tr afirmar, declarar; exponer, manifestar; plantear (un problema)

state·ly ['stetlɪ] adj (comp -lier; super -liest) imponente, majestuoso

statement ['stetmənt] s declaración; exposición, informe m, relación; (com) estado de cuentas

state of mind s estado de ánimo

state'room' s camarote m; (rr) compartimiento particular

states·man ['stetsmən] s (pl -men [mən]) estadista m, hombre m de estado

static ['stætɪk] adj estático; (rad) atmosférico ‖ s (rad) parásitos atmosféricos

station ['steʃən] s estación; condición, situación ‖ tr estacionar, apostar

station agent s jefe m de estación

stationary ['steʃən͵erɪ] adj estacionario

station break s (rad) descanso, intermedio

stationer ['steʃənər] s papelero

stationery ['steʃən͵erɪ] s efectos de escritorio; papel m para cartas

stationery store s papelería

station house s cuartelillo de policía

station identification s (rad & telv) indicativo de la emisora

sta'tion·mas'ter s jefe m de estación

station wagon s rubia, coche m rural, vagoneta

statistical [stə'tɪstɪkəl] adj estadístico

statistician [͵stætɪs'tɪʃən] s estadístico

statistics [stə'tɪstɪks] ssg (science) estadística; spl (data) estadística o estadísticas

statue ['stætʃu] s estatua

statuesque [͵stætʃu'esk] adj escultural

stature ['stætʃər] s estatura, talla; carácter m, habilidad

status ['stetəs] s condición, estado; situación social, legal o profesional; (prestige or superior rank) categoría

status seeking s esfuerzo por adquirir categoría

status symbol s símbolo de categoría social

statute ['stætʃut] s estatuto, ley f

statutory ['stætʃu͵torɪ] adj estatutario, legal

staunch [stɔntʃ] o [stantʃ] adj & tr var de **stanch**

stave [stev] s (of a barrel) duela; (of a ladder) peldaño; (mus) pentagrama m ‖ v (pret & pp staved o stove [stov]) tr romper, destrozar; (to break a hole in) desfondar; **to stave off** mantener a distancia; evitar, impedir, diferir

stay [ste] s morada, permanencia, estancia; suspensión; (of a corset) ballena, varilla; apoyo, sostén m; (law) espera; (naut) estay m ‖ tr aplazar, detener; poner freno a ‖ intr quedar, quedarse, permanecer; parar, hospedarse; habitar; **to stay up** no acostarse, velar

stay'-at-home' adj & s hogareño

stead [sted] s lugar m; **in his stead** en su lugar, en lugar de él; **to stand in good stead** ser de provecho, ser ventajoso

stead'fast' adj fijo; resuelto; constante

stead·y ['stedɪ] adj (comp -ier; super -iest) constante, fijo, firme, seguro; regular, uniforme; resuelto; asentado, serio ‖ v (pret & pp -ied) tr estabilizar, reforzar; calmar (los nervios) ‖ intr estabilizarse; calmarse

steak [stek] s lonja, tajada; biftec m

steal [stil] s (coll) hurto, robo ‖ v (pret stole [stol]; pp stolen) tr hurtar, robar; atraer, cautivar ‖ intr hurtar, robar; **to steal away** escabullirse; **to steal into** meterse a hurtadillas en; **to steal upon** aproximarse sin ruido a

stealth [stelθ] s cautela, recato; **by stealth** a hurtadillas

steam [stim] adj de vapor ‖ s vapor m; vaho, humo; **to get up steam** dar presión; **to let off steam** descargar vapor; (fig) desahogarse ‖ tr cocer al vapor; saturar de vapor; empañar (p.ej., las ventanas) ‖ intr echar vapor, emitir vapor; evaporarse; funcionar o marchar a vapor; **to steam ahead** avanzar por medio del vapor; (fig) hacer grandes progresos

steam'boat' s buque m de vapor

steamer ['stimər] s vapor m

steamer rug s manta de viaje

steamer trunk s baúl m de camarote

steam heat s calefacción por vapor

steam roller s apisonadora movida a vapor; (coll) fuerza arrolladora

steam'ship' s vapor m, buque m de vapor

steam shovel s pala mecánica de vapor

steam table s plancha caliente

steed [stid] s caballo; (high-spirited horse) corcel m

steel [stil] adj acerado; (business, industry) siderúrgico; (fig) duro, frío ‖ s acero; (for striking fire from flint; for sharpening knives) eslabón m ‖ tr acerar; **to steel oneself** acerarse

steel wool s virutillas de acero, estopa de acero

steelyard ['stil͵jard] o ['stiljərd] s romana

steep [stip] adj escarpado, empinado;

(price) alto, excesivo ‖ *tr* empapar, remojar; **steeped in** absorbido en

steeple ['stipəl] *s* aguja, campanario

stee'ple·chase' *s* carrera de campanario, carrera de obstáculos

stee'ple·jack' *s* escalatorres *m*

steer [stɪr] *s* buey *m* ‖ *tr* conducir, gobernar, guiar ‖ *intr* conducirse; **to steer clear of** (coll) evitar, eludir

steerage ['stɪrɪdʒ] *s* dirección; (naut) proa, entrepuente *m*

steerage passenger *s* (naut) pasajero de entrepuente

steering wheel *s* (aut) volante *m;* (naut) rueda del timón

stem [stem] *s (of a goblet)* pie *m; (of a pipe, of a feather)* cañón *m; (of a column)* fuste *m; (of a watch)* botón *m; (of a key)* espiga, tija; *(of a word)* tema *m;* (bot) tallo, vástago; **from stem to stern** de proa a popa ‖ *v (pret & pp* **stemmed***; ger* **stemming***) tr (to remove the stem from)* desgranar; *(to check)* detener, refrenar; *(to plug)* estancar; hacer frente a; rendir *(la marea)* ‖ *intr* nacer, provenir; **to stem from** originarse en, provenir de

stem'-wind'er *s* remontuar *m*

stench [stentʃ] *s* hedor *m,* hediondez *f*

sten·cil ['stensəl] *s* cartón picado; *(work produced by it)* estarcido ‖ *v (pret & pp* **-ciled** o **-cilled***; ger* **-ciling** o **-cilling***) tr* estarcir

stenographer [stə'nɑgrəfər] *s* estenógrafo

stenography [stə'nɑgrəfɪ] *s* estenografía

step [step] *s* paso; *(of staircase)* grada, peldaño; *(footprint)* huella, pisada; *(of carriage)* estribo. *(measure, démarche)* gestión, medida; (mus) intervalo; **step by step** paso a paso; **to watch one's step** proceder con cautela, andarse con tiento ‖ *v (pret & pp* **stepped***; ger* **stepping***) tr* escalonar; **to step off** medir a pasos ‖ *intr* dar un paso, dar pasos; caminar, ir; (coll) andar de prisa; **to step on it** (coll) acelerar la marcha, darse prisa; **to step on the starter** pisar el arranque

step'broth'er *s* medio hermano, hermanastro

step'child' *s (pl* **-children** [,tʃɪldrən]*)* hijastro

step'daugh'ter *s* hijastra

step'fa'ther *s* padrastro

step'lad'der *s* escala, escalera de tijera

step'moth'er *s* madrastra

steppe [step] *s* estepa

stepping stone *s* estriberón *m,* pasadera; (fig) escabel *m,* escabel *m*

step'sis'ter *s* media hermana, hermanastra

step'son' *s* hijastro

stere·o ['stɛrɪ,o] o ['stɪrɪ,o] *adj* (coll) estereofónico; (coll) estereoscópico ‖ *s (pl* **-os**) (coll) música estereofónica, disco estereofónico; (coll) radiodifusión estereofónica; (coll) fotografía estereofónica

stereotyped ['stɛrɪ·ə,taɪpt] o ['stɪrɪ·ə,taɪpt] *adj* estereotipado

sterile ['stɛrɪl] *adj* estéril

sterilize ['stɛrɪ,laɪz] *tr* esterilizar

sterling ['stʌrlɪŋ] *adj* fino, de ley; verdadero, genuino, puro, excelente ‖ *s* libras esterlinas; plata de ley; vajilla de plata

stern [stʌrn] *adj* austero, severo; decidido, firme ‖ *s* popa

stethoscope ['stɛθə,skop] *s* estetoscopio

stevedore ['stivə,dor] *s* estibador *m*

stew [stju] o [stu] *s* guisado, estofado ‖ *tr* guisar, estofar ‖ *intr* abrasarse; (coll) estar apurado

steward ['stju·ərd] o ['stu·ərd] *s* mayordomo; administrador *m; (of ship or plane)* camarero

stewardess ['stju·ərdɪs] o ['stu·ərdɪs] *s* mayordoma; *(of ship or plane)* camarera; *(of plane)* azafata, aeromoza

stewed fruit *s* compota de frutas

stewed tomatoes *spl* puré *m* de tomates

stick [stɪk] *s* palo, palillo; bastón *m,* vara; *(of dynamite)* barra; (naut) mástil *m,* verga; (typ) componedor *m* ‖ *v (pret & pp* **stuck** [stʌk]*) tr* picar, punzar; apuñalar; clavar, hincar; pegar; (coll) confundir; **to stick out** asomar *(la cabeza);* sacar *(la lengua);* **to stick up** *(in order to rob)* (slang) asaltar, atracar ‖ *intr* estar prendido, estar hincado; pegarse; agarrarse *(la pintura);* encastillarse *(p.ej., una ventana);* resaltar, sobresalir; continuar, persistir; permanecer; atascarse; **to stick out** salir *(p.ej., el pañuelo del bolsillo);* sobresalir, proyectarse; velar *(un escollo);* resultar evidente; **to stick together** (coll) quedarse unidos, no abandonarse; **to stick up** destacarse; estar de punta *(el pelo);* **to stick up for** (coll) defender

sticker ['stɪkər] *s* etiqueta engomada, marbete engomado; punta, espina; (coll) problema arduo

sticking plaster *s* esparadrapo

stick'pin' *s* alfiler *m* de corbata

stick'-up' *s* (slang) asalto, atraco

stick·y ['stɪkɪ] *adj (comp* **-ier***; super* **-iest***)* pegajoso; (coll) húmedo, mojado; *(weather)* bochornoso

stiff [stɪf] *adj* tieso; entorpecido, entumecido; arduo, difícil; *(price)* (coll) excesivo ‖ *s* (slang) cadáver *m*

stiff collar *s* cuello almidonado

stiffen ['stɪfən] *tr* atiesar; endurecer; espesar ‖ *intr* atiesarse; endurecerse; espesarse; obstinarse

stiff neck *s* torticolis *m;* obstinación

stiff-necked ['stɪf,nɛkt] *adj* terco, obstinado

stiff shirt *s* camisola

stifle ['staɪfəl] *tr* ahogar, sofocar; apagar, suprimir

stig·ma ['stɪgmə] *s (pl* **-mas** o **-mata** [mətə]*)* estigma *m*

stigmatize ['stɪgmə,taɪz] *tr* estigmatizar

stilet·to [stɪ'lɛto] *s (pl* **-tos**) estilete *m,* puñal *m*

still [stɪl] *adj* inmóvil, quieto, tranquilo; callado, silencioso; (*wine*) no espumoso ‖ *adv* tranquilamente; silenciosamente; aún, todavía ‖ *conj* con todo, sin embargo ‖ *s* alambique *m*, destiladera; destilería; fotografía de lo inmóvil; (*poet*) silencio ‖ *tr* acallar; amortiguar; calmar ‖ *intr* callar; calmarse

still'birth' *s* parto muerto

still'born' *adj* nacido muerto

still life *s* (*pl* **still lifes** o **still lives**) bodegón *m*, naturaleza muerta

stilt [stɪlt] *s* zanco; (*in the water*) pilote *m*

stilted ['stɪltɪd] *adj* elevado; hinchado, pomposo, tieso

stimulant ['stɪmjələnt] *adj* & *s* estimulante *m*, excitante *m*

stimulate ['stɪmjə‚let] *tr* estimular

stimu·lus ['stɪmjələs] *s* (*pl* **-li** [‚laɪ]) estímulo

sting [stɪŋ] *s* picadura; aguijón *m* ‖ *v* (*pret* & *pp* **stung** [stʌŋ]) *tr* picar; aguijonear ‖ *intr* picar

stin·gy ['stɪndʒi] *adj* (*comp* **-gier**; *super* **-giest**) mezquino, tacaño

stink [stɪŋk] *s* hedor *m*, mal olor *m* ‖ *v* (*pret* **stank** [stæŋk] o **stunk** [stʌŋk]; *pp* **stunk**) *tr* dar mal olor a ‖ *intr* heder, oler muy mal; **to stink of** heder a; (*slang*) poseer (*p.ej.*, *dinero*) en un grado que da asco

stint [stɪnt] *s* faena, tarea ‖ *tr* limitar, restringir ‖ *intr* ser económico, ahorrar con mezquindad

stipend ['staɪpənd] *s* estipendio

stipulate ['stɪpjə‚let] *tr* estipular

stir [stʌr] *s* agitación, meneo; alboroto, tumulto; **to create a stir** meter ruido ‖ *v* (*pret* & *pp* **stirred**; *ger* **stirring**) *tr* agitar, mover; revolver; conmover, excitar; atizar, avivar (*el fuego*); remover (*un líquido*); **to stir up** revolver; despertar; conmover; fomentar (*discordias*) ‖ *intr* bullirse, moverse

stirring ['stʌrɪŋ] *adj* conmovedor, emocionante

stirrup ['stʌrəp] o ['stɪrəp] *s* estribo

stitch [stɪtʃ] *s* puntada, punto; pedazo de tela; punzada, dolor *m* punzante; (*coll*) poquito; **to be in stitches** (coll) desternillarse de risa ‖ *tr* coser, bastear, hilvanar ‖ *intr* coser

stock [stak] *adj* común, regular; banal, vulgar; bursátil; ganadero, del ganado; (*theat*) de repertorio ‖ *s* surtido; capital *f* comercial; acciones, valores *mpl*; (*of meat*) caldo; (*of a tree*) tronco; (*of an anvil*) cepo; (*of a rifle*) caja, culata; (*of a tree*; *of a family*) cepa; mango, manija; palo, madero; leño; (*livestock*) ganado; (*theat*) programa *m*, repertorio; **in stock** en existencia; **out of stock** agotado; **to take stock** hacer el inventario; **to take stock in** (coll) dar importancia a, confiar en ‖ *tr* abastecer, surtir; tener existencias de; acopiar, acumular; poblar (*un estanque, una colmena, etc.*)

stockade [sta'ked] *s* estacada, empalizada ‖ *tr* empalizar

stock'breed'er *s* criador *m* de ganado

stock'bro'ker *s* bolsista *mf*, corredor *m* de bolsa

stock car *s* (aut) coche *m* de serie; (rr) vagón *m* para el ganado

stock company *s* (com) sociedad anónima; (theat) teatro de repertorio

stock dividend *s* acción liberada

stock exchange *s* bolsa

stock'hold'er *s* accionista *mf*, tenedor *m* de acciones

stockholder of record *s* accionista *mf* que como tal figura en el libro-registro de la compañía

Stockholm ['stakhom] *s* Estocolmo

stocking ['stakɪŋ] *s* media

stock market *s* bolsa, mercado de valores; **to play the stock market** jugar a la bolsa

stock'pile' *s* reserva de materias primas ‖ *tr* acumular (*materias primas*) ‖ *intr* acumular materias primas

stock raising *s* ganadería

stock'room' *s* almacén *m*; sala de exposición

stock split *s* reparto de acciones gratis

stock·y ['staki] *adj* (*comp* **-ier**; *super* **-iest**) bajo, grueso y fornido

stock'yard' *s* corral *m* de concentración de ganado

stoic ['sto·ɪk] *adj* & *s* estoico

stoke [stok] *tr* atizar, avivar (*el fuego*); alimentar, cebar (*el horno*)

stoker ['stokər] *s* fogonero

stolid ['stalɪd] *adj* impasible, insensible

stomach ['stʌmək] *s* estómago; apetito; deseo, inclinación ‖ *tr* tragar; **to not be able to stomach** (coll) no poder tragar

stone [ston] *s* piedra; (*of fruit*) hueso; (pathol) mal *m* de piedra ‖ *tr* lapidar, apedrear; deshuesar (*la fruta*)

stone'-broke' *adj* arrancado, sin blanca

stone'-deaf' *adj* sordo como una tapia

stone'ma'son *s* albañil *m*

stone quarry *s* cantera, pedrera

stone's throw *s* tiro de piedra; **within a stone's throw** a tiro de piedra

ston·y ['stoni] *adj* (*comp* **-ier**; *super* **-iest**) pedregoso; duro, empedernido

stool [stul] *s* escabel *m*, taburete *m*; sillico, retrete *m*; (*bowel movement*) cámara, evacuación

stoop [stup] *s* encorvada, inclinación; escalinata de entrada ‖ *intr* doblarse, inclinarse, encorvarse; andar encorvado; humillarse, rebajarse

stoop-shouldered ['stup‚ʃoldərd] *adj* cargado de espaldas

stop [stap] *s* parada, alto; estada, estancia; cesación, fin *m*, suspensión; cerradura, tapadura; impedimento, obstáculo; freno; tope *m*, retén *m*; (*in writing*; *in telegrams*) punto; (*of a guitar*) llave *f*, traste *m*; **to put a stop to** poner fin a ‖ *v* (*pret* & *pp* **stopped**; *ger* **stopping**) *tr* parar, detener; acabar, terminar; estorbar, obstruir; interceptar; suspender; cerrar, tapar; rechazar (*un golpe*); retener (*un sueldo o parte de él*); **to stop up** cegar, obstruir, tapar ‖ *intr* parar, pararse, detenerse; quedarse; permanecer; alojarse, hospedarse; acabarse, terminarse; **to stop** + *ger* cesar de + *inf*, dejar de + *inf*

stop′cock′ *s* llave *f* de cierre, llave de paso

stop′gap′ *adj* provisional || *s* substituto provisional

stop light *s* luz *f* de parada

stop′o′ver *s* parada intermedia, escala; billete *m* de parada intermedia

stoppage ['stɑpɪdʒ] *s* parada, detención; (*of work*) paro; interrupción; suspensión; obstáculo; (*of wages*) retención; (pathol) obstrucción

stopper ['stɑpər] *s* tapón *m*; taco, tarugo

stop sign o **stop signal** *s* señal *f* de alto, señal de parada

stop watch *s* reloj *m* de segundos muertos, cronómetro

storage ['stɔrɪdʒ] *s* almacenaje *m*; (*costs*) derechos de almacenaje

storage battery *s* (elec) acumulador *m*

store [stɔr] *s* tienda, almacén *m*; **I know what is in store for you** sé lo que le espera; **to set store by** dar mucha importancia a || *tr* abastecer; tener guardado, almacenar; **to store away** acumular

store′house′ *s* almacén *m*, depósito; (*e.g., of wisdom*) (fig) mina

store′keep′er *s* tendero, almacenista *mf*

store′room′ *s* cuarto de almacenar; (*for furniture*) guardamuebles *m*; (naut) despensa

stork [stɔrk] *s* cigüeña; **to have a visit from the stork** recibir la cigüeña

storm [stɔrm] *s* borrasca, tempestad, tormenta; (mil) asalto; (naut) borrasca; (fig) tempestad, tumulto; **to take by storm** tomar por asalto || *tr* asaltar || *intr* tempestear; precipitarse

storm cloud *s* nubarrón *m*

storm door *s* contrapuerta, guardapuerta

storm sash *s* contravidriera

storm troops *spl* tropas de asalto

storm window *s* guardaventana, sobrevidriera

storm·y ['stɔrmi] *adj* (*comp* **-ier**; *super* **-iest**) borrascoso, tempestuoso; (*session, meeting, etc.*) tumultuoso

sto·ry ['stɔri] *s* (*pl* **-ries**) historia, cuento, anécdota; enredo, trama; (coll) mentira; piso, alto || *v* (*pret & pp* **-ried**) *tr* historiar

sto′ry·tel′ler *s* narrador *m*; (coll) mentiroso

stout [staut] *adj* corpulento, gordo, robusto; animoso; leal; terco || *s* cerveza obscura fuerte

stove [stov] *s* (*for heating a house or room*) estufa; (*for cooking*) hornillo, cocina de gas, cocina eléctrica

stove′pipe′ *s* tubo de estufa, tubo de hornillo; (*hat*) (coll) chistera, chimenea

stow [sto] *tr* guardar, meter, esconder; (naut) arrumar, estibar || *intr* — **to stow away** embarcarse clandestinamente, esconderse en un barco o avión

stowage ['sto·ɪdʒ] *s* arrumaje *m*, estiba

stow′a·way′ *s* llovido, polizón *m*

str. *abbr* **strait, steamer**

straddle ['strædəl] *s* esparrancamiento || *tr* montar a horcajadas; (coll) tratar de favorecer a ambas partes en (*p.ej., un pleito*) || *intr* ponerse a horcajadas; (coll) tratar de favorecer a ambas partes

strafe [strɑf] o [stref] *s* (slang) bombardeo violento || *tr* (slang) bombardear violentamente

straggle ['strægəl] *intr* errar, vagar; andar perdido, extraviarse; separarse; estar esparcido

straight [stret] *adj* derecho; recto; erguido; (*hair*) lacio; continuo, seguido; honrado, sincero; correcto; decidido, intransigente; (*e.g., whiskey*) solo; **to set a person straight** mostrar el camino a una persona; dar consejo a una persona; mostrar a una persona el modo de proceder || *adv* derecho; sin interrupción; sinceramente; exactamente; en seguida; **straight ahead** todo seguido, derecho; **to go straight** (coll) enmendarse

straighten ['stretən] *tr* enderezar; poner en orden || *intr* enderezarse

straight face *s* cara seria

straight′for′ward *adj* franco, sincero; honrado

straight off *adv* luego, en seguida

straight razor *s* navaja barbera

straight′way′ *adv* luego, en seguida

strain [stren] *s* tensión, tirantez *f*; esfuerzo muy grande; fatiga excesiva, agotamiento; (*of a muscle*) torcedura; aire *m*, melodía; (*of a family or lineage*) cepa; linaje *m*, raza; rasgo racial; genio, vena; huella, rastro || *tr* estirar; torcer o torcerse (*p.ej., la muñeca*); forzar (*p.ej., los nervios, la vista*); apretar; deformar; colar, tamizar || *intr* esforzarse; deformarse; colarse, tamizarse; filtrarse; exprimirse (*un jugo*); resistirse; **to strain at** hacer grandes esfuerzos por

strained [strend] *adj* (*smile*) forzado; (*friendship*) tirante

strainer ['strenər] *s* colador *m*

strait [stret] *s* estrecho; **straits** estrecho; **to be in dire straits** estar en el mayor apuro, hallarse en gran estrechez

strait jacket *s* camisa de fuerza

strait-laced ['stret,lest] *adj* gazmoño

strand [strænd] *s* playa; filamento; (*of rope or cable*) torón *m*, ramal *m*; (*of pearls*) hilo; pelo || *tr* deshebrar; retorcer trenzar (*cuerda, cable, etc.*); dejar extraviado; (naut) varar

stranded ['strændɪd] *adj* desprovisto, desamparado; (*ship*) encallado; (*rope or cable*) trenzado, retorcido

strange [strendʒ] *adj* extraño, singular; nuevo, desconocido; novel, no acostumbrado

stranger ['strendʒər] *s* forastero; visitador *m;* intruso; desconocido; principiante *mf*

strangle ['stræŋgəl] *tr* estrangular; reprimir, suprimir ‖ *intr* estrangularse

strap [stræp] *s (of leather)* correa; *(of cloth, metal, etc.)* banda, tira; *(to sharpen a razor)* asentador *m* ‖ *v (pret & pp strapped; ger strapping) tr* atar o liar con correa, banda o tira; azotar con una correa; fajar, vendar; asentar *(una navaja)*

strap'hang'er *s* (coll) pasajero colgado

stratagem ['strætədʒəm] *s* estratagema *f*

strategic(al) [strə'tidʒɪk(əl)] *adj* estratégico

strategist ['strætɪdʒɪst] *s* estratega *m*

strate·gy ['strætɪdʒɪ] *s (pl* -gies) estrategia

strati·fy ['strætɪˌfaɪ] *v (pret & pp -fied) tr* estratificar ‖ *intr* estratificarse

stratosphere ['strætəˌsfɪr] o ['stretəˌsfɪr] *s* estratosfera

stra·tum ['stretəm] o ['strætəm] *s (pl -ta* [tə] o *-tums)* estrato; *(e.g., of society)* clase *f*

straw [strɔ] *adj* pajizo; baladí, de poca importancia; falso; ficticio ‖ *s* paja; *(for drinking)* pajita; **I don't care a straw** no se me da un bledo; **to be the last straw** ser el colmo, no faltar más

straw'ber'ry *s (pl -*ries) fresa

straw hat *s* sombrero de paja; *(with low flat crown)* canotié *m*

straw man *s* figura de paja; *(figurehead)* testaferro; testigo falso

straw vote *s* voto informativo

stray [stre] *adj* extraviado, perdido; aislado, suelto ‖ *s* animal extraviado o perdido ‖ *intr* extraviarse, perderse

streak [strik] *s* lista, raya; vena, veta; rasgo, traza; *(of light)* rayo; *(of good luck)* racha; (coll) tiempo muy breve; **like a streak** (coll) como un rayo ‖ *tr* listar, rayar; abigarrar ‖ *intr* rayarse; (coll) andar o pasar como un rayo

stream [strim] *s (current)* corriente *f;* arroyo, río; chorro, flujo; *(of people)* torrente *m;* *(e.g., of automobiles)* desfile *m* ‖ *intr* correr, manar *(un líquido);* chorrear; flotar, ondear; salir a torrentes

streamer ['strimər] *s* flámula, banderola; cinta ondeante; rayo de luz

streamlined ['strim,laɪnd] *adj* aerodinámico, perfilado

stream'lin'er *s* tren aerodinámico de lujo

street [strit] *adj* callejero ‖ *s* calle *f*

street'car' *s* tranvía *m*

street cleaner *s* basurero; *(device)* barredera

street clothes *spl* traje *m* de calle

street floor *s* piso bajo

street lamp *s* farol *m* (de la calle)

street sprinkler ['sprɪŋklər] *s* carricuba, carro de riego, regadera

street'walk'er *s* cantonera, carrerista

strength [strɛŋθ] *s* fuerza; intensidad;

(of spirituous liquors) graduación; (com) tendencia a la subida; (mil) número; **on the strength of** fundándose en, confiando en

strengthen ['strɛŋθən] *tr* fortificar, reforzar; confirmar ‖ *intr* fortificarse, reforzarse

strenuous ['strɛnju·əs] *adj* estrenuo, enérgico, vigoroso; arduo, difícil

stress [strɛs] *s* tensión, fuerza; compulsión; acento; (mech) tensión; **to lay stress on** hacer hincapié en ‖ *tr* someter a esfuerzo; hacer hincapié en; acentuar

stress accent *s* acento prosódico

stretch [strɛtʃ] *s* estiramiento, estirón *m;* *(distance in time or space)* trecho; *(section of road)* tramo; extensión; *(of the imagination)* esfuerzo; *(confinement in jail)* (slang) condena; **at a stretch** de un tirón ‖ *tr* estirar; extender; tender; forzar, violentar; (fig) estirar *(el dinero);* **to stretch a point** hacer una concesión; **to stretch oneself** desperezarse ‖ *intr* estirarse; extenderse; tenderse; desperezarse; **to stretch out** (coll) echarse

stretcher ['strɛtʃər] *s (for gloves)* ensanchador *m;* *(for a painting)* bastidor *m;* *(to carry sick or wounded)* camilla

stretch'er-bear'er *s* camillero

strew [stru] *v (pret* strewed; *pp* strewed o strewn) *tr* derramar, esparcir; sembrar, salpicar; polvorear

stricken ['strɪkən] *adj* afligido; inhabilitado; herido; **stricken in years** debilitado por los años

strict [strɪkt] *adj* estricto, riguroso; *(exacting)* severo

stricture ['strɪktʃər] *s* crítica severa; (pathol) estrictura

stride [straɪd] *s* zancada, tranco; **to hit one's stride** alcanzar la actividad o velocidad acostumbrada; **to make great (o rapid) strides** avanzar a grandes pasos; **to take in one's stride** hacer sin esfuerzo ‖ *v (pret* strode [strod]; *pp* stridden ['strɪdən]) *tr* cruzar de un tranco; montar a horcajadas ‖ *intr* dar zancadas, caminar a paso largo, andar a trancos

strident ['straɪdənt] *adj* estridente

strife [straɪf] *s* contienda; rivalidad

strike [straɪk] *s (blow)* golpe *m;* *(stopping of work)* huelga; *(discovery of ore, oil, etc.)* descubrimiento repentino; golpe *m* de fortuna; **to go on strike** ir a la huelga ‖ *v (pret & pp* struck [strʌk]) *tr* golpear; pulsar *(una tecla);* herir, percutir; topar, dar con; acuñar *(monedas);* echar *(raíces);* frotar, rayar, encender *(un fósforo);* descubrir repentinamente *(mineral, aceite, etc.);* cerrar *(un trato);* arriar *(las velas);* dar *(la hora);* asumir, tomar *(una postura);* borrar, cancelar; impresionar; atraer *(la atención);* **to strike it rich** descubrir un buen filón, tener un golpe de fortuna ‖ *intr* dar, sonar *(una campana, un reloj);* declararse en huelga;

(mil) dar el asalto; **to strike out** ponerse en marcha, echar camino adelante

strike'break'er s rompehuelgas m, esquirol m

striker ['straɪkər] s golpeador m; huelguista mf

striking ['straɪkɪŋ] adj impresionante, llamativo, sorprendente; en huelga

striking power s potencia de choque

string [strɪŋ] s cuerdecilla; (of pearls; of lies) sarta; (of beans) hebra; (of onions or garlic) ristra; (row) hilera; (mus) cuerda; (limitation, proviso) (coll) condición; **strings** instrumentos de cuerda; **to pull strings** tocar resortes || v (pret & pp **strung** [strʌŋ]) tr enhebrar, ensartar; atar con cuerdas; proveer de cuerdas; colgar de una cuerda; tender (un cable, un alambre); encordar (un violín, una raqueta); colocar en fila; (slang) engañar, burlar; **to string along** (slang) traer al retortero; **to string up** (coll) ahorcar

string bean s habichuela verde, judía verde

stringed instrument [strɪŋd] s instrumento de cuerda

stringent ['strɪndʒənt] adj riguroso, severo, estricto; convincente

string quartet s cuarteto de cuerdas

strip [strɪp] s tira; (of metal) lámina; (of land) faja || v (pret & pp **stripped**; ger **stripping**) tr desnudar; despojar; desforrar; deshacer (la cama); estropear (el engranaje, un tornillo); desvenar (tabaco); descortezar; **to strip of** despojar de || intr desnudarse; despojarse; descortezarse

stripe [straɪp] s banda, lista, raya; gaya; cinta, franja; (mil & nav) galón m; índole f, tipo; **to win one's stripes** ganar los entorchados || tr listar, rayar; gayar

strip mining s mineraje m a tajo abierto

strive [straɪv] v (pret **strove** [strov]; pp **striven** ['strɪvən]) intr esforzarse; luchar

stroke [strok] s golpe m; (of bell or clock) campanada; (of pen) plumada; (of brush) pincelada, brochada; (of arms in swimming) brazada; (in a game) jugada; (caress with hand) caricia; (with a racket) raquetazo; (of a piston) carrera, embolada; (of a paddle) palada; (of an oar) remada; (of lightning) rayo; (line, mark) raya; (of good luck) golpe m; (of wit) agudeza, chiste m; (of genius) rasgo; ataque m de parálisis; **at the stroke of** (e.g., five) al dar las (p.ej., cinco); **to not do a stroke of work** no dar golpe, no levantar paja del suelo || tr frotar suavemente, acariciar con la mano

stroll [strol] s paseo; **to take a stroll** dar un paseo || intr pasear, pasearse; callejear, errar, vagar

stroller ['strolər] s paseante mf; cochecito para niños

strong [strɔŋ] o [strɑŋ] adj fuerte,

resistente; recio, robusto; intenso; (stock market) firme; enérgico; marcado; picante; rancio

strong'box' s cofre m fuerte, caja de caudales

strong drink s bebida alcohólica, bebida fuerte

strong'hold' s plaza fuerte

strong man s (e.g., in a circus) hércules m; (leader, good planner) alma, promotor m; (dictator) hombre m fuerte

strong-minded ['strɔŋ‚maɪndɪd] o ['strɑŋ‚maɪndɪd] adj independiente; de inteligencia vigorosa; (e.g., woman) hombruna

strontium ['strɑnʃɪ‚əm] s estroncio

strop [strɑp] s suavizador m || v (pret & pp **stropped**; ger **stropping**) tr suavizar, afilar

strophe ['strofɪ] s estrofa

structure ['strʌktʃər] s estructura; edificio

struggle ['strʌgəl] s lucha; esfuerzo, forcejeo || intr luchar; esforzarse, forcejear

strum [strʌm] v (pret & pp **strummed**; ger **strumming**) tr arañar (un instrumento músico) sin arte || intr cencerrear; **to strum on** rasguear

strumpet ['strʌmpɪt] s ramera

strut [strʌt] s (brace, prop) riostra, tornapunta; contoneo, pavoneo || v (pret & pp **strutted**; ger **strutting**) intr contonearse, pavonearse

strychnine ['strɪknaɪn] o ['strɪknɪn] s estricnina

stub [stʌb] s fragmento, trozo; (of a cigar) colilla; (of a tree) tocón m; (of a pencil) cabo; (of a check) talón m || v (pret & pp **stubbed**; ger **stubbing**) tr — **to stub one's toe** dar un tropezón

stubble ['stʌbəl] s rastrojo; (of beard) cañón m

stubborn ['stʌbərn] adj terco, testarudo, obstinado; porfiado; intratable

stucco ['stʌko] s (pl **-coes** o **-cos**) estuco || tr estucar

stuck'-up' adj (coll) estirado, orgulloso

stud [stʌd] s tachón m; botón m de camisa; montante m, pie derecho; clavo de adorno; (bolt) espárrago; caballeriza; (of mares) yeguada || v (pret & pp **studded**; ger **studding**) tr tachonar

stud bolt s espárrago

stud'book' s registro genealógico de caballos

student ['stjudənt] o ['studənt] adj estudiantil || s estudiante mf; (person who investigates) estudioso

student body s estudiantado, alumnado

stud'horse' s caballo padre, caballo semental

studied ['stʌdɪd] adj premeditado, hecho adrede; (affected) estudiado

studi·o ['stjudɪ‚o] o ['studɪ‚o] s (pl **-os**) estudio, taller m; (mov & rad) estudio

studious ['stjudɪ‚əs] o ['studɪ‚əs] adj estudioso; asiduo, solícito

stud·y ['stʌdɪ] s (pl **-ies**) estudio; solicitud; meditación profunda; (e.g., *of a professor*) gabinete *m*, estudio ‖ *v* (*pret & pp* **-ied**) *tr & intr* estudiar

stuff [stʌf] *s* materia; género, paño, tela; muebles *mpl*, baratijas; medicina; fruslerías; cosa, cosas ‖ *tr* rellenar; henchir, llenar; atascar, cerrar, tapar; embutir; (*with food*) atracar; meter sin orden, llenar sin orden; disecar (*un animal muerto*) ‖ *intr* atracarse, hartarse

stuffed shirt *s* (slang) tragavirotes *m*

stuffing ['stʌfɪŋ] *s* relleno

stuff·y ['stʌfi] *adj* (*comp* **-ier**; *super* **-iest**) sofocante, mal ventilado; aburrido, sin interés; (*prim*) (coll) relamido

stumble ['stʌmbəl] *intr* tropezar, dar un traspié; moverse a tropezones; hablar a tropezones; **to stumble on** o **upon** tropezar con

stumbling block *s* escollo, tropezadero

stump [stʌmp] *s* (*of a tree, arm, etc.*) tocón *m*; (*of an arm*) muñón *m*; (*of a tooth*) raigón *m*; (*of a cigar*) colilla; (*of a tail*) rabo; paso pesado; fragmento, resto; tribuna pública; (*for shading drawings*) esfumino ‖ *tr* recorrer (*el país*) pronunciando discursos políticos; (coll) confundir, dejar sin habla; esfumar

stump speaker *s* orador callejero

stump speech *s* arenga electoral

stun [stʌn] *v* (*pret & pp* **stunned**; *ger* **stunning**) *tr* atolondrar, aturdir

stunning ['stʌnɪŋ] *adj* (coll) pasmoso, estupendo, pistonudo, elegante

stunt [stʌnt] *s* atrofia. (*underdeveloped creature*) engendro; (coll) suerte acrobática; (coll) faena, hazaña, proeza ‖ *tr* atrofiar ‖ *intr* (coll) hacer suertes acrobáticas

stunt flying *s* vuelo acrobático

stunt man *s* (mov) doble *m* que hace suertes peligrosas

stupe·fy ['stjupɪ,faɪ] o ['stupɪ,faɪ] *v* (*pret & pp* **-fied**) *tr* dejar estupefacto, pasmar; causar estupor a

stupendous [stju'pɛndəs] o [stu'pɛndəs] *adj* estupendo; enorme

stupid ['stjupɪd] o ['stupɪd] *adj* estúpido

stupor ['stjupər] o ['stupər] *s* estupor *m*, modorra

stur·dy ['stʌrdi] *adj* (*comp* **-dier**; *super* **-diest**) fuerte, robusto, fornido; firme, tenaz

sturgeon ['stʌrdʒən] *s* esturión *m*

stutter ['stʌtər] *s* tartamudeo ‖ *tr* decir tartamudeando ‖ *intr* tartamudear

sty [staɪ] *s* (*pl* **sties**) pocilga, zahúrda; (pathol) orzuelo

style [staɪl] *s* estilo; moda; elegancia; **to live in great style** vivir en gran lujo ‖ *tr* intitular, nombrar

stylish ['staɪlɪʃ] *adj* de moda, elegante

styptic pencil ['stɪptɪk] *s* lápiz estíptico

Styx [stɪks] *s* Estigia

suave [swɑv] o [swev] *adj* suave; afable, fino, zalamero, pulido

sub. *abbr* **subscription, substitute, suburban**

subaltern [səb'ɔltərn] *adj & s* subalterno

subconscious [səb'kɑnʃəs] *adj* subconsciente ‖ *s* subconsciencia

subconsciousness [səb'kɑnʃəsnɪs] *s* subconsciencia

subdeb ['sʌb,dɛb] *s* tobillera

subdivide ['sʌbdɪ,vaɪd] o [,sʌbdɪ-'vaɪd] *tr* subdividir ‖ *intr* subdividirse

subdue [səb'dju] o [səb'du] *tr* sojuzgar, subyugar; amansar, dominar; suavizar

subdued [səb'djud] o [səb'dud] *adj* sojuzgado; sumiso; (*e.g., light*) suave

subheading ['sʌb,hɛdɪŋ] *s* subtítulo

subject ['sʌbdʒɪkt] *adj* sujeto; súbdito ‖ *s* asunto, materia, tema *m*; (*person in his relationship to a ruler or government*) súbdito; (gram, med, philos) sujeto ‖ [səb'dʒɛkt] *tr* sujetar, someter, sojuzgar

subject index *s* índice *m* de materias

subjection [səb'dʒɛkʃən] *s* sumisión, sometimiento

subjective [səb'dʒɛktɪv] *adj* subjetivo

subject matter *s* asunto, materia

subjugate ['sʌbdʒə,get] *tr* subyugar

subjunctive [səb'dʒʌŋktɪv] *adj & s* subjuntivo

sub·let ['sʌb'lɛt] o ['sʌb,lɛt] *v* (*pret & pp* **-let**; *ger* **-letting**) *tr* realquilar, subarrendar

submachine gun [,sʌbmə'ʃin] *s* subfusil *m* ametrallador

submarine ['sʌbmə,rin] *adj & s* submarino ‖ *tr* (coll) atacar o hundir con un submarino

submarine chaser ['tʃesər] *s* cazasubmarinos *m*

submerge [səb'mʌrdʒ] *tr* sumergir ‖ *intr* sumergirse

submersion [səb'mʌrʒən] o [səb'mʌrʃən] *s* sumersión

submission [səb'mɪʃən] *s* sumisión

submissive [səb'mɪsɪv] *adj* sumiso

sub·mit [səb'mɪt] *v* (*pret & pp* **-mitted**; *ger* **-mitting**) *tr* someter; proponer, permitirse decir ‖ *intr* someterse

subordinate [səb'ɔrdɪnɪt] *adj & s* subordinado ‖ [səb'ɔrdɪ,net] *tr* subordinar

subornation of perjury [,sʌbər'neʃən] *s* (law) soborno de testigo

subplot ['sʌb,plɑt] *s* trama secundaria

subpoena o **subpena** [sʌb'pinə] o [sə'pinə] *s* comparendo ‖ *tr* mandar comparecer

sub rosa [sʌb'rozə] *adv* en secreto, en confianza

subscribe [səb'skraɪb] *tr* subscribir ‖ *intr* subscribir; subscribirse, abonarse; **to subscribe to** subscribirse a, abonarse a (*una publicación periódica*); subscribir (*una opinión*)

subscriber [səb'skraɪbər] *s* abonado

subsequent ['sʌbsɪkwənt] *adj* subsiguiente, posterior

subservient [səb'sʌrvɪ·ənt] *adj* servil; subordinado; útil

subside [səb'saɪd] *intr* calmarse; acabarse, cesar; bajar (*el nivel del agua*); amainar (*el viento*)

subsidize ['sʌbsɪ‚daɪz] *tr* subsidiar, subvencionar; (*to bribe*) sobornar
subsi‧dy ['sʌbsɪdi] *s* (*pl* -dies) subsidio, subvención
subsist [səb'sɪst] *intr* subsistir
subsistence |seb'sɪstəns] *s* subsistencia
substance ['sʌbstəns] *s* substancia
substandard [sʌb'stændərd] *adj* inferior al nivel normal
substantial [səb'stænʃəl] *adj* considerable, importante; fuerte, sólido; acomodado, rico; esencial; (*food*) substancial
substantiate [səb'stænʃɪ‚et] *tr* comprobar, establecer, verificar
substantive ['sʌbstəntɪv] *adj* & *s* substantivo
substation ['sʌb‚steʃən] *s* (elec) subcentral *f*
substitute ['sʌbstɪ‚tjut] o ['sʌbstɪ‚tut] *adj* substitutivo || *s* (*person*) substituto; (*thing, substance*) substitutivo; (mil) reemplazo || *tr* poner (*a una persona o cosa*) en lugar de otra || *intr* actuar de substituto; **to substitute for** substituir (with personal *a*)
substitution [‚sʌbstɪ'tjuʃən] o [‚sʌbstɪ'tuʃən] *s* empleo o uso (de una persona o cosa en lugar de otra); (chem, law, math) substitución; (coll) imitación fraudulenta
subterranean [‚sʌbtə'renɪ‧ən] *adj* & *s* subterráneo
subtitle ['sʌb‚taɪtəl] *s* subtítulo || *tr* subtitular
subtle ['sʌtəl] *adj* sutil; astuto; insidioso
subtle‧ty ['sʌtəlti] *s* (*pl* -ties) sutileza; agudeza; distinción sutil
subtract [səb'trækt] *tr* substraer; (math) substraer, restar
suburb ['sʌbɑrb] *s* suburbio, arrabal *m;* **the suburbs** las afueras, los barrios externos
subvention [səb'venʃən] *s* subvención || *tr* subvencionar
subversive [səb'vʌrsɪv] *adj* subversivo || *s* subversor *m*
subvert [səb'vʌrt] *tr* subvertir
subway ['sʌb‚we] *s* galería subterránea; metro, ferrocarril subterráneo
succeed [sək'sid] *tr* suceder (*a una persona o cosa*) || *intr* tener buen éxito
success [sək'ses] *s* buen éxito
successful [sək'sesfəl] *adj* feliz, próspero; acertado; logrado
succession [sək'seʃən] *s* sucesión; **in succession** seguidos, uno tras otro
successive [sək'sesɪv] *adj* sucesivo
succor ['sʌkər] *s* socorro || *tr* socorrer
succotash ['sʌkə‚tæʃ] *s* guiso de maíz tierno y habas
succumb [sə'kʌm] *intr* sucumbir
such [sʌtʃ] *adj* & *pron* indef tal, semejante; **such a** tal, semejante; **such a** + *adj* un tan + *adj;* **such as** quienes, los que
suck [sʌk] *s* chupada; mamada || *tr* chupar; mamar; aspirar (*el aire*)
sucker ['sʌkər] *s* chupador *m;* mamón

m; (bot & mach) chupón *m;* (coll) bobo, primo
suckle ['sʌkəl] *tr* lactar; criar, educar
suckling pig ['sʌklɪŋ] *s* lechón *m,* cerdo de leche
suction ['sʌkʃən] *adj* aspirante || *s* succión
sudden ['sʌdən] *adj* súbito, repentino; **all of a sudden** de repente
suds [sʌdz] *spl* jabonadura; (coll) espuma, cerveza
sue [su] o [sju] *tr* demandar; pedir; (law) procesar || *intr* (law) poner pleito, entablar juicio; **to sue for damages** demandar por daños y perjuicios; **to sue for peace** pedir la paz
suede [swed] *s* gamuza, ante *m*
suet ['su‧ɪt] o ['sju‧ɪt] *s* sebo
suffer ['sʌfər] *tr* & *intr* sufrir, padecer
sufferance ['sʌfərəns] *s* tolerancia; paciencia; **on sufferance** por tolerancia
suffering ['sʌfərɪŋ] *adj* doliente || *s* dolencia, sufrimiento
suffice [sə'faɪs] *intr* bastar, ser suficiente
sufficient [sə'fɪʃənt] *adj* suficiente
suffix ['sʌfɪks] *s* sufijo
suffocate ['sʌfə‚ket] *tr* sofocar || *intr* sofocarse
suffrage ['sʌfrɪdʒ] *s* sufragio; aprobación, voto favorable
suffragette [‚sʌfrə'dʒet] *s* sufragista (*mujer*)
suffuse [sə'fjuz] *tr* saturar, bañar
sugar ['ʃugər] *adj* azucarero || *s* azúcar *m* || *tr* azucarar
sugar beet *s* remolacha azucarera
sugar bowl *s* azucarero
sugar cane *s* caña de azúcar
sug'ar-coat' *tr* azucarar; (fig) endulzar, dorar
suggest [səg'dʒest] *tr* sugerir
suggestion [səg'dʒestʃən] *s* sugestión, sugerencia; sombra, traza ligera
suggestive [səg'dʒestɪv] *adj* sugestivo; sicaliptico
suicidal [‚su‧ɪ'saɪdəl] o [‚sju‧ɪ'saɪdəl] *adj* suicida
suicide ['su‧ɪ‚saɪd] o ['sju‧ɪ‚saɪd] *s* (*act*) suicidio; (*person*) suicida *mf;* **to commit suicide** suicidarse
suit [sut] o [sjut] *s* traje *m,* terno; (*of a lady*) traje *m* sastre; (*group forming a set*) juego; (*of cards*) palo; petición, súplica; cortejo, galanteo; (law) pleito, proceso; **to follow suit** servir del palo; seguir la corriente || *tr* adaptar, ajustar; adaptarse a; sentar, ir o venir bien a; favorecer, satisfacer; **to suit oneself** hacer (*uno*) lo que le guste || *intr* convenir, ser a propósito
suitable ['sutəbəl] o ['sjutəbəl] *adj* apropiado, conveniente, adecuado
suit'case' *s* maleta, valija
suite [swit] *s* comitiva, séquito; (*group forming a set*) juego; serie *f;* (*of rooms*) crujía; habitación salón; (mus) suite *f*
suiting ['sutɪŋ] o ['sjutɪŋ] *s* corte *m* de traje
suit of clothes *s* traje completo (*de hombre*)

suitor ['sutər] o ['sjutər] s pretendiente m; (law) demandante mf

sulfa drugs ['sʌlfə] spl medicamentos sulfas

sulfate ['sʌlfet] s sulfato

sulfide ['sʌlfaɪd] s sulfuro

sulfite ['sʌlfaɪt] s sulfito

sulfur ['sʌlfər] s (chem) azufre m; véase **sulphur**

sulfuric [sʌl'fjurɪk] adj sulfúrico

sulfur mine s azufrera

sulfurous ['sʌlfərəs] adj sulfuroso || ['sʌlfərəs] o [sʌl'fjurəs] adj (chem) sulfuroso

sulk [sʌlk] s murria || intr amorrarse, enfurruñarse

sulk·y ['sʌlki] adj (comp -ier; super -iest) enfurruñado, murrio, resentido

sullen ['sʌlən] adj hosco, malhumorado, taciturno, triste

sul·ly ['sʌli] v (pret & pp -lied) tr empañar, manchar

sulphur ['sʌlfər] adj azufrado || s azufre m; color de azufre || tr azufrar

sultan ['sʌltən] s sultán m

sul·try ['sʌltri] adj (comp -trier; super -triest) bochornoso, sofocante

sum [sʌm] s suma; (coll) problema m de aritmética || v (pret & pp summed; ger summing) tr sumar; to **sum up** sumar, resumir

sumac o **sumach** [ʃ'ʃumæk] o ['sumæk] s zumaque m

summarize ['sʌmə,raɪz] tr resumir

summa·ry ['sʌməri] adj sumario || s (pl -ries) sumario, resumen m

summer ['sʌmər] adj estival, veraniego || s verano, estío || intr veranear

summer resort s lugar m de veraneo

summersault ['sʌmər,sɔlt] s salto mortal || intr dar un salto mortal

summer school s escuela de verano

summery ['sʌməri] adj estival, veraniego

summit ['sʌmɪt] s cima, cumbre f

summit conference s conferencia en la cumbre

summon ['sʌmən] tr convocar, llamar; evocar; (law) citar, emplazar

summons ['sʌmənz] s orden f, señal f; (law) citación, emplazamiento f || tr (coll) citar, emplazar

sumptuous ['sʌmptʃu·əs] adj suntuoso

sun [sʌn] s sol m; to **have a place in the sun** ocupar su puesto en el mundo || v (pret & pp sunned; ger sunning) tr asolear || intr asolearse

sun bath s baño de sol

sun'beam' s rayo de sol

sun'bon'net s papalina

sun'burn' s quemadura de sol || v (pret & pp -burned o burnt) tr quemar al sol || intr quemarse al sol

sundae ['sʌndi] s helado con frutas, jarabes o nueces

Sunday ['sʌndi] adj dominical; (used or worn on Sunday) dominguero || s domingo

Sunday best s (coll) trapos de cristianar, ropa dominguera

Sunday's child s niño nacido de pies, niño mimado de la fortuna

Sunday school s escuela dominical, doctrina dominical

sunder ['sʌndər] tr separar; romper

sun'di'al s reloj m de sol, cuadrante m solar

sun'down' s puesta del sol

sundries ['sʌndriz] spl artículos diversos

sundry ['sʌndri] adj diversos, varios

sun'flow'er s girasol m, tornasol m

sun'glass'es spl gafas de sol, gafas para el sol

sunken ['sʌŋkən] adj hundido, sumido

sun lamp s lámpara de rayos ultravioletas

sun'light' s luz f del sol

sun'lit' adj iluminado por el sol

sun·ny ['sʌni] adj (comp -nier; super -niest) de sol; asoleado; brillante, resplandeciente; alegre, risueño; to **be sunny** hacer sol

sunny side s sol m; (fig) lado bueno, lado favorable

sun porch s solana

sun'rise' s salida del sol; **from sunrise to sunset** de sol a sol

sun'set' s puesta del sol

sun'shade' s quitasol m, sombrilla; toldo; visera contra el sol

sun'shine' s claridad del sol; alegría; **in the sunshine** al sol

sun'spot' s mancha solar

sun'stroke' s insolación

sup. abbr **superior**, **supplement**

sup [sʌp] v (pret & pp supped; ger supping) intr cenar

superannuated [,supər'ænju,etɪd] adj jubilado, inhabilitado por ancianidad o enfermedad; fuera de moda

superb [su'pʌrb] o [sə'pʌrb] adj soberbio, estupendo, magnífico

supercar·go ['supər,kargo] s (pl -goes o -gos) (naut) sobrecargo

supercharge [,supər'tʃardʒ] tr sobrealimentar

supercilious [,supər'sɪlɪ·əs] adj arrogante, altanero, desdeñoso

superficial [,supər'fɪʃəl] adj superficial

superfluous [su'pʌrflu·əs] adj superfluo

superhuman [,supər'hjumən] adj sobrehumano

superimpose [,supərɪm'poz] tr sobreponer

superintendent [,supərɪn'tendənt] s superintendente mf

superior [sə'pɪrɪ·ər] o [su'pɪrɪ·ər] adj superior; indiferente, sereno; arrogante; (typ) volado || s superior m

superiority [sə,pɪrɪ'arɪti] o [su,pɪrɪ'arɪti] s superioridad; indiferencia, serenidad; arrogancia

superlative [sə'pʌrlətɪv] o [su'pʌrlə-tɪv] adj & s superlativo

super·man ['supər,mæn] s (pl -men [,men]) sobrehombre m, superhombre m

supermarket ['supər,markɪt] s supermercado

supernatural [,supər'nætʃərəl] adj sobrenatural

superpose [,supər'poz] tr sobreponer, superponer

supersede [ˌsupərˈsid] *tr* reemplazar; desalojar

supersonic [ˌsupərˈsɑnɪk] *adj* supersónico ‖ **supersonics** *ssg* supersónica

superstitious [ˌsupərˈstɪʃəs] *adj* supersticioso

supervene [ˌsupərˈvin] *intr* sobrevenir

supervise [ˈsupərˌvaɪz] *tr* superintender, supervisar, dirigir

supervisor [ˈsupərˌvaɪzər] *s* superintendente *mf*, supervisor *m*, dirigente *mf*

supp. *abbr* **supplement**

supper [ˈsʌpər] *s* cena

supplant [səˈplænt] *tr* reemplazar

supple [ˈsʌpəl] *adj* flexible; dócil

supplement [ˈsʌplɪmənt] *s* suplemento ‖ [ˈsʌplɪˌment] *tr* suplir, completar

suppliant [ˈsʌplɪˌənt] *adj & s* suplicante *mf*

supplication [ˌsʌplɪˈkeʃən] *s* súplica

sup·ply [səˈplaɪ] *s* (*pl* **-plies**) suministro, provisión; surtido, repuesto; oferta, existencia; **supplies** pertrechos, provisiones, víveres *mfj*; artículos, efectos ‖ *v* (*pret & pp* **-plied**) *tr* suministrar, aprovisionar; reemplazar

supply and demand *spl* oferta y demanda

support [səˈport] *s* apoyo, soporte *m*, sostén *m*; sustento ‖ *tr* apoyar, soportar, sostener; sustentar; aguantar

supporter [səˈportər] *s* partidario, (*jockstrap*) suspensorio; faja abdominal, faja medical

suppose [səˈpoz] *tr* suponer; creer; **to be supposed to** deber; **to suppose so** creer que sí

supposed [səˈpozd] *adj* supuesto

supposition [ˌsʌpəˈzɪʃən] *s* suposición

suppos·i·to·ry [səˈpazɪˌtori] *s* (*pl* **-ries**) supositorio

suppress [səˈpres] *tr* suprimir

suppression [səˈpreʃən] *s* supresión

suppurate [ˈsʌpjəˌret] *intr* supurar

supreme [səˈprim] o [suˈprim] *adj* supremo

supt. *abbr* **superintendent**

surcharge [ˈsʌrˌtʃɑrdʒ] *s* sobrecarga ‖ [ˌsʌrˈtʃɑrdʒ] o [ˈsʌrˌtʃɑrdʒ] *tr* sobrecargar

sure [ʃur] *adj* seguro; **to be sure** seguramente, sin duda ‖ *adv* (coll) seguramente, claro; **sure enough** efectivamente

sure thing *adv* (slang) seguramente ‖ *interj* ¡claro!, ¡seguro! ‖ *s* (slang) sacabocados *m*

sure·ty [ˈʃurti] o [ˈʃurɪti] *s* (*pl* **-ties**) seguridad, garantía, fianza

surf [sʌrf] *s* cachones *mpl*, olas que rompen en la playa

surface [ˈsʌrfɪs] *adj* superficial ‖ *s* superficie *f* ‖ *tr* alisar, allanar; recubrir ‖ *intr* emerger (*p.ej., un submarino*)

surface mail *s* correo por vía ordinaria

surf'board' *s* patín *m* de mar

surfeit [ˈsʌrfɪt] *s* exceso; hartura, hastío; empacho, indigestión ‖ *tr* atracar, hastiar; encebadar (*las bestias*) ‖ *intr* atracarse, hastiarse; encebadarse

surf'-rid'ing *s* patinaje *m* sobre las olas

surge [sʌrdʒ] *s* oleada; (elec) sobretensión ‖ *intr* agitarse, ondular

surgeon [ˈsʌrdʒən] *s* cirujano

surger·y [ˈsʌrdʒəri] *s* (*pl* **-ies**) cirugía; sala de operaciones

surgical [ˈsʌrdʒɪkəl] *adj* quirúrgico

sur·ly [ˈsʌrli] *adj* (*comp* **-lier**; *super* **-liest**) áspero, rudo, hosco, insolente

surmise [sərˈmaɪz] o [ˈsʌrmaɪz] *s* conjetura, suposición ‖ [sərˈmaɪz] *tr & intr* conjeturar, suponer

surmount [sərˈmaunt] *tr* levantarse sobre; aventajar, sobrepujar; superar; coronar

surname [ˈsʌrˌnem] *s* apellido; (*added name*) sobrenombre *m* ‖ *tr* apellidar; sobrenombrar

surpass [sərˈpæs] o [sərˈpas] *tr* aventajar, sobrepasar

surplice [ˈsʌrplɪs] *s* sobrepelliz *f*

surplus [ˈsʌrpləs] *adj* sobrante, excedente ‖ *s* sobrante *m*, exceso; (com) superávit *m*

surprise [sərˈpraɪz] *adj* inesperado, improviso ‖ *s* sorpresa; **to take by surprise** coger por sorpresa ‖ *tr* sorprender

surprise package *s* sorpresa

surprise party *s* reunión improvisada para felicitar por sorpresa a una persona

surprising [sərˈpraɪzɪŋ] *adj* sorprendente

surrender [səˈrendər] *s* rendición ‖ *tr* rendir ‖ *intr* rendirse

surrender value *s* (ins) valor *m* de rescate

surreptitious [ˌsʌrepˈtɪʃəs] *adj* subrepticio

surround [səˈraund] *tr* cercar, rodear, circundar; (mil) sitiar

surrounding [səˈraundɪŋ] *adj* circundante, circunstante ‖ **surroundings** *spl* alrededores *mpl*, contornos; ambiente *m*, medio

surtax [ˈsʌrˌtæks] *s* impuesto complementario

surveillance [sərˈveləns] o [sərˈveljəns] *s* vigilancia

survey [ˈsʌrve] *s* estudio, examen *m*, inspección, reconocimiento; agrimensura, medición, plano; levantamiento de planos; (*of opinion*) encuesta; (*of literature*) bosquejo ‖ [sərˈve] o [ˈsʌrve] *tr* estudiar, examinar, inspeccionar, reconocer; medir; levantar el plano de ‖ *intr* levantar el plano

surveyor [sərˈve·ər] *s* inspector *m*; agrimensor *m*

survival [sərˈvaɪvəl] *s* supervivencia

survive [sərˈvaɪv] *tr* sobrevivir a (*otra persona; algún acontecimiento*) ‖ *intr* sobrevivir

surviving [sərˈvaɪvɪŋ] *adj* sobreviviente

survivor [sərˈvaɪvər] *s* sobreviviente *mf*

survivorship [sərˈvaɪvərˌʃɪp] *s* (law) sobrevivencia

susceptible [səˈseptɪbəl] *adj* susceptible; (*to love*) enamoradizo

suspect [ˈsʌspekt] o [səsˈpekt] *adj &*

s sospechoso ‖ [səs'pɛkt] *tr* sospechar

suspend [səs'pɛnd] *tr* suspender ‖ *intr* dejar de obrar; suspender pagos

suspenders [səs'pɛndərz] *spl* tirantes *mpl*

suspense [səs'pɛns] *s* suspenso, suspensión; duda, incertidumbre; indecisión, irresolución; ansiedad

suspension bridge [səs'pɛn/ən] *s* puente *m* colgante

suspicion [səs'pɪ/ən] *s* sospecha, suspicacia; sombra, traza ligera

suspicious [səs'pɪ/əs] *adj* (*inclined to suspect*) suspicaz; (*subject to suspicion*) sospechoso

sustain [səs'ten] *tr* sostener, sustentar; apoyar, defender; confirmar, probar; sufrir (*p.ej.*, *un daño*, *una pérdida*)

sustenance ['sʌstɪnəns] *s* sustento, alimentos; sostenimiento

sutler ['sʌtlər] *s* (mil) vivandero

swab [swab] *s* escobón *m*, estropajo; (naut) lampazo; (surg) tapón *m* de algodón ‖ *v* (*pret & pp* swabbed; *ger* swabbing) *tr* fregar, limpiar; (naut) lampacear; (surg) limpiar con algodón

swaddle ['swadəl] *tr* empañar, fajar

swaddling clothes *spl* pañales *mpl*

swagger ['swægər] *adj* (coll) muy elegante ‖ *s* fanfarronada; contoneo, paso jactancioso ‖ *intr* fanfarronear; contonear

swain [swen] *s* (*lad*) zagal; galán *m*, amante *m*

swallow ['swalo] *s* trago; (orn) golondrina ‖ *tr* tragar, deglutir; (fig) tragar, tragarse ‖ *intr* tragar, deglutir

swallow-tailed coat ['swalo,teld] *s* frac *m*

swal'low·wort' *s* vencetósigo

swamp [swamp] *s* pantano, marisma ‖ *tr* encharcar, inundar; (*e.g.*, *with work*) abrumar

swamp·y ['swampɪ] *adj* (*comp* -ier; *super* -iest) pantanoso

swan [swan] *s* cisne *m*

swan dive *s* salto de ángel

swank [swæŋk] *adj* (slang) elegante, vistoso ‖ *s* (slang) elegancia vistosa

swan knight *s* caballero del cisne

swan's-down ['swanz,daun] *s* plumón *m* de cisne; moletón *m*, paño de vicuña

swan song *s* canto del cisne

swap [swap] *s* (coll) trueque *m*, cambalache *m* ‖ *v* (*pret & pp* swapped; *ger* swapping) *tr & intr* trocar, cambalachear

swarm [sworm] *s* enjambre *m* ‖ *intr* enjambrar; volar en enjambres; hormiguear (*una multitud de gente o animales*)

swarth·y ['swɔrðɪ] o ['swɔrθɪ] *adj* (*comp* -ier; *super* -iest) atezado, carinegro, moreno

swashbuckler ['swaʃ,bʌklər] *s* espadachín *m*, matasiete *m*, valentón *m*

swat [swat] *s* (coll) golpe violento ‖ *v* (*pret & pp* swatted; *ger* swatting) *tr* (coll) golpear con fuerza; (coll) aporrear, aplastar (*una mosca*)

sway [swe] *s* oscilación, vaivén *m*; dominio, imperio ‖ *tr* hacer oscilar; conmover; disuadir; gobernar, dominar ‖ *intr* oscilar; desviarse; tambalear, flaquear

swear [swer] *v* (*pret* swore [swor]; *pp* sworn [sworn]) *tr* jurar; juramentar; prestar (*juramento*); **to swear in** to-mar juramento a; **to swear off** jurar renunciar a; **to swear out** obtener mediante juramento ‖ *intr* jurar; **to swear at** maldecir; **to swear by** jurar por; poner toda su confianza en; **to swear to** prestar juramento a; declarar bajo juramento; jurar + *inf*

sweat [swet] *s* sudor *m* ‖ *v* (*pret & pp* sweat o sweated) *tr* sudar (*agua por los poros*; *la ropa*); (slang) hacer sudar; **to sweat it out** (slang) aguantarlo hasta el fin ‖ *intr* sudar

sweater ['swetər] *s* suéter *m*

sweat·y ['swetɪ] *adj* (*comp* -ier; *super* -iest) sudoroso

Swede [swid] *s* sueco

Sweden ['swidən] *s* Suecia

Swedish ['swidɪʃ] *adj & s* sueco

sweep [swip] *s* barrido; alcance *m*, extensión; (*of wind*) soplo; (*of a well*) cigoñal *m* ‖ *v* (*pret & pp* swept [swept]) *tr* barrer; arrastrar; rozar, tocar; recorrer con la mirada, los dedos, etc. ‖ *intr* barrer; pasar rápidamente; extenderse; precipitarse; andar con paso majestuoso

sweeper ['swipər] *s* (*person*) barrendero; (*machine for sweeping streets*) barredera; barredera de alfombra; (nav) dragaminas *m*

sweeping ['swipɪŋ] *adj* arrebatador; comprensivo, extenso, vasto ‖ **sweep-ings** *spl* barreduras

sweep'-sec'ond *s* segundero central

sweep'stakes' *ssg* o *spl* lotería en la cual una persona gana todas las apuestas; carrera que decide todas las apuestas; premio en las carreras de caballos

sweet [swit] *adj* dulce; oloroso; melodioso, grato al oído; fresco; bonito, lindo; amable; querido; **to be sweet on** (coll) estar enamorado de ‖ *adv* dulcemente; **to smell sweet** tener buen olor ‖ **sweets** *spl* dulces *mpl*, golosinas

sweet'bread' *s* lechecillas, mollejas

sweet'bri'er *s* eglantina

sweeten ['switən] *tr* azucarar, endulzar; suavizar; purificar ‖ *intr* azucararse, endulzarse; suavizarse

sweet'heart' *s* enamorado o enamorada; amiga querida; galán *m*, cortejo

sweet marjoram *s* mejorana

sweet'meats' *spl* dulces *mpl*, confites *mpl*, confitura

sweet pea *s* guisante *m* de olor

sweet potato *s* batata, camote *m*

sweet-scented ['swit,sentɪd] *adj* oloroso, perfumado

sweet tooth *s* gusto por los dulces

sweet-toothed ['swit,tuθt] *adj* dulcero, goloso

sweet william *s* clavel *m* de ramillete, minutisa

swell [swel] *adj* (coll) muy elegante; (slang) de órdago, magnífico ‖ *s* hinchazón *f*; bulto; marejada; oleaje *m*; (*of a crowd of people*) oleada; (coll) petimetre *m*, pisaverde *m* ‖ *v* (*pret* **swelled**; *pp* **swelled** o **swollen** ['swolən]) *tr* hinchar, inflar; abultar, aumentar; elevar, levantar; (fig) hinchar, engreír ‖ *intr* hincharse; abultarse, aumentar, crecer; elevarse, levantarse; embravecerse (*el mar*); (fig) hincharse, engreírse

swelled head *s* entono; **to have a swelled head** estar muy pagado de sí mismo, creerse gran cosa

swelter ['sweltər] *intr* sofocarse de sudor

swept'back' wing *s* (aer) ala en flecha

swerve [swʌrv] *s* viraje *m*, desvío brusco ‖ *tr* desviar ‖ *intr* desviarse, torcer

swift [swift] *adj* rápido, veloz; pronto; repentino ‖ *adv* rápidamente, velozmente ‖ *s* vencejo

swig [swig] *s* (coll) chisguete, tragantada ‖ *v* (*pret & pp* **swigged**; *ger* **swigging**) *tr & intr* (coll) beber a grandes tragos

swill [swil] *s* basura, inmundicia; tragantada ‖ *tr* beber a grandes tragos; emborrachar ‖ *intr* beber a grandes tragos; emborracharse

swim [swim] *s* natación; **the swim** (*in affairs, society, etc.*) (coll) la corriente ‖ *v* (*pret* **swam** [swæm]; *pp* **swum** [swʌm]; *ger* **swimming**) *tr* pasar a nado ‖ *intr* nadar; deslizarse, escurrirse; padecer vahídos; dar vueltas (*la cabeza*); **to swim across** atravesar a nado

swimmer ['swimər] *s* nadador *m*

swimming pool *s* piscina

swimming suit *s* traje *m* de baño

swindle ['swindəl] *s* estafa, timo ‖ *tr & intr* estafar, timar

swine [swain] *s* cerdo, puerco; *spl* ganado porcino

swing [swiŋ] *s* balance *m*, oscilación, vaivén *m*; (*device used for recreation*) columpio; hamaca; turno, período; fuerza, ímpetu *m*; (*trip*) jira; (box) golpe *m* de lado; (mus) ritmo constantemente repetido; **in full swing** en plena marcha ‖ *v* (*pret & pp* **swung** [swʌŋ]) *tr* blandir (*p.ej., un arma*); menear (*los brazos*); hacer oscilar; columpiar; manejar con éxito ‖ *intr* oscilar; balancearse; columpiar; estar colgado; dar una vuelta; **to swing open** abrirse de pronto (*una puerta*)

swinging door ['swiŋiŋ] *s* batiente *m* oscilante, puerta de vaivén

swinish ['swainiʃ] *adj* porcuno, (fig) cochino, puerco

swipe [swaip] *s* (coll) golpe *m* fuerte ‖ *tr* (coll) dar un golpe fuerte a; (slang) hurtar, robar

swirl [swʌrl] *s* remolino, torbellino ‖ *tr* hacer girar ‖ *intr* arremolinarse, remolinar; girar

swish [swiʃ] *s* (*e.g., of a whip*) chasquido; (*of a dress*) crujido ‖ *tr* chasquear (*el látigo*) ‖ *intr* chasquear; crujir (*un vestido*)

Swiss [swis] *adj & s* suizo

Swiss chard [tʃɑrd] *s* acelga

Swiss cheese *s* Gruyère *m*, queso suizo

Swiss Guards *spl* guardia suiza

switch [switʃ] *s* bastoncillo, latiguillo; latigazo; coletazo; (*false hair*) trenza postiza, moño postizo; (elec) llave *f*, interruptor *m*, conmutador *m*; (rr) agujas ‖ *tr* azotar, fustigar; (elec) conmutar; (rr) desviar; **to switch off** (elec) cortar, desconectar; **to switch on** (elec) cerrar (*el circuito*); (elec) encender, poner (*la luz, la radio, etc.*) ‖ *intr* cambiarse, moverse; desviarse

switch'back' *s* vía en zigzag

switch'board' *s* cuadro de distribución

switching engine *s* locomotora de maniobras

switch•man ['switʃmən] *s* (*pl* -**men** [mən]) agujetero, guardagujas *m*

switch'yard' *s* patio de maniobras

Switzerland ['switsərlənd] *s* Suiza

swiv•el ['swivəl] *s* eslabón giratorio ‖ *v* (*pret & pp* -**eled** o -**elled**; *ger* -**eling** o -**elling**) *intr* girar sobre un eje

swivel chair *s* silla giratoria

swoon [swun] *s* desmayo ‖ *intr* desmayarse

swoop [swup] *s* descenso súbito; (*of a bird of prey*) calada ‖ *intr* bajar rápidamente, precipitarse; abatirse (*p.ej., el ave de rapiña*)

sword [sord] *s* espada; **at swords' points** enemistados a sangre y fuego; **to put to the sword** pasar al filo de la espada, pasar a cuchillo

sword belt *s* cinturón *m*

sword'fish' *s* pez *m* espada

sword handler *s* (taur) mozo de estoques

sword rattling *s* fanfarronería

swords•man ['sordzmən] *s* (*pl* -**men** [mən]) espada *m*; esgrimidor *m*

sword swallower ['swalo•ər] *s* tragasable *m*

sword thrust *s* estocada, golpe *m* de espada

sworn [sworn] *adj* (*enemy*) jurado

sycophant ['sikəfənt] *s* adulador *m*; parásito

sycosis [sai'kosis] *s* (pathol) sicosis *f*

syll. *abbr* **syllable**

syllable ['siləbəl] *s* sílaba

syllogism ['silə,dʒizəm] *s* silogismo

sylph [silf] *s* sílfide *f*

sym. *abbr* **symbol, symmetrical, symphony, symptom**

symbol ['simbəl] *s* símbolo

symbolic(al) [sim'bɑlik(əl)] *adj* simbólico

symbolize ['simbə,laiz] *tr* simbolizar

symmetric(al) [si'metrik(əl)] *adj* simétrico

symme•try ['simitri] *s* (*pl* -**tries**) simetría

sympathetic [,simpə'θetik] *adj* compasivo; favorablemente dispuesto

sympathize ['simpə,θaiz] *intr* compadecerse; **to sympathize with** compadecerse de; comprender

sympa·thy [ˈsɪmpəθi] s (pl **-thies**) compasión, conmiseración; **to be in sympathy with** estar de acuerdo con, ser partidario de; **to extend one's sympathy to** dar el pésame a

symphonic [sɪmˈfɑnɪk] adj sinfónico

sympho·ny [ˈsɪmfəni] s (pl **-nies**) sinfonía

symposi·um [sɪmˈpozɪ·əm] s (pl **-a** [ə]) coloquio

symptom [ˈsɪmptəm] s síntoma m

syn. abbr **synonym, synonymous**

synagogue [ˈsɪnə‚gɑg] o [ˈsɪnə‚gɑg] s sinagoga

synchronize [ˈsɪŋkrə‚naɪz] tr & intr sincronizar

synchronous [ˈsɪŋkrənəs] adj sincrónico

syncope [ˈsɪŋkə‚pi] s (phonet) síncopa

syndicate [ˈsɪndɪkɪt] s sindicato || [ˈsɪndɪ‚ket] tr sindicar || intr sindicarse

synonym [ˈsɪnənɪm] s sinónimo

synonymous [sɪˈnɑnɪməs] adj sinónimo

synop·sis [sɪˈnɑpsɪs] s (pl **-ses** [siz]) sinopsis f

syntax [ˈsɪntæks] s sintaxis f

synthe·sis [ˈsɪnθɪsɪs] s (pl **-ses** [‚siz]) síntesis f

synthesize [ˈsɪnθɪ‚saɪz] tr sintetizar

synthetic(al) [sɪnˈθɛtɪk(əl)] adj sintético

syphilis [ˈsɪfɪlɪs] s sífilis f

Syria [ˈsɪrɪ·ə] s Siria

Syrian [ˈsɪrɪ·ən] adj & s sirio

syringe [sɪˈrɪndʒ] o [ˈsɪrɪndʒ] s jeringa; (fountain syringe) mangueta; (syringe fitted with needle for hypodermic injections) jeringuilla || tr jeringar

syrup [ˈsɪrəp] o [ˈsʌrəp] s almíbar m; (with fruit juices or medicinal substances) jarabe m

system [ˈsɪstəm] s sistema m

systematic(al) [‚sɪstəˈmætɪk(əl)] adj sistemático

systematize [ˈsɪstəmə‚taɪz] tr sistematizar

systole [ˈsɪstəli] s sístole f

T

T, t [ti] vigésima letra del alfabeto inglés

t. abbr **teaspoon, temperature, tenor, tense, territory, town**

T. abbr **Territory, Testament**

tab [tæb] s apéndice m, proyección; marbete m; **to keep tab on** (coll) tener a la vista; **to pick up the tab** (coll) pagar la cuenta

tab·by [ˈtæbi] s (pl **-bies**) gato atigrado; gata; solterona; chismosa

tabernacle [ˈtæbər‚nækəl] s tabernáculo

table [ˈtebəl] s mesa; (list, catalogue; index of a book) tabla; **to set the table** poner la mesa; **to turn the tables** volver las tornas; **under the table** completamente emborrachado || tr aplazar la discusión de

tab·leau [ˈtæblo] s (pl **-leaus** o **-leaux** [loz]) cuadro vivo

ta'ble·cloth' s mantel m

table d'hôte [ˈtɑbəlˈdot] s mesa redonda; comida a precio fijo

ta'ble·land' s meseta

table linen s mantelería

table manners spl modales mpl que uno tiene en la mesa

table of contents s índice m de materias, tabla de materias

ta'ble·spoon' s cuchara de sopa

tablespoonful [ˈtebəl‚spun‚ful] s cucharada

tablet [ˈtæblɪt] s (writing pad) bloc m; (slab) lápida, placa; (lozenge, pastille) comprimido, tableta

table talk s conversación de sobremesa

table tennis s tenis de mesa

ta'ble·ware' s servicio de mesa, artículos para la mesa

tabloid [ˈtæblɔɪd] s periódico sensacional

taboo [təˈbu] adj prohibido || s tabú m || tr prohibir

tabulate [ˈtæbjə‚let] tr tabular

tabulator [ˈtæbjə‚letər] s tabulador m

tacit [ˈtæsɪt] adj tácito

taciturn [ˈtæsɪ‚tʌrn] adj taciturno

tack [tæk] s tachuela; nuevo plan de acción; (naut) virada; (sew) hilván m || tr clavar con tachuelas; añadir; unir; (naut) virar; (sew) hilvanar || intr cambiar de plan; (naut) virar

tackle [ˈtækəl] s avíos, enseres mpl; (naut) poleame m || tr atacar, embestir; emprender

tack·y [ˈtæki] adj (comp **-ier;** super **-iest**) pegajoso; (coll) desaliñado

tact [tækt] s tacto, juicio, tino

tactful [ˈtæktfəl] adj discreto, político

tactical [ˈtæktɪkəl] adj táctico

tactician [tækˈtɪʃən] s táctico

tactics [ˈtæktɪks] ssg (mil) táctica || spl táctica

tactless [ˈtæklɪs] adj indiscreto

tad'pole' s renacuajo

taffeta [ˈtæfɪtə] s tafetán m

taffy [ˈtæfi] s arropía, melcocha; (coll) lisonja, zalamería

tag [tæg] s etiqueta, marbete m; herrete m; pingajo; mechón m; vedija; (curlicue in writing) ringorrango; **to play tag** jugar al tócame tú || v (pret & pp **tagged;** ger **tagging**) tr pegar un marbete a; marcar con marbete || intr (coll) seguir de cerca

tag end s cabo flojo; retal m, retazo

Tagus [ˈtegəs] s Tajo

tail [tel] adj de cola || s cola; **tails** (of a coin) cruz f; (coll) frac m; **to turn**

tail mostrar los talones || *tr* atar, juntar || *intr* formar cola; **to tail after** pisar los talones a

tail assembly *s* (aer) empenaje *m*, planos de cola

tail end *s* cola, extremo; conclusión; **at the tail end** al final

tail'light' *s* faro trasero; (rr) disco de cola

tailor ['telər] *s* sastre *m* || *tr* entallar (*un traje*) || *intr* ser sastre

tailoring ['telərɪŋ] *s* sastrería, costura

tai'lor-made' suit *s* traje *m* de sastre, traje hecho a la medida

tail'piece' *s* apéndice *m*, cabo; (*of stringed instrument*) (mus) cordal *m*; (typ) florón *m*

tail'race' *s* cauce *m* de salida; (min) canal *m* de desechos

tail spin *s* (aer) barrena picada

tail wind *s* (aer) viento de cola; (naut) viento en popa

taint [tent] *s* mancha; corrupción, infección || *tr* manchar; corromper, inficionar

take [tek] *s* toma; presa, redada; (mov) toma; (slang) entradas, ingresos || *v* (*pret* **took** [tʊk]; *pp* **taken**) *tr* tomar; (*to carry off with one*) llevarse; (*to remove*) quitar; quedarse con (*p.ej., una compra en una tienda*); comer (*una pieza, en el juego de ajedrez y en el de damas*); dar (*un paso, un salto, un paseo*); hacer (*un viaje; ejercicio*); seguir (*un consejo; una asignatura*); sacar (*una fotografía*); calzar, usar (*cierto tamaño de zapatos o guantes*); estudiar (*p.ej., historia, francés, matemáticas*); echar (*una siesta*); tomar (*un tren, autobús, tranvía*); aguantar, tolerar; soportar; **to take amiss** llevar a mal; **to take apart** descomponer, desarmar, desmontar; **to take down** bajar; descolgar; poner por escrito, tomar nota de; desmontar; (*to humble*) quitar los humos a; **to take for** tomar por, p.ej., **I took you for someone else** le tomé por otra persona; **to take from** quitar a; **to take in** acoger, admitir; (*to welcome into one's home, one's company*) recibir; (*to encompass*) abarcar, comprender; ganar (*dinero*); visitar (*los puntos de interés*); (*to win over by flattery or deceit*) cazar; meter (*p.ej., las costuras de una prenda de vestir*); **to take it that** suponer que; **to take off** quitarse (*p.ej., el sombrero*); descontar; (coll) imitar, parodiar; **to take on** tomar, contratar; empezar; cargar con; tomar sobre sí; desafiar; **to take out** sacar; pasear (*p.ej., a un niño, un caballo*); omitir; extraer, separar; **to take place** tener lugar; **to take up** subir; levantar; apretar; coger; recoger; emprender, comenzar; tomar posesión de (*un cargo, un puesto*); tomar, estudiar; ocupar, llenar (*un espacio*) || *intr* arraigar, prender; cuajar; actuar, obrar; salir, resultar; adherirse; pegar; (coll) tener éxito; **to take after** parecerse a; **to take off**

levantarse; salir; (aer) despegar; **to take up with** (coll) estrechar amistad con; (coll) vivir con; **to take well** (coll) sacar buen retrato

take'-off' *s* (aer) despegue *m*; (coll) imitación burlesca, parodia

talcum powder ['tælkəm] *s* polvos de talco; talco en polvo

tale [tel] *s* cuento, relato; embuste *m*, mentira

tale'bear'er *s* chismoso, cuentista *mf*

talent ['tælənt] *s* talento; gente *f* de talento

talented ['tæləntɪd] *adj* talentoso

talent scout *s* buscador *m* de nuevas figuras

talk [tɔk] *s* charla, plática; (*gossip*) fábula, comidilla; (*lecture*) conferencia; **to cause talk** dar que hablar || *tr* hablar; convencer hablando; **to talk up** ensalzar || *intr* hablar; parlar (*el loro*); **to talk on** discutir (*un asunto*); hablar sin parar; continuar hablando; **to talk up** elevar la voz, osar hablar

talkative ['tɔkətɪv] *adj* hablador, locuaz

talker ['tɔkər] *s* hablador *m*; orador *m*; charlatán *m*, parlón *m*

talkie ['tɔki] *s* (coll) cine hablado

talking doll ['tɔkɪŋ] *s* muñeca parlante

talking film *s* película hablada

talking machine *s* máquina parlante

talking picture *s* cine hablado, cine parlante

tall [tɔl] *adj* alto; (coll) exagerado

tallow ['tælo] *s* sebo

tal·ly ['tæli] *s* (*pl* **-lies**) cuenta || *v* (*pret* & *pp* **-lied**) *tr* echar la cuenta de || *intr* echar la cuenta; concordar, corresponder, conformarse

tally sheet *s* hoja en que se anota una cuenta

talon ['tælən] *s* garra

tambourine [,tæmbə'rin] *s* pandereta

tame [tem] *adj* manso, domesticado; dócil, sumiso; insípido || *tr* amansar, domesticar; domar (*a un animal salvaje*); someter; captar (*una caída de agua*)

tamp [tæmp] *tr* atacar (*un barreno*); apisonar

tamper ['tæmpər] *s* (*person*) apisonador *m*; (*ram*) pisón *m* || *intr* entremeterse; **to tamper with** manosear, tocar ajando; tratar de forzar (*una cerradura*); falsificar (*un documento*); corromper (*p.ej., a un testigo*)

tampon ['tæmpɑn] *s* (surg) tapón *m* || *tr* (surg) taponar

tan [tæn] *adj* requemado, tostado; de color de canela; marrón; café (Am) || *v* (*pret* & *pp* **tanned**; *ger* **tanning**) *tr* adobar, curtir, zurrar; quemar, tostar; (coll) zurrar, dar una paliza a

tang [tæŋ] *s* sabor *m* u olor *m* fuerte y picante; dejo, gustillo; (*ringing sound*) tañido

tangent ['tændʒənt] *adj* tangente || *s* tangente *f*; **to fly off at a tangent** tomar súbitamente nuevo rumbo, cambiar de repente

tangerine [ˌtændʒəˈrin] s mandarina

tangible [ˈtændʒɪbəl] adj palpable, tangible

Tangier |tænˈdʒɪr| s Tánger f

tangle |ˈtæŋgəl| s enredo, maraña, lío || tr enredar, enmarañar || intr enredarse, enmarañarse

tank [tæŋk] s tanque m, depósito; (mil) tanque, carro de combate; (rr) ténder m; (heavy drinker) (slang) bodega

tank car s (rr) carro cuba, vagón m tanque

tanker [ˈtæŋkər] s barco tanque, buque m cisterna; avión-nodriza m

tank farming s quimicultura, cultivo hidropónico

tank truck s camión m tanque

tanner [ˈtænər] s curtidor m

tanner·y [ˈtænəri] s (pl -ies) curtiduría, tenería

tantalize [ˈtæntəˌlaɪz] tr atormentar con falsas promesas

tantamount [ˈtæntəˌmaʊnt] adj equivalente

tantrum [ˈtæntrəm] s berrinche m, rabieta

tap [tæp] s golpecito, palmadita; canilla, espita; grifo; (elec) toma; (mach) macho de terraja; **on tap** sacado del barril, servido al grifo; listo, a mano; **taps** (signal to put out lights) (mil) silencio || v (pret & pp **tapped**; ger **tapping**) tr dar golpecitos o un golpecito a o en; espitar, poner (la espita); sacar o tomar (quitando la espita); sangrar (un árbol); intervenir (un teléfono); derivar (electricidad); aterrajar (tuercas) || intr dar golpecitos

tap dance s zapateado

tap'-dance' intr zapatear

tape [tep] s cinta || tr proveer de cinta; medir con cinta; (coll) grabar en cinta magnetofónica

tape measure s cinta de medir

taper [ˈtepər] s cerilla, velita larga y delgada || tr ahusar || intr ahusarse; ir disminuyendo

tape'-re·cord' tr grabar sobre cinta

tape recorder [rɪˈkɔrdər] s magnetófono, grabadora de cinta

tapes·try [ˈtæpɪstri] s (pl -tries) tapiz m || v (pret & pp -tried) tr tapizar

tape'worm' s solitaria, lombriz solitaria

tappet [ˈtæpɪt] s (aut) alzaválvulas m, taqué m

tap'room' s bodegón m, taberna

tap water s agua de grifo

tap wrench s volvedor m de machos

tar [tɑr] s alquitrán m; (coll) marinero || v (pret & pp **tarred**; ger **tarring**) tr alquitranar; **to tar and feather** embrear y emplumar

tar·dy [ˈtɑrdi] adj (comp -dier; super -diest) tardío

target [ˈtɑrgɪt] s blanco

target area s zona a batir

target practice s tiro al blanco

tariff [ˈtærɪf] adj arancelario || s (duties) arancel m; (rates in general) tarifa

tarnish [ˈtɑrnɪʃ] s deslustre m || tr deslustrar || intr deslustrarse

tar paper s papel alquitranado

tarpaulin |tɑrˈpɔlɪn| s alquitranado, encerado, empegado

tar·ry [ˈtɑri] adj alquitranado, embreado || [ˈtæri] v (pret & pp -ried) intr detenerse, quedarse; tardar

tart [tɑrt] adj acre, agrio; (fig) áspero, mordaz || s tarta; (coll) puta

task [tæsk] o [tɑsk] s tarea; **to bring** o **take to task** llamar a capítulo

task'mas'ter s amo, superintendente mf; ordenancista mf, tirano

tassel [ˈtæsəl] s borla; (bot) penacho

taste [test] s gusto, sabor m; sorbo, trago; muestra; gusto, buen gusto; **in bad taste** de mal gusto; **in good taste** de buen gusto; **to acquire a taste for** tomar gusto a || tr gustar; (to sample) probar || intr saber; **to taste of** saber a

tasteless [ˈtestlɪs] adj desabrido, insípido; de mal gusto

tast·y [ˈtesti] adj (comp -ier; super -iest) (coll) sabroso; (coll) de buen gusto

tatter [ˈtætər] s andrajo, harapo, guiñapo || tr hacer andrajos

tattered [ˈtætərd] adj andrajoso, haraposo

tattle [ˈtætəl] s charla; habladuría || intr charlar; chismear, murmurar

tat'tle·tale adj revelador || s cuentista mf, chismoso

tattoo [tæˈtu] s tatuaje m; (mil) retreta || tr tatuar o tatuarse

taunt [tɔnt] o [tɑnt] s mofa, pulla || tr provocar con insultos

taut [tɔt] adj tieso, tirante

tavern [ˈtævərn] s taberna; mesón m, posada

taw·dry [ˈtɔdri] adj (comp -drier; super -driest) cursi, charro, vistoso

taw·ny [ˈtɔni] adj (comp -nier; super -niest) leonado

tax [tæks] s contribución, impuesto || tr poner impuestos a (una persona); poner impuestos sobre (la propiedad); abrumar, cargar; agotar (la paciencia de uno)

taxable [ˈtæksəbəl] adj imponible

taxation [tækˈseʃən] s imposición de contribuciones; contribuciones, impuestos

tax collector s recaudador m de impuestos

tax cut s reducción de impuestos

tax evader [ɪˈvedər] s burlador m de impuestos

tax'-ex·empt' adj exento de impuesto

tax·i [ˈtæksi] s (pl -is) taxi m || v (pret & pp -ied; ger -iing o -ying) tr (aer) carretear || intr ir en taxi; (aer) carretear, taxear

tax'i·cab' s taxi m

taxi dancer s taxista f

taxi driver s taxista mf

tax'i·plane' s avioneta de alquiler

taxi stand s parada de taxis

tax'pay'er s contribuyente mf

tax rate s tipo impositivo

t.b. abbr tuberculosis

tbs. o **tbsp.** *abbr* tablespoon, tablespoons

tea [ti] *s* té *m*; *(medicinal infusion)* tisana; caldo de carne

tea bag *s* muñeca

tea ball *s* huevo del té

tea'cart' *s* mesita de té *(con ruedas)*

teach [titʃ] *v (pret & pp* **taught** [tɔt]) *tr & intr* enseñar

teacher ['titʃər] *s* maestro, instructor *m*; *(such as adversity)* (fig) maestra

teacher's pet *s* alumno mimado

teaching ['titʃɪŋ] *adj* docente ‖ *s* enseñanza; doctrina

teaching aids *spl* material *m* auxiliar de instrucción

teaching staff *s* personal *m* docente

tea'cup' *s* taza para té

tea dance *s* té *m* bailable

teak [tik] *s* teca

tea'ket'tle *s* tetera

team [tim] *s (e.g., of horses)* tiro, tronco; *(of oxen)* yunta; *(sport)* equipo ‖ *tr* enganchar, uncir, enyugar ‖ *intr* — **to team up** asociarse, unirse; formar un equipo

team'mate' *s* compañero de equipo, equipier *m*

teamster ['timstər] *s (of horses)* tronquista *m*; *(of a truck)* camionista *m*

team'work' *s* espíritu de equipo; trabajo de equipo

tea'pot' *s* tetera

tear [tɪr] *s* lágrima; **to burst into tears** romper a llorar; **to fill with tears** arrasarse *(los ojos)* de o en lágrimas; **to hold back one's tears** beberse las lágrimas; **to laugh away one's tears** convertir las lágrimas en risas ‖ [ter] *s* desgarro, rasgón *m* ‖ [ter] *v (pret* **tore** [tor]; *pp* **torn** [torn]) *tr* desgarrar, rasgar; acongojar, afligir; mesarse *(los cabellos)*; **to tear apart** romper en dos; **to tear down** derribar *(un edificio)*; desarmar *(una máquina)*; **to tear off** desgajar; **to tear up** romper *(p.ej., un papel)* ‖ *intr* desgarrarse, rasgarse; **to tear along** correr a toda velocidad

tear bomb [tɪr] *s* bomba lacrimógena

tearful ['tɪrfəl] *adj* lacrimoso

tear gas [tɪr] *s* gas lacrimógeno

tear-jerker ['tɪr,dʒʌrkər] *s (slang)* drama *m* o cine *m* que arrancan lágrimas

tear-off ['ter,ɔf] o ['ter,ɑf] *adj* exfoliador

tea'room' *s* salón *m* de té

tear sheet [ter] *s* hoja del anunciante

tease [tiz] *tr* embromar, azuzar

tea'spoon' *s* cucharilla, cucharita

teaspoonful ['ti,spun,ful] *s* cucharadita

teat [tit] *s* teta, pezón *m*

tea time *s* hora del té

technical ['tɛknɪkəl] *adj* técnico

technical·ty [,tɛknɪ'kælɪti] *s (pl* **-ties)** detalle técnico

technician [tɛk'nɪʃən] *s* técnico

technics ['tɛknɪks] *ssg* técnica

technique [tɛk'nik] *s* técnica

Teddy bear ['tɛdi] *s* oso de juguete, oso de trapo

tedious ['tidɪəs] o ['tidʒəs] *adj* tedioso, enfadoso

teem [tim] *intr* hormiguear; llover a cántaros; **to teem with** hervir de

teeming ['timɪŋ] *adj* hormigueante; *(rain)* torrencial

teen age [tin] *s* edad de 13 a 19 años

teen-ager ['tin,edʒər] *s* joven *mf* de 13 a 19 años de edad

teens [tinz] *spl* números ingleses que terminan en -teen (de 13 a 19); edad de 13 a 19 años; **to be in one's teens** tener de 13 a 19 años

tee-ny ['tini] *adj (comp* **-nier;** *super* **-niest)** (coll) diminuto, pequeñito

teeter ['titər] *s* vaivén *m*, balanceo ‖ *intr* balancear, oscilar

teethe [tið] *intr* endentecer

teething ['tiðɪŋ] *s* dentición

teething ring *s* chupador *m*

teetotaler [ti'totələr] *s* teetotalista *mf*, nefalista *mf*, abstemio

tel. *abbr* telegram, telegraph, telephone

tele-cast ['tɛlɪ,kæst] o ['tɛlɪ,kɑst] *s* teledifusión ‖ *v (pret & pp* **-cast** o **-casted)** *tr & intr* teledifundir

telegram ['tɛlɪ,græm] *s* telegrama *m*

telegraph ['tɛlɪ,græf] o ['tɛlɪ,grɑf] *s* telégrafo ‖ *tr & intr* telegrafiar

telegrapher [tɪ'lɛgrəfər] *s* telegrafista *mf*

telegraph pole *s* poste *m* de telégrafo

Telemachus [tɪ'lɛməkəs] *s* Telémaco

telemeter [tɪ'lɛmɪtər] *s* telémetro ‖ *tr* telemetrar

telemetry [tɪ'lɛmɪtri] *s* telemetría

telephone ['tɛlɪ,fon] *s* teléfono ‖ *tr & intr* telefonear

telephone booth *s* locutorio, cabina telefónica

telephone call *s* llamada telefónica

telephone directory *s* anuario telefónico, guía telefónica

telephone exchange *s* estación telefónica, central *f* de teléfonos

telephone operator *s* telefonista *mf*

telephone receiver *s* receptor telefónico

telephone table *s* mesita portateléfono

teleprinter ['tɛlɪ,prɪntər] *s* teleimpresor *m*

telescope ['tɛlɪ,skop] *s* telescopio ‖ *tr* telescopar ‖ *intr* telescoparse

teletype ['tɛlɪ,taɪp] *s* teletipo ‖ *tr & intr* transmitir por teletipo

teleview ['tɛlɪ,vju] *tr & intr* ver por televisión

televiewer ['tɛlɪ,vju·ər] *s* televidente *mf*, telespectador *m*

televise ['tɛlɪ,vaɪz] *tr* televisar

television ['tɛlɪ,vɪʒən] *adj* televisor ‖ *s* televisión

television screen *s* pantalla televisora

television set *s* televisor *m*, telerreceptor *m*

tell [tɛl] *v (pret & pp* **told** [told]) *tr* decir; *(to narrate; to count)* contar; determinar; conocer, distinguir; **I told you so!** ¡por algo te lo dije!; **to tell someone to** + *inf* decirle a uno que + *subj* ‖ *intr* hablar; surtir efecto; **to tell on** dejarse ver en *(p.ej., la salud de uno)*; (coll) denunciar

teller ['tɛlər] s narrador m; (of a bank) cajero; (of votes) escrutador m

temper ['tɛmpər] s temple m, natural m, genio; cólera, mal genio; (of steel, glass, etc.) temple m; **to keep one's temper** dominar su mal genio; **to lose one's temper** encolerizarse, perder la paciencia || tr templar || intr templarse

temperament ['tɛmpərəmənt] s disposición; temperamento sensible o excitable

temperamental [ˌtɛmpərə'mɛntəl] adj temperamental

temperance ['tɛmpərəns] s templanza

temperate ['tɛmpərɪt] adj templado

temperature ['tɛmpərət/ər] s temperatura

tempest ['tɛmpɪst] s tempestad

tempestuous [tɛm'pɛst/u·əs] adj tempestuoso

temple ['tɛmpəl] s (place of worship) templo; (side of forehead) sien f; (sidepiece of spectacles) gafa

tem·po ['tɛmpo] s (pl -pos o -pi [pi]) (mus) tiempo; (fig) ritmo (p.ej., de la vida)

temporal ['tɛmpərəl] adj temporal

temporary ['tɛmpəˌrɛri] adj temporáneo, temporario, provisional, interino

temporize ['tɛmpəˌraɪz] intr contemporizar, temporizar

tempt [tɛmpt] tr tentar

temptation [tɛmp'te/ən] s tentación

tempter ['tɛmptər] s tentador m

tempting ['tɛmptɪŋ] adj tentador

ten [tɛn] adj & pron diez || s diez m; **ten o'clock** las diez

tenable ['tɛnəbəl] adj defendible

tenacious [tɪ'ne/əs] adj tenaz

tenacity [tɪ'næsɪti] s tenacidad

tenant ['tɛnənt] s arrendatario, inquilino; morador m, residente mf

tend [tɛnd] tr cuidar, vigilar; servir || intr tender, dirigirse; **to tend to** atender a; **to tend to** + inf tender a + inf

tenden·cy ['tɛndənsi] s (pl -cies) tendencia

tender ['tɛndər] adj tierno; (painfully sensitive) dolorido || n oferta; (naut) alijador m, falúa; (rr) ténder m || tr ofrecer, tender

tender-hearted ['tɛndər'hɑrtɪd] adj compasivo, tierno de corazón

ten'der-loin' s filete m || **Tenderloin** s barrio de mala vida

tenderness ['tɛndərnɪs] s ternura, terneza; sensibilidad

tendon ['tɛndən] s tendón m

tendril ['tɛndrɪl] s zarcillo

tenement ['tɛnɪmənt] s habitación, vivienda; casa de vecindad

tenement house s casa de vecindad

tenet ['tɛnɪt] s dogma m, credo, principio

tennis ['tɛnɪs] s tenis m

tennis court s campo de tenis

tennis player s tenista mf

tenor ['tɛnər] s tenor m, carácter m, curso, tendencia; (mus) tenor

tense [tɛns] adj tenso, tieso; (person; situation) (fig) tenso; (relations) tirante || s (gram) tiempo

tension ['tɛn/ən] s tensión; ansia, congoja, esfuerzo mental; (in personal or diplomatic relations) tirantez f

tent [tɛnt] s tienda; tienda de campaña

tentacle ['tɛntəkəl] s tentáculo

tentative ['tɛntətɪv] adj tentativo

tenth [tɛnθ] adj & s décimo || s (in dates) diez m

tenuous ['tɛnju·əs] adj tenue; (thin in consistency) raro

tenure ['tɛnjər] s (of property) tenencia; (of an office) ejercicio; (protection from dismissal) inamovilidad

tepid ['tɛpɪd] adj tibio

tercet ['tʌrsɪt] s terceto

term [tʌrm] s término; (of imprisonment) condena; semestre m, período escolar; (of the presidency of the U.S.A.) mandato, período; **terms** condiciones || tr llamar, nombrar

termagant ['tʌrməgənt] s mujer regañona, mujer de mal genio

terminal ['tʌrmɪnəl] adj terminal || s término, fin m; (elec) terminal m; (rr) estación de fin de línea

terminate ['tʌrmɪˌnet] tr & intr terminar

termination [ˌtʌrmɪ'ne/ən] s terminación

terminus ['tʌrmɪnəs] s término; (rr) estación de cabeza, estación extrema

termite ['tʌrmaɪt] s termite m, comeién m

terrace ['tɛrəs] s terraza; (flat roof of a house) azotea

terra firma ['tɛrə 'fʌrmə] s tierra firme; **on terra firma** sobre suelo firme

terrain [tɛ'ren] s terreno

terrestrial [tə'trɛstrɪ·əl] adj terrestre

terrible ['tɛrɪbəl] adj terrible; muy desagradable

terrific [tə'rɪfɪk] adj terrífico; (coll) enorme, intenso, brutal

terri·fy ['tɛrɪˌfaɪ] v (pret & pp -fied) tr aterrorizar, atemorizar

territo·ry ['tɛrɪˌtori] s (pl -ries) territorio

terror ['tɛrər] s terror m

terrorize ['tɛrəˌraɪz] tr aterrorizar; imponerse a, mediante el terror

terry cloth ['tɛri] s albornoz m

terse [tʌrs] adj breve, sucinto

tertiary ['tʌr/ɪˌɛri] o ['tʌr/əri] adj terciario

Test. abbr **Testament**

test [tɛst] s prueba, ensayo; examen m || tr probar, poner a prueba; examinar

testament ['tɛstəmənt] s testamento

test flight s vuelo de ensayo

testicle ['tɛstɪkəl] s testículo

testi·fy ['tɛstɪˌfaɪ] v (pret & pp -fied) tr & intr testificar

testimonial [ˌtɛstɪ'moni·əl] s recomendación, certificado; (expression of esteem, gratitude, etc.) homenaje m

testimo·ny ['tɛstɪˌmoni] s (pl -nies) testimonio

test pilot s (aer) piloto de pruebas

test tube s probeta, tubo de ensayo

tether ['tɛðər] *s* atadura, traba; **at the end of one's tether** al límite de las posibilidades o la paciencia de uno ‖ *tr* apersogar

tetter ['tɛtər] *s* empeine *m*

text [tɛkst] *s* texto; tema *m*, lema *m*

text'book' *s* libro de texto

textile ['tɛkstɪl] o ['tɛkstaɪl] *adj* & *s* textil *m*

texture ['tɛkstʃər] *s* textura

Thai ['tɑ-i] o ['taɪ] *adj* & *s* tailandés *m*

Thailand ['taɪlənd] *s* Tailandia

Thales ['θeliz] *s* Tales *m*

Thalia [θə'laɪ-ə] *s* Talía

Thames [tɛmz] *s* Támesis *m*

than [ðæn] *conj* que, p.ej., **he is richer than I** es más rico que yo; (*before a numeral*) de, p.ej., **more than twenty** más de veinte; (*before a verb*) de lo que, p.ej., **the crop is larger than was expected** la cosecha es mayor de lo que se esperaba; (*before a verb with direct object understood*) de (de la, de los, de las) que, p.ej., **they sent us more coffee than we ordered** nos enviaron más café del que pedimos

thank [θæŋk] *tr* agradecer, dar las gracias a; **to thank someone for something** agradecerle a uno una cosa ‖ **thanks** *spl* gracias; **thanks to** gracias a, merced a ‖ **thanks** *interj* ¡gracias!

thankful ['θæŋkfəl] *adj* agradecido

thankless ['θæŋklɪs] *adj* ingrato

thanksgiving [,θæŋks'gɪvɪŋ] *s* acción de gracias

Thanksgiving Day *s* (U.S.A.) día *m* de acción de gracias

that [ðæt] *adj dem* (*pl* those) ese; aquel; **that one** ése: aquél ‖ *pron dem* (*pl* those) ése; aquél; eso; aquello ‖ *pron rel* que, quien; el cual, el que ‖ *adv* tan; **that far** tan lejos; hasta allí; **that many** tantos; **that much** tanto ‖ *conj* que; para que

thatch [θætʃ] *s* barda, paja; techo de paja ‖ *tr* cubrir de paja, techar con paja, bardar

thaw [θɔ] *s* deshielo, derretimiento ‖ *tr* deshelar, derretir ‖ *intr* deshelarse, derretirse

the [ðə], [ðɪ] o [ði] *art def* el ‖ *adv* cuanto, p.ej., **the more the merrier** cuanto más mejor; **the more . . . the more** cuanto más . . . tanto más

theater ['θi-ətər] *s* teatro

the'ater-go'er *s* teatrero

theater news *s* actualidad escénica

theater page *s* noticiario teatral

theatrical [θɪ'ætrɪkəl] *adj* teatral

Thebes [θibz] *s* Tebas *f*

thee [ði] *pron pers* (archaic, poet, Bib) te; ti; **with thee** contigo

theft [θɛft] *s* hurto, robo

their [ðɛr] *adj poss* su; el . . . de ellos

theirs [ðɛrz] *pron poss* el suyo, el de ellos

them [ðɛm] *pron pers* los; ellos; **to them** les; a ellos

theme [θim] *s* tema *m*; (mus) tema *m*

theme song *s* (mus) tema *m* central; (rad) sintonía

them·selves' *pron pers* ellos mismos; sí, sí mismos; se, p.ej., **they enjoyed themselves** se divirtieron; **with themselves** consigo

then [ðɛn] *adv* entonces; después, luego, en seguida; además, también; **by then** para entonces; **from then on** desde entonces, de allí en adelante; **then and there** ahí mismo

thence [ðɛns] *adv* desde allí; desde entonces; por eso

thence'forth' *adv* de allí en adelante; desde entonces

theolo·gy [θi'ɑlədʒi] *s* (*pl* -gies) teología

theorem ['θi-ərəm] *s* teorema *m*

theo·ry ['θi-əri] *s* (*pl* -ries) teoría

therapeutic [,θɛrə'pjutɪk] *adj* terapéutico ‖ **therapeutics** *ssg* terapéutica

thera·py ['θɛrəpi] *s* (*pl* -pies) terapia

there [ðɛr] *adv* allí, allá; **there is** o **there are** hay; aquí tiene Vd.

there'a·bouts' *adv* por allí; cerca, aproximadamente

there·af'ter *adv* de allí en adelante, después de eso

there·by' *adv* con eso; así, de tal modo; por allí cerca

therefore ['ðɛrfor] *adv* por lo tanto, por consiguiente

there·in' *adv* en esto, en eso; en ese respecto

there·of' *adv* de ello, de eso

Theresa [tə'risə] o [tə'resə] *s* Teresa

there·u·pon' *adv* sobre eso, encima de eso; por consiguiente; en seguida

thermistor [θər'mɪstər] *s* (elec) termistor *m*

thermocouple ['θʌrmo,kʌpəl] *s* (elec) termopar *m*

thermodynamic [,θʌrmodaɪ'næmɪk] *adj* termodinámico ‖ **thermodynamics** *ssg* termodinámica

thermometer [θər'mɑmɪtər] *s* termómetro

thermonuclear [,θʌrmo'njuklɪ-ər] o [,θʌrmo'nukli-ər] *adj* termonuclear

Thermopylae [θər'mɑpɪ,li] *s* las Termópilas

thermos bottle ['θʌrməs] *s* termos *m*, botella termos

thermostat ['θʌrmə,stæt] *s* termóstato

thesau·rus [θɪ'sɔrəs] *s* (*pl* -ri [raɪ]) tesoro; (*dictionary or the like*) tesauro, tesoro

these [ðiz] *pl de* **this**

the·sis ['θisɪs] *s* (*pl* -ses [siz]) tesis *f*

Thespis ['θɛspɪs] *s* Tespis *m*

Thessaly ['θɛsəli] *s* la Tesalia

they [ðe] *pron pers* ellos, ellas

thick [θɪk] *adj* espeso; grueso; denso; (coll) estúpido; (coll) íntimo ‖ *s* espesor *m*; **the thick of** (e.g., a crowd) lo más denso de; (e.g., a battle) lo más reñido de; **through thick and thin** contra viento y marea

thicken ['θɪkən] *tr* espesar ‖ *intr* espesarse; complicarse (*el enredo*)

thicket ['θɪkɪt] *s* espesura, matorral *m*, soto

thick-headed ['θɪk'hɛdɪd] *adj* (coll) torpe, estúpido

thick'-set' *adj* grueso, rechoncho

thief [θif] s (pl **thieves** [θivz]) ladrón m

thieve [θiv] intr hurtar, robar

thiev·er·y ['θivəri] s (pl -ies) latrocinio, hurto, robo

thigh [θaɪ] s muslo

thigh'bone' s hueso del muslo, fémur m

thimble ['θɪmbəl] s dedal m

thin [θɪn] adj (comp **thinner**; super **thinnest**) delgado, flaco, tenue; (cloth, paper, sole of shoe, etc.) fino; (hair) ralo; (broth) aguado; (excuse) débil; claro, ligero, escaso || v (pret & pp **thinned**; ger **thinning**) tr adelgazar, enflaquecer; enrarecer; aclarar; aguar; desleír (los colores) || intr adelgazarse, enflaquecerse; enrarecerse; **to thin out** ralear (el pelo)

thine [ðaɪn] adj poss (archaic & poet) tu || pron poss (archaic & poet) tuyo; el tuyo

thing [θɪŋ] s cosa; **of all things!** ¡qué sorpresa!; **to be the thing** ser la última moda; **to be the thing to do** ser lo que debe hacerse; **to see things** ver visiones, padecer alucinaciones

think [θɪŋk] v (pret & pp **thought** [θɔt]) tr pensar; **to think it over** pensarlo; **to think nothing of** tener en poco; creer fácil; no dar importancia a; **to think of** pensar de, p.ej., **what do you think of this book?** ¿qué piensa Vd. de este libro?; **to think up** imaginar; inventar (p.ej., una excusa) || intr pensar; **to think not** creer que no; **to think of** (to turn one's thoughts to) pensar en; pensar (un número, un naipe, etc.); **to think so** creer que sí; **to think well of** tener buena opinión de

thinker ['θɪŋkər] s pensador m

third [θʌrd] adj tercero || s (in a series) tercero; (one of three equal parts) tercio; (in dates) tres m

third degree s (coll) interrogatorio bajo tortura

third rail s (rr) tercer carril m, carril de toma

thirst [θʌrst] s sed f || intr tener sed; **to thirst for** tener sed de

thirst·y ['θʌrsti] adj (comp -ier; super -iest) sediento; **to be thirsty** tener sed

thirteen ['θʌr'tin] adj, pron & s trece m

thirteenth ['θʌr'tinθ] adj & s (in a series) decimotercero; (part) trezavo || s (in dates) trece m

thirtieth ['θʌrtɪ·ɪθ] adj & s (in a series) trigésimo; (part) treintavo || s (in dates) treinta m

thir·ty ['θʌrti] adj & pron treinta || s (pl -ties) treinta m

this [ðɪs] adj dem (pl **these**) este; **this one** éste || pron dem (pl **these**) éste; esto || adv tan

thistle ['θɪsəl] s cardo

thither ['θɪðər] o ['ðɪðər] adv allá, hacia allá

Thomas ['tɑməs] s Tomás m

thong [θɔŋ] o [θɑŋ] s correa

tho·rax ['θoræks] s (pl -raxes o -races [rə,siz]) tórax m

thorn [θɔrn] s espina

thorn·y ['θɔrni] adj (comp -ier; super -iest) espinoso; (difficult) (fig) espinoso

thorough ['θʌro] adj cabal, completo; concienzudo, cuidadoso

thor'ough·bred' adj de pura sangre; bien nacido || s pura sangre m; persona bien nacida

thor'ough·fare' s vía pública; **no thoroughfare** se prohibe el paso

thor'ough·go'ing adj cabal, completo, esmerado, perfecto

thoroughly ['θʌroli] adv a fondo

those [ðoz] pl de **that**

thou [ðau] pron pers (archaic, poet & Bib) tú || tr & intr tutear

though [ðo] adv sin embargo || conj aunque, bien que; **as though** como si

thought [θɔt] s pensamiento

thoughtful ['θɔtfəl] adj pensativo; atento, considerado

thoughtless ['θɔtlɪs] adj irreflexivo; descuidado; inconsiderado

thought transference s transmisión del pensamiento

thousand ['θauzənd] adj & s mil m; **a thousand** u **one thousand** mil m

thousandth ['θauzəndθ] adj & s milésimo

thralldom ['θrɔldəm] s esclavitud, servidumbre

thrash [θræʃ] tr (agr) trillar; azotar, zurrar; **to thrash out** decidir después de una discusión cabal || intr trillar; agitarse, menearse

thread [θred] s hilo; (mach) filete m, rosca; (of a speech, of life) hilo; **to lose the thread of** perder el hilo de || tr enhebrar, enhilar; ensartar (p.ej., cuentas); (mach) aterrajar, filetear

thread'bare' adj raído; gastado, usado, viejo

threat [θret] s amenaza

threaten ['θretən] tr & intr amenazar

threatening ['θretənɪŋ] adj amenazante

three [θri] adj & pron tres || s tres m; **three o'clock** las tres

three'-cor'nered adj triangular; (hat) de tres picos

three hundred adj & pron trescientos || s trescientos m

threepence ['θrepəns] o ['θrɪpəns] s suma de tres peniques; moneda de tres peniques

three'-ply' adj de tres capas

three R's [ɑrz] spl lectura, escritura y aritmética, primeras letras

three'score' adj tres veintenas de

thren·o·dy ['θrenədi] s (pl -dies) treno

thresh [θreʃ] tr (agr) trillar; **to thresh out** decidir después de una discusión cabal || intr trillar; agitarse, menearse

threshing machine s máquina trilladora

threshold ['θreʃold] s umbral m; (physiol, psychol & fig) umbral, limen m; **to be on the threshold of** estar en los umbrales de; **to cross the threshold** atravesar o pisar los umbrales

thrice [θraɪs] adv tres veces; repetidamente, sumamente

thrift [θrɪft] s economía, parquedad

thrift·y ['θrɪftɪ] adj (comp -ier; super -iest) económico, parco; próspero

thrill [θrɪl] s emoción viva || tr emocionar, conmover || intr emocionarse, conmoverse

thriller ['θrɪlər] s cuento o pieza de teatro espeluznante

thrilling ['θrɪlɪŋ] adj emocionante; espeluznante

thrive [θraɪv] v (pret thrived o throve [θrov]; pp thrived o thriven ['θrɪvən]) intr medrar, prosperar

throat [θrot] s garganta; **to clear one's throat** aclarar la voz

throb [θrɑb] s latido, palpitación, pulsación || v (pret & pp throbbed; ger throbbing) intr latir, palpitar, pulsar

throe [θro] s congoja, dolor m; **throes** angustia, agonía; esfuerzo penoso

throne [θron] s trono

throng [θrɔŋ] o [θrɑŋ] s gentío, tropel m, muchedumbre || intr agolparse, apiñarse

throttle ['θrɑtəl] s válvula reguladora; (of a locomotive) regulador m; (of an automobile) acelerador m || tr ahogar, sofocar; impedir, suprimir; (mach) regular, **to throttle down** reducir la velocidad de

through [θru] adj directo, sin paradas; acabado, terminado, **to be through with** haber terminado; no querer ocuparse más de || adv a través de un lado a otro; completamente || prep por, a través de; por medio de; a causa de; todo lo largo de

through·out' adv por todas partes; en todos respectos; desde el principio hasta el fin || prep por todo . . .; durante todo . . .; a lo largo de

through'way' s carretera de peaje de acceso limitado

throw [θro] s echada, tirada, lance m; cobertor ligero || v (pret threw [θru]; pp thrown) tr arrojar, echar, lanzar; tirar (los dados); lanzar (una mirada); desarzonar (a un jinete); proyectar (una sombra); tender (un puente); perder con premeditación (un juego, una carrera), **to throw away** tirar; malgastar; perder, no aprovechar; **to throw to** añadir, dar de más; **to throw out** arrojar, botar, desechar; echar a la calle; **to throw over** abandonar, dejar || intr arrojar, echar, lanzar, **to throw up** vomitar

thrum [θrʌm] v (pret & pp thrummed; ger thrumming) intr teclear, zangarrear; **to thrum on** rasguear

thrush [θrʌʃ] s tordo

thrust [θrʌst] s empuje m; acometida; (with horns) cornada; (with dagger) puñalada; (with sword) estocada; (with knife) cuchillada || v (pret & pp thrust) tr empujar, acometer; clavar, hincar; atravesar, traspasar

thud [θʌd] s baque m, ruido sordo || v (pret & pp thudded; ger thudding) tr & intr golpear con ruido sordo

thug [θʌg] s ladrón m, asesino

thumb [θʌm] s pulgar m, dedo gordo;

all thumbs (coll) desmañado, chapucero, torpe; **to twiddle one's thumbs** menear ociosamente los pulgares; no hacer nada; **under the thumb of** bajo la férula de || tr manosear sin cuidado; ensuciar con los dedos; hojear (un libro) con el pulgar; **to thumb a ride** pedir ser llevado en automóvil indicando la dirección con el pulgar; **to thumb one's nose at** (coll) señalar (a una persona) poniendo el pulgar sobre la nariz en son de burla; (coll) tratar con sumo desprecio

thumb index s escalerilla, índice m con pestañas

thumb'print' s impresión del pulgar || tr marcar con impresión del pulgar

thumb'screw' s tornillo de mariposa, tornillo de orejas

thumb'tack' s chinche m

thump [θʌmp] s golpazo, porrazo || tr golpear, aporrear || intr caer con golpe pesado; andar con pasos pesados; latir (el corazón) con golpes pesados

thumping ['θʌmpɪŋ] adj (coll) enorme, pesado

thunder ['θʌndər] s trueno; (of applause) estruendo; amenaza || tr fulminar (p.ej., censuras, amenazas) || intr tronar; **to thunder against** tronar contra

thun'der·bolt' s rayo

thun'der·clap' s tronido

thunderous ['θʌndərəs] adj atronador, tronitoso

thun'der·show'er s chubasco con truenos

thun'der·storm' s tronada

thun'der·struck' adj atónito, estupefacto, pasmado

Thursday ['θʌrzdɪ] s jueves m

thus [ðʌs] adv así; **thus far** hasta aquí, hasta ahora

thwack [θwæk] s golpe m, porrazo || tr golpear, pegar

thwart [θwɔrt] adj transversal, oblicuo || adv de través || tr desbaratar, impedir, frustrar

thy [ðaɪ] adj poss (archaic & poet) tu

thyme [taɪm] s tomillo

thyroid gland ['θaɪrɔɪd] s glándula tiroides

tuyself [ðaɪ'self] pron (archaic & poet) tú mismo; ti mismo; te; ti

tiara [taɪ'ɑrə] o [taɪ'ɛrə] s (papal miter) tiara; (female adornment) diadema f

tick [tɪk] s tictac m; funda (de almohada o colchón); (coll) crédito; (ent) garrapata; **on tick** (coll) al fiado || intr hacer tictac; latir (el corazón)

ticker ['tɪkər] s teleimpresor m de cinta; (slang) reloj m; (slang) corazón m

ticker tape s cinta de teleimpresor

ticket ['tɪkɪt] s billete m; boleto (Am); (theat) entrada, localidad; (for wrong parking) (coll) aviso de multa; (of a political party) (U.S.A.) lista de candidatos; **that's the ticket** (coll) eso es, eso es lo que se necesita

ticket agent *s* taquillero
ticket collector *s* revisor *m*
ticket office *s* taquilla, despacho de billetes
ticket scalper ['skælpər] *s* revendedor *m* de billetes de teatro
ticket window *s* taquilla, ventanilla
ticking ['tɪkɪŋ] *s* cutí *m*, terliz *m*
tickle ['tɪkəl] *s* cosquillas || *tr* cosquillear; gustar, satisfacer; divertir || *intr* cosquillear
ticklish ['tɪklɪʃ] *adj* cosquilloso; difícil, delicado; inseguro
tick-tock ['tɪk ,tɑk] *s* tictac *m*
tidal wave ['taɪdəl] *s* aguaje *m*, ola de marea; (*e.g., of popular indignation*) ola
tidbit ['tɪd,bɪt] *s* buen bocado, bocadito
tiddlywinks ['tɪdli,wɪŋks] *s* juego de la pulga
tide [taɪd] *s* marea; temporada; **to go against the tide** ir contra la corriente; **to stem the tide** rendir la marea || *tr* llevar, hacer flotar; **to tide over** ayudar un poco; superar (*una dificultad*)
tide'wa'ter *adj* *s* agua de marea; orilla del mar
tidings ['taɪdɪŋz] *spl* noticias, informes *mpl*
ti·dy ['taɪdi] *adj* (*comp* **-dier;** *super* **-diest**) aseado, limpio, pulcro, ordenado || *s* (*pl* **-dies**) pañito bordado, cubierta de respaldar || *v* (*pret* & *pp* **-died**) *tr* asear, limpiar, arreglar, poner en orden || *intr* asearse
tie [taɪ] *s* atadura; lazo, nudo; (*worn on neck*) corbata; (*in games and elections*) empate *m;* (*mus*) ligado; (rr) traviesa || *v* (*pret* & *pp* **tied;** *ger* **tying**) *tr* atar, liar; enlazar; hacer (*la corbata*); confinar, limitar; empatar (*p.ej., una elección*); empatársela a (*una persona*); **to be tied up** estar ocupado; **to tie down** confinar, limitar; **to tie up** atar; envolver; obstruir (*el tráfico*) || *intr* atar; empatar o empatarse (*dos candidatos, dos equipos*)
tie'pin' *s* alfiler *m* de corbata
tier [tɪr] *s* fila, ringlera; (theat) fila de palcos
tiger ['taɪgər] *s* tigre *m*
tiger lily *s* azucena atigrada
tight [taɪt] *adj* apretado, estrecho, ajustado; bien cerrado, hermético, compacto, denso; fijo, firme, sólido; (com) escaso; (sport) casi igual; (coll) agarrado, tacaño; (slang) borracho || *adv* firmemente; **to hold tight** mantener fijo; agarrarse bien ||
tights *spl* traje *m* de malla
tighten ['taɪtən] *tr* apretar; atiesar, estirar || *intr* apretarse; atiesarse, estirarse
tight-fisted ['taɪt'fɪstɪd] *adj* agarrado, tacaño
tight'-fit'ting *adj* ceñido, muy ajustado
tight'rope' *s* cuerda tirante
tight squeeze *s* (coll) brete *m*, aprieto
tigress ['taɪgrɪs] *s* tigresa
tile [taɪl] *s* azulejo; (*for floors*) bal-

dosa; (*for roofs*) teja || *tr* azulejar; embaldosar; tejar
tile roof *s* tejado (de tejas)
till [tɪl] *prep* hasta || *conj* hasta que || *s* cajón *m* o gaveta del dinero || *tr* labrar, cultivar
tilt [tɪlt] *s* inclinación; justa, torneo; **full tilt** a toda velocidad || *tr* inclinar; asestar (*una lanza*) || *intr* inclinarse; justar, tornear; luchar; **to tilt at** luchar con, arremeter contra; protestar contra
timber ['tɪmbər] *s* madera de construcción; madero, viga; bosque *m*, árboles *mpl* de monte
tim'ber-land' *s* bosque *m* maderable
timber line *s* límite *m* de la vegetación, límite del bosque maderable
timbre ['tɪmbər] *s* (phonet & phys) timbre *m*
time [taɪm] *s* tiempo; hora, p.ej., **time to eat** hora de comer; vez, p.ej., **five times** cinco veces; rato, p.ej., **a nice time** un buen rato; (*period for payment*) plazo; horas de trabajo; sueldo; tiempo de parir, término del embarazo; última hora; (phot) tiempo de exposición; **for the time being** por ahora, por el momento; **on time** a tiempo, a la hora debida; (*in installments*) a plazos; **to bide one's time** esperar la hora propicia; **to do time** (coll) cumplir una condena; **to have a good time** darse buen tiempo; **to have no time for** no poder tolerar; **to lose time** atrasarse (*el reloj*); **to make time** avanzar con rapidez; **to pass the time of day** saludarse (*dos personas*); **to take one's time** no darse prisa, ir despacio; **what time is it?** ¿qué hora es? || *tr* calcular el tiempo de; medir el tiempo de; (sport) cronometrar
time bomb *s* bomba-reloj *f*
time'card' *s* hoja de presencia, tarjeta registradora
time clock *s* reloj *m* registrador
time exposure *s* exposición de tiempo
time fuse *s* espoleta de tiempos
time'keep'er *s* alistador *m* de tiempo; reloj *m;* (sport) cronometrador *m*, juez *m* de tiempo
time·ly ['taɪmli] *adj* (*comp* **-lier;** *super* **-liest**) oportuno
time'piece' *s* reloj *m*
time signal *s* señal horaria
time'ta'ble *s* horario, itinerario
time'work' *s* trabajo a jornal
time'worn' *adj* gastado por el tiempo
time zone *s* huso horario
timid ['tɪmɪd] *adj* tímido
timing gears ['taɪmɪŋ] *spl* engranaje *m* de distribución, mando de las válvulas
timorous ['tɪmərəs] *adj* tímido, miedoso
tin [tɪn] *s* (*element*) estaño; (*tin plate*) hojalata; (*cup, box, etc.*) lata || *v* (*pret* & *pp* **tinned;** *ger* **tinning**) *tr* estañar; (*to pack in cans*) enlatar; recubrir de hojalata
tin can *s* lata, envase *m* de hojalata
tincture ['tɪŋktʃər] *s* tintura

tin cup s taza de hojalata
tinder ['tɪndər] s yesca
tin'der-box' s lumbres fpl, yesquero; persona muy excitable; semillero de violencia
tin foil s hojuela de estaño, papel m de estaño
ting-a-ling ['tɪŋə,lɪŋ] s tilín m
tinge [tɪndʒ] s matiz m, tinte m; dejo, gustillo || v (ger **tingeing** o **tinging**) tr matizar, teñir; dar gusto o sabor a
tingle ['tɪŋgəl] s comezón f, picazón f || intr sentir comezón; zumbar (los oídos); (e.g., with enthusiasm) estremecerse
tin hat s (coll) yelmo de acero
tinker ['tɪŋkər] s calderero remendón; chapucero || intr ocuparse vanamente
tinkle ['tɪŋkəl] s retintín m || tr hacer retiñir || intr retiñir
tin plate s hojalata
tin roof s tejado de hojalata
tinsel ['tɪnsəl] s oropel m; (e.g., for a Christmas tree) lentejuelas de hojas de estaño
tin'smith' s hojalatero
tin soldier s soldadito de plomo
tint [tɪnt] s tinte m, matiz m || tr teñir, matizar, colorar ligeramente
tin'ware' s objetos de hojalata
tin'type' s ferrotipo
ti-ny ['taɪni] adj (comp **-nier;** super **-niest**) diminuto, menudo, pequeñito
tip [tɪp] s extremo, extremidad; (of shoestring) herrete m; (of arrow) casquillo; (of umbrella) regatón m; (of tongue) punta; (of shoe) puntera; (of cigarette) embocadura; inclinación; golpecito; soplo, aviso confidencial; (fee) propina f || v (pret & pp **tipped;** ger **tipping**) tr herretear; inclinar, ladear; volcar; golpear ligeramente; dar propina a; informar por debajo de cuerda; tocarse (el sombrero) con los dedos; quitarse (el sombrero en señal de cortesía); **to tip in** (typ) encañonar (un pliego) || intr dar una propina o propinas; inclinarse, ladearse; volcarse
tip'cart' s volquete m
tip'-off' s (coll) informe dado por debajo de cuerda
tipped'-in' adj (bb) fuera de texto
tipple ['tɪpəl] intr beborrotear
tip'staff' s vara de justicia; alguacil m de vara
tip-sy ['tɪpsi] adj (comp **-sier;** super **-siest**) achispado
tip'toe' s punta del pie; **on tiptoe** de puntillas; alerta; furtivamente || v (pret & pp **-toed;** ger **-toeing**) intr andar de puntillas
tirade ['taɪred] s diatriba, invectiva
tire [taɪr] s neumático, llanta de goma; (of metal) calce m, llanta || tr cansar; aburrir, fastidiar || intr (to be tiresome) cansar; (to get tired) cansarse; aburrirse, fastidiarse
tire chain s cadena de llanta, cadena antirresbaladiza
tired [taɪrd] adj cansado, rendido
tire gauge s indicador m de presión de inflado

tireless ['taɪrlɪs] adj incansable, infatigable
tire pressure s presión de inflado
tire pump s bomba para inflar neumáticos
tiresome ['taɪrsəm] adj cansado, aburrido, pesado
tissue ['tɪʃu] s tejido fino; papel m de seda; (biol & fig) tejido
tissue paper s papel m de seda
titanium [taɪ'teni-əm] o [tɪ'teni-əm] s titanio
tithe [taɪð] s décimo, décima parte; (tax paid to church) diezmo || tr diezmar
Titian ['tɪʃən] adj castaño rojizo || s el Ticiano
title ['taɪtəl] s título; (sport) campeonato || tr titular
title deed s título de propiedad
ti'tle-hold'er s titulado; (sport) campeón m
title page s portada, frontispicio
title rôle s (theat) papel m principal (el que corresponde al título de la obra)
titter ['tɪtər] s risita ahogada, risita disimulada || intr reír a medias, reír con disimulo
titular ['tɪtʃələr] adj titular; nominal
tn. abbr **ton**
to [tu], [tʊ] o [tə] adv hacia adelante; **to and fro** de una parte a otra, de aquí para allá; **to come to** volver en sí || prep a, para; **he is going to Madrid** va a Madrid; **they gave something to the beggar** dieron algo al pobre; **we are learning to dance** aprendemos a bailar; para, p.ej., **he is reading to himself** lee para sí; por, p.ej., **work to do** trabajo por hacer; hasta, p.ej., **to a certain extent** hasta cierto punto; en, p.ej., **from door to door** de puerta en puerta; con, p.ej., **kind to her** amable con ella; segun, p.ej., **to my way of thinking** según mi modo de pensar; menos, p.ej., **five minutes to ten** las diez menos cinco
toad [tod] s sapo
toad'stool' s agárico, seta; seta venenosa
to-and-fro ['tu-ənd'fro] adj alternativo, de vaivén
toast [tost] s tostadas; (drink) brindis m; **a piece of toast** una tostada || tr tostar; brindar a o por || intr tostarse; brindar
toaster ['tostər] s (of bread) tostador m; brindador m
toast'mas'ter s el que presenta a los oradores en un banquete, maestro de ceremonias
tobac-co [tə'bæko] s (pl **-cos**) tabaco
tobacco pouch s petaca
toboggan [tə'bɑgən] s tobogán m || intr deslizarse en tobogán
tocsin ['tɑksɪn] s campana de alarma; campana de alarma
today [tʊ'de] adv & s hoy
toddle ['tɑdəl] s pasitos vacilantes || intr andar con pasitos vacilantes; hacer pinitos (un niño o un enfermo)

tod·dy ['tadı] s (pl -dies) ponche m

to-do [tə'du] s (coll) alharaca, alboroto

toe [to] s dedo del pie; (of stocking) punta || v (pret & pp toed; ger toeing) tr — to toe the line o the mark ponerse a la raya; obrar como se debe

toe'nail' s uña del dedo del pie

tog [tag] s (coll) prenda de vestir

together [tu'geðər] adv juntamente; juntos; al mismo tiempo; sin interrupción; de acuerdo; to bring together reunir; confrontar; reconciliar; to call together convocar; to go together ir juntos; ser novios; hacer juego; to stick together (coll) quedarse unidos, no abandonarse

toil [tɔɪl] s afán m, fatiga; faena, obra laboriosa; toils red f, lazo || intr atrafagar; moverse con fatiga

toilet ['tɔɪlɪt] s tocado, atavío; (dressing table) tocador m; retrete m, inodoro, excusado; to make one's toilet asearse, acicalarse

toilet articles spl artículos de tocador

toilet paper s papel higiénico

toilet powder s polvos de tocador

toilet soap s jabón m de olor, jabón de tocador

toilet water s agua de tocador

token ['tokən] s señal f, prueba; prenda, recuerdo; (used as money) ficha, tanto; by the same token por el mismo motivo; in token of en señal de

tolerance ['talərəns] s tolerancia

tolerate ['talə,ret] tr tolerar

toll [tol] s (of bells) doble m; (to pass along a road or over a bridge) peaje m; (to use a canal) derechos de paso; (to use a telephone) tarifa; (number of victims) baja, mortalidad || tr tocar a muerto (una campana); llamar con toque de difuntos || intr doblar

toll bridge s puente m de peaje

toll call s (telp) llamada a larga distancia

toll'gate' s barrera de peaje

toma·to [tə'meto] o [tə'mato] s (pl -toes) (plant) tomatera o tomate m; (fruit) tomate

tomb [tum] s tumba, sepulcro

tomboy ['tam,bɔɪ] s moza retozona, muchacha traviesa

tomb'stone' s piedra o lápida sepulcral

tomcat ['tam,kæt] s gato macho

tome [tom] s tomo; libro grueso

tomorrow [tu'maro] o [tu'mɔro] adv mañana || s mañana m; the day after tomorrow pasado mañana

tom-tom ['tam,tam] s tantán m

ton [tʌn] s tonelada; tons (coll) montones mpl

tone [ton] s tono || tr entonar || intr armonizar; to tone down moderarse; to tone up reforzarse

tone poem s poema sinfónico

tongs [tɔŋz] o [taŋz] spl tenazas; (e.g., for sugar) tenacillas

tongue [tʌŋ] s (anat) lengua; (of a wagon) vara, lanza; (of a belt buckle) tarabilla; (of shoe) lengua, lengüeta; (language) lengua, idioma

m; to hold one's tongue morderse la lengua

tongue twister ['twɪstər] s trabalenguas m

tonic ['tanık] adj & s tónico

tonic accent s acento prosódico

tonight [tu'naɪt] adv & s esta noche

tonnage ['tʌnɪdʒ] s tonelaje m

tonsil ['tansəl] s tonsila, amígdala

tonsillitis [,tansı'laɪtıs] s tonsilitis f, amigdalitis f

ton·y ['toni] adj (comp -ler; super -iest) (slang) elegante, aristocrático

too [tu] adv (also) también; (more than enough) demasiado; too bad! ¡qué lástima!; too many demasiados; too much demasiado

tool [tul] s herramienta; (person used for one's own ends) instrumento || tr trabajar con herramienta; (bb) filetear, estampar

tool bag s bolsa de herramientas

tool'mak'er s tallador m de herramientas, herrero de herramientas

toot [tut] s (of horn) toque m; (of klaxon) bocinazo; (of locomotive) pitazo; (coll) parranda || tr sonar; to toot one's own horn cantar sus propias alabanzas || intr sonar

tooth [tuθ] s (pl teeth [tiθ]) diente m

tooth'ache' s dolor m de muelas

tooth'brush' s cepillo de dientes

toothless ['tuθlıs] adj desdentado

tooth paste s pasta dentífrica

tooth'pick' s limpiadientes m, mondadientes m, palillo

tooth powder s polvo dentífrico

top [tap] s (of a mountain, tree, etc.) cima; (of a mountain; high point) cumbre f; (of a tree) copa; (of a barrel, box, etc.) tapa; (of a page) principio; (of a table) tablero; (of a wall) coronamiento; (of a bathing suit) camiseta; (of a carriage or auto) toldo; (toy) peón m, peonza; (naut) cofa; at the top of en lo alto de; (e.g., one's class) a la cabeza de; at the top of one's voice a voz en grito; from top to bottom de arriba abajo; de alto a bajo; completamente; on top of en lo alto de; encima de, the tops (slang) la flor de la canela; to sleep like a top dormir como un leño || v (pret & pp topped; ger topping) tr coronar, rematar; cubrir; aventajar, superar; descopar (p.ej., un árbol)

topaz ['topæz] s topacio

top billing s cabecera de cartel

top'coat' s sobretodo; abrigo de entretiempo

toper ['topər] s borrachín m

top hat s chistera, sombrero de copa

top'-heav'y adj más pesado arriba que abajo

topic ['tapık] s asunto, materia, tema m

top'knot' s moño

top'mast' s (naut) mastelero

top'most' adj (el) más alto

topogra·phy [tə'pagrəfi] s (pl -phies) topografía

topple ['tapəl] tr derribar, volcar ||

intr derribarse, volcarse; caerse, venirse abajo

top priority *s* máxima prioridad

topsail ['tɑpsəl] o ['tɑp,sel] *s* (naut) gavia

top'soil' *s* capa superficial del suelo

topsy-turvy ['tɑpsɪ'tʌrvi] *adj* desbarajustado || *adv* en cuadro, patas arriba || *s* desbarajuste *m*

torch [tɔrtʃ] *s* antorcha; lámpara de bolsillo; **to carry the torch for** (slang) amar desesperadamente

torch'bear'er *s* hachero; (fig) adicto, partidario

torch'light' *s* luz *f* de antorcha

torch song *s* canción lenta y melancólica de amor no correspondido

torment [ˈtɔrment] *s* tormento || [tɔr'ment] *tr* atormentar

torna•do [tɔr'nedo] *s* (*pl* -does o -dos) tornado, tromba terrestre

torpe•do [tɔr'pido] *s* (*pl* -does) torpedo || *tr* torpedear

torrent [ˈtɑrənt] o [ˈtɔrənt] *s* torrente *m*

torrid [ˈtɑrɪd] o [ˈtɔrɪd] *adj* tórrido

tor•so [ˈtɔrso] *s* (*pl* -sos) torso

tortoise [ˈtɔrtəs] *s* tortuga

tortoise shell *s* carey *m*

torture [ˈtɔrtʃər] *s* tortura || *tr* torturar, atormentar

toss [tɔs] o [tɑs] *s* echada; alcance *m* de una echada || *tr* arrojar, echar; lanzar al aire; agitar, menear; levantar airosamente (*la cabeza*); lanzar (*p.ej., un comentario*); echar a cara o cruz; **to toss off** hacer muy rápidamente; tragar de un golpe || *intr* agitarse, menearse; **to toss and turn** (*in bed*) revolverse, dar vueltas

toss'-up' *s* cara o cruz; probabilidad igual

tot [tɑt] *s* párvulo, peque *m*, chiquitín *m*

to•tal [ˈtotəl] *adj* total; (*e.g., loss*) completo || *s* total *m* || *v* (*pret & pp* -taled o -talled; *ger* -taling o -talling) *tr* ascender a, sumar

totter [ˈtɑtər] *s* tambaleo || *intr* tambalear; estar para desplomarse

touch [tʌtʃ] *s* (*act*) toque *m*; (*sense*) tacto, tiento; (*of piano, pianist, typewriter, typist*) tacto; (*of an illness*) ramo, ataque ligero; pizca, poquito; **to get in touch with** ponerse en comunicación o contacto con; **to lose one's touch** perder el tiento || *tr* tocar; conmover, enternecer; probar (*vino, licor*); (*for a loan*) (slang) pedir prestado a, dar un sablazo a; **to touch up** retocar || *intr* tocar; **to touch at** tocar en (*un puerto*)

touching [ˈtʌtʃɪŋ] *adj* conmovedor, enternecedor || *prep* tocante a

touch typewriting *s* escritura al tacto

touch•y [ˈtʌtʃi] *adj* (*comp* -ier; *super* -iest) quisquilloso, enojadizo

tough [tʌf] *adj* correoso; tenaz; difícil; gamberro; (*e.g., luck*) malo || *s* gamberro, guapetón *m*

toughen [ˈtʌfən] *tr* hacer correoso; hacer tenaz; dificultar || *intr* ponerse

correoso; hacerse tenaz; hacerse difícil

tour [tur] *s* jira, paseo, vuelta; viaje largo; **on tour** de jira, de viaje || *tr* viajar por, recorrer || *intr* viajar por distracción o diversión

touring car [ˈturɪŋ] *s* coche *m* de turismo

tourist [ˈturɪst] *adj* turístico || *s* turista *mf*

tournament [ˈturnəmənt] o [ˈtʌrnəmənt] *s* torneo

tourney [ˈturni] o [ˈtʌrni] *s* torneo || *intr* tornear

tourniquet [ˈturnɪ,ket] o [ˈtʌrnɪ,ke] *s* torniquete *m*

tousle [ˈtauzəl] *tr* despeinar, enmarañar

tow [to] *s* remolque *m*; (*e.g., of hemp*) estopa; **to take in tow** dar remolque a; (fig) encargarse de || *tr* remolcar

towage [ˈto-ɪdʒ] *s* remolque *m*; derechos de remolque

toward(s) [tord(z)] o [tə'word(z)] *prep* (*in the direction of*) hacia; (*with regard to*) para con; (*a certain hour*) cerca de, a eso de

tow'boat' *s* remolcador *m*

tow•el [ˈtau-əl] *s* toalla || *v* (*pret & pp* -eled o -elled; *ger* -eling o -elling) *tr* secar con toalla

towel rack *s* toallero

tower [ˈtau-ər] *s* torre *f* || *intr* encumbrarse, empinarse

towering [ˈtau-ərɪŋ] *adj* encumbrado; sobresaliente; excesivo

towing service [ˈto-ɪŋ] *s* servicio de grúa

tow'line' *s* cable *m* de remolque, sirga

town [taun] *s* población, pueblo, villa; **in town** a la ciudad, en la ciudad

town clerk *s* escribano municipal

town council *s* concejo municipal

town crier *s* pregonero público

town hall *s* ayuntamiento, casa de ayuntamiento

towns'folk' *spl* vecinos del pueblo

township [ˈtaun/ɪp] *s* sexmo; terreno público de seis millas en cuadro

towns•man [ˈtaunzmən] *s* (*pl* -men [mən]) ciudadano, vecino; conciudadano, paisano

towns'peo'ple *spl* vecinos del pueblo

town talk *s* comidilla o hablillas del pueblo

tow'path' *s* camino de sirga

tow plane *s* avión *m* de remolque

tow'rope' *s* cuerda de remolque

tow truck *s* camión-grúa *m*

toxic [ˈtɑksɪk] *adj & s* tóxico

toy [tɔɪ] *adj* de juguete || *s* juguete *m*; (*trifle*) bagatela; (*trinket*) dije *m*, bujería || *intr* jugar; divertirse; **to toy with** jugar con (*los sentimientos de una persona*); acariciar (*una idea*)

toy bank *s* alcancía, hucha

toy soldier *s* soldado de juguete

trace [tres] *s* huella, rastro; indicio, vestigio; (*of harness*) tirante *m*; pizca || *tr* rastrear; trazar (*p.ej., una curva*; *los rasgos de una persona o cosa*); averiguar el paradero de; remontar al origen de

trache·a ['treki·ə] s (pl -ae [ˌi]) tráquea

track [træk] s (of foot) huella; (of a wheel) rodada, carril m; (of a boat) estela; (of railroad) vía; (of an airplane, a hurricane) trayectoria; (of a tractor) llanta de oruga; camino, senda; (course followed by a boat) derrota; (of ideas, events, etc.) sucesión; (sport) pista; **to keep track** of no perder de vista, no olvidar; **to lose track of** perder de vista; olvidar; **to make tracks** dejar pisadas; irse muy de prisa ‖ tr rastrear; seguir la huella o la pista de; dejar pisadas en, manchar pisando; **to track down** seguir y capturar; averiguar el origen de

tracking ['trækɪŋ] s seguimiento (de vehículos espaciales)

tracking station s estación de seguimiento

trackless trolley ['træklɪs] s filobús m, trolebús m

track meet s concurso de carreras y saltos

track'walk'er s guardavía m

tract [trækt] s espacio, tracto; folleto; (anat) canal m, sistema m

traction ['trækʃən] s tracción

traction company s empresa de tranvías

tractor ['træktər] s tractor m

trade [tred] s comercio; negocio, trato; trueque m, canje m; (calling, job) oficio; clientela, parroquia; (e.g., in slaves) trata ‖ tr cambiar, trocar; **to trade in** dar como parte del pago; **to trade off** cambalachear; ‖ intr comerciar; comprar; **to trade in** comerciar en; **to trade on** aprovecharse de

trade'mark' s marca de fábrica, marca registrada

trade name s nombre m comercial, razón f social; nombre de fábrica

trader ['tredər] s traficante mf

trade school s escuela de artes y oficios

trades·man ['tredzmən] s (pl -men [mən]) tendero; comerciante m; (Brit) artesano

trades union o **trade union** s sindicato, gremio de obreros

trade unionist s sindicalista mf

trade winds spl vientos alisios

trading post ['tredɪŋ] s factoría; (in stock exchange) puesto de compraventa

trading stamp s sello de premio, sello de descuento

tradition [trə'dɪʃən] s tradición

traduce [trə'djus] o [trə'dus] tr calumniar

traf·fic ['træfɪk] s tráfico, comercio; tráfico, circulación; (e.g., in slaves) trata ‖ v (pret & pp **-ficked**; ger **-ficking**) intr traficar

traffic circle s glorieta de tráfico

traffic court s juzgado de tráfico

traffic jam s embotellamiento, tapón m de tráfico

traffic light s luz f de tráfico, semáforo

traffic sign o **signal** s señal f de tráfico

traffic ticket s aviso de multa

tragedian [trə'dʒidɪ·ən] s trágico

trage·dy ['trædʒɪdi] s (pl -dies) tragedia

tragic ['trædʒɪk] adj trágico

trail [trel] s rastro, huella, pista; (path through rough country) trocha, senda, vereda; (of a gown) cola; (of smoke, a rocket, etc.) estela ‖ tr arrastrar; seguir la pista de; andar detrás de, llevar (p.ej., barro) con los pies ‖ intr arrastrar; rezagarse; arrastrarse, trepar (una planta); **to trail off** desaparecer poco a poco

trailer ['trelər] s remolque m, coche-habitación m, casa rodante; planta rastrera

trailing arbutus ['trelɪŋ] s epigea rastrera

train [tren] s (of railway cars; of waves) tren m; (of thought) hilo ‖ tr adiestrar; guiar (las plantas); (sport) entrenar ‖ intr adiestrarse; (sport) entrenarse

trained nurse s enfermera graduada

trainer ['trenər] s (sport) entrenador m

training ['trenɪŋ] s adiestramiento; instrucción; (sport) entrenamiento

training school s escuela práctica; reformatorio

training ship s buque m escuela

trait [tret] s característica, rasgo

traitor ['tretər] s traidor m

traitress ['tretrɪs] s traidora

trajecto·ry [trə'dʒɛktəri] s (pl -ries) trayectoria

tramp [træmp] s vagabundo; marcha pesada, ruido de pisadas ‖ tr pisar con fuerza; recorrer a pie ‖ intr andar a pie; vagabundear

trample ['træmpəl] tr pisotear ‖ intr — **to trample on** o sumo pisotear

tramp steamer s vapor volandero

trance [træns] s trans, s arrobamiento; rapto; estado hipnótico

tranquil ['træŋkwɪl] adj tranquilo

tranquilize ['træŋkwɪˌlaɪz] tr & intr tranquilizar

tranquilizer ['træŋkwɪˌlaɪzər] s tranquilizante m

tranquillity [træŋ'kwɪlɪti] s tranquilidad

transact [træn'zækt] o [træns'ækt] tr tramitar; llevar a cabo

transaction [træn'zækʃən] o [træns-'ækʃən] s tramitación, transacción

transatlantic [ˌtrænsət'læntɪk] adj & s transatlántico

transcend [træn'sɛnd] tr exceder, superar ‖ intr sobresalir

transcribe [træn'skraɪb] tr transcribir

transcript ['trænskrɪpt] s trasunto, traslado; (educ) hoja de estudios, certificado de estudios

transcription [træn'skrɪpʃən] s transcripción

transept ['trænsɛpt] s crucero, transepto

trans·fer ['trænsfər] s traslado; transbordo; contraseña o billete m de transferencia ‖ [træns'fʌr] o ['trænsfər] v (pret & pp **-ferred**; ger

-ferring) *tr* trasladar, transferir; transbordar ‖ *intr* cambiar de tren, tranvía, etc.

transfix [træns'fɪks] *tr* espetar, traspasar; dejar atónito

transform [træns'fɔrm] *tr* transformar ‖ *intr* transformarse

transformer [træns'fɔrmər] *s* transformador *m*

transfusion [træns'fju/ən] *s* transfusión; (med) transfusión de la sangre

transgress [træns'grɛs] *tr* transgredir, violar; exceder, traspasar (*p.ej., los límites de la prudencia*) ‖ *intr* pecar, prevaricar

transgression [træns'grɛ/ən] *s* transgresión; pecado, prevaricación

transient ['træn/ənt] *adj* pasajero, transitorio; de tránsito ‖ *s* transeúnte *mf*

transistor [træn'zɪstər] *s* transistor *m*

transit [ɪ'trænsɪt] o [ɪ'trænzɪt] *s* tránsito

transitive [ɪ'trænsɪtɪv] *adj* transitivo ‖ *s* verbo transitivo

transitory [ɪ'trænsɪ‚tori] *adj* transitorio

translate [træns'let] o ['trænslet] *tr* (*from one language to another*) traducir; (*from one place to another*) trasladar ‖ *intr* traducirse

translation [træns'le/ən] *s* traducción; traslación

translator [træns'letər] *s* traductor *m*

transliterate [træns'lɪtə‚ret] *tr* transcribir

translucent [træns'lusənt] *adj* translúcido

transmission [træns'mɪ/ən] *s* transmisión; (aut) cambio de marchas, cambio de velocidades

transmis·sion-gear' box *s* caja de cambio de marchas, caja de velocidades

trans·mit [træns'mɪt] *v* (*pret & pp* -mitted; *ger* -mitting) *tr & intr* transmitir

transmitter [træns'mɪtər] *s* transmisor *m*

transmitting set *s* aparato transmisor

transmitting station *s* estación transmisora, emisora

transmute [træns'mjut] *tr & intr* transmutar

transom [trænsəm] *s* (*crosspiece*) travesaño; (*window over door*) montante *m*; (*of ship*) yugo de popa

transparen·cy [træns'pɛrənsi] *s* (*pl* -cies) transparencia

transparent [træns'pɛrənt] *adj* transparente

transpire [træns'paɪr] *intr* transpirar; (*to become known, leak out*) transpirar; (coll) acontecer, tener lugar

transplant [træns'plænt] o ['trænsplɑnt] *tr* transplantar ‖ *intr* transplantarse

transport ['trænspɔrt] *s* transporte *m*; (aer & naut) transporte *m*; rapto, éxtasis *m*, transporte *m* ‖ [træns'pɔrt] *tr* transportar

transportation [‚trænspɔr'te/ən] *s* transporte *m*; (U.S.A.) pasaje *m*, billete *m* de viaje

transport worker *s* transportista *mf*

transpose [træns'poz] *tr* transponer; (mus) transportar

trans·ship [træns'/ɪp] *v* (*pret & pp* -shipped; *ger* -shipping) *tr* transbordar

transshipment [træns'/ɪpmənt] *s* transbordo

trap [træp] *s* trampa; (*double-curved pipe*) sifón *m*; coche ligero de dos ruedas; (sport) lanzaplatos *m* ‖ *v* (*pret & pp* trapped; *ger* trapping) *tr* entrampar; atrapar (*a un ladrón*)

trap door *s* escotillón *m*, trampa; (theat) escotillón *m*, pescante *m*

trapeze [trə'piz] *s* trapecio

trapezoid ['træpɪ‚zɔɪd] *s* trapecio

trapper [ɪ'træpər] *s* cazador *m* de alforja

trappings [ɪ'træpɪŋz] *spl* (*adornments*) adornos, atavíos; (*of a horse's harness*) jaeces *mpl*

trap'shoot'ing *s* tiro al vuelo

trash [træ/] *s* broza, basura, desecho; (*junk*) cachivaches *mpl*; (*nonsense*) disparates *mpl*; (*worthless people*) gentuza

trash can *s* basurero

travail [ɪ'trævel] o [trə'vel] *s* afán *m*, labor *f*, pena; dolores *mpl* del parto

trav·el [ɪ'trævəl] *s* viaje *m*; el viajar; (mach) recorrido ‖ *v* (*pret & pp* -eled o -elled; *ger* -eling o -elling) *tr* viajar por; recorrer ‖ *intr* viajar; andar, recorrer

travel bureau *s* oficina de turismo

traveler [ɪ'trævələr] *s* viajero; (*salesman*) viajante *m*

traveler's check *s* cheque *m* de viajeros

traveling expenses *spl* gastos de viaje

traveling salesman *s* viajante *m*, agente viajero

traverse [ɪ'trævərs] o [trə'vʌrs] *tr* atravesar; recorrer, pasar por

traves·ty [ɪ'trævɪsti] *s* (*pl* -ties) parodia ‖ *v* (*pret & pp* -tied) *tr* parodiar

trawl [trɔl] *s* red barredera, espinel *m*, palangre *m* ‖ *tr & intr* pescar a la rastra

tray [tre] *s* bandeja; (chem & phot) cubeta

treacherous ['tret/ərəs] *adj* traicionero, traidor; incierto, poco seguro

treacher·y ['tret/əri] *s* (*pl* -ies) traición, alevosía

tread [trɛd] *s* (*stepping*) pisada; (*of stairs*) grada, huella, peldaño; (*of stilts*) horquilla; (*of a tire*) banda de rodamiento; (*of shoe*) suela; (*of an egg*) meaje, galladura ‖ *v* (*pret* trod [trɑd]; *pp* trodden ['trɑdən] o trod) *tr* pisar, pisotear; abrumar, agobiar ‖ *intr* andar, caminar

treadle ['trɛdəl] *s* pedal *m*

tread'mill' *s* rueda de andar; (*futile drudgery*) noria

treas. *abbr* treasurer, treasury

treason ['trizən] *s* traición

treasonable ['trizənəbəl] *adj* traicionero, traidor

treasure ['trɛʒər] *s* tesoro ‖ *tr* atesorar

treasurer ['trɛʒərər] *s* tesorero

treasur·y ['trɛʒəri] *s* (*pl* -ies) tesorería; tesoro

treat [trit] s convite m; (to a drink) convidada; (something providing particular enjoyment) regalo, deleite m || tr tratar; convidar, regalar; curar (a un enfermo) || intr tratar; convidar, regalar; **to treat of** tratar de

treatise ['tritɪs] s tratado

treatment ['tritmənt] s tratamiento

trea·ty ['triti] s (pl -ties) tratado

treble ['trebəl] adj (threefold) tresdoble, triple; sobreagudo; (mus) atiplado; (mus) de tiple || s (person) tiple mf; (voice) tiple m || tr triplicar || intr triplicarse

tree [tri] s árbol m

tree farm s monte m tallar

treeless ['trilɪs] adj pelado, sin árboles

tree'top' s copa, cima de árbol

trellis ['trelɪs] s enrejado, espaldera; emparrado

tremble ['trembəl] s temblor m, estremecimiento || intr temblar, estremecerse

tremendous [trɪ'mendəs] adj tremendo

tremor ['tremər] o ['trimər] s temblor m

trench [trentʃ] s foso, zanja; (for irrigation) acequia; (mil) trinchera

trenchant ['trentʃənt] adj mordaz, punzante; enérgico, bien definido

trench coat s trinchera

trench mortar s (mil) lanzabombas m

trench'-plow' tr (agr) desfondar

trend [trend] s curso, dirección, tendencia || intr dirigirse, tender

trespass ['trespəs] s entrada sin derecho; infracción, violación; culpa, pecado || intr entrar sin derecho; pecar; **no trespassing** prohibida la entrada; **to trespass against** pecar contra; **to trespass on** entrar sin derecho en; infringir, violar; abusar de (p.ej., la paciencia de uno)

tress [tres] s (braid of hair) trenza; (curl) bucle m, rizo

trestle ['tresəl] s caballete m; puente m o viaducto de caballetes

trial ['traɪəl] s ensayo, prueba; aflicción, desgracia; (law) juicio, proceso, vista; **on trial** a prueba; (law) en juicio; **to bring to trial** enjuiciar

trial and error s método de tanteos

trial balloon s globo sonda; **to send up a trial balloon** (fig) lanzar un globo sonda

trial by jury s juicio por jurado

trial jury s jurado procesal

trial order s (com) pedido de ensayo

triangle ['traɪ,æŋgəl] s triángulo

tribe [traɪb] s tribu f

tribunal [trɪ'bjunəl] o [traɪ'bjunəl] s tribunal m

tribune ['trɪbjun] s tribuna

tributar·y ['trɪbjə,teri] adj tributario || s (pl -ies) tributario

tribute ['trɪbjut] s tributo

trice [traɪs] s momento, instante m; **in a trice** en un periquete

trick [trɪk] s ardid m, artimaña; (knack) maña; (feat) suerte f; (prank) travesura, burla, chasco; tanda, turno, ilusión; (feat with cards) truco; (cards in one round) baza; (coll) chiquita; **to be up to one's old tricks** hacer de las suyas; **to play a dirty trick on** hacer una mala jugada a || tr trampear; burlar, engañar; ataviar

tricker·y ['trɪkəri] s (pl -ies) tramperia, malas mañas

trickle ['trɪkəl] s chorro delgado, goteo || intr escurrir, gotear; pasar gradual e irregularmente

trickster ['trɪkstər] s tramposo, embustero

trick·y ['trɪki] adj (comp -ier; super -iest) tramposo, engañoso; difícil; (animal) vicioso; (ticklish to deal with) delicado

tricorn ['traɪkɔrn] adj & s tricornio

tried [traɪd] adj fiel, probado, seguro

trifle ['traɪfəl] s bagatela, friolera, fruslería; (trinket) bagatela, baratija || tr — **to trifle away** malgastar || intr estar ocioso, holgar; **to trifle with** manosear; jugar con, burlarse de

trifling ['traɪflɪŋ] adj frívolo, fútil, ligero; insignificante, trivial

trifocal [traɪ'fokəl] adj trifocal || s lente f trifocal; **trifocals** anteojos trifocales

trig. abbr **trigonometric, trigonometry**

trigger ['trɪgər] s (e.g., of a gun) disparador m, gatillo; (of any device) disparador || tr poner en movimiento, provocar

trigonometry [,trɪgə'nɑmɪtri] s trigonometría

trill [trɪl] s trinado, trino; (made with voice, esp. of birds) gorjeo; (phonet) vibración || tr decir o cantar gorjeando; pronunciar con vibración || intr trinar; gorjear

trillion ['trɪljən] s (U.S.A.) billón m; (Brit) trillón m

trilo·gy ['trɪlədʒi] s (pl -gies) trilogía

trim [trɪm] adj (comp **trimmer**; super **trimmest**) acicalado, compuesto, elegante || s condición, estado; buena condición; adorno, atavío; traje m, vestido; (of sails) orientación || v (pret & pp **trimmed**; ger **trimming**) tr ajustar, adaptar, arreglar, componer; adornar, decorar; decorar, enguirnaldar (el árbol de Navidad); recortar, cortar ligeramente (el pelo); despabilar (una lámpara o vela); mondar, podar (árboles, plantas); acepillar, desbastar; (naut) orientar (las velas); (coll) derrotar, vencer; (coll) regañar

trimming ['trɪmɪŋ] s adorno, guarnición; franja, orla; (coll) paliza, zurra; (coll) derrota; **trimmings** accesorios, arrequives mpl; recortes mpl

trini·ty ['trɪnɪti] s (pl -ties) (group of three) trinca || **Trinity** s Trinidad

trinket ['trɪŋkɪt] s (small ornament) dije m; (trivial object) baratija, bujería, chuchería

tri·o ['tri-o] s (pl -os) (group of three) terna, trío; (mus) trío

trip [trɪp] s viaje m; jira, recorrido;

(*stumble*) tropiezo; (*act of causing a person to stumble*) traspié *m*, zancadilla; (*blunder*) desliz *m* ‖ *v* (*pret & pp* tripped; *ger* tripping) *tr* trompicar, echar la zancadilla a; detener, estorbar; inclinar; coger en falta; coger en una mentira ‖ *intr* ir con paso rápido y ligero; brincar, saltar, correr; tropezar; **to trip over** tropezar con, contra o en

tripe [traip] *s* callos, mondongo; (*slang*) disparate *m*, barbaridad

trip'ham'mer *s* martillo pilón

triphthong [ˈtrifθɔŋ] o [ˈtrifθaŋ] *s* triptongo

triple [ˈtripəl] *adj & s* triple *m* ‖ *tr* triplicar ‖ *intr* triplicarse

triplet [ˈtriplit] *s* (*offspring*) trillizo; (*stanza of three lines*) terceto; (*mus*) terceto, tresillo

triplicate [ˈtriplikit] *adj & s* triplicado; **in triplicate** por triplicado ‖ [ˈtriplɪˌket] *tr* triplicar

tripod [ˈtraipɑd] *m* trípode *m*

triptych [ˈtriptik] *s* tríptico

trite [trait] *adj* gastado, trillado, trivial

triumph [ˈtraiəmf] *s* triunfo ‖ *intr* triunfar; **to triumph over** triunfar de

triumphal arch [traiˈʌmfəl] *s* arco triunfal

triumphant [traiˈʌmfənt] *adj* triunfante

trivia [ˈtrivi·ə] *spl* bagatelas, trivialidades

trivial [ˈtrivi·əl] *adj* trivial, insignificante

triviali·ty [ˌtriviˈælɪti] *s* (*pl* -ties) trivialidad

Trojan [ˈtrodʒən] *adj & s* troyano

Trojan horse *s* caballo de Troya

Trojan War *s* guerra de Troya

troll [trol] *tr & intr* pescar a la cacea

trolley [ˈtrali] *s* polea o arco de trole; tranvía *m*

trolley bus *s* trolebús *m*

trolley car *s* coche *m* de tranvía

trolley pole *s* trole *m*

trolling [ˈtroliŋ] *s* cacea, pesca a la cacea

trollop [ˈtraləp] *s* (*slovenly woman*) cochina; mujer *f* de mala vida

trombone [ˈtrɑmbon] *s* trombón *m*

troop [trup] *s* tropa; (*of actors*) compañía; (*of cavalry*) escuadrón *m* ‖ *intr* agruparse; marcharse en tropel

trooper [ˈtrupər] *s* soldado de caballería; corcel *m* de guerra; policía *m* de a caballo; (*ship*) transporte *m;* **to swear like a trooper** jurar como un carretero

tro·phy [ˈtrofi] *s* (*pl* -phies) trofeo; (*any memento*) recuerdo

tropic [ˈtrɑpik] *adj* tropical ‖ *s* trópico

tropical [ˈtrɑpikəl] *adj* tropical

tropics o **Tropics** [ˈtrɑpiks] *spl* zona tropical

troposphere [ˈtrɑpəˌsfir] *s* troposfera

trot [trɑt] *s* trote *m* ‖ *v* (*pret & pp* trotted) *ger* trotting) *tr* hacer trotar; **to trot out** (*slang*) sacar para mostrar ‖ *intr* trotar

troth [troθ] o [troθ] *s* fe *f;* verdad;

esponsales *mpl;* **in troth** en verdad; **to plight one's troth** prometer fidelidad; dar palabra de casamiento

troubadour [ˈtrubəˌdor] o [ˈtrubəˌdur] *adj* trovadoresco ‖ *s* trovador *m*

trouble [ˈtrʌbəl] *s* apuro, dificultad; confusión, estorbo; conflicto; inquietud, preocupación; pena, molestia; mal *m*, enfermedad; (*of a mechanical nature*) avería, falla, pana; **not to be worth the trouble** no valer la pena; **that's the trouble** ahí está el busilis; **the trouble is that . . .** lo malo es que . . .; **to be in trouble** estar en un aprieto; **to be looking for trouble** buscar tres pies al gato; **to get into trouble** enredarse, meterse en líos; **to take the trouble to** tomarse la molestia de ‖ *tr* apurar; confundir, estorbar; inquietar, preocupar; apenar, afligir; incomodar, molestar; dar que hacer a; **to be troubled with** padecer de; **to trouble oneself** molestarse ‖ *intr* apurarse; inquietarse, preocuparse; molestarse, darse molestia; **to trouble to** molestarse en

trouble lamp *s* lámpara de socorro

trou'ble·mak'er *s* perturbador *m*, alborotador *m*

troubleshooter [ˈtrʌbəlˌʃutər] *s* localizador *m* de averías; (*in disputes*) componedor *m*

troubleshooting [ˈtrʌbəlˌʃutiŋ] *s* localización de averías; (*of disputes*) composición, arbitraje *m*

troublesome [ˈtrʌbəlsəm] *adj* molesto, pesado, gravoso; impertinente; perturbador

trouble spot *s* lugar *m* de conflicto

trough [trɔf] o [traf] *s* (*e.g., to knead bread*) artesa; (*for water for animals*) abrevadero; (*for feeding animals*) comedero; (*under eaves*) canal *f;* (*between two waves*) seno

troupe [trup] *s* compañía de actores o de circo

trousers [ˈtrauzərz] *spl* pantalones *mpl*

trous·seau [truˈso] o [ˈtruso] *s* (*pl* -seaux o -seaus) ajuar *m* de novia, equipo de novia

trout [traut] *s* trucha

trouvère [truˈvɛr] *s* trovero

trowel [ˈtrau·əl] *s* paleta, llana

Troy [trɔi] *s* Troya

truant [ˈtru·ənt] *s* novillero; **to play truant** hacer novillos

truce [trus] *s* tregua

truck [trʌk] *s* carro; vagoneta; camión *m;* autocamión *m;* (*to be moved by hand*) carretilla; (*of locomotive or car*) carretón *m;* hortalizas para el mercado; (*coll*) desperdicios; (*coll*) negocio, relaciones ‖ *tr* acarrear

truck driver *s* camionista *mf*

truck garden *s* huerto de hortalizas (*para el mercado*)

truculent [ˈtrʌkjələnt] o [ˈtrukjələnt] *adj* truculento

trudge [trʌdʒ] *intr* caminar, ir a pie; **to trudge along** marchar con pena y trabajo

true [tru] *adj* verdadero; exacto; constante, uniforme; fiel. leal; alineado; a plomo, a nivel; **to come true** hacerse realidad; **true to life** conforme a la realidad

true copy *s* copia fiel

true-hearted ['tru ,hɑrtɪd] *adj* fiel, leal, sincero

true'love' *s* fiel amante *mf;* (bot) hierba de París

truelove knot *s* lazo de amor

truffle ['trʌfəl] o ['trufəl] *s* trufa

truism ['tru·ɪzəm] *s* perogrullada, verdad trillada

truly ['truli] *adv* verdaderamente; efectivamente; fielmente; **truly yours** de Vd. atto. y S.S., su seguro servidor

trump [trʌmp] *s* triunfo; (coll) buen chico, buena chica; **no trump** sin triunfo || *tr* matar con un triunfo; aventajar, sobrepujar; **to trump up** forjar, inventar *(para engañar)* || *intr* triunfar

trumpet ['trʌmpɪt] *s* trompeta; trompeta acústica; **to blow one's own trumpet** cantar sus propias alabanzas || *tr* pregonar a son de trompeta || *intr* trompetear

truncheon ['trʌntʃən] *s* cachiporra, bastón *m* de mando

trunk [trʌŋk] *s (of living body, tree, family, railroad)* tronco *m; (chest for clothes, etc.)* baúl *m; (of an automobile)* portaequipaje *m; (of elephant)* trompa; **trunks** taparrabo

trunk hose *spl* trusas

truss [trʌs] *s (framework)* armadura; haz *m*, paquete *m*, lío; *(for holding back a hernia)* braguero || *tr* armar; empaquetar; espetar; apretar *(barriles)*

trust [trʌst] *s* confianza; esperanza; cargo, custodia; depósito; crédito; obligación; (econ) trust *m*, cartel *m*; (law) fideicomiso; **in trust** en confianza; en depósito; **on trust** a crédito, al fiado || *tr* confiar; confiar en; vender a crédito a || *intr* confiar; fiar; **to trust in** fiarse a o de

trust company *s* banco fideicomisario, banco de depósitos

trustee [trʌs'ti] *s* administrador *m*, comisario; regente (universitario); *(of an estate)* fideicomisario

trusteeship [trʌs'tiʃɪp] *s* cargo de administrador, fideicomisario; *(of the UN)* fideicomiso

trustful ['trʌstfəl] *adj* confiado

trust'wor'thy *adj* confiable, fidedigno

trust·y ['trʌsti] *adj (comp -ier; super -iest)* honrado, fidedigno || *s (pl -ies)* presidiario fidedigno *(que se ha merecido ciertos privilegios)*

truth [truθ] *s* verdad; **in truth** a la verdad, en verdad

truthful ['truθfəl] *adj* verídico, veraz

try [traɪ] *s (pl* tries) ensayo, intento, prueba || *v (pret & pp* tried) *tr* ensayar, intentar, probar; comprobar, verificar; cansar; exasperar, irritar; (law) procesar *(a una persona)*; (law) ver *(un pleito)*; **to try on** probarse *(una prenda de vestir)* || *intr*

ensayar, probar; esforzarse; **to try to** tratar de, intentar

trying ['traɪ·ɪŋ] *adj* cansado, molesto, irritante; penoso

tryst [trɪst] o [traɪst] *s* cita; lugar *m* de cita

tub [tʌb] *s* cuba, tina; (coll) baño; *(clumsy boat)* (coll) carcamán *m*, trompo; *(fat person)* (coll) cuba

tube [tjub] o [tub] *s* tubo; túnel *m; (of a tire)* cámara; (coll) ferrocarril subterráneo

tuber ['tjubər] o ['tubər] *s* tubérculo

tubercle ['tjubərkəl] o ['tubərkəl] *s* tubérculo

tuberculosis [tju,bɑrkjə'losɪs] o [tu,bɑrkjə'losɪs] *s* tuberculosis *f*

tuck [tʌk] *s* alforza || *tr* alforzar; **to tuck away** encubrir, ocultar; **to tuck in** arropar, enmantar; meter *(p.ej., la ropa de cama);* **to tuck up** arremangar *(un vestido);* guarnecer *(la cama)*

tucker ['tʌkər] *s* escote *m* || *tr* — **to tucker out** (coll) agotar, cansar

Tuesday ['tjuzdi] o ['tuzdi] *s* martes *m*

tuft [tʌft] *s (of feathers, hair, etc.)* penacho, copete *m;* manojo, racimo, ramillete *m;* borla || *tr* empenachar || *intr* crecer formando mechones

tug [tʌg] *s* estirón *m*, tirón *m; (boat)* remolcador *m* || *v (pret & pp* tugged; *ger* tugging) *tr* arrastrar, tirar con fuerza de; remolcar *(un barco)* || *intr* tirar con fuerza esforzarse, luchar

tug'boat' *s* remolcador *m*

tug of war *s* lucha de la cuerda

tuition [tju'ɪʃən] o [tu'ɪʃən] *s* enseñanza precio de la enseñanza

tulip ['tjulɪp] o ['tulɪp] *s* tulipán *m*

tumble ['tʌmbəl] *s* caída, tumbo; *(somersault)* voltereta, tumba; confusión, desorden *m* || *intr* caerse, rodar; voltear; derribarse, volcarse; brincar, dar saltos; *(into bed)* echarse, *(to catch on)* (slang) caer, comprender; **to tumble down** desplomarse, hundirse, venirse abajo

tum'ble-down' *adj* destartalado, desvencijado

tumbler ['tʌmblər] *s (for drinking)* vaso; *(person who performs bodily feats)* volatinero; *(self-righting toy)* dominguillo, tentemozo

tumor ['tjumər] o ['tumər] *s* tumor *m*

tumult ['tjumʌlt] o ['tumʌlt] *s* tumulto

tun [tʌn] *s* barril *m*, tonel *m; (measure of capacity for wine)* tonelada

tuna ['tunə] *s* atún *m*

tune [tjun] o [tun] *s* tonada, aire *m; (manner of acting or speaking)* tono; **in tune** afinado; afinadamente; **out of tune** desafinado; desafinadamente; **to change one's tune** mudar de tono || *tr* acordar, afinar; (rad) sintonizar; **to tune in** (rad) sintonizar; **to tune out** (rad) desintonizar; **to tune up** poner a punto; poner a tono *(un motor de automóvil)*

tungsten ['tʌŋstən] *s* tungsteno

tunic ['tjunɪk] o ['tunɪk] *s* túnica

tuning coil *s* (rad) bobina de sintonía

tuning fork s diapasón m
Tunis ['tjunɪs] o ['tunɪs] s Túnez (ciudad)
Tunisia [tju'nɪʒə] o [tu'nɪʒə] s Túnez (país)
Tunisian [tju'nɪʒən] o [tu'nɪʒən] adj & s tunecino
tun·nel ['tʌnəl] s túnel m; (min) galería ‖ v (pret & pp -neled o -nelled; ger -neling o -nelling) tr construir un túnel a través de o debajo de
turban ['tʌrbən] s turbante m
turbid ['tʌrbɪd] adj turbio
turbine ['tʌrbɪn] o ['tʌrbaɪn] s turbina
turbojet ['tʌrbo,dʒet] s turborreactor m; avión m de turborreacción
turboprop ['tʌrbo,prɑp] s turbopropulsor m; avión m de turbopropulsión
turbulent ['tʌrbjələnt] adj turbulento
tureen [tu'rin] o [tju'rin] s sopera
turf [tʌrf] s (surface layer of grassland) césped m; terrón m de césped; (peat) turba; **the turf** el hipódromo; las carreras de caballos
turf·man ['tʌrfmən] s (pl -men [mən]) turfista m
Turk [tʌrk] s turco
turkey ['tʌrki] s pavo ‖ **Turkey** s Turquía
turkey vulture s aura
Turkish ['tʌrkɪʃ] adj & s turco
Turkish towel s toalla rusa
turmoil ['tʌrmɔɪl] s alboroto, disturbio, tumulto
turn [tʌrn] s vuelta; (time of action) turno; (change of direction) virada; (bend) recodo, (walk) paseo corto; (of a spiral, roll of wire, etc.) espira; aspecto; inclinación; vahído, vértigo; giro, expresión; servicio; (coll) sacudida, susto; **at every turn** a cada paso; **in turn** por turno; **to be one's turn** tocarle a uno, p.ej., **it's your turn** le toca a Vd.; **to take turns** alternar, turnar; **to wait one's turn** aguardar turno, esperar vez ‖ tr volver; dar vuelta a (p.ej., una llave); torcer (p.ej., el tobillo); doblar (la esquina); dirigir (p.ej., los ojos); (to make sour) agriar; (on a lathe) tornear; tener (p.ej., veinte años cumplidos); **to turn against** predisponer en contra de; **to turn around** volver, voltear; torcer (las palabras de una persona); **to turn aside** desviar; **to turn away** desviar, despedir, **to turn back** devolver; hacer retroceder; retrasar (el reloj); **to turn down** doblar hacia abajo; invertir; rechazar, rehusar; bajar (p.ej., el gas); **to turn in** doblar hacia adentro; entregar; **to turn off** apagar (la luz, la radio); cortar (el agua, gas, etc.); cerrar (la llave del agua, gas, etc.; la radio, la televisión); interrumpir (la corriente eléctrica); **to turn on** encender (la luz); poner (la luz, la radio, etc.); abrir (la llave del agua, gas, etc.); establecer (la corriente eléctrica); **to turn out** despedir; echar al campo (a los animales); volver al revés; apa-

gar (la luz); hacer, fabricar; **to turn up** doblar hacia arriba; levantar; arremangar (p.ej., las mangas); volver (un naipe); poner más alto o más fuerte (la radio); abrir la llave de (p.ej., el gas) ‖ intr volver, p.ej., **the road turns to the right** el camino vuelve a la derecha; virar (un automóvil, un avión, etc.); (to revolve) girar; volverse (p.ej., la conversación; la opinión; ciertos licores); **to turn against** cobrar aversión a; rebelarse contra; **to turn around** dar vuelta; **to turn aside** o **away** desviarse; alejarse; **to turn back** volver, regresar; retroceder; **to turn down** doblarse hacia abajo; invertirse; **to turn in** doblarse hacia adentro; replegarse; recogerse, volver a casa; (coll) recogerse, acostarse; **to turn into** entrar en; convertirse en; **to turn on** volverse contra; depender de; versar sobre; ocuparse de; **to turn out badly** salir mal; **to turn out right** acabar bien; **to turn out to be** venir a ser; resultar, salir; **to turn over** volcar, derribarse (un vehículo); **to turn up** doblarse hacia arriba; levantarse; acontecer; aparecer
turn'coat' s tránsfuga mf, apóstata mf, renegado; **to become a turncoat** volver la casaca, cambiarse la camisa
turn'down' adj (collar) caído ‖ s rechazamiento
turning point s punto de transición, punto decisivo
turnip ['tʌrnɪp] s nabo; (cheap watch) (slang) calentador m; (slang) tipo
turn'key' s carcelero, llavero de cárcel
turn of life s menopausia
turn of mind s natural m, inclinación
turn'out' s (gathering of people) concurrencia; (number attending a show, etc.) entrada; (side track or passage) apartadero; (amount produced) producción; (array, outfit) equipaje m; carruaje m de lujo
turn'o'ver s (spill, upset) vuelco; cambio de personal; movimiento de mercancías, ciclo de compra y venta
turn'pike' s carretera de peaje
turnstile ['tʌrn,staɪl] s torniquete m
turn'ta'ble s (of phonograph) placa giratoria; plato giratorio; (rr) placa giratoria, plataforma giratoria
turpentine ['tʌrpən,taɪn] s trementina
turpitude ['tʌrpɪ,tjud] o ['tʌrpɪ,tud] s torpeza, infamia, vileza
turquoise ['tʌrkɔɪz] o ['tʌrkwɔɪz] s turquesa
turret ['tʌrɪt] s torrecilla; (archit) torreón m; (nav) torreta
turtle ['tʌrtəl] s tortuga; **to turn turtle** derribarse patas arriba
tur'tle-dove' s tórtola
Tuscan ['tʌskən] adj & s toscano
Tuscany ['tʌskəni] s la Toscana
tusk [tʌsk] s colmillo
tussle ['tʌsəl] s agarrada ‖ intr agarrarse, asirse, reñir
tutor ['tjutər] o ['tutər] s maestro particular; (guardian) tutor m ‖ tr dar enseñanza particular a ‖ intr

dar enseñanza particular; (coll) tomar lecciones particulares

tuxe·do [tʌk'sido] s (pl **-dos**) esmoquin m, smoking m

TV abbr **television**

twaddle ['twɑdəl] s charla, tonterías, música celestial || intr charlar, decir tonterías

twang [twæŋ] s (of musical instrument) tañido; (of voice) timbre m nasal || tr tocar con un tañido; decir con timbre nasal || intr hablar por la nariz

twang·y [twæŋi] adj (comp **-ier**; super **-iest**) (device) tañente; (person, voice) gangoso

tweed [twid] s mezcla de lana; traje m de mezcla de lana; **tweeds** ropa de mezcla de l na

tweet [twit] s pío || intr piar

tweeter ['twitɔr] s altavoz m para audiofrecuencias elevadas

tweezers ['twizɔrz] spl bruselas, pinzas, tenacillas

twelfth [twelfθ] adj & s (in a series) duodécimo; (part) dozavo || s (in dates) doce m

Twelfth'-night' s la víspera del día de Reyes; la noche del día de Reyes

twelve [twelv] adj & pron doce || s doce m; **twelve o'clock** las doce

twentieth ['twenti·ɪθ] adj & s (in a series) vigésimo; (part) veintavo || s (in dates) veinte m

twen·ty [twenti] adj & pron veinte || s (pl **-ties**) veinte m

twice [twais] adv dos veces

twice'-told' adj dicho dos veces; trillado, sabido

twiddle ['twidəl] tr menear o revolver ociosamente

twig [twig] s ramito; **twigs** leña menuda

twilight ['twai‚lait] adj crepuscular || s crepúsculo

twill [twil] s tela cruzada; (pattern of weave) cruzado || tr cruzar

twin [twin] adj & s gemelo

twine [twain] s guita, cuerda, bramante m || tr enroscar, retorcer || intr enroscarse, retorcerse

twinge [twindʒ] s punzada, dolor agudo

twin'jet' plane s avión m birreactor

twinkle ['twiŋkəl] s centelleo; (of eye) pestañeo; instante m || intr centellear; pestañear; moverse rápidamente

twin'-screw' adj (naut) de doble hélice

twirl [twʌrl] s vuelta, giro || tr hacer girar; (baseball) lanzar (la pelota) || intr dar vueltas, girar; piruetear

twist [twist] s torcedura; enroscadura; curva, recodo; giro, vuelta; propensión, prejuicio; (of mind or disposition) sesgo || tr torcer; retorcer; enroscar; hacer girar; entrelazar; desviar; (to give a different meaning to) torcer || intr torcerse; retorcerse; enroscarse; dar vueltas; entrelazarse;

desviarse; serpentear; **to twist and turn** (in bed) dar vueltas

twit [twit] v (pret & pp **twitted**; ger **twitting**) tr reprender (a uno) recordando algo desagradable o poniéndole en ridículo

twitch [twitʃ] s crispatura; ligero temblor || intr crisparse; temblar (p.ej., los párpados)

twitter ['twitɔr] s gorjeo; risita sofocada; inquietud || intr gorjear; reír sofocadamente; temblar de inquietud

two [tu] adj & pron dos || s dos m; **to put two and two together** atar cabos, sacar la conclusión evidente; **two o'clock** las dos

two'-cy'cle adj (mach) de dos tiempos

two'-cyl'inder adj (mach) de dos cilindros

two-edged ['tu‚edʒd] adj de dos filos

two hundred adj & pron doscientos || s doscientos m

twosome ['tusəm] s pareja; pareja de jugadores; juego de dos

two'-time' tr (slang) engañar en amor, ser infiel a (una persona del otro sexo)

tycoon [tai'kun] s (coll) magnate m

type [taip] s tipo; (piece) (typ) tipo, letra; (pieces collectively) (typ) letra; letras impresas, letras escritas a máquina || tr escribir a máquina, tipiar; representar, simbolizar || intr escribir a máquina

type'face' s tipo de letra

type'script' s material escrito a máquina

typesetter ['taip‚setɔr] s (typ) cajista mf; (typ) máquina de componer

type'write' v (pret **-wrote** [‚rot]; pp **-written** [‚ritən]) tr & intr escribir a máquina, tipiar

type'writ'er s máquina de escribir; tipista mf

typewriter ribbon s cinta para máquinas de escribir

type'writ'ing s mecanografía; trabajo hecho con máquina de escribir

typhoid fever ['taifɔid] s fiebre tifoidea

typhoon [tai'fun] s tifón m

typical ['tipikəl] adj típico

typi·fy ['tipi‚fai] v (pret & pp **-fied**) tr simbolizar; ser ejemplo o modelo de

typist ['taipist] s mecanógrafo, tipista mf

typographic(al) [‚taipə'græfik(əl)] adj tipográfico

typographical error s error m de imprenta

typography [tai'pɑgrəfi] s tipografía

tyrannic(al) [ti'rænik(əl)] o [tai-'rænik(əl)] adj tiránico

tyrannous ['tirənəs] adj tirano

tyran·ny ['tirəni] s (pl **-nies**) tiranía

tyrant ['tairənt] s tirano

ty·ro ['tairo] s (pl **-ros**) tirón m, novicio

U

U, u [ju] vigésima primera letra del alfabeto inglés

U. *abbr* **University**

ubiquitous [ju'bɪkwɪtəs] *adj* ubicuo

udder ['ʌdər] *s* ubre *f*

ugliness ['ʌglɪnɪs] *s* fealdad; (coll) malhumor *m*

ug·ly ['ʌgli] *adj* (comp **-lier**; super **-liest**) feo; (coll) malhumorado

ugly mug *s* (slang) carantamaula

Ukraine ['jukren] o [ju'kren] *s* Ucrania

Ukrainian [ju'krenɪ-ən] *adj & s* ucraniano, ucranio

ulcer ['ʌlsər] *s* llaga, úlcera; (corrupting influence) (fig) llaga

ulcerate ['ʌlsə,ret] *tr* ulcerar || *intr* ulcerarse

ulterior [ʌl'tɪrɪ-ər] *adj* ulterior; (concealed) escondido, oculto

ultimate ['ʌltɪmɪt] *adj* último

ultima·tum [,ʌltɪ'metəm] *s* (pl **-tums** o **-ta** [tə]) ultimátum *m*

ultimo ['ʌltɪ,mo] *adv* de o en el mes próximo pasado

ultrahigh [,ʌltrə'haɪ] *adj* (electron) ultraelevado

ultraviolet [,ʌltrə'vaɪ-əlɪt] *adj & s* ultravioleta, ultraviolado

umbilical cord [ʌm'bɪlɪkəl] *s* cordón *m* umbilical

umbrage ['ʌmbrɪdʒ] *s* — **to take umbrage at** resentirse de o por

umbrella [ʌm'brelə] *s* paraguas *m*; (mil) sombrilla protectora

umbrella man *s* paragüero

umbrella stand *s* paragüero

umlaut ['umlaut] *s* inflexión vocálica, metafonía; (mark) diéresis *f* || *tr* inflexionar; escribir con diéresis

umpire ['ʌmpaɪr] *s* árbitro || *tr & intr* arbitrar

UN ['ju'en] *s* (letterword) ONU *f*

unable [ʌn'ebəl] *adj* incapaz, imposibilitado; **to be unable to** no poder

unabridged [,ʌnə'brɪdʒd] *adj* sin abreviar, íntegro

unaccented [ʌn'æksentɪd] o [,ʌnæk-'sentɪd] *adj* inacentuado

unaccountable [,ʌnə'kauntəbəl] *adj* inexplicable; irresponsable

unaccounted-for [,ʌnə'kauntɪd,fɔr] *adj* inexplicado; no hallado

unaccustomed [,ʌnə'kʌstəmd] *adj* (unusual) desacostumbrado; inhabituado

unafraid [,ʌnə'fred] *adj* sin miedo

unaligned [,ʌnə'laɪnd] *adj* no empeñado

unanimity [,junə'nɪmɪti] *s* unanimidad

unanimous [ju'nænɪməs] *adj* unánime

unanswerable [ʌn'ænsərəbəl] *adj* incontestable; (argument) incontrastable

unappreciative [,ʌnə'priʃɪ,etɪv] *adj* ingrato, desagradecido

unapproachable [,ʌnə'protʃəbəl] *adj* inabordable; incomparable, único

unarmed [ʌn'armd] *adj* desarmado, inerme

unascertainable [ʌn,æsər'tenəbəl] *adj* inaveriguable

unasked [ʌn'æskt] o [ʌn'askt] *adj* no solicitado; no convidado

unassembled [,ʌnə'sembəld] *adj* desmontado, desarmado

unassuming [,ʌnə'sumɪŋ] o [,ʌnə-'sjumɪŋ] *adj* modesto, sencillo

unattached [,ʌnə'tætʃt] *adj* independiente; (loose) suelto; (not engaged to be married) no prometido; (law) no embargado; (mil & nav) de reemplazo

unattainable [,ʌnə'tenəbəl] *adj* inasequible, inalcanzable

unattractive [,ʌnə'træktɪv] *adj* poco atrayente, desairado

unavailable [,ʌnə'veləbəl] *adj* indisponible

unavailing [,ʌnə'velɪŋ] *adj* ineficaz, inútil, vano

unavoidable [,ʌnə'vɔɪdəbəl] *adj* inevitable, ineluctable

unaware [,ʌnə'wer] *adj* — **to be unaware of** no estar al corriente de || *adv* de improviso; sin saberlo

unawares [,ʌnə'werz] *adv* (unexpectedly) de improviso; (unknowingly) sin saberlo

unbalanced [ʌn'bælənst] *adj* desequilibrado

unbandage [ʌn'bændɪdʒ] *tr* desvendar

un·bar [ʌn'bar] *v* (pret & pp **-barred**; ger **-barring**) *tr* desatrancar

unbearable [ʌn'berəbəl] *adj* inaguantable

unbeatable [ʌn'bitəbəl] *adj* imbatible

unbecoming [,ʌnbɪ'kʌmɪŋ] *adj* inconveniente, indecente; que sienta mal

unbelievable [,ʌnbɪ'livəbəl] *adj* increíble

unbending [ʌn'bendɪŋ] *adj* inflexible

unbiased o **unbiassed** [ʌn'baɪ-əst] *adj* imparcial

un·bind [ʌn'baɪnd] *v* (pret & pp **-bound** ['baund]) *tr* desatar

unbleached [ʌn'blitʃt] *adj* sin blanquear

unbolt [ʌn'bolt] *tr* desatrancar (p.ej., una puerta); (to remove the bolts from) desempernar

unborn [ʌn'bɔrn] *adj* no nacido, por nacer, futuro

unbosom [ʌn'buzəm] *tr* confesar, descubrir (sus pensamientos, sus secretos); **to unbosom oneself** abrir su pecho, desahogarse

unbound [ʌn'baund] *adj* (book) sin encuadernar

unbreakable [ʌn'brekəbəl] *adj* irrompible

unbuckle [ʌn'bʌkəl] *tr* deshebillar

unburden [ʌn'bʌrdən] *tr* descargar; **to unburden oneself of** desahogarse de

unburied [ʌn'berɪd] *adj* insepulto

unbutton [ʌn'bʌtən] *tr* desabotonar

uncalled-for [ʌn'kɔld,fɔr] *adj* innecesario, no justificado; insolente

uncanny [ʌn'kæni] *adj* espectral, misterioso; extraordinario, maravilloso

uncared-for !ʌn'kerd,fər] *adj* desamparado, descuidado, abandonado

unceasing [ʌn'sisɪŋ] *adj* incesante

unceremonious [,ʌnserɪ'moni-əs] *adj* inceremonioso

uncertain [ʌn'sʌrtən] *adj* incierto

uncertain-ty [ʌn'sʌrtanti] *s* (*pl* -ties) incertidumbre

unchain [ʌn'tʃen] *tr* desencadenar

unchangeable [ʌn'tʃendʒəbəl] *adj* incambiable, inmutable

uncharted [ʌn'tʃɑrtɪd] *adj* inexplorado

unchecked [ʌn'tʃɛkt] *adj* no verificado; no refrenado; desenfrenado

uncivilized [ʌn'sɪvɪ,laɪzd] *adj* incivilizado

unclad [ʌn'klæd] *adj* desvestido

unclaimed [ʌn'klemd] *adj* sin reclamar; (*mail*) rechazado, sobrante

unclasp [ʌn'klæsp] o [ʌn'klɑsp] *tr* desabrochar

unclassified [ʌn'klæsɪ,faɪd] *adj* no clasificado; no clasificado como secreto

uncle ['ʌŋkəl] *s* tío

unclean [ʌn'klin] *adj* desaseado, sucio

un-clog [ʌn'klag] *v* (*pret* & *pp* -clogged; *ger* -clogging) *tr* desatrancar

unclouded [ʌn'klaudɪd] *adj* despejado

uncollectible [,ʌnkə'lektɪbəl] *adj* incobrable

uncomfortable [ʌn'kʌmfərtəbəl] *adj* incómodo

uncommitted [,ʌnkə'mɪtɪd] *adj* no empeñado, no comprometido

uncommon [ʌn'kamən] *adj* raro, poco común

uncompromising [ʌn'kamprə,maɪzɪŋ] *adj* intransigente

unconcerned [,ʌnkən'sʌrnd] *adj* despreocupado, indiferente

unconditional [,ʌnkən'dɪʃənəl] *adj* incondicional

uncongenial [,ʌnkən'dʒini-əl] *adj* antipático; incompatible; desagradable

unconquerable [ʌn'kaŋkərəbəl] *adj* inconquistable

unconquered [ʌn'kaŋkərd] *adj* invicto

unconscionable [ʌn'kanʃənəbəl] *adj* inescrupuloso; desrazonable, excesivo

unconscious [ʌn'kanʃəs] *adj* inconsciente; (*temporarily deprived of consciousness*) desmayado; (*unintentional*) involuntario

unconsciousness [ʌn'kanʃəsnɪs] *s* inconsciencia; desmayo

unconstitutional [,ʌnkanstɪ'tjuʃənəl] o [,ʌnkanstɪ'tuʃənəl] *adj* inconstitucional

uncontrollable [,ʌnkən'troləbəl] *adj* ingobernable; (*laughter*) inextinguible

unconventional [,ʌnkən'vɛnʃənəl] *adj* no convencional

uncork [ʌn'kɔrk] *tr* destapar, descorchar

uncouth [ʌn'kuθ] *adj* desgarbado, torpe, rústico

uncover [ʌn'kʌvər] *tr* descubrir

unction ['ʌŋkʃən] *s* (*anointing*) unción; suavidad hipócrita

unctuous ['ʌŋkt/u-əs] *adj* untuoso; zalamero

uncultivated [ʌn'kʌltɪ,vetɪd] *adj* inculto (*que no está cultivado; rústico, grosero*)

uncultured [ʌn'kʌltʃərd] *adj* inculto, rústico, grosero

uncut [ʌn'kʌt] *adj* sin cortar; (*book or magazine*) intonso

undamaged [ʌn'dæmɪdʒd] *adj* indemne, ileso

undaunted [ʌn'dɔntɪd] *adj* impávido, denodado

undecided [,ʌndɪ'saɪdɪd] *adj* indeciso

undefeated [,ʌndɪ'fitɪd] *adj* invicto

undefended [,ʌndɪ'fɛndɪd] *adj* indefenso

undefiled [,ʌndɪ'faɪld] *adj* inmaculado, impoluto

undeniable [,ʌndɪ'naɪ-əbəl] *adj* innegable

under ['ʌndər] *adj* inferior; (*clothing*) interior || *adv* debajo; más abajo; **to go under** hundirse; (*to fail*) fracasar || *prep* bajo, debajo de; inferior a; **under full sail** a vela llena; **under lock and key** bajo llave; **under oath** bajo juramento; **under penalty of death** so pena de muerte; **under sail** a vela; **under separate cover** por separado, bajo cubierta separada; **under steam** bajo presión; **under the hand and seal of** firmado y sellado por; **under the nose of** (coll) en las barbas de; **under the weather** (coll) algo indispuesto; **under way** en camino

un'der·age' *adj* menor de edad

un'der·bid' *v* (*pret* & *pp* -bid; *ger* -bidding) *tr* ofrecer menos que

un'der·brush' *s* maleza

un'der·car'riage *s* carro inferior; (aer) tren *m* de aterrizaje

un'der·clothes' *s* ropa interior

un'der·con·sump'tion *s* infraconsumo

un'der·cov'er *adj* secreto

underdeveloped [,ʌndərdɪ'veləpt] *adj* subdesarrollado

un'der·dog' *s* víctima, perdidoso; **the underdogs** los de abajo

underdone ['ʌndər,dʌn] *adj* a medio asar, soasado

un'der·es'ti·mate' *tr* subestimar

un'der·gar'ment *s* prenda de vestir interior

un'der·go' *v* (*pret* -went; *pp* -gone) *tr* experimentar; sufrir, padecer

un'der·grad'uate *adj* no graduado; (*course*) para el bachillerato || *s* alumno no graduado de universidad

un'der·ground' *adj* subterráneo; clandestino || *adv* bajo tierra; ocultamente || *s* ferrocarril subterráneo; movimiento de resistencia

un'der·growth' *s* maleza

underhanded ['ʌndər'hændɪd] *adj* clandestino, taimado, disimulado

un'der·line' o **un'der·line'** *tr* subrayar

underling ['ʌndərlɪŋ] *s* subordinado, secuaz *m* servil

un'der·mine' *tr* socavar, minar

underneath [ˌʌndərˈniθ] *adj* inferior, más bajo || *adv* debajo || *prep* debajo de || *s* parte baja, superficie *f* inferior

undernourished [ˌʌndərˈnʌrɪʃt] *adj* desnutrido

un·der·nour·ish·ment *s* desnutrición

un'der·pass' *s* paso inferior

un·der·pay' *s* pago insuficiente || *v* (*pret* & *pp* **-paid**) *tr* & *intr* pagar insuficientemente

un·der·pin' *v* (*pret* & *pp* **-pinned**) *ger* **-pinning**) *tr* apuntalar, socalzar

underprivileged [ˌʌndərˈprɪvɪlɪdʒd] *adj* desheredado, desamparado

un'der·rate' *tr* menospreciar

un'der·score' *tr* subrayar

un'der·sea' *adj* submarino || **un'der·sea'** *adv* debajo de la superficie del mar

un'der·sec're·tar'y *s* (*pl* **-ies**) subsecretario

un'der·sell' *v* (*pret* & *pp* **-sold**) *tr* vender a menor precio que; (*for less than the actual value*) malbaratar

un'der·shirt' *s* camiseta

undersigned [ˈʌndərˌsaɪnd] *adj* infrascrito, subscrito

un'der·skirt' *s* enaguas, refajo

un'der·stand' *v* (*pret* & *pp* **-stood**) *tr* entender, comprender; sobrentender, subentender (*una cosa que no está expresa*) || *intr* entender, comprender

understandable [ˌʌndərˈstændəbəl] *adj* comprensible

understanding [ˌʌndərˈstændɪŋ] *adj* entendedor; (*tolerant, sympathetic*) comprensivo || *s* comprensión; (*intellectual faculty, mind*) entendimiento; (*agreement*) acuerdo; **to come to an understanding** llegar a un acuerdo

un'der·stud'y *s* (*pl* **-ies**) sobresaliente *mf*

un'der·take' *v* (*pret* **-took**; *pp* **-taken**) *tr* emprender; (*to agree to perform*) comprometerse a

undertaker [ˌʌndərˈtekər] o [ˈʌndərˌtekər] *s* empresario || [ˈʌndərˌtekər] *s* empresario de pompas fúnebres, director *m* de funeraria

undertaking [ˌʌndərˈtekɪŋ] *s* (*task*) empresa; (*pledge*) empeño || [ˈʌndərˌtekɪŋ] *s* (*business of funeral director*) funeraria

un'der·tak'ing establishment *s* funeraria, empresa de pompas fúnebres

un'der·tone' *s* voz baja; (*background sound*) fondu; color apagado

un'der·tow' *s* (*countercurrent below surface*) contracorriente *f*; (*on the beach*) resaca

un'der·wear' *s* ropa interior

un'der·world' *s* (*criminal world*) inframundo, bajos fondos sociales; (*the earth*) mundo terrenal; (*pagan world of the dead*) averno, infierno; (*world under the water*) mundo submarino; (*opposite side of earth*) antípodas

un'der·write' o **un'der·write'** *v* (*pret* **-wrote**; *pp* **-written**) *tr* subscribir; (*to insure*) asegurar

un'der·writ'er *s* subscritor *m*; asegurador *m*; compañía aseguradora

undeserved [ˌʌndɪˈzʌrvd] *adj* inmerecido

undesirable [ˌʌndɪˈzaɪrəbəl] *adj* & *s* indeseable *mf*

undetachable [ˌʌndɪˈtætʃəbəl] *adj* inamovible

undignified [ʌnˈdɪgnɪˌfaɪd] *adj* poco digno, poco grave, indecoroso

undiscernible [ˌʌndɪˈzʌrnɪbəl] o [ˌʌndɪˈsʌrnəbəl] *adj* imperceptible, invisible

un·do' *v* (*pret* **-did**; *pp* **-done**) *tr* deshacer; anular, borrar; arruinar

undoing [ʌnˈduɪŋ] *s* destrucción, pérdida, ruina

undone [ʌnˈdʌn] *adj* sin hacer, por hacer; **to come undone** deshacerse, desatarse; **to leave nothing undone** no dejar nada por hacer

undoubtedly [ʌnˈdaʊtɪdlɪ] *adv* indudablemente, sin duda

undramatic [ˌʌndrəˈmætɪk] *adj* poco dramático

undress [ˈʌnˌdrɛs] o [ʌnˈdrɛs] *s* traje *m* de casa; vestido de calle; (*mil*) traje de cuartel || [ˈʌnˈdrɛs] *tr* desnudar; desvendar (*una herida*) || desnudarse

undrinkable [ʌnˈdrɪŋkəbəl] *adj* impotable

undue [ʌnˈdju] o [ʌnˈdu] *adj* indebido

undulate [ˈʌndjəˌlet] *intr* ondular

unduly [ʌnˈdjulɪ] o [ʌnˈdulɪ] *adv* indebidamente

undying [ʌnˈdaɪɪŋ] *adj* imperecedero

unearned increment [ʌnˈʌrnd] *s* plusvalía

unearth [ʌnˈʌrθ] *tr* desenterrar

unearthly [ʌnˈʌrθlɪ] *adj* sobrenatural; fantástico, espectral; extraordinario

uneasy [ʌnˈizɪ] *adj* (*worried*) inquieto; (*constrained*) encogido, embarazado

uneatable [ʌnˈitəbəl] *adj* incomible

uneconomic(al) [ˌʌnikəˈnɑmɪk(əl)] o [ˌʌnɛkəˈnɑmɪk(əl)] *adj* antieconómico

uneducated [ʌnˈɛdjəˌketɪd] *adj* ineducado, sin instrucción

unemployed [ˌʌnɛmˈplɔɪd] *adj* desocupado, desempleado, improductivo

unemployment [ˌʌnɛmˈplɔɪmənt] *s* desocupación, desempleo

unemployment insurance *s* seguro de desemple o desocupación, seguro contra el paro obrero

unending [ʌnˈɛndɪŋ] *adj* interminable

unequal [ʌnˈikwəl] *adj* desigual; **to be unequal to** (*a task*) no estar a la altura de

unequaled o **unequalled** [ʌnˈikwəld] *adj* inigualado

unerring [ʌnˈʌrɪŋ] o [ʌnˈɛrɪŋ] *adj* infalible, seguro

unessential [ˌʌnɛˈsɛnʃəl] *adj* no esencial

uneven [ʌnˈivən] *adj* desigual; (*number*) impar

unexceptionable [ˌʌnɛkˈsɛpʃənəbəl] *adj* intachable, irreprensible

unexpected [ˌʌnɛkˈspɛktɪd] *adj* inesperado

unexplained [ˌʌnɛkˈsplend] *adj* inexplicado

unexplored [ˌʌnek'splord] *adj* inexplorado

unexposed [ˌʌnek'spozd] *adj* (phot) inexpuesto

unfading [ʌn'fediŋ] *adj* inmarcesible

unfailing [ʌn'feliŋ] *adj* indefectible; (*inexhaustible*) inagotable

unfair [ʌn'fer] *adj* injusto; desleal, doble, falso; (sport) sucio

unfaithful [ʌn'feθfəl] *adj* infiel

unfamiliar [ˌʌnfə'miljər] *adj* poco familiar; poco familiarizado

unfasten [ʌn'fæsən] o [ʌn'fɑsən] *tr* desatacar, desatar, soltar

unfathomable [ʌn'fæðəmabəl] *adj* insondable

unfavorable [ʌn'fevərabəl] *adj* desfavorable

unfeathered [ʌn'feðərd] *adj* implume

unfeeling [ʌn'filiŋ] *adj* insensible

unfetter [ʌn'fetər] *tr* desencadenar

unfilled [ʌn'fɪld] *adj* no lleno; por cumplir, pendiente

unfinished [ʌn'fɪnɪʃt] *adj* sin acabar; imperfecto, mal acabado; (*business*) pendiente

unfit [ʌn'fɪt] *adj* impropio, incapaz, inhábil; inservible, inútil

unfold [ʌn'fold] *tr* desplegar ‖ *intr* desplegarse

unforeseeable [ˌʌnfor'si-əbəl] *adj* imprevisible

unforeseen [ˌʌnfor'sin] *adj* imprevisto

unforgettable [ˌʌnfər'getəbəl] *adj* inolvidable

unforgivable [ˌʌnfər'givəbəl] *adj* imperdonable

unfortunate [ʌn'fɔrtʃənɪt] *adj & s* desgraciado

unfounded [ʌn'faundɪd] *adj* infundado

unfreeze [ʌn'friz] *tr* deshelar; desbloquear (*el crédito*)

unfriendly [ʌn'frendli] *adj* inamistoso; desfavorable

unfruitful [ʌn'frutfəl] *adj* infructuoso

unfulfilled [ˌʌnfəl'fɪld] *adj* incumplido

unfurl [ʌn'fʌrl] *tr* desplegar, extender

unfurnished [ʌn'fʌrnɪʃt] *adj* desamueblado

ungainly [ʌn'genli] *adj* desgarbado, desmañado

ungentlemanly [ʌn'dʒɛntəlmənli] *adj* poco caballeroso, descortés

ungird [ʌn'gʌrd] *tr* desceñir

ungodly [ʌn'gɑdli] *adj* impío, irreligioso; (*dreadful*) (coll) atroz

ungracious [ʌn'greʃəs] *adj* descortés; desagradable

ungrammatical [ˌʌngrə'mætɪkəl] *adj* ingramatical

ungrateful [ʌn'gretfəl] *adj* ingrato, desagradecido

ungrudgingly [ʌn'grʌdʒɪŋli] *adj* de buena gana, sin quejarse

unguarded [ʌn'gɑrdɪd] *adj* indefenso; descuidado; (*moment*) de inadvertencia

unguent [ˈʌŋgwənt] *s* ungüento

unhandy [ʌn'hændi] *adj* inmanejable; (*awkward*) desmañado

unhappiness [ʌn'hæpɪnɪs] *s* infelicidad

unhappy [ʌn'hæpi] *adj* (*comp* -**pier**;

super -**piest**) infeliz; (*unlucky*) desgraciado; (*fateful*) aciago

unharmed [ʌn'hɑrmd] *adj* indemne

unharmonious [ˌʌnhɑr'moni-əs] *adj* inarmónico

unharness [ʌn'hɑrnɪs] *tr* desenjaezar, desguarnecer; desenganchar

unhealthy [ʌn'helθi] *adj* malsano

unheard-of [ʌn'hʌrd,ɑv] *adj* inaudito

unhinge [ʌn'hɪndʒ] *tr* desgonzar; (fig) desequilibrar, trastornar

unhitch [ʌn'hɪtʃ] *tr* desenganchar

unholy [ʌn'holi] *adj* (*comp* -**lier**; *super* -**liest**) impío, malo, profano

unhook [ʌn'hʊk] *tr* desabrochar; desenganchar; (*to take down from a hook*) descolgar

unhoped-for [ʌn'hopt,fər] *adj* inesperado, no esperado

unhorse [ʌn'hɔrs] *tr* desarzonar

unhurt [ʌn'hʌrt] *adj* incólume, ileso

unicorn [ˈjunɪ,kɔrn] *s* unicornio

unification [ˌjunɪfɪ'keʃən] *s* unificación

uniform [ˈjunɪ,fɔrm] *adj & s* uniforme *m* ‖ *tr* uniformar

uniformity [ˌjunɪ'fɔrmiti] *s* (*pl* -**ties**) uniformidad

unify [ˈjunɪ,faɪ] *v* (*pret & pp* -**fied**) *tr* unificar

unilateral [ˌjunɪ'lætərəl] *adj* unilateral

unimpeachable [ˌʌnɪm'pitʃəbəl] *adj* irrecusable, intachable

unimportant [ˌʌnɪm'pɔrtənt] *adj* poco importante

uninhabited [ˌʌnɪn'hæbɪtɪd] *adj* inhabitado

uninspired [ˌʌnɪn'spaɪrd] *adj* sin inspiración; aburrido, fastidioso

unintelligent [ˌʌnɪn'tɛlɪdʒənt] *adj* ininteligente

unintelligible [ˌʌnɪn'tɛlɪdʒɪbəl] *adj* ininteligible

uninterested [ʌn'ɪntrɪstɪd] o [ʌn'ɪntə,restɪd] *adj* desinteresado

uninteresting [ʌn'ɪntrɪstɪŋ] o [ʌn'ɪntə,restɪŋ] *adj* poco interesante

uninterrupted [ˌʌnɪntə'rʌptɪd] *adj* ininterrumpido

union [ˈjunjən] *s* unión; (*organization of workmen*) gremio obrero, sindicato; unión matrimonial

unionize [ˈjunjə,naɪz] *tr* agremiar ‖ *intr* agremiarse

union shop *s* taller *m* de obreros agremiados

union suit *s* traje *m* interior de una sola pieza

unique [ju'nik] *adj* único

unison [ˈjunɪsən] o [ˈjunɪzən] *s* unisonancia; **in unison (with)** al unísono (de)

unit [ˈjunɪt] *adj* unitario ‖ *s* unidad; (mach & elec) grupo

unite [ju'naɪt] *tr* unir ‖ *intr* unirse

united [ju'naɪtɪd] *adj* unido

United Kingdom *s* Reino Unido

United Nations *spl* Naciones Unidas

United States *adj* estadounidense ‖ **the United States** *s* los Estados Unidos *mpl*; Estados Unidos *msg*

unity [ˈjunɪti] *s* (*pl* -**ties**) unidad

univ. *abbr* **universal, university**

universal [‚juni'vʌrsəl] *adj* universal
universal joint *s* cardán *m*, junta universal
universe ['juni‚vʌrs] *s* universo
universi•ty [‚juni'vʌrsiti] *adj* universitario || *s* (*pl* -ties) universidad
unjust [ʌn'dʒʌst] *adj* injusto
unjustified [ʌn'dʒʌsti‚faɪd] *adj* injustificado
unkempt [ʌn'kempt] *adj* despeinado
unkind [ʌn'kaɪnd] *adj* poco amable; duro, despiadado
unknowable [ʌn'no-əbəl] *adj* inconocible, insabible
unknowingly [ʌn'no-ɪŋli] *adv* desconocidamente, sin saberlo
unknown [ʌn'non] *adj* desconocido, ignoto, incógnito || *s* desconocido; (math) incógnita
unknown quantity *s* (math & fig) incógnita
unknown soldier *s* soldado desconocido
unlace [ʌn'les] *tr* desenlazar; desatar (*los cordones del zapato*)
unlatch [ʌn'lætʃ] *tr* abrir levantando el picaporte
unlawful [ʌn'lɔfəl] *adj* ilegal
unleash [ʌn'liʃ] *tr* destraillar; soltar, desencadenar
unleavened [ʌn'levənd] *adj* ázimo
unless [ʌn'les] *conj* a menos que, a no ser que
unlettered [ʌn'letərd] *adj* iletrado, indocto; sin rotular; (*illiterate*) analfabeto
unlike [ʌn'laɪk] *adj* desemejante; desemejante de; (*poles of a magnet*) (elec) de nombres contrarios; (elec) de signo contrario || *prep* a diferencia de
unlikely [ʌn'laɪkli] *adj* improbable
unlimber [ʌn'lɪmbər] *tr* preparar para la acción || *intr* prepararse para la acción
unlined [ʌn'laɪnd] *adj* (*coat*) sin forro; (*paper*) sin rayar; (*face*) sin arrugas
unload [ʌn'lod] *tr* descargar; (coll) deshacerse de || *intr* descargar
unloading [ʌn'lodɪŋ] *s* descarga, descargue *m*
unlock [ʌn'lɑk] *tr* abrir (*p.ej., una puerta*); (typ) desapretar
unloose [ʌn'lus] *tr* aflojar, soltar, desatar
unloved [ʌn'lʌvd] *adj* desamado
unlovely [ʌn'lʌvli] *adj* desgraciado
unluck•y [ʌn'lʌki] *adj* (*comp* -ier; *super* -iest) desgraciado, desdichado; aciago, nefasto, de mala suerte
un•make [ʌn'mek] *v* (*pret & pp* -made ['med]) *tr* deshacer; destruir
unmanageable [ʌn'mænɪdʒəbəl] *adj* inmanejable
unmanly [ʌn'mænli] *adj* afeminado; bajo, cobarde
unmannerly [ʌn'mænərli] *adj* descortés, malcriado
unmarketable [ʌn'mɑrkɪtəbəl] *adj* incomerciable
unmarriageable [ʌn'mærɪdʒəbəl] *adj* incasable
unmarried [ʌn'mærɪd] *adj* soltero
unmask [ʌn'mæsk] o [ʌn'mɑsk] *tr*

desenmascarar || *intr* desenmascararse
unmatchable [ʌn'mætʃəbəl] *adj* incomparable, sin igual; (*price*) incompetible
unmerciful [ʌn'mʌrsɪfəl] *adj* despiadado, inclemente
unmesh [ʌn'meʃ] *tr* desengranar || *intr* desengranarse
unmindful [ʌn'maɪndfəl] *adj* desatento, descuidado; **to be unmindful of** olvidar, no pensar en
unmistakable [‚ʌnmɪs'tekəbəl] *adj* inequívoco, inconfundible
unmixed [ʌn'mɪkst] *adj* puro, sin mezcla
unmoor [ʌn'mur] *tr* desamarrar (*un buque*); desaferrar (*las áncoras*)
unmoved [ʌn'muvd] *adj* fijo, inmoto; impasible
unmuzzle [ʌn'mʌzəl] *tr* desbozalar
unnatural [ʌn'nætʃərəl] *adj* innatural; (*artificial, forced*) afectado; anormal; inhumano
unnecessary [ʌn'nesə‚seri] *adj* innecesario
unnerve [ʌn'nʌrv] *tr* acobardar, trastornar
unnoticeable [ʌn'notɪsəbəl] *adj* imperceptible
unnoticed [ʌn'notɪst] *adj* inadvertido
unobliging [‚ʌnə'blaɪdʒɪŋ] *adj* poco servicial, poco amable
unobserved [‚ʌnəb'zʌrvd] *adj* inadvertido, sin ser visto
unobtainable [‚ʌnəb'tenəbəl] *adj* inencontrable, inasequible
unobtrusive [‚ʌnəb'trusɪv] *adj* discreto, reservado
unoccupied [ʌn'ɑkjə‚paɪd] *adj* libre, vacante; (*not busy*) desocupado
unofficial [‚ʌnə'fɪʃəl] *adj* extraoficial, oficioso
unopened [ʌn'opənd] *adj* sin abrir; (*book*) no cortado
unorthodox [ʌn'ɔrθə‚dɑks] *adj* inortodoxo
unpack [ʌn'pæk] *tr* desembalar, desempaquetar
unpalatable [ʌn'pælətəbəl] *adj* desabrido, ingustable
unparalleled [ʌn'pærə‚leld] *adj* incomparable, sin par, sin igual
unpardonable [ʌn'pardənəbəl] *adj* imperdonable
unpatriotic [‚ʌnpetri'ɑtɪk] o [‚ʌnpætri'ɑtɪk] *adj* antipatriótico
unperceived [‚ʌnpər'sivd] *adj* inadvertido
unperturbable [‚ʌnpər'tʌrbəbəl] *adj* infracto, imperturbable
unpleasant [ʌn'plezənt] *adj* antipático, desagradable
unpopular [ʌn'pɑpjələr] *adj* impopular
unpopularity [ʌn‚pɑpjə'læriti] *s* impopularidad
unprecedented [ʌn'presi‚dentɪd] *adj* sin precedente, inaudito
unprejudiced [ʌn'predʒədɪst] *adj* sin prejuicios, imparcial
unpremeditated [‚ʌnpri'medi‚tetɪd] *adj* impremeditado

unprepared [,ʌnprɪ'perd] *adj* desprevenido; falto de preparación

unprepossessing [,ʌnpripə'zesɪŋ] *adj* poco atrayente

unpresentable [,ʌnprɪ'zentəbəl] *adj* impresentable

unpretentious [,ʌnprɪ'tenʃəs] *adj* modesto, sencillo

unprincipled [ʌn'prɪnsɪpəld] *adj* sin principios, sin conciencia

unproductive [,ʌnprə'dʌktɪv] *adj* improductivo

unprofitable [ʌn'prɑfɪtəbəl] *adj* no provechoso, inútil

unpronounceable [,ʌnprə'naʊnsəbəl] *adj* impronunciable

unpropitious [,ʌnprə'pɪʃəs] *adj* impropicio

unpublished [ʌn'pʌblɪʃt] *adj* inédito

unpunished [ʌn'pʌnɪʃt] *adj* impune

unpurchasable [ʌn'pʌrtʃəsəbəl] *adj* incomprable

unquenchable [ʌn'kwentʃəbəl] *adj* inextinguible

unquestionable [ʌn'kwestʃənəbəl] *adj* incuestionable

unrav-el [ʌn'rævəl] *v* (*pret & pp* -**eled** o -**elled**; *ger* -**eling** o -**elling**) *tr* deshebrar; desenredar, desenmarañar ‖ *intr* desenredarse, desenmarañarse

unreachable [ʌn'ritʃəbəl] *adj* inalcanzable

unreal [ʌn'ri-əl] *adj* irreal

unreali·ty [,ʌnrɪ'ælɪti] *s* (*pl* -**ties**) irrealidad

unreasonable [ʌn'rizənəbəl] *adj* irrazonable, desrazonable

unrecognizable [ʌn'rekəg,naɪzəbəl] *adj* irreconocible

unreel [ʌn'ril] *tr* desenrollar ‖ *intr* desenrollarse

unrefined [,ʌnrɪ'faɪnd] *adj* no refinado, impuro; grosero, rudo, tosco

unrelenting [,ʌnrɪ'lentɪŋ] *adj* inexorable, inflexible, implacable

unreliable [,ʌnrɪ'laɪ-əbəl] *adj* indigno de confianza, informal

unremitting [,ʌnrɪ'mɪtɪŋ] *adj* constante, incesante; infatigable

unrenewable [,ʌnrɪ'nju-əbəl] o [,ʌnrɪ-'nu-əbəl] *adj* irrenovable; (com) improrrogable

unrented [ʌn'rentɪd] *adj* desalquilado

unrepentant [,ʌnrɪ'pentənt] *adj* impenitente

unrequited love [,ʌnrɪ'kwaɪtɪd] *s* amor no correspondido

unresponsive [,ʌnrɪ'spɑnsɪv] *adj* insensible, frío, desinteresado

unrest [ʌn'rest] *s* intranquilidad, inquietud; alboroto, desorden *m*

un·rig [ʌn'rɪg] *v* (*pret & pp* -**rigged**; *ger* -**rigging**) *tr* (naut) desaparejar

unrighteous [ʌn'raɪtʃəs] *adj* injusto, malvado, vicioso

unripe [ʌn'raɪp] *adj* inmaturo, verde; prematuro, precoz

unrivaled o **unrivalled** [ʌn'raɪvəld] *adj* sin rival, sin par

unroll [ʌn'rol] *tr* desenrollar, desplegar

unromantic [,ʌnro'mæntɪk] *adj* poco romántico

unruffled [ʌn'rʌfəld] *adj* tranquilo, sereno

unruly [ʌn'ruli] *adj* ingobernable, indómito, revoltoso

unsaddle [ʌn'sædəl] *tr* desensillar (*un caballo*); desarzonar (*al jinete*)

unsafe [ʌn'sef] *adj* inseguro, peligroso

unsaid [ʌn'sed] *adj* callado, no dicho

unsalable [ʌn'seləbəl] *adj* invendible

unsanitary [ʌn'sænɪ,teri] *adj* antihigiénico, insalubre

unsatisfactory [ʌn,sætɪs'fæktəri] *adj* insatisfactorio, poco satisfactorio

unsatisfied [ʌn'sætɪs,faɪd] *adj* insatisfecho

unsavory [ʌn'sevəri] *adj* desabrido; (fig) infame, deshonroso

unscathed [ʌn'skeðd] *adj* ileso, sano y salvo

unscientific [,ʌnsaɪ-ən'tɪfɪk] *adj* anticientífico

unscrew [ʌn'skru] *tr* destornillar ‖ *intr* destornillarse

unscrupulous [ʌn'skrupjələs] *adj* inescrupuloso

unseal [ʌn'sil] *tr* desellar; (fig) abrir

unseasonable [ʌn'sizənəbəl] *adj* intempestivo, inoportuno

unseaworthy [ʌn'si,wʌrði] *adj* innavegable

unseemly [ʌn'simli] *adj* impropio, indecoroso, indigno

unseen [ʌn'sin] *adj* invisible, oculto

unselfish [ʌn'selfɪʃ] *adj* desinteresado, generoso, altruísta

unsettled [ʌn'setəld] *adj* inhabitado, despoblado; sin residencia fija; indeciso; descompuesto; (bills) por pagar

unshackle [ʌn'ʃækəl] *tr* desherrar, desencadenar

unshaken [ʌn'ʃekən] *adj* imperturbado

unshapely [ʌn'ʃepli] *adj* desproporcionado, mal formado

unshatterable [ʌn'ʃætərəbəl] *adj* inastillable

unshaven [ʌn'ʃevən] *adj* sin afeitar

unsheathe [ʌn'ʃið] *tr* desenvainar

unshod [ʌn'ʃɑd] *adj* descalzo; (*horse*) desherrado

unshrinkable [ʌn'ʃrɪŋkəbəl] *adj* inencogible

unsightly [ʌn'saɪtli] *adj* feo, de aspecto malo, repugnante

unsinkable [ʌn'sɪŋkəbəl] *adj* insumergible

unskilled [ʌn'skɪld] *adj* inexperto

unskilled laborer *s* bracero, peón *m*

unskillful [ʌn'skɪlfəl] *adj* desmañado

unsnarl [ʌn'snɑrl] *tr* desenredar

unsociable [ʌn'so/əbəl] *adj* insociable, huraño

unsold [ʌn'sold] *adj* invendido

unsolder [ʌn'sɑdər] *tr* desoldar; (fig) desunir, separar

unsophisticated [,ʌnsə'fɪstɪ,ketɪd] *adj* ingenuo, natural, sencillo

unsound [ʌn'saʊnd] *adj* poco firme; falso, erróneo; (decayed) podrido; (sleep) ligero

unsown [ʌn'son] *adj* yermo, no sembrado

unspeakable [ʌn'spikəbəl] *adj* indecible, inefable; (*atrocious, infamous*) incalificable

unsportsmanlike [ʌn'spɔrtsmən ˌlaɪk] *adj* antideportivo

unstable [ʌn'stebəl] *adj* inestable

unsteady [ʌn'stɛdɪ] *adj* inseguro, inestable; irresoluto, inconstante; poco juicioso

unstinted [ʌn'stɪntɪd] *adj* no escatimado, generoso, liberal

unstitch [ʌn'stɪtʃ] *tr* descoser

un·stop [ʌn'stɑp] *v* (*pret* & *pp* **-stopped**; *ger* **-stopping**) *tr* destaponar

unstressed [ʌn'strɛst] *adj* sin énfasis; (*syllable*) inacentuado

unstrung [ʌn'strʌŋ] *adj* nervioso, trastornado

unsuccessful [ˌʌnsək'sɛsfəl] *adj* (*person*) desairado; (*undertaking*) impróspero; **to be unsuccessful** no tener éxito

unsuitable [ʌn'sutəbəl] o [ʌn'sjutəbəl] *adj* inadecuado, inconveniente

unsurpassable [ˌʌnsər'pæsəbəl] o [ˌʌnsər'pɑsəbəl] *adj* insuperable

unsuspected [ˌʌnsəs'pɛktɪd] *adj* insospechado

unswerving [ʌn'swɜrvɪŋ] *adj* firme, inmutable, resoluto

unsymmetrical [ˌʌnsɪ'mɛtrɪkəl] *adj* asimétrico, disimétrico

unsympathetic [ˌʌnsɪmpə'θɛtɪk] *adj* incompasivo, indiferente

unsystematic(al) [ˌʌnsɪstə'mætɪk(əl)] *adj* poco sistemático, sin sistema

untactful [ʌn'tæktfəl] *adj* indiscreto, falto de tacto

untamed [ʌn'temd] *adj* indomado, bravío

untangle [ʌn'tæŋgəl] *tr* desenredar, desenmarañar

unteachable [ʌn'titʃəbəl] *adj* indócil

untenable [ʌn'tɛnəbəl] *adj* insostenible

unthankful [ʌn'θæŋkfəl] *adj* ingrato, desagradecido

unthinkable [ʌn'θɪŋkəbəl] *adj* impensable

unthinking [ʌn'θɪŋkɪŋ] *adj* irreflexivo, desatento; irracional, instintivo

untidy [ʌn'taɪdɪ] *adj* desaseado, desaliñado

un·tie [ʌn'taɪ] *v* (*pret* & *pp* **-tied**; *ger* **-tying**) *tr* desatar; deshacer (*un nudo, una cuerda*); (*to free from restraint*) soltar; resolver || *intr* desatarse

until [ʌn'tɪl] *prep* hasta || *conj* hasta que; **to wait until** aguardar a que, esperar a que

untillable [ʌn'tɪləbəl] *adj* incultivable

untimely [ʌn'taɪmlɪ] *adj* intempestivo

untiring [ʌn'taɪrɪŋ] *adj* incansable

untold [ʌn'told] *adj* nunca dicho; (*uncounted*) innumerable, incalculable

untouchable [ʌn'tʌtʃəbəl] *adj* intangible || *s* intocable *mf*

untouched [ʌn'tʌtʃt] *adj* intacto; íntegro; impasible; no mencionado

untoward [ʌn'tord] *adj* desfavorable; indecoroso

untrammeled o **untrammelled** [ʌn'træməld] *adj* libre, sin trabas

untried [ʌn'traɪd] *adj* no probado, no ensayado

untroubled [ʌn'trʌbləd] *adj* tranquilo, sosegado

untrue [ʌn'tru] *adj* falso; infiel

untrustworthy [ʌn'trʌst ˌwɜrðɪ] *adj* indigno de confianza

untruth [ʌn'truθ] *s* falsedad, mentira

untruthful [ʌn'truθfəl] *adj* falso, mentiroso

untwist [ʌn'twɪst] *tr* destorcer || *intr* destorcerse

unused [ʌn'juzd] *adj* inutilizado, no usado; nuevo; **unused to** [ʌn'juzdtu] o [ʌn'justu] *adj* no acostumbrado a

unusual [ʌn'juʒʊ·əl] *adj* inusual, insólito

unutterable [ʌn'ʌtərəbəl] *adj* indecible, inexpresable

unvanquished [ʌn'væŋkwɪʃt] *adj* invicto

unvarnished [ʌn'vɑrnɪʃt] *adj* sin barnizar; (fig) sencillo, sin adornos

unveil [ʌn'vel] *tr* quitar el velo a; descubrir, develar, inaugurar (*una estatua*) || *intr* quitarse el velo

unveiling [ʌn'velɪŋ] *s* develación, inauguración

unventilated [ʌn'vɛntɪ ˌletɪd] *adj* sin ventilar

unvoice [ʌn'vɔɪs] *tr* afonizar, ensordecer || *intr* afonizarse, ensordecerse

unwanted [ʌn'wɑntɪd] *adj* indeseado

unwarranted [ʌn'wɑrəntɪd] *adj* injustificado; no autorizado; sin garantía

unwary [ʌn'werɪ] *adj* incauto, imprudente

unwavering [ʌn'wevərɪŋ] *adj* firme, determinado, resuelto

unwelcome [ʌn'wɛlkəm] *adj* mal acogido; importuno, molesto

unwell [ʌn'wɛl] *adj* indispuesto, enfermo; (coll) menstruante

unwholesome [ʌn'holsəm] *adj* insalubre

unwieldy [ʌn'wildɪ] *adj* inmanejable, abultado, pesado

unwilling [ʌn'wɪlɪŋ] *adj* desinclinado, maldispuesto, renuente

unwillingly [ʌn'wɪlɪŋlɪ] *adv* de mala gana

un·wind [ʌn'waɪnd] *v* (*pret* & *pp* **-wound** ['waund]) *tr* desenvolver || *intr* desenvolverse; distenderse (*el muelle del reloj*)

unwise [ʌn'waɪz] *adj* indiscreto, malaconsejado

unwished-for [ʌn'wɪʃt ˌfɔr] *adj* indeseado

unwitting [ʌn'wɪtɪŋ] *adj* inadvertido, inconsciente

unwonted [ʌn'wʌntɪd] *adj* poco común, raro, insólito

unworldly [ʌn'wɜrldlɪ] *adj* no terrenal, no mundano, espiritual

unworthy [ʌn'wɜrðɪ] *adj* indigno, desmerecedor

un·wrap [ʌn'ræp] *v* (*pret* & *pp* **-wrapped**; *ger* **-wrapping**) *tr* desenvolver, desempapelar

unwrinkle [ʌn'rɪŋkəl] *tr* desarrugar || *intr* desarrugarse

unwritten [ʌn'rɪtən] *adj* no escrito; (*blank*) en blanco; oral

unyielding [ʌn'jildɪŋ] *adj* firme, inflexible; terco, reacio

unyoke [ʌn'jok] *tr* desuncir

up [ʌp] *adj* ascendente; alto, elevado; derecho, en pie; terminado; cumplido; levantado de la cama; **to be up and about** estar levantado (*el que estaba enfermo*) ‖ *s* subida; **ups and downs** altibajos, vicisitudes ‖ *adv* arriba; en el aire; hacia arriba; al norte; **to be up** estar levantado; vencer (*un plazo*); **to be up in arms** estar sobre las armas; protestar vehementemente; **to be up to a person** tocarle a una persona; **to get up** levantarse; **to go up** subir; **to keep up** mantener; continuar; mantenerse firme; **to keep up with** correr parejas con; **up above** allá arriba; **up against it** (*slang*) en apuros; **up to** hasta; (*capable of*) a la altura de; (*informed of*) al corriente de; (*scheming*) armando, tramando; **what is up?** ¿qué pasa? ‖ *prep* subiendo; **up the river** río arriba; **up the street** calle arriba

up-and-coming ['ʌpən'kʌmɪŋ] *adj* (coll) prometedor

up-and-doing ['ʌpən'du·ɪŋ] *adj* (coll) emprendedor

up-and-up ['ʌpən'ʌp] *s* — **on the up-and-up** (coll) mejorándose; (coll) abiertamente, sin dolo

up·braid' *tr* regañar, reprender

upbringing ['ʌp·brɪŋɪŋ] *s* educación, crianza

up'coun'try *adv* (coll) hacia el interior, tierra adentro ‖ *s* (coll) interior *m* del país

up·date' *tr* poner al día

upheaval [ʌp'hivəl] *s* trastorno, cataclismo

up'hill' *adj* ascendente; arduo, difícil, penoso ‖ **up·hill'** *adv* cuesta arriba

up·hold' *v* (*pret & pp* **-held**) *tr* levantar; apoyar, sostener; defender

upholster [ʌp'holstər] *tr* tapizar

upholsterer [ʌp'holstərər] *s* tapicero

upholster·y [ʌp'holstəri] *s* (*pl* **-ies**) tapicería

up'keep' *s* conservación, manutención; gastos de conservación, gastos de entretenimiento

upland ['ʌplənd] o ['ʌplænd] *adj* alto, elevado ‖ *s* tierra alta, terreno elevado

up'lift' *s* (*lifting*) elevación, levantamiento; mejora social; (*moral or spiritual improvement*) edificación ‖ **up·lift'** *tr* elevar, levantar; edificar

upon [ə'pɑn] *prep* en, sobre, encima de; **upon** + *ger* al + *inf*, p.ej., **upon arriving** al llegar; **upon my word!** ¡por mi palabra!

upper ['ʌpər] *adj* alto, superior; (*country*) interior; (*clothing*) exterior ‖ *s* (*of shoe*) pala; **on one's uppers** con las suelas gastadas; (coll) andrajoso, pobre, sin blanca

upper berth *s* litera alta, cama alta

upper case *s* (typ) caja alta

upper classes *spl* altas clases

upper hand *s* dominio, ventaja; **to have the upper hand** tener vara alta

upper middle class *s* alta burguesía

up'per·most' *adj* (el) más alto; (el) principal ‖ *adv* en lo más alto; primero, en primer lugar

uppish ['ʌpɪʃ] *adj* (coll) copetudo, arrogante

up·raise' *tr* levantar

up'right' *adj* derecho, vertical; probo, recto ‖ *adv* verticalmente ‖ *s* montante *m*

uprising [ʌp'raɪzɪŋ] o ['ʌp·raɪzɪŋ] *s* insurrección, levantamiento

up'roar' *s* alboroto, conmoción, tumulto

uproarious [ʌp'rorɪ·əs] *adj* tumultuoso; (*noisy*) ruidoso; (*funny*) muy cómico

up·root' *tr* desarraigar

up·set' o **up'set'** *adj* (*overturned*) volcado; trastornado; indispuesto ‖ **up'set'** *s* (*overturn*) vuelco; (*unexpected defeat*) contratiempo; (*disturbance*) trastorno; (*illness*) indisposición, enfermedad ‖ **up·set'** *v* (*pret & pp* **-set**; *ger* **-setting**) *tr* volcar; trastornar; indisponer ‖ *intr* volcar

upset price *s* precio mínimo fijado en una subasta

upsetting [ʌp'setɪŋ] *adj* desconcertante

up'shot' *s* conclusión, resultado; esencia, quid *m*

up'side' *s* parte *f* superior, lado superior; **on the upside** (*said of prices*) subiendo

upside down *adv* al revés, lo de arriba abajo, patas arriba; en confusión, revuelto; **to turn upside down** volcar; trastornar; volcarse; trastornarse

up'stage' *adj* situado al fondo de la escena; (coll) altanero, arrogante ‖ *adv* al fondo de la escena ‖ **up'stage'** *tr* (coll) mirar por encima del hombro, desairar

up'stairs' *adj* de arriba ‖ *adv* arriba ‖ *s* piso superior, pisos superiores

upstanding [ʌp'stændɪŋ] *adj* derecho; gallardo; probo, recto

up'start' *adj* & *s* advenedizo

up'stream' *adv* aguas arriba, río arriba

up'stroke' *s* carrera ascendente

up'swing' *s* movimiento hacia arriba; mejora notable; **on the upswing** mejorando notablemente

up'-to-date' *adj* corriente; reciente, moderno; de última hora, de última moda

up'-to-the-min'ute *adj* al día, de actualidad

up'town' *adj* de la parte alta de la ciudad ‖ *adv* en la parte alta de la ciudad

up train *s* tren *m* ascendente

up'trend' *s* tendencia al alza

up'turn' *s* alza, subida, mejora

upturned [ʌp'tʌrnd] *adj* revuelto; (*part of clothing*) arremangado; (*nose*) respingada

upward ['ʌpwərd] *adj* ascendente ‖ *adv* hacia arriba; **upward of** más de

Ural ['jurəl] *adj* ural || **Urals** *spl* Urales *mpl*

uranium [ju'reni·əm] *s* uranio

urban ['ʌrbən] *adj* urbano *(perteneciente a la ciudad)*

urbane [ʌr'ben] *adj* urbano *(atento, cortés)*

urbanite ['ʌrbə,naɪt] *s* ciudadano

urbanity [ʌr'bænɪti] *s* urbanidad

urbanize ['ʌrbə,naɪz] *tr* urbanizar

urchin ['ʌrtʃɪn] *s* pilluelo, galopín *m*

ure·thra [ju'riθrə] *s (pl* **-thras** o **-thrae** [θri]) uretra

urge [ʌrdʒ] *s* impulso, estímulo || *tr* apremiar, impeler, estimular; pedir instantemente; *(to try to persuade)* instar || *intr* instar

urgen·cy ['ʌrdʒənsi] *s (pl* **-cies)** urgencia; instancia, apremio

urgent ['ʌrdʒənt] *adj* urgente; apremiante

urinal ['jurɪnəl] *s (receptacle)* orinal *m; (place)* urinario

urinary ['jurɪ,neri] *adj* urinario

urinate ['jurɪ,net] *tr* orinar *(p.ej., sangre)* || *intr* orinar, orinarse

urine ['jurɪn] *s* orina, orines *mpl*

urn [ʌrn] *s (decorative vase)* jarrón *m*; cafetera o tetera con grifo; *(to hold ashes of the dead after cremation)* urna

urology [ju'ralədʒi] *s* urología

Uruguay ['jurə,gwe] o ['jurə,gwaɪ] *s* el Uruguay

Uruguayan [,jurə'gwe·ən] o [,jurə'gwaɪ·ən] *adj & s* uruguayo

us [ʌs] *pron pers* nos; nosotros; **to us** nos; a nosotros

U.S.A. *abbr* **United States of America, United States Army, Union of South Africa**

usable ['juzəbəl] *adj* aprovechable, utilizable

usage ['jusɪdʒ] o ['juzɪdʒ] *s* usanza; *(e.g., of a language)* uso

use [jus] *s* uso, empleo; utilidad; **in use** en uso; **out of use** desusado; **to be of no use** no servir para nada; **to have no use for** no necesitar; **no servirse de;** (coll) tener en poco; **to make use of** servirse de || [juz] *tr* usar, emplear, servirse de; **to use badly**

maltratar; **to use up** agotar, consumir || *intr* (empléase sólo en el pretérito y se traduce al español con el pretérito imperfecto o el verbo **soler**), p.ej., **I used to go out for a walk every evening** salía de paseo todas las tardes o solía salir de paseo todas las tardes

used [juzd] *adj (customarily employed; worn, partly worn-out; accustomed)* usado; **used to** ['juzdtu] o ['justu] acostumbrado a

useful ['jusfəl] *adj* útil

usefulness ['jusfəlnɪs] *s* utilidad

useless ['juslɪs] *adj* inservible, inútil

user ['juzər] *s* usuario

usher ['ʌʃər] *s (in a theater)* acomodador *m; (doorkeeper)* ujier *m*, portero || *tr* acomodar; **to usher in** anunciar, introducir

U.S.S.R. *abbr* **Union of Soviet Socialist Republics**

usual ['juʒu·əl] *adj* usual, acostumbrado; **as usual** como de costumbre

usually ['juʒu·əli] *adv* usualmente, de ordinario

usurp [ju'zʌrp] *tr* usurpar

usu·ry ['juʒəri] *s (pl* **-ries)** usura

utensil [ju'tensɪl] *s* utensilio

uter·us ['jutərəs] *s (pl* **-i** [,aɪ]) útero

utilitarian [,jutɪlɪ'teri·ən] *adj* utilitario

util·ty [ju'tɪlɪti] *s (pl* **-ties)** utilidad; empresa de servicio público

utilize ['jutɪ,laɪz] *tr* utilizar

utmost ['ʌt,most] *adj* sumo, extremo, último; más grande, mayor posible; más lejano || *s* — **the utmost** lo sumo, lo mayor, lo más; **to the utmost** a lo sumo, a más no poder; **to do one's utmost** hacer todo lo posible

utopia [ju'topi·ə] *s* utopía

utopian [ju'topi·ən] *adj* utópico, utopista || *s* utopista *mf*

utter ['ʌtər] *adj* total, absoluto || *tr* proferir, pronunciar; dar *(un suspiro)*

utterance ['ʌtərəns] *s* expresión, pronunciación; declaración

utterly ['ʌtərli] *adj* completamente, totalmente, absolutamente

uxoricide [ʌk'sɔrɪ,saɪd] *s (husband)* uxoricida *m; (act)* uxoricidio

uxorious [ʌk'sɔrɪ·əs] *adj* uxorio

V

V, v [vi] vigésima segunda letra del alfabeto inglés

v. *abbr* **verb, verse, versus, vide** (Lat) see, voice, volt, volume

V. *abbr* **Venerable, Vice, Viscount, Volunteer**

vacan·cy ['vekənsi] *s (pl* **-cies)** *(emptiness; gap, opening)* vacío; *(unfilled position or job)* vacancia, vacante *f*, vacío; piso vacante; cargo vacante

vacant ['vekənt] *adj (empty)* vacío; *(having no occupant; untenanted)*

vacante; *(expression, look)* vago; distraído

vacate ['veket] *tr* dejar vacante; anular, invalidar, revocar || *intr (to move out)* desalojar; (coll) irse, marcharse

vacation [ve'keʃən] *s* vacaciones; **on vacation** de vacaciones || *intr* tomar vacaciones

vacationist [ve'keʃənɪst] *s* vacacionista *mf*

vacation with pay *s* vacaciones retribuídas

vaccinate ['væksɪ ,net] *tr* vacunar
vaccination [,væksɪ'ne/ən] *s* vacunación
vaccine [væk'sin] *s* vacuna
vacillate ['væsɪ ,let] *intr* vacilar
vacillating ['væsɪ ,letɪŋ] *adj* vacilante
vacu·ity [væ'kju·ɪti] *s* (*pl* **-ties**) vacuidad
vacu·um ['vækju·əm] *s* (*pl* **-ums** o **-a** [ə]) vacío || *tr* (coll) limpiar
vacuum cleaner *s* aspirador *m* de polvo
vacuum tank *s* (aut) aspirador *m* de gasolina, nodriza
vacuum tube *s* tubo de vacío
vagabond ['vægə ,bɑnd] *adj & s* vagabundo
vagar·y [və'geri] *s* (*pl* **-ies**) capricho
vagran·cy ['vegrənsɪ] *s* (*pl* **-cies**) vagabundaje *m*
vagrant ['vegrənt] *adj & s* vagabundo
vague [veg] *adj* vago
vain [ven] *adj* vano; (*conceited*) vanidoso; **in vain** en vano
vainglorious [ven'glorɪ·əs] *adj* vanaglorioso
valance ['væləns] *s* (*across the top of a window*) guardamalleta; (*drapery*) doselera
vale [vel] *s* valle *m*
valedictorian [,vælɪdɪk'torɪ·ən] *s* alumno que pronuncia el discurso de despedida al fin del curso
valedicto·ry [,vælɪ'dɪktərɪ] *adj* de despedida || *s* (*pl* **-ries**) discurso de despedida
valence ['veləns] *s* (chem) valencia
valentine ['vælən ,taɪn] *s* tarjeta amorosa o jocosa del día de San Valentín
Valentine Day *s* día m de los corazones, día de los enamorados (*14 de febrero*)
vale of tears *s* valle *m* de lágrimas
valet ['vælɪt] o ['væle] *s* ayuda *m*, paje *m*
valiant ['væljənt] *adj* valiente, valeroso
valid ['vælɪd] *adj* válido, valedero
validate ['vælɪ ,det] *tr* validar; (sport) homologar
validation [,vælɪ'de/ən] *s* validación; (sport) homologación
validi·ty [və'lɪdɪtɪ] *s* (*pl* **-ties**) validez *f*
valise [və'lis] *s* maleta
valley ['vælɪ] *s* valle *m*; (*of roof*) lima hoya
valor ['vælər] *s* valor *m*, ánimo
valorous ['vælərəs] *adj* valeroso
valuable ['vælju·əbəl] o ['væljəbəl] *adj* (*having monetary value*) valioso; (*highly thought of*) estimable || **valuables** *spl* alhajas, objetos de valor
value ['vælju] *s* valor *m*; (*return for one's money in a purchase*) (coll) adquisición, inversión, p.ej., **an excellent value** una adquisición excelente || *tr* (*to think highly of*) estimar; (*to set a price for*) valuar, valuar
valueless ['væljulɪs] *adj* sin valor
valve [vælv] *s* válvula; (*of mollusk*) valva; (mus) llave *f*
valve cap *s* capuchón *m*
valve gears *spl* distribución
valve'-in-head' engine *s* motor *m* con válvulas en cabeza

valve lifter ['lɪftər] *s* levantaválvulas *m*
valve seat *s* asiento de válvula
valve spring *s* muelle *m* de válvula
valve stem *s* vástago de válvula
vamp [væmp] *s* (*of shoe*) empella; (*patchwork*) remiendo; (*woman who preys on men*) (slang) mujer *f* fatal, vampiresa || *tr* poner empella a (*un zapato*); remendar; (*to concoct*) componer, enmendar; (jazz) improvisar (*un acompañamiento*); (slang) seducir (*una mujer mundana a un hombre*)
vampire ['væmpaɪr] *s* vampiro; (*woman who preys on men*) mujer *f* fatal, vampiresa
van [væn] *s* carro de carga, camión *m* de mudanzas; (mil & fig) vanguardia; (Brit) furgón *m* de equipajes
vanadium [və'nedɪ·əm] *s* vanadio
vandal ['vændəl] *adj & s* vándalo || **Vandal** *adj & s* vándalo
vandalism ['vændə ,lɪzəm] *s* vandalismo
vane [ven] *s* (*weathervane*) veleta; (*of windmill*) aspa; (*of propeller or turbine*) paleta; (*of feather*) barba
vanguard ['væn ,gɑrd] *s* (mil & fig) vanguardia; **in the vanguard** a vanguardia
vanilla [və'nɪlə] *s* vainilla
vanish ['vænɪ/] *intr* desvanecerse
vanishing cream ['vænɪ/ɪŋ] *s* crema desvanecedora
vani·ty ['vænɪtɪ] *s* (*pl* **-ties**) vanidad; (*dressing table*) tocador *m*; (*vanity case*) estuche *m* de afeites
vanity case *s* estuche *m* de afeites, neceser *m* de belleza
vanquish ['væŋkwɪ/] *tr* vencer, rendir
vantage ground ['væntɪdʒ] *s* posición ventajosa
vapid ['væpɪd] *adj* insípido
vapor ['vepər] *s* vapor *m* (*el visible; exhalación, vaho, niebla, etc.*)
vaporize ['vepə ,raɪz] *tr* vaporizar || *intr* vaporizarse
vaporous ['vepərəs] *adj* vaporoso
vapor trail *s* (aer) estela de vapor, rastro de condensación
var. *abbr* **variant**
variable ['verɪ·əbəl] *adj & s* variable *f*
variance ['verɪ·əns] *s* diferencia, variación; **at variance with** en desacuerdo con
variant ['verɪ·ənt] *adj & s* variante *f*
variation [,verɪ'e/ən] *s* variación
varicose ['værɪ ,kos] *adj* varicoso
varicose vein *s* (pathol) varice *f*
varied ['verɪd] *adj* variado, vario
variegated ['verɪ·ə ,getɪd] o ['verɪ ,getɪd] *adj* abigarrado, variado
varie·ty [və'raɪ·ɪti] *s* (*pl* **-ties**) variedad
variety show *s* variedades
variola [və'raɪ·ələ] *s* (pathol) viruela
various ['verɪ·əs] *adj* (*several; of different kinds*) varios; (*many-sided; many-colored*) vario
varnish ['vɑrnɪ/] *s* barniz *m*; (fig) capa, apariencia || *tr* barnizar; (fig) dar apariencia falsa a
varsi·ty ['vɑrsɪti] *adj* (sport) universi-

tario ‖ s (pl -ties) (sport) equipo principal de la universidad

var·y ['veri] v (pret & pp -ied) tr & intr variar

vase [ves] o [vez] s florero, jarrón m

vaseline ['væsə,lin] s (trademark) vaselina

vassal ['væsəl] adj & s vasallo

vast [væst] o [vɑst] adj vasto

vastly ['væstli] o ['vɑstli] adv enormemente

vastness ['væstnıs] o ['vɑstnıs] s vastedad

vat [væt] s cuba, tina

vaudeville ['vodvıl] o ['vɔdəvıl] s variedades; (light theatrical piece interspersed with songs) zarzuela

vault [vɔlt] s (underground chamber) bodega; (of a bank) cámara acorazada; (burial chamber) sepultura, tumba; (firmament) bóveda celeste; (leap) salto; (archit) bóveda ‖ tr abovedar; saltar ‖ intr saltar

vaunt [vɔnt] o [vɑnt] s jactancia ‖ tr jactarse de ‖ intr jactarse

veal [vil] s ternera, carne f de ternera

veal chop s chuleta de ternera

vedette [vı'det] s buque m escucha; centinela m de avanzada

veer [vır] s viraje m ‖ tr virar ‖ intr virar; (naut) llamar (el viento)

vegetable ['vedʒıtəbəl] adj vegetal ‖ s (plant) vegetal m; (edible part of plant) hortaliza, legumbre f

vegetable garden s huerto de hortalizas, huerto de verduras

vegetable soup s menestra, sopa de hortalizas

vegetarian [,vedʒı'terı·ən] adj & s vegetariano

vehemence ['vi·ıməns] s vehemencia

vehement ['vi·ımənt] adj vehemente

vehicle ['vi·ıkəl] s vehículo

vehicular traffic [vı'hıkjələr] s circulación rodada

veil [vel] s velo; to take the veil tomar el velo ‖ tr velar (cubrir con un velo; cubrir, disimular)

vein [ven] s vena; (streak) veta; (distinctive quality) rasgo ‖ tr vetear

velar ['vilər] adj & s velar f

vellum ['veləm] s vitela; papel m vitela

veloci·ty [vı'lasıti] s (pl -ties) velocidad

velvet ['velvıt] adj de terciopelo ‖ s terciopelo; (slang) ganancia limpia

velveteen [,velvı'tin] s velludillo

velvety ['velvıti] adj aterciopelado

Ven. abbr Venerable

vend [vend] tr vender como buhonero

vending machine s distribuidor automático

vendor ['vendər] s vendedor m, buhonero

veneer [və'nır] s chapa, enchapado; (fig) apariencia ‖ tr enchapar

venerable ['venərəbəl] adj venerable

venerate ['venə,ret] tr venerar

venereal [vı'nırı·əl] adj venéreo

Venetia [vı'nıʃı·ə] o [vı'nıʃə] s Venecia (provincia)

Venetian [vı'nıʃən] adj & s veneciano

Venetian blind s persiana

Venezuela [,venı'zwilə] s Venezuela

Venezuelan [,venı'zwilən] adj & s venezolano

vengeance ['vendʒəns] s venganza; with a vengeance con furia, con violencia; excesivamente, con creces

vengeful [ˈvendʒfəl] adj vengativo

Venice ['venıs] s Venecia (ciudad)

venire [vı'naırı] s (law) auto de convocación del jurado

venison ['venısən] o ['venızən] s carne f de venado

venom ['venəm] s veneno

venomous ['venəməs] adj venenoso

vent [vent] s agujero, orificio; (outlet) salida; to give vent to dar libre curso a ‖ tr proveer de abertura; desahogar, expresar; to vent one's spleen descargar la bilis

vent'hole' s respiradero

ventilate ['ventı,let] tr ventilar

ventilator ['ventı,letər] s ventilador m

ventricle ['ventrıkəl] s ventrículo

ventriloquism [ven'trılə,kwızəm] s ventriloquia

ventriloquist [ven'trıləkwıst] s ventrílocuo

venture ['ventʃər] s empresa arriesgada; at a venture a la buena ventura ‖ tr aventurar ‖ intr aventurarse; to venture on arriesgarse en

venturesome ['ventʃərsəm] adj (bold, daring) aventurero; (hazardous) aventurado

venturous ['ventʃərəs] adj (bold, daring) aventurero; (hazardous) aventurado, arriesgado

venue ['venju] s (law) lugar m del crimen; (law) lugar donde se reúne el jurado; change of venue (law) traslado de jurisdicción

Venus ['vinəs] s (astr) Venus m; (myth) Venus f; (very beautiful woman) Venus f

veracious [vı're/əs] adj veraz

veraci·ty [vı'ræsıti] s (pl -ties) veracidad

veranda o verandah [və'rændə] s terraza, veranda, galería

verb [vʌrb] adj verbal ‖ s verbo

verbatim [vər'betım] adj textual ‖ adv palabra por palabra, al pie de la letra

verbena [vər'binə] s (bot) verbena

verbiage ['vʌrbı·ıdʒ] s palabrería, verbosidad

verbose [vər'bos] adj verboso

verdant ['vʌrdənt] adj verde; cándido, sencillo

verdict ['vʌrdıkt] s veredicto, fallo

verdigris ['vʌrdı,gris] s verdete m

verdure ['vʌrdʒər] s verdor m

verge [vʌrdʒ] s borde m, límite m; (of a column) fuste m; báculo; (eccl) cetro; on the verge of al borde de; a punto de; within the verge of al alcance de ‖ intr — to verge on o upon llegar casi hasta, rayar en

verification [,verıfı'ke/ən] s verificación

veri·fy ['verı,faı] v (pret & pp -fied) tr verificar, comprobar; (law) afirmar bajo juramento

verily ['verɪlɪ] *adv* verdaderamente, en verdad

veritable ['verɪtəbəl] *adj* verdadero

vermicelli [ˌvɑrmɪ'selɪ] *s* fideos

vermilion [vər'mɪljən] *adj* bermejo || *s* bermellón *m*

vermin ['vɑrmɪn] *ssg (objectionable person)* sabandija || *spl (objectionable animals or persons)* sabandijas

vermouth [vər'muθ] o ['vɑrmuθ] *s* vermú *m*

vernacular [vər'nækjələr] *adj* vernáculo || *s* lenguaje vernáculo; idioma *m* corriente; *(language peculiar to a class or profession)* jerga

veronica [və'rɑnɪkə] *s* (bot & taur) verónica; lienzo de la Verónica

Versailles [ver'saɪ] *s* Versalles

versatile ['vɑrsətɪl] *adj (person)* de muchas habilidades; *(informed on many subjects)* polifacético, universal; *(device or tool)* útil para muchas cosas

verse [vɑrs] *s* verso; *(in the Bible)* versículo

versed [vɑrst] *adj* versado; **to become versed in** versarse en

versification [ˌvɑrsɪfɪ'keʃən] *s* versificación

versi-fy ['vɑrsɪˌfaɪ] *v (pret & pp -fied) tr & intr* versificar

version ['vɑrʒən] *s* versión

ver-so ['vɑrso] *s (pl -sos) (e.g., of a coin)* reverso; *(typ)* verso

versus ['vɑrsəs] *prep* contra

verte-bra ['vɑrtɪbrə] *s (pl -brae [ˌbri] o -bras)* vértebra

vertebrate ['vɑrtɪˌbret] *adj & s* vertebrado

ver-tex ['vɑrteks] *s (pl -texes o -tices [tɪˌsiz]) (top, summit)* ápice *m*; *(geom)* vértice *m*

vertical ['vɑrtɪkəl] *adj & s* vertical *f*

vertical hold *s* (telv) bloqueo vertical

vertical rudder *s* (aer) timón *m* de dirección

verti-go ['vɑrtɪˌgo] *s (pl -gos o -goes)* vértigo

verve [vɑrv] *s* brío, ánimo, vigor *m*

very ['verɪ] *adj* mismísimo; *(sheer, utter)* mero, puro; *(actual)* verdadero || *adv* muy; mucho, p.ej., **to be very hungry** tener mucha hambre

vesicle ['vesɪkəl] *s* vesícula

vesper ['vespər] *s* tarde *f*, caída de la tarde; oración de la tarde; canción de la tarde; **vespers** (eccl) vísperas || **Vesper** *s* Véspero

vesper bell *s* campana que llama a vísperas

vessel ['vesəl] *s* vasija, recipiente *m*; *(ship)* bajel *m*, embarcación, buque *m*; (anat) vaso

vest [vest] *s (of man's suit)* chaleco; *(jabot)* chorrera; *(undershirt)* camiseta || *tr* vestir; **to vest in** conceder *(p.ej., poder)* a; **to vest with** investir de || *intr* vestirse; **to vest in** pasar a

vested interests *spl* intereses creados

vestibule ['vestɪˌbjul] *s* vestíbulo, zaguán *m*

vestige ['vestɪdʒ] *s* vestigio

vestment ['vestmənt] *s* vestidura

vest'-pock'et *adj* de bolsillo, en miniatura; diminuto

ves-try ['vestrɪ] *s (pl -tries)* sacristía; *(chapel)* capilla; junta parroquial; reunión de la junta parroquial

vestry-man ['vestrɪmən] *s (pl -men [mən])* miembro de la junta parroquial

Vesuvius [vɪ'suvɪ-əs] o [vɪ'sjuvɪ-əs] *s* el Vesubio

vet. *abbr* **veteran, veterinary**

vetch [vetʃ] *s* arveja, veza; *(grass pea)* almorta

veteran ['vetərən] *adj & s* veterano

veterinarian [ˌvetərɪ'nerɪ-ən] *s* veterinario

veterinar-y ['vetərɪˌnerɪ] *adj* veterinario || *s (pl -ies)* veterinario

veterinary medicine *s* veterinaria, medicina veterinaria

ve-to ['vito] *s (pl -toes)* veto || *tr* vetar

vex [veks] *tr* vejar, molestar

vexation [vek'seʃən] *s* vejación, molestia

v.g. *abbr* **verbi gratia** (Lat) **for example**

via ['vaɪ-ə] *prep* vía, p.ej., **via Lisbon** vía Lisboa

viaduct ['vaɪ-əˌdʌkt] *s* viaducto

vial ['vaɪ-əl] *s* redoma, frasco pequeño

viati-cum ['vaɪ'ætɪkəm] *s (pl -cums o -ca [kə])* (eccl) viático

viand ['vaɪ-ənd] *s* vianda, manjar *m*

vibrate ['vaɪbret] *tr & intr* vibrar

vibration [vaɪ'breʃən] *s* vibración

vicar ['vɪkər] *s* vicario

vicarage ['vɪkərɪdʒ] *s* casa del vicario; *(duties of vicar)* vicaría

vicarious [vaɪ'kerɪ-əs] o [vɪ'kerɪ-əs] *adj* substituto; *(punishment)* sufrido por otro; *(power, authority)* delegado; *(enjoyment)* reflejado

vice [vaɪs] *s* vicio

vice'-ad'miral *s* vicealmirante *m*

vice'-pres'ident *s* vicepresidente *m*

viceroy ['vaɪsrɔɪ] *s* virrey *m*

vice versa ['vaɪsɪ 'vɑrsə] o ['vaɪs 'vɑrsə] *adv* viceversa

vicini-ty [vɪ'sɪnɪtɪ] *s (pl -ties)* vecindad

vicious ['vɪʃəs] *adj* vicioso; *(dog)* bravo; *(horse)* arisco

victim ['vɪktɪm] *s* víctima

victimize ['vɪktɪˌmaɪz] *tr* hacer víctima; engañar, estafar

victor ['vɪktər] *s* vencedor *m*

victorious [vɪk'torɪ-əs] *adj* victorioso

victo-ry ['vɪktərɪ] *s (pl -ries)* victoria

victuals ['vɪtəlz] *spl* vituallas, provisiones de boca

vid. *abbr* **vide** (Lat) **see**

video signal ['vɪdɪˌo] *s* señal *f* de vídeo

video tape *s* cinta grabada de televisión

vid'eo-tape' recording *s* videograbación

vie [vaɪ] *v (pret & pp vied; ger vying) intr* competir, emular, rivalizar

Vien-nese [ˌviɪ-ə'niz] *adj* vienés || *s (pl -nese)* vienés *m*

Vietnam-ese [vɪˌetnə'miz] *adj* vietnamés || *s (pl -ese)* vietnamés *m*

view [vju] *s* vista; *(purpose)* intento, propósito, vista; **to be on view** estar expuesto *(p.ej., un cadáver)*; **to keep in view** no perder de vista; no olvidar, tener presente; **to take a dim view of** no entusiasmarse por, mirar escépticamente; **with a view to** con vistas a ‖ *tr* ver, mirar; considerar, contemplar; examinar, inspeccionar

viewer ['vju·ər] *s* espectador *m;* telespectador *m*, televidente *mf;* proyector *m* de transparencias; mirador *m* de transparencias

view finder *s* (phot) visor *m*

view'point' *s* punto de vista

vigil ['vɪdʒɪl] *s* vigilia; **to keep vigil** velar

vigilance ['vɪdʒɪləns] *s* vigilancia

vigilant ['vɪdʒɪlənt] *adj* vigilante

vignette [vɪn'jet] *s* viñeta

vigor ['vɪgər] *s* vigor *m*

vigorous ['vɪgərəs] *adj* vigoroso

vile [vaɪl] *adj* vil; *(disgusting)* asqueroso, repugnante; *(weather)* muy malo

vili·fy ['vɪlɪ,faɪ] *v* (*pret & pp* **-fied**) *tr* difamar, denigrar

villa ['vɪlə] *s* villa, quinta

village ['vɪlɪdʒ] *s* aldea

villager ['vɪlɪdʒər] *s* aldeano

villain ['vɪlən] *s* malvado; *(of a play)* malo, traidor *m*

villainous ['vɪlənəs] *adj* malvado

villain·y ['vɪləni] *s* (*pl* **-ies**) maldad, perfidia

vim [vɪm] *s* fuerza, brío, vigor *m*

vinaigrette [,vɪnə'gret] *s* vinagrera

vinaigrette sauce *s* vinagreta

vindicate ['vɪndɪ,ket] *tr* vindicar, exculpar

vindictive [vɪn'dɪktɪv] *adj* vengativo

vine [vaɪn] *s* *(creeping or climbing plant)* enredadera; *(grape plant)* vid *f,* parra

vine'dress'er *s* viñador *m*, viticultor *m*

vinegar ['vɪnɪgər] *s* vinagre *m*

vinegarish ['vɪnɪgərɪ/] *adj* avinagrado

vinegary ['vɪnɪgəri] *adj* vinagroso

vineyard ['vɪnjərd] *s* viña, viñedo

vineyardist ['vɪnjərdɪst] *s* viñador *m*, viticultor *m*

vintage ['vɪntɪdʒ] *s* vendimia; vino de buena cosecha; (coll) categoría, clase *f*

vintager ['vɪntɪdʒər] *s* vendimiador *m*

vintage wine *s* vino de buena cosecha

vintage year *s* año de buen vino

vintner ['vɪntnər] *s* vinatero

vinyl ['vaɪnɪl] *o* ['vɪnɪl] *s* vinilo

violate ['vaɪ·ə,let] *tr* violar

violence ['vaɪ·ələns] *s* violencia

violent ['vaɪ·ələnt] *adj* violento

violet ['vaɪ·əlɪt] *adj* violado ‖ *s* (color) violeta *m*, violado; *(dye)* violeta *m;* (bot) violeta *f*

violin [,vaɪ·ə'lɪn] *s* violín *m*

violinist [,vaɪ·ə'lɪnɪst] *s* violinista *mf*

violoncellist [,vaɪ·ələn't/elɪst] *o* [,vi·ələn't/elɪst] *s* violoncelista *mf*

violoncel·lo [,vaɪ·ələn't/elo] *o* [,vi·ələn't/elo] *s* (*pl* **-los**) violoncelo

viper ['vaɪpər] *s* víbora

vira·go [vɪ'rego] *s* (*pl* **-goes** *o* **-gos**) mujer de mal genio

virgin ['vʌrdʒɪn] *adj & s* virgen *f*

virgin birth *s* parto virginal de María Santísima; (zool) partenogénesis *f*

Virginia creeper [vər'dʒɪnɪ·ə] *s* (bot) guau *m*

virginity [vər'dʒɪnɪti] *s* virginidad

virility [vɪ'rɪlɪti] *s* virilidad

virology [vaɪ'rɒlədʒi] *s* virología

virtual ['vʌrt/u·əl] *adj* virtual

virtue ['vʌrt/u] *s* virtud

virtuosi·ty [,vʌrt/u'ɒsɪti] *s* (*pl* **-ties**) virtuosismo

virtu·oso [,vʌrt/u'oso] *s* (*pl* **-sos** *o* **-si** [si]) virtuoso

virtuous ['vʌrt/u·əs] *adj* virtuoso

virulence ['vɪrjələns] *s* virulencia

virulent ['vɪrjələnt] *adj* virulento

virus ['vaɪrəs] *s* virus *m*

Vis. *abbr* **Viscount**

visa ['vizə] *s* visa ‖ *tr* visar

visage ['vɪzɪdʒ] *s* cara, semblante *m;* aspecto, apariencia

vis-à-vis [,vizə'vi] *adj* enfrentados ‖ *adv* frente a frente ‖ *prep* enfrente de; respecto de

viscera ['vɪsərə] *spl* vísceras

viscount ['vaɪkaunt] *s* vizconde *m*

viscountess ['vaɪkauntɪs] *s* vizcondesa

viscous ['vɪskəs] *adj* viscoso

vise [vaɪs] *s* tornillo, torno

visé ['vize] *o* [vi'ze] *s & tr* var de **visa**

visible ['vɪzɪbəl] *adj* visible

Visigoth ['vɪzɪ,gɒθ] *s* visigodo

vision ['vɪʒən] *s* visión; *(sense of sight)* vista

visionar·y ['vɪʒə,neri] *adj* visionario ‖ *s* (*pl* **-ies**) visionario

visit ['vɪzɪt] *s* visita ‖ *tr* visitar; afligir, acometer; enviar (p.ej., *castigo, venganza*) ‖ *intr* hacer visitas; visitarse *(dos o más personas)*

visitation [,vɪzɪ'te/ən] *s* visitación; gracia del cielo, castigo del cielo

visiting card *s* tarjeta de visita

visiting hours *spl* horas de visita

visiting nurse *s* enfermera ambulante

visitor ['vɪzɪtər] *s* visitante *mf*

visor ['vaɪzər] *s* visera; *(disguise)* máscara

vista ['vɪstə] *s* vista, panorama *m*

visual ['vɪʒu·əl] *adj* visual

visual acuity *s* agudeza visual

visualize ['vɪʒu·ə,laɪz] *tr* representarse en la mente; hacer visible

vital ['vaɪtəl] *adj* vital; *(deadly)* mortal ‖ **vitals** *spl* partes *fpl* vitales, órganos vitales

vitality [vaɪ'tælɪti] *s* vitalidad

vitalize ['vaɪtə,laɪz] *tr* vitalizar

vitamin ['vaɪtəmɪn] *s* vitamina

vitiate ['vɪ/ɪ,et] *tr* viciar

vitreous ['vɪtrɪ·əs] *adj* vítreo

vitriolic [,vɪtrɪ'ɒlɪk] *adj* (chem) vitriólico; *(fig)* cáustico, mordaz

vituperable [vaɪ'tupərəbəl] *o* [vaɪ'tjupərəbəl] *adj* vituperable

vituperate [vaɪ'tupə,ret] *o* [vaɪ'tjupə,ret] *tr* vituperar

viva ['vivə] *interj* ¡viva! ‖ *s* viva *m*

vivacious [vaɪ've/əs] *o* [vaɪ'we/əs] *adj* vivaz, vivaracho

vivaci·ty [vɪ'væsɪti] *o* [vaɪ'væsɪti] *s* (*pl* **-ties**) vivacidad, animación

viva voce ['vaɪvə 'vosi] *adv* de viva voz

vivid ['vɪvɪd] *adj* vivo (*intenso; brillante; expresivo*)

vivi·fy ['vɪvɪ‚faɪ] *v* (*pret & pp* **-fied**) *tr* vivificar

vivisection [‚vɪvɪ'sɛkʃən] *s* vivisección

vixen ['vɪksən] *s* vulpeja; mujer regañona y colérica

viz. *abbr* **videlicet** (Lat) **namely, to wit**

vizier [vɪ'zɪr] o ['vɪzjər] *s* visir *m*

vocabular·y [vo'kæbjə‚lɛri] *s* (*pl* **-ies**) vocabulario

vocal ['vokəl] *adj* vocal; (*inclined to express oneself freely*) expresivo

vocalist ['vokəlɪst] *s* vocalista *mf*

vocation [vo'keʃən] *s* vocación; empleo, ocupación

vocative ['vakətɪv] *s* vocativo

vociferate [vo'sɪfə‚ret] *intr* vociferar

vociferous [vo'sɪfərəs] *adj* clamoroso, vociglero

vogue [vog] *s* boga, moda; **in vogue** en boga, de moda

voice [vɔɪs] *s* voz *f*; **in a loud voice** en alta voz; **in a low voice** en voz baja; **with one voice** a una voz ‖ *tr* expresar; sonorizar (*una consonante sorda*) ‖ *intr* sonorizarse

voiceless ['vɔɪslɪs] *adj* sin voz; mudo; silencioso; (*phonet*) sordo

void [vɔɪd] *adj* (*empty*) vacío; (*useless*) vano; (*law*) inválido, nulo; **void of** desprovisto de ‖ *s* vacío; (*gap*) hueco ‖ *tr* vaciar; evacuar (*el vientre*); anular ‖ *intr* excretar

voile [vɔɪl] *s* espumilla

vol. *abbr* **volume**

volatile ['valətɪl] *adj* volátil

volatilize ['valətɪ‚laɪz] *tr* volatilizar ‖ *intr* volatilizarse

volcanic [val'kænɪk] *adj* volcánico

volca·no [val'keno] *s* (*pl* **-noes** o **-nos**) volcán *m*

volition [vo'lɪʃən] *s* voluntad; **of one's own volition** por su propia voluntad

volley ['vali] *s* (*of stones, bullets, etc.*) descarga, lluvia; (*mil*) descarga; (*tennis*) voleo ‖ *tr & intr* volear

vol'ley-ball' *s* volibol *m*

volplane ['val‚plen] *s* vuelo planeado ‖ *intr* planear

volt [volt] *s* voltio

voltage ['voltɪdʒ] *s* voltaje *m*

voltage divider *s* (rad) divisor *m* de voltaje

voltaic [val'te·ɪk] *adj* voltaico

volte-face [volt'fas] *s* cambio de dirección; cambio de opinión

volt'me'ter *s* voltímetro

voluble ['valjəbəl] *adj* locuaz, hablador

volume ['valjəm] *s* (*book; bulk; mass, e.g., of water*) volumen *m*; (*each book in a set*) tomo; (*degree of loudness*) volumen sonoro; (geom) volumen *m*; **to speak volumes** ser muy significativo; ser muy expresivo

voluminous [və'lumɪnəs] *adj* voluminoso

voluntar·y ['valən‚tɛri] *adj* voluntario ‖ *s* (*pl* **-ies**) (eccl) solo de órgano

volunteer [‚valən'tɪr] *adj* s voluntario ‖ *tr* ofrecer (*sus servicios*) ‖ *intr* ofrecerse; servir como voluntaria; **to volunteer to** + *inf* ofrecerse a + *inf*

voluptuar·y [və'lʌptʃu‚ɛri] *adj* voluptuoso ‖ *s* (*pl* **-ies**) voluptuoso, sibarita *mf*

voluptuous [və'lʌptʃu·əs] *adj* voluptuoso

volute [və'lut] *s* voluta

vomit ['vamɪt] *s* vómito; (*emetic*) vomitivo ‖ *tr & intr* vomitar

voodoo ['vudu] *adj* voduísta ‖ *s* (*practice*) vodú *m*; (*person*) voduísta *mf*

voracious [və'reʃəs] *adj* voraz

voracity [və'ræsɪti] *s* voracidad

vor·tex ['vɔrtɛks] *s* (*pl* **-texes** o **-tices** [tɪ‚siz]) vórtice *m*

vota·ry ['votəri] *s* (*pl* **-ries**) persona ligada por votos solemnes; aficionado, partidario

vote [vot] *s* (*formal expression of choice; right to vote; person who votes*) voto; (*act of voting; votes considered together*) votación; **to put to the vote** poner a votación; **to tally the votes** regular los votos ‖ *tr* votar (*sí, no*); **to vote down** derrotar por votación; **to vote in** elegir por votación ‖ *intr* votar

vote getter ['gɛtər] *s* acaparador *m* de votos; (*slogan*) consigna que gana votos

voter ['votər] *s* votante *mf*

voting machine ['votɪŋ] *s* máquina registradora de votos

votive ['votɪv] *adj* votivo

votive offering *s* voto, exvoto

vouch [vautʃ] *tr* garantizar ‖ *intr* — **to vouch for** responder de (*una cosa*); responder por (*una persona*)

voucher ['vautʃər] *s* garante *mf*; (*certificate*) comprobante *m*

vouch·safe' *tr* conceder, otorgar; permitir ‖ *intr* — **to vouchsafe to** + *inf* dignarse + *inf*

voussoir [vu'swar] *s* dovela

vow [vau] *s* voto; **to take vows** tomar el hábito religioso ‖ *tr* votar (*p.ej., un cirio a la Virgen*); jurar (*venganza*) ‖ *intr* votar; **to vow to** hacer votos de

vowel ['vau·əl] *s* vocal *f*

voyage ['vɔɪ·ɪdʒ] *s* travesía, trayecto; (*any journey*) viaje *m* ‖ *tr* atravesar (*p.ej., el mar*) ‖ *intr* viajar

voyager ['vɔɪ·ɪdʒər] *s* pasajero, navegante *mf*, viajero

V.P. *abbr* **Vice-President**

vs. *abbr* **versus**

Vul. *abbr* **Vulgate**

vulcanize ['vʌlkə‚naɪz] *tr* vulcanizar

vulg. *abbr* **vulgar**

Vulg. *abbr* **Vulgate**

vulgar ['vʌlgər] *adj* grosero; (*popular, common; vernacular*) vulgar

vulgari·ty [vʌl'gærɪti] *s* (*pl* **-ties**) grosería

Vulgar Latin *s* latín vulgar, latín rústico

Vulgate ['vʌlget] *s* Vulgata

vulnerable ['vʌlnərəbəl] *adj* vulnerable

vulture ['vʌltʃər] *s* buitre *m*; (*American vulture*) catartes *m*, aura (*buitre americano*)

W

W, w ['dʌbəl,ju] vigésima tercera
letra del alfabeto inglés

w *abbr* watt

w. *abbr* week, west, wide, wife

W. *abbr* Wednesday, west

wad [wɑd] *s* (*of cotton*) bolita, tapón
m; (*of papers*) fajo, lío; (*in a gun*)
taco || *v* (*pret & pp* **wadded;** *ger*
wadding) *tr* emborrar, rellenar; atacar (*una escopeta*)

waddle ['wɑdəl] *s* anadeo || *intr* ana-
dear

wade [wed] *intr* andar sobre terreno
cubierto de agua; andar descalzo por
la orilla; chapotear (*los niños*) con
los pies desnudos; **to wade into** (coll)
embestir con violencia, (coll) meter
el hombro a; **to wade through** (coll)
avanzar con dificultad por; (coll)
leer con dificultad

wading bird ['wedɪŋ] *s* ave zancuda

wafer ['wefər] *s* (*for sealing letters;
pill*) oblea; (*thin, crisp cake*) hostia;
(eccl) hostia

waffle ['wɑfəl] *s* barquillo

waffle iron *s* barquillero

waft [wæft] o [wɑft] *tr* llevar por el
aire; llevar por encima del agua ||
intr flotar

wag [wæg] *s* (*of head*) meneo; (*of tail*)
coleada; (*jester*) bromista *mf* || *v*
(*pret & pp* **wagged;** *ger* **wagging**) *tr*
menear (*la cabeza, la cola*) || *intr*
menearse

wage [wedʒ] *s* salario; **wages** galardón
m, premio || *tr* hacer (*la guerra*)

wage earner ['ˌʌrnər] *s* asalariado

wager ['wedʒər] *s* apuesta; **to lay a
wager** hacer una apuesta || *tr & intr*
apostar

wage'work'er *s* asalariado

waggish ['wægɪʃ] *adj* divertido, gracioso; (*person*) bromista

Wagnerian [vɑg'nɪrɪ·ən] *adj & s* vag-
neriano

wagon ['wægən] *s* carro, furgón *m*, carretón *m*; **on the wagon** (slang) sin
tomar bebidas alcohólicas; **to hitch
one's wagon to a star** poner el tiro
muy alto

wag'tail' *s* aguanieves *m*, aguzanieves
m

waif [wef] *s* (*foundling*) expósito; animal extraviado o abandonado; (*stray
child*) granuja *m*

wail [wel] *s* gemido, lamento || *intr*
gemir, lamentar

wain-scot ['wenskət] o ['wenskɑt] *s*
arrimadillo, friso de madera || *v*
(*pret & pp* **-scoted** o **-scotted;** *ger*
-scoting o **-scotting**) *tr* poner arrimadillo o friso de madera a

waist [west] *s* (*of human body; corresponding part of garment*) talle *m*,
cintura; (*garment*) corpiño, jubón *m*,
blusa

waist'band' *s* pretina

waist'cloth' *s* taparrabo

waistcoat ['west,kot] o ['weskət] *s*
chaleco

waist'line' *s* cintura

wait [wet] *s* espera; **to have a good
wait** (coll) esperar sentado; **to lie in
wait for** acechar emboscado || *tr* —
to wait one's turn esperar vez || *intr*
esperar, aguardar; **to wait for** esperar, aguardar; **to wait on** atender,
despachar (*a los parroquianos en una
tienda*); servir (*a una persona a la
mesa*); **to wait until** esperar a que

waiter ['wetər] *s* camarero, mozo de
restaurante, (trar) bandeja

waiting list *s* lista de espera

waiting room *s* (*of station*) sala de espera; (*of doctor's office*) antesala

waitress ['wetrɪs] *s* camarera, moza de
restaurante

waive [wev] *tr* renunciar a (*un derecho*); diferir, poner a un lado

waiver ['wevər] *s* renuncia

wake [wek] *s* (*watch by the body of a
dead person*) velatorio; (*of a boat or
other moving object*) estela; **in the
wake of** siguiendo inmediatamente;
de resultas de || *v* (*pret* **waked** o
woke [wok]; *pp* **waked**) *tr* despertar
|| *intr* — **to wake** darse cuenta de;
to wake up despertar

wakeful ['wekfəl] *adj* desvelado

wakefulness ['wekfəlnɪs] *s* desvelo

waken ['wekən] *tr & intr* despertar

wale [wel] *s* verdugón *m*

Wales [welz] *s* Gales, el país de Gales

walk [wɔk] *s* (*act*) paseo; (*distance*)
caminata; (*way of walking, bearing*)
andar *m*, paso; (*of a horse*) andadura; (*place to walk animals*) cercado; empleo, cargo, carrera; **at a
walk** al paso de una persona; **to go
for a walk** salir a pasear; **to take a
walk** dar un paseo || *tr* pasear (*a un
niño, un caballo*): caminar (*recorrer
caminando*); hacer ir al paso (*un caballo*); **to walk off** quitarse (*n.ej., un
dolor de cabeza*) caminando || *intr*
andar, caminar, ir a pie; (*to stroll*)
pasear; **to walk away from** alejarse
caminando de; **to walk off with** cargar con, llevarse; **to walk out** salir
repentinamente; declararse en huelga; **to walk out on** (coll) dejar aira-
damente

walkaway ['wɔkə,we] *s* (coll) triunfo
fácil

walker ['wɔkər] *s* caminante *mf*; (*pedestrian*) peatón *m*; (*gocart*) andaderas

walkie-talkie ['wɔki'tɔki] *s* (rad) trans-
misor-receptor *m* portátil

walking papers *spl* (coll) despedida de
un empleo

walking stick *s* bastón *m*

walk'-on' *s* (theat) parte *f* de por medio

walk'out' *s* (coll) huelga

walk'o'ver *s* (coll) triunfo fácil

wall [wɔl] *s* muro; (*between rooms; of
a pipe, boiler, etc.*) pared *f*; (*of a*

fortification) muralla; **to drive to the wall** poner entre la espada y la pared; **to go to the wall** rendirse; fracasar || *tr* murar, amurallar (*una ciudad, un castillo*); emparedar (*a un criminal*); **to wall up** cerrar con muro

wall'board' *s* cartón *m* tabla

wallet ['wɑlɪt] *s* cartera de bolsillo

wall'flow'er *s* alhelí *m*; **to be a wallflower** (coll) comer pavo, planchar el asiento

Walloon [wɑ'lun] *adj & s* valón *m*

wallop ['wɑləp] *s* (coll) golpazo, puñetazo || *tr* (coll) golpear fuertemente; (coll) vencer cabalmente

wallow ['wɑlo] *s* revuelco; (*place*) revolcadero || *intr* revolcarse; (*e.g., in wealth*) nadar

wall'pa'per *s* papel *m* de empapelar, papel pintado || *tr* empapelar

walnut ['wɔlnət] *s* (*tree and wood*) nogal *m*; nuez *f* de nogal

walrus ['wɔlrəs] o ['wɑlrəs] *s* morsa

Walter ['wɔltər] *s* Gualterio

waltz [wɔlts] *s* vals *m* || *tr* hacer valsar; (coll) conducir directamente || *intr* valsar

wan [wɑn] *adj* (*comp* **wanner;** *super* **wannest**) pálido, macilento; débil

wand [wɑnd] *s* vara; (*of deviner or magician*) varilla de virtudes

wander ['wɑndər] *tr* recorrer a la ventura || *intr* errar, vagar; extraviarse, perderse; **to wander around** errar de una parte a otra

wanderer ['wɑndərər] *s* vagabundo; peregrino

wan'der-lust' *s* ansia de viajar

wane [wen] *s* decadencia, declinación; menguante *f* de la luna; **on the wane** decayendo, declinando; menguando (*la luna*) || *intr* decaer, declinar; menguar (*la luna*)

wangle ['wæŋgəl] *tr* (*to obtain by scheming*) (coll) mamar o mamarse; (coll) adulterar, falsear (*cuentas*); **to wangle one's way out of** (coll) salir con maña de || *intr* (*to get along by scheming*) (coll) sacudirse

want [wɑnt] o [wɔnt] *s* deseo; necesidad; carencia; **for want of** a falta de; **to be in want** pasar necesidad || *tr* desear; necesitar; carecer de || *intr* desear; necesitar; **to want for** necesitar; carecer de

want ad *s* anuncio clasificado

wanton ['wɑntən] *adj* inconsiderado, desconsiderado; insensible, perverso; disoluto, licencioso; lascivo; cabezudo

war [wɔr] *s* guerra; **to go to war** declarar la guerra; (*as a soldier*) ir a la guerra; **to wage war** hacer la guerra || *v* (*pret & pp* **warred;** *ger* **warring**) *intr* guerrear; **to war on** guerrear con, hacer la guerra a

warble ['wɔrbəl] *s* gorjeo, trino || *intr* gorjear, trinar

warbler ['wɔrblər] *s* pájaro cantor; curruca de cabeza negra

war cloud *s* amenaza de guerra

ward [wɔrd] *s* (*person, usually a minor, under protection of another*) pupilo; (*guardianship*) custodia, tutela; (*of a city*) barrio, distrito; (*of a hospital*) cuadra, crujía; (*of a lock*) guarda || *tr* — **to ward off** parar, desviar

warden ['wɔrdən] *s* guardián *m*; (*of a jail*) alcaide *m*, carcelero; (*of a church*) capiller *m*; (*in charge of fire prevention*) vigía *m*

ward heeler *s* muñidor *m*

ward'robe' *s* (*closet or cabinet for holding clothes*) guardarropa *m*; (*stock of clothing for a person*) vestuario; (theat) guardarropía

wardrobe trunk *s* baúl ropero

ward'room' *s* (nav) cámara de oficiales

ware [wer] *s* loza; **wares** efectos, artículos de comercio, mercancías

war effort *s* esfuerzo bélico

ware'house' *s* almacén *m*; (*for furniture*) guardamuebles *m*

warehouse-man ['wer,hausmən] *s* (*pl* **-men** [mən]) almacenista *m*; guardaalmacén *m*

war'fare' *s* guerra

war'head' *s* punta de combate

war horse *s* corcel *m* de guerra; (coll) veterano

warily ['werɪli] *adv* cautelosamente

wariness ['werɪnɪs] *s* cautela

war'like' *adj* guerrero

war loan *s* empréstito de guerra

war lord *s* jefe *m* militar

warm [wɔrm] *adj* (*being moderately hot*) caliente; (*neither hot nor cold*) templado; (*clothing*) abrigador; (*climate, region*) caluroso; (*color*) cálido; (fig) caluroso, cordial; **to be warm** (*said of a person*) tener calor; (*said of the weather*) hacer calor || *tr* calentar, acalorar; (fig) animar, acalorar; **to warm up** recalentar (*p.ej., la comida*); hacer más amistoso || *intr* calentarse; **to warm up** templar (*el tiempo*); (*with work or exercise*) acalorarse; **to warm up to** cobrar afecto a

warm-blooded ['wɔrm'blʌdɪd] *adj* apasionado, ardiente; (*animals*) de sangre caliente

war memorial *s* monumento a los caídos

warmer ['wɔrmər] *s* calentador *m*

warm-hearted ['wɔrm'hɑrtɪd] *adj* afectuoso, de buen corazón

warming pan *s* mundillo

warmonger ['wɔr,mʌŋgər] *s* belicista *mf*

war mother *s* madrina de guerra

warmth [wɔrmθ] *s* calor *m*; ardor *m*, entusiasmo; cordialidad

warm'-up' *s* calentón *m*

warn [wɔrn] *tr* advertir, avisar; (*to exhort*) amonestar; (*to advise*) aconsejar

warning *adj* de aviso || *s* advertencia, aviso

War of the Roses *s* guerra de las dos Rosas

warp [wɔrp] *s* (*of a fabric*) urdimbre *f*; (*of a board*) comba, alabeo; aberración mental; (naut) espía || *tr* combar, alabear; pervertir (*el juicio* *de una persona*); (naut) mover con espía ‖ *intr* combarse, alabearse; (naut) espiar

war'path' *s* — **to be on the warpath** prepararse para la guerra; estar buscando pendencia

war'plane' *s* avión *m* de guerra

warrant ['warənt] o ['worənt] *s* garantía, promesa; (*for arrest*) orden *f* de prisión; (*before a judge*) citación; cédula, certificado ‖ *tr* garantizar, prometer; autorizar; justificar

warrantable ['warəntəbəl] o ['worəntəbəl] *adj* garantizable; justificable

warrant officer *s* suboficial *m* de las clases

warren ['warən] o ['worən] *s* (*where rabbits breed*) conejera; barrio densamente poblado

warrior ['worjər] o ['warjər] *s* guerrero

Warsaw ['worsɔ] *s* Varsovia

war'ship' *s* buque *m* de guerra

wart [wort] *s* verruga

war'time' *s* tiempo de guerra

war'-torn' *adj* devastado por la guerra

war to the death *s* guerra a muerte

war-y ['weri] *adj* (*comp* **-ier**; *super* **-iest**) cauteloso

wash [waʃ] o [wɔʃ] *s* lavado; (*clothes washed or to be washed*) jabonado; (*dirty water*) lavazas; loción; (*place where surf breaks*) batiente *m*; (aer) estela turbulenta ‖ *tr* lavar; fregar (*los platos*); bañar, mojar; **to wash away** quitar lavando; derrubiar (*las aguas corrientes la tierra de las riberas*) ‖ *intr* lavarse; lavar la ropa; batir (*el agua*); derrubiarse

washable ['waʃəbəl] o ['wɔʃəbəl] *adj* lavable

wash and wear *adj* de lava y pon

wash'ba'sin *s* jofaina, palangana

wash'bas'ket *s* cesto de la colada

wash'board' *s* tabla de lavar; (*baseboard*) rodapié *m*

wash'bowl' *s* jofaina, palangana

wash'cloth' *s* paño para lavarse

wash'day' *s* día *m* de la colada

washed-out ['waʃt,aut] o ['wɔʃt,aut] *adj* desteñido; (coll) debilitado, rendido

washed-up ['waʃt,ʌp] o ['wɔʃt,ʌp] *adj* (coll) agotado, deslomado

washer ['waʃər] o ['wɔʃər] *s* lavador *m*; (*machine*) lavadora; (*ring of metal placed under head of bolt*) arandela; (*ring of rubber, etc. to keep a spigot from leaking*) zapatilla; (phot) lavador

wash'er-wom'an *s* (*pl* **-wom'en**) lavandera

wash goods *spl* tejidos lavables

washing ['waʃɪŋ] o ['wɔʃɪŋ] *s* (*act of washing*); *washed clothes or clothes to be washed*) lavado; **washings** (*dirty water; abraded material*) lavadura

washing machine *s* lejiadora, lavadora mecánica

washing soda *s* sal *f* de sosa

wash'out' *s* derrubio; derrumbe *m*; (coll) desilusión, fracaso

wash'rag' *s* paño para lavarse; paño de cocina

wash'room' *s* gabinete *m* de aseo, lavabo

wash'stand' *s* lavamanos *m*

wash'tub' *s* cuba de colada, tina de lavar

wash water *s* lavazas

wasp [wasp] *s* avispa

waste [west] *s* derroche *m*, desgaste *m*; (*garbage*) basura, despojo; (*wild region*) despoblado, yermo; (*of time*) pérdida; (*useless by-products*) desperdicios; excremento, (*for wiping machinery*) hilacha de algodón; **to lay waste** devastar, poner a fuego y sangre ‖ *tr* malgastar, perder ‖ *intr* — **to waste away** consumirse

waste'bas'ket *s* papelera

wasteful ['westfəl] *adj* derrochador, manirroto; devastador, destructivo

waste paper *s* papeles usados, papel de desecho, papel viejo

waste pipe *s* tubo de desagüe

waste products *spl* desperdicios; materia excretada

wastrel ['westrəl] *s* derrochador *m*, malgastador *m*; pródigo, perdido

watch [watʃ] *s* reloj *m* (*de bolsillo o de pulsera*); (*lookout*) vigía *m*; (mil) vigilia; (naut) guardia; **to be on the watch for** estar a la mira de; **to keep watch over** velar ‖ *tr* (*to look at*) mirar; (*to oversee*) velar, vigilar, guardar; tener cuidado con ‖ *intr* mirar; (*to keep awake*) velar; **to watch for** acechar; **to watch out** tener cuidado; **to watch out for** estar a la mira de; tener cuidado con; guardarse de; **to watch over** velar, vigilar

watch'case' *s* caja de reloj

watch charm *s* dije *m*

watch crystal *s* cristal *m* de reloj

watch'dog' *s* perro de guarda, perro guardián; (fig) guardián *m* fiel

watchful ['watʃfəl] *adj* desvelado, vigilante

watchfulness ['watʃfəlnɪs] *s* desvelo, vigilancia

watch'mak'er *s* relojero

watch-man ['watʃmən] *s* (*pl* **-men** [mən]) vigilante *m*, velador *m*

watch night *s* noche vieja; oficio de noche vieja

watch pocket *s* relojera

watch strap *s* pulsera

watch'tow'er *s* atalaya, vigía

watch'word' *s* santo y seña; (*slogan*) lema *m*

water ['wɔtər] o ['watər] *s* agua; **of the first water** de lo mejor; **to back water** ciar; **to carry water on both shoulders** nadar entre dos aguas; **to fish in troubled waters** pescar en río revuelto; **to hold water** (coll) ser bien fundado; **to make water** (*to urinate*) hacer aguas; (naut) hacer agua; **to pour o throw cold water on** echar un jarro de agua (fría) a ‖ *tr* regar, rociar; abrevar (*el ganado*), aguar (*el vino*); proveer de agua ‖ *intr* abrevarse (*el ganado*); tomar agua (*una locomotora*); llorar (*los ojos*)

water carrier *s* aguador *m*

water closet *s* excusado, retrete *m*, váter *m*

water color *s* acuarela

wa'ter-course' *s* corriente *f* de agua; lecho de corriente

water cress *s* berzo

water cure *s* cura de aguas

wa'ter-fall' *s* cascada, caída de agua

water front *s* terreno ribereño

water gap *s* garganta, hondonada

water hammer *s* golpe *m* de ariete

water heater *s* calentador *m* de agua

water ice *s* sorbete *m*

watering can *s* regadera

watering place *s* aguadero; balneario

watering pot *s* regadera

watering trough *s* abrevadero

water jacket *s* camisa de agua

water lily *s* ninfea, nenúfar *m*

water line *s* línea de agua, línea de flotación; nivel *m* de agua

water main *s* cañería de agua

wa'ter-mark' *s* (*in paper*) filigrana; marca de nivel de agua

wa'ter-mel'on *s* sandía

water meter *s* contador *m* de agua

water pipe *s* cañería de agua

water polo *s* polo de agua

water power *s* fuerza de agua, hulla blanca

wa'ter-proof' *adj* & *s* impermeable *m*

wa'ter-shed' *s* divisoria de aguas; (*drainage area*) cuenca

water ski *s* esquí acuático

wa'ter-spout' *s* (*to carry water from roof*) canalón *m*; (*funnel of wet air extending from cloud to surface of water*) manga de agua, tromba marina

wa'ter-sup-ply' system *s* fontanería

wa'ter-tight' *adj* estanco, hermético; (*fig*) seguro

water tower *s* arca de agua

water wagon *s* (mil) carro de agua; **on the water wagon** (slang) sin tomar bebidas alcohólicas

wa'ter-way' *s* vía de agua, vía fluvial; (naut) canalizo

water wheel *s* rueda de agua; turbina de agua; (*of steamboat*) rueda de paletas

water wings *spl* nadaderas

wa'ter-works' *s* estación de bombas

watery ['wɔtəri] o ['watəri] *adj* acuoso; (*said of the eyes*) lagrimoso, lloroso; insípido; húmedo, mojado

watt [wat] *s* vatio

wattage ['watɪdʒ] *s* vatiaje *m*

watt'-hour' *s* (*pl* watt-hours) vatiohora

wattle ['watəl] *s* (*of bird*) barba; (*of fish*) barbilla

watt'me'ter *s* vatímetro

wave [wev] *s* onda; (*of hair*) onda, ondulación; (*e.g., of heat or cold*) ola; (*e.g., of strikes*) oleaje *m*; señal hecha con la mano || *tr* blandir (*la espada*); ondear, ondular (*el cabello*); hacer señal con (*la mano*); decir (*adiós*) con la mano; **to wave**

aside rechazar || *intr* ondear u ondearse; hacer señal con la mano

wave motion *s* movimiento ondulatorio

waver ['wevər] *intr* oscilar; (*to hesitate*) vacilar, titubear; (*to totter*) tambalear

wav-y ['wevi] *adj* (*comp* -ier; *super* -iest) undoso, ondoso; (*water*) ondulado; (*hair*) ondeado

wax [wæks] *s* cera; **to be wax in one's hands** ser como una cera || *tr* encerar; cerotear (*el hilo*) || *intr* hacerse, volverse; crecer (*la luna*)

wax paper *s* papel encerado, papel parafinado

wax taper *s* cerilla

wax'works' *s* museo de cera

way [we] *s* vía, camino; dirección, sentido; manera, modo; costumbre, hábito; **across the way** enfrente; **a good way** un buen trecho; **all the way** hasta el fin del camino; **any way** de cualquier modo; **by the way** a propósito; **in a way** hasta cierto punto; **in every way** en todos respectos; **in this way** de este modo; **on the way to** camino de, rumbo a; **on the way out** saliendo; desapareciendo; **out of the way** hecho, despachado; inconveniente, impropio; a un lado, apartado; fuera de lo común; **that way** por allí; de ese modo; **this way** por aquí; de este modo; **to be in the way** estorbar; **to feel one's way** tantear el camino; proceder con tiento; **to force one's way** abrirse paso por fuerza; **to get out of the way** quitarse de en medio; (*to finish*) quitarse de encima; **to give way** ceder, retroceder; romperse (*una cuerda*); fracasar; **to give way to** entregarse a; **to go out of one's way** dar un rodeo; dar un rodeo innecesario; darse molestia; **to have one's way** salirse con la suya; **to keep out of the way** no obstruir el paso; **to know one's way around** saber entendérselas; **to know one's way to** conocer el camino a, saber ir a; **to lead the way** enseñar el camino; ir o entrar primero; **to lose one's way** perder el camino, extraviarse; **to make one's way** avanzar; hacer carrera, acreditarse; **to make way for** dar paso a, hacer lugar para; **to mend one's ways** mudar de vida; **to not know which way to turn** no saber dónde meterse; **to put out of the way** alejar, apartar; quitar de en medio; **to see one's way to** ver el modo de; **to take one's way** irse, marcharse; **to wend one's way** seguir camino; **to wind one's way through** serpentear por; **to wing one's way** ir volando; **under way** en marcha, en camino; **way in** entrada; **way out** salida; **ways** maneras, modales *mpl*; (*for launching a ship*) anguilas; **which way?** ¿por dónde?; ¿cómo?

way'bill' *s* hoja de ruta

wayfarer ['we,ferər] *s* caminante *mf*

way'lay' *v* (*pret* & *pp* -laid') *tr* detener de improviso; (*to attack from ambush*) insidiar, asaltar

way'side' s borde m del camino; **to fall by the wayside** (to disappear) caer en el camino; fracasar

way station s apeadero

way train s tren m ómnibus

wayward ['wewərd] adj díscolo, voluntarioso; voltario, caprichoso

w.c. abbr **water closet, without charge**

we [wi] pron pers nosotros

weak [wik] adj débil, flaco; (vowel; verb) débil

weaken ['wikən] tr debilitar, enflaquecer || intr debilitarse, enflaquecerse

weakling ['wiklɪŋ] s alfeñique m, canijo

weak-minded ['wik'maɪndɪd] adj irresoluto; simple, mentecato

weakness ['wiknɪs] s debilidad, flaqueza; lado débil; afición, gusto

weal [wil] s verdugón m

wealth [wɛlθ] s riqueza

wealth·y ['wɛlθi] adj (comp -ier; super -iest) rico

wean [win] tr destetar; **to wean away from** apartar gradualmente de

weanling ['winlɪŋ] adj & s destetado

weapon ['wɛpən] s arma

wear [wer] s (act of wearing) uso; (clothing) ropa; estilo, moda; (wasting away from use) desgaste m, deterioro; (lasting quality) durabilidad; **for all kinds of wear** a todo llevar; **for everyday wear** para todo trote || v (pret **wore** [wor]; pp **worn** [worn]) tr llevar, traer, llevar puesto; calzar (cierto tamaño de zapato o guante); (to waste away by use) desgastar, deteriorar; (to tire) agotar, cansar; **to wear out** consumir, gastar; agotar, cansar; abusar de (la hospitalidad de una persona) || intr desgastarse, deteriorarse; **to wear off** pasar, desaparecer; **to wear out** gastarse, usarse; **to wear well** durar, ser duradero

wear and tear s uso y desgaste

weariness ['wirinɪs] s cansancio; aburrimiento

wearing apparel ['werɪŋ] s ropaje m, prendas de vestir

wearisome ['wirisəm] adj aburrido, cansado, fastidioso

wea·ry ['wiri] adj (comp -rier; super -riest) cansado || v (pret & pp -ried) tr cansar || intr cansarse

weasel ['wizəl] s comadreja

weaseler ['wizələr] s pancista mf

weasel words spl palabras ambiguas

weather ['wɛðər] s tiempo; mal tiempo; **to be under the weather** (coll) no estar muy católico; (coll) estar borracho || tr aguantar (el temporal, la adversidad)

weather-beaten ['wɛðər,bitən] adj curtido por la intemperie

weather bureau s meteo f, servicio meteorológico

weath'er·cock' s veleta; (fickle person) (fig) veleta

weather forecasting s pronóstico del tiempo, previsión del tiempo

weather·man ['wɛðər,mæn] s (pl -men [,mɛn]) meteorologista m, pronosticador m del tiempo

weather report s parte meteorológico

weather stripping ['strɪpɪŋ] s burlete m, cierre hermético

weather vane s veleta

weave [wiv] s tejido || v (pret **wove** [wov] o **weaved**; pp **wove** o **woven** ['wovən]) tr tejer; **to weave one's way** avanzar zigzagueando || intr tejer; zigzaguear

weaver ['wivər] s tejedor m

web [wɛb] s tejido, tela; (of spider) tela; (between toes of birds and other animals) membrana; (of an iron rail) alma; (fig) tejido, tela, enredo

web-footed ['wɛb,futid] adj palmípedo, de pie palmeado

wed [wɛd] v (pret & pp **wed** o **wedded**; ger **wedding**) tr (to join in marriage) casar; casarse con || intr casarse

wedding ['wɛdɪŋ] adj nupcial || s bodas, nupcias, matrimonio

wedding cake s pastel m de boda

wedding day s día m de bodas

wedding march s marcha nupcial

wedding night s noche f de bodas

wedding ring s anillo nupcial

wedge [wɛdʒ] s cuña || tr acuñar, apretar con cuña

wed'lock' s matrimonio

Wednesday ['wɛnzdi] s miércoles m

wee [wi] adj pequeñito, diminuto

weed [wid] s mala hierba; (coll) tabaco; **weeds** ropa de luto (especialmente, de una viuda) || tr desherbar, escardar

weeding hoe s escardillo

weed killer s matamalezas m, herbicida m

week [wik] s semana; **week in week out** semana tras semana

week'day' s día m laborable

week'end' s fin m de semana || intr pasar el fin de semana

week·ly ['wikli] adj semanal || adv cada semana || s (pl -lies) revista semanal, semanario

weep [wip] v (pret & pp **wept** [wɛpt]) tr llorar (p.ej., la muerte de una persona); derramar (lágrimas) || intr llorar

weeper ['wipər] s llorón m; (hired mourner) llorona, plañidera

weeping willow s sauce m llorón

weep·y ['wipi] adj (comp -ier; super -iest) (coll) lloroso

weevil ['wivəl] s gorgojo

weft [wɛft] s (yarns running across warp) trama; (fabric) tejido

weigh [we] tr pesar; (naut) levantar (el ancla) || intr pesar; **to weigh in** pesarse (un jockey)

weight [wet] s peso; (of scales, clock, gymnasium, etc.) pesa; **to lose weight** rebajar de peso; **to put on weight** ponerse gordo; **to throw one's weight around** (coll) hacer valer su poder || tr cargar, gravar; (statistically) ponderar

weightless ['wetlɪs] adj ingrávido

weightlessness ['wetlɪsnɪs] s ingravidez f

weight·y ['weti] adj (comp -ier; super

-lest) (*heavy*) pesado; (*troublesome*) gravoso; importante, influyente

weir [wɪr] *s* presa, vertedero; (*for catching fish*) pescadera

weird [wɪrd] *adj* misterioso, sobrenatural, espectral; extraño, raro

welcome ['wɛlkəm] *adj* bienvenido; grato, agradable; **you are welcome** (*i.e., gladly received*) sea Vd. bienvenido; (*in answer to thanks*) no hay de qué; **you are welcome to it** está a la disposición de Vd.; **you are welcome to your opinion** piense Vd. lo que quiera || *interj* ¡bienvenido! || *s* bienvenida, buena acogida || *tr* dar la bienvenida a; acoger con gusto, recibir con amabilidad

weld [wɛld] *s* autógena; (bot) gualda || *tr* soldar con autógena; (fig) unir || *intr* soldarse

welder ['wɛldər] *s* soldador *m*; (*machine*) soldadora

welding ['wɛldɪŋ] *s* autógena, soldadura autógena

wel'fare *s* bienestar *m*; (*effort to improve living conditions of the underprivileged*) asistencia, beneficencia; **to be on welfare** vivir de la asistencia pública

welfare state *s* gobierno socializante, estado de beneficencia

well [wɛl] *adj* bien; bien de salud || *adv* bien; pues; pues bien; **as well** también; **as well as** así como; además de || *interj* ¡vaya! || *s* pozo; (*natural source of water*) fuente *f*, manantial *m* || *intr* — **to well up** salir a borbotones

well-appointed ['wɛlə'pɔɪntɪd] *adj* bien amueblado, bien equipado

well-attended ['wɛlə'tɛndɪd] *adj* muy concurrido

well-behaved ['wɛlbɪ'hevd] *adj* de buena conducta

well'-be'ing *s* bienestar *m*

well'born' *adj* bien nacido

well-bred ['wɛl'brɛd] *adj* cortés, bien criado

well-disposed ['wɛldɪs'pozd] *adj* bien dispuesto

well-done ['wɛl'dʌn] *adj* bien hecho; (*meat*) bien asado

well-fixed ['wɛl'fɪkst] *adj* (coll) acaudalado

well-formed ['wɛl'fɔrmd] *adj* bien formado; (*nose*) perfilado

well-founded ['wɛl'faundɪd] *adj* bien fundado

well-groomed ['wɛl'grumd] *adj* de mucho aseo, atildado

well-heeled ['wɛl'hild] *adj* (coll) acomodado; **to be well-heeled** (coll) tener bien cubierto el riñón

well-informed ['wɛlɪn'fɔrmd] *adj* versado, bien enterado

well-intentioned ['wɛlɪn'tɛnʃənd] *adj* bien intencionado

well-kept ['wɛl'kɛpt] *adj* bien cuidado, bien atendido; (*secret*) bien guardado

well-known ['wɛl'non] *adj* bien conocido; familiar

well-meaning ['wɛl'minɪŋ] *adj* bien intencionado

well-nigh ['wɛl'naɪ] *adv* casi

well'-off' *adj* adinerado, acaudalado

well-preserved ['wɛlprɪ'zɑrvd] *adj* bien conservado

well-read ['wɛl'rɛd] *adj* leído, muy leído

well-spent ['wɛl'spɛnt] *adj* (*money, youth, life*) bien empleado

well-spoken ['wɛl'spokən] *adj* (*person*) bienhablado; (*word*) bien dicho

well'spring' *s* fuente *f*, manantial *m*; fuente inagotable

well sweep *s* cigoñal *m*

well-tempered ['wɛl'tɛmpərd] *adj* bien templado

well-thought-of ['wɛl'θɔt,av] *adj* bien mirado

well-timed ['wɛl'taɪmd] *adj* oportuno

well-to-do ['wɛltə'du] *adj* adinerado, acaudalado

well-wisher ['wɛl'wɪʃər] *s* amigo, favorecedor *m*

well-worn ['wɛl'worn] *adj* trillado, vulgar

welsh [wɛlʃ] *intr* (slang) dejar de cumplir; **to welsh on** (slang) dejar de cumplir con || **Welsh** *adj* galés || *s* (*language*) galés *m*; **the Welsh** los galeses

Welsh·man ['wɛlʃmən] *s* (*pl* -men [mən]) galés *m*

Welsh rabbit o **rarebit** ['rɛrbɪt] *s* tostada cubierta de queso derretido en cerveza

welt [wɛlt] *s* (*finish along a seam*) ribete *m*; (*of a shoe*) vira; (*wale from a blow*) verdugón *m*

welter ['wɛltər] *s* confusión, conmoción; (*a tumbling about*) revuelco || *intr* revolcar

wel'ter·weight' *s* (box) peso mediano ligero

wen [wɛn] *s* lobanillo

wench [wɛntʃ] *s* muchacha, jovencita; moza, criada

wend [wɛnd] *tr* — **to wend one's way** dirigir sus pasos, seguir su camino

west [wɛst] *adj* occidental, del oeste || *adv* al oeste, hacia el oeste || *s* oeste *m*

western ['wɛstərn] *adj* occidental || *s* película del Oeste

West Indies ['ɪndiz] *spl* Indias Occidentales

westward ['wɛstwərd] *adv* hacia el oeste

wet [wɛt] *adj* (*comp* wetter; *super* wettest) mojado; (*damp*) húmedo; (*paint*) fresco; (*weather*) lluvioso; (coll) antiprohibicionista || *s* (coll) antiprohibicionista *mf* || *v* (*pret* & *pp* wet o wetted; *ger* wetting) *tr* mojar || *intr* mojarse

wet'back' *s* mojado

wet battery *s* pila húmeda

wet blanket *s* aguafiestas *mf*

wet goods *spl* caldos

wet nurse *s* ama de cría o de leche

w.f. *abbr* wrong font

w.g. *abbr* wire gauge

whack [hwæk] *s* (coll) golpe ruidoso;

(coll) prueba, tentativa || *tr* (coll) golpear ruidosamente

whale [hwel] *s* ballena; (*sperm whale*) cachalote *m*; **a whale at** (coll) un as de; **a whale for** (coll) un genio para; **a whale of a difference** (coll) una enorme diferencia; **a whale of a meal** (coll) una comida brutal || *tr* (coll) azotar || *intr* pescar ballenas

whale'bone' *s* ballena

wharf [hwɔrf] *s* (*pl* **wharves** [hwɔrvz] o **wharfs**) muelle *m*, embarcadero

what [hwɑt] *pron interr* qué; cuál; **what else?** ¿qué más?; **what if . . .?** ¿y si . . .?, ¿qué le parece si?; **what of it?** ¿qué importa? || *pron rel* lo que; **what's what** lo que hay, toda la verdad || *adj interr* qué || *adj rel* el . . . que, la . . . que, etc. || *interj* qué; **what a . . .!** qué . . . más o tan, p.ej., **what a beautiful day!** ¡qué día más (o tan) hermoso!

what·ev'er *pron* cualquiera; todo lo que || *adj* cualquier, cualquier . . . que

what'not' *s* juguetero

what's-his-name ['hwɑtsɪz,nem] *s* (coll) el señor fulano

wheal [hwil] *s* roncha

wheat [hwit] *s* trigo

wheedle ['hwidəl] *tr* engatusar; conseguir por medio de halagos

wheel [hwil] *s* rueda; (coll) bicicleta; **at the wheel** en el volante || *tr* pasear (*a un niño*) en un cochecito; conducir (*a un enfermo*) en una silla de ruedas || *intr* (coll) ir en bicicleta; **to wheel about** o **around** dar una vuelta; cambiar de opinión

wheelbarrow ['hwil,bæro] *s* carretilla

wheel base *s* batalla, paso, distancia entre ejes

wheel chair *s* silla de ruedas, cochecillo para inválidos

wheeler-dealer ['hwilər'dilər] *s* (slang) negociante *m* de gran influencia e independencia

wheel horse *s* caballo de varas; (fig) esclavo (*el que trabaja mucho y cumple con sus obligaciones*)

wheelwright ['hwil,raɪt] *s* carpintero de carretas

wheeze [hwiz] *s* resuello ruidoso || *intr* resollar produciendo un silbido

whelp [hwelp] *s* cachorro || *intr* parir

when [hwen] *adv* cuándo *o* *conj* cuando

whence [hwens] *adv* de dónde; por lo tanto || *conj* de donde

when·ev'er *conj* siempre que, cada vez que

where [hwer] *adv* dónde; adónde || *conj* donde; adonde

whereabouts ['hwerə,bauts] *s* paradero

whereas [hwer'æz] *conj* mientras que, al paso que; considerando || *s* considerando

where·by' *adv* por medio del cual

wherefore ['hwerfor] *adv* por qué, para qué; por eso, por tanto || *conj* por lo cual || *s* motivo, razón *f*

where·from' *adv* de donde

where·in' *adv* dónde, en qué || *conj* donde; en lo cual

where·of' *adv* de qué || *conj* de que; de lo cual

where·up·on' *adv* con lo cual, después de lo cual

wherever [hwer'evər] *conj* dondequiera que

wherewithal ['hwerwɪð,ɔl] *s* cumquibus *m*, medios

whet [hwet] *v* (*pret & pp* **whetted**; *ger* **whetting**) *tr* afilar, aguzar; despertar, estimular; abrir (*el apetito*)

whether ['weðər] *conj* si; **whether or no** en todo caso, de todas maneras; **whether or not** si . . . o no, ya sea que . . . o no

whet'stone' *s* piedra de afilar

whey [hwe] *s* suero de la leche

which [hwɪtʃ] *pron interr* cuál; **which is which** cuál es el uno y cuál el otro || *pron rel* que, el (la, etc.) que || *adj interr* qué; cuál, cuál de los (las) || *adj rel* el (la, etc.) . . . que

which·ev'er *pron rel* cualquiera || *adj rel* cualquier; **whichever ones** cualesquiera

whiff [hwɪf] *s* soplo; fumada; olorcillo; acceso, arranque *m*; **to get a whiff of** percibir un olor fugaz de || *intr* soplar (*el viento*); echar bocanadas (*el que fuma*)

while [hwaɪl] *conj* mientras, mientras que || *s* rato; **a long while** largo rato; **a while ago** hace un rato; **between whiles** de vez en cuando || *tr* — **to while away** entretener (*el tiempo*); pasar (*p.ej., la tarde*) de un modo entretenido

whim [hwɪm] *s* capricho, antojo

whimper ['hwɪmpər] *s* lloriqueo || *tr* decir lloriqueando || *intr* lloriquear

whimsical ['hwɪmzɪkəl] *adj* caprichoso, extravagante, fantástico

whine [hwaɪn] *s* gimoteo, quejido || *intr* gimotear, quejarse

whin·ny ['hwɪnɪ] *s* (*pl* **-nies**) relincho || *v* (*pret & pp* **-nied**) *intr* relinchar

whip [hwɪp] *s* látigo, zurriago; huevos batidos con nata || *v* (*pret & pp* **whipped** o **whipt**: *ger* **whipping**) *tr* azotar, zurriagar, fustigar; batir (*huevos y nata*); (coll) derrotar, vencer; **to whip off** (coll) escribir de prisa; **to whip out** sacar de repente; **to whip up** (coll) preparar de prisa; (coll) avivar, excitar

whip'cord' *s* tralla; tejido fuerte con costurones diagonales

whip hand *s* mano *f* del látigo; (*upper hand*) vara alta

whip'lash' *s* tralla

whipped cream *s* nata, crema batida

whipper-snapper ['hwɪpər,snæpər] *s* arrapiezo, mequetrefe *m*

whippet ['hwɪpɪt] *s* perro lebrel

whipping boy ['hwɪpɪŋ] *s* cabeza de turco, víctima inocente

whipping post *s* poste *m* de flagelación

whippoorwill [,hwɪpər'wɪl] *s* chotacabras norteamericano (*Caprimulgus vociferus*)

whir [hwʌr] *s* zumbido || *v* (*pret & pp*

whirred; *ger* **whirring**) *intr* girar zumbando

whirl [hwʌrl] *s* vuelta, giro; remolino; (*of events, parties, etc.*) serie *f* interminable || *tr & intr* remolinear; **my head whirls** siento vértigo

whirligig ['hwʌrlɪ,gɪg] *s* (ent) escribano del agua; tiovivo; (*pinwheel*) rehilandera, molinete *m;* peonza

whirl'pool' *s* remolino, vorágine *f*

whirl'wind' *s* torbellino, manga de viento

whirlybird ['hwʌrlɪ,bʌrd] *s* (coll) helicóptero

whish [hwɪʃ] *s* zumbido suave || *intr* zumbar suavemente

whisk [hwɪsk] *s* escobilla; toque ligero || *tr* barrer, cepillar; **to whisk out of sight** escamotear || *intr* moverse rápidamente

whisk broom *s* escobilla

whiskers ['hwɪskərz] *spl* barbas; (*on side of face*) patillas; (*of cat*) bigotes *mpl*

whiskey ['hwɪskɪ] *adj* (*voice*) (coll) aguardentoso || *s* whisky *m*

whisper ['hwɪspər] *s* cuchicheo; (*of leaves*) susurro; **in a whisper** en voz baja || *tr* susurrar, decir al oído || *intr* cuchichear, hablar al oído; susurrar (*p.ej., las hojas*); (*to gossip*) susurrar, murmurar

whisperer ['hwɪspərər] *s* susurrón *m*

whispering ['hwɪspərɪŋ] *adj & s* (*gossiping*) susurrón *m*

whist [hwɪst] *s* whist *m* (*juego de naipes*)

whistle ['hwɪsəl] *s* (*sound*) silbido, silbo; (*device*) silbato, pito; **to wet one's whistle** (coll) remojar la palabra || *tr* silbar (*p.ej., una canción*) || *intr* silbar; **to whistle for** llamar con un silbido; (coll) tener que componérselas sin

whistle stop *s* apeadero, pueblecito

whit [hwɪt] *s* — **not a whit** ni pizca; **to not care a whit** no importarle a (*uno*) un bledo

white [hwaɪt] *adj* blanco || *s* blanco; (*of an egg*) clara; **whites** (pathol) pérdidas blancas, flujo blanco

white'caps' *spl* cabrillas, palomas

white coal *s* hulla blanca

white'-col'lar *adj* oficinesco

white feather *s* — **to show the white feather** mostrarse cobarde

white goods *spl* tejidos de algodón; ropa blanca; aparatos electrodomésticos

white-haired ['hwaɪt,herd] *adj* de pelo blanco; (*gray-haired*) cano; (coll) favorito, predilecto

white heat *s* blanco, calor blanco; (fig) viva agitación

white lead [led] *s* albayalde *m*

white lie *s* mentirilla, mentira inocente u oficiosa

white meat *s* pechuga, carne *f* de la pechuga del ave

whiten ['hwaɪtən] *tr* blanquear, emblanquecer || *intr* blanquear, emblanquecerse; palidecer

whiteness ['hwaɪtnɪs] *s* blancura

white plague *s* peste blanca (*tuberculosis*)

white slavery *s* trata de blancas

white tie *s* corbatín blanco; traje *m* de etiqueta

white'wash' *s* jalbegue *m*, lechada; (*e.g., of a scandal*) encubrimiento || *tr* jalbegar, enjalbegar, encalar; absolver sin justicia; encubrir (*un escándalo*)

whither ['hwɪðər] *adv* adónde || *conj* adonde

whitish ['hwaɪtɪʃ] *adj* blanquecino, blancuzco

whitlow ['hwɪtlo] *s* panadizo, uñero

Whitsuntide ['hwɪtsən,taɪd] *s* semana de Pentecostés

whittle ['hwɪtəl] *tr* sacar pedazos a (*un trozo de madera*); **to whittle away o down** reducir poco a poco

whiz o whizz [hwɪz] *s* silbido, zumbido; (slang) perito, fenómeno || *v* (*pret & pp* **whizzed**; *ger* **whizzing**) *intr* — **to whiz by** rehilar, silbar; pasar como una flecha

who [hu] *pron interr* quién; **who else?** ¿quién más?; **who goes there?** (mil) ¿quién vive?; **who's who** quién es el uno y quién el otro; **quiénes son gente de importancia** || *pron rel* que, quien; el (la, etc.) que

whoa [hwo] o [wo] *interj* ¡so!

who·ev'er *pron rel* quienquiera que, cualquiera que

whole [hol] *adj* todo, entero; (*intact*) ileso; (*not scattered or dispersed*) único, p.ej., **the whole interest for him was the child he was raising** el único interés para él era el niño que educaba; **made out of the whole cloth** enteramente falso o imaginario || *s* conjunto, todo; **as a whole** en conjunto; **on the whole** en general; **por la mayor parte**

wholehearted ['hol,hɑrtɪd] *adj* sincero, cordial

whole note *s* (mus) semibreve *f*

whole'sale' *adj & adv* al por mayor || *s* venta al por mayor || *tr* vender al por mayor || *intr* vender al por mayor; venderse al por mayor

wholesaler ['hol,selər] *s* comerciante *mf* al por mayor

wholesome ['holsəm] *adj* (*conducive to good health*) saludable; (*in good health*) fresco, rollizo

wholly ['holi] *adv* enteramente, completamente

whom [hum] *pron interr* a quién || *pron rel* que, a quien; al (a la, etc.) que

whom·ev'er *pron rel* a quienquiera que

whoop [hup] o [hwup] *s* ululato || *tr* — **to whoop it up** (slang) armar una gritería || *intr* ulular

whooping cough ['hupɪŋ] o ['hwupɪŋ] *s* tos ferina, tos convulsiva

whopper ['hwɑpər] *s* (coll) enormidad; (coll) mentirón *m*

whopping ['hwɑpɪŋ] *adj* (coll) enorme, grandísimo

whore [hor] *s* puta || *intr* — **to whore around** putañear, putear

whortleber·ry ['hwʌrtəl,beri] s (pl -ries) arándano

whose [huz] pron interr de quién || pron rel de quien, cuyo

why [hwaɪ] adv por qué; **why not?** ¿cómo no? || s (pl whys) porqué m || interj ¡toma!; **why, certainly!** ¡desde luego!, ¡por supuesto!; **why, yes!** ¡claro!, ¡pues sí!

wick [wɪk] s mecha, pabilo

wicked ['wɪkɪd] adj malo; (mischievous) travieso, revoltoso; (vicious) arisco; ofensivo

wicker ['wɪkər] adj mimbroso || s mimbre m & f

wicket ['wɪkɪt] s (small door in a larger one) portillo, postigo; (small opening in a door) ventanillo; (ticket window) taquilla; (gate to regulate flow of water) compuerta; (cricket) meta; (croquet) aro

wide [waɪd] adj ancho; de ancho; (sense of a word) amplio, lato || adv de par en par; enteramente; lejos; **wide of the mark** lejos del blanco; fuera de propósito

wide'-an'gle adj granangular

wide'-a·wake' adj despabilado

widen ['waɪdən] tr ensanchar || intr ensancharse

wide'-o'pen adj abierto de par en par; **to be wide-open** estar (p.ej., una ciudad) abierta a los jugadores

wide'spread' adj (arms, wings) extendido; difundido, extenso

widow ['wɪdo] s viuda; (cards) baceta || tr dejar viuda

widower ['wɪdo·ər] s viudo

widowhood ['wɪdo,hud] s viudez f

widow's mite s limosna que da un pobre

widow's pension s viudedad

widow's weeds spl luto de viuda

width [wɪdθ] s anchura

wield [wild] tr esgrimir, manejar (la espada); ejercer (el poder)

wife [waɪf] s (pl wives [waɪvz]) esposa, mujer f

wig [wɪg] s peluca

wiggle ['wɪgəl] s meneo rápido || tr menear rápidamente || intr menearse rápidamente

wig'wag' s comunicación con banderas || v (pret & pp -wagged; ger -wagging) tr menear; mandar (informes) moviendo banderas || intr menearse; señalar con banderas

wigwam ['wɪgwam] s choza cónica (de los pieles rojas)

wild [waɪld] adj (not domesticated; growing without cultivation; uncivilized) salvaje; (unrestrained) descabellado; (frantic, mad) frenético; (riotous) desenfrenado, revoltoso; extravagante; (bullet, shot) perdido; **wild about** loco por || adv disparatadamente; **to run wild** crecer locamente; estar sin gobierno || s desierto, yermo; **wilds** monte m, despoblado

wild boar s jabalí m

wild card s comodín m

wild'cat' s gato montés; lince m; empresa arriesgada

wildcat strike s huelga no autorizada por el sindicato

wilderness ['wɪldərnɪs] s desierto, yermo

wild'fire' s fuego fatuo; fucilazo; **to spread like wildfire** ser un reguero de pólvora, correr como pólvora en reguero

wild flower s flor f del campo

wild goose s ganso bravo

wild'-goose' chase s caza de grillos

wild'life' s animales mf salvajes

wild oats spl excesos de la juventud, mocedad; **to sow one's wild oats** llevar (los mozos) una vida de excesos

wild olive s acebuche m

wile [waɪl] s ardid m, engaño; (cunning) astucia || tr engatusar; **to wile away** entretener (el tiempo); pasar (p.ej., la tarde)

will [wɪl] s voluntad; (law) testamento; **at will** a voluntad || tr querer; (to bequeath) legar || intr querer; **do as you will** haga Vd. lo que quiera || v (pret & cond would) v aux **he will arrive at six o'clock** llegará a las seis; **he will go for days without smoking** pasa días enteros sin fumar

willful ['wɪlfəl] adj voluntarioso

willfulness ['wɪlfəlnɪs] s voluntariedad

William ['wɪljəm] s Guillermo

willing ['wɪlɪŋ] adj dispuesto; gustoso, pronto; espontáneo; **willing or unwilling** que quiera, que no quiera

willingly ['wɪlɪŋli] adv de buena gana, de buena voluntad

willingness ['wɪlɪŋnɪs] s buena gana, buena voluntad

will-o'-the-wisp ['wɪləðə'wɪsp] s fuego fatuo; ilusión, quimera

willow ['wɪlo] s sauce m

willowy ['wɪlo·i] adj (pliant) juncal, mimbreño; (slender, graceful) juncal, cimbreño, esbelto; lleno de sauces

will power s fuerza de voluntad

willy-nilly ['wɪli'nɪli] adv de grado o por fuerza

wilt [wɪlt] tr marchitar || intr marchitarse

wil·y ['waɪli] adj (comp -ier; super -iest) artero, engañoso; astuto

wimple ['wɪmpəl] s griñón m, impla

win [wɪn] s (coll) éxito, triunfo || v (pret & pp won [wʌn]; ger winning) tr ganar; to win over ganar, conquistar || intr ganar; **to win out** ganar; (coll) tener éxito

wince [wɪns] s sobresalto || intr sobresaltarse

winch [wɪntʃ] s maquinilla, torno; (handle, crank) manubrio

wind [wɪnd] s viento; (gas in intestines) (coll) viento; (breath) respiración, resuello; **to break wind** ventosear; **to get wind of** saber de, tener noticia de; **to sail close to the wind** (naut) ceñir el viento; **to take the wind out of one's sails** apagarle a uno los fuegos || tr dejar sin aliento || [waɪnd] v (pret & pp wound [waund]) *tr* (*to coil; to wrap up*) arrollar, envolver; devanar (*alambre*); ovillar (*hilo*); torcer (*hebras*); hacer girar (*un manubrio*); dar cuerda a (*un reloj*); **to wind one's way through** serpentear por; **to wind up** arrollar, envolver; (coll) poner punto final a || *intr* serpentear (*un camino*)

windbag ['wɪnd,bæg] *s* (*of bagpipe*) odre *m*; (coll) charlatán *m*, palabrero

windbreak ['wɪnd,brek] *s* guardavientos *m*

wind cone [wɪnd] *s* (aer) cono de viento

winded ['wɪndɪd] *adj* falto de respiración, sin resuello

windfall ['wɪnd,fɔl] *s* fruta caída del árbol; fortunón *m*, cosa llovida del cielo

winding sheet ['waɪndɪŋ] *s* sudario, mortaja

winding stairs *spl* escalera de caracol

wind instrument [wɪnd] *s* (mus) instrumento de viento

windlass ['wɪndləs] *s* maquinilla, torno

windmill ['wɪnd,mɪl] *s* (*mill operated by wind*) molino de viento; (*modern wind-driven source of power*) aeromotor *m*; (*pinwheel*) molinete *m*; **to tilt at windmills** luchar con los molinos de viento

window ['wɪndo] *s* ventana; (*of ticket office; of envelope*) ventanilla; (*of coach, automobile*) ventanilla, portezuela

window dresser *s* escaparatista *mf*

window dressing *s* adorno de escaparates

window frame *s* marco de ventana

win'dow-pane' *s* cristal *m* o vidrio de ventana

window screen *s* alambrera, sobrevidriera

window shade *s* visillo, transparente *m* de resorte

win'dow-shop' *v* (*pret & pp* -shopped; *ger* -shopping) *intr* mirar los escaparates sin comprar

window shutter *s* contraventana

window sill *s* repisa de ventana

windpipe ['wɪnd,paɪp] *s* tráquea

windshield ['wɪnd,ʃild] *s* parabrisa *m*

windshield washer *s* lavaparabrisas *m*

windshield wiper *s* limpiaparabrisas *m*

wind sock *s* (aer) cono de viento

windstorm ['wɪnd,stɔrm] *s* ventarrón *m*

wind-up ['waɪnd,ʌp] *s* conclusión; (sport) final *f* de partido

windward ['wɪndwərd] *s* barlovento; **to turn to windward** barloventear

Windward Islands *spl* islas de Barlovento

Windward Passage *s* paso de los Vientos

wind·y ['wɪndi] *adj* (*comp* -ier; *super* -iest) ventoso; (*unsubstantial*) vacío; palabrero, ampuloso; **it is windy** hace viento

wine [waɪn] *s* vino || *tr* obsequiar con vino || *intr* beber vino

wine cellar *s* bodega

wine'glass' *s* copa para vino

winegrower ['waɪn,gro·ər] *s* vinicultor *m*

winegrowing ['waɪn,gro·ɪŋ] *s* vinicultura

wine press *s* lagar *m*

winer·y ['waɪnəri] *s* (*pl* -ies) lagar *m*

wine'skin' *s* odre *m*

winetaster ['waɪn,testər] *s* catavinos *m*

wing [wɪŋ] *s* ala; facción, bando; (theat) bastidor *m*; **to take wing** alzar el vuelo || *tr* herir en el ala; **to wing one's way** avanzar volando

wing chair *s* sillón *m* de orejas

wing collar *s* cuello de pajarita

wing nut *s* tuerca de aletas

wing'spread' *s* envergadura

wink [wɪŋk] *s* guiño; **to not sleep a wink** no pegar los ojos; **to take forty winks** (coll) descabezar el sueño || *tr* guiñar (*el ojo*) || *intr* guiñar; (*to blink*) parpadear, pestañear; **to wink at** guiñar el ojo a; fingir no ver

winner ['wɪnər] *s* ganador *m*, vencedor *m*; premiado

winning ['wɪnɪŋ] *adj* triunfante, victorioso; atrayente, simpático || **winnings** *spl* ganancias

winnow ['wɪno] *tr* aventar; entresacar || *intr* aletear

winsome ['wɪnsəm] *adj* atrayente, simpático, engañador; alegre

winter ['wɪntər] *adj* invernal || *s* invierno || *intr* invernar

win'ter·green' *s* gaulteria, té *m* del Canadá; esencia de gaulteria

win·try ['wɪntri] *adj* (*comp* -trier; *super* -triest) invernal, invernizo; helado, frío

wipe [waɪp] *tr* frotar para limpiar; enjugar (*la cara, el sudor, las manos*); **to wipe away** enjugar (*lágrimas*); **to wipe off** quitar frotando; **to wipe out** (coll) borrar, cancelar; (coll) aniquilar, destruir; (coll) enjugar (*deudas, un déficit*)

wiper ['waɪpər] *s* paño, trapo; (elec) contacto deslizante

wire [waɪr] *s* (*thread of metal*) alambre *m*; telégrafo; telegrama *m*; teléfono; **to pull wires** (coll) tocar resortes || *tr* alambrar; telegrafiar || *intr* telegrafiar

wire cutter *s* cortaalambres *m*

wire entanglement *s* (mil) alambrado

wire gauge *s* calibrador *m* de alambre

wire-haired ['waɪr,herd] *adj* de pelo áspero

wireless ['waɪrlɪs] *adj* inalámbrico, sin hilos

wire nail *s* punta de París, clavo de alambre

wire pulling ['pʊlɪŋ] *s* (coll) empleo de resortes

wire recorder *s* grabadora de alambre

wire screen *s* alambrera, tela de alambre

wire'tap' *v* (*pret & pp* -tapped; *ger* -tapping) *tr* intervenir (*una conversación telefónica*)

wiring ['waɪrɪŋ] *s* (elec) alambraje *m*

wir·y ['waɪri] *adj* (*comp* -ier; *super*

-iest) alambrino; cimbreante; nervudo; vibrante

wisdom ['wɪzdəm] s sabiduría, cordura

wisdom tooth s muela cordal, muela del juicio

wise [waɪz] adj sabio, cuerdo; (step, decision) acertado, juicioso; **to be wise to** (slang) conocer el juego de; **to get wise** (coll) caer en el chiste || s modo, manera; **in no wise** de ningún modo

wiseacre ['waɪz,ekər] s sabihondo

wise'crack' s (slang) cuchufleta || intr (slang) cuchufletear

wise guy s (slang) sabelotodo

wish [wɪʃ] s deseo; **to make a wish** pensar algo que se desea || tr desear; dar (los buenos días) || intr desear; **to wish for** desear, anhelar

wish'bone' s espoleta, hueso de la suerte

wishful ['wɪʃfəl] adj deseoso

wishful thinking s optimismo a ultranza; **to indulge in wishful thinking** forjarse ilusiones

wistful ['wɪstfəl] adj melancólico, tristón, pensativo

wit [wɪt] s agudeza; (person) chistoso; (keen mental power) juicio; **to be at one's wits' end** no saber qué hacer; **to have the wit** to tener el tino de; **to live by one's wits** vivir del cuento

witch [wɪtʃ] s bruja, hechicera; (old hag) bruja

witch'craft' s brujería

witches' Sabbath s aquelarre m

witch hazel s (shrub) nogal m de la brujería, planta del sortilegio; (liquid) hamamelina, hazelina

with [wɪð] o [wɪθ] prep con; de

with-draw v (pret -drew; pp -drawn) tr retirar || intr retirarse

withdrawal [wɪð'drɔ·əl] o [wɪθ'drɔ·əl] s retirada

wither ['wɪðər] tr marchitar; (fig) aplastar, confundir || intr marchitarse; confundirse

with-hold v (pret & pp -held) tr retener; suspender (pago); negar (un permiso)

withholding tax s impuesto deducido del sueldo

with-in' adv dentro || prep dentro de; al alcance de; poco menos de; con un margen de

with-out' adv fuera || prep fuera de; (lacking, not with) sin; **to do without** pasar sin; **without** + ger sin + inf, p.ej., **he left without saying goodbye** salió sin despedirse; **sin que** + subj, p.ej., **he came in without anyone seeing him** entró sin que nadie le viese

with-stand' v (pret & pp -stood) tr aguantar, resistir

witness ['wɪtnɪs] s testigo mf; **in witness whereof** en fe de lo cual; **to bear witness** dar testimonio || intr (to be present at) presenciar; (to attest) atestiguar, testimoniar; firmar como testigo

witness stand s banquillo o estrado de los testigos

witticism ['wɪtɪ,sɪzəm] s agudeza, dicho agudo, ocurrencia

wittingly ['wɪtɪŋli] adv a sabiendas

wit-ty ['wɪti] adj (comp -tier; super -tiest) agudo, ingenioso; (person) ocurrente, chistoso

wizard ['wɪzərd] s brujo, hechicero; (coll) as m, experto

wizardry ['wɪzərdri] s hechicería, magia

wizened ['wɪzənd] adj acartonado, arrugado

wk. abbr **week**

w.l. abbr **wave length**

woad [wod] s hierba pastel

wobble ['wabəl] s bamboleo, tambaleo || intr bambolear, tambalear; bailar (una silla); (fig) vacilar, ser inconstante

wob-bly ['wabli] adj (comp -blier; super -bliest) bamboleante, inseguro; vacilante

woe [wo] s aflicción, miseria, infortunio || interj — woe is me! ¡ay de mí!

woebegone ['wobɪ,gɔn] o ['wobɪ,gɑn] adj cariacontecido, triste

woeful ['wofəl] adj triste, miserable; (of poor quality) malo, pésimo

wolf [wulf] s (pl wolves [wulvz]) lobo; persona cruel, persona mafiosa; (coll) tenorio; **to cry wolf** dar falsa alarma; **to keep the wolf from the door** ponerse a cubierto del hambre || tr & intr comer vorazmente, engullir

wolf'hound' s galgo lobero

wolfram ['wulfrəm] s (element) volframio; (mineral) volframita

wolf's-bane o **wolfsbane** ['wulfs,ben] s matalobos m

woman ['wumən] s (pl women ['wɪmɪn]) mujer f

womanhood ['wumən,hud] s el sexo femenino; las mujeres

womanish ['wumənɪʃ] adj mujeril; (effeminate) afeminado

wom'an-kind' s el sexo femenino

womanly ['wumənli] adj (comp -lier; super -liest) femenil, mujeriego

woman suffrage s sufragismo

woman-suffragist ['wumən'sʌfrədʒɪst] s sufragista mf

womb [wum] s útero; (fig) seno

womenfolk ['wɪmɪn,fok] spl las mujeres

wonder ['wʌndər] s (something strange or surprising) maravilla; (feeling of surprise) admiración; (something strange, miracle) milagro; **for a wonder** cosa extraña; **no wonder that . . .** no es mucho que . . .; **to work wonders** hacer milagros || tr preguntarse || intr admirarse, maravillarse; **to wonder at** admirarse de, maravillarse con o de

wonder drugs spl drogas milagrosas

wonderful ['wʌndərfəl] adj maravilloso

won'der-land' s tierra de las maravillas; reino de las hadas

wonderment ['wʌndərmənt] s asombro, sorpresa

wont [wʌnt] o [wɔnt] adj acostum-

brado; **to be wont to** acostumbrar ‖
s costumbre, hábito

wonted ['wɑntɪd] o ['wɔntɪd] *adj*
acostumbrado, habitual

woo [wu] *tr* cortejar (*a una mujer*);
tratar de conquistar; tratar de persuadir

wood [wud] *s* madera; (*for making a
fire*) leña; barril *m* de madera; **out
of the woods** (coll) fuera de peligro;
(coll) libre de dificultades; **to take to
the woods** andar a monte; **woods**
bosque *m*

woodbine ['wud,baɪn] *s* (*honeysuckle*)
madreselva; (*Virginia creeper*) guau
m

wood carving *s* labrado de madera

wood'chuck' *s* marmota de América

wood'cock' *s* becada, coalla, chocha

wood'cut' *s* (typ) grabado en madera

wood'cut'ter *s* leñador *m*

wooded ['wudɪd] *adj* arbolado, enselvado

wooden ['wudən] *adj* de madera, hecho de madera; torpe, estúpido; sin
ánimo

wood engraving *s* (typ) grabado en
madera

wooden-headed ['wudən,hedɪd] *adj*
(coll) torpe, estúpido

wooden leg *s* pata de palo

wooden shoe *s* zueco

wood grouse *s* gallo de bosque

woodland ['wudlənd] *adj* selvático ‖ *s*
bosque *m*, monte *m*

woodland scene *s* (paint) boscaje *m*

wood-man ['wudmən] *s* (*pl* -**men**
[mən]) leñador *m*

woodpecker ['wud,pekər] *s* carpintero, pájaro carpintero; (*green woodpecker*) picamaderos *m*

wood'pile' *s* montón *m* de leña

wood screw *s* tirafondo

wood'shed' *s* leñero

woods-man ['wudzmən] *s* (*pl* -**men**
[mən]) leñador *m*

wood'wind' *s* (mus) instrumento de
viento de madera

wood'work' *s* (*working in wood*) ebanistería, obra de carpintería; (*things
made of wood*) maderaje *m*

wood'work'er *s* ebanista *mf*, carpintero

wood'worm' *s* carcoma

wood-y ['wudi] *adj* (*comp* -**ier**; *super*
-**iest**) arbolado, enselvado; (*like
wood*) leñoso

wooer ['wu-ər] *s* pretendiente *m*,
galán *m*

woof [wuf] *s* (*yarns running across
warp*) trama; (*fabric*) tejido

woofer ['wufər] *s* altavoz *m* para audiofrecuencias bajas

wool [wul] *s* lana

woolen ['wulən] *adj* de lana, hecho de
lana ‖ *s* tejido de lana; **woolens** lanerías

woolgrower ['wul,gro-ər] *s* criador *m*
de ganado lanar

wool-ly ['wuli] *adj* (*comp* -**lier**; *super*
-**liest**) lanoso, lanudo; borroso, confuso

word [wʌrd] *s* palabra; **to be as good
as one's word** cumplir lo prometido;

to have a word with hablar cuatro
palabras con; **to have word from**
recibir noticias de; **to keep one's
word** cumplir su palabra; **to leave
word** dejar dicho; **to send word that**
mandar decir que; **words** (*a quarrel*)
palabras mayores; (*text of a song*)
letra ‖ *tr* redactar, formular ‖ **Word**
s (theol) Verbo

word count *s* recuento de vocabulario

word formation *s* (gram) formación de
palabras

wording ['wʌrdɪŋ] *s* fraseología, estilo

word order *s* (gram) orden *m* de colocación

word'stock' *s* vocabulario, léxico

word-y ['wʌrdi] *adj* (*comp* -**ier**; *super*
-**iest**) verboso

work [wʌrk] *s* (*exertion; labor, toil*)
trabajo; (*result of exertion; human
output; engineering structure*) obra;
(sew) labor *f*; **at work** trabajando;
(*not at home*) en la oficina, en el
taller, en la tienda; **out of work** sin
trabajo, desempleado; **to shoot the
works** (slang) echar el resto; **works**
fábrica; mecanismo; (*of clock*) movimiento ‖ *tr* hacer trabajar; trabajar, obrar (*la madera, el hierro*);
obrar (*un milagro*); explotar (*una
mina*); **to work up** preparar: estimular, excitar ‖ *intr* trabajar; funcionar,
marchar (*un aparato, un motor*);
obrar (*p.ej., un remedio*); **to work
loose** aflojarse; **to work out** resolverse

workable ['wʌrkəbəl] *adj* (*feasible*)
practicable, (*that can be worked*)
laborable

work'bench' *s* banco de trabajo, banco
de taller

work'book' *s* (*manual of instructions*)
libro de reglas; libro de ejercicios

work'box' *s* caja de herramientas; (*for
needlework*) caja de labor

work'day' *adj* de cada día; ordinario,
vulgar ‖ *s* día *m* de trabajo; (*number of hours of work*) jornada

worked-up ['wʌrkt'ʌp] *adj* muy conmovido, sobreexcitado, exaltado

worker ['wʌrkər] *s* trabajador *m*,
obrero

work force *s* mano *f* de obra, personal
obrero

work'horse' *s* caballo de carga; (*tireless worker*) yunque *m*

work'house' *s* taller penitenciario;
(Brit) asilo de pobres

working class *s* clase obrera

work'ing-girl' *s* trabajadora joven

working hours *spl* horas de trabajo

working-man ['wʌrkɪŋ,mæn] *s* (*pl*
-**men** [,mɛn]) *s* obrero, trabajador *m*

working-woman ['wʌrkɪŋ,wumən] *s*
(*pl* -**women** [,wɪmɪn]) obrera, trabajadora

work-man ['wʌrkmən] *s* (*pl* -**men**
[mən]) obrero, trabajador *m*; (*skilled
worker*) artífice *m*

workmanship ['wʌrkmən,ʃɪp] *s* destreza en el trabajo; (*work executed*)
hechura, obra

work of art *s* obra de arte

work'out' s ensayo, prueba; (physical exercise) ejercicio
work'room' s (for manual work) obrador m, taller m; (study) gabinete m de trabajo
work'shop' s obrador m, taller m
work stoppage s paro
world [wʌrld] adj mundial ‖ s mundo; **a world of** la mar de; **half the world** (a lot of people) medio mundo; **since the world began** desde que el mundo es mundo; **the other world** el otro mundo; **to bring into the world** echar al mundo; **to see the world** ver mundo; **to think the world of** tener un alto concepto de
world affairs spl asuntos internacionales
world·ly ['wʌrldli] adj (comp -lier; super -liest) mundano
world'ly-wise' adj que tiene mucho mundo
world's fair s exposición mundial
World War s Guerra Mundial
world'-wide' adj global, mundial
worm [wʌrm] s gusano; **worms** (pathol) lombrices fpl ‖ tr limpiar de lombrices; **to worm a secret out of a person** arrancar mañosamente un secreto a una persona; **to worm one's way** into insinuarse en
worm-eaten ['wʌrm,itən] adj carcomido; (fig) decaído, desgastado
worm gear s engranaje m de tornillo sin fin
worm'wood' s (Artemisia) ajenjo; (Artemisia absinthium) ajenjo del campo o ajenjo mayor; (something bitter or grievous) (fig) ajenjo
worm·y ['wʌrmi] adj (comp -ier; super -iest) gusaniento, gusanoso; (worm-eaten) carcomido; (groveling) rastrero, servil
worn [worn] adj roto, raído, gastado
worn'-out' adj muy gastado, inservible; (by toil, illness) consumido, rendido
worrisome ['wʌrisəm] adj inquietante; (inclined to worry) aprensivo, inquieto
wor·ry ['wʌri] s (pl -ries) inquietud, preocupación; (cause of anxiety) molestia ‖ v (pret & pp -ried) tr inquietar, preocupar; (to harass, pester) acosar, molestar; **to be worried** estar inquieto ‖ intr inquietarse, preocuparse; **don't worry** pierda Vd. cuidado
worse [wʌrs] adj & adv comp peor; **worse and worse** de mal en peor
worsen ['wʌrsən] tr & intr empeorar
wor·ship ['wʌrʃip] s adoración, culto; **your worship** vuestra merced ‖ v (pret & pp -shiped o -shipped; ger -shiping o -shipping) tr & intr adorar, venerar
worshiper o **worshipper** ['wʌrʃipər] s adorador m, devoto
worst [wʌrst] adj & adv super peor ‖ s (lo) peor; **at worst** en las peores circunstancias; **if worst comes to worst** si pasa lo peor; **to get the worst of** llevar la peor parte, salir perdiendo

worsted ['wustid] adj de estambre ‖ s estambre m; tela de estambre
wort [wʌrt] s (bot) hierba, planta; mosto de cerveza
worth [wʌrθ] adj del valor de; digno de; **to be worth** valer; tener una fortuna de; **to be worth + ger** valer la pena de + inf; **to be worth while** valer la pena; **ser de mérito** ‖ s valor m; mérito; **a dollar's worth of** un dólar de
worthless ['wʌrθlis] adj sin valor, inútil, inservible; (person) despreciable
worth'while' adj de mérito, digno de atención
wor·thy ['wʌrði] adj (comp -thier; super -thiest) digno; benemérito, meritorio ‖ s (pl -thies) benemérito; (hum & iron) personaje m
would [wud] v aux she said she would do it dijo que lo haría; **he would come if he could** vendría si pudiese; **he would go for days without smoking** pasaba días enteros sin fumar; **would that . . .!** ¡ojalá que . . .!
would'-be' adj llamado; supuesto ‖ s presumido
wound [wund] s herida ‖ tr herir
wounded ['wundid] adj herido ‖ **the wounded** los heridos
wow [wau] s (of phonograph record) ululación; (slang) éxito rotundo ‖ tr (slang) entusiasmar
wrack [ræk] s naufragio; vestigio; (fucaceous seaweed) varec m; **to go to wrack and ruin** desvencijarse; ir al desastre
wraith [reθ] s fantasma m, espectro
wrangle ['ræŋɡəl] s pendencia, riña ‖ intr pelotear, reñir
wrap [ræp] s abrigo, manto ‖ v (pret & pp wrapped; ger wrapping) tr envolver; **to be wrapped up in** (fig) estar prendado de; **to wrap up** envolver; (in clothing) arropar; (coll) concluir ‖ intr — **to wrap up** arroparse
wrapper ['ræpər] s bata, peinador m; (of newspaper or magazine) faja; (of tobacco) capa
wrapping paper ['ræpiŋ] s papel m de envolver, papel de embalar
wrath [ræθ] o [rɑθ] s cólera, ira; venganza
wrathful ['ræθfəl] o ['rɑθfəl] adj colérico, iracundo
wreak [rik] tr descargar (la cólera); infligir (venganza)
wreath [riθ] s (pl wreaths [riðz]) guirnalda; corona funeraria; (worn as a mark of honor or victory) corona de laurel; (of smoke) espiral f
wreathe [rið] tr enguirnaldar; ceñir, envolver; tejer (una guirnalda) ‖ intr elevarse en espirales (el humo)
wreck [rek] s destrucción, ruina; naufragio; catástrofe f, desastre m; despojos, restos; (of one's hopes) naufragio; **to be a wreck** estar hecho un cascajo, estar hecho una ruina ‖ tr destruir, arruinar; hacer

naufragar; hacer chocar, descarrilar (*un tren*)

wrecking ball *s* bola rompedora

wrecking car *s* (aut) camión *m* de auxilio; (rr) carro de grúa

wrecking crane *s* grúa de auxilio

wren [rɛn] *s* buscareta, coletero, rey *m* de zarza

wrench [rɛntʃ] *s* llave *f*; (*pull*) arranque *m*, tirón *m*; (*twist of a joint*) esguince *m* ‖ *tr* torcerse (*p.ej., la muñeca*); (fig) torcer (*el sentido de una oración*)

wrest [rɛst] *tr* arrebatar, arrancar violentamente

wrestle [ˈrɛsəl] *s* lucha; partido de lucha ‖ *intr* luchar

wrestling match [ˈrɛslɪŋ] *s* partido de lucha

wretch [rɛtʃ] *s* miserable *mf*

wretched [ˈrɛtʃɪd] *adj* miserable; (*poor, worthless*) malísimo, pésimo

wriggle [ˈrɪgəl] *s* culebreo, meneo serpentino ‖ *tr* menear rápidamente ‖ *intr* culebrear, ondular; **to wriggle out of** escabullirse de

wrig-gly [ˈrɪglɪ] *adj* (*comp* **-glier**; *super* **-gliest**) retorciéndose; (fig) evasivo, tramoyista

wring [rɪŋ] *v* (*pret & pp* **wrung** [rʌŋ]) *tr* torcer; retorcer (*las manos*); exprimir (*el zumo, la ropa, etc.*); sacar por fuerza (*la verdad*); arrancar (*dinero*); **to wring out** exprimir (*la ropa*)

wringer [ˈrɪŋər] *s* exprimidor *m*

wrinkle [ˈrɪŋkəl] *s* arruga; (*clever trick or idea*) (coll) ardid *m*, truco ‖ *tr* arrugar ‖ *intr* arrugarse

wrin-kly [ˈrɪŋklɪ] *adj* (*comp* **-klier**; *super* **-kliest**) arrugado

wrist [rɪst] *s* muñeca

wrist'band' *s* bocamanga, puño

wrist watch *s* reloj *m* de pulsera

writ [rɪt] *s* escrito, escritura; (law) mandato, orden *f*

write [raɪt] *v* (*pret* **wrote** [rot]; *pp* **written** [ˈrɪtən]) *tr* escribir; **to write down** poner por escrito; bajar el precio de; **to write off** cancelar (*una deuda*); **to write up** describir extensamente por escrito; (*to ballyhoo*) dar bombo a ‖ *intr* escribir; **to write back** contestar por carta

writer [ˈraɪtər] *s* escritor *m*

writer's cramp *s* grafoespasmo

write'-up' *s* (*favorable report*) bombo; (com) valoración excesiva

writhe [raɪð] *intr* contorcerse, retorcerse

writing [ˈraɪtɪŋ] *s* el escribir; (*something written*) escrito; profesión de escritor; **at this writing** al escribir ésta; **in one's own writing** de su puño y letra; **to put in writing** poner por escrito

writing desk *s* escritorio

writing materials *spl* recado de escribir

writing paper *s* papel *m* de escribir, papel de cartas

written accent [ˈrɪtən] *s* acento ortográfico

wrong [rɔŋ] o [raŋ] *adj* injusto; malo; erróneo, equivocado; impropio; **no . . . que se busca**, *p.ej.*, **this is the wrong house** ésta no es la casa que se busca; **no . . . que se necesita**, *p.ej.*, **this is the wrong train** éste no es el tren que se necesita; **no . . . que debe**, *p.ej.*, **he is going the wrong way** no sigue el camino que debe; **in the wrong place** mal colocado; **to be wrong** no tener razón; tener la culpa; **to be wrong with** pasar algo a, *p.ej.*, **something is wrong with the motor** algo le pasa al motor ‖ *adv* mal; sin razón; al revés; **to go wrong** ir por mal camino; darse a la mala vida ‖ *s* daño, perjuicio; agravio, injusticia; error *m*; **to be in the wrong** no tener razón; tener la culpa; **to do wrong** obrar mal ‖ *tr* agraviar, hacer daño a, ofender, ser injusto con

wrongdoer [ˈrɔŋˌduˑər] o [ˈraŋˌduˑər] *s* malhechor *m*

wrongdoing [ˈrɔŋˌduˑɪŋ] o [ˈraŋˌduˑɪŋ] *s* malhecho, maldad

wrong number *s* (telp) número equivocado

wrong side *s* contrahaz *f*, revés *m*; (*of the street*) lado contrario; **to get out of bed on the wrong side** levantarse del lado izquierdo; **wrong side out** al revés

wrought iron [rɔt] *s* hierro dulce

wrought'-up' *adj* muy conmovido, sobreexcitado, exaltado

wry [raɪ] *adj* (*comp* **wrier**; *super* **wriest**) torcido; desviado, pervertido; irónico, burlón

wry'neck' *s* (orn) torcecuello; (pathol) torticolis *m*

wt. *abbr* **weight**

X

X, x [ɛks] vigésima cuarta letra del alfabeto inglés

Xanthippe [zænˈtɪpɪ] *s* Jantipa

Xavier [ˈzævɪˑər] o [ˈzevɪˑər] *s* Javier *m*

xebec [ˈzibɛk] *s* (naut) jabeque *m*

xenia [ˈzinɪˑə] *s* xenia

xenon [ˈzinan] o [ˈzenan] *s* xenón *m*

xenophobe [ˈzenəˌfob] *s* xenófobo

xenophobia [ˌzenəˈfobɪˑə] *s* xenofobia

Xenophon [ˈzenəfən] *s* Jenofonte *m*

Xerxes [ˈzʌrksiz] *s* Jerjes *m*

Xmas [ˈkrɪsməs] *s* Navidad

X ray s rayo X; (*photograph*) radiograma m

X-ray ['ɛks͵re] adj radiográfico || ['ɛks're] tr radiografiar; tratar por medio de los rayos X

xylograph ['zaɪlə͵græf] o ['zaɪlə͵græf] s xilografía

xylography [zaɪ'lɑgrəfi] s xilografía

xylophone ['zaɪlə͵fon] s (mus) xilófono

Y

Y, y [waɪ] vigésima quinta letra del alfabeto inglés

y. abbr **yard, year**

yacht [jɑt] s yate m

yacht club s club náutico

yak [jæk] s (zool) yac m

yam [jæm] s ñame m; (*sweet potato*) boniato, camote m

yank [jæŋk] s (coll) tirón m || tr (coll) sacar de un tirón || intr (coll) dar un tirón

Yankee ['jæŋki] adj & s yanqui mf

Yankeedom ['jæŋkidəm] s Yanquilandia; los yanquis

yap [jæp] s ladrido corto; (slang) charla necia y ruidosa || v (*pret* & *pp* **yapped**; *ger* **yapping**) intr ladrar con ladrido corto; (slang) charlar necia y ruidosamente

yard [jɑrd] s cercado, patio; (*measure*) yarda; (naut) verga; (rr) patio

yard'arm' s (naut) penol m

yard goods spl géneros de pieza

yard'mas'ter s (rr) superintendente m de patio

yard'stick' s yarda, vara de medir; (fig) criterio, norma

yarn [jɑrn] s hilado, hilaza; (coll) cuento increíble, burlería

yarrow ['jæro] s milenrama

yaw [jɔ] s (naut) guiñada; **yaws** (pathol) frambesia || intr (naut) guiñar

yawl [jɔl] s (naut) bote m; (naut) queche m

yawn [jɔn] s bostezo || intr bostezar; abrirse desmesuradamente

yd. abbr **yard**

yea [je] adv & s sí m

yean [jin] intr parir (la oveja, la cabra, etc.)

year [jɪr] s año; **to be . . . years old** cumplir . . . años; **year in, year out** año tras año

year'book' s anuario

yearling ['jɪrlɪŋ] adj & s primal m

yearly ['jɪrli] adj anual || adv anualmente

yearn [jʌrn] intr suspirar; **to yearn for** suspirar por, anhelar por

yearning ['jʌrnɪŋ] s anhelo, deseo ardiente

yeast [jist] s levadura

yeast cake s levadura comprimida, pastilla de levadura

yell [jɛl] s grito, voz f || tr decir a gritos || intr gritar, dar voces

yellow ['jɛlo] adj amarillo; (*cowardly*) (coll) blanco; (*journalism*) sensacional || s amarillo; yema de huevo || intr amarillecer

yellowish ['jɛlo͵ɪʃ] adj amarillento

yellow jacket s avispón m

yellowness ['jɛlonɪs] s amarillez f

yellow streak s vena de cobarde

yelp [jɛlp] s gañido || intr gañir

yeo-man ['jomən] s (*pl* -men [mən]) (naut) pañolero; (naut) oficinista m de a bordo; (Brit) labrador acomodado

yeoman of the guard s (Brit) alabardero de palacio, continuo

yeoman's service s ayuda leal

yes [jɛs] adv sí || s sí m; **to say yes** dar el sí || v (*pret* & *pp* **yessed**; *ger* **yessing**) tr decir sí a || intr decir sí

yes man s (coll) sacristán de amén

yesterday ['jɛstərdi] o ['jɛstər͵de] adj & s ayer m

yet [jɛt] adv todavía, aún; **as yet** hasta ahora; **not yet** todavía no || conj sin embargo

yew tree [ju] s tejo

yield [jild] s producción, rendimiento; (*crop*) cosecha; (*income produced*) rédito || tr producir, rendir, redituar || intr entregarse, rendirse, someterse; acceder, ceder, consentir; producir

yodeling o **yodelling** ['jodəlɪŋ] s tirolesa

yoke [jok] s (*pair of draft animals*) yunta; (*device to join a pair of draft animals*) yugo; (fig) yugo; (*of a shirt*) hombrillo; (elec) culata; **to throw off the yoke** sacudir el yugo || tr uncir

yokel ['jokəl] s patán m

yolk [jok] s yema

yonder ['jɑndər] adj aquel, de más allá || adv allá, más allá

yore [jor] s — **of yore** antaño, antiguamente

you [ju] pron pers usted, ustedes; le, la, les; **with you** consigo || pron indef se, p.ej., **you go in this way** se entra por aquí

young [jʌŋ] adj (comp **younger** ['jʌŋgər]; super **youngest** ['jʌŋgɪst]) joven || **the young** los jóvenes, la gente joven

young hopeful s joven m de esperanzas

young people spl jóvenes mpl, gente f joven

youngster ['jʌŋstər] s jovencito; (*child*) chico, chiquillo

your [jur] adj poss su, el (o su) de Vd. o Vds.

yours [jurz] pron poss suyo; de Vd., de Vds.; el suyo; el de Vd., el de Vds.; **of yours** suyo; de Vd., de

Vds.; **yours truly** su seguro servidor; (coll) este cura (*yo*)
your·self [jur'self] *pron pers* (*pl* **-selves** ['selvz]) usted mismo; sí, sí mismo; se, p.ej., **you enjoyed yourself** se divirtió Vd.
youth [juθ] *s* (*pl* **youths** [juθs] o [juðz]) juventud; (*person*) jovenzuelo; jovenzuelos, jóvenes *mpl*
youthful ['juθfəl] *adj* juvenil, mocil
yowl [jaul] *s* aullido, alarido ‖ *intr* aullar, dar alaridos

yr. *abbr* **year**
Yugoslav ['jugo'slɑv] *adj* & *s* yugoeslavo
Yugoslavia ['jugo'slɑvɪ·ə] *s* Yugoeslavia
Yule [jul] *s* la Navidad; la pascua de Navidad
Yule log *s* nochebueno, leño de nochebuena
Yuletide ['jul,taɪd] *s* la pascua de Navidad

Z

Z, z [zi] vigésima sexta letra del alfabeto inglés
za·ny ['zeni] *adj* (*comp* **-nier**; *super* **-niest**) cómico, gracioso, chiflado ‖ *s* (*pl* **-nies**) bufón *m*, payaso; mentecato
zeal [zil] *s* celo, entusiasmo
zealot ['zelət] *s* fanático, entusiasta *mf*
zealotry ['zelətri] *s* fanatismo
zealous ['zeləs] *adj* celoso, entusiasta
zebra ['zibrə] *s* cebra
zebu ['zibju] *s* cebú *m*
zenith ['ziniθ] *s* cenit *m*
zephyr ['zefər] *s* céfiro
zeppelin ['zepəlɪn] *s* zepelín *m*
ze·ro ['ziro] *s* (*pl* **-ros** o **-roes**) cero
zero gravity *s* gravedad nula
zest [zest] *s* entusiasmo; (*agreeable and piquant flavor*) gusto, sabor *m*
Zeus [zus] *s* Zeus *m*
zig·zag ['zɪg,zæg] *adj* & *adv* en zigzag ‖ *s* zigzag *m*, ziszas *m* ‖ *v* (*pret* & *pp* **-zagged**; *ger* **-zagging**) *intr* zigzaguear
zinc [zɪŋk] *s* cinc *m*
zinc etching *s* cincograbado
zinnia ['zɪnɪ·ə] *s* rascamoño

Zionism ['zaɪ·ə,nɪzəm] *s* sionismo
zip [zɪp] *s* (coll) silbido, zumbido; (coll) energía, brío ‖ *v* (*pret* & *pp* **zipped**; *ger* **zipping**) *tr* cerrar con cierre relámpago, abrir con cierre relámpago; (coll) llevar con rapidez; **to zip up** dar gusto a ‖ *intr* silbar, zumbar; (coll) moverse con energía; **to zip by** (coll) pasar rápidamente
zipper ['zɪpər] *s* cierre *m* relámpago, cierre cremallera; chanclo con cierre relámpago
zircon ['zɑrkɑn] *s* circón *m*
zirconium [zər'konɪ·əm] *s* circonio
zither ['zɪθər] *s* (mus) cítara
zodiac ['zodɪ,æk] *s* zodíaco
zone [zon] *s* zona; distrito postal ‖ *tr* dividir en zonas
zoölogic(al) [,zo·ə'lɑdʒɪk(əl)] *adj* zoológico
zoölogist [zo'ɑlədʒɪst] *s* zoólogo
zoölogy [zo'ɑlədʒi] *s* zoología
zoom [zum] *s* zumbido; (aer) empinada ‖ *tr* (aer) empinar ‖ *intr* zumbar; (aer) empinarse
zoöphyte ['zo·ə,faɪt] *s* zoófito
Zu·lu ['zulu] *adj* zulú ‖ *s* (*pl* **-lus**) zulú *mf*